HOBSON-JOBSON

HOBSON-JOBSON

A GLOSSARY OF COLLOQUIAL ANGLO-INDIAN WORDS AND PHRASES, AND OF KINDRED TERMS, ETYMOLOGICAL, HISTORICAL, GEOGRAPHICAL AND DISCURSIVE

BY COL. HENRY YULE, R.E., C.B.
AND A. C. BURNELL, PH.D., C.I.E.

NEW EDITION EDITED BY
WILLIAM CROOKE, B.A.

GYAN

Published by

GYAN

Gyan Publishing House
5, Ansari Road
Daryaganj, New Delhi-110002
Phone: 011-47034999, 9811692060
E-mail: books@gyanbooks.com

Distribution Network
gyanbooks.com
India, USA, Canada, UK, Australia, France

ISBN : 978-81-212-3557-0 (PB)
First Published, London, 1903

2nd Impression 2020

Printed at: Gyan Press, Delhi.

Hobson-Jobson
Author: William Crooke

A GLOSSARY

OF

ANGLO-INDIAN COLLOQUIAL WORDS AND PHRASES

AND OF

KINDRED TERMS

HOBSON-JOBSON

A GLOSSARY OF COLLOQUIAL ANGLO-INDIAN WORDS AND PHRASES, AND OF KINDRED TERMS, ETYMOLOGICAL, HISTORICAL, GEOGRAPHICAL AND DISCURSIVE

BY COL. HENRY YULE, R.E., C.B.
AND A. C. BURNELL, PH.D., C.I.E.

NEW EDITION EDITED BY
WILLIAM CROOKE, B.A.

LONDON
JOHN MURRAY, ALBEMARLE STREET
1903

[*Dedication to Sir George Udny Yule, C.B., K.C.S.I.*]

G. U. Y.

FRATRI OPTIMO DILECTISSIMO

AMICO JUCUNDISSIMO

HOC TRIUM FERME LUSTRORUM

OBLECTAMENTUM ET SOLATIUM

NEC PARVI LABORIS OPUS

ABSOLUTUM TANDEM

SENEX SENI

DEDICAT

H. Y.

PREFACE.

THE objects and scope of this work are explained in the Introductory Remarks which follow the Preface. Here it is desired to say a few words as to its history.

The book originated in a correspondence between the present writer, who was living at Palermo, and the late lamented ARTHUR BURNELL, of the Madras Civil Service, one of the most eminent of modern Indian scholars, who during the course of our communications was filling judicial offices in Southern and Western India, chiefly at Tanjore. We had then met only once—at the India Library; but he took a kindly interest in work that engaged me, and this led to an exchange of letters, which went on after his return to India. About 1872—I cannot find his earliest reference to the subject—he mentioned that he was contemplating a vocabulary of Anglo-Indian words, and had made some collections with that view. In reply it was stated that I likewise had long been taking note of such words, and that a notion similar to his own had also been at various times floating in my mind. And I proposed that we should combine our labours.

I had not, in fact, the linguistic acquirements needful for carrying through such an undertaking alone; but I had gone through an amount of reading that would largely help in instances and illustrations, and had also a strong natural taste for the kind of work.

This was the beginning of the portly double-columned edifice which now presents itself, the completion of which my friend has not lived to see. It was built up from our joint contributions till his untimely death in 1882, and since then almost daily additions have continued to be made to the material and to the structure. The subject, indeed, had taken so comprehensive a shape, that it was becoming difficult to say where its limits lay, or why it should ever end, except for the old reason which had received such poignant illustration: *Ars longa, vita brevis.* And so it has been wound up at last.

The work has been so long the companion of my *horae subsicivae*, a thread running through the joys and sorrows of so many years, in the search for material first, and then in their handling and adjustment to the edifice—for their careful building up has been part of my duty from the beginning, and the whole of the matter has, I suppose, been written and re-written with my own hand at least four times—and the work has been one of so much interest to dear friends, of whom not a few are no longer here to welcome its appearance in print,* that I can hardly speak of the work except as mine.

Indeed, in bulk, nearly seven-eighths of it is so. But BURNELL contributed so much of value, so much of the essential; buying, in the search for illustration, numerous rare and costly books which were not otherwise accessible to him in India; setting me, by his example, on lines of research with which I should have else possibly remained unacquainted; writing letters with such fulness, frequency, and interest on the details of the work up to the summer of his death; that the measure of bulk in contribution is no gauge of his share in the result.

In the *Life of Frank Buckland* occur some words in relation to the church-bells of Ross, in Herefordshire, which may with some aptness illustrate our mutual relation to the book:

> "It is said that the Man of Ross" (John Kyrle) "was present at the casting of the tenor, or great bell, and that he took with him an old silver tankard, which, after drinking claret and sherry, he threw in, and had cast with the bell."

John Kyrle's was the most precious part of the metal run into the mould, but the shaping of the mould and the larger part of the material came from the labour of another hand.

At an early period of our joint work BURNELL sent me a fragment of an essay on the words which formed our subject, intended as the basis of an introduction. As it stands, this is too incomplete to print, but I have made use of it to some extent, and given some extracts from it in the Introduction now put forward.†

---

* The dedication was sent for press on 6th January; on the 13th, G. U. Y. departed to his rest.

† Three of the mottoes that face the title were also sent by him.

The alternative title (*Hobson-Jobson*) which has been given to this book (not without the expressed assent of my collaborator), doubtless requires explanation.

A valued friend of the present writer many years ago published a book, of great acumen and considerable originality, which he called *Three Essays*, with no Author's name; and the resulting amount of circulation was such as might have been expected. It was remarked at the time by another friend that if the volume had been entitled *A Book, by a Chap*, it would have found a much larger body of readers. It seemed to me that *A Glossary* or *A Vocabulary* would be equally unattractive, and that it ought to have an alternative title at least a little more characteristic. If the reader will turn to *Hobson-Jobson* in the Glossary itself, he will find that phrase, though now rare and moribund, to be a typical and delightful example of that class of Anglo-Indian *argot* which consists of Oriental words highly assimilated, perhaps by vulgar lips, to the English vernacular; whilst it is the more fitted to our book, conveying, as it may, a veiled intimation of dual authorship. At any rate, there it is; and at this period my feeling has come to be that such *is* the book's name, nor could it well have been anything else.

In carrying through the work I have sought to supplement my own deficiencies from the most competent sources to which friendship afforded access. Sir JOSEPH HOOKER has most kindly examined almost every one of the proof-sheets for articles dealing with plants, correcting their errors, and enriching them with notes of his own. Another friend, Professor ROBERTSON SMITH, has done the like for words of Semitic origin, and to him I owe a variety of interesting references to the words treated of, in regard to their occurrence, under some cognate form, in the Scriptures. In the early part of the book the Rev. GEORGE MOULE (now Bishop of Ningpo), then in England, was good enough to revise those articles which bore on expressions used in China (not the first time that his generous aid had been given to work of mine). Among other friends who have been ever ready with assistance I may mention Dr. REINHOLD ROST, of the India Library; General ROBERT MACLAGAN, R.E.; Sir GEORGE BIRDWOOD, C.S.I.; Major-General R. H. KEATINGE, V.C., C.S.I.; Professor TERRIEN DE LA COUPERIE; and Mr. E. COLBORNE BABER, at present Consul-General in Corea. Dr. J. A. H. MURRAY, editor of the great English Dictionary, has also been most kind and courteous in the interchange of communications, a circumstance which will account for a few cases in which the passages cited in both works are the same.

My first endeavour in preparing this work has been to make it accurate; my next to make it—even though a Glossary—interesting. In a work intersecting so many fields, only a fool could imagine that he had not fallen into many mistakes; but these when pointed out, may be amended. If I have missed the other object of endeavour, I fear there is little to be hoped for from a second edition.

H. YULE.

5th January 1886.

PREFACE TO THE SECOND EDITION.

THE twofold hope expressed in the closing sentence of Sir Henry Yule's Preface to the original Edition of this book has been amply justified. More recent research and discoveries have, of course, brought to light a good deal of information which was not accessible to him, but the general accuracy of what he wrote has never been seriously impugned—while those who have studied the pages of *Hobson-Jobson* have agreed in classing it as unique among similar works of reference, a volume which combines interest and amusement with instruction, in a manner which few other Dictionaries, if any, have done.

In this edition of the *Anglo-Indian Glossary* the original text has been reprinted, any additions made by the Editor being marked by square brackets. No attempt has been made to extend the vocabulary, the new articles being either such as were accidentally omitted in the first edition, or a few relating to words which seemed to correspond with the general scope of the work. Some new quotations have been added, and some of those included in the original edition have been verified and new references given. An index to words occurring in the quotations has been prepared.

I have to acknowledge valuable assistance from many friends. Mr. W. W. SKEAT has read the articles on Malay words, and has supplied many notes. Col. Sir R. TEMPLE has permitted me to use several of his papers on Anglo-Indian words, and has kindly sent me advance sheets of that portion of the Analytical Index to the first edition by Mr. C. PARTRIDGE, which is being published in the *Indian Antiquary*. Mr. R. S. WHITEWAY has given me numerous extracts from Portuguese writers; Mr. W. FOSTER, quotations from unpublished records in the India Office; Mr. W. IRVINE, notes on the later Moghul period. For valuable suggestions and information on disputed points I am indebted to Mr.

H. Beveridge, Sir G. Birdwood, Mr. J. Brandt, Prof. E. G. Browne, Mr. M. Longworth Dames, Mr. G. R. Dampier, Mr. Donald Ferguson, Mr. C. T. Gardner, the late Mr. E. J. W. Gibb, Prof. H. A. Giles, Dr. G. A. Grierson, Mr. T. M. Horsfall, Mr. L. W. King, Mr. J. L. Myres, Mr. J. Platt, jun., Prof. G. U. Pope, Mr. V. A. Smith, Mr. C. H. Tawney, and Mr. J. Weir.

W. CROOKE.

14*th November* 1902.

CONTENTS.

INTRODUCTORY REMARKS.

WORDS of Indian origin have been insinuating themselves into English ever since the end of the reign of Elizabeth and the beginning of that of King James, when such terms as *calico, chintz*, and *gingham* had already effected a lodgment in English warehouses and shops, and were lying in wait for entrance into English literature. Such outlandish guests grew more frequent 120 years ago, when, soon after the middle of last century, the numbers of Englishmen in the Indian services, civil and military, expanded with the great acquisition of dominion then made by the Company; and we meet them in vastly greater abundance now.

Vocabularies of Indian and other foreign words, in use among Europeans in the East, have not unfrequently been printed. Several of the old travellers have attached the like to their narratives; whilst the prolonged excitement created in England, a hundred years since, by the impeachment of Hastings and kindred matters, led to the publication of several glossaries as independent works; and a good many others have been published in later days. At the end of this Introduction will be found a list of those which have come under my notice, and this might no doubt be largely added to.*

Of modern Glossaries, such as have been the result of serious labour, all, or nearly all, have been of a kind purely technical, intended to facilitate the comprehension of official documents by the explanation of terms used in the Revenue department, or in other branches of Indian administration. The most notable examples are (of brief and occasional character), the Glossary appended to the famous *Fifth Report* of the Select Committee of 1812, which was compiled by Sir Charles Wilkins; and (of a far more vast and comprehensive sort), the late Professor Horace Hayman Wilson's *Glossary of Judicial and Revenue Terms* (4to, 1855) which leaves far behind every other attempt in that kind.†

That kind is, however, not ours, as a momentary comparison of a page or two in each Glossary would suffice to show. Our work indeed, in the long course of its compilation, has gone through some modification and enlargement of scope; but hardly such as in any degree to affect its distinctive character, in which something has been aimed at differing in form from any work known to us. In its original conception it was intended to deal with all that class of words which, not in general pertaining to the technicalities of administration, recur constantly in the daily intercourse of the English in India, either as expressing ideas really not provided for by

---

* See Note A. at end of Introduction.

† Professor Wilson's work may perhaps bear re-editing, but can hardly, for its purpose, be superseded. The late eminent Telugu scholar, Mr. C. P. Brown, interleaved, with criticisms and addenda, a copy of Wilson, which is now in the India Library. I have gone through it, and borrowed a few notes, with acknowledgment by the initials C. P. B. The amount of improvement does not strike me as important.

our mother-tongue, or supposed by the speakers (often quite erroneously) to express something not capable of just denotation by any English term. A certain percentage of such words have been carried to England by the constant reflux to their native shore of Anglo-Indians, who in some degree imbue with their notions and phraseology the circles from which they had gone forth. This effect has been still more promoted by the currency of a vast mass of literature, of all qualities and for all ages, dealing with Indian subjects; as well as by the regular appearance, for many years past, of Indian correspondence in English newspapers, insomuch that a considerable number of the expressions in question have not only become familiar in sound to English ears, but have become naturalised in the English language, and are meeting with ample recognition in the great Dictionary edited by Dr. Murray at Oxford.

Of words that seem to have been admitted to full franchise, we may give examples in *curry*, *toddy*, *veranda*, *cheroot*, *loot*, *nabob*, *teapoy*, *sepoy*, *cowry;* and of others familiar enough to the English ear, though hardly yet received into citizenship, *compound*, *batta*, *pucka*, *chowry*, *baboo*, *mahout*, *aya*, *nautch*,* first-*chop*, competition-*wallah*, *griffin*, &c. But beyond these two classes of words, received within the last century or so, and gradually, into half or whole recognition, there are a good many others, long since fully assimilated, which really originated in the adoption of an Indian word, or the modification of an Indian proper name. Such words are the three quoted at the beginning of these remarks, *chintz*, *calico*, *gingham*, also *shawl*, *bamboo*, *pagoda*, *typhoon*, *monsoon*, *mandarin*, *palanquin*,† &c., and I may mention among further examples which may perhaps surprise my readers, the names of three of the boats of a man-of-war, viz. the *cutter*, the *jolly-boat*, and the *dingy*, as all (probably) of Indian origin.‡ Even phrases of a different character—slang indeed, but slang generally supposed to be vernacular as well as vulgar—*e.g.* '*that is the cheese*';‡ or supposed to be vernacular and profane—*e.g.* 'I don't care a *dam*'‡—are in reality, however vulgar they may be, neither vernacular nor profane, but phrases turning upon innocent Hindustani vocables.

We proposed also, in our Glossary, to deal with a *selection* of those administrative terms, which are in such familiar and quotidian use as to form part of the common Anglo-Indian stock, and to trace all (so far as possible) to their true origin—a matter on which, in regard to many of the words, those who hourly use them are profoundly ignorant—and to follow them down by quotation from their earliest occurrence in literature.

A particular class of words are those indigenous terms which have been adopted in scientific nomenclature, botanical and zoological. On these Mr. Burnell remarks:—

"The first Indian botanical names were chiefly introduced by Garcia de Orta (*Colloquios*, printed at Goa in 1563), C. d'Acosta (*Tractado*, Burgos, 1578), and Rhede van Drakenstein (*Hortus Malabaricus*, Amsterdam, 1682). The Malay names were chiefly introduced by Rumphius (*Herbarium Am-*

* *Nautch*, it may be urged, *is* admitted to full franchise, being used by so eminent a writer as Mr. Browning. But the fact that his use is entirely *misuse*, seems to justify the classification in the text (see GLOSS., s.v.). A like remark applies to *compound*. See for the tremendous fiasco made in its intended use by a most intelligent lady novelist, the last quotation s.v. in GLOSS.

† GLOSS., s.v. (note p. 659, col. *a*), contains quotations from the Vulgate of the passage in Canticles iii. 9, regarding King Solomon's *ferculum* of Lebanon cedar. I have to thank an old friend for pointing out that the word *palanquin* has, in this passage, received solemn sanction by its introduction into the Revised Version.

‡ See these words in GLOSS.

boinense, completed before 1700, but not published till 1741). The Indian zoological terms were chiefly due to Dr. F. Buchanan, at the beginning of this century. Most of the N. Indian botanical words were introduced by Roxburgh."

It has been already intimated that, as the work proceeded, its scope expanded somewhat, and its authors found it expedient to introduce and trace many words of Asiatic origin which have disappeared from colloquial use, or perhaps never entered it, but which occur in old writers on the East. We also judged that it would add to the interest of the work, were we to investigate and make out the pedigree of a variety of geographical names which are or have been in familiar use in books on the Indies; take as examples *Bombay*, *Madras*, *Guardafui*, *Malabar*, *Moluccas*, *Zanzibar*, *Pegu*, *Sumatra*, *Quilon*, *Seychelles*, *Ceylon*, *Java*, *Ava*, *Japan*, *Doab*, *Punjab*, &c., illustrating these, like every other class of word, by quotations given in chronological series.

Other divagations still from the original project will probably present themselves to those who turn over the pages of the work, in which we have been tempted to introduce sundry subjects which may seem hardly to come within the scope of such a glossary.

The words with which we have to do, taking the most extensive view of the field, are in fact organic remains deposited under the various currents of external influence that have washed the shores of India during twenty centuries and more. Rejecting that derivation of *elephant* * which would connect it with the Ophir trade of Solomon, we find no existing Western term traceable to that episode of communication; but the Greek and Roman commerce of the later centuries has left its fossils on both sides, testifying to the intercourse that once subsisted. *Agallochum*, *carbasus*, *camphor*, *sandal*, *musk*, *nard*, *pepper* (*πέπερι*, from Skt. *pippali*, 'long pepper'), *ginger* (*ζιγγίβερις*, see under *Ginger*), *lac*, *costus*, *opal*, *malabathrum* or *folium indicum*, *beryl*, *sugar* (*σάκχαρ*, from Skt. *sarkara*, Prak. *sakkara*), *rice* (*ὄρυζα*, but see s.v.), were products or names, introduced from India to the Greek and Roman world, to which may be added a few terms of a different character, such as *Βραχμᾶνες*, *Σαρμάνες* (*śramaṇas*, or Buddhist ascetics), *ξύλα σαγαλῖνα καὶ σασαμῖνα* (logs of teak and shīsham), the *σάγγαρα* (rafts) of the Periplus (see *Jangar* in Gloss.); whilst *dīnāra*, *dramma*, perhaps *kastīra* ('tin,' *κασσίτερος*), *kastūrī* ('musk,' *καστόριον*, properly a different, though analogous animal product), and a very few more, have remained in Indian literature as testimony to the same intercourse.†

The trade and conquests of the Arabs both brought foreign words to India and picked up and carried westward, in form more or less corrupted, words of Indian origin, some of which have in one way or other become part of the heritage of all succeeding foreigners in the East. Among terms which are familiar items in the Anglo-Indian colloquial, but which had, in some shape or other, found their way at an early date into use on the shores of the Mediterranean, we may instance *bazaar*, *cazee*, *hummaul*, *brinjaul*, *gingely*, *safflower*, *grab*, *maramut*, *dewaun* (dogana, douane, &c.). Of others which are found in medieval literature, either West-Asiatic or European, and which still have a place in Anglo-Indian or English vocabulary, we may mention *amber*-gris, *chank*, *junk*, *jogy*, *kincob*, *kedgeree*, *fanam*, *calay*, *bankshall*, *mudiliar*, *tindal*, *cranny*.

---

* See this word in Gloss.

† See A. Weber, in *Indian Antiquary*, ii. 143 *seqq*. Most of the other Greek words, which he traces in Sanskrit, are astronomical terms derived from books.

The conquests and long occupation of the Portuguese, who by the year 1540 had established themselves in all the chief ports of India and the East, have, as might have been expected, bequeathed a large number of expressions to the European nations who have followed, and in great part superseded them. We find instances of missionaries and others at an early date who had acquired a knowledge of Indian languages, but these were exceptional.* The natives in contact with the Portuguese learned a bastard variety of the language of the latter, which became the *lingua franca* of intercourse, not only between European and native, but occasionally between Europeans of different nationalities. This Indo-Portuguese dialect continued to serve such purposes down to a late period in the last century, and has in some localities survived down nearly to our own day.† The number of people in India claiming to be of Portuguese descent was, in the 17th century, very large. Bernier, about 1660, says :—

"For he (Sultan Shujā', Aurangzeb's brother) much courted all those *Portugal* Fathers, Missionaries, that are in that Province. . . . And they were indeed capable to serve him, it being certain that in the kingdom of *Bengale* there are to be found not less than eight or nine thousand families of *Franguis, Portugals*, and these either Natives or Mesticks." (*Bernier*, E.T. of 1684, p. 27.)

A. Hamilton, whose experience belonged chiefly to the end of the same century, though his book was not published till 1727, states :—

"Along the Sea-coasts the *Portuguese* have left a Vestige of their Language, tho' much corrupted, yet it is the Language that most *Europeans* learn first to qualify them for a general Converse with one another, as well as with the different inhabitants of *India*." (*Preface*, p. xii.)

Lockyer, who published 16 years before Hamilton, also says :—

"This they (the *Portugueze*) may justly boast, they have established a kind of *Lingua Franca* in all the Sea Ports in *India*, of great use to other *Europeans*, who would find it difficult in many places to be well understood without it." (*An Account of the Trade in India*, 1711, p. 286.)

The early Lutheran Missionaries in the South, who went out for the S.P.C.K., all seem to have begun by learning Portuguese, and in their diaries speak of preaching occasionally in Portuguese.‡ The foundation of this *lingua franca* was the Portuguese of the beginning of the 16th century ; but it must have soon degenerated, for by the beginning of the last century it had lost nearly all trace of inflexion.§

It may from these remarks be easily understood how a large number of

* Varthema, at the very beginning of the 16th century, shows some acquaintance with Malayālam, and introduces pieces of conversation in that language. Before the end of the 16th century, printing had been introduced at other places besides Goa, and by the beginning of the 17th, several books in Indian languages had been printed at Goa, Cochin, and Ambalakkādu.—(A. B.)

† "At Point de Galle, in 1860, I found it in common use, and also, somewhat later, at Calecut."—(A. B.)

‡ See "Notices of Madras and Cuddalore, &c., by the earlier Missionaries." Longman, 1858, *passim*. See also *Manual*, &c. in BOOK-LIST, *infra* p. xxxix. Dr Carey, writing from Serampore as late as 1800, says that the children of Europeans by native women, whether children of English, French, Dutch, or Danes, were all called Portuguese. *Smith's Life of Carey*, 152.

§ See Note B. at end of Introductory Remarks. "Mr. Beames remarked some time ago that most of the names of places in South India are greatly disfigured in the forms used by Europeans. This is because we have adopted the Portuguese orthography. Only in this way it can be explained how Kolladam has become *Côleroon*, Solamandalam, *Coromandel*, and Tuttukkudi, *Tuticorin*." (A. B.) Mr. Burnell was so impressed with the excessive corruption of S. Indian names, that he would hardly ever willingly venture any explanation of them, considering the matter all too uncertain.

our Anglo-Indian colloquialisms, even if eventually traceable to native sources (and especially to Mahratti, or Dravidian originals) have come to us through a Portuguese medium, and often bear traces of having passed through that alembic. Not a few of these are familiar all over India, but the number current in the South is larger still. Some other Portuguese words also, though they can hardly be said to be recognized elements in the Anglo-Indian colloquial, have been introduced either into Hindustani generally, or into that shade of it which is in use among natives in habitual contact with Europeans. Of words which are essentially Portuguese, among Anglo-Indian colloquialisms, persistent or obsolete, we may quote *goglet, gram, plantain, muster, caste, peon, padre, mistry* or *maistry, almyra, aya, cobra, mosquito, pomfret, cameez, palmyra,* still in general use; *picotta, rolong, pial, fogass, margosa,* preserved in the South; *batel, brab, foras, oart, vellard* in Bombay; *joss, compradore, linguist* in the ports of China; and among more or less obsolete terms, *Moor,* for a Mahommedan, still surviving under the modified form *Moorman,* in Madras and Ceylon; *Gentoo,* still partially kept up, I believe, at Madras in application to the Telugu language, *mustees, castees, bandeja* ('a tray'), *Kittysol* ('an umbrella,' and this survived ten years ago in the Calcutta customs tariff), *cuspadore* ('a spittoon'), and *covid* ('a cubit or ell'). Words of native origin which bear the mark of having come to us through the Portuguese may be illustrated by such as *palanquin, mandarin, mangelin* (a small weight for pearls, &c.) *monsoon, typhoon, mango, mangosteen, jack-fruit, batta, curry, chop, congee, coir, cutch, catamaran, cassanar, nabob, avadavat, betel, areca, benzoin, corge, copra.** A few examples of Hindustani words borrowed from the Portuguese are *chābī* ('a key'), *bāola* ('a portmanteau'), *bāltī* ('a bucket'), *martol* ('a hammer'), *tauliya* ('a towel,' Port. *toalha*), *sābūn* ('soap'), *bāsan* ('plate' from Port. *bacia*), *līlām* and *nīlām* ('an auction'), besides a number of terms used by Lascars on board ship.

The Dutch language has not contributed much to our store. The Dutch and the English arrived in the Indies contemporaneously, and though both inherited from the Portuguese, we have not been the heirs of the Dutch to any great extent, except in Ceylon, and even there Portuguese vocables had already occupied the colloquial ground. *Petersilly,* the word in general use in English families for 'parsley,' appears to be Dutch. An example from Ceylon that occurs to memory is *burgher.* The Dutch admitted people of mixt descent to a kind of citizenship, and these were distinguished from the pure natives by this term, which survives. *Burgher* in Bengal means 'a rafter,' properly *bargā.* A word spelt and pronounced in the same way had again a curiously different application in Madras, where it was a corruption of *Vaḍagar,* the name given to a tribe in the Nilgherry hills;—to say nothing of Scotland, where Burghers and Antiburghers were Northern tribes (*veluti* Gog *et* Magog!) which have long been condensed into elements of the United Presbyterian Church——!

Southern India has contributed to the Anglo-Indian stock words that are in hourly use also from Calcutta to Peshawur (some of them already noted under another cleavage), *e.g. betel, mango, jack, cheroot, mungoose, pariah, bandicoot, teak, patcharee, chatty, catechu, tope* ('a grove'), *curry, mulligatawny, congee. Mamooty* (a digging tool) is familiar in certain branches of the

* The nasal termination given to many Indian words, when adopted into European use, as in *palanquin, mandarin,* &c., must be attributed mainly to the Portuguese; but it cannot be entirely due to them. For we find the nasal termination of *Achīn,* in Mahommedan writers (see p. 3), and that of *Cochin* before the Portuguese time (see p. 225), whilst the conversion of *Pasei,* in Sumatra, into *Pacem,* as the Portuguese call it, is already indicated in the *Basma* of Marco Polo.

service, owing to its having long had a place in the nomenclature of the Ordnance department. It is Tamil, *manvĕtti*, 'earth-cutter.' Of some very familiar words the origin remains either dubious, or matter only for conjecture. Examples are *hackery* (which arose apparently in Bombay), *florican*, *topaz*.

As to Hindustani words adopted into the Anglo-Indian colloquial the subject is almost too wide and loose for much remark. The habit of introducing these in English conversation and writing seems to prevail more largely in the Bengal Presidency than in any other, and especially more than in Madras, where the variety of different vernaculars in use has tended to make their acquisition by the English less universal than is in the north that of Hindustani, which is so much easier to learn, and also to make the use in former days of Portuguese, and now of English, by natives in contact with foreigners, and of French about the French settlements, very much more common than it is elsewhere. It is this bad habit of interlarding English with Hindustani phrases which has so often excited the just wrath of high English officials, not accustomed to it from their youth, and which (*e.g.*) drew forth in orders the humorous indignation of Sir Charles Napier.

One peculiarity in this use we may notice, which doubtless exemplifies some obscure linguistic law. Hindustani *verbs* which are thus used are habitually adopted into the quasi-English by converting the imperative into an infinitive. Thus to *bunow*, to *lugow*, to *foozilow*, to *puckarow*, to *dumbcow*, to *sumjow*, and so on, almost *ad libitum*, are formed as we have indicated.*

It is curious to note that several of our most common adoptions are due to what may be most especially called the Oordoo (*Urdū*) or 'Camp' language, being terms which the hosts of Chinghiz brought from the steppes of North Eastern Asia—*e.g.* "The old *Bukshee* is an awful *bahadur*, but he keeps a first-rate *bobachee*." That is a sentence which might easily have passed without remark at an Anglo-Indian mess-table thirty years ago—perhaps might be heard still. Each of the outlandish terms embraced in it came from the depths of Mongolia in the thirteenth century. *Chick* (in the sense of a cane-blind), *daroga*, *oordoo* itself, are other examples.

With the gradual assumption of administration after the middle of last century, we adopted into partial colloquial use an immense number of terms, very many of them Persian or Arabic, belonging to technicalities of revenue and other departments, and largely borrowed from our Mahommedan predecessors. Malay has contributed some of our most familiar expressions, owing partly to the ceaseless rovings among the Eastern coasts of the Portuguese, through whom a part of these reached us, and partly doubtless to the fact that our early dealings and the sites of our early factories lay much more on the shores of the Eastern Archipelago than on those of Continental India. *Paddy*, *godown*, *compound*, *bankshall*, *rattan*, *durian*, *a-muck*, *prow*, and *cadjan*, *junk*, *crease*, are some of these. It is true that several of them may be traced eventually to Indian originals, but it seems not the less certain that we got them through the Malay, just as we got words already indicated through the Portuguese.

We used to have a very few words in French form, such as *boutique* and *mort-de-chien*. But these two are really distortions of Portuguese words.

A few words from China have settled on the Indian shores and been adopted by Anglo-India, but most of them are, I think, names of fruits or

* The first five examples will be found in GLOSS. *Banāo*, is imperative of *banā-nā*, 'to fabricate'; *lagāo* of *lagā-nā*, 'to lay alongside,' &c.; *sumjhāo*, of *samjhā-nā*, 'to cause to understand,' &c.

other products which have been imported, such as *loquot*, *leechee*, *chow-chow*, *cumquat*, *ginseng*, &c. and (recently) *jinrickshaw*. For it must be noted that a considerable proportion of words much used in Chinese ports, and often ascribed to a Chinese origin, such as *mandarin*, *junk*, *chop*, *pagoda*, and (as I believe) *typhoon* (though this is a word much debated) are not Chinese at all, but words of Indian languages, or of Malay, which have been precipitated in Chinese waters during the flux and reflux of foreign trade.

Within my own earliest memory Spanish dollars were current in England at a specified value if they bore a stamp from the English mint. And similarly there are certain English words, often obsolete in Europe, which have received in India currency with a special stamp of meaning; whilst in other cases our language has formed in India new compounds applicable to new objects or shades of meaning. To one or other of these classes belong *outcry*, *buggy*, *home*, *interloper*, *rogue* (-elephant), *tiffin*, *furlough*, *elk*, *roundel* ('an umbrella,' obsolete), *pish-pash*, *earth-oil*, *hog-deer*, *flying-fox*, *garden-house*, *musk-rat*, *nor-wester*, *iron-wood*, *long-drawers*, *barking-deer*, *custard-apple*, *grass-cutter*, &c.

Other terms again are corruptions, more or less violent, of Oriental words and phrases which have put on an English mask. Such are *maund*, *fool's rack*, *bearer*, *cot*, *boy*, *belly-band*, *Penang-lawyer*, *buckshaw*, *goddess* (in the Malay region, representing Malay *gādīs*, 'a maiden'), *compound*, *college-*pheasant, *chopper*, *summer-head*,* *eagle-wood*, *jackass-*copal, *bobbery*, *Upper Roger* (used in a correspondence given by Dalrymple, for *Yuva Raja*, the 'Young King,' or Caesar, of Indo-Chinese monarchies), *Isle-o'-Bats* (for Allahābād or *Ilahābāz* as the natives often call it), *hobson-jobson* (see Preface), *St. John's*. The last proper name has at least three applications. There is "St. John's" in Guzerat, viz. *Sanjān*, the landing-place of the Parsee immigration in the 8th century; there is another "St. John's" which is a corruption of *Shang-Chuang*, the name of that island off the southern coast of China whence the pure and ardent spirit of Francis Xavier fled to a better world: there is the group of "St. John's Islands" near Singapore, the chief of which is properly Pulo-*Sikajang*.

Yet again we have hybrids and corruptions of English fully accepted and adopted as Hindustani by the natives with whom we have to do, such as *simkin*, *port-shrāb*, *brandy-pānī*, *apīl*, *rasīd*, *tumlet* (a tumbler), *gilās* ('glass,' for drinking vessels of sorts), *rail-ghārī*, *lumber-dār*, *jail-khāna*, *bottle-khāna*, *buggy-khāna*, 'et omne quod exit in' *khāna*, including *gymkhāna*, a very modern concoction (q.v.), and many more.

Taking our subject as a whole, however considerable the philological interest attaching to it, there is no disputing the truth of a remark with which Burnell's fragment of intended introduction concludes, and the application of which goes beyond the limit of those words which can be considered to have 'accrued as additions to the English language': "Considering the long intercourse with India, it is noteworthy that the additions which have thus accrued to the English language are, from the intellectual standpoint, of no intrinsic value. Nearly all the borrowed words refer to material facts, or to peculiar customs and stages of society, and, though a few of them furnish allusions to the penny-a-liner, they do not represent new ideas."

It is singular how often, in tracing to their origin words that come within the field of our research, we light upon an absolute dilemma, or bifurcation, *i.e.* on two or more sources of almost equal probability, and in themselves

* This is in the Bombay ordnance nomenclature for a large umbrella. It represents the Port. *sombrero!*

entirely diverse. In such cases it may be that, though the use of the word *originated* from one of the sources, the existence of the other has invigorated that use, and contributed to its eventual diffusion.

An example of this is *boy*, in its application to a native servant. To this application have contributed both the old English use of *boy* (analogous to that of *puer*, *garçon*, *Knabe*) for a camp-servant, or for a slave, and the Hindī-Marāṭhī *bhoi*, the name of a caste which has furnished palanquin and umbrella-bearers to many generations of Europeans in India. The habitual use of the word by the Portuguese, for many years before any English influence had touched the shores of India (*e.g. bóy de sombrero, bóy d'aguoa, bóy de palanquy*), shows that the earliest source was the Indian one.

Cooly, in its application to a carrier of burdens, or performer of inferior labour, is another example. The most probable origin of this is from a *nomen gentile*, that of the *Kolīs*, a hill-people of Guzerat and the Western Ghats (compare the origin of *slave*). But the matter is perplexed by other facts which it is difficult to connect with this. Thus, in S. India, there is a Tamil word *kūli*, in common use, signifying 'daily hire or wages,' which H. H. Wilson regards as the true origin of the word which we call *cooly*. Again, both in Oriental and Osmali Turkish, *kol* is a word for a slave, and in the latter also there is *kūleh*, 'a male slave, a bondsman.' *Khol* is, in Tibetan also, a word for a slave or servant.

Tank, for a reservoir of water, we are apt to derive without hesitation, from *stagnum*, whence Sp. *estanc*, old Fr. *estang*, old Eng. and Lowland Scotch *stank*, Port. *tanque*, till we find that the word is regarded by the Portuguese themselves as Indian, and that there is excellent testimony to the existence of *tānkā* in Guzerat and Rajputana as an indigenous word, and with a plausible Sanskrit etymology.

Veranda has been confidently derived by some etymologists (among others by M. Defrémery, a distinguished scholar) from the Pers. *barāmada*, 'a projection,' a balcony; an etymology which is indeed hardly a possible one, but has been treated by Mr. Beames (who was evidently unacquainted with the facts that do make it hardly possible) with inappropriate derison, he giving as the unquestionable original a Sanskrit word *baraṇḍa*, 'a portico.' On this Burnell has observed that the word does not belong to the older Sanskrit, but is only found in comparatively modern works. Be that as it may, it need not be doubted that the word *veranda*, as used in England and France, was imported from India, *i.e.* from the usage of Europeans in India; but it is still more certain that either in the same sense, or in one closely allied, the word existed, quite independent of either Sanskrit or Persian, in Portuguese and Spanish, and the manner in which it occurs in the very earliest narrative of the Portuguese adventure to India (*Roteiro do Viagem de Vasco da Gama*, written by one of the expedition of 1497), confirmed by the Hispano-Arabic vocabulary of Pedro de Alcalà, printed in 1505, preclude the possibility of its having been adopted by the Portuguese from intercourse with India.

Mangrove, John Crawfurd tells us, has been adopted from the Malay *manggi-manggi*, applied to trees of the genus *Rhizophora*. But we learn from Oviedo, writing early in the sixteenth century, that the name *mangle* was applied by the natives of the Spanish Main to trees of the same, or a kindred genus, on the coast of S. America, which same *mangle* is undoubtedly the parent of the French *manglier*, and not improbably therefore of the English form *mangrove*.*

* Mr. Skeat's *Etym. Dict.* does not contain *mangrove.* [It will be found in his *Concise Etymological Dict.* ed. 1901.]

The words *bearer*, *mate*, *cotwal*, partake of this kind of dual or doubtful ancestry, as may be seen by reference to them in the Glossary.

Before concluding, a word should be said as to the orthography used in the Glossary.

My intention has been to give the headings of the articles under the most usual of the popular, or, if you will, vulgar quasi-English spellings, whilst the Oriental words, from which the headings are derived or corrupted, are set forth under precise transliteration, the system of which is given in a following "Nota Bene." When using the words and names in the course of discursive elucidation, I fear I have not been consistent in sticking either always to the popular or always to the scientific spelling, and I can the better understand why a German critic of a book of mine, once upon a time, remarked upon the *etwas schwankende yulische Orthographie*. Indeed it is difficult, it never will for me be possible, in a book for popular use, to adhere to one system in this matter without the assumption of an ill-fitting and repulsive pedantry. Even in regard to Indian proper names, in which I once advocated adhesion, with a small number of exceptions, to scientific precision in transliteration, I feel much more inclined than formerly to sympathise with my friends Sir William Muir and General Maclagan, who have always favoured a large and liberal recognition of popular spelling in such names. And when I see other good and able friends following the scientific Will-o'-the-Wisp into such bogs as the use in English composition of *sipâhî* and *jangal*, and *verandah*—nay, I have not only heard of *bagî*, but have recently seen it—instead of the good English words 'sepoy,' and 'jungle,' 'veranda,' and 'buggy,' my dread of pedantic usage becomes the greater.*

For the spelling of *Mahratta*, *Mahratti*, I suppose I must apologize (though something is to be said for it), *Marāṭhī* having established itself as orthodox.

NOTE A.—LIST OF GLOSSARIES.

1. Appended to the **Roteiro de Vasco da Gama** (see Book-list, p. xliii.) is a Vocabulary of 138 Portuguese words with their corresponding word in the *Lingua de Calicut*, *i.e.* in Malayālam.

2. Appended to the **Voyages**, &c., du Sieur **de la Boullaye-le-Gouz** (Book-list, p. xxxii.), is an *Explication de plusieurs mots dont l'intelligence est nécessaire au Lecteur* (pp. 27).

3. Fryer's New Account (Book-list, p. xxxiv.) has an *Index Explanatory*, including *Proper Names*, *Names of Things*, and *Names of Persons* (12 pages).

4. "**Indian Vocabulary**, to which is prefixed the Forms of Impeachment." 12mo. Stockdale, 1788 (pp. 136).

5. "An **Indian Glossary**, consisting of some Thousand Words and Forms commonly used in the East Indies . . . . extremely serviceable in assisting Strangers to acquire with Ease and Quickness the Language of that Country." By **T. T. Robarts**, Lieut., &c., of the 3rd Regt. Native Infantry, E.I. Printed for Murray & Highley, Fleet Street, 1800. 12mo. (not paged).

6. "A **Dictionary of Mohammedan Law**, Bengal Revenue Terms, Shanscrit, Hindoo, and other words used in the East Indies, with full explanations, the leading word used in each article being printed in a new Nustaluk Type," &c. By **S. Rousseau**. London, 1802. 12mo. (pp. lxiv.-287). Also 2nd ed. 1805.

---

* 'Buggy' of course is not an Oriental word at all, except as adopted from us by Orientals. I call *sepoy*, *jungle*, and *veranda*, good English words; and so I regard them, just as good as *alligator*, or *hurricane*, or *canoe*, or *Jerusalem* artichoke, or *cheroot*. What would my friends think of spelling these in English books as *alagarto*, and *huracan*, and *canoa*, and *girasole*, and *shuruṭṭu*?

7. **Glossary** prepared for the **Fifth Report** (see Book-list, p. xxxiv.), by Sir **Charles Wilkins.** This is dated in the preface "E. I. House, 1813." The copy used is a Parliamentary reprint, dated 1830.

8. The Folio compilation of the **Bengal Regulations**, published in 1828-29, contains in each volume a Glossarial Index, based chiefly upon the Glossary of Sir C. Wilkins.

9. In 1842 a preliminary "**Glossary of Indian Terms**," drawn up at the E. I. House by Prof. H. H. Wilson, 4to, unpublished, with a blank column on each page "for Suggestions and Additions," was circulated in India, intended as a basis for a comprehensive official Glossary. In this one the words are entered in the vulgar spelling, as they occur in the documents.

10. The only important result of the circulation of No. 9. was "**Supplement to the Glossary of Indian Terms,** A—J." By **H. M. Elliot**, Esq., Bengal Civil Service. Agra, 1845. 8vo. (pp. 447).

This remarkable work has been revised, re-arranged, and re-edited, with additions from Elliot's notes and other sources, by Mr. **John Beames**, of the Bengal Civil Service, under the title of "**Memoirs on the Folk-Lore and Distribution of the Races** of the North-Western Provinces of India, being an amplified edition of" (the above). 2 vols. 8vo. Trübner, 1869.

11. To "**Morley's Analytical Digest** of all the Reported Cases Decided in the Supreme Courts of Judicature in India," Vol. I., 1850, there is appended a "Glossary of Native Terms used in the Text" (pp. 20).

12. In "**Wanderings of a Pilgrim**" (Book-list, p. xlvi.), there is a Glossary of some considerable extent (pp. 10 in double columns).

13. "The **Zillah Dictionary** in the Roman character, explaining the Various Words used in Business in India." By **Charles Philip Brown**, of the Madras Civil Service, &c. Madras, 1852. Imp. 8vo. (pp. 132).

14. "A **Glossary of Judicial and Revenue** Terms, and of Useful Words occurring in Official Documents, relating to the Administration of the Government of British India, from the Arabic, Persian, Hindústání, Sanskrit, Hindí, Bengálí, Uriyá, Maráthí, Guzaráthí, Telugu, Karnáta, Támil, Mayalálam, and other languages. By **H. H. Wilson**, M.A., F.R.S., Boden Professor, &c." London, 1855. 4to. (pp. 585, besides copious Index).

15. A useful folio Glossary published by Government at Calcutta between 1860 and 1870, has been used by me and is quoted in the present GLOSS. as "Calcutta Glossary." But I have not been able to trace it again so as to give the proper title.

16. **Ceylonese Vocabulary.** See Book-list, p. xxxi.

17. "**Kachahri Technicalities,** or A Glossary of Terms, Rural, Official, and General, in Daily Use in the Courts of Law, and in Illustration of the Tenures, Customs, Arts, and Manufactures of Hindustan." By **Patrick Carnegy**, Commissioner of Rai Bareli, Oudh. 8vo. 2nd ed. Allahabad, 1877 (pp. 361).

18. "A **Glossary of Indian Terms,** containing many of the most important and Useful Indian Words Designed for the Use of Officers of Revenue and Judicial Practitioners and Students." Madras, 1877. 8vo. (pp. 255).

19. "**A Glossary of Reference** on Subjects connected with the Far East" (China and Japan). By **H. A. Giles.** Hong-Kong, 1878, 8vo. (pp. 182).

20. "**Glossary of Vernacular Terms** used in Official Correspondence in the Province of **Assam.**" Shillong, 1879. (Pamphlet).

21. "**Anglo-Indian Dictionary.** A Glossary of such Indian Terms used in English, and such English or other non-Indian terms as have obtained special meanings in India." By **George Clifford Whitworth,** Bombay Civil Service. London, 8vo, 1885 (pp. xv.—350).

Also the following minor Glossaries contained in Books of Travel or History:—

22. In "**Cambridge's Account** of the War in India," 1761 (Book-list, p. xxx.); 23. In "**Grose's Voyage,**" 1772 (Book-list, p. xxxv.); 24. In **Carraccioli's "Life of Clive"** (Book-list, p. xxx.); 25. In "**Bp. Heber's Narrative**" (Book-list, p. xxxvi.); 26. In **Herklot's "Qanoon-e-Islam** (Book-list, p. xxxv.); [27. In "**Verelst's View of Bengal,**" 1772; 28. "**The Malayan Words in English,**" by C. P. G. Scott, reprinted from the Journal of the American Oriental Society: New Haven, 1897; 29. "**Manual of the Administration of the Madras Presidency,**" Vol. III. Glossary, Madras, 1893. The name of the author of this, the most valuable book of the kind recently published in India, does not appear upon the title-page. It is believed to be the work of C. D. Macleane; 30. A useful Glossary of Malayālam words will be found in **Logan, "Manual of Malabar."**]

NOTE B.—THE INDO-PORTUGUESE PATOIS

(BY A. C. BURNELL.)

The phonetic changes of Indo-Portuguese are few. *F* is substituted for *p*; whilst the accent varies according to the race of the speaker.* The vocabulary varies, as regards the introduction of native Indian terms, from the same cause.

Grammatically, this dialect is very singular:

1. All traces of genders are lost—*e.g.* we find *sua povo* (Mat. i. 21); *sua nome* (Id. i. 23); *sua filho* (Id. i. 25); *sua filhos* (Id. ii. 18); *sua olhos* (Acts, ix. 8); *o dias* (Mat. ii. 1); *o rey* (Id. ii. 2); *hum voz tinha ouvido* (Id. ii. 18).
2. In the plural, *s* is rarely added; generally, the plural is the same as the singular.
3. The genitive is expressed by *de*, which is not combined with the article—*e.g. conforme de o tempo* (Mat. ii. 16); *Depois de o morte* (Id. ii. 19).
4. The definite article is unchanged in the plural: *como o discipulos* (Acts, ix. 19).
5. The pronouns still preserve some inflexions: *Eu, mi; nos, nossotros; minha, nossos*, &c.; *tu, ti, vossotros; tua, vossos; Elle, ella, ellotros, elles, sua, suas, lo, la.*
6. The verb substantive is (present) *tem*, (past) *timha*, and (subjunctive) *seja*.
7. Verbs are conjugated by adding, for the present, *te* to the only form, viz., the infinitive, which loses its final *r*. Thus, *te falla; te faze; te vi.* The past is formed by adding *ja*—e.g. *ja falla; ja olha.* The future is formed by adding *ser*. To express the infinitive, *per* is added to the Portuguese infinitive deprived of its *r*.

---

* Unfortunately, the translators of the Indo-Portuguese New Testament have, as much as possible, preserved the Portuguese orthography.

NOTA BENE

IN THE USE OF THE GLOSSARY

(A.) The dates attached to quotations are not always quite consistent. In beginning the compilation, the dates given were those of the *publication* quoted; but as the date of the *composition*, or of the use of the word in question, is often much earlier than the date of the book or the edition in which it appears, the system was changed, and, where possible, the date given is that of the actual use of the word. But obvious doubts may sometimes rise on this point.

The dates of *publication* of the works quoted will be found, if required, from the Book List, following this *Nota bene*.

(B.) The system of transliteration used is substantially the same as that modification of Sir William Jones's which is used in Shakespear's *Hindustani Dictionary*. But—

The first of the three Sanskrit sibilants is expressed by (*ś*), and, as in Wilson's Glossary, no distinction is marked between the Indian aspirated *k*, *g*, and the Arabic gutturals *kh*, *gh*. Also, in words transliterated from Arabic, the sixteenth letter of the Arabic alphabet is expressed by (*ṭ*). This is the same type that is used for the cerebral Indian (*ṭ*). Though it can hardly give rise to any confusion, it would have been better to mark them by distinct types. The fact is, that it was wished at first to make as few demands as possible for distinct types, and, having begun so, change could not be made.

The fourth letter of the Arabic alphabet is in several cases represented by (*th*) when Arabic use is in question. In Hindustani it is pronounced as (*s*).

Also, in some of Mr. Burnell's transliterations from S. Indian languages, he has used (R) for the peculiar Tamil hard (*r*), elsewhere (r), and (γ) for the Tamil and Malayālam (*k*) when preceded and followed by a vowel.

LIST OF FULLER TITLES OF BOOKS QUOTED IN THE GLOSSARY

Abdallatif. Relation de l'Egypte. *See* **De Sacy, Silvestre.**

Abel-Rémusat. Nouveaux Mélanges Asiatiques. 2 vols. 8vo. Paris, 1829.

Abreu, A. de. **Desc. de Malaca,** from the *Parnaso Portuguez.*

Abulghazi. H. des Mogols et des Tatares, par Aboul Ghazi, with French transl. by Baron Desmaisons. 2 vols. 8vo. St. Petersb., 1871.

Academy, The. A Weekly Review, &c. London.

Acosta, Christ. Tractado de las Drogas y Medecinas de las Indias Orientales. 4to. Burgos, 1578.

—— E. Hist. Rerum a Soc. Jesu in Oriente gestarum. Paris, 1572.

—— Joseph de. Natural and Moral History of the Indies, E.T. of Edward Grimstone, 1604. Edited for HAK. Soc. by C. Markham. 2 vols. 1880.

Adams, Francis. Names of all Minerals, Plants, and Animals described by the Greek authors, &c. (Being a Suppl. to Dunbar's Greek Lexicon.)

Aelian. Claudii Aeliani, De Natura Animalium, Libri XVII.

Āin. Āin-i-Akbari, The, by Abul Fazl 'Allami, tr. from the orig. Persian by H. Blochmann, M.A. Calcutta. 1873. Vol. i.; [vols. ii. and iii. translated by Col. H. S. Jarrett; Calcutta, 1891-94].

The MS. of the remainder disappeared at Mr. Blochmann's lamented death in 1878; a deplorable loss to Oriental literature.

—— (Orig.). The same. Edited in the **original** Persian by H. Blochmann, M.A. 2 vols. 4to. Calcutta, 1872. Both these were printed by the Asiatic Society of Bengal.

Aitchison, C. U. Collection of Treaties, Engagements, and Sunnuds relating to India and Neighbouring Countries, 8 vols. 8vo. Revised ed., Calcutta, 1876-78.

Ajaib-al-Hind. *See* **Merveilles.**

Albirûnî. Chronology of Ancient Nations E.T. by Dr. C. E. Sachau (Or. Transl. Fund). 4to. 1879.

Alcalà, Fray Pedro de. Vocabulista Arauigo en letra Castellana. Salamanca, 1505.

Ali Baba, Sir. Twenty-one Days in India, being the Tour of (by G. Aberigh Mackay). London, 1880.

[**Ali,** Mrs Meer Hassan, Observations on the Mussulmauns of India. 2 vols. London, 1832.

[**Allardyce,** A. The City of Sunshine. Edinburgh. 3 vols. 1877.

[**Allen,** B. C. Monograph on the Silk Cloths of Assam. Shillong, 1899.]

Amari. I Diplomi Arabi del R. Archivio Fiorentino. 4to. Firenze, 1863.

Anderson, Philip, A.M. The English in Western India, &c. 2nd ed. Revised. 1856.

Andriesz, G. Beschrijving der Reyzen. 4to. Amsterdam, 1670.

Angria Tulagee. Authentic and Faithful History of that Arch-Pyrate. London, 1756.

Annaes Maritimos. 4 vols. 8vo. Lisbon, 1840-44.

Anquetil du Perron. Le Zendavesta. 3 vols. Discours Preliminaire, &c. (in first vol.). 1771.

Aragon, Chronicle of King James of. E.T. by the late John Forster, M.P. 2 vols. imp. 8vo. [London, 1883.]

Arbuthnot, Sir A. Memoir of Sir T. Munro, prefixed to ed. of his Minutes. 2 vols. 1881.

Arch. Port. Or. Archivo Portuguez Oriental. A valuable and interesting collection published at Nova Goa, 1857 *seqq.*

Archivio Storico Italiano.

The quotations are from two articles in the *Appendice* to the early volumes, viz.:

(1) Relazione di Leonardo da Ca' Masser sopra il Commercio dei Portoghesi nell' India (1506). App. Tom. II. 1845.

(2) Lettere di Giov. da Empoli, e la Vita di Esso, scritta da suo zio (1530). App. Tom. III. 1846.

Arnold, Edwin. The Light of Asia (as told in Verse by an Indian Buddhist). 1879.

Assemani, Joseph Simonius, Syrus Maronita. Bibliotheca Orientalis Clementino-Vaticana. 3 vols. in 4, folio. Romae, 1719-1728.

Ayeen Akbery. By this spelling are distinguished quotations from the tr. of Francis Gladwin, first published at Calcutta in 1783. Most of the quotations are from the London edition, 2 vols. 4to. 1800.

Baber. Memoirs of Zehir-ed-din Muhammed Baber, Emperor of Hindustan. . . . Translated partly by the late John Leyden, Esq., M.D., partly by William Erskine, Esq., &c. London and Edinb., 4to. 1826.

Baboo and other Tales, descriptive of Society in India. Smith & Elder. London, 1834. (By Augustus Prinsep, B.C.S., a brother of James and H. Thoby Prinsep.)

Bacon, T. First Impressions of Hindustan. 2 vols. 1837.

Baden Powell. Punjab Handbook, vol. ii. Manufactures and Arts. Lahore, 1872.

Bailey, Nathan. *Diction. Britannicum*, or a more Compleat Universal Etymol. English Dict. &c. The whole Revis'd and Improv'd by N. B., Φιλόλογος. Folio. 1730.

Baillie, N. B. E. Digest of Moohummudan Law applied by British Courts in India. 2 vols. 1865-69.

Baker, Mem. of Gen. Sir W. E., R.E., K.C.B. Privately printed. 1882.

Balbi, Gasparo. Viaggio dell' Indie Orientali. 12mo. Venetia, 1590.

Baldaeus, P. Of this writer Burnell used the Dutch ed., Naauwkeurige Beschryvinge van Malabar en Choromandel, folio, 1672, and —— Ceylon, folio, 1672.

I have used the German ed., containing in one volume seriatim, Wahrhaftige Ausführliche Beschreibung der beruhmten Ost-Indischen Kusten Malabar und Coromandel, als auch der Insel Zeylon . . . benebst einer . . . Entdeckung der Abgöterey der Ost-Indischen Heyden. . . . Folio. Amsterdam, 1672.

Baldelli-Boni. Storia del Milione. 2 vols. Firenze, 1827.

Baldwin, Capt. J. H. Large and Small Game of Bengal and the N.W. Provinces of India. 1876.

Balfour, Dr. E. **Cyclopaedia of India**. [3rd ed. London, 1885.]

[**Ball**, J. D. Things Chinese, being Notes on various Subjects connected with China. 3rd ed. London, 1900.

Ball, V. Jungle Life in India, or the Journeys and Journals of an Indian Geologist. London, 1880.]

Banarus, Narrative of Insurrection at, in 1781. 4to. Calcutta, 1782. Reprinted at Roorkee, 1853.

Bányan Tree, The. A Poem. Printed for private circulation. Calcutta, 1856.

(The author was Lt.-Col. R. A. Yule, 9th Lancers, who fell before Delhi, June 19, 1857.)

Barbaro, Iosafa. Viaggio alla Tana, &c. In *Ramusio*, tom. ii. Also E.T. by W. Thomas, Clerk of Council to King Edward VI., embraced in Travels to Tana and Persia, Hak. Soc., 1873.

N.B.—It is impossible to discover from Lord Stanley of Alderley's Preface whether this was a reprint, or printed from an unpublished MS.

Barbier de Méynard, Dictionnaire Géogr. Hist. et Littér. de la Perse, &c. Extrait . . . de Yaqout. Par C. B. de M. Large 8vo. Paris, 1861.

Barbosa. A Description of the Coasts of E. Africa and Malabar in the beginning of the 16th century. By Duarte Barbosa. Transl. &c., by Hon. H. E. J. Stanley. Hak. Soc., 1866.

—— **Lisbon Ed.** Livro de Duarte Barbosa. Being No. VII. in Collecção de Noticias para a Historia e Geografia, &c. Publ. pela Academia Real das Sciencias, tomo ii. Lisboa, 1812.

—— Also in tom. ii. of Ramusio.

Barretto. Relation de la Province de Malabar. Fr. tr. 8vo. Paris, 1646.

Originally pub. in Italian. Roma, 1645.

Barros, João de. Decadas de Asia, Dos feitos que os Portuguezes fizeram na Conquista e Descubrimento das Terras e Mares do Oriente.

Most of the quotations are taken from the edition in 12mo., Lisboa, 1778, issued along with Couto in 24 vols.

The first Decad was originally printed in 1552, the 2nd in 1553, the 3rd in 1563, the 4th as completed by Lavanha in 1613 (Barbosa-Machado, Bibl. Lusit. ii. pp. 606-607, as corrected by Figanière, *Bibliogr. Hist. Port.* p. 169). A. B.

In some of Burnell's quotations he uses the 2nd ed. of Decs. i. to iii. (1628), and the 1st ed. of Dec. iv. (1613). In these there is apparently no division into chapters, and I have transferred the references to the edition of 1778, from which all my own quotations are made, whenever I could identify the passages, having myself no convenient access to the older editions.

Barth, A. Les Religions de l'Inde. Paris, 1879.

Also English translation by Rev. T. Wood. Trübner's Or. Series. 1882.

Bastian, Adolf, Dr. Die Völker des Oestlichen Asien, Studien und Reisen. 8vo. Leipzig, 1866—Jena, 1871.

Beale, Rev. Samuel. Travels of **Fah-hian** and Sung-yun, Buddhist Pilgrims from China to India. Sm. 8vo. 1869.

Beames, John. **Comparative Grammar** of the Modern Aryan Languages of India &c. 3 vols. 8vo. 1872-79.

—— See also in *List of Glossaries*.

Beatson, Lt.-Col. A. View of the Origin and Conduct of the War with Tippoo Sultaun. 4to. London, 1800.

[**Belcher**, Capt. Sir E. Narrative of the Voyage of H.M.S. Samarang, during the years 1843-46, employed surveying the Islands of the Eastern Archipelago. 2 vols. London, 1846.]

Bellew, H. W. Journal of a Political Mission to Afghanistan in 1857 under Major Lumsden. 8vo. 1862.

——— [The Races of Afghanistan, being A Brief Account of the Principal Nations inhabiting that Country. Calcutta and London, 1880.]

Belon, Pierre, du Mans. **Les Observations** de Plvsievrs Singularités et Choses memorables, trouuées en Grece, Asie, Iudée, Egypte, Arabie, &c. Sm. 4to. Paris, 1554.

Bengal, Descriptive Ethnology of, by Col. E. T. Dalton. Folio. Calcutta, 1872.

Bengal Annual, or Literary Keepsake, 1831-32.

Bengal Obituary. Calcutta, 1848. This was I believe an extended edition of De Rozario's 'Complete Monumental Register,' Calcutta, 1815. But I have not been able to recover trace of the book.

Benzoni, Girolamo. The Travels of, (1542-56), orig. Venice, 1572. Tr. and ed. by Admiral W. H. Smyth, HAK. SOC. 1857.

[**Berncastle**, J. Voyage to China, including a Visit to the Bombay Presidency. 2 vols. London, 1850.]

Beschi, Padre. *See* **Gooroo Paramarttan.**

[**Beveridge**, H. The District of Bakarganj, its History and Statistics. London, 1876.]

Bhotan and the History of the Dooar War. By Surgeon **Rennie**, M.D. 1866.

Bird's Guzerat. The Political and Statistical History of Guzerat, transl. from the Persian of Ali Mohammed Khan. Or. Tr. Fund. 8vo. 1835.

Bird, Isabella (now Mrs. Bishop). The **Golden Chersonese**, and the Way Thither. 1883.

Bird's Japan. Unbeaten Tracks in J. by Isabella B. 2 vols. 1880.

Birdwood (Sir) George, C.S.I., M.D. The Industrial Arts of India. 1880.

[——— Report on The Old Records of the India Office, with Supplementary Note and Appendices. Second Reprint. London, 1891.

[——— and Foster, W. The First Letter Book of the East India Company, 1600-19. London, 1893.]

[**Blacker**, Lt.-Col. V. Memoir of the British Army in India in 1817-19. 2 vols. London, 1821.

[**Blanford**, W. T. The Fauna of British India: Mammalia. London, 1888-91.

Blumentritt, Ferd. **Vocabular** einzelner Ausdrücke und Redensarten, welche dem Spanischen der Philippinschen Inseln eigenthümlich sind. Druck von Dr. Karl Pickert in Leitmeritz. 1882.

Bluteau, Padre D. Raphael. Vocabulario Portuguez Latino, Aulico, Anatomico, Architectonico, (and so on to Zoologico) . . . Lisboa, 1712-21. 8 vols. folio, with 2 vols. of Supplemento, 1727-28.

Bocarro. Decáda 13 da Historia da India, composta por Antonio B. (Published by the Royal Academy of Lisbon). 1876.

Bocarro. Detailed Report (Portuguese) upon the Portuguese Forts and Settlements in India, **MS.** transcript in India Office. Geog. Dept. from B.M. Sloane MSS. No. 197, fol. 172 *seqq.* Date 1644.

Bocharti Hierozoicon. In vol. i. of Opera Omnia, 3 vols. folio. Lugd. Bat. 1712.

Bock, Carl. Temples and Elephants. 1884.

Bogle. *See* **Markham's Tibet.**

Boileau, A. H. E. (Bengal Engineers). **Tour through the Western States of Rajwara** in 1835. 4to. Calcutta, 1837.

Boldensele, Gulielmus de. **Itinerarium** in the *Thesaurus* of *Canisius*, 1604. v. pt. ii. p. 95, also in ed. of same by *Basnage*, 1725, iv. 337; and by C. L. Grotefend in *Zeitschrift* des Histor. Vereins für Nieder Sachsen, Jahrgang 1852. Hannover, 1855.

Bole Pongis, by H. M. Parker. 2 vols. 8vo. 1851.

Bombay. A Description of the Port and Island of, and Hist. Account of the Transactions between the English and Portuguese concerning it, from the year 1661 to the present time. 12mo. Printed in the year 1724.

[**Bond**, E. A. Speeches of the Manager and Counsel in the Trial of Warren Hastings. 4 vols. London, 1859-61.]

Bongarsii, Gesta Dei der Francos. Folio. Hanoviae, 1611.

Bontius, Jacobi B. Hist. Natural et Medic. Indiae Orientalis Libri Sex. Printed with **Piso**, q.v.

[**Bose**, S. C. The Hindoos as they are: A Description of the Manners, Customs, and Inner Life of Hindoo Society in Bengal. Calcutta, 1881.

Bosquejo das Possessões, &c. See p. 809*b*.

[**Boswell**, J. A. C. Manual of the Nellore District. Madras, 1887.]

Botelho, Simão. Tombo do Estado da India. 1554. Forming a part of the **Subsidios**, q.v.

Bourchier, Col. (Sir George). Eight Months' Campaign against the Bengal Sepoy Army. 8vo. London, 1858.

Bowring, Sir John. The Kingdom and People of **Siam**. 2 vols. 8vo. 1857.

Boyd, Hugh. The Indian Observer, with Life, Letters, &c. By L. D. Campbell. London, 1798.

Briggs, H. Cities of Gujarashtra; their Topography and History Illustrated. 4to. Bombay, 1849.

Brigg's Firishta. H. of the Rise of the Mahomedan Power in India. Translated from the Orig. Persian of Mahomed Kasim Firishta. By John Briggs, Lieut-Col. Madras Army. 4 vols. 8vo. 1829.

[**Brinckman, A.** The Rifle in Cashmere: A Narrative of Shooting Expeditions. London, 1862.]

Brooks, T. Weights, Measures, Exchanges, &c., in East India. Small 4to. 1752.

Broome, Capt. Arthur. Hist. of the Rise and Progress of the **Bengal Army.** 8vo. 1850. Only vol. i. published.

Broughton, T. D. Letters written in a Mahratta Camp during the year 1809. 4to. 1813. [New ed. London, 1892.]

Bruce's Annals. Annals of the Honourable E. India Company. (1600-1707-8.) By John Bruce, Esq., M.P., F.R.S. 3 vols. 4to. 1810.

Brugsch Bey (Dr. Henry). Hist. of Egypt under the Pharaohs from the Monuments. E.T. 2nd ed. 2 vols. 1881.

Buchanan, Claudius, D.D. **Christian Researches** in Asia. 11th ed. 1819. Originally pubd. 1811.

Buchanan Hamilton, Fr. The Fishes of the Ganges River and its Branches. Oblong folio. Edinburgh, 1822.

[——— Also *see* **Eastern India.**

[**Buchanan,** Dr. Francis (afterwards Hamilton). A Journey . . . through . . . Mysore, Canara and Malabar . . . &c. 3 vols. 4to. 1807.]

Burckhardt, J. L. See p. 315*a*.

Burke, The **Writings** and Correspondence of the Rt. Hon. Edmund. 8 vols. 8vo. London, 1852.

Burman, The: His Life and Notions. By Shway Yoe. 2 vols. 1882.

Burnes, Alexander. Travels into Bokhara. 3 vols. 2nd ed. 1835.

[**Burnes, J.** A Visit to the Court of Scinde. London, 1831.]

Burnouf, Eugène. Introduction à l'Histoire du **Bouddhisme Indien.** (Vol. i. alone published.) 4to. 1844.

Burton, Capt. R. F. **Pilgrimage** to El Medina and Mecca. 3 vols. 1855-56.

[——— Memorial Edition. 2 vols. London, 1893.]

——— **Scinde,** or the Unhappy Valley. 2 vols. 1851.

——— **Sind Revisited.** 2 vols. 1877.

——— **Camoens.** *Os Lusiadas,* Englished by R. F. Burton. 2 vols. 1880. And 2 vols. of Life and Commentary, 1881.

——— **Goa** and the Blue Mountains. 1851.

[——— The Book of the Thousand Nights and a Night, translated from the Arabic by Capt. Sir R. F. Burton, edited by L. C. Smithers. 12 vols. London, 1894.]

Busbequii, A. Gislenii. Omnia quae extant. Amstelod. Elzevir. 1660.

[**Busteed,** H. E. Echoes of Old Calcutta. 3rd ed. Calcutta, 1857.

[**Buyers,** Rev. W. Recollections of Northern India. London, 1848.]

Cadamosto, Luiz de. **Navegação Primeira.** In Collecção de Noticias of the Academia Real das Sciencias. Tomo II. Lisboa, 1812.

Caldwell, Rev. Dr. (afterwards Bishop). A **Comparative Grammar** of the Dravidian or South Indian Family of Languages. 2nd ed. Revd. and Enlarged, 1875.

Caldwell, Right Rev. Bishop. Pol. and Gen. History of the District of **Tinnevelly.** Madras, 1881.

———, Dr. R. (now Bishop). Lectures on **Tinnevelly Missions.** 12mo. London, 1857.

Ca' Masser. Relazione di Lionardo in **Archivio Storico Italiano,** q.v.

Cambridge, R. Owen. An Account of the **War in India** between the English and French, on the Coast of Coromandel (1750-1760). 4to. 1761.

Cameron, J. Our Tropical Possessions in Malayan India. 1865.

Camões, Luiz de. **Os Lusiadas.** Folio ed. of 1720, and Paris ed., 8vo., of 1847 are those used.

[**Campbell,** Maj.-Gen. John. A Personal Narrative of Thirteen Years' Service among the Wild Tribes of Khondistan. London, 1864.

[**Campbell,** Col. W. The Old Forest Ranger. London, 1853.]

Capmany, Ant. Memorias Hist. sobre la Marina, Comercio, y Artes de Barcelona. 4 vols. 4to. Madrid, 1779.

Cardim, T. Relation de la Province du **Japon,** du Malabar, &c. (trad. du Portug.). Tournay, 1645.

[**Carey,** W. H. The Good Old Days of Honble. John Company. 2 vols. Simla, 1882.]

Carletti, Francesco. Ragionamenti di— Fiorentino, sopra le cose da lui vedute ne' suoi Viaggi, &c. (1594-1606). First published in Firenze, 1701. 2 vols. in 12mo.

Carnegy, Patrick. See *List of Glossaries.*

Carpini, Joannes de Plano. Hist. Mongalorum, ed. by D'Avezac, in Recueil de Voyages et de Mémoires de la Soc. de Géographie, tom. iv. 1837.

Carraccioli, C. Life of Lord Clive. 4 vols. 8vo. No date (c. 1785).

It is not certain who wrote this ignoble book, but the author must have been in India.

Castanheda, Fernão Lopez de. Historia do descobrimento e conquista da India.

The original edition appeared at Coimbra, 1551-1561 (in 8 vols. 4to and folio), and was reprinted at Lisbon in

1833 (8 vols. sm. 4to). This last ed. is used in quotations of the Port. text.
Castanheda was the first writer on Indian affairs (*Barbosa Machado, Bibl. Lusit.*, ii. p. 30. See also *Figanière, Bibliographia Hist. Port.*, pp. 165-167).
He went to Goa in 1528, and died in Portugal in 1559.

Castañeda. The First Booke of the Historie of the Discouerie and Conquest of the East Indias. . . . Transld. into English by N. L.(itchfield), Gentleman. 4to. London, 1582.
The translator has often altered the spelling of the Indian words, and his version is very loose, comparing it with the printed text of the Port. in the ed. of 1833. It is possible, however, that Litchfield had the first ed. of the first book (1551) before him, whereas the ed. of 1833 is a reprint of 1554. (A.B.).

Cathay and the Way Thither. By H. Yule, HAK. SOC. 8vo. 2 vols. (Continuously paged.) 1866.

[**Catrou**, F. F. A History of the Mogul Dynasty in India. London, 1826.]

Cavenagh, Lt.-Gen. Sir Orfeur. **Reminiscences** of an Indian Official. 8vo. 1884.

Ceylonese Vocabulary. List of Native Words commonly occurring in Official Correspondence and other Documents. Printed by order of the Government. Columbo, June 1869.

[**Chamberlain, B. H.** Things Japanese, being Notes on Various Subjects connected with Japan. 3rd ed. London, 1898.]

Chardin, Voyages en Perse. Several editions are quoted, *e.g.* Amsterdam, 4 vols. 4to, 1735; by Langlès, 10 vols. 8vo. 1811.

Charnock's Hist. of **Marine Architecture.** 2 vols. 1801.

Charters, &c., of the **East India Company** (a vol. in India Office without date).

Chaudoir, Baron Stan. Aperçu sur les Monnaies Russes, &c. 4to. St. Pétersbourg, 1836-37.

[**Chevers**, N. A. A Manual of Medical Jurisprudence for India. Calcutta, 1870.]

Childers, R. A **Dictionary** of the **Pali** Language. 1875.

Chitty, S. C. **The Ceylon Gazetteer.** Ceylon, 1834.

Chow Chow, being Selections from a Journal kept in India, &c., by Viscountess Falkland. 2 vols. 1857.

Cieza de Leon, Travels of Pedro. Ed. by C. Markham. HAK. SOC. 1864.

Clarke, Capt. H. W., R.E. Translation of the **Sikandar Nāma** of Nizāmī. London, 1881.

Clavijo. Itineraire de l'Ambassade Espagnole à Samarcande, in 1403-1406 (original Spanish, with Russian version by I. Sreznevevsky). St. Petersburg, 1881.

——— Embassy of Ruy Gonzalez de, to the Court of Timour. E.T. by C. Markham. HAK. SOC. 1859.

Cleghorn, Dr. Hugh. Forests and Gardens of S. India. 8vo. 1861.

Coast of Coromandel: Regulations for the Hon. Comp.'s Black Troops on the. 1787.

Cobarruvias, Tesoro de la Lengua Castellana o Española, compvesto per el Licenciado Don Sebastian de. Folio. Madrid, 1611.

Cocks, Richard. Diary of ———, Cape-Merchant in the English Factory at Japan (first published from the original MS. in the B. M. and Admiralty). Edited by Edward Maunde Thompson, 2 vols. HAK. SOC. 1883.

Cogan. *See* **Pinto.**

Colebrooke, Life of, forming the first vol. of the collection of his Essays, by his son, Sir E. Colebrooke. 1873.

Collet, S. The Brahmo Year-Book. Brief Records of Work and Life in the Theistic Churches of India. London, 1876 *seqq.*

Collingwood, C. Rambles of a Naturalist on Shores and Waters of the China Sea. 8vo. 1868.

Colomb, Capt. R.N. Slave-catching in the Indian Ocean. 8vo. 1873.

Colonial Papers. *See* **Sainsbury.**

Competition-wallah, Letters of a (by G. O. Trevelyan). 1864.

Complete Hist. of the War in India (Tract). 1761.

Conti, Nicolo. *See* **Poggius**; also see **India in the XVth Century.**

[**Cooper**, T. T. The Mishmee Hills, an Account of a Journey made in an Attempt to penetrate Thibet from Assam, to open out new Routes for Commerce. London, 1873.]

Cordiner, Rev. J. A. Description of **Ceylon**, &c. 2 vols. 4to. 1807.

Cornwallis, Correspondence of Charles, First Marquis. Edited by C. Ross. 3 vols. 1859.

Çorrea, Gaspar, Lendas da India por. This most valuable, interesting, and detailed chronicle of Portuguese India was not published till in our own day it was issued by the Royal Academy of Lisbon—4 vols. in 7, in 4to, 1858-1864. The author went to India apparently with Jorge de Mello in 1512, and at an early date began to make notes for his history. The latest year that he mentions as having in it written a part of his history is 1561. The date of his death is not known.
Most of the quotations from Correa, begun by Burnell and continued by me, are from this work published in Lisbon. Some are, however, taken from "The **Three Voyages of Vasco da Gama** and his Viceroyalty, from the Lendas da India of Gaspar Correa," by the Hon. E. J. Stanley (now Lord Stanley of Alderley). HAK. SOC. 1869.

Coryat, T. **Crudities.** Reprinted from the ed. of 1611. 3 vols. 8vo. 1776.

Couto, Diogo de. The edition of the **Decadas** da Asia quoted habitually is that of 1778 (see **Barros**). The 4th Decade (Couto's first) was published first in 1602, fol.; the 5th, 1612; the 6th, 1614; the 7th, 1616; the 8th, 1673; 5 books of the 12th, Paris, 1645. The 9th was first published in an edition issued in 1736; and 120 pp. of the 10th (when, is not clear). But the whole of the 10th, in ten books, is included in the publication of 1778. The 11th was lost, and a substitute by the editor is given in the ed. of 1778. Couto died 10th Dec. 1616.

——— **Dialogo** do Soldado Pratico (written in 1611, printed at Lisbon under the title Observações, &c., 1790).

Cowley, Abraham. His Six Books of **Plants**. In Works, folio ed. of 1700.

Crawfurd, John. **Descriptive Dict.** of the Indian Islands and adjacent countries. 8vo. 1856.

——— **Malay Dictionary**, A Grammar and Dict. of the Malay Language. Vol. i. Dissertation and Grammar. Vol. ii. Dictionary. London, 1852.

——— Journal of an Embassy to Siam and Cochin China. 2nd ed. 2 vols. 1838. (First ed. 4to, 1828.)

——— Journal of an Embassy to the Court of **Ava** in 1827. 4to. 1829.

[**Crooke**, W. The Popular Religion and Folk-lore of Northern India. 1st ed. 1 vol. Allahabad, 1893; 2nd ed. 2 vols. London, 1896.

[——— The Tribes and Castes of the North-Western Provinces and Oudh, 4 vols. Calcutta, 1896.]

Cunningham, Capt. Joseph Davy, B.E. History of the Sikhs, from the Rise of the Nation to the Battles of the Sutlej. 8vo. 2nd ed. 1853. (1st ed. 1849.)

Cunningham, Major Alex., B.E. **Ladak**, Physical, Statistical, and Historical. 8vo. 1854.

Cunningham, M.-Gen., R.E., C.S.I. (the same). Reports of the Archaeological Survey of India. Vol. i., Simla, 1871. Vol. xix., Calcutta, 1885.

Cyclades, The. By J. Theodore **Bent**. 8vo. 1885.

Dabistan, The; or, School of Manners. Transl. from the Persian by David Shea and Anthony Troyer. (Or. Tr. Fund.) 3 vols. Paris, 1843.

D'Acunha, **Dr**. Gerson. Contributions to the Hist. of Indo-**Portuguese Numismatics**. 4 fascic. Bombay, 1880 *seqq.*

Da Gama. *See* **Roteiro** and **Correa**.

D'Albuquerque, Afonso. Commentarios. Folio. Lisboa, 1557.

——— **Commentaries**, transl. and edited by Walter de Grey **Birch**. HAK. SOC. 4 vols. 1875-1884.

Dalrymple, A. The **Oriental Repertory** (originally published in numbers, 1791-97), then at the expense of the E.I. Co. 2 vols. 4to. 1808.

Damiani a Göes, Diensis Oppugnatio. Ed. 1602.

——— De Bello Cambaico.

——— **Chronica.**

Dampier's Voyages. (Collection including sundry others). 4 vols. 8vo. London, 1729.

[**Danvers**, F. C., and Foster W. Letters received by the E.I. Co. from its Servants in the East. 4 vols. London, 1896-1900.]

D'Anville. **Eclaircissemens** sur la Carte de l'Inde. 4to. Paris, 1753.

Darmesteter, James. Ormazd et Ahriman. 1877.

——— The Zendavesta. (Sacred Books of the East, vol. iv.) 1880.

Davidson, Col. C. J. (Bengal Engineers). Diary of Travels and Adventures in Upper India. 2 vols. 8vo. 1843.

Davies, T. Lewis O., M.A. A **Supplemental English Glossary**. 8vo. 1881.

Davis, Voyages and Works of John. Ed. by A. H. Markham. HAK. SOC. 1880.

[**Davy**, J. An Account of the Interior of Ceylon. London, 1821.]

Dawk Bungalow, The; or, Is his appointment pucka? (By G. O. Trevelyan). In Fraser's Mag., 1866, vol. lxiii. pp. 215-231 and pp. 382-391.

Day, Dr. Francis. The **Fishes of India.** 2 vols. 4to. 1876-1878.

De Bry, J. F. and J. "Indien Orientalis." 10 parts, 1599-1614.

The quotations from this are chiefly such as were derived through it by Mr. Burnell from Linschoten, before he had a copy of the latter. He notes from the *Biog. Univ.* that Linschoten's text is altered and re-arranged in De Bry, and that the Collection is remarkable for endless misprints.

De Bussy, Lettres de M., de Lally et autres. Paris, 1766.

De Candolle, Alphonse. **Origine** des Plantes Cultivées. 8vo. Paris, 1883.

De Castro, D. João de. Primeiro Roterio da Costa da India, desde Goa até Dio. Segundo MS. Autografo. Porto, 1843.

De Castro. Roteiro de Dom Joam, do Viagem que fizeram os Portuguezes ao Mar Roxo no Anno de 1541. Paris, 1833.

De Gubernatis, Angelo. Storia dei **Viaggiatori Italiani** nelle Indie Orientali. Livorno, 1875. 12mo. There was a previous issue containing much less matter.

De la Boullaye-le-Gouz, Voyages et Observations du Seigneur, Gentilhomme Angevin. Sm. 4to. Paris, 1653, and 2nd ed. 1657.

De la Loubère. Historical Relation of **Siam** by M. E.T. 2 vols. folio in one. 1693.

Della Tomba, Marco. Published by De Gubernatis. Florence, 1878.

Della Valle, Pietro. Viaggi de ——, il Pellegrino, descritti, da lui medesimo in Lettere Familiari . . . (1614 - 1626). Originally published at Rome, 1650-53. The Edition quoted is that published at Brighton (but printed at Turin), 1843. 2 vols. in small 8vo.

[—— From the O.E. Tr. of 1664, by G. Havers. 2 vols. ed. by E. Grey. HAK. SOC. 1891.]

Dellon. Relation de l'**Inquisition de Goa.** 1688. Also E.T., Hull, 1812.

De Monfart, H. An Exact and Curious Survey of all the East Indies, even to Canton, the chiefe citie of China. Folio. 1615. (A worthless book.)

De Morga, Antonio. **The Philippine Islands,** ed. by Hon. E. J. Stanley. HAK. SOC. 1868.

[**Dennys,** N.B. Descriptive Dictionary of British Malaya. London, 1894.]

De Orta, Garcia. *See* **Garcia.**

De Sacy, Silvestre. Chrestomathie Arabe. 2nd ed. 3 vols. Paris, 1826-27.

Desideri, P. Ipolito. MS. transcript of his Narrative of a residence in Tibet, belonging to the Hakluyt Society. 1714-1729.

Diccionario della Lengua **Castellana** compuesto por l'Academia Real. 6 vols. folio. Madrid, 1726-1739.

Dicty. of Words used in the **East Indies.** 2nd ed. 1805. (List of Glossaries, No. 6.).

Diez, Friedrich. **Etymologisches Wörterbuch** der Romanischen Sprachen. 2te. Ausgabe. 2 vols. 8vo. Bonn, 1861-62.

Dilemma, The. (A novel, by Col. G. Chesney, R.E.) 3 vols. 1875.

Dipavanso. The Dipavamso: edited and translated by H. Oldenberg. London, 1879.

Diplomi Arabi. *See* **Amari.**

Dirom. Narrative of the Campaign in India which terminated the War with Tippoo Sultan in 1792. 4to. 1793.

D'Ohsson, Baron C. Hist. des Mongols. La Haye et Amsterdam. 1834. 4 vols.

Dom Manuel of Portugal, **Letter of.** Reprint of old Italian version, by A. Burnell. 1881.
Also Latin in **Grynaeus,** Novus Orbis.

Dorn, Bernhard. **Hist. of the Afghans,** translated from the Persian of Neamet 'Allah. In Two Parts. 4to. (Or. Tr. Fund.) 1829-1836.

Dosabhai Framji. Hist. of the **Parsis.** 2 vols. 8vo. 1884.

Dostoyeffski. 1881. *See* p. 833*b*.

Douglas, Revd. Carstairs. Chinese-English Dictionary of the Vernacular or Spoken Language of Amoy. Imp. 8vo. London, 1873.

[**Douglas,** J. **Bombay** and Western India. 2 vols. London, 1893.]

Dowson. *See* **Elliot.**

Dozy and Engelmann. Glossaire des Mots Espagnols et Portugais derivés de l'Arabe, par R. D. et W. H. F. 2nd ed. Leide, 1869.

—— **Oosterlingen.** Verklarende Lijst der Nederlandsche Woorden die mit het Arabsch, Hebreeuwsch, Chaldeeuwsch, Perzisch, en Turksch afkomstig zijn, door R. Dozy. S' Gravenhage, 1867. (Tract.)

—— Supplément aux Dictionnaires Arabes. 2 vols. 4to.

Drake, The World Encompassed by Sir Francis (orig. 1628). Edited by W. S. W. Vaux. HAK. SOC. 1856.

Drummond, R. Illustrations of the Grammatical parts of Guzarattee, Mahrattee, and English Languages. Folio. Bombay, 1808.

Dry Leaves from Young Egypt, by an ex-Political (E. B. Eastwick). 1849.

Dubois, Abbé J. Desc. of the Character, Manners, &c., of the People of India. E.T. from French MS. 4to. 1817.

[**Dufferin** and **Ava,** Marchioness of. Our Viceregal Life in India. New edition. London, 1890.]

Dunn. A **New Directory** for the East Indies. London, 1780.

Du Tertre, P. Hist. Générale des **Antilles** Habitées par les François. Paris, 1667.

Eastern India, The History, Antiquities, Topography and Statistics of. By Montgomery Martin (in reality compiled entirely from the papers of Dr. **Francis Buchanan,** whose name does not appear at all in a very diffuse title-page!) 3 vols. 8vo. 1838.

Echoes of Old Calcutta, by H. E. Busteed. Calcutta, 1882. [3rd ed. Calcutta, 1897.]

[**Eden,** Hon. E. Up the Country. 2 vols. London, 1866.]

Eden, R. A. **Hist. of Trauayle,** &c. R. Jugge. Small 4to. 1577.

Edrisi. Géographie. (Fr. Tr.) par Amedée Jaubert. 2 vols. 4to. Paris, 1836. (Soc. de Géogr.)

[**Edwardes,** Major H. B. A Year on the Punjab Frontier. 2 vols. London, 1851.

[**Egerton,** Hon. W. An Illustrated Handbook of Indian Arms, being a Classified and Descriptive Catalogue of the Arms exhibited at the India Museum. London, 1880.]

Elgin, Lord. Letters and Journals of James Eighth Earl of E. Edited by T. Walrond. 1872.

Elliot. The Hist. of India as told by its own Historians. Edited from the Posth. Papers of Sir H. M. Elliot, K.C.B., by Prof. John **Dowson.** 8 vols. 8vo. 1867-1877.

Elliot, Sir Walter. Coins of S. India, belonging to the new ed. of Numismata Orientalia. Not yet issued (Nov. 1885).

Elphinstone, The Hon. **Mount-Stewart**, Life of, by Sir Edward Colebrooke, Bart. 2 vols. 8vo. 1884.

Elphinstone, The Hon. Mount-Stewart. Account of the Kingdom of **Caubool**. New edition. 2 vols. 8vo. 1839.

Emerson Tennent. An Account of the Island of **Ceylon**, by Sir James. 2 vols. 8vo. [3rd ed. 1859.] 4th ed. 1860.

Empoli, Giovanni da. Letters, in **Archivio** Storico Italiano, q.v.

Eredia. *See* **Godinho.**

Evelyn, John, Esq., F.R.S., The **Diary** of, from 1641 to 1705-6. (First published and edited by Mr. W. Bray in 1818.)

Fahian, or **Fah-hian.** *See* **Beale.**

Fallon, S. W. New Hindustani-English Dictionary. Banāras (Benares), 1879.

Fankwae, or Canton before Treaty Days: by an Old Resident. 1881.

Faria y Sousa (Manoel). **Asia Portuguesa.** 3 vols. folio. 1666-1675.

——— E.T. by Capt. J. Stevens. 3 vols. 8vo. 1695.

Favre, P. **Dictionnaire** Malais-Français et Français-Malais, 4 vols. Vienne, 1875-80.

Fayrer, (Sir) Joseph. **Thanatophidia** of India, being a Description of the Venomous Snakes of the Indian Peninsula. Folio. 1872.

Federici (or Fedrici). Viaggio de M. Cesare de F.— nell' India Orientale et oltra l'India. In Venetia, 1587. Also in vol. iii. of Ramusio, ed. 1606.

Ferguson. A Dictionary of the Hindostan Language. 4to. London, 1773.

Fergusson, James, D.C.L., F.R.S. Hist. of **Indian** and Eastern **Architecture**. 8vo. 1875.

[**Ferrier**, J. P. Caravan Journeys in Persia, Afghanistan, Turkestan, and Beloochistan. London, 1856.]

Fifth Report from the Select Committee of the House of Commons on the Affairs of the E.I. Company. Folio. 1812.

Filet, G. F. Plant-kundig Woordenboek voor Nederlandsch Indie. Leiden, 1876.

Firishta, Scott's. Ferishta's H. of the Dekkan from the great Mahommedan Conquests. Tr. by Capt. J. Scott. 2 vols. 4to. Shrewsbury, 1794.

——— **Briggs's.** *See* **Briggs.**

Flacourt, Hist. de la Grande isle **Madagascar**, composée par le Sieur de. 4to. 1658.

Flückiger. *See* **Hanbury.**

Fonseca, Dr. J. N. da. **Hist.** and Archæological Sketch of the City of **Goa**. 8vo. Bombay, 1878.

Forbes, A. Kinloch. *See* **Râs Mâlâ.**

[**Forbes**, Capt. C. J. F. S. British Burmah, and its People, being Sketches of Native Manners, Customs, and Religion. London, 1878.]

Forbes, Gordon S. Wild Life in Canara and Ganjam. 1885.

Forbes, James. Oriental Memoirs. 4 vols. 4to. 1813. [2nd ed. 2 vols. 1834.]

Forbes, H. O. A Naturalist's Wanderings in the Indian Archipelago. 1885.

Forbes Watson's Nomenclature. A List of Indian Products, &c., by J. F. W., M.A., M.D., &c. Part II., largest 8vo. 1872.

[——— The Textile Manufactures and the Costumes of the People of India. London, 1866.]

Forrest, Thomas. Voyage from Calcutta to the **Mergui** Archipelago, &c., by ——, Esq. 4to. London, 1792.

——— Voyage to **New Guinea** and the Moluccas from Balambangan, 1774-76. 4to. 1779.

Forster, George. **Journey** from Bengal to England. 2 vols. 8vo. London, 1808. Original ed., Calcutta, 1790.

Forsyth, Capt. J. Highlands of Central India, &c. 8vo. London, 1872. [2nd ed. London, 1899.]

Forsyth, Sir T. Douglas. Report of his **Mission** to Yarkund in 1873. 4to. Calcutta, 1875.

[**Foster.** *See* **Danvers**, F. C.

[**Francis**, E. B. Monograph on Cotton Manufacture in the Punjab. Lahore, 1884.

[**Francis**, Sir P. The Francis Letters, ed. by Beata Francis and Eliza Keary. 2 vols. London, 1901.]

Fraser, James Baillie. Journal of a Tour through Part of the Snowy Range of the Himālā Mountains. 4to. 1820.

[——— The Persian Adventurer. 3 vols. London, 1830.]

Frere, Miss M. **Deccan Days**, or Hindoo Fairy Legends current in S. India, 1868.

Frescobaldi, Lionardo. **Viaggi** in Terra Santa di L. F. ed. altri. Firenze, 1862; very small.

Friar Jordanus. *See* **Jordanus.**

Fryer, John, M.D. A New Account of **East India** and Persia, in 8 Letters; being 9 years Travels. Begun 1672. And Finished 1681. Folio. London, 1698.

No work has been more serviceable in the compilation of the Glossary.

Fullarton, Col. View of English Interests in India. 1787.

Galland, Antoine. Journal pendant son Séjour à Constantinople, 1672-73. Annoté par Ch. Schefer. 2 vols. 8vo. Paris, 1881.

Galvano, A. Discoveries of the World, with E.T. by Vice-Admiral Bethune, C.B. Hak. Soc., 1863.

Garcia. **Colloquios** dos Simples e Drogas e Cousas Medecinaes da India, e assi de Algumas Fructas achadas nella . . .

compostos pelo Doutor **Garcia de Orta.** Physico del Rei João 3°. 2a edição. Lisboa, 1872.

(Printed nearly page for page with the original edition, which was printed at Goa by João de Eredem in 1563.) A most valuable book, full of curious matter and good sense.

Garcin de Tassy. Particularités de la Religion Musulmane dans l'Inde. Paris, 1851.

Garden, In my Indian. By Phil. Robinson. 2nd ed. 1878.

Garnier, Francis. **Voyage d'Exploration** en Indo-Chine. 2 vols. 4to and two atlases. Paris, 1873.

Gildemeister. Scriptorum Arabum de Rebus Indicis Loci et Opuscula Inedita. Bonn, 1838.

Giles, Herbert A. Chinese Sketches. 1876.

——. *See List of Glossaries.*

Gill, Captain William. The **River of Golden Sand,** The Narrative of a Journey through China and Eastern Tibet to Burmah. 2 vols. 8vo. 1880. [Condensed ed., London, 1883.]

Gleig, Rev. G. R. Mem. of Warren Hastings. 3 vols. 8vo. 1841.

—— *See* **Munro.**

Glossographia, by T. B. (Blount). Folio ed. 1674.

Gmelin. Reise durch Siberien. 1773.

Godinho de Eredia, Malaca, L'Inde Meridionale et le Cathay, MS. orig. autographe de, reproduit et traduit par L. Janssen. 4to. Bruxelles, 1882.

Gooroo Pararmattan, writtten in Tamil by P. Beschi; E.T. by Babington. 4to. 1822.

Gouvea, A. de. Iornada do Arcebispo de Goa, D. Frey Aleixo de Menezes . . . quando foy as Serras de Malabar, &c. Sm. folio. Coimbra, 1606.

[**Gover,** C. E. The Folk-Songs of Southern India. Madras, 1871.]

Govinda Sámanta, or the History of a Bengal Ráiyat. By the Rev. Lál Behári Day, Chinsurah, Bengal. 2 vols. London, 1874.

Graham, Maria. Journal of a Residence in India. 4to. Edinburgh, 1812.

An excellent book.

Grainger, James. The Sugar-Cane, a Poem in 4 books, with notes. 4to. 1764.

Gramatica Indostana. Roma, 1778.

See p. 417*b*.

Grand Master, The, or Adventures of Qui Hi, by Quiz. 1816.

One of those would-be funny mountains of doggerel, begotten by the success of Dr Syntax, and similarly illustrated.

Grant, Colesworthy. Rural Life in Bengal. Letters from an artist in India to his Sisters in England. [The author died in Calcutta, 1883.] Large 8vo. 1860.

Grant, Gen. Sir Hope. Incidents in the Sepoy War, 1857-58. London, 1873.

Grant-Duff, Mount-Stewart Elph. Notes of an Indian Journey. 1876.

Greathed, Hervey. Letters written during the Siege of Delhi. 8vo. 1858.

[**Gribble,** J. D. B. Manual of Cuddapah. Madras, 1875.

[**Grierson,** G. A. Bihār Peasant Life. Calcutta, 1885.

[**Grigg,** H. B. Manual of the Nilagiri District. Madras, 1880.]

Groeneveldt. Notes on the Malay Archipelago, &c. From Chinese sources. Batavia, 1876.

Grose, Mr. A **Voyage** to the **East Indies,** &c. &c. In 2 vols. A new edition. 1772.

The first edition seems to have been pub. in 1766. I have never seen it. [The 1st ed., of which I possess a copy, is dated 1757.]

[**Growse,** F. S. Mathurá, a District Memoir. 3rd ed. Allahabad, 1883.]

Guerreiro, Fernan. **Relacion** Annual de las cosas que han hecho los Padres de la Comp. de J. . . . en (1)600 y (1)601, traduzida de Portuguez par Colaço. Sq. 8vo. Valladolid, 1604.

Gundert, Dr. Malayālam and English Dictionary. Mangalore, 1872.

Haafner, M. J. **Voyages** dans la Péninsule Occid. de l'Inde et dans l'Ile de Ceilan. Trad. du Hollandois par M. J. 2 vols. 8vo. Paris, 1811.

[**Hadi,** S. M. A Monograph on Dyes and Dyeing in the North-Western Provinces and Oudh. Allahabad, 1896.]

Hadley. *See* under **Moors, The,** in the Glossary.

Haeckel, Ernest. A Visit to Ceylon. E.T. by Clara Bell. 1883.

Haex, David. Dictionarium Malaico-Latinum et Latino-Malaicum. Romae, 1631.

Hajji Baba of Ispahan. Ed. 1835 and 1851. Originally pubd. 1824. 2 vols.

—— in England. Ed. in 1 vol. 1835 and 1850. Originally pubd. 1828. 2 vols.

Hakluyt. The references to this name are, with a very few exceptions, to the reprint, with many additions, in 5 vols. 4to. 1807.

Several of the additions are from travellers subsequent to the time of Richard Hakluyt, which gives an odd aspect to some of the quotations.

Halhed, N. B. **Code** of Gentoo Laws. 4to. London, 1776.

Hall, Fitz Edward. Modern English, 1873.

Hamilton, Alexander, Captain. A New Account of the East Indies.

The original publication (2 vols. 8vo.) was at Edinburgh, 1727; again published, London, 1744. I fear the quotations are from both; they differ to a small extent in the pagination. [Many of the references have now been checked with the edition of 1744.]

Hamilton, Walter. **Hindustan.** Geographical, Statistical, and Historical Description of Hindustan and the Adjacent Countries. 2 vols. 4to. London, 1820.

Hammer-Purgstall, Joseph. Geschichte der Goldenen Horde. 8vo. Pesth, 1840.

Hanbury and Flückiger. Pharmacographia: A Hist. of the Principal Drugs of Vegetable Origin. Imp. 8vo. 1874. There has been a 2nd ed.

Hanway, Jonas. Hist. Acc. of the British Trade over the Caspian Sea, with a Journal of **Travels**, &c. 4 vols. 4to. 1753.

[**Harcourt**, Capt. A. F. P. The Himalayan Districts of Kooloo, Lahoul, and Spiti. London, 1871.]

Hardy, Revd. Spence. Manual of **Buddhism** in its Modern Development.
The title-page in my copy says 1860, but it was first published in 1853.

Harrington, J. H. Elementary **Analysis** of the Laws and Regulations enacted by the G.-G. in C. at Fort William. 3 vols. folio. 1805-1817.

Haug, Martin. **Essays** on the Sacred Language, Writings, and Religion of the Parsis. 8vo. 1878.

Havart, Daniel, M.D. Op- en Ondergang van Coromandel. 4to. Amsterdam, 1693.

Hawkins. The Hawkins' Voyages. Hak. Soc. Ed. by C. Markham. 1878.

Heber, Bp. Reginald. **Narrative** of a Journey through the Upper Provinces of India. 3rd ed. 3 vols. 1878.
But most of the quotations are from the edition of 1844 (Colonial and Home Library). 2 vols. Double columns.

Hedges, Diary of Mr. (afterwards Sir) William, in Bengal, &c., 1681-1688.
The earlier quotations are from a MS. transcription, by date; the later, paged, from its sheets printed by the Hak. Soc. (still unpublished). [Issued in 2 vols., Hak. Soc. 1886.]

Hehn, V. **Kulturpflanzen** und **Hausthiere** in ihren Uebergang aus Asien nach Griechenland und Italien so wie in das übrige Europa. 4th ed. Berlin, 1883.

Heiden, T. Vervaerlyke Schipbreuk, 1675.

Herbert, Sir Thomas. Some Yeares **Travels** into Divers Parts of Asia and Afrique. Revised and Enlarged by the Author. Folio, 1638. Also 3rd ed. 1665.

Herklots, G. B. **Qanoon-e-Islam.** 1832. 2nd ed. Madras, 1863.

Heylin, Peter. **Cosmographie**, in 4 Books (paged as sep. volumes), folio, 1652.

Heyne, Benjamin. **Tracts** on India. 4to 1814.

Hodges, William. Travels in India during the Years 1780-83. 4to. 1793.

[**Hoey**, W. A Monograph on Trade and Manufactures in Northern India, Lucknow. 1880.]

Hoffmeister. Travels. 1848.

Holland, Philemon. The Historie of the World, commonly called The Natvrall Historie of **C. Plinivs** Secvndvs. . . . Tr. into English by P. H., Doctor in Physic. 2 vols. Folio. London, 1601.

Holwell, J. Z. Interesting **Historical Events** Relative to the Province of Bengal and the Empire of Indostan, &c. Part I. 2nd ed. 1766. Part II. 1767.

Hooker (Sir) Jos. Dalton. Himalayan Journals. Notes of a Naturalist, &c. 2 vols. Ed. 1855.

[**Hoole**, E. Madras, Mysore, and the South of India, or a Personal Narrative of a Mission to those Countries from 1820 to 1828. London, 1844.]

Horsburgh's India Directory. Various editions have been used.

Houtman. Voyage. *See* **Spielbergen.** I believe this is in the same collection.

Huc et Gabet. Souvenirs d'un Voyage dans la Tartarie, le Thibet, et la Chine pendant les Années 1844, 1845, et 1846. 2 vols. 8vo. Paris 1850. [E.T. by W. Hazlitt. 2 vols. London, 1852.]

[**Hügel**, Baron Charles. Travels in Kashmir and the Panjab, with notes by Major T. B. Jervis. London, 1845.

[**Hughes**, T. P. A Dictionary of Islam. London, 1885.]

Hulsius. Collection of Voyages, 1602-1623.

Humāyūn. Private **Mem.** of the Emperor. Tr. by Major C. Stewart. (Or. Tr. Fund.) 4to. 1832.

Humboldt, W. von. Die Kawi Sprache auf der Insel Java. 3 vols. 4to. Berlin, 1836-38.

Hunter, W. W. **Orissa.** 2 vols. 8vo. 1872.

Hyde, Thomas. Syntagma Dissertationum, 2 vols. 4to. Oxon., 1767.

Hydur Naik, Hist. of, by Meer Hussein Ali Khan Kirmani. Trd. by Col. W. Miles. (Or. Tr. Fund). 8vo. 1842.

[**Ibbetson**, D. C. J. Outlines of Panjab Ethnography. Calcutta, 1883.]

Ibn Baithar. Heil und Nahrungsmittel von Abu Mohammed Abdallah . . . bekannt unter dem Namen Ebn Baithar. (Germ. Transl. by Dr. Jos. v. Sontheimer). 2 vols. large 8vo. Stuttgart, 1840.

Ibn Batuta. Voyages d'Ibn Batoutah, Texte Arabe, accompagné d'une Traduction par C. De Frémery et le Dr. B. R. Sanguinetti (Société Asiatique). 4 vols. Paris, 1853-58.

Ibn Khallikan's Biographical Dictionary. Tr. from the Arabic by Baron McGuckin de Slane. 4 vols. 4to. Paris, 1842-71.

India in the XVth Century. Being a Coll. of Narratives of Voyages to India, &c. Edited by R. H. Major, Esq., F.S.A. Hak. Soc. 1857.

Indian Administration of Lord Ellenborough. Ed. by Lord Colchester. 8vo. 1874.

Indian Antiquary, The, a Journal of Oriental Research. 4to. Bombay, 1872, and succeeding years till now.

Indian Vocabulary. See *List of Glossaries.*

Intrigues of a Nabob. By H. F. Thompson. *See* under **Nabob** in GLOSSARY.

Isidori Hispalensis Opera. Folio. Paris, 1601.

Ives, Edward. A **Voyage** from England to India in the year 1754, &c. 4to. London, 1773.

Jacquemont Victor. **Correspondance** avec sa Famille, &c. (1828-32). 2 vols. Paris, 1832.

——— (English Translation.) 2 vols. 1834.

Jagor, F. Ost-Indische Handwerk und Gewerbe. 1878.

Jahanguier, **Mem.** of the Emperor, tr. by Major D. Price (Or. Tr. Fund). 4to. 1829.

Jal, A. **Archéologie Navale.** 2 vols. large 8vo. Paris, 1840.

Japan. A Collection of Documents on Japan, with comment. by Thomas Rundall, Esq. HAK. Soc. 1850.

Jarric, P. (S.J.). Rerum Indicarum **Thesaurus.** 3 vols. 12mo. Coloniae, 1615-16.

Jenkins, E. The Coolie. 1871.

Jerdon's Birds. The Birds of India, being a Natural Hist. of all the Birds known to inhabit Continental India, &c. Calcutta, 1862.

The quotations are from the Edition issued by Major Godwin Austen. 2 vols. (in 3). Calcutta, 1877.

——— **Mammals.** The Mammals of India, A Nat. Hist. of all the Animals known to inhabit Continental India. By T. C. Jerdon, Surgeon-Major Madras Army. London, 1874.

[**Johnson**, D. Sketches of Field Sports as followed by the Natives of India. London, 1822.]

Joinville, Jean Sire de. **Hist. de Saint Louis**, &c. Texte et Trad. par M. Natalis de Wailly. Large 8vo. Paris, 1874.

Jones, Mem. of the Life, Writings, and Correspondence of **Sir William.** By Lord Teignmouth. Orig. ed., 4to., 1804. That quoted is—2nd ed. 8vo., 1807.

Jordanus, **Friar**, **Mirabilia** Descripta (c. 1328). HAK. Soc. 1863.

J. Ind. Arch. Journal of the Indian Archipelago, edited by Logan. Singapore, 1847, *seqq.*

Julien, Stanislas. *See* **Pèlerins.**

Kaempfer Engelbert. Hist. Naturelle, Civile et Ecclesiastique du Japon. Folio. La Haye. 1729.

——— **Am. Exot.** Amœnitatum Exoticarum . . . Fasciculi V. . . . Auctore Engelberto Kæmpfero, D. Sm. 4to. Lemgoviæ, 1712.

Khozeh Abdulkurreem, Mem. of, tr. by **Gladwin.** Calcutta, 1788.

Kinloch, A. A. Large Game Shooting in Thibet and the N.W.P. 2nd Series. 4to. 1870.

Kinneir, John Macdonald. Geogr. Memoir of the **Persian Empire.** 4to. 1813.

[**Kipling**, J. L. Beast and Man in India, a Popular Sketch of Indian Animals in their Relations with the People. London, 1892.]

Kircher, Athan. **China** Monumentis, &c. Illustrata. Folio. Amstelod. 1667.

Kirkpatrick, Col. Account of **Nepaul**, 4to. 1811.

Klaproth, Jules. **Magasin Asiatique.** 2 vols. 8vo. 1825.

Knox, Robert. An Historical Relation of the Island of **Ceylon** in the East Indies, &c. Folio. London, 1681.

Kuzzilbash, The (By J. B. Fraser). 3 vols. 1828.

La Croze, M. V. **Hist. du Christianisme** des Indes. 12mo. A la Haye, 1724.

La Roque. Voyage to Arabia the Happy, &c. E.T. London, 1726. (French orig. London, 1715.)

La Rousse, **Dictionnaire Universel** du XIXe Siècle. 16 vols. 4to. 1864-1878.

Lane's Modern Egyptians, ed. 2 vols. 1856.

——— Do., ed. 1 vol. 8vo. 1860.

——— **Arabian Nights**, 3 vols. 8vo. 1841.

[**Le Fanu**, H. Manual of the Salem District. 2 vols. Madras, 1883.]

Leland, C. G. **Pidgin-English** Sing-song, 16mo. 1876.

[**Leman**, G. D. Manual of the Ganjam District. Madras, 1882.]

Lembrança de Cousas da India em 1525, forming the last part of **Subsidios**, q.v.

Letter to a Proprietor of the E. India Company. (Tract.) 1750.

Letters of Simpkin the Second on the Trial of Warren Hastings. London, 1791.

Letters from Madras during the years 1836-1839. By a Lady. [Julia Charlotte Maitland.] 1843.

Lettres Edifiantes et Curieuses. 1st issue in 34 Recueils. 12mo. 1717 to 1774. 2nd do. re-arranged, 26 vols. 1780-1783.

Leunclavius. Annales Sultanorum Othmanidarum. Folio ed. 1650.

An earlier ed. 4to. Francof. 1588, in the B. M., has autograph notes by Jos. Scaliger.

Lewin, Lt.-Col. T. A Fly on the Wheel, or How I helped to Govern India. 8vo. 1885. An excellent book.

[——— The Wild Races of South-Eastern India. London, 1870.]

Leyden, John. Poetical Remains, with Memoirs of his Life, by Rev. J. **Morton.** London, 1819.

(Burnell has quoted from a reprint at Calcutta of the Life, 1823.)

Life in the Mofussil, by an Ex-Civilian. 2 vols. 8vo. 1878.

Light of Asia, or the Great Renunciation. As told in verse by an Indian Buddhist. By **Edwin Arnold**. 1879.

Lindsays, Lives of The, or a Mem. of the House of Crawford and Balcarres. By Lord Lindsay. 3 vols. 8vo. 1849.

Linschoten. Most of the quotations are from the old English version: Iohn Hvighen van Linschoten, his Discours of Voyages into Ye Easte and Weste Indies. Printed at London by Iohn Wolfe, 1598—either from the black-letter folio, or from the reprint for the HAK. Soc. (2 vols. 1885), edited by Mr. Burnell and Mr. P. Tiele. If not specified, they are from the former.

The original Dutch is: "Itinerarie Voyage ofter Schipvaert van Jan Huygen van Linschoten." To T'Amstelredam, 1596.

Littré, E. Dict. de la Langue Française. 4 vols. 4to., 1873-74, and 1 vol. SUPPT., 1877.

Livros das Monções. (Collecçao de Monumentos Ineditos). Publd. by R. Academy of Lisbon. 4to. Lisbon, 1880.

[**Lloyd**, Sir W. Gerard. Capt. A. A Narrative of a Journey from Caunpoor to the Boorendo Pass in the Himalaya Mountains. 2 vols. London, 1840.]

Lockyer, Charles. An Account of the Trade in India, &c. London, 1711.

[**Logan**, W. Malabar. 3 vols. Madras, 1887-91.]

Long, Rev. James. Selections from Unpublished Records of Government (Fort William) for the years 1748-1767. Calcutta, 1869.

Lord. Display of two forraigne Sects in the East Indies. 1. A Discouerie of the Sect of the Banians. 2. The Religion of the Persees. Sm. 4to. 1630.

Lowe, Lieut. C. R. History of the Indian Navy. 2 vols. 8vo. 1877.

Lubbock, Sir John. Origin of Civilisation. 1870.

Lucena, P. João de. Hist da Vida do Padre F. de Xavier. Folio. Lisbon, 1600.

Ludolphus, Job. Historia Aethiopica Francof. ad Moenum. Folio. 1681.

Luillier. Voyage du Sieur, aux Grandes Indes. 12mo. Paris, 1705. Also E. T., 1715.

Lutfullah. Autobiog. of a Mahomedan Gentleman. Ed. by E. B. Eastwick. 1857.

Macarius. Travels of the Patriarch. E.T. by F. C. Belfour (Or. Trans. Fund). 4to. 1829.

McCrindle, J. W. Ancient India as described by Megasthenes and Arrian. 8vo. 1877.

——— Transl. of the Periplus Maris Erythraei, and of Arrian's Voyage of Nearchus. 1879.

M'Crindle, J. W. Ancient India as described by Ktesias the Knidian. 1882.

——— Ancient India as described by Ptolemy. 1885.

[——— The Invasion of India by Alexander the Great. New ed. London, 1896.]

Macdonald, D., M.D. A Short Account of the Fisheries of the Bombay Presidency (prepared for the great Fisheries Exhibition of 1883).

Macgregor, Col. (now Sir Charles). A Journey through Khorassan. 2 vols. 1875.

Mackenzie. Storms and Sunshine of a Soldier's Life. By Mrs. Colin Mackenzie. 2 vols. 8vo. 1882.

[——— Life in the Mission, the Camp, and the Zenáná, or Six Years in India. 2nd ed. London, 1854.]

Mackenzie Collection. Desc. Catalogue of. By H. H. Wilson. 2 vols. 8vo. Calcutta, 1828.

Mackintosh, Capt. A. An Account of the Origin and Present Condition of the Tribe of Ramoosies, &c. Bombay, 1833.

[**Maclagan**, E. D. Monograph on the Gold and Silver Works of the Punjab. Lahore, 1890.]

MacLennan, J. F. An Inquiry into the origin of the form of Capture in Marriage Ceremonies. Edinburgh, 1865.

[**McMahon**, Lieut.-Col. A. R. The Karens of the Golden Chersonese. London, 1876.]

McNair, Major. Perak and the Malays. 1878.

Madras, or Fort St. George. Dialogues written originally in the Naruga or Gentou language. By B. S. V. Halle, 1750. (German).

Maffeus, Joannes Petrus, E. S. J. Historiarum Indicarum Libri XVI. Ed. Vienna, 1751.

——— also Selectarum Epistolarum ex India Libri IV. Folio. (Hist. first pubd. at Florence, 1588).

Maine, Sir Henry S. Village Communities. 3rd ed. 1876.

——— Early History of Institutions. 1875.

Makrizi. Hist. des Sultans Mamlouks de l'Egypte par . . . trad. par M. Quatremère. (Or. Transl. Fund). 2 vols. 4to. 1837-1842.

Malaca Conquistada pelo Grande Af. de Alboquerque. A Poem by Fr. de Sa de Menezes. 4to. 1634.

Malcolm, Sir John. Hist. of Central India. 1st ed. 1823; 2nd, 1824; 3rd, 1832. 2 vols.

——— Hist. of Persia. 2 vols. 4to. 1815. [New ed. 2 vols. 1829.]

——— Life of Robert, Lord Clive. 3 vols. 1836.

Malcolm's Anecdotes of the Manners and Customs of London during the 18th Century. 4to. 1808.

Mandelslo, Voyages and Travels of J. A., into the E. Indies, E.T. 1669. Folio.

Manning. *See* **Markham's Tibet.**

Manual ou Breue Instructção que serue por Uso D'as Crianças, que Aprendem Ler, e comêçam rezar nas Escholas Portuguezas, que são em India Oriental; e especialmente na Costa dos Malabaros que se chama Coromandel. Anno 1713. (In Br. Museum. No place or Printer. It is a Protestant work, no doubt of the first Danish missionaries of the S.P.G. It contains a prayer "A oração por a Illustrissima Companhia da India Oriental.")

Manual of the Geology of India. Large 8vo. 2 parts by Medlicott and Blanford. Calcutta, 1879. Part 3 by V. Ball, M.A. Economic Geology, 1881.

Marcel Devic. Dictionnaire Etymologique des Mots d'origine orientale. In the Supplemental Vol. of Littré. 1877.

Marini. Hist. Nouuelle et Cvrievse des Royaumes de Tunquin et de Lao. Trad. de l'Italien. Paris, 1666.

Marino Sanudo. Secretorum Fidelium Crucis. *See* **Bongarsius**, of whose work it forms the 2nd part.

Markham, C. R., C.B. Travels in Peru and India. 1862.

——— Clavijo. Narr. of Embassy of Ruy Gonzalez de C. to the Court of Timour (1403-6). Tra. and Ed. by C. R. M. Hak. Soc. 1859.

———**'s Tibet.** Narrative of the Mission of G. Bogle to Tibet; and of the Journey of Thomas Manning to Lhasa. 8vo. 1876.

[——— A Memoir of the Indian Surveys. 2nd ed. London, 1878.]

Marmol, El Veedor Lvys de. Descripcion General de **Africa**; Libro Tercero, y Segundo Volumen de la Primera parte. En Granada, 1573.

Marre. Kata-Kata Malayou, ou Recueil des Mots Malais Françisés, par Avis-Marre (Ext. from Compte Rendu du Congrès Prov. des Orientalistes). Paris, 1875.

Marsden, W. Memoirs of a Malayan Family, transl. from the original by, (O. T. F.). 1830.

——— **History of Sumatra.** 2nd ed. 4to. 1784; 3rd ed. 4to. 1811.

——— **Dictionary** of the Malayan Language. In two Parts. 4to. 1812.

——— A Brief Mem. of his Life and Writings. Written by Himself. 4to. 1838.

Martinez de la Puente. Compendio de los Descubrimentos, Conquistas y Guerras de la India Oriental y sus Islas. Sq. 8vo. Madrid, 1681.

[**Mason**, F. Burmah, its People and Natural Productions. Rangoon, 1860.

[**Maspero**, G. The Dawn of Civilisation. Egypt and Chaldaea. Ed. by A. H. Sayce. London, 1894.]

Mas'udi. Maçoudi, Les Prairies d'Or, par Barbier de Meynard et Pavet de Courteille. 9 vols. 8vo. 1861-1877.

[**Mateer**, S. The Land of Charity: A Descriptive Account of Travancore and its People. London, 1871.]

Matthioli, P. A. Commentary on Dioscorides. The edition chiefly used is an old French transl. Folio. Lyon, 1560.

Maundeville, Sir John. Ed. by Halliwell. 8vo. 1866.

Max Havelaar door Multatuli (E. Douwes Dekker). 4th ed. Amsterdam, 1875. This is a novel describing Society in Java, but especially the abuses of rural administration. It was originally published c. 1860, and made a great noise in Java and the mother country. It was translated into English a few years later.

[**Mayne**, J. D. A Treatise on Hindu Law and Custom. 2nd ed. Madras, 1880.]

Mehren, M. A. F. Manuel de la Cosmographie du Moyen Age (tr. de l'Arabe de Chemseddîn Dimichqî). Copenhague, &c. 1874.

Memoirs of the Revolution in Bengal. (Tract.) 1760.

Mendoza, Padre Juan Gonzales de. The work was first published at Rome in 1585: Historia de las cossas mas notables, Ritos y Costumbres del Gran Reyno de la **China** (&c.) . . . hecho y ordenado por el mvy R. P. Maestro Fr. Joan Gonzalez de Mendoça, &c. The quotations are from the Hak. Soc.'s reprint, 2 vols. (1853), of R. Parke's E.T., entitled "The Historie of the Great and Mightie Kingdome of China" (&c). London, 1588.

Meninski, F. à M. **Thesaurus** Linguarum Orientalium. 4 vols. folio. Vienna, 1670. New ed. Vienna, 1780.

Merveilles de l'Inde, Livre des. Par MM. Van der Lith et Devic. 4to. Leide, 1883.

Middleton's Voyage, Sir H. Last East India V. to Bantam and the Maluco Islands, 1604. 4to. London, 1606; also reprint Hak. Soc. 1857.

Milburn, Wm. Oriental Commerce, &c. 2 vols. 4to. 1813. [New ed. 1 vol. 1825.]

Miles. *See* **Hydur Ali** and **Tipú.**

Mill, James. Hist. of **British India.** Originally published 3 vols. 4to. 1817. Edition used in 8vo, edited and completed by H. H. Wilson. 9 vols. 1840.

Milman, Bishop. Memoir of, by Frances Maria Milman. 8vo. 1879.

Millingen. Wild Life among the Koords. 1870.

Minsheu, John. The Guide into the Tongues, &c. The 2nd ed. folio. 1627.

Minto, Lord, in India. Life and Letters of Gilbert Elliot, first Earl of Minto from 1807 to 1814, while Governor-General of India. Edited by his great niece, the Countess of Minto. 8vo. 1880.

Minto Life of Gilbert Elliot, by Countess of Minto. 3 vols. 1874.

Mirat-i-Ahmedi. *See* **Bird's Guzerat.**

Miscellanea Curiosa (Norimbergae). *See* pp. 957*a*, and 23*b*.

Mission to Ava. Narrative of the M. sent to the Court of A. in 1855. By Capt. H. Yule, Secretary to the Envoy, Major Phayre. 1858.

Mocquet, Jean. Voyages en Afrique, Asie, Indes Orientales et Occidentales. Paris, 1617. The edition quoted is of 1645.

Mohit, The, by Sidi Ali Kapudan. Translated Extracts, &c., by Joseph v. Hammer-Purgstall, in J. A. S. Soc. Bengal. Vols. III. and V. [Also see **Sidi Ali.**]

Molesworth's Dicty. Maráthí and English. 2nd ed. 4to. Bombay 1857.

Money, William. **Java,** or How to Manage a Colony. 2 vols. 1860. (I believe Mr. Money was not responsible for the vulgar second title.)

Moor, Lieut. E. **Narrative** of the operations of Capt. Little's Detachment, &c. 4to. 1794.

Moore, Thomas. Lalla Rookh. 1817.

[**Morier,** J. A Journey through Persia, Armenia and Asia Minor, to Constantinople, in the years 1808 and 1809. London, 1812.]

Morton, Life of Leyden. *See* **Leyden.**

Mountain, Mem. and Letters of Col. Armine S. H. 1857.

Muir, Sir William. Annals of the Early **Caliphate,** from original sources. 1883.

[**Mukharji,** T. N. Art-Manufactures of India. Calcutta, 1888.]

Müller, Prof. Max. Lectures on the Science of Language. 1st Ser. 1861. 2nd Ser. 1864.

——— Hibbert Lectures on the Origin and Growth of Religion, as illustrated by the Religions of India. 1878.

[**Mundy,** Gen. G. C. Pen and Pencil Sketches in India. 3rd ed. London, 1858.]

Munro, Sir T. Life of M.-Gen., by the Rev. G. R. **Gleig.** 3 vols. 1830. (At first 2 vols., then a 3rd vol. of additional letters.)

——— His **Minutes,** &c., edited by Sir A. Arbuthnot, with a Memoir. 2 vols. 8vo. 1881.

Munro, Capt. Innes. **Narrative** of Military Operations against the French, Dutch, and Hyder Ally Cawn, 1780-84. 4to. 1789.

Munro, Surgeon Gen., C.B. **Reminiscences** of Military Service with the 93rd Highlanders. 1883. (An admirable book of its kind.)

Napier, General Sir Charles. Records of the Indian Command of, comprising all his General Orders, &c. Compiled by John Mawson. Calcutta, 1851.

[**Neale,** F. A. Narrative of a Residence at the Capital of the Kingdom of Siam, with a Description of the Manners, Customs, and Laws of the modern Siamese. London, 1852.

[**N.E.D.** A New English Dictionary on Historical Principles: founded mainly on the Materials collected by the Philological Society: edited by J. H. Murray and H. Bradley. 5 vols. Oxford. 1888-1902.]

Nelson, J. H., M.A. The **Madura** Country, a Manual. Madras, 1868.

Niebuhr, Carsten. **Voyage en Arabie,** &c. 2 vols. 4to. Amsterdam, 1774.

——— **Desc. de l'Arabie,** 4to. Amsterdam, 1774.

Nieuhof, Joan. Zee-en Lant Reize. 2 vols. folio. 1682.

Norbert, Père (O.S.F.). **Mémoires** Historiques presentés au Souverain Pontife Benoit XIV. sur les Missions des Indes Orientales (A bitter enemy of the Jesuits). 2 vols. 4to. Luques (Avignon). 1744. A 3rd vol. London, 1750; also 4 pts. (4 vols.) 12mo. Luques, 1745.

Notes and Extracts from the Govt. Records in Fort St. George (1670-1681). Parts I., II., III. Madras, 1871-73.

N. & E. Notices et Extraits des Manuscrits de la Bibliothèque du Roi (and afterwards *Nationale, Impériale, Royale,* &c.). 4to. Paris, 1787, *et seqq.*

Notices of Madras and Cuddalore in the Last Century, from the Journals and Letters of the Earlier Missionaries (Germans) of the S.P.C.K. Small 8vo. 1858. A very interesting little work.

Novus orbis Regionum ac Insularum Veteribus Incognitarum, &c. Basiliae apud Io. Hervagium. 1555, folio. Orig. ed., 1537.

Nunes, A. Livro dos Pesos da Ymdia, e assy Medidas e Moedas. 1554. Contained in **Subsidios,** q.v.

Oakfield, or Fellowship in the East. By **W. D. Arnold,** late 58th Reg. B.N.I. 2 vols. 2nd ed. 1854. The 1st ed. was apparently of the same year.

Observer, The Indian. *See* **Boyd.**

[**Oliphant,** L. Narrative of the Earl of Elgin's Mission to China and Japan in the years 1857-8-9. 2 vols. Edinburgh, 1859.

[**Oppert,** G. The Original Inhabitants of Bharatavarṣa or India. Westminster, 1893.

[**Oriental Sporting Magazine,** June 1828 to June 1833, reprint. 2 vols. London, 1873.]

Orme, Robert. **Historical Fragments** of the Mogul Empire, &c. This was first published by Mr. Orme in 1782. But a more complete ed. with sketch of his life,

&c., was issued after his death. 4to. 1805.

Orme, Robert. **Hist. of the Military Transactions** of the British Nation in Indostan. 3 vols. 4to. The dates of editions are as follows: Vol. I., 1763; 2nd ed., 1773; 3rd ed., 1781. Vol. II. (in two Sections commonly called Vols. II. and III.), 1778. Posthumous edition of the complete work, 1805. These all in 4to. Reprint at Madras, large 8vo. 1861-62.

Osbeck. A Voyage to China and the E. Indies. Tr. by J. R. Forster. 2 vols. 1771.

Osborne, Hon. W. G. **Court and Camp of Runjeet Singh.** 8vo. 1840.

Ousely, Sir William. **Travels** in Various Countries of the East. 3 vols. 4to. 1819-23.

Ovington, Rev. F. A Voyage to Suratt in the year 1689. London, 1696.

[**Owen**, Capt. W. F. W. Narrative of Voyages to explore the Shores of Africa, Arabia, and Madagascar. 2 vols. London, 1833.]

Palgrave, W. Gifford. Narrative of a Year's Journey through Central and Western **Arabia**. 2 vols. 1865. [New ed. 1 vol. 1868.]

Pallegoix. Monseigneur. **Description** du Royaume Thai ou **Siam**. 2 vols. 1854.

[**Palmer**, Rev. A. S. Folk-etymology. London, 1882.]

Pandurang Hari, or Memoirs of a Hindoo, originally published by Whitaker. 3 vols. 1826. The author was Mr. Hockley of the Bo. C.S. of whom little is known. The quotations are partly from the reissue by H. S. King & Co. in 1873, with a preface by Sir Bartle Frere, 2 vols. small 8vo.; but Burnell's apparently from a 1-vol. issue in 1877. [See 4 Ser. N. & Q. xi. 439, 527. The quotations have now been given from the ed. of 1873.]

Panjab Notes and Queries, a monthly Periodical, ed. by Capt. R. C. Temple. 1883 *seqq.* [Continued as "**North Indian Notes and Queries**," ed. by W. Crooke. 5 vols. 1891-96.]

Paolino, Fra P. da S. Bartolomeo. **Viaggio** alle Indiè Orientali. 4to. Roma, 1796.

Paolino, E.T. by J. R. Forster. 8vo. 1800.

[**Pearce**, N. Life and Adventures in Abyssinia, ed. J. J. Halls. 2 vols. London, 1831.]

Pegolotti, Fr. Balducci. **La Pratica di Mercatura**, written c. 1343; publd. by Gian Francisco Pagnini del Ventura of Volterra in his work Della Decima, &c. Lisbone e Lucca (really Florence), 1765-66. 4 vols. 4to. Of this work it constitutes the 3rd volume. Extracts translated in Cathay and the Way Thither, q.v. The 5th volume is a similar work by **G. Uzzano**, written c. 1440.

Pèlerins Bouddhistes, by **Stanislas, Julien.** Vol. I. Vie et Voyages de Hiouen Thsang. Vols. II. and III. Mémoires des Contrées Occidentales. Paris. 1857.

[**Pelly**, Col. Sir L. The Miracle Play of Hasan and Husain, collected from Oral Tradition, ed. A. N. Wollaston. 2 vols. London, 1879.]

Pemberton, Major R. B. **Report** on the Eastern Frontier of British India. 8vo. Calcutta, 1835.

Pennant's (T.) **View of Hindoostan**, India extra Gangem, China, and Japan. 4 vols. 4to. 1798-1800.

Percival, R. An Account of the Island of **Ceylon**. 2 vols. 1833.

Peregrinatoris Medii Aevi **Quatuor.** Recensuit J. C. M. Laurent. Lipsiae. 1864.

Peregrine Pultuney. A Novel. 3 vols. 1844. (Said to be written by the late Sir John Kaye.)

Periplus Maris Erythraei (I have used sometimes C. Müller in the Geog. Graeci Minores, and sometimes the edition of B. Fabricius, Leipzig, 1883).

Petis de la Croix. Hist. de **Timur-bec**, &c. 4 vols. 12mo. Delf. 1723.

Philalethes, The **Boscawen's Voyage** to Bombay. 1750.

Philippi, R.P.F., de Sanctma. Trinitate, **Itinerarium** Orientale, &c. 1652.

Phillips, Sir Richard. **A Million of Facts.** Ed. 1837. [This Million of Facts contains innumerable absurdities.

Phillips, Mr. An Account of the Religion, Manners, and the Learning of the People of Malabar. 16mo. London, 1717.

Pictet, Adolphe. **Les Origines** Indo-Européenes. 2 vols. imp. 8vo. 1859-1863.

Pigafetta, and other contemporary Writers. The first Voyage round the World by **Magellan**, translated from the accounts of——. By Lord Stanley of Alderley. HAK. Soc. 1874.

Pilot, The English, by Thornton. Part III. Folio. 1711.

Pinto, **Fernam Mendez. Peregrinação** de — por elle escrita, &c. Folio. Originally published at Lisbon, 1614.

Pinto (Cogan's). The Voyages and Adventures of Fernand Mendez P., A Portugal, &c. Done into English by H. C. Gent. Folio. London, 1653.

Pioneer & Pioneer Mail. (Daily and Weekly Newspapers published at Allahabad.)

Piso, Gulielmus, de Indiae utriusque Re Naturali et Medicâ. Folio. Amsterdam, 1658. See *Bontius*, whose book is attached.

[**Platts**, J. T. A Dictionary of Urdū, Classical Hindī, and English. London, 1884.]

Playfair, G. **Taleef-i-Shereef**, or Indian Materia Medica. Tr. from the original by. Calcutta, 1883.

Poggius De Varietate Fortunae. The quotations under this reference are from the reprint of what pertains to the travels of Nicolo Conti in Dr. Friedr. Kuntsmann's *Die Kenntniss Indiens*. München. 1863.

Pollok, Lt.-Col. **Sport in British Burmah**, Assam, and the Jynteah Hills. 2 vols. 1879.

Polo, The Book of Ser Marco, the Venetian. Newly Tr. and Ed. by Colonel Henry Yule, C.B. In 2 vols. 1871. 2nd ed., revised, with new matter and many new Illustrations. 1875.

Price, Joseph. *Tracts.* 3 vols. 8vo. 1783.

Pridham, C. An Hist., Pol. and Stat. Ac. of Ceylon and its Dependencies. 2 vols. 8vo. 1849.

Primor e Honra da Vida Soldadesca no estado da India. Fr. A. Freyre (1580). Lisbon, 1630.

Pringle (Mrs.) M.A. A Journey in East Africa. 1880.

[**Pringle**, A.T. Selections from the Consultations of the Agent, Governor, and Council of Fort St. George, 1681. 4th Series. Madras, 1893.

——— The Diary and Consultation Book of the Agent, Governor, and Council of Fort St. George. 1st Series, 1682-85. 4 vols. (in progress). Madras, 1894-95.]

Prinsep's Essays. Essays on Indian Antiquities of the late James Prinsep . . . to which are added his **Useful Tables** ed. . . . by **Edward Thomas.** 2 vols. 8vo. 1858.

Prinsep, H. T. Hist. of Political and Military Transactions in India, during the Adm. of the Marquess of Hastings. 2 vols. 1825.

Propagation of the Gospel in the East. In Three Parts. Ed. of 1718. An English Translation of the letters of the first Protestant Missionaries **Ziegenbalg** and **Plutscho.**

Prosper Alpinus. Hist. Aegypt. Naturalis et Rerum Aegyptiarum Libri. 3 vols. sm. 4to. Lugd. Bat. 1755.

Punjab Plants, comprising Botanical and Vernacular Names and Uses, by J. L. **Stewart.** Lahore, 1869.

Punjaub Trade Report. Report on the Trade and Resources of the Countries on the N.W. Boundary of British India. By **R. H. Davies**, Sec. to Govt. Punjab. Lahore, 1862.

Purchas, his **Pilgrimes**, &c. 4 vols. folio. 1625-26. The Pilgrimage is often bound as Vol. V. It is really a separate work.

——— His Pilgrimage, or Relations of the World, &c. The 4th ed. folio. 1625. The 1st ed. is of 1614.

Pyrard de Laval, François. Discours du **Voyage** des Français aux Indes Orientales, 1615-16. 2 pts. in 1 vol. 1619 in 2 vols. 12mo. Also published, 2 vols. 4to in 1679 as Voyage de Franc. Pyrard de Laval. This is most frequently quoted.

There is a smaller first sketch of 1611, under the name "Discours des Voyages des Francais aux Indes Orientales." [Ed. for HAK. Soc. by A. Gray and H. C. P. Bell, 1887-89.]

Qanoon-e-Islam. See **Herklots.**

Raffles' Hist. of Java. [2nd. ed. 2 vols. London, 1830.]

[**Raikes**, C. Notes on the North-Western Provinces of India. London, 1852.

[**Rájendralála Mitra**, Indo-Aryans. Contributions towards the Elucidation of their Ancient and Mediæval History. 2 vols. London, 1881.]

Raleigh, Sir W. The Discourse of the Empire of **Guiana.** Ed. by Sir R. Schomburgk. HAK. Soc. 1850.

Ramāyana of Tulsi Dās. Translated by **F. Growse.** 1878. [Revised ed. 1 vol. Allahabad, 1883.]

Ramusio, G. B. Delle **Navigationi** e Viaggi. 3 vols. folio, in Venetia. The editions used by me are Vol. I., 1613; Vol. II., 1606; Vol. III., 1556; except a few quotations from C. Federici, which are from Vol. III. of 1606, in the B. M.

Rashiduddin, in Quatremère, **Histoire des Mongols** de la Perse, par Raschid-el-din, trad. &c., par M. **Quatremère.** Atlas folio. 1836.

Râs Mâlâ, or Hindoo Annals of the Province of Goozerat. By Alex. Kinloch Forbes, H.E.I.C.C.S. 2 vols. 8vo. London, 1856.

Also a New Edition in one volume, 1878.

Rates and Valuatioun of Merchandize **(Scotland).** Published by the Treasury. Edinb. 1867.

Ravenshaw, J. H. Gaur, its Ruins and Inscriptions. 4to. 1878.

Raverty, Major H. G. **Ṭabakāt-i-Nāsiri**, E.T. 2 vols. 8vo. London, 1881.

Rawlinson's Herodotus. 4 vols. 8vo. 4th edition. 1880.

Ray, Mr. John. **A Collection** of Curious Travels and Voyages. In Two Parts (includes **Rauwolff**). The second edition. 2 vols. 1705.

——— Historia Plantarum. Folio. *See* p. 957*a*.

——— Synopsis Methodica Animalium Quadrupedum et Serpentini Generis, &c. Auctore Joanne Raio, F.R.S. Londini, 1693.

Raynal, Abbé W. F. **Histoire Philosophique** et Politique des Etablissements des Européens dans les deux Indes. (First published, Amsterdam, 1770. 4 vols. First English translation by J. Justamond, London, 1776.) There were an immense number of editions of the original, with modifications, and a second English version by the same Justamond in 6 vols. 1798.

Reformer, A True. (By Col. George **Chesney**, R.E.). 3 vols. 1873.

Regulations for the Hon. **Company's Troops** on the Coast of **Coromandel**, by M.-Gen. Sir A. Campbell, K.B., &c. &c. Madras, 1787.

Reinaud. Fragmens sur l'Inde, in *Journ. Asiatique*, Ser. IV. tom. iv.

——— *See* **Relation.**

——— **Mémoire** sur l'Inde. 4to. 1849.

Relation des **Voyages faites par les Arabes** et les Persans . . . trad., &c., par M. Reinaud. 2 sm. vols. Paris, 1845.

Rennell, Major James. **Memoir** of a **Map** of Hindoostan, or the Mogul Empire. 3rd edition. 4to. 1793.

Resende, Garcia de. **Chron.** del Rey dom João II. Folio. Evora, 1554.

[**Revelations**, the, of an **Orderly**. By Paunchkouree Khan. Benares, 1866.]

Rhede, H., van Drakenstein. **Hortus Malabaricus.** 6 vols. folio. Amstelod. 1686.

Rhys Davids. Buddhism. S.P.C.K. *No date* (more shame to S.P.C.K.).

Ribeiro, J. **Fadalidade Historica.** (1685.) First published recently.

[**Rice**, B. L. Gazetteer of Mysore. 2 vols. London, 1897.

[**Riddell**, Dr. R. Indian Domestic Economy. 7th ed. Calcutta, 1871.

[**Risley**, H. H. The Tribes and Castes of Bengal. 2 vols. Calcutta, 1891.]

Ritter, Carl. **Erdkunde.** 19 vols. in 21. Berlin, 1822-1859.

Robinson Philip. *See* **Garden, in My Indian.**

Rochon, Abbé. *See* p. 816*a*.

[**Roe**, Sir T. Embassy to the Court of the Great Mogul, 1615-19. Ed. by W. Foster. Hak. Soc. 2 vols. 1899.]

Roebuck, T. An English and Hindoostanee **Naval Dictionary.** 12mo. Calcutta, 1811. *See* **Small.**

Rogerius, Abr. **De open Deure** tot het Verborgen Hyedendom. 4to. Leyden, 1651.

Also sometimes quoted from the French version, viz. :—

Roger, Abraham. **La Porte Ouverte . . .** ou la Vraye Representation, &c. 4to. Amsterdam, 1670.

The author was the first Chaplain at Pulicat (1631-1641), and then for some years at Batavia (see Havart, p. 132). He returned home in 1647 and died in 1649, at Gouda (Pref. p. 3). The book was brought out by his widow. Thus, at the time that the English Chaplain **Lord** (q.v.) was studying the religion of the Hindus at Surat, the Dutch Chaplain Roger was doing the same at Pulicat. The work of the last is in every way vastly superior to the former. It was written at Batavia (see p. 117), and, owing to its publication after his death, there are a few misprints of Indian words. The author had his information from a Brahman named Padmanaba (*Padmanābha*), who knew Dutch, and who gave him a Dutch translation of Bhartrihari's Satakas, which is printed at the end of the book. It is the first translation from Sanskrit into an European language (A.B.).

Roteiro da Viagem de Vasco da Gama em MCCCCXCVII. 2a edição. Lisboa, 1861. The 1st ed. was published in 1838. The work is inscribed to Alvaro Velho. See Figanière, *Bibliog. Hist. Port.* p. 159. (Note by A.B.).

——— *See* **De Castro.**

Rousset Léon. A Travers la Chine. 8vo. Paris, 1878.

[**Row**, T. V. Manual of Tanjore District. Madras, 1883.]

Royle, J. F., M.D. An Essay on the Antiquity of **Hindoo Medicine.** 8vo. 1837.

——— Illustrations of the **Botany** and other branches of Nat. History of the **Himalayas**, and of the Floras of Cashmere. 2 vols. folio. 1839.

Rubruk, Wilhelmus de. **Itinerarium** in **Recueil de Voyages** et de Mémoires de la Soc. de Géographie. Tom. iv. 1837.

Rumphius (Geo. Everard Rumphf.). Herbarium Amboinense. 7 vols. folio. Amstelod. 1741. (He died in 1693.)

Russell, Patrick. An Account of Indian **Snakes** collected on the coast of Coromandel. 2 vols. folio. 1803.

Rycaut, Sir Paul. Present State of the Ottoman Empire. Folio, 1687. Appended to ed. of **Knollys' Hist.** of the Turks.

Saar, Johann Jacob, Ost-Indianische **Fünf-zehn-Jährige Kriegs-Dienste** (&c.). (1644-1659.) Folio. Nürnberg, 1672.

Sacy, Silvestre de. Relation de l'Egypte. *See* **Abdallatif.**

——— **Chrestomathie Arabe.** 2de Ed. 3 vols. 8vo. Paris, 1826-27.

Sadik Isfahani, The Geographical Works of. Translated by J. C. from original Persian MSS., &c. Oriental Translation Fund, 1832.

Sainsbury, W. Noel. **Calendar** of State Papers, **East Indies.** Vol. I., 1862 (1513-1616); Vol. II., 1870 (1617-1621); Vol. III., 1878 (1622-1624); Vol. IV., 1884 (1625-1629). An admirable work.

Sanang Setzen. Geschichte der Ost-Mongolen . . . von Ssanang Ssetzen Chungtaidschi der Ordus. aus dem Mongol . . . von Isaac Jacob Schmidt. 4to. St. Petersburg, 1829.

[**Sanderson**, G. P. Thirteen Years among the Wild Beasts of India, 3rd ed. London, 1882.]

Sangermano, Rev. Father. A description of the **Burmese Empire.** Translated by W. Tandy, D.D. (Or. Transl. Fund). 4to. Rome, 1833.

San Roman, Fray A. **Historia General** de la India Oriental. Folio. Valladolid, 1603.

Sassetti, Lettere, contained in **De Gubernatis**, q.v.

Saty. Rev. The Saturday Review, London weekly newspaper.

Schiltberger, Johann. The Bondage and **Travels** of. Tr. by Capt. J. Buchan Telfer, R.N. HAK. SOC. 1879.

Schouten, Wouter. Oost-Indische **Voyagie**, &c. t'Amsterdam, 1676.

This is the Dutch original rendered in German as **Walter Schulzen**, q.v.

[**Schrader**, O. Prehistoric Antiquities of the Aryan Peoples. Tr. by F. B. Jevons. London, 1890.]

Schulzen, Walter. Ost-Indische Reise-Beschreibung. Folio. Amsterdam, 1676. See **Schouten.**

Schuyler, Eugene. **Turkistan.** 2 vols. 8vo. 1876.

[**Scott**, J. G. and J. P. Hardiman. Gazetteer of Upper Burma and the Shan States. 5 vols. Rangoon, 1900.]

Scrafton, Luke. **Reflexions** on the Government of Hindostan, with a Sketch of the Hist. of Bengal. 1770.

Seely, Capt. J. B. The **Wonders of Ellora.** 8vo. 1824.

Seir Mutaqherin, or a View of Modern Times, being a History of India from the year 1118 to 1195 of the Hedjirah. From the Persian of Gholam Hussain Khan. 2 vols. in 3. 4to. Calcutta, 1789.

Seton-Karr, W. S., aud Hugh Sandeman. **Selections** from Calcutta Gazettes (1784-1823). 5 vols. 8vo. (The 4th and 5th by H. S.) Calcutta, 1864-1869.

Shaw, Robert. Visits to **High Tartary**, Yarkand, and Kâshghâr, 1871.

Shaw, Dr. T. Travels or Observations relating to several Parts of **Barbary** and the Levant. 2nd ed. 1757. (Orig. ed. is of 1738).

Shelvocke's Voyage. A V. round the World, by the Way of the Great South Sea, Perform'd in the Years 1719, 20, 21, 22. By Capt. George S. London, 1726.

Sherring, Revd., M.A. Hindu Tribes and Castes. 3 vols. 4to. Calcutta, 1872-81.

Sherwood, Mrs. **Stories** from the Church Catechism. Ed. 1873. This work was originally published about 1817, but I cannot trace the exact date. It is almost unique as giving some view of the life of the non-commissioned ranks of a British regiment in India, though of course much is changed since its date.

Sherwood, Mrs., The Life of, chiefly Autobiographical. 1857.

Shipp, John. Memoirs of the Extraordinary Military Career of . . . written by Himself. 2nd ed. (First ed., 1829). 3 vols. 8vo. 1830.

Sibree, Revd. J. The **Great African Island.** 1880.

Sidi 'Ali. The **Mohit**, by S. A. Kapudan. Exts. translated by Joseph v. Hammer, in *J. As. Soc. Bengal*, Vols. III. & V.

——— **Relation** des **Voyages** de, nommé ordinairement Katibi Roumi, trad. sur la version allemande de M. Diez par M. Moris in *Journal Asiatique*, Ser. I. tom. ix.

[——— The Travels and Adventures of the Turkish Admiral. Trans. by A. Vambéry. London, 1899.]

Sigoli, Simone. **Viaggio** al Monte Sinai. See **Frescobaldi.**

Simpkin. See *Letters.*

[**Skeat**, W. W. Malay Magic, being an Introduction to the Folklore and Popular Religion of the Malay Peninsula. 8vo. London, 1900.

[**Skinner**, Capt. T. Excursions in India, including a Walk over the Himalaya Mountains to the Sources of the Jumna and the Ganges, 2nd ed. 2 vols. London, 1833.]

Skinner, Lt.-Col. James, Military Memoirs of. Ed. by J. B. Fraser. 2 vols. 1851.

Sleeman, Lt.-Col. (Sir Wm.). **Ramaseeana** and Vocabulary of the Peculiar Language of the Thugs. 8vo. Calcutta, 1836.

——— **Rambles and Recollections** of an Indian Official. 2 vols. large 8vo. 1844. An excellent book. [New ed. in 2 vols., by V. A. Smith, in Constable's Oriental Miscellany. London, 1893.]

[——— A Journey through the Kingdom of Oudh in 1849-50. 2 vols. London, 1858.]

Small, Rev. G. A **Laskari** Dictionary. 12mo., 1882 (being an enlarged ed. of **Roebuck**, q.v.).

Smith, R. **Bosworth. Life of Lord Lawrence.** 2 vols. 8vo. 1883.

Smith, Major L. F. Sketch of the **Regular Corps** in the service of Native Princes. 4to. Tract. Calcutta, N.D. London. 1805.

[**Society** in India, by an Indian Officer. 2 vols. London, 1841.

Society, Manners, Tales, and Fictions of India. 3 vols. London, 1844.]

Solvyns, F. B. **Les Hindous.** 4 vols. folio. Paris, 1808.

Sonnerat. Voyages aux Indes Orientales et à la Chine. 2 vols. 4to. 1781. Also 3 vols. 8vo. 1782.

Sousa, P. Francesco de. **Oriente Conquistado** a Jesus Christo pelos Padres da Companha de Jesus. Folio. Lisbon. 1710. Reprint of Pt. I., at Bombay, 1881.

Southey, R. **Curse of Kehama.** 1810. In Collected Works.

Spielbergen van Waerwijck, **Voyage of.** (Four Voyages to the E. Indies from 1594 to 1604, in Dutch.) 1646.

Sprenger, Prof. Aloys. Die **Post und Reise-Routen** des Orients. 8vo. Leipzig, 1864.

[**Stanford** Dictionary, the, of Anglicised Words and Phrases, by C. A. M. Fennell. Cambridge, 1892.]

Stanley's Vasco da Gama. *See* **Correa.**

Staunton, Sir G. **Authentic Account** of Lord Macartney's Embassy to the Emperor of China. 2 vols. 4to. 1797.

Stavorinus. Voyage to the E. Indies. Tr. from Dutch by S. H. Wilcocke. 3 vols. 1798.

Stedman, J. G. Narrative of a Five Years' Expedition against the Revolted Negroes in Surinam. 2 vols. 4to. 1806.

Stephen, Sir James F. Story of **Nuncomar** and Impey. 2 vols. 1885.

Stokes, M. **Indian Fairy Tales.** Calcutta, 1879.

Strangford, Viscount, Select Writings of. 2 vols. 8vo. 1869.

St. Pierre, B. de. **La Chaumière Indienne.** 1791.

[**Stuart,** H. A. *See* **Sturrock,** J.

[**Sturrock,** J. and Stuart, H. A. Manual of S. Canara. 2 vols. Madras, 1894-95.]

Subsidios para a Historia da India Portugueza. (Published by the Royal Academy of Lisbon.) Lisbon, 1878.

Sulivan, Capt. G. L., R.A. **Dhow Chasing** in Zanzibar Waters, and on the Eastern Coast of Africa. 1873.

Surgeon's Daughter. By Sir **Walter Scott.** 1827. Reference by chapter.

Symes, Major Michael. Account of an **Embassy to** the Kingdom of Ava, in the year 1795. 4to. 1800.

Taranatha's Geschichte des Buddhismus in India. Germ. Tr. by A. Schiefner. St. Petersburg, 1869.

Tavernier, J. B. Les Six Voyages en Turquie, en Perse, et aux Indes. 2 vols. 4to. Paris, 1676.

——— E.T., which is generally that quoted, being contained in Collections of Travels, &c.; being the Travels of Monsieur Tavernier, Bernier, and other great men. In 2 vols. folio. London, 1684. [Ed. by V. A. Ball. 2 vols. London, 1889.]

Taylor, Col. Meadows. **Story of My Life.** 8vo. (1877). 2nd ed. 1878.

[**Taylor,** J. A Descriptive and Historical Account of the Cotton Manufacture of Dacca, in Bengal. London, 1851.]

Teignmouth, Mem. of **Life** of John Lord, by his Son, Lord Teignmouth. 2 vols. 1843.

Teixeira, P. Pedro. Relaciones . . . de los Reyes de Persia, de los Reyes de Harmuz, y de un Viage dende la India Oriental hasta Italia por terra (all three separately paged). En Amberes, 1610.

Tennent, Sir Emerson. *See* **Emerson.**

Tenreiro, Antonio. **Itinerario** . . . como da India veo por terra a estes Reynos. Orig. ed. Coimbra, 1560. Edition quoted (by Burnell) seems to be of Lisbon, 1762.

Terry. A **Voyage to East India,** &c. Observed by Edward Terry, then Chaplain to the Right Hon. Sir Thomas Row, Knt., Lord Ambassador to the Great Mogul. Reprint, 1777. Ed. 1655.

——— An issue without the Author's name, printed at the end of the E.T. of the Travels of Sig. Pietro della Valle into East India, &c. 1665.

——— Also a part in Purchas, Vol. II.

Thevenot, Melchizedek. (**Collection**). Relations de divers Voyages Curieux. 2nd ed. 2 vols. folio. 1696.

Thevenot, J. de. **Voyages** en Europe, Asie et Afrique. 2nd ed. 5 vols. 12mo. 1727.

Thevet, André. **Cosmographie** Universelle. Folio. Paris, 1575.

Thevet. Les Singularitez de la **France Antarticque,** autrement nommée Amerique. Paris, 1558.

Thomas, H. S. **The Rod in India.** 8vo. Mangalore, 1873.

Thomas, Edward. **Chronicles of the Pathán Kings** of Dehli. 8vo. 1871.

Thomson, Dr. T. **Western Himalaya and Tibet.** 8vo. London, 1852.

Thomson, J. The **Straits of Malacca,** Indo-China, and China. 8vo. 1875.

Thornhill, Mark. **Personal Adventures,** &c., in the Mutiny. 8vo. 1884.

[——— Haunts and Hobbies of an Indian Official. London, 1899.]

Thunberg, C. P., M.D. **Travels** in Europe, Africa, and Asia, made between the years 1770 and 1779. E.T. 4 vols. 8vo. 1799.

Timour, Institutes of. E.T. by Joseph White. 4to. Oxford, 1783.

Timur, Autobiographical **Memoirs of.** E.T. by Major C. Stewart (Or. Tr. Fund). 4to. 1830.

Tippoo Sultan, Select **Letters** of. E.T. by Col. W. Kirkpatrick. 4to. 1811.

Tipú Sultán, Hist. of, by Hussein Ali Khan Kirmani. E.T. by Miles. (Or. Tr. Fund.) 8vo. 1864.

Tod, Lieut.-Col. James. **Annals** and Antiquities of Rajasthan. 2 vols. 4to. 1829. [Reprinted at Calcutta. 2 vols. 1884.]

Tohfut-ul-Mujahideen (Hist. of the Mahomedans in Malabar). Trd. by Lieut. M. J. Rowlandson. (Or. Tr. Fund.) 8vo. 1833. (Very badly edited.)

Tom Cringle's Log. Ed. 1863. (Originally published in Blackwood, c. 1830-31.)

Tombo do Estado da India. *See* **Subsidios** and **Botelho.**

Tr. Lit. Soc. Bo. Transactions of the Literary Society of Bombay. 3 vols. 4to. London, 1819-23.

Trevelyan, G. O. *See* **Competition-Wallah** and **Dawk-Bungalow.**

Tribes on My Frontier. Bombay, 1883.

Trigautius. De Christiana Expeditione apud Sinas. 4to. Lugduni, 1616.

Turnour's (Hon. George) **Mahawanso.** The M. in Roman characters with the translation subjoined, &c. (Only one vol. published.) 4to. Ceylon, 1837.

Tylor, E. B. **Primitive Culture.** 2 vols. 8vo. 1871.

[——— Anahuac; or Mexico and the Mexicans, Ancient and Modern. London, 1861.]

Tyr, Guillaume de, et ses Continuateurs—Texte du XIII. Siècle—par M. Paulin. Paris. 2 vols. large 8vo. 1879-80.

[**Tytler,** A. F. Considerations on the Present Political State of India. 2 vols. London, 1815.]

Uzzano, G. A book of *Pratica della Mercatura* of 1440, which forms the 4th vol. of *Della Decima*. *See* **Pegolotti.**

Valentia, Lord. Voyages and Travels to India, &c. 1802-1806. 3 vols. 4to. 1809.

Valentijn. Oud en Niew **Oost-Indien.** 6 vols. folio—often bound in 8 or 9. Amsterdam, 1624-6.

[**Vámbéry,** A. Sketches of Central Asia. Additional Chapters on my Travels, Adventures, and on the Ethnology of Central Asia. London, 1868.]

Van Braam Houckgeist (**Embassy** to China), E.T. London, 1798.

Van den Broecke, Pieter. Reysen naer Oost Indien, &c. Amsterdam, edns. 1620 ? 1634, 1646, 1648.

Vander Lith. *See* **Merveilles.**

Vanity Fair, a Novel without a Hero, **Thackeray's.** This is usually quoted by chapter. If by page, it is from ed. 1867. 2 vols. 8vo.

Vansittart H. **A Narrative** of the Transactions in Bengal, 1760-1764. 3 vols. 8vo. 1766.

Van Twist, Jehan; Gewesen Overhooft van de Nederlandsche comtooren *Amadabat, Cambaya, Brodera,* en *Broitchia,* **Generall Beschrijvinge** van Indien, &c. t'Amsteledam, 1648.

Varthema, Lodovico di. The **Travels** of. Tr. from the orig. Italian Edition of 1510 by T. Winter Jones, F.S.A., and edited, &c., by George Percy Badger. HAK. SOC. 1863.

This is the edn. quoted with a few exceptions. Mr. Burnell writes:

"We have also used the second edition of the original (?) Italian text (12mo. Venice, 1517). A third edition appeared at Milan in 1523 (4to.), and a fourth at Venice in 1535. This interesting Journal was translated into English by Eden in 1576 (8vo.), and Purchas (ii. pp. 1483-1494) gives an abridgement; it is thus one of the most important sources."

Neither Mr. Winter Jones nor my friend Dr. Badger, in editing Varthema, seem to have been aware of the disparagement cast on his veracity in the famous Colloquios of Garcia de Orta (f. 29*v*. and f. 30). These affect his statements as to his voyages in the further East; and deny his ever having gone beyond Calicut and Cochin; a thesis which it would not be difficult to demonstrate out of his own narrative.

[**Verelst,** H. A View of the Rise, Progress, and Present State of the English Government in Bengal, including a Reply to the Misrepresentations of Mr. Bolts, and other Writers. London, 1772.]

Vermeulen, Genet. Oost Indische **Voyage.** 1677.

Vigne, G. **Travels** in Kashmir, Ladakh, &c. 2 vols. 8vo. 1842.

Vincenzo Maria. Il **Viaggio** all' Indie orientali del P. . . . Procuratore Generale de' Carmelitani Scalzi. Folio. Roma, 1672.

Vitriaci, Jacobi (Jacques de Vitry). Hist. Jherosolym. *See* **Bongars.**

Vocabulista in **Arabico.** (Edited by C. Schiaparelli.) Firenze, 1871.

Voigt. Hortus Suburbanus Calcuttensis. 8vo. Calcutta, 1845.

Von Harff, Arnold. **Pilgerfahrt** des Ritters (1496-1499). From MSS. Cöln, 1860.

Voyage to the East Indies in 1747 and 1748. . . . Interspersed with many useful and curious Observations and Anecdotes. 8vo. London, 1762.

Vüllers, J. A. **Lexicon** Persico-Latinum. 2 vols. and Suppt. Bonnae ad Rhenum. 1855-67.

Wallace, A. R. The Malay Archipelago. 7th ed. 1880.

[**Wallace,** Lieut. Fifteen Years in India, or Sketches of a Soldier's Life. London, 1822.]

Wanderings of a Pilgrim in Search of the Picturesque (by Fanny Parkes). 2 vols. imp. 8vo. 1850.

Ward, W. **A View of the** History, Literature, and Religion of the **Hindoos.** 3rd ed. 4 vols. 8vo. London, 1817-1820.

In the titles of first 2 vols. publd. in 1817, this ed. is stated to be in 2 vols. In those of the 3rd and 4th, 1820, it is stated to be in 4 vols. This arose from some mistake, the author being absent in India when the first two were published.

The work originally appeared at Serampore, 1811, 4 vols. 4to, and an abridged ed. *ibid.* 1 vol. 4to. 1815.

Waring, E. J. The **Tropical Resident** at Home, &c. 8vo. 1866.

Wassaf, Geschichte Wassafs, Persisch herausgegeben, und Deutsch übersetzt, von Joseph **Hammer-Purgstall.** 4to. Wien, 1856.

Watreman, W. **The Fardle of Facions.** London, 1555. Also reprinted in the Hakluyt of 1807.

[**Watt**, G. A Dictionary of the Economic Products of India. 10 vols. Calcutta, 1889-93.]

Wellington Despatches. The Edn. quoted is usually that of 1837.

Welsh, Col. James. **Military Reminiscences** . . . of nearly 40 years' Active Service in the E. Indies. 2 vols. 8vo. 1830. (An excellent book.)

Wheeler, J. T. Madras in the Olden Time . . . compiled from Official Records. 3 vols. sm. sq. 8vo. 1861.

——— **Early Records** of British India. Calcutta, 1878. 2nd ed. 1879.

Wheler, Rev. **Sir George.** Journey into Greece. Folio. 1682.

Witney (Prof. W. D.) **Oriental and Linguistical Studies.** 2 vols. New York, 1873-74.

Widows, Hindoo. Papers relating to E.I. Affairs; printed by order of Parliament. Folio. 1821.

[**Wilkinson**, R. J. A Malay-English Dictionary. Part I. Singapore, 1901.]

Wilks, Col. Mark. **Historical Sketches** of the South of India in an Attempt to trace the Hist of Mysoor. 3 vols. 4to. 1810-17. 2nd ed., 2 vols. 8vo. Madras, 1869.

Williams, Monier. **Religious Thought** and Life in India. Part I., 1883.

[——— Brāhmanism and Hindūism. 4th ed. London, 1891.]

Williams, S. Wells. **Chinese Commercial Guide.** 4th ed. Canton, 1856.

Williamson, V. M. The East India Vade Mecum, by Capt. Thomas Williamson (the author of *Oriental Field Sports*). 2 vols. 8vo. 1810.

Williamson, Capt. T. **Oriental Field Sports.** Atlas folio. 1807.

Wills, C. T. In the Land of the Lion and the Sun, or **Modern Persia.** 1883.

[**Wilson**, A. The Abode of Snow, Observations on a Journey from Chinese Tibet to the Indian Caucasus. Edinburgh, 1875.]

Wilson, John, D.D., Life of, by George Smith, LL.D. 1878.

[——— Indian Caste. 2 vols. Bombay, 1877.]

Wolff, J. Travels and Adventures. 2 vols. London, 1860.]

Wollaston, A. N. **English-Persian Dictionary.** 8vo. 1882.

Wright, T. **Early Travels** in Palestine, edited with Notes. (Bohn.) 1848.

Wright, T. Domestic Manners and Sentiments in England in the Middle Ages. 1862.

Wyllie, J. W. S. **Essays** on the External Policy of India. Edited by Dr. W. W. Hunter. 1875.

Wytfliet. Histoire des Indes. Fo., 3 pts. Douay. 1611.

Xaverii, Scti. Francisci. Indiarum Apostoli **Epistolarum** Libri Quinque. Pragae, 1667.

Xavier, St. Francis, Life and Letters of, by Rev. H. I. **Coleridge** (S.J.). 2 vols. 8vo. 1872.

[**Yusuf Ali**, A. A Monograph on Silk Fabrics produced in the North-Western Provinces and Oudh. Allahabad, 1900.]

Zedler, J. H. Grosses Vollständliges Universal Lexicon. 64 vols. folio. Leipzig, 1732-1750; and Supplement, 4 vols. 1751-1754.

Ziegenbalg. *See* **Propagation of the Gospel.**

CORRIGENDA.

PAGE. COL.

32 *b*.—**Apollo Bunder.** Mr. S. M. Edwardes (*History of Bombay, Town and Island, Census Report*, 1901, p. 17) derives this name from 'Pallav Bandar,' 'the Harbour of Clustering Shoots.'

274 *a*.—**Crease.** 1817. "the Portuguese commander requested permission to see the **Cross** which Janiere wore. . . ."—*Rev. R. Fellowes, History of Ceylon*, chap. v. quoted in 9 ser. *N. & Q.* I. 85.

276 *b*.—*For* "Porus" *read* "Portus."

380 *b*.—*For* "It is probable that what that geographer . . ." *read* "It is probable from what . . ."

499 *b*.—The reference to **Bao** was accidentally omitted. The word is Peguan *bā* (pronounced *bā-a*), "a monastery." The quotation from Sangermano (p. 88) runs: "There is not any village, however small, that has not one or more large wooden houses, which are a species of convent, by the Portuguese in India called **Bao.**"

511 *a*.—*For* "**Adawlvt**" *read* "**Adawlat.**"

565 *a*.—Mr. Edwardes (*op. cit.* p. 5) derives **Mazagong** from Skt. *matsya-grāma*, "fish-village," due to "the pungent odour of the fish, which its earliest inhabitants caught, dried and ate."

655 *b*.—*For* "Steven's" *read* "Stevens'."

678 *a*.—Mr. Edwardes (*op. cit.* p. 15) derives **Parell** from *pādel*, "the Tree-Trumpet Flower" (*Bignonia suaveolens*).

816 *a*.—*For* "*shā-bāsh*" *read* "*shāh-bāsh*."

858 *b*.—*Far* "**Sowar**" *read* "**Sonar,** a goldsmith."

920 *b*.—**Tiffin** add:

1784.—"Each temperate day
With health glides away,
No **Triffings*** our forenoons profane."
—*Memoirs of the Late War in Asia*, by *An Officer of Colonel Baillie's Detachment*, ii. *Appendix*, *p.* 293.

1802.—"I suffered a very large library to be useless whence I might have extracted that which would have been of more service to me than running about to **Tiffins** and noisy parties."—*Metcalfe*, to *J. W. Sherer*, in *Kaye*, *Life of Lord Metcalfe*, I. 81.

* [In note "Luncheons."]

A GLOSSARY

OF

ANGLO-INDIAN COLLOQUIAL TERMS AND PHRASES OF ANALOGOUS ORIGIN.

ABADA, s. A word used by old Spanish and Portuguese writers for a 'rhinoceros,' and adopted by some of the older English narrators. The origin is a little doubtful. If it were certain that the word did not occur earlier than c. 1530–40, it would most probably be an adoption from the Malay *badak*, 'a rhinoceros.' The word is not used by Barros where he would probably have used it if he knew it (see quotation under **GANDA**); and we have found no proof of its earlier existence in the language of the Peninsula; if this should be established we should have to seek an Arabic origin in such a word as *abadat*, *ābid*, fem. *ābida*, of which one meaning is (*v. Lane*) 'a wild animal.' The usual form *abada* is certainly somewhat in favour of such an origin. [Prof. Skeat believes that the *a* in *abada* and similar Malay words represents the Arabic article, which was commonly used in Spanish and Portuguese prefixed to Arabic and other native words.] It will be observed that more than one authority makes it the female rhinoceros, and in the dictionaries the word is feminine. But so Barros makes *Ganda*. [Mr W. W. Skeat suggests that the female was the more dangerous animal, or the one most frequently met with, as is certainly the case with the crocodile.]

1541.—"Mynes of Silver, Copper, Tin, and Lead, from whence great quantities thereof were continually drawn, which the Merchants carried away with Troops of Elephants and Rhinoceroses (*em cafilas de elefantes e* **badas**) for to transport into the Kingdoms of *Sornau*, by us called *Siam*, *Passiloco*, *Sarady*, (*Savady* in orig.), *Tangu*, *Prom*, *Calaminham* and other Provinces . . . ."—*Pinto* (orig. cap. xli.) in *Cogan*, p. 49. The kingdoms named here are Siam (see under **SARNAU**); Pitchalok and Sawatti (now two provinces of Siam); Taungu and Prome in B. Burma; Calaminham, in the interior of Indo-China, more or less fabulous.

1544.—"Now the King of Tartary was fallen upon the city of *Pequin* with so great an army as the like had never been seen since *Adam's* time; in this army . . . were seven and twenty Kings, under whom marched 1,800,000 men . . . . with four score thousand Rhinoceroses" (*donde partirão com oitenta mil* **badas**).—*Ibid.* (orig. cap. cvii.) in *Cogan*, p. 149.

[1560.—See quotation under **LAOS**.]

1585.—"It is a very fertile country, with great stoare of prouisioun; there are elephants in great number and **abadas**, which is a kind of beast so big as two great buls, and hath vppon his snowt a little horne."—*Mendoza*, ii. 311.

1592.—"We sent commodities to their king to barter for Amber-greese, and for the hornes of **Abath**, whereof the Kinge onely hath the traffique in his hands. Now this **Abath** is a beast that hath one horne only in her forehead, and is thought to be the female Vnicorne, and is highly esteemed of all the Moores in those parts as a most soveraigne remedie against poyson."—*Barker* in *Hakl.* ii. 591.

1598.—"The **Abada**, or Rhinoceros, is not in India,* but onely in *Bengala* and *Patane*."—*Linschoten*, 88. [Hak. Soc. ii. 8.]

"Also in *Bengala* we found great numbers of the beasts which in Latin are called *Rhinocerotes*, and of the Portingalles **Abadas**."—*Ibid.* 28. [Hak. Soc. i. 96.]

c. 1606.—". . . ove portano le loro mercanzie per venderle a' Cinesi, particolarmente . . . molti corni della **Bada**, detto Rinoceronte . . ."—*Carletti*, p. 199.

1611.—"**Bada**, a very fierce animal, called by another more common name *Rhinoceros*. In our days they brought to the King Philip II., now in glory, a **Bada** which was long at Madrid, having his horn sawn off, and being blinded, for fear he should hurt anybody. . . . The name of **Bada** is one imposed by the Indians themselves; but assuming that

* *i.e.*, not on the W. coast of the Peninsula, called *India* especially by the Portuguese. See under **INDIA**.

there is no language but had its origin from the Hebrew in the confusion of tongues . . . it will not be out of the way to observe that **Bada** is an Hebrew word, from *Badad*, 'solus, solitarius,' for this animal is produced in desert and very solitary places."—*Cobarruvias*, s. v.

1613.—"And the woods give great timber, and in them are produced elephants, **badas** . . ."—*Godinho de Eredia*, 10 *v.*

1618.—"A China brought me a present of a cup of **abado** (or black unecorns horne) with sugar cakes."—*Cocks's Diary*, ii. 56.

1626.—On the margin of Pigafetta's *Congo*, as given by Purchas (ii. 1001), we find: "Rhinoceros or **Abadas**."

1631.—"Lib. v. cap. 1. De **Abada** seu Rhinocerote."—*Bontii Hist. Nat. et Med.*

1726.—"**Abada**, s. f. La hembra del Rhinoceronte."—*Dicc. de la Lengua Castellana.*

ABCÁREE, ABKARY. H. from P. *āb-kārī*, the business of distilling or selling (strong) waters, and hence elliptically the excise upon such business. This last is the sense in which it is used by Anglo-Indians. In every district of India the privilege of selling spirits is farmed to contractors, who manage the sale through retail shopkeepers. This is what is called the '**Abkary** System.' The system has often been attacked as promoting tippling, and there are strong opinions on both sides. We subjoin an extract from a note on the subject, too long for insertion in integrity, by one of much experience in Bengal—Sir G. U. Yule.

June, 1879.—"Natives who have expressed their views are, I believe, unanimous in ascribing the increase of drinking to our **Abkaree** system. I don't say that this is putting the cart before the horse, but they are certainly too forgetful of the increased means in the country, which, if not the sole cause of the increased consumption, has been at least a very large factor in that result. I myself believe that more people drink now than formerly; but I knew one gentleman of very long and intimate knowledge of Bengal, who held that there was as much drinking in 1820 as in 1860."

In any case exaggeration is abundant. All Sanskrit literature shows that tippling is no absolute novelty in India. [See the article on "Spirituous Drinks in Ancient India," by Rajendralala Mitra, *Indo-Aryans*, i. 389 *seqq.*]

1790.—"In respect to **Abkarry**, or Tax on Spirituous Liquors, which is reserved for Taxation . . . it is evident that we cannot establish a general rate, since the quantity of consumption and expense of manufacture, etc., depends upon the vicinity of principal stations. For the amount leviable upon different Stills we must rely upon officers' local knowledge. The public, indeed, cannot suffer, since, if a few stills are suppressed by over-taxation, drunkenness is diminished."—In a *Letter from Board of Revenue* (Bengal) to Government, 12th July. MS. in *India Office.*

1797.—"The stamps are to have the words '**Abcaree** licenses' inscribed in the Persian and Hindu languages and character."—*Bengal Regulations*, x. 33.

ABIHÓWA. Properly P. *āb-o-hawā*, 'water and air.' The usual Hindustani expression for 'climate.'

1786.—"What you write concerning the death of 500 Koorgs from small-pox is understood . . . . they must be kept where the climate [**āb-o-hawā**] may best agree with them."—*Tippoo's Letters*, 269.

ABYSSINIA, n.p. This geographical name is a 16-century Latinisation of the Arabic *Habash*, through the Portuguese *Abex*, bearing much the same pronunciation, minus the aspirate. [See **HUBSHEE.**]

[1598.—"The countrey of the **Abexynes**, at Prester John's land."—*Linschoten*, Hak. Soc. i. 38.

1617.—"He sent mee to buy three **Abassines**."—*Sir T. Roe, Travels*, Hak. Soc. ii. 445.]

A. C. (*i.e.* 'after compliments'). In official versions of native letters these letters stand for the omitted formalities of native compliments.

ACHÁNOCK, n.p. H. *Chānak* and *Achānak*. The name by which the station of **Barrackpore** is commonly known to Sepoys and other natives. Some have connected the name with that of Job *Charnock*, or, as A. Hamilton calls him, **Channock**, the founder of Calcutta, and the quotations render this probable. Formerly the Cantonment of Secrole at Benares was also known, by a transfer no doubt, as *Chhotā* (or 'Little') **Achānak**. Two additional remarks may be relevantly made: (1) Job's name was certainly *Charnock*, and not *Channock*. It is distinctly signed "Job Charnock," in a MS. letter from the factory at "Chutta," *i.e.* Chuttanuttee (or Calcutta) in the India Office records, which I have seen. (2) The map in Valentijn which shows the village of **Tsjannok**, though published in 1726, was apparently compiled by Van der

Broecke in 1662. Hence it is not probable that it took its name from Job Charnock, who seems to have entered the Company's service in 1658. When he went to Bengal we have not been able to ascertain. [See *Diary of Hedges*, edited by Sir H. Yule, ii., xcix. In some "Documentary Memoirs of Job Charnock," which form part of vol. lxxv. (1888) of the Hakluyt Soc., Job is said to have "arrived in India in 1655 or 1656."]

1677.—"The ship *Falcone* to go up the river to Hughly, or at least to **Channock.**" —Court's Letter to Ft. St. Geo. of 12th December. In *Notes and Extracts*, Madras, 1871, No. 1., p. 21 ; see also p. 23.

1711.—"**Chanock**-Reach hath two shoals, the upper one in **Chanock**, and the lower one on the opposite side . . . . you must from below *Degon* as aforesaid, keep the starboard shore aboard until you come up with a Lime-Tree . . . . and then steer over with **Chanock** Trees and house between the two shoals, until you come mid-river, but no nearer the house."—*The English Pilot*, 55.

1726.—"'t stedeken **Tsjannock.**"—*Valentijn*, v. 153. In Val.'s map of Bengal also, we find opposite to *Oegli* (Hoogly), **Tsjannok**, and then *Collecatte*, and *Calcula*.

1758.—"Notwithstanding these solemn assurances from the Dutch it was judged expedient to send a detachment of troops . . . . to take possession of Tanna Fort and **Charnoc's** Battery opposite to it."—Narrative of Dutch attempt in the Hoogly, in *Malcolm's Life of Clive*, ii. 76.

1810.—"The old village of **Achanock** stood on the ground which the post of Barrackpore now occupies."—*M. Graham*, 142.

1848.—"From an oral tradition still prevalent among the natives at Barrackpore . . . we learn that Mr. Charnock built a bungalow there, and a flourishing bazar arose under his patronage, before the settlement. of Calcutta had been determined on. Barrackpore is at this day best known to the natives by the name of **Chanock.**"—*The Bengal Obituary*, Calc. p. 2.

ACHÁR, s. P. *āchār*, Malay *ăchār*, adopted in nearly all the vernaculars of India for acid and salt relishes. By Europeans it is used as the equivalent of 'pickles,' and is applied to all the stores of Crosse and Blackwell in that kind. We have adopted the word through the Portuguese ; but it is not impossible that Western Asiatics got it originally from the Latin *acetaria*.—(See *Plin. Hist. Nat.* xix. 19).

1563.—"And they prepare a conserve of it (*Anacardium*) with salt, and when it is green (and this they call **Achar**), and this is sold in the market just as olives are with us."—*Garcia*, f. 17.

1596.—Linschoten in the Dutch gives the word correctly, but in the English version (Hak. Soc. ii. 26) it is printed *Machar*.

[1612.—"**Achar** none to be had except one jar."—*Danvers, Letters*, i. 230.]

1616.—"Our *jurebasso's* (**Juribasso**) wife came and brought me a small jarr of **Achar** for a present, desyring me to exskews her husband in that he abcented hymselfe to take phisik."—*Cocks*, i. 135.

1623.—"And all these preserved in a way that is really very good, which they call **acciao.**"—*P. della Valle*, ii. 708. [Hak. Soc. ii. 327.]

1653.—"**Achar** est vn nom Indistanni, ou Indien, que signifie des mangues, ou autres fruits confis avec de la moutarde, de l'ail, du sel, et du vinaigre à l'Indienne."—*De la Boullaye-le-Gouz*, 531.

1687.—"**Achar** I presume signifies sauce. They make in the *East Indies*, especially at *Siam* and *Pegu*, several sorts of **Achar**, as of the young tops of Bamboes, &c. Bambo-*Achar* and Mango-*Achar* are most used."—*Dampier*, i. 391.

1727.—"And the Soldiery, Fishers, Peasants, and Handicrafts (of Goa) feed on a little Rice boiled in Water, with a little bit of Salt Fish, or **Atchaar**, which is pickled Fruits or Roots."—*A. Hamilton*, i. 252. [And see under **KEDGEREE.**]

1783.—We learn from Forrest that limes, salted for sea-use against scurvy, were used by the *Chulias* (**Choolia**), and were called **atchar** (*Voyage to Mergui*, 40). Thus the word passed to Java, as in next quotation :

1768-71.—"When green it (the mango) is made into **attjar**; for this the kernel is taken out, and the space filled in with ginger, pimento, and other spicy ingredients, after which it is pickled in vinegar." —*Stavorinus*, i. 237.

ACHEEN, n.p. (P. *Āchīn* [Tam. *Attai*, Malay *Acheh*, *Achih*] 'a wood-leech'). The name applied by us to the State and town at the N.W. angle of Sumatra, which was long, and especially during the 16th and 17th centuries, the greatest native power on that Island. The proper Malay name of the place is *Acheh*. The Portuguese generally called it *Achem* (or frequently by the adhesion of the genitive preposition, *Dachem*, so that Sir F. Greville below makes two kingdoms), but our **Acheen** seems to have been derived from mariners of the P. Gulf or W. India, for we find the name so given (*Āchīn*) in the *Āīn-i-Akbari*, and in the Geog. Tables of Ṣādiḳ Isfahānī. This form may have been suggested by a jingling analogy, such as Orientals love, with Māchīn (**Macheen**). See also under **LOOTY**.

1549.—"Piratarum **Acenorum** nec periculum nec suspicio fuit."—*S. Fr. Xav. Epistt.* 337.

1552.—"But after Malacca was founded, and especially at the time of our entry into India, the Kingdom of Pacem began to increase in power, and that of Pedir to diminish. And that neighbouring one of **Achem**, which was then insignificant, is now the greatest of all."—*Barros*, III. v. 8.

1563.—

"Occupado tenhais na guerra infesta
Ou do sanguinolento,
Taprobanico* **Achem**, que ho mar molesta
Ou do Cambaico occulto imiguo nosso."
Camões, Ode prefixed to Garcia de Orta.

c. 1569.—"Upon the headland towards the West is the Kingdom of **Assi**, governed by a Moore King."—*Cæsar Frederike*, tr. in *Hakluyt*, ii. 355.

c. 1590.—"The *zabád* (civet), which is brought from the harbour-town of Sumatra, from the territory of **Achín**, goes by the name of *Sumatra-zabád*, and is by far the best."—*Āīn*, i. 79.

1597.—". . . . . do Pegu como do **Dachem**."—*King's Letter*, in *Arch. Port. Or.* fasc. 3, 669.

1599.—"The iland of Sumatra, or Taprobuna, is possessed by many Kynges, enemies to the Portugals; the cheif is the Kinge of **Dachem**, who besieged them in Malacca. . . The Kinges of **Acheyn** and Tor (read *Jor* for *Johore*) are in lyke sort enemies to the Portugals."—*Sir Fulke Greville* to Sir F. Walsingham (in *Bruce*, i. 125).

[1615.—"It so proved that both Ponleema and Governor of Tecoo was come hither for **Achein**."—*Foster, Letters*, iv. 3.

1623.—"**Acem** which is Sumatra."—*P. della Valle*, Hak. Soc. ii. 287.]

c. 1635.—"**Achín** (a name equivalent in rhyme and metre to 'Máchín') is a well-known island in the Chinese Sea, near to the equinoctial line."—*Ṣādiḳ Isfahānī* (Or. Tr. F.), p. 2.

1780.—"**Archin**." See quotation under **BOMBAY MARINE**.

1820.—"In former days a great many junks used to frequent **Achin**. This trade is now entirely at an end."—*Crawfurd, H. Ind. Arch.* iii. 182.

ADAM'S APPLE. This name (*Pomo d'Adamo*) is given at Goa to the fruit of the *Mimusops Elengi*, Linn. (*Birdwood*); and in the 1635 ed. of Gerarde's *Herball* it is applied to the Plantain. But in earlier days it was applied to a fruit of the Citron kind.—(See *Marco Polo*, 2nd ed., i. 101), and the following:

c. 1580.—"In his hortis (of Cairo) ex arboribus virescunt mala citria, aurantia, limonia sylvestria et domestica **poma Adami** vocata."—*Prosp. Alpinus*, i. 16.

c. 1712.—"It is a kind of lime or citron tree . . . it is called **Pomum Adami**, because it has on its rind the appearance of two bites, which the simplicity of the ancients imagined to be the vestiges of the impression which our forefather made upon the forbidden fruit. . . ." *Bluteau*, quoted by Tr. of *Alboquerque*, Hak. Soc. i. 100. The fruit has nothing to do with *zamboa*, with which Bluteau and Mr. Birch connect it. See **JAMBOO**.

ADATI, s. A kind of piece-goods exported from Bengal. We do not know the proper form or etymology. It may have been of half-width (from H. *ādhā*, 'half'). [It may have been half the ordinary length, as the Salampore (**Salempoory**) was half the length of the cloth known in Madras as *Punjum*. (*Madras Man. of Ad.* iii. 799). Also see Yule's note in *Hedges' Diary*, ii. ccxl.]

1726.—"*Casseri* (probably *Kasiāri* in Midnapur Dist.) supplies many *Taffatshelas* (**Alleja, Shalee**), *Ginggangs*, *Allegias*, and **Adathays**, which are mostly made there."—*Valentijn*, v. 159.

1813.—Among piece-goods of Bengal: "**Addaties**, Pieces 700" (*i.e.* pieces to the ton).—*Milburn*, ii. 221.

ADAWLUT, s. Ar.—H.—*'adālat*, 'a Court of Justice,' from *'adl*, 'doing justice.' Under the Mohammedan government there were 3 such courts, viz., *Nizāmat* **'Adālat**, *Dīwānī* **Adālat**, and *Faujdārī* **'Adālat**, so-called from the respective titles of the officials who nominally presided over them. The first was the chief Criminal Court, the second ä Civil Court, the third a kind of Police Court. In 1793 regular Courts were established under the British Government, and then the *Sudder* **Adawlut** (*Ṣadr 'Adālat*) became the chief Court of Appeal for each Presidency, and its work was done by several European (Civilian) Judges. That Court was, on the criminal side, termed *Nizamut Adawlat*, and on the civil side *Dewanny Ad.* At Madras and Bombay, *Foujdarry* was the style adopted in lieu of *Nizamut*. This system ended in 1863, on the introduction of the Penal Code, and the institution of the High Courts on their

* This alludes to the mistaken notion, as old as N. Conti (c. 1440), that Sumatra = *Taprobane*.

present footing. (On the original history and constitution of the Courts see *Fifth Report*, 1812, p. 6.)

What follows applies only to the Bengal Presidency, and to the administration of justice under the Company's Courts beyond the limits of the Presidency town. Brief particulars regarding the history of the Supreme Courts and those Courts which preceded them will be found under **SUPREME COURT**.

The grant, by Shāh 'Ālam, in 1765, of the Dewanny of Bengal, Behar, and Orissa to the Company, transferred all power, civil and military, in those provinces, to that body. But no immediate attempt was made to undertake the direct detailed administration of either revenue or justice by the agency of the European servants of the Company. Such superintendence, indeed, of the administration was maintained in the prior acquisitions of the Company—viz., in the Zemindary of Calcutta, in the Twenty-four Pergunnas, and in the Chucklas (**Chucklah**) or districts of Burdwan, Midnapoor, and Chittagong, which had been transferred by the Nawab, Kāsim 'Ali Khān, in 1760; but in the rest of the territory it was confined to the agency of a Resident at the Moorshedabad Durbar, and of a 'Chief' at Patna. Justice was administered by the Mohammedan courts under the native officials of the Dewanny.

In 1770, European officers were appointed in the districts, under the name of *Supervisors*, with powers of control over the natives employed in the collection of the Revenue and the administration of justice, whilst local councils, with superior authority in all branches, were established at Moorshedabad and Patna. It was not till two years later that, under express orders from the Court of Directors, the effective administration of the provinces was undertaken by the agency of the Company's covenanted servants. At this time (1772) Courts of Civil Justice (*Mofussil Dewanny Adawlut*) were established in each of the Districts then recognised. There were also District Criminal Courts (*Foujdary Adawlut*) held by **Cazee** or **Mufty** under the superintendence, like the Civil Court, of the Collectors, as the Supervisors were now styled; whilst Superior Courts (*Sudder Dewanny, Sudder Nizamut* **Adawlut**) were established at the Presidency, to be under the superintendence of three or four members of the Council of Fort William.

In 1774 the Collectors were recalled, and native 'Amils (**Aumil**) appointed in their stead. Provincial Councils were set up for the divisions of Calcutta, Burdwan, Dacca, Moorshedabad, Dinagepore, and Patna, in whose hands the superintendence, both of revenue collection and of the administration of civil justice, was vested, but exercised by the members in rotation.

The state of things that existed under this system was discreditable. As Courts of Justice the provincial Councils were only "colourable imitations of courts, which had abdicated their functions in favour of their own subordinate (native) officers, and though their decisions were nominally subject to the Governor-General in Council, the Appellate Court was even a more shadowy body than the Courts of first instance. The Court never sat at all, though there are some traces of its having at one time decided appeals on the report of the head of the **Khalsa**, or native exchequer, just as the Provincial Council decided them on the report of the Cazis and Muftis." *

In 1770 the Government resolved that Civil Courts, independent of the Provincial Councils, should be established in the six divisions named above,† each under a civilian judge with the title of Superintendent of the *Dewanny Adawlut*; whilst to the Councils should still pertain the trial of causes relating to the public revenue, to the demands of zemindars upon their tenants, and to boundary questions. The appeal from the District Courts still lay to the Governor-General and his Council, as forming the Court of *Sudder Dewanny*; but that this might be real, a judge was appointed its head in the person of Sir Elijah Impey, the Chief Justice of the Supreme Court, an appointment which became famous. For it was represented as a transaction intended to compromise the acute dis-

* *Sir James Stephen*, in *Nuncomar and Impey*, ii. 221.

† These six were increased in 1781 to eighteen.

sensions which had been going on between that Court and the Bengal Government, and in fact as a bribe to Impey. It led, by an address from the House of Commons, to the recall of Impey, and constituted one of the charges in the abortive impeachment of that personage. Hence his charge of the Sudder Dewanny ceased in November, 1782, and it was resumed in form by the Governor-General and Council.

In 1787, the first year of Lord Cornwallis's government, in consequence of instructions from the Court of Directors, it was resolved that, with an exception as to the Courts at Moorshedabad, Patna, and Dacca, which were to be maintained independently, the office of judge in the Mofussil Courts was to be attached to that of the collection of the revenue; in fact, the offices of Judge and Collector, which had been divorced since 1774, were to be reunited. The duties of Magistrate and Judge became mere appendages to that of Collector; the administration of justice became a subordinate function; and in fact all Regulations respecting that administration were passed in the Revenue Department of the Government.

Up to 1790 the criminal judiciary had remained in the hands of the native courts. But this was now altered; four Courts of Circuit were created, each to be superintended by two civil servants as judges; the *Sudder Nizamut Adawlut* at the Presidency being presided over by the Governor-General and the members of Council.

In 1793 the constant succession of revolutions in the judicial system came to something like a pause, with the entire reformation which was enacted by the Regulations of that year. The Collection of Revenue was now entirely separated from the administration of justice; Zillah Courts under European judges were established (Reg. iii.) in each of 23 Districts and 3 cities, in Bengal, Behar, and Orissa; whilst Provincial Courts of Appeal, each consisting of three judges (Reg. v.), were established at Moorshedabad, Patna, Dacca, and Calcutta. From these Courts, under certain conditions, further appeal lay to the Sudder Dewanny **Adawluts** at the Presidency.

As regarded criminal jurisdiction, the judges of the Provincial Courts were also (Reg. ix., 1793) constituted Circuit Courts, liable to review by the *Sudder Nizamut*. Strange to say, the impracticable idea of placing the duties of both of the higher Courts, civil and criminal, on the shoulders of the executive Government was still maintained, and the Governor-General and his Council were the constituted heads of the *Sudder Dewanny* and *Sudder Nizamut*. This of course continued as unworkable as it had been; and in Lord Wellesley's time, eight years later, the two *Sudder Adawluts* were reconstituted, with three regular judges to each, though it was still ruled (Reg. ii., 1801) that the chief judge in each Court was to be a member of the Supreme Council, not being either the Governor-General or the Commander-in-Chief. This rule was rescinded by Reg. x. of 1805.

The number of Provincial and Zillah Courts was augmented in after years with the extension of territory, and additional Sudder Courts, for the service of the Upper Provinces, were established at Allahabad in 1831 (Reg. vi.), a step which may be regarded as the inception of the separation of the N.W. Provinces into a distinct Lieutenant-Governorship, carried out five years later. But no change that can be considered at all organic occurred again in the judiciary system till 1862; for we can hardly consider as such the abolition of the Courts of Circuit in 1829 (Reg. i.), and that of the Provincial Courts of Appeal initiated by a section in Reg. v. of 1831, and completed in 1833.

1822.—"This refers to a traditional story which Mr. Elphinstone used to relate .... During the progress of our conquests in the North-West many of the inhabitants were encountered flying from the newly-occupied territory. 'Is Lord Lake coming?' was the enquiry. 'No,' was the reply, 'the **Adawlut** is coming.'"—*Life of Ephinstone*, ii. 131.

1826.—"The **adawlut** or Court-house was close by."—*Pandurang Hari*, 271 [ed. 1873, ii. 90].

ADIGAR, s. Properly *adhikār*, from Skt. *adhikārin*, one possessing authority; Tam. *adhikāri*, or *-kāren*. The title was formerly in use in South India, and perhaps still in the native States of Malabar, for a rural headman. [See quot. from Logan below.] It was also in Ceylon (*adikārama, adikār*) the title of chief minister of the Candyan Kings. See **PATEL**.

1544.—"Fac te comem et humanum cum isti Genti praebeas, tum praesertim magistratibus eorum et Praefectis Pagorum, quos **Adigares** vocant."—*S. Fr. Xav. Epistt.* 113.

1583.—"Mentre che noi erauamo in questa città, l'assalirono sù la mezza notte all' improuiso, mettendoui il fuoco. Erano questi d'una città uicina, lontana da S. Thomè, doue stanno i Portoghesi, un miglio, sotto la scorta d'un loro Capitano, che risiede in detta città . . . et questo Capitano è da loro chiamato **Adicario**."—*Balbi*, f. 87.

1681.—"There are two who are the greatest and highest officers in the land. They are called **Adigars**; I may term them Chief Judges."—*Knox*, 48.

1726.—"**Adigaar**. This is as it were the second of the *Dessave*."—*Valentijn* (Ceylon), *Names of Officers*, &c., 9.

1796.—"In Malabar esiste oggidi l'uffizio . . . . molti *Káriakárer* o ministri; molti **Adhigári** o ministri d'un distretto . . . "—*Fra Paolino*, 237.

1803.—"The highest officers of State are the **Adigars** or Prime Ministers. They are two in number."—*Percival's Ceylon*, 256.

[1810-17.—"Announcing in letters . . . . his determination to exercise the office of Serv **Adikar**."—*Wilks, Mysoor*, i. 264.

1887.—"Each *amsam* or parish has now besides the **Adhikāri** or man of authority, headman, an accountant."—*Logan, Man. of Malabar*, i. 90.]

ADJUTANT, s. A bird so called (no doubt) from its comical resemblance to a human figure in a stiff dress pacing slowly on a parade-ground. It is the H. *haṛgīlā*, or gigantic crane, and popular scavenger of Bengal, the *Leptoptilus argala* of Linnæus. The H. name is by some dictionaries derived from a supposed Skt. word *haḍḍa-gila*, 'bone-swallower.' The compound, however appropriate, is not to be found in Böhtlingk and Roth's great Dictionary. The bird is very well described by Aelian, under the name of Κήλα, which is perhaps a relic of the still preserved vernacular one. It is described by another name, as one of the peculiarities of India, by Sultan Baber. See **PELICAN**.

"The feathers known as Marabou or Comercolly feathers, and sold in Calcutta, are the tail-coverts of this, and the *Lept. Javanica*, another and smaller species" (*Jerdon*). The name *marabout* (from the Ar. *murābit*, 'quiet,' and thence 'a hermit,' through the Port. *marabuto*) seems to have been given to the bird in Africa on like reason to that of adjutant in India. [Comercolly, properly Kumārkhāli, is a town in the Nadiya District, Bengal. See *Balfour, Cycl.* i. 1082.]

c. A.D. 250.—"And I hear that there is in India a bird *Kēla*, which is 3 times as big as a bustard; it has a mouth of a frightful size, and long legs, and it carries a huge crop which looks like a leather bag; it has a most dissonant voice, and whilst the rest of the plumage is ash-coloured, the tail-feathers are of a pale (or greenish) colour."—*Aelian, de Nat. Anim.* xvi. 4.

c. 1530.—"One of these (fowls) is the *dīng*, which is a large bird. Each of its wings is the length of a man; on its head and neck there is no hair. Something like a bag hangs from its neck; its back is black, its breast white; it frequently visits Kābul. One year they caught and brought me a *dīng*, which became very tame. The flesh which they threw it, it never failed to catch in its beak, and swallowed without ceremony. On one occasion it swallowed a shoe well shod with iron; on another occasion it swallowed a good-sized fowl right down, with its wings and feathers."—*Baber*, 321.

1754.—"In the evening excursions . . . . we had often observed an extraordinary species of birds, called by the natives *Argill* or *Hargill*, a native of Bengal. They would majestically stalk along before us, and at first we took them for Indians naked. . . . The following are the exact marks and dimensions. . . . The wings extended 14 feet and 10 inches. From the tip of the bill to the extremity of the claw it measured 7 feet 6 inches. . . . In the craw was a *Terapin* or land-tortoise, 10 inches long; and a large black male cat was found entire in its stomach."—*Ives*, 183-4.

1798.—"The next is the great Heron, the *Argali* or **Adjutant**, or Gigantic Crane of Latham. . . . It is found also in Guinea."—*Pennant's View of Hindostan*, ii. 156.

1810.—"Every bird saving the vulture, the **Adjutant** (or *argeelah*) and kite, retires to some shady spot."—*Williamson, V. M.* ii. 3.

[1880.—Ball (*Jungle Life*, 82) describes the "snake-stone" said to be found in the head of the bird.]

AFGHÁN, n.p. P.—H—*Afghān*. The most general name of the predominant portion of the congeries of tribes beyond the N.W. frontier of India, whose country is called from them *Afghānistān*. In England one often hears the country called *Afgunist-un*, which is a mispronunciation painful to an Anglo-Indian ear, and even *Af'gann*, which is a still more excruciating solecism. [The common local pronunciation of the name is *Aoghān*, which accounts for some of the forms below. Bellew insists on the distinction between the

Afghān and the Pathān (**PUTTAN**). "The Afghan is a Pathan merely because he inhabits a Pathan country, and has to a great extent mixed with its people and adopted their language" (*Races of Af.*, p. 25). The name represents Skt. *asvaka* in the sense of a 'cavalier,' and this reappears scarcely modified in the Assakani or Assakeni of the historians of the expedition of Alexander.]

c. 1020.—". . . **Afgháns** and Khiljis . . ." —'*Utbi* in *Elliot*, ii. 24; see also 50, 114.

c. 1265.—"He also repaired the fort of Jalálí, which he garrisoned with **Afgháns**." —*Tárikh-i-Firozsháhi* in do. iii. 106.

14th cent.—The **Afghans** are named by the continuator of Rashiduddin among the tribes in the vicinity of Herat (see *N. & E.* xiv. 494).

1504.—"The **Afghans**, when they are reduced to extremities in war, come into the presence of their enemy with grass between their teeth; being as much as to say, 'I am your ox.'" *—*Baber*, 159.

c. 1556.—"He was afraid of the **Afgháns**." —*Sidi 'Ali*, in *J. As.*, 1st S., ix. 201.

1609.—"**Agwans** and *Potans*." — *W. Finch*, in *Purchas*, i. 521.

c. 1665.—"Such are those petty Sovereigns, who are seated on the Frontiers of Persia, who almost never pay him anything, no more than they do to the King of Persia. As also the *Balouches* and **Augans**, and other Mountaineers, of whom the greatest part pay him but a small matter, and even care but little for him: witness the Affront they did him, when they stopped his whole Army by cutting off the Water . . . . when he passed from *Atek* on the River *Indus* to **Caboul** to lay siege to **Kandahar** . . . ."—*Bernier*, E. T. 64 [ed. *Constable*, 205].

1676.—"The people called **Augans** who inhabit from *Candahar* to *Caboul* . . a sturdy sort of people, and great robbers in the night-time."—*Tavernier*, E. T. ii. 44; [*ed. Ball*, i. 92].

1767.—"Our final sentiments are that we have no occasion to take any measures against the **Afghans**' King if it should appear he comes only to raise contributions, but if he proceeds to the eastward of Delhi to make an attack on your allies, or threatens the peace of Bengal, you will concert such measures with Sujah Dowla as may appear best adapted for your mutual defence." —*Court's Letter*, Nov. 20. In *Long*, 486; also see **ROHILLA**.

1838.—"Professor Dorn . . . . discusses severally the theories that have been maintained of the descent of the **Afghauns**: 1st, from the Copts; 2nd, the Jews; 3rd, the Georgians; 4th, the Toorks; 5th, the Moguls; 6th, the Armenians: and he mentions more cursorily the opinion that they are descended from the Indo-Scythians, Medians, Sogdians, Persians, and Indians: on considering all which, he comes to the rational conclusion, that they cannot be traced to any tribe or country beyond their present seats and the adjoining mountains."—*Elphinstone's Caubool*, ed. 1839, i. 209.

* This symbolical action was common among *beldars* (Bildar), or native *navvies*, employed on the Ganges Canal many years ago, when they came before the engineer to make a petition. But besides grass in mouth, the beldar stood *on one leg*, with hands joined before him.

AFRICO, n.p. A negro slave.

1682.—"Here we met with ye Barbadoes Merchant . . . . James Cock, Master, laden with Salt, Mules, and **Africos**."—*Hedges, Diary*, Feb. 27. [Hak. Soc. i. 16.]

[**AGAM**, adj. A term applied to certain cloths dyed in some particular way. It is the Ar. *'ajam* (lit. "one who has an impediment or difficulty in speaking Arabic"), a foreigner, and in particular, a Persian. The adj. *'ajamī* thus means "foreign" or "Persian," and is equivalent to the Greek *βάρβαρος* and the Hind. *mlećcha*. Sir G. Birdwood (*Rep. on Old Rec.*, p. 145) quotes from Hieronimo di Santo Stefano (1494-99), "in company with some Armenian and *Azami* merchants": and (*ibid.*) from Varthema: "It is a country of very great traffic in merchandise, and particularly with the Persians and *Azamini*, who come so far as there."]

[1614.—"Kerseys, **Agam** colours."—*Foster, Letters*, ii. 237.

1614.—"Persia will vent five hundred cloths and one thousand kerseys, **Agam** colours, per annum."—*Ibid.* ii. 237.]

AGAR-AGAR, s. The Malay name of a kind of sea-weed (*Spherococcus lichenoïdes*). It is succulent when boiled to a jelly; and is used by the Chinese with birdsnest (*q.v.*) in soup. They also employ it as a glue, and apply it to silk and paper intended to be transparent. It grows on the shores of the Malay Islands, and is much exported to China.—(See *Crawfurd, Dict. Ind. Arch.*, and *Milburn*, ii. 304).

AGDAUN, s. A hybrid H. word from H. *āg* and P. *dān*, made in imitation of *pīk-dān*, *kalam-dān*, *shama-dān* ('spittoon, pencase, candlestick'). It means a small vessel for holding fire to light a cheroot.

ĀG-GĀRI, s. H. 'Fire carriage.' In native use for a railway train.

AGUN-BOAT, s. A hybrid word for a steamer, from H. *agan*, 'fire,' and Eng. *boat*. In Bombay *Ag-bōt* is used.

1853.—" . . . . **Agin boat**."—*Oakfield*, i. 84.

[**AJNĀS**, s. Ar. plur. of *jins*, 'goods, merchandise, crops,' etc. Among the Moguls it was used in the special sense of pay in kind, not in cash.]

[c. 1665.—"It (their pay) is, however, of a different kind, and not thought so honourable, but the *Rouzindars* are not subject, like the *Mansebdars* (**Munsubdar**) to the **Agenas**; that is to say, are not bound to take, at a valuation, carpets, and other pieces of furniture, that have been used in the King's palace, and on which an unreasonable value is sometimes set."—*Bernier* (ed. *Constable*), 215-6.]

AK, s. H. *āk* and *ark*, in Sindi *ăk*: the prevalent name of the *madār* (**MUDDAR**) in Central and Western India. It is said to be a popular belief (of course erroneous) in Sind, that Akbar was so called after the *āk*, from his birth in the desert. [Ives (488) calls it **Ogg**.] The word appears in the following popular rhyme quoted by Tod (*Rajasthan*, i. 669):—

> Ak-rā jhoprā,
> Phok-rā bār,
> Bajra-rā rotī,
> Mot'h-rā dāl:
> Dekho Rājā terī Mārwār.
> (For houses hurdles of *madār*,
> For hedges heaps of withered thorn,
> Millet for bread, horse-peas for pulse:
> Such is thy kingdom, Raja of Mārwār!)

AKALEE, or *Nihang* ('the naked one'), s. A member of a body of zealots among the Sikhs, who take this name 'from being worshippers of Him who is without time, eternal' (*Wilson*). Skt. *a* privative, and *kāl*, 'time.' The Akālis may be regarded as the Wahābis of Sikhism. They claim their body to have been instituted by Guru Govind himself, but this is very doubtful. Cunningham's view of the order is that it was the outcome of the struggle to reconcile warlike activity with the abandonment of the world; the founders of the Sikh doctrine rejecting the inert asceticism of the Hindu sects. The Akālis threw off all subjection to the earthly government, and acted as the censors of the Sikh community in every rank. Runjeet Singh found them very difficult to control. Since the annexation of the Panjab, however, they have ceased to give trouble. The **Akalee** is distinguished by blue clothing and steel armlets. Many of them also used to carry several steel *chakras* (**CHUCKER**) encircling their turbans. [See *Ibbetson, Panjab Ethnog.*, 286; *Maclagan*, in *Panjab Census Rep.*, 1891, i. 166.]

1832.—"We received a message from the **Acali** who had set fire to the village. . . . These fanatics of the Seik creed acknowledge no superior, and the ruler of the country can only moderate their frenzy by intrigues and bribery. They go about everywhere with naked swords, and lavish their abuse on the nobles as well as the peaceable subjects. . . . They have on several occasions attempted the life of Runjeet Singh."—*Burnes, Travels*, ii. 10-11.

1840.—"The **Akalis** being summoned to surrender, requested a conference with one of the attacking party. The young Khan bravely went forward, and was straightway shot through the head."—*Mrs Mackenzie, Storms and Sunshine*, i. 115.

AKYÁB, n.p. The European name of the seat of administration of the British province of Arakan, which is also a port exporting rice largely to Europe. The name is never used by the natives of Arakan (of the Burmese race), who call the town *Tsit-htwé*, 'Crowd (in consequence of) War.' This indicates how the settlement came to be formed in 1825, by the fact of the British force encamping on the plain there, which was found to be healthier than the site of the ancient capital of the kingdom of Arakan, up the valley of the Arakan or Kaladyne R. The name **Akyáb** had been applied, probably by the Portuguese, to a neighbouring village, where there stands, about 1½ miles from the present town, a pagoda covering an alleged relique of Gautama (a piece of the lower jaw, or an induration of the throat), the name of which pagoda, taken from the description of relique, is *Au-kyait-dau*, and of this **Akyáb** was probably a corruption. The present town and cantonment occupy dry land of very recent formation, and the high ground on which the pagoda stands must have stood on the shore at no distant date, as appears from the finding of a small anchor there about 1835. The village adjoining the pagoda must then have stood at the mouth of the Arakan R., which was much frequented by the Portuguese and the Chittagong people in the 16th and 17th centuries, and thus probably became known to them by a name taken from the Pagoda.—(From a note by *Sir Arthur Phayre.*) [Col. Temple writes—"The only derivation which strikes me as plausible, is from the Agyattaw Phaya, near which, on the island of Sittwé, a Cantonment was formed after the first Burmese war, on the abandonment of Mrohaung or Arakan town in 1825, on account of sickness among the troops stationed there. The word Agyattaw is spelt Akhyap-taw, whence probably the modern name."]

[1826.—"It (the despatch) at length arrived this day (3rd Dec. 1826), having taken two months in all to reach us, of which forty-five days were spent in the route from **Akyab** in Aracan."—*Crawfurd, Ava*, 289.]

ALA-BLAZE PAN, s. This name is given in the Bombay Presidency to a tinned-copper stew-pan, having a cover, and staples for straps, which is carried on the march by European soldiers, for the purpose of cooking in, and eating out of. Out on picnics a larger kind is frequently used, and kept continually going, as a kind of *pot-au-feu*. [It has been suggested that the word may be a corr. of some French or Port. term—Fr. *braiser*; Port. *brazeiro*, 'a fire-pan,' *braza*, 'hot coals.']

ALBACORE, s. A kind of rather large sea-fish, of the Tunny genus (*Thynnus albacora*, Lowe, perhaps the same as *Thynnus macropterus*, Day); from the Port. *albacor* or *albecora*. The quotations from Ovington and Grose below refer it to *albo*, but the word is, from its form, almost certainly Arabic, though Dozy says he has not found the word in this sense in Arabic dictionaries, which are very defective in the names of fishes (p. 61). The word *albacora* in Sp. is applied to a large early kind of fig, from Ar. *al-bākūr*, 'praecox' (Dozy), Heb. *bikkūra*, in Micah vii. 1.—See *Cobarruvias*, s. v. *Albacora*. [The *N.E.D.* derives it from Ar. *al-bukr*, 'a young camel, a heifer,' whence Port. *bacoro*, 'a young pig.' Also see Gray s note on *Pyrard*, i. 9.]

1579.—'These (flying fish) have two enemies, the one in the sea, the other in the aire. In the sea the fish which is called **Albocore**, as big as a salmon."—*Letter from Goa, by T. Stevens*, in *Hakl.* ii. 583.

1592.—"In our passage over from S. Laurence to the maine, we had exceeding great store of Bonitos and **Albocores**."—*Barker*, in *Hakl.* ii. 592.

1696.—"We met likewise with shoals of **Albicores** (so call'd from a piece of white Flesh that sticks to their Heart) and with multitudes of Bonettoes, which are named from their Goodness and Excellence for eating; so that sometimes for more than twenty Days the whole Ship's Company have feasted on these curious fish."—*Ovington*, p. 48.

c. 1760.—"The **Albacore** is another fish of much the same kind as the Bonito . . from 60 to 90 pounds weight and upward. The name of this fish too is taken from the Portuguese, importing its white colour."—*Grose*, i. 5.

ALBATROSS, s. The great sea-bird (*Diomedea exulans*, L.), from the Port. *alcatraz*, to which the forms used by Hawkins and Dampier, and by Flacourt (according to Marcel Devic) closely approach. [*Alcatras* 'in this sense altered to *albi-*, *albe-*, *albatross* (perhaps with etymological reference to *albus*, "white," the albatross being white, while the *alcatras* was black.') *N.E.D.* s.v.] The Port. word properly means 'a pelican.' A reference to the latter word in our Glossary will show another curious misapplication. Devic states that *alcatruz* in Port. means 'the bucket of a Persian wheel,'* representing the Ar. *al-kādūs*, which is again from κάδος. He supposes that the pelican may have got this name in the same way that it is called in ordinary Ar. *sakka*, 'a water-carrier.' It has been pointed out by Dr Murray, that the *alcatruz* of some of the earlier voyagers, *e.g.*, of Davis below, is not the *Diomedea*, but the Man-of-War (or Frigate) Bird (*Fregatus aquilus*). Hawkins, at p. 187 of the work quoted, describes, without naming, a bird which is evidently the modern albatross. In the quotation from Mocquet again, *alcatruz* is applied to some smaller sea-bird. The passage from Shelvocke is that which suggested to Coleridge "The Ancient Mariner."

1564.—"The 8th December we ankered by a small Island called **Alcatrarsa**, wherein at our going a shoare, we found nothing but sea-birds, as we call them Ganets, but by the Portugals called **Alcatrarses**, who for that cause gave the said Island the same name."—*Hawkins* (Hak. Soc.), 15.

* Also see Dozy, s. v. *alcaduz*. *Alcadus*, according to Cobarruvias, is in Sp. one of the earthen pots of the *noria* or Persian wheel.

1593.—"The dolphins and bonitoes are the houndes, and the **alcatrarces** the hawkes, and the flying fishes the game."—*Ibid.* 152.

1604.—"The other foule called **Alcatrarzi** is a kind of Hawke that liueth by fishing. For when the Bonitos or Dolphines doe chase the flying fish vnder the water .... this **Alcatrarzi** flyeth after them like a Hawke after a Partridge."—*Davis* (Hak. Soc.), 158.

c. 1608-10.—"**Alcatraz** sont petis oiseaux ainsi comme estourneaux."—*Mocquet, Voyages*, 226.

1672.—"We met with those feathered Harbingers of the Cape .... **Albetrosses** .... they haue great Bodies, yet not proportionate to their Wings, which mete out twice their length."—*Fryer*, 12.

1690.—"They have several other Signs, whereby to know when they are near it, as by the Sea Fowl they meet at Sea, especially the **Algatrosses**, a very large long-winged Bird."—*Dampier*, i. 531.

1719.—"We had not had the sight of one fish of any kind, since we were come Southward of the Streights of *Le Mair*, nor one sea-bird, except a disconsolate black **Albitross**, who accompanied us for several days, hovering about us as if he had lost himself, till *Hatley* (my second Captain) observing, in one of his melancholy fits, that this bird was always hovering near us, imagin'd from his colour, that it might be some ill omen. .... But be that as it would, he after some fruitless attempts, at length shot the **Albitross**, not doubting (perhaps) that we should have a fair wind after it. . . ."—*Shelvocke's Voyage*, 72, 73.

1740.—". . . . a vast variety of sea-fowl, amongst which the most remarkable are the *Penguins*; they are in size and shape like a goose, but instead of wings they have short stumps like fins .... their bills are narrow like those of an **Albitross**, and they stand and walk in an erect posture. From this and their white bellies, *Sir John Narborough* has whimsically likened them to little children standing up in white aprons."—*Anson's Voyage*, 9th ed. (1756), p. 68.

1754.—"An **albatrose**, a sea-fowl, was shot off the Cape of Good Hope, which measured 17½ feet from wing to wing."—*Ives*, 5.

1803.—

"At length did cross an **Albatross**;
Thorough the fog it came;
As if it had been a Christian soul
We hailed it in God's name."

The Ancient Mariner.

c. 1861.—

"Souvent pour s'amuser, les hommes d'équipage
Prennent des **albatros**, vastes oiseaux des mers,
Qui suivent, indolents compagnons de voyage,
Le navire glissant sur les gouffres amers."

Baudelaire, L'Albatros.

ALCATIF, s. This word for 'a carpet' was much used in India in the 16th century, and is treated by some travellers as an Indian word. It is not however of Indian origin, but is an Arabic word (*ḳatīf*, 'a carpet with long pile') introduced into Portugal through the Moors.

c. 1540.—"There came aboard of Antonio de Faria more than 60 *batels*, and *balloons*, and *manchuas* (q. q. v.) with awnings and flags of silk, and rich **alcatifas**."—*Pinto*, ch. lxviii. (orig.).

1560.—"The whole tent was cut in a variety of arabesques, inlaid with coloured silk, and was carpeted with rich **alcatifas**."—*Tenreiro, Itin.*, c. xvii.

1578.—"The windows of the streets by which the Viceroy passes shall be hung with carpets (**alcatifadas**), and the doors decorated with branches, and the whole adorned as richly as possible."—*Archiv. Port. Orient.*, fascic. ii. 225.

[1598.—"Great store of rich Tapestrie, which are called **alcatiffas**."—*Linschoten*, Hak. Soc. i. 47.]

1608-10.—"Quand elles vont à l'Eglise on les porte en palanquin .... le dedans est d'vn grand tapis de Perse, qu'ils appellent **Alcatif** ...."—*Pyrard*, ii. 62; [Hak. Soc. ii. 102].

1648.—". . . . many silk stuffs, such as satin, contenijs (**Cuttanee**) attelap (read *attelas*), **alegie** .... *ornijs* [H. *orhnī*, 'A woman's sheet'] of gold and silk for women's wear, gold **alacatijven** . . . ."—*Van Twist*, 50.

1726.—"They know nought of chairs or tables. The small folks eat on a mat, and the rich on an **Alcatief**, or carpet, sitting with their feet under them, like our Tailors."—*Valentijn*, v. *Chorom*, 55.

ALCORANAS, s. What word does Herbert aim at in the following? [The Stanf. Dict. regards this as quite distinct from *Alcorān*, the Korān, or sacred book of Mohammedans (for which see *N.E.D.* s.v.), and suggests *Al-qorūn*, 'the horns,' or *al-qirān*, 'the vertices.']

1665.—"Some (mosques) have their **Alcorana's** high, slender, round steeples or towers, most of which are terrassed near the top, like the Standard in Cheapside, but twice the height."—*Herbert, Travels*, 3rd ed. 164.

ALCOVE, s. This English word comes to us through the Span. *alcova* and Fr. *alcove* (old Fr. *aucube*), from Ar. *al-ḳubbàh*, applied first to a kind of tent (so in Hebr. *Numbers* xxv. 8) and then to a vaulted building or recess. An edifice of Saracenic construction at Palermo is still known as *La Cuba*; and another, a domed tomb, as *La Cubola*. Whatever be the true formation of the last word, it seems to have given us, through the Italian, *Cupola*. [Not so in *N.E.D.*]

1738.—"**Cubba**, commonly used for the vaulted tomb of *marab-butts*" [Adjutant.]—*Shaw's Travels*, ed. 1757, p. 40.

ALDEA, s. A village; also a villa. Port. from the Ar. *al-ḍai'a*, 'a farm or villa.' Bluteau explains it as 'Povoção menor que lugar.' Lane gives among other and varied meanings of the Ar. word: 'An estate consisting of land or of land and a house, ... land yielding a revenue.' The word forms part of the name of many towns and villages in Spain and Portugal.

1547.—"The Governor (of Baçaem) Dom João de Castro, has given and gives many **aldeas** and other grants of land to Portuguese who served and were wounded at the fortress of Dio, and to others of long service. . . . ."—*Simão Botelho, Cartas* 3.

[1609.—"**Aldeas** in the Country."—*Danvers, Letters*, i. 25.]

1673.—"Here . . . in a sweet Air, stood a Magnificent Rural Church; in the way to which, and indeed all up and down this Island, are pleasant **Aldeas**, or villages and hamlets that . . . swarm with people."—*Valentijn*, v. (*Malabar*), 11.

1753.—"Les principales de ces qu'on appelle **Aldées** (terme que les Portugals ont mis en usage dans l'Inde) autour de Pondichéri et dans sa dependance sont . . ."—*D'Anville, Éclaircissemens*, 122.

1780.—"The Coast between these is filled with **Aldees**, or villages of the Indians."—*Dunn, N. Directory*, 5th ed., 110.

1782.—"Il y a aussi quelques **Aldées** considérables, telles que Navar et Portenove, qui appartiennent aux Princes du pays."—*Sonnerat, Voyage*, i. 37.

ALEPPEE, n.p. On the coast of Travancore; properly Alappuli. [Mal. *alappuzha*, 'the broad river'—(*Mad. Adm. Man. Gloss.* s.v.)].

[**ALFANDICA**, s. A custom-house and resort for foreign merchants in an oriental port. The word comes through the Port. *alfandega*, Span. *fundago*, Ital. *fondaco*, Fr. *fondeque* or *fondique*, from Ar. *al-funduk*, 'the inn,' and this from Gk. πανδοκεῖον or πανδοχεῖον, 'a pilgrim's hospice.']

[c. 1610.—"The conveyance of them thence to the **alfandigue**."—*Pyrard della Valle*, Hak. Soc. i. 361.]

[1615.—"The Iudge of the **Alfandica** came to invite me."—*Sir T. Roe, Embassy*, Hak. Soc. i. 72.]

[1615.—"That the goods of the English may be freely landed after dispatch in the **Alfandiga**."—*Foster, Letters*, iv. 79.]

ALGUADA, n.p. The name of a reef near the entrance to the Bassein branch of the Irawadi R., on which a splendid lighthouse was erected by Capt. Alex. Fraser (now Lieut.-General Fraser, C.B.) of the Engineers, in 1861-65. See some remarks and quotations under **NEGRAIS**.

ALJOFAR, s. Port. 'seed-pearl.' Cobarruvias says it is from Ar. *al-jauhar*, 'jewel.'

1404.—"And from these bazars (*alcacerias*) issue certain gates into certain streets, where they sell many things, such as cloths of silk and cotton, and *sendals*, and *tafetanas*, and silk, and pearl (**alxofar**)."—*Clavijo*, § lxxxi. (comp. *Markham*, 81).

1508.—"The **aljofar** and pearls that (your Majesty) orders me to send you I cannot have as they have them in Ceylon and in Caille, which are the sources of them: I would buy them with my blood, and with my money, which I have only from your giving. The Sinabaffs (*sinabafos*), **porcelain** vases (*porcellanas*), and wares of that sort are further off. If for my sins I stay here longer I will endeavour to get everything. The slave girls that you order me to send you must be taken from prizes,* for the heathen women of this country are black, and are mistresses to everybody by the time they are ten years old."—*Letter of the Viceroy D. Francisco d'Almeida to the King*, in *Correa*, i. 908-9.

[1665.—"As it (the idol) was too deformed, they made hands for it of the small pearls which we call 'pearls by the ounce.'"—*Tavernier*, ed. *Ball*, ii. 228.]

ALLAHABAD, n.p. This name, which was given in the time of Akbar to the old Hindu Prayāg or Prāg (**PRAAG**) has been subjected to a variety of corrupt pronunciations, both European and native. *Illahābāz* is a not uncommon native form, converted by Europeans into *Halabas*, and further by English soldiers formerly into *Isle o' bats*. And the *Illiabad*, which we find in the Hastings charges, survives in the *Elleeabad* still heard occasionally.

* Query, from captured vessels containing foreign (non-Indian) women? The words are as follows: "*As escravas que me diz que lhe mande, tomãose de prezas, que as Gentias d'esta terra são pretas, e mancebas do mundo como chegão a dez annos.*"

c. 1666.—"La Province de **Halabas** s'appelloit autrefois *Purop* (**Poorub**)."—*Thevenot*, v. 197.

[,, "**Elabas** (where the Gemna (Jumna) falls into the Ganges."—*Bernier* (ed. *Constable*), p. 36.]

1726.—"This exceptionally great river (Ganges) . . . . comes so far from the N. to the S. . . . . and so further to the city **Halabas**."—*Valentijn*.

1753.—"Mais ce qui interesse davantage dans la position de **Helabas**, c'est d'y retrouver celle de l'ancienne *Palibothra*. Aucune ville de l'Inde ne paroit égaler *Palibothra* ou *Palimbothra*, dans l'Antiquité. . . . C'est satisfaire une curiosité géographique bien placée, que de retrouver l'emplacement d'une ville de cette considération: mais j'ai lieu de croire qu'il faut employer quelque critique, dans l'examen des circonstances que l'Antiquité a fourni sur ce point. . . . Je suis donc persuadé, qu'il ne faut point chercher d'autre emplacement à Palibothra que celui de la ville d'**Helabas**. . . . ."—*D'Anville, Eclaircissemens*, pp. 53-55.

(Here D'Anville is in error. But see Rennell's *Memoir*, pp. 50-54, which clearly identifies Palibothra with **Patna**.)

1786.—" . . . . an attack and invasion of the Rohillas . . . . which nevertheless the said Warren Hastings undertook at the very time when, under the pretence of the difficulty of defending Corah and **Illiabad**, he sold these provinces to Sujah Dowla."—*Articles of Charge*, &c., in *Burke*, vi. 577.

,, "You will see in the letters from the Board . . . . a plan for obtaining **Illabad** from the Vizier, to which he had spirit enough to make a successful resistance."—*Cornwallis*, i. 238.

ALLEJA, s. This appears to be a stuff from Turkestan called (Turki) **alchah**, **alajah**, or **alăchah**. It is thus described: "a silk cloth 5 yards long, which has a sort of wavy line pattern running in the length on either side." (*Baden-Powell's Punjab Handbook*, 66). [Platts in his Hind. Dict. gives *ilăcha*, "a kind of cloth woven of silk and thread so as to present the appearance of cardamoms (*ilăchī*)." But this is evidently a folk etymology. Yusuf Ali (*Mon. on Silk Fabrics*, 95) accepts the derivation from *Alcha* or *Alăcha*, and says it was probably introduced by the Moguls, and has historical associations with Agra, where alone in the N.W.P. it is manufactured. "This fabric differs from the *Doriya* in having a substantial texture, whereas the *Doriya* is generally flimsy. The colours are generally red, or bluish-red, with white stripes." In some of the western Districts of the Panjab various kinds of fancy cotton goods are described as *Lacha*. (*Francis, Mon. on Cotton*, p. 8). It appears in one of the trade lists (see **PIECE-GOODS**) as *Elatches*.]

c. 1590.—"The improvement is visible . . . . *secondly* in the *Safid* **Alchahs** also called *Tarhdārs* . . ."—*Āīn*, i. 91. (Blochmann says: "*Alchah* or *Alăchah*, any kind of corded stuff. *Tarhdār* means *corded*.")

[1612.—"Hold the **Allesas** at 50 Rs."—*Danvers, Letters*, i. 205.]

1613.—"The *Nabob* bestowed upon him 850 *Mamoodies*, 10 fine *Baftas*, 30 *Topseiles* and 30 **Allizaes**."—*Dowton*, in *Purchas*, i. 504. "*Topseiles* are *Tafçilah* (*a stuff from Mecca*)."—*Āīn*, i. 93. [See **ADATI, PIECE-GOODS**].

1615.—"1 pec. **alleia** of 30 Rs. . . . "—*Cocks's Diary*, i. 64.

1648.—See *Van Twist* above, under **ALCATIF**. And 1673, see *Fryer* under **ATLAS**.

1653.—"**Alaias** (Alajas) est vn mot Indien, qui signifie des toiles de cotton et de soye: meslée de plusieurs couleurs."—*De la Boullaye-le-Gouz*, ed. 1657, p. 532.

[c. 1666.—"**Alachas**, or silk stuffs interwoven with gold and silver."—*Bernier* (ed. *Constable*), p. 120-21.]

1690.—"It (Suratt) is renown'd . . . . both for rich Silks, such as Atlasses, Cuttanees, Sooseys, Culgars, **Allajars** . . . . "—*Ovington*, 218.

1712.—"An **Allejah** petticoat striped with green and gold and white."—Advert. in *Spectator*, cited in *Malcolm, Anecdotes*, 429.

1726.—"Gold and silver **Allegias**."—*Valentijn* (*Surat*), iv. 146.

1813.—"**Allachas** (pieces to the ton) 1200."—*Milburn*, ii. 221.

1885.—"The cloth from which these pyjamas are made (in Swāt) is known as **Alacha**, and is as a rule manufactured in their own houses, from 2 to 20 threads of silk being let in with the cotton; the silk as well as the cotton is brought from Peshawur and spun at home."—*M'Nair's Report on Explorations*, p. 5.

ALLIGATOR, s. This is the usual Anglo-Indian term for the great lacertine amphibia of the rivers. It was apparently in origin a corruption, imported from S. America, of the Spanish *el* or *al lagarto* (from Lat. *lacerta*), 'a lizard.' The "Summary of the Western Indies" by Pietro Martire d'Angheria, as given in Ramusio, recounting the last voyage of Columbus, says that, in a certain river, "they sometimes encountered those crocodiles which they call **Lagarti**; these make away when they see the Christians, and in making away they leave behind them an odour more fragrant than musk." (*Ram.* iii.

f. 17*v.*). Oviedo, on another page of the same volume, calls them "**Lagarti o dragoni**" (f. 62).

Bluteau gives "**Lagarto**, *Crocodilo*" and adds: "In the Oriente Conquistado (Part I. f. 823) you will find a description of the Crocodile under the name of *Lagarto*."

One often, in Anglo-Indian conversation, used to meet with the endeavour to distinguish the two well-known species of the Ganges as *Crocodile* and **Alligator**, but this, like other applications of popular and general terms to mark scientific distinctions, involves fallacy, as in the cases of 'panther, leopard,' 'camel, dromedary,' 'attorney, solicitor,' and so forth. The two kinds of Gangetic crocodile were known to Aelian (c. 250 A.D.), who writes: "It (the Ganges) breeds two kinds of crocodiles; one of these is not at all hurtful, while the other is the most voracious and cruel eater of flesh; and these have a horny prominence on the top of the nostril. These latter are used as ministers of vengeance upon evil-doers; for those convicted of the greatest crimes are cast to them; and they require no executioner."

1493.—"In a small adjacent island . . . our men saw an enormous kind of lizard (**lagarto** *muy grande*), which they said was as large round as a calf, and with a tail as long as a lance . . . . but bulky as it was, it got into the sea, so that they could not catch it."—*Letter of Dr. Chanca*, in *Select Letters of Columbus* by Major, Hak. Soc. 2nd ed., 43.

1539.—"All along this River, that was not very broad, there were a number of Lizards (**lagartos**), which might more properly be called Serpents . . . . with scales upon their backs, and mouths two foot wide . . . . . there be of them that will sometimes get upon an **almadia** . . . . and overturn it with their tails, swallowing up the men whole, without dismembering of them."—*Pinto*, in Cogan's tr. 17 (*orig.* cap. xiv.).

1552.—" . . . . aquatic animals such as . . . . very great lizards (**lagartos**), which in form and nature are just the crocodiles of the Nile."—*Barros*, I. iii. 8.

1568.—"In this River we killed a monstrous **Lagarto**, or Crocodile . . . he was 23 foote by the rule, headed like a hogge. . . . . "—*Iob Hortop*, in *Hakl*. iii. 580.

1579.—"We found here many good commodities . . . . . besides **alagartoes**, munckeyes, and the like."—*Drake, World Encompassed*, Hak. Soc. 112.

1591.—"In this place I have seen very great water **aligartos** (which we call in English crocodiles), seven yards long."—*Master Antonie Knivet*, in *Purchas*, iv. 1228.

1593.—"In this River (of Guayaquill) and all the Rivers of this Coast, are great abundance of **Alagartoes** . . . . persons of credit have certified to me that as small fishes in other Rivers abound in scoales, so the *Alagartoes* in this . . . . . "—*Sir Richard Hawkins*, in *Purchas*, iv. 1400.

c. 1593.—

"And in his needy shop a tortoise hung,
An **alligator** stuff'd, and other skins
Of ill-shaped fishes. . ."—

Romeo & Juliet, v. 1.

1595.—"Vpon this river there were great store of fowle . . . . . but for **lagartos** it exceeded, for there were thousands of those vgly serpents; and the people called it for the abundance of them, the riuer of **Lagartos** in their language."—*Raleigh, The Discoverie of Guiana*, in *Hakl*. iv. 137.

1596.—"Once he would needs defend a rat to be *animal rationale* . . . . because she eate and gnawd his bookes . . . . And the more to confirme it, because everie one laught at him . . . . the next rat he seaz'd on hee made an anatomie of, and read a lecture of 3 dayes long upon everie artire or musckle, and after hanged her over his head in his studie in stead of an apothecarie's crocodile or dride **Alligatur**."—*T. Nashe's 'Have with you to Saffron Walden.'* Repr. in J. Payne Collier's *Misc. Tracts*, p. 72.

1610.—"These Blackes . . . told me the River was full of **Aligatas**, and if I saw any I must fight with him, else he would kill me."—*D. Midleton*, in *Purchas*, i. 244.

1613.—" . . . . mais avante . . . . por distancia de 2 legoas, esta o fermoso ryo de Cassam de **lagarthos** o crocodillos."—*Godinho de Eredia*, 10.

1673.—"The River was full of **Aligators** or Crocodiles, which lay basking in the Sun in the Mud on the River's side."—*Fryer*, 55.

1727.—"I was cleaning a vessel . . . . and had Stages fitted for my People to stand on . . . . and we were plagued with five or six **Allegators**, which wanted to be on the Stage."—*A. Hamilton*, ii. 133.

1761.—

" . . . . else that sea-like Stream
(Whence Traffic pours her bounties on mankind)
Dread **Alligators** would alone possess."

Grainger, Bk. ii.

1881.—"The Hooghly alone has never been so full of sharks and **alligators** as now. We have it on undoubted authority that within the past two months over a hundred people have fallen victims to these brutes."—*Pioneer Mail*, July 10th.

ALLIGATOR-PEAR, s. The fruit of the *Laurus persea*, Lin., *Persea gratissima*, Gaertn. The name as here given is an extravagant, and that of *avocato* or *avogato* a more moderate, corruption of *aguacate* or *ahuacatl* (see below), which appears to have been the native name in Central America, still surviving there. The Quichua name is *palta*, which is used as well as *aguacaté* by Cieza de Leon, and also by Joseph de Acosta. Grainger (*Sugarcane*, Bk. I.) calls it "rich *sabbaca*," which he says is "the Indian name of the *avocato*, *avocado*, *avigato*, or as the English corruptly call it, *alligator pear*. The Spaniards in S. America call it *Aguacate*, and under that name it is described by Ulloa." In French it is called **avocat**. The praise which Grainger, as quoted below, "liberally bestows" on this fruit, is, if we might judge from the specimens occasionally met with in India, absurd. With liberal pepper and salt there may be a remote suggestion of marrow: but that is all. Indeed it is hardly a fruit in the ordinary sense. Its common sea name of 'midshipman's butter' [or 'subaltern's butter'] is suggestive of its merits, or demerits.

Though common and naturalised throughout the W. Indies and E. coasts of tropical S. America, its actual native country is unknown. Its introduction into the Eastern world is comparatively recent; not older than the middle of 18th century. Had it been worth eating it would have come long before.

1532-50.—"There are other fruits belonging to the country, such as fragrant pines and plantains, many excellent *guavas*, *caymitos*, **aguacates**, and other fruits."—*Cieza de Leon*, 16.

1608.—"The *Palta* is a great tree, and carries a faire leafe, which hath a fruite like to great peares; within it hath a great stone, and all the rest is soft meate, so as when they are full ripe, they are, as it were, butter, and have a delicate taste."—*Joseph de Acosta*, 250.

c. 1660.—

"The **Aguacat** no less is *Venus* Friend
(To th' *Indies Venus* Conquest doth extend)
A fragrant Leaf the **Aguacata** bears;
Her Fruit in fashion of an Egg appears,
With such a white and spermy Juice it swells
As represents moist Life's first Principles."

Cowley, Of Plantes, v.

1680.—"This Tavoga is an exceeding pleasant Island, abounding in all manner of fruits, such as Pine-apples . . . . **Albecatos**, Pears, Mammes."—*Capt. Sharpe*, in *Dampier*, iv.

1685.—"The **Avogato** Pear-tree is as big as most Pear-trees . . . and the Fruit as big as a large Lemon. . . . The Substance in the inside is green, or a little yellowish, and soft as Butter. . . ."—*Dampier*, i. 203.

1736.—"**Avogato**, *Baum*. . . . This fruit itself has no taste, but when mixt with sugar and lemon juice gives a wholesome and tasty flavour."—*Zeidler's Lexicon*, s.v.

1761.—

"And thou green **avocato**, charm of sense,
Thy ripen'd marrow liberally bestows't."

Grainger, Bk. I.

1830.—"The **avocada**, with its Brobdignag pear, as large as a purser's lantern."—*Tom Cringle*, ed. 1863, 40.

[1861.—"There is a well-known West Indian fruit which we call an **avocado** or **alligator pear**."—*Tylor, Anahuac*, 227.]

1870.—"The **aguacate** or **Alligator** pear."—*Squier, Honduras*, 142.

1873.—"Thus the fruit of the *Perseu gratissima* was called **Ahucatl'** by the ancient Mexicans; the Spaniards corrupted it to **avocado**, and our sailors still further to '**Alligator pears**.'"—*Belt's Nicaragua*, 107.

[ALLYGOLE, ALIGHOL, ALLYGOOL, ALLEEGOLE, s. H.—P. '*aligol*, from *'ālī* 'lofty, excellent,' Skt. *gola*, a troop; a nondescript word used for "irregular foot in the Maratha service, without discipline or regular arms. According to some they are so named from charging in a dense mass and invoking 'Ali, the son-in-law of Mohammed, being chiefly Mohammedans."—(*Wilson*.)

1796.—"The Nezibs (**Nujeeb**) are matchlockmen, and according to their different casts are called **Allegoles** or Rohillas; they are indifferently formed of high-cast Hindoos and Musselmans, armed with the country Bandook (**bundook**), to which the ingenuity of De Boigne had added a Bayonet."—*W. H. Tone, A Letter on the Maratta People*, p. 50.

1804.—"**Alleegole**, A sort of chosen light infantry of the Rohilla Patans: sometimes the term appears to be applied to troops supposed to be used generally for desperate service."—*Fraser, Military Memoirs of Skinner*, ii. 71 note, 75, 76.

1817.—"The **Allygools** answer nearly the same description."—*Blacker, Mem. of Operations in India*, p. 22.]

ALMADIA, s. This is a word introduced into Portuguese from Moorish Ar. *al-ma'dīya*. Properly it means 'a raft' (see *Dozy*, s.v.). But it is generally used by the writers on India for a canoe, or the like small native boat.

1514.—"E visto che non veniva nessuno ambasciata, solo venia molte **abadie**, cioè barche, a venderci galline. . . ."—*Giov. da Empoli*, in *Archiv. Stor. Ital.*, p. 59.

[1539.—See quotation from Pinto under **ALLIGATOR**.

c. 1610.—"Light vessels which they call **almadia**."—*Pyrard della Valle*, Hak. Soc. i. 122; and also see under **DONEY**.]

1644.—"Huma **Almadia** pera serviço do dito Baluarte, com seis marinheiros que cada hum ven-se hum x(erafi)m por mes . . . . xs 72."—*Expenses of Diu*, in *Bocarro* (Sloane MSS. 197, fol. 175).

ALMANACK, s. On this difficult word see Dozy's Oosterlingen and *N.E.D.* In a passage quoted by Eusebius from Porphyry (*Praep. Evangel.* t. iii. ed. Gaisford) there is mention of Egyptian calendars called ἀλμενιχιανά. Also in the *Vocabular Arauigo* of Pedro de Alcala (1505) the Ar. *Manāk* is given as the equivalent of the Span. **almanaque**, which seems to show that the Sp. Arabs did use *manākh* in the sense required, probably having adopted it from the Egyptian, and having assumed the initial *al* to be their own article.

ALMYRA, s. H. *almārī*. A wardrobe, chest of drawers, or like piece of (closed) furniture. The word is in general use, by masters and servants in Anglo-Indian households, in both N. and S. India. It has come to us from the Port. **almario**, but it is the same word as Fr. *armoire*, Old E. *ambry* [for which see *N.E.D.*] &c., and Sc. *awmry*, orginating in the Lat. *armarium*, or *-ria*, which occurs also in L. Gr. as ἀρμαρή, ἀρμάριον.

c. B.C. 200.—"Hoc est quod olim clanculum ex **armario** te surripuisse aiebas uxori tuae . . . ."—*Plautus, Men.* iii. 3.

A.D. 1450.—"Item, I will my chambre prestes haue . . . . the thone of thame the to **almer**, & the tothir of yame the tother **almar** whilk I ordnyd for kepyng of vestmentes."—*Will of Sir T. Cumberlege*, in *Academy*, Sept. 27, 1879, p. 231.

1589.—"—— item ane langsettle, item ane **almarie**, ane Kist, ane sait burde . . . ."—*Ext. Records Burgh of Glasgow*, 1876, 130.

1878.—"Sahib, have you looked in Mr Morrison's **almirah**?"—*Life in Mofussil*, i. 34.

ALOES, s. The name of aloes is applied to two entirely different substances: **a.** the drug prepared from the inspissated bitter juice of the **Aloë** *Socotrina*, Lam. In this meaning (a) the name is considered (*Hanbury and Flückiger, Pharmacographia*, 616) to be derived from the Syriac *'elwai* (in P. *alwā*). **b. Aloes**-wood, the same as **Eagle-wood**. This is perhaps from one of the Indian forms, through the Hebrew (pl. forms) *ahālim*, *akhālim* and *ahālōth*, *akhālōth*. Neither Hippocrates nor Theophrastus mentions aloes, but Dioscorides describes two kinds of it (*Mat. Med.* iii. 3). "It was probably the Socotrine aloes with which the ancients were most familiar. Eustathius says the aloe was called ἱερὰ, from its excellence in preserving life (ad. *Il.* 630). This accounts for the powder of aloes being called *Hiera picra* in the older writers on Pharmacy."—(*Francis Adams, Names of all Minerals, Plants, and Animals desc. by the Greek authors*, etc.)

(a) c. A.D. 70.—"The best **Aloe** (Latin the same) is brought out of India. . . . Much use there is of it in many cases, but principally to loosen the bellie; being the only purgative medicine that is comfortable to the stomach. . . ."—*Pliny*, Bk. xxvii (*Ph. Holland*, ii. 212).

(b) "Ἦλθε δὲ καὶ Νικόδημος . . . . φέρων μίγμα σμύρνης καὶ ἀλόης ὡσεὶ λίτρας ἑκατόν."—*John* xix. 39.

c. A.D. 545.—"From the remoter regions, I speak of Tzinista and other places, the imports to Taprobane are silk **Aloes**-wood (ἀλόη), cloves, sandal-wood, and so forth."—*Cosmas*, in *Cathay*, p. clxxvii.

[c. 1605.—"In wch Iland of **Allasakatrina** are good harbors faire depth and good Anchor ground." — *Discription* in *Birdwood, First Letter Book*, 82. (Here there is a confusion of the name of the island Socotra with that of its best-known product —*Aloes Socotrina*).]

1617.—". . . . a kind of lignum **Allowaies**."—*Cocks's Diary*, i. 309 [and see i. 3].

ALOO, s. Skt. - H. *ālū*. This word is now used in Hindustani and other dialects for the 'potato.' The original Skt. is said to mean the esculent root *Arum campanulatum*.

ALOO BOKHARA, s. P. *ālū-bokhāra*, 'Bokh. plum'; a kind of prune commonly brought to India by the Afghan traders.

[c. 1666.—"Usbec being the country which principally supplies Delhi with . . . . many loads of dry fruit, as **Bokara** prunes. . . ."—*Bernier*, ed. Constable, 118.]

1817.—
"Plantains, the golden and the green,
Malaya's nectar'd mangosteen;
Prunes of Bokhara, and sweet nuts
From the far groves of Samarkand."
Moore, Lalla Rookh.

ALPEEN, s. H. *alpīn*, used in Bombay. A common pin, from Port. *alfinete* (*Panjab N. & Q.*, ii. 117).

AMAH, s. A wet nurse; used in Madras, Bombay, China and Japan. It is Port. *ama* (comp. German and Swedish *amme*).

1839.—". . . . A sort of good-natured housekeeper-like bodies, who talk only of ayahs and **amahs**, and bad nights, and babies, and the advantages of Hodgson's ale while they are nursing: seeming in short devoted to 'suckling fools and chronicling small beer.'"—*Letters from Madras*, 294. See also p. 106.

AMBAREE, s. This is a P. word (*'amārī*) for a **Howdah**, and the word occurs in Colebrooke's letters, but is quite unusual now. Gladwin defines *Amaree* as "an umbrella over the Howdeh" (*Index to Ayeen*, i.). The proper application is to a canopied howdah, such as is still used by native princes.

[c. 1661.—"Aurengzebe felt that he might venture to shut his brother up in a covered **embary**, a kind of closed litter in which women are carried on elephants."—*Bernier* (ed. *Constable*), 69.]

c. 1665.—"On the day that the King went up the Mountain of *Pire-ponjale* . . . being followed by a long row of elephants, upon which sat the Women in *Mikdembers* and **Embarys** . . . ."—*Bernier*, E.T. 130 [ed. *Constable*, 407].

1798.—"The Rajah's *Sowarree* was very grand and superb. He had twenty elephants, with richly embroidered **ambarrehs**, the whole of them mounted by his sirdars, —he himself riding upon the largest, put in the centre."—*Skinner*, *Mem*. i. 157.

1799.—"Many of the largest Ceylon and other Deccany Elephants bore **ambáris** on which all the chiefs and nobles rode, dressed with magnificence, and adorned with the richest jewels."—*Life of Colebrooke*, p. 164.

1805.—"**Amaury**, a canopied seat for an elephant. An open one is called *Houza* or *Howda*."—*Dict. of Words used in E. Indies*, 2nd ed. 21.

1807.—"A royal tiger which was started in beating a large cover for game, sprang up so far into the **umbarry** or state howdah, in which Sujah Dowlah was seated, as to leave little doubt of a fatal issue."—*Williamson, Orient. Field Sports*, 15.

B

AMBARREH, s. Dekh. Hind. and Mahr. *ambārā*, *ambārī* [Skt. *amla-vāṭika*], the plant *Hibiscus cannabinus*, affording a useful fibre.

AMBOYNA, n.p. A famous island in the Molucca Sea, belonging to the Dutch. The native form of the name is **Ambun** [which according to Marsden means 'dew'].

[1605.—"He hath sent hither his forces which hath expelled all the Portingalls out of the fforts they here hould att **Ambweno** and Tydore."—*Birdwood, First Letter Book*, 68.]

AMEEN, s. The word is Ar. *amīn*, meaning 'a trustworthy person,' and then an inspector, intendant, &c. In India it has several uses as applied to native officials employed under the Civil Courts, but nearly all reducible to the definition of *fide-commissarius*. Thus an **ameen** may be employed by a Court to investigate accounts connected with a suit, to prosecute local enquiries of any kind bearing on a suit, to sell or to deliver over possession of immovable property, to carry out legal process as a bailiff, &c. The name is also applied to native assistants in the duties of land-survey. But see *Sudder Ameen* (**SUDDER**).

[1616.—"He declared his office of **Amin** required him to hear and determine differences."—*Foster, Letters*, iv. 351.]

1817.—"Native officers called **aumeens** were sent to collect accounts, and to obtain information in the districts. The first incidents that occurred were complaints against these **aumeens** for injurious treatment of the inhabitants. . . ."—*Mill. Hist.*, ed. 1840, iv. 12.

1861.—"Bengallee dewans, once pure, are converted into demons; **Ameens**, once harmless, become tigers; magistrates, supposed to be just, are converted into oppressors."—Peterson, *Speech for Prosecution in Nil Durpan case.*

1878.—"The **Ameen** employed in making the partition of an estate."—*Life in the Mofussil*, i. 206.

1882.—"A missionary . . . . might, on the other hand, be brought to a standstill when asked to explain all the terms used by an **amin** or valuator who had been sent to fix the judicial rents."—*Saty. Rev.*, Dec. 30, p. 866.

AMEER, s. Ar. *Amīr* (root *amr*, 'commanding,' and so) 'a commander, chief, or lord,' and, in Ar. application, any kind of chief from the *Amīru' l-mūminīn*, 'the Amīr of the Faithful' *i.e.* the Caliph, downwards. The word in this form perhaps first became familiar as applied to the Princes of Sind, at the time of the conquest of that Province by Sir C. J. Napier. It is the title affected by many Musulman sovereigns of various calibres, as the Amīr of Kābul, the Amīr of Bokhārā, &c. But in sundry other forms the word has, more or less, taken root in European languages since the early Middle Ages. Thus it is the origin of the title 'Admiral,' now confined to generals of the sea service, but applied in varying forms by medieval Christian writers to the **Amīrs**, or lords, of the court and army of Egypt and other Mohammedan States. The word also came to us again, by a later importation from the Levant, in the French form, **Emir** or **Emer**.—See also **Omrah**, which is in fact *Umarā*, the pl. of *Amīr*. Byzantine writers use Ἀμὲρ, Ἀμηρᾶς, Ἀμυρᾶς, Ἀμηραῖος, &c. (See *Ducange*, *Gloss. Græcit.*) It is the opinion of the best scholars that the forms *Amiral*, *Ammiraglio*, *Admiral* &c., originated in the application of a Low Latin termination *-alis* or *-alius*, though some doubt may still attach to this question. (See Marcel Devic, s.v. *Amiral*, and Dozy, Oosterlingen, s.v. *Admiraal* [and *N.E.D.* s.v. *Admiral*]. The *d* in admiral probably came from a false imagination of connection with *admirari*.

1250.—"Li grand **amiraus** des galies m'envoia querre, et me demanda si j'estoie cousins le roy; et je le di que nanin. . . ."—*Joinville*, p. 178. This passage illustrates the sort of way in which our modern use of the word **admiral** originated.

c. 1345.—"The Master of the Ship is like a great **amīr**; when he goes ashore the archers and the blackamoors march before him with javelins and swords, with drums and horns and trumpets."—*Ibn Batuta*, iv. 93.

Compare with this description of the Commander of a Chinese Junk in the 14th century, A. Hamilton's of an English Captain in Malabar in the end of the 17th:

"Captain Beawes, who commanded the *Albemarle*, accompanied us also, carrying a Drum and two Trumpets with us, so as to make our Compliment the more solemn."—i. 294.

And this again of an "interloper" skipper at Hooghly, in 1683:

1683.—"Alley went in a splendid Equipage, habitted in scarlet richly laced. Ten Englishmen in Blue Capps and Coats edged with Red, all armed with Blunderbusses, went before his pallankeen, 80 (? 8) *Peons* before them, and 4 Musicians playing on the Weights with 2 Flaggs, before him, like an Agent . . ."—*Hedges*, Oct. 8 (Hak. Soc. i. 123).

1384.—"Il Soldano fu cristiano di Grecia, e fu venduto per schiavo quando era fanciullo a uno **ammiraglio**, come tu dicessi 'capitano di guerra.'"—*Frescobaldi*, p. 39.

[1510.—See quotation from *Varthema* under **XERAFINE**.]

1615.—"The inhabitants (of Sidon) are of sundry nations and religions; governed by a succession of Princes whom they call **Emers**; descended, as they say, from the Druses."—*Sandys, Iourney*, 210.

AMOY, n.p. A great seaport of Fokien in China, the name of which in Mandarin dialect is *Hia-men*, meaning 'Hall Gate,' which is in the Changchau dialect *A-mui*ⁿ. In some books of the last century it is called *Emwy* and the like. It is now a Treaty-Port.

1687.—"**Amoy** or Anhay, which is a city standing on a Navigable River in the Province of Fokien in China, and is a place of vast trade."—*Dampier*, i. 417. (This looks as if Dampier confounded the name of *Amoy*, the origin of which (as generally given) we have stated, with that of *An-hai*, one of the connected ports, which lies to the N.E., about 30 m., as the crow flies, from Amoy).

1727.—"There are some curiosities in **Amoy**. One is a large Stone that weighs above forty Tuns . . . . in such an Equilibrium, that a Youth of twelve Years old can easily make it move."—*A. Hamilton*, ii. 243.

AMSHOM, s. Malayāl. *aṁśam*, from Skt. *āṁśah*, 'a part,' defined by Gundert as "part of a Talook, formerly called *hobili*, greater than a *taṛa*." [Logan (*Man. Malabar*, i. 87) speaks of the *amsam* as a 'parish.'] It is further explained in the following quotation:—

1878.—"The **amshom** is really the smallest revenue division there is in Malabar, and is generally a tract of country some square miles in extent, in which there is no such thing as a village, but a series of scattered homesteads and farms, where the owner of the land and his servants reside . . . . separate and apart, in single separate huts, or in scattered collections of huts."—*Report of Census Com. in India*.

A MUCK, to run, v. There is we believe no room for doubt that, to us at least, this expression came from the Malay countries, where both the phrase and the practice are still familiar. Some valuable remarks on the phenomenon, as prevalent among the Malays, were contributed by Dr Oxley of Singapore to the *Journal of the Indian Archipelago*, vol. iii. p. 532; see a quotation below. [Mr W. W. Skeat writes—"The best explanation of the fact is perhaps that it was the Malay national method of committing suicide, especially as one never hears of Malays committing suicide in any other way. This form of suicide may arise from a wish to die fighting and thus avoid a 'straw death, a cow's death'; but it is curious that women and children are often among the victims, and especially members of the suicide's own family. The act of running **a-muck** is probably due to causes over which the culprit has some amount of control, as the custom has now died out in the British Possessions in the Peninsula, the offenders probably objecting to being caught and tried in cold blood. I remember hearing of only about two cases (one by a Sikh soldier) in about six years. It has been suggested further that the extreme monotonous heat of the Peninsula may have conduced to such outbreaks as those of Running **amuck** and Latah.]

The word is by Crawfurd ascribed to the Javanese, and this is his explanation:

"*Amuk* (J.). An *a-muck*; to run *a-muck*; to tilt; to run furiously and desperately at any one; to make a furious onset or charge in combat."—(*Malay Dict.*) [The standard Malay, according to Mr Skeat, is rather *amok* (*mengāmok*).]

Marsden says that the word rarely occurs in any other than the verbal form *mengāmuk*, 'to make a furious attack' (*Mem. of a Malayan Family*, 96).

There is reason, however, to ascribe an Indian origin to the term; whilst the practice, apart from the term, is of no rare occurrence in Indian history. Thus Tod records some notable instances in the history of the Rājputs. In one of these (1634) the eldest son of the Raja of Mārwār ran *a-muck* at the court of Shāh Jahān, failing in his blow at the Emperor, but killing five courtiers of eminence before he fell himself. Again, in the 18th century, Bījai Singh, also of Mārwār, bore strong resentment against the Tālpura prince of Hyderabad, Bījar Khān, who had sent to demand from the Rājput tribute and a bride. A Bhattī and a Chondāwat offered their services for vengeance, and set out for Sind as envoys. Whilst Bījar Khān read their credentials, muttering, 'No mention of the bride!' the Chondāwat buried a dagger in his heart, exclaiming 'This for the bride!' 'And this for the tribute!' cried the Bhattī, repeating the blow. The pair then plied their daggers right and left, and 26 persons were slain before the envoys were hacked to pieces (*Tod*, ii. 45 & 315).

But it is in Malabar that we trace the apparent origin of the Malay term in the existence of certain desperadoes who are called by a variety of old travellers **amouchi** or **amuco**. The nearest approach to this that we have been able to discover is the Malayālam *amar-kkan*, 'a warrior' (from *amar*, 'fight, war'). [The proper Malayālam term for such men was *Chaver*, literally those who took up or devoted themselves to death.] One of the special applications of this word is remarkable in connection with a singular custom in Malabar. After the **Zamorin** had reigned 12 years, a great assembly was held at Tirunāvāyi, when that Prince took his seat surrounded by his dependants, fully armed. Any one might then attack him, and the assailant, if successful in killing the Zamorin, got the throne. This had often happened. [For a full discussion of this custom see *Frazer*, *Golden Bough*, 2nd ed., ii. 14 sq.] In 1600 thirty such assailants were killed in the enterprise. Now these men were called *amar-kkār* (pl. of *amar-kkan*, see *Gundert* s.v.). These men evidently ran *a-muck* in the true Malay sense; and quotations below will show other illustrations from Malabar which confirm the idea that both name and practice originated in Continental India. There is indeed a difficulty as to the derivation here indicated, in the fact that the *amuco* or *amouchi* of European writers on Malabar seems by no means close enough to *amarkkan*, whilst it is so close to the Malay *āmuk*; and on this further light may be hoped for. The identity between the **amoucos** of Malabar and the **amuck** runners of the Malay peninsula is clearly shown by the passage from *Correa* given below. [Mr Whiteway adds—"Gouvea (1606) in his *Iornada* (ch. 9, Bk. ii.) applies the word **amouques** to certain Hindus whom he saw in S. Malabar near Quilon, whose duty it was to defend the Syrian Christians with their lives. There are reasons for thinking that the worthy priest got hold of the story of a cock and a bull; but in any case the Hindus referred to were really Jangadas."] (See **JANCADA**).

De Gubernatis has indeed suggested that the word *amouchi* was derived from the Skt. *amokshya*, 'that cannot be loosed'; and this would be very consistent with several of the passages which we shall quote, in which the idea of being 'bound by a vow' underlies the conduct of the persons to whom the term was applicable both in Malabar and in the Archipelago. But *amokshya* is a word unknown to Malayālam, in such a sense at least.

We have seen *a-muck* derived from the Ar. *aḥmak*, 'fatuous' [(*e.g. Ball, Jungle Life*, 358).] But this is etymology of the kind which scorns history.

The phrase has been thoroughly naturalised in England since the days of Dryden and Pope. [The earliest quotation for "running *amuck*" in the N.E.D. is from Marvell (1672).]

c. 1430.—Nicolo Conti, speaking of the greater Islands of the Archipelago under the name of the Two Javas, does not use the word, but describes a form of the practice:—

"Homicide is here a jest, and goes without punishment. Debtors are made over to their creditors as slaves; and some of these, preferring death to slavery, will with drawn swords rush on, stabbing all whom they fall in with of less strength than themselves, until they meet death at the hands of some one more than a match for them. This man, the creditors then sue in Court for the dead man's debt."—In *India in the XVth C.* 45.

1516.—"There are some of them (Javanese) who if they fall ill of any severe illness vow to God that if they remain in health they will of their own accord seek another more honourable death for his service, and as soon as they get well they take a dagger in their hands, and go out into the streets and kill as many persons as they meet, both men, women, and children, in such wise that they go like mad dogs, killing until they are killed. These are called **Amuco**. And as soon as they see them begin this work, they cry out, saying **Amuco, Amuco**, in order that people may take care of themselves, and they kill them with dagger and spear thrusts."—*Barbosa*, Hak. Soc. 194. This passage seems to show that the word *amuk* must have been commonly used in Malay countries before the arrival of the Portuguese there, c. 1511.

1539.—". . . The Tyrant (*o Rey Ache*) sallied forth in person, accompanied with 5000 resolute men (*cinco mil* **Amoucos**) and charged the *Bataes* very furiously."—*Pinto* (orig. cap. xvii.) in *Cogan*, p. 20.

1552.—De Barros, speaking of the capture of the Island of Beth (*Beyt*, off the N.W. point of Kāthiāwār) by Nuno da Cunha in 1531, says: "But the natives of Guzarat stood in such fear of Sultan Badur that they would not consent to the terms. And so, like people determined on death, all that night they shaved their heads (this is a superstitious practice of those who despise life, people whom they call in India **Amaucos**) and betook themselves to their mosque, and there devoted their persons to death . . . . and as an earnest of this vow, and an example of this resolution, the Captain ordered a great fire to be made, and cast into it his wife, and a little son that he had, and all his household and his goods, in fear lest anything of his should fall into our possession." Others did the like, and then they fell upon the Portuguese.—Dec. IV. iv. 13.

c. 1561.—In war between the Kings of Calicut and Cochin (1503) two princes of Cochin were killed. A number of these desperadoes who have been spoken of in the quotations were killed. . . . "But some remained who were not killed, and these went in shame, not to have died avenging their lords . . . . these were more than 200, who all, according to their custom, shaved off all their hair, even to the eyebrows, and embraced each other and their friends and relations, as men about to suffer death. In this case they are as madmen—known as **amoucos**—and count themselves as already among the dead. These men dispersed, seeking wherever they might find men of Calicut, and among these they rushed fearless, killing and slaying till they were slain. And some of them, about twenty, reckoning more highly of their honour, desired to turn their death to better account; and these separated, and found their way secretly to Calicut, determined to slay the king. But as it became known that they were **amoucos**, the city gave the alarm, and the King sent his servants to slay them as they slew others. But they like desperate men played the devil (*fazião diabruras*) before they were slain, and killed many people, with women and children. And five of them got together to a wood near the city, which they haunted for a good while after, making robberies and doing much mischief, until the whole of them were killed."—*Correa*, i. 364-5.

1566.—"The King of *Cochin* . . . . . hath a great number of gentlemen which he calleth **Amocchi**, and some are called *Nairi*: these two sorts of men esteem not their lives anything, so that it may be for the honour of their King."—*M. Cæsar Frederike* in *Purchas*, ii. 1708. [See *Logan, Man. Malabar*, i. 138.]

1584.—"Their forces (in Cochin) consist in a kind of soldiers whom they call amocchi, who are under obligation to die at the King's pleasure, and all soldiers who in war lose their King or their general lie under this obligation. And of such the King makes use in urgent cases, sending them to die fighting."—Letter of *F. Sassetti* to *Francesco I.*, Gd. D. of Tuscany, in *De Gubernatis*, 154.

c. 1584.—"There are some also who are called **Amocchi** . . . . who being weary of living, set themselves in the way with a weapon in their hands, which they call a *Crise*, and kill as many as they meete with, till somebody killeth them; and this they doe for the least anger they conceive, as desperate men."—*G. Balbi* in *Purchas*, ii. 1724.

1602.—De Couto, speaking of the Javanese: "They are chivalrous men, and of such determination that for whatever offence may be offered them they make themselves **amoucos** in order to get satisfaction thereof. And were a spear run into the stomach of such an one he would still press forward without fear till he got at his foe."—*Dec.* IV. iii. 1.

,, In another passage (*ib.* vii. 14) De Couto speaks of the **amoucos** of Malabar just as Della Valle does below. In *Dec.* VI. viii. 8 he describes how, on the death of the King of Pimenta, in action with the Portuguese, "nearly 4000 Nairs made themselves **amoucos** with the usual ceremonies, shaving their heads on one side, and swearing by their pagoda to avenge the King's death."

1603.—"Este es el genero de milicia de la India, y los Reyes señalan mas o menos **Amoyos** (ò **Amacos**, que todo es uno) para su guarda ordinaria."—*San Roman, Historia*, 48.

1604.—"Auia hecho vna junta de **Amocos**, con sus ceremonias para venir a morir adonde el Panical auia sedo muerto."—*Guerrero, Relacion*, 91.

1611.—"**Viceroy**. What is the meaning of **amoucos**? **Soldier**. It means men who have made up their mind to die in killing as many as they can, as is done in the parts about Malaca by those whom they call **amoucos** in the language of the country."—*Couto, Dialogo do Soldado Pratico*, 2nd part, p. 9.—(Printed at Lisbon in 1790).

1615.—"Hos inter Nairos genus est et ordo quem **Amocas** vocant quibus ob studium rei bellicae praecipua laus tribuitur, et omnium habentur validissimi."—*Jarric, Thesaurus*, i. 65.

1624.—"Though two kings may be at war, either enemy takes great heed not to kill the King of the opposite faction, nor yet to strike his umbrella, wherever it may go . . . for the whole kingdom of the slain or wounded king would be bound to avenge him with the complete destruction of the enemy, or all, if needful, to perish in the attempt. The greater the king's dignity among these people, the longer period lasts this obligation to furious revenge . . . . this period or method of revenge is termed **Amoco**, and so they say that the **Amoco** of the Samori lasts one day; the **Amoco** of the king of Cochin lasts a life-time; and so of others."—*P. della Valle*, ii. 745 [Hak. Soc., ii. 380 *seq.*].

1648.—"Derrière ces palissades s'estoit caché un coquin de Bantamois qui estoit revenu de la Mecque et jouoit à **Moqua** . . . . il court par les rues et tue tous ceux qu'il rencontre. . . ."—*Tavernier, V. des Indes, liv.* iii. ch. 24 [Ed. *Ball*, ii. 361 seq.].

1659.—"I saw in this month of February at Batavia the breasts torn with red-hot tongs off a black Indian by the executioner; and after this he was broken on the wheel from below upwards. This was because through the evil habit of eating opium (according to the godless custom of the Indians) he had become mad and raised the cry of *Amocle* (misp. for **Amock**) . . . in which mad state he had slain five persons. . . . This was the third **Amock**-cryer whom I saw during that visit to Batavia (a few months) broken on the wheel for murder."

* * * * *

. . . . . "Such a murderer and **Amock**-runner has sometimes the fame of being an invincible hero because he has so manfully repulsed all who tried to seize him. . . . . So the Netherlands Government is compelled when such an **Amock**-runner is taken alive to punish him in a terrific manner."—*Walter Schulzens Ost-Indische Reise-Beschreibung* (German ed.), Amsterdam, 1676, pp. 19-20 and 227.

1672.—"Every community (of the Malabar Christians), every church has its own **Amouchi**, which . . . . are people who take an oath to protect with their own lives the persons and places put under their safeguard, from all and every harm."—*P. Vicenzo Maria*, 145.

,, "If the Prince is slain the **amouchi**, who are numerous, would avenge him desperately. If he be injured they put on festive raiment, take leave of their parents, and with fire and sword in hand invade the hostile territory, burning every dwelling, and slaying man, woman, and child, sparing none, until they themselves fall."—*Ibid.* 237-8.

1673.—"And they (the Mohammedans) are hardly restrained from running **a muck** (which is to kill whoever they meet, till they be slain themselves), especially if they have been at *Hodge* [**Hadgee**] a Pilgrimage to Mecca."—*Fryer*, 91.

1687.—Dryden assailing Burnet:—

"Prompt to assault, and careless of defence,
Invulnerable in his impudence,
He dares the World; and eager of a name,
He thrusts about and justles into fame.
Frontless and satire-proof, he scours the streets
And runs an **Indian Muck** at all he meets."

The Hind and the Panther, line 2477.

1689.—"Those that run these are called **Amouki**, and the doing of it *Running a* **Muck**."—*Ovington*, 237.

1712.—"**Amouco** (Termo da India) val o mesmo que homem determinado e apostado que despreza a vida e não teme a morte."—*Bluteau*, s.v.

1727.—"I answered him that I could no longer bear their Insults, and, if I had not Permission in three Days, I would **run a Muck** (which is a mad Custom among the *Mallayas* when they become desperate)."—*A. Hamilton*, ii. 231.

1737.—
"Satire's my weapon, but I'm too discreet
To **run a muck**, and tilt at all I meet."
Pope, Im. of Horace, B. ii. Sat. i. 69.

1768-71.—"These acts of indiscriminate murder are called by us **mucks**, because the perpetrators of them, during their frenzy, continually cry out **amok, amok**, which signifies *kill, kill*. . ."—*Stavorinus*, i. 291.

1783.—At Bencoolen in this year (1760)—"the Count (d'Estaing) afraid of an insurrection among the Buggesses . . . . invited several to the Fort, and when these had entered the Wicket was shut upon them; in attempting to disarm them, they *mangamoed*, that is **ran a muck**; they drew their cresses, killed one or two Frenchmen, wounded others, and at last suffered themselves, for supporting this point of honour."—*Forrest's Voyage to Mergui*, 77.

1784.—"It is not to be controverted that these desperate acts of indiscriminate murder, called by us **mucks**, and by the natives *mongamo*, do actually take place, and frequently too, in some parts of the east (in Java in particular)."—*Marsden, H. of Sumatra*, 239.

1788.—"We are determined to **run a muck** rather than suffer ourselves to be forced away by these Hollanders."—*Mem. of a Malayan Family*, 66.

1798.—"At Batavia, if an officer take one of these **amoks**, or **mohawks**, as they have been called by an easy corruption, his reward is very considerable; but if he kill them, nothing is added to his usual pay. . ."—*Translator of Stavorinus*, i. 294.

1803.—"We cannot help thinking, that one day or another, when they are more full of opium than usual, they (the Malays) will **run a muck** from Cape Comorin to the Caspian."—*Sydney Smith*, Works, 3rd ed., iii. 6.

1846.—"On the 8th July, 1846, Sunan, a respectable Malay house-builder in Penang, **ran amok** . . . . killed an old Hindu woman, a Kling, a Chinese boy, and a Kling girl about three years old . . . . and wounded two Hindus, three Klings, and two Chinese, of whom only two survived. . . . On the trial Sunan declared he did not know what he was about, and persisted in this at the place of execution. . . . The **amok** took place on the 8th, the trial on the 13th, and the execution on the 15th July,—all within 8 days."—*J. Ind. Arch.*, vol. iii. 460-61.

1849.—"A man sitting quietly among his friends and relatives, will without provocation suddenly start up, weapon in hand, and slay all within his reach. . . . Next day when interrogated . . . . the answer has invariably been, "The Devil entered into me, my eyes were darkened, I did not know what I was about." I have received the same reply on at least 20 different occasions; on examination of these monomaniacs, I have generally found them labouring under some gastric disease, or troublesome ulcer. . . . The Bugis, whether from revenge or disease, are by far the most addicted to run **amok**. I should think three-fourths of all the cases I have seen have been by persons of this nation."—*Dr T. Oxley*, in *J. Ind. Archip.*, iii. 532.

[1869.—"Macassar is the most celebrated place in the East for 'running **a muck**.'"—Wallace, *Malay Archip.* (ed. 1890), p. 134.]

[1870.—For a full account of many cases in India, see *Chevers, Med. Jurisprudence*, p. 781 seqq.]

1873.—"They (the English) . . . . crave governors who, not having bound themselves beforehand to '**run amuck**,' may give the land some chance of repose."—*Blackwood's Magazine*, June, p. 759.

1875.—"On being struck the Malay at once stabbed Arshad with a *kriss*; the blood of the people who had witnessed the deed was aroused, they ran **amok**, attacked Mr Birch, who was bathing in a floating bath close to the shore, stabbed and killed him."—*Sir W. D. Jervois* to the E. of Carnarvon, Nov. 16, 1875.

1876.—"Twice over, while we were wending our way up the steep hill in Galata, it was our luck to see a Turk '**run a muck**' . . . . nine times out of ten this frenzy is feigned, but not always, as for instance in the case where a priest took to running *a-muck* on an Austrian Lloyd's boat on the Black Sea, and after killing one or two passengers, and wounding others, was only stopped by repeated shots from the Captain's pistol."—*Barkley, Five Years in Bulgaria*, 240-41.

1877.—The *Times* of February 11th mentions a fatal **muck** run by a Spanish sailor, Manuel Alves, at the Sailors' Home, Liverpool; and the *Overland Times of India* (31st August) another run by a sepoy at Meerut.

1879.—"Running **a-muck** does not seem to be confined to the Malays. At Ravenna, on Monday, when the streets were full of people celebrating the festa of St John the Baptist, a maniac rushed out, snatched up a knife from a butcher's stall and fell upon everyone he came across . . . . before he was captured he wounded more or less seriously 11 persons, among whom was one little child."—*Pall Mall Gazette*, July 1.

,, "Captain Shaw mentioned . . . that he had known as many as 40 people being injured by a single '**amok**' runner. When the cry '**amok! amok!**' is raised, people fly to the right and left for shelter, for after the blinded madman's *kris* has once 'drunk blood,' his fury becomes ungovernable, his sole desire is to kill; he strikes here and there; he stabs fugitives in the back, his *kris* drips blood, he rushes on yet more wildly, blood and murder in his course; there are shrieks and groans, his bloodshot eyes start from their sockets, his frenzy gives him unnatural strength; then all of a sudden he drops, shot through the heart, or from sudden exhaustion, clutching his bloody *kris*."—*Miss Bird, Golden Chersonese*, 356.

ANACONDA, s. This word for a great python, or boa, is of very obscure origin. It is now applied in scientific zoology as the specific name of a great S. American water-snake. Cuvier has "**L'Anacondo** (*Boa scytale et murina*, L.—*Boa aquatica*, Prince Max.)," (*Règne Animal*, 1829, ii. 78). Again, in the Official Report prepared by the Brazilian Government for the Philadelphia Exhibition of 1876, we find: "Of the genus Boa . . . . we may mention the . . . . *sucuriù* or *sucuriuba* (B. **anaconda**), whose skins are used for boots and shoes and other purposes." And as the subject was engaging our attention we read the following in the *St James' Gazette* of April 3, 1882:—"A very unpleasant account is given by a Brazilian paper, the *Voz do Povo* of Diamantino, of the proceedings of a huge water-snake called the *sucuruyu*, which is to be found in some of the rivers of Brazil. . . . A slave, with some companions, was fishing with a net in the river, when he was suddenly seized by a *sucuruyu*, who made an effort with his hinder coils to carry off at the same time another of the fishing party." We had naturally supposed the name to be S. American, and its S. American character was rather corroborated by our finding in Ramusio's version of Pietro Martire d'Angheria such S. American names as *Anacauchoa* and *Anacaona*. Serious doubt was however thrown on the American origin of the word when we found that Mr H. W. Bates entirely disbelieved it, and when we failed to trace the name in any older books about S. America.

In fact the oldest authority that we have met with, the famous John Ray, distinctly assigns the name, and the serpent to which the name properly belonged, to Ceylon. This occurs in his *Synopsis Methodica Animalium Quadrupedum et Serpentini Generis*, Lond. 1693. In this he gives a Catalogue of Indian Serpents, which he had received from his friend Dr Tancred Robinson, and which the latter had noted *e Museo Leydensi*. No. 8 in this list runs as follows:—

"8. *Serpens Indicus Bubalinus*, **Anacandaia** Zeylonensibus, id est Bubalorum aliorumque jumentorum membra conterens," p. 332.

The following passage from St Jerome, giving an etymology, right or wrong, of the word *boa*, which our naturalists now limit to certain great serpents of America, but which is often popularly applied to the pythons of E. Asia, shows a remarkable analogy to Ray's explanation of the name *Anacandaia*:—

c. A.D. 395-400.—"Si quidem draco mirae magnitudinis, quos gentili sermone *Boas* vocant, *ab eo quod tam grandes sint ut* boves *glutire soleant*, omnem late vastabat provinciam, et non solum armenta et pecudes sed agricolas quoque et pastores tractos ad se vi spiritus absorbebat."—In *Vita Scti. Hilarionis Eremitae*, Opera Scti. Eus. Hieron. Venetiis, 1767, ii. col. 35.

Ray adds that on this No. 8 should be read what D. Cleyerus has said in the *Ephem. German.* An 12. obser. 7, entitled: *De Serpente magno Indiae Orientalis Urobubalum deglutiente*. The serpent in question was 25 feet long. Ray quotes in abridgment the description of its treatment of the buffalo; how, if the resistance is great, the victim is dragged to a tree, and compressed against it; how the noise of the crashing bones is heard as far as a cannon: how the crushed carcass is covered with saliva, etc. It is added that the country people (apparently this is in Amboyna) regard this great serpent as most desirable food.

The following are extracts from Cleyer's paper, which is, more fully cited, *Miscellanea Curiosa, sive Ephimeridum Medico-Physicarum Germanicarum Academiae Naturae Curiosorum*, Dec. ii.—Annus Secundus, Anni MDCLXXXIII. Norimbergae. Anno MDCLXXXIV. pp. 18-20. It is illustrated by a formidable but inaccurate picture showing the serpent seizing an ox (not a buffalo) by the muzzle, with huge teeth. He tells how he dissected a great snake that he bought from a huntsman in which he found a whole stag of middle age, entire in skin and every part;

and another which contained a wild goat with great horns, likewise quite entire; and a third which had swallowed a porcupine armed with all his "sagittiferis aculeis." In Amboyna a woman great with child had been swallowed by such a serpent. . . .

"Quod si animal quoddam robustius renitatur, ut spiris anguinis enecari non possit, serpens crebris cum animali convolutionibus caudâ suâ proximam arborem in auxilium et robur corporis arripit eamque circumdat, quo eo fortius et valentius gyris suis animal comprimere, suffocare, et demum enecare possit . . . ."

"Factum est hoc modo, ut (quod ex fide dignissimis habeo) in Regno Aracan . . . . talis vasti corporis anguis prope flumen quoddam, cum Uro-bubalo, sive sylvestri bubalo aut uro . . . . immani spectaculo congredi visus fuerit, eumque dicto modo occiderit; quo conflictu et plusquam hostili amplexu fragor ossium in bubalo comminutorum ad distantiam tormenti bellici majoris . . . . a spectatoribus sat eminus stantibus exaudiri potuit. . . ."

The natives said these great snakes had poisonous fangs. These Cleyer could not find, but he believes the teeth to be in some degree venomous, for a servant of his scratched his hand on one of them. It swelled, greatly inflamed, and produced fever and delirium:

"Nec prius cessabant symptomata, quam Serpentinus lapis (see **SNAKE-STONE**) quam Patres Jesuitae hic componunt, vulneri adaptatus omne venenum extraheret, et ubique symptomata convenientibus antidotis essent profligata."

Again, in 1768, we find in the *Scots Magazine*, App. p. 673, but quoted from "London pap. Aug. 1768," and signed by *R. Edwin*, a professed eye-witness, a story with the following heading: "Description of the **Anaconda**, a monstrous species of serpent. In a letter from an English gentleman, many years resident in the Island of Ceylon in the East Indies. . . . The Ceylonese seem to know the creature well; they call it **Anaconda**, and talked of eating its flesh when they caught it." He describes its seizing and disposing of an enormous "tyger." The serpent darts on the "tyger" from a tree, attacking first with a bite, then partially crushing and dragging it to the tree . . . . "winding his body round both the tyger and the tree with all his violence, till the ribs and other bones began to give way . . . . each giving a loud crack when it burst . . . . the poor creature all this time was living, and at every loud crash of its bones gave a houl, not loud, yet piteous enough to pierce the cruelest heart."

Then the serpent drags away its victim, covers it with slaver, swallows it, etc. The whole thing is very cleverly told, but is evidently a romance founded on the description by "D. Cleyerus," which is quoted by Ray. There are no tigers in Ceylon. In fact, "R. Edwin" has developed the Romance of the Anaconda out of the description of D. Cleyerus, exactly as "Mynheer Försch" some years later developed the Romance of the Upas out of the older stories of the poison tree of Macassar. Indeed, when we find "Dr Andrew Cleyer" mentioned among the early relators of these latter stories, the suspicion becomes strong that both romances had the same author, and that "R. Edwin" was also the true author of the wonderful story told under the name of Foersch. (See further under **UPAS**.)

In Percival's *Ceylon* (1803) we read: "Before I arrived in the island I had heard many stories of a monstrous snake, so vast in size as to devour tigers and buffaloes, and so daring as even to attack the elephant" (p. 303). Also, in Pridham's *Ceylon and its Dependencies* (1849, ii. 750-51): "Pimbera or **Anaconda** is of the genus Python, Cuvier, and is known in English as the rock-snake." Emerson Tennent (*Ceylon*, 4th ed., 1860, i. 196) says: "The great python (the 'boa' as it is commonly designated by Europeans, the '**anaconda**' of Eastern story) which is supposed to crush the bones of an elephant, and to swallow a tiger" . . . . It may be suspected that the letter of "R. Edwin" was the foundation of all or most of the stories alluded to in these passages. Still we have the authority of Ray's friend that Anaconda, or rather *Anacondaia*, was at Leyden applied as a Ceylonese name to a specimen of this python. The only interpretation of this that we can offer is Tamil *ānai-kondra* [*ānaik-koṇḍa*], "which killed an elephant"; an appellative, but not a name. We have no authority for the application of this appellative to a snake, though the passages quoted from Percival, Pridham, and Tennent are all suggestive of such stories, and the interpretation of the name *anacondaia* given to Ray: "*Bubalorum* . . . membra conterens," is at least quite analogous as an appellative. It may be added that in Malay **anakanda** signifies "one that is well-born," which does not help us. . . [Mr Skeat is unable to trace the word in Malay, and rejects the derivation from *anakanda* given above. A more plausible explanation is that given by Mr D. Ferguson (8 Ser. *N. & Q.* xii. 123), who derives *anacandaia* from Singhalese *Henakandayâ* (*hena*, 'lightning'; *kanda*, 'stem, trunk,') which is a name for the whip-snake (*Passerita mycterizans*), the name of the smaller reptile being by a blunder transferred to the greater. It is at least a curious coincidence that Ogilvy (1670) in his "*Description of the African Isles*" (p. 690), gives: "*Anakandef*, a sort of small snakes," which is the Malagasy *Anakandîfy*, 'a snake.']

1859.—"The skins of **anacondas** offered at Bangkok come from the northern provinces."—*D. O. King*, in *J. R. G. Soc.*, xxx. 184.

ANANAS, s. The Pine-apple (*Ananassa sativa*, Lindl.; *Bromelia Ananas*, L.), a native of the hot regions of Mexico and Panama. It abounded, as a cultivated plant, in Hispaniola and all the islands according to Oviedo. The Brazilian *Nana*, or perhaps *Nanas*, gave the Portuguese *Ananas* or *Ananaz*. This name has, we believe, accompanied the fruit whithersoever, except to England, it has travelled from its home in America. A pine was brought home to Charles V., as related by J. D'Acosta below. The plant is stated to have been first, in Europe, cultivated at Leyden about 1650 (?). In England it first fruited at Richmond, in Sir M. Decker's garden, in 1712.* But its diffusion in the East was early and rapid. To one who has seen the hundreds of acres covered with pine-apples on the islands adjoining Singapore, or their profusion in a seemingly wild state in the valleys of the Kasia country on the eastern borders of Bengal, it is hard to conceive of this fruit as introduced in modern times from another hemisphere. But, as in the case of tobacco, the name bewrayeth its true origin, whilst the large natural family of plants to which it belongs is exclusively American. The names given by Oviedo, probably those of Hispaniola, are *Iaiama* as a general name, and *Boniana* and *Aiagua* for two species. Pine-apples used to cost a **pardao** (a coin difficult to determine the value of in those days) when first introduced in Malabar, says Linschoten, but "now there are so many grown in the country, that they are good cheape" (91); [Hak. Soc. ii. 19]. Athanasius Kircher, in the middle of the 17th century, speaks of the *ananas* as produced in great abundance in the Chinese provinces of Canton, Kiangsu and Fuhkien. In Ibn Muhammad Wali's *H. of the Conquest of Assam*, written in 1662, the pine-apples of that region are commended for size and flavour. In the last years of the preceding century Carletti (1599) already commends the excellent *ananas* of Malacca. But even some 20 or 30 years earlier the fruit was grown profusely in W. India, as we learn from Chr. d'Acosta (1578). And we know from the *Āīn* that (about 1590) the *ananas* was habitually served at the table of Akbar, the price of one being reckoned at only 4 *dams*, or $\frac{1}{10}$ of a rupee; whilst Akbar's son Jahāngīr states that the fruit came from the sea-ports in the possession of the Portuguese.—(See *Āīn*, i. 66-68.)

In Africa too, this royal fruit has spread, carrying the American name along with it. "The Mānānāzi † or pine-apple," says Burton, "grows luxuriantly as far as 3 marches from the coast (of Zanzibar). It is never cultivated, nor have its qualities as a fibrous plant been discovered." (*J.R.G.S.* xxix. 35). On the Ile Ste Marie, of Madagascar, it grew in the first half of the 17th century as *manasse* (*Flacourt*, 29).

Abul Faẕl, in the *Āīn*, mentions that the fruit was also called *kaṭhal-i-safarī*, or 'travel jack-fruit,' "because young plants put into a vessel may be taken on travels and will yield fruits." This seems a nonsensical pre-

* The *English Cyclop.* states on the authority of the Sloane MSS. that the pine was brought into England by the Earl of Portland, in 1690. [See *Encyl. Brit.*, 9th ed., xix. 106.]

† *M* is here a Suāhili prefix. See *Bleek's Comp. Grammar*, 189.

text for the name, especially as another American fruit, the Guava, is sometimes known in Bengal as the *Safarī-ām*, or 'travel mango.' It has been suggested by one of the present writers that these cases may present an uncommon use of the word *safarī* in the sense of 'foreign' or 'outlandish,' just as Clusius says of the pine-apple in India, "*peregrinus* est hic fructus," and as we begin this article by speaking of the *ananas* as having 'travelled' from its home in S. America. In the *Tesoro* of Cobarruvias (1611) we find "*Çafari*, cosa de Africa o Argel, como grenada" ('a thing from Africa or Algiers, such as a pomegranate'). And on turning to *Dozy and Eng.* we find that in Saracenic Spain a renowned kind of pomegranate was called *rommān safarī*: though this was said to have its name from a certain *Safar ibn-Obaid al Kilāi*, who grew it first. One doubts here, and suspects some connection with the Indian terms, though the link is obscure. The lamented Prof. Blochmann, however, in a note on this suggestion, would not admit the possibility of the use of *safarī* for 'foreign.' He called attention to the possible analogy of the Ar. *safarjal* for 'quince.' [Another suggestion may be hazarded. There is an Ar. word, *āsāfiriy*, which the dicts. define as 'a kind of olive.' Burton (*Ar. Nights*, iii. 79) translates this as 'sparrow-olives,' and says that they are so called because they attract sparrows (*āsāfīr*). It is perhaps possible that this name for a variety of olive may have been transferred to the pine-apple, and on reaching India, have been connected by a folk etymology with *safarī* applied to a 'travelled' fruit.] In Macassar, according to Crawfurd, the *ananas* is called *Pandang*, from its strong external resemblance, as regards fruit and leaves, to the *Pandanus*. Conversely we have called the latter *screw-pine*, from its resemblance to the *ananas*, or perhaps to the pine-cone, the original owner of the name. Acosta again (1578) describes the *Pandanus odoratissima* as the 'wild *ananas*,' and in Malayālam the pine-apple is called by a name meaning 'pandanus-jack-fruit.'

The term *ananas* has been Arabized, among the Indian pharmacists at least, as *'aīn-un-nās* 'the eye of man'; in Burmese *nan-na-si*, and in Singhalese and Tamil as *annāsi* (see *Moodeen Sheriff*).

We should recall attention to the fact that pine-apple was good English long before the discovery of America, its proper meaning being what we have now been driven (for the avoiding of confusion) to call a *pine-cone*. This is the only meaning of the term 'pine-apple' in Minsheu's *Guide into Tongues* (2nd ed. 1627). And the *ananas* got this name from its strong resemblance to a pine-cone. This is most striking as regards the large cones of the Stone-Pine of S. Europe. In the following three first quotations 'pine-apple' is used in the old sense:

1563.—"To all such as die so, the people erecteth a chappell, and to each of them a pillar and pole made of *Pine-apple* for a perpetuall monument."—*Reports of Japan*, in *Hakl.* ii. 567.

" "The greater part of the quadrangle set with savage trees, as Okes, Chesnuts, Cypresses, *Pine-apples*, Cedars."—*Reports of China*, tr. by *R. Willes*, in *Hakl.* ii. 559.

1577.—"In these islandes they found no trees knowen vnto them, but *Pine-apple* trees, and Date trees, and those of marueylous heyght, and exceedyng hardé."—*Peter Martyr*, in Eden's *H. of Trauayle*, fol. 11.

Oviedo, in *H. of the* (Western) *Indies*, fills 2½ folio pages with an enthusiastic description of the *pine-apple* as first found in Hispaniola, and of the reason why it got this name (*pina* in Spanish, *pigna* in Ramusio's Italian, from which we quote). We extract a few fragments.

1535.—"There are in this iland of Spagnuolo certain thistles, each of which bears a *Pigna*, and this is one of the most beautiful fruits that I have seen. . . . It has all these qualities in combination, viz. beauty of aspect, fragrance of colour, and exquisite flavour. The Christians gave it the name it bears (*Pigna*) because it is, in a manner, like that. But the *pine-apples* of the Indies of which we are speaking are much more beautiful than the *pigne* [*i.e.* pine-cones] of Europe, and have nothing of that hardness which is seen in those of Castile, which are in fact nothing but wood," &c.—*Ramusio*, iii. f. 135 v.

1564.—"Their pines be of the bigness of two fists, the outside whereof is of the making of a *pine-apple* [*i.e.* pine-cone], but it is softe like the rinde of a cucomber, and the inside eateth like an apple, but it is more delicious than any sweet apple sugared."—*Master John Hawkins*, in *Hakl.* iii. 602.

1575.—"Aussi la plus part des Sauuages s'en nourrissent vne bonne partie de l'année, comme aussi ils font d'vne autre espece de fruit, noñé **Nana**, qui est gros coñe vne moyenne citrouille, et fait autour comme vne pomme de pin. . . ."—*A. Thevet, Cosmographie Vniverselle*, liv. xxii. ff. 935 *v.*, 936 (with a pretty good cut).

1590.—"The Pines, or Pine-apples, are of the same fashion and forme outwardly to those of Castille, but within they wholly differ. . . One presented one of these Pine-apples to the Emperour Charles the fift, which must have cost much paine and care to bring it so farre, with the plant from the Indies, yet would he not trie the taste."—*Jos. de Acosta*, E. T. of 1604 (Hak. Soc.), 236-7.

1595.—". . . with diuers sortes of excellent fruits and rootes, and great abundance of *Pinas*, the princesse of fruits that grow vnder the Sun."—*Ralegh, Disc. of Guiana* (Hak. Soc.), 73.

c. 1610.—"**Ananats**, et plusieurs autres fruicts."—*P. de Laval*, i. 236 [Hak. Soc. i. 328].

1616.—"The **ananas** or Pine, which seems to the taste to be a pleasing compound, made of strawberries, claret-wine, rose-water, and sugar, well tempered together."—*Terry*, in *Purchas*, ii. 1469.

1623.—"The **ananas** is esteemed, and with reason, for it is of excellent flavour, though very peculiar, and rather acid than otherwise, but having an indescribable dash of sweetness that renders it agreeable. And as even these books (Clusius, &c.) don't mention it, if I remember rightly, I will say in brief that when you regard the entire fruit externally, it looks just like one of our pine-cones (*pigna*), with just such scales, and of that very colour."—*P. della Valle*, ii. 582 [Hak. Soc., i. 135].

1631.—Bontius thus writes of the fruit:—

"Qui legitis Cynaras, atque Indica dulcia fraga,
Ne nimis haec comedas, fugito hinc, latet anguis in herbâ."
Lib. vi. cap. 50, p. 145.

1661.—"I first saw the famous *Queen Pine* brought from Barbados and presented to his Majestie; but the first that were ever seen in England were those sent to Cromwell House foure years since."—*Evelyn's Diary*, July 19.

[c. 1665.—"Among other fruits, they preserve large citrons, such as we have in Europe, a certain delicate root about the length of sarsaparilla, that common fruit of the Indies called *amba*, another called **ananas** . . . ."—*Bernier* (ed. *Constable*), 438.]

1667.—"Ie peux à très-juste titre appeller l'**Ananas** le Roy des fruits, parcequ'il est le plus beau, et le meilleur de tous ceux qui sont sur la terre. C'est sans doute pour cette raison le Roy des Roys luy a mis une couronne sur la teste, qui est comme une marque essentielle de sa Royaute, puis qu'à la cheute du pere, il produit un ieune Roy qui luy succede en toutes ses admirables qualitez."—*P. Du Tertre, Hist. Gén. des Antilles Habitées par les François*, ii. 127.

1668.—"Standing by his Majesty at dinner in the Presence, there was of that rare fruit call'd the *King-pine*, grown in the Barbadoes and the West indies, the first of them I have ever seene. His Majesty having cut it up was pleas'd to give me a piece off his owne plate to taste of, but in my opinion it falls short of those ravishing varieties of deliciousness describ'd in Capt. Ligon's history and others."—*Evelyn*, July 19.

1673.—"The fruit the English call *Pine-Apple* (the Moors **Ananas**) because of the Resemblance."—*Fryer*, 182.

1716.—"I had more reason to wonder that night at the King's table" (at Hanover) "to see a present from a gentleman of this country . . . . what I thought, worth all the rest, two ripe **Ananasses**, which to my taste are a fruit perfectly delicious. You know they are naturally the growth of the Brazil, and I could not imagine how they came here but by enchantment."—*Lady M. W. Montagu*, Letter XIX.

1727.—

"Oft in humble station dwells
Unboastful worth, above fastidious pomp;
Witness, thou best **Anana**, thou the pride
Of vegetable life, beyond whate'er
The poets imaged in the golden age."
Thomson, Summer.

The poet here gives the word an unusual form and accent.

c. 1730.—"They (the Portuguese) cultivate the skirts of the hills, and grow the best products, such as sugar-cane, *pine-apples*, and rice."—*Khāfī Khān*, in *Elliot*, vii. 345.

A curious question has been raised regarding the *ananas*, similar to that discussed under **CUSTARD-APPLE**, as in the existence of the pine-apple to the Old World, before the days of Columbus.

In Prof. Rawlinson's *Ancient Monarchies* (i. 578), it is stated in reference to ancient Assyria: "Fruits . . . . were highly prized; amongst those of most repute were pomegranates, grapes, citrons, and apparently pine-apples." A foot-note adds: "The representation is so exact that I can hardly doubt the pine-apple being intended. Mr Layard expresses himself on this point with some hesitation (*Nineveh and Babylon*, p. 338)." The cut given is something like the conventional figure of a pine-apple, though it seems to us by no means very exact as such. Again, in Winter Jones's tr. of Conti (c. 1430) in *India in the 15th Century*, the traveller, speaking of a place called *Panconia* (read

Pauconia apparently Pegu) is made to say: "they have *pine-apples*, oranges, chestnuts, melons, but small and green, white sandal-wood and camphor."

We cannot believe that in either place the object intended was the *Ananas*, which has carried that American name with it round the world. Whatever the Assyrian representation was intended for, Conti seems to have stated, in the words *pinus habent* (as it runs in Poggio's Latin) merely that they had pine-trees. We do not understand on what ground the translator introduced *pine-apples*. If indeed any fruit was meant, it might have been that of the screw-pine, which though not eaten might perhaps have been seen in the bazars of Pegu, as it is used for some economical purposes. But *pinus* does not mean a fruit at all. 'Pine-cones' even would have been expressed by *pineas* or the like. [A reference to Mr L. W. King was thus answered: "The identity of the tree with the date-palm is, I believe, acknowledged by all naturalists who have studied the trees on the Assyrian monuments, and the 'cones' held by the winged figures have obviously some connection with the trees. I think it was Prof. Tylor of Oxford (see *Academy*, June 8, 1886, p. 283) who first identified the ceremony with the fertilization of the palm, and there is much to be said for his suggestion. The date-palm was of very great use to the Babylonians and Assyrians, for it furnished them with food, drink, and building materials, and this fact would explain the frequent repetition on the Assyrian monuments of the ceremony of fertilisation. On the other hand, there is no evidence, so far as I know, that the pine-apple was extensively grown in Assyria." Also see *Maspero*, *Dawn of Civ.* 556 *seq.*; on the use of the pine-cone in Greece, *Fraser*, *Pausanias*, iii. 65.]

ANCHEDIVA, ANJEDIVA, n.p. A small island off the W. coast of India, a little S. of Carwar, which is the subject of frequent and interesting mention in the early narratives. The name is interpreted by Malayālim as *añju-dīvu*, 'Five Islands,' and if this is correct belongs to the whole group. This may, however, be only an endeavour to interpret an old name, which is perhaps traceable in Ἀιγιδίων Νῆσος of Ptolemy. It is a remarkable example of the slovenliness of English professional map-making that Keith Johnston's *Royal Atlas* map of India contains no indication of this famous island. [The *Times Atlas* and Constable's *Hand Atlas* also ignore it.] It has, between land surveys and sea-charts, been omitted altogether by the compilers. But it is plain enough in the Admiralty charts; and the way Mr Birch speaks of it in his translation of Alboquerque as an "Indian seaport, no longer marked on the maps," is odd (ii. 168).

c. 1345.—Ibn Batuta gives no name, but Anjediva is certainly the island of which he thus speaks: "We left behind us the island (of Sindābūr or Goa), passing close to it, and cast anchor by a small island near the mainland, where there was a temple, with a grove and a reservoir of water. When we had landed on this little island we found there a *Jogi* leaning against the wall of a *Budkhānah* or house of idols."—*Ibn Batuta*, iv. 63.

The like may be said of the *Roteiro* of V. da Gama's voyage, which likewise gives no name, but describes in wonderful correspondence with Ibn Batuta; as does Correa, even to the *Jogi*, still there after 150 years!

1498.—"So the Captain-Major ordered Nicolas Coello to go in an armed boat, and see where the water was; and he found in the same island a building, a church of great ashlar-work, which had been destroyed by the Moors, as the country people said, only the chapel had been covered with straw, and they used to make their prayers to three black stones in the midst of the body of the chapel. Moreover they found, just beyond the church, a *tanque* of wrought ashlar, in which we took as much water as we wanted; and at the top of the whole island stood a great *tanque* of the depth of 4 fathoms, and moreover we found in front of the church a beach where we careened the ship."—*Roteiro*, 95.

1510.—"I quitted this place, and went to another island which is called **Anzediva**. . . There is an excellent port between the island and the mainland, and very good water is found in the said island."—*Varthema*, 120.

c. 1552.—"Dom Francesco de Almeida arriving at the Island of **Anchediva**, the first thing he did was to send João Homem with letters to the factors of Cananor, Cochin, and Coulão. . . ."—*Barros*, I. viii. 9.

c. 1561.—"They went and put in at **Angediva**, where they enjoyed themselves much; there were good water springs, and there was in the upper part of the island a tank built with stone, with very good water, and much wood; . . . there were no inhabitants, only a beggar man whom they called *Joguedes* . . . ."—*Correa*, Hak. Soc. 239.

1727.—"In January, 1664, my Lord (Marlborough) went back to England . . . . and left Sir Abraham with the rest, to pass the westerly Monsoons, in some Port on the Coast, but being unacquainted, chose a desolate Island called **Anjadwa**, to winter at. . . . Here they stayed from April to October, in which time they buried above 200 of their Men."—*A. Hamilton*, i. 182. At p. 274 the name is printed more correctly **Anjediva**.

ANDAMAN, n.p. The name of a group of islands in the Bay of Bengal, inhabited by tribes of a negrito race, and now partially occupied as a convict settlement under the Government of India. The name (though perhaps obscurely indicated by Ptolemy—see H. Y. in *P.R.G.S.* 1881, p. 665) first appears distinctly in the Ar. narratives of the 9th century. [The Ar. dual form is said to be from *Agamitae*, the Malay name of the aborigines.] The persistent charge of cannibalism seems to have been unfounded. [See E. H. Man, *On the Aboriginal Inhabitants of the Andaman Islands*, Intro. xiii. 45.]

A.D. 851.—"Beyond are two islands divided by a sea called **Andāmān**. The natives of these isles devour men alive; their hue is black, their hair woolly; their countenance and eyes have something frightful in them . . . . they go naked, and have no boats. . . . ."—*Relation des Voyages*, &c. par *Reinaud*, i. 8.

c. 1050.—These islands are mentioned in the great Tanjore temple-inscription (11th cent.) as *Tīmaittīvu*, 'Islands of Impurity,' inhabited by cannibals.

c. 1292.—"**Angamanain** is a very large Island. The people are without a King and are idolators, and are no better than wild beasts . . . . they are a most cruel generation, and eat everybody that they can catch if not of their own race."—*Marco Polo*, Bk. iii. c. 13.

c. 1430.—". . . leaving on his right hand an island called **Andemania**, which means the island of Gold, the circumference of which is 800 miles. The inhabitants are cannibals. No travellers touch here unless driven to do so by bad weather, for when taken they are torn to pieces and devoured by these cruel savages."—*Conti*, in *India in XV. Cent.*, 8.

c. 1566.—"Da Nicubar sinò a Pegu é vna catena d'Isole infinite, delle quali molte sono habitate da gente seluaggia, e chiamansi **Isole d'Andeman** . . . . e se per disgratia si perde in queste Isole qualche naue, come già se n'ha perso, non ne scampa alcuno, che tutti gli amazzano, e mangiano."—*Cesare de' Federici*, in *Ramusio*, iii. 391.

1727.—"The Islands opposite the Coast of *Tanacerin* are the **Andemans**. They lie about 80 leagues off, and are surrounded by many dangerous Banks and Rocks; they are all inhabited with *Canibals*, who are so fearless that they will swim off to a Boat if she approach near the shore, and attack her with their wooden Weapons . . . ."—*A. Hamilton*, ii. 65.

ANDOR, s. Port. 'a litter,' and used in the old Port. writers for a palankin. It was evidently a kind of **Muncheel** or **Dandy**, *i.e.* a slung hammock rather than a palankin. But still, as so often is the case, comes in another word to create perplexity. For *andas* is, in Port., a bier or a *litter*, appearing in Bluteau as a genuine Port. word, and the use of which by the writer of the Roteiro quoted below shows that it is so indeed. And in defining **Andor** the same lexicographer says: "A portable vehicle in India, in those regions where they do not use beasts, as in Malabar and elsewhere. It is a kind of contrivance like an uncovered *Andas*, which men bear on their shoulders, &c. . . . Among us **Andor** is a machine with four arms in which images or reliques of the saints are borne in processions." This last term is not, as we had imagined an old Port. word. It is Indian, in fact Sanskrit, *hindola*, 'a swing, a swinging cradle or hammock,' whence also Mahr. *hiṇḍolā*, and H. *hiṇḍolā* or *haṇḍolā*. It occurs, as will be seen, in the old Ar. work about Indian wonders, published by MM. Van der Lith and Marcel Devic. [To this Mr Skeat adds that in Malay **andor** means 'a buffalo-sledge for carting rice,' &c. It would appear to be the same as the Port. word, though it is hard to say which is the original.]

1013.—"Le même m'a conté qu'à Sérendīb, les rois et ceux qui se comportent à la façon des rois, se font porter dans le **handoul** (*handūl*) qui est semblable à une litière, soutenu sur les épaules de quelques piétons."—*Kitāb 'Ajāīb-al Hind*, p. 118.

1498.—"After two days had passed he (the Catual [**Cotwal**]) came to the factory in an **andor** which men carried on their shoulders, and these (*andors*) consist of great canes which are bent overhead and arched, and from these are hung certain cloths of a half fathom wide, and a fathom and a half long, and at the ends are pieces of wood to bear the cloth which hangs from the cane; and laid over the cloth there is a great mattrass of the same size, and this all made of silk-stuff wrought with gold-thread, and with many decorations and fringes and tassels; whilst the ends of the cane are mounted with silver, all very gorgeous, and rich, like the lords who travel so."—*Correa*, i. 102.

1498.—"Alii trouveram ao capitam mor humas **andas** d'omeens em que os onrrados, custumam em a quella terra d'andar, e alguns mercadores se as querem ter pagam por ello a elrey certa cousa."—*Roteiro*, pp. 54-55. *I.e.* "There they brought for the Captain-Major certain **andas**, borne by men, in which the persons of distinction in that country are accustomed to travel, and if any merchants desire to have the same they pay to the King for this a certain amount."

1505.—"Il Re se fa portare in vna Barra quale chiamono **Andora** portata da homini." —*Italian version of Dom Manuel's Letter* to the K. of Castille. (Burnell's Reprint) p. 12.

1552.—"The Moors all were on foot, and their Captain was a valiant Turk, who as being their Captain, for the honour of the thing was carried in an **Andor** on the shoulders of 4 men, from which he gave his orders as if he were on horseback."—*Barros*, II. vi. viii.

[1574.—See quotation under **PUNDIT**.]

1623.—Della Valle describes three kinds of shoulder-borne vehicles in use at Goa: (1) *reti* or nets, which were evidently the simple hammock, **muncheel** or **dandy**; (2) the **andor**; and (3) the palankin. "And these two, the palankins and the **andors**, also differ from one another, for in the **andor** the cane which sustains it is, as it is in the *reti*, straight; whereas in the palankin, for the greater convenience of the inmate, and to give more room for raising his head, the cane is arched upward like this, Ω. For this purpose the canes are bent when they are small and tender. And those vehicles are the most commodious and honourable that have the curved canes, for such canes, of good quality and strength to bear the weight, are not numerous; so they sell for 100 or 120 **pardaos** each, or about 60 of our *scudi*."—*P. della Valle*, ii. 610.

c. 1760.—"Of the same nature as palankeens, but of a different name, are what they call **andolas** . . . . these are much cheaper, and less esteemed."—*Grose*, i. 155.

ANDRUM, s. Malayāl. *āndram*. The form of hydrocele common in S. India. It was first described by Kaempfer, in his *Decas*, Leyden, 1694. —(See also his *Amoenitates Exoticae*, Fascic. iii. pp. 557 *seqq.*)

ANGELY-WOOD, s. Tam. *anjilī-*, or *anjalī-maram*; *artocarpus hirsuta* Lam. [in Malabar also known as *Iynee* (*āyini*) (*Logan*, i. 39)]. A wood of great value on the W. Coast, for shipbuilding, house-building, &c.

c. 1550.—"In the most eminent parts of it (Siam) are thick Forests of **Angelin** wood, whereof thousands of ships might be made." —*Pinto*, in *Cogan*, p. 285; see also p. 64.

1598.—"There are in India other wonderfull and thicke trees, whereof Shippes are made: there are trees by Cochiin, that are called **Angelina**, whereof certaine scutes or skiffes called Tones [**Doney**] are made . . . . it is so strong and hard a woode that Iron in tract of time would bee consumed thereby by reason of the hardness of the woode."—*Linschoten*, ch. 58 [Hak. Soc. ii. 56].

1644.—"Another thing which this province of Mallavar produces, in abundance and of excellent quality, is timber, particularly that called **Angelim**, which is most durable, lasting many years, insomuch that even if you desire to build a great number of ships, or vessels of any kind . . . . you may make them all in a year."—*Bocarro*, MS. f. 315.

ANGENGO, n.p. A place on the Travancore coast, the site of an old English Factory; properly said to be *Añju-tengu*, *Añchutennu*, Malayāl; the trivial meaning of which would be "five cocoa-nuts." This name gives rise to the marvellous rhapsody of the once famous Abbé Raynal, regarding "Sterne's Eliza," of which we quote below a few sentences from the 3½ pages of close print which it fills.

1711.—". . . **Anjengo** is a small Fort belonging to the *English East India Company*. There are about 40 Soldiers to defend it . . . most of whom are *Topazes*, or mungrel Portuguese."—*Lockyer*, 199.

1782.—"Territoire d'**An'inga**; tu n'es rien; mais tu as donné naissance à Eliza. Un jour, ces entrepôts . . . ne subsisteront plus . . . mais si mes écrits ont quelque durée, le nom d'**Anjinga** restera dans le mémoire des hommes . . . **Anjinga**, c'est à l'influence de ton heureux climat qu'elle devoit, sans doute, cet accord presqu'incompatible de volupté et de décence qui accompagnoit toute sa personne, et qui se mêloit à tous ses mouvements, &c., &c."—*Hist. Philosophique des Deux Indes*, ii. 72-73.

ANICUT, s. Used in the irrigation of the Madras Presidency for the dam constructed across a river to fill and regulate the supply of the channels drawn off from it; the cardinal work in fact of the great irrigation systems. The word, which has of late years become familiar all over India, is the Tam. comp. *anai-kaṭṭu*, 'Dam-building.'

1776.—"Sir — We have received your letter of the 24th. If the Rajah pleases to go to the **Anacut**, to see the repair of the bank, we can have no objection, but it will not be convenient that you should leave the garrison at present."—*Letter from Council at Madras* to Lt.-Col. Harper, Comm. at Tanjore, in *E. I. Papers*, 1777, 4to, i. 836.

1784.—"As the cultivation of the Tanjore country appears, by all the surveys and reports of our engineers employed in that service, to depend altogether on a supply of water by the Cauvery, which can only be secured by keeping the **Anicut** and banks in repair, we think it necessary to repeat to you our orders of the 4th July, 1777, on the subject of these repairs."—*Desp. of Court of Directors*, Oct. 27th, as amended by Bd. of Control, in *Burke*, iv. 104.

1793.—"The **Annicut** is no doubt a *judicious building*, whether the work of *Solar Rajah* or anybody else."—*Correspondence between A. Ross, Esq., and G. A. Ram, Esq., at Tanjore*, on the subject of furnishing water to the N. Circars. In *Dalrymple, O. R.*, ii. 459.

1862.—"The upper Coleroon **Anicut** or weir is constructed at the west end of the Island of Seringham."—*Markham, Peru & India*, 426.

[1883.—"Just where it enters the town is a large stone dam called Fischer's **Anaikat**."—*Lefanu, Man. of Salem*, ii. 32.]

ANILE, NEEL, s. An old name for indigo, borrowed from the Port. *anil*. They got it from the Ar. *al-nīl*, pron. *an-nīl*; *nīl* again being the common name of indigo in India, from the Skt. *nīla*, 'blue.' The vernacular (in this instance Bengali) word appears in the title of a native satirical drama *Nīl-Darpan*, 'The Mirror of Indigo (planting),' famous in Calcutta in 1861, in connection with a *cause célèbre*, and with a sentence which discredited the now extinct Supreme Court of Calcutta in a manner unknown since the days of Impey.

"*Neel-walla*" is a phrase for an Indigo-planter [and his Factory is "*Neel-kothee*"].

1501.—Amerigo Vespucci, in his letter from the Id. of Cape Verde to Lorenzo di Piero Francesco de' Medici, reporting his meeting with the Portuguese Fleet from India, mentions among other things brought "**anib** and tuzia," the former a manifest transcriber's error for *anil*.—In *Baldelli Boni, 'Il Milione,'* p. lvii.

1516.—In Barbosa's price list of Malabar we have:

"**Anil** nadador (i.e. floating; see *Garcia* below) very good,
per *farazola* . . . . *fanams* 30.
Anil loaded, with much sand,
per *farazola* . . . *fanams* 18 to 20."
In *Lisbon Collection*, ii. 393.

1525.—"A load of **anyll** in cakes which weighs 3½ maunds, 353 tangas."—*Lembrança*, 52.

1563.—"**Anil** is not a medicinal substance but an article of trade, so we have no need to speak thereof. . . . The best is pure and clear of earth, and the surest test is to burn it in a candle . . . . others put it in water, and if it floats then they reckon it good."—*Garcia*, f. 25 v.

1583.—"**Neel**, the churle 70 duckats, and a churle is 27 rottles and a half of Aleppo."—*Mr Iohn Newton*, in *Hakl.* ii. 378.

1583.—"They vse to pricke the skinne, and to put on it a kind of **anile**, or blacking which doth continue alwayes."—*Fitch*, in *Hakl.* ii. 395.

c. 1610.—". . . l'**Anil** ou Indique, qui est vne teinture bleüe violette, dont il ne s'en trouue qu'à Cambaye et Suratte."—*Pyrard de Laval*, ii. 158; [Hak. Soc. ii. 246].

[1614.—"I have 30 fardels **Anil** Geree." *Foster, Letters*, ii. 140. Here *Geree* is probably H. *jaṛī* (from *jaṛ*, 'the root'), the crop of indigo growing from the stumps of the plants left from the former year.]

1622.—"E conforme a dita pauta se dispachará o dito **anil** e canella."—In *Archiv. Port. Orient.*, fasc. 2, 240.

1638.—"Les autres marchandises, que l'on y débite le plus, sont . . . . du sel ammoniac, et de l'indigo, que ceux de pais appellent **Anil**."—*Mandelslo*, Paris, 1659, 138.

1648.—". . . . and a good quantity of **Anil**, which, after the place where most of it is got, is called *Chirchees* Indigo."—*Van Twist*, 14. Sharkej or Sirkej, 5 m. from Ahmedabad. "Cirquez Indigo" (1624) occurs in *Sainsbury*, iii. 442. It is the "*Sercase*" of Forbes [*Or. Mem.* 2nd ed. ii. 204]. The Dutch, about 1620, established a factory there on account of the indigo. Many of the Sultans of Guzerat were buried there (*Stavorinus*, iii. 109). Some account of the "Sarkhej *Rozas*," or Mausolea, is given in H. Brigg's *Cities of Gujarâshtra* (Bombay, 1849, pp. 274, *seqq.*). ["Indigo of Bian (Biana) *Sicchese*" (1609), *Danvers, Letters*, i. 28; "Indico, of Laher, here worth viij[s] the pounde *Serchis*."—*Birdwood, Letter Book*, 287.]

1653.—"Indico est un mot Portugais, dont l'on appelle une teinture bleüe qui vient des Indes Orientales, qui est de contrabande en France, les Turqs et les Arabes la nomment **Nil**."—*De la Boullaye-le-Gouz*, 543.

[1670.—"The neighbourhood of Delhi produces **Anil** or Indigo."—*Bernier* (ed. *Constable*), 283.]

ANNA, s. Properly H. *ānā*, *ānah*, the 16th part of a rupee. The term belongs to the Mohammedan monetary system (**RUPEE**). There is no coin of one *anna* only, so that it is a money of account only. The term *anna* is used in denoting a corresponding fraction of any kind of property, and especially in regard to coparcenary shares in land, or shares in a speculation. Thus a one-*anna* share is $\frac{1}{16}$ of such right, or a share of $\frac{1}{16}$ in the speculation; a four-*anna* is $\frac{1}{4}$, and so on. In some parts of India the term is used as subdivision ($\frac{1}{16}$) of the current land measure. Thus, in Saugor, the *anna*=16 *rūsīs*, and is itself $\frac{1}{16}$ of a *kancha* (*Elliot, Gloss.* s.v.). The term is also sometimes applied colloquially to persons of mixt parentage. 'Such a one has at least 2 *annas* of dark blood,' or 'coffee-colour.' This may be compared with the Scotch expression that a person of deficient intellect 'wants twopence in the shilling.'

1708.—"Provided . . . that a debt due from Sir Edward Littleton . . . of 80,407 Rupees and Eight **Annas** Money of *Bengal*, with Interest and Damages to the said English Company shall still remain to them. . ."—*Earl of Godolphin's Award* between the Old and the New E. I. Co., in *Charters*, &c., p. 358.

1727.—"The current money in Surat:
Bitter Almonds go 32 to a *Pice*:
1 **Annoe** is . . . . 4 Pice.
1 Rupee . . . . . 16 **Annoes**.
* * * * *
In Bengal their Accounts are kept in *Pice*:
12 to an Annoe.
16 **Annoes** to a Rupee."
A. Hamilton, ii. App. pp. 5, 8.

ANT, WHITE, s. The insect (*Termes bellicosus* of naturalists) not properly an ant, of whose destructive powers there are in India so many disagreeable experiences, and so many marvellous stories. The phrase was perhaps taken up by the English from the Port. *formigas branchas*, which is in Bluteau's Dict. (1713, iv. 175). But indeed exactly the same expression is used in the 14th century by our medieval authority. It is, we believe, a fact that these insects have been established at Rochelle in France, for a long period, and more recently at St. Helena. They exist also at the Convent of Mt. Sinai, and a species in Queensland.

A.D. c. 250.—It seems probable that Aelian speaks of White Ants.—"But the Indian ants construct a kind of heaped-up dwellings, and these not in depressed or flat positions easily liable to be flooded, but in lofty and elevated positions. . ."—*De Nat. Animal.* xvi. cap. 15.

c. 1328.—"Est etiam unum genus parvissimarum *formicarum* sicut lana *albarum*, quarum durities dentium tanta est quod etiam ligna rodunt et venas lapidum; et quotquot breviter inveniunt siccum super terram, et pannos laneos, et bombycinos laniant; et faciunt ad modum muri crustam unam de arenâ minutissimâ, ita quod sol non possit eas tangere; et sic remanent coopertae; verum est quod si contingat illam crustam frangi, et solem eas tangere, quam citius moriuntur.—*Fr. Jordanus*, p. 53.

1679.—"But there is yet a far greater inconvenience in this Country, which proceeds from the infinite number of **white Emmets**, which though they are but little, have teeth so sharp, that they will eat down a wooden Post in a short time. And if great care be not taken in the places where you lock up your Bales of Silk, in four and twenty hours they will eat through a Bale, as if it had been saw'd in two in the middle."—*Tavernier's Tunquin*, E. T., p. 11.

1688.—"Here are also abundance of Ants of several sorts, and Wood-lice, called by the English in the East Indies, **White Ants**."—*Dampier*, ii. 127.

1713.—"On voit encore des fourmis de plusieurs espèces; la plus pernicieuse est celle que les Européens ont nommé **fourmi blanche**."—*Lettres Edifiantes*, xii. 98.

1727.—"He then began to form Projects how to clear Accounts with his Master's Creditors, without putting anything in their Pockets. The first was on 500 chests of *Japon* Copper . . . . and they were brought into Account of Profit and Loss, for so much eaten up by the **White Ants**."—*A. Hamilton*, ii. 169.

1751.—". . . . concerning the Organ, we sent for the Revd. Mr. Bellamy, who declared that when Mr. Frankland applied to him for it that he told him that it was not in his power to give it, but wished it was removed from thence, as Mr. Pearson informed him it was eaten up by the **White Ants**."—*Ft. Will. Cons.*, Aug. 12. In *Long*, 25.

1789.—"The **White Ant** is an insect greatly dreaded in every house; and this is not to be wondered at, as the devastation it occasions is almost incredible."—*Munro, Narrative*, 31.

1876.—"The metal cases of his baggage are disagreeably suggestive of **White Ants**, and such omnivorous vermin."—*Sat. Review*, No. 1057, p. 6.

APĪL, s. Transfer of Eng. 'Appeal'; in general native use, in connection with our Courts.

1872.—"There is no Sindi, however wild, that cannot now understand '**Rasíd**' (receipt) [**Raseed**] and '**Apīl**' (appeal)."—*Burton, Sind Revisited*, i. 283.

APOLLO BUNDER, n.p. A well-known wharf at Bombay. A street near it is called Apollo Street, and a gate of the Fort leading to it 'the Apollo

Gate.' The name is said to be a corruption, and probably is so, but of what it is a corruption is not clear. The quotations given afford different suggestions, and Dr Wilson's dictum is entitled to respect, though we do not know what *pālawā* here means. Sir G. Birdwood writes that it used to be said in Bombay, that *Apollo-bandar* was a corr. of *palwa*-bandar, because the pier was the place where the boats used to land *palwa* fish. But we know of no fish so called; it is however possible that the *palla* or *Sable-fish* (**Hilsa**) is meant, which is so called in Bombay, as well as in Sind. [The *Āīn* (ii. 338) speaks of "a kind of fish called *palwah* which comes up into the Indus from the sea, unrivalled for its fine and exquisite flavour," which is the **Hilsa.**] On the other hand we may observe that there was at Calcutta in 1748 a frequented tavern called the Apollo (see *Long*, p. 11). And it is not impossible that a house of the same name may have given its title to the Bombay street and wharf. But Sir Michael Westropp's quotation below shows that *Pallo* was at least the native representation of the name more than 150 years ago. We may add that a native told Mr W. G. Pedder, of the Bombay C.S., from whom we have it, that the name was due to the site having been the place where the "*poli*" cake, eaten at the Holi festival, was baked. And so we leave the matter.

[1823.—"Lieut. Mudge had a tent on **Apollo**-green for astronomical observations." —*Owen, Narrative*, i. 327.]

1847.—"A little after sunset, on 2nd Jan. 1843, I left my domicile in Ambrolie, and drove to the **Pálawá bandar**, which receives from our accommodative countrymen the more classical name of *Apollo* pier." —*Wilson, Lands of the Bible*, p. 4.

1860.—"And atte what place ye Knyghte came to Londe, theyre ye ffolke . . . . worschyppen II Idolys in cheefe. Ye ffyrste is **Apollo**, wherefore yē cheefe londynge place of theyr Metropole is hyght **Apollo-Bundar**. . . ."—Ext. from a MS. of Sir John Mandeville, lately discovered. (A friend here queries: 'By Mr. Shapira?')

1877.—"This bunder is of comparatively recent date. Its name '**Apollo**' is an English corruption of the native word *Pallow* (fish), and it was probably not extended and brought into use for passenger traffic till about the year 1819. . . ."—*Maclean, Guide to Bombay*, 167. The last work adds a note: "Sir Michael Westropp gives a different derivation. . . . : *Polo*, a corruption of *Pálwa*, derived from *Pál*, which *inter alia* means a fighting vessel, by which kind of craft the locality was probably frequented. From *Pálwa* or *Pálwar*, the bunder now called Apollo is supposed to take its name. In the memorial of a grant of land, dated 5th Dec., 1743, the *pākhādē* in question is called *Pallo*."—*High Court Reports*, iv. pt. 3.

[1880.—"His mind is not prehensile like the tail of the **Apollo Bundar**."—*Aberigh-Mackay, Twenty-one Days in India*, p. 141.]

APRICOT, s. *Prunus Armeniaca*, L. This English word is of curious origin, as Dozy expounds it. The Romans called it *Malum Armeniacum*, and also (*Persicum?*) *praecox*, or 'early.' Of this the Greeks made πραικόκκιον, &c., and the Arab conquerors of Byzantine provinces took this up as *birkōk* and *barkōk*, with the article *al-barkōk*, whence Sp. *albarcoque*, Port. *albricoque*, *alboquorque*, Ital. *albercocca*, *albicocca*, Prov. *aubricot*, *ambricot*, Fr. *abricot*, Dutch *abricock*, *abrikoos*, Eng. *apricock*, **apricot**. Dozy mentions that Dodonaeus, an old Dutch writer on plants, gives the vernacular name as *Vroege Persen*, 'Early Peaches,' which illustrates the origin. In the Cyprus bazars, apricots are sold as χρυσόμηλα; but the less poetical name of '*kill-johns*' is given by sailors to the small hard kinds common to St. Helena, the Cape, China, &c. *Zard ālū* [**aloo**] (Pers.) 'yellow-plum' is the common name in India.

1615.—"I received a letter from Jorge Durois . . . with a baskit of **aprecockes** for my selfe. . ."—*Cocks's Diary*, i. 7.

1711.—"**Apricocks**—the Persians call *Kill Franks*, because Europeans not knowing the Danger are often hurt by them."—*Lockyer*, p. 231.

1738.—"The common **apricot** . . . is . . . known in the Frank language (in Barbary) by the name of *Matza Franca*, or the Killer of Christians."—*Shaw's Travels*, ed. 1757, p. 144.

ARAB, s. This, it may be said, in Anglo-Indian always means 'an Arab horse.'

1298.—"Car il va du port d'Aden en Inde moult grant quantité de bons destriers **arrabins** et chevaus et grans roncins de ij selles."—*Marco Polo*, Bk. iii. ch. 36. [See *Sir H. Yule's* note, 1st ed., vol. ii. 375.]

1338.—"Alexandre descent du destrier **Arrabis**."—*Rommant d'Alexandre* (Bodl. MS.).

c. 1590.—"There are fine horses bred in every part of the country; but those of Cachh excell, being equal to **Arabs**."—*Āīn*, i. 133.

1825.—"**Arabs** are excessively scarce and dear; and one which was sent for me to look at, at a price of 800 rupees, was a skittish, cat-legged thing."—*Heber*, i. 189 (ed. 1844).

c. 1844.—A local magistrate at Simla had returned from an unsuccessful investigation. An acquaintance hailed him next day: 'So I hear you came back *re infectâ?*' 'No such thing,' was the reply; 'I came back on my grey **Arab**!'

1856.—
". . . . the true blood-royal of his race,
The silver **Arab** with his purple veins
Translucent, and his nostrils caverned wide,
And flaming eye. . . ."
The Banyan Tree.

ARAKAN, ARRACAN, n.p. This is an European form, perhaps through Malay [which Mr Skeat has failed to trace], of *Rakhaing*, the name which the natives give themselves. This is believed by Sir Arthur Phayre [see *Journ. As. Soc. Ben.* xii. 24 *seqq.*] to be a corruption of the Skt. *rākshasa*, Pali *rakkhaso*, *i.e.* 'ogre' or the like, a word applied by the early Buddhists to unconverted tribes with whom they came in contact. It is not impossible that the Ἀργυρῆ of Ptolemy, which unquestionably represents Arakan, may disguise the name by which the country is still known to foreigners; at least no trace of the name as 'Silver-land' in old Indian Geography has yet been found. We may notice, without laying any stress upon it, that in Mr. Beal's account of early Chinese pilgrims to India, there twice occurs mention of an Indo-Chinese kingdom called *O-li-ki-lo*, which transliterates fairly into some name like *Argyrē*, and not into any other yet recognisable (see *J.R.A.S.* (N.S.) xiii. 560, 562).

c. 1420-30.—"Mari deinceps cum mense integro ad ostium **Rachani** fluvii pervenisset."—*N. Conti*, in *Poggius, De Varietate Fortunae.*

1516.—"Dentro fra terra del detto regno di Verma, verso tramontana vi è vn altro regno di Gentili molto grande . . . . confina similmente col regno di Bēgala e col regno di Aua, e chiamasi **Aracan**."—*Barbosa*, in *Ramusio*, i. 316.

[c. 1535.—"*Arquam*": See **CAPELAN**.]

1545.—"They told me that coming from India in the ship of Jorge Manhoz (who was a householder in Goa), towards the Port of Chatigaon in the kingdom of Bengal, they were wrecked upon the shoals of **Racaon** owing to a badly-kept watch."—*Pinto*, cap. clxvii.

1552.—"Up to the Cape of Negraes . . . will be 100 leagues, in which space are these populated places, Chocoriá, Bacalá, **Arracão** City, capital of the kingdom so styled. . . ."—*Barros*, I. ix. 1.

1568.—"Questo Re di **Rachan** ha il suo stato in mezzo la costa, tra il Regno di Bengala e quello di Pegù, ed è il maggiore nemico che habbia il Re del Pegù."—*Cesare de' Federici*, in *Ramusio*, iii. 396.

1586.—". . . . Passing by the Island of Sundiua, Porto grande, or the Countrie of Tippera, the Kingdom of **Recon** and *Mogen* (**Mugg**) . . . . our course was S. and by E. which brought vs to the barre of Negrais."—*R. Fitch*, in *Hakl.* ii. 391.

c. 1590.—"To the S.E. of Bengal is a large country called **Arkung** to which the Bunder of Chittagong properly belongs."—*Gladwin's Ayeen*, ed. 1800, ii. 4. [Ed. *Jarrett*, ii. 119] in orig. (i. 388) **Arkhang**.

[1599.—**Arracan**. See **MACAO**.

[1608.—**Rakhang**. See **CHAMPA**.

[c. 1069.—**Aracan**. See **PROME**.

[1659.—**Aracan**. See **TALAPOIN**.]

1660.—"Despatches about this time arrived from Mu'azzam Khān, reporting his successive victories and the flight of Shuja to the country of **Rakhang**, leaving Bengal undefended."—*Khāfī Khān*, in *Elliot*, vii. 254.

[c. 1660.—"The Prince . . . . sent his eldest son, Sultan Banque, to the King of **Racan**, or Mog."—*Bernier* (ed. *Constable*), 109.]

c. 1665.—"Knowing that it is impossible to pass any Cavalry by Land, no, not so much as any Infantry, from *Bengale* into **Rakan**, because of the many channels and rivers upon the Frontiers . . . he (the Governor of Bengal) thought upon this experiment, viz. to engage the *Hollanders* in his design. He therefore sent a kind of Ambassador to Batavia."—*Bernier*, E. T., 55 [(ed. *Constable*, 180)].

1673.—". . . . A mixture of that Race, the most accursedly base of all Mankind who are known for their Bastard-brood lurking in the Islands at the Mouths of the Ganges, by the name of **Racanners**."—*Fryer*, 219. (The word is misprinted *Buccaneers*; but see Fryer's *Index*.)

1726.—"It is called by some Portuguese **Orrakan**, by others among them **Arrakaon**, and by some again **Rakan** (after its capital) and also Mog (**Mugg**)."—*Valentijn*, v. 140.

1727.—"**Arackan** has a Conveniency of a noble spacious River."—*A. Hamilton*, ii. 30.

ARBOL TRISTE, s. The tree or shrub, so called by Port. writers, appears to be the *Nyctanthes arbor tristis*, or *Arabian jasmine* (N. O. *Jasmineae*), a native of the drier parts of India.

[The quotations explain the origin of the name.]

[c. 1610.—"Many of the trees they call **tristes**, of which they make saffron."—*Pyrard de Laval*, Hak. Soc., i. 411.

,, "That tree called **triste**, which is produced in the East Indies, is so named because it blooms only at night."—*Ibid.* ii. 362; and see Burnell's *Linschoten*, Hak. Soc. ii. 58-62.

1624.—"I keep among my baggage to show the same in Italy, as also some of the tree **trifoe** (in orig. *Arbor Trisoe*, a misprint for *Tristo*) with its odoriferous flowers, which blow every day and night, and fall at the approach of day.—*P. della Valle*, Hak. Soc. ii. 406.]

ARCOT, n.p. *Arkāt*, a famous fortress and town in the Madras territory, 65 miles from Madras. The name is derived by Bp. Caldwell from Tam. *ārkād*, the 'Six Forests,' confirmed by the Tam-Fr. Dict. which gives a form *ārukādu*='Six forêts' ["the abode of six Rishis in former days. There are several places of this name in the southern districts besides the town of Arcot near Vellore. One of these in Tanjore would correspond better than that with Harkatu of Ibn Batuta, who reached it on the first evening of his march inland after landing from Ceylon, apparently on the shallow coast of Madura or Tanjore."—*Madras Ad. Man.* ii. 211]. Notwithstanding the objection made by Maj.-Gen. Cunningham in his *Geog. of Ancient India*, it is probable that Arcot is the Ἀρκατοῦ βασίλειον Σῶρα of Ptolemy, 'Arkatu, residence of K. Sora.'

c. 1346.—"We landed with them on the beach, in the country of Ma'bar . . . . we arrived at the fortress of **Harkātū**, where we passed the night."—*Ibn Batuta*, iv. 187, 188.

1785.—"It may be said that this letter was written by the Nabob of **Arcot** in a moody humour. . . . Certainly it was; but it is in such humours that the truth comes out."—*Burke's Speech*, Feb. 28th.

ARECA, s. The seed (in common parlance the nut) of the palm *Areca catechu*, L., commonly, though somewhat improperly, called 'betel-nut'; the term **Betel** belonging in reality to the leaf which is chewed along with the *areca*. Though so widely cultivated, the palm is unknown in a truly indigenous state. The word is Malayāl. *aḍakka* [according to Bp. Caldwell, from *adai* 'close arrangement of the cluster,' *kay*, 'nut' *N.E.D.*], and comes to us through the Port.

1510.—"When they eat the said leaves (betel), they eat with them a certain fruit which is called *coffolo*, and the tree of the said *coffolo* is called **Arecha**."—*Varthema*, Hak. Soc., 144.

1516.—"There arrived there many zambucos [**Sambook**] . . . . . with **areca**."—*Barbosa*, Hak. Soc., 64.

1521.—"They are always chewing **Arecca**, a certaine Fruit like a Peare, cut in quarters and rolled up in leaves of a Tree called *Bettre* (or *Vettele*), like Bay leaves; which having chewed they spit forth. It makes the mouth red. They say they doe it to comfort the heart, nor could live without it."—*Pigafetta*, in *Purchas*, i. 38.

1548.—"In the *Renda do Betel*, or Betel duties at Goa are included Betel, **arequa**, jacks, green ginger, oranges, lemons, figs, coir, mangos, citrons."—*Botelho*, *Tombo*, 48. The Port. also formed a word *ariqueira* for the tree bearing the nuts.

1563.—". . . and in Malabar they call it *pac* (Tam. *pāk*); and the Nairs (who are the gentlemen) call it **areca**."—*Garcia D'O.*, f. 91 *b*.

c. 1566.—"Great quantitie of **Archa**, which is a fruite of the bignesse of nutmegs, which fruite they eate in all these parts of the Indies, with the leafe of an Herbe, which they call *Bettell*."—*C. Frederike*, transl. in *Hakl.* ii. 350.

1586.—"Their friends come and bring gifts, cocos, figges, **arrecaes**, and other fruits."—*Fitch*, in *Hakl.*, ii. 395.

[1624.—"And therewith they mix a little ashes of sea-shells and some small pieces of an Indian nut sufficiently common, which they here call *Foufel*, and in other places **Areca**; a very dry fruit, seeming within like perfect wood; and being of an astringent nature they hold it good to strengthen the Teeth."—*P. della Valle*, Hak. Soc. i. 36. Mr Grey says: "As to the Port. name, *Foufel* or *Fofel*, the origin is uncertain. In Sir J. Maundeville's Travels it is said that black pepper "is called *Fulful*," which is probably the same word as "*Foufel*." But the Ar. *Fawfal* or *Fufal* is 'betel-nut.']

1689.—". . . . the *Neri* which is drawn from the **Arequies** Tree in a fresh earthen vessel, is as sweet and pleasant as Milk"—*Ovington*, 237. [*Neri*=H. and Mahr. *nīr*, 'sap,' but *neri* is, we are told, Guzerati for toddy in some form.]

ARGEMONE MEXICANA. This American weed (N.O. *Papaveraceae*) is notable as having overrun India, in every part of which it seems to be familiar. It is known by a variety of names, *Firinghī dhatūra*, gamboge thistle, &c. [See Watt, *Dict. Econ. Prod.*, i. 306 *seqq.*]

ARGUS PHEASANT, s. This name, which seems more properly to belong to the splendid bird of the Malay Peninsula (*Argusanus giganteus*, Tem., *Pavo argus*, Lin.), is confusingly applied in Upper India to the Himālayan horned pheasant *Ceriornis* (Spp. *satyra*, and *melanocephala*) from the round white eyes or spots which mark a great part of the bird's plumage.—See remark under **MOONAUL**.

ARRACK, RACK, s. This word is the Ar. *'araḳ*, properly 'perspiration,' and then, first the exudation or sap drawn from the date palm (*'araḳ al-tamar*); secondly any strong drink, 'distilled spirit,' 'essence,' etc. But it has spread to very remote corners of Asia. Thus it is used in the forms *ariki* and *arki* in Mongolia and Manchuria, for spirit distilled from grain. In India it is applied to a variety of common spirits; in S. India to those distilled from the fermented sap of sundry palms; in E. and N. India to the spirit distilled from cane-molasses, and also to that from rice. The Turkish form of the word, *rāḳi*, is applied to a spirit made from grape-skins; and in Syria and Egypt to a spirit flavoured with aniseed, made in the Lebanon. There is a popular or slang Fr. word, *riquiqui*, for brandy, which appears also to be derived from *araḳī* (*Marcel Devic*). Humboldt (*Examen*, &c., ii. 300) says that the word first appears in Pigafetta's Voyage of Magellan; but this is not correct.

c. 1420.—"At every *yam* (post-house) they give the travellers a sheep, a goose, a fowl . . . . **'arak**. . . ."—*Shah Rukh's Embassy to China*, in N. & E., xiv. 396.

1516.—"And they bring cocoa-nuts, **hurraca** (which is something to drink) . . . ."—*Barbosa*, Hak. Soc. 59.

1518.—"—que todos os mantimentos asy de pão, como vinhos, **orracas**, arrozes, carnes, e pescados."—In *Archiv. Port. Orient.*, fasc. 2, 57.

1521.—"When these people saw the politeness of the captain, they presented some fish, and a vessel of palm-wine, which they call in their language **uraca**. . . ."—*Pigafetta*, Hak. Soc. 72.

1544.—"Manueli a cruce . . . . commendo ut plurimum invigilet duobus illis Christianorum Carearum pagis, diligenter attendere . . . . nemo potu **Orracae** se inebriet . . . si ex hoc deinceps tempore Punicali **Orracha** potetur, ipsos ad mihi suo gravi damno luituros."—*Scti. Fr. Xar. Epistt.*, p. 111.

1554.—"And the excise on the *orraquas* made from palm-trees, of which there are three kinds, viz., *çura*, which is as it is drawn; **orraqua**, which is *çura* once boiled (*cozida*, qu. distilled?); *sharab* (*xarao*) which is boiled two or three times and is stronger than *orraqua*."—*S. Botelho, Tombo*, 50.

1563.—"One kind (of coco-palm) they keep to bear fruit, the other for the sake of the *çura*, which is *vino mosto;* and this when it has been distilled they call **orraca**."—*Garcia D'O.*, f. 67. (The word *surā*, used here, is a very ancient importation from India, for Cosmas (6th century) in his account of the coco-nut, confounding (it would seem) the milk with the toddy of that palm, says: "The *Argellion* is at first full of a very sweet water, which the Indians drink from the nut, using it instead of wine. This drink is called *rhoncosura*, and is extremely pleasant." It is indeed possible that the **rhonco** here may already be the word *arrack*).

1605.—"A Chines borne, but now turned Iauan, who was our next neighbour . . . . and brewed **Aracke** which is a kind of hot drinke, that is vsed in most of these parts of the world, instead of Wine. . ."—*E. Scot*, in *Purchas*, i. 173.

1631.—". . . . jecur . . . . a potu istius maledicti **Arac**, non tantum in temperamento immutatum, sed etiam in substantiâ suâ corrumpitur."—*Jac. Bontius*, lib. ii. cap. vii. p. 22.

1687.—"Two jars of **Arack** (made of rice as I judged) called by the Chinese *Samshu* [**Samshoo**]."—*Dampier*, i. 419.

1719.—"We exchanged some of our wares for opium and some **arrack**. . . ."—*Robinson Crusoe*, Pt. II.

1727.—"Mr Boucher had been 14 Months soliciting to procure his *Phirmaund;* but his repeated Petitions . . . . had no Effect. But he had an *Englishman*, one *Swan*, for his Interpreter, who often took a large Dose of **Arrack**. . . . Swan got pretty near the King (Aurungzeb) . . . . and cried with a loud Voice in the Persian Language that his Master wanted Justice done him" (see **DOAI**).—*A. Hamilton*, i. 97.

Rack is a further corruption; and **rack-punch** is perhaps not quite obsolete.

1603.—"We taking the But-ends of Pikes and Halberts and Faggot-sticks, drave them into a **Racke**-house."—*E. Scot*, in *Purchas*, i. 184.

Purchas also has **Vraca** and other forms; and at i. 648 there is mention of a strong kind of spirit called **Rack**-*apee* (Malay *āpi*= 'fire'). See **FOOL'S RACK**.

1616.—"Some small quantitie of Wine, but not common, is made among them; they call it **Raack**, distilled from Sugar and a spicie Rinde of a Tree called *Iagra* [**Jaggery**]."—*Terry*, in *Purchas*, ii. 1470.

1622.—"We'll send him a jar of **rack** by next conveyance."—Letter in *Sainsbury*, iii. 40.

1627.—"Java hath been fatal to many of the English, but much through their own distemper with **Rack**."—*Purchas, Pilgrimage*, 693.

1848.—"Jos . . . finally insisted upon having a bowl of **rack punch**. . . . That bowl of **rack punch** was the cause of all this history."—*Vanity Fair*, ch. vi.

ARSENAL, s. An old and ingenious etymology of this word is *arx navalis*. But it is really Arabic. Hyde derives it from *tars-khānah*, 'domus terroris,' contracted into *tarsānah*, the form (as he says) used at Constantinople (*Syntagma Dissertt.*, i. 100). But it is really the Ar. *dār-al-ṣinā'a*, 'domus artificii,' as the quotations from Mas'ūdī clearly show. The old Ital. forms *darsena*, *darsinale* corroborate this, and the Sp. *ataraçana*, which is rendered in Ar. by Pedro de Alcala, quoted by Dozy, as *dar a cinaa*.—(See details in *Dozy, Oosterlingen*, 16-18.)

A.D. 943-4.—"At this day in the year of the Hijra 332, Rhodes (*Rodas*) is an arsenal (*dār-ṣinā'a*) where the Greeks build their war-vessels."—*Mas'ūdī*, ii. 423. And again "*dār-ṣinā'at al marākib*," 'an arsenal of ships,' iii. 67.

1573.—"In this city (Fez) there is a very great building which they call **Daraçana**, where the Christian captives used to labour at blacksmith's work and other crafts under the superintendence and orders of renegade headmen . . . here they made cannon and powder, and wrought swords, cross-bows, and arquebusses."—*Marmol, Desc. General de Affrica*, lib. iii. f. 92.

1672.—"On met au **Tershana** deux belles galères à l'eau."—*Antoine Galland, Journ.*, i. 80.

ART, EUROPEAN. We have heard much, and justly, of late years regarding the corruption of Indian art and artistic instinct by the employment of the artists in working for European patrons, and after European patterns. The copying of such patterns is no new thing, as we may see from this passage of the brightest of writers upon India whilst still under Asiatic government.

c. 1665.—". . . . not that the Indians have not wit enough to make them successful in Arts, they doing very well (as to some of them) in many parts of India, and it being found that they have inclination enough for them, and that some of them make (even without a Master) very pretty workmanship and imitate so well our work of Europe, that the difference thereof will hardly be discerned."—*Bernier*, E. T., 81-82 [ed. *Constable*, 254].

ARTICHOKE, s. The genealogy of this word appears to be somewhat as follows: The Ar. is **al-ḥarshūf** (perhaps connected with *ḥarash*, 'rough-skinned') or *al-kharshūf*; hence Sp. **alcarchofa** and It. *carcioffo* and *arciocco*, Fr. *artichaut*, Eng. *artichoke*.

c. 1348.—"The Incense (benzoin) tree is small . . . . its branches are like those of a thistle or an artichoke (**al-kharshaf**)."—*Ibn Batuta*, iv. 240. **Al-kharshaf** in the published text. The spelling with *ḥ* instead of *kh* is believed to be correct (see *Dozy*, s.v. *Alcarchofa*); [also see *N.E.D.* s.v. *Artichoke*].

ARYAN, adj. Skt. *Ārya*, 'noble.' A term frequently used to include all the races (Indo-Persic, Greek, Roman, Celtic, Sclavonic, &c.) which speak languages belonging to the same family as Sanskrit. Much vogue was given to the term by Pictet's publication of *Les Origines Indo-Européennes, ou les Aryas Primitifs* (Paris, 1859), and this writer seems almost to claim the name in this sense as his own (see quotation below). But it was in use long before the date of his book. Our first quotation is from Ritter, and there it has hardly reached the full extent of application. Ritter seems to have derived the use in this passage from Lassen's *Pentapotamia*. The word has in great measure superseded the older term *Indo-Germanic*, proposed by F. Schlegel at the beginning of the last century. The latter is, however, still sometimes used, and M. Hovelacque, especially, prefers it. We may observe here that the connection which evidently exists between the several languages classed together as Aryan cannot be regarded, as it was formerly, as warranting an assumption of identity of race in all the peoples who speak them.

It may be noted as curious that among the Javanese (a people so remote in blood from what we understand by Aryan), the word *ārya* is commonly used as an honorary prefix to the names of men of rank; a survival of the ancient Hindu influence on the civilisation of the island.

The earliest use of *Aryan* in an ethnic sense is in the Inscription on the tomb of Darius, in which the king calls himself an Aryan, and of Aryan descent, whilst Ormuzd is in the Median version styled, 'God of the Aryans'

B.C. c. 486.—"*Adam Dáryavush Khsháyathiya vazarka . . . . Pársa, Pársahiyá putra*, **Ariya**, **Ariya** *chitra.*" *i.e.* "I (am) Darius, the Great King, the King of Kings, the King of all inhabited countries, the King of this great Earth far and near, the son of Hystaspes, an Achaemenian, a Persian, an **Arian**, of *Arian* descent."—In *Rawlinson's Herodotus*, 3rd ed., iv. 250.

"These Medes were called anciently by all people **Arians**, but when Medêa, the Colchian, came to them from Athens, they changed their name."—*Herodot.*, vii. 62 (Rawlins).

1835.—"Those eastern and proper Indians, whose territory, however, Alexander never touched by a long way, call themselves in the most ancient period *Arians* (**Arier**) (*Manu*, ii. 22, x. 45), a name coinciding with that of the ancient Medes."—*Ritter*, v. 458.

1838.—See also *Ritter*, viii. 17 seqq.; and Potto's art. in *Ersch & Grueber's Encyc.*, ii. 18, 46.

1850.—"The **Aryan** tribes in conquering India, urged by the Brahmans, made war against the Turanian demon-worship, but not always with complete success."—*Dr. J. Wilson*, in *Life*, 450.

1851.—"We must request the patience of our readers whilst we give a short outline of the component members of the great **Arian** family. The first is the Sanskrit. . . . The second branch of the Arian family is the Persian. . . . There are other scions of the Arian stock which struck root in the soil of Asia, before the Arians reached the shores of Europe. . ."—(*Prof. Max Müller*) *Edinburgh Review*, Oct. 1851, pp. 312-313.

1853.—"Sur les sept premières civilisations, qui sont celles de l'ancien monde, six appartiennent, en partie au moins, à la race **ariane**."—*Gobineau, De l'Inégalité des Races Humaines*, i. 364.

1855.—"I believe that all who have lived in India will bear testimony . . . . that to natives of India, of whatever class or caste, Mussulman, Hindoo, or Parsee, '**Aryan** or Tamulian,' unless they have had a special training, our European paintings, prints, drawings, and photographs, plain or coloured, if they are landscapes, are absolutely unintelligible."—*Yule, Mission to Ava*, 59 (publ. 1858).

1858.—"The **Aryan** tribes—for that is the name they gave themselves, both in their old and new homes—brought with them institutions of a simplicity almost primitive."—*Whitney, Or. & Ling. Studies*, ii. 5.

1861.—"Latin, again, with Greek, and the Celtic, the Teutonic, and Slavonic languages, together likewise with the ancient dialects of India and Persia, must have sprung from an earlier language, the mother of the whole Indo-European or **Aryan** family of speech."—*Prof. Max Müller, Lectures*, 1st Ser. 32.

We also find the verb *Aryanize*:

1858.—"Thus all India was brought under the sway, physical or intellectual and moral, of the alien race; it was thoroughly **Aryanized**."—*Whitney, u. s.* 7.

ASHRAFEE, s. Arab. *ashrafī*, 'noble,' applied to various gold coins (in analogy with the old English 'noble'), especially to the *dīnār* of Egypt, and to the Gold **Mohur** of India.—See **XERAFINE**.

c. 1550.—"There was also the sum of 500,000 Falory **ashrafies** equal in the currency of Persia to 50,000 royal Irak tomāns."—*Mem. of Humayun*, 125. A note suggests that *Falory*, or *Flori*, indicates *florin*.

ASSAM, n.p. The name applied for the last three centuries or more to the great valley of the Brahmaputra River, from the emergence of its chief sources from the mountains till it enters the great plain of Bengal. The name *Āsām* and sometimes *Āshām* is a form of *Āhām* or *Āhom*, a dynasty of Shan race, who entered the country in the middle ages, and long ruled it. Assam politically is now a province embracing much more than the name properly included.

c. 1590.—"The dominions of the Rajah of **Asham** join to Kamroop; he is a very powerful prince, lives in great state, and when he dies, his principal attendants, both male and female, are voluntarily buried alive with his corpse."—*Gladwin's Ayeen* (ed. 1800) ii. 3; [*Jarrett*, trans. ii. 118].

1682.—"Ye Nabob was very busy dispatching and vesting divers principal officers sent with all possible diligence with recruits for their army, lately overthrown in **Asham** and *Sillet*, two large plentiful countries 8 days' journey distant from this city (Dacca)."—*Hedges, Diary*, Oct. 29th; [Hak. Soc. i. 43].

1770.—"In the beginning of the present century, some Bramins of Bengal carried their superstitions to **Asham**, where the people were so happy as to be guided solely by the dictates of natural religion."—*Raynal* (tr. 1777) i. 420.

1788.—"M. Chevalier, the late Governor of Chandernagore, by permission of the King, went up as high as the capital of **Assam**, about the year 1762."—*Rennell's Mem.*, 3rd ed. p. 299.

ASSEGAY, s. An African throwing-spear. Dozy has shown that this is Berber *zaghāya*, with the Ar. article prefixed (p. 223). Those who use it often seem to take it for a S. African or Eastern word. So Godinho de Eredia seems to use it as if Malay (f. 21*v*). [Mr Skeat remarks that the nearest word in Malay is *seligi*, explained by Klinkert as 'a short wooden throwing-spear,' which is possibly that referred to by G. de Eredia.]

c. 1270.—"There was the King standing with three 'exortins' (or men of the guard) by his side armed with javelins [*ab lur* **atzagayes**"].—*Chronicle of K. James of Aragon*, tr. by Mr. Foster, 1883, i. 173.

c. 1444.—" . . . They have a quantity of **azagaias**, which are a kind of light darts." —*Cadamosto, Navegação primeira*, 32.

1552.—"But in general they all came armed in their fashion, some with **azagaias** and shields and others with bows and quivers of arrows."—*Barros*, I. iii. 1.

1572.—
"Hum de escudo embraçado, e de **azagaia**,
Outro de arco encurvado, e setta ervada."
Camões, i. 86.

By Burton:
"this, targe on arm and **assegai** in hand,
that, with his bended bow, and venom'd reed."

1586.—"I loro archibugi sono belli, e buoni, come i nostri, e le lance sono fatte con alcune canne piene, e forti, in capo delle quali mettono vn ferro, come uno di quelli delle nostri **zagaglie**."—*Balbi*, 111.

1600.—"These they use to make Instruments of wherewith to fish . . . . as also to make weapons, as Bows, Arrowes, Aponers, and **Assagayen**."—*Disc. of Guinea*, from the Dutch, in *Purchas*, ii. 927.

1608.—"Doncques voyant que nous ne pouvions passer, les deux hommes sont venu en nageant auprès de nous, et ayans en leurs mains trois Lancettes ou **Asagayes**."—*Houtman*, 5*b*.

[1648.—"The ordinary food of these Cafres is the flesh of this animal (the elephant), and four of them with their **Assegais** (in orig. **ageagayes**), which are a kind of short pike, are able to bring an elephant to the ground and kill it."—*Tavernier* (ed. *Ball*), ii. 161, cf. ii. 295.]

1666.—"Les autres armes offensives (in India) sont l'arc et la flèche, le javelot ou **zagaye** . . . ."—*Thevenot*, v. 132 (ed. 1727).

1681.—" . . . . encontraron diez y nueve hombres bazos armados con dardas, y **azagayas**, assi llaman los Arabes vnas lanças pequeñas arrojadizas, y pelearon con ellos." —*Martinez de la Puente, Compendio*, 87.

1879.—
"Alert to fight, athirst to slay,
They shake the dreaded **assegai**,
And rush with blind and frantic will
On all, when few, whose force is skill."
Isandlana, by *Ld. Stratford de Redcliffe*, *Times*, March 29.

ATAP, ADAP, s. Applied in the Malayo-Javanese regions to any palm-fronds used in thatching, commonly to those of the **Nipa** (*Nipa fruticans*, Thunb.). [*Atap*, according to Mr Skeat, is also applied to any roofing; thus tiles are called *atap batu*, 'stone *ataps*.'] The Nipa, "although a wild plant, for it is so abundant that its culture is not necessary, it is remarkable that its name should be the same in all the languages from Sumatra to the Philippines."—(*Crawfurd, Dict. Ind. Arch.* 301). **Atĕp** is Javanese for 'thatch.'

1672.—"**Atap** or leaves of Palm-trees . . . ."—*Baldaeus, Ceylon*, 164.

1690.—"**Adapol** (quae folia sunt sicca et vetusta) . . . ."—*Rumphius, Herb. Amb.* i. 14.

1817.—"In the maritime districts, **ātap** or thatch is made . . . . from the leaves of the *nipa*."—*Raffles, Java*, i. 166; [2nd ed. i. 186].

1878.—"The universal roofing of a Perak house is **Attap** stretched over bamboo rafters and ridge-poles. This *attap* is the dried leaf of the nipah palm, doubled over a small stick of bamboo, or *nibong*."—*McNair, Perak, &c.*, 164.

ATLAS, s. An obsolete word for 'satin,' from the Ar. *aṭlas*, used in that sense, literally 'bare' or 'bald' (comp. the Ital. *raso* for 'satin'). The word is still used in German. [The *Draper's Dict.* (s.v.) says that "a silk stuff wrought with threads of gold and silver, and known by this name, was at one time imported from India." Yusuf Ali (*Mon. on Silk Fabrics*, p. 93) writes: "*Atlas* is the Indian satin, but the term *satan* (corrupted from the English) is also applied, and sometimes specialised to a thicker form of the fabric. This fabric is always substantial, *i.e.* never so thin or netted as to be semi-transparent; more of the weft showing on the upper surface than of the warp."]

1284.—"Cette même nuit par ordre du Sultan quinze cents de ses Mamlouks furent revêtus de robes d'**atlas** rouges brodées. . ." —*Makrizi*, t. ii. pt. i. 69.

,, "The Sultan Mas'ūd clothed his dogs with trappings of **aṭlas** of divers colours, and put bracelets upon them."—*Fakhrī*, p. 68.

1505.—"Raso por seda rasa."—**Atlās**, *Vocabular Arauigo of Fr. P. de Alcala*.

1673.—"They go Rich in Apparel, their Turbats of Gold, Damask'd Gold **Atlas** Coats to their Heels, Silk, *Alajah* or Cuttanee breeches."—*Fryer*, 196.

1683.—"I saw ye *Taffaties* and **Atlasses** in ye Warehouse, and gave directions concerning their several colours and stripes."—*Hedges, Diary*, May 6; [Hak. Soc. i. 85].

1689.—(Surat) "is renown'd for . . . . rich Silks, such as **Atlasses** . . . . and for Zarbafts [**Zerbaft**]. . . ."—*Ovington*, 218.

1712.—In the *Spectator* of this year are advertised "a purple and gold **Atlas** gown" and "a scarlet and gold **Atlas** petticoat edged with silver."—Cited in *Malcolm's Anecdotes* (1808), 429.

1727.—"They are exquisite in the Weaver's Trade and Embroidery, which may be seen in the rich **Atlasses** . . . . made by them."—*A. Hamilton*, i. 160.

c. 1750-60.—"The most considerable (manufacture) is that of their **atlasses** or satin flowered with gold and silver."—*Grose*, i. 117.

Note.—I saw not long ago in India a Polish Jew who was called Jacob **Atlas**, and he explained to me that when the Jews (about 1800) were forced to assume surnames, this was assigned to his grandfather, because he wore a black satin gaberdine!—(*A. B.* 1879.)

ATOLL, s. A group of coral islands forming a ring or chaplet, sometimes of many miles in diameter, inclosing a space of comparatively shallow water, each of the islands being on the same type as the *atoll*. We derive the expression from the Maldive islands, which are the typical examples of this structure, and where the form of the word is *atoḷu*. [P. de Laval (Hak. Soc. i. 93) states that the provinces in the Maldives were known as *Atollon*.] It is probably connected with the Singhalese *ätul*, 'inside'; [or *etula*, as Mr Gray (*P. de Laval*, Hak. Soc. i. 94) writes the word. The *Mad. Admin. Man.* in the *Glossary* gives Malayāl. *attālam*, 'a sinking reef']. The term was made a scientific one by Darwin in his publication on Coral Reefs (see below), but our second quotation shows that it had been generalised at an earlier date.

c. 1610.—"Estant au milieu d'vn **Atollon**, vous voyez autour de vous ce grand banc de pierre que jay dit, qui environne et qui defend les isles contre l'impetuosité de la mer."—*Pyrard de Laval*, i. 71 (ed. 1679); [Hak. Soc. i. 94].

1732.—"**Atollon**, a name applied to such a place in the sea as exhibits a heap of little islands lying close together, and almost hanging on to each other."—*Zeidler's* (German) *Universal Lexicon*, s.v.

1842.—"I have invariably used in this volume the term **atoll**, which is the name given to these circular groups of coral islets by their inhabitants in the Indian Ocean, and is synonymous with 'lagoon-island.'"—*Darwin, The Structure, &c., of Coral Reefs*, 2.

AUMIL, s. Ar. and thence H. *'āmil* (noun of agency from *'amal*, 'he performed a task or office,' therefore 'an agent'). Under the native governments a collector of Revenue; also a farmer of the Revenue invested with chief authority in his District. Also

AUMILDAR. Properly *'amaldār*, 'one holding office'; (Ar. *'amal*, 'work,' with P. term of agency). A factor or manager. Among the Mahrattas the *'Amaldār* was a collector of revenue under varying conditions—(See details in *Wilson*). The term is now limited to Mysore and a few other parts of India, and does not belong to the standard system of any Presidency. The word in the following passage looks as if intended for *'amaldār*, though there is a term *Māldār*, 'the holder of property.'

1680.—"The **Mauldar** or *Didwan* [**Dewan**] that came with the *Ruccas* [**Roocka**] from Golcondah sent forward to Lingappa at Conjiveram."—*Ft. St. Geo. Cons.*, 9th Novr. No. III., 38.

c. 1780.—". . . . having detected various frauds in the management of the **Amuldar** or renter . . . . (M. Lally) paid him 40,000 rupees."—*Orme*, iii. 496 (ed. 1803).

1793.—"The **aumildars**, or managers of the districts."—*Dirom*, p. 56.

1799.—"I wish that you would desire one of your people to communicate with the **Amildar** of Soondah respecting this road."—*A. Wellesley* to T. Munro, in *Munro's Life*, i. 335.

1804.—"I know the character of the Peshwah, and his ministers, and of every Mahratta **amildar** sufficiently well . . . ."—*Wellington*, iii. 38.

1809.—"Of the **aumil** I saw nothing."—*Ld. Valentia*, i. 412.

AURUNG, s. H. from P. *aurang*, 'a place where goods are manufactured, a depôt for such goods.' During the Company's trading days this term was applied to their factories for the purchase, on advances, of native piece-goods, &c.

1778.—". . . . Gentoo-factors in their own pay to provide the investments at the different **Aurungs** or cloth markets in the province."—*Orme*, ii. 51.

1789.—"I doubt, however, very much whether he has had sufficient experience in the commercial line to enable him to manage so difficult and so important an **aurung** as Luckipore, which is almost the only one of any magnitude which supplies the species of coarse cloths which do not interfere with the British manufacture."—*Cornwallis*. i. 435.

AVA, n.p. The name of the city which was for several centuries the capital of the Burmese Empire, and was applied often to that State itself. This name is borrowed, according to Crawfurd, from the form *Awa* or *Awak* used by the Malays. The proper Burmese form was *Eng-wa*, or 'the Lake-Mouth,' because the city was built near the opening of a lagoon into the Irawadi; but this was called, even by the Burmese, more popularly *A-wā*, 'The Mouth.' The city was founded A.D. 1364. The first European occurrence of the name, so far as we know, is (c. 1440) in the narrative of Nicolo Conti, and it appears again (no doubt from Conti's information) in the great World-Map of Fra Mauro at Venice (1459).

c. 1430.—"Having sailed up this river for the space of a month he arrived at a city more noble than all the others, called **Ava**, and the circumference of which is 15 miles." —*Conti*, in *India in the XVth Cent.* 11.

c. 1490.—"The country (Pegu) is distant 15 days' journey by land from another called **Ava** in which grow rubies and many other precious stones."—*Hier. di Sto. Stefano*, u. s. p. 6.

1516.—"Inland beyond this Kingdom of Pegu . . . . there is another Kingdom of Gentiles which has a King who resides in a very great and opulent city called **Ava**, 8 days' journey from the sea; a place of rich merchants, in which there is a great trade of jewels, rubies, and spinel-rubies, which are gathered in this Kingdom."—*Barbosa*, 186.

c. 1610.—". . . .The King of **Ová** having already sent much people, with cavalry, to relieve Porão (Prome), which marches with the Pozão (?) and city of **Ová** or **Anvá**, (which means 'surrounded on all sides with streams') . . ."—*Antonio Bocarro, Decada*, 150.

1726.—"The city **Ava** is surpassing great. . . . One may not travel by land to Ava, both because this is permitted by the Emperor to none but envoys, on account of the Rubies on the way, and also because it is a very perilous journey on account of the tigers."—*Valentijn, V.* (*Chorom.*) 127.

AVADAVAT, s. Improperly for *Amadavat*. The name given to a certain pretty little cage-bird (*Estrelda amandava*, L. or 'Red Wax-Bill') found throughout India, but originally brought to Europe from *Aḥmadābād* in Guzerat, of which the name is a corruption. We also find Aḥmadābād represented by *Madava*: as in old maps *Astarābād* on the Caspian is represented by *Strava* (see quotation from *Correa* below). [One of the native names for the bird is *lāl*, 'ruby,' which appears in the quotation from Mrs. Meer Hassan Ali below.]

1538.—". . . . o qual veyo **d'Amadava** principall cidade do reino."—In *S. Botelho, Tombo*, 228.

1546.—"The greater the resistance they made, the more of their blood was spilt in their defeat, and when they took to flight, we gave them chase for the space of half a league. And it is my belief that as far as the will of the officers and lascarys went, we should not have halted on this side of **Madavá**; but as I saw that my people were much fatigued, and that the Moors were in great numbers, I withdrew them and brought them back to the city."—D. João de Castro's despatch to the City of Goa respecting the victory at Diu.—*Correa*, iv. 574.

1648.—"The capital (of Guzerat) lies in the interior of the country and is named *Hamed-Ewat, i.e.* the City of King *Hamed* who built it; nowadays they call it *Amadavar* or **Amadabat**."—*Van Twist*, 4.

1673.—"From **Amidavad**, small Birds, who, besides that they are spotted with white and Red no bigger than Measles, the principal Chorister beginning, the rest in Consort, Fifty in a Cage, make an admirable Chorus."—*Fryer*, 116.

[1777.—". . . a few presents now and then —china, shawls, congou tea, **avadavats**, and Indian crackers."—*The School for Scandal*, v. i.]

1813.—". . . . **amadavats**, and other songsters are brought thither (Bombay) from Surat and different countries."—*Forbes, Or. Mem.* i. 47. [The 2nd ed. (i. 32) reads **amadavads**.]

[1832.—"The *lollah*, known to many by the name of **haver-dewatt**, is a beautiful little creature, about one-third the size of a hedge-sparrow."—*Mrs Meer Hassan Ali, Observat.* ii. 54.]

AVATAR, s. Skt. *Avatāra*, an incarnation on earth of a divine Being. This word first appears in Baldaeus (1672) in the form **Autaar** (*Afgoderye*, p. 52), which in the German version generally quoted in this book takes the corrupter shape of *Altar*.

[c. 1590.—"In the city of Sambal is a temple called Hari Mandal (the temple of Vishnu) belonging to a Brahman, from among whose descendants the tenth **avatar** will appear at this spot."—*Āīn*, tr. Jarrett, ii. 281.]

1672.—"Bey den Benjanen haben auch diese zehen Verwandlungen den Namen daas sie **Altare** heissen, und also hat Mats *Altar* als dieser erste, gewähret 2500 Jahr." —*Baldaeus*, 472.

1784.—"The ten **Avatárs** or descents of the deity, in his capacity of Preserver."—*Sir W. Jones*, in *Asiat. Res.* (reprint) i. 234.

1812.—"The **Awatars** of Vishnu, by which are meant his descents upon earth, are usually counted ten. . . ."—*Maria Graham*, 49.

1821.—"The Irish **Avatar**."—*Byron*.

1845.—"In Vishnu-land what **Avatar**?"—*Browning, Dramatic Romances, Works*, ed. 1870, iv. pp. 209, 210.

1872.—". . . . all which cannot blind us to the fact that the Master is merely another **avatar** of Dr Holmes himself."—*Sat. Review*, Dec. 14, p. 768.

1873.—"He . . . builds up a curious History of Spiritualism, according to which all matter is mediately or immediately the **avatar** of some Intelligence, not necessarily the highest."—*Academy*, May 15th, 172*b*.

1875.—"Balzac's **avatars** were a hundred-fold as numerous as those of Vishnu."—*Ibid.*, April 24th, p. 421.

AVERAGE, s. Skeat derives this in all its senses from L. Latin *averia*, used for cattle; for his deduction of meanings we must refer to his Dictionary. But it is worthy of consideration whether *average*, in its special marine use for a proportionate contribution towards losses of those whose goods are cast into the sea to save a ship, &c., is not directly connected with the Fr. *avarie*, which has quite that signification. And this last Dozy shows most plausibly to be from the Ar. '*awār*, spoilt merchandise.' [This is rejected by the *N.E.D.*, which concludes that the Ar. '*awār* is "merely a mod. Arabic translation and adaptation of the Western term in its latest sense."] Note that many European words of trade are from the Arabic; and that *avarie* is in Dutch *avarij*, *averij*, or *haverij*.—(See Dozy, *Oosterlingen*.)

AYAH, s. A native lady's-maid or nurse-maid. The word has been adopted into most of the Indian vernaculars in the forms *āya* or *āyā*, but it is really Portuguese (f. **aia**, 'a nurse, or governess'; m. *aio*, 'the governor of a young noble'). [These again have been connected with L. Latin *aidus*, Fr. *aide*, 'a helper.']

1779.—"I was sitting in my own house in the compound, when the **iya** came down and told me that her mistress wanted a candle."—*Kitmutgar's evidence*, in the case of *Grand v. Francis*. Ext. in *Echoes of Old Calcutta*, 225.

1782.—(A Table of Wages):—
"*Consumah*.........10 (rupees a month).
* * * * * *
Eyah.................5."—*India Gazette*, Oct. 12.

1810.—"The female who attends a lady while she is dressing, etc., is called an **Ayah**."—*Williamson, V. M.* i. 337.

1826.—"The lieutenant's visits were now less frequent than usual; one day, however, he came . . . . and on leaving the house I observed him slip something, which I doubted not was money, into the hand of the **Ayah**, or serving woman, of Jane."—*Pandurang Hari*, 71; [ed. 1873, i. 99].

1842.—"Here (at Simla) there is a great preponderence of Mahometans. I am told that the guns produced absolute consternation, visible in their countenances. One **Ayah** threw herself upon the ground in an agony of despair. . . . I fired 42 guns for Ghuzni and Cabul; the 22nd (42nd?) gun—which announced that all was finished—was what overcame the Mahometans."—*Lord Ellenborough*, in *Indian Administration* 295. This stuff was written to the great Duke of Wellington!

1873.—"The white-robed **ayah** flits in and out of the tents, finding a home for our various possessions, and thither we soon retire."—*Fraser's Mag.*, June, i. 99.

1879.—"He was exceedingly fond of his two children, and got for them servants; a man to cook their dinner, and an **ayah** to take care of them."—*Miss Stokes, Indian Fairy Tales*, 7.

B

BABA, s. This is the word usually applied in Anglo-Indian families, by both Europeans and natives, to the children—often in the plural form, *bābā lōg* (*lōg*='folk'). The word is not used by the natives among themselves in the same way, at least not habitually: and it would seem as if our word *baby* had influenced the use. The word *bābā* is properly Turki='father'; sometimes used to a child as a term of endearment (or forming part of such a term, as in the P. *Bābā-jān*, 'Life of your Father'). Compare the Russian use of *batushka*. [*Bābājī* is a common form of address to a Faḳīr, usually a member of one of the Musulman sects. And hence it is used generally as a title of respect.]

[1685.—"A Letter from the Pettepolle **Bobba**."—*Pringle, Diary, Fort St. Geo.* iv. 92.]

1826.—"I reached the hut of a Gossein . . . and reluctantly tapped at the wicket, calling, 'O **Baba**, O Maharaj.'"—*Pandurang Hari* [ed. 1873, i. 76].

[1880.—"While **Sunny Baba** is at large, and might at any time make a raid on Mamma, who is dozing over a novel on the spider chair near the mouth of the thermantidote, the Ayah and Bearer dare not leave their charge." — *Aberigh-Mackay, Twenty-one Days*, p. 94.]

BABAGOOREE, s. H. *Bābāghūrī*, the white agate (or chalcedony ?) of Cambay. [For these stones see *Forbes, Or. Mem.* 2nd ed. i. 323 : *Tavernier*, ed. *Ball*, i. 68.] It is apparently so called from the patron saint or martyr of the district containing the mines, under whose special protection the miners place themselves before descending into the shafts. Tradition alleges that he was a prince of the great Ghori dynasty, who was killed in a great battle in that region. But this prince will hardly be found in history.

1516.—"They also find in this town (Limadura in Guzerat) much chalcedony, which they call **babagore**. They make beads with it, and other things which they wear about them."—*Barbosa*, 67.

1554.—"In this country (Guzerat) is a profusion of **Bābāghūrī** and carnelians ; but the best of these last are those coming from Yaman."—*Sidi 'Ali Kapudān*, in *J.A.S.B.* v. 463.

1590.—"By the command of his Majesty grain weights of **bābāghūrī** were made, which were used in weighing."—*Āīn*, i. 35, and note, p. 615 (*Blochmann*).

1818.—"On the summit stands the tomb . . . . of the titular saint of the country, **Baba Ghor**, to whom a devotion is paid more as a deity than as a saint. . . ."—*Copland*, in *Tr. Lit. Soc. Bo.*, i. 294.

1849.—Among ten kinds of carnelians specified in H. Briggs's *Cities of Gujarāshtra* we find "**Bawa Gori** Akik, a veined kind."—p. 183.

BABBS, n.p. This name is given to the I. of Perim, in the St. of Babelmandel, in the quotation from Ovington. It was probably English sea-slang only. [Mr Whiteway points out that this is clearly from *albabo*, the Port. form of the Ar. word. João de Castro in Roteiro (1541), p. 34, says : "This strait is called by the neighbouring people, as well as those who dwell on the shores of the Indian Ocean, **Albabo**, which in Arabic signifies 'gates.'"]

[1610.—"We attempting to work up to the **Babe**."—*Danvers, Letters*, i. 52.]

[1611.—"There is at the **Babb** a ship come from Swahell."—*Ibid.* i. 111.]

1690.—"The **Babbs** is a small island opening to the *Red Sea*. . . . Between this and the Main Land is a safe Passage. . ."—*Ovington*, 458.

[1769.—"Yet they made no estimation of the currents without the **Babs**"; (note), "This is the common sailors' phrase for the Straits of Babelmandel."—*Bruce, Travels to discover the Source of the Nile*, ed. 1790, Bk. i. cap. ii.]

BABER, BHABUR, s. H. *bābar*, *bhābar*. A name given to those districts of the N.W. Provinces which lie immediately under the Himālaya to the dry forest belt on the talus of the hills, at the lower edge of which the moisture comes to the surface and forms the wet forest belt called Tarāī. (See **TERAI**.) The following extract from the report of a lecture on Indian Forests is rather a happy example of the danger of "a little learning" to a reporter :

1877.—"Beyond that (the Tarāī) lay another district of about the same breadth, called in the native dialect the **Bahadar**. That in fact was a great filter-bed of sand and vegetation."—*London Morning Paper of 26th May*.

BABI-ROUSSA, s. Malay *babi* * ('hog') *rūsa* ('stag'). The 'Stag-hog,' a remarkable animal of the swine genus (*Sus babirussa*, L. ; *Babirussa alfurus*, F. Cuvier), found in the island of Bourou, and some others of the I. Archipelago, but nowhere on continental Asia. Yet it seems difficult to apply the description of Pliny below, or the name and drawing given by Cosmas, to any other animal. The 4-horned swine of Aelian is more probably the African Wart-hog, called accordingly by F. Cuvier *Phacochoerus Aeliani*.

c. A.D. 70.—"The wild bores of India have two bowing fangs or tuskes of a cubit length, growing out of their mouth, and as many out of their foreheads like calves hornes."—*Pliny*, viii. 52 (*Holland's Tr.* i. 231).

c. 250. "*Λέγει δὲ Δίνων ἐν 'Αιθιωπίᾳ γίνεσθαι . . . . ὗς τετράκερως.*"—*Aelian, De Nat. Anim.* xvii. 10.

c. 545.—"The *Choirelaphus* ('Hog-stag') I have both seen and eaten."—*Cosmas Indicopleustes*, in *Cathay*, &c., p. clxxv.

1555.—"There are *hogs also with hornes*, and parats which prattle much which they call *noris* (**Lory**)."—*Galvano, Discoveries of the World*, Hak. Soc. 120.

* This word takes a ludicrous form in *Dampier* : "All the Indians who spake Malayan . . . . lookt on those *Meangians* as a kind of Barbarians ; and upon any occasion of dislike, would call them *Bobby*, that is Hogs."—i. 515.

1658.—"Quadrupes hoc inusitatatae figurae monstrosis bestiis ascribunt Indi quod adversae speciei animalibus, Porco scilicet et Cervo, pronatum putent . . . . ita ut primo intuitu quatuor cornibus juxta se positis videatur armatum hoc animal **Baby-Roussa**."—*Piso*, App. to *Bontius*, p. 61.

[1869.—"The wild pig seems to be of a species peculiar to the island (Celebes); but a much more curious animal of this family is the **Babirusa** or Pig-deer, so named by the Malays from its long and slender legs, and curved tusks resembling horns. This extraordinary creature resembles a pig in general appearance, but it does not dig with its snout, as it feeds on fallen fruits. . . . . Here again we have a resemblance to the Wart-hogs of Africa, whose upper canines grow outwards and curve up so as to form a transition from the usual mode of growth to that of the *Babirusa*. In other respects there seems no affinity between these animals, and the *Babirusa* stands completely isolated, having no resemblance to the pigs of any other part of the world."—*Wallace, Malay Archip.* (ed. 1890), p. 211, *seqq*.

BABOO, s. Beng. and H. *Bābū* [Skt. *vapra*, 'a father']. Properly a term of respect attached to a name, like *Master* or *Mr.*, and formerly in some parts of Hindustan applied to certain persons of distinction. Its application as a term of respect is now almost or altogether confined to Lower Bengal (though C. P. Brown states that it is also used in S. India for 'Sir, My lord, your Honour'). In Bengal and elsewhere, among Anglo-Indians, it is often used with a slight savour of disparagement, as characterizing a superficially cultivated, but too often effeminate, Bengali. And from the extensive employment of the class, to which the term was applied as a title, in the capacity of clerks in English offices, the word has come often to signify 'a native clerk who writes English.'

1781.—"I said . . . From my youth to this day I am a servant to the English. I have never gone to any Rajahs or **Bauboos** nor will I go to them."—Depn. of *Doond Sing*, Commandant. In *Narr. of Insurn. at Banaras* in 1781. Calc. 1782. Reprinted at Roorkee, 1853. App., p. 165.

1782.—"*Cantoo* **Baboo**" appears as a subscriber to a famine fund at Madras for 200 Sicca Rupees.—*India Gazette*, Oct. 12.

1791.

"Here Edmund was making a monstrous ado,
About some bloody Letter and Conta **Bah-Booh**."*

Letters of Simkin the Second, 147.

[* "Mr Burke's method of pronouncing it."]

1803.—". . . Calling on Mr. Neave I found there **Baboo** Dheep Narrain, brother to Oodit Narrain, Rajah at Benares."—*Lord Valentia's Travels*, i. 112.

1824.—". . . the immense convent-like mansion of some of the more wealthy **Baboos**. . ."—*Heber*, i. 31, ed. 1844.

1834.—"The **Baboo** and other Tales, descriptive of Society in India."—Smith & Elder, London. (By Augustus Prinsep.)

1850.—"If instruction were sought for from them (the Mohammedan historians) we should no longer hear bombastic **Baboos**, enjoying under our Government the highest degree of personal liberty . . . rave about patriotism, and the degradation of their present position."—*Sir H. M. Elliot*, Orig. Preface to *Mahom. Historians of India*, in Dowson's ed., I. xxii.

c. 1866.

"But I'd sooner be robbed by a tall man who showed me a yard of steel,
Than be fleeced by a sneaking **Baboo**, with a peon and badge at his heel."

Sir A. C. Lyall, The Old Pindaree.

1873.—"The pliable, plastic, receptive **Baboo** of Bengal eagerly avails himself of this system (of English education) partly from a servile wish to please the *Sahib logue*, and partly from a desire to obtain a Government appointment."—*Fraser's Mag.*, August, 209.

[1880.—"English officers who have become de-Europeanised from long residence among undomesticated natives. . . . Such officials are what Lord Lytton calls White **Baboos**."—*Aberigh-Mackay, Twenty-one Days*, p. 104.]

N.B.—In Java and the further East *bābū* means a nurse or female servant (Javanese word).

BABOOL, s. H. *babūl*, *babūr* (though often mispronounced *bābul*, as in two quotations below); also called *kīkar*. A thorny mimosa common in most parts of India except the Malabar Coast; the *Acacia arabica*, Willd. The Bhils use the gum as food.

1666.—"L'eau de Vie de ce Païs . . . . qu'on y boit ordinairement, est faicte de *jagre* ou sucre noir, qu'on met dans l'eau avec de l'écorce de l'arbre **Baboul**, pour y donner quelque force, et ensuite on les distile ensemble."—*Thevenot*, v. 50.

1780.—"Price Current. *Country Produce*: **Bable** Trees, large, 5 pc. each tree."—*Hickey's Bengal Gazette*, April 29. [This is *bāblā*, the Bengali form of the word.]

1824.—"Rampoor is . . . chiefly remarkable for the sort of fortification which surrounds it. This is a high thick hedge . . . of bamboos . . . faced on the outside by a formidable underwood of cactus and **bâbool**."—*Heber*, ed. 1844, i. 290.

1849.—"Look at that great tract from Deesa to the Hāla mountains. It is all sand; sometimes it has a little ragged clothing of **bābul** or milk-bush."—*Dry Leaves from Young Egypt*, 1.

BABOON, s. This, no doubt, comes to us through the Ital. *babuino*; but it is probable that the latter word is a corruption of Pers. *maimūn* ['the auspicious one'], and then applied by way of euphemism or irony to the baboon or monkey. It also occurs in Ital. under the more direct form of *maimone* in *gatto-maimone*, 'cat-monkey,' or rather 'monkey-cat.' [The *N.E.D.* leaves the origin of the word doubtful, and does not discuss this among other suggested derivations.]

BACANORE and **BARCELORE**, nn.pp. Two ports of Canara often coupled together in old narratives, but which have entirely disappeared from modern maps and books of navigation, insomuch that it is not quite easy to indicate their precise position. But it would seem that Bacanore, Malayāl. *Vakkanūr*, is the place called in Canarese *Bārkūr*, the *Barcoor-pettah* of some maps, in lat. 13° 28½'. This was the site of a very old and important city, "the capital of the Jain kings of Tulava . . . and subsequently a stronghold of the Vijiyanagar Rajas."—*Imp. Gazet.* [Also see Stuart, *Man. S. Canara*, ii. 264.]

Also that *Barcelore* is a Port. corruption of *Basrūr* [the Canarese *Basarūru*, 'the town of the waved-leaf fig tree.' (*Mad. Adm. Man. Gloss*, s.v.).] It must have stood immediately below the 'Barsilur Peak' of the Admiralty charts, and was apparently identical with, or near to, the place called Seroor in Scott's Map of the Madras Presidency, in about lat. 13° 55'. [See Stuart, *ibid.* ii. 242. Seroor is perhaps the *Shirūr* of Mr Stuart (*ibid.* p. 243).]

c. 1330.—"Thence (from Hannaur) the traveller came to **Bāsarūr**, a small city. . . ." —*Abulfeda*, in *Gildemeister*, 184.

c. 1343.—"The first town of Mulaibār that we visited was **Abu-Sarūr**, which is small, situated on a great estuary, and abounding in coco-nut trees. . . . Two days after our departure from that town we arrived at **Fākanūr**, which is large and situated on an estuary. One sees there an abundance of sugar-cane, such as has no equal in that country."—*Ibn Batuta*, iv. 77-78.

c. 1420.—"Duas praeterea ad maritimas urbes, alteram **Pachamuriam** . . . nomine, xx diebus transiit."—*Conti*, in *Poggius de Var. Fort.* iv.

1501.—"**Bacanut**," for Bacanur, is named in Amerigo Vespucci's letter, giving an account of Da Gama's discoveries, first published by Baldelli Boni, *Il Milione*, pp. liii. *seqq.*

1516.—"Passing further forward . . . . along the coast, there are two little rivers on which stand two places, the one called **Bacanor**, and the other **Bracalor**, belonging to the kingdom of Narsyngua and the province of Tolinate (*Tulu-nāḍa*, *Tuluva* or S. Canara). And in them is much good rice grown round about these places, and this is loaded in many foreign ships and in many of Malabar. . . ."—*Barbosa*, in Lisbon Coll. 294.

1548.—"The Port of the River of **Barcalor** pays 500 loads (of rice as tribute)."—*Botelho*, *Tombo*, 246.

1552.—"Having dispatched this vessel, he (V. da Gama) turned to follow his voyage, desiring to erect the *padrão* (votive pillar) of which we have spoken; and not finding a place that pleased him better, he erected one on certain islets joined (as it were) to the land, giving it the name of Sancta Maria, whence these islands are now called Saint Mary's Isles, standing between **Bacanor** and Baticalá, two notable places on that coast."—*De Barros*, I. iv. 11.

" ". . . the city Onor, capital of the kingdom, Baticalá, Bendor, **Bracelor**, **Bacanor**."—*Ibid.* I. ix. 1.

1726.—"In **Barseloor** or **Basseloor** have we still a factory . . . a little south of Basseloor lies **Baquanoor** and the little River Vier."—*Valentijn*, v. (Malabar) 6.

1727.—"The next town to the Southward of *Batacola* [**Batcul**] is **Barceloar**, standing on the Banks of a broad River about 4 Miles from the Sea . . . . The Dutch have a Factory here, only to bring up Rice for their Garrisons . . . . **Baccanoar** and *Molkey* lie between **Barceloar** and *Mangalore*, both having the benefit of Rivers to export the large quantities of Rice that the Fields produce."—*A. Hamilton*, i. 284-5. [*Molkey* is *Mulki*, see Stuart, *op. cit.* ii. 259.]

1780.—"St Mary's Islands lie along the coast N. and S. as far as off the river of **Bacanor**, or Callianpoor, being about 6 leagues . . . In lat. 13° 50' N., 5 leagues from *Bacanor*, runs the river **Barsalor**."—*Dunn's N. Directory*, 5th ed. 105.

1814.—"**Barcelore**, now frequently called Cundapore."—*Forbes*, *Or. Mem.* iv. 109, also see 113; [2nd ed. II. 464].

BACKDORE, s. H. *bāg-ḍor* ('bridle-cord'); a halter or leading rein.

BACKSEE. Sea H. *bāksī*: nautical 'aback,' from which it has been formed (*Roebuck*).

BADEGA, n.p. The Tamil *Vadagar, i.e.* 'Northerners.' The name has at least two specific applications:

a. To the Telegu people who invaded the Tamil country from the kingdom of Vijayanagara (the **Bisnaga** or **Narsinga** of the Portuguese and old travellers) during the later Middle Ages, but especially in the 16th century. This word first occurs in the letters of St. Francis Xavier (1544), whose Parava converts on the Tinnevelly Coast were much oppressed by these people. The *Badega* language of Lucena, and other writers regarding that time, is the Telegu. The Badagas of St. Fr. Xavier's time were in fact the emissaries of the Nāyaka rulers of Madura, using violence to exact tribute for those rulers, whilst the Portuguese had conferred on the Paravas "the somewhat dangerous privilege of being Portuguese subjects."—See *Caldwell, H. of Tinnevelly*, 69 *seqq.*

1544.—"Ego ad Comorinum Promontorium contendo eòque naviculas deduco xx. cibariis onustas, ut miseris illis subveniam Neophytis, qui **Bagadarum** (read **Badagarum**) acerrimorum Christiani nominis hostium terrore perculsi, relictis vicis, in desertas insulas se abdiderunt."—*S. F. Xav. Epistt.* I. vi., ed. 1677.

1572.—"Gens est in regno Bisnagae quos **Badagas** vocant."— *E. Acosta*, 4 *b.*

1737.—"In eâ parte missionis Carnatensis in quâ *Telougou*, ut aiunt, lingua viget, seu inter **Badagos**, quinque annos versatus sum; neque quamdiu viguerunt vires ab illâ dilectissimâ et sanctissimâ Missione Pudecherium veni."—In *Norbert*, iii. 230.

1875.—"Mr C. P. Brown informs me that the early French missionaries in the Guntur country wrote a vocabulary 'de la langue Talenga, dite vulgairement le **Badega**.'"—*Bp. Caldwell, Dravidian Grammar*, Intr. p. 33.

b. To one of the races occupying the Nilgiri Hills, speaking an old Canarese dialect, and being apparently a Canarese colony, long separated from the parent stock.—(See *Bp. Caldwell's Grammar*, 2nd ed., pp. 34, 125, &c.) [The best recent account of this people is that by Mr Thurston in *Bulletin of the Madras Museum*, vol. ii. No. 1.] The name of these people is usually in English corrupted to **Burghers**.

BADGEER, s. P. *bād-gīr*, 'wind-catch.' An arrangement acting as a windsail to bring the wind down into a house; it is common in Persia and in Sind. [It is the *Bādhanj* of Arabia, and the *Malkaf* of Egypt (*Burton, Ar. Nights*, i. 237; *Lane, Mod. Egypt*, i. 23.]

1298.—"The heat is tremendous (at Hormus), and on that account the houses are built with ventilators (*ventiers*) to catch the wind. These ventilators are placed on the side from which the wind comes, and they bring the wind down into the house to cool it."—*Marco Polo*, ii. 450.

[1598.—A similar arrangement at the same place is described by *Linschoten*, i. 51, Hak. Soc.]

1682.—At Gamron (**Gombroon**) "most of the houses have a square tower which stands up far above the roof, and which in the upper part towards the four winds has ports and openings to admit air and catch the wind, which plays through these, and ventilates the whole house. In the heat of summer people lie at night at the bottom of these towers, so as to get good rest."—*Nieuhof, Zee en Lant-Reize*, ii. 79.

[1798.—"The air in it was continually refreshed and renewed by a cool-sail, made like a funnel, in the manner of M. du Hamel."—*Stavorinus, Voyage*, ii. 104.]

1817.
"The *wind-tower* on the Emir's dome
Can scarcely win a breath from heaven."
Moore, Fire-worshippers.

1872.—". . . . **Badgirs** or windcatchers. You see on every roof these diminutive screens of wattle and dab, forming acute angles with the hatches over which they project. Some are moveable, so as to be turned to the S.W. between March and the end of July, when the monsoon sets in from that quarter."—*Burton's Sind Revisited*, 254.

1881.—"A number of square turrets stick up all over the town; these are **badgirs** or ventilators, open sometimes to all the winds, sometimes only to one or two, and divided inside like the flues of a great chimney, either to catch the draught, or to carry it to the several rooms below."—*Pioneer Mail, March 8th.*

BADJOE, BAJOO, s. The Malay jacket (Mal. *bājū*) [of which many varieties are described by Dennys (*Disc. Dict.* p. 107)].

[c. 1610.—"The women (Portuguese) take their ease in their smocks or **Bajus**, which are more transparent and fine than the most delicate crape of those parts."—*Pyrard de Laval*, Hak. Soc. ii. 112.]

1784.—"Over this they wear the **badjoo**, which resembles a morning gown, open at the neck, but fastened close at the wrist, and half-way up the arm."—*Marsden, H. of Sumatra*, 2nd ed. 44.

1878.—"The general Malay costume . . . . consists of an inner vest, having a collar to button tight round the neck, and the **baju**, or jacket, often of light coloured dimity, for undress."—*McNair*, 147.

1883.—"They wear above it a short-sleeved jacket, the **baju**, beautifully made, and often very tastefully decorated in fine needlework."—*Miss Bird, Golden Chersonese*, 139.

BAEL, s. H. *bel*, Mahr. *bail*, from Skt. *vilva*, the Tree and Fruit of *Aegle marmelos* (Correa), or 'Bengal Quince,' as it is sometimes called, after the name (*Marmelos de Benguala*) given it by Garcia de Orta, who first described the virtues of this fruit in the treatment of dysentery, &c. These are noticed also by P. Vincenzo Maria and others, and have always been familiar in India. Yet they do not appear to have attracted serious attention in Europe till about the year 1850. It is a small tree, a native of various parts of India. The dried fruit is now imported into England.—(See *Hanbury and Flückiger*, 116); [*Watt, Econ. Dict.* i. 117 *seqq.*]. The shelly rind of the *bel* is in the Punjab made into carved snuff-boxes for sale to the Afghans.

1563.—"And as I knew that it was called **beli** in Baçaim, I enquired of those native physicians which was its proper name, *cirifole* or *beli*, and they told me that *cirifole* [*śriphala*] was the physician's name for it."—*Garcia De O.*, ff. 221 *v.*, 222.

[1614.—"One jar of **Byle** at ru. 5 per maund."—*Foster, Letters*, iii. 41.]

1631.—Jac. Bontius describes the **bel** as *malum cydonium* (*i.e.* a quince), and speaks of its pulp as good for dysentery and the *cholerae immanem orgasmum.*—Lib. vi. cap. viii.

1672.—"The **Bili** plant grows to no greater height than that of a man [this is incorrect], all thorny . . . . the fruit in size and hardness, and nature of rind, resembles a pomegranate, dotted over the surface with little dark spots equally distributed. . . . With the fruit they make a decoction, which is a most efficacious remedy for dysenteries or fluxes, proceeding from excessive heat. . ."—*P. Vincenzo*, 353.

1879.—". . . On this plain you will see a large **bél**-tree, and on it one big **bél**-fruit."—*Miss Stokes, Indian Fairy Tales*, 140.

BAFTA, s. A kind of calico, made especially at Baroch; from the Pers. *bāfta*, 'woven.' The old Baroch *baftas* seem to have been fine goods. Nothing is harder than to find intelligible explanations of the distinction between the numerous varieties of cotton stuffs formerly exported from India to Europe under a still greater variety of names; names and trade being generally alike obsolete. *Baftas* however survived in the Tariffs till recently. [*Bafta* is at present the name applied to a silk fabric. (See quotation from *Yusuf Ali* below.) In Bengal, Charpata and Noakhali in the Chittagong Division were also noted for their cotton *baftas* (*Birdwood, Industr. Arts*, 249).]

1598.—"There is made great store of Cotton Linnen of diuers sort . . . **Boffetas.**"—*Linschoten*, p. 18. [Hak. Soc. i. 60.]

[1605-6.—"*Patta Kassa* of the ffinest *Totya*, **Baffa.**"—*Birdwood, First Letter Book*, 73. We have also "Black **Baffatta.**"—*Ibid.* 74.]

[1610.—"**Baffata**, the corge Rs. 100."—*Danvers, Letters*, i. 72.]

1612.—"**Baftas** or white Callicos, from twentie to fortie Royals the *corge.*"—*Capt. Saris*, in *Purchas*, i. 347.

1638.—". . . tisserans qui y font cette sorte de toiles de cotton, que l'on appelle **baftas**, qui sont les plus fines de toutes celles qui se font dans la Prouince de Guzaratta."—*Mandelslo*, 128.

1653.—"**Baftas** est un nom Indien qui signifie des toiles fort serrées de cotton, lesquelles la pluspart viennent de Baroche, ville du Royaume de Guzerat, appartenant au Grand Mogol."—*De la B. le Gouz*, 515.

1665.—"The **Baftas**, or Calicuts painted red, blue, and black, are carried white to *Agra* and *Amadabad*, in regard those cities are nearest the places where the *Indigo* is made that is us'd in colouring."—*Tavernier*, (E. T.) p. 127; [ed. *Ball*, ii. 5].

1672.—"*Broach* **Baftas**, broad and narrow."—*Fryer*, 86.

1727.—"The *Baroach* **Baftas** are famous throughout all India, the country producing the best Cotton in the World."—*A. Hamilton*, i. 144.

1875.—In the Calcutta Tariff valuation of this year we find Piece Goods, Cotton:

* * * *

Baftahs, score, Rs. 30.

[1900.—"Akin to the *pot thāns* is a fabric known as **Bafta** (literally woven), produced in Benares; body pure silk, with *butis* in *kalabatun* or cloth; . . . used for *angarkhas*, *kots*, and women's *paijamas* (Musulmans)."—*Yusuf Ali, Mon. on Silk Fabrics*, 97.]

It is curious to find this word now current on Lake Nyanza. The burial of King Mtesa's mother is spoken of:

1883.—"The chiefs half filled the nicely-padded coffin with **bufta** (bleached calico) . . . after that the corpse and then the coffin was filled up with more **bufta**. . . ."—In *Ch. Missy. Intelligencer*, N.S., viii. p. 543.

BAHAR, s. Ar. *bahār*, Malayāl. *bhāram*, from Skt. *bhāra*, 'a load.' A weight used in large trading transactions; it varied much in different localities; and though the name is of

Indian origin it was naturalised by the Arabs, and carried by them to the far East, being found in use, when the Portuguese arrived in those seas, at least as far as the Moluccas. In the Indian islands the *bahār* is generally reckoned as equal to 3 **peculs** (q.v.), or 400 avoirdupois. But there was a different *bahār* in use for different articles of merchandise; or, rather, each article had a special surplus allowance in weighing, which practically made a different *bahār* (see **PICOTA**). [Mr. Skeat says that it is now uniformly equal to 400 lbs. av. in the British dominions in the Malay Peninsula; but Klinkert gives it as the equivalent of 12 *pikuls* of **Agar-agar**; 6 of cinnamon; 3 of **Tripang.**]

1498.—". . . and begged him to send to the King his Lord a **bagar** of cinnamon, and another of clove . . . for sample" (*a mostra*).—*Roteiro de V. da Gama*, 78.

1506.—"In Cananor el suo Re si è zentil, e qui nasce zz. (*i.e. zenzeri* or 'ginger'); ma li zz. pochi e non cusi boni come quelli de Colcut, e suo peso si chiama **baar**, che sono K. (Cantari) 4 da Lisbona."—*Relazione di Leonardo Ca' Masser*, 26.

1510.—"If the merchandise about which they treat be spices, they deal by the *bahar*, which **bahar** weighs three of our *cantari*."—*Varthema*, p. 170.

1516.—"It (Malacca) has got such a quantity of gold, that the great merchants do not estimate their property, nor reckon otherwise than by *bahars* of gold, which are 4 quintals to each **bahar**."—*Barbosa*, 193.

1552.—"300 **bahares** of pepper."—*Castanheda*, ii. 301. Correa writes **bares**, as does also Couto.

1554.—"The **baar** of nuts (*noz*) contains 20 faraçolas, and 5 maunds more of **picota**; thus the *baar*, with its *picota*, contains 20½ faraçolas. . . ."—*A. Nunes*, 6.

c. 1569.—"After this I saw one that would have given a **barre** of Pepper, which is two Quintals and a halfe, for a little Measure of water, and he could not have it."—*C. Fredericke*, in *Hakl.* ii. 358.

1598.—"Each **Bhar** of *Sunda* weigheth 330 *catten* of China."—*Linschoten*, 34: [Hak. Soc. i. 113].

1606.—". . . their came in his company a Portugall Souldier, which brought a Warrant from the Capitaine to the Gouernor of *Manillia*, to trade with vs, and likewise to giue *John Rogers*, for his pains a **Bahar** of Cloues."—*Middleton's Voyage*, D. 2. *b*.

1613.—"Porque os naturaes na quelle tempo possuyão muytos **bâres** de ouro."—*Godinho de Eredia*, 4 *v*.

[1802.—"That at the proper season for gathering the pepper and for a *Pallam* weighing 13 rupees and 1½ *Viessam* 120 of which are equal to a *Tulam* or *Maund* weighing 1,732 rupees, calculating, at which standard for one **barom** or *Candy* the Sircar's price is Rs. 120."—*Procl. at Malabar*, in *Logan*, iii. 348. This makes the **barom** equal to 650 lbs.]

BAHAUDUR, s. H. *Bahādur*, 'a hero, or champion.' It is a title affixed commonly to the names of European officers in Indian documents, or when spoken of ceremoniously by natives (*e.g.* "Jones Ṣāhib *Bahādur*"), in which use it may be compared with "the gallant officer" of Parliamentary courtesy, or the *Illustrissimo Signore* of the Italians. It was conferred as a title of honour by the Great Mogul and by other native princes [while in Persia it was often applied to slaves (Burton, *Ar. Nights*, iii. 114)]. Thus it was particularly affected to the end of his life by Hyder Ali, to whom it had been given by the Raja of Mysore (see quotation from John Lindsay below [and Wilks, *Mysoor*, Madras reprint, i. 280]). *Bahādur* and *Sirdār Bahādur* are also the official titles of members of the 2nd and 1st classes respectively of the Order of British India, established for native officers of the army in 1837. [The title of *Rāē Bahādur* is also conferred upon Hindu civil officers.]

As conferred by the Court of Delhi the usual gradation of titles was (ascending):—1. *Bahādur*; 2. *Bahādur Jang*; 3. *Bahādur ud-Daulah*; 4. *Bahādur ul-mulk*. At Hyderabad they had also *Bahādur ul-Umrā* (*Kirkpatrick*, in *Tippoo's Letters*, 354). [Many such titles of Europeans will be found in *North Indian N. & Q.*, i. 35, 143, 179; iv. 17.]

In Anglo-Indian colloquial parlance the word denotes a haughty or pompous personage, exercising his brief authority with a strong sense of his own importance; a *don* rather than a swaggerer. Thackeray, who derived from his Indian birth and connections a humorous felicity in the use of Anglo-Indian expressions, has not omitted this serviceable word. In that brilliant burlesque, the *Memoirs of Major Gahagan*, we have the Mahratta traitor *Bobachee Bahauder*. It is said also that Mr Canning's malicious wit bestowed on Sir John Malcolm, who was not less great as a talker than as a soldier and statesman, the title, not included in the

Great Mogul's repertory, of *Bahauder Jaw.**

Bahādur is one of the terms which the hosts of Chingiz Khan brought with them from the Mongol Steppes. In the Mongol genealogies we find Yesugai *Bahādur*, the father of Chingiz, and many more. Subutai *Bahādur*, one of the great soldiers of the Mongol host, twice led it to the conquest of Southern Russia, twice to that of Northern China. In Sanang Setzen's poetical annals of the Mongols, as rendered by I. J. Schmidt, the word is written *Baghatur*, whence in Russian *Bogatir* still survives as a memento probably of the Tartar domination, meaning 'a hero or champion.' It occurs often in the old Russian epic ballads in this sense; and is also applied to Samson of the Bible. It occurs in a Russian chronicler as early as 1240, but in application to Mongol leaders. In Polish it is found as *Bohatyr*, and in Hungarian as *Bátor*,—this last being in fact the popular Mongol pronunciation of *Baghatur*. In Turki also this elision of the guttural extends to the spelling, and the word becomes *Bātur*, as we find it in the Dicts. of Vambéry and Pavet de Courteille. In Manchu also the word takes the form of *Baturu*, expressed in Chinese characters as *Pa-tu-lu*;† the Kirghiz has it as *Batyr;* the Altai-Tataric as *Paattyr*, and the other dialects even as *Magathyr*. But the singular history of the word is not yet entirely told. Benfey has suggested that the word originated in Skt. *bhaga-dhara* ('happiness-possessing').‡ But the late lamented Prof. A. Schiefner, who favoured us with a note on the subject, was strongly of opinion that the word was rather a corruption "through dissimulation of the consonant," of the Zend *bagha-puthra* 'Son of God,' and thus but another form of the famous term **Faghfūr**, by which the old Persians rendered the Chinese *Tien-tsz* ('Son of Heaven'), applying it to the Emperor of China.

* At Lord Wellesley's table, Major Malcolm mentioned as a notable fact that he and three of his brothers had once met together in India. "Impossible, Malcolm, quite impossible!" said the Governor-General. Malcolm persisted. "No, no," said Lord Wellesley, "if four Malcolms had met, we should have heard the noise all over India!"

† See *Chinese Recorder*, 1876, vii. 324, and *Kovalefski's Mongol Dict.* No. 1058.

‡ *Orient und Occident*, i. 187.

1280-90.—In an eccentric Persian poem purposely stuffed with Mongol expressions, written by Purbahā Jāmī in praise of Arghūn Khān of Persia, of which Hammer has given a German translation, we have the following:—

"The Great Kaan names thee his *Ulugh-Bitekchī* [Great Secretary],
Seeing thou art *bitekchi* and **Behādir** to boot;
O Well-beloved, the *yarlīgh* [rescript] that thou dost issue is obeyed
By Turk and Mongol, by Persian, Greek, and Barbarian!"
Gesch. der Gold. Horde, 461.

c. 1400.—"I ordained that every Ameer who should reduce a Kingdom, or defeat an army, should be exalted by three things: by a title of honour, by the *Tugh* [Yak's tail standard], and by the *Nakkāra* [great kettle drum]; and should be dignified by the title of **Bahaudur.**"—*Timour's Institutes*, 283; see also 291-293.

1404.—"E elles le dixeron q̃ aquel era uno de los valiẽtes e **Bahadures** q'en el linage del Señor auia."—*Clavijo*, § lxxxix.

" "E el home q̃ este haze e mas vino beue dizen que es **Bahadur**, que dizen elles por homem rezio."—Do. § cxii.

1407.—"The Prince mounted, escorted by a troop of **Bahadurs**, who were always about his person."—*Abdurrazāk's Hist.* in *Not. et Ext.* xiv. 126.

1536.—(As a proper name.) "Itaq̃ ille potentissimus Rex **Badur**, Indiae universae terror, a quo nonulli regnũ Pori maximi quōdam regis teneri affirmant. . . ."—Letter from *John III. of Portugal* to Pope Paul III.

Hardly any native name occurs more frequently in the Portuguese Hist. of India than this of *Badur*—viz. Bahādur Shāh, the warlike and powerful king of Guzerat (1526-37), killed in a fray which closed an interview with the Viceroy, Nuno da Cunha, at Diu.

1754.—"The *Kirgeese Tartars* . . . are divided into three *Hordas*, under the Government of a *Khan*. That part which borders on the Russian dominions was under the authority of *Jean Beek*, whose name on all occasions was honoured with the title of **Bater.**"—*Hanway*, i. 239. The name *Jean Beek* is probably *Janībek*, a name which one finds among the hordes as far back as the early part of the 14th century (see *Ibn Batuta*, ii. 397).

1759.—"From Shah Alum **Bahadre**, son of Alum Guire, the Great Mogul, and successor of the Empire, to Colonel Sabut Jung **Bahadre**" (*i.e.* Clive).—Letter in *Long*, p. 163.

We have said that the title *Behauder* (*Bahādur*) was one by which Hyder Ali of Mysore was commonly known in his day. Thus in the two next quotations:

1781.—"Sheikh Hussein upon the guard tells me that our army has beat the **Behauder** [*i.e.* Hyder Ali], and that peace was making. Another sepoy in the afternoon tells us that the **Behauder** had destroyed our army, and was besieging Madras."—*Captivity of Hon. John Lindsay*, in *Lives of the Lindsays*, iii. 296.

1800.—"One lac of **Behaudry** pagodas." —*Wellington*, i. 148.

1801.—"Thomas, who was much in liquor, now turned round to his *sowars*, and said—'Could any one have stopped Sahib **Bahaudoor** at this gate but one month ago?' 'No, no,' replied they; on which——"—*Skinner, Mil. Mem.* i. 236.

1872.—". . . the word '**Bahádur**' . . . (at the Mogul's Court) . . . was only used as an epithet. Ahmed Shah used it as a title and ordered his name to be read in the Friday prayer as 'Mujahid ud dín Muhammad Abú naçr Ahmad Sháh **Bahádur**. Hence also '*Kampani* **Bahadur**,' the name by which the E. I. Company is still known in India. The modern 'Khan **Bahádur**' is, in Bengal, by permission assumed by Muhammedan Deputy Magistrates, whilst Hindu Deputy Magistrates assume 'Rái **Bahádur**'; it stands, of course, for 'Khán-i-**Bahádur**,' 'the courageous Khán.' The compound, however, is a modern abnormal one; for 'Khán' was conferred by the Dihli Emperors, and so also 'Bahádur' and 'Bahádur Khán,' but not 'Khán Bahádur.'"—*Prof. Blochmann*, in *Ind. Antiquary*, i. 261.

1876.—"Reverencing at the same time bravery, dash, and boldness, and loving their freedom, they (the Kirghiz) were always ready to follow the standard of any **batyr**, or hero, . . . who might appear on the stage."—*Schuyler's Turkistan*, i. 33.

1878.—"Peacock feathers for some of the subordinate officers, a yellow jacket for the successful general, and the bestowal of the Manchoo title of **Baturu**, or 'Brave,' on some of the most distinguished brigadiers, are probably all the honours which await the return of a triumphal army. The reward which fell to the share of 'Chinese Gordon' for the part he took in the suppression of the Taiping rebellion was a yellow jacket, and the title of *Baturu* has lately been bestowed on Mr Mesny for years of faithful service against the rebels in the province of Kweichow."—*Saturday Rev.*, Aug. 10, p. 182.

" "There is nothing of the great **bahawder** about him."—*Athenaeum*, No. 2670, p. 851.

1879.—"This strictly prohibitive Proclamation is issued by the Provincial Administrative Board of Likim . . . and Chang, Brevet-Provincial Judge, chief of the Foochow Likim Central Office, Taot'ai for special service, and **Bat'uru** with the title of 'Awe-inspiring Brave'"—Transl. of *Proclamation against the cultivation of the Poppy* in Foochow, July 1879.

BAHIRWUTTEEA, s. Guj. *bāhirwatū*. A species of outlawry in Guzerat; *bāhirwatīā*, the individual practising the offence. It consists "in the Rajpoots or **Grassias** making their ryots and dependants quit their native village, which is suffered to remain waste; the *Grassia* with his brethren then retires to some asylum, whence he may carry on his depredations with impunity. Being well acquainted with the country, and the redress of injuries being common cause with the members of every family, the *Bahirwutteea* has little to fear from those who are not in the immediate interest of his enemy, and he is in consequence enabled to commit very extensive mischief."—*Col. Walker*, quoted in *Forbes, Rās Māla*, 2nd ed., p. 254-5. Col. Walker derives the name from *bāhir*, 'out,' and *wāt*, 'a road.' [Tod, in a note to the passage quoted below, says "this term is a compound of *bār* (*bāhir*) and *wuttan* (*waṭan*), literally *ex patriâ*."]

[1829.—"This petty chieftain, who enjoyed the distinctive epithet of outlaw (*barwattia*), was of the Sonigurra clan." . . .—*Pers. Narr.*, in *Annals of Raj.* (Calcutta reprint), i. 724.]

The origin of most of the brigandage in Sicily is almost what is here described in Kattiwār.

BAIKREE, s. The Bombay name for the **Barking-deer**. It is Guzarātī *bekrī*; and acc. to Jerdon and [Blandford, *Mammalia*, 533] Mahr. *bekra* or *bekar*, but this is not in Molesworth's Dict. [Forsyth (*Highlands of C. I.*, p. 470) gives the Gond and Korku names as *Bherki*, which may be the original].

1879.—"Any one who has shot **baikri** on the spurs of the Ghats can tell how it is possible unerringly to mark down these little beasts, taking up their position for the day in the early dawn."—*Overl. Times of India*, Suppt. May 12, 7*b*.

BAJRA, s. H. *bājrā* and *bājrī* (*Penicillaria spicata*, Willden.). One of the tall millets forming a dry crop in many parts of India. Forbes calls it *bahjeree* (*Or. Mem.* ii. 406; [2nd ed. i. 167), and *bajeree* (i. 23)].

1844.—"The ground (at Maharajpore) was generally covered with **bajree**, full 5 or 6 feet high."—*Lord Ellenborough*, in *Ind. Admin.* 414.

BĀKIR-KHĀNĪ, s. P.—H. *bāqir-khānī*; a kind of cake. almost exactly resembling pie-crust, said to owe its name to its inventor, *Bāqir Khān*.

[1871.—"The best kind (of native cakes) are **baka kanah** and '*sheer mahl*' (Sheer-maul)."—*Riddell, Ind. Domest. Econ.* 386.]

BALÁCHONG, BLACHONG, s. Malay *balāchān*; [acc. to Mr Skeat the standard Malay is *blachan*, in full *belachan*.] The characteristic condiment of the Indo-Chinese and Malayan races, composed of prawns, sardines, and other small fish, allowed to ferment in a heap, and then mashed up with salt. [Mr Skeat says that it is often, if not always, trodden out like grapes.] Marsden calls it 'a species of caviare,' which is hardly fair to caviare. It is the *ngāpi* (**Ngapee**) of the Burmese, and *trāsi* of the Javanese, and is probably, as Crawfurd says, the Roman *garum*. One of us, who has witnessed the process of preparing *ngāpi* on the island of Negrais, is almost disposed to agree with the Venetian Gasparo Balbi (1583), who says "he would rather smell a dead dog, to say nothing of eating it" (f. 125*v*). But when this experience is absent it may be more tolerable.

1688.—Dampier writes it **Balachaun**, ii. 28.

1727.—"*Bankasay* is famous for making **Ballichang**, a Sauce made of dried Shrimps, Cod-pepper, Salt, and a Sea-weed or Grass, all well mixed and beaten up to the Consistency of thick Mustard."—*A. Hamilton*, ii. 194. The same author, in speaking of Pegu, calls the like sauce *Prock* (44), which was probably the Talain name. It appears also in Sonnerat under the form *Prox* (ii. 305).

1784.—"**Blachang** . . . is esteemed a great delicacy among the Malays, and is by them exported to the west of India. . . . It is a species of caviare, and is extremely offensive and disgusting to persons who are not accustomed to it."—*Marsden's H. of Sumatra*, 2nd ed. 57.

[1871.—Riddell (*Ind. Domest. Econ.* p. 227) gives a receipt for **Ballachong**, of which the basis is prawns, to which are added chillies, salt, garlic, tamarind juice, &c.]

1883.—". . . **blachang**—a Malay preparation much relished by European lovers of decomposed cheese. . ."—*Miss Bird, Golden Chersonese*, 96.

BALAGHAUT, used as n.p.; P. *bālā*, 'above,' H. Mahr., &c., *ghāt*, 'a pass,'—the country 'above the passes,' *i.e.* above the passes over the range of mountains which we call the "Western **Ghauts**." The mistaken idea that *ghāt* means 'mountains' causes Forbes to give a nonsensical explanation, cited below. The expression may be illustrated by the old Scotch phrases regarding "below and above the Pass" of so and so, implying Lowlands and Highlands.

c. 1562.—"All these things were brought by the Moors, who traded in pepper which they brought from the hills where it grew, by land in Bisnega, and **Balagate**, and Cambay."—*Correa*, ed. Ld. Stanley, Hak. Soc. p. 344.

1563.—"*R.* Let us get on horseback and go for a ride; and as we go you shall tell me what is the meaning of *Nizamosha* (**Nizamaluco**), for you often speak to me of such a person.

"*O.* I will tell you now that he is King in the **Bagalate** (misprint for *Balagate*), whose father I have often attended medically, and the son himself sometimes. From him I have received from time to time more than 12,000 **pardaos**; and he offered me a salary of 40,000 pardaos if I would visit him for so many months every year, but I would not accept."—*Garcia de Orta*, f. 33*v*.

1598.—"This high land on the toppe is very flatte and good to build upon, called **Balagatte**."—*Linschoten*, 20; [Hak. Soc. i. 65; cf. i. 235].

,, "**Ballagate**, that is to say, above the hill, for *Balla* is above, and *Gate* is a hill. . . ."—*Ibid.* 49; [Hak. Soc. i. 169].

1614.—"The coast of Coromandel, **Balagatt** or Telingana."—*Sainsbury*, i. 301.

1666.—"**Balagate** est une des riches Provinces du Grand Mogol. . . . Elle est au midi de celle de Candich."—*Thevenot*, v. 216.

1673.—". . . opening the ways to **Baligaot**, that Merchants might with safety bring down their Goods to Port."—*Fryer*, 78.

c. 1760.—"The **Ball-a-gat** Mountains, which are extremely high, and so called from *Bal*, mountain, and *gatt*, flat [!], because one part of them affords large and delicious plains on their summit, little known to Europeans."—*Grose*, i. 231.

This is nonsense, but the following are also absurd misdescriptions:—

1805.—"**Bala Ghaut**, the higher or upper *Gaut* or *Ghaut*, a range of mountains so called to distinguish them from the Payen Ghauts, the lower Ghauts or Passes."—*Dict. of Words used in E. Indies*, 28.

1813.—"In some parts this tract is called the **Balla-Gaut**, or high mountains; to distinguish them from the lower Gaut, nearer the sea."—*Forbes, Or. Mem.* i. 206; [2nd ed. i. 119].

BALASORE, n.p. A town and district of Orissa; the site of one of the earliest English factories in the "**Bay**," established in **1642**, and then an important seaport; supposed to be properly *Bāleśvara*, Skt. *bāla*, 'strong,' *īśvara*, 'lord,' perhaps with reference to Krishna. Another place of the same name in Madras, an isolated peak, 6762' high, lat. 11° 41' 43", is said to take its name from the Asura Bana.

1676.—
"When in the vale of **Balaser** I fought,
And from Bengal the captive Monarch brought."
Dryden, Aurungzebe, ii. 1.

1727.—"The Sea-shore of **Balasore** being very low, and the Depths of Water very gradual from the Strand, make Ships in **Ballasore** Road keep a good Distance from the Shore; for in 4 or 5 Fathoms, they ride 3 Leagues off."—*A. Hamilton*, i. 397.

BALASS, s. A kind of ruby, or rather a rose-red spinelle. This is not an Anglo-Indian word, but it is a word of Asiatic origin, occurring frequently in old travellers. It is a corruption of *Balakhshī*, a popular form of *Badakhshī*, because these rubies came from the famous mines on the Upper Oxus, in one of the districts subject to Badakhshān. [See *Vambéry, Sketches*, 255; *Ball, Tavernier*, i. 382 *n*.]

c. 1350.—"The mountains of Badakhshān have given their name to the Badakhshi ruby, vulgarly called *al*-**Balakhsh**."—*Ibn Batuta*, iii. 59, 394.

1404.—"Tenia (Tamerlan) vestido vna ropa et vn paño de seda raso sin lavores e ẽ la cabeça tenia vn sombrero blãco alto con un **Balax** en cima e con aljofar e piedras."—*Clavijo*, § cx.

1516.—"These **balasses** are found in Balaxayo, which is a kingdom of the mainland near Pegu and Bengal."—*Barbosa*, 213. This is very bad geography for Barbosa, who is usually accurate and judicious, but it is surpassed in much later days.

1581.—"I could never understand from whence those that be called **Balassi** come."—*Caesar Fredericke*, in *Hakl*. ii. 372.

[1598.—"The **Ballayeses** are likewise sold by weight."—*Linschoten*, Hak. Soc. ii. 156.]

1611.—"Of **Ballace** Rubies little and great, good and bad, there are single two thousand pieces" (in Akbar's treasury).—*Hawkins*, in *Purchas*, i. 217.

[1616.—"Fair pearls, **Ballast** rubies."—*Foster*, *Letters*, iv. 243.]

1653.—"Les Royaumes de Pegou, d'où viennent les rubis **balets**."—*De la Boullaye-le-Gouz*, 126.

1673.—"The last sort is called a **Ballace** Ruby, which is not in so much esteem as the Spinell, because it is not so well coloured."—*Fryer*, 215.

1681.—". . . ay ciertos **balaxes**, que llmana candidos, que son como los diamantes."—*Martinez de la Puente*, 12.

1689.—". . . The **Balace** Ruby is supposed by some to have taken its name from *Palatium*, or Palace; . . . . the most probable Conjecture is that of *Marcus Paulus Venetus*, that it is borrow'd from the Country, where they are found in greatest Plentie. . . ."—*Ovington*, 588.

BALCONY, s. Not an Anglo-Indian word, but sometimes regarded as of Oriental origin; a thing more than doubtful. The etymology alluded to by Mr. Schuyler and by the lamented William Gill in the quotations below, is not new, though we do not know who first suggested it. Neither do we know whether the word *balagani*, which Erman (*Tr. in Siberia*, E. T. i. 115) tells us is the name given to the wooden booths at the Nijnei Fair, be the same P. word or no. Wedgwood, Littré, [and the *N.E.D.*] connect *balcony* with the word which appears in English as *balk*, and with the Italian *balco*, 'a scaffolding' and the like, also used for 'a box' at the play. *Balco*, as well as *palco*, is a form occurring in early Italian. Thus Franc. da Buti, commenting on Dante (1385-87), says: "*Balco* è luogo alto doue si monta e scende." Hence naturally would be formed *balcone*, which we have in Giov. Villani, in Boccaccio and in Petrarch. Manuzzi (*Vocabolario It.*) defines *balcone* as = *finestra* (?).

It may be noted as to the modern pronunciation that whilst ordinary mortals (including among verse-writers Scott and Lockhart, Tennyson and Hood) accent the word as a dactyl (*bālcŏnȳ*), the *crême de la crême*, if we are not mistaken, makes it, or did in the last generation make it, as Cowper does below, an amphibrach (*băłcōnȳ*): "Xanthus his name with those of heavenly birth, But called Scamander by the sons of earth!" [According to the *N.E.D.* the present pronunciation, "which," said Sam. Rogers, "makes me sick," was established about 1825.]

c. 1348.—"E al continuo v'era pieno di belle donne a' **balconi**."—*Giov. Villani*, x. 132-4.

c. 1340-50.—
"Il figliuol di Latona avea già nove
Volte guardato dal **balcon** sovrano,
Per quella, ch'alcun tempo mosse
I suoi sospir, ed or gli altrui commove in vano."
Petrarca, Rime, Pte. i. Sonn. 35, ed. Pisa, 1805.

c. 1340-50.—

"Ma si com' uom talor che piange, a parte
Vede cosa che gli occhi, e 'l cor alletta,
Così colei per ch'io son in prigione
Standosi ad un **balcone**,
Che fù sola a' suoi di cosa perfetta
Cominciai a mirar con tale desío
Che me stesso, e 'l mio mal pose in oblío:
I'era in terra, e 'l cor mio in Paradiso."
Petrarca, Rime, Pte. ii. Canzone 4.

1645-52.—"When the King sits to do Justice, I observe that he comes into the **Balcone** that looks into the Piazza."—*Tavernier*, E. T. ii. 64; [ed. *Ball*, i. 152].

1667.—"And be it further enacted, That in the Front of all Houses, hereafter to be erected in any such Streets as by Act of Common Council shall be declared to be High Streets, **Balconies** Four Foot broad with Rails and Bars of Iron . . . shall be placed. . . ."—Act 19 Car. II., cap. 3, sect. 13. (Act for Rebuilding the City of London.)

1783.

"At Edmonton his loving wife
From the **balcōny** spied
Her tender husband, wond'ring much
To see how he did ride."
John Gilpin.

1805.—

"For from the lofty **balcōny**,
Rung trumpet, shalm and psaltery."
Lay of the Last Minstrel.

1833.—

"Under tower and **balcōny**,
By garden-wall and gallery,
A gleaming shape she floated by,
Dead pale between the houses high."
Tennyson's Lady of Shalott.

1876.—"The houses (in Turkistan) are generally of but one story, though sometimes there is a small upper room called *bala-khana* (P. *bala*, upper, and *khana*, room) whence we get our **balcony**."—*Schuyler's Turkistan*, i. 120.

1880.—"*Bālā khānā* means 'upper house,' or 'upper place,' and is applied to the room built over the archway by which the *chăppă khānă* is entered, and from it, by the way, we got our word '**Balcony**.'"—MS. Journal in Persia of *Captain W. J. Gill*, R.E.

BALOON, BALLOON, &c., s. A rowing vessel formerly used in various parts of the Indies, the basis of which was a large canoe, or 'dug-out.' There is a Mahr. word *balyānw*, a kind of barge, which is probably the original. [See *Bombay Gazetteer*, xiv. 26.]

1539.—"E embarcando-se . . . partio, eo forão accompanhando dez ou doze **balões** ate a Ilha de Upe. . . ."—*Pinto*, ch. xiv.

1634.—

"Neste tempo da terra para a armada
Balões, e cal' luzes cruzar vimos. . ."
Malaca Conquistada, iii. 44.

1673.—"The President commanded his own **Baloon** (a Barge of State, of Two and Twenty Oars) to attend me."—*Fryer*, 70.

1755.—"The Burmas has now Eighty **Ballongs**, none of which as [*sic*] great Guns."—Letter from *Capt. R. Jackson*, in *Dalrymple Or. Repert.* i. 195.

1811.—"This is the simplest of all boats, and consists merely of the trunk of a tree hollowed out, to the extremities of which pieces of wood are applied, to represent a stern and prow; the two sides are boards joined by rottins or small bambous without nails; no iron whatsoever enters into their construction. . . . The **Balaums** are used in the district of Chittagong."—*Solvyns*, iii.

BALSORA, BUSSORA, &c., n.p. These old forms used to be familiar from their use in the popular version of the Arabian Nights after Galland. The place is the sea-port city of *Basra* at the mouth of the Shat-al-'Arab, or United Euphrates and Tigris. [Burton (*Ar. Nights*, x. 1) writes *Bassorah.*]

1298.—"There is also on the river as you go from Baudas to Kisi, a great city called **Bastra** surrounded by woods in which grow the best dates in the world."—*Marco Polo*, Bk. i. ch. 6.

c. 1580.—"**Balsara**, altrimente detta **Bassora**, è una città posta nell' Arabia, la quale al presente e signoreggiata dal Turco . . . è città di gran negocio di spetiarie, di droghe, e altre merci che uengono di Ormus; è abondante di dattoli, risi, e grani."—*Balbi*, f. 32*f*.

[1598.—"The town of **Balsora**; also **Bassora**."—*Linschoten*, Hak. Soc. i. 45.]

1671.—

"From Atropatia and the neighbouring plains
Of Adiabene, Media, and the south
Of Susiana to **Balsara's** Haven. . ."
Paradise Regained, iii.

1747.—"He (the Prest. of Bombay) further advises us that they have wrote our Honble. Masters of the Loss of Madrass by way of **Bussero**, the 7th of November."—*Ft. St. David Consn.*, 8th January 1746-7. MS. in India Office.

[Also see **CONGO.**]

BALTY, s. H. *bāltī*, 'a bucket,' [which Platts very improbably connects with Skt. *vāri*, 'water'], is the Port. *balde*.

BÁLWAR, s. This is the native servant's form of 'barber,' shaped by the 'striving after meaning' as *bālwār*, for *bālwālā*, *i.e.* 'capillarius,' 'hair-man.' It often takes the further form **bāl-būr,** another factitious hybrid, shaped by P. *būrīdan*, 'to cut,' quasi 'hair-cutter.' But though now obsolete, there was also (see both *Meninski* and *Vullers* s.v.) a Persian word *bărbăr*, for a barber or surgeon, from which came this Turkish term "Le *Berber*-bachi, qui fait la barbe au Pacha," which we find (c. 1674) in the Appendix to the journal of Antoine Galland, pubd. at Paris, 1881 (ii. 190). It looks as if this must have been an early loan from Europe.

BAMBOO, s. Applied to many gigantic grasses, of which *Bambusa arundinacea* and *B. vulgaris* are the most commonly cultivated; but there are many other species of the same and allied genera in use; natives of tropical Asia, Africa, and America. This word, one of the commonest in Anglo-Indian daily use, and thoroughly naturalised in English, is of exceedingly obscure origin. According to Wilson it is Canarese *bănbŭ* [or as the *Madras Admin. Man.* (*Gloss.* s.v.) writes it, *bombu*, which is said to be "onomatopaeic from the crackling and explosions when they burn"]. Marsden inserts it in his dictionary as good Malay. Crawfurd says it is certainly used on the west coast of Sumatra as a native word, but that it is elsewhere unknown to the Malay languages. The usual Malay word is *buluh*. He thinks it more likely to have found its way into English from Sumatra than from Canara. But there is evidence enough of its familiarity among the Portuguese before the end of the 16th century to indicate the probability that we adopted the word, like so many others, through them. We believe that the correct Canarese word is *banwu*. In the 16th century the form in the Concan appears to have been *mambu*, or at least it was so represented by the Portuguese. Rumphius seems to suggest a quaint *onomatopoeia*: "vehementissimos edunt ictus et sonitus, quum incendio comburuntur, quando notum ejus nomen *Bambu*, *Bambu*, facile exauditur."—(*Herb. Amb.* iv. 17.) [Mr. Skeat writes: "Although *buluh* is the standard Malay, and *bambu* apparently introduced, I think *bambu* is the form used in the low Javanese vernacular, which is quite a different language from high Javanese. Even in low Javanese, however, it may be a borrowed word. It looks curiously like a trade corruption of the common Malay word *samambu*, which means the well-known 'Malacca cane,' both the bamboo and the Malacca cane being articles of export. Klinkert says that the *samambu* is a kind of rattan, which was used as a walking-stick, and which was called the Malacca cane by the English. This Malacca cane and the rattan 'bamboo cane' referred to by Sir H. Yule must surely be identical. The fuller Malay name is actually *rotan samambu*, which is given as the equivalent of *Calamus Scipionum*, Lour. by Mr. Ridley in his Plant List (*J.R.A.S.*, July 1897).]

The term applied to *ṭăbāshīr* (**Tabasheer**), a siliceous concretion in the bamboo, in our first quotation seems to show that *bambu* or *mambu* was one of the words which the Portuguese inherited from an earlier use by Persian or Arab traders. But we have not been successful in finding other proof of this. With reference to *sakkar-mambu* Ritter says: "That this drug (*Tabashir*), as a product of the bamboo-cane, is to this day known in India by the name of *Sacar Mambu* is a thing which no one needs to be told" (ix. 334). But in fact the name seems now entirely unknown.

It is possible that the Canarese word is a vernacular corruption, or development, of the Skt. *vaṇśa* [or *vambha*], from the former of which comes the H. *bāṇs*. *Bamboo* does not occur, so far as we can find, in any of the *earlier* 16th-century books, which employ *canna* or the like.

In England the term *bamboo-cane* is habitually applied to a kind of walking-stick, which is formed not from any bamboo but from a species of *rattan*. It may be noted that some 30 to 35 years ago there existed along the high road between Putney Station and West Hill a garden fence of bamboos of considerable extent; it often attracted the attention of one of the present writers.

1563.—"The people from whom it (*tabashir*) is got call it *sacar*-**mambum** . . . because the canes of that plant are called by the Indians **mambu**."—*Garcia*, f. 194.

1578.—"Some of these (canes), especially in Malabar, are found so large that the people make use of them as boats (*embarcaciones*) not opening them out, but cutting one of the canes right across and using the natural knots to stop the ends, and so a couple of naked blacks go upon it . . . each of them at his own end of the **mambu** [in orig. *mābu*] (so they call it), being provided with two paddles, one in each hand . . . . and so upon a cane of this kind the folk pass across, and sitting with their legs clinging naked."—*C. Acosta, Tractado*, 296.

Again:

". . . and many people on that river (of Cranganor) make use of these canes in place of boats, to be safe from the numerous Crocodiles or *Caymoins* (as they call them) which are in the river (which are in fact great and ferocious lizards)" [*lagartos*].—*Ibid.* 297.

These passages are curious as explaining, if they hardly justify, Ctesias, in what we have regarded as one of his greatest bounces, viz. his story of Indian canes big enough to be used as boats.

1586.—"All the houses are made of canes, which they call **Bambos**, and bee covered with Strawe."—*Fitch*, in *Hakl.* ii. 391.

1598.—". . . a thicke reede as big as a man's legge, which is called **Bambus.**"—*Linschoten*, 56; [Hak. Soc. i. 195].

1608.—"Iava multas producit arundines grossas, quas **Manbu** vocant."—*Prima Pars Desc. Itin. Navalis in Indiam* (Houtman's *Voyage*), p. 36.

c. 1610.—"Les Portugais et les Indiens ne se seruent point d'autres bastons pour porter leurs palanquins ou litieres. Ils l'appellent partout **Bambou.**"—*Pyrard*, i. 237; [Hak. Soc. i. 329].

1615.—"These two kings (of Camboja and Siam) have neyther Horses, nor any fiery Instruments: but make use only of bowes, and a certaine kind of pike, made of a knottie wood like Canes, called **Bambuc**, which is exceeding strong, though pliant and supple for vse."—*De Monfart*, 33.

1621.—"These Forts will better appeare by the Draught thereof, herewith sent to your Worships, inclosed in a **Bamboo.**"—Letter in *Purchas*, i. 699.

1623.—"Among the other trees there was an immense quantity of **bambù**, or very large Indian canes, and all clothed and covered with pretty green foliage that went creeping up them."—*P. della Valle*, ii. 640; [Hak. Soc. ii. 220].

c. 1666.—"Cette machine est suspendue à une longue barre que l'on appelle **Pambou.**"—*Thevenot*, v. 162. (This spelling recurs throughout a chapter describing palankins, though elsewhere the traveller writes *bambou*.)

1673.—"A **Bambo**, which is a long hollow cane."—*Fryer*, 34.

1727.—"The City (Ava) tho' great and populous, is only built of **Bambou** canes."—*A. Hamilton*, ii. 47.

1855.—"When I speak of bamboo huts, I mean to say that post and walls, wall-plates and rafters, floor and thatch and the withes that bind them, are all of bamboo. In fact it might almost be said that among the Indo-Chinese nations the staff of life is *a* **Bamboo.** Scaffolding and ladders, landing-jetties, fishing apparatus, irrigation-wheels and scoops, oars, masts and yards, spears and arrows, hats and helmets, bow, bow-string and quiver, oil-cans, water-stoups and cooking-pots, pipe-sticks, conduits, clothes-boxes, pan-boxes, dinner-trays, pickles, preserves, and melodious musical instruments, torches, footballs, cordage, bellows, mats, paper, these are but a few of the articles that are made from the bamboo."—*Yule, Mission to Ava*, p. 153. To these may be added, from a cursory inspection of a collection in one of the museums at Kew, combs, mugs, sun-blinds, cages, grotesque carvings, brushes, fans, shirts, sails, teapots, pipes and harps.

Bamboos are sometimes popularly distinguished (after a native idiom) as male and female; the latter embracing all the common species with hollow stems, the former title being applied to a certain kind (in fact, a sp. of a distinct genus, *Dendrocalamus strictus*), which has a solid or nearly solid core, and is much used for bludgeons (see **LATTEE**) and spear-shafts. It is remarkable that this popular distinction by sex was known to Ctesias (c. B.C. 400) who says that the Indian reeds were divided into male and female, the male having no ἐντερώνην.

One of the present writers has seen (and partaken of) rice cooked in a joint of bamboo, among the Khyens, a hill-people of Arakan. And Mr Markham mentions the same practice as prevalent among the Chunchos and savage aborigines on the eastern slopes of the Andes (*J. R. Geog. Soc.* xxv. 155). An endeavour was made in Pegu in 1855 to procure the largest obtainable bamboo. It was a little over 10 inches in diameter. But Clusius states that he had seen two great specimens in the University at Leyden, 30 feet long and from 14 to 16 inches in diameter. And E. Haeckel, in his *Visit to Ceylon* (1882), speaks of bamboo-stems at Peridenia, "each from a foot to two feet thick." We can obtain no corroboration of anything approaching 2 feet.—[See Gray's note on *Pyrard*, Hak. Soc. i. 330.]

BAMÓ, n.p. Burm. *Bha-maw*, Shan *Manmaw*; in Chinese *Sin-Kai*, 'New-market.' A town on the upper Irawadi, where one of the chief routes from China abuts on that river; regarded as the early home of the Karens. [(*McMahon, Karens of the Golden Cher.*, 103.)] The old Shan town of Bamó was on the Tapeng R., about 20 m. east of the Irawadi, and it is supposed that the English factory alluded to in the quotations was there.

[1684.—"A Settlement at **Bammoo** upon the confines of China."—*Pringle, Madras Cons.*, iii. 102.]

1759.—"This branch seems formerly to have been driven from the Establishment at *Prammoo*."—*Dalrymple, Or. Rep.*, i. 111.

BANANA, s. The fruit of *Musa paradisaica*, and *M. sapientum* of Linnaeus, but now reduced to one species under the latter name by R. Brown. This word is not used in India, though one hears it in the Straits Settlements. The word itself is said by De Orta to have come from Guinea; so also Pigafetta (see below). The matter will be more conveniently treated under **PLANTAIN**. Prof. Robertson Smith points out that the coincidence of this name with the Ar. *banān*, 'fingers or toes,' and *banāna*, 'a single finger or toe,' can hardly be accidental. The fruit, as we learn from Muḳaddasī, grew in Palestine before the Crusades; and that it is known in literature only as *mauz* would not prove that the fruit was not somewhere popularly known as 'fingers.' It is possible that the Arabs, through whom probably the fruit found its way to W. Africa, may have transmitted with it a name like this; though historical evidence is still to seek. [Mr. Skeat writes: "It is curious that in Norwegian and Danish (and I believe in Swedish), the exact Malay word *pisang*, which is unknown in England, is used. Prof. Skeat thinks this may be because we had adopted the word *banana* before the word *pisang* was brought to Europe at all."]

1563.—"The Arab calls these *musa* or *amusa*; there are chapters on the subject in Avicenna and Serapion, and they call them by this name, as does Rasis also. Moreover, in Guinea they have these figs, and call them **bananas**."—*Garcia*, 93*v*.

1598.—"Other fruits there are termed **Banana**, which we think to be the *Muses* of Egypt and Soria . . . but here they cut them yearly, to the end they may bear the better."—Tr. of *Pigafetta's Congo*, in Harleian Coll. ii. 553 (also in *Purchas*, ii. 1008.)

c. 1610.—"Des *bannes* (marginal rubric **Bannanes**) que les Portugais appellent figues d'Inde, and aux Maldives *Quella*."—*Pyrard de Laval*, i. 85; [Hak. Soc. i. 113]. The Maldive word is here the same as H. *kelā* (Skt. *kadala*).

1673.—"**Bonanoes**, which are a sort of *Plantain*, though less, yet much more grateful."—*Fryer*, 40.

1686.—"The **Bonano** tree is exactly like the Plantain for shape and bigness, not easily distinguishable from it but by the Fruit, which is a great deal smaller."—*Dampier*, i. 316.

BANCHOOT, BETEECHOOT, ss. Terms of abuse, which we should hesitate to print if their odious meaning were not obscure "to the general." If it were known to the Englishmen who sometimes use the words, we believe there are few who would not shrink from such brutality. Somewhat similar in character seem the words which Saul in his rage flings at his noble son (1 Sam. xx. 30).

1638.—"L'on nous monstra à vne demy lieue de la ville vn sepulchre, qu'ils appellent **Bety-chuit**, c'est à dire la vergogne de la fille decouverte."—*Mandelslo*, Paris, 1659, 142. See also *Valentijn*, iv. 157.

There is a handsome tomb and mosque to the N. of Ahmedabad, erected by Hajji Malik Bahā-ud-dīn, a wazīr of Sultan Mohammed Bigara, in memory of his wife *Bībī Achut* or *Achhūt*; and probably the vile story to which the 17th-century travellers refer is founded only on a vulgar misrepresentation of this name.

1648.—"**Bety-chuit**; dat is (onder eerbredinge gesproocken) in onse tale te seggen, u Dochters Schaemelheyt."—*Van Twist*, 16.

1792.—"The officer (of Tippoo's troops) who led, on being challenged in Moors answered (*Agari que logue*), 'We belong to the advance'—the title of Lally's brigade, supposing the people he saw to be their own Europeans, whose uniform also is red; but soon discovering his mistake the commandant called out (*Feringhy* **Banchoot!**—*chelow*) 'they are the rascally English! Make off'; in which he set the corps a ready example."—*Dirom's Narrative*, 147.

BANCOCK, n.p. The modern capital of Siam, properly *Bang-kok*; see explanation by Bp. Pallegoix in quotation. It had been the site of forts erected on the ascent of the Menam to the old capital Ayuthia, by Constantine Phaulcon in 1675; here the modern city was established as the seat of government in 1767, after the capture of Ayuthia (see **JUDEA**) by the Burmese in that year. It is uncertain if the first quotation refer to **Bancock**.

1552.—". . . and **Bamplacot**, which stands at the mouth of the Menam."—*Barros*, I. ix. 1.

1611.—"They had arrived in the Road of *Syam* the fifteenth of August, and cast Anchor at three fathome high water. . . . The Towne lyeth some thirtie leagues vp along the Riuer, whither they sent newes of their arrivall. The Sabander (see **SHAHBUNDER**) and the Governor of **Mancock** (a place scituated by the Riuer), came backe with the Messengers to receiue his Majesties Letters, but chiefly for the presents expected."—*P. Williamson Floris*, in *Purchas*, i. 321.

1727.—The Ship arrived at **Bencock**, a Castle about half-way up, where it is customary for all Ships to put their Guns ashore."—*A. Hamilton*, i. 363.

1850.—"Civitas regia tria habet nomina: . . . *ban măkōk*, per contractionem **Bangkōk**, pagus oleastrorum, est nomen primitivum quod hodie etiam vulgo usurpatur."—*Pallegoix*, *Gram. Linguae Thai.*, Bangkok, 1850, p. 167.

BANDANNA, s. This term is properly applied to the rich yellow or red silk handkerchief, with diamond spots left white by pressure applied to prevent their receiving the dye. The etymology may be gathered from Shakespear's Dict., which gives "*Bāndhnū*: 1. A mode of dyeing in which the cloth is tied in different places, to prevent the parts tied from receiving the dye; . . . 3. A kind of silk cloth" A class or caste in Guzerat who do this kind of preparation for dyeing are called *Bandhārā* (*Drummond*). [Such handkerchiefs are known in S. India as **Pulicat** handkerchiefs. Cloth dyed in this way is in Upper India known as *Chūnrī*. A full account of the process will be found in *Journ. Ind. Art*, ii. 63, and *S. M. Hadi's Mon. on Dyes and Dyeing*, p. 35.]

c. 1590.—"His Majesty improved this department in four ways. . . . *Thirdly*, in stuffs as . . . **Bándhnún**, *Chhînt*, *Alchah*."—*Āīn*, i. 91.

1752.—"The Cossembazar merchants having fallen short in gurrahs, plain taffaties, ordinary **bandannoes**, and chappas."—In *Long*, 31.

1813.—"**Bandannoes** . . . 800."—*Milburn* (List of Bengal Piece-goods, and no. to the ton), ii. 221.

1848.—"Mr Scape, lately admitted partner into the great Calcutta House of Fogle, Fake, and Cracksman . . . taking Fake's place, who retired to a princely Park in Sussex (the Fogles have long been out of the firm, and Sir Horace Fogle is about to be raised to the peerage as Baron **Bandanna**), . . . two years before it failed for a million, and plunged half the Indian public into misery and ruin."—*Vanity Fair*, ii. ch. 25.

1866.—"'Of course,' said Toogood, wiping his eyes with a large red **bandana** handkerchief. 'By all means, come along, Major.' The major had turned his face away, and he also was weeping."—*Last Chronicle of Barset*, ii. 362.

1875.—"In Calcutta Tariff Valuations: 'Piece goods silk: **Bandanah** Choppahs, per piece of 7 handkerchiefs . . . score . . . 115 *Rs.*"

BANDAREE, s. Mahr. *Bhaṇḍārī*, the name of the caste or occupation. It is applied at Bombay to the class of people (of a low caste) who tend the coco-palm gardens in the island, and draw toddy, and who at one time formed a local militia. [It has no connection with the more common *Bhâṇḍârî*, 'a treasurer or storekeeper.']

1548.—". . . . certain duties collected from the **bandarys** who draw the toddy (*sura*) from the aldeas. . . ."—*S. Botelho*, *Tombo*, 203.

1644.—"The people . . . are all Christians, or at least the greater part of them consisting of artizans, carpenters, *chaudaris* (this word is manifestly a mistranscription of **bandaris**), whose business is to gather nuts from the coco-palms, and *corumbis* (see **KOONBEE**) who till the ground. . . ."—*Bocarro, MS.*

1673.—"The President . . . if he go abroad, the **Bandarines** and Moors under two Standards march before him."—*Fryer*, 68.

" ". . . besides 60 Field-pieces ready in their Carriages upon occasion to attend the Militia and **Bandarines**."—*Ibid.* 66.

c. 1760.—"There is also on the island kept up a sort of militia, composed of the land-tillers, and **bandarees**, whose living depends chiefly on the cultivation of the coco-nut trees."—*Grose*, i. 46.

1808.—". . . whilst on the **Brab** trees the cast of **Bhundarees** paid a due for extracting the liquor."—*Bombay Regulation*, i. of 1808, sect. vi. para. 2.

1810.—"Her husband came home, laden with toddy for distilling. He is a **bandari** or toddy-gatherer."—*Maria Graham*, 26.

c. 1836.—"Of the **Bhundarees** the most remarkable usage is their fondness for a peculiar species of long trumpet, called *Bhongalee*, which, ever since the dominion of the Portuguese, they have had the privilege of carrying and blowing on certain State occasions."—*R. Murphy*, in *Tr. Bo. Geog. Soc.* i. 131.

1883.—"We have received a letter from one of the large **Bhundarries** in the city, pointing out that the tax on toddy trees is now Rs. 18 (? *Rs.* 1, 8 *as.*) per tapped toddy tree per annum, whereas in 1872 it was only

Re. 1 per tree; . . . he urges that the Bombay toddy-drawers are entitled to the privilege of practising their trade free of license, in consideration of the military services rendered by their ancestors in garrisoning Bombay town and island, when the Dutch fleet advanced towards it in 1670."—*Times of India* (*Mail*), July 17th.

BANDEJAH, s. Port. *bandeja*, 'a salver,' 'a tray to put presents on.' We have seen the word used only in the following passages:—

1621.—"We and the Hollanders went to vizet Semi Dono, and we carid hym a bottell of strong water, and an other of Spanish wine, with a great box (or **bandeja**) of sweet bread."—*Cocks's Diary*, ii. 143.

[1717.—"Received the *Phirmaund* (see **FIRMAUN**) from Captain Boddam in a **bandaye** couered with a rich piece of Atlass (see **ATLAS**)."—*Hedges, Diary*, Hak. Soc. ii. ccclx.]

1747.—"Making a small Cott (see **COT**) and a rattan **Bandijas** for the Nabob . . . . (Pagodas) 4: 32: 21."—*Acct. Expenses at Fort St. David*, Jany., *MS. Records in India Office*.

c. 1760.—"(*Betel*) in large companies is brought in ready made up on Japan chargers, which they call from the Portuguese name, **Bandejahs**, something like our tea-boards."—*Grose*, i. 237.

1766.—"To Monurbad Dowla Nabob—

	R.	A.	P.
1 Pair Pistols .	216	0	0
2 China **Bandazes**	172	12	9"

—*Lord Clive's Durbar Charges*, in *Long*, 433.

Bandeja appears in the *Manilla Vocabular* of Blumentritt as used there for the present of cakes and sweetmeats, tastefully packed in an elegant basket, and sent to the priest, from the wedding feast. It corresponds therefore to the Indian *ḍāli* (see **DOLLY**).

BANDEL, n.p. The name of the old Portuguese settlement in Bengal about a mile above Hoogly, where there still exists a monastery, said to be the oldest church in Bengal (see *Imp. Gazeteer*). The name is a Port. corruption of *bandar*, 'the wharf'; and in this shape the word was applied among the Portuguese to a variety of places. Thus in Correa, under 1541-42, we find mention of a port in the Red Sea, near the mouth, called *Bandel dos Malemos* ('of the Pilots'). Chittagong is called *Bandel de Chatigão* (*e.g.* in *Bocarro*, p. 444), corresponding to *Bandar Chātgām* in the Autobiog. of Jahāngīr (*Elliot*, vi. 326). [In the Diary of Sir T. Roe (see below) it is applied to **Gombroon**], and in the following passage the original no doubt runs *Bandar-i-Hūghlī* or *Hūglī-Bandar*.

[1616.—"To this Purpose took **Bandell** theyr foort on the Mayne."—*Sir T. Roe*, Hak. Soc. i. 129.]

1631.—". . . these Europeans increased in number, and erected large substantial buildings, which they fortified with cannons, muskets, and other implements of war. In due course a considerable place grew up, which was known by the name of **Port of Hūglī**."—*'Abdul Hamīd*, in *Elliot*, vii. 32.

1753.—". . . les établissements formés pour assurer leur commerce sont situés sur les bords de cette rivière. Celui des Portugais, qu'ils ont appelé **Bandel**, en adoptant le terme Persan de *Bender*, qui signifie port, est aujourd'hui reduit à peu de chose . . et il est presque çontigu à Ugli en remontant."—*D'Anville, Eclaircissemens*, p. 64.

1782.—"There are five European factories within the space of 20 miles, on the opposite banks of the river Ganges in Bengal; Houghly, or **Bandell**, the Portuguese Presidency; Chinsura, the Dutch; Chandernagore, the French; Sirampore, the Danish; and Calcutta, the English."—*Price's Observations*, &c., p. 51. In *Price's Tracts*, i.

BANDICOOT, s. Corr. from the Telegu *pandi-kokku*, lit. 'pig-rat.' The name has spread all over India, as applied to the great rat called by naturalists *Mus malabaricus* (Shaw), *Mus giganteus* (Hardwicke), *Mus bandicota* (Bechstein), [*Nesocia bandicota* (Blanford, p. 425)]. The word is now used also in Queensland, [and is the origin of the name of the famous *Bendigo* gold-field (3 ser. *N. & Q.* ix. 97)].

c. 1330.—"In Lesser India there be some rats as big as foxes, and venomous exceedingly."—*Friar Jordanus*, Hak. Soc. 29.

c. 1343.—"They imprison in the dungeons (of Dwaigīr, *i.e.* Daulatābād) those who have been guilty of great crimes. There are in those dungeons enormous rats, bigger than cats. In fact, these latter animals run away from them, and can't stand against them, for they would get the worst of it. So they are only caught by stratagem. I have seen these rats at Dwaigīr, and much amazed I was!"—*Ibn Batuta*, iv. 47.

Fryer seems to exaggerate worse than the Moor:

1673.—"For Vermin, the strongest huge Rats as big as our Pigs, which burrow under the Houses, and are bold enough to venture on Poultry."—*Fryer*, 116.

The following surprisingly confounds two entirely different animals:

1789.—"The **Bandicoot**, or musk rat, is another troublesome animal, more indeed from its offensive smell than anything else."—*Munro, Narrative*, 32. See **MUSK-RAT**.

[1828.—"They be called **Brandy-cutes**."—*Or. Sporting Mag.* i. 128.]

1879.—"I shall never forget my first night here (on the Cocos Islands). As soon as the Sun had gone down, and the moon risen, thousands upon thousands of rats, in size equal to a **bandicoot**, appeared."—*Pollok, Sport in B. Burmah*, &c., ii. 14.

1880.—"They (wild dogs in Queensland) hunted Kangaroo when in numbers . . . . but usually preferred smaller and more easily obtained prey, as rats, **bandicoots**, and 'possums.'"—*Blackwood's Mag.*, Jan., p. 65.

[1880.—"In England the Collector is to be found riding at anchor in the **Bandicoot** Club."—*Aberigh-Mackay, Twenty-one Days*, 87.]

BANDICOY, s. The colloquial name in S. India of the fruit of *Hibiscus esculentus*; Tamil *veṇḍai-khāi*, *i.e.* unripe fruit of the *veṇḍai*, called in H. *bhenḍi*. See **BENDY**.

BANDO! H. imperative *bāndho*, 'tie or make fast.' "This and probably other Indian words have been naturalised in the docks on the Thames frequented by Lascar crews. I have heard a London lighter-man, in the Victoria Docks, throw a rope ashore to another Londoner, calling out, **Bando!**"—(*M.-Gen. Keatinge.*)

BANDY, s. A carriage, bullock-carriage, buggy, or cart. This word is usual in both the S. and W. Presidencies, but is unknown in Bengal, and in the N.W.P. It is the Tamil *vanḍi*, Telug. *banḍi*, 'a cart or vehicle.' The word, as *bendi*, is also used in Java. [Mr Skeat writes—"Klinkert has Mal. *bendi*, 'a chaise or caleche,' but I have not heard the word in standard Malay, though Clifford and Swett. have *bendu*, 'a kind of sedan-chair carried by men,' and the commoner word *tandu* 'a sedan-chair or litter,' which I have heard in Selangor. Wilkinson says that *kereta* (*i.e. kreta bendi*) is used to signify any two-wheeled vehicle in Johor."]

1791.—"To be sold, an elegant new and fashionable **Bandy**, with copper panels, lined with Morocco leather."—*Madras Courier*, 29th Sept.

1800.—"No wheel-carriages can be used in Canara, not even a buffalo-**bandy**."—Letter of *Sir T. Munro*, in *Life*, i. 243.

1810.—"None but open carriages are used in Ceylon; we therefore went in **bandies**, or, in plain English, *gigs*."—*Maria Graham*, 88.

1826.—"Those persons who have not European coachmen have the horses of their . . . '**bandies**' or gigs, led by these men. . . . Gigs and hackeries all go here (in Ceylon) by the name of *bandy*."—*Heber* (ed. 1844), ii. 152.

1829.—"A mighty solemn old man, seated in an open **bundy** (read *bandy*) (as a gig with a head that has an opening behind is called) at Madras."—*Mem. of Col. Mountain*, 2nd ed. 84.

1860.—"Bullock **bandies**, covered with cajans met us."—*Tennent's Ceylon*, ii. 146.

1862.—"At Coimbatore I bought a **bandy** or country cart of the simplest construction."—*Markham's Peru and India*, 393.

BANG, BHANG, s. H. *bhāng*, the dried leaves and small stalks of hemp (*i.e. Cannabis indica*), used to cause intoxication, either by smoking, or when eaten mixed up into a sweetmeat (see **MAJOON**). *Hashīsh* of the Arabs is substantially the same; Birdwood says it "consists of the tender tops of the plants after flowering." [*Bhang* is usually derived from Skt. *bhanga*, 'breaking,' but Burton derives both it and the Ar. *banj* from the old Coptic *Nibanj*, "meaning a preparation of hemp; and here it is easy to recognise the Homeric *Nepenthe*."

"On the other hand, not a few apply the word to the henbane (*hyoscyamus niger*) so much used in mediæval Europe. The Kámús evidently means henbane, distinguishing it from Hashísh *al harāfish*, 'rascal's grass,' *i.e.* the herb Pantagruelion. . . The use of Bhang doubtless dates from the dawn of civilisation, whose earliest social pleasures would be inebriants. Herodotus (iv. c. 75) shows the Scythians burning the seeds (leaves and capsules) in worship and becoming drunk upon the fumes, as do the S. African Bushmen of the present day."—(*Arab. Nights*, i. 65.)]

1563.—"The great Sultan Badur told Martim Affonzo de Souza, for whom he had a great liking, and to whom he told all his secrets, that when in the night he had a desire to visit Portugal, and the Brazil, and Turkey, and Arabia, and Persia, all he had to do was to eat a little **bangue**. . . ."—*Garcia*, f. 26.

1578.—"**Bangue** is a plant resembling hemp, or the Cannabis of the Latins . . . the Arabs call this **Bangue** '*Axis*'" (*i.e.* Hashīsh).—*C. Acosta*, 360-61.

1598.—"They have . . . . also many kinds of Drogues, as Amfion, or Opium, Camfora, **Bangue** and Sandall Wood."—*Linschoten*, 19; [Hak. Soc. i. 61; also see ii. 115].

1606.—"O mais de tẽpo estava cheo de **bangue**."—*Gouvea*, 93.

1638.—"Il se fit apporter vn petit cabinet d'or . . . . dont il tira deux layettes, et prit dans l'vne de l'*offion*, ou opium, et dans l'autre du **bengi**, qui est vne certaine drogue ou poudre, dont ils se seruent pour s'exciter à la luxure."—*Mandelslo*, Paris, 1659, 150.

1685.—"I have two sorts of the **Bangue**, which were sent from two several places of the East Indies; they both differ much from our Hemp, although they seem to differ most as to their magnitude."—*Dr. Hans Sloane to Mr. Ray*, in *Ray's Correspondence*, 1848, p. 160.

1673.—"**Bang** (a pleasant intoxicating Seed mixed with Milk). . . ."—*Fryer*, 91.

1711.—"**Bang** has likewise its Vertues attributed to it; for being used as Tea, it inebriates, or exhilarates them according to the Quantity they take."—*Lockyer*, 61.

1727.—"Before they engage in a Fight, they drink **Bang**, which is made of a Seed like Hemp-seed, that has an intoxicating Quality."—*A. Hamilton*, i. 131.

1763.—"Most of the troops, as is customary during the agitations of this festival, had eaten plentifully of **bang**. . . ."—*Orme*, i. 194.

1784.—". . . it does not appear that the use of **bank**, an intoxicating weed which resembles the hemp of Europe, . . . is considered even by the most rigid (Hindoo) a breach of the law."—*G. Forster, Journey*, ed. 1808, ii. 291.

1789.—"A shop of **Bang** may be kept with a capital of no more than two shillings, or one rupee. It is only some mats stretched under some tree, where the *Bangeras* of the town, that is, the vilest of mankind, assemble to drink **Bang**."—Note on *Seir Mutaqherin*, iii. 308.

1868.—

"The Hemp—with which we used to hang
Our prison pets, yon felon gang,—
In Eastern climes produces **Bang**,
Esteemed a drug divine.
As Hashish dressed, its magic powers
Can lap us in Elysian bowers;
But sweeter far our social hours,
O'er a flask of rosy wine."

Lord Neaves.

BANGED—is also used as a participle, for 'stimulated by *bang*,' *e.g.* "*banged* up to the eyes."

BANGLE, s. H. *bangrī* or *baṅgṛī*. The original word properly means a ring of coloured glass worn on the wrist by women; [the *chūrī* of N. India;] but *bangle* is applied to any native ring-bracelet, and also to an *anklet* or ring of any kind worn on the ankle or leg. Indian silver bangles on the wrist have recently come into common use among English girls.

1803.—"To the *cutwahl* he gave a heavy pair of gold **bangles**, of which he considerably enhanced the value by putting them on his wrists with his own hands."—Journal of *Sir J. Nicholls*, in note to *Wellington Despatches*, ed. 1837, ii. 373.

1809.—"**Bangles**, or bracelets."—*Maria Graham*, 13.

1810.—"Some wear . . . a stout silver ornament of the ring kind, called a **bangle**, or *karrah* [*kaṛā*] on either wrist."—*Williamson, V. M.* i. 305.

1826.—"I am paid with the silver **bangles** of my enemy, and his cash to boot."—*Pandurang Hari*, 27; [ed. 1873, i. 36].

1873.—"Year after year he found some excuse for coming up to Sirmoori—now a proposal for a tax on **bangles**, now a scheme for a new mode of Hindustani pronunciation."—*The True Reformer*, i. 24.

BANGUN, s.—See **BRINJAUL**.

BANGUR, s. Hind. *bāngar*. In Upper India this name is given to the higher parts of the plain country on which the towns stand—the older alluvium—in contradistinction to the *khādar* [**Khādir**] or lower alluvium immediately bordering the great rivers, and forming the limit of their inundation and modern divagations; the *khādar* having been cut out from the *bāngar* by the river. Medlicott spells *bhāngar* (*Man. of Geol. of India*, i. 404).

BANGY, BANGHY, &c. s. H. *bahaṅgī*, Mahr. *baṅgī*; Skt. *vihaṅgamā*, and *vihaṅgikā*.

a. A shoulder-yoke for carrying loads, the yoke or bangy resting on the shoulder, while the load is apportioned at either end in two equal weights, and generally hung by cords. The milkmaid's yoke is the nearest approach to a survival of the bangy-staff in England. Also such a yoke with its pair of baskets or boxes.—(See **PITARRAH**).

b. Hence a parcel post, carried originally in this way, was called **bangy** or dawk-**bangy**, even when the primitive mode of transport had long become obsolete. "A **bangy** parcel" is a parcel received or sent by such post.

a.—

1789.—

"But I'll give them 2000, with **Bhanges** and *Coolies*,
With elephants, camels, with hackeries and *doolies*."

Letters of Simpkin the Second, p. 57.

1803.—"We take with us indeed, in six **banghys**, sufficient changes of linen."—*Ld. Valentia*, i. 67.

1810.—"The **bangy**-*wollah*, that is the bearer who carries the **bangy**, supports the bamboo on his shoulder, so as to equipoise the baskets suspended at each end."—*Williamson, V. M.* i. 323.

[1843.—"I engaged eight bearers to carry my palankeen. Besides these I had four **banghy**-*burdars*, men who are each obliged to carry forty pound weight, in small wooden or tin boxes, called *petarrahs*."—*Traveller's account, Carey, Good Old Days*, ii. 91.]

b.—

c. 1844.—"I will forward with this by **bhangy** *dâk* a copy of Capt. Moresby's Survey of the Red Sea."—*Sir G. Arthur*, in *Ind. Admin. of Lord Ellenborough*, p. 221.

1873.—"The officers of his regiment . . . subscribed to buy the young people a set of crockery, and a plated tea and coffee service (got up by **dawk banghee** . . . at not much more than 200 per cent. in advance of the English price."—*The True Reformer*, i. 57.

BANJO, s. Though this is a West- and not East-Indian term, it may be worth while to introduce the following older form of the word:

1764.—

"Permit thy slaves to lead the choral dance
To the wild **banshaw's** melancholy sound."—*Grainger*, iv.

See also *Davies*, for example of **banjore**, [and *N.E.D* for **banjer**].

BANKSHALL, s. **a.** A warehouse. **b.** The office of a Harbour Master or other Port Authority. In the former sense the word is still used in S. India; in Bengal the latter is the only sense recognised, at least among Anglo-Indians; in Northern India the word is not in use. As the Calcutta office stands on the *banks* of the Hoogly, the name is, we believe, often accepted as having some indefinite reference to this position. And in a late work we find a positive and plausible, but entirely unfounded, explanation of this kind, which we quote below. In Java the word has a specific application to the open hall of audience, supported by wooden pillars without walls, which forms part of every princely residence. The word is used in Sea Hindustani, in the forms *bansār*, and *bangsāl* for a 'store-room' (*Roebuck*).

Bankshall is in fact one of the oldest of the words taken up by foreign traders in India. And its use not only by Correa (c. 1561) but by King John (1524), with the regularly-formed Portuguese plural of words in *-al*, shows how early it was adopted by the Portuguese. Indeed, Correa does not even explain it, as is his usual practice with Indian terms.

More than one serious etymology has been suggested:—(1). Crawfurd takes it to be the Malay word *bangsal*, defined by him in his Malay Dict. thus: "(J.) A shed; a storehouse; a workshop; a porch; a covered passage" (see *J. Ind. Archip.* iv. 182). [Mr Skeat adds that it also means in Malay 'half-husked paddy,' and 'fallen timber, of which the outer layer has rotted and only the core remains.'] But it is probable that the Malay word, though marked by Crawfurd ("J.") as Javanese in origin, is a corruption of one of the two following:

(2) Beng. *bankaśāla*, from Skt. *baṇik* or *vaṇik*, 'trade,' and *śāla*, 'a hall.' This is Wilson's etymology.

(3). Skt. *bhāndaśāla*, Canar. *bhandaśāle*, Malayāl. *pāṇḍiśāla*, Tam. *paṇḍaśālai* or *paṇḍakaśālai*, 'a storehouse or magazine.'

It is difficult to decide which of the two last is the original word; the prevalence of the second in S. India is an argument in its favour; and the substitution of *g* for *ḍ* would be in accordance with a phonetic practice of not uncommon occurrence.

a.—

c. 1345.—"For the *bandar* there is in every island (of the Maldives) a wooden building, which they call **bajanṣār** [evidently for *banjaṣār*, *i.e.* Arabic spelling for *bangaṣār*] where the Governor . . . collects all the goods, and there sells or barters them."—*Ibn Batuta*, iv. 120.

[1520.—"Collected in his **bamgasal**" (in the Maldives).—*Doc. da Torre do Tombo*, p. 452.]

1524.—A grant from K. John to the City of Goa, says: "that henceforward even if no market rent in the city is collected from the **bacacés**, viz. those at which are sold honey, oil, butter, *betre* (*i.e.* betel), spices, and cloths, for permission to sell such things in the said *bacacés*, it is our pleasure that they shall sell them freely." A note says: "Apparently the word should be *bacaçaes*, or **bancacaes**, or *bangaçaes*, which then signified any place to sell things, but now particularly a wooden house."—*Archiv. Portug. Or.*, Fasc. ii. 43.

1561.—". . . in the **bengaçaes**, in which stand the goods ready for shipment."—*Correa, Lendas*, i. 2, 260.

1610.—The form and use of the word have led P. Teixeira into a curious confusion (as it would seem) when, speaking of foreigners at Ormus, he says: "hay muchos gentiles, Baneanes [see **BANYAN**], **Bangasalys**, y Cambayatys"—where the word in italics probably represents *Bangalys*, *i.e.* Bengālis (*Rel. de Harmuz*, 18).

c. 1610.—"Le facteur du Roy chrestien des Maldiues tenoit sa **banquesalle** ou plustost cellier, sur le bord de la mer en l'isle de Malé."—*Pyrard de Laval*, ed. 1679, i. 65; [Hak. Soc. i. 85; also see i. 267].

1613.—"The other settlement of Yler . . . with houses of wood thatched extends . . . to the fields of Tanjonpacer, where there is a **bangasal** or sentry's house without other defense."—*Godinho de Eredia*, 6.

1623.—"**Bangsal**, a shed (or barn), or often also a roof without walls to sit under, sheltered from the rain or sun."—*Gaspar Willens, Vocabularium*, &c., ins' Gravenhaage; repr. Batavia, 1706.

1734-5.—"Paid the **Bankshall** Merchants for the house poles, country **reapers**, &c., necessary for housebuilding."—In *Wheeler*, iii. 148.

1748.—"A little below the town of Wampo . . . These people (*compradores*) build a house for each ship. . . . They are called by us **banksalls**. In these we deposit the rigging and yards of the vessel, chests, water-casks, and every thing that incommodes us aboard."—*A Voyage to the E. Indies* in 1747 and 1748 (1762), p. 294. It appears from this book (p. 118) that the place in Canton River was known as **Banksall Island**.

1750-52.—"One of the first things on arriving here (Canton River) is to procure a **bancshall**, that is, a great house, constructed of bamboo and mats . . . in which the stores of the ship are laid up."—*A Voyage*, &c., by *Olof Toreen* . . . in a series of letters to Dr Linnæus, Transl. by J. R. Forster (with Osbeck's Voyage), 1771.

1783.—"These people (*Chulias*, &c., from India, at Achin) . . . on their arrival immediately build, by contract with the natives, houses of bamboo, like what in China at Wampo is called **bankshall**, very regular, on a convenient spot close to the river."—*Forrest, V. to Mergui*, 41.

1788.—"**Banksauls**—Storehouses for depositing ships' stores in, while the ships are unlading and refitting."—*Indian Vocab.* (Stockdale).

1813.—"The East India Company for seventy years had a large **banksaul**, or warehouse, at Mirzee, for the reception of the pepper and sandalwood purchased in the dominions of the Mysore Rajah."—*Forbes, Or. Mem.* iv. 109.

1817.—"The **bāngsal** or *mendōpo* is a large open hall, supported by a double row of pillars, and covered with shingles, the interior being richly decorated with paint and gilding."—*Raffles, Java* (2nd ed.), i. 93. The Javanese use, as in this passage, corresponds to the meaning given in Jansz, Javanese Dict.: "**Bangsal**, Vorstelijke Zitplaats" (Prince's Sitting-place).

b.—

[1614.—"The custom house or **banksall** at Masulpatam."—*Foster, Letters*, ii. 86.]

1623.—"And on the Place by the sea there was the Custom-house, which the Persians in their language call **Benksal**, a building of no great size, with some open outer porticoes."—*P. della Valle*, ii. 465.

1673.—". . . Their **Bank Solls**, or Custom House Keys, where they land, are Two; but mean, and shut only with ordinary Gates at Night."—*Fryer*, 27.

1683.—"I came ashore in Capt. Goyer's Pinnace to ye **Bankshall**, about 7 miles from Ballasore."—*Hedges, Diary*, Feb. 2; [Hak. Soc. i. 65].

1687.—"The Mayor and Aldermen, etc., do humbly request the Honourable President and Council would please to grant and assign over to the Corporation the petty dues of **Banksall** Tolls."—In *Wheeler*, i. 207.

1727.—"Above it is the *Dutch* **Bankshall**, a Place where their Ships ride when they cannot get further up for the too swift Currents."—*A. Hamilton*, ii. 6.

1789.—"And that no one may plead ignorance of this order, it is hereby directed that it be placed constantly in view at the **Bankshall** in the English and country languages."—*Procl. against Slave-Trading* in *Seton-Karr*, ii. 5.

1878.—"The term '**Banksoll**' has always been a puzzle to the English in India. It is borrowed from the Dutch. The 'Soll' is the Dutch or Danish 'Zoll,' the English 'Toll.' The **Banksoll** was then the place on the 'bank' where all tolls or duties were levied on landing goods."—*Talboys Wheeler, Early Records of B. India*, 196. (Quite erroneous, as already said; and *Zoll* is not Dutch.)

BANTAM, n.p. The province which forms the western extremity of Java, properly *Bāntan*. [Mr Skeat gives *Bantan*, Crawfurd, *Bantân*.] It formed an independent kingdom at the beginning of the 17th century, and then produced much pepper (no longer grown), which caused it to be greatly frequented by European traders. An English factory was established here in 1603, and continued till 1682, when the Dutch succeeded in expelling us as interlopers.

[1615.—"They were all valued in my invoice at **Bantan**."—*Foster, Letters*, iv. 93.]

1727.—"The only Product of **Bantam** is Pepper, wherein it abounds so much, that they can export 10,000 Tuns per annum."—*A. Hamilton*, ii. 127.

BANTAM FOWLS, s. According to Crawfurd, the dwarf poultry which we call by this name were imported from Japan, and received the name "not from the place that produced them, but from that where our voyagers first found them."—(*Desc. Dict.* s.v. *Bantam*). The following evidently in Pegu describes Bantams:

1586.—"They also eat certain cocks and hens called *lorine*, which are the size of a turtle-dove, and have feathered feet; but so pretty, that I never saw so pretty a bird. I brought a cock and hen with me as far as Chaul, and then, suspecting they might be taken from me, I gave them to the Capuchin fathers belonging to the Madre de Dios."—*Balbi*, f. 125*v*, 126.

1673.—"From Siam are brought hither little *Champore* Cocks with ruffled Feet, well armed with Spurs, which have a strutting Gate with them, the truest mettled in the World."—*Fryer*, 116.

[1703.—"Wilde cocks and hens . . . much like the small sort called *Champores*, severall of which we have had brought us from Camboja."—*Hedges, Diary*, Hak. Soc. ii. cccxxxiii.

This looks as if they came from **Champa** (q. v.).

(1) BANYAN, s. **a.** A Hindu trader, and especially of the Province of Guzerat, many of which class have for ages been settled in Arabian ports and known by this name; but the term is often applied by early travellers in Western India to persons of the Hindu religion generally. **b.** In Calcutta also it is (or perhaps rather was) specifically applied to the native brokers attached to houses of business, or to persons in the employment of a private gentleman doing analogous duties (now usually called **sircar**).

The word was adopted from *Vāṇiya*, a man of the trading caste (in Gujarāti *vāṇiyo*), and that comes from Skt. *vaṇij*, 'a merchant.' The terminal nasal may be a Portuguese addition (as in *palanquin, mandarin, Bassein*), or it may be taken from the plural form *vāṇiyān*. It is probable, however, that the Portuguese found the word already in use by the Arab traders. Sidi 'Ali, the Turkish Admiral, uses it in precisely the same form, applying it to the Hindus generally; and in the poem of Sassui and Panhu, the Sindian Romeo and Juliet, as given by Burton in his *Sindh* (p. 101), we have the form *Wāṇiyān*. P. F. Vincenzo Maria, who is quoted below absurdly alleges that the Portuguese called these Hindus of Guzerat **Bagnani**, because they were always washing themselves ". . . chiamati da Portughesi *Bagnani*, per la frequenza e superstitione, con quale si lauano piu volte il giorno" (251). See also Luillier below. The men of this class profess an extravagant respect for animal life; but after Stanley brought home Dr. Livingstone's letters they became notorious as chief promoters of slave-trade in Eastern Africa. A. K. Forbes speaks of the mediæval **Wānias** at the Court of Anhilwāra as "equally gallant in the field (with Rajputs), and wiser in council . . . already in profession puritans of peace, but not yet drained enough of their fiery Kshatri blood."—(*Rās Māla*, i. 240; [ed. 1878, 184].)

Bunya is the form in which *vāṇiya* appears in the Anglo-Indian use of Bengal, with a different shade of meaning, and generally indicating a grain-dealer.

1516.—"There are three qualities of these Gentiles, that is to say, some are called Razbuts . . . others are called **Banians**, and are merchants and traders."—*Barbosa*, 51.

1552.—". . . Among whom came certain men who are called **Baneanes** of the same heathen of the Kingdom of Cambaia . . . coming on board the ship of Vasco da Gama, and seeing in his cabin a pictorial image of Our Lady, to which our people did reverence, they also made adoration with much more fervency. . . ."—*Barros*, Dec., I. liv. iv. cap. 6.

1555.—"We may mention that the inhabitants of Guzerat call the unbelievers **Banyāns**, whilst the inhabitants of Hindustan call them Hindū."—*Sidi 'Ali Kapudān*, in J. As., 1ère S. ix. 197-8.

1563.—"*R.* If the fruits were all as good as this (mango) it would be no such great matter in the **Baneanes**, as you tell me, not to eat flesh. And since I touch on this matter, tell me, prithee, who are these **Baneanes** . . . who do not eat flesh? . . ." —*Garcia*, f. 136.

1608.—"The Gouernour of the Towne of *Gandeuee* is a **Bannyan**, and one of those kind of people that obserue the Law of Pythagoras."—*Jones*, in *Purchas*, i. 231.

[1610.—"**Baneanes.**" See quotation under **BANKSHALL, a.**]

1623.—"One of these races of Indians is that of those which call themselves *Vanià*, but who are called, somewhat corruptly by the Portuguese, and by all our other Franks, **Banians**; they are all, for the most part, traders and brokers."—*P. della Valle*, i. 486-7; [and see i. 78 Hak. Soc.]

1630.—"A people presented themselves to mine eyes, cloathed in linnen garments, somewhat low descending, of a gesture and garbe, as I may say, maidenly and well nigh effeminate; of a countenance shy, and somewhat estranged; yet smiling out a glosed and bashful familiarity. . . . I asked what manner of people these were, so strangely notable, and notably strange. Reply was made that they were **Banians.**" —*Lord, Preface.*

1665.—"In trade these **Banians** are a thousand times worse than the *Jews;* more expert in all sorts of cunning tricks, and more maliciously mischievous in their revenge."—*Tavernier*, E. T. ii. 58; [ed. *Ball*, i. 136, and see i. 91].

c. 1666.—"Aussi chacun a son **Banian** dans les Indes, et il y a des personnes de qualité qui leur confient tout ce qu'ils ont . . . ."—*Thevenot*, v. 166. This passage shows in anticipation the transition to the Calcutta use (b., below).

1672.—"The inhabitants are called Guizeratts and **Benyans.**"—*Baldaeus*, 2.

,, "It is the custom to say that to make one **Bagnan** (so they call the Gentile Merchants) you need three Chinese, and to make one Chinese three Hebrews."—*P. F. Vincenzo di Maria*, 114.

1673.—"The **Banyan** follows the Soldier, though as contrary in Humour as the Antipodes in the same Meridian are opposite to one another. . . . In Cases of Trade they are not so hide-bound, giving their Consciences more Scope, and boggle at no Villainy for an Emolument."—*Fryer*, 193.

1677.—"In their letter to Ft. St. George, 15th March, the Court offer £20 reward to any of our servants or soldiers as shall be able to speak, write, and translate the **Banian** language, and to learn their arithmetic."—In Madras *Notes and Exts.*, No. I. p. 18.

1705.—" . . . ceux des premieres castes, comme les **Baignans.**"—*Luillier*, 106.

1813.—" . . . it will, I believe, be generally allowed by those who have dealt much with **Banians** and merchants in the larger trading towns of India, that their moral character cannot be held in high estimation."—*Forbes, Or. Mem.* ii. 456.

1877.—"Of the *Wani*, **Banyan**, or trade-caste there are five great families in this country."—*Burton, Sind Revisited*, ii. 281.

b.—

1761.—"We expect and positively direct that if our servants employ **Banians** or black people under them, they shall be accountable for their conduct."—*The Court of Directors*, in *Long*, 254.

1764.—"*Resolutions and Orders.* That no Moonshee, Linguist, **Banian**, or Writer, be allowed to any officer, excepting the Commander-in-Chief."—*Ft. William Proc.*, in *Long*, 382.

1775.—"We have reason to suspect that the intention was to make him (Nundcomar) **Banyan** to General Clavering, to surround the General and us with the Governor's creatures, and to keep us totally unacquainted with the real state of the Government."—*Minute by Clavering, Monson, and Francis, Ft. William*, 11th April. In *Price's Tracts*, ii. 138.

1780.—"We are informed that the Juty Wallahs or Makers and Vendors of Bengal Shoes in and about Calcutta . . . intend sending a Joint Petition to the Supreme Council . . . on account of the great decay of their Trade, entirely owing to the Luxury of the Bengalies, chiefly the **Bangans** (*sic*) and Sarcars, as there are scarce any of them to be found who does not keep a Chariot, Phaeton, Buggy or Pallanquin, and some all four . . ."—In *Hicky's Bengal Gazette*, June 24th.

1783.—"Mr. Hastings' **bannian** was, after this auction, found possessed of territories yielding a rent of £140,000 a year."—*Burke, Speech on E. I. Bill*, in *Writings*, &c., iii. 490.

1786.—"The said Warren Hastings did permit and suffer his own **banyan** or principal black steward, named Canto Baboo, to hold farms . . . to the amount of 13 lacs of rupees per annum."—*Art. agst. Hastings, Burke*, vii. 111.

,, "A practice has gradually crept in among the **Banians** and other rich men of Calcutta, of dressing some of their servants . . . nearly in the uniform of the Honourable Company's Sepoys and Lascars. . . ."—*Notification*, in *Seton Karr*, i. 122.

1788.—"**Banyan**—A Gentoo servant employed in the management of commercial affairs. Every English gentleman at Bengal has a **Banyan** who either acts of himself, or as the substitute of some great man or black merchant."—*Indian Vocabulary* (Stockdale).

1810.—"The same person frequently was **banian** to several European gentlemen; all of whose concerns were of course accurately known to him, and thus became the subject of conversation at those meetings the **banians** of Calcutta invariably held. . . ."—*Williamson, V. M.* i. 189.

1817.—"The European functionary . . . has first his **banyan** or native secretary."—*Mill, Hist.* (ed. 1840), iii. 14. Mr. Mill does not here accurately interpret the word.

(2). **BANYAN,** s. An undershirt, originally of muslin, and so called as resembling the body garment of the Hindus; but now commonly applied to under body-clothing of elastic cotton, woollen, or silk web. The following quotations illustrate the stages by which the word reached its present application. And they show that our predecessors in India used to adopt the native or **Banyan** costume in their hours of ease. C. P. Brown defines **Banyan** as "a *loose dressing-gown*, such as Hindu tradesmen wear." Probably this may have been the original use; but it is never so employed in Northern India.

1672.—"It is likewise ordered that both Officers and Souldiers in the Fort shall, both on every Sabbath Day, and on every day when they exercise, *weare English apparel;* in respect the garbe is most becoming as Souldiers, and correspondent to their profession."—*Sir W. Langhorne's Standing Order*, in *Wheeler*, iii. 426.

1731.—"The Ensign (as it proved, for his first appearance, being undressed and in his **banyon** coat, I did not know him) came off from his cot, and in a very haughty manner cried out, 'None of your disturbance, Gentlemen.'"—In *Wheeler*, iii. 109.

1781.—"I am an Old Stager in this Country, having arrived in Calcutta in the Year 1736. . . . Those were the days, when Gentlemen studied *Ease* instead of *Fashion;* when even the Hon. Members of the Council met in **Banyan Shirts, Long Drawers** (q.v.), and Conjee (**Congee**) caps; with a Case Bottle of good old Arrack, and a Gouglet of Water placed on the Table, which the Secretary (a Skilful Hand) frequently converted into Punch . . ."—Letter from *An Old Country Captain*, in *India Gazette*, Feb. 24th.

[1773.—In a letter from Horace Walpole to the Countess of Upper Ossory, dated April 30th, 1773 (*Cunningham's* ed., v. 459) he describes a ball at Lord Stanley's, at which two of the dancers, Mr. Storer and Miss Wrottesley, were dressed "in **banians** with furs, for winter, cock and hen." It would be interesting to have further details of these garments, which were, it may be hoped, different from the modern **Banyan.**]

1810.—". . . an undershirt, commonly called a **banian**."—*Williamson, V.M.* i. 19.

(3) **BANYAN,** s. See **BANYAN-TREE.**

BANYAN-DAY, s. This is sea-slang for a *jour maigre*, or a day on which no ration of meat was allowed; when (as one of our quotations above expresses it) the crew had "to observe the Law of Pythagoras."

1690.—"Of this (*Kitchery* or **Kedgeree**, q.v.) the *European* Sailors feed in these parts once or twice a Week, and are forc'd at those times to a Pagan Abstinence from Flesh, which creates in them a perfect Dislike and utter Detestation to those **Bannian Days,** as they commonly call them."—*Ovington*, 310, 311.

BANYAN-FIGHT, s. Thus:

1690.—"This Tongue Tempest is termed there a **Bannian-Fight,** for it never rises to blows or bloodshed."—*Ovington*, 275. Sir G. Birdwood tells us that this is a phrase still current in Bombay.

BANYAN-TREE, also elliptically **Banyan,** s. The Indian Fig-Tree (*Ficus Indica*, or *Ficus bengalensis*, L.), called in H. *bar* [or *bargat*, the latter the "*Bourgade*" of Bernier (ed. *Constable*, p. 309).] The name appears to have been first bestowed popularly on a famous tree of this species growing near **Gombroon** (q.v.), under which the *Banyans* or Hindu traders settled at that port, had built a little pagoda. So says Tavernier below. This original *Banyan-tree* is described by P. della Valle (ii. 453), and by Valentijn (v. 202). P. della Valle's account (1622) is extremely interesting, but too long for quotation. He calls it by the Persian name, *lūl*. The tree still stood, within half a mile of the English factory, in 1758, when it was visited by Ives, who quotes Tickell's verses given below. [Also see **CUBEER BURR.**]

c. A.D. 70.—"First and foremost, there is a Fig-tree there (in India) which beareth very small and slender figges. The propertie of this Tree, is to plant and set it selfe without mans helpe. For it spreadeth out with mightie armes, and the lowest water-boughes underneath, do bend so downeward to the very earth, that they touch it againe, and lie upon it: whereby, within one years space they will take fast root in the ground, and put foorth a new Spring round about the Mother-tree: so as these braunches, thus growing, seeme like a traile or border of arbours most curiously and artificially made," &c.—*Plinies Nat. Historie*, by *Philemon Holland*, i. 360.

1624.—

". . . The goodly bole being got
To certain cubits' height, from every side
The boughs decline, which, taking root afresh,
Spring up new boles, and these spring new, and newer,
Till the whole tree become a porticus,
Or arched arbour, able to receive
A numerous troop."

Ben Jonson, Neptune's Triumph.

c. 1650.—"Cet Arbre estoit de même espece que celuy qui est a une lieue du Bander, et qui passe pour une merveille; mais dans les Indes il y en a quantité. Les Persans l'appellent *Lul*, les Portugais *Arber de Reys*, et les Francais **l'Arbre des Banianes;** parce que les Banianes ont fait bâtir dessous une Pagode avec un carvansera accompagné de plusieurs petits étangs pour se laver."—*Tavernier, V. de Perse*, liv. v. ch. 23. [Also see ed. *Ball*, ii. 198.]

c. 1650.—"Near to the City of *Ormus* was a **Bannians tree,** being the only tree that grew in the Island."—*Tavernier*, Eng. Tr. i. 255.

c. 1666.—"Nous vimes à cent ou cent cinquante pas de ce jardin, l'arbre *War* dans toute son etenduë. On l'appelle aussi *Ber*, et **arbre des Banians,** et *arbre des racines* . . . ."—*Thevenot*, v. 76.

1667.—

"The fig-tree, not that kind for fruit renown'd;
But such as at this day, to Indians known,
In Malabar or Decan spreads her arms
Branching so broad and long, that in the ground
The bended twigs take root, and daughters grow
About the mother-tree, a pillar'd shade
High over-arch'd, and echoing walks between." *Paradise Lost*, ix. 1101.

[Warton points out that Milton must have had in view a description of the Banyan-tree in *Gerard's Herbal* under the heading "of the arched Indian fig-tree."]

1672.—"*Eastward of Surat* two *Courses*, *i.e.* a League, we pitched our Tent under a Tree that besides its Leafs, the Branches bear its own Roots, therefore called by the *Portugals, Arbor de Raiz;* For the Adoration the *Banyans* pay it, the **Banyan-Tree**."—*Fryer*, 105.

1691.—"About a (Dutch) mile from Gamron . . . stands a tree, heretofore described by Mandelslo and others. . . . Beside this tree is an idol temple where the **Banyans** do their worship."—*Valentijn*, v. 267-8.

1717.—

"The fair descendants of thy sacred bed
Wide-branching o'er the Western World shall spread,
Like the fam'd **Banian Tree**, whose pliant shoot
To earthward bending of itself takes root,
Till like their mother plant ten thousand stand
In verdant arches on the fertile land;
Beneath her shade the tawny Indians rove,
Or hunt at large through the wide-echoing grove."
Tickell, Epistle from a Lady in England to a Lady in Avignon.

1726.—"On the north side of the city (Surat) is there an uncommonly great Pichar or *Waringin** tree. . . The Portuguese call this tree Albero de laiz, *i.e.* Root-tree. . . . Under it is a small chapel built by a *Benyan*. . . . Day and night lamps are alight there, and **Benyans** constantly come in pilgrimage, to offer their prayers to this saint."—*Valentijn*, iv. 145.

1771.—". . . being employed to construct a military work at the fort of Triplasore (afterwards called Marsden's Bastion) it was necessary to cut down a **banyan-tree** which so incensed the brahmans of that place, that they found means to poison him" (*i.e.* Thomas Marsden of the Madras Engineers).—*Mem. of W. Marsden*, 7-8.

1809.—"Their greatest enemy (*i.e.* of the buildings) is the **Banyan-Tree**."—*Ld. Valentia*, i. 396.

* *Waringin* is the Javanese name of a sp. kindred to the banyan, *Ficus benjamina*, L.

1810.—

"In the midst an aged **Banian** grew.
It was a goodly sight to see
That venerable tree,
For o'er the lawn, irregularly spread,
Fifty straight columns propt its lofty head;
And many a long depending shoot,
Seeking to strike its root,
Straight like a plummet grew towards the ground,
Some on the lower boughs which crost their way,
Fixing their bearded fibres, round and round,
With many a ring and wild contortion wound;
Some to the passing wind at times, with sway
Of gentle motion swung;
Others of younger growth, unmoved, were hung
Like stone-drops from the cavern's fretted height."
Southey, Curse of Kehama, xiii. 51.

[Southey takes his account from *Williamson, Orient. Field Sports*, ii. 113.]

1821.—

"Des **banians** touffus, par les brames adorés,
Depuis longtemps la langueur nous implore,
Courbés par le midi, dont l'ardeur les dévore,
Ils étendent vers nous leurs rameaux altérés."
Casimir Delavigne, Le Paria, iii. 6.

A note of the publishers on the preceding passage, in the edition of 1855, is diverting:

"Un journaliste allemand a accusé M. Casimir Delavigne d'avoir pris pour un arbre une secte religieuse de l'Inde. . . ." The German journalist was wrong here, but he might have found plenty of matter for ridicule in the play. Thus the Brahmins (men) are *Akebar* (!), *Idamore* (!!), and *Empsael* (!!!); their women *Néala* (?), *Zaïde* (!), and *Mirza* (!!).

1825.—"Near this village was the finest **banyan-tree** which I had ever seen, literally a grove rising from a single primary stem, whose massive secondary trunks, with their straightness, orderly arrangement, and evident connexion with the parent stock, gave the general effect of a vast vegetable organ. The first impression which I felt on coming under its shade was, 'What a noble place of worship!'"—*Heber*, ii. 93 (ed. 1844).

1834.—"Cast forth thy word into the everliving, everworking universe; it is a seed-grain that cannot die; unnoticed to-day, it will be found flourishing as a **banyan-grove**—(perhaps alas! as a hemlock forest) after a thousand years."—*Sartor Resartus*.

1856.—

". . . its pendant branches, rooting in the air,
Yearn to the parent earth and grappling fast,

Grow up huge stems again, which shooting forth
In massy branches, these again despatch
Their drooping heralds, till a labyrinth
Of root and stem and branch commingling, forms
A great cathedral, aisled and choired in wood."

The **Banyan Tree**, a Poem.

1865.—"A family tends to multiply families around it, till it becomes the centre of a tribe, just as the **banyan** tends to surround itself with a forest of its own offspring."—*Maclennan, Primitive Marriage*, 269.

1878.—". . . des **banyans** soutenus par des racines aëriennes et dont les branches tombantes engendrent en touchant terre des sujets nouveaux."—*Rev. des Deux Mondes*, Oct. 15, p. 832.

BĀRASINHĀ, s. The H. name of the widely-spread *Cervus Wallichii*, Cuvier. This H. name ('12-horn') is no doubt taken from the number of tines being approximately twelve. The name is also applied by sportsmen in Bengal to the *Rucervus Duvaucellii*, or *Swamp-Deer*. [See *Blanford, Mamm.* 538 *seqq.*].

[1875.—"I know of no flesh equal to that of the ibex; and the *navo*, a species of gigantic antelope of Chinese Tibet, with the **barra-singh**, a red deer of Kashmir, are nearly equally good."—*Wilson, Abode of Snow*, 91.]

[**BARBER'S BRIDGE**, n.p. This is a curious native corruption of an English name. The bridge in Madras, known as **Barber's Bridge**, was built by an engineer named Hamilton. This was turned by the natives into *Ambuton*, and in course of time the name *Ambuton* was identified with the Tamil *ambattan*, 'barber,' and so it came to be called *Barber's Bridge*.—See *Le Fanu, Man. of the Salem Dist.* ii. 169, note.]

• **BARBICAN**, s. This term of mediæval fortification is derived by Littré, and by Marcel Devic, from Ar. *barbakh*, which means a sewer-pipe or water-pipe. And *one* of the meanings given by Littré is, "une ouverture longue et étroite pour l'écoulement des eaux." Apart from the possible, but untraced, history which this alleged meaning may involve, it seems probable, considering the usual meaning of the word as 'an outwork before a gate,' that it is from Ar. P. *bāb-khāna*, 'gate-house.' This etymology was suggested in print about 50 years ago by one of the present writers,* and confirmed to his mind some years later, when in going through the native town of Cawnpore, not long before the Mutiny, he saw a brand-new double-towered gateway, or gate-house, on the face of which was the inscription in Persian characters: "*Bāb-Khāna*-i-Mahommed Bakhsh," or whatever was his name, *i.e.* "The **Barbican** of *Mahommed Bakhsh.*" [The *N.E.D.* suggests P. *barbar-khānah*, 'house on the wall,' it being difficult to derive the Romanic forms in *bar-* from *bāb-khāna*.]

The editor of the Chron. of K. James of Aragon (1833, p. 423) says that *barbacana* in Spain means a second, outermost and lower wall; *i.e.* a fausse-braye. And this agrees with facts in that work, and with the definition in Cobarruvias; but not at all with Joinville's use, nor with V.-le-Duc's explanation.

c. 1250.—"Tuit le baron . . s'acorderent que en un tertre . . . féist l'en une forteresse qui fust bien garnie de gent, si qui se li Tur fesoient saillies . . cell tore fust einsi come **barbacane** (orig. '*quasi antemurale*') de l'oste."—The Med. Fr. tr. of *William of Tyre*, ed. *Paul Paris*, i. 158.

c. 1270.—". . . on condition of his at once putting me in possession of the albarrana tower . . . and should besides make his Saracens construct a **barbacana** round the tower."—*James of Aragon*, as above.

1309.—"Pour requerre sa gent plus sauvement, fist le roys faire une **barbaquane** devant le pont qui estoit entre nos dous os, en tel maniere que l'on pooit entrer de dous pars en la **barbaquane** à cheval."—*Joinville*, p. 162.

1552.—"Lourenço de Brito ordered an intrenchment of great strength to be dug, in the fashion of a **barbican** (**barbacã**) outside the wall of the fort . . . on account of a well, a stone-cast distant. . ."—*Barros*, II. i. 5.

c. 1870.—"*Barbacane.* Défense extérieure protégeant une entrée, et permettant de réunir un assez grand nombre d'hommes pour disposer des sorties ou protéger une retraite."—*Viollet-le-Duc, H. d'une Forteresse*, 361.

BARBIERS, s. This is a term which was formerly very current in the East, as the name of a kind of paralysis, often occasioned by exposure to chills. It began with numbness and imperfect command of the power of movement, sometimes also affecting the muscles of the neck and power of

* In a Glossary of Military Terms, appended to *Fortification for Officers of the Army and Students of Military History*, Edinburgh, Blackwood, 1851.

articulation, and often followed by loss of appetite, emaciation, and death. It has often been identified with **Beri-beri**, and medical opinion seems to have come back to the view that the two are *forms* of one disorder, though this was not admitted by some older authors of the last century. The allegation of Lind and others, that the most frequent subjects of *barbiers* were Europeans of the lower class who, when in drink, went to sleep in the open air, must be contrasted with the general experience that *beri-beri* rarely attacks Europeans. The name now seems obsolete.

1673.—"Whence follows Fluxes, Dropsy, Scurvy, **Barbiers** (which is an enervating (*sic*) the whole Body, being neither able to use hands or Feet), Gout, Stone, Malignant and Putrid Fevers."—*Fryer*, 68.

1690.—"Another Distemper with which the Europeans are sometimes afflicted, is the **Barbeers**, or a deprivation of the Vse and Activity of their Limbs, whereby they are rendered unable to move either Hand or Foot."—*Ovington*, 350.

1755.—(If the land wind blow on a person sleeping) "the consequence of this is always dangerous, as it seldom fails to bring on a fit of the **Barbiers** (as it is called in this country), that is, a total deprivation of the use of the limbs."—*Ives*, 77.

[c. 1757.—"There was a disease common to the lower class of Europeans, called the **Barbers**, a species of palsy, owing to exposure to the land winds after a fit of intoxication."—In *Carey, Good Old Days*, ii. 266.]

1768.—"The **barbiers**, a species of palsy, is a disease most frequent in India. It distresses chiefly the lower class of Europeans, who when intoxicated with liquors frequently sleep in the open air, exposed to the land winds."—*Lind* on *Diseases of Hot Climates*, 260. (See **BERIBERI**.)

BARGANY, BRAGANY, H. *bāra-kānī*. The name of a small silver coin current in W. India at the time of the Portuguese occupation of Goa, and afterwards valued at 40 *reis* (then about 5¼*d.*). The name of the coin was apparently a survival of a very old system of coinage-nomenclature. *Kānī* is an old Indian word, perhaps Dravidian in origin, indicating ¼ of ¼ of ¼, or 1-64th part. It was applied to the *jital* (see **JEETUL**) or 64th part of the mediæval Delhi silver *tanka*—this latter coin being the prototype in weight and position of the Rupee, as the *kānī* therefore was of the modern Anglo-Indian pice (= 1-64th of a Rupee). There were in the currency of Mohammed Tughlak (1324-1351) of Delhi, aliquot parts of the *tanka*, *Dokānīs*, *Shash-kānīs*, *Hasht-kānīs*, *Dwāzda-kānīs*, and *Shānzda-kānīs*, representing, as the Persian numerals indicate, pieces of 2, 6, 8, 12, and 16 *kānīs* or *jitals*. (See *E. Thomas, Pathan Kings of Delhi*, pp. 218-219.) Other fractional pieces were added by Fīroz Shāh, Mohammed's son and successor (see *Id.* 276 *seqq.* and quotation under c. 1360, below). Some of these terms long survived, *e.g. do-kānī* in localities of Western and Southern India, and in Western India in the present case the *bārakānī* or 12 *kānī*, a vernacular form of the *dwāzda-kānī* of Mohammed Tughlak.

1330.—"Thousands of men from various quarters, who possessed thousands of these copper coins . . . now brought them to the treasury, and received in exchange gold *tankas* and silver *tankas* (**Tanga**), *shash-gānīs* and *du-gānīs*, which they carried to their homes."—*Tārīkh-i-Fīroz-Shāhi*, in *Elliot*, iii. 240-241.

c. 1350—"Sultan Fīroz issued several varieties of coins. There was the gold *tanka* and the silver *tanka*. There were also distinct coins of the respective value of 48, 25, 24, 12, 10, 8 and 6, and one *jital*, known as *chihal-o-hasht-gānī*, *bist-o-panjgānī*, *bist-o-chahār-gānī*, *dwāzdah-gānī*, *dah-gānī*, *hasht-gānī*, *shāsh-gānī*, and *yak jital*."—*Ibid.* 357-358.

1510.—**Barganym**, in quotation from Correa under **Pardao**.

1554.—"E as *tamgas* brancas que se recebem dos foros, são de 4 **barganis** a *tamga*, e de 24 leaes o **bargany**. . . *i.e.* "And the white *tangas* that are received in payment of land revenues are at the rate of 4 **barganis** to the *tanga*, and of 24 *leals* to the **bargany**."—*A. Nunez*, in *Subsidios*, p. 31.

" "*Statement of the Revenues which the King our Lord holds in the Island and City of Guoa.*

"Item—The Islands of *Tiçoary*, and *Divar*, and that of *Chorão*, and *Johão*, all of them, pay in land revenue (*de foro*) according to ancient custom 36,474 white *tanguas*, 3 **barguanis**, and 21 *leals*, at the tale of 3 **barguanis** to the *tangua* and 24 *leals* to the **barguanim**, the same thing as 24 *bazarucos*, amounting to 14,006 *pardaos*, 1 *tangua* and 47 *leals*, making 4,201,916 ⅗ *reis*. The Isle of Tiçoary (**Salsette**) is the largest, and on it stands the city of Guoa; the others are much smaller and are annexed to it, they being all contiguous, only separated by rivers."—*Botelho, Tombo, ibid.* pp. 46-7.

1584.—"They vse also in Goa amongst the common sort to bargain for coals, wood, lime and such like, at so many **braganines**, accounting 24 *basaruchies* for one *braganine*, albeit there is no such money stamped."—*Barret*, in *Hakl.* ii. 411; (but it is copied from *G. Balbi's* Italian, f. 71*v*).

BARGEER, s. H. from P. *bārgīr*. A trooper of irregular cavalry who is not the owner of his troop horse and arms (as is the normal practice (see **SILLADAR**), but is either put in by another person, perhaps a native officer in the regiment, who supplies horses and arms and receives the man's full pay, allowing him a reduced rate, or has his horse from the State in whose service he is. The P. word properly means 'a load-taker,' 'a baggage horse.' The transfer of use is not quite clear. ["According to a man's reputation or connections, or the number of his followers, would be the rank (*mansab*) assigned to him. As a rule, his followers brought their own horses and other equipment; but sometimes a man with a little money would buy extra horses, and mount relations or dependants upon them. When this was the case, the man riding his own horse was called, in later parlance, a *silaḥdār* (literally, 'equipment-holder'), and one riding somebody else's horse was a *bārgīr* ('burden-taker')."—*W. Irvine, The Army of the Indian Moghuls, J.R.A.S.* July 1896, p. 539.]

1844.—"If the man again has not the cash to purchase a horse, he rides one belonging to a native officer, or to some privileged person, and becomes what is called his **bargeer** . . . ."—*Calcutta Rev.*, vol ii. p. 57.

BARKING-DEER, s. The popular name of a small species of deer (*Cervulus aureus*, Jerdon) called in H. *kākar*, and in Nepal *ratwā*; also called *Ribfaced-Deer*, and in Bombay **Baikree**. Its common name is from its call, which is a kind of short bark, like that of a fox but louder, and may be heard in the jungles which it frequents, both by day and by night. —(*Jerdon*).

[1873.—"I caught the cry of a little **barking-deer.**"—*Cooper, Mishmee Hills*, 177.]

BARODA, n.p. Usually called by the Dutch and older English writers *Brodera*; proper name according to the *Imp. Gazetteer*, *Wadodra*; a large city of Guzerat, which has been since 1732 the capital of the Mahratta dynasty of Guzerat, the Gaikwārs. (See **GUICOWAR**).

1552.—In Barros, "Cidade de **Barodar**," IV. vi. 8.

1555.—"In a few days we arrived at *Barūj*; some days after at **Baloudra**, and then took the road towards *Champaīz* (read *Champanīr*?)."—*Sidī 'Alī*, p. 91.

1606.—"That city (Champanel) may be a day's journey from **Deberadora** or **Barodar**, which we commonly call **Verdora**."—*Couto*, IV. ix. 5.

[1614.—"We are to go to Amadavar, Cambaia and **Brothera**."—*Foster, Letters*, ii. 213; also see iv. 197.]

1638.—"La ville de **Brodra** est située dans une plaine sablonneuse, sur la petite riviere de *Wasset*, a trente *Cos*, ou quinze lieües de *Broitschea*."—*Mandelslo*, 130.

1813.—**Brodera**, in *Forbes, Or. Mem.*, iii. 268; [2nd ed. ii. 282, 389].

1857.—"The town of **Baroda**, originally *Barpatra* (or a bar leaf, *i.e.* leaf of the *Ficus indica*, in shape), was the first large city I had seen."—*Autob. of Lutfullah*, 39.

BAROS, n.p. A fort on the West Coast of Sumatra, from which the chief export of Sumatra camphor, so highly valued in China, long took place. [The name in standard Malay is, according to Mr Skeat, *Barus*.] It is perhaps identical with the *Panṣūr* or *Fanṣūr* of the Middle Ages, which gave its name to the *Fanṣūrī* camphor, famous among Oriental writers, and which by the perpetuation of a misreading is often styled *Ḳaiṣūrī* camphor, &c. (See **CAMPHOR**, and *Marco Polo*, 2nd ed. ii. 282, 285 *seqq.*) The place is called **Barrowse** in the *E. I. Colonial Papers*, ii. 52, 153.

1727.—"**Baros** is the next place that abounds in Gold, Camphire, and Benzoin, but admits of no foreign Commerce."—*A. Hamilton*, ii. 113.

BARRACKPORE, n.p. The auxiliary Cantonment of Calcutta, from which it is 15 m. distant, established in 1772. Here also is the country residence of the Governor-General, built by Lord Minto, and much frequented in former days before the annual migration to Simla was established. The name is a hybrid. (See **ACHANOCK**).

BARRAMUHUL, n.p. H. *Bāra-mahall*, 'Twelve estates'; an old designation of a large part of what is now the district of Salem in the Madras Presidency. The identification of the Twelve Estates is not free from difficulty; [see a full note in *Le Fanu's Man. of Salem*, i. 83, *seqq.*].

1881.—"The **Baramahal** and Dindigal was placed under the Government of Madras; but owing to the deficiency in that Presidency of civil servants possessing a competent knowledge of the native languages, and to the unsatisfactory manner in which the revenue administration of the older possessions of the Company under the Madras Presidency had been conducted, Lord Cornwallis resolved to employ military officers for a time in the management of the Baramahl."—*Arbuthnot, Mem. of Sir T. Munro*, xxxviii.

BASHAW, s. The old form of what we now call *pasha*, the former being taken from *bāshā*, the Ar. form of the word, which is itself generally believed to be a corruption of the P. *pādishāh*. Of this the first part is Skt. *patis*, Zend. *paitis*, Old P. *pati*, 'a lord or master' (comp. Gr. δεσπότης). *Pechah*, indeed, for 'Governor' (but with the *ch* guttural) occurs in I. Kings x. 15, II. Chron. ix. 14, and in Daniel iii. 2, 3, 27. Prof. Max Müller notices this, but it would seem merely as a curious coincidence.—(See *Pusey on Daniel*, 567.)

1554.—"Hujusmodi **Bassarum** sermonibus reliquorum Turcarum sermones congruebant."—*Busbeq.* Epist. ii. (p. 124).

1584.—

"Great kings of Barbary and my portly **bassas**."

Marlowe, Tamburlane the Great, 1st Part, iii. 1.

c. 1590.—"Filius alter Osmanis, Vrchanis frater, alium non habet in Annalibus titulum, quam Alis **bassa**: quod *bassae* vocabulum Turcis caput significat."—*Lennclavius, Annales Sultanorum Othmanidarum*, ed. 1650, p. 402. This etymology connecting *bāshā* with the Turkish *bāsh*, 'head,' must be rejected.

c. 1610.—"Un **Bascha** estoit venu en sa Cour pour luy rendre compte du tribut qu'il luy apportoit; mais il fut neuf mois entiers à attendre que celuy qui a la charge . . . eut le temps et le loisir de le compter . . ." *Pyrard de Laval* (of the Great Mogul), ii. 161.

1702.—" . . . The most notorious injustice we have suffered from the Arabs of Muscat, and the **Bashaw** of Judda."—In *Wheeler*, ii. 7.

1727.—"It (Bagdad) is now a prodigious large City, and the Seat of a *Beglerbeg*. . . . The **Bashaws** of *Bassora, Comera*, and *Musol* (the ancient Nineveh) are subordinate to him."—*A. Hamilton*, i. 78.

BASIN, s. H. *besan*. Pease-meal, generally made of **Gram** (q. v.) and used, sometimes mixed with ground orange-peel or other aromatic substance, to cleanse the hair, or for other toilette purposes.

[1832.—"The attendants present first the powdered peas, called **basun**, which answers the purpose of soap."—*Mrs. Meer Hassan Ali, Observations*, i. 328.]

BASSADORE, n.p. A town upon the island of **Kishm** in the Persian Gulf, which belonged in the 16th century to the Portuguese. The place was ceded to the British Crown in 1817, though the claim now seems dormant. The permission for the English to occupy the place as a naval station was granted by Saiyyid Sultan bin Aḥmad of 'Omān, about the end of the 18th century; but it was not actually occupied by us till 1821, from which time it was the depôt of our Naval Squadron in the Gulf till 1882. The real form of the name is, according to Dr. Badger's transliterated map (in *H. of Imâns, &c. of Omân*), *Bāsīdū*.

1673.—"At noon we came to **Bassatu**, an old ruined town of the Portugals, fronting Congo."—*Fryer*, 320.

BASSAN, s. H. *bāsan*, 'a dinner-plate'; from Port *bacia* (*Panjab N. & Q.* ii. 117).

BASSEIN, n.p. This is a corruption of three entirely different names, and is applied to various places remote from each other.

(1) *Wasāi*, an old port on the coast, 26 m. north of Bombay, called by the Portuguese, to whom it long pertained, **Baçaim** (*e.g. Barros*, I. ix. 1).

c. 1565.—"Dopo Daman si troua **Basain** con molte ville . . . ne di questa altro si caua che risi, frumenti, e molto ligname."—*Cesare de' Federici* in *Ramusio*, iii. 387*v*.

1756.—"Bandar **Bassai**."—*Mirat-i-Ahmadi*, Bird's tr., 129.

1781.—"General Goddard after having taken the fortress of **Bessi**, which is one of the strongest and most important fortresses under the Mahratta power. . . ."—*Seir Mutaqherin*, iii. 327.

(2) A town and port on the river which forms the westernmost delta-arm of the Irawadi in the Province of Pegu. The Burmese name **Bathein**, was, according to Prof. Forchammer, a change, made by the Burmese conqueror Alompra, from the former

name *Kuthein* (*i.e. Kusein*), which was a native corruption of the old name *Kusima* (see **COSMIN**). We cannot explain the old European corruption *Persaim*. [It has been supposed that the name represents the *Besynga* of Ptolemy (*Geog.* ii. 4; see *M'Crindle* in *Ind. Ant.* xiii. 372); but (*ibid.* xxii. 20) Col. Temple denies this on the ground that the name **Bassein** does not date earlier than about 1780. According to the same authority (*ibid.* xxii. 19), the modern Burmese name is *Patheng*, by ordinary phonetics used for *Putheng*, and spelt *Pusin* or *Pusim*. He disputes the statement that the change of name was made by Alaungp'aya or Alompra. The Talaing pronunciation of the name is *Pasem* or *Pasim*, according to dialect.]

[1781.—"Intanto piaciutto era alla Congregazione di Propagando che il Regno di Ava fosse allora coltivato nella fede da' Sacerdoti secolari di essa Congregazione, e a' nostri destino li Regni di **Battiam**, Martaban, e Pegu."—*Quirini, Percoto*, 93.

[1801.—"An ineffectual attempt was made to repossess and defend **Bassien** by the late Chekey or Lieutenant."—*Symes, Mission*, 16.]

The form **Persaim** occurs in *Dalrymple*, (1759) (*Or. Repert.*, i. 127 and *passim*).

(3) *Basim*, or properly *Wāsim*; an old town in Berar, the chief place of the district so-called. [See *Berar Gazett.* 176.]

BATÁRA, s. This is a term applied to divinities in old Javanese inscriptions, &c., the use of which was spread over the Archipelago. It was regarded by W. von Humboldt as taken from the Skt. *avatāra* (see **AVATAR**); but this derivation is now rejected. The word is used among R. C. Christians in the Philippines now as synonymous with 'God'; and is applied to the infant Jesus (*Blumentritt, Vocabular*). [Mr. Skeat (*Malay Magic*, 86 *seqq.*) discusses the origin of the word, and prefers the derivation given by Favre and Wilkin, Skt. *bhaṭṭāra*, 'lord.' A full account of the "*Petara*, or Sea Dyak gods," by Archdeacon J. Perham, will be found in *Roth, Natives of Sarawak*, I. 168 *seqq.*]

BATAVIA, n.p. The famous capital of the Dutch possessions in the Indies; occupying the site of the old city of Jakatra, the seat of a Javanese kingdom which combined the present Dutch Provinces of Bantam, Buitenzorg, Krawang, and the Preanger Regencies.

1619.—"On the day of the capture of Jakatra, 30th May 1619, it was certainly time and place to speak of the Governor-General's dissatisfaction that the name of **Batavia** had been given to the Castle."—*Valentijn*, iv. 489.

The Governor-General, Jan Pietersen Coen, who had taken Jakatra, desired to have called the new fortress *New Hoorn*, from his own birth-place, Hoorn, on the Zuider Zee.

c. 1649.—"While I stay'd at **Batavia**, my Brother dy'd; and it was pretty to consider what the *Dutch* made me pay for his Funeral."—*Tavernier* (E.T.), i. 203.

BATCUL, BATCOLE, BATECALA, &c., n.p. *Bhatkal.* A place often named in the older narratives. It is on the coast of Canara, just S. of Pigeon Island and Hog Island, in lat. 13° 59′, and is not to be confounded (as it has been) with **BEITCUL**.

1328.—". . . there is also the King of **Batigala**, but he is of the Saracens."—*Friar Jordanus*, p. 41.

1510.—The "**Bathecala**, a very noble city of India," of Varthema (119), though misplaced, must we think be this place and not **Beitcul**.

1548.—"Trelado (*i.e.* 'Copy') do Contrato que o Gouernador Gracia de Saa fez com a Raynha de **Batecalaa** por não aver Reey e ela reger o Reeyno."—In *S. Botelho, Tombo*, 242.

1599.—". . . part is subject to the Queene of **Baticola**, who selleth great store of pepper to the Portugals, at a towne called Onor. . ."—*Sir Fulke Greville* to Sir Fr. Walsingham, in *Bruce's Annals*, i. 125.

1618.—"The fift of March we anchored at **Batachala**, shooting three Peeces to give notice of our arriuall. . ."—*Wm. Hore*, in *Purchas*, i. 657. See also *Sainsbury*, ii. p. 374.

[1624.—"We had the wind still contrary, and having sail'd three other leagues, at the usual hour we cast anchor near the Rocks of **Baticala**."—*P. della Valle*, Hak. Soc. ii. 390.]

1727.—"The next Sea-port, to the Southward of *Onoar*, is **Batacola**, which has the *vestigia* of a very large city. . . ."—*A. Hamilton*, i. 282.

[1785.—"**Byte Koal**." See quotation under **DHOW**.]

BATEL, BATELO, BOTELLA, s. A sort of boat used in Western India, Sind, and Bengal. Port. *batell*, a word which occurs in the *Roteiro de V. da Gama*, 91 [cf. **PATTELLO**].

[1686.—"About four or five hundred houses burnt down with a great number of their **Bettilos**, Boras and boats."—*Hedges, Diary*, Hak. Soc. ii. 55.]

1838.—"The **Botella** may be described as a Dow in miniature. . . It has invariably a square flat stern, and a long grab-like head."—*Vaupell*, in *Trans. Bo. Geog. Soc.* vii. 98.

1857.—"A Sindhi **battéla**, called *Rahmati*, under the Tindal Kasim, laden with dry fish, was about to proceed to Bombay."—*Lutfullah*, 347. See also *Burton, Sind Revisited* (1877), 32, 33.

[1900.—"The Sheikh has some fine war-vessels, called **batils**."—*Bent, Southern Arabia*, 8.]

BATTA, s. Two different words are thus expressed in Anglo-Indian colloquial, and in a manner confounded.

a. H. *bhata* or *bhātā*: an extra allowance made to officers, soldiers, or other public servants, when in the field, or on other special grounds; also subsistence money to witnesses, prisoners, and the like. Military **Batta**, originally an occasional allowance, as defined, grew to be a constant addition to the pay of officers in India, and constituted the chief part of the excess of Indian over English military emoluments. The question of the right to *batta* on several occasions created great agitation among the officers of the Indian army, and the measure of economy carried out by Lord William Bentinck when Governor-General (G. O. of the Gov.-Gen. in Council, 29th November 1828) in the reduction of full *batta* to half *batta*, in the allowances received by all regimental officers serving at stations within a certain distance of the Presidency in Bengal (viz. Barrackpore, Dumdum, Berhampore, and Dinapore) caused an enduring bitterness against that upright ruler.

It is difficult to arrive at the origin of this word. There are, however several Hindi words in rural use, such as *bhāt*, *bhantā*, 'advances made to ploughmen without interest,' and *bhaṭṭa*, *bhanṭā*, 'ploughmen's wages in kind,' with which it is possibly connected. It has also been suggested, without much probability, that it may be allied to *bahut*, 'much, excess,' an idea entering into the meaning of both **a** and **b**. It is just possible that the familiar military use of the term in India may have been influenced by the existence of the European military term *bât* or *bât-money*. The latter is from *bât*, 'a pack-saddle,' [Late Lat. *bastum*], and implies an allowance for carrying baggage in the field. It will be seen that one writer below seems to confound the two words.

b. H. *baṭṭā* and *bāṭṭā*: agio, or difference in exchange, discount on coins not current, or of short weight. We may notice that Sir H. Elliot does not recognize an absolute separation between the two senses of **Batta**. His definition runs thus: "Difference of exchange; anything extra; an extra allowance; discount on uncurrent, or short-weight coins; usually called **Batta**. The word has been supposed to be a corruption of *Bharta*, increase, but it is a pure Hindi vocable, and is more usually applied to discount than to premium."—(*Supp. Gloss.* ii. 41.) [Platts, on the other hand, distinguishes the two words—*Baṭṭa*, Skt. *vritta*, 'turned,' or *varta*, 'livelihood'—"Exchange, discount, difference of exchange, deduction, &c.," and *Bhaṭṭa*, Skt. *bhakta* 'allotted,'—"advances to ploughmen without interest; ploughman's wages in kind."] It will be seen that we have early Portuguese instances of the word apparently in both senses.

The most probable explanation is that the word (and I may add, the thing) originated in the Portuguese practice, and in the use of the Canarese word *bhatta*, Mahr, *bhāt*, 'rice' in 'the husk,' called by the Portuguese *bate* and *bata*, for a maintenance allowance.

The word *batty*, for what is more generally called *paddy*, is or was commonly used by the English also in S. and W. India (see *Linschoten*, *Lucena* and *Fryer* quoted s.v. **Paddy**, and *Wilson's Glossary*, s.v. *Bhatta*).

The practice of giving a special allowance for *mantimento* began from a very early date in the Indian history of the Portuguese, and it evidently became a recognised augmentation of pay, corresponding closely to our *batta*, whilst the quotation from Botelho below shows also that *bata* and *mantimento* were used, more or less interchangeably, for this allowance. The correspondence with our Anglo-Indian *batta* went very far, and a case singularly parallel to the discontent raised in the Indian army by the reduction of full-*batta* to half-*batta* is spoken of by Correa (iv. 256). The *mantimento* had been paid all the year round, but the Governor, Martin Afonso de Sousa, in 1542, "desiring," says the historian, "a way to curry favour for himself, whilst going against the people and sending his soul to hell," ordered that in future the *mantimento* should be paid only during the 6 months of **Winter** (*i.e.* of the rainy season), when the force was on shore, and not for the other 6 months when they were on board the cruisers, and received rations. This created great bitterness, perfectly analogous in depth and in expression to that entertained with regard to Lord W. Bentinck and Sir John Malcolm, in 1829. Correa's utterance, just quoted, illustrates this, and a little lower down he adds: "And thus he took away from the troops the half of their *mantimento* (*half their batta*, in fact), and whether he did well or ill in that, he'll find in the next world."—(See also *ibid.* p. 430).

The following quotations illustrate the Portuguese practice from an early date:

1502.—"The Captain-major . . . between officers and men-at-arms, left 60 men (at Cochin), to whom the factor was to give their pay, and every month a *cruzado* of *mantimento*, and to the officers when on service 2 *cruzados*. . . ."—*Correa*, i. 328.

1507.—(In establishing the settlement at Mozambique) "And the Captains took counsel among themselves, and from the money in the chest, paid the force each a *cruzado* a month for *mantimento*, with which the men greatly refreshed themselves. . . ." —*Ibid.* 786.

1511.—"All the people who served in Malaca, whether by sea or by land, were paid their pay for six months in advance, and also received monthly *two cruzados* of *mantimento*, cash in hand" (*i.e.* they had *double batta*).—*Ibid.* ii. 267.

a.

1548.—"And for 2 *ffarazes* (see **FARASH**) 2 pardaos a month for the two and 4 tangas for **bata**." . . .—*S. Botelho, Tombo*, 233. The editor thinks this is for *bate*, *i.e. paddy*. But even if so it is used exactly like **batta** or maintenance money. A following entry has: "To the constable 38,920 reis a year, in which is comprised maintenance (*mantimento*)."

1554.—An example of **batee** for rice will be found s. v. **MOORAH**.

The following quotation shows *battee* (or *batty*) used at Madras in a way that also indicates the original identity of *batty*, 'rice,' and **batta**, 'extra allowance':—

1680.—"The *Peons* and *Tarryars* (see **TALIAR**) sent in quest of two soldiers who had deserted from the garrison returned with answer that they could not light of them, whereupon the Peons were turned out of service, but upon Verona's intercession were taken in again, and fined each one month's pay, and to repay the money paid them for **Battee**. . . ."—*Ft. St. Geo. Consn.*, Feb. 10. In *Notes and Exts.* No. iii. p. 3.

1707.—". . . that they would allow **Batta** or subsistence money to all that should desert us."—In *Wheeler*, ii. 63.

1765.—". . . orders were accordingly issued . . . that on the 1st January, 1766, the double **batta** should cease. . . ."—*Caraccioli's Clive*, iv. 160.

1789.—". . . **batta**, or as it is termed in England, *bât* and forage money, which is here, in the field, almost double the peace allowance."—*Munro's Narrative*, p. 97.

1799.—"He would rather live on half-pay, in a garrison that could boast of a fives court, than vegetate on *full* **batta**, where there was none."—*Life of Sir T. Munro*, i. 227.

The following shows Batty used for rice in Bombay:

[1813.—Rice, or **batty**, is sown in June." —*Forbes, Or. Mem.* 2nd ed. i. 23.]

1829.—"*To the Editor of the Bengal Hurkaru.*—Sir,—Is it understood that the Wives and daughters of officers on *half* **batta** are included in the order to mourn for the Queen of Wirtemberg; or will *half*-mourning be considered sufficient for them?"—Letter in above, dated 15th April 1829.

1857.—"They have made me a K.C.B. I may confess to you that I would much rather have got a year's **batta**, because the latter would enable me to leave this country a year sooner."—*Sir Hope Grant*, in *Incidents of the Sepoy War.*

b.—

1554.—"And gold, if of 10 *mates* or 24 carats, is worth 10 cruzados the tael . . . if of 9 *mates*, 9 cruzados; and according to whatever the *mates* may be it is valued; but moreover it has its **batao**, *i.e.* its shroffage (*çarrafagem*) or agio (*caibo*) varying with the season."—*A. Nunes*, 40.

1680.—"The payment or receipt of **Batta** or **Vatum** upon the exchange of Pollicat for Madras pagodas prohibited, both coines being of the same **Matt** and weight, upon pain of forfeiture of 24 pagodas for every offence together with the loss of the **Batta**." —*Ft. St. Geo. Consn.*, Feb. 10. In *Notes and Exts.*, p. 17.

1760.—"The Nabob receives his revenues in the **siccas** of the current year only . . . and all **siccas** of a lower date being esteemed, like the coin of foreign provinces, only a merchandize, are bought and sold at a certain discount called **batta**, which rises and falls like the price of other goods in the market. . . ."—*Ft. Wm. Cons.*, June 30, in *Long*, 216.

1810.—". . . he immediately tells master that the **batta**, *i.e.* the exchange, is altered."—*Williamson, V. M.* i. 203.

BATTAS, BATAKS, &c. n.p. [the latter, according to Mr. Skeat, being the standard Malay name]; a nation of Sumatra, noted especially for their singular cannibal institutions, combined with the possession of a written character of their own and some approach to literature.

c. 1430.—"In ejus insulae, quam dicunt **Bathech**, parte, anthropophagi habitant . . . capita humana in thesauris habent, quae ex hostibus captis abscissa, esis carnibus recondunt, iisque utuntur pro nummis."—*Conti*, in *Poggius, De Var. Fort.* lib. iv.

c. 1539.—"This Embassador, that was Brother-in-law to the King of **Battas** . . . brought him a rich Present of Wood of Aloes, Calambaa, and five quintals of Benjamon in flowers."—*Cogan's Pinto*, 15.

c. 1555.—"This Island of Sumatra is the first land wherein we know man's flesh to be eaten by certaine people which liue in the mountains, called **Bacas** (read **Batas**), who vse to gilde their teethe."—*Galvano, Discoveries of the World*, Hak. Soc. 108.

1586.—"Nel regno del Dacin sono alcuni luoghi, ne' quali sì ritrouano certe genti, che mangiano le creature humane, e tali genti, si chaimano **Batacchi**, e quando frà loro i padri, e i madri sono vechhi, si accordano i vicinati di mangiarli, e li mangiano."—*G. Balbi*, f. 130.

1613.—"In the woods of the interior dwelt Anthropophagi, eaters of human flesh . . . and to the present day continues that abuse and evil custom among the **Battas** of Sumatra."—*Godinho de Eredia*, f. 23*v*.

[The fact that the Battas are cannibals has recently been confirmed by Dr. Volz and H. von Autenrieth (*Geogr. Jour.*, June 1898, p. 672.]

BAWUSTYE, s. Corr. of *bobstay* in Lascar dialect (*Roebuck*).

BAY, The, n.p. In the language of the old Company and its servants in the 17th century, *The* **Bay** meant the Bay of Bengal, and their factories in that quarter.

1683.—"And the Councell of the **Bay** is as expressly distinguished from the Councell of Hugly, over which they have noe such power."—In *Hedges*, under Sept. 24. [Hak. Soc. i. 114.]

1747.—"We have therefore laden on her 1784 Bales . . . which we sincerely wish may arrive safe with You, as We do that the Gentlemen at the **Bay** had according to our repeated Requests, furnished us with an earlier conveyance . . ."—*Letter from Ft. St. David*, 2nd May, to the Court (MS. in India Office).

BAYA, s. H. *baiā* [*bayā*], the Weaver-bird, as it is called in books of Nat. Hist., *Ploceus baya*, Blyth (Fam. *Fringillidae*). This clever little bird is not only in its natural state the builder of those remarkable pendant nests which are such striking objects, hanging from eaves or palm-branches; but it is also docile to a singular degree in domestication, and is often exhibited by itinerant natives as the performer of the most delightful tricks, as we have seen, and as is detailed in a paper of Mr Blyth's quoted by Jerdon. "The usual procedure is, when ladies are present, for the bird on a sign from its master to take a cardamom or sweetmeat in its bill, and deposit it between a lady's lips. . . . A miniature cannon is then brought, which the bird loads with coarse grains of powder one by one . . . it next seizes and skilfully uses a small ramrod: and then takes a lighted match from its master, which it applies to the touch-hole." Another common performance is to scatter small beads on a sheet; the bird is provided with a needle and thread, and proceeds in the prettiest way to thread the beads successively. [The quotation from Abul Fazl shows that these performances are as old as the time of Akbar and probably older still.]

[c. 1590.—"The **baya** is like a wild sparrow but yellow. It is extremely intelligent, obedient and docile. It will take small coins from the hand and bring them to its master, and will come to a call from a long distance. Its nests are so ingeniously constructed as to defy the rivalry of clever artificers."—*Āīn* (trans. Jarrett), iii. 122.]

1790.—"The young Hindu women of Banáras . . . wear very thin plates of gold, called *tica's*, slightly fixed by way of ornament between the eyebrows; and when they pass through the streets, it is not uncommon for the youthful libertines, who amuse themselves with training **Bayā's**, to give them a sign, which they understand, and to send them to pluck the pieces of gold from the foreheads of their mistresses."—*Asiat. Researches*, ii. 110.

[1813.—Forbes gives a similar account of the nests and tricks of the **Baya**.—*Or. Mem.*, 2nd ed. i. 33.]

BAYADÈRE, s. A Hindu dancing-girl. The word is especially used by French writers, from whom it has been sometimes borrowed as if it were a genuine Indian word, particularly characteristic of the persons in question. The word is in fact only a Gallicized form of the Portuguese *bailadeira*, from *bailar*, to dance. Some 50 to 60 years ago there was a famous ballet called *Le dieu et la* **bayadère**, and under this title *Punch* made one of the most famous hits of his early days by presenting a cartoon of Lord Ellenborough as the **Bayadère** dancing before the idol of Somnāth ; [also see **DANCING-GIRL**].

1513.—"There also came to the ground many dancing women (*molheres* **bailadeiras**) with their instruments of music, who make their living by that business, and these danced and sang all the time of the banquet . . ."—*Correa*, ii. 364.

1526.—"XLVII. The dancers and danceresses (bayladores e **bayladeiras**) who come to perform at a village shall first go and perform at the house of the principal man of the village" (*Gancar*, see **GAUM**).—*Foral de usos costumes dos Gancares e Lavradores de esta Ilha de Goa*, in *Arch. Port. Or.*, fascic. 5, 132.

1598.—"The heathenish whore called **Balliadera**, who is a dancer."—*Linschoten*, 74 ; [Hak. Soc. i. 264].

1599.—"In hâc icone primum proponitur *Inda* **Balliadera**, id est saltatrix, quae in publicis ludis aliisque solennitatibus saltando spectaculum exhibet."—*De Bry*, Text to pl. xii. in vol. ii. (also see p. 90, and vol. vii. 26), etc.

[c. 1676.—"All the **Baladines** of Gombroon were present to dance in their own manner according to custom."—*Tavernier*, ed. *Ball*, ii. 335.]

1782.—"Surate est renommé par ses **Bayadères**, dont le véritable nom est *Déédassi :* celui de *Bayadères* que nous leur donnons, vient du mot **Balladeiras**, qui signifie en Portugais *Danseuses*."—*Sonnerat*, i. 7.

1794.—"The name of **Balliadere**, we never heard applied to the dancing girls ; or saw but in Raynal, and 'War in Asia, by an Officer of Colonel Baillie's Detachment ;' it is a corrupt Portuguese word."—*Moor's Narrative of Little's Detachment*, 356.

1825.—"This was the first specimen I had seen of the southern **Bayadère**, who differ considerably from the nâch girls of northern India, being all in the service of different temples, for which they are purchased young."—*Heber*, ii. 180.

c. 1836.—"On one occasion a rumour reached London that a great success had been achieved in Paris by the performance of a set of Hindoo dancers, called **Les Bayadères**, who were supposed to be priestesses of a certain sect, and the London theatrical managers were at once on the *qui vive* to secure the new attraction . . . My father had concluded the arrangement with the Bayadères before his brother managers arrived in Paris. Shortly afterwards, the Hindoo priestesses appeared at the Adelphi. They were utterly uninteresting, wholly unattractive. My father lost £2000 by the speculation ; and in the family they were known as the '**Buy-em-dears**' ever after."—*Edmund Yates, Recollections*, i. 29, 30 (1884).

BAYPARREE, BEOPARRY, s. H. *bepārī*, and *byopārī* (from Skt. *vyāpārin*) ; a trader, and especially a petty trader or dealer.

A friend long engaged in business in Calcutta (Mr J. F. Ogilvy, of Gillanders & Co.) communicates a letter from an intelligent Bengalee gentleman, illustrating the course of trade in country produce before it reaches the hands of the European shipper :

1878.—" . . . the enhanced rates . . . do not practically benefit the producer in a marked, or even in a corresponding degree ; for the lion's share goes into the pockets of certain intermediate classes, who are the growth of the above system of business.

"Following the course of trade as it flows into Calcutta, we find that between the cultivators and the exporter these are : 1st. The **Bepparree**, or petty trader ; 2nd. The *Aurut-dar ;** and 3rd. The **Mahajun**, interested in the Calcutta trade. As soon as the crops are cut, **Bepparree** appears upon the scene ; he visits village after village, and goes from homestead to homestead, buying there, or at the village marts, from the **ryots** ; he then takes his purchases to the *Aurut-dar*, who is stationed at a centre of trade, and to whom he is perhaps under advances, and from the *Aurut-dar* the Calcutta Mahajun obtains his supplies . . . for eventual despatch to the capital. There is also a fourth class of dealers called *Phoreas*, who buy from the Mahajun and sell to the European exporter. Thus, between the cultivator and the shipper there are so many middlemen, whose participation in the trade involves a multiplication of profits, which goes a great way towards enhancing the price of commodities before they reach the shipper's hands."—*Letter from Baboo Nobokissin Ghose.* [Similar details for Northern India will be found in *Hoey, Mon. Trade and Manufactures of Lucknow*, 59 *seqq*.]

BAZAAR, s. H. &c. From P. *bāzār*, a permanent market or street of shops. The word has spread westward into

* *Aurut-dar* is *ārhat-dār*, from H. *ārhat*, 'agency' ; *phorea*=H. *phaṛiyā*, 'a retailer.'

Arabic, Turkish, and, in special senses, into European languages, and eastward into India, where it has generally been adopted into the vernaculars. The popular pronunciation is *bāzār*. In S. India and Ceylon the word is used for a single shop or stall kept by a native. The word seems to have come to S. Europe very early. F. Balducci Pegolotti, in his Mercantile Handbook (c. 1340) gives **Bazarra** as a Genoese word for 'market-place' (*Cathay*, &c. ii. 286). The word is adopted into Malay as *pāsār*, [or in the poems *pasara*].

1474.—Ambrose Contarini writes of Kazan, that it is "walled like Como, and with **bazars** (*bazzari*) like it."—*Ramusio*, ii. f. 117.

1478.—Josafat Barbaro writes: "An Armenian Choza Mirech, a rich merchant in the **bazar**" (*bazarro*).—*Ibid.* f. 111*v*.

1563.—". . . **bazar**, as much as to say the place where things are sold."—*Garcia*, f. 170.

1564.—A privilege by Don Sebastian of Portugal gives authority "to sell garden produce freely in the **bazars** (*bazares*), markets, and streets (of Goa) without necessity for consent or license from the farmers of the garden produce, or from any other person whatsoever."—*Arch. Port. Or.*, fasc. 2, 157.

c. 1566.—"La Pescaria delle Perle . . . si fa ogn' anno . . . e su la costa all' in contro piantano vna villa di case, e **bazarri** di paglia."—*Cesare de' Federici*, in *Ramusio*, iii. 390.

1606.—". . . the Christians of the **Bazar**."—*Gouvea*, 29.

1610.—"En la Ville de Cananor il y a vn beau marché tous les jours, qu'ils appellent **Basare**."—*Pyrard de Laval*, i. 325; [Hak. Soc. i. 448].

[1615.—"To buy pepper as cheap as we could in the **busser**."—*Foster*, *Letters*, iii. 114.]

[,, "He forbad all the **bezar** to sell us victuals or else. . ."—*Ibid.* iv. 80.]

[1623.—"They call it **Bezari Kelan**, that is the Great Merkat. . ."—*P. della Valle*, Hak. Soc. i. 96. (P. *Kalān*, 'great').]

1638.—"We came into a **Bussar**, or very faire Market place."—*W. Bruton*, in *Hakl.* v. 50.

1666.—"Les **Bazards** ou Marchés sont dans une grande rue qui est au pié de la montagne."—*Thevenot*, v. 18.

1672.—". . . Let us now pass the Pale to the Heathen Town (of Madras) only parted by a wide Parrade, which is used for a **Buzzar** or Mercate-place."—*Fryer*, 38.

[1826.—"The Kotwall went to the **bazaar-master**."—*Pandurang Hari*, ed. 1873, p. 156.]

1837.—"Lord, there is a honey **bazar**, repair thither."—*Turnour's* transl. of *Mahawanso*, 24.

1873.—"This, remarked my handsome Greek friend from Vienna, is the finest wife-**bazaar** in this part of Europe. . . . Go a little way east of this, say to Roumania, and you will find wife-**bazaār** completely undisguised, the ladies seated in their carriages, the youths filing by, and pausing before this or that beauty, to bargain with papa about the dower, under her very nose."—*Fraser's Mag. N. S.* vii. p. 617 (*Vienna*, by *M. D. Conway*).

BDELLIUM, s. This aromatic gum-resin has been identified with that of the *Balsamodendron Mukul*, Hooker, inhabiting the dry regions of Arabia and Western India; *gugal* of Western India, and *mokl* in Arabic, called in P. *bo-i-jahūdān* (Jews' scent). What the Hebrew *bdolah* of the R. Phison was, which was rendered *bdellium* since the time of Josephus, remains very doubtful. Lassen has suggested *musk* as possible. But the argument is only this: that Dioscorides says some called bdellium μάδελκον; that μάδελκον perhaps represents *Madālaka*, and though there is no such Skt. word as *madālaka*, there *might* be *madāraka*, because there is *madāra*, which means some perfume, no one knows what! (*Ind. Alterth.* i. 292.) Dr. Royle says the Persian authors describe the **Bdellium** as being the product of the Doom palm (see *Hindu Medicine*, p. 90). But this we imagine is due to some ambiguity in the sense of *mokl*. [See the authorities quoted in *Encycl. Bibl.* s.v. **Bdellium** which still leave the question in some doubt.]

c. A.D. 90.—"In exchange are exported from Barbarice (Indus Delta) costus, **bdella**. . . ."—*Periplus*, ch. 39.

c. 1230.—"**Bdallyūn.** A Greek word which as some learned men think, means 'The Lion's Repose.' This plant is the same as *mokl*."—*Ebn El-Baithār*, i. 125.

1612.—"**Bdellium**, the pund . . . xxs."—Rates and Valuatiouns (*Scotland*), p. 298.

BEADALA, n.p. Formerly a port of some note for native craft on the Rāmnād coast (Madura district) of the Gulf of Manar, *Vadaulay* in the Atlas of India. The proper name seems to be *Vēdālai*, by which it is mentioned in Bishop Caldwell's *Hist. of Tinnevelly* (p. 235), [and which is derived from Tam. *vedu*, 'hunting,' and *al*, 'a banyan-tree' (*Mad. Adm. Man. Gloss.*

p. 953)]. The place was famous in the Portuguese History of India for a victory gained there by Martin Affonso de Sousa (*Capitão Mór do Mar*) over a strong land and sea force of the Zamorin, commanded by a famous Mahommedan Captain, whom the Portuguese called Pate Marcar, and the Tuhfat-al Mujāhidīn calls 'Ali Ibrahīm Markār, 15th February, 1538. Barros styles it "one of the best fought battles that ever came off in India." This occurred under the viceroyalty of Nuno da Cunha, not of Stephen da Gama, as the allusions in Camões seem to indicate. Captain Burton has too hastily identified *Beadala* with a place on the coast of Malabar, a fact which has perhaps been the cause of this article (see *Lusiads*, Commentary, p. 477).

1552.—"Martin Affonso, with this light fleet, on which he had not more than 400 soldiers, went round Cape Comorin, being aware that the enemy were at **Beadalá** . . ."—*Barros*, Dec. IV., liv. viii. cap. 13.

1562.—"The Governor, departing from Cochym, coasted as far as Cape Comoryn, doubled that Cape, and ran for **Beadalá**, which is a place adjoining the Shoals of **Chilao** [**Chilaw**] . . ."—*Correa*, iv. 324.

c. 1570.—"And about this time Alee Ibrahim Murkar, and his brother-in-law Kunjee-Alee-Murkar, sailed out with 22 grabs in the direction of Kaeel, and arriving off **Bentalah**, they landed, leaving their grabs at anchor. . . . But destruction overtook them at the arrival of the Franks, who came upon them in their galliots, attacking and capturing all their grabs. . . . Now this capture by the Franks took place in the latter part of the month of Shaban, in the year 944 [end of January, 1538]."—*Tohfut-ul-Mujahideen*, tr. by Rowlandson, 141.

1572.—

"E despois junto ao Cabo Comorim
Huma façanha faz esclarecida,
A frota principal do Samorim,
Que destruir o mundo não duvida,
Vencerá co o furor do ferro e fogo;
Em si verá **Beadâla** o martio jogo."
Camões, x. 65.

By Burton (but whose misconception of the locality has here affected his translation):

"then *well nigh reached* the Cape 'clept Comorin,
another wreath of Fame by him is won;
the strongest squadron of the Samorim
who doubted not to see the world undone,
he shall destroy with rage of fire and steel:
Be'adálá's self his martial yoke shall feel."

1814.—"**Vaidálai**, a pretty populous village on the coast, situated 13 miles east of Mutupetta, inhabited chiefly by Musulmans and Shánárs, the former carrying on a wood trade."—*Account of the Prov. of Ramnad*, from Mackenzie Collections in *J. R. As. Soc.* iii. 170.

BEAR-TREE, BAIR, &c. s. H. *ber*, Mahr. *bora*, in Central Provinces *bor*, [Malay *bedara* or *bidara China*,] (Skt. *badara* and *vadara*) *Zizyphus jujuba*, Lam. This is one of the most widely diffused trees in India, and is found wild from the Punjab to Burma, in all which region it is probably native. It is cultivated from Queensland and China to Morocco and Guinea. "Sir H. Elliot identifies it with the lotus of the ancients, but although the large juicy product of the garden *Zizyphus* is by no means bad, yet, as Madden quaintly remarks, one might eat any quantity of it without risk of forgetting home and friends."—(*Punjab Plants*, 43.)

1563.—"*O.* The name in Canarese is *bor*, and in the Decan **bér**, and the Malays call them *vidaras*, and they are better than ours; yet not so good as those of Balagate . . . . which are very tasty."—*Garcia De O.*, 33

[1609.—"Here is also great quantity of gum-lack to be had, but is of the tree called **Ber**, and is in grain like unto red mastic."—*Danvers, Letters*, i. 30.]

BEARER, s. The word has two meanings in Anglo-Indian colloquial: **a.** A palanquin-carrier; **b.** (In the Bengal Presidency) a domestic servant who has charge of his master's clothes, household furniture, and (often) of his ready money. The word in the latter meaning has been regarded as distinct in origin, and is stated by Wilson to be a corruption of the Bengali *vehārā* from Skt. *vyavahāri*, a domestic servant. There seems, however, to be no *historical* evidence for such an origin, *e.g.* in any habitual use of the term *vehārā*, whilst as a matter of fact the domestic bearer (or *sirdār-bearer*, as he is usually styled by his fellow-servants, often even when he has no one under him) was in Calcutta, in the penultimate generation when English gentlemen still kept palankins, usually just what this literally implies, viz. the head-man of a set of palankin-bearers. And throughout the Presidency the **bearer**, or valet, still, as a rule, belongs to the caste of *Kahārs* (see **KUHAR**), or palki-bearers. [See **BOY**.]

a.—

c. 1760.—". . . The poles which . . . are carried by six, but most commonly four **bearers**."—*Grose*, i. 153.

1768-71.—"Every house has likewise . . . one or two sets of **berras**, or palankeen-bearers."—*Stavorinus*, i. 523.

1771.—"Le bout le plus court du Palanquin est en devant, et porté par deux **Beras**, que l'on nomme **Boys** à la Côte (c'est a-dire *Garçons, Serviteurs*, en Anglois). Le long bout est par derrière et porte par trois **Beras**."—*Anquetil du Perron, Desc. Prelim.* p. xxiii. *note*.

1778.—"They came on foot, the town having neither horses nor palankin-**bearers** to carry them, and Colonel Coote received them at his headquarters. . . ."—*Orme*, iii. 719.

1803.—"I was . . . detained by the scarcity of **bearers**."—*Lord Valentia*, i. 372.

b.—

1782.—". . . imposition . . . that a gentleman should pay a rascal of a *Sirdar* **Bearer** monthly wages for 8 or 10 men . . . out of whom he gives 4, or may perhaps indulge his master with 5, to carry his palankeen."—*India Gazette*, Sept. 2.

c. 1815.—"*Henry and his* **Bearer**."—(Title of a well-known book of Mrs. Sherwood's.)

1824.—". . . I called to my *sirdar*-**bearer** who was lying on the floor, outside the bedroom."—*Seely, Ellora*, ch. i.

1831.—". . . le grand maître de ma garde-robe, *sirdar* **beehrah**."—*Jacquemont, Correspondance*, i. 114.

1876.—"My **bearer** who was to go with us (Eva's ayah had struck at the last moment and stopped behind) had literally girt up his loins, and was loading a diminutive mule with a miscellaneous assortment of brass pots and blankets."—*A True Reformer*, ch. iv.

BEEBEE, s. H. from P. *bībī*, a lady. [In its contracted form *bī*, it is added as a title of distinction to the names of Musulman ladies.] On the principle of degradation of titles which is so general, this word in application to European ladies has been superseded by the hybrids *Mem-Sāhib*, or *Madam-Sāhib*, though it is often applied to European maid-servants or other Englishwomen of that rank of life. [It retains its dignity as the title of the *Bībī* of Cananore, known as *Bībī Valiya*, Malayāl., 'great lady,' who rules in that neighbourhood and exercises authority over three of the islands of the Laccadives, and is by race a Moplah Mohammedan.] The word also is sometimes applied to a prostitute. It is originally, it would seem, Oriental Turki. In Pavet de Courteille's Dict. we have "*Bībī*, dame, épouse légitime" (p. 181). In W. India the word is said to be pronounced *bobo* (see *Burton's Sind*). It is curious that among the Sákaláva of Madagascar the wives of chiefs are termed *biby*; but there seems hardly a possibility of this having come from Persia or India. [But for Indian influence on the island, see *Encycl. Britt.* 9th ed. xv. 174.] The word in Hova means 'animal.'—(*Sibree's Madagascar*, p. 253.)

[c. 1610.—"Nobles in blood . . . . call their wives **Bybis**."—*Pyrard de Laval*, Hak. Soc. i. 217.]

1611.—". . . the title **Bibi** . . . is in Persian the same as among us, sennora, or doña."—*Teixeira, Relacion . . . de Hormuz*. 19.

c. 1786.—"The word *Lowndika*, which means the son of a slave-girl, was also continually on the tongue of the Nawaub, and if he was angry with any one he called him by this name; but it was also used as an endearing fond appellation to which was attached great favour,* until one day, Ali Zumán Khan . . . represented to him that the word was low, discreditable, and not fit for the use of men of knowledge and rank. The Nawaub smiled, and said, 'O friend, you and I are both the sons of slave women, and the two Husseins only (on whom be good wishes and Paradise!) are the sons of a **Bibi**."—*Hist. of Hydur Naik*, tr. by Miles, 486.

[1793.—"I, **Beebee Bulea**, the Princess of Cannanore and of the Laccadives Islands, &c., do acknowledge and give in writing that I will pay to the Government of the English East India Company the moiety of whatever is the produce of my country. . . ."—*Engagement* in *Logan, Malabar*, iii. 181.]

BEECH-DE-MER, s. The old trade way of writing and pronouncing the name, *bicho-de-mar* (borrowed from the Portuguese) of the sea-slug or *holothuria*, so highly valued in China. [See menu of a dinner to which the Duke of Connaught was invited, in *Ball, Things Chinese*, 3rd ed. p. 247.] It is split, cleaned, dried, and then carried to the Straits for export to China, from the Maldives, the Gulf

* The "Bahadur" could hardly have read Don Quixote! But what a curious parallel presents itself! When Sancho is bragging of his daughter to the "Squire of the Wood," and takes umbrage at the free epithet which the said Squire applies to her (= *laundikā* and more); the latter reminds him of the like term of apparent abuse (hardly reproduceable here) with which the mob were wont to greet a champion in the bull-ring after a deft spear-thrust, meaning only the highest fondness and applause!—Part ii. ch. 13.

of Manar, and other parts of the Indian seas further east. The most complete account of the way in which this somewhat important article of commerce is prepared, will be found in the *Tijdschrift voor Nederlandsch Indie*, Jaarg, xvii. pt. i. See also **SWALLOW** and **TRIPANG**.

BEECHMÁN, also **MEECHILMÁN**, s. Sea-H. for 'midshipman.' (*Roebuck*).

BEEGAH, s. H. *bīghā*. The most common Hindu measure of land-area, and varying much in different parts of India, whilst in every part that has a *bīghā* there is also certain to be a *pucka beegah* and a *kutcha beegah* (vide **CUTCHA** and **PUCKA**), the latter being some fraction of the former. The *beegah* formerly adopted in the Revenue Survey of the N.W. Provinces, and in the Canal Department there, was one of 3025 sq. yards or ⅝ of an acre. This was apparently founded on Akbar's *beegah*, which contained 3600 sq. *Ilāhi gaz*, of about 33 inches each. [For which see Āīn, trans. *Jarrett*, ii. 62.] But it is now in official returns superseded by the English acre.

1763.—"I never seized a **beega** or *beswa* ($\frac{1}{20}$ *bīghā*) belonging to Calcutta, nor have I ever impressed your gomastahs." . . *Nawāb Kāsim 'Ali*, in *Gleig's Mem. of Hastings*, i. 129.

1823.—"A **Begah** has been computed at one-third of an acre, but its size differs in almost every province. The smallest *Begah* may perhaps be computed at one-third, and the largest at two-thirds of an acre."—Malcolm's *Central India*, ii. 15.

1877.—"The Resident was gratified at the low rate of assessment, which was on the general average eleven annas or 1*s*. 4½*d*. per **beegah**, that for the Nizam's country being upwards of four rupees."—*Meadows Taylor, Story of my Life*, ii. 5.

BEEGUM, BEGUM, &c. s. A Princess, a Mistress, a Lady of Rank; applied to Mahommedan ladies, and in the well-known case of the *Beegum Sumroo* to the professedly Christian (native) wife of a European. The word appears to be Or. Turki. *bīgam*, [which some connect with Skt. *bhaga*, 'lord,'] a feminine formation from *Beg*, 'chief, or lord,' like *Khānum* from *Khān*; hence P. *begam*. [*Beg* appears in the early travellers as *Beage*.]

[1614.—"Narranse saith he standeth bound before **Beage** for 4,800 and odd mamoodies."—*Foster, Letters*, ii. 282.]

[1505.—"**Begum**." See quotation under **KHANUM**.]

[1617.—"Their Company that offered to rob the **Beagam's** junck."—*Sir T. Roe*, Hak. Soc. ii. 454.]

1619.—"Behind the girl came another **Begum**, also an old woman, but lean and feeble, holding on to life with her teeth, as one might say."—*P. della Valle*, Hak. Soc. ii. 6.

1653.—"**Begun**, Reine, ou espouse du Schah."—*De la Boullaye le Gouz*, 127.

[1708.—"They are called for this reason '**Begom**,' which means Free from Care or Solicitude" (as if P. *be-gham*, 'without care'!) —*Catrou, H. of the Mogul Dynasty in India*, E. T., 287.]

1787.—"Among the charges (against Hastings) there is but one engaged, two at most—the **Begum's** to Sheridan; the Rannee of Goheed (Gohud) to Sir James Erskine. So please your palate."—*Ed. Burke* to Sir G. Elliot. *L. of Ld. Minto*, i. 119.

BEEJOO, s. Or 'Indian badger,' as it is sometimes called, H. *bījū* [*bijjū*], *Mellivora indica*, Jerdon, [*Blanford, Mammalia*, 176]. It is also often called in Upper India the *Grave-digger*, [*gorkhodo*] from a belief in its bad practices, probably unjust.

BEER, s. This liquor, imported from England, [and now largely made in the country], has been a favourite in India from an early date. *Porter* seems to have been common in the 18th century, judging from the advertisements in the *Calcutta Gazette*; and the *Pale Ale* made, it is presumed, expressly for the India market, appears in the earliest years of that publication. That expression has long been disused in India, and *beer*, simply, has represented the thing. Hodgson's at the beginning of this century, was the beer in almost universal use, replaced by Bass, and Allsopp, and of late years by a variety of other brands. [Hodgson's ale is immortalised in *Bon Gualtier*.]

1638.—". . . the Captain . . . was well provided with . . . excellent good Sack, *English* **Beer**, French Wines, *Arak*, and other refreshments."—*Mandelslo, E. T.*, p. 10.

1690.—(At Surat in the English Factory) . . . . *Europe* Wines and *English* **Beer**, because of their former acquaintance with our Palates, are most coveted and most desirable Liquors, and tho' sold at high

Rates, are yet purchased and drunk with pleasure."—*Ovington*, 395.

1784.—"London Porter and *Pale Ale*, light and excellent . . . 150 Sicca Rs. per hhd. . . ."—In *Seton-Karr*, i. 39.

1810.—"Porter, pale-ale and table-beer of great strength, are often drank after meals."—*Williamson, V. M.* i. 122.

1814.—

"What are the luxuries they boast them here?
The lolling couch, the joys of bottled beer."

From '*The Cadet*, a Poem in 6 parts, &c. by a late resident in the East.' This is a most lugubrious production, the author finding nothing to his taste in India. In this respect it reads something like a caricature of "Oakfield," without the noble character and sentiment of that book. As the Rev. Hobart Caunter, the author seems to have come to a less doleful view of things Indian, and for some years he wrote the letter-press of the "Oriental Annual."

BEER, COUNTRY. At present, at least in Upper India, this expression simply indicates ale made in India (see **COUNTRY**) as at Masūri, Kasauli, and Ootacamund Breweries. But it formerly was (and in Madras perhaps still is) applied to ginger-beer, or to a beverage described in some of the quotations below, which must have become obsolete early in the last century. A drink of this nature called *Sugar-beer* was the ordinary drink at Batavia in the 17th century, and to its use some travellers ascribed the prevalent unhealthiness. This is probably what is described by Jacob Bontius in the first quotation:

1631.—There is a recipe given for a **beer** of this kind, "not at all less good than Dutch beer. . . . Take a hooped cask of 30 *amphorae* (?), fill with pure river water; add 2lb. black Java sugar, 4oz. tamarinds, 3 lemons cut up, cork well and put in a cool place. After 14 hours it will boil as if on a fire," &c.—*Hist. Nat. et Med. Indiae Orient.*, p. 8. We doubt the result anticipated.

1789.—"They use a pleasant kind of drink, called **Country-beer,** with their victuals; which is composed of toddy . . . porter, and brown-sugar; is of a brisk nature, but when cooled with saltpetre and water, becomes a very refreshing draught."—*Munro, Narrative*, 42.

1810.—"A temporary beverage, suited to the very hot weather, and called **Country-beer,** is in rather *general* use, though water artificially cooled is commonly drunk during the repasts."—*Williamson, V. M.* ii. 122.

BEER-DRINKING. Up to about 1850, and a little later, an ordinary exchange of courtesies at an Anglo-Indian dinner-table in the provinces, especially a mess-table, was to ask a guest, perhaps many yards distant, to "drink beer" with you; in imitation of the English custom of drinking wine together, which became obsolete somewhat earlier. In Western India, when such an invitation was given at a mess-table, two tumblers, holding half a bottle each, were brought to the inviter, who carefully divided the bottle between the two, and then sent one to the guest whom he invited to drink with him.

1848.—"'He aint got distangy manners, dammy,' Bragg observed to his first mate; 'he wouldn't do at Government House, Roper, where his Lordship and Lady William was as kind to me . . . and asking me at dinner to **take beer** with him before the Commander-in-Chief himself . . .'"—*Vanity Fair*, II. ch. xxii.

1853.—"First one officer, and then another, asked him to **drink beer** at mess, as a kind of tacit suspension of hostilities."—*Oakfield*, ii. 52.

BEETLEFAKEE, n.p. "In some old Voyages coins used at Mocha are so called. The word is *Bait-ul-fākiha*, the 'Fruit-market,' the name of a bazar there." So C. P. Brown. The place is in fact the Coffee-mart of which Hodeida is the port, from which it is about 30 m. distant inland, and 4 marches north of Mocha. And the name is really *Bait-al-Faḳīh*, 'The House of the Divine,' from the tomb of the Saint Aḥmad Ibn Mūsā, which was the nucleus of the place.—(See *Ritter*, xii. 872; see also **BEETLEFACKIE,** *Milburn*, i. 96.)

1690.—"Coffee . . . grows in abundance at **Beetle-fuckee** . . . and other parts."—*Ovington*, 465.

1710.—"They daily bring down coffee from the mountains to **Betelfaquy,** which is not above 3 leagues off, where there is a market for it every day of the week."—(*French*) *Voyage to Arabia the Happy*, E. T., London, 1726, p. 99.

1770.—"The tree that produces the Coffee grows in the territory of **Betel-faqui,** a town belonging to Yemen."—*Raynal* (tr. 1777), i. 352.

BEGAR, BIGARRY, s. H. *begārī*, from P. *begār*, 'forced labour' [*be* 'without,' *gār* (for *kār*), 'one who works']; a person pressed to carry a load, or do other work really or professedly for public service. In some provinces *begār* is the forced labour, and *bigārī* the pressed man; whilst in Karnāta, *begārī* is the performance of the lowest village offices without money payment, but with remuneration in grain or land (*Wilson*). C. P. Brown says the word is Canarese; but the P. origin is hardly doubtful.

[1519.—"It happened that one day sixty **bigairis** went from the Comorin side towards the fort loaded with oyster-shells."—*Castanheda*, Bk. V. ch. 38.]

[1525.—"The inhabitants of the villages are bound to supply **begarins** who are workmen."—*Archiv. Port. Orient.* Fasc. V. p. 126.]

[1535.—"Telling him that they fought like heroes and worked (at building the fort) like **bygairys.**"—*Correa*, iii. 625.]

1554.—"And to 4 **begguaryns**, who serve as water carriers to the Portuguese and others in the said intrenchment, 15 leals a day to each. . . ."—*S. Botelho, Tombo*, 78.

1673.—"*Gocurn*, whither I took a Pilgrimage, with one other of the Factors, Four Peons, and Two **Biggereens**, or Porters only."—*Fryer*, 158.

1800.—"The **bygarry** system is not bearable: it must be abolished entirely."—*Wellington*, i. 244.

1815.—*Aitchison's Indian Treaties*, &c., contains under this year numerous *sunnuds* issued, in Nepāl War, to Hill Chiefs, stipulating for attendance when required with "**begarees** and sepoys."—ii. 339 *seqq.*

1882.—"The Malauna people were some time back ordered to make a practicable road, but they flatly refused to do anything of the kind, saying they had never done any **begâr** labour, and did not intend to do any."—(*ref. wanting.*)

BEHAR, n.p. H. *Bihār*. That province of the Mogul Empire which lay on the Ganges immediately above Bengal, was so called, and still retains the name and character of a province, under the Lieutenant-Governor of Bengal, and embracing the ten modern districts of Patna, Sāran, Gāya, Shāhābād, Tirhut, Champāran, the Santāl Parganas, Bhāgalpūr, Monghyr, and Purnīah. The name was taken from the old city of **Bihār**, and that derived its title from being the site of a famous **Vihāra** in Buddhist times. In the later days of Mahommedan rule the three provinces of Bengal, Behar and Orissa were under one Subadar, viz. the Nawāb, who resided latterly at Murshidābād.

[c. 1590.—"Sarkar of **Behar**; containing 46 Mahals. . ."—*Āīn* (tr. *Jarrett*), ii. 153.]

F

[1676.—"Translate of a letter from Shausteth Caukne (Shaista Khan) . . . in answer to one from Wares Cawne, Great Chancellor of the Province of **Bearra** about the English."—In *Birdwood, Rep.* 80].

The following is the first example we have noted of the occurrence of the three famous names in combination:

1679.—"On perusal of several letters relating to the procuring of the Great Mogul's Phyrmaund for trade, custome free, in the Bay of Bengall, the Chief in Council at Hugly is ordered to procure the same, for the English to be Customs free in **Bengal**, **Orixa** and **Bearra**. . ."—*Ft. St. Geo. Cons.*, 20th Feb. in *Notes and Exts.*, Pt. ii. p. 7.

BEHUT, n.p. H. *Behat*. One of the names, and in fact the proper name, of the Punjab river which we now call Jelum (*i.e. Jhīlam*) from a town on its banks: the *Hydaspes* or *Bidaspes* of the ancients. Both *Behat* and the Greek name are corruptions, in different ways, of the Skt. name *Vitastā*. Sidi 'Alī (p. 200) calls it the river of *Bahra*. Bahra or Bhera was a district on the river, and the town and taḥsīl still remain, in Shahpur Dist. [It "is called by the natives of Kaśmīr, where it rises, the *Bedasta*, which is but a slightly-altered form of its Skt. name, the *Vitastā*, which means 'wide-spread.'"—*McCrindle, Invasion of India*, 93 *seqq.*]

BEIRAMEE, **BYRAMEE**, also **BYRAMPAUT**, s. P. *bairam*, *bairamī*. The name of a kind of cotton stuff which appears frequently during the flourishing period of the export of these from India; but the exact character of which we have been unable to ascertain. In earlier times, as appears from the first quotation, it was a very fine stuff. [From the quotation dated 1609 below, they appear to have resembled the fine linen known as "Holland" (for which see *Draper's Dict.* s.v.).]

c. 1343.—Ibn Batuta mentions, among presents sent by Sultan Mahommed Tughlak of Delhi to the great Kaan, "100 suits of raiment called **bairamīyah**, *i.e.* of a cotton stuff, which were of unequalled beauty, and were each worth 100 dīnārs [rupees]."—iv. 2.

[1498.—"20 pieces of white stuff, very fine, with gold embroidery which they call **Beyramies**."—*Correa*, Hak. Soc. 197.]

1510.—"Fifty ships are laden every year in this place (Bengala) with cotton and silk stuffs . . . that is to say **bairam**."—*Varthema*, 212.

[1513.—"And captured two Chaul ships laden with **beirames**."—*Albuquerque, Cartas*, p. 166.]

1554.—"From this country come the muslins called Candaharians, and those of Daulatābād, Berūpātri, and **Bairami**."—*Sidi 'Ali*, in *J.A.S.B.*, v. 460.

" "And for 6 **beirames** for 6 surplices, which are given annually . . . which may be worth 7 pardaos."—*S. Botelho, Tombo*, 129.

[1609.—"A sort of cloth called **Byramy** resembling Holland cloths."—*Danvers, Letters*, i. 29.]

[1610.—"**Bearams** white will vent better than the black."—*Ibid.* i. 75].

1615.—"10 pec. **byrams** nill (see **ANILE**) of 51 Rs. per corg. . . ."—*Cocks's Diary*, i. 4.

[1648.—"**Beronis.**" Quotation from Van Twist, s. v. **GINGHAM.**]

[c. 1700.—"50 blew **byrampants**" (read **byrampauts**, H. *pāt*, 'a length of cloth'). —In *Notes and Queries*, 7th Ser. ix. 29.]

1727.—"Some Surat *Baftaes* dyed blue, and some **Berams** dyed red, which are both coarse cotton cloth."—*A. Hamilton*, ii. 125.

1813.—"**Byrams** of sorts," among Surat piece-goods, in *Milburn*, i. 124.

BEITCUL, n.p. We do not know how this name should be properly written. The place occupies the isthmus connecting Carwar Head in Canara with the land, and lies close to the Harbour of Carwar, the inner part of which is *Beitcul Cove*.

1711.—"Ships may ride secure from the South West Monsoon at *Batte Cove* (qu. **BATTECOLE**?), and the River is navigable for the largest, after they have once got in." —*Lockyer*, 272.

1727.—"The *Portugueze* have an Island called Anjediva [see **ANCHEDIVA**] . . . about two miles from **Batcoal**."—*A. Hamilton*, i. 277.

BELGAUM, n.p. A town and district of the Bombay Presidency, in the S. Mahratta country. The proper name is said to be Canarese *Vennugrāmā*, 'Bamboo-Town.' [The name of a place of the same designation in the Vizagapatam district in Madras is said to be derived from Skt. *bila-grāma*, 'cave-village.'—*Mad. Admin. Man. Gloss.* s.v.] The name occurs in De Barros under the form "Cidade de **Bilgan**" (Dec. IV., liv. vii. cap 5).

BENAMEE, adj. P.—H. *be-nāmī*, 'anonymous'; a term specially applied to documents of transfer or other contract in which the name entered as that of one of the chief parties (*e.g.* of a purchaser) is not that of the person really interested. Such transactions are for various reasons very common in India, especially in Bengal, and are not by any means necessarily fradulent, though they have often been so. ["There probably is no country in the world except India, where it would be necessary to write a chapter 'On the practice of putting property into a false name."—(*Mayne, Hindu Law*, 373).] In the Indian Penal Code (Act XLV. of 1860), sections 421-423, "on fraudulent deeds and dispositions of Property," appear to be especially directed against the dishonest use of this *benamee* system.

It is alleged by C. P. Brown on the authority of a statement in the *Friend of India* (without specific reference) that the proper term is *banāmī*, adopted from such a phrase as *banāmī chiṭṭhī*, 'a transferable note of hand,' such notes commencing, '*ba-nām-i-fulāna*,' 'to the name or address of' (Abraham Newlands). This is conceivable, and probably true, but we have not the evidence, and it is opposed to all the authorities: and in any case the present form and interpretation of the term *benāmī* has become established.

1854.—"It is very much the habit in India to make purchases in the name of others, and from whatever causes the practice may have arisen, it has existed for a series of years: and these transactions are known as '**Benamee** transactions'; they are noticed at least as early as the year 1778, in Mr. Justice Hyde's Notes."—*Ld. Justice Knight Bruce*, in Moore's Reports of Cases on Appeal before the P. C., vol. vi. p. 72.

"The presumption of the Hindoo law, in a joint undivided family, is that the whole property of the family is joint estate . . . where a purchase of real estate is made by a Hindoo in the name of one of his sons, the presumption of the Hindoo law is in favour of its being a **benamee** purchase, and the burthen of proof lies on the party in whose name it was purchased, to prove that he was solely entitled."—*Note by the Editor of above Vol.*, p. 53.

1861.—"The decree Sale law is also one chief cause of that nuisance, the **benamee** system. . . . It is a peculiar contrivance for getting the benefits and credit of property, and avoiding its charges and liabilities. It consists in one man holding land, nominally for himself, but really in secret trust for another, and by ringing the changes between the two . . . relieving the land from being attached for any liability personal to the proprietor."—*W. Money, Java*, ii. 261.

1862.—"Two ingredients are necessary to make up the offence in this section (§ 423 of Penal Code). First a fraudulent intention, and secondly a false statement as to the consideration. The mere fact that an assignment has been taken in the name of a person not really interested, will not be sufficient. Such . . . known in Bengal as **benamee** transactions . . . have nothing necessarily fraudulent."—*J. D. Mayne's Comm. on the Penal Code*, Madras 1862, p. 257.

BENARES, n.p. The famous and holy city on the Ganges. H. *Banāras* from Skt. *Vārānasī*. The popular Pundit etymology is from the names of the streams *Varanā* (mod. *Barnā*) and *Āsī*, the former a river of some size on the north and east of the city, the latter a rivulet now embraced within its area ; [or from the mythical founder, *Rājā Bānār*]. This origin is very questionable. The name, as that of a city, has been (according to Dr. F. Hall) familiar to Sanscrit literature since B.C. 120. The Buddhist legends would carry it much further back, the name being in them very familiar.

[c. 250 A.D.—". . . and the **Errenysis** from the Mathai, an Indian tribe, unite with the Ganges."—*Aelian, Indika*, iv.]

c. 637.—"The Kingdom of *P'o-lo-nis-se* (**Vârânaçi** *Bénarès*) is 4000 *li* in compass. On the west the capital adjoins the Ganges. . . ."—*Hiouen Thsang*, in *Pèl. Boudd.* ii. 354.

c. 1020.—"If you go from Bárí on the banks of the Ganges, in an easterly direction, you come to Ajodh, at the distance of 25 parasangs ; thence to the great Benares (**Bānāras**) about 20."—*Al-Birūnī*, in *Elliot*, i. 56.

1665.—"**Banarou** is a large City, and handsomely built ; the most part of the Houses being either of Brick or Stone . . . but the inconveniency is that the Streets are very narrow."—*Tavernier*, E. T., ii. 52 ; [ed. *Ball*, i. 118. He also uses the forms **Benarez** and **Banarous**, *Ibid.* ii. 182, 225].

BENCOOLEN, n.p. A settlement on the West Coast of Sumatra, which long pertained to England, viz. from 1685 to 1824, when it was given over to Holland in exchange for Malacca, by the Treaty of London. The name is a corruption of Malay *Bangkaulu*, and it appears as *Mangkoulou* or *Wénkouléou* in Pauthier's Chinese geographical quotations, of which the date is not given (*Marc. Pol.*, p. 566, note). The English factory at Bencoolen was from 1714 called Fort Marlborough.

1501.—"**Bencolu**" is mentioned among the ports of the East Indies by Amerigo Vespucci in his letter quoted under **BACANORE**.

1690.—"We . . . were forced to bear away to **Bencouli**, another English Factory on the same Coast. . . . It was two days before I went ashoar, and then I was importuned by the Governour to stay there, to be Gunner of the Fort."—*Dampier*, i. 512.

1727.—"**Bencolon** is an English colony, but the European inhabitants not very numerous."—*A. Hamilton*, ii. 114.

1788.—"It is nearly an equal absurdity, though upon a smaller scale, to have an establishment that costs nearly 40,000*l*. at **Bencoolen**, to facilitate the purchase of one cargo of pepper."—*Cornwallis*, i. 390.

BENDAMEER, n.p. Pers. *Bandamīr*. A popular name, at least among foreigners, of the River Kur (*Araxes*) near Shiraz. Properly speaking, the word is the name of a dam constructed across the river by the Amīr Fanā Khusruh, otherwise called Aded-ud-daulah, a prince of the Buweih family (A.D. 965), which was thence known in later days as the *Band-i-Amīr*, "The Prince's Dam." The work is mentioned in the Geog. Dict. of Yāķūt (c. 1220) under the name of *Sikru Fannā-Khusrah Khurrah* and *Kirdu Fannā Khusrah* (see *Barb. Meynard, Dict. de la Perse*, 313, 480). Fryer repeats a rigmarole that he heard about the miraculous formation of the dam or bridge by **Band Haimero** (!) a prophet, "wherefore both the Bridge and the Plain, as well as the River, by Boterus is corruptly called **Bindamire**" (*Fryer*, 258).

c. 1475.—"And from thense, a daies iorney, ye come to a great bridge vpon the **Byndamyr**, which is a notable great ryver. This bridge they said Salomon caused to be made."—*Barbaro* (Old E. T.), Hak. Soc. 80.

1621.—". . . having to pass the Kur by a longer way across another bridge called **Bend' Emir**, which is as much as to say the Tie (*ligatura*), or in other words the Bridge, of the Emir, which is two leagues distant from Chehil minar . . . and which is so called after a certain Emir Hamza the Dilemite who built it. . . . Fra Filippo Ferrari, in his Geographical Epitome, attributes the name of *Bendemir* to the river, but he is wrong, for *Bendemir* is the name of the bridge and not of the river."—*P. della Valle*, ii. 264.

1686.—"Il est bon d'observer, vue le commun Peuple appelle le **Bend-Emir** en cet endroit *ab pulneu*, c'est à dire le Fleuve du Pont Neuf ; qu'on ne l'appelle par son nom de **Bend-Emir** que proche de la *Digue*, qui lui a fait donner ce nom."—*Chardin* (ed. 1711), ix. 45.

1809.—"We proceeded three miles further, and crossing the River **Bend-emir**, entered the real plain of Merdasht."—*Morier* (First Journey), 124. See also (1811) 2nd Journey, pp. 73-74, where there is a view of the *Band-Amir*.

1813.—"The river **Bund Emeer**, by some ancient Geographers called the *Cyrus*,* takes its present name from a dyke (in Persian a *bund*) erected by the celebrated Ameer Azad-a-Doulah Delemi."—*Macdonald Kinneir, Geog. Mem. of the Persian Empire*, 59.

1817.—

"There's a bower of roses by **Bendameer's** stream,
And the nightingale sings round it all the day long."—*Lalla Rookh*.

1850.—"The water (of Lake Neyriz) . . . is almost entirely derived from the Kur (known to us as the **Bund Amir** River) . . ."—*Abbott*, in *J.R.G.S.*, xxv. 73.

1878.—We do not know whether the **Band-i-Amīr** is identical with the quasi-synonymous *Pul-i-Khān* by which Col. Macgregor crossed the Kur on his way from Shiraz to Yezd. See his *Khorassan*, i. 45.

BENDÁRA, s. A term used in the Malay countries as a title of one of the higher ministers of state—Malay *bandahāra*, Jav. *bendårå*, 'Lord.' The word enters into the numerous series of purely honorary Javanese titles, and the etiquette in regard to it is very complicated. (See *Tijdschr. v. Nederl. Indie*, year viii. No. 12, 253 *seqq.*). It would seem that the title is properly *bāṇḍārā*, 'a treasurer,' and taken from the Skt. *bhāṇḍārin*, 'a steward or treasurer.' Haex in his Malay-Latin Dict. gives *Bandàri*, 'Oeconomus, quaestor, expenditor.' [Mr. Skeat writes that Clifford derives it from *Benda-hara-an*, 'a treasury,' which he again derives from Malay *benda*, 'a thing,' without explaining *hara*, while Wilkinson with more probability classes it as Skt.]

1509.—"Whilst Sequeira was consulting with his people over this matter, the King sent his **Bendhara** or Treasure-Master on board."—*Valentijn*, v. 322.

1539.—"There the **Bandara** (*Bendara*) of *Malaca*, (who is as it were Chief Justicer among the Mahometans), (*o supremo no mando, na honra e ne justica dos mouros*) was present in person by the express commandment of *Pedro de Faria* for to entertain him."—*Pinto* (orig. cap. xiv.), in *Cogan*, p. 17.

1552.—"And as the **Bendara** was by nature a traitor and a tyrant, the counsel they gave him seemed good to him."—*Castanheda*, ii. 359, also iii. 433.

1561.—"Então manson . . . que dizer que matára o seu **bandara** polo mao conselho que lhe deve."—*Correa, Lendas*, ii. 225.

[1610.—An official at the Maldives is called *Rana*-**bandery** *Tacourou*, which Mr. Gray interprets—Singh. *ran*, 'gold,' *bandhara*, 'treasury,' *ṭhakkura*, Skt., 'an idol.'—*Pyrard de Laval*, Hak. Soc. i. 58.]

1613.—"This administration (of Malacca) is provided for a three years' space with a governor . . . and with royal officers of revenue and justice, and with the native **Bendara** in charge of the government of the lower class of subjects and foreigners."—*Godinho de Eredia*, 6v.

1631.—"There were in Malaca five principal officers of dignity . . . the second is **Bendará**, he is the superintendent of the executive (*veador da fazenda*) and governs the Kingdom: sometimes the *Bendará* holds both offices, that of Puduca raja and of **Bendará**." — *D'Alboquerque, Commentaries* (orig.), 358-359.

1634.—

"O principal sogeito no governo
De Mahomet, e privanca, era o **Bendára**,
Magistrado supremo."

Malaca Conquistada, iii. 6.

1726.—"**Bandares** or *Adassing* are those who are at the Court as Dukes, Counts, or even Princes of the Royal House."—*Valentijn* (Ceylon), *Names of Officers, &c.*, 8.

1810.—"After the Raja had amused himself with their speaking, and was tired of it . . . the **bintara** with the green eyes (for it is the custom that the eldest **bintara** should have green shades before his eyes, that he may not be dazzled by the greatness of the Raja, and forget his duty) brought the books and packets, and delivered them to the **bintara** with the black *baju*, from whose hands the Raja received them, one by one, in order to present them to the youths."—A *Malay's* account of a visit to Govt. House, Calcutta, transl. by Dr. Leyden in *Maria Graham*, p. 202.

1883.—"In most of the States the reigning prince has regular officers under him, chief among whom . . . the **Bandahara** or treasurer, who is the first minister. . ."—*Miss Bird, The Golden Chersonese*, 26.

BENDY, BINDY, s.: also **BANDICOY** (q. v.), the form in S. India ; H. *bhinḍī*, [*bhenḍī*], Dakh. *bhenḍī*, Mahr. *bhenḍā*; also in H. *rāmturāī*; the fruit of the plant *Abelmoschus esculentus*, also *Hibiscus esc.* It is called in Arab. *bāmiyah* (*Lane, Mod. Egypt*, ed. 1837, i. 199: [5th ed. i. 184: *Burton, Ar.*

* "The Greeks call it the *Araxes*, Khondamīr the *Kur*."

Nights, xi. 57]), whence the modern Greek μπάμια. In Italy the vegetable is called *corni de' Greci*. The Latin name *Abelmoschus* is from the Ar. *ḥabb-ul-mushk*, 'grain of musk' (*Dozy*).

1810.—"The **bendy**, called in the West Indies *okree*, is a pretty plant resembling a hollyhock; the fruit is about the length and thickness of one's finger . . . when boiled it is soft and mucilaginous."—*Maria Graham*, 24.

1813.—"The **banda** (*Hibiscus esculentus*) is a nutritious oriental vegetable."—*Forbes, Or. Mem.* i. 32; [2nd ed. i. 22].

1880.—"I recollect the West Indian *Ookroo* . . . being some years ago recommended for introduction in India. The seed was largely advertised, and sold at about 8s. the ounce to eager horticulturists, who . . . found that it came up nothing other than the familiar **bendy**, the seed of which sells at Bombay for 1*d*. the ounce. Yet . . . *ookroo* seed continued to be advertised and sold at 8*s*. the ounce. . . ."—*Note* by *Sir G. Birdwood*.

BENDY-TREE, s. This, according to Sir G. Birdwood, is the *Thespesia populnea*, Lam. [*Watt, Econ. Dict.* vi. pt. iv. 45 *seqq.*], and gives a name to the '*Bendy Bazar*' in Bombay. (See **PORTIA**.)

BENGAL, n.p. The region of the Ganges Delta and the districts immediately above it; but often in English use with a wide application to the whole territory garrisoned by the Bengal army. This name does not appear, so far as we have been able to learn, in any Mahommedan or Western writing before the latter part of the 13th century. In the earlier part of that century the Mahommedan writers generally call the province *Lakhnaotī*, after the chief city, but we have also the old form *Bang*, from the indigenous *Vanga*. Already, however, in the 11th century we have it as *Vangālam* on the Inscription of the great Tanjore Pagoda. This is the oldest occurrence that we can cite.

The alleged *City* of *Bengala* of the Portuguese which has greatly perplexed geographers, probably originated with the Arab custom of giving an important foreign city or seaport the name of the country in which it lay (compare the city of *Solmandala*, under **COROMANDEL**). It long kept a place in maps. The last occurrence that we know of is in a chart of 1743, in Dalrymple's Collection, which identifies it with Chittagong, and it may be considered certain that Chittagong was the place intended by the older writers (see *Varthema* and *Ovington*). The former, as regards his visiting *Banghella*, deals in fiction—a thing clear from internal evidence, and expressly alleged, by the judicious Garcia de Orta: "As to what you say of Ludovico Vartomano, I have spoken, both here and in Portugal, with men who knew him here in India, and they told me that he went about here in the garb of a Moor, and then reverted to us, doing penance for his sins; and that the man never went further than Calecut and Cochin."—*Colloquios*, f. 30.

c. 1250.—"Muhammad Bakhtiyár . . . returned to Behár. Great fear of him prevailed in the minds of the infidels of the territories of Lakhnauti, Behar, **Bang**, and Kámrúp."—*Tabakát-i-Násiri*, in *Elliot*, ii. 307.

1298.—"**Bangala** is a Province towards the south, which up to the year 1290 . . . had not yet been conquered. . . ." (&c.).—*Marco Polo*, Bk. ii. ch. 55.

c. 1300.—". . . then to Bijalár (but better reading **Bangālā**), which from of old is subject to Delhi . . . ."—*Rashīduddīn*, in *Elliot*, i. 72.

c. 1345.—". . . we were at sea 43 days and then arrived in the country of **Banjāla**, which is a vast region abounding in rice. I have seen no country in the world where provisions are cheaper than in this; but it is muggy, and those who come from Khorāsān call it 'a hell full of good things.'"—*Ibn Batuta*, iv. 211. (But the Emperor Aurungzebe is alleged to have "emphatically styled it the *Paradise of Nations*."—Note in *Stavorinus*, i. 291.)

c. 1350.—

"*Shukr shikan shawand hama ṭūṭiān-i-Hind*
Zīn ḳand-i-Pārsī kih ba **Bangāla** *mi rawad.*" *Ḥāfiz.*

i.e.,

"Sugar nibbling are all the parrots of Ind
From this Persian candy that travels to **Bengal**" (viz. his own poems).

1498.—"**Bemgala**: in this Kingdom are many Moors, and few Christians, and the King is a Moor . . . in this land are many cotton cloths, and silk cloths, and much silver; it is 40 days with a fair wind from Calicut."—*Roteiro de V. da Gama*, 2nd ed. p. 110.

1506.—"A **Banzelo**, el suo Re è Moro, e li se fa el forzo de' panni de gotton. . ."—*Leonardo do Ca' Masser*, 28.

1510.—"We took the route towards the city of **Banghella** . . . one of the best that I had hitherto seen."—*Varthema*, 210.

1516.—"... the Kingdom of **Bengala**, in which there are many towns. ... Those of the interior are inhabited by Gentiles subject to the King of Bengala, who is a Moor; and the seaports are inhabited by Moors and Gentiles, amongst whom there is much trade and much shipping to many parts, because this sea is a gulf ... and at its inner extremity there is a very great city inhabited by Moors, which is called **Bengala**, with a very good harbour." —*Barbosa*, 178-9.

c. 1590.—"**Bungaleh** originally was called **Bung**; it derived the additional *al* from that being the name given to the mounds of earth which the ancient Rajahs caused to be raised in the low lands, at the foot of the hills."—*Ayeen Akbery*, tr. *Gladwin*, ii. 4 (ed. 1800); [tr. *Jarrett*, ii. 120].

1690.—"Arracan ... is bounded on the *North-West* by the Kingdom of *Bengala*, some Authors making *Chatigam* to be its first Frontier City; but *Teixeira*, and generally the *Portuguese* Writers, reckon that as a City of **Bengala**; and not only so, but place the City of *Bengala* it self ... more South than *Chatigam*. Tho' I confess a late *French* Geographer has put *Bengala* into his Catalogue of imaginary Cities. .."—*Ovington*, 554.

BENGAL, s. This was also the designation of a kind of piece-goods exported from that country to England, in the 17th century. But long before, among the Moors of Spain, a fine muslin seems to have been known as *al-bangala*, surviving in Spanish *albengala*. (See *Dozy and Eng.* s. v.) [What were called "*Bengal* Stripes" were striped ginghams brought first from Bengal and first made in Great Britain at Paisley. (*Draper's Dict.* s. v.). So a particular kind of silk was known as "*Bengal* wound," because it was "rolled in the rude and artless manner immemorially practised by the natives of that country." (*Milburn*, in *Watt*, *Econ. Dict.* vi. pt. 3, 185.) See *N.E.D.* for examples of the use of the word as late as Lord Macaulay.]

1696.—"Tis granted that **Bengals** and stain'd Callicoes, and other *East India* Goods, do hinder the Consumption of Norwich stuffs ...."—*Davenant, An Essay on the East India Trade*, 31.

BENGALA, s. This is or was also applied in Portuguese to a sort of cane carried in the army by sergeants, &c. (*Bluteau*).

BENGALEE, n.p. A native of Bengal [**Baboo**]. In the following early occurrence in Portuguese, *Bengala* is used:

1552.—"In the defence of the bridge died three of the King's captains and Tuam Bandam, to whose charge it was committed, a *Bengali* (**Bengala**) by nation, and a man sagacious and crafty in stratagems rather than a soldier (cavalheiro)."—*Barros*, II., vi. iii.

[1610.—"**Bangasalys**." See quotation from Teixeira under **BANKSHALL**.]

A note to the *Seir Mutaqherin* quotes a Hindustani proverb: **Bangālī** *jangālī*, *Kashmīrī bepīrī*, *i.e.* 'The Bengalee is ever an entangler, the Cashmeeree without religion.'

[In modern Anglo-Indian parlance the title is often applied in provinces other than Bengal to officers from N. India. The following from Madras is a curious early instance of the same use of the word:—

[1699.—"Two **Bengalles** here of Council." —*Hedges, Diary*, Hak. Soc. ii. cclxvii.]

BENIGHTED, THE, adj. An epithet applied by the denizens of the other Presidencies, in facetious disparagement to Madras. At Madras itself "all Carnatic fashion" is an habitual expression among older English-speaking natives, which appears to convey a similar idea. (See **MADRAS, MULL**.)

1860.—"... to ye Londe of St Thomé. It ys ane darke Londe, & ther dwellen ye Cimmerians whereof speketh Homerus Poeta in hys Odysseia & to thys Daye thei clepen Tenebrosi, or Ye **Benyghted** ffolke." —*Fragments of Sir J. Maundevile, from a MS. lately discovered.*

BENJAMIN, BENZOIN, &c., s. A kind of incense, derived from the resin of the *Styrax benzoin*, Dryander, in Sumatra, and from an undetermined species in Siam. It got from the Arab traders the name *lubān-Jāwī*, *i.e.* 'Java Frankincense,' corrupted in the Middle Ages into such forms as we give. The first syllable of the Arabic term was doubtless taken as an article—*lo bengioi*, whence *bengioi*, *benzoin*, and so forth. This etymology is given correctly by De Orta, and by Valentijn, and suggested by Barbosa in the quotation below. Spanish forms are *benjui*, *menjui*; Modern Port. *beijoim*, *beijuim*; Ital. *belzuino*, &c. The terms *Jāwā*, *Jāwī* were applied by the Arabs to the Malay countries generally (especially

Sumatra) and their products. (See *Marco Polo*, ii. 266; [*Linschoten*, Hak. Soc. ii. 96] and the first quotation here.)

c. 1350.—"After a voyage of 25 days we arrived at the Island of Jāwa (here Sumatra) which gives its name to the *Jāwī* incense (**al-lubān al-Jāwī**)."—*Ibn Batuta*, iv. 228.

1461.—"Have these things that I have written to thee next thy heart, and God grant that we may be always at peace. The presents (herewith): **Benzoi**, rotoli 30. Legno Aloë, rotoli 20. Due paja di tapeti. . ."—Letter from the *Soldan of Egypt* to the Doge Pasquale Malipiero, in the Lives of the Doges, *Muratori, Rerum Italicarum Scriptores*, xxii. col. 1170.

1498.—"*Xarnauz* . . . is from Calecut 50 days' sail with a fair wind (see **SARNAU**) . . . in this land there is much **beijoim**, which costs iii cruzados the *farazalla*, and much *aloee* which costs xxv cruzados the farazalla" (see **FRAZALA**).—*Roteiro da Viagem de V. da Gama*, 109-110.

1516.—"**Benjuy**, each farazola lx, and the very good lxx fanams."—*Barbosa* (Tariff of Prices at Calicut), 222.

" "**Benjuy**, which is a resin of trees which the Moors call *luban javi*."—*Ibid.* 188.

1539.—"Cinco quintais de **beijoim** de boninas."*—*Pinto*, cap. xiii.

1563.—"And all these species of **benjuy** the inhabitants of the country call *cominham*,† but the Moors call them **louan jaoy**, *i.e.* 'incense of Java' . . . for the Arabs call incense *louan*."—*Garcia*, f. 29*v*.

1584.—"**Belzuinum** mandolalo* from Sian and Baros. Belzuinum, burned, from Bonnia" (Borneo?).—*Barret*, in *Hakl.* ii. 413.

1612.—"**Beniamin**, the pund iiii *li.*"—*Rates and Valuatioun of Merchandize* (Scotland), pub. by the Treasury, Edin. 1867, p. 298.

BENUA, n.p. This word, Malay *banuwa*, [in standard Malay, according to Mr. Skeat, *benuwa* or *benua*], properly means 'land, country,' and the Malays use *orang-banuwa* in the sense of aborigines, applying it to the wilder tribes of the Malay Peninsula. Hence "Benuas" has been used by Europeans as a proper name of those tribes.—See *Crawfurd, Dict. Ind. Arch.* sub voce.

1613.—"The natives of the interior of Viontana (**Ujong-tana**, q. v.) are properly those **Banuas**, black anthropophagi, and hairy, like satyrs."—*Godinho de Eredia*, 20.

* On *benjuy de boninas* ("of flowers"), see *De Orta*, ff. 28, 30, 31. And on *benjuy de amendoada* or *mandolalo* (*mandolado?* "of almond") *id.* 30*v*.

† *Kamañan* or *Kamiñan* in Malay and Javanese.

BERBERYN, BARBERYN, n.p. Otherwise called *Beruwala*, a small port with an anchorage for ships and a considerable coasting trade, in Ceylon, about 35 m. south of Columbo.

c. 1350.—"Thus, led by the Divine mercy, on the morrow of the Invention of the Holy Cross, we found ourselves brought safely into port in a harbour of Seyllan, called **Pervilis**, over against Paradise."—*Marignolli*, in *Cathay*, ii. 357.

c. 1618.—"At the same time Barreto made an attack on **Berbelim**, killing the Moorish modeliar [**Modelliar**] and all his kinsfolk."—*Bocarro, Decada*, 713.

1780.—"**Barbarien** Island."—*Dunn, New Directory*, 5th ed. 77.

1836.—"**Berberyn** Island. . . . There is said to be an anchorage north of it, in 6 or 7 fathoms, and a small bay further in . . . where small craft may anchor."—*Horsburgh*, 5th ed. 551.

[1859.—Tennent in his map (*Ceylon*, 3rd ed.) gives **Barberyn, Barbery, Barberry.**]

BERIBERI, s. An acute disease, obscure in its nature and pathology, generally but not always presenting dropsical symptoms, as well as paralytic weakness and numbness of the lower extremities, with oppressed breathing. In cases where debility, oppression, anxiety and dyspnœa are extremely severe, the patient sometimes dies in 6 to 30 hours. Though recent reports seem to refer to this disease as almost confined to natives, it is on record that in 1795, in Trincomalee, 200 Europeans died of it.

The word has been alleged to be Singhalese *beri* [the *Mad. Admin. Man. Gloss.* s. v. gives *baribari*], 'debility.' This kind of reduplication is really a common Singhalese practice. It is also sometimes alleged to be a W. Indian Negro term; and other worthless guesses have been made at its origin. The Singhalese origin is on the whole most probable [and is accepted by the *N.E.D.*]. In the quotations from Bontius and Bluteau, the disease described seems to be that formerly known as **Barbiers**. Some authorities have considered these diseases as quite distinct, but Sir Joseph Fayrer, who has paid attention to *beriberi* and written upon it (see *The Practitioner*, January 1877), regards Barbiers as "the dry form of *beri-beri*," and Dr. Lodewijks, quoted below, says briefly that "the Barbiers of some French writers is incontestably the same disease." (On this it is necessary to remark that the use of the term *Barbiers* is by no means confined to French writers, as a glance at the quotations under that word will show). The disease prevails endemically in Ceylon, and in Peninsular India in the coast-tracts, and up to 40 or 60 m. inland; also in Burma and the Malay region, including all the islands, at least so far as New Guinea, and also Japan, where it is known as *kakké*: [see *Chamberlain, Things Japanese*, 3rd ed. p. 238 *seqq.*]. It is very prevalent in certain Madras Jails. The name has become somewhat old-fashioned, but it has recurred of late years, especially in hospital reports from Madras and Burma. It is frequently epidemic, and some of the Dutch physicians regard it as infectious. See a pamphlet, **Beri-Beri** *door J. A. Lodewijks, ondofficier van Gezondheit bij het Ned. Indische Leger*, Harderwijk, 1882. In this pamphlet it is stated that in 1879 the total number of *beri-beri* patients in the military hospitals of Netherlands-India, amounted to 9873, and the deaths among these to 1682. In the great military hospitals at Achin there died of *beri-beri* between 1st November 1879, and 1st April 1880, 574 persons, of whom the great majority were *dwangarbeiders, i.e.* 'forced labourers.' These statistics show the extraordinary prevalence and fatality of the disease in the Archipelago. Dutch literature on the subject is considerable.

Sir George Birdwood tells us that during the Persian Expedition of 1857 he witnessed *beri-beri* of extraordinary virulence, especially among the East African stokers on board the steamers. The sufferers became dropsically distended to a vast extent, and died in a few hours.

In the second quotation *scurvy* is evidently meant. This seems much allied by *causes* to *beriberi* though different in character.

[1568.—"Our people sickened of a disease called **berbere**, the belly and legs swell, and in a few days they die, as there died many, ten or twelve a day."—*Couto*, viii. ch. 25.]

c. 1610.—"Ce ne fut pas tout, car i'eus encor ceste fascheuse maladie de *louende* que les Portugais appellent autrement **berber** et les Hollandais *scurbut*."—*Mocquet*, 221.

1613.—"And under the orders of the said General André Furtado de Mendoça, the discoverer departed to the court of Goa, being ill with the malady of the **berebere**, in order to get himself treated."—*Godinho de Eredia*, f. 58.

1631.—". . . Constat frequenti illorum usu, praesertim liquoris *saguier* dicti, non solum diarrhaeas . . . sed et paralysin **Beriberi** dictam hinc natam esse."—*Jac. Bontii*, Dial. iv. See also Lib. ii. cap. iii., and Lib. iii. p. 40.

1659.—"There is also another sickness which prevails in Banda and Ceylon, and is called **Barberi**; it does not vex the natives so much as foreigners."—*Sarr*, 37.

1682.—"The Indian and Portuguese women draw from the green flowers and cloves, by means of firing with a still, a water or spirit of marvellous sweet smell . . . especially is it good against a certain kind of paralysis called **Berebery**."—*Nieuhof, Zee en Lant-Reize*, ii. 33.

1685.—"The Portuguese in the Island suffer from another sickness which the natives call **béri-béri**."—*Ribeiro*, f. 55.

1720.—"**Berebere** (termo da India). Huma *Paralysia* bastarde, ou entorpecemento, com que fica o corpo como tolhido." —*Bluteau, Dict.* s. v.

1809.—"A complaint, as far as I have learnt, peculiar to the island (Ceylon), the **berri-berri**; it is in fact a dropsy that frequently destroys in a few days."—*Ld. Valentia*, i. 318.

1835.—(On the Maldives) ". . . the crew of the vessels during the survey . . . suffered mostly from two diseases; the **Beri-beri** which attacked the Indians only, and generally proved fatal."—*Young and Christopher*, in *Tr. Ro. Geog. Soc.*, vol. i.

1837.—"Empyreumatic oil called *oleum nigrum*, from the seeds of *Celastrus nutans* (*Malkungnee*) described in Mr. Malcolmson's able prize Essay on the Hist. and Treatment of **Beriberi** . . . the most efficacious remedy in that intractable complaint."—*Royle on Hindu Medicine*, 46.

1880.—"A malady much dreaded by the Japanese, called *Kakké*. . . . It excites a most singular dread. It is considered to be the same disease as that which, under the name of **Beriberi**, makes such havoc at times on crowded jails and barracks."—*Miss Bird's Japan*, i. 288.

1882.—"**Berbá**, a disease which consists in great swelling of the abdomen."—*Blumentritt, Vocabular*, s. v.

1885.—"Dr. Wallace Taylor, of Osaka, Japan, reports important discoveries respecting the origin of the disease known as **beri-beri**. He has traced it to a microscopic spore largely developed in rice. He has finally detected the same organism in the earth of certain alluvial and damp localities." —*St. James's Gazette*, Aug. 9th.

Also see Report on Prison Admin. in Br. Burma, for 1878, p. 26.

BERYL, s. This word is perhaps a very ancient importation from India to the West, it having been supposed that its origin was the Skt. *vaidūrya*, Prak. *velūriya*, whence [Malay *baiduri* and *biduri*], P. *billaur*, and Greek *βήρυλλος*. Bochart points out the probable identity of the two last words by the transposition of *l* and *r*. Another transposition appears to have given Ptolemy his 'Ορούδια ὄρη (for the Western Ghats), representing probably the native *Vaidūrya* mountains. In Ezekiel xxvii. 13, the Sept. has *βηρύλλιον*, where the Hebrew now has *tarshīsh*, [another word with probably the same meaning being *shohsm* (see Professor Ridgeway in *Encycl. Bibl.* s.v. *Beryl*)]. Professor Max Müller has treated of the possible relation between *vaidūrya* and *vidāla*, 'a cat,' and in connection with this observes that "we should, at all events, have learnt the useful lesson that the chapter of accidents is sometimes larger than we suppose."—(*India, What can it Teach us?*" p. 267). This is a lesson which many articles in our book suggest; and in dealing with the same words, it may be indicated that the resemblance between the Greek *αἴλουρος*, *bilāur*, a common H. word for a cat, and the P. *billaur*, 'beryl,' are at least additional illustrations of the remark quoted.

c. A.D. 70.—"**Beryls** . . . from India they come as from their native place, for seldom are they to be found elsewhere. . . . Those are best accounted of which carrie a sea-water greene."—*Pliny*, Bk. XXXVII. cap. 20 (in *P. Holland*, ii. 613).

c. 150.—"Πυννάτα ἐν ᾗ βήρυλλος."—*Ptolemy*, l. vii.

BETEL, s. The leaf of the *Piper betel*, L., chewed with the dried **areca**-nut (which is thence improperly called *betel-nut*, a mistake as old as **Fryer**—1673,—see p. 40), *chunam*, etc., by the natives of India and the Indo-Chinese countries. The word is Malayāl. *vettila*, *i.e. veru + ila* = 'simple or mere leaf,' and comes to us through the Port. *betre* and *betle*. **Pawn** (q.v.) is the term more generally used by modern Anglo-Indians. In former times the *betel-leaf* was in S. India the subject of a monopoly of the E. I. Co.

1298.—"All the people of this city (Cael) as well as of the rest of India, have a custom of perpetually keeping in the mouth a certain leaf called *Tembul* . . . . the lords and gentlefolks and the King have these leaves prepared with camphor and other aromatic spices, and also mixt with quicklime. . . ."—*Marco Polo*, ii. 358. See also *Abdurrazzāk*, in *India in XV. Cent.*, p. 32.

1498.—In Vasco da Gama's *Roteiro*, p. 59, the word used is *atombor*, *i.e. al-tambūl* (Arab.) from the Skt. *tāmbūla*. See also *Acosta*, p. 139. [See **TEMBOOL**.]

1510.—"This **betel** resembles the leaves of the sour orange, and they are constantly eating it."—*Varthema*, p. 144.

1516.—"We call this **betel** Indian leaf."*—*Barbosa*, 73.

[1521.— '**Bettre** (or **vettele**)." See under **ARECA**.]

1552.—". . . . at one side of the bed . . . stood a man . . . who held in his hand a gold plate with leaves of **betelle**. . . ."—*De Barros*, Dec. I. liv. iv. cap. viii.

1563.—"We call it **betre**, because the first land known by the Portuguese was Malabar, and it comes to my remembrance that in Portugal they used to speak of their coming not to *India*, but to Calecut . . . . insomuch that in all the names that occur, which are not Portuguese, are Malabar, like **betre**."—*Garcia*, f. 37*g*.

1582.—The transl. of *Castañeda* by N. L. has **betele** (f. 35), and also **vitele** (f. 44).

1585.—A King's letter grants the revenue from betel (**betre**) to the bishop and clergy of Goa.—In *Arch. Port. Or.*, fasc. 3, p. 38.

1615.—"He sent for Coco-Nuts to give the Company, himselfe chewing **Bittle** and lime of Oyster-shels, with a Kernell of Nut called *Arracca*, like an Akorne, it bites in the mouth, accords rheume, cooles the head, strengthens the teeth, & is all their Phisicke."—*Sir T. Roe*, in *Purchas*, i. 537; [with some trifling variations in *Foster's* ed. (Hak. Soc.) i. 19].

1623.—"Celebratur in universo oriente radix quaedam vocata **Betel**, quam Indi et reliqui in ore habere et mandere consueverunt, atque ex eâ mansione mire recreantur, et ad labores tolerandos, et ad languores discutiendos . . . . videtur autem esse ex *narcoticis*, quia magnopere denigrat dentes."—*Bacon*, *Historia Vitae et Mortis*, ed. Amst. 1673, p. 97.

1672.—"They pass the greater part of the day in indolence, occupied only with talk, and chewing **Betel** and Areca, by which means their lips and teeth are always stained."—*P. di Vincenzo Maria*, 232.

1677.—The Court of the E. I. Co. in a letter to Ft. St. George, Dec. 12, disapprove of allowing "Valentine Nurse 20 Rupees a month for diet, 7 Rs. for house-rent, 2 for a cook, 1 for **Beetle**, and 2 for a Porter, which is a most extravagant rate, which we shall not allow him or any other."—*Notes and Exts.*, No. i. p. 21.

1727.—"I presented the Officer that

* *Folium indicum* of the druggist is, however, not *betel*, but the leaf of the wild cassia (see **MALABATHRUM**.)

waited on me to the Sea-side (at Calicut) with 5 zequeens for a feast of **bettle** to him and his companions."—*A. Hamilton*, i. 306.

BETTEELA, BEATELLE, &c., s. The name of a kind of muslin constantly mentioned in old trading-lists and narratives. This seems to be a Sp. and Port. word *beatilla* or *beatilha*, for 'a veil,' derived, according to Cobarruvias, from "certain *beatas*, who invented or used the like." *Beata* is a *religieuse*. ["The **Betilla** is a certain kind of white E. I. chintz made at Masulipatam, and known under the name of *Organdi*."—*Mad. Admin. Man. Gloss.* p. 233.]

[1566.—A score **Byatilhas**, which were worth 200 pardaos."—*Correa*, iii. 479.]

1572.—

"Vestida huma camisa preciosa
Trazida de delgada **beatilha**,
Que o corpo crystallino deixa ver-se;
Que tanto bem não he para esconder-se."

Camões, vi. 21.

1598.—". . . this linnen is of divers sorts, and is called Serampuras, Cassas, Comsas, **Beattillias**, Satopassas, and a thousand such names."—*Linschoten*, 28; [Hak. Soc. i. 95; and cf. i. 56].

1685.—"To servants, 3 pieces **beteelaes**."—In *Wheeler*, i. 149.

1727.—"Before *Aurungzeb* conquered *Visiapore*, this country (Sundah) produced the finest **Betteelas** or Muslins in India."—*A. Hamilton*, i. 264.

[1788.—"There are various kinds of muslins brought from the East Indies, chiefly from Bengal: **Betelles**, &c."—*Chambers' Cycl.*, quoted in 3 ser. *Notes & Q.* iv. 88.]

BEWAURIS, adj. P.—H. *be-wāris*, 'without heir.' Unclaimed, without heir or owner.

BEYPOOR, n.p. Properly *Veppūr*, or *Bēppūr*, [derived from Malayāl. *veppu*, 'deposit,' *ur*, 'village,' a place formed by the receding of the sea, which has been turned into the Skt. form *Vāyupura*, 'the town of the Wind-god']. The terminal town of the Madras Railway on the Malabar coast. It stands north of the river; whilst the railway station is on the S. of the river—(see **CHALIA**). Tippoo Sahib tried to make a great port of Beypoor, and to call it Sultanpatnam. [It is one of the many places which have been suggested as the site of Ophir (*Logan, Malabar*, i. 246), and is probably the *Belliporto* of Tavernier, "where there was a fort which the Dutch had made with palms" (ed. *Ball*, i. 235).]

1572.—

"Chamará o Samorim mais gente nova;
Virão Reis de **Bipur**, e de Tanor. . ."

Camões, x. 14.

1727.—"About two Leagues to the Southward of *Calecut*, is a fine River called **Baypore**, capable to receive ships of 3 or 400 Tuns."—*A. Hamilton*, i. 322.

BEZOAR, s. This word belongs, not to the A.-Indian colloquial, but to the language of old oriental trade and *materia medica*. The word is a corruption of the P. name of the thing, *pādzahr*, 'pellens venenum,' or *pāzahr*. The first form is given by Meninski as the etymology of the word, and this is accepted by Littré [and the *N.E.D.*]. The quotations of Littré from Ambrose Paré show that the word was used generically for 'an antidote,' and in this sense it is used habitually by Avicenna. No doubt the term came to us, with so many others, from Arab medical writers, so much studied in the Middle Ages, and this accounts for the *b*, as Arabic has no *p*, and writes *bāzahr*. But its usual application was, and is, limited to certain hard concretions found in the bodies of animals, to which antidotal virtues were ascribed, and especially to one obtained from the stomach of a wild goat in the Persian province of Lar. Of this animal and the *bezoar* an account is given in Kaempfer's *Amoenitates Exoticae*, pp. 398 *seqq.* The *Bezoar* was sometimes called **Snake-Stone**, and erroneously supposed to be found in the head of a snake. It may have been called so really because, as Ibn Baithar states, such a stone was laid upon the bite of a venomous creature (and was believed) to extract the poison. Moodeen Sheriff, in his Suppt. to the Indian Pharmacopœia, says there are various *bezoars* in use (in native *mat. med.*), distinguished according to the animal producing them, as a goat-, camel-, fish-, and snake-*bezoar*; the last quite distinct from **Snake-Stone** (q.v.).

[A false Bezoar stone gave occasion for the establishment of one of the great distinctions in our Common Law, viz. between actions founded upon contract, and those founded upon wrongs: *Chandelor* v. *Lopus* was decided in 1604 (reported in 2. *Croke*, and in *Smith's Leading Cases*). The head-note runs—

"The defendant sold to the plaintiff a stone, which he affirmed to be a Bezoar stone, but which proved not to be so. No action lies against him, unless he either knew that it was not a Bezoar stone, or warranted it to be a Bezoar stone" (quoted by *Gray*, *Pyrard de Laval*, Hak. Soc. ii. 484).]

1516.—Barbosa writes **pajar**.

[1528.—"Near this city (Lara) in a small mountain are bred some animals of the size of a buck, in whose stomach grows a stone they call **bazar**."—*Tenreiro*, ch. iii. p. 14.]

[1554.—Castanheda (I. ch. 46) calls the animal whence bezoar comes *bagoldaf*, which he considers an Indian word.]

c. 1580.—". . . adeo ut ex solis **Bezahar** nonnulla vasa conflata viderim, maxime apud eos qui a venenis sibi cavere student."—*Prosper Alpinus*, Pt. i. p. 56.

1599.—"Body o' me, a shrewd mischance. Why, had you no unicorn's horn, nor **bezoar's** stone about you, ha?"—*B. Jonson*, *Every Man out of his Humour*, Act v. sc. 4.

[,, "**Bezar** sive **bazar**"; see quotation under **MACE**.]

1605.—The King of Bantam sends K. James I. "two **beasar** stones."—*Sainsbury*, i. 143.

1610.—"The Persian calls it, *par excellence*, **Pazahar**, which is as much as to say 'antidote' or more strictly 'remedy of poison or venom,' from *Zahar*, which is the general name of any poison, and *pá*, 'remedy'; and as the Arabic lacks the letter *p*, they replace it by *b*, or *f*, and so they say, instead of *Pázahar*, *Bázahar*, and we with a little additional corruption **Bezar**."—*P. Teixeira*, *Relaciones*, &c., p. 157.

1613.—". . . . elks, and great snakes, and apes of **bazar** stone, and every kind of game birds."—*Godinho de Eredia*, 10*v*.

1617.—". . . late at night I drunke a little **bezas** stone, which gave me much paine most parte of night, as though 100 Wormes had byn knawing at my hart; yet it gave me ease afterward."—*Cocks's Diary*, i. 301; [in i. 154 he speaks of "**beza** stone"].

1634.—Bontius claims the etymology just quoted from Teixeira, erroneously, as his own.—Lib. iv. p. 47.

1673.—"The Persians then call this stone **Pazahar**, being a compound of *Pa* and *Zahar*, the first of which is *against*, and the other is *Poyson*."—*Fryer*, 238.

,, "The Monkey **Bezoars** which are long, are the best. . . ."—*Ibid.* 212.

1711.—"In this animal (Hog-deer of Sumatra, apparently a sort of chevrotain or *Tragulus*) is found the bitter **Bezoar**, called *Pedra di Porco Siacca*, valued at ten times its Weight in Gold."—*Lockyer*, 49.

1826.—"What is spikenard? what is *mumiai*? what is **pahzer**? compared even to a twinkle of a royal eye-lash?"—*Hajji Baba*, ed. 1835, p. 148.

BHAT, s. H. &c. *bhāt* (Skt. *bhaṭṭa*, a title of respect, probably connected with *bhartri*, 'a supporter or master'), a man of a tribe of mixed descent, whose members are professed genealogists and poets; a bard. These men in Rājputāna and Guzerat had also extraordinary privileges as the guarantors of travellers, whom they accompanied, against attack and robbery. See an account of them in *Forbes's Rās Mālā*, I. ix. &c., reprint 558 *seqq.*; [for Bengal, *Risley*, *Tribes & Castes*, i. 101 *seqq.*; for the N.W.P., *Crooke*, *Tribes & Castes*, ii. 20 *seqq.*

[1554.—"**Bats**," see quotation under **RAJPUT**.]

c. 1555.—"Among the infidel Bānyāns in this country (Guzerat) there is a class of *literati* known as **Bāts**. These undertake to be guides to traders and other travellers . . . when the caravans are waylaid on the road by *Rāshbūts*, *i.e.* Indian horsemen, coming to pillage them, the *Bāt* takes out his dagger, points it at his own breast, and says: 'I have become surety! If aught befals the caravan I must kill myself!' On these words the Rāshbūts let the caravan pass unharmed."—*Sidi 'Ali*, 95.

[1623.—"Those who perform the office of Priests, whom they call **Boti**."—*P. della Valle*, Hak. Soc. i. 80.]

1775.—"The Hindoo rajahs and Mahratta chieftains have generally a **Bhaut** in the family, who attends them on public occasions . . . sounds their praise, and proclaims their titles in hyperbolical and figurative language . . . many of them have another mode of living; they offer themselves as security to the different governments for payment of their revenue, and the good behaviour of the Zemindars, patels, and public farmers; they also become guarantees for treaties between native princes, and the performance of bonds by individuals."—*Forbes*, *Or. Mem.* ii. 89; [2nd ed. i. 377; also see ii. 258]. See **TRAGA**.

1810.—"India, like the nations of Europe, had its minstrels and poets, concerning whom there is the following tradition: At the marriage of Siva and Parvatty, the immortals having exhausted all the amusements then known, wished for something new, when Siva, wiping the drops of sweat from his brow, shook them to earth, upon which the **Bawts**, or Bards, immediately sprang up."—*Maria Graham*, 169.

1828.—"A '**Bhat**' or Bard came to ask a gratuity."—*Heber*, ed. 1844, ii. 53.

BHEEL, n.p. Skt. *Bhilla*; H. *Bhīl*. The name of a race inhabiting the hills and forests of the Vindhya, Malwa, and of the N.-Western Deccan, and believed to have been the aborigines of Rājputāna; some have supposed them to be the Φυλλῖται of Ptolemy. They are closely allied to the **Coolies** (q. v.) of Guzerat, and are believed to belong to the *Kolarian* division of Indian aborigines. But no distinct Bhīl language survives.

1785.—"A most infernal yell suddenly issued from the deep ravines. Our guides informed us that this was the noise always made by the **Bheels** previous to an attack."—*Forbes, Or. Mem.* iii. 480.

1825.—"All the **Bheels** whom we saw to-day were small, slender men, less broad-shouldered . . . and with faces less Celtic than the Puharees of the Rajmahal. . . . Two of them had rude swords and shields, the remainder had all bows and arrows."—*Heber*, ed. 1844, ii. 75.

BHEEL, s. A word used in Bengal —*bhīl*: a marsh or lagoon; same as **Jeel** (q. v.)

[1860.—"The natives distinguish a lake so formed by a change in a river's course from one of usual origin or shape by calling the former a *bowr*—whilst the latter is termed a **Bheel**."—*Grant, Rural Life in Bengal*, 35.]

1879.—"Below Shouy-doung there used to be a big **bheel**, wherein I have shot a few duck, teal, and snipe."—*Pollok, Sport in B. Burmah*, i. 26.

BHEESTY, s. The universal word in the Anglo-Indian households of N. India for the domestic (corresponding to the *saḳḳā* of Egypt) who supplies the family with water, carrying it in a **mussuck**, (q.v.), or goatskin, slung on his back. The word is P. *bihishtī*, a person of *bihisht* or paradise, though the application appears to be peculiar to Hindustan. We have not been able to trace the history of this term, which does not apparently occur in the *Āīn*, even in the curious account of the way in which water was cooled and supplied in the Court of Akbar (*Blochmann*, tr. i. 55 *seqq.*), or in the old travellers, and is not given in Meninski's lexicon. Vullers gives it only as from Shakespear's Hindustani Dict. [The trade must be of ancient origin in India, as the leather bag is mentioned in the Veda and Manu (*Wilson, Rig Veda*, ii. 28; *Institutes*, ii. 79.) Hence Col. Temple (*Ind. Ant.*, xi. 117) suggests that the word is Indian, and connects it with the Skt. *vish*, 'to sprinkle.'] It is one of the fine titles which Indian servants rejoice to bestow on one another, like *Mehtar*, *Khalīfa*, &c. The title in this case has some justification. No class of men (as all Anglo-Indians will agree) is so diligent, so faithful, so unobtrusive, and uncomplaining as that of the *bihishtīs*. And often in battle they have shown their courage and fidelity in supplying water to the wounded in face of much personal danger.

[c. 1660.—"Even the menials and carriers of water belonging to that nation (the Pathāns) are high-spirited and war-like."—*Bernier*, ed. *Constable*, 207.]

1773.—"**Bheestee**, Waterman" (etc.)—*Fergusson, Dict. of the Hindostan Language*, &c.

1781.—"I have the happiness to inform you of the fall of Bijah Gurh on the 9th inst. with the loss of only 1 sepoy, 1 **beasty**, and a cossy (? **Cossid**) killed . . ."—Letter in *India Gazette* of Nov. 24th.

1782.—(Table of Wages in Calcutta),

Consummah	. . . .	10 Rs.
Kistmutdar	. . . .	6 ,,
Beasty	. . . .	5 ,,

India Gazette, Oct. 12.

Five Rupees continued to be the standard wage of a *bihishtī* for full 80 years after the date given.

1810.—". . . If he carries the water himself in the skin of a goat, prepared for that purpose, he then receives the designation of **Bheesty**."—*Williamson, V.M.* i. 229.

1829.—"Dressing in a hurry, find the drunken **bheesty** . . . has mistaken your boot for the goglet in which you carry your water on the line of march."—*Camp Miseries*, in *John Shipp*, ii. 149. N.B.—We never knew a drunken *bheesty*.

1878.—"Here comes a seal carrying a porpoise on its back. No! it is only our friend the **bheesty**."—*In my Indian Garden*, 79.

[1898

"Of all them black-faced crew,
The finest man I knew
Was our regimental **bhisti**, Ganga Din."
R. Kipling, Barrack-room Ballads, p. 23.]

BHIKTY, s. The usual Calcutta name for the fish *Lates calcarifer*. See **COCKUP**.

[**BHOOSA**, s. H. Mahr. *bhus, bhusa*; the husks and straw of various kinds of corn, beaten up into chaff by the feet of the oxen on the threshing-floor; used as the common food of cattle all over India.

[1829.—"Every commune is surrounded with a circumvallation of thorns . . . and the stacks of **bhoos**, or 'chaff,' which are placed at intervals, give it the appearance of a respectable fortification. These *bhoos* stacks are erected to provide provender for the cattle in scanty rainy seasons."—*Tod, Annals*, Calcutta reprint, i. 737.]

[**BHOOT**, s. H. &c., *bhūt, bhūta*, Skt. *bhūta*, 'formed, existent,' the common term for the multitudinous ghosts and demons of various kinds by whom the Indian peasant is so constantly beset.]

[1623.—"All confessing that it was **Buto**, *i.e.* the Devil."—*P. della Valle*, Hak. Soc. ii. 341.]

[1826.—"The sepoys started up, and cried '**B,hooh**, *b,hooh, arry arry*.' This cry of 'a ghost' reached the ears of the officer, who bid his men fire into the tree, and that would bring him down, if there."—*Pandurang Hari*, ed. 1873, i. 107.]

BHOUNSLA, n.p. Properly *Bhoslah* or *Bhonslah*, the surname of Sivaji, the founder of the Mahratta empire. It was also the surname of Parsoji and Raghuji, the founders of the Mahratta dynasty of Berar, though not of the same family as Sivaji.

1673.—"Seva Gi, derived from an Ancient Line of Rajahs, of the Cast of the **Bounceloes**, a Warlike and Active Offspring."—*Fryer*, 171.

c. 1730.—"At this time two *parganas*, named Púna and Súpa, became the *jagír* of Sáhú **Bhoslah**. Sívají became the manager. . . . He was distinguished in his tribe for courage and intelligence; and for craft and trickery he was reckoned a sharp son of the devil."—*Kháfī Khán*, in *Elliot*, vii. 257.

1780.—"It was at first a particular tribe governed by the family of **Bhosselah**, which has since lost the sovereignty."—*Seir Mutaqherin*, iii. 214.

1782.—". . . le **Bonzolo**, les Marates, et les Mogols."—*Sonnerat*, i. 60.

BHYACHARRA, s. H. *bhayāchārā*. This is a term applied to settlements made with the village as a community, the several claims and liabilities being regulated by established customs, or special traditional rights. Wilson interprets it as "fraternal establishments." [This hardly explains the tenure, at least as found in the N.W.P., and it would be difficult to do so without much detail. In its perhaps most common form each man's holding is the measure of his interest in the estate, irrespective of the share to which he may be entitled by ancestral right.]

BICHÁNA, s. Bedding of any kind. H. *bichhānā*.

1689.—"The Heat of the Day is spent in Rest and Sleeping . . . sometimes upon Cotts, and sometimes upon **Bechanahs**, which are thick Quilts."—*Ovington*, 313.

BIDREE, BIDRY, s. H. *Bidrī*; the name applied to a kind of ornamental metal-work, made in the Deccan, and deriving its name from the city of Bīdar (or Bedar), which was the chief place of manufacture. The work was, amongst natives, chiefly applied to hooka-bells, rose-water bottles and the like. The term has acquired vogue in England of late amongst amateurs of "art manufacture." The ground of the work is pewter alloyed with one-fourth copper: this is inlaid (or damascened) with patterns in silver; and then the pewter ground is blackened. A short description of the manufacture is given by Dr. G. Smith in the *Madras Lit. Soc. Journ.*, N.S. i. 81-84; [by Sir G. Birdwood, *Indust. Arts*, 163 *seqq.*; *Journ. Ind. Art*, i. 41 *seqq.*] The ware was first descrbed by B. Heyne in 1813.

BILABUNDY, s. H. *bilabandī*. An account of the revenue settlement of a district, specifying the name of each *mahal* (estate), the farmer of it, and the amount of the rent (*Wilson*). In the N.W.P. it usually means an arrangement for securing the payment of revenue (*Elliot*). C. P. Brown says, quoting Raikes (p. 109), that the word is *bila-bandī*, 'hole-stopping,' viz. stopping those vents through which the coin of the proprietor might ooze out. This, however, looks very like a 'striving after meaning,' and Wilson's suggestion that it is a corruption of *behrī-bandī*, from *behrī*, 'a share,' 'a quota,' is probably right.

[1858.—"This transfer of responsibility, from the landholder to his tenants, is called '*Jumog Lagána*,' or transfer of *jumma*. The assembly of the tenants, for the purpose of such adjustment, is called *zunjeer bundee*, or linking together. The adjustment thus made is called the **bilabundee**."—*Sleeman, Journey through Oudh*, i. 208.]

BILAYUT, BILLAÏT, &c. n.p. Europe. The word is properly Ar. *Wilāyat*, 'a kingdom, a province,' variously used with specific denotation, as the Afghans term their own country often by this name; and in India again it has come to be employed for distant Europe. In Sicily *Il Regno* is used for the interior of the island, as we use *Mofussil* in India. *Wilāyat* is the usual form in Bombay.

BILAYUTEE PAWNEE, BILÁTEE PANEE. The adject. *bilāyatī* or *wilāyatī* is applied specifically to a variety of exotic articles, *e.g.* *bilāyatī baingan* (see **BRINJAUL**), to the tomato, and most especially *bilāyatī pānī*, 'European water,' the usual name for soda-water in Anglo-India.

1885.—"'But look at us English,' I urged, 'we are ordered thousands of miles away from home, and we go without a murmur.' 'It is true, *Khudawund*,' said Gunga Pursad, 'but you *sahebs* drink **English-water** (soda-water), and the strength of it enables you to bear up under all fatigues and sorrows.' His idea (adds Mr. Knighton) was that the effervescing force of the soda-water, and the strength of it which drove out the cork so violently, gave strength to the drinker of it."—*Times of India Mail*, Aug. 11, 1885.

BILDÁR, s. H. from P. *beldār*, 'a spade-wielder,' an excavator or digging labourer. Term usual in the Public Works Department of Upper India for men employed in that way.

1847.—

"Ye Lyme is alle oute! Ye Masouns lounge aboute!
Ye **Beldars** have alle strucke, and are smoaking atte their Eese!
Ye Brickes are alle done! Ye Kyne are Skynne and Bone,
And ye Threasurour has bolted with xii thousand Rupeese!"

Ye Dreme of an Executive Engineere.

BILOOCH, BELOOCH, n.p. The name (*Balūch or Bilūch*) applied to the race inhabiting the regions west of the Lower Indus, and S.E. of Persia, called from them *Bilūchistān;* they were dominant in Sind till the English conquest in 1843. [Prof. Max Müller (*Lectures*, i. 97, note) identified the name with Skt. *mlechcha*, used in the sense of the Greek βάρβαρος for a despised foreigner.]

A.D. 643.—"In the year 32 H. 'Abdulla bin 'A'mar bin Rabi' invaded Kirmán and took the capital Kuwáshír, so that the aid of 'the men of Kúj and **Balúj**' was solicited in vain by the Kirmánis."—In *Elliot*, i. 417.

c. 1200.—"He gave with him from Kandahār and Lār, mighty **Balochis**, servants. . . with nobles of many castes, horses, elephants, men, carriages, charioteers, and chariots."—*The Poem of Chand Bardāi*, in *Ind. Ant.* i. 272.

c. 1211.—"In the desert of Khabis there was a body . . . of **Buluchís** who robbed on the highway. . . . These people came out and carried off all the presents and rarities in his possession."—*'Utbi*, in *Elliot*, ii. 193.

1556.—"We proceeded to Gwādir, a trading town. The people here are called **Balūj**; their prince was Malik Jalaluddīn, son of Malik Dīnār."—*Sidi 'Ali*, p. 73.

[c. 1590.—"This tract is inhabited by an important **Baloch** tribe called Kalmani."—*Āīn*, trans. *Jarret*, ii. 337.]

1613.—The **Boloches** are of Mahomet's Religion. They deale much in Camels, most of them robbers. . . ."—*N. Whittington*, in *Purchas*, i. 485.

1648.—"Among the Machumatists next to the Pattans are the **Blotias** of great strength" [? *Wilāyatī*].—*Van Twist*, 58.

1727.—"They were lodged in a *Caravanseray*, when the **Ballowches** came with about 300 to attack them; but they had a brave warm Reception, and left four Score of their Number dead on the Spot, without the loss of one *Dutch* Man."—*A. Hamilton*, i. 107.

1813.—*Milburn* calls them **Bloaches** (*Or. Com.* i. 145).

1844.—"Officers must not shoot Peacocks: if they do the **Belooches** will shoot officers —at least so they have threatened, and M.-G. Napier has not the slightest doubt but that they will keep their word. There are no wild peacocks in Scinde,—they are all private property and sacred birds, and no man has any right whatever to shoot them."—*Gen. Orders* by *Sir C. Napier*.

BINKY-NABOB, s. This title occurs in documents regarding Hyder and Tippoo, *e.g.* in Gen. Stewart's desp. of 8th March 1799: "Mohammed Rezza, the Binky Nabob." [Also see *Wilks*, *Mysoor*, Madras reprint, ii. 346.] It is properly *benkī-nawāb*, from Canarese *benkī*, 'fire,' and means the Commandant of the Artillery.

BIRD OF PARADISE. The name given to various beautiful birds of the family *Paradiseidae*, of which many species are now known, inhabiting N. Guinea and the smaller islands adjoining it. The largest species was called by Linnæus *Paradisaea apoda*, in allusion to the fable that these birds had no feet (the dried skins brought for sale to the Moluccas having usually none attached to them). The name *Manucode* which Buffon adopted for these birds occurs in the form *Manucodiata* in some of the following quotations. It is a corruption of the Javanese name *Manuk-devata*, 'the Bird of the Gods,' which our popular term renders with sufficient accuracy. [The Siamese word for 'bird,' according to Mr. Skeat, is *nok*, perhaps from *manok*.]

c. 1430.—"In majori Java avis præcipua reperitur sine pedibus, instar palumbi, pluma levi, cauda oblonga, semper in arboribus quiescens: caro non editur, pellis et cauda habentur pretiosiores, quibus pro ornamento capitis utuntur."—*N. Conti*, in *Poggius de Varietate Fortunae*, lib. iv.

1552.—"The Kings of the said (Moluccas) began only a few years ago to believe in the immortality of souls, taught by no other argument than this, that they had seen a most beautiful little bird, which never alighted on the ground or on any other terrestrial object, but which they had sometimes seen to come from the sky, that is to say, when it was dead and fell to the ground. And the Machometan traders who traffic in those islands assured them that this little bird was **a native of Paradise**, and that *Paradise* was the place where the souls of the dead are; and on this account the princes attached themselves to the sect of the Machometans, because it promised them many marvellous things regarding this place of souls. This little bird they called by the name of *Manucodiata*. . . ."—Letter of *Maximilian of Transylvania*, Sec. to the Emp. Charles V., in *Ramusio*, i. f. 351*v*; see also f. 352.

c. 1524.—"He also (the K. of Bachian) gave us for the King of Spain two most beautiful dead birds. These birds are as large as thrushes; they have small heads, long beaks, legs slender like a writing pen, and a span in length; they have no wings, but instead of them long feathers of different colours, like plumes; their tail is like that of the thrush. All the feathers, except those of the wings (?), are of a dark colour; they never fly except when the wind blows. They told us that these **birds** *come from the terrestrial* **Paradise**, and they call them '*bolon dinata*,' [*burung-dewata*, same as Javanese *Manuk-dewata, supra*] that is, divine birds."—*Pigafetta*, Hak. Soc. 143.

1598.—". . . in these Ilands (Moluccas) onlie is found the bird, which the Portingales call *Passaros de Sol*, that is Foule of the Sunne, the Italians call it *Manu codiatas*, and the Latinists *Paradiseas*, by us called **Paradice birdes**, for ye beauty of their feathers which passe al other birds: these birds are never seene alive, but being dead they are found vpon the Iland; they flie, as it is said, alwaies into the Sunne, and keepe themselues continually in the ayre . . . for they haue neither feet nor wings, but onely head and bodie, and the most part tayle. . . ."—*Linschoten*, 35; [Hak. Soc. i. 118].

1572.—

"Olha cá pelos mares do Oriente
As infinitas ilhas espalhadas
* * * * * * *
Aqui as aureas aves, que não decem
Nunca á terra, e só mortas aparecem."
Camões, x. 132.

Eng-shed by Burton:

"Here see o'er oriental seas bespread
infinite island-groups and alwhere strewed * * * *
here dwell the golden fowls, whose home is air,
and never earthward save in death may fare."

1645.—". . . the male and female *Manucodiatae*, the male having a hollow in the back, in which 'tis reported the female both layes and hatches her eggs."—*Evelyn's Diary*, 4th Feb.

1674.—

"The strangest long-wing'd hawk that flies,
That like a **Bird of Paradise**,
Or herald's martlet, has no legs . . . ."
Hudibras, Pt. ii. cant. 3.

1591.—"As for the story of the *Manucodiata* or **Bird of Paradise**, which in the former Age was generally received and accepted for true, even by the Learned, it is now discovered to be a fable, and rejected and exploded by all men" (*i.e.* that it has no feet).—*Ray*, *Wisdom of God Manifested in the Works of the Creation*, ed. 1692, Pt. ii. 147.

1705.—"The **Birds of Paradice** are about the bigness of a Pidgeon. They are of varying Colours, and are never found or seen alive; neither is it known from whence they come . . . ."—*Funnel*, in *Dampier's Voyages*, iii. 266-7.

1868.—"When seen in this attitude, the **Bird of Paradise** really deserves its name, and must be ranked as one of the most beautiful and wonderful of living things."—*Wallace, Malay Archip.*, 7th ed., 464.

BIRDS' NESTS. The famous edible nests, formed with mucus, by certain swiftlets, *Collocalia nidifica*, and *C. linchi*. Both have long been known on the eastern coasts of the B. of Bengal, in the Malay Islands [and, according to Mr. Skeat in the islands of the Inland Sea (*Tale Sap*) at Singora]. The former is also now known to visit Darjeeling, the Assam Hills, the Western Ghats, &c., and to breed on the islets off Malabar and the Concan.

BISCOBRA, s. H. *biskhoprā* or *biskhaprā*. The name popularly applied to a large lizard alleged, and commonly believed, to be mortally venomous. It is very doubtful whether there is any real lizard to which this name applies, and it may be taken as certain that there is none in India with the qualities attributed. It is probable that the name does carry to many the terrific character which the ingenious author of *Tribes on My Frontier* alleges. But the name has nothing to do with either *bis* in the sense of 'twice,' or *cobra* in that of 'snake.' The first element is no doubt **bish,** (q.v.) 'poison,' and the second is probably *khoprā*, 'a shell or skull.' [See *J. L. Kipling, Beast and Man in India* (p. 317), who gives the scientific name as *varanus dracaena*, and says that the name *biscobra* is sometimes applied to the lizard generally known as the *ghorpad*, for which see **GUANA.**]

1883.—"But of all the things on earth that bite or sting, the palm belongs to the **biscobra**, a creature whose very name seems to indicate that it is twice as bad as the cobra. Though known by the terror of its name to natives and Europeans alike, it has never been described in the Proceedings of any learned Society, nor has it yet received a scientific name. . . . The awful deadliness of its bite admits of no question, being supported by countless authentic instances. . . The points on which evidence is required are—first, whether there is any such animal; second, whether, if it does exist, it is a snake with legs, or a lizard without them."—*Tribes on my Frontier*, p. 205.

BISH, BIKH, &c., n. H. from Skt. *visha*, 'poison.' The word has several specific applications, as **(a)** to the poison of various species of aconite, particularly *Aconitum ferox*, otherwise more specifically called in Skt. *vatsanābha*, 'calf's navel,' corrupted into *bachnābh* or *bachnāg*, &c. But it is also applied **(b)** in the Himālaya to the effect of the rarefied atmosphere at great heights on the body, an effect which there and over Central Asia is attributed to poisonous emanations from the soil, or from plants; a doctrine somewhat naïvely accepted by Huc in his famous narrative. The Central Asiatic (Turki) expression for this is *Esh*, 'smell.'

a.—

1554.—"Entre les singularités que le consul de Florentins me monstra, me feist gouster vne racine que les Arabes nomment *Bisch*: laquelle me causa si grande chaleur en la bouche, qui me dura deux iours, qu'il me sembloit y auoir du feu. . . . Elle est bien petite comme vn petit naueau: les autres (*auteurs?*) l'ont nommée *Napellus* . . ."—*Pierre Belon, Observations, &c.*, f. 97.

b.—

1624.—Antonio Andrada in his journey across the Himālaya, speaking of the sufferings of travellers from **the poisonous emanations.**—See *Ritter, Asien.*, iii. 444.

1661-2.—"Est autem Langur mons omnium altissimus, ita ut in summitate ejus viatores vix respirare ob aëris subtilitatim queant: neque is ob **virulentas** nonnullarum **herbarum exhalationes** aestivo tempore, sine manifesto vitae periculo transire possit."—*PP. Dorville and Grueber*, in *Kircher, China Illustrata*, 65. It is curious to see these intelligent Jesuits recognise the true cause, but accept the fancy of their guides as an additional one!

(?) "La partie supérieure de cette montagne est remplie **d'exhalaisons pestilentielles.**"—*Chinese Itinerary to Hlassa*, in *Klaproth, Magasin Asiatique*, ii. 112.

1812.—"Here begins the **Esh**—this is a Turkish word signifying Smell . . . it implies something the odour of which induces indisposition; far from hence the breathing of horse and man, and especially of the former, becomes affected."—*Mir Izzet Ullah*, in *J. R. As. Soc.* i. 283.

1815.—"Many of the coolies, and several of the Mewattee and Ghoorkha sepoys and chuprasees now lagged, and every one complained of the **bis** or poisoned wind. I now suspected that the supposed poison was nothing more than the effect of the rarefaction of the atmosphere from our great elevation."—*Fraser, Journal of a Tour, &c.*, 1820, p. 442.

1819.—"The difficulty of breathing which at an earlier date Andrada, and more recently Moorcroft had experienced in this region, was confirmed by Webb; the Butias themselves felt it, and call it **bis ki huwa**, *i.e.* poisonous air; even horses and yaks . . . suffer from it."—*Webb's Narrative*, quoted in *Ritter, Asien.*, ii. 532, 649.

1845.—"Nous arrivâmes à neuf heures au pied du Bourhan-Bota. La caravane s'arrêta un instant . . . on se montrait avec anxiété un gaz subtil et léger, qu'on nommait **vapeur pestilentielle,** et tout le monde paraissait abattu et découragé . . . Bientot les chevaux se refusent à porter leurs cavaliers, et chacun avance à pied et à petits pas . . . tous les visages blémissent, on sent le cœur s'affadir, et les jambes ne pouvent plus fonctionner . . . Une partie de la troupe, par mesure de prudence s'arrêta . . . le reste par prudence aussi épuisa tous les efforts pour arriver jusqu'au bout, et ne pas mourir asphyxié au milieu de cet air chargé d'acide carbonique," &c., *Huc et Gabet*, ii. 211: [E. T., ii. 114].

[BISMILLAH, intj., lit. "In the name of God"; a pious ejaculation used by Mahommedans at the commencement of any undertaking. The ordinary form runs—*Bi-'smi 'llāhi 'r-raḥmāni 'r-raḥīm*, *i.e.* "In the name of God, the Compassionate, the Merciful," is of Jewish origin, and is used at the commencement of meals, putting on new clothes, beginning any new work, &c. In the second form, used at the time of going into battle or slaughtering animals, the allusion to the attribute of mercy is omitted.

[1535.—"As they were killed after the Portuguese manner without the **bysmela**, which they did not say over them."—*Correa*, iii. 746.]

BISNAGAR, BISNAGA, BEEJANUGGER, n.p. These and other forms stand for the name of the ancient city which was the capital of the most important Hindu kingdom that existed in the peninsula of India, during the later Middle Ages, ruled by the *Rāya* dynasty. The place is now known as *Humpy* (*Hampī*), and is entirely in ruins. [The modern name is corrupted from *Pampa*, that of the river near which it stood. (*Rice*, *Mysore*, ii. 487.)] It stands on the S. of the Tungabhadra R., 36 m. to the N.W. of Bellary. The name is a corruption of *Vijayanagara* (City of Victory), or *Vidyanagara* (City of learning), [the latter and earlier name being changed into the former (*Rice*, *Ibid.* i. 342, note).] Others believe that the latter name was applied only since the place, in the 13th century, became the seat of a great revival of Hinduism, under the famous Sayana Mādhava, who wrote commentaries on the Vedas, and much besides. Both the city and the kingdom were commonly called by the early Portuguese **Narsinga** (q.v.), from *Narasimha* (c. 1490-1508), who was king at the time of their first arrival. [Rice gives his dates as 1488-1508.]

c. 1420.—"Profectus hinc est procul a mari milliaribus trecentis, ad civitatem ingentem, nomine **Bizenegaliam**, ambitu milliarum sexaginta, circa praeruptos montes sitam."—*Conti*, in *Poggius de Var. Fortunae*, iv.

1442.—". . . the chances of a maritime voyage had led Abd-er-razzak, the author of this work, to the city of **Bidjanagar**. He saw a place extremely large and thickly peopled, and a King possessing greatness and sovereignty to the highest degree, whose dominion extends from the frontier of Serendib to the extremity of the county of Kalbergah—from the frontiers of Bengal to the environs of Malabar."—*Abdurrazzāk*, in *India in XV. Cent.*, 22.

c. 1470.—"The Hindu sultan Kadam is a very powerful prince. He possesses a numerous army, and resides on a mountain at **Bichenegher**."—*Athan. Nikitin*, in *India in XV. Cent.*, 29.

1516.—"45 leagues from these mountains inland, there is a very great city, which is called **Bijanagher**. . . ."—*Barbosa*, 85.

1611.—"Le Roy de **Bisnagar**, qu'on appelle aussi quelquefois le Roy de Narzinga, est puissant."—*Wytfliet*, *H. des Indes*, ii. 64.

BISON, s. The popular name, among Southern Anglo-Indian sportsmen, of the great wild-ox called in Bengal *gaur* and *gavial* (*Gavaeus gaurus*, Jerdon); [*Bos gaurus*, Blanford]. It inhabits sparsely all the large forests of India, from near Cape Comorin to the foot of the Himālayas (at least in their Eastern portion), and from Malabar to Tenasserim.

1881.—"Once an unfortunate native superintendent or *mistari* [**Maistry**] was pounded to death by a savage and solitary **bison**."—*Saty. Review*, Sept. 10, p. 335.

BLACAN-MATEE, n.p. This is the name of an island adjoining Singapore, which forms the beautiful 'New Harbour' of that port; Malay *bĕlākang*, or *blakang-māti*, lit. 'Dead-Back island,' [of which, writes Mr. Skeat, no satisfactory explanation has been given. According to Dennys (*Discr. Dict.*, 51), "one explanation is that the Southern, or as regards Singapore, hinder, face was so unhealthy that the Malays gave it a designation signifying by *onomatopoea* that death was to be found behind its ridge"]. The island (*Blacan-mati*) appears in one of the charts of Godinho de Eredia (1613) published in his *Malaca*, &c. (Brussels, 1882), and though, from the excessive looseness of such old charts, the island seems too far from Singapore, we are satisfied after careful comparison with the modern charts that the island now so-called is intended.

BLACK, s. Adj. and substantive denoting natives of India. Old-fashioned, and heard, if still heard, only from the lower class of Europeans; even in the last generation its habitual use was chiefly confined to these, and to old officers of the Queen's Army.

[1614.—"The 5th ditto came in a ship from Mollacco with 28 Portugals and 36 **Blacks**."—*Foster*, *Letters*, ii. 31.]

1676.—"We do not approve of your sending any persons to St. Helena against their wills. One of them you sent there makes a great complaint, and we have ordered his liberty to return again if he desires it; for we know not what effect it may have if complaints should be made to the King that we send away the natives; besides that it is against our inclination to buy any **blacks**, and to transport them from their wives and children without their own consent."—*Court's Letter to Ft. St. Geo.*, in *Notes and Exts.* No. i. p. 12.

1747.—"Vencatachlam, the Commanding Officer of the Black Military, having behaved very commendably on several occasions against the French; In consideration thereof *Agreed* that a Present be made him of Six hundred Rupees to buy a Horse, that it may encourage him to act in like manner."—*Ft. St. David Cons.*, Feb. 6. (MS. Record, in India Office).

1750.—"Having received information that some **Blacks** residing in this town were dealing with the French for goods proper for the Europe market, we told them if we found any proof against any residing under your Honors' protection, that such should suffer our utmost displeasure."—*Ft. Wm. Cons.*, Feb. 4, in *Long*, 24.

1753.—"John Wood, a free merchant, applies for a pass which, if refused him, he says 'it will reduce a free merchant to the condition of a foreigner, or indeed of the meanest **black** fellow.'"—*Ft. Wm. Cons.*, in *Long*, p. 41.

1761.—"You will also receive several private letters from Hastings and Sykes, which must convince me as Circumstances did me at the time, that the Dutch forces were not sent with a View only of defending their own Settlements, but absolutely with a Design of disputing our Influence and Possessions; certain Ruin must have been the Consequence to the East India Company. They were raising **black** Forces at Patna, Cossimbazar, Chinsura, &c., and were working Night and day to compleat a Field Artillery . . . all these preparations previous to the commencement of Hostilities plainly prove the Dutch meant to act offensively not defensively."—*Holograph Letter from Clive* (unpublished) *in the* India Office Records. *Dated* Berkeley Square, and *indorsed* "27th Decr. 1761."

1762.—"The **Black** inhabitants send in a petition setting forth the great hardship they labour under in being required to sit as arbitrators in the Court of Cutcherry."—*Ft. Wm. Cons.*, in *Long*, 277.

1782.—See quotation under **Sepoy**, from *Price*.

" "... the 35th Regiment, commanded by Major Popham, which had lately behaved in a mutinous manner . . . was broke with infamy. . . . The **black** officers with halters about their necks, and the sepoys stript of their coats and turbands were drummed out of the Cantonments."—*India Gazette*, March 30.

1787.—"As to yesterday's particular charge, the thing that has made me most inveterate and unrelenting in it is only that it related to cruelty or oppression inflicted on two **black** ladies. . . ."—*Lord Minto*, in *Life, &c.*, i. 128.

1789.—"I have just learned from a Friend at the India House, y[t] the object of Treves' ambition at present is to be appointed to the *Adaulet* of Benares, w[h] is now held by a **Black** named Alii Caun. Understanding that most of the *Adaulets* are now held by Europeans, and as I am informed y[t] it is the intention y[t] the Europeans are to be so placed in future, I s[hd] be vastly happy if without committing any injustice you c[d] place young Treves in y[t] situation."—*George P. of Wales*, to Lord Cornwallis, in *C.'s Corresp.* ii. 29.

1832-3.—"And be it further enacted that . . . in all captures which shall be made by H. M.'s Army, Royal Artillery, provincial, **black**, or other troops. . . ."—*Act* 2 & 3 Will. IV., ch. 53, sec. 2.

The phrase is in use among natives, we know not whether originating with them, or adopted from the usage of the foreigner. But *Kālā ādmī* '**black man**,' is often used by them in speaking to Europeans of other natives. A case in point is perhaps worth recording. A statue of Lord William Bentinck, on foot, and in bronze, stands in front of the Calcutta Town Hall. Many years ago a native officer, returning from duty at Calcutta to Barrackpore, where his regiment was, reported himself to his adjutant (from whom we had the story in later days). 'Anything new, Sūbadār, Sāhib?' said the Adjutant. 'Yes,' said the Sūbadār, 'there is a figure of the former Lord Sahib arrived.' 'And what do you think of it?' '*Sāhib*,' said the Sūbadār, '*abhi hai* kālā ādmī *kā sā, jab potā ho jaegā jab achchhā hogā!*' ('It is now just like a native—'a **black man**'); when the whitewash is applied it will be excellent.'

In some few phrases the term has become crystallised and semi-official. Thus the native dressers in a hospital were, and possibly still are, called **Black Doctors.**

1787.—"The Surgeon's assistant and **Black Doctor** take their station 100 paces in the rear, or in any place of security to which the Doolies may readily carry the wounded."—*Regulations for the H. C.'s Troops on the Coast of Coromandel.*

In the following the meaning is special:

1788.—"*For Sale.* That small upper-roomed Garden House, with about 5 biggahs (see **BEEGAH**) of ground, on the road leading from Cheringhee to the Burying Ground, which formerly belonged to the

Moravians; it is very private, from the number of trees on the ground, and having lately received considerable additions and repairs, is well adapted for a **Black** *Family.* ☞ Apply to Mr. Camac."—*In Seton-Karr*, i. 282.

BLACK ACT. This was the name given in odium by the non-official Europeans in India to Act XI., 1836, of the Indian Legislature, which laid down that no person should by reason of his place of birth or of his descent be, in any civil proceeding, excepted from the jurisdiction of the Courts named, viz.: Sudder Dewanny Adawlut, Zillah and City Judge's Courts, Principal Sudder Ameens, Sudder Ameens, and Moonsiff's Court, or, in other words, it placed European subjects on a level with natives as to their subjection in civil causes to all the Company's Courts, including those under Native Judges. This Act was drafted by T. B. Macaulay, then Legislative Member of the Governor-General's Council, and brought great abuse on his head. Recent agitation caused by the "Ilbert Bill," proposing to make Europeans subject to native magistrates in regard to police and criminal charges, has been, by advocates of the latter measure, put on all fours with the agitation of 1836. But there is much that discriminates the two cases.

1876.—"The motive of the scurrility with which Macaulay was assailed by a handful of sorry scribblers was his advocacy of the Act, familiarly known as the **Black Act**, which withdrew from British subjects resident in the provinces their so called privilege of bringing civil appeals before the Supreme Court at Calcutta."—*Trevelyan's Life of Macaulay*, 2nd ed., i. 398.

[**BLACK BEER**, s. A beverage mentioned by early travellers in Japan. It was probably not a malt liquor. Dr. Aston suggests that it was *kuro-hi*, a dark-coloured *saké* used in the service of the Shinto gods.

[1616.—"One jar of **black beer**."—*Foster, Letters*, iv. 270.]

BLACK-BUCK, s. The ordinary name of the male antelope (*Antilope bezoartica*, Jerdon) [*A. cervicapra*, Blanford], from the dark hue of its back, by no means however literally black.

1690.—"The *Indians* remark, *'tis* September's *Sun which caused the black lines on the Antelopes' Backs*."—*Ovington*, 139.

BLACK COTTON SOIL. — (See **REGUR**.)

[**BLACK JEWS**, a term applied to the Jews of S. India; see 2 ser. *N. & Q.*, iv. 4. 429; viii. 232, 418, 521; *Logan, Malabar*, i. 246 *seqq*.]

BLACK LANGUAGE. An old-fashioned expression, for Hindustani and other vernaculars, which used to be common among officers and men of the Royal Army, but was almost confined to them.

BLACK PARTRIDGE, s. The popular Indian name of the common francolin of S.E. Europe and Western Asia (*Francolinus vulgaris*, Stephens), notable for its harsh quasi-articulate call, interpreted in various parts of the world into very different syllables. The rhythm of the call is fairly represented by two of the imitations which come nearest one another, viz. that given by Sultan Baber (Persian): '*Shīr dāram, shakrak*' ('I've got milk and sugar'!) and (Hind.) one given by Jerdon: '*Lahsan piyāz adrak*' ('Garlic, onion, and ginger'!) A more pious one is: *Khudā terī ḳudrat*, 'God is thy strength!' Another mentioned by Capt. Baldwin is very like the truth: 'Be quick, pay your debts!' But perhaps the Greek interpretation recorded by Athenaeus (ix. 39) is best of all: τρὶς τοῖς κακούργοις κακά 'Three-fold ills to the ill-doers!' see *Marco Polo*, Bk. i. ch. xviii. and note 1; [*Burton, Ar. Nights*, iii. 234, iv. 17].

BLACK TOWN, n.p. Still the popular name of the native city of Madras, as distinguished from the Fort and southern suburbs occupied by the English residents, and the bazars which supply their wants. The term is also used at Bombay.

1673.—Fryer calls the native town of Madras "the Heathen Town," and "the Indian Town."

1727.—"The **Black Town** (of Madras) is inhabited by *Gentows*, *Mahometans*, and *Indian Christians*. . . . It was walled in towards the Land, when Governor *Pit* ruled it."—*A. Hamilton*, i. 367.

1780.—"Adjoining the glacis of Fort St. George, to the northward, is a large town commonly called the **Black Town**, and which is fortified sufficiently to prevent any surprise by a body of horse."—*Hodges*, p. 6.

1780.—". . . Cadets upon their arrival in the country, many of whom . . . are obliged to take up their residence in dirty punch-houses in the **Black Town**. . ."—*Munro's Narrative*, 22.

1782.—"When Mr. Hastings came to the government he added some new regulations . . . divided the **black** and white **town** (Calcutta) into 35 wards, and purchased the consent of the natives to go a little further off."—*Price, Some Observations, &c.*, p. 60. In *Tracts*, vol. i.

[1813.—"The large bazar, or the street in the **Black Town**, (Bombay) . . . contained many good Asiatic houses."—*Forbes, Or. Mem.*, 2nd ed., i. 96. Also see quotation (1809) under **BOMBAY**.]

1827.—"Hartley hastened from the **Black Town**, more satisfied than before that some deceit was about to be practised towards Menie Gray."—*Walter Scott, The Surgeon's Daughter*, ch. xi.

BLACK WOOD. The popular name for what is in England termed 'rose-wood'; produced chiefly by several species of *Dalbergia*, and from which the celebrated carved furniture of Bombay is made. [The same name is applied to the Chinese ebony used in carving (*Ball, Things Chinese*, 3rd ed., 107).] (See **SISSOO**.)

[1615.—"Her lading is **Black Wood**, I think ebony."—*Cocks's Diary*, Hak. Soc. i. 35.

[1813.—"**Black wood** furniture becomes like heated metal."—*Forbes, Or. Mem.*, 2nd ed., i. 106.]

1879.—(In Babylonia). "In a mound to the south of the mass of city ruins called Jum-juma, Mr. Rassam discovered the remains of a rich hall or palace . . . the cornices were of painted brick, and the roof of rich Indian **blackwood**."—*Athenaeum*, July 5, 22.

BLANKS, s. The word is used for 'whites' or 'Europeans' (Port. *branco*) in the following, but we know not if anywhere else in English:

1718.—"The Heathens . . . too shy to venture into the Churches of the **Blanks** (so they call the Christians), since these were generally adorned with fine cloaths and all manner of proud apparel."—(*Ziegenbalg and Plutscho*), *Propagation of the Gospel, &c.* Pt. I., 3rd ed., p. 70.

[**BLATTY**, adj. A corr. of *wilāyatī*, 'foreign' (see **BILAYUT**). A name applied to two plants in S. India, the *Sonneratia acida*, and *Hydrolea zeylanica* (see *Mad. Admin. Man. Gloss.* s. v.). In the old records it is applied to a kind of cloth. Owen (*Narrative*, i. 349) uses **Blat** as a name for the land-wind in Arabia, of which the origin is perhaps the same.

[1610.—"**Blatty**, the corge Rs. 060."—*Danvers, Letters*, i. 72.]

BLIMBEE, s. Malayāl. *vilimbi*; H. *belambū* [or *bilambū*;] Malay. *bălimbing* or *belimbing*. The fruit of *Averrhoa bilimbi*, L. The genus was so called by Linnæus in honour of Averrhoes, the Arab commentator on Aristotle and Avicenna. It embraces two species cultivated in India for their fruits; neither known in a wild state. See for the other **CARAMBOLA**.

BLOOD-SUCKER, s. A harmless lizard (*Lacerta cristata*) is so called, because when excited it changes in colour (especially about the neck) from a dirty yellow or grey, to a dark red.

1810.—"On the morn, however, I discovered it to be a large lizard, termed a **blood-sucker**."—*Morton's Life of Leyden*, 110.

[1813.—"The large seroor, or lacerta, commonly called the **bloodsucker**."—*Forbes, Or. Mem.* i. 110 (2nd ed.).]

BOBACHEE, s. A cook (male). This is an Anglo-Indian vulgarisation of *bāwarchī*, a term originally brought, according to Hammer, by the hordes of Chingiz Khan into Western Asia. At the Mongol Court the *Bāwarchī* was a high dignitary, 'Lord Sewer' or the like (see *Hammer's Golden Horde*, 235, 461). The late Prof. A. Schiefner, however, stated to us that he could not trace a Mongol origin for the word, which appears to be Or. Turki. [Platts derives it from P. *bāwar*, 'confidence.']

c. 1333.—"Chaque émir a un **bâwerdjy**, et lorsque la table a éte dressée, cet officier s'assied devant son maître . . . le *bâwerdjy* coupe la viande en petits morceaux. Ces gens-là possèdent une grande habileté pour dépecer la viande."—*Ibn Batuta*, ii. 407.

c. 1590.—**Bāwarchī** is the word used for cook in the original of the *Āīn* (*Blochmann's* Eng. Tr. i. 58).

1810.—". . . the dripping . . . is returned to the meat by a bunch of feathers . . . tied to the end of a short stick. This little neat, *cleanly*, and cheap dripping-ladle, answers admirably; it being in the power of the **babachy** to baste any part with great precision."—*Williamson, V. M.* i. 238.

1866.—

"And every night and morning
The **bobachee** shall kill
The sempiternal *moorghee*,
And we'll all have a grill."

The Dawk Bungalow, 223.

BOBACHEE CONNAH, s. H. *Bāwarchī-khāna*, 'Cook-house,' *i.e.* Kitchen; generally in a cottage detached from the residence of a European household.

[1829.—"In defiance of all **Bawurchee-khana** rules and regulations."—*Or. Sport Mag.*, i. 118.]

BOBBERY, s. For the origin see **BOBBERY-BOB**. A noise, a disturbance, a row.

[1710.—"And beat with their hand on the mouth, making a certain noise, which we Portuguese call **babare**. **Babare** is a word composed of *baba*, 'a child' and *are*, an adverb implying 'to call.'"—*Oriente Conquistado*, vol ii.; *Conquista*, i. div. i. sec. 8.]

1830.—"When the band struck up (my Arab) was much frightened, made **bobbery**, set his foot in a hole and nearly pitched me."—*Mem. of Col. Mountain*, 2nd ed., 106.

1866.—"But what is the meaning of all this **bobbery**?"—*The Dawk Bungalow*, p. 387.

Bobbery is used in 'pigeon English,' and of course a Chinese origin is found for it, viz. *pa-pi*, Cantonese, 'a noise.' [The idea that there is a similar English word (see 7 ser. *N. & Q.*, v. 205, 271, 338, 415, 513) is rejected by the *N.E.D.*]

BOBBERY-BOB! interj. The Anglo-Indian colloquial representation of a common exclamation of Hindus when in surprise or grief—'**Bāp-rē!** or **Bap-rē Bāp**,' 'O Father!' (we have known a friend from north of Tweed whose ordinary interjection was 'My great-grandmother!'). Blumenroth's *Philippine Vocabulary* gives *Nacú!* = *Madre mia*, as a vulgar exclamation of admiration.

1782.—"Captain Cowe being again examined . . . if he had any opportunity to make any observations concerning the execution of Nundcomar? said, he had; that he saw the whole except the immediate act of execution . . . there were 8 or 10,000 people assembled; who at the moment the Rajah was turned off, dispersed suddenly, crying '**Ah-bauparee!**' leaving nobody about the gallows but the Sheriff and his attendants, and a few European spectators. He explains the term **Ah-baup-aree**, to be an exclamation of the black people, upon the appearance of anything very alarming, and when they are in great pain."—*Price's* 2nd *Letter to E. Burke*, p. 5. In *Tracts*, vol. ii.

„ "If an Hindoo was to see a house on fire, to receive a smart slap on the face, break a china basin, cut his finger, see two Europeans boxing, or a sparrow shot, he would call out **Ah-baup-aree!**"—From *Report of Select Committee of H. of C., Ibid.* pp. 9-10.

1834.—"They both hastened to the spot, where the man lay senseless, and the syce by his side muttering **Bāpre bāpre**."—*The Baboo*, i. 48.

1863-64.—"My men soon became aware of the unwelcome visitor, and raised the cry, 'A bear, a bear!'

"**Ahi! bap-re-bap!** Oh, my father! go and drive him away,' said a timorous voice from under a blanket close by."—*Lt.-Col. Lewin, A Fly on the Wheel*, 142.

BOBBERY-PACK, s. A pack of hounds of different breeds, or (oftener) of no breed at all, wherewith young officers hunt jackals or the like; presumably so called from the noise and disturbance that such a pack are apt to raise. And hence a 'scratch pack' of any kind, as a 'scratch match' at cricket, &c. (See a quotation under **BUNOW**.)

1878.—" . . . on the mornings when the '**bobbera**' **pack** went out, of which Macpherson was 'master,' and I 'whip,' we used to be up by 4 A.M."—*Life in the Mofussil*, i. 142.

The following occurs in a letter received from an old Indian by one of the authors, some years ago:

"What a Cabinet —— has put together! —a regular **bobbery-pack**."

BOCCA TIGRIS, n.p. The name applied to the estuary of the Canton River. It appears to be an inaccurate reproduction of the Portuguese *Boca do Tigre*, and that to be a rendering of the Chinese name *Hu-mēn*, "Tiger Gate." Hence in the second quotation *Tigris* is supposed to be the name of the river.

1747.—"At 8 o'clock we passed the **Bog of Tygers**, and at noon the Lyon's Tower."—*A Voy. to the E. Indies in* 1747 *and* 1748.

1770.—"The City of Canton is situated on the banks of the **Tigris**, a large river. . . ."—*Raynal* (tr. 1771), ii. 258.

1782.—". . . . à sept lieues de la **bouche du Tigre**, on apperçoit la Tour du Lion."—*Sonnerat, Voyage*, ii. 234.

[1900.—"The launch was taken up the Canton River and abandoned near the **Bocca Tigris** (the Bogue)."—*The Times*, 29 Oct.]

BOCHA, s. H. *bochā*. A kind of chair-palankin formerly in use in Bengal, but now quite forgotten.

1810.—"Ladies are usually conveyed about Calcutta . . . in a kind of palanquin called a **bochah** . . . being a compound of our sedan chair with the body of a chariot. . . . I should have observed that most of the gentlemen residing at Calcutta ride in **bochahs**."—*Williamson, V. M.* i. 322.

BOGUE, n.p. This name is applied by seamen to the narrows at the mouth of the Canton River, and is a corruption of *Boca*. (See **BOCCA TIGRIS**.)

BOLIAH, BAULEAH, s. Beng. *bāūlīa*. A kind of light accommodation boat with a cabin, in use on the Bengal rivers. We do not find the word in any of the dictionaries. Ives, in the middle of the 18th century, describes it as a boat very long, but so narrow that only one man could sit in the breadth, though it carried a multitude of rowers. This is not the character of the boat so called now. [Buchanan Hamilton, writing about 1820, says: "The **bhauliya** is intended for the same purpose, [conveyance of passengers], and is about the same size as the *Pansi* (see **PAUNCHWAY**). It is sharp at both ends, rises at the ends less than the *Pansi*, and its tilt is placed in the middle, the rowers standing both before and behind the place of accommodation of passengers. On the Kosi, the *Bhauliya* is a large fishing-boat, carrying six or seven men." (*Eastern India*, iii. 345.) Grant (*Rural Life*, p. 5) gives a drawing and description of the modern boat.]

1757.—"To get two **bolias**, a Goordore, and 87 dandies from the Nazir."—*Ives*, 157.

1810.—"On one side the picturesque boats of the natives, with their floating huts; on the other the **bolios** and pleasure-boats of the English."—*Maria Graham*, 142.

1811.—"The extreme lightness of its construction gave it incredible . . . . speed. An example is cited of a Governor General who in his **Bawaleea** performed in 8 days the voyage from Lucknow to Calcutta, a distance of 400 marine leagues."—*Solvyns*, iii. The drawing represents a very light skiff, with only a small kiosque at the stern.

1824.—"We found two **Bholiahs**, or large row-boats, with convenient cabins. . . ."—*Heber*, i. 26.

1834.—"Rivers's attention had been attracted by seeing a large **beauliah** in the act of swinging to the tide."—*The Baboo*, i. 14.

BOLTA, s. A turn of a rope; sea H. from Port. *volta* (*Roebuck*).

BOMBASA, n.p. The Island of Mombasa, off the E. African Coast, is so called in some old works. *Bombāsī* is used in Persia for a negro slave; see quotation.

1516.—". . . another island, in which there is a city of the Moors called **Bombaza**, very large and beautiful."—*Barbosa*, 11. See also *Colonial Papers* under 1609, i. 188.

1883.—". . . the **Bombassi**, or coal-black negro of the interior, being of much less price, and usually only used as a cook."—*Wills, Modern Persia*, 326.

BOMBAY, n.p. It has been alleged, often and positively (as in the quotations below from Fryer and Grose), that this name is an English corruption from the Portuguese *Bombahia*, 'good bay.' The grammar of the alleged etymon is bad, and the history is no better; for the name can be traced long before the Portuguese occupation, long before the arrival of the Portuguese in India. C. 1430, we find the islands of Mahim and *Mumba*-Devi, which united form the existing island of Bombay, held, along with Salsette, by a Hindu Rāī, who was tributary to the Mohammedan King of Guzerat. (See *Rās Mālā*, ii. 350); [ed. 1878, p. 270]. The same form reappears (1516) in Barbosa's Tana-*Mayambu* (p. 68), in the *Estado da India* under 1525, and (1563) in Garcia de Orta, who writes both *Mombaim* and *Bombaim*. The latter author, mentioning the excellence of the areca produced there, speaks of himself having had a grant of the island from the King of Portugal (see below). It is customarily called *Bombaim* on the earliest English Rupee coinage. (See under **RUPEE**.) The shrine of the goddess **Mumba**-*Devī* from whom the name is supposed to have been taken, stood on the Esplanade till the middle of the 17th century, when it was removed to its present site in the middle of what is now the most frequented part of the native town.

1507.—"Sultan Mahommed Bigarrah of Guzerat having carried an army against Chaiwal, in the year of the Hijra 913, in order to destroy the Europeans, he effected his designs against the towns of Bassai (see **BASSEIN**) and **Manbai**, and returned to his own capital. . . ."—*Mirat-i-Ahmedi* (Bird's transl.), 214-15.

1508.—"The Viceroy quitted Dabul, passing by Chaul, where he did not care to go in, to avoid delay, and anchored at **Bombaim**, whence the people fled when they saw the fleet, and our men carried off many cows, and caught some blacks whom they found hiding in the woods, and of these they took away those that were good, and killed the rest."—*Correa*, i. 926.

1516.—". . . a fortress of the before-named King (of Guzerat), called Tana-**mayambu**, and near it is a Moorish town, very pleasant, with many gardens . . . a town of very great Moorish mosques, and temples of worship of the Gentiles . . . it is likewise a sea port, but of little trade."—*Barbosa*, 69. The name here appears to combine, in a common oriental fashion, the name of the adjoining town of Thana (see **TANA**) and Bombay.

1525.—"E a Ilha de **Mombayn**, que no forall velho estaua em catorze mill e quatro cento fedeas . . . j̃ xii ij. iiii.ᶜ fedeas.

"E os anos otros estaua arrendada por mill trezentos setenta e cinque pardaos . . . j iii.ᶜ lxxv. pardaos.

"Foy aforada a mestre Dioguo pelo dito governador, por mill quatro centos trinta dous pardaos méo . . . j̃ iiij.ᶜ xxxij. pardaos méo."—*Tombo do Estada da India*, 160-161.

1531.—"The Governor at the island of **Bombaim** awaited the junction of the whole expedition, of which he made a muster, taking a roll from each captain, of the Portuguese soldiers and sailors and of the captive slaves who could fight and help, and of the number of musketeers, and of other people, such as servants. And all taken together he found in the whole fleet some 3560 soldiers (*homens d'armas*), counting captains and gentlemen; and some 1450 Portuguese seamen, with the pilots and masters; and some 2000 soldiers who were Malabars and Goa Canarines; and 8000 slaves fit to fight; and among these he found more than 3000 musketeers (*espingardeiros*), and 4000 country seamen who could row (*marinheiros de terra remeiros*), besides the mariners of the junks who were more than 800; and with married and single women, and people taking goods and provisions to sell, and menial servants, the whole together was more than 30,000 souls. . . ."—*Correa*, iii. 392.

1538.—"The Isle of **Bombay** has on the south the waters of the bay which is called after it, and the island of **Chaul**; on the N. the island of **Salsete**; on the east Salsete also; and on the west the Indian Ocean. The land of this island is very low, and covered with great and beautiful groves of trees. There is much game, and abundance of meat and rice, and there is no memory of any scarcity. Nowadays it is called the island of **Boa-Vida**; a name given to it by Hector da Silveira, because when his fleet was cruising on this coast his soldiers had great refreshment and enjoyment there."—*J. de Castro, Primeiro Roteiro*, p. 81.

1552.—". . . a small stream called *Bate* which runs into the Bay of **Bombain**, and which is regarded as the demarcation between the Kingdom of Guzurate and the Kingdom of Decan."—*Barros*, I. ix. 1.

1552.—"The Governor advanced against **Bombaym** on the 6th February, which was moreover the very day on which Ash Wednesday fell."—*Couto*, IV., v. 5.

1554.—"Item of Mazaguao 8500 *fedeas*.

"Item of **Monbaym**, 17,000 *fedeas*.

"Rents of the land surrendered by the King of Canbaya in 1543, from 1535 to 1548."—*S. Botelho, Tombo*, 139.

1563.—". . . and better still is (that the **areca**) of **Mombaim**, an estate and island which the King our Lord has graciously granted me on perpetual lease."*—*Garcia De Orta*, f. 91*v*.

,, "SERVANT. Sir, here is Simon Toscano, your tenant at **Bombaim**, who has brought this basket of mangoes for you to make a present to the Governor; and he says that when he has moored his vessel he will come here to put up."—*Ibid.* f. 134*v*.

1644.—"*Description of the Port of* **Mombaym**. . . . The Viceroy Conde de Linhares sent the 8 councillors to fortify this Bay, so that no European enemy should be able to enter. These Ministers visited the place, and were of opinion that the width (of the entrance) being so great, becoming even wider and more unobstructed further in, there was no place that you could fortify so as to defend the entrance. . . ."—*Bocarro*, MS. f. 227.

1666.—"Ces Tchérons . . . . demeurent pour la plupart à Baroche, à **Bambaye** et à Amedabad."—*Thevenot*, v. 40.

,, "De Bacaim à **Bombaiim** il y a six lieues."—*Ibid.* 248.

1673.—"December the Eighth we paid our Homage to the Union-flag flying on the Fort of **Bombaim**."—*Fryer*, 59.

,, "Bombaim . . . ventures furthest out into the Sea, making the Mouth of a spacious Bay, whence it has its Etymology; **Bombaim**, quasi *Boon bay*."—*Ibid.* 62.

1676.—"Since the present King of *England* married the Princess of *Portugall*, who had in Portion the famous Port of **Bombeye** . . . they coin both Silver, Copper, and Tinn."—*Tavernier*, E. T., ii. 6.

1677.—"Quod dicta Insula de **Bombaim**, una cum dependentiis suis, nobis ab origine bonâ fide ex pacto (sicut oportuit) tradita non fuerit."—*King Charles II.* to the Viceroy L. de Mendoza Furtado, in *Descn., &c. of the Port and Island of* **Bombay**, 1724, p. 77.

1690.—"This Island has its Denomination from the Harbour, which . . . was originally called **Boon Bay**, *i.e.* in the *Portuguese* Language, a Good Bay or Harbour."—*Ovington*, 129.

* "Terra e ilha de que El-Rei nosso senhor me fez mercê, aforada em fatiota." *Em fatiota* is a corruption apparently of *emphyteuta*, *i.e.* properly the person to whom land was granted on a lease such as the Civil Law called *emphyteusis*. "The emphyteuta was a perpetual lessee who paid a perpetual rent to the owner."—*English Cycl.* s.v. *Emphyteusis*.

1711.—Lockyer declares it to be impossible, with all the Company's Strength and Art, to make **Bombay** "a Mart of great Business."—P. 83.

c. 1760.—". . . one of the most commodious bays perhaps in the world, from which distinction it received the denomination of **Bombay**, by corruption from the Portuguese *Buona-Bahia*, though now usually written by them **Bombaim**."—*Grose*, i. 29.

1770.—"No man chose to settle in a country so unhealthy as to give rise to the proverb *That at* **Bombay** *a man's life did not exceed two monsoons*."—*Raynal* (E. T., 1777), i. 389.

1809.—"The largest pagoda in **Bombay** is in the Black Town. . . . It is dedicated to *Momba Devee* . . . who by her images and attributes seems to be Parvati, the wife of Siva."—*Maria Graham*, 14.

BOMBAY BOX-WORK. This well-known manufacture, consisting in the decoration of boxes, desks, &c., with veneers of geometrical mosaic, somewhat after the fashion of Tunbridge ware, is said to have been introduced from Shiraz to Surat more than a century ago, and some 30 years later from Surat to Bombay. The veneers are formed by cementing together fine triangular prisms of ebony, ivory, green-stained ivory, stag's horn, and tin, so that the sections when sawn across form the required pattern, and such thin sections are then attached to the panels of the box with strong glue.

BOMBAY DUCK.—See **BUMMELO.**

BOMBAY MARINE. This was the title borne for many years by the meritorious but somewhat depressed service which in 1830 acquired the style of the "Indian Navy," and on 30th April, 1863, ceased to exist. The detachments of this force which took part in the China War (1841-42) were known to their brethren of the Royal Navy, under the temptation of alliteration, as the "Bombay Buccaneers." In their earliest employment against the pirates of Western India and the Persian Gulf, they had been known as "the **Grab** Service." But, no matter for these names, the history of this Navy is full of brilliant actions and services. We will quote two noble examples of public virtue:

(1) In July 1811, a squadron under Commodore John Hayes took two large junks issuing from Batavia, then under blockade. These were lawful prize, laden with Dutch property, valued at £600,000. But Hayes knew that such a capture would create great difficulties and embarrassments in the English trade at Canton, and he directed the release of this splendid prize.

(2) 30th June 1815, Lieut. Boyce in the brig 'Nautilus' (180 tons, carrying ten 18-pr. carronades, and four 9-prs.) encountered the U. S. sloop-of-war 'Peacock' (539 tons, carrying twenty 32-pr. carronades, and two long 18-prs.). After he had informed the American of the ratification of peace, Boyce was peremptorily ordered to haul down his colours, which he answered by a flat refusal. The 'Peacock' opened fire, and a short but brisk action followed, in which Boyce and his first lieutenant were shot down. The gallant Boyce had a special pension from the Company (£435 in all) and lived to his 93rd year to enjoy it.

We take the facts from the History of this Navy by one of its officers, Lieut. C. R. Low (i. 294), but he erroneously states the pension to have been granted by the U.S. Govt.

1780.—"The Hon. Company's schooner, Carinjar, with Lieut. Murry Commander, of the **Bombay Marines**, is going to Archin (*sic*, see **ACHEEN**) to meet the Ceres and the other Europe ships from Madrass, to put on board of them the St. Helena stores."—*Hicky's Bengal Gazette*, April 8th.

BONITO, s. A fish (*Thynnus pelamys*, Day) of the same family (*Scombridae*) as mackerel and tunny, very common in the Indian seas. The name is Port., and apparently is the adj. **bonito,** 'fine.'

c. 1610.—"On y pesche vne quantité admirable de gros poissons, de sept ou huit sortes, qui sont néantmoins quasi de mesme race et espece . . . commes **bonites**, albachores, daurades, et autres."—*Pyrard*, i. 137.

1615.—"**Bonitoes** and albicores are in colour, shape, and taste much like to Mackerils, but grow to be very large."—*Terry*, in *Purchas*, ii. 1464.

c. 1620.—

"How many sail of well-mann'd ships
As the **Bonito** does the Flying-fish
Have we pursued. . . ."

Beaum. & Flet., *The Double Marriage*, ii. 1.

c. 1760.—"The fish undoubtedly takes its name from relishing so well to the taste of the Portuguese . . . that they call it

Bonito, which answers in our tongue to delicious."—*Grose*, i. 5.

1764.—
"While on the yard-arm the harpooner sits,
Strikes the **boneta**, or the shark ensnares."—*Grainger*, B. ii.

1773.—"The Captain informed us he had named his ship the **Bonnetta**, out of gratitude to Providence; for once . . . the ship in which he then sailed was becalmed for five weeks, and during all that time, numbers of the fish **Bonnetta** swam close to her, and were caught for food; he resolved therefore that the ship he should next get should be called the *Bonnetta*."—*Boswell, Journal of a Tour, &c.*, under Oct. 16, 1773.

BONZE, s. A term long applied by Europeans in China to the Buddhist clergy, but originating with early visitors to Japan. Its origin is however not quite clear. The Chinese *Fán-sēng*, 'a religious person' is in Japanese *bonzi* or *bonzô;* but Köppen prefers *fă-sze*, 'Teacher of the Law,' pron. in Japanese *bo-zi* (*Die Rel. des Buddha*, i. 321, and also Schott's *Zur Litt. des Chin. Buddhismus*, 1873, p. 46). It will be seen that some of the old quotations favour one, and some the other, of these sources. On the other hand, *Bandhya* (for Skt. *vandya*, 'to whom worship or reverence is due, very reverend') seems to be applied in Nepal to the Buddhist clergy, and Hodgson considers the Japanese bonze (*bonzô ?*) traceable to this. (*Essays*, 1874, p. 63.) The same word, as *bandhe* or *bande*, is in Tibetan similarly applied.—(See *Jaeschke's Dict.*, p. 365.) The word first occurs in Jorge Alvarez's account of Japan, and next, a little later, in the letters of St. Francis Xavier. Cocks in his Diary uses forms approaching *boze*.

1549.—"I find the common secular people here less impure and more obedient to reason than their priests, whom they call **bonzos**."—*Letter of St. F. Xavier*, in *Coleridge's Life*, ii. 238.

1552.—"Erubescunt enim, et incredibiliter confunduntur **Bonzii**, ubi male cohaerere, ac pugnare inter sese ea, quae docent, palam ostenditur."—*Scti. Fr. Xaverii Epistt.* V. xvii., ed. 1667.

1572.—". . . sacerdotes . . . qui ipsorum linguâ **Bonzii** appellantur."—*E. Acosta*, 58.

1585.—"They have amongst them (in Japan) many priests of their idols whom they call **Bonsos**, of the which there be great convents."—*Parkes's Tr. of Mendoza* (1589), ii. 300.

1590.—"This doctrine doe all they embrace, which are in China called *Cen*, but with us at Iapon are named **Bonzi**."—*An Exct. Treatise of the Kingd. of China, &c., Hakl.* ii. 580.

c. 1606.—"Capt. Saris has **Bonzees**."—*Purchas*, i. 374.

1618.—"And their is 300 **boze** (or pagon pristes) have alowance and mentaynance for eaver to pray for his sole, in the same sorte as munkes and fryres use to doe amongst the Roman papistes."—*Cocks's Diary*, ii. 75; [in i. 117, **bose**]; **bosses** (i. 143).

[1676.—"It is estimated that there are in this country (Siam) more than 200,000 priests called **Bonzes**."—*Tavernier*, ed. *Ball*, ii. 293.]

1727.—". . . or perhaps make him fadge in a *China* **bonzee** in his Calendar, under the name of a Christian Saint."—*A. Hamilton*, i. 253.

1794-7.—
"Alike to me encas'd in Grecian bronze
Koran or Vulgate, Veda, Priest, or **Bonze**."
Pursuits of Literature, 6th ed., p. 335.

c. 1814.—
"While Fum deals in Mandarins, **Bonzes**, Bohea—
Peers, Bishops, and Punch, Hum—are sacred to thee."
T. Moore, Hum and Fum.

[(1) **BORA, BOORA**, s. Beng. *bhada*, a kind of cargo-boat used in the rivers of Bengal.

[1675.—"About noone overtook the eight **boraes**."—*Hedges, Diary*, Hak. Soc. ii. ccxxxvii.

[1680.—"The **boora** . . . being a very floaty light boat, rowinge with 20 to 30 Owars, these carry Salt Peeter and other goods from Hugly downewards, and some trade to Dacca with salt; they also serve for tow boats for ye ships bound up or downe ye river."—*Ibid.* ii. 15.]

(2) **BORA**, s. H. and Guz. *bohrā* and *bohorā*, which H. H. Wilson refers to the Skt. *vyavahārī*, 'a trader, or man of affairs,' from which are formed the ordinary H. words *byoharā*, *byohariyā* (and a Guzerati form which comes very near *bohorā*). This is confirmed by the quotation from Nurullah below, but it is not quite certain. Dr. John Wilson (see below) gives an Arabic derivation which we have been unable to verify. [There can be no reasonable doubt that this is incorrect.]

There are two classes of Bohrās belonging to different Mohammedan sects, and different in habit of life.

1. The Shī'a *Bohrās*, who are essentially townspeople, and especially congregate in Surat, Burhanpur, Ujjain, &c. They are those best known far and wide by the name, and are usually devoted to trading and money-lending.

Their original seat was in Guzerat, and they are most numerous there, and in the Bombay territory generally, but are also to be found in various parts of Central India and the N.-W. Provinces, [where they are all Hindus]. The word in Bombay is often used as synonymous with pedlar or **boxwallah.** They are generally well-to-do people, keeping very cleanly and comfortable houses. [See an account of them in *Forbes, Or. Mem.* i. 470 *seqq.* 2nd ed.] These **Bohras** appear to form one of the numerous Shī'a sects, akin in character to, and apparently of the same origin as, the Ismāīlīyah (or *Assassins* of the Middle Ages), and claim as their original head and doctor in India one Ya'ḳūb, who emigrated from Egypt, and landed in Cambay A.D. 1137. But the chief seat of the doctrine is alleged to have been in Yemen, till that country was conquered by the Turks in 1538. A large exodus of the sect to India then took place. Like the Ismāīlīs they attach a divine character to their Mullah or chief Pontiff, who now resides at Surat. They are guided by him in all things, and they pay him a percentage on their profits. But there are several sectarian subdivisions: *Dāūdi* Bohrās, *Sulaimāni* Bohrās, &c. [See *Forbes, Rās Mālā,* ed. 1878, p. 264 *seqq.*]

2. The Sunni *Bohrās.* These are very numerous in the Northern Concan and Guzerat. They are essentially peasants, sturdy, thrifty, and excellent cultivators, retaining much of Hindu habit; and are, though they have dropped caste distinctions, very exclusive and "denominational" (as the *Bombay Gazetteer* expresses it). Exceptionally, at Pattan, in Baroda State, there is a rich and thriving community of trading Bohrās of the Sunni section; they have no intercourse with their Shī'a namesakes.

The history of the Bohrās is still very obscure; nor does it seem ascertained whether the two sections were originally one. Some things indicate that the Shī'a Bohrās may be, in accordance with their tradition, in some considerable part of foreign descent, and that the Sunni Bohrās, who are unquestionably of Hindu descent, may have been native converts of the foreign immigrants, afterwards forcibly brought over to Sunnism by the Guzerat Sultans. But all this must be said with much reserve. The history is worthy of investigation.

The quotation from Ibn Batuta, which refers to Gandari on the Baroda river, south of Cambay, alludes most probably to the Bohrās, and may perhaps, though not necessarily, indicate an origin for the name different from either of those suggested.

c. 1343.—"When we arrived at Kandahār . . . we received a visit from the principal Musulmans dwelling at his (the pagan King's) Capital, such as the *Children of Khojah* **Bohrah,** among whom was the Nākhoda Ibrahīm, who had 6 vessels belonging to him."—*Ibn Batuta,* iv. 58.

c. 1620.—Nurullah of Shuster, quoted by Colebrooke, speaks of this class as having been converted to Islam 300 years before. He says also: "Most of them subsist by commerce and mechanical trades; as is indicated by the name **Bohrah,** which signifies 'merchant' in the dialect of Gujerat."—In *As. Res.,* vii. 338.

1673.—". . . The rest (of the Mohammedans) are adopted under the name of the Province or Kingdom they are born in, as *Mogul* . . . or Schisms they have made, as *Bilhim, Jemottee,* and the lowest of all is **Borrah.**"—*Fryer,* 93.

c. 1780.—"Among the rest was the whole of the property of a certain Muhammad Mokrim, a man of the **Bohra** tribe, the Chief of all the merchants, and the owner of three or four merchant ships."—*H. of Hydur Naik,* 383.

1810.—"The **Borahs** are an inferior set of travelling merchants. The inside of a *Borah's* box is like that of an English country shop, spelling-books, prayer-books, lavender water, eau de luce, soap, tapes, scissors, knives, needles, and thread make but a small part of the variety."—*Maria Graham,* 33.

1825.—"The **Boras** (at Broach) in general are unpopular, and held in the same estimation for parsimony that the Jews are in England."—*Heber,* ed. 1844, ii. 119; also see 72.

1853.—"I had the pleasure of baptizing Ismail Ibraim, the first **Bohorá** who, as far as we know, has yet embraced Christianity in India. . . . He appears thoroughly divorced from Muhammad, and from 'Ali the son-in-law of Muhammad, whom the *Bohorás* or *Initiated,* according to the meaning of the Arabic word, from which the name is derived, esteem as an improvement on his father-in-law, having a higher degree of inspiration, which has in good measure, as they imagine, manifested itself among his successors, recognised by the **Bohoras** and by the Ansariyah, Ismaeliyah, Drus, and Metawileh of Syria. . . ."—*Letter of Dr. John Wilson,* in *Life,* p. 456.

1863.—". . . India, between which and the north-east coast of Africa, a considerable trade is carried on, chiefly by **Borah** merchants of Guzerat and Cutch."—*Badger, Introd. to Varthema*, Hak. Soc. xlix.

BORNEO, n.p. This name, as applied to the great Island in its entirety, is taken from that of the capital town of the chief Malay State existing on it when it became known to Europeans, *Bruné*, *Burné*, *Brunai*, or *Burnai*, still existing and known as *Brunei*.

1516.—"In this island much camphor for eating is gathered, and the Indians value it highly. . . . This island is called **Borney**."—*Barbosa*, 203-4.

1521.—"The two ships departed thence, and running among many islands came on one which contained much cinnamon of the finest kind. And then again running among many islands they came to the Island of **Borneo**, where in the harbour they found many junks belonging to merchants from all the parts about Malacca, who make a great mart in that **Borneo**."—*Correa*, ii. 631.

1584.—"Camphora from **Brimeo** (misreading probably for **Bruneo**) neare to China."—*Barret*, in *Hakl.* ii. 412.

[1610.—"**Bornelaya** are with white and black quarls, like checkers, such as Polingknytsy are."—*Danvers, Letters*, i. 72.]

The cloth called **Bornelaya** perhaps took its name from this island.

[" "There is brimstone, pepper, **Bournesh** camphor."—*Danvers, Letters*, i. 79.]

1614.—In *Sainsbury*, i. 313 [and in *Foster, Letters*, ii. 94], it is written **Burnea**.

1727.—"The great island of **Bornew** or **Borneo**, the largest except *California* in the known world."—*A. Hamilton*, ii. 44.

BORO-BODOR, or **-BUDUR**, n.p. The name of a great Buddhistic monument of Indian character in the district of Kadū in Java; one of the most remarkable in the world. It is a quasi-pyramidal structure occupying the summit of a hill, which apparently forms the core of the building. It is quadrangular in plan, the sides, however, broken by successive projections; each side of the basement, 406 feet. Including the basement, it rises in six successive terraces, four of them forming corridors, the sides of which are panelled with bas-reliefs, which Mr. Fergusson calculated would, if extended in a single line, cover three miles of ground. These represent scenes in the life of Sakya Muni, scenes from the Jātakas, or pre-existences of Sakya, and other series of Buddhistic groups. Above the corridors the structure becomes circular, rising in three shallower stages, bordered with small dagobas (72 in number), and a large dagoba crowns the whole. The 72 dagobas are hollow, built in a kind of stone lattice, and each contains, or has contained, within, a stone Buddha in the usual attitude. In niches of the corridors also are numerous Buddhas larger than life, and about 400 in number. Mr. Fergusson concludes from various data that this wonderful structure must date from A.D. 650 to 800.

This monument is not mentioned in Valentijn's great History of the Dutch Indies (1726), nor does its name ever seem to have reached Europe till Sir Stamford Raffles, the British Lieut.-Governor of Java, visited the district in January 1814. The structure was then covered with soil and vegetation, even with trees of considerable size. Raffles caused it to be cleared, and drawings and measurements to be made. His *History of Java*, and Crawford's *Hist. of the Indian Archipelago*, made it known to the world. The Dutch Government, in 1874, published a great collection of illustrative plates, with a descriptive text.

The meaning of the name by which this monument is known in the neighbourhood has been much debated. Raffles writes it *Bóro Bódo* [*Hist. of Java*, 2nd ed., ii. 30 *seqq.*]. [Crawfurd, *Descr. Dict.* (s.v.), says: "*Boro* is, in Javanese, the name of a kind of fish-trap, and *budor* may possibly be a corruption of the Sanscrit *buda*, 'old.'"] The most probable interpretation, and accepted by Friedrich and other scholars of weight, is that of '*Myriad Buddhas*.' This would be in some analogy to another famous Buddhist monument in a neighbouring district, at Brambánan, which is called *Chandi Sewu*, or the "Thousand Temples," though the number has been really 238.

BOSH, s. and interj. This is alleged to be taken from the Turkish *bosh*, signifying "empty, vain, useless, void of sense, meaning or utility" (*Redhouse's Dict.*). But we have not been able to trace its history or first appearance in English. [According to the *N.E.D.* the word seems to have come into use about 1834 under the influence of Morier's novels, *Ayesha*, *Hajji Baba*,

&c. For various speculations on its origin see 5 ser. *N. & Q.* iii. 114, 173, 257.

[1843.—"The people flatter the Envoy into the belief that the tumult is **Bash** (nothing)."—*Lady Sale, Journal*, 47.]

BOSMÁN, BOCHMÁN, s. Boatswain. Lascar's H. (*Roebuck*).

BOTICKEER, s. Port. *botiqueiro.* A shop or stall-keeper. (See **BOUTIQUE**.)

1567.—"Item, pareceo que . . . os **botiqueiros** não tenhão as **buticas** apertas nos dias de festa, senão depois la messa da terça."—Decree 31 of Council of Goa, in *Archiv. Port. Orient.*, fasc. 4.

1727.—". . . he past all over, and was forced to relieve the poor **Botickeers** or Shopkeepers, who before could pay him Taxes."—*A. Hamilton*, i. 268.

BO TREE, s. The name given in Ceylon to the Pipal tree (see **PEEPUL**) as reverenced by the Buddhists; Singh. *bo-gās.* See in *Emerson Tennent* (*Ceylon*, ii. 632 *seqq.*), a chronological series of notices of the Bo-tree from B.C. 288 to A.D. 1739.

1675.—"Of their (the Veddas') worship there is little to tell, except that like the Cingaleze, they set round the high trees **Bogas**, which our people call *Pagod-trees*, with a stone base and put lamps upon it."—*Ryklof Van Goens*, in *Valentijn* (Ceylon), 209.

1681.—"I shall mention but one Tree more as famous and highly set by as any of the rest, if not more so, tho' it bear no fruit, the benefit consisting chiefly in the Holiness of it. This tree they call **Bogahah**; we the *God-tree.*"—*Knox*, 18.

BOTTLE-TREE, s. Qu. *Adansonia digitata*, or 'baobab'? Its aspect is somewhat suggestive of the name, but we have not been able to ascertain. [It has also been suggested that it refers to the **Babool**, on which the **Baya**, often builds its nest. "These are formed in a very ingenious manner, by long grass woven together in the shape of a **bottle**." (*Forbes, Or. Mem.*, 2nd ed., i. 33.]

1880.—"Look at this prisoner slumbering peacefully under the suggestive **bottle-tree.**"—*Ali Baba*, 153.

[**BOUND-HEDGE**, s. A corruption of *boundary-hedge*, and applied in old military writers to the thick plantation of bamboo or prickly-pear which used to surround native forts.

1792.—"A **Bound Hedge**, formed of a wide belt of thorny plants (at Seringapatam)."—*Wilks, Historical Sketches*, iii. 217.]

BOUTIQUE, s. A common word in Ceylon and the Madras Presidency (to which it is now peculiar) for a small native shop or booth: Port. *butica* or *boteca.* From Bluteau (Suppt.) it would seem that the use of *butica* was peculiar to Portuguese India.

[1548.—**Buticas.** See quotation under **SIND.**]

1554.—". . . nas quaes **buticas** ninguem pode vender senão os que se concertam com o Rendeiro."—*Botelho, Tombo do Estado da India*, 50.

c. 1561.—"The Malabars who sold in the **botecas.**"—*Correa*, i. 2, 267.

1739.—"That there are many **battecas** built close under the Town-wall."—*Remarks on Fortfns. of Fort St. George*, in *Wheeler*, iii. 188.

1742.—In a grant of this date the word appears as **Butteca.**—*Selections from Records of S. Arcot District*, ii. 114.

1767.—"Mr. Russell, as Collector-General, begs leave to represent to the Board that of late years the Street by the river side . . . has been greatly encroached upon by a number of **golahs**, little straw huts, and **boutiques**. . ."—In *Long*, 501.

1772.—". . . a **Boutique** merchant having died the 12th inst., his widow was desirous of being burnt with his body."—*Papers relating to E. I. Affairs*, 1821, p. 268.

1780.—"You must know that Mrs. Henpeck . . . is a great buyer of Bargains, so that she will often go out to the Europe Shops and the **Boutiques**, and lay out 5 or 600 Rupees in articles that we have not the least occasion for."—*India Gazette*, Dec. 9.

1782.—"For Sale at No. 18 of the range **Botiques** to the northward of Lyon's Buildings, where **musters** (q.v.) may be seen. . ." *India Gazette*, Oct. 12.

1834.—"The **boutiques** are ranged along both sides of the street."—*Chitty, Ceylon Gazetteer*, 172.

BOWLA, s. A portmanteau. H. *bāolā*, from Port. *baul*, and *bahu*, 'a trunk.'

BOWLY, BOWRY, s. H. *bāolī*, and *bāorī*, Mahr. *bāvaḍī.* C. P. Brown (*Zillah Dict.* s.v.) says it is the Telegu *bāviḍi*; *bāvī* and *bāviḍi*, = 'well.' This is doubtless the same word, but in all its forms it is probably connected with Skt. *vavra*, 'a hole, a well,' or with *vāpi*, 'an oblong reservoir, a pool or lake.' There is also in Singhalese *væva*, 'a lake or pond,' and in inscriptions *vaviya.* There is again Maldivian *weu*, 'a well,' which comes near the Guzerati forms mentioned below. A great and deep rectangular well (or tank dug down to the springs), furnished with a descent to the water by means of long flights of steps, and generally with landings and *loggie* where travellers may rest in the shade. This kind of structure, almost peculiar to Western and Central India, though occasionally met with in Northern India also, is a favourite object of private native munificence, and though chiefly beneath the level of the ground, is often made the subject of most effective architecture. Some of the finest specimens are in Guzerat, where other forms of the word appear to be *wāo* and *wāīn*. One of the most splendid of these structures is that at Asārwa in the suburbs of Ahmedabad, known as the Well of Dhāī (or 'the Nurse') Harīr, built in 1485 by a lady of the household of Sultan Mohammed Bigara (that famous 'Prince of Cambay' celebrated by Butler—see under **CAMBAY**), at a cost of 3 lakhs of rupees. There is an elaborate model of a great Guzerati *bāolī* in the Indian Museum at S. Kensington.

We have seen in the suburbs of Palermo a regular *bāolī*, excavated in the tufaceous rock that covers the plain. It was said to have been made at the expense of an ancestor of the present proprietor (Count Ranchibile) to employ people in a time of scarcity.

c. 1343.—"There was also a **bāīn**, a name by which the Indians designate a very spacious kind of well, revetted with stone, and provided with steps for descent to the water's brink. Some of these wells have in the middle and on each side pavilions of stone, with seats and benches. The Kings and chief men of the country rival each other in the construction of such reservoirs on roads that are not supplied with water."—*Ibn Batuta*, iv. 13.

1526.—"There was an empty space within the fort (of Agra) between Ibrahim's palace and the ramparts. I directed a large **wâin** to be constructed on it, ten gez by ten. In the language of Hindostân they denominate a large well having a staircase down it **wâin**."—*Baber, Mem.*, 342.

1775.—"Near a village called Sevasee Contra I left the line of march to sketch a remarkable building . . . on a near approach I discerned it to be a well of very superior workmanship, of that kind which the natives call **Bhouree** or **Bhoulie**."—*Forbes, Or. Mem.* ii. 102; [2nd ed. i. 387].

1808.—"'Who-so digs a well deserves the love of creatures and the grace of God,' but a **Vavidee** is said to value 10 *Kooas* (or wells) because the water is available to bipeds without the aid of a rope."—*R. Drummond, Illustrations of Guzerattee, &c.*

1825.—"These **boolees** are singular contrivances, and some of them extremely handsome and striking. . . ."—*Heber*, ed. 1844, ii. 37.

1856.—"The **wāv** (Sansk. *wápeeká*) is a large edifice of a picturesque and stately as well as peculiar character. Above the level of the ground a row of four or five open pavilions at regular distances from each other . . . is alone visible. . . . The entrance to the **wāv** is by one of the end pavilions."—*Forbes, Rās Mālā*, i. 257; [reprint 1878, p. 197].

1876.—"To persons not familiar with the East such an architectural object as a **bowlee** may seem a strange perversion of ingenuity, but the grateful coolness of all subterranean apartments, especially when accompanied by water, and the quiet gloom of these recesses, fully compensate in the eyes of the Hindu for the more attractive magnificence of the ghâts. Consequently the descending flights of which we are now speaking, have often been more elaborate and expensive pieces of architecture than any of the buildings aboveground found in their vicinity."—*Fergusson, Indian and Eastern Architecture*, 486.

BOXWALLAH, s. Hybrid H. *Bakas*- (*i.e.* box) *wālā*. A native itinerant pedlar, or *packman*, as he would be called in Scotland by an analogous term. The *Boxwālā* sells cutlery, cheap nick-nacks, and small wares of all kinds, chiefly European. In former days he was a welcome visitor to small stations and solitary bungalows. The **Borā** of Bombay is often a *boxwālā*, and the *boxwālā* in that region is commonly called *Borā*. (See **BORA**.)

BOY, s.

a. A servant. In Southern India and in China a native personal servant is so termed, and is habitually summoned with the vocative '**Boy**!' The same was formerly common in Jamaica and other W. I. Islands. Similar uses are familiar of *puer* (*e.g.* in the Vulgate *Dixit Giezi* puer *Viri Dei*. II Kings v. 20), Ar. *walad*, *παιδάριον*, *garçon*, *knave* (Germ. *Knabe*); and this same word is used for a camp-servant in Shakespeare, where Fluelen says: "Kill the **Poys** and the luggage! 'tis expressly against the laws of arms."—See also *Grose's Mil. Antiquities*, i. 183, and Latin quotation from Xavier under **Conicopoly**. The word, however, came to be especially used for 'Slave-boy,' and applied to slaves of any age. The Portuguese used *moço* in the same way. In 'Pigeon English' also 'servant' is *Boy*, whilst 'boy' in our ordinary sense is discriminated as '*smallo-boy*!'

b. A Palankin-bearer. From the name of the caste, Telug. and Malayāl. *bōyi*, Tam. *bōvi*, &c. Wilson gives *bhoi* as H. and Mahr. also. The word is in use northward at least to the Nerbudda R. In the Konkan, people of this class are called *Kahār bhūī* (see *Ind. Ant.* ii. 154, iii. 77). P. Paolino is therefore in error, as he often is, when he says that the word *boy* as applied by the English and other Europeans to the coolies or *facchini* who carry the dooly, "has nothing to do with any Indian language." In the first and third quotations (under **b**), the use is more like **a**, but any connection with English at the dates seems impossible.

a.—

1609.—"I bought of them a *Portugall* **Boy** (which the Hollanders had given unto the King) . . . hee cost mee fortie-five Dollers."—*Keeling*, in *Purchas*, i. 196.

,, "My **Boy** Stephen Grovenor."—*Hawkins*, in *Purchas*, 211. See also 267, 296.

1681.—"We had a *black* **boy** my Father brought from Porto Nova to attend upon him, who seeing his Master to be a Prisoner in the hands of the People of his own Complexion, would not now obey his Command."—*Knox*, 124.

1696.—"Being informed where the Chief man of the Choultry lived, he (Dr. Brown) took his sword and pistol, and being followed by his **boy** with another pistol, and his horse keeper. . . ."—In *Wheeler*, i. 300.

1784.—"*Eloped.* From his master's House at Moidapore, a few days since, A Malay Slave **Boy**."—In *Seton-Karr*, i. 45; see also pp. 120, 179.

1836.—"The real Indian ladies lie on a sofa, and if they drop their handkerchief, they just lower their voices and say **Boy**! in a very gentle tone."—*Letters from Madras*, 38.

1866.—"Yes, Sahib, I Christian **Boy**. Plenty poojah do. Sunday time never no work do."—*Trevelyan, The Dawk Bungalow*, p. 226.

Also used by the French in the East:

1872.—"Mon **boy** m'accompagnait pour me servir à l'occasion de guide et d'interprète."—*Rev. des Deux Mondes*, xcviii. 957.

1875.—"He was a faithful servant, or **boy**, as they are here called, about forty years of age."—*Thomson's Malacca*, 228.

1876.—"A Portuguese **Boy** . . . from Bombay."—*Blackwood's Mag.*, Nov., p. 578.

b.—

1554.—(At Goa) "also to a *naique*, with 6 *peons* (*piães*) and a *mocadam* with 6 torch-bearers (*tochās*), one umbrella **boy** (*hum* **bóy** *do sombreiro*), two washermen (*mainatos*), 6 water-carriers (**bóys** *d'agoa*) all serving the governor . . . in all 280 pardaos and 4 tangas annually, or 84,240 reis."—*S. Botelho, Tombo*, 57.

[1563.—"And there are men who carry this umbrella so dexterously to ward off the sun, that although their master trots on his horse, the sun does not touch any part of his body, and such men are called in India **boi**."—*Barros*, Dec. 3, Bk. x. ch. 9.]

1591.—A proclamation of the viceroy, Matthias d'Alboquerque, orders: "that no person, of what quality or condition soever, shall go in a *palanquim* without my express licence, save they be over 60 years of age, to be first proved before the Auditor-General of Police . . . and those who contravene this shall pay a penalty of 200 cruzados, and persons of mean estate the half, the *palanquys* and their belongings to be forfeited, and the **bois** or mouços who carry such *palanquys* shall be condemned to his Majesty's galleys."—*Archiv. Port. Orient.*, fasc. 3, 324.

1608-10.—". . . faisans les graues et obseruans le *Sossiego* à l'Espagnole, ayans tousiours leur **boay** qui porte leur parasol, sans lequel ils n'osent sortir de logis, ou autrement on les estimeroit *picaros* et miserables."—*Mocquet, Voyages*, 305.

1610.—". . . autres Gentils qui sont comme Crocheteurs et Porte-faix, qu'ils appellent **Boye**, c'est a dire Bœuf pour porter quelque pesāt faix que ce soit."—*Pyrard de Laval*, ii. 27; [Hak. Soc. ii. 44. On this Mr. Gray notes: "Pyrard's fanciful interpretation 'ox,' Port. *boi*, may be due either to himself or to some Portuguese friend who would have his joke. It is repeated by Boullaye-de-Gouz (p. 211), who finds a parallel indignity in the use of the term *mulets* by the French gentry towards their chair-men."]

1673.—"We might recite the Coolies . . . and *Palenkeen* **Boys**; by the very Heathens esteemed a degenerate Offspring of the *Holencores* (see **HALALCORE**)."—*Fryer*, 34.

1720.—"**Bois**. In Portuguese India are those who carry the *Andores* (see **ANDOR**), and in Salsete there is a village of them which pays its dues from the fish which they sell, buying it from the fishermen of the shores."—*Bluteau, Dict.* s.v.

1755-60.—". . . Palankin-**boys**."—*Ives*, 50.

1778.—"**Boys** *de pàlanquim*, Kàhàr."—*Gramatica Indostanà* (Port.), Roma, 86.

1782.—". . . un bambou arqué dans le milieu, qui tient au palanquin, and sur les bouts duquel se mettent 5 ou 6 porteurs qu'on appelle **Boués.**"—*Sonnerat, Voyage*, i. 58.

1785.—"The **boys** with Colonel Lawrence's palankeen having straggled a little out of the line of march, were picked up by the Morattas."—*Carraccioli, Life of Clive*, i. 207.

1804.—"My palanquin **boys** will be laid on the road on Monday."—*Wellington*, iii. 553.

1809.—"My **boys** were in high spirits, laughing and singing through the whole night."—*Ld. Valentia*, i. 326.

1810.—"The palankeen-bearers are called **Bhois**, and are remarkable for strength and swiftness."—*Maria Graham*, 128.

BOYA, s. A buoy. Sea H. (*Roebuck*). [Mr. Skeat adds: "The Malay word is also *boya* or *bai-rop*, which latter I cannot trace."]

[**BOYANORE, BAONOR**, s. A corr. of the Malayāl. *Vāllunavar*, 'Ruler.'

[1887.—"Somewhere about 1694-95 . . . the Kadattunād Raja, known to the early English as the **Boyanore** or **Baonor** of Badagara, was in semi-independent possession of Kaduttanād, that is, of the territory lying between the Mahé and Kōtta rivers."—*Logan, Man. of Malabar*, i. 345.]

BRAB, s. The Palmyra Tree (see **PALMYRA**) or *Borassus flabelliformis*. The Portuguese called this Palmeira **brava** ('wild' palm), whence the English corruption. The term is unknown in Bengal, where the tree is called 'fan-palm,' 'palmyra,' or by the H. name *tāl* or *tār*.

1623.—"The book is made after the fashion of this country, *i.e.* not of paper which is seldom or never used, but of palm leaves, viz. of the leaves of that which the Portuguese call *palmum* **brama** (*sic*), or wild palm."—*P. della Valle*, ii. 681; [Hak. Soc. ii. 291].

c. 1666.—"Tous les Malabares écrivent comme nous de gauche à droit sur les feuilles des *Palmeras* **Bravas.**"—*Thevenot*, v. 268.

1673.—"Another Tree called **Brabb**, bodied like the Cocoe, but the leaves grow round like a Peacock's Tail set upright."—*Fryer*, 76.

1759.—"**Brabb**, so called at Bombay: *Palmira* on the coast; and *Tall* at Bengal."—*Ives*, 458.

c. 1760.—"There are also here and there interspersed a few **brab**-trees, or rather wild palm-trees (the word *brab* being derived from **Brabo**, which in Portuguese signifies wild) . . . the chief profit from that is the toddy."—*Grose*, i. 48.

[1808.—See quotation under **BANDAREE.**]

1809.—"The *Palmyra* . . . here called the **brab**, furnishes the best leaves for thatching, and the dead ones serve for fuel."—*Maria Graham*, 5.

BRAHMIN, BRAHMAN, BRAMIN, s. In some parts of India called *Bahman*; Skt. *Brāhmaṇa*. This word now means a member of the priestly caste, but the original meaning and use were different. Haug. (*Brahma und die Brahmanen*, pp. 8-11) traces the word to the root *brih*, 'to increase,' and shows how it has come to have its present signification. The older English form is **Brachman**, which comes to us through the Greek and Latin authors.

c. B.C. 330.—". . . τῶν ἐν Ταξίλοις σοφιστῶν ἰδεῖν δύο φησί, **Βραχμᾶνας** ἀμφοτέρους, τὸν μὲν πρεσβύτερον ἐξυρημένον, τὸν δὲ νεώτερον κομήτην, αμφοτέροις δ' ακολουθεῖν μαθητάς . . ."—*Aristobulus*, quoted in *Strabo*, xv. c. 61.

c. B.C. 300.—"Ἄλλην δὲ διαίρεσιν ποιεῖται περὶ τῶν φιλοσόφων δύο γένη φάσκων, ὧν τοὺς μὲν **Βραχμᾶνας** καλεῖ, τοὺς δὲ Γαρμάνας [Σαρμάνας?]"—From *Megasthenes*, in *Strabo*, xv. c. 59.

c. A.D. 150.—"But the evil stars have not forced the **Brahmins** to do evil and abominable things; nor have the good stars persuaded the rest of the (Indians) to abstain from evil things."—*Bardesanes*, in *Cureton's Spicilegium*, 18.

c. A.D. 500.—"**Βραχμᾶνες**; Ἰνδικὸν ἔθνος σοφώτατον οὓς καὶ βράχμας καλοῦσιν."—*Stephanus Byzantinus.*

1298.—Marco Polo writes (pl.) **Abraiaman** or *Abraiamin*, which seems to represent an incorrect Ar. plural (*e.g. Abrāhamīn*) picked up from Arab sailors; the correct Ar. plural is *Barāhima*.

1444.—Poggio taking down the reminiscences of Nicolo Conti writes **Brammones.**

1555.—"Among these is ther a people called **Brachmanes**, whiche (as Didimus their Kinge wrote unto Alexandre . . .) live a pure and simple life, led with no likerous lustes of other mennes vanities."—*W. Watreman, Fardle of Faciouns.*

1572.—

"**Brahmenes** são os seus religiosos,
Nome antiguo, e de grande preeminencia:
Observam os preceitos tão famosos
D'hum, que primeiro poz nomo á sciencia."
Camões, vii. 40.

1578.—Acosta has **Bragmen.**

1582.—"Castañeda, tr. by N. L.," has **Bramane.**

1630.—"The **Bramanes** . . . Origen, cap. 13 & 15, affirmeth to bee descended from Abraham by Cheturah, who seated themselves in India, and that so they were called **Abrahmanes.**"—*Lord, Desc. of the Banian Rel.*, 71.

1676.—

"Comes he to upbraid us with his innocence?
Seize him, and take this preaching **Brachman** hence."
Dryden, Aurungzebe, iii. 3.

1688.—"The public worship of the pagods was tolerated at Goa, and the sect of the **Brachmans** daily increased in power, because these Pagan priests had bribed the Portuguese officers."—*Dryden, Life of Xavier.*

1714.—"The Dervis at first made some scruple of violating his promise to the dying **brachman.**"—*The Spectator*, No. 578.

BRAHMINY BULL, s. A bull devoted to Siva and let loose; generally found frequenting Hindu bazars, and fattened by the run of the Bunyas' shops. The term is sometimes used more generally (*Brahminy* bull, -ox, or -cow) to denote the humped Indian ox as a species.

1872.—"He could stop a huge **Bramini bull**, when running in fury, by catching hold of its horns."—*Govinda Samanta*, i. 85.

[1889.—"Herbert Edwards made his mark as a writer of the **Brahminee Bull Letters** in the Delhi Gazette."—*Calcutta Rev.*, app. xxii.]

BRAHMINY BUTTER, s. This seems to have been an old name for **Ghee** (q.v.). In MS. "Acct. Charges, Dieting, &c., at Fort St. David for Nov.—Jany., 1746-47," in India Office, we find:

"**Butter** . . . . *Pagodas* 2 2 0
Brahminy do. ,, 1 34 0."

BRAHMINY DUCK, s. The common Anglo-Indian name of the handsome bird *Casarca rutila* (Pallas), or 'Ruddy Shieldrake'; constantly seen on the sandy shores of the Gangetic rivers in single pairs, the pair almost always at some distance apart. The Hindi name is *chakwā*, and the *chakwā-chakwī* (male and female of the species) afford a commonplace comparison in Hindi literature for faithful lovers and spouses. "The Hindus have a legend that two lovers for their indiscretion were transformed into Brahminy Ducks, that they are condemned to pass the night apart from each other, on opposite banks of the river, and that all night long each, in its turn, asks its mate if it shall come across, but the question is always met by a negative—"Chakwa, shall I come?" "No, Chakwi." "Chakwi, shall I come?" "No, Chakwa." —(*Jerdon.*) The same author says the bird is occasionally killed in England.

BRAHMINY KITE, s. The *Milvus Pondicerianus* of Jerdon, *Haliastur Indus*, Boddaert. The name is given because the bird is regarded with some reverence by the Hindus as sacred to Vishnu. It is found throughout India.

c. 1328.—"There is also in this India a certain bird, big, like a **Kite**, having a white head and belly, but all red above, which boldly snatches fish out of the hands of fishermen and other people, and indeed [these birds] go on just like dogs."—*Friar Jordanus*, 36.

1673.—" . . . 'tis Sacrilege with them to kill a Cow or Calf; but highly piacular to shoot a **Kite**, *dedicated to the* **Brachmins**, for which Money will hardly pacify."—*Fryer*, 33.

[1813.—"We had a still bolder and more ravenous enemy in the hawks and **brahminee kites.**"—*Forbes, Or. Mem.*, 2nd ed., ii. 162.]

BRAHMO-SOMÁJ, s. The Bengali pronunciation of Skt. *Brahma Samāja*, 'assembly of Brahmists'; Brahma being the Supreme Being according to the Indian philosophic systems. The reform of Hinduism so called was begun by Ram Mohun Roy (*Rāma Mohana Rāī*) in 1830. Professor A. Weber has shown that it does not constitute an independent Indian movement, but is derived from European Theism. [Also see *Monier-Williams, Brahmanism*, 486.]

1876.—"The **Brahmo Somaj**, or Theistic Church of India, is an experiment hitherto unique in religious history."—*Collet, Brahmo Year-book*, 5.

BRANDUL, s. 'Backstay,' in Sea H. Port. *brandal* (*Roebuck*).

BRANDY COORTEE, -COATEE, s. Or sometimes simply *Brandy*. A corruption of *bārānī*, 'a cloak,' literally *pluviale*, from P. *bārān*, 'rain.' **Bārānī-kurtī** seems to be a kind of hybrid shaped by the English word *coat*, though *kurtā* and *kurtī* are true P. words for various forms of jacket or tunic.

[1754.—"Their women also being not less than 6000, were dressed with great coats (these are called **baranni**) of crimson cloth, after the manner of the men, and not to be distinguished at a distance; so that the whole made a very formidable appearance."—*H. of Nadir Shah*, in *Hanway*, 367.]

1788.—"**Barrannee**—a cloak to cover one from the rain."—*Ind. Vocab.* (Stockdale).

[The word **Bārānī** is now commonly used to describe those crops which are dependent on the annual rains, not on artificial irrigation.

[1900.—"The recent rain has improved the **barani** crops."—*Pioneer Mail*, 19th Feb.]

BRANDYPAWNEE, s. Brandy and water; a specimen of genuine *Urdū*, *i.e.* Camp jargon, which hardly needs interpretation. H. *panī*, 'water.' Williamson (1810) has *brandy-shraub-pauny* (*V. M.* ii. 123).

[1854.—"I'm sorry to see you gentlemen drinking **brandy-pawnee**," says he; "it plays the deuce with our young men in India."—*Thackeray, Newcomes*, ch. i.]

1866.—"The **brandy pawnee** of the East, and the 'sangaree' of the West Indies, are happily now almost things of the past, or exist in a very modified form."—*Waring, Tropical Resident*, 177.

BRASS, s. A brace. Sea dialect.—(*Roebuck*.)

[**BRASS-KNOCKER**, s. A term applied to a *réchauffé* or serving up again of yesterday's dinner or supper. It is said to be found in a novel by Winwood Reade called *Liberty Hall*, as a piece of Anglo-Indian slang; and it is supposed to be a corruption of *bāsī khāna*, H. 'stale food'; see 5 ser. *N. & Q.*, 34, 77.]

BRATTY, s. A word, used only in the South, for cakes of dry cow-dung, used as fuel more or less all over India. It is Tam. *varaṭṭi*, [or *virāṭṭi*], 'dried dung.' Various terms are current elsewhere, but in Upper India the most common is *uplā*.—(Vide **OOPLA**).

BRAVA, n.p. A sea-port on the east coast of Africa, lat. 1° 7′ N., long. 44° 3′, properly **Barāwa**.

1516.—". . . a town of the Moors, well walled, and built of good stone and white-wash, which is called **Brava**. . . . It is a place of trade, which has already been destroyed by the Portuguese, with great slaughter of the inhabitants. . . ."—*Barbosa*, 15.

BRAZIL-WOOD, s. This name is now applied in trade to the dye-wood imported from Pernambuco, which is derived from certain species of *Caesalpinia* indigenous there. But it originally applied to a dye-wood of the same genus which was imported from India, and which is now known in trade as **Sappan** (q.v.). [It is the *andam* or *bakkam* of the Arabs (*Burton, Ar. Nights*, iii. 49).] The history of the word is very curious. For when the name was applied to the newly discovered region in S. America, probably, as Barros alleges, because it produced a dye-wood similar in character to the **brazil** of the East, the trade-name gradually became appropriated to the S. American product, and was taken away from that of the E. Indies. See some further remarks in *Marco Polo*, 2nd ed., ii. 368-370 [and *Encycl. Bibl.* i. 120].

This is alluded to also by *Camões* (x. 140):

"But here where Earth spreads wider, ye shall claim
realms by the *ruddy Dye-wood* made renown'd;
these of the 'Sacred Cross' shall win the name:
by your first Navy shall that world be found." *Burton*.

The medieval forms of *brazil* were many; in Italian it is generally *verzi*, *verzino*, or the like.

1330.—"And here they burn the **brazil-wood** (*verzino*) for fuel . . ."—*Fr. Odoric*, in *Cathay*, &c., p. 77.

1552.—". . . when it came to the 3d of May, and Pedralvares was about to set sail, in order to give a name to the land thus newly discovered, he ordered a very great Cross to be hoisted at the top of a tree, after mass had been said at the foot of the tree, and it had been set up with the solemn benediction of the priests, and then he gave the country the name of *Sancta Cruz*. . . . But as it was through the symbol of the Cross that the Devil lost his dominion over us . . . as soon as the red wood called **Brazil** began to arrive from that country, he wrought that *that* name should abide in the mouth of the people, and that the name of *Holy Cross* should be lost, as if the name of a wood for colouring cloth were of more moment than that wood which imbues all the sacraments with the tincture of salvation, which is the Blood of Jesus Christ."—*Barros*, I. v. 2.

1554.—"The baar (**Bahar**) of **Brazil** contains 20 faraçolas (see **FRAZALA**), weighing it in a coir rope, and there is no *picotaa* (see **PICOTA**)"—*A. Nunes*, 18.

1641.—"We went to see the Rasp-house where the lusty knaves are compelled to labour, and the rasping of **Brazill** and Logwood is very hard labour."—*Evelyn's Diary, August* [19].

BREECH-CANDY, n.p. A locality on the shore of Bombay Island to the north of Malabar Hill. The true name, as Dr. Murray Mitchell tells me, is believed to be *Burj-khāḍī*, 'the Tower of the Creek.'

BRIDGEMÁN, s. Anglo-Sepoy H. *brijmān*, denoting a military *prisoner*, of which word it is a quaint corruption.

BRINJARRY, s. Also **BINJARREE, BUNJARREE,** and so on. But the first form has become classical from its constant occurrence in the Indian Despatches of Sir A. Wellesley. The word is properly H. *banjārā*, and Wilson derives it from Skt. *banij*, 'trade,' *kāra*, 'doer.' It is possible that the form *brinjārā* may have been suggested by a supposed connection with the Pers. *birinj*, 'rice.' (It is alleged in the *Dict. of Words used in the E. Indies*, 2nd ed., 1805, to be derived from *brinj*, 'rice,' and *ara*, 'bring'!) The *Brinjarries* of the Deccan are dealers in grain and salt, who move about, in numerous parties with cattle, carrying their goods to different markets, and who in the days of the Deccan wars were the great resource of the commissariat, as they followed the armies with supplies for sale. They talk a kind of Mahratta or Hindi patois. Most classes of Banjārās in the west appear to have a tradition of having first come to the Deccan with Moghul camps as commissariat carriers. In a pamphlet called *Some Account of the Bunjarrah Class*, by N. R. Cumberlege, *District Sup. of Police, Basein, Berar* (Bombay, 1882; [*North Indian N. & Q.* iv. 163 *seqq.*]), the author attempts to distinguish between *brinjarees* as 'grain-carriers,' and *bunjarrahs*, from *bunjār*, 'waste land' (meaning *banjar* or *bānjar*). But this seems fanciful. In the N.-W. Provinces the name is also in use, and is applied to a numerous tribe spread along the skirt of the Himālaya from Hardwār to Gorakhpur, some of whom are settled, whilst the rest move about with their cattle, sometimes transporting goods for hire, and sometimes carrying grain, salt, lime, forest produce, or other merchandise for sale. [See *Crooke, Tribes and Castes*, i. 149 *seqq.*] **Vanjārās**, as they are called about Bombay, used to come down from Rajputāna and Central India, with large droves of cattle, laden with grain, &c., taking back with them salt for the most part. These were not mere carriers, but the actual dealers, paying ready money, and they were orderly in conduct.

c. 1505.—"As scarcity was felt in his camp (Sultan Sikandar Lodi's) in consequence of the non-arrival of the **Banjáras**, he despatched 'Azam Humáyun for the purpose of bringing in supplies."—*Ni'amat Ullah*, in *Elliot*, v. 100 (written c. 1612).

1516.—"The Moors and Gentiles of the cities and towns throughout the country come to set up their shops and cloths at Cheul . . . they bring these in great caravans of domestic oxen, with packs, like donkeys, and on the top of these long white sacks placed crosswise, in which they bring their goods; and one man drives 30 or 40 beasts before him."—*Barbosa*, 71.

1563.—". . . This King of Dely took the Balagat from certain very powerful gentoos, whose tribe are those whom we now call **Venezaras**, and from others dwelling in the country, who are called *Colles*; and all these, Colles, and *Venezaras*, and Reisbutos, live by theft and robbery to this day."—*Garcia De O.*, f. 34.

c. 1632.—"The very first step which Mohabut Khan [Khān Khānān] took in the Deccan, was to present the **Bunjaras** of Hindostan with elephants, horses, and cloths; and he collected (by these conciliatory measures) so many of them that he had one chief *Bunjara* at Agrah, another in Goojrat, and another above the Ghats, and established the advanced price of 10 *sers* per rupee (in his camp) to enable him to buy it cheaper."—MS. *Life of Mohabut Khan* (*Khan Khanan*), in *Briggs's* paper quoted below, 183.

1638.—"Il y a dans le Royaume de *Cuncam* vn certain peuple qu'ils appellent **Venesars**, qui achettent le bled et le ris . . . pour le reuendre dans *l'Indosthan* . . . ou ils vont auec des *Caffilas* ou *Caravances* de cinq ou six, et quelque fois de neuf ou dix mille bestes de somme. . . ."—*Mandelslo*, 245.

1793.—"Whilst the army halted on the 23rd, accounts were received from Captain Read . . . that his convoy of **brinjarries** had been attacked by a body of horse."—*Dirom*, 2.

1800.—"The **Binjarries** I look upon in the light of servants of the public, of whose grain I have a right to regulate the sale . . . always taking care that they have a proportionate advantage."—*A. Wellesley*, in *Life of Sir T. Munro*, i. 264.

" "The **Brinjarries** drop in by degrees."—*Wellington*, i. 175.

1810.—"Immediately facing us a troop of **Brinjarees** had taken up their residence for the night. These people travel from one end of India to the other, carrying salt, grain, assafœtida, almost as necessary to an army as salt."—*Maria Graham*, 61.

1813.—"We met there a number of **Vanjarrahs**, or merchants, with large droves of oxen, laden with valuable articles from the interior country, to commute for salt on the sea-coast."—*Forbes, Or. Mem.* i. 206; [2nd ed. i. 118; also see ii. 276 *seqq.*].

" "As the Deccan is devoid of a single navigable river, and has no roads that admit of wheel-carriages, the whole of this extensive intercourse is carried on by laden bullocks, the property of that class of people known as **Bunjaras**."—*Acc. of Origin, Hist., and Manners of . . . Bunjāras*, by *Capt. John Briggs*, in *Tr. Lit. Soc. Bo.* i. 61.

1825.—"We passed a number of **Brinjarrees** who were carrying salt. . . . They . . . had all bows . . . arrows, sword and shield. . . . Even the children had, many of them, bows and arrows suited to their strength, and I saw one young woman equipped in the same manner."—*Heber*, ii. 94.

1877.—"They were **brinjarries**, or carriers of grain, and were quietly encamped at a village about 24 miles off; trading most unsuspiciously in grain and salt."—*Meadows Taylor, Life*, ii. 17.

BRINJAUL, s. The name of a vegetable called in the W. Indies the *Egg-plant*, and more commonly known to the English in Bengal under that of *bangun* (prop. *baingan*). It is the *Solanum Melongena*, L., very commonly cultivated on the shores of the Mediterranean as well as in India and the East generally. Though not known in a wild state under this form, there is no reasonable doubt that *S. Melongena* is a derivative of the common Indian *S. insanum*, L. The word in the form *brinjaul* is from the Portuguese, as we shall see. But probably there is no word of the kind which has undergone such extraordinary variety of modifications, whilst retaining the same meaning, as this. The Skt. is *bhanṭākī*, H. *bhānṭā*, *baigan*, *baingan*, P. *badingān*, *badilgān*, Ar. *badinjān*, Span. *alberengena*, *berengena*, Port. *beringela*, *bringiela*, **bringella**, Low Latin *melangolus*, *merangolus*, Ital. *melangola*, *melanzana*, *mela insana*, &c. (see *P. della Valle*, below), French *aubergine* (from *alberengena*), *melongène*, *merangène*, and provincially *belingène*, *albergaine*, *albergine*, *albergame*. (See *Marcel Devic*, p. 46.) Littré, we may remark, explains (*dormitante Homero?*) *aubergine* as '*espèce de morelle*,' giving the etym. as "diminutif de *auberge*" (in the sense of a kind of peach). *Melongena* is no real Latin word, but a factitious rendering of *melanzana*, or, as Marcel Devic says, "Latin du botaniste." It looks as if the Skt. word were the original of all. The H. *baingan* again seems to have been modified from the P. *badingān*, [or, as Platts asserts, direct from the Skt. *vanga*, *vangana*, 'the plant of Bengal,'] and *baingan* also through the Ar. to have been the parent of the Span. *berengena*, and so of all the other European names except the English 'egg-plant.' The Ital. *mela insana* is the most curious of these corruptions, framed by the usual effort after meaning, and connecting itself with the somewhat indigestible reputation of the vegetable as it is eaten in Italy, which is a fact. When cholera is abroad it is considered (*e.g.* in Sicily) to be an act of folly to eat the *melanzana*. There is, however, behind this, some notion (exemplified in the quotation from *Lane's Mod. Egypt.* below) connecting the *badinjān* with madness. [*Burton, Ar. Nights*, iii. 417.] And it would seem that the old Arab medical writers give it a bad character as an article of diet. Thus Avicenna says the *badinjān* generates melancholy and obstructions. To the N. O. *Solanaceae* many poisonous plants belong.

The word has been carried, with the vegetable, to the Archipelago, probably by the Portuguese, for the Malays call it *berinjalā*. [On this Mr. Skeat writes: "The Malay form *brinjal*, from the Port., not *berinjalā*, is given by Clifford and Swettenham, but it cannot be established as a Malay word, being almost certainly the Eng. *brinjaul* done into Malay. It finds no place in Klinkert, and the native Malay word, which is the only word used in pure Peninsular Malay, is *terong* or *trong*. The form *berinjalā*, I believe, must have come from the Islands if it really exists."]

1554.—(At Goa). "And the excise from garden stuff under which are comprised these things, viz.: Radishes, beetroot, garlick, onions green and dry, green tamarinds, lettuces, *conbalinguas*, ginger, oranges, dill, coriander, mint, cabbage, salted mangoes, **brinjelas**, lemons, gourds, citrons, cucumbers, which articles none may sell in retail except the Rendeiro of this excise, or some one who has got permission from him. . . ."—*S. Botelho, Tombo*, 49.

c. 1580.—"Trifolium quoquè virens comedunt *Arabes*, mentham *Judaei* crudam, . . . **mala insana** . . ."—*Prosper Alpinus*, i. 65.

1611.—"We had a market there kept

upon the Strand of diuers sorts of prouisions, towit . . . **Pallingenies**, cucumbers . . ."—*N. Downton*, in *Purchas*, i. 298.

1616.—"It seems to me to be one of those fruits which are called in good Tuscan *petronciani*, but which by the Lombards are called **melanzane**, and by the vulgar at Rome *marignani;* and if my memory does not deceive me, by the Neapolitans in their patois *molegnane*."—*P. della Valle*, i. 197.

1673.—"The Garden . . . planted with Potatoes, Yawms, **Berenjaws**, both hot plants . . ."—*Fryer*, 104.

1738.—"Then follow during the rest of the summer, *calabashas* . . . . **bedin-janas**, and tomatas."—*Shaw's Travels*, 2nd ed. 1757, p. 141.

c. 1740.—"This man (Balaji Rao), who had become absolute in Hindostan as well as in Decan, was fond of bread made of Badjrah . . . he lived on raw **Bringelas**, on unripe mangoes, and on raw red pepper."—*Seir Mutaqherin*, iii. 229.

1782.—Sonnerat writes **Béringédes**.—i. 186.

1783.—Forrest spells **brinjalles** (*V. to Mergui*, 40); and (1810) Williamson **biringal** (*V. M.* i. 133). Forbes (1813), **bringal** and **berenjal** (*Or. Mem.* i. 32) [in 2nd ed. i. 22, **bungal**,] ii. 50; [in 2nd ed. i. 348].

1810.—"I saw last night at least two acres covered with **brinjaal**, a species of Solanum."—*Maria Graham*, 24.

1826.—"A plate of poached eggs, fried in sugar and butter; a dish of **badenjâns**, slit in the middle and boiled in grease."—*Hajji Baba*, ed. 1835, p. 150.

1835.—"The neighbours unanimously declared that the husband was mad. . . . One exclaimed: 'There is no strength nor power but in God! God restore thee!' Another said: 'How sad! He was really a worthy man.' A third remarked: '**Badingâns** are very abundant just now.'"—*Lane, Mod. Egyptians*, ed. 1860, 299.

1860.—"Amongst other triumphs of the native cuisine were some singular, but by no means inelegant *chefs d'œuvre*, **brinjals** boiled and stuffed with savoury meats, but exhibiting ripe and undressed fruit growing on the same branch."—*Tennent's Ceylon*, ii. 161. This dish is mentioned in the Sanskrit Cookery Book, which passes as by King Nala. It is managed by wrapping part of the fruit in wet cloths whilst the rest is being cooked.

BROACH, n.p. *Barōch*, an ancient and still surviving city of Guzerat, on the River Nerbudda. The original forms of the name are *Bhrigu-kachchha*, and *Bhāru-Kachchha*, which last form appears in the Sunnar Cave Inscription No. ix., and this was written with fair correctness by the Greeks as Βαρυγάζα and Βαργόση. "Illiterate Guzerattees would in attempting to articulate *Bhreeghoo-Kshetra* (*sic*), lose the half in coalescence, and call it *Barigache*."—*Drummond, Illus. of Guzerattee*, &c.

c. B.C. 20.—"And then laughing, and stript naked, anointed and with his loin-cloth on, he leaped upon the pyre. And this inscription was set upon his tomb: *Zarmanochēgas the Indian from* **Bargósē** *having rendered himself immortal after the hereditary custom of the Indians lieth here*."—*Nicolaus Damascenus*, in *Strabo*, xv. 72. [Lassen takes the name Zarmanochēgas to represent the Skt. *Śrâmanâcharya*, teacher of the *Śrâmanas*, from which it would appear that he was a Buddhist priest.]

c. A.D. 80.—"On the right, at the very mouth of the gulf, there is a long and narrow strip of shoal. . . . And if one succeeds in getting into the gulf, still it is hard to hit the mouth of the river leading to **Barygaza**, owing to the land being so low . . . and when found it is difficult to enter, owing to the shoals of the river near the mouth. On this account there are at the entrances fishermen employed by the King . . . to meet ships as far off as Syrastrene, and by these they are piloted up to Barygaza."—*Periplus*, sect. 43. It is very interesting to compare Horsburgh with this ancient account. "From the sands of Swallow to Broach a continued bank extends along the shore, which at Broach river projects out about 5 miles. . . . The tide flows here . . . velocity 6 knots . . . rising nearly 30 feet. . . . On the north side of the river, a great way up, the town of **Broach** is situated; vessels of considerable burden may proceed to this place, as the channels are deep in many places, but too intricate to be navigated without a pilot."—*India Directory* (*in loco*).

c. 718.—**Barús** is mentioned as one of the places against which Arab attacks were directed.—See *Elliot*, i. 441.

c. 1300.—". . . a river which lies between the Sarsut and Ganges . . . has a south-westerly course till it falls into the sea near **Bahrúch**."—*Al-Birūni*, in *Elliot*, i. 49.

A.D. 1321.—"After their blessed martyrdom, which occurred on the Thursday before Palm Sunday, in Thana of India, I baptised about 90 persons in a certain city called **Parocco**, 10 days' journey distant therefrom . . ."—*Friar Jordanus*, in *Cathay*, &c., 226.

1552.—"A great and rich ship said to belong to Meleque Gupij, Lord of **Baroche**."—*Barros*, II. vi. 2.

1555.—"Sultan Ahmed on his part marched upon **Barūj**."—*Sidī 'Ali*, 85.

[1615.—"It would be necessary to give credit unto two or three Guzzaratts for some cloth to make a voyage to **Burrouse**."—*Foster, Letters*, iv. 94.]

1617.—"We gave our host . . . a peece of *backar* **baroche** to his children to make them 2 coates."—*Cocks's Diary*, i. 330. [*Backar* here seems to represent a port connected with Broach, called in the *Āīn* (ii. 243) *Bhankora* or *Bhakor*; Bayley gives *Bhakorah* as a village on the frontier of Gujerat.]

1623.—"Before the hour of complines . . . we arrived at the city of **Barochi**, or **Behrug** as they call it in Persian, under the walls of which, on the south side, flows a river called Nerbedà."—*P. della Valle*, ii. 529; [Hak. Soc. i. 60].

1648.—In *Van Twist* (p. 11), it is written **Broichia**.

[1676.—"From Surat to **Baroche**, 22 coss."—*Tavernier*, ed *Ball*, i. 66.]

1756.—"Bandar of **Bhrōch**."—(Bird's tr. of) *Mirat-i-Ahmadi*, 115.

1803.—"I have the honour to enclose . . . papers which contain a detailed account of the . . . capture of **Baroach**." — *Wellington*, ii. 289.

BUCK, v. To prate, to chatter, to talk much and egotistically. H. *baknā*. [A *buck-stick* is a chatterer.]

1880.—"And then . . . he **bucks** with a quiet stubborn determination that would fill an American editor, or an Under Secretary of State with despair. He belongs to the 12-foot-tiger school, so perhaps he can't help it."—*Ali Baba*, 164.

BUCKAUL, s. Ar. H. *baḳḳāl*, 'a shopkeeper;' a *bunya* (q. v. under **BANYAN**). In Ar. it means rather a 'second-hand' dealer.

[c. 1590.—"There is one cast of the Vaiśyas called Banik, more commonly termed Baniya (grain-merchant). The Persians name them **bakkál**. . . ."—*Āīn*, *tr. Jarrett*, iii. 118.]

1800.—". . . a **buccal** of this place told me he would let me have 500 bags tomorrow."—*Wellington*, i. 196.

1826.—"Should I find our neighbour the **Baqual** . . . at whose shop I used to spend in sweetmeats all the copper money that I could purloin from my father."—*Hajji Baba*, ed. 1835, 295.

BUCKSHAW, s. We have not been able to identify the fish so called, or the true form of the name. Perhaps it is only H. *bachchā*, Mahr. *bachchā* (P. *bacha*, Skt. *vatsa*), 'the young of any creature.' But the Konkani Dict. gives '*boussa*—peixe pequeno de qualquer sorte,' 'little fish of any kind.' This is perhaps the real word; but it also may represent *bachcha*. The practice of manuring the coco-palms with putrid fish is still rife, as residents of the Government House at Parell never forget. The fish in use is refuse **bummelo** (q. v.). [The word is really the H. *bachhua*, a well-known edible fish which abounds in the Ganges and other N. Indian rivers. It is either the *Pseudoutropius garua*, or P. *murius* of Day, *Fish. Ind.*, nos. 474 or 471; *Fau. Br. Ind.* i. 141, 137.]

1673.—". . . Cocoe Nuts, for Oyl, which latter they dunging with (**Bubsho**) Fish, the Land-Breezes brought a poysonous Smell on board Ship."—*Fryer*, 55. [Also see *Wheeler*, *Early Rec.*, 40.]

1727.—"The Air is somewhat unhealthful, which is chiefly imputed to their dunging their Cocoa-nut trees with **Buckshoe**, a sort of small Fishes which their Sea abounds in."—*A. Hamilton*, i. 181.

c. 1760.—". . . manure for the coco-nut-tree . . . consisting of the small fry of fish, and called by the country name of **Buckshaw**."—*Grose*, i. 31.

[1883.—"*Mahsīr*, rohū and **batchwa** are found in the river Jumna."—*Gazetteer of Delhi District*, 21.]

BUCKSHAW, s. This is also used in *Cocks's Diary* (i. 63, 99) for some kind of Indian piece-goods, we know not what. [The word is not found in modern lists of piece-goods. It is perhaps a corruption of Pers. *bukchah*, 'a bundle,' used specially of clothes. Tavernier (see below) uses the word in its ordinary sense.

[1614.—"Percalla, **Boxshaes**." — *Foster*, *Letters*, ii. 88.

[1615.—"80 pieces **Boxsha** gingams"; "Per **Puxshaws**, double piece, at 9 mas."—*Ibid.* iii. 156; iv. 50.

[1665.—"I went to lie down, my **bouchha** being all the time in the same place, half under the head of my bed and half outside."—*Tavernier*, ed. *Ball*, ii. 166.]

BUCKSHEESH, BUXEES, s. P. through P.—H. *bakhshish*. Buonamano, Trinkgeld, pourboire; we don't seem to have in England any exact equivalent for the word, though the thing is so general; 'something for (the driver)' is a poor expression; *tip* is accurate, but is slang; gratuity is official or dictionary English.

[1625.—"**Bacsheese** (as they say in the Arabicke tongue) that is gratis freely."—*Purchas*, ii. 1340 [N.E.D.].

1759.—"To Presents:—

	R.	A.	P.
2 Pieces of flowered Velvet	532	7	0
1 ditto of Broad Cloth . .	50	0	0
Buxis to the Servants . .	50	0	0"

Cost of Entertainment to Jugget Set. In *Long*, 190.

c. 1760.—"... **Buxie** money."—*Ives*, 51.

1810.—"... each mile will cost full one rupee (*i.e.* 2*s.* 6*d.*), besides various little disbursements by way of **buxees**, or presents, to every set of bearers."—*Williamson, V. M.* ii. 235.

1823.—"These Christmas-boxes are said to be an ancient custom here, and I could almost fancy that our name of *box* for this particular kind of present . . . is a corruption of **buckshish**, a gift or gratuity, in Turkish, Persian, and Hindoostanee."—*Heber*, i. 45.

1853.—"The relieved bearers opened the shutters, thrust in their torch, and their black heads, and most unceremoniously demanded **buxees**."—*W. Arnold, Oakfield*, i. 239.

BUCKYNE, s. H. *bakāyan*, the tree *Melia sempervivens*, Roxb. (N. O. *Meliaceae*). It has a considerable resemblance to the *nīm* tree (see **NEEM**); and in Bengali is called *mahā-nīm*, which is also the Skt. name, *mahānimba*. It is sometimes erroneously called Persian Lilac.

BUDDHA, BUDDHISM, BUDDHIST. These words are often written with a quite erroneous assumption of precision *Bhudda*, &c. All that we shall do here is to collect some of the earlier mentions of Buddha and the religion called by his name.

c. 200.—"Εἰσὶ δὲ τῶν Ἰνδῶν οἱ τοῖς Βούττα πειθόμενοι παραγγέλμασιν· ὃν δι' ὑπερβολὴν σεμνότητος εἰς θεὸν τετιμήκασι." *Clemens Alexandrinus*, Strōmatōn, Liber I. (Oxford ed., 1715, i. 359).

c. 240.—"Wisdom and deeds have always from time to time been brought to mankind by the messengers of God. So in one age they have been brought to mankind by the messenger called **Buddha** to India, in another by Zarâdusht to Persia, in another by Jesus to the West. Thereupon this revelation has come down, this prophecy in this last age, through me, Mânî, the messenger of the God of truth to Babylonia."—The Book of *Mānī*, called *Shābūrkān*, quoted by *Albirūnī*, in his *Chronology*, tr. by Sachau, p. 190.

c. 400.—"Apud Gymnosophistas Indiae quasi per manus hujus opinionis auctoritas traditur, quod **Buddam** principem dogmatis eorum, e latere suo virgo generaret. Nec hoc mirum de barbaris, quum Minervam quoque de capite Jovis, et Liberum patrem de femore ejus procreatos, docta finxit Graecia."—*St. Jerome, Adv. Jovinianum*, Lib. i. ed. Vallarsii, ii. 309:

c. 440.—". . . Τηνικαῦτα γαρ τὸ Ἐμπεδοκλέους τοῦ παρ' Ἕλλησι φιλοσόφου δόγμα, διὰ τοῦ Μανιχαίου χριστιανισμὸν ὑπεκρίνατο . . . τούτου δὲ τοῦ Σκυθιανοῦ μαθητὴς γίνεται Βούδδας, πρότερον Τερέβινθος καλούμενος . . . κ. τ. λ." (see the same matter from *Georgius Cedrenus* below).—*Socratis, Hist. Eccles.* Lib. I. cap. 22.

c. 840.—"An certè Bragmanorum sequemur opinionem, ut quemadmodum illi sectae suae auctorem **Bubdam**, per virginis latus narrant exortum, ita nos Christum fuisse praedicemus? Vel magis sic nascitur Dei sapientia de virginis cerebro, quomodo Minerva de Jovis vertice, tamquam Liber Pater de femore? Ut Christicolam de virginis partu non solennis natura, vel auctoritas sacrae lectionis, sed superstitio Gentilis, et commenta perdoceant fabulosa."—*Ratramni Corbeiensis L. de Nativitate Xti.*, cap. iii. in *L. D'Achery, Spicilegium*, tom. i. p. 54, Paris, 1723.

c. 870.—"The Indians give in general the name of **budd** to anything connected with their worship, or which forms the object of their veneration. So, an idol is called *budd*."—*Bilâduri*, in *Elliot*, i. 123.

c. 904.—"**Budāsaf** was the founder of the Sabaean Religion . . . he preached to mankind renunciation (of this world) and the intimate contemplation of the superior worlds. . . . There was to be read on the gate of the Naobihar * at Balkh an inscription in the Persian tongue of which this is the interpretation: 'The words of **Budāsaf**: In the courts of kings three things are needed, Sense, Patience, Wealth.' Below had been written in Arabic: '**Budāsaf** lies. If a free man possesses any of the three, he will flee from the courts of Kings.'"—*Mas'ūdī*, iv. 45 and 49.

1000.—"... pseudo-prophets came forward, the number and history of whom it would be impossible to detail. . . . The first mentioned is **Bûdhâsaf**, who came forward in India."—*Albirûnî, Chronology*, by Sachau, p. 186. This name given to Buddha is specially interesting as showing a step nearer the true *Bodhisattva*, the origin of the name Ἰωάσαφ, under which Buddha became a Saint of the Church, and as elucidating Prof. Max Müller's ingenious suggestion of that origin (see *Chips*, &c., iv. 184; see also *Academy*, Sept. 1, 1883, p. 146).

c. 1030.—"A stone was found there in the temple of the great **Budda** on which an inscription . . . purporting that the temple had been founded 50,000 years ago. . . ."—*Al 'Utbi*, in *Elliot*, ii. 39.

c. 1060.—"This madman then, Manēs (also called Scythianus) was by race a Brachman, and he had for his teacher **Budas**, formerly called Terebinthus, who having been brought up by Scythianus in the learning of the Greeks became a follower of the sect of Empedocles (who said there were two first principles opposed to one another), and when he entered Persia declared that he had been born of a virgin, and had been brought up among the hills . . . and this **Budas** (alias Terebinthus) did perish, crushed by an unclean spirit."—*Georg. Cedrenus, Hist. Comp.*,

* Naobihār = Nava-Vihāra ('New Buddhist Monastery') is still the name of a district adjoining Balkh.

Bonn ed., 455 (old ed. i. 259). This wonderful jumble, mainly copied, as we see, from Socrates (*supra*), seems to bring Buddha and Manes together. "Many of the ideas of Manicheism were but fragments of Buddhism."—*E. B. Cowell*, in *Smith's Dict. of Christ. Biog.*

c. 1190.—"Very grieved was Sārang Deva. Constantly he performed the worship of the Arihant; the **Buddhist** religion he adopted; he wore no sword."—*The Poem of Chand Bardai*, paraphr. by *Beames*, in *Ind. Ant.* i. 271.

1610.—". . . This Prince is called in the histories of him by many names: his proper name was *Dramâ Rajo;* but that by which he has been known since they have held him for a saint is the **Budao**, which is as much as to say 'Sage' . . . and to this name the Gentiles throughout all India have dedicated great and superb Pagodas."—*Couto*, Dec. V., liv. vi. cap. 2.

[1615.—"The image of **Dibottes**, with the hudge collosso or bras imadg (or rather idoll) in it."—*Cocks's Diary*, i. 200.]

c. 1666.—"There is indeed another, a seventh Sect, which is called **Bauté**, whence do proceed 12 other different sects; but this is not so common as the others, the Votaries of it being hated and despised as a company of irreligious and atheistical people, nor do they live like the rest."—*Bernier*, E. T., ii. 107; [ed. *Constable*, 336].

1685.—"Above all these they have one to whom they pay much veneration, whom they call **Bodu**; his figure is that of a man."—*Ribeiro*, f. 40*b*.

1728.—"Before Gautama **Budhum** there have been known 26 *Budhums*—viz.: . . . ." —*Valentijn*, v. (Ceylon) 369.

1753.—"Edrisi nous instruit de cette circonstance, en disant que le *Balahar* est adorateur de **Bodda**. Les Brahmènes du Malabar disent que c'est le nom que Vishtnu a pris dans une de ses apparitions, et on connoît Vishtnu pour une des trois principales divinités Indiennes. Suivant St. Jerôme et St. Clément d'Alexandrie, **Budda** ou **Butta** est le legislateur des Gymno-Sophistes de l'Inde. La secte des **Shamans** ou Samanéens, qui est demeurée la dominante dans tous les royaumes d'au delà du Gange, a fait de **Budda** en cette qualité son objet d'adoration. C'est la première des divinités Chingulaises ou de Ceilan, selon Ribeiro. Samano-Codom (see **GAUTAMA**), la grande idole des Siamois, est par eux appelé Putti."—*D'Anville, Éclaircissemens*, 75. What knowledge and apprehension, on a subject then so obscure, is shown by this great Geographer! Compare the pretentious ignorance of the flashy Abbé Raynal in the quotations under 1770.

1770.—"Among the deities of the second order, particular honours are paid to **Buddou**, who descended upon earth to take upon himself the office of mediator between God and mankind."—*Raynal* (tr. 1777), i. 91.

"The *Budzoists* are another sect of Japan, of which **Budzo** was the founder. . . . The spirit of *Budzoism* is dreadful. It breathes nothing but penitence, excessive fear, and cruel severity."—*Ibid.* i. 138. Raynal in the two preceding passages shows that he was not aware that the religions alluded to in Ceylon and in Japan were the same.

1779.—"Il y avoit alors dans ces parties de l'Inde, et principalement à la Côte de Coromandel et à Ceylan, un Culte dont on ignore absolument les Dogmes; le Dieu **Baouth**, dont on ne connoit aujourd'hui, dans l'Inde que le Nom et l'objet de ce Culte; mais il est tout-à-fait aboli, si ce n'est, qu'il se trouve encore quelques familles d'Indiens séparées et méprisées des autres Castes, qui sont restées fidèles à **Baouth**, et qui ne reconnoissent pas la religion des Brames."—*Voyage de M. Gentil*, quoted by *W. Chambers*, in *As. Res.* i. 170.

1801.—"It is generally known that the religion of **Bouddhou** is the religion of the people of *Ceylon*, but no one is acquainted with its forms and precepts. I shall here relate what I have heard upon the subject." —*M. Joinville*, in *As. Res.* vii. 399.

1806.—". . . The head is covered with the cone that ever adorns the head of the Chinese deity Fo, who has been often supposed to be the same as **Boudah**."—*Salt, Caves of Salsette*, in *Tr. Lit. Soc. Bo.* i. 50.

1810.—"Among the **Bhuddists** there are no distinct castes."—*Maria Graham*, 89.

It is remarkable how many poems on the subject of Buddha have appeared of late years. We have noted:

1. **Buddha**, *Epische Dichtung in Zwanzig Gesängen, i.e.* an Epic Poem in 20 cantos (in *ottava rima*). Von Joseph Vittor Widmann, Bern. 1869.

2. *The Story of* **Gautama Buddha** *and his Creed:* An Epic by Richard Phillips, Longmans, 1871. This is also printed in octaves, but each octave consists of 4 heroic couplets.

3. *Vasadavatta*, a **Buddhist** *Idyll;* by Dean Plumtre. Republished in *Things New and Old*, 1884. The subject is the story of the Courtesan of Mathura ("Vāsavadattā and Upagupta"), which is given in Burnouf's *Introd. a l'Histoire du Buddhisme Indien*, 146-148; a touching story, even in its original crude form.

It opens:

"Where proud **Mathoura** rears her hundred towers. . . ."

The Skt. Dict. gives indeed as an alternative *Mathūra*, but *Mathūra* is the usual name, whence Anglo-Ind. **Muttra**.

4. The brilliant Poem of Sir Edwin Arnold, called *The Light of Asia, or the Great Renunciation, being the Life and*

Teaching of **Gautama,** *Prince of India, and Founder of* **Buddhism,** *as told in verse by an Indian* **Buddhist,** 1879.

BUDGE-BUDGE, n. p. A village on the Hooghly R., 15 m. below Calcutta, where stood a fort which was captured by Clive when advancing on Calcutta to recapture it, in December, 1756. The *Imperial Gazetteer* gives the true name as *Baj-baj,* [but Hamilton writes *Bhuja-bhuj*].

1756.—"On the 29th *December,* at six o'clock in the morning, the admiral having landed the Company's troops the evening before at *Mayapour,* under the command of Lieutenant-Colonel Clive, cannonaded **Bougee Bougee** Fort, which was strong and built of mud, and had a wet ditch round it." —*Ives,* 99.

1757.—The Author of *Memoir of the Revolution in Bengal* calls it **Busbudgia**; (1763), Luke Scrafton **Budge Boodjee.**

BUDGEROW, s. A lumbering keelless barge, formerly much used by Europeans travelling on the Gangetic rivers. Two-thirds of the length aft was occupied by cabins with Venetian windows. Wilson gives the word as H. and B. *bajrā;* Shakespear gives H. *bajrā* and *bajra,* with an improbable suggestion of derivation from *bajar,* 'hard or heavy.' Among Blochmann's extracts from Mahommedan accounts of the conquest of Assam we find, in a detail of Mīr Jumla's fleet in his expedition of 1662, mention of 4 *bajras* (*J. As. Soc. Ben.* xli. pt. i. 73). The same extracts contain mention of war-sloops called *bach'haris* (pp. 57, 75, 81), but these last must be different. *Bajra* may possibly have been applied in the sense of 'thunder-bolt.' This may seem unsuited to the modern budgerow, but is not more so than the title of 'lightning-darter' is to the modern **Burkundauze** (q.v.)! We remember how Joinville says of the approach of the great galley of the Count of Jaffa:—"*Sembloit que foudre cheist des ciex.*" It is however perhaps more probable that *bajrā* may have been a variation of *baglā.* And this is especially suggested by the existence of the Portuguese form *pajeres,* and of the Ar. form *bagara* (see under **BUGGALOW**). Mr. Edye, Master Shipwright of the Naval Yard in Trincomalee, in a paper on the Native Craft of India and Ceylon, speaks of the **Baggala** or **Budgerow,** as if he had been accustomed to hear the words used indiscriminately. (See *J. R. A. S.,* vol. i. p. 12). [There is a drawing of a modern Budgerow in *Grant, Rural Life,* p. 5.]

c. 1570.—"Their barkes be light and armed with oares, like to Foistes . . . and they call these barkes **Bazaras** and Patuas" (in Bengal).—*Cæsar Fredericke,* E. T. in *Hakl.* ii. 358.

1662.—(Blochmann's Ext. as above).

1705.—". . . des **Bazaras** qui sont de grands bateaux."—*Luillier,* 52.

1723.—"Le lendemain nous passâmes sur les **Bazaras** de la compagnie de France."—*Lett. Edif.* xiii. 269.

1727.—". . . in the evening to recreate themselves in Chaises or Palankins; . . . or by water in their **Budgeroes,** which is a convenient Boat."—*A. Hamilton,* ii. 12.

1737.—"Charges, **Budgrows** . . . Rs. 281. 6. 3."—MS. *Account from Ft. William,* in India Office.

1780.—"A gentleman's **Bugerow** was drove ashore near Chaun-paul Gaut . . ." —*Hicky's Bengal Gazette,* May 13th.

1781.—"The boats used by the natives for travelling, and also by the Europeans, are the **budgerows,** which both sail and row."—*Hodges,* 39.

1783.—". . . his boat, which, though in Kashmire (it) was thought magnificent, would not have been disgraced in the station of a Kitchen-tender to a Bengal **budgero.**"—*G. Forster, Journey,* ii. 10.

1784.—"I shall not be at liberty to enter my **budgerow** till the end of July, and must be again at Calcutta on the 22nd of October."—*Sir W. Jones,* in *Mem.* ii. 38.

1785.—"Mr. Hastings went aboard his **Budgerow,** and proceeded down the river, as soon as the tide served, to embark for Europe on the Berrington."—In *Seton-Karr,* i. 86.

1794.—"By order of the Governor-General in Council . . . will be sold the Hon'ble Company's **Budgerow,** named the Sonamookhee* . . . the Budgerow lays in the nullah opposite to Chitpore."—*Ibid.* ii. 114.

1830.—

"Upon the bosom of the tide
Vessels of every fabric ride;
The fisher's skiff, the light canoe,
* * * * * *
The **Bujra** broad, the *Bholia* trim,
Or *Pinnaces* that gallant swim,
With favouring breeze—or dull and slow
Against the heady current go . . . ."

H. H. Wilson, in *Bengal Annual,* 29.

* This (*Sonamukhi,* 'Chrysostoma') has continued to be the name of the Viceroy's river yacht (probably) to this day. It was so in Lord Canning's time, then represented by a barge adapted to be towed by a steamer.

BUDGROOK, s. Port. *bazarucco*. A coin of low denomination, and of varying value and metal (copper, tin, lead, and tutenague), formerly current at Goa and elsewhere on the Western Coast, as well as at some other places on the Indian seas. It was also adopted from the Portuguese in the earliest English coinage at Bombay. In the earliest Goa coinage, that of Albuquerque (1510), the *leal* or *bazarucco* was equal to 2 *reis*, of which *reis* there went 420 to the gold *cruzado* (*Gerson da Cunha*). The name appears to have been a native one in use in Goa at the time of the conquest, but its etymology is uncertain. In Van Noort's Voyage (1648) the word is derived from *bāzār*, and said to mean 'market-money' (perhaps *bāzār-rūka*, the last word being used for a copper coin in Canarese). [This view is accepted by Gray in his notes on *Pyrard* (Hak. Soc. ii. 68), and by Burnell (*Linschoten*, Hak. Soc. ii. 143). The *Madras, Admin. Man. Gloss.* (s.v.) gives the Can. form as *bajāra-rokkha*, 'market-money.'] C. P. Brown (MS. notes) makes the word = *badaga-rūka*, which he says would in Canarese be 'base-penny,' and he ingeniously quotes Shakspeare's "beggarly denier," and Horace's "*vilem assem.*" This is adopted in substance by Mr. E. Thomas, who points out that *rukā* or *rukkā* is in Mahratti (see *Molesworth*, s.v.) one-twelfth of an anna. But the words of Khāfi Khān below suggest that the word may be a corruption of the P. *buzurg*, 'big,' and according to Wilson, *budrūkh* (s.v.) is used in Mahratti as a dialectic corruption of *buzūrg*. This derivation may be partially corroborated by the fact that at Mocha there is, or was formerly, a coin (which had become a money of account only, 80 to the dollar) called *kabīr*, *i.e.* 'big' (see *Ovington*, 463, and *Milburn*, i. 98). If we could attach any value to Pyrard's spelling—*bousuruques*—this would be in favour of the same etymology; as is also the form *besorg* given by Mandelslo. [For a full examination of the value of the *budgrook* based on the most recent authorities, see *Whiteway, Rise of the Port. Power*, p. 68.]

1554.—*Bazarucos* at Maluco (Moluccas) 50=1 tanga, at 60 reis to the tanga, 5 tangas =1 pardao. "Os quaes bazarucos se faz comta de 200 caixas" (*i.e.* to the tanga).—*A. Nunes*, 41.

[1584.—**Basaruchies**, *Barret*, in *Hakl.* See **SHROFF.**]

1598.—"They pay two **Basarukes**, which is as much as a Hollander's Doit. . . . It is molten money of badde Tinne."—*Linschoten*, 52, 69; [Hak. Soc. i. 180, 242].

1609.—"Le plus bas argent, sont **Basarucos** . . . et sont fait de mauvais Estain."—*Houtmann*, in *Navigation des Hollandois*, i. 53*v*.

c. 1610.—"Il y en a de plusieurs sortes. La premiere est appellée **Bousuruques**, dont il en faut 75 pour une *Tangue*. Il y a d'autre **Bousuruques** vieilles, dont il en faut 105 pour le Tangue. . . . Il y a de cette monnoye qui est de fer; et d'autre de *callin*, metal de Chine" (see **CALAY**).—*Pyrard*, ii. 39; see also 21; [Hak. Soc. ii. 33, 68].

1611.—"Or a Viceroy coins false money; for so I may call it, as the people lose by it. For copper is worth 40 *xerafims* (see **XERAFINE**) the hundred weight, but they coin the **basaruccos** at the rate of 60 and 70. The Moors on the other hand, keeping a keen eye on our affairs, and seeing what a huge profit there is, coin there on the mainland a great quantity of **basarucos**, and gradually smuggle them into Goa, making a pitful of gold."—*Couto, Dialogo do Soldado Pratico*, 138.

1638.—"They have (at Gombroon) a certain Copper Coin which they call **Besorg**, whereof 6 make a *Peys*, and 10 *Peys* make a *Chay* (*Shāhī*) which is worth about 5*d*. English."—*V. and Tr. of J. A. Mandelslo into the E. Indies*, E. T. 1669, p. 8.

1672.—"Their coins (at **Tanor** in Malabar) . . . of Copper, a **Buserook**, 20 of which make a Fanam."—*Fryer*, 53. [He also spells the word **Basrook**. See quotation under **REAS.**]

1677.—"Rupees, Pices and **Budgrooks.**"—*Letters Patent of Charles II.* in *Charters of the E. I. Co.*, p. 111.

1711.—"The **Budgerooks** (at Muskat) are mixt Mettle, rather like Iron than anything else, have a Cross on one side, and were coin'd by the Portuguese. Thirty of them make a silver *Mamooda*, of about Eight Pence Value."—*Lockyer*, 211.

c. 1720-30.—"They (the Portuguese) also use bits of copper which they call *buzurg*, and four of these **buzurgs** pass for a *fulūs*."—*Khāfi Khān*, in *Elliot*, v. 345.

c. 1760.—"At Goa the sceraphim is worth 240 Portugal *reas*, or about 16*d*. sterling; 2 *reas* make a **basaraco**, 15 **basaracos** a *vintin*, 42 *vintins* a *tanga*, 4 *tangas* a *paru*, 2½ *parues* a pagoda of gold."—*Grose*, i. 282.

1838.—"Only eight or ten loads (of coffee) were imported this year, including two loads of 'Kopes' (see **COPECK**), the copper currency of Russia, known in this country by the name of **Bughrukcha**. They are converted to the same uses as copper."—*Report from Kabul*, by *A. Burnes*; in *Punjab Trade Report*, App. p. iii.

This may possibly contain some indication of the true form of this obscure word, but I have derived no light from it myself. The *budgrook* was apparently current at Muscat down to the beginning of last century (see *Milburn*, i. 116).

BUDLEE, s. A substitute in public or domestic service. H. *badlī*, 'exchange; a person taken in exchange; a *locum tenens*'; from Ar. *badal*, 'he changed.' (See **MUDDLE**.)

BUDMÁSH, s. One following evil courses; Fr. *mauvais sujet*; It. *malandrino*. Properly *bad-ma'āsh*, from P. *bad*, 'evil,' and Ar. *ma'āsh*, 'means of livelihood.'

1844.—". . . the reputation which John Lawrence acquired . . . by the masterly manœuvring of a body of police with whom he descended on a nest of gamblers and cut-throats, '**budmashes**' of every description, and took them all prisoners."—*Bosworth Smith's Life of Ld. Lawrence*, i. 178.

1866.—"The truth of the matter is that I was foolish enough to pay these **budmashes** beforehand, and they have thrown me over." —*The Dawk Bungalow*, by *G. O. Trevelyan*, in *Fraser*, p. 385.

BUDZAT, s. H. from P. *badzāt*, 'evil race,' a low fellow, 'a bad lot,' a blackguard.

1866.—"*Cholmondeley*. Why the shaitan didn't you come before, you lazy old **budzart**?"—*The Dawk Bungalow*, p. 215.

BUFFALO, s. This is of course originally from the Latin *bubalus*, which we have in older English forms, *buffle* and *buff* and *bugle*, through the French. The present form probably came from India, as it seems to be the Port. *bufalo*. The proper meaning of *bubalus*, according to Pliny, was not an animal of the ox-kind (βούβαλις was a kind of African antelope); but in Martial, as quoted, it would seem to bear the vulgar sense, rejected by Pliny.

At an early period of our connection with India the name of *buffalo* appears to have been given erroneously to the common Indian ox, whence came the still surviving misnomer of London shops, '*buffalo* humps.' (See also the quotation from *Ovington*.) The *buffalo* has no hump. Buffalo *tongues* are another matter, and an old luxury, as the third quotation shows. The ox having appropriated the name of the buffalo, the true Indian domestic buffalo was differentiated as the '*water buffalo*,' a phrase still maintained by the British soldier in India. This has probably misled Mr. Blochmann, who uses the term '*water buffalo*,' in his excellent English version of the *Āīn* (*e.g.* i. 219). We find the same phrase in *Barkley's Five Years in Bulgaria*, 1876: "Besides their bullocks every well-to-do Turk had a drove of *water-buffaloes*" (32). Also in *Collingwood's Rambles of a Naturalist* (1868), p. 43, and in *Miss Bird's Golden Chersonese* (1883), 60, 274. [The unscientific use of the word as applied to the American Bison is as old as the end of the 18th century (see *N.E.D.*).]

The domestic buffalo is apparently derived from the wild buffalo (*Bubalus arni*, Jerd.; *Bos bubalus*, Blanf.), whose favourite habitat is in the swampy sites of the Sunderbunds and Eastern Bengal, but whose haunts extend north-eastward to the head of the Assam valley, in the Terai west to Oudh, and south nearly to the Godavery; not beyond this in the Peninsula, though the animal is found in the north and north-east of Ceylon.

The domestic buffalo exists not only in India but in Java, Sumatra, and Manilla, in Mazanderan, Mesopotamia, Babylonia, Adherbijan, Egypt, Turkey, and Italy. It does not seem to be known how or when it was introduced into Italy.—(See *Hehn*.) [According to the *Encycl. Britt.* (9th ed. iv. 442), it was introduced into Greece and Italy towards the close of the 6th century.]

c. A.D. 70.—"Howbeit that country bringeth forth certain kinds of goodly great wild bœufes: to wit the Bisontes, mained with a collar, like Lions; and the Vri [Urus], a mightie strong beast, and a swift, which the ignorant people call *Buffles* (**bubalos**), whereas indeed the *Buffle* is bred in Affrica, and carieth some resemblance of a calfe rather, or a Stag."—*Pliny*, by *Ph. Hollande*, i. 199-200.

c. A.D. 90.—

"Ille tulit geminos facili cervice juvencos
Illi cessit atrox **bubalus** atque bison."
Martial, De Spectaculis, xxiv.

c. 1580.—"Veneti mercatores linguas **Bubalorum**, tanquam mensis optimas, sale conditas, in magna copia Venetias mittunt." —*Prosperi Alpini, Hist. Nat. Aegypti*, P. I. p. 228.

1585.—"Here be many Tigers, wild **Bufs**, and great store of wilde Foule. . ."—*R. Fitch*, in *Hakl.* ii. 389.

"Here are many wilde **buffes** and Elephants."—*Ibid.* 394.

"The King (Akbar) hath . . . as they doe credibly report, 1000 Elephants, 30,000 horses, 1400 tame deere, 800 concubines; such store of ounces, tigers, **Buffles**, cocks and Haukes, that it is very strange to see." —*Ibid.* 386.

1589.—"They doo plough and till their ground with kine, **bufalos**, and bulles."—*Mendoza's China*, tr. by *Parkes*, ii. 56.

[c. 1590.—Two methods of snaring the **buffalo** are described in *Āīn, Blochmann*, tr. i. 293.]

1598.—"There is also an infinite number of wild **buffs** that go wandering about the desarts."—*Pigafetta, E. T.* in *Harleian Coll. of Voyages*, ii. 546.

[1623.—"The inhabitants (of Malabar) keep Cows, or **buffalls**."—*P. della Valle*, Hak. Soc. ii. 207.]

1630.—"As to Kine and **Buffaloes** . . . they besmeare the floores of their houses with their dung, and thinke the ground sanctified by such pollution."—*Lord, Discoverie of the Banian Religion*, 60-61.

1644.—"We tooke coach to Livorno, thro' the Great Duke's new Parke, full of huge corke-trees; the underwood all myrtills, amongst which were many **buffalos** feeding, a kind of wild ox, short nos'd, horns reversed."—*Evelyn*, Oct. 21.

1666.—". . . it produces Elephants in great number, oxen and **buffaloes**" (*bufaros*). —*Faria y Souza*, i. 189.

1689.—". . . both of this kind (of Oxen), and the **Buffaloes**, are remarkable for a big piece of Flesh that rises above Six Inches high between their Shoulders, which is the choicest and delicatest piece of Meat upon them, especially put into a dish of Palau."—*Ovington*, 254.

1808.—". . . the **Buffala** milk, and curd, and butter simply churned and clarified, is in common use among these Indians, whilst the dainties of the Cow Dairy is prescribed to valetudinarians, as Hectics, and preferred by vicicous (*sic*) appetites, or impotents alone, as that of the caprine and assine is at home." —*Drummond, Illus. of Guzerattee*, &c.

1810.—

"The tank which fed his fields was there. . .
There from the intolerable heat
The **buffaloes** retreat;
Only their nostrils raised to meet the air,
Amid the shelt'ring element they rest."
Curse of Kehama ix. 7.

1878.—"I had in my possession a head of a cow **buffalo** that measures 13 feet 8 inches in circumference, and 6 feet 6 inches between the tips—the largest **buffalo** head in the world."—*Pollok, Sport in Br. Burmah*, &c., i. 107.

BUGGALOW, s. Mahr. *baglā, bagalā.* A name commonly given on the W. coast of India to Arab vessels of the old native form. It is also in common use in the Red Sea (*bakalā*) for the larger native vessels, all built of teak from India. It seems to be a corruption of the Span. and Port. *bajel, baxel, baixel, baxella*, from the Lat. *vascellum* (see *Diez, Etym. Wörterb.* i. 439, s. v.). Cobarruvias (1611) gives in his Sp. Dict. "*Baxel*, quasi *vasel*" as a generic name for a vessel of any kind going on the sea, and quotes St. Isidore, who identifies it with *phaselus*, and from whom we transcribe the passage below. It remains doubtful whether this word was introduced into the East by the Portuguese, or had at an earlier date passed into Arabic marine use. The latter is most probable. In *Correa* (c. 1561) this word occurs in the form *pajer*, pl. *pajeres* (*j* and *x* being interchangeable in Sp. and Port. See *Lendas*, i. 2, pp. 592, 619, &c.). In Pinto we have another form. Among the models in the Fisheries Exhibition (1883), there was "A *Zaroogat* or **Bagarah** from Aden." [On the other hand Burton (*Ar. Nights*, i. 119) derives the word from the Ar. *baghlah*, 'a she-mule.' Also see **BUDGEROW**.]

c. 636.—"*Phaselus* est navigium quod nos corrupte **baselum** dicimus. De quo Virgilius: *Pictisque phaselis.*"—*Isodorus Hispalensis, Originum et Etymol.* lib. xix.

c. 1539.—"Partida a nao pera Goa, Fernão de Morais . . . seguio sua viage na volta do porto de Dabul, onde chegou ao outro dia as nove horas, e tomando nelle hũ **paguel** de Malavares, carregado de algodao e de pimenta, poz logo a tormento o Capitano e o piloto delle, os quaes confessarão. . . ."—*Pinto*, ch. viii.

1842.—"As store and horse boats for that service, Capt. Oliver, I find, would prefer the large class of native **buggalas**, by which so much of the trade of this coast with Scinde, Cutch . . . is carried on."—*Sir G. Arthur*, in *Ind. Admin. of Lord Ellenborough*, 222.

[1900. — "His tiny **baggala**, which mounted ten tiny guns, is now employed in trade."—*Bent, Southern Arabia*, 8.]

BUGGY, s. In India this is a (two-wheeled) gig with a hood, like the gentleman's cab that was in vogue in London about 1830-40, before broughams came in. Latham puts a (?) after the word, and the earliest examples that he gives are from the second quarter of this century (from Praed and I. D'Israeli). Though we trace the word much further back, we have not discovered its birthplace or etymology. The word, though used in England, has never been very common there; it is better known both in

Ireland and in America. Littré gives *boghei* as French also. The American *buggy* is defined by Noah Webster as "a light, one-horse, four-wheel vehicle, usually with one seat, and with or without a calash-top." Cuthbert Bede shows (*N. & Q.* 5 ser. v. p. 445) that the adjective 'buggy' is used in the Eastern Midlands for 'conceited.' This suggests a possible origin. "When the Hunterian spelling-controversy raged in India, a learned Member of Council is said to have stated that he approved the change until ——— ——— began to spell *buggy* as *bagī*. Then he gave it up."—(*M.-G. Keatinge.*) I have recently seen this spelling in print. [The *N.E.D.* leaves the etymology unsettled, merely saying that it has been connected with *bogie* and *bug*. The earliest quotation given is that of 1773 below.]

1773.—"Thursday 3d (June). At the sessions at Hicks's Hall two boys were indicted for driving a post-coach and four against a single horse-chaise, throwing out the driver of it, and breaking the chaise to pieces. Justice Welch, the Chairman, took notice of the frequency of the brutish custom among the post drivers, and their insensibility in making it a matter of sport, ludicrously denominating mischief of this kind 'Running down the **Buggies**.'—The prisoners were sentenced to be confined in Newgate for 12 months."—*Gentleman's Magazine*, xliii. 297.

1780.—

"Shall D(*onal*)d come with Butts and tons
And knock down Epegrams and Puns?
With Chairs, old Cots, and **Buggies** trick ye?
Forbid it, Phœbus, and forbid it, Hicky!"
In *Hicky's Bengal Gazette*, May 13th.

„ "... go twice round the Race-Course as hard as we can set legs to ground, but we are beat hollow by Bob Crochet's Horses driven by Miss Fanny Hardheart, who in her career oversets Tim Capias the Attorney in his **Buggy**. . . ."—In *India Gazette*, Dec. 23rd.

1782.—"Wanted, an excellent **Buggy** Horse about 15 Hands high, that will trot 15 miles an hour."—*India Gazette*, Sept. 14.

1784.—"For sale at Mr. Mann's, Rada Bazar. A Phaeton, a four-spring'd **Buggy**, and a two-spring'd ditto. . . ."—*Calcutta Gazette*, in *Seton-Karr*, i. 41.

1793.—"For sale. A good **Buggy** and Horse. . . ."—*Bombay Courier*, Jan. 20th.

1824.—". . . the Archdeacon's **buggy** and horse had every appearance of issuing from the back-gate of a college in Cambridge on Sunday morning."—*Heber*, i. 192 (ed. 1844).

[1837.—"The vehicles of the place (Monghir), amounting to four **Buggies** (that is a foolish term for a cabriolet, but as it is the only vehicle in use in India, and as *buggy* is the only name for said vehicle, I give it up), . . . were assembled for our use."—*Miss Eden, Up the Country*, i. 14.]

c. 1838.—"But substitute for him an average ordinary, uninteresting Minister; obese, dumpy . . . with a second-rate wife —dusty, deliquescent— . . . or let him be seen in one of those Shem-Ham-and-Japhet **buggies**, made on Mount Ararat soon after the subsidence of the waters. . . ."—*Sydney Smith*, 3rd Letter to Archdeacon Singleton.

1848.—"'Joseph wants me to see if his—his **buggy** is at the door.'

"'What is a **buggy**, papa?'

"'It is a one-horse palanquin,' said the old gentleman, who was a wag in his way."—*Vanity Fair*, ch. iii.

1872.—"He drove his charger in his old **buggy**."—*A True Reformer*, ch. i.

1878.—"I don't like your new Bombay **buggy**. With much practice I have learned to get into it, I am hanged if I can ever get out."—*Overland Times of India*, 4th Feb.

1879.—"Driven by that hunger for news which impels special correspondents, he had actually ventured to drive in a 'spider,' apparently a kind of **buggy**, from the Tugela to Ginglihovo."—*Spectator*, May 24th.

BUGIS, n.p. Name given by the Malays to the dominant race of the island of Celébes, originating in the S.-Western limb of the island; the people calling themselves *Wugi*. But the name used to be applied in the Archipelago to native soldiers in European service, raised in any of the islands. Compare the analogous use of **Telinga** (q.v.) formerly in India.

[1615.—"All these in the kingdom of Macassar . . . besides **Bugies**, Mander and Tollova."—*Foster, Letters*, iii. 152.]

1656.—"Thereupon the *Hollanders* resolv'd to unite their forces with the **Bouquises**, that were in rebellion against their Soveraign."—*Tavernier*, E. T. ii. 192.

1688.—"These **Buggasses** are a sort of warlike trading Malayans and mercenary soldiers of India. I know not well whence they come, unless from Macassar in the Isle of Celebes."—*Dampier*, ii. 108.

[1697.—". . . with the help of **Buggesses**. . . ."—*Hedges, Diary*, Hak. Soc. ii. cxvii.]

1758.—"The Dutch were commanded by Colonel Roussely, a French soldier of fortune. They consisted of nearly 700 Europeans, and as many **buggoses**, besides country troops."—*Narr. of Dutch attempt in Hoogly*, in *Malcolm's Clive*, ii. 87.

1783.—"**Buggesses**, inhabitants of Celebes."—*Forrest, Voyage to Mergui*, p. 59.

1783.—"The word **Buggess** has become among Europeans consonant to soldier, in the east of India, as Sepoy is in the West." —*Ibid.* 78.

1811.—"We had fallen in with a fleet of nine **Buggese** prows, when we went out towards Pulo Mancap."—*Lord Minto in India*, 279.

1878.—"The **Bugis** are evidently a distinct race from the Malays, and come originally from the southern part of the Island of Celebes."—*McNair, Perak*, 130.

BULBUL, s. The word *bulbul* is originally Persian (no doubt intended to imitate the bird's note), and applied to a bird which does duty with Persian poets for the nightingale. Whatever the Persian *bulbul* may be correctly, the application of the name to certain species in India "has led to many misconceptions about their powers of voice and song," says Jerdon. These species belong to the family *Brachipodidae*, or short-legged thrushes, and the true *bulbuls* to the sub-family *Pycnonotinae*, *e.g.* genera *Hypsipetes*, *Hemixos*, *Alcurus*, *Criniger*, *Ixos*, *Kelaartia*, *Rubigula*, *Brachipodius*, *Otocompsa*, *Pycnonotus* (*P. pygaeus*, common Bengal Bulbul; *P. haemorhous*, common Madras Bulbul). Another sub-family, *Phyllornithinae*, contains various species which Jerdon calls *green Bulbuls*.

[A lady having asked the late Lord Robertson, a Judge of the Court of Session, "What sort of animal is the *bull-bull*?" he replied, "I suppose, Ma'am, it must be the mate of the *coo-coo*."—3rd ser., *N. & Q.* v. 81.]

1784.—"We are literally lulled to sleep by Persian nightingales, and cease to wonder that the **Bulbul**, with a thousand tales, makes such a figure in Persian poetry."—*Sir W. Jones*, in *Memoirs*, &c., ii. 37.

1813.—"The **bulbul** or Persian nightingale. . . . I never heard one that possessed the charming variety of the English nightingale . . . whether the Indian **bulbul** and that of Iran entirely correspond I have some doubts."—*Forbes, Oriental Memoirs*, i. 50; [2nd ed. i. 34].

1848.—"'It is one's nature to sing and the other's to hoot,' he said, laughing, 'and with such a sweet voice as you have yourself, you must belong to the **Bulbul** faction." —*Vanity Fair*, ii. ch. xxvii.

BULGAR, BOLGAR, s. P. *bulghār*. The general Asiatic name for what we call 'Russia leather,' from the fact that the region of manufacture and export was originally **Bolghār** on the Volga, a kingdom which stood for many centuries, and gave place to Kazan in the beginning of the 15th century. The word was usual also among Anglo-Indians till the beginning of last century, and is still in native Hindustani use. A native (mythical) account of the manufacture is given in *Baden-Powell's Punjab Handbook*, 1872, and this fanciful etymology: "as the scent is derived from soaking in the pits (*ghār*), the leather is called *Balghār*" (p. 124).

1298.—"He bestows on each of those 12,000 Barons . . . likewise a pair of boots of **Borgal**, curiously wrought with silver thread."—*Marco Polo*, 2nd ed. i. 381. See also the note on this passage.

c. 1333.—"I wore on my feet boots (or stockings) of wool; over these a pair of linen lined, and over all a thin pair of **Borghāli**, *i.e.* of horse-leather lined with wolf skin."—*Ibn Batuta*, ii. 445.

[1614.—"Of your **Bullgaryan** hides there are brought hither some 150."—*Foster, Letters*, iii. 67.]

1623.—Offer of Sheriff Freeman and Mr. Coxe to furnish the Company with "**Bulgary** red hides."—*Court Minutes*, in *Sainsbury*, iii. 184.

1624.—"Purefy and Hayward, Factors at Ispahan to the E. I. Co., have bartered morse-teeth and '**bulgars**' for carpets."—*Ibid.* p. 268.

1673.—"They carry also **Bulgar**-Hides, which they form into Tanks to bathe themselves."—*Fryer*, 398.

c. 1680.—"Putting on a certain dress made of **Bulgar**-leather, stuffed with cotton."—*Seir Mutaqherin*, iii. 387.

1759.—Among expenses on account of the Nabob of Bengal's visit to Calcutta we find:

"To 50 pair of **Bulger** Hides at 13 per pair, Rs. 702 : 0 : 0."—*Long*, 193.

1786.—Among "a very capital and choice assortment of Europe goods" we find "**Bulgar** Hides."—*Cal. Gazette*, June 8, in *Seton-Karr*, i. 177.

1811.—"Most of us furnished at least one of our servants with a kind of bottle, holding nearly three quarts, made of **bulghár** . . . or Russia-leather."—*W. Ousely's Travels*, i. 247.

In Tibetan the word is **bulhari**.

BULKUT, s. A large decked ferry-boat; from Telug. *balla*, a board. (C. P. Brown).

BULLUMTEER, s. Anglo-Sepoy dialect for '*Volunteer*.' This distinctive title was applied to certain regiments of the old Bengal Army, whose terms of enlistment embraced service beyond sea; and in the days of that army various ludicrous stories were current in connection with the name.

BUMBA, s. H. *bamba*, from Port. *bomba*, 'a pump.' Haex (1631) gives: "*Bomba*, organum pneumaticum quo aqua hauritur," as a Malay word. This is incorrect, of course, as to the origin of the word, but it shows its early adoption into an Eastern language. The word is applied at Ahmedabad to the water-towers, but this is modern; [and so is the general application of the word in N. India to a canal distributary].

1572.—

"Alija, disse o mestre rijamente,
Alija tudo ao mar, não falte acordo
Vão outros dar á **bomba**, não cessando;
A' **bomba** que nos imos alagando.'"
Camões, vi. 72.

By Burton:

"'Heave!' roared the Master with a mighty roar,
'Heave overboard your all, together's the word!
Others go work the pumps, and with a will:
The pumps! and sharp, look sharp, before she fill!'"

BUMMELO, s. A small fish, abounding on all the coasts of India and the Archipelago; *Harpodon nehereus* of Buch. Hamilton; the specific name being taken from the Bengali name *nehare*. The fish is a great delicacy when fresh caught and fried. When dried it becomes the famous Bombay Duck (see **DUCKS, BOMBAY**), which is now imported into England.

The origin of either name is obscure. Molesworth gives the word as Mahratti with the spelling *bombīl*, or *bombīla* (p. 595 *a*). *Bummelo* occurs in the Supp. (1727) to Bluteau's Dict. in the Portuguese form *bambulim*, as "the name of a very savoury fish in India." The same word *bambulim* is also explained to mean '*humas pregas na saya a moda*,' 'certain plaits in the fashionable ruff,' but we know not if there is any connection between the two. The form *Bombay Duck* has an analogy to *Digby Chicks* which are sold in the London shops, also a kind of dried fish, pilchards we believe, and the name may have originated in imitation of this or some similar English name. [The *Digby Chick* is said to be a small herring cured in a peculiar manner at *Digby*, in Lincolnshire: but the Americans derive them from *Digby* in Nova Scotia; see 8 ser. *N. & Q.* vii. 247.]

In an old chart of Chittagong River (by B. Plaisted, 1764, published by A. Dalrymple, 1785) we find a point called *Bumbello Point*.

1673.—"Up the Bay a Mile lies Massigoung, a great Fishing-Town, peculiarly notable for a Fish called **Bumbelow**, the Sustenance of the Poorer sort."—*Fryer*, 67.

1785.—"My friend General Campbell, Governor of Madras, tells me that they make Speldings in the East Indies, particularly at Bombay, where they call them **Bumbaloes**."—Note by *Boswell* in his *Tour to the Hebrides*, under August 18th, 1773.

1810.—"The **bumbelo** is like a large sand-eel; it is dried in the sun, and is usually eaten at breakfast with kedgeree."—*Maria Graham*, 25.

1813.—Forbes has **bumbalo**; *Or. Mem.*, i. 53; [2nd ed., i. 36].

1877.—"**Bummalow** or *Bolil*, the dried fish still called 'Bombay Duck.'"—*Burton, Sind Revisited*, i. 68.

BUNCUS, BUNCO, s. An old word for cheroot. Apparently from the Malay *bungkus*, 'a wrapper, bundle, thing wrapped.'

1711.—"Tobacco . . . for want of Pipes they smoke in **Buncos**, as on the *Coromandel* Coast. A **Bunco** is a little Tobacco wrapt up in the Leaf of a Tree, about the Bigness of one's little Finger, they light one End, and draw the Smoke thro' the other . . . these are curiously made up, and sold 20 or 30 in a bundle."—*Lockyer*, 61.

1726.—"After a meal, and on other occasions it is one of their greatest delights, both men and women, old and young, to eat *Pinang* (areca), and to smoke tobacco, which the women do with a **Bongkos**, or dry leaf rolled up, and the men with a *Gorregorri* (a little can or flower pot) whereby they both manage to pass most of their time."—*Valentijn*, v. *Chorom.*, 55. [*Gorregorri* is Malay *guri-guri*, 'a small earthenware pot, also used for holding provisions' (*Klinkert*).]

" (In the retinue of Grandees in Java):

"One with a coconut shell mounted in gold or silver to hold their tobacco or **bongkooses** (*i.e.* tobacco in rolled leaves)."—*Valentijn*, iv. 61.

c. 1760.—"The tobacco leaf, simply rolled up, in about a finger's length, which they call a **buncus**, and is, I fancy, of the same make as what the West Indians term a segar; and of this the Gentoos chiefly make use."—*Grose*, i. 146.

BUND, s. Any artificial embankment, a dam, dyke, or causeway. H. *band*. The root is both Skt. (*bandh*) and P., but the common word, used as it is without aspirate, seems to have come from the latter. The word is common in Persia (*e.g.* see **BENDAMEER**). It is also naturalised in the Anglo-Chinese ports. It is there applied especially to the embanked quay along the shore of the settlements. In Hong Kong alone this is called (not *bund*, but) *praia* (Port. 'shore' [see **PRAYA**]), probably adopted from Macao.

1810.—"The great **bund** or dyke."—*Williamson, V. M.* ii. 279.

1860.—"The natives have a tradition that the destruction of the **bund** was effected by a foreign enemy."—*Tennent's Ceylon*, ii. 504.

1875.—"... it is pleasant to see the Chinese ... being propelled along the **bund** in their hand carts."—*Thomson's Malacca*, &c., 408.

1876.—"... so I took a stroll on Tien-Tsin **bund**."—*Gill, River of Golden Sand*, i. 28.

BUNDER, s. P. *bandar*, a landing-place or quay; a seaport; a harbour; (and sometimes also a custom-house). The old Ital. *scala*, mod. *scalo*, is the nearest equivalent in most of the senses that occurs to us. We have (c. 1565) the *Mīr-bandar*, or Port Master, in Sind (*Elliot*, i. 277) [cf. **Shabunder**]. The Portuguese often wrote the word **bandel**. **Bunder** is in S. India the popular native name of **Masulipatam**, or *Machli-bandar*.

c. 1344.—"The profit of the treasury, which they call **bandar**, consists in the right of buying a certain portion of all sorts of cargo at a fixed price, whether the goods be only worth that or more; and this is called the *Law of the Bandar*."—*Ibn Batuta*, iv. 120.

c. 1346.—"So we landed at the **bandar**, which is a large collection of houses on the sea-shore."—*Ibid.* 228.

1552.—"Coga-atar sent word to Affonzo d'Alboquerque that on the coast of the main land opposite, at a port which is called **Bandar** Angon ... were arrived two ambassadors of the King of Shiraz."—*Barros*, II. ii. 4.

[1616.—"Besides the danger in intercepting our boats to and from the shore, &c., their firing from the **Banda** would be with much difficulty."—*Foster, Letters*, iv. 328.]

1673.—"We fortify our Houses, have **Bunders** or Docks for our Vessels, to which belong Yards for Seamen, Soldiers, and Stores."—*Fryer*, 115.

1809.—"On the new **bunder** or pier."—*Maria Graham*, 11.

[1847, 1860.—See quotations under **APOLLO BUNDER**.]

BUNDER-BOAT, s. A boat in use on the Bombay and Madras coast for communicating with ships at anchor, and also much employed by officers of the civil departments (Salt, &c.) in going up and down the coast. It is rigged as Bp. Heber describes, with a cabin amidships.

1825.—"We crossed over ... in a stout boat called here a **bundur boat**. I suppose from '*bundur*' a harbour, with two masts, and two lateen sails. ..."—*Heber*, ii. 121, ed. 1844.

BUNDOBUST, s. P.-H.—*band-o-bast*, lit. 'tying and binding.' Any system or mode of regulation; discipline; a revenue settlement.

[1768.—"Mr. Rumbold advises us ... he proposes making a tour through that province ... and to settle the **Bandobust** for the ensuing year."—*Letter to the Court of Directors*, in *Verelst, View of Bengal*, App. 77.]

c. 1843.—"There must be *bahut achch'hā bandobast* (*i.e.* very good order or discipline) in your country," said an aged Khānsamā (in Hindustani) to one of the present writers. "When I have gone to the Sandheads to meet a young gentleman from *Bilāyat*, if I gave him a cup of tea, '*tānki tānki*,' said he. Three months afterwards this was all changed; bad language, violence, no more *tānki*."

1880.—"There is not a more fearful wild-fowl than your travelling M.P. This unhappy creature, whose mind is a perfect blank regarding *Faujdāri* and **Bandobast**. ..."—*Ali Baba*, 181.

BUNDOOK, s. H. *bandūk*, from Ar. *bunduk*. The common H. term for a musket or matchlock. The history of the word is very curious. *Bunduḳ*, pl. *banādiḳ*, was a name applied by the Arabs to filberts (as some allege) because they came from Venice (*Banadiḳ*, comp. German *Venedig*). The name was transferred to the nut-like pellets shot from cross-bows, and thence the cross-bows or arblasts were called *bunduḳ*, elliptically for *kaus al-b.*, 'pellet-bow.' From cross-bows the name was transferred again to fire-arms, as in the parallel case of *arquebus*. [Al-Bandukāni, 'the man of the pellet-bow,' was one of the names by which the Caliph Hārūn-al-Rashīd was known, and Al Zahir Baybars al-Bandukdāri, the fourth Baharite Soldan (A.D. 1260-77) was so entitled because he had been slave to a Bandukdār, or Master of Artillery (*Burton, Ar. Nights*, xii. 38).]

[1875.—"**Bandūqis**, or orderlies of the Maharaja, carrying long guns in a loose red cloth cover."—*Drew, Jummoo and Kashmir*, 74.]

BUNGALOW, s. H. and Mahr. *banglā*. The most usual class of house occupied by Europeans in the interior of India; being on one story, and covered by a pyramidal roof, which in the normal bungalow is of thatch, but may be of tiles without impairing its title to be called a *bungalow*. Most of the houses of officers in Indian cantonments are of this character. In reference to the style of the house, *bungalow* is sometimes employed in contradistinction to the (usually more pretentious) *pucka house;* by which latter term is implied a masonry house with a terraced roof. A *bungalow* may also be a small building of the type which we have described, but of temporary material, in a garden, on a terraced roof for sleeping in, &c., &c. The word has also been adopted by the French in the East, and by Europeans generally in Ceylon, China, Japan, and the coast of Africa.

Wilson writes the word *bānglā*, giving it as a Bengālī word, and as probably derived from *Banga*, Bengal. This is fundamentally the etymology mentioned by Bp. Heber in his *Journal* (see below), and that etymology is corroborated by our first quotation, from a native historian, as well as by that from F. Buchanan. It is to be remembered that in Hindustan proper the adjective 'of or belonging to Bengal' is constantly pronounced as *bangălā* or *banglā*. Thus one of the eras used in E. India is distinguished as the *Banglā* era. The probability is that, when Europeans began to build houses of this character in Behar and Upper India, these were called *Banglā* or 'Bengal-fashion' houses; that the name was adopted by the Europeans themselves and their followers, and so was brought back to Bengal itself, as well as carried to other parts of India. ["In Bengal, and notably in the districts near Calcutta, native houses to this day are divided into *ath-chala*, *chau-chala*, and *Bangala*, or eight-roofed, four-roofed, and Bengali, or common huts. The first term does not imply that the house has eight coverings, but that the roof has four distinct sides with four more projections, so as to cover a verandah all round the house, which is square. The *Bangala*, or Bengali house, or *bungalow* has a sloping roof on two sides and two gable ends. Doubtless the term was taken up by the first settlers in Bengal from the native style of edifice, was materially improved, and was thence carried to other parts of India. It is not necessary to assume that the first bungalows were erected in Behar." (*Saturday Rev.*, 17th April 1886, in a review of the first ed. of this book).]

A.H. 1041=A.D. 1633.—"Under the rule of the Bengalis (*darahd-i-Bangālīyān*) a party of Frank merchants, who are inhabitants of Sundíp, came trading to Sátgánw. One kos above that place they occupied some ground on the banks of the estuary. Under the pretence that a building was necessary for their transactions in buying and selling, they erected several houses in the **Bengálí** style."—*Bādshāhnāma*, in *Elliot*, vii. 31.

c. 1680.—In the tracing of an old Dutch chart in the India Office, which may be assigned to about this date, as it has no indication of Calcutta, we find at Hoogly: "*Ougli . . . Hollantze Logie* . . . **Bangelaer** *of Speelhuys*," *i.e.* "Hoogly . . . Dutch Factory . . . **Bungalow**, or Pleasure-house."

1711.—"*Mr. Herring, the Pilot's, Directions for bringing of Ships down the River of Hughley.*

"From *Gull Gat* all along the *Hughley* Shore until below the *New Chaney* almost as far as the *Dutch* **Bungelow** lies a Sand. . . ."—*Thornton, The English Pilot*, Pt. III. p. 54.

1711.—"*Natty* **Bungelo** or *Nedds* **Bangalla** River lies in this Reach (Tanna) on the Larboard side. . ."—*Ibid.* 56. The place in the chart is *Nedds* **Bengalla**, and seems to have been near the present Akra on the Hoogly.

1747.—"Nabob's Camp near the Hedge of the Bounds, building a **Bangallaa**, raising Mudd Walls round the Camp, making Gun Carriages, &c. . . . (Pagodas) 55 : 10 : 73."—*Acct. of Extraordinary Charges* . . . January, at *Fort St. David, MS. Records in India Office.*

1758.—"I was talking with my friends in Dr. Fullerton's **bangla** when news came of Ram Narain's being defeated."—*Seir Mutaqherin*, ii. 103.

1780.—"To be Sold or Let, A Commodious **Bungalo** and out Houses . . . situated on the Road leading from the Hospital to the Burying Ground, and directly opposite to the Avenue in front of Sir Elijah Impey's House. . . ."—*The India Gazette*, Dec. 23.

1781-83.—"**Bungelows** are buildings in India, generally raised on a base of brick, one, two, or three feet from the ground, and consist of only one story: the plan of them usually is a large room in the center for an eating and sitting room, and rooms at each corner for sleeping; the whole is covered with one general thatch, which comes low to each side; the spaces between the angle rooms are *viranders* or open porticoes . . . sometimes the center *viranders* at each end are converted into rooms."—*Hodges, Travels*, 146.

1784.—"To be let at Chinsurah . . . That large and commodious House. . . . The outbuildings are—a warehouse and two large *bottle-connahs*, 6 store-rooms, a cook-room, and a garden, with a **bungalow** near the house."—*Cal. Gazette*, in *Seton-Karr*, i. 40.

1787.—"At Barrackpore many of the **Bungalows** much damaged, though none entirely destroyed."—*Ibid.* p. 213.

1793.—". . . the **bungalo**, or Summer-house. . . ."—*Dirom*, 211.

" "For Sale, a **Bungalo** situated between the two Tombstones, in the Island of Coulaba."—*Bombay Courier*, Jan. 12.

1794.—"The candid critic will not however expect the parched plains of India, or **bungaloes** in the land-winds, will hardly tempt the Aonian maids wont to disport on the banks of Tiber and Thames. . . ."—*Hugh Boyd*, 170.

1809.—"We came to a small **bungalo** or garden-house, at the point of the hill, from which there is, I think, the finest view I ever saw."—*Maria Graham*, 10.

c. 1810.—"The style of private edifices that is proper and peculiar to Bengal consists of a hut with a pent roof constructed of two sloping sides which meet in a ridge forming the segment of a circle. . . . This kind of hut, it is said, from being peculiar to Bengal, is called by the natives **Banggolo**, a name which has been somewhat altered by Europeans, and applied by them to all their buildings in the cottage style, although none of them have the proper shape, and many of them are excellent brick houses."—*Buchanan's Dinagepore* (in *Eastern India*, ii. 922).

1817.—"The *Yorŭ-bangala* is made like two thatched houses or **bangalas**, placed side by side. . . . These temples are dedicated to different gods, but are not now frequently seen in Bengal."—*Ward's Hindoos*, Bk. II. ch. i.

c. 1818.—"As soon as the sun is down we will go over to the Captain's **bungalow**."—*Mrs Sherwood, Stories*, &c., ed. 1873, p. 1. The original editions of this book contain an engraving of "The Captain's Bungalow at Cawnpore" (c. 1811-12), which shows that no material change has occurred in the character of such dwellings down to the present time.

1824.—"The house itself of Barrackpore . . . barely accommodates Lord Amherst's own family; and his aides-de-camp and visitors sleep in bungalows built at some little distance from it in the Park. **Bungalow**, a corruption of Bengalee, is the general name in this country for any structure in the cottage style, and only of one floor. Some of these are spacious and comfortable dwellings. . . ."—*Heber*, ed. 1844, i. 33.

1872.—"L'emplacement du **bungalou** avait été choisi avec un soin tout particulier."—*Rev. des Deux Mondes*, tom., xcviii. 930.

1875.—"The little groups of officers dispersed to their respective **bungalows** to dress and breakfast."—*The Dilemma*, ch. i.

[In Oudh the name was specially applied to Fyzabad.

[1858.—"Fyzabad . . . was founded by the first rulers of the reigning family, and called for some time **Bungalow**, from a bungalow which they built on the verge of the stream."—*Sleeman, Journey through the Kingdom of Oudh*, i. 137.]

BUNGALOW, DAWK-, s. A rest-house for the accommodation of travellers, formerly maintained (and still to a reduced extent) by the paternal care of the Government of India. The *matériel* of the accommodation was humble enough, but comprised the things essential for the weary traveller—shelter, a bed and table, a bath-room, and a servant furnishing food at a very moderate cost. On principal lines of thoroughfare these bungalows were at a distance of 10 to 15 miles apart, so that it was possible for a traveller to make his journey by marches without carrying a tent. On some less frequented roads they were 40 or 50 miles apart, adapted to a night's run in a palankin.

1853.—"**Dâk-bungalows** have been described by some Oriental travellers as the 'Inns of India.' Playful satirists!"—*Oakfield*, ii. 17.

1866.—"The **Dawk Bungalow**; or, Is his Appointment Pucka?"—By *G. O. Trevelyan*, in *Fraser's Magazine*, vol. 73, p. 215.

1878.—"I am inclined to think the value of life to a **dak bungalow** fowl must be very trifling."—*In my Indian Garden*, 11.

BUNGY, s. H. *bhangī*. The name of a low caste, habitually employed as sweepers, and in the lowest menial offices, the man being a house sweeper and dog-boy, [his wife an **Ayah**]. Its members are found throughout Northern and Western India, and every European household has a servant of this class. The colloquial application of the term *bungy* to such servants is however peculiar to Bombay, [but the word is commonly used in the N.W.P. but always with a contemptuous significance]. In the Bengal Pry. he is generally called **Mehtar** (q.v.), and by politer natives Halālkhor (see **HALALCORE**), &c. In Madras *totī* (see **TOTY**) is the usual word; [in W. India *Dher* or *Dheḍ*]. Wilson suggests that the caste name may be derived from *bhang* (see **BANG**), and this is possible enough, as the class is generally given to strong drink and intoxicating drugs.

1826.—"The *Kalpa* or Skinner, and the **Bunghee**, or Sweeper, are yet one step below the *Dher*."—*Tr. Lit. Soc. Bombay*, iii. 362.

BUNOW, s. and v. H. *banāo*, used in the sense of 'preparation, fabrication,' &c., but properly the imperative of *banānā*, 'to make, prepare, fabricate.' The Anglo-Indian word is applied to anything fictitious or factitious, 'a cram, a shave, a sham'; or, as a verb, to the manufacture of the like. The following lines have been found among old papers belonging to an officer who was at the Court of the Nawāb Sa'ādat 'Ali at Lucknow, at the beginning of the last century:—

"Young Grant and Ford the other day
Would fain have had some Sport,
But Hound nor Beagle none had they,
Nor aught of Canine sort.
A luckless *Parry* * came most pat
When Ford—'we've Dogs enow!
Here *Maitre—Kawn aur Doom ko Kaut Juld!* Terrier **bunnow**!' †

"So Saadut with the like design
(I mean, to form a Pack)
To * * * * * t gave a Feather fine
And Red Coat to his Back;
A Persian Sword to clog his side,
And Boots Hussar *sub-nyah*,‡
Then eyed his Handiwork with Pride,
Crying *Meejir myn* **bunnayah** !!!" §

"Appointed to be said or sung in all Mosques, Mutts, Tuckeahs, or Eedgahs within the Reserved Dominions." ‖

1853.—"You will see within a week if this is anything more than a **banau**."—*Oakfield*, ii. 58.

[1870.—"We shall be satisfied with choosing for illustration, out of many, one kind of **benowed** or prepared evidence."—*Chevers, Med. Jurisprud.*, 86.]

* *I.e.* Pariah dog.

† "Mehtar! cut his ears and tail, quick; *fabricate* a Terrier!"

‡ All new.

§ "See, *I* have *fabricated* a Major!"

‖ The writer of these lines is believed to have been Captain Robert Skirving, of Croys, Galloway, a brother of Archibald Skirving, a Scotch artist of repute, and the son of Archibald Skirving, of East Lothian, the author of a once famous ballad on the battle of Prestonpans. Captain Skirving served in the Bengal army from about 1780 to 1806, and died about 1840.

BURDWÁN, n.p. A town 67 m. N.W. of Calcutta — *Bardwān*, but in its original Skt. form *Vardhamāna*, 'thriving, prosperous,' a name which we find in Ptolemy (*Bardamana*), though in another part of India. Some closer approximation to the ancient form must have been current till the middle of 18th century, for Holwell, writing in 1765, speaks of "*Burdwan*, the principal town of *Burdomaan*" (*Hist. Events*, &c., i. 112; see also 122, 125).

BURGHER. This word has three distinct applications.

a. s. This is only used in Ceylon. It is the Dutch word *burger*, 'citizen.' The Dutch admitted people of mixt descent to a kind of citizenship, and these people were distinguished by this name from pure natives. The word now indicates any persons who claim to be of partly European descent, and is used in the same sense as '*half-caste*' and '*Eurasian*' in India Proper. [In its higher sense it is still used by the Boers of the Transvaal.]

1807.—"The greater part of them were admitted by the Dutch to all the privileges of citizens under the denomination of **Burghers**."—*Cordiner, Desc. of Ceylon.*

1877.—"About 60 years ago the **Burghers** of Ceylon occupied a position similar to that of the Eurasians of India at the present moment."—*Calcutta Review*, cxvii. 180-1.

b. n.p People of the **Nilgherry** Hills, properly *Baḍagas*, or 'Northerners.'—See under **BADEGA**.

c. s. A rafter, H. *bargā*.

BURKUNDAUZE, s. An armed retainer; an armed policeman, or other armed unmounted employé of a civil department; from Ar.-P. *barkandāz*, 'lightning-darter,' a word of the same class as *jān-bāz*, &c. [Also see **BUXERRY**.]

1726.—"2000 men on foot, called **Bircandes**, and 2000 pioneers to make the road, called *Bieldars* (see **BILDAR**)."—*Valentijn*, iv. *Suratte*, 276.

1793.—"Capt. Welsh has succeeded in driving the Bengal **Berkendosses** out of Assam."—*Cornwallis*, ii. 207.

1794.—"Notice is hereby given that persons desirous of sending escorts of **burkundazes** or other armed men, with merchandise, are to apply for passports."—In *Seton-Karr*, ii. 139.

[1832.—"The whole line of march is guarded in each procession by **burkhandhars** (matchlock men), who fire singly, at intervals, on the way."—*Mrs Meer Hassan Ali*, i. 87.]

BURMA, BURMAH (with **BURMESE**, &c.) n.p. The name by which we designate the ancient kingdom and nation occupying the central basin of the Irawadi River. "British Burma" is constituted of the provinces conquered from that kingdom in the two wars of 1824-26 and 1852-53, viz. (in the first) Arakan, Martaban, Tenasserim, and (in the second) Pegu. [Upper Burma and the Shan States were annexed after the third war of 1885.]

The name is taken from **Mran-mā**, the national name of the Burmese people, which they themselves generally pronounce *Bam-mā*, unless when speaking formally and emphatically. Sir Arthur Phayre considers that this name was in all probability adopted by the Mongoloid tribes of the Upper Irawadi, on their conversion to Buddhism by missionaries from Gangetic India, and is identical with that (*Brām-mā*) by which the first and holy inhabitants of the world are styled in the (Pali) Buddhist Scriptures. *Brahma-desa* was the term applied to the country by a Singhalese monk returning thence to Ceylon, in conversation with one of the present writers. It is however the view of Bp. Bigandet and of Prof. Forchhammer, supported by considerable arguments, that *Mran*, *Myan*, or *Myen* was the original name of the Burmese people, and is traceable in the names given to them by their neighbours; *e.g.* by Chinese *Mien* (and in Marco Polo); by Kakhyens, *Myen* or *Mren*; by Shans, *Mān*; by Sgaw Karens, *Payo*; by Pgaw Karens, *Payān*; by Paloungs, *Parān*, &c.* Prof. F. considers that Mran-*mā* (with this honorific suffix) does not date beyond the 14th century. [In *J. R A. Soc.* (1894, p. 152 *seqq.*), Mr. St John suggests that the word *Myamma* is derived from *myan*, 'swift,' and *ma*, 'strong,' and was taken as a soubriquet by the people at some early date, perhaps in the time of Anawrahta, A.D. 1150.]

* Forchhammer argues further that the original name was Ran or Yan, with *m'*, *mā*, or *pa* as a pronominal accent.

1516.—"Having passed the Kingdom of Bengale, along the coast which turns to the South, there is another Kingdom of Gentiles, called **Berma**. . . . They frequently are at war with the King of Peigu. We have no further information respecting this country, because it has no shipping."—*Barbosa*, 181.

[,, "**Verma**." See quotation under **ARAKAN**.

[1538.—"But the war lasted on and the **Bramās** took all the kingdom."—*Correa*, iii. 851.]

1543.—"And folk coming to know of the secrecy with which the force was being despatched, a great desire took possession of all to know whither the Governor intended to send so large an armament, there being no Rumis to go after, and nothing being known of any other cause why ships should be despatched in secret at such a time. So some gentlemen spoke of it to the Governor, and much importuned him to tell them whither they were going, and the Governor, all the more bent on concealment of his intentions, told them that the expedition was going to Pegu to fight with the **Bramas** who had taken that Kingdom."—*Ibid.* iv. 298.

c. 1545.—"*How the King of* **Bramâ** *undertook the conquest of this kingdom of Sião* (Siam), *and of what happened till his arrival at the City of Odiâ.*"—*F. M. Pinto* (orig.) cap. 185.

[1553.—"**Bremá**." See quotation under **JANGOMAY**.]

1606.—"Although one's whole life were wasted in describing the superstitions of these Gentiles—the Pegus and the **Bramas**—one could not have done with the half, therefore I only treat of some, in passing, as I am now about to do."—*Couto*, viii. cap. xii.

[1639.—"His (King of Pegu's) Guard consists of a great number of Souldiers, with them called **Brahmans**, is kept at the second Port."—*Mandelslo, Travels*, E. T. ii. 118.]

1680.—"ARTICLES of COMMERCE to be proposed to the King of **Barma** and Pegu, in behalfe of the English Nation for the settling of a Trade in those countrys."—*Ft. St. Geo. Cons.*, in *Notes and Exts.*, iii. 7.

1727.—"The Dominions of **Barma** are at present very large, reaching from *Moravi* near *Tanacerin*, to the Province of *Yunan* in *China*."—*A. Hamilton*, ii. 41.

1759.—"The **Bûraghmahs** are much more numerous than the Peguese and more addicted to commerce; even in Pegu their numbers are 100 to 1."—Letter in *Dalrymple*, *O. R.*, i. 99. The writer appears desirous to convey by his unusual spelling some accurate reproduction of the name as he had heard it. His testimony as to the predominance of Burmese in Pegu, at that date even, is remarkable.

[1763.—"**Burmah.**" See quotation under **MUNNEEPORE.**

[1767.—"**Buraghmagh.**" See quotation under **SONAPARANTA.**

[1782.—"**Bahmans.**" See quotation under **GAUTAMA.**]

1793.—"**Burmah** borders on Pegu to the north, and occupies both banks of the river as far as the frontiers of China."—*Rennell's Memoir*, 297.

[1795.—"**Birman.**" See quotation under **SHAN.**

[c. 1819.—"In fact in their own language, their name is not **Burmese**, which we have borrowed from the Portuguese, but **Biamma.**"—*Sangermano*, 36.]

BURRA-BEEBEE, s. H. *barī bībī*, 'Grande dame.' This is a kind of slang word applied in Anglo-Indian society to the lady who claims precedence at a party. [Nowadays *Barī Mem* is the term applied to the chief lady in a Station.]

1807.—"At table I have hitherto been allowed but one dish, namely the **Burro Bebee**, or lady of the highest rank."—*Lord Minto in India*, 29.

1848.—"The ladies carry their **burrahbibiship** into the steamers when they go to England. . . . My friend endeavoured in vain to persuade them that whatever their social importance in the 'City of Palaces,' they would be but small folk in London."—*Chow Chow*, by *Viscountess Falkland*, i. 92.

[**BURRA-DIN**, s. H. *barā-din*. A 'great day,' the term applied by natives to a great festival of Europeans, particularly to Christmas Day.

[1880.—"This being the **Burra Din**, or great day, the fact of an animal being shot was interpreted by the men as a favourable augury."—*Ball, Jungle Life*, 279.]

BURRA-KHANA, s. H. *barā khānā*, 'big dinner'; a term of the same character as the two last, applied to a vast and solemn entertainment.

[1880.—"To go out to a **burra khana**, or big dinner, which is succeeded in the same or some other house by a larger evening party."—*Wilson, Abode of Snow*, 51.]

BURRA SAHIB. H. *barā*, 'great'; 'the great *Ṣāḥib* (or Master),' a term constantly occurring, whether in a family to distinguish the father or the elder brother, in a station to indicate the Collector, Commissioner, or whatever officer may be the recognised head of the society, or in a department to designate the head of that department, local or remote.

[1889.—"At any rate a few of the great lords and ladies (**Burra Sahib** and **Burra Mem Sahib**) did speak to me without being driven to it."—*Lady Dufferin*, 34.]

BURRAMPOOTER, n.p. Properly (Skt.) *Brahmaputra* ('the son of Brahmā'), the great river *Brahmputr* of which Assam is the valley. Rising within 100 miles of the source of the Ganges, these rivers, after being separated by 17 degrees of longitude, join before entering the sea. There is no distinct recognition of this great river by the ancients, but the *Diardanes* or *Oidanes*, of Curtius and Strabo, described as a large river in the remoter parts of India, abounding in dolphins and crocodiles, probably represents this river under one of its Skt. names, *Hlādini*.

1552.—Barros does not mention the name before us, but the Brahmaputra seems to be the river of *Caor*, which traversing the kingdom so called (**Gour**) and that of **Comotay**, and that of *Cirote* (see **SILHET**), issues above *Chatigão* (see **CHITTAGONG**), in that notable arm of the Ganges which passes through the island of Sornagam.

c. 1590.—"There is another very large river called **Berhumputter**, which runs from Khatai to Coach (see **COOCH BEHAR**) and from thence through Bazoohah to the sea."—*Ayeen Akberry* (Gladwin) ed. 1800, ii. 6; [ed. *Jarrett*, ii. 121].

1726.—"Out of the same mountains we see . . . a great river flowing which . . . divides into two branches, whereof the easterly one on account of its size is called the Great **Barrempooter.**"—*Valentijn*, v. 154.

1753.—"Un peu au-dessous de Daka, le Gange est joint par une grosse rivière, qui sort de la frontière du Tibet. Le nom de **Bramanpoutre** qu'on lui trouve dans quelques cartes est une corruption de celui de **Brahmaputren**, qui dans le langage du pays signifie tirant son origine de Brahma."—*D'Anville, Eclaircissemens*, 62.

1767.—"Just before the Ganges falls into ye Bay of Bengall, it receives the **Barramputrey** or Assam River. The Assam River is larger than the Ganges . . . it is a perfect Sea of fresh Water after the Junction of the two Rivers. . . ."—*MS. Letter* of *James Rennell*, d. 10th March.

1793.—". . . till the year 1765, the **Burrampooter**, as a capital river, was unknown in Europe. On tracing this river in 1765, I was no less surprised at finding it rather larger than the Ganges, than at its course previous to its entering Bengal. . . . I could no longer doubt that the **Burrampooter** and Sanpoo were one and the same river."—*Rennell, Memoir*, 3rd ed. 356.

BURREL, s. H. *bharal; Ovis nahura*, Hodgson. The blue wild sheep of the Himālaya. [*Blanford, Mamm.* 499, with illustration.]

BURSAUTEE, s. H. *barsātī*, from *barsāt*, 'the Rains.'

a. The word properly is applied to a disease to which horses are liable in the rains, pustular eruptions breaking out on the head and fore parts of the body.

[1828.—"That very extraordinary disease, the **bursattee**."—*Or. Sport. Mag.*, reprint, 1873, i. 125.

[1832.—"Horses are subject to an infectious disease, which generally makes its appearance in the rainy season, and therefore called **burrhsaatie**."—*Mrs Meer Hassan Ali*, ii. 27.]

b. But the word is also applied to a waterproof cloak, or the like. (See **BRANDY COORTEE.**)

1880.—"The scenery has now been arranged for the second part of the Simla season . . . and the appropriate costume for both sexes is the decorous **bursatti**."—*Pioneer Mail*, July 8.

BUS, adv. P.-H. *bas*, 'enough.' Used commonly as a kind of interjection: 'Enough! Stop! *Ohe jam satis! Basta, basta!*' Few Hindustani words stick closer by the returned Anglo-Indian. The Italian expression, though of obscure etymology, can hardly have any connection with *bas*. But in use it always feels like a mere expansion of it!

1853.—"'And if you pass,' say my dear good-natured friends, 'you may get an appointment. **Bus**! (you see my Hindostanee knowledge already carries me the length of that emphatic monosyllable). . . .'"—*Oakfield*, 2nd ed. i. 42.

BUSHIRE, n.p. The principal modern Persian seaport on the Persian Gulf; properly *Abūshahr*.

1727.—"Bowchier is also a Maritim Town. . . . It stands on an Island, and has a pretty good Trade."—*A. Hamilton*, i. 90.

BUSTEE, s. An inhabited quarter, a village. H. *bastī*, from Skt. *vas*= 'dwell.' Many years ago a native in Upper India said to a European assistant in the Canal Department: "You Feringis talk much of your country and its power, but we know that the whole of you come from five villages" (*pānch* **basti**). The word is applied in Calcutta to the separate groups of huts in the humbler native quarters, the sanitary state of which has often been held up to reprobation.

[1889.—"There is a dreary **bustee** in the neighbourhood which is said to make the most of any cholera that may be going."—*R. Kipling, City of Dreadful Night*, 54.]

BUTLER, s. In the Madras and Bombay Presidencies this is the title usually applied to the head-servant of any English or quasi-English household. He generally makes the daily market, has charge of domestic stores, and superintends the table. As his profession is one which affords a large scope for feathering a nest at the expense of a foreign master, it is often followed at Madras by men of comparatively good caste. (See **CONSUMAH.**)

1616.—"Yosky the **butler**, being sick, asked lycense to goe to his howse to take phisick."—*Cocks*, i. 135.

1689.—". . . the **Butlers** are enjoin'd to take an account of the Place each Night, before they depart home, that they (the Peons) might be examin'd before they stir, if ought be wanting."—*Ovington*, 393.

1782.—"Wanted a Person to act as Steward or **Butler** in a Gentleman's House, *he must understand Hairdressing*."—*India Gazette*, March 2.

1789.—"No person considers himself as comfortably accommodated without entertaining a *Dubash* at 4 pagodas per month, a **Butler** at 3, a Peon at 2, a Cook at 3, a Compradore at 2, and kitchen boy at 1 pagoda."—*Munro's Narrative of Operations*, p. 27.

1873.—"Glancing round, my eye fell on the pantry department . . . and the **butler** trimming the reading lamps."—*Camp Life in India, Fraser's Mag.*, June, 696.

1879.—". . . the moment when it occurred to him (*i.e.* the Nyoung-young Prince of Burma) that he ought really to assume the guise of a Madras **butler**, and be off to the Residency, was the happiest inspiration of his life."—*Standard*, July 11.

BUTLER-ENGLISH. The broken English spoken by native servants in the Madras Presidency; which is not very much better than the **Pigeon-English** of China. It is a singular dialect; the present participle (*e.g.*) being used for the future indicative, and the preterite indicative being formed by 'done'; thus *I telling*= 'I will tell'; *I done tell* = 'I have told'; *done come* = 'actually arrived.' Peculiar meanings are also attached to words; thus *family* = 'wife.' The oddest characteristic about this jargon is (or was) that masters used it in speaking to their servants as well as servants to their masters.

BUXEE, s. A military paymaster; H. *bakhshī*. This is a word of complex and curious history.

In origin it is believed to be the Mongol or Turki corruption of the Skt. *bhikshu*, 'a beggar,' and thence a Buddhist or religious mendicant or member of the ascetic order, bound by his discipline to obtain his daily food by begging.* *Bakshi* was the word commonly applied by the Tartars of the host of Chingiz and his successors, and after them by the Persian writers of the Mongol era, to the regular Buddhist clergy; and thus the word appears under various forms in the works of medieval European writers from whom examples are quoted below. Many of the class came to Persia and the west with Hulākū and with Bātū Khān; and as the writers in the Tartar camps were probably found chiefly among the *bakshis*, the word underwent exactly the same transfer of meaning as our *clerk*, and came to signify a *literatus*, scribe or secretary. Thus in the Latino-Perso-Turkish vocabulary, which belonged to Petrarch and is preserved at Venice, the word *scriba* is rendered in Comanian, *i.e.* the then Turkish of the Crimea, as *Bacsi*. The change of meaning did not stop here.

Abu'l-Fazl in his account of Kashmīr (in the *Āīn*, [ed. *Jarrett*, iii. 212]) recalls the fact that *bakhshī* was the title given by the learned among Persian and Arabic writers to the Buddhist priests whom the Tibetans styled *lāmās*. But in the time of Baber, say circa 1500, among the Mongols the word had come to mean *surgeon*; a change analogous again, in some measure, to our colloquial use of *doctor*. The modern Mongols, according to Pallas, use the word in the sense of 'Teacher,' and apply it to the most venerable or learned priest of a community. Among the Kirghiz Kazzāks, who profess Mahommedanism, it has come to bear the character which Marco Polo more or less associates with it, and means a mere conjurer or medicine-man; whilst in Western Turkestan it signifies a 'Bard' or 'Minstrel.' [Vambéry in his *Sketches of Central Asia* (p. 81) speaks of a *Bakhshi* as a troubadour.]

By a further transfer of meaning, of which all the steps are not clear, in another direction, under the Mohammedan Emperors of India the word *bakhshi* was applied to an officer high in military administration, whose office is sometimes rendered 'Master of the Horse' (of horse, it is to be remembered, the whole substance of the army consisted), but whose duties sometimes, if not habitually, embraced those of Paymaster-General, as well as, in a manner, of Commander-in-Chief, or Chief of the Staff. [Mr. Irvine, who gives a detailed account of the Bakhshi under the latter Moguls (*J. R. A. Soc.*, July 1896, p. 539 *seqq.*), prefers to call him Adjutant-General.] More properly perhaps this was the position of the *Mīr Bakhshī*, who had other *bakhshīs* under him. *Bakhshīs* in military command continued in the armies of the Mahrattas, of Hyder Ali, and of other native powers. But both the Persian spelling and the modern connection of the title with *pay* indicate a probability that some confusion of association had arisen between the old Tartar title and the P. *bakhsh*, 'portion,' *bakhshīdan*, 'to give,' *bakhshīsh*, 'payment.' In the early days of the Council of Fort William we find the title **Buxee** applied to a European Civil officer, through whom payments were made (see *Long* and *Seton-Karr*, passim). This is obsolete, but the word is still in the Anglo-Indian Army the recognised designation of a *Paymaster*.

This is the best known existing use of the word. But under some Native Governments it is still the designation of a high officer of state. And according to the *Calcutta Glossary* it has been used in the N.W.P. for 'a collector of a house tax' (?) and the like; in Bengal for 'a superintendent of peons'; in Mysore for 'a treasurer,' &c. [In the N.W.P. the *Bakhshī*, popularly known to natives as '*Bakhshī Tikkas*,' 'Tax Bakhshi,' is the person in charge

* In a note with which we were favoured by the late Prof. Anton Schiefner, he expressed doubts whether the *Bakshi* of the Tibetans and Mongols was not of early introduction through the Uigurs from some other corrupted Sanskrit word, or even of præ-buddhistic derivation from an Iranian source. We do not find the word in Jaeschke's Tibetan Dictionary.

of one of the minor towns which are not under a Municipal Board, but are managed by a *Panch*, or body of assessors, who raise the income needed for watch and ward and conservancy by means of a graduated house assessment.] See an interesting note on this word in *Quatremère, H. des Mongols*, 184 *seqq.*; also see *Marco Polo*, Bk. i. ch. 61, note.

1298.—"There is another marvel performed by those **Bacsi**, of whom I have been speaking as knowing so many enchantments. . . ."—*Marco Polo*, Bk. I. ch. 61.

c. 1300.—"Although there are many **Bakhshis**, Chinese, Indian and others, those of Tibet are most esteemed."—*Rashiduddín*, quoted by *D'Ohsson*, ii. 370.

c. 1300.—"Et sciendum, quod Tartar quosdam homines super omnes de mundo honorant: **boxitas**, scilicet quosdam pontifices ydolorum."—*Ricoldus de Montecrucis*, in *Peregrinatores*, *IV.* p. 117.

c. 1308.—"Ταῦτα γὰρ Κουτζίμπαξις ἐπανήκων πρὸς βασιλέα διεβεβαίου· πρῶτος δὲ τῶν ἱερομάγων, τοὔνομα τοῦτο ἐξελληνίζεται."—*Georg. Pachymeres de Andronico Palaeologo, Lib.* vii. The last part of the name of this *Kutzimpaxis*, 'the first of the sacred magi,' appears to be **Bakhshi**; the whole perhaps to be *Khoja*-**Bakhshi**, or *Kūchin-Bakhshi*.

c. 1340.—"The Kings of this country sprung from Jinghiz Khan . . . followed exactly the *yassah* (or laws) of that Prince and the dogmas received in his family, which consisted in revering the sun, and conforming in all things to the advice of the **Bakshis**."—*Shihābuddīn*, in *Not. et Extr.* xiii. 237.

1420.—"In this city of Kamcheu there is an idol temple 500 cubits square. In the middle is an idol lying at length, which measures 50 paces. . . . Behind this image . . . figures of **Bakshis** as large as life. . . ."—*Shah Rukh's Mission to China*, in *Cathay*, i. cciii.

1615.—"Then I moved him for his favor for an *English* Factory to be Resident in the Towne, which hee willingly granted, and gave present order to the **Buxy**, to draw a *Firma* both for their comming vp, and for their residence."—*Sir T. Roe*, in *Purchas*, i. 541; [Hak. Soc. i. 93.]

c. 1660.—". . . obliged me to take a Salary from the *Grand Mogol* in the quality of a Phisitian, and a little after from *Danechmend-Kan*, the most knowing man of *Asia*, who had been **Bakchis**, or Great Master of the Horse."—*Bernier*, E.T. p. 2; [ed. *Constable*, p. 4].

1701.—"The friendship of the **Buxie** is not so much desired for the post he is now in, but that he is of a very good family, and has many relations near the King."—In *Wheeler*, i. 378.

1706-7.—"So the Emperor appointed a nobleman to act as the **bakshí** of Kám Bakhsh, and to him he intrusted the Prince, with instructions to take care of him. The **bakshí** was Sultan Hasan, otherwise called Mír Malang."—*Dowson's Elliot*, vii. 385.

1711.—"To his Excellency Zulfikar Khan Bahadur, Nurzerat Sing (*Nasrat-Jang?*) **Backshee** of the whole Empire."—*Address of a Letter from President and Council of Fort St. George*, in *Wheeler*, ii. 160.

1712.—"Chan Dhjehaan . . . first **Baksi** general, or Muster-Master of the horsemen."—*Valentijn*, iv. (Suratte), 295.

1753.—"The **Buxey** acquaints the Board he has been using his endeavours to get sundry artificers for the Negrais."—In *Long*, 43.

1756.—Barth. Plaisted represents the bad treatment he had met with for "strictly adhering to his duty during the **Buxy**-ship of Messrs. Bellamy and Kempe"; and "the abuses in the post of **Buxy**."—*Letter to the Hon. the Court of Directors, &c.*, p. 3.

1763.—"The **buxey** or general of the army, at the head of a select body, closed the procession."—*Orme*, i. 26 (reprint).

1766.—"The **Buxey** lays before the Board an account of charges incurred in the **Buxey Connah** . . . for the relief of people saved from the *Falmouth*."—*Ft. William, Cons.*, *Long*, 457.

1793.—"The **bukshey** allowed it would be prudent in the Sultan not to hazard the event."—*Dirom*, 50.

1804.—"A **buckshee** and a body of horse belonging to this same man were opposed to me in the action of the 5th; whom I daresay that I shall have the pleasure of meeting shortly at the Peshwah's durbar."—*Wellington*, iii. 80.

1811.—"There appear to have been different descriptions of **Buktshies** (in Tippoo's service). The **Buktshies** of Kushoons were a sort of commissaries and paymasters, and were subordinate to the *sipahdâr*, if not to the Resâladâr, or commandant of a battalion. The **Meer Buktshy**, however, took rank of the Sipahdâr. The **Buktshies** of the *Ehsham* and **Jyshe** were, I believe, the superior officers of these corps respectively."—Note to *Tippoo's Letters*, 165.

1823.—"In the Mahratta armies the prince is deemed the Sirdar or Commander; next to him is the **Bukshee** or Paymaster, who is vested with the principal charge and responsibility, and is considered accountable for all military expenses and disbursements."—*Malcolm, Central India*, i. 534.

1827.—"Doubt it not—the soldiers of the Beegum Mootee Mahul . . . are less hers than mine. I am myself the **Bukshee** . . . and her Sirdars are at my devotion."—*Walter Scott, The Surgeon's Daughter*, ch. xii.

1861.—"To the best of my memory he was accused of having done his best to urge the people of Dhar to rise against our Government, and several of the witnesses deposed to this effect; amongst them the **Bukshi**."—*Memo. on Dhar*, by *Major McMullen*.

1874.—"Before the depositions were taken down, the gomasta of the planter drew aside the **Bakshi**, who is a police-officer next to the darogá."—*Govinda Samanta*, ii. 235.

BUXERRY, s. A matchlock man; apparently used in much the same sense as **Burkundauze** (q.v.) now obsolete. We have not found this term excepting in documents pertaining to the middle decades of 18th century in Bengal; [but see references supplied by Mr. Irvine below;] nor have we found any satisfactory etymology. *Buxo* is in Port. a gun-barrel (Germ. *Buchse*); which suggests some possible word *buxeiro*. There is however none such in Bluteau, who has, on the other hand, "*Butgeros*, an Indian term; artillery-men, &c.," and quotes from *Hist. Orient.* iii. 7: "*Butgeri* sunt hi qui quinque tormentis praeficiuntur." This does not throw much light. *Bajjar*, 'thunderbolt,' may have given vogue to a word in analogy to P. *barḳ-andāz*, 'lightning-darter,' but we find no such word. As an additional conjecture, however, we may suggest *Baksāris*, from the possible circumstance that such men were recruited in the country about *Baksār* (*Buxar*), *i.e.* the *Shāhābād* district, which up to 1857 was a great recruiting ground for sepoys. [There can be no doubt that this last suggestion gives the correct origin of the word. *Buchanan Hamilton, Eastern India*, i. 471, describes the large number of men who joined the native army from this part of the country.]

[1690.—The Mogul army was divided into three classes—*Suwārān*, or mounted men; *Topkhānah*, artillery; *Aḥshām*, infantry and artificers.

["*Aḥshām—Bandūqchī-i-jangī—Baksariyah wa Bundelah Aḥshām*, *i.e.* regular matchlock-men, **Baksariyahs** and Bundelahs."—*Dastūr-ul-'amal*, written about 1690-1; *B. Museum MS.*, No. 1641, fol. 58*b*.]

1748.—"Ordered the Zemindars to send **Buxerries** to clear the boats and bring them up as Prisoners."—*Ft. William Cons.*, April, in *Long*, p. 6.

" "We received a letter from . . . Council at Cossimbazar . . . advising of their having sent Ensign McKion with all the Military that were able to travel, 150 **buxerries**, 4 field pieces, and a large quantity of ammunition to Cutway."—*Ibid.* p. 1.

1749.—"Having frequent reports of several straggling parties of this banditti plundering about this place, we on the 2d November ordered the Zemindars to entertain one hundred **buxeries** and fifty pike-men over and above what were then in pay for the protection of the outskirts of your Honor's town."—*Letter to Court*, Jan. 13, *Ibid.* p. 21.

1755.—"Agreed, we despatch Lieutenant John Harding of a command of soldiers 25 **Buxaries** in order to clear these boats if stopped in their way to this place."—*Ibid.* 55.

" "In an account for this year we find among charges on behalf of William Wallis, Esq., Chief at Cossimbazar:

	Rs.
"'4 **Buxeries** . . .	20 (year) . 240.'"

MS. Records in India Office.

1761.—"The 5th they made their last effort with all the Sepoys and **Buxerries** they could assemble."—In *Long*, 254.

" "The number of **Buxerriés** or matchlockmen was therefore augmented to 1500."—*Orme* (reprint), ii. 59.

" "In a few minutes they killed 6 **buxerries**."—*Ibid.* 65; see also 279.

1772.—"**Bucksserrias**. Foot soldiers whose common arms are only sword and target."—*Glossary in Grose's Voyage*, 2nd ed. [This is copied, as Mr. Irvine shows, from the Glossary of 1757 prefixed to *An Address to the Proprietors of E. I. Stock*, in *Holwell's Indian Tracts*, 3rd ed., 1779.]

1788.—"**Buxerries**—Foot soldiers, whose common arms are swords and targets or spears."—*Indian Vocabulary* (Stockdale's).

1850.—"Another point to which Clive turned his attention . . . was the organization of an efficient native regular force. . . . Hitherto the native troops employed at Calcutta . . . designated **Buxarries** were nothing more than *Burkandāz*, armed and equipped in the usual native manner."—*Broome, Hist. of the Rise and Progress of the Bengal Army*, i. 92.

BYDE, or **BEDE HORSE**, s. A note by Kirkpatrick to the passage below from *Tippoo's Letters* says *Byde Horse* are "the same as *Pindârehs*, *Looties*, and *Kuzzâks*" (see **PINDARRY**, **LOOTY**, **COSSACK**). In the *Life of Hyder Ali* by Hussain 'Ali Khān Kirmāni, tr. by Miles, we read that Hyder's Kuzzaks were under the command of "Ghazi Khan **Bede**." But whether this leader was so called from leading the "**Bede**" Horse, or gave his name to them, does not appear. Miles has the highly intelligent note: 'Bede is another name for (Kuzzak): Kirkpatrick supposed the word Bede meant infantry, which, I believe, it does not' (p. 36). The quotation from the *Life of Tippoo* seems to indicate that it was the name of a caste. And we find in *Sherring's Indian Tribes and Castes*, among those of Mysore, mention of the **Bedar** as a tribe, probably of huntsmen, dark, tall, and warlike. Formerly many were employed as soldiers, and served in Hyder's wars (iii. 153; see also the same tribe in the S. Mahratta country, ii. 321). Assuming *-ar* to be a plural sign, we have here probably the "**Bedes**" who gave their name to these plundering horse. The **Bedar** are mentioned as one of the predatory classes of the peninsula, along with Marawars, Kallars, Ramūsis (see **RAMOOSY**), &c., in Sir Walter Elliot's paper (*J. Ethnol. Soc.*, 1869, N.S. pp. 112-13). But more will be found regarding them in a paper by the late Gen. Briggs, the translator of Ferishta's Hist. (*J. R. A. Soc.* xiii.). Besides Bedar, **Bednor** (or Nagar) in Mysore seems to take its name from this tribe. [See *Rice, Mysore*, i. 255.]

1758.—". . . The Cavalry of the Rao . . . received such a defeat from Hydur's **Bedes** or Kuzzaks that they fled and never looked behind them until they arrived at Goori Bundar."—*Hist. of Hydur Naik*, p. 120.

1785.—"**Byde Horse**, out of employ, have committed great excesses and depredations in the Sircar's dominions."—*Letters of Tippoo Sultan*, 6.

1802.—"The Kakur and Chapao horse . . . (Although these are included in the **Bede** tribe, they carry off the palm even from them in the arts of robbery) . . ."—*H. of Tipú*, by *Hussein 'Ali Khan Kirmāni*, tr. by Miles, p. 76.

[**BYLEE**, s. A small two-wheeled vehicle drawn by two oxen. H. *bahal*, *bahlī*, *bailī*, which has no connection, as is generally supposed, with *bail*, 'an ox'; but is derived from the Skt. *vah*, 'to carry.' The *bylee* is used only for passengers, and a larger and more imposing vehicle of the same class is the **Rut**. There is a good drawing of a Panjab *bylee* in *Kipling's Beast and Man* (p. 117); also see the note on the quotation from Forbes under **HACKERY**.

[1841.—"A native **bylee** will usually produce, in gold and silver of great purity, ten times the weight of precious metals to be obtained from a general officer's equipage."—*Society in India*, i. 162.

[1854.—"Most of the party . . . were in a barouch, but the rich man himself [one of the Muttra Seths] still adheres to the primitive conveyance of a **bylis**, a thing like a footboard on two wheels, generally drawn by two oxen, but in which he drives a splendid pair of white horses, sitting cross-legged the while!"—*Mrs Mackenzie, Life in the Mission*, &c., ii. 205.]

C

CABAYA, s. This word, though of Asiatic origin, was perhaps introduced into India by the Portuguese, whose writers of the 16th century apply it to the surcoat or long tunic of muslin, which is one of the most common native garments of the better classes in India. The word seems to be one of those which the Portuguese had received in older times from the Arabic (*kabā*, 'a vesture'). From Dozy's remarks this would seem in Barbary to take the form *kabāya*. Whether from Arabic or from Portuguese, the word has been introduced into the Malay countries, and is in common use in Java for the light cotton surcoat worn by Europeans, both ladies and gentlemen, in dishabille. The word is not now used in India Proper, unless by the Portuguese. But it has become familiar in Dutch, from its use in Java. [Mr. Gray, in his notes to *Pyrard* (i. 372), thinks that the word was introduced before the time of the Portuguese, and remarks that **kabaya** in Ceylon means a coat or jacket worn by a European or native.]

c. 1540.—"There was in her an Embassador who had brought *Hidalcan* [**Idalcan**] a very rich **Cabaya** . . . which he would not accept of, for that thereby he would not acknowledge himself subject to the Turk."—*Cogan's Pinto*, pp. 10-11.

1552.—". . . he ordered him then to bestow a **cabaya**."—*Castanheda*, iv. 438. See also Stanley's *Correa*, 132.

1554.—"And moreover there are given to these Kings (Malabar Rajas) when they come to receive these allowances, to each of them a **cabaya** of silk, or of scarlet, of 4 cubits, and a cap or two, and two sheath-knives."—*S. Botelho, Tombo*, 26.

1572.—

"Luzem da fina purpura as **cabayas**,
Lustram os pannos da tecida seda."
Camões, ii. 93.

"**Cabaya** de damasco rico e dino
Da Tyria cor, entre elles estimada."
Ibid. 95.

In these two passages Burton translates *caftan*.

1585.—"The King is apparelled with a **Cabie** made like a shirt tied with strings on one side."—*R. Fitch*, in *Hakl.*, ii. 386.

1598.—"They wear sometimes when they go abroad a thinne cotton linnen gowne called **Cabaia**. . . ."—*Linschoten*, 70; [Hak. Soc. i. 247].

c. 1610.—"Cette jaquette ou soutane, qu'ils appellent *Libasse* (P. *libās*, 'clothing') ou **Cabaye**, est de toile de Cotton fort fine et blanche, qui leur va jusqu'aux talons."—*Pyrard de Laval*, i. 265; [Hak. Soc. i. 372].

[1614.—"The white **Cabas** which you have with you at Bantam would sell here." —*Foster, Letters*, ii. 44.]

1645.—"Vne **Cabaye** qui est vne sorte de vestement comme vne large soutane couverte par le devant, à manches fort larges."—*Cardim, Rel. de la Prov. du Japon*, 56.

1689.—"It is a distinction between the *Moors* and *Bannians*, the *Moors* tie their **Caba's** always on the Right side, and the *Bannians* on the left. . . ."—*Ovington*, 314. This distinction is still true.

1860.—"I afterwards understood that the dress they were wearing was a sort of native garment, which there in the country they call *sarong* or **kabaai**, but I found it very unbecoming."—*Max Havelaar*, 43. [There is some mistake here, **sarong** and *Kabaya* are quite different.]

1878.—"Over all this is worn (by Malay women) a long loose dressing-gown style of garment called the **kabaya**. This robe falls to the middle of the leg, and is fastened down the front with circular brooches."—*McNair, Perak*, &c., 151.

CABOB, s. Ar.-H. *kabāb*. This word is used in Anglo-Indian households generically for roast meat. [It usually follows the name of the dish, *e.g. murghī kabāb*, 'roast fowl'.] But specifically it is applied to the dish described in the quotations from Fryer and Ovington.

c. 1580.—"Altero modo . . . ipsam (carnem) in parva frustra dissectam, et veruculis ferreis acuum modo infixam, super crates ferreas igne supposito positam torrefaciunt, quam succo limonum aspersam avidè esitant."—*Prosper Alpinus*, Pt. i. 229.

1673.—"**Cabob** is Rostmeat on Skewers, cut in little round pieces no bigger than a Sixpence, and Ginger and Garlick put between each."—*Fryer*, 404.

1689.—"**Cabob**, that is Beef or Mutton cut in small pieces, sprinkled with salt and pepper, and dipt with Oil and Garlick, which have been mixt together in a dish, and then roasted on a Spit, with sweet Herbs put between and stuff in them, and basted with Oil and Garlick all the while."—*Ovington*, 397.

1814.—"I often partook with my Arabs of a dish common in Arabia called **Kabob** or **Kab-ab**, which is meat cut into small pieces and placed on thin skewers, alternately between slices of onion and green ginger, seasoned with pepper, salt, and Kian, fried in ghee, to be ate with rice and dholl."—*Forbes, Or. Mem.* ii. 480; [2nd ed. ii. 82; in i. 315 he writes **Kebabs**].

[1876.—". . . *kavap* (a name which is naturalised with us as **Cabobs**), small bits of meat roasted on a spit. . . ."—*Schuyler, Turkistan*, i. 125.]

CABOOK, s. This is the Ceylon term for the substance called in India **Laterite** (q.v.), and in Madras by the native name **Moorum** (q.v.). The word is perhaps the Port. *cabouco* or *cavouco*, 'a quarry.' It is not in Singh. Dictionaries. [Mr. Ferguson says that it is a corruption of the Port. *pedras de cavouco*, 'quarry-stones,' the last word being by a misapprehension applied to the stones themselves. The earliest instance of the use of the word he has met with occurs in the *Travels* of Dr. Aegidius Daalmans (1687-89), who describes **kaphok** stone as 'like small pebbles lying in a hard clay, so that if a large square stone is allowed to lie for some time in the water, the clay dissolves and the pebbles fall in a heap together; but if this stone is laid in good mortar, so that the water cannot get at it, it does good service' (*J. As. Soc. Ceylon*, x. 162). The word is not in the ordinary Singhalese Dicts., but A. Mendis Gunasekara in his Singhalese Grammar (1891), among words derived from the Port., gives *kabuk-gal* (*cabouco*), *cabook* (stone), 'laterite.']

1834.—"The soil varies in different situations on the Island. In the country round Colombo it consists of a strong red clay, or marl, called **Cabook**, mixed with sandy ferruginous particles."—*Ceylon Gazetteer*, 33.

" "The houses are built with **cabook**, and neatly whitewashed with chunam."—*Ibid.* 75.

1860.—"A peculiarity which is one of the first to strike a stranger who lands at Galle or Colombo is the bright red colour of the streets and roads . . . and the ubiquity of the fine red dust which penetrates every crevice and imparts its own tint to every neglected article. Natives resident in these localities are easily recognisable elsewhere by the general hue of their dress. This is occasioned by the prevalence . . . of *laterite*, or, as the Singhalese call it, **cabook**."—*Tennent's Ceylon*, i. 17.

CABUL, CAUBOOL, &c., n.p. This name (*Kābul*) of the chief city of N. Afghanistan, now so familiar, is perhaps traceable in Ptolemy, who gives in that same region a people called Καβολῖται, and a city called Κάβουρα. Perhaps, however, one or both may be corroborated by the νάρδος Καβαλίτη of the Periplus. The accent of Kābul is most distinctly on the first and long syllable, but English mouths are very perverse in error here. Moore accents the last syllable :

"... pomegranates full
Of melting sweetness, and the pears
And sunniest apples that **Caubul**
In all its thousand gardens bears."
Light of the Harem.

Mr. Arnold does likewise in *Sohrab and Rustam :*

"But as a troop of pedlars from **Cabool**,
Cross underneath the Indian Caucasus. . . ."

It was told characteristically of the late Lord Ellenborough that, after his arrival in India, though for months he heard the name correctly spoken by his councillors and his staff, he persisted in calling it *Căbōol* till he met Dost Mahommed Khan. After the interview the Governor-General announced as a new discovery, from the Amir's pronunciation, that *Cābŭl* was the correct form.

1552.—Barros calls it "a Cidade **Cabol**, Metropoli dos Mogoles."—IV. vi. 1.

[c. 1590.—"The territory of **Kábul** comprises twenty Tumáns."—*Āīn*, tr. *Jarrett*, ii. 410.]

1856.—

"Ah **Cabul** ! word of woe and bitter shame ;
Where proud old England's flag, dishonoured, sank
Beneath the Crescent ; and the butcher knives
Beat down like reeds the bayonets that had flashed
From Plassey on to snow-capt Caucasus,
In triumph through a hundred years of war."
The Banyan Tree, a Poem.

CACOULI, s. This occurs in the App. to the *Journal d'Antoine Galland*, at Constantinople in 1673 : "Dragmes de **Cacouli**, drogue qu'on use dans le Cahue," *i.e.* in coffee (ii. 206). This is Pers. Arab. *kākula* for Cardamom, as in the quotation from Garcia. We may remark that *Kākula* was a place somewhere on the Gulf of Siam, famous for its fine aloes-wood (see *Ibn Batuta*, iv. 240-44). And a bastard kind of Cardamom appears to be exported from Siam, *Amomum xanthoides*, Wal.

1563.—"O. Avicena gives a chapter on the **cacullá**, dividing it into the *bigger* and the *less* . . . calling one of them *cacollá quebir*, and the other *cacollá ceguer* [Ar. *kabīr*, *ṣaghīr*], which is as much as to say *greater cardamom* and *smaller cardamom*."—*Garcia De O.*, f. 47*v*.

1759.—"These Vakeels . . . stated that the Rani (of Bednore) would pay a yearly sum of 100,000 *Hoons* or Pagodas, besides a tribute of other valuable articles, such as *Foful* (betel), Dates, Sandal-wood, **Kakul** . . . black pepper, &c."—*Hist. of Hydur Naik*, 133.

CADDY, s. *i.e.* tea-caddy. This is possibly, as Crawfurd suggests, from **Catty** (q.v.), and may have been originally applied to a small box containing a *catty* or two of tea. The suggestion is confirmed by this advertisement :

1792.—"By R. Henderson . . . A Quantity of Tea in Quarter Chests and **Caddies**, imported last season. . . ."—*Madras Courier*, Dec. 2.

CADET, s. (From Prov. *capdet*, and Low Lat. *capitettum*, [dim. of *caput*, 'head'] Skeat). This word is of course by no means exclusively Anglo-Indian, but it was in exceptionally common and familiar use in India, as all young officers appointed to the Indian army went out to that country as *cadets*, and were only promoted to ensigncies and posted to regiments after their arrival—in olden days sometimes a considerable time after their arrival. In those days there was a building in Fort William known as the 'Cadet Barrack' ; and for some time early in last century the cadets after their arrival were sent to a sort of college at Baraset ; a system which led to no good, and was speedily abolished.

1763.—"We should very gladly comply with your request for sending you young persons to be brought up as assistants in the Engineering branch, but as we find it extremely difficult to procure such, you will do well to employ any who have a talent that way among the **cadets** or others."—*Court's Letter*, in *Long*, 290.

1769.—"Upon our leaving England, the **cadets** and **writers** used the great cabin promiscuously ; but finding they were troublesome and quarrelsome, we brought a Bill into the house for their ejectment."—*Life of Lord Teignmouth*, i. 15.

1781.—"The **Cadets** of the end of the years 1771 and beginning of 1772 served in the country four years as **Cadets** and carried the musket all the time."—Letter in *Hicky's Bengal Gazette*, Sept. 29.

CADJAN, s. Jav. and Malay *kājāng*, [or according to Mr. Skeat, *kajang*], meaning 'palm-leaves,' especially those of the **Nipa** (q.v.) palm, dressed for thatching or matting. Favre's Dict. renders the word *feuilles entrelacées*. It has been introduced by foreigners into S. and W. India, where it is used in two senses :

a. Coco-palm leaves matted, the common substitute for thatch in S. India.

1673.—"... flags especially in their Villages (by them called **Cajans**, being Cocoe-tree branches) upheld with some few sticks, supplying both Sides and Coverings to their Cottages."—*Fryer*, 17. In his Explanatory Index Fryer gives '**Cajan**, a bough of a Toddy-tree.'

c. 1680.—"Ex iis (foliis) quoque rudiores mattae, **Cadjang** vocatae, conficiuntur, quibus aedium muri et navium orae, quum frumentum aliquod in iis deponere velimus, obteguntur."—*Rumphius*, i. 71.

1727.—"We travelled 8 or 10 miles before we came to his (the Cananore Raja's) Palace, which was built with Twigs, and covered with **Cadjans** or Cocoa-nut Tree Leaves woven together."—*A. Hamilton*, i: 296.

1809.—"The lower classes (at Bombay) content themselves with small huts, mostly of clay, and roofed with **cadjan**."—*Maria Graham*, 4.

1860.—"Houses are timbered with its wood, and roofed with its plaited fronds, which under the name of **cadjans**, are likewise employed for constructing partitions and fences."—*Tennent's Ceylon*, ii. 126.

b. A strip of fan-palm leaf, *i.e.* either of the **Talipot** (q.v.) or of the **Palmyra**, prepared for writing on; and so a document written on such a strip. (See **OLLAH**.)

1707.—"The officer at the Bridge Gate bringing in this morning to the Governor a **Cajan** letter that he found hung upon a post near the Gate, which when translated seemed to be from a body of the Right Hand Caste."—In *Wheeler*, ii. 78.

1716.—"The President acquaints the Board that he has intercepted a villainous letter or **Cajan**."—*Ibid.* ii. 231.

1839.—"At Rajahmundry . . . the people used to sit in our reading room for hours, copying our books on their own little **cadjan** leaves."—*Letters from Madras*, 275.

CADJOWA, s. [P. *kajāwah*]. A kind of frame or pannier, of which a pair are slung across a camel, sometimes made like litters to carry women or sick persons, sometimes to contain sundries of camp equipage.

1645.—"He entered the town with 8 or 10 camels, the two **Cajavas** or Litters on each side of the Camel being close shut. . . . But instead of Women, he had put into every **Cajava** two Souldiers."—*Tavernier*, E. T. ii. 61; [ed. *Ball*, i. 144].

1790.—"The camel appropriated to the accommodation of passengers, carries two persons, who are lodged in a kind of pannier, laid loosely on the back of the animal. This pannier, termed in the Persic **Kidjahwah**, is a wooden frame, with the sides and bottom of netted cords, of about 3 feet long and 2 broad, and 2 in depth . . . the journey being usually made in the night-time, it becomes the only place of his rest. . . . Had I been even much accustomed to this manner of travelling, it must have been irksome; but a total want of practice made it excessively grievous."—*Forster's Journey*, ed. 1808, ii. 104-5.

CAEL, n.p. Properly *Kāyal* [Tam. *kāyu*, 'to be hot'], 'a lagoon' or 'backwater.' Once a famous port near the extreme south of India at the mouth of the Tamraparni R., in the Gulf of Manaar, and on the coast of Tinnevelly, now long abandoned. Two or three miles higher up the river lies the site of *Korkai* or *Kolkai*, the Κόλχοι ἐμπόριον of the Greeks, each port in succession having been destroyed by the retirement of the sea. Tutikorin, six miles N., may be considered the modern and humbler representative of those ancient marts; [see *Stuart, Man. of Tinnevelly*, 38 *seqq.*].

1298.—"**Cail** is a great and noble city. . . . It is at this city that all the ships touch that come from the west."—*Marco Polo*, Bk. iii. ch. 21.

1442.—"The Coast, which includes Calicut with some neighbouring ports, and which extends as far as Kabel (read **Kāyel**) a place situated opposite the Island of Serendib. . . ."—*Abdurrazzāk*, in *India in the XVth Cent.*, 19.

1444.—"Ultra eas urbs est **Cahila**, qui locus margaritas . . . producit."—*Conti*, in *Poggius, De Var. Fortunae.*

1498.—"Another Kingdom, **Caell**, which has a Moorish King, whilst the people are Christian. It is ten days from Calecut by sea . . . here there be many pearls."—*Roteiro de V. da Gama*, 108.

1514.—"Passando oltre al Cavo Comedi (C. Comorin), sono gentili; e intra esso e **Gael** è dove si pesca le perle."—*Giov. da Empoli*, 79.

1516.—"Further along the coast is a city called **Cael**, which also belongs to the King of Coulam, peopled by Moors and Gentoos, great traders. It has a good harbour, whither come many ships of Malabar; others of Charamandel and Benguala."—*Barbosa*, in *Lisbon Coll.*, 357-8.

CAFFER, CAFFRE, COFFREE, &c., n.p. The word is properly the

Ar. *Kāfir*, pl. *Kofra*, 'an infidel, an unbeliever in Islām.' As the Arabs applied this to Pagan negroes, among others, the Portuguese at an early date took it up in this sense, and our countrymen from them. A further appropriation in one direction has since made the name specifically that of the black tribes of South Africa, whom we now call, or till recently did call, **Caffres**. It was also applied in the Philippine Islands to the Papuas of N. Guinea, and the Alfuras of the Moluccas, brought into the slave-market.

In another direction the word has become a quasi-proper name of the (more or less) fair, and non-Mahommedan, tribes of Hindu-Kush, sometimes called more specifically the *Siāh-posh* or 'black-robed' **Cafirs**.

The term is often applied malevolently by Mahommedans to Christians, and this is probably the origin of the mistake pervading some of the early Portuguese narratives, especially the *Roteiro of Vasco da Gama*, which described many of the Hindu and Indo-Chinese States as being Christian.*

[c. 1300.—"**Kāfir**." See under **LACK**.]

c. 1404.—Of a people near China: "They were Christians after the manner of those of Cathay."—*Clavijo* by *Markham*, 141.

" And of India: "The people of India are Christians, the Lord and most part of the people, after the manner of the Greeks; and among them also are other Christians who mark themselves with fire in the face, and their creed is different from that of the others; for those who thus mark themselves with fire are less esteemed than the others. And among them are Moors and Jews, but they are subject to the Christians."—*Clavijo*, (orig.) § cxxi.; comp. *Markham*, 153-4. Here we have (1) the confusion of **Caffer** and Christian; and (2) the confusion of Abyssinia (*India Tertia* or *Middle India* of some medieval writers) with India Proper.

c. 1470.—"The sea is infested with pirates, all of whom are **Kofars**, neither Christians nor Mussulmans; they pray to stone idols, and know not Christ."—*Athan. Nitikin*, in *India in the XVth Cent.*, p. 11.

1552.—". . . he learned that the whole people of the Island of S. Lourenço . . . were black **Cafres** with curly hair like those of Mozambique."—*Barros*, II. i. 1.

* Thus: "*Chomandarla* (*i.e.* Coromandel) he de Christãoos e o rey Christãoo." So also *Ceylam Camatarra*, *Melequa* (Malacca), *Peguo*, &c., are all described as Christian states with Christian kings. Also the so-called Indian Christians who came on board Da Gama at Melinde seem to have been Hindu banians.

1563.—"In the year 1484 there came to Portugal the King of Benin, a **Caffre** by nation, and he became a Christian."—*Stanley's Correa* p. 8.

1572.—

"Verão os **Cafres** asperos e avaros
Tirar a linda dama seus vestidos."
Camões, v. 47.

By Burton:

"shall see the **Caffres**, greedy race and fere
"strip the fair Ladye of her raiment torn."

1582.—"These men are called **Cafres** and are Gentiles."—*Castañeda* (by N.L.), f. 42*b*.

c. 1610.—"Il estoit fils d'vn **Cafre** d'Ethiopie, et d'vne femme de ces isles, ce qu'on appelle Mulastre."—*Pyrard de Laval*, i. 220; [Hak. Soc. i. 307].

[c. 1610.—". . . a Christian whom they call **Caparou**."—*Ibid.*, Hak. Soc. i. 261.]

1614.—"That knave Simon the **Caffro**, not what the writer took him for—he is a knave, and better lost than found."—*Sainsbury*, i. 356.

[1615.—"Odola and Gala are **Capharrs** which signifieth misbelievers."—*Sir T. Roe*, Hak. Soc. i. 23.]

1653.—". . . toy mesme qui passe pour vn **Kiaffer**, ou homme sans Dieu, parmi les Mausulmans."—*De la Boullaye-le-Gouz*, 310 (ed. 1657).

c. 1665.—"It will appear in the sequel of this History, that the pretence used by *Aureng-Zebe*, his third Brother, to cut off his (*Dara's*) head, was that he was turned **Kafer**, that is to say, an Infidel, of no Religion, an Idolater."—*Bernier*, E. T. p. 3; [ed. *Constable*, p. 7].

1673.—"They show their Greatness by their number of Sumbreeroes and **Cofferies**, whereby it is dangerous to walk late."—*Fryer*, 74.

" "Beggars of the Musslemen Cast, that if they see a Christian in good Clothes . . . are presently upon their Punctilios with God Almighty, and interrogate him, Why he suffers him to go afoot and in Rags, and this **Coffery** (Unbeliever) to vaunt it thus?"—*Ibid.* 91.

1678.—"The Justices of the Choultry to turn Padry Pasquall, a Popish Priest, out of town, not to return again, and if it proves to be true that he attempted to seduce Mr. Mohun's **Coffre** Franck from the Protestant religion."—*Ft. St. Geo. Cons.* in *Notes and Exts.*, Pt. i. p. 72.

1759.—"Blacks, whites, **Coffries**, and even the natives of the country (Pegu) have not been exempted, but all universally have been subject to intermittent Fevers and Fluxes" (at Negrais).—In *Dalrymple*, *Or. Rep.* i. 124.

" Among expenses of the Council at Calcutta in entertaining the Nabob we find "Purchasing a **Coffre** boy, Rs. 500."—In *Long*, 194.

1781.—"*To be sold by Private Sale*.—Two **Coffree** Boys, who can play remarkably well on the French Horn, about 18 Years of Age: belonging to a Portuguese Paddrie lately deceased. For particulars apply to the. Vicar of the Portuguese Church, Calcutta, March 17th, 1781."—*The India Gazette or Public Advertiser*, No. 19.

1781.—"Run away from his Master, a good-looking **Coffree** Boy, about 20 years old, and about 6 *feet* 7 *inches in height*. . . . *When he went off he had a high toupie*."—*Ibid*. Dec. 29.

1782.—"On Tuesday next will be sold three **Coffree** Boys, two of whom play the French Horn . . . a three-wheel'd Buggy, and a variety of other articles."—*India Gazette*, June 15.

1799.—"He (Tippoo) had given himself out as a Champion of the Faith, who was to drive the English **Caffers** out of India."—Letter in *Life of Sir T. Munro*, i. 221.

1800.—"The **Caffre** slaves, who had been introduced for the purpose of cultivating the lands, rose upon their masters, and seizing on the boats belonging to the island, effected their escape."—*Symes, Embassy to Ava*, p. 10.

c. 1866.—

"And if I were forty years younger, and
my life before me to choose,
I wouldn't be lectured by **Kafirs**, or
swindled by fat Hindoos."

Sir A. C. Lyall, The Old Pindaree.

CAFILA, s. Arab. *ḳāfila*; a body or convoy of travellers, a **Caravan** (q.v.). Also used in some of the following quotations for a sea convoy.

1552.—"Those roads of which we speak are the general routes of the **Cafilas**, which are sometimes of 3,000 or 4,000 men . . . for the country is very perilous because of both hill-people and plain-people, who haunt the roads to rob travellers."—*Barros*, IV. vi. 1.

1596.—"The ships of *Chatins* (see **CHETTY**) of these parts are not to sail along the coast of Malavar or to the north except in a **cafilla**, that they may come and go more securely, and not be cut off by the Malavars and other corsairs."—*Proclamation of Goa Viceroy*, in *Archiv. Port. Or.*, fasc. iii. 661.

[1598.—"Two **Caffylen**, that is companies of people and Camelles."—*Linschoten*, Hak. Soc. ii. 159.]

[1616.—"A **cafilowe** consisting of 200 broadcloths," &c.—*Foster, Letters*, iv. 276.]

[1617.—"By the failing of the Goa **Caffila**."—*Sir T. Roe*, Hak. Soc. ii. 402.]

1623.—"Non navigammo di notte, perchè la **cafila** era molto grande, al mio parere di più di ducento vascelli."—*P. della Valle*, ii. 587; [and comp. Hak. Soc. i. 18].

1630.—". . . some of the Raiahs . . . making Outroades prey on the **Caffaloes** passing by the Way. . . ."—*Lord, Banian's Religion*, 81.

1672.—"Several times yearly numerous **cafilas** of merchant barques, collected in the Portuguese towns, traverse this channel (the Gulf of Cambay), and these always await the greater security of the full moon. It is also observed that the vessels which go through with this voyage should not be joined and fastened with iron, for so great is the abundance of loadstone in the bottom, that indubitably such vessels go to pieces and break up."—*P. Vincenzo*, 109. A curious survival of the old legend of the Loadstone Rocks.

1673.—" . . . Time enough before the **Caphalas** out of the Country come with their Wares."—*Fryer*, 86.

1727.—"*In Anno* 1699, a pretty rich **Caffila** was robbed by a Band of 4 or 5000 villains . . . which struck Terror on all that had commerce at *Tatta*."—*A. Hamilton*, i. 116.

1867.—"It was a curious sight to see, as was seen in those days, a carriage enter one of the northern gates of Palermo preceded and followed by a large convoy of armed and mounted travellers, a kind of **Kafila**, that would have been more in place in the opening chapters of one of James's romances than in the latter half of the 19th century."—*Quarterly Review*, Jan., 101-2.

CAFIRISTAN, n.p. P. *Kāfiristān*, the country of *Kāfirs*, *i.e.* of the pagan tribes of the Hindu Kush noticed in the article **Caffer**.

c. 1514.—"In Cheghânserâi there are neither grapes nor vineyards; but they bring the wines down the river from **Kaferistân**. . . . So prevalent is the use of wine among them that every **Kafer** has a *khig*, or leathern bottle of wine about his neck; they drink wine instead of water."—*Autobiog. of Baber*, p. 144.

[c. 1590.—The **Káfirs** in the Túmáns of Alishang and Najrao are mentioned in the *Āīn*, tr. *Jarrett*, ii. 406.]

1603.—" . . . they fell in with a certain pilgrim and devotee, from whom they learned that at a distance of 30 days' journey there was a city called **Capperstam**, into which no Mahomedan was allowed to enter . . ."—*Journey of Bened. Goës*, in *Cathay*, &c. ii. 554.

CAIMAL, s. A Nair chief; a word often occurring in the old Portuguese historians. It is Malayāl. *kaimal*.

1504.—"So they consulted with the Zamorin, and the Moors offered their agency to send and poison the wells at Cochin, so as to kill all the Portuguese, and also to send Nairs in disguise to kill any of our people that they found in the palm-woods, and away from the town. . . . And meanwhile the Mangate **Caimal**, and the **Caimal** of Primbalam, and the **Caimal** of Diamper, seeing that the Zamorin's affairs were going from bad to worse, and that the castles which the Italians were making were all wind and nonsense, that it was already August when ships might be arriving from Portugal . . . departed to their own estates with a multitude of their followers, and sent to the King of Cochin their **ollas** of allegiance."—*Correa*, i. 482.

1566.—" . . . certain lords bearing title, whom they call **Caimals**" (*caimães*).—*Damian de Goës, Chron. del Rei Dom Emmanuel*, p. 49.

1606.—"The Malabars give the name of **Caimals** (*Caimães*) to certain great lords of vassals, who are with their governments haughty as kings; but most of them have confederation and alliance with some of the great kings, whom they stand bound to aid and defend . . ."—*Gouvea*, f. 27*v*.

1634.—
"Ficarão seus **Caimais** prezos e mortos."
Malaca Conquistada, v. 10.

CAIQUE, s. The small skiff used at Constantinople, Turkish *ḳāïḳ*. Is it by accident, or by a radical connection through Turkish tribes on the Arctic shores of Siberia, that the Greenlander's *kayak* is so closely identical? [The *Stanf. Dict.* says that the latter word is Esquimaux, and recognises no connection with the former.]

CAJAN, s. This is a name given by Sprengel (*Cajanus indicus*), and by Linnæus (*Cytisus cajan*), to the leguminous shrub which gives **dhall** (q.v.). A kindred plant has been called *Dolichos catjang*, Willdenow. We do not know the origin of this name. The *Cajan* was introduced to America by the slave-traders from Africa. De Candolle finds it impossible to say whether its native region is India or Africa. (See **DHALL, CALAVANCE.**) [According to Mr. Skeat the word is Malay. *poko'kachang*, 'the plant which gives beans,' quite a different word from *kajang* which gives us **Cadjan.**]

CAJEPUT, s. The name of a fragrant essential oil produced especially in Celebes and the neighbouring island of Bouro. A large quantity is exported from Singapore and Batavia. It is used most frequently as an external application, but also internally, especially (of late) in cases of cholera. The name is taken from the Malay *kayu-putih, i.e.* '*Lignum album.*' Filet (see p. 140) gives six different trees as producing the oil, which is derived from the distillation of the leaves. The chief of these trees is *Melaleuca leucadendron*, L., a tree diffused from the Malay Peninsula to N.S. Wales. The drug and tree were first described by Rumphius, who died 1693. (See *Hanbury and Flückiger*, 247 [and *Wallace, Malay Arch.*, ed. 1890, p. 294].)

CAKSEN, s. This is Sea H. for *Coxswain* (*Roebuck*).

CALALUZ, s. A kind of swift rowing vessel often mentioned by the Portuguese writers as used in the Indian Archipelago. We do not know the etymology, nor the exact character of the craft. [According to Mr. Skeat, the word is Jav. *kelulus*, *kalulus*, spelt *keloeles* by Klinkert, and explained by him as a kind of vessel. The word seems to be derived from *loeloes*, 'to go right through anything,' and thus the literal translation would be 'the threader,' the reference being, as in the case of most Malay boat names, to the special figure-head from which the boat was supposed to derive its whole character.]

[1513.—**Calauz**, according to Mr. Whiteway, is the form of the word in *Andrade's Letter to Albuquerque of Feb. 22nd.*—*India Office MS.*]

1525.—"4 great *lancharas*, and 6 **calaluzes** and *manchuas* which row very fast."—*Lembrança*, 8.

1539.—"The King (of Achin) set forward with the greatest possible despatch, a great armament of 200 rowing vessels, of which the greater part were *lancharas, joangas*, and **calaluzes**, besides 15 high-sided junks."—*F. M. Pinto*, cap. xxxii.

1552.—"The King of Siam . . . ordered to be built a fleet of some 200 sail, almost all *lancharas* and **calaluzes**, which are rowing-vessels."—*Barros*, II. vi. 1.

1613.—"And having embarked with some companions in a **caleluz** or rowing vessel. . . ."—*Godinho de Eredia*, f. 51.

CALAMANDER WOOD, s. A beautiful kind of rose-wood got from a Ceylon tree (*Diospyros quaesita*). Tennent regards the name as a Dutch corruption of *Coromandel* wood (i. 118), and Drury, we see, calls one of the ebony-trees (*D. melanoxylon*) "Coromandel-ebony." Forbes Watson gives as Singhalese names of the wood *Calumidiriya*, *Kalumederiye*, &c., and the term *Kalumadīriya* is given with this meaning in Clough's Singh. Dict.; still in absence of further information, it may remain doubtful if this be not a borrowed word. It may be worth while to observe that, according to Tavernier, [ed. *Ball*, ii. 4] the "painted calicoes" or "chites" of Masulipatam were called "*Calmendar*, that is to say, done with a pencil" (*Ḳalam-dār?*), and possibly this appellation may have been given by traders to a delicately veined wood. [The *N.E.D.* suggests that the Singh. terms quoted above may be adaptations from the Dutch.]

1777.—"In the Cingalese language **Calaminder** is said to signify a black flaming tree. The heart, or woody part of it, is extremely handsome, with whitish or pale yellow and black or brown veins, streaks and waves."—*Thunberg*, iv. 205-6.

1813.—"**Calaminder** wood" appears among Ceylon products in *Milburn*, i. 345.

1825.—"A great deal of the furniture in Ceylon is made of ebony, as well as of the **Calamander** tree . . . which is become scarce from the improvident use formerly made of it."—*Heber* (1844), ii. 161.

1834.—"The forests in the neighbourhood afford timber of every kind (**Calamander** excepted)."—*Chitty, Ceylon Gazetteer*, 198.

CALAMBAC, s. The finest kind of aloes-wood. Crawfurd gives the word as Javanese, *kalambak*, but it perhaps came with the article from **Champa** (q.v.).

1510.—"There are three sorts of aloes-wood. The first and most perfect sort is called **Calampat**."—*Varthema*, 235.

1516.—". . . It must be said that the very fine **calembuco** and the other eagle-wood is worth at Calicut 1000 maravedis the pound."—*Barbosa*, 204.

1539.—"This Embassador, that was Brother-in-law to the King of the Batas . . . brought him a rich Present of Wood of Aloes, **Calambaa**, and 5 quintals of Benjamon in flowers."—*F. M. Pinto*, in Cogan's tr. p. 15 (orig. cap. xiii.).

1551.—(Campar, in Sumatra) "has nothing but forests which yield aloeswood, called in India **Calambuco**."—*Castanheda*, bk. iii. cap. 63, p. 218, quoted by *Crawfurd*, Des. Dic. 7.

1552.—"Past this kingdom of Camboja begins the other Kingdom called Campa (**Champa**), in the mountains of which grows the genuine aloes-wood, which the Moors of those parts call **Calambuc**."—*Barros*, I. ix. 1.

[c. 1590.—"**Kalanbak** (calembic) is the wood of a tree brought from **Zírbád**; it is heavy and full of veins. Some believe it to be the raw wood of aloes."—*Āīn*, ed. *Blochmann*, i. 81.

[c. 1610.—"From this river (the Ganges) comes that excellent wood **Calamba**, which is believed to come from the Earthly Paradise."—*Pyrard de Laval*, Hak. Soc. i. 335.]

1613.—"And the **Calamba** is the most fragrant *medulla* of the said tree."—*Godinho de Eredia*, f. 15*v*.

[1615.—"Lumra (a black gum), gumlack, **collomback**."—*Foster*, *Letters*, iv. 87.]

1618.—"We opened the ij chistes which came from Syam with **callamback** and silk, and waid it out."—*Cocks's Diary*, ii. 51.

1774.—"Les Mahometans font de ce **Kalambac** des chapelets qu'ils portent à la main par amusement. Ce bois quand il est échauffé ou un peu frotté, rend un odeur agréable."—*Niebuhr, Desc. de l'Arabie*, 127.

See **EAGLE-WOOD** and **ALOES**.

CALASH, s. French *calèche*, said by Littré to be a Slav word, [and so *N.E.D.*]. In Bayly's Dict. it is *calash* and *caloche*. [The *N.E.D.* does not recognise the latter form; the former is as early as 1679]. This seems to have been the earliest precursor of the **buggy** in Eastern settlements. Bayly defines it as 'a small open chariot.' The quotation below refers to Batavia, and the President in question was the Prest. of the English Factory at Chusan, who, with his council, had been expelled from China, and was halting at Batavia on his way to India.

1702.—"The Shabander riding home in his **Calash** this Morning, and seeing the President sitting without the door at his Lodgings, alighted and came and Sat with the President near an hour . . . what moved the Shabander to speak so plainly to the President thereof he knew not, But observed that the Shahbander was in his Glasses at his first alighting from his **Calash**."—*Procgs.* "Munday, 30th March," *MS. Report in India Office*.

CALAVANCE, s. A kind of bean; acc. to the quotation from Osbeck, *Dolichos sinensis*. The word was once common in English use, but seems forgotten, unless still used at sea. Sir Joseph Hooker writes: "When I was in the Navy, haricot beans were in constant use as a substitute for potatoes and in Brazil and elsewhere, were called **Calavances**. I do not remember whether they were the seed of *Phaseolus lunatus* or *vulgaris*, or of *Dolichos sinensis*, alias *Catjang*" (see **CAJAN**). The word comes from the Span. *garbanzos*, which De Candolle mentions as Castilian for '*pois chiche*,' or *Cicer arietinum*, and as used also in Basque under the form *garbantzua*,

[or *garbatzu*, from *garau*, 'seed,' *antzu*, 'dry,' *N.E.D.*]

1620.—". . . from hence they make their provition in aboundance, viz. beefe and porke . . . **garvances**, or small peaze or beanes. . . ."—*Cocks's Diary*, ii. 311.

c. 1630.—". . . in their Canoos brought us . . . green pepper, **caravance**, Buffols, Hens, Eggs, and other things."—*Sir T. Herbert*, ed. 1665, p. 350.

1719.—"I was forc'd to give them an extraordinary meal every day, either of *Farina* or **calavances**, which at once made a considerable consumption of our water and firing."—*Shelvocke's Voyage*, 62.

1738.—"But **garvanços** are prepared in a different manner, neither do they grow soft like other pulse, by boiling. . . ."—*Shaw's Travels*, ed. 1757, p. 140.

1752.—". . . **Callvanses** (*Dolichos sinensis*)."—*Osbeck*, i. 304.

1774.—"When I asked any of the men of Dory why they had no gardens of plantains and **Kalavansas** . . . I learnt . . . that the Haraforas supply them."—*Forrest, V. to N. Guinea*, 109.

1814.—"His Majesty is authorised to permit for a limited time by Order in Council, the Importation from any Port or Place whatever of . . . any Beans called Kidney, French Beans, Tares, Lentiles, **Callivances**, and all other sorts of Pulse."—Act 54 Geo. III. cap. xxxvi.

CALAY, s. Tin; also v., to tin copper vessels—H. *ḳala'ī karnā*. The word is Ar. *ḳala'ī*, 'tin,' which according to certain Arabic writers was so called from a mine in India called *ḳala'*. In spite of the different initial and terminal letters, it seems at least possible that the place meant was the same that the old Arab geographers called *Kalah*, near which they place mines of tin (*al-ḳala'ī*), and which was certainly somewhere about the coast of Malacca, possibly, as has been suggested, at *Kadah* * or as we write it, **Quedda**. [See *Āīn*, tr. *Jarrett*, iii 48.] The tin produce of that region is well known. *Kalang* is indeed also a name of tin in Malay, which may have been the true origin of the word before us. It may be added that the small State of Salangor between Malacca and Perak was formerly known as *Nagri*-**Kalang**, or the 'Tin Country,' and that the place on the coast where the British Resident lives is called **Klang** (see *Miss Bird, Golden Chersonese*, 210, 215). The Portuguese have the forms *calaim* and *calin*, with the nasal termination so frequent in their Eastern borrowings. Bluteau explains *calaim* as 'Tin of India, finer than ours.' The old writers seem to have hesitated about the identity with tin, and the word is confounded in one quotation below with **Tootnague** (q.v.). The French use *calin*. In the P. version of the Book of Numbers (ch. xxxi. v. 22) *ḳala'ī* is used for 'tin.' See on this word Quatremère in the *Journal des Savans*, Dec. 1846.

c. 920.—"Kalah is the focus of the trade in aloeswood, in camphor, in sandalwood, in ivory, in the lead which is called **al-Kala'i**."—*Relation des Voyages, &c.*, i. 94.

c. 1154.—"Thence to the Isles of Lankiāliūs is reckoned two days, and from the latter to the Island of Kalah 5. . . . There is in this last island an abundant mine of tin (**al-Kala'i**). The metal is very pure and brilliant."—*Edrisi*, by *Jaubert*, i. 80.

1552.—"—Tin, which the people of the country call **Calem**."—*Castanheda*, iii. 213. It is mentioned as a staple of Malacca in ii. 186.

1606.—"That all the chalices which were neither of gold, nor silver, nor of tin, nor of **calaim**, should be broken up and destroyed."—*Gouvea, Synodo*, f. 29*b*.

1610.—"They carry (to Hormuz) . . . clove, cinnamon, pepper, cardamom, ginger, mace, nutmeg, sugar, **calayn**, or tin."—*Relaciones de P. Teixeira*, 382.

c. 1610.—". . . money . . . not only of gold and silver, but also of another metal, which is called **calin**, which is white like tin, but harder, purer, and finer, and which is much used in the Indies."—*Pyrard de Laval* (1679) i. 164; [Hak. Soc. i. 234, with Gray's note].

1613.—"And he also reconnoitred all the sites of mines, of gold, silver, mercury, tin or **calem**, and iron and other metals . . ."—*Godinho de Eredia*, f. 58.

[1644.—"**Callaym.**" See quotation under **TOOTNAGUE.**]

1646.—". . . il y a (*i.e.* in Siam) plusieurs minieres de **calain**, qui est vn metal metoyen, entre le plomb et l'estain."—*Cardim, Rel. de la Prov. de Japon*, 163.

1726.—"The goods exported hither (from Pegu) are . . . **Kalin** (a metal coming very near silver) . . ."—*Valentijn*, v. 128.

1770.—"They send only one vessel (viz. the Dutch to Siam) which transports Javanese horses, and is freighted with sugar, spices, and linen; for which they receive in return **calin**, at 70 livres 100 weight."—*Raynal* (tr. 1777), i. 208.

1780.—". . . the port of Quedah; there is a trade for **calin** or tutenague . . . to

* It may be observed, however, that *kwāla* in Malay indicates the estuary of a navigable river, and denominates many small ports in the Malay region. The *Kalah* of the early Arabs is probably the Κῶλι πόλις of Ptolemy's Tables.

export to different parts of the Indies."—In *Dunn, N. Directory*, 338.

1794-5.—In the *Travels to China* of the younger Deguignes, **Calin** is mentioned as a kind of tin imported into China from Batavia and Malacca.—iii. 367.

CALCUTTA, n.p. B. *Kalikātā*, or *Kalikattā*, a name of uncertain etymology. The first mention that we are aware of occurs in the *Āīn-i-Akbari*. It is well to note that in some early charts, such as that in Valentijn, and the oldest in the *English Pilot*, though Calcutta is not entered, there is a place on the Hoogly *Calcula*, or *Calcuta*, which leads to mistake. It is far below, near the modern Fulta. [With reference to the quotations below from Luillier and Sonnerat, Sir H. Yule writes (*Hedges, Diary*, Hak. Soc. ii. xcvi.): "In Orme's *Historical Fragments*, Job Charnock is described as 'Governor of the Factory at Golgot near Hughley.' This name Golgot and the corresponding Golghāt in an extract from Muhabbat Khān indicate the name of the particular locality where the English Factory at Hugli was situated. And some confusion of this name with that of Calcutta may have led to the curious error of the Frenchman Luiller and Sonnerat, the former of whom calls Calcutta *Golgouthe*, while the latter says: 'Les Anglais prononcent et ecrivent *Golgota*.'"]

c. 1590.—"**Kalikatā** *wa Bakoya wa Barbakpūr*, 3 *Mahal*."—*Āīn*. (orig.) i. 408; [tr. *Jarrett*, ii. 141].

[1688.—"Soe myself accompanyed with Capt. Haddock and the 120 soldiers we carryed from hence embarked, and about the 20th September arrived at **Calcutta**."—*Hedges, Diary*, Hak. Soc. ii. lxxix.]

1698.—"This avaricious disposition the English plied with presents, which in 1698 obtained his permission to purchase from the Zemindar . . . the towns of Sootanutty, **Calcutta**, and Goomopore, with their districts extending about 3 miles along the eastern bank of the river."—*Orme*, repr. ii. 71.

1702.—"The next Morning we pass'd by the *English* Factory belonging to the old Company, which they call **Golgotha**, and is a handsome Building, to which were adding stately Warehouses."—*Voyage to the E. Indies, by Le Sieur Luillier*, E. T. 1715, p. 259.

1726.—"The ships which sail thither (to Hugli) first pass by the English Lodge in **Collecatte**, 9 miles (Dutch miles) lower down than ours, and after that the French one called *Chandarnagor*. . . ."—*Valentijn*, v. 162.

1727.—"The Company has a pretty good Hospital at **Calcutta**, where many go in to undergo the Penance of Physic, but few come out to give an Account of its Operation. . . . One Year I was there, and there were reckoned in August about 1200 *English*, some Military, some Servants to the Company, some private Merchants residing in the Town, and some Seamen belong to Shipping lying at the Town, and before the beginning of *January* there were 460 Burials registred in the Clerk's Books of Mortality."—*A. Hamilton*, ii. 9 and 6.

c. 1742.—"I had occasion to stop at the city of Firáshdánga (Chandernagore) which is inhabited by a tribe of Frenchmen. The city of **Calcutta**, which is on the other side of the water, and inhabited by a tribe of English who have settled there, is much more extensive and thickly populated. . . ."—*'Abdul Karīm Khān*, in *Elliot*, viii. 127.

1753.—"Au dessous d'Ugli immédiatement, est l'établissement Hollandois de **Shinsura**, puis **Shandernagor**, établissement François, puis la loge Danoise (Serampore), et plus bas, sur la rivage opposé, qui est celui de la gauche en descendant, Banki-bazar, où les Ostendois n'ont pû se maintenir; enfin **Colicotta** aux Anglois, à quelques lieues de Banki-bazar, et du même côté."—*D'Anville, Eclaircissemens*, 64. With this compare: "Almost opposite to the *Danes* Factory is *Banke-banksal*, a Place where the Ostend Company settled a Factory, but, in *Anno* 1723, they quarrelled with the *Fouzdaar* or Governor of *Hughly*, and he forced the *Ostenders* to quit. . . ."—*A. Hamilton*, ii. 18.

1782.—"Les Anglais pourroient retirer aujourd'hui des sommes immenses de l'Inde, s'ils avoient eu l'attention de mieux composer le conseil suprême de **Calecuta**." *—*Sonnerat, Voyage*, i. 14.

CALEEFA, s. Ar. *Khalīfa*, the Caliph or Vice-gerent, a word which we do not introduce here in its high Mahommedan use, but because of its quaint application in Anglo-Indian households, at least in Upper India, to two classes of domestic servants, the tailor and the cook, and sometimes to the barber and farrier. The first is *always* so addressed by his fellow-servants (*Khalīfa-jī*). In South India the cook is called **Maistry**, *i.e. artiste*. In Sicily, we may note, he is always called *Monsù* (!) an indication of what ought to be his nationality. The root of the word *Khalīfa*, according to Prof. Sayce, means 'to change,' and another

* "Capitale des établissements Anglais dans le Bengale. *Les Anglais prononcent et écrivent* **Golgota**" (!)

derivative, *khālif*, 'exchange or agio' is the origin of the Greek κολλύβος (*Princ. of Philology*, 2nd ed., 213).

c. 1253.—"... vindrent marcheant en l'ost qui nous distrent et conterent que li roys des Tartarins avoit prise la citei de Baudas et l'apostole des Sarrazins ... lequel on apeloit le **calife** de Baudas. . . ."—*Joinville*, cxiv.

1298.—"Baudas is a great city, which used to be the seat of the **Calif** of all the Saracens in the world, just as Rome is the seat of the Pope of all the Christians."—*Marco Polo*, Bk. I. ch. 6.

1552.—"To which the Sheikh replied that he was the vassal of the Soldan of Cairo, and that without his permission who was the sovereign **Califa** of the Prophet Mahamed, he could hold no communication with people who so persecuted his followers. . . ."—*Barros*, II. i. 2.

1738.—"Muzeratty, the late **Kaleefa**, or lieutenant of this province, assured me that he saw a bone belonging to one of them (ancient stone coffins) which was near two of their *drass* (*i.e.* 36 inches) in length."—*Shaw's Travels in Barbary*, ed. 1757, p. 30.

1747.—'As to the house, and the patrimonial lands, together with the appendages of the murdered minister, they were presented by the **Qhalif** of the age, that is by the Emperor himself, to his own daughter."—*Seir Mutaqherin*, iii. 37.

c. 1760 (?).—

"I hate all Kings and the thrones they sit on,
From the King of France to the **Caliph** of Britain."

These lines were found among the papers of Pr. Charles Edward, and supposed to be his. But Lord Stanhope, in the 2nd ed. of his *Miscellanies*, says he finds that they are slightly altered from a poem by Lord Rochester. This we cannot find. [The original lines of Rochester (*Poems on State Affairs*, i. 171) run:

"I hate all Monarchs, and the thrones they sit on,
From the Hector of France to the Cully of Britain."]

[1813.—"The most skilful among them (the wrestlers) is appointed **khuleefu**, or superintendent for the season. . . ."—*Broughton, Letters*, ed. 1892, p. 164.]

CALEEOON, CALYOON, s. P. *kaliyūn*, a water-pipe for smoking; the Persian form of the **Hubble-Bubble** (q.v.).

[1812.—"A Persian visit, when the guest is a distinguished personage, generally consists of three acts: first, the **kaleoun**, or water pipe. . . ."—*Morier, Journey through Persia*, &c., p. 13.]

1828.—"The elder of the men met to smoke their **calleoons** under the shade."—*The Kuzzilbash*, i. 59.

[1880.—"**Kalliúns**." See quotation under **JULIBDAR**.]

CALICO, s. Cotton cloth, ordinarily of tolerably fine texture. The word appears in the 17th century sometimes in the form of *Calicut*, but possibly this may have been a purism, for *calicoe* or *callico* occurs in English earlier, or at least more commonly in early voyages. [*Callaca* in 1578, *Draper's Dict.* p. 42.] The word may have come to us through the French *calicot*, which though retaining the *t* to the eye, does not do so to the ear. The quotations sufficiently illustrate the use of the word and its origin from Calicut. The fine cotton stuffs of Malabar are already mentioned by Marco Polo (ii. 379). Possibly they may have been all brought from beyond the Ghauts, as the Malabar cotton, ripening during the rains, is not usable, and the cotton stuffs now used in Malabar all come from Madura (see *Fryer* below; and *Terry* under **CALICUT**). The Germans, we may note, call the turkey *Calecutische Hahn*, though it comes no more from Calicut than it does from Turkey. [See **TURKEY**.]

1579.—"3 great and large Canowes, in each whereof were certaine of the greatest personages that were about him, attired all of them in white Lawne, or cloth of **Calecut**."—*Drake, World Encompassed*, Hak. Soc. 139.

1591.—"The commodities of the shippes that come from Bengala bee . . . fine **Calicut** cloth, *Pintados*, and Rice."—*Barker's Lancaster*, in *Hakl.* ii. 592.

1592.—"The **calicos** were book-**calicos**, **calico** launes, broad white **calicos**, fine starched **calicos**, coarse white **calicos**, browne coarse **calicos**."—*Desc. of the Great Carrack Madre de Dios.*

1602.—"And at his departure gaue a robe, and a Tucke of **Calico** wrought with gold."—*Lancaster's Voyage*, in *Purchas*, i. 153.

1604.—"It doth appear by the abbreviate of the Accounts sent home out of the Indies, that there remained in the hands of the Agent, Master Starkey, 482 fardels of **Calicos**."—In *Middleton's Voyage*, Hak. Soc. App. iii. 13.

,, "I can fit you, gentlemen, with fine **callicoes** too, for doublets; the only sweet fashion now, most delicate and courtly: a meek gentle **callico**, cut upon two double affable taffatas; all most neat, feat, and unmatchable."—*Dekker, The Honest Whore*, Act. II. Sc. v.

1605.—". . . about their loynes they (the

Javanese) weare a kind of **Callico**-cloth."—*Edm. Scot, ibid.* 165.

1608.—"They esteem not so much of money as of **Calecut** clothes, Pintados, and such like stuffs."—*Iohn Davis, ibid.* 136.

1612.—"**Calico** copboord claiths, the piece . . . xls."—*Rates and Valuatiouns*, &c. (Scotland), p. 294.

1616.—"Angarezia . . . inhabited by Moores trading with the Maine, and other three Easterne Ilands with their Cattell and fruits, for **Cālicoes** or other linnen to cover them."—*Sir T. Roe*, in *Purchas*; [with some verbal differences in Hak. Soc. i. 17].

1627.—"**Calicoe**, *tela delicata Indica.* H. Calicúd, *dicta* à Calecút, *Indiae regione ubi conficitur.*"—*Minsheu*, 2nd ed., s.v.

1673.—"Staple Commodities are **Calicuts**, white and painted."—*Fryer*, 34.

,, "Calecut for Spice . . . and no Cloath, though it give the name of **Calecut** to all in India, it being the first Port from whence they are known to be brought into Europe."—*Ibid.* 86.

1707.—"The Governor lays before the Council the insolent action of Captain Leaton, who on Sunday last marched part of his company . . . over the Company's **Calicoes** that lay a dyeing."—Minute in *Wheeler*, ii. 48.

1720.—Act 7 Geo. I. cap. vii. "An Act to preserve and encourage the woollen and silk manufacture of this kingdom, and for more effectual employing of the Poor, by prohibiting the Use and Wear of all printed, painted, stained or dyed **Callicoes** in Apparel, Houshold Stuff, Furniture, or otherwise. . . ."—*Stat. at Large*, v. 229.

1812.—

"Like Iris' bow down darts the painted clue,
Starred, striped, and spotted, yellow, red, and blue,
Old **calico**, torn silk, and muslin new."
Rejected Addresses (*Crabbe*).

CALICUT, n.p. In the Middle Ages the chief city, and one of the chief ports of Malabar, and the residence of the **Zamorin** (q.v.). The name *Kōḻikōḍu* is said to mean the 'Cock-Fortress.' [Logan (*Man. Malabar*, i. 241 note) gives *koli*, 'fowl,' and *kottu*, 'corner or empty space,' or *kotta*, 'a fort.' There was a legend, of the Dido type, that all the space within cock-crow was once granted to the Zamorin.]

c. 1343.—"We proceeded from Fandaraina to **Kalikūt**, one of the chief ports of Mulībār. The people of Chīn, of Java, of Sailān, of Mahal (Maldives), of Yemen, and Fārs frequent it, and the traders of different regions meet there. Its port is among the greatest in the world."—*Ibn Batuta*, iv. 89.

c. 1430.—"**Colliculthiam** deinceps petiit, urbem maritimam, octo millibus passuum ambitu, nobile totius Indiae emporium, pipere, lacca, gingibere, cinnamomo crassiore,* kebulis, zedoaria fertilis."—*Conti*, in *Poggius, De Var. Fortunae.*

1442.—"**Calicut** is a perfectly secure harbour, which like that of Ormuz brings together merchants from every city and from every country."—*Abdurrazzāk*, in *India in XVth Cent.*, p. 13.

c. 1475.—"**Calecut** is a port for the whole Indian sea. . . . The country produces pepper, ginger, colour plants, muscat [nutmeg?], cloves, cinnamon, aromatic roots, *adrach* [green ginger] . . . and everything is cheap, and servants and maids are very good."—*Ath. Nikitin.*, *ibid.* p. 20.

1498.—"We departed thence, with the pilot whom the king gave us, for a city which is called **Qualecut.**"—*Roteiro de V. da Gama*, 49.

1572.—

"Já fóra de tormenta, e dos primeiros
Mares, o temor vão do peito voa;
Disse alegre o Piloto Melindano,
'Terra he de **Calecut**, se não me engano.'"
Camões, vi. 92.

By Burton:

"now, 'scaped the tempest and the first sea-dread,
fled from each bosom terrors vain, and cried
the Melindanian Pilot in delight,
'Calecut-land, if aught I see aright!'"

1616.—"Of that wool they make divers sorts of *Callico*, which had that name (as I suppose) from **Callicutts**, not far from Goa, where that kind of cloth was first bought by the Portuguese."—*Terry*, in *Purchas*. [In ed. 1777, p. 105, **Callicute**.]

CALINGULA, s. A sluice or escape. Tam. *kalingal*; much used in reports of irrigation works in S. India.

[1883.—"Much has been done in the way of providing sluices for minor channels of supply, and **calingulahs**, or water weirs for surplus vents."—*Venkasami Row, Man. of Tanjore*, p. 332.]

CALPUTTEE, s. A caulker; also the process of caulking; H. and Beng. *kālāpattī* and *kalāpāttī*, and these no doubt from the Port. *calafate*. But this again is oriental in origin, from the Arabic *kālāfat*, the 'process of caulking.' It is true that Dozy (see p. 376) and also Jal (see his *Index*, ii. 589) doubt the last derivation, and are disposed to connect the Portuguese

* Not 'a larger kind of cinnamon,' or 'cinnamon which is known there by the name of *crassa*' (*canellae quae* grossae *appellantur*), as Mr. Winter Jones oddly renders, but *canella grossa*, *i.e.* 'coarse' cinnamon, alias *cassia*.

and Spanish words, and the Italian *calafattare*, &c., with the Latin *calefacere*, a view which M. Marcel Devic rejects. The latter word would apply well enough to the process of *pitching* a vessel as practised in the Mediterranean, where we have seen the vessel careened over, and a great fire of thorns kindled under it to keep the pitch fluid. But caulking is not pitching; and when both form and meaning correspond so exactly, and when we know so many other marine terms in the Mediterranean to have been taken from the Arabic, there does not seem to be room for reasonable doubt in this case. The Emperor Michael V. (A.D. 1041) was called *καλαφάτης*, because he was the son of a caulker (see *Ducange*, *Gloss. Graec.*, who quotes *Zonaras*).

1554. — (At Mozambique) . . . "To two **calafattes** . . . of the said brigantines, at the rate annually of 20,000 [*reis* each, with 9000 *reis* each for maintenance and 6 measures of millet to each, of which no count is taken."—*Simão Botelho*, *Tombo*, 11.

c. 1620.—"S'il estoit besoin de **calfader** le Vaisseau . . . on y auroit beaucoup de peine dans ce Port, principalement si on est constraint de se seruir des Charpentiers et des **Calfadeurs** du Pays; parce qu'ils dependent tous du Gouverneur de Bombain." —*Routier* . . . *des Indes Orient.*, par Aleixo da Motta, in Thevenot's Collection.

CALUAT, s. This in some old travels is used for Ar. *khilwat*, 'privacy, a private interview' (*C. P. Brown*, *MS.*).

1404.—"And this Garden they call *Talicia*, and in their tongue they call it **Calbet**."—*Clavijo*, § cix. Comp. *Markham*, 130.

[1670.—"Still deeper in the square is the third tent, called **Caluet-Kane**, the retired spot, or the place of the privy Council."—*Bernier*, ed. *Constable*, 361.]

1822.—"I must tell you what a good fellow the little Raja of Tallaca is. When I visited him we sat on two musnads without exchanging one single word, in a very respectable durbar; but the moment we retired to a **Khilwut** the Raja produced his Civil and Criminal Register, and his Minute of demands, collections and balances for the 1st quarter, and began explaining the state of his country as eagerly as a young Collector."—*Elphinstone*, in *Life*, ii. 144.

[1824.—"The **khelwet** or private room in which the doctor was seated."—*Hajji Baba*, p. 87.]

CALUETE, CALOETE, s. The punishment of impalement; Malayāl. *kaluekki* (pron. *etti*). [See **IMPALE.**]

1510.—"The said wood is fixed in the middle of the back of the malefactor, and passes through his body . . . this torture is called '**uncalvet.**'"—*Varthema*, 147.

1582.—"The Capitaine General for to encourage them the more, commanded before them all to pitch a long staffe in the ground, the which was made sharp at ye one end. The same among the Malabars is called **Calvete**, upon ye which they do execute justice of death, unto the poorest or vilest people of the country."—*Castañeda*, tr. by N. L., ff. 142*v*, 143.

1606.—"The Queen marvelled much at the thing, and to content them she ordered the sorcerer to be delivered over for punishment, and to be set on the **caloete**, which is a very sharp stake fixed firmly in the ground . . ." &c.—*Gouvea*, f. 47*v*; see also f. 163.

CALYAN, n.p. The name of more than one city of fame in W. and S. India; Skt. *Kalyāna*, 'beautiful, noble, propitious.' One of these is the place still known as *Kalyān*, on the Ulas river, more usually called by the name of the city, 33 m. N.E. of Bombay. This is a very ancient port, and is probably the one mentioned by Cosmas below. It appears as the residence of a donor in an inscription on the Kanheri caves in Salsette (see *Fergusson and Burgess*, p. 349). Another **Kalyāna** was the capital of the Chalukyas of the Deccan in the 9th-12th centuries. This is in the Nizam's district of Naldrūg, about 40 miles E.N.E. of the fortress called by that name. A third **Kalyāna** was a port of Canara, between Mangalore and Kundapur, in lat. 13° 28′ or thereabouts, on the same river as **Bacanore** (q.v.). [This is apparently the place which Tavernier (ed. *Ball*, ii. 206) calls *Callian Bondi* or *Kalyān Bandar*.] The quotations refer to the first Calyan.

c. A.D. 80-90.—"The local marts which occur in order after Barygaza are Akabaru, Suppara, **Kalliena**, a city which was raised to the rank of a regular mart in the time of Saraganes, but, since Sandanes became its master, its trade has been put under restrictions; for if Greek vessels, even by accident, enter its ports, a guard is put on board, and they are taken to Barygaza."—*Periplus*, § 52.

c. A.D. 545.—"And the most notable places of trade are these: Sindu, Orrhotha, **Kalliana**, Sibor. . . ."—*Cosmas*, in *Cathay*, *&c.*, p. clxxviii.

1673.—"On both sides are placed stately *Aldeas*, and dwellings of the *Portugal Fidalgos*; till on the Right, within a Mile or more of **Gullean**, they yield possession to the neighbouring *Seva Gi*, at which City (the key this way into that Rebel's Country),

Wind and Tide favouring us, we landed."—*Fryer*, p. 123.

1825.—"Near Candaulah is a waterfall . . . its stream winds to join the sea, nearly opposite to Tannah, under the name of the **Callianee** river."—*Heber*, ii. 137.

Prof. Forchhammer has lately described the great remains of a Pagoda and other buildings with inscriptions, near the city of Pegu, called **Kalyāni**.

CAMBAY, n.p. Written by Mahommedan writers *Kanbāyat*, sometimes *Kinbāyat*. According to Col. Tod, the original Hindu name was *Khambavati*, 'City of the Pillar'; [the *Mad. Admin. Man. Gloss.* gives *stambha-tīrtha*, 'sacred pillar pool']. Long a very famous port of Guzerat, at the head of the Gulf to which it gives its name. Under the Mahommedan Kings of Guzerat it was one of their chief residences, and they are often called Kings of Cambay. Cambay is still a feudatory State under a Nawab. The place is in decay, owing partly to the shoals, and the extraordinary rise and fall of the tides in the Gulf, impeding navigation. [See *Forbes, Or. Mem.* 2nd ed. i. 313 *seqq.*].

c. 951.—"From **Kambáya** to the sea about 2 parasangs. From Kambáya to Súrabáya (?) about 4 days."—*Istakhri*, in *Elliot*, i. 30.

1298.—"**Cambaet** is a great kingdom. . . . There is a great deal of trade. . . . Merchants come here with many ships and cargoes. . . ."—*Marco Polo*, Bk. iii. ch. 28.

1320.—"Hoc vero Oceanum mare in illis partibus principaliter habet duos portus: quorum vnus nominatur *Mahabar*, et alius **Cambeth**."—*Marino Sanudo*, near beginning.

c. 1420.—"**Cambay** is situated near to the sea, and is 12 miles in circuit; it abounds in spikenard, lac, indigo, myrabolans, and silk."—*Conti*, in *India in XVth Cent.*, 20.

1498.—"In which Gulf, as we were informed, there are many cities of Christians and Moors, and a city which is called **Quambaya**."—*Roteiro*, 49.

1506.—"In **Combea** è terra de Mori, e il suo Re è Moro; el è una gran terra, e li nasce turbiti, e spigonardo, e milo (read *nilo*—see **ANIL**), lache, corniole, calcedonie, gotoni. . . ."—*Rel. di Leonardo Ca' Masser*, in *Archivio Stor. Italiano*, App.

1674.—

"The Prince of **Cambay's** daily food
Is asp and basilisk and toad,
Which makes him have so strong a breath,
Each night he stinks a queen to death."
Hudibras, Pt. ii. Canto i.

Butler had evidently read the stories of Mahmūd Bigara, Sultan of Guzerat, in Varthema or Purchas.

CAMBOJA, n.p. An ancient kingdom in the eastern part of Indo-China, once great and powerful: now fallen, and under the 'protectorate' of France, whose Saigon colony it adjoins. The name, like so many others of Indo-China since the days of Ptolemy, is of Skt. origin, being apparently a transfer of the name of a nation and country on the N.W. frontier of India, *Kamboja*, supposed to have been about the locality of Chitral or Kafiristan. Ignoring this, fantastic Chinese and other etymologies have been invented for the name. In the older Chinese annals (c. 1200 B.C.) this region had the name of *Fu-nan*; from the period after our era, when the kingdom of Camboja had become powerful, it was known to the Chinese as *Chin-la*. Its power seems to have extended at one time westward, perhaps to the shores of the B. of Bengal. Ruins of extraordinary vastness and architectural elaboration are numerous, and have attracted great attention since M. Mouhot's visit in 1859; though they had been mentioned by 16th century missionaries, and some of the buildings when standing in splendour were described by a Chinese visitor at the end of the 13th century. The Cambojans proper call themselves *Khmer*, a name which seems to have given rise to singular confusions (see **COMAR**). The gum **Gamboge** (*Cambodiam* in the early records [*Birdwood, Rep. on Old Rec.*, 27]) so familiar in use, derives its name from this country, the chief source of supply.

c. 1161.—". . . although . . . because the belief of the people of Rámánya (Pegu) was the same as that of the Buddha-believing men of Ceylon. . . . Parakrama the king was living in peace with the king of Rámánya—yet the ruler of Rámánya . . . forsook the old custom of providing maintenance for the ambassadors . . . saying: 'These messengers are sent to go to **Kámboja**,' and so plundered all their goods and put them in prison in the Malaya country. . . . Soon after this he seized some royal virgins sent by the King of Ceylon to the King of **Kámboja**. . . ."—Ext. from *Ceylonese Annals*, by *T. Rhys Davids*, in *J.A.S.B.* xli. Pt. i. p. 198.

1295.—"Le pays de Tchin-la. . . Les gens du pays le nomment **Kan-phou-tchi**. Sous la dynastie actuelle, les livres sacrés des Tibétains nomment ce pays **Kan-phou-**

tchi. . . ."—*Chinese Account of Chinla*, in *Abel Rémusat, Nouv. Mél.* i. 100.

c. 1535.—"Passing from Siam towards China by the coast we find the kingdom of Cambaia (read **Camboia**) . . . the people are great warriors . . . and the country of **Camboia** abounds in all sorts of victuals . . . in this land the lords voluntarily burn themselves when the king dies. . . ."—*Sommario de' Regni*, in *Ramusio*, i. f. 336.

1552.—"And the next State adjoining Siam is the kingdom of **Camboja**, through the middle of which flows that splendid river the Mecon, the source of which is in the regions of China. . . ."—*Barros*, Dec. I. Liv. ix. cap. 1.

1572.—

"Vês, passa por **Camboja** Mecom rio,
Que capitão das aguas se interpreta. . . ."
Camões, x. 127.

[1616.—"22 cattes **camboja** (gamboge)."—*Foster, Letters*, iv. 188.]

CAMEEZE, s. This word (*kamīs*) is used in colloquial H. and Tamil for 'a shirt.' It comes from the Port. *camisa*. But that word is directly from the Arab *kamīṣ*, 'a tunic.' Was St. Jerome's Latin word an earlier loan from the Arabic, or the source of the Arabic word? probably the latter; [so *N.E.D.* s.v. *Camise*]. The Mod. Greek Dict. of Sophocles has *καμίσιον*. *Camesa* is, according to the *Slang Dictionary*, used in the cant of English thieves; and in more ancient slang it was made into '*commission*.'

c. 400.—"Solent militantes habere lineas quas **Camisias** vocant, sic aptas membris et adstrictas corporibus, ut expediti sint vel ad cursum, vel ad praelia . . . quocumque necessitas traxerit."—*Scti. Hieronymi Epist.* (lxiv.) *ad Fabiolam*, § 11.

1404.—"And to the said Ruy Gonzalez he gave a big horse, an ambler, for they prize a horse that ambles, furnished with saddle and bridle, very well according to their fashion; and besides he gave him a **camisa** and an umbrella" (see **SOMBRERO**).—*Clavijo*, § lxxxix.; *Markham*, 100.

1464.—"to William and Richard my sons, all my fair **camises**. . . ."—*Will of Richard Strode*, of Newnham, Devon.

1498.—"That a very fine **camysa**, which in Portugal would be worth 300 *reis*, was given here for 2 *fanons*, which in that country is the equivalent of 30 *reis*, though the value of 30 *reis* is in that country no small matter."—*Roteiro de V. da Gama*, 77.

1573.—"The richest of all (the shops in Fez) are where they sell **camisas**. . . ."—*Marmol. Desc. General de Affrica*, Pt. I. Bk. iii. f. 87*v*.

CAMP, s. In the Madras Presidency [as well as in N. India] an official not at his headquarters is always addressed as 'in Camp.'

CAMPHOR, s. There are three camphors:—

a. The Bornean and Sumatran camphor from *Dryobalanops aromatica*.

b. The camphor of China and Japan, from *Cinnamomum Camphora*. (These are the two chief camphors of commerce; the first immensely exceeding the second in market value: see *Marco Polo*, Bk. iii. ch. xi. Note 3.)

c. The camphor of *Blumea balsamifera*, D.C., produced and used in China under the name of *ngai* camphor.

The relative ratios of value in the Canton market may be roundly given as **b**, 1; **c**, 10; **a**, 80.

The first Western mention of this drug, as was pointed out by Messrs Hanbury and Flückiger, occurs in the Greek medical writer Aëtius (see below), but it probably came through the Arabs, as is indicated by the *ph*, or *f* of the Arab *kāfūr*, representing the Skt. *karpūra*. It has been suggested that the word was originally Javanese, in which language *kāpūr* appears to mean both 'lime' and 'camphor.'

Moodeen Sheriff says that *kāfūr* is used (in Ind. Materia Medica) for 'amber.' *Tābashīr* (see **TABASHEER**), is, according to the same writer, called *bāns-kāfūr* 'bamboo-camphor'; and *ras-kāfūr* (mercury-camphor) is an impure subchloride of mercury. According to the same authority, the varieties of camphor now met with in the bazars of S. India are—1. *kāfūr-i-ḳaiṣūrī*, which is in Tamil called *pach'ch'ai* (*i.e.* crude *karuppuram*; 2. *Sūratī kāfūr*; 3. *chīnī*; 4. *batai* (from the *Batta* country?). The first of these names is a curious instance of the perpetuation of a blunder, originating in the misreading of loose Arabic writing. The name is unquestionably *fanṣūrī*, which carelessness as to points has converted into *ḳaiṣūrī* (as above, and in *Blochmann's Āīn*, i. 79). The camphor *alfanṣūrī* is mentioned as early as by Avicenna, and by Marco Polo, and came from a place called *Pansūr* in Sumatra, perhaps the same as Barus, which has now long given its name to the costly Sumatran drug.

A curious notion of Ibn Batuta's

(iv. 241) that the camphor of Sumatra (and Borneo) was produced in the inside of a cane, filling the joints between knot and knot, may be explained by the statement of Barbosa (p. 204), that the Borneo camphor as exported was packed in tubes of bamboo. This camphor is by Barbosa and some other old writers called 'eatable camphor' (*da mangiare*), because used in medicine and with betel.

Our form of the word seems to have come from the Sp. *alcanfor* and *canfora*, through the French *camphre*. Dozy points out that one Italian form retains the truer name *cafura*, and an old German one (Mid. High Germ.) is *gaffer* (*Oosterl.* 47).

c. A.D. 540.—"Hygromyri cōfectio, olei salca lib. ij, opobalsami lib. i., spicænardi, folij singu. unc. iiii. carpobalsami, arna-bonis, amomi, ligni aloes, sing. unc. ij. mastichae, moschi, sing. scrup. vi. quod si etiã **caphura** non deerit ex ea unc. ij adjicito. . . ."—*Aetii Amideni*, Librorum xvi. Tomi Dvo . . . Latinitate donati, Basil, MDXXXV., Liv. xvi. cap. cxx.

c. 940.—"These (islands called al-Ramīn) abound in gold mines, and are near the country of Kansūr, famous for its **camphor**. . . ."—*Maṣ'ūdī*, i. 338. The same work at iii. 49, refers back to this passage as "the country of *Manṣūrah*." Probably Maṣ'ūdī wrote correctly *Fanṣūrah*.

1298.—"In this kingdom of *Fansur* grows the best *camphor* in the world, called **Camfera** *Fansuri*."—*Marco Polo*, bk. iii. ch. xi.

1506.—". . . e de li (Tenasserim) vien pevere, canella . . . **camfora** *da manzar* e de *quella non se manza* . . ." (*i.e.* both camphor to eat and not to eat, or Sumatra and China camphor).—*Leonardo Ca' Masser*.

c. 1590.—"The **Camphor** *tree* is a large tree growing in the ghauts of Hindostan and in China. A hundred horsemen and upwards may rest in the shade of a single tree. . . . Of the various kinds of camphor the best is called *Ribāhi* or *Qaiçūri*. . . . In some books camphor in its natural state is called . . . *Bhimsīnī*."—*Āīn*, *Blochmann* ed. i. 78-9. [*Bhimsīnī* is more properly *bhimsenī*, and takes its name from the demi-god Bhīmsen, second son of Pandu.]

1623.—"In this shipp we have laden a small parcell of **camphire** of *Barouse*, being in all 60 *catis*."—*Batavian Letter*, pubd. in *Cocks's Diary*, ii. 343.

1726.—"The Persians name the Camphor of Baros, and also of Borneo to this day **Kafur** *Canfuri*, as it also appears in the printed text of Avicenna . . . and *Bellunensis* notes that in some MSS. of the author is found **Kafur Fansuri**. . . ."—*Valentijn*, iv. 67.

1786.—"The **Camphor** Tree has been recently discovéred in this part of the Sircar's country. We have sent two bottles of the essential oil made from it for your use."—*Letter of Tippoo*, *Kirkpatrick*, p. 231.

1875.—

"**Camphor**, Bhimsaini (barus), valuation . . . . . . 1lb. 80 rs.
Refined cake . . . 1 cwt. 65 rs."
Table of Customs Duties on Imports into Br. India up to 1875.

The first of these is the fine Sumatran camphor; the second at $\frac{1}{138}$ of the price is China camphor.

CAMPOO, s. H. *kampū*, corr. of the English '*camp*,' or more properly of the Port. '*campo*.' It is used for 'a camp,' but formerly was specifically applied to the partially disciplined brigades under European commanders in the Mahratta service.

[1525.—Mr. Whiteway notes that Castanheda (bk. vi. ch. ci. p. 217) and Barros (iii. 10, 3) speak of a ward of Malacca as **Campu** *China*; and de Eredia (1613) calls it **Campon** *China*, which may supply a link between **Campoo** and *Kampung*. (See **COMPOUND**).

1803.—"Begum Sumroo's **Campoo** has come up the ghauts, and I am afraid . . . joined Scindiah yesterday. Two deserters . . . declared that Pohlman's **Campoo** was following it."—*Wellington*, ii. 264.

1883.—". . . its unhappy plains were swept over, this way and that, by the cavalry of rival Mahratta powers, Mogul and Rohilla horsemen, or **cāmpos** and *pultuns* (battalions) under European adventurers. . . ."—*Quarterly Review*, April, p. 294.

CANARA, n.p. Properly *Kannaḍa*. This name has long been given to that part of the West coast which lies below the Ghauts, from Mt. Dely northward to the Goa territory; and now to the two British districts constituted out of that tract, viz. N. and S. Canara. This appropriation of the name, however, appears to be of European origin. The name, probably meaning 'black country' [Dravid. *kar*, 'black,' *nādu*, 'country'], from the black cotton soil prevailing there, was properly synonymous with *Karnātaka* (see **CARNATIC**), and apparently a corruption of that word. Our quotations show that throughout the sixteenth century the term was applied to the country above the Ghauts, sometimes to the whole kingdom of **Narsinga** or Vijayanagar (see **BISNAGAR**). Gradually, and probably owing to local application at Goa, where the natives seem to have been from the first known to the Portuguese as *Canarijs*, a term which in the old Portuguese works means the Konkani people and language of Goa, the name became appropriated to the low country on the coast between Goa and Malabar, which was subject to the kingdom in question, much in the same way that the name *Carnatic* came at a later date to be misapplied on the other side of the Peninsula.

The *Kanara* or Canarese language is spoken over a large tract above the Ghauts, and as far north as Bidar (see *Caldwell, Introd.* p. 33). It is only one of several languages spoken in the British districts of Canara, and that only in a small portion, viz. near Kundāpur. *Tuḷu* is the chief language in the Southern District. **Kanadam** occurs in the great Tanjore inscription of the 11th century.

1516.—"Beyond this river commences the Kingdom of Narsinga, which contains five very large provinces, each with a language of its own. The first, which stretches along the coast to Malabar, is Tulinate (*i.e. Tuḷu-nādu*, or the modern district of S. Canara); another lies in the interior . . . ; another has the name of Telinga, which confines with the Kingdom of Orisa; another is **Canari**, in which is the great city of Bisnaga; and then the Kingdom of Charamendel, the language of which is Tamul."—*Barbosa*. This passage is exceedingly corrupt, and the version (necessarily imperfect) is made up from three—viz. Stanley's English, from a Sp. MS., Hak. Soc. p. 79; the Portuguese of the Lisbon Academy, p. 291; and Ramusio's Italian (i. f. 299*v*).

c. 1535.—"The last Kingdom of the First India is called the Province **Canarim**; it is bordered on one side by the Kingdom of Goa and by Anjadiva, and on the other side by Middle India or Malabar. In the interior is the King of Narsinga, who is chief of this country. The speech of those of **Canarim** is different from that of the Kingdom of Decan and of Goa."—Portuguese *Summary of Eastern Kingdoms*, in *Ramusio*, i. f. 330.

1552.—"The third province is called **Canará**, also in the interior. . . ."—*Castanheda*, ii. 50.

And as applied to the language :—

"The language of the Gentoos is **Canará**."—*Ibid.* 78.

1552.—"The whole coast that we speak of back to the Ghaut (*Gate*) mountain range . . . they call Concan, and the people properly Concanese (*Conquenijs*), though our people call them **Canarese** (*Canarijs*). . . . And as from the Ghauts to the sea on the west of the Decan all that strip is called Concan, so from the Ghauts to the sea on the west of **Canará**, always excepting that stretch of 46 leagues of which we have spoken [north of Mount Dely] which belongs to the same *Canará*, the strip which stretches to Cape Comorin is called Malabar."—*Barros*, Dec. I. liv. ix. cap. 1.

1552.—". . . The Kingdom of **Canará**, which extends from the river called Gate, north of Chaul, to Cape Comorin (so far as concerns the interior region east of the Ghats) . . . and which in the east marches with the kingdom of Orisa; and the Gentoo Kings of this great Province of **Canará** were those from whom sprang the present Kings of Bisnaga."—*Ibid.* Dec. II. liv. v. cap. 2.

1572.—

"Aqui se enxerga lá do mar undoso
Hum monte alto, que corre longamente
Servindo ao Malabar de forte muro,
Com que do **Canará** vive seguro."
Camões, vii. 21.

Englished by Burton :

"Here seen yonside where wavy waters play
a range of mountains skirts the murmuring main
serving the Malabar for mighty mure,
who thus from him of **Canará** dwells secure."

1598.—"The land itselfe is called Decan, and also **Canara**."—*Linschoten*, 49; [Hak. Soc. i. 169].

1614.—"Its proper name is *Charnathaca*, which from corruption to corruption has come to be called **Canara**."—*Couto*, Dec. VI. liv. v. cap. 5.

In the following quotations the term is applied, either inclusively or exclusively, to the territory which we *now* call Canara :—

1615.—"**Canara**. Thence to the Kingdome of the **Cannarins**, which is but a little one, and 5 dayes journey from *Damans*. They are tall of stature, idle, for the most part, and therefore the greater theeves."—*De Monfart*, p. 23.

1623.—"Having found a good opportunity, such as I desired, of getting out of Goa, and penetrating further into India, that is more to the south, to **Canara**. . . ." *P. della Valle*, ii. 601; [Hak. Soc. ii. 168].

1672.—"The strip of land **Canara**, the inhabitants of which are called **Canarins**, is fruitful in rice and other food-stuffs."—*Baldaeus*, 98. There is a good map in this work, which shows 'Canara' in the modern acceptation.

1672.—"*Description of* **Canara** *and Journey to Goa*.—This kingdom is one of the finest in India, all plain country near the sea, and even among the mountains all peopled." —*P. Vincenzo Maria*, 420. Here the title seems used in the modern sense, but the same writer applies *Canara* to the whole Kingdom of Bisnagar.

1673.—"At Mirja the Protector of **Canora** came on board."—*Fryer* (margin), p. 57.

1726.—"The Kingdom **Canara** (under

which Onor, Batticala, and Garcopa are dependent) comprises all the western lands lying between Walkan (*Konkan?*) and Malabar, two great coast countries."—*Valentijn*, v. 2.

1727.—"The country of **Canara** is generally governed by a Lady, who keeps her Court at a Town called *Baydour*, two Days journey from the Sea."—*A. Hamilton*, i. 280.

CANARIN, n.p. This name is applied in some of the quotations under **Canara** to the people of the district now so called by us. But the Portuguese applied it to the (*Konkani*) people of Goa and their language. Thus a Konkani grammar, originally prepared about 1600 by the Jesuit, Thomas Estevão (Stephens, an Englishman), printed at Goa, 1640, bears the title *Arte da Lingoa* **Canarin**. (See A. B(urnell) in *Ind. Antiq.* ii. 98).

[1823.—"**Canareen**, an appellation given to the Creole Portuguese of Goa and their other Indian settlements."—*Owen, Narrative*, i. 191.]

CANAUT, CONAUT, CONNAUGHT, s. H. from Ar. *ḳanāt*, the side wall of a tent, or canvas enclosure. [See **SURRAPURDA**.]

[1616.—"High **cannattes** of a coarse stuff made like arras."—*Sir T. Roe, Diary*, Hak. Soc. ii. 325.]

,, "The King's Tents are red, reared on poles very high, and placed in the midst of the Camp, covering a large Compasse, encircled with **Canats** (made of red calico stiffened with Canes at every breadth) standing upright about nine foot high, guarded round every night with Souldiers."—*Terry*, in *Purchas*, ii. 1481.

c. 1660.—"And (what is hard enough to believe in *Indostan*, where the Grandees especially are so jealous . . .) I was so near to the wife of this Prince (Dara), that the cords of the **Kanates** . . , which enclosed them (for they had not so much as a poor tent), were fastened to the wheels of my chariot."—*Bernier*, E. T. 29; [ed. *Constable*, 89].

1792.—"They passed close to Tippoo's tents: the **canaut** (misprinted **canaul**) was standing, but the green tent had been removed."—*T. Munro*, in *Life*, iii. 73.

1793.—"The **canaut** of canvas . . . was painted of a beautiful sea-green colour."—*Dirom*, 230.

[c. 1798.—"On passing a skreen of Indian **connaughts**, we proceeded to the front of the Tusbeah Khanah."—*Asiatic Res.*, iv. 444.]

1817.—"A species of silk of which they make tents and **kanauts**."—*Mill*, ii. 201.

1825.—Heber writes **connaut**.—Orig. ed. ii. 257.

[1838.—"The **khenauts** (the space between the outer covering and the lining of our tents)."—*Miss Eden, Up the Country* ii. 63.]

CANDAHAR, n.p. *Ḳandahār*. The application of this name is now exclusively to (a) the well-known city of Western Afghanistan, which is the object of so much political interest. But by the Ar. geographers of the 9th to 11th centuries the name is applied to (b) the country about Peshāwar, as the equivalent of the ancient Indian *Gandhāra*, and the *Gandaritis* of Strabo. Some think the name was transferred to (a) in consequence of a migration of the people of Gandhāra carrying with them the begging-pot of Buddha, believed by Sir H. Rawlinson to be identical with a large sacred vessel of stone preserved in a mosque of Candahar. Others think that Candahar may represent *Alexandropolis* in Arachosia. We find a third application of the name (c) in Ibn Batuta, as well as in earlier and later writers, to a former port on the east shore of the Gulf of Cambay, Ghandhar in the Broach District.

a.—1552.—"Those who go from Persia, from the kingdom of Horaçam (Khorasan), from Bohára, and all the Western Regions, travel to the city which the natives corruptly call **Candar**, instead of Scandar, the name by which the Persians call Alexander. . . ."—*Barros*, IV. vi. 1.

1664.—"All these great preparations give us cause to apprehend that, instead of going to *Kachemire*, we be not led to besiege that important city of **Kandahar**, which is the Frontier to Persia, Indostan, and Usbeck, and the Capital of an excellent Country."—*Bernier*, E. T., p. 113; [ed. *Constable*, 352].

1671.—

"From Arachosia, from **Candaor** east,
And Margiana to the Hyrcanian cliffs
Of Caucasus. . . ."
Paradise Regained, iii. 316 *seqq.*

b.—c. 1030.—". . . thence to the river Chandráha (Chináb) 12 (parasangs); thence to Jailam on the West of the Báyat (or Hydaspes) 18; thence to Waihind, capital of **Kandahár** . . . 20; thence to Parsháwar 14. . . ."—*Al-Birūni*, in *Elliot*, i. 63 (corrected).

c.—c. 1343.—"From Kinbāya (Cambay) we went to the town of Kāwi (*Kānvi*, opp. Cambay), on an estuary where the tide rises and falls . . . thence to **Kandahār**, a considerable city belonging to the Infidels, and situated on an estuary from the sea."—*Ibn Batuta*, iv. 57-8.

1516.—"Further on . . . there is another place, in the mouth of a small river, which is called **Guendari**. . . . And it is a very good town, a seaport."—*Barbosa*, 64.

1814.—"**Candhar**, eighteen miles from the wells, is pleasantly situated on the banks of a river; and a place of considerable trade; being a great thoroughfare from the sea coast to the Gaut mountains."—*Forbes, Or. Mem.* i. 206; [2nd ed. i. 116].

CANDAREEN, s. In Malay, to which language the word apparently belongs, *kandūrī*. A term formerly applied to the hundredth of the Chinese ounce or weight, commonly called by the Malay name *tāhil* (see **TAEL**). Fryer (1673) gives the Chinese weights thus:—

1 *Cattee* is nearest 16 *Taies*
1 *Teen* (Taie?) is 10 *Mass*
1 *Mass* in Silver is 10 **Quandreens**
1 **Quandreen** is 10 *Cash*
733 *Cash* make 1 *Royal*
1 grain English weight is 2 cash.

1554.—"In Malacca the weight used for gold, musk, &c., the *cate*, contains 20 *taels*, each tael 16 *mazes*, each maz 20 **cumduryns**; also 1 paual 4 mazes, each maz 4 *cupongs*; each cupong 5 **cumduryns**."—*A. Nunes*, 39.

1615.—"We bought 5 greate square postes of the Kinges master carpenter; cost 2 *mas* 6 **condrins** per peece."—*Cocks*, i. 1.

(1) **CANDY**, n.p. A town in the hill country of Ceylon, which became the deposit of the sacred tooth of Buddha at the beginning of the 14th century, and was adopted as the native capital about 1592. Chitty says the name is unknown to the natives, who call the place *Mahā nuvera*, 'great city.' The name seems to have arisen out of some misapprehension by the Portuguese, which may be illustrated by the quotation from Valentijn.

c. 1530.—"And passing into the heart of the Island, there came to the Kingdom of **Candia**, a certain Friar Pascoal with two companions, who were well received by the King of the country Javira Bandar . . . in so much that he gave them a great piece of ground, and everything needful to build a church, and houses for them to dwell in."—*Couto*, Dec. VI. liv. iv. cap. 7.

1552.—". . . and at three or four places, like the passes of the Alps of Italy, one finds entrance within this circuit (of mountains) which forms a Kingdom called **Cande**."—*Barros*, Dec. III. Liv. ii. cap. 1.

1645.—"Now then as soon as the Emperor was come to his Castle in **Candi** he gave order that the 600 captive Hollanders should be distributed throughout his country among the peasants, and in the City."—*J. J. Saar's 15-Jährige Kriegs-Dienst*, 97.

1681.—"The First is the City of *Candy*, so generally called by the *Christians*, probably from *Conde*, which in the *Chingulays* Language signifies *Hills*, for among them it is situated, but by the Inhabitants called *Hingodagul-neure*, as much as to say 'The City of the *Chingulay* people,' and *Mauneur*, signifying the 'Chief or Royal City.'"—*R. Knox*, p. 5.

1726.—"**Candi**, otherwise *Candia*, or named in Cingalees *Conde Ouda*, *i.e.* the high mountain country."—*Valentijn* (*Ceylon*), 19.

(2) **CANDY**, s. A weight used in S. India, which may be stated roughly at about 500 lbs., but varying much in different parts. It corresponds broadly with the Arabian **Bahar** (q.v.), and was generally equivalent to 20 **Maunds**, varying therefore with the maund. The word is Mahr. and Tel. *khaṇḍi*, written in Tam. and Mal. *kaṇḍi*, or Mal. *kanti*, [and comes from the Skt. *khaṇḍ*, 'to divide.' A **Candy** of land is supposed to be as much as will produce a *candy* of grain, approximately 75 acres]. The Portuguese write the word *candil*.

1563.—"A **candil** which amounts to 522 pounds" (*arrateis*).—*Garcia*, f. 55.

1598.—"One **candiel** (v.l. *candiil*) is little more or less than 14 bushels, wherewith they measure Rice, Corne, and all graine."—*Linschoten*, 69; [Hak. Soc. i. 245].

1618.—"The **Candee** at this place (Batecala) containeth neere 500 pounds."—*W. Hore*, in *Purchas*, i. 657.

1710.—"They advised that they have supplied Habib Khan with ten **candy** of country gunpowder."—In *Wheeler*, ii. 136.

c. 1760.—Grose gives the Bombay **candy** as 20 maunds of 28 lbs. each=560 lbs.; the Surat ditto as 20 maunds of $37\frac{1}{3}$ lbs.=$746\frac{2}{3}$ lbs.; the Anjengo ditto 560 lbs.; the Carwar ditto 575 lbs.; the Coromandel ditto at 500 lbs. &c.

(3) **CANDY (SUGAR-)**. This name of crystallized sugar, though it came no doubt to Europe from the P.-Ar. *ḳand* (P. also *shakar ḳand*; Sp. *azucar cande*; It. *candi* and *zucchero candito*; Fr. *sucre candi*) is of Indian origin. There is a Skt. root *khaṇḍ*, 'to break,' whence *khaṇḍa*, 'broken,' also applied in various compounds to granulated and candied sugar. But there is also Tam. *kar-kaṇḍa*, *kala-kaṇḍa*, Mal. *kaṇḍi*, *kalkaṇḍi*, and *kalkaṇṭu*, which may have been the direct source of the P. and Ar. adoption of the word, and perhaps

its original, from a Dravidian word = 'lump.' [The Dravidian terms mean 'stone-piece.']

A German writer, long within last century (as we learn from Mahn, quoted in Diez's Lexicon), appears to derive **candy** from Candia, "because most of the sugar which the Venetians imported was brought from that island" —a fact probably invented for the nonce. But the writer was the same wiseacre who (in the year 1829) characterised the book of Marco Polo as a "clumsily compiled ecclesiastical fiction disguised as a Book of Travels" (see *Introduction* to *Marco Polo*, 2nd ed. pp. 112-113).

c. 1343.—"A centinajo si vende giengiovo, cannella, lacca, incenso, indaco . . . verzino scorzuto, zucchero . . . **zucchero candi** . . . porcellane . . . costo . . ."—*Pegolotti*, p. 134.

1461.—". . . Un ampoletto di balsamo. Teriaca bossoletti 15. Zuccheri Moccari (?) panni 42. **Zuccheri canditi**, scattole 5. . . ."—*List of Presents from Sultan of Egypt to the Doge*. (See under **BENJAMIN**.)

c. 1596.—"White sugar candy (**kandī** *safed*) . . . 5½ *dams* per *ser*."—*Āīn*, i. 63.

1627.—"**Sugar Candie**, or Stone Sugar." —*Minshew*, 2nd ed. s.v.

1727.—"The Trade they have to China is divided between them and *Surat* . . . the Gross of their own Cargo, which consists in Sugar, **Sugar-candy**, Allom, and some Drugs . . . are all for the *Surat* Market."— *A. Hamilton*, i. 371.

CANGUE, s. A square board, or portable pillory of wood, used in China as a punishment, or rather, as Dr. Wells Williams says, as a kind of censure, carrying no disgrace; strange as that seems to us, with whom the essence of the pillory is disgrace. The frame weighs up to 30 lbs., a weight limited by law. It is made to rest on the shoulders without chafing the neck, but so broad as to prevent the wearer from feeding himself. It is generally taken off at night (*Giles*, [and see *Gray, China*, i. 55 *seqq.*]).

The *Cangue* was introduced into China by the Tartar dynasty of Wei in the 5th century, and is first mentioned under A.D. 481. In the *Kwang-yun* (a Chin. Dict. published A.D. 1009) it is called *kanggiai* (modern mandarin *hiang-hiai*), *i.e.* 'Neck-fetter.' From this old form probably the Anamites have derived their word for it, *gong*, and the Cantonese *k'ang-ka*, 'to wear the *Cangue*,' a survival (as frequently happens in Chinese vernaculars) of an ancient term with a new orthography. It is probable that the Portuguese took the word from one of these latter forms, and associated it with their own *canga*, 'an ox-yoke,' or 'porter's yoke for carrying burdens.' [This view is rejected by the *N.E.D.* on the authority of Prof. Legge, and the word is regarded as derived from the Port. form given above. In reply to an enquiry, Prof. Giles writes: "I am entirely of opinion that the word is from the Port., and not from any Chinese term."] The thing is alluded to by F. M. Pinto and other early writers on China, who do not give it a name.

Something of this kind was in use in countries of Western Asia, called in P. *doshāka* (*bilignum*). And this word is applied to the Chinese *cangue* in one of our quotations. *Doshāka*, however, is explained in the lexicon *Burhān-i-Kāṭi* as 'a piece of timber with two branches placed on the neck of a criminal' (*Quatremère*, in *Not. et Extr.* xiv. 172, 173).

1420.—". . . made the ambassadors come forward side by side with certain prisoners. . . . Some of these had a *doshāka* on their necks."—*Shah Rukh's Mission to China*, in *Cathay*, p. cciv.

[1525.—Castanheda (Bk. VI. ch. 71, p. 154) speaks of women who had come from Portugal in the ships without leave, being tied up in a **caga** and whipped.]

c. 1540.—". . . Ordered us to be put in a horrid prison with fetters on our feet, manacles on our hands, and *collars* on our necks. . . ."—*F. M. Pinto*, (orig.) ch. lxxxiv.

1585.—"Also they doo lay on them a certaine covering of timber, wherein remaineth no more space of hollownesse than their bodies doth make: thus they are vsed that are condemned to death."—*Mendoza* (tr. by Parke, 1599), Hak. Soc. i. 117-118.

1696.—"He was imprisoned, **congoed**, tormented, but making friends with his Money . . . was cleared, and made Under-Customer. . . ."—*Bowyer's Journal* at Cochin China, in *Dalrymple, Or. Rep.* i. 81.

[1705.—"All the people were under confinement in separate houses and also in **congass**"—*Hedges, Diary*, Hak. Soc. ii. cccxl.]

" "I desir'd several Times to wait upon the Governour; but could not, he was so taken up with over-halling the Goods, that came from *Pulo Condore*, and weighing the Money, which was found to amount to 21,300 Tale. At last upon the 28th, I was obliged to appear as a Criminal in **Congas**, before the Governour and his Grand Council, attended with all the Slaves in the **Congas.**" —Letter from *Mr. James Conyngham*, survivor of the Pulo Condore massacre, in *Lockyer*, p. 93. Lockyer adds: "I understood the **Congas** to be Thumbolts" (p. 95).

1727.—"With his neck in the **congoes** which are a pair of Stocks made of bamboos." —*A. Hamilton*, ii. 175.

1779.—"Aussitôt on les mit tous trois en prison, des chaines aux pieds, une **cangue** au cou."—*Lettres Edif.* xxv. 427.

1797.—"The punishment of the *cha*, usually called by Europeans the **cangue**, is generally inflicted for petty crimes."—*Staunton, Embassy*, &c., ii. 492.

1878.—". . . frapper sur les joues a l'aide d'une petite lame de cuir ; c'est, je crois, la seule correction infligée aux femmes, car je n'en ai jamais vu aucune porter la **cangue.**" —*Léon Rousset, A Travers la Chine*, 124.

CANHAMEIRA, CONIMERE, [COONIMODE], n.p. *Kanyimedu* [or *Kunimedu*, Tam. *kūni*, 'humped,' *medu*, 'mound']; a place on the Coromandel coast, which was formerly the site of European factories (1682-1698) between Pondicherry and Madras, about 13 m. N. of the former.

1501.—In Amerigo Vespucci's letter from C. Verde to Lorenzo de' Medici, giving an account of the Portuguese discoveries in India, he mentions on the coast, before *Mailepur*, "**Conimal.**"—In *Baldelli-Boni*, Introd. to *Il Milione*, p. liii.

1561.—"On this coast there is a place called **Canhameira,** where there are so many deer and wild cattle that if a man wants to buy 500 deer-skins, within eight days the blacks of the place will give him delivery, catching them in snares, and giving two or three skins for a fanam."—*Correa*, ii. 772.

1680.—"It is resolved to apply to the Soobidar of Sevagee's Country of Chengy for a Cowle to settle factories at Cooraboor (?) and **Coonemerro**, and also at Porto Novo, if desired."—*Ft. St. Geo. Consns.*, 7th Jan., in *Notes and Exts.*, No. iii. p. 44.

[1689.—"We therefore conclude it more safe and expedient that the Chief of **Conimere** . . . do go and visit Rama Raja."—In *Wheeler, Early Rec.*, p. 97.]

1727.—"**Connymere** or **Conjemeer** is the next Place, where the *English* had a Factory many Years, but, on their purchasing Fort St. *David*, it was broken up. . . . At present its name is hardly seen in the Map of Trade." —*A. Hamilton*, i. 357.

1753.—"De Pondicheri, à Madras, la côte court en général nord-nord-est quelques degrés est. Le premier endroit de remarque est **Congi-medu,** vulgairement dit **Congimer,** à quatre lieues marines plus que moins de Pondicheri."—*D'Anville*, p. 123.

CANNANORE, n.p. A port on the coast of northern Malabar, famous in the early Portuguese history, and which still is the chief British military station on that coast, with a European regiment. The name is *Kannūr* or *Kannanūr*, 'Krishna's Town.' [The *Madras Gloss.* gives Mal. *kannu*, 'eye,' *ur*, 'village,' *i.e.* 'beautiful village.']

c. 1506.—"In **Cananor** il suo Re si è zentil, e qui nasce zz. (*i.e. zenzari*, 'ginger'); ma li zz. pochi e non cusi boni come quelli de Colcut."—*Leonardo Ca' Masser*, in *Archivio Storico Ital.*, Append.

1510.—"**Canonor** is a fine and large city, in which the King of Portugal has a very strong castle. . . . This Canonor is a port at which horses which come from Persia disembark."—*Varthema*, 123.

1572.—

"Chamará o Samorim mais gente nova
* * * * * *
Fará que todo o Nayre em fim se mova
Que entre Calecut jaz, e **Cananor.**"
Camões, x. 14.

By Burton:

"The Samorin shall summon fresh allies;
* * * * * *
lo! at his bidding every Nayr-man hies,
that dwells 'twixt Calecut and **Cananor.**"

[1611.—"The old Nahuda Mahomet of **Cainnor** goeth aboard in this boat."—*Danvers, Letters*, i. 95.]

CANONGO, s. P. *kānūn-go*, *i.e.* 'Law-utterer' (the first part being Arab. from Gr. κανών). In upper India, and formerly in Bengal, the registrar of a *tahsīl*, or other revenue subdivision, who receives the reports of the *patwārīs*, or village registrars.

1758.—"Add to this that the King's **Connegoes** were maintained at our expense, as well as the Gomastahs and other servants belonging to the Zemindars, whose accounts we sent for."—*Letter to Court*, Dec. 31, in *Long*, 157.

1765.—"I have to struggle with every difficulty that can be thrown in my way by ministers, *mutseddies*, **congoes** (!), &c., and their dependents."—Letter from *F. Sykes*, in *Carraccioli's Life of Clive*, i. 542.

CANTEROY, s. A gold coin formerly used in the S.E. part of Madras territory. It was worth 3 rs. Properly *Kanthiravi hun* (or pagoda) from *Kanthiravā Rāyā*, 'the lion-voiced,' [Skt. *kantha*, 'throat,' *rava*, 'noise'], who ruled in Mysore from 1638 to 1659 (*C. P. Brown, MS.*; [*Rice, Mysore*, i. 803]. See *Dirom's Narrative*, p. 279, where the revenues of the territory taken from Tippoo in 1792 are stated in **Canteray** pagodas.

1790.—"The full collections amounted to five Crores and ninety-two lacks of **Canteroy** pagodas of 3 Rupees each."—*Dalrymple, Or. Rep.* i. 237.

1800.—"Accounts are commonly kept in Canter'raia *Palams*, and in an imaginary money containing 10 of these, by the Musulmans called *chucrams* [see **CHUCKRUM**], and by the English **Canteroy** Pagodas. . . ."—*Buchanan's Mysore*, i. 129.

CANTON, n.p. The great seaport of Southern China, the chief city of the Province of Kwang-tung, whence we take the name, through the Portuguese, whose older writers call it *Cantão*. The proper name of the city is *Kwang-chau-fu*. The Chin. name *Kwang-tung* (='Broad East') is an ellipsis for "capital of the E. Division of the Province *Liang-Kwang* (or 'Two Broad Realms')."—(*Bp. Moule*).

1516.—"So as this went on Fernão Peres arrived from Pacem with his cargo (of pepper), and having furnished himself with necessaries set off on his voyage in June 1516 . . . they were 7 sail altogether, and they made their voyage with the aid of good pilots whom they had taken, and went without harming anybody touching at certain ports, most of which were subject to the King of China, who called himself the Son of God and Lord of the World. Fernão Peres arrived at the islands of China, and when he was seen there came an armed squadron of 12 junks, which in the season of navigation always cruized about, guarding the sea, to prevent the numerous pirates from attacking the ships. Fernão Peres knew about this from the pilots, and as it was late, and he could not double a certain island there, he anchored, sending word to his captains to have their guns ready for defence if the Chins desired to fight. Next day he made sail towards the island of Veniaga, which is 18 leagues from the city of **Cantão**. It is on that island that all the traders buy and sell, without licence from the rulers of the city. . . . And 3 leagues from that island of Veniaga is another island, where is posted the Admiral or Captain-Major of the Sea, who immediately on the arrival of strangers at the island of Veniaga reports to the rulers of **Cantão**, who they are, and what goods they bring or wish to buy; that the rulers may send orders what course to take."—*Correa*, ii. 524.

c. 1535.—". . . queste cose . . . vanno alla China con li lor giunchi, e a **Camton**, che è Città grande. . . ."—*Sommario de' Regni, Ramusio*, i. f. 337.

1585.—"The Chinos do vse in their pronunciation to terme their cities with this sylable, Fu, that is as much as to say, citie, as Taybin fu, **Canton** fu, and their townes with this syllable, Cheu."—*Mendoza*, Parke's old E. T. (1588) Hak. Soc. i. 24.

1727.—"**Canton** or *Quantung* (as the Chinese express it) is the next maritime Province."—*A. Hamilton*, ii. 217.

CANTONMENT, s. (Pron. *Cantoonment*, with accent on penult.). This English word has become almost appropriated as Anglo-Indian, being so constantly used in India, and so little used elsewhere. It is applied to military stations in India, built usually on a plan which is originally that of a standing camp or 'cantonment.'

1783.—"I know not the full meaning of the word **cantonment**, and a camp this singular place cannot well be termed; it more resembles a large town, very many miles in circumference. The officers' bungalos on the banks of the Tappee are large and convenient," &c.—*Forbes*, Letter in *Or. Mem.* describing the "Bengal Cantonments near Surat." iv. 239.

1825.—"The fact, however, is certain . . . the **cantonments** at Lucknow, nay Calcutta itself, are abominably situated. I have heard the same of Madras; and now the lately-settled **cantonment** of Nusseerabad appears to be as objectionable as any of them."—*Heber*, ed. 1844, ii. 7.

1848.—"Her ladyship, our old acquaintance, is as much at home at Madras as at Brussels—in the **cantonment** as under the tents."—*Vanity Fair*, ii. ch. 8.

CAPASS, s. The cotton plant and cotton-wool. H. *kapās*, from Skt. *karpasa*, which seems as if it must be the origin of κάρπασος, though the latter is applied to flax.

1753.—". . . They cannot any way conceive the musters of 1738 to be a fit standard for judging by them of the cloth sent us this year, as the **copass** or country cotton has not been for these two years past under nine or ten rupees. . . ."—*Ft. Wm. Cons.*, in *Long*, 40.

[1813.—"Guzerat cows are very fond of the **capaussia**, or cotton-seed."—*Forbes, Or. Mem.* 2nd ed. ii. 35.]

CAPEL, s. Malayāl. *kappal*, 'a ship.' This word has been imported into Malay, *kāpal*, and Javanese. [It appears to be still in use on the W. Coast; see *Bombay Gazetteer*, xiii. (2) 470.]

1498.—In the vocabulary of the language of Calicut given in the *Roteiro de V. de Gamā* we have—

"*Naoo;* **capell**."—p. 118.

1510.—"Some others which are made like ours, that is in the bottom, they call **capel**."—*Varthema*, 154.

CAPELAN, n.p. This is a name which was given by several 16th-century travellers to the mountains in Burma from which the rubies purchased at Pegu were said to come; the idea of their distance, &c., being very vague. It is not in our power to say what name was intended. [It was perhaps *Kyat-pyen.*] The real position of the 'ruby-mines' is 60 or 70 m. N.E. of Mandalay. [See Ball's *Tavernier*, ii. 99, 465 *seqq.*]

1506.—"... e qui è uno porto appresso uno loco che si chiama **Acaplen**, dove li se trova molti rubini, e spinade, e zoie d'ogni sorte."—*Leonardo di Ca' Masser*, p. 28.

1510.—"The sole merchandise of these people is jewels, that is, rubies, which come from another city called **Capellan**, which is distant from this (Pegu) 30 days' journey."—*Varthema*, 218.

1516.—"Further inland than the said Kingdom of Ava, at five days journey to the south-east, is another city of Gentiles ... called **Capelan**, and all round are likewise found many and excellent rubies, which they bring to sell at the city and fair of Ava, and which are better than those of Ava."—*Barbosa*, 187.

c. 1535.—"This region of Arquam borders on the interior with the great mountain called **Capelangam**, where are many places inhabited by a not very civilised people. These carry musk and rubies to the great city of Ava, which is the capital of the Kingdom of Arquam. ..."—*Sommario de Regni*, in *Ramusio*, i. 334*v*.

c. 1660.—"... A mountain 12 days journey or thereabouts, from *Siren* towards the North-east; the name whereof is **Capelan**. In this mine are found great quantities of Rubies."—*Tavernier* (E. T.) ii. 143; [ed. *Ball*, ii. 99].

Phillip's Mineralogy (according to Col. Burney) mentions the locality of the ruby as "the **Capelan** mountains, sixty miles from Pegue, a city in Ceylon!"—(*J. As. Soc. Bengal*, ii. 75). This writer is certainly very loose in his geography, and Dana (ed. 1850) is not much better: "The best ruby sapphires occur in the **Capelan** mountains, near Syrian, a city of Pegu."—*Mineralogy*, p. 222.

CAPUCAT, n.p. The name of a place on the sea near Calicut, mentioned by several old authors, but which has now disappeared from the maps, and probably no longer exists. The proper name is uncertain. [It is the little port of Kāppatt or Kappaṭṭangadi (Mal. *kāval*, 'guard,' *pātu*, 'place,') in the Cooroombranaud Taluka of the Malabar District. (*Logan, Man. of Malabar*, i. 73). The *Madras Gloss.* calls it *Caupaud.* Also see Gray, *Pyrard*, i. 360.]

1498.—In the *Roteiro* it is called **Capua**.

1500.—"This being done the Captain-Major (Pedralvares Cabral) made sail with the foresail and mizen, and went to the port of **Capocate** which was attached to the same city of Calecut, and was a haven where there was a great loading of vessels, and where many ships were moored that were all engaged in the trade of Calicut. ..."—*Correa*, i. 207.

1510.—"... another place called **Capogatto**, which is also subject to the King of Calecut. This place has a very beautiful palace, built in the ancient style."—*Varthema*, 133-134.

1516.—"Further on ... is another town, at which there is a small river, which is called **Capucad**, where there are many country-born Moors, and much shipping."—*Barbosa*, 152.

1562.—"And they seized a great number of grabs and vessels belonging to the people of **Kabkad**, and the new port, and Calicut, and Funan [*i.e. Ponany*], these all being subject to the Zamorin."—*Tohfat-ul-Mujahideen*, tr. by *Rowlandson*, p. 157. The want of editing in this last book is deplorable.

CARACOA, CARACOLLE, KARKOLLEN, &c., s. Malay *kōra-kōra* or *kūra-kūra*, which is [either a transferred use of the Malay *kūra-kūra*, or *ku-kūra*, 'a tortoise,' alluding, one would suppose, either to the shape or pace of the boat, but perhaps the tortoise was named from the boat, or the two words are independent; or from the Ar. *ḳurḳūr*, pl. *ḳarāḳīr*, 'a large merchant vessel.' Scott (s.v. *Coracora*), says: "In the absence of proof to the contrary, we may assume *kora-kora* to be native Malayan."] Dozy (s.v. *Carraca*) says that the Ar. *ḳura-ḳūra* was, among the Arabs, a merchant vessel, sometimes of very great size. Crawfurd describes the Malay *kura-kura*, as 'a large kind of sailing vessel'; but the quotation from Jarric shows it to have been the Malay galley. Marre (*Kata-Kata Malayou*, 87) says: "The Malay **kora-kora** is a great row-boat; still in use in the Moluccas. Many measure 100 feet long and 10 wide. Some have as many as 90 rowers."

c. 1330.—"We embarked on the sea at Lādhikiya in a big *ḳurḳūra* belonging to Genoese people, the master of which was called Martalamin."—*Ibn Batuta*, ii. 254.

1349.—"I took the sea on a small *ḳurḳūra* belonging to a Tunisian."—*Ibid.* iv. 327.

1606.—"The foremost of these galleys or **Caracolles** recovered our Shippe, wherein was the King of Tarnata."—*Middleton's Voyage*, E. 2.

,, ". . . Nave conscensâ, quam linguâ patriâ **caracora** noncupant. Navigii genus est oblõgum, et angustum, triremis instar, velis simul et remis impellitur."—*Jarric, Thesaurus*, i. 192.

[1613.—"**Curra-curra.**" See quotation under **ORANKAY.**]

1627.—"They have Gallies after their manner, formed like Dragons, which they row very swiftly, they call them **karkollen.**"—*Purchas, Pilgrimage*, 606.

1659.—"They (natives of Ceram, &c.) hawked these dry heads backwards and forwards in their **korrekorres** as a special rarity."—*Walter Schultzen's Ost-Indische Reise, &c.*, p. 41.

1711.—"Les Philippines nomment ces batimens **caracoas.** C'est vne espèce de petite galère à rames et à voiles."—*Lettres Edif.* iv. 27.

1774.—"A **corocoro** is a vessel generally fitted with outriggers, having a high arched stem and stern, like the points of a half moon. . . . The Dutch have fleets of them at Amboyna, which they employ as guarda-costos."—*Forrest, Voyage to N. Guinea*, 23. Forrest has a plate of a **corocoro**, p. 64.

[1869.—"The boat was one of the kind called **kora-kora**, quite open, very low, and about four tons burden. It had out-riggers of bamboo, about five off each side, which supported a bamboo platform extending the whole length of the vessel. On the extreme outside of this sat the twenty rowers, while within was a convenient passage fore and aft. The middle of the boat was covered with a thatch-house, in which baggage and passengers are stowed; the gunwale was not more than a foot above water, and from the great side and top weight, and general clumsiness, these boats are dangerous in heavy weather, and are not infrequently lost."—*Wallace, Malay Arch.*, ed. 1890, p. 266.]

CARAFFE, s. Dozy shows that this word, which in English we use for a water-bottle, is of Arabic origin, and comes from the root *gharaf*, 'to draw' (water), through the Sp. *garrâfa*. But the precise Arabic word is not in the dictionaries. (See under **CARBOY.**)

CARAMBOLA, s. The name given by various old writers on Western India to the beautiful acid fruit of the tree (*N.O. Oxalideae*) called by Linn. from this word, *Averrhoa carambola*. This name was that used by the Portuguese. De Orta tells us that it was the Malabar name. The word *karanbal* is also given by Molesworth as the Mahratti name; [another form is *karambela*, which comes from the Skt. *karmara* given below in the sense of 'food-appetizer']. In Upper India the fruit is called *kamranga, kamrakh*, or *khamrak* (Skt. *karmara, karmāra, karmaraka, karmaranga*).* (See also **BLIMBEE.**) Why a cannon at billiards should be called by the French *carambolage* we do not know. [If Mr. Ball be right, the fruit has a name, Cape-Gooseberry, in China which in India is used for the Tiparry.—*Things Chinese*, 3rd ed. 253.]

c. 1530.—"Another fruit is the **Kermerik.** It is fluted with five sides," &c.—*Erskine's Baber*, 325.

1563.—"*O.* Antonia, pluck me from that tree a **Carambola** or two (for so they call them in Malavar, and we have adopted the Malavar name, because that was the first region where we got acquainted with them).

"*A.* Here they are.

"*R.* They are beautiful; a sort of sour-sweet, not *very* acid.

"*O.* They are called in Canarin and Decan *camariz*, and in Malay *balimba* . . . they make with sugar a very pleasant conserve of these. . . . Antonia! bring hither a preserved **carambola.**"—*Garcia*, ff. 46*v*, 47.

1598.—"There is another fruite called **Carambolas**, which hath 8 (5 really) corners, as bigge as a smal aple, sower in eating, like vnripe plums, and most vsed to make Conserues. (*Note by Paludanus*). The fruite which the Malabars and Portingales call **Carambolas**, is in Decan called **Camarix**, in Canar, *Camarix* and *Carabeli*; in Malaio, *Bolumba*, and by the Persians **Chamaroch.**"—*Linschoten*, 96; [Hak. Soc. ii. 33].

1672.—"The **Carambola** . . . as large as a pear, all sculptured (as it were) and divided into ribs, the ridges of which are not round but sharp, resembling the heads of those iron maces that were anciently in use."—*P. Vincenzo Maria*, 352.

1878.—". . . the oxalic **Kamrak.**"—*In my Indian Garden*, 50.

[1900.—". . . that most curious of fruits, the **carambola**, called by the Chinese the *yong-t'o*, or foreign peach, though why this name should have been selected is a mystery, for when cut through, it looks like a star with five rays. By Europeans it is also known as the *Cape gooseberry.*"—*Ball, Things Chinese*, 3rd ed. p. 253.]

CARAT, s. Arab *ḳirrāt*, which is taken from the Gr. κεράτιον, a bean of the κερατεία or carob tree (*Ceratonia siliqua*, L.). This bean, like the Indian *rati* (see **RUTTEE**) was used as a weight, and thence also it gave name to a coin

* Sir J. Hooker observes that the fact that there is an acid and a sweet-fruited variety (*blimbee*) of this plant indicates a very old cultivation.

of account, if not actual. To discuss the carat fully would be a task of extreme complexity, and would occupy several pages.

Under the name of *siliqua* it was the 24th part of the golden solidus of Constantine, which was again = $\frac{1}{6}$ of an ounce. Hence this carat was = $\frac{1}{144}$ of an ounce. In the passage from St. Isidore quoted below, the *cerates* is distinct from the *siliqua*, and = $1\frac{1}{2}$ *siliquae*. This we cannot explain, but the *siliqua Graeca* was the *κεράτιον*; and the *siliqua* as $\frac{1}{24}$ of a solidus is the parent of the *carat* in all its uses. [See Prof. Gardner, in Smith, *Dict. Ant.* 3rd ed. ii. 675.] Thus we find the *carat* at Constantinople in the 14th century = $\frac{1}{24}$ of the *hyperpera* or Greek *bezant*, which was a debased representative of the solidus; and at Alexandria $\frac{1}{24}$ of the Arabic *dīnār*, which was a purer representative of the solidus. And so, as the Roman *uncia* signified $\frac{1}{12}$ of any unit (compare *ounce*, *inch*), so to a certain extent *carat* came to signify $\frac{1}{24}$. Dictionaries give Arab. *ḳirrāt* as "$\frac{1}{24}$ of an ounce." Of this we do not know the evidence. The *English Cyclopaedia* (s.v.) again states that "the *carat* was originally the 24th part of the *marc*, or half-pound, among the French, from whom the word came." This sentence perhaps contains more than one error; but still both of these allegations exhibit the *carat* as $\frac{1}{24}$th part. Among our goldsmiths the term is still used to measure the proportionate quality of gold; pure gold being put at 24 *carats*, gold with $\frac{1}{12}$ alloy at 22 *carats*, with $\frac{1}{4}$ alloy at 18 *carats*, &c. And the word seems also (like **Anna**, q.v.) sometimes to have been used to express a proportionate scale in other matters, as is illustrated by a curious passage in Marco Polo, quoted below.

The *carat* is also used as a weight for diamonds. As $\frac{1}{144}$ of an ounce troy this ought to make it $3\frac{1}{3}$ grains. But these carats really run $151\frac{1}{2}$ to the ounce troy, so that the diamond *carat* is $3\frac{1}{6}$ grs. nearly. This we presume was adopted direct from some foreign system in which the carat *was* $\frac{1}{144}$ of the local ounce. [See Ball, *Tavernier*, ii. 447.]

c. A.D. 636.—"Siliqua vigesima quarta pars solidi est, ab arboris semine vocabulum tenens. **Cerates** oboli pars media est siliquā habens unam semis. Hanc latinitas semiobulū vocat; **Cerates** autem Graece, Latine siliqua cornuū interpretatur. Obulus siliquis tribus appenditur, habens *cerates* duos, calcos quatuor."—*Isidori Hispalensis Opera* (ed. Paris, 1601), p. 224.

1298.—"The Great Kaan sends his commissioners to the Province to select four or five hundred . . . of the most beautiful young women, according to the scale of beauty enjoined upon them. The commissioners . . . assemble all the girls of the province, in presence of appraisers appointed for the purpose. These carefully survey the points of each girl. . . . They will then set down some as estimated at 16 **carats**, some at 17, 18, 20, or more or less, according to the sum of the beauties or defects of each. And whatever standard the Great Kaan may have fixed for those that are to be brought to him, whether it be 20 carats or 21, the commissioners select the required number from those who have attained to that standard."—*Marco Polo*, 2nd ed. i. 350-351.

1673.—"A stone of one **Carrack** is worth 10*l*."—*Fryer*, 214.

CARAVAN, s. P. *karwān*; a convoy of travellers. The Ar. *ḳāfila* is more generally used in India. The word is found in French as early as the 13th century (*Littré*). A quotation below shows that the English transfer of the word to a wheeled conveyance for travellers (now for goods also) dates from the 17th century. The abbreviation *van* in this sense seems to have acquired rights as an English word, though the altogether analogous *bus* is still looked on as slang.

c. 1270.—"Meanwhile the convoy (la **caravana**) from Tortosa . . . armed seven vessels in such wise that any one of them could take a galley if it ran alongside."—*Chronicle of James of Aragon*, tr. by *Foster*, i. 379.

1330.—"De hac civitate recedens cum **caravanis** et cum quadam societate, ivi versus Indiam Superiorem."—*Friar Odoric*, in *Cathay*, &c., ii. App. iii.

1384.—"Rimonda che l'avemo, vedemo venire una grandissima **carovana** di cammelli e di Saracini, che recavano spezierie delle parti d' India."—*Frescobaldi*, 64.

c. 1420.—"Is adolescens ab Damasco Syriae, ubi mercaturae gratiâ erat, perceptâ prius Arabum linguâ, in coetu mercatorum —hi sexcenti erant—quam vulgo **caroanam** dicunt. . . ."—*N. Conti*, in *Poggius de Varietate Fortunae*.

1627.—"A **Caravan** is a convoy of souldiers for the safety of merchants that trauell in the East Countreys."—*Minshew*, 2nd ed. s.v.

1674.—"**Caravan** or **Karavan** (Fr. *caravane*) a Convoy of Souldiers for the safety of Merchants that travel by Land. Also of late corruptly used with us for a kind of

Waggon to carry passengers to and from London."—*Glossographia*, &c., by J. E.

CARAVANSERAY, s. P. *karwānsarāī*; a **Serai** (q.v.) for the reception of **Caravans** (q.v.).

1404.—"And the next day being Tuesday, they departed thence and going about 2 leagues arrived at a great house like an Inn, which they call **Carabansaca** (read *-sara*), and here were Chacatays looking after the Emperor's horses."—*Clavijo*, § xcviii. Comp. *Markham*, p. 114.

[1528.—"In the Persian language they call these houses **carvancaras**, which means resting-place for caravans and strangers." —*Tenreiro*, ii. p. 11.]

1554.—"I'ay à parler souuent de ce nom de **Carbachara**: . . . Ie ne peux le nommer autrement en François, sinon vn **Carbachara**: et pour le sçauoir donner à entendre, il fault supposer qu'il n'y a point d'hostelleries es pays ou domaine le Turc, ne de lieux pour se loger, sinon dedens celles maisons publiques appellée **Carbachara**. . . ."—*Observations* par *P. Belon*, f. 59.

1564.—"Hic diverti in diversorium publicum, **Caravasarai** Turcae vocant . . . vastum est aedificium . . . in cujus medio patet area ponendis sarcinis et camelis."—*Busbequii*, *Epist.* i. (p. 35).

1619.—". . . a great bazar, enclosed and roofed in, where they sell stuffs, cloths, &c. with the House of the Mint, and the great **caravanserai**, which bears the name of *Lala Beig* (because Lala Beig the Treasurer gives audiences, and does his business there) and another little **caravanserai**, called that of the *Ghilac* or people of Ghilan."—*P. della Valle* (from Ispahan), ii. 8; [comp. Hak. Soc. i. 95].

1627.—"At *Band Ally* we found a neat **Carravansraw** or Inne . . . built by mens charity, to give all civill passengers a resting place *gratis*; to keepe them from the injury of theeves, beasts, weather, &c."—*Herbert*, p. 124.

CARAVEL, s. This often occurs in the old Portuguese narratives. The word is alleged to be not Oriental, but Celtic, and connected in its origin with the old British *coracle*; see the quotation from Isidore of Seville, the indication of which we owe to Bluteau, s.v. The Portuguese *caravel* is described by the latter as a 'round vessel' (*i.e.* not long and sharp like a galley), with lateen sails, ordinarily of 200 tons burthen. The character of swiftness attributed to the *caravel* (see both Damian and Bacon below) has suggested to us whether the word has not come rather from the Persian Gulf—Turki *ḳarāwul*, 'a scout, an outpost, a vanguard.' Doubtless there are difficulties. [The *N.E.D.* says that it is probably the dim. of Sp. *caraba.*] The word is found in the following passage, quoted from the Life of St. Nilus, who died c. 1000, a date hardly consistent with Turkish origin. But the Latin translation is by Cardinal Sirlet, c. 1550, and the word may have been changed or modified:—

"Cogitavit enim in unaquaque Calabriae regione perficere navigia. . . . Id autem non ferentes Russani cives . . . simul irruentes ac tumultuantes navigia combusserunt et eas quae **Caravellae** appellantur secuerunt." —In the Collection of *Martene* and *Durand*, vi. col. 930.

c. 638.—"**Carabus**, parua scafa ex vimine facta, quae contexta crudo corio genus navigii praebet."—*Isidori Hispal. Opera.* (Paris, 1601), p. 255.

1492.—"So being one day importuned by the said Christopher, the Catholic King was persuaded by him that nothing should keep him from making this experiment; and so effectual was this persuasion that they fitted out for him a ship and two **caravels**, with which at the beginning of August 1492, with 120 men, sail was made from Gades."—*Summary of the H. of the Western Indies*, by *Pietro Martire* in *Ramusio*, iii. f. 1.

1506.—"Item traze della Mina d'oro de Ginea ogn anno ducati 120 mila che vien ogni mise do' **caravelle** con ducati 10 mila." —*Leonardo di Ca' Masser*, p. 30.

1549.—"Viginti et quinque agiles naues, quas et **caravellas** dicimus, quo genere nauium soli Lusitani utuntur."—*Damiani a Goës, Diensis Oppugnatio*, ed. 1602, p. 289.

1552.—"Ils lâchèrent les bordées de leurs **Karawelles**; ornèrent leurs vaisseaux de pavillons, et s'avancèrent sur nous."—*Sidi Ali*, p. 70.

c. 1615.—"She may spare me her mizen and her bonnets; I am a **carvel** to her."—*Beaum. & Flet.*, *Wit without Money*, i. 1.

1624.—"Sunt etiam naves quaedam nunciae quae ad officium celeritatis apposite exstructae sunt (quas **caruellas** vocant)."—*Bacon, Hist. Ventorum.*

1883.—"The deep-sea fishing boats called *Machoās* . . . are **carvel** built, and now generally iron fastened. . . ."—*Short Account of Bombay Fisheries*, by *D. G. Macdonald*, M.D.

CARBOY, s. A large glass bottle holding several gallons, and generally covered with wicker-work, well known in England, where it is chiefly used to convey acids and corrosive liquids in bulk. Though it is not an Anglo-Indian word, it comes (in the form *ḳarāba*) from Persia, as Wedgwood has pointed out. Kaempfer, whom we quote from his description of the wine trade at Shiraz, gives an exact etching of a carboy. Littré mentions that the late M. Mohl referred **caraffe** to the same original; but see that word. *Karāba* is no doubt connected with Ar. *ḳirba*, 'a large leathern milk-bottle.'

1712.—"Vasa vitrea, alia sunt majora, ampullacea et circumducto scirpo tunicata, quae vocant **Karabà** . . . Venit *Karaba* una apud vitriarios duobus mamudi, raro carius."—*Kaempfer, Amoen. Exot.* 379.

1754.—"I delivered a present to the Governor, consisting of oranges and lemons, with several sorts of dried fruits, and six **karboys** of Isfahan wine."—*Hanway*, i. 102.

1800.—"Six **corabahs** of rose-water."—*Symes, Emb. to Ava*, p. 488.

1813.—"**Carboy** of Rosewater. . . ."—*Milburn*, ii. 330.

1875.—"People who make it (Shiraz Wine) generally bottle it themselves, or else sell it in huge bottles called '**Kuraba**' holding about a dozen quarts."—*Macgregor, Journey through Khorassan, &c.*, 1879, i. 37.

CARCANA, CARCONNA, s. H. from P. *kārkhāna*, 'a place where business is done'; a workshop; a departmental establishment such as that of the commissariat, or the artillery park, in the field.

1663.—"There are also found many raised Walks and Tents in sundry Places, that are the offices of several Officers. Besides these there are many great Halls that are called **Kar-Kanays**, or places where Handy-craftsmen do work."—*Bernier*, E. T. 83; [ed. *Constable*, 258].

c. 1756.—"In reply, Hydur pleaded his poverty . . . but he promised that as soon as he should have established his power, and had time to regulate his departments (**Kārkhānajāt**), the amount should be paid."—*Hussein Ali Khan, History of Hydur Naik*, p. 87.

1800.—"The elephant belongs to the **Karkana**, but you may as well keep him till we meet."—*Wellington*, i. 144.

1804.—"If the (bullock) establishment should be formed, it should be in regular **Karkanas**."—*Ibid.* iii. 512.

CARCOON, s. Mahr. *kārkūn*, 'a clerk,' H.—P. *kār-kun*, (*faciendorum factor*) or 'manager.'

[c. 1590.—"In the same way as the **karkun** sets down the transactions of the assessments, the *muḳaddam* and the *patwārī* shall keep their respective accounts."—*Āīn*, tr. *Jarrett*, ii. 45.

[1615.—"Made means to the **Corcone** or Scrivano to help us to the copia of the King's licence."—*Foster, Letters*, iii. 122.

[1616.—"Addick Raia Pongolo, **Corcon** of this place."—*Ibid.* iv. 167.]

1826.—"My benefactor's chief **carcoon** or clerk allowed me to sort out and direct despatches to officers at a distance who belonged to the command of the great Sawant Rao."—*Pandurang Hari*, 21; [ed. 1873, i. 28.]

CARÉNS, n.p. Burm. *Ka-reng*, [a word of which the meaning is very uncertain. It is said to mean 'dirty-feeders,' or 'low-caste people,' and it has been connected with the *Kirāta* tribe (see the question discussed by *McMahon, The Karens of the Golden Chersonese*, 43 *seqq.*)]. A name applied to a group of non-Burmese tribes, settled in the forest and hill tracts of Pegu and the adjoining parts of Burma, from Mergui in the south, to beyond Toungoo in the north, and from Arakan to the Salwen, and beyond that river far into Siamese territory. They do not know the name *Kareng*, nor have they one name for their own race; distinguishing, among these whom we call Karens, three tribes, *Sgaw*, *Pwo*, and *Bghai*, which differ somewhat in customs and traditions, and especially in language. "The results of the labours among them of the American Baptist Mission have the appearance of being almost miraculous, and it is not going too far to state that the cessation of blood feuds, and the peaceable way in which the various tribes are living . . . and have lived together since they came under British rule, is far more due to the influence exercised over them by the missionaries than to the measures adopted by the English Government, beneficial as these doubtless have been" (*Br. Burma Gazetteer*, [ii. 226]). The author of this excellent work should not, however, have admitted the quotation of Dr. Mason's fanciful notion about the identity of Marco Polo's *Carajan* with Karen, which is totally groundless.

1759.—"There is another people in this country called **Carianners**, whiter than either (Burmans or Peguans), distinguished into *Buraghmah* and *Pegu* **Carianners**; they live in the *woods*, in small Societies, of ten or twelve *houses*; are not wanting in industry, though it goes no further than to procure them an annual subsistence."—In *Dalrymple, Or. Rep.* i. 100.

1799—"From this reverend father (V. Sangermano) I received much useful information. He told me of a singular description of people called **Carayners** or **Carianers**, that inhabit different parts of the country, particularly the western provinces of Dalla and Bassein, several societies of whom also dwell in the district adjacent to Rangoon. He represented them as a simple, innocent race, speaking a language distinct from that of the Birmans, and entertaining rude notions of religion. . . . They are timorous, honest, mild in their manners, and exceedingly hospitable to strangers."—*Symes*, 207.

c. 1819.—"We must not omit here the **Carian**, a good and peaceable people, who live dispersed through the forests of Pegù, in small villages consisting of 4 or 5 houses . . . they are totally dependent upon the despotic government of the Burmese." —*Sangermano*, p. 34.

CARICAL, n.p. Etymology doubtful; Tam. *Karaikkāl*, [which is either *kāṟai*, 'masonry' or 'the plant, thorny webera': *kāl*, 'channel' (*Madras Adm. Man.* ii. 212, *Gloss.* s.v.)]. A French settlement within the limits of Tanjore district.

CARNATIC, n.p. *Karṇāṭaka* and *Kārṇāṭaka*, Skt. adjective forms from *Karṇāṭa* or *Kārṇāṭa*, [Tam. *kar*, 'black,' *nādu*, 'country']. This word in native use, according to Bp. Caldwell, denoted the Telegu and Canarese people and their language, but in process of time became specially the appellation of the people speaking Canarese and their language (*Drav. Gram.* 2nd ed. Introd. p. 34). The Mahommedans on their arrival in S. India found a region which embraces Mysore and part of Telingāna (in fact the kingdom of Vijayanagara), called the *Karṇāṭaka* country, and this was identical in application (and probably in etymology) with the **Canara** country (q.v.) of the older Portuguese writers. The *Karṇāṭaka* became extended, especially in connection with the rule of the Nabobs of Arcot, who partially occupied the Vijayanagara territory, and were known as Nawābs of the *Karṇāṭaka*, to the country below the Ghauts, on the eastern side of the Peninsula, just as the other form *Canara* had become extended to the country below the Western Ghauts; and eventually among the English the term *Carnatic* came to be understood in a sense more or less restricted to the eastern low country, though never quite so absolutely as Canara has become restricted to the western low country. The term *Carnatic* is now obsolete.

c. A.D. 550.—In the *Brihat-Sanhitā* of Varāhamihira, in the enumeration of peoples and regions of the south, we have in Kern's translation (*J. R. As. Soc.* N.S. v. 83) *Karnatic;* the original form, which is not given by Kern, is **Karnāta**.

c. A.D. 1100.—In the later Sanskrit literature this name often occurs, *e.g.* in the *Kathasaritsāgara*, or 'Ocean of Rivers of Stories,' a collection of tales (in verse) of the beginning of the 12th century, by Somadeva, of Kashmir; but it is not possible to attach any very precise meaning to the word as there used. [See refs. in *Tawney*, tr. ii. 651.]

A.D. 1400.—The word also occurs in the inscriptions of the Vijayanagara dynasty, *e.g.* in one of A.D. 1400.—(*Elem. of S. Indian Palaeography*, 2nd ed. pl. xxx.)

1608.—"In the land of **Karṇāṭa** and Vidyānagara was the King Mahendra."—*Taranatha's H. of Buddhism*, by *Schiefner*, p. 267.

c. 1610.—"The Zamindars of Singaldip (Ceylon) and **Karnátak** came up with their forces and expelled Sheo Rai, the ruler of the Dakhin."—*Firishta*, in *Elliot*, vi. 549.

1614.—See quotation from Couto under **CANARA**.

[1623.—"His Tributaries, one of whom was the Queen of **Curnat**."—*P. della Valle*, Hak. Soc. ii. 314.]

c. 1652.—"Gandicot is one of the strongest Cities in the Kingdom of **Carnatica**."—*Tavernier*, E. T. ii. 98; [ed. *Ball*, i. 284].

c. 1660.—"The Ráís of the **Karnátik**, Mahratta (country), and Telingana, were subject to the Ráí of Bidar."—*'Amal-i-Sálih*, in *Elliot* vii. 126

1673.—"I received this information from the natives, that the **Canatick** country reaches from *Gongola* to the *Zamerhin's* Country of the *Malabars* along the Sea, and inland up to the Pepper Mountains of *Sunda* . . . *Bedmure*, four Days Journey hence, is the Capital City."—*Fryer*, 162, in Letter IV., *A Relation of the* **Canatick** *Country*.—Here he identifies the "Canatick" with Canara below the Ghauts.

So also the coast of Canara seems meant in the following:—

c. 1760.—"Though the navigation from the **Carnatic** coast to Bombay is of a very short run, of not above six or seven degrees. . . ."—*Grose*, i. 232.

" "The **Carnatic** or province of Arcot . . . its limits now are greatly inferior to those which bounded the ancient **Carnatic**; for the Nabobs of Arcot have never extended their authority beyond the river Gondegama to the north; the great chain of mountains to the west; and the branches of the Kingdom of Trichinopoli, Tanjore, and Maissore to the south; the sea bounds it on the east."—*Ibid.* II. vii.

1762.—"Siwaee Madhoo Rao . . . with this immense force . . . made an incursion into the **Karnatic** Balaghaut."—*Hussein Ali Khan, History of Hydur Naik*, 148.

1792.—"I hope that our acquisitions by this peace will give so much additional strength and compactness to the frontier of our possessions, both in the **Carnatic**, and on the coast of Malabar, as to render it difficult for any power above the Ghauts to invade us."—*Lord Cornwallis's* Despatch from Seringapatam, in *Seton-Karr*, ii. 96.

1826.—"Camp near Chillumbrum (**Carnatic**), March 21st." This date of a letter of Bp. Heber's is probably one of the latest instances of the use of the term in a natural way.

CARNATIC FASHION. See under **BENIGHTED**.

(1). **CARRACK**, n.p. An island in the upper part of the Persian Gulf, which has been more than once in British occupation. Properly **Khārak**. It is so written in *Jaubert's Edrisi* (i. 364, 372). But Dr. Badger gives the modern Arabic as *el-Khārij*, which would represent old P. *Khārig*.

c. 830.—"**Kharek** . . . cette isle qui a un farsakh en long et en large, produit du blé, des palmiers, et des vignes."—*Ibn Khurdādba*, in *J. As.* ser. vi. tom. v. 283.

c. 1563.—"Partendosi da Basora si passa 200 miglia di Golfo co'l mare a banda destra sino che si giunge nell' isola di **Carichi**. . . ." —*C. Federici*, in *Ramusio*, iii. 386*v*.

1727.—"The Islands of **Carrick** ly, about West North West, 12 Leagues from *Bowchier*."—*A. Hamilton*, i. 90.

1758.—"The Baron . . . immediately sailed for the little island of **Karec**, where he safely landed; having attentively surveyed the spot he at that time laid the plan, which he afterwards executed with so much success."—*Ives*, 212.

(2). **CARRACK**, s. A kind of vessel of burden from the Middle Ages down to the end of the 17th century. The character of the earlier *carrack* cannot be precisely defined. But the larger cargo-ships of the Portuguese in the trade of the 16th century were generally so styled, and these were sometimes of enormous tonnage, with 3 or 4 decks. Charnock (*Marine Architecture*, ii. p. 9) has a plate of a Genoese carrack of 1542. He also quotes the description of a Portuguese carrack taken by Sir John Barrough in 1592. It was of 1,600 tons burden, whereof 900 merchandize; carried 32 brass pieces and between 600 and 700 passengers (?); was built with 7 decks. The word (L. Lat.) *carraca* is regarded by Skeat as properly *carrica*, from *carricare*, It. *caricare*, 'to lade, to charge.' This is possible; but it would be well to examine if it be not from the Ar. *ḥarākah*, a word which the dictionaries explain as 'fire-ship'; though this is certainly not always the meaning. Dozy is inclined to derive *carraca* (which is old in Sp. he says) from *ḳarāḳir*, the pl. of *ḳurḳūr* or *ḳurḳūra* (see **CARACOA**). And *ḳurḳūra* itself he thinks may have come from *carricare*, which already occurs in St. Jerome. So that Mr. Skeat's origin is possibly correct. [The *N.E.D.* refers to *carraca*, of which the origin is said to be uncertain.] Ibn Batuta uses the word twice at least for a state barge or something of that kind (see *Cathay* p. 499, and *Ibn Bat.* ii. 116; iv. 289) The like use occurs several times in *Makrizi* (*e.g.* I. i. 143; I. ii. 66; and II. i. 24). Quatremère at the place first quoted observes that the *ḥarākah* was not a fire ship in our sense, but a vessel with a high deck from which fire could be thrown; but that it could also be used as a transport vessel, and was so used on sea and land.

1338.—". . . after that we embarked at Venice on board a certain **carrack**, and sailed down the Adriatic Sea."—*Friar Pasqual*, in *Cathay*, &c., 231.

1383.—"Eodem tempore venit in magnâ tempestate ad Sandevici portum navis quam dicunt **carika** (mirae) magnitudinis, plena divitiis, quae facile inopiam totius terrae relevare potuisset, si incolarum invidia permisisset."—*T. Walsingham, Hist. Anglic.*, by *H. T. Riley*, 1864, ii. 83-84.

1403.—"The prayer being concluded, and the storm still going on, a light like a candle appeared in the cage at the mast-head of the **carraca**, and another light on the spar that they call bowsprit (*bauprés*) which is fixed in the forecastle; and another light like a candle *in una vara de espinelo* (?) over the poop, and these lights were seen by as many as were in the **carrack**, and were called up to see them, and they lasted awhile and then disappeared, and all this while the storm did not cease, and by-and-by all went to sleep except the steersman and certain sailors of the watch."—*Clavijo*, § xiii. Comp. *Markham*, p. 13.

1548.—"De Thesauro nostro munitionum artillariorum, Tentorum, Pavilionum, pro Equis navibus **caracatis**, Galeis et aliis navibus quibuscumque. . . ."—Act of Edw. VI. in *Rymer*, xv. 175.

1552.—"Ils avaient 4 barques, grandes comme des *ḳarrāḳa*. . . ."—*Sidi 'Ali*, p. 67.

1566-68.—". . . about the middle of the month of Ramazan, in the year 974, the inhabitants of Funan and Fandreeah [*i.e.* Ponany and **Pandarāni**, q.v.], having sailed out of the former of these ports in a fleet of 12 grabs, captured a **caracca** belonging to the Franks, which had arrived from Bengal, and which was laden with rice and sugar . . . in the year 976 another party . . . in a fleet of 17 grabs . . . made capture off Shaleeat (see **CHALIA**) of a large **caracca**, which had sailed from Cochin, having on board nearly 1,000 Franks. . . ."—*Tohfut-ul-Mujahideen*, p. 159.

1596.—"It comes as farre short as . . . a cocke-boate of a **Carrick**."—*T. Nash, Have with you to Saffron Walden*, repr. by *J. P. Collier*, p. 72.

1613.—"They are made like **carracks**, only strength and storage."—*Beaum. & Flet., The Coxcomb*, i. 3.

1615.—"After we had given her chase for about 5 hours; her colours and bulk discovered her to be a very great Portugal **carrack** bound for Goa."—*Terry*, in *Purchas*; [ed. 1777, p. 34].

1620.—"The harbor at Nangasaque is the best in all Japon, wheare there may be 1000 seale of shipps ride landlockt, and the greatest shipps or **carickes** in the world . . . ride before the towne within a cable's length of the shore in 7 or 8 fathom water at least."—*Cocks, Letter to Batavia*, ii. 313.

c. 1620.—"Il faut attendre là des Pilotes du lieu, que les Gouverneurs de Bombaim et de Marsagão ont soin d'envoyer tout à l'heure, pour conduire le Vaisseau à Turumba [*i.e.* Trombay] où les **Caraques** ont coustume d'hyverner."—*Routier . . . des Indes Or.*, by *Aleixo da Motta*, in *Thevenot*.

c. 1635.—

"The bigger Whale, like some huge **carrack** lay
Which wanted Sea room for her foes to play. . . ."
Waller, Battle of the Summer Islands.

1653.—". . . pour moy il me vouloit loger en son Palais, et que si i'auois la volonté de retourner a Lisbone par mer, il me feroit embarquer sur les premieres **Karaques**. . . ."—*De la Boullaye-le-Gouz*, ed. 1657, p. 213.

1660.—"And further, That every Merchant Denizen who shall hereafter ship any Goods or Merchandize in any **Carrack** or Galley shall pay to your Majesty all manner of Customs, and all the Subsidies aforesaid, as any Alien born out of the Realm."—Act 12 Car. II. cap. iv. s. iv. (Tonnage and Poundage).

c. 1680.—"To this City of the floating . . . which foreigners, with a little variation from *carroços*, call **carracas**."—*Vieira*, quoted by *Bluteau*.

1684.—". . . there was a **Carack** of Portugal cast away upon the Reef having on board at that Time 4,000,000 of Guilders in Gold . . . a present from the King of Siam to the King of Portugal."—*Cowley*, 32, in *Dampier's Voyages*, iv.

CARRAWAY, s. This word for the seed of *Carum carui*, L., is (probably through Sp. *alcaravea*) from the Arabic *karawiyā*. It is curious that the English form is thus closer to the Arabic than either the Spanish, or the French and Italian *carvi*, which last has passed into Scotch as *carvy*. But the Arabic itself is a corruption [not immediately, *N.E.D.*] of Lat. *careum*, or Gr. *κάρον* (*Dozy*).

CARTMEEL, s. This is, at least in the Punjab, the ordinary form that 'mail-cart' takes among the natives. Such inversions are not uncommon. Thus Sir David Ochterlony was always called by the Sepoys *Loni-okhtar*. In our memory an officer named *Holroyd* was always called by the Sepoys *Roydāl*, [and *Brownlow*, *Lobrūn*. By another curious corruption *Mackintosh* becomes *Makkhanī-tosh*, 'buttered toast'!]

CARTOOCE, s. A cartridge; *kārtūs*, Sepoy H.; [comp. **TOSTDAUN**].

CARYOTA, s. This is the botanical name (*Caryota urens*, L.) of a magnificent palm growing in the moister forest regions, as in the Western Ghauts and in Eastern Bengal, in Ceylon, and in Burma. A conspicuous character is presented by its enormous bipinnate leaves, somewhat resembling colossal bracken-fronds, 15 to 25 feet long, 10 to 12 in width; also by the huge pendent clusters of its inflorescence and seeds, the latter like masses of rosaries 10 feet long and upwards. It affords much **Toddy** (q.v.) made into spirit and sugar, and is the tree chiefly affording these products in Ceylon, where it is called *Kitul*. It also affords a kind of sago, and a woolly substance found at the foot of the leaf-stalks is sometimes used for caulking, and forms a good tinder. The sp. name *urens* is derived from the acrid, burning taste of the fruit. It is called, according to Brandis, the *Mhār*-palm in Western India. We know of no Hindustani or familiar Anglo-Indian name. [Watt, (*Econ. Dict.* ii. 206) says that it is known in Bombay as the *Hill* or *Sago* palm. It has penetrated in Upper India as far as Chunār.] The name *Caryota* seems taken from Pliny, but his application is to a kind of date-palm; his statement that it afforded the best wine of the East probably suggested the transfer.

c. A.D. 70.—"Ab his **caryotae** maxume celebrantur, et cibo quidem et suco uberrimae, ex quibus praecipua vina orienti, iniqua capiti, unde pomo nomen."—*Pliny*, xiii. § 9.

1681.—"The next tree is the *Kettule*. It groweth straight, but not so tall or big as a *Coker-Nut-Tree;* the inside nothing but a white pith, as the former. It yieldeth a sort of Liquor . . . very sweet and pleasing to the Pallate. . . . The which Liquor they boyl and make a kind of brown sugar called *Jaggory* [see **JAGGERY**], &c."—*Knox*, p. 15.

1777.—"The **Caryota** *urens*, called the Saguer tree, grew between Salatiga and Kopping, and was said to be the real tree from which sago is made."—*Thunberg*, E. T. iv. 149. A mistake, however.

1861.—See quotation under **PEEPUL**.

CASH, s. A name applied by Europeans to sundry coins of low value in various parts of the Indies. The word in its original form is of extreme antiquity, "Skt. *karsha* . . . a weight of silver or gold equal to $\frac{1}{400}$ of a *Tulā*" (*Williams, Skt. Dict.;* and see also a Note on the *Kārsha*, or rather *kārshāpaṇa*, as a copper coin of great antiquity, in *E. Thomas's Pathân Kings of Delhi*, 361-362). From the Tam. form *kāsu*, or perhaps from some Konkani form which we have not traced, the Portuguese seem to have made *caixa*, whence the English *cash*. In Singalese also *kāsi* is used for 'coin' in general. The English term was appropriated in the monetary system which prevailed in S. India up to 1818; thus there was a copper coin for use in Madras struck in England in 1803, which bears on the reverse, "XX Cash." A figure of this coin is given in *Ruding*. Under this system 80 cash=1 fanam, 42 fanams=1 star pagoda. But from an early date the Portuguese had applied *caixa* to the small money of foreign systems, such as those of the Malay Islands, and especially to that of the Chinese. In China the word *cash* is used, by Europeans and their hangers-on, as the synonym of the Chinese *le* and *tsien*, which are those coins made of an alloy of copper and lead with a square hole in the middle, which in former days ran 1000 to the *liang* or **tael** (q.v.), and which are strung in certain numbers on cords. [This type of money, as was recently pointed out by Lord Avebury, is a survival of the primitive currency, which was in the shape of an axe.] Rouleaux of coin thus strung are represented on the surviving bank-notes of the Ming dynasty (A.D. 1368 onwards), and probably were also on the notes of their Mongol predecessors.

The existence of the distinct English word *cash* may probably have affected the form of the corruption before us. This word had a European origin from It. *cassa*, French *caisse*, 'the money-chest': this word in book-keeping having given name to the heading of account under which actual disbursements of coin were entered (see *Wedgwood* and *N.E.D.* s.v.). In Minsheu (2nd ed. 1627) the present sense of the word is not attained. He only gives "a tradesman's **Cash**, or Counter to keepe money in."

1510.—"They have also another coin called **cas**, 16 of which go to a *tare* of silver."—*Varthema*, 130.

" "In this country (Calicut) a great number of apes are produced, one of which is worth 4 **casse**, and one **casse** is worth a *quattrino*."—*Ibid*. 172. (Why a monkey should be worth 4 *casse* is obscure.)

1598.—"You must understand that in *Sunda* there is also no other kind of money than certaine copper mynt called **Caixa**, of the bignes of a Hollādes doite, but not half so thicke, in the middle whereof is a hole to hang it on a string, for that commonlie they put two hundreth or a thousand vpon one string."—*Linschoten*, 34; [Hak. Soc. i. 113].

1600.—"Those (coins) of Lead are called **caxas**, whereof 1600 make one mas."—*John Davis*, in *Purchas*, i. 117.

1609.—"Ils (les Chinois) apportent la monnoye qui a le cours en toute l'isle de Iava, et Isles circonvoisines, laquelle en lãgue Malaique est appellee **Cas**. . . . Cette monnoye est jettée en moule en Chine, a la Ville de Chincheu."—*Houtman*, in *Nav. des Hollandois*, i. 30*b*.

[1621.—"In many places they threw abroad **Cashes** (or brasse money) in great quantety."—*Cocks, Diary*, ii. 202.]

1711.—"Doodoos and **Cash** are Copper Coins, eight of the former make one Fanham, and ten of the latter one Doodoo."—*Lockyer*, 8. [*Doodoo* is the Tel. *duddu*, Skt. *dvi*, 'two'; a more modern scale is: 2 *dooggaunies*=1 *doody:* 3 *doodies*=1 *anna*.—*Mad. Gloss.* s.v.]

1718.—"**Cass** (a very small coin, eighty whereof make one Fano)."—*Propagation of the Gospel in the East*, ii. 52.

1727.—"At Atcheen they have a small coin of leaden Money called **Cash**, from

12 to 1600 of them goes to one *Mace*, or *Masscie*."—*A. Hamilton*, ii. 109.

c. 1750-60.—"At Madras and other parts of the coast of Coromandel, 80 **casches** make a fanam, or 3d. sterling; and 36 fanams a silver pagoda, or 7s. 8d. sterling."—*Grose*, i. 282.

1790.—"So far am I from giving credit to the late Government (of Madras) for œconomy, in not making the necessary preparations for war, according to the positive orders of the Supreme Government, after having received the most gross insult that could be offered to any nation! I think it very possible that every **Cash** of that ill-judged saving may cost the company a crore of rupees."—Letter of *Lord Cornwallis* to E. J. Hollond, Esq., see the *Madras Courier*, 22nd Sept. 1791.

[1792.—"Whereas the sum of Raheties 1223, 6 fanams and 30 **khas** has been deducted."—Agreement in *Logan*, *Malabar*, iii. 226.]

1813.—At Madras, according to Milburn, the coinage ran:

"10 **Cash**=1 *doodee*; 2 *doodees*=1 pice; 8 *doodees*=1 single fanam," &c.

The following shows a singular corruption, probably of the Chinese *tsien*, and illustrates how the striving after meaning shapes such corruptions:—

1876.—"All money transactions (at Manwyne on the Burman-Chinese frontier) are effected in the copper coin of China called '*change*,' of which about 400 or 500 go to the rupee. These coins are generally strung on cord," &c.—*Report on the Country through which the Force passed to meet the Governor*, by *W. J. Charlton, M.D.*

An intermediate step in this transformation is found in Cocks's *Japan Journal*, *passim*, *e.g.*, ii. 89:

"But that which I tooke most note of was of the liberalitee and devotion of these heathen people, who thronged into the Pagod in multetudes one after another to cast money into a littel chapell before the idalles, most parte . . . being *gins* or brass money, whereof 100 of them may vallie som 10d. str., and are about the bignes of a 3d. English money."

CASHEW, s. The tree, fruit, or nut of the *Anacardium occidentale*, an American tree which must have been introduced early into India by the Portuguese, for it was widely diffused apparently as a wild tree long before the end of the 17th century, and it is described as an Indian tree by Acosta, who wrote in 1578. Crawfurd also speaks of it as abundant, and in full bearing, in the jungly islets of Hastings Archipelago, off the coast of Camboja (*Emb. to Siam, &c.*, i. 103) [see *Teele's* note on *Linschoten*, Hak. Soc. ii. 27]. The name appears to be S. American, *acajou*, of which an Indian form, *kājū*, [and Malay *gajus*], have been made. The so-called fruit is the fleshy top of the peduncle which bears the nut. The oil in the shell of the nut is acrid to an extraordinary degree, whilst the kernels, which are roasted and eaten, are quite bland. The tree yields a gum imported under the name of *Cadju* gum.

1578.—"This tree gives a fruit called commonly **Caiu**; which being a good stomachic, and of good flavour, is much esteemed by all who know it. . . . This fruit does not grow everywhere, but is found in gardens at the city of Santa Cruz in the Kingdom of Cochin."—*C. Acosta*, *Tractado*, 324 *seqq.*

1598.—"**Cajus** groweth on trees like apple-trees, and are of the bignes of a Peare."—*Linschoten*, p. 94; [Hak. Soc. ii. 28].

[1623.—*P. della Valle*, Hak. Soc. i. 135, calls it **cagiu**.]

1658.—In *Piso*, *De Indiae utriusque Re Naturali et Medicâ*, Amst., we have a good cut of the tree as one of Brasil, called *Acaibaa* "et fructus ejus **Acaju**."

1672.—". . . il **Cagiu**. . . . Questo è l'Amandola ordinaria dell' India, per il che se ne raccoglie grandissima quantità, essendo la pianta fertilissima e molto frequente, ancora nelli luoghi più deserti et inculti."—*Vincenzo Maria*, 354.

1673.—Fryer describes the tree under the name *Cheruse* (apparently some mistake), p. 182.

1764.— ". . . Yet if
The **Acajou** haply in the garden bloom..."
Grainger, iv.

[1813.—Forbes calls it "the *chashew*-apple," and the "*cajew*-apple."—*Or. Mem.* 2nd ed. i. 232, 238.]

c. 1830.—"The **cashew**, with its apple like that of the cities of the Plain, fair to look at, but acrid to the taste, to which the far-famed nut is appended like a bud."—*Tom Cringle*, ed. 1863, p. 140.

1875.—"**Cajoo** kernels."—*Table of Customs Duties imposed in Br. India up to* 1875.

CASHMERE, n.p. The famous valley province of the Western Himālaya, H. and P. *Kashmīr*, from Skt. *Kaśmīra*, and sometimes *Kāśmīra*, alleged by Burnouf to be a contraction of *Kaśyapamīra*. [The name is more probably connected with the *Khasa* tribe.] Whether or not it be the *Kaspatyrus* or *Kaspapyrus* of Herodotus, we believe it undoubtedly to be the *Kaspeiria* (kingdom) of Ptolemy.

Several of the old Arabian geographers write the name with the guttural *ḳ*, but this is not so used in modern times.

c. 630.—"The Kingdom of **Kia-shi-mi-lo** (*Kaśmīra*) has about 7000 *li* of circuit. On all sides its frontiers are surrounded by mountains; these are of prodigious height; and although there are paths affording access to it, these are extremely narrow."—*Hwen T'sang* (*Pèl. Bouddh.*) ii. 167.

c. 940.—"**Kashmīr** . . . is a mountainous country, forming a large kingdom, containing not less than 60,000 or 70,000 towns or villages. It is inaccessible except on one side, and can only be entered by one gate."—*Mas'ūdi*, i. 373.

1275.—"**Kashmīr**, a province of India, adjoining the Turks; and its people of mixt Turk and Indian blood excel all others in beauty."—*Zakarīya Kazvīni*, in *Gildemeister*, 210.

1298.—"**Keshimur** also is a province inhabited by a people who are idolaters and have a language of their own . . . this country is the very source from which idolatry has spread abroad."—*Marco Polo*, i. 175.

1552.—"The Mogols hold especially towards the N.E. the region Sogdiana, which they now call **Queximir**, and also Mount Caucasus which divides India from the other Provinces."—*Barros*, IV. vi. 1.

1615.—"**Chishmeere**, the chiefe Citie is called *Sirinakar*."—*Terry*, in *Purchas*, ii. 1467; [so in *Roe's* Map, vol. ii. Hak. Soc. ed.; **Chismer** in *Foster*, *Letters*, iii. 283].

1664.—"From all that hath been said, one may easily conjecture, that I am somewhat charmed with **Kachemire**, and that I pretend there is nothing in the world like it for so small a kingdom."—*Bernier*, E. T. 128; [ed. *Constable*, 400].

1676.—

"A trial of your kindness I must make;
Though not for mine, so much as virtue's sake,
The Queen of **Cassimere** . . ."

Dryden's Aurungzebe, iii. 1.

1814.—"The shawls of **Cassimer** and the silks of Iran."—*Forbes*, *Or. Mem.* iii. 177; [2nd ed. ii. 232]. (See **KERSEYMERE**.)

CASIS, CAXIS, CACIZ, &c., s. This Spanish and Portuguese word, though Dozy gives it only as *prêtre chrétien*, is frequently employed by old travellers, and writers on Eastern subjects, to denote Mahommedan divines (*mullas* and the like). It may be suspected to have arisen from a confusion of two Arabic terms—*ḳāḍi* (see **CAZEE**) and *ḳashīsh* or *ḳasīs*, 'a Christian Presbyter' (from a Syriac root signifying *senuit*). Indeed we sometimes find the precise word *ḳashīsh* (*Caxix*) used by Christian writers as if it were the special title of a Mahommedan theologian, instead of being, as it really is, the special and technical title of a Christian priest (a fact which gives Mount Athos its common Turkish name of *Kashīsh Dāgh*). In the first of the following quotations the word appears to be applied by the Mussulman historian to *pagan* priests, and the word for churches to pagan temples. In the others, except that from Major Millingen, it is applied by Christian writers to Mahommedan divines, which is indeed its recognised signification in Spanish and Portuguese. In Jarric's *Thesaurus* (Jesuit Missions, 1606) the word *Cacizius* is constantly used in this sense.

c. 1310.—"There are 700 churches (*kalīsīa*) resembling fortresses, and every one of them overflowing with presbyters (**ḳashīshān**) without faith, and monks without religion."—*Description of the Chinese City of Khanzai* (Hangchau) in *Wasāf's History* (see also *Marco Polo*, ii. 196).

1404.—"The town was inhabited by Moorish hermits called **Caxixes**; and many people came to them on pilgrimage, and they healed many diseases."—*Markham's Çlavijo*, 79.

1514.—"And so, from one to another, the message passed through four or five hands, till it came to a **Gazizi**, whom we should call a bishop or prelate, who stood at the King's feet. . . ."—Letter of *Giov. de Empoli*, in *Archiv. Stor. Ital.* Append. p. 56.

1538.—"Just as the Cryer was offering to deliver me unto whomsoever would buy me, in comes that very **Cacis** Moulana, whom they held for a Saint, with 10 or 11 other **Cacis** his Inferiors, all Priests like himself of their wicked sect."—*F. M. Pinto* (tr. by H. C.), p. 8.

1552.—**Caciz** in the same sense used by *Barros*, II. ii. 1.

[1553.—See quotation from *Barros* under **LAR**.

[1554.—"Who was a **Caciz** of the Moors, which means in Portuguese an ecclesiastic."—*Castañeda*, Bk. I. ch. 7.]

1561.—"The King sent off the Moor, and with him his **Casis**, an old man of much authority, who was the principal priest of his Mosque."—*Correa*, by *Ld. Stanley*, 113.

1567.—". . . The Holy Synod declares it necessary to remove from the territories of His Highness all the infidels whose office it is to maintain their false religion, such as are the **cācizes** of the Moors, and the preachers of the Gentoos, *jogues*, sorcerers, (*feiticeiros*), *jousis*, *grous* (*i.e. joshis* or astrologers, and *gurūs*), and whatsoever others make a business of religion among the infidels, and so also the bramans and *paibus*

(? *prabhūs*, see **PURVOE**)."—*Decree 6 of the Sacred Council of Goa*, in *Arch. Port. Or.* fasc. 4.

1580.—". . . e foi sepultado no campo per **Cacises**."—*Primor e Honra*, &c., f. 13*v*.

1582.—"And for pledge of the same, he would give him his sonne, and one of his chief chaplaines, the which they call **Cacis**."—*Castañeda*, by N. L.

1603.—"And now those initiated priests of theirs called *Cashishes* (**Casciscis**) were endeavouring to lay violent hands upon his property."—*Benedict Goës*, in *Cathay*, &c., ii. 568.

1648.—"Here is to be seen an admirably wrought tomb in which a certain **Casis** lies buried, who was the *Pedagogue* or Tutor of a King of *Guzuratte*."—*Van Twist*, 15.

1672.—"They call the common priests **Casis**, or by another name *Schierifi* (see **SHEREEF**), who like their bishops are in no way distinguished in dress from simple laymen, except by a bigger turban . . . and a longer mantle. . . ."—*P. Vincenzo Maria*, 55.

1688.—"While they were thus disputing, a **Caciz**, or doctor of the law, joined company with them."—*Dryden, L. of Xavier, Works*, ed. 1821, xvi. 68.

1870.—"A hierarchical body of priests, known to the people (Nestorians) under the names of **Kieshishes** and *Abunas*, is at the head of the tribes and villages, entrusted with both spiritual and temporal powers."—*Millingen, Wild Life among the Koords*, 270.

CASSANAR, CATTANAR, s. A priest of the Syrian Church of Malabar; Malayāl. *kattanār*, meaning originally 'a chief,' and formed eventually from the Skt. *kartṛi*.

1606.—"The Christians of St. Thomas call their priests **Caçanares**."—*Gouvea*, f. 28*b*. This author gives **Catatiara** and **Caçaneira** as feminine forms, 'a Cassanar's wife.' The former is Malayāl. *kàttatti*, the latter a Port. formation.

1612.—"A few years ago there arose a dispute between a Brahman and a certain **Cassanar** on a matter of jurisdiction."—*P. Vincenzo Maria*, 152.

[1887.—"Mgr. Joseph . . . consecrated as a bishop . . . a **Catenar**."—*Logan, Man. of Malabar*, i. 211.]

CASSAY, n.p. A name often given in former days to the people of **Munneepore** (Manipur), on the eastern frontier of Bengal. It is the Burmese name of this people, *Kasé*, or as the Burmese pronounce it, *Kathé*. It must not be confounded with **Cathay** (q.v.) with which it has nothing to do. [See **SHAN**.]

1759.—In *Dàlrymple's Orient. Repert.* we find **Cassay** (i. 116).

1795.—"All the troopers in the King's service are natives of **Cassay**, who are much better horsemen than the Burmans."—*Symes*, p. 318.

CASSOWARY, s. The name of this great bird, of which the first species known (*Casuarius galeatus*) is found only in Ceram Island (*Moluccas*), is Malay *kasavārī* or *kasuārī*; [according to Scott, the proper reading is *kasuwārī*, and he remarks that no Malay Dict. records the word before 1863]. Other species have been observed in N. Guinea, N. Britain, and N. Australia.

[1611.—"St. James his Ginny Hens, the **Cassawarway** moreover."—(*Note by Coryat.*) "An East Indian bird at St. James in the keeping of Mr. Walker, that will carry no coales, but eat them as whot you will."—*Peacham*, in *Paneg. verses* on Coryat's *Crudities*, sig. 1. 3r. (1776); quoted by Scott.]

1631.—"De Emeu, vulgo **Casoaris**. In insula Ceram, aliisque Moluccensibus vicinis insulis, celebris haec avis reperitur."—*Jac. Bontii*, lib. v. c. 18.

1659.—"This aforesaid bird **Cossebàres** also will swallow iron and lead, as we once learned by experience. For when our Connestabel once had been casting bullets on the Admiral's Bastion, and then went to dinner, there came one of these **Cossebâres** on the bastion, and swallowed 50 of the bullets. And . . . next day I found that the bird after keeping them a while in his maw had regularly cast up again all the 50."—*J. J. Saar*, 86.

1682.—"On the islands Sumatra (?) Banda, and the other adjoining islands of the Moluccas there is a certain bird, which by the natives is called *Emeu* or *Eme*, but otherwise is commonly named by us **Kasuaris**."—*Nieuhof*, ii. 281.

1705.—"The **Cassawaris** is about the bigness of a large Virginia Turkey. His head is the same as a Turkey's; and he has a long stiff hairy Beard upon his Breast before, like a Turkey. . . ."—*Funnel*, in *Dampier*, iv. 266.

CASTE, s. "The artificial divisions of society in India, first made known to us by the Portuguese, and described by them under their term *caste*, signifying 'breed, race, kind,' which has been retained in English under the supposition that it was the native name" (*Wedgwood*, s.v.). [See the extraordinary derivation of Hamilton below.] Mr. Elphinstone prefers to write "*Cast*."

We do not find that the early Portuguese writer Barbosa (1516) applies the word *casta* to the divisions of Hindu society. He calls these divisions in Narsinga and Malabar so many *leis de gentios, i.e.* 'laws' of the heathen, in the sense of sectarian rules of life. But he uses the word *casta* in a less technical way, which shows how it should easily have passed into the technical sense. Thus, speaking of the King of Calicut: "This King keeps 1000 women, to whom he gives regular maintenance, and they always go to his court to act as the sweepers of his palaces . . . these are ladies, and of good family" (*estas saom fidalgas e de boa* **casta**.—In *Coll. of Lisbon Academy*, ii. 316). So also Castanheda: "There fled a knight who was called Fernão Lopez, *homem de boa* **casta**" (iii. 239). In the quotations from Barros, Correa, and Garcia de Orta, we have the word in what we may call the technical sense.

c. 1444.—"Whence I conclude that this race (**casta**) of men is the most agile and dexterous that there is in the world."—*Cadamosto, Navegação*, i. 14.

1552.—"The Admiral . . . received these Naires with honour and joy, showing great contentment with the King for sending his message by such persons, saying that he expected this coming of theirs to prosper, as there did not enter into the business any man of the **caste** of the Moors."—*Barros*, I. vi. 5.

1561.—"Some of them asserted that they were of the **caste** (*casta*) of the Christians."—*Correa, Lendas*, i. 2, 685.

1563.—"One thing is to be noted . . . that no one changes from his father's trade, and all those of the same **caste** (*casta*) of shoemakers are the same."—*Garcia*, f. 213*b*.

1567.—"In some parts of this Province (of Goa) the Gentoos divide themselves into distinct races or **castes** (*castas*) of greater or less dignity, holding the Christians as of lower degree, and keep these so superstitiously that no one of a higher caste can eat or drink with those of a lower. . . ."—Decree 2nd of the *Sacred Council of Goa*, in *Archiv. Port. Orient.*, fasc. 4.

1572.—

"Dous modos ha de gente; porque a nobre
Nairos chamados são, e a menos dina
Poleas tem por nome, a quem obriga
A lei não misturar a **castà** antiga."—
Camões, vii. 37.

By Burton:

"Two modes of men are known; the nobles know
the name of Nayrs, who call the lower **Caste**
Poléas, whom their haughty laws contain
from intermingling with the higher strain."

1612.—"As regards the **castes** (*castas*) the great impediment to the conversion of the Gentoos is the superstition which they maintain in relation to their **castes**, and which prevents them from touching, communicating, or mingling with others, whether superior or inferior; these of one observance with those of another."—*Couto*, Dec. V. vi. 4. See also as regards the Portuguese use of the word, *Gouvea*, ff. 103, 104, 105, 106*b*, 129*b*; *Synodo*, 18*b*, &c.

1613.—"The Banians kill nothing; there are thirtie and odd severall **Casts** of these that differ something in Religion, and may not eat with each other."—*N. Withington*, in *Purchas*, i. 485; see also *Pilgrimage*, pp. 997, 1003.

1630. — "The common *Bramane* hath eighty two **Casts** or Tribes, assuming to themselves the name of that tribe. . . ."—*Lord's Display of the Banians*, p. 72.

1673.—"The mixture of **Casts** or Tribes of all India are distinguished by the different modes of binding their Turbats."—*Fryer*, 115.

c. 1760.—"The distinction of the Gentoos into their tribes or **Casts**, forms another considerable object of their religion."—*Grose*, i. 201.

1763—"The **Casts** or tribes into which the Indians are divided, are reckoned by travellers to be eighty-four."—*Orme* (ed. 1803), i. 4.

[1820.—"The Kayasthas (pronounced Kaists, hence the word **caste**) follow next."—*W. Hamilton, Descr. of Hindostan*, i. 109.]

1878—"There are thousands and thousands of these so-called **Castes**; no man knows their number, no man can know it; for the conception is a very flexible one, and moreover new **castes** continually spring up and pass away."—*F. Jagor, Ost-Indische Handwerk und Gewerbe*, 13.

Castes are, according to Indian social views, either high or low.

1876.—"**Low-caste** Hindoos in their own land are, to all ordinary apprehension, slovenly, dirty, ungraceful, generally unacceptable in person and surroundings. . . . Yet offensive as is the *low-caste* Indian, were I estate-owner, or colonial governor, I had rather see the lowest Pariahs of the low, than a single trim, smooth-faced, smooth-wayed, clever **high-caste** Hindoo, on my lands or in my colony."—*W. G. Palgrave*, in *Fortnightly Rev.*, cx. 226.

In the Madras Pres. *castes* are also '*Right-hand*' and '*Left-hand*.' This distinction represents the agricultural classes on the one hand, and the artizans, &c., on the other, as was pointed out by F. W. Ellis. In the old days of Ft. St. George, faction-fights between the two were very common, and the terms *right-hand* and *left-hand* castes occur early in the old records of that settlement, and frequently in Mr. Talboys Wheeler's extracts from them. They are mentioned by Couto. [See *Nelson, Madura*, Pt. ii. p. 4; *Oppert. Orig. Inhab.* p. 57.]

Sir Walter Elliot considers this feud to be "nothing else than the occasional outbreak of the smouldering antagonism between Brahmanism and Buddhism, although in the lapse of ages both parties have lost sight of the fact. The points on which they split now are mere trifles, such as parading on horse-back or in a palankeen in procession, erecting a **pandal** or marriage-shed on a given number of pillars, and claiming to carry certain flags, &c. The right-hand party is headed by the Brahmans, and includes the Parias, who assume the van, beating their tom-toms when they come to blows. The chief of the left-hand are the Panchalars [*i.e.* the Five Classes, workers in metal and stone, &c.], followed by the Pallars and workers in leather, who sound their long trumpets and engage the Parias." (In *Journ. Ethnol. Soc.* N.S. 1869, p. 112.)

1612.—"From these four **castes** are derived 196; and those again are divided into two parties, which they call *Valanga* and *Elange* [Tam. *valangai, idangai*], which is as much as to say 'the right hand' and 'the left hand. . ."—*Couto*, u. s.

The word is current in French:

1842.—"Il est clair que les **castes** n'ont jamais pu exister solidement sans une veritable conservation religieuse."—*Comte, Cours de Phil. Positive*, vi. 505.

1877.—"Nous avons aboli les **castes** et les privilèges, nous avons inscrit partout le principe de l'égalité devant la loi, nous avons donné le suffrage à tous, mais voilà qu'on réclame maintenant l'égalité des conditions."—*E. de Laveleye, De la Propriété*, p. iv.

Caste is also applied to breeds of animals, as 'a **high-caste** Arab.' In such cases the usage may possibly have come directly from the Port. *alta casta, casta baixa*, in the sense of breed or strain.

CASTEES, s. Obsolete. The Indo-Portuguese formed from *casta* the word *castiço*, which they used to denote children born in India of Portuguese parents; much as *creole* was used in the W. Indies.

1599.—"Liberi vero nati in Indiâ, utroque parente Lusitano, **castisos** vocantur, in omnibus fere Lusitanis similes, colore tamen modicum differunt, ut qui ad gilvum non nihil deflectant. Ex **castisis** deinde nati magis magisque gilvi fiunt, a parentibus et *mesticis* magis deflectentes; porro et *mesticis* nati per omnia indigenis respondent, ita ut in tertiâ generatione Lusitani reliquis Indis sunt simillimi."—*De Bry*, ii. 76; (*Linschoten* [Hak. Soc. i. 184]).

1638.—"Les habitans sont ou **Castizes**, c'est à dire Portugais naturels, et nez de pere et de mere Portugais, ou *Mestizes*, c'est à dire, nez d'vn pere Portugais et d'vne mere Indienne."—*Mandelslo.*

1653.—"Les **Castissos** sont ceux qui sont nays de pere et mere reinols (**Reinol**); ce mot vient de Casta, qui signifie Race, ils sont mesprizez des Reynols. . . ."—*Le Gouz, Voyages*, 26 (ed. 1657).

1661.—"Die Stadt (Negapatam) ist zimlich volksreich, doch mehrentheils von Mastyсen **Castycen**, und Portugesichen Christen."—*Walter Schulze*, 108.

1699.—"**Castees** wives at Fort St. George."—*Census of English on the Coast*, in *Wheeler*, i. 356.

1701-2.—In the MS. *Returns of Persons in the Service of the Rt. Honble. the E. I. Company*, in the India Office, for this year, we find, "4th (in Council) Matt. Empson, Sea Customer, marry'd **Castees**," and under 1702, "13. Charles Bugden . . . marry'd **Casteez.**"

1726.—". . . or the offspring of the same by native women, to wit *Mistices* and **Castices**, or blacks . . . and Moors."—*Valentijn*, v. 3.

CASUARINA, s. A tree (*Casuarina muricata*, Roxb.—*N. O. Casuarineae*) indigenous on the coast of Chittagong and the Burmese provinces, and southward as far as Queensland. It was introduced into Bengal by Dr. F. Buchanan, and has been largely adopted as an ornamental tree both in Bengal and in Southern India. The tree has a considerable superficial resemblance to a larch or other finely-feathered conifer, making a very acceptable variety in the hot plains, where real pines will not grow. [The name, according to Mr. Scott, appears to be based on a Malayan name associating the tree with the **Cassowary**, as Mr. Skeat suggests from the resemblance of its needles to the quills of the bird.]

1861.—See quotation under **PEEPUL.**

1867.—"Our road lay chiefly by the sea-coast, along the white sands, which were fringed for miles by one grand continuous line or border of **casuarina** trees."—*Lt.-Col. Lewin, A Fly on the Wheel*, 362.

1879.—"It was lovely in the white moonlight, with the curving shadows of palms on the dewy grass, the grace of the drooping **casuarinas**, the shining water, and the long drift of surf. . . ."—*Miss Bird, Golden Chersonese*, 275.

CATAMARAN, s. Also **CUTMURRAM, CUTMURAL.** Tam. *kattu*, 'binding,' *maram*, 'wood.' A raft formed of three or four logs of wood lashed together. The Anglo-Indian accentuation of the last syllable is not correct.

1583.—"Seven round timbers lashed together for each of the said boats, and of the said seven timbers five form the bottom; one in the middle longer than the rest makes a cutwater, and another makes a poop which is under water, and on which a man sits. . . These boats are called **Gatameroni**."—*Balbi, Viaggio*, f. 82.

1673.—"Coasting along some **Cattamarans** (Logs lashed to that advantage that they waft off all their Goods, only having a Sail in the midst and Paddles to guide them) made after us. . . ."—*Fryer*, 24.

1698.—"Some time after the **Cattamaran** brought a letter. . . ."—In *Wheeler*, i. 334.

1700.—"Un pecheur assis sur un **catimaron**, c'est à dire sur quelques grosses pièces de bois liées ensemble en manière de radeau."—*Lett. Edif.* x. 58.

c. 1780.—"The wind was high, and the ship had but two anchors, and in the next forenoon parted from that by which she was riding, before that one who was coming from the shore on a **Catamaran** could reach her."—*Orme*, iii. 300.

1810.—Williamson (*V. M.* i. 65) applies the term to the rafts of the Brazilian fishermen.

1836.—"None can compare to the **Catamarans** and the wonderful people that manage them . . . each **catamaran** has one, two, or three men . . . they sit crouched upon their heels, throwing their paddles about very dexterously, but very unlike rowing."—*Letters from Madras*, 34.

1860.—"The **Cattamaran** is common to Ceylon and Coromandel."—*Tennent, Ceylon*, i. 442.

[During the war with Napoleon, the word came to be applied to a sort of fire-ship. "Great hopes have been formed at the Admiralty (in 1804) of certain vessels which were filled with combustibles and called **catamarans**."—(*Ld. Stanhope, Life of Pitt*, iv. 218.) This may have introduced the word in English and led to its use as 'old cat' for a shrewish hag.]

CATECHU, also **CUTCH** and **CAUT**, s. An astringent extract from the wood of several species of Acacia (*Acacia catechu*, Willd.), the *khair*, and *Acacia suma*, Kurz, *Ac. sundra*, D. C. and probably more. The extract is called in H. *kath*, [Skt. *kvath*, 'to decoct'], but the two first commercial names which we have given are doubtless taken from the southern forms of the word, *e.g.* Can. *kāchu*, Tam. *kāsu*, Malay *kachu*. De Orta, whose judgments are always worthy of respect, considered it to be the *lycium* of the ancients, and always applied that name to it; but Dr. Royle has shown that *lycium* was an extract from certain species of *berberis*, known in the bazars as *rasōt*. Cutch is first mentioned by Barbosa, among the drugs imported into Malacca. But it remained unknown in Europe till brought from Japan about the middle of the 17th century. In the 4th ed. of Schröder's *Pharmacop. Medico-chymica*, Lyons, 1654, it is briefly described as *Catechu* or *Terra Japonica*, "*genus terrae exoticae*" (*Hanbury and Flückiger*, 214). This misnomer has long survived.

1516.—". . . drugs from Cambay; amongst which there is a drug which we do not possess, and which they call *puchô* (see **PUTCHOCK**) and another called **cachô**."—*Barbosa*, 191.

1554.—"The bahar of **Cate**, which here (at Ormuz) they call **cacho**, is the same as that of rice."—*A. Nunes*, 22.

1563.—"Colloquio XXXI. Concerning the wood vulgarly called **Cate**; and containing profitable matter on that subject."—*Garcia*, f. 125.

1578.—"The Indians use this **Cate** mixt with Areca, and with Betel, and by itself without other mixture."—*Acosta, Tract.* 150.

1585.—Sassetti mentions **catu** as derived from the *Khadira* tree, *i.e.* in modern Hindi the *Khair* (Skt. *khadira*).

[1616.—"010 bags **Catcha**."—*Foster, Letters*, iv. 127.]

1617.—"And there was rec. out of the *Adviz*, viz. . . 7 hhds. drugs **cacha**; 5 hampers pochok" (see **PUTCHOCK**).—*Cocks's Diary*, i. 294.

1759.—"*Hortal* [see **HURTAUL**] and **Cotch**, Earth-oil, and Wood-oil."—*List of Burma Products in Dalrymple, Oriental Repert.* i. 109.

c. 1760.—"To these three articles (betel, areca, and chunam) is often added for luxury what they call **cachoonda**, a Japan-earth, which from perfumes and other mixtures, chiefly manufactured at Goa, receives such improvement as to be sold to advantage when re-imported to Japan. . . . Another addition too they use of what they call **Catchoo**, being a blackish granulated perfumed composition. . . ."—*Grose*, i. 238.

1813.—". . . The peasants manufacture **catechu**, or *terra Japonica*, from the *Keiri* [*khair*] tree (*Mimosa catechu*) which grows wild on the hills of Kankana, but in no other part of the Indian Peninsula" [erroneous].—*Forbes, Or. Mem.* i. 303; [2nd ed. i. 193].

CATHAY, n.p. China; originally Northern China. The origin of the name is given in the quotation below from the Introduction to Marco Polo. In the 16th century, and even later, from a misunderstanding of the medieval travellers, Cathay was supposed to be a country north of China, and is so represented in many maps. Its identity with China was fully recognised by P. Martin Martini in his *Atlas Sinensis*; also by Valentijn, iv. *China*, 2.

1247.—"**Kitai** autem . . . homines sunt pagani, qui habent literam specialem . . . homines benigni et humani satis esse videantur. Barbam non habent, et in dispositione faciei satis concordant cum Mongalis, non tamen sunt in facie ita lati . . . meliores artifices non inveniuntur in toto mundo . . . terra eorum est opulenta valde."—*J. de Plano Carpini, Hist. Mongalorum*, 653-4.

1253.—"Ultra est magna **Cataya**, qui antiquitus, ut credo, dicebantur Seres. . . . Isti Catai sunt parvi homines, loquendo multum aspirantes per nares et . . . habent parvam aperturam oculorum," &c.—*Itin. Wilhelmi de Rubruk*, 291-2.

c. 1330.—"**Cathay** is a very great Empire, which extendeth over more than c. days' journey, and it hath only one lord. . . ."—*Friar Jordanus*, p. 54.

1404.—"E lo mas alxofar [see **ALJOFAR**] que en el mundo se ha, se pesia e falla en aq̃l mar del **Catay**."—*Clavijo*, f. 32.

1555.—"The Yndians called **Catheies** have eche man many wiues."—*Watreman, Fardle of Facioũns*, M. ii.

1598.—"In the lande lying westward from China, they say there are white people, and the land called **Cathaia**, where (as it is thought) are many Christians, and that it should confine and border upon *Persia*."—*Linschoten*, 57; [Hak. Soc. i. 126].

[1602.—". . . and arriued at any porte within the dominions of the kingdomes of **Cataya**, China, or Japan."—*Birdwood, First Letter Book*, 24. Here *China* and *Cataya* are spoken of as different countries. Comp. *Birdwood, Rep. on Old Rec.*, 168 note.]

Before 1633.—

"I'll wish you in the Indies or **Cataia**. . . ."
Beaum. & Fletch., The Woman's Prize, iv. 5.

1634.—

"Domadores das terras e dos mares
Não so im Malaca, Indo e Perseu streito
Mas na China, **Catai**, Japão estranho
Lei nova introduzindo em sacro banho."
Malaca Conquistada.

1664.—"'Tis not yet twenty years, that there went caravans every year from *Kachemire*, which crossed all those mountains of the great *Tibet*, entred into Tartary, and arrived in about three months at **Cataja**. . . ."—*Bernier*, E. T., 136; [ed. *Constable*, 425].

1842.—

"Better fifty years of Europe
than a cycle of **Cathay**."
Tennyson, Locksley Hall.

1871.—"For about three centuries the Northern Provinces of China had been detached from native rule, and subject to foreign dynasties; first to the *Khitan* . . . whose rule subsisted for 200 years, and originated the name of *Khitai*, Khata, or **Cathay**, by which for nearly 1000 years China has been known to the nations of Inner Asia, and to those whose acquaintance with it was got by that channel."—*Marco Polo, Introd.* ch. ii.

CAT'S-EYE, s. A stone of value found in Ceylon. It is described by Dana as a form of chalcedony of a greenish grey, with glowing internal reflections, whence the Portuguese call it *Olho de gato*, which our word translates. It appears from the quotation below from Dr. Royle that the *Beli oculus* of Pliny has been identified with the *cat's-eye*, which may well be the case, though the odd circumstance noticed by Royle may be only a curious coincidence. [The phrase *billī kī ānkh* does not appear in *Platt's Dict.* The usual name is *lahsaniyā*, 'like garlic.' The Burmese are said to call it *kyoung*, 'a cat.']

c. A.D. 70.—"The stone called *Belus eye* is white, and hath within it a black apple, the mids whereof a man shall see to glitter like gold. . . ."—*Holland's Plinie*, ii. 625.

c. 1340.—"Quaedam regiones monetam non habent, sed pro ea utuntur lapidibus quos dicimus **Cati Oculos**."—*Conti*, in *Poggius, De Var. Fortunae*, lib. iv.

1516.—"And there are found likewise other stones, such as **Olho de gato**, Chrysolites, and amethysts, of which I do not treat because they are of little value."—*Barbosa*, in *Lisbon Acad.*, ii. 390.

1599.—"Lapis insuper alius ibi vulgaris est, quem Lusitani **olhos de gatto**, id est, *oculum felinum* vocant, propterea quod cum eo et colore et facie conveniat. Nihil autem aliud quam *achates* est."—*De Bry*, iv. 84 (after *Linschoten*); [Hak. Soc. i. 61, ii. 141].

1672.—"The **Cat's-eyes**, by the Portuguese called *Olhos de Gatos*, occur in *Zeylon*, *Cambaya*, and *Pegu*; they are more esteemed by the Indians than by the Portuguese; for some Indians believe that if a man wears this stone his power and riches will never diminish, but always increase."—*Baldaeus*, Germ. ed. 160.

1837.—"Beli oculus, mentioned by Pliny, xxxvii. c. 55, is considered by Hardouin to be equivalent to œil de chat—named in India *billi ke ankh.*"—*Royle's Hindu Medicine*, p. 103.

CATTY, s.

a. A weight used in China, and by the Chinese introduced into the Archipelago. The Chinese name is *kin* or *chin.* The word *kātī* or *katī* is Malayo-Javanese. It is equal to 16 taels, *i.e.* 1⅓ lb. avoird. or 625 grammes. This is the weight fixed by treaty; but in Chinese trade it varies from 4 oz. to 28 oz.; the lowest value being used by tea-vendors at Peking, the highest by coal-merchants in Honan.

[1554.—"**Cate.**" See quotation under **PECUL.**]

1598.—"Everie **Catte** is as much as 20 Portingall ounces."—*Linschoten*, 34; [Hak. Soc. i. 113].

1604.—"Their pound they call a **Cate** which is one and twentie of our ounces."—*Capt. John Davis*, in *Purchas*, i. 123.

1609.—"Offering to enact among them the penaltie of death to such as would sel one **cattie** of spice to the Hollanders."—*Keeling*, *ibid.* i. 199.

1610.—"And (I prayse God) I have aboord one hundred thirtie nine Tunnes, six **Cathayes**, one quarterne two pound of nutmegs and sixe hundred two and twenty suckettes of Mace, which maketh thirtie sixe Tunnes, fifteene **Cathayes** one quarterne, one and twentie pound."—*David Midleton*, *ibid.* i. 247. In this passage, however, *Cathayes* seems to be a strange blunder of Purchas or his copyist for *Cwt. Suckette* is probably Malay *sukat*, "a measure, a stated quantity." [The word appears as *suckell* in a letter of 1615 (*Foster*, iii. 175). Mr. Skeat suggests that it is a misreading for **Pecul.** *Sukat*, he says, means 'to measure anything' (indefinitely), but is never used for a definite measure.]

b. The word **catty** occurs in another sense in the following passage. A note says that "*Catty* or more literally *Kuttoo* is a Tamil word signifying **batta**" (q.v.). But may it not rather be a clerical error for *batty*?

1659.—"If we should detain them longer we are to give them **catty.**"—Letter in *Wheeler*, i. 162.

CATUR, s. A light rowing vessel used on the coast of Malabar in the early days of the Portuguese. We have not been able to trace the name to any Indian source, [unless possibly Skt. *chatura*, 'swift']. Is it not probably the origin of our '*cutter*'? We see that Sir R. Burton in his Commentary on Camoens (vol. iv. 391) says: "*Catur* is the Arab. *katīreh*, a small craft, our 'cutter.'" [This view is rejected by the *N.E.D.*, which regards it as an English word from 'to cut.'] We cannot say when *cutter* was introduced in marine use. We cannot find it in Dampier, nor in *Robinson Crusoe*; the first instance we have found is that quoted below from *Anson's Voyage.* [The *N.E.D.* has nothing earlier than 1745.]

Bluteau gives *catur* as an Indian term indicating a small war vessel, which in a calm can be aided by oars. Jal (*Archéologie Navale*, ii. 259) quotes Witsen as saying that the *Caturi* or **Almadias** were Calicut vessels, having a length of 12 to 13 paces (60 to 65 feet), sharp at both ends, and curving back, using both sails and oars. But there was a larger kind, 80 feet long, with only 7 or 8 feet beam.

1510.—"There is also another kind of vessel. . . . These are all made of one piece . . . sharp at both ends. These ships are called **Chaturi**, and go either with a sail or oars more swiftly than any galley, *fusta*, or brigantine."—*Varthema*, 154.

1544.—". . . navigium majus quod vocant **caturem.**"—*Scti. Franc. Xav. Epistolae*, 121.

1549.—"Naves item duas (quas Indi **catures** vocant) summâ celeritate armari jussit, vt oram maritimam legentes, hostes commeatu prohiberent."—*Goës, de Bello Cambaico*, 1331.

1552.—"And this winter the Governor sent to have built in Cochin thirty **Catures**, which are vessels with oars, but smaller than brigantines."—*Castanheda*, iii. 271.

1588.—"Cambaicam oram Jacobus Lacteus duobos **caturibus** tueri jussus. . . ."—*Maffei*, lib. xiii. ed. 1752, p. 283.

1601.—"Biremes, seu **Cathuris** quam plurimae conduntur in Lassaon, Javae civitate. . . ."—*De Bry*, iii. 109 (where there is a plate, iii. No. xxxvii.).

1688.—"No man was so bold to contradict the man of God; and they all went to the Arsenal. There they found a good and sufficient bark of those they call **Catur**, besides seven old foysts."—*Dryden, Life of Xavier*, in *Works*, 1821, xvi. 200.

1742.—". . . to prevent even the possibility of the galeons escaping us in the night, the two **Cutters** belonging to the *Centurion* and the *Gloucester* were both manned and sent in shore. . . ."—*Anson's Voyage*, 9th ed. 1756, p. 251. **Cutter** also occurs pp. 111, 129, 150, and other places.

CAUVERY, n.p. The great river of S. India. Properly Tam. *Kāviri*, or rather *Kāveri*, and Sanscritized *Kāvērī*. The earliest mention is that of Ptolemy, who writes the name (after the Skt. form) Χάβηρος (sc. ποταμός). The Καμάρα of the Periplus (c. A.D. 80-90) probably, however, represents the same name, the Χαβηρὶς ἐμποριόν of Ptolemy. The meaning of the name has been much debated, and several plausible but unsatisfactory explanations have been given. Thus the Skt. form *Kāvērī* has been explained from that language by *kāvēra* 'saffron.' A river in the Tamil country is, however, hardly likely to have a non-mythological Skt. name. The Cauvery in flood, like other S. Indian rivers, assumes a reddish hue. And the form *Kāvēri* has been explained by Bp. Caldwell as possibly from the Dravidian *kāvi*, 'red ochre' or *kā* (*kā-va*), 'a grove,' and *ēr-u*, Tel. 'a river,' *ēr-i*, Tam. 'a sheet of water'; thus either 'red river' or 'grove river.' [The *Madras Admin. Gloss.* takes it from *kā*, Tam. 'grove,' and *ēri*, Tam. 'tank,' from its original source in a garden tank.] *Kā-viri*, however, the form found in inscriptions, affords a more satisfactory Tamil interpretation, viz. *Kā - viri*, 'grove-extender,' or developer. Any one who has travelled along the river will have noticed the thick groves all along the banks, which form a remarkable feature of the stream.

c. 150 A.D.—

"Χαβήρου ποταμοῦ ἐκβολάι
Χαβηρὶς ἐμποριόν."—*Ptolemy*, lib. vii. 1.

The last was probably represented by *Kaveripatan*.

c. 545.—"Then there is Sieledēba, *i.e.* Taprobane . . . and then again on the Continent, and further back, is Marallo, which exports conch-shells; **Kaber**, which exports alabandinum."—*Cosmas, Topog. Christ.* in *Cathay*, &c. clxxviii.

1310-11.—"After traversing the passes, they arrived at night on the banks of the river **Kānobari**, and bivouacked on the sands."—*Amīr Khusrū*, in *Elliot*, ii. 90.

The *Cauvery* appears to be ignored in the older European account and maps.

CAVALLY, s. This is mentioned as a fish of Ceylon by *Ives*, 1775 (p. 57). It is no doubt the same that is described in the quotation from Pyrard [see *Gray's* note, Hak. Soc. i. 388]. It may represent the genus *Equula*, of which 12 spp. are described by Day (*Fishes of India*, pp. 237-242), two being named by different zoologists E. *caballa*. But Dr. Day hesitates to identify the fish now in question. The fish mentioned in the fourth and fifth quotations may be the same species; but that in the fifth seems doubtful. Many of the spp. are extensively sun-dried, and eaten by the poor.

c. 1610.—"Ces Moucois pescheurs prennent entr'autres grande quantité d'vne sorte de petit poisson, qui n'est pas plus grande que la main et large comme vn petit bremeau. Les Portugais l'appellent Pesche **cauallo.** Il est le plus commun de toute ceste coste, et c'est de quoy ils font le plus grand trafic; car ils le fendent par la moitié, ils le salent, et le font secher au soleil."—*Pyrard de Laval*, i. 278; see also 309; [Hak. Soc. i. 427; ii. 127, 294, 299].

1626.—"The Ile inricht us with many good things; Buffols, . . . oysters, Breams, **Cavalloes**, and store of other fish."—*Sir T. Herbert*, 28.

1652.—"There is another very small fish vulgarly called **Cavalle**, which is good enough to eat, but not very wholesome."—*Philippus a Sanct. Trinitate*, in Fr. Tr. 383.

1796.—"The *ayla*, called in Portuguese **cavala**, has a good taste when fresh, but when salted becomes like the herring."—*Fra Paolini*, E. T., p. 240.

1875.—"*Çaranx denter* (Bl. Schn.). This fish of wide range from the Mediterranean to the coast of Brazil, at St. Helena is known as the **Cavalley**, and is one of the best table fish, being indeed the salmon of St. Helena. It is taken in considerable numbers, chiefly during the summer months, around the coast, in not very deep water: it varies in length from nine inches up to two or three feet."—*St. Helena*, by *J. C. Melliss*, p. 106.

CAWNEY, CAWNY, s. Tam. *kāni*, 'property,' hence 'land,' [from Tam. *kan*, 'to see,' what is known and recognised,] and so a measure of land used in the Madras Presidency. It varies, of course, but the standard *Cawny* is considered to be = 24 *manai* or **Grounds** (q.v.), of 2,400 sq. f. each, hence 57,600 sq. f. or ac. 1·322. This is the only sense in which the word is used in the Madras dialect of the Anglo-Indian tongue. The 'Indian Vocabulary' of 1788 has the word in the form **Connys**, but with an unintelligible explanation.

1807.—"The land measure of the *Jaghire* is as follows: 24 Adies square=1 Culy; 100 Culies=1 **Canay**. Out of what is called charity however the Culy is in fact a Bamboo 26 Adies or 22 feet 8 inches in length . . . the *Ady* or Malabar foot is therefore $10\frac{46}{100}$ inches nearly; and the customary **canay** contains 51,375 sq. feet, or $1\frac{18}{100}$ acres nearly; while the proper **canay** would only contain 43,778 feet."—*F. Buchanan, Mysore, &c.* i. 6.

CAWNPORE, n.p. The correct name is *Kānhpur*, 'the town of Kānh, Kanhaiya or Krishna.' The city of the Doab so called, having in 1891 a population of 188,712, has grown up entirely under British rule, at first as the bazar and dependence of the cantonment established here under a treaty made with the Nabob of Oudh in 1766, and afterwards as a great mart of trade.

CAYMAN, s. This is not used in India. It is an American name for an alligator; from the Carib *acayuman* (*Littré*). But it appears formerly to have been in general use among the Dutch in the East. [It is one of those words "which the Portuguese or Spaniards very early caught up in one part of the world, and naturalised in another." (*N.E.D.*)].

1530.—"The country is extravagantly hot; and the rivers are full of **Caimans**, which are certain water-lizards (*lagarti*)." —*Nunno de Guzman*, in *Ramusio*, iii. 339.

1598.—"In this river (Zaire or Congo) there are living divers kinds of creatures, and in particular, mighty great crocodiles, which the country people there call **Caiman**."—*Pigafetta*, in Harleian Coll. of Voyages, ii. 533.

This is an instance of the way in which we so often see a word belonging to a different quarter of the world undoubtingly ascribed to Africa or Asia, as the case may be. In the next quotation we find it ascribed to India.

1631.—"Lib. v. cap. iii. De Crocodilo qui per totam Indiam **cayman** audit."—*Bontius, Hist. Nat. et Med.*

1672.—"The figures so represented in Adam's footsteps were . . . 41. The King of the **Caimans** or Crocodiles."—*Baldaeus* (*Germ. ed.*), 148.

1692.—"Anno 1692 there were 3 newly arrived soldiers . . . near a certain gibbet that stood by the river outside the boom, so sharply pursued by a **Kaieman** that they were obliged to climb the gibbet for safety whilst the creature standing up on his hind feet reached with his snout to the very top of the gibbet."—*Valentijn*, iv. 231.

CAYOLAQUE, s. *Kayu*='wood,' in Malay. *Laka* is given in Crawfurd's Malay Dict. as "name of a red wood used as incense, *Myristica iners*." In his *Descr. Dict.* he calls it the "*Tanarius major*; a tree with a red-coloured wood, a native of Sumatra, used in dyeing and in pharmacy. It is an article of considerable native trade, and is chiefly exported to China" (p. 204). [The word, according to Mr. Skeat, is probably *kayu*, 'wood,' *lakh*, 'red dye' (see **LAC**), but the combined form is not in Klinkert, nor are these trees in Ridley's plant list. He gives *Laka-laka* or *Malaka* as the name of the *phyllanthus emblica*.]

1510.—"There also grows here a very great quantity of **lacca** for making red colour, and the tree of this is formed like our trees which produce walnuts."—*Varthema*, p. 238.

c. 1560.—"I being in Cantan there was a rich (bed) made wrought with Iuorie, and of a sweet wood which they call **Cayolaque**, and of *Sandalum*, that was prized at 1500 Crownes."—*Gaspar Da Cruz*, in *Purchas*, iii. 177.

1585.—"Euerie morning and euening they do offer vnto their idolles frankensence, benjamin, wood of aguila, and **cayolaque**, the which is maruelous sweete. . . ."—*Mendoza's China*, i. 58.

CAZEE, KAJEE, &c., s. Arab. *ḳāḍī*, 'a judge,' the letter *zwād* with which it is spelt being always pronounced in India like a *z*. The form *Cadi*, familiar from its use in the old version of the Arabian Nights, comes to us from the Levant. The word with the article, *al-ḳāḍī*, becomes in Spanish *alcalde*;* not *alcaide*, which is from *ḳā'id*, 'a chief'; nor *alguacil*, which is from *wazīr*. So Dozy and Engelmann, no doubt correctly. But in Pinto, cap. 8, we find "ao *guazil* da justiça q̃ em elles he como corregedor entre nos"; where *guazil* seems to stand for *ḳāẓī*.

It is not easy to give an accurate account of the position of the *Ḳāẓī* in British India, which has gone through variations of which a distinct record cannot be found. But the following outline is believed to be substantially correct.

* Dr. R. Rost observes to us that the Arabic letter *zwād* is pronounced by the Malays like *ll* (see also *Crawfurd's Malay Grammar*, p. 7). And it is curious to find a transfer of the same letter into Spanish as *ld*. In Malay *ḳāḍī* becomes *kālī*.

Under **Adawlut** I have given a brief sketch of the history of the judiciary under the Company in the Bengal Presidency. Down to 1790 the greater part of the administration of criminal justice was still in the hands of native judges, and other native officials of various kinds, though under European supervision in varying forms. But the native judiciary, except in positions of a quite subordinate character, then ceased. It was, however, still in substance Mahommedan law that was administered in criminal cases, and also in civil cases between Mahommedans as affecting succession, &c. And a *Kāzī* and a *Muftī* were retained in the Provincial Courts of Appeal and Circuit as the exponents of Mahommedan law, and the deliverers of a formal **Futwa.** There was also a *Kāzī-al-Ḳozāt*, or chief *Kāzī* of Bengal, Behar and Orissa, attached to the Sudder Courts of Dewanny and Nizamut, assisted by two *Muftīs*, and these also gave written *futwas* on references from the District Courts.

The style of *Kāzī* and *Muftī* presumably continued in formal existence in connection with the Sudder Courts till the abolition of these in 1862; but with the earlier abolition of the Provincial Courts in 1829-31 it had quite ceased, in this sense, to be familiar. In the District Courts the corresponding exponents were in English officially designated **Law-officers**, and, I believe, in official vernacular, as well as commonly among Anglo-Indians, **Moolvees** (q.v.).

Under the article **LAW-OFFICER**, it will be seen that certain trivial cases were, at the discretion of the magistrate, referred for disposal by the Law-officer of the district. And the latter, from this fact, as well as, perhaps, from the tradition of the elders, was in some parts of Bengal popularly known as 'the *Kāzī*.' "In the Magistrate's office," writes my friend Mr. Seton-Karr, "it was quite common to speak of this case as referred to the joint magistrate, and that to the *Chhoṭā Sāhib* (the Assistant), and that again to the *Kāzī*."

But the duties of the *Kāzī* popularly so styled and officially recognised, had, almost from the beginning of the century, become limited to certain notarial functions, to the performance and registration of Mahommedan marriages, and some other matters connected with the social life of their co-religionists. To these functions must also be added as regards the 18th century and the earlier years of the 19th, duties in connection with distraint for rent on behalf of Zemindars. There were such *Kāzīs* nominated by Government in towns and pergunnas, with great variation in the area of the localities over which they officiated. The Act XI. of 1864, which repealed the laws relating to law-officers, put an end also to the appointment by Government of *Kāzīs*. But this seems to have led to inconveniences which were complained of by Mahommedans in some parts of India, and it was enacted in 1880 (Act XII., styled "The *Kāzīs* Act") that with reference to any particular locality, and after consultation with the chief Musulman residents therein, the Local Government might select and nominate a *Kāzī* or *Kāzīs* for that local area (see **FUTWA, LAW-OFFICER, MUFTY**).

1338.—"They treated me civilly and set me in front of their mosque during their Easter; at which mosque, on account of its being their Easter, there were assembled from divers quarters a number of their **Cadini**, *i.e.* of their bishops."—Letter of *Friar Pascal*, in *Cathay, &c.*, 235.

c. 1461.—

"Au tems que Alexandre regna
Ung hom, nommé Diomedès
Devant luy, on luy amena
Engrilloné poulces et detz
Comme ung larron; car il fut des
Escumeurs que voyons courir
Si fut mys devant le **cadès**,
Pour estre jugé à mourir."

Gd. Testament de Fr. Villon.

[c. 1610.—"The Pandiare is called **Cady** in the Arabic tongue."—*Pyrard de Laval*, Hak. Soc. i. 199.]

1648.—"The Government of the city (Ahmedabad) and surrounding villages rests with the Governor *Coutewael*, and the Judge (whom they call **Casgy**)."—*Van Twist*, 15.

[1670.—"The Shawbunder, **Cozzy**."—*Hedges, Diary*, Hak. Soc. ii. ccxxix.]

1673.—"Their Law-Disputes, they are soon ended; the Governor hearing; and the **Cadi** or Judge determining every Morning."—*Fryer*, 32.

" "The **Cazy** or Judge . . . marries them."—*Ibid.* 94.

1683.—". . . more than that 3000 poor men gathered together, complaining with full mouths of his exaction and injustice towards them: some demanding Rupees 10, others Rupees 20 per man, which Bulchund very generously paid them in the **Cazee's** presence. . . ."—*Hedges*, Nov. 5; [Hak. Soc. i. 134; **Cazze** in i. 85].

1684.—"*January* 12.—From Cassumbazar 'tis advised ye Merchants and Picars appeal again to ye **Cazee** for Justice against Mr. Charnock. Ye **Cazee** cites Mr. Charnock to appear. . . ."—*Ibid.* i. 147.

1689.—"A **Cogee** . . . who is a Person skilled in their Law."—*Ovington*, 206.

Here there is perhaps a confusion with **Coja.**

1727.—"When the Man sees his Spouse, and likes her, they agree on the Price and Term of Weeks, Months, or Years, and then appear before the **Cadjee** or Judge."—*A. Hamilton*, i. 52.

1763.—"The **Cadi** holds court in which are tried all disputes of property."—*Orme*, i. 26 (ed. 1803).

1773.—"That they should be mean, weak, ignorant, and corrupt, is not surprising, when the salary of the principal judge, the **Cazi**, does not exceed Rs. 100 per month."—*From* Impey's *Judgment in the Patna Cause*, quoted by *Stephen*, ii. 176.

1790.—"*Regulations for the Court of Circuit.*

"24. That each of the Courts of Circuit be superintended by two covenanted civil servants of the Company, to be denominated Judges of the Courts of Circuit . . . assisted by a **Kazi** and a Mufti."—*Regns. for the Adm. of Justice in the Foujdarry or Criminal Courts in Bengal, Bahar, and Orissa.* Passed by the G.-G. in C., Dec. 3, 1790.

"32. . . . The charge against the prisoner, his confession, which is always to be received with circumspection and tenderness . . . &c. . . . being all heard and gone through in his presence and that of the **Kazi** and Mufti of the Court, the **Kazi** and Mufti are then to write at the bottom of the record of the proceedings held in the trial, the *futwa* or law as applicable to the circumstances of the case. . . . The Judges of the Court shall attentively consider such *futwa*, &c."—*Ibid.*

1791.—"The Judges of the Courts of Circuit shall refer to the **Kazi** and Mufti of their respective Courts all questions on points of law . . . regarding which they may not have been furnished with specific instructions from the G.-G. in C. or the *Nizamut Adawlut*. . . ."—*Regn. No. XXXV.*

1792.—Revenue Regulation of July 20, No. lxxv., empowers Landholders and Farmers of Land to distrain for Arrears of Rent or Revenue. The "**Kazi** of the Pegunnah" is the official under the Collector, repeatedly referred to as regulating and carrying out the distraint. So, again, in *Regn.* XVII. of 1793.

1793.—"lxvi. The Nizamut Adaulat shall continue to be held at Calcutta.

"lxvii. The Court shall consist of the Governor-General, and the members of the Supreme Council, assisted by the head **Cauzy** of Bengal, Behar, and Orissa, and two Muftis." (This was already in the Regulations of 1791.)—*Regn. IX. of* 1793. See also quotation under **MUFTY.**

1793.—"I. **Cauzies** are stationed at the Cities of Patna, Dacca, and Moorshedabad, and the principal towns, and in the pergunnahs, for the purpose of preparing and attesting deeds of transfer, and other law papers, celebrating marriages, and performing such religious duties or ceremonies prescribed by the Mahommedan law, as have been hitherto discharged by them under the British Government."—*Reg. XXXIX. of* 1793.

1803.—Regulation XLVI. regulates the appointment of **Cauzy** in towns and pergunnahs, "for the purpose of preparing and attesting deeds of transfer, and other law papers, celebrating marriages," &c., but makes no allusion to judicial duties.

1824.—"Have you not learned this common saying—'Every one's teeth are blunted by acids except the **cadi's**, which are by sweets.'"—*Hajji Baba*, ed. 1835, p. 316.

1864.—"Whereas it is unnecessary to continue the offices of Hindoo and Mahomedan **Law-Officers**, and is inexpedient that the appointment of **Cazee**-*ool-Cozaat*, or of City, Town, or Pergunnah **Cazees** should be made by Government, it is enacted as follows:—

* * *

"II. Nothing contained in this Act shall be construed so as to prevent a **Cazee**-*ool-Cozaat* or other **Cazee** from performing, when required to do so, any duties or ceremonies prescribed by the Mahomedan Law."—*Act No. XI. of* 1864.

1880.—". . . whereas by the usage of the Muhammadan community in some parts of India the presence of **Kázís** appointed by the Government is required at the celebration of marriages. . . ."—*Bill introduced into the Council of Gov.-Gen.*, January 30, 1880.

" "An Act for the appointment of persons to the office of **Kází.**

"Whereas by the preamble to Act No. XI. of 1864 . . . it was (among other things declared inexpedient, &c.) . . . and whereas by the usage of the Muhammadan community in some parts of India the presence of **Kázís** appointed by the Government is required at the celebration of marriages and the performance of certain other rites and ceremonies, and it is therefore expedient that the Government should again be empowered to appoint such persons to the office of **Kází**; It is hereby enacted . . ."—*Act No. XII. of* 1880.

1885.—"To come to something more specific. 'There were instances in which men of the most venerable dignity, persecuted without a cause by extortioners, died of rage and shame in the gripe of the vile alguazils of Impey' [Macaulay's *Essay on Hastings*].

"Here we see one **Cazi** turned into an indefinite number of 'men of the most venerable dignity'; a man found guilty by legal process of corruptly oppressing a helpless widow into 'men of the most venerable dignity' persecuted by extortioners without a cause; and a guard of sepoys, with which the Supreme Court had nothing to do, into 'vile alguazils of Impey.'"—*Stephen, Story of Nuncomar*, ii. 250-251.

Cazee also is a title used in Nepal for Ministers of State.

1848.—"**Kajees**, Counsellors, and mitred Lamas were there, to the number of twenty, all planted with their backs to the wall, mute and motionless as statues."—*Hooker's Himalayan Journals*, ed. 1855, i. 286.

1868.—"The Durbar (of Nepal) have written to the four **Kajees** of Thibet enquiring the reason."—Letter from *Col. R. Lawrence*, dated 1st April, regarding persecution of R. C. Missions in Tibet.

1873.—

"Ho, lamas, get ye ready,
Ho, **Kazis**, clear the way;
The chief will ride in all his pride
To the Rungeet Stream to-day."

Wilfrid Heeley, A Lay of Modern Darjeeling.

CEDED DISTRICTS, n.p. A name applied familiarly at the beginning of the last century to the territory south of the Tungabhadra river, which was ceded to the Company by the Nizam in 1800, after the defeat and death of Tippoo Sultan. This territory embraced the present districts of Bellary, Cuddapah, and Karnúl, with the Palnãd, which is now a subdivision of the Kistna District. The name perhaps became best known in England from *Gleig's Life of Sir Thomas Munro*, that great man having administered these provinces for 7 years.

1873.—"We regret to announce the death of Lieut.-General Sir Hector Jones, G.C.B., at the advanced age of 86. The gallant officer now deceased belonged to the Madras Establishment of the E. I. Co.'s forces, and bore a distinguished part in many of the great achievements of that army, including the celebrated march into the **Ceded Districts** under the Collector of Canara, and the campaign against the Zemindar of Madura."—*The True Reformer*, p. 7 ("wrot serkestick").

CELÉBES, n.p. According to Crawfurd this name is unknown to the natives, not only of the great island itself, but of the Archipelago generally, and must have arisen from some Portuguese misunderstanding or corruption. There appears to be no general name for the island in the Malay language, unless *Tanah Bugis*, 'the Land of the Bugis people' [see **BUGIS**]. It seems sometimes to have been called the Isle of Macassar. In form *Celebes* is apparently a Portuguese plural, and several of their early writers speak of *Celebes* as a *group* of islands. Crawfurd makes a suggestion, but not very confidently, that *Pulo sālabih*, 'the islands over and above,' might have been vaguely spoken of by the Malays, and understood by the Portuguese as a name. [Mr. Skeat doubts the correctness of this explanation: "The standard Malay form would be *Pulau Sălĕbih*, which in some dialects might be *Să-lĕbis*, and this may have been a variant of *Si-Lĕbih*, a man's name, the *si* corresponding to the def. art. in the Germ. phrase '*der* Hans.' Numerous Malay place-names are derived from those of people."]

1516.—"Having passed these islands of Maluco . . . at a distance of 130 leagues, there are other islands to the west, from which sometimes there come white people, naked from the waist upwards. . . . These people eat human flesh, and if the King of Maluco has any person to execute, they beg for him to eat him, just as one would ask for a pig, and the islands from which they come are called **Celebe**."—*Barbosa*, 202-3.

c. 1544.—"In this street (of Pegu) there were six and thirty thousand strangers of two and forty different Nations, namely. . . *Papuaas*, **Selebres**, *Mindanaos* . . . and many others whose names I know not."—*F. M. Pinto*, in *Cogan's* tr., p. 200.

1552.—"In the previous November (1529) arrived at Ternate D. Jorge de Castro who came from Malaca by way of Borneo in a junk . . . and going astray passed along the *Isle of Macaçar*. . ."—*Barros*, Dec. IV. i. 18.

" "The first thing that the Samarao did in this was to make Tristão de Taide believe that in the **Isles of the Celebes**, and of the *Macaçares* and in that of Mindinão there was much gold."—*Ibid.* vi. 25.

1579.—"The 16 Day (December) wee had sight of the Iland **Celebes** or **Silebis**."—*Drake, World Encompassed* (Hak. Soc.), p. 150.

1610.—"At the same time there were at Ternate certain ambassadors from the *Isles of the Macaçás* (which are to the west of those of Maluco—the nearest of them about 60 leagues). . . These islands are many, and joined together, and appear in the sea-charts thrown into one very big island, extending, as the sailors say, North and South, and having near 100 leagues of compass. And this island imitates the shape of a big locust, the head of which (stretching to the south to 5½ degrees) is formed by the **Cellebes** (*são os Çellebes*), which have a King over them. . . . These islands are ruled by many Kings, differing in language, in laws, and customs. . . ."—*Couto*, Dec. V. vii. 2.

CENTIPEDE, s. This word was perhaps borrowed directly from the Portuguese in India (*centopèa*). [The *N.E.D.* refers it to Sp.]

1662.—"There is a kind of worm which the Portuguese call *un* **centopè**, and the Dutch also 'thousand-legs' (*tausend-bein*)."—*T. Saal*, 68.

CERAM, n.p. A large island in the Molucca Sea, the *Serung* of the Malays. [Klinkert gives the name *Seran*, which Mr. Skeat thinks more likely to be correct.]

CERAME, CARAME, &c., s. The Malayālim *śrāmbi*, a gatehouse with a room over the gate, and generally fortified. This is a feature of temples, &c., as well as of private houses, in Malabar [see *Logan*, i. 82]. The word is also applied to a chamber raised on four posts. [The word, as Mr. Skeat notes, has come into Malay as *sarambi* or *serambi*, 'a house veranda.']

[1500.—"He was taken to a **cerame**, which is a one-storied house of wood, which the King had erected for their meeting-place."—*Castañeda*, Bk. I. cap. 33, p. 103.]

1551.—". . . where stood the **çarame** of the King, which is his temple. . . ."—*Ibid.* iii. 2.

1552. — "Pedralvares . . . was carried ashore on men's shoulders in an **andor** till he was set among the Gentoo Princes whom the Çamorin had sent to receive him at the beach, whilst the said Çamorin himself was standing within sight in the **cerame** awaiting his arrival."—*Barros*, I. v. 5.

1557.—The word occurs also in D'Alboquerque's Commentaries (*Hak. Soc.* tr. i. 115), but it is there erroneously rendered "jetty."

1566. — "Antes de entrar no **Cerame** vierão receber alguns senhores dos que ficarão com el Rei."—*Dam. de Goes, Chron.* 76 (ch. lviii.).

CEYLON, n.p. This name, as applied to the great island which hangs from India like a dependent jewel, becomes usual about the 13th century. But it can be traced much earlier. For it appears undoubtedly to be formed from *Sinhala* or *Sīhala*, 'lions' abode,' the name adopted in the island itself at an early date. This, with the addition of 'Island,' *Sīhala-dvīpa*, comes down to us in Cosmas as Σιελεδίβα. There was a Pali form *Sīhalan*, which, at an early date, must have been colloquially shortened to *Silan*, as appears from the old Tamil name *Ilam* (the Tamil having no proper sibilant), and probably from this was formed the *Sarandīp* and *Sarandīb* which was long the name in use by mariners of the Persian Gulf.

It has been suggested by Mr. Van der Tuuk, that the name *Sailan* or *Silan* was really of Javanese origin, as *sela* (from Skt. *śilā*, 'a rock, a stone') in Javanese (and in Malay) means 'a precious stone,' hence *Pulo Selan* would be 'Isle of Gems.' ["This," writes Mr. Skeat, "is possible, but it remains to be proved that the gem was not named after the island (*i.e.* 'Ceylon stone'). The full phrase in standard Malay is *batu Sēlan*, where *batu* means 'stone.' Klinkert merely marks *Sailan* (Ceylon) as Persian."] The island was really called anciently *Ratnadvīpa*, 'Isle of Gems,' and is termed by an Arab historian of the 9th century *Jazīrat-al yākūt*, 'Isle of Rubies.' So that there is considerable plausibility in Van der Tuuk's suggestion. But the genealogy of the name from *Sīhala* is so legitimate that the utmost that can be conceded is the possibility that the Malay form *Selan* may have been shaped by the consideration suggested, and may have influenced the general adoption of the form *Sailān*, through the predominance of Malay navigation in the Middle Ages.

c. 362.—"Unde nationibus Indicis certatim cum donis optimates mittentibus ante tempus, ab usque Divis et **Serendivis**."—*Ammianus Marcellinus*, XXI. vii.

c. 430.—"The island of Lanka was called **Sihala** after the Lion; listen ye to the narration of the island which I (am going to) tell: 'The daughter of the Vanga King cohabited in the forest with a lion.'"—*Dīpavanso*, IX. i. 2.

c. 545.—"This is the great island in the ocean, lying in the Indian Sea. By the Indians it is called **Sielediba**, but by the Greeks Taprobane."—*Cosmas*, Bk. xi.

851.—"Near **Sarandīb** is the pearl-fishery. *Sarandīb* is entirely surrounded by the sea."—*Relation des Voyages*, i. p. 5.

c. 940.—"Mas'ūdi proceeds: In the Island **Sarandīb**, I myself witnessed that when the King was dead, he was placed on a chariot with low wheels so that his hair dragged upon the ground."—In *Gildemeister*, 154.

c. 1020.—"There you enter the country of Lárán, where is Jaimúr, then Malia, then Kánji, then Darúd, where there is a great gulf in which is **Sinkaldíp** (*Sinhala dvīpa*), or the island of **Sarandíp**."—*Al Birūnī*, as given by *Rashiduddin*, in *Elliot*, i. 66.

1275.—"The island **Sailan** is a vast island between China and India, 80 parasangs in circuit. . . . It produces wonderful things, sandal-wood, spikenard, cinnamon, cloves, brazil, and various spices. . . ."—*Kazvīnī*, in *Gildemeister*, 203.

1298.—"You come to the island of **Seilan**, which is in good sooth the best island of its size in the world."—*Marco Polo*, Bk. iii. ch. 14.

c. 1300.—"There are two courses . . . from this place (Ma'bar); one leads by sea to Chín and Máchín, passing by the island of **Sílán**."—*Rashiduddin*, in *Elliot*, i. 70.

1330.—"There is another island called **Sillan**. . . . In this . . . there is an exceeding great mountain, of which the folk relate that it was upon it that Adam mourned for his son one hundred years."—*Fr. Odoric*, in *Cathay*, i. 98.

c. 1337.—"I met in this city (Brussa) the pious sheikh 'Abd-Allah-al-Misrī, the Traveller. He was a worthy man. He made the circuit of the earth, except he never entered China, nor the island of **Sarandīb**, nor Andalusia, nor the Sūdān. I have excelled him, for I have visited those regions."—*Ibn Batuta*, ii. 321.

c. 1350.—". . . I proceeded to sea by **Seyllan**, a glorious mountain opposite to Paradise. . . . 'Tis said the sound of the waters falling from the fountain of Paradise is heard there."—*Marignolli*, in *Cathay*, ii. 346.

c. 1420.—"In the middle of the Gulf there is a very noble island called **Zeilam**, which is 3000 miles in circumference, and on which they find by digging, rubies, saffires, garnets, and those stones which are called cats'-eyes."—*N. Conti*, in *India in the XVth Century*, 7.

1498.—". . . much ginger, and pepper, and cinnamon, but this is not so fine as that which comes from an island which is called **Cillam**, and which is 8 days distant from Calicut."—*Roteiro de V. da Gama*, 88.

1514.—"Passando avanti intra la terra e il mare si truova l'isola di **Zolan** dove nasce la cannella. . . ."—*Giov. da Empoli*, in *Archiv. Stor. Ital.*, Append. 79.

1516.—"Leaving these islands of Mahal-diva . . . there is a very large and beautiful island which the Moors, Arabs, and Persians call **Ceylam**, and the Indians call it Ylinarim."—*Barbosa*, 166.

1586.—"This **Ceylon** is a brave Iland, very fruitful and fair."—*Hakl.* ii. 397.

[1605.—"Heare you shall buie theis Comodities followinge of the Inhabitants of **Selland**."—*Birdwood, First Letter Book*, 84.

[1615.—"40 tons of cinnamon of **Celand**."—*Foster, Letters*, iii. 277.

[„ "Here is arrived a ship out of Holland . . . at present turning under **Silon**."—*Ibid.* iv. 34.]

1682.—". . . having run 35 miles North without seeing **Zeilon**."—*Hedges, Diary*, July 7; [Hak. Soc. i. 28].

1727.—A. Hamilton writes **Zeloan** (i. 340, &c.), and as late as 1780, in *Dunn's Naval Directory*, we find **Zeloan** throughout.

1781.—"We explored the whole coast of **Zelone**, from Pt. Pedro to the Little Basses, looked into every port and spoke to every vessel we saw, without hearing of French vessels."—*Price's Letter to Ph. Francis*, in *Tracts*, i. 9.

1830.—

"For dearer to him are the shells that sleep
By his own sweet native stream,
Than all the pearls of **Serendeep**,
Or the Ava ruby's gleam!
Home! Home! Friends—health—repose,
What are Golconda's gems to those?"
Bengal Annual.

CHABEE, s. H. *chābī*, *chābhī*, 'a key,' from Port. *chave*. In Bengali it becomes *sābī*, and in Tam. *sāvī*. In Sea-H. 'a fid.'

CHABOOTRA, s. H. *chabūtrā* and *chābūtara*, a paved or plastered platform, often attached to a house, or in a garden.

c. 1810.—"It was a burning evening in June, when, after sunset, I accompanied Mr. Sherwood to Mr. Martin's bungalow. . . . We were conducted to the **Cherbuter** . . . this **Cherbuter** was many feet square, and chairs were set for the guests."—*Autobiog. of Mrs. Sherwood*, 345.

1811.—". . . the **Chabootah** or Terrace."—*Williamson, V. M.* ii. 114.

1827.—"The splendid procession, having entered the royal gardens, approached through a long avenue of lofty trees, a **chabootra** or platform of white marble canopied by arches of the same material."—*Sir W. Scott, The Surgeon's Daughter*, ch. xiv:

1834.—"We rode up to the **Chabootra**, which has a large enclosed court before it, and the Darogha received us with the respect which my showy escort claimed."—*Mem. of Col. Mountain*, 133:

CHACKUR, s. P.—H. *chākar*, 'a servant.' The word is hardly ever now used in Anglo-Indian households except as a sort of rhyming amplification to *Naukar* (see **NOKUR**): "*Naukar-chākar*," the whole following. But in a past generation there was a distinction made between *naukar*, the superior servant, such as a *munshī*, a *gomāshta*, a *chobdār*, a *khānsama*, &c., and *chākar*, a menial servant. Williamson gives a curious list of both classes, showing what a large Calcutta household embraced at the beginning of last century (*V. M.* i. 185-187).

1810.—"Such is the superiority claimed by the *nokers*, that to ask one of them 'whose **chauker** he is?' would be considered a gross insult."—*Williamson*, i. 187.

CHALIA, CHALÉ, n.p. *Chālyam*, *Chāliyam*, or *Chālayam;* an old port of Malabar, on the south side of the Beypur [see **BEYPOOR**] R., and opposite Beypur. The terminal station of the Madras Railway is in fact where Chālyam was. A plate is given in the *Lendas* of Correa, which makes this plain. The place is incorrectly alluded to as *Kalyān* in *Imp. Gazetteer*, ii. 49; more correctly on next page as *Chalium*. [See *Logan, Malabar*, i. 75.]

c. 1330.—See in *Abulfeda*, "**Shāliyāt**, a city of Malabar."—*Gildemeister*, 185.

c. 1344.—"I went then to **Shālyāt**, a very pretty town, where they make the stuffs that bear its name [see **SHALEE**]. . . . Thence I returned to Kalikut."—*Ibn Batuta*, iv. 109.

1516.—"Beyond this city (Calicut) towards the south there is another city called **Chalyani**, where there are numerous Moors, natives of the country, and much shipping."—*Barbosa*, 153.

c. 1570.—"And it was during the reign of this prince that the Franks erected their fort at **Shaleeat** . . . it thus commanded the trade between Arabia and Calicut, since between the last city and *Shaleeat* the distance was scarcely 2 parasangs."—*Tohfut-ul-Mujahideen*, p. 129.

1572.—

"A Sampaio feroz succederá
Cunha, que longo tempe tem o leme:
De **Chale** as torres altas erguerá
Em quanto Dio illustre delle treme."

Camões, x. 61.

By Burton:

"Then shall succeed to fierce Sampaio's powers
Cunha, and hold the helm for many a year,
building of **Chale**-town the lofty towers,
while quakes illustrious Diu his name to hear."

[c. 1610.—". . . crossed the river which separates the Calecut kingdom from that of a king named **Chaly**."—*Pyrard de Laval*, Hak. Soc. i. 368.]

1672.—"Passammo Cinacotta situata alla bocca del fiume **Ciali**, doue li Portughesi hebbero altre volte Fortezza."—*P. Vincenzo Maria*, 129.

CHAMPA, n.p. The name of a kingdom at one time of great power and importance in Indo-China, occupying the extreme S.E. of that region. A limited portion of its soil is still known by that name, but otherwise as the Binh-Thuān province of Cochin China. The race inhabiting this portion, *Chams* or *Tsiams*, are traditionally said to have occupied the whole breadth of that peninsula to the Gulf of Siam, before the arrival of the *Khmer* or Kambojan people. It is not clear whether the people in question took their name from Champa, or Champa from the people; but in any case the *form* of Champa is Sanskrit, and probably it was adopted from India like Kamboja itself and so many other Indo-Chinese names. The original *Champā* was a city and kingdom on the Ganges, near the modern Bhāgalpur. And we find the Indo-Chinese Champa in the 7th century called *Mahā-champā*, as if to distinguish it. It is probable that the Ζάβα or Ζάβαι of Ptolemy represents the name of this ancient kingdom; and it is certainly the *Sanf* or *Chanf* of the Arab navigators 600 years later; this form representing *Champ* as nearly as is possible to the Arabic alphabet.

c. A.D. 640.—". . . plus loin à l'est, le royaume de *Mo-ho-tchen-po*" (**Mahāchampā**).—*Hiouen Thsang*, in *Pèlerins Bouddh.* iii. 83.

851.—"Ships then proceed to the place called **Sanf** (or **Chanf**) . . . there fresh water is procured; from this place is exported the aloes-wood called **Chanfi**. This is a kingdom."—*Relation des Voyages*, &c., i. 18.

1298.—"You come to a country called **Chamba**, a very rich region, having a King of its own. The people are idolaters, and pay a yearly tribute to the Great Kaan . . . there are a very great number of Elephants in this Kingdom, and they have lign-aloes in great abundance."—*Marco Polo*, Bk. iii. ch. 5.

c. 1300.—"Passing on from this, you come to a continent called **Jampa**, also subject to the Kaan. . . ."—*Rashīduddīn*, in *Elliot*, i. 71.

c. 1328.—"There is also a certain part of India called **Champa**. There, in place of horses, mules, asses, and camels, they make use of elephants for all their work."—*Friar Jordanus*, 37.

1516.—"Having passed this island (Borney) . . . towards the country of Ansiam and China, there is another great island of Gentiles called **Champa**; which has a King and language of its own, and many elephants. . . . There also grows in it aloes-wood."—*Barbosa*, 204.

1552.—"Concorriam todolos navegantes dos mares Occidentaes da India, e dos Orientaes a ella, que são as regiões di Sião, China, **Choampa**, Cambòja. . . ."—*Barros*, ii. vi. 1.

1572.—

"Ves, corre a costa, que **Champa** se chama
Cuja mata he do pao cheiroso ornada."
Camões, x. 129.

By Burton:

"Here courseth, see, the callèd **Champa** shore,
with woods of odorous wood 'tis deckt and dight."

1608.—". . . thence (from Assam) eastward on the side of the northern mountains are the Nangata [*i.e.* Nāga] lands, the Land of Pukham lying on the ocean, Balgu [Baigu? *i.e.* Pegu], the land Rakhang, Hamsavati, and the rest of the realm of Munyang; beyond these **Champa**, Kamboja, etc. All these are in general named *Koki*."—*Taranatha* (Tibetan) *Hist. of Buddhism*, by *Schiefner*, p. 262. The preceding passage is of great interest as showing a fair general knowledge of the kingdoms of Indo-China on the part of a Tibetan priest, and also as showing that Indo-China was recognised under a general name, viz. *Koki*.

1696.—"Mr. Bowyear says the Prince of **Champa** whom he met at the *Cochin Chinese Court* was very polite to him, and strenuously exhorted him to introduce the English to the dominions of *Champa*."—In *Dalrymple's Or. Repert.* i. 67.

CHAMPANA, s. A kind of small vessel. (See **SAMPAN**.)

CHANDAUL, s. H. *Chanḍāl*, an outcaste, 'used generally for a man of the lowest and most despised of the mixt tribes' (*Williams*); 'properly one sprung from a Sudra father and Brahman mother' (*Wilson*). [The last is the definition of the *Āīn* (ed. *Jarrett*, iii. 116). Dr. Wilson identifies them with the *Kandali* or *Gondali* of Ptolemy (*Ind. Caste*, i. 57).]

712.—"You have joined those **Chandáls** and coweaters, and have become one of them."—*Chach-Nāmah*, in *Elliot*, i. 193.

[1810.—"**Chandela**," see quotation under **HALALCORE**.]

CHANDERNAGORE, n.p. The name of the French settlement on the Hoogly, 24 miles by river above Calcutta, originally occupied in 1673. The name is alleged by Hunter to be properly *Chandan(a)-nagara*, 'Sandalwood City,' but the usual form points rather to *Chandra-nagara*, 'Moon City.' [Natives prefer to call it *Farash-danga*, or 'The gathering together of Frenchmen.']

1727.—"He forced the Ostenders to quit their Factory, and seek protection from the French at **Charnagur**. . . . They have a few private Families dwelling near the Factory, and a pretty little Church to hear Mass in, which is the chief Business of the French in Bengal."—*A. Hamilton*, ii. 18.

[1753.—"**Shandernagor**." See quotation under **CALCUTTA**.]

CHANK, CHUNK, s. H. *sankh*, Skt. *sankha*, a large kind of shell (*Turbinella rapa*), prized by the Hindus, and used by them for offering libations, as a horn to blow at the temples, and for cutting into armlets and other ornaments. It is found especially in the Gulf of Manaar, and the *Chank* fishery was formerly, like that of the pearl-oysters, a Government monopoly (see *Tennent's Ceylon*, ii. 556, and the references). The abnormal *chank*, with its spiral opening to the right, is of exceptional value, and has been sometimes priced, it is said, at a lakh of rupees!

c. 545.—"Then there is Sielediba, *i.e.* Taprobane . . . and then again on the continent, and further back is *Marallo*, which exports **conch**-shells (κοχλίους)."—*Cosmas*, in *Cathay*, I. clxxviii.

851.—"They find on its shores (of Ceylon) the pearl, and the **shank**, a name by which they designate the great shell which serves for a trumpet, and which is much sought after."—*Reinaud, Relations*, i. 6.

1563.—". . . And this **chanco** is a ware for the Bengal trade, and formerly it produced more profit than now. . . . And there was formerly a custom in Bengal that no virgin in honour and esteem could be corrupted unless it were by placing bracelets of **chanco** on her arms; but since the Patans came in this usage has more or less ceased; and so the *chanco* is rated lower now. . . ."—*Garcia*, f. 141.

1644.—"What they chiefly bring (from Tuticorin) are cloths called *cachas** . . . a large quantity of **Chanquo**; these are large shells which they fish in that sea, and which supply Bengal, where the blacks make of them bracelets for the arm; also the biggest and best fowls in all these Eastern parts."—*Bocarro*, *MS.* 316.

1672.—"Garroude flew in all haste to Brahma, and brought to Kisna the **chianko**, or *kinkhorn*, twisted to the right."—*Baldaeus*, Germ. ed. 521.

* These are probably the same as Milburn, under Tuticorin, calls *ketchies*. We do not know the proper name. [See **Putton Ketchies**, under **PIECE-GOODS**.]

1673.—"There are others they call **chanquo**; the shells of which are the Mother of Pearl."—*Fryer*, 322.

1727.—"It admits of some Trade, and produces Cotton, Corn, coars Cloth, and **Chonk**, a Shell-fish in shape of a Periwinkle, but as large as a Man's Arm above the Elbow. In *Bengal* they are saw'd into Rings for Ornaments to Women's Arms."—*A. Hamilton*, i. 131.

1734.—"Expended towards digging a foundation, where **chanks** were buried with accustomed ceremonies."—In *Wheeler*, iii. 147.

1770.—"Upon the same coast is found a shell-fish called **xanxus**, of which the Indians at Bengal make bracelets."—*Raynal* (tr. 1777) i. 216.

1813.—"A **chank** opening to the right hand is highly valued . . . always sells for its weight in gold."—*Milburn*, i. 357.

[1871.—"The conch or **chunk** shell."—*Mateer, Land of Charity*, 92.]

1875.—

"**Chanks.**	Large for Cameos.	Valuation per 100	10 Rs.
	White, live	,, ,,	6 ,,
	,, dead	,, ,,	3 ,,

Table of Customs Duties on Imports into British India up to 1875.

CHARPOY, s. H. *chārpāī*, from P. *chihār-pāī* (*i.e.* four-feet), the common Indian bedstead, sometimes of very rude materials, but in other cases handsomely wrought and painted. It is correctly described in the quotation from Ibn Batuta.

c. 1350.—"The beds in India are very light. A single man can carry one, and every traveller should have his own bed, which his slave carries about on his head. The bed consists of four conical legs, on which four staves are laid; between they plait a sort of ribbon of silk or cotton. When you lie on it you need nothing else to render the bed sufficiently elastic."—iii. 380.

c. 1540.—"Husain Khan Tashtdár was sent on some business from Bengal. He went on travelling night and day. Whenever sleep came over him he placed himself on a bed (**chahār-pāī**) and the villagers carried him along on their shoulders."—MS. quoted in *Elliot*, iv. 418.

1662.—"Turbans, long coats, trowsers, shoes, and sleeping on **chárpáis**, are quite unusual."—*H. of Mir Jumla's Invasion of Assam*, transl. by *Blochmann, J.A.S.B.* xli. pt. i. 80.

1876.—"A syce at Mozuffernuggar, lying asleep on a **charpoy** . . . was killed by a tame buck goring him in the side . . . it was supposed in play."—*Baldwin, Large and Small Game of Bengal*, 195.

1883.—"After a gallop across country, he would rest on a **charpoy**, or country bed, and hold an impromptu *levee* of all the village folk."—*C. Raikes*, in *L. of L. Lawrence*, i. 57.

CHATTA, s. An umbrella; H. *chhātā*, *chhatr*; Skt. *chhatra*.

c. 900.—"He is clothed in a waist-cloth, and holds in his hand a thing called a **Jatra**; this is an umbrella made of peacock's feathers."—*Reinaud, Relations*, &c. 154.

c. 1340.—"They hoist upon these elephants as many **chatrās**, or umbrellas of silk, mounted with many precious stones, and with handles of pure gold."—*Ibn Batuta*, iii. 228.

c. 1354.—"But as all the Indians commonly go naked, they are in the habit of carrying a thing like a little tent-roof on a cane handle, which they open out at will as a protection against sun and rain. This they call a **chatyr**. I brought one home to Florence with me. . . ."—*John Marignolli*, in *Cathay*, &c. p. 381.

1673.—"Thus the chief Naik with his loud Musick . . . an Ensign of Red, Swallow-tailed, several **Chitories**, little but rich *Kitsolls* (which are the Names of several Countries for Umbrelloes). . . ."—*Fryer*, 160.

[1694.—"3 **chatters**."—*Hedges, Diary*, Hak. Soc. ii. cclxv.

[1826.—"Another as my **chitree**-burdar or umbrella-carrier."—*Pandurang Hari*, ed. 1873, i. 28.]

CHATTY, s. An earthen pot, spheroidal in shape. It is a S. Indian word, but is tolerably familiar in the Anglo-Indian parlance of N. India also, though the H. **Ghurra** (*gharā*) is more commonly used there. The word is Tam. *shaṭi*, *shaṭṭi*, Tel. *chatti*, which appears in Pali as *chāḍi*.

1781.—"In honour of His Majesty's birthday we had for dinner fowl cutlets and a flour pudding, and drank his health in a **chatty** of sherbet."—*Narr. of an Officer of Baillie's Detachment*, quoted in *Lives of the Lindsays*, iii. 285.

1829.—"The **chatties** in which the women carry water are globular earthen vessels, with a bell-mouth at top."—*Mem. of Col. Mountain*, 97.

CHAW, s. For *chā*, *i.e.* **Tea** (q.v.).

1616.—"I sent . . . a silver **chaw** pot and a fan to Capt. China wife."—*Cocks's Diary*, i. 215.

CHAWBUCK, s. and v. A whip; to whip. An obsolete vulgarism from P. *chābuk*, 'alert'; in H. 'a horse-whip.' It seems to be the same as the *sjambok* in use at the Cape, and apparently carried from India (see the quotation from Van Twist). [Mr.

Skeat points out that Klinkert gives *chambok* or *sambok*, as Javanese forms, the standard Malay being *chabok* or *chabuk;* and this perhaps suggests that the word may have been introduced by Malay grooms once largely employed at the Cape.]

1648. "... Poor and little thieves are flogged with a great whip (called **Siamback**) several days in succession."—*Van Twist*, 29.

1673.—"Upon any suspicion of default he has a Black Guard that by a **Chawbuck**, a great Whip, extorts Confession."—*Fryer*, 98.

1673.—"The one was of an Armenian, **Chawbucked** through the City for selling of Wine."—*Ibid*. 97.

1682.—"... Ramgivan, our *Vekeel* there (at Hugly) was sent for by Permesuradass, Bulchund's servant, who immediately clapt him in prison. Ye same day was brought forth and slippered; the next day he was beat on ye soles of his feet, ye third day **Chawbuckt**, and ye 4th drub'd till he could not speak, and all to force a writing in our names to pay Rupees 50,000 for custome of ye Silver brought out this year."—*Hedges, Diary*, Nov. 2; [Hak. Soc. i. 45].

[1684-5.—"Notwithstanding his being a great person was soon stripped and **chawbuckt**."—*Pringle, Madras Consns.* iv. 4.]

1688.—"Small offenders are only whipt on the Back, which sort of Punishment they call **Chawbuck**."—*Dampier*, ii. 138.

1699.—"The Governor of Surrat ordered the cloth Broker to be tyed up and **chawbucked**."—*Letter from General and Council at Bombay to E. I. C.* (in Record Office), 23rd March, 1698-9.

1726.—"Another Pariah he **chawbucked** 25 blows, put him in the Stocks, and kept him there an hour."—*Wheeler*, ii. 410.

1756.—"... a letter from Mr. Hastings ... says that the Nabob to engage the Dutch and French to purchase also, had put peons upon their Factories and threatened their *Vaquills* with the **Chaubac**."—In *Long*, 79.

1760.—"Mr. Barton, laying in wait, seized Benautrom Chattogee opposite to the door of the Council, and with the assistance of his bearer and his peons tied his hands and his feet, swung him upon a bamboo like a hog, carried him to his own house, there with his own hand **chawbooked** him in the most cruel manner, almost to the deprivation of life; endeavoured to force beef into his mouth, to the irreparable loss of his Bramin's caste, and all this without giving ear to, or suffering the man to speak in his own defence. ..."—*Fort Wm. Consn.*, in *Long*, 214-215.

1784.—
"The sentinels placed at the door
Are for our security bail;
With Muskets and **Chaubucks** secure,
They guard us in Bangalore Jail."
Song, by a *Gentleman of the Navy* (prisoner with Hyder) in *Seton-Karr*, i. 18.

1817.—"... ready to prescribe his favourite regimen of the **Chabuk** for every man, woman, or child who dared to think otherwise."—*Lalla Rookh.*

CHAWBUCKSWAR, s. H. from P. *chābuk-suwār*, a rough-rider.

[1820.—"As I turned him short, he threw up his head, which came in contact with mine and made my **chabookswar** exclaim, *Ali mudat*. 'the help of Ali.'"—*Tod, Personal Narr*. Calcutta rep. ii. 723.

[1892.—"A sort of high-stepping caper is taught, the **chabuksowar** (whip-rider), or breaker, holding, in addition to the bridle, cords tied to the fore fetlocks."—*Kipling, Beast and Man in India*, 171.]

CHEBULI. The denomination of one of the kinds of **Myrobolans** (q.v.) exported from India. The true etymology is probably *Kābulī*, as stated by Thevenot, *i.e.* 'from Cabul.'

c. 1343.—"**Chebuli** *mirabolani*."—*List of Spices*, &c., in *Pegolotti* (Della Decima, iii. 303).

c. 1665.—"De la Province de Caboul ... les Mirabolans croissent dans les Montagnes et c'est la cause pourquoi les Orientaux les appelent **Cabuly**."—*Thevenot*, v. 172.

CHEECHEE, adj. A disparaging term applied to half-castes or **Eurasians** (q.v.) (corresponding to the **Lip-lap** of the Dutch in Java) and also to their manner of speech. The word is said to be taken from *chī* (Fie!), a common native (S. Indian) interjection of remonstrance or reproof, supposed to be much used by the class in question. The term is, however, perhaps also a kind of onomatopœia, indicating the mincing pronunciation which often characterises them (see below). It should, however, be added that there are many well-educated East Indians who are quite free from this mincing accent.

1781.—
"Pretty little Looking-Glasses,
Good and cheap for **Chee-chee** Misses."
Hicky's Bengal Gazette, March 17.

1873.—"He is no favourite with the pure native, whose language he speaks as his own in addition to the hybrid minced English (known as **chee-chee**), which he also employs."—*Fraser's Magazine*, Oct., 437.

1880.—"The Eurasian girl is often pretty and graceful. ... 'What though upon her lips there hung The accents of her **tchi-tchi** tongue.'"—*Sir Ali Baba*, 122.

1881.—"There is no doubt that the '**Chee Chee** twang,' which becomes so objectionable to every Englishman before he has been long in the East, was originally learned in the convent and the Brothers' school, and will be clung to as firmly as the queer turns of speech learned in the same place."—*St. James's Gazette*, Aug. 26.

CHEENAR, s. P. *chīnār*, the Oriental Plane (*Platanus orientalis*) and *platanus* of the ancients; native from Greece to Persia. It is often by English travellers in Persia miscalled *sycamore* from confusion with the common British tree (*Acer pseudo-platanus*), which English people also habitually miscall *sycamore*, and Scotch people miscall *plane-tree!* Our quotations show how old the confusion is. The tree is not a native of India, though there are fine *chīnārs* in Kashmere, and a few in old native gardens in the Punjab, introduced in the days of the Moghul emperors. The tree is the *Arbre Sec* of Marco Polo (see 2nd ed. vol. i. 131, 132). *Chīnārs* of especial vastness and beauty are described by Herodotus and Pliny, by Chardin and others. At Buyukdereh near Constantinople, is still shown the Plane under which Godfrey of Boulogne is said to have encamped. At Tejrīsh, N. of Teheran, Sir H. Rawlinson tells us that he measured a great *chīnār* which has a girth of 108 feet at 5 feet from the ground.

c. 1628.—"The gardens here are many . . . abounding in lofty pyramidall cypresses, broad-spreading **Chenawrs**. . . ."—*Sir T. Herbert*, 136.

1677.—"We had a fair Prospect of the City (Ispahan) filling the one half of an ample Plain, few Buildings . . . shewing themselves by reason of the high **Chinors**, or Sicamores shading the choicest of them. . . ."—*Fryer*, 259.

,, "We in our Return cannot but take notice of the famous Walk between the two Cities of *Jelfa* and *Ispahaun;* it is planted with two rows of Sycamores (which is the tall Maple, not the Sycamore of *Alkair*)."—*Ibid.* 286.

1682.—"At the elegant villa and garden at Mr. Bohun's at Lee. He shewed me the **Zinnar** tree or platanus, and told me that since they had planted this kind of tree about the Citty of Ispahan . . . the plague . . . had exceedingly abated of its mortal effects."—*Evelyn's Diary*, Sept. 16.

1726.—". . . the finest road that you can imagine . . . planted in the middle with 135 **Sennaar** trees on one side and 132 on the other."—*Valentijn*, v. 208.

1783.—"This tree, which in most parts of Asia is called the **Chinaur**, grows to the size of an oak, and has a taper straight trunk, with a silver-coloured bark, and its leaf, not unlike an expanded hand, is of a pale green."—*G. Forster's Journey*, ii. 17.

1817.— ". . . they seem
Like the **Chenar**-tree grove, where winter throws
O'er all its tufted heads its feathery snows."
Mokanna.

[1835.—". . . the island Char **chúnar** . . . a skilful monument of the Moghul Emperor, who named it from the four plane trees he planted on the spot."—*Hügel, Travels in Kashmir*, 112.

[1872.—"I . . . encamped under some enormous **chunar** or oriental plane trees."—*Wilson, Abode of Snow*, 370.]

Chīnār is alleged to be in Badakhshān applied to a species of poplar.

CHEENY, s. See under **SUGAR**.

1810.—"The superior kind (of raw sugar) which may often be had nearly white . . . and sharp-grained, under the name of **cheeny**."—*Williamson, V. M.* ii. 134.

CHEESE, s. This word is well known to be used in modern English slang for "anything good, first-rate in quality, genuine, pleasant, or advantageous" (*Slang Dict.*). And the most probable source of the term is P. and H. *chīz*, 'thing.' For the expression used to be common among Anglo-Indians, *e.g.*, "My new Arab is the real *chīz*"; "These cheroots are the real *chīz*," *i.e.* the real thing. The word may have been an Anglo-Indian importation, and it is difficult otherwise to account for it. [This view is accepted by the *N.E.D.;* for other explanations see 1 ser. *N. & Q.* viii. 89; 3 ser. vii. 465, 505.]

CHEETA, s. H. *chītā*, the *Felis jubata*, Schreber, [*Cynaelurus jubatus*, Blanford], or 'Hunting Leopard,' so called from its being commonly trained to use in the chase. From Skt. *chitraka*, or *chitrakāya*, lit. 'having a speckled body.'

1563.—". . . and when they wish to pay him much honour they call him *Ráo;* as for example Chita-Ráo, whom I am acquainted with; and this is a proud name, for **Chita** signifies 'Ounce' (or panther) and this *Chita*-Rao means 'King as strong as a Panther.'"—*Garcia*, f. 36.

c. 1596.—"Once a leopard (**chīta**) had been caught, and without previous training, on a mere hint by His Majesty, it brought in the prey, like trained leopards."—*Āīn-i-Akbarī*, ed. *Blochmann*, i. 286.

1610.—Hawkins calls the **Cheetas** at Akbar's Court 'ounces for game.'—In *Purchas*, i. 218.

[1785.—"The **Cheetah**-connah, the place where the Nabob's panthers and other animals for hunting are kept."—*Forbes, Or. Mem.* 2nd ed. ii. 450.]

1862.—"The true **Cheetah**, the Hunting Leopard of India, does not exist in Ceylon." —*Tennent*, i. 140.

1879.—"Two young **cheetahs** had just come in from Bombay; one of these was as tame as a house-cat, and like the puma, purred beautifully when stroked."—"*Jamrack's*," in *Sat. Review*, May 17, p. 612.

It has been ingeniously suggested by Mr. Aldis Wright that the word *cheater*, as used by Shakspere, in the following passage, refers to this animal:—

Falstaff: "He's no swaggerer, Hostess; a *tame* **cheater** i' faith; you may stroke him gently as a puppy greyhound; he'll not swagger."—2nd Part *King Henry IV.* ii. 4.

Compare this with the passage just quoted from the *Saturday Review!* And the interpretation would rather derive confirmation from a parallel passage from Beaumont & Fletcher:

". . . if you give any credit to the juggling rascal, you are worse than simple widgeons, and will be drawn into the net by this decoy-duck, this *tame* **cheater**."—*The Fair Maid of the Inn*, iv. 2.

But we have not been able to trace any possible source from which Shakspere could have derived the name of the animal at all, to say nothing of the familiar use of it. [The *N.E.D.* gives no support to the suggestion.]

CHELING, CHELI, s. The word is applied by some Portuguese writers to the traders of Indian origin who were settled at Malacca. It is not found in the Malay dictionaries, and it is just possible that it originated in some confusion of *Quelin* (see **KLING**) and *Chuli* (see **CHOOLIA**), or rather of *Quelin* and *Chetin* (see **CHETTY**).

1567.—"From the cohabitation of the **Chelins** of Malaqua with the Christians in the same street (even although in divers houses) spring great offences against God our Lord."—*Decrees of the Sacred Council of Goa*, in *Archiv. Port. Orient.*, Dec. 23.

1613.—"E depois daquelle porto aberto e franqueado aportarão mercadores de Choromandel; mormente aquelles **chelis** com roupas. . . ."—*Godinho de Eredia*, 4v.

,, "This settlement is divided into two parishes, S. Thome and S. Estevão, and that part of S. Thome called *Campon* **Chelim** extends from the shore of the *Jaos* Bazar to the N.W. and terminates at the Stone Bastion; in this part dwell the **Chelis** of Choromandel."—*Godinho de Eredia*, 5v. See also f. 22, [and under **CAMPOO**].

CHELINGO, s. Arab. *shalandī*, [whence Malayāl. *chalanti*, Tam. *shalangu*;] "*djalanga*, qui va sur l'eau; *chalangue*, barque, bateau dont les planches sont clouées" (*Dict. Tam. Franc.*, Pondichéry, 1855). This seems an unusual word, and is perhaps connected through the Arabic with the medieval vessel *chelandia*, *chelandria*, *chelindras*, *chelande*, &c., used in carrying troops and horses. [But in its present form the word is S. Indian.]

1726.—". . . as already a **Chialeng** (a sort of small native row-boat, which is used for discharging and loading cargo). . . ."—*Valentijn*, *V. Chor.* 20.

1746.—
"**Chillinga** hire . . . . . 0 22 0"
Account charges at Fort St. David, Decr. 31, MS. in India Office.

1761.—"It appears there is no more than one frigate that has escaped; therefore don't lose an instant to send us **chelingoes** upon **chelingoes** loaded with rice. . . ."—*Lally to Raymond at Pulicat.* In *Comp. H. of the War in India* (Tract), 1761, p. 85.

,, "No more than one frigate has escaped; lose not an instant in sending **chelingoes** upon **chelingoes** loaded with rice."—*Carraccioli's Life of Clive*, i. 58.

CHEROOT, s. A cigar; but the term has been appropriated specially to cigars truncated at both ends, as the Indian and Manilla cigars always were in former days. The word is Tam. *shuruttu*, [Mal. *churuttu*,] 'a roll (of tobacco).' In the South cheroots are chiefly made at Trichinopoly and in the Godavery Delta, the produce being known respectively as **Trichies** and **Lunkas**. The earliest occurrence of the word that we know is in Father Beschi's Tamil story of Parmartta Guru (c. 1725). On p. 1 one of the characters is described as carrying a firebrand to light his *pugaiyailai shshuruttu*, 'roll (cheroot) of tobacco.' [The *N.E.D.* quotes **cherootta** in 1669.] Grose (1750-60), speaking of Bombay, whilst describing the cheroot does not use that word, but another which is, as far as we know, entirely obsolete in British India, viz. **Buncus** (q.v.).

1759.—In the expenses of the Nabob's entertainment at Calcutta in this year we find:

"60 lbs. of Masulipatam **cheroots**, Rs. 500."—In *Long*, 194.

1781.—". . . am tormented every day by a parcel of gentlemen coming to the end of my berth to talk politics and smoke **cheroots**—advise them rather to think of mending the holes in their old shirts, like me."—*Hon. J. Lindsay* (in *Lives of the Lindsays*), iii. 297.

,, "Our evening amusements instead of your stupid Harmonics, was playing Cards and Backgammon, chewing Beetle and smoking **Cherutes.**"—*Old Country Captain*, in *India Gazette*, Feby. 24.

1782.—"Le tabac y réussit très bien; les **chiroutes** de Manille sont renommées dans toute l'Inde par leur goût agréable; aussi les Dames dans ce pays fument-elles toute la journée."—*Sonnerat, Voyage*, iii. 43.

1792.—"At that time (c. 1757) I have seen the officers mount guard many's the time and oft . . . neither did they at that time carry your fusees, but had a long Pole with an iron head to it. . . . With this in one Hand and a **Chiroot** in the other you saw them saluting away at the Main Guard."—*Madras Courier*, April 3.

1810.—"The lowest classes of Europeans, as also of the natives . . . frequently smoke **cheroots**, exactly corresponding with the Spanish *segar*, though usually made rather more bulky."—*Williamson, V. M.* i. 499.

1811.—"Dire que le **T'cherout** est la cigarre, c'est me dispenser d'en faire la description."—*Solvyns*, iii.

[1823.—"He amused himself by smoking several **carrotes.**"—*Owen, Narr.* ii. 50.]

1875.—"The meal despatched, all who were not on duty lay down . . . almost too tired to smoke their **cheroots** before falling asleep."—*The Dilemma*, ch. xxxvii.

CHERRY FOUJ, s. H. *charī-fauj?* This curious phrase occurs in the quotations, the second of which explains its meaning. I am not certain what the first part is, but it is most probably *charī*, in the sense of 'movable,' 'locomotive,' so that the phrase was equivalent to 'flying brigade.' [It may possibly be *charhī*, for *charhnī*, in the sense of 'preparation for battle.'] It was evidently a technicality of the Mahratta armies.

1803.—"The object of a **cherry fouj**, without guns, with two armies after it, must be to fly about and plunder the richest country it can find, not to march through exhausted countries, to make revolutions in cities."—*Elphinstone*, in *Life*, i. 59.

1809.—"Two detachments under . . . Mahratta chiefs of some consequence, are now employed in levying contributions in different parts of the Jypoor country. Such detachments are called **churee fuoj**; they are generally equipped very lightly, with but little artillery; and are equally formidable in their progress to friend and foe."—*Broughton, Letters from a Mahratta Camp*, 128; [ed. 1892, p. 96].

CHETTY, s. A member of any of the trading castes in S. India, answering in every way to the **Banyans** of W. and N. India. Malayāl. *chetti*, Tam. *shetti*, [Tel. *setti*, in Ceylon *seddi*]. These have all been supposed to be forms from the Skt. *śreshti;* but C. P. Brown (MS.) denies this, and says "*Shetti*, a shop-keeper, is plain Telegu," and quite distinct from *śreshti*. [The same view is taken in the *Madras Gloss.*] Whence then the H. *Seth* (see **SETT**)? [The word was also used for a 'merchantman': see the quotations from Pyrard on which Gray notes: "I do not know any other authority for the use of the word for merchantships, though it is analogous to our 'merchantmen.'"]

c. 1349.—The word occurs in Ibn Batuta (iv. 259) in the form **ṣāti**, which he says was given to very rich merchants in *China;* and this is one of his questionable statements about that country.

1511.—"The great Afonso Dalboquerque . . . determined to appoint Ninachatu, because he was a Hindoo, Governor of the Quilins (**Cheling**) and **Chetins.**"—*Comment. of Af. Dalboq.*, Hak. Soc. iii. 128; [and see quotation from *ibid.* iii. 146, under **KLING**].

1516.—"Some of these are called **Chettis**, who are Gentiles, natives of the province of Cholmender."—*Barbosa*, 144.

1552.—". . . whom our people commonly call **Chatis**. These are men with such a genius for merchandise, and so acute in every mode of trade, that among our people when they desire either to blame or praise any man for his subtlety and skill in merchant's traffic they say of him, 'he is a **Chatim**'; and they use the word **chatinar** for 'to trade,'—which are words now very commonly received among us."—*Barros*, I. ix. 3.

c. 1566.—"Ui sono uomini periti che si chiamano **Chitini**, li quali metteno il prezzo alle perle."—*Cesare Federici*, in *Ramusio*, iii. 390.

1596.—"The vessels of the **Chatins** of these parts never sail along the coast of Malavar nor towards the north, except in a *cafilla*, in order to go and come more securely, and to avoid being cut off by the Malavars and other corsairs, who are continually roving in those seas."—*Viceroy's Proclamation at Goa*, in *Archiv. Port. Or.*, fasc. 3, 661.

1598.—"The Souldiers in these dayes give themselves more to be **Chettijns** [var. lect. **Chatiins**] and to deale in Marchandise, than to serve the King in his Armado."—*Linschoten*, 58; [Hak. Soc. i. 202].

[,, "Most of these vessels were **Chetils**, that is to say, merchantmen."—*Pyrard de Laval*, Hak. Soc. i. 345.

[c. 1610.—"Each is composed of fifty or sixty war galiots, without counting those of **chetie**, or merchantmen."—*Pyrard de Laval*, Hak. Soc. ii. 117.]

1651.—"The **Sitty** are merchant folk."—*Rogerius*, 8.

1686.—". . . And that if the **Chetty** Bazaar people do not immediately open their shops, and sell their grain, etc., as usually, that the goods and commodities in their several ships be confiscated."—In *Wheeler*, i. 152.

1726.—"The **Sittis** are merchant folk and also porters. . . ."—*Valentijn*, *Choro.* 88.

" "The strength of a Bramin is Knowledge; the strength of a King is Courage; the strength of a *Bellale* (or Cultivator) is Revenue; the strength of a **Chetti** is Money."—*Apophthegms of Ceylon*, tr. in *Valentijn*, v. 390.

c. 1754.—"**Chitties** are a particular kind of merchants in Madras, and are generally very rich, but rank with the *left-hand cast*."—*Ives*, 25.

1796.—"**Cetti**, mercanti astuti, diligenti, laboriosi, sobrii, frugali, ricchi."—*Fra Paolino*, 79.

[**CHEYLA**, s. "Originally a H. word (*chelā*, Skt. *chetaka*, *chedaka*) meaning 'a servant,' many changes have been rung upon it in Hindu life, so that it has meant a slave, a household slave, a family retainer, an adopted member of a great family, a dependant relative and a soldier in its secular senses; a follower, a pupil, a disciple and a convert in its ecclesiastical senses. It has passed out of Hindu usage into Muhammadan usage with much the same meanings and ideas attached to it, and has even meant a convert from Hinduism to Islam." (*Col. Temple*, in *Ind. Ant.*, July, 1896, pp. 200 *seqq.*). In Anglo-Indian usage it came to mean a special battalion made up of prisoners and converts.

[c. 1596.—"The **Chelahs** or Slaves. His Majesty from religious motives dislikes the name *bandah* or slave. . . . He therefore calls this class of men **Chelahs**, which Hindi term signifies a faithful disciple."—*Āīn*, *Blochmann*, i. 253 *seqq.*

[1791.—"(The Europeans) all were bound on the parade and rings (*boly*) the badge of slavery were put into their ears. They were then incorporated into a battalion of **Cheylas**."—In *Seton-Karr*, ii. 311.

[1795.—". . . a Havildar . . . compelled to serve in one of his **Chela** Corps."—*Ibid.* ii. 407.]

CHIAMAY, n.p. The name of an imaginary lake, which in the maps of the 16th century, followed by most of those of the 17th, is made the source of most of the great rivers of Further India, including the Brahmaputra, the Irawadi, the Salwen, and the Menam. Lake Chiamay was the counterpart of the African lake of the same period which is made the source of all the great rivers of Africa, but it is less easy to suggest what gave rise to this idea of it. The actual name seems taken from the State of **Zimmé** (see **JANGOMAY**) or Chiang-mai.

c. 1544.—"So proceeding onward, he arrived at the Lake of *Singipamor*, which ordinarily is called **Chiammay**. . . ."—*F. M. Pinto*, *Cogan's* tr., p. 271.

1552.—"The Lake of **Chiamai**, which stands to the northward, 200 leagues in the interior, and from which issue six notable streams, three of which combining with others form the great river which passes through the midst of Siam, whilst the other three discharge into the Gulf of Bengala."—*Barros*, I. ix. 1.

1572.—

"Olha o rio Menão, que se derrama
Do grande lago, que **Chiamai** se chama."
Camões, x. 125.

1652.—"The Countrey of these Brames . . . extendeth Northwards from the neerest *Peguan* Kingdomes . . . watered with many great and remarkable Rivers, issuing from the Lake **Chiamay**, which though 600 miles from the Sea, and emptying itself continually into so many Channels, contains 400 miles in compass, and is nevertheless full of waters for the one or the other."—*P. Heylin's Cosmographie*, ii. 238.

CHICANE, CHICANERY, ss. These English words, signifying pettifogging, captious contention, taking every possible advantage in a contest, have been referred to Spanish *chico*, 'little,' and to Fr. *chic*, *chicquet*, 'a little bit,' as by Mr. Wedgwood in his *Dict. of Eng. Etymology*. See also quotation from *Saturday Review* below. But there can be little doubt that the words are really traceable to the game of *chaugān*, or horse-golf. This game is now well known in England under the name of **Polo** (q.v.). But the recent introduction under that name is its second importation into Western Europe. For in the Middle Ages it came from Persia to Byzantium, where it was popular under a modification of its Persian name (verb τζυκανίζειν, playing ground τζυκανιστήριον), and from Byzantium it passed, as a pedestrian game, to Languedoc, where it was called, by a further modification, *chicane* (see

Ducange, Dissertations sur l'Histoire de St. Louis, viii., and his *Glossarium Graecitatis*, s.v. τζυκανίζειν; also *Ouseley's Travels*, i. 345). The analogy of certain periods of the game of golf suggests how the figurative meaning of *chicaner* might arise in taking advantage of the petty accidents of the surface. And this is the strict meaning of *chicaner*, as used by military writers.

Ducange's idea was that the Greeks had borrowed both the game and the name from France, but this is evidently erroneous. He was not aware of the Persian *chaugān*. But he explains well how the tactics of the game would have led to the application of its name to "those tortuous proceedings of pleaders which we old practitioners call *barres*." The indication of the Persian origin of both the Greek and French words is due to W. Ouseley and to Quatremère. The latter has an interesting note, full of his usual wealth of Oriental reading, in his translation of Makrizi's *Mameluke Sultans*, tom. i. pt. i. pp. 121 *seqq.*

The preceding etymology was put forward again in Notes upon Mr. Wedgwood's Dictionary published by one of the present writers in *Ocean Highways*, Sept. 1872, p. 186. The same etymology has since been given by Littré (s.v.), who says: "Dès lors, la série des sens est: jeu de mail, puis action de disputer la partie, et enfin manœuvres processives"; [and is accepted by the *N.E.D.* with the reservation that "evidence actually connecting the French with the Greek word appears not to be known"].

The P. forms of the name are *chaugān* and *chauigān*; but according to the *Bahāri 'Ajam* (a great Persian dictionary compiled in India, 1768) the primitive form of the word is *chulgān* from *chūl*, 'bent,' which (as to the form) is corroborated by the Arabic *sawljān*. On the other hand, a probable origin of *chaugān* would be an Indian (Prakrit) word, meaning 'four corners' [Platts gives *chaugāna*, 'four-fold'], viz. as a name for the polo-ground. The *chulgān* is possibly a 'striving after meaning.' The meanings are according to Vüllers (1) any stick with a crook; (2) such a stick used as a drumstick; (3) a crook from which a steel ball is suspended, which was one of the royal insignia, otherwise called *kaukaba* [see *Blochmann, Āīn*, vol. i. plate ix. No. 2.]; (4) (The golf-stick, and) the game of horse-golf.

The game is now quite extinct in Persia and Western Asia, surviving only in certain regions adjoining India, as is specified under **Polo**. But for many centuries it was the game of kings and courts over all Mahommedan Asia. The earliest Mahommedan historians represent the game of *chaugān* as familiar to the Sassanian kings; Ferdusi puts the *chaugān*-stick into the hands of Siāwūsh, the father of Kai Khusrū or Cyrus; many famous kings were devoted to the game, among whom may be mentioned Nūruddīn the Just, Atābek of Syria and the great enemy of the Crusaders. He was so fond of the game that he used (like Akbar in after days) to play it by lamp-light, and was severely rebuked by a devout Mussulman for being so devoted to a mere amusement. Other zealous *chaugān*-players were the great Saladin, Jalāluddīn Mankbarni of Khwārizm, and Malik Bībars, Marco Polo's "Bendocquedar Soldan of Babylon," who was said more than once to have played *chaugān* at Damascus and at Cairo within the same week. Many illustrious persons also are mentioned in Asiatic history as having met their death by accidents in the *maidān*, as the *chaugān*-field was especially called; *e.g.* Kutbuddīn Ībak of Delhi, who was killed by such a fall at Lahore in (or about) 1207. In Makrizi (I. i. 121) we read of an Amīr at the Mameluke Court called Husāmuddīn Lajīn 'Azīzī the *Jukāndār* (or Lord High Polo-stick).

It is not known when the game was conveyed to Constantinople, but it must have been not later than the beginning of the 8th century.* The fullest description of the game as played there is given by Johannes Cinnamus (c. 1190), who does not however give the barbarian name:

"The winter now being over and the gloom cleared away, he (the Emperor Manuel Comnenus) devoted himself to a certain sober exercise which from the first had been the custom of the Emperors and their sons to practise. This is the manner thereof. A party of young men divide into two equal bands, and in a flat space which has been

* The court for *chaugān* is ascribed by Codinus (see below) to Theodosius Parvus. This could hardly be the son of Arcadius (A.D. 408-450), but rather Theodosius III. (716-718).

measured out purposely they cast a leather ball in size somewhat like an apple; and setting this in the middle as if it were a prize to be contended for they rush into the contest at full speed, each grasping in his right hand a stick of moderate length which comes suddenly to a broad rounded end, the middle of which is closed by a network of dried catgut. Then each party strives who shall first send the ball beyond the goal planted conspicuously on the opposite side, for whenever the ball is struck by the netted sticks through the goal at either side, that gives the victory to the other side. This is the kind of game, evidently a slippery and dangerous one. For a player must be continually throwing himself right back, or bending to one side or the other, as he turns his horse short, or suddenly dashes off at speed, with such strokes and twists as are needed to follow up the ball. . . . And thus as the Emperor was rushing round in furious fashion in this game, it so happened that the horse which he rode came violently to the ground. He was prostrate below the horse, and as he struggled vainly to extricate himself from its incumbent weight his thigh and hand were crushed beneath the saddle and much injured. . . ."—In Bonn ed. pp. 263-264.

We see from this passage that at Byzantium the game was played with a kind of racket, and not with a polo-stick.

We have not been able to find an instance of the medieval French *chicane* in this sense, nor does Littré's Dictionary give any. But Ducange states positively that in his time the word in this sense survived in Languedoc, and there could be no better evidence. From Henschel's *Ducange* also we borrow a quotation which shows *chuca*, used for some game of ball, in French-Latin, surely a form of *chaugān* or *chicane*.

The game of *chaugān*, the ball (*gū* or *gavī*) and the playing-ground (*maidān*) afford constant metaphors in Persian literature.

c. 820.—"If a man dream that he is on horseback along with the King himself, or some great personage, and that he strikes the ball home, or wins the **chukān** (ἤτοι τζυκανίζει) he shall find grace and favour thereupon, conformable to the success of his ball and the dexterity of his horse." Again: "If the King dream that he has won in the **chukān** (ὅτι ἐτζυκάνιζεν) he shall find things prosper with him."—*The Dream Judgments of Achmet Ibn Seirim*, from a MS. Greek version quoted by *Ducange* in *Gloss. Graecitatis.*

c. 940. — Constantine Porphyrogenitus, speaking of the rapids of the *Danapris* or Dnieper, says: "ὁ δὲ τοῦτο φραγμὸς τοσοῦτον ἐστι στενὸς ὅσον τὸ πλάτος τοῦ τζυκανιστηρίου" ("The defile in this case is as narrow as the width of the *chukan*-ground.").—*De Adm. Imp.*, cap. ix. (Bonn ed. iii. 75).

969.—"Cumque inquisitionis sedicio non modica petit pro Constantino . . . ex ea parte qua **Zucanistri** magnitudo portenditur, Constantinus crines solutus per cancellos caput exposuit, suaque ostensione populi mox tumultum sedavit."—*Liudprandus*, in *Pertz, Mon. Germ.*, iii. 333.

". . . he selected certain of his medicines and drugs, and made a *goff-stick* (**jaukan**?) [Burton, 'a bat'] with a hollow handle, into which he introduced them; after which . . . he went again to the King . . . and directed him to repair to the horse-course, and to play with the ball and *goff-stick*. . . ."—*Lane's Arabian Nights*, i. 85-86; [*Burton*, i. 43].

c. 1030-40.—"Whenever you march . . . you must take these people with you, and you must . . . not allow them to drink wine or to play at **chaughān**."—*Baihaki*, in *Elliot*, ii. 120.

1416.—"Bernardus de Castro novo et nonnulli alii in studio Tholosano studentes, ad ludum lignobolini sive **Chucarum** luderunt pro vino et volema, qui ludus est quasi ludus billardi," &c.—MS. quoted in *Henschel's Ducange.*

c. 1420.—"The Τζυκανιστήριον was founded by Theodosius the Less . . . Basilius the Macedonian extended and levelled the Τζυκανιστήριον."—*Georgius Codinus de Antiq. Constant.*, Bonn ed. 81-82.

1516.—Barbosa, speaking of the Mahommedans of Cambay, says: "Saom tam ligeiros e manhosos na sela que a cavalo jogaom ha **choqua**, ho qual joguo eles tem antre sy na conta em que nos temos ho das canas"—(Lisbon ed. 271); *i.e.* "They are so swift and dexterous in the saddle that they play **choca** on horseback, a game which they hold in as high esteem as we do that of the canes" (*i.e.* the *jereed*).

1560.—"They (the Arabs) are such great riders that they play tennis on horseback" (*que jogão a* **choca** *a cavallo*).—*Tenreiro, Itinerario*, ed. 1762, p. 359.

c. 1590.—"His Majesty also plays at **chaugán** in dark nights. . . the balls which are used at night are set on fire. . . . For the sake of adding splendour to the games . . . His Majesty has knobs of gold and silver fixed to the tops of the *chaugān* sticks. If one of them breaks, any player that gets hold of the pieces may keep them."—*Āīn-i-Akbarī*, i. 298; [ii. 303].

1837.—"The game of **choughan** mentioned by Baber is still played everywhere in Tibet; it is nothing but 'hockey on horseback,' and is excellent fun."—*Vigne*, in *J. A. S. Bengal*, vi. 774.

In the following I would say, in justice to the great man whose words are quoted, that *chicane* is used in the quasi-military sense of taking every possible advantage of the ground in a contest:

1761.—"I do suspect that some of the great Ones have had hopes given to them that the Dutch may be induced to join us in this war against the Spaniards,—if such an Event should take place I fear some sacrifices will be made in the East Indies—I pray God my suspicions may be without foundation. I think Delays and **Chicanery** is allowable against those who take Advantage of the times, our Distresses, and situation." — *Unpublished Holograph Letter from Lord Clive*, in India Office Records. *Dated* Berkeley Square, and indorsed 27th Decr. 1761.

1881.—"One would at first sight be inclined to derive the French *chic* from the English 'cheek'; but it appears that the English is itself the derived word, *chic* being an old Romance word signifying *finesse*, or subtlety, and forming the root of our own word **chicanery**." — *Sat. Rev.*, Sept. 10, p. 326 (Essay on French Slang).

CHICK, s.

a. H.—P. *chik;* a kind of screen-blind made of finely-split bamboo, laced with twine, and often painted on the outer side. It is hung or framed in doorways or windows, both in houses and in tents. The thing [which is described by Roe,] may possibly have come in with the Mongols, for we find in Kovalefski's Mongol Dict. (2174) "*Tchik=Natte.*" The Āīn (i. 226) has *chigh*. *Chicks* are now made in London, as well as imported from China and Japan. *Chicks* are described by Clavijo in the tents of Timour's chief wife:

1404.—"And this tent had two doors, one in front of the other, and the first doors were of certain thin coloured wands, joined one to another like in a hurdle, and covered on the outside with a texture of rose-coloured silk, and finely woven; and these doors were made in this fashion, in order that when shut the air might yet enter, whilst those within could see those outside, but those outside could not see those who were within."—§ cxxvi.

[1616.—His wives "whose Curiositye made them breake little holes in a grate of reede that hung before it to gaze on mee."—*Sir T. Roe*, Hak. Soc. ii. 321.]

1673.—"Glass is dear, and scarcely purchaseable . . . therefore their Windows are usually folding doors, screened with **Cheeks** or latises."—*Fryer*, 92.

The pron. *cheek* is still not uncommon among English people:—"The Coach where the Women were was covered with **cheeks**, a sort of hanging Curtain, made with Bents variously coloured with Lacker, and Checquered with Packthred so artificially that you see all without, and yourself within unperceived."—*Fryer*, 83.

1810.—"**Cheeks** or Screens to keep out the glare."—*Williamson, V. M.* ii. 43.

1825.—"The **check** of the tent prevents effectually any person from seeing what passes within. . . ." — *Heber* (ed. 1844), i. 192.

b. Short for *chickeen*, a sum of four rupees. This is the Venetian *zecchino*, *cecchino*, or *sequin*, a gold coin long current on the shores of India, and which still frequently turns up in treasure-trove, and in hoards. In the early part of the 15th century Nicolo Conti mentions that in some parts of India, Venetian ducats, *i.e.* sequins, were current (p. 30). And recently, in fact in our own day, *chick* was a term in frequent Anglo-Indian use, *e.g.* "I'll bet you a **chick**."

The word *zecchino* is from the *Zecca*, or Mint at Venice, and that name is of Arabic origin, from *sikka*, 'a coining die.' The double history of this word is curious. We have just seen how in one form, and by what circuitous secular journey, through Egypt, Venice, India, it has gained a place in the Anglo-Indian Vocabulary. By a directer route it has also found a distinct place in the same repository under the form **Sicca** (q.v.), and in this shape it still retains a ghostly kind of existence at the India Office. It is remarkable how first the spread of Saracenic power and civilisation, then the spread of Venetian commerce and coinage, and lastly the spread of English commerce and power, should thus have brought together two words identical in origin, after so widely divergent a career.

The sequin is sometimes called in the South *shānārcash*, because the Doge with his sceptre is taken for the *Shānār*, or toddy-drawer climbing the palm-tree! [See *Burnell*, *Linschoten*, i. 243.] (See also **VENETIAN**.)

We apprehend that the gambling phrases '*chicken*-stakes' and '*chicken*-hazard' originate in the same word.

1583.—"**Chickinos** which be pieces of Golde woorth seuen shillings a piece sterling."—*Caesar Frederici*, in *Hakl.* ii. 343.

1608.—"When I was there (at Venice) a **chiquiney** was worth eleven livers and twelve sols."—*Çoryat's Çrudities*, ii. 68.

1609.—"Three or four thousand **chequins** were as pretty a proportion to live quietly on, and so give over."—*Pericles, P. of Tyre*, iv. 2.

1612.—"The Grand Signiors Custome of this Port Moha is worth yearly unto him 1500 **chicquenes**."—*Saris*, in *Purchas*, i. 348.

[1616. — "Shee tooke **chickenes** and royalls for her goods."—*Sir T. Roe*, Hak. Soc. i. 228.]

1623.—"Shall not be worth a **chequin**, if it were knock'd at an outcry."—*Beaum. & Flet.*, *The Maid in the Mill*, v. 2.

1689. — "Four Thousand **Checkins** he privately tied to the flooks of an Anchor under Water."—*Ovington*, 418.

1711.—"He (the Broker) will charge 32 *Shahees per* **Chequeen** when they are not worth 31½ in the Bazar."—*Lockyer*, 227.

1727.—"When my Barge landed him, he gave the Cockswain five **Zequeens**, and loaded her back with Poultry and Fruit."—*A. Hamilton*, i. 301; ed. 1744, i. 303.

1767.—"Received . . .

* * * * *

"**Chequins** 5 at 5. Arcot Rs. 25 0 0"

* * * * *

Lord Clive's Account of his Voyage to India, in *Long*, 497.

1866.—

"Whenever master spends a **chick**,
I keep back two rupees, Sir."

Trevelyan, The Dawk Bungalow.

1875.—"'Can't do much harm by losing twenty **chicks**,' observed the Colonel in Anglo-Indian *argot*."—*The Dilemma*, ch. x.

CHICKEN, s. Embroidery; **Chickenwalla**, an itinerant dealer in embroidered handkerchiefs, petticoats, and such like. P. *chikin* or *chikīn*, 'art needlework.' [At Lucknow, the chief centre of the manufacture, this embroidery was formerly done in silk; the term is now applied to hand-worked flowered muslin. (See *Hoey, Monograph*, 88, *Yusuf Ali*, 69.)]

CHICKORE, s. The red-legged partridge, or its close congener *Caccabis chukor*, Gray. It is common in the Western Himālaya, in the N. Punjab, and in Afghanistan. The *francolin* of Moorcroft's Travels is really the *chickore*. The name appears to be Skt. *chakora*, and this disposes of the derivation formerly suggested by one of the present writers, as from the Mongol *tsokhor*, 'dappled or pied' (a word, moreover, which the late Prof. Schiefner informed us is only applied to horses). The name is sometimes applied to other birds. Thus, according to Cunningham, it is applied in Ladak to the Snow-cock (*Tetraogallus Himalayensis*, Gray), and he appears to give *chá-kor* as meaning 'white-bird' in Tibetan. Jerdon gives 'snow *chukor*' and 'strath-*chukor*' as sportsmen's names for this fine bird. And in Bengal Proper the name is applied, by local English sportsmen, to the large handsome partridge (*Ortygornis gularis*, Tem.) of Eastern Bengal, called in H. *kaiyah* or *ban-tītar* ('forest partridge'). See *Jerdon*, ed. 1877, ii. 575. Also the birds described in the extract from Mr. Abbott below do not appear to have been *caccabis* (which he speaks of in the same journal as 'red-legged partridge'). And the use of the word by Persians (apparently) is notable; it does not appear in Persian dictionaries. There is probably some mistake. The birds spoken of may have been the Large Sand-grouse (*Pterocles arenarius*, Pal.), which in both Persia and Afghanistan is called by names meaning 'Black-breast.'

The belief that the *chickore* eats fire, mentioned in the quotation below, is probably from some verbal misconception (quasi *ātish-khōr*?). [This is hardly probable as the idea that the partridge drinks the moonbeams is as old as the Brahma Vaivarta Purāna: "O Lord, I drink in with the partridges of my eyes thy face full of nectar, which resembles the full moon of autumn." Also see *Katha Sarit Sāgara*, tr. by Mr. Tawney (ii. 243), who has kindly given the above references.] Jerdon states that the Afghans call the bird the 'Fire-eater.'

c. 1190.—". . . plantains and fruits, Koils, **Chakors**, peacocks, Sarases, beautiful to behold."—The *Prithirája Rásan of Chand Bardái*, in *Ind. Ant.* i. 273.

In the following passage the word **cator** is supposed by the editor to be a clerical error for *çacor* or *chacor*.

1298.—"The Emperor has had several little houses erected in which he keeps in mew a huge number of **cators**, which are what we call the Great Partridge."—*Marco Polo* (2nd ed.), i. 287.

1520.—"Haidar Alemdâr had been sent by me to the Kafers. He met me below the Pass of Bâdîj, accompanied by some of their chiefs, who brought with them a few skins of wine. While coming down the Pass, he saw prodigious numbers of **Chikûrs**."—*Baber*, 282.

1814.—". . . partridges, quails, and a bird which is called Cupk by the Persians and Afghauns, and the hill **Chikore** by the Indians, and which I understand is known in Europe by the name of the Greek Partridge."—*Elphinstone's Caubool*, ed. 1839, i. 192; ["the same bird which is called **Chicore** by the natives and fire-eater by the English in Bengal."—*Ibid.* ii. 95].

c. 1815.—"One day in the fort he found a hill-partridge enclosed in a wicker basket. . . . This bird is called the **chuckoor**, and is said to eat fire."—*Mrs. Sherwood, Autobiog.*, 440.

1850.—"A flight of birds attracted my attention; I imagine them to be a species of bustard or grouse—black beneath and with much white about the wings—they were beyond our reach; the people called them **Chukore.**"—*K. Abbott, Notes during a Journey in Persia*, in *J. R. Geog. Soc.* xxv. 41.

CHILAW, n.p. A place on the west coast of Ceylon, an old seat of the pearl-fishery. The name is a corruption of the Tam. *salābham*, 'the diving'; in Singhalese it is *Halavatta.* The name was commonly applied by the Portuguese to the whole aggregation of shoals (*Baixos de* **Chilao**) in the Gulf of Manaar, between Ceylon and the coast of Madura and Tinnevelly.

1543.—"Shoals of **Chilao.**" See quotation under **BEADALA.**

1610.—"La pesqueria de **Chilao** . . . por hazerse antiguamente in un puerto del mismo nombre en la isla de Seylan . . . llamado asi por ista causa; por que **chilao**, en lengua Chengala, . . . quiere dezir *pesqueria.*"—*Teixeira*, Pt. ii. 29.

CHILLUM, s. H. *chilam;* "the part of the *hukka* (see **HOOKA**) which contains the tobacco and charcoal balls, whence it is sometimes loosely used for the pipe itself, or the act of smoking it" (*Wilson*). It is also applied to the replenishment of the bowl, in the same way as a man asks for "another glass." The tobacco, as used by the masses in the hubble-bubble, is cut small and kneaded into a pulp with *goor*, *i.e.* molasses, and a little water. Hence actual contact with glowing charcoal is needed to keep it alight.

1781.—"Dressing a hubble-bubble, per week at 3 **chillums** a day.

fan 0, *dubs* 3, *cash* 0."

—*Prison Experiences in Captivity of Hon. J. Lindsay*, in *Lives of Lindsays*, iii.

1811.—"They have not the same scruples for the **Chillum** as for the rest of the Hooka, and it is often lent . . . whereas the very proposition for the Hooka gives rise frequently to the most ridiculous quarrels."—*Solvyns*, iii.

1828.—"Every sound was hushed but the noise of that wind . . . and the occasional bubbling of my *hookah*, which had just been furnished with another **chillum.**"—*The Kuzzilbash*, i. 2.

1829.—"Tugging away at your hookah, find no smoke; a thief having purloined your silver **chelam** and **surpoose.**"—*John Shipp*, ii. 159.

1848.—"Jos however . . . could not think of moving till his baggage was cleared, or of travelling until he could do so with his **chillum.**"—*Vanity Fair*, ii. ch. xxiii.

CHILLUMBRUM, n.p. A town in S. Arcot, which is the site of a famous temple of Siva, properly *Shidamburam.* Etym. obscure. [Garstin (*Man. S. Arcot*, 400) gives the name as *Chedambram*, or more correctly *Chittambalam*, 'the atmosphere of wisdom.']

1755.—"Scheringham (Seringam), **Schalembron**, et Gengy m'offroient également la retraite après laquelle je soupirois."—*Anquetil du Perron, Zendav. Disc. Prelim.* xxviii.

CHILLUMCHEE, s. H. *chilamchī*, also *silfchī*, and *silpchī*, of which *chilamchī* is probably a corruption. A basin of brass (as in Bengal), or tinned copper (as usually in the West and South) for washing hands. The form of the word seems Turkish, but we cannot trace it.

1715.—"We prepared for our first present, viz., 1000 gold mohurs . . . the unicorn's horn . . . the astoa (?) and **chelumgie** of Manilla work. . . ."—In *Wheeler*, ii. 246.

1833.—"Our supper was a *peelaw* . . . when it was removed a **chillumchee** and goblet of warm water was handed round, and each washed his hands and mouth."—*P. Gordon, Fragment of the Journal of a Tour*, &c.

1851.—"When a **chillumchee** of water *sans* soap was provided, 'Have you no soap?' Sir C. Napier asked——"—*Mawson, Indian Command of Sir C. Napier.*

1857.—"I went alone to the Fort Adjutant, to report my arrival, and inquire to what regiment of the Bengal army I was likely to be posted.

"'Army!—regiment!' was the reply. 'There is *no* Bengal Army; it is all in revolt. . . . Provide yourself with a camp-bedstead, and a **chillumchee**, and wait for orders.'

"I saluted and left the presence of my superior officer, deeply pondering as to the possible nature and qualities of a **chillumchee**, but not venturing to enquire further."—*Lt.-Col. Lewin, A Fly on the Wheel*, p. 3.

There is an Anglo-Indian tradition, which we would not vouch for, that one of the orators on the great Hastings trial depicted the oppressor on some occasion, as "grasping his *chillum* in one hand and his **chillumchee** in the other."

The latter word is used chiefly by Anglo-Indians of the Bengal Presidency and their servants. In Bombay the article has another name. And it is told of a gallant veteran of the old Bengal Artillery, who was full of "Presidential" prejudices, that on hearing the Bombay army commended by a brother officer, he broke out in just wrath: "The Bombay Army! Don't talk to me of the Bombay Army! They call a **chillumchee** a *gindy!*——THE BEASTS!"

CHILLY, s. The popular Anglo-Indian name of the pod of red pepper (*Capsicum fruticosum* and *C. annuum*, Nat. Ord. *Solanaceae*). There can be little doubt that the name, as stated by Bontius in the quotation, was taken from *Chili* in S. America, whence the plant was carried to the Indian Archipelago, and thence to India.

[1604.—"Indian pepper. . . . In the language of Cusco, it is called Vchu, and in that of Mexico, **chili**."—*Grimston*, tr. *D'Acosta, H. W. Indies*, I. Bk. iv. 239 (*Stanf. Dict.*)]

1631.—". . . eos addere fructum Ricini Americani, quod **lada Chili** Malaii vocant, quasi dicas Piper e **Chile**, Brasiliae contermina regione."—*Jac. Bontii*, Dial. V. p. 10.

Again (lib. vi. cap. 40, p. 131) Bontius calls it '*piper Chilensis*,' and also 'Ricinus Braziliensis.' But his commentator, Piso, observes that Ricinus is quite improper; "vera Piperis sive Capsici Braziliensis species apparet." Bontius says it was a common custom of natives, and even of certain Dutchmen, to keep a piece of **chilly** continually chewed, but he found it intolerable.

1848.—"'Try a **chili** with it, Miss Sharp,' said Joseph, really interested. 'A **chili**?' said Rebecca, gasping. 'Oh yes!' . . . 'How fresh and green they look,' she said, and put one into her mouth. It was hotter than the curry; flesh and blood could bear it no longer."—*Vanity Fair*, ch. iii.

CHIMNEY-GLASS, s. Gardener's name, on the Bombay side of India, for the flower and plant *Allamanda cathartica* (*Sir G. Birdwood*).

CHINA, n.p. The European knowledge of this name in the forms *Thinae* and *Sinae* goes back nearly to the Christian era. The famous mention of the *Sinim* by the prophet Isaiah would carry us much further back, but we fear the possibility of that referring to the Chinese must be abandoned, as must be likewise, perhaps, the similar application of the name *Chinas* in ancient Sanskrit works. The most probable origin of the name—which is essentially a name applied by *foreigners* to the country—as yet suggested, is that put forward by Baron F. von Richthofen, that it comes from *Jih-nan*, an old name of Tongking, seeing that in Jih-nan lay the only port which was open for foreign trade with China at the beginning of our era, and that that province was then included administratively within the limits of China Proper (see *Richthofen*, *China*, i. 504-510; the same author's papers in the *Trans. of the Berlin Geog. Soc.* for 1876; and a paper by one of the present writers in *Proc. R. Geog. Soc.*, November 1882.)

Another theory has been suggested by our friend M. Terrien de la Couperie in an elaborate note, of which we can but state the general gist. Whilst he quite accepts the suggestion that Kiao-chi or Tongking, anciently called *Kiao-ti*, was the *Kattigara* of Ptolemy's authority, he denies that *Jih-nan* can have been the origin of Sinae. This he does on two chief grounds: (1) That Jih-nan was not Kiao-chi, but a province a good deal further south, corresponding to the modern province of *An* (*Nghé Ane*, in the map of M. Dutreuil de Rhins, the capital of which is about 2° 17′ in lat. S. of Hanoi). This is distinctly stated in the Official Geography of Annam. *An* was one of the twelve provinces of Cochin China proper till 1820-41, when, with two others, it was transferred to Tongking. Also, in the Chinese Historical Atlas, Jih-nan lies in Chen-Ching, *i.e.* Cochin-China. (2) That the ancient pronunciation of Jih-nan, as indicated by the Chinese authorities of the Han period, was *Nit-nam*. It is still pronounced in Sinico-Annamite (the most archaic of the Chinese dialects) *Nhut-nam*, and in Cantonese *Yat-nam*. M. Terrien further points out that the export of Chinese goods, and the traffic with the south and west, was for several centuries B.C. monopolised by the State of *Tsen* (now pronounced in Sinico-Annamite *Chen*, and in Mandarin *Tien*), which corresponded to the centre and west of modern Yun-nan. The *She-ki* of Szema Tsien (B.C. 91), and the Annals of the Han Dynasty afford interesting information on this subject. When the Emperor Wu-ti, in consequence of Chang-Kien's information brought back from Bactria, sent envoys to find the route followed by the traders of Shuh (*i.e.* Sze-chuen) to India, these envoys were detained by Tang-Kiang, King of Tsen, who objected to their exploring trade-routes through his territory, saying haughtily: "Has the Han a greater dominion than ours?"

M. Terrien conceives that as the only communication of this Tsen State with the Sea would be by the Song-Koi R., the emporium of sea-trade with that State would be at its mouth, viz. at Kiaoti or Kattigara. Thus, he considers, the name of *Tsen*, this powerful and arrogant State, the monopoliser of trade-routes, is in all probability that which spread far and wide the name of *Chīn*, *Sīn*, *Sinae*, *Thinae*, and preserved its predominance in the mouths of foreigners, even when, as in the 2nd century of our era, the great Empire of the Han has extended over the Delta of the Song-Koi.

This theory needs more consideration than we can now give it. But it will doubtless have discussion elsewhere, and it does not disturb Richthofen's identification of Kattigara.

[Prof. Giles regards the suggestions of Richthofen and T. de la Couperie as mere guesses. From a recent reconsideration of the subject he has come to the conclusion that the name may possibly be derived from the name of a dynasty, *Ch'in* or *Ts'in*, which flourished B.C. 255-207, and became widely known in India, Persia, and other Asiatic countries, the final *a* being added by the Portuguese.]

c. A.D. 80-89.—"Behind this country (*Chrysē*) the sea comes to a termination somewhere in **Thin**, and in the interior of that country, quite to the north, there is a very great city called **Thinae**, from which raw silk and silk thread and silk stuffs are brought overland through Bactria to Barygaza, as they are on the other hand by the Ganges River to Limyricē. It is not easy, however, to get to this **Thin**, and few and far between are those who come from it. . . ."—*Periplus Maris Erythraei*; see Müller, *Geog. Gr. Min.* i. 303.

c. 150—"The inhabited part of our earth is bounded on the east by the Unknown Land which lies along the region occupied by the easternmost races of Asia Minor, the **Sinae** and the natives of Sericē. . . ."—*Claudius Ptolemy*, Bk. vii. ch. 5.

c. 545.—"The country of silk, I may mention, is the remotest of all the Indies, lying towards the left when you enter the Indian Sea, but a vast distance further off than the Persian Gulf or that island which the Indians call Selediba, and the Greeks Taprobane. **Tzinitza** (elsewhere **Tzinista**) is the name of the Country, and the Ocean compasses it round to the left, just as the same Ocean compasses Barbari (*i.e.* the Somāli Country) round to the right. And the Indian philosophers called Brachmans tell you that if you were to stretch a straight cord from **Tzinitza** through Persia to the Roman territory, you would just divide the world in halves."—*Cosmas, Topog. Christ.*, Bk. II.

c. 641.—"In 641 the King of Magadha (Behar, &c.) sent an ambassador with a letter to the Chinese Court. The emperor . . . in return directed one of his officers to go to the King . . . and to invite his submission. The King Shiloyto (Siladitya) was all astonishment. 'Since time immemorial,' he asked his officer, 'did ever an ambassador come from *Mohochintan*?' . . . The Chinese author remarks that in the tongue of the barbarians the Middle Kingdom is called *Mohochintan* (Mahā-**Chīna**-sthāna)."—From *Cathay*, &c., lxviii.

781.—"Adam Priest and Bishop and Pope of **Tzinesthan**. . . . The preachings of our Fathers to the King of **Tzinia**."—*Syriac Part* of the *Inscription of Singanfu*.

11th Century.—The "King of China" (**Shina***ttarashan*) appears in the list of provinces and monarchies in the great Inscription of the Tanjore Pagoda.

1128.—"**Chīna** and *Mahā***chīna** appear in a list of places producing silk and other cloths, in the *Abhilashitārthachintāmani* of the Chālukya King."—*Somesvaradiva* (*MS.*)* Bk. III. ch. 6.

1298.—"You must know the Sea in which lie the Islands of those parts is called the Sea of **Chin**. . . . For, in the language in those Isles, when they say **Chin**, 'tis Manzi they mean."—*Marco Polo*, Bk. III. ch. iv.

* It may be well to append here the whole list which I find on a scrap of paper in Dr. Burnell's handwriting (Y):

Pohālapura.
Chīnavallī.
Avantikshetra (*Ujjain*).
Nāgapaṭṭana (*Negapatam?*)
Pāṇḍyadeśa (*Madura*).
Allikākara.
Simhaladvīpa (*Ceylon*).
Gopākasthāna (! ?).
Gujaṇasthāna.
Thāṇaka (*Thana?*)
Aṇitavāta (*Anhilvād*).
Sunāpura.
Mūlasthāna (*Multan*).
Toṭṭideśa.
Pañchapaṭṭaṇa.
Chīna.
Mahāchīna.
Kalingadeśa (*Telugu Country*).
Vaṅgadeśa (*Bengal*).

c. 1300.—"Large ships, called in the language of **Chin** 'junks,' bring various sorts of choice merchandize and cloths. . . ."—*Rashíduddín*, in *Elliot.* i. 69.

1516.—". . . there is the Kingdom of **China**, which they say is a very extensive dominion, both along the coast of the sea, and in the interior. . . ."—*Barbosa*, 204.

1563.—"*R.* Then Ruelius and Mathiolus of Siena say that the best camphor is from **China**, and that the best of all Camphors is that purified by a certain barbarian King whom they call King (of) **China**.

"*O.* Then you may tell Ruelius and Mathiolus of Siena that though they are so well acquainted with Greek and Latin, there's no need to make such a show of it as to call every body 'barbarians' who is not of their own race, and that besides this they are quite wrong in the fact . . . that the King of China does not occupy himself with making camphor, and is in fact one of the greatest Kings known in the world."—*Garcia De Orta*, f. 45*b*.

c. 1590.—"Near to this is Pegu, which former writers called **Cheen**, accounting this to be the capital city."—*Ayeen*, ed. 1800, ii. 4; [tr. *Jarrett*, ii. 119]. (See **MACHEEN**.)

CHINA, s. In the sense of porcelain this word (*Chīnī*, &c.) is used in Asiatic languages as well as in English. In English it does not occur in Minshew (2nd ed. 1627), though it does in some earlier publications. [The earliest quotation in *N.E.D.* is from *Cogan's Pinto*, 1653.] The phrase *China-dishes* as occurring in Drake and in Shakspere, shows how the word took the sense of porcelain in our own and other languages. The phrase *China-dishes* as first used was analogous to *Turkey-carpets.* But in the latter we have never lost the geographical sense of the adjective. In the word *turquoises*, again, the phrase was no doubt originally *pierres turquoises*, or the like, and here, as in *china dishes*, the specific has superseded the generic sense. The use of *arab* in India for an Arab horse is analogous to *china.* The word is used in the sense of a *china dish* in *Lane's Arabian Nights*, iii. 492; [Burton, I. 375].

851.—"There is in China a very fine clay with which they make vases transparent like bottles; water can be seen inside of them. These vases are made of clay."—*Reinaud, Relations*, i. 34.

c. 1350.—"**China**-ware (*al-fakhkhār al-***Sīnīy**) is not made except in the cities of Zaitūn and of Sīn Kalān. . . ."—*Ibn Batuta*, iv. 256.

c. 1530.—"I was passing one day along a street in Damascus, when I saw a slave-boy let fall from his hands a great China dish (*ṣaḥfat min al-bakhkhār al-***Sīnīy**) which they call in that country *sahn.* It broke, and a crowd gathered round the little Mameluke."—*Ibn Batuta*, i. 238.

c. 1567.—"Le mercantie ch'andauano ogn' anno da Goa a Bezeneger erano molti caualli Arabi . . . e anche *pezze di* **China**, zafaran, e scarlatti."—*Cesare de' Federici*, in *Ramusio*, iii. 389.

1579.—". . . we met with one ship more loaden with linnen, China silke, and **China dishes**. . . ."—*Drake, World Encompassed*, in Hak. Soc. 112.

c. 1580.—"Usum vasorum aureorum et argenteorum Aegyptii rejecerunt, ubi murrhina vasa adinvenere; quae ex India afferuntur, et ex ea regione quam **Sini** vocant, ubi conficiuntur ex variis lapidibus, praecipueque ex jaspide."—*Prosp. Alpinus*, Pt. I. p. 55.

c. 1590.—"The gold and silver dishes are tied up in red cloths, and those in Copper and **China** (*chīnī*) in white ones."—*Āīn*, i. 58.

c. 1603.—". . . as it were in a fruit-dish, a dish of some threepence, your honours have seen such dishes; they are not **China** dishes, but very good dishes."—*Measure for Measure*, ii. 1.

1608-9.—"A faire **China** dish (which cost ninetie Rupias, or forty-five Reals of eight) was broken."—*Hawkins*, in *Purchas*, i. 220.

1609.—"He has a lodging in the Strand for the purpose, or to watch when ladies are gone to the **China**-house, or the Exchange, that he may meet them by chance and give them presents. . . ."

"Ay, sir: his wife was the rich **China**-woman, that the courtiers visited so often."—*Ben Jonson, Silent Woman*, i. 1.

1615.—

". . . Oh had I now my Wishes,
Sure you should learn to make their **China**
Dishes."

Doggrel prefixed to *Coryat's Crudities*.

c. 1690.—Kaempfer in his account of the Persian Court mentions that the department where porcelain and plate dishes, &c., were kept and cleaned was called **Chīn-khāna**, 'the China-closet'; and those servants who carried in the dishes were called **Chīnīkash**.—*Amoen. Exot.*, p. 125.

1711.—"Purselaine, or **China**-ware is so tender a Commodity that good Instructions are as necessary for Package as Purchase."—*Lockyer*, 126.

1747.—"The Art of Cookery made Plain and Easy; which far Exceeds any Thing of the Kind yet Published. By a Lady. London. Printed for the Author, and Sold by Mrs. Asburn a **China** Shop Woman, Corner of Fleet Ditch, MDCCXLVII." This the title of the original edition of Mrs. Glass's Cookery, as given by G. A. Sala, in *Illd. News*, May 12, 1883.

1876.—"Schuyler mentions that the best native earthenware in Turkistan is called **Chīnī**, and bears a clumsy imitation of a Chinese mark"—(see *Turkistan*, i. 187.)

For the following interesting note on the Arabic use we are indebted to Professor Robertson Smith:—

Ṣīnīya is spoken of thus in the Latāifo'l-ma'ārif of al-Th'ālibī, ed. De Jong, Leyden, 1867, a book written in A.D. 990. "The Arabs were wont to call all elegant vessels and the like **Sīnīya** (*i.e.* Chinese), whatever they really were, because of the specialty of the Chinese in objects of vertu; and this usage remains in the common word *ṣawānī* (pl. of *ṣīnīya*) to the present day."

So in the *Tajāribo'l-Omam* of Ibn Maskowaih (Fr. Hist. Ar. ii. 457), it is said that at the wedding of Mamūn with Būrān "her grandmother strewed over her 1000 pearls from a **sīnīya** of gold." In Egypt the familiar round brass trays used to dine off, are now called *ṣīnīya* (vulgo *ṣanīya*), [the *ṣīnī*, *ṣenī* of N. India] and so is a European saucer.

The expression *ṣīnīyat al ṣīn*, "A Chinese *ṣīnīya*," is quoted again by De Goeje from a poem of Abul-shibl Agānī, xiii. 27. [See **SNEAKER.**]

[CHINA-BEER, s. Some kind of liquor used in China, perhaps a variety of *saké*.

[1615.—"I carid a jarr of **China** Beare."—*Cocks's Diary*, i. 34.]

CHINA-BUCKEER, n.p. One of the chief Delta-mouths of the Irawadi is so called in marine charts. We have not been able to ascertain the origin of the name, further than that Prof. Forchhammer, in his *Notes on the Early Hist. and Geog. of Br. Burma* (p. 16), states that the country between Rangoon and Bassein, *i.e.* on the west of the Rangoon River, bore the name of *Pokhara*, of which *Buckeer* is a corruption. This does not explain the *China*.

CHINA-ROOT, s. A once famous drug, known as *Radix Chinae* and *Tuber Chinae*, being the tuber of various species of *Smilax* (N. O. *Smilaceae*, the same to which sarsaparilla belongs). It was said to have been used with good effect on Charles V. when suffering from gout, and acquired a great repute. It was also much used in the same way as sarsaparilla. It is now quite obsolete in England, but is still held in esteem in the native pharmacopœias of China and India.

1563.—"*R.* I wish to take to Portugal some of the **Root** or Wood of **China**, since it is not a contraband drug. . . .

"*O.* This wood or root grows in China, an immense country, presumed to be on the confines of Muscovy . . . and because in all these regions, both in China and in Japan, there exists the *morbo napolitano*, the merciful God hath willed to give them this root for remedy, and with it the good physicians there know well the treatment."—*Garcia*, f. 177.

c. 1590.—"Sircar Silhet is very mountainous. . . . **China-Root** (*chob-chīnī*) is produced here in great plenty, which was but lately discovered by some Turks."—*Ayeen Akb.*, by *Gladwin*, ii. 10; [ed. *Jarrett*, ii. 124].

1598.—"The **roote of China** is commonlie vsed among the Egyptians . . . specially for a consumption, for the which they seeth the roote China in broth of a henne or cocke, whereby they become whole and faire of face."—*Dr. Paludanus*, in *Linschoten*, 124, [Hak. Soc. ii. 112].

c. 1610.—"Quant à la verole. . . . Ils la guerissent sans suer avec du **bois d'Eschine.** . . ."—*Pyrard de Laval*, ii. 9 (ed. 1679); [Hak. Soc. ii. 13; also see i. 182].

[c. 1690.—"The caravans returned with musk, **China-wood** (*bois de Chine*)."—*Bernier*, ed. *Constable*, p. 425.]

CHINAPATAM, n.p. A name sometimes given by the natives to Madras. The name is now written *Shennai-Shenna-ppatanam*, Tam., in Tel. *Chennapattanamu*, and the following is the origin of that name according to the statement given in W. Hamilton's *Hindostan*.

On "this part of the Coast of Coromandel . . . the English . . . possessed no fixed establishment until A.D. 1639, in which year, on the 1st of March, a grant was received from the descendants of the Hindoo dynasty of Bijanagur, then reigning at Chandergherry, for the erection of a fort. This document from Sree Rung Rayeel expressly enjoins, that the town and fort to be erected at Madras shall be called after his own name, *Sree Rungà Rayapatam;* but the local governor or Naik, Damerla Vencatadri, who first invited Mr. Francis Day, the chief of Armagon, to remove to Madras, had previously intimated to him that he would have the new English establishment founded in the name of his father Chennappa, and the name of Chenappapatam continues to be universally applied to the town of Madras by the natives of that division of the south of India named Dravida."—(Vol. ii. p. 413).

Dr. Burnell doubted this origin of the name, and considered that the actual name could hardly have been formed from that of Chenappa. It is possible that some name similar to

Chinapatan was borne by the place previously. It will be seen under **MADRAS** that Barros curiously connects the Chinese with St. Thomé. To this may be added this passage from the English translation of *Mendoza's China*, the original of which was published in 1585, the translation by R. Parke in 1588:—

"... it is plainely seene that they did come with the shipping vnto the Indies ... so that at this day there is great memory of them in the Ilands Philippinas and on the cost of Coromande, which is the cost against the Kingdome of Norsinga towards the sea of Bengala (misprinted *Cengala*); *whereas is a town called vnto this day* the Soile of the Chinos *for that they did reedifie and make the same*"—(i. 94).

I strongly suspect that this was *Chinapatam*, or Madras. [On the other hand, the popular derivation is accepted in the *Madras Gloss.*, p. 163. The gold plate containing the grant of Sri Ranga Rāja is said to have been kept by the English for more than a century, till its loss in 1746 at the capture of Madras by the French.—(*Wheeler, Early Rec.*, 49).]

1780.—"The Nawaub sent him to **Cheena Pattun** (Madras) under the escort of a small party of light Cavalry."—*H. of Hydur Naik*, 395.

CHINCHEW, CHINCHEO, n.p. A port of Fuhkien in China. Some ambiguity exists as to the application of the name. In English charts the name is now attached to the ancient and famous port of Chwan-chau-fu (*Thsiouan-chéou-fou* of French writers), the Zayton of Marco Polo and other medieval travellers. But the Chincheo of the Spaniards and Portuguese to this day, and the *Chinchew* of older English books, is, as Mr. G. Phillips pointed out some years ago, not Chwan-chau-fu, but *Chang-chau-fu*, distant from the former some 80 m. in a direct line, and about 140 by navigation. The province of Fuhkien is often called *Chincheo* by the early Jesuit writers. Changchau and its dependencies seem to have constituted the ports of Fuhkien with which Macao and Manilla communicated, and hence apparently they applied the same name to the port and the province, though Chang-chau was never the official capital of Fukhien (see *Encyc. Britann.*, 9th ed. s.v. and references there). **Chincheos** is used for "people of Fuhkien" in a quotation under **COMPOUND**.

1517.—"... in another place called **Chincheo**, where the people were much richer than in Canton (*Cantão*). From that city used every year, before our people came to Malaca, to come to Malaca 4 junks loaded with gold, silver, and silk, returning laden with wares from India."—*Correa*, ii. 529.

CHIN-CHIN. In the "pigeon English" of Chinese ports this signifies 'salutation, compliments,' or 'to salute,' and is much used by Englishmen as slang in such senses. It is a corruption of the Chinese phrase *ts'ing-ts'ing*, Pekingese *ch'ing-ch'ing*, a term of salutation answering to 'thank-you,' 'adieu.' In the same vulgar dialect *chin-chin joss* means religious worship of any kind (see **JOSS**). It is curious that the phrase occurs in a quaint story told to William of Rubruck by a Chinese priest whom he met at the Court of the Great Kaan (see below). And it is equally remarkable to find the same story related with singular closeness of correspondence out of "the Chinese books of Geography" by Francesco Carletti, 350 years later (in 1600). He calls the creatures **Zinzin** (*Ragionamenti di F. C.*, pp. 138-9).

1253.—"One day there sate by me a certain priest of Cathay, dressed in a red cloth of exquisite colour, and when I asked him whence they got such a dye, he told me how in the eastern parts of Cathay there were lofty cliffs on which dwelt certain creatures in all things partaking of human form, except that their knees did not bend. ... The huntsmen go thither, taking very strong beer with them, and make holes in the rocks which they fill with this beer. ... Then they hide themselves and these creatures come out of their holes and taste the liquor, and call out '**Chin Chin.**'"—*Itinerarium*, in *Rec. de Voyages*, &c., iv. 328.

Probably some form of this phrase is intended in the word used by Pinto in the following passage, which Cogan leaves untranslated:—

c. 1540.—"So after we had saluted one another after the manner of the Country, they went and anchored by the shore" (in orig. "*despois de se fazerem as suas e as nossas salvas a* **Charachina** *como entre este gente se custuma.*")—In *Cogan*, p. 56; in orig. ch. xlvii.

1795.—"The two junior members of the Chinese deputation came at the appointed hour. ... On entering the door of the marquee they both made an abrupt stop, and resisted all solicitation to advance to chairs that had been prepared for them, until I should first be seated; in this dilemma, Dr. Buchanan, who had visited China, advised me what was to be done; I immediately seized on the foremost, whilst the Doctor himself grappled with the second; thus we soon fixed them in their seats, both parties during the struggle, repeating **Chin Chin, Chin Chin**, the Chinese term of salutation."—*Symes, Embassy to Ava*, 295.

1829.—"One of the Chinese servants came to me and said, 'Mr. Talbot **chin-chin** you come down.'"—*The Fankwae at Canton*, p. 20.

1880.—"But far from thinking it any shame to deface our beautiful language, the English seem to glory in its distortion, and will often ask one another to come to 'chow-chow' instead of dinner; and send their '**chin-chin**,' even in letters, rather than their compliments; most of them ignorant of the fact that '*chow-chow*' is no more Chinese than it is Hebrew; that '*chin-chin*,' though an expression used by the Chinese, does not in its true meaning come near to the 'good-bye, old fellow,' for which it is often used, or the compliments for which it is frequently substituted."—*W. Gill, River of Golden Sand*, i. 156; [ed. 1883, p. 41].

CHINSURA, n.p. A town on the Hoogly River, 26 miles above Calcutta, on the west bank, which was the seat of a Dutch settlement and factory down to 1824, when it was ceded to us by the Treaty of London, under which the Dutch gave up Malacca and their settlements in continental India, whilst we withdrew from Sumatra. [The place gave its name to a kind of cloth, *Chinechuras* (see **PIECE-GOODS**).]

1684.—"This day between 3 and 6 o'clock in the Afternoon, Capt. Richardson and his Sergeant, came to my house in ye **Chinchera**, and brought me this following message from ye President. . . ."—*Hedges, Diary*, Hak. Soc. i. 166.

1705.—"La Loge appellée Chamdernagor est une très-belle Maison située sur le bord d'un des bras du fleuve de Gange. . . . À une lieue de la Loge il y a une grande Ville appellée **Chinchurat**. . . ."—*Luillier*, 64-65.

1726.—"The place where our Lodge (or Factory) is is properly called **Sinternu** [*i.e.* Chinsura] and not Hoogli (which is the name of the village)."—*Valentijn*, v. 162.

1727.—"**Chinchura**, where the Dutch Emporium stands . . . the Factors have a great many good Houses standing pleasantly on the River-Side; and all of them have pretty Gardens."—*A. Hamilton*, ii. 20; ed. 1744, ii. 18.

[1753.—"**Shinshura.**" See quotation under **CALCUTTA**.]

CHINTS, CHINCH, s. A bug. This word is now quite obsolete both in India and in England. It is a corruption of the Portuguese *chinche*, which again is from *cimex*. Mrs. Trollope, in her once famous book on the Domestic Manners of the Americans, made much of a supposed instance of affected squeamishness in American ladies, who used the word *chintses* instead of *bugs*. But she was ignorant of the fact that *chints* was an old and proper name for the objectionable exotic insect, 'bug' being originally but a figurative (and perhaps a polite) term, 'an object of disgust and horror' (*Wedgwood*). Thus the case was exactly the opposite of what she chose to imagine; *chints* was the real name, *bug* the more or less affected euphonism.

1616.—"In the night we were likewise very much disquieted with another sort, called *Musqueetoes*, like our Gnats, but some-what less; and in that season we were very much troubled with **Chinches**, another sort of little troublesome and offensive creatures, like little *Tikes*: and these annoyed us two wayes; as first by their biting and stinging, and then by their stink."—*Terry*, ed. 1665, p. 372; [ed. 1777, p. 117].

1645.—". . . for the most part the bedsteads in Italy are of forged iron gilded, since it is impossible to keepe the wooden ones from the **chimices**."—*Evelyn's Diary*, Sept. 29.

1673.—". . . Our Bodies broke out into small fiery Pimples . . . augmented by Muskeetoe-Bites, and **Chinces** raising Blisters on us."—*Fryer*, 35.

" "**Chints** are venomous, and if squeezed leave a most Poysonous Stench."—*Ibid.* 189.

CHINTZ, s. A printed or spotted cotton cloth; Port. *chita*; Mahr. *chīt*, and H. *chīnt*. The word in this last form occurs (c. 1590) in the *Āīn-i-Akbarī* (i. 95). It comes apparently from the Skt. *chitra*, 'variegated, speckled.' The best *chintzes* were bought on the Madras coast, at Masulipatam and Sadras. The French form of the word is *chite*, which has suggested the possibility of our *sheet* being of the same origin. But *chite* is apparently of Indian origin, through the Portuguese, whilst *sheet* is much older than the Portuguese communication with India. Thus (1450) in Sir T. Cumberworth's will he directs his "wreched body to be beryd in a *chitte* with owte any kyste" (*Academy*, Sept. 27, 1879, p. 230).

The resemblance to the Indian forms in this is very curious.

1614.—"... **chintz** and chadors...."—*Peyton*, in *Purchas*, i. 530.

[1616.—"3 per **Chint** bramport."—*Cocks's Diary*, i. 171.

[1623.—"Linnen stamp'd with works of sundry colours (which they call **cit**)."—*P. della Valle*, Hak. Soc. i. 45.]

1653.—"**Chites** en Indou signifie des toilles imprimeés."—*De la Boullaye-le-Gouz*, ed. 1647, p. 536.

c. 1666.—"Le principal trafic des Hollandois à Amedabad, est de **chites**, qui sont de toiles peintes."—*Thevenot*, v. 35. In the English version (1687) this is written **schites** (iv. ch. v.).

1676.—"**Chites** or Painted Calicuts, which they call *Calmendar*, that is done with a pencil, are made in the Kingdom of Golconda, and particularly about *Masulipatam*."—*Tavernier*, E.T., p. 126; [ed. *Ball*, ii. 4].

1725.—"The returns that are injurious to our manufactures, or growth of our own country, are printed calicoes, **chintz**, wrought silks, stuffs, of herba, and barks."—*Defoe*, *New Voyage round the World*. *Works*, Oxford, 1840, p. 161.

1726.—"The Warehouse Keeper reported to the Board, that the **chintzes**, being brought from painting, had been examined at the sorting godown, and that it was the general opinion that both the cloth and the paintings were worse than the musters."—In *Wheeler*, ii. 407.

c. 1733.—

"No, let a charming **chintz** and Brussels lace
Wrap my cold limbs, and shade my lifeless face."
Pope, *Moral Essays*, i. 248.

"And, when she sees her friend in deep despair,
Observes how much a **Chintz** exceeds Mohair...."
Ibid. ii. 170.

1817.—"Blue cloths, and **chintzes** in particular, have always formed an extensive article of import from Western India."—*Raffles*, *H. of Java*, i. 86; [2nd ed. i. 95, and comp. i. 190].

In the earlier books about India some kind of *chintz* is often termed **pintado** (q.v.). See the phraseology in the quotation from Wheeler above.

This export from India to Europe has long ceased. When one of the present writers was Sub-Collector of the Madras District (1866-67), chintzes were still figured by an old man at Sadras, who had been taught by the Dutch, the cambric being furnished to him by a Madras **Chetty** (q.v.). He is now dead, and the business has ceased; in fact the colours for the process are no longer to be had.* The former *chintz* manufactures of Pulicat are mentioned by *Correa*, *Lendas*, ii. 2, p. 567. Havart (1693) mentions the manufacture at Sadras (i. 92), and gives a good description of the process of painting these cloths, which he calls **chitsen** (iii. 13). There is also a very complete account in the *Lettres Édifiantes*, xiv. 116 *seqq.*

In Java and Sumatra *chintzes* of a very peculiar kind of marbled pattern are still manufactured by women, under the name of *bātik*.

CHIPE, s. In Portuguese use, from Tamil *shippi*, 'an oyster.' The pearl-oysters taken in the pearl-fisheries of Tuticorin and Manār.

[1602.—"And the fishers on that coast gave him as tribute one day's oysters (*hum dia de* **chipo**), that is the result of one day's pearl fishing."—*Couto*, Dec. 7, Bk. VIII. ch. ii.]

1685.—"The **chipe**, for so they call those

* I leave this passage as Dr. Burnell wrote it. But though limited to a specific locality, of which I doubt not it was true, it conveys an idea of the entire extinction of the ancient chintz production which I find is not justified by the facts, as shown in a most interesting letter from Mr. Purdon Clarke, C.S.I., of the India Museum. One kind is still made at Masulipatam, under the superintendence of Persian merchants, to supply the Ispahan market and the "Moghul" traders at Bombay. At Pulicat very peculiar chintzes are made, which are entirely *Kalam Kārī* work, or hand-painted (apparently the word now used instead of the *Calmendār* of Tavernier,—see above, and under **CALAMANDER**). This is a work of infinite labour, as the ground has to be stopped off with wax almost as many times as there are colours used. At Combaconum Sarongs (q.v.) are printed for the Straits. Very bold printing is done at Wālājāpet in N. Arcot, for sale to the Moslem at Hyderabad and Bangalore.

An anecdote is told me by Mr. Clarke which indicates a caution as to more things than chintz printing. One particular kind of chintz met with in S. India, he was assured by the vendor, was printed at W——; but he did not recognize the locality. Shortly afterwards, visiting for the second time the city of X. (we will call it), where he had already been assured by the collector's native aids that there was no such manufacture, and showing the stuff, with the statement of its being made at W——, 'Why,' said the collector, 'that is where I live!' Immediately behind his bungalow was a small bazar, and in this the work was found going on, though on a small scale.

Just so we shall often find persons "who have been in India, and on the spot"—asseverating that at such and such a place there are no missions or no converts; whilst those who have cared to know, know better.—(H. Y.)

[For Indian chintzes, see Forbes Watson, *Textile Manufactures*, 90 *seqq.*; Mukharji, *Art Manufactures of India*, 348 *seqq.*; S. H. Hadi, *Mon. on Dyes and Dyeing in the N.W.P. and Oudh*, 44 *seqq.*; Francis, *Mon. on Punjab Cotton Industry*, 6.]

oysters which their boats are wont to fish."—*Ribeiro*, f. 63.

1710.—"Some of these oysters or **chepis**, as the natives call them, produce pearls, but such are rare, the greater part producing only seed pearls (*aljofres*) [see **ALJOFAR**]." *Sousa, Oriente Conquist.* ii. 243.

CHIRETTA, s. H. *chirāītā*, Mahr. *kirāītā*. A Himalayan herbaceous plant of the order *Gentianaceae* (*Swertia Chirata*, Ham.; *Ophelia Chirata*, Griesbach; *Gentiana Chirayita*, Roxb.; *Agathetes chirayta*, Don.), the dried twigs of which, infused, afford a pure bitter tonic and febrifuge. Its Skt. name *kirāta-tikta*, 'the bitter plant of the *Kirātas*,' refers its discovery to that people, an extensively-diffused forest tribe, east and north-east of Bengal, the Κιῤῥάδαι of the Periplus, and the people of the Κιῤῥάδια of Ptolemy. There is no indication of its having been known to G. de Orta.

[1773.—"*Kol Meg* in Bengal; **Creat** in Bombay. . . . It is excessively bitter, and given as a stomachic and vermifuge."—*Ives*, 471.]

1820.—"They also give a bitter decoction of the neem (*Melia azadirachta*) and **chereeta**."—*Acc. of the Township of Luny*, in *Trans. Lit. Soc. of Bombay*, ii. 232.

1874.—"**Chiretta** has long been held in esteem by the Hindus. . . . In England it began to attract some attention about 1829; and in 1839 was introduced into the Edinburgh Pharmacopœia. The plant was first described by Roxburgh in 1814."—*Hanbury and Flückiger*, 392.

CHIT, CHITTY, s. A letter or note; also a certificate given to a servant, or the like; a pass. H. *chiṭṭhī*; Mahr. *chiṭṭī*. [Skt. *chitra*, 'marked.'] The Indian Portuguese also use *chito* for *escrito* (*Bluteau*, Supplement). The Tamil people use *shīt* for a ticket, or for a playing-card.

1673.—"I sent one of our Guides, with his Master's **Chitty**, or Pass, to the Governor, who received it kindly."—*Fryer*, 126.

[1757.—"If Mr. Ives is not too busie to honour this **chitt** which nothing but the greatest uneasiness could draw from me."—*Ives*, 134.]

1785.—". . . Those Ladies and Gentlemen who wish to be taught that polite Art (drawing) by Mr. Hone, may know his terms by sending a **Chit**. . . ."—In *Seton-Karr*, i. 114.

1786.—"You are to sell rice, &c., to every merchant from Muscat who brings you a **chitty** from Meer Kāzim."—*Tippoo's Letters*, 284.

1787.—"Mrs. Arend . . . will wait upon any Lady at her own house on the shortest notice, by addressing a **chit** to her in Chattawala Gully, opposite Mr. Motte's old house, Tiretta's bazar."—Advt. in *Seton-Karr*, i. 226.

1794.—"The petty but constant and universal manufacture of **chits** which prevails here."—*Hugh Boyd*, 147.

1829.—"He wanted a **chithee** or note, for this is the most note-writing country under heaven; the very Drum-major writes me a note to tell me about the mails."—*Mem. of Col. Mountain*, 2nd ed., 80.

1839.—"A thorough Madras lady . . . receives a number of morning visitors, takes up a little worsted work; goes to tiffin with Mrs. C., unless Mrs. D. comes to tiffin with her, and writes some dozens of **chits**. . . . These incessant **chits** are an immense trouble and interruption, but the ladies seem to like them."—*Letters from Madras*, 284.

CHITCHKY, s. A curried vegetable mixture, often served and eaten with meat curry. Properly Beng. *chhechkī*.

1875.—". . . **Chhenchki**, usually called *tarkāri* in the Vardhamāna District, a sort of hodge-podge consisting of potatoes, brinjals, and tender stalks. . . ."—*Govinda Samanta*, i. 59.

CHITTAGONG, n.p. A town, port, and district of Eastern Bengal, properly written *Chatgānw* (see **PORTO PIQUENO**). Chittagong appears to be the *City of Bengala* of Varthema and some of the early Portuguese. (See **BANDEL, BENGAL**).

c. 1346.—"The first city of Bengal that we entered was **Sudkāwān**, a great place situated on the shore of the great Sea."—*Ibn Batuta*, iv. 212.

1552.—"In the mouths of the two arms of the Ganges enter two notable rivers, one on the east, and one on the west side, both bounding this kingdom (of Bengal); the one of these our people call the River of **Chatigam**, because it enters the Eastern estuary of the Ganges at a city of that name, which is the most famous and wealthy of that Kingdom, by reason of its Port, at which meets the traffic of all that Eastern region."—*De Barros*, Dec. IV. liv. ix. cap. i.

[1586.—"**Satagam**." See quotation under **HING**.]

1591.—"So also they inform me that Antonio de Sousa Goudinho has served me well in *Bemgualla*, and that he has made tributary to this state the Isle of Sundiva, and has taken the fortress of **Chataguão** by force of arms."—*King's Letter*, in *Archivio Port. Orient.*, fasc. iii. 257.

1598.—"From this River Eastward 50 miles lyeth the towne of **Chatigan**, which is the chief towne of Bengala."—*Linschoten*, ch. xvi.; [Hak. Soc. i. 94].*

c. 1610.—Pyrard de la Val has **Chartican**, i. 234; [Hak. Soc. i. 326].

1727.—"**Chittagoung**, or, as the Portuguese call it, **Xatigam**, about 50 Leagues below Dacca."—*A. Hamilton*, ii. 24; ed. 1744, ii. 22.

17—.—"**Chittigan**" in Orme (reprint), ii. 14.

1786.—"The province of **Chatigan** (vulgarly **Chittagong**) is a noble field for a naturalist. It is so called, I believe, from the *chatag*,† which is the most beautiful little bird I ever saw."—*Sir W. Jones*, ii. 101.

Elsewhere (p. 81) he calls it a "Montpelier." The derivation given by this illustrious scholar is more than questionable. The name seems to be really a form of the Sanskrit *Chaturgrāma* (= *Tetrapolis*), [or according to others of *Saptagrāma*, 'seven villages'], and it is curious that near this position Ptolemy has a *Pentapolis*, very probably the same place. *Chaturgrāma* is still the name of a town in Ceylon, lat. 6°, long. 81°.

CHITTLEDROOG, n.p. A fort S.W. of Bellary; properly *Chitra Durgam*, Red Hill (or Hill-Fort, or ['picturesque fort']) called by the Mahommedans *Chītaldurg* (C. P. B.).

CHITTORE, n.p. *Chītor*, or *Chītorgarh*, a very ancient and famous rock fortress in the Rajput State of Mewār. It is almost certainly the Τιάτουρα of Ptolemy (vii. 1).

1533.—"Badour (*i.e.* Bahādur Shāh) . . . in Champanel . . . sent to carry off a quantity of powder and shot and stores for the attack on **Chitor**, which occasioned some delay because the distance was so great."—*Correa*, iii. 506.

1615.—"The two and twentieth (Dec.), Master Edwards met me, accompanied with Thomas Coryat, who had passed into India on foote, fiue *course* to **Cytor**, an ancient Citie ruined on a hill, but so that it appeares a Tombe (Towne?) of wonderfull magnificence. . . ."—*Sir Thomas Roe*, in *Purchas*, i. 540; [Hak. Soc. i. 102; "**Cetor**" in i. 111, "**Chytor**" in ii. 540].

[1813.—". . . a tribute . . . imposed by Muhadajee Seendhiya for the restitution of **Chuetohrgurh**, which he had conquered from the Rana."—*Broughton*, *Letters*, ed. 1892, p. 175.]

CHOBDAR, s. H. from P. *chobdār*, 'a stick-bearer.' A frequent attendant of Indian nobles, and in former days of Anglo-Indian officials of rank. They are still a part of the state of the Viceroy, Governors, and Judges of the High Courts. The *chobdārs* carry a staff overlaid with silver.

1442.—"At the end of the hall stand **tchobdars** . . . drawn up in line."—*Abdur-Razzāk*, in *India in the XV. Cent.* 25.

1673.—"If he (the President) move out of his Chamber, the *Silver Staves* wait on him."—*Fryer*, 68.

1701.—". . . Yesterday, of his own accord, he told our Linguists that he had sent four **Chobdars** and 25 men, as a safeguard."—In *Wheeler*, i. 371.

1788.—"**Chubdár** . . . Among the Nabobs he proclaims their praises aloud, as he runs before their palankeens."—*Indian Vocabulary* (Stockdale's).

1793.—"They said a **Chubdar**, with a silverstick, one of the Sultan's messengers of justice, had taken them from the place, where they were confined, to the public Bazar, where their hands were cut off."—*Dirom*, *Narrative*, 235.

1798.—"The chief's **Chobedar** . . . also endeavoured to impress me with an ill opinion of these messengers."—*G. Forster's Travels*, i. 222.

1810.—"While we were seated at breakfast, we were surprised by the entrance of a **Choabdar**, that is, a servant who attends on persons of consequence, runs before them with a silver stick, and keeps silence at the doors of their apartments, from which last office he derives his name."—*Maria Graham*, 57.

This usually accurate lady has been here misled, as if the word were *chup-dār*, 'silence-keeper,' a hardly possible hybrid.

CHOBWA, s. Burmese *Tsaubwa*, Siamese *Chao*, 'prince, king,' also *Chaohpa* (compounded with *hpa*, 'heaven'), and in Cushing's Shan Dicty. and cacography, *sow*, 'lord, master,' *sowhpa*, a 'hereditary prince.' The word *chu-hu*, for 'chief,' is found applied among tribes of Kwang-si, akin to the Shans, in A.D. 1150 (*Prof. T. de la Couperie*). The designation of the princes of the Shan States on the east of Burma, many of whom are (or were till lately) tributary to Ava.

* There is no reason to suppose that Linschoten had himself been to Chittagong. My friend, Dr. Burnell, in his (posthumous) edition of Linschoten for the Hakluyt Society has confounded *Chātigam* in this passage with *Satgaon*—see **Porto Piqueno** (H. Y.).

† The *chātak* which figures in Hindu poetry, is, according to the dictionaries, *Cuculus melanoleucos*, which must be the pied cuckoo, *Coccystes melanoleucos*, Gm., in Jerdon; but this surely cannot be Sir William's "most beautiful little bird he ever saw"?

1795.—"After them came the **Chobwaas**, or petty tributary princes: these are personages who, before the Birmans had extended their conquests over the vast territories which they now possess, had held small independent sovereignties which they were able to maintain so long as the balance of power continued doubtful between the Birmans, Peguers, and Siamese."—*Symes*, 366.

1819.—"All that tract of land . . . is inhabited by a numerous nation called Sciam, who are the same as the Laos. Their kingdom is divided into small districts under different chiefs called **Zaboà**, or petty princes."—*Sangermano*, 34.

1855.—"The **Tsaubwas** of all these principalities, even where most absolutely under Ava, retain all the forms and appurtenances of royalty."—*Yule, Mission to Ava*, 303.

[1890.—"The succession to the throne primarily depends upon the person chosen by the court and people being of princely descent—all such are called **chow** or prince." —*Hallet, A Thousand Miles on an Elephant*, p. 32.]

CHOGA, s. Turki *choghā*. A long sleeved garment, like a dressing-gown (a purpose for which Europeans often make use of it). It is properly an Afghan form of dress, and is generally made of some soft woollen material, and embroidered on the sleeves and shoulders. In Bokhara the word is used for a furred robe. ["In Tibetan *ch'uba;* in Turki *juba*. It is variously pronounced *chuba, juba* or *chogha* in Asia, and *shuba* or *shubka* in Russia" (*J.R.A.S.*, N.S. XXIII. 122)].

1883.—"We do not hear of 'shirt-sleeves' in connection with Henry (Lawrence), so often as in John's case; we believe *his* favourite dishabille was an Afghan **choga**, which like charity covered a multitude of sins."—*Qu. Review*, No. 310, on *Life of Lord Lawrence*, p. 303.

CHOKIDAR, s. A watchman. Derivative in Persian form from **Choky**. The word is usually applied to a private watchman; in some parts of India he is generally of a thieving tribe, and his employment may be regarded as a sort of blackmail to ensure one's property. [In N. India the village *Chaukīdār* is the rural policeman, and he is also employed for watch and ward in the smaller towns.]

1689.—"And the Day following the **Chocadars**, or Souldiers were remov'd from before our Gates."—*Ovington*, 416.

1810.—"The **chokey-dar** attends during the day, often performing many little offices, . . . at night parading about with his spear, shield, and sword, and assuming a most terrific aspect, until all the family are asleep; when HE GOES TO SLEEP TOO."—*Williamson, V. M.* i. 295.

c. 1817.—"The birds were scarcely beginning to move in the branches of the trees, and there was not a servant excepting the **chockedaurs**, stirring about any house in the neighbourhood, it was so early."—*Mrs. Sherwood's Stories*, &c. (ed. 1873), 243.

1837.—"Every village is under a *potail*, and there is a *pursau* or priest, and **choukeednop** (sic!) or watchman."—*Phillips, Million of Facts*, 320.

1864.—The church book at Peshawar records the death there of "The Revd. I—— L——l, who on the night of the —th ——, 1864, when walking in his veranda was shot by his own **chokidar**"—to which record the hand of an injudicious friend has added: "Well done, thou good and faithful servant!" (The exact words will now be found in the late Mr. E. B. Eastwick's *Panjāb Handbook*, p. 279).

CHOKRA, s. Hind. *chhokrā*, 'a boy, a youngster'; and hence, more specifically, a boy employed about a household, or a regiment. Its chief use in S. India is with the latter. (See **CHUCKAROO.**)

[1875.—"He was dubbed 'the **chokra**,' or simply 'boy.'"—*Wilson, Abode of Snow*, 136.]

CHOKY, s. H. *chaukī*, which in all its senses is probably connected with Skt. *chatur*, 'four'; whence *chatushka*, 'of four,' 'four-sided,' &c.

a. (Perhaps first a shed resting on four posts); a station of police; a lock-up; also a station of palankin bearers, horses, &c., when a post is laid; a customs or toll-station, and hence, as in the first quotation, the dues levied at such a place; the act of watching or guarding.

[1535.—"They only pay the **choqueis** coming in ships from the Moluccas to Malacca, which amounts to 3 parts in 10 for the owner of the ship for *choque*, which is freight; that which belongs to His Highness pays nothing when it comes in ships. This *choque* is as far as Malacca, from thence to India is another freight as arranged between the parties. Thus when cloves are brought in His Highness's ships, paying the third and the *choquies*, there goes from every 30 bahars 16 to the King, our Lord."—*Arrangement made by Nuno da Cunha*, quoted in *Botelho Tombo*, p. 113. On this Mr. Whiteway remarks: "By this arrangement the King of Portugal did not ship any cloves of his own at the Moluccas, but he took one-third of every shipment free, and on the balance he took one-third as **Choky**, which is, I imagine, in lieu of customs."]

c. 1590.—"Mounting guard is called in Hindi **Chauki**."—*Āīn*, i. 257.

1608.—"The Kings Custome called **Chukey**, is eight bagges upon the hundred bagges."—*Saris*, in *Purchas*, i. 391.

1664.—"Near this Tent there is another great one, which is called **Tchaukykane**, because it is the place where the Omrahs keep guard, every one in his turn, once a week twenty-four hours together."—*Bernier*, E.T., 117; [ed. *Constable*, 363].

1673.—"We went out of the Walls by Broach Gate . . . where, as at every gate, stands a **Chocky**, or Watch to receive Toll for the Emperor. . . ."—*Fryer*, 100.

" "And when they must rest, if they have no Tents, they must shelter themselves under Trees . . . unless they happen on a **Chowkie**, *i.e.*, a Shed where the Customer keeps a Watch to take Custom."—*Ibid.* 410.

1682.—"About 12 o'clock Noon we got to ye **Chowkee**, where after we had shown our *Dustick* and given our present, we were dismissed immediately."—*Hedges, Diary*, Dec. 17; [Hak. Soc. i. 58].

1774.—"Il più difficile per viaggiare nell' Indostan sono certi posti di guardie chiamate **Cioki** . . . questi **Cioki** sono insolentissimi."—*Della Tomba*, 33.

1810.—". . . **Chokies**, or patrol stations." —*Williamson, V. M.*, i. 297.

This word has passed into the English slang vocabulary in the sense of 'prison.'

b. A chair. This use is almost peculiar to the Bengal Presidency. Dr. John Muir [*Orig. Skt. Texts*, ii. 5] cites it in this sense, as a Hindi word which has no resemblance to any Skt. vocable. Mr. Growse, however, connects it with *chatur*, 'four' (*Ind. Antiq.*, i. 105). See also beginning of this article. *Chau* is the common form of 'four' in composition, *e.g. chaubandi*, (*i.e.* 'four fastening') the complete shoeing of a horse; *chaupahra* ('four watches') all night long; *chaupār*, 'a quadruped'; *chaukaṭ* and *chaukhaṭ* ('four timber'), a frame (of a door, &c.). So *chaukī* seems to have been used for a square-framed stool, and thence a chair.

1772.—"Don't throw yourself back in your *burra* **chokey**, and tell me it won't do. . . ." —*W. Hastings to G. Vansittart*, in *Gleig*, i. 238.

c. 1782.—"As soon as morning appeared he (Haidar) sat down on his chair (**chauki**) and washed his face."—*H. of Hydur Naik*, 505.

CHOLERA, and **CHOLERA MORBUS**, s. The Disease. The term 'cholera,' though employed by the old medical writers, no doubt came, as regards its familiar use, from India. Littré alleges that it is a mistake to suppose that the word *cholera* (χολέρα) is a derivative from χολή, 'bile,' and that it really means 'a gutter,' the disease being so called from the symptoms. This should, however, rather be ἀπὸ τῶν χολάδων, the latter word being anciently used for the intestines (the etym. given by the medical writer, Alex. Trallianus). But there is a discussion on the subject in the modern ed. of *Stephani Thesaurus*, which indicates a conclusion that the derivation from χολή is probably right; it is that of Celsus (see below). [The *N.E.D.* takes the same view, but admits that there is some doubt.] For quotations and some particulars in reference to the history of this terrible disease, see under **MORT-DE-CHIEN**.

c. A.D. 20.—"Primoque facienda mentio est **cholerae**; quia commune id stomachi atque intestinorum vitium videri potest . . . intestina torquentur, bilis supra infraque erumpit, primum aquae similis: deinde ut in eâ recens caro tota esse videatur, interdum alba, nonnunquam nigra vel varia. Ergo eo nomine morbum hunc χολέραν Graeci nominârunt. . . ." &c.—*A. C. Celsi Med. Libri* VIII. iv. xi.

c. A.D. 100.—"ΠΕΡῚ ΧΟΛΈΡΗΣ . . . θάνατος ἐπώδυνος καὶ οἴκτιστος σπασμῷ καὶ πνιγὶ καὶ ἐμέσῳ κενῷ."—*Aretaeus, De Causis et signis acutorum morborum*, ii. 5.

Also Θεραπεία Χολερῆς, *in De Curatione Morb. Ac.* ii. 4.

1563.—"*R.* Is this disease the one which kills so quickly, and from which so few recover? Tell me how it is called among us, and among them, and its symptoms, and the treatment of it in use?

"*O.* Among us it is called **Collerica passio**. . . ."—*Garcia*, f. 74*v*.

[1611.—"As those ill of **Colera**."—*Couto, Dialogo de Soldado Pratico*, p. 5.]

1673.—"The Diseases reign according to the Seasons. . . . In the extreme Heats, **Cholera Morbus**."—*Fryer*, 113-114.

1832.—"Le **Choléra Morbus**, dont vous me parlez, n'est pas inconnu à Cachemire." —*Jacquemont, Corresp.* ii. 109.

CHOLERA HORN. See **COLLERY**.

CHOOLA, s. H. *chūlhā, chūlhī, chūlā*, fr. Skt. *chulli*. The extemporized cooking-place of clay which a native of India makes on the ground to prepare his own food; or to cook that of his master.

1814.—"A marble corridor filled up with **choolas**, or cooking-places, composed of mud, cowdung, and unburnt bricks."—*Forbes, Or. Mem.* iii. 120; [2nd ed. ii. 193].

CHOOLIA, s. *Chūliā* is a name given in Ceylon and in Malabar to a particular class of Mahommedans, and sometimes to Mahommedans generally. There is much obscurity about the origin and proper application of the term. [The word is by some derived from Skt. *chūḍa*, the top-knot which every Hindu must wear, and which is cut off on conversion to Islam. In the same way in the Punjab, *chotīkat*, 'he that has had his top-knot cut off,' is a common form of abuse used by Hindus to Musulman converts; see *Ibbetson, Panjab Ethnog.* p. 240.] According to Sonnerat (i. 109), the Chulias are of Arab descent and of Shīa profession. [The *Madras Gloss.* takes the word to be from the kingdom of *Chola* and to mean a person of S. India.]

c. 1345.—"... the city of Kaulam, which is one of the finest of Malibār. Its bazars are splendid, and its merchants are known by the name of **Ṣūlia** (*i.e. Chūlia*)."—*Ibn Batuta*, iv. 99.

1754.—"**Chowlies** are esteemed learned men, and in general are merchants."—*Ives*, 25.

1782.—"We had found ... less of that foolish timidity, and much more disposition to intercourse in the **Choliars** of the country, who are Mahommedans and quite distinct in their manners...."—*Hugh Boyd, Journal of a Journey of an Embassy to Candy*, in *Misc. Works* (1800), i. 155.

1783.—"During Mr. Saunders's government I have known **Chulia** (Moors) vessels carry coco-nuts from the Nicobar Islands to Madras."—*Forrest, Voyage to Mergui*, p. v.

" "**Chulias** and Malabars (the appellations are I believe synonymous)."—*Ibid.* 24.

1836.—"Mr. Boyd ... describes the Moors under the name of **Cholias**, and Sir Alexander Johnston designates them by the appellation *Lubbies* (see **LUBBYE**). These epithets are, however, not admissible, for the former is only confined to a particular sect among them, who are rather of an inferior grade; and the latter to the priests who officiate."—*Casie Chitty*, in *J. R. A. Soc.* iii. 338.

1879.—"There are over 15,000 Klings, **Chuliahs**, and other natives of India."—*Miss Bird, Golden Chersonese*, 254.

CHOP, s. Properly a seal-impression, stamp, or brand; H. *chhāp*; the verb (*chhāpnā*) being that which is now used in Hindustani to express the art of printing (books).

The word *chhāp* seems not to have been traced back with any accuracy beyond the modern vernaculars. It has been thought possible (at least till the history should be more accurately traced) that it might be of Portuguese origin. For there is a Port. word *chapa*, 'a thin plate of metal,' which is no doubt the original of the Old English *chape* for the metal plate on the sheath of a sword or dagger.* The word in this sense is not in the Portuguese Dictionaries; but we find 'homem *chapado*,' explained as 'a man of notable worth or excellence,' and Bluteau considers this a metaphor 'taken from the *chapas* or plates of metal on which the kings of India caused their letters patent to be engraven.' Thus he would seem to have regarded, though perhaps erroneously, the *chhāpā* and the Portuguese *chapa* as identical. On the other hand, Mr. Beames entertains no doubt that the word is genuine Hindi, and connects it with a variety of other words signifying *striking*, or *pressing*. And Thompson in his *Hindi Dictionary* says that *chhāppā* is a technical term used by the Vaishnavas to denote the sectarial marks (lotus, trident, &c.), which they delineate on their bodies. Fallon gives the same meaning, and quotes a Hindi verse, using it in this sense. We may add that while *chhāpā* is used all over the N.W.P. and Punjab for printed cloths, Drummond (1808) gives *chhāpanīya*, *chhapārā*, as words for 'Stampers or Printers of Cloth' in Guzerati, and that the passage quoted below from a Treaty made with an ambassador from Guzerat by the Portuguese in 1537, uses the word *chapada* for struck or coined, exactly as the modern Hindi verb *chhāpnā* might be used.† *Chop*, in writers

* Thus, in Shakspeare, "This is Monsieur Parolles, the gallant militarist ... that had the whole theorie of war in the knot of his scarf, the practice in the *chape* of his dagger."—*All's Well that Ends Well*, iv. 3. And, in the Scottish *Rates and Valuatiouns*, under 1612:

"Lockattis and *Chapes* for daggers."

† "... e quanto á moeda, ser *chapada de sua sica* (by error printed *sita*), pois já lhe concedea, que todo o proveyto serya del Rey de Portuguall, como soya a ser dos Reis dos Guzarates, e ysto nas terras que nos tiuermos em Canbaya, e a nós quisermos bater."—Treaty (1537) in *S. Botelho, Tombo*, 226.

prior to the last century, is often used for the seal itself. "Owen Cambridge says the *Mohr* was the great seal, but the small or privy seal was called a '**chop**' or 'stamp.'" (*C. P. Brown*).

The word *chop* is hardly used now among Anglo-Indians in the sense of seal or stamp. But it got a permanent footing in the 'Pigeon English' of the Chinese ports, and thence has come back to England and India, in the phrase "*first*-**chop**," *i.e.* of the first *brand* or quality.

The word **chop** (*chāp*) is adopted in Malay [with the meanings of seal-impression, stamp, to seal or stamp, though there is, as Mr. Skeat points out, a pure native word *tera* or *tra*, which is used in all these senses;] and **chop** has acquired the specific sense of a passport or licence. The word has also obtained a variety of applications, including that just mentioned, in the *lingua franca* of foreigners in the China seas. Van Braam applies it to a tablet bearing the Emperor's name, to which he and his fellow envoys made **kotow** on their first landing in China (*Voyage*, &c., Paris, An vi., 1798, i. 20-21). Again, in the same jargon, a **chop** of tea means a certain number of chests of tea, all bearing the same brand. **Chop**-*houses* are customs stations on the Canton River, so called from the chops, or seals, used there (*Giles, Glossary*). **Chop**-*dollar* is a dollar *chopped*, or stamped with a private mark, as a guarantee of its genuineness (*ibid.*). (Dollars similarly marked had currency in England in the first quarter of last century, and one of the present writers can recollect their occasional occurrence in Scotland in his childhood). The *grand* **chop** is the port clearance granted by the Chinese customs when all dues have been paid (*ibid.*). All these have obviously the same origin; but there are other uses of the word in China not so easily explained, *e.g. chop*, for 'a hulk'; *chop-boat* for a lighter or cargo-boat.

In Captain Forrest's work, quoted below, a golden badge or decoration, conferred on him by the King of Achin, is called a **chapp** (p. 55). The portrait of Forrest, engraved by Sharp, shows this badge, and gives the inscription, translated: "Capt. Thomas Forrest, Orancayo [see **ORANKAY**] of the Golden Sword. This **chapp** was conferred as a mark of honour in the city of Atcheen, belonging to the Faithful, by the hands of the Shabander [see **SHAHBUNDER**] of Atcheen, on Capt. Thomas Forrest."

[1534.—"The Governor said that he would receive nothing save under his **chapa**." "Until he returned from Badur with his reply and the **chapa** required."—*Correa*, iii. 585.]

1537.—"And the said Nizamamede Zamom was present and then before me signed, and swore on his Koran (*moçafo*) to keep and maintain and fulfil this agreement entirely . . . and he sealed it with his seal" (*e o* **chapo** *de sua* **chapa**).—Treaty above quoted, in *S. Botelho, Tombo*, 228.

1552.—". . . ordered . . . that they should allow no person to enter or to leave the island without taking away his **chapa**. . . . And this **chapa** was, as it were, a seal."—*Castanheda*, iii. 32.

1614.—"The King (of Achen) sent us his **Chop**."—*Milward*, in *Purchas*, i. 526.

1615.—"Sailed to Acheen; the King sent his **Chope** for them to go ashore, without which it was unlawful for any one to do so."—*Sainsbury*, i. 445.

[„ "2 chistes plate . . . with the rendadors **chape** upon it."—*Cocks's Diary*, i. 219.]

1618.—"Signed with my **chop**, the 14th day of May (*sic*), in the Yeare of our Prophet Mahomet 1027."—Letter from Gov. of Mocha, in *Purchas*, i. 625.

1673.—"The Custom-house has a good Front, where the chief Customer appears certain Hours to **chop**, that is to mark Goods outward-bound."—*Fryer*, 98.

1678.—". . . sending of our *Vuckeel* this day to Compare the Coppys with those sent, in order to yᵉ **Chaup**, he refused it, alledging that they came without yᵉ Visiers **Chaup** to him. . . ."—*Letter* (in India Office) *from Dacca Factory* to Mr. Matthias Vincent (Ft. St. George?).

1682.—"To Rajemaul I sent ye old Duan . . .'s Perwanna, **Chopt** both by the Nabob and new Duan, for its confirmation."—*Hedges, Diary*, Hak. Soc. i. 37.

1689.—"Upon their **Chops** as they call them in India, or Seals engraven, are only Characters, generally those of their Name."—*Ovington*, 251.

1711.—"This (Oath at Acheen) is administered by the Shabander . . . lifting, very respectfully, a short Dagger in a Gold Case, like a Scepter, three times to their Heads; and it is called receiving the **Chop** for Trade."—*Lockyer*, 35.

1715.—"It would be very proper also to put our **chop** on the said Books."—In *Wheeler*, ii. 224.

c. 1720.—"Here they demanded tax and toll; felt us all over, not excepting our mouths, and when they found nothing, stamped a **chop** upon our arms in red paint; which was to serve for a pass."—*Zesteen*

Jaarige Reize . . . door *Jacob de Bucquoy*, Haarlem, 1757.

1727.—"On my Arrival (at Acheen) I took the **Chap** at the great River's Mouth, according to Custom. This *Chap* is a Piece of Silver about 8 ounces Weight, made in Form of a Cross, but the cross Part is very short, that we . . . put to our Fore-head, and declare to the Officer that brings the *Chap*, that we come on an honest Design to trade."—*A. Hamilton*, ii. 103.

1771.—". . . with **Tiapp** or passports."—*Osbeck*, i. 181.

1782.—". . . le Pilote . . . apporte avec lui leur **chappe**, ensuite il adore et consulte son Poussa, puis il fait lever l'ancre."—*Sonnerat*, ii. 233.

1783.—"The bales (at Acheen) are immediately opened; 12 in the hundred are taken for the king's duty, and the remainder being marked with a certain mark (**chapp**) may be carried where the owner pleases."—*Forrest, V. to Mergui*, 41.

1785.—"The only pretended original produced was a manifest forgery, for it had not the **chop** or smaller seal, on which is engraved the name of the Mogul."—*Carraccioli's Clive*, i. 214.

1817.—". . . and so great reluctance did he (the Nabob) show to the ratification of the Treaty, that Mr. Pigot is said to have seized his **chop**, or seal, and applied it to the paper."—*Mill's Hist.* iii. 340.

1876.—"'*First* **chop**! tremendously pretty too,' said the elegant Grecian, who had been paying her assiduous attention."—*Daniel Deronda*, Bk. I. ch. x.

1882.—"On the edge of the river facing the 'Pow-shan' and the Creek Hongs, were **Chop** *houses*, or branches of the Hoppo's department, whose *duty* it was to prevent smuggling, but whose *interest* it was to aid and facilitate the shipping of silks . . . at a considerable reduction on the Imperial tariff."—*The Fankwae at Canton*, p. 25.

The writer last quoted, and others before him, have imagined a Chinese origin for **chop**, *e.g.*, as "from *chah*, 'an official note from a superior,' or *chah*, 'a contract, a diploma, &c.,' both having at Canton the sound *chăp*, and between them covering most of the 'pigeon' uses of *chop*" (Note by *Bishop Moule*). But few of the words used by Europeans in Chinese trade are really Chinese, and we think it has been made clear that *chop* comes from India.

CHOP-CHOP. Pigeon-English (or -Chinese) for 'Make haste! look sharp!' This is supposed to be from the Cantonese, pron. *kăp-kăp*, of what is in the Mandarin dialect *kip-kip*. In the Northern dialects *kwai-kwai*, 'quick-quick' is more usual (*Bishop Moule*). [Mr. Skeat compares the Malay *chepat-chepat*, 'quick-quick.']

CHOPPER.

a. H. *chhappar*, 'a thatched roof.'

[1773.—". . . from their not being provided with a sufficient number of boats, there was a necessity for crouding a large party of *Sepoys* into one, by which the **chuppar**, or upper slight deck broke down."—*Ives*, 174.]

1780.—"About 20 Days ago a Villian was detected here setting fire to Houses by throwing the *Tickeea** of his Hooka on the **Choppers**, and was immediately committed to the *Phouzdar's* Prison. . . . On his tryal . . . it appering that he had more than once before committed the same Nefarieus and abominable Crime, he was sentenced to have his left Hand, and right Foot cut off. . . . It is needless to expatiate on the Efficacy such exemplary Punishments would be of to the Publick in general, if adopted on all similar occasions. . . ."—Letter from Moorshedabad, in *Hicky's Bengal Gazette*, May 6.

1782.—"With Mr. Francis came the Judges of the Supreme Court, the Laws of England, partial oppression, and licentious liberty. The common felons were cast loose, . . . the merchants of the place told that they need not pay duties . . . and the natives were made to know that they might erect their **chappor** huts in what part of the town they pleased."—*Price, Some Observations*, 61.

1810.—"**Chuppers**, or grass thatches."—*Williamson, V. M.* i. 510.

c. 1817.—"These cottages had neat **choppers**, and some of them wanted not small gardens, fitly fenced about."—*Mrs. Sherwood's Stories*, ed. 1873, 258.

[1832.—"The religious devotee sets up a **chupha**-hut without expence."—*Mrs. Meer Haṣsan Ali*, ii. 211.]

[b. In Persia, a corr. of P. *chār-pā*, 'on four feet, a quadruped' and thence a mounted post and posting.

1812.—"Eight of the horses belong to the East India Company, and are principally employed in carrying **choppers** or couriers to Shiraz."—*Morier, Journey through Persia*, &c., p. 64.

1883.—"By this time I had begun to pique myself on the rate I could get over the ground 'en **chuppar**.'"—*Wills, In the Land of the Lion and the Sun*, ed. 1891, p. 259.]

CHOPPER-COT, a. Much as this looks like a European concoction, it is

* H. *Tikiyā* is a little cake of charcoal placed in the bowl of the hooka, or hubble-bubble.

a genuine H. term, *chhappar khāṭ*, 'a bedstead with curtains.'

1778.—"Leito com armação. **Châpâr cátt.**"—*Grammatica Indostana*, 128.

c. 1809.—"Bedsteads are much more common than in Puraniya. The best are called *Palang*, or **Chhapar Khat** . . . they have curtains, mattrasses, pillows, and a sheet. . . ."—*Buchanan, Eastern India*, ii. 92.

c. 1817.—"My husband chanced to light upon a very pretty **chopper-cot**, with curtains and everything complete."—*Mrs. Sherwood's Stories*, ed. 1873, 161. (See **COT**.)

CHOPSTICKS, s. The sticks used in pairs by the Chinese in feeding themselves. The Chinese name of the article is '*kwai-tsz*,' 'speedy-ones.' "Possibly the inventor of the present word, hearing that the Chinese name had this meaning, and accustomed to the phrase *chop-chop* for 'speedily,' used *chop* as a translation" (*Bishop Moule*). [Prof. Giles writes: "The *N.E.D.* gives incorrectly *kwai-tze*, *i.e.* 'nimble boys,' 'nimble ones.' Even Sir H. Yule is not without blemish. He leaves the aspirate out of *kwai*, of which the official orthography is now *k'uai-k'uai-tzŭ*, 'hasteners,' the termination *-ers* bringing out the value of *tzŭ*, an enclitic particle, better than 'ones.' Bishop Moule's suggestion is on the right track. I think, however, that **chopstick** came from a Chinaman, who of course knew the meaning of *k'uai* and applied it accordingly, using the 'pidgin' word **chop** as the, to him, natural equivalent."]

c. 1540.—". . . his young daughters, with their brother, did nothing but laugh to see us feed ourselves with our hands, for that is contrary to the custome which is observed throughout the whole empire of *China*, where the Inhabitants at their meat carry it to their mouthes with two little sticks made like a pair of Cizers" (this is the translator's folly; it is really *com duos paos feitos como fusos*—"like spindles)."—*Pinto*, orig. cap. lxxxiii., in *Cogan*, p. 103.

[1598.—"Two little peeces of blacke woode made round . . . these they use instead of forkes."—*Linschoten*, Hak. Soc. i. 144.]

c. 1610.—". . . ont comme deux petites spatules de bois fort bien faites, qu'ils tiennent entre leurs doigts, et prennent avec cela ce qu'ils veulent manger, si dextrement, que rien plus."—*Mocquet*, 346.

1711—"They take it very dexterously with a couple of small **Chopsticks**, which serve them instead of Forks."—*Lockyer*, 174.

1876.—"Before each there will be found a pair of **chopsticks**, a wine-cup, a small saucer for soy . . . and a pile of small pieces of paper for cleaning these articles as required."—*Giles, Chinese Sketches*, 153-4.

CHOTA-HAZRY, s. H. *chhoṭī hāzirī*, vulg. *hāzrī*, 'little breakfast'; refreshment taken in the early morning, before or after the morning exercise. The term (see **HAZREE**) was originally peculiar to the Bengal Presidency. In Madras the meal is called 'early tea.' Among the Dutch in Java, this meal consists (or did consist in 1860) of a large cup of tea, and a large piece of cheese, presented by the servant who calls one in the morning.

1853.—"After a bath, and hasty ante-breakfast (which is called in India '**a little breakfast**') at the Euston Hotel, he proceeded to the private residence of a man of law."—*Oakfield*, ii. 179.

1866.—"There is one small meal . . . it is that commonly known in India by the Hindustani name of **chota-hāziri**, and in our English colonies as '**Early Tea.**' . . ."—*Waring, Tropical Resident*, 172.

1875.—"We took **early tea** with him this morning."—*The Dilemma*, ch. iii.

CHOUL, CHAUL, n.p. A seaport of the Concan, famous for many centuries under various forms of this name, *Cheṅwal* properly, and pronounced in Konkani *Tseṁwal* (*Sinclair, Ind. Ant.* iv. 283). It may be regarded as almost certain that this was the Σιμυλλα of Ptolemy's Tables, called by the natives, as he says, Τιμουλα. It may be fairly conjectured that the true reading of this was Τιμουλα, or Τιέμουλα. We find the sound *ch* of Indian names apparently represented in Ptolemy by τι (as it is in Dutch by *tj*). Thus Τιάτουρα = *Chitor*, Τιάσταvης = *Chashṭana*; here Τιμουλα = *Cheṅwal*; while Τιάγουρα and Τιαύσπα probably stand for names like *Chagara* and *Chauspa*. Still more confidently *Cheṅwal* may be identified with the *Saimur* (Chaimur) or Jaimur of the old Arab. Geographers, a port at the extreme end of Lār or Guzerat. At Choul itself there is a tradition that its antiquity goes back beyond that of Suali (see **SWALLY**), Bassein, or Bombay. There were memorable sieges of Choul in 1570-71, and again in 1594, in which the Portuguese successfully resisted Mahommedan attempts to capture the place. Dr. Burgess identifies the ancient Σήμυλλα rather with a place called *Chembur*, on the island of Trombay, which lies immediately east of the island of Bombay; but till more evidence is adduced we see no reason to adopt this.* Choul seems now to be known as Revadanda. Even the name is not to be found in the *Imperial Gazetteer*. *Rewadanda* has a place in that work, but without a word to indicate its connection with this ancient and famous port. Mr. Gerson d'Acunha has published in the *J. Bo. Br. As. Soc.*, vol. xii., *Notes on the H. and Ant. of Chaul.*

A.D. c. 80–90.—"Μετὰ δὲ Καλλιέναν ἄλλα ἐμπόρια τοπικὰ, Σήμυλλα, καὶ Μανδαγόρα. . . ."—*Periplus.*

A.D. c. 150.—"Σίμυλλα ἐμπόριον (καλούμενον ὑπὸ τῶν ἐγχωρίων Τίμουλα)."—*Ptol.* i. cap. 17.

A.D. 916. "The year 304 I found myself in the territory of *Saimūr* (or **Chaimūr**), belonging to Hind and forming part of the province of Lār. . . . There were in the place about 10,000 Mussulmans, both of those called *baiāsirah* (half-breeds), and of natives of Sirāf, Omān, Basrah, Bagdad, &c."—*Maṣ'ūdi*, ii. 86.

[1020.—"**Jaimúr.**" See quotation under **LAR.**]

c. 1150.—"**Saimūr**, 5 days from Sindān, is a large, well-built town."—*Edrisi*, in *Elliot*, i. [85].

c. 1470.—"We sailed six weeks in the *tava* till we reached **Chivil**, and left Chivil on the seventh week after the great day. This is an Indian country."—*Ath. Nikitin*, 9, in *India in XVth. Cent.*

1510.—"Departing from the said city of Combeia, I travelled on until I arrived at another city named **Cevul (Chevul)** which is distant from the above-mentioned city 12 days' journey, and the country between the one and the other of these cities is called Guzerati."—*Varthema*, 113.

1546.—Under this year D'Acunha quotes from Freire d'Andrada a story that when the Viceroy required 20,000 **pardaos** (q.v.) to send for the defence of Diu, offering in pledge a wisp of his mustachio, the women of **Choul** sent all their earrings and other jewellery, to be applied to this particular service.

1554.—"The ports of Mahaim and **Sheúl** belong to the Deccan."—*The Mohit*, in *J.A.S.B.*, v. 461.

1584.—"The 10th of November we arrived at **Chaul** which standeth in the firme land. There be two townes, the one belonging to the Portugales, and the other to the Moores."—*R. Fitch*, in Hakl. ii. 384.

c. 1630.—"After long toil . . . we got to **Choul**; then we came to Daman."—*Sir T. Herbert*, ed. 1665, p. 42.

1635.—"**Chíval**, a seaport of Deccan."—*Sádik Isfaháni*, 88.

1727.—"**Chaul**, in former Times, was a noted Place for Trade, particularly for fine embroidered Quilts; but now it is miserably poor."—*A. Hamilton*, i. 243.

1782.—"That St. Lubin had some of the Mahratta officers on board of his ship, at the port of **Choul** . . . he will remember as long as he lives, for they got so far the ascendancy over the political Frenchman, as to induce him to come into the harbour, and to land his cargo of military stores . . . not one piece of which he ever got back again, or was paid sixpence for."—*Price's Observations on a Late Publication*, &c., 14. In *Price's Tracts*, vol. i.

CHOULTRY, s. Peculiar to S. India, and of doubtful etymology; Malayāl. *chāwaṭī*, Tel. *chāwaḍi*, [*tsāvaḍi*, *chau*, Skt. *chatur*, 'four,' *vāṭa*, 'road, a place where four roads meet]. In W. India the form used is *chowry* or *chowree* (Dakh. *chāoṛī*). A hall, a shed, or a simple *loggia*, used by travellers as a resting-place, and also intended for the transaction of public business. In the old Madras Archives there is frequent mention of the "Justices of the **Choultry**." A building of this kind seems to have formed the early Court-house.

1673.—"Here (at Swally near Surat) we were welcomed by the Deputy President . . . who took care for my Entertainment, which here was rude, the place admitting of little better Tenements than Booths stiled by the name of **Choultries**."—*Fryer*, 82.

,, "Maderas . . . enjoys some **Choultries** for Places of Justice."—*Ibid.* 39.

1683.—". . . he shall pay for every slave so shipped . . . 50 pagodas to be recovered of him in the **Choultry** of Madraspattanam."—*Order of Madras Council*, in *Wheeler*, i. 136.

1689.—"Within less than half a Mile, from the Sea (near Surat) are three **Choultries** or Convenient Lodgings made of Timber."—*Ovington*, 164.

1711.—"Besides these, five Justices of the **Choultry**, who are of the Council, or chief Citizens, are to decide Controversies, and punish offending Indians."—*Lockyer*, 7.

1714.—In the MS. List of Persons in the Service, &c. (India Office Records), we have:—

"Josiah Cooke ffactor Register of the **Choultry**, £15."

1727.—"There are two or three little **Choulteries** or Shades built for Patients to rest in."—*A. Hamilton*, ch. ix.; [i. 95].

* See *Fergusson & Burgess, Cave Temples*, pp. 168 & 349. See also Mr. James Campbell's excellent *Bombay Gazetteer*, xiv. 52, where reasons are stated against the view of Dr. Burgess.

[1773.—"A **Choltre** is not much unlike a large summer-house, and in general is little more than a bare covering from the inclemency of the weather. Some few indeed are more spacious, and are also endowed with a salary to support a servant or two, whose business is to furnish all passengers with a certain quantity of rice and fresh water."—*Ives*, 67.]

1782.—"Les fortunes sont employées à bâtir des **Chauderies** sur les chemins."—*Sonnerat*, i. 42.

1790.—"On ne rencontre dans ces voyages aucune auberge ou hôtellerie sur la route; mais elles sont remplacées par des lieux de repos appelées **schultris** (*chauderies*), qui sont des bâtimens ouverts et inhabités, où les voyageurs ne trouvent, en général, qu'un toit. . . ."—*Haafner*, ii. 11.

1809.—"He resides at present in an old **Choultry** which has been fitted up for his use by the Resident."—*Ld. Valentia*, i. 356.

1817.—"Another fact of much importance is, that a Mahomedan Sovereign was the first who established **Choultries**."—*Mill's Hist.* ii. 181.

1820.—"The **Chowree** or town-hall where the public business of the township is transacted, is a building 30 feet square, with square gable-ends, and a roof of tile supported on a treble row of square wooden posts."—*Acc. of Township of Loony*, in *Tr. Lit. Soc. Bombay*, ii. 181.

1833.—"Junar, 6th Jan. 1833. . . . We at first took up our abode in the **Chawadi**, but Mr. Escombe of the C. S. kindly invited us to his house."—*Smith's Life of Dr. John Wilson*, 156.

1836.—"The roads are good, and well supplied with **choultries** or taverns" (!)—*Phillips, Million of Facts*, 319.

1879.—"Let an organised watch . . . be established in each village . . . armed with good **tulwars**. They should be stationed each night in the village **chouri**."—*Overland Times of India*, May 12, Suppl. 7*b*.

See also **CHUTTRUM**.

CHOULTRY PLAIN, n.p. This was the name given to the open country formerly existing to the S.W. of Madras. *Choultry Plain* was also the old designation of the Hd. Quarters of the Madras Army; equivalent to "Horse Guards" in Westminster (C. P. B. MS.).

1780.—"Every gentleman now possessing a house in the fort, was happy in accommodating the family of his friend, who before had resided in **Choultry Plain**. *Note*. The country near Madras is a perfect flat, on which is built, at a small distance from the fort, a small *choultry*."—*Hodges, Travels*, 7.

CHOUSE, s. and v. This word is originally Turk. *chāush*, in former days a sergeant-at-arms, herald, or the like. [Vambéry (*Sketches*, 17) speaks of the *Tchaush* as the leader of a party of pilgrims.] Its meaning as 'a cheat,' or 'to swindle' is, apparently beyond doubt, derived from the anecdote thus related in a note of W. Gifford's upon the passage in Ben Jonson's *Alchemist*, which is quoted below. "In 1609 Sir Robert Shirley sent a messenger or *chiaus* (as our old writers call him) to this country, as his agent, from the Grand Signor and the Sophy, to transact some preparatory business. Sir Robert followed him, at his leisure, as ambassador from both these princes; but before he reached England, his agent had *chiaused* the Turkish and Persian merchants here of 4000*l*., and taken his flight, unconscious perhaps that he had enriched the language with a word of which the etymology would mislead Upton and puzzle Dr. Johnson."—Ed. of *Ben Jonson*, iv. 27. "In Kattywar, where the native chiefs employ Arab mercenaries, the **Chaus** still flourishes as an officer of a company. When I joined the Political Agency in that Province, there was a company of Arabs attached to the Residency under a *Chaus*." (*M.-Gen. Keatinge*). [The *N.E.D.* thinks that "Gifford's note must be taken with reserve." The *Stanf. Dict.* adds that Gifford's note asserts that two other *Chiauses* arrived in 1618-1625. One of the above quotations proves his accuracy as to 1618. Perhaps, however, the particular fraud had little to do with the modern use of the word. As Jonson suggests, *chiaus* may have been used for 'Turk' in the sense of 'cheat'; just as *Cataian* stood for 'thief' or 'rogue.' For a further discussion of the word see *N. & Q.*, 7 ser. vi. 387; 8 ser. iv. 129.]

1560.—"Cum vero me taederet inclusionis in eodem diversorio, ago cum meo **Chiauso** (genus id est, ut tibi scripsi alias, multiplicis apud Turcas officii, quod etiam ad oratorum custodiam extenditur) ut mihi liceat aere meo domum conducere. . . ."—*Busbeq. Epist.* iii. p. 149.

1610.—"*Dapper*. . . . What do you think of me, that I am a **chiaus**?

Face. What's that?

Dapper. The Turk was here.

As one would say, do you think I am a Turk?

* * * * *

Face. Come, noble doctor, pray thee let's prevail;
This is the gentleman, and he's no **chiaus**."
Ben. Jonson, The Alchemist, Act I. sc. i.

1638.—
"*Fulgoso.* Gulls or Moguls,
Tag, rag, or other, hogen-mogen, vanden,
Ship-jack or **chouses**. Whoo! the brace are flinched.
The pair of shavers are sneak'd from us, Don. . . ."
Ford, The Lady's Trial, Act II. sc. i.

1619.—"Con gli ambasciatori stranieri che seco conduceva, cioè l'Indiano, di Sciah Selim, un **ciausc** Turco ed i Moscoviti. . . ."—*P. della Valle*, ii. 6.

1653.—"**Chiaoux** en Turq est vn Sergent du Diuan, et dans la campagne la garde d'vne Karauane, qui fait le guet, se nomme aussi **Chiaoux**, et cet employ n'est pas autrement honeste."—*Le Gouz*, ed. 1657, p. 536.

1659.—
"*Conquest.* We are
In a fair way to be ridiculous.
What think you? **Chiaus'd** by a scholar."
Shirley, Honoria & Mammon, Act II. sc. iii.

1663.—"The Portugals have **choused** us, it seems, in the Island of Bombay in the East Indys; for after a great charge of our fleets being sent thither with full commission from the King of Portugal to receive it, the Governour by some pretence or other will not deliver it to Sir Abraham Shipman."—*Pepys, Diary*, May 15; [ed. *Wheatley* iii. 125].

1674.—
"When geese and pullen are seduc'd
And sows of sucking pigs are **chows'd**."
Hudibras, Pt. II. canto 3.

1674.—
"Transform'd to a Frenchman by my art;
He stole your cloak, and pick'd your pocket,
Chows'd and caldes'd ye like a blockhead." *Ibid.*

1754.—"900 **chiaux**: they carried in their hand a baton with a double silver crook on the end of it; . . . these frequently chanted moral sentences and encomiums on the SHAH, occasionally proclaiming also his victories as he passed along."—*Hanway*, i. 170.

1762.—"Le 27ᵉ d'Août 1762 nous entendîmes un coup de canon du chateau de Kâhira, c'étoit signe qu'un **Tsjaus** (courier) étoit arrivé de la grande caravane."—*Niebuhr, Voyage*, i. 171.

1826.—"We started at break of day from the northern suburb of Ispahan, led by the **chaoushes** of the pilgrimage. . . ."—*Hajji Baba*, ed. 1835, p. 6.

CHOW-CHOW, s. A common application of the *Pigeon*-English term in China is to mixed preserves; but, as the quotation shows, it has many uses; the idea of mixture seems to prevail. It is the name given to a book by Viscountess Falkland, whose husband was Governor of Bombay. There it seems to mean 'a medley of trifles.' **Chow** is in 'pigeon' applied to food of any kind. ["From the erroneous impression that dogs form one of the principal items of a Chinaman's diet, the common variety has been dubbed the '**chow** dog'" (*Ball, Things Chinese*, p. 179).] We find the word **chow-chow** in Blumentritt's *Vocabular* of Manilla terms: "*Chau-chau*, a Tagal dish so called."

1858.—"The word **chow-chow** is suggestive, especially to the Indian reader, of a mixture of things, 'good, bad, and indifferent,' of sweet little oranges and bits of bamboo stick, slices of sugar-cane and rinds of unripe fruit, all concocted together, and made upon the whole into a very tolerable confection. . . .

"Lady Falkland, by her happy selection of a name, to a certain extent deprecates and disarms criticism. We cannot complain that her work is without plan, unconnected, and sometimes trashy, for these are exactly the conditions implied in the word **chow-chow**."—*Bombay Quarterly Review*, January, p. 100.

1882.—"The variety of uses to which the compound word '**chow-chow**' is put is almost endless. . . . A 'No. 1 *chow-chow*' thing signifies utterly worthless, but when applied to a breakfast or dinner it means 'unexceptionably good.' A '*chow-chow*' cargo is an assorted cargo; a 'general shop' is a '*chow-chow*' shop . . . one (factory) was called the '*chow-chow*,' from its being inhabited by divers Parsees, Moormen, or other natives of India."—*The Fankwae*, p. 63.

CHOWDRY, s. H. *chaudharī*, lit. 'a holder of four'; the explanation of which is obscure: [rather Skt. *chakradharin*, 'the bearer of the discus as an ensign of authority']. The usual application of the term is to the headman of a craft in a town, and more particularly to the person who is selected by Government as the agent through whom supplies, workmen, &c., are supplied for public purposes. [Thus the *Chaudharī* of carters provides carriage, the *Chaudharī* of Kahārs bearers, and so on.] Formerly, in places, to the headman of a village; to certain holders of lands; and in Cuttack it was, under native rule, applied to a district Revenue officer. In a paper of 'Explanations of Terms' furnished to the Council at Fort William by Warren Hastings, then Resident at Moradbagh (1759), **chowdrees** are defined as "Landholders in the next rank to Zemindars." (In *Long*, p. 176.) [Comp. **VENDU-MASTER.**] It is also an honorific title given by servants to one of their number, usually, we believe, to the *mālī* [see **MOLLY**], or gardener—as *khalīfa* to the cook and tailor, *jama'dār* to the *bhishtī*, *mehtar* to the sweeper, *sirdār* to the bearer.

c. 1300.—"... The people were brought to such a state of obedience that one revenue officer would string twenty ... **chaudharis** together by the neck, and enforce payment by blows."—*Ziā-ud-dīn Barnī*, in *Elliot*, iii. 183.

c. 1343.—"The territories dependent on the capital (Delhi) are divided into hundreds, each of which has a **Jauthari**, who is the Sheikh or chief man of the Hindus."—*Ibn Batuta*, iii. 388.

[1772.—"**Chowdrahs**, land-holders, in the next rank to Zemeendars."—*Verelst, View of Bengal*, Gloss. s.v.]

1788.—"**Chowdry.** — A Landholder or Farmer. Properly he is above the Zemindar in rank; but, according to the present custom of Bengal, he is deemed the next to the Zemindar. Most commonly used as the principal purveyor of the markets in towns or camps."—*Indian Vocabulary* (Stockdale's).

CHOWK, s. H. *chauk*. An open place or wide street in the middle of a city where the market is held; [as, for example, the *Chāndnī Chauk* of Delhi]. It seems to be adopted in Persian, and there is an Arabic form *Sūḳ*, which, it is just possible, may have been borrowed and Arabized from the present word. The radical idea of *chauk* seems to be "four ways" [Skt. *chatushka*], the crossing of streets at the centre of business. Compare *Carfax*, and the *Quattro Cantoni* of Palermo. In the latter city there is a market place called Piazza Ballarò, which in the 16th century a chronicler calls *Seggeballarath*, or as Amari interprets, *Sūḳ*-Balharā.

[1833.—"The Chandy **Choke**, in Delhi ... is perhaps the broadest street in any city in the East."—*Skinner, Excursions in India*, i. 49.]

CHOWNEE, s. The usual native name, at least in the Bengal Presidency, for an Anglo-Indian **cantonment** (q.v.). It is H. *chhāonī*, 'a thatched roof,' *chhāonā*, *chhānā*, v. 'to thatch.'

[1829.—"The Regent was at the **chaoni**, his standing camp at Gagrown, when this event occurred."—*Tod, Annals* (Calcutta reprint), ii. 611.]

CHOWRINGHEE, n.p. The name of a road and quarter of Calcutta, in which most of the best European houses stand; *Chaurangī*.

1789.—"The houses ... at **Chowringee** also will be much more healthy."—*Seton-Karr*, ii. 205.

1790.—"To dig a large tank opposite to the **Cheringhee** Buildings."—*Ibid.* 13.

1791.—"Whereas a robbery was committed on Tuesday night, the first instant, on the **Chowringhy** Road."—*Ibid.* 54.

1792.—"*For Private Sale.* A neat, compact and new built garden house, pleasantly situated at **Chouringy**, and from its contiguity to Fort William, peculiarly well calculated for an officer; it would likewise be a handsome provision for a native lady, or a child. The price is 1500 sicca rupees."—*Ibid.* ii. 541.

1803.—"**Chouringhee**, an entire village of palaces, runs for a considerable length at right angles with it, and altogether forms the finest view I ever beheld in any city."—*Ld. Valentia*, i. 236.

1810.—"As I enjoyed Calcutta much less this time ... I left it with less regret. Still, when passing the **Chowringhee** road the last day, I—

'Looked on stream and sea and plain
As what I ne'er might see again.'"

Elphinstone, in *Life*, i. 231.

1848.—"He wished all Cheltenham, all **Chowringhee**, all Calcutta, could see him in that position, waving his hand to such a beauty, and in company with such a famous buck as Rawdon Crawley, of the Guards."—*Vanity Fair*, ed. 1867, i. 237.

CHOWRY, s.

(a.) See **CHOULTRY**.

(b.) H. *chaṅwar*, *chaunrī*; from Skt. *chamara*, *chāmara*. The bushy tail of the Tibetan **Yak** (q.v.), often set in a costly decorated handle to use as a fly-flapper, in which form it was one of the insignia of ancient Asiatic royalty. The tail was also often attached to the horse-trappings of native warriors; whilst it formed from remote times the standard of nations and nomad tribes of Central Asia. The Yak-tails and their uses are mentioned by Aelian, and by Cosmas (see under **YAK**). Allusions to the *chāmara*, as a sign of royalty, are frequent in Skt. books and inscriptions, *e.g.* in the Poet Kalidāsa (see transl. by Dr. Mill in

J. As. Soc. Beng. i. 342; the *Amarakosha*, ii. 7, 31, &c.). The common Anglo-Indian expression in the 18th century appears to have been "**Cow-tails**" (q.v.). And hence Bogle in his Journal, as published by Mr. Markham, calls *Yaks* by the absurd name of "*cow-tailed cows*," though "horse-tailed cows" would have been more germane!

c. A.D. 250.—"Βοῶν δε γένη δύο, δρομικούς τε καὶ ἄλλους ἀγρίους δεινῶς· ἐκ τουτῶν γε τῶν βοῶν καὶ τὰς μυιοσόβας ποιοῦνται, καὶ τὸ μὲν σῶμα παμμέλανες εἶσιν οἵδε· τὰς δὲ οὐρὰς ἔχουσι λευκὰς ἰσχυρῶς."—*Aelian. de Nat. An.* xv. 14.

A.D. 634-5.—". . . with his armies which were darkened by the spotless **chāmaras** that were waved over them."—*Aihole Inscription.*

c. 940.—"They export from this country the hair named *al-zamar* (or al-**chamar**) of which those fly-flaps are made, with handles of silver or ivory, which attendants hold over the heads of kings when giving audience."—*Maṣ'ūdī*, i. 385. The expressions of *Maṣ'ūdī* are aptly illustrated by the Assyrian and Persepolitan sculptures. (See also *Marco Polo*, bk. iii. ch. 18; *Nic. Conti*, p. 14, in *India in the XVth Century*).

1623.—"For adornment of their horses they carried, hung to the cantles of their saddles, great tufts of a certain white hair, long and fine, which they told me were the tails of certain wild oxen found in India."—*P. della Valle*, ii. 662; [Hak. Soc. ii. 260].

1809.—"He also presented me in trays, which were as usual laid at my feet, two beautiful **chowries**."—*Lord Valentia*, i. 428.

1810.—"Near Brahma are Indra and Indranee on their elephant, and below is a female figure holding a *chamara* or **chowree**."—*Maria Graham*, 56.

1827.—"A black female slave, richly dressed, stood behind him with a **chowry**, or cow's tail, having a silver handle, which she used to keep off the flies."—*Sir W. Scott, The Surgeon's Daughter*, ch. x.

CHOWRYBURDAR, s. The servant who carries the **Chowry**. H. P. *chaunrī-bardār*.

1774.—"The Deb-Rajah on horseback . . . a **chowra-burdar** on each side of him."—*Bogle*, in *Markham's Tibet*, 24.

[1838.—". . . the old king was sitting in the garden with a **chowrybadar** waving the flies from him."—*Miss Eden, Up the Country*, i. 138.]

CHOWT, CHOUT, s. Mahr. *chauth*, 'one fourth part.' The blackmail levied by the Mahrattas from the provincial governors as compensation for leaving their districts in immunity from plunder. The term is also applied to some other exactions of like ratio (see *Wilson*).

[1559.—Mr. Whiteway refers to *Couto* (Dec. VII. bk. 6, ch. 6), where this word is used in reference to payments made in 1559 in the time of D. Constantine de Bragança, and in papers of the early part of the 17th century the King of the **Chouteas** is frequently mentioned.]

1644.—"This King holds in our lands of Daman a certain payment which they call **Chouto**, which was paid him long before they belonged to the Portuguese, and so after they came under our power the payment continued to be made, and about these exactions and payments there have risen great disputes and contentions on one side and another."—*Bocarro* (MS.).

1674.—"Messengers were sent to Bassein demanding the **chout** of all the Portuguese territory in these parts. The *chout* means the fourth part of the revenue, and this is the earliest mention we find of the claim."—*Orme's Fragments*, p. 45.

1763-78.—"They (the English) were . . . not a little surprised to find in the letters now received from Balajerow and his agent to themselves, and in stronger terms to the Nabob, a peremptory demand of the **Chout** or tribute due to the King of the Morattoes from the Nabobship of Arcot."—*Orme*, ii. 228-9.

1803.—"The Peshwah . . . cannot have a right to two **choutes**, any more than to two revenues from any village in the same year."—*Wellington Desp.* (ed. 1837), ii. 175.

1858.—". . . They (the Mahrattas) were accustomed to demand of the provinces they threatened with devastation a certain portion of the public revenue, generally the fourth part; and this, under the name of the **chout**, became the recognized Mahratta tribute, the price of the absence of their plundering hordes."—*Whitney, Oriental and Ling. Studies*, ii. 20-21.

CHOYA, CHAYA, CHEY, s. A root, [generally known as **chayroot**,] (*Hedyotis umbellata*, Lam., *Oldenlandia umb.*, L.) of the Nat. Ord. *Cinchonaceae*, affording a red dye, sometimes called 'India Madder,' ['Dye Root,' 'Rameshwaram Root']; from Tam. *shāyaver*, Malayāl. *chāyaver* (*chāya*, 'colour,' *ver*, 'root'). It is exported from S. India, and was so also at one time from Ceylon. There is a figure of the plant in *Lettres Edif.* xiv. 164.

c. 1566.—"Also from *S. Tome* they layd great store of red yarne, of bombast died with a roote which they call **saia**, as aforesayd, which colour will never out."—*Caesar Frederike*, in *Hakl.* [ii. 354].

1583.—"Ne vien anchora di detta **saia** da un altro luogo detto Petopoli, e se ne tingono parimente in S. Thomè."—*Balbi*, f. 107.

1672.—"Here groweth very good **Zaye**." —*Baldaeus, Ceylon.*

[1679.—" . . . if they would provide mustors of **Chae** and White goods. . . ." —*Memoriall of S. Master*, in *Kistna Man.*, p. 131.]

1726.—"**Saya** (a dye-root that is used on the *Coast* for painting chintzes)."—*Valentijn, Chor.* 45.

1727.—"The Islands of *Diu* (near Masulipatam) produce the famous *Dye* called **Shaii**. It is a Shrub growing in Grounds that are overflown with the Spring tides." —*A. Hamilton*, i. 370; [ed. 1744, i. 374].

1860.—"The other productions that constituted the exports of the Island were sapan-wood to Persia; and **choya**-roots, a substitute for Madder, collected at Manaar . . . for transmission to Surat."—*Tennent's Ceylon*, ii. 54-55. See also *Chitty's Ceylon Gazetteer* (1834), p. 40.

CHUCKAROO, s. English soldier's lingo for **Chokra** (q.v.)

CHUCKER. From H. *chakar, chakkar, chakrā*, Skt. *chakra*, 'a wheel or circle.'

(**a.**) s. A quoit for playing the English game; but more properly the sharp quoit or discus which constituted an ancient Hindu missile weapon, and is, or was till recently, carried by the Sikh fanatics called *Akālī* (see **AKALEE**), generally encircling their peaked turbans. The thing is described by Tavernier (E. T. ii. 41: [ed. *Ball*, i. 82]) as carried by a company of Mahommedan Fakīrs whom he met at Sherpūr in Guzerat. See also *Lt.-Col. T. Lewin, A Fly*, &c., p. 47: [*Egerton, Handbook*, Pl. 15, No. 64].

1516.—"In the Kingdom of Dely . . . they have some steel wheels which they call **chacarani**, two fingers broad, sharp outside like knives, and without edge inside; and the surface of these is the size of a small plate. And they carry seven or eight of these each, put on the left arm; and they take one and put it on the finger of the right hand, and make it spin round many times, and so they hurl it at their enemies." —*Barboṣa*, 100-101.

1630.—"In her right hand shee bare a **chuckerey**, which is an instrument of a round forme, and sharp-edged in the superficies thereof . . . and slung off, in the quickness of his motion, it is able to deliuer or conuey death to a farre remote enemy." —*Lord, Disc. of the Banian Religion*, 12.

(**b**) v. and s. To lunge a horse. H. *chakarnā* or *chakar karnā*. Also 'the lunge.'

1829.—"It was truly tantalizing to see those fellows **chŭckering** their horses, not more than a quarter of a mile from our post."—*John Shipp*, i. 153.

[(**c.**) In Polo, a 'period.'

[1900.—"Two bouts were played to-day . . . In the opening **chukker** Capt. —— carried the ball in."—*Overland Mail*, Aug. 13.]

CHUCKERBUTTY, n.p. This vulgarized Bengal Brahman name is, as Wilson points out, a corruption of *chakravarttī*, the title assumed by the most exalted ancient Hindu sovereigns, an universal Emperor, whose chariot-wheels rolled over all (so it is explained by some).

c. 400.—"Then the Bikshuni Uthala began to think thus with herself, 'To-day the King, ministers, and people are all going to meet Buddha . . . but I—a woman—how can I contrive to get the first sight of him?' Buddha immediately, by his divine power, changed her into a holy **Chakravartti** Raja."—*Travels of Fah-hian, tr. by Beale*, p. 63.

c. 460.—"On a certain day (Asoka), having . . . ascertained that the supernaturally gifted . . . Nága King, whose age extended to a *Kappo*, had seen the four Buddhas . . . he thus addressed him: 'Beloved, exhibit to me the person of the omniscient being of infinite wisdom, the **Chakkawatti** of the doctrine.'"—*The Mahawanso*, p. 27.

1856.—"The importance attached to the possession of a white elephant is traceable to the Buddhist system. A white elephant of certain wonderful endowments is one of the seven precious things, the possession of which marks the *Maha* **Chakravartti** *Raja* . . . the holy and universal sovereign, a character which appears once in a cycle."—*Mission to the Court of Ava* (Major's Phayre's), 1858, p. 154.

CHUCKLAH, s. H. *chaklā*, [Skt. *chakra*, 'a wheel']. A territorial subdivision under the Mahommedan government, thus defined by Warren Hastings, in the paper quoted under **CHOWDRY**:

1759.—"The jurisdiction of a *Phojdar* (see **FOUJDAR**), who receives the rents from the Zemindars, and accounts for them with the Government."

1760.—"In the treaty concluded with the Nawáb Meer Mohummud Cásim Khán, on the 27th Sept. 1760, it was agreed that . . . the English army should be ready to assist him in the management of all affairs, and that the lands of the **chuklahs** (districts) of Burdwan, Midnapore and Chittagong, should be assigned for all the charges of the company and the army. . . ."—*Harington's Analysis of the Laws and Regulations*, vol. i. Calcutta, 1805-1809, p. 5.

CHUCKLER, s. Tam. and Malayāl. *shakkili*, the name of a very low caste, members of which are tanners or cobblers, like the *Chamārs* (see **CHUMAR**) of Upper India. But whilst the latter are reputed to be a very dark caste, the *Chucklers* are fair (see *Elliot's Gloss.* by *Beames*, i. 71, and *Caldwell's Gram.* 574). [On the other hand the *Madràs Gloss.* (s.v.) says that as a rule they are of "a dark black hue."] Colloquially in S. India *Chuckler* is used for a native shoemaker.

c. 1580.—"All the Gentoos (*Gentios*) of those parts, especially those of Bisnaga, have many castes, which take precedence one of another. The lowest are the **Chaquivilis**, who make shoes, and eat all unclean flesh. . . ."—*Primor e Honra*, &c., f. 95.

1759.—"**Shackelays** are shoemakers, and held in the same despicable light on the Coromandel Coast as the Niaddes and Pullies on the *Malabar*."—*Ives*, 26.

c. 1790.—"Aussi n'est-ce que le rébut de la classe méprisée des parrias; savoir les **tschakelís** ou cordonniers et les *vettians* ou fossoyeurs, qui s'occupent de l'enterrement et la combustion des morts."—*Haafner*, ii. 60.

[1844.—". . . the **chockly**, who performs the degrading duty of executioner. . . ."—*Society, Manners, &c., of India*, ii. 282.]

1869.—"The *Komatis* or mercantile caste of Madras by long established custom, are required to send an offering of betel to the **chucklers**, or shoemakers, before contracting their marriages."—*Sir W. Elliot*, in *J. Ethn. Soc.*, N. S. vol. i. 102.

CHUCKMUCK, s. H. *chakmak*. 'Flint and steel.' One of the titles conferred on Haidar 'Ali before he rose to power was '**Chakmak** *Jang*, 'Firelock of War'? See *H. of Hydur Naik*, 112.

CHUCKRUM, s. An ancient coin once generally current in the S. of India, Malayāl. *chakram*, Tel. *chakramu*; from Skt. *chakra* (see under **CHUCKER**). It is not easy to say what was its value, as the statements are inconsistent: nor do they confirm Wilson's, that it was equal to one-tenth of a pagoda. [According to the *Madras Gloss.* (s.v.) it bore the same relation to the gold **Pagoda** that the **Anna** does to the **Rupee**, and under it again was the copper **Cash**, which was its sixteenth.] The denomination survives in Travancore, [where 28½ go to one rupee. (*Ibid.*)]

1554.—"And the fanoms of the place are called **chocrões**, which are coins of inferior gold; they are worth 12⅓ or 12¼ to the *pardao* of gold, reckoning the *pardao* at 360 *reis*."—*A. Nunez, Livro dos Pesos*, 36.

1711.—"The Enemy will not come to any agreement unless we consent to pay 30,000 **chuckrums**, which we take to be 16,600 and odd pagodas."—In *Wheeler*, ii. 165.

1813.—Milburn, under Tanjore, gives the **chuckrum** as a coin equal to 20 Madras, or ten gold fanams. 20 Madras fanams would be ⅜ of a pagoda.

[From the difficulty of handling these coins, which are small and round, they are counted on a **chuckrum** board as in the case of the **Fanam** (q.v.).]

CHUDDER, s. H. *chādar*, a sheet, or square piece of cloth of any kind; the ample sheet commonly worn as a mantle by women in N. India. It is also applied to the cloths spread over Mahommedan tombs. Barbosa (1516) and Linschoten (1598) have *chautars*, *chautares*, as a kind of cotton piece-goods, but it is certain that this is not the same word. *Chowtars* occur among Bengal piece-goods in *Milburn*, ii. 221. [The word is *chautár*, 'anything with four threads,' and it occurs in the list of cotton cloths in the *Āīn* (i. 94). In a letter of 1610 we have "*Chautares* are white and well requested" (*Danvers, Letters*, i. 75); "*Chauters* of Agra" (*Foster, Letters*, ii. 45); Cocks has "fine *Casho* or *Chowter*" (*Diary*, i. 86); and in 1615 they are called "*Cowter*" (*Foster*, iv. 51).]

1525.—"**Chader** of Cambaya."—*Lembrança*, 56.

[c. 1610.—"From Bengal comes another sort of hanging, of fine linen painted and ornamented with colours in a very agreeable fashion; these they call **iader**."—*Pyrard de Laval*, Hak. Soc. i. 222.]

1614.—"Pintados, chints and **chadors**."—*Peyton*, in *Purchas*, i. 530.

1673.—"The habit of these water-nymphs was fine **Shudders** of lawn embroidered on the neck, wrist, and skirt with a border of several coloured silks or threads of gold."—*Herbert*, 3rd ed. 191.

1832.—"**Chuddur** . . . a large piece of cloth or sheet, of one and a half or two breadths, thrown over the head, so as to cover the whole body. Men usually sleep rolled up in it."—*Herklots, Qanoon-e-Islam*, xii.-xiii.

1878.—"Two or three women, who had been chattering away till we appeared, but who, on seeing us, drew their '**chadders**' . . . round their faces, and retired to the further end of the boat."—*Life in the Mofussil*, i. 79.

The **Rampore Chudder** is a kind of shawl, of the Tibetan shawl-wool, of uniform colour without pattern, made originally at Rāmpur on the Sutlej; and of late years largely imported into England: [(see the *Panjab Mono. on Wool*, p. 9). Curiously enough a claim to the derivation of the title from Rāmpur, in Rohilkhand, N.W.P. is made in the *Imperial Gazetteer*, 1st ed. (s.v.).]

CHUL! CHULLO! v. in imperative; 'Go on! Be quick.' H. *chalo!* imper. of *chalnā*, to go, go speedily. [Another common use of the word in Anglo-Indian slang is—"It won't **chul**," 'it won't answer, succeed.']

c. 1790.—"Je montai de très-bonne heure dans mon palanquin.—**Tschollo** (c'est-à-dire, marche), crièrent mes **coulis**, et aussitôt le voyage commença."—*Haafner*, ii. 5.

[**CHUMAR**, s. H. *Chamār*, Skt. *charma-kāra*, 'one who works in leather,' and thus answering to the **Chuckler** of S. India; an important caste found all through N. India, whose primary occupation is tanning, but a large number are agriculturists and day labourers of various kinds.

[1823.—"From this abomination, beef-eating . . . they [the Bheels] only rank above the **Choomars**, or shoemakers, who feast on dead carcases, and are in Central India, as elsewhere, deemed so unclean that they are not allowed to dwell within the precincts of the village."—*Malcolm, Central India*, 2nd ed. ii. 179.]

CHUMPUK, s. A highly ornamental and sacred tree (*Michelia champaca*, L., also *M. Rheedii*), a kind of magnolia, whose odorous yellow blossoms are much prized by Hindus, offered at shrines, and rubbed on the body at marriages, &c. H. *champak*, Skt. *champaka*. Drury strangely says that the name is "derived from *Champa*, an island between Cambogia and Cochin China, where the tree grows." *Champa* is *not* an island, and certainly derives its Sanskrit name from India, and did *not* give a name to an Indian tree. The tree is found wild in the Himālaya from Nepāl, eastward; also in Pegu and Tenasserim, and along the Ghauts to Travancore. The use of the term *champaka* extends to the Philippine Islands. [Mr. Skeat notes that it is highly prized by Malay women, who put it in their hair.]

1623.—"Among others they showed me a flower, in size and form not unlike our lily, but of a yellowish white colour, with a sweet and powerful scent, and which they call **champà** [ciampá]."—*P. della Valle*, ii. 517; [Hak. Soc. i. 40].

1786.—"The walks are scented with blossoms of the **champac** and nagisar, and the plantations of pepper and coffee are equally new and pleasing."—*Sir W. Jones*, in *Mem.*, &c., ii. 81.

1810.—"Some of these (birds) build in the sweet-scented **champaka** and the mango."—*Maria Graham*, 22.

1819.—

"The wandering airs they faint
On the dark, the silent stream;
And the **chumpak's** odours fail
Like sweet thoughts in a dream."
Shelley, Lines to an Indian Air.

1821.—

"Some **chumpak** flowers proclaim
it yet divine."
Medwin, Sketches in Hindoostan, 73.

CHUNÁM, s. Prepared lime; also specially used for fine polished plaster. Forms of this word occur both in Dravidian languages and Hind. In the latter *chūnā* is from Skt. *chūrṇa*, 'powder'; in the former it is somewhat uncertain whether the word is, or is not, an old derivative from the Sanskrit. In the first of the following quotations the word used seems taken from the Malayāl. *chuṇṇāmba*, Tam. *shuṇṇāmbu*.

1510.—"And they also eat with the said leaves (betel) a certain lime made from oyster shells, which they call **cionama**."—*Varthema*, 144.

1563.—". . . so that all the names you meet with that are not Portuguese are Malabar; such as *betre* (betel), **chuna**, which is lime. . . ."—*Garcia*. f. 37*g*.

c. 1610.—". . . l'vn porte son éventail, l'autre la boëte d'argent pleine de betel, l'autre une boëte ou il y a du **chunan**, qui est de la chaux."—*Pyrard de Laval*, ii. 84; [Hak. Soc. ii. 135].

1614.—"Having burnt the great idol into **chunah**, he mixed the powdered lime with *pān* leaves, and gave it to the Rājpūts that they might eat the objects of their worship."—*Firishta*, quoted by *Quatremère, Not. et Ext.*, xiv. 510.

1673.—"The Natives chew it (Betel) with **Chinam** (Lime of calcined Oyster Shells)."—*Fryer*, 40.

1687.—"That stores of Brick, Iron, Stones, and **Chenam** be in readiness to make up any breach."—*Madras Consultations*, in *Wheeler*, i. 168.

1689.—"**Chinam** is Lime made of Cockle-shells, or Lime-stone; and Pawn is the Leaf of a Tree."—*Ovington*, 123.

1750-60.—"The flooring is generally composed of a kind of loam or stucco, called **chunam**, being a lime made of burnt shells."—*Grose*, i. 52.

1763.—"In the *Chuckleh* of Silet for the space of five years . . . my phoasdar and the Company's gomastah shall jointly prepare **chunam**, of which each shall defray all expenses, and half the **chunam** so made shall be given to the Company, and the other half shall be for my use."—*Treaty of Mir Jaffir with the Company*, in *Carraccioli's L. of Clive*, i. 64.

1809.—"The row of **chunam** pillars which supported each side . . . were of a shining white."—*Ld. Valentia*, i. 61.

CHUNÁM, TO, v. To set in mortar; or, more frequently, to plaster over with chunam.

1687.—". . . to get what great jars he can, to put wheat in, and **chenam** them up, and set them round the fort curtain."—In *Wheeler*, i. 168.

1809.—". . . having one . . . room . . . beautifully **chunammed**."—*Ld. Valentia*, i. 386.

Both noun and verb are used also in the Anglo-Chinese settlements.

CHUNÁRGURH, n.p. A famous rock-fort on the Ganges, above Benares, and on the right bank. The name is believed to be a corr. of *Charana-giri*, 'Foot Hill,' a name probably given from the actual resemblance of the rock, seen in longitudinal profile, to a human foot. [There is a local legend that it represents the foot of Vishnu. A native folk etymology makes it a corr. of *Chandālgarh*, from some legendary connection with the Bhangi tribe (see **CHANDAUL**). (See *Crooke, Tribes and Castes*, i. 263.)]

[1768.—"Sensible of the vast importance of the fort of **Chunar** to Sujah al Dowlah . . . we have directed Col. Barker to reinforce the garrison. . . ."—*Letter to Court of Directors*, in *Verelst*, App. 78.

[1785.—"**Chunar**, called by the natives Chundalghur. . . ."—*Forbes, Or. Mem.* 2nd ed. ii. 442.]

CHUPATTY, s. H. *chapātī*, an unleavened cake of bread (generally of coarse wheaten meal), patted flat with the hand, and baked upon a griddle; the usual form of native bread, and the staple food of Upper India. (See **HOPPER**).

1615.—Parson Terry well describes the thing, but names it not: "The ordinary sort of people eat bread made of a coarse grain, but both toothsome and wholesome and hearty. They make it up in broad cakes, thick like our oaten cakes; and then bake it upon small round iron hearths which they carry with them."—In *Purchas*, ii. 1468.

1810.—"**Chow-patties**, or bannocks."—*Williamson, V. M.* ii. 348.

1857.—"From village to village brought by one messenger and sent forward by another passed a mysterious token in the shape of one of those flat cakes made from flour and water, and forming the common bread of the people, which in their language, are called **chupatties**."—*Kaye's Sepoy War*, i. 570. [The original account of this by the Correspondent of the '*Times*,' dated "Bombay, March 3, 1857," is quoted in 2 ser. *N. & Q.* iii. 365.]

There is a tradition of a noble and gallant Governor-General who, when compelled to rough it for a day or two, acknowledged that "*chuprassies* and *masaulchies* were not such bad diet," meaning **Chupatties** and **Mussalla**.

CHUPKUN, s. H. *chapkan*. The long frock (or cassock) which is the usual dress in Upper India of nearly all male natives who are not actual labourers or indigent persons. The word is probably of Turki or Mongol origin, and is perhaps identical with the *chakman* of the *Āīn* (i. 90), a word still used in Turkistan. [Vambéry, (*Sketches*, 121 *seqq.*) describes both the *Tchapan* or upper coat and the *Tchekmen* or gown.] Hence Beames's connection of *chapkan* with the idea of *chap* as meaning compressing or clinging [Platts *chapaknā*, 'to be pressed'], "a tightly-fitting coat or cassock," is a little fanciful. (*Comp. Gram.* i. 212 *seq.*) Still this idea may have shaped the corruption of a foreign word.

1883.—"He was, I was going to say, in his shirt-sleeves, only I am not sure that he wore a shirt in those days—I think he had a **chupkun**, or native under-garment."—*C. Raikes*, in *L. of Ld. Lawrence*, i. 59.

CHUPRA, n.p. *Chaprā*, [or perhaps rather *Chhaprā*, 'a collection of straw huts,' (see **CHOPPER**),] a town and head-quarter station of the District Sāran in Bahār, on the north bank of the Ganges.

1665.—"The Holland Company have a House there (at Patna) by reason of their trade in Salt Peter, which they refine at a great Town called **Choupar** . . . 10 leagues above Patna."—*Tavernier*, E. T. ii. 53; [ed. *Ball*, i. 122].

1726.—"**Sjoppera** (*Chupra*)."—*Valentijn*, *Chorom.*, &c., 147.

CHUPRASSY, s. H. *chaprāsī*, the bearer of a *chaprās*, *i.e.* a badge-plate inscribed with the name of the office to which the bearer is attached. The *chaprāsī* is an office-messenger, or henchman, bearing such a badge on a cloth or leather belt. The term belongs to the Bengal Presidency. In Madras **Peon** is the usual term; in Bombay **Puttywalla**, (H. *paṭṭīwālā*), or "man of the belt." The etymology of *chaprās* is obscure; [the popular account is that it is a corr. of P. *chap-o-rāst*, 'left and right']; but see *Beames* (*Comp. Gram.* i. 212), who gives *buckle* as the original meaning.

1865.—"I remember the days when every servant in my house was a **chuprassee**, with the exception of the Khansaumaun and a Portuguese Ayah."—*The Dark Bungalow*, p. 389.

c. 1866.—

"The big Sahib's tent has gone from under the Peepul tree,
With his horde of hungry **chuprassees**, and oily sons of the quill—
I paid them the bribe they wanted, and Sheitan will settle the bill."

Sir A. C. Lyall, The Old Pindaree.

1877.—"One of my **chuprassies** or messengers . . . was badly wounded."—*Meadows Taylor*, *Life*, i. 227.

1880.—"Through this refractory medium the people of India see their rulers. The **Chuprassie** paints his master in colours drawn from his own black heart. Every lie he tells, every insinuation he throws out, every demand he makes, is endorsed with his master's name. He is the arch-slanderer of our name in India."—*Ali Baba*, 102-3.

CHURR, s. H. *char*, Skt. *char*, 'to move.' "A sand-bank or island in the current of a river, deposited by the water, claims to which were regulated by the Bengal Reg. xi. 1825" (*Wilson*). A *char* is new alluvial land deposited by the great rivers as the floods are sinking, and covered with grass, but not necessarily insulated. It is remarkable that Mr. Marsh mentions a very similar word as used for the same thing in Holland. "New sandbank land, covered with grasses, is called in Zeeland *schor*" (*Man and Nature*, p. 339). The etymologies are, however, probably quite apart.

1878.—"In the dry season all the various streams . . . are merely silver threads winding among innumerable sandy islands, the soil of which is specially adapted for the growth of Indigo. They are called **Churs**."—*Life in the Mofussil*, ii. 3 *seq.*

CHURRUCK, s. A wheel or any rotating machine; particularly applied to simple machines for cleaning cotton. Pers. *charkh*, 'the celestial sphere,' 'a wheel of any kind,' &c. Beng. *charak* is apparently a corruption of the Persian word, facilitated by the nearness of the Skt. *chakra*, &c.

—— **POOJAH**. Beng. *charak-pūjā* (see **POOJA**). The Swinging Festival of the Hindus, held on the sun's entrance into Aries. The performer is suspended from a long yard, traversing round on a mast, by hooks passed through the muscle over the blade-bones, and then whirled round so as to fly out centrifugally. The chief seat of this barbarous display is, or latterly was, in Bengal, but it was formerly prevalent in many parts of India. [It is the **Shirry** (Ca. and Tel. *sidi*, Tam. *shedil*, Tel. *sidi*, 'a hook') of S. India.] There is an old description in Purchas's *Pilgrimage*, p. 1000; also (in Malabar) in *A. Hamilton*, i. 270; [at Ikkeri, *P. della Valle*, Hak. Soc. ii. 259]; and (at Calcutta) in Heber's *Journal*, quoted below.

c. 1430.—"Alii ad ornandos currus perforato latere, fune per corpus immisso se ad currum suspendunt, pendentesque et ipsi exanimati idolum comitantur; id optimum sacrificium putant et acceptissimum deo."—*Conti*, in *Poggius*, *De Var. Fortunae*, iv.

[1754.—See a long account of the Bengal rite in *Ives*, 27 *seqq.*]

1824.—"The Hindoo Festival of '**Churruck Poojah**' commenced to-day, of which, as my wife has given an account in her journal, I shall only add a few particulars."—*Heber*, ed. 1844, i. 57.

CHURRUS, s.

a. H. *charas*. A simple apparatus worked by oxen for drawing water from a well, and discharging it into irrigation channels by means of pulley ropes, and a large bag of hide (H. *charsā*, Skt. *charma*). [See the description in *Forbes*, *Or. Mem.* 2nd ed. i. 153. Hence the area irrigated from a well.]

[1829.—"To each **Churrus**, *chursa*, or skin of land, there is attached twenty-five beeghas of irrigated land." — *Tod*, *Annals* (Calcutta repr.), ii. 688.]

b. H. *charus*, [said to be so called because the drug is collected by men who walk with leather aprons through the field]. The resinous exudation of the hemp-plant (*Cannabis Indica*), which is the basis of intoxicating preparations (see **BANG, GUNJA**).

[1842.—"The Moolah sometimes smoked the intoxicating drug called **Chirs**."—*Elphinstone*, *Caubul*, i. 344.]

CHUTKARRY, CHATTAGAR, in S. India, a half-caste; Tam. *shatti-kar*, 'one who wears a waistcoat' (*C. P. B*).

CHUTNY, s. H. *chatnī*. A kind of strong relish, made of a number of condiments and fruits, &c., used in India, and more especially by Mahommedans, and the merits of which are now well known in England. For native *chutny* recipes, see *Herklots*, *Qanoon-e-Islam*, 2nd ed. xlvii. *seqq.*

1813.—"The **Chatna** is sometimes made with cocoa-nut, lime-juice, garlic, and chillies, and with the pickles is placed in deep leaves round the large cover, to the number of 30 or 40."—*Forbes*, *Or. Mem.* ii. 50 *seq.*; [2nd ed. i. 348].

1820.—"**Chitnee, Chatnee**, some of the hot spices made into a paste, by being bruised with water, the 'kitchen' of an Indian peasant."—*Acc. of Township of Loony*, in *Tr. Lit. Soc. Bombay*, ii. 194.

CHUTT, s. H. *chhat*. The proper meaning of the vernacular word is 'a roof or platform.' But in modern Anglo-Indian its usual application is to the coarse cotton sheeting, stretched on a frame and whitewashed, which forms the usual ceiling of rooms in thatched or tiled houses; properly *chādar-chhat*, 'sheet-ceiling.'

CHUTTANUTTY, n.p. This was one of the three villages purchased for the East India Company in 1686, when the agents found their position in Hugli intolerable, to form the settlement which became the city of Calcutta. The other two villages were Calcutta and Govindpūr. Dr. Hunter spells it *Sūtanatī*, but the old Anglo-Indian orthography indicates *Chatānatī* as probable. In the letter-books of the Factory Council in the India Office the earlier letters from this establishment are lost, but down to 27th March, 1700, they are dated from "**Chuttanutte**"; on and after June 8th, from "Calcutta"; and from August 20th in the same year from "Fort William" in Calcutta. [See *Hedges, Diary*, Hak. Soc. ii. lix.] According to Major Ralph Smyth, Chatānatī occupied "the site of the present native town," *i.e.* the northern quarter of the city. Calcutta stood on what is now the European commercial part; and Govindpūr on the present site of Fort William.*

1753.—"The Hoogly Phousdar demanding the payment of the ground rent for 4 months from January, namely:—

	R.	A.	P.
Sootaloota, Calcutta. .	325	0	0
Govindpoor, Picar . .	70	0	0
Govindpoor, Calcutta .	33	0	0
Buxies	1	8	0

Agreed that the President do pay the same out of cash."—*Consn. Ft. William*, April 30, in *Long*, 43.

CHUTTRUM, s. Tam *shattiram*, which is a corruption of Skt. *sattra*, 'abode.' In S. India a house where pilgrims and travelling members of the higher castes are entertained and fed gratuitously for a day or two. [See **CHOULTRY, DHURMSALLA.**]

1807.—"There are two distinct kinds of buildings confounded by Europeans under the name of *Choultry*. The first is that called by the natives **Chaturam**, and built for the accommodation of travellers. These . . . have in general pent roofs . . . built in the form of a square enclosing a court. . . . The other kind are properly built for the reception of images, when these are carried in procession. These have flat roofs, and consist of one apartment only, and by the natives are called *Mandapam*. . . . Besides the **Chaturam** and the *Mandapam*, there is another kind of building which by Europeans is called *Choultry;* in the Tamul language it is called *Tany Pundal*, or Water Shed . . . small buildings where weary travellers may enjoy a temporary repose in the shade, and obtain a draught of water or milk."—*F. Buchanan*, *Mysore*, i. 11, 15.

* *Stat. and Geog. Rep. of the 24 Pergunnahs District*, Calcutta, 1857, p. 57.

CINDERELLA'S SLIPPER. A Hindu story on the like theme appears among the Hala Kanara MSS. of the Mackenzie Collection:—

"*Suvarnadevi* having dropped her slipper in a reservoir, it was found by a fisherman of *Kusumakesari*, who sold it to a shopkeeper, by whom it was presented to the King *Ugrabáhu*. The Prince, on seeing the beauty of the slipper, fell in love with the wearer, and offered large rewards to any person who should find and bring her to him. An old woman undertook the task, and succeeded in tracing the shoe to its owner. . . ."—*Mackenzie Collection*, by *H. H. Wilson*, ii. 52. [The tale is not uncommon in Indian folk-lore. See *Miss Cox, Cinderella* (Folk-lore Soc.), ii. 91, 183, 465, &c.]

CINTRA ORANGES. See **ORANGE** and **SUNGTARA.**

CIRCARS, n.p. The territory to the north of the Coromandel Coast, formerly held by the Nizam, and now forming the districts of Kistna, Godávari, Vizagapatam, Ganjám, and a part of Nellore, was long known by the title of "*The Circars*," or "*Northern Circars*" (*i.e.* Governments), now officially obsolete. The Circars of Chicacole (now Vizagapatam Dist.), Rajamandri and Ellore (these two embraced now in Godávari Dist.), with Condapilly (now embraced in Kistna Dist.), were the subject of a grant from the Great Mogul, obtained by Clive in 1765, confirmed by treaty with the Nizam in 1766. Gantūr (now also included in Kistna Dist.) devolved eventually by the same treaty (but did not come permanently under British rule till 1803. [For the history see *Madras Admin. Man.* i. 179.] C. P. Brown says the expression "The Circars" was first used by the French, in the time of Bussy. [Another name for the Northern Circars was the *Carling* or *Carlingo* country, apparently a corr. of *Kalinga* (see **KLING**), see Pringle, *Diary, &c., of Ft. St. George*, 1st ser. vol. 2, p. 125. (See **SIRCAR.**)]

1758.—"Il est à remarquer qu'après mon départ d'Ayder Abad, Salabet Zingue a nommé un *Phosdar*, ou Gouverneur, pour les quatres **Cerkars.**"—*Mémoire*, by Bussy, in *Lettres de MM. de Bussy, de Lally et autres*, Paris, 1766, p. 24.

1767.—"Letter from the Chief and Council at Masulipatam . . . that in consequence of orders from the President and Council of Fort St. George for securing and sending away all vagrant Europeans that might be met with in the **Circars,** they have embarked there for this place. . . ."—*Fort William Consn.*, in *Long*, 476 *seq.*

1789.—"The most important public transaction . . . is the surrender of the Guntoor **Circar** to the Company, by which it becomes possessed of the whole Coast, from Jaggernaut to Cape Comorin. The Nizam made himself master of that province, soon after Hyder's invasion of the Carnatic, as an equivalent for the arrears of *peshcush*, due to him by the Company for the other **Circars.**"—*Letter of T. Munro*, in *Life* by *Gleig*, i. 70.

1823.—"Although the **Sirkárs** are our earliest possessions, there are none, perhaps, of which we have so little accurate knowledge in everything that regards the condition of the people."—*Sir T. Munro*, in *Selections, &c.*, by *Sir A. Arbuthnot*, i. 204.

We know from the preceding quotation what Munro's spelling of the name was.

1836.—"The district called the **Circars,** in India, is part of the coast which extends from the Carnatic to Bengal. . . . The domestic economy of the people is singular; they inhabit villages (!!), and all labour is performed by public servants paid from the public stock."—*Phillips, Million of Facts*, 320.

1878.—"General Sir J. C., C.B., K.C.S.I. He entered the Madras Army in 1820, and in 1834, according to official despatches, displayed 'active zeal, intrepidity, and judgment' in *dealing with the savage tribes in Orissa known as the* **Circars**"(!!!).—*Obituary Notice* in *Homeward Mail*, April 27.

CIVILIAN, s. A term which came into use about 1750-1770, as a designation of the covenanted European servants of the E. I. Company, not in military employ. It is not used by Grose, c. 1760, who was himself of such service at Bombay. [The earliest quotation in the *N.E.D.* is of 1766 from *Malcolm's L. of Clive*, 54.] In Anglo-Indian parlance it is still appropriated to members of the covenanted Civil Service [see **COVENANTED SERVANTS**]. The *Civil* Service is mentioned in *Carraccioli's L. of Clive*, (c. 1785), iii. 164. From an early date in the Company's history up to 1833, the members of the Civil Service were classified during the first five years as **Writers** (q.v.), then to the 8th year as **Factors** (q.v.); in the 9th and 11th as *Junior Merchants;* and thenceforward as *Senior Merchants.* These names were relics of the original commercial character of the E. I. Company's transactions, and had long ceased to have any practical meaning at the time of their abolition in 1833, when the Charter Act (3 & 4 Will. IV. c. 85), removed the last traces of the Company's commercial existence.

1848.—(Lady O'Dowd's) "quarrel with Lady Smith, wife of Minos Smith the puisne Judge, is still remembered by some at Madras, when the Colonel's lady snapped her fingers in the Judge's lady's face, and said *she'd* never walk behind ever a beggarly **civilian**."—*Vanity Fair*, ed. 1867, ii. 85.

1872.—"You bloated **civilians** are never satisfied, retorted the other."—*A True Reformer*, i. 4.

CLASSY, CLASHY, s. H. *khalāsī*, usual etym. from Arab *khalāṣ*. A tent-pitcher; also (because usually taken from that class of servants) a man employed as chain-man or staff-man, &c., by a surveyor; a native sailor; or **Matross** (q.v.). *Khalāṣ* is constantly used in Hindustani in the sense of 'liberation'; thus, of a prisoner, a magistrate says '*khalāṣ karo*,' 'let him go.' But it is not clear how *khalāsī* got its ordinary Indian sense. It is also written *khalāshī*, and Vullers has an old Pers. word *khalāsha* for 'a ship's rudder.' A learned friend suggests that this may be the real origin of *khalāsī* in its Indian use. [*Khalāṣ* also means the 'escape channel of a canal,' and *khalāsī* may have been originally a person in charge of such a work.]

1785.—"A hundred **clashies** have been sent to you from the presence."—*Tippoo's Letters*, 171.

1801.—"The sepoys in a body were to bring up the rear. Our left flank was to be covered by the sea, and our right by Gopie Nath's men. Then the **clashies** and other armed followers."—*Mt. Stewart Elphinstone*, in *Life*, i. 27.

1824.—"If the tents got dry, the **clashees** (tent-pitchers) allowed that we might proceed in the morning prosperously."—*Heber*, ed. 1844, i. 194.

CLEARING NUT, WATER FILTER NUT, s. The seed of *Strychnos potatorum*, L.; a tree of S. India; [known in N. India as *nirmalā*, *nirmalī*, 'dirt-cleaner']. It is so called from its property of clearing muddy water, if well rubbed on the inside of the vessel which is to be filled.

CLOVE, s. The flower-bud of *Caryophyllum aromaticum*, L., a tree of the Moluccas. The modern English name of this spice is a kind of ellipsis from the French *clous de girofles*, 'Nails of Girofles,' *i.e.* of *garofala*, *caryophylla*, &c., the name by which this spice was known to the ancients; the full old English name was similar, 'clove gilloflour,' a name which, cut in two like a polypus, has formed two different creatures, the clove (or *nail*) being assigned to the spice, and the 'gillyflower' to a familiar clove-smelling flower. The comparison to nails runs through many languages. In Chinese the thing is called *ting-hiang*, or 'nail-spice'; in Persian *mekhak*, 'little nails,' or 'nailkins,' like the German *Nelken*, *Nägelchen*, and *Gewürtz-nagel* (spice nail).

[1602-3.—"Alsoe be carefull to gett together all the **cloues** you can."—*Birdwood, First Letter Book*, 36.]

COAST, THE, n.p. This term in books of the 18th century means the 'Madras or Coromandel Coast,' and often 'the Madras Presidency.' It is curious to find Παραλία, "the Shore," applied in a similar specific way, in Ptolemy, to the coast near Cape Comorin. It will be seen that the term "*Coast* Army," for "Madras Army," occurs quite recently. The Persian rendering of *Coast* Army by *Bandarī* below is curious.

1781.—"Just imported from the **Coast** . . . a very fine assortment of the following cloths."—*India Gazette*, Sept. 15.

1793.—"Unseduced by novelty, and uninfluenced by example, the belles of the **Coast** have courage enough to be unfashionable . . . and we still see their charming tresses flow in luxuriant ringlets."—*Hugh Boyd*, 78.

1800.—"I have only 1892 **Coast** and 1200 Bombay sepoys."—*Wellington*, i. 227.

1802.—"From Hydurabád also, Colonels Roberts and Dalrymple, with 4000 of the *Bunduri* or **coast** sipahees."—*H. of Reign of Tipú Sultán*, E. T. by *Miles*, p. 253.

1879.—"Is it any wonder then, that the **Coast** Army has lost its ancient renown, and that it is never employed, as an army should be, in fighting the battles of its country, or its employers?"—*Pollok, Sport in Br. Burmah*, &c., i. 26.

COBANG. See **KOBANG.**

COBILY MASH, s. This is the dried **bonito** (q.v.), which has for ages been a staple of the Maldive Islands. It is still especially esteemed in Achin and other Malay countries. The name is explained below by Pyrard as 'black fish,' and he is generally to be depended on. But the first accurate elucidation has been given by Mr. H. C. P. Bell, of the Ceylon C. S., in the *Indian Antiquary* for Oct. 1882, p. 294; see also Mr. Bell's *Report on Maldive Islands*, Colombo, 1882, p. 93, where there is an account of the preparation. It is the Maldive *kalu-bili-mās*, 'black-bonito-fish.' The second word corresponds to the Singhalese *balayā*.

c. 1345.—"Its flesh is red, and without fat, but it smells like mutton. When caught each fish is cut in four, slightly boiled, and then placed in baskets of palm-leaf, and hung in the smoke. When perfectly dry it is eaten. From this country it is exported to India, China, and Yemen. It is called **Kolb-al-mās**."—*Ibn Batuta* (on Maldives), iv. 112, also 311.

1578.—". . . They eat it with a sort of dried fish, which comes from the Islands of Maledivia, and resembles jerked beef, and it is called **Comalamasa**."—*Acosta*, 103.

c. 1610.—"Ce poisson qui se prend ainsi, s'apelle generalement en leur langue **cobolly masse**, c'est à dire du poisson noir. . . . Ils le font cuire en de l'eau de mer, et puis le font secher au feu sur des clayes, en sorte qu'estant sec il se garde fort long-temps."—*Pyrard de Laval*, i. 138; see also 141; [Hak. Soc. i. 190 (with *Gray's* note) and 194].

1727.—"The Bonetta is caught with Hook and Line, or with nets . . . they cut the Fish from the Back-bone on each Side, and lay them in a Shade to dry, sprinkling them sometimes with Sea Water. When they are dry enough . . . they wrap them up in Leaves of Cocoa-nut Trees, and put them a Foot or two under the Surface of the Sand, and with the Heat of the Sun, they become baked as hard as Stock-fish, and Ships come from *Atcheen* . . . and purchase them with Gold-dust. I have seen **Comelamash** (for that is their name after they are dried) sell at *Atcheen* for 8L. *Sterl.* per 1000."—*A. Hamilton*, i. 347; [ed. 1744, i. 350].

1783.—"Many Maldivia boats come yearly to Atcheen, and bring chiefly dried *bonnetta* in small pieces about two or three ounces; this is a sort of staple article of commerce, many shops in the *Bazar* deal in it only, having large quantities piled up, put in matt bags. It is when properly cured, hard like horn in the middle; when kept long the worm gets to it."—*Forrest, V. to Mergui*, 45.

1813.—"The fish called **Commel mutch**, so much esteemed in Malabar, is caught at Minicoy."—*Milburn*, i. 321, also 336.

1841.—"The Sultan of the Maldiva Islands sends an agent or minister every year to the government of Ceylon with presents consisting of . . . a considerable quantity of dried fish, consisting of *bonitos*, *albicores*, and fish called by the inhabitants of the Maldivas the black fish, or **comboli mas**."—*J. R. As. Soc.* vi. 75.

The same article contains a Maldivian vocabulary, in which we have "Bonito or goomulmutch . . . *kannelimas*" (p. 49). Thus we have in this one paper *three* corrupt forms of the same expression, viz. **comboli mas**, **kanneli mas**, and **goomulmutch**, all attempts at the true Maldivian term **kalu-bili-mās**, 'black bonito fish.'

COBRA DE CAPELLO, or simply **COBRA**, s. The venomous snake *Naja tripudians*. *Cobra* [Lat. *colubra*] is Port. for 'snake'; *cobra de capello*, 'snake of (the) hood.' [In the following we have a curious translation of the name: "Another sort, which is called **Chapel-snakes**, because they keep in Chapels or Churches, and sometimes in Houses" (*A Relation of Two Several Voyages made into the East Indies*, by *Christopher Fryke*, Surg. . . . London, 1700, p. 291).]

1523.—"A few days before, **cobras de capello** had been secretly introduced into the fort, which bit some black people who died thereof, both men and women; and when this news became known it was perceived that they must have been introduced by the hand of some one, for since the fort was made never had the like been heard of."—*Correa*, ii. 776.

1539.—"Vimos tãbẽ aquy grande soma de **cobras de capello**, da grossura da coxa de hũ homẽ, e tão peçonhentas em tanto estremo, que dizião os negros que se chegarão cõ a baba da boca a qualquer cousa viva, logo em proviso cahia morta em terra . . ."—*Pinto*, cap. xiv.

,, ". . . Adders that were copped on the crowns of their heads, as big as a man's thigh, and so venomous, as the *Negroes* of the country informed us, that if any living thing came within the reach of their breath, it dyed presently. . . ."—*Cogan's Transl.*, p. 17.

1563.—"In the beautiful island of Ceylon . . . there are yet many serpents of the kind which are vulgarly called **Cobras de capello**; and in Latin we may call them *regulus serpens*."—*Garcia*, f. 156.

1672.—"In Jafnapatam, in my time, there lay among others in garrison a certain High German who was commonly known as the Snake-Catcher; and this man was summoned by our Commander . . . to lay hold of a **Cobre Capel** that was in his Chamber. And this the man did, merely holding his hat before his eyes, and seizing it with his hand, without any damage. . . . I had my suspicions that this was done by some devilry . . . but he maintained that it was all by natural means. . . ."—*Baldaeus* (Germ. ed.), 25.

Some forty-nine or fifty years ago a staff-sergeant at Delhi had a bull-dog that used to catch cobras in much the same way as this High-Dutchman did.

1710.—"The Brother Francisco Rodriguez persevered for the whole 40 days in these exercises, and as the house was of clay, and his cell adjoined the garden, it was invaded by **cobra de capelo**, and he made report of this inconvenience to the Father-Rector. But his answer was that *these* were not the snakes that did spiritual harm; and so left the Brother in the same cell. This and other admirable instances have always led me to doubt if S. Paul did not communicate to his Paulists in India the same virtue as of the tongues of S. Paul,* for the snakes in these parts are so numerous and so venomous, and though our Missionaries make such long journeys through wild uncultivated places, there is no account to this day that any Paulist was ever bitten."—*F. de Souza, Oriente Conquistado*, Conq. i. Div. i. cap. 73.

1711.—Bluteau, in his great Port. Dict., explains **Cobra de Capello** as a "reptile (*bicho*) of Brazil." But it is only a slip; what is further said shows that he meant to say India.

c. 1713.—"En secouant la peau de cerf sur laquelle nous avons coutume de nous asseoir, il en sortit un gros serpent de ceux qu'on appelle en Portugais **Cobra-Capel**."—*Lettres Edif.*, ed. 1781, xi. 83.

1883.—"In my walks abroad I generally carry a strong, supple walking cane. . . . Armed with it, you may rout and slaughter the hottest-tempered **cobra** in Hindustan. Let it rear itself up and spread its spectacled head-gear and bluster as it will, but one rap on the side of its head will bring it to reason."—*Tribes on my Frontier*, 198-9.

COBRA LILY, s. The flower *Arum campanulatum*, which stands on its curving stem exactly like a cobra with a reared head.

COBRA MANILLA, or **MINELLE**, s. Another popular name in S. India for a species of venomous snake, perhaps a little uncertain in its application. Dr. Russell says the *Bungarus caeruleus* was sent to him from Masulipatam, with the name *Cobra Monil*, whilst Günther says this name is given in S. India to the *Daboia Russellii*, or *Tic*-**Polonga** (q.v.) (see *Fayrer's Thanatophidia*, pp. 11 and 15). [The *Madras Gloss.* calls it the *chain-viper*, *Daboia elegans*.] One explanation of the name is given in the quotation from Lockyer. But the name is really Mahr. *maṇer*, from Skt. *maṇi*, 'a jewel.' There are judicious remarks in a book lately quoted, regarding the popular names and popular stories of snakes, which apply, we suspect, to all the quotations under the following heading:

"There are names in plenty . . . but they are applied promiscuously to any sort of snake, real or imaginary, and are therefore of no use. The fact is, that in real life, as distinguished from romance, snakes are so seldom seen, that no one who does not make a study of them can know one from the other."*—*Tribes on my Frontier*, 197.

1711.—"The **Cobra Manilla** has its name from a way of Expression common among the *Nears* on the *Malabar* Coast, who speaking of a quick Motion . . . say, in a Phrase peculiar to themselves, *Before they can pull a* Manilla *from their Hands*. A Person bit with this Snake, dies immediately; or before one can take a *Manilla* off. A **Manilla** is a solid piece of Gold, of two or three ounces Weight, worn in a Ring round the Wrist."—*Lockyer*, 276.

[1773.—"The **Covra Manilla**, is a small bluish snake of the size of a man's little finger, and about a foot long, often seen about old walls."—*Ives*, 43.]

1780.—"The most dangerous of those reptiles are the **coverymanil** and the green snake. The first is a beautiful little creature, very lively, and about 6 or 7 inches long. It creeps into all private corners of houses, and is often found coiled up betwixt the sheets, or perhaps under the pillow of one's bed. Its sting is said to inflict immediate death, though I must confess, for my own part, I never heard of any dangerous accident occasioned by it."—*Munro's Narrative*, 34.

1810.—". . . Here, too, lurks the small bright speckled **Cobra manilla**, whose fangs convey instant death."—*Maria Graham*, 23.

1813.—"The **Cobra minelle** is the smallest and most dangerous; the bite occasions a speedy and painful death."—*Forbes, Or. Mem.* i. 42; [2nd ed. i. 27].

COCHIN, n.p. A famous city of Malabar, Malayāl. *Kochchi*, ['a small place'] which the nasalising, so usual with the Portuguese, converted into *Cochim* or *Cochin*. We say "the Portuguese" because we seem to owe so many nasal terminations of words in Indian use to them; but it is evident that the real origin of this nasal was in *some* cases anterior to their arrival, as in the present case (see the first quotations), and in that of **Acheen** (q.v.). Padre Paolino says the town was called after the small river "Cocci" (as he writes it). It will be seen that

* *Lingue di San Paolo* is a name given to fossil sharks' teeth, which are commonly found in Malta, and in parts of Sicily.

* I have seen more snakes in a couple of months at the Bagni di Lucca, than in any two years passed in India.—H. Y.

Conti in the 15th century makes the same statement.

c. 1430.—"Relictâ Coloënâ ad urbem **Cocym**, trium dierum itinere transiit, quinque millibus passuum ambitu supra ostium fluminis, a quo et nomen."—*N. Conti* in *Poggius, de Variet. Fortunae*, iv.

1503.—"Inde Franci ad urbem **Cocen** profecti, castrum ingens ibidem construxere, et trecentis praesidiariis viris bellicosis munivere. . . ."—*Letter of Nestorian Bishops from India, in Assemani*, iii. 596.

1510.—"And truly he (the K. of Portugal) deserves every good, for in India and especially in **Cucin**, every fête day ten and even twelve Pagans and Moors are baptised."—*Varthema*, 296.

[1562.—"**Cochym.**" See under **BEADALA.**]

1572.—

"Vereis a fortaleza sustentar-se
De Cananor con pouca força e gente
* * * *
E vereis em **Cochin** assinalar-se
Tanto hum peito soberbo, e insolente*
Que cithara ja mais cantou victoria,
Que assi mereça eterno nome e gloria."
Camões, ii. 52.

By Burton:

"Thou shalt behold the Fortalice hold out
of Cananor with scanty garrison
* * * *
shalt in **Cochin** see one approv'd so stout,
who such an arr'gance of the sword hath shown,
no harp of mortal sang a similar story,
digne of e'erlasting name, eternal glory."

[1606.—"Att **Cowcheen** which is a place neere Callicutt is stoare of pepper. . . ."—*Birdwood, First Letter Book*, 84.

[1610.—"**Cochim** bow worth in Surat as sceala and kannikee."—*Danvers, Letters*, i. 74.]

1767.—"From this place the Nawaub marched to **Koochi-Bundur**, from the inhabitants of which he exacted a large sum of money."—*H. of Hydur Naik*, 186.

COCHIN-CHINA, n.p. This country was called by the Malays *Kuchi*, and apparently also, to distinguish it from *Kuchi* of India (or Cochin), **Kuchi-China**, a term which the Portuguese adopted as **Cauchi-China**; the Dutch and English from them. *Kuchi* occurs in this sense in the Malay traditions called *Sijara Malayu* (see *J. Ind. Archip.*, v. 729). In its origin this word *Kuchi* is no doubt a foreigner's form of the Annamite *Kuu-chön* (Chin. *Kiu-Ching*, South Chin. *Kau-Chen*), which was the ancient name of the province Thanh'-hoa, in which the city of Huë has been the capital since 1398.*

1516.—"And he (Fernão Peres) set sail from Malaca . . . in August of the year 516, and got into the Gulf of **Concam china**, which he entered in the night, escaping by miracle from being lost on the shoals. . . ."—*Correa*, ii. 474.

[1524.—"I sent Duarte Coelho to discover **Canchim China**."—*Letter of Albuquerque to the King*, India Office MSS., *Corpo Chronologico*, vol. i.]

c. 1535.—"This King of **Cochinchina** keeps always an ambassador at the court of the King of China; not that he does this of his own good will, or has any content therein, but because he is his vassal."—*Sommario de' Regni*, in *Ramusio*, i. 336*v*.

c. 1543.—"Now it was not without much labour, pain, and danger, that we passed these two Channels, as also the River of *Ventinau*, by reason of the Pyrats that usually are encountred there, nevertheless we at length arrived at the Town of *Manaquilen*, which is scituated at the foot of the Mountains of *Chomay* (*Çomhay* in orig.), upon the Frontiers of the two Kingdoms of China, and **Cauchenchina** (*da China e do* **Cauchim** in orig.), where the Ambassadors were well received by the Governor thereof."—*Pinto*, E. T., p. 166 (orig. cap. cxxix.).

c. 1543.—"CAPITULO CXXX. *Do recebimento que este Rey da* **Cauchenchina** *fez ao Embaixador da Tartaria na villa de Fanau grem.*"—*Pinto*, original.

1572.—

"Ves, **Cauchichina** esta de oscura fama,
E de Ainão vê a incognita enseada."
Camões, x. 129.

By Burton:

"See **Cauchichina** still of note obscure
and of Ainam yon undiscovered Bight."

1598.—"This land of **Cauchinchina** is devided into two or three Kingdomes, which are vnder the subiection of the King of *China*, it is a fruitfull countrie of all necessarie prouisiouns and Victuals."—*Linschoten*, ch. 22; [Hak. Soc. i. 124].

1606.—"Nel Regno di **Coccincina**, che . . . è alle volte chiamato dal nome di *Anan*, vi sono quattordici Provincie piccole. . . ."—*Viaggi di Carletti*, ii. 138.

[1614.—"The **Cocchichinnas** cut him all in pieces."—*Foster, Letters*, ii. 75.

[1616.—"27 pecull of lignum aloes of **Cutcheinchenn**."—*Ibid.* iv. 213.]

* Duarte Pacheco Pereira, whose defence of the Fort at Cochin (c. 1504) against a great army of the Zamorin's, was one of the great feats of the Portuguese in India. [*Comm. Alboquerque*, Hak. Soc. i. 5.]

* MS. communication from Prof. Terrien de la Couperie.

1652.—"**Cauchin-China** is bounded on the West with the Kingdomes of *Brama;* on the East, with the Great Realm of *China;* on the North extending towards *Tartary;* and on the South, bordering on *Camboia.*"—*P. Heylin, Cosmographie*, iii. 239.

1727.—"**Couchin-china** has a large Sea-coast of about 700 Miles in Extent . . . and it has the Conveniency of many good Harbours on it, tho' they are not frequented by Strangers."—*A. Hamilton*, ii. 208; [ed. 1744].

COCHIN-LEG. A name formerly given to elephantiasis, as it prevailed in Malabar. [The name appears to be still in use (*Boswell, Man. of Nellore*, 33). Linschoten (1598) describes it in *Malabar* (Hak. Soc. i. 288), and it was also called "St. Thomas's leg" (see an account with refs. in *Gray, Pyrard de Laval*, Hak. Soc. i. 392).]

1757.—"We could not but take notice at this place (Cochin) of the great number of the **Cochin**, or Elephant **legs**."—*Ives*, 193.

1781.—". . . my friend Jack Griskin, enclosed in a buckram Coat of the 1745, with a **Cochin Leg**, hobbling the Allemand. . . ."—Letter from an *Old Country Captain*, in *India Gazette*, Feb. 24.

1813.—"**Cochin-Leg**, or elephantiasis."—*Forbes, Or Mem.* i. 327; [2nd ed. i. 207].

COCKATOO, s. This word is taken from the Malay *kākātūwa*. According to Crawfurd the word means properly 'a vice,' or 'gripe,' but is applied to the bird. It seems probable, however, that the name, which is asserted to be the natural cry of the bird, may have come with the latter from some remoter region of the Archipelago, and the name of the tool may have been taken from the bird. This would be more in accordance with usual analogy. [Mr. Skeat writes: "There is no doubt that Sir H. Yule is right here and Crawfurd wrong. *Kakak tuwa* (or *tua*) means in Malay, if the words are thus separated, 'old sister,' or 'old lady.' I think it is possible that it may be a familiar Malay name for the bird, like our 'Polly.' The final *k* in *kakak* is a mere click, which would easily drop out."]

1638.—"Il y en a qui sont blancs . . . et sont coeffés d'vne houpe incarnate . . . l'on les appelle **kakatou**, à cause de ce mot qu'ils prononcent en leur chant assez distinctement."—*Mandelslo* (Paris, 1669), 144.

1654.—"Some rarities of naturall things, but nothing extraordinary save the skin of a *jaccall*, a rarely colour'd **jacatoo** or prodigious parrot. . . ."—*Evelyn's Diary*, July 11.

1673.—". . . **Cockatooas** and Newries (see **LORY**) from Bantem."—*Fryer*, 116.

1705.—"The **Crockadore** is a Bird of various Sizes, some being as big as a Hen, and others no bigger than a Pidgeon. They are in all Parts exactly of the shape of a Parrot. . . . When they fly wild up and down the Woods they will call **Crockadore, Crockadore**; for which reason they go by that name."—*Funnel*, in *Dampier*, iv. 265-6.

1719.—"Maccaws, **Cokatoes**, plovers, and a great variety of other birds of curious colours."—*Shelvocke's Voyage*, 54-55.

1775.—"At Sooloo there are no Loories, but the **Cocatores** have yellow tufts."—*Forrest, V. to N. Guinea*, 295.

[1843.—". . . saucy **Krocotoas**, and gaudy-coloured Loris."—*Belcher, Narr. of Voyage of Samarang*, i. 15.]

COCKROACH, s. This objectionable insect (*Blatta orientalis*) is called by the Portuguese *cacalacca*, for the reason given by Bontius below; a name adopted by the Dutch as *kakerlak*, and by the French as *cancrelat*. The Dutch also apply their term as a slang name to half-castes. But our word seems to have come from the Spanish, *cucaracha*. The original application of this Spanish name appears to have been to a common insect found under water-vessels standing on the ground, &c. (apparently *Oniscus*, or woodlouse); but as *cucaracha de Indias* it was applied to the insect now in question (see *Dicc. de la Lengua Castellana*, 1729).

1577.—"We were likewise annoyed not a little by the biting of an Indian fly called **Cacaroch**, a name agreeable to its bad condition; for living it vext our flesh; and being kill'd smelt as loathsomely as the French punaise, whose smell is odious."—*Herbert's Travels*, 3rd ed., 332-33.

[1598.—"There is a kind of beast that flyeth, twice as big as a Bee, and is called *Baratta* (Blatta)."—*Linschoten*, Hak. Soc. i. 304.]

1631.—"Scarabaeos autem hos Lusitani *Caca-laccas* vocant, quod ova quae excludunt, colorem et laevorem Laccae factitiae (*i.e.* of sealing-wax) referant."—*Jac. Bontii*, lib. v. cap 4.

1764.—

"... from their retreats
Cockroaches crawl displeasingly abroad."
Grainger, Bk. i.

c. 1775.—"Most of my shirts, books, &c., were gnawed to dust by the *blatta* or **cockroach**, called *cackerlakke* in Surinam."—*Stedman*, i. 203.

COCKUP, s. An excellent table-fish, found in the mouths of tidal rivers in most parts of India. In Calcutta it is generally known by the Beng. name of *begtī* or *bhiktī* (see **BHIKTY**), and it forms the daily breakfast dish of half the European gentlemen in that city. The name may be a corruption, we know not of what; or it may be given from the erect sharp spines of the dorsal fin. [The word is a corr. of the Malay (*ikan*) *kakap*, which Klinkert defines as a palatable sea-fish, *Lates nobilis*, the more common form being *siyakap*.] It is *Lates calcarifer* (Günther) of the group *Percina*, family *Percidae*, and grows to an immense size, sometimes to eight feet in length.

COCO, COCOA, COCOA-NUT, and (vulg.) **COKER-NUT**, s. The tree and nut *Cocos nucifera*, L.; a palm found in all tropical countries, and the only one common to the Old and New Worlds.

The etymology of this name is very obscure. Some conjectural origins are given in the passages quoted below. Ritter supposes, from a passage in Pigafetta's *Voyage of Magellan*, which we cite, that the name may have been indigenous in the Ladrone Islands, to which that passage refers, and that it was first introduced into Europe by Magellan's crew. On the other hand, the late Mr. C. W. Goodwin found in ancient Egyptian the word *kuku* used as "the name of the fruit of a palm 60 cubits high, which fruit contained water." (*Chabas, Mélanges Êgyptologiques*, ii. 239.) It is hard, however, to conceive how this name should have survived, to reappear in Europe in the later Middle Ages, without being known in any intermediate literature.*

The more common etymology is that which is given by Barros, Garcia de Orta, Linschoten, &c., as from a Spanish word *coco* applied to a monkey's or other grotesque face, with reference to the appearance of the base of the shell with its three holes. But after all may the term not have originated in the old Span. *coca*, 'a shell' (presumably Lat. *concha*), which we have also in French *coque?* properly an egg-shell, but used also for the shell of any nut. (See a remark under **COPRAH**.)

The Skt. *narikila* [*nārikera*, *nārikela*] has originated the Pers. *nārgīl*, which Cosmas grecizes into ἀργελλίον, [and H. *nāriyal*].

Medieval writers generally (such as *Marco Polo, Fr. Jordanus*, &c.) call the fruit the *Indian Nut*, the name by which it was known to the Arabs (*al jauz-al-Hindī*). There is no evidence of its having been known to classical writers, nor are we aware of any Greek or Latin mention of it before Cosmas. But Brugsch, describing from the Egyptian wall-paintings of c. B.C. 1600, on the temple of Queen Hashop, representing the expeditions by sea which she sent to the Incense Land of Punt, says: "Men never seen before, the inhabitants of this divine land, showed themselves on the coast, not less astonished than the Egyptians. They lived on pile-buildings, in little dome-shaped huts, the entrance to which was effected by a ladder, under the shade of cocoa-palms laden with fruit, and splendid incense-trees, on whose boughs strange fowls rocked themselves, and at whose feet herds of cattle peacefully reposed." (*H. of Egypt*, 2nd ed. i. 353; [*Maspero, Struggle of the Nations*, 248].)

c. A.D. 70.—"In ipsâ quidem Aethiopiâ fricatur haec, tanta est siccitas, et farinae modo spissatur in panem. Gignitur autem in frutice ramis cubitalibus, folio latiore, pomo rotundo majore quam mali amplitudine, **coicas** vocant."—*Pliny*, xiii. § 9.

A.D. 545.—"Another tree is that which bears the *Argell, i.e.* the great *Indian Nut*."—*Cosmas*, in *Cathay*, &c., clxxvi.

1292.—"The *Indian Nuts* are as big as melons, and in colour green, like gourds. Their leaves and branches are like those of the date-tree."—*John of Monte Corvino*, in do., p. 213.

c. 1328.—"First of these is a certain tree called *Nargil;* which tree every month in the year sends out a beautiful frond like [that of] a [date-] palm tree, which frond or branch produces very large fruit, as big as a man's head. . . . And both flowers and fruit are produced at the same time, beginning with the first month, and going up gradually to the twelfth. . . . The fruit is that which we call *nuts of India*."—*Friar Jordanus*, 15 *seq.* The wonder of the coco-palm is so often noticed in this form by medieval writers, that doubtless in their

* It may be noted that Theophrastus describes under the names of κύκας and κόϊξ a palm of Ethiopia, which was perhaps the *Doom* palm of Upper Egypt (*Theoph. H. P.* ii. 6, 10). Schneider, the editor of Theoph., states that Sprengel identified this with the coco-palm. See the quotation from Pliny below.

minds they referred it to that "tree of life, which bare twelve manner of fruit, and yielded her fruit every month" (*Apocal.* xxii. 2).

c. 1340.—"Le *nargīl*, appelé autrement *noix d'Inde*, auquel on ne peut comparer aucun autre fruit, est vert et rempli d'huile." —*Shihābbuddīn Dimishkī*, in *Not. et Exts.* xiii. 175.

c. 1350.—"Wonderful fruits there are, which we never see in these parts, such as the *Nargil*. Now the Nargil is the *Indian Nut*."—*John Marignolli*, in *Cathay*, p. 352.

1498-99.—"And we who were nearest boarded the vessel, and found nothing in her but provisions and arms; and the provisions consisted of **coquos** and of four jars of certain cakes of palm-sugar, and there was nothing else but sand for ballast."—*Roteiro de Vasco da Gama*, 94.

1510.—Varthema gives an excellent account of the tree; but he uses only the Malayāl. name *tenga*. [Tam. *tennai*, *ten*, 'south' as it was supposed to have been brought from Ceylon.]

1516.—"These trees have clean smooth stems, without any branch, only a tuft of leaves at the top, amongst which grows a large fruit which they call *tenga*. . . . We call these fruits **quoquos**."—*Barbosa*, 154 (collating Portuguese of *Lisbon Academy*, p. 346).

1519.—"**Cocas** (*coche*) are the fruits of palm-trees, and as we have bread, wine, oil, and vinegar, so in that country they extract all these things from this one tree." —*Pigafetta*, *Viaggio intorno il Mondo*, in *Ramusio*, i. f. 356.

1553.—"Our people have given it the name of **coco**, a word applied by women to anything with which they try to frighten children; and this name has stuck, because nobody knew any other, though the proper name was, as the Malabars call it, *tenga*, or as the Canarins call it, *narle*."—*Barros*, Dec. III. liv. iii. cap. 7.

c. 1561.—Correa writes **coquos**.—I. i. 115.

1563.—". . . We have given it the name of **coco**, because it looks like the face of a monkey, or of some other animal."—*Garcia*, 66*b*.

"That which we call **coco**, and the Malabars *Temga*."—*Ibid.* 67*b*.

1578.—"The Portuguese call it **coco** (because of those three holes that it has)."—*Acosta*, 98.

1598.—"Another that bears the Indian nuts called **Coecos**, because they have within them a certain shell that is like an ape; and on this account they use in Spain to show their children a **Coecota** when they would make them afraid."—English trans. of *Pigafetta's Congo*, in *Harleian Coll.* ii. 553.

The parallel passage in De Bry runs: "Illas quoque quae nuces Indicas **coceas**, id est *Simias* (intus enim simiae caput referunt) dictas palmas appellant."—i. 29.

Purchas has various forms in different narratives: **Cocus** (i. 37); **Cokers**, a form which still holds its ground among London stall-keepers and costermongers (i. 461, 502); **coquer-nuts** (*Terry*, in ii. 1466); **coco** (ii. 1008); **coquo** (*Pilgrimage*, 567), &c.

[c. 1610.—"None, however, is more useful than the **coco** or Indian nut, which they (in the Maldives) call **roul** (Malē, *rū*)."—*Pyrard de Laval*, Hak. Soc. i. 113.]

c. 1690.—Rumphius, who has **cocus** in Latin, and **cocos** in Dutch, mentions the derivation already given as that of Linschoten and many others, but proceeds:—

"Meo vero judicio verior et certior vocis origo invenienda est, plures enim nationes, quibus hic fructus est notus, *nucem* appellant. Sic dicitur Arabicè *Gauzos-Indi* vel *Geuzos-Indi*, h. e. Nux Indica. . . . Turcis *Cock-Indi* eadem significatione, unde sine dubio Æthiopes, Africani, eorumque vicini Hispani ac Portugalli **coquo** deflexerunt. Omnia vero ista nomina, originem suam debent Hebraicae voci *Egoz* quae nucem significat."—*Herb. Amboin.* i. p. 7.

,, ". . . in India Occidentali **Kokernoot** vocatus. . . ."—*Ibid.* p. 47.

One would like to know where Rumphius got the term *Cock-Indi*, of which we can find no trace.

1810.—

"What if he felt no wind? The air was still.
That was the general will
Of Nature . . . . . .
Yon rows of rice erect and silent stand,
The shadow of the **Cocoa's** lightest plume
Is steady on the sand."
Curse of Kehama, iv. 4.

1881.—"Among the popular French slang words for 'head' we may notice the term '**coco**,' given—like our own 'nut'—on account of the similarity in shape between a cocoa-nut and a human skull:—

"'Mais de ce franc picton de table
Qui rend spirituel, aimable,
Sans vous alourdir le **coco**,
Je m'en fourre à gogo.'—H. Valère."
Sat. Review, Sept. 10, p. 326.

The *Dict. Hist. d'Argot* of Lorédan Larchey, from which this seems taken, explains *picton* as 'vin supérieur.'

COCO-DE-MER, or **DOUBLE COCO-NUT**, s. The curious twin fruit so called, the produce of the *Lodoicea Sechellarum*, a palm growing only in the Seychelles Islands, is cast up on the shores of the Indian Ocean, most frequently on the Maldive Islands, but occasionally also on Ceylon and S. India, and on the coasts of Zanzibar, of Sumatra, and some others of the Malay Islands. Great virtues as medicine and antidote were supposed to reside in these fruits, and extravagant prices were paid for them. The story goes that a "country captain," expecting to make his fortune, took a cargo of these nuts from the Seychelles Islands to Calcutta, but the only result was to destroy their value for the future.

The old belief was that the fruit was produced on a palm growing below the sea, whose fronds, according to Malay seamen, were sometimes seen in quiet bights on the Sumatran coast, especially in the Lampong Bay. According to one form of the story among the Malays, which is told both by Pigafetta and by Rumphius, there was but one such tree, the fronds of which rose above an abyss of the Southern Ocean, and were the abode of the monstrous bird Garuda (or Rukh of the Arabs—see **ROC**).* The tree itself was called *Pausengi*, which Rumphius seems to interpret as a corruption of *Buwa-zangi*, "Fruit of Zang" or E. Africa. [Mr. Skeat writes: "Rumphius is evidently wrong. . . . The first part of the word is '*Pau*,' or '*Pauh*,' which is perfectly good Malay, and is the name given to various species of mango, especially the wild one, so that '*Pausengi*' represents (not '*Buwa*,' but) '*Pauh Janggi*,' which is to this day the universal Malay name for the tree which grows, according to Malay fable, in the central whirlpool or Navel of the Seas. Some versions add that it grows upon a sunken bank (*tĕbing runtoh*), and is guarded by dragons. This tree figures largely in Malay romances, especially those which form the subject of Malay shadow-plays (vide *infra*, Pl. 23, for an illustration of the Pauh Janggi and the Crab). Rumphius' explanation of the second part of the name (*i.e. Janggi*) is, no doubt, quite correct."—*Malay Magic*, pp. 6 *seqq.*).] They were cast up occasionally on the islands off the S.W. coast of Sumatra; and the wild people of the islands brought them for sale to the Sumatran marts, such as Padang and Priamang. One of the largest (say about 12 inches across) would sell for 150 rix dollars. But the Malay princes coveted them greatly, and would sometimes (it was alleged) give a laden junk for a single nut. In India the best known source of supply was from the Maldive Islands. [In India it is known as *Daryāī nāriyal*, or 'cocoa-nut of the sea,' and this term has been in Bombay corrupted into *jaharī* (*zahrī*) or 'poisonous,' so that the fruit is incorrectly regarded as dangerous to life. The hard shell is largely used to make Fakīrs' water-bowls.]

The medicinal virtues of the nut were not only famous among all the peoples of the East, including the Chinese, but are extolled by Piso and by Rumphius, with many details. The latter, learned and laborious student of nature as he was, believed in the submarine origin of the nut, though he discredited its growing on a great palm, as no traces of such a plant had ever been discovered on the coasts. The fame of the nut's virtues had extended to Europe, and the Emperor Rudolf II. in his later days offered in vain 4000 florins to purchase from the family of Wolfert Hermanszen, a Dutch Admiral, one that had been presented to that commander by the King of Bantam, on the Hollander's relieving his capital, attacked by the Portuguese, in 1602.

It will be seen that the Maldive name of this fruit was *Tāva-kārhī*. The latter word is 'coco-nut,' but the meaning of *tāva* does not appear from any Maldive vocabulary. [The term is properly *Tāva'karhi*, 'the hard-shelled nut,' (*Gray*, on *Pyrard de Laval*, Hak. Soc. i. 231).] Rumphius states that a book in 4to (*totum opusculum*) was published on this nut, at Amsterdam in 1634, by Augerius Clutius, M.D. [In more recent times the nut has become famous as the subject of curious speculations regarding it by the late Gen. Gordon.]

1522.—"They also related to us that beyond Java Major . . . there is an enormous tree named *Campanganghi*, in which dwell certain birds named Garuda, so large that they take with their claws, and carry away flying, a buffalo and even an elephant, to the place of the tree. . . . The fruit of this tree is called *Buapanganghi*, and is larger than a water-melon . . . it was understood that those fruits which are frequently found in the sea came from that place."—*Pigafetta*, Hak. Soc. p. 155.

1553.—". . . it appears . . . that in some places beneath the salt-water there grows

* This mythical story of the unique tree producing this nut curiously shadows the singular fact that *one* island only (Praslin) of that secluded group, the Seychelles, bears the *Lodoicea* as an indigenous and spontaneous product. (See *Sir L. Pelly*, in *J.R.G.S.*, xxxv. 232.)

another kind of these trees, which gives a fruit bigger than the coco-nut; and experience shows that the inner husk of this is much more efficacious against poison than the Bezoar stone."—*Barros*, III. iii. 7.

1563.—"The common story is that those islands were formerly part of the continent, but being low they were submerged, whilst these palm-trees continued *in situ*; and growing very old they produced such great and very hard coco-nuts, buried in the earth which is now covered by the sea. . . . When I learn anything in contradiction of this I will write to you in Portugal, and anything that I can discover here, if God grant me life; for I hope to learn all about the matter when, please God, I make my journey to Malabar. And you must know that these cocos come joined two in one, just like the hind quarters of an animal."—*Garcia*, f. 70-71.

1572.—

"Nas ilhas de Maldiva nasce a planta
No profundo das aguas soberana,
Cujo pomo contra o veneno urgente
He tido por antidoto excellente."

Camões, x. 136.

c. 1610.—"Il est ainsi d'vne certaine noix que la mer iette quelques fois à bord, qui est grosse comme la teste d'vn homme qu'on pourroit comparer à deux gros melons ioints ensemble. Ils la nomment *Tauarcarré*, et ils tiennent que cela vient de quelques arbres qui sont sous la mer . . . quand quelqu'vn deuient riche tout à coup et en peu de temps, on dit communement qu'il a trouué du *Tauarcarré* ou de l'ambre."—*Pyrard de Laval*, i. 163; [Hak. Soc. i. 230].

? 1650.—In Piso's *Mantissa Aromatica*, &c., there is a long dissertation, extending to 23 pp., *De Tavarcare seu Nuce Medicâ Maldivensium*.

1678.—"P.S. Pray remember ye **Coquer nutt** Shells (doubtless *Coco-de-Mer*) and long nulls (?) formerly desired for ye Prince."—*Letter from Dacca*, quoted under **CHOP**.

c. 1680.—"Hic itaque **Calappus marinus*** non est fructus terrestris qui casu in mare procidit . . . uti *Garcias ab Orta* persuadere voluit, sed fructus est in ipso crescens mari, cujus arbor, quantum scio, hominum oculis ignota et occulta est."—*Rumphius*, Lib. xii. cap. 8.

1763.—"By Durbar charges paid for the following presents to the Nawab, as per Order of Consultation, the 14th October, 1762.

* * * * * *

1 **Sea cocoa nut**.........Rs. 300 0 0."

In *Long*, 308.

1777.—"Cocoa-nuts from the Maldives, or as they are called the **Zee Calappers**, are said to be annually brought hither (to Colombo) by certain messengers, and presented, among other things, to the Governor. The kernel of the fruit . . . is looked upon here as a very efficacious antidote or a sovereign remedy against the Flux, the Epilepsy and Apoplexy. The inhabitants of the Maldives call it *Tavarcare*. . . ."—*Travels of Charles Peter Thunberg, M.D.* (E.T.) iv. 209.

[1833.—"The most extraordinary and valuable production of these islands (Seychelles) is the **Coco Do Mar**, or Maldivia nut, a tree which, from its singular character, deserves particular mention. . . ."—*Owen, Narrative*, ii. 166 *seqq*.]

1882.—"Two minor products obtained by the islanders from the sea require notice. These are ambergris (M. *goma*, *mávaharu*) and the so-called '**sea-cocoanut**' (M. *távakárhi*) . . . rated at so high a value in the estimation of the Maldive Sultans as to be retained as part of their royalties."—*H. C. P. Bell* (Ceylon C. S.), *Report on the Maldive Islands*, p. 87.

1883.—". . . sailed straight into the **coco-de-mer** valley, my great object. Fancy a valley as big as old Hastings, quite full of the great yellow stars! It was almost too good to believe. . . . Dr. Hoad had a nut cut down for me. The outside husk is shaped like a mango. . . . It is the inner nut which is double. I ate some of the jelly from inside; there must have been enough to fill a soup-tureen—of the purest white, and not bad."—(*Miss North*) in *Pall Mall Gazette*, Jan. 21, 1884.

CODAVASCAM, n.p. A region with this puzzling name appears in the Map of Blaeu (c. 1650), and as *Ryk van Codavascan* in the Map of Bengal in Valentijn (vol. v.), to the E. of Chittagong. Wilford has some Wilfordian nonsense about it, connecting it with the Τοκοσάννα R. of Ptolemy, and with a Touascan which he says is mentioned by the "Portuguese writers" (in such case a criminal mode of expression). The name was really that of a Mahommedan chief, "hum Principe Mouro, grande Senhor," and "Vassalo del Rey de Bengála." It was probably "Khodābakhsh Khān." His territory must have been south of Chittagong, for one of his towns was *Chacuriá*, still known as *Chakiria* on the Chittagong and Arakan Road, in lat 21° 45′. (See *Barros*, IV. ii. 8. and IV. ix. 1; and *Couto*, IV. iv. 10; also *Correa*, iii. 264-266, and again as below:—

1533.—"But in the city there was the Rumi whose foist had been seized by Dimião Bernaldes; being a soldier (*lascarym*) of the King's, and seeing the present (offered by the Portuguese) he said: My lord, these are crafty robbers; they get into a country with their wares, and pretend to buy and sell, and make friendly gifts, whilst they go

* *Kalāpā*, or *Klāpā*, is the Javanese word for coco-nut palm, and is that commonly used by the Dutch.

spying out the land and the people, and then come with an armed force to seize them, slaying and burning . . . till they become masters of the land. . . . And this Captain-Major is the same that was made prisoner and ill-used by **Codavascão** in Chatigão, and he is come to take vengeance for the ill that was done him."—*Correa*, iii. 479.

COFFEE, s. Arab. *kahwa*, a word which appears to have been originally a term for wine.* [So in the *Arab. Nights*, ii. 158, where Burton gives the derivation as *akhá*, fastidire fecit, causing disinclination for food. In old days the scrupulous called coffee *ḳihwah* to distinguish it from *ḳahwah*, wine.] It is probable, therefore, that a somewhat similar word was twisted into this form by the usual propensity to strive after meaning. Indeed, the derivation of the name has been plausibly traced to *Kaffa*, one of those districts of the S. Abyssinian highlands (Enarea and Kaffa) which appear to have been the original habitat of the Coffee plant (*Coffea arabica*, L.); and if this is correct, then *Coffee* is nearer the original than *Ḳahwa*. On the other hand, *Ḳahwa*, or some form thereof, is in the earliest mentions appropriated to the drink, whilst some form of the word *Bunn* is that given to the plant, and *Būn* is the existing name of the plant in Shoa. This name is also that applied in Yemen to the coffee-berry. There is very fair evidence in Arabic literature that the use of coffee was introduced into Aden by a certain Sheikh Shihābuddīn Dhabḥānī, who had made acquaintance with it on the African coast, and who died in the year H. 875, *i.e.* A.D. 1470, so that the introduction may be put about the middle of the 15th century, a time consistent with the other negative and positive data.† From Yemen it spread to Mecca (where there arose after some years, in 1511, a crusade against its use as unlawful), to Cairo, to Damascus and Aleppo, and to Constantinople, where the first coffee-house was established in 1554. [It is said to have been introduced into S. India some two centuries ago by a Mahommedan pilgrim, named Bābā Būdan, who brought a few seeds with him from Mecca: see *Grigg, Nilagiri Man.* 483; *Rice, Mysore*, i. 162.] The first European mention of coffee seems to be by Rauwolff, who knew it in Aleppo in 1573. [See 1 ser. *N. & Q.* I. 25 *seqq.*] It is singular that in the *Observations* of Pierre Belon, who was in Egypt, 1546-49, full of intelligence and curious matter as they are, there is no indication of a knowledge of coffee.

* It is curious that Ducange has a L. Latin word *cahua*, 'vinum album et debile.'

† See the extract in De Sacy's *Chrestomathie Arabe* cited below. Playfair, in his history of Yemen, says coffee was first introduced from Abyssinia by Jamāluddīn Ibn Abdalla, Kāḍī of Aden, in the middle of the 15th century: the person differs, but the time coincides.

1558.—Extrait du Livre intitulé: "Les Preuves le plus fortes en faveur de la legitimité de l'usage du Café (**Kahwa**); par le Scheikh Abd-Alkader Ansari Djézéri Hanbali, fils de Mohammed."—In *De Sacy, Chrest. Arabe*, 2nd ed. i. 412.

1573.—"Among the rest they have a very good Drink, by them called **Chaube**, that is almost black as Ink, and very good in Illness, chiefly that of the Stomach; of this they drink in the Morning early in open places before everybody, without any fear or regard, out of *China* cups, as hot as they can; they put it often to their Lips, but drink but little at a Time, and let it go round as they sit. In the same water they take a Fruit called *Bunru*, which in its Bigness, Shape, and Colour, is almost like unto a Bay-berry, with two thin Shells . . . they agree in the Virtue, Figure, Looks, and Name with the *Buncho* of Avicen,* and *Bancha* of *Rasis ad Almans.* exactly; therefore I take them to be the same."—*Rauwolff*, 92.

c. 1580. — "Arborem vidi in viridario Halydei Turcae, cujus tu iconem nunc spectabis, ex qua semina illa ibi vulgatissima, *Bon* vel *Ban* appellata, producuntur; ex his tum Aegyptii tum Arabes parant decoctum vulgatissimum, quod vini loco ipsi potant, venditurque in publicis œnopoliis, non secus quod apud nos vinum: illique ipsum vocant **Caova**. . . . Avicenna de his seminibus meminit."* — *Prosper Alpinus*, ii. 36.

1598.—In a note on the use of tea in Japan, Dr. Paludanus says: "The Turkes holde almost the same mañer of drinking of their *Chaona* (read **Chaoua**), which they make of a certaine fruit, which is like unto the *Bakelaer*,† and by the Egyptians called *Bon* or *Ban*; they take of this fruite one pound and a halfe, and roast them a little in the fire, and then sieth them in twentie poundes of water, till the half be consumed away; this drinke they take everie morning fasting in their chambers, out of an earthen pot, being verie hote, as we doe here drinke *aqua composita* in the morning; and they say that it strengtheneth them and maketh them warm, breaketh wind, and openeth any

* There seems no foundation for this.

† *i.e. Bacca Lauri*; laurel berry.

stopping."—In *Linschoten*, 46; [Hak. Soc. i. 157].

c. 1610.—"La boisson la plus commune c'est de l'eau, ou bien du vin de Cocos tiré le mesme iour. On en fait de deux autres sortes plus delicates; l'vne est chaude, composée de l'eau et de miel de Cocos, avec quantité de poivre (dont ils vsent beaucoup en toutes leurs viandes, et ils le nomment *Pasme*) et d'vne autre graine appellée **Cahoa**. . . ."—*Pyrard de Laval*, i. 128; [Hak. Soc. i. 172].

[1611.—"Buy some **coho** pots and send me."—*Danvers, Letters*, i. 122; "**coffao** pots."—*Ibid.* i. 124.]

1615.—"They have in steed of it (wine) a certaine drinke called **Caahiete** as black as Inke, which they make with the barke of a tree (!) and drinke as hot as they can endure it."—*Monfart*, 28.

,, ". . . passano tutto il resto della notte con mille feste e bagordi; e particolarmente in certi luoghi pubblici . . . bevendo di quando in quando a sorsi (per chè è calda che cuoce) più d'uno scodellino di certa loro acqua nera, che chiamano **cahue**; la quale, nelle conversazioni serve a loro, appunto come a noi il giuoco dello sbaraglino" (*i.e.* backgammon). — *P. della Valle* (from Constant.), i. 51. See also pp. 74-76.

[,, "**Cohu**, blake liquor taken as hotte as may be endured."—*Sir T. Roe*, Hak. Soc. i. 32.]

1616.—"Many of the people there (in India), who are strict in their Religion, drink no Wine at all; but they use a Liquor more wholesome than pleasant, they call **Coffee**; made by a black Seed boyld in water, which turnes it almost into the same colour, but doth very little alter the taste of the water (!): notwithstanding it is very good to help Digestion, to quicken the Spirits, and to cleanse the Blood."—*Terry*, ed. of 1665, p. 365.

1623. — "Turcae habent etiam in usu herbae genus quam vocant **Caphe** . . . quam dicunt haud parvum praestans illis vigorem, et in animas (*sic*) et in ingenio; quae tamen largius sumpta mentem movet et turbat. . . ." —*F. Bacon, Hist. Vitae et Mortis*, 25.

c. 1628.—"They drink (in Persia) . . . above all the rest, **Coho or Copha**: by Turk and Arab called **Caphe** and **Cahua**: a drink imitating that in the Stigian lake, black, thick, and bitter: destrain'd from Bunchy, Bunnu, or Bay berries; wholsome they say, if hot, for it expels melancholy . . . but not so much regarded for those good properties, as from a Romance that it was invented and brew'd by Gabriel . . . to restore the decayed radical Moysture of kind hearted *Mahomet*. . . ."—*Sir T. Herbert, Travels*, ed. 1638, p. 241.

[1631.—"**Caveah.**" See quotation under **TEA.**]

c. 1637.—"There came in my time to the Coll: (Balliol) one Nathaniel Conopios out of Greece, from Cyril the Patriarch of Constantinople. . . . He was the first I ever saw drink **coffee**, which custom came not into England till 30 years after."—*Evelyn's Diary*, [May 10].

1673.—"Every one pays him their congratulations, and after a dish of **Coho** or Tea, mounting, accompany him to the Palace."—*Fryer*, 225.

,, "Cependant on l'apporta le **cavé**, le parfum, et le sorbet."—*Journal d'Antoine Galland*, ii. 124.

[1677.—"**Cave.**" See quotation under **TEA.**]

1690.—"For Tea and **Coffee** which are judg'd the privileg'd Liquors of all the *Mahometans*, as well *Turks*, as those of *Persia, India*, and other parts of *Arabia*, are condemn'd by them (the Arabs of Muscatt) as unlawful Refreshments, and abominated as Bug-bear Liquors, as well as Wine."—*Ovington*, 427.

1726.—"A certain gentleman, M. Paschius, maintains in his Latin work published at Leipzig in 1700, that the parched corn (1 Sam. xxv. 18) which Abigail presented with other things to David, to appease his wrath, was nought else but **Coffi**-beans."—*Valentijn*, v. 192.

COIMBATORE, n.p. Name of a District and town in the Madras Presidency. *Koyammutūru*; [*Kōni*, the local goddess so called, *muttu*, 'pearl,' *ūr*, 'village'].

COIR, s. The fibre of the coco-nut husk, from which rope is made. But properly the word, which is Tam. *kayiru*, Malayāl. *kāyar*, from v. *kāyāru*. 'to be twisted,' means 'cord' itself (see the accurate *Al-Birūnī* below). The former use among Europeans is very early. And both the fibre and the rope made from it appear to have been exported to Europe in the middle of the 16th century. The word appears in early Arabic writers in the forms *kānbar* and *kanbār*, arising probably from some misreading of the diacritical points (for *ḳaiyar*, and *ḳaiyār*). The Portuguese adopted the word in the form *cairo*. The form *coir* seems to have been introduced by the English in the 18th century. [The *N.E.D.* gives *coire* in 1697; *coir* in 1779.] It was less likely to be used by the Portuguese because *coiro* in their language is 'leather.' And Barros (where quoted below) says allusively of the rope: "*parece feito de coiro* (leather) encolhendo e estendendo a vontade do mar," contracting and stretching with the movement of the sea.

c. 1030.—"The other islands are called *Dīva Ḳanbār* from the word **Ḳanbār** signifying the cord plaited from the fibre of the coco-tree with which they stitch their ships together."—*Al-Birūnī*, in *J. As.*, Ser. iv. tom. viii. 266.

c. 1346.—"They export . . . cowries and **kanbar**; the latter is the name which they give to the fibrous husk of the coco-nut. . . . They make of it twine to stitch together the planks of their ships, and the cordage is also exported to China, India, and Yemen. This *ḳanbar* is better than hemp."—*Ibn Batuta*, iv. 121.

1510.—"The Governor (Alboquerque) . . . in Cananor devoted much care to the preparation of cables and rigging for the whole fleet, for what they had was all rotten from the rains in Goa River; ordering that all should be made of **coir** (*cairo*), of which there was great abundance in Cananor; because a Moor called Mamalle, a chief trader there, held the whole trade of the Maldive islands by a contract with the kings of the isles . . . so that this Mòor came to be called the Lord of the Maldives, and that all the **coir** that was used throughout India had to be bought from the hands of this Moor. . . . The Governor, learning this, sent for the said Moor, and ordered him to abandon this island trade and to recall his factors. . . . The Moor, not to lose such a profitable business, . . . finally arranged with the Governor that the Isles should not be taken from him, and that he in return would furnish for the king 1000 *bahars* (*barés*) of coarse **coir**, and 1000 more of fine **coir**, each *bahar* weighing 4½ *quintals*; and this every year, and laid down at his own charges in Cananor and Cochym, gratis and free of all charge to the King (not being able to endure that the Portuguese should frequent the Isles at their pleasure)."—*Correa*, ii. 129-30.

1516.—"These islands make much cordage of palm-trees, which they call **cayro**."—*Barbosa*, 164.

c. 1530.—"They made ropes of **coir**, which is a thread which the people of the country make of the husks which the coco-nuts have outside."—*Correa*, by *Stanley*, 133.

1553.—"They make much use of this **cairo** in place of nails; for as it has this quality of recovering its freshness and swelling in the sea-water, they stitch with it the planking of a ship's sides, and reckon them then very secure."—*De Barros*, Dec. III. liv. iii. cap. 7.

1563.—"The first rind is very tough, and from it is made **cairo**, so called by the Malabars and by us, from which is made the cord for the rigging of all kinds of vessels."—*Garcia*, f. 67*v*.

1582.—"The Dwellers therein are Moores; which trade to Sofala in great Ships that have no Decks, nor nailes, but are sowed with **Cayro**."—*Castañeda* (by N. L.), f. 14*b*.

c. 1610.—"This revenue consists in . . . **Cairo**, which is the cord made of the coco-tree."—*Pyrard de Laval*, i. 172; [Hak. Soc. i. 250].

1673.—"They (the Surat people) have not only the **Cair**-yarn made of the Cocoe for cordage, but good Flax and Hemp."—*Fryer*, 121.

c. 1690.—"Externus nucis cortex putamen ambiens, quum exsiccatus, et stupae similis . . . dicitur . . . Malabarice **Cairo**, quod nomen ubique usurpatur ubi lingua Portugallica est in usu. . . ."—*Rumphius*, i. 7.

1727.—"Of the Rind of the Nut they make **Cayar**, which are the Fibres of the Cask that environs the Nut spun fit to make Cordage and Cables for Shipping."—*A. Hamilton*, i. 296; [ed. 1744, i. 298].

[1773.—". . . these they call **Kiar** Yarns."—*Ives*, 457.]

COJA, s. P. *khojah* for *khwājah*, a respectful title applied to various classes: as in India especially to eunuchs; in Persia to wealthy merchants; in Turkistan to persons of sacred families.

c. 1343.—"The chief mosque (at Kaulam) is admirable; it was built by the merchant **Khojah** Muhaddhab."—*Ibn. Batuta*, iv. 100.

[1590.—"**Hoggia**." See quotation under **TALISMAN**.

[1615.—"The Governor of Suratt is displaced, and **Hoyja** Hassan in his room."—*Foster, Letters*, iv. 16.

[1708.—"This grave is made for **Hodges** Shaughsware, the chiefest servant to the King of Persia for twenty years. . . ."—Inscription on the tomb of "*Coya Shawsware, a Persin in St. Botolph's Churchyard, Bishopsgate*," *New View of London*, p. 169.]

1786.—"I also beg to acquaint you I sent for Retafit Ali Khân, the **Cojah** who has the charge of (the women of Oudh Zenanah) who informs me it is well grounded that they have sold everything they had, even the clothes from their backs, and now have no means to subsist."—Capt. Jaques in *Articles of Charge*, &c., *Burke*, vii. 27.

1838.—"About a century back Khan **Khojah**, a Mohamedan ruler of Kashghar and Yarkand, eminent for his sanctity, having been driven from his dominions by the Chinese, took shelter in Badakhshan."—*Wood's Oxus*, ed. 1872, p. 161.

COLAO, s. Chin. *koh-lao*. 'Council Chamber Elders' (*Bp. Moule*). A title for a Chinese Minister of State, which frequently occurs in the Jesuit writers of the 17th century.

COLEROON, n.p. The chief mouth, or delta-branch, of the Kāveri River (see **CAUVERY**). It is a Portuguese corruption of the proper name *Kol̤l̤idam*, vulg. *Kolladam*. This name, from Tam. *kōl*, 'to receive,' and '*iḍam*,' 'place,' perhaps answers to the fact of this channel having been originally an escape formed at the construction of the great Tanjore irrigation works in the 11th century. In full flood the Coleroon is now, in places, nearly a mile wide, whilst the original stream of the Kāveri disappears before reaching the sea. Besides the etymology and the tradition, the absence of notice of the Coleroon in Ptolemy's Tables is (*quantum valeat*) an indication of its modern origin. As the sudden rise of floods in the rivers of the Coromandel coast often causes fatal accidents, there seems a curious popular tendency to connect the names of the rivers with this fact. Thus *Kŏllidam*, with the meaning that has been explained, has been commonly made into *Kollidam*, 'Killing-place.' [So the *Madras Gloss.* which connects the name with a tradition of the drowning of workmen when the Srirangam temple was built, but elsewhere (ii. 213) it is derived from Tam. *kollāyi*, 'a breach in a bank.'] Thus also the two rivers *Pennar* are popularly connected with *pinam*, 'corpse.' Fra Paolino gives the name as properly *Colárru*, and as meaning 'the River of Wild Boars.' But his etymologies are often wild as the supposed Boars.

1553.—De Barros writes **Coloran**, and speaks of it as a place (*lugar*) on the coast, not as a river.—Dec. I. liv. ix. cap. 1.

1672.—"From *Trangebar* one passes by *Trinilivaas* to **Colderon**; here a Sandbank stretches into the sea which is very dangerous."—*Baldaeus*, 150. (He does not speak of it as a *River* either.)

c. 1713.—"Les deux Princes . . . se liguèrent contre l'ennemi commun, à fin de le contraindre par la force des armes à rompre une digue si préjudiciable à leurs Etats. Ils faisoient déjà de grands preparatifs, lorsque le fleuve **Coloran** vengea par lui-même (comme on s'exprimoit ici) l'affront que le Roi faisoit a ses eaux en les retenant captives."—*Lettres Edifiantes*, ed. 1781, xi. 180.

1753.—". . . en doublant le Cap Callamedu, jusqu'à la branche du fleuve Caveri qui porte le nom de **Colh-ram**, et dont l'embouchure est la plus septentrionale de celles du Caveri."—*D'Anville*, 115.

c. 1760.—". . . the same river being written **Collarum** by M. la Croze, and *Collodham* by Mr. Ziegenbalg."—*Grose*, i. 281.

1761.—"Clive dislodged a strong body of the Nabob's troops, who had taken post at Sameavarem, a fort and temple situated on the river **Kalderon**."—*Complete H. of the War in India, from* 1749 to 1761 (Tract), p. 12.

1780.—"About 3 leagues north from the river Triminious [? Tirumullavāsel], is that of **Coloran**. Mr. Michelson calls this river *Danecottu*."—*Dunn, N. Directory*, 138.

The same book has "**Coloran** or **Colderoon.**"

1785.—"Sundah Saheb having thrown some of his wretched infantry into a temple, fortified according to the Indian method, upon the river **Kaldaron**, Mr. Clive knew there was no danger in investing it."—*Carraccioli's Life of Clive*, i. 20.

COLLECTOR, s. The chief administrative official of an Indian Zillah or District. The special duty of the office is, as the name intimates, the Collection of Revenue; but in India generally, with the exception of Bengal Proper, the Collector, also holding controlling magisterial powers, has been a small pro-consul, or kind of *préfet*. This is, however, much modified of late years by the greater definition of powers, and subdivision of duties everywhere. The title was originally no doubt a translation of *tahsīldār*. It was introduced, with the office, under Warren Hastings, but the Collector's duties were not formally settled till 1793, when these appointments were reserved to members of the covenanted Civil Service.

1772.—"The Company having determined to stand forth as *dewan*, the Supervisors should now be designated **Collectors.**"—Reg. of 14th May, 1772.

1773.—"Do not laugh at the formality with which we have made a law to change their name from *supervisors* to **collectors**. You know full well how much the world's opinion is governed by names."—*W. Hastings* to *Josias Dupre*, in *Gleig*, i. 267.

1785.—"The numerous **Collectors** with their assistants had hitherto enjoyed very moderate allowances from their employers."—*Letter in Colebrooke's Life*, p. 16.

1838.—"As soon as three or four of them get together they speak about nothing but 'employment' and 'promotion' . . . and if left to themselves, they sit and conjugate the verb 'to collect': 'I am a **Collector**—He was a *Collector*—We shall be *Collectors*—You ought to be a *Collector*—They would have been *Collectors*.'"—*Letters from Madras*, 146.

1848.—"Yet she could not bring herself to suppose that the little grateful gentle governess would dare to look up to such a magnificent personage as the **Collector** of Boggleywallah."—*Thackeray, Vanity Fair*, ch. iv.

1871.—"There is no doubt a decay of discretionary administration throughout India . . . it may be taken for granted that in earlier days **Collectors** and Commissioners changed their rules far oftener than does the Legislature at present."—*Maine, Village Communities*, 214.

1876.—"These 'distinguished visitors' are becoming a frightful nuisance; they think that **Collectors** and Judges have nothing to do but to act as their guides, and that Indian officials have so little work, and suffer so much from *ennui*, that even ordinary thanks for hospitality are unnecessary; they take it all as their right."—Ext. of a *Letter from India*.

COLLEGE-PHEASANT, s. An absurd enough corruption of *kālij*; the name in the Himālaya about Simla and Mussooree for the birds of the genus *Gallophasis* of Hodgson, intermediate between the pheasants and the Jungle-fowls. "The group is composed of at least three species, two being found in the Himalayas, and one in Assam, Chittagong and Arakan." (*Jerdon*).

[1880.—"These, with **kalege** pheasants, afforded me some very fair sport."—*Ball, Jungle Life*, 538.

[1882.—"Jungle-fowl were plentiful, as well as the black **khalege** pheasant."—*Sanderson, Thirteen Years among Wild Beasts*, 147.]

COLLERY, CALLERY, &c. s. Properly Bengali *khālāṛī*, 'a salt-pan, or place for making salt.'

[1767.—". . . rents of the **Collaries**, the fifteen Dees, and of Calcutta town, are none of them included in the estimation I have laid before you."—*Verelst, View of Bengal*, App. 223.]

1768.—". . . the Collector-general be desired to obtain as exact an account as he possibly can, of the number of **colleries** in the Calcutta purgunnehs."—In *Carraccioli's L. of Clive*, iv. 112.

COLLERY, n.p. The name given to a non-Aryan race inhabiting part of the country east of Madura. Tam. *kallaṛ*, 'thieves.' They are called in Nelson's *Madura*, [Pt. ii. 44 *seqq.*] *Kallans*; *Kallan* being the singular, *Kallar* plural.

1763.—"The Polygar Tondiman . . . likewise sent 3000 **Colleries**; these are a people who, under several petty chiefs, inhabit the woods between Trichinopoly and Cape Comorin; their name in their own language signifies Thieves, and justly describes their general character."—*Orme*, i. 208.

c. 1785.—"**Colleries**, inhabitants of the woods under the Government of the Tondiman."—*Carraccioli, Life of Clive*, iv. 561.

1790.—"The country of the **Colleries** . . . extends from the sea coast to the confines of Madura, in a range of sixty miles by fifty-five."—*Cal. Monthly Register* or *India Repository*, i. 7.

COLLERY-HORN, s. This is a long brass horn of hideous sound, which is often used at native funerals in the Peninsula, and has come to be called, absurdly enough, *Cholera-horn!*

[1832.—"*Toorree* or *Toorrtooree*, commonly designated by Europeans **collery horn**, consists of three pieces fixed into one another, of a semi-circular shape."—*Herklots, Qanoon-e-Islam*, ed. 1863, p. liv. App.]

1879.—". . . an early start being necessary, a happy thought struck the Chief Commissioner, to have the Amildar's **Cholera-horn** men out at that hour to sound the reveillé, making the round of the camp."—*Madras Mail*, Oct. 7.

COLLERY-STICK, s. This is a kind of throwing-stick or boomerang used by the **Colleries**.

1801.—"It was he first taught me to throw the spear, and hurl the **Collery-stick**, a weapon scarcely known elsewhere, but in a skilful hand capable of being thrown to a certainty to any distance within 100 yards."—*Welsh's Reminiscences*, i. 130.

Nelson calls these weapons "*Vallari Thadis* or boomerangs."—*Madura*, Pt. ii. 44. [The proper form seems to be Tam. *valai tādi*, 'curved stick'; more usually Tam. *kallardādi, tādi*, 'stick.'] See also Sir Walter Elliot in *J. Ethnol. Soc.*, N. S., i. 112, *seq.*

COLOMBO, n.p. Properly *Kolumbu*, the modern capital of Ceylon, but a place of considerable antiquity. The derivation is very uncertain; some suppose it to be connected with the adjoining river *Kalani*-gangi. The name *Columbum*, used in several medieval narratives, belongs not to this place but to *Kaulam* (see **QUILON**).

c. 1346.—"We started for the city of **Kalanbū**, one of the finest and largest cities of the island of Serendīb. It is the residence of the Wazīr Lord of the Sea (*Hākim-al-Bahr*), Jālastī, who has with him about 500 Habshis."—*Ibn Batuta*, iv. 185.

1517.—"The next day was Thursday in Passion Week; and they, well remembering this, and inspired with valour, said to the King that in fighting the Moors they would be insensible to death, which they greatly desired rather than be slaves to the Moors. . . . There were not 40 men in all, whole and sound for battle. And one brave man made a cross on the tip of a cane, which he set in front for standard, saying that God was his Captain, and that was his Flag, under which they should march deliberately against **Columbo**, where the Moor was with his forces."—*Correa*, ii. 521.

1553.—"The King, Don Manuel, because . . . he knew . . . that the King of **Columbo**, who was the true Lord of the Cinnamon, desired to possess our peace and friendship, wrote to the said Affonso d'Alboquerque, who was in the island in person, that if he deemed it well, he should establish a fortress in the harbour of **Columbo**, so as to make sure the offers of the King."—*Barros*, Dec. III. liv. ii. cap. 2.

COLUMBO ROOT, CALUMBA ROOT, is stated by Milburn (1813) to be a staple export from Mozambique, being in great esteem as a remedy for dysentery, &c. It is *Jateorhiza palmata*, Miers; and the name *Kalumb* is of E. African origin (*Hanbury and Flückiger*, 23). [The *N.E.D.* takes it from **Colombo**, 'under a false impression that it was supplied from thence.'] The following quotation is in error as to the name:

c. 1779.—"**Radix Colombo** . . . derives its name from the town of Columbo, from whence it is sent with the ships to Europe (?); but it is well known that this root is neither found near Columba, nor upon the whole island of Ceylon. . . ."—*Thunberg, Travels*, iv. 185.

1782.—"Any person having a quantity of fresh sound **Columbia Root** to dispose of, will please direct a line. . . ."—*India Gazette*, Aug. 24.

[1809.—"An Account of the Male Plant, which furnishes the Medicine generally called **Columbo** or **Colomba** Root."—*Asiat. Res.* x. 385 *seqq.*]

1850.—"Caoutchouc, or India-rubber, is found in abundance . . . (near Tette) . . . and **calumba**-root is plentiful. . . . The India-rubber is made into balls for a game resembling 'fives,' and **calumba**-root is said to be used as a mordant for certain colours, but not as a dye itself."—*Livingstone, Expedition to the Zambezi*, &c., p. 32.

COMAR, n.p. This name (Ar. *al-Ḳumār*), which appears often in the old Arab geographers, has been the subject of much confusion among modern commentators, and probably also among the Arabs themselves; some of the former (*e.g.* the late M. Reinaud) confounding it with C. Comorin, others with Kāmrūp (or Assam). The various indications, *e.g.* that it was on the continent, and facing the direction of Arabia, *i.e.* the west; that it produced most valuable aloes-wood; that it lay a day's voyage, or three days' voyage, west of Ṣanf or **Champa** (q.v.), and from ten to twenty days' sail from Zābaj (or Java), together with the name, identify it with **Camboja**, or *Khmer*, as the native name is (see *Reinaud, Rel. des Arabes*, i. 97, ii. 48, 49; *Gildemeister*, 156 *seqq.*; *Ibn Batuta*, iv. 240; *Abulfeda*, *Cathay and the Way Thither*, 519, 569). Even the sagacious De Orta is misled by the Arabs, and confounds *alcomari* with a product of Cape Comorin (see *Colloquios*, f. 120*v*.).

CÓMATY, s. Telug. and Canar. *kōmati*, 'a trader,' [said to be derived from Skt. *go*, 'eye,' *mushti*, 'fist,' from their vigilant habits]. This is a term used chiefly in the north of the Madras Presidency, and corresponding to **Chetty**, [which the males assume as an affix].

1627.—"The next Tribe is there termed **Committy**, and these are generally the Merchants of the Place who by themselves or their servants, travell into the Countrey, gathering up Callicoes from the weavers, and other commodities, which they sell againe in greater parcels."—*Purchas, Pilgrimage*, 997.

[1679.—"There came to us the Factory this day a Dworfe an Indian of the **Comitte** Cast, he was he said 30 years old . . . we measured him by the rule 46 inches high, all his limbs and his body streight and equall proportioned, of comely face, his speech small equalling his stature. . . ."—*Streynsham Master*, in *Kistna Man.* 142.

[1869.—"**Komatis**." See quotation under **CHUCKLER**.]

COMBACONUM, n.p., written *Kumbakonam*. Formerly the seat of the Chola dynasty. Col. Branfill gives, as the usual derivation, Skt. *Kumbhakona*, 'brim of a water-pot'; [the *Madras Gloss.* Skt. *kumbha*, *kona*, 'lane'] and this form is given in *Williams's Skt. Dict.* as 'name of a town.' The fact that an idol in the Saiva temple at Combaconam is called *Kumbheśvaram* ('Lord of the water-pot') may possibly be a justification of this etymology. But see general remarks on S. Indian names in the Introduction.

COMBOY. A sort of skirt or kilt of white calico, worn by Singhalese of both sexes, much in the same way as the Malay **Sarong**. The derivation which Sir E. Tennent (*Ceylon*, i. 612, ii. 107) gives of the word is quite inadmissible. He finds that a Chinese author describes the people of Ceylon as wearing a cloth made of *koo-pei*, *i.e.* of cotton; and he assumes therefore that those people call their own dress by a Chinese name for cotton! The word, however, is not real Singhalese; and we can have no doubt that it is the proper name **Cambay**. *Paños de Cãbaya* are mentioned early as used in Ceylon (*Castanheda*, ii. 78), and *Cambays* by Forrest (*Voyage to Mergui*, 79). In the *Government List of Native Words* (Ceylon, 1869) the form used in the Island is actually *Kambāya*. A picture of the dress is given by Tennent (*Ceylon*, i. 612). It is now usually of white, but in mourning black is used.

1615.—"Tansho Samme, the Kinges kinsman, brought two pec. **Cambaia** cloth."—*Cocks's Diary*, i. 15.

[1674-5.—"**Cambaja** Brawles."—*Invoice in Birdwood, Report on Old Recs.*, p. 42.]

1726.—In list of cloths purchased at Porto Novo are "**Cambayen**."—*Valentijn, Chorom.* 10.

[1727.—"**Cambaya** Lungies." See quotation under **LOONGHEE**.]

COMMERCOLLY, n.p. A small but well-known town of Lower Bengal in the Nadiya District; properly *Kumār-khālī* ['Prince's Creek']. The name is familiar in connection with the feather trade (see **ADJUTANT**).

COMMISSIONER, s. In the Bengal and Bombay Presidencies this is a grade in the ordinary administrative hierarchy; it does not exist in Madras, but is found in the Punjab, Central Provinces, &c. The Commissioner is over a *Division* embracing several Districts or Zillahs, and stands between the Collectors and Magistrates of these Districts on the one side, and the Revenue Board (if there is one) and the Local Government on the other. In the Regulation Provinces he is always a member of the Covenanted Civil Service; in Non-Regulation Provinces he may be a military officer; and in these the District officers immediately under him are termed 'Deputy Commissioners.'

COMMISSIONER, CHIEF. A high official, governing a Province inferior to a Lieutenant-Governorship, in direct subordination to the Governor-General in Council. Thus the Punjab till 1859 was under a Chief Commissioner, as was Oudh till 1877 (and indeed, though the offices are united, the Lieut.-Governor of the N.W. Provinces holds also the title of Chief Commissioner of Oudh). The Central Provinces, Assam, and Burma are other examples of Provinces under Chief Commissioners.

COMORIN, CAPE, n.p. The extreme southern point of the Peninsula of India; a name of great antiquity. No doubt Wilson's explanation is perfectly correct; and the quotation from the Periplus corroborates it. He says: "*Kumārī*, . . . a young girl, a princess; a name of the goddess Durgā, to whom a temple dedicated at the extremity of the Peninsula has long given to the adjacent cape and coast the name of *Kumārī*, corrupted to Comorin. . . ." The Tamil pronunciation is *Kumări*.

c. 80-90.—"Another place follows called Κομὰρ, at which place is (* * *) and a port;* and here those who wish to consecrate the remainder of their life come and bathe, and there remain in celibacy. The same do women likewise. For it is related that the goddess there tarried a while and bathed."—*Periplus*, in Müller's *Geog. Gr. Min.* i. 300.

c. 150.—"Κομαρία ἄκρον καὶ πόλις."—*Ptol.* [viii. 1 § 9].

1298.—"**Comari** is a country belonging to India, and there you may see something of the North Star, which we had not been able to see from the Lesser Java thus far."—*Marco Polo*, Bk. III. ch. 23.

c. 1330.—"The country called Ma'bar is said to commence at the Cape **Kumhari**, a name applied both to a town and a mountain."—*Abulfeda*, in *Gildemeister*, 185.

[1514.—"**Comedis**." See quotation under **MALABAR**.]

1572.—

"Ves corre a costa celebre Indiana
Para o Sul até o cabo **Comori**
Ja chamado Cori, que Taprobana
(Que ora he Ceilão) de fronte tem de si."
Camões, v. 107.

Here Camões identifies the ancient Κῶρυ or Κῶλις with Comorin. These are in Ptolemy distinct, and his *Kory* appears to be the point of the Island of Rāmeśvaram from which the passage to Ceylon was shortest. This, as *Kōlis*, appears in various forms in other geographers as the extreme seaward point of India, and in the geographical poem of Dionysius it is described as towering to a stupendous height above the waves. Mela regards *Colis* as the

* There is here a doubtful reading. The next paragraph shows that the word should be κομαρεί. [We should also read for βριάριον, φρούριον, a watch-post, citadel.]

turning point of the Indian coast, and even in Ptolemy's Tables his *Kōry* is further south than *Komaria*, and is the point of departure from which he discusses distances to the further East (see *Ptolemy*, Bk. I. capp. 13, 14; also see Bishop Caldwell's *Comp. Grammar*, *Introd.*, p. 103). It is thus intelligible how comparative geographers of the 16th century identified *Kōry* with C. Comorin.

In 1864 the late venerated Bishop Cotton visited C. Comorin in company with two of his clergy (both now missionary bishops). He said that having bathed at Hardwār, one of the most northerly of Hindu sacred places, he should like to bathe at this, the most southerly. Each of the chaplains took one of the bishop's hands as they entered the surf, which was heavy; so heavy that his right-hand aid was torn from him, and had not the other been able to hold fast, Bishop Cotton could hardly have escaped.*

[1609.—"... very strong cloth and is called *Cacha de* **Comoree.**"—*Danvers*, *Letters*, i. 29.

[1767.—"The pagoda of the **Cunnacomary** belonging to Tinnevelly."—Treaty, in *Logan*, *Malabar*, iii. 117.]

1817.—

"... Lightly latticed in
With odoriferous woods of **Comorin.**"
Lalla Rookh, *Mokanna.*

This probably is derived from D'Herbelot, and involves a confusion often made between *Comorin* and **Comar**—the land of aloes-wood.

COMOTAY, COMATY, n.p. This name appears prominently in some of the old maps of Bengal, *e.g.* that embraced in the *Magni Mogolis Imperium* of Blaeu's great Atlas (1645-50). It represents *Kāmata*, a State, and *Kāmatapur*, a city, of which most extensive remains exist in the territory of Koch Bihār in Eastern Bengal (see **COOCH BEHAR**). These are described by Dr. Francis Buchanan, in the book published by Montgomery Martin under the name of *Eastern India* (vol. iii. 426 *seqq.*). The city stood on the west bank of the River Darlā, which formed the defence on the east side, about 5 miles in extent. The whole circumference of the enclosure is estimated by Buchanan at 19 miles, the remainder being formed by a rampart which was (c. 1809) "in general about 130 feet in width at the base, and from 20 to 30 feet in perpendicular height."

1553.—"Within the limits in which we comprehend the kingdom of Bengala are those kingdoms subject to it . . . lower down towards the sea the kingdom of **Comotaij.**"—*Barros*, IV. ix. 1.

[c. 1596.—**Kamtah.**" See quotation under **COOCH BEHAR.**]

1873.—"During the 15th century, the tract north of Rangpúr was in the hands of the Rájahs of **Kámata**. . . . **Kámata** was invaded, about 1498 A.D., by Husain Sháh."—*Blochmann*, in *J. As. Soc. Bengal*, xiii. pt. i. 240.

COMPETITION-WALLAH, s. A hybrid of English and Hindustani, applied in modern Anglo-Indian colloquial to members of the Civil Service who have entered it by the competitive system first introduced in 1856. The phrase was probably the invention of one of the older or Haileybury members of the same service. These latter, whose nominations were due to interest, and who were bound together by the intimacies and *esprit de corps* of a common college, looked with some disfavour upon the children of Innovation. The name was readily taken up in India, but its familiarity in England is probably due in great part to the "Letters of a **Competition-wala,**" written by one who had no real claim to the title, Sir G. O. Trevelyan, who was later on member for Hawick Burghs, Chief Secretary for Ireland, and author of the excellent *Life* of his uncle, Lord Macaulay.

The second portion of the word, *wālā*, is properly a Hindi adjectival affix, corresponding in a general way to the Latin *-arius*. Its usual employment as affix to a substantive makes it frequently denote "agent, doer, keeper, man, inhabitant, master, lord, possessor, owner," as Shakespear vainly tries to define it, and as in Anglo-Indian usage is popularly assumed to be its meaning. But this kind of denotation is incidental; there is no real limitation to such meaning. This is demonstrable from such phrases as *Kābul-wālā ghorā*, 'the Kabulian horse,' and from the common form of village nomenclature in the Panjāb, *e.g. Mīr-Khān-wālā*, *Ganda-Singh-wālā*, and so forth, implying the village established by Mir-Khan or Ganda-Singh. In the three immediately following quotations, the second and third exhibit a strictly idiomatic use of *wālā*, the first an incorrect English use of it.

* I had this from one of the party, my respected friend Bishop Caldwell.—H. Y.

1785.—
"Tho' then the Bostonians made such a fuss,
Their example ought not to be followed by us,
But I wish that a band of good Patriot-**wallahs** . . ."—In *Seton-Karr*, i. 93.

,, In this year Tippoo Sahib addresses a rude letter to the Nawāb of Shānūr (or Savanūr) as "The Shahnoor**wâlah**."—*Select Letters of Tippoo*, 184.

1814.—"Gungadhur Shastree is a person of great shrewdness and talent. . . . Though a very learned shastree, he affects to be quite an Englishman, walks fast, talks fast, interrupts and contradicts, and calls the Peshwa and his ministers 'old fools' and . . . 'dam rascals.' He mixes English words with everything he says, and will say of some one (Holkar for instance): *Bhot tricks***walla** *tha, laiken barra akulkund*, Kukhye *tha*, ('He was very tricky, but very sagacious; he was cock-eyed')."—*Elphinstone*, in *Life*, i. 276.

1853.—"'No, I'm a Suffolk-walla.'"—*Oakfield*, i. 66.

1864.—"The stories against the **Competition-wallahs**, which are told and fondly believed by the Haileybury men, are all founded more or less on the want of *savoir faire*. A collection of these stories would be a curious proof of the credulity of the human mind on a question of class against class."—*Trevelyan*, p. 9.

1867.—"From a deficiency of civil servants . . . it became necessary to seek reinforcements, not alone from Haileybury, . . . but from new recruiting fields whence volunteers might be obtained . . . under the pressure of necessity, such an exceptional measure was sanctioned by Parliament. Mr. Elliot, having been nominated as a candidate by Campbell Marjoribanks, was the first of the since celebrated list of the **Competition-wallahs**."—Biog. Notice prefixed to vol. i. of *Dowson's Ed. of Elliot's Historians of India*, p. xxviii.

The exceptional arrangement alluded to in the preceding quotation was authorised by 7 Geo. IV. cap. 56. But it did not involve competition; it only authorised a system by which writerships could be given to young men who had not been at Haileybury College, on their passing certain test examinations, and they were ranked according to their merit in passing such examinations, but below the writers who had left Haileybury at the preceding half-yearly examination. The first examination under this system was held 29th March, 1827, and Sir H. M. Elliot headed the list. The system continued in force for five years, the last examination being held in April, 1832. In all 83 civilians were nominated in this way, and, among other well-known names, the list included H. Torrens, Sir H. B. Harington, Sir R. Montgomery, Sir J. Cracroft Wilson, Sir T. Pycroft, W. Tayler, the Hon. E. Drummond.

1878.—"The **Competition-Wallah**, at home on leave or retirement, dins perpetually into our ears the greatness of India. . . . We are asked to feel awestruck and humbled at the fact that Bengal alone has 66 millions of inhabitants. We are invited to experience an awful thrill of sublimity when we learn that the area of Madras far exceeds that of the United Kingdom."—*Sat. Rev.*, June 15, p. 750.

COMPOUND, s. The enclosed ground, whether garden or waste, which surrounds an Anglo-Indian house. Various derivations have been suggested for this word, but its history is very obscure. The following are the principal suggestions that have been made:—*

(*a.*) That it is a corruption of some supposed Portuguese word.
(*b.*) That it is a corruption of the French *campagne*.
(*c.*) That it is a corruption of the Malay word *kampung*, as first (we believe) indicated by Mr. John Crawfurd.

(a.) The Portuguese origin is assumed by Bishop Heber in passages quoted below. In one he derives it from *campaña* (for which, in modern Portuguese at least, we should read *campanha*); but *campanha* is not used in such a sense. It seems to be used only for 'a campaign,' or for the Roman *Campagna*. In the other passage he derives it from *campao* (*sic*), but there is no such word.

It is also alleged by Sir Emerson Tennent (*infra*), who suggests *campinho*; but this, meaning 'a small plain,' is not used for compound. Neither is the latter word, nor any word suggestive of it, used among the Indo-Portuguese.

In the early Portuguese histories of India (*e.g. Castanheda*, iii. 436, 442; vi. 3) the words used for what we term *compound*, are *jardim*, *patio*, *horta*. An examination of all the passages of the Indo-Portuguese Bible,

* On the origin of this word for a long time different opinions were held by my lamented friend Burnell and by me. And when we printed a few specimens in the *Indian Antiquary*, our different arguments were given in brief (see *I. A.*, July 1879, pp. 202, 203). But at a later date he was much disposed to come round to the other view, insomuch that in a letter of Sept. 21, 1881, he says: "*Compound* can, I think, after all, be Malay *Kampong*; take these lines from a Malay poem"—then giving the lines which I have transcribed on the following page. I have therefore had no scruple in giving the same unity to this article that had been unbroken in almost all other cases.—H. Y.

where the word might be expected to occur, affords only *horta*.

There is a use of *campo* by the Italian Capuchin P. Vincenzo Maria (Roma, 1672), which we thought at first to be analogous: "Gionti alla porta della città (Aleppo) . . . arrivati al *Campo* de' Francesi; doue è la Dogana . . ." (p. 475). We find also in Rauwolff's *Travels* (c. 1573), as published in English by the famous John Ray: "Each of these nations (at Aleppo) have their peculiar *Champ* to themselves, commonly named after the Master that built it . . ."; and again: "When . . . the *Turks* have washed and cleansed themselves, they go into their Chappells, which are in the Middle of their great *Camps* or *Carvatschars* . . ." (p. 84 and p. 259 of Ray's 2nd edition). This use of *Campo*, and *Champ*, has a curious kind of analogy to *compound*, but it is probably only a translation of *Maidān* or some such Oriental word.

(b.) As regards *campagne*, which once commended itself as probable, it must be observed that nothing like the required sense is found among the seven or eight classes of meaning assigned to the word in *Littré*.

The word *campo* again in the Portuguese of the 16th century seems to mean always, or nearly always, a *camp*. We have found only one instance in those writers of its use with a meaning in the least suggestive of *compound*, but in this its real meaning is 'site': "queymou a cidade toda ate não ficar mais que ho *campo* em que estevera." ("They burned the whole city till nothing remained but the site on which it stood"—*Castanheda*, vi. 130). There is a special use of *campo* by the Portuguese in the Further East, alluded to in the quotation from Pallegoix's *Siam*, but that we shall see to be only a representation of the Malay *Kampung*. We shall come back upon it. [See quotation from *Correa*, with note, under **FACTORY**.]

(c.) The objection raised to *kampung* as the origin of *compound* is chiefly that the former word is not so used in Java by either Dutch or natives, and the author of *Max Havelaar* expresses doubt if *compound* is a Malay or Javanese word at all (pp. 360-361). *Erf* is the usual word among the Dutch. In Java *kampung* seems to be used only for a native village, or for a particular ward or quarter of a town.

But it is impossible to doubt that among the English in our Malay settlements **compound** is used in this sense in speaking English, and *kampung* in speaking Malay. *Kampung* is also used by the Malays themselves, in our settlements, in this sense. All the modern dictionaries that we have consulted give this sense among others. The old *Dictionarium Malaico-Latinum* of David Haex (Romae, 1631) is a little vague:

"**Campon,** coniunctio, vel conuentus. Hinc viciniae et parua loca, *campon* etiam appellantur."

Crawfurd (1852): "**Kampung** . . . an enclosure, a space fenced in; a village; a quarter or subdivision of a town."

Favre (1875): "Maison avec un terrain qui l'entoure."

Pijnappel (1875), *Maleisch-Hollandisch Woordenboek:* "**Kampoeng**—Omheind Erf, Wijk, Buurt, Kamp," *i.e.* "Ground hedged round, village, hamlet, *camp*."

And also, let it be noted, the Javanese Dict. of *P. Jansz* (*Javaansch-Nederlandsch Woordenboek*, Samarang, 1876): "**Kampoeng** — Omheind erf van Woningen; wijk die onder een hoofd staat," *i.e.* "Enclosed ground of dwellings; village which is under one Headman."

Marre, in his *Kata-Kata Malayou* (Paris, 1875), gives the following expanded definition: "Village palissadé, ou, dans une ville, quartier séparé et généralement clos, occupé par des gens de même nation, Malays, Siamois, Chinois, Bouguis, &c. Ce mot signifie proprement un enclos, une encеinte, et par extension quartier clos, faubourg, ou village palissadé. Le mot *Kampong* désigne parfois aussi une maison d'une certaine importance avec le terrain clos qui en dépend, et qui l'entoure" (p. 95).

We take Marsden last (*Malay Dictionary*, 1812) because he gives an illustration: "**Kampong,** an enclosure, a place surrounded with a paling; a fenced or fortified village; a quarter, district, or suburb of a city; a collection of buildings. *Membûat* [to make] *rumah* [house] *serta* *dañgan* [together with] **kampong**-*nia* [compound thereof], to erect a house with its enclosure . . . *Ber-Kampong*, to assemble, come together; *meñgampong*, to collect, to bring together." The Reverse Dictionary gives: "YARD, *alaman*, **Kampong.**" [See also many further references much to the same effect in Scott, *Malayan Words*, p. 123 *seqq.*]

In a Malay poem given in the *Journal of the Ind. Archipelago*, vol i. p. 44, we have these words:—

" *Trûslâh ka* **kampong** *s'orange Saudâgar.*"

[" Passed to the *kampong* of a Merchant."]

and

" *Titâh bâgindâ rajâ sultânì*
Kámpong *śiápá garângun ìnì.*"

[" Thus said the Prince, the Raja Sultani,
Whose *kampong* may this be?"]

These explanations and illustrations render it almost unnecessary to add in corroboration that a friend who held office in the Straits for twenty years assures us that the word **kampung** is habitually used, in the Malay there spoken, as the equivalent of the Indian **compound.** If this was the case 150 years ago in the English settlements at Bencoolen and elsewhere (and we know from Marsden that it *was* so 100 years ago), it does not matter whether such a use of *kampung* was correct or not, *compound* will have been a natural corruption of it. Mr. E. C. Baber, who lately spent some time in our Malay settlements on his way from China, tells me (H. Y.) that the frequency with which he heard *kampung* applied to the 'compound,' convinced him of this etymology, which he had before doubted greatly.

It is not difficult to suppose that the word, if its use originated in our Malay factories and settlements, should have spread to the continental Presidencies, and so over India.

Our factories in the Archipelago were older than any of our settlements in India Proper. The factors and writers were frequently moved about, and it is conceivable that a word so much wanted (for no English word now in use *does* express the idea satisfactorily) should have found ready acceptance. In fact the word, from like causes, *has* spread to the ports of China and to the missionary and mercantile stations in tropical Africa, East and West, and in Madagascar.

But it may be observed that it was possible that the word *kampung* was itself originally a corruption of the Port. *campo*, taking the meaning first of *camp*, and thence of an enclosed area, or rather that in some less definable way the two words reacted on each other. The Chinese quarter at Batavia—*Kampong Tzina*—is commonly called in Dutch '*het Chinesche* Kamp' or '*het* Kamp *der Chinezen.*' *Kampung* was used at Portuguese Malacca in this way at least 270 years ago, as the quotation from Godinho de Eredia shows. The earliest Anglo-Indian example of the word **compound** is that of 1679 (below). In a quotation from Dampier (1688) under **Cot**, where *compound* would come in naturally, he says '*yard.*'

1613.—(At Malacca). "And this settlement is divided into 2 parishes, S. Thomé and S. Stephen, and that part of S. Thomé called **Campon** *Chelim* extends from the shore of the *Jaos* bazar to N.W., terminating at the Stone Bastion; and in this dwell the *Chelis* of Coromandel. . . . And the other part of S. Stephen's, called **Campon** *China*, extends from the said shore of the *Jaos* Bazar, and mouth of the river to the N.E., . . . and in this part, called **Campon** *China*, dwell the *Chincheos* . . . and foreign traders, and native fishermen."—*Godinho de Eredia*, i. 6. In the plans given by this writer, we find different parts of the city marked accordingly, as **Campon** *Chelim*, **Campon** *China*, **Campon** *Bendara* (the quarter where the native magistrate, the **Bendāra** lived). [See also **CHELING** and **CAMPOO.**]

1679.—(At Pollicull near Madapollam), "There the Dutch have a Factory of a large **Compounde,** where they dye much blew cloth, having above 300 jars set in the ground for that work; also they make many of their best paintings there."—*Fort St. Geo. Consns.* (on Tour), April 14. In *Notes and Extracts*, Madras 1871.

1696.—"The 27th we began to unlade, and come to their custom-houses, of which there are *three*, in a *square* **Compound** of about 100 paces over each way. . . . The goods being brought and set in *two Rows* in the middle of the *square* are one by one opened before the *Mandareens.*"—*Mr. Bowyear's Journal at Cochin China*, dated Foy-Foe, April 30. *Dalrymple, Or. Rep.* i. 79.

1772.—"YARD (before or behind a house), Aungâun. Commonly called a **Compound.**"—Vocabulary in *Hadley's Grammar*, 129. (See under **MOORS.**)

1781.—
" In common usage here a *chit*
Serves for our business or our wit.
Bankshal's a place to lodge our ropes,
And Mango orchards all are *Topes*.
Godown usurps the ware-house place,
Compound denotes each walled space.
To *Dufterkhanna, Ottor, Tanks,*
The English language owes no thanks;
Since Office, Essence, Fish-pond shew
We need not words so harsh and new.
Much more I could such words expose,
But *Ghauts* and *Dawks* the list shall close;
Which in plain English is no more
Than Wharf and Post expressed before."
India Gazette, March 3.

,, ". . . will be sold by Public Auction . . . all that Brick Dwelling-house, Godowns, and **Compound**."—*Ibid.*, April 21.

1788.—"**Compound**—The court-yard belonging to a house. A corrupt word."—The *Indian Vocabulary*, London, Stockdale.

1793.—"To be sold by Public Outcry . . . the House, Out Houses, and **Compound**," &c.—*Bombay Courier*, Nov. 2.

1810.—"The houses (at Madras) are usually surrounded by a field or **compound**, with a few trees or shrubs, but it is with incredible pains that flowers or fruit are raised."—*Maria Graham*, 124.

,, "When I entered the great gates, and looked around for my palankeen . . . and when I beheld the beauty and extent of the **compound** . . . I thought that I was no longer in the world that I had left in the East."—*An Account of Bengal, and of a Visit to Government House* (at Calcutta) *by Ibrahim the son of Candu the Merchant, ibid.* p. 198. This is a Malay narrative translated by Dr. Leyden. Very probably the word translated **compound** was *kampung*, but that cannot be ascertained.

1811.—"Major Yule's attack was equally spirited, but after routing the enemy's force at **Campong** Malayo, and killing many of them, he found the bridge on fire, and was unable to penetrate further."—*Sir S. Auchmuty's Report of the Capture of Fort Cornelis.*

c. 1817.—"When they got into the **compound**, they saw all the ladies and gentlemen in the verandah waiting."—*Mrs. Sherwood's Stories*, ed. 1863, p. 6.

1824.—"He then proceeded to the rear **compound** of the house, returned, and said, 'It is a tiger, sir.'"—*Seely, Wonders of Ellora*, ch. i.

,, ". . . The large and handsome edifices of Garden Reach, each standing by itself in a little woody lawn (a '**compound**' they call it here, by an easy corruption from the Portuguese word *campaña* . . .)."—*Heber*, ed. 1844, i. 28.

1848.—"Lady O'Dowd, too, had gone to her bed in the nuptial chamber, on the ground floor, and had tucked her mosquito curtains round her fair form, when the guard at the gates of the commanding officer's **compound** beheld Major Dobbin, in the moonlight, rushing towards the house with a swift step."—*Vanity Fair*, ed. 1867, ii. 93.

1860.—"Even amongst the English, the number of Portuguese terms in daily use is remarkable. The grounds attached to a house are its '**compound**,' *campinho*."—*Emerson Tennent, Ceylon*, ii. 70.

[1869.—"I obtained the use of a good-sized house in the **Campong** Sirani (or Christian village)."—*Wallace, Malay Archip.*, ed. 1890, p. 256.]

We have found this word singularly transformed in a passage extracted from a modern novel:

1877.—"When the Rebellion broke out at other stations in India, I left our own **compost**."—*Sat. Review*, Feb. 3, p. 148.

A little learning is a dangerous thing!

The following shows the adoption of the word in West Africa.

1880.—From West Afr. Mission, Port Lokkoh, Mr. A. Burchaell writes: "Every evening we go out visiting and preaching the Gospel to our Timneh friends in their **compounds**."—*Proceedings of C. M. Society* for 1878-9, p. 14.

COMPRADORE, COMPODORE, &c., s. Port. *comprador*, 'purchaser,' from *comprar*, 'to purchase.' This word was formerly in use in Bengal, where it is now quite obsolete; but it is perhaps still remembered in Madras, and it is common in China. In Madras the *compradore* is (or was) a kind of house-steward, who keeps the household accounts, and purchases necessaries. In China he is much the same as a **Butler** (q.v.). A new building was to be erected on the Bund at Shanghai, and Sir T. Wade was asked his opinion as to what style of architecture should be adopted. He at once said that for Shanghai, a great Chinese commercial centre, it ought to be **Compradoric**!

1533.—"Antonio da Silva kept his own counsel about the (threat of) war, because during the delay caused by the exchange of messages, he was all the time buying and selling by means of his **compradores**."—*Correa*, iii. 562.

1615.—"I understand that yesterday the Hollanders cut a slave of theirs a-peeces for theft, per order of justice, and thrust their **comprador** (or cats buyer) out of dores for a lecherous knave. . . ."—*Cocks's Diary*, i. 19.

1711.—"Every Factory had formerly a **Compradore**, whose Business it was to buy in Provisions and other Necessarys. But the Hoppos have made them all such Knaves. . . ."—*Lockyer*, 108.

[1748.—"**Compradores.**" See quotation under **BANKSHALL.**]

1754.—"**Compidore.** The office of this servant is to go to market and bring home small things, such as fruit, &c."—*Ives*, 50.

1760-1810.—"All river-pilots and ships' **Compradores** must be registered at the office of the Tung-che at Macao."—'*Eight Regulations*,' from the *Fankwae at Canton* (1882), p. 28.

1782.—"Le **Comprador** est celui qui fournit généralement tout ce dont on a besoin, excepté les objets de cargaison; il y en a un pour chaque Nation: il approvisionne la loge, et tient sous lui plusieurs commis chargés de la fourniture des vaisseaux."—*Sonnerat* (ed. 1782), ii. 236.

1785.—"**Compudour** . . . Sicca Rs. 3."—In *Seton-Karr*, i. 107 (Table of Wages).

1810.—"The **Compadore**, or *Kurz-burdar*, or *Butler-Konnah-Sircar*, are all designations for the same individual, who acts as purveyor. . . . This servant may be considered as appertaining to the order of sircars, of which he should possess all the cunning."—*Williamson, V. M.* i. 270.

See **SIRCAR.** The obsolete term *Kurz-burdar* above represents *Kharach-bardār* "in charge of (daily) expenditure."

1840.—"About 10 days ago . . . the Chinese, having kidnapped our **Compendor**, Parties were sent out to endeavour to recover him."—*Mem. Col. Mountain*, 164.

1876.—"We speak chiefly of the educated classes, and not of 'boys' and **compradores**, who learn in a short time both to touch their caps, and wipe their noses in their masters' pocket-handkerchiefs." — *Giles, Chinese Sketches*, [p. 15].

1876.—

"An' Massa Coe feel velly sore
An' go an' scold he **compradore**."
Leland, Pidgin English Sing-Song, 26.

1882.—"The most important Chinese within the Factory was the **Compradore** . . . all Chinese employed in any factory, whether as his own 'pursers,' or in the capacity of servants, cooks, or coolies, were the **Compradore's** own people."—*The Fankwae*, p. 53.

CONBALINGUA, s. The common pumpkin, [*cucurbita pepo*. The word comes from the Malayāl., Tel. or Can. *kumbalam*; *kumbalanu*, the pumpkin].

1510.—"I saw another kind of fruit which resembled a pumpkin in colour, is two spans in length, and has more than three fingers of pulp . . . and it is a very curious thing, and it is called **Comolanga**, and grows on the ground like melons."—*Varthema*, 161.

[1554.—"**Conbalinguas.**" See quotation under **BRINJAUL.**]

[c. 1610.—Couto gives a tradition of the origin of the kingdom of Pegu, from a fisherman who was born of a certain flower; "they also say that his wife was born of a **Combalenga**, which is an apple (*pomo*) very common in India of which they make several kinds of preserve, so cold that it is used in place of sugar of roses; and they are of the size and fashion of large melons; and there are some so large that it would be as much as a lad could do to lift one by himself. This apple the Pegús call *Sapua*."—Dec. xii. liv. v. cap. iii.]

c. 1690.—"In Indiae insulis quaedam quoque Cucurbitae et Cucumeris reperiuntur species ab Europaeis diversae . . . harumque nobilissima est **Comolinga**, quae maxima est species Indicarum cucurbitarum."—*Rumphius, Herb. Amb.* v. 395.

CONCAN, n.p. Skt. *konkana*, [Tam. *konkaṇam*], the former in the Pauranic lists the name of a people; Hind. *Konkan* and *Kokan*. The low country of Western India between the Ghauts and the sea, extending, roughly speaking, from Goa northward to Guzerat. But the modern Commissionership, or Civil Division, embraces also North Canara (south of Goa). In medieval writings we find frequently, by a common Asiatic fashion of coupling names, *Kokan-* or *Konkan-Tana*; **Tana** having been a chief place and port of Konkan.

c. 70 A.D.—The **Cocondae** of Pliny are perhaps the *Konkaṇas*.

404.—"In the south are Ceylon (Lankâ) . . . **Konkan** . . ." &c.—*Bṛhat Sanhita*, in *J.R.A.S.*, N.S. v. 83.

c. 1300.—"Beyond Guzerat are **Konkân** and *Tāna*; beyond them the country of Malībār."—*Rashīduddīn*, in *Elliot*, i. 68.

c. 1335.—"When he heard of the Sultan's death he fled to a Kafir prince called Burabra, who lived in the inaccessible mountains between Daulatabad and **Kūkan**-*Tāna*."—*Ibn Batuta*, iii. 335.

c. 1350.—In the *Portulano Mediceo* in the Laurentian Library we have '**Cocin***tana*,' and in the Catalan Map of 1375 '**Cocin***taya*.'

1553.—"And as from the Ghauts (*Gate*) to the Sea, on the west of the Decan, all that strip is called **Concan**, so also from the Ghauts to the Sea, on the West of Canara (leaving out those forty and six leagues just spoken of, which are also parts of this same Canara), that strip which extends to Cape Comorin . . . is called Malabar. . . ."—*Barros*, I. ix. 1.

[1563.—"**Cuncam.**" See quotation under **GHAUT.**]

1726.—"The kingdom of this Prince is commonly called Visiapoer, after its capital, . . . but it is properly called **Cunkan.**"—*Valentijn*, iv. (*Suratte*), 243; [also see under **DECCAN**].

c. 1732.—"Goa, in the Adel Shāhi **Kokan**."—*Khāfī Khān*, in *Elliot*, vii. 211.

1804.—"I have received your letter of the 28th, upon the subject of the landing of 3 French officers in the **Konkan**; and I have taken measures to have them arrested."—*Wellington*, iii. 33.

1813.—". . . **Concan** or **Cokun** . . ."—*Forbes, Or. Mem.* i. 189; [2nd ed. i. 102].

1819.—Mr. W. Erskine, in his Account of Elephanta, writes **Kokan**.—*Tr. Lit. Soc. Bomb.*, i. 249.

CONFIRMED, p. Applied to an officer whose hold of an appointment is made permanent. In the Bengal Presidency the popular term is **pucka**; (q.v.); (also see **CUTCHA**).

[1805.—"It appears not unlikely that the Government and the Company may **confirm** Sir G. Barlow in the station to which he has succeeded. . . ."—In *L. of Colebrooke*, 223.]

1886.—". . . one Marsden, who has paid his addresses to my daughter—a young man in the Public Works, who (would you believe it, Mr. Cholmondeley?) has not even been **confirmed**.

"*Cholm.* The young heathen!"

Trevelyan, The Dawk Bungalow, p. 220.

CONGEE, s. In use all over India for the water in which rice has been boiled. The article being used as one of invalid diet, the word is sometimes applied to such slops generally. *Congee* also forms the usual starch of Indian washermen. [A *conjee*-cap was a sort of starched night-cap, and Mr. Draper, the husband of Sterne's Eliza, had it put on by Mrs. Draper's rival when he took his afternoon nap. (*Douglas, Glimpses of Old Bombay*, pp. 86, 201.)] It is from the Tamil *kanji*, 'boilings.' *Congee* is known to Horace, though reckoned, it would seem, so costly a remedy that the miser patient would as lief die as be plundered to the extent implied in its use:

"... Hunc medicus multum celer atque fidelis
Excitat hoc pacto . . .
. . . 'Agedum; sume hoc *ptisanarium Oryzae*.'
'Quanti emptae?' 'Parvo.' '*Quanti* ergo.' 'Octussibus.' 'Eheu!
Quid refert, morbo, an furtis pereamve rapinis?'"

Sat. II. iii. 147 *seqq.*

c. A.D. 70.—(Indi) "maxime quidem **oryza** gaudent, ex qua **tisanam** conficiunt quam reliqui mortales ex hordeo."—*Pliny*, xviii. § 13.

1563.—"They give him to drink the water squeezed out of rice with pepper and cummin (which they call **canje**)."—*Garcia*, f. 76*b*.

1578.—". . . **Canju**, which is the water from the boiling of rice, keeping it first for some hours till it becomes acid. . . ."—*Acosta, Tractado*, 56.

1631.—"Potus quotidianus itaque sit decoctum oryzae quod **Candgie** Indi vocant."—*Jac. Bontii*, Lib. II. cap. iii.

1672.—". . . la **cangia**, ordinaria colatione degl' Indiani . . . quale colano del riso mal cotto."—*P. Vinc. Maria*, 3rd ed., 379.

1673.—"They have . . . a great smooth Stone on which they beat their Cloaths till clean; and if for Family use, starch them with **Congee**."—*Fryer*, 200.

1680.—"Le dejeûné des noirs est ordinairement du **Cangé**, qui est une eau de ris epaisse."—*Dellon, Inquisition at Goa*, 136.

1796.—"**Cagni**, [boiled rice water, which the Europeans call **Cangi**, is given free of all expenses, in order that the traveller may quench his thirst with a cooling and wholesome beverage."—*P. Paulinus, Voyage*, p. 70.

"Can't drink as it is hot, and can't throw away as it is **Kanji**."—*Ceylon Proverb, Ind. Ant.* i. 59.

CONGEE-HOUSE, CONJEE-HOUSE, s. The 'cells' (or temporary lock-up) of a regiment in India; so called from the traditionary regimen of the inmates; [in N. India commonly applied to a cattle-pound].

1835.—"All men confined for drunkenness should, if possible, be confined by themselves in the **Congee-House**, till sober."—G. O., quoted in *Mawson's Records of the Indian Command of Sir C. Napier*, 101 note.

CONGEVERAM, n.p. An ancient and holy city of S. India, 46 m. S.W. of Madras. It is called *Kachchi* in Tamil literature, and *Kachchipuram* is probably represented by the modern name. [The *Madras Gloss.* gives the indigenous name as *Cutchy* (*Kachchi*), meaning 'the heart-leaved moon-seed plant,' *tinospera cordifolia*, from which the Skt. name *Kanchipura*, 'shining city,' is corrupted.]

c. 1030.—See **Kanchi** in Al-Birūnī, under **MALABAR**.

1531.—"Some of them said that the whole history of the Holy House (of St. Thomas) was written in the house of the Pagoda which is called **Camjeverão**, twenty leagues distant from the Holy House, of which I will tell you hereafter. . . ."—*Correa*, iii. 424.

1680.—"Upon a report that Podela Lingapa had put a stop to all the Dutch business of Policat under his government, the agent sent Braminy spys to **Conjee Voram** and to Policat."—*Ft. St. Geo. Cons.* Aug. 30. In *Notes and Exts.* No. iii. 32.

CONGO-BUNDER, CONG, n.p. *Kung bandar;* a port formerly of some consequence and trade, on the north shore of the Persian Gulf, about 100 m. west of Gombroon. The Portuguese had a factory here for a good many years after their expulsion from Ormus, and under treaty with Persia, made in 1625, had a right of pearl-fishing at Bahrein and a claim to half of the customs of Cong. These claims seem to have been gradually disregarded, and to have had no effect after about 1670, though the Portuguese would appear to have still kept up some pretext of monopoly of rights there in 1677 (see *Chardin*, ed. 1735, i. 348, and *Bruce's Annals of the E.I.C.*, iii. 393). Some confusion is created by the circumstance that there is another place on the same coast, called *Kongūn*, which possessed a good many vessels up to 1859, when it was destroyed by a neighbouring chief (see *Stiffe's P. Gulf Pilot*, 128). And this place is indicated by A. Hamilton (below) as the great mart for Bahrein pearls, which Fryer and others assign to what is evidently *Cong*.

1652.—"Near to the place where the Euphrates falls from Balsara [see **BALSORA**] into the Sea, there is a little Island, where the Barques generally come to an Anchor. . . . There we stay'd four days, whence to Bandar-**Congo** it is 14 days Sail. . . . This place would be a far better habitation for the Merchants than *Ormus*, where it is very unwholsom and dangerous to live. But that which hinders the Trade from Bandar-**Congo** is, because the Road to *Lar* is so bad. . . . The 30th, we hir'd a Vessel for *Bander-Abassi*, and after 3 or 4 hours Sailing we put into a Village . . . in the Island of *Keckmishe*" (see **KISHM**).—*Tavernier*, E.T. i. 94.

1653.—"**Congue** est vne petite ville fort agreable sur le sein Persique à trois journées du Bandar Abbassi tirant à l'Ouest dominée par le Schah . . . les Portugais y ont vn Feitour (see **FACTOR**) qui prend la moitié de la Doüane, et donne la permission aux barques de nauiger, en luy payant vn certain droit, parceque toutes ces mers sont tributaires de la generalité de Mascati, qui est à l'entrée du sein Persique. . . . Cette ville est peuplée d'Arabes, de Parsis et d'Indous qui ont leur Pagodes et leur Saincts hors la ville."—*De la Boullaye-le-Gouz*, ed. 1657, p. 284.

1677.—"*A Voyage to* **Congo** *for Pearl.*—Two days after our Arrival at Gombroon, I went to **Congo**. . . . At noon we came to *Bassatu* (see **BASSADORE**), an old ruined Town of the Portugals, fronting **Congo** . . . **Congo** is something better built than Gombroon, and has some small Advantage of the Air" (Then goes off about pearls).—*Fryer*, 320.

1683.—"One Haggerston taken by ye said President into his Service, was run away with a considerable quantity of Gold and Pearle, to ye amount of 30,000 Rupees, intrusted to him at Bussera (see **BALSORA**) and **Cong**, to bring to Surrat, to save Freight and Custom."—*Hedges, Diary*, i. 96 *seq.*

1685. — "*May* 27. — This afternoon it pleased God to bring us in safety to **Cong** Road. I went ashore immediately to Mr. Brough's house (Supra Cargo of ye *Siam Merchant*), and lay there all night."—*Ibid.* i. 202.

1727.—"*Congoun* stands on the South side of a large River, and makes a pretty good figure in Trade; for most of the Pearl that are caught at *Bareen*, on the *Arabian* Side, are brought hither for a Market, and many fine Horses are sent thence to *India*, where they generally sell well. . . . The next maritim town, down the Gulf, is **Cong**, where the *Portuguese* lately had a Factory, but of no great Figure in Trade, tho' that Town has a small Trade with *Banyans* and *Moors* from *India*." (Here the first place is *Kongun*, the second one *Kung*).—*A. Hamilton*, i. 92 *seq.*; [ed. 1744].

CONICOPOLY, s. Literally 'Account-Man,' from Tam. *kanakka*, 'account' or 'writing,' and *pillai*, 'child' or 'person.' ["The *Kanakar* are usually addressed as '*Pillay*,' a title of respect common to them and the agricultural and shepherd castes" (*Madras Man.* ii. 229).] In Madras, a native clerk or writer, [in particular a shipping clerk. The corresponding Tel. term is **Curnum**].

1544.—"Duc eò tecum . . . domesticos tuos; pueros et aliquem **Conacapulam** qui norit scribere, cujus manu exaratas relinquere posses in quovis loco precationes a Pueris et aliis Catechumenis ediscendas."—*Scti. Franc. Xavier, Epist.*, pp. 160 *seq.*

1584.—"So you must appoint in each village or station fitting teachers and **Canacopoly**, as we have already arranged, and these must assemble the children every day at a certain time and place, and teach and drive into them the elements of reading and religion."—*Ditto*, in *Coleridge's L.* of him, ii. 24.

1578.—"At Tanor in Malabar I was acquainted with a Nayre **Canacopóla**, a writer in the Camara del Rey at Tanor . . . who every day used to eat to the weight of 5 drachms (of opium), which he would take in my presence."—*Acosta, Tractado*, 415.

c. 1580.—"One came who worked as a clerk, and said he was a poor **canaquapolle**, who had nothing to give."—*Primor e Honra*, &c., f. 94.

1672.—"Xaverius set everywhere teachers called **Canacappels.**"—*Baldaeus, Ceylon*, 377.

1680.—"The Governour, accompanyed with the Councell and severall Persons of the factory, attended by six files of Soldyers, the Company's Peons, 300 of the Washers, the Pedda Naigue, the **Cancoply** of the Towne and of the grounds, went the circuit of Madras ground, which was described by the **Cancoply** of the grounds, and lyes so intermixed with others (as is customary in these Countrys) that 'tis impossible to be knowne to any others, therefore every Village has a **Cancoply** and a Parryar, who are imployed in this office, which goes from Father to Son for ever."—*Ft. St. Geo. Consn.* Sept. 21. In *Notes and Exts.*, No. iii. 34.

1718.—"Besides this we maintain seven **Kanakappel**, or Malabarick writers."—*Propagation of the Gospel in the East*, Pt. ii. 55.

1726.—"The **Conakapules** (commonly called **Kannekappels**) are writers."—*Valentijn, Choro.* 88.

[1749.—"**Canacapula**," in *Logan, Malabar*, iii. 52.

[1750.—"**Conicoplas**," *ibid.* iii. 150.

[1773.—"**Conucopola.** He keeps your accounts, pays the rest of the servants their wages, and assists the Dubash in buying and selling. At Bengal he is called secretary. . . ."—*Ives*, 49.]

CONSOO-HOUSE, n.p. At Canton this was a range of buildings adjoining the foreign Factories, called also the 'Council Hall' of the foreign Factories. It was the property of the body of Hong merchants, and was the place of meeting of these merchants among themselves, or with the chiefs of the Foreign houses, when there was need for such conference (see *Fankwae*, p. 23). The name is probably a corruption of 'Council.' Bp. Moule, however, says: "The name is likely to have come from *kung-su*, the public hall, where a *kung-sz'*, a 'public company,' or guild, meets."

CONSUMAH, KHANSAMA, s. P. *Khānsāmān*; 'a house-steward.' In Anglo-Indian households in the Bengal Presidency, this is the title of the chief table servant and provider, now always a Mahommedan. [See **BUTLER.**] The literal meaning of the word is 'Master of the household gear'; it is not connected with *khwān*, 'a tray,' as Wilson suggests. The analogous word *Mīr-sāmān* occurs in *Elliot*, vii. 153. The Anglo-Indian form **Consumer** seems to have been not uncommon in the 18th century, probably with a spice of intention. From tables quoted in *Long*, 182, and in *Seton-Karr*, i. 95, 107, we see that the wages of a "**Consumah**, Christian, Moor, or Gentoo," were at Calcutta, in 1759, 5 rupees a month, and in 1785, 8 to 10 rupees.

[1609.—"Emersee Nooherdee being called by the **Cauncamma.**"—*Danvers, Letters*, i. 24.]

c. 1664.—"Some time after . . . she chose for her **Kane-saman**, that is, her Steward, a certain *Persian* called *Nazerkan*, who was a young Omrah, the handsomest and most accomplished of the whole Court."—*Bernier*, E.T., p. 4; [ed. *Constable*, p. 13].

1712.—"They were brought by a great circuit on the River to the **Chansamma** or Steward (Dispenser) of the aforesaid *Mahal*."—*Valentijn*, iv. (*Suratte*) 288.

1759.—"DUSTUCK *or* ORDER, *under the* **Chan Sumaun**, *or* Steward's *Seal, for the Honourable Company's holding the King's* [*i.e.* the Great Mogul's] *fleet.*"

* * * * *

"At the back of this is the seal of Zecah al Doulat Tidaudin Caun Bahadour, who is **Caun Samaun**, or Steward to his Majesty, whose prerogative it is to grant this Order."—*R. Owen Cambridge*, pp. 231 *seq.*

1788.—"After some deliberation I asked the **Khansaman**, what quantity was remaining of the clothes that had been brought from Iran to camp for sale, who answered that there were 15,000 jackets, and 12,000 pairs of long drawers."—*Mem. of Khojeh Abdulkurreem*, tr. by *Gladwin*, 55.

1810.—"The **Kansamah** may be classed with the house-steward, and butler; both of which offices appear to unite in this servant."—*Williamson, V. M.*, i. 199.

1831.—"I have taught my **khansama** to make very light iced punch."—*Jacquemont, Letters*, E.T., ii. 104.

COOCH AZO, or **AZO** simply, n.p. *Koch Hājo*, a Hindu kingdom on the banks of the Brahmaputra R., to the E. of Koch Bihār, annexed by Jahāngīr's troops in 1637. See *Blochmann* in *J.A.S.B.* xli. pt. i. 53, and xlii. pt. i. 235. In Valentijn's map of Bengal (made c. 1660) we have *Cos Assam* with *Azo* as capital, and *T'Ryk van Asoe*, a good way south and east of Silhet.

1753.—"Ceste rivière (Brahmapoutra), en remontant, conduit à Rangamati et à **Azoo**, qui font la frontière de l'état du Mogol. **Azoo** est une forteresse que l'Emir Jemla, sous le règne d'Aorengzèbe, reprit sur le roi d'Asham, comme une dependance de Bengale."—*D'Anville*, p. 62.

COOCH BEHAR, n.p. *Koch Bihār*, a native tributary State on the N.E. of Bengal, adjoining Bhotan and the Province of Assam. The first part of the name is taken from that of a tribe, the *Koch*, apparently a forest race who founded this State about the 15th century, and in the following century obtained dominion of considerable extent. They still form the majority of the population, but, as usual in such circumstances, give themselves a Hindu pedigree, under the name of *Rājbansi*. [See *Risley, Tribes and Castes of Bengal*, i. 491 *seqq.*] The site of the ancient monarchy of Kāmrūp is believed to have been in Koch Bihār, within the limits of which there are the remains of more than one ancient city. The second part of the name is no doubt due to the memory of some important **Vihara**, or Buddhist Monastery, but we have not found information on the subject. [Possibly the ruins at Kamatapur, for which see *Buchanan Hamilton, Eastern India*, iii. 426 *seqq.*]

1585.—"I went from Bengala into the countrey of **Couche**, which lieth 25 dayes iourny Northwards from Tanda."—*R. Fitch*, in *Hakl.* ii. 397.

c. 1596.—"To the north of Bengal is the province of **Coach**, the Chief of which commands 1,000 horse, and 100,000 foot. Kamroop, which is also called Kamroo and Kamtah (see **COMOTAY**) makes a part of his dominions."—*Ayeen* (by *Gladwin*), ed. 1800, ii. 3; [ed. *Jarrett*, ii. 117].

1726.—"**Cos Bhaar** is a Kingdom of itself, the King of which is sometimes subject to the Great Mogol, and sometimes throws his yoke off."—*Valentijn*, v. 159.

1774.—"The country about Bahar is low. Two *kos* beyond **Bahar** we entered a thicket . . . frogs, watery insects and dank air . . . 2 miles farther on we crossed the river which separates the **Kuch Bahar** country from that of the Deb Rajah, in sal canoes. . . ."—*Bogle*, in *Markham's Tibet*, &c., 14 *seq.*

(But Mr. Markham spoils all the original spelling. We may be sure Bogle did not write *kos*, nor "*Kuch Bahar*," as Mr. M. makes him do.)

1791.—"The late Mr. George Bogle . . . travelled by way of **Coos-Beyhar**, Tassasudon, and Paridrong, to Chanmanning the then residence of the Lama."—*Rennell* (3rd ed.), 301.

COOJA, s. P. *kūza*; an earthenware water-vessel (not long-necked, like the *surāḥī*—see **SERAI**). It is a word used at Bombay chiefly, [but is not uncommon among Mahommedans in N. India].

[1611.—"One sack of **cusher** to make coho."—*Danvers, Letters*, i. 128.

[1871.—"Many parts of India are celebrated for their **coojahs** or guglets, but the finest are brought from Bussorah, being light, thin, and porous, made from a whitish clay."—*Riddell, Indian Domestic Economy*, 7th ed., p. 362.]

1883.—"They (tree-frogs) would perch pleasantly on the edge of the water **cooja**, or on the rim of a tumbler."—*Tribes on my Frontier*, 118.

COOK-ROOM, s. Kitchen; in Anglo-Indian establishments always detached from the house.

1758.—"We will not in future admit of any expenses being defrayed by the Company either under the head of **cook-rooms**, gardens, or other expenses whatever."—*The Court's Letter*, March 3, in *Long*, 130.

1878.—"I was one day watching an old female monkey who had a young one by her side to whom she was giving small bits of a piece of bread which she had evidently just received from my **cook-room**."—*Life in the Mofussil*, ii. 44.

COOLCURNEE, s. This is the title of the village accountant and writer in some of the central and western parts of India. Mahr. *kulkarṇī*, apparently from *kula*, 'tribe,' and *karaṇa*, writer, &c., the *patwārī* of N. India (see under **CRANNY, CURNUM**). [*Kula* "in the revenue language of the S. appears to be applied especially to families, or individual heads of families, paying revenue" (*Wilson*).]

c. 1590.—". . . in this Soobah (Berar) . . . a chowdry they call *Deysmuck*; a *Canoongou* with them is *Deyspandeh*; a *Mokuddem* . . . they style *Putiel*; and a *Putwaree* they name **Kulkurnee**."—*Gladwin's Ayeen Akbery*, ii. 57; [ed. *Jarrett*, ii. 228].

[1826.—"You potails, **coolcunnies**, &c., will no doubt . . . contrive to reap tolerable harvests."—*Pandurang Hari*, ed. 1873, ii. 47.]

COOLICOY, s. A Malay term, properly *kulit-kayu*, 'skin-wood,' explained in the quotation:

1784.—"The **coolitcayo** or **coolicoy**. . . . This is a bark procured from some particular trees. (It is used for matting the sides of houses, and by Europeans as *dunnage* in pepper cargoes.)"—*Marsden's H. of Sumatra*, 2nd ed. 51.

COOLIN, adj. A class of Brāhmans of Bengal Proper, who make extraordinary claims to purity of caste and exclusiveness. Beng. *kulīnas*, from Skt. *kula*, 'a caste or family,' *kulīna*, 'belonging to a noble family.' They are much sought in marriage for the daughters of Brāhmans of less exalted pretensions, and often take many brides for the sake of the presents they receive. The system is one of the greatest abuses in Bengali Hinduism. [*Risley, Tribes and Castes of Bengal*, i. 146 *seqq.*]

1820.—"Some inferior **Koolēēnūs** marry many wives; I have heard of persons having 120; many have 15 or 20, and others 40 and 50 each. Numbers procure a subsistence by this excessive polygamy. . . ."—*Ward*, i. 81.

COOLUNG, COOLEN, and in W. India **CULLUM**, s. Properly the great grey crane (*Grus cinerea*), H. *kulang* (said by the dictionaries to be Persian, but Jerdon gives Mahr. *kallam*, and Tel. *kulangi*, *kolangi*, which seem against the Persian origin), [and Platts seems to connect it with Skt. *kurankara*, the Indian crane, *Ardea Sibirica* (*Williams*)]. Great companies of these are common in many parts of India, especially on the sands of the less frequented rivers; and their clanging, trumpet-like call is often heard as they pass high overhead at night.

"Ille gruum . . .
Clamor in aetheriis dispersus nubibus austri." (*Lucr.* iv. 182 *seq.*).

The name, in the form *Coolen*, is often misapplied to the Demoiselle Crane (*Anthropoides virgo*, L.), which is one of the best of Indian birds for the table (see *Jerdon*, ed. 1877, ii. 667, and last quotation below). The true *Coolung*, though inferior, is tolerably good eating. This bird, which is now quite unknown in Scotland, was in the 15th century not uncommon there, and was a favourite dish at great entertainments (see *Accts. of L. H. Treasurer of Scotland*, i. ccv.).

1698.—"Peculiarly Brand-geese, **Colum**, and *Serass*, a species of the former."—*Fryer*, 117.

c. 1809.—"Large flocks of a crane called **Kolong**, and of another called Saros (*Ardea Antigone*—see **CYRUS**), frequent this district in winter. . . . They come from the north in the beginning of the cold season, and retire when the heats commence."—*Buchanan's Rungpoor*, in *Eastern India*, iii. 579.

1813.—"Peacocks, partridges, quails, doves, and green-pigeons supplied our table, and with the addition of two stately birds, called the *Sahras* and **cullum**, added much to the animated beauty of the country."—*Forbes, Or. Mem.* ii. 29; [2nd ed. i. 331].

1883.—"Not being so green as I was, I let the tempting herd of antelopes pass, but the **kullum** I cannot resist. They are feeding in thousands at the other end of a large field, and to reach them it will only be necessary to crawl round behind the hedge for a quarter of a mile or so. But what will one not do with roast **kullum** looming in the vista of the future?"—*Tribes on my Frontier*, p. 162.

"*** N.B.—I have applied the word **kullum**, as everybody does, to the demoiselle crane, which, however, is not properly the **kullum** but the *Koonja*."—*Ibid.* p. 171.

COOLY, s. A hired labourer, or burden-carrier; and, in modern days especially, a labourer induced to emigrate from India, or from China, to labour in the plantations of Mauritius, Réunion, or the West Indies, sometimes under circumstances, especially in French colonies, which have brought the cooly's condition very near to slavery. In Upper India the term has frequently a specific application to the lower class of labourer who carries earth, bricks, &c., as distinguished from the skilled workman, and even from the digger.

The original of the word appears to have been a *nomen gentile*, the name (**Koli**) of a race or caste in Western India, who have long performed such offices as have been mentioned, and whose savagery, filth, and general degradation attracted much attention in former times, [see *Hamilton, Descr. of Hindostan* (1820), i. 609]. The application of the word would thus be analogous to that which has rendered the name of a *Slav*, captured and made a bondservant, the word for such a bondservant in many European tongues. According to Dr. H. V. Carter the *Kolīs* proper are a true hill-people, whose especial locality lies in the Western Ghāts, and in the northern extension of that range, between 18° and 24° N. lat. They exist in large numbers in Guzerat, and in the Konkan, and in the adjoining districts of the Deccan, but not beyond these limits (see *Ind. Antiquary*, ii. 154). [But they are possibly kinsfolk of the *Kols*, an important Dravidian race in Bengal and the

N.W.P. (see *Risley, T. and C. of Bengal*, ii. 101; *Crooke, T. C. of N.W.P.* iii. 294).] In the *Rās Mālā* [ed. 1878, p. 78 *seqq.*] the *Koolies* are spoken of as a tribe who lived long near the Indus, but who were removed to the country of the Null (the Nal, a brackish lake some 40 m. S.W. of Ahmedabad) by the goddess Hinglāj.

Though this explanation of the general use of the term *Cooly* is the most probable, the matter is perplexed by other facts which it is difficult to trace to the same origin. Thus in S. India there is a Tamil and Can. word *kūli* in common use, signifying 'hire' or 'wages,' which Wilson indeed regards as the true origin of *Cooly*. [Oppert (*Orig. Inhab. of Bharatavarsa*, p. 131) adopts the same view, and disputing the connection of *Cooly* with *Koli* or *Kol*, regards the word as equivalent to 'hired servant' and originating in the English Factories on the E. coast.] Also in both Oriental and Osmanli Turkish *kol* is a word for a slave, whilst in the latter also *kūleh* means 'a male slave, a bondsman' (*Redhouse*). *Khol* is in Tibetan also a word for a servant or slave (Note from A. Schiefner; see also Jäschke's *Tibetan Dict.*, 1881, p. 59). But with this the Indian term seems to have no connection. The familiar use of *Cooly* has extended to the Straits Settlements, Java, and China, as well as to all tropical and sub-tropical colonies, whether English or foreign.

In the quotations following, those in which the race is distinctly intended are marked with an *.

*1548.—"And for the duty from the **Colés** who fish at the sea-stakes and on the river of Bacaim. . . ."—*S. Botelho, Tombo*, 155.

*1553.—"Soltan Badur . . . ordered those pagans to be seized, and if they would not become Moors, to be flayed alive, saying that was all the black-mail the **Collijs** should get from Champanel."—*Barros*, Dec. IV. liv. v. cap. 7.

*1563.—"These **Colles** . . . live by robbing and thieving at this day."—*Garcia*, f. 34.

*1584.—"I attacked and laid waste nearly fifty villages of the **Kolís** and Grassias, and I built forts in seven different places to keep these people in check."—*Tabakāt-i-Akbarī*, in *Elliot*, v. 447.

*1598.—"Others that yet dwell within the countrie called **Colles**: which *Colles* . . . doe yet live by robbing and stealing. . . ."—*Linschoten*, ch. xxvii.; [Hak. Soc. i. 166].

*1616.—"Those who inhabit the country villages are called **Coolees**; these till the ground and breed up cattle."—*Terry*, in *Purchas*; [ed. 1777, p. 180].

* "The people called **Collees or Quillees**."—In *Purchas*, i. 436.

1630.—"The husbandmen or inferior sort of people called the **Coulies**."—*Lord's Display*, &c., ch. xiii.

1638.—"He lent us horses to ride on, and **Cowlers** (which are Porters) to carry our goods."—*W. Bruton*, in Hakl. v. 49.

In this form there was perhaps an indefinite suggestion of the *cowl-staff* used in carrying heavy loads.

1644.—"In these lands of Damam the people who dwell there as His Majesty's Vassals are heathen, whom they call **Collis**, and all the *Padres* make great complaints that the owners of the *aldeas* do not look with favour on the conversion of these heathen **Collis**, nor do they consent to their being made Christians, lest there thus may be hindrance to the greater service which is rendered by them when they remain heathen."—*Bocarro* (*Port. MS.*).

*1659.—"To relate how I got away from those Robbers, the **Koullis** . . . how we became good Friends by the means of my Profession of Physick . . . I must not insist upon to describe."—*Bernier*, E.T., p. 30; [ed. *Constable*, 91].

*c. 1666.—"Nous rencontrâmes quantité de **Colys**, qui sont gens d'une Caste ou tribut des Gentils, qui n'ont point d'habitation arrêtée, mais qui vont de village en village et portent avec eux tout leur ménage."—*Thevenot*, v. 21.

*1673.—"The Inhabitants of Ramnagur are the Salvages called **Coolies**. . . ."—*Fryer*, 161.

" "**Coolies**, Frasses, and Holencores, are the Dregs of the People."—*Ibid.* 194.

1680.—". . . It is therefore ordered forthwith that the drum be beat to call all **coolies**, carpenters. . . ."—*Official Memo.* in *Wheeler*, i. 129.

*c. 1703.—"The Imperial officers . . . sent . . . ten or twelve *sardārs*, with 13,000 or 14,000 horse, and 7,000 or 8,000 trained **Kolís** of that country."—*Khāfī Khān*, in *Elliot*, vii. 375.

1711.—"The better sort of people travel in Palankeens, carry'd by six or eight **Cooleys**, whose Hire, if they go not far from Town, is threepence a Day each."—*Lockyer*, 26.

1726.—"**Coeli's.** Bearers of all sorts of Burdens, goods, Andols (see **ANDOR**) and Palankins. . . ."—*Valentijn*, vol. v., *Names*, &c., 2.

*1727.—"Goga . . . has had some Mud Wall Fortifications, which still defend them from the Insults of their Neighbours the **Coulies**."—*A. Hamilton*, i: 141; [ed. 1744, i. 142].

1755.—"The Families of the **Coolies** sent to the Negrais complain that Mr. Brook has paid to the Head **Cooley** what money those who died there left behind them."—In *Long*, 54.

1785.—". . . the officers were obliged to have their baggage transported upon men's heads over an extent of upwards of 800 miles, at the rate of 5*l.* per month for every **couley** or porter employed."—*Carraccioli's L. of Clive*, i. 243 *seq.*

1789.—"If you should ask a common **cooly** or porter, what cast he is of, he will answer, the same as Master, *pariar-cast.*"—*Munro's Narrative*, 29.

1791.—". . . deux relais de vigoreux **coulis**, ou porteurs, de quatre hommes chacun. . . ."—*B. de St. Pierre, La Chaumière Indienne*, 15.

[1798.—"The Resident hopes all distinctions between the **Cooley** and Portuguese inhabitants will be laid aside."—*Procl.* in *Logan, Malabar*, iii. 302.]

*1813.—"Gudgerah, a large populous town surrounded by a wall, to protect it from the depredations of the **Coolees**, who are a very insolent set among the numerous and probably indigenous tribes of freebooters, and robbers in this part of India."—*Forbes, Orient. Mem.* iii. 63; [2nd ed. ii. 160; also see i. 146].

1817.—"These (Chinese) emigrants are usually employed as **coolees** or labourers on their first arrival (in Java)."—*Raffles, H. of Java*, i. 205.

*1820.—"In the profession of thieving the **Koolees** may be said to act *con amore.* A **Koolee** of this order, meeting a defenceless person in a lane about dusk, would no more think of allowing him to pass unplundered than a Frenchman would a woman without bowing to her; it may be considered a point of honour of the caste."—*Tr. Lit. Soc. Bo.* iii. 335.

*1825.—"The head man of the village said he was a *Kholee*, the name of a degenerate race of Rajpoots in Guzerat, who from the low occupations in which they are generally employed have (under the corrupt name of **Coolie**) given a name, probably through the medium of the Portuguese, to bearers of burdens all over India."—*Heber*, ed. 1844, ii. 92.

1867.—"Bien que de race différente les **Coolies** et les Chinois sont comportés à peu-près de même."—*Quatrefages, Rapport sur le Progrès de l'Anthropologie*, 219.

1871.—"I have hopes for the **Coolies** in British Guiana, but it will be more sure and certain when the immigration system is based on better laws."—*Jenkins, The Coolie.*

1873.—"The appellant, the Hon. Julian Pauncefote, is the Attorney-General for the Colony (Hong Kong) and the respondent Hwoka-Sing is a **Coolie** or labourer, and a native of China."—*Report of Case before Jud. Com. of Privy Council.*

,, "A man (Col. Gordon) who had wrought such wonders with means so modest as a levy of **Coolies** . . . needed, we may be sure, only to be put to the highest test to show how just those were who had marked him out in his Crimean days as a youth whose extraordinary genius for war could not be surpassed in the army that lay before Sebastopol."—*Sat. Review*, Aug. 16, 203.

1875.—"A long row of cottages, evidently pattern-built . . . announced the presence of **Coolies**, Indian or Chinese."—*Palgrave, Dutch Guiana*, ch. i.

The word **Cooly** has passed into English thieves' jargon in the sense of 'a soldier' (v. *Slang Dict.*).

COOMKEE, adj., used as *sub.* This is a derivative from P. *kumak*, 'aid,' and must have been widely diffused in India, for we find it specialised in different senses in the extreme West and East, besides having in both the general sense of 'auxiliary.'

[(a) In the Moghul army the term is used for auxiliary troops.

[c. 1590.—"Some troops are levied occasionally to strengthen the *munsubs*, and they are called **Kummeky** (or auxiliaries)."—*Gladwin, Ayeen Akbery*, ed. 1800, i. 188; in *Blochmann*, i. 232, **Kumakis**.

[1858.—"The great landholders despise them (the ordinary levies) but respect the **Komukee** corps. . . ."—*Sleeman, Journey through Oudh*, i. 30.]

(b) **Kumakī**, in N. and S. Canara, is applied to a defined portion of forest, from which the proprietor of the village or estate has the privilege of supplying himself with wood for house-building, &c. (except from the reserved kinds of wood), with leaves and twigs for manure, fodder, &c. (See **COOMRY**). [The system is described by Sturrock, *Man. S. Canara*, i. 16, 224 *seqq.*]

(c). **Koomkee**, in Bengal, is the technical name of the female elephant used as a decoy in capturing a male.

1807.—"When an elephant is in a proper state to be removed from the *Keddah*, he is conducted either by **koomkies** (*i.e.* decoy females) or by tame males."—*Williamson, Oriental Field Sports*, folio ed., p. 30.

[1873.—"It was an interesting sight to see the captive led in between two **khoonkies** or tame elephants."—*Cooper, Mishmee Hills*, 88.

[1882.—"Attached to each elephant hunting party there must be a number of tame elephants, or **Koonkies**, to deal with the wild elephants when captured."—*Sanderson, Thirteen Years*, 70.]

COOMRY, s. [Can. *kumari*, from Mahr. *kumbarī*, 'a hill slope of poor soil.'] *Kumari* cultivation is the S. Indian (especially in Canara), [*Sturrock, S. Canara Man.* i. 17], appellation of that system pursued by hill-people in many parts of India and its frontiers, in which a certain tract of forest is cut down and burnt, and the ground planted with crops for one or two seasons, after which a new site is similarly treated. This system has many names in different regions; in the east of Bengal it it known as *jhūm* (see **JHOOM**); in Burma as *toungyyan*; [in parts of the N.W.P. *dahya*, Skt. *daha*, 'burning'; *ponam* in Malabar; *ponacaud* in Salem]. We find *kumried* as a quasi-English participle in a document quoted by the High Court, Bombay, in a judgment dated 27th January, 1879, p. 227.

1883.—"*Kumaki* (**Coomkee**) and **Kumari** privileges stand on a very different platform. The former are perfectly reasonable, and worthy of a civilised country. . . . As for *Kumari* privileges, they cannot be defended before the tribunal of reason as being really good for the country, but old custom is old custom, and often commands the respect of a wise government even when it is indefensible."—*Mr. Grant Duff's Reply to an Address at Mangalore, 15th October.*

COONOOR, n.p. A hill-station in the Neilgherries. *Kunnur*, 'Hill-Town.' [The *Madras Gloss.* gives Can. *Kunnūru*, Skt. *kunna*, 'small,' Can. *ūru*, 'village.']

COORG, n.p. A small hill State on the west of the table-land of Mysore, in which lies the source of the Cauvery, and which was annexed to the British Government, in consequence of cruel misgovernment in 1834. The name is a corruption of *Kŏḍagu*, of which Gundert says: "perhaps from *kodu*, 'steep,' or Tamil *kaḍaga*, 'west.'" [For various other speculations on the derivation, see *Oppert, Original Inhabit.*, 162 *seqq.* The *Madras Gloss.* seems to refer it to Skt. *kroḍadeśa*, 'hog-land,' from "the tradition that the inhabitants had nails on hands and feet like a boar."] *Coorg* is also used for a native of the country, in which case it stands for *Kŏḍaga*.

COORSY, s. H.—from Ar.—*kursī* [which is used for the stand on which the Korán is laid]. It is the word usually employed in Western India for 'a chair,' and is in the Bengal Presidency a more dignified term than *chaukī* (see **CHOKY**). *Kursī* is the Arabic form, borrowed from the Aramaic, in which the emphatic state is *kursĕyā*. But in Hebrew the word possesses a more original form with *ss* for *rs* (*kisse*, the usual word in the O. T. for 'a throne'). The original sense appears to be 'a covered seat.'

1781.—"It happened, at this time, that the Nawaub was seated on his **koorsi**, or chair, in a garden, beneath a banyan tree."—*Hist. of Hydur Naik*, 452.

COOSUMBA, s. H. *kusum*, *kusumbha*, **Safflower**, q.v. But the name is applied in Rajputana and Guzerat to the tincture of opium, which is used freely by Rājputs and others in those territories; also (according to Shakespear) to an infusion of **Bang** (q.v.).

[1823.—"Several of the Rajpoot Princes West of the Chumbul seldom hold a Durbar without presenting a mixture of liquid opium, or, as it is termed, '**kusoombah**,' to all present. The minister washes his hands in a vessel placed before the Rawul, after which some liquid opium is poured into the palm of his right hand. The first in rank who may be present then approaches and drinks the liquid."—*Malcolm, Mem. of Central India*, 2d ed. ii. 146, note.]

COOTUB, THE, n.p. The *Kuṭb Minār*, near Delhi, one of the most remarkable of Indian architectural antiquities, is commonly so called by Europeans. It forms the minaret of the Great Mosque, now long in ruins, which Kuṭb-uddīn Ibak founded A.D. 1191, immediately after the capture of Delhi, and which was built out of the materials of numerous Hindu temples, as is still manifest. According to the elaborate investigation of Gen. A. Cunningham [*Arch. Rep.* i. 189 *seqq.*], the magnificent Minār was begun by Kuṭb-uddīn Ībak about 1200, and completed by his successor Shamsuddīn Īyaltimish about 1220. The tower has undergone, in its upper part, various restorations. The height as it now stands is 238 feet 1 inch. The traditional name of the tower no doubt had reference to the name of its founder, but also there may have been a reference to the contemporary Saint, Kuṭb-uddīn Ūshī, whose tomb is close by; and perhaps also to the meaning of the name Kuṭb-uddīn, 'The Pole or

Axle of the Faith,' as appropriate to such a structure.

c. 1330.—"Attached to the mosque (of Delhi) is a tower for the call to prayer which has no equal in the whole world. It is built of red stone, with about 360 steps. It is not square, but has a great number of angles, is very massive at the base, and very lofty, equalling the Pharos of Alexandria."—*Abulfeda*, in *Gildemeister*, 190.

c. 1340.—"In the northern court of the mosque stands the minaret (*al-ṣauma'a*), which is without a parallel in all the countries of Islām. . . . It is of surpassing height; the pinnacle is of milk-white marble, and the globes which decorate it are of pure gold. The aperture of the staircase is so wide that elephants can ascend, and a person on whom I could rely told me that when the minaret was a-building, he saw an elephant ascend to the very top with a load of stones."—*Ibn Batuta*, iii. 151.

The latter half of the last quotation is fiction.

1663.—"At two Leagues off the City on Agra's side, in a place by the Mahumetans called *Koja Kotubeddine*, there is a very ancient Edifice which hath been a Temple of Idols. . . ."—*Bernier*, E.T. 91.

It is evident from this that Bernier had not then visited the *Kuṭb*. [Constable in his tr. reads "*Koia Kotub-eddine*," by which he understands *Koh-i-Kuṭab-uddīn*, the hill or eminence of the Saint, p. 283.]

1825.—"I will only observe that the **Cuttab** Minar . . . is really the finest tower I have ever seen, and must, when its spire was complete, have been still more beautiful."—*Heber*, ed. 1844, i. 308.

COPECK, s. This is a Russian coin, $\frac{1}{100}$ of a ruble. The degeneration of coin denominations is often so great that we may suspect this name to preserve that of the *dīnār Kopekī* often mentioned in the histories of Timur and his family. *Kopek* is in Turki, 'dog,' and Charmoy explains the term as equivalent to *Abū-kalb*, 'Father of a dog,' formerly applied in Egypt to Dutch crowns (*Löwenthaler*) bearing a lion. There could not be Dutch coins in Timur's time, but some other Frank coin bearing a lion may have been so called, probably Venetian. A Polish coin with a lion on it was called by a like name (see *Macarius*, quoted below, p. 169). Another etymology of *kopek* suggested (in *Chaudoir*, *Aperçu des Monnaies Russes*) is from Russ. *kopié*, *kopyé*, a pike, many old Russian coins representing the Prince on horseback with a spear. [This is accepted by the *N.E.D.*] **Kopeks** are mentioned in the reign of Vassili III., about the middle of the 15th century, but only because regularly established in the coinage c. 1536. [See **TANGA**.]

1390.—(Timour resolved) "to visit the venerated tomb of Sheikh Maslahat . . . and with that intent proceeded to Tāshkand . . . he there distributed as alms to worthy objects, 10,000 *dīnārs* **kopakī**. . . ."—*Sharīfuddīn*, in Extracts by *M. Charmoy*, *Mem. Acad. St. P.*, vi. S., tome iii. p. 363, also note, p. 135.

1535.—"It was on this that the Grand Duchess Helena, mother of Ivan Vassilievitch, and regent in his minority, ordered, in 1535, that these new *Dengui* should be melted down and new ones struck, at the rate of 300 *dengui*, or 3 Roubles of Moscow à la grivenka, in **Kopeks**. . . . From that time accounts continued to be kept in *Roubles*, **Kopeks**, and *Dengui*."—*Chaudoir*, *Aperçu*.

c. 1655.—"The pension in lieu of provisions was, for our Lord the Patriarch 25 **copecks** daily."—*Travels of the Patriarch Macarius*, Or. Tr. Fund, i. 281.

1783.—"The **Copeck** of Russia, a copper coin, in name and apparently in value, is the same which was current in Tartary during the reign of Timur."—*Forster's Journey*, ed. 1808, ii. 332.

COPPERSMITH, s. Popular name both in H. (*tambayat*) and English of the crimson-breasted barbet (*Xantholaema indica*, Latham). See the quotation from Jerdon.

1862.—"It has a remarkably loud note, which sounds like *took-took-took*, and this it generally utters when seated on the top of some tree, nodding its head at each call, first to one side and then to another. . . . This sound and the motion of its head, accompanying it, have given origin to the name of '**Coppersmith**.' . . ."—*Jerdon*, ed. 1877, i. 316.

1879.—

"... In the mango-sprays
The sun-birds flashed; alone at his green forge
Toiled the loud **Coppersmith**. . . ."
The Light of Asia, p. 20.

1883.—"For the same reason *mynas* seek the tope, and the 'blue jay,' so-called, and the little green **coppersmith** hooting ventriloquistically."—*Tribes on my Frontier*, 154.

COPRAH, s. The dried kernel of the coco-nut, much used for the expression of its oil, and exported largely from the Malabar ports. The Portuguese probably took the word from the Malayāl. *koppara*, which is, however, apparently borrowed from the H. *khoprā*, of the same meaning. The latter is connected by some with *khapnā*, 'to dry up.' Shakespear however, more probably, connects *khoprā*, as well as *khoprī*, 'a skull, a shell,' and *khappar*, 'a skull,' with Skt. *kharpara*, having also the meaning of 'skull.' Compare with this a derivation which we have suggested (s.v.) as possible of **coco** from old Fr. and Span. *coque, coco*, 'a shell'; and with the slang use of *coco* there mentioned.

1563.—"And they also dry these cocos . . . and these dried ones they call **copra**, and they carry them to Ormuz, and to the Balaghat."—*Garcia, Colloq.* f. 68*b*.

1578.—"The kernel of these cocos is dried in the sun, and is called **copra**. . . . From this same *copra* oil is made in presses, as we make it from olives."—*Acosta*, 104.

1584.—"**Chopra**, from Cochin and Malabar. . . ."—*Barret*, in *Hakl.* ii. 413.

1598.—"The other Oyle is prest out of the dried Cocus, which is called **Copra**. . . ." —*Linschoten*, 101. See also (1602), *Couto*, Dec. I. liv. iv. cap. 8; (1606) *Gouvea*, f. 62*b*; [(1610) *Pyrard de Laval*, Hak. Soc. ii. 384 (reading *kuppara* for *suppara*);] (c. 1690) *Rumphius, Herb. Amb.* i. 7.

1727.—"That tree (coco-nut) produceth . . . **Copera**, or the Kernels of the Nut dried, and out of these Kernels there is a very clear Oil exprest."—*A. Hamilton*, i. 307; [ed. 1744, i. 308].

1860.—"The ordinary estimate is that one thousand full-grown nuts of Jaffna will yield 525 pounds of **Copra** when dried, which in turn will produce 25 gallons of cocoa-nut oil."—*Tennent, Ceylon*, ii. 531.

1878.—It appears from Lady Brassey's *Voyage in the Sunbeam* (5th ed. 248) that this word is naturalised in Tahiti.

1883.—"I suppose there are but few English people outside the trade who know what **copra** is; I will therefore explain:—it is the white pith of the ripe cocoa-nut cut into strips and dried in the sun. This is brought to the trader (at New Britain) in baskets varying from 3 to 20 lbs. in weight; the payment . . : was a thimbleful of beads for each pound of copra. . . . The nut is full of oil, and on reaching Europe the copra is crushed in mills, and the oil pressed from it . . . half the oil sold as 'olive-oil' is really from the cocoa-nut."—*Wilfred Powell, Wanderings in a Wild Country*, p. 37.

CORAL-TREE, s. *Erythrina indica*, Lam., so called from the rich scarlet colour of its flowers.

[1860.—"There are . . . two or three species of the genus *Erythrina* or **Coral Tree**. A small species of *Erythrina*, with reddish flowers, is famous in Buddhist mythology as the tree around which the Devas dance till they are intoxicated in Sudra's (? Indra's) heaven." *Mason's Burmah*, p. 531.—*McMahon, Karens of the Golden Chersonese*, p. 11.]

CORCOPALI, s. This is the name of a fruit described by Varthema, Acosta, and other old writers, the identity of which has been the subject of much conjecture. It is in reality the *Garcinia indica*, Choisy (N. O. *Guttiferae*), a tree of the Concan and Canara, which belongs to the same genus as the mangosteen, and as the tree affording the gamboge (see **CAMBOJA**) of commerce. It produces an agreeable, acid, purple fruit, which the Portuguese call *brindões*. From the seeds a fatty oil is drawn, known as *kokun butter*. The name in Malayāl. is *kodukka*, and this possibly, with the addition of *puli*, 'acid,' gave rise to the name before us. It is stated in the *English Cyclopaedia* (*Nat. Hist.* s.v. *Garcinia*) that in Travancore the fruit is called by the natives *gharka pulli*, and in Ceylon *goraka*. Forbes Watson's 'List of Indian Productions' gives as synonyms of the *Garcinia cambogia* tree '*karka-puliemaram?*' Tam.; '*kurka-pulie*,' Mal.; and '*goraka-gass*,' Ceyl. [The *Madras Gloss.* calls it *Mate mangosteen*, a ship term meaning 'cook-room mangosteen'; Can. *murginahuli*, 'twisted tamarind'; Mal. *punampuli*, 'stiff tamarind.'] The *Cyclopædia* also contains some interesting particulars regarding the uses in Ceylon of the *goraka*. But this Ceylon tree is a different species (*G. Gambogia*, Desrous). Notwithstanding its name it does not produce gamboge; its gum being insoluble in water. A figure of *G. indica* is given in *Beddome's Flora Sylvatica*, pl. lxxxv. [A full account of *Kokam butter* will be found in *Watt, Econ. Dict.* iii. 467 *seqq.*]

1510.—"Another fruit is found here fashioned like a melon, and it has divisions after that manner, and when it is cut, three or four grains which look like grapes, or birdcherries, are found inside. The tree which bears this fruit is of the height of a quince tree, and forms its leaves in the same manner. This fruit is called **Corcopal**; it is extremely good for eating, and excellent as a medicine."—*Varthema* (transl. modified from), Hak. Soc. 167.

1578.—"**Carcapuli** is a great tree, both lofty and thick; its fruit is in size and aspect like an orange without a rind, all divided in lobes. . . ."—*Acosta, Tractado*, 357.

(This author gives a tolerable cut of the

fruit; there is an inferior plate in Debry, iv. No. xvii.).

1672.—"The plant **Carcapuli** is peculiar to Malabar. . . . The ripe fruit is used as ordinary food; the unripe is cut in pieces and dried in the sun, and is then used all the year round to mix in dishes, along with tamarind, having an excellent flavour, of a tempered acidity, and of a very agreeable and refreshing odour. The form is nearly round, of the size of an apple, divided into eight equal lobes of a yellow colour, fragrant and beautiful, and with another little fruitlet attached to the extremity, which is perfectly round," &c., &c.—*P. Vincenzo Maria*, 356.

CORGE, COORGE, &c., s. A mercantile term for 'a score.' The word is in use among the trading Arabs and others, as well as in India. It is established in Portuguese use apparently, but the Portuguese word is almost certainly of Indian origin, and this is expressly asserted in some Portuguese Dictionaries (*e.g. Lacerda's*, Lisbon, 1871). *Korī* is used exactly in the same way by natives all over Upper India. Indeed, the vulgar there in numeration habitually say *do korī*, *tīn korī*, for 40, 60, and so forth. The first of our quotations shows the word in a form very closely allied to this, and explaining the transition. Wilson gives Telugu *khorjam*, "a bale or lot of 20 pieces, commonly called a *corge*." [The *Madras Gloss.* gives Can. *korji*, Tel. *khorjam*, as meaning either a measure of capacity, about 44 maunds, or a Madras town cloth measure of 20 pieces.] But, unless a root can be traced, this may easily be a corruption of the trade-word. Littré explains *corge* or *courge* as "Paquet de toile de coton des Indes"; and Marcel Devic says: "C'est vraisemblablement l'Arabe *khordj*" — which means a saddlebag, a portmanteau. Both the definition and the etymology seem to miss the essential meaning of *corge*, which is that of a *score*, and not that of a packet or bundle, unless by accident.

1510.—"If they be stuffs, they deal by **curia**, and in like manner if they be jewels. By a **curia** is understood twenty."—*Varthema*, 170.

1525.—"A **corjá** dos quotonyas grandes vale (250) tamgas."—*Lembrança, das Cousas da India*, 48.

1554.—"The nut and mace when gathered were bartered by the natives for common kinds of cloth, and for each **korja** of these . . . they gave a *bahar* of mace . . . and seven *bahars* of the nut."—*Castanheda*, vi. 8.

[1605-6.—"Note the **cody** or **corge** is a bondell or set nomber of 20 pieces."—*Birdwood, First Letter Book*, 80.]

1612.—"White callicos from twentie to fortie Royals the **Corge** (a **Corge** being twentie pieces), a great quantitie."—*Capt. Saris*, in *Purchas*, i. 347.

1612-13.—"They returning brought doune the Mustraes of everie sort, and the prices demanded for them per **Corge**."—*Downton*, in *Purchas*, i. 299.

1615.—

"6 pec. whit *baftas* of 16 and 17 Rs....**corg.**
6 pec. blew *byrams*, of 15 Rs. ....**corg.**
6 pec. red *zelas*, of 12 Rs. ....**corg.**"
Cocks's Diary, i. 75.

1622.—Adam Denton . . . admits that he made "90 **corge** of Pintadoes" in their house at Patani, but not at their charge.—*Sainsbury*, iii. 42.

1644.—"To the Friars of St. Francis for their regular yearly allowance, a cow every week, 24 candies of wheat, 15 sacks of rice *girasol*, 2 sacks of sugar, half a candy of *sero* (qu. *sevo*, 'tallow,' 'grease,'?) ½ candy of coco-nut oil, 6 maunds of butter, 4 **corjas** of cotton stuffs, and 25,920 rés for dispensary medicines (*mezinhas de bottica*)."—*Bocarro, MS.* f. 217.

c. 1670.—"The *Chites* . . . which are made at *Lahor* . . . are sold by **Corges**, every *Corge* consisting of twenty pieces. . . ."—*Tavernier, On the Commodities of the Domns. of the Great Mogul*, &c., E.T. p. 58; [ed. *Ball*, ii. 5].

1747.—"Another Sett of Madrass Painters . . . being examined regarding what Goods were Remaining in their hands upon the Loss of Madrass, they acknowledge to have had 15 **Corge** of Chints then under their Performance, and which they acquaint us is all safe . . . but as they have lost all their Wax and Colours, they request an Advance of 300 Pagodas for the Purchase of more. . . ."—*Consns. Fort St. David*, Aug. 13. *MS. Records* in India Office.

c. 1760.—"At Madras . . . 1 **gorge** is 22 pieces."—*Grose*, i. 284.

" "No washerman to demand for 1 **corge** of pieces more than 7 *pun* of cowries."—In *Long*, 239.

1784.—In a Calcutta Lottery-list of prizes we find "55 **corge** of Pearls."—In *Seton-Karr*, i. 33.

[c. 1809.—"To one **korj** or 20 pieces of Tunzebs . . . 50 rs."—*Buchanan Hamilton, Eastern India*, i. 398.]

1810.—"I recollect about 29 years back, when marching from Berhampore to Cawnpore with a detachment of European recruits, seeing several **coarges** (of sheep) bought for their use, at 3 and 3½ rupees! at the latter rate 6 sheep were purchased for a rupee . . . five pence each."—*Williamson, V. M.* i. 293.

1813.—"**Corge** is 22 at Judda."—*Milburn*, i. 93.

CORINGA, n.p. *Koringa*; probably a corruption of *Kalinga* [see **KLING**]. [The *Madras Gloss.* gives the Tel. *korangi*, 'small cardamoms.'] The name of a seaport in Godāvari Dist. on the northern side of the Delta. ["The only place between Calcutta and Trincomalee where large vessels used to be docked."—*Morris, Godavery Man.*, p. 40.]

CORLE, s. Singh. *kōrale*, a district.

1726.—"A *Coraal* is an overseer of a **Corle** or District. . . ."—*Valentijn, Names of Native Officers in the Villages of Ceylon*, 1.

CORNAC, s. This word is used, by French writers especially, as an Indian word, and as the equivalent of **Mahout** (q.v.), or driver of the elephant. Littré defines: "*Nom qu'on donne* dans les Indes *au conducteur d'un eléphant,*" &c., &c., adding: "Etym. Sanskrit *karnikin, éléphant.*" "Dans les Indes" is happily vague, and the etymology worthless. Bluteau gives **Cornâca**, but no etymology. In Singhalese *Kūrawa*='Elephant Stud.' (It is not in the Singhalese Dict., but it is in the official *Glossary of Terms*, &c.), and our friend Dr. Rost suggests *Kūrawa-nāyaka*, 'Chief of the *Kūrawa*' as a probable origin. This is confirmed by the form *Cournakea* in Valentijn, and by another title which he gives as used for the head of the Elephant Stable at Matura, viz. *Gagi-naicke* (*Names*, &c., p. 11), *i.e. Gaji-nāyaka*, from *Gaja*, 'an elephant.' [The *N.E.D.* remarks that some authorities give for the first part of the word Skt. *kari*, 'elephant.']

1672.—"There is a certain season of the year when the old elephant discharges an oil at the two sides of the head, and at that season they become like mad creatures, and often break the neck of their **carnac** or driver."—*Baldaeus*, Germ. ed. 422. (See **MUST**.)

1685.—"O **cornaca** q̃ estava de baixo delle tinha hum laço que metia em hũa das mãos ao bravo."—*Ribeiro*, f. 49*b*.

1712.—"The aforesaid author (P. Fr. Gaspar de S. Bernardino in his Itinerary), relates that in the said city (Goa), he saw three Elephants adorned with jewels, adoring the most Holy Sacrament at the Sè Gate on the Octave of Easter, on which day in India they make the procession of *Corpus Domini*, because of the calm weather. I doubt not that the **Cornacas** of these animals had taught them to perform these acts of apparent adoration. But at the same time there appears to be Religion and Piety innate in the Elephant." *—In *Bluteau*, s.v. *Elephante*.

1726.—"After that (at Mongeer) one goes over a great walled area, and again through a gate, which is adorned on either side with a great stone elephant with a **Carnak** on it."—*Valentijn*, v. 167.

,, "**Cournakeas**, who stable the new-caught elephants, and tend them."—*Valentijn, Names*, &c., 5 (in vol. v.).

1727.—"As he was one Morning going to the River to be washed, with his **Carnack** or Rider on his Back, he chanced to put his Trunk in at the Taylor's Window."—*A. Hamilton*, ii. 110; [ed. 1744, ii. 109]. This is the only instance of English use that we know (except Mr. Carl Bock's; and he is not an Englishman, though his book is in English). It is the famous story of the Elephant's revenge on the Tailor.

[1831.—"With the same judgment an elephant will task his strength, without human direction. 'I have seen,' says M. D'Obsonville, 'two occupied in beating down a wall which their **cornacs** (keepers) had desired them to do. . . .'"—*Library of Entertaining Knowledge, Quadrupeds*, ii. 157.]

1884.—"The **carnac**, or driver, was quite unable to control the beast, which roared and trumpeted with indignation."—*C. Bock, Temples and Elephants*, p. 22.

COROMANDEL, n.p. A name which has been long applied by Europeans to the Northern Tamil Country, or (more comprehensively) to the eastern coast of the Peninsula of India from Pt. Calimere northward to the mouth of the Kistna, sometimes to Orissa. It corresponds pretty nearly to the *Maabar* of Marco Polo and the Mahommedan writers of his age, though that is defined more accurately as from C. Comorin to Nellore.

Much that is fanciful has been written on the origin of this name. Tod makes it *Kūrū-mandala*, the Realm of the Kūrūs (*Trans. R. As. Soc.* iii. 157). Bp. Caldwell, in the first edition of his *Dravidian Grammar*, suggested that European traders might have taken this familiar name from that of *Karumanal* ('black sand'), the name of a small village on the coast north of Madras, which is habitually pronounced and written *Coromandel* by European residents at Madras. [The same suggestion was made earlier (see *Wilks, Hist. Sketches*, ed. 1869, i. 5,

* "This elephant is a very pious animal"—a German friend once observed in India, misled by the double sense of his vernacular *fromm* ('harmless, tame' as well as 'pious or innocent').

note)]. The learned author, in his second edition, has given up this suggestion, and has accepted that to which we adhere. But Mr. C. P. Brown, the eminent Telugu scholar, in repeating the former suggestion, ventures positively to assert: "The earliest Portuguese sailors pronounced this *Coromandel*, and called the whole coast by this name, which was unknown to the Hindus";* a passage containing in three lines several errors. Again, a writer in the *Ind. Antiquary* (i. 380) speaks of this supposed origin of the name as "pretty generally accepted," and proceeds to give an imaginative explanation of how it was propagated. These etymologies are founded on a corrupted form of the name, and the same remark would apply to *Kharamaṇḍalam*, the 'hot country,' which Bp. Caldwell mentions as one of the names given, in Telugu, to the eastern coast. Padre Paolino gives the name more accurately as *Ciola* (*i.e. Chola*) *maṇḍalam*, but his explanation of it as meaning the Country of *Cholam* (or *juwārī—Sorghum vulgare*, Pers.) is erroneous. An absurd etymology is given by Teixeira (*Relacion de Harmuz*, 28; 1610). He writes: "*Choromãdel* or Choro Bãdel, *i.e.* Rice Port, because of the great export of rice from thence." He apparently compounds H. *chaul*, *chāwal*, 'cooked rice' (!) and **bandel**, *i.e.* **bandar** (q.v.) 'harbour.' This is a very good type of the way etymologies are made by some people, and then confidently repeated.

The name is in fact **Chôṛamaṇḍala**, the Realm of *Chôṛa*; this being the Tamil form of the very ancient title of the Tamil Kings who reigned at Tanjore. This correct explanation of the name was already given by D'Anville (see *Éclaircissemens*, p. 117), and by W. Hamilton in 1820 (ii. 405), by Ritter, quoting him in 1836 (*Erdkunde*, vi. 296); by the late M. Reinaud in 1845 (*Relation*, &c., i. lxxxvi.); and by Sir Walter Elliot in 1869 (*J. Ethnol. Soc.* N.S. i. 117). And the name occurs in the forms **Cholamaṇḍalam** or **Solamandalam** on the great Temple inscription of Tanjore (11th century), and in an inscription of A.D. 1101 at a temple dedicated to Varāhasvāmi near the Seven Pagodas. We have other quite analogous names in early inscriptions, *e.g.* *Īlamaṇḍalam* (Ceylon), *Cheramaṇḍalam*, *Tondaimaṇḍalam*, &c.

Chola, as the name of a Tamil people and of their royal dynasty appears as *Choḍa* in one of Asoka's inscriptions, and in the Telugu inscriptions of the Chālukya dynasty. Nor can we doubt that the same name is represented by Σῶρα of Ptolemy who reigned at Ἀρκατοῦ (Arcot), Σώρ-ναξ who reigned at Ὄρθουρα (Wariūr), and the Σῶραι νομάδες who dwelt inland from the site of Madras.†

The word *Soli*, as applied to the Tanjore country, occurs in Marco Polo (Bk. iii. ch. 20), showing that *Chola* in some form was used in his day. Indeed *Soli* is used in Ceylon.‡ And although the *Choromandel* of Baldaeus and other Dutch writers is, as pronounced in their language, ambiguous or erroneous, Valentijn (1726) calls the country *Sjola*, and defines it as extending from Negapatam to Orissa, saying that it derived its name from a certain kingdom, and adding that *mandalam* is 'kingdom.'§ So that this respectable writer had already distinctly indicated the true etymology of *Coromandel*.

Some old documents in Valentijn speak of the 'old city of Coromandel.' It is not absolutely clear what place was so called (probably by the Arabs in their fashion of calling a chief town by the name of the country), but the indications point almost certainly to Negapatam.‖

The oldest European mention of the name is, we believe, in the *Roteiro de Vasco da Gama*, where it appears as **Chomandarla**. The short Italian narrative of Hieronymo da Sto. Stefano is, however, perhaps earlier still, and he curiously enough gives the name in exactly the modern form "Coromandel," though perhaps his *C*

* *J.R.A.S.*, N.S. v. 148. He had said the same in earlier writings, and was apparently the original author of this suggestion. [But see above.]

† See Bp. Caldwell's *Comp. Gram.*, 18, 95, &c.

‡ See *Tennent*, i. 395.

§ "This coast bears commonly the corrupted name of *Choromandel*, and is now called only thus; but the right name is *Sjola-mandalam*, after *Sjola*, a certain kingdom of that name, and *mandalam*, 'a kingdom,' one that used in the old times to be an independent and mighty empire."—*Val.* v. 2.

‖ *e.g.* 1675.—"Hence the country . . . has become very rich, wherefore the Portuguese were induced to build a town on the site of the old Gentoo (*Jentiefze*) city *Chiormandelan*."—Report on the Dutch Conquests in Ceylon and S. India, by *Rykloof Van Goens* in *Valentijn*, v. (Ceylon) 234.

had originally a *cedilla* (*Ramusio*, i. f. 345*v*.). These instances suffice to show that the name was not given by the Portuguese. Da Gama and his companions knew the east coast only by hearsay, and no doubt derived their information chiefly from Mahommedan traders, through their "Moorish" interpreter. That the name was in familiar Mahommedan use at a later date may be seen from Rowlandson's Translation of the *Tohfat-ul-Mujāhidīn*, where we find it stated that the Franks had built fortresses "at Meelapoor (*i.e. Mailapur* or San Tomé) and Nagapatam, and other ports of **Solmundul**," showing that the name was used by them just as we use it (p. 153). Again (p. 154) this writer says that the Mahommedans of Malabar were cut off from extra-Indian trade, and limited "to the ports of Guzerat, the Concan, *Solmondul*, and the countries about Kaeel." At page 160 of the same work we have mention of "**Coromandel** and other parts," but we do not know how this is written in the original Arabic. Varthema (1510) has **Ciormandel**, *i.e. Chormandel*, but which Eden in his translation (1577, which probably affords the earliest English occurrence of the name) deforms into **Cyromandel** (f. 396*b*). [Albuquerque in his *Cartas* (see p. 135 for a letter of 1513) has **Choromandell** *passim*.] Barbosa has in the Portuguese edition of the Lisbon Academy, **Charamandel**; in the Span. MS. translated by Lord Stanley of Alderley, **Cholmendel** and *Cholmender*. D'Alboquerque's *Commentaries* (1557), Mendez Pinto (c. 1550) and Barros (1553) have **Choromandel**, and Garcia De Orta (1563) **Charamandel**. The ambiguity of the *ch*, soft in Portuguese and Spanish, but hard in Italian, seems to have led early to the corrupt form *Coromandel*, which we find in Parkes's *Mendoza* (1589), and **Coromandyll**, among other spellings, in the English version of Castanheda (1582). Cesare Federici has in the Italian (1587) **Chiaramandel** (probably pronounced soft in the Venetian manner), and the translation of 1599 has **Coromandel**. This form thenceforward generally prevails in English books, but not without exceptions. A Madras document of 1672 in Wheeler has **Cormandell**, and so have the early Bengal records in the India Office; Dampier (1689) has **Coromondel** (i. 509); Lockyer (1711) has "the Coast of **Cormandel**"; A. Hamilton (1727) **Chormondel** (i. 349); ed. 1744, i. 351; and a paper of about 1759, published by Dalrymple, has "**Choromandel** Coast" (*Orient. Repert.* i. 120-121). The poet Thomson has **Cormandel**:

> "all that from the tract
> Of woody mountains stretch'd through gorgeous Ind
> Fall on *Cormandel's* Coast or Malabar."
>
> *Summer.*

The Portuguese appear to have adhered in the main to the correcter form **Choromandel**: *e.g. Archivio Port. Oriental*, fasc. 3, p. 480, and *passim*. A Protestant Missionary Catechism, printed at Tranquebar in 1713 for the use of Portuguese schools in India has: "na costa dos Malabaros que se chama **Cormandel**." Bernier has "la côte de **Koromandel**" (Amst. ed. ii. 322). W. Hamilton says it is written *Choramandel* in the Madras Records until 1779, which is substantially correct. In the MS. "List of Persons in the Service of the Rt. Honble. E. I. Company in Fort St. George and other places on the Coast of **Choromandell**," preserved in the Indian Office, that spelling continues down to 1778. In that year it is changed to **Coromandel**. In the French translation of Ibn Batuta (iv. 142) we find *Coromandel*, but this is only the perverse and misleading manner of Frenchmen, who make Julius Caesar cross from "France" to "England." The word is *Ma'bar* in the original. [Alboquerque (*Comm.* Hak. Soc. i. 41) speaks of a violent squall under the name of *vara de Coromandel*.]

CORPORAL FORBES, s. A soldier's grimly jesting name for *Cholera Morbus*.

1829.—"We are all pretty well, only the regiment is sickly, and a great quantity are in hospital with the **Corporal Forbes**, which carries them away before they have time to die, or say who comes there."—In *Shipp's Memoirs*, ii. 218.

CORRAL, s. An enclosure as used in Ceylon for the capture of wild elephants, corresponding to the **Keddah** of Bengal. The word is Sp. *corral*, 'a court,' &c., Port. *curral*. 'a cattle-pen, a paddock.' The Americans have the same word, direct from the Spanish, in common use for a cattle-pen; and they have formed a verb 'to *corral*,' *i.e.* to enclose in a pen, to pen. The word *kraal* applied to native camps and villages at the Cape of Good Hope appears to be the same word introduced there by the Dutch. The word *corral* is explained by Bluteau: "A receptacle for any kind of cattle, with railings round it and no roof, in which respect it differs from *Corte*, which is a building with a roof." Also he states that the word is used especially in churches for *septum nobilium feminarum*, a pen for ladies.

c. 1270.—"When morning came, and I rose and had heard mass, I proclaimed a council to be held in the open space (**corral**) between my house and that of Montaragon."—*Chron. of James of Aragon*, tr. by *Foster*, i. 65.

1404.—"And this mosque and these chapels were very rich, and very finely wrought with gold and azure, and enamelled tiles (*azulejos*); and within there was a great **corral**, with trees and tanks of water."—*Clavijo*, § cv. Comp. *Markham*, 123.

1672.—"About Mature they catch the Elephants with **Coraals**" (*Coralen*, but sing. *Coraal*).—*Baldaeus, Ceylon*, 168.

1860.—In Emerson Tennent's *Ceylon*, Bk. VIII. ch. iv. the **corral** is fully described.

1880.—"A few hundred pounds expended in houses, and the erection of **coralls** in the neighbourhood of a permanent stream will form a basis of operations." (In Colorado.) —*Fortnightly Rev.*, Jan., 125.

CORUNDUM, s. This is described by Dana under the species Sapphire, as including the grey and darker coloured opaque crystallised specimens. The word appears to be Indian. Shakespear gives Hind. *kurand*, Dakh. *kurund*. Littré attributes the origin to Skt. *kuruvinda*, which Williams gives as the name of several plants, but also as 'a ruby.' In Telugu we have *kuruvindam*, and in Tamil *kurundam* for the substance in present question; the last is probably the direct origin of the term.

c. 1666.—"Cet emeri blanc se trouve par pierres dans un lieu particulier du Roiaume, et s'apelle **Corind** en langue Telengui."—*Thevenot*, v. 297.

COSMIN, n.p. This name is given by many travellers in the 16th and 17th centuries to a port on the western side of the Irawadi Delta, which must have been near **Bassein**, if not identical with it. Till quite recently this was all that could be said on the subject, but Prof. Forchhammer of Rangoon has now identified the name as a corruption of the classical name formerly borne by Bassein, viz. *Kusima* or *Kusumanagara*, a city founded about the beginning of the 5th century. *Kusimamandala* was the western province of the Delta Kingdom which we know as Pegu. The Burmese corrupted the name of *Kusuma* into *Kusmein* and *Kothein*, and Alompra after his conquest of Pegu in the middle of the 18th century, changed it to *Bathein*. So the facts are stated substantially by Forchhammer (see *Notes on Early Hist. and Geog. of Br. Burma*, No. 2, p. 12); though familiar and constant use of the word *Persaim*, which appears to be a form of *Bassein*, in the English writings of 1750-60, published by Dalrymple (*Or. Repertory*, *passim*), seems hardly consistent with this statement of the origin of *Bassein*. [Col. Temple (*Ind. Ant.* xxii. 19 *seqq.*; *J. R. A. S.* 1893, p. 885) disputes the above explanation. According to him the account of the change of name by Alompra is false history; the change from initial *p* to *k* is not isolated, and the word *Bassein* itself does not date beyond 1780.]

The last publication in which *Cosmin* appears is the "Draught of the River Irrawaddy or Irabatty," made in 1796, by Ensign T. Wood of the Bengal Engineers, which accompanies Symes's *Account* (London, 1800). This shows both *Cosmin*, and *Persaim* or *Bassein*, some 30 or 40 miles apart. But the former was probably taken from an older chart, and from no actual knowledge.

c. 1165.—"Two ships arrived at the harbour **Kusuma** in Aramana, and took in battle and laid waste country from the port Sapattota, over which Kurttipurapam was governor."—*J.A.S. Bengal*, vol. xli. pt. i. p. 198.

1516.—"Anrique Leme set sail right well equipped, with 60 Portuguese. And pursuing his voyage he captured a junk belonging to Pegu merchants, which he carried off towards Martaban, in order to send it with a cargo of rice to Malaca, and so make a great profit. But on reaching the coast he could not make the port of Martaban, and had to make the mouth of the River of Pegu. . . . Twenty leagues from the bar there is another city called **Cosmim**, in which merchants buy and sell and do business. . . ."—*Correa*, ii. 474.

1545.—". . . and 17 persons only out of 83 who were on board, being saved in the boat, made their way for 5 days along the coast; intending to put into the river of **Cosmim**, in the kingdom of Pegu, there to embark for India (*i.e.* Goa) in the king's lacker ship. . . ."—*F. M. Pinto*, ch. cxlvii.

1554.—"**Cosmym** . . . the currency is the same in this port that is used in Peguu, for this is a seaport by which one goes to Peguu."—*A. Nunez*, 38.

1566.—"In a few days they put into **Cosmi**, a port of Pegu, where presently they gave out the news, and then all the Talapoins came in haste, and the people who were dwelling there."—*Couto*, Dec. viii. cap. 13.

c. 1570.—"They go it vp the riuer in foure daies . . . with the flood, to a City called **Cosmin** . . . whither the Customer of Pegu comes to take the note or markes of euery man. . . . Nowe from **Cosmin** to the citie Pegu . . . it is all plaine and a goodly Country, and in 8 dayes you may make your voyage."—*Cæsar Frederike*, in *Hakl.* ii. 366-7.

1585.—"So the 5th October we came to **Cosmi**, the territory of which, from side to side is full of woods, frequented by parrots, tigers, boars, apes, and other like creatures."—*G. Balbi*, f. 94.

1587.—"We entered the barre of Negrais, which is a braue barre, and hath 4 fadomes water where it hath least. Three dayes after we came to **Cosmin**, which is a very pretie towne, and standeth very pleasantly, very well furnished with all things . . . the houses are all high built, set vpon great high postes . . . for feare of the Tygers, which be very many."—*R. Fitch*, in *Hakl.* ii. 390.

1613.—"The Portuguese proceeded without putting down their arms to attack the Banha Dela's (position), and destroyed it entirely, burning his factory and compelling him to flee to the kingdom of Prom, so that there now remained in the whole realm of Pegu only the Banho of **Cosmim** (a place adjoining Negrais) calling himself vassal of the King of Arracan."—*Bocarro*, 132.

COSPETIR, n.p. This is a name which used greatly to perplex us on the 16th and 17th century maps of India, *e.g.* in Blaeu's Atlas (c. 1650), appearing generally to the west of the Ganges Delta. Considering how the geographical names of different ages and different regions sometimes get mixed up in old maps, we at one time tried to trace it to the Κασπάτυρος of Herodotus, which was certainly going far afield! The difficulty was solved by the sagacity of the deeply-lamented Prof. Blochmann, who has pointed out (*J. As. Soc. Beng.*, xlii. pt. i. 224) that Cospetir represents the Bengali genitive of **Gajpati**, 'Lord of Elephants,' the traditional title of the Kings of Orissa. The title *Gajpati* was that one of the Four Great Kings who, according to Buddhist legend, divided the earth among them in times when there was no *Chakravartti*, or Universal Monarch (see **CHUCKERBUTTY**). *Gajapati* rules the South; *Aśvapati* (Lord of Horses) the North; *Chhatrapati* (Lord of the Umbrella) the West; *Narapati* (Lord of Men) the East. In later days these titles were variously appropriated (see *Lassen*, ii. 27 *seq.*). And Akbar, as will be seen below, adopted these names, with others of his own devising, for the suits of his pack of cards. There is a Raja *Gajpati*, a chief Zamindar of the country north of Patna, who is often mentioned in the wars of Akbar (see *Elliot*, v. 399 and *passim*, vi. 55, &c.) who is of course not to be confounded with the Orissa Prince.

c. 700 (?).—"In times when there was no *Chakravartti* King . . . Chen-pu (*Sambadvīpa*) was divided among four lords. The southern was the Lord of Elephants (**Gajapati**), &c. . . ."—Introd. to *Si-yu-ki* (in *Pèlerins Bouddh.*), ii. lxxv.

1553.—"On the other or western side, over against the Kingdom of Orixa, the Bengalis (*os Bengalos*) hold the Kingdom of **Cospetir**, whose plains at the time of the risings of the Ganges are flooded after the fashion of those of the River Nile."—*Barros*, Dec. IV. ix. cap. I.

This and the next passage compared show that Barros was not aware that *Cospetir* and *Gajpati* were the same.

" "Of this realm of Bengala, and of other four realms its neighbours, the Gentoos and Moors of those parts say that God has given to each its peculiar gift: to Bengala infantry numberless; to the Kingdom of Orixa elephants; to that of Bisnaga men most skilful in the use of sword and shield; to the Kingdom of Dely multitudes of cities and towns; and to Cou a vast number of horses. And so naming them in this order they give them these other names, viz.: *Espaty*, **Gaspaty**, Noropaty, Buapaty, and Coapaty."—*Barros*, *ibid.* [These titles appear to be *Aśvapati*, "Lord of Horses"; **Gajapati**; *Narapati*, "Lord of Men"; *Bhūpati*, "Lord of Earth"; *Gopati*, "Lord of Cattle."]

c. 1590.—"His Majesty (Akbar) plays with the following suits of cards. 1st. *Ashwapati*, the lord of horses. The highest card represents a King on horseback, resembling the King of Dihli. . . . 2nd. **Gajpati**, the King whose power lies in the number of his elephants, as the ruler of Orisah. . . . 3rd.

Narpati, a King whose power lies in his infantry, as is the case with the rulers of Bijápúr," &c.—*Āīn*, i. 306.

c. 1590.—"Orissa contains one hundred and twenty-nine brick forts, subject to the command of **Gujeputty**."—*Ayeen* (by *Gladwin*), ed. 1800, ii. 11; [ed. *Jarrett*, ii. 126].

1753.—"Herodote fait aussi mention d'une ville de *Caspatyrus* située vers le haut du fleuve Indus, ce que Mercator a cru correspondre à une denomination qui existe dans la Géographie moderne, sans altération marquée, savoir **Cospetir**. La notion qu'on a de **Cospetir** se tire de l'historien Portugais Jean de Barros . . . la situation n'est plus celle qui convient à *Caspatyrus*."—*D'Anville*, 4 *seq*.

COSS, s. The most usual popular measure of distance in India, but like the *mile* in Europe, and indeed like the mile within the British Islands up to a recent date, varying much in different localities.

The Skt. word is *krośa*, which also is a measure of distance, but originally signified 'a call,' hence the distance at which a man's call can be heard.*

In the Pali vocabulary called *Abhidhānappadīpikā*, which is of the 12th century, the word appears in the form *koss;* and nearly this, *kos*, is the ordinary Hindi. *Kuroh* is a Persian form of the word, which is often found in Mahommedan authors and in early travellers. These latter (English) often write **course**. It is a notable circumstance that, according to Wrangell, the Yakuts of N. Siberia reckon distance by *kiosses* (a word which, considering the Russian way of writing Turkish and Persian words, must be identical with *kos*). With them this measure is "indicated by the time necessary to cook a piece of meat." *Kioss* is = to about 5 *versts*, or 1⅔ miles, in hilly or marshy country, but on plain ground to 7 *versts*, or 2⅓ miles.† The Yakuts are a Turk people, and their language is a Turki dialect. The suggestion arises whether the form *kos* may not have come with the Mongols into India, and modified the previous *krośa?* But this is met by the existence of the word *kos* in Pali, as mentioned above.

In ancient Indian measurement, or estimation, 4 *krośas* went to the *yojana*. Sir H. M. Elliot deduced from distances in the route of the Chinese pilgrim Fa-hian that the *yojana* of his age was as nearly as possible 7 miles. Cunningham makes it 7½ or 8, Fergusson 6; but taking Elliot's estimate as a mean, the ancient *kos* would be 1¾ miles.

The *kos* as laid down in the *Āīn* [ed. *Jarrett*, iii. 414] was of 5000 *gaz* [see **GUDGE**]. The official decision of the British Government has assigned the length of Akbar's *Ilāhī gaz* as 33 inches, and this would make Akbar's *kos* = 2 m. 4 f. 183⅓ yards. Actual measurement of road distances between 5 pair of Akbar's *kos-minārs*,* near Delhi, gave a mean of 2 m. 4 f. 158 yards.

In the greater part of the Bengal Presidency the estimated *kos* is about 2 miles, but it is much less as you approach the N.W. In the upper part of the Doab, it is, with fair accuracy, 1¼ miles. In Bundelkhand again it is nearly 3 m. (*Carnegy*), or, according to Beames, even 4 m. [In Madras it is 2¼ m., and in Mysore the *Sultānī kos* is about 4 m.] Reference may be made on this subject to Mr. Thomas's ed. of *Prinsep's Essays*, ii. 129; and to Mr. Beames's ed. of Elliot's *Glossary* ("*The Races of the N.-W. Provinces*," ii. 194). The latter editor remarks that in several parts of the country there are two kinds of *kos*, a *pakkā* and a *kachchā kos*, a double system which pervades all the weights and measures of India; and which has prevailed also in many other parts of the world [see **PUCKA**].

c. 500.—"A *garyūtih* (or league—see **GOW**) is two **krosas**."—*Amarakosha*, ii. 2, 18.

c. 600.—"The descendant of Kukulstha (*i.e.* Rāma) having gone half a **krośa**. . . ."—*Raghuvamsā*, xiii. 79.

c. 1340.—"As for the mile it is called among the Indians al-**Kurūh**."—*Ibn Batuta*, iii. 95.

" "The Sultan gave orders to assign me a certain number of villages. . . .

* "It is characteristic of this region (central forests of Ceylon) that in traversing the forest they calculate their march, not by the eye, or by measures of distance, but by sounds. Thus a '*dog's cry*' indicates a quarter of a mile; a '*cock's crow*,' something more; and a '*hoo*' implies the space over which a man can be heard when shouting that particular monosyllable at the pitch of his voice."—*Tennent's Ceylon*, ii. 582. In S. Canara also to this day such expressions as "a horn's blow," "a man's call," are used in the estimation of distances. [See under **GOW**.]

† *Le Nord de la Sibérie*, i. 82.

* ". . . that Royal Alley of Trees planted by the command of *Jehan-Guire*, and continued by the same order for 150 leagues, with little Pyramids or Turrets erected every half league."—*Bernier*, E.T. 91; [ed. *Constable*, 284].

They were at a distance of 16 **Kurūhs** from Dihlī."—*Ibn Batuta*, 388.

c. 1470.—"The Sultan sent ten viziers to encounter him at a distance of ten **Kors** (a *kor* is equal to 10 versts). . . ."—*Ath. Nikitin*, 26, in *India in the XVth Cent.*

" "From Chivil to Jooneer it is 20 **Kors**; from Jooneer to Beder 40; from Beder to Kulongher, 9 **Kors**; from Beder to Koluberg, 9."—*Ibid.* p. 12.

1528.—"I directed Chikmâk Beg, by a writing under the royal hand and seal, to measure the distance from Agra to Kâbul; that at every nine **kos** he should raise a minâr or turret, twelve *gez* in height, on the top of which he was to construct a pavilion. . . ."—*Baber*, 393.

1537.—". . . that the King of Portugal should hold for himself and all his descendants, from this day forth for aye, the Port of the City of Mangualor (in Guzerat) with all its privileges, revenues, and jurisdiction, with 2½ **coucees** round about. . . ."—*Treaty in S. Botelho, Tombo*, 225.

c. 1550.—"Being all unmanned by their love of Raghoba, they had gone but two **Kos** by the close of day, then scanning land and water they halted."—*Rāmāyana* of *Tulsī Dās*, by *Growse*, 1878, p. 119.

[1604.—"At the rate of four *coss* (**Coces**) the league by the calculation of the Moors."—*Couto*, Dec. XII., Bk. I. cap. 4.]

1616.—"The three and twentieth arrived at Adsmeere, 219 **Courses** from Brampoore, 418 English miles, the **Courses** being longer than towards the Sea."—*Sir T. Roe*, in *Purchas*, i. 541; [Hak. Soc. i. 105].

" "The length of these forenamed Provinces is North-West to South-East, at the least 1000 **Courses**, every Indian **Course** being two English miles."—*Terry*, in *Purchas*, ii. 1468.

1623.—"The distance by road to the said city they called seven **cos**, or **corū**, which is all one; and every *cos* or *corū* is half a *ferseng* or league of Persia, so that it will answer to a little less than two Italian [English] miles."—*P. della Valle*, ii. 504; [Hak. Soc.i. 23].

1648.—". . . which two **Coss** are equivalent to a Dutch mile."—*Van Twist, Gen. Beschrijv.* 2.

1666.—". . . une **cosse** qui est la mesure des Indes pour l'espace des lieux, est environ d'une demi-lieue."—*Thevenot*, v. 12.

COSSACK, s. It is most probable that this Russian term for the military tribes of various descent on what was the S. frontier of the Empire has come originally from *kazzāk*, a word of obscure origin, but which from its adoption in Central Asia we may venture to call Turki. [*Schuyler, Turkistan*, i. 8.] It appears in Pavet de Courteille's *Dict. Turk-Oriental* as "*vagabond; aventurier . . .; onagre que ses compagnons chassent loin d'eux.*" But in India it became common in the sense of 'a predatory horseman' and freebooter.

1366.—"On receipt of this bad news I was much dispirited, and formed to myself three plans; 1st. That I should turn **Cossack**, and never pass 24 hours in one place, and plunder all that came to hand."—*Mem. of Timūr*, tr. by *Stewart*, p. 111.

[1609.—In a Letter from the Company to the factors at Bantam mention is made of one "Sophony **Cosuke**," or as he is also styled in the Court Minutes "the Russe."—*Birdwood, First Letter Book*, 288.]

1618.—"**Cossacks** (*Cosacchi*) . . . you should know, is not the name of a nation, but of a collection of people of various countries and sects (though most of them Christians) who without wives or children, and without horses, acknowledge obedience to no prince; but dwelling far from cities in fastnesses among the woods or mountains, or rivers . . . live by the booty of their swords . . . employ themselves in perpetual inroads and cruisings by land and sea to the detriment of their nearest enemies, *i.e.* of the Turks and other Mahometans. . . . As I have heard from them, they promise themselves one day the capture of Constantinople, saying that Fate has reserved for them the liberation of that country, and that they have clear prophecies to that effect."—*P. della Valle*, i. 614 *seq.*

c. 1752.—"His **kuzzaks** . . . were likewise appointed to surround and plunder the camp of the French. . . ."—*Hist. of Hydur Naik*, tr. by *Miles*, p. 36.

1813.—"By the bye, how do Clarke's friends the **Cossacks**, who seem to be a band of Circassians and other Sarmatians, come to be called by a name which seems to belong to a great Toorkee tribe on the banks of the Jaxartes? **Kuzzauk** is used about Delhi for a highwayman. Can it be (as I have heard) an Arabic *Mobaligh* (exaggeration) from *kizk* (plunder) applied to all predatory tribes?"—*Elphinstone*, in *Life*, i. 264.

1819.—"Some dashing leader may . . . gather a predatory band round his standard, which, composed as it would be of desperate adventurers, and commanded by a professional **Kuzzauk**, might still give us an infinite deal of trouble."—*Ibid.* ii. 68.

c. 1823.—"The term **Cossack** is used because it is the one by which the Mahrattas describe their own species of warfare. In their language the word **Cossâkee** (borrowed like many more of their terms from the Moghuls) means predatory."—*Malcolm, Central India*, 3d ed. i. 69.

COSSID, s. A courier or running messenger; Arab. *ḳāṣid.*

1682.—"I received letters by a **Cossid** from Mr. Johnson and Mr. Catchpoole, dated ye 18th instant from *Muxoodavad*, Bulchund's residence."—*Hedges, Diary*, Dec. 20th; [Hak. Soc. i. 58].

[1687.—"Haveing detained the **Cossetts** 4 or 5 Daies."—*Ibid.* ii. lxix.]

1690.—"Therefore December the 2d. in the evening, word was brought by the Broker to our President, of a **Cosset's** Arrival with Letters from Court to the *Vacinavish*, injoyning our immediate Release."—*Ovington*, 416.

1748.—"The Tappies [dâk runners] on the road to Ganjam being grown so exceedingly indolent that he has called them in, being convinced that our packets may be forwarded much faster by **Cassids** [mounted postmen *]."—In *Long*, p. 3.

c. 1759.—"For the performance of this arduous . . . duty, which required so much care and caution, intelligencers of talent, and **Kasids** or messengers, who from head to foot were eyes and ears . . . were stationed in every quarter of the country."—*H. of Hydur Naik*, 126.

1803.—"I wish that you would open a communication by means of **cossids** with the officer commanding a detachment of British troops in the fort of Songhur."—*Wellington*, ii. 159.

COSSIMBAZAR, n.p. Properly *Kāsimbāzār*. A town no longer existing, which closely adjoined the city of Murshīdābād, but preceded the latter. It was the site of one of the most important factories of the East India Company in their mercantile days, and was indeed a chief centre of all foreign trade in Bengal during the 17th century. ["In 1658 the Company established a factory at Cossimbazaar, '**Castle Bazaar**.'"—(*Birdwood Rep. on Old Rec.* 219.)] Fryer (1673) calls it **Castle Buzzar** (p. 38).

1665.—"That evening I arrived at **Casen-Basar**, where I was welcom'd by Menheir *Arnold van Wachtendonk*, Director of all *Holland*-Factories in Bengal."—*Tavernier*, E.T., ii. 56; [ed. *Ball*, i. 131. *Bernier* (E.T. p. 141; ed. *Constable*, 440) has *Kassem-Bazar*; in the map, p. 454, *Kasembazar*.]

1676.—"**Kassembasar**, a Village in the Kingdom of *Bengala*, sends abroad every year two and twenty thousand Bales of Silk; every Bale weighing a hunder'd pound."—*Tavernier*, E.T. ii. 126; [*Ball*, ed. ii. 2].

[1678.—"**Cassumbazar**." See quotation under **DADNY**.]

COSSYA, n.p. More properly *Kāsia*, but now officially *Khāsi*; in the language of the people themselves *ki-Kāsi*, the first syllable being a prefix denoting the plural. The name of a hill people of Mongoloïd character, occupying the mountains immediately north of Silhet in Eastern Bengal. Many circumstances in relation to this people are of high interest, such as their practice, down to our own day, of erecting rude stone monuments of the *menhir* and *dolmen* kind, their law of succession in the female line, &c. Shillong, the modern seat of administration of the Province of Assam, and lying midway between the proper valley of Assam and the plain of Silhet, both of which are comprehended in that government, is in the Kāsia country, at a height of 4,900 feet above the sea. The Kāsias seem to be the people encountered near Silhet by Ibn Batuta as mentioned in the quotation:

c. 1346.—"The people of these mountains resemble Turks (*i.e.* Tartars), and are very strong labourers, so that a slave of their race is worth several of another nation."—*Ibn Batuta*, iv. 216. [See **KHASYA**.]

1780.—"The first thing that struck my observation on entering the arena was the similarity of the dresses worn by the different tribes of **Cusseahs** or native Tartars, all dressed and armed agreeable to the custom of the country or mountain from whence they came."—*Hon. R. Lindsay*, in *Lives of the Lindsays*, iii. 182.

1789.—"We understand the **Cossyahs** who inhabit the hills to the north-westward of Sylhet, have committed some very daring acts of violence."—In *Seton-Karr*, ii. 218.

1790.—"Agreed and ordered, that the Trade of Sylhet . . . be declared entirely free to all the natives . . . under the following Regulations:—1st. That they shall not supply the **Cossyahs** or other Hill-people with Arms, Ammunition or other articles of Military store. . . ."—In *Seton-Karr*, ii. 31.

COSTUS. (See **PUTCHOCK**.)

COT, s. A light bedstead. There is a little difficulty about the true origin of this word. It is universal as a sea-term, and in the South of India. In Northern India its place has been very generally taken by **charpoy** (q.v.), and *cot*, though well understood, is not in such prevalent European use as it formerly was, except as applied to barrack furniture, and among soldiers and their families. Words with this last characteristic have very frequently been introduced

* This gloss is a mistake.

from the south. There are, however, both in north and south, vernacular words which may have led to the adoption of the term *cot* in their respective localities. In the north we have H. *khāṭ* and *khaṭwā*, both used in this sense, the latter also in Sanskrit; in the south, Tam. and Malayāl. *kaṭṭil*, a form adopted by the Portuguese. The quotations show, however, no *Anglo-Indian* use of the word in any form but *cot*.

The question of origin is perhaps further perplexed by the use of *quatre* as a Spanish term in the West Indies (see *Tom Cringle* below). A Spanish lady tells us that *catre*, or *catre de tigera* ("scissors-cot") is applied to a bedstead with X-trestles. *Catre* is also common Portuguese for a wooden bedstead, and is found as such in a dictionary of 1611. These forms, however, we shall hold to be of Indian origin; unless it can be shown that they are older in Spain and Portugal than the 16th century. The form *quatre* has a curious analogy (probably accidental) to *chārpāī*.

1553.—"The Camarij (Zamorin) who was at the end of a house, placed on a bedstead, which they call **catle**. . . ."—*De Barros*, Dec. I. liv. iv. cap. viii.

1557.—"The king commanded his men to furnish a tent on that spot, where the interview was to take place, all carpeted inside with very rich tapestries, and fitted with a sofa (**catle**) covered over with a silken cloth."—*Alboquerque*, Hak. Soc. ii. 204.

1566.—"The king was set on a **catel** (the name of a kind of field bedstead) covered with a cloth of white silk and gold. . . ."—*Damian de Goës, Chron. del R. Dom Emanuel*, 48.

1600.—"He retired to the hospital of the sick and poor, and there had his cell, the walls of which were of coarse palm-mats. Inside there was a little table, and on it a crucifix of the wood of St. Thomé, covered with a cloth, and a breviary. There was also a **catre** of coir, with a stone for pillow; and this completes the inventory of the furniture of that house."—*Lucena, V. do P. F. Xavier*, 199.

[1613.—"Here hired a **catele** and 4 men to have carried me to Agra."—*Danvers, Letters*, i. 277.

[1634.—"The better sort sleepe upon **cots**, or Beds two foot high, matted or done with girth-web."—*Sir T. Herbert, Trav.* 149. N.E.D.]

1648.—"Indian bedsteads or **Cadels**."—*Van Twist*, 64.

1673.—". . . where did sit the King in State on a **Cott** or Bed."—*Fryer*, 18.

1678.—"Upon being thus abused the said Serjeant Waterhouse commanded the corporal Edward Short, to tie Savage down on his **cot**."—In *Wheeler*, i. 106.

1685.—"I hired 12 stout fellows . . . to carry me as far as Lar in my **cott** (Palankeen fashion). . . ."—*Hedges, Diary*, July 29; [Hak Soc. i. 203].

1688.—"In the East Indies, at Fort St. George, also Men take their **Cotts** or little Field-Beds and put them into the Yards, and go to sleep in the Air."—*Dampier's Voyages*, ii. Pt. iii.

1690.—". . . the **Cot** or Bed that was by . . ."—*Ovington*, 211.

1711.—In Canton Price Current: "Bamboo **Cotts** for Servants each . . . 1 mace."—*Lockyer*, 150.

1768-71.—"We here found the body of the deceased, lying upon a **kadel**, or couch."—*Stavorinus*, E.T., i. 442.

1794.—"Notice is hereby given that sealed proposals will be received . . . for supplying . . . the different General Hospitals with clothing, **cotts**, and bedding."—In *Seton-Karr*, ii. 115.

1824.—"I found three of the party insisted upon accompanying me the first stage, and had despatched their camp-**cots**."—*Seely, Ellora*, ch. iii.

c. 1830.—"After being . . . furnished with food and raiment, we retired to our **quatres**, a most primitive sort of couch, with a piece of canvas stretched over it."—*Tom Cringle's Log*, ed. 1863, p. 100.

1872.—"As Badan was too poor to have a **khāt**, that is, a wooden bedstead with tester frames and mosquito curtains."—*Govinda Samanta*, i. 140.

COTAMALUCO, n.p. The title by which the Portuguese called the kings of the Golconda Dynasty, founded, like the other Mahommedan kingdoms of S. India, on the breaking up of the Bāhmani kingdom of the Deccan. It was a corruption of *Ḳuṭb-ul-Mulk*, the designation of the founder, retained as the style of the dynasty by Mahommedans as well as Portuguese (see extract from *Akbar-nāma* under **IDALÇAN**).

1543.—"When **Idalcan** heard this reply he was in great fear . . . and by night made his escape with some in whom he trusted (very few they were), and fled in secret, leaving his family and his wives, and went to the territories of the *Izam Maluco* (see **NIZAMALUCO**), his neighbour and friend . . . and made matrimonial ties with the *Izam Maluco*; marrying his daughter, on which they arranged together; and there also came into this concert the **Madremaluco**, and **Cotamaluco**, and the

Verido, who are other great princes, marching with Izam Maluco, and connected with him by marriage."—*Correa*, iv. 313 *seq.*

1553.—"The Captains of the Kingdom of the Decan added to their proper names other honorary ones which they affected more, one calling himself *Iniza Malmulco*, which is as much as to say 'Spear of the State,' *Cota Malmulco*, *i.e.* 'Fortress of the State,' *Adelchan*, 'Lord of Justice'; and we, corrupting these names, call them **Nizamaluco, Cotamaluco,** and **Hidalchan.**"—*Barros*, IV. iv. 16; [and see *Linschoten*, Hak. Soc. i. 172]. These same explanations are given by Garcia de Orta (*Colloquios*, f. 36*v*), but of course the two first are quite wrong. *Iniza Malmulco*, as Barros here writes it, is Ar. *An-Nizām ul Mulk*, "The Administrator of the State," not from P. *neza*, "a spear." **Cotamaluco** is *Kutb-ul-Mulk*, Ar. "the Pivot (or Pole-star) of the State," not from H. *koṭā*, "a fort."

COTIA, s. A fast-sailing vessel, with two masts and lateen sails, employed on the Malabar coast. *Koṭṭiya* is used in Malayāl.; [the *Madras Gloss.* writes the word *kotyeh*, and says that it comes from Ceylon;] yet the word hardly appears to be Indian. Bluteau however appears to give it as such (iii. 590).

1552.—"Among the little islands of Goa he embarked on board his fleet, which consisted of about a dozen **cotias**, taking with him a good company of soldiers."—*Castanheda*, iii. 25. See also pp. 47, 48, 228, &c.

c. 1580.—"In the gulf of Nagunā . . . I saw some **Çutiás.**"—*Primor e Honra*, &c., f. 73.

1602.—". . . embarking his property on certain **Cotias**, which he kept for that purpose."—*Couto*, Dec. IV. liv. i. cap. viii.

COTTA, s. H. *kaṭṭhā*. A small land-measure in use in Bengal and Bahar, being the twentieth part of a Bengal *bīghā* (see **BEEGAH**), and containing eighty square yards.

[1767.—"The measurement of land in Bengal is thus estimated: 16 *Gundas* make 1 **Cotta**; 20 **Cottas**, 1 *Bega*, or about 16,000 square feet."—*Verelst*, *View of Bengal*, 221, note.]

1784.—". . . An upper roomed House standing upon about 5 **cottahs** of ground. . . ."—*Seton-Karr*, i. 34.

COTTON, s. We do not seem to be able to carry this familiar word further back than the Ar. *ḳuṭn*, *kuṭun*, or *ḳuṭunn*, having the same meaning, whence Prov. *coton*, Port. *cotão*, It. *cotone*, Germ. *Kattun*. The Sp. keeps the Ar. article, *algodon*, whence old Fr. *auqueton* and *hoqueton*, a coat quilted with cotton. It is only by an odd coincidence that Pliny adduces a like-sounding word in his account of the *arbores lanigerae*: "ferunt mali *cotonei* amplitudine cucurbitas, quae maturitate ruptae ostendunt lanuginis pilas, ex quibus vestes pretioso linteo faciunt"—xii. 10 (21). [On the use and cultivation of cotton in the ancient world, see the authorities collected by *Frazer*, *Pausanias*, iii. 470, *seqq.*]

[1830.—"The dress of the great is on the Persian model; it consists of a shirt of **kuttaun** (a kind of linen of a wide texture, the best of which is imported from Aleppo, and the common sort from Persia). . . ."—*Elphinstone's Caubul*, i. 351.]

COTTON-TREE, SILK. (See **SEEMUL.**)

COTWAL, CUTWAUL, s. A police-officer; superintendent of police; native town magistrate. P. *kotwāl*, 'a seneschal, a commandant of a castle or fort.' This looks as if it had been first taken from an Indian word, *kotwālā*; [Skt. *koṭha-* or *koshṭha pālā* 'castle-porter']; but some doubt arises whether it may not have been a Turki term. In Turki it is written *kotāul*, *kotāwal*, and seems to be regarded by both Vambéry and Pavet de Courteille as a genuine Turki word. V. defines it as: "*Ketaul*, garde de forteresse, chef de la garnison; nom d'un tribu d'Ozbegs;" P. "*kotāwal*, *kotāwāl*, gardien d'une citadelle." There are many Turki words of analogous form, as *karāwal*, 'a vidette,' *bakāwal*, 'a table-steward,' *yasāwal*, 'a chamberlain,' *tangāwal*, 'a patrol,' &c. In modern Bokhara *Kataul* is a title conferred on a person who superintends the Amir's buildings (*Khanikoff*, 241). On the whole it seems probable that the title was originally Turki, but was shaped by Indian associations.

[The duties of the *Kotwāl*, as head of the police, are exhaustively laid down in the *Āīn* (*Jarrett*, ii. 41). Amongst other rules: "He shall amputate the hand of any who is the pot-companion of an executioner, and the finger of such as converse with his family."] The office of *Kotwāl* in Western and Southern India, technically speaking, ceased about 1862, when the new police system (under Act, India, V. of 1861, and corresponding local

Acts) was introduced. In Bengal the term has been long obsolete. [It is still in use in the N.W.P. to designate the chief police officer of one of the larger cities or cantonments.]

c. 1040.—"Bu-Ali **Kotwal** (of Ghazni) returned from the Khilj expedition, having adjusted matters." — *Baihaki*, in *Elliot*, ii. 151.

1406-7. — "They fortified the city of Astarābād, where Abul Leïth was placed with the rank of **Kotwal**."—*Abdurrazāk*, in *Not. et Extr.* xiv. 123.

1553. — "The message of the Camorij arriving, Vasco da Gama landed with a dozen followers, and was received by a noble person whom they called **Catual**. . . ." —*Barros*, Dec. I. liv. iv. ch. viii.

1572.—

"Na praya hum regedor do Regno estava
Que na sua lingua **Catual** se chama."
Camões, vii. 44.

By Burton:

"There stood a Regent of the Realm ashore,
a chief, in native parlance '**Cat'ual**' hight."

also the plural:

"Mas aquelles avaros **Catuais**
Que o Gentilico povo governavam."
Ibid. viii. 56.

1616.—Roe has **Cutwall** *passim*; [*e.g.* Hak. Soc. i. 90. &c.].

1727.—"Mr. Boucher being bred a Druggist in his youth, presently knew the Poison, and carried it to the **Cautwaul** or Sheriff, and showed it."—*A. Hamilton*, ii. 199. [In ed. 1744, ii. 199, **cautwal**].

1763.—"The **Catwal** is the judge and executor of justice in criminal cases."—*Orme* (ed. 1803), i. 26.

1812.—". . . an officer retained from the former system, denominated **cutwal**, to whom the general police of the city and regulation of the market was entrusted."—*Fifth Report*, 44.

1847.—"The **Kutwal** . . . seems to have done his duty resolutely and to the best of his judgment."—*G. O.* by *Sir C. Napier*, 121.

[1880.—"The son of the Raja's **Kotwal** was the prince's great friend."—*Miss Stokes*, *Indian Fairy Tales*, 209.]

COUNSILLEE, s. This is the title by which the natives in Calcutta generally designate English barristers. It is the same use as the Irish one of *Counsellor*, and a corruption of that word.

COUNTRY, adj. This term is used colloquially, and in trade, as an adjective to distinguish articles produced in India (generally with a sub-indication of disparagement), from such as are imported, and especially imported from Europe. Indeed **Europe** (q.v.) was, and still occasionally is, used as the contrary adjective. Thus, '**country** harness' is opposed to '**Europe** harness'; '*country*-born' people are persons of European descent, but born in India; '*country* horses' are Indian-bred in distinction from **Arabs**, **Walers** (q.v.), English horses, and even from 'stud-breds,' which are horses reared in India, but from foreign sires; '*country* ships' are those which are owned in Indian ports, though often officered by Europeans; *country* bottled beer is beer imported from England in cask and bottled in India; ['*country*-wound' silk is that reeled in the crude native fashion]. The term, as well as the H. *desī*, of which *country* is a translation, is also especially used for things grown or made in India as substitutes for certain foreign articles. Thus the *Cicca disticha* in Bombay gardens is called '*Country* gooseberry'; *Convolvulus batatas*, or sweet potato, is sometimes called the '*country* potato.' It was, equally with our quotidian root which has stolen its name, a foreigner in India, but was introduced and familiarised at a much earlier date. Thus again *desī bādām*, or '*country* almond,' is applied in Bengal to the nut of the *Terminalia Catappa*. On *desī*, which is applied, among other things, to silk, the great Ritter (*dormitans Homerus*) makes the odd remark that *desī* is just *Seide* reversed! But it would be equally apposite to remark that *Trigon*-ometry is just *Country*-ometry reversed!

Possibly the idiom may have been taken up from the Portuguese, who also use it, *e.g.* '*açafrao da* terra,' '*country* saffron,' *i.e.* **safflower**, otherwise called bastard saffron, the term being sometimes applied to turmeric. But the source of the idiom is general, as the use of *desī* shows. Moreover the Arabic *baladī*, having the same literal meaning, is applied in a manner strictly analogous, including the note of disparagement, insomuch that it has been naturalised in Spanish as indicating 'of little or no value.' Illustrations of the mercantile use of *beledi* (*i.e. baladī*) will be found in a note to *Marco Polo*, 2nd ed. ii. 370. For the Spanish use we may quote the Dict.

of Cobarruvias (1611): "*Baladi*, the thing which is produced at less cost, and is of small duration and profit." (See also *Dozy* and *Engelmann*, 232 *seq.*)

1516.—"*Beledyn* ginger grows at a distance of two or three leagues all round the city of Calicut. . . . In Bengal there is also much ginger of the **country** (*Gengivre Beledi*)."—*Barbosa*, 221 *seq.*

[1530.—"I at once sent some of these **country** men (*homeens valadis*) to the Thanas."—*Alboquerque, Cartas*, p. 148.]

1582.—"The Nayres maye not take anye **Countrie** women, and they also doe not marrie."—*Castañeda*, (by N. L.), f. 36.

[1608.—"The **Country** here are at dissension among themselves." — *Danvers, Letters*, i. 20.]

1619. — "The twelfth in the morning Master *Methwold* came from *Messalipatam* in one of the **Countrey** Boats."—*Pring*, in *Purchas*, i. 638.

1685.—"The inhabitants of the Gentoo Town, all in arms, bringing with them also elephants, kettle-drums, and all the **Country** music."—*Wheeler*, i. 140.

1747.—"It is resolved and ordered that a Serjeant with two Troopers and a Party of **Country** Horse, to be sent to Markisnah Puram to patroll. . . ."—*Ft. St. David Council of War*, Dec. 25. *MS. Records* in India Office.

1752.—"Captain Clive did not despair . . . and at ten at night sent one Shawlum, a serjeant who spoke the **country** languages, with a few sepoys to reconnoitre."—*Orme*, i. 211 (ed. 1803).

1769.—"I supped last night at a **Country** Captain's; where I saw for the first time a specimen of the Indian taste."—*Teignmouth, Mem.* i. 15.

1775.—"The Moors in what is called **Country** ships in East India, have also their chearing songs; at work in hoisting, or in their boats a rowing."—*Forrest, V. to N. Guinea*, 305.

1793.—"The jolting springs of **country**-made carriages, or the grunts of **country**-made carriers, commonly called *palankeen-boys*."—*Hugh Boyd*, 146.

1809.—"The Rajah had a drawing of it made for me, on a scale, by a **country** Draftsman of great merit."—*Ld. Valentia*, i. 356.

" "... split **country** peas . . ."—*Maria Graham*, 25.

1817.—"Since the conquest (of Java) a very extensive trade has been carried on by the English in **country** ships."—*Raffles, H. of Java*, i. 210.

[1882. — "There was a **country** - born European living in a room in the bungalow." —*Sanderson, Thirteen Years*, 256.]

COUNTRY-CAPTAIN, s. This is in Bengal the name of a peculiar dry kind of curry, often served as a breakfast dish. We can only conjecture that it was a favourite dish at the table of the skippers of '*country* ships,' who were themselves called '*country* captains,' as in our first quotation. In Madras the term is applied to a *spatchcock* dressed with onions and curry stuff, which is probably the original form. [Riddell says: "**Country-captain.**—Cut a fowl in pieces; shred an onion small and fry it brown in butter; sprinkle the fowl with fine salt and curry powder and fry it brown; then put it into a stewpan with a pint of soup; stew it slowly down to a half and serve it with rice" (*Ind. Dom. Econ.* 176).]

1792.—"But now, Sir, a **Country Captain** is not to be known from an ordinary man, or a Christian, by any certain mark whatever."—*Madras Courier*, April 26.

c. 1825.—"The local name for their business was the 'Country Trade,' the ships were '**Country** Ships,' and the masters of them '**Country Captains.**' Some of my readers may recall a dish which was often placed before us when dining on board these vessels at Whampoa, viz. '**Country Captain.**'"—*The Fankwae at Canton* (1882), p. 33.

COURSE, s. The drive usually frequented by European gentlemen and ladies at an Indian station.

1853.—"It was curious to Oakfield to be back on the Ferozepore **course**, after a six months' interval, which seemed like years. How much had happened in these six months!"—*Oakfield*, ii. 124.

COURTALLUM, n.p. The name of a town in Tinnevelly [used as an European sanatorium (*Stuart, Man. of Tinnevelly*, 96)]; written in vernacular *Kuttālam*. We do not know its etymology. [The *Madras Gloss.* gives *Trikūtāchala*, Skt., the 'Three-peaked Mountain.']

COVENANTED SERVANTS. This term is specially applied to the regular Civil Service of India, whose members used to enter into a formal covenant with the East India Company, and do now with the Secretary of State for India. Many other classes of servants now go out to India under a variety of contracts and covenants, but the term in question continues to be appropriated as before. [See **CIVILIAN.**]

1757.—"There being a great scarcity of **covenanted servants** in Calcutta, we have entertained Mr. Hewitt as a monthly writer . . . and beg to recommend him to be covenanted upon this Establishment."—Letter in *Long*, 112.

COVID, s. Formerly in use as the name of a measure, varying much locally in value, in European settlements not only in India but in China, &c. The word is a corruption, probably an Indo-Portuguese form, of the Port. *covado*, a cubit or ell.

[1612.—"A long **covad** within 1 inch of our English yard, wherewith they measure cloth, the short **covad** is for silks, and containeth just as the Portuguese **covad**."—*Danvers, Letters*, i. 241.

[1616. — "Clothes of gould : . . were worth 100 rupies a **cobde**."—*Sir T. Roe*, Hak: Soc. i. 203.

[1617.—Cloth "here affoorded at a rupie and two in a **cobdee** vnder ours."—*Ibid.* ii. 409.]

1672.—"Measures of Surat are only two; the Lesser and the Greater **Coveld** [probably misprint for *Coveed*], the former of 27 inches English, the latter of 36 inches English."—*Fryer*, 206.

1720.—"Item. I leave 200 pagodas for a tomb to be erected in the burial place in form as follows. Four large pillars, each to be six **covids** high, and six *covids* distance one from the other; the top to be arched, and on each pillar a cherubim; and on the top of the arch the effigy of Justice."—*Testament of Charles Davers, Merchant*, in *Wheeler*, ii. 338.

[1726.—"**Cobidos.**" See quotation under **LOONGHEE.**]

c. 1760.—According to Grose the **covid** at Surat was 1 yard English [the greater *coveed* of Fryer], at Madras ½ a yard; but he says also: "At Bengal the same as at Surat and Madras."

1794.—"To be sold, on very reasonable terms, About 3000 **covits** of 2-inch *Calicut* Planks."—*Bombay Courier*, July 19.

The measure has long been forgotten under this name in Bengal, though used under the native name *hāth*. From Milburn (i. 334, 341, &c.) it seems to have survived on the West Coast in the early part of last century, and possibly may still linger.

[1612.—"½ corge of pintados of 4 **hastas** the piece."—*Danvers, Letters*, i. 232.]

COVIL, s. Tam. *kō-v-il*, 'God-house,' a Hindu temple; and also (in Malabar) a palace, [also in the form *Colghum*, for *Kovilagam*]. In colloquial use in S. India and Ceylon. In S. India it is used, especially among the French, for 'a church'; also among the uneducated English.

[1796.—"I promise to use my utmost endeavours to procure for this Raja the **colghum** of Pychi for his residence. . . ."—Treaty, in *Logan, Malabar*, iii. 254.]

COWCOLLY, n.p. The name of a well-known lighthouse and landmark at the entrance of the Hoogly, in Midnapur District. Properly, according to Hunter, *Geonkhālī*. In Thornton's *English Pilot* (pt. iii. p. 7, of 1711) this place is called **Cockoly**.

COW-ITCH, s. The irritating hairs on the pod of the common Indian climbing herb *Mucuna pruriens*, D.C., N. O. *Leguminosae*, and the plant itself. Both pods and roots are used in native practice. The name is doubtless the Hind. *kewānch* (Skt. *kapikachchhu*), modified in Hobson-Jobson fashion, by the 'striving after meaning.'

[1773.—"**Cow-itch.** This is the down found on the outside of a pod, which is about the size and thickness of a man's little finger, and of the shape of an Italian S."—*Ives*, 494.]

COWLE, s. A lease, or grant in writing; a safe-conduct, amnesty, or in fact any written engagement. The Emperor Sigismund gave *Cowle* to John Huss—and broke it. The word is Ar. *kaul*, 'word, promise, agreement,' and it has become technical in the Indian vernaculars, owing to the prevalence of Mahommedan Law.

[1611.—"We desired to have a **cowl** of the Shahbunder to send some persons aland."—*Danvers, Letters*, i. 133.

[1613.—"Procured a **cowl** for such ships as should come."—*Foster, Letters*, ii. 17.]

1680.—"A **Cowle** granted by the Right Worshipful Streynsham Master, Esq., Agent and Governour for affairs of the Honorable East India Company in ffort St. George at Chinapatnam, by and with the advice of his Councell to all the Pegu Ruby Marchants. . . ."—*Fort St. George Cons.* Feb. 23, in *Notes and Extracts*, No. iii. p. 10.

1688.—"The President has by private correspondence procured a **Cowle** for renting the Town and customs of S. Thomé."—*Wheeler*, i. 176.

1758.—"The Nawaub . . . having mounted some large guns on that hill . . . sent to the Killadar a **Kowl-nama**, or a summons and terms for his surrender."—*H. of Hydur Naik*, 123.

1780.—"This **Caoul** was confirmed by another King of Gingy . . . of the Bramin Caste."—*Dunn, New Directory*, 140.

Sir A. Wellesley often uses the word in his Indian letters. Thus:

1800.—"One tandah of brinjarries . . . has sent to me for **cowle**. . . ."—*Wellington Desp.* (ed. 1837), i. 59.

1804.—"On my arrival in the neighbourhood of the *pettah* I offered **cowle** to the inhabitants."—*Ibid.* ii. 193.

. **COWRY**, s. Hind. *kaurī* (*kauḍī*), Mahr. *kavaḍī*, Skt. *kaparda*, *kapardika*. The small white shell, *Cypraea moneta*, current as money extensively in parts of S. Asia and of Africa.

By far the most ancient mention of shell currency comes from Chinese literature. It is mentioned in the famous "Tribute of Yü" (or *Yü-Kung*); in the *Shu-King* (about the 14th cent. B.C.); and in the "Book of Poetry" (*Shi-King*), in an ode of the 10th cent. B.C. The Chinese seem to have adopted the use from the aborigines in the East and South; and they extended the system to tortoise-shell, and to other shells, the cowry remaining the unit. In 338 B.C., the King of Tsin, the supply of shells failing, suppressed the cowry currency, and issued copper coin, already adopted in other States of China. The usurper Wang Mang, who ruled A.D. 9-23, tried to revive the old systems, and issued rules instituting, in addition to the metallic money, ten classes of tortoise-shell and five of smaller shells, the value of all based on the *cowry*, which was worth 3 cash.* [Cowries were part of the tribute paid by the aborigines of Puanit to Metesouphis I. (*Maspero, Dawn of Civ.*, p. 427).]

The currency of cowries in India does not seem to be alluded to by any Greek or Latin author. It is mentioned by Mas'ūdī (c. 943), and their use for small change in the Indo-Chinese countries is repeatedly spoken of by Marco Polo, who calls them *pourcelaines*, the name by which this kind of shell was known in Italy (*porcellane*) and France. When the Mahommedans conquered Bengal, early in the 13th century, they found the ordinary currency composed exclusively of cowries, and in some remote districts this continued to the beginning of the last century. Thus, up to 1801, the whole revenue of the Silhet District, amounting then to Rs. 250,000, was collected in these shells, but by 1813 the whole was realised in specie. Interesting details in connection with this subject are given by the Hon. Robert Lindsay, who was one of the early Collectors of Silhet (*Lives of the Lindsays*, iii. 170).

The Sanskrit vocabulary called *Trikāṇḍaśesha* (iii. 3, 206) makes 20 *kapardika* (or *kauṛīs*) = ¼ *paṇa*; and this value seems to have been pretty constant. The cowry table given by Mr. Lindsay at Silhet, circa 1778, exactly agrees with that given by Milburn as in Calcutta use in the beginning of last century, and up to 1854 or thereabouts it continued to be the same:

4 *kauṛis* = 1 *ganda*
20 *gandas* = 1 *paṇ*
4 *paṇ* = 1 *āna*
4 *ānas* = 1 *kāhan*, or about ¼ rupee.

This gives about 5120 cowries to the Rupee. We have not met with any denomination of currency in actual use below the cowry, but it will be seen that, in a quotation from Mrs. Parkes, two such are indicated. It is, however, Hindu idiosyncracy to indulge in imaginary submultiples as well as imaginary multiples. (See a parallel under **LACK**).

In Bastar, a secluded inland State between Orissa and the Godavery, in 1870, the following was the prevailing table of cowry currency, according to Sir W. Hunter's *Gazetteer*:

28 *kauris* = 1 *borī*
12 *boris* = 1 *dugānī*
12 *dugānīs* = 1 Rupee, *i.e.* 2880 cowries.

Here we may remark that both the *paṇ* in Bengal, and the *dugānī* in this secluded Bastar, were originally the names of pieces of money, though now in the respective localities they represent only certain quantities of cowries. (For *paṇ*, see under **FANAM**; and as regards *dugānī*, see *Thomas's Patan Kings of Delhī*, pp. 218 *seq.*). ["Up to 1865 *bee-a* or cowries were in use in Siam; the value of these was so small that from 800 to 1500 went to a *fuang* (7½ cents.)."—*Hallett, A Thousand Miles on an Elephant*, p. 164. Mr. Gray has an interesting note on cowries in

* Note communicated by Professor Terrien de la Couperie.

his ed. of *Pyrard de Laval*, Hak. Soc. i. 236 *seqq.*]

Cowries were at one time imported into England in considerable quantities for use in the African slave-trade. "For this purpose," says Milburn, "they should be small, clean, and white, with a beautiful gloss" (i. 273). The duty on this importation was £53, 16*s.* 3*d.* per cent. on the sale value, with ¼ added for war-tax. In 1803, 1418 cwt. were sold at the E. I. auctions, fetching £3,626; but after that few were sold at all. In the height of slave-trade, the great mart for cowries was at Amsterdam, where there were spacious warehouses for them (see the *Voyage*, &c., quoted 1747).

c. A.D. 943.—"Trading affairs are carried on with *cowries* (*al-wada'*), which are the money of the country."—*Maṣ'ūdī*, i. 385.

c. 1020.—"These isles are divided into two classes, according to the nature of their chief products. The one are called *Dewa-Kaudha*, 'the Isles of the **Cowries**,' because of the **Cowries** that they collect on the branches of coco-trees planted in the sea."—*Albirūnī*, in *J. As.*, Ser. IV. tom. iv. 266.

c. 1240.—"It has been narrated on this wise that as in that country (Bengal), the **kauri** [shell] is current in place of silver, the least gift he used to bestow was a *lak* of **kauṛis**. The Almighty mitigate his punishment [in hell]!"—*Ṭabaḳāt-i-Nāṣiri*, by *Raverty*, 555 *seq.*

c. 1350.—"The money of the Islanders (of the Maldives) consists of *cowries* (*al-wada'*). They so style creatures which they collect in the sea, and bury in holes dug on the shore. The flesh wastes away, and only a white shell remains. 100 of these shells are called *siyāh*, and 700 *fāl*; 12,000 they call *kutta*; and 100,000 *bustū*. Bargains are made with these cowries at the rate of 4 *bustū* for a gold dīnār. [This would be about 40,000 for a rupee.] Sometimes the rate falls, and 12 *bustū* are exchanged for a gold dīnār. The islanders barter them to the people of Bengal for rice, for they also form the currency in use in that country. . . . These cowries serve also for barter with the negroes in their own land. I have seen them sold at Mālī and Gūgū [on the Niger] at the rate of 1150 for a gold dīnār."—*Ibn Batuta*, iv. 122.

c. 1420.—"A man on whom I could rely assured me that he saw the people of one of the chief towns of the Said employ as currency, in the purchase of low-priced articles of provision, **kaudas**, which in Egypt are known as *wada*, just as people in Egypt use *fals*."—*Makrizi, S. de Sacy, Chrest. Arabe*, 2nd ed. i. 252.

[1510.—Mr. Whiteway writes: "In an abstract of an unpublished letter of Alboquerque which was written about 1510, and abstracted in the following year, occurs this sentence:—'The merchandize which they carry from Cairo consists of snails (*caracoes*) of the Twelve Thousand Islands.' He is speaking of the internal caravan-trade of Africa, and these snails must be **cowries**."]

1554.—At the Maldives: "**Cowries** 12,000 make one *cota*; and 4½ *cotas* of average size weigh one *quintal*; the big ones something more."—*A. Nunes*, 35.

" "In these isles . . . are certain white little shells which they call **cauris**."—*Castanheda*, iv. 7.

1561.—"Which vessels (*Gundras*, or palm-wood boats from the Maldives) come loaded with coir and **caury**, which are certain little white shells found among the Islands in such abundance that whole vessels are laden with them, and which make a great trade in Bengala, where they are current as money."—*Correa*, I. i. 341.

1586.—"In Bengal are current those little shells that are found in the islands of Maldiva, called here **courim**, and in Portugal *Buzio*."—*Sassetti*, in *De Gubernatis*, 205.

[c. 1590.—"Four kos from this is a well, into which if the bone of any animal be thrown it petrifies, like a **cowrie** shell, only smaller."—*Āīn*, ed. *Jarrett*, ii. 229.]

c. 1610.—"Les marchandises qu'ils portent le plus souvent sont ces petites coquilles des Maldives, dont ils chargent tous les ans grand nombre de nauires. Ceux des Maldives les appellent *Boly*, et les autres Indiens **Caury**."—*Pyrard de Laval*, i. 517; see also p. 165; [Hak. Soc. i. 438; also comp. i. 78, 157, 228, 236, 240, 250, 299; *Boly* is Singh. *bella*, a cowry].

c. 1664.—". . . lastly, it (Indostan) wants those little *Sea-cockles* of the Maldives, which serve for common Coyne in *Bengale*, and in some other places: . . ."—*Bernier*, E.T. 63; [ed. *Constable*, 204].

[c. 1665.—"The other small money consists of shells called **Cowries**, which have the edges inverted, and they are not found in any other part of the world save only the Maldive Islands. . . . Close to the sea they give up to 80 for the *paisa*, and that diminishes as you leave the sea, on account of carriage; so that at Agra you receive but 50 or 55 for the *paisa*."—*Tavernier*, ed. *Ball*, i. 27 *seq.*]

1672.—"**Cowreys**, like sea-shells, come from Siam, and the Philippine Islands."—*Fryer*, 86.

1683.—"The Ship Britannia—from the Maldiva Islands, arrived before the Factory . . . at their first going ashore, their first salutation from the natives was a shower of Stones and Arrows, whereby 6 of their Men were wounded, which made them immediately return on board, and by ye mouths of their Guns forced them to a complyance, and permission to load what **Cowries** they would at Markett Price; so that in a few days time they sett sayle from thence for Surrat with above 60 Tunn of **Cowryes**."—*Hedges, Diary*, July 1; [Hak. Soc. i. 96].

1705.—". . . **Coris**, qui sont des petits coquillages."—*Luillier*, 245.

1727.—"The **Couries** are caught by putting Branches of Cocoa-nut trees with their Leaves on, into the Sea, and in five or six Months the little Shell-fish stick to those leaves in Clusters, which they take off, and digging Pits in the Sand, put them in and cover them up, and leave them two or three Years in the Pit, that the Fish may putrefy, and then they take them out of the Pit, and barter them for Rice, Butter, and Cloth, which Shipping bring from *Ballasore* in *Orisa* near *Bengal*, in which Countries **Couries** pass for Money from 2500 to 3000 for a Rupee, or half a Crown *English*."—*A. Hamilton* [ed. 1744], i. 349.

1747.—"Formerly 12,000 weight of these **cowries** would purchase a cargo of five or six hundred Negroes: but those lucrative times are now no more; and the Negroes now set such a value on their countrymen, that there is no such thing as having a cargo under 12 or 14 tuns of cowries.

"As payments of this kind of specie are attended with some intricacy, the Negroes, though so simple as to sell one another for shells, have contrived a kind of copper vessel, holding exactly 108 pounds, which is a great dispatch to business."—*A Voyage to the Id. of Ceylon on board a Dutch Indiaman in the year* 1747, &c. &c. Written by a Dutch Gentleman. Transl. &c. London, 1754, pp. 21 *seq.*

1749.—"The only Trade they deal in is **Cowries** (or Blackamoor's Teeth as they call them in England), the King's sole Property, which the sea throws up in great abundance."—*The Boscawen's Voyage to Bombay*, by *Philalethes* (1750), p. 52.

1753.—"Our Hon'ble Masters having expressly directed ten tons of **couries** to be laden in each of their ships homeward bound, we ordered the Secretary to prepare a protest against Captain Cooke for refusing to take any on board the Admiral Vernon."—In *Long*, 41.

1762.—"The trade of the salt and *butty wood* in the Chucla of Sillett, has for a long time been granted to me, in consideration of which I pay a yearly rent of 40,000 *caouns* * of **cowries**. . . ."—Native Letter to Nabob, in *Van Sittart*, i. 203.

1770.—". . . millions of millions of lires, pounds, rupees, and **cowries**."—*H. Walpole's Letters*, v. 421.

1780.—"We are informed that a Copper Coinage is now on the Carpet . . . it will be of the greatest utility to the Public, and will totally abolish the trade of **Cowries**, which for a long time has formed so extensive a field for deception and fraud. A greviance (*sic*) the poor has long groan'd under."—*Hicky's Bengal Gazette*, April 29.

1786.—In a Calcutta Gazette the rates of payment at Pultah Ferry are stated in Rupees, Annas, *Puns*, and *Gundas* (*i.e.* of *Cowries*, see above).—In *Seton-Karr*, i. 140.

* *Kāhan*, see above=1280 cowries.

1791.—"Notice is hereby given, that on or before the 1st November next, sealed proposals of Contract for the remittance in Dacca of the cowries received on account of the Revenues of Sylhet . . . will be received at the Office of the Secretary to the Board of Revenue. . . . All persons who may deliver in proposals, are desired to specify the rates per cowan or *cowans* of **cowries** (see *kāhan* above) at which they will engage to make the remittance proposed."—In *Seton-Karr*, ii. 53.

1803.—"I will continue to pay, without demur, to the said Government, as my annual *peshkush* or tribute, 12,000 *kahuns* of **cowries** in three instalments, as specified herein below."—*Treaty Engagement* by the Rajah of Kitta Keonghur, a Tributary subordinate to Cuttack, 16th December, 1803.

1833.—"May 1st. Notice was given in the Supreme Court that Messrs. Gould and Campbell would pay a dividend at the rate of nine *gundahs*, one **cowrie**, one *cawg*, and eighteen *teel*, in every sicca rupee, on and after the 1st of June. A curious dividend, not quite a farthing in the rupee!" *—*The Pilgrim* (by Fanny Parkes), i. 273.

c. 1865.—"Strip him stark naked, and cast him upon a desert island, and he would manage to play heads and tails for **cowries** with the sea-gulls, if land-gulls were not to be found."—*Zelda's Fortune*, ch. iv.

1883.—"Johnnie found a lovely **cowrie** two inches long, like mottled tortoise-shell, walking on a rock, with its red fleshy body covering half its shell, like a jacket trimmed with chenille fringe."—*Letter* (of Miss North's) *from Seychelle Islands*, in *Pall Mall Gazette*, Jan. 21, 1884.

COWRY, s. Used in S. India for the yoke to carry burdens, the **Bangy** (q.v.) of N. India. In Tamil, &c., *kāvadi*, [*kāvu*, 'to carry on the shoulder,' *tadi*, 'pole'].

[1853.—"**Cowrie** baskets . . . a circular ratan basket, with a conical top, covered with green oil-cloth, and secured by a brass padlock."—*Campbell*, *Old Forest Ranger*, 3rd ed. 178.]

COWTAILS, s. The name formerly in ordinary use for what we now more euphoniously call **chowries** (q.v.).

c. 1664.—"These Elephants have then also . . . certain **Cow-tails** of the great *Tibet*, white and very dear, hanging at their

* A *Kāg* would seem here to be equivalent to ¼ of a cowry. Wilson, with (?) as to its origin [perhaps P. *kāk*, 'minute'], explains it as "a small division of money of account, less than a *ganda* of Kauris." *Til* is properly the sesamum seed, applied in Bengal, Wilson says, "in account to $\frac{1}{20}$ of a kauri." The Table would probably thus run: 20 *til*=1 *kāg*, 4 *kāg*=1 *kauri*, and so forth. And 1 rupee=409,600 til!

Ears like great Mustachoes. . . ."—*Bernier*, E.T., 84; [ed. *Constable*, 261].

1665.—"Now that this King of the Great Tibet knows, that *Aureng-Zebe* is at *Kachemire*, and threatens him with War, he hath sent to him an Ambassador, with Presents of the Countrey, as Chrystal, and those dear White **Cow-tails**. . . ."—*Ibid.* 135; [ed. *Constable*, 422].

1774.—"To send one or more pair of the cattle which bear what are called **cowtails**." —*Warren Hastings*, Instruction to Bogle, in *Markham's Tibet*, 8.

,, "There are plenty of **cowtailed** cows (!), but the weather is too hot for them to go to Bengal."—*Bogle, ibid.* 52. 'Cow-tailed cows' seem analogous to the 'dismounted mounted infantry' of whom we have recently heard in the Suakin campaign.

1784.—In a 'List of Imports probable from Tibet,' we find "**Cow Tails**."—In *Seton-Karr*, i. 4.

,, "From the northern mountains are imported a number of articles of commerce. . . . The principal . . . are . . . musk, **cowtails**, honey. . . ."—*Gladwin's Ayeen Akbery* (ed. 1800) ii. 17; [ed. *Jarrett*, ii. 172].

CRAN, s. Pers. *krān*. A modern Persian silver coin, worth about a franc, being the tenth part of a **Tomaun**.

1880.—"A couple of mules came clattering into the courtyard, driven by one muleteer. Each mule carried 2 heavy sacks . . . which jingled pleasantly as they were placed on the ground. The sacks were afterwards opened in my presence, and contained no less than 35,000 silver **krans**. The one muleteer without guard had brought them across the mountains, 170 miles or so, from Tehran."—MS. Letter from *Col. Bateman-Champain, R.E.*

[1891.—"I on my arrival took my servants' accounts in tomauns and **kerans**, afterwards in *kerans* and shaies, and at last in *kerans* and puls."—*Wills, Land of the Lion*, 63.]

CRANCHEE, s. Beng. H. *karānchī*. This appears peculiar to Calcutta, [but the word is also used in N. India]. A kind of ricketty and sordid carriage resembling, as Bp. Heber says below, the skeleton of an old English hackney-coach of 1800-35 (which no doubt was the model), drawn by wretched ponies, harnessed with rope, and standing for native hire in various parts of the city.

1823.—". . . a considerable number of '**caranchies**,' or native carriages, each drawn by two horses, and looking like the skeletons of hackney coaches in our own country."—*Heber*, i. 28 (ed. 1844).

1834.—"As Lady Wroughton guided her horse through the crowd to the right, a **kuranchy**, or hackney-coach, suddenly passed her at full speed."—*The Baboo*, i. 228.

CRANGANORE, n.p. Properly (according to Dr. Gundert), *Koḍuṅṅāllūr*, more generally *Koḍuṅgalūr*; [the *Madras Gloss.* gives Mal. *Kotannallūr*, *kota*, 'west,' *kovil*, 'palace,' *ūr*, 'village']. An ancient city and port of Malabar, identical with the *Mūyiri-kkoḍu* of an ancient copper-plate inscription,* with the Μουζιρίς of Ptolemy's Tables and the Periplus, and with the *Muziris primum emporium Indiae* of Pliny (Bk. vi. cap. 23 or 26), [see *Logan, Malabar*, i. 80]. "The traditions of Jews, Christians, Brahmans, and of the *Kérala Ulpatti* (legendary History of Malabar) agree in making Kodungalūr the residence of the Perumāls (ancient sovereigns of Malabar), and the first resort of Western shipping" (Dr. Gundert in *Madras Journal*, vol. xiii. p. 120). It was apparently the earliest settlement of Jew and Christian immigrants. It is prominent in all the earlier narratives of the 16th century, especially in connection with the Malabar Christians; and it was the site of one of the seven churches alleged in the legends of the latter to have been founded by St. Thomas.† Cranganor was already in decay when the Portuguese arrived. They eventually established themselves there with a strong fort (1523), which the Dutch took from them in 1662. This fort was dismantled by Tippoo's troops in 1790, and there is now hardly a trace left of it. In Baldaeus (*Malabar und Coromandel*, p. 109, Germ. ed.) there are several good views of Cranganore as it stood in the 17th century. [See **SHINKALI**.]

c. 774. A.D.—"We have given as eternal possession to Iravi Corttan, the lord of the town, the brokerage and due customs . . . namely within the river-mouth of **Codangalur**."—*Copper Charter*, see *Madr. Journ.* xiii. And for the date of the inscription, *Burnell*, in *Ind. Antiq.* iii. 315.

(Before 1500, see as in above quotation, p. 334.).—"I Erveh Barmen . . . sitting this day in **Canganúr**. . . ." (*Madras Journal*, xiii. pt. ii. p. 12). This is from an old Hebrew translation of the 8th century copper-grant to the Jews, in which the Tamil has "The

* See *Madras Journal*, xiii. 127.

† *Ind. Ant.* iii. 309.

king . . . Sri Bhaskara Ravi Varman . . . on the day when he was pleased to sit in Muyiri-kōdu. . . ."—thus identifying *Muyiri* or *Muziris* with Cranganore, an identification afterwards verified by tradition ascertained on the spot by Dr. Burnell.

1498.—"**Quorongoliz** belongs to the Christians, and the king is a Christian; it is 3 days distant from Calecut by sea with fair wind; this king could muster 4,000 fighting men; here is much pepper. . . ."—*Roteiro de Vasco da Gama*, 108.

1503.—"Nostra autem regio in qua Christiani commorantur Malabar appellatur, habetque xx circiter urbes, quarum tres celebres sunt et firmæ, **Carongoly**, *Palor*, et *Colom*, et aliæ illis proximæ sunt."—Letter of *Nestorian Bishops* on mission to India, in *Assemani*, iii. 594.

1516.—". . . a place called **Crongolor**, belonging to the King of Calicut . . . there live in it Gentiles, Moors, Indians, and Jews, and Christians of the doctrine of St. Thomas."—*Barbosa*, 154.

c. 1535.—"**Crancanor** fu antichamente honorata, e buon porto, tien molte genti . . . la città e grande, ed honorata con grã traffico, auãti che si facesse Cochin, cõ la venuta di Portoghesi, nobile."—*Sommario de' Regni*, &c. *Ramusio*, i. f. 332*v*.

1554.—"Item . . . paid for the maintenance of the boys in the College, which is kept in **Cranguanor**, by charter of the King our Lord, annually 100 000 *reis*. . . ."—*S. Botelho, Tombo*, &c., 27.

c. 1570.—". . . prior to the introduction of Islamism into this country, a party of Jews and Christians had found their way to a city of Malabar called **Cadungaloor**."—*Tohfat-ul-Mujahideen*, 47.

1572.—

"A hum Cochin, e a outro Cananor,
A qual Chale, a qual a ilha da pimenta,
A qual Coulão, a qual dá **Cranganor**,
E os mais, a quem o mais serve e contenta. . . ." *Camões*, vii. 35.

1614.—"The Great Samorine's Deputy came aboord . . . and . . . earnestly persuaded vs to stay a day or two, till he might send to the Samorine, then at **Crangelor**, besieging a Castle of the Portugals."—*Peyton*, in *Purchas*, i. 531.

c. 1806.—"In like manner the Jews of **Kranghír** (Cranganore), observing the weakness of the Sámuri . . . made a great many Mahomedans drink the cup of martyrdom. . . ."—*Muhabbat Khán* (writing of events in 16th century), in *Elliot*, viii. 388.

CRANNY, s. In Bengal commonly used for a clerk writing English, and thence vulgarly applied generically to the East Indians, or half-caste class, from among whom English copyists are chiefly recruited. The original is Hind. *karānī*, *kirānī*, which Wilson derives from Skt. *karan*, 'a doer.'

S

Karana is also the name of one of the (so-called) mixt castes of the Hindus, sprung from a Sudra mother and Vaisya father, or (according to some) from a pure Kshatriya mother by a father of degraded Kshatriya origin. The occupation of the members of this mixt caste is that of writers and accountants; [see *Risley, Tribes and Castes of Bengal*, i. 424 *seqq.*].

The word was probably at one time applied by natives to the junior members of the Covenanted Civil Service —"Writers," as they were designated. See the quotations from the "*Seir Mutaqherin*" and from Hugh Boyd. And in our own remembrance the "Writers' Buildings" in Calcutta, where those young gentlemen were at one time quartered (a range of apartments which has now been transfigured into a splendid series of public offices, but, wisely, has been kept to its old name), was known to the natives as *Karānī kī Bārik*.

c. 1350.—"They have the custom that when a ship arrives from India or elsewhere, the slaves of the Sultan . . . carry with them complete suits . . . for the *Rabban* or skipper, and for the **kirānī**, who is the ship's clerk."—*Ibn Batuta*, ii. 198.

" "The second day after our arrival at the port of Kailūkari, the princess escorted the *nakhodāh* (or skipper), the **kirānī**, or clerk. . . ."—*Ibid.* iv. 250.

c. 1590.—"The **Karrání** is a writer who keeps the accounts of the ship, and serves out the water to the passengers."—*Āīn* (*Blochmann*), i. 280.

c. 1610.—"Le Secretaire s'apelle **carans** . . ."—*Pyrard de Laval*, i. 152; [Hak. Soc. i. 214].

[1611.—"Doubt you not but it is too true, howsoever the **Cranny** flatters you with better hopes."—*Danvers, Letters*, i. 117, and see also i. 190.

[1684. — "Ye Noceda and **Cranee**."—*Pringle, Diary of Ft. St. George*, iii. 111.]

c. 1781.—"The gentlemen likewise, other than the Military, who are in high offices and employments, have amongst themselves degrees of service and work, which have not come minutely to my knowledge; but the whole of them collectively are called **Carranis**."—*Seir Mutaqherin*, ii. 543.

1793.—"But, as Gay has it, example gains where precept fails. As an encouragement therefore to my brother **crannies**, I will offer an instance or two, which are remembered as good Company's jokes."—*Hugh Boyd, The Indian Observer*, 42.

1810.—"The **Cranny**, or clerk, may be either a native Armenian, a native Portuguese, or a Bengallee."—*Williamson, V. M.* i. 209.

1834.—"Nazir, see bail taken for 2000 rupees. The **Crany** will write your evidence, Captain Forrester."—*The Baboo*, i. 311

It is curious to find this word explained by an old French writer, in almost the modern application to East Indians. This shows that the word was used at Goa in something of its Hindu sense of one of mixt blood.

1653.—"Les **karanes** sont engendrez d'vn Mestis, et d'vne Indienne, lesquels sont oliaustres. Ce mot de **Karanes** vient a mon advis de *Kara*, qui signifie en Turq la terre, ou bien la couleur noire, comme si l'on vouloit dire par **karanes** les enfans du païs, ou bien les noirs: ils ont les mesmes aduantages dans leur professions que les autres Mestis."—*De la Boullaye-le-Gouz*, ed. 1657, p. 226. Compare in *M. Polo*, Bk. I., ch. 18, his statement about the **Caraonas**, and note thereon.

CRAPE, s. This is no Oriental word, though crape comes from China. It is the French *crêpe*, *i.e.* *crespe*, Lat. *crispus*, meaning frizzed or minutely curled. As the word is given in a 16th century quotation by Littré, it is probable that the name was first applied to a European texture. [Its use in English dates from 1633, according to the *N.E.D.*]

"I own perhaps I might desire
Some shawls of true Cashmere—
Some narrowy **crapes** of China silk,
Like wrinkled skins, or scalded milk."
O. W. Holmes, '*Contentment*.'

CREASE, CRIS, &c., s. A kind of dagger, which is the characteristic weapon of the Malay nations; from the Javanese name of the weapon, adopted in Malay, *krīs*, *kirīs*, or *kres* (see *Favre, Dict. Javanais-Français*, 137*b*, *Crawfurd's Malay Dict.* s.v., *Jansz, Javaansch-Nederl. Woordenboek*, 202). The word has been generalised, and is often applied to analogous weapons of other nations, as 'an Arab *crease*,' &c. It seems probable that the H. word *kirich*, applied to a straight sword, and now almost specifically to a sword of European make, is identical with the Malay word *krīs*. See the form of the latter word in Barbosa, almost exactly *kirich*. Perhaps Turki *kīlīçh* is the original. [Platts gives Skt. *kṛiti*, 'a sort of knife or dagger.'] If Reinaud is right in his translation of the Arab *Relations* of the 9th and 10th centuries, in correcting a reading, otherwise unintelligible, to *khrī*, we shall have a very early adoption of this word by Western travellers. It occurs, however, in a passage relating to Ceylon.

c. 910.—"Formerly it was common enough to see in this island a man of the country walk into the market grasping in his hand a **khrī**, *i.e.* a dagger peculiar to the country, of admirable make, and sharpened to the finest edge. The man would lay hands on the wealthiest of the merchants that he found, take him by the throat, brandish his dagger before his eyes, and finally drag him outside of the town. . . ."—*Relation*, &c., *par Reinaud*, p. 156; and see Arabic text, p. 120, near bottom.

It is curious to find the **cris** adopted by Alboquerque as a piece of state costume. When he received the ambassadors of Sheikh Ismael, *i.e.* the Shāh of Persia, Ismael Sūfī, at Ormuz, we read:

1515.—"For their reception there was prepared a dais of three steps . . . which was covered with carpets, and the Governor seated thereon in a decorated chair, arrayed in a tunic and surcoat of black damask, with his collar, and his golden **cris**, as I described before, and with his big, long snow-white beard; and at the back of the dais the captains and gentlemen, handsomely attired, with their swords girt, and behind them their pages with lances and targets, and all uncovered."—*Correa*, ii. 423.

The portrait of Alboquerque in the 1st vol. of Mr. Birch's Translation of the Commentaries, realises the snow-white beard, tunic, and black surcoat, but the *cris* is missing. [The Malay **Creese** is referred to in iii. 85.]

1516.—"They are girt with belts, and carry daggers in their waists, wrought with rich inlaid work, these they call **querix**."—*Barbosa*, 193.

1552.—"And the quartermaster ran up to the top, and thence beheld the son of Timuta raja to be standing over the Captain Major with a **cris** half drawn."—*Castanheda*, ii. 363.

1572.—

". . . assentada
Lá no gremio da Aurora, onde nasceste,
Opulenta Malaca nomeada!
As settas venenosas que fizeste!
Os **crises**, com que já te vejo armáda. . . ."
Camões, x. 44.

By Burton:

". . . so strong thy site
there on Aurora's bosom, whence they rise,
thou Home of Opulence, Malacca hight!
The poysoned arrows which thine art supplies,
the **krises** thirsting, as I see, for fight. . . ."

1580.—A vocabulary of "Wordes of the naturall language of Iaua" in the voyage of

Sir Fr. Drake, has **Cricke**, 'a dagger.'—*Hakl.* iv. 246.

[1584.—"**Crise.**" See quotation under **A MUCK.**]

1586-88.—"The custom is that whenever the King (of Java) doth die . . . the wives of the said King . . . every one with a dagger in her hand (which dagger they call a **crese**, and is as sharp as a razor) stab themselves to the heart."—*Cavendish*, in *Hakl.* iv. 337.

1591.—"Furthermore I enjoin and order in the name of our said Lord . . . that no servant go armed whether it be with staves or daggers, or **crisses.**"—Procl. of *Viceroy Mathias d'Alboquerque* in *Archiv. Port. Oriental*, fasc. 3, p. 325.

1598.—"In the Western part of the Island (Sumatra) is Manancabo where they make Poinyards, which in India are called **Cryses**, which are very well accounted and esteemed of."—*Linschoten*, 33; [with some slight differences of reading, Hak. Soc. i. 110].

1602.—". . . Chinesische Dolchen, so sie **Cris** nennen."—*Hulsius*, i. 33.

c. 1610.—"Ceux-là ont d'ordinaire à leur costé vn poignard ondé qui s'apelle **cris**, et qui vient d'Achen en Sumatra, de Iaua, et de la Chine."—*Pyrard de Laval*, i. 121; [Hak. Soc. i. 164]; also see ii. 101; [ii. 162, 170].

1634.—"Malayos **crises**, Arabes alfanges."—*Malaca Conquistada*, ix. 32.

1686.—"The **Cresset** is a small thing like a Baggonet which they always wear in War or Peace, at Work or Play, from the greatest of them to the poorest or meanest person."—*Dampier*, i. 337.

1690.—"And as the Japanners . . . rip up their Bowels with a **Cric**. . . ."—*Ovington*, 173.

1727.—"A Page of twelve Years of Age . . . (said) that he would shew him the Way to die, and with that he took a **Cress**, and ran himself through the body."—*A. Hamilton*, ii. 99; [ed. 1744, ii. 98].

1770.—"The people never go without a poniard which they call **cris**."—*Raynal* (tr. 1777), i. 97.

c. 1850-60.—"They (the English) chew hashish, cut themselves with poisoned **creases** . . . taste every poison, buy every secret."—*Emerson, English Traits* [ed. 1866, ii. 59].

The Portuguese also formed a word **crisada**, a blow with a **cris** (see *Castanheda*, iii. 379). And in English we find a verb to '*crease*'; see in *Purchas*, i. 532, and this:

1604.—"This Boyhog we tortured not, because of his confession, but **crysed** him."—*Scot's Discourse of Iava*, in *Purchas*, i. 175.

[1704.—"At which our people . . . were most of them **creezed**."—*Yule, Hedges' Diary*, Hak. Soc. ii. cccxxxvii.]

Also in *Braddel's Abstract of the Sijara Malayu*:

"He was in consequence **creased** at the shop of a sweetmeat seller, his blood flowed on the ground, but his body disappeared miraculously."—*Sijara Malayu*, in *J. Ind. Arch.* v. 318.

CREDERE, DEL. An old mercantile term.

1813.—"**Del credere**, or guaranteeing the responsibility of persons to whom goods were sold—commission ⅔ per cent."—*Milburn*, i. 235.

CREOLE, s. This word is never used by the English in India, though the mistake is sometimes made in England of supposing it to be an Anglo-Indian term. The original, so far as we can learn, is Span. *criollo*, a word of uncertain etymology, whence the French *créole*, a person of European blood but colonial birth. See *Skeat*, who concludes that *criollo* is a negro corruption of *criadillo*, dim. of *criado*, and is='little nursling.' *Criados*, *criadas*, according to Pyrard de Laval, [Hak. Soc. ii. 89 *seq.*] were used at Goa for male and female servants. And see the passage quoted under **NEELAM** from Correa, where the words 'apparel and servants' are in the original '*todo o fato e* criados.'

1782.—"Mr. Macintosh being the son of a Scotch Planter by a French **Creole**, of one of the West India Islands, is as swarthy and ill-looking a man as is to be seen on the Portugueze Walk on the Royal Exchange."—*Price's Observations*, &c. in *Price's Tracts*, i. 9.

CROCODILE, s. This word is seldom used in India; **alligator** (q.v.) being the term almost invariably employed.

c. 1328.—"There be also **coquodriles**, which are vulgarly called *calcatix* [Lat. *calcatrix*, 'a cockatrice']. . . . These animals be like lizards, and have a tail stretched over all like unto a lizard's," &c.—*Friar Jordanus*, p. 19.

1590.—"One **Crocodile** was so huge and greedy that he devoured an *Alibamba*, that is a chained company of eight or nine slaves; but the indigestible Iron paid him his wages, and murthered the murtherer."—*Andrew Battel* (West Africa), in *Purchas*, ii. 985.

[1870.—". . . I have been compelled to amputate the limbs of persons seized by **crocodiles** (*Mugger*). . . . The Alligator (*gharial*) sometimes devours children. . . ."—*Chevers, Med. Jurispr. in India*, 366 *seq.*].

CRORE, s. One hundred *lakhs*, *i.e.* 10,000,000. Thus a crore of rupees was for many years almost the exact equivalent of a million sterling. It had once been a good deal more, and has now been for some years a good deal less. The H. is *karoṛ*, Skt. *koṭi*.

c. 1315.—"Kales Dewar, the ruler of Ma'bar, enjoyed a highly prosperous life. . . . His coffers were replete with wealth, insomuch that in the city of Mardī (Madura) there were 1200 **crores** of gold deposited, every *crore* being equal to a thousand laks, and every lak to one hundred thousand dinārs."—*Wassāf*, in *Elliot*, iii. 52. N.B.—The reading of the word *crore* is however doubtful here (see note by Elliot *in loco*). In any case the value of *crore* is misstated by Wassāf.

c. 1343.—"They told me that a certain Hindu farmed the revenue of the city and its territories (Daulatābād) for 17 **karōr** . . . as for the **karōr** it is equivalent to 100 *laks*, and the *lak* to 100,000 dīnārs."—*Ibn Batuta*, iv. 49.

c. 1350.—"In the course of three years he had misappropriated about a **kror** of *tankas* from the revenue."—*Ziā-uddīn-Barnī*, in *Elliot*, iii. 247.

c. 1590.—"Zealous and upright men were put in charge of the revenues, each over one **Krōr** of dams." (These, it appears, were called **krōris**.)—*Āīn-i-Akbari*, i. 13.

1609.—"The King's yeerely Income of his Crowne Land is fiftie **Crou** of *Rupias*, every **Crou** is an hundred *Leckes*, and every *Lecke* is an hundred thousand *Rupias*."—*Hawkins*, in *Purchas*, i. 216.

1628.—"The revenue of all the territories under the Emperors of Delhi amounts, according to the Royal registers, to six *arbs* and thirty **krors** of *dāms*. One *arb* is equal to a hundred **krors** (a *kror* being ten millions) and a hundred *Krors* of *dāms* are equivalent to two *krors* and fifty *lacs* of rupees."—*Muhammad Sharīf Hanafi*, in *Elliot*, vii. 138.

1690.—"The *Nabob* or Governour of *Bengal* was reputed to have left behind him at his Death, twenty **Courous** of Roupies: A **kourou** is an hundred thousand lacks."—*Ovington*, 189.

1757.—"In consideration of the losses which the English Company have sustained . . . I will give them one **crore** of rupees."—*Orme*, ii. 162 (ed. 1803).

c. 1785.—"The revenues of the city of Decca, once the capital of Bengal, at a low estimation amount annually to two **kherore**."—*Carraccioli's Life of Clive*, i. 172.

1797. — "An Englishman, for H. E.'s amusement, introduced the elegant European diversion of a race in sacks by old women: the Nabob was delighted beyond measure, and declared that though he had spent a **crore** of rupees : . . in procuring amusement, he had never found one so pleasing to him."—*Teignmouth, Mem.* i. 407.

1879.—
"'Tell me what lies beyond our brazen gates.'
Then one replied, 'The city first, fair Prince!
* * * * * *
And next King Bimbasâra's realm, and then
The vast flat world with **crores on crores** of folk.'"
Sir E. Arnold, The Light of Asia, iii.

[**CRORI**, s. "The possessor or collector of a **kror**, or ten millions, of any given kind of money; it was especially applied as an official designation, under the Mohammedan government, to a collector of revenue to the extent of a **kror** of dāms, or 250,000 rupees, who was also at various times invested with the general superintendence of the lands in his district, and the charge of the police." (*Wilson*.)

[c. 1590.—See quotation under **CRORE**.

[1675. — "Nor does this exempt them from *pishcashing* the Nabob's **Crewry** or Governour:"—*Yule, Hedges' Diary*, Hak. Soc. ii. ccxxxix.]

[**CROTCHEY, KURACHEE**, properly *Karāchi*, the sea-port and chief town of the province of Sind, which is a creation of the British rule, no town appearing to have existed on the site before 1725. In As Suyūti's *History of the Caliphs* (E.T. p. 229) the capture of Kīrakh or Kīraj is mentioned. Sir H. M. Elliot thinks that this place was probably situated in if not named from Kachh. Jarrett (*Āīn*, ii. **344**, note) supposes this to be Karāchi, which Elliot identified with the Krokala of Arrian. Here, according to Curtius, dwelt the Arabioi or Arabitai. The harbour of Karāchi was possibly the Porus Alexandri, where Nearchus was detained by the monsoon for twenty-four days (see *McCrindle, Ancient India*, **167**, **262**).

[1812.—"From **Crotchey** to Cape Monze the people call themselves Balouches."—*Morier, Journey through Persia*, p. 5.

[1839.—". . . spices of all kinds, which are carried from Bombay . . . to **Koratchee** or other ports in Sind." — *Elphinstone's Caubul*, i. 384.]

CROW-PHEASANT, s. The popular Anglo-Indian name of a somewhat ignoble bird (Fam. *Cuculidae*), common all over the plains of India, in Burma, and the Islands, viz. *Cen-*

tropus rufipennis, Illiger. It is held in India to give omens.

1878.—"The **crow-pheasant** stalks past with his chestnut wings drooping by his side." — *Phil. Robinson, In My Indian Garden*, 7.

1883.—"There is that ungainly object the *coucal*, **crow-pheasant**, jungle-crow, or whatever else you like to call the miscellaneous thing, as it clambers through a creeper-laden bush or spreads its reddish-bay wings and makes a slow voyage to the next tree. To judge by its appearance only it might be a crow developing for a peacock, but its voice seems to have been borrowed from a black-faced monkey."—*Tribes on my Frontier*, 155.

CUBEB, s. The fruit of the *Piper Cubeba*, a climbing shrub of the Malay region. [Its Hind. name *kabāb chīnī* marks its importation from the East by Chinese merchants.] The word and the articles were well known in Europe in the Middle Ages, the former being taken directly from the Arab. *kabābah*. It was used as a spice like other peppers, though less common. The importation into Europe had become infinitesimal, when it revived in last century, owing to the medicinal power of the article having become known to our medical officers during the British occupation of Java (1811-15). Several particulars of interest will be found in *Hanbury and Flückiger's Pharmacog.* 526, and in the notes to *Marco Polo*, ii. 380.

c. 943.—"The territories of this Prince (the Maharaja of the Isles) produce all sorts of spices and aromatics. . . . The exports are camphor, lign-aloes, clove, sandal-wood, betel-nut, nutmeg, cardamom, **cubeb** (*al-kabābah*). . . ."—*Maṣ'ūdi*, i. 341 *seq.*

13th cent.—
"Theo canel and the licoris
And swete savoury meynte I wis,
Theo gilofre, **quybibe** and mace. . . ."
King Alesaunder, in *Weber's Metr. Rom.*, i. 279.

1298.—"This Island (Java) is of surpassing wealth, producing black pepper, nutmegs, spikenard, galingale, **cubebs**, cloves. . . ."—*Marco Polo*, ii. 254.

c. 1328.—"There too (in *Jaua*) are produced **cubebs**, and nutmegs, and mace, and all the other finest spices except pepper."—*Friar Jordanus*, 31.

c. 1340.—"*The following are sold by the pound.* Raw silk; saffron; clove-stalks and cloves; **cubebs**; lign-aloes. . . ."—*Pegolotti*, in *Cathay*, &c., p. 305.

" "**Cubebs** are of two kinds, *i.e.* domestic and wild, and both should be entire and light, and of good smell; and the domestic are known from the wild in this way, that the former are a little more brown than the wild; also the domestic are round, whilst the wild have the lower part a little flattened underneath like flattened buttons."—*Pegolotti*, in *Cathay*, &c.; in orig. 374 *seq.*

c. 1390.—"Take fresh pork, seethe it, chop it small, and grind it well; put to it hard yolks of eggs, well mixed together, with dried currants, powder of cinnamon, and maces, **cubebs**, and cloves whole."—*Recipe* in *Wright's Domestic Manners*, 350.

1563.—"*R.* Let us talk of **cubebs**; although, according to Sepulveda, we seldom use them alone, and only in compounds.

"*O.* 'Tis not so in India; on the contrary they are much used by the Moors soaked in wine . . . and in their native region, which is Java, they are habitually used for coldness of stomach; you may believe me they hold them for a very great medicine."—*Garcia*, f. 80-80*v*.

1572. — "The Indian physicians use **Cubebs** as cordials for the stomach. . . ."—*Acosta*, p. 138.

1612.—"**Çubebs**, the pound . . . xvi. s."—*Rates and Valuatioun* (Scotland).

1874.—"In a list of drugs to be sold in the . . . city of Ulm, A.D. 1596, **cubebs** are mentioned . . . the price for half an ounce being 8 *kreuzers*."—*Hanb. & Flück.* 527.

CUBEER BURR, n.p. This was a famous banyan-tree on an island of the Nerbudda, some 12 m. N.E. of Baroch, and a favourite resort of the English there in the 18th century. It is described by Forbes in his *Or. Mem.* i. 28; [2nd ed. i. 16, and in *Pandurang Hari*, ed. 1873, ii. 137 *seqq.*]. Forbes says that it was thus called by the Hindus in memory of a favourite saint (no doubt Kabīr). Possibly, however, the name was merely the Ar. *kabīr*, 'great,' given by some Mahommedan, and misinterpreted into an allusion to the sectarian leader.

[1623.—"On an other side of the city, but out of the circuit of the houses, in an open place, is seen a great and fair tree, of that kind which I saw in the sea coasts of Persia, near Ormuz, called there *Lul*, but here *Ber*."—*P. della Valle*, Hak. Soc. i. 35. Mr. Grey identifies this with the **CUBEER BURR**.]

1818.—"The popular tradition among the Hindus is that a man of great sanctity named **Kubeer**, having cleaned his teeth, as is practised in India, with a piece of stick, stuck it into the ground, that it took root, and became what it now is."—*Copland*, in *Tr. Lit. Soc. Bo.* i. 290.

CUCUYA, CUCUYADA, s. A cry of alarm or warning; Malayāl. *kūkkuya*, 'to cry out'; not used by English. but found among Portuguese writers, who formed *cucuyada* from the native word, as they did *Crisada* from *kris* (see **CREASE**). See *Correa, Lendas*, ii. 2. 926. See also quotation from Tennent, under **COSS**, and compare Australian *cooey*.

1525.—"On this immediately some of his Nairs who accompanied him, desired to smite the Portuguese who were going through the streets; but the Regedor would not permit it; and the **Caimal** approaching the King's palace, without entering to speak to the King, ordered those cries of theirs to be made which they call **cucuyadas**, and in a few minutes there gathered together more than 2000 Nairs with their arms. . . ."—*Correa*, ii. 926.

1543.—"At the house of the pagod there was a high enclosure-wall of stone, where the Governor collected all his people, and those of the country came trooping with bows and arrows and a few matchlocks, raising great cries and **cucuyadas**, such as they employ to call each other to war, just like cranes when they are going to take wing."—*Ibid.* iv. 327.

CUDDALORE, n.p. A place on the marine backwater 16 m. S. of Pondicherry, famous in the early Anglo-Indian history of Coromandel. It was settled by the Company in 1682-3, and Fort St. David's was erected there soon after. Probably the correct name is *Kaḍal-ūr*, 'Sea-Town.' [The *Madras Gloss.* gives Tam. *kūḍal*, 'junction,' *ūr*, 'village,' because it stands on the confluence of the Kadilam and Paravanar Rivers.]

[1773.—"Fort St. David is . . . built on a rising ground, about a mile from the Black-Town, which is called **Cuddalore**."—*Ives*, p. 18.]

CUDDAPAH, n.p. Tel. *kaḍapa*, ['threshold,' said to take its name from the fact that it is situated at the opening of the pass which leads to the holy town of Tripatty (*Gribble, Man. of Cuddapah*, p. 3); others connect it with Skt. *kripa*, 'pity,' and the Skt. name is *Kripanagara*]. A chief town and district of the Madras Presidency. It is always written *Kurpah* in Kirkpatrick's Translation of *Tippoo's Letters*, [and see Wilks, *Mysore*, ed. 1869, i. 303]. It has been suggested as possible that it is the ΚΑΡΙΓΗ (for ΚΑΡΙΠΗ) of Ptolemy's Tables. [**Kurpah** indigo is quoted on the London market.]

1768.—"The chiefs of Shanoor and **Kirpa** also followed the same path."—*H. of Hydur Naik*, 189.

CUDDOO, s. A generic name for pumpkins, [but usually applied to the musk-melon, *cucurbita moschata* (Watt, *Econ. Dict.* ii. 640)]. Hind. *Kaddū*.

[1870.—"Pumpkin, Red and White—Hind. **Kuddoo**. This vegetable grows in great abundance in all parts of the Deccan."—*Riddell, Ind. Dom. Econ.* 568.]

CUDDY, s. The public or captain's cabin of an Indiaman or other passenger ship. We have not been able to trace the origin satisfactorily. It must, however, be the same with the Dutch and Germ. *kajute*, which has the same signification. This is also the Scandinavian languages, Sw. in *kajuta*, Dan. *kahyt*, and Grimm quotes *kajute*, "Casteria," from a vocabulary of Saxon words used in the first half of 15th century. It is perhaps originally the same with the Fr. *cahute*, 'a hovel,' which Littré quotes from 12th century as *quahute*. Ducange has L. Latin *cahua*, 'casa, tugurium,' but a little doubtfully. [Burton (*Ar. Nights*, xi. 169) gives P. *kadah*, 'a room,' and compares **Cumra**. The *N.E.D.* leaves the question doubtful.]

1726.—"Neither will they go into any ship's **Cayuyt** so long as they see any one in the Skipper's cabin or on the half-deck." *Valentijn, Chorom. (and Pegu)*, 134.

1769.—"It was his (the Captain's) invariable practice on Sunday to let down a canvas curtain at one end of the **cuddy** . . . and to read the church service,—a duty which he considered a complete clearance of the sins of the preceding week."—*Life of Lord Teignmouth*, i. 12.

1848.—"The youngsters among the passengers, young Chaffers of the 150th, and poor little Ricketts, coming home after his third fever, used to draw out Sedley at the **cuddy**-table, and make him tell prodigious stories about himself and his exploits against tigers and Napoleon."—*Vanity Fair*, ed. 1867, ii. 255.

CULGEE, s. A jewelled plume surmounting the *sirpesh* or aigrette upon the turban. Shakespear gives *kalghī* as a Turki word. [Platts gives *kalghā*, *kalghī*, and refers it to Skt. *kalāśa*, 'a spire.']

c. 1514.—"In this manner the people of Bârân catch great numbers of herons. The **Kilki**-*saj* ['Plumes worn on the cap or turban on great occasions.' Also see *Punjab Trade Report*, App., p. ccxv.] are of the heron's feathers."—*Baber*, 154.

1715.—"John Surman received a vest and **Culgee** set with precious stones."—*Wheeler*, ii. 246.

1759.—"To present to Omed Roy, viz. :—

1 **Culgah**	1200 0 0
1 Surpage (*sirpesh*, or aigrette) .	600 0 0
1 Killot (see **Killut**)	250 0 0"

—*Expenses of Nabob's Entertainment.* In *Long*, 193.

1786.—"Three **Kulgies**, three *Surpaishes* (see **Sirpech**), and three *Puduks* (?) [*padak*, H. 'a badge, a flat piece of gold, a neck ornament'] of the value of 36,320 rupees have been despatched to you in a casket."—*Tippoo's Letters*, 263.

[1892.—Of a Banjara ox—"Over the beast's forehead is a shaped frontlet of cotton cloth bordered with patterns in colour with pieces of mirror sewn in, and crowned by a **kalgi** or aigrette of peacock feather tips."—*L. Kipling, Beast and Man in India*, 147.

[The word was also applied to a rich silk cloth imported from India.

[1714.—In a list of goods belonging to sub-governors of the South Sea C.—"A pair of **culgee** window curtains."—2 *ser. Notes & Q.* VI. 244.]

CULMUREEA, KOORMUREEA, s. Nautical H. *kalmarīya*, 'a calm,' taken direct from Port. *calmaria* (*Roebuck*).

CULSEY, s. According to the quotation a weight of about a **candy** (q.v.). We have traced the word, which is rare, also in Prinsep's Tables (ed. *Thomas*, p. 115), as a measure in Bhūj, *kalsī*. And we find R. Drummond gives it: "*Kulsee* or *Culsy* (Guz.). A weight of sixteen maunds" (the Guzerat maunds are about 40 lbs., therefore *kalsi*=about 640 lbs.). [The word is probably Skt. *kalaśi*, 'a water jar,' and hence a grain measure. The *Madras Gloss.* gives Can. *kalasi* as a measure of capacity holding 14 **Seers**.]

1813.—"So plentiful are mangos . . . that during my residence in Guzerat they were sold in the public markets for one rupee the **culsey**; or 600 pounds in English weight."—*Forbes, Orient. Mem.* i. 30; [2d. ed. i. 20].

CUMBLY, CUMLY, CUMMUL, s. A blanket; a coarse woollen cloth. Skt. *kambala*, appearing in the vernaculars in slightly varying forms, *e.g.* H. *kamlī*. Our first quotation shows a curious attempt to connect this word with the Arab. *ḥammāl*, 'a porter' (see **HUMMAUL**), and with the camel's hair of John Baptist's raiment. The word is introduced into Portuguese as *cambolim*, 'a cloak.'

c. 1350.—"It is customary to make of those fibres wet-weather mantles for those rustics whom they call *camalls*,* whose business it is to carry burdens, and also to carry men and women on their shoulders in palankins (*lecticis*). . . . A garment, such as I mean, of this **camall** cloth (and not camel cloth) I wore till I got to Florence. . . . No doubt the raiment of John the Baptist was of that kind. For, as regards *camel's hair*, it is, next to silk, the softest stuff in the world, and never could have been meant. . . ."—*John Marignolli*, in *Cathay*, 366.

1606.—"We wear nothing more frequently than those **cambolins**."—*Gouvea*, f. 132.

[c. 1610.—"Of it they make also good store of cloaks and capes, called by the Indians *Mansaus*, and by the Portuguese 'Ormus **cambalis**.'"—*Pyrard de Laval*, Hak. Soc. ii. 240.]

1673.—"Leaving off to wonder at the natives quivering and quaking after Sunset wrapping themselves in a **combly** or Hair-Cloth."—*Fryer*, 54.

1690.—"**Camlees**, which are a sort of Hair Coat made in Persia. . . ."—*Ovington*, 455.

1718.—"But as a body called the **Cammul**-*poshes*, or blanket wearers, were going to join Qhandaoran, their commander, they fell in with a body of troops of Mahratta horse, who forbade their going further."—*Seir Mutaqherin*, i. 143.

1781.—"One **comley** as a covering . . . 4 *fanams*, 6 *dubs*, 0 *cash*."—*Prison Expenses* of Hon. J. Lindsay, *Lives of Lindsays*, iii.

1798.—". . . a large black **Kummul**, or blanket."—*G. Forster, Travels*, i. 194.

1800.—"One of the old gentlemen, observing that I looked very hard at his **cumly**, was alarmed lest I should think he possessed numerous flocks of sheep."—Letter of *Sir T. Munro*, in *Life*, i. 281.

1813.—Forbes has **cameleens**.—*Or. Mem.* i. 195; [2d. ed. i. 108].

CUMMERBUND, s. A girdle. H. from P. *kamar-band*, *i.e.* 'loin-band.' Such an article of dress is habitually worn by domestic servants, peons, and irregular troops; but any waist-belt is so termed.

[1534.—"And tying on a **cummerbund** (*camarabando*) of yellow silk."—*Correa*, iii. 588. *Camarabandes* in *Dalboquerque, Comm.*, Hak. Soc. iv. 104.]

1552.—"The Governor arriving at Goa received there a present of a rich cloth of Persia which is called **comarbãdos**, being of gold and silk."—*Castanheda*, iii. 396.

* *Camalli* (=*facchini*) survives from the Arabic in some parts of Sicily.

1616.—"The nobleman of Xaxma sent to have a sample of gallie pottes, jugges, podingers, lookinglasses, table bookes, chint bramport, and **combarbands**, with the prices."—*Cocks's Diary*, i. 147.

1638.—"Ils serrent la veste d'vne ceinture, qu'ils appellent **Commerbant**."—*Mandelslo*, 223.

1648.—"In the middle they have a well adjusted girdle, called a **Commerbant**."—*Van Twist*, 55.

1727.—"They have also a fine Turband, embroidered Shoes, and a Dagger of Value, stuck into a fine **Cummerband**, or Sash."—*A. Hamilton*, i. 229; [ed. 1744, ii. 233].

1810.—"They generally have the turbans and **cummer-bunds** of the same colour, by way of livery."—*Williamson, V. M.* i. 274.

[1826.—"My white coat was loose, for want of a **kumberbund**."—*Pandurang Hari*, ed. 1873, i. 275.]

1880.—". . . The Punjab seems to have found out Manchester. A meeting of native merchants at Umritsur . . . describes the effects of a shower of rain on the English-made turbans and **Kummerbunds** as if their heads and loins were enveloped by layers of starch."—*Pioneer Mail*, June 17.

CUMQUOT, s. The fruit of *Citrus japonica*, a miniature orange, often sent in jars of preserved fruits, from China. *Kumkwat* is the Canton pronunciation of *kin-kü*, 'gold orange,' the Chinese name of the fruit.

CUMRA, s. H. *kamrā*, from Port. *camara*; a chamber, a cabin. [In Upper India the drawing-room is the *gol kamrā*, so called because one end of it is usually semi-circular.]

CUMRUNGA, s. See **CARAMBOLA**.

CUMSHAW, s. Chin. Pigeon-English for **bucksheesh** (q.v.), or a present of any kind. According to Giles it is the Amoy pron. (*kam-siā*) of two characters signifying 'grateful thanks.' Bp. Moule suggests *kan-siu* (or Cantonese) *kăm-sau*, 'thank-gift.'

1879.—". . . they pressed upon us, blocking out the light, uttering discordant cries, and clamouring with one voice, **Kum-sha**, *i.e.* backsheesh, looking more like demons than living men."—*Miss Bird's Golden Chersonese*, 70.

1882.—"As the ship got under weigh, the Compradore's **cumshas**, according to 'olo custom,' were brought on board . . . dried lychee, Nankin dates . . . baskets of oranges, and preserved ginger."—*The Fankwae*, 103.

CUNCHUNEE, s. H. *kanchanī*. A dancing-girl. According to Shakespear, this is the feminine of a caste, *Kanchan*, whose women are dancers. But there is doubt as to this: [see Crooke, *Tribes and Castes, N.W.P.* iv. 364, for the *Kanchan* caste.] *Kanchan* is 'gold'; also a yellow pigment, which the women may have used; see quot. from Bernier. [See **DANCING-GIRL**.]

[c. 1590.—"The Kanjari; the men of this class play the Pakhāwaj, the Rabāb, and the Tāla, while the women sing and dance. His Majesty calls them **Kanchanis**."—*Āīn*, ed. *Jarrett*, iii. 257.]

c. 1660.—"But there is one thing which seems to me a little too extravagant . . . the publick Women, I mean not those of the Bazar, but those more retired and considerable ones that go to the great marriages at the houses of the *Omrahs* and Mansebdars to sing and dance, those that are called **Kenchen**, as if you should say the *guilded* the *blossoming* ones. . . ."—*Bernier*, E.T. 88; [ed. *Constable*, 273 *seq.*].

c. 1661.—"On regala dans le Serrail, toutes ces Dames Etrangères, de festins et des dances des **Quenchenies**, qui sont des femmes et des filles d'une Caste de ce nom, qui n'ont point d'autre profession que celle de la danse."—*Thevenot*, v. 151.

1689.—"And here the Dancing Wenches, or **Quenchenies**, entertain you, if you please."—*Ovington*, 257.

1799.—"In the evening the **Canchanis** . . . have exhibited before the Prince and court."—Diary in *Life of Colebrooke*, 153.

1810.—"The dancing-women are of different kinds . . . the *Meeraseens* never perform before assemblies of men. . . . The **Kunchenee** are of an opposite stamp; they dance and sing for the amusement of the male sex."—*Williamson, V. M.* i. 386.

CURIA MURIA, n.p. The name of a group of islands off the S.E. coast of Arabia (*Kharyān Maryān*, of Edrisi).

1527.—"Thus as they sailed, the ship got lost upon the shore of Fartaque in (the region of) **Curia Muria**; and having swum ashore they got along in company of the Moors by land to Calayata, and thence on to Ormuz."—*Correa*, iii. 562; see also i. 366.

c. 1535.—"Dopo Adem è Fartaque, e le isole **Curia, Muria**. . . ."—*Sommario de' Regni*, in *Ramusio*, f. 325.

1540.—"We letted not to discover the Isles of **Curia, Muria**, and *Avedalcuria* (in orig. *Abedalcuria*)."—*Mendez Pinto*, E.T. p. 4.

[1553.—See quotation under **ROSALGAT**.]

1554.—". . . it is necessary to come forth between Súkara and the islands **Khúr** or **Múria** (*Khōr Mōriyā*)."—*The Mohit*, in *Jour. As. Soc. Beng.* v. 459.

[1833.—"The next place to Saugra is **Koorya Moorya Bay**, which is extensive, and has good soundings throughout; the islands are named Jibly, Hallanny, Soda, and Haskee."—*Owen, Narr.* i. 348.]

1834.—"The next place to Saugra is **Koorya Moorya** Bay."—*J. R. Geog. Soc.* ii. 208.

CURNUM, s. Tel. *karaṇamu;* a village accountant, a town-clerk. Acc. to Wilson from Skt. *karaṇa;* (see **CRANNY**). [It corresponds to the Tam. *kanakan* (see **CONICOPOLY**).]

1827.—"Very little care has been taken to preserve the survey accounts. Those of several villages are not to be found. Of the remainder only a small share is in the Collector's cutcherry, and the rest is in the hands of **curnums**, written on **cadjans**."—*Minute by Sir T. Munro*, in *Arbuthnot*, i. 285.

CUROUNDA, s. H. *karaundā*. A small plum-like fruit, which makes good jelly and tarts, and which the natives pickle. It is borne by *Carissa carandas*, L., a shrub common in many parts of India (N.O. *Apocynaceae*).

[1870.—Riddell gives a receipt for **kurunder** jelly, *Ind. Dom. Econ.* 338.]

[CURRIG JEMA, adj. A corr. of H. *khārij jama*, "separated or detached from the rental of the State, as lands exempt from rent, or of which the revenue has been assigned to individuals or institutions" (*Wilson*).

[1687.—". . . that whenever they have a mind to build Factorys, satisfying for the land where it was **Currig Jema**, that is over measure, not entred in the King's books, or paying the usuall and accustomed Rent, no Government should molest them."—*Yule, Hedges, Diary*, Hak. Soc. ii. lxiii.]

CURRUMSHAW HILLS, n.p. This name appears in Rennell's Bengal Atlas, applied to hills in the Gaya district. It is ingeniously supposed by F. Buchanan to have been a mistake of the geographer's, in taking *Karna-Chaupār* ('Karna's place of meeting or teaching'), the name of an ancient ruin on the hills in question, for *Karnachau Pahār* (*Pahār* = Hill).—(*Eastern India*, i. 4).

CURRY, s. In the East the staple food consists of some cereal, either (as in N. India) in the form of flour baked into unleavened cakes, or boiled in the grain, as rice is. Such food having little taste, some small quantity of a much more savoury preparation is added as a relish, or 'kitchen,' to use the phrase of our forefathers. And this is in fact the proper office of *curry* in native diet. It consists of meat, fish, fruit, or vegetables, cooked with a quantity of bruised spices and turmeric [see **MUSSALLA**]; and a little of this gives a flavour to a large mess of rice. The word is Tam. *kari*, *i.e.* 'sauce'; [*kari*, v. 'to eat by biting']. The Canarese form *karil* was that adopted by the Portuguese, and is still in use at Goa. It is remarkable in how many countries a similar dish is habitual; *pilāo* [see **PILLAU**] is the analogous mess in Persia, and *kuskussu* in Algeria; in Egypt a dish well known as *ruzz mufalfal* [Lane, *Mod. Egypt*, ed. 1871, i. 185], or "peppered rice." In England the proportions of rice and "kitchen" are usually reversed, so that the latter is made to constitute the bulk of the dish.

The oldest indication of the Indian cuisine in this kind, though not a very precise one, is cited by Athenaeus from Megasthenes: "Among the Indians, at a banquet, a table is set before each individual . . . and on the table is placed a golden dish on which they throw, first of all, boiled rice . . . . and then they add many sorts of meat dressed after the Indian fashion" (*Athen.*, by *Yonge*, iv. 39). The earliest precise mention of *curry* is in the Mahavanso (c. A.D. 477), where it is said of Kassapo that "he partook of rice dressed in butter, with its full accompaniment of *curries*." This is Turnour's translation, the original Pali being *sūpa*.

It is possible, however, that the kind of *curry* used by Europeans and Mahommedans is not of purely Indian origin, but has come down from the spiced cookery of medieval Europe and Western Asia. The medieval spiced dishes in question were even coloured like curry. Turmeric, indeed, called by Garcia de Orta, *Indian saffron*, was yet unknown in Europe, but it was represented by saffron and sandalwood. A notable incident occurs in the old English poem of King Richard, wherein the Lion-heart feasts on the head of a Saracen—

"soden full hastily
With powder and with spysory,
And with saffron of good colour."

Moreover, there is hardly room for doubt that *capsicum* or red pepper (see **CHILLY**) was introduced into India by the Portuguese (see *Hanbury and Flückiger*, 407); and this spice constitutes the most important ingredient in modern curries. The Sanskrit books of cookery, which cannot be of any considerable antiquity, contain many recipes for curry without this ingredient. A recipe for curry (*caril*) is given, according to Bluteau, in the Portuguese *Arte de Cozinha*, p. 101. This must be of the 17th century.

It should be added that *kari* was, among the people of S. India, the name of only one form of 'kitchen' for rice, viz. of that in consistency resembling broth, as several of the earlier quotations indicate. Europeans have applied it to all the savoury concoctions of analogous spicy character eaten with rice. These may be divided into three classes—viz. (1), that just noticed; (2), that in the form of a stew of meat, fish or vegetables; (3), that called by Europeans 'dry curry.' These form the successive courses of a Hindu meal in S. India, and have in the vernaculars several discriminating names.

In Java the Dutch, in their employment of curry, keep much nearer to the original Hindu practice. At a breakfast, it is common to hand round with the rice a dish divided into many sectoral spaces, each of which contains a different kind of curry, more or less liquid.

According to the *Fankwae at Canton* (1882), the word is used at the Chinese ports (we presume in talking with Chinese servants) in the form **käärle** (p. 62).

1502.—"Then the Captain-major commanded them to cut off the hands and ears of all the crews, and put all that into one of the small vessels, into which he ordered them to put the friar, also without ears or nose or hands, which he ordered to be strung round his neck with a palm-leaf for the King, on which he told him to have a curry (**caril**) made to eat of what his friar brought him."—*Correa, Three Voyages*, Hak. Soc. 331. The "Friar" was a Brahman, in the dress of a friar, to whom the odious ruffian Vasco da Gama had given a safe-conduct.

1563.—"They made dishes of fowl and flesh, which they call **caril**."—*Garcia*, f. 68.

c. 1580.—"The victual of these (renegade soldiers) is like that of the barbarous people; that of Moors all *bringe* [*birinj*, 'rice']; that of Gentoos rice-**carril**."—*Primor e Honra*, &c., f. 9*v*.

1598.—"Most of their fish is eaten with rice, which they seeth in broth, which they put upon the rice, and is somewhat soure, as if it were sodden in gooseberries, or unripe grapes, but it tasteth well, and is called **Carriel** [v.l. **Carriil**], which is their daily meat."—*Linschoten*, 88; [Hak. Soc. ii. 11]. This is a good description of the ordinary tamarind curry of S. India.

1606.—"Their ordinary food is boiled rice with many varieties of certain soups which they pour upon it, and which in those parts are commonly called **caril**."—*Gouvea*, 61*b*.

1608-1610.—". . . me disoit qu'il y auoit plus de 40 ans, qu'il estoit esclaue, et auoit gagné bon argent à celuy qui le possedoit; et toute fois qu'il ne luy donnoit pour tout viure qu'vne mesure de riz cru par iour sans autre chose . . . et quelquefois deux *baseruques*, qui sont quelque deux deniers (see **BUDGROOK**), pour auoir du **Caril** à mettre auec le riz."—*Mocquet, Voyages*, 337.

1623.—"In India they give the name of **caril** to certain messes made with butter, with the kernel of the coco-nut (in place of which might be used in our part of the world milk of almonds) . . . with spiceries of every kind, among the rest cardamom and ginger . . . with vegetables, fruits, and a thousand other condiments of sorts; . . . and the Christians, who eat everything, put in also flesh or fish of every kind, and sometimes eggs . . . with all which things they make a kind of broth in the fashion of our *guazzetti* (or hotch-potches) . . . and this broth with all the said condiments in it they pour over a good quantity of rice boiled simply with water and salt, and the whole makes a most savoury and substantial mess."—*P. della Valle*, ii. 709; [Hak. Soc. ii. 328.]

1681.—"Most sorts of these delicious Fruits they gather before they be ripe, and boyl them to make **Carrees**, to use the Portuguese word, that is somewhat to eat with and relish their Rice."—*Knox*, p. 12. This perhaps indicates that the English *curry* is formed from the Port. *caris*, plural of *caril*.

c. 1690.—"Curcuma in Indiâ tam ad cibum quam ad medecinam adhibetur, Indi enim . . . adeo ipsi adsueti sunt ut cum cunctis admiscent condimentis et piscibus, praesertim autem isti quod **karri** ipsis vocatur."—*Rumphius*, Pars Vta. p. 166.

c. 1759-60.—"The **currees** are infinitely various, being a sort of fricacees to eat with rice, made of any animals or vegetables."—*Grose*, i. 150.

1781.—"To-day have **curry** and rice for my dinner, and plenty of it as C——, my messmate, has got the gripes, and cannot eat his share."—*Hon. J. Lindsay's Imprisonment*, in *Lives of Lindsays*, iii. 296.

1794-97.—

"The Bengal squad he fed so wondrous nice,
Baring his **currie** took, and Scott his rice."

Pursuits of Literature, 5th ed., p. 287.

This shows that **curry** was not a domesticated dish in England at the date of publication. It also is a sample of what the wit was that ran through so many editions!

c. 1830.—"J'ai substitué le lait à l'eau pour boisson . . . c'est une sorte de contre-poison pour l'essence de feu que forme la sauce enragée de mon sempiternel cari."—*Jacquemont, Correspondance*, i. 196.

1848.—"Now we have seen how Mrs. Sedley had prepared a fine **curry** for her son."—*Vanity Fair*, ch. iv.

1860.—". . . Vegetables, and especially farinaceous food, are especially to be commended. The latter is indeed rendered attractive by the unrivalled excellence of the Singhalese in the preparation of innumerable **curries**, each tempered by the delicate creamy juice expressed from the flesh of the cocoa-nut, after it has been reduced to a pulp."—*Tennent's Ceylon*, i. 77. N.B. Tennent is misled in supposing (i. 437) that chillies are mentioned in the Mahavanso. The word is *maricha*, which simply means "pepper," and which Turnour has translated erroneously (p. 158).

1874.—"The craving of the day is for quasi-intellectual food, not less highly peppered than the **curries** which gratify the faded stomach of a returned Nabob."—*Blackwood's Magazine*, Oct. 434.

The Dutch use the word as **Kerrie** or **Karrie**; and **Kari** *à l'Indienne* has a place in French cartes.

CURRY-STUFF, s. Onions, chillies, &c.; the usual material for preparing curry, otherwise **mussalla** (q.v.), represented in England by the preparations called *curry-powder* and *curry-paste*.

1860.—". . . with plots of esculents and **curry-stuffs** of every variety, onions, chillies, yams, cassavas, and sweet potatoes."—*Tennent's Ceylon*, i. 463.

CUSBAH, s. Ar.—H. *ḳaṣba, ḳaṣaba*; the chief place of a **pergunnah** (q.v.).

1548.—"And the **caçabe** of *Tanaa* is rented at 4450 *pardaos*."—*S. Botelho, Tombo*, 150.

[c. 1590.—"In the fortieth year of his Majesty's reign, his dominions consisted of one hundred and five *Sircars*, sub-divided into two thousand seven hundred and thirty-seven **kusbahs**."—*Ayeen*, tr. *Gladwin*, ii. 1; *Jarrett*, ii. 115.]

1644.—"On the land side are the houses of the Vazador (?) or Possessor of the **Casabe**, which is as much as to say the town or *aldea* of Mombaym (**Bombay**). This town of Mombaym is a small and scattered affair."—*Bocarro, MS.* fol. 227.

c. 1844-45.—"In the centre of the large **Cusbah** of Streevygoontum exists an old mud fort, or rather wall of about 20 feet high, surrounding some 120 houses of a body of people calling themselves *Kotie Vellalas*,—that is 'Fort Vellalas.' Within this wall no police officer, warrant or Peon ever enters. . . . The females are said to be kept in a state of great degradation and ignorance. They never pass without the walls alive; when dead they are carried out by night in sacks."—Report by *Mr. E. B. Thomas*, Collector of Tinnevelly, quoted in *Lord Stanhope's Miscellanies*, 2nd Series, 1872, p. 132.

CUSCUSS, CUSS, s. Pers.—H. *khaskhas*. The roots of a grass [called in N. India *senthā* or *tīn*,] which abounds in the drier parts of India, *Anatherum muricatum* (Beauv.), *Andropogon muricatus* (Retz), used in India during the hot dry winds to make screens, which are kept constantly wet, in the window openings, and the fragrant evaporation from which greatly cools the house (see **TATTY**). This device seems to be ascribed by Abul Fazl to the invention of Akbar. These roots are well known in France by the name *vetyver*, which is the Tam. name *veṭṭivēru*, 'the root which is dug up.' In some of the N. Indian vernaculars *khaskhas* is 'a poppy-head'; [but this is a different word, Skt. *khaskhasa*, and compare P. *khashkhash*].

c. 1590.—"But they (the Hindus) were notorious for the want of cold water, the intolerable heat of their climate. . . . His Majesty remedied all these evils and defects. He taught them how to cool water by the help of saltpetre. . . . He ordered mats to be woven of a cold odoriferous root called **Khuss** . . . and when wetted with water on the outside, those within enjoy a pleasant cool air in the height of summer."—*Ayeen* (*Gladwin*, 1800), ii. 196; [ed. *Jarrett*, iii. 9].

1663.—"**Kas** *kanays*." See quotation under **TATTY**.

1810.—"The **Kuss-Kuss** . . . when fresh, is rather fragrant, though the scent is somewhat terraceous."—*Williamson, V. M.* i. 235.

1824.—"We have tried to keep our rooms cool with 'tatties,' which are mats formed of the **Kuskos**, a peculiar sweet-scented grass. . . ."—*Heber*, ed. 1844, i. 59.

It is curious that the coarse grass which covers the more naked parts of the Islands of the Indian Archipelago appears to be called *kusu-kusu* (*Wallace*, 2nd ed. ii. 74). But we know not if there is any community of origin in these names.

[1832.—"The sirrakee (*sirkī*) and sainturh (*senthā*) are two specimens of one genus of jungle grass, the roots of which are called secundah (*sirkanda*) or **khus-khus.**"—*Mrs. Meer Hasan Ali, Observations*, &c., ii. 208.]

In the sense of poppy-seed or poppy-head, this word is P.; De Orta says Ar.; [see above.]

1563.—". . . at Cambaiete, seeing in the market that they were selling poppy-heads big enough to fill a *canada*, and also some no bigger than ours, and asking the name, I was told that it was *caxcax* (**cashcash**)—and that in fact is the name in Arabic—and they told me that of these poppies was made opium (*amfião*), cuts being made in the poppy-head, so that the opium exudes."—*Garcia De Orta*, f. 155.

1621.—"The 24th of April public proclamation was made in Ispahan by the King's order . . . that on pain of death, no one should drink *cocnur*, which is a liquor made from the husk of the capsule of opium, called by them **khash-khash.**"—*P. della Valle*, ii. 209; [*cocnur* is P. *koknār*].

CUSPADORE, s. An old term for a spittoon. Port. *cuspadeira*, from *cuspir*, [Lat. *conspuere*], to spit. *Cuspidor* would be properly *qui multum spuit*.

[1554.—Speaking of the greatness of the Sultan of Bengal, he says to illustrate it—"From the camphor which goes with his spittle when he spits into his gold spittoon (**cospidor**) his chamberlain has an income of 2000 cruzados."—*Castanheda*, Bk. iv. ch. 83.]

1672.—"Here maintain themselves three of the most powerful lords and Naiks of this kingdom, who are subject to the Crown of Velour, and pay it tribute of many hundred Pagodas . . . viz. *Vitipa-naik* of *Madura*, the King's **Cuspidoor**-bearer, 200 Pagodas, *Cristapa-naik* of *Chengier*, the King's *Betel*-server, 200 pagodas, the *Naik* of *Tanjouwer*, the King's Warder and Umbrella carrier, 400 Pagodas. . . ."—*Baldaeus*, Germ. ed. 153.

1735.—In a list of silver plate we have "5 **cuspadores.**"—*Wheeler*, iii. 139.

1775.—"Before each person was placed a large brass salver, a black earthen pot of water, and a brass **cuspadore.**"—*Forrest, V. to N. Guinea*, &c. (at Magindanao), 235.

[1900.—"The royal **cuspadore**" is mentioned among the regalia at Selangor, and a "**cuspadore**" (*ketor*) is part of the marriage appliances.—*Skeat, Malay Magic*, 26, 374.]

CUSTARD-APPLE, s. The name in India of a fruit (*Anona squamosa*, L.) originally introduced from S. America, but which spread over India during the 16th century. Its commonest name in Hindustan is *sharīfa*, *i.e.* 'noble'; but it is also called *Sītap'hal*, *i.e.* 'the Fruit of Sītā,' whilst another *Anona* ('bullock's heart,' *A. reticulata*, L., the custard-apple of the W. Indies, where both names are applied to it) is called in the south by the name of her husband *Rāma*. And the *Sītap'hal* and *Rāmp'hal* have become the subject of Hindu legends (see *Forbes, Or. Mem.* iii. 410). The fruit is called in Chinese *Fan-li-chi*, *i.e.* foreign **leechee.**

A curious controversy has arisen from time to time as to whether this fruit and its congeners were really imported from the New World, or were indigenous in India. They are not mentioned among Indian fruits by Baber (c. A.D. 1530), but the translation of the *Āīn* (c. 1590) by Prof. Blochmann contains among the "Sweet Fruits of Hindustan," *Custard-apple* (p. 66). On referring to the original, however, the word is *sadāp'hal* (*fructus perennis*), a Hind. term for which Shakespear gives many applications, not one of them the *anona*. The *bel* is one (*Aegle marmelos*), and seems as probable as any (see **BAEL**). The custard-apple is not mentioned by Garcia de Orta (1563), Linschoten (1597), or even by P. della Valle (1624). It is not in Bontius (1631), nor in Piso's commentary on Bontius (1658), but is described as an American product in the West Indian part of Piso's book, under the Brazilian name *Araticu*. Two species are described as common by P. Vincenzo Maria, whose book was published in 1672. Both the custard-apple and the sweet-sop are fruits now generally diffused in India; but of their having been imported from the New World, the name *Anona*, which we find in Oviedo to have been the native West Indian name of one of the species, and which in various corrupted shapes is applied to them over different parts of the East, is an indication. Crawfurd, it is true, in his Malay Dictionary explains *nona* or *buah-* ("fruit") *nona* in its application to the custard-apple as *fructus virginalis*, from *nona*, the term applied in the Malay countries (like *missy* in India) to an unmarried European lady. But in the face of the American word this becomes out of the question.

It is, however, a fact that among the Bharhut sculptures, among the carvings dug up at Muttra by General Cunningham, and among the copies from wall-paintings at Ajanta (as pointed out by Sir G. Birdwood in 1874, (see *Athenaeum*, 26th October), [*Bombay Gazetteer*, xii. 490]) there is a fruit represented which is certainly very like a custard-apple (though an abnormally big one), and not very like anything else yet pointed out. General Cunningham is convinced that it is a custard-apple, and urges in corroboration of his view that the Portuguese in introducing the fruit (which he does not deny) were merely bringing coals to Newcastle; that he has found extensive tracts in various parts of India covered with the wild custard-apple; and also that this fruit bears an indigenous Hindi name, *ātā* or *āt*, from the Sanskrit *ātripya*.

It seems hard to pronounce about this *ātripya*. A very high authority, Prof. Max Müller, to whom we once referred, doubted whether the word (meaning 'delightful') ever existed in real Sanskrit. It was probably an artificial name given to the fruit, and he compared it aptly to the factitious Latin of *aureum malum* for "orange," though the latter word really comes from the Sanskrit *nāranga*. On the other hand, *ātripya* is quoted by Rāja Rādhakant Deb, in his Sanskrit dictionary, from a medieval work, the *Dravyaguna*. And the question would have to be considered how far the MSS. of such a work are likely to have been subject to modern interpolation. Sanskrit names have certainly been invented for many objects which were unknown till recent centuries. Thus, for example, Williams gives more than one word for *cactus*, or prickly pear, a class of plants which was certainly introduced from America (see *Vidara* and *Viśvasaraka*, in his Skt. Dictionary).

A new difficulty, moreover, arises as to the indigenous claims of *ātā*, which is the name for the fruit in Malabar as well as in Upper India. For, on turning for light to the splendid works of the Dutch ancients, Rheede and Rumphius, we find in the former (*Hortus Malabaricus*, part iv.) a reference to a certain author, 'Recchus de Plantis Mexicanis,' as giving a drawing of a custard-apple tree, the name of which in Mexico was *ahaté* or *até*, "fructu apud Mexicanos praecellenti arbor nobilis" (the expressions are noteworthy, for the popular Hindustani name of the fruit is *sharīfa* = "nobilis"). We also find in a Manilla Vocabulary that *ate* or *atte* is the name of this fruit in the Philippines. And from Rheede we learn that in Malabar the *ātā* was sometimes called by a native name meaning "the Manilla jack-fruit"; whilst the *Anona reticulata*, or sweet-sop, was called by the Malabars "the *Parangi* (*i.e. Firingi* or Portuguese) jack-fruit."

These facts seem to indicate that probably the *ātā* and its name came to India from Mexico *viâ* the Philippines, whilst the *anona* and its name came to India from Hispaniola *viâ* the Cape. In the face of these probabilities the argument of General Cunningham from the existence of the tree in a wild state loses force. The fact is undoubted and may be corroborated by the following passage from "*Observations on the nature of the Food of the Inhabitants of South India*," 1864, p. 12:—"I have seen it stated in a botanical work that this plant (*Anona sq.*) is not indigenous, but introduced from America, or the W. Indies. If so, it has taken most kindly to the soil of the Deccan, for the jungles are full of it": [also see *Watt, Econ. Dict.* ii. 259 *seq.*, who supports the foreign origin of the plant]. The author adds that the wild custard-apples saved the lives of many during famine in the Hyderabad country. But on the other hand, the *Argemone Mexicana*, a plant of unquestioned American origin, is now one of the most familiar weeds all over India. The cashew (*Anacardium occidentale*), also of American origin, and carrying its American name with it to India, not only forms tracts of jungle now (as Sir G. Birdwood has stated) in Canara and the Concan (and, as we may add from personal knowledge, in Tanjore), but was described by P. Vincenzo Maria, more than two hundred and twenty years ago, as then abounding in the wilder tracts of the western coast.

The question raised by General Cunningham is an old one, for it is alluded to by Rumphius, who ends by leaving it in doubt. We cannot say that we have seen any satisfactory suggestion of another (Indian) plant as that represented in the ancient sculpture of Bharhut. [Dr. Watt says: "They may prove to be conventional representations of the jack-fruit tree or some other allied plant; they are not unlike the flower-heads of the sacred *kadamba* or *Anthocephalus*," (*loc. cit.* i. 260)]. But it is well to get rid of fallacious arguments on either side.

In the "*Materia Medica of the Hindus* by Udoy Chand Dutt, with a Glossary by G. King, M.B., Calc. 1877," we find the following synonyms given:—

"*Anona squamosa:* Skt. *Gandagatra;* Beng. *Ātā;* Hind. *Sharīfa*, and *Sītāphal.*"

"*Anona reticulata:* Skt. *Lavali;* Beng. *Lonā.*" *

1672.—"The plant of the *Atta* in 4 or 5 years comes to its greatest size . . . the fruit . . . under the rind is divided into so many wedges, corresponding to the external compartments. . . The pulp is very white, tender, delicate, and so delicious that it unites to agreeable sweetness a most delightful fragrance like rose-water . . . and if presented to one unacquainted with it he would certainly take it for a blamange. . . . The *Anona*," &c., &c.—*P. Vincenzo Maria*, pp. 346-7.

1690.—"They (Hindus) feed likewise upon Pine-Apples, **Custard-apples**, so called because they resemble a Custard in Colour and Taste. . . ."—*Ovington*, 303.

c. 1830.—". . . the **custard-apple**, like russet bags of cold pudding."—*Tom Cringle's Log*, ed. 1863, p. 140.

1878.—"The gushing **custard-apple** with its crust of stones and luscious pulp."—*Ph Robinson, In my Indian Garden*, [49].

CUSTOM, s. Used in Madras as the equivalent of **Dustoor**, **Dustoory**, of which it is a translation. Both words illustrate the origin of *Customs* in the solemn revenue sense.

1683.—"Threder and Barker positively denied ye overweight, ye Merchants proved it by their books; but ye skeyne out of every draught was confest, and claimed as their due, having been always the **custom**."—*Hedges, Diary*, Hak. Soc. i. 83.

1768-71.—"Banyans, who . . . serve in this capacity without any fixed pay, but they know how much more they may charge upon every rupee, than they have in reality paid, and this is called **costumado**."—*Stavorinus*, E.T., i. 522.

CUSTOMER, s. Used in old books of Indian trade for the native official who exacted duties. [The word was in common use in England from 1448 to 1748; see *N.E.D.*]

[1609.—"His houses . . . are seized on by the **Customer**."—*Danvers, Letters*, i. 25; and comp. *Foster, ibid.* ii. 225.

[1615.—"The **Customer** should come and visitt them."—*Sir T. Roe*, Hak. Soc. i. 44.]

1682.—"The several affronts, insolences, and abuses dayly put upon us by Boolchund, our chief **Customer**.—*Hedges, Diary*, [Hak. Soc. i. 33].

CUTCH, s. See **CATECHU**.

CUTCH, n.p. Properly *Kachchh*, a native State in the West of India, immediately adjoining Sind, the Rājput ruler of which is called the *Rāo*. The name does not occur, as far as we have found, in any of the earlier Portuguese writers, nor in Linschoten, [but the latter mentions the gulf under the name of *Jaqueta* (Hak. Soc. i. 56 *seq.*)]. The Skt. word *kachchha* seems to mean a morass or low, flat land.

c. 1030.—"At this place (Mansura) the river (Indus) divides into two streams, one empties itself into the sea in the neighbourhood of the city of Lúhárání, and the other branches off to the east to the borders of **Kach**."—*Al-Birūnī*, in *Elliot*, i. 49.

Again, "**Kach**, the country producing gum" (*i.e. mukal* or *bdellium*), p. 66.

The port mentioned in the next three extracts was probably *Mandavi* (this name is said to signify "Custom-House"; [*mandwī*, 'a temporary hut,' is a term commonly applied to a bazaar in N. India].

1611.—"**Cuts**-*nagore*, a place not far from the River of Zinde."—*Nic. Dounton*, in *Purchas*, i. 307.

[1612.—"The other ship which proved of **Cuts**-*nagana*."—*Danvers, Letters*, i. 179.]

c. 1615.—"Francisco Sodre . . . who was serving as captain-major of the fortress of Dio, went to **Cache**, with twelve ships and a *sanguicel*, to inflict chastisement for the arrogance and insolence of these blacks ("... *pela soberbia e desaforos d'estes negros.* . . ."—"Of these niggers!"), thinking that he might do it as easily as Gaspar de Mello had punished those of Por."—*Bocarro*, 257.

[c. 1661.—"Dara . . . traversing with speed the territories of the Raja **Katche** soon reached the province of Guzarate. . . ."—*Bernier*, ed. *Constable*, 73.]

1727.—"The first town on the south side of the Indus is **Cutch**-*naggen*."—*A. Hamilton*, i. 131; [ed. 1744].

* Sir Joseph Hooker observes that the use of the terms Custard-apple, Bullock's heart, and Sweet-sop has been so indiscriminate or uncertain that it is hardly possible to use them with unquestionable accuracy.

CUTCH GUNDAVA, n.p. *Kachchh Gandāva* or *Kachchī*, a province of Biluchistan, under the Khan of Kela't, adjoining our province of Sind; a level plain, subject to inordinate heat in summer, and to the visitation of the *simūm.* Across the northern part of this plain runs the railway from Sukkur to Sibi. *Gandāva*, the chief place, has been shown by Sir H. Elliot to be the *Kandābīl* or *Kandhābel* of the Arab geographers of the 9th and 10th centuries. The name in its modern shape, or what seems intended for the same, occurs in the Persian version of the *Chachnāmah*, or H. of the Conquest of Sind, made in A.D. 1216 (see *Elliot*, i. 166).

CUTCHA, KUTCHA, adj. Hind. *kachchā*, 'raw, crude, unripe, uncooked.' This word is with its opposite *pakkā* (see **PUCKA**) among the most constantly recurring Anglo-Indian colloquial terms, owing to the great variety of metaphorical applications of which both are susceptible. The following are a few examples only, but they will indicate the manner of use better than any attempt at comprehensive definition:—

A **cutcha** *Brick* is a sun-dried brick.	A **pucka** *Brick* is a properly kiln-burnt brick.
,, *House* is built of mud, or of sun-dried brick.	,, *House* is of burnt brick or stone with lime, and generally with a terraced plaster roof.
,, *Road* is earthwork only.	,, *Road* is a Macadamised one.
,, *Appointment* is acting or temporary.	,, *Appointment* is permanent.
,, *Settlement* is one where the land is held without lease.	,, *Settlement* is one fixed for a term of years.
,, *Account* or *Estimate*, is one which is rough, superficial, and untrustworthy.	,, *Account*, or *Estimate*, is carefully made, and claiming to be relied on.
,, *Maund*, or *Seer*, is the smaller, where two weights are in use, as often happens.	,, *Maund*, or *Seer*, is the larger of two in use.
,, *Major* is a brevet or local Major.	,, *Major*, is a regimental Major.
,, *Colour* is one that won't wash.	,, *Colour*, is one that will wash.
,, *Fever* is a simple ague or a light attack.	,, *Fever*, is a dangerous remittent or the like (what the Italians call *pernizziosa*).
,, *Pice* generally means one of those amorphous coppers, current in up-country bazars at varying rates of value.	,, *Pice*; a double copper coin formerly in use; also a proper pice (=¼ anna) from the Govt. mints.
,, *Coss*—see analogy under *Maund* above.	,, *Coss*—see under *Maund* above.
,, *Roof*. A roof of mud laid on beams; or of thatch, &c.	,, *Roof*; a terraced roof made with cement.
,, *Scoundrel*, a limp and fatuous knave.	,, *Scoundrel*, one whose motto is "Thorough."
,, *Seam* (*silāī*) is the tailor's tack for trying on.	,, *Seam* is the definite stitch of the garment.

1763.—"Il parait que les **catcha** cosses sont plus en usage que les autres cosses dans le gouvernement du Decan."—*Lettres Edifiantes*, xv. 190.

1863.—"In short, in America, where they cannot get a *pucka* railway they take a **kutcha** one instead. This, I think, is what we must do in India."—*Lord Elgin*, in *Letters and Journals*, 432.

Captain Burton, in a letter dated Aug. 26, 1879, and printed in the "*Academy*" (p. 177), explains the gypsy word *gorgio*, for a Gentile or non-Rommany, as being **kachhā** or **cutcha.** This may be, but it does not carry conviction.

CUTCHA-PUCKA, adj. This term is applied in Bengal to a mixt kind of building in which burnt brick is used, but which is cemented with mud instead of lime-mortar.

CUTCHÉRRY, and in Madras **CUTCHERY**, s. An office of administration, a court-house. Hind. *kachahrī*; used also in Ceylon. The word is not usually now, in Bengal, applied to a merchant's counting-house, which is called **dufter**, but it *is* applied to the office of an Indigo-Planter or a Zemindar, the business in which is more like that of a Magistrate's or Collector's Office. In the service of Tippoo Sahib **cutcherry** was used in peculiar senses besides the ordinary one. In the civil administration it seems to have been used for something like what we should now call *Department* (see *e.g. Tippoo's Letters,* 292); and in the army for a division or large brigade (*e.g. ibid.* 332; and see under **JYSHE** and quotation from *Wilks* below).

1610.—"Over against this seat is the **Cichery** or Court of Rolls, where the King's Viseer sits every morning some three houres, by whose hands passe all matters of Rents, Grants, Lands, Firmans, Debts, &c."—*Hawkins,* in *Purchas,* i. 439.

1673.—"At the lower End the Royal Exchange or **Queshery** . . . opens its folding doors."—*Fryer,* 261.

[1702. — "But not makeing an early escape themselves were carried into the **Cacherra** or publick Gaol."—*Hedges, Diary,* Hak. Soc. ii. cvi.]

1763. — "The Secretary acquaints the Board that agreeably to their orders of the 9th May, he last Saturday attended the Court of **Cutcherry**, and acquainted the Members with the charge the President of the Court had laid against them for non-attendance."—In *Long,* 316.

,, "The protection of our Gomastahs and servants from the oppression and jurisdiction of the Zemindars and their **Cutcherries** has been ever found to be a liberty highly essential both to the honour and interest of our nation."—From the Chief and Council at Dacca, in *Van Sittart,* i. 247.

c. 1765.—"We can truly aver that during almost five years that we presided in the **Cutchery** Court of *Calcutta,* never any murder or atrocious crime came before us but it was proved in the end a *Bramin* was at the bottom of it."—*Holwell, Interesting Historical Events,* Pt. II. 152.

1783.—"The moment they find it true that the English Government shall remain as it is, they will divide sugar and sweetmeats among all the people in the **Cutcheree**; then every body will speak sweet words."—*Native Letter,* in *Forbes, Or. Mem.* iv. 227.

1786.—"You must not suffer any one to come to your house; and whatever business you may have to do, let it be transacted in our **Kuchurry**."—*Tippoo's Letters,* 303.

1791.—"At Seringapatam General Matthews was in confinement. James Skurry was sent for one day to the **Kutcherry** there, and some pewter plates with marks on them were shown to him to explain; he saw on them words to this purport, 'I am indebted to the Malabar Christians on account of the Public Service 40,000 Rs.; the Company owes me (about) 30,000 Rs.; I have taken *Poison* and am now within a short time of *Death;* whoever communicates this to the Bombay Govt. or to my wife will be amply rewarded. (Signed) Richard Matthews.'"—*Narrative of Mr. William Drake, and other Prisoners* (in Mysore), in *Madras Courier,* 17th Nov.

c. 1796.—". . . the other Asof Mirán Hussein, was a low fellow and a debauchee, . . . who in different . . . towns was carried in his pálkí on the shoulders of dancing girls as ugly as demons to his **Kutcheri** or hall of audience."—*H. of Tipú Sultán,* E.T. by *Miles,* 246.

,, ". . . the favour of the Sultan towards that worthy man (Dundia Wágh) still continued to increase . . . but although, after a time, a **Kutcheri**, or brigade, was named after him, and orders were issued for his release, it was to no purpose."—*Ibid.* 248.

[c. 1810.—"Four appears to have been the fortunate number (with Tippoo; four companies (*yeuz*), one battalion (*teep*), four *teeps* one *cushoon* (see **KOSHOON**): . . . four *cushoons,* one **Cutcherry**. The establishment . . . of a *cutcherry* . . . 5,688, but these numbers fluctuated with the Sultaun's caprices, and at one time a *cushoon,* with its cavalry attached, was a legion of about 3,000."—*Wilks, Mysore,* ed. 1869, ii. 132.]

1834.—"I mean, my dear Lady Wroughton, that the man to whom Sir Charles is most heavily indebted, is an officer of his own **Kucheree**, the very sircar who cringes to you every morning for orders."—*The Baboo,* ii. 126.

1860.—"I was told that many years ago, what remained of the Dutch records were removed from the record-room of the Colonial Office to the **Cutcherry** of the Government Agent."—*Tennent's Ceylon,* i. xxviii.

1873.—"I'd rather be out here in a tent any time . . . than be stewing all day in a stuffy **Kutcherry** listening to Ram Buksh and Co. perjuring themselves till they are nearly white in the face."—*The True Reformer,* i. 4.

1883.—"Surrounded by what seemed to me a mob of natives, with two or three dogs at his feet, talking, writing, dictating,—in short doing **Cutcherry**."—*C. Raikes,* in *Bosworth Smith's Lord Lawrence,* i. 59.

CUTCHNAR, s. Hind. *kachnār,* Skt. *kānchanāra* (*kānchana,* 'gold') the beautiful flowering tree *Bauhinia variegata,* L., and some other species of the same genus (N. O. *Leguminosae*).

1855. — "Very good fireworks were exhibited . . . among the best was a sort of maypole hung round with minor fireworks which went off in a blaze and roll of smoke, leaving disclosed a tree hung with quivering flowers of purple flame, evidently intended to represent the **Kachnar** of the Burmese forests."—*Yule, Mission to Ava,* 95.

CUTTACK, n.p. The chief city of Orissa, and district immediately attached. From Skt. *kataka*, 'an army, a camp, a royal city.' This name *Al-kataka* is applied by Ibn Batuta in the 14th century to Deogīr in the Deccan (iv. 46), or at least to a part of the town adjoining that ancient fortress.

c. 1567.—"Citta di **Catheca**."—*Cesare Federici*, in *Ramusio*, iii. 392. [**Catecha**, in *Hakl.* ii. 358].

[c. 1590.—"Attock on the Indus is called *Atak Benares* in contra distinction to *Katak Benares* in Orissa at the opposite extremity of the Empire."—*Āīn*, ed. *Jarrett*, ii. 311.]

1633.—"The 30 of April we set forward in the Morning for the City of **Coteka** (it is a city of seven miles in compasse, and it standeth a mile from Malcandy where the Court is kept."—*Bruton*, in *Hakl.* v. 49.

1726.—"**Cattek**."—*Valentijn*, v. 158.

CUTTANEE, s. Some kind of piece-goods, apparently either of silk or mixed silk and cotton. *Kuttān*, Pers., is flax or linen cloth. This is perhaps the word. [*Kattan* is now used in India for the waste selvage in silk weaving, which is sold to Patwas, and used for stringing ornaments, such as *joshans* (armlets of gold or silver beads) *bāzūbands* (armlets with folding bands), &c. (*Yusuf Ali, Mon. on Silk Fabrics*, 66).] **Cutanees** appear in Milburn's list of Calcutta piece-goods.

[1598.—"**Cotonias**, which are like canvas." —*Linschoten*, Hak. Soc. i. 60.]

[1648. — "**Contenijs**." See under **ALCATIF**.

[1673.—"**Cuttanee** breeches." See under **ATLAS**.

[1690.—". . . rich Silks, such as Atlasses, **Cuttanees**. . . ."—See under **ALLEJA**.

[1734. — "They manufacture . . . in cotton and silk called **Cuttenees**."—*A. Hamilton*, i. 126; ed. 1744.]

CUTTRY. See **KHUTTRY**.

CYRUS, SYRAS, SARUS, &c. A common corruption of Hind. *sāras*, [Skt. *sarasa*, the 'lake bird,'] or (corruptly) *sārhans*, the name of the great gray crane, *Grus Antigone*, L., generally found in pairs, held almost sacred in some parts of India, and whose "fine trumpet-like call, uttered when alarmed or on the wing, can be heard a couple of miles off" (*Jerdon*). [The British soldier calls the bird a "*Serious*," and is fond of shooting him for the pot.]

1672. — ". . . peculiarly Brand-geese, Colum [see **COOLUNG**], and **Serass**, a species of the former."—*Fryer*, 117.

1807.—"The *argeelah* as well as the **cyrus**, and all the aquatic tribe are extremely fond of snakes, which they . . . swallow down their long throats with great despatch."—*Williamson, Or. Field Sports*, 27.

[1809.—"**Saros**." See under **COOLUNG**.]

1813.—In Forbes's *Or. Mem.* (ii. 277 *seqq.*; [2nd ed. i. 502 *seqq.*]), there is a curious story of a **Cyrus** or **Sahras** (as he writes it) which Forbes had tamed in India, and which nine years afterwards recognised its master when he visited General Conway's menagerie at Park Place near Henley.

1840.—"Bands of gobbling pelicans" (see this word, probably **ADJUTANTS** are meant) "and groups of tall **cyruses** in their half-Quaker, half-lancer plumage, consulted and conferred together, in seeming perplexity as to the nature of our intentions." —*Mrs. Mackenzie, Storms and Sunshine of a Soldier's Life*, i. 108.

D

DABUL, n.p. *Dābhol*. In the later Middle Ages a famous port of the Konkan, often coupled with **Choul** (q.v.), carrying on extensive trade with the West of Asia. It lies in the modern dist. of Ratnagiri, in lat. 17° 34′, on the north bank of the Anjanwel or Vashishti R. In some maps (*e.g.* A. Arrowsmith's of 1816, long the standard map of India), and in W. Hamilton's *Gazetteer*, it is confounded with Dāpoli, 12 m. north, and not a seaport.

c. 1475.—"**Dabyl** is also a very extensive seaport, where many horses are brought from Mysore,* Rabast [Arabistan? *i.e.* Arabia], Khorassan, Turkistan, Neghostan." —*Nikitin*, p. 20. "It is a very large town, the great meeting-place for all nations living along the coast of India and of Ethiopia."—*Ibid.* 30.

1502.—"The gale abated, and the caravels reached land at **Dabul**, where they rigged their lateen sails, and mounted their artillery."—*Correa, Three Voyages of V. da Gama*, Hak. Soc. 308.

1510.—"Having seen Cevel and its customs, I went to another city, distant from it two days journey, which is called **Dabuli**. . . . There are Moorish merchants here in very great numbers."—*Varthema*, 114.

* *Mysore* is nonsense. As suggested by Sir J. Campbell in the *Bombay Gazetteer, Misr* (Egypt) is probably the word.

1516.—"This **Dabul** has a very good harbour, where there always congregate many Moorish ships from various ports, and especially from Mekkah, Aden, and Ormuz with horses, and from Cambay, Diu, and the Malabar country."—*Barbosa*, 72.

1554.—"23d Voyage, from **Dābul** to Aden."—*The Mohit*, in *J. As. Soc. Beng.*, v. 464.

1572.—See *Camões*, x. 72.

[c. 1665.—"The King of Bijapur has three good ports in this kingdom: these are Rajapur, **Dabhol**, and Kareputtun."—*Tavernier*, ed. *Ball*, i. 181 *seq.*]

DACCA, n.p. Properly *Dhākā*, ['the wood of *ḍhāk* (see **DHAWK**) trees'; the *Imp. Gaz.* suggests Dhakeswarī, 'the concealed goddess']. A city in the east of Bengal, once of great importance, especially in the later Mahommedan history; famous also for the "*Dacca* muslins" woven there, the annual advances for which, prior to 1801, are said to have amounted to £250,000. [*Taylor, Descr. and Hist. Account of the Cotton Manufacture of Dacca in Bengal*]. **Dāka** is throughout Central Asia applied to all muslins imported through Kabul.

c. 1612.—". . . liberos Osmanis assecutus vivos cepit, eosque cum elephantis et omnibus thesauris defuncti, post quam **Daeck** Bengalae metropolim est reversus, misit ad regem."—*De Laet*, quoted by *Blochmann*, *Āīn*, i. 521.

[c. 1617.—"**Dekaka**" in *Sir T. Roe's* List, Hak. Soc. ii. 538.]

c. 1660.—"The same Robbers took *Sultan-Sujah* at **Daka**, to carry him away in their Galeasses to *Rakan*. . . ."—*Bernier*, E.T. 55; [ed. *Constable*, 109].

1665.—"**Daca** is a great Town, that extends itself only in length; every one coveting to have an House by the Ganges side. The length . . . is above two leagues. . . . These Houses are properly no more than paltry Huts built up with *Bambouc's*, and daub'd over with fat Earth."—*Tavernier*, E.T. ii. 55; [ed. *Ball*, i. 128].

1682.—"The only expedient left was for the Agent to go himself in person to the *Nabob* and *Duan* at **Decca**."—*Hedges, Diary*, Oct. 9; [Hak. Soc. i. 33].

DACOIT, DACOO, s. Hind. *dakait*, *ḍākāyat*, *ḍākū*; a robber belonging to an armed gang. The term, being current in Bengal, got into the Penal Code. By law, to constitute *dacoity*, there must be five or more in the gang committing the crime. Beames derives the word from *ḍākna*, 'to shout,' a sense not in Shakespear's Dict. [It is to be found in Platts, and Fallon gives it as used in E. H. It appears to be connected with Skt. *dashṭa*, 'pressed together.']

1810.—"**Decoits**, or water-robbers."—*Williamson, V. M.* ii. 396.

1812.—"**Dacoits**, a species of depredators who infest the country in gangs."—*Fifth Report*, p. 9.

1817.—"The crime of **dacoity**" (that is, robbery by gangs), says Sir Henry Strachey, ". . . has, I believe, increased greatly since the British administration of justice."—*Mill, H. of B. I.*, v. 466.

1834.—"It is a conspiracy! a false warrant!—they are **Dakoos**! **Dakoos**!!"—*The Baboo*, ii. 202.

1872.—"Daroga! Why, what has he come here for? I have not heard of any **dacoity** or murder in the Village."—*Govinda Samanta*, i. 264.

DADNY, s. H. *dādnī*, [P. *dādan*, 'to give']; an advance made to a craftsman, a weaver, or the like, by one who trades in the goods produced.

1678.—"Wee met with Some trouble About ye Investment of Taffaties wch hath Continued ever Since, Soe y^t wee had not been able to give out any **daudne** on Muxadavad Side many weauours absenting themselves. . . ."—*MS. Letter* of 3d June, from *Cassumbazar Factory*, in India Office.

1683.—"Chuttermull and Deepchund, two Cassumbazar merchants this day assured me Mr. Charnock gives out all his new *Sicca Rupees* for **Dadny** at 2 per cent., and never gives the Company credit for more than 1¼ rupee—by which he gains and putts in his own pocket Rupees ¾ per cent. of all the money he pays, which amounts to a great Summe in ye Yeare: at least £1,000 sterling."—*Hedges, Diary*, Oct. 2; [Hak. Soc. i. 121, also see i. 83].

1748.—"The Sets being all present at the Board inform us that last year they dissented to the employment of Fillick Chund, Gosserain, Occore, and Otteram, they being of a different caste, and consequently they could not do business with them, upon which they refused **Dadney**, and having the same objection to make this year, they propose taking their shares of the **Dadney**."—*Ft. William Cons.*, May 23. In *Long*, p. 9.

1772.—"I observe that the Court of Directors have ordered the *gomastahs* to be withdrawn, and the investment to be provided by **Dadney** merchants."—*Warren Hastings* to J. Purling, in *Gleig*, i. 227.

DAGBAIL, s. Hind. from Pers. *dāgh-i-bel*, 'spade-mark.' The line dug to trace out on the ground a camp, or a road or other construction. As the central line of a road, canal, or railroad it is the equivalent of English 'lockspit.'

DAGOBA, s. Singhalese *dāgaba*, from Pali *dhātugabbha*, and Sansk. *dhātu-garbha*, 'Relic-receptacle'; applied to any dome-like Buddhist shrine (see **TOPE**, **PAGODA**). Gen. Cunningham alleges that the *Chaitya* was usually an empty tope dedicated to the Adi-Buddha (or Supreme, of the quasi-Theistic Buddhists), whilst the term *Dhātu-garbha*, or *Dhagoba*, was properly applied only to a *tope* which was an actual relic-shrine, or repository of ashes of the dead (*Bhilsa Topes*, 9). ["The Shan word '*Htat*,' or '*Tat*,' and the Siamese '*Sat-oop*,' for a pagoda placed over portions of Gaudama's body, such as his flesh, teeth, and hair, is derived from the Sanskrit '*Dhātu-garba*,' a relic shrine" (*Hallett, A Thousand Miles*, 308).]

We are unable to say who first introduced the word into European use. It was well known to William von Humboldt, and to Ritter; but it has become more familiar through its frequent occurrence in Fergusson's *Hist. of Architecture*. The only surviving example of the native use of this term on the Continent of India, so far as we know, is in the neighbourhood of the remains of the great Buddhist establishments at Nalanda in Behar. See quotation below.

1806.—"In this irregular excavation are left two **dhagopes**, or solid masses of stone, bearing the form of a cupola."—*Salt, Caves of Salsette*, in *Tr. Lit. Soc. Bo.* i. 47, pub. 1819.

1823.—". . . from the centre of the screens or walls, projects a **daghope**."—*Des. of Caves near Nasick*, by *Lt.-Col. Delamaine* in *As. Journal*, N.S. 1830, vol. iii. 276.

1834.—". . . Mihindu-Kumara . . . preached in that island (Ceylon) the Religion of Buddha, converted the aforesaid King, built **Dagobas** (Dagops, *i.e.* sanctuaries under which the relics or images of Buddha are deposited) in various places."—*Ritter, Asien*, Bd. iii. 1162.

1835.—"The Temple (cave at Nāsik) . . . has no interior support, but a rock-ceiling richly adorned with wheel-ornaments and lions, and in the end-niche a **Dagop** . . ." —*Ibid.* iv. 683.

1836.—"Although the **Dagops**, both from varying size and from the circumstance of their being in some cases independent erections and in others only elements of the internal structure of a temple, have very different aspects, yet their character is universally recognised as that of closed masses devoted to the preservation or concealment of sacred objects."—*W. v. Humboldt, Kawi-Sprache*, i. 144.

1840.—"We performed *pradakshina* round the **Dhagobs**, reclined on the living couches of the devotees of Nirwan."—Letter of *Dr. John Wilson*, in *Life*, 282.

1853.—"At the same time he (Sakya) foresaw that a **dágoba** would be erected to Kantaka on the spot. . . ."—*Hardy, Manual of Buddhism*, 160.

1855.—"All kinds and forms are to be found . . . the bell-shaped pyramid of dead brickwork in all its varieties . . . the bluff knob-like dome of the Ceylon **Dagobas**. . . ."—*Yule, Mission to Ava*, 35.

1872.—"It is a remarkable fact that the line of mounds (at Nalanda in Bihar) still bears the name of '**dagop**' by the country people. Is not this the **dágoba** of the Páli annals?"—*Broadley, Buddh. Remains of Bihār*, in *J.A.S.B.* xli., Pt. i. 305.

DAGON, n.p. A name often given by old European travellers to the place now called Rangoon, from the great Relic-shrine or **dagoba** there, called *Shwé* (Golden) *Dagôn*. Some have suggested that it is a corruption of *dagoba*, but this is merely guesswork. In the Talaing language *tă'kkūn* signifies 'athwart,' and, after the usual fashion, a legend had grown up connecting the name with the story of a tree lying 'athwart the hill-top,' which supernaturally indicated where the sacred relics of one of the Buddhas had been deposited (see *J.A.S.B.* xxviii. 477). Prof. Forchhammer recently (see *Notes on Early Hist. and Geog. of B. Burma*, No. 1) explained the true origin of the name. Towns lying near the sacred site had been known by the successive names of *Asitañña-nagara* and *Ukkalanagara*. In the 12th century the last name disappears and is replaced by *Trikumbha-nagara*, or in Pali form *Tikumbha-nagara*, signifying '3-Hill-city.'* The Kalyāni inscription near Pegu contains both forms. *Tikumbha* gradually in popular utterance became *Tikum*, *Tăkum*, and *Tăkun*, whence **Dagôn**. The classical name of the great Dagoba is *Tikumbha-cheti*, and this is still in daily Burman use.

* *Kumbha* means an earthen pot, and also the "frontal globe on the upper part of the forehead of the elephant." The latter meaning was, according to Prof. Forchhammer, that intended, being applied to the hillocks on which the town stood, because of their form. But the Burmese applied it to 'alms-bowls,' and invented a legend of Buddha and his two disciples having buried their alms-bowls at this spot.

When the original meaning of the word *Tăkum* had been effaced from the memory of the Talaings, they invented the fable alluded to above in connection with the word *tă'kkūn*. [This view has been disputed by Col. Temple (*Ind. Ant.*, Jan. 1893, p. 27). He gives the reading of the Kalyāni inscription as *Tigumpanagara* and goes on to say: "There is more in favour of this derivation (from *dagoba*) than of any other yet produced. Thus we have *dāgaba*, Singhalese, admittedly from *dhātugabbha*, and as far back as the 16th century we have a persistent word *tigumpa* or *digumpa* (*dagon, digon*) in Burma with the same meaning. Until a clear derivation is made out, it is, therefore, not unsafe to say that *dagon* represents some medieval Indian current form of *dhātugabbha*. This view is supported by a word *gompa*, used in the Himālayas about Sikkim for a Buddhist shrine, which looks *primâ facie* like the remains of some such word as *gabbha*, the latter half of the compound *dhātugabbha*. . . . Neither *Trikumbha-nagara* in Skt. nor *Tikumbha-nagara* in Pali would mean 'Three-hill-city,' *kumbha* being in no sense a 'hill' which is *kūta*, and there are not three hills on the site of the Shwe-Dagon Pagoda at Rangoon."]

c. 1546.—"He hath very certaine intelligence, how the Zemindoo hath raised an army, with an intent to fall upon the Towns of **Cosmin** and Dalaa (**DALA**), and to gain all along the rivers of **Digon** and *Meidoo*, the whole Province of *Danapluu*, even to *Ansedaa* (hod. Donabyu and Henzada)."—*F. M. Pinto*, tr. by H. C. 1653, p. 288.

c. 1585.—"After landing we began to walk, on the right side, by a street some 50 paces wide, all along which we saw houses of wood, all gilt, and set off with beautiful gardens in their fashion, in which dwell all the Talapoins, which are their Friars, and the rulers of the *Pagode* or **Varella** of **Dogon**."—*Gasparo Balbi*, f. 96.

c. 1587.—"About two dayes iourney from Pegu there is a Varelle (see **VARELLA**) or Pagode, which is the pilgrimage of the Pegues: it is called **Dogonne**, and is of a wonderfulle bignesse and all gilded from the foot to the toppe."—*R. Fitch*, in *Hakl.* ii. 398, [393].

c. 1755.—**Dagon** and **Dagoon** occur in a paper of this period in *Dalrymple's Oriental Repertory*, i. 141, 177; [Col. Temple adds: "The word is always **Digon** in Flouest's account of his travels in 1786 (*T'aung Pao*, vol. i. *Les Francais en Birmanie au xviiie Siècle. passim*). It is always **Digon** (except once: "**Digone** capitale del Pegù," p. 149) in Quirini's *Vità di Monsignor G. M. Percoto*, 1781; and it is **Digon** in a map by Antonio Zultae e figli Venezia, 1785. Symes, *Embassy to Ava*, 1803 (pp. 18, 23) has **Dagon**. Crawfurd, 1829, *Embassy to Ava* (pp. 346-7), calls it **Dagong**. There is further a curious word, "Too **Degon**," in one of Mortier's maps, 1740."]

DAIBUL, n.p. See **DIULSIND**.

DAIMIO, s. A feudal prince in Japan. The word appears to be approximately the Jap. pronunciation of Chin. *taiming*, 'great name.' ["The Daimyōs were the territorial lords and barons of feudal Japan. The word means literally 'great name.' Accordingly, during the Middle Ages, warrior chiefs of less degree, corresponding, as one might say, to our knights or baronets, were known by the correlative title of *Shōmyō*, that is, 'small name.' But this latter fell into disuse. Perhaps it did not sound grand enough to be welcome to those who bore it" (*Chamberlain, Things Japanese*, 101 *seq.*).]

DAISEYE, s. This word, representing *Desai*, repeatedly occurs in Kirkpatrick's *Letters of Tippoo* (*e.g.* p. 196) for a local chief of some class. See **DESSAYE**.

DALA, n.p. This is now a town on the (west) side of the river of Rangoon, opposite to that city. But the name formerly applied to a large province in the Delta, stretching from the Rangoon River westward.

1546.—See *Pinto*, under **DAGON**.

1585.—"The 2d November we came to the city of **Dala**, where among other things there are 10 halls full of elephants, which are here for the King of Pegu, in charge of various attendants and officials."—*Gasp. Balbi*, f. 95.

DALAWAY, s. In S. India the Commander-in-chief of an army; [Tam. *talavāy*, Skt. *dala*, 'army,' *vah*, 'to lead']; Can. and Mal. *dhalavāy* and *dalavāyi*. Old Can. *dhaḷa*, H. *dal*, 'an army.'

1615.—"Caeterum **Deleuaius** . . . vehementer à rege contendit, ne cōmitteret vt vllum condenda noua hac urbe Arcomaganensis portus antiquissimus detrimentum caperet."—*Jarric, Thesaurus*, i. p. 179.

1700.—"Le **Talavai**, c'est le nom qu'on donne au Prince, qui gouverne aujourd'hui le Royaume sous l'autorité de la Reine."—*Lettres Edif.* x. 162. See also p. 173 and xi. 90.

c. 1747.—"A few days after this, the **Dulwai** sent for Hydur, and seating him on a musnud with himself, he consulted with him on the re-establishment of his own affairs, complaining bitterly of his own distress for want of money."—*H. of Hydur Naik*, 44. (See also under **DHURNA**.)

1754.—"You are imposed on, I never wrote to the Maissore King or **Dalloway** any such thing, nor they to me; nor had I a knowledge of any agreement between the Nabob and the **Dallaway**."—*Letter from Gov. Saunders* of Madras to French Deputies in *Cambridge's Acct. of the War*, App. p. 29.

1763-78.—"He (Haidar) has lately taken the King (Mysore) out of the hands of his Uncle, the **Dalaway**."—*Orme*, iii. 636.

[1810.—"Two manuscripts . . . preserved in different branches of the family of the ancient **Dulwoys** of Mysoor."—*Wilks, Mysore*, Pref. ed. 1869, p. xi.]

DALOYET, DELOYET, s. An armed attendant and messenger, the same as a **Peon**. H. *ḍhalait, ḍhalāyat*, from *ḍhāl*, 'a shield.' The word is never now used in Bengal and Upper India.

1772.—"Suppose every farmer in the province was enjoined to maintain a number of good serviceable bullocks . . . obliged to furnish the Government with them on a requisition made to him by the Collector in writing (not by sepoys, **delects** (*sic*), or hercarras" (see **HURCARRA**).—*W. Hastings*, to G. Vansittart, in *Gleig*, i. 237.

1809.—"As it was very hot, I immediately employed my **delogets** to keep off the crowd."—*Ld. Valentia*, i. 339. The word here and elsewhere in that book is a misprint for *deloyets*.

DAM, s. H. *dām*. Originally an actual copper coin, regarding which we find the following in the *Āīn*, i. 31, ed. *Blochmann*:—"1. The *Dám* weighs 5 *tánks*, *i.e.* 1 *tolah*, 8 *máshas*, and 7 *surkhs*; it is the fortieth part of a rupee. At first this coin was called *Paisah*, and also *Bahloli*; now it is known under this name (*dám*). On one side the place is given where it was struck, on the other the date. For the purpose of calculation, the *dám* is divided into 25 parts, each of which is called a *jétal*. This imaginary division is only used by accountants.

"2. The *adhelah* is half of a *dám*. 3. The *Páulah* is a quarter of a *dám*. 4. The *damrí* is an eighth of a *dám*."

It is curious that Akbar's revenues were registered in this small currency, viz. in *laks* of *dāms*. We may compare the Portuguese use of *reis* [see **REAS**].

The tendency of denominations of coins is always to sink in value. The *jetal* [see **JEETUL**], which had become an imaginary money of account in Akbar's time, was, in the 14th century, a real coin, which Mr. E. Thomas, chief of Indian numismatologists, has unearthed [see *Chron. Pathan Kings*, 231]. And now the *dām* itself is imaginary. According to Elliot the people of the N.W.P. not long ago calculated 25 *dāms* to the *paisā*, which would be 1600 to a rupee. Carnegy gives the Oudh popular currency table as:

26 *kauris*	=	1 *damrī*
1 *damrī*	=	3 dām
20 ,,	=	1 *ānā*
25 *dām*	=	1 pice.

But the Calcutta Glossary says the *dām* is in Bengal reckoned $\frac{1}{20}$ of an *ānā*, *i.e.* 320 to the rupee. ["Most things of little value, here as well as in Bhagalpur (writing of Behar) are sold by an imaginary money called *Takā*, which is here reckoned equal to two *Paysas*. There are also imaginary monies called *Chadām* and *Damrī*; the former is equal to 1 *Paysa* or 25 cowries, the latter is equal to one-eighth of a *Paysa*" (*Buchanan, Eastern Ind.* i. 382 *seq.*)]. We have not in our own experience met with any reckoning of *dāms*. In the case of the *damrī* the denomination has increased instead of sinking in relation to the *dām*. For above we have the *damrī*=3 *dāms*, or according to Elliot (*Beames*, ii. 296)= 3¼ *dāms*, instead of ⅛ of a *dām* as in Akbar's time. But in reality the *damrī's* absolute value has remained the same. For by Carnegy's table 1 rupee or 16 anas would be equal to 320 *damrīs*, and by the *Āīn*, 1 rupee $=40\times8$ *damrīs*=320 *damrīs*. *Damrī* is a common enough expression for the infinitesimal in coin, and one has often heard a Briton in India say: "No, I won't give a *dumree!*" with but a vague notion what a *damrī* meant, as in Scotland we have heard, "I won't give a *plack*," though certainly the speaker could not have stated the value of that ancient coin. And this leads to the suggestion that a like expression, often heard from coarse talkers in England as well as in India, originated in the latter country, and that whatever profanity there may be in the animus, there is none in the etymology, when such an one blurts out "I don't care a *dām!*" *i.e.* in other words, "I don't care a brass farthing!"

If the Gentle Reader deems this a far-fetched suggestion, let us back it by a second. We find in Chaucer (*The Miller's Tale*):

"——ne raught he not a *kers*,"

which means, "he recked not a *cress*" (*ne flocci quidem*); an expression which is also found in Piers Plowman:

"Wisdom and witte is nowe not worthe a *kerse*."

And this we doubt not has given rise to that other vulgar expression, "I don't care a curse";—curiously parallel in its corruption to that in illustration of which we quote it.

[This suggestion about *dām* was made by a writer in *Asiat. Res.*, ed. 1803, vii. 461: "This word was perhaps in use even among our forefathers, and may innocently account for the expression '*not worth a fig*,' or a *dam*, especially if we recollect that *ba-dam*, an *almond*, is to-day current in some parts of India as small money. Might not dried figs have been employed anciently in the same way, since the Arabic word *fooloos*, a *halfpenny*, also denotes a *cassia bean*, and the root *fuls* means the scale of a fish. Mankind are so apt, from a natural depravity, that 'flesh is heir to,' in their use of words, to pervert them from their original sense, that it is not a convincing argument against the present conjecture our using the word *curse* in vulgar language in lieu of *dam*." The *N.E.D.* disposes of the matter: "The suggestion is ingenious, but has no basis in fact." In a letter to Mr. Ellis, Macaulay writes: "How they settle the matter I care not, as the Duke says, one *twopenny damn*"; and Sir G. Trevelyan notes: "It was the Duke of Wellington who invented this oath, so disproportioned to the greatness of its author." (*Life*, ed. 1878, ii. 257.)]

1628.—"The revenue of all the territories under the Emperors of Delhi amounts, according to the Royal registers, to 6 *arbs* and 30 *krors* of **dāms**. One *arb* is equal to 100 *krors* (a *kror* being 10,000,000), and a hundred *krors* of **dams** are equal to 2 *krors* and 50 *lacs* of rupees."—*Muhammad Sharīf Hanīfi*, in *Elliot*, vii. 138.

c. 1840.—"Charles Greville saw the Duke soon after, and expressing the pleasure he had felt in reading his speech (commending the conduct of Capt. Charles Elliot in China), added that, however, many of the party were angry with it; to which the Duke replied,—'I know they are, and I don't care a **damn**. I have no time to do what is right.'

"A *twopenny damn* was, I believe, the form usually employed by the Duke, as an expression of value: but on the present occasion he seems to have been less precise."—*Autobiography of Sir Henry Taylor*, i. 296. The term referred to seems curiously to preserve an unconscious tradition of the pecuniary, or what the idiotical jargon of our time calls the 'monetary,' estimation contained in the expression.

1881.—"A Bavarian printer, jealous of the influence of capital, said that 'Cladstone baid millions of money to the beeble to fote for him, and Beegonsfeel would not bay them a **tam**, so they fote for Cladstone.'"—*A Socialistic Picnic*, in *St. James's Gazette*, July 6.

[1900.—"There is not, I dare wager, a single bishop who cares one 'twopenny-halfpenny **dime**' for any of that plenteousness for himself."—*H. Bell*, Vicar of Muncaster, in *Times*, Aug. 31.]

DAMAN, n.p. *Damān*, one of the old settlements of the Portuguese which they still retain, on the coast of Guzerat, about 100 miles north of Bombay; written by them *Damão*.

1554.—". . . the pilots said: 'We are here between Diu and **Daman**; if the ship sinks here, not a soul will escape; we must make sail for the shore."—*Sidi 'Ali*, 80.

[1607-8.—"Then that by no means or ships or men can goe saffelie to Suratt, or theare expect any quiett trade for the many dangers likelie to happen vnto them by the Portugals Cheef Comanders of Diu and **Demon** and places there aboute. . . ."—*Birdwood, First Letter Book*, 247.]

1623.—"Il capitano . . . sperava che potessimo esser vicini alla città di **Daman**; laqual esta dentro il golfo di Cambaia a man destra. . . ."—*P. della Valle*, ii. 499 [Hak. Soc. i. 15].

DAMANI, s. Applied to a kind of squall. (See **ELEPHANTA**.)

DAMMER, s. This word is applied to various resins in different parts of India, chiefly as substitutes for pitch. The word appears to be Malayo-Javanese *damar*, used generically for resins, a class of substances the origin of which is probably often uncertain. [Mr. Skeat notes that the Malay *damar* means rosin and a torch made of rosin, the latter consisting of a regular cylindrical case, made of bamboo or other suitable material, filled to the top with rosin and ignited.] To one of the *dammer*-producing trees in the Archipelago the name *Dammara alba*, Rumph. (N. O. *Coniferae*), has been given, and this furnishes the 'East India Dammer' of English varnish-makers. In Burma the *dammer* used is derived from at least three different genera of the N. O. *Dipterocarpeae;* in Bengal it is derived from the *sāl* tree (see **SAUL-WOOD**) (*Shorea robusta*) and other *Shoreae*, as well as by importation from transmarine sources. In S. India "white *dammer*," "*Dammer* Pitch," or *Piney* resin, is the produce of *Vateria indica*, and "black *dammer*" of *Canarium strictum;* in Cutch the *dammer* used is stated by Lieut. Leech (*Bombay Selections*, No. xv. p. 215-216) to be made from *chandrūz* (or *chandras* =copal) boiled with an equal quantity of oil. This is probably Fryer's 'rosin taken out of the sea' (*infra*). [On the other hand Mr. Pringle (*Diary, &c., Fort St. George*, 1st ser. iv. 178) quotes Crawfurd (*Malay Archip.* i. 455): (Dammer) "exudes through the bark, and is either found adhering to the trunk and branches in large lumps, or in masses on the ground, under the trees. As these often grow near the sea-side or on banks of rivers, the damar is frequently floated away and collected at different places as drift"; and adds: "The dammer used for caulking the *masula* boats at Madras when Fryer was there, may have been, and probably was, imported from the Archipelago, and the fact that the resin was largely collected as drift may have been mentioned in answer to his enquiries."] Some of the Malay *dammer* also seems, from Major M'Nair's statement, to be, like copal, fossil. [On this Mr. Skeat says: "It is true that it is sometimes dug up out of the ground, possibly because it may form on the roots of certain trees, or because a great mass of it will fall and partially bury itself in the ground by its own weight, but I have never heard of its being found actually fossilised, and I should question the fact seriously."]

The word is sometimes used in India [and by the Malays, see above] for 'a torch,' because torches are formed of rags dipped in it. This is perhaps the use which accounts for Haex's explanation below.

1584. — "*Demnar* (for **demmar**) from Siacca and Blinton" (*i.e.* Siak and Billiton). —*Barret*, in *Hakl.* ii. 43.

1631. — In *Haex's Malay Vocabulary:* "**Damar**, Lumen quod accenditur."

1673. — "The Boat is not strengthened with Knee-Timbers as ours are, the bended Planks are sowed together with Rope-yarn of the Cocoe, and calked with **Dammar** (a sort of Rosin taken out of the sea)."—*Fryer*, 37.

" "The long continued Current from the Inland Parts (at Surat) through the vast Wildernesses of huge Woods and Forests, wafts great Rafts of Timber for Shipping and Building: and **Damar** for Pitch, the finest sented Bitumen (if it be not a gum or Rosin) I ever met with."—*Ibid.* 121.

1727.—"**Damar**, a gum that is used for making Pitch and Tar for the use of Shipping."—*A. Hamilton*, ii. 73; [ed. 1744, ii. 72].

c. 1755. "A **Demar**-Boy (Torch-boy)."—*Ives*, 50.

1878. — "This **dammar**, which is the general Malayan name for resin, is dug out of the forests by the Malays, and seems to be the fossilised juices of former growth of jungle."—*McNair, Perak*, &c., 188.

1885.—"The other great industry of the place (in Sumatra) is **dammar** collecting. This substance, as is well known, is the resin which exudes from notches made in various species of coniferous and dipterocarpous trees . . . out of whose stem . . . the native cuts large notches up to a height of 40 or 50 feet from the ground. The tree is then left for 3 or 4 months when, if it be a very healthy one, sufficient **dammar** will have exuded to make it worth while collecting; the yield may then be as much as 94 Amsterdam pounds."—*H. O. Forbes, A Naturalist's Wanderings*, p. 135.

DANA, s. H. *dāna*, literally 'grain,' and therefore the exact translation of **gram** in its original sense (q.v.). It is often used in Bengal as synonymous with gram, thus: "Give the horse his *dāna*." We find it also in this specific way by an old traveller:

1616.—"A kind of graine called **Donna**, somewhat like our Pease, which they boyle, and when it is cold give them mingled with course Sugar, and twise or thrise in the Weeke, Butter to scoure their Bodies."—*Terry*, in *Purchas*, ii. 1471.

DANCING-GIRL, s. This, or among the older Anglo-Indians, *Dancing-Wench*, was the representative of the (Portuguese *Bailadeira*) **Bayadère**, or **Nautch**-girl (q.v.), also **Cunchunee.** In S. India dancing-girls are all Hindus, [and known as *Devadāsī* or *Bhogam-dāsī;*] in N. India they are both Hindu, called *Rāmjanī* (see **RUM-JOHNNY**), and Mussulman, called

Kanchanī (see **CUNCHUNEE**). In Dutch the phrase takes a very plain-spoken form, see quotation from Valentijn; [others are equally explicit, *e.g.* Sir T. Roe (Hak. Soc. i. 145) and P. della Valle, ii. 282.]

1606.—See description by *Gouvea*, f. 39.

1673. — "After supper they treated us with the **Dancing Wenches**, and good soops of Brandy and Delf Beer, till it was late enough."—*Fryer*, 152.

1701. — "The Governor conducted the Nabob into the Consultation Room . . . after dinner they were diverted with the **Dancing Wenches**."—In *Wheeler*, i. 377.

1726.—"Wat de **dans-Hoeren** (anders *Dewataschi* **(Deva-dāsī)** . . . genaamd, en an de Goden hunner Pagoden als getrouwd) belangd."—*Valentijn, Chor.* 54.

1763-78.—"Mandelslow tells a story of a Nabob who cut off the heads of a set of **dancing girls** . . . because they did not come to his palace on the first summons."—*Orme*, i. 28 (ed. 1803).

1789.—". . . **dancing girls** who display amazing agility and grace in all their motions."—*Munro, Narrative*, 73.

c. 1812.—"I often sat by the open window, and there, night after night, I used to hear the songs of the unhappy **dancing girls**, accompanied by the sweet yet melancholy music of the *cithāra*."—*Mrs. Sherwood's Autobiog.* 423.

[1813. — Forbes gives an account of the two classes of **dancing girls**, those who sing and dance in private houses, and those attached to temples.—*Or. Mem.* 2nd ed. i. 61.]

1815. — "**Dancing girls** were once numerous in Persia; and the first poets of that country have celebrated the beauty of their persons and the melody of their voices."—*Malcolm, H. of Persia*, ii. 587.

1838.—"The Maharajah sent us in the evening a new set of **dancing girls**, as they were called, though they turned out to be twelve of the ugliest old women I ever saw."—*Osborne, Court and Camp of Runjeet Singh*, 154.

1843. — "We decorated the Temples of the false gods. We provided the **dancing girls**. We gilded and painted the images to which our ignorant subjects bowed down."—*Macaulay's Speech on the Somnauth Proclamation.*

DANDY, s.

(a). A boatman. The term is peculiar to the Gangetic rivers. H. and Beng. *ḍānḍi*, from *ḍānḍ* or *ḍanḍ*, 'a staff, an oar.'

1685.—"Our **Dandees** (or boatmen) boyled their rice, and we supped here."—*Hedges, Diary*, Jan. 6; [Hak. Soc. i. 175].

1763.—"The oppressions of your officers were carried to such a length that they put a stop to all business, and plundered and seized the **Dandies** and Mangies' [see **MANJEE**] vessel."—*W. Hastings* to the Nawab, in *Long*, 347.

1809.—"Two naked **dandys** paddling at the head of the vessel."—*Ld. Valentia*, i. 67.

1824.—"I am indeed often surprised to observe the difference between my **dandees** (who are nearly the colour of a black tea-pot) and the generality of the peasants whom we meet."—*Bp. Heber*, i. 149 (ed. 1844).

—— **(b)**. A kind of ascetic who carries a staff. Same etymology. See *Solvyns*, who gives a plate of such an one.

[1828.—". . . the **Dandi** is distinguished by carrying a small *Dand*, or wand, with several processes or projections from it, and a piece of cloth dyed with red ochre, in which the Brahmanical cord is supposed to be enshrined, attached to it."—*H. H. Wilson, Sketch of the Religious Sects of the Hindus*, ed. 1861, i. 193.]

—— **(c)**. H. same spelling, and same etymology. A kind of vehicle used in the Himālaya, consisting of a strong cloth slung like a hammock to a bamboo staff, and carried by two (or more) men. The traveller can either sit sideways, or lie on his back. It is much the same as the Malabar **muncheel** (q.v.), [and P. della Valle describes a similar vehicle which he says the Portuguese call *Rete* (Hak. Soc. i. 183)].

[1875.—"The nearest approach to travelling in a **dandi** I can think of, is sitting in a half-reefed top-sail in a storm, with the head and shoulders above the yard."—*Wilson, Abode of Snow*, 103.]

1876.—"In the lower hills when she did not walk she travelled in a **dandy**."—*Kinloch, Large Game Shooting in Thibet*, 2nd S., p. vii.

DANGUR, n.p. H. *Ḍhāngar*, the name by which members of various tribes of Chūtiā Nāgpūr, but especially of the Orāons, are generally known when they go out to distant provinces to seek employment as labourers ("coolies"). A very large proportion of those who emigrate to the tea-plantations of E. India, and also to Mauritius and other colonies, belong to the Orāon tribe. The etymology of the term *Dhāngar* is doubtful. The late Gen. Dalton says: "It is a word that from its apparent derivation (*dāng* or *dhāng*, 'a hill') may mean any hill-man; but amongst several tribes of the Southern tributary Maháls, the terms Dhángar and Dhángarin mean the youth of the two sexes, both in highland and lowland villages, and it cannot be considered the national designation of any particular tribe" (*Descriptive Ethnology of Bengal*, 245) [and see *Risley, Tribes and Castes*, i. 219].

DARCHEENEE, s. P. *dār-chīnī*, 'China-stick,' *i.e.* cinnamon.

1563. — ". . . The people of Ormuz, because this bark was brought for sale there by those who had come from China, called it **dar-chini**, which in Persian means 'wood of China,' and so they sold it in Alexandria. . . ."—*Garcia*, f. 59-60.

1621. — "As for cinnamon which you wrote was called by the Arabs **dartzeni**, I assure you that the *dar-sini*, as the Arabs say, or **dar-chini** as the Persians and Turks call it, is nothing but our ordinary *canella*." —*P. della Valle*, ii. 206-7.

DARJEELING, DĀRJĪLING, n.p. A famous sanitarium in the Eastern Himālaya, the cession of which was purchased from the Raja of Sikkim in 1835; a tract largely added to by annexation in 1849, following on an outrage committed by the Sikkim Minister in imprisoning Dr. (afterwards Sir) Joseph Hooker and the late Dr. A. Campbell, Superintendent of Darjeeling. The sanitarium stands at 6500 to 7500 feet above the sea. The popular Tibetan spelling of the name is, according to Jaeshcke, *rDor-rje-glin*, 'Land of the *Dorje*,' *i.e.* 'of the Adamant or thunderbolt,' the ritual sceptre of the Lamas. But 'according to several titles of books in the Petersburg list of MSS. it ought properly to be spelt *Dar-rgyas-glin*' (*Tib. Eng. Dict.* p. 287).

DARÓGA, s. P. and H. *dārogha*. This word seems to be originally Mongol (see *Kovalevsky's Dict.* No. 1672). In any case it is one of those terms brought by the Mongol hosts from the far East. In their nomenclature it was applied to a Governor of a province or city, and in this sense it continued to be used under Timur and his immediate successors. But it is the tendency of official titles, as of denominations of coin, to descend in value; and that of *dārogha* has in later days been bestowed on a variety of humbler persons. Wilson defines the word thus: "The chief native officer in various departments under the native government, a superintendent, a manager: but in later times he is especially the head of a police, customs, or excise station." Under the British Police system, from 1793 to 1862-63, the *Darogha* was a local Chief of Police, or Head Constable, [and this is still the popular title in the N.W.P. for the officer in charge of a Police Station.] The word occurs in the sense of a Governor in a Mongol inscription, of the year 1314, found in the Chinese Province of Shensi, which is given by Pauthier in his *Marc. Pol.*, p. 773. The Mongol Governor of Moscow, during a part of the Tartar domination in Russia, is called in the old Russian Chronicles *Doroga* (see *Hammer, Golden Horde*, 384). And according to the same writer the word appears in a Byzantine writer (unnamed) as Δάρηγας (*ibid.* 238-9). The Byzantine form and the passages below of 1404 and 1665 seem to imply some former variation in pronunciation. But Clavijo has also **derroga** in § clii.

c. 1220.—"Tuli Khan named as **Darugha** at Merv one called Barmas, and himself marched upon Nishapur."—*Abulghāzi*, by *Desmaisons*, 135.

1404.—"And in this city (Tauris) there was a kinsman of the Emperor as Magistrate thereof, whom they call **Derrega**, and he treated the said Ambassadors with much respect."—*Clavijo*, § lxxxii. Comp. *Markham*, 90.

1441. — ". . . I reached the city of Kerman. . . . The **deroghah** (governor) the Emir Hadji Mohamed Kaiaschirin, being then absent. . . ."—*Abdurrazzāk*, in *India in the XVth Cent.*, p. 5.

c. 1590. — "The officers and servants attached to the Imperial Stables. 1. The *Atbegi*. . . . 2. The **Dāroghah**. There is one appointed for each stable. . . ."—*Āīn*, tr. *Blochmann*, i. 137.

1621.—"The 10th of October, the **darogā**, or Governor of Ispahan, Mir Abdulaazim, the King's son-in-law, who, as was afterwards seen in that charge of his, was a downright madman. . . ."—*P. della Valle*, ii. 166.

1665.—"There stands a **Derega**, upon each side of the River, who will not suffer any person to pass without leave."—*Tavernier*, E.T., ii. 52; [ed. *Ball*, i. 117].

1673.—"The **Droger**, or Mayor of the City, or Captain of the Watch, or the Rounds; It is his duty to preside with the Main Guard a-nights before the Palace-gates."—*Fryer*, 339.

1673.—"The **Droger** being Master of his Science, persists; what comfort can I reap from your Disturbance?"—*Fryer*, 389.

1682.—"I received a letter from Mr. Hill at Rajemaul advising ye **Droga** of ye Mint would not obey a Copy, but required at least a sight of ye Originall."—*Hedges, Diary*, Dec. 14; [Hak. Soc. i. 57].

c. 1781.—"About this time, however, one day being very angry, the **Darogha**, or master of the mint, presented himself, and asked the Nawaub what device he would have struck on his new copper coinage. Hydur, in a violent passion, told him to stamp an obscene figure on it."—*Hydur Naik*, tr. by *Miles*, 488.

1812.—"Each division is guarded by a **Darogha**, with an establishment of armed men."—*Fifth Report*, 44.

DATCHIN, s. This word is used in old books of Travel and Trade for a steelyard employed in China and the Archipelago. It is given by Leyden as a *Malay* word for 'balance,' in his *Comp. Vocab. of Barma, Malay and Thai*, Serampore, 1810. It is also given by Crawfurd as *ḍachin*, a Malay word from the Javanese. There seems to be no doubt that in Peking dialect *ch'eng* is 'to weigh,' and also '*steelyard*'; that in Amoy a small steelyard is called *ch'in*; and that in Canton dialect the steelyard is called *t'okch'ing*. Some of the Dictionaries also give *ta 'chêng*, 'large steelyard.' *Datchin* or *dotchin* may therefore possibly be a Chinese term; but considering how seldom traders' words are really Chinese, and how easily the Chinese monosyllables lend themselves to plausible combinations, it remains probable that the Canton word was adopted from foreigners. It has sometimes occurred to us that it might have been adopted from *Achin* (d'Achin); see the first quotation. [The *N.E.D.*, following Prof. Giles, gives it as a corruption of the Cantonese name *toh-ch'ing* (in Court dialect *to-ch'êng*) from *toh* 'to measure,' *ch'ing*, 'to weigh.' Mr. Skeat notes: "The standard Malay is *daching*, the Javanese *dachin* (v. *Klinkert*, s.v.). He gives the word as of Chinese origin, and the probability is that the English word is from the Malay, which in its turn was borrowed from the Chinese. The final suggestion, *d'Achin*, seems out of the question.] Favre's *Malay Dict.* gives (in French) "**daxing** (Ch. *pa-tchen*), steelyard, balance," also "*ber*-**daxing**, to weigh," and Javan. "**daxin**, a weight of 100 kātis." Gericke's *Javan. Dict.* also gives "**datsin**-Picol," with a reference to Chinese. [With reference to Crawfurd's statement quoted above, Mr. Pringle (*Diary, Ft. St. George*, 1st ser. iv. 179) notes that Crawfurd had elsewhere adopted the view that the yard and the designation of it originated in China and passed from thence to the Archipelago (*Malay Archip.* i. 275). On the whole, the Chinese origin seems most probable.]

1554.—At Malacca. "The *baar* of the great **Dachem** contains 200 cates, each *cate* weighing two *arratels*, 4 ounces, 5 eighths, 15 grains, 3 tenths. . . . The Baar of the little **Dachem** contains 200 cates; each cate weighing two arratels."—*A. Nunes*, 39.

[1684-5.—". . . he replyed That he was now Content yt ye Honble Company should solely enjoy ye Customes of ye Place on condition yt ye People of ye Place be free from all dutys & Customes and yt ye Profitt of ye **Dutchin** be his. . . ."—*Pringle, Diary, Ft. St. Geo.* 1st ser. iv. 12.]

1696.—"For their **Dotchin** and *Ballance* they use that of Japan."—*Bowyear's Journal at Cochin-China*, in *Dalrymple, O. R.* i. 88.

1711.—"Never weigh your Silver by their **Dotchins**, for they have usually two Pair, one to receive, the other to pay by."—*Lockyer*, 113.

" "In the **Dotchin**, an expert Weigher will cheat two or three *per cent.* by placing or shaking the Weight, and minding the Motion of the Pole only."—*Ibid.* 115.

" ". . . every one has a *Chopchin* and **Dotchin** to cut and weigh silver."—*Ibid.* 141.

1748.—"These scales are made after the manner of the Roman balance, or our English Stilliards, called by the Chinese *Litang*, and by us **Dot-chin**."—*A Voyage to the E. Indies in* 1747 *and* 1748, &c., London, 1762, p. 324. The same book has, in a short vocabulary, at p. 265, "English scales or **dodgeons** . . . Chinese *Litang*."

DATURA, s. This Latin-like name is really Skt. *dhattūra*, and so has passed into the derived vernaculars. The widely-spread *Datura Stramonium*, or Thorn-apple, is well known over Europe, but is not regarded as indigenous to India; though it appears to be wild in the Himālaya from Kashmīr to Sikkim. The Indian species, from which our generic name has been borrowed, is *Datura alba*, Nees (see *Hanbury and Flückiger*, 415) (*D. fastuosa*, L.). Garcia de Orta mentions the common use of this by thieves in India. Its effect on the victim was to produce temporary alienation of mind, and violent laughter, permitting the thief to act unopposed. He describes his own practice in dealing with such cases, which he had always found successful. *Datura* was also often given as a practical joke, whence the Portuguese called it *Burladora* ('Joker'). De Orta strongly disapproves of such pranks. The criminal use of *datura* by a class of Thugs is rife in our own time. One of the present writers has judicially convicted many. Coolies returning with fortunes from the colonies often become the victims of such crimes. [See details in *Chevers, Ind. Med. Jurispr.* 179 *seqq.*]

1563.—"*Maidservant.* A black woman of the house has been giving **datura** to my mistress; she stole the keys, and the jewels that my mistress had on her neck and in her jewel box, and has made off with a black man. It would be a kindness to come to her help."—*Garcia, Colloquios*, f. 83.

1578.—"They call this plant in the Malabar tongue *unmata caya* [*ummata-kāya*] . . . in Canarese **Datyro**. . . ."—*Acosta*, 87.

c. 1580.—"Nascitur et . . . **Datura** Indorum, quarum ex seminibus Latrones bellaria parant, quae in caravanis mercatoribus exhibentes largumque somnum, profundumque inducentes aurum gemmasque surripiunt et abeunt."—*Prosper Alpinus*, Pt. I. 190-1.

1598.—"They name [have] likewise an hearbe called **Deutroa**, which beareth a seede, whereof bruising out the sap, they put it into a cup, or other vessell, and give it to their husbands, eyther in meate or drinke, and presently therewith the Man is as though hee were half out of his wits."—*Linschoten*, 60; [Hak. Soc. i. 209].

1608-10.—"Mais ainsi de mesme les femmes quand elles sçauent que leurs maris en entretiennent quelqu'autre, elles s'en desfont par poison ou autrement, et se seruent fort à cela de la semence de **Datura**, qui est d'vne estrange vertu. Ce *Datura* ou **Duroa**, espece de *Stramonium*, est vne plante grande et haute qui porte des fleurs blanches en Campane, comme le *Cisampelo*, mais plus grande."—*Mocquet, Voyages*, 312.

[1610.—"In other parts of the Indies it is called **Dutroa**."—*Pyrard de Laval*, Hak. Soc. ii. 114.

[1621.—"Garcias ab Horto . . . makes mention of an hearb called **Datura**, which, if it be eaten, for 24 hours following, takes away all sense of grief, makes them incline to laughter and mirth."—*Burton, Anatomy of Mel.*, Pt. 2, Sec. 5 Mem. I. Subs. 5.]

1673.—"**Dutry**, the deadliest sort of *Solarium* (*Solanum*) or *Nightshade*."—*Fryer*, 32.

1676.—

"Make lechers and their punks with **dewtry**
Commit fantastical advowtry."
Hudibras, Pt. iii. Canto 1.

1690.—"And many of them (the Moors) take the liberty of mixing **Dutra** and Water together to drink . . . which will intoxicate almost to Madness."—*Ovington*, 235.

1810.—"The **datura** that grows in every part of India."—*Williamson, V. M.* ii. 135.

1874.—"**Datūra.** This plant, a native of the East Indies, and of Abyssinia, more than a century ago had spread as a naturalized plant through every country in Europe except Sweden, Lapland, and Norway, through the aid of gipsy quacks, who used the seed as anti-spasmodics, or for more questionable purposes."—*R. Brown* in *Geog. Magazine*, i. 371. *Note.*—The statements derived from *Hanbury and Flückiger* in the beginning of this article disagree with this view, both as to the origin of the European *Datura* and the identity of the Indian plant. The doubts about the birthplace of the various species of the genus remain in fact undetermined. [See the discussion in *Watt, Econ. Dict.* iii. 29 *seqq.*]

DATURA, YELLOW, and YELLOW THISTLE. These are Bombay names for the *Argemone mexicana*, *fico del inferno* of Spaniards, introduced accidentally from America, and now an abundant and pestilent weed all over India.

DAWK, s. H. and Mahr. *ḍāk*, 'Post,' *i.e.* properly transport by relays of men and horses, and thence 'the mail' or letter-post, as well as any arrangemen for travelling, or for transmitting articles by such relays. The institution was no doubt imitated from the *barīd*, or post, established throughout the empire of the Caliphs by Mo'āwia. The *barīd* is itself connected with the Latin *verēdus*, and *verēdius*.

1310.—"It was the practice of the Sultan (Alá-uddín) when he sent an army on an expedition to establish posts on the road, wherever posts could be maintained. . . . At every half or quarter *kos* runners were posted . . . the securing of accurate intelligence from the court on one side and the army on the other was a great public benefit."—*Ziā-uddīn Barnī*, in *Elliot*, iii. 203.

c. 1340.—"The foot-post (in India) is thus arranged: every mile is divided into three equal intervals which are called **Dāwah**, which is as much as to say 'the third part of a mile' (the mile itself being called in India *Koruh*). At every third of a mile there is a village well inhabited, outside of which are three tents where men are seated ready to start. . . ."—*Ibn Batuta*, iii. 95.

c. 1340.—"So he wrote to the Sultan to announce our arrival, and sent his letter by the **dāwah**, which is the foot post, as we have told you. . . ."—*Ibid.* 145.

,, "At every mile (*i.e. Korūh* or *coss*) from Delhi to Daulatabād there are three **dāwah** or posts."—*Ibid.* 191-2. It seems probable that this **dāwah** is some misunderstanding of **ḍāk**.

,, "There are established, between the capital and the chief cities of the different territories, posts placed at certain distances from each other, which are like the post-relays in Egypt and Syria . . . but the distance between them is not more than four bowshots or even less. At each of these posts ten swift runners are stationed . . . as soon as one of these men receives a letter he runs off as rapidly as possible. . . . At each of these post stations there are mosques, where prayers are said, and where the traveller can find shelter, reservoirs full of good water, and markets . . . so that there is very little necessity for carrying water, or food, or tents."—*Shahābuddīn Dimishkī*, in *Elliot*, iii. 581.

1528.—". . . that every ten *kos* he should erect a *yam*, or post-house, which they call a **dâk-choki**, for six horses. . . ."—*Baber*, 393.

c. 1612.—"He (Akbar) established posts throughout his dominions, having two horses and a set of footmen stationed at every five coss. The Indians call this establishment '**Dak** *chowky*.'"—*Firishta*, by *Briggs*, ii. 280-1.

1657.—"But when the intelligence of his (Dara-Shekoh's) officious meddling had spread abroad through the provinces by the **dák** *chauki*. . . ."—*Khāfī Khān*, in *Elliot*, vii. 214.

1727.—"The Post in the Mogul's Dominions goes very swift, for at every Caravanseray, which are built on the High-roads, about ten miles distant from one another, Men, very swift of Foot, are kept ready. . . . And these Curriers are called **Dog** *Chouckies*."—*A. Hamilton*, i. 149; [ed. 1744, i. 150].

1771.—"I wrote to the Governor for permission to visit Calcutta by the **Dawks**. . . ."—Letter in the *Intrigues of a Nabob*, &c., 76.

1781.—"I mean the absurd, unfair, irregular and dangerous Mode, of suffering People to paw over their Neighbours' Letters at the **Dock**. . . ."—Letter in *Hicky's Bengal Gazette*, Mar. 24.

1796.—"The Honble. the Governor-General in Council has been pleased to order the re-establishment of **Dawk** *Bearers* upon the new road from Calcutta to Benares and Patna. . . . The following are the rates fixed. . . .

"From Calcutta to Benares. . . . Sicca Rupees 500."

In *Seton-Karr*, ii. 185.

1809.—"He advised me to proceed immediately by **Dawk**. . . ."—*Ld. Valentia*, i. 62.

1824.—"The **dāk** or post carrier having passed me on the preceding day, I dropped a letter into his leathern bag, requesting a friend to send his horse on for me."—*Seely*, *Wonders of Ellora*, ch. iv. A letter so sent by the post-runner, in the absence of any receiving office, was said to go "*by outside* **dawk**."

1843.—"JAM: You have received the money of the British for taking charge of the **dawk**; you have betrayed your trust, and stopped the **dawks**. . . . If you come in and make your salám, and promise fidelity to the British Government, I will restore to you your lands . . . and the superintendence of the **dawks**. If you refuse I will wait till the hot weather has gone past, and then I will carry fire and sword into your territory . . . and if I catch you, I will hang you as a rebel."—*Sir C. Napier* to the Jam of the Jokees (in *Life of Dr. J. Wilson*, p. 440).

1873.—". . . the true reason being, Mr Barton declared, that he was too stingy to pay her **dawk**."—*The True Reformer*, i. 63.

DAWK, s. Name of a tree. See **DHAWK**.

DAWK, To lay a, v. To cause relays of bearers, or horses, to be posted on a road. As regards palankin bearers this used to be done either through the post-office, or through local **chowdries** (q.v.) of bearers. During the mutiny of 1857-58, when several young surgeons had arrived in India, whose services were urgently wanted at the front, it is said that the Head of the Department to which they had reported themselves, directed them immediately to '**lay a dawk.**' One of them turned back from the door, saying: 'Would you explain, Sir; for you might just as well tell me to lay an egg!'

DAWK BUNGALOW. See under **BUNGALOW.**

DAYE, DHYE, s. A wet-nurse; used in Bengal and N. India, where this is the sense now attached to the word. Hind. *dāī*, Skt. *dātrikā*; conf. Pers. *dāyah*, a nurse, a midwife. The word also in the earlier English Regulations is applied, Wilson states, to "a female commissioner employed to interrogate and swear native women of condition, who could not appear to give evidence in a Court."

[1568.—"No Christian shall call an infidel **Daya** at the time of her labour."—*Archiv. Port. Orient.* fasc. iv. p. 25.]

1578.—"The whole plant is commonly known and used by the **Dayas**, or as we call them *comadres*" ("gossips," midwives).—*Acosta, Tractado*, 282.

1613.—"The medicines of the Malays . . . ordinarily are roots of plants . . . horns and claws and stones, which are used by their leeches, and for the most part by **Dayas**, which are women physicians, excellent herbalists, apprentices of the schools of Java Major."—*Godinho de Eredia*, f. 37.

1782.—In a Table of monthly Wages at Calcutta, we have:—

"**Dy** (Wet-nurse) 10 Rs."

India Gazette, Oct. 12.

1808.—"If the bearer hath not strength what can the **Daee** (midwife) do?"—Guzerati Proverb, in *Drummond's Illustrations*, 1803.

1810.—"The **Dhye** is more generally an attendant upon native ladies."—*Williamson, V.M.* i. 341.

1883.—". . . the '**dyah**' or wet-nurse is looked on as a second mother, and usually provided for for life."—*Wills, Modern Persia*, 326.

[1887.—"I was much interested in the **Dhais** ('midwives') class."—*Lady Dufferin, Viceregal Life in India*, 337.]

DEANER, s. This is not Anglo-Indian, but it is a curious word of English Thieves' cant, signifying 'a shilling.' It seems doubtful whether it comes from the Italian *danaro* or the Arabic **dīnār** (q.v.); both eventually derived from the Latin *denarius*.

DEBAL, n.p. See **DIUL-SIND**.

DECCAN, n.p. and adj. Hind. *Dakhin, Dakkhin, Dakhan, Dakkhan; dakkhiṇa*, the Prakr. form of Skt. *dakshiṇa*, 'the South'; originally 'on the right hand'; compare *dexter*, *δεξιος*. The Southern part of India, the Peninsula, and especially the Table-land between the Eastern and Western Ghauts. It has been often applied also, politically, to specific States in that part of India, *e.g.* by the Portuguese in the 16th century to the Mahommedan Kingdom of Bījapur, and in more recent times by ourselves to the State of Hyderabad. In Western India the **Deccan** stands opposed to the **Concan** (q.v.), *i.e.* the table-land of the interior to the maritime plain; in Upper India the **Deccan** stands opposed to **Hindūstān**, *i.e.* roundly speaking, the country south of the Nerbudda to that north of it. The term frequently occurs in the Skt. books in the form *dakshiṇāpatha* ('Southern region,' whence the Greek form in our first quotation), and *dakshīṇātya* ('Southern'—qualifying some word for 'country'). So, in the *Pañchatantra*: "There is in the Southern region (*dakshīṇātya janapada*) a town called Mihilāropya."

c. A.D. 80-90.—"But immediately after Barygaza the adjoining continent extends from the North to the South, wherefore the region is called **Dachinabadēs** (Δαχιναβάδης), for the South is called in their tongue **Dachanos** (Δάχανος)."—*Periplus M.E., Geog. Gr. Min.* i. 254.

1510.—"In the said city of **Decan** there reigns a King, who is a Mahommedan."—*Varthema*, 117. (Here the term is applied to the city and kingdom of Bījapur).

1517.—"On coming out of this Kingdom of Guzarat and Cambay towards the South, and the inner parts of India, is the Kingdom of **Dacani**, which the Indians call **Decan**."—*Barbosa*, 69.

1552.—"Of **Decani** or **Daquẽ** as we now call it."—*Castanheda*, ii. 50.

,, "He (Mahmūd Shāh) was so powerful that he now presumed to style himself King of Canara, giving it the name of **Decan**. And the name is said to have been given to it from the combination of different nations contained in it, because **Decanij** in their language signifies 'mongrel.'"—*De Barros*, Dec. II. liv. v. cap. 2. (It is difficult to discover what has led astray here the usually well-informed De Barros).

1608.—"For the *Portugals* of *Daman* had wrought with an ancient friend of theirs a *Raga*, who was absolute Lord of a Prouince (betweene *Daman*, *Guzerat*, and **Decan**) called Cruly, to be readie with 200 Horsemen to stay my passage."—*Capt. W. Hawkins*, in *Purchas*, i. 209.

[1612.—"The **Desanins**, a people bordering on them (Portuguese) have besieged six of their port towns."—*Danvers, Letters*, i. 258.]

1616.—". . . his son Sultan Coron, who he designed, should command in **Deccan**."—*Sir T. Roe*.

[,, "There is a resolution taken that Sultan Caronne shall go to the **Decan** Warres."—*Ibid.* Hak. Soc. i. 192.

[1623.—"A Moor of **Dacàn**."—*P. della Valle*, Hak. Soc. ii. 225.]

1667.—

"But such as at this day, to Indians known,
In Malabar or **Decan** spreads her arms."

Paradise Lost, ix. [1102-3].

1726.—"**Decan** [as a division] includes **Decan**, *Cunkam*, and *Balagutta*."—*Valentijn*, v. 1.

c. 1750.—". . . alors le Nababe d'Arcate, tout petit Seigneur qu'il étoit, comparé au Souba du **Dekam** dont il n'étoit que le Fermier traiter (*sic*) avec nous comme un Souverain avec ses sujets."—Letter of M. Bussy, in *Cambridge's War in India*, p. xxix.

1870.—"In the **Deccan** and in Ceylon trees and bushes near springs, may often be seen covered with votive flowers."—*Lubbock, Origin of Civilization*, 200. N.B.—This is a questionable statement as regards the Deccan.

DECCANY, adj., also used as subst. Properly *dakhinī, dakkhinī, dakhnī*. Coming from the **Deccan**. A (Mahommedan) inhabitant of the Deccan. Also the very peculiar dialect of Hindustani spoken by such people.

1516.—"The **Decani** language, which is the natural language of the country."—*Barbosa*, 77.

1572.— ". . .
Decanys, Orias, que e esperança
Tem de sua salvação nas resonantes
Aguas do Gange. . . ." —*Camões*, vii. 20.

1578.—"The **Decanins** (call the Betel-leaf) *Pan*."—*Acosta*, 139.

c. 1590.—"Hence **Dak'hinīs** are notorious in Hindústán for stupidity. . . ."—Author quoted by *Blochmann, Āīn*, i. 443.

[1813.—". . . and the **Decanne**-bean (*butea superba*) are very conspicuous."—*Forbes, Or. Mem.* 2nd. ed. i. 195.]

1861.—
"Ah, I rode a **Deccanee** charger, with a saddle-cloth gold laced,
And a Persian sword, and a twelve-foot spear, and a pistol at my waist."
Sir A. C. Lyall, The Old Pindaree.

DECK, s. A look, a peep. Imp. of Hind. *dekh-nā*, 'to look.'

[1830.—"When on a sudden, coming to a check, Thompson's mahout called out, '**Dekh**! Sahib, **Dekh**!'"—*Or. Sporting Mag.*, ed. 1873, i. 350.]

1854.—". . . these formed the whole assemblage, with the occasional exception of some officer, stopping as he passed by, returning from his morning ride 'just to have a **dekh** at the steamer.' . . ."—*W. Arnold, Oakfield*, i. 85.

DEEN, s. Ar. Hind. *dīn*, 'the faith.' The cry of excited Mahommedans, *Dīn, Dīn!*

c. 1580.—". . . crying, as is their way, **Dim, Dim**, *Mafamede*, so that they filled earth and air with terror and confusion."—*Primor e Honra*, &c., f. 19.

[c. 1760.—"The sound of **ding** Mahomed."—Orme, *Military Trans.* Madras reprint, ii. 339.

[1764.—"When our seapoys observed the enemy they gave them a **ding** or huzza."—*Carraccioli, Life of Clive* i. 57.]

DELHI, n.p. The famous capital of the great Moghuls, in the latter years of that family; and the seat under various names of many preceding dynasties, going back into ages of which we have no distinct record. *Dillī* is, according to Cunningham, the old Hindu form of the name; *Dihlī* is that used by Mahommedans. According to *Panjab Notes and Queries* (ii. 117 *seq.*), *Dilpat* is traditionally the name of the Dillī of Prithvī Rāj. *Dil* is an old Hindi word for an eminence; and this is probably the etymology of *Dilpat* and *Dillī*. The second quotation from Correa curiously illustrates the looseness of his geography. [The name has become unpleasantly familiar in connection with the so-called '*Delhi boil*,' a form of Oriental sore, similar to Biskra Button, Aleppo Evil, Lahore or Multan Sore (see *Delhi Gazetteer*, 15, note).]

1205.—(Muhammad Ghori marched) "towards **Dehli** (may God preserve its prosperity, and perpetuate its splendour!), which is among the chief (mother) cities of Hind."—*Hasan Nizāmi*, in *Elliot*, ii. 216.

c. 1321.—"Hanc terram (Tana, near Bombay) regunt Sarraceni, nunc subjacentes dal **dili**. . . . Audiens ipse imperator dol **Dali** . . . misit et ordinavit ut ipse Lomelic penitus caperetur. . . ."—*Fr. Odoric.* See *Cathay*, &c., App., pp. v. and x.

c. 1330.—"**Dilli** . . . a certain traveller relates that the brick-built walls of this great city are loftier than the walls of Hamath; it stands in a plain on a soil of mingled stones and sand. At the distance of a parasang runs a great river, not so big, however, as Euphrates."—*Abulfeda*, in *Gildemeister*, 189 *seq.*

c. 1334.—"The wall that surrounds **Dihlī** has no equal. . . . The city of **Dihlī** has 28 gates . . ." &c.—*Ibn Batuta*, iii. 147 *seqq.*

c. 1375.—The *Carta Catalana* of the French Library shows *ciutat de* **Dilli** and also *Lo Rey Dilli*, with this rubric below it: "*Aci esta un soldā gran e podaros molt rich. Aquest soldā ha* DCC *orifans e* C *millia homens à cavall sot lo seu imperi. Ha encora paons sens nombre. . . .*"

1459.—Fra Mauro's great map at Venice shows **Deli** *cittade grandissima*, and the rubrick *Questa cittade nobilissima zà dominava tuto el paese del* **Deli** *over India Prima.*

1516.—"This king of **Dely** confines with Tatars, and has taken many lands from the King of Cambay; and from the King of

Dacan, his servants and captains with many of his people, took much, and afterwards in time they revolted, and set themselves up as kings."—*Barbosa*, p. 100.

1533.—"And this kingdom to which the Badur proceeded was called the **Dely**; it was very great, but it was all disturbed by wars and the risings of one party against another, because the King was dead, and the sons were fighting with each other for the sovereignty."—*Correa*, iii. 506.

,, "This Kingdom of **Dely** is the greatest that is to be seen in those parts, for one point that it holds is in Persia, and the other is in contact with the Loochoos (*os Lequios*) beyond China."—*Ibid.* iii. 572.

c. 1568.—"About sixteen yeeres past this King (of Cuttack), with his Kingdome, were destroyed by the King of Pattane, which was also King of the greatest part of Bengala . . . but this tyrant enioyed his Kingdome but a small time, but was conquered by another tyrant, which was the great Mogol King of Agra, **Delly**, and of all Cambaia."—*Caesar Frederike* in *Hakl.* ii. 358.

1611.—"On the left hand is seene the carkasse of old **Dely**, called the nine castles and fiftie-two gates, now inhabited onely by *Googers*. . . . The city is 2^c betweene Gate and Gate, begirt with a strong wall, but much ruinate. . . ."—*W. Finch*, in *Purchas*, i. 430.

DELING, s. This was a kind of hammock conveyance, suspended from a pole, mentioned by the old travellers in Pegu. The word is not known to Burmese scholars, and is perhaps a Persian word. Meninski gives "*deleng*, adj. *pendulus*, *suspensus*." The *thing* seems to be the Malayālam *Manchīl*. (See **MUNCHEEL** and **DANDY**).

1569.—"Carried in a closet which they call **Deling**, in the which a man shall be very well accommodated, with cushions under his head."—*Çaesar Frederike*, in *Hakl.* ii. 367.

1585.—"This **Delingo** is a strong cotton cloth doubled, . . . as big as an ordinary rug, and having an iron at each end to attach it by, so that in the middle it hangs like a pouch or purse. These irons are attached to a very thick cane, and this is borne by four men. . . . When you go on a journey, a cushion is put at the head of this **Delingo**, and you get in, and lay your head on the cushion," &c.—*Gasparo Balbi*, f. 99*b*.

1587.—"From Cirion we went to Macao, which is a pretie towne, where we left our boats and *Paroes*, and in the morning taking **Delingeges**, which are a kind of Coches made of cords and cloth quilted, and carried vpon a stang betweene 3 and 4 men: we came to Pegu the same day."—*R. Fitch*, in *Hakl.* ii. 391.

DELLY, MOUNT, n.p. Port. *Monte D'Eli.* A mountain on the Malabar coast which forms a remarkable object from seaward, and the name of which occurs sometimes as applied to a State or City adjoining the mountain. It is prominently mentioned in all the old books on India, though strange to say the Map of India in Keith Johnstone's Royal Atlas has neither name nor indication of this famous hill. [It is shown in Constable's Hand Atlas.] It was, according to Correa, the first Indian land seen by Vasco da Gama. The name is Malayāl. *Eli mala*, 'High Mountain.' Several erroneous explanations have however been given. A common one is that it means 'Seven Hills.' This arose with the compiler of the local Skt. *Mahātmya* or legend, who rendered the name *Saptaṣaila*, 'Seven Hills,' confounding *ēli* with *ēḻu*, 'seven,' which has no application. Again we shall find it explained as 'Rat-hill'; but here *ĕli* is substituted for *ēli*. [The *Madras Gloss.* gives the word as Mal. *ezhimala*, and explains it as 'Rat-hill,' "because infested by rats."] The position of the town and port of Ely or Hili mentioned by the older travellers is a little doubtful, but see *Marco Polo*, notes to Bk. III. ch. xxiv. The *Ely-Maide* of the Peutingerian Tables is not unlikely to be an indication of Ely.

1298.—"Eli is a Kingdom towards the west, about 300 miles from Comari. . . . There is no proper harbour in the country, but there are many rivers with good estuaries, wide and deep."—*Marco Polo*, Bk. III. ch. 24.

c. 1330.—"Three days journey beyond this city (Manjarūr, *i.e.* Mangalore) there is a great hill which projects into the sea, and is descried by travellers from afar, the promontory called **Hili**."—*Abulfeda*, in *Gildemeister*, 185.

c. 1343.—"At the end of that time we set off for **Hili**, where we arrived two days later. It is a large well-built town on a great bay (or estuary) which big ships enter."—*Ibn Batuta*, iv. 81.

c. 1440.—"Proceeding onwards he . . . arrived at two cities situated on the sea shore, one named Pacamuria, and the other **Helly**."—*Nicolo Conti*, in *India in the XVth Cent.* p. 6.

1516.—"After passing this place along the coast is the Mountain **Dely**, on the edge of the sea; it is a round mountain, very lofty, in the midst of low land; all the ships of the Moors and the Gentiles . . .

sight this mountain . . . and make their reckoning by it."—*Barbosa*, 149.

c. 1562.—"In twenty days they got sight of land, which the pilots foretold before that they saw it, this was a great mountain which is on the coast of India, in the Kingdom of Cananor, which the people of the country in their language call the mountain **Dely**, *elly* meaning 'the rat,'* and they call it Mount **Dely**, because in this mountain there are so many rats that they could never make a village there."—*Correa, Three Voyages*, &c., Hak. Soc. 145.

1579.—". . . Malik Ben Habeeb . . . proceeded first to Quilon . . . and after erecting a mosque in that town and settling his wife there, he himself journeyed on to [Hīlī Marāwī]. . . ."—Rowlandson's Tr. of *Tohfut-ul-Mujahideen*, p. 54. (Here and elsewhere in this ill-edited book *Hīlī Marāwī* is read and printed *Hubaee Murawee*).

[1623.—". . . a high Hill, inland near the seashore, call'd Monte **Deli**."—*P. della Valle*, Hak. Soc. ii. 355].

1638.—"Sur le midy nous passames à la veüe de **Monte-Leone**, qui est vne haute montagne dont les Malabares descouurent de loin les vaisseaux, qu'ils peuuent attaquer avec aduantage."—*Mandelslo*, 275.

1727.—"And three leagues south from **Mount Delly** is a spacious deep River called Balliapatam, where the English Company had once a Factory for Pepper."—*A. Hamilton*, i. 291; [ed. 1744, ii. 293].

1759.—"We are further to remark that the late troubles at Tellicherry, which proved almost fatal to that settlement, took rise from a dispute with our linguist and the Prince of that Country, relative to lands he, the linguist, held at **Mount Dilly**."—*Court's Letter* of March 23. In *Long*, 198.

DELOLL, s. A broker; H. from Ar. *dallāl*; the literal meaning being one who directs (the buyer and seller to their bargain). In Egypt the word is now also used in particular for a broker of old clothes and the like, as described by Lane below. (See also under **NEELÁM**.)

[c. 1665.—"He spared also the house of a deceased **Delale** or Gentile broker, of the Dutch."—*Bernier*, ed. *Constable*, 188. In the first English trans. this passage runs: "He has also regard to the House of the Deceased *De Lale*."]

1684.—"Five **Delolls**, or Brokers, of Decca, after they had been with me went to Mr. Beard's chamber. . . ."—*Hedges, Diary*, July 25; [Hak. Soc. i. 152].

1754.—"Mr. Baillie at Jugdea, accused by these villains, our **dulols**, who carried on for a long time their most flagrant rascality. The **Dulols** at Jugdea found to charge the Company 15 per cent. beyond the price of the goods."—*Fort Wm. Cons.* In *Long*, p. 50.

1824.—"I was about to answer in great wrath, when a **dalal**, or broker, went by, loaded with all sorts of second-hand clothes, which he was hawking about for sale."—*Hajji Baba*, 2d ed. i. 183; [ed. 1851, p. 81].

1835.—"In many of the sooks in Cairo, auctions are held . . . once or twice a week. They are conducted by '**dellâls**' (or brokers). . . . The '**dellâls**' carry the goods up and down, announcing the sums bidden by the cries of 'haráq.'"—*Lane, Mod. Egyptians*, ed. 1860, p. 317; [5th ed. ii. 13].

* A correction is made here on Lord Stanley's translation.

DEMIJOHN, s. A large glass bottle holding 20 or 30 quarts, or more. The word is not Anglo-Indian, but it is introduced here because it has been supposed to be the corruption of an Oriental word, and suggested to have been taken from the name of *Damaghān* in Persia. This looks plausible (compare the Persian origin of **carboy**, which is another name for just the same *thing*), but no historical proof has yet been adduced, and it is doubted by Mr. Marsh in his *Notes on Wedgwood's Dictionary*, and by Dozy (*Sup. aux Dict. Arabes*). It may be noticed, as worthy of further enquiry, that Sir T. Herbert (192) speaks of the abundance and cheapness of *wine* at Damaghān. Niebuhr, however, in a passage quoted below, uses the word as an Oriental one, and in a note on the 5th ed. of Lane's *Mod. Egyptians*, 1860, p. 149, there is a remark quoted from Hammer-Purgstall as to the omission from the detail of domestic vessels of two whose names have been adopted in European languages, viz. the *garra* or *jarra*, a water 'jar,' and the *demigān* or *demijān*, '*la dame-jeanne*.' The word is undoubtedly known in modern Arabic. The *Moḥīt* of B. Bistānī, the chief modern native lexicon, explains *Dāmijāna* as 'a great glass vessel, big-bellied and narrow-necked, and covered with wicker-work; a Persian word.'* The vulgar use the forms *damajāna* and *damanjāna*. *Dame-jeanne* appears in *P. Richelet, Dict. de la Langue Franc.* (1759), with this definition: "[*Lagena amplior*] Nom que les matelots donnent à une grande bouteille couverte

* Probably not much stress can be laid on this last statement. [The *N.E.D.* thinks that the Arabic word came from the West].

de natte." It is not in the great Castilian Dict. of 1729, but it is in those of the last century, *e.g.* Dict. of the Span. Academy, ed. 1869. "*Damajuana*, f. Prov(incia de) And(alucia, CASTAÑA . . ."—and *castaña* is explained as a "great vessel of glass or terra cotta, of the figure of a chestnut, and used to hold liquor." [See *N.E.D.* which believes the word adopted from *dame-jeanne*, on the analogy of 'Bellarmine' and 'Greybeard.']

1762.—"Notre vin étoit dans de grands flacons de verre (**Damasjanes**) dont chacun tenoit près de 20 bouteilles."—*Niebuhr, Voyage*, i. 171.

DENGUE, s. The name applied to a kind of fever. The term is of West Indian, not East Indian, origin, and has only become known and familiar in India within the last 30 years or more. The origin of the name which seems to be generally accepted is, that owing to the stiff unbending carriage which the fever induced in those who suffered from it, the negroes in the W. Indies gave it the name of '*dandy* fever'; and this name, taken up by the Spaniards, was converted into *dengy* or *dengue*. [But according to the *N.E.D.* both '*dandy*' and '*dengue*' are corruptions of the Swahili term, *ka dinga pepo*, 'sudden cramp-like seizure by an evil spirit.'] Some of its usual characteristics are the great suddenness of attack; often a red eruption; pain amounting sometimes to anguish in head and back, and shifting pains in the joints; excessive and sudden prostration; after-pains of rheumatic character. Its epidemic occurrences are generally at long intervals.

Omitting such occurrences in America and in Egypt, symptoms attach to an epidemic on the Coromandel coast about 1780 which point to this disease; and in 1824 an epidemic of the kind caused much alarm and suffering in Calcutta, Berhampore, and other places in India. This had no repetition of equal severity in that quarter till 1871-72, though there had been a minor visitation in 1853, and a succession of cases in 1868-69. In 1872 it was so prevalent in Calcutta that among those in the service of the E. I. Railway Company, European and native, prior to August in that year, 70 per cent. had suffered from the disease; and whole households were sometimes attacked at once. It became endemic in Lower Bengal for several seasons. When the present writer (H. Y.) left India (in 1862) the name **dengue** may have been known to medical men, but it was quite unknown to the lay European public.

1885.—THE CONTAGION OF DENGUE FEVER. "In a recent issue (March 14th, p. 551) under the heading '**Dengue** Fever in New Caledonia,' you remark that, although there had been upwards of nine hundred cases, yet, 'curiously enough,' there had not been one death. May I venture to say that the 'curiosity' would have been much greater had there been a death? For, although this disease is one of the most infectious, and as I can testify from unpleasant personal experience, one of the most painful that there is, yet death is a very rare occurrence. In an epidemic at Bermuda in 1882, in which about five hundred cases came under my observation, not one death was recorded. In that epidemic, which attacked both whites and blacks impartially, inflammation of the cellular tissue, affecting chiefly the face, neck, and scrotum, was especially prevalent as a sequela, none but the lightest cases escaping. I am not aware that this is noted in the text-books as a characteristic of the disease; in fact, the descriptions in the books then available to me, differed greatly from the disease as I then found it, and I believe that was the experience of other medical officers at the time. . . . During the epidemic of **dengue** above mentioned, an officer who was confined to his quarters, convalescing from the disease, wrote a letter home to his father in England. About three days after the receipt of the letter, that gentleman complained of being ill, and eventually, from his description, had a rather severe attack of what, had he been in Bermuda, would have been called dengue fever. As it was, his medical attendant was puzzled to give a name to it. The disease did not spread to the other members of the family, and the patient made a good recovery.—*Henry J. Barnes*, Surgeon, Medical Staff, Fort Pitt, Chatham." From *British Medical Journal*, April 25.

DEODAR, s. The *Cedrus deodara*, Loud., of the Himālaya, now known as an ornamental tree in England for some seventy-five years past. The finest specimens in the Himālaya are often found in clumps shadowing a small temple. The **Deodar** is now regarded by botanists as a variety of *Cedrus Libani*. It is confined to the W. Himālaya from Nepāl to Afghanistan; it reappears as the Cedar of Lebanon in Syria, and on through Cyprus and Asia Minor; and emerges once more in Algeria, and thence westwards to the Riff Mountains in Morocco, under the name of *C. Atlantica.* The word occurs in Avicenna, who speaks of the *Deiudar* as yielding a kind of turpentine (see below). We may note that an article called *Deodar-wood Oil* appears in Dr. Forbes Watson's "List of Indian Products" (No. 2941) [and see *Watt, Econ. Dict.* ii. 235].

Deodar is by no means the universal name of the great Cedar in the Himālay. It is called so (*Dewdār*, *Diār*, or *Dyār* [*Drew, Jummoo*, 100]) in Kashmīr, where the *deodār* pillars of the great mosque of Srinagar date from A.D. 1401. The name, indeed (*devadāru*, 'timber of the gods'), is applied in different parts of India to different trees, and even in the Himālaya to more than one. The list just referred to (which however has not been revised critically) gives this name in different modifications as applied also to the pencil Cedar (*Juniperus excelsa*), to *Guatteria* (or *Uvaria*) *longifolia*, to *Sethia Indica*, to *Erythroxylon areolatum*, and (on the Rāvī and Sutlej) to *Cupressus torulosa.*

The **Deodār** first became known to Europeans in the beginning of the last century, when specimens were sent to Dr. Roxburgh, who called it a *Pinus.* Seeds were sent to Europe by Capt. Gerard in 1819; but the first that grew were those sent by the Hon. W. Leslie Melville in 1822.

c. 1030.—"**Deiudar** (or rather **Diudar**) est ex genere abhel (*i.e.* juniper) quae dicitur pinus Inda, et *Syr deiudar* (Milk of Deodar) est ejus lac (turpentine)."—*Avicenna*, Lat. Transl. p. 297.

c. 1220.—"He sent for two trees, one of which was a . . . white poplar, and the other a **deodár**, that is a fir. He planted them both on the boundary of Kashmīr."—*Chach Nâmah* in *Elliot*, i. 144.

DERRISHACST, adj. This extraordinary word is given by C. B. P. (MS.) as a corruption of P. *daryā-shikast*, 'destroyed by the river.'

DERVISH, s. P. *darvesh*; a member of a Mahommedan religious order. The word is hardly used now among Anglo-Indians, *fakīr* [see **FAKEER**] having taken its place. On the Mahommedan confraternities of this class, see *Herklots*, 179 *seqq.*; *Lane, Mod. Egyptians*, *Brown's Dervishes*, or *Oriental Spiritualism*; *Capt. E. de Neven, Les Khouan, Ordres Religieux chez les Musulmans* (Paris, 1846).

c. 1540.—"The dog *Coia Acem* . . . crying out with a loud voyce, that every one might hear him. . . . *To them, To them, for as we are assured by the Book of Flowers, wherein the Prophet* Noby *doth promise eternal delights to the* **Daroezes** *of the House of* Mecqua, *that he will keep his word both with you and me, provided that we bathe ourselves in the blood of these dogs without Law!*"—*Pinto* (cap. lix.), in *Cogan*, 72.

1554.—"Hic multa didicimus à monachis Turcicis, quos **Dervis** vocant."—*Busbeq. Epist.* I. p. 93.

1616.—"Among the *Mahometans* are many called **Dervises**, which relinquish the World, and spend their days in Solitude."—*Terry*, in *Purchas*, ii. 1477.

[c. 1630.—"**Deruissi.**" See **TALISMAN.**]

1653.—"Il estoit **Dervische** ou Fakir et menoit une vie solitaire dans les bois."—*De la Boullaye-le-Gouz*, ed. 1657, p. 182.

1670.—"Aureng-Zebe . . . was reserved, crafty, and exceedingly versed in dissembling, insomuch that for a long time he made profession to be a *Fakire*, that is, Poor, **Dervich**, or Devout, renouncing the World." *Bernier*, E.T. 3; [ed. *Constable*, 10].

1673.—"The **Dervises** professing Poverty, assume this Garb here (*i.e.* in Persia), but not with that state they ramble up and down in India."—*Fryer*, 392.

DESSAYE, s. Mahr. *deśāī*; in W. and S. India a native official in charge of a district, often held hereditarily; a petty chief. (See **DISSAVE.**)

1590-91.—". . . the **Desayes**, Mukaddams, and inhabitants of several parganahs made a complaint at Court."—Order in *Mirat-i-Ahmadi* (Bird's Tr.), 408.

[1811.—"**Daiseye.**"—*Kirkpatrick, Letters of Tippoo*, p. 196.]

1883.—"The **Desai** of Sawantwari has arrived at Delhi on a visit. He is accompanied by a European Assistant Political Officer and a large following. From Delhi His Highness goes to Agra, and visits Calcutta before returning to his territory, *viâ* Madras."—*Pioneer Mail*, Jan. 24.

The regular title of this chief appears to be *Sar-Deśāī.*

DESTOOR, s. A Parsee priest; P. *dastūr*, from the Pahlavi *dastôbar*, 'a prime minister, councillor of State . . . a high priest, a bishop of the Parsees; a custom, mode, manner' (*Haug, Old Pahlavi and Pazand Glossary*). [See **DUSTOOR.**]

1630.—". . . their **Distoree** or high priest. . . ."—*Lord's Display*, &c., ch. viii.

1689.—"The highest Priest of the *Persies* is called **Destoor**, their ordinary Priests *Daroos*, or *Hurboods* [**HERBED**]."—*Ovington*, 376.

1809.—"The **Dustoor** is the chief priest of his sect in Bombay."—*Maria Graham*, 36.

1877.—". . . le **Destour** de nos jours, pas plus que le Mage d'autrefois, ne soupçonne les phases successives que sa religion a traversées."—*Darmesteter, Ormazd et Ahriman*, 4.

DEUTI, DUTY, s. H. *diuṭī, dewṭī, deoṭi*, Skt. *dīpa*, 'a lamp'; a lamp-stand, but also a link-bearer.

c. 1526.—(In Hindustan) "instead of a candle or torch, you have a gang of dirty fellows whom they call **Deûtis**, who hold in their hand a kind of small tripod, to the side of one leg of which . . . they fasten a pliant wick. . . . In their right hand they hold a gourd . . . and whenever the wick requires oil, they supply it from this gourd. . . . If their emperors or chief nobility at any time have occasion for a light by night, these filthy **Deûtis** bring in their lamp . . . and there stand holding it close by his side." —*Baber*, 333.

1681.—"Six men for **Dutys**, *Rundell* (see **ROUNDEL**), and Kittysole (see **KITTYSOLL**)."—List of Servants allowed at Madapollam Factory. *Ft. St. George Cons.*, Jan. 8. In *Notes and Exts.* No. ii. p. 72.

DEVA-DĀSĪ, s. H. 'Slave-girl of the gods'; the official name of the poor girls who are devoted to dancing and prostitution in the idol-temples, of Southern India especially. "The like existed at ancient Corinth under the name of ἱερόδουλοι, which is nearly a translation of the Hindi name . . . (see *Strabo*, viii. 6)." —*Marco Polo*, 2nd ed. ii. 338. These appendages of Aphrodite worship, borrowed from Phœnicia, were the same thing as the *kĕdēshōth* repeatedly mentioned in the Old Testament, *e.g. Deut.* xxiii. 18: "Thou shalt not bring the wages of a *kĕdēsha* . . . into the House of Jehovah." [See *Cheyne*, in *Encycl. Bibl.* ii. 1964 *seq.*] Both male and female ἱερόδουλοι are mentioned in the famous inscription of Citium in Cyprus (*Corp. Inscr. Semit.* No. 86); the latter under the name of *'alma*, curiously near that of the modern Egyptian *'ālima*. (See **DANCING-GIRL**.)

1702.—"Peu de temps après je baptisai une **Deva-Dachi**, ou *Esclave Divine*, c'est ainsi qu'on appelle les femmes dont les Prêtres des idoles abusent, sous prétexte que leurs dieux les demandent."—*Lettres Edifiantes*, x. 245.

c. 1790.—"La principale occupation des **devedaschies**, est de danser devant l'image de la divinité qu'elles servent, et de chanter ses louanges, soit dans son temple, soit dans les rues, lorsqu'on porte l'idole dans des processions. . . ."—*Haafner* ii. 105.

1868.—"The **Dâsis**, the dancing girls attached to Pagodas. They are each of them married to an idol when quite young. Their male children . . . have no difficulty in acquiring a decent position in society. The female children are generally brought up to the trade of their mothers. . . . It is customary with a few castes to present their superfluous daughters to the Pagodas. . . ." —*Nelson's Madura*, Pt. 2, p. 79.

DEVIL, s. A petty whirlwind, or circular storm, is often so called. (See **PISACHEE, SHAITAN, TYPHOON**.)

[1608-10.—"Often you see coming from afar great whirlwinds which the sailors call **dragons**."—*Pyrard de Laval*, Hak. Soc. i. 11.

[1813.—". . . we were often surrounded by the little whirlwinds called *bugulas*, or **Devils**."—*Forbes, Or. Mem.* 2nd ed. i. 118.]

DEVIL-BIRD, s. This is a name used in Ceylon for a bird believed to be a kind of owl—according to Haeckel, quoted below, the *Syrnium Indrani* of Sykes, or Brown Wood Owl of Jerdon. Mr. Mitford, quoted below, however, believes it to be a *Podargus*, or Nighthawk.

c. 1328.—"Quid dicam? **Diabolus** ibi etiam loquitur, saepe et saepius, hominibus, nocturnis temporibus, sicut ego audivi."—*Jordani Mirabilia*, in *Rec. de Voyages*, iv. 53.

1681.—"This for certain I can affirm, That oftentimes the **Devil** doth cry with an audible Voice in the Night; 'tis very shrill, almost like the barking of a Dog. This I have often heard myself; but never heard that he did anybody any harm. . . . To believe that this is the Voice of the Devil these reasons urge, because there is no Creature known to the Inhabitants, that cry like it, and because it will on a sudden depart from one place, and make a noise in another, quicker than any fowl could fly; and because the very Dogs will tremble and shake when they hear it."—*Knox's Ceylon*, 78.

1849.—"**Devil's Bird** (Strix Gaulama or Ulama, *Singh.*). A species of owl. The wild and wailing cry of this bird is considered a sure presage of death and misfortune, unless measures be taken to avert its infernal threats, and refuse its warning. Though often heard even on the tops of their houses, the natives maintain that it has never been caught or distinctly seen, and they consider it to be one of the most annoying of the evil spirits which haunt their country."—*Pridham's Ceylon*, p. 737-8.

1860.—"The **Devil-Bird**, is not an owl . . . its ordinary note is a magnificent clear shout like that of a human being, and which can be heard at a great distance. It has another cry like that of a hen just caught, but the sounds which have earned for it its bad name . . . are indescribable, the most appalling that can be imagined, and scarcely to be heard without shuddering; I can only compare it to a boy in torture, whose screams are being stopped by being strangled."—*Mr. Mitford's Note* in *Tennent's Ceylon*, i. 167.

1881.—"The uncanny cry of the **devil-bird**, *Syrnium Indrani* . . ."—*Haeckel's Visit to Ceylon*, 235.

DEVIL'S REACH, n.p. This was the old name of a reach on the Hoogly R. a little above Pulta (and about 15 miles above Calcutta). On that reach are several groups of **dewals**, or idol-temples, which probably gave the name.

1684.—"August 28.—I borrowed the late Dutch Fiscall's Budgero (see **BUDGEROW**), and went in Company with Mr. Beard, Mr. Littleton" (etc.) "as far as y^e^ **Devill's Reach**, where I caused ye tents to be pitched in expectation of ye President's arrivall and lay here all night."—*Hedges, Diary*, Hak. Soc. i. 156.

1711.—"From the lower Point of **Devil's Reach** you must keep mid-channel, or nearest the Starboard Shore, for the Larboard is shoal until you come into the beginning of *Pulta* or *Poutto* Reach, and there abreast of a single great Tree, you must edge over to the East Shore below Pulta."—*The English Pilot*, 54.

DEVIL WORSHIP. This phrase is a literal translation of *bhūta-pūjā*, *i.e.* worship of *bhūtas* [see **BHOOT**], a word which appears in slightly differing forms in various languages of India, including the Tamil country. A *bhūta*, or as in Tamil more usually, *pēy*, is a malignant being which is conceived to arise from the person of anyone who has come to a violent death. This superstition, in one form or another, seems to have formed the religion of the Dravidian tribes of S. India before the introduction of Brahmanism, and is still the real religion of nearly all the low castes in that region, whilst it is often patronized also by the higher castes. These superstitions, and especially the demonolatrous rites called 'devil-dancing,' are identical in character with those commonly known as *Shamanism* [see **SHAMAN**], and which are spread all over Northern Asia, among the red races of America, and among a vast variety of tribes in Ceylon and in Indo-China, not excluding the Burmese. A full account of the demon-worship of Tinnevelly was given by Bp. Caldwell in a small pamphlet on the "Tinnevelly Shanars" (Madras 1849), and interesting evidence of its identity with the Shamanism of other regions will be found in his *Comparative Grammar* (2nd ed. 579 *seqq.*); see also *Marco Polo*, 2nd ed. ii. 79 *seq.*; [Oppert. *Orig. Inhabit. of Bharatavarśa*, 554 *seqq.*]

DÉWAL, DÉWÁLÉ, s. H. *dewal*, Skt. *deva-ālaya*; a Temple or pagoda. This, or *Dewalgarh*, is the phrase commonly used in the Bombay territory for a Christian church. In Ceylon **Déwálé** is a temple dedicated to a Hindu god.

1681.—"The second order of Priests are those called *Koppuhs*, who are the Priests that belong to the Temples of the other Gods (*i.e.* other than *Boddou*, or Buddha). Their Temples are called **Dewals**."—*Knox, Ceylon*, 79.

[1797.—"The Company will settle . . . the **dewal** or temple charge."—Treaty, in *Logan, Malabar*, iii. 285.

[1813.—"They plant it (the nayna tree) near the **dewals** or Hindoo temples, improperly called Pagodas."—*Forbes, Or. Mem.* 2nd ed. i. 15].

DEWALEEA, s. H. *diwāliyā*, 'a bankrupt,' from *diwālā*, 'bankruptcy,' and that, though the etymology is disputed, is alleged to be connected with *dīpa*, 'a lamp'; because "it is the custom . . . when a merchant finds himself failing, or failed, to set up a blazing lamp in his house, shop, or office, and abscond therefrom for some time until his creditors are satisfied by a disclosure of his accounts or dividend of assets."—*Drummond's Illustrations* (s.v.).

DEWALLY, s. H. *diwālī*, from Skt. *dīpa-ālikā*, 'a row of lamps,' *i.e.* an illumination. An autumnal feast attributed to the celebration of various divinities, as of Lakshmī and of Bhavānī, and also in honour of Krishna's slaying of the demon Naraka, and the release of 16,000 maidens, his prisoners. It is held on the last two days of the dark half of the month *Aśvina* or *Aśan*, and on the new moon and four following days of *Karttika*, *i.e.*

usually some time in October. But there are variations of Calendar in different parts of India, and feasts will not always coincide, *e.g.* at the three Presidency towns, nor will any curt expression define the dates. In Bengal the name *Diwālī* is not used; it is *Kālī Pūjā*, the feast of that grim goddess, a midnight festival on the most moonless nights of the month, celebrated by illuminations and fireworks, on land and river, by feasting, carousing, gambling, and sacrifice of goats, sheep, and buffaloes.

1613.—". . . no equinoctio da entrada de libra, dià chamado **Divâly**, tem tal privilegio e vertude que obriga falar as arvores, plantas e ervas. . . ."—*Godinho de Eredia*, f. 38*v*.

[1623.—"October the four and twentieth was the **Davàli**, or Feast of the Indian Gentiles."—*P. della Valle*, Hak. Soc. ii. 206.]

1651.—"In the month of *October*, eight days after the full moon, there is a feast held in honour of Vistnou, which is called **Dipáwali**."—*A. Rogerius, De Open-Deure*.

[1671. — "In October they begin their yeare with great feasting, Jollity, Sending Presents to all they have any busynes with, which time is called **Dually**." — *Hedges, Diary*, Hak. Soc. ii. cccxiv.]

1673.—"The first New Moon in October is the Banyan's **Dually**."—*Fryer*, 110.

1690.—". . . their Grand Festival Season, called the **Dually** Time."—*Ovington*, 401.

1820.—"The **Dewalee**, **Deepaullee**, or Time of Lights, takes place 20 days after the **Dussera**, and lasts three days; during which there is feasting, illumination, and fireworks."—*T. Coats*, in *Tr. Lit. Soc. Bo.*, ii. 211.

1843.—"Nov. 5. The **Dīwālī**, happening to fall on this day, the whole river was bright with lamps. . . . Ever and anon some votary would offer up his prayers to Lakshmi the *Fortuna*, and launch a tiny raft bearing a cluster of lamps into the water,—then watch it with fixed and anxious gaze. If it floats on till the far distance hides it, thrice happy he . . . but if, caught in some wild eddy of the stream, it disappears at once, so will the bark of his fortunes be engulphed in the whirlpool of adversity."—*Dry Leaves from Young Egypt*, 84.

1883. — "The **Dīvālī** is celebrated with splendid effect at Benares. . . . At the approach of night small earthen lamps, fed with oil, are prepared by millions, and placed quite close together, so as to mark out every line of mansion, palace, temple, minaret, and dome in streaks of fire." — *Monier Williams, Religious Thought and Life in India*, 432.

DEWAUN, s. The chief meanings of this word in Anglo-Indian usage are: (1) Under the Mahommedan Governments which preceded us, "the head financial minister, whether of the state or a province . . . charged, in the latter, with the collection of the revenue, the remittance of it to the imperial treasury, and invested with extensive judicial powers in all civil and financial causes" (*Wilson*). It was in this sense that the grant of the **Dewauny** (q.v.) to the E. I. Company in 1765 became the foundation of the British Empire in India. (2) The prime minister of a native State. (3) The chief native officer of certain Government establishments, such as the Mint; or the native manager of a Zemindary. (4) (In Bengal) a native servant in confidential charge of the dealings of a house of business with natives, or of the affairs of a large domestic establishment. These meanings are perhaps all reducible to one conception, of which 'Steward' would be an appropriate expression. But the word has had many other ramifications of meaning, and has travelled far.

The Arabian *dīwān* is, according to Lane, an Arabicized word of Persian origin (though some hold it for pure Arabic), and is in original meaning nearly equivalent to Persian *daftar* (see **DUFTER**), *i.e.* a collection of written leaves or sheets (forming a book for registration); hence 'a register of accounts'; a 'register of soldiers or pensioners'; a 'register of the rights or dues of the State, or relating to the acts of government, the finances and the administration'; also any book, and especially a collection of the poems of some particular poet. It was also applied to signify 'an account'; then a 'writer of accounts'; a 'place of such writers of accounts'; also a 'council, court, or tribunal'; and in the present day, a 'long seat formed of a mattress laid along the wall of a room, with cushions, raised or on the floor'; or 'two or more of such seats.' Thus far (in this paragraph) we abstract from Lane.

The Arabian historian Bilāḍurī (c. 860) relates as to the first introduction of the *dīwān* that, when 'Omar was discussing with the people how to divide the enormous wealth derived from the conquests in his time, Walīd bin Hishām bin Moghaira said to the caliph, 'I have been in Syria, and saw that its kings make a **dīwān**; do thou the like.' So 'Omar accepted his advice, and sent for two men of the Persian tongue, and said to them: 'Write down the people according to their rank' (and corresponding pensions).*

We must observe that in the Mahommedan States of the Mediterranean the word *dīwān* became especially applied to the Custom-house, and thus passed into the Romance languages as *aduana, douane, dogana,* &c. Littré indeed avoids any decision as to the etymology of *douane,* &c. And Hyde (Note on Abr. Peritsol, in *Syntagma Dissertt.* i. 101) derives *dogana* from *docân* (*i.e.* P. *dukān,* '*officina,* a shop'). But such passages as that below from Ibn Jubair, and the fact that, in the medieval Florentine treaties with the Mahommedan powers of Barbary and Egypt, the word *dīwān* in the Arabic texts constantly represents the *dogana* of the Italian, seem sufficient to settle the question (see *Amari, Diplomi Arabi del Real Archivio,* &c.; *e.g.* p. 104, and (Latin) p. 305, and in many other places).† The Spanish Dict. of Cobarruvias (1611) quotes Urrea as saying that "from the Arabic noun **Diuanum,** which signifies the house where the duties are collected, we form *diuana,* and thence *adiuana,* and lastly *aduana.*"

At a later date the word was re-imported into Europe in the sense of a hall furnished with Turkish couches and cushions, as well as of a couch of this kind. Hence we get *cigar*-**divans,** *et hoc genus omne.* The application to certain collections of poems is noticed above. It seems to be especially applied to assemblages of short poems of homogeneous character. Thus the *Odes* of Horace, the *Sonnets* of Petrarch, the *In Memoriam* of Tennyson, answer to the character of **Dīwān** so used. Hence also Goethe took the title of his *West-Östliche Diwan.*

c. A. D. 636.—". . . in the Caliphate of Omar the spoil of Syria and Persia began in ever-increasing volume to pour into the treasury of Medina, where it was distributed almost as soon as received. What was easy in small beginnings by equal sharing or discretionary preference, became now a heavy task. . . . At length, in the 2nd or 3rd year of his Caliphate, Omar determined that the distribution should be regulated on a fixed and systematic scale. . . . To carry out this vast design, a Register had to be drawn and kept up of every man, woman, and child, entitled to a stipend from the State. . . . The Register itself, as well as the office for its maintenance and for pensionary account, was called the **Dewân** or Department of the Exchequer."—*Muir's Annals,* &c., pp. 225-9.

As Minister, &c.

[1610.—"We propose to send you the copy hereof by the old scrivano of the **Aduano.**"—*Danvers, Letters,* i. 51.

[1616.—"Sheak Isuph **Dyvon** of Amadavaz."—*Foster, Letters,* iv. 311.]

1690.—"Fearing miscarriage of ye Originall *ffarcuttee* [*fārigh-khaṭṭī,* Ar. 'a deed of release,' variously corrupted in Indian technical use] we have herewith Sent you a Coppy Attested by Hugly Cazee, hoping ye **Duan** may be Sattisfied therewith."—MS. Letter in India Office, from *Job Charnock* and others at Chuttanutte to Mr. Ch. Eyre at Ballasore.

c. 1718. — "Even the **Divan** of the Qhalissah Office, who is, properly speaking, the Minister of the finances, or at least the accomptant general, was become a mere cypher, or a body without a soul."—*Seir Mutaqherin,* i. 110.

1762.—"A letter from Dacca states that the Hon'ble Company's **Dewan** (Manikchand) died on the morning of this letter. . . . As they apprehend he has died worth a large sum of money which the Government's people (*i.e.* of the Nawāb) may be desirous to possess to the injury of his lawful heirs, they request the protection of the flag . . . to the family of a man who has served the Company for upwards of 30 years with care and fidelity."—*Ft. Wm. Cons.,* Nov. 29. In *Long,* 283.

1766.—"There then resided at his Court a *Gentoo* named *Allum Chund,* who had been many years **Dewan** to Soujah Khan, by whom he was much revered for his great age, wisdom, and faithful services."—*Holwell, Hist. Events,* i. 74.

1771.—"By our general address you will be informed that we have to be dissatisfied with the administration of Mahomet Reza Cawn, and will perceive the expediency of our divesting him of the rank and influence he holds as Naib **Duan** of the Kingdom of Bengal."—*Court of Directors to W. Hastings,* in *Gleig,* i. 121.

1783.—"The Committee, with the best intentions, best abilities, and steadiest of application, must after all be a tool in the hands of their **Duan.**"—*Teignmouth, Mem.* i. 74.

* We owe this quotation, as well as that below from Ibn Jubair, to the kindness of Prof. Robertson Smith. On the proceedings of 'Omar see also Sir Wm. Muir's *Annals of the Early Caliphate* in the chapter quoted below.

† At p. 6 there is an Arabic letter, dated A.D. 1200, from Abdurrahmān ibn 'Ali Tāhir, '*al-nazir ba-dīwān Ifriḳiya,*' inspector of the dogana of Africa. But in the Latin version this appears as *Rector omnium Christianorum qui veniunt in totam provinciam de Africa* (p. 276). In another letter, without date, from Yusuf ibn Mahommed *Sāhib dīwān Tunis wal-Mahdia,* Amari renders 'preposto della dogana di Tunis,' &c. (p. 311).

1834.—"His (Raja of Ulwar's) **Dewanjee**, Balmochun, who chanced to be in the neighbourhood, with 6 Risalas of horse . . . was further ordered to go out and meet me." —*Mem. of Col. Mountain*, 132.

[1861.—See quotation under **AMEEN.**]

In the following quotations the identity of *dīwān* and *douane* or *dogana* is shown more or less clearly.

A. D. 1178.—"The Moslem were ordered to disembark their goods (at Alexandria), and what remained of their stock of provisions; and on the shore were officers who took them in charge, and carried all that was landed to the **Dīwān**. They were called forward one by one; the property of each was brought out, and the **Dīwān** was straitened with the crowd. The search fell on every article, small or great; one thing got mixt up with another, and hands were thrust into the midst of the packages to discover if anything were concealed in them. Then, after this, an oath was administered to the owners that they had nothing more than had been found. Amid all this, in the confusion of hands and the greatness of the crowd many things went a-missing. At length the passengers were dismissed after a scene of humiliation and great ignominy, for which we pray God to grant an ample recompense. But this, past doubt, is one of the things kept hidden from the great Sultan Salāh-ud-dīn, whose well-known justice and benevolence are such that, if he knew it, he would certainly abolish the practice" [*viz.* as regards Mecca pilgrims].* —*Ibn Jubair*, orig. in *Wright's* ed., p. 36.

c. 1340.—"**Doana** *in all the cities of the Saracens*, in Sicily, in Naples, and throughout the Kingdom of Apulia . . . *Dazio* at Venice; *Gabella* throughout Tuscany; . . . *Costuma* throughout the Island of England. . . . All these names mean *duties* which have to be paid for goods and wares and other things, imported to, or exported from, or passed through the countries and places detailed."—*Francesco Balducci Pegolotti*, see *Cathay*, &c., ii. 285-6.

c. 1348.—"They then order the skipper to state in detail all the goods that the vessel contains. . . . Then everybody lands, and the keepers of the custom-house (*al*-**dīwān**) sit and pass in review whatever one has."—*Ibn Batuta*, iv. 265.

The following medieval passage in one of our note-books remains a fragment without date or source:

(?).—"Multi quoque Saracenorum, qui vel in apothecis suis mercibus vendendis praeerunt, vel in **Duanis** fiscales. . . ."

1440.—The Handbook of Giovanni da Uzzano, published along with Pegolotti by Pagnini (1765-66) has for custom-house **Dovana**, which corroborates the identity of *Dogana* with *Dīwān*.

A Council Hall:

1367.—"Hussyn, fearing for his life, came down and hid himself under the tower, but his enemies . . . surrounded the mosque, and having found him, brought him to the (**Dyvan**-*Khane*) Council Chamber."—*Mem. of Timūr*, tr. by *Stewart*, p. 130.

1554. — "Utcunque sit, cum mane in **Divanum** (is concilii vt alias dixi locus est) imprudens omnium venisset. . . ."—*Busbequii Epistolae*, ii. p. 138.

A place, fitted with mattresses, &c., to sit in:

1676.—"On the side that looks towards the River, there is a **Divan**, or a kind of out-jutting Balcony, where the King sits."—*Tavernier*, E.T. ii. 49; [ed. *Ball*, i. 108].

[1785.—"It seems to have been intended for a **Duan Konna**, or eating room."—*Forbes, Or. Mem.* 2nd ed. ii. 393.]

A Collection of Poems:

1783.—"One (writer) died a few years ago at Benares, of the name of Souda, who composed a **Dewan** in Moors."—*Teignmouth, Mem.* i. 105.

DEWAUNY, DEWANNY, &c., s. Properly, *dīwānī*; popularly, *dewānī*. The office of *dīwān* (**Dewaun**); and especially the right of receiving as *dīwān* the revenue of Bengal, Behar, and Orissa, conferred upon the E. I. Company by the Great Mogul Shāh 'Ālam in 1765. Also used sometimes for the territory which was the subject of that grant.

1765.—(Lord Clive) "visited the Vezir, and having exchanged with him some sumptuous entertainments and curious and magnificent presents, he explained the project he had in his mind, and asked that the Company should be invested with the *Divanship* (no doubt in orig. **Dīwānī**) of the three provinces. . . ."—*Seir Mutaqherin*, ii. 384.

1783.—(The opium monopoly) "is stated to have begun at Patna so early as the year 1761, but it received no considerable degree of strength until the year 1765; when the acquisition of the **Duanne** opened a wide field for all projects of this nature."—*Report of a Committee on Affairs of India*, in *Burke's Life and Works*, vi. 447.

* The present generation in England can have no conception how closely this description applies to what took place at many an English port before Sir Robert Peel's great changes in the import tariff. The present writer, in landing from a P. & O. steamer at Portsmouth in 1843, after four or five days' quarantine in the Solent, had to go through *five to six hours* of such treatment as Ibn Jubair describes, and his feelings were very much the same as the Moor's.—[H. Y.]

DEWAUNY, DEWANNY, adj. Civil, as distinguished from Criminal; *e.g.* *Dīwānī 'Adālat* as opposite to *Faujdārī Adālat.* (See **ADAWLUT**). The use of *Diwānī* for civil as opposed to criminal is probably modern and Indian. For Kaempfer in his account of the Persian administration at the end of the 17th century, has: "**Diwaen** *begì*, id est, *Supremus* criminalis *Judicii Dominus* . . . de latrociniis et homicidiis non modo in hâc Regiâ metropoli, verùm etiam in toto Regno disponendi facultatem habet."—*Amoenit. Exot.* 80.

DHALL, DOLL, s. Hind. *dāl*, a kind of pulse much used in India, both by natives as a kind of porridge, and by Europeans as an ingredient in **kedgeree** (q.v.), or to mix with rice as a breakfast dish. It is best represented in England by what are called 'split pease.' The proper *dāl*, which Wilson derives from the Skt. root *dal*, 'to divide' (and which thus corresponds in meaning also to 'split pease'), is, according to the same authority, *Phaseolus aureus:* but, be that as it may, the *dāls* most commonly in use are varieties of the shrubby plant *Cajanus Indicus*, Spreng., called in Hind. *arhar*, *rahar*, &c. It is not known where this is indigenous; [De Candolle thinks it probably a native of tropical Africa, introduced perhaps 3,000 years ago into India;] it is cultivated throughout India. The term is also applied occasionally to other pulses, such as *mūng*, *urd*, &c. (See **MOONG, OORD.**) It should also be noted that in its original sense *dāl* is not the name of a particular pea, but the generic name of pulses prepared for use by being broken in a hand-mill; though the peas named are those commonly used in Upper India in this way.

1673.—"At their coming up out of the Water they bestow the largess of Rice or **Doll** (an Indian Bean)."—*Fryer*, 101.

1690.—"*Kitcheree* . . . made of **Dol**, that is, a small round Pea, and Rice boiled together, and is very strengthening, tho' not very savoury."—*Ovington*, 310.

1727.—"They have several species of Legumen, but those of **Doll** are most in use, for some **Doll** and Rice being mingled together and boiled, make *Kitcheree*."—*A. Hamilton*, i. 162; [ed. 1744].

1776.—"If a person hath bought the seeds of . . . **doll** . . . or such kinds of Grain, without Inspection, and in ten Days discovers any Defect in that Grain, he may return such Grain."—*Halhed, Code*, 178.

1778.—". . . the essential articles of a Sepoy's diet, rice, **doll** (a species of pea), ghee (an indifferent kind of butter), &c., were not to be purchased."—*Acc. of the Gallant Defence made at Mangalore.*

1809.—". . . **dol**, split country peas."—*Maria Graham*, 25.

[1813.—"Tuar (*cytisus cajan*, Lin.) . . . is called **Dohll**. . . ."—*Forbes, Or. Mem.* 2nd ed. ii. 35.]

DHAWK, s. Hind. *dhāk;* also called *palās.* A small bushy tree, *Butea frondosa* (N. O. *Leguminosae*), which forms large tracts of jungle in the Punjab, and in many dry parts of India. Its deep orange flowers give a brilliant aspect to the jungle in the early part of the hot weather, and have suggested the occasional name of 'Flame of the Forest.' They are used for dyeing *basanto*, *basantī*, a fleeting yellow; and in preparing *Holī* (see **HOOLY**) powder. The second of the two Hindī words for this tree gave a name to the famous village of *Plassy* (*Palāśī*), and also to ancient Magadha or Behār as *Palāśa* or *Parāśa*, whence *Parāśiya*, a man of that region, which, if Gen. Cunningham's suggestion be accepted, was the name represented by the *Prasii* of Strabo, Pliny, and Arrian, and the *Pharrasii* of Curtius (*Anc. Geog. of India*, p. 454). [The derivation of the word from Skt. *Prāchyās* 'Inhabitants of the east country,' is supported by McCrindle, *Ancient India*, 365 *seq.* So the *dhāk* tree possibly gave its name to **Dacca**].

1761.—"The pioneers, agreeably to orders, dug a ditch according to custom, and placed along the brink of it an abattis of **dhák** trees, or whatever else they could find."—*Saiyid Ghulām 'Ali*, in *Elliot*, viii. 400.

DHOBY, DOBIE, s. A washerman; H. *dhobī*, [from *dhonā*, Skt. *dhāv*, 'to wash.'] In colloquial Anglo-Indian use all over India. A common H. proverb runs: *Dhobī kā kuttā kā sā, na ghar kā na ghāṭ kā*, *i.e.* "Like a **Dhoby's** dog belonging neither to the house nor to the river side." [**Dhoby's** itch is a troublesome cutaneous disease supposed to be communicated by clothes from the wash, and **Dhoby's** earth is a whitish-grey sandy efflorescence, found in many places, from which by boiling and the addition of quicklime an alkali of considerable strength is obtained.

[c. 1804.—"**Dobes.**" See under **DIRZEE**].

DHOOLY, DOOLIE, s. A covered litter; Hind. *ḍolī*. It consists of a cot *or frame*, suspended by the four corners from a bamboo pole, and is carried by two or four men (see figure in *Herklots, Qanoon-e-Islam*, pl. vii. fig. 4). *Doli* is from *ḍolnā*, 'to swing.' The word is also applied to the meat- (or milk-) safe, which is usually slung to a tree, or to a hook in the verandah. As it is lighter and cheaper than a palankin it costs less both to buy or hire and to carry, and is used by the poorer classes. It also forms the usual ambulance of the Indian army. Hence the familiar story of the orator in Parliament who, in celebrating a battle in India, spoke of the "ferocious *Doolies* rushing down from the mountain and carrying off the wounded"; a story which, to our regret, we have not been able to verify. [According to one account the words were used by Burke: "After a sanguinary engagement, the said Warren Hastings had actually ordered ferocious *Doolys* to seize upon the wounded" (2nd ser. *Notes & Queries*, iv. 367).

[But Burke knew too much of India to make this mistake. In the *Calcutta Review* (Dec. 1846, p. 286, footnote) Herbert Edwardes, writing on the first Sikh War, says: "It is not long since a member of the British Legislature, recounting the incidents of one of our Indian fights, informed his countrymen that 'the ferocious *Dūlī*' rushed from the hills and carried off the wounded soldiers."] *Dūla* occurs in *Ibn Batuta*, but the translators render '*palankin*,' and do not notice the word.

c. 1343.—"The principal vehicle of the people (of Malabar) is a **dūla**, carried on the shoulders of slaves and hired men. Those who do not ride in a *dūla*, whoever they may be, go on foot."—*Ibn Batuta*, iv. 73.

c. 1590.—"The *Kahárs* or *Pálkí-bearers*. They form a class of foot servants peculiar to India. With their *pálkís* . . . and **dúlís**, they walk so evenly that the man inside is not inconvenienced by any jolting."—*Āīn*, i. 254; [and see the account of the *sukhāsan*, *ibid.* ii. 122].

1609.—"He turned *Moore*, and bereaved his elder Brother of this holde by this stratageme. He invited him and his women to a Banket, which his Brother requiting with like inuitation of him and his, in steed of women he sends choice Souldiers well appointed, and close couered, two and two in a **Dowle**."—*Hawkins*, in *Purchas*, i. 435.

1662.—"The Rájah and the Phúkans travel in singhásans, and chiefs and rich people in **dúlís**, made in a most ridiculous way."—*Mir Jumlah's Invasion of Asam*, tr. by *Blochmann*, in *J. As. Soc. Ben.*, xli., pt. I. 80.

1702.—". . . un **Douli**, c'est une voiture moins honorable que le palanquin."—*Lettres Edif.* xi. 143.

c. 1760.—"**Doolies** are much of the same material as the *andolas* [see **ANDOR**]; but made of the meanest materials."—*Grose*, i. 155.

c. 1768.—". . . leaving all his wounded . . . on the field of battle, telling them to be of good cheer, for that he would send **Doolies** for them from Astara. . . ."—*H. of Hydur Naik*, 226.

1774.—"If by a **dooley**, chairs, or any other contrivance they can be secured from the fatigues and hazards of the way, the expense is to be no objection."—*Letter of W. Hastings*, in *Markham's Tibet*, 18.

1785.—"You must despatch **Doolies** to Dhârwâr to bring back the wounded men."—*Letters of Tippoo*, 133.

1789.—". . . **doolies**, or sick beds, which are a mean representation of a palanquin: the number attached to a corps is in the proportion of one to every ten men, with four bearers to each."—*Munro, Narrative*, 184.

1845.—"Head Qrs., Kurrachee, 27 Decr., 1845.

"The Governor desires that it may be made known to the **Doolee**-*wallas* and Camel-men, that no increase of wages shall be given to them. They are very highly paid. If any man deserts, the Governor will have him pursued by the police, and if caught he shall be hanged."—*G. O. by Sir Charles Napier*, 113.

1872.—"At last . . . a woman arrived from Dargánagar with a **dúlí** and two bearers, for carrying Málâti."—*Govinda Samanta*, ii. 7.

1880.—"The consequence of holding that this would be a Trust enforceable in a Court of Law would be so monstrous that persons would be probably startled . . . if it be a Trust, then every one of those persons in England or in India—from persons of the highest rank down to the lowest **dhoolie**-*bearer*, might file a bill for the administration of the Trust."—*Ld. Justice James*, Judgment on the Kirwee and Banda Prize Appeal, 13th April.

1883.—"I have great pleasure here in bearing my testimony to the courage and devotion of the Indian **dhooly**-bearers. I . . . never knew them shrink from the dangers of the battle-field, or neglect or forsake a wounded European. I have several times seen one of these bearers killed and many of them disabled while carrying a wounded soldier out of action."—*Surgeon-*

General Munro, C.B., Reminiscences of Mil. Service with the 93rd Sutherland Highlanders, p. 193.

DHOON, s. Hind. *dūn*. A word in N. India specially applied to the flat valleys, parallel to the base of the Himālaya, and lying between the rise of that mountain mass and the low tertiary ranges known as the sub-Himālayan or **Siwālik** Hills (q.v.), or rather between the interior and exterior of these ranges. The best known of these valleys is the *Dūn* of Dehra, below Mussooree, often known as "the **Dhoon**"; a form of expression which we see by the second quotation to be old.

1526.—"In the language of Hindustân they call a *Jûlga* (or dale) Dûn. The finest running water in Hindustân is that in this **Dûn**."—*Baber*, 299.

1654-55.—"Khalilu-lla Khan . . . having reached the **Dún**, which is a strip of country lying outside of Srínagar, 20 *kos* long and 5 broad, one extremity of its length being bounded by the river Jumna, and the other by the Ganges."—*Shâh-Jahân-Nâma*, in *Elliot*, vii. 106.

1814.—"*Me voici* in the far-famed **Dhoon**, the *Tempe* of Asia. . . . The fort stands on the summit of an almost inaccessible mountain . . . it will be a tough job to take it; but by the 1st proximo I think I shall have it, *auspice Deo*."—In *Asiatic Journal*, ii. 151; ext. of letter from Sir Rollo Gillespie before Kalanga, dated 29th Oct. He fell next day.

1879.—"The Sub-Himalayan Hills . . . as a general rule . . . consist of two ranges, separated by a broad flat valley, for which the name '*dūn*' (**Doon**) has been adopted. . . . When the outer of these ranges is wanting, as is the case below Naini Tal and Darjiling, the whole geographical feature might escape notice, the inner range being confounded with the spurs of the mountains."—*Manual of the Geology of India*, 521.

DHOTY, s. Hind. *dhotī*. The loin-cloth worn by all the respectable Hindu castes of Upper India, wrapt round the body, the end being then passed between the legs and tucked in at the waist, so that a festoon of calico hangs down to either knee. [It is mentioned, not by name, by Arrian (*Indika*, 16) as "an under garment of cotton which reaches below the knee, half way to the ankle"; and the Orissa *dhotī* of 1200 years ago, as shown on the monuments, does not differ from the mode of the present time, save that men of rank wore a jewelled girdle with a pendant in front. (*Rajendralala Mitra, Indo-Aryans*, i. 187).] The word *duttee* in old trade lists of cotton goods is possibly the same; [but at the present time a coarse cotton cloth woven by Dhers in Surat is known as *Doti*.]

[1609.—"Here is also a strong sort of cloth called **Dhootie**."—*Danvers, Letters*, i. 29.

[1614.—"20 corge of strong **Dutties**, such as may be fit for making and mending sails."—*Forster, Letters*, ii. 219.

[1615.—"200 peeces **Dutts**." — *Cocks's Diary*, i. 83.]

1622.—"Price of calicoes, **duttees** fixed."

* * * * *

"List of goods sold, including diamonds, pepper, bastas, (read *baftas*), **duttees**, and silks from Persia."—*Court Minutes*, &c., in *Sainsbury*, iii. 24.

1810.—". . . a **dotee** or waist-cloth."—*Williamson, V. M.* i. 247.

1872.—"The human figure which was moving with rapid strides had no other clothing than a **dhuti** wrapped round the waist, and descending to the knee-joints."—*Govinda Samanta*, i. 8.

DHOW, DOW, s. The last seems the more correct, though not perhaps the more common. The term is common in Western India, and on various shores of the Arabian sea, and is used on the E. African coast for craft in general (see *Burton*, in *J.R.G.S.* xxix. 239); but in the mouths of Englishmen on the western seas of India it is applied specially to the old-fashioned vessel of Arab build, with a long **grab** stem, *i.e.* rising at a long slope from the water, and about as long as the keel, usually with one mast and lateen-rig. There are the lines of a *dow*, and a technical description, by Mr. Edie, in *J. R. As. Soc.*, vol. i. p. 11. The slaving *dow* is described and illustrated in Capt. Colomb's *Slave-catching in the Indian Ocean*; see also Capt. W. F. Owen's *Narrative* (1833), p. 385, [i. 384 *seq.*]. Most people suppose the word to be Arabic, and it is in (Johnson's) Richardson (*dāo*) as an Arabic word. But no Arabic scholar whom we have consulted admits it to be genuine Arabic. Can it possibly have been taken from Pers. *dav*, 'running'? [The *N.E.D.* remarks that if *Tava* (in *Ath. Nikitin*, below) be the same, it would tend to localise the word at Ormus in the Persian Gulf.] Capt. Burton identifies it with the word *zabra* applied in the *Roteiro* of Vasco's Voyage (p. 37) to a native vessel at Mombasa. But *zabra* or *zavra* was apparently a Basque name for a kind of craft in Biscay (see s.v. *Bluteau*, and the *Dicc. de la Lingua Castel.*, vol. vi. 1739). *Dāo* or *Dāva* is indeed in Molesworth's *Mahr. Dict.* as a word in that language, but this gives no assurance of origin. Anglo-Indians on the west coast usually employ *dhow* and *buggalow* interchangeably. The word is used on Lake V. Nyanza.

c. 1470.—"I shipped my horses in a **Tava**, and sailed across the Indian Sea in ten days to Moshkat."—*Ath. Nikitin*, p. 8, in *India in XVth Cent.*

" "So I imbarked in a **tava**, and settled to pay for my passage to Hormuz two pieces of gold."—*Ibid.* 30.

1785.—"A **Dow**, the property of Rutn Jee and Jeewun Doss, merchants of *Muscat*, having in these days been dismasted in a storm, came into Byte Koal (see **BATCUL**), a seaport belonging to the Sircar. . . ."—*Tippoo's Letters*, 181.

1786.—"We want 10 shipwrights acquainted with the construction of **Dows**. Get them together and despatch them hither."—*Tippoo* to his Agent at Muskat, *ibid.* 234.

1810.—"Close to Calcutta, it is the busiest scene we can imagine; crowded with ships and boats of every form,—here a fine English East Indiaman, there a grab or a **dow** from Arabia."—*Maria Graham*, 142.

1814.—"The different names given to these ships (at Jedda), as *Say*, *Seume*, *Merkeb*, *Sambouk* [see **SAMBOOK**], **Dow**, denote their size; the latter only, being the largest, perform the voyage to India."—*Burckhardt*, *Tr. in Arabia*, 1829, 4to, p. 22.

1837.—"Two young princes . . . nephews of the King of Hinzuan or Joanna . . . came in their own **dhow** on a visit to the Government."—*Smith, Life of Dr. J. Wilson*, 253.

1844.—"I left the hospitable village of Takaungu in a small boat, called a '**Daw**' by the Suahilis . . . the smallest sea-going vessel."—*Krapf*, p. 117.

1865.—"The goods from Zanzibar (to the Seychelles) were shipped in a **dhow**, which ran across in the month of May; and this was, I believe, the first native craft that had ever made the passage."—*Pelly*, in *J.R.G.S.* xxxv. 234.

1873.—"If a pear be sharpened at the thin end, and then cut in half longitudinally, two models will have been made, resembling in all essential respects the ordinary slave **dhow**."—*Colomb*, 35.

" "**Dhow** Chasing in Zanzibar Waters and on the Eastern Coast of Africa . . . by Capt. G. L. Sulivan, R.N.," 1873.

1880.—"The third division are the Mozambiques or African slaves, who have been brought into the country from time immemorial by the Arab slave-trading **dhows**."—*Sibree's Great African Island*, 182.

1883.—"**Dhau** is a large vessel which is falling into disuse. . . . Their origin is in the Red Sea. The word is used vaguely, and is applied to baghlas (see **BUGGALOW**)."—*Bombay Gazetteer*, xiii. 717 *seq.*

DHURMSALLA, s. H. and Mahr. *dharm-śālā*, 'pious edifice'; a rest-house for wayfarers, corresponding to the S. Indian **Choultry** or **Chuttrum** (q.v.).

1826.—"We alighted at a **durhmsallah** where several horsemen were assembled."—*Pandurang Hari*, 254; [ed. 1873, ii. 66].

DHURNA, TO SIT, v. In H. *dharnā denā* or *baiṭhnā*, Skt. *dhri*, 'to hold.' A mode of extorting payment or compliance with a demand, effected by the complainant or creditor sitting at the debtor's door, and there remaining without tasting food till his demand shall be complied with, or (sometimes) by threatening to do himself some mortal violence if it be not complied with. Traces of this custom in some form are found in many parts of the world, and Sir H. Maine (see below) has quoted a remarkable example from the Irish Brehon Laws. There was a curious variety of the practice, in arrest for debt, current in S. India, which is described by Marco Polo and many later travellers (see *M. P.*, 2nd ed., ii. 327, 335, [and for N. India, *Crooke, Pop. Rel. and Folklore*, ii. 42, *seq.*]). The practice of *dharnā* is made an offence under the Indian Penal Code. There is a systematic kind of *dharnā* practised by classes of beggars, *e.g.* in the Punjab by a class called *Tasmīwālās*, or 'strap-riggers,' who twist a leather strap round the neck, and throw themselves on the ground before a shop, until alms are given; [*Dorīwālās*, who threaten to hang themselves: *Dandīwālās*, who rattle sticks, and stand cursing till they get alms; *Urimārs*, who simply stand before a shop all day, and *Gurzmārs* and *Chharimārs*, who cut themselves with knives and spiked clubs] (see *Ind. Antiq.* i. 162, [*Herklots, Qanoon-e-Islam*, ed. 1863, p. 193 *seq.*]. It appears from Elphinstone (below) that the custom sometimes received the Ar.

Pers. name of *takāẓa*, 'dunning' or 'importunity.'

c. 1747.—"While Nundi Raj, the Dulwai (see **DALAWAY**), was encamped at Sutti Mangul, his troops, for want of pay, placed him in **Dhurna**. . . . Hurree Singh, forgetting the ties of salt or gratitude to his master, in order to obtain his arrears of pay, forbade the sleeping and eating of the Dulwai, by placing him in **Dhurna** . . . and that in so great a degree as even to stop the water used in his kitchen. The Dulwai, losing heart from this rigour, with his clothes and the vessels of silver and gold used in travelling, and a small sum of money, paid him off and discharged him."—*H. of Hydur Naik*, 41 *seq.*

c. 1794.—"The practice called **dharna**, which may be translated caption, or arrest." —*Sir J. Shore*, in *As. Res.* iv. 144.

1808.—"A remarkable circumstance took place yesterday. Some Sirdars put the Maharaja (Sindia) in **dhurna**. He was angry, and threatened to put them to death. Bhugwunt Ras Byse, their head, said, 'Sit still; put us to death.' Sindia was enraged, and ordered him to be paid and driven from camp. He refused to go. . . . The bazaars were shut the whole day; troops were posted to guard them and defend the tents. . . . At last the mutineers marched off, and all was settled."—*Elphinstone's Diary*, in *Life*, i. 179 *seq.*

1809.—"Seendhiya (*i.e.* Sindia), who has been lately plagued by repeated **D'hurnas**, seems now resolved to partake also in the active part of the amusement: he had permitted this same Patunkur, as a signal mark of favour, to borrow 50,000 rupees from the *Khasgee*, or private treasury. . . . The time elapsed without the agreement having been fulfilled; and Seendhiya immediately dispatched the treasurer to sit **D'hurna** on his behalf at Patunkur's tents." —*Broughton, Letters from a Mahratta Camp*, 169 *seq.*; [ed. 1892, 127].

[1812.—Morier (*Journey through Persia*, 32) describes similar proceedings by a Dervish at Bushire.]

1819.—"It is this which is called *tukaza* * by the Mahrattas. . . . If a man have demand from (? upon) his inferior or equal, he places him under restraint, prevents his leaving his house or eating, and even compels him to sit in the sun until he comes to some accommodation. If the debtor were a superior, the creditor had first recourse to supplications and appeals to the honour and sense of shame of the other party; he laid himself on his threshold, threw himself in his road, clamoured before his door, or he employed others to do this for him; he would even sit down and fast before the debtor's door, during which time the other was compelled to fast also; or he would appeal to the gods, and invoke their curses upon the person by whom he was injured." —*Elphinstone*, in *Life*, ii. 87.

* Ar. *takāẓā*, dunning or importunity.

1837.*—"Whoever voluntarily causes or attempts to cause any person to do anything which that person is not legally bound to do . . . by inducing . . . that person to believe that he . . . will become . . . by some act of the offender, an object of the divine displeasure if he does not do the thing . . . shall be punished with imprisonment of either description for a term which may extend to one year, or with fine, or with both.

Illustrations.

"(*a*) A. sits **dhurna** at Z.'s door with the intention of causing it to be believed that by so sitting he renders Z. an object of divine displeasure. A. has committed the offence defined in this section.

"(*b*) A. threatens Z. that unless Z. performs a certain act A. will kill one of A.'s own children, under such circumstances that the killing would be believed to render Z. an object of the divine displeasure. A. has committed the offence described in this section."—*Indian Penal Code*, 508, in Chap. XXII., *Criminal Intimidation, Insult, and Annoyance.*

1875.—"If you have a legal claim against a man of a certain rank and you are desirous of compelling him to discharge it, the Senchus Mor tells you 'to fast upon him.' . . . The institution is unquestionably identical with one widely diffused throughout the East, which is called by the Hindoos 'sitting **dharna**.' It consists in sitting at the debtor's door and starving yourself till he pays. From the English point of view the practice has always been considered barbarous and immoral, and the Indian Penal Code expressly forbids it. It suggests, however, the question—what would follow if the debtor simply allowed the creditor to starve? Undoubtedly the Hindoo supposes that some supernatural penalty would follow; indeed, he generally gives definiteness to it by retaining a Brahmin to starve himself vicariously, and no Hindoo doubts what would come of causing a Brahmin's death." —*Maine, Hist. of Early Institutions*, 40. See also 297-304.

1885.—"One of the most curious practices in India is that still followed in the native states by a Brahman creditor to compel payment of his debt, and called in Hindi **dharnā**, and in Sanskrit *ācharita*, 'customary proceeding,' or *Prāyopaveçana*, 'sitting down to die by hunger.' This procedure has long since been identified with the practice of 'fasting upon' (*troscud for*) a debtor to God or man, which is so frequently mentioned in the Irish so-called Brehon Laws. . . . In a MS. in the Bodleian . . . there is a Middle-Irish legend which tells how St. Patrick 'fasted upon' Loegaire, the unbelieving over-king of Ireland. Loegaire's pious queen declares

* This is the date of the Penal Code, as originally submitted to Lord Auckland, by T. B. Macaulay and his colleagues; and in that original form this passage is found as § 283, and in chap. xv. of *Offences relating to Religion and Caste.*

that she will not eat anything while Patrick is fasting. Her son Enna seeks for food. 'It is not fitting for thee,' says his mother, 'to eat food while Patrick is fasting upon you.' . . . It would seem from this story that in Ireland the wife and children of the debtor, and, *a fortiori*, the debtor himself, had to fast so long as the creditor fasted."—*Letter from Mr. Whitley Stokes*, in *Academy*, Sept. 12th.

A striking story is told in Forbes's *Rās Māla* (ii. 393 *seq.*; [ed. 1878, p. 657]) of a farther proceeding following upon an unsuccessful **dharnā**, put in practice by a company of Chārans, or bards, in Kathiawār, to enforce payment of a debt by a chief of Jailā to one of their number. After fasting three days in vain, they proceeded from **dharnā** to the further rite of **trāgā** (q.v.). Some hacked their own arms; others decapitated three old women of their party, and hung their heads up as a garland at the gate. Certain of the women cut off their own breasts. The bards also pierced the throats of four of the older men with spikes, and took two young girls and dashed their brains out against the town-gate. Finally the Chāran creditor soaked his quilted clothes in oil, and set fire to himself. As he burned to death he cried out, 'I am now dying, but I will become a headless ghost (*Kavīs*) in the Palace, and will take the chief's life, and cut off his posterity!'

DIAMOND HARBOUR, n.p. An anchorage in the Hoogly below Calcutta, 30 m. by road, and 41 by river. It was the usual anchorage of the old Indiamen in the mercantile days of the E. I. Company. In the oldest charts we find the "Diamond Sand," on the western side of what is now called Diamond Harbour, and on some later charts, Diamond Point.

1683.—"We anchored this night on ye head of ye **Diamond** Sand.

"*Jan.* 26. This morning early we weighed anchor . . . but got no further than the Point of Kegaria Island" (see **KEDGEREE**). —*Hedges, Diary*, Hak. Soc. i. 64. (See also **ROGUE'S RIVER**.)

DIDWAN, s. P. *dīdbān, dīdwān*, 'a look-out,' 'watchman,' 'guard,' 'messenger.'

[1679.—See under **AUMILDAR, TRIPLICANE**.

[1680.—See under **JUNCAMEER**.

[1683-4.—". . . three yards of Ordinary Broadcloth and five Pagodas to the **Dithwan** that brought the Phirmaund. . . ."—*Pringle, Diary of Ft. St. Geo.*, 1st ser. iii. 4.]

DIGGORY, DIGRĪ, DEGREE, s. Anglo-Hindustani of law-court jargon for 'decree.'

[1866.—"This is grand, thought bold Bhuwanee Singh, **diggree** *to pāh, lekin roopyea to morpāss bah*, 'He has got his decree, but I have the money.'"—*Confessions of an Orderly*, 138.]

DIKK, s. Worry, trouble, botheration; what the Italians call *seccatura*. This is the Anglo-Indian use. But the word is more properly adjective, Ar.-P.-H. *dik, dikk*, 'vexed, worried,' and so *dikk honā*, 'to be worried.' [The noun *dikk-dārī*, 'worry,' in vulgar usage, has become an adjective.]

1873.—

"And Beaufort learned in the law,
And Atkinson the Sage,
And if his locks are white as snow,
'Tis more from **dikk** than age!"
Wilfrid Heeley, A Lay of Modern Darjeeling.

[1889.—"Were the Company's pumps to be beaten by the vagaries of that **dikhdari**, Tarachunda nuddee?"—*R. Kipling, In Black and White*, 52.]

DINAPORE, n.p. A well-known cantonment on the right bank of the Ganges, being the station of the great city of Patna. The name is properly *Dānāpur*. Ives (1755) writes *Dunapoor* (p. 167). The cantonment was established under the government of Warren Hastings about 1772, but we have failed to ascertain the exact date. [Cruso, writing in 1785, speaks of the cantonments having cost the Company 25 lakhs of rupees. (*Forbes, Or. Mem.* 2nd ed. ii. 445). There were troops there in 1773 (*Gleig, Life of Warren Hastings*, i. 297.]

DĪNĀR, s. This word is not now in any Indian use. But it is remarkable as a word introduced into Skt. at a comparatively early date. "The names of the Arabic pieces of money . . . are all taken from the coins of the Lower Roman Empire. Thus, the copper piece was called *fals* from *follis*; the silver *dirham* from *drachma*, and the gold **dīnār**, from *denarius*, which, though properly a silver coin, was used generally to denote coins of other metals, as the *denarius aeris*, and the *denarius auri*, or *aureus*" (*James Prinsep, in Essays*, &c., ed. by *Thomas*, i. 19). But it was long before the rise of Islām that the knowledge and name of the *denarius* as applied to a gold coin had reached India. The inscription on the east gate of the great tope at Sanchi is probably the oldest instance preserved, though the date of that is a matter greatly disputed. But in the *Amarakosha* (c. A.D. 500) we have '**dīnāre** *'pi cha nishkah*,' *i.e.* 'a *nishkah* (or gold coin) is the same as **dīnāra**.' And in the *Kalpasūtra* of Bhadrabāhu (of about the same age) § 36, we have 'dīnāra *mālaya*,' 'a necklace of **dīnārs**,' mentioned (see *Max Müller* below). The *dīnār* in modern Persia is a very small imaginary coin, of which 10,000 make a **tomaun** (q.v.). In the Middle Ages we find Arabic writers applying the term *dīnār* both to the staple gold coin (corresponding to the gold mohr of more modern times) and to the staple silver coin (corresponding to what has been called since the 16th century the rupee). [Also see *Yule, Cathay*, ii. 439 *seqq.* See **DEANER.**]

A.D. (?) "The son of Amuka . . . having made salutation to the eternal gods and goddesses, has given a piece of ground purchased at the legal rate; also five temples, and twenty-five (thousand ?) **dínárs** . . . as an act of grace and benevolence of the great emperor Chandragupta."—*Inscription on Gateway at Sanchi* (*Prinsep's Essays*, i. 246).

A.D. (?) "Quelque temps après, à Pataliputra, un autre homme devoué aux Brahmanes renversa une statue de Bouddha aux pieds d'un mendiant, qui la mit en pièces. Le roi (Açoka) . . . fit proclamer cet ordre: Celui qui m'apportera la tête d'un mendiant brahmanique, recevra de moi un **Dînâra**."—Tr. of *Divya avadâna*, in *Burnouf*, *Int. à l'Hist. du Bouddhisme Indien*, p. 422.

c. 1333.—"The *lak* is a sum of 100,000 **dīnārs** (*i.e.* of silver); this sum is equivalent to 10,000 **dīnārs** of gold, Indian money; and the Indian (gold) **dīnār** is worth 2½ **dīnārs** in money of the West (*Maghrab*)."—*Ibn Batuta*, iii. 106.

1859.—"Cosmas Indicopleustes remarked that the Roman denarius was received all over the world;* and how the denarius came to mean in India a gold ornament we may learn from a passage in the 'Life of Mahâvîra.' There it is said that a lady had around her neck a string of grains and golden **dinars**, and Stevenson adds that the custom of stringing coins together, and adorning with them children especially, is still very common in India."—*Max Müller, Hist. of Sanskrit Literature*, 247.

DINGY, DINGHY, s. Beng. *dingī*; [H. *dingī*, *dengī*, another form of *dongī*, Skt. *drona*, 'a trough.'] A small boat or skiff; sometimes also 'a canoe,' *i.e.* dug out of a single trunk. This word is not merely Anglo-Indian; it has become legitimately incorporated in the vocabulary of the British navy, as the name of the smallest ship's boat; [in this sense, according to the *N.E.D.*, first in *Midshipman Easy* (1836)]. *Dingā* occurs as the name of some kind of war-boat used by the Portuguese in the defence of Hugli in 1631 ("Sixty-four large **dingas**"; *Elliot*, vii. 34). The word *dingī* is also used for vessels of size in the quotation from Tippoo. Sir J. Campbell, in the *Bombay Gazetteer*, says that *dhangī* is a large vessel belonging to the Mekrān coast; the word is said to mean 'a log' in Bilūchī. In Guzerat the larger vessel seems to be called *dangā*; and besides this there is *dhangī*, like a canoe, but *built*, not dug out.

[1610.—"I have brought with me the pinnace and her **ginge** for better performance."—*Danvers, Letters*, i. 61.]

1705.—". . . pour aller à terre on est obligé de se servir d'un petit Bateau dont les bords sont très hauts, qu'on appelle **Dingues**. . . ."—*Luiller*, 39.

1785.—"Propose to the merchants of *Muscat* . . . to bring hither, on the **Dingies**, such horses as they may have for sale; which, being sold to us, the owner can carry back the produce in rice."—*Letters of Tippoo*, 6.

1810.—"On these larger pieces of water there are usually canoes, or **dingies**."—*Williamson, V.M.* ii. 59.

[1813.—"The Indian pomegranates . . . are by no means equal to those brought

* The passage referred to is probably that where Cosmas relates an adventure of his friend Sopatrus, a trader in Taprobane, or Ceylon, at the king's court. A Persian present brags of the power and wealth of his own monarch. Sopatrus says nothing till the king calls on him for an answer. He appeals to the king to compare the Roman gold denarius (called by Cosmas νόμισμα), and the Persian silver drachma, both of which were at hand, and to judge for himself which suggested the greater monarch. "Now the *nomisma* was a coin of right good ring and fine ruddy gold, bright in metal and elegant in execution, for such coins are picked on purpose to take thither, whilst the *miliaresion* (or drachma), to say it in one word, was of silver, and of course bore no comparison with the gold coin," &c. In another passage he says that elephants in Taprobane were sold at from 50 to 100 *nomismata* and more, which seems to imply that the gold *denarii* were actually current in Ceylon. See the passages at length in *Cathay*, &c., pp. clxxix-clxxx.

from Arabia by the Muscat **dingeys**."—*Forbes, Or. Mem.* 2nd ed. i. 468.]

1878.—"I observed among a crowd of **dinghies**, one contained a number of native commercial agents."—*Life in the Mofussil*, i. 18.

DIRZEE, s. P. *darzī*, H. *darzī* and vulgarly *darjī*; [*darz*, 'a rent, seam.'] A tailor.

[1623.—"The street, which they call **Terzi** Caravanserai, that is the Tayler's Inn."—*P. della Valle*, Hak. Soc. i. 95.]

c. 1804.—"In his place we took other servants, **Dirges** and *Dobes*, and a *Sais* for Mr. Sherwood, who now got a pony."—*Mrs. Sherwood, Autobiog.* 283.

1810.—"The **dirdjees**, or taylors, in Bombay, are Hindoos of respectable caste."—*Maria Graham*, 30.

DISPATCHADORE, s. This curious word was apparently a name given by the Portuguese to certain officials in Cochin-China. We know it only in the document quoted:

1696.—"The 23 I was sent to the Under-**Dispatchadore**, who I found with my *Scrutore* before him. I having the *key*, he desired me to open it."—*Bowyear's Journal at Cochin China*, in *Dalrymple, Or. Rep.* i. 77; also "was made *Under-Customer* or **Despatchadore**" (*ibid.* 81); and again: "The Chief **Dispatchadore** of the Strangers" (84).

DISSAVE, DISSAVA, &c., s. Singh. *disāva* (Skt. *deśa*, 'a country,' &c.), 'Governor of a Province,' under the Candyan Government. *Disave*, as used by the English in the gen. case, adopted from the native expression *disave mahatmya*, 'Lord of the Province.' It is now applied by the natives to the Collector or "Government Agent." (See **DESSAYE**.)

1681.—"Next under the *Adigars* are the **Dissauva's** who are Governours over provinces and counties of the land."—*Knox*, p. 50.

1685.—". . . un **Dissava** qui est comme un General Chingulais, ou Gouverneur des armées d'une province."—*Ribeyro* (Fr. tr.), 102.

1803.—". . . the **Dissauvas** . . . are governors of the corles or districts, and are besides the principal military commanders."—*Percival's Ceylon*, 258.

1860.—". . . the **dissave** of Oovah, who had been sent to tranquillize the disturbed districts, placed himself at the head of the insurgents" (in 1817).—*Tennent's Ceylon*, ii. 91.

DITCH, DITCHER. Disparaging sobriquets for Calcutta and its European citizens, for the rationale of which see **MAHRATTA DITCH**.

DIU, n.p. A port at the south end of Peninsular Guzerat. The town stands on an island, whence its name, from Skt. *dvīpa*. The Portuguese were allowed to build a fort here by treaty with Bahādur Shāh of Guzerat, in 1535. It was once very famous for the sieges which the Portuguese successfully withstood (1538 and 1545) against the successors of Bahādur Shāh [see the account in *Linschoten*, Hak. Soc. i. 37 *seq.*]. It still belongs to Portugal, but is in great decay. [Tavernier (ed. *Ball*, ii. 35) dwells on the advantages of its position.]

c. 700.—Chinese annals of the T'ang dynasty mention **Tiyu** as a port touched at by vessels bound for the Persian Gulf, about 10 days before reaching the Indus. See *Deguignes*, in *Mém. de l'Acad. Inscript.* xxxii. 367.

1516.—". . . there is a promontory, and joining close to it is a small island which contains a very large and fine town, which the Malabars call **Diuxa** and the Moors of the country call it **Diu**. It has a very good harbour," &c.—*Barbosa*, 59.

1572.—

"Succeder-lhe-ha alli Castro, que o estandarte
Portuguez terá sempre levantado,
Conforme successor ao succedido;
Que hum ergue **Dio**, outro o defende erguido." *Camões*, x. 67.

By Burton:

"Castro succeeds, who Lusias estandard
shall bear for ever in the front to wave;
Successor the Succeeded's work who endeth;
that buildeth **Diu**, this builded **Diu** defendeth."

1648.—"At the extremity of this Kingdom, and on a projecting point towards the south lies the city **Diu**, where the Portuguese have 3 strong castles; this city is called by both Portuguese and Indians **Dive** (the last letter, *e*, being pronounced somewhat softly), a name which signifies 'Island.'"—*Van Twist*, 13.

1727.—"**Diu** is the next Port. . . . It is one of the best built Cities, and best fortified by Nature and Art, that I ever saw in India, and its stately Buildings of free Stone and Marble, are sufficient Witnesses of its ancient Grandeur and Opulency; but at present not above one-fourth of the City is inhabited."—*A. Hamilton*, i. 137; [ed. 1744, i. 136].

DIUL-SIND, n.p. A name by which Sind is often called in early European narratives, taken up by the authors, no doubt, like so many other prevalent names, from the Arab traders who had preceded them. *Dewal* or *Daibul* was a once celebrated city and seaport of Sind, mentioned by all the old Arabian geographers, and believed to have stood at or near the site of modern *Karāchī*. It had the name from a famous temple (*devālya*), probably a Buddhist shrine, which existed there, and which was destroyed by the Mahommedans in 711. The name of *Dewal* long survived the city itself, and the specific addition of *Sind* or *Sindī* being added, probably to distinguish it from some other place of resembling name, the name of *Dewal-Sind* or *Sindi* came to be attached to the delta of the Indus.

c. 700.—The earliest mention of Dewal that we are aware of is in a notice of Chinese Voyages to the Persian Gulf under the T'ang dynasty (7th and 8th centuries) quoted by Deguignes. In this the ships, after leaving *Tiyu* (**Diu**) sailed 10 days further to another **Tiyu** near the great river *Milan* or *Sinteu*. This was, no doubt, **Dewal** near the great *Mihrān* or *Sindhu*, *i.e.* Indus.—*Mém. de l'Acad. des Insc.* xxxii. 367.

c. 880.—"There was at **Debal** a lofty temple (*budd*) surmounted by a long pole, and on the pole was fixed a red flag, which when the breeze blew was unfurled over the city . . . Muhammad informed Hajjáj of what he had done, and solicited advice. . . . One day a reply was received to this effect:—'Fix the manjaník . . . call the manjaník-master, and tell him to aim at the flagstaff of which you have given a description.' So he brought down the flagstaff, and it was broken; at which the infidels were sore afflicted."—*Bilādurī*, in *Elliot*, i. 120.

c. 900.—"From Nármasírá to **Debal** is 8 days' journey, and from **Debal** to the junction of the river Mihrán with the sea, is 2 parasangs."—*Ibn Khordádbah*, in *Elliot*, i. 15.

976.—"The City of **Debal** is to the west of the Mihrán, towards the sea. It is a large mart, and the port not only of this, but of the neighbouring regions. . . ."—*Ibn Haukal*, in *Elliot*, i. 37.

c. 1150.—"The place is inhabited only because it is a station for the vessels of Sind and other countries . . . ships laden with the productions of 'Umán, and the vessels of China and India come to **Debal**."—*Idrisi*, in *Elliot*, i. p. 77.

1228.—"All that country down to the seashore was subdued. Malik Sinán-ud-dín Habsh, chief of **Dewal** and **Sind**, came and did homage to the Sultan."—*Ṭabaḳāt-i-Nāsiri*, in *Elliot*, ii. 326.

[1513.—"And thence we had sight of **Diulcindy**."—*Albuquerque, Cartas*, p. 239.]

1516.—"Leaving the Kingdom of Ormuz . . . the coast goes to the South-east for 172 leagues as far as **Diulcinde**, entering the Kingdom of **Ulcinde**, which is between Persia and India."—*Barbosa*, 49.

1553.—"From this Cape Jasque to the famous river Indus are 200 leagues, in which space are these places Guadel, Calara, Calamente, and **Diul**, the last situated on the most westerly mouth of the Indus."—*De Barros*, Dec. I. liv. ix. cap. i.

c. 1554.—"If you guess that you may be drifting to Jaked . . . you must try to go to Karaushī, or to enter Khur (the estuary of) **Diúl Sind**."—*The Mohit*, in *J. As. Soc. Ben.* v. 463.

" "He offered me the town of Lahori," *i.e.* **Diuli Sind**, but as I did not accept it I begged him for leave to depart."—*Sidi 'Ali Kapudān*, in *Journ. As.* 1st Ser. tom. ix. 131.

[1557.—Couto says that the Italians who travelled overland before the Portuguese discovered the sea route 'found on the other side on the west those people called **Diulis**, so called from their chief city named **Diul**, where they settled, and whence they passed to **Cinde**.']

1572.—

"Olha a terra de **Ulcinde** fertilissima
E de Jaquete a intima enseada."

Camões, x. cvi.

1614.—"At **Diulsinde** the *Expedition* in her former Voyage had deliuered Sir Robert Sherley the Persian Embassadour."—*Capt. W. Peyton*, in *Purchas*, i. 530.

[1616.—"The riuer Indus doth not powre himself into the sea by the bay of Cambaya, but far westward, at **Sindu**."—*Sir T. Roe*, Hak. Soc. i. 122.]

1638.—"Les Perses et les Arabes donnent au Royaume de *Sindo* le nom de **Diul**."—*Mandelslo*, 114.

c. 1650.—**Diul** is marked in Blaeu's great Atlas on the W. of the most westerly mouth of the Indus.

c. 1666.—". . . la ville la plus Méridionale est **Diul**. On la nomme encore **Diul-Sind**, et autrefois on l'a appellée **Dobil**. . . . Il y a des Orientaux qui donnent le nom de **Diul** au Païs de Sinde."—*Thevenot*, v. 158.

1727.—"All that shore from *Jasques* to *Sindy*, inhabited by uncivilized People, who admit of no Commerce with Strangers, tho' Guaddel and **Diul**, two Sea-ports, did about a Century ago afford a good Trade."—*A. Hamilton*, i. 115; [ed. 1744].

1753.—"Celui (le bras du Sind) de la droite, après avoir passé à Fairuz, distant ce Mansora de trois journées selon Edrisi, se rend à *Debil* ou **Divl**, au quel nom on ajoûte quelque fois celui de **Sindi**. . . . La ville est situće sur une langue de terre en forme de peninsule, d'où je pense que lui vient son nom actuel de **Diul** ou *Divl*, formé du mot Indien *Div*, qui signifie une île. D'Herbelot . . . la confond avec *Diu*, dont la situation est à l'entrée du Golfe de Cambaye."—*D'Anville*, p. 40.

DOAB, s. and n.p. P.—H. *doāb*, 'two waters,' *i.e.* 'Mesopotamia,' the tract between two confluent rivers. In Upper India, when used absolutely, the term always indicates the tract between the Ganges and Jumna. Each of the like tracts in the Punjab has its distinctive name, several of them compounded of the names of the limiting rivers, *e.g. Rīchnā Doāb*, between Rāvī and Chenāb, *Jech Doāb*, between Jelam and Chenāb, &c. These names are said to have been invented by the Emperor Akbar. [*Āīn*, ed. *Jarrett*, ii. 311 *seq.*] The only *Doāb* known familiarly by that name in the south of India is the *Raichūr Doāb* in the Nizam's country, lying between the Kistna and Tungabhadra.

DOAI! DWYE! Interj. Properly H. *dohāī*, or *dūhāī*, Gujarātī *dawāhī*, an exclamation (hitherto of obscure etymology) shouted aloud by a petitioner for redress at a Court of Justice, or as any one passes who is supposed to have it in his power to aid in rendering the justice sought. It has a kind of analogy, as Thevenot pointed out over 200 years ago, to the old Norman *Haro! Haro! viens à mon aide, mon Prince!* * but does not now carry the privilege of the Norman cry; though one may conjecture, both from Indian analogies and from the statement of Ibn Batuta quoted below, that it once did. Every Englishman in Upper India has often been saluted by the calls of, '**Dohāi** *Khudāwand kī!* **Dohāi** *Mahārāj!* **Dohāi** *Kompanī Bahādur!*' 'Justice, my Lord! Justice, O King! Justice, O Company!'—perhaps in consequence of some oppression by his followers, perhaps in reference to some grievance with which he has no power to interfere. "Until 1860 no one dared to ignore the appeal of **dohāī** to a native Prince within his territory. I have heard a serious charge made against a person for calling the **dohāī** needlessly" (*M.-Gen. Keatinge*).

* It will be seen that the Indian cry also appeals to the Prince expressly. It was the good fortune of one of the present writers (A. B.) to have witnessed the call of Haro! brought into serious operation at Jersey.

X

Wilson derives the exclamation from *do*, 'two' or repeatedly, and *hāi* 'alas,' illustrating this by the phrase '*dohāī tihāī karnā*,' 'to make exclamation (or invocation of justice) twice and thrice.' [Platts says, *do-hāy*, Skt. *hrī-hāhā*,' a crying twice "alas!"] This phrase, however, we take to be merely an example of the 'striving after meaning,' usual in cases where the real origin of the phrase is forgotten. We cannot doubt that the word is really a form of the Skt. *droha*, 'injury, wrong.' And this is confirmed by the form in Ibn Batuta, and the Mahr. *durāhi*; "an exclamation or expression used in prohibiting in the name of the Raja. . . implying an imprecation of his vengeance in case of disobedience" (*Molesworth's Dict.*); also Tel. and Canar. *durāi*, 'protest, prohibition, caveat, or veto in arrest of proceedings' (*Wilson and C. P. B., MS.*)

c. 1340.—"It is a custom in India that when money is due from any person who is favoured by the Sultan, and the creditor wants his debt settled, he lies in wait at the Palace gate for the debtor, and when the latter is about to enter he assails him with the exclamation **Darōhai** *us-Sultan!* 'O Enemy of the Sultan.—I swear by the head of the King thou shalt not enter till thou hast paid me what thou owest.' The debtor cannot then stir from the spot, until he has satisfied the creditor, or has obtained his consent to the respite."—*Ibn Batuta*, iii. 412. The signification assigned to the words by the Moorish traveller probably only shows that the real meaning was unknown to his Musulman friends at Delhi, whilst its form strongly corroborates our etymology, and shows that it still kept close to the Sanskrit.

1609.—"He is severe enough, but all helpeth not; for his poore Riats or clownes complaine of Iniustice done them, and cry for justice at the King's hands."—*Hawkins*, in *Purchas*, i. 223.

c. 1666.—"Quand on y veut arrêter une personne, on crie seulement **Doa** *padecha*; cette clameur a autant de force que celle de haro en Normandie; et si on defend à quelqu'un de sortir, du lieu où il est, en disant **Doa** *padecha*, il ne peut partir sans se rendre criminel, et il est obligé de se presentir à la Justice."—*Thevenot*, v. 61.

1834.—"The servant woman began to make a great outcry, and wanted to leave the ship, and cried **Dohaee** to the Company, for she was murdered and kidnapped."—*The Baboo*, ii. 242.

DOAR, n.p. A name applied to the strip of moist land, partially cultivated with rice, which extends at the foot of the Himālaya mountains to Bhotan. It corresponds to the **Terai** further west; but embraces the conception of the passes or accesses to the hill country from this last verge of the plain, and is apparently the Skt. *dvāra*, a gate or entrance. [The E. **Dwars** of Goalpara District, and the W. **Dwars** of Jalpaiguri were annexed in 1864 to stop the raids of the Bhutias.]

DOBUND, s. This word is not in the Hind. Dicts. (nor is it in Wilson), but it appears to be sufficiently elucidated by the quotation:

1787.—"That the power of Mr. Fraser to make **dobunds**, or new and additional embankments in aid of the old ones . . . was a power very much to be suspected, and very improper to be entrusted to a contractor who had already covenanted to keep the old *pools* in perfect repair," &c.—*Articles against W. Hastings*, in *Burke*, vii. 98.

DOLLY, s. Hind. *ḍālī*. A complimentary offering of fruit, flowers, vegetables, sweetmeats and the like, presented usually on one or more trays; also the daily basket of garden produce laid before the owner by the *Mālī* or gardener ("The *Molly* with his *dolly*"). The proper meaning of *ḍālī* is a 'branch' or 'twig' (Skt. *ḍār*); then a 'basket,' a 'tray,' or a 'pair of trays slung to a yoke,' as used in making the offerings. Twenty years ago the custom of presenting *ḍālīs* was innocent and merely complimentary; but, if the letter quoted under 1882 is correct, it must have grown into a gross abuse, especially in the Punjab. [The custom has now been in most Provinces regulated by Government orders.]

[1832.—"A **Dhaullie** is a flat basket, on which is arranged in neat order whatever fruit, vegetables, or herbs are at the time in season."—*Mrs. Meer Hassan Ali, Observations*, i. 333.]

1880.—"Brass dishes filled with pistachio nuts are displayed here and there; they are the oblations of the would-be visitors. The English call these offerings **dollies**; the natives **dáli**. They represent in the profuse East the visiting cards of the meagre West." —*Ali Baba*, 84.

1882.—"I learn that in Madras **dallies** are restricted to a single gilded orange or lime, or a tiny sugar pagoda, and Madras officers who have seen the *bushels* of fruit, nuts, almonds, sugar-candy . . . &c., received by single officials in a single day in the N.W. Provinces, and in addition the number of bottles of brandy, champagne, liquors, &c., received along with all the preceding in the Punjab, have been . . . astounded that such a practice should be countenanced by Government." — *Letter in Pioneer Mail*, March 15.

DOME, DHOME; in S. India commonly **Dombaree, Dombar**, s. Hind. *Ḍōm* or *Ḍōmrā*. The name of a very low caste, representing some old aboriginal race, spread all over India. In many places they perform such offices as carrying dead bodies, removing carrion, &c. They are often musicians; in Oudh sweepers; in Champāran professional thieves (see *Elliot's Races of the N.W.P.*, [*Risley, Tribes and Castes of Bengal*, s.v.]). It is possible, as has been suggested by some one, that the Gypsy *Romany* is this word.

c. 1328.—"There be also certain others which be called **Dumbri** who eat carrion and carcases; who have absolutely no object of worship; and who have to do the drudgeries of other people, and carry loads."—*Friar Jordanus*, Hak. Soc. p. 21.

1817.—"There is yet another tribe of vagrants, who are also a separate sect. They are the class of mountebanks, buffoons, posture-masters, tumblers, dancers, and the like. . . . The most dissolute body is that of the **Dumbars** or **Dumbaru**."—*Abbé Dubois*, 468.

DONDERA HEAD, n.p. The southernmost point of Ceylon; called after a magnificent Buddhist shrine there, much frequented as a place of pilgrimage, which was destroyed by the Portuguese in 1587. The name is a corruption of *Dewa-nagara*, in Elu (or old Singalese) *Dewu-nuwara*; in modern Singalese *Dewuṅdara* (*Ind. Antiq.* i. 329). The place is identified by Tennent with Ptolemy's "Dagana, sacred to the moon." Is this name in any way the origin of the opprobrium 'dunderhead'? [The *N.E.D.* gives no countenance to this, but leaves the derivation doubtful; possibly akin to *dunner*]. The name is so written in *Dunn's Directory*, 5th ed. 1780, p. 59; also in a chart of the Bay of Bengal, without title or date in Dalrymple's Collection.

1344.—"We travelled in two days to the city of **Dīnawar**, which is large, near the sea, and inhabited by traders. In a vast temple there, one sees an idol which bears the same name as the city. . . . The city and its revenues are the property of the idol."—*Ibn Batuta*, iv. 184.

[1553.—"**Tanabaré**." See under **GALLE, POINT DE.**]

DONEY, DHONY, s. In S. India, a small native vessel, properly formed (at least the lower part of it) from a single tree. Tamil. *tōṇi*. Dr. Gundert suggests as the origin Skt. *droṇa*, 'a wooden vessel.' But it is perhaps connected with the Tamil *tonduga*, 'to scoop out'; and the word would then be exactly analogous to the Anglo-American 'dug-out.' In the *J.R.A.S.* vol. i. is a paper by Mr. Edye, formerly H.M.'s Master Shipwright in Ceylon, on the native vessels of South India, and among others he describes the **Doni** (p. 13), with a drawing to scale. He calls it "a huge vessel of ark-like form, about 70 feet long, 20 feet broad, and 12 feet deep; with a flat bottom or keel part, which at the broadest place is 7 feet; . . . the whole equipment of these rude vessels, as well as their construction, is the most coarse and unseaworthy that I have ever seen." From this it would appear that the *doney* is no longer a 'dug-out,' as the suggested etymology, and Pyrard de Laval's express statement, indicate it to have been originally.

1552.—Castanheda already uses the word as Portuguese: "foy logo cõtra ho **tône**."—iii. 22.

1553.—"Vasco da Gama having started . . . on the following day they were becalmed rather more than a league and a half from Calicut, when there came towards them more than 60 **tonés**, which are small vessels, crowded with people."—*Barros*, I. iv., xi.

1561.—The word constantly occurs in this form (**toné**) in *Correa*, *e.g.* vol. i. pt. 1, 403, 502, &c.

[1598.—". . . certaine scutes or Skiffes called **Tones**."—*Linschoten*, Hak. Soc. ii. 56.]

1606.—There is a good description of the vessel in *Gouvea*, f. 29.

c. 1610.—"Le basteau s'appelloit **Donny**, c'est à dire oiseau, pource qu'il estoit proviste de voiles."—*Pyrard de Laval*, i. 65; [Hak. Soc. i. 86].

,, "La plupart de leurs vaisseaux sont d'une seule piece, qu'ils appellent **Tonny**, et les Portugais Almediés (**Almadia**)."—*Ibid.* i. 278; [Hak. Soc. i. 389].

1644.—"They have in this city of Cochin certain boats which they call **Tones**, in which they navigate the shallow rivers, which have 5 or 6 palms of depth, 15 or 20 cubits in length, and with a broad *parana* of 5 or 6 palms, so that they build above an upper story called *Bayleu*, like a little house, thatched with *Ola* (**Ollah**), and closed at the sides. This contains many passengers, who go to amuse themselves on the rivers, and there are spent in this way many thousands of cruzados."—*Bocarro MS.*

1666.—". . . with 110 *paraos*, and 100 *catures* (see **PROW, CATUR**) and 80 **tonees** of broad beam, full of people . . . the enemy displayed himself on the water to our caravels."—*Faria y Sousa, Asia Portug.* i. 66.

1672.—". . . four fishermen from the town came over to us in a **Tony**."—*Baldaeus, Ceylon* (Dutch ed.), 89.

[1821.—In *Travels on Foot through the Island of Ceylon*, by J. Haafner, translated from the Dutch (*Phillip's New Voyages and Travels*, v. 6, 79), the words "*thonij*," "*thony's*" of the original are translated **Funny, Funnies**; this is possibly a misprint for **Tunnies**, which appears on p. 66 as the rendering of "*thonij's*." See *Notes and Queries*, 9th ser. iv. 183.]

1860.—"Amongst the vessels at anchor (at Galle) lie the dows of the Arabs, the Patamars of Malabar, the **dhoneys** of Coromandel."—*Tennent's Ceylon*, ii. 103.

DOOB, s. H. *dūb*, from Skt. *dūrvā*. A very nutritious creeping grass (*Cynodon dactylon*, Pers.), spread very generally in India. In the hot weather of Upper India, when its growth is scanty, it is eagerly sought for horses by the 'grass-cutters.' The natives, according to Roxburgh, quoted by Drury, cut the young leaves and make a cooling drink from the roots. The popular etymology, from *dhūp*, 'sunshine,' has no foundation. Its merits, its lowly gesture, its spreading quality, give it a frequent place in native poetry.

1810.—"The **doob** is not to be found everywhere; but in the low countries about Dacca . . . this grass abounds; attaining to a prodigious luxuriance."—*Williamson, V. M.* i. 259.

DOOCAUN, s. Ar. *dukkān*, Pers. and H. *dukān*, 'a shop'; *dukāndār*, 'a shopkeeper.'

1554.—"And when you buy in the *dukāns* (*nos* **ducões**), they don't give picotaa (see **PICOTA**), and so the Dukándárs (*os* **Ducamdares**) gain. . . ."—*A. Nunes*, 22.

1810.—"L'estrade elevée sur laquelle le marchand est assis, et d'où il montre sa marchandise aux acheteurs, est proprement ce qu'on appelle **dukān**; mot qui signifie, suivant son étymologie, une *estrade* ou *plateforme, sur laquelle on se peut tenir assis*, et que nous traduisons improprement par boutique."—Note by *Silvestre de Sacy*, in *Relation de l'Egypte*, 304.

[1832.—"The **Dukhauns** (shops) small, with the whole front open towards the street."—*Mrs. Meer Hassan Ali, Observations*, ii. 36.]

1835.—"The shop (**dookkán**) is a square recess, or cell, generally about 6 or 7 feet high. . . . Its floor is even with the top of a *mus̀tabah*, or raised seat of stone or brick, built against the front."—*Lane's Mod. Egyptians*, ed. 1836, ii. 9.

DOOMBUR, s. The name commonly given in India to the fat-tailed sheep, breeds of which are spread over West Asia and East Africa. The word is properly Pers. *dunba, dumba; dumb*, 'tail,' or especially this fat tail. The old story of little carts being attached to the quarters of these sheep to bear their tails is found in many books, but it is difficult to trace any modern evidence of the fact. We quote some passages bearing on it :

c. A.D. 250.—"The tails of the sheep (of India) reach to their feet. . . . The shepherds . . . cut open the tails and take out the tallow, and then sew it up again. . . ."—*Aelian, De Nat. Animal.* iv. 32.

1298.—"Then there are sheep here as big as asses; and their tails are so large and fat, that one tail shall weigh some 30 lbs. They are fine fat beasts, and afford capital mutton."—*Marco Polo*, Bk. i. ch. 18.

1436.—"Their iiijth kinde of beasts are sheepe, which be unreasonable great, longe legged, longe woll, and great tayles, that waie about xij*l.* a piece. And some such I have seene as have drawen a wheele aftre them, their tailes being holden vp."—*Jos. Barbaro*, Hak. Soc. 21.

c. 1520.—"These sheep are not different from others, except as regards the tail, which is very large, and the fatter the sheep is the bigger is his tail. Some of them have tails weighing 10 and 20 pounds, and that will happen when they get fat of their own accord. But in Egypt many persons make a business of fattening sheep, and feed them on bran and wheat, and then the tail gets so big that the sheep can't stir. But those who keep them tie the tail on a kind of little cart, and in this way they move about. I saw one sheep's tail of this kind at Asiot, a city of Egypt 150 miles from Cairo, on the Nile, which weighed 80 lbs., and many people asserted that they have seen such tails that weighed 150 lbs."—*Leo Africanus*, in *Ramusio*, i. f. 92*v*.

[c. 1610.—"The tails of rams and ewes are wondrous big and heavy; one we weighed (in the Island of St. Lawrence) turned 28 pounds."—*Pyrard de Laval*, i. 36.

[1612.—"Goodly Barbary sheep with great rumps."—*Danvers, Letters*, i. 178.]

1828.—"We had a **Doomba** ram at Prag. The *Doomba* sheep are difficult to keep alive in this climate."—*Wanderings of a Pilgrim*, i. 28.

1846.—"I was informed by a person who possessed large flocks, and who had no reason to deceive me, that sometimes the tail of the Tymunnee **doombas** increased to such a size, that a cart or small truck on wheels was necessary to support the weight, and that without it the animal could not wander about; he declared also that he had produced tails in his flock which weighed 12 *Tabreezi munds*, or 48 *seers puckah*, equal to about 96 *lbs.*"—*Captain Hutton*, in *Jour. As. Soc. Beng.* xv. 160.

DOOPUTTY, s. Hind. *do-pattah, dupattā*, &c. A piece of stuff of 'two breadths,' a sheet. "The principal or only garment of women of the lower orders" (in Bengal—*Wilson*). ["Formerly these pieces were woven narrow, and joined alongside of one another to produce the proper width; now, however, the *dupatta* is all woven in one piece. This is a piece of cloth worn entire as it comes from the loom. It is worn either round the head or over the shoulders, and is used by both men and women, Hindu and Muhammadan" (*Yusuf Ali, Mon. on Silk*, 71).] Applied in S. India by native servants, when speaking their own language, to European bed-sheets.

[1615.—". . . **dubeties** gouzerams."—*Foster, Letters*, iii. 156.]

DOORGA POOJA, s. Skt. *Durgā-pūjā*, 'Worship of Durga.' The chief Hindu festival in Bengal, lasting for 10 days in September—October, and forming the principal holiday-time of all the Calcutta offices. (See **DUSSERA**.) [The common term for these holidays nowadays is 'the **Poojahs**.']

c. 1835.—

"And every **Doorga Pooja** would good Mr. Simms explore
The famous river Hoogly up as high as Barrackpore."
Lines in honour of the late Mr. Simms, Bole Ponjis, 1857, ii. 220.

[1900.—"Calcutta has been in the throes of the **Pujahs** since yesterday."—*Pioneer Mail*, Oct. 5.]

DOORSUMMUND, n.p. *Dūrsamand*; a corrupt form of *Dvāra-Samudra* (Gate of the Sea), the name of the capital of the Balālās, a medieval dynasty in S. India, who ruled a country generally corresponding with Mysore. [See *Rice, Mysore*, ii. 353.] The city itself is identified with the fine ruins at Halabīdu [Hale-bīdu, 'old capital'], in the Hassan district of Mysore.

c. 1300.—"There is another country called Deogir. Its capital is called **Dúrú Samundúr**."—*Rashīduddīn*, in *Elliot*, i. 73. (There is confusion in this.)

1309.—"The royal army marched from this place towards the country of **Dúr Samun**."—*Wassāf*, in *Elliot*, iii. 49.

1310.—"On Sunday, the 23rd . . . he took a select body of cavalry with him, and on the 5th Shawwāl reached the fort of **Dhúr Samund**, after a difficult march of 12 days."—*Amīr Khusrū, ibid.* 88. See also *Notices et Extraits*, xiii. 171.

DORADO, s. Port. A kind of fish; apparently a dolphin (not the cetaceous animal so called). The *Coryphaena hippurus* of Day's *Fishes* is called by Cuvier and Valenciennes *C. dorado*. See also quotation from Drake. One might doubt, because of the praise of its flavour in Bontius, whilst Day only says of the *C. hippurus* that "these dolphins are eaten by natives." Fryer, however, uses an expression like that of Bontius:—"The Dolphin is extolled beyond these,"—*i.e.* Bonito and Albicore (p. 12).

1578.—"When he is chased of the *Bonito*, or great mackrel (whom the **Aurata** or Dolphin also pursueth)."—*Drake, World Encompassed*, Hak. Soc. 32.

1631.—"Pisces **Dorados** dicti a Portugalensibus, ab aureo quem ferunt in cute colore . . . hic piscis est longe optimi saporis, *Bonitas* bonitate excellens."—*Jac. Bontii*, Lib. V. cap. xix. 73.

DORAY, DURAI, s. This is a South Indian equivalent of **Sāhib** (q.v.); Tel. *dora*, Tam. *turai*, 'Master.' *Sinnaturai*, 'small gentleman' is the equivalent of *Chhoṭa Sāhib*, a junior officer; and Tel. *dorasāni*, Tam. *turaisāni* (corruptly *doresāni*) of 'Lady' or 'Madam.'

1680.—"The delivery of three Iron guns to the **Deura** of Ramacole at the rate of 15 *Pagodas* per *candy* is ordered . . . which is much more than what they cost."—*Fort St. Geo. Cons.*, Aug. 5. In *Notes and Extracts*, No. iii. p. 31.

1837.—"The Vakeels stand behind their masters during all the visit, and discuss with them all that A— says. Sometimes they tell him some barefaced lie, and when they find he does not believe it, they turn to me grinning, and say, 'Ma'am, the **Doory** plenty cunning gentlyman.'"—*Letters from Madras*, 86.

1882.—"The appellation by which Sir T. Munro was most commonly known in the Ceded Districts was that of 'Colonel **Dora**.' And to this day it is considered a sufficient answer to inquiries regarding the reason for any Revenue Rule, that i was laid down by the Colonel **Dora**."—*Arbuthnot's Memoir of Sir T. M.*, p. xcviii.

"A village up the Godavery, on the left bank, is inhabited by a race of people known as **Doraylu**, or 'gentlemen.' That this is the understood meaning is shown by the fact that their women are called **Doresandlu**, *i.e.* 'ladies.' These people rifle their arrow feathers, *i.e.* give them a spiral." (Reference lost.) [These are perhaps the Kois, who are called by the Telingas *Koidhoras*, "the word *dhora* meaning 'gentleman' or Sahib."—(*Central Prov. Gaz.* 500; also see *Ind. Ant.* viii. 34)].

DORIA, s. H. *ḍoriyā*, from *ḍor*, *ḍorī*, 'a cord or leash'; a dog-keeper.

1781.—"Stolen . . . The Dog was taken out of Capt. Law's Baggage Boat . . . by the **Durreer** that brought him to Calcutta."—*India Gazette*, March 17.

[**Doriya** is also used for a kind of cloth. "As the characteristic pattern of the *chārkhāna* is a check, so that of the **doriya** is stripes running along the length of the *thān*, *i.e.* in warp threads. The **doriya** was originally a cotton fabric, but it is now manufactured in silk, silk-and-cotton, *tasar*, and other combinations" (*Yusuf Ali*, *Mon. on Silk*, 94).

[c. 1590.—In a list of cotton cloths, we have "**Doriyah**, per piece, 6R. to 2M."—*Āīn*, i. 95.

[1683.—". . . 3 pieces **Dooreas**."—*Hedges, Diary*, Hak. Soc. i. 94.]

DOSOOTY, s. H. *do-sūtī*, *do-sūtā*, 'double thread,' a kind of cheap cotton stuff woven with threads doubled.

[1843.—"The other pair (of travelling baskets) is simply covered with **dosootee** (a coarse double-threaded cotton)."—*Davidson, Diary in Upper India*, i. 10.]

DOUBLE-GRILL, s. Domestic H. of the kitchen for 'a devil' in the culinary sense.

DOUR, s. A foray, or a hasty expedition of any kind. H. *daur*, 'a run.' Also to **dour**, 'to run,' or 'to make such an expedition.'

1853.—"'Halloa! Oakfield,' cried Perkins, as he entered the mess tent . . . 'don't look down in the mouth, man; Attok taken, Chutter Sing **dauring** down like the devil—march to-morrow. . . .'"—*Oakfield*, ii. 67.

DOW, s. H. *dāo*, [Skt. *dātra*, *dā*, 'to cut']. A name much used on the Eastern frontier of Bengal as well as by Europeans in Burma, for the hewing knife or bill, of various forms, carried by the races of those regions, and used both for cutting jungle and as a sword. *Dhā* is the true Burmese name for their weapon of this kind, but we do not know if there is any relation but an accidental one with the Hind. word. [See drawing in *Egerton, Handbook of Indian Arms*, p. 84.]

[1870.—"The **Dao** is the hill knife. . . . It is a blade about 18 inches long, narrow at the haft, and square and broad at the tip; pointless, and sharpened on one side only. The blade is set in a handle of wood; a bamboo root is considered the best. The fighting **dao** is differently shaped; this is a long pointless sword, set in a wooden or ebony handle; it is very heavy, and a blow of almost incredible power can be given by one of these weapons. . . . The weapon is identical with the '*parang latok*' of the Malays. . . ."—*Lewin, Wild Races of S.E. India*, 35 *seq.*

DOWLE, s. H. *ḍaul, ḍaulā.* The ridge of clay marking the boundary between two rice fields, and retaining the water; called commonly in S. India a *bund.* It is worth noting that in Sussex *doole* is "a small conical heap of earth, to mark the bounds of farms and parishes in the downs" (*Wright, Dict. of Obs. and Prov. English*). [The same comparison was made by Sir H. Elliot (*Supp. Gloss*, s.v. *Doula*); the resemblance is merely accidental; see *N.E.D.* s.v. *Dool.*]

1851.—"In the N.W. corner of Suffolk, where the country is almost entirely open, the boundaries of the different parishes are marked by earthen mounds from 3 to 6 feet high, which are known in the neighbourhood as **dools.**"—*Notes and Queries*, 1st Series, vol. iv. p. 161.

DOWRA, s. A guide. H. *dauṛāhā, daurahā, dauṛā*, 'a village runner, a guide,' from *dauṛnā*, 'to run,' Skt. *drava*, 'running.'

1827.—"The vidette, on his part, kept a watchful eye on the **Dowrah**, a guide supplied at the last village."—*Sir W. Scott, The Surgeon's Daughter*, ch. xiii.

[**DRABI, DRABY**, s. The Indian camp-followers' corruption of the English '*driver.*'

[1900.—"The mule race for **Drabis** and grass-cutters was entertaining."—*Pioneer Mail*, March 16.]

DRAVIDIAN, adj. The Skt. term *Drāviḍa* seems to have been originally the name of the Conjevaram Kingdom (4th to 11th cent. A.D.), but in recent times it has been used as equivalent to 'Tamil.' About A.D. 700 Kumārila Bhaṭṭa calls the language of the South *Andhradrāviḍa-bhāshā*, meaning probably, as Bishop Caldwell suggests, what we should now describe as '*Telegu-Tamil*-language.' Indeed he has shown reason for believing that *Tamil* and *Drāviḍa*, of which *Dramiḍa* (written *Tiramiḍa*), and *Dramila* are old forms, are really the same word. [Also see *Oppert, Orig. Inhab.* 25 *seq.*, and *Dravira*, in a quotation from Al-biruni under **MALABAR.**] It may be suggested as posssible that the *Tropina* of Pliny is also the same (see below). Dr. Caldwell proposed *Dravidian* as a convenient name for the S. Indian languages which belong to the Tamil family, and the cultivated members of which are Tamil, Malayālam, Canarese, Tulu, Kuḍagu (or Coorg), and Telegu; the uncultivated Tuḍa, Kōta, Gōnḍ, Khonḍ, Orāon, Rājmahāli. [It has also been adopted as an enthnological term to designate the non-**Aryan** races of India (see *Risley, Tribes and Castes of Bengal*, i. Intro. xxxi.).]

c. A.D. 70.—"From the mouth of Ganges where he entereth into the sea unto the cape Calingon, and the town Dandagula, are counted 725 miles; from thence to **Tropina** where standeth the chiefe mart or towne of merchandise in all India, 1225 miles. Then to the promontorie of Perimula they reckon 750 miles, from which to the towne abovesaid Patale . . . 620."—*Pliny*, by *Phil. Holland*, vi. chap. xx.

A.D. 404.—In a south-western direction are the following tracts . . . Surashtrians, Bâdaras, and **Drâviḍas.**—*Varâha-mihira*, in *J.R.A.S.*, 2nd ser. v. 84.

" "The eastern half of the Narbadda district . . . the Pulindas, the eastern half of the **Drâvidas** . . . of all these the Sun is the Lord."—*Ibid.* p. 231.

c. 1045.—"Moreover, chief of the sons of Bharata, there are, the nations of the South, the **Drâviḍas** . . . the Karnâtakas, Mâhishakas. . . ."—*Vishnu Purâna*, by *H. H. Wilson*, 1865, ii. 177 *seq.*

1856.—"The idioms which are included in this work under the general term '**Dravidian**' constitute the vernacular speech of the great majority of the inhabitants of S. India."—*Çaldwell, Comp. Grammar of the Dravidian Languages*, 1st ed.

1869.—"The people themselves arrange their countrymen under two heads; five termed *Panch-gaura*, belonging to the Hindi, or as it is now generally called, the Aryan group, and the remaining five, or *Panch-Dravida*, to the Tamil type."—*Sir W. Elliot*, in *J. Ethn. Soc.* N.S. i. 94.

DRAWERS, LONG, s. An old-fashioned term, probably obsolete except in Madras, equivalent to **pyjāmas** (q.v.).

1794.—"The contractor shall engage to supply . . . every patient . . . with . . . a clean gown, cap, shirt, and **long drawers**."—In *Seton-Karr*, ii. 115.

DRESSING-BOY, DRESS-BOY, s. Madras term for the servant who acts as valet, corresponding to the **bearer** (q.v.) of N. India.

1837.—See *Letters from Madras*, 106.

DRUGGERMAN, s. Neither this word for an 'interpreter,' nor the Levantine *dragoman*, of which it was a quaint old English corruption, is used in Anglo-Indian colloquial; nor is the Arab *tarjumān*, which is the correct form, a word usual in Hindustāni. But the character of the two former words seems to entitle them not to be passed over in this Glossary. The Arabic is a loan-word from Aramaic *targĕmān, metargĕmān*, 'an interpreter'; the Jewish *Targums*, or Chaldee paraphrases of the Scriptures, being named from the same root. The original force of the Aramaic root is seen in the Assyrian *ragāmu*, 'to speak,' *rigmu*, 'the word.' See *Proc. Soc. Bibl. Arch.*, 1883, p. 73, and *Delitsch, The Hebrew Lang. viewed in the Light of Assyrian Research*, p. 50. In old Italian we find a form somewhat nearer to the Arabic. (See quotation from Pegolotti below.)

c. 1150?.—"Quorum lingua cum praenominato Iohanni, Indorum patriarchae, nimis esset obscura, quod neque ipse quod Romani dicerent, neque Romani quod ipse diceret intelligerent, interprete interposito, quem Achivi **drogomanum** vocant, de mutuo statu Romanorum et Indicae regionis ad invicem querere coeperunt."—*De Adventu Patriarchae Indorum*, printed in *Zarncke, Der Priester Johannes*, i. 12. Leipzig, 1879.

[1252.—"Quia meus **Turgemanus** non erat sufficiens."—*W. de Rubruk*, p. 154.]

c. 1270.—"After this my address to the assembly, I sent my message to Elx by a dragoman (**trujaman**) of mine."—*Chron. of James of Aragon*, tr. by *Foster*, ii. 538.

Villehardouin, early in the 13th century, uses **drughement**, [and for other early forms see *N.E.D.* s.v. *Dragoman*.]

c. 1309.—"Il avoit gens illec qui savoient le Sarrazinnois et le françois que l'on apelle **drugemens**, qui enromancoient le Sarrazinnois au Conte Perron."—*Joinville*, ed. *de Wailly*, 182.

c. 1343.—"And at Tana you should furnish yourself with dragomans (**turcimanni**)."—*Pegolotti's Handbook*, in *Cathay*, &c., ii. 291, and App. iii.

1404.—". . . el maestro en Theologia dixo por su **Truximan** que dixesse al Señor q̃ aquella carta que su fijo el rey le embiara non la sabia otro leer, salvo el. . . ."—*Clavijo*, 446.

1585.—". . . e dopo m'esservi prouisto di vn buonissimo **dragomano**, et interprete, fu inteso il suono delle trombette le quali annuntiauano l'udienza del Rè" (di Pegù).—*Gasparo Balbi*, f. 102*v*.

1613.—"To the *Trojan* Shoare, where I landed Feb. 22 with fourteene *English* men more, and a Iew or **Druggerman**."—*T. Coryat*, in *Purchas*, ii. 1813.

1615.—"E dietro, a cavallo, i **dragomanni**, cioè interpreti della repubblica e con loro tutti i **dragomanni** degli altri ambasciatori ai loro luoghi."—*P. della Valle*, i. 89.

1738.—
"Till I cried out, you prove yourself so able,
Pity! you was not **Druggerman** at Babel!
For had they found a linguist half so good,
I make no question that the Tower had stood."—*Pope*, after *Donne, Sat.* iv. 81.

Other forms of the word are (from Span. *trujaman*) the old French *truchement*, Low-Latin *drocmandus, turchimannus*, Low Greek δραγούμανος, &c.

DRUMSTICK, s. The colloquial name in the Madras Presideny for the long slender pods of the *Moringa pterygosperma*, Gaertner, the **Horse-Radish Tree** (q.v.) of Bengal.

c. 1790.—"Mon domestique étoit occupé à me préparer un plat de *morungas*, qui sont une espèce de fèves longues, auxquelles les Européens ont donné, à cause de leur forme, le nom de **baguettes à tambour**. . ."—*Haafner*, ii. 25.

DUB, s. Telugu *dabbu*, Tam. *idappu*; a small copper coin, the same as the *doody* (see **CASH**), value 20 *cash*; whence it comes to stand for money in general. It is curious that we have also an English *provincial* word, "*Dubs*=money, E. Sussex" (*Holloway, Gen. Dict. of Provincialisms*, Lewes, 1838). And the slang 'to dub up,' for to pay up, is common (see *Slang Dict.*).

1781.—"In "Table of Prison Expenses and articles of luxury only to be attained by the opulent, after a length of saving" (*i.e.* in captivity in Mysore), we have—

"Eight cheroots . . . 0 1 0.

"The prices are in *fanams*, **dubs**, and cash. The fanam changes for 11 *dubs* and 4 cash."—In *Lives of the Lindsays*, iii.

c. 1790.—"J'eus pour quatre **dabous**, qui font environ cinq sous de France, d'excellent poisson pour notre souper."—*Haafner*, ii. 75.

DUBASH, DOBASH, DEBASH, s. H. *dubhāshiyā*, *dobāshī* (lit. 'man of two languages'), Tam. *tupāshi*. An interpreter; obsolete except at Madras, and perhaps there also now, at least in its original sense; [now it is applied to a **dressing-boy** or other servant with a European.] The *Dubash* was at Madras formerly a usual servant in every household; and there is still one attached to each mercantile house, as the broker transacting business with natives, and corresponding to the Calcutta **banyan** (q.v.). According to Drummond the word has a peculiar meaning in Guzerat: "A *Doobasheeo* in Guzerat is viewed as an evil spirit, who by telling lies, sets people by the ears." This illustrates the original meaning of *dubash*, which might be rendered in Bunyan's fashion as Mr. Two-Tongues.

[1566.—"Bring **toopaz** and interpreter, Antonio Fernandes."—*India Office MSS.* Gaveta's agreement with the jangadas of the fort of Quilon, Aug. 13.

[1664.—"Per nossa conta a ambos por manilha 400 fanoim e ao **tupay** 50 fanoim." —*Letter of Zamorin*, in *Logan*, *Malabar*, iii. 1.]

1673.—"The Moors are very grave and haughty in their Demeanor, not vouchsafing to return an Answer by a slave, but by a **Deubash**."—*Fryer*, 30.

[1679.—"The **Dubass** of this Factory having to regaine his freedom."—*S. Master*, in *Man. of Kistna Dist.* 133.]

1693.—"The chief **Dubash** was ordered to treat . . . for putting a stop to their proceedings."—*Wheeler*, i. 279.

1780.—"He ordered his **Dubash** to give the messenger two pagodas (sixteen shillings);—it was poor reward for having received two wounds, and risked his life in bringing him intelligence."—Letter of *Sir T. Munro*, in *Life*, i. 26.

1800.—"The **Dubash** here ought to be hanged for having made difficulties in collecting the rice."—Letter of *Sir A. Wellesley*, in *do.* 259.

c. 1804.—"I could neither understand them nor they me; but they would not give me up until a **Debash**, whom Mrs. Sherwood had hired . . . came to my relief with a palanquin."—*Autobiog. of Mrs. Sherwood*, 272.

1809.—"He (Mr. North) drove at once from the coast the tribe of Aumils and **Debashes**."—*Ld. Valentia*, i. 315.

1810.—"In this first boat a number of **debashes** are sure to arrive."—*Williamson*, *V. M.* i. 133.

" "The **Dubashes**, then all powerful at Madras, threatened loss of caste, and absolute destruction to any Bramin who should dare to unveil the mysteries of their sacred language."—*Morton's Life of Leyden*, 30.

1860.—"The moodliars and native officers . . . were superseded by Malabar **Dubashes**, men aptly described as enemies to the religion of the Singhalese, strangers to their habits, and animated by no impulse but extortion."—*Tennent's Ceylon*, ii. 72.

DUBBEER, s. P.—H. *dabīr*, 'a writer or secretary.' It occurs in Pehlevi as *debīr*, connected with the old Pers. *dipi*, 'writing.' The word is quite obsolete in Indian use.

1760.—"The King . . . referred the adjustment to his **Dubbeer**, or minister, which, amongst the Indians, is equivalent to the Duan of the Mahomedan Princes."—*Orme*, ii. § ii. 601.

DUBBER, s. Hind. (from Pers.) *dabbah*; also, according to Wilson, Guzerāti *dabaro*; Mahr. *dabara*. A large oval vessel, made of green buffalo-hide, which, after drying and stiffening, is used for holding and transporting *ghee* or oil. The word is used in North and South alike.

1554.—"Butter (*á mámteiga*, *i.e.* ghee) sells by the maund, and comes hither (to Ormuz) from Bacoraa and from Reyxel (see **RESHIRE**); the most (however) that comes to Ormuz is from Diul and from Mamgalor, and comes in certain great jars of hide, **dabaas**."—*A. Nunes*, 23.

1673.—"Did they not boil their Butter it would be rank, but after it has passed the Fire they keep it in **Duppers** the year round."—*Fryer*, 118.

1727.—(From the Indus Delta.) "They export great quantities of Butter, which they gently melt and put up in Jars called **Duppas**, made of the Hides of Cattle, almost in the Figure of a Glob, with a Neck and Mouth on one side."—*A. Hamilton*, i. 126; [ed. 1744, i. 127].

1808.—"*Purbhoodas Shet* of Broach, in whose books a certain Mahratta Sirdar is said to stand debtor for a Crore of Rupees . . . in early life brought . . . *ghee* in **dubbers** upon his own head hither from Baroda, and retailed it . . . in open Bazar."—*R. Drummond*, *Illustrations*, &c.

1810.—"... **dubbahs** or bottles made of green hide."—*Williamson, V. M.* ii. 139.

1845.—"I find no account made out by the prisoner of what became of these **dubbas** of *ghee.*"—G. O. by *Sir C. Napier*, in *Sind*, 35.

DUCKS, s. The slang distinctive name for gentlemen belonging to the Bombay service; the correlative of the **Mulls** of Madras and of the **Qui-His** of Bengal. It seems to have been taken from the term next following.

1803. — "I think they manage it here famously. They have neither the comforts of a Bengal army, nor do they rough it, like the **Ducks**."—*Elphinstone*, in *Life*, i. 53.

1860.—"Then came Sire Jhone by Waye of Baldagh and Hormuz to yē Costys of Ynde . . . And atte what Place yē Knyghte came to Londe, theyre yē ffolke clepen 𝔇𝔲𝔠𝔨𝔶𝔰 (quasi DUCES INDIAE)."—Extract from a MS. of the *Travels of Sir John Maundevill* in the E. Indies, lately discovered (Calcutta).

[In the following the word is a corruption of the Tam. *tūkku*, a weight equal to 1¼ viss, about 3 lbs. 13 oz.

[1787.—"We have fixed the produce of each vine at 4 **ducks** of wet pepper."—*Purwannah of Tippoo Sultan*, in *Logan, Malabar*, iii. 125.]

DUCKS, BOMBAY. See **BUMMELO.**

1860.—"A fish nearly related to the salmon is dried and exported in large quantities from Bombay, and has acquired the name of **Bombay Ducks**."—*Mason, Burmah*, 273.

DUFFADAR, s. Hind. (from Arabo-Pers.) *daf'adār*, the exact rationale of which name it is not easy to explain, [*daf'a*, 'a small body, a section,' *daf'adār*, 'a person in charge of a small body of troops']. A petty officer of native police (*v.* **burkundauze**, v.); and in regiments of Irregular Cavalry, a non-commissioned officer corresponding in rank to a corporal or **naik**.

1803.—"The pay . . . for the **duffadars** ought not to exceed 35 rupees."—*Wellington*, ii. 242.

DUFTER, s. Ar.—H. *daftar*. Colloquially 'the office,' and interchangeable with **cutcherry**, except that the latter generally implies an office of the nature of a Court. *Daftarkhāna* is more accurate, [but this usually means rather a record-room where documents are stored]. The original Arab. *daftar* is from the Greek διφθέρα = *membranum*, 'a parchment,' and thin 'paper' (whence also *diphtheria*), and was applied to loose sheets filed on a string, which formed the record of accounts; hence *daftar* becomes 'a register,' a public record. In Arab. any account-book is still a *daftar*, and in S. India *daftar* means a bundle of connected papers tied up in a cloth, [the *basta* of Upper India].

c. 1590.—"Honest experienced officers upon whose forehead the stamp of correctness shines, write the agreement upon loose pages and sheets, so that the transaction cannot be forgotten. These loose sheets, into which all *sanads* are entered, are called the **daftar**."—*Āīn*, i. 260, and see *Blochmann's* note there.

[1757.—". . . that after the expiration of the year they take a discharge according to custom, and that they deliver the accounts of their Zemindarry agreeable to the stated forms every year into the **Dufter** Cana of the Sircar. . . ."—*Sunnud for the Company's Zemindarry*, in *Verelst, View of Bengal*, App. 147.]

DUFTERDAR, s. Ar. — P. — H. *daftardār*, is or was "the head native revenue officer on the Collector's and Sub-Collector's establishment of the Bombay Presidency" (*Wilson*). In the provinces of the Turkish Empire the **Daftardār** was often a minister of great power and importance, as in the case of Mahommed Bey Daftardār, in Egypt in the time of Mahommed 'Ali Pasha (see *Lane's Mod. Egyptns.*, ed. 1860, pp. 127-128). The account of the constitution of the office of *Daftardār* in the time of the Mongol conqueror of Persia, Hulāgū, will be found in a document translated by Hammer-Purgstall in his *Gesch. der Goldenen Horde*, 497-501.

DUFTERY, s. Hind. *daftarī*. A servant in an Indian office (Bengal), whose business it is to look after the condition of the records, dusting and binding them; also to pen-mending, paper-ruling, making of envelopes, &c. In Madras these offices are done by a **Moochy**. [For the military sense of the word in Afghanistan, see quotation from *Ferrier* below.]

1810.—"The **Duftoree** or office-keeper attends solely to those general matters in an office which do not come within the notice of the *crannies*, or clerks."—*Williamson, V. M.* i. 275.

[1858.—"The whole Afghan army consists of the three divisions of Kabul, Kandahar, and Herat; of these, the troops called **Defteris** (which receive pay), present the following effective force."—*Ferrier, H. of the Afghans*, 315 *seq.*]

DUGGIE, s. A word used in the Pegu teak trade, for a long squared timber. Milburn (1813) says: "**Duggies** are timbers of teak from 27 to 30 feet long, and from 17 to 24 inches square." Sir A. Phayre believes the word to be a corruption of the Burmese *htāp-gyī*. The first syllable means the 'cross-beam of a house,' the second, 'big'; hence 'big-beam.'

DUGONG, s. The cetaceous mammal, *Halicore dugong*. The word is Malay *dūyung*, also Javan. *duyung;* Macassar, *ruyung*. The etymology we do not know. [The word came to us from the name *Dugung*, used in the Philippine island of Leyte, and was popularised in its present form by Buffon in 1765. See *N.E.D.*]

DUMBCOW, v., and **DUMBCOWED**, participle. To brow-beat, to cow; and cowed, brow-beaten, set-down. This is a capital specimen of Anglo-Indian dialect. *Dam khānā*, 'to eat one's breath,' is a Hind. idiom for 'to be silent.' Hobson-Jobson converts this into a transitive verb, to *damkhāo*, and both spelling and meaning being affected by English suggestions of sound, this comes in Anglo-Indian use to imply *cowing* and *silencing*. [A more probable derivation is from Hind. *dhamkānā*,' 'to chide, scold, threaten, to repress by threats or reproof' (*Platts, H. Dict.*).]

DUMDUM, n.p. The name of a military cantonment 4½ miles N.W. of Calcutta, which was for seventy years (1783-1853) the head-quarters of that famous corps the Bengal Artillery. The name, which occurs at intervals in Bengal, is no doubt P.—H. *damdama*, 'a mound or elevated battery.' At Dumdum was signed the treaty which restored the British settlements after the re-capture of Calcutta in 1757. [It has recently given a name to the **dumdum** or expanding bullet, made in the arsenal there.]

[1830.—Prospectus of the "**Dumdum** Golfing Club."—"We congratulate them on the prospect of seeing that noble and gentleman-like game established in Bengal."—*Or. Sport. Mag.*, reprint 1873, i. 407.

1848.—"'Pooh! nonsense,' said Joe, highly flattered. 'I recollect, sir, there was a girl at **Dumdum**, a daughter of Cutler of the Artillery . . . who made a dead set at me in the year '4.'"—*Vanity Fair*, i. 25, ed. 1867.

[1886.—"The Kiranchi (see **CRANCHEE**) has been replaced by the ordinary **Dumdummer**, or Pálki carriage ever since the year 1856."—*Sat. Review*, Jan. 23.

[1900.—"A modern murderer came forward proudly with the **dumdum**."—*Ibid.* Aug. 4.]

DUMPOKE, s. A name given in the Anglo-Indian kitchen to a baked dish, consisting usually of a duck, boned and stuffed. The word is Pers. *dampukht*, 'air-cooked,' *i.e.* baked. A recipe for a dish so called, as used in Akbar's kitchen, is in the first quotation:

c. 1590.—"**Dampukht.** 10 sers meat; 2 s. ghi; 1 s. onions; 11 m. fresh ginger; 10 m. pepper; 2 d. cardamoms."—*Āīn*, i. 61.

1673.—"These eat highly of all Flesh **Dumpoked**, which is baked with Spice in Butter."—*Fryer*, 93.

" "Baked Meat they call **Dumpoke** which is dressed with sweet Herbs and Butter, with whose Gravy they swallow Ricedry Boiled."—*Ibid.* 404.

1689.—". . . and a **dumpoked** Fowl, that is boil'd with Butter in any small Vessel, and stuft with Raisins and Almonds is another (Dish)."—*Ovington*, 397.

DUMREE, s. Hind. *damṛī*, a copper coin of very low value, not now existing. (See under **DAM**).

1823.—In Malwa "there are 4 *cowries* to a *gunda;* 3 *gundas* to a **dumrie**; 2 *dumries* to a *chedaum;* 3 *dumries* to a *tun***dumrie**; and 4 *dumries* to an *adillah* or half pice."—*Malcolm, Central India*, 2nd ed. ii. 194; [86 note].

DUNGAREE, s. A kind of coarse and inferior cotton cloth; the word is not in any dictionary that we know. [Platts gives H. *dungrī*, 'a coarse kind of cloth.' The *Madras Gloss.* gives Tel. *dangidi*, which is derived from Dāngidi, a village near Bombay. Molesworth in his *Mahr. Dict.* gives: "*Doṅgarī Kāpaṛ*. a term originally for the common country cloth sold in the quarter contiguous to the *Doṅgarī Killa* (Fort George, Bombay), applied now to poor and low-priced cotton cloth. Hence in the corruption *Dun-*

garie." He traces the word to *ḍongarī*, "a little hill." Dungaree is woven with two or more threads together in the web and woof. The finer kinds are used for clothing by poor people; the coarser for sails for native boats and tents. The same word seems to be used of silk (see below).]

1613.—"We traded with the *Naturalls* for Cloves . . . by bartering and exchanging cotton cloth of *Cambay* and *Coromandell* for Cloves. The sorts requested, and prices that they yeelded. *Candakeens* of *Barochie*, 6 Cattees of Cloves. . . . **Dongerijns**, the finest, twelve."—*Capt. Saris*, in *Purchas*, i. 363.

1673.—"Along the Coasts are Bombaim . . . Carwar for **Dungarees** and the weightiest pepper."—*Fryer*, 86.

[1812.—"The Prince's Messenger . . . told him, 'Come, now is the time to open your purse-strings; you are no longer a merchant or in prison; you are no longer to sell **Dungaree**' (a species of coarse linen)."—*Morier, Journey through Persia*, 26.]

1813.—"**Dungarees** (pieces to a ton) 400."—*Milburn*, ii. 221.

[1859.—"In addition to those which were real . . . were long lines of sham batteries, known to sailors as **Dungaree** forts, and which were made simply of coarse cloth or canvas, stretched and painted so as to resemble batteries."—*L. Oliphant, Narr. of Ld. Elgin's Mission*, ii. 6.]

1868.—"Such **dungeree** as you now pay half a rupee a yard for, you could then buy from 20 to 40 yards per rupee."—*Miss Frere's Old Deccan Days*, p. xxiv.

[1900.—"From this thread the **Dongari** Tasar is prepared, which may be compared to the organzine of silk, being both twisted and doubled."—*Yusuf Ali, Mem. on Silk*, 35.]

DURBAR, s. A Court or Levee. Pers. *darbār*. Also the Executive Government of a Native State (*Carnegie*). "In Kattywar, by a curious idiom, the chief himself is so addressed: 'Yes, **Durbar**'; 'no, **Durbar**,' being common replies to him."—(*M.-Gen. Keatinge*).

1609.—"On the left hand, thorow another gate you enter into an inner court where the King keepes his **Darbar**."—*Hawkins*, in *Purchas*, i. 432.

1616.—"The tenth of Ianuary, I went to Court at foure in the euening to the **Durbar**, which is the place where the *Mogoll* sits out daily, to entertaine strangers, to receiue Petitions and Presents, to giue commands, to see and to be seene."—*Sir T. Roe*, in *Purchas*, i. 541; [with some slight differences of reading, in Hak. Soc. i. 106].

1633.—"This place they call the **Derba** (or place of Councill) where Law and Justice was administered according to the Custome of the Countrey."—*W. Bruton*, in *Hakl.* v. 51.

c. 1750.—". . . il faut se rappeller ces tems d'humiliations où le Francois étoient forcés pour le bien de leur commerce, d'aller timidement porter leurs presens et leurs hommages à de petis chefs de Bourgades que nous n'admetons aujourd'hui à nos **Dorbards** que lorsque nos intérêts l'exigent."—Letter of *M. de Bussy*, in *Cambridge's Account*, p. xxix.

1793.—"At my **durbar** yesterday I had proof of the affection entertained by the natives for Sir William Jones. The Professors of the Hindu Law, who were in the habit of attendance upon him, burst into unrestrained tears when they spoke to me."—*Teignmouth, Mem.* i. 289.

1809.—"It was the **durbar** of the native Gentoo Princes."—*Ld. Valentia*, i. 362.

[1826.—". . . a **Durbar**, or police-officer, should have men in waiting. . . ."—*Pandurang Hari*, ed. 1873, i. 126.]

1875.—"Sitting there in the centre of the **durbar**, we assisted at our first nautch."—*Sir M. E. Grant Duff*, in *Contemp. Rev.*, July.

[1881.—"Near the centre (at Amritsar) lies the sacred tank, from whose midst rises the **Darbar** Sahib, or great temple of the Sikh faith."—*Imperial Gazetteer*, i. 186.]

DURGAH, s. P. *dargāh*. Properly a royal court. But the habitual use of the word in India is for the shrine of a (Mahommedan) Saint, a place of religious resort and prayer.

1782.—"Adjoining is a **durgaw** or burial place, with a view of the river."—*Hodges*, 102.

1807.—"The **dhurgaw** may invariably be seen to occupy those scites pre-eminent for comfort and beauty."—*Williamson, Oriental Field Sports*, 24.

1828.—". . . he was a relation of the . . . superior of the **Durgah**, and this is now a sufficient protection."—*The Kuzzilbash*, ii. 273.

DURIAN, DORIAN, s. Malay *duren*, Molucca form *duriyān*, from *durī*, 'a thorn or prickle, [and *ān*, the common substantival ending; Mr. Skeat gives the standard Malay as *duriyan* or *durian*]; the great fruit of the tree (N. O. *Bombaceae*) called by botanists *Durio zibethinus*, D. C. The tree appears to be a native of the Malay Peninsula, and the nearest islands; from which it has been carried to Tenasserim on one side and to Mindanao on the other.

The earliest European mention of this fruit is that by Nicolo Conti. The passage is thus rendered by Winter Jones: "In this island (Sumatra) there also grows a green fruit which they call *duriano*, of the size of a cucumber. When opened five fruits are found within, resembling oblong oranges. The taste varies like that of cheese." (In *India in the XVth Cent.*, p. 9.) We give the original Latin of Poggio below, which must be more correctly rendered thus: "They have a green fruit which they call *durian*, as big as a water-melon. Inside there are five things like elongated oranges, and resembling thick butter, with a combination of flavours." (See *Carletti*, below).

The *dorian* in Sumatra often forms a staple article of food, as the **jack** (q.v.) does in Malabar. By natives and old European residents in the Malay regions in which it is produced the *dorian* is regarded as incomparable, but novices have a difficulty in getting over the peculiar, strong, and offensive odour of the fruit, on account of which it is usual to open it away from the house, and which procured for it the inelegant Dutch nickname of *stancker*. "When that aversion, however, is conquered, many fall into the taste of the natives, and become passionately fond of it." (*Crawfurd, H. of Ind. Arch.* i. 419.) [Wallace (*Malay Arch.* 57) says that he could not bear the smell when he "first tried it in Malacca, but in Borneo I found a ripe fruit on the ground, and, eating it out of doors, I at once became a confirmed Durian eater . . . the more you eat of it the less you feel inclined to stop. In fact to eat Durians is a new sensation, worth a voyage to the East to experience."] Our forefathers had not such delicate noses, as may be gathered from some of the older notices. A Governor of the Straits, some forty-five years ago, used to compare the *Dorian* to 'carrion in custard.'

c. 1440.—"Fructum viridem habent nomine **durianum**, magnitudine cucumeris, in quo sunt quinque veluti malarancia oblonga, varii saporis, instar butyri coagulati."—*Poggii, de Varietate Fortunae*, Lib. iv.

1552.—"**Durions**, which are fashioned like artichokes" (!)—*Castanheda*, ii. 355.

1553.—"Among these fruits was one kind now known by the name of **durions**, a thing greatly esteemed, and so luscious that the Malacca merchants tell how a certain trader came to that port with a ship load of great value, and he consumed the whole of it in guzzling **durions** and in gallantries among the Malay girls."—*Barros*, II. vi. i.

1563.—"A gentleman in this country (Portuguese India) tells me that he remembers to have read in a Tuscan version of Pliny, '*nobiles* **durianes**.' I have since asked him to find the passage in order that I might trace it in the Latin, but up to this time he says he has not found it."—*Garcia*, f. 85.

1588.—"There is one that is called in the Malacca tongue **durion**, and is so good that I have heard it affirmed by manie that have gone about the worlde, that it doth exceede in savour all others that ever they had seene or tasted. . . . Some do say that have seene it that it seemeth to be that wherewith Adam did transgresse, being carried away by the singular savour."—*Parke's Mendoza*, ii. 318.

1598.—'**Duryoen** is a fruit ỹt only groweth in Malacca, and is so much comẽded by those which have proued ye same, that there is no fruite in the world to bee compared with it."—*Linschoten*, 102; [Hak. Soc. i. 51].

1599.—The **Dorian**, Carletti thought, had a smell of onions, and he did not at first much like it, but when at last he got used to this he liked the fruit greatly, and thought nothing of a simple and natural kind could be tasted which possessed a more complex and elaborate variety of odours and flavours than this did. — See *Viaggi*, Florence, 1701; Pt. II. p. 211.

1601.—"**Duryoen** . . . ad apertionem primam . . . putridum coepe redolet, sed dotem tamen divinam illam omnem gustui profundit."—*Debry*, iv. 33.

[1610.—"The **Darion** tree nearly resembles a pear tree in size."—*Pyrard de Laval*, Hak. Soc. ii. 366.]

1615.—"There groweth a certaine fruit, prickled like a ches-nut, and as big as one's fist, the best in the world to eate, these are somewhat costly, all other fruits being at an easie rate. It must be broken with force and therein is contained a white liquor like vnto creame, never the lesse it yields a very vnsauory sent like to a rotten oynion, and it is called **Esturion**" (probably a misprint).—*De Monfart*, 27.

1727.— 'The **Durean** is another excellent Fruit, but offensive to some People's Noses, for it smells very like . . . but when once tasted the smell vanishes."—*A. Hamilton*, ii. 81; [ed. 1744, ii. 80].

1855.—"The fetid **Dorian**, prince of fruits to those who like it, but chief of abominations to all strangers and novices, does not grow within the present territories of Ava, but the King makes great efforts to obtain a supply in eatable condition from the Tenasserim Coast. King Tharawadi used to lay post-horses from Martaban to Ava, to bring his odoriferous delicacy."—*Yule, Mission to Ava*, 161.

1878.—"The **Durian** will grow as large as a man's head, is covered closely with terribly sharp spines, set hexagonally upon its hard skin, and when ripe it falls; if it should strike any one under the tree, severe injury or death may be the result."—*M'Nair, Perak*, 60.

1885.—"I proceeded . . . under a continuous shade of tall **Durian** trees from 35 to 40 feet high. . . . In the flowering time it was a most pleasant shady wood; but later in the season the chance of a fruit now and then descending on one's head would be less agreeable." *Note.*—"Of this fruit the natives are passionately fond; . . . and the elephants flock to its shade in the fruiting time; but, more singular still, the tiger is said to devour it with avidity."—*Forbes, A Naturalist's Wanderings*, p. 240.

DURJUN, s. H. *darjan*, a corr. of the English *dozen*.

DURWAUN, s. H. from P. *darwān*, *darbān*. A doorkeeper. A domestic servant so called is usual in the larger houses of Calcutta. He is porter at the gate of the **compound** (q.v.).

[c. 1590.—"The **Darbáns**, or Porters. A thousand of these active men are employed to guard the palace."—*Āīn*, i. 258.]

c. 1755.—"**Derwan.**"—List of servants in *Ives*, 50.

1781.—(After an account of an alleged attempt to seize Mr. Hicky's *Darwān*). "Mr. Hicky begs leave to make the following remarks. That he is clearly of opinion that these horrid Assassins wanted to dispatch him whilst he lay a sleep, as a **Door-van** is well known to be the alarm of the House, to prevent which the Villians wanted to carry him off,—and their precipitate flight the moment they heard Mr. Hicky's Voice puts it past a Doubt."—Reflections on the consequence of the late attempt made to Assassinate the Printer of the original *Bengal Gazette* (in the same, April 14).

1784.—"Yesterday at daybreak, a most extraordinary and horrid murder was committed upon the **Dirwan** of Thomas Martin, Esq."—In *Seton-Karr*, i. 12.

" "In the entrance passage, often on both sides of it, is a raised floor with one or two open cells, in which the **Darwans** (or doorkeepers) sit, lie, and sleep—in fact dwell."—*Calc. Review*, vol. lix. p. 207.

DURWAUZA-BUND. The formula by which a native servant in an Anglo-Indian household intimates that his master or mistress cannot receive a visitor—'Not at home'—without the untruth. It is elliptical for *darwāza band hai*, 'the door is closed.'

[1877.—"When they did not find him there, it was **Darwaza bund.**"—*Allardyce, The City of Sunshine*, i. 125.]

DUSSERA, DASSORA, DASEHRA, s. Skt. *daśaharā*, H. *dasharā*, Mahr. *dasrā*; the '*nine-nights*' (or ten days') festival in October, also called *Durgā-pūjā* (see **DOORGA-P.**). In the west and south of India this holiday, taking place after the close of the wet season, became a great military festival, and the period when military expeditions were entered upon. The Mahrattas were alleged to celebrate the occasion in a way characteristic of them, by destroying a village! The popular etymology of the word and that accepted by the best authorities, is *daś*, 'ten (sins)' and *har*, 'that which takes away (or expiates).' It is, perhaps, rather connected with the ten days' duration of the feast, or with its chief day being the 10th of the month (*Aśvina*); but the origin is decidedly obscure.

c. 1590.—"The autumn harvest he shall begin to collect from the **Deshereh**, which is another Hindoo festival that also happens differently, from the beginning of Virgo to the commencement of Libra."—*Ayeen*, tr. *Gladwin*, ed. 1800, i. 307; [tr. *Jarrett*, ii. 46].

1785.—"On the anniversary of the **Dusharah** you will distribute among the Hindoos, composing your escort, a goat to every ten men."—*Tippoo's Letters*, 162.

1799.—"On the Institution and Ceremonies of the Hindoo Festival of the **Dusrah**," published (1820) in *Trans. Bomb. Lit. Soc.* iii. 73 *seqq.* (By Sir John Malcolm.)

1812.—"The Courts . . . are allowed to adjourn annually during the Hindoo festival called **dussarah**."—*Fifth Report*, 37.

1813.—"This being the **desserah**, a great Hindoo festival . . . we resolved to delay our departure and see some part of the ceremonies."—*Forbes, Or. Mem.* iv. 97; [2nd ed. ii. 450].

DUSTOOR, DUSTOORY, s. P.—H. *dastūr*, 'custom' [see **DESTOOR**,] *dastūrī*, 'that which is customary.' That commission or percentage on the money passing in any cash transaction which, with or without acknowledgment or permission, sticks to the fingers of the agent of payment. Such 'customary' appropriations are, we believe, very nearly as common in England as in India; a fact of which newspaper correspondence from time to time makes us aware, though Europeans in India, in condemning the natives, often forget, or are ignorant of this. In India the practice is perhaps more distinctly recognised, as the word denotes. Ibn Batuta tells us that at the Court of Delhi, in his time (c. 1340), the custom was for the officials to deduct 1/10 of every sum which the Sultan ordered to be paid from the treasury (see *I. B.* pp. 408, 426, &c.).

[1616.—"The **dusturia** in all bought goodes . . . is a great matter."—*Sir T. Roe*, Hak. Soc. ii. 350.]

1638.—"Ces vallets ne sont point nourris au logis, mais ont leurs gages, dont ils s'entretiennent, quoy qu'ils ne montent qu'à trois ou quatre Ropias par moys . . . mais ils ont leur tour du baston, qu'ils appellent **Testury**, qu'ils prennent du consentement du Maistre de celuy dont ils achettent quelque chose."—*Mandelslo*, Paris, 1659, 224.

[1679.—"The usuall **Dustoore** shall be equally divided."—*S. Master*, in *Kistna Man.* 136.]

1680.—"It is also ordered that in future the *Vakils* (see **VAKEEL**), *Mutsuddees* (see **MOOTSUDDY**), or Writers of the *Tagadgeers*,* *Dumiers*, (?)† or overseers of the Weavers, and the **Picars** and **Podars** shall not receive any monthly wages, but shall be content with the **Dustoor** . . . of a quarter anna in the rupee, which the merchants and weavers are to allow them. The **Dustoor** may be divided twice a year or oftener by the Chief and Council among the said employers."—*Ft. St. Geo. Cons.*, Dec. 2. In *Notes and Extracts*, No. II. p. 61.

1681.—"For the farme of **Dustoory** on cooley hire at Pagodas 20 per annum received a part . . . (Pag.) 13 00 0."—*Ibid.* Jan. 10; *Ibid.* No. III. p. 45.

[1684.—"The Honble. Comp. having order'd . . . that the **Dustore** upon their Investment . . . be brought into the Generall Books."—*Pringle, Diary, Ft. St. Geo.* 1st ser. iii. 69.]

1780.—"It never can be in the power of a superintendent of Police to reform the numberless abuses which servants of every Denomination have introduced, and now support on the Broad Basis of **Dustoor**."—*Hicky's Bengal Gazette*, April 29.

1785.—"The Public are hereby informed that no Commission, Brokerage, or **Dustoor** is charged by the Bank, or permitted to be taken by any Agent or Servant employed by them."—In *Seton-Karr*, i. 130.

1795.—"All servants belonging to the Company's Shed have been strictly prohibited from demanding or receiving any fees or **dastoors** on any pretence whatever."—*Ibid.* ii. 16.

1824.—"The profits however he made during the voyage, and by a **dustoory** on all the alms given or received . . . were so considerable that on his return some of his confidential disciples had a quarrel with him."—*Heber*, ed. 1844, i. 198.

1866.—". . . of all taxes small and great the heaviest is **dustooree**."—*Trevelyan, Dawk Bungalow*, 217.

* *Tagādāgīr*, under the Mahrattas, was an officer who enforced the State demands against defaulting cultivators (*Wilson*); and no doubt it was here an officer similarly employed to enforce the execution of contracts by weavers and others who had received advances. It is a corruption of Pers. *takāzagīr*, from Ar. *takāzā*, importunity (see quotation of 1819, under **DHURNA**).

[† Mr. F. Brandt suggests that this word may be Telegu *Thumiar*, *tūmu* being a measure of grain, and possibly the "Dumiers" may have been those entitled to receive the *dustooree* in grain.]

DUSTUCK, s. P. *dastak*, ['a little hand, hand-clapping to attract attention, a notice']. A pass or permit. The *dustucks* granted by the Company's covenanted servants in the early half of the 18th century seems to have been a constant instrument of abuse, or bone of contention, with the native authorities in Bengal. [The modern sense of the word in N. India is a notice of the revenue demand served on a defaulter.]

1716.—"A passport or **dustuck**, signed by the President of Calcutta, should exempt the goods specified from being visited or stopped."—*Orme*, ed. 1803, ii. 21.

1748.—"The Zemindar near Pultah having stopped several boats with English **Dusticks** and taken money from them, and disregarding the Phousdar's orders to clear them. . . ."—In *Long*, 6.

[1762.—"**Dusticks**." See **WRITER**.]

1763.—"The dignity and benefit of our **Dustucks** are the chief badges of honour, or at least interest, we enjoy from our *Phirmaund*."—From the Chief and Council at Dacca, in *Van Sittart*, i. 210.

[1769.—"**Dusticks**." See under **HOSBOLHOOKUM**.

[1866.—"It is a practice of the Revenue Courts of the **sircar** to issue **Dustuck** for the malgoozaree the very day the **kist** (instalment) became due."—*Confessions of an Orderly*, 132.]

DWARKA, n.p. More properly *Dvārakā* or *Dvārikā*, quasi ἑκατόμπυλος, 'the City with many gates,' a very sacred Hindu place of pilgrimage, on the extreme N.W. point of peninsular Guzerat; the alleged royal city of Krishna. It is in the small State called Okha, which Gen. Legrand Jacob pronounces to be "barren of aught save superstition and piracy" (*Tr. Bo. Geog. Soc.* vii. 161). *Dvārikā* is, we apprehend, the βαράκη of

Ptolemy. Indeed, in an old Persian map, published in *Indian Antiq.* i. 370, the place appears, transcribed as *Bharraky*.

c. 1590.—"The *Fifth Division* is Jugget (see **JACQUETE**), which is also called **Daurka**. Kishen came from Mehtra, and dwelt at this place, and died here. This is considered as a very holy spot by the Brahmins."—*Ayeen*, by *Gladwin*, ed. 1800, ii. 76; [ed. *Jarrett*, ii. 248].

E

EAGLE-WOOD, s. The name of an aromatic wood from Camboja and some other Indian regions, chiefly trans-gangetic. It is the "odorous wood" referred to by Camões in the quotation under **CHAMPA**. We have somewhere read an explanation of the name as applied to the substance in question, because this is flecked and mottled, and so supposed to resemble the plumage of an eagle! [*Burton, Ar. Nights*, iv. 395; *Linschoten*, Hak. Soc. i. 120, 150.] The word is in fact due to a corrupt form of the Skt. name of the wood, *agaru, aguru*. A form, probably, of this is *aγil, akil*, which Gundert gives as the Malayāl. word.* From this the Portuguese must have taken their *aguila*, as we find it in Barbosa (below), or *pao* (wood) *d'aguila*, made into *aquila*, whence French *bois d'aigle*, and Eng. **eagle-wood**. The Malays call it *Kayū* (wood)-*gahru*, evidently the same word, though which way the etymology flowed it is difficult to say. [Mr. Skeat writes: "the question is a difficult one. Klinkert gives *garu* (*garoe*) and *gaharu* (*gaharoe*), whence the trade names '*Garrow*' and '*Garroo*'; and the modern standard Malay certainly corresponds to Klinkert's forms, though I think *gaharu* should rather be written *gharu, i.e.* with an aspirated *g*, which is the way the Malays pronounce it. On the other hand, it seems perfectly clear that there must have been an alternative modern form *agaru*, or perhaps even *aguru*, since otherwise such trade names as '*ugger*' and (?) '*tugger*' could not have arisen. They can scarcely have come from the Skt. In Ridley's *Plant List* we have *gaharu* and *gagaheu*, which is the regular abbreviation of the reduplicated form *gahru-gahru* identified as *Aquilaria Malaccensis, Lam.*"] [See **CAMBULAC**.]

The best quality of this wood, once much valued in Europe as incense, is the result of disease in a tree of the N. O. *Leguminosae*, the *Aloexylon agallochum*, Loureiro, growing in Camboja and S. Cochin China, whilst an inferior kind, of like aromatic qualities, is produced by a tree of an entirely different order, *Aquilaria agallocha*, Roxb. (N. O. *Aquilariaceae*), which is found as far north as Silhet.*

Eagle-wood is another name for aloes-wood, or **aloes** (q.v.) as it is termed in the English Bible. [See *Encycl. Bibl.* i. 120 *seq.*] It is curious that Bluteau, in his great Portuguese *Vocabulario*, under *Pao d'Aguila*, jumbles up this *aloes-wood* with Socotrine Aloes. Ἀγάλλοχον was known to the ancients, and is described by Dioscorides (c. A.D. 65). In *Liddell and Scott* the word is rendered "the bitter aloe"; which seems to involve the same confusion as that made by Bluteau.

Other trade-names of the article given by Forbes Watson are *Garrow*- and *Garroo*-wood, *agla*-wood, *ugger*-, and *tugger*- (?) wood.

1516.—
"*Das Dragoarias, e preços que ellas valem em Calicut* . . .

* * * * *

Aguila, cada Farazola (see **FRAZALA**) de 300 a 400 (*fanams*)
Lenho aloes verdadeiro, negro, pesado, e muito fino val 1000 (*fanams*)."†—*Barbosa* (Lisbon), 393.

1563.—"*R.* And from those parts of which you speak, comes the true lign-aloes? Is it produced there?

"*O.* Not the genuine thing. It is indeed true that in the parts about C. Comorin and in Ceylon there is a wood with a scent (which we call **aguila** *brava*), as we have many another wood with a scent. And at one time that wood used to be exported to Bengala under the name of **aguila** *brava*; but since then the Bengalas have got more knowing, and buy it no longer. . . ."—*Garcia*, f. 119*v.*-120.

* Royle says "*Malayan agila*," but this is apparently a misprint for *Malayālam*.

* We do not find information as to which tree produces the eagle-wood sold in the Tenasserim bazars. [It seems to be *A. agallocha*: see *Watt, Econ. Dict.* i. 279 *seq.*]

† This *lign aloes*, "genuine, black, heavy, very choice," is presumably the fine kind from Champa: the *aguila* the inferior product.

1613.—"... A aguila, arvore alta e grossa, de folhas como a Olyveira."—*Godinho de Eredia*, f. 15*v*.

1774.—"*Kinnâmon* ... *Oud el bochor*, et *Agadj oudi*, est le nom hébreu, arabe, et turc d'un bois nommé par les Anglois **Agal-wood**, et par les Indiens de Bombay **Agar**, dont on a deux diverses sortes, savoir: *Oud mawârdi*, c'est la meilleure. *Oud Kakulli*, est la moindre sorte."—*Niebuhr, Des. de l'Arabie*, xxxiv.

1854.—(In Cachar) "the **eagle-wood**, a tree yielding **uggur** oil, is also much sought for its fragrant wood, which is carried to Silhet, where it is broken up and distilled."—*Hooker, Himalayan Journals*, ed. 1855, ii. 318.

The existence of the **aguila** tree (*dārakht-i-'ūd*) in the Silhet hills is mentioned by Abu'l Fazl (*Gladwin's Ayeen*, ii. 10; [ed. *Jarrett*, ii. 125]; orig. i. 391).

EARTH-OIL, s. Petroleum, such as that exported from Burma. .. The term is a literal translation of that used in nearly all the Indian vernaculars. The chief sources are at *Ye-nan-gyoung* on the Irawadi, lat. c. 20° 22′.

1755.—"Raynan-Goung ... at this Place there are about 200 Families, who are chiefly employed in getting **Earth-oil** out of Pitts, some five miles in the Country."—*Baker*, in *Dalrymple's Or. Rep.* i. 172.

1810.—"Petroleum, called by the natives **earth-oil** ... which is imported from Pegu, Ava, and the Arvean (read Aracan) Coast."—*Williamson, V.M.* ii. 21-23.

ECKA, s. A small one-horse carriage used by natives. It is Hind. *ekkā*, from *ek*, 'one.' But we have seen it written *acre*, and punned upon as quasi-*acher*, by those who have travelled by it! [Something of the kind was perhaps known in very early times, for Arrian (*Indika*, xvii.) says: "To be drawn by a single horse is considered no distinction." For a good description with drawing of the *ekka*, see *Kipling, Beast and Man in India*, 190 *seq.*]

1811.—"... perhaps the simplest carriage that can be imagined, being nothing more than a chair covered with red cloth, and fixed upon an axle-tree between two small wheels. The **Ekka** is drawn by one horse, who has no other harness than a girt, to which the shaft of the carriage is fastened."—*Solvyns*, iii.

1834.—"One of those native carriages called **ekkas** was in waiting. This vehicle resembles in shape a meat-safe, placed upon the axletree of two wheels, but the sides are composed of hanging curtains instead of wire pannels."—*The Baboo*, ii. 4.

[1843.—"**Ekhees**, a species of single horse carriage, with cloth hoods, drawn by one pony, were by no means uncommon."—*Davidson, Travels in Upper India*, i. 116.]

EED, s. Arab. *'Īd*. A Mahommedan holy festival, but in common application in India restricted to two such, called there the *barī* and *chhoṭī* (or Great and Little) *'Īd*. The former is the commemoration of Abraham's sacrifice, the victim of which was, according to the Mahommedans, Ishmael. [See Hughes, *Dict. of Islam*, 192 *seqq.*] This is called among other names, *Bakr-'Īd*, the 'Bull *'Īd*,' *Bakarah 'Īd*, 'the cow festival,' but this is usually corrupted by ignorant natives as well as Europeans into *Bakrī-'Id* (Hind. *bakrā*, f. *bakrī*, 'a goat'). The other is the *'Īd* of the *Ramazān*, *viz.* the termination of the annual fast; the festival called in Turkey *Bairam*, and by old travellers sometimes the "Mahommedan Easter."

c. 1610.—"Le temps du ieusne finy on celebre vne grande feste, et des plus solennelles qu'ils ayent, qui s'appelle **ydu**."—*Pyrard de Laval*, i. 104; [Hak. Soc. i. 140].

[1671.—"They have allsoe a great feast, which they call **Buckery Eed**."—In *Yule, Hedges' Diary*, Hak. Soc. ii. cccx.]

1673.—"The New Moon before the New Year (which commences at the *Vernal Equinox*), is the Moors **Æde**, when the Governor in no less Pomp than before, goes to sacrifice a Ram or He-Goat, in remembrance of that offered for *Isaac* (by them called *Ishauh*); the like does every one in his own House, that is able to purchase one, and sprinkle their blood on the sides of their Doors."—*Fryer*, 108. (The passage is full of errors.)

1860.—"By the Nazim's invitation we took out a party to the palace at the *Bakri* **Eed** (or Feast of the Goat), in memory of the sacrifice of Isaac, or, as the Moslems say, of Ishmael."—*Mrs. Mackenzie, Storms and Sunshine*, &c., ii. 255 *seq.*

1869.—"Il n'y a proprement que deux fêtes parmi les Musulmans sunnites, celle de la rupture du jeûne de *Ramazan*, **'Id** *fito*, et celle des victimes **'Id** *curbân*, nommée aussi dans l'Inde *Bacr* **'Id**, fête du *Taureau*, ou simplement **'Id**, la fête par excellence, laquelle est établie en mémoire du sacrifice d'Ismael."—*Garcin de Tassy, Rel. Mus. dans l'Inde*, 9 *seq.*

EEDGAH, s. Ar.—P. *'Īdgāh*, 'Place of *'Īd*.' (See **EED**.) A place of assembly and prayer on occasion of Musulman festivals. It is in India usually a platform of white plastered brickwork, enclosed by a low wall on three sides, and situated outside of a town or village. It is a marked characteristic of landscape in Upper India. [It is also known as *Namāzgāh*, or 'place of prayer,' and a drawing of one is given by *Herklots, Qanoon-e-Islam*, Pl. iii. fig. 2.]

1792.—"The commanding nature of the ground on which the **Eed-Gah** stands had induced Tippoo to construct a redoubt upon that eminence."—*Ld. Cornwallis*, Desp. from Seringapatam, in *Seton-Karr*, ii. 89.

[1832.—". . . Kings, Princes and Nawaubs . . . going to an appointed place, which is designated the **Eade-Garrh.**"—*Mrs. Meer Hassan Ali, Observations*, i. 262.

[1843.—"In the afternoon . . . proceeded in state to the **Eed Gao**, a building at a small distance, where Mahommedan worship was performed."—*Davidson, Travels in Upper India*, i. 53.]

EKTENG, adj. The native representation of the official designation '*acting*' applied to a substitute, especially in the Civil Service. The manner in which the natives used to explain the expression to themselves is shown in the quotation.

1883.—"Lawrence had been only 'acting' there; a term which has suggested to the minds of the natives, in accordance with their pronunciation of it, and with that striving after meaning in syllables which leads to so many etymological fallacies, the interpretation **ek-tang**, 'one-leg,' as if the temporary incumbent had but one leg in the official stirrup."—H. Y. in *Quarterly Review* (on *Bosworth Smith's Life of Lord Lawrence*), April, p. 297.

ELCHEE, s. An ambassador. Turk. *īlchī*, from *īl*, a (nomad) tribe, hence the representative of the *īl*. It is a title that has attached itself particularly to Sir John Malcolm, and to Sir Stratford Canning, probably because they were personally more familiar to the Orientals among whom they served than diplomatists usually are.

1404.—"And the people who saw them approaching, and knew them for people of the Emperor's, being aware that they were come with some order from the great Lord, took to flight as if the devil were after them; and those who were in their tents selling their wares, shut them up and also took to flight, and shut themselves up in their houses, calling out to one another, **Elchi!** which is as much as to say 'Ambassadors!' For they knew that with ambassadors coming they would have a black day of it; and so they fled as if the devil had got among them."—*Clavijo*, xcvii. Comp. *Markham*, p. 111.

[1599.—"I came to the court to see a Morris dance, and a play of his **Elchies.**"—*Hakluyt, Voyages*, II. ii. 67 (*Stanf. Dict.*).]

1885.—"No historian of the Crimean War could overlook the officer (Sir Hugh Rose) who, at a difficult crisis, filled the post of the famous diplomatist called the great **Elchi** by writers who have adopted a tiresome trick from a brilliant man of letters."—*Sat. Review*, Oct. 24.

ELEPHANT, s. This article will be confined to notes connected with the various suggestions which have been put forward as to the origin of the word—a sufficiently ample subject.

The oldest occurrence of the word (ἐλέφας—φαντος) is in Homer. With him, and so with Hesiod and Pindar, the word means 'ivory.' Herodotus first uses it as the name of the animal (iv. 191). Hence an occasional, probably an erroneous, assumption that the word ἐλέφας originally meant only the material, and not the beast that bears it.

In Persian the usual term for the beast is *pīl*, with which agree the Aramaic *pīl* (already found in the Chaldee and Syriac versions of the O. T.), and the Arabic *fīl*. Old etymologists tried to develop *elephant* out of *fīl*; and it is natural to connect with it the Spanish for 'ivory' (*marfil*, Port. *marfim*), but no satisfactory explanation has yet been given of the first syllable of that word. More certain is the fact that in early Swedish and Danish the word for 'elephant' is *fil*, in Icelandic *fill*; a term supposed to have been introduced by old traders from the East *viâ* Russia. The old Swedish for 'ivory' is *filsben*.*

The oldest Hebrew mention of ivory is in the notice of the products brought to Solomon from Ophir, or India. Among these are ivory tusks—*shen-habbim*, *i.e.* 'teeth of *habbīm*,' a word which has been interpreted as from Skt. *ibha*, elephant.† But it is entirely doubtful what this *habbīm*, occurring here only, really means.‡ We know

* *Pīlu*, for elephant, occurs in certain Sanskrit books, but it is regarded as a foreign word.

† See *Lassen*, i. 313; *Max Müller's Lectures on Sc. of Language*, 1st S. p. 189.

‡ "As regards the interpretation of *habbim*, a ἅπαξ λεγ., in the passage where the state of the text, as shown by comparison with the LXX, is very unsatisfactory, it seems impossible to say anything that can be of the least use in clearing

from other evidence that ivory was known in Egypt and Western Asia for ages before Solomon. And in other cases the Hebrew word for ivory is simply *shen*, corresponding to *dens Indus* in Ovid and other Latin writers. In Ezekiel (xxvii. 15) we find *karnoth shen*='cornua dentis.' The use of the word '*horns*' does not necessarily imply a confusion of these great curved tusks with horns; it has many parallels, as in Pliny's, "*cum arbore exacuant limentque* cornua *elephanti*" (xviii. 7); in Martial's "*Indicoque* cornu" (i. 73); in Aelian's story, as alleged by the Mauritanians, that the elephants there shed their *horns* every ten years ("δεκάτῳ ἔτει πάντως τὰ κέρατα ἐκπεσεῖν"—xiv. 5); whilst Cleasby quotes from an Icelandic saga '*olifant*-horni' for 'ivory.'

We have mentioned Skt. *ibha*, from which Lassen assumes a compound *ibhadantā* for ivory, suggesting that this, combined by early traders with the Arabic article, formed *al-ibhadantā*, and so originated ἐλέφαντος. Pott, besides other doubts, objects that *ibhadantā*, though the name of a plant (*Tiaridium indicum*, Lehm.), is never actually a name of ivory.

Pott's own etymology is *alaf-hindi*, 'Indian ox,' from a word existing in sundry resembling forms, in Hebrew and in Assyrian (*alif*, *alap*).* This has met with favour; though it is a little hard to accept any form like *Hindī* as earlier than Homer.

Other suggested origins are Pictet's from *airāvata* (lit. 'proceeding from water'), the proper name of the elephant of Indra, or Elephant of the Eastern Quarter in the Hindu Cosmology.† This is felt to be only too ingenious, but as improbable. It is, however, suggested, it would seem independently, by Mr. Kittel (*Indian Antiquary*, i. 128), who supposes the first part of the word to be Dravidian, a transformation from *āne*, 'elephant.'

up the origin of *elephant*. The O. T. speaks so often of ivory, and never again by this name, that *habbim* must be either a corruption or some trade-name, presumably for some special kind of ivory. Personally, I believe it far more likely that *habbim* is at bottom the same as *hobnim* (ebony?) associated with *shen* in Ezekiel xxvii. 15, and that the passage once ran 'ivory and ebony'" (*W. Robertson Smith*); [also see *Encycl. Bibl.* ii. 2297 *seq.*].

* See *Zeitschr. für die Kie Kunde des Morgs*, iv. 12 *seqq.*; also *Ebehr. Schrader* in *Zeitsch. d. M. Gesellsch.* xxvii. 706 *seqq.*; [*Encycl. Bibl.* ii. 1262].

† In *Journ. As.*, ser. iv. tom. ii.

Pictet, finding his first suggestion not accepted, has called up a Singhalese word *aliya*, used for 'elephant,' which he takes to be from *āla*, 'great'; thence *aliya*, 'great creature'; and proceeding further, presents a combination of *āla*, 'great,' with Skt. *phata*, sometimes signifying 'a tooth,' thus *ali-phaṭa*, 'great tooth'=*elephantus*.*

Hodgson, in *Notes on Northern Africa* (p. 19, quoted by Pott), gives *elef ameqran* ('Great Boar,' *elef* being 'boar') as the name of the animal among the Kabyles of that region, and appears to present it as the origin of the Greek and Latin words.

Again we have the Gothic *ulbandus*, 'a camel,' which has been regarded by some as the same word with *elephantus*. To this we shall recur.

Pott, in his elaborate paper already quoted, comes to the conclusion that the choice of etymologies must lie between his own *alaf-hindī* and Lassen's *al-ibha-dantā*. His paper is 50 years old, but he repeats this conclusion in his *Wurzel-Wörterbüch der Indo-Germanische Sprachen*, published in 1871,† nor can I ascertain that there has been any later advance towards a true etymology. Yet it can hardly be said that either of the alternatives carries conviction.

Both, let it be observed, apart from other difficulties, rest on the assumption that the knowledge of ἐλέφας, whether as fine material or as monstrous animal, came from India, whilst nearly all the other or less-favoured suggestions point to the same assumption.

But knowledge acquired, or at least taken cognizance of, since Pott's latest reference to the subject, puts us in possession of the new and surprising fact that, even in times which we are entitled to call historic, the elephant existed wild, far to the westward of India, and not very far from the eastern extremity of the Mediterranean. Though the fact was indicated from the wall-paintings by Wilkinson some 65 years ago,‡ and has more recently been amply displayed in historical works which have circulated by scores in popular libraries, it

* In *Kuhn's Zeitschr. für Vergleichende Sprachkunst*, iv. 128-131.

† Detmold, pp. 950-952.

‡ See *Topography of Thebes, with a General View of Egypt*, 1835, p. 158.

is singular how little attention or interest it seems to have elicited.*

The document which gives precise Egyptian testimony to this fact is an inscription (first interpreted by Ebers in 1873) † from the tomb of Amenemhib, a captain under the great conqueror Thotmes III. [Thūtmosis], who reigned B.C. c. 1600. This warrior, speaking from his tomb of the great deeds of his master, and of his own right arm, tells how the king, in the neighbourhood of *Ni*, hunted 120 elephants for the sake of their tusks; and how he himself (Amenemhib) encountered the biggest of them, which had attacked the sacred person of the king, and cut through its trunk. The elephant chased him into the water, where he saved himself between two rocks; and the king bestowed on him rich rewards.

The position of *Ni* is uncertain, though some have identified it with Nineveh.‡ [Maspero writes: "Nīi, long confounded with Nineveh, after Champolion (*Gram. égyptienne*, p. 150), was identified by Lenormant (*Les Origines*, vol. iii. p. 316 *et seq.*) with Ninus Vetus, Membidj, and by Max Müller (*Asien und Europa*, p. 267) with Balis on the Euphrates: I am inclined to make it Kefer-Naya, between Aleppo and Turmanīn" (*Struggle of the Nations*, 144, note).] It is named in another inscription between *Arinath* and *Akerith*, as, all three, cities of *Naharain* or Northern Mesopotamia, captured by Amenhotep II., the son of Thotmes III. Might not *Ni* be Nisibis? We shall find that Assyrian inscriptions of later date have been interpreted as placing elephant-hunts in the land of Harran and in the vicinity of the Chaboras.

If then these elephant-hunts may be located on the southern skirts of Taurus, we shall more easily understand how a tribute of elephant-tusks should have been offered at the court of Egypt by the people of *Rutennu* or Northern Syria, and also by the people of the adjacent *Asebi* or Cyprus, as we find repeatedly recorded on the Egyptian monuments, both in hieroglyphic writing and pictorially.*

What the stones of Egypt allege in the 17th cent. B.C., the stones of Assyria 500 years afterwards have been alleged to corroborate. The great inscription of Tighlath-Pileser I., who is calculated to have reigned about B.C. 1120-1100, as rendered by Lotz, relates:

> "Ten mighty Elephants
> Slew I in Harran, and on the banks of the Haboras.
> Four Elephants I took alive;
> Their hides,
> Their teeth, and the live Elephants
> I brought to my city Assur." †

The same facts are recorded in a later inscription, on the broken obelisk of Assurnazirpal from Kouyunjik, now in the Br. Museum, which commemorates the deeds of the king's ancestor, Tighlath Pileser.‡

In the case of these Assyrian inscriptions, however, *elephant* is by no means an undisputed interpretation. In the famous quadruple *test* exercise on this inscription in 1857, which gave the death-blow to the doubts which some sceptics had emitted as to the genuine character of the Assyrian interpretations, Sir H. Rawlinson, in this passage, rendered the animals slain and taken alive as *wild buffaloes*. The ideogram given as *teeth* he had not interpreted. The question is argued at length by Lotz in the work already quoted, but it is a question for cuneiform experts, dealing, as it does, with the interpretation of more than one *ideogram*, and enveloped as yet in uncertainties. It is to be observed, that in 1857 Dr. Hincks, one of the four test-translators,§ had rendered the passage almost exactly as Lotz has done 23 years later, though I cannot see that Lotz makes any allusion to this fact. [See *Encycl. Bibl.* ii. 1262.] Apart from arguments as to decipherment and ideograms, it is certain that probabilities are much affected by the publication of the Egyptian inscription

* See *e.g. Brugsch's Hist. of the Pharaohs*, 2d ed. i. 396-400; and *Canon Rawlinson's Egypt*, ii. 235-6.

† In *Z. für Aegypt. Spr. und Aetferth.* 1873, pp. 1-9, 63, 64; also tr. by Dr. Birch in *Records of the Past*, vol. ii. p. 59 (*no date*, more shame to S. Bagster & Sons); and again by Ebers, revised in Z.D.M.G., 1876, pp. 391 *seqq.*

‡ See Canon Rawlinson's *Egypt*, u.s.

* For the painting see *Wilkinson's Ancient Egyptians*, edited by Birch, vol. i. pl. 11 b, which shows the Rutennu bringing a chariot and horses, a bear, an elephant, and ivory tusks, as tribute to Thotmes III. For other records see *Brugsch*, E.T., 2nd ed. i. 381, 384, 404.

† *Die Inschriften Tighlathpileser's I., . . . mit Übersetzung und Kommentar von Dr. Wilhelm Lotz*, Leipzig, 1880, p. 53; [and see Maspero, *op. cit.* 661 *seq.*].

‡ *Lotz, loc. cit.* p. 197.

§ See *J.R. As. Soc.* vol. xviii.

of Amenhoteb, which gives a greater plausibility to the rendering 'elephant' than could be ascribed to it in 1857. And should it eventually be upheld, it will be all the more remarkable that the sagacity of Dr. Hincks should then have ventured on that rendering.

In various suggestions, including Pott's, besides others that we have omitted, the etymology has been based on a transfer of the name of the ox, or some other familiar quadruped. There would be nothing extraordinary in such a transfer of meaning. The reference to the *bos Luca** is trite; the Tibetan word for ox (*glan*) is also the word for 'elephant'; we have seen how the name 'Great Boar' is alleged to be given to the elephant among the Kabyles; we have heard of an elephant in a menagerie being described by a Scotch rustic as 'a muckle sow'; Pausanias, according to Bochart, calls rhinoceroses 'Aethiopic bulls' [Bk. ix. 21, 2]. And let me finally illustrate the matter by a circumstance related to me by a brother officer who accompanied Sir Neville Chamberlain on an expedition among the turbulent Pathan tribes c. 1860. The women of the villages gathered to gaze on the elephants that accompanied the force, a stranger sight to them than it would have been to the women of the most secluded village in Scotland. 'Do you see these?' said a soldier of the Frontier Horse; 'do you know what they are? These are the Queen of England's buffaloes that give 5 maunds (about 160 quarts) of milk a day!'

Now it is an obvious suggestion, that if there were elephants on the skirts of Taurus down to B.C. 1100, or even (taking the less questionable evidence) down only to B.C. 1600, it is highly improbable that the Greeks would have had to seek a name for the animal, or its tusk, from Indian trade. And if the Greeks had a vernacular name for the elephant, there is also a probability, if not a presumption, that some tradition of this name would be found, *mutatis mutandis*, among other Aryan nations of Europe.

Now may it not be that ἐλέφας—φαντος in Greek, and *ulbandus* in Moeso-Gothic, represent this vernacular name? The latter form is exactly the modification of the former which Grimm's law demands. Nor is the word confined to Gothic. It is found in the Old H. German (*olpentâ*); in Anglo-Saxon (*olfend, oluend*, &c.); in Old Swedish (*aelpand, alwandyr, ulfwald*); in Icelandic (*ulfaldi*). All these Northern words, it is true, are used in the sense of *camel*, not of *elephant*. But instances already given may illustrate that there is nothing surprising in this transfer, all the less where the animal originally indicated had long been lost sight of. Further, Jülg, who has published a paper on the Gothic word, points out its resemblance to the Slav forms *welbond*, *welblond*, or *wielblad*, also meaning 'camel' (compare also Russian *verbliud*). This, in the last form (*wielblad*), may, he says, be regarded as resolvable into 'Great beast.' Herr Jülg ends his paper with a hint that in this meaning may perhaps be found a solution of the origin of *elephant* (an idea at which Pictet also transiently pointed in a paper referred to above), and half promises to follow up this hint; but in thirty years he has not done so, so far as I can discover. Nevertheless it is one which may yet be pregnant.

Nor is it inconsistent with this suggestion that we find also in some of the Northern languages a second series of names designating the elephant—not, as we suppose *ulbandus* and its kin to be, common vocables descending from a remote age in parallel development—but adoptions from Latin at a much more recent period. Thus, we have in Old and Middle German *Elefant* and *Helfant*, with *elfenbein* and *helfenbein* for ivory; in Anglo-Saxon, *ylpend, elpend*, with shortened forms *ylp* and *elp*, and *ylpenban* for ivory; whilst the Scandinavian tongues adopt and retain *fil*. [The *N.E.D.* regards the derivation as doubtful, but considers the theory of Indian origin improbable.

[A curious instance of misapprehension is the use of the term '*Chain elephants*.' This is a misunderstanding

* "Inde *boves Lucas* turrito corpore tetros,
Anguimanos, belli docuerunt volnera Pœnei
Sufferre, et magnas Martis turbare catervas."
Lucretius, v. 1301-3.

Here is the origin of Tennyson's 'serpent-hands' quoted under HATTY. The title *bos Luca* is explained by St. Isidore:

"Hos *boves Lucanos* vocabant antiqui Romani: *boves* quia nullum animal grandius videbant: *Lucanos* quia in Lucania illos primus Pyrrhus in prœlio objecit Romanis."—*Isid. Hispal.* lib. xii. *Originum*, cap. 2.

of the ordinary locution *zanjīr-i-fīl* when speaking of elephants. *Zanjīr* is literally a 'chain,' but is here akin to our expressions, a 'pair,' 'couple,' 'brace' of anything. It was used, no doubt, with reference to the iron chain by which an elephant is hobbled. In an account 100 elephants would be entered thus: *Fīl, Zanjīr,* 100. (See **NUMERICAL AFFIXES.**)]

[1826.—"Very frequent mention is made in Asiatic histories of *chain*-**elephants**; which always mean elephants trained for war; but it is not very clear why they are so denominated."—*Ranking, Hist. Res. on the Wars and Sports of the Mongols and Romans,* 1826, Intro. p. 12.]

ELEPHANTA.

a. n.p. An island in Bombay Harbour, the native name of which is *Ghārāpurī* (or sometimes, it would seem, shortly, *Purī*), famous for its magnificent excavated temple, considered by Burgess to date after the middle of the 8th cent. The name was given by the Portuguese from the life-size figure of an elephant, hewn from an isolated mass of trap-rock, which formerly stood in the lower part of the island, not far from the usual landing-place. This figure fell down many years ago, and was often said to have disappeared. But it actually lay *in situ* till 1864-5, when (on the suggestion of the late Mr. W. E. Frere) it was removed by Dr. (now Sir) George Birdwood to the Victoria Gardens at Bombay, in order to save the relic from destruction. The elephant had originally a smaller figure on its back, which several of the earlier authorities speak of as a young elephant, but which Mr. Erskine and Capt. Basil Hall regarded as a tiger. The horse mentioned by Fryer remained in 1712; it had disappeared apparently before Niebuhr's visit in 1764. [Compare the recovery of a similar pair of elephant figures at Delhi, *Cunningham, Archaeol. Rep.* i. 225 *seqq.*]

c. 1321.—"In quod dum sic ascendissem, in xxviii. dietis me transtuli usque ad Tanam . . . haec terra multum bene est situata. . . . Haec terra antiquitus fuit valde magna. Nam ipsa fuit terra regis Pori, qui cum rege Alexandro praelium maximum commisit."—*Friar Odoric,* in *Cathay,* &c., App. p. v.

We quote this because of its relation to the passages following. It seems probable that the alleged connection with Porus and Alexander may have grown out of the name *Puri* or *Pori.*

[1539.—Mr. Whiteway notes that in João de Crastro's Log of his voyage to Diu will be found a very interesting account with measurements of the **Elephanta** Caves.]

1548.—"And the Isle of Pory, which is that of the **Elephant** (*do Alyfante*), is leased to João Pirez by arrangements of the said Governor (dom João de Crastro) for 150 pardaos."—*S. Botelho, Tombo,* 158.

1580.—"At 3 hours of the day we found ourselves abreast of a cape called Bombain, where is to be seen an ancient Roman temple, hollowed in the living rock. And above the said temple are many tamarind-trees, and below it a living spring, in which they have never been able to find bottom. The said temple is called **Alefante**, and is adorned with many figures, and inhabited by a great multitude of bats; and here they say that Alexander Magnus arrived, and for memorial thereof caused this temple to be made, and further than this he advanced not."—*Gasparo Balbi,* f. 62*v*.-63.

1598.—"There is yet an other Pagode, which they hold and esteem for the highest and chiefest Pagode of all the rest, which standeth in a little Iland called *Pory;* this Pagode by the Portingalls is called the Pagode of the **Elephant**. In that Iland standeth an high hill, and on the top thereof there is a hole, that goeth down into the hill, digged and carved out of the hard rock or stones as big as a great cloyster . . . round about the wals are cut and formed, the shapes of Elephants, Lions, tigers, & a thousand such like wilde and cruel beasts. . . ."—*Linschoten,* ch. xliv.; [Hak. Soc. i. 291].

1616.—Diogo de Couto devotes a chapter of 11 pp. to his detailed account "*do muito notável e espantoso Pagode do* **Elefante**." We extract a few paragraphs:

"This notable and above all others astonishing Pagoda of the **Elephant** stands on a small islet, less than half a league in compass, which is formed by the river of Bombain, where it is about to discharge itself southward into the sea. It is so called because of a great **elephant** of stone, which one sees in entering the river. They say that it was made by the orders of a heathen king called Banasur, who ruled the whole country inland from the Ganges. . . . On the left side of this chapel is a doorway 6 palms in depth and 5 in width, by which one enters a chamber which is nearly square and very dark, so that there is nothing to be seen there; and with this ends the fabric of this great pagoda. It has been in many parts demolished; and what the soldiers have left is so maltreated that it is grievous to see destroyed in such fashion one of the Wonders of the World. It is now 50 years since I went to see this marvellous Pagoda; and as I did not then visit it with such curiosity as I should now feel in doing so, I failed to remark many particulars which exist no longer. But I do remember me to have seen a certain Chapel, not to be seen now, open on the whole façade (which was more than 40 feet in length), and which along the rock formed a plinth the whole length of the edifice, fashioned like our altars both as to breadth and height; and on this plinth were many remarkable things to be seen. Among others I remember to have noticed the story of Queen Pasiphae and the bull; also the Angel with naked sword thrusting forth from below a tree two beautiful figures of a man and a woman, who were naked, as the Holy Scripture paints for us the appearance of our first parents Adam and Eve."—*Couto*, Dec. VII. liv. iii. cap. xi.

1644.—". . . an islet which they call **Ilheo do Ellefanté**. . . . In the highest part of this Islet is an eminence on which there is a mast from which a flag is unfurled when there are prows (*paros*) about, as often happens, to warn the small unarmed vessels to look out. . . . There is on this island a pagoda called that of the Elephant, a work of extraordinary magnitude, being cut out of the solid rock," &c.—*Bocarro, MS.*

1673.—". . . We steered by the south side of the Bay, purposely to touch at **Elephanto**, so called from a monstrous Elephant cut out of the main Rock, bearing a young one on its Back; not far from it the Effigies of a Horse stuck up to the Belly in the Earth in the Valley; from thence we clambered up the highest Mountain on the Island, on whose summit was a miraculous Piece hewed out of solid Stone: It is supported with 42 *Corinthian* Pillars," &c.—*Fryer*, 75.

1690. — "At 3 Leagues distance from *Bombay* is a small Island called **Elephanta**, from the Statue of an Elephant cut in Stone. . . . Here likewise are the just dimensions of a Horse Carved in Stone, so lively . . . that many have rather Fancyed it, at a distance, a living Animal. . . . But that which adds the most Remarkable Character to this Island, is the fam'd *Pagode* at the top of it; so much spoke of by the *Portuguese*, and at present admir'd by the present Queen Dowager, that she cannot think any one has seen this part of India, who comes not Freighted home with some Account of it."—*Ovington*, 158-9.

1712.—"The island of **Elephanta** . . . takes its name from an elephant in stone, with another on its back, which stands on a small hill, and serves as a sea mark. . . . As they advanced towards the pagoda through a smooth narrow pass cut in the rock, they observed another hewn figure which was called Alexander's horse."—From an account written by *Captain Pyke*, on board the Stringer East Indiaman, and illd. by drawings. *Read by A. Dalrymple to the Soc. of Antiquaries*, 10th Feb. 1780, and pubd. in *Archaeologia*, vii. 323 *seqq.* One of the plates (xxi.) shows the elephant having on its back distinctly a small elephant, whose proboscis comes down into contact with the head of the large one.

1727.—"A league from thence is another larger, called **Elephanto**, belonging to the *Portugueze*, and serves only to feed some Cattle. I believe it took its name from an Elephant carved out of a great black Stone, about Seven Foot in Height."—*A. Hamilton*, i. 240; [ed. 1744, i. 241].

1760.—"Le lendemain, 7 Decembre, des que le jour parut, je me transportai au bas de la seconde montagne, en face de Bombaye, dans un coin de l'Isle, où est l'Elephant qui a fait donner à Galipouri le nom d'**Elephante**. L'animal est de grandeur naturelle, d'une pierre noire, et detachée du sol, et paroit porter son petit sur son dos." —*Anquetil du Perron*, I. ccccxxiii.

1761.—". . . The work I mention is an artificial cave cut out of a solid Rock, and decorated with a number of pillars, and gigantic statues, some of which discover ye work of a skilful artist; and I am inform'd by an acquaintance who is well read in ye antient history, and has minutely considered ye figures, that it appears to be ye work of King Sesostris after his Indian Expedition." —MS. Letter of *James Rennell*.

1764. — "Plusieurs Voyageurs font bien mention du vieux temple Payen sur la petite Isle **Elephanta** près de Bombay, mais ils n'en parlent qu'en passant. Je le trouvois si curieux et si digne de l'attention des Amateurs d'Antiquités, que j'y fis trois fois le Voyage, et que j'y dessinois tout ce que s'y trouve de plus remarquable. . . ."—*Carsten Niebuhr*, *Voyaye*, ii. 25.

" "Pas loin du Rivage de la Mer, et en pleine Campagne, on voit encore un Elephant d'une pierre dure et noiratre . . . La Statue . . . porte quelque chose sur le dos, mais que le tems a rendu entièrement meconnoissable. . . . Quant au Cheval dont Ovington et Hamilton font mention je ne l'ai pas vu."—*Ibid.* 33.

1780.—"That which has principally attracted the attention of travellers is the small island of **Elephanta**, situated in the east side of the harbour of Bombay. . . . Near the south end is the figure of an elephant rudely cut in stone, from which the island has its name. . . . On the back are the remains of something that is said to have formerly represented a young elephant, though no traces of such a resemblance are now to be found."—*Account*, &c. By *Mr. William Hunter*, Surgeon in the E. Indies, *Archaeologia*, vii. 286.

1783. — In vol. viii. of the *Archaeologia*, p. 251, is another account in a letter from Hector Macneil, Esq. He mentions "the elephant cut out of stone," but not the small elephant, nor the horse.

1795.—"*Some Account of the Caves in the Island of* **Elephanta**. *By J. Goldingham*, Esq." (No date of paper). In *As. Researches*, iv. 409 *seqq.*

1813.—*Account of the Cave Temple of* **Elephanta** . . . by *Wm. Erskine*, *Trans. Bombay Lit. Soc.* i. 198 *seqq.* Mr. Erskine says in regard to the figure on the back of the large elephant: "The remains of its paws, and also the junction of its belly with the larger animal, were perfectly distinct; and the appearance it offered is represented on the annexed drawing made by Captain Hall (Pl. II.),* who from its appearance conjectured that it must have been a tiger rather than an elephant; an idea in which I feel disposed to agree."—*Ibid.* 208.

b. s. A name given, originally by the Portuguese, to violent storms occurring at the termination, though some travellers describe it as at the setting-in, of the Monsoon. [The Portuguese, however, took the name from the H. *hathiyā*, Skt. *hastā*, the 13th lunar Asterism, connected with *hastin*, an elephant, and hence sometimes called 'the sign of the elephant.' The *hathiyā* is at the close of the Rains.]

1554.—"The *Damani*, that is to say a violent storm arose; the kind of storm is known under the name of the **Elephant**; it blows from the west."—*Sidi 'Ali*, p. 75.

[1611.—"The storm of **Ofante** doth begin."—*Danvers, Letters*, i. 126.]

c. 1616.—"The 20th day (August), the night past fell a storme of raine called the **Oliphant**, vsuall at going out of the raines."—*Sir T. Roe*, in *Purchas*, i. 549; [Hak. Soc. i. 247].

1659.—"The boldest among us became dismayed; and the more when the whole culminated in such a terrific storm that we were compelled to believe that it must be that yearly raging tempest which is called the **Elephant**. This storm, annually, in September and October, makes itself heard in a frightful manner, in the Sea of Bengal."—*Walter Schulze*, 67.

c. 1665.—"Il y fait si mauvais pour le Vaisseaux au commencement de ce mois à cause d'un Vent d'Orient qui y souffle en ce tems-là avec violence, et qui est toujours accompagnè de gros nuages qu'on appelle **Elephans**, parce-qu'ils en ont la figure. . . ."—*Thevenot*, v. 38.

1673.—"Not to deviate any longer, we are now winding about the *South-West* part of Ceilon; where we have the **Tail of the Elephant** full in our mouth; a constellation by the *Portugals* called **Rabo del Elephanto**, known for the breaking up of the *Munsoons*, which is the last Flory this season makes."—*Fryer*, 48.

[1690.—"The Mussoans (**Monsoon**) are rude and Boisterous in their departure, as well as at their coming in, which two seasons are called the **Elephant** in India, and just before their breaking up, take their farewell for the most part in very rugged puffing weather."—*Ovington*, 137].

1756.—"9th (October). We had what they call here an **Elephanta**, which is an excessive hard gale, with very severe thunder, lightning and rain, but it was of short continuance. In about 4 hours there fell . . . 2 (inches)."—*Ives*, 42.

c. 1760.—"The setting in of the rains is commonly ushered in by a violent thunderstorm, generally called the **Elephanta**."—*Grose*, i. 33.

* It is not easy to understand the bearing of the drawing in question.

ELEPHANT-CREEPER, s. *Argyreia speciosa*, Sweet. (N. O. *Convolvulaceae*). The leaves are used in native medicine as poultices, &c.

ELK, s. The name given by sportsmen in S. India, with singular impropriety, to the great stag *Rusa Aristotelis*, the *sāmbar* (see **SAMBRE**) of Upper and W. India.

[1813.—"In a narrow defile . . . a male **elk** (*cervus alces*, Lin.) of noble appearance, followed by twenty-two females, passed majestically under their platform, each as large as a common-sized horse."—*Forbes, Or. Mem.* 2nd ed. i. 506.]

ELL'ORA, (though very commonly called **Ellóra**), n.p. Properly *Elurā*, [Tel. *elu*, 'rule,' *ūru*, 'village,'] otherwise *Vērulē*, a village in the Nizam's territory, 7 m. from Daulatābād, which gives its name to the famous and wonderful rock-caves and temples in its vicinity, excavated in the crescent-shaped scarp of a plateau, about 1½ m. in length. These works are Buddhist (ranging from A.D. 450 to 700), Brahminical (c. 650 to 700), and Jain (c. 800-1000).

c. 1665.—"On m'avoit fait a Sourat grande estime des Pagodes d'**Elora** . . . (and after describing them) . . . Quoiqu'il en soit, si l'on considère cette quantité de Temples spacieux, remplis de pilastres et de colonnes, et tant de milliers de figures, et le tout taillé dans le roc vif, on peut dire avec verité que ces ouvrages surpassent la force humaine; et qu'au moins les gens du siècle dans lequel ils ont été faits, n'étoient pas tout-à-fait barbares."—*Thevenot*, v. p. 222.

1684.—"Muhammad Shāh Malik Júná, son of Tughlik, selected the fort of Deogir as a central point whereat to establish the seat of government, and gave it the name of Daulatábád. He removed the inhabitants of Delhí thither. . . . Ellora is only a short distance from this place. At some very remote period a race of men, as if by magic, excavated caves high up among the defiles of the mountains. These rooms extended over a breadth of one *kos*. Carvings of various designs and of correct execution adorned all the walls and ceilings; but the outside of the mountain is perfectly level, and there is no sign of any dwelling. From the long period of time these Pagans remained masters of this territory, it is reasonable to conclude, although historians differ, that to them is to be attributed the construction of these places."—*Sākī Musta-'idd Khān, Ma-āṣir-i-'Ālamgīrī*, in *Elliot*, vii. 189 *seq.*

1760.—"Je descendis ensuite par un sentier frayé dans le roc, et après m'être muni de deux Brahmes que l'on me donna pour fort instruits je commencai la visite de ce que j'appelle les Pagodes d'**Eloura**."—*Anquetil du Perron*, I. ccxxxiii.

1794.—"*Description of the Caves . . . on the Mountain, about a Mile to the Eastward of the town of* **Ellora**, *or as called on the spot, Verrool.*" (By Sir C. W. Malet.) In *As. Researches*, vi. 38 *seqq.*

1803.—"*Hindoo Excavations in the Mountain of . . .* **Ellora** *in Twenty-four Views. . . . Engraved from the Drawings of* James Wales, *by and under the direction of* Thomas Daniell."

ELU, HELU, n.p. This is the name by which is known an ancient form of the Singhalese language from which the modern vernacular of Ceylon is immediately derived, "and to which" the latter "bears something of the same relation that the English of to-day bears to Anglo-Saxon. Fundamentally Elu and Singhalese are identical, and the difference of form which they present is due partly to the large number of new grammatical forms evolved by the modern language, and partly to an immense influx into it of Sanskrit nouns, borrowed, often without alteration, at a comparatively recent period. . . . The name **Elu** is no other than *Sinhala* much corrupted, standing for an older form, *Hĕla* or *Hĕlu*, which occurs in some ancient works, and this again for a still older, *Sĕla*, which brings us back to the Pali *Sihala*." (*Mr. R. C. Childers*, in *J.R.A.S.*, N.S., vii. 36.) The loss of the initial sibilant has other examples in Singhalese. (See also under **CEYLON**.)

EMBLIC *Myrobalans*. See under **MYROBALANS**.

ENGLISH-BAZAR, n.p. This is a corruption of the name (*Angrezābād* = 'English-town') given by the natives in the 17th century to the purlieus of the factory at Malda in Bengal. Now the Head-quarters Station of Malda District.

1683.—"I departed from Cassumbazar with designe (God willing) to visit ye factory at **Englesavad**."—*Hedges, Diary*, May 9; [Hak. Soc. i. 86; also see i. 71].

1878.—"These ruins (Gaur) are situated about 8 miles to the south of Angrézābád (**English Bázár**), the civil station of the district of Máldah. . . ."—*Ravenshaw's Gaur*, p. 1.

[**ESTIMAUZE**, s. A corruption of the Ar.—P. *iltimās*, 'a prayer, petition, humble representation.'

[1687.—"The Arzdest (**Urz**) with the **Estimauze** concerning your twelve articles which you sent to me arrived."—In *Yule, Hedges' Diary*, Hak. Soc. ii. lxx.]

EURASIAN, a. A modern name for persons of mixt European and Indian blood, devised as being more euphemistic than **Half-caste** and more precise than *East-Indian*. ["No name has yet been found or coined which correctly represents this section. **Eurasian** certainly does not. When the European and Anglo-Indian Defence Association was established 17 years ago, the term *Anglo-Indian*, after much consideration, was adopted as best designating this community."—(*Procs. Imperial Anglo-Indian Ass.*, in *Pioneer Mail*, April 13, 1900.)]

[1844.—"*The* **Eurasian** Belle," *in a few Local Sketches by J. M.*, Calcutta.—6th ser. *Notes and Queries*, xii. 177.

[1866.—See quotation under **KHUDD**.]

1880.—"The shovel-hats are surprised that the **Eurasian** does not become a missionary or a schoolmaster, or a policeman, or something of that sort. The native papers say, 'Deport him'; the white prints say, 'Make him a soldier'; and the *Eurasian* himself says, 'Make me a Commissioner, give me a pension.'"—*Ali Baba*, 123.

EUROPE, adj. Commonly used in India for "European," in contradistinction to **country** (q.v.) as qualifying goods, viz. those imported from Europe. The phrase is probably obsolescent, but still in common use. "Europe shop" is a shop where European goods of sorts are sold in an up-country station. The first quotation applies the word to a *man*. [A "*Europe* morning" is lying late in bed, as opposed to the Anglo-Indian's habit of early rising.]

1673.—"The Enemies, by the help of an **Europe** Engineer, had sprung a Mine to blow up the Castle."—*Fryer*, 87.

[1682-3.—"Ordered that a sloop be sent to Conimero with **Europe** goods. . . ."—*Pringle, Diary, Ft. St. Geo.*, 1st ser. ii. 14.]

1711.—"On the arrival of a **Europe** ship, the Sea-Gate is always throng'd with People." —*Lockyer*, 27.

1781.—"Guthrie and Wordie take this method of acquainting the Public that they intend quitting the **Europe** Shop Business." —*India Gazette*, May 26.

1782.—"To be Sold, a magnificent **Europe** Chariot, finished in a most elegant manner, and peculiarly adapted to this Country."—*Ibid.* May 11.

c. 1817.—"Now the **Europe** shop into which Mrs. Browne and Mary went was a very large one, and full of all sorts of things. One side was set out with **Europe** caps and bonnets, ribbons, feathers, sashes, and what not."—*Mrs. Sherwood's Stories*, ed. 1873, 23.

1866.—"*Mrs. Smart.* Ah, Mr. Cholmondeley, I was called the **Europe** Angel."—*The Dawk Bungalow*, 219.

[1888.—"I took a '**European** morning' after having had three days of going out before breakfast. . . ."—*Lady Dufferin, Viceregal Life*, 371.]

EYSHAM, EHSHÂM, s. Ar. *aḥshām*, pl. of *ḥashm*, 'a train or retinue.' One of the military technicalities affected by Tippoo; and according to Kirkpatrick (*Tippoo's Letters*, App. p. cii.) applied to garrison troops. Miles explains it as "Irregular infantry with swords and matchlocks." (See his tr. of *H. of Hydur Naik*, p. 398, and tr. of *H. of Tipú Sultan*, p. 61). [The term was used by the latter Moghuls (see Mr. Irvine below).

[1896.—"In the case of the **Ahshām**, or troops belonging to the infantry and artillery, we have a little more definite information under this head."—*W. Irvine, Army of the Indian Moghuls*, in *J.R.A.S.*, July 1896, p. 528.]

F

FACTOR, s. Originally a commercial agent; the executive head of a **factory**. Till some 55 years ago the *Factors* formed the third of the four classes into which the covenanted civil servants of the Company were theoretically divided, viz. Senior Merchants, Junior Merchants, **factors** and **writers**. But these terms had long ceased to have any relation to the occupation of these officials, and even to have any application at all except in the nominal lists of the service. The titles, however, continue (through *vis inertiae* of administration in such matters) in the classified lists of the Civil Service for years after the abolition of the last vestige of the Company's trading character, and it is not till the publication of the E. I. Register for the first half of 1842 that they disappear from that official publication. In this the whole body appears without any classification; and in that for the second half of 1842 they are divided into six classes, first class, second class, &c., an arrangement which, with the omission of the 6th class, still continues. Possibly the expressions *Factor*, *Factory*, may have been adopted from the Portuguese *Feitor*, *Feitoria*. The formal authority for the classification of the civilians is quoted under 1675.

1501.—"With which answer night came on, and there came aboard the Captain Mór that Christian of Calecut sent by the **Factor** (*feitor*) to say that Cojebequi assured him, and he knew it to be the case, that the King of Calecut was arming a great fleet.' —*Correa*, i. 250.

1582.—"The **Factor** and the Catuall having seen these parcels began to laugh thereat."—*Castañeda*, tr. by N. L., f. 46*b*.

1600.—"Capt. Middleton, John Havard, and Francis Barne, elected the three principal **Factors**. John Havard, being present, willingly accepted."—*Sainsbury*, i. 111.

c. 1610.—"Les Portugais de Malaca ont des commis et **facteurs** par toutes ces Isles pour le trafic."—*Pyrard de Laval*, ii. 106. [Hak. Soc. ii. 170].

1653.—"**Feitor** est vn terme Portugais signifiant vn Consul aux Indes."—*De la Boullaye-le-Gouz*, ed. 1657, p. 538.

1666.—"The Viceroy came to Cochin, and there received the news that Antonio de Sà, **Factor** (*Fator*) of Coulam, with all his officers, had been slain by the Moors."—*Faria y Sousa*, i. 35.

1675-6.—"For the advancement of our Apprentices, we direct that, after they have served the first five yeares, they shall have £10 per annum, for the last two yeares; and having served these two yeares, to be entertayned one year longer, as **Writers**, and have Writers' Sallary: and having served that yeare, to enter into ye degree of **Factor**, which otherwise would have been ten yeares. And knowing that a distinction of titles is, in many respects necessary, we do order that when the Apprentices have served their times, they be stiled *Writers;* and when the Writers have served their times, they be stiled **Factors**, and Factors having served their times to be stiled *Merchants;* and Merchants having served their times to be stiled *Senior Merchants*."—*Ext. of Court's Letter* in *Bruce's Annals of the E.I. Co.*, ii. 374-5.

1689.—"These are the chief Places of Note and Trade where their Presidents and Agents reside, for the support of whom, with their Writers and **Factors**, large Privileges and Salaries are allowed."—*Ovington*, 386. (The same writer tells us that *Factors* got £40 a year; junior Factors, £15; Writers, £7. Peons got 4 rupees a month. P. 392.)

1711. — Lockyer gives the salaries at Madras as follows: "The Governor, £200 and £100 gratuity; 6 Councillors, of whom the chief (2nd?) had £100, 3d. £70, 4th. £50, the others £40, which was the salary of 6 Senior Merchants. 2 Junior Merchants £30 per annum; 5 **Factors**, £15; 10 Writers, £5; 2 Ministers, £100; 1 Surgeon, £36.

* * * * * * *

"Attorney-General has 50 Pagodas per *Annum* gratuity.

"Scavenger 100 do."

* * * * * * *

(p. 14.)

c. 1748.—"He was appointed to be a Writer in the Company's Civil Service, becoming . . . after the first five (years) a **factor**."—*Orme, Fragments*, viii.

1781.—"Why we should have a Council and Senior and Junior Merchants, **factors** and writers, to load one ship in the year (at Penang), and to collect a very small revenue, appears to me perfectly incomprehensible."—*Corresp. of Ld. Cornwallis*, i. 390.

1786.—In a notification of Aug. 10th, the subsistence of civil servants out of employ is fixed thus:—

A Senior Merchant—£400 sterling per ann.
A Junior Merchant—£300 " "
Factors and Writers—£200 " "
In *Seton-Karr*, i. 131.

FACTORY, s. A trading establishment at a foreign port or mart (see preceding).

1500. — "And then he sent ashore the Factor Ayres Correa with the ship's carpenters . . . and sent to ask the King for timber . . . all which the King sent in great sufficiency, and he sent orders also for him to have many carpenters and labourers to assist in making the houses; and they brought much plank and wood, and palm-trees which they cut down at the Point, so that they made a great Campo,* in which they made houses for the Captain Mór, and for each of the Captains, and houses for the people, and they made also a separate large house for the **factory** (*feitoria*)."—*Correa*, i. 168.

1582.—". . . he sent a Nayre . . . to the intent hee might remaine in the **Factorye**."—*Castañeda* (by N. L.), ff. 54*b*.

1606.—"In which time the *Portingall* and Tydoryan Slaves had sacked the towne, setting fire to the **factory**."—*Middleton's Voyage*, G. (4).

1615.—"The King of Acheen desiring that the Hector should leave a merchant in his country . . . it has been thought fit to settle a **factory** at Acheen, and leave Juxon and Nicolls in charge of it."—*Sainsbury*, i. 415.

1809.—"The **factory**-house (at Cuddalore) is a chaste piece of architecture, built by my relative Diamond Pitt, when this was the chief station of the British on the Coromandel Coast."—*Ld. Valentia*, i. 372.

We add a list of the Factories established by the E. I. Company, as complete as we have been able to compile. We have used *Milburn*, *Sainsbury*, the "*Charters of the E. I. Company*," and "*Robert Burton, The English Acquisitions in Guinea and East India*, 1728," which contains (p. 184) a long list of English Factories. It has not been possible to submit our list as yet to proper criticism. The letters attached indicate the authorities, viz. M. Milburn, S. Sainsbury, C. Charters, B. Burton. [For a list of the Hollanders' Factories in 1613 see *Danvers, Letters*, i. 309.]

In Arabia, the Gulf, and Persia.

Judda, B.	Muscat, B.
Mocha, M.	Kishm, B.
Aden, M.	Bushire, M.
Shahr, B.	Gombroon, C.
Durga (?), B.	Bussorah, M.
Dofar, B.	Shiraz, C.
Maculla, B.	Ispahan, C.

In Sind.—Tatta (?).

In Western India.

Cutch, M.	Barcelore, M.
Cambay, M.	Mangalore, M.
Brodera (Baroda), M.	Cananore, M.
Broach, C.	Dhurmapatam, M.
Ahmedabad, C.	Tellecherry, C.
Surat and Swally, C.	Calicut, C.
Bombay, C.	Cranganore, M.
Raybag (?), M.	Cochin, M.
Rajapore, M.	Porca, M.
Carwar, C.	Carnoply, M.
Batikala, M.	Quilon, M.
Honore, M.	Anjengo, C.

Eastern and Coromandel Coast.

Tuticorin, M.	Masulipatam, C., S.
Callimere, B.	Madapollam, C.
Porto Novo, C.	Verasheron (?), M.
Cuddalore (Ft. St. David), C. (qy. Sadras?)	Ingeram (?), M.
	Vizagapatam, C.
	Bimlipatam, M.
Fort St. George, C.M.	Ganjam, M.
Pulicat, M.	Manickpatam, B.
Pettipoli, C., S.	Arzapore (?), B.

Bengal Side.

Balasore, C. (and Jelasore?)	Malda, C.
	Berhampore, M.
Calcutta (Ft. William and Chuttanuttee, C.)	Patna, C.
	Lucknow, C.
	Agra, C.
Hoogly, C.	Lahore, M.
Cossimbazar, C.	Dăcca, C.
Rajmahal, C.	Chittagong?

* This use of *campo* is more like the sense of **Compound** (q.v.) than in any instance we had found when completing that article.

Indo-Chinese Countries.

Pegu, M.	Ligore, M.
Tennasserim (*Trinacore*, B.)	Siam, M., S. (Judea, *i.e.* Yuthia).
Quedah, M.	Camboja, M.
Johore, M.	Cochin China, M.
Pahang, M.	Tonquin, C.
Patani, S.	

In China.

Macao, M., S.	Tywan (in Formosa), M.
Amoy, M.	
Hoksieu (*i.e.* Fu-chow), M.	Chusan, M. (and Ning-po ?).

In Japan.—Firando, M.

Archipelago.

In Sumatra.

Acheen, M.	Indrapore, C.
Passaman, M.	Tryamong, C.
Ticoo, M. (qu. same as Ayer Dickets, B. ?)	(B. has also, in Sumatra, Ayer Borma, Eppon, and Bamola, which we cannot identify.)
Sillebar, M.	
Bencoolen, C.	
Jambi, M., S.	Indraghiri, S.

In Java.

Bantam, C.	Jacatra (since Batavia), M.
Japara, M., S.	

In Borneo.

Banjarmasin, M.	Brunei, M.
Succadana, M.	

In Celebes, &c.

Macassar, M., S.	Pulo Roon (?), M., S.
Banda, M.	Puloway, S.
Lantar, S.	Pulo Condore, M.
Neira, S.	Magindanao, M.
Rosingyn, S.	Machian, (3), S.
Ṣelaman, S.	Moluccas, S.
Amboyna, M.	

Camballo (in Ceram), Hitto, Larica (or Luricca), and Looho, or Lugho, are mentioned in S. (iii. 303) as sub-factories of Amboyna.

[**FAGHFÚR**, n.p. "The common Moslem term for the Emperors of China; in the Kamus the first syllable is Zammated (Fugh); in Al-Maṣ'udi (chap. xiv.) we find **Baghfúr** and in Al-Idrisi **Baghbúgh**, or **Baghbún**. In Al-Asma'i *Bagh*=god or idol (Pehlewi and Persian); hence according to some Baghdád (?) and Bághistán, a pagoda (?). Sprenger (*Al-Maṣ'udi*, p. 327) remarks that **Baghfúr** is a literal translation of Tien-tse, and quotes Visdelou: "pour mieux faire comprendre de quel ciel ils veulent parler, ils poussent la généalogie (of the Emperor) plus loin. Ils lui donnent le ciel pour père, la terre pour mère, le soleil pour frère aîné, et la lune pour sœur aînée."—*Burton, Arabian Nights*, vi. 120-121.]

FAILSOOF, s. Ar.—H. *failsūf*, from φιλόσοφος. But its popular sense is a 'crafty schemer,' an 'artful dodger.' **Filosofo**, in Manilla, is applied to a native who has been at college, and returns to his birthplace in the provinces, with all the importance of his acquisitions, and the affectation of European habits (*Blumentritt, Vocabular.*).

FAKEER, s. Hind. from Arab. *faḳīr* ('poor'). Properly an indigent person, but specially 'one poor in the sight of God,' applied to a Mahommedan religious mendicant, and then, loosely and inaccurately, to Hindu devotees and naked ascetics. And this last is the most ordinary Anglo-Indian use.

1604.—"**Fokers** are men of good life, which are only given to peace. Leo calls them Hermites; others call them *Talbies* and Saints."—*Collection of things . . . of Barbarie*, in *Purchas*, ii. 857.

" "*Muley Boferes* sent certaine **Fokers**, held of great estimation amongst the *Moores*, to his brother *Muley Sidan*, to treate conditions of Peace."—*Ibid.*

1633.—"Also they are called **Fackeeres**, which are religious names."—*W. Bruton*, in *Hakl.* v. 56.

1653.—"**Fakir** signifie pauure en Turq et Persan, mais en Indien signifie . . . vne espece de Religieux Indou, qui foullent le monde aux pieds, et ne s'habillent que de haillons qu'ils ramassent dans les ruës."—*De la Boullaye-le-Gouz*, ed. 1657, 538.

c. 1660.—"I have often met in the Field, especially upon the Lands of the Rajas, whole squadrons of these **Faquires**, altogether naked, dreadful to behold. Some held their Arms lifted up . . .; others had their terrible Hair hanging about them . . .; some had a kind of *Hercules's* Club; others had dry and stiff Tiger-skins over their Shoulders. . . ."—*Bernier*, E.T. p. 102; [ed. *Constable*, 317].

1673.—"**Fakiers** or Holy Men, abstracted from the World, and resigned to God."—*Fryer*, 95.

[1684.—"The **Ffuckeer** that Killed ye Boy at Ennore with severall others . . . were brought to their tryalls. . . ."—*Pringle, Diary, Ft. St. Geo.* 1st ser. iii. 111.]

1690.—"They are called **Faquirs** by the Natives, but *Ashmen* commonly by us, because of the abundance of Ashes with which they powder their Heads."—*Ovington*, 350.

1727.—"Being now settled in Peace, he invited his holy Brethren the **Fakires**, who are very numerous in India, to come to Agra and receive a new Suit of Clothes."—*A. Hamilton*, i. 175; [ed. 1744, ii. 177].

1763.—"Received a letter from Dacca dated 29th Novr., desiring our orders with regard to the **Fakirs** who were taken prisoners at the retaking of Dacca."—*Ft. William Cons.* Dec. 5, in *Long*, 342. On these latter *Fakirs*, see under **SUNYASEE.**

1770.—"Singular expedients have been tried by men jealous of superiority to share with the Bramins the veneration of the multitude; this has given rise to a race of monks known in India by the name of **Fakirs.**"—*Raynal* (tr. 1777), i. 49.

1774.—"The character of a **fakir** is held in great estimation in this country."—*Bogle*, in *Markham's Tibet*, 23.

1856.—

"There stalks a row of Hindoo devotees,
Bedaubed with ashes, their foul matted hair
Down to their heels; their blear eyes fiercely scowl
Beneath their painted brows. On this side struts
A Mussulman **Fakeer**, who tells his beads,
By way of prayer, but cursing all the while
The heathen."—*The Banyan Tree.*

1878.—"Les mains abandonnées sur les genoux, dans une immobilité de **fakir.**"—*Alph. Daudet, Le Nabob*, ch. vi.

FALAUN, s. Ar. *falān*, *fulān*, and H. *fulāna*, *falāna*, 'such an one,' 'a certain one'; Span. and Port. *fulano*, Heb. *Fuluni* (Ruth iv. 1). In Elphinstone's *Life* we see that this was the term by which he and his friend Strachey used to indicate their master in early days, and a man whom they much respected, Sir Barry Close. And gradually, by a process of Hobson-Jobson, this was turned into **Forlorn.**

1803.—"The General (A. Wellesley) is an excellent man to have a peace to make. . . . I had a long talk with him about **such a one**; he said he was a very sensible man."—*Op. cit.* i. 81.

1824.—"This is the old ghaut down which we were so glad to retreat with old **Forlorn.**"—ii. 164. See also i. 56, 108, 345, &c.

FANÁM, s. The denomination of a small coin long in use in S. India, Malayāl. and Tamil *paṇam*, 'money,' from Skt. *paṇa*, [rt. *paṇ*, 'to barter']. There is also a Dekhani form of the word, *falam*. In Telugu it is called *rūka*. The form *fanam* was probably of Arabic origin, as we find it long prior to the Portuguese period. The *fanam* was anciently a gold coin, but latterly of silver, or sometimes of base gold. It bore various local values, but according to the old Madras monetary system, prevailing till 1818, 42 *fanams* went to one star pagoda, and a Madras *fanam* was therefore worth about 2d. (see *Prinsep's Useful Tables*, by E. Thomas, p. 18). The weights of a large number of ancient *fanams* given by Mr. Thomas in a note to his *Pathan Kings of Delhi* show that the average weight was 6 grs. of gold (p. 170). *Fanams* are still met with on the west coast, and as late as 1862 were received at the treasuries of Malabar and Calicut. As the coins were very small they used to be counted by means of a small board or dish, having a large number of holes or pits. On this a pile of *fanams* was shaken, and then swept off, leaving the holes filled. About the time named Rs. 5000 worth of gold *fanams* were sold off at those treasuries. [Mr. Logan names various kinds of fanams: the *vīrāy*, or gold, of which 4 went to a rupee; new *vīrāy*, or gold, 3½ to a rupee; in silver, 5 to a rupee; the *rāsī fanam*, the most ancient of the indigenous *fanams*, now of fictitious value; the *sultānī fanam* of Tippoo in 1790-92, of which 3½ went to a rupee (*Malabar*, ii. Gloss. clxxix.).]

c. 1344.—"A hundred **fānām** are equal to 6 golden *dīnārs*" (in Ceylon).—*Ibn Batuta*, iv. 174.

c. 1348.—"And these latter (Malabar Christians) are the Masters of the public steelyard, from which I derived, as a perquisite of my office as Pope's Legate, every month a hundred gold **fan**, and a thousand when I left."—*John Marignolli*, in *Cathay*, 343.

1442.—"In this country they have three kinds of money, made of gold mixed with alloy . . . the third called **fanom**, is equivalent in value to the tenth part of the last mentioned coin" (*partāb*, vid. **pardao**).—*Abdurrazāk*, in *India in the XVth Cent.* p. 26.

1498.—"Fifty **fanoeens**, which are equal to 3 cruzados."—*Roteiro de V. da Gama*, 107.

1505.—"Quivi spendeno ducati d'auro veneziani e monete di auro et argento e metalle, chiamano vna moneta de argento **fanone**. XX vagliono vn ducato. *Tara* e vn altra moneta de metale. XV vagliono vn **Fanone.**"—Italian version of *Letter from Dom Manuel of Portugal* (Reprint by A. Burnell, 1881), p. 12.

1510.—"He also coins a silver money called *tare*, and others of gold, 20 of which go to a *pardao*, and are called **fanom.** And of these small coins of silver, there go sixteen to a **fanom.**"—*Varthema*, Hak. Soc. 130.

[1515.—"They would take our cruzados at 19 **fanams.**"—Albuquerque's Treaty with the Samorin, *Alguns Documentos da Torre do Tombo*, p. 373.]

1516.—"Eight fine rubies of the weight of one **fanão** . . . are worth **fanões** 10."—*Barbosa* (Lisbon ed.), 384.

1553.—"In the ceremony of dubbing a knight he is to go with all his kinsfolk and friends, in pomp and festal procession, to the House of the King . . . and make him an offering of 60 of those pieces of gold which they call **Fanões**, each of which may be worth 20 *reis* of our money."—*De Barros*, Dec. I. liv. ix. cap. iii.

1582.—In the English transl. of 'Castañeda' is a passage identical with the preceding, in which the word is written "**Fannon.**"—Fol. 36*b*.

" . "In this city of Negapatan aforesaid are current certain coins called **fannò**. . . . They are of base gold, and are worth in our money 10 soldi each, and 17 are equal to a *zecchin* of Venetian gold."—*Gasp. Balbi*, f. 84*v*.

c. 1610.—"Ils nous donnent tous les jours a chacun un **Panan**, qui est vne pièce d'or monnoye du Roy qui vaut environ quatre sols et demy."—*Pyrard de Laval*, i. 250; [Hak. Soc. i. 350; in i. 365 **Panants**].

[c. 1665.—". . . if there is not found in every thousand oysters the value of 5 **fanos** of pearls—that is to say a half ecu of our money,—it is accepted as a proof that the fishing will not be good. . . ."—*Tavernier*, ed. *Ball*, ii. 117 *seq*.]

1678.—"2. Whosoever shall profane the name of God by swearing or cursing, he shall pay 4 **fanams** to the use of the poore for every oath or curse."—*Orders agreed on by the Governor and Council of Ft. St. Geo. Oct. 28. In Notes and Exts.* No. i. 85.

1752.—"N.B. 36 **Fanams** to a Pagoda, is the exchange, by which all the servants belonging to the Company receive their salaries. But in the Bazar the general exchange in Trade is 40 to 42."—*T. Brooks*, p. 8.

1784.—This is probably the word which occurs in a "Song by a Gentleman of the Navy when a Prisoner in Bangalore Jail" (temp. Hyder 'Ali).

"Ye Bucks of Seringapatam,
Ye Captives so cheerful and gay;
How sweet with a golden **sanam**
You spun the slow moments away."
In *Seton-Karr*, i. 19.

1785.—"You are desired to lay a silver **fanam**, a piece worth three pence, upon the ground. This, which is the smallest of all coins, the elephant feels about till he finds."—*Caraccioli's Life of Clive*, i. 288.

1803.—"The pay I have given the boatmen is one gold **fanam** for every day they do not work, and two gold **fanams** for every day they do."—From *Sir A. Wellesley*, in *Life of Munro*, i. 342.

FAN-PALM, s. The usual application of this name is to the *Borassus flabelliformis*, L. (see **BRAB**, **PALMYRA**), which is no doubt the type on which our ladies' fans have been formed. But it is also sometimes applied to the **Talipot** (q.v.); and it is exceptionally (and surely erroneously) applied by Sir L. Pelly (*J.R.G.S.* xxxv. 232) to the "Traveller's Tree," *i.e.* the Madagascar *Ravenala* (*Urania speciosa*).

FANQUI, s. Chin. *fan-kwei*, 'foreign demon'; sometimes with the affix *tsz* or *tsŭ*, 'son'; the popular Chinese name for Europeans. ["During the 15th and 16th centuries large numbers of black slaves of both sexes from the E. I. Archipelago were purchased by the great houses of Canton to serve as gate-keepers. They were called 'devil slaves,' and it is not improbable that the term 'foreign devil,' so freely used by the Chinese for foreigners, may have had this origin."—*Ball, Things Chinese*, 535.]

FARÁSH, FERÁSH, FRASH, s. Ar.—H. *farrāsh*, [*farsh*, 'to spread (a carpet')]. A menial servant whose proper business is to spread carpets, pitch tents, &c., and, in fact, in a house, to do housemaid's work; employed also in Persia to administer the bastinado. The word was in more common use in India two centuries ago than now. One of the highest hereditary officers of Sindhia's Court is called the **Farāsh-khāna-wālā**. [The same word used for the tamarisk tree (*Tamarix gallica*) is a corr. of the Ar. *farās*.]

c. 1300.—"Sa grande richesce apparut en un paveillon que li roys d'Ermenie envoia au roy de France, qui valoit bien cinq cens livres; et li manda li roy de Hermenie que uns **ferrais** au Soudanc dou Coyne li avoit donnei. **Ferrais** est cil qui tient les paveillons au Soudanc et qui li nettoie ses mesons."—*Jehan, Seigneur de Joinville*, ed. *De Wailly*, p. 78.

c. 1513.—"And the gentlemen rode . . . upon horses from the king's stables, attended by his servants whom they call **farazes**, who groom and feed them."—*Correa, Lendas*, II. i. 364.

(Here it seems to be used for **Syce** (q.v.) or groom).

[1548.—"**Ffarazes.**" See under **BATTA**, a.]

c. 1590.—"Besides, there are employed 1000 **Farráshes**, natives of Irán, Turán, and Hindostán."—*Āīn*, i. 47.

1648.—"The **Frassy** for the Tents."—*Van Twist*, 86.

1673.—"Where live the **Frasses** or Porters also."—*Fryer*, 67.

1764.—(Allowances to the Resident at Murshīdābād).

* * * * *

"Public servants as follows:—1 *Vakeel*, 2 *Moonshees*, 4 *Chobdars*, 2 *Jemadars*, 20 *Peons*, 10 *Mussalchees*, 12 *Bearers*, 2 *Chowry Bearers*, and such a number of **Frosts** and *Lascars* as he may have occasion for removing his tents."—In *Long*, 406.

[1812.—"Much of course depends upon the chief of the **Feroshes** or tent-pitchers, called the **Ferosh**-*Bashee*, who must necessarily be very active."—*Morier, Journey through Persia*, 70.]

1824.—"Call the **ferashes** . . . and let them beat the rogues on the soles of their feet, till they produce the fifty ducats."—*Hajji Baba* (ed. 1835), 40.

[1859.—

"The Sultan rises and the dark **Ferrash**
Strikes and prepares it for another guest."
FitzGerald, Omar Khayyam, xlv.]

FEDEA, FUDDEA, s. A denomination of money formerly current in Bombay and the adjoining coast; Mahr. *p'hadyā* (qu. Ar. *fidya*, ransom?). It constantly occurs in the account statements of the 16th century, *e.g.* of Nunez (1554) as a money of account, of which 4 went to the silver *tanga*, [see **TANGA**] 20 to the **Pardao**. In Milburn (1813) it is a *pice* or copper coin, of which 50 went to a rupee. Prof. Robertson Smith suggests that this may be the Ar. denomination of a small coin used in Egypt, *fadda* (*i.e.* 'silverling'). It may be an objection that the letter *zwād* used in that word is generally pronounced in India as a *z*. The *faḍḍa* is the Turkish *pāra*, $\frac{1}{40}$ of a piastre, an infinitesimal value now. [Burton (*Arabian Nights*, xi. 98) gives 2000 *faddahs* as equal about 1s. 2*d.*] But, according to Lane, the name was originally given to half-dirhems, coined early in the 15th century, and these would be worth about 5$\frac{3}{4}$*d.* The *fedea* of 1554 would be about 4$\frac{1}{4}$*d.* This rather indicates the identity of the names.

FERÁZEE, s Properly Ar. *farāizī*, from *farāiz* (pl. of *farz*) 'the divine ordinances.' A name applied to a body of Mahommedan Puritans in Bengal, kindred to the Wahābis of Arabia. They represent a reaction and protest against the corrupt condition and pagan practices into which Mahommedanism in Eastern India had fallen, analogous to the former decay of native Christianity in the south (see **MALABAR RITES**). This reaction was begun by Hajji Sharīyatullah, a native of the village of Daulatpūr, in the district of Farīdpūr, who was killed in an agrarian riot in 1831. His son Dūdū Mīyān succeeded him as head of the sect. Since his death, some 35 years ago, the influence of the body is said to have diminished, but it had spread very largely through Lower Bengal. The *Farāizī* wraps his **dhoty** (q.v.) round his loins, without crossing it between his legs, a practice which he regards as heathenish, as a Bedouin would.

FEROZESHUHUR, FEROSHUHR, PHERŪSHAHR, n.p. The last of these appears to be the correct representation of this name of the scene of the hard-fought battle of 21st-22nd December, 1845. For, according to Col. R. C. Temple, the Editor of *Panjab Notes and Queries*, ii. 116 (1885), the village was named after *Bhāī Pherū*, a Sikh saint of the beginning of the century, who lies buried at Mīān-ke-Taḥṣīl in Lahore District.

FETISH, s. A natural object, or animal, made an object of worship. From Port. *fetiço*, *feitiço*, or *fetisso* (old Span. *fechizo*), apparently from *factitius*, signifying first 'artificial,' and then 'unnatural,' 'wrought by charms,' &c. The word is not Anglo-Indian; but it was at an early date applied by the Portuguese to the magical figures, &c., used by natives in Africa and India, and has thence been adopted into French and English. The word has of late years acquired a special and technical meaning, chiefly through the writings of Comte. [See *Jevons, Intr. to the Science of Rel.* 166 *seqq.*] Raynouard (*Lex. Roman.*) has *fachurier*, *fachilador*, for 'a sorcerer,' which he places under *fat*, *i.e. fatum*, and cites old Catalan *fadador*, old Span. *hadador*, and then Port. *feiticeiro*, &c. But he has mixed up the derivatives of two different words, *fatum* and *factitius*. Prof. Max Müller quotes, from Muratori, a work of 1311 which has: "incantationes, sacrilegia, auguria, vel malefica, quae *facturae* seu praestigia vulgariter appellantur." And

Raynouard himself has in a French passage of 1446: "par leurs sorceries et *faictureries*."

1487.—"E assi lhe (a el Rey de Beni) mandou muitos e santos conselhos pera tornar á Fé de Nosso Senhor . . . mandandolhe muito estranhar suas idolotrias e **feitiçarias**, que em suas terras os negros tinhão e usão."—*Garcia, Resende, Chron. of Dom. João II.* ch. lxv.

c. 1539.—"E que jà por duas vezes o tinhão tẽtado cõ arroydo **feytiço**, só a fim de elle sayr fora, e o matarem na briga . . ." —*Pinto*, ch. xxxiv.

1552.—"They have many and various idolatries, and deal much in charms (**feitiçoes**) and divinations."—*Castanheda*, ii. 51.

1553.—"And as all the nation of this Ethiopia is much given to sorceries (**feitiços**) in which stands all their trust and faith . . . and to satisfy himself the more surely of the truth about his son, the king ordered a **feitiço** which was used among them (in Congo). This **feitiço** being tied in a cloth was sent by a slave to one of his women, of whom he had a suspicion."—*Barros*, I. iii. 10.

1600.—"If they find any **Fettisos** in the way as they goe (which are their idolatrous gods) they give them some of their fruit."—In *Purchas*, ii. 940, see also 961.

1606.—"They all determined to slay the Archbishop . . . they resolved to do it by another kind of death, which they hold to be not less certain than by the sword or other violence, and that is by sorceries (**feytiços**), making these for the places by which he had to pass."—*Gouvea*, f. 47.

1613.—"As **feiticeiras** usão muyto de rayzes de ervas plantas e arvores e animaes pera **feitiços** e transfigurações. . . ."—*Godinho de Eredia*, f. 38.

1673.—"We saw several the Holy Office had branded with the names of **Fetisceroes** or Charmers, or in English Wizards."—*Fryer*, 155.

1690.—"They (the Africans) travel nowhere without their **Fateish** about them." —*Ovington*, 67.

1878.—"The word **fetishism** was never used before the year 1760. In that year appeared an anonymous book called *Du Culte des Dieux* **Fétiches**, *ou Parallèle de l'Ancienne Religion de l'Egypte avec la Rel. actuelle de la Nigritie.*" It is known that this book was written by . . . the well known President de Brosses. . . . Why did the Portuguese navigators . . . recognise at once what they saw among the Negroes of the Gold Coast as **feitiços**? The answer is clear. Because they themselves were perfectly familiar with a **feitiço**, an amulet or talisman."—*Max Müller, Hibbert Lectures*, 56-57.

FIREFLY, s. Called in South Indian vernaculars by names signifying 'Lightning Insect.'

A curious question has been discussed among entomologists, &c., of late years, viz. as to the truth of the alleged rhythmical or synchronous flashing of fireflies when visible in great numbers. Both the present writers can testify to the fact of a distinct effect of this kind. One of them can never forget an instance in which he witnessed it, twenty years or more before he was aware that any one had published, or questioned, the fact. It was in descending the Chāndor Ghāt, in Nāsik District of the Bombay Presidency, in the end of May or beginning of June 1843, during a fine night preceding the rains. There was a large amphitheatre of forest-covered hills, and every leaf of every tree seemed to bear a firefly. They flashed and intermitted throughout the whole area in apparent rhythm and sympathy. It is, we suppose, possible that this may have been a deceptive impression, though it is difficult to see how it could originate. The suggestions made at the meetings of the Entomological Society are utterly unsatisfactory to those who have observed the phenomenon. In fact it may be said that those suggested explanations only assume that the *soi-disant* observers did not observe what they alleged. We quote several independent testimonies to the phenomenon.

1579.—"Among these trees, night by night, did show themselues an infinite swarme of fierie seeming wormes flying in the aire, whose bodies (no bigger than an ordinarie flie) did make a shew, and giue such light as euery twigge on euery tree had beene a lighted candle, or as if that place had beene the starry spheare."—*Drake's Voyage*, by *F. Fletcher*, Hak. Soc. 149.

1675.—"We . . . left our Burnt Wood on the Right-hand, but entred another made us better Sport, deluding us with false Flashes, that you would have thought the Trees on a Flame, and presently, as if untouch'd by **Fire**, they retained their wonted Verdure. The Coolies beheld the Sight with Horror and Amazement . . . where we found an Host of **Flies**, the Subject both of our Fear and Wonder. . . . This gave my Thoughts the Contemplation of that Miraculous Bush crowned with Innocent Flames, . . . the Fire that consumes everything seeming rather to dress than offend it."—*Fryer*, 141-142.

1682.—"**Fireflies** (*de vuur-vliegen*) are so called by us because at eventide, whenever they fly they burn so like fire, that from a distance one fancies to see so many lanterns; in fact they give light enough to write by.

. . . They gather in the rainy season in great multitudes in the bushes and trees, and live on the flowers of the trees. There are various kinds."—*Nieuhoff*, ii. 291.

1764.—
"Ere **fireflies** trimmed their vital lamps,
and ere
Dun Evening trod on rapid Twilight's
heel,
His knell was rung."—*Grainger*, Bk. I.

1824.—
"Yet mark! as fade the upper skies,
Each thicket opes ten thousand eyes.
Before, behind us, and above,
The **fire-fly** lights his lamp of love,
Retreating, chasing, sinking, soaring,
The darkness of the copse exploring."
Heber, ed. 1844, i. 258.

1865.—"The bushes literally swarm with **fireflies**, which flash out their intermittent light almost contemporaneously; the effect being that for an instant the exact outline of all the bushes stands prominently forward, as if lit up with electric sparks, and next moment all is jetty dark—darker from the momentary illumination that preceded. These flashes succeed one another every 3 or 4 seconds for about 10 minutes, when an interval of similar duration takes place; as if to allow the insects to regain their electric or phosphoric vigour."—*Cameron Our Tropical Possessions in Malayan India*, 80-81.

The passage quoted from Mr. Cameron's book was read at the Entom. Soc. of London in May 1865, by the Rev. Hamlet Clarke, who added that:

"Though he was utterly unable to give an explanation of the phenomenon, he could so far corroborate Mr. Cameron as to say that he had himself witnessed this simultaneous flashing; he had a vivid recollection of a particular glen in the Organ Mountains where he had on several occasions noticed the contemporaneous exhibition of their light by numerous individuals, as if they were acting in concert."

Mr. McLachlan then suggested that this might be caused by currents of wind, which by inducing a number of the insects simultaneously to change the direction of their flight, might occasion a momentary concealment of their light.

Mr. Bates had never in his experience received the impression of any simultaneous flashing. . . . he regarded the contemporaneous flashing as an illusion produced probably by the swarms of insects flying among foliage, and being continually, but only momentarily, hidden behind the leaves. —*Proc. Entom. Soc. of London*, 1865, pp. 94-95.

Fifteen years later at the same Society:

"Sir Sidney Saunders stated that in the South of Europe (Corfu and Albania) the simultaneous flashing of *Luciola italica*, with intervals of complete darkness for some seconds, was constantly witnessed in the dark summer nights, when swarming myriads were to be seen. . . . He did not concur in the hypothesis propounded by Mr. McLachlan . . . the flashes are certainly intermittent . . . the simultaneous character of these coruscations among vast swarms would seem to depend upon an instinctive impulse to emit their light at certain intervals as a protective influence, which intervals became assimilated to each other by imitative emulation. But whatever be the causes . . . the fact itself was incontestable."—*Ibid.* for 1880, Feby. 24, p. ii.; see also p. vii.

1868.—"At Singapore . . . the little luminous beetle commonly known as the **firefly** (Lampyris, sp. ign.) is common . . . clustered in the foliage of the trees, instead of keeping up an irregular twinkle, every individual shines simultaneously at regular intervals, as though by a common impulse; so that their light pulsates, as it were, and the tree is for one moment illuminated by a hundred brilliant points, and the next is almost in total darkness. The intervals have about the duration of a second, and during the intermission only one or two remain luminous."—*Collingwood, Rambles of a Naturalist*, p. 255.

1880.—"HARBINGERS OF THE MONSOON. —One of the surest indications of the approach of the monsoon is the spectacle presented nightly in the Mawul taluka, that is, at Khandalla and Lanoli, where the trees are filled with myriads of **fireflies**, which flash their phosphoric light simultaneously. Each tree suddenly flashes from bottom to top. Thousands of trees presenting this appearance simultaneously, afford a spectacle beautiful, if not grand, beyond conception. This little insect, the female of its kind, only appears and displays its brilliant light immediately before the monsoon."—*Deccan Herald.* (From *Pioneer Mail*, June 17).

FIRINGHEE, s. Pers. *Farangī*, *Firingī*; Ar. *Al-Faranj*, *Ifranjī*, *Firanjī*, *i.e.* a Frank. This term for a European is very old in Asia, but when now employed by natives in India is either applied (especially in the South) specifically to the Indian-born Portuguese, or, when used more generally, for 'European,' implies something of hostility or disparagement. (See *Sonnerat* and *Elphinstone* below.) In South India the Tamil *P'arangi*, the Singhalese *Parangi*, mean only 'Portuguese,' [or natives converted by the Portuguese, or by Mahommedans, any

European (*Madras Gloss.* s.v.). St. Thomas's Mount is called in Tam. *Parangi Malai*, from the original Portuguese settlement]. *Piringi* is in Tel. = 'cannon,' (C. B. P.), just as in the medieval Mahommedan historians we find certain mangonels for sieges called *maghribī* or 'Westerns.' [And so *Farhangī* or *Phirangī* is used for the straight cut and thrust swords introduced by the Portuguese into India, or made there in imitation of the foreign weapon (*Sir W. Elliot, Ind. Antiq.* xv. 30)]. And it may be added that Baber, in describing the battle of Pānipat (1526) calls his artillery *Farangīha* (see *Autob.* by Leyden and Erskine, p. 306, note. See also paper by Gen. R. Maclagan, R.E., on early Asiatic fire-weapons, in *J.A.S. Beng.* xlv. Pt. i. pp. 66-67).

c. 930.—"The **Afranjah** are of all those nations the most warlike . . . the best organised, the most submissive to the authority of their rulers."—*Maṣ'ūdī*, iii. 66.

c. 1340.—"They call **Franchi** all the Christians of these parts from Romania westward."—*Pegolotti*, in *Cathay*, &c., 292.

c. 1350.—"—— **Franks**. For so they term us, not indeed from France, but from Frank-land (non a *Franciâ* sed a *Franquiâ*)."—*Marignolli*, *ibid.* 336.

In a Chinese notice of the same age the horses carried by Marignolli as a present from the Pope to the Great Khan are called "horses of the kingdom of **Fulang**," *i.e.* of *Farang* or Europe.

1384.—"E quello nominare **Franchi** procede da' Franceschi, che tutti ci appellano Franceschi."—*Frescobaldi*, *Viaggio*, p. 23.

1436.—"At which time, talking of *Cataio*, he told me howe the chief of that Princes corte knewe well enough what the **Franchi** were. . . . Thou knowest, said he, how neere wee bee unto Capha, and that we practise thither continually . . . adding this further, We Cataini have twoo eyes, and yow **Franchi** one, whereas yow (torneng him towards the Tartares that were wth him) have neuer a one. . . ."—*Barbaro*, Hak. Soc. 58.

c. 1440.—"Hi nos **Francos** appellant, aiuntque cum ceteras gentes coecas vocent, se duobis oculis, nos unico esse, superiores existimantes se esse prudentiâ."—*Conti*, in *Poggius, de Var. Fortunae*, iv.

1498.—"And when he heard this he said that such people could be none other than **Francos**, for so they call us in those parts."—*Roteiro de V. da Gama*, 97.

1560.—"Habitão aqui (Tabriz) duas nações de Christãos . . . e huns delles a qui chamão **Franques**, estes tem o costume e fé, como nos . . . e outros são Armenos."—*A. Tenreiro, Itinerario*, ch. xv.

1565.—"Suddenly news came from Thatta that the **Firingis** had passed Lahori Bandar, and attacked the city."—*Tárikh-i-Táhiri*, in *Elliot*, i. 276.

c. 1610.—"La renommée des François a esté telle par leur conquestes en Orient, que leur nom y est demeuré pour memoire éternelle, en ce qu'encore aujourd'huy par toute l'Asie et Afrique on appelle du nom de **Franghi** tous ceux qui viennent d'Occident."—*Mocquet*, 24.

[1614.—". . . including us within the word **Franqueis**."—*Foster*, *Letters*, ii. 299.]

1616.—". . . alii *Cafres* et *Cafaros* eos dicunt, alii **Francos**, quo nomine omnes passim Christiani . . . dicuntur."—*Jarric*, *Thesaurus*, iii. 217.

[1623.—"**Franchi**, or Christians."—*P. della Valle*, Hak. Soc. ii. 251.]

1632.—". . . he shew'd two Passes from the Portugals which they call by the name of **Fringes**."—*W. Bruton*, in *Hakluyt*, v. 32.

1648.—"Mais en ce repas-là tout fut bien accommodé, et il y a apparence qu'un cuisinier **Frangui** s'en estoit mélé."—*Tavernier*, *V. des Indes*, iii. ch. 22; [ed. *Ball*, ii. 335].

1653.—"**Frenk** signifie en Turq vn Europpeen, ou plustost vn Chrestien ayant des cheueux et vn chapeau comme les François, Anglois. . . ."—*De la Boullaye-le-Gouz*, ed. 1657, 538.

c. 1660.—"The same Fathers say that this King (Jehan-Guire), to begin in good earnest to countenance the Christian Religion, designed to put the whole Court into the habit of the **Franqui**, and that after he had . . . even dressed himself in that fashion, he called to him one of the chief Omrahs . . . this Omrah . . . having answered him very seriously, that it was a very dangerous thing, he thought himself obliged to change his mind, and turned all to raillery."—*Bernier*, E.T. 92; [ed. *Constable*, 287; also see p. 3].

1673.—"The Artillery in which the **Fringis** are Listed; formerly for good Pay, now very ordinary, having not above 30 or 40 Rupees a month."—*Fryer*, 195.

1682.—". . . whether I had been in Turky and Arabia (as he was informed) and could speak those languages . . . with which they were pleased, and admired to hear from a **Frenge** (as they call us)."—*Hedges*, *Diary*, Oct. 29; [Hak. Soc. i. 44].

1712.—"*Johan Whelo, Serdaar* **Frengiaan**, or Captain of the Europeans in the Emperor's service. . . ."—*Valentijn*, iv. (Suratte) 295.

1755.—"By **Feringy** I mean all the black *mustee* (see **MUSTEES**) Portuguese Christians residing in the settlement as a people distinct from the natural and proper subjects of Portugal; and as a people who sprung originally from Hindoos or Mussulmen."—*Holwell*, in *Long*, 59.

1774.—"He said it was true, but everybody was afraid of the **Firingies**."—*Bogle*, in *Markham's Tibet*, 176.

1782.—"Ainsi un Européen est tout ce que les Indiens connoissent de plus méprisable ; ils le nomment **Parangui**, nom qu'ils donnèrent aux Portugais, lorsque ceux-ci abordèrent dans leur pays, et c'est un terme qui marque le souverain mépris qu'ils ont pour toutes les nations de l'Europe."—*Sonnerat*, i. 102.

1791.—". . . il demande à la passer (la nuit) dans un des logemens de la pagoda ; mais on lui refusa d'y coucher, à cause qu'il étoit **frangui**."—*B. de St. Pierre, Chaumière Indienne*, 21.

1794.—"**Feringee**. The name given by the natives of the Decan to Europeans in general, but generally understood by the English to be confined to the Portuguese."—*Moor's Narrative*, 504.

[1820.—"In the southern quarter (of Backergunje) there still exist several original Portuguese colonies. . . . They are a meagre, puny, imbecile race, blacker than the natives, who hold them in the utmost contempt, and designate them by the appellation of *Caula* **Ferenghies**, or black Europeans."—*Hamilton, Descr. of Hindostan*, i. 133 ; for an account of the Feringhis of Sibpur, see *Beveridge, Bākarganj*, 110.]

1824.—"'Now Hajji,' said the ambassador. . . . 'The **Franks** are composed of many, many nations. As fast as I hear of one hog, another begins to grunt, and then another and another, until I find that there is a whole herd of them.'"—*Hajji Baba*, ed. 1835, p. 432.

1825.—"Europeans, too, are very little known here, and I heard the children continually calling out to us, as we passed through the villages, '**Feringhee**, *ue* **Feringhee**!'"—*Heber*, ii. 43.

1828.—"Mr. Elphinstone adds in a note that in India it is a positive affront to call an Englishman a **Feringhee**."—*Life of E.* ii. 207.

c. 1861.—

"There goes my lord the **Feringhee**, who talks so civil and bland,
But raves like a soul in Jehannum if I don't quite understand—
He begins by calling me Sahib, and ends by calling me fool. . . ."

Sir A. C. Lyall, The Old Pindaree.

The Tibetans are said to have corrupted **Firinghee** into **Pelong** (or *Philin*). But Jaeschke disputes this origin of *Pelong*.

FIRMAUN, s. Pers. *farmān*, 'an order, patent, or passport,' der. from *farmūdan*, 'to order.' Sir T. Roe below calls it *firma*, as if suggestive of the Italian for 'signature.'

[1561.—". . . wrote him a letter called **Firmao**. . . ."—*Castanheda*, Bk. viii. ch. 99.

[1602.—"They said that he had a **Firmao** of the Grand Turk to go overland to the Kingdom of (Portugal). . . ."—*Couto*, Dec. viii. ch. 15.]

1606.—"We made our journey having a **Firman** (*Firmão*) of safe conduct from the same Soltan of Shiraz."—*Gouvea*, f. 140*b*.

[1614.—"But if possible, bring their chaps, their **Firms**, for what they say or promise."—*Foster, Letters*, ii. 28.]

1616.—"Then I moued him for his favour for an *English* Factory to be resident in the Towne, which hee willingly granted, and gave present order to the Buxy to draw a **Firma** . . . for their residence."—*Sir T. Roe*, in *Purchas*, i. 541 ; [Hak. Soc. i. 93 ; also see i. 47].

1648.—"The 21st April the Bassa sent me a **Firman** or Letter of credentials to all his lords and Governors."—*T. Van den Broecke*, 32.

1673.—"Our Usage by the **Pharmaund** (or charters) granted successively from their Emperors, is kind enough, but the better because our Naval Power curbs them."—*Fryer*, 115.

1683.—"They (the English) complain, and not without a Cause ; they having a **Phirmaund**, and Hodgee Sophee Caun's *Perwannas* thereon, in their hands, which cleared them thereof ; and to pay Custome now they will not consent, but will rather withdraw their trading. Wherefore their desire is that for 3,000 rup. *Piscash* (as they paid formerly at Hugly) and 2,000 r. more yearly on account of *Jidgea*, which they are willing to pay, they may on that condition have a grant to be Custome Free."—*Nabob's Letter to Vizier* (MS.), in *Hedges' Diary*, July 18 ; [Hak. Soc. i. 101].

1689.—". . . by her came Bengal Peons who brought in several letters and a **firmaun** from the new Nabob of Bengal."—*Wheeler*, i. 213.

c. 1690.—"Now we may see the Mogul's Stile in his **Phirmaund** to be sent to Surat, as it stands translated by the Company's Interpreter."—*A. Hamilton*, i. 227 ; [ed. 1744, i. 230].

FISCAL, s. Dutch *Fiscaal;* used in Ceylon for 'Sheriff' ; a relic of the Dutch rule in the island. [It was also used in the Dutch settlements in Bengal (see quotation from *Hedges*, below). "In Malabar the Fiscal was a Dutch Superintendent of Police, Justice of the Peace and Attorney General in criminal cases. The office and title of Fiscal was retained in British Cochin till 1860, when the designation was changed into Tahsildar and Sub-Magistrate." — (*Logan, Malabar*, iii. *Gloss.* s.v.)]

[1684.—". . . the late Dutch **Fiscall's** Budgero. . . ."—See quotation from *Hedges*, under **DEVIL'S REACH**.]

FLORICAN, FLORIKIN, s. A name applied in India to two species of small bustard, the 'Bengal Florican' (*Sypheotides bengalensis*, Gmelin), and the Lesser Florican (*S. auritus*, Latham), the *līkh* of Hind., a word which is not in the dictionaries. [In the N.W.P. the common name for the Bengal Florican is *charas*, P. *charz*. The name *Curmoor* in Bombay (see quotation from *Forbes* below) seems to be *khar-mor*, the 'grass peacock.' Another Mahr. name, *tanamora*, has the same meaning.] The origin of the word **Florican** is exceedingly obscure; see *Jerdon* below. It looks like Dutch. [The *N.E.D.* suggests a connection with *Flanderkin*, a native of Flanders.] Littré has: "**Florican** . . . Nom à Ceylon d'un grand échassier que l'on présume être un grue." This is probably mere misapprehension in his authority.

1780.—"The **floriken**, a most delicious bird of the buzzard (*sic!*) kind."—*Munro's Narrative*, 199.

1785.—
"A **floriken** at eve we saw
And kill'd in yonder glen,
When lo! it came to table raw,
And rouzed (*sic*) the rage of Ben."
In *Seton-Karr*, i. 98.

1807.—"The **floriken** is a species of the bustard. . . . The cock is a noble bird, but its flight is very heavy and awkward . . . if only a wing be broken . . . he will run off at such a rate as will baffle most spaniels. . . . There are several kinds of the **floriken** . . . the *bastard floriken* is much smaller. . . . Both kinds . . . delight in grassy plains, keeping clear of heavy cover."—*Williamson, Oriental Field Sports*, 104.

1813.—"The **florican** or curmoor (*Otis houbara*, Lin.) exceeds all the Indian wild fowl in delicacy of flavour."—*Forbes, Or. Mem.* ii. 275; [2nd ed. i. 501].

1824.—". . . bringing with him a brace of **florikens**, which he had shot the previous day. I had never seen the bird before; it is somewhat larger than a blackcock, with brown and black plumage, and evidently of the bustard species."—*Heber*, i. 258.

1862.—"I have not been able to trace the origin of the Anglo-Indian word '**Florikin**,' but was once informed that the Little Bustard in Europe was sometimes called *Flanderkin*. Latham gives the word '*Flercher*' as an English name, and this, apparently, has the same origin as *Florikin*."—*Jerdon's Birds*, 2nd ed. ii. 625. (We doubt if Jerdon has here understood Latham correctly. What Latham writes is, in describing the *Passarage Bustard*, which, he says, is the size of the *Little Bustard*: "Inhabits India. Called Passarage Plover. . . . I find that it is known in India by the name of *Oorail*; by some of the English called *Flercher*." (*Suppt. to Gen. Synopsis of Birds*, 1787, 229.) Here we understand "the English" to be the English in India, and *Flercher* to be a clerical error for some form of "*floriken*." [*Flercher* is not in *N.E.D.*]

1875.—"In the rains it is always matter of emulation at Rajkot, who shall shoot the first purple-crested **florican**." — *Wyllie's Essays*, 358.

FLOWERED-SILVER. A term applied by Europeans in Burma to the standard quality of silver used in the ingot currency of Independent Burma, called by the Burmese *yowet-nī* or 'Red-leaf.' The English term is taken from the appearance of stars and radiating lines, which forms on the surface of this particular alloy, as it cools in the crucible. The Ava standard is, or was, of about 15 per cent. alloy, the latter containing, besides copper, a small proportion of lead, which is necessary, according to the Burmese, for the production of the flowers or stars (see *Yule, Mission to Ava*, 259 *seq.*).

[1744.—"Their way to make **flower'd Silver** is, when the Silver and Copper are mix'd and melted together, and while the Metal is liquid, they put it into a Shallow Mould, of what Figure and Magnitude they please, and before the Liquidity is gone, they blow on it through a small wooden Pipe, which makes the Face, or Part blown upon, appear with the Figures of Flowers or Stars, but I never saw any *European* or other Foreigner at Pegu, have the Art to make those Figures appear, and if there is too great a Mixture of Alloy, no Figures will appear."—*A. Hamilton*, ed. 1744, ii. 41.]

FLY, s. The sloping, or roof part of the canvas of a tent is so called in India; but we have not traced the origin of the word; nor have we found it in any English dictionary. [The *N.E.D.* gives the primary idea as "something attached by the edge," as a strip on a garment to cover the button-holes.] A tent such as officers generally use has two *flies*, for better protection from sun and rain. The vertical canvas walls are called *Kanāt* (see **CANAUT**). [Another sense of the word is "a quick-travelling carriage" (see quotation in Forbes below).]

[1784.—"We all followed in **fly-palanquins**."—*Sir J. Day*, in *Forbes, Or. Mem.* ii. 88.]

1810.—"The main part of the operation of pitching the tent, consisting of raising the **flies**, may be performed, and shelter afforded, without the walls, &c., being present."—*Williamson, V. M.* ii. 452.

1816.—

"The cavalcade drew up in line,
Pitch'd the marquee, and went to dine.
The bearers and the servants lie
Under the shelter of the **fly.**"

The Grand Master, or Adventures of Qui Hi, p. 152.

1885.—"After I had changed my riding-habit for my one other gown, I came out to join the general under the **tent-fly**. . . ."—*Boots and Saddles*, by *Mrs. Custer*, p. 42 (American work).

FLYING-FOX, s. Popular name of the great bat (*Pteropus Edwardsi*, Geoff). In the daytime these bats roost in large colonies, hundreds or thousands of them pendent from the branches of some great *ficus*. Jerdon says of these bats: "If water is at hand, a tank, or river, or the sea, they fly cautiously down and touch the water, but I could not ascertain if they took a sip, or merely dipped part of their bodies in" (*Mammals of India*, p. 18). The truth is, as Sir George Yule has told us from his own observation, that the bat in its skimming flight dips its breast in the water, and then imbibes the moisture from its own wet fur. Probably this is the first record of a curious fact in natural history. "I have been positively assured by natives that on the Odeypore lake in Rajputana, the crocodiles rise to catch these bats, as they follow in line, touching the water. Fancy fly-fishing for crocodile with such a fly!" (*Communication from M.-Gen. R. H. Keatinge.*) [On the other hand Mr. Blanford says: "I have often observed this habit: the head is lowered, the animal pauses in its flight, and the water is just touched, I believe, by the tongue or lower jaw. I have no doubt that some water is drunk, and this is the opinion of both Tickell and M'Master. The former says that flying-foxes in confinement drink at all hours, lapping with their tongues. The latter has noticed many other bats drink in the evening as well as the flying-foxes." (*Mammalia of India*, 258).]

1298.—". . . all over India the birds and beasts are entirely different from ours, all but . ... the Quail. . . . For example, they have bats—I mean those birds that fly by night and have no feathers of any kind; well, their birds of this kind are as big as a goshawk!"—*Marco Polo*, Bk. iii. ch. 17.

c. 1328:—"There be also bats really and truly as big as kites. These birds fly nowhither by day, but only when the sun sets. Wonderful! By day they hang themselves up on trees by the feet, with their bodies downwards, and in the daytime they look just like big fruit on the tree." — *Friar Jordanus*, p. 19.

1555.—"On the road we occasionally saw trees whose top reached the skies, and on which one saw marvellous bats, whose wings stretched some 14 palms. But these bats were not seen on every tree."—*Sidi 'Ali*, 91.

[c. 1590.—Writing of the Sarkār of Kābul, 'Abul Fazl says: "There is an animal called a **flying-fox**, which flies upward about the space of a yard." This is copied from Baber, and the animal meant is perhaps the flying squirrel.—*Āīn*, ed. *Jarrett*, ii. 406.

[1623.—"I saw Batts as big as Crows."—*P. della Valle*, Hak. Soc. i. 103.]

1813.—"The enormous bats which darken its branches frequently exceed 6 feet in length from the tip of each wing, and from their resemblance to that animal are not improperly called **flying-foxes**." — *Forbes, Or. Mem.* iii. 246; [2nd ed. ii. 269].

[1869.—"They (in Batchian) are almost the only people in the Archipelago who eat the great fruit-eating bats called by us '**flying foxes**' . . . they are generally cooked with abundance of spices and condiments, and are really very good eating, something like hare."—*Wallace, Malay Archip.*, ed. 1890, p. 256.]

1882.—". . . it is a common belief in some places that emigrant coolies hang with heads downward, like **flying-foxes**, or are ground in mills for oil."—*Pioneer Mail*, Dec. 13, p. 579.

FOGASS, s. A word of Port. origin used in S. India; *fogaça*, from *fogo*, 'fire,' a cake baked in embers. It is composed of minced radish with chillies, &c., used as a sort of curry, and eaten with rice.

1554.—". . . fecimus iter per amoenas et non infrugiferas Bulgarorum convalles: quo fere tempore pani usu sumus subcinericio, **fugacias** vocant."—*Busbequii Epist.* i. p. 42.

FOLIUM INDICUM. (See **MALABATHRUM.**) The article appears under this name in Milburn (1813, i. 283), as an article of trade.

FOOL'S RACK, s. (For *Rack* see **ARRACK.**) *Fool Rack* is originally, as will be seen from Garcia and Acosta, the name of the strongest distillation from *toddy* or *sura*, the 'flower' (*p'hūl*, in H. and Mahr.) of the spirit. But the 'striving after meaning' caused the English corruption of this name to be applied to a peculiarly abominable and pernicious spirit, in which, according to the statement of various old writers, the stinging sea-blubber was mixed, or even a distillation of the same, with a view of making it more ardent.

1563.—". . . this çura they distil like brandy (*agua ardente*): and the result is a liquor like brandy; and a rag steeped in this will burn as in the case of brandy; and this fine spirit they call **fula**, which means 'flower'; and the other quality that remains they call **orraca**, mixing with it a small quantity of the first kind. . . ."—*Garcia*, f. 67.

1578.—". . . la qual (*sura*) en vasos despues distilan, para hazer agua ardiente, de la qual una, a que ellos llaman **Fula**, que quiere dezir 'flor,' es mas fina . . . y la segunda, que llaman **Orraca**, no tanto."—*Acosta*, p. 101.

1598.—"This *Sura* being [beeing] distilled, is called **Fula** or Nipe [see **NIPA**], and is as excellent *aqua vitae* as any is made in *Dort* of their best renish [rennish] wine, but this is of the finest kinde of distillation."—*Linschoten*, 101; [Hak. Soc. ii. 49].

1631.—"DURAEUS: . . . Apparet te etiam a vino adusto, nec Arac Chinensi, abhorrere? BONTIUS. Usum commendo, abusum abominor . . . at cane pejus et angue vitandum est quod Chinenses avarissimi simul et astutissimi bipedum, mixtis Holothuriis in mari fluctuantibus, parant . . . eaque tam exurentis sunt caloris ut solo attactu vesicas in cute excitent. . . ."—*Jac. Bontii, Hist. Nat. et Med. Ind., Dial.* iii.

1673.—"Among the worst of these (causes of disease) **Fool Rack** (Brandy made of *Blubber*, or *Carvil*, by the *Portugals*, because it swims always in a Blubber, as if nothing else were in it; but touch it, and it stings like nettles; the latter, because sailing on the Waves it bears up like a *Portuguese Carvil* (see **CARAVEL**): It is, being taken, a Gelly, and distilled causes those that take it to be **Fools**. . . ."—*Fryer*, 68-69.

[1753.—". . . that fiery, single and simple distilled spirit, called **Fool**, with which our seamen were too frequently intoxicated."—*Ives*, 457.

[1868.—"The first spirit that passes over is called '**phúl**.'"—*B. H. Powell, Handbook, Econ. Prod. of Punjab*, 311.]

FOOZILOW, TO, v. The imperative *p'huslāo* of the H. verb *p'huslānā*, 'to flatter or cajole,' used, in a common Anglo-Indian fashion (see **BUNNOW**, **PUCKAROW**, **LUGOW**), as a verbal infinitive.

FORAS LANDS, s. This is a term peculiar to the island of Bombay, and an inheritance from the Portuguese. They are lands reclaimed from the sea, by the construction of the **Vellard** (q.v.) at **Breech-Candy**, and other embankments, on which account they are also known as 'Salt Batty [see **BATTA**] (*i.e.* rice) -grounds.' The Court of Directors, to encourage reclamation, in 1703 authorised these lands to be leased rent-free to the reclaimers for a number of years, after which a small quit-rent was to be fixed. But as individuals would not undertake the maintenance of the embankments, the Government stepped in and constructed the Vellard at considerable expense. The lands were then let on terms calculated to compensate the Government. The tenure of the lands, under these circumstances, for many years gave rise to disputes and litigation as to tenant-right, the right of Government to resume, and other like subjects. The lands were known by the title **Foras**, from the peculiar tenure, which should perhaps be *Foros*, from *foro*, 'a quit-rent.' The Indian Act VI. of 1851 arranged for the termination of these differences, by extinguishing the disputed rights of Government, except in regard to lands taken up for public purposes, and by the constitution of a Foras Land Commission to settle the whole matter. This work was completed by October 1853. The roads from the Fort crossing the "Flats," or **Foras Lands**, between Malabar Hill and Parell were generally known as "the **Foras** Roads"; but this name seems to have passed away, and the Municipal Commissioners have superseded that general title by such names as Clerk Road, Bellasis Road, Falkland Road. One name, 'Comattee-poora **Forest** Road,' perhaps preserves the old generic title under a disguise.

Forasdārs are the holders of **Foras Lands**. See on the whole matter *Bombay Selections*, No. III., New Series, 1854. The following quaint quotation is from a petition of Forasdārs of Mahim and other places regarding some points in the working of the Commission:

1852.—". . . that the case with respect to the old and new salt batty grounds, may it please your Honble. Board to consider deeply, is totally different, because in their original state the grounds were not of the nature of other sweet waste grounds on the island, let out as **foras**, nor these grounds were of that state as one could saddle himself at the first undertaking thereof with leases or grants even for that smaller rent as the **foras** is under the denomination of foras is same other denomination to it, because the depth of these grounds at the time when sea-water was running over them was so much that they were a perfect sea-bay, admitting fishing-boats to float towards Parell."—In *Selections*, as above, p. 29.

FOUJDAR, PHOUSDAR, &c., s. Properly a military commander (P. *fauj*, 'a military force,' *fauj-dār*, 'one holding such a force at his disposal'), or a military governor of a district. But in India, an officer of the Moghul Government who was invested with the charge of the police, and jurisdiction in criminal matters. Also used in Bengal, in the 18th century, for a criminal judge. In the *Āīn*, a *Faujdār* is in charge of several pergunnahs under the *Sipāh-sālār*, or Viceroy and C.-in-Chief of the Subah (*Gladwin's Ayeen*, i. 294; [*Jarrett*, ii. 40]).

1683.—"The **Fousdar** received another Perwanna directed to him by the Nabob of Decca . . . forbidding any merchant whatsoever trading with any *Interlopers*."—*Hedges, Diary*, Nov. 8; [Hak. Soc. i. 136].

[1687.—"Mullick Burcoordar **Phousdardar** of Hughly."—*Ibid.* ii. lxv.]

1690.—". . . If any Thefts or Robberies are committed in the Country, the **Fousdar**, another officer, is oblig'd to answer for them. . . ."—*Ovington*, 232.

1702.—". . . Perwannas directed to all **Foujdars**."—*Wheeler*, i. 405.

[1727.—"**Fouzdaar**." See under **HOOGLY**.]

1754.—"The **Phousdar** of Vellore . . . made overtures offering to acknowledge Mahomed Ally."—*Orme*, i. 372.

1757.—"**Phousdar**. . . ."—*Ives*, 157.

1783.—"A complaint was made that Mr. Hastings had sold the office of **phousdar** of Hoogly to a person called Khân Jehân Khân, on a corrupt agreement."—*11th Report on Affairs of India*, in *Burke*, vi. 545.

1786.—". . . the said **phousdar** (of Hoogly) had given a receipt of bribe to the patron of the city, meaning Warren Hastings, to pay him annually 36,000 rupees a year."—*Articles agst. Hastings*, in *Ibid.* vii. 76.

1809.—"The **Foojadar**, being now in his capital, sent me an excellent dinner of fowls, and a pillau."—*Ld. Valentia*, i. 409.

1810.—

"For ease the harass'd **Foujdar** prays
When crowded Courts and sultry days
Exhale the noxious fume,
While poring o'er the cause he hears
The lengthened lie, and doubts and fears
The culprit's final doom."

Lines by Warren Hastings.

1824.—"A messenger came from the '**Foujdah**' (chatellain) of Suromunuggur, asking why we were not content with the quarters at first assigned to us."—*Heber*, i. 232. The form is here plainly a misreading; for the Bishop on next page gives **Foujdar**.

FOUJDARRY, PHOUSDARRY, s. P. *faujdārī*, a district under a *faujdār* (see **FOUJDAR**); the office and jurisdiction of a *faujdār*; in Bengal and Upper India, 'police jurisdiction,' 'criminal' as opposed to 'civil' justice. Thus the chief criminal Court at Madras and Bombay, up to 1863, was termed the **Foujdary** Adawlut, corresponding to the *Nizamut Adawlut* of Bengal. (See **ADAWLUT**.)

[1802.—"The Governor in Council of Fort St. George has deemed it to be proper at this time to establish a Court of **Fozdarry** Adaulut."—*Procl.* in *Logan, Malabar*, ii. 350; iii. 351.]

FOWRA, s. In Upper India, a mattock or large hoe; the tool generally employed in digging in most parts of India. Properly speaking (H.) *phāorā*. (See **MAMOOTY**.)

[1679.—(Speaking of diamond digging) "Others with iron **pawraes** or spades heave it up to a heap."—*S. Master*, in *Kistna Man.* 147.

[1848.—"On one side Bedullah and one of the grasscutters were toiling away with **fowrahs**, a kind of spade-pickaxe, making water-courses."—*Mrs. Mackenzie, Life in the Mission*, i. 373.]

1880.—"It so fell out the other day in Cawnpore, that, when a *patwari* endeavoured to remonstrate with some cultivators for taking water for irrigation from a pond, they knocked him down with the handle of a **phaora** and cut off his head with the blade, which went an inch or more into the ground, whilst the head rolled away several feet."—*Pioneer Mail*, March 4.

FOX, FLYING. (See **FLYING-FOX**.)

FRAZALA, FARASOLA, FRAZIL, FRAIL, s. Ar. *fārsala*, a weight formerly much used in trade in the Indian seas. As usual, it varied much locally, but it seems to have run from 20 to 30 lbs., and occupied a place intermediate between the (smaller) maund and the **Bahar**; the *fārsala* being generally equal to ten (small) maunds, the *bahār* equal to 10, 15, or 20 *fārsalas*. See *Barbosa* (Hak. Soc.) 224; *Milburn*, i. 83, 87, &c.; *Prinsep's Useful Tables*, by Thomas, pp. 116, 119.

1510.—"They deal by **farasola**, which *farasola* weighs about twenty-five of our lire."—*Varthema*, p. 170. On this Dr.

Badger notes: "*Farasola* is the plural of *fārsala* . . . still in ordinary use among the Arabs of the Red Sea and Persian Gulf; but I am unable to verify (its) origin." Is the word, which is sometimes called *frail*, the same as a *frail*, or basket, of figs? And again, is it possible that *fārsala* is the same word as '*parcel*,' through Latin *particella*? We see that this is Sir R. Burton's opinion (*Camōens*, iv. 390; [*Arab. Nights*, vi. 312]). [The *N.E.D.* says: "O. F. *frayel* of unknown origin."]

[1516.—"Farazola." See under **EAGLE-WOOD.**]

1554.—"The *baar* (see **BAHAR**) of cloves in Ormuz contains 20 **faraçola**, and besides these 20 ffaraçolas it contains 3 maunds (*mãos*) more, which is called *picottaa* (see **PICOTA**)."—*A. Nunez*, p. 5.

[1611.—"The weight of Mocha 25 lbs. 11 oz. every **frasula**, and 15 frasulas makes a bahar."—*Danvers, Letters*, i. 123.]

1793.—"Coffee per **Frail** . . . Rs. 17."—*Bombay Courier*, July 20.

FREGUEZIA, s. This Portuguese word for 'a parish' appears to have been formerly familiar in the west of India.

c. 1760.—"The island . . . still continues divided into three Roman Catholic parishes, or **Freguezias**, as they call them; which are *Bombay*, *Mahim*, and *Salvaçam*."—*Grose*, i. 45.

FULEETA, s. Properly P. *palīta* or *fatīla*, 'a slow-match,' as of a match-lock, but its usual colloquial Anglo-Indian application is to a cotton slow-match used to light cigars, and often furnished with a neat or decorated silver tube. This kind of cigar-light is called at Madras **Ramasammy** (q.v.).

FULEETA-PUP, s. This, in Bengal, is a well-known dish in the repertory of the ordinary native cook. It is a corruption of '*fritter-puff*'!

FURLOUGH, s. This word for a soldier's leave has acquired a peculiar citizenship in Anglo-Indian colloquial, from the importance of the matter to those employed in Indian service. It appears to have been first made the subject of systematic regulation in 1796. The word seems to have come to England from the Dutch *Verlof*, 'leave of absence,' in the early part of the 17th century, through those of our countrymen who had been engaged in the wars of the Netherlands. It is used by Ben Jonson, who had himself served in those wars:

1625.—
"*Pennyboy, Jun.* Where is the deed? hast
thou it with thee?
Picklock. No.
It is a thing of greater consequence
Than to be borne about in a black box
Like a Low-Country **vorloffe**, or Welsh
brief."
The Staple of News, Act v. sc. 1.

FURNAVEESE, n.p. This once familiar title of a famous Mahratta Minister (*Nana Furnaveese*) is really the Persian *fard-navīs*, 'statement writer,' or secretary.

[1824.—"The head civil officer is the **Furnavese** (a term almost synonymous with that of minister of finance) who receives the accounts of the renters and collectors of revenue."—*Malcolm, Central India*, 2nd ed. i. 531.]

FUSLY, adj. Ar.—P. *faṣlī*, relating to the *faṣl*, season or crop. This name is applied to certain solar eras established for use in revenue and other civil transactions, under the Mahommedan rule in India, to meet the inconvenience of the lunar calendar of the Hijra, in its want of correspondence with the natural seasons. Three at least of these eras were established by Akbar, applying to different parts of his dominions, intended to accommodate themselves as far as possible to the local calendars, and commencing in each case with the Hijra year of his accession to the throne (A.H. 963 = A.D. 1555-56), though the month of commencement varies. [See *Āīn*, ed. *Jarrett*, ii. 30.] The *Faṣlī* year of the Deccan again was introduced by Shāh Jehān when settling the revenue system of the Mahratta country in 1636; and as it starts with the Hijra date of that year, it is, in numeration, two years in advance of the others.

Two of these *faṣlī* years are still in use, as regards revenue matters, viz. the *Faṣlī* of Upper India, under which the *Faṣlī* year 1286 began 2nd April 1878; and that of Madras, under which *Faṣlī* year 1286 began 1st July 1877.

FUTWA, s. Ar. *fatwā*. The decision of a council of men learned in Mahommedan law, on any point of Moslem law or morals. But technically and specifically, the deliverance of a Mahommedan law-officer on a case put before him. Such a deliverance was, as a rule, given officially and in writing, by such an officer, who was attached to the Courts of British India up to a little later than the middle of last century, and it was more or less a basis of the judge's decision. (See more particularly under **ADAWLUT**, **CAZEE** and **LAW-OFFICER**.)

1796.—"In all instances wherein the **Futwah** of the **Law-officers** of the *Nizamut-Adaulat* shall declare the prisoners liable to more severe punishment than under the evidence, and all the circumstances of the case shall appear to the Court to be just and equitable. . . ."—*Regn. VI.* of 1796, § ii.

1836.—"And it is hereby enacted that no Court shall, on a Trial of any person accused of the offence made punishable by this Act require any **Futwa** from any Law-Officer. . . ."—*Act XXX. of* 1836, *regarding Thuggee*, § iii.

G

GALEE, s. H. *gālī*, abuse; bad language.

[1813. — ". . . the grossest **galee**, or abuse, resounded throughout the camp."—*Broughton, Letters from a Mahr. Camp.*, ed. 1892, p. 205.

[1877.—"You provoke me to give you **gali** (abuse), and then you cry out like a neglected wife." — *Allardyce, The City of Sunshine*, ii. 2.]

GALLEECE, s. Domestic Hindustani *gālīs*, 'a pair of braces,' from the old-fashioned *gallows*, now obsolete, except in Scotland, [S. Ireland and U.S.,] where the form is *gallowses*.

GALLE, POINT DE, n.p. A rocky cape, covering a small harbour and a town with old fortifications, in the S.W. of Ceylon, familiar to all Anglo-Indians for many years as a coaling-place of mail-steamers. The Portuguese gave the town for crest a cock (*Gallo*), a legitimate pun. The serious derivations of the name are numerous. Pridham says that it is *Galla*, 'a Rock,' which is probable. But Chitty says it means 'a Pound,' and was so called according to the Malabars (*i.e.* Tamil people) from ". . . this part of the country having been anciently set aside by Ravana for the breeding of his cattle" (*Ceylon Gazetteer*, 1832, p. 92). Tennent again says it was called after a tribe, the *Gallas*, inhabiting the neighbouring district (see ii. 105, &c.). [Prof. Childers (5 *ser. Notes & Queries*, iii. 155) writes: "In Sinhalese it is *Gālla*, the etymology of which is unknown; but in any case it can have nothing to do with 'rock,' the Sinhalese for which is *gala* with a short *a* and a single *l*."] Tennent has been entirely misled by Reinaud in supposing that Galle could be the *Kala* of the old Arab voyages to China, a port which certainly lay in the Malay seas. (See **CALAY**.)

1518.—"He tried to make the port of Columbo, before which he arrived in 3 days, but he could not make it because the wind was contrary, so he tacked about for 4 days till he made the port of **Galle**, which is in the south part of the island, and entered it with his whole squadron; and then our people went ashore killing cows and plundering whatever they could find."—*Correa*, ii. 540.

1553. — "In which Island they (the Chinese), as the natives say, left a language which they call *Chingálla*, and the people themselves *Chingállas*, particularly those who dwell from **Ponta de Gálle** onwards, facing the south and east. For adjoining that point they founded a City called Tanabaré (see **DONDERA HEAD**), of which a large part still stands; and from being hard by that **Cape of Gálle**, the rest of the people, who dwelt from the middle of the Island upwards, called the inhabitants of this part *Chingálla*, and their language the same, as if they would say language or people of the *Chins* of *Gálle*."—*Barros*, III. ii. cap. 1. (This is, of course, all fanciful.)

[1554.—"He went to the port of **Gabaliquama**, which our people now call **Porto de Gale**."—*Castanheda*, ii. ch. 23.]

c. 1568.—"Il piotta s'ingannò per cioché il **Capo di Galli** dell' Isola di Seilan butta assai in mare." — *Cesare de' Federici*, in *Ramusio*, iii. 396*v*.

1585.—"Dopo haver nauigato tre giorni senza veder terra, al primo di Maggio fummo in vista di **Punta di Gallo**, laquale è assai pericolosa da costeggiare."—*G. Balbi*, f. 19.

1661. — "Die Stadt **Punto-Gale** ist im Jahr 1640 vermittelst Gottes gnadigem Seegen durch die Tapferkeit des Commandanten Jacob Koster den Neiderländen zu teil geworden."—*W. Schulze*, 190.

1691.—"We passed by Cape Comoryn, and came to **Puntogale**."—*Valentijn*, ii. 540.

GALLEGALLE, s. A mixture of lime and linseed oil, forming a kind of mortar impenetrable to water (Shakespear), Hind. *galgal*.

1621.—"Also the justis, Taccomon Done, sent us word to geve ouer making **gallegalle** in our howse we hired of China Capt., because the white lyme did trowble the player or singing man, next neighbour. . . ." —*Cocks's Diary*, ii. 190.

GALLEVAT, s. The name applied to a kind of galley, or war-boat with oars, of small draught of water, which continued to be employed on the west coast of India down to the latter half of the 18th century. The work quoted below under 1717 explains the *galley-watts* to be "large boats like Gravesend Tilt-boats; they carry about 6 Carvel-Guns and 60 men at small arms, and Oars; They sail with a Peak Sail like the Mizen of a Man-of-War, and row with 30 or 40 Oars. . . They are principally used for landing Troops for a Descent. . . ." (p. 22). The word is highly interesting from its genealogical tree; it is a descendant of the great historical and numerous family of the *Galley* (galley, galiot, galleon, galeass, galleida, galeoncino, &c.), and it is almost certainly the immediate parent of the hardly less historical *Jolly-boat*, which plays so important a part in British naval annals. [Prof. Skeat takes *jolly-boat* to be an English adaptation of Danish *jolle*, 'a yawl'; Mr. Foster remarks that *jollyvatt* as an English word, is at least as old as 1495-97 (*Oppenheim, Naval Accounts and Inventories, Navy Rec. Soc.* viii. 193) (*Letters*, iii. 296).] If this be true, which we can hardly doubt, we shall have three of the boats of the British man-of-war owing their names (*quod minime reris!*) to Indian originals, viz. the *Cutter*, the *Dingy*, and the *Jolly-boat* to **catur, dingy** and **gallevat**. This last derivation we take from Sir J. Campbell's *Bombay Gazetteer* (xiii. 417), a work that one can hardly mention without admiration. This writer, who states that a form of the same word, *galbat*, is now generally used by the natives in Bombay waters for large foreign vessels, such as English ships and steamers, is inclined to refer it to *jalba*, a word for a small boat used on the shores of the Red Sea (see *Dozy and Eng.*, p. 276), which appears below in a quotation from Ibn Batuta, and which vessels were called by the early Portuguese *gelvas*. Whether this word is the parent of *galley* and its derivatives, as Sir J. Campbell thinks, must be very doubtful, for *galley* is much older in European use than he seems to think, as the quotation from Asser shows. The word also occurs in Byzantine writers of the 9th century, such as the Continuator of Theophanes quoted below, and the Emperor Leo. We shall find below the occurrence of *galley* as an Oriental word in the form *jalia*, which looks like an Arabized adoption from a Mediterranean tongue. The Turkish, too, still has *ḳālyūn* for a ship of the line, which is certainly an adoption from *galeone*. The origin of *galley* is a very obscure question. Amongst other suggestions mentioned by Diez (*Etym. Worterb.*, 2nd ed. i. 198-199) is one from γαλεός, a shark, or from γαλεώτης, a sword-fish—the latter very suggestive of a galley with its aggressive beak; another is from γάλη, a word in Hesychius, which is the apparent origin of '*gallery*.' It is possible that *galeota*, *galiote*, may have been taken directly from the shark or sword-fish, though in imitation of the *galea* already in use. For we shall see below that *galiot* was used for a pirate. [The *N.E.D.* gives the European synonymous words, and regards the ultimate etymology of *galley* as unknown.]

The word *gallevat* seems to come directly from the *galeota* of the Portuguese and other S. European nations, a kind of inferior galley with only one bank of oars, which appears under the form *galion* in Joinville, *infra* (not to be confounded with the *galleons* of a later period, which were larger vessels), and often in the 13th and 14th centuries as *galeota*, *galiotes*, &c. It is constantly mentioned as forming part of the Portuguese fleets in India. Bluteau defines *galeota* as "a small galley with one mast, and with 15 or 20 benches a side, and one oar to each bench."

a. *Galley*.

c. 865.—"And then the incursion of the Russians (τῶν Ῥῶς) afflicted the Roman territory (these are a Scythian nation of rude and savage character), devastating Pontus . . . and investing the City itself when Michael was away engaged in war with the Ishmaelites. . . . So this incursion of these people afflicted the empire on the one hand, and on the other the advance of the fleet on Crete, which with some 20 cymbaria, and 7 **galleys** (γαλέας), and taking with it cargo-vessels also, went about, descending sometimes on the Cyclades Islands, and sometimes on the whole coast (of the main) right up to Proconnesus."—*Theophanis Continuatio*, Lib. iv. 33-34.

A.D. 877. — "Crescebat insuper diebus singulis perversorum numerus; adeo quidem, ut si triginta ex eis millia una die necarentur, alii succedebant numero duplicato. Tunc rex Aelfredus jussit cymbas et **galeas**, id est longas naves, fabricari per regnum, ut navali proelio hostibus adventantibus obviaret." — *Asser, Annales Rer. Gest. Aelfredi Magni*, ed. *West*, 1722, p. 29.

c. 1232. — "En cele navie de Genevois avoit soissante et dis **galeis**, mout bien armées; cheuetaine en estoient dui grant home de Gene. . . ."—*Guillaume de Tyr*, Texte Français, ed. *Paulin Paris*, i. 393.

1243.—Under this year Matthew Paris puts into the mouth of the Archbishop of York a punning couplet which shows the difference of accent with which **galea** in its two senses was pronounced:

"In terris galeas, in aquis formido **galeîas**:
Inter eas et eas consulo cautus eas."

1249.—"Lors s'esmut notre **galie**, et alames bien une grant lieue avant que li uns ne parlast à l'autre. . . . Lors vint messires Phelippes de Monfort en un **galion**,* et escria au roy: 'Sires, sires, parlés à vostre frere le conte de Poitiers, qui est en cel autre vessel.' Lors escria li roys: 'Alume, alume!'"—*Joinville*, ed. *de Wailly*, p. 212.

1517.—"At the Archinale ther (at Venice) we saw in makyng iiii^{xx} (*i.e.* 80) new **galyes** and **galye** Bastards, and **galye** Sotyltes, besyd they that be in viage in the haven."—*Torkington's Pilgrimage*, p. 8.

1542.—"They said that the Turk had sent orders to certain lords at Alexandria to make him up **galleys** (*galés*) in wrought timber, to be sent on camels to Suez; and this they did with great diligence . . . insomuch that every day a **galley** was put together at Suez . . . where they were making up 50 **galleys**, and 12 **galeons**, and also small rowing-vessels, such as **caturs**, much swifter than ours."—*Correa*, iv. 237.

b. *Jalia.*

1612.—". . . and coming to Malaca and consulting with the General they made the best arrangements that they could for the enterprise, adding a flotilla . . . sufficient for any need, for it consisted of seven **Galeots**, a *calamute* (?), a **sanguicel**, five *bantins*,† and one **jalia**."—*Bocarro*, 101.

1615. — "You must know that in 1605 there had come from the Reino (*i.e.* Portugal) one Sebastian Gonçalves Tibau . . . of humble parentage, who betook himself to Bengal and commenced life as a soldier; and afterwards became a factor in cargoes of salt (which forms the chief traffic in those parts), and acquiring some capital in this business, with that he bought a **jalia**, a kind of vessel that is there used for fighting and trading at once."—*Ibid.* 431.

* *Galeon* is here the galliot of later days. See above.

† "A kind of boat," is all that Crawfurd tells.—*Malay Dict.* s.v. ["*Banting*, a native sailing-vessel with two masts"—Williamson, *Malay Dict.*: "*Bantieng*, soort van boot met twee masten."—Van Eysinga, *Malay-Dutch Dict.*]

1634.—"Many others (of the Firingis) who were on board the *ghrâbs*, set fire to their vessels, and turned their faces towards hell. Out of the 64 large *dingas*, 57 *ghrâbs*, and 200 **jaliyas**, one *ghrâb* and two **jaliyas** escaped." — Capture of Hoogly in 1634, *Bādshāh Nāma*, in *Elliot*, vii. 34.

c. *Jalba, Jeloa*, &c.

c. 1330.—"We embarked at this town (Jedda) on a vessel called **jalba** which belonged to Rashīd-eddīn al-alfī al-Yamanī, a native of Ḥabsh."—*Ibn Batuta*, ii. 158. The Translators comment: "A large boat or gondola made of planks stitched together with coco-nut fibre."

1518.—"And Merocem, Captain of the fleet of the Grand Sultan, who was in Cambaya . . . no sooner learned that Goa was taken . . . than he gave up all hopes of bringing his mission to a fortunate termination, and obtained permission from the King of Cambaya to go to Judá . . . and from that port set out for Suez in a shallop" (**gelua**).—*Alboquerque*, Hak. Soc. iii. 19.

1538.—". . . before we arrived at the Island of Rocks, we discerned three vessels on the other side, that seemed to us to be **Geloas**, or *Terradas*, which are the names of the vessels of that country."—*Pinto*, in *Cogan*, p. 7.

[1611.—"Messengers will be sent along the coast to give warning of any **jelba** or ship approaching."—*Danvers, Letters*, i. 94.]

1690.—"In this is a Creek very convenient for building Grabbs or **Geloas**."—*Ovington*, 467.

d. *Galliot.*

In the first quotation we have *galiot* in the sense of "pirate."

c. 1232.—"L'en leur demanda de quel terre; il respondirent de Flandres, de Hollande et de Frise; et ce estoit voirs que il avoient esté **galiot** et ulague de mer, bien huit anz; or s'estoient repenti et pour penitence venoient en pelerinage en Jerusalem."—*Guill. de Tyr*, as above, p. 117.

1337.—". . . que elles doivent partir pour uenir au seruice du roy le jer J. de may l'an 337 au plus tart e doiuent couster les d. 40 galées pour quatre mois 144000 florins d'or, payez en partie par la compagnie des Bardes . . . et 2000 autres florins pour viretons et 2 **galiotes**."—*Contract with Genoese for Service of Philip of Valois*, quoted by *Jal*, ii. 337.

1518.—"The Governor put on great pressure to embark the force, and started from Cochin the 20th September, 1518, with 17 sail, besides the Goa foists, taking 3 **galleys** (*galés*) and one **galeota**, two brigantines (*bargantys*), four caravels, and the rest round ships of small size."—*Correa*, ii. 539.

1548.—". . . pera a **gualveta** em que ha d'andar o alcaide do maar."—*S. Botelho, Tombo*, 239.

1552.—"As soon as this news reached the Sublime Porte the Sandjak of Katif was ordered to send Murad-Beg to take command of the fleet, enjoining him to leave in the port of Bassora one or two ships, five galleys, and a **galiot.**"—*Sidi 'Ali*, p. 48.

,, "They (the Portuguese) had 4 ships as big as carracks, 3 *ghurābs* or great (rowing) vessels, 6 Portuguese caravels and 12 smaller ghurabs, *i.e.* **galiots** with oars." —*Ibid.* 67-68. Unfortunately the translator does not give the original Turkish word for *galiot.*

c. 1610.—"Es grandes Galeres il y peut deux et trois cens hommes de guerre, et en d'autres grandes **Galiotes**, qu'ils nomment *Fregates*, il y en peut cent. . . ."—*Pyrard de Laval*, ii. 72; [Hak. Soc. ii. 118].

[1665.—"He gave a sufficient number of **galiotes** to escort them to sea."—*Tavernier*, ed. *Ball*, i. 193.]

1689.—"He embarked about the middle of October in the year 1542, in a **galiot**, which carried the new Captain of Comorin." —*Dryden, Life of Xavier.* (In *Works*, ed. 1821, xvi. 87.)

e. *Gallevat.*

1613.—"Assoone as I anchored I sent Master *Molineux* in his Pinnasse, and Master *Spooner*, and *Samuell Squire* in my **Gellywatte** to sound the depths within the sands."—*Capt. N. Downton*, in *Purchas*, i. 501. This illustrates the origin of *Jolly-boat.*

[1679.—"I know not how many **Galwets.**" —In *Hedges, Diary*, Hak. Soc. ii. clxxxiv.]

1717.—"Besides the Salamander Fire-ship, Terrible Bomb, six **Galleywatts** of 8 guns, and 60 men each, and 4 of 6 guns and 50 men each."—*Authentic and Faithful History of that Arch-Pyrate Tulajee Angria* (1756), p. 47.

c. 1760.—"Of these armed boats called **Gallevats**, the Company maintains also a competent number, for the service of their marine."—*Grose*, ii. 62.

1763.—"The **Gallevats** are large row-boats, built like the grab, but of smaller dimensions, the largest rarely exceeding 70 tons; they have two masts . . . they have 40 or 50 stout oars, and may be rowed four miles an hour."—*Orme*, i. 409.

[1813.—". . . here they build vessels of all sizes, from a ship of the line to the smallest grabs and **gallivats**, employed in the Company's services."—*Forbes. Or Mem.* 2nd ed. i. 94-5.]

GAMBIER, s. The extract of a climbing shrub (*Uncaria Gambier*, Roxb.? *Nauclea Gambier*, Hunter; N.O. *Rubiaceae*) which is a native of the regions about the Straits of Malacca, and is much grown in plantations in Singapore and the neighbouring islands. The substance in chemical composition and qualities strongly resembles **cutch** (q.v.), and the names *Catechu* and *Terra Japonica* are applied to both. The plant is mentioned in Debry, 1601 (iii. 99), and by Rumphius, c. 1690 (v. 63), who describes its use in mastication with betel-nut; but there is no account of the catechu made from it, known to the authors of the *Pharmacographia*, before 1780. Crawfurd gives the name as Javanese, but Hanbury and Flückiger point out the resemblance to the Tamil name for catechu, *Katta Kāmbu* (*Pharmacographia*, 298 *seqq.*). [Mr. Skeat points out that the standard Malay name is *gambir*, of which the origin is uncertain, but that the English word is clearly derived from it.]

GANDA, s. This is the H. name for a rhinoceros, *gaiṇḍa*, *geṇḍa* from Skt. *gaṇḍa* (giving also *gaṇḍaka*, *gaṇḍānga*, *gajendra*). The note on the passage in Barbosa by his Hak. Soc. editor is a marvel in the way of error. The following is from a story of Correa about a battle between "Bober Mirza" (*i.e.* Sultan Baber) and a certain King "Cacandar" (Sikandar?), in which I have been unable to trace even what events it misrepresents. But it keeps Fernan Mendez Pinto in countenance, as regards the latter's statement about the advance of the King of the Tartars against Peking with four score thousand rhinoceroses!

"The King Cacandar divided his army into five battles well arrayed, consisting of 140,000 horse and 280,000 foot, and in front of them a battle of 800 elephants, which fought with swords upon their tusks, and on their backs castles with archers and musketeers. And in front of the elephants 80 rhinoceroses (**gandas**), like that which went to Portugal, and which they call *bichá* (?); these on the horn which they have over the snout carried three-pronged iron weapons with which they fought very stoutly . . . and the Mogors with their arrows made a great discharge, wounding many of the elephants and the **gandas**, which as they felt the arrows, turned and fled, breaking up the battles. . . ."—*Correa*, iii. 573-574.

1516.—"The King (of Guzerat) sent a **Ganda** to the King of Portugal, because they told him that he would be pleased to see her."—*Barbosa*, 58.

1553.—"And in return for many rich presents which this Diogo Fernandez carried to the King, and besides others which the King sent to Affonso Alboquerque, there was an animal, the biggest which

Nature has created after the elephant, and the great enemy of the latter . . . which the natives of the land of Cambaya, whence this one came, call **Ganda**, and the Greeks and Latins Rhinoceros. And Affonso d'Alboquerque sent this to the King Don Manuel, and it came to this Kingdom, and it was afterwards lost on its way to Rome, when the King sent it as a present to the Pope."—*Barros*, Dec. II. liv. x. cap. 1. [Also see *d'Alboquerque*, Hak. Soc. iv. 104 *seq.*].

GANTON, s. This is mentioned by some old voyagers as a weight or measure by which pepper was sold in the Malay Archipelago. It is presumably Malay *gantang*, defined by Crawfurd as "a dry measure, equal to about a gallon." [Klinkert has: "*gantang*, a measure of capacity 5 *katis* among the Malays; also a gold weight, formerly 6 *suku*, but later 1 *bongkal*, or 8 *suku*." *Gantang-gantang* is 'cartridge-case.']

1554.—"Also a candy of Goa, answers to 140 **gamtas**, equivalent to 15 *paraas*, 30 *medidas* at 42 medidas to the paraa."—*A. Nunes*, 39.

[1615.—". . . 1000 **gantans** of pepper."—*Foster*, *Letters*, iii. 168.]

,, "I sent to borow 4 or five **gantas** of oyle of Yasemon Dono. . . . But he returned answer he had non, when I know, to the contrary, he bought a parcell out of my handes the other day."—*Cocks's Diary*, i. 6.

GANZA, s. The name given by old travellers to the metal which in former days constituted the inferior currency of Pegu. According to some it was lead; others call it a mixt metal. Lead in rude lumps is still used in the bazars of Burma for small purchases. (*Yule*, *Mission to Ava*, 259.) The word is evidently Skt. *kaṉsa*, 'bell-metal,' whence Malay *gangsa*, which last is probably the word which travellers picked up.

1554.—"In this Kingdom of Pegu there is no coined money, and what they use commonly consists of dishes, pans, and other utensils of service, made of a metal like *frosyleyra* (?), broken in pieces; and this is called **gamça**. . . ."—*A. Nunes*, 38.

,, ". . . vn altra statua cosi fatta di **Ganza**; che è vn metallo di che fanno le lor monete, fatte di rame e di piombo mescolati insieme."—*Çesare Federici*, in *Ramusio*, iii. 394*v*.

c. 1567.—"The current money that is in this Citie, and throughout all this kingdom, is called **Gansa** or **Ganza**, which is made of copper and lead. It is not the money of the king, but every man may stampe it that will. . . ."—*Caesar Frederick*, E.T., in *Purchas*, iii. 1717-18.

1726.—"Rough Peguan **Gans** (a brass mixt with lead). . . ."—*Valentijn*, *Chor.* 34.

1727.—"Plenty of **Ganse** or Lead, which passeth all over the Pegu Dominions, for Money."—*A. Hamilton*, ii. 41; [ed. 1744, ii. 40].

GARCE, s. A cubic measure for rice, &c., in use on the Madras coast, as usual varying much in value. Buchanan (*infra*) treats it as a weight. The word is Tel. *gārisa*, *gārise*, Can. *garasi*, Tam. *karisai*. [In Chingleput salt is weighed by the *Garce* of 124 maunds, or nearly 5·152 tons (*Crole*, *Man.* 58); in Salem, 400 *Markals* (see **MERCALL**) are 185·2 cubic feet, or 18 quarters English (*Le Fanu*, *Man.* ii. 329); in Malabar, 120 *Paras* of 25 Macleod seers, or 10,800 lbs. (*Logan*, *Man.* ii. clxxix.). As a superficial measure in the N. Circars, it is the area which will produce one *Garce* of grain.]

[1684-5.—"A Generall to Conimeer of this day date enordring them to provide 200 **gars** of salt. . . ."—*Pringle*, *Diary Ft. St. Geo.* 1st ser. iv. 40, who notes that a still earlier use of the word will be found in *Notes and Exts.* i. 97.]

1752.—"Grain Measures.
1 Measure weighs about 26 lb. 1 oz. avd.
8 Do. is 1 *Mercal* 21 ,, ,,
3200 Do. is 400 do., or
1 **Garse** 8400 ,, ,,"
Brooks, Weights and Measures, &c., p. 6.

1759.—". . . a **garce** of rice. . . ."—In *Dalrymple*, *Or. Rep.* i. 120.

1784.—"The day that advice was received . . . (of peace with Tippoo) at Madras, the price of rice fell there from 115 to 80 pagodas the **garce**."—In *Seton-Karr*, i. 13.

1807.—"The proper native weights used in the Company's Jaghire are as follows: 10 *Vara hun* (Pagodas)=1 *Polam*, 40 *Polams* =1 *Visay*, 8 *Visay* (Vees)=1 *Manungu*, 20 *Manungus* (Maunds)=1 *Baruays*, 20 *Baruays* (Candies)=1 *Gursay*, called by the English **Garse**. The *Vara hun* or Star *Pagoda* weighs 52¾ grains, therefore the *Visay* is nearly three pounds avoirdupois (see **VISS**); and the **Garse** is nearly 1265 lbs."—*F. Buchanan*, *Mysore*, &c., i. 6.

By this calculation, the **Garse** should be 9600 lbs. instead of 1265 as printed.

GARDEE, s. A name sometimes given, in 18th century, to native soldiers disciplined in European fashion, *i.e.* **sepoys** (q.v.). The *Indian Vocabulary* (1788) gives: "**Gardee**—a tribe inhabiting the provinces of Bijapore, &c., esteemed good foot soldiers." The word may be only a corruption of 'guard,' but probably the origin assigned in the second quotation may be well founded; 'Guard' may have shaped the corruption of *Gharbi*. The old Bengal sepoys were commonly known in the N.W. as *Purbias* or Easterns (see **POORUB**). [Women in the Amazon corps at Hyderabad (Deccan), known as the *Zafar Paltan*, or 'Victorious Battalion,' were called **gardunee** (*Gārdanī*), the feminine form of *Gārad* or *Guard*.]

1762.—"A coffre who commanded the Telingas and **Gardees** . . . asked the horseman whom the horse belonged to?"—*Native Letter*, in *Van Sittart*, i. 141.

1786.—". . . originally they (Sipahis) were commanded by Arabians, or those of their descendants born in the Canara and Concan or Western parts of India, where those foreigners style themselves *Gharbies* or Western. Moreover these corps were composed mostly of Arabs, Negroes, and Habissinians, all of which bear upon that coast the same name of *Gharbi*. . . . In time the word *Gharbi* was corrupted by both the French and Indians into that of **Gardi**, which is now the general name of Sipahies all over India save Bengal . . . where they are stiled *Talingas*."—Note by Transl. of *Seir Mutaqherin*, ii. 93.

[1815.—"The women composing them are called **Gardunees**, a corruption of our word *Guard*."—*Blacker, Mem. of the Operations in India* in 1817-19, p. 213 note.]

GARDENS, GARDEN-HOUSE, s. In the 18th century suburban villas at Madras and Calcutta were so called. 'Garden Reach' below Fort William took its name from these.

1682.—"Early in the morning I was met by Mr. Littleton and most of the Factory, near Hugly, and about 9 or 10 o'clock by Mr. Vincent near the Dutch **Garden**, who came attended by severall Boats and Budgerows guarded by 35 Firelocks, and about 50 Rashpoots and Peons well armed."—*Hedges, Diary*, July 24; [Hak. Soc. i. 32].

1685.—"The whole Council . . . came to attend the President at the **garden-house**. . . ."—*Pringle, Diary, Fort St. Geo.* 1st ser. iv. 115; in *Wheeler*, i. 139.

1747.—"In case of an Attack at the **Garden House**, if by a superior Force they should be oblig'd to retire, according to the orders and send a Horseman before them to advise of the Approach. . . ."—*Report of Council of War at Fort St. David*, in *India Office MS. Records*.

1758.—"The guard of the redoubt retreated before them to the **garden-house**." —*Orme*, ii. 303.

,, "Mahomed Isoof . . . rode with a party of horse as far as Maskelyne's **garden**."—*Ibid*. iii. 425.

1772.—"The place of my residence at present is a **garden-house** of the Nabob, about 4 miles distant from Moorshedabad." —*Teignmouth, Mem*. i. 34.

1782.—"A body of Hyder's horse were at St. Thomas's Mount on the 29th ult. and Gen. Munro and Mr. Brodie with great difficulty escaped from the General's **Gardens**. They were pursued by Hyder's horse within a mile of the Black Town."—*India Gazette*, May 11.

1809.—"The gentlemen of the settlement live entirely in their **garden-houses**, as they very properly call them."—*Ld. Valentia*, i. 389.

1810.—". . . Rural retreats called **Garden-houses**."—*Williamson, V. M*. i. 137.

1873.—"To let, or for sale, Serle's **Gardens** at Adyar.—For particulars apply," &c.—*Madras Mail*, July 3.

GARRY, GHARRY, s. H. *gārī*, a cart or carriage. The word is used by Anglo-Indians, at least on the Bengal side, in both senses. Frequently the species is discriminated by a distinctive prefix, as *palkee-garry* (palankin carriage), *sej-garry* (chaise), *rel-garry* (railway carriage), &c. [The modern *dawk-garry* was in its original form called the "Equirotal Carriage," from the four wheels being of equal dimensions. The design is said to have been suggested by Lord Ellenborough. (See the account and drawing in *Grant, Rural Life in Bengal*, 3 *seq*.).]

1810.—"The common **g'horry** . . . is rarely, if ever, kept by any European, but may be seen plying for hire in various parts of Calcutta."—*Williamson, V. M*. i. 329.

1811.—The **Gary** is represented in Solvyns's engravings as a two-wheeled *rath* [see **RUT**] (*i.e.* the primitive native carriage, built like a light hackery) with two ponies.

1866.—"My husband was to have met us with a two-horse **gharee**."—*Trevelyan, Dawk Bungalow*, 384.

[1892.—"The *brūm* **gārī**, brougham; the *fitton* **gārī**, phaeton or barouche; the *vāgnūt*, waggonette, are now built in most large towns. . . . The *vāgnūt* seems likely to be the carriage of the future, because of its capacity."—*R. Kipling, Beast and Man in India*, 193.]

GAUM, GONG, s. A village, H. *gāon*, from Skt. *grāma*.

1519.—"In every one of the said villages, which they call **guãoos**."—*Goa Proclam*. in *Arch. Port. Orient*., fasc. 5, 38.

Gāonwār occurs in the same vol. (p. 75), under the forms *gancare* and *guancare*, for the village heads in Port. India.

GAURIAN, adj. This is a convenient name which has been adopted of late years as a generic name for the existing Aryan languages of India, *i.e.* those which are radically sprung from, or cognate to, the Sanskrit. The name (according to Mr. E. L. Brandreth) was given by Prof. Hoernle; but it is in fact an adoption and adaptation of a term used by the Pundits of Northern India. They divide the colloquial languages of (civilised) India into the 5 *Gauṛas* and 5 *Drāviras* [see **DRAVIDIAN**]. The *Gauṛas* of the Pundits appear to be (1) Bengalee (*Bangālī*) which is the proper language of *Gauḍa*, or Northern Bengal, from which the name is taken (see **GOUR** c.), (2) Oriya, the language of Orissa, (3) Hindī, (4) Panjābī, (5) Sindhī; their *Drāvira* languages are (1) Telinga, (2) Karṇāṭaka (Canarese), (3) Marāṭhī, (4) Gurjara (Gujarātī), (5) Drāvira (Tamil). But of these last (3) and (4) are really to be classed with the Gauṛian group, so that the latter is to be considered as embracing 7 principal languages. Kashmīrī, Singhalese, and the languages or dialects of Assam, of Nepaul, and some others, have also been added to the list of this class.

The extraordinary analogies between the changes in grammar and phonology from Sanskrit in passing into those Gaurian languages, and the changes of Latin in passing into the Romance languages, analogies extending into minute details, have been treated by several scholars; and a very interesting view of the subject is given by Mr. Brandreth in vols. xi. and xii. of the *J.R.A.S.*, N.S.

GAUTAMA, n.p. The surname, according to Buddhist legend, of the Sakya tribe from which the Buddha Sakya Muni sprang. It is a derivative from *Gotama*, a name of "one of the ancient Vedic bard-families" (*Oldenberg*). It is one of the most common names for Buddha among the Indo-Chinese nations. The *Sommona*-**codom** of many old narratives represents the Pali form of *S'ramaṇa Gautama*, "The Ascetic Gautama."

1545.—"I will pass by them of the sect of **Godomem**, who spend their whole life in crying day and night on those mountains, **Godomem, Godomem**, and desist not from it until they fall down stark dead to the ground."—*F. M. Pinto*, in *Cogan*, p. 222.

c. 1590.—See under **Godavery** passage from *Āīn*, where **Gotam** occurs.

1686.—"J'ai cru devoir expliquer toutes ces choses avant que de parler de *Sommono*-**khodom** (c'est ainsi que les Siamois appellent le Dieu qu'ils adorent à present)."—*Voy. de Siam, Des Pères Jesuites*, Paris, 1686, p. 397.

1687-88.—"Now tho' they say that several have attained to this Felicity (*Nireupan, i.e.* Nirvana) . . . yet they honour only one alone, whom they esteem to have surpassed all the rest in Vertue. They call him *Sommona*-**Codom**; and they say that **Codom** was his Name, and that Sommona signifies in the *Balie* Tongue a *Talapoin* of the Woods."—*Hist. Rel. of Siam*, by *De La Loubere*, E.T. i. 130.

[1727.—". . . inferior Gods, such as *Somma* **Cuddom**. . . ."—*A. Hamilton*, ed. 1744, ii. 54.]

1782.—"Les Pegouins et les Bahmans. . . . Quant à leurs Dieux, ils en comptent sept principaux. . . . Cependant ils n'en adorent qu'un seul, qu'ils appellent **Godeman**. . . ." —*Sonnerat*, ii. 299.

1800.—"**Gotma**, or **Goutum**, according to the Hindoos of India, or **Gaudma** among the inhabitants of the more eastern parts, is said to have been a philosopher . . . he taught in the Indian schools, the heterodox religion and philosophy of Boodh. The image that represents Boodh is called Gautama, or **Goutum**. . . ."—*Symes, Embassy*, 299.

1828.—"The titles or synonymes of Buddha, as they were given to me, are as follow: "**Kotamo** (*Gautama*) . . . *Somana*-**kotamo**, agreeably to the interpretation given me, means in the Pali language, the priest **Gautama**."—*Crawfurd, Emb. to Siam*, p. 367.

GAVEE, s. Topsail. Nautical jargon from Port. *gavea*, the top. (*Roebuck*).

GAVIAL, s. This is a name adopted by zoologists for one of the alligators of the Ganges and other Indian rivers, *Gavialis gangeticus*, &c. It is the less dangerous of the Gangetic saurians, with long, slender, subcylindrical jaws expanding into a protuberance at the muzzle. The name must have originated in some error, probably a clerical one, for the true word is Hind. *ghariyāl*, and *gavial* is nothing. The term (*gariyālī*) is used by Baber (p. 410), where the translator's note says: "The **geriali** is the round-mouthed crocodile," words which seem to indicate the *magar* (see **MUGGUR**) (*Crocodilus biporcatus*) not the *ghariyāl*.

c. 1809.—"In the Brohmoputro as well as in the Ganges there are two kinds of crocodile, which at Goyalpara are both called *Kumir*; but each has a specific name. The *Crocodilus Gangeticus* is called **Ghoriyal**, and the other is called *Bongcha*."—*Buchanan's Rungpoor*, in *Eastern India*, iii. 581-2.

GAZAT, s. This is domestic Hind. for 'dessert.' (*Panjab N. & Q.* ii. 184).

GECKO, s. A kind of house lizard. The word is not now in Anglo-Indian use; it is a naturalist's word; and also is French. It was no doubt originally an onomatopoeia from the creature's reiterated utterance. Marcel Devic says the word is adopted from Malay *gekok* [*gēkoq*]. This we do not find in Crawfurd, who has *tăké*, *tăkék*, and *goké*, all evidently attempts to represent the utterance. In Burma the same, or a kindred lizard, is called *tokté*, in like imitation.

1631.—Bontius seems to identify this lizard with the **Guana** (q.v.), and says its bite is so venomous as to be fatal unless the part be immediately cut out, or cauterized. This is no doubt a fable. "Nostratis ipsum animal apposito vocabulo **gecco** vocant; quippe non secus ac *Coccyx* apud nos suum cantum iterat, etiam *gecko* assiduo sonat, prius edito stridore qualem Picus emittit."—Lib. V. cap. 5, p. 57.

1711.—"**Chaccos**, as Cuckoos receive their Names from the Noise they make. . . . They are much like lizards, but larger. 'Tis said their Dung is so venomous," &c.—*Lockyer*, 84.

1727.—"They have one dangerous little Animal called a **Jackoa**, in shape almost like a Lizard. It is very malicious . . . and wherever the Liquor lights on an Animal Body, it presently cankers the Flesh."—*A. Hamilton*, ii. 131; [ed. 1744, ii. 136].

This is still a common belief. (See **BISCOBRA**).

1883.—"This was one of those little house lizards called **geckos**, which have pellets at the ends of their toes. They are not repulsive brutes like the garden lizard, and I am always on good terms with them. They have full liberty to make use of my house, for which they seem grateful, and say chuck, chuck, chuck."—*Tribes on My Frontier*, 38.

GENTOO, s. and adj. This word is a corruption of the Portuguese *Gentio*, 'a gentile' or heathen, which they applied to the Hindus in contradistinction to the *Moros* or 'Moors,' *i.e.* Mahommedans. [See **MOOR**.] Both terms are now obsolete among English people, except perhaps that *Gentoo* still lingers at Madras in the sense **b**; for the terms *Gentio* and *Gentoo* were applied in two senses:

a. To the Hindūs generally.

b. To the Telugu-speaking Hindūs of the Peninsula specially, and to their language.

The reason why the term became thus specifically applied to the Telugu people is probably because, when the Portuguese arrived, the Telugu monarchy of Vijayanagara, or Bijanagar (see **BISNAGAR, NARSINGA**) was dominant over great part of the Peninsula. The officials were chiefly of Telugu race, and thus the people of this race, as the most important section of the Hindūs, were *par excellence* the *Gentiles*, and their language the Gentile language. Besides these two specific senses, *Gentio* was sometimes used for *heathen* in general. Thus in F. M. Pinto: "A very famous Corsair who was called Hinimilau, a Chinese by nation, and who from a *Gentio* as he was, had a little time since turned Moor. . . ."—Ch. L.

a.—

1548.—"The *Religiosos* of this territory spend so largely, and give such great alms at the cost of your Highness's administration that it disposes of a good part of the funds. . . . I believe indeed they do all this in real zeal and sincerity . . . but I think it might be reduced a half, and all for the better; for there are some of them who often try to make Christians by force, and worry the **Gentoos** (*jentios*) to such a degree that it drives the population away."—*Simao Botelho Çartas*, 35.

1563.—". . . Among the *Gentiles* (**Gentios**) Rão is as much as to say 'King.'"—*Garcia*, f. 35*b*.

" "This ambergris is not so highly valued among the Moors, but it is highly prized among the **Gentiles**."—*Ibid.* f. 14.

1582.—"A **gentile** . . . whose name was Canaca."—*Castañeda*, trans. by N. L., f. 31.

1588.—In a letter of this year to the Viceroy, the King (Philip II.) says he "understands the **Gentios** are much the best persons to whom to farm the *alfandegas* (customs, &c.), paying well and regularly, and it does not seem contrary to canon-law to farm to them, but on this he will consult the learned."—In *Arch. Port. Orient.* fasc. 3, 135.

c. 1610.—"Ils (les Portugais) exercent ordinairement de semblables cruautez lors qu'ils sortent en trouppe le long des costes, bruslans et saccageans ces pauures **Gentils** qui ne desirent que leur bonne grace, et leur amitié mais ils n'en ont pas plus de pitié pour cela."—*Mocquet*, 349.

1630.—". . . which **Gentiles** are of two sorts . . . first the purer **Gentiles** . . . or else the impure or vncleane *Gentiles* . . . such are the husbandmen or inferior sort of people called the *Coulees*."—*H. Lord, Display*, &c., 85.

1673.—"The finest Dames of the **Gentues** disdained not to carry Water on their Heads."—*Fryer*, 116.

,, "**Gentues**, the Portuguese idiom for *Gentiles*, are the Aborigines."—*Ibid*. 27.

1679.—In Fort St. Geo. Cons. of 29th January, the **Black Town** of Madras is called "the **Gentue** Town."—*Notes and Exts.*, No. ii. 3.

1682.—"This morning a **Gentoo** sent by Bulchund, Governour of Hugly and Cassumbazar, made complaint to me that Mr. Charnock did shamefully — to ye great scandal of our Nation — keep a **Gentoo** woman of his kindred, which he has had these 19 years."—*Hedges, Diary*, Dec. 1.; [Hak. Soc. i. 52].

1683. — "The ceremony used by these **Gentu's** in their sicknesse is very strange; they bring ye sick person . . . to ye brinke of ye River Ganges, on a *Cott*. . . ."—*Ibid*. May 10; [Hak. Soc. i. 86].

In Stevens's Trans. of *Faria y Sousa* (1695) the Hindus are still called *Gentiles*. And it would seem that the English form **Gentoo** did not come into general use till late in the 17th century.

1767.—"In order to transact Business of any kind in this Countrey you must at least have a Smattering of the Language. . . . The original Language of this Countrey (or at least the earliest we know of) is the Bengala or **Gentoo**; this is commonly spoken in all parts of the Countrey. But the politest Language is the Moors or Mussulmans, and Persian."—*MS. Letter of James Rennell*.

1772.—"It is customary with the **Gentoos**, as soon as they have acquired a moderate fortune, to dig a pond."—*Teignmouth, Mem.* i. 36.

1774. — "When I landed (on Island of Bali) the natives, who are **Gentoos**, came on board in little canoes, with outriggers on each side."—*Forrest, V. to N. Guinea*, 169.

1776. — "A Code of **Gentoo** Laws or Ordinations of the Pundits. From a Persian Translation, made from the original written in the Shanskrit Language. London, Printed in the Year 1776."—(Title of Work by Nathaniel Brassey Halhed.)

1778. — "The peculiar patience of the **Gentoos** in Bengal, their affection to business, and the peculiar cheapness of all productions either of commerce or of necessity, had concurred to render the details of the revenue the most minute, voluminous, and complicated system of accounts which exist in the universe."—*Orme*, ii. 7 (Reprint).

1781.—"They (Syrian Christians of Travancore) acknowledged a **Gentoo** Sovereign, but they were governed even in temporal concerns by the bishop of Angamala."—*Gibbon*, ch. xlvii.

1784.—"Captain Francis Swain Ward, of the Madras Establishment, whose paintings and drawings of **Gentoo** Architecture, &c., are well known."—In *Seton-Karr*, i. 31.

1785.—"I found this large concourse (at Chandernagore) of people were gathered to see a **Gentoo** woman burn herself with her husband."—*Ibid*. i. 90.

,, "The original inhabitants of India are called **Gentoos**."—*Carraccioli's Life of Clive*, i. 122.

1803.—"*Peregrine*. O mine is an accommodating palate, hostess. I have swallowed burgundy with the French, hollands with the Dutch, sherbet with a Turk, sloe-juice with an Englishman, and water with a simple **Gentoo**."—*Colman's John Bull*, i. sc. 1.

1807.—"I was not prepared for the entire nakedness of the **Gentoo** inhabitants."—*Lord Minto in India*, 17.

b.—

1648. — "The Heathen who inhabit the kingdom of *Golconda*, and are spread all over India, are called **Jentives**."— *Van Twist*, 59.

1673.—"Their Language they call generally **Gentu** . . . the peculiar Name of their Speech is *Telinga*."—*Fryer*, 33.

1674. — "50 Pagodas gratuity to John Thomas ordered for good progress in the **Gentu** tongue, both speaking and writing."—*Fort St. Geo. Cons.*, in *Notes and Exts.* No. i. 32.

[1681.—"He hath the **Gentue** language."—In *Yule, Hedges' Diary*, Hak. Soc. ii. cclxxxiv.]

1683.—"Thursday, 21st June. . . . The Hon. Company having sent us a Law with reference to the Natives . . . it is ordered that the first be translated into Portuguese, **Gentoo**, Malabar, and Moors, and proclaimed solemnly by beat of drum."—*Madras Consultation*, in *Wheeler*, i. 314.

1719.—"Bills of sale wrote in **Gentoo** on Cajan leaves, which are entered in the Register kept by the Town Conicoply for that purpose."—*Ibid*. ii. 314.

1726.—"The proper vernacular here (Golconda) is the **Gentoos** (*Jentiefs*) or Telingaas."—*Valentijn, Chor*. 37.

1801.—"The **Gentoo** translation of the Regulations will answer for the Ceded Districts, for even . . . the most Canarine part of them understand **Gentoo**."—*Munro*, in *Life*, i. 321.

1807.—"A Grammar of the **Gentoo** language, as it is understood and spoken by the **Gentoo** People, residing north and north-westward of Madras. By a Civil Servant under the Presidency of Fort St. George, many years resident in the Northern Circars. Madras. 1807."

1817.—The third grammar of the Telugu language, published in this year, is called a '**Gentoo** Grammar.'

1837.—"I mean to amuse myself with learning **Gentoo**, and have brought a Moonshee with me. **Gentoo** is the language of this part of the country [Godavery delta], and one of the prettiest of all the dialects." —*Letters from Madras*, 189.

GHAUT, s. Hind. *ghāt*.

a. A landing-place; a path of descent to a river; the place of a ferry, &c. Also a quay or the like.

b. A path of descent from a mountain; a mountain pass; and hence

c., n.p. The mountain ranges parallel to the western and eastern coasts of the Peninsula, through which the *ghāts* or passes lead from the table-lands above down to the coast and lowlands. It is probable that foreigners hearing these tracts spoken of respectively as the country above and the country below the *Ghāts* (see **BALAGHAUT**) were led to regard the word *Ghāts* as a proper name of the mountain range itself, or (like De Barros below) as a word signifying *range*. And this is in analogy with many other cases of mountain nomenclature, where the name of a pass has been transferred to a mountain chain, or where the word for 'a pass' has been mistaken for a word for 'mountain range.' The proper sense of the word is well illustrated from Sir A. Wellesley, under **b.**

a.—

1809.—"The *dandys* there took to their paddles, and keeping the beam to the current the whole way, contrived to land us at the destined **gaut**."—*Ld. Valentia*, i. 185.

1824.—"It is really a very large place, and rises from the river in an amphitheatral form . . . with many very fine **ghâts** descending to the water's edge."—*Heber*, i. 167.

b.—

c. 1315.—"In 17 more days they arrived at Gurganw. During these 17 days the **Ghâts** were passed, and great heights and depths were seen amongst the hills, where even the elephants became nearly invisible." —*Amír Khusrū*, in *Elliot*, iii. 86.

This passage illustrates how the transition from **b** to **c** occurred. The *Ghāts* here meant are not a range of mountains so called, but, as the context shows, the passes among the Vindhya and Sātpūra hills. Compare the two following, in which 'down the *ghauts*' and 'down the *passes*' mean exactly the same thing, though to many people the former expression will suggest 'down through a range of mountains called the Ghauts.'

1803.—"The enemy are down the **ghauts** in great consternation."—*Wellington*, ii. 333.

" "The enemy have fled northward, and are getting down the *passes* as fast as they can."—*M. Elphinstone*, in *Life* by *Colebrooke*, i. 71.

1826.—"Though it was still raining, I walked up the Bohr **Ghât**, four miles and a half, to Candaulah."—*Heber*, ii. 136, ed. 1844. That is, up one of the Passes, from which Europeans called the mountains themselves "the **Ghauts**."

The following passage indicates that the great Sir Walter, with his usual sagacity, saw the true sense of the word in its geographical use, though misled by books to attribute to the (so-called) 'Eastern Ghauts' the character that belongs to the Western only.

1827.—". . . they approached the **Ghauts**, those tremendous mountain passes which descend from the table-land of Mysore, and through which the mighty streams that arise in the centre of the Indian Peninsula find their way to the ocean."—*The Surgeon's Daughter*, ch. xiii.

c.—

1553.—"The most notable division which Nature hath planted in this land is a chain of mountains, which the natives, by a generic appellation, because it has no proper name, call **Gate**, which is as much as to say *Serra*." —*De Barros*, Dec. I. liv. iv. cap. vii.

1561.—"This *Serra* is called **Gate**."—*Correa, Lendas*, ii. 2, 56.

1563.—"The *Cuncam*, which is the land skirting the sea, up to a lofty range which they call **Guate**."—*Garcia*, f. 34*b*.

1572.—
"Da terra os Naturaes lhe chamam **Gate**,
Do pe do qual pequena quantidade
Se estende hũa fralda estreita, que combate
Do mar a natural ferocidade. . . ."
Camões, vii. 22.

Englished by Burton:

"The country-people call this range the **Ghaut**,
and from its foot-hills scanty breadth there be,
whose seaward-sloping coast-plain long hath fought
'gainst Ocean's natural ferocity. . . ."

1623.—"We commenced then to ascend the mountain-(range) which the people of the country call **Gat**, and which traverses in the middle the whole length of that part of India which projects into the sea, bathed on the east side by the Gulf of Bengal, and on the west by the Ocean, or Sea of Goa."—*P. della Valle*, ii. 32; [Hak. Soc. ii. 222].

1673.—"The Mountains here are one continued ridge . . . and are all along called **Gaot.**"—*Fryer*, 187.

1685.—"On les appelle, *montagnes de* **Gatte**, c'est comme qui diroit montagnes de montagnes, *Gatte* en langue du pays ne signifiant autre chose que montagne" (quite wrong).—*Ribeyro, Ceylan*, (Fr. Transl.), p. 4.

1727.—"The great Rains and Dews that fall from the Mountains of **Gatti**, which ly 25 or 30 leagues up in the Country."—*A. Hamilton*, i. 282; [ed. 1744, ii. 285].

1762.—"All the South part of India save the Mountains of **Gate** (a string of Hills in ye country) is level Land the Mould scarce so deep as in England. . . . As you make use of every expedient to drain the water from your tilled ground, so the Indians take care to keep it in theirs, and for this reason sow only in the level grounds."—*MS. Letter of James Rennell*, March 21.

1826.—"The mountains are nearly the same height . . . with the average of Welsh mountains. . . . In one respect, and only one, the **Ghâts** have the advantage,—their precipices are higher, and the outlines of the hills consequently bolder."—*Heber*, ed. 1844, ii. 136.

GHEE, s. Boiled butter; the universal medium of cookery throughout India, supplying the place occupied by oil in Southern Europe, and more; [the *samn* of Arabia, the *raughan* of Persia]. The word is Hind. *ghī*, Skt. *ghrita*. A short but explicit account of the mode of preparation will be found in the *English Cyclopaedia* (Arts and Sciences), s.v.; [and in fuller detail in *Watt, Econ. Dict.* iii. 491 *seqq.*].

c. 1590.—"Most of them (Akbar's elephants) get 5 s. (ers) of sugar, 4 s. of **ghí**, and half a *man* of rice mixed with chillies, cloves, &c."—*Āīn-i-Akbarī*, i. 130.

1673.—"They will drink milk, and boil'd butter, which they call **Ghe.**"—*Fryer*, 33.

1783.—"In most of the prisons [of Hyder 'Ali] it was the custom to celebrate particular days, when the funds admitted, with the luxury of plantain fritters, a draught of sherbet, and a convivial song. On one occasion the old Scotch ballad, 'My wife has ta'en the gee,' was admirably sung, and loudly encored. . . . It was reported to the Kelledar (see **KILLADAR**) that the prisoners said and sung throughout the night of nothing but **ghee.** . . . The Kelledar, certain that discoveries had been made regarding his malversations in that article of garrison store, determined to conciliate their secrecy by causing an abundant supply of this unaccustomed luxury to be thenceforth placed within the reach of their farthing purchases."—*Wilks, Hist. Sketches*, ii. 154.

1785.—"The revenues of the city of Decca . . . amount annually to two kherore (see **CRORE**), proceeding from the customs and duties levied on **ghee.**"—*Carraccioli L. of Clive*, i. 172.

1817.—"The great luxury of the Hindu is butter, prepared in a manner peculiar to himself, and called by him **ghee.**"—*Mill, Hist.* i. 410.

GHILZAI, n.p. One of the most famous of the tribes of Afghanistan, and probably the strongest, occupying the high plateau north of Kandahar, and extending (roundly speaking) eastward to the Sulimānī mountains, and north to the Kābul River. They were supreme in Afghanistan at the beginning of the 18th century, and for a time possessed the throne of Ispahan. The following paragraph occurs in the article Afghanistan, in the 9th ed. of the *Encyc. Britan.*, 1874 (i. 235), written by one of the authors of this book:—

"It is remarkable that the old Arab geographers of the 10th and 11th centuries place in the Ghilzai country" (*i.e.* the country now occupied by the Ghilzais, or nearly so) "a people called **Khilijis**, whom they call a tribe of Turks, to whom belonged a famous family of Delhi Kings. The probability of the identity of the **Khilijis** and **Ghilzais** is obvious, and the question touches others regarding the origin of the Afghans; but it does not seem to have been gone into."

Nor has the writer since ever been able to go into it. But whilst he has never regarded the suggestion as more than a probable one, he has seen no reason to reject it. He may add that on starting the idea to Sir Henry Rawlinson (to whom it seemed new), a high authority on such a question, though he would not accept it, he made a candid remark to the effect that the Ghilzais had undoubtedly a very Turk-like aspect. A belief in this identity was, as we have recently noticed, entertained by the traveller Charles Masson, as is shown in a passage quoted below. And it has also been maintained by Surgeon-Major Bellew, in his *Races of Afghanistan* (1880), [who (p. 100) refers the name to *Khilichī*, a swordsman. The folk etymology of De Guignes and D'Herbelot is *Kall*, 'repose,' *atz*, 'hungry,' given to an officer by Ogouz Khān, who delayed on the road to kill game for his sick wife].

All the accounts of the Ghilzais indicate great differences between them and the other tribes of Afghanistan; whilst there seems nothing impossible, or even unlikely, in the partial assimilation of a Turki tribe in the course of centuries to the Afghans who surround them, and the consequent assumption of a quasi-Afghan genealogy. We do not find that Mr. Elphinstone makes any explicit reference to the question now before us. But two of the notes to his *History* (5th ed. p. 322 and 384) seem to indicate that it was in his mind. In the latter of these he says: "The Khiljis . . . though Turks by descent . . . had been so long settled among the Afghans that they had almost become identified with that people; but they probably mixed more with other nations, or at least with their Turki brethren, and would be more civilized than the generality of Afghan mountaineers." The learned and eminently judicious William Erskine was also inclined to accept the identity of the two tribes, doubting (but perhaps needlessly) whether the Khiliji had been really of Turki race. We have not been able to meet with any translated author who mentions both Khiliji and Ghilzai. In the following quotations all the earlier refer to Khiliji, and the later to Ghilzai. Attention may be called to the expressions in the quotation from Zīauddīn Barnī, as indicating some great difference between the Turk proper and the Khiliji even then. The language of Baber, again, so far as it goes, seems to indicate that by his time the Ghilzais were regarded as an Afghan clan.

c. 940.—"Hajjāj had delegated 'Abdarrahmān ibn Mahommed ibn al-Ash'ath to Sijistān, Bost and Rukhāj (Arachosia) to make war on the Turk tribes diffused in those regions, and who are known as Ghūz and **Khulj** . . ."—*Maṣ'ūdi*, v. 302.

c. 950.—"The **Khalaj** is a Turki tribe, which in ancient times migrated into the country that lies between India and the parts of Sijistān beyond the Ghūr. They are a pastoral people and resemble the Turks in their natural characteristics, their dress and their language."—*Istakhri*, from *De Goeje's* text, p. 245.

c. 1030.—"The Afghâns and **Khiljís** having submitted to him (Sabaktigín), he admitted thousands of them . . . into the ranks of his armies."—*Al-'Utbi.*, in *Elliot*, ii. 24.

c. 1150.—"The Khilkhs (read **Khilij**) are people of Turk race, who, from an early date invaded this country (Dāwar, on the banks of the Helmand), and whose dwellings are spread abroad to the north of India and on the borders of Ghaur and of Western Sijistān. They possess cattle, wealth, and the various products of husbandry; they all have the aspect of Turks, whether as regards features, dress, and customs, or as regards their arms and manner of making war. They are pacific people, doing and thinking no evil."—*Edrisi*, i. 457.

1289.—"At the same time Jalálu-d dín (Khilji), who was *'Ariz-i-mamálik* (Muster-master-general), had gone to Bahárpúr, attended by a body of his relations and friends. Here he held a muster and inspection of the forces. He came of a race different from that of the Turks, so he had no confidence in them, nor would the Turks own him as belonging to the number of their friends. . . . The people high and low . . . were all troubled by the ambition of the **Khiljis**, and were strongly opposed to Jalálu-d dín's obtaining the crown. . . . Sultán Jalálu-d dín Fíroz **Khilji** ascended the throne in the . . . year 688 A.H. . . . The people of the city (of Delhi) had for 80 years been governed by sovereigns of Turk extraction, and were averse to the succession of the *Khiljis* . . . they were struck with admiration and amazement at seeing the *Khiljis* occupying the throne of the Turks, and wondered how the throne had passed from the one to the other."—*Ziáu-d-dín Barní*, in *Elliot*, iii. 134-136.

14th cent.—The continuator of Rashídud-dín enumerates among the tribes occupying the country which we now call Afghanistan, *Ghūris*, *Herawis*, *Nigudaris*, *Sejzis*, **Khilij**, Balūch and Afghāns. See *Notices et Extraits*, xiv. 494.

c. 1507.—"I set out from Kábul for the purpose of plundering and beating up the quarters of the **Ghiljis** . . . a good farsang from the Ghilji camp, we observed a blackness, which was either owing to the Ghiljis being in motion, or to smoke. The young and inexperienced men of the army all set forward full speed; I followed them for two kos, shooting arrows at their horses, and at length checked their speed. When five or six thousand men set out on a pillaging party, it is extremely difficult to maintain discipline. . . . A minaret of skulls was erected of the heads of these Afghans."—*Baber*, pp. 220-221; see also p. 225.

[1753.—"The **Cligis** knowing that his troops must pass thro' their mountains, waited for them in the defiles, and successively defeated several bodies of Mahommed's army."—*Hanway*, *Hist. Acc.* iii. 24.]

1842.—"The **Ghilji** tribes occupy the principal portion of the country between Kándahár and Ghazní. They are, moreover, the most numerous of the Afghân tribes, and if united under a capable chief might . . . become the most powerful. . . . They are brave and warlike, but have a sternness of disposition amounting to ferocity. . . . Some of the inferior Ghiljís are so violent in their intercourse with strangers that they can scarcely be considered in the light of human beings, while no language can describe the terrors of a transit through their country, or the indignities which have to be endured. . . . The Ghiljis, although considered, and calling themselves, Afghâns, and moreover employing the Pashto, or Afghân dialect, are undoubtedly a mixed race.

"The name is evidently a modification or corruption of **Khaljí** or **Khilají**, that of a great Turkí tribe mentioned by Sherífudín in his history of Taimúr. . . ."—*Ch. Masson, Narr. of various Journeys*, &c., ii. 204, 206, 207.

1854.—"The Ghúri was succeeded by the **Khiljí** dynasty; also said to be of Turki extraction, but which seems rather to have been of Afghán race; and it may be doubted if they are not of the **Ghiljí** Afgháns."—*Erskine, Báber and Humáyun*, i. 404.

1880.—"As a race the **Ghilji** mix little with their neighbours, and indeed differ in many respects, both as to internal government and domestic customs, from the other races of Afghanistan . . . the great majority of the tribe are pastoral in their habits of life, and migrate with the seasons from the lowlands to the highlands with their families and flocks, and easily portable black hair tents. They never settle in the cities, nor do they engage in the ordinary handicraft trades, but they manufacture carpets, felts, &c., for domestic use, from the wool and hair of their cattle. . . . Physically they are a remarkably fine race . . . but they are a very barbarous people, the pastoral class especially, and in their wars excessively savage and vindictive.

"Several of the **Ghilji** or Ghilzai-clans are almost wholly engaged in the carrying trade between India and Afghanistan, and the Northern States of Central Asia, and have been so for many centuries."—*Races of Afghanistan*, by *Bellew*, p. 103.

GHOUL, s. Ar. *ghūl*, P. *ghōl*. A goblin, ἔμπουσα, or man-devouring demon, especially haunting wildernesses.

c. 70.—"In the deserts of Affricke yee shall meet oftentimes with fairies,* appearing in the shape of men and women; but they vanish soone away, like fantasticall illusions."—*Pliny*, by *Ph. Holland*, vii. 2.

c. 940.—"The Arabs relate many strange stories about the **Ghūl** and their transformations. . . . The Arabs allege that the two feet of the **Ghūl** are ass's feet. . . . These Ghūl appeared to travellers in the night, and at hours when one meets with no one on the road; the traveller taking them for some of their companions followed them, but the Ghūl led them astray, and caused them to lose their way."—*Maṣ'ūdī*, iii. 314 *seqq.* (There is much more after the copious and higgledy-piggledy Plinian fashion of this writer.)

* There is no justification for this word in the Latin.

c. 1420.—"In exitu deserti . . . rem mirandam dicit contigisse. Nam cum circiter mediam noctem quiescentes magno murmure strepituque audito suspicarentur omnes, Arabes praedones ad se spoliandos venire . . . viderunt plurimas equitum turmas transeuntium. . . . Plures qui id antea viderant, daemones (**ghūls**, no doubt) esse per desertum vagantes asseruere."—*Nic. Conti*, in *Poggio*, iv.

1814.—"The Afghauns believe each of the numerous solitudes in the mountains and desarts of their country to be inhabited by a lonely daemon, whom they call *Ghoolee Beeabaun* (the **Goule** or Spirit of the Waste); they represent him as a gigantic and frightful spectre (who devours any passenger whom chance may bring within his haunts."—*Elphinstone's Caubul*, ed. 1839, i. 291.

[**GHURRA**, s. Hind. *ghaṛa*, Skt. *ghaṭa*. A water-pot made of clay, of a spheroidal shape, known in S. India as the **chatty**.

[1827.—". . . . the Rajah sent . . . 60 **Gurrahs** (earthen vessels holding a gallon) of sugar-candy and sweetmeats."—*Mundy, Pen and Pencil Sketches*, 66.]

GHURRY, GURREE, s. Hind. *ghaṛī*. A clepsydra or water-instrument for measuring time, consisting of a floating cup with a small hole in it, adjusted so that it fills and sinks in a fixed time; also the gong by which the time so indicated is struck. This latter is properly *ghaṛiyāl*. Hence also a clock or watch; also the 60th part of a day and night, equal therefore to 24 minutes, was in old Hindu custom the space of time indicated by the clepsydra just mentioned, and was called a *ghaṛī*. But in Anglo-Indian usage, the word is employed for 'an hour,' [or some indefinite period of time]. The water-instrument is sometimes called **Pun-Ghurry** (*panghaṛī quasi pānī-ghaṛī*); also the Sun-dial, **Dhoop-Ghurry** (*dhūp*, 'sunshine'); the hour-glass, **Ret-Ghurry** (*ret*, *retā*, 'sand').

(Ancient).—"The magistrate, having employed the first four **Ghurries** of the day in bathing and praying, . . . shall sit upon the Judgment Seat."—*Code of the Gentoo Laws* (*Halhed*, 1776), 104.

[1526.—"**Gheri.**" See under **PUHUR**.

[c. 1590.—An elaborate account of this method of measuring time will be found in *Āīn*, ed. *Jarrett*, iii. 15 *seq.*

[1616.—"About a **guary** after, the rest of my company arrived with the money."—*Foster, Letters*, iv. 343.]

1633.—"First they take a great Pot of Water . . . and putting therein a little Pot (this lesser pot having a small hole in the bottome of it), the water issuing into it having filled it, then they strike on a great plate of brasse, or very fine metal, which stroak maketh a very great sound; this stroak or parcell of time they call a *Goome*, the small Pot being full they call a **Gree**, 8 **grees** make a *Par*, which *Par* (see **PUHUR**) is three hours by our accompt."—*W. Bruton*, in *Hakl.* v. 51.

1709.—"Or un **gari** est une de leurs heures, mais qui est bien petite en comparaison des nôtres; car elle n'est que de vingt-neuf minutes et environ quarante-trois secondes."(?)—*Lettres Edif.* xi. 233.

1785.—"We have fixed the *Coss* at 6,000 *Guz*, which distance must be travelled by the postmen in a **Ghurry** and a half. . . . If the letters are not delivered according to this rate . . . you must flog the *Hurkârehs* belonging to you."—*Tippoo's Letters*, 215.

[1869.—Wallace describes an instrument of this kind in use on board a native vessel. "I tested it with my watch and found that it hardly varied a minute from one hour to another, nor did the motion of the vessel have any effect upon it, as the water in the bucket of course kept level."—*Wallace, Malay Archip.*, ed. 1890, p. 314.]

GINDY, s. The original of this word belongs to the Dravidian tongues; Malayāl. *kiṇḍi*; Tel. *giṇḍi*; Tam. *kinni*, from v. *kiṇu*, 'to be hollow'; and the original meaning is a basin or pot, as opposed to a flat dish. In Malabar the word is applied to a vessel resembling a coffee-pot without a handle, used to drink from. But in the Bombay dialect of H., and in Anglo-Indian usage, *giṇḍi* means a wash-hand basin of tinned copper, such as is in common use there (see under **CHILLUMCHEE**).

1561.—". . . **guindis** of gold. . . ."—*Correa, Lendas*, II. i. 218.

1582.—"After this the Capitaine Generall commanded to discharge theyr Shippes, which were taken, in the whiche was bound store of rich Merchaundize, and amongst the same these peeces following:

"Foure great **Guyndes** of silver. . . ."
Castañeda, by N. L., f. 106.

1813.—"At the English tables two servants attend after dinner, with a **gindey** and ewer, of silver or white copper."—*Forbes, Or. Mem.* ii. 397; [2nd ed. ii. 30; also i. 333].

1851.—". . . a tinned bason, called a **gendee**. . . ."—*Burton, Scinde, or the Unhappy Valley*, i. 6.

GINGALL, JINJALL, s. H. *janjāl*, 'a swivel or wall-piece'; a word of uncertain origin. [It is a corruption of the Ar. *jazā'il* (see **JUZAIL**).] It is in use with Europeans in China also.

1818.—"There is but one gun in the fort, but there is much and good sniping from matchlocks and **gingals**, and four Europeans have been wounded."—*Elphinstone, Life*, ii. 31.

1829.—"The moment the picket heard them, they fired their long **ginjalls**, which kill a mile off."—*Shipp's Mem.* iii. 40.

[1900.—"**Gingals**, or **Jingals**, are long tapering guns, six to fourteen feet in length, borne on the shoulders of two men and fired by a third. They have a stand, or tripod, reminding one of a telescope. . . ."—*Ball, Things Chinese*, 38.]

GINGELI, GINGELLY, &c. s. The common trade name for the seed and oil of *Sesamum indicum*, v. *orientale*. There is a H. [not in *Platts' Dict.*] and Mahr. form *jinjalī*, but most probably this also is a trade name introduced by the Portuguese. The word appears to be Arabic *al-juljulān*, which was pronounced in Spain *al-jonjolīn* (*Dozy* and *Engelmann*, 146-7), whence Spanish *aljonjolí*, Italian *giuggiolino*, *zerzelino*, &c., Port. *girgelim*, *zirzelim*, &c., Fr. *jugeoline*, &c., in the Philippine Islands *ajonjoli*. The proper H. name is *til*. It is the σήσαμον of Dioscorides (ii. 121), and of Theophrastus (*Hist. Plant.* i. 11). [See *Watt, Econ. Dict.* VI. ii. 510 *seqq.*]

1510.—"Much grain grows here (at Zeila) . . . oil in great quantity, made not from olives, but from **zerzalino**."—*Varthema*, 86.

1552.—"There is a great amount of **gergelim**."—*Castanheda*, 24.

[1554.—". . . oil of **Jergelim** and quoquo (**Coco**)."—*Botelho, Tombo*, 54.]

1599.—". . . Oyle of **Zezeline**, which they make of a Seed, and it is very good to eate, or to fry fish withal."—*C. Fredericke*, ii. 358.

1606.—"They performed certain anointings of the whole body, when they baptized, with oil of coco-nut, or of **gergelim**."—*Gouvea*, f. 39.

c. 1610.—"I'achetay de ce poisson frit en l'huile de **gerselin** (petite semence comme nauete dont ils font huile) qui est de tres-mauvais goust."—*Mocquet*, 232.

[1638.—Mr. Whiteway notes that "in a letter of Amra Rodriguez to the King, of Nov. 30 (India Office MSS. *Book of the Monssons*, vol. iv.), he says: 'From Masulipatam to the furthest point of the Bay of Bengal runs the coast which we call that of **Gergilim**.' They got Gingeli thence, I suppose."]

c. 1661.—"La gente più bassa adopra un' altro olio di certo seme detto **Telselin**, che è una spezie del di setamo, ed è alquanto amarognolo."—*Viag. del. P. Gio. Grueber*, in *Thevenot, Voyages Divers*.

1673.—"Dragmes de Soussamo ou graine de **Georgeline**."—App. to *Journal d'Ant. Galland*, ii. 206.

1675.—"Also much Oil of *Sesamos* or **Jujoline** is there expressed, and exported thence."—*T. Heiden, Vervaerlyke Schipbreuk*, 81.

1726.—"From Orixa are imported hither (Pulecat), with much profit, Paddy, also . . . **Gingeli**-seed Oil. . . ."—*Valentijn, Chor.* 14.

„ "An evil people, gold, a drum, a wild horse, an ill conditioned woman, sugar-cane, **Gergelim**, a Bellale (or cultivator) without foresight—all these must be wrought sorely to make them of any good."—Native Apophthegms translated in *Valentijn*, v. (*Ceylon*) 390.

1727.—"The Men are bedaubed all over with red Earth, or Vermilion, and are continually squirting **gingerly** Oyl at one another."—*A. Hamilton*, i. 128; [ed. 1744, i. 130].

1807.—"The oil chiefly used here, both for food and unguent, is that of *Sesamum*, by the English called **Gingeli**, or sweet oil."—*F. Buchanan, Mysore*, &c. i. 8.

1874.—"We know not the origin of the word **Gingeli**, which Roxburgh remarks was (as it is now) in common use among Europeans."—*Hanbury & Flückiger*, 426.

1875.—"Oils, **Jinjili** or Til. . . ."—*Table of Customs Duties, imposed on Imports into B. India*, up to 1875.

1876.—"There is good reason for believing that a considerable portion of the olive oil of commerce is but the **Jinjili**, or the ground-nut, oil of India, for besides large exports, of both oils to Europe, several thousand tons of the sesamum seed, and ground-nuts in smaller quantities, are exported annually from the south of India to France, where their oil is expressed, and finds its way into the market, as olive oil."—*Suppl. Report on Supply of Drugs to India*, by Dr. Paul, India Office, March, 1876.

GINGER, s. The root of *Zingiber officinale*, Roxb. We get this word from the Arabic *zānjabīl*, Sp. *agengibre* (*al-zānjabīl*), Port. *gingibre*, Latin *zingiber*, Ital. *zenzero*, *gengiovo*, and many other old forms.

The Skt. name is *sriñgavera*, professedly connected with *sriñga*, 'a horn,' from the antler-like form of the root. But this is probably an introduced word shaped by this imaginary etymology. Though ginger is cultivated all over India, from the Himālaya to the extreme south,* the best is grown in Malabar, and in the language of that province (Malayālam) green ginger is called *inchi* and *inchi-ver*, from *inchi*, 'root.' *Inchi* was probably in an earlier form of the language *siñchi* or *chiñchi*, as we find it in Canarese still *sūnti*, which is perhaps the true origin of the H. *sonth* for 'dry ginger,' [more usually connected with Skt. *sunthi*, *sunth*, 'to dry'].

It would appear that the Arabs, misled by the form of the name, attributed *zānjabīl* or *zinjabīl*, or ginger, to the coast of *Zinj* or Zanzibar; for it would seem to be ginger which some Arabic writers speak of as 'the plant of Zinj.' Thus a poet quoted by Kazwīnī enumerates among the products of India the *shajr al-Zānij* or *Arbor Zingitana*, along with shisham-wood, pepper, steel, &c. (see *Gildemeister*, 218). And Abulfeda says also: "At Melinda is found the plant of Zinj" (*Geog.* by *Reinaud*, i. 257). In Marino Sanudo's map of the world also (c. 1320) we find a rubric connecting *Zinziber* with *Zinj*. We do not indeed find ginger spoken of as a product of eastern continental Africa, though Barbosa says a large quantity was produced in Madagascar, and Varthema says the like of the Comoro Islands.

* "Rheede says: 'Etiam in sylvis et desertis reperitur' (*Hort. Mal.* xi. 10). But I am not aware of any botanist having found it wild. I suspect that no one has looked for it."—*Sir J. D. Hooker.*

c. A.D. 65.—"Ginger (Ζιγγίβερις) is a special kind of plant produced for the most part in Troglodytic Arabia, where they use the green plant in many ways, as we do rue (πήγανον), boiling it and mixing it with drinks and stews. The roots are small, like those of *cyperus*, whitish, and peppery to the taste and smell. . . ."—*Dioscorides*, ii. cap. 189.

c. A.D. 70.—"This pepper of all kinds is most biting and sharpe. . . . The blacke is more kindly and pleasant. . . . Many have taken Ginger (which some call Zimbiperi and others **Zingiberi**) for the root of that tree; but it is not so, although in tast it somewhat resembleth pepper. . . . A pound of **Ginger** is commonly sold at Rome for 6 deniers. . . ."—*Pliny*, by *Ph. Holland*, xii. 7.

c. 620-30.—"And therein shall they be given to drink a cup of wine, mixed with the water of **Zenjebil**. . . ."—*The Koran*, ch. lxxvi. (by *Sale*).

c. 940.—"Andalusia possesses considerable silver and quicksilver mines. . . . They export from it also saffron, and roots of ginger (? *'arūḳ al-***zanjabīl**)."—*Maṣ'ūdi*, i. 367.

1298.—"Good ginger (**gengibre**) also grows here (at Coilum—see **QUILON**), and it is known by the same name of *Coilumin*, after the country."—*Marco Polo*, Bk. III. ch. 22.

c. 1343.—"Giengiovo si è di piu maniere, cioe *belledi* (see **COUNTRY**), e *colombino*, e *micchino*, e detti nomi portano per le contrade, onde sono nati ispezialmente il *colombino* e il *micchino*, che primieramente il belledi nasce in molte contrade dell' India, e il colombino nasce nel Isola del Colombo d' India, ed ha la scorza sua piana, e delicata, e cenerognola; e il micchino viene dalle contrade del Mecca . . . e ragiona che il buono giengiovo dura buono 10 anni," &c.—*Pegolotti*, in *Della Decima*, iii. 361.

c. 1420.—"His in regionibus (Malabar) **gingiber** oritur, quod *belledi* (see **COUNTRY**), *gebeli* et *neli** vulgo appellatur. Radices sunt arborum duorum cubitorum altitudine, foliis magnis instar enulae (elecampane), duro cortice, veluti arundinum radices, quae fructum tegunt; ex eis extrahitur gingiber, quod immistum cineri, ad solemque expositum, triduo exsiccatur."—*N. Conti*, in *Poggio*.

1580.—In a list of drugs sold at Ormuz we find **Zenzeri** da buli (presumably from **Dabul.**)
,, mordaci
,, Mecchini
,, beledi
Zenzero condito in giaga (preserved in **Jaggery**?)—*Gasparo Balbi*, f. 54.

GINGERLY, s. A coin mentioned as passing in Arabian ports by *Milburn* (i. 87, 91). Its country and proper name are doubtful. [The following quotations show that **Gingerlee** or **Gergelin** was a name for part of the E. coast of India, and Mr. Whiteway (see **GINGELI**) conjectures that it was so called because the oil was produced there.] But this throws no light on the gold coin of Milburn.

1680-81.—"The form of the pass given to ships and vessels, and Register of Passes given (18 in all), bound to Jafnapatam, Manilla, Mocha, **Gingerlee**, Tenasserim, &c."—*Fort St. Geo. Cons. Notes and Exts.*, App. No. iii. p. 47.

1701.—The *Carte Marine depuis Suratte jusqu'au Detroit de Malaca*, par le R. Père P. P. Tachard, shows the coast tract between *Vesegapatam* and *Iagrenate* as **Gergelin.**

1753.—"Some authors give the Coast between the points of Devi and Gaudewari, the name of the Coast of **Gergelin**. The Portuguese give the name of **Gergelim** to the plant which the Indians call *Ellu*, from which they extract a kind of oil."—*D'Anville*, 134.

[Mr. Pringle (*Diary Fort St. Geo.* 1st ser. iii. 170) identifies the *Gingerly* Factory with Vizagapatam. See also i. 109; ii. 99.]

* *Gebeli*, Ar. "of the hills." *Neli* is also read *dely*, probably for *d'Ely* (see **DELY, MOUNT**). The Ely ginger is mentioned by Barbosa (p. 220).

GINGHAM, s. A kind of stuff, defined in the *Draper's Dictionary* as made from cotton yarn dyed before being woven. The Indian ginghams were apparently sometimes of cotton mixt with some other material. The origin of this word is obscure, and has been the subject of many suggestions. Though it has long passed into the English language, it is on the whole most probable that, like **chintz** and **calico**, the term was one originating in the Indian trade.

We find it hardly possible to accept the derivation, given by Littré, from "*Guingamp*, ville de Bretagne, où il y a des fabriques de tissus." This is also alleged, indeed, in the *Encycl. Britannica*, 8th ed., which states, under the name of Guingamp, that there are in that town manufactures of *ginghams*, to which the town gives its name. [So also in 9th ed.] We may observe that the productions of Guingamp, and of the Côtes-du-Nord generally, are of *linen*, a manufacture dating from the 15th century. If it could be shown that *gingham* was either originally applied to linen fabrics, or that the word occurs before the Indian trade began, we should be more willing to admit the French etymology as possible.

The *Penny Cyclopaedia* suggests a derivation from *guingois*, 'awry.' "The variegated, striped, and crossed patterns may have suggested the name."

'Civilis,' a correspondent of *Notes and Queries* (5 ser. ii. 366, iii. 30) assigns the word to an Indian term, *ginghām*, a stuff which he alleges to be in universal use by Hindu women, and a name which he constantly found, when in judicial employment in Upper India, to be used in inventories of stolen property and the like. He mentions also that in Sir G. Wilkinson's *Egypt*, the word is assigned to an Egyptian origin. The alleged Hind. word is unknown to us and to the dictionaries; if used as 'Civilis' believes, it was almost certainly borrowed from the English term.

It is likely enough that the word came from the Archipelago. Jansz's *Javanese Dict.* gives "*ginggang*, a sort of striped or chequered East Indian *lijnwand*," the last word being applied to cotton as well as linen stuffs, equivalent to French *toile*. The verb *ginggang* in Javanese is given as meaning 'to separate, to go away,' but this seems to throw no light on the matter; nor can we connect the name with that of a place on the northern coast of Sumatra, a little E. of Acheen, which we have seen written *Gingham* (see *Bennett's Wanderings*, ii. 5, 6; also *Elmore, Directory to India and China Seas*, 1802, pp. 63-64). This place appears prominently as *Gingion* in a chart by W. Herbert, 1752. Finally, Bluteau gives the following:—"**Guingam.** So in some parts of the kingdom (Portugal) they call the excrement of the Silkworm, *Bombicis excrementum.* **Guingão.** A certain stuff which is made in the territories of the Mogul. *Beirames*, **guingoens**, *Canequis*, &c. (*Godinho, Viagam da India*, 44)." Wilson gives *kindan* as the Tamil equivalent of *gingham*, and perhaps intends to suggest that it is the original of this word. The *Tamil Dict.* gives "*kindan*, a kind of coarse cotton cloth, striped or chequered." [The *Madras Gloss.* gives Can. *ginta*, Tel. *gintena*, Tam. *kindan*, with the meaning of "double-thread texture." The *N.E.D.*, following Scott, *Malayan Words in English*, 142 *seq.*, accepts the Javanese derivation as given above: "Malay *ginggang* . . . a striped or checkered cotton fabric known to Europeans in the East as '*gingham*.' As an adjective, the word means, both in Malay and Javanese, where it seems to be original, 'striped.' The full expression is *kāin ginggang*, 'striped cloth' (*Grashuis*). The Tamil '*kindan*, a kind of coarse cotton cloth, striped or chequered' (quoted in *Yule*), cannot be the source of the European forms, nor, I think, of the Malayan forms. It must be an independent word, or a perversion of the Malayan term." On the other hand, Prof. Skeat rejects the Eastern derivation on the ground that "no one explains the spelling. The right explanation is simply that *gingham* is an old English spelling of *Guingamp*. See the account of the 'towne of Gyngham' in the *Paston Letters*, ed. *Gairdner*, iii. 357." (8th ser. *Notes and Queries*, iv. 386.)]

c. 1567.—Cesare Federici says there were at Tana many weavers who made "*ormesini e* **gingani** di lana e di bombaso"—ginghams of wool and cotton.—*Ramusio*, iii. 387*v*.

1602.—"With these toils they got to Arakan, and took possession of two islets which stood at the entrance, where they immediately found on the beach two sacks of mouldy biscuit, and a box with some **ginghams** (*guingões*) in it."—*De Couto*, Dec. IV. liv. iv. cap. 10.

1615.—"Captain Cock is of opinion that the **ginghams**, both white and browne, which yow sent will prove a good commodity in the Kinge of Shashmahis cuntry, who is a Kinge of certaine of the most westermost ilandes of Japon . . . and hath conquered the ilandes called The Leques."—*Letter appd. to Cocks's Diary*, ii. 272.

1648.—"The principal names (of the stuffs) are these: **Gamiguins, Baftas**, *Chelas* (see **PIECE-GOODS**), *Assamanis* (*asmānī ?* sky-blues), *Madafoene, Beronis* (see **BEIRAMEE**), *Tricandias, Chittes* (see **CHINTZ**), *Langans* (see **LUNGOOTY?**), *Toffochillen* (*Tafsīla*, a gold stuff from Mecca; see **ADATI, ALLEJA**), *Dotias* (see **DHOTY**)."—*Van Twist*, 63.

1726.—In a list of cloths at Pulicat:

"*Gekeperde* **Ginggangs** (Twilled ginghams)
Ditto *Chialones* (shaloons?)"—*Valentijn*, *Chor.* 14.

Also

"Bore (?) **Gingganes** driedraad."—v. 128.

1770.—"Une centaine de balles de mouchoirs, de pagnes, et de **guingans**, d'un très beau rouge, que les Malabares fabriquent à Gaffanapatam, où ils sont établis depuis très longtemps."—*Raynal, Hist. Philos.*, ii. 15, quoted by *Littré*.

1781.—"The trade of Fort St. David's consists in longcloths of different colours, sallamporees, morees, dimities, **Ginghams**, and succatoons."—*Carraccioli's L. of Clive*, i. 5. [Mr. Whiteway points out that this is taken word for word from *Hamilton, New Account* (i. 355), who wrote 40 years before.]

,, "*Sadras* est renommé par ses **guingans**, ses toiles peintes; et *Paliacate* par ses mouchoirs."—*Sonnerat*, i. 41.

1793.—"Even the **gingham** waistcoats, which striped or plain have so long stood their ground, must, I hear, ultimately give way to the stronger **kerseymere** (q.v.)."—*Hugh Boyd, Indian Observer*, 77.

1796.—"**Guingani** are cotton stuffs of Bengal and the Coromandel coast, in which the cotton is interwoven with thread made from certain barks of trees."—*Fra Paolino, Viaggio*, p. 35.

GINGI, JINJEE, &c., n.p. Properly *Chenji*, [*Shenji*; and this from Tam. *shingi*, Skt. *sringi*, 'a hill']. A once celebrated hill-fortress in S. Arcot, 50 [44] m. N.E. of Cuddalore, 35 m. N.W. from Pondicherry, and at one time the seat of a Mahratta principality. It played an important part in the wars of the first three-quarters of the 18th century, and was held by the French from 1750 to 1761. The place is now entirely deserted.

c. 1616.—"And then they were to publish a proclamation in Negapatam, that no one was to trade at Tevenapatam, at Porto Novo, or at any other port of the Naik of **Ginja**, or of the King of Massulapatam, because these were declared enemies of the state, and all possible war should be made on them for having received among them the Hollanders. . . ."—*Bocarro*, p. 619.

1675.—"Approve the treaty with the Cawn [see **KHAN**] of **Chengie**."—*Letter from Court to Fort St. Geo.* In *Notes and Exts.*, No. i. 5.

1680.—"Advice received . . . that Santogee, a younger brother of Sevagee's, had seized upon Rougnaut Pundit, the Soobidar of **Chengy** Country, and put him in irons."—*Ibid.* No. iii. 44.

1752.—"It consists of two towns, called the Great and Little **Gingee**. . . . They are both surrounded by one wall, 3 miles in circumference, which incloses the two towns, and five mountains of ragged rock, on the summits of which are built 5 strong forts. . . . The place is inaccessible, except from the east and south-east. . . . The place was well supplied with all manner of stores, and garrisoned by 150 Europeans, and sepoys and black people in great numbers. . . ."—*Cambridge, Account of the War*, &c., 32-33.

GINSENG, s. A medical root which has an extraordinary reputation in China as a restorative, and sells there at prices ranging from 6 to 400 dollars an ounce. The plant is *Aralia Ginseng*, Benth. (N.O. *Araliaceae*). The second word represents the Chinese name *Jên-Shên*. In the literary style the drug is called simply *Shên*. And possibly *Jên*, or 'Man,' has been prefixed on account of the forked radish, man-like aspect of the root. European practitioners do not recognise its alleged virtues. That which is most valued comes from Corea, but it grows also in Mongolia and Manchuria. A kind much less esteemed, the root of *Panax quinquefolium*, L., is imported into China from America. A very closely-allied plant occurs in the Himālaya, *A. Pseudo-Ginseng*, Benth. *Ginseng* is first mentioned by Alv. Semedo (Madrid, 1642). [See *Ball, Things Chinese*, 268 *seq.*, where Dr. P. Smith seems to believe that it has some medicinal value.]

GIRAFFE, s. English, not Anglo-Indian. Fr. *girafe*, It. *giraffa*, Sp. and Port. *girafa*, old Sp. *azorafa*, and these from Ar. *al-zarāfa*, a cameleopard. The Pers. *surnāpa, zurnāpa*, seems to be a form curiously divergent of the same word, perhaps nearer the original. The older Italians sometimes make *giraffa* into *seraph*. It is not impossible that the latter word, in its biblical use, may be radically connected with *giraffe*.

The oldest mention of the animal is in the Septuagint version of Deut. xiv. 5, where the word *zămăr*, rendered in the English Bible 'chamois,' is translated καμηλοπάρδαλις; and so also in the Vulgate *camelopardalus*, [probably the 'wild goat' of the Targums, not the *giraffe* (*Encycl. Bibl.* i. 722)]. We quote some other ancient notices of the animal, before the introduction of the word before us:

c. B.C. 20.—"The animals called *camelopards* (καμηλοπαρδάλεις) present a mixture of both the animals comprehended in this appellation. In size they are smaller than camels, and shorter in the neck; but in the distinctive form of the head and eyes. In the curvature of the back again they have some resemblance to a camel; but in colour and hair, and in the length of tail, they are like panthers."—*Diodorus*, ii. 51.

c. A.D. 20.—"*Camelleopards* (καμηλοπαρδάλεις) are bred in these parts, but they do not in any respect resemble leopards, for their variegated skin is more like the streaked and spotted skin of fallow deer. The hinder quarters are so very much lower than the fore quarters, that it seems as if the animal sat upon its rump. . . . It is not, however, a wild animal, but rather like a domesticated beast; for it shows no sign of a savage disposition."—*Strabo*, Bk. XVI. iv. § 18, E.T. by *Hamilton* and *Falconer*.

c. A.D. 210.—Athenaeus, in the description which he quotes of the wonderful procession of Ptolemy Philadelphus at Alexandria, besides many other strange creatures, details 130 Ethiopic sheep, 20 of Eubœa, 12 white *koloi*, 26 Indian oxen, 8 Aethiopic, a huge white bear, 14 pardales and 16 panthers, 4 lynxes, 3 *arkēloi*, one *camèlopardalis*, 1 Ethiopic Rhinoceros.—Bk. V. cap. xxxii.

c. A.D. 520.—

"Ἔννεπέ μοι κἀκεῖνα, πολύθροος Μοῦσα λιγεῖα,
μικτὰ φύσιν θηρῶν, διχόθεν κεκερασμένα, φῦλα,
πάρδαλιν αἰολόνωτον ὁμοῦ ξυνήν τε κάμηλον.

* * * * * * *

Δειρὴ οἱ ταναὴ, στικτὸν δέμας, οὔατα βαιὰ,
ψιλὸν ὕπερθε κάρη, δολιχοὶ πόδες εὐρέα ταρσὰ,
κώλων δ' οὐκ ἴσα μέτρα, πόδες τ' οὐ πάμπαν ὁμοῖοι,
ἀλλ' οἱ πρόσθεν ἔασιν ἀρείονες, ὑστάτιοι δὲ
πολλὸν ὀλιζότεροι."—κ. τ. λ.

Oppiani Cynegetica, iii. 461 *seqq.*

c. 380.—"These also presented gifts, among which besides other things a certain species of animal, of nature both extraordinary and wonderful. In size it was equal to a camel, but the surface of its skin marked with flower-like spots. Its hinder parts and the flanks were low, and like those of a lion, but the shoulders and fore-legs and chest were much higher in proportion than the other limbs. The neck was slender, and in regard to the bulk of the rest of the body was like a swan's throat in its elongation. The head was in form like that of a camel, but in size more than twice that of a Libyan ostrich. . . . Its legs were not moved alternately, but by pairs, those on the right side being moved together, and those on the left together, first one side and then the other. . . . When this creature appeared the whole multitude was struck with astonishment, and its form suggesting a name, it got from the populace, from the most prominent features of its body, the improvised name of *camelopardalis*."—*Heliodorus, Aethiopica*, x. 27.

c. 940.—"The most common animal in those countries is the *giraffe* (**Zarāfa**) . . . some consider its origin to be a variety of the camel; others say it is owing to a union of the camel with the panther: others in short that it is a particular and distinct species, like the horse, the ass, or the ox, and not the result of any cross-breed. . . . In Persian the giraffe is called *Ushturgāo* ('camel-cow'). It used to be sent as a present from Nubia to the kings of Persia, as in later days it was sent to the Arab princes, to the first khālifs of the house of 'Abbās, and to the Wālis of Misr. . . . The origin of the giraffe has given rise to numerous discussions. It has been noticed that the panther of Nubia attains a great size, whilst the camel of that country is of low stature, with short legs," &c., &c.—*Maṣ'ūdī*, iii. 3-5.

c. 1253.—"Entre les autres joiaus que il (le Vieil de la Montagne) envoia au Roy, li envoia un oliphant de cristal mout bien fait, et une beste que l'on appelle **orafle**, de cristal aussi."—*Joinville*, ed. *de Wailly*, 250.

1271.—"In the month of Jumada II. a female giraffe in the Castle of the Hill (at Cairo) gave birth to a young one, which was nursed by a cow."—*Makrizi* (by *Quatremère*), i. pt. 2, 106.

1298.—"Mais bien ont **giraffes** assez qui naissent en leur pays."—*Marco Polo*, *Pauthier's* ed., p. 701.

1336.—"Vidi in Kadro (Cairo) animal **geraffan** nomine, in anteriori parte multum elevatum, longissimum collum habens, ita ut de tecto domus communis altitudinis comedere possit. Retro ita demissum est ut dorsum ejus manu hominis tangi possit. Non est ferox animal, sed ad modum jumenti pacificum, colore albo et rubeo pellem habens ordinatissime decoratam."—*Gul. de Boldensele*, 248-249.

1384.—"Ora racconteremo della **giraffa** che bestia ella è. La giraffa è fatta quasi come lo struzzolo, salvo che l'imbusto suo non ha penne ('just like an ostrich, except that it has no feathers on its body'!) anzi ha lana branchissima . . . ella è veramente a vedere una cosa molto contraffatta."—*Simone Sigoli, V. al Monte Sinai*, 182.

1404.—"When the ambassadors arrived in the city of Khoi, they found in it an ambassador, whom the Sultan of Babylon had sent to Timour Bey. . . . He had also with him 6 rare birds and a beast called **jornufa** . . ." (then follows a very good description).—*Clavijo*, by *Markham*, pp. 86-87.

c. 1430.—"Item, I have also been in Lesser India, which is a fine Kingdom. The capital is called Dily. In this country are many elephants, and animals called **surnasa** (for *surnafa*), which is like a stag, but is a tall animal and has a long neck, 4 fathoms in length or longer."—*Schiltberger*, Hak. Soc. 47.

1471.—"After this was brought foorthe a giraffa, which they call **Girnaffa**, a beaste as long legged as a great horse, or rather more; but the hinder legges are halfe a foote shorter than the former," &c. (The Italian in *Ramusio*, ii. f. 102, has "vna **Zirapha**, la quale essi chiamano Zirnapha ouer **Giraffa**.")—*Josafa Barbaro*, in *Venetians in Persia*, Hak. Soc. 54.

1554.—"Il ne fut onc que les grands seigneurs quelques barbares qu'ilz aient esté, n'aimassent qu'on leurs presentast les bestes d'estranges pais. Aussi en auons veu plusieurs au chasteau du Caire . . . entre lesquelles est celle qu'ilz nomment vulgairement **Zurnapa**."—*P. Belon*, f. 118. It is remarkable to find Belon adopting this Persian form in Egypt.

GIRJA, s. This is a word for a Christian church, commonly used on the Bengal side of India, from Port. *igreja*, itself a corruption of *ecclesia*. Khāfī Khān (c. 1720) speaking of the Portuguese at Hoogly, says they called their places of worship *Kalīsā* (*Elliot*, vii. 211). No doubt *Kalīsā*, as well as *igreja*, is a form of *ecclesia*, but the superficial resemblance is small, so it may be suspected that the Musulman writer was speaking from book-knowledge only.

1885.—"It is related that a certain Maulvī, celebrated for the power of his curses, was called upon by his fellow religionists to curse a certain church built by the English in close proximity to a *Masjid*. Anxious to stand well with them, and at the same time not to offend his English rulers, he got out of the difficulty by cursing the building thus:

'**Gir jā ghar! Gir jā ghar! Gir jā!**'
(*i.e.*) 'Fall down, house! Fall down, house! Fall down!' or simply
'Church-house! Church-house! Church!'"
—*W. J. D'Gruyther*, in *Panjab Notes and Queries*, ii. 125.

The word is also in use in the Indian Archipelago:

1885.—"The village (of Wai in the Moluccas) is laid out in rectangular plots. . . . One of its chief edifices is the **Gredja**, whose grandeur quite overwhelmed us; for it is far more elaborately decorated than many a rural parish church at home."—*H. O. Forbes, A Naturalist's Wanderings*, p. 294.

GOA, n.p. Properly *Gowa*, *Gova*, Mahr. *Goven*, [which the *Madras Gloss.* connects with Skt. *go*, 'a cow,' in the sense of the 'cowherd country']. The famous capital of the Portuguese dominions in India since its capture by Albuquerque in 1510. In earlier history and geography the place appears under the name of **Sindābūr** or **Sandābūr** (Sundāpūr?) (q.v.). *Govā* or *Kuva* was an ancient name of the southern Konkan (see in *H. H. Wilson's Works, Vishnu Purana*, ii. 164, note 20). We find the place called by the Turkish admiral Sidi 'Ali **Gowai**-*Sandābūr*, which may mean "Sandābūr of Gova."

1391.—In a copper grant of this date (S. 1313) we have mention of a chief city of Kankan (see **CONCAN**) called **Gowa** and **Gowāpūra**. See the grant as published by Major Legrand Jacob in *J. Bo. Br. R. As. Soc.* iv. 107. The translation is too loose to make it worth while to transcribe a quotation; but it is interesting as mentioning the reconquest of Goa from the *Turushkas*, *i.e.* Turks or foreign Mahommedans. We know from Ibn Batuta that Mahommedan settlers at Hunāwar had taken the place about 1344.

1510 (but referring to some years earlier). "I departed from the city of Dabuli aforesaid, and went to another island which is about a mile distant from the mainland and is called **Goga**. . . . In this island there is a fortress near the sea, walled round after our manner, in which there is sometimes a captain who is called Savaiu, who has 400 mamelukes, he himself being also a mameluke."—*Varthema*, 115-116.

c. 1520.—"In the Island of *Tissoury*, in which is situated the city of **Goa**, there are 31 **aldeas**, and these are as follows. . . ."—In *Archiv. Port. Orient.*, fasc. 5.

c. 1554.—"At these words (addressed by the Vizir of Guzerat to a Portuguese Envoy) my wrath broke out, and I said: 'Malediction! You have found me with my fleet gone to wreck, but please God in his mercy, before long, under favour of the Pādshāh, you shall be driven not only from Hormuz, but from Diu and **Gowa** too!'"—*Sidi 'Ali Kapudān*, in *J. Asiat.* Ser. I. tom. ix. 70.

1602.—"The island of **Goa** is so old a place that one finds nothing in the writings of the Canaras (to whom it always belonged) about the beginning of its population. But we find that it was always so frequented by strangers that they used to have a proverbial saying: 'Let us go and take our ease among the cool shades of **Goe** *moat*,' which in the old language of the country means 'the cool fertile land.'"—*Couto*, IV. x. cap. 4.

1648.—"All those that have seen *Europe* and *Asia* agree with me that the Port of **Goa**, the Port of *Constantinople*, and the Port of *Toulon*, are three of the fairest Ports of all our vast continent."—*Tavernier*, E.T. ii. 74; [ed. *Ball*, i. 186].

GOA PLUM. The fruit of *Parinarium excelsum*, introduced at Goa from Mozambique, called by the Portuguese *Matomba*. "The fruit is almost pure brown sugar in a paste" (*Birdwood, MS.*).

GOA POTATO. *Dioscorea aculeata* (*Birdwood, MS.*).

GOA POWDER. This medicine, which in India is procured from Goa only, is invaluable in the virulent eczema of Bombay, and other skin diseases. In eczema it sometimes acts like magic, but smarts like the cutting of a knife. It is obtained from *Andira Araroba* (N.O. *Leguminosae*), a native (we believe) of S. America. The active principle is Chrysophanic acid (*Commn. from Sir G. Birdwood*).

GOA STONE. A factitious article which was in great repute for medical virtues in the 17th century. See quotation below from Mr. King. Sir G. Birdwood tells us it is still sold in the Bombay Bazar.

1673.—"The *Paulistines* enjoy the biggest of all the Monasteries at St. Roch; in it is a Library, an Hospital, and an Apothecary's Shop well furnished with Medicines, where *Gasper Antonio*, a Florentine, a Lay-Brother of the Order, the Author of the **Goa-Stones**, brings them in 50,000 *Xerephins*, by that invention Annually; he is an Old Man, and almost Blind."—*Fryer*, 149-150.

1690.—"The double excellence of this Stone (snake-stone) recommends its worth very highly . . . and much excels the deservedly famed *Gaspar Antoni*, or **Goa Stone**."—*Ovington*, 262.

1711.—"**Goa Stones** or *Pedra de Gasper Antonio*, are made by the Jesuits here: They are from ¼ to 8 Ounces each; but the Sise makes no Difference in the Price: We bought 11 Ounces for 20 *Rupees*. They are often counterfeited, but 'tis an easie Matter for one who has seen the right Sort, to discover it. . . . *Manooch's* Stones at Fort St. George come the nearest to them . . . both Sorts are deservedly cried up for their Vertues."—*Lockyer*, 268.

1768-71.—"Their medicines are mostly such as are produced in the country. Amongst others, they make use of a kind of little artificial stone, that is manufactured at **Goa**, and possesses a strong aromatic scent. They give scrapings of this, in a little water mixed with sugar, to their patients."—*Stavorinus*, E.T. i. 454.

1867.—"The **Goa-Stone** was in the 16th (?) and 17th centuries as much in repute as the Bezoar, and for similar virtues . . . It is of the shape and size of a duck's egg, has a greyish metallic lustre, and though hard, is friable. The mode of employing it was to take a minute dose of the powder scraped from it in one's drink every morning . . . So precious was it esteemed that the great usually carried it about with them in a casket of gold filigree."—*Nat. Hist. of Gems*, by *C. W. King, M.A.*, p. 256.

—**GOBANG**, s. The game introduced some years ago from Japan. The name is a corr. of Chinese *K'i-p'an*, 'checker-board.'

[1898.—"**Go**, properly *gomoku narabe*, often with little appropriateness termed 'checkers' by European writers, is the most popular of the indoor pastimes of the Japanese,—a very different affair from the simple game known to Europeans as **Goban** or **Gobang**, properly the name of the board on which **go** is played."—*Chamberlain, Things Japanese*, 3rd ed., 190 *seq.*, where a full account of the game will be found.]

GODAVERY, n.p. Skt. *Godāvarī*, 'giving kine.' Whether this name of northern etymology was a corruption of some indigenous name we know not. [The Dravidian name of the river is *Goday* (Tel. *gode*, 'limit'), of which the present name is possibly a corruption.] It is remarkable how the Godavery is ignored by writers and map-makers till a comparatively late period, with the notable exception of D. João de Castro, in a work, however, not published till **1843**. Barros, in his trace of the coasts of the Indies (Dec. I. ix. cap. 1), mentions **Gudavarij** as a place adjoining a cape of the same name (which appears in some much later charts as C. *Gordewar*), but takes no notice of the great river, so far as we are aware, in any part of his history. Linschoten also speaks of the *Punto de* **Guadovaryn**, but not of the river. Nor does his map show the latter, though showing the Kistna distinctly. The small general map of India in "*Cambridge's Acc. of the War in India*," 1761, confounds the sources of the Godavery with those of the Mahanadi (of Orissa) and carries the latter on to combine with the western rivers of the Ganges Delta. This was evidently the prevailing view until Rennell published the first edition of his *Memoir* (1783), in which he writes:

"The Godavery river, or Gonga **Godowry**, commonly called *Ganga* in European maps, and sometimes *Gang* in Indian histories, has generally been represented as the same river with that of Cattack.

"As we have no authority that I can find for supposing it, the opinion must have been taken up, on a supposition that there was no opening between the mouths of the Kistna and Mahanadee (or Cattack river) of magnitude sufficient for such a river as the Ganga" (pp. 74-75) [also *ibid.* 2nd ed. 244]. As to this error see also a quotation from D'Anville under **KEDGEREE**. It is probable that what that geographer says in his *Éclaircissemens*, p. 135, that he had no real idea of the Godavery. That name occurs in his book only as "la pointe de **Gaudewari**." This point, he says, is about E.N.E. of the "river of Narsapur," at a distance of about 12 leagues; "it is a low land, intersected by several river-arms, forming the mouths of that which the maps, esteemed to be most correct, call *Wenseron;* and the river of Narsapur is itself one of those arms, according to a MS. map in my possession." Narsaparam is the name of a taluk on the westernmost delta branch, or Vasishta Godāvarī [see *Morris, Man. of Godavery Dist.*, 193]. *Wenseron* appears on a map in Baldaeus (1672), as the name of one of the two mouths of the Eastern or Gautamī Godāvarī, entering the sea near Coringa. It is perhaps the same name as *Injaram* on that branch, where there was an English Factory for many years.

In the neat map of "Regionum Choromandel, Golconda, et Orixa," which is in Baldaeus (1672), there is no indication of it whatever except as a short inlet from the sea called **Gondewary**.

1538.—"The noblest rivers of this province (*Daquem* or Deccan) are six in number, to wit: Crusna (*Krishna*), in many places known as Hinapor, because it passes by a city of this name (*Hindapūr ?*); Bivra (read *Bima ?*); these two rivers join on the borders of the Deccan and the land of **Canara** (q.v.), and after traversing great distances enter the sea in the Oria territory; Malaprare (*Malprabha ?*); **Guodavam** (read **Guodavari**) otherwise called Gangua; Purnadi; Tapi. Of these the Malaprare enters the sea in the Oria territory, and so does the **Guodavam**; but Purnadi and Tapi enter the Gulf of Cambay at different points."—*João de Castro, Primeiro Roteiro da Costa da India*, pp. 6, 7.

c. 1590.—"Here (in Berar) are rivers in abundance; especially the Ganga of Gotam, which they also call **Godovārī**. The Ganga of Hindustan they dedicate to Mahadeo, but this Ganga to Gotam. And they tell wonderful legends of it, and pay it great adoration. It has its springs in the Sahyā Hills near Trimbak, and passing through the Wilāyat of Ahmadnagar, enters Berār and thence flows on to Tilingāna."—*Āīn-i-Akbari* (orig.) i. 476; [ed. *Jarrett*, ii. 228.] We may observe that the most easterly of the Delta branches of the Godavery is still called *Gautami*.

GODDESS, s. An absurd corruption which used to be applied by our countrymen in the old settlements in the Malay countries to the young women of the land. It is Malay *gādīs*, 'a virgin.'

c. 1772.—

"And then how strange, at night opprest
By toils, with songs you're lulled to rest;
Of rural **goddesses** the guest,
Delightful!"

W. Marsden, in *Memoirs*, 14.

1784.—"A lad at one of these entertainments, asked another his opinion of a **gaddees** who was then dancing. 'If she were plated with gold,' replied he, 'I would not take her for my concubine, much less for my wife.'"—*Marsden's H. of Sumatra*, 2nd ed., 230.

GODOWN, s. A warehouse for goods and stores; an outbuilding used for stores; a store-room. The word is in constant use in the Chinese ports as well as in India. The H. and Beng. *gudām* is apparently an adoption of the Anglo-Indian word, not its original. The word appears to have passed to the continent of India from the eastern settlements, where the Malay word **gadong** is used in the same sense of 'store-room,' but also in that of 'a house built of brick or stone.' Still the word appears to have come primarily from the South of India, where in Telugu *giḍangi*, *giḍḍangi*, in Tamil *kiḍangu*, signify 'a place where goods lie,' from *kiḍu*, 'to lie.' It appears in Singhalese also as *gudāma*. It is a fact that many common Malay and Javanese words are Tamil, or only to be explained by Tamil. Free intercourse between the Coromandel Coast and the Archipelago is very ancient, and when the Portuguese first appeared at Malacca they found there numerous settlers from S. India (see s.v. **KLING**). Bluteau gives the word as *palavra da India*, and explains it as a "logea quasi debaixo de chão" ("almost under ground"), but this is seldom the case.

[1513.—". . . in which all his rice and a **Gudam** full of mace was burned."—*Letter of F. P. Andrade to Albuquerque*, Feb. 22, India Office, MSS. *Çorpo Chronologico*, vol. I.

[1552.—"At night secretly they cleared their **Gudams**, which are rooms almost under ground, for fear of fire."—*Barros*, Dec. II. Bk. vi. ch. 3.]

1552.—". . . and ordered them to plunder many **godowns** (*gudoes*) in which there was such abundance of clove, nutmeg, mace, and sandal wood, that our people could not transport it all till they had called in the people of Malacca to complete its removal."—*Castanheda*, iii. 276-7.

1561.—". . . **Godowns** (*Gudões*), which are strong houses of stone, having the lower part built with lime."—*Correa*, II. i. 236. (The last two quotations refer to events in 1511.)

1570.—". . . but the merchants have all one house or *Magazon*, which house they call **Godon**, which is made of brickes."—*Caesar Frederike*, in *Hakl.*

1585.—"In the Palace of the King (at Pegu) are many magazines both of gold and of silver. . . . Sandalwood, and lign-aloes, and all such things, have their *gottons* (**gottoni**), which is as much as to say separate chambers."—*Gasparo Balbi*, f. 111.

[c. 1612.—". . . if I did not he would take away from me the key of the **gadong**."—*Danvers*, *Letters*, i. 195.]

1613.—"As fortelezas e fortificações de Malayos ordinariamente erão aedifficios de matte entaypado, de que havia muytas casas e armenyas ou **godoens** que são aedifficios sobterraneos, em que os mercadores recolhem as roupas de Choromandel per il perigo de fogo."—*Godinho de Eredia*, 22.

1615.—"We paid Jno. Dono 70 *taies* or plate of bars in full payment of the fee symple of the **gadonge** over the way, to westward of English howse, whereof 100 *taies* was paid before."—*Cocks's Diary*, i. 39; [in i. 15 **gedonge**].

[,, "An old ruined brick house or **godung**."—*Foster*, *Letters*, iii. 109.

[,, "The same goods to be locked up in the **gaddones**."—*Ibid.* iii. 159.]

1634.—

"Virão das ruas as secretas minas
* * * * *
Das abrazadas casas as ruinas,
E das riquezas os **gudões** desertos."

Malacca Conquistada, x. 61.

1680.—"Rent Rowle of Dwelling Houses, **Goedowns**, etc., within the Garrison in Christian Town."—In *Wheeler*, i. 253-4.

1683.—"I went to ye Bankshall to mark out and appoint a Plat of ground to build a **Godown** for ye Honble. Company's Salt Petre."—*Hedges*, *Diary*, March 5; [Hak. Soc. i. 67].

1696.—"Monday, 3rd August. The Choultry Justices having produced examinations taken by them concerning the murder of a child in the Black town, and the robbing of a **godown** within the walls:—it is ordered that the Judge-Advocate do cause a session to be held on Tuesday the 11th for the trial of the criminals."—*Official Memorandum*, in *Wheeler*, i. 303.

[1800.—"The cook-room and **Zodoun** at the Laul Baug are covered in."—*Wellington*, i. 66.]

1809.—"The Black Hole is now part of a **godown** or warehouse: it was filled with goods, and I could not see it."—*Ld. Valentia*, i. 237.

1880.—"These '**Godowns**' . . . are one of the most marked features of a Japanese town, both because they are white where all else is gray, and because they are solid where all else is perishable."—*Miss Bird's Japan*, i. 264.

GOGLET, GUGLET. s. A water-bottle, usually earthenware, of globular body with a long neck, the same as what is called in Bengal more commonly a *surāhī* (see **SERAI, b., KOOZA**). This is the usual form now; the article described by Linschoten and Pyrard, with a sort of cullender mouth and pebbles shut inside, was somewhat different. Corrupted from the Port. *gorgoleta*, the name of such a vessel. The French have also in this sense *gargoulette*, and a word *gargouille*, our medieval *gurgoyle*; all derivations from *gorga*, *garga*, *gorge*, 'the throat,' found in all the Romance tongues. *Tom Cringle* shows that the word is used in the W. Indies.

1598.—"These cruses are called **Gorgoletta**."—*Linschoten*, 60; [Hak. Soc. i. 207].

1599.—In *Debry*, vii. 28, the word is written **Gorgolane**.

c. 1610.—"Il y a une pièce de terre fort delicate, et toute percée de petits trous façonnez, et au dedans y a de petites pierres qui ne peuvent sortir, c'est pour nettoyer le vase. Ils appellent cela **gargoulette**: l'eau n'en sorte que peu à la fois."—*Pyrard de Laval*, ii. 43; [Hak Soc. ii. 74, and see i. 329].

[1616.—". . . 6 **Gorgoletts**."—*Foster, Letters*, iv. 198.]

1648.—"They all drink out of **Gorgelanes**, that is out of a Pot with a Spout, without setting the Mouth thereto."—*T. Van Spilbergen's Voyage*, 37.

c. 1670.—"Quand on est à la maison on a des **Gourgoulettes** ou aiguières d'une certaine pierre poreuse."—*Bernier* (ed. Amst.), ii. 214; [and comp. ed. *Constable*, 356].

1688.—"L'on donne à chacun de ceux que leur malheur conduit dans ces saintes prisons, un pot de terre plein d'eau pour se laver, un autre plus propre de ceux qu'on appelle **Gurguleta**, aussi plein d'eau pour boire."—*Dellon, Rel. de l'Inquisition de Goa*, 135.

c. 1690.—"The Siamese, Malays, and Macassar people have the art of making from the larger coco-nut shells most elegant drinking vessels, cups, and those other receptacles for water to drink called **Gorgelette**, which they set with silver, and which no doubt by the ignorant are supposed to be made of the precious Maldive cocos."—*Rumphius*, I. iii.

1698.—"The same way they have of cooling their Liquors, by a wet cloth wrapped about their **Gurgulets** and Jars, which are vessels made of a porous Kind of Earth."—*Fryer*, 47.

1726.—"However, they were much astonished that the water in the **Gorgolets** in that tremendous heat, especially out of doors, was found quite cold."—*Valentijn, Choro.* 59.

1766.—"I perfectly remember having said that it would not be amiss for General Carnac to have a man with a **Goglet** of water ready to pour on his head, whenever he should begin to grow warm in debate."—*Lord Clive, Consn. Fort William*, Jan. 29. In *Long*, 406.

1829.—"Dressing in a hurry, find the drunken bheesty . . . has mistaken your boot for the **goglet** in which you carry your water on the line of march."—*Shipp's Memoirs*, ii. 149.

c. 1830.—"I was not long in finding a bottle of very tolerable rum, some salt junk, some biscuit, and a **goglet**, or porous earthen jar of water, with some capital cigars."—*Tom Cringle*, ed. 1863, 152.

1832.—"Murwan sent for a woman named Joada, and handing her some virulent poison folded up in a piece of paper, said, 'If you can throw this into Hussun's **gugglet**, he on drinking a mouthful or two of water will instantly bring up his liver piece-meal.'"—*Herklots, Qanoon-e-Islam*, 156.

1855.—"To do it (gild the Rangoon Pagoda) they have enveloped the whole in an extraordinary scaffolding of bamboos, which looks as if they had been enclosing the pagoda in basketwork to keep it from breaking, as you would do with a water **goglet** for a *dāk* journey."—In *Blackwood's Mag.*, May, 1856.

GOGO, GOGA, n.p. A town on the inner or eastern shore of Kattywar Peninsula, formerly a seaport of some importance, with an anchorage sheltered by the Isle of Peram (the *Beiram* of the quotation from Ibn Batuta). Gogo appears in the Catalan map of 1375. Two of the extracts will show how this unhappy city used to suffer at the hands of the Portuguese. Gogo is now superseded to a great extent by Bhaunagar, 8 m. distant.

1321.—"Dated from **Caga** the 12th day of October, in the year of the Lord 1321."—*Letter of Fr. Jordanus*, in *Cathay*, &c. i. 228.

c. 1343.—"We departed from Beiram and arrived next day at the city of **Kūka**, which is large, and possesses extensive bazars. We anchored 4 miles off because of the ebb tide."—*Ibn Batuta*, iv. 60.

1531.—"The Governor (Nuno da Cunha) . . . took counsel to order a fleet to remain behind to make war upon Cambaya, leaving Antonio de Saldanha with 50 sail, to wit: 4 galeons, and the rest galleys and galeots, and rowing-vessels of the King's, with some private ones eager to remain, in the greed for prize. And in this fleet there stayed 1000 men with good will for the plunder before them, and many honoured gentlemen and captains. And running up the Gulf they came to a city called **Goga**, peopled by rich merchants; and the fleet entering by the river ravaged it by fire and sword, slaying much people. . . "—*Correa*, iii. 418.

[c. 1590.—"**Ghogeh.**" See under **SURATH.**]

1602.—". . . the city of **Gogá**, which was one of the largest and most opulent in traffic, wealth and power of all those of Cambaya. . . . This city lies almost at the head of the Gulf, on the western side, spreading over a level plain, and from certain ruins of buildings still visible, seems to have been in old times a very great place, and under the dominion of certain foreigners."—*Couto*, IV. vii. cap. 5.

1614.—"The passage across from Surrate to **Goga** is very short, and so the three fleets, starting at 4 in the morning, arrived there at nightfall. . . . The next day the Portuguese returned ashore to burn the city . . . and entering the city they set fire to it in all quarters, and it began to blaze with such fury that there was burnt a great quantity of merchandize (*fazendas de porte*), which was a huge loss to the Moors. . . . After the burning of the city they abode there 3 days, both captains and soldiers content with the abundance of their booty, and the fleet stood for Dio, taking, besides the goods that were on board, many boats in tow laden with the same."—*Bocarro, Decada*, 333.

[c. 1660.—"A man on foot going by land to a small village named the **Gauges**, and from thence crossing the end of the Gulf, can go from Diu to Surat in four or five days. . . ."—*Tavernier*, ed. *Ball*, ii. 37.]

1727.—"**Goga** is a pretty large Town . . . has some Trade. . . . It has the Conveniences of a Harbour for the largest Ships, though they lie dry on soft Mud at low Water."—*A. Hamilton*, i. 143.

GOGOLLA, GOGALA, n.p. This is still the name of a village on a peninsular sandy spit of the mainland, opposite to the island and fortress of Diu, and formerly itself a fort. It was known in the 16th century as the *Villa dos Rumes*, because Melique Az (Malik Ayāz, the Mahom. Governor), not much trusting the Rumes (*i.e.* the Turkish Mercenaries), "or willing that they should be within the Fortress, sent them to dwell there." (*Barros*, II. iii. cap. 5).

1525.—"Paga **dyo** e **gogolla** a el Rey de Cambaya treze layques em tangas . . . xiij laiques."—*Lembrança*, 34.

1538.—In *Botelho, Tombo*, 230, 239, we find "Alfandegua de **Guogualaa**."

1539.—". . . terminating in a long and narrow tongue of sand, on which stands a fort which they call **Gogala**, and the Portuguese the *Villa dos Rumes.* On the point of this tongue the Portuguese made a beautiful round bulwark."—*João de Castro, Primeiro Roteiro*, p. 218.

GOLAH, s. Hind. *golā* (from *gol*, 'round'). A store-house for grain or salt; so called from the typical form of such store-houses in many parts of India, viz. a circular wall of mud with a conical roof. [One of the most famous of these is the *Golā* at Patna, completed in 1786, but never used.]

[1785.—"We visited the **Gola**, a building intended for a public granary."—In *Forbes, Or. Mem.* 2nd ed. ii. 445.]

1810.—"The **golah**, or warehouse."—*Williamson, V. M.* ii. 343.

1878.—"The villagers, who were really in want of food, and maddened by the sight of those **golahs** stored with grain, could not resist the temptation to help themselves."—*Life in the Mofussil*, ii. 77.

GOLD MOHUR FLOWER, s. *Caesalpinia pulcherrima*, Sw. The name is a corruption of the H. *gulmor*, which is not in the dictionaries, but is said to mean 'peacock-flower.'

[1877.—"The crowd began to press to the great **Gool-mohur tree.**"—*Allardyce, City of Sunshine*, iii. 207.]

GOLE, s. The main body of an army in array; a clustered body of troops; an irregular squadron of horsemen. P.—H. *ghol;* perhaps a confusion with the Arab. *jaul* (*gaul*), 'a troop': [but Platts connects it with Skt. *kula*, 'an assemblage'].

1507.—"As the right and left are called Beranghâr and Sewanghâr . . . and are not included in the centre which they call **ghûl**, the right and left do not belong to the **ghûl**."—*Baber*, 227.

1803.—"When within reach, he fired a few rounds, on which I formed my men into two **gholes**. . . . Both **gholes** attempted to turn his flanks, but the men behaved ill, and we were repulsed."—*Skinner, Mil. Mem.* i. 298.

1849.—"About this time a large **gole** of horsemen came on towards me, and I proposed to charge; but as they turned at once from the fire of the guns, and as there was a *nullah* in front, I refrained from advancing after them."—*Brigadier Lockwood, Report of 2nd Cavalry Division at Battle of Goojerât.*

GOMASTA, GOMASHTAH, s. Hind. from Pers. *gumāshtah*, part. 'appointed, delegated.' A native agent or factor. In Madras the modern application is to a clerk for vernacular correspondence.

1747.—"As for the Salem Cloth they beg leave to defer settling any Price for that sort till they can be advised from the **Goa Masters** (!) in that Province."—*Ft. St. David Consn.*, May 11. MS. Records in India Office.

1762.—"You will direct the gentleman, **Gomastahs**, *Muttasuddies* (see **MOOTSUDDY**), and *Moonshies*, and other officers of the English Company to relinquish their farms, *taalucs* (see **TALOOK**), **gunges**, and **golahs**."—*The Nabob to the Governor*, in *Van Sittart*, i. 229.

1776.—"The Magistrate shall appoint some one person his **gomastah** or Agent in each Town."—*Halhed's Code*, 55.

1778.—"The Company determining if possible to restore their investment to the former condition . . . sent **gomastahs**, or Gentoo factors in their own pay."—*Orme*, ed. 1803, ii. 57.

c. 1785.—"I wrote an order to my **gomastah** in the factory of Hughly."—*Carraccioli's Life of Clive*, iii. 448.

1817.—"The banyan hires a species of broker, called a **Gomastah**, at so much a month."—*Mill's Hist.* iii. 13.

1837.—". . . (The Rajah) sent us a very good breakfast; when we had eaten it, his **gomashta** (a sort of secretary, at least more like that than anything else) came to say . . ."—*Letters from Madras*, 128.

GOMBROON, n.p. The old name in European documents of the place on the Persian Gulf now known as *Bandar 'Abbās*, or *'Abbāsī*. The latter name was given to it when Shāh 'Abbās, after the capture and destruction of the island city of Hormuz, established a port there. The site which he selected was the little town of **Gamrūn**. This had been occupied by the Portuguese, who took it from the 'King of Lar' in 1612, but two years later it was taken by the Shāh. The name is said (in the *Geog. Magazine*, i. 17) to be Turkish, meaning 'a Custom House.' The word alluded to is probably *gumruk*, which has that meaning, and which is again, through Low Greek, from the Latin *commercium*. But this etymology of the name seems hardly probable. That indicated in the extract from A. Hamilton below is from Pers. *ḳamrūn*, 'a shrimp,' or Port. *camarão*, meaning the same.

The first mention of Gombroon in the E. I. Papers seems to be in 1616, when Edmund Connok, the Company's chief agent in the Gulf, calls it "*Gombraun*, the best port in all Persia," and "that hopeful and glorious port of Gombroon" (*Sainsbury*, i. 484-5; [*Foster, Letters*, iv. 264]). There was an English factory here soon after the capture of Hormuz, and it continued to be maintained in 1759, when it was taken by the Comte d'Estaing. The factory was re-established, but ceased to exist a year or two after.

[1565.—"*Bamdel* **Gombruc**, so-called in Persian and Turkish, which means Customhouse."—*Mestre Afonso's Overland Journey, Ann. Maritim. e Colon.* ser. 4. p. 217.]

1614.—(The Captain-major) "under orders of Dom Luis da Gama returned to succour **Comorão**, but found the enemy's fleet already there and the fort surrendered. . . . News which was heard by Dom Luis da Gama and most of the people of Ormuz in such way as might be expected, some of the old folks of Ormuz prognosticating at once that in losing **Comorão** Ormuz itself would be lost before long, seeing that the former was like a barbican or outwork on which the rage of the Persian enemy spent itself, giving time to Ormuz to prepare against their coming thither."—*Bocarro, Decada*, 349.

1622.—"That evening, at two hours of the night, we started from below that fine tree, and after travelling about a league and a half . . . we arrived here in **Combrù**, a place of decent size and population on the sea-shore, which the Persians now-a-days, laying aside as it were the old name, call the 'Port of Abbas,' because it was wrested from the Portuguese, who formerly possessed it, in the time of the present King Abbas."—*P. della Valle*, ii. 413; [in Hak. Soc. i. 3, he calls it **Combu**].

c. 1630.—"**Gumbrown** (or *Gomroon*, as some pronounce it) is by most Persians Κατ' ἐξοχὴν cald *Bander* or the Port Towne . . . some (but I commend them not) write it *Gamrou*, others *Gomrow*, and other-some *Cummeroon*. . . . A Towne it is of no Antiquity, rising daily out of the ruines of late glorious (now most wretched) *Ormus*."—*Sir T. Herbert*, 121.

1673.—"The Sailors had stigmatized this place of its Excessive Heat, with this sarcastical Saying, *That there was but an Inch-Deal between* **Gomberoon** *and Hell*."—*Fryer*, 224.

Fryer in another place (marginal rubric, p. 331) says: "**Gombroon** ware, made of Earth, the best next China." Was this one of the sites of manufacture of the Persian porcelain now so highly prized? ["The main varieties of this Perso-Chinese ware are the following:—(1) A sort of semi-porcelain, called by English dealers, quite without reason, '*Gombroon* ware,' which is pure white and semi-transparent, but, unlike Chinese porcelain, is soft and friable where not protected by the glaze."—*Ency. Brit.* 9th ed. xix. 621.]

1727.—"This **Gombroon** was formerly a Fishing Town, and when *Shaw Abass* began to build it, had its Appellation from the Portugueze, in Derision, because it was a good place for catching Prawns and Shrimps, which they call **Camerong**."—*A. Hamilton*, i. 92; [ed. 1744, i. 93].

1762.—"As this officer (Comte d'Estaing) . . . broke his parole by taking and destroying our settlements at **Gombroon**, and upon the west Coast of Sumatra, at a time when he was still a prisoner of war, we have laid before his Majesty a true state of the case."—In *Long*, 288.

GOMUTÍ, s. Malay *gumuti* [Scott gives *gāmūti*]. A substance resembling horsehair, and forming excellent cordage (the *cabos negros* of the Portuguese —*Marre, Kata-Kata Malayou*, p. 92), sometimes improperly called **coir** (q.v.), which is produced by a palm growing in the Archipelago, *Arenga saccharifera*, Labill. (*Borassus Gomutus*, Lour.). The tree also furnishes *kalams* or reed-pens for writing, and the material for the poisoned arrows used with the blow-tube. The name of the palm itself in Malay is *anau*. (See **SAGWIRE**.) There is a very interesting account of this palm in *Rumphius, Herb. Amb.*, i. pl. xiii. Dampier speaks of the fibre thus:

1686.—". . . There is another sort of Coire cables . . . that are black, and more strong and lasting, and are made of Strings that grow like Horse-hair at the Heads of certain Trees, almost like the Coco-trees. This sort comes mostly from the Island of Timor."—i. 295.

GONG, s. This word appears to be Malay (or, according to Crawfurd, originally Javanese), *gong* or *agong*. ["The word *gong* is often said to be Chinese. Clifford and Swettenham so mark it; but no one seems to be able to point out the Chinese original" (*Scott, Malayan Words in English*, 53).] Its well-known application is to a disk of thin bell-metal, which when struck with a mallet, yields musical notes, and is used in the further east as a substitute for a bell. ["The name *gong, agong*, is considered to be imitative or suggestive of the sound which the instrument produces" (*Scott, loc. cit.* 51).] Marcel Devic says that the word exists in all the languages of the Archipelago; [for the variants see *Scott, loc. cit.*]. He defines it as meaning "instrument de musique aussi appelé *tam-tam*"; but see under **TOM-TOM**. The great drum, to which Dampier applies the name, was used like the metallic *gong* for striking the hour. Systems of *gongs* variously arranged form harmonious musical instruments among the Burmese, and still more elaborately among the Javanese.

The word is commonly applied by Anglo-Indians also to the H. *ghanṭā* (*ganṭa*, Dec.) or *gharī*, a thicker metal disc, not musical, used in India for striking the hour (see **GHURRY**). The *gong* being used to strike the hour, we find the word applied by Fryer (like *gurry*) to the hour itself, or interval denoted.

c. 1590.—"In the morning before day the Generall did strike his **Gongo**, which is an instrument of War that soundeth like a Bell."—(This was in Africa, near Benguela). *Advent. of Andrew Battel*, in *Purchas*, ii. 970.

1673.—"They have no Watches nor Hour-Glasses, but measure Time by the dropping of Water out of a Brass Bason, which holds a **Ghong**, or less than half an Hour; when they strike once distinctly, to tell them it's the First **Ghong**, which is renewed at the Second **Ghong** for Two, and so Three at the End of it till they come to Eight; when they strike on the Brass Vessel at their liberty to give notice the *Pore* (see **PUHUR**) is out, and at last strike One leisurely to tell them it is the First *Pore*."—*Fryer*, 186.

1686. — "In the Sultan's Mosque (at Mindanao) there is a great Drum with but one Head, called a **Gong**; which is instead of a Clock. This **Gong** is beaten at 12 a Clock, at 3, 6, and 9."—*Dampier*, i. 333.

1726.—"These **gongs** (gongen) are beaten very gently at the time when the Prince is going to make his appearance."—*Valentijn*, iv. 58.

1750-52.—"Besides these (in China) they have little drums, great and small kettle drums, **gungungs** or round brass basons like frying pans."—*Olof Toreen*, 248.

1817.—
"War music bursting out from time to time
With **gong** and tymbalon's tremendous chime."—*Lalla Rookh, Mokanna.*

Tremendous sham poetry!

1878.—". . . le nom plébéien . . . sonna dans les salons. . . . Comme un coup de cymbale, un de ces **gongs** qui sur les théâtres de féerie annoncent les apparitions fantastiques."—*Alph. Daudet, Le Nabab*, ch. 4.

GOODRY, s. A quilt; H. *gudrī*. [The *gudṛī*, as distinguished from the *razāi* (see **ROZYE**), is the bundle of rags on which Faḳīrs and the very poorest people sleep.]

1598.—"They make also faire couerlits, which they call **Godoriins** [or] Colchas, which are very faire and pleasant to the eye, stitched with silke; and also of cotton of all colours and stitchinges."—*Linschoten*, ch. 9; [Hak. Soc. i. 61].

c. 1610.—"Les matelats et les couvertures sont de soye ou de toille de coton façonnée à toutes sortes de figures et couleur. Ils appellent cela **Gouldrins**."—*Pyrard de Laval*, ii. 3; [Hak. Soc. ii. 4].

1653.—"**Goudrin** est vn terme Indou et Portugais, qui signifie des couuertures picquées de cotton."—*De la Boullaye-le-Gouz*, ed. 1657, p. 539.

[1819.—"He directed him to go to his place, and take a **godhra** of his (a kind of old patched counterpane of shreds, which Fuqueers frequently have to lie down upon and throw over their shoulders)."—*Tr. Lit. Soc. Bo.* i. 113.]

GOOGUL, s. H. *gugal, guggul*, Skt. *guggula, guggulu*. The aromatic gum-resin of the *Balsamodendron Mukul*, Hooker (*Amyris agallocha*, Roxb.), the *muḳl* of the Arabs, and generally supposed to be the **bdellium** of the ancients. It is imported from the Beyla territory, west of Sind (see *Bo. Govt. Selections* (N.S.), No. xvii. p. 326).

1525.—(Prices at Cambay). "**Gugall** d'orumuz (the maund), 16 *fedeas*."—*Lembrança*, 43.

1813.—"**Gogul** is a species of bitumen much used at Bombay and other parts of India, for painting the bottom of ships."—*Milburn*, i. 137.

GOOJUR, n.p. H. *Gūjar*, Skt. *Gurjjara*. The name of a great Hindu clan, very numerous in tribes and in population over nearly the whole of Northern India, from the Indus to Rohilkhand. In the Delhi territory and the Doab they were formerly notorious for thieving propensities, and are still much addicted to cattle-theft; and they are never such steady and industrious cultivators as the *Jāts*, among whose villages they are so largely interspersed. In the Punjab they are Mahommedans. Their extensive diffusion is illustrated by their having given name to Gujarāt (see **GOOZERAT**) as well as to *Gujrāt* and *Gujrānwāla* in the Punjab. And during the 18th century a great part of Sahāranpūr District in the Northern Doab was also called *Gujrāt* (see *Elliot's Races*, by *Beames*, i. 99 *seqq.*).

1519.—"In the hill-country between Nilāb and Behreh . . . and adjoining to the hill-country of Kashmīr, are the Jats, **Gujers**, and many other men of similar tribes."—*Memoirs of Baber*, 259.

[1785.—"The road is infested by tribes of banditti called **googurs** and mewatties."—In *Forbes, Or. Mem.* 2nd ed. II. 426.]

GOOLAIL, s. A pellet-bow. H. *gulel*, probably from Skt. *guḍa, gula*, the pellet used. [It is the Arabic *Kaus-al-bandūk*, by using which the unlucky Prince in the First Kalandar's Tale got into trouble with the Wazīr (*Burton, Arab. Nights*, i. 98).]

1560.—Busbeck speaks of being much annoyed with the multitude and impudence of kites at Constantinople: "ego interim cum **manuali balista** post columnam sto, modo hujus, modo illius caudae vel alarum, ut casus tulerit, pinnas testaceis globis verberans, donec mortifero ictu unam aut alteram percussam decutio. . . ."—*Busbeq. Epist.* iii. p. 163.

[c. 1590.—"From the general use of pellet bows which are fitted with bowstrings, sparrows are very scarce (in Kashmir)."—*Āīn*, ed. *Jarrett*, ii. 351. In the original *kamān-i-guroha, guroha*, according to *Steingass, Dict.*, being "a ball . . . ball for a cannon, balista, or cross-bow."]

1600.—"O for a *stone-bow* to hit him in the eye."—*Twelfth Night*, ii. 5.

1611.—
"Children will shortly take him for a wall,
And set their *stone-bows* in his forehead."
Beaum. & Flet., A King and No King, V.

[1870.—"The **Gooleil-bans**, or pellet-bow, generally used as a weapon against crows, is capable of inflicting rather severe injuries."—*Chevers, Ind. Med. Jurisprudence*, 337.]

GOOLMAUL, GOOLMOOL, s. H. *gol-māl*, 'confusion, jumble'; *gol-māl karnā*, 'to make a mess.'

[1877.—"The boy has made such a **golmol** (uproar) about religion that there is a risk in having anything to do with him."—*Allardyce, City of Sunshine*, ii. 106.]

[**GOOMTEE**, n.p. A river of the N.W.P., rising in the Shāhjahānpur District, and flowing past the cities of Lucknow and Jaunpur, and joining the Ganges between Benares and

Ghāzipur. The popular derivation of the name, as in the quotation, is, as if *Ghūmtī*, from H. *ghūmnā*, 'to wind,' in allusion to its winding course. It is really from Skt. *gomati*, 'rich in cattle.'

[1848.—"The **Ghumti**, which takes its name from its windings . . ."—*Buyers, Recoll. of N. India*, 240.]

GOONT, s. H. *gūnth*, *gūṭh*. A kind of pony of the N. Himālayas, strong but clumsy.

c. 1590.—"In the northern mountainous districts of Hindustan a kind of small but strong horses is bred, which is called **gut**; and in the confines of Bengal, near Kúch, another kind of horses occurs, which rank between the *gut* and Turkish horses, and are called *tánghan* (see **TANGUN**); they are strong and powerful."—*Āīn*, i. 133; [also see ii. 280].

1609.—"On the further side of *Ganges* lyeth a very mighty Prince, called *Raiaw Rodorow*, holding a mountainous Countrey . . . thence commeth much Muske, and heere is a great breed of a small kind of Horse, called **Gunts**, a true travelling scale-cliffe beast."—*W. Finch*, in *Purchas*, i. 438.

1831.—"In Cashmere I shall buy, without regard to price, the best **ghounte** in Tibet."—*Jacquemont's Letters*, E.T. i. 238.

1838.—"Give your **gūnth** his head and he will carry you safely . . . any horse would have struggled, and been killed; these **gūnths** appear to understand that they must be quiet, and their master will help them."—*Fanny Parkes, Wanderings of a Pilgrim*, ii. 226.

GOORKA, GOORKALLY, n.p. H. *Gurkhā*, *Gurkhālī*. The name of the race now dominant in Nepāl, and taking their name from a town so called 53 miles W. of Khatmandu. [The name is usually derived from the Skt. *go-raksha*, 'cow-keeper.' For the early history see *Wright, H. of Nepāl*, 147]. They are probably the best soldiers of modern India, and several regiments of the Anglo-Indian army are recruited from the tribe.

1767.—"I believe, Sir, you have before been acquainted with the situation of Nīpal, which has long been besieged by the **Goorcully** Rajah."—*Letter from Chief at Patna*, in *Long*, 526.

[,, "The Rajah being now dispossessed of his country, and shut up in his capital by the Rajah of **Goercullah**, the usual channel of commerce has been obstructed."—*Letter from Council to E.I. Co.*, in *Verelst, View of Bengal*, App. 36.]

GOOROO, s. H. *gurū*, Skt. *guru*; a spiritual teacher, a (Hindu) priest.

(Ancient).—"That brahman is called **guru** who performs according to rule the rites on conception and the like, and feeds (the child) with rice (for the first time)."—*Manu*, ii. 142.

c. 1550.—"You should do as you are told by your parents and your **Guru**."—*Rāmāyana* of Tulsī Dās, by *Growse* (1878), 43.

[1567.—"**Grous**." See quotation under **CASIS**.]

1626.—"There was a famous Prophet of the Ethnikes, named **Goru**."—*Purchas, Pilgrimage*, 520.

1700.—". . . je suis fort surpris de voir à la porte . . . le Pénitent au colier, qui demandoit à parler au **Gourou**."—*Lettres Edif.*, x. 95.

1810.—"Persons of this class often keep little schools . . . and then are designated **gooroos**; a term implying that kind of respect we entertain for pastors in general."—*Williamson, V. M.* ii. 317.

1822.—"The Adventures of the **Gooroo** Paramartan; a tale in the Tamul Language" (translated by B. Babington from the original of Padre Beschi, written about 1720-1730), London.

1867.—"Except the **guru** of Bombay, no priest on earth has so large a power of acting on every weakness of the female heart as a Mormon bishop at Salt Lake."—*Dixon's New America*, 330.

GOORUL, s. H. *gūral*, *goral*; the Himālayan chamois; *Nemorhoedus Goral* of Jerdon. [*Cemas Goral* of Blanford (*Mammalia*, 516).]

[1821.—"The flesh was good and tasted like that of the **ghorul**, so abundant in the hilly belt towards India."—*Lloyd & Gerard's Narr.*, ii. 112.

[1886.—"On Tuesday we went to a new part of the hill to shoot '**gurel**,' a kind of deer, which across a khud, looks remarkably small and more like a hare than a deer."—*Lady Dufferin, Viceregal Life*, 235.]

[**GOORZEBURDAR**, s. P. *gurz-bardār*, 'a mace-bearer.'

[1663.—"Among the Kours and the Mansebdars are mixed many **Gourze-berdars**, or mace-bearers chosen for their tall and handsome persons, and whose business it is to preserve order in assemblies, to carry the King's orders, and execute his commands with the utmost speed."—*Bernier*, ed. *Constable*, 267.

[1717.—"Everything being prepared for the **Goorzeburdar's** reception."—In *Yule, Hedges' Diary*, Hak. Soc. ii. ccclix.

[1727.—"**Goosberdar**. See under **HOSBOLHOOKUM**.]

GOOZERAT, GUZERAT, n.p. The name of a famous province in Western India, Skt. *Gurjjara, Gurjjara-rāshtra*, Prakrit passing into H. and Mahr. *Gujarāt, Gujrāt*, taking its name from the Gūjar (see **GOOJUR**) tribe. The name covers the British Districts of Surat, Broach, Kaira, Panch Mahals, and Ahmedābād, besides the territories of the Gaekwar (see **GUICOWAR**) of Baroda, and a multitude of native States. It is also often used as including the peninsula of Kāthiāwāṛ or Surāshtra, which alone embraces 180 petty States.

c. 640.—Hwen T'sang passes through *Kiu-chi-lo, i.e.* **Gurjjara**, but there is some difficulty as to the position which he assigns to it.—*Pèlerins Bouddh.*, iii. 166; [*Çunningham, Arch. Rep.* ii. 70 *seqq.*].

1298.—"**Gozurat** is a great Kingdom. . . . The people are the most desperate pirates in existence. . . ."—*Marco Polo*, Bk. iii. ch. 26.

c. 1300.—"**Guzerat**, which is a large country, within which are Kambáy, Somnát, Kanken-Tána, and several other cities and towns."—*Rashiduddín*, in *Elliot*, i. 67.

1300.—"The Sultan despatched Ulugh Khán to Ma'bar and **Gujarát** for the destruction of the idol-temple of Somnát, on the 20th of Jumádá'-l awwal, 698 H. . . ."—*Amīr Khusrū*, in *Elliot*, iii. 74.

[c. 1330.—"**Juzrat.**" See under **LAR.**]

1554.—"At last we made the land of **Guchrát** in Hindustan."—*Sidi 'Ali*, p. 79.

The name is sometimes used by the old writers for the people, and especially for the Hindu merchants or **banyans** (q.v.) of Guzerat. See *Sainsbury*, i. 445 and *passim*.

[c. 1605.—"And alsoe the **Guzatts** do saile in the Portugalls shipps in euery porte of the East Indies . . ."—*Birdwood, First Letter Book*, 85.]

GOOZUL-KHANA, s. A bath-room; H. from Ar.—P. *ghusl-khāna*, of corresponding sense. The apartment so called was used by some of the Great Moghuls as a place of private audience.

1616.—"At eight, after supper he comes down to the **guzelcan** (v.l. **gazelcan**), a faire Court wherein in the middest is a Throne erected of freestone."—*Sir T. Roe*, in *Purchas*, ii.; [Hak. Soc. i. 106].

" "The thirteenth, at night I went to the **Gussell Chan**, where is best opportunitie to doe business, and tooke with me the *Italian*, determining to walk no longer in darknesse, but to prooue the King. . . ."—*Ibid.* p. 543; [in Hak. Soc. i. 202, **Guzelchan**; in ii. 459, **Gushel choes**].

c. 1660.—"The grand hall of the *Am-Kas* opens into a more retired chamber, called the **gosel-kane**, or the place to wash in. But few are suffered to enter there. . . . There it is where the king is seated in a chair . . . and giveth a more particular Audience to his officers."—*Bernier*, E.T. p. 85; [ed. *Constable*, 265; *ibid.* 361 **goslekane**].

GOPURA, s. The meaning of the word in Skt. is 'city-gate,' *go* 'eye,' *pura*, 'city.' But in S. India the *gopuram* is that remarkable feature of architecture, peculiar to the Peninsula, the great pyramidal tower over the entrance-gate to the precinct of a temple. See *Fergusson's Indian and Eastern Architecture*, 325, &c. [The same feature has been reproduced in the great temple of the Seth at Brindāban, which is designed on a S. Indian model. (*Growse, Mathura*, 260).] This feature is not, in any of the S. Indian temples, older than the 15th or 16th cent., and was no doubt adopted for purposes of defence, as indeed the *Śilpa-śāstra* ('Books of Mechanical Arts') treatises imply. This fact may sufficiently dispose of the idea that the feature indicates an adoption of architecture from ancient Egypt.

1862.—"The **gopurams** or towers of the great pagoda."—*Markham, Peru and India*, 408.

GORA, s. H. *gorā*, 'fair-complexioned.' A white man; a European soldier; any European who is not a **sahib** (q.v.). Plural *gorā-lōg*, 'white people.'

[1861.—"The cavalry . . . rushed into the lines . . . declaring that the **Gora Log** (the European soldiers) were coming down upon them."—*Cave Browne, Punjab and Delhi*, i. 243.]

GORAWALLAH, s. H. *ghoṛā-wālā, ghoṛā*, 'a horse.' A groom or horsekeeper; used at Bombay. On the Bengal side **syce** (q.v.) is always used, on the Madras side **horsekeeper** (q.v.).

1680.—**Gurrials**, apparently for *ghoṛā-wālās* (*Gurrials* would be alligators, **Gavial**), are allowed with the horses kept with the Hoogly Factory.—See *Fort St. Geo. Consns. on Tour*, Dec. 12, in *Notes and Exts.*, No. ii. 63.

c. 1848.—"On approaching the different points, one knows Mrs. —— is at hand, for her **Gorahwallas** wear green and gold *puggries*."—*Chow-Chow*, i. 151.

GORAYT, s. H. *goreṭ, goraiṭ*, [which has been connected with Skt. *ghur*, 'to shout']; a village watchman and messenger, [in the N.W.P. usually of a lower grade than the **chokidar**, and not, like him, paid a cash wage, but remunerated by a piece of rent-free land; one of the village establishment, whose special duty it is to watch crops and harvested grain].

[c. 1808.—"Fifteen messengers (**gorayits**) are allowed ¼ ser on the man of grain, and from 1 to 5 bigahs of land each."—*Buchanan, Eastern India*, ii. 231.]

GORDOWER, GOORDORE, s. A kind of boat in Bengal, described by Ives as "a vessel pushed on by paddles." Etym. obscure. *Ghuṛdauṛ* is a horse-race, a race-course; sometimes used by natives to express any kind of open-air assemblage of Europeans for amusement. [The word is more probably a corr. of P. *girdāwā*, 'a patrol'; *girdāwar*, 'all around, a supervisor,' because such boats appear to be used in Bengal by officials on their tours of inspection.]

1757.—"To get two bolias (see **BOLIAH**), a **goordore**, and 87 **dandies** (q.v.) from the Nazir."—*Ives*, 157.

GOSAIN, GOSSYNE, &c. s. H. and Mahr. *Gosāīn, Gosāī, Gosāvī, Gusā'īn*, &c., from Skt. *Goswāmī*, 'Lord of Passions' (lit. 'Lord of cows'), *i.e.* one who is supposed to have subdued his passions and renounced the world. Applied in various parts of India to different kinds of persons not necessarily celibates, but professing a life of religious mendicancy, and including some who dwell together in convents under a superior, and others who engage in trade and hardly pretend to lead a religious life.

1774.—"My hopes of seeing Teshu Lama were chiefly founded on the **Gosain**."—*Bogle*, in *Markham's Tibet*, 46.

c. 1781.—"It was at this time in the hands of a **Gosine**, or Hindoo Religious."—*Hodges*, 112. (The use of this barbarism by Hodges is remarkable, common as it has become of late years.)

[1813.—"Unlike the generality of Hindoos, these **Gosaings** do not burn their dead . . ." *Forbes, Or. Mem.* 2nd ed. i. 312-3; in i. 544 he writes **Gosannee.**]

1826.—"I found a lonely cottage with a light in the window, and being attired in the habit of a **gossein**, I did not hesitate to request a lodging for the night."—*Pandurang Hari*, 399; [ed. 1873, ii. 275].

GOSBECK, COSBEAGUE, s. A coin spoken of in Persia (at Gombroon and elsewhere). From the quotation from Fryer it appears that there was a *Goss* and a *Gosbegi*, corresponding to Herbert's double and single *Cozbeg*. Mr. Wollaston in his *English-Persian Dict.* App. p. 436, among "Moneys now current in Persia," gives "5 *dīnār* =1 **ghāz**; also a nominal money." The *ghāz*, then, is the name of a coin (though a coin no longer), and **ghāz-begī** was that worth 10 *dīnārs*. Marsden mentions a copper coin, called *kazbegi*=50 (nominal) *dīnārs*, or about 3½*d.* (*Numism. Orient.*, 456.) But the value in *dīnārs* seems to be in error. [Prof. Browne, who referred the matter to M. Husayn Kuli Khān, Secretary of the Persian Embassy in London, writes: "This gentleman states that he knows no word *ghāzī-beg*, or *gāzī-beg*, but that there was formerly a coin called *ghāz*, of which 5 went to the *shāhī*; but this is no longer used or spoken of." The *ghāz* was in use at any rate as late as the time of Hajji Baba; see below.]

[1615.—"The chiefest money that is current in Persia is the *Abase*, which weigheth 2 *metzicales*. The second is the *mamede*, which is half an *abesse*. The third is the *shahey* and is a quarter of an *abbesse*. In the *rial* of eight are 13 *shayes*. In the *cheken* of Venetia 20 *shayes*. In a *shaye* are 2½ *bisties* or **casbeges** 10. One *bistey* is 4 **casbeges** or 2 *tanges*. The *Abasse*, *momede* and *Shahey* and *bistey* are of silver; the rest are of copper like to the *pissas* of India."—*Foster, Letters*, iii. 176.]

c. 1630.—"The *Abbasee* is in our money sixteene pence; *Larree* ten pence; *Mamoodee* eight pence; *Bistee* two pence; double **Cozbeg** one penny; single **Cozbeg** one half-penny; *Fluces* are ten to a **Cozbeg**."—*Sir T. Herbert*, ed. 1638, p. 231.

1673.—"A Banyan that seemingly is not worth a **Gosbeck** (the lowest coin they have)."—*Fryer*, 113. See also p. 343.

" "10 **cosbeagues** is 1 Shahee; 4 Shahees is one Abassee or 16*d.*"—*Ibid.* 211.

" "Brass money with characters,
Are a **Goss**, ten whereof compose a Shahee,
A **Gosbeege**, five of which go to a Shahee."
Ibid. 407.

1711.—"10 **Coz**, or *Pice*, a Copper Coin, are 1 Shahee."—*Lockyer*, 241.

1727.—"1 *Shahee* is . . . 10 **Gaaz** or **Cosbegs**."—*A. Hamilton*, ii. 311; [ed. 1744].

1752.—"10 **cozbaugues** or Pice (a Copper Coin) are 1 Shatree" (read *Shahee*).—*Brooks*, p. 37. See also in *Hanway*, vol. i. p. 292, **Kazbegie**; [in ii. 21, **Kazbekie**].

[1824.—"But whatever profit arose either from these services, or from the spoils of my monkey, he alone was the gainer, for I never touched a **ghauz** of it."—*Hajji Baba*, 52 *seq.*]

1825.—"A toman contains 100 mamoodies; a new abassee, 2 mamoodies or 4 shakees . . . a shakee, 10 **coz** or **cozbaugues**, a small copper coin."—*Milburn*, 2nd ed. p. 95.

GOSHA, adj. Used in some parts, as an Anglo-Indian technicality, to indicate that a woman was secluded, and cannot appear in public. It is short for P. *gosha-nishīn*, 'sitting in a corner'; and is much the same as *parda-nishīn* (see **PURDAH**).

GOUNG, s. Burm. *gaung*; a village head man. ["Under the Thoogyee were *Rwa*-**goung**, or heads of villages, who aided in the collection of the revenue and were to some extent police officials." (*Gazetteer of Burma*, i. 480.)]

a. **GOUR**, s. H. *gāur*, *gāuri gāē*, (but not in the dictionaries), [Platts gives *gaur*, Skt. *gaura*, 'white, yellowish, reddish, pale red']. The great wild ox, *Gavaeus Gaurus*, Jerd.; [*Bos gaurus*, Blanford (*Mammalia*), 484 *seq.*], the same as the **Bison** (q.v.). [The classical account of the animal will be found in *Forsyth, Highlands of Central India*, ed. 1889, pp. 109 *seqq.*]

1806.—"They erect strong fences, but the buffaloes generally break them down. . . . They are far larger than common buffaloes. There is an account of a similar kind called the **Gore**; one distinction between it and the buffalo is the length of the hoof."—*Elphinstone*, in *Life*, i. 156.

b. **GOUR**, s. Properly Can. *gauḍ*, *gauṛ*, *gauḍa*. The head man of a village in the Canarese-speaking country; either as corresponding to **patel**, or to the **Zemindar** of Bengal. [See *F. Buchanan, Mysore*, i. 268; *Rice, Mysore*, i. 579.]

c. 1800.—"Every Tehsildary is farmed out in villages to the **Gours** or head-men." —In *Munro's Life*, iii. 92.

c. **GOUR**, n.p. *Gaur*, the name of a medieval capital of Bengal, which lay immediately south of the modern civil station of Malda, and the traces of which, with occasional Mahommedan buildings, extend over an immense area, chiefly covered with jungle. The name is a form of the ancient *Gauḍa*, meaning, it is believed, 'the country of sugar,' a name applied to a large part of Bengal, and specifically to the portion where those remains lie. It was the residence of a Hindu dynasty, the Senas, at the time of the early Mahommedan invasions, and was popularly known as *Lakhnāotī*; but the reigning king had transferred his seat to Nadiya (70 m. above Calcutta) before the actual conquest of Bengal in the last years of the 12th century. Gaur was afterwards the residence of several Mussulman dynasties. [See *Ravenshaw, Gaur, its Ruins and Inscriptions*, 1878.]

1536.—"But Xercansor [Shīr Khān Sūr, afterwards King of Hindustan as Shīr Shāh] after his success advanced along the river till he came before the city of **Gouro** to besiege it, and ordered a lodgment to be made in front of certain verandahs of the King's Palace which looked upon the river; and as he was making his trenches certain Rumis who were resident in the city, desiring that the King should prize them highly (*d'elles fizesse cabedal*) as he did the Portuguese, offered their service to the King to go and prevent the enemy's lodgment, saying that he should also send the Portuguese with them."—*Correa*, iii. 720.

[1552.—"**Caor.**" See under **BURRAMPOOTER.**]

1553.—"The chief city of the Kingdom (of Bengala) is called **Gouro**. It is situated on the banks of the Ganges, and is said to be 3 of our leagues in length, and to contain 200,000 inhabitants. On the one side it has the river for its defence, and on the landward faces a wall of great height . . . the streets are so thronged with the concourse and traffic of people . . . that they cannot force their way past . . . a great part of the houses of this city are stately and well-wrought buildings."—*Barros*, IV. ix. cap. 1.

1586.—"From Patanaw I went to Tanda which is in the land of the **Gouren**. It hath in times past been a kingdom, but is now subdued by Zelabdin Echebar . . ."—*R. Fitch*, in *Hakluyt*, ii. 389.

1683.—"I went to see ye famous Ruins of a great Citty and Pallace called [of] **GOWRE** . . . we spent 3½ hours in seeing ye ruines especially of the Pallace which has been . . . in my judgment considerably bigger and more beautifull than the Grand Seignor's Seraglio at Constantinople or any other Pallace that I have seen in Europe."—*Hedges, Diary*, May 16; [Hak. Soc. i. 88].

GOVERNOR'S STRAITS, n.p. This was the name applied by the Portuguese (*Estreito do Gobernador*) to the Straits of Singapore, *i.e.* the straits south of that island (or New Strait). The reason of the name is given in our first quotation. The Governor in question was the Spaniard Dom João da Silva.

1615.—"The Governor sailed from Manilha in March of this year with 10 galleons and 2 galleys. . . . Arriving at the Straits of Sincapur, * * * and passing by a new strait which since has taken the name of **Estreito do Governador**, there his galleon grounded on the reef at the point of the strait, and was a little grazed by the top of it."—*Bocarro*, 428.

1727.—"Between the small *Carimon* and *Tanjong-bellong* on the Continent, is the entrance of the Streights of *Sincapure* before mentioned, and also into the **Streights of Governadore**, the largest and easiest Passage into the *China* Seas."—*A. Hamilton*, ii. 122.

1780.—"Directions for sailing from Malacca to Pulo Timoan through **Governor's Straits**, commonly called the Straits of Sincapour."—*Dunn's N. Directory*, 5th ed. p. 474. See also *Lettres Edif.*, 1st ed. ii. 118.

1841.—"Singapore Strait, called **Governor Strait**, or New Strait, by the French and Portuguese."—*Horsburgh*, 5th ed. ii. 264.

GOW, GAOU, s. Dak. H. *gau*. An ancient measure of distance preserved in S. India and Ceylon. In the latter island, where the term still is in use, the *gawwa* is a measure of about 4 English miles. It is Pali *gāvuta*, one quarter of a *yojana*, and that again is the Skt. *gavyūti* with the same meaning. There is in Molesworth's *Mahr. Dictionary*, and in *Wilson*, a term *gaukos* (see **COSS**), 'a land measure' (for which read 'distance measure'), the distance at which the lowing of a cow may be heard. This is doubtless a form of the same term as that under consideration, but the explanation is probably modern and incorrect. The *yojana* with which the *gau* is correlated, appears etymologically to be 'a yoking,' viz. "the stage, or distance to be gone in one harnessing without unyoking" (*Williams*); and the lengths attributed to it are very various, oscillating from 2½ to 9 miles, and even to 8 *krośas* (see **COSS**). The last valuation of the *yojana* would correspond with that of the *gau* at ¼.

c. 545.—"The great Island (Taprobane), according to what the natives say, has a length of 300 **gaudia**, and a breadth of the same, *i.e.* 900 miles."—*Cosmas Indicopleustes*, (in *Cathay*, clxxvii.).

1623.—"From Garicota to Tumbre may be about a league and a half, for in that country distances are measured by **gaù**, and each **gaù** is about two leagues, and from Garicòta to Tumbre they said was not so much as a **gaù** of road."—*P. della Valle*, ii. 638; [Hak. Soc. ii. 230].

1676.—"They measure the distances of places in India by **Gos** and *Costes*. A **Gos** is about 4 of our common leagues, and a *Coste* is one league."—*Tavernier*, E.T. ii. 30; [ed. *Ball*, i. 47].

1860.—"A **gaou** in Ceylon expresses a somewhat indeterminate length, according to the nature of the ground to be traversed, a **gaou** across a mountainous country being less than one measured on level ground, and a **gaou** for a loaded cooley is also permitted to be shorter than for one unburthened, but on the whole the average may be taken *under four miles*."—*Tennent's Ceylon*, 4th ed. i. 467.

GRAB, s. This name, now almost obsolete, was applied to a kind of vessel which is constantly mentioned in the sea- and river-fights of India, from the arrival of the Portuguese down to near the end of the 18th century. That kind of etymology which works from inner consciousness would probably say: "This term has always been a puzzle to the English in India. The fact is that it was a kind of vessel much used by corsairs, who were said to *grab* all that passed the sea. Hence," &c. But the real derivation is different.

The Rev. Howard Malcom, in a glossary attached to his *Travels*, defines it as "a square-rigged Arab vessel, having a projecting stern (stem?) and no bowsprit; it has two masts." Probably the application of the term may have deviated variously in recent days. [See *Bombay Gazetteer*, xiii. pt. i. 348.] For thus again in *Solwyns* (*Les Hindous*, vol. i.) a *grab* is drawn and described as a ship with three masts, a sharp prow, and a bowsprit. But originally the word seems, beyond question, to have been an Arab name for a *galley*. The proper word is Arab. *ghorāb*, 'a raven,' though adopted into Mahratti and Konkani as *gurāb*. Jal says, quoting Reinaud, that *ghorāb* was the name given by the Moors to the true galley, and cites Hyde for the *rationale* of the name. We give Hyde's words below. Amari, in a work quoted below (p. 397), points out the analogous *corvetta* as perhaps a transfer of *ghurāb*:

1181.—"A vessel of our merchants . . . making sail for the city of Tripoli (which God protect) was driven by the winds on the shore of that country, and the crew being in want of water, landed to procure it, but the people of the place refused it unless some corn were sold to them. Meanwhile there came a **ghurāb** from Tripoli . . . which took and plundered the crew, and seized all the goods on board the vessel." *—*Arabic Letter from* Ubaldo, *Archbishop and other authorities of Pisa, to the Almohad Caliph* Abu Yak'ub Yusuf, in *Amari, Diplomi Arabi*, p. 8.

The Latin contemporary version runs thus:

"Cum quidam nostri cari cives de Siciliâ cum carico frumenti ad Tripolim venirent, tempestate maris et vi ventorum compulsi, ad portum dictum Macri devenerunt; ibique aquâ deficiente, et cum pro eâ auriendâ irent, Barbarosi non permiserunt eos . . . nisi prius eis de frumento venderent. Cumque inviti eis de frumento venderent *galea* vestra de Tripoli armata," &c.—*Ibid.* p. 269.

c. 1200.—**Ghurāb**, Cornix, Corvus, galea.

* * * * *

Galea, Ghurāb, Gharbān. — *Vocabulista Arabico* (from Riccardian Library), pubd. Florence, 1871, pp. 148, 404.

1343.—"Jalansi . . . sent us off in company with his son, on board a vessel called *al-'Ukairi*, which is like a **ghorāb**, only more roomy. It has 60 oars, and when it engages is covered with a roof to protect the rowers from the darts and stone-shot." —*Ibn Batuta*, iv. 59.

1505.—In the *Vocabulary* of Pedro de Alcala, *galera* is interpreted in Arabic as **gorâb.**

1554. — In the narrative of Sidi 'Ali Kapudān, in describing an action that he fought with the Portuguese near the Persian Gulf, he says the enemy's fleet consisted of 4 barques as big as **carracks** (q.v.), 3 great **ghurābs**, 6 Karāwals (see **CARAVEL**) and 12 smaller **ghurābs**, or galliots (see **GALLEVAT**) with oars.—In *J. As.*, ser. 1. tom. ix. 67-68.

[c. 1610.—"His royal galley called by them Ogate **Gourabe** (*gourabe* means 'galley,' and *ogate* 'royal')."—*Pyrard de Laval*, Hak. Soc. i. 312.]

1660.—"Jani Beg might attack us from the hills, the **ghrābs** from the river, and the men of Sihwān from the rear, so that we should be in a critical position."—*Mohammed M'asum*, in *Elliot*, i. 250. The word occurs in many pages of the same history.

[1679.—"My Selfe and Mr. Gapes **Grob** the stern most."—In *Hedges, Diary*, Hak. Soc. ii. clxxxiv.]

1690.—"*Galera* . . . ab Arabibus tam Asiaticis quam Africanis vocatur . . . **Ghorâb**, *i.e.* Corvus, quasi piceâ nigredine, rostro extenso, et velis remisque sicut alis volans galera: unde et Vlacho Graece dicitur Μέλαινα."—*Hyde, Note on Peritsol*, in *Synt. Dissertt.* i. 97.

1673.—"Our Factors, having concerns in the cargo of the ships in this Road, loaded two **Grobs** and departed."—*Fryer*, 153.

1727.—"The *Muskat* War . . . obliges them (the Portuguese) to keep an *Armada* of five or six Ships, besides small Frigates and **Grabs** of War."—*A. Hamilton*, i. 250; [ed. 1744, ii. 253].

1750-52.—"The ships which they make use of against their enemies are called **goerabbs** by the Dutch, and **grabbs** by the English, have 2 or 3 masts, and are built like our ships, with the same sort of rigging, only their prows are low and sharp as in gallies, that they may not only place some cannons in them, but likewise in case of emergency for a couple of oars, to push the **grabb** on in a calm."—*Olof Toreen, Voyage*, 205.

c. 1754.—"Our E. I. Company had here (Bombay) one ship of 40 guns, one of 20, one **Grab** of 18 guns, and several other vessels."—*Ives*, 43. Ives explains "Ketches, which they call **grabs**." This shows the meaning already changed, as no galley could carry 18 guns.

c. 1760.—"When the Derby, Captain Ansell, was so scandalously taken by a few of Angria's **grabs**."—*Grose*, i. 81.

1763.—"The **grabs** have rarely more than two masts, though some have three; those of three are about 300 tons burthen; but the others are not more than 150: they are built to draw very little water, being very broad in proportion to their length, narrowing, however, from the middle to the end, where instead of bows they have a prow, projecting like that of a Mediterranean galley."—*Orme* (reprint), i. 408-9.

1810.—"Here a fine English East Indiaman, there a **grab**, or a dow from Arabia." —*Maria Graham*, 142.

,, "This **Glab** (*sic*) belongs to an Arab merchant of Muscat. The Nakhodah, an Abyssinian slave."—*Elphinstone*, in *Life*, i. 232.

[1820.—"We had scarce set sail when there came in a **ghorab** (a kind of boat) the Cotwal of Surat . . ."—*Trans. Lit. Soc. Bo.* ii. 5.]

1872.—"Moored in its centre you saw some 20 or 30 **ghurábs** (grabs) from Maskat, Baghlahs from the Persian Gulf, Kotiyahs from Kach'h, and Pattimars or Batelas from the Konkan and Bombay."—*Burton, Sind Revisited*, i. 83.

GRAM, s. This word is properly the Portuguese *grão*, *i.e.* 'grain,' but it has been specially appropriated to that kind of vetch (*Cicer arietinum*, L.) which is the most general grain-(rather pulse-) food of horses all over India, called in H. *chanā*. It is the Ital. *cece*, Fr. *pois chiche*, Eng. *chick-pea* or *Egypt. pea*, much used in France and S.

* From Amari's Italian version.

Europe. This specific application of *grão* is also Portuguese, as appears from Bluteau. The word *gram* is in some parts of India applied to other kinds of pulse, and then this application of it is recognised by qualifying it as *Bengal gram*. (See remarks under **CALAVANCE**.) The plant exudes oxalate of potash, and to walk through a gram-field in a wet morning is destructive to shoe-leather. The natives collect the acid.

[1513.—"And for the food of these horses (exported from the Persian Gulf) the factor supplied **grãos**." — *Albuquerque, Cartas*, p. 200, Letter of Dec. 4.

[1554.—(Describing Vijayanagar.) "There the food of horses and elephants consists of **grãos**, rice and other vegetables, cooked with *jagra*, which is palm-tree sugar, as there is no barley in that country."—*Castanheda*, Bk. ii. ch. 16.

[c. 1610.—"They give them also a certain **grain** like lentils."—*Pyrard de Laval*, Hak. Soc. ii. 79.]

1702.—". . . he confessing before us that their allowance three times a week is but a quart of rice and **gram** together for five men a day, but promises that for the future it shall be rectified."—In *Wheeler*, ii. 10.

1776.—". . . Lentils, **gram** . . . mustard seed."—*Halhed's Code*, p. 8 (pt. ii.).

1789.—". . . **Gram**, a small kind of pulse, universally used instead of oats."—*Munro's Narrative*, 85.

1793.—". . . **gram**, which it is not customary to give to bullocks in the Carnatic."—*Dirom's Narrative*, 97.

1804.—"The **gram** alone, for the four regiments with me, has in some months cost 50,000 pagodas."—*Wellington*, iii. 71.

1865.—"But they had come at a wrong season, **gram** was dear, and prices low, and the sale concluded in a dead loss."—*Palgrave's Arabia*, 290.

GRAM-FED, adj. Properly the distinctive description of mutton and beef fattened upon gram, which used to be the pride of Bengal. But applied figuratively to any 'pampered creature.'

c. 1849.—"By an old Indian I mean a man full of curry and of bad Hindustani, with a fat liver and no brains, but with a self-sufficient idea that no one can know India except through long experience of brandy, champagne, **gram-fed** mutton, cheroots and hookahs."—*Sir C. Napier*, quoted in *Bos. Smith's Life of Ld. Lawrence*, i. 338.

1880.—"I missed two persons at the Delhi assemblage in 1877. All the **gram-fed** secretaries and most of the alcoholic chiefs were there; but the famine-haunted villagers and the delirium-shattered opium-eating Chinaman, who had to pay the bill, were not present."—*Ali Baba*, 127.

GRANDONIC. (See **GRUNTHUM** and **SANSKRIT**).

GRASS-CLOTH. s. This name is now generally applied to a kind of cambric from China made from the *Chuma* of the Chinese (*Boehmaria nivea*, Hooker, the *Rhea*, so much talked of now), and called by the Chinese *sia-pu*, or 'summer-cloth.' We find grass-cloths often spoken of by the 16th century travellers, and even later, as an export from Orissa and Bengal. They were probably made of *Rhea* or some kindred species, but we have not been able to determine this. Cloth and nets are made in the south from the Neilgherry nettle (*Girardinia heterophylla*, D. C.)

c. 1567.—"**Cloth of herbes** (*panni d'erba*), which is a kinde of silke, which groweth among the woodes without any labour of man."—*Caesar Frederike*, in *Hakl*. ii. 358.

1585.—"Great store of the **cloth** which is made from **Grasse**, which they call *yerua*" (in Orissa).—*R. Fitch*, in *Hakl*. ii. 387.

[1598.—See under **SAREE**.

[c. 1610.—"Likewise is there plenty of silk, as well that of the silkworm as of the (silk) *herb*, which is of the brightest yellow colour, and brighter than silk itself."—*Pyrard de Laval*, Hak. Soc. i. 328.]

1627.—"Their manufactories (about Balasore) are of Cotton . . . Silk, and Silk and Cotton *Romals* . . . ; and of **Herba** (a Sort of tough **Grass**) they make *Ginghams*, *Pinascos*, and several other Goods for Exportation."—*A. Hamilton*, i. 397; [ed. 1744].

1813.—Milburn, in his List of Bengal Piece-Goods, has **Herba** *Taffaties* (ii. 221).

GRASS-CUTTER, s. This is probably a corruption representing the H. *ghāskhodā* or *ghāskāṭā*, 'the digger, or cutter, of grass'; the title of a servant employed to collect grass for horses, one such being usually attached to each horse besides the **syce or horse-keeper**. In the north the *grasscutter* is a man; in the south the office is filled by the horsekeeper's wife. *Ghās-kat* is the form commonly used by Englishmen in Upper India speaking Hindustani; but *ghasiyārā* by those aspiring to purer language. The former term appears in *Williamson's V. M.* (1810) as *gauskot* (i. 186), the latter in *Jacquemont's Correspondence* as *grassyara.* No grasscutters are mentioned as attached to the stables of Akbar; only a money allowance for grass. The antiquity of the Madras arrangement is shown by a passage in Castanheda (1552): " . . . he gave him a horse, and a boy to attend to it, and a *female slave* to see to its fodder."—(ii. 58.)

1789.—" . . . an Horsekeeper and **Grass-cutter** at two pagodas."—*Munro's Narr.* 28.

1793.—"Every horse . . . has two attendants, one who cleans and takes care of him, called the horse-keeper, and the other the **grasscutter**, who provides for his forage."—*Dirom's Narr.* 242.

1846.—"Every horse has a man and a maid to himself—the maid cuts grass for him; and every dog has a boy. I inquired whether the cat had any servants, but I found he was allowed to wait upon himself."—*Letters from Madras,* 37.

[1850.—"Then there are our servants . . . four Saises and four **Ghascuts** . . ."—*Mrs. Mackenzie, Life in the Mission,* ii. 253.]

1875.—"I suppose if you were to pick up . . . a **grasscutter's** pony to replace the one you lost, you wouldn't feel that you had done the rest of the army out of their rights."—*The Dilemma,* ch. xxxvii.

[**GRASSHOPPER FALLS,** n.p. An Anglo-Indian corruption of the name of the great waterfall on the Sheravati River in the Shimoga District of Mysore, where the river plunges down in a succession of cascades, of which the principal is 890 feet in height. The proper name of the place is *Gersoppa,* or *Gerusappe,* which takes its name from the adjoining village; *geru,* Can., 'the marking nut plant' (*semecarpus anacardium,* L.), *soppu,* 'a leaf.' See *Mr. Grey's* note on *P. della Valle,* Hak. Soc. ii. 218.]

GRASS-WIDOW, s. This slang phrase is applied in India, with a shade of malignity, to ladies living apart from their husbands, especially as recreating at the Hill stations, whilst the husbands are at their duties in the plains.

We do not know the origin of the phrase. In the *Slang Dictionary* it is explained: "An unmarried mother; a deserted mistress." But no such opprobrious meanings attach to the Indian use. In *Notes and Queries,* 6th ser. viii. 414, will be found several communications on this phrase. [Also see *ibid.* x. 436, 526; xi. 178; 8th ser. iv. 37, 75.] We learn from these that in *Moor's Suffolk Words and Phrases,* **Grace-Widow** occurs with the meaning of an unmarried mother. Corresponding to this, it is stated also, is the N.S. (?) or Low German *gras-wedewe.* The Swedish *Gräsänka* or *-enka* also is used for 'a low dissolute married woman living by herself.' In Belgium a woman of this description is called *haecke-wedewe,* from *haecken,* 'to feel strong desire' (to 'hanker'). And so it is suggested *grüsenka* is contracted from *grädesenka,* from *gradig,* 'esuriens' (greedy, in fact). In Danish Dict. *graesenka* is interpreted as a woman whose betrothed lover is dead. But the German *Stroh-Wittwe,* 'straw-widow' (which Flügel interprets as 'mock widow'), seems rather inconsistent with the suggestion that *grass-widow* is a corruption of the kind suggested. A friend mentions that the masc. *Stroh-Wittwer* is used in Germany for a man whose wife is absent, and who therefore dines at the eating-house with the young fellows. [The *N.E.D.* gives the two meanings: 1. An unmarried woman who has cohabited with one or more men; a discarded mistress; 2. A married woman whose husband is absent from her. "The etymological notion is obscure, but the parallel forms disprove the notion that the word is a 'corruption' of *grace-widow.* It has been suggested that in sense 1. *grass* (and G. *stroh*) may have been used with opposition to bed. Sense 2. may have arisen as an etymologizing interpretation of the compound after it had ceased to be generally understood; in Eng. it seems to have first appeared as Anglo-Indian." The French equivalent, *Veuve de Malabar,* was in allusion to Lemierre's tragedy, produced in 1770.]

1878.—"In the evening my wife and I went out house-hunting; and we pitched upon one which the newly incorporated body of Municipal Commissioners and the Clergyman (who was a **Grass-widower,** his wife being at home) had taken between them."—*Life in the Mofussil,* ii. 99-100.

1879.—The Indian newspaper's "typical official rises to a late breakfast—probably on herrings and soda-water—and dresses tastefully for his round of morning calls, the last on a **grass-widow,** with whom he has a *tête-à-tête* tiffin, where 'pegs' alternate with champagne."—*Simla Letter* in *Times,* Aug. 16.

1880.—"The **Grass-widow** in Nephelococcygia."—*Sir Ali Baba*, 169.

,, "Pleasant times have these Indian **grass-widows**!"—*The World*, Jan. 21, 13.

GRASSIA, s. *Grās* (said to mean 'a mouthful') is stated by Mr. Forbes in the *Rās Mālā* (p. 186) to have been in old times usually applied to alienations for religious objects; but its prevalent sense came to be the portion of land given for subsistence to cadets of chieftains' families. Afterwards the term *grās* was also used for the blackmail paid by a village to a turbulent neighbour as the price of his protection and forbearance, and in other like meanings. "Thus the title of *grassia*, originally an honourable one, and indicating its possessor to be a cadet of the ruling tribe, became at last as frequently a term of opprobrium, conveying the idea of a professional robber" (*Ibid.* Bk. iv. ch. 3); [ed. 1878, p. 568].

[1584.—See under **COOLY**.]

c. 1665.—"Nous nous trouvâmes au Village de Bilpar, dont les Habitans qu'on nomme **Gratiates**, sont presque tous Voleurs."—*Thevenot*, v. 42.

1808.—"The **Grasias** have been shewn to be of different Sects, Casts, or families, viz., 1st, Colees and their Collaterals; 2nd, Rajpoots; 3rd, Syed Mussulmans; 4th, Mole-Islams or modern Mahomedans. There are besides many others who enjoy the free usufruct of lands, and permanent emolument from villages, but those only who are of the four aforesaid warlike tribes seem entitled by prescriptive custom. . . to be called **Grassias**."—*Drummond, Illustrations*.

1813.—"I confess I cannot now contemplate my extraordinary deliverance from the **Gracia** machinations without feelings more appropriate to solemn silence, than expression."—*Forbes, Or. Mem.* iii. 393; [conf. 2nd ed. ii. 357].

1819.—"**Grassia**, from **Grass**, a word signifying 'a mouthful.' This word is understood in some parts of Mekran, Sind, and Kutch; but I believe not further into Hindostan than Jaypoor."—*Mackmurdo*, in *Tr. Lit. Soc. Bo.* i. 270. [On the use in Central India, see *Tod, Annals*, i. 175; *Malcolm, Central India*, i. 508.]

GRAVE-DIGGER. (See **BEEJOO**.)

GREEN-PIGEON. A variety of species belonging to the sub.-fam. *Treroninae*, and to genera *Treron*, *Crocopus*, *Osmotreron*, and *Sphenocercus*, bear this name. The three first following quotations show that these birds had attracted the attention of the ancients.

c. 180.—"Daimachus, in his History of India, says that **pigeons** of an **apple-green** colour are found in India."—*Athenaeus*, ix. 51.

c. A.D. 250.—"They bring also **greenish** (ὠχρὰς) **pigeons** which they say can never be tamed or domesticated."—*Aelian, De Nat. Anim.* xv. 14.

,, "There are produced among the Indians . . . **pigeons** of a pale **green colour** (χλωρόπτιλοι); any one seeing them for the first time, and not having any knowledge of ornithology, would say the bird was a parrot and not a pigeon. They have legs and bill in colour like the partridges of the Greeks."—*Ibid.* xvi. 2.

1673.—"Our usual diet was (besides Plenty of Fish) Water-Fowl, Peacocks, **Green Pidgeons**, Spotted Deer, Sabre, Wild Hogs, and sometimes Wild Cows."—*Fryer*, 176.

1825.—"I saw a great number of peafowl, and of the beautiful **greenish pigeon** common in this country . . ."—*Heber*, ii. 19.

GREY PARTRIDGE. The common Anglo-Indian name of the Hind. *tītar*, common over a great part of India, *Ortygornis Ponticeriana*, Gmelin. "Its call is a peculiar loud shrill cry, and has, not unaptly, been compared to the word *Pateela-pateela-pateela*, quickly repeated but preceded by a single note, uttered two or three times, each time with a higher intonation, till it gets, as it were, the key-note of its call."—*Jerdon*, ii. 566.

GRIBLEE, s. A graplin or grapnel. Lascars' language (*Roebuck*).

GRIFFIN, GRIFF, s.; **GRIFFISH**, adj. One newly arrived in India, and unaccustomed to Indian ways and peculiarities; a Johnny Newcome. The origin of the phrase is unknown to us. There was an Admiral *Griffin* who commanded in the Indian seas from Nov. 1746 to June 1748, and was not very fortunate. Had his name to do with the origin of the term? The word seems to have been first used at Madras (see *Boyd*, below). [But also see the quotation from *Beaumont & Fletcher*, below.] Three references below indicate the parallel terms formerly used by the Portuguese at Goa, by the Dutch in the Archipelago, and by the English in Ceylon.

[c. 1624.—"Doves beget doves, and eagles eagles, Madam: a citizen's heir, though never so rich, seldom at the best proves a gentleman."—*Beaumont & Fletcher, Honest Man's Fortune*, Act III. sc. 1, vol. iii. p. 389, ed. *Dyce*. Mr. B. Nicolson (3 ser. *Notes and Queries*, xi. 439) points out that Dyce's MS. copy, licensed by Sir Henry Herbert in 1624, reads "proves but a **griffin** gentleman." Prof. Skeat (*ibid.* xi. 504) quoting from *Piers Plowman*, ed. *Wright*, p. 96, "*Gryffyn* the Walshe," shows that *Griffin* was an early name for a Welshman, apparently a corruption of *Griffith*. The word may have been used abroad to designate a raw Welshman, and thus acquired its present sense.]

1794.—"As I am little better than an unfledged **Griffin**, according to the fashionable phrase here" (Madras).—*Hugh Boyd*, 177.

1807.—"It seems really strange to a **griffin**—the cant word for a European just arrived."—*Ld. Minto, in India*, 17.

1808.—"At the Inn I was tormented to death by the impertinent persevering of the black people; for every one is a beggar, as long as you are reckoned a **griffin**, or a new-comer."—*Life of Leyden*, 107.

1836.—"I often tire myself . . . rather than wait for their dawdling; but Mrs. Staunton laughs at me and calls me a '**Griffin**,' and says I must learn to have patience and save my strength."—*Letters from Madras*, 38.

" "... he was living with bad men, and saw that they thought him no better than themselves, but only more **griffish** . . ."—*Ibid.* 53.

1853.—"There were three more cadets on the same steamer, going up to that great **griff** depot, Oudapoor."—*Oakfield*, i. 38.

1853.—

"'Like drill?'

"'I don't dislike it much now: the goose-step was not lively.'

"'Ah, they don't give **griffs** half enough of it now-a-days; by Jove, Sir, when I was a **griff**'—and thereupon . . ."—*Ibid.* i. 62.

[1900.—"Ten Rangoon sportsmen have joined to import ponies from Australia on the **griffin** system, and have submitted a proposal to the Stewards to frame their events to be confined to **griffins** at the forthcoming autumn meeting."—*Pioneer Mail*, May 18.]

The **griffin** at Goa also in the old days was called by a peculiar name. (See **REINOL**.)

1631.—"Haec exanthemata (prickly heat-spots) magis afficiunt recenter advenientes ut et Mosquitarum puncturae . . . ita ut derididiculum ergo hic inter nostrates dicterium enatum sit, eum qui hoc modo affectus sit, esse **Orang Barou**, quod novitium hominem significat."—*Jac. Bontii, Hist. Nat.*, &c., ii. cap. xviii. p. 33.

Here **orang barou** is Malay **orang-baharu**, *i.e.* 'new man'; whilst *Orang-lama*, 'man of long since,' is applied to old colonials. In connection with these terms we extract the following:—

c. 1790.—"Si je n'avois pas été un *oorlam*, et si un long séjour dans l'Inde ne m'avoit pas accoutumé à cette espèce de fleau, j'aurois certainement souffert l'impossible durant cette nuit."—*Haafner*, ii. 26-27.

On this his editor notes:

"*Oorlam* est un mot Malais corrumpu; il faut dire *Orang-lama*, ce qui signifie une personne qui a déjà été long-temps dans un endroit, ou dans un pays, et c'est par ce nom qu'on designe les Européens qui ont habité depuis un certain temps dans l'Inde. Ceux qui ne font qu'y arriver, sont appelés *Baar;* denomination qui vient du mot Malais **Orang-Baru** . . . un homme nouvellement arrivé."

[1894.—"In the *Standard*, Jan. 1, there appears a letter entitled 'Ceylon Tea-Planting—a Warning,' and signed 'An Ex-**creeper**.' The correspondent sends a cutting from a recent issue of a Ceylon daily paper—a paragraph headed '**Creepers** Galore.' From this extract it appears that **Creeper** is the name given in Ceylon to paying pupils who go out there to learn tea-planting."—*Mr. A. L. Mayhew*, in 8 ser. *Notes and Queries*, v. 124.]

GROUND, s. A measure of land used in the neighbourhood of Madras. [Also called *Munny*, Tam. *manai*.] (See under **CAWNY**.)

GRUFF, adj. Applied to bulky goods. Probably the Dutch *grof*, 'coarse.'

[1682-3.—". . . that for every Tunne of Saltpetre and all other **Groffe** goods I am to receive nineteen pounds."—*Pringle, Diary, Ft. St. Geo.* 1st ser. vol. ii. 3-4.]

1750.—". . . all which could be called Curtins, and some of the Bastions at *Madrass*, had Warehouses under them for the Reception of Naval Stores, and other **gruff** Goods from Europe, as well as Salt Petre from *Bengal*."—*Letter to a Propr. of the E. I. Co.*, p. 52.

1759.—"Which by causing a great export of rice enhances the price of labour, and consequently of all other **gruff**, piece-goods and raw silk."—In *Long*, 171.

1765.—". . . also *foole sugar*, lump *jaggre*, ginger, long pepper, and *piply-mol* . . . articles that usually compose the **gruff** cargoes of our outward-bound shipping."—*Holwell, Hist. Events*, &c., i. 194.

1783.—"What in India is called a **gruff** (bulky) cargo."—*Forrest, Voyage to Mergui*, 42.

GRUNTH, s. Panjābī *Granth*, from Skt. *grantha*, lit. 'a knot,' leaves tied together by a string. 'The Book,' *i.e.* the Scripture of the Sikhs, containing the hymns composed or compiled by their leaders from Nānak (1469-1539) onwards. The *Granth* has been translated by Dr. Trumpp, and published, at the expense of the Indian Government.

1770.—"As the young man (Nānak) was early introduced to the knowledge of the most esteemed writings of the Mussulmen . . . he made it a practice in his leisure hours to translate literally or virtually, as his mind prompted him, such of their maxims as made the deepest impression on his heart. This was in the idiom of Pendjab, his maternal language. Little by little he strung together these loose sentences, reduced them into some order, and put them in verses. . . . His collection became numerous; it took the form of a book which was entitled **Grenth.**"—*Seir Mutaqherin*, i. 89.

1798.—"A book entitled the **Grunth** . . . is the only typical object which the Sicques have admitted into their places of worship."—*G. Forster's Travels*, i. 255.

1817.—"The fame of Nannak's book was diffused. He gave it a new name, **Kirrunt.**"—*Mill's Hist.* ii. 377.

c. 1831.—". . . Au centre du quel est le temple d'or où est gardé le **Grant** ou livre sacré des Sikes."—*Jacquemont, Correspondance*, ii. 166.

[1838.—"There was a large collection of priests, sitting in a circle, with the **Grooht**, their holy book, in the centre . . ."—*Miss Eden, Up the Country*, ii. 7.]

GRUNTHEE, s. Panj. *granthī* from *granth* (see **GRUNTH**). A sort of native chaplain attached to Sikh regiments. [The name *Granthī* appears among the Hindi mendicant castes of the Panjab in *Mr. Maclagan's Census Rep.*, 1891, p. 300.]

¶**GRUNTHUM**, s. This (*grantham*) is a name, from the same Skt. word as the last, given in various odd forms to the Sanskrit language by various Europeans writing in S. India during the 16th and 17th centuries. The term properly applied to the character in which the Sanskrit books were written.

1600.—"In these verses is written, in a particular language, called **Gerodam**, their Philosophy and Theology, which the Bramens study and read in Universities all over India."—*Lucena, Vida do Padre F. Xavier*, 95.

1646.—"Cette langue correspond à la nostre Latine, parceque les seules Lettrés l'apprennent; il se nomment **Guirindans.**"—*Barretto, Rel. de la Prov. de la Malabar*, 257.

1727.—". . . their four law-books, *Sama Vedam*, *Urukku Vedam*, *Edirwarna Vedam*, and *Adir Vedam*, which are all written in the **Girandams**, and are held in high esteem by the Bramins."—*Valentijn*, v. (*Ceylon*), 399.

,, "**Girandam** (by others called **Kerendum**, and also *Sanskrits*) is the language of the Bramins and the learned."—*Ibid.* 386.

1753.—"Les Indiens du pays se donnent le nom de *Tamules*, et on sait que la langue vulgaire différente du Sanskret, et du **Grendam**, qui sont les langues sacrées, porte le même nom."—*D'Anville.* 117.

GUANA, IGUANA, s. This is not properly an Indian term, nor the name of an Indian species, but, as in many other cases, it has been applied by transfer from superficially resembling *genera* in the new Indies, to the old. The great lizards, sometimes called *guanas* in India, are apparently *monitors*. It must be observed, however, that approximating Indian names of lizards have helped the confusion. Thus the large monitor to which the name *guana* is often applied in India, is really called in Hindi *goh* (Skt. *godhā*), Singhalese *goyā*. The true *iguana* of America is described by Oviedo in the first quotation under the name of *iuana*. [The word is Span. *iguana*, from Carib *iwana*, written in early writers *hiuana*, *igoana*, *iuanna* or *yuana*. See *N.E.D.* and *Stanf. Dict.*]

c. 1535.—"There is in this island an animal called **Iuana**, which is here held to be amphibious (*neutrale*), *i.e.* doubtful whether fish or flesh, for it frequents the rivers and climbs the trees as well. . . . It is a Serpent, bearing to one who knows it not a horrid and frightful aspect. It has the hands and feet like those of a great lizard, the head much larger, but almost of the same fashion, with a tail 4 or 5 palms in length. . . . And the animal, formed as I have described, is much better to eat than to look at," &c.—*Oviedo*, in *Ramusio*, iii. f. 156*v*, 157.

c. 1550.—"We also used to catch some four-footed animals called **iguane**, resembling our lizards in shape . . . the females are most delicate food."—*Girolàmi Benzoni*, p. 140.

1634.—"De Lacertae quâdam specie, Incolis **Liguan**. Est . . . genus venenosissimum," &c.—*Jac. Bontii*, Lib. v. cap. 5. p. 57. (See **GECKO**.)

1673.—"**Guiana**, a Creature like a Crocodile, which Robbers use to lay hold on by their Tails, when they clamber Houses."—*Fryer*, 116.

1681.—Knox, in his *Ceylon*, speaks of two creatures resembling the Alligator—one called *Kobbera* **guion**, 5 or 6 feet long, and not eatable; the other called *tolla* **guion**, very like the former, but "which is eaten, and reckoned excellent meat . . . and I suppose it is the same with that which in the W. Indies is called the **guiana**" (pp. 30, 31). The names are possibly Portuguese, and *Kobberaguion* may be *Cobra-***guana**.

1704.—"The **Guano** is a sort of Creature some of which are found on the land, some in the water . . . stewed with a little Spice they make good Broth."—*Funnel*, in *Dampier*, iv. 51.

1711.—"Here are Monkeys, **Gaunas**, Lissards, large Snakes, and Alligators."—*Lockyer*, 47.

1780.—"They have here an amphibious animal called the **guana**, a species of the crocodile or alligator, of which soup is made equal to that of turtle. This I take upon hearsay, for it is to me of all others the most loathsome of animals, not less so than the toad."—*Munro's Narrative*, 36.

c. 1830.—"Had I known I was dining upon a **guana**, or large wood-lizard, I scarcely think I would have made so hearty a meal."—*Tom Cringle* (ed. 1863), 178.

1879.—"Captain Shaw asked the Imaum of one of the mosques of Malacca about alligator's eggs, a few days ago, and his reply was, that the young that went down to the sea became alligators, and those that came up the river became **iguanas**."—*Miss Bird, Golden Chersonese*, 200.

1881.—"The chief of Mudhol State belongs to the Bhonslá family. . . . The name, however, has been entirely superseded by the second designation of *Ghorpade*, which is said to have been acquired by one of the family who managed to scale a fort previously deemed impregnable, by fastening a cord around the body of a *ghorpad* or **iguana**."—*Imperial Gazetteer*, vi. 437.

1883.—"Who can look on that anachronism, an iguana (I mean the large *monitor* which Europeans in India generally call an **iguana**, sometimes a **guano**!) basking, four feet long, on a sunny bank . . ."—*Tribes on My Frontier*, 36.

1885.—"One of my moonshis, José Prethoo, a Concani of one of the numerous families descended from Xavier's converts, gravely informed me that in the old days **iguanas** were used in gaining access to besieged places; for, said he, a large **iguana**, sahib, is so strong that if 3 or 4 men laid hold of its tail he could drag them up a wall or tree!"—*Gordon Forbes, Wild Life in Canara*, 56.

GUARDAFUI, CAPE, n.p. The eastern horn of Africa, pointing towards India. We have the name from the Portuguese, and it has been alleged to have been so called by them as meaning, 'Take you heed!' (*Gardez-vous*, in fact.) But this is etymology of the species that so confidently derives 'Bombay' from *Boa Bahia*. Bruce, again (see below), gives dogmatically an interpretation which is equally unfounded. We must look to history, and not to the 'moral consciousness' of anybody. The country adjoining this horn of Africa, the *Regio Aromatum* of the ancients, seems to have been called by the Arabs *Hafūn*, a name which we find in the *Periplus* in the shape of *Opōnē*. This name *Hafūn* was applied to a town, no doubt the true *Opōnē*, which Barbosa (1516) mentions under the name of *Afuni*, and it still survives in those of two remarkable promontories, viz. the Peninsula of *Rās Hafūn* (the *Chersonnesus* of the *Periplus*, the *Zingis* of Ptolemy, the Cape *d'Affui* and *d'Orfui* of old maps and nautical directories), and the cape of **Jard-Hafūn** (or according to the Egyptian pronunciation, *Gard-Hafūn*), *i.e.* **Guardafui**. The nearest possible meaning of *jard* that we can find is 'a wide or spacious tract of land without herbage.' Sir R. Burton (*Commentary on Camõens*, iv. 489) interprets *jard* as = Bay, "from a break in the dreadful granite wall, lately provided by Egypt with a lighthouse." The last statement is unfortunately an error. The intended light seems as far off as ever. [There is still no lighthouse, and shipowners differ as to its advantage; see answer by Secretary of State, in House of Commons, *Times*, March 14, 1902.] We cannot judge of the ground of his interpretation of *jard*.

An attempt has been made to connect the name *Hafūn* with the Arabic *af'a*, 'pleasant odours.' It would then, be the equivalent of the ancient *Reg. Aromatum*. This is tempting, but very questionable. We should have mentioned that Guardafui is the site of the mart and Promontory of the Spices described by the author of the *Periplus* as the furthest point and abrupt termination of the continent of *Barbarice* (or eastern Africa), towards the Orient (τὸ τῶν Ἀρωματῶν ἐμπόριον καὶ ἀκρωτήριον τελευταῖον τῆς βαρβαρικῆς ἠπείρου πρὸς ἀνατολὴν ἀποκόπον).

According to C. Müller our *Guardafui* is called by the natives *Rās Aser*; their *Rās Jardafūn* being a point some 12

m. to the south, which on some charts is called *Rās Shenarif*, and which is also the Τάβαι of the *Periplus* (*Geog. Gr. Minores*, i. 263).

1516.—"And that the said ships from his ports (K. of Coulam's) shall not go inwards from the Strait and Cape of **Guoardaffuy**, nor go to Adem, except when employed in our obedience and service . . . and if any vessel or *Zambuque* is found inward of the Cape of **Guoardaffuy** it shall be taken as good prize of war."—*Treaty between Lopo Soares and the K. of Caulam*, in *Botelho, Tombo*, 33.

" "After passing this place (*Afuni*) the next after it is *Cape* **Guardafun**, where the coast ends, and trends so as to double towards the Red Sea."—*Barbosa*, 16.

c. 1530.—"This province, called of late Arabia, but which the ancients called *Trogloditica*, begins at the Red Sea and the country of the Abissines, and finishes at Magadasso . . . others say it extends only to the Cape of **Guardafuni**."—*Sommario de' Regni*, in *Ramusio*, i. f. 325.

1553.—"Vicente Sodre, being despatched by the King, touched at the Island of Çocotora, where he took in water, and thence passed to the Cape of **Guardafu**, which is the most easterly land of Africa."—*De Barros*, I. vii. cap. 2.

1554.—"If you leave Dábúl at the end of the season, you direct yourselves W.S.W. till the pole is four inches and an eighth, from thence true west to **Kardafún**."—*Sidi 'Ali Kapudān, The Mohit*, in *J. As. Soc. Ben.*, v. 464.

" "You find such whirlpools on the coasts of **Kardafūn**. . . ."—The same, in his narrative, *Journ. As.* ser. 1. tom. ix. p. 77.

1572.—

"O Cabo vê já Aromata chamado,
E agora **Guardafú**, dos moradores,
Onde começa a boca do affamado
Mar Roxo, que do fundo toma as cores."
Camões, x. 97.

Englished by Burton:

"The Cape which Antients 'Aromatic' clepe
behold, yclept by Moderns **Guardafú**;
where opes the Red Sea mouth, so wide and deep,
the Sea whose ruddy bed lends blushing hue."

1602.—"Eitor da Silveira set out, and without any mishap arrived at the Cape of **Gardafui**."—*Couto*, IV. i. 4.

1727.—"And having now travell'd along the Shore of the Continent, from the Cape of *Good Hope* to Cape **Guardafoy**, I'll survey the Islands that lie in the Ethiopian Sea."—*A. Hamilton*, i. 15; [ed. 1744].

1790.—"The Portuguese, or Venetians, the first Christian traders in these parts, have called it **Gardefui**, which has no signification in any language. But in that part of the country where it is situated, it is called **Gardefan** and means the *Straits of Burial*, the reason of which will be seen afterwards."—*Bruce's Travels*, i. 315.

[1823.—". . . we soon obtained sight of Cape **Gardafui**. . . . It is called by the natives *Ras Assere*, and the high mountain immediately to its south is named *Gibel* **Jordafoon**. . . . Keeping about nine miles off shore we rounded the peninsula of **Hafoon**. . . . **Hafoon** appears like an island, and belongs to a native Somauli prince. . . ."—*Owen, Narr.* i. 353.]

GUAVA, s. This fruit (*Psidium Guayava*, L., Ord. *Myrtaceae*; Span. *guayava*, Fr. *goyavier*, [from Brazilian *guayaba*, *Stanf. Dict.*]), *Guayabo pomifera Indica* of Caspar Bauhin, *Guayava* of Joh. Bauhin, strangely appears by name in Elliot's translation from Amīr Khosrū, who flourished in the 13th century: "He who has placed only *guavas* and quinces in his throat, and has never eaten a plantain, will say it is like so much jujube" (iii. 556). This must be due to some ambiguous word carelessly rendered. The fruit and its name are alike American. It appears to be the *guaiabo* of Oviedo in his *History of the Indies* (we use the Italian version in *Ramusio*, iii. f. 141*v*). There is no mention of the *guava* in either De Orta or Acosta. *Amrūd*, which is the commonest Hindustani (Pers.) name for the guava, means properly 'a pear'; but the fruit is often called *safarī ām*, 'journey mango' (respecting which see under **ANANAS**). And this last term is sometimes vulgarly corrupted into *supārī ām* (areca-mango!). In the Deccan (according to Moodeen Sheriff) and all over Guzerat and the Central Provinces (as we are informed by M.-Gen. Keatinge), the fruit is called *jām*, Mahr. *jamba*, which is in Bengal the name of *Syzigium jambolanum* (see **JAMOON**), and in Guzerāti *jāmrūd*, which seems to be a factitious word in imitation of *āmrūd*.

The guava, though its claims are so inferior to those of the pine-apple (indeed except to stew, or make jelly, it is *nobis judicibus*, an utter impostor), [Sir Joseph Hooker annotates: "You never ate good ones!"] must have spread like that fruit with great rapidity. Both appear in Blochmann's transl. of the *Āīn* (i. 64) as served at Akbar's table; though when the guava is named among the fruits of Tūrān, doubts again arise as to the fruit intended, for the word used, *amrūd*, is ambiguous. In 1688 Dampier mentions guavas at Achin, and in Cochin China. The tree, like the custard-apple, has become wild in some parts of India. See *Davidson*, below.

c. 1550.—"The **guaiava** is like a peach-tree, with a leaf resembling the laurel . . . the red are better than the white, and are well-flavoured."—*Girol. Benzoni*, p. 88.

1658.—There is a good cut of the **guava**, as *guaiaba*, in *Piso*, pp. 152-3.

1673.—". . . flourish pleasant Tops of Plantains, Cocoes, **Guiavas**, a kind of Pear."—*Fryer*, 40.

1676.—"The N.W. part is full of **Guaver** Trees of the greatest variety, and their Fruit the largest and best tasted I have met with."—*Dampier*, ii. 107.

1685.—"The **Guava** . . . when the Fruit is ripe, it is yellow, soft, and very pleasant. It bakes well as a Pear."—*Ibid.* i. 222.

c. 1750-60.—"Our guides too made us distinguish a number of **goyava**, and especially plumb-trees."—*Grose*, i. 20.

1764.—

"A wholesome fruit the ripened **guava** yields,
Boast of the housewife."
Grainger, Bk. i.

1843.—"On some of these extensive plains (on the Mohur R. in Oudh) we found large orchards of the wild **Guava** . . . strongly resembling in their rough appearance the pear-trees in the hedges of Worcestershire."—*Col. C. J. Davidson, Diary of Travels*, ii. 271.

GUBBER, s. This is some kind of gold ducat or sequin; Milburn says 'a Dutch ducat.' It may have adopted this special meaning, but could hardly have held it at the date of our first quotation. The name is probably *gabr* (*dīnār-i-gabr*), implying its being of *infidel* origin.

c. 1590.—"Mirza Jani Beg Sultán made this agreement with his soldiers, that every one who should bring in an enemy's head should receive 500 **gabars**, every one of them worth 12 *mirís* . . . of which 72 went to one *tanka*."—*Táríkh-i-Táhirí*, in *Elliot*, i. 287.

1711.—"Rupees are the most current Coin; they have Venetians, **Gubbers**, Muggerbees, and Pagodas."—*Lockyer*, 201.

,, "When a Parcel of Venetian Ducats are mixt with others the whole goes by the name of *Chequeens* at Surat, but when they are separated, one sort is called Venetians, and all the others **Gubbers** indifferently."—*Ibid.* 242.

1762.—"*Gold and Silver Weights:*

	oz.	dwts.	grs.
100 Venetian Ducats .	11	0	5
10 (100?) **Gubbers** . .	10	17	12."

Brooks, Weights and Measures.

GUBBROW, v. To bully, to dumbfound, and perturb a person. Made from *ghabrāo*, the imperative of *ghabrānā*. The latter, though sometimes used transitively, is more usually neuter, 'to be dumbfounded and perturbed.'

GUDDA, s. A donkey, literal and metaphorical. H. *gadhā*: [Skt. *gardabha*, 'the roarer']. The coincidence of the Scotch *cuddy* has been attributed to a loan from H. through the gypsies, who were the chief owners of the animal in Scotland, where it is not common. On the other hand, this is ascribed to a nickname *Cuddy* (for Cuthbert), like the English *Neddy*, similarly applied. [So the *N.E.D.* with hesitation.] A Punjab proverbial phrase is *gadōn khurkī*, "Donkeys' rubbing" their sides together, a sort of 'claw me and I'll claw thee.'

GUDDY, GUDDEE, s. H. *gaddī*, Mahr. *gādī*. 'The Throne.' Properly it is a cushion, a throne in the Oriental sense, *i.e.* the seat of royalty, "a simple sheet, or mat, or carpet on the floor, with a large cushion or pillow at the head, against which the great man reclines" (*Wilson*). "To be placed on the **guddee**" is to succeed to the kingdom. The word is also used for the pad placed on an elephant's back.

[1809.—"Seendhiya was seated nearly in the centre, on a large square cushion covered with gold brocade; his back supported by a round bolster, and his arms resting upon two flat cushions; all covered with the same costly material, and forming together a kind of throne, called a **musnud**, or **guddee**."—*Broughton, Letters from a Mahratta Camp*, ed. 1892, p. 28.]

GUDGE, s. P.—H. *gaz*, and corr. *gaj*; a Persian yard measure or thereabouts; but in India applied to measures of very varying lengths, from the *hāth*, or natural cubit, to the English yard. In the *Āīn* [ed. *Jarrett*, ii. 58 *seqq.*] Abu'l Fazl details numerous *gaz* which had been in use under the Caliphs or in India, varying from 18 inches English (as calculated by

J. Prinsep) to 52⅛. The *Ilāhī gaz* of Akbar was intended to supersede all these as a standard; and as it was the basis of all records of land-measurements and rents in Upper India, the determination of its value was a subject of much importance when the revenue surveys were undertaken about 1824. The results of enquiry were very discrepant, however, and finally an arbitrary value of 33 inches was assumed. The *bīghā* (see **BEEGAH**), based on this, and containing 3600 square *gaz*=⅝ of an acre, is the standard in the N.W.P., but statistics are now always rendered in acres. See *Gladwin's Ayeen* (1800) i. 302, *seqq.*; *Prinsep's Useful Tables*, ed. Thomas, 122; [*Madras Administration Manual*, ii. 505.]

[1532.—". . . and if in quantity the measure and the weight, and whether ells, roods or **gazes**."—*Archiv. Port. Orient.* f. 5, p. 1562.]

1754.—"Some of the townsmen again demanded of me to open my bales, and sell them some pieces of cloth; but . . . I rather chose to make several of them presents of 2¼ **gaz** of cloth, which is the measure they usually take for a coat."—*Hanway*, i. 125.

1768-71.—"A **gess** or **goss** is 2 *cobidos*, being at Chinsurah 2 feet and 10 inches Rhineland measure." — *Stavorinus*, E.T. i. 463.

1814.—"They have no measures but the **gudge**, which is from their elbow to the end of the middle finger, for measuring length." *Pearce, Acc. of the Ways of the Abyssinians*, in *Tr. Lit. Soc. Bo.* ii. 56.

GUICOWAR, n.p. *Gāekwār*, the title of the Mahratta kings of Guzerat, descended from Dāmāji and Pīlāji Gāekwār, who rose to distinction among Mahratta warriors in the second quarter of the 18th century. The word means 'Cowherd.'

[1813.—"These princes were all styled **Guickwar**, in addition to their family name . . . the word literally means a cow-keeper, which, although a low employment in general, has, in this noble family among the Hindoos, who venerate that animal, become a title of great importance."—*Forbes, Or. Mem.* 2nd ed. i. 375.]

GUINEA-CLOTHS, GUINEA-STUFFS, s. Apparently these were piece-goods bought in India to be used in the West African trade. [On the other hand, Sir G. Birdwood identifies them with **gunny** (*Report on old Recs.*, 224). The manufacture still goes on at Pondicherry.] These are presumably the *Negros-tücher* of Baldaeus (1672), p. 154.

[1675.—"**Guinea-stuffs**," in *Birdwood, ut supra.*]

1726.—We find in a list of cloths purchased by the Dutch Factory at Porto Novo, **Guinees Lywaat**, and *Negros-Kleederen* ('Guinea linens and Negro's clothing').—See *Valentijn, Chorom.* 9.

1813.—"The demand for Surat piece-goods has been much decreased in Europe . . . and from the abolition of the slave trade, the demand for the African market has been much reduced . . . **Guinea stuffs**, 4½ yards each (per ton) 1200 (pieces)."—*Milburn*, i. 289.

[1878.—"The chief trades of Pondicherry are, spinning, weaving and dyeing the cotton stuffs known by the name of **Guinees**."—*Garstin, Man. of S. Arcot*, 426.]

[**GUINEA DEER**, s. An old name for some species of Chevrotain, in the quotation probably the *Tragulus meminna* or Mouse Deer (*Blanford, Mammalia*, 555).

[1755.—"Common deer they have here (in Ceylon) in great abundance, and also **Guinea Deer**."—*Ives*, 57.]

GUINEA-FOWL. There seems to have been, in the 16th century, some confusion between turkeys and Guinea-fowl. See however under **TURKEY**. The Guinea-fowl is the *Meleagris* of Aristotle and others, the *Afra avis* of Horace.

GUINEA-PIG, s. This was a nickname given to midshipmen or apprentices on board Indiamen in the 18th century, when the command of such a vessel was a sure fortune, and large fees were paid to the captain with whom the youngsters embarked. Admiral Smyth, in his *Sailor's Handbook*, 1867, defines: 'The younger midshipmen of an Indiaman.'

[1779.—"I promise you, to me it was no slight penance to be exposed during the whole voyage to the half sneering, satirical looks of the mates and **guinea-pigs**."—*Macintosh, Travels*, quoted in *Carey, Old Days*, i. 73.]

GUINEA-WORM, s. A parasitic worm (*Filaria Medinensis*) inhabiting the subcutaneous cellular tissue of man, frequently in the leg, varying from 6 inches to 12 feet in length, and common on the Pers. Gulf, in Upper Egypt, Guinea, &c. It is found in some parts of W. India. "I have known," writes M.-Gen. Keatinge, "villages where half the people were maimed by it after the rains. Matunga, the Head Quarters of the Bombay Artillery, was abandoned, in great measure, on account of this pest." [It is the disease most common in the Damoh District (*C. P. Gazetteer*, 176, *Sleeman, Rambles, &c.*, ed. *V. A. Smith*, i. 94). It is the *rāshta*, *reshta* of Central Asia (*Schuyler, Turkistan*, i. 147; *Wolff, Travels*, ii. 407).] The reason of the name is shown by the quotation from Purchas respecting its prevalence in Guinea. The disease is graphically described by Agatharchides in the first quotation.

B.C. c. 113.—"Those about the Red Sea who are stricken with a certain malady, as Agatharchides relates, besides being afflicted with other novel and unheard-of symptoms, of which one is that small snake-like worms (δρακόντια μικρὰ) eat through the legs and arms, and peep out, but when touched instantly shrink back again, and winding among the muscles produce intolerable burning pains."—In Dubner's ed. of *Plutarch*, iv. 872, viz. *Table Discussions*, Bk. VIII. Quest. ix. 3.

1600.—"The wormes in the legges and bodies trouble not euery one that goeth to those Countreys, but some are troubled with them and some are not"—(a full account of the disease follows).—*Descn. of* **Guinea**, in *Purchas*, ii. 963.

c. 1630.—"But for their water . . . I may call it *Aqua Mortis* . . . it ingenders small long worms in the legges of such as use to drink it . . . by no potion, no unguent to be remedied: they have no other way to destroy them, save by rowling them about a pin or peg, not unlike the treble of Theorbo."—*Sir T. Herbert*, p. 128.

1664.—". . . nor obliged to drink of those naughty waters . . . full of nastiness of so many people and beasts . . . that do cause such fevers, which are very hard to cure, and which breed also certain very dangerous worms in the legs . . . they are commonly of the bigness and length of a small Vial-string . . . and they must be drawn out little by little, from day to day, gently winding them about a little twig about the bigness of a needle, for fear of breaking them."—*Bernier*, E.T. 114; [ed. *Constable*, 355].

1676.—"**Guinea Worms** are very frequent in some Places of the West Indies . . . I rather judge that they are generated by drinking bad water."—*Dampier*, ii. 89-90.

1712.—"Haec vita est Ormusiensium, imò civium totius littoris Persici, ut perpetuas in corpore calamitates ferant ex coeli intemperie: modo sudore diffluunt; modo vexantur furunculis; nunc cibi sunt, mox aquae inopes; saepè ventis urentibus, semper sole torrente, squalent et quis omnia recenseat? Unum ex aerumnis gravioribus induco: nimirum *Lumbricorum* singulare genus, quod non in intestinis, sed in musculis per corporis ambitum natales invenit. Latini medici vermem illum nomine donant τοῦ δρακοντίου, s. *Dracunculi*. . . . **Guineenses** nigritae linguâ suâ . . . vermes illos vocant *Ickòn*, ut produnt reduces ex aurifero illo Africae littore. . . ."—*Kaempfer, Amoen. Exot.*, 524-5. Kaempfer speculates as to why the old physicians called it *dracunculus*; but the name was evidently taken from the δρακόντιον of Agatharchides, quoted above.

1768.—"The less dangerous diseases which attack Europeans in Guinea are, the dry belly-ache, and a worm which breeds in the flesh. . . . Dr. Rouppe observes that the disease of the **Guinea-worm** is infectious."—*Lind on Diseases of Hot Climates*, pp. 53, 54.

1774.—See an account of this pest under the name of "*le ver des nerfs* (Vena Medinensis)," in *Niebuhr, Desc. de l'Arabie*, 117. The name given by Niebuhr is, as we learn from Kaempfer's remarks, *'araḳ Medīnī*, the Medina nerve (rather than vein).

[1821.—"The doctor himself is just going off to the Cape, half-dead from the Kotah fever; and, as if that were not enough, the *narooa*, or **guinea-worm**, has blanched his cheek and made him a cripple."—*Tod, Annals*, ed. 1884, ii. 743.]

GUJPUTTY, n.p. (See **COSPETIR.**)

GUM-GUM, s. We had supposed this word to be an invention of the late Charles Dickens, but it seems to be a real Indian, or Anglo-Indian, word. The nearest approximation in Shakespear's Dict. is *gamak*, 'sound of the kettledrum.' But the word is perhaps a Malay plural of *gong* originally; see the quotation from *Osbeck*. [The quotations from *Bowdich* and *Medley* (from *Scott, Malay Words*, p. 53) perhaps indicate an African origin.]

[1659.—". . . The roar of great guns, the sounding of trumpets, the beating of drums, and the noise of the **gomgommen** of the Indians."—From the account of the Dutch attack (1659) on a village in Ceram, given in *Wouter Schouten, Reistogt nadr en door Oostindiën*, 4th ed. 1775, i. 55. In the Dutch version, "en het geraas van de **gomgommen** der Indiäanen." The French of 1707 (i. 92) has "au bruit du canon, des trompettes, des tambour et des **gomgommes** Indiennes."

[1731.—"One of the Hottentot Instruments of Musick is common to several Negro Nations, and is called both by Negroes and Hottentots, **gom-gom** . . . is a Bow of Iron, or Olive Wood, strung with twisted Sheep-Gut or Sinews."—*Medley*, tr. *Kolben's Cape of Good Hope*, i. 271.]

c. 1750-60.—"A music far from delightful, consisting of little drums they call **Gum-gums**, cymbals, and a sort of fife."—*Grose*, i. 139.

1768-71.—"They have a certain kind of musical instruments called **gom-goms**, consisting in hollow iron bowls, of various sizes and tones, upon which a man strikes with an iron or wooden stick . . . not unlike a set of bells."—*Stavorinus*, E.T. i. 215. See also p. 65.

1771.—"At night we heard a sort of music, partly made by insects, and partly by the noise of the **Gungung**."—*Osbeck*, i. 185.

[1819.—"The **gong-gongs** and drums were beat all around us."—*Bowdich, Mission to Ashantee*, i. 7, 136.]

1836.—"'Did you ever hear a tom-tom, Sir?' sternly enquired the Captain . . .

'A what?' asked Hardy, rather taken aback.

'A tom-tom.'

'Never!'

'Nor a **gum-gum**?'

'Never!'

'What *is* a **gum-gum**?' eagerly enquired several young ladies."—*Sketches by Boz, The Steam Excursion*.

[**GUNGE**, s. Hind. *ganj*, 'a store, store-house, market.'

[1762.—See under **GOMASTA**.

[1772.—"**Gunge**, a market principally for grain."—*Verelst, View of Bengal*, Gloss. s.v.

[1858.—"The term **Gunge** signifies a range of buildings at a place of traffic, for the accommodation of merchants and all persons engaged in the purchase and sale of goods, and for that of their goods and of the shopkeepers who supply them."—*Sleeman, Journey through Oudh*, i. 278.]

GUNJA, s. Hind. *gānjhā*, *gānjā*. The flowering or fruiting shoots of the female plant of Indian hemp (*Cannabis sativa*, L., formerly distinguished as *C. indica*), used as an intoxicant. (See **BANG**.)

[c. 1813.—"The natives have two proper names for the hemp (*Cannabis sativa*), and call it **Gangja** when young, and *Siddhi* when the flowers have fully expanded."—*Buchanan, Eastern India*, ii. 865.]

1874.—"In odour and the absence of taste, **ganjá** resembles *bhang*. It is said that after the leaves which constitute *bhang* have been gathered, little shoots sprout from the stem, and that these, picked off and dried, form what is called **ganjá**."—*Hanbury & Flückiger*, 493.

GUNNY, GUNNY-BAG, s. From Skt. *goṇī*, 'a sack'; Hind. and Mahr. *goṇ*, *goṇī*, 'a sack, sacking.' The popular and trading name of the coarse sacking and sacks made from the fibre of **jute**, much used in all Indian trade. *Ṭāṭ* is a common Hind. name for the stuff. [With this word Sir G. Birdwood identifies the forms found in the old records—"*Guiny* Stuffes (1671)," "*Guynie* stuffs," "*Guinea* stuffs," "*Gunnys*" (*Rep. on Old Records*, 26, 38, 39, 224); but see under **GUINEA-CLOTHS**.]

c. 1590.—"Sircar Ghoraghat produces raw silk, **gunneys**, and plenty of *Tanghion* horses."—*Gladwin's Ayeen*, ed. 1800, ii. 9; [ed. *Jarrett*, ii. 123]. (But here, in the original, the term is *pārchah-i-ṭāṭband*.)

1693.—"Besides the aforenamed articles **Goeny-sacks** are collected at Palicol."—*Havart* (3), 14.

1711.—"When Sugar is pack'd in double **Goneys**, the outer Bag is always valued in Contract at 1 or 1½ *Shahee*."—*Lockyer*, 244.

1726.—In a list of goods procurable at *Daatzerom*: "**Goeni-zakken** (Gunny bags)."—*Valentijn, Chor.* 40.

1727.—"Sheldon . . . put on board some rotten long Pepper, that he could dispose of in no other Way, and some damaged **Gunnies**, which are much used in Persia for embaling Goods, when they are good in their kind."—*A. Hamilton*, ii. 15; [ed. 1744].

1764.—"Baskets, **Gunny bags**, and *dubbers* . . . Rs. 24."—In *Long*, 384.

1785.—"We enclose two *parwanehs* . . . directing them each to despatch 1000 **goonies** of grain to that person of mighty degree."—*Tippoo's Letters*, 171.

1885.—"The land was so covered with them (plover) that the hunters shot them with all kind of arms. We counted 80 birds in the **gunny**-sack that three of the soldiers brought in."—*Boots and Saddles*, by *Mrs. Custer*, p. 37. (American work.)

GUNTA, s. Hind. *ghanṭā*, 'a bell or gong.' This is the common term for expressing an European hour in modern Hindūstānī. [See **PANDY**.]

GUP, s. Idle gossip. P.—H. *gap*, 'prattle, tattle.' The word is perhaps an importation from Tūrān. Vámbéry gives Orient. Turki *gep*, *geb*, 'word, saying, talk'; which, however, Pavet de Courteille suggests to be a corruption from the Pers. *guftan*, 'to say'; of which, indeed, there is a form *guptan*. [So Platts, who also compares Skt. *jalpa*, which is the Bengali *golpo*, 'babble.'] See quotation from Schuyler showing the use in Turkistan. The word is perhaps best known in England through an unamiable account of society in S.

India, published under the name of "**Gup**," in 1868.

1809-10.—"They (native ladies) sit on their cushions from day to day, with no other . . . amusement than hearing the '**gúp-gup**,' or gossip of the place."—*Mrs. Sherwood's Autobiog.* 357.

1876.—"The first day of mourning goes by the name of **gup**, *i.e.* commemorative talk."—*Schuyler's Turkistan*, i. 151.

GUREEBPURWUR, GURREEB-NUWAUZ, ss. Ar.—P. *Gharībpārwar*, *Gharībnawāz*, used in Hind. as respectful terms of address, meaning respectively 'Provider of the Poor!' 'Cherisher of the Poor!'

1726.—"Those who are of equal condition bend the body somewhat towards each other, and lay hold of each other by the beard, saying **Grab-anemoas**, *i.e.* I wish you the prayers of the poor."—*Valentijn*, *Chor.* 109, who copies from *Van Twist* (1648), p. 55.

1824.—"I was appealed to loudly by both parties, the soldiers calling on me as '**Ghureeb purwur**,' the Goomashta, not to be outdone, exclaiming 'Donai, Lord Sahib! Donai! Rajah!'" (Read *Dohāī* and see **DOAI**).—*Heber*, i. 266. See also p. 279.

1867.—"'**Protector of the poor!**' he cried, prostrating himself at my feet, 'help thy most unworthy and wretched slave! An unblest and evil-minded alligator has this day devoured my little daughter. She went down to the river to fill her earthen jar with water, and the evil one dragged her down, and has devoured her. Alas! she had on her gold bangles. Great is my misfortune!'"—*Lt-Col. Lewin, A Fly on the Wheel*, p. 99.

GURJAUT, n.p. The popular and official name of certain forest tracts at the back of Orissa. The word is a hybrid, being the Hind. *gaṛh*, 'a fort,' Persianised into a plural *gaṛhjāt*, in ignorance of which we have seen, in quasi-official documents, the use of a further English plural, *Gurjauts* or *gaṛhjāts*, which is like 'fortses.' [In the quotation below, the writer seems to think it a name of a class of people.] This manner of denominating such tracts from the isolated occupation by fortified posts seems to be very ancient in that part of India. We have in Ptolemy and the *Periplus* *Ḍosarēnē* or *Dēsarēnē*, apparently representing Skt. *Daśārṇa*, quasi *daśan ṛiṇa*, 'having Ten Forts,' which the lists of the *Bṛhat Sanhitā* shew us in this part of India (*J.R. As. Soc.*, N.S., v. 83). The forest tract behind Orissa is called in the grant of an Orissa king, *Nava Koti*, 'the Nine Forts' (*J.A.S.B.* xxxiii. 84); and we have, in this region, further in the interior, the province of *Chattīsgaṛh*, '36 Forts.'

[1820.—"At present nearly one half of this extensive region is under the immediate jurisdiction of the British Government; the other possessed by tributary zemindars called **Ghurjauts**, or hill chiefs. . . ."—*Hamilton, Description of Hindostan*, ii. 32.]

GURRY.

a. A little fort; Hind. *gaṛhī*. Also **Gurr**, *i.e.* *gaṛh*, 'a fort.'

b. See **GHURRY**.

a.—

1693.—". . . many of his Heathen Nobles, only such as were befriended by strong **Gurrs**, or Fastnesses upon the Mountains. . . ."—*Fryer*, 165.

1786.—". . . The Zemindars in 4 pergunnahs are so refractory as to have forfeited (read *fortified*) themselves in their **gurries**, and to refuse all payments of revenue."—*Articles against W. Hastings*, in *Burke*, vii. 59.

[1835.—"A shot was at once fired upon them from a high **Ghurree**."—*Forbes, Rās Mālā*, ed. 1878, p. 521.]

GUTTA PERCHA, s. This is the Malay name *Gatah Pertja*, *i.e.* 'Sap of the Percha,' *Dichopsis Gutta*, Benth. (*Isonandra Gutta*, Hooker; N.O. *Sapotaceae*). Dr. Oxley writes (*J. Ind. Archip.* i. 22) that *percha* is properly the name of a tree which produces a spurious article; the real *gutta p.* is produced by the *túbau*. [Mr. Maxwell (*Ind. Ant.* xvii. 358) points out that the proper reading is *taban*.] The product was first brought to notice in 1843 by Dr. Montgomery. It is collected by first ringing the tree and then felling it, and no doubt by this process the article will speedily become extinct. The history of G. P. is, however, far from well known. Several trees are known to contribute to the exported article; their juices being mixed together. [Mr. Scott (*Malay Words*, 55 *seqq.*) writes the word *getah percha*, or *getah perchah*, 'gum of percha,' and remarks that it has been otherwise explained as meaning 'gum of Sumatra,' "there being another word *percha*, a name of Sumatra, as well as a third word *percha*, 'a rag, a remnant.'" Mr. Maxwell (*loc. cit.*) writes: "It is still uncertain whether there is a gutta-producing tree called *Percha* by the Malays. My experience is that they give the name of *Perchah* to that kind of *getah taban* which hardens into strips in boiling. These are stuck together and made into balls for export."]

[1847.—"**Gutta Percha** is a remarkable example of the rapidity with which a really useful invention becomes of importance to the English public. A year ago it was almost unknown, but now its peculiar properties are daily being made more available in some new branch of the useful or ornamental arts."—*Mundy, Journal*, in *Narrative of Events in Borneo and Celebes*, ii. 342 *seq.* (quoted by *Scott, loc. cit.*).]

1868.—"The late Mr. d'Almeida was the first to call the attention of the public to the substance now so well known as **gutta-percha.** At that time the *Isonandra Gutta* was an abundant tree in the forests of Singapore, and was first known to the Malays, who made use of the juice which they obtained by cutting down the trees. . . . Mr. d'Almeida . . . acting under the advice of a friend, forwarded some of the substance to the Society of Arts. There it met with no immediate attention, and was put away uncared for. A year or two afterwards Dr. Montgomery sent specimens to England, and bringing it under the notice of competent persons, its value was at once acknowledged. . . . The sudden and great demand for it soon resulted in the disappearance of all the **gutta-percha** trees on Singapore Island."—*Collingwood, Rambles of a Naturalist*, pp. 268-9.

ᵗGUZZY, s. Pers. and Hind. *gazī*; perhaps from its having been woven of a *gaz* (see **GUDGE**) in breadth. A very poor kind of cotton cloth.

1701.—In a price list for Persia we find: "**Gesjes** Bengaals."—*Valentijn*, v. 303.

1784.—"It is suggested that the following articles may be proper to compose the first adventure (to Tibet): . . . **Guzzie**, or coarse Cotton Cloths, and Otterskins. . . ."—In *Seton-Karr*, i. 4.

[1866.—". . . common unbleached fabrics . . . used for packing goods, and as a covering for the dead. . . These fabrics in Bengal pass under the names of *Garrha* and **Guzee.**"—*Forbes Watson, Textile Manufactures*, 83.]

GWALIOR, n.p. Hind. *Gwālīār*. A very famous rock-fortress of Upper India, rising suddenly and picturesquely out of a plain (or shallow valley rather) to a height of 300 feet, 65 m. south of Agra, in lat. 26° 13′. Gwalior may be traced back, in Gen. Cunningham's opinion, to the 3rd century of our era. It was the seat of several ancient Hindu dynasties, and from the time of the early Mahommedan sovereigns of Delhi down to the reign of Aurangzīb it was used as a state-prison. Early in the 18th century it fell into the possession of the Mahratta family of Sindhia, whose residence was established to the south of the fortress, in what was originally a camp, but has long been a city known by the original title of *Lashkar* (camp). The older city lies below the northern foot of the rock. Gwalior has been three times taken by British arms: (1) escaladed by a force under the command of Major Popham in 1780, a very daring feat;* (2) by a regular attack under Gen. White in 1805; (3) most gallantly in June 1858, by a party of the 25th Bombay N. I. under Lieutenants Rose and Waller, in which the former officer fell. After the two first captures the fortress was restored to the Sindhia family. From 1858 it was retained in our hands, but in December 1885 it was formally restored to the Mahārājā Sindhia.

The name of the fortress, according to Gen. Cunningham (*Archaeol. Survey*, ii. 335), is derived from a small Hindū shrine within it dedicated to the hermit *Gwāli* or *Gwāli-pā*, after whom the fortress received the name of *Gwāli-āwar*, contracted into *Gwālīār*.

c. 1020.—"From Kanauj, in travelling south-east, on the western side of the Ganges, you come to Jajáhotí, at a distance of 30 parasangs, of which the capital is Kajuráha. In that country are the two forts of **Gwáliár** and Kálinjar. . . ."—*Al-Bīrūnī*, in *Elliot*, i. 57-8.

1196.—The royal army marched "towards **Gālewār**, and invested that fort, which is the pearl of the necklace of the castles of Hind, the summit of which the nimble-footed wind from below cannot reach, and on the bastions of which the clouds have never cast their shade. . . ."—*Hasan Nizāmī*, in *Elliot*, ii. 227.

c. 1340.—"The castle of **Gālyūr**, of which we have been speaking, is on the top of a high hill, and appears, so to speak, as if it were itself cut out of the rock. There is no other hill adjoining; it contains reservoirs

* The two companies which escaladed were led by Captain Bruce, a brother of the Abyssinian traveller. "It is said that the spot was pointed out to Popham by a cowherd, and that the whole of the attacking party were supplied with grass shoes to prevent them from slipping on the ledges of rock. There is a story also that the cost of these grass-shoes was deducted from Popham's pay, when he was about to leave India as a major-general, nearly a quarter of a century afterwards."—*Cunningham, Arch. Surv.* ii. 340.

of water, and some 20 wells walled round are attached to it: on the walls are mounted mangonels and catapults. The fortress is ascended by a wide road, traversed by elephants and horses. Near the castle-gate is the figure of an elephant carved in stone, and surmounted by a figure of the driver. Seeing it from a distance one has no doubt about its being a real elephant. At the foot of the fortress is a fine city, entirely built of white stone, mosques and houses alike; there is no timber to be seen in it, except that of the gates."—*Ibn Batuta*, ii. 193.

1526.—"I entered **Guâliâr** by the Hâtipûl gate. . . . They call an elephant *hâti*, and a gate *pûl*. On the outside of this gate is the figure of an elephant, having two elephant drivers on it. . . ."—*Baber*, p. 383.

[c. 1590.—"**Gualiar** is a famous fort, in which are many stately buildings, and there is a stone elephant over the gate. The air and water of this place are both esteemed good. It has always been celebrated for fine singers and beautiful women. . . ."—*Ayeen*, *Gladwin*, ed. 1800, ii. 38; ed. *Jarrett*, ii. 181.]

1610.—"The 31 to **Gwalere**, 6 c., a pleasant Citie with a Castle. . . . On the West side of the Castle, which is a steep craggy cliffe of 6 c. compasse at least (divers say eleven). . . . From hence to the top, leads a narrow stone cawsey, walled on both sides; in the way are three gates to be passed, all exceeding strong, with Courts of guard to each. At the top of all, at the entrance of the last gate, standeth a mightie Elephant of stone very curiously wrought. . . ."—*Finch*, in *Purchas*, i. 426-7.

1616.—"23. **Gwalier**, the chief City so called, where the Mogol hath a very rich Treasury of Gold and Silver kept in this City, within an exceeding strong Castle, wherein the King's *Prisoners* are likewise kept. The Castle is continually guarded by a very strong Company of Armed Souldiers."—*Terry*, ed. 1665, p. 356.

[,, "**Kualiar**," in *Sir T. Roe's List*, Hak. Soc. ii. 539.]

c. 1665.—"For to shut them up in **Goualeor**, which is a Fortress where the Princes are ordinarily kept close, and which is held impregnable, it being situated upon an inaccessible Rock, and having within itself good water, and provision enough for a Garison; *that* was not an easie thing."—*Bernier* E.T. 5; [ed. *Constable*, 14].

c. 1670.—"Since the Mahometan Kings became Masters of this Countrey, this Fortress of **Goualeor** is the place where they secure Princes and great Noblemen. *Chaiehan* coming to the Empire by foul-play, caus'd all the Princes and Lords whom he mistrusted, to be seiz'd one after another, and sent them to the Fortress of **Goualeor**; but he suffer'd them all to live and enjoy their estates. *Aureng-zeb* his Son acts quite otherwise; for when he sends any great Lord to this place, at the end of nine or ten days he orders him to be poison'd; and this he does that the people may not exclaim against him for a bloody Prince."—*Tavernier*, E.T. ii. 35; [ed. *Ball*, i. 63].

GYAUL (properly **GAYĀL**), [Skt. *go*, 'an ox'], s. A large animal (*Gavaeus frontalis*, Jerd., *Bos f.* Blanford, *Mammalia*, 487) of the ox tribe, found wild in various forest tracts to the east of India. It is domesticated by the Mishmis of the Assam valley, and other tribes as far south as Chittagong. In Assam it is called *Mithan*.

[c. 1590.—In Arakan, "cows and buffaloes there are none, but there is an animal which has somewhat of the characteristics of both, piebald and particoloured whose milk the people drink."—*Āīn*, ed. *Jarrett*, ii. 119.]

1824.—"In the park several uncommon animals are kept. Among them the **Ghyal**, an animal of which I had not, to my recollection, read any account, though the name was not unknown to me. It is a very noble creature, of the ox or buffalo kind, with immensely large horns. . . ."—*Heber*, i. 34.

1866-67.—"I was awakened by an extraordinary noise, something between a bull's bellow and a railway whistle. What was it? We started to our feet, and Fuzlah and I were looking to our arms when Adupah said, 'It is only the **guyal** calling; Sahib! Look, the dawn is just breaking, and they are opening the village gates for the beasts to go out to pasture.'

"These **guyal** were beautiful creatures, with broad fronts, sharp wide-spreading horns, and mild melancholy eyes. They were the indigenous cattle of the hills domesticated by these equally wild Lushais. . . ."—*Lt.-Col. T. Lewin, A Fly on the Wheel*, &c., p. 303.

GYELONG, s. A Buddhist priest in Tibet. Tib. *dGe-sLong*, *i.e.* 'beggar of virtue,' *i.e.* a *bhikshu* or mendicant friar (see under **BUXEE**); but latterly a priest who has received the highest orders. See *Jaeschke*, p. 86.

1784.—"He was dressed in the festival habit of a **gylong** or priest, being covered with a scarlet satin cloak, and a gilded mitre on his head."—*Bogle*, in *Markham's Tibet*, 25.

GYM-KHANA, s. This word is quite modern, and was unknown 40 years ago. The first use that we can trace is (on the authority of Major John Trotter) at Rūrkī in 1861, when a *gymkhana* was instituted there. It is a factitious word, invented, we believe, in the Bombay Presidency, and probably based upon *gend-khāna* ('ball-house'), the name usually given in Hind. to an English racket-court. It is applied to a place of public resort at a station, where the needful facilities for athletics and games of sorts are provided, including (when that was in fashion) a skating-rink, a lawn-tennis ground, and so forth. The *gym* may have been simply a corruption of *gend* shaped by *gym*nastics, [of which the English public school short form *gym* passed into Anglo-Indian jargon]. The word is also applied to a meeting for such sports; and in this sense it has travelled already as far as Malta, and has since become common among Englishmen abroad. [The suggestion that the word originated in the P.—H. *jamā'at-khana*, 'a place of assemblage,' is not probable.]

1877.—"Their proposals are that the Cricket Club should include in their programme the games, &c., proposed by the promoters of a **gymkhana** Club, so far as not to interfere with cricket, and should join in making a rink and lawn-tennis, and badminton courts, within the cricket-ground enclosure."—*Pioneer Mail*, Nov. 3.

1879.—"Mr. A—— F—— can always be depended on for epigram, but not for accuracy. In his letters from Burma he talks of the **Gymkhana** at Rangoon as a sort of *establissement* [*sic*] where people have pleasant little dinners. In the 'Oriental Arcadia,' which Mr. F—— tells us is flavoured with naughtiness, people may do strange things, but they do *not* dine at **Gymkhanas**."—*Ibid*. July 2.

1881.—"R. E. **Gymkhana** at Malta, for Polo and other Ponies, 20th June, 1881."—Heading in *Royal Engineer Journal*, Aug. 1, p. 159.

1883.—"I am not speaking of Bombay people with their clubs and **gymkhanas** and other devices for oiling the wheels of existence. . . ."—*Tribes on My Frontier*, 9.

GYNEE, s. H. *gainī*. A very diminutive kind of cow bred in Bengal. It is, when well cared for, a beautiful creature, is not more than 3 feet high, and affords excellent meat. It is mentioned by Aelian:

c. 250.—"There are other bullocks in India, which to look at are no bigger than the largest goats; these also are yoked, and run very swiftly."—*De Nat. Anim.*, xv. 24.

c. 1590.—"There is also a species of oxen called **gaini**, small like *gūt* (see **GOONT**) horses, but very beautiful."—*Āīn*, i. 149.

[1829.—". . . I found that the said tiger had feasted on a more delicious morsel,—a nice little **Ghinee**, a small cow."—*Mem. of John Shipp*, iii. 132.]

1832.—"We have become great farmers, having sown our crop of oats, and are building outhouses to receive some 34 dwarf cows and oxen (**gynees**) which are to be fed up for the table."—*F. Parkes, Wanderings of a Pilgrim*, i. 251.

H

HACKERY, s. In the Bengal Presidency this word is now applied only to the common native bullock-cart used in the slow draught of goods and materials. But formerly in Bengal, as still in Western India and Ceylon, the word was applied to lighter carriages (drawn by bullocks) for personal transport. In Broughton's *Letters from a Mahratta Camp* (p. 156; [ed. 1892, p. 117]) the word is used for what in Upper India is commonly called an **ekka** (q.v.), or light native pony-carriage; but this is an exceptional application. Though the word is used by Englishmen almost universally in India, it is unknown to natives, or if known is regarded as an English term; and its origin is exceedingly obscure. The word seems to have originated on the west side of India, where we find it in our earliest quotations. It is probably one of those numerous words which were long in use, and undergoing corruption by illiterate soldiers and sailors, before they appeared in any kind of literature. Wilson suggests a probable Portuguese origin, *e.g.* from *acarretar*, 'to convey in a cart.' It is possible that the mere Portuguese article and noun '*a carreta*' might have produced the Anglo-Indian *hackery*. Thus in Correa, under 1513, we have a description of the Surat hackeries; "and the carriages (*as carretas*) in which he and the Portuguese travelled, were elaborately wrought, and furnished with silk hangings, covering them from the sun; and these carriages (*as carretas*) run so smoothly (the country consisting of level plains) that the people travelling in them sleep as tranquilly as on the ground" (ii. 369).

But it is almost certain that the origin of the word is the H. *chhakra*, 'a two-wheeled cart'; and it may be noted that in old Singhalese *çhakka*, 'a cart-wheel,' takes the forms *haka* and *saka* (see *Kuhn, On Oldest Aryan Elements of Singhalese*, translated by D. Ferguson in *Indian Ant.* xii. 64). [But this can have no connection with *chhakra*, which represents Skt. *śakaṭa*, 'a waggon.']

1673.—"The Coach wherein I was breaking, we were forced to mount the Indian **Hackery**, a Two-wheeled Chariot, drawn by swift little Oxen."—*Fryer*, 83. [For these swift oxen, see quot. from Forbes below, and from Aelian under **GYNEE**].

1690.—"Their **Hackeries** likewise, which are a kind of Coach, with two Wheels, are all drawn by Oxen."—*Ovington*, 254.

1711.—"The Streets (at Surat) are wide and commodious; otherwise the **Hackerys**, which are very common, would be an Inconveniency. These are a sort of Coaches drawn by a Pair of Oxen."—*Lockyer*, 259.

1742.—"The bridges are much worn, and out of repair, by the number of **Hackaries** and other carriages which are continually passing over them."—In *Wheeler*, iii. 262.

1756.—"The 11th of July the Nawab arrived in the city, and with him Bundoo Sing, to whose house we were removed that afternoon in a **hackery**."—*Holwell*, in *Wheeler's Early Records*, 249.

c. 1760.—"The **hackrees** are a conveyance drawn by oxen, which would at first give an idea of slowness that they do not deserve . . . they are open on three sides, covered a-top, and are made to hold two people sitting cross-legged."—*Grose*, i. 155-156.

1780.—"A **hackery** is a small covered carriage upon two wheels drawn by bullocks, and used generally for the female part of the family."—*Hodges, Travels*, 5.

c. 1790.—"Quant aux palankins et **hakkaries** (voitures à deux roues), on les passe sur une double **sangarie**" (see **JANGAR**).—*Haafner*, ii. 173.

1793.—"To be sold by Public Auction . . . a new Fashioned **Hackery**."—*Bombay Courier*, April 13.

1798.—"At half-past six o'clock we each got into a **hackeray**."—*Stavorinus*, tr. by *Wilcocks*, iii. 295.

1811.—Solvyns draws and describes the **Hackery** in the modern Bengal sense.

" "Il y a cependant quelques endroits où l'on se sert de charettes couvertes à deux roues, appelées **hickeris**, devant lesquelles on attèle des bœufs, et qui servent à voyager."—Editor of *Haafner, Voyages*, ii. 3.

1813.—"Travelling in a light **hackaree**, at the rate of five miles an hour."—*Forbes, Or. Mem.* iii. 376; [2nd ed. ii. 352; in i. 150, **hackeries**, ii. 253, **hackarees**]. Forbes's engraving represents such an ox-carriage as would be called in Bengal a *bailī* (see **BYLEE**).

1829.—"The genuine vehicle of the country is the **hackery**. This is a sort of wee tent, covered more or less with tinsel and scarlet, and bells and gilding, and placed upon a clumsy two-wheeled carriage with a pole that seems to be also a kind of boot, as it is at least a foot deep. This is drawn by a pair of white bullocks."—*Mem. of Col. Mountain*, 2nd ed., 84.

1860.—"Native gentlemen, driving fast trotting oxen in little **hackery** carts, hastened home from it."—*Tennent's Ceylon*, ii. 140.

[**HADDY**, s. A grade of troops in the Mogul service. According to Prof. Blochmann (*Āīn*, i. 20, note) they corresponded to our "Warranted officers." "Most clerks of the Imperial offices, the painters of the Court, the foremen in Akbar's workshops, &c., belonged to this corps. They were called *Aḥadīs*, or single men, because they stood under Akbar's immediate orders." And Mr. Irvine writes: "Midway between the nobles or leaders (*mansabdārs*) with the horsemen under them (*tābīnān*) on the one hand, and the *Aḥshām* (see **EYSHAM**), or infantry, artillery, and artificers on the other, stood the *Aḥadī*, or gentleman trooper. The word is literally 'single' or 'alone' (A. *aḥad*, 'one'). It is easy to see why this name was applied to them; they offered their services singly, they did not attach themselves to any chief, thus forming a class apart from the *tābīnān*; but as they were horsemen, they stood equally apart from the specialised services included under the remaining head of *Aḥshām*." (*J. R. As. Soc.*, July 1896, p. 545.)

[c. 1590.—"Some soldiers are placed under the care and guidance of *one* commander. They are called **Ahadis**, because they are fit for a harmonious *unity*."—*Āīn*, ed. *Blochmann*, i. 231.

[1616.—"The Prince's **Haddy** . . . betrayed me."—*Sir T. Roe*, Hak. Soc. ii. 383.

[1617.—"A **Haddey** of horse sent down to see it effected."—*Ibid.* ii. 450.

[c. 1625.—"The day after, one of the King's **Haddys** finding the same."—*Coryat*, in *Purchas*, i. 600.]

HADGEE, s. Ar. *Ḥājj*, a pilgrim to Mecca; from *ḥajj*, the pilgrimage, or visit to a venerated spot. Hence *Ḥājjī* and *Ḥājī* used colloquially in Persian and Turkish. Prof. Robertson Smith writes: "There is current confusion about the word *ḥājj*. It is originally the participle of *ḥajj*, 'he went on the *ḥajj*.' But in modern use *ḥājij* is used as part., and *ḥājj* is the title given to one who has made the pilgrimage. When this is prefixed to a name, the double *j* cannot be pronounced without inserting a short vowel and the *a* is shortened; thus you say '*el-Hajjĕ* Soleimān,' or the like. The incorrect form *Hājjī* is however used by Turks and Persians."

[1609.—"Upon your order, if **Hoghee** Careen so please, I purpose to delve him 25 pigs of lead."—*Danvers, Letters*, i. 26.

[c. 1610.—"Those who have been to Arabia . . . are called **Agy**."—*Pyrard de Laval*, Hak. Soc. i. 165.

[c. 1665.—"*Aureng-Zebe* once observed perhaps by way of joke, that *Sultan Sujah* was become at last an **Agy** or pilgrim."—*Bernier*, ed. *Constable*, 113.

[1673.—"**Hodge**, a Pilgrimage to Mecca." (See under **A MUCK**.)

[1683.—"**Hodgee** Sophee Caun." See under **FIRMAUN**.]

1765.—"**Hodgee** acquired this title from his having in his early years made a pilgrimage to **Hodge** (or the tomb of *Mahommed* at *Mecca*)."—*Holwell, Hist. Events*, &c., i. 59.

[c. 1833.—"The very word in Hebrew *Khog*, which means 'festival,' originally meant 'pilgrimage,' and corresponds with what the Arabs call **hatch**. . . ."—*Travels of Dr. Wolff*, ii. 155.]

HÁKIM, s. H. from Ar. *ḥākim*, 'a judge, a ruler, a master'; 'the authority.' The same Ar. root *ḥakm*, 'bridling, restraining, judging,' supplies a variety of words occurring in this Glossary, viz. *Hākim* (as here); *Hakīm* (see **HUCKEEM**); *Ḥukm* (see **HOOKUM**); *Ḥikmat* (see **HICKMAT**).

[1611.—"Not standing with his greatness to answer every **Haccam**, which is as a Governor or petty King."—*Danvers, Letters*, i. 158. In *ibid.* i. 175, **Hackum** is used in the same way.]

1698.—"**Hackum**, a Governor."—*Fryer's Index Explanatory*.

c. 1861.—
"Then comes a settlement **Hakim**, to teach
me to plough and weed—
I sowed the cotton he gave me—but first
I boiled the seed. . . ."

Sir A. C. Lyall, The Old Pindaree.

HALÁLCORE, s. Lit. Ar.—P. *ḥalāl-khor*, 'one who eats what is lawful,' [*ḥalāl* being the technical Mahommedan phrase for the slaying of an animal to be used for food according to the proper ritual], applied euphemistically to a person of very low caste, a sweeper or scavenger, implying 'to whom all is lawful food.' Generally used as synonymous with **bungy** (q.v.). [According to Prof. Blochmann, "*Halālkhūr*, *i.e.* one who eats that which the ceremonial law allows, is a euphemism for *ḥarāmkhūr*, one who eats forbidden things, as pork, &c. The word *ḥalālkhūr* is still in use among educated Muhammadans; but it is doubtful whether (as stated in the *Āīn*) it was Akbar's invention." (*Āīn*, i. 139 note.)]

1623.—"Schiah Selim nel principio . . . si sdegnò tanto, che poco mancò che per dispetto non la desse per forza in matrimonio ad uno della razza che chiamano **halal chor**, quasi dica 'mangia lecito,' cioè che ha per lecito di mangiare ogni cosa. . . ." (See other quotation under **HAREM**).—*P. della Valle*, ii. 525; [Hak. Soc. i. 54].

1638.—". . . sont obligez de se purifier depuis la teste i'usqu'aux pieds si quelqu'vn de ces gens qu'ils appellent **Alchores**, leur a touché."—*Mandelslo*, Paris, 1659, 219.

1665.—"Ceux qui ne parlent que Persan dans les Indes, les appellent **Halalcour**, c'est à dire celui qui se donne la liberté de manger de tout ce qu'il lui plait, ou, selon quelques uns, celui qui mange ce qu'il a légitimement gagné. Et ceux qui approuvent cette dernière explication, disent qu'autrefois **Halalcours** s'appellent *Haramcours*, mangeurs de Viande defenduës."—*Thevenot*, v. 190.

1673.—"That they should be accounted the Offscum of the People, and as base as the **Holencores** (whom they account so, because they defile themselves by eating anything)."—*Fryer*, 28; [and see under **BOY, b**].

1690.—"The **Halalchors** . . . are another Sort of Indians at Suratt, the most contemptible, but extremely necessary to be there."—*Ovington*, 382.

1763.—"And now I must mention the **Hallachores**, whom I cannot call a Tribe, being rather the refuse of all the Tribes. These are a set of poor unhappy wretches, destined to misery from their birth. . . ."—*Reflexions*, &c., by *Luke Scrafton*, Esq., 7-8. It was probably in this passage that Burns (see below) picked up the word.

1783.—"That no **Hollocore**, Derah, or Chandala caste, shall upon any consideration come out of their houses after 9 o'clock in the morning, lest they should taint the air, or touch the superior Hindoos in the streets."—*Mahratta Proclamation at Baroch*, in *Forbes, Or. Mem.* iv. 232.

1786.—"When all my schoolfellows and youthful compeers (those misguided few excepted who joined, to use a Gentoo phrase, the **hallachores** of the human race) were striking off with eager hope and earnest intent, in some one or other of the many paths of a busy life, I was 'standing idle in the market-place.'"—*Letter of Robert Burns*, in A. Cunningham's ed. of *Works and Life*, vi. 63.

1788.—The *Indian Vocabulary* also gives **Hallachore.**

1810.—"For the meaner offices we have a **Hallalcor** or Chandela (one of the most wretched Pariahs)."—*Maria Graham*, 31.

HALÁLLCUR. V. used in the imperative for infinitive, as is common in the Anglo-Indian use of H. verbs, being Ar.—H. *ḥalāl-kar*, 'make lawful,' *i.e.* put (an animal) to death in the manner prescribed to Mahommedans, when it is to be used for food.

[1855.—"Before breakfast I bought a moderately sized sheep for a dollar. Shaykh Hamid '**halaled**' (butchered) it according to rule. . . ."—*Burton, Pilgrimage*, ed. 1893, i. 255.]

1883.—"The diving powers of the poor duck are exhausted. . . . I have only . . . to seize my booty, which has just enough of life left to allow Peer Khan to **make it halal**, by cutting its throat in the name of Allah, and dividing the webs of its feet."—*Tribes on My Frontier*, 167.

HALF-CASTE, s. A person of mixt European and Indian blood. (See **MUSTEES; EURASIAN.**)

1789.—"Mulattoes, or as they are called in the East Indies, **half-casts.**"—*Munro's Narrative*, 51.

1793.—"They (the Mahratta Infantry) are commanded by **half-cast** people of Portuguese and French extraction, who draw off the attention of the spectators from the bad clothing of their men, by the profusion of antiquated lace bestowed on their own."—*Dirom, Narrative*, ii.

1809.—"The Padre, who is a **half-cast** Portuguese, informed me that he had three districts under him."—*Ld. Valentia*, i. 329.

1828.—"An invalid sergeant . . . came, attended by his wife, a very pretty young **half-caste.**"—*Heber*, i. 298.

1875.—"Othello is black—the very tragedy lies there; the whole force of the contrast, the whole pathos and extenuation of his doubts of Desdemona, depend on this blackness. Fechter makes him a **half-caste.**"—*G. H. Lewes, On Actors and the Art of Acting.*

HANGER, s. The word in this form is not in Anglo-Indian use, but (with the Scotch *whinger*, Old Eng. *whinyard*, Fr. *cangiar*, &c., other forms of the same) may be noted here as a corruption of the Arab. *khanjar*, 'a dagger or short falchion.' This (vulg. **cunjur**) is the Indian form. [According to the *N.E.D.* though '*hanger*' has sometimes been employed to translate *khanjar* (probably with a notion of etymological identity) there is no connection between the words.] The *khanjar* in India is a large double-edged dagger with a very broad base and a slight curve. [See drawings in *Egerton, Handbook of Indian Arms*, pl. X. Nos. 504, 505, &c.]

1574.—"Patrick Spreull . . . being persewit be Johne Boill Chepman . . . in invadyng of him, and stryking him with ane **quhinger** . . . throuch the quhilk the said Johnes neis wes woundit to the effusioun of his blude."—*Exts. from Records of the Burgh of Glasgow* (1876), p. 2.

1601.—"The other day I happened to enter into some discourse of a **hanger**, which I assure you, both for fashion and workmanship was most peremptory beautiful and gentlemanlike. . . ."—*B. Jonson, Every Man in His Humour*, i. 4.

[c. 1610.—"The islanders also bore their arms, viz., **alfanges** (*al-khanjar*) or scimitars."—*Pyrard de Laval*, Hak. Soc. i. 43.]

1653.—"**Gangeard** est en Turq, Persan et Indistanni vn poignard courbé."—*De la Boullaye-le-Gouz*, ed. 1657, p. 539.

1672.—". . . il s'estoit emporté contre elle jusqu'à un tel excès qu'il luy avoit porté quelques coups de **Cangiar** dans les mamelles. . . ."—*Journal d'Ant. Galland*, i. 177.

1673.—". . . **handjar** de diamants. . . ."—*App.* to *do.* ii. 189.

1676.—

"His pistol next he cock'd anew
And out his nutbrown **whinyard** drew."
Hudibras, Canto iii.

1684.—"The Souldiers do not wear **Hangers** or Scimitars like the *Persians*, but broad Swords like the Switzers. . . ."—*Tavernier*, E.T. ii. 65; [ed. *Ball*, i. 157].

1712.—"His Excy . . . was presented by the Emperor with a Hindoostany **Candjer**, or dagger, set with fine stones."—*Valentijn*, iv. (Suratte), 286.

[1717.—"The 23rd ultimo, John Surman received from his Majesty a horse and a **Cunger**. . . ."—In *Wheeler, Early Records*, 183.]

1781.—"I fancy myself now one of the most formidable men in Europe; a blunderbuss for Joe, a pair of double barrels to stick in my belt, and a cut and thrust **hanger** with a little pistol in the hilt, to hang by my side."—*Lord Minto, in Life*, i. 56.

" "Lost out of a buggy on the Road between Barnagur and Calcutta, a steel mounted **Hanger** with a single guard."—*Hicky's Bengal Gazette*, June 30.

1883.—". . . by *farrashes*, the carpet-spreader class, a large **canjar**, or curved dagger, with a heavy ivory handle, is carried; less for use than as a badge of office."—*Wills, Modern Persia*, 326.

HANSALERI, s. Table-servant's Hind. for 'horse-radish'! "A curious corruption, and apparently influenced by *saleri*, 'celery'"; (*Mr. M. L. Dames*, in *Panjab N. and Q.* ii. 184).

HANSIL, s. A hawser, from the English (*Roebuck*).

HANSPEEK, USPUCK, &c., s. Sea Hind. *Aspak*. A handspike, from the English.

HARAKIRI, s. This, the native name of the Japanese rite of suicide committed as a point of honour or substitute for judicial execution, has long been interpreted as "happy despatch," but what the origin of this curious error is we do not know. [The *N.E.D.* s.v. *dispatch*, says that it is humorous.] The real meaning is realistic in the extreme, viz., *hara*, 'belly,' *kiri*, 'to cut.'

[1598.—"And it is often seene that they **rip** their own **bellies** open."—*Linschoten*, Hak. Soc. i. 153.

[1615.—"His mother **cut** her own **belly**."—*Foster*, *Letters*, iv. 45.]

1616.—"Here we had news how Galsa Same was to passe this way to morrow to goe to a church near Miaco, called Coye; som say to **cut his bellie**, others say to be shaved a prist and to remeane theare the rest of his dais."—*Cocks's Diary*, i. 164.

1617.—"The King demanded 800 *tais* from Shosque Dono, or else to **cut his belly**, whoe, not having it to pay, did it."—*Ibid.* 337, see also ii. 202.

[1874.—See the elaborate account of the rite in *Mitford*, *Tales of Old Japan*, 2nd ed. 329 *seqq.* For a similar custom among the Karens, see *M'Mahon*, *Karens of the Golden Chersonese*, 294.]

HARAMZADA, s. A scoundrel; literally 'misbegotten'; a common term of abuse. It is Ar.—P. *ḥarāmzāda*, 'son of the unlawful.' *Ḥarām* is from a root signifying *sacer* (see under **HAREM**), and which appears as Hebrew in the sense of 'devoting to destruction,' and of 'a ban.' Thus in Numbers xxi. 3: "They utterly destroyed them and their cities; and he called the name of the place *Hormah*." [See *Encycl. Bibl.* i. 468; ii. 2110.]

[1857.—"I am no advocate for slaying Shahzadas or any such-like **Haramzadas** without trial."—*Bosworth Smith*, *L. of Ld. Lawrence*, ii. 251.]

HAREM, s. Ar. *ḥaram*, *ḥarīm*, *i.e.* *sacer*, applied to the women of the family and their apartment. This word is not now commonly used in India, **zenana** (q.v.) being the common word for 'the women of the family,' or their apartments.

1298.—". . . car maintes homes emorurent e mantes dames en furent veves . . . e maintes autres dames ne furent à toz jorz mès en plores et en lermes: ce furent les meres et les **araines** de homes qe hi morurent."—*Marco Polo*, in Old Text of *Soc. de Géographie*, 251.

1623.—"Non so come sciah Selim ebbe notizia di lei e s'innamorò. Volle condurla nel suo **haram** o *gynaeceo*, e tenerla quivi appresso di sè come una delle altre concubine; ma questa donna (Nurmahal) che era sopra modo astuta . . . ricusò."—*P. della Valle*, ii. 525; [Hak. Soc. i. 53].

1630.—"This Duke here and in other seralios (or **Harams** as the Persians term them) has above 300 concubines."—*Herbert*, 139.

1676.—"In the midst of the large Gallery is a Nich in the Wall, into which the King descends out of his **Haram** by a private pair of Stairs."—*Tavernier*, E.T. ii. 49; [ed. *Ball*, i. 101].

1726.—"On the Ganges also lies a noble fortress, with the Palace of the old Emperor of Hindostan, with his **Hharaam** or women's apartment. . . ."—*Valentijn*, v. 168.

[1727.—"The King . . . took his Wife into his own **Harran** or Seraglio. . . ."—*A. Hamilton*, ed. 1744, i. 171.

[1812.—"Adjoining to the Chel Sitoon is the **Harem**; the term in Persia is applied to the establishments of the great, *zenana* is confined to those of inferior people."—*Morier*, *Journey through Persia*, &c., 166.]

HARRY, s. This word is quite obsolete. Wilson gives *Hārī* as Beng. 'A servant of the lowest class, a sweeper.' [The word means 'a collector of bones,' Skt. *hadda*, 'a bone'; for the caste, see *Risley*, *Tribes of Bengal*, i. 314 *seqq.*] M.-Gen. Keatinge remarks that they are the goldsmiths of Assam; they are village watchmen in Bengal. (See under **PYKE**.) In two of the quotations below, *Harry* is applied to a *woman*, in one case employed to carry water. A female servant of this description is not now known among English families in Bengal.

1706.—
"2 Tendells (see **TINDAL**) . 6 0 0
* * * * *
1 *Hummummee* * . . . 2 0 0

* I.e. *hamāmī*, a bath attendant. Compare the *Hummums* in Covent Garden.

* * * * *

4 **Manjees** 10 0 0
5 *Dandees* (see **DANDY**) . 8 0 0
* * * * *
5 **Harrys** 9 8 0
* * * * *

List of Men's Names, &c., immediately in the Service of the Honble. the Vnited Compy. *in their Factory of* Fort William, Bengall, *November*, 1706" (MS. in India Office).

c. 1753.—Among the expenses of the Mayor's Court at Calcutta we find: "A **harry** . . . Rs. 1."—*Long*, 43.

c. 1754.—"A **Harry** or water-wench. . . ." (at Madras).—*Ives*, 50.

[„ "**Harries** are the same at Bengal, as *Frosts* (see **FARASH**) are at Bombay. Their women do all the drudgery at your houses, and the men carry your Palanquin." —*Ibid.* 26.]

„ In a tariff of wages recommended by the "Zemindars of Calcutta," we have: "**Harry**-woman to a Family . . . 2 Rs."—In *Seton-Karr*, i. 95.

1768-71.—"Every house has likewise . . . a **harry**-maid or *matarani* (see **MATRANEE**) who carries out the dirt; and a great number of slaves, both male and female."—*Stavorinus*, i. 523.

1781.—"2 **Harries** or Sweepers . . . 6 Rs.
* * * * *
2 *Beesties* . . . 8 Rs."

Establishment . . . under the Chief Magistrate of Banaris, in Appendix to *Narr. of Insurrection there*, Calcutta, 1782.

[1813.—"He was left to view a considerable time, and was then carried by the **Hurries** to the Golgotha."—*Forbes, Or. Mem.* 2nd ed. ii. 131.]

HATTY, s. Hind. *hāthī*, the most common word for an elephant; from Skt. *hasta*, 'the hand,' and *hastī*, 'the elephant,' come the Hind. words *hāth* and *hāthī*, with the same meanings. The analogy of the elephant's trunk to the hand presents itself to Pliny:

"Mandunt ore; spirant et bibunt odoranturque haud inproprie appellatâ **manu**." —viii. 10

and to Tennyson:

"... camels knelt
Unbidden, and the brutes of mountain back
That carry kings in castles, bow'd black knees
Of homage, ringing with their **serpent hands**,
To make her smile, her golden ankle-bells."
Merlin and Vivien.

c. 1526.—"As for the animals peculiar to Hindustân, one is the elephant, as the Hindustânis call it **Hathì**, which inhabits the district of Kalpi, the more do the wild elephants increase in number. That is the tract in which the elephant is chiefly taken." —*Baber*, 315. This notice of Baber's shows how remarkably times have changed. No elephants now exist anywhere near the region indicated. [On elephants in Hindustan, see *Blochmann's Āīn*, i. 618].

[1838.—"You are of course aware that we habitually call elephants **Hotties**, a name that might be safely applied to every other animal in India, but I suppose the elephants had the first choice of names and took the most appropriate."—*Miss Eden, Up the Country*, i. 269.]

HATTYCHOOK, s. Hind. *hāthī-chak*, servant's and gardener's Hind. for the globe artichoke; [the Jerusalem artichoke is *hāthīpīch*]. This is worth producing, because our word (**artichoke**) is itself the corruption of an Oriental word thus carried back to the East in a mangled form.

HAUT, s.

a. Hind. *hāth*, (the hand or forearm, and thence) 'a cubit,' from the elbow to the tip of the middle finger; a measure of 18 inches, and sometimes more.

[1614.—"A godown 10 **Hast** high."—*Foster, Letters*, ii. 112.

[c. 1810.—"... even in the measurements made by order of the collectors, I am assured, that the only standards used were the different Kazis' arms, which leaves great room for fraud. . . . All persons measuring cloth know how to apply their arm, so as to measure a cubit of 18 inches with wonderful exactness."—*Buchanan, Eastern India*, ii. 576.]

b. Hind. *hāt*, Skt. *haṭṭa*, 'a market held on certain days.'

[1800.—"In this Carnatic . . . there are no fairs like the **hauts** of Bengal."—*Buchanan, Mysore*, i. 19.

[1818.—"The Hindoos have also market days (**hătūs**), when the buyers and sellers assemble, sometimes in an open plain, but in general in market places."—*Ward, Hindoos*, i. 151.]

HAVILDAR, s. Hind. *ḥavildār*. A sepoy non-commissioned officer, corresponding to a sergeant, and wearing the chevrons of a sergeant. This dating from about the middle of the 18th century is the only modern use of the term in that form. It is a corruption of Pers. *ḥawāladār*, or *ḥawāldār*, 'one holding an office of trust'; and in this form it had, in other times, a variety of applications to different charges and subordinate officers. Thus among the Mahrattas the commandant of a fort was so styled; whilst in

Eastern Bengal the term was, and perhaps still is, applied to the holder of a *ḥawāla*, an intermediate tenure between those of zemindar and ryot.

1672.—Regarding the **Cowle** obtained from the Nabob of Golcondah for the Fort and Town of Chinapatnam. 11,000 Pagodas to be paid in full of all demands for the past, and in future Pagodas 1200 per annum rent, "and so to hold the Fort and Town free from any **Avildar** or **Divân's** People, or any other imposition for ever."—*Fort St. George Consn.*, April 11, in *Notes and Exts.*, No. i. 25.

1673.—"We landed at about Nine in the Morning, and were civilly treated by the Customer in his *Choultry*, till the **Havildar** could be acquainted of my arrival."—*Fryer*, 123.

[1680.—"**Avaldar.**" See under **JUNCAMEER.**]

1696.—". . . the **havildar** of St. Thomé and Pulecat."—*Wheeler*, i. 308.

[1763.—"Three *avaldars* (**avaldares**) or receivers."—India Office MSS. *Conselho, Ultramarino*, vol. i.

[1773.—"One or two Hircars, one **Havildah**, and a company of sepoys. . . ."—*Ives*, 67.]

1824.—"Curreem Musseeh was, I believe, a **havildar** in the Company's army, and his sword and sash were still hung up, with a not unpleasing vanity, over the desk where he now presided as catechist."—*Heber*, i. 149.

HAVILDAR'S GUARD, s. There is a common way of cooking the fry of fresh-water fish (a little larger than whitebait) as a breakfast dish, by frying them in rows of a dozen or so, spitted on a small skewer. On the Bombay side this dish is known by the whimsical name in question.

HAZREE, s. This word is commonly used in Anglo-Indian households in the Bengal Presidency for 'breakfast.' It is not clear how it got this meaning. [The earlier sense was religious, as below.] It is properly *ḥāzirī*, 'muster,' from the Ar. *ḥāzir*, 'ready or present.' (See **CHOTA-HAZRY**.)

[1832.—"The Sheeahs prepare **hazree** (breakfast) in the name of his holiness Abbas Allee Ullum-burdar, Hosein's step-brother; *i.e.* they cook *polaoo*, *rotee*, curries, &c., and distribute them."—*Herklots, Qanoon-e-Islam*, ed. 1863, p. 183.]

HENDRY KENDRY, n.p. Two islands off the coast of the Concan, about 7 m. south of the entrance to Bombay Harbour, and now belonging to Kolāba District. The names, according to Ph. Anderson, are *Haneri* and *Khaneri*; in the Admy. chart they are *Oonari*, and *Khundari*. They are also variously written (the one) *Hundry*, *Ondera*, *Hunarey*, *Henery*, and (the other) *Kundra*, *Cundry*, *Cunarey*, *Kenery*. The real names are given in the *Bombay Gazetteer* as *Underi* and *Khanderi*. Both islands were piratically occupied as late as the beginning of the 19th century. Khanderi passed to us in 1818 as part of the Peshwa's territory; Underi lapsed in 1840. [Sir G. Birdwood (*Rep. on Old Records*, 83), describing the "Consultations" of 1679, writes: "At page 69, notice of 'Sevagee' fortifying 'Hendry Kendry,' the twin islets, now called Henery (*i.e. Vondarī*, 'Mouse-like,' *Kenery* (*i.e. Khandarī*), *i.e.* 'Sacred to Khandaroo.'" The former is thus derived from Skt. *undaru*, *unduru*, 'a rat'; the latter from Mahr. *Khanderāv*, 'Lord of the Sword,' a form of Śiva.]

1673.—"These islands are in number seven; viz. *Bombaim*, *Canorein*, *Trumbay*, *Elephanto*, the *Putachoes*, *Munchumbay*, and *Kerenjau*, with the Rock of **Henry Kenry**. . . ."—*Fryer*, 61.

1681.—"Although we have formerly wrote you that we will have no war for **Hendry Kendry**, yet all war is so contrary to our constitution, as well as our interest, that we cannot too often inculcate to you our aversion thereunto."—*Court of Directors to Surat*, quoted in *Anderson's Western India*, p. 175.

1727.—". . . four Leagues south of *Bombay*, are two small Islands **Undra**, and **Cundra**. The first has a Fortress belonging to the *Sedee*, and the other is fortified by the *Sevajee*, and is now in the Hands of *Connajee Angria*."—*A. Hamilton*, i. 243; [ed. 1744].

c. 1760.—"At the harbor's mouth lie two small fortified rocks, called **Henara** and **Canara**. . . . These were formerly in the hands of Angria, and the *Siddees*, or Moors, which last have long been dispossest of them."—*Grose*, i. 58.

HERBED, s. A Parsee priest, not specially engaged in priestly duties. Pers. *hirbad*, from Pahlavi *aêrpat*.

1630.—"The **Herbood** or ordinary Churchman."—*Lord's Display*, ch. viii.

HICKMAT, s. Ar.—H. *ḥikmat*; an ingenious device or contrivance. (See under **HAKIM**.)

1838.—"The house has been roofed in, and my relative has come up from Meerut, to have the slates put on after some peculiar **hikmat** of his own."—*Wanderings of a Pilgrim*, ii. 240.

HIDGELEE, n.p. The tract so called was under native rule a *chakla*, or district, of Orissa, and under our rule formerly a *zilla* of Bengal; but now it is a part of the Midnapūr Zilla, of which it constitutes the S.E. portion, viz. the low coast lands on the west side of the Hoogly estuary, and below the junction of the Rūpnārāyan. The name is properly *Hijilī*; but it has gone through many strange phases in European records.

1553.—"The first of these rivers (from the E. side of the Ghauts) rises from two sources to the east of Chaul, about 15 leagues distant, and in an altitude of 18 to 19 degrees. The river from the most northerly of these sources is called *Crusna*, and the more southerly *Benkora*, and when they combine they are called *Ganga*: and this river discharges into the illustrious stream of the Ganges between the two places called **Angeli** and Picholda in about 22 degrees."—*Barros*, I. ix. 1.

1586.—"An haven which is called **Angeli** in the Country of Orixa."—*Fitch*, in *Hakl.* ii. 389.

1686.—"Chanock, on the 15th December (1686) . . . burned and destroyed all the magazines of salt, and granaries of rice, which he found in the way between Hughley and the island of **Ingelee**."—*Orme* (reprint), ii. 12.

1726.—"**Hingeli**."—*Valentijn*, v. 158.

1727.—". . . inhabited by Fishers, as are also **Ingellie** and **Kidgerie** (see **KEDGEREE**), two neighbouring Islands on the West Side of the Mouth of the Ganges."—*A. Hamilton*, i. 275; [ed. 1744, ii. 2].

1758.—In apprehension of a French Fleet the Select Committee at Fort William recommend: "That the pagoda at **Ingelie** should be washed black, the great tree at the place cut down, and the buoys removed."—In *Long*, 153.

1784.—"Ships laying at **Kedgeree**, **Ingellee**, or any other parts of the great River."—In *Seton-Karr*, i. 37.

HILSA, s. Hind. *hilsā*, Skt. *ilīśa*, *illiśa*; a rich and savoury fish of the shad kind (*Clupea ilisha*, Day), called in books the 'sable-fish' (a name, from the Port. *savel*, quite obsolete in India) and on the Indus *pulla* (*palla*). The large shad which of late has been commonly sold by London fishmongers in the beginning of summer, is very near the *hilsa*, but not so rich. The *hilsa* is a sea-fish, ascending the river to spawn, and is taken as high as Delhi on the Jumna, as high as Mandalay on the Irawadi (*Day*). It is also taken in the Guzerat rivers, though not in the short and shallow streams of the Concan, nor in the Deccan rivers, from which it seems to be excluded by the rocky obstructions. It is the special fish of Sind under the name of *palla*, and monopolizes the name of fish, just as salmon does on the Scotch rivers (*Dr. Macdonald's Acct. of Bombay Fisheries*, 1883).

1539.—". . . A little Island, called *Apofingua* (*Ape-Fingan*) . . . inhabited by poor people who live by the fishing of *shads* (*que vive de la pescaria dos* **saveis**)."—*Pinto* (orig. cap. xviii.), *Cogan*, p. 22.

1613.—"Na quella costa marittima occidental de Viontana (*Ujong-Tana*, Malay Peninsula) habitavão Saletes pescadores que não tinhão outro tratto . . . salvo de sua pescarya de **saveis**, donde so aproveitarão das ovas chamado *Turabos* passados por salmeura."—*Eredia de Godinho*, 22. [On this Mr. Skeat points out that "Saletes pescadores" must mean "Fishermen of the Straits" (Mal. *selat*, "straits"); and when he calls them "*Turabos*" he is trying to reproduce the Malay name of this fish, *terubok* (pron. *trubo*).]

1810.—"The **hilsah** (or sable-fish) seems to be midway between a mackerel and a salmon."—*Williamson, V. M.* ii. 154-5.

1813.—Forbes calls it the *sable* or *salmon*-fish, and says "it a little resembles the European fish (salmon) from which it is named."—*Or. Mem.* i. 53; [2nd ed. i. 36].

1824.—"The fishery, we were told by these people, was of the '**Hilsa**' or 'Sable-fish.'"—*Heber*, ed. 1844, i. 81.

HIMALÝA, n.p. This is the common pronunciation of the name of the great range

"Whose snowy ridge the roving Tartar bounds,"

properly *Himălăya*, 'the Abode of Snow'; also called *Himavat*, 'the Snowy'; *Himagiri* and *Himaśaila*; *Himādri*, *Himakūta*, &c., from various forms of which the ancients made *Imaus*, *Emōdus*, &c. Pliny had got somewhere the true meaning of the name: ". . . a montibus Hemodis, quorum promontorium Imaus vocatur *nivosum* significante . . ." (vi. 17). We do not know how far back the use of the modern name is to be found. [The references in early Hindu literature are collected by *Atkinson* (*Hima-*

layan Gazetteer, ii. 273 *seqq.*).] We do not find it in Baber, who gives *Siwālak* as the Indian name of the mountains (see **SIWALIK**). The oldest occurrence we know of is in the *Āīn*, which gives in the Geographical Tables, under the Third Climate, *Koh-i-***Himālah** (orig. ii. 36); [ed. *Jarrett*, iii. 69]). This is disguised in Gladwin's version by a wrong reading into *Kerdehmaleh* (ed. 1800, ii. 367).* This form (**Himmaleh**) is used by Major Rennell, but hardly as if it was yet a familiar term. In Elphinstone's Letters **Himāleh** or some other spelling of that form is always used (see below). When we get to Bishop Heber we find **Himalaya**, the established English form.

1822.—"What pleases me most is the contrast between your present enjoyment, and your former sickness and despondency. Depend upon it England will turn out as well as **Hemaleh**."—*Elphinstone* to Major Close, in *Life*, ii. 139; see also i. 336, where it is written **Himalleh**.

HINDEE, s. This is the Pers. adjective form from *Hind*, 'India,' and illustration of its use for a native of India will be found under **HINDOO**. By Europeans it is most commonly used for those dialects of Hindustani speech which are less modified by P. vocables than the usual Hindustani, and which are spoken by the rural population of the N.W. Provinces and its outskirts. The earliest literary work in Hindi is the great poem of Chand Bardai (c. 1200), which records the deeds of Prithirāja, the last Hindu sovereign of Delhi. [On this literature see Dr. G. A. Grierson, The *Modern Vernacular Literature of Hindustān*, in *J.A.S.B.* Part I., 1888.] The term **Hinduwī** appears to have been formerly used, in the Madras Presidency, for the Marāṭhī language. (See a note in *Sir A. Arbuthnot's* ed. of *Munro's Minutes*, i. 133.)

* *Hemāchal* and *Hemakūt* also occur in the Āīn (see *Gladwin*, ii. 342, 343; [ed. *Jarrett*, iii. 30, 31]). *Karāchal* is the name used by Ibn Batuta in the 14th century, and by Al-Birūni 300 years earlier. 17th century writers often call the Himālaya the "Mountains of Nuggur-Cote" (q.v.). [Mr. Tawney writes: "We have in Rig Veda (x. 121) *ime himavanto parvatāh*, 'these snowy mountains,' spoken of as abiding by the might of Prajāpati. In the Bhagavadgītā, an episode of the Mahābhārata, Krishṇa says that he is 'the *Himālaya* among stable things,' and the word *Himālaya* is found in the Kumāra Sambhava of Kālidāsa, about the date of which opinions differ. Perhaps the Greek Ιμαος is *himavat*; 'Ημωδὸς, *himādri*."]

HINDKĪ, HINDEKĪ, n.p. This modification of the name is applied to people of Indian descent, but converted to Islam, on the Peshawar frontier, and scattered over other parts of Afghanistan. They do the banking business, and hold a large part of the trade in their hands.

[1842.—"The inhabitants of Peshawer are of Indian origin, but speak Pushtoo as well as **Hindkee**."—*Elphinstone, Caubul*, i. 74.]

HINDOO, n.p. P. *Hindū*. A person of Indian religion and race. This is a term derived from the use of the Mahommedan conquerors (see under **INDIA**). The word in this form is Persian; *Hindī* is that used in Arabic, *e.g.*

c. 940.—"An inhabitant of Mansūra in Sind, among the most illustrious and powerful of that city . . . had brought up a young Indian or Sindian slave (**Hindī** aw Sindī)."—*Maṣ'ūdī*, vi. 264.

In the following quotation from a writer in Persian observe the distinction made between **Hindū** and *Hindī*:

c. 1290.—"Whatever live **Hindú** fell into the King's hands was pounded into bits under the feet of elephants. The Musalmáns, who were *Hindís* (country born), had their lives spared."—*Amīr Khosrū*, in *Elliot*, iii. 539.

1563.—". . . moreover if people of Arabia or Persia would ask of the men of this country whether they are Moors or Gentoos, they ask in these words: 'Art thou Mosalman or **Indu**?'"—*Garcia*, f. 137*b*.

1653.—"Les **Indous** gardent soigneusement dans leurs Pagodes les Reliques de Ram, Schita (Sita), et les autres personnes illustres de l'antiquité."—*De la Boullaye-le-Gouz*, ed. 1657, 191.

Hindu is often used on the Peshawar frontier as synonymous with *bunya* (see under **BANYAN**). A soldier (of the tribes) will say: 'I am going to the **Hindu**,' *i.e.* to the *bunya* of the company.

HINDOO KOOSH, n.p. *Hindū-Kūsh*; a term applied by our geographers to the whole of the Alpine range which separates the basins of the Kabul River and the Helmand from that of the Oxus. It is, as Rennell points out, properly that part of the range immediately north of Kabul, the *Caucasus* of the historians of Alexander, who crossed and recrossed it somewhere not far from the longitude of that city. The real origin of the name is not known; [the most plausible explanation is perhaps that it is a corruption of *Indicus Caucasus*]. It is, as far as we know, first used in literature by Ibn Batuta, and the explanation of the name which he gives, however doubtful, is still popular. The name has been by some later writers modified into Hindu *Koh* (mountain), but this is factitious, and throws no light on the origin of the name.

c. 1334.—"Another motive for our stoppage was the fear of snow; for there is midway on the road a mountain called **Hindū-Kūsh**, *i.e.* 'the Hindu-Killer,' because so many of the slaves, male and female, brought from India, die in the passage of this mountain, owing to the severe cold and quantity of snow."—*Ibn Batuta*, iii. 84.

1504.—"The country of Kâbul is very strong, and of difficult access. . . . Between Balkh, Kundez, and Badakshân on the one side, and Kâbul on the other, is interposed the mountain of **Hindû-kûsh**, the passes over which are seven in number."—*Baber*, p. 139.

1548.—"From this place marched, and entered the mountains called **Hindū-Kush**."—*Mem. of Emp. Humayun*, 89.

,, "It was therefore determined to invade Badakhshan . . . The Emperor, passing over the heel of the **Hindū-Kush**, encamped at Shergirán."—*Tabakāt-i-Akbarī*, in *Elliot*, v. 223.

1753.—"Les montagnes qui donnent naissance à l'Indus, et à plusieurs des rivières qu'il reçoit, se nomment **Hendou Kesh**, et c'est l'histoire de Timur qui m'instruit de cette denomination. Elle est composée du nom d'*Hendou* ou *Hind*, qui désigne l'Inde . . . et de *kush* ou *kesh* . . . que je remarque être propre à diverses montagnes."—*D'Anville*, p. 16.

1793. — "The term Hindoo - Kho, or **Hindoo-Kush**, is not applied to the ridge throughout its full extent; but seems confined to that part of it which forms the N.W. boundary of Cabul; and this is the INDIAN CAUCASUS of Alexander."—*Rennell*, *Mem.* 3rd ed. 150.

1817.— ". . . those
Who dwell beyond the everlasting snows
Of **Hindoo Koosh**, in stormy freedom
bred."—*Mokanna*.

HINDOSTAN, n.p. Pers. *Hindūstān*. **(a)** 'The country of the Hindūs,' India. In modern native parlance this word indicates distinctively **(b)** India north of the Nerbudda, and exclusive of Bengal and Behar. The latter provinces are regarded as *pūrb* (see **POORUB**), and all south of the Nerbudda as *Dakhan* (see **DECCAN**). But the word is used in older Mahommedan authors just as it is used in English school-books and atlases, viz. as **(a)** the equivalent of India Proper. Thus Baber says of Hindustān: "On the East, the South, and the West it is bounded by the Ocean" (310).

a.—

1553.—". . . and so the Persian nation adjacent to it give it as at present its proper name that of **Indostān**."—*Barros*, I. iv. 7.

1563.—". . . and common usage in Persia, and Coraçone, and Arabia, and Turkey, calls this country **Industam** . . . for *istām* is as much as to say 'region,' and *indu* 'India.'"—*Garcia*, f. 137*b*.

1663.—"And thus it came to pass that the Persians called it **Indostan**."— *Faria y Sousa*, i. 33.

1665. — "La derniere parti est la plus connüe: c'est celle que l'on appelle **Indostan**, et dont les bornes naturelles au Couchant et au Levant, sont le Gange et l'Indus."—*Thevenot*, v. 9.

1672.—"It has been from old time divided into two parts, *i.e.* the Eastern, which is India beyond the Ganges, and the Western India within the Ganges, now called **Indostan**."—*Baldaeus*, 1.

1770.—"By **Indostan** is properly meant a country lying between two celebrated rivers, the Indus and the Ganges. . . . A ridge of mountains runs across this long tract from north to south, and dividing it into two equal parts, extends as far as Cape Comorin."—*Raynal* (tr.), i. 34.

1783.—"In Macassar **Indostan** is called *Neegree Telinga*."—*Forrest, V. to Mergui*, 82.

b.—

1803.—"I feared that the dawk direct through **Hindostan** would have been stopped."—*Wellington*, ed. 1837, ii. 209.

1824.—"One of my servants called out to them,—'Aha! dandee folk, take care! You are now in **Hindostan**! The people of this country know well how to fight, and are not afraid."—*Heber*, i. 124. See also pp. 268, 269.

In the following stanza of the good bishop's the application is apparently the same; but the accentuation is excruciating—'Hindóstan,' as if rhyming to 'Boston.'

1824.—
"Then on! then on! where duty leads,
My course be onward still,
O'er broad **Hindostan's** sultry meads,
Or bleak Almora's hill."—*Ibid.* 113.

1884.—"It may be as well to state that Mr. H. G. Keene's forthcoming *History of Hindustan* . . . will be limited in its scope to the strict meaning of the word '**Hindustan**'=India north of the Deccan."—*Academy*, April 26, p. 294.

HINDOSTANEE, s. *Hindūstānī*, properly an adjective, but used substantively in two senses, viz. **(a)** a native of Hindustān, and **(b)** (*Hindūstānī zabān*) 'the language of that country,' but in fact the language of the Mahommedans of Upper India, and eventually of the Mahommedans of the Deccan, developed out of the Hindi dialect of the Doab chiefly, and of the territory round Agra and Delhi, with a mixture of Persian vocables and phrases, and a readiness to adopt other foreign words. It is also called **Oordoo**, *i.e.* the language of the Urdū ('Horde') or Camp. This language was for a long time a kind of Mahommedan *lingua franca* over all India, and still possesses that character over a large part of the country, and among certain classes. Even in Madras, where it least prevails, it is still recognised in native regiments as the language of intercourse between officers and men. Old-fashioned Anglo-Indians used to call it the **Moors** (q.v.).

a.—

1653.—(applied to a native.) "**Indistanni** est vn Mahometan noir des Indes, ce nom est composé de *Indou*, Indien, et *stan*, habitation."—*De la Boullaye-le-Gouz*, ed. 1657, 543.

b.—

1616.—"After this he (Tom Coryate) got a great mastery in the **Indostan**, or more vulgar language; there was a woman, a landress, belonging to my Lord Embassador's house, who had such a freedom and liberty of speech, that she would sometimes scould, brawl, and rail from the sun-rising to the sun-set; one day he undertook her in her own language. And by eight of the clock he so silenced her, that she had not one word more to speak."—*Terry, Extracts relating to T. C.*

1673.—"The Language at Court is *Persian*, that commonly spoke is **Indostan** (for which they have no proper Character, the written Language being called *Banyan*), which is a mixture of *Persian* and *Sclavonian*, as are all the dialects of India."—*Fryer*, 201. This intelligent traveller's reference to Sclavonian is remarkable, and shows a notable perspicacity, which would have delighted the late Lord Strangford, had he noticed the passage.

1677.—In Court's letter of 12th Dec. to Ft. St. Geo. they renew the offer of a reward of £20, for proficiency in the Gentoo or **Indostan** languages, and sanction a reward of £10 each for proficiency in the Persian language, "and that fit persons to teach the said language be entertained."—*Notes and Exts.*, No. i. 22.

1685.—". . . so applyed myself to a Portuguese mariner who spoke **Indostan** (ye current language of all these Islands)" [Maldives]."—*Hedges, Diary*, March 9; [Hak. Soc. i. 191].

1697.—"Questions addressed to Khodja Movaad, Ambassador from Abyssinia.

* * * * *

4.—"What language he, in his audience made use of?

"The **Hindustani** language (*Hindoestanze taal*), which the late Hon. Paulus de Roo, then Secretary of their Excellencies the High Government of Batavia, interpreted."—*Valentijn*, iv. 327.

[1699.—"He is expert in the **Hindorstand** or Moores Language."—In *Yule, Hedges' Diary*, Hak. Soc. ii. cclxvii.]

1726.—"The language here is **Hindustans** or **Moors** (so 'tis called there), though he who can't speak any Arabic and Persian passes for an ignoramus."—*Valentijn, Chor.* i. 37.

1727.—"This Persian . . . and I, were discoursing one Day of my Affairs in the **Industan** Language, which is the established Language spoken in the Mogul's large Dominions."—*A. Hamilton*, ii. 183; [ed. 1744, ii. 182].

1745.—"Benjamini Schulzii Missionarii Evangelici, Grammatica **Hindostanica** . . . Edidit, et de suscipiendâ barbaricarum linguarum culturâ praefatus est D. Jo. Henr. Callenberg, Halae Saxoniae."—Title from Catalogue of M. Garcin de Tassy's Books, 1879. This is the earliest we have heard of.

1763.—"Two of the Council of Pondicherry went to the camp, one of them was well versed in the **Indostan** and Persic languages, which are the only tongues used in the Courts of the Mahomedan Princes."—*Orme*, i. 144 (ed. 1803).

1772.—"Manuscripts have indeed been handed about, ill spelt, with a confused mixture of Persian, **Indostans**, and Bengals."—Preface to *Hadley's Grammar*, xi. (See under **MOORS**.)

1777.—"Alphabetum Brammhanicum seu **Indostanum**."—*Romae.*

1778.—"Grammatica **Indostana**—A mais Vulgar—Que se practica no Imperio do gram Mogol—Offerecida—Aos muitos Reverendos—Padres Missionarios—Do dito Imperio. Em Roma MDCCLXXVIII—Na Estamperia da Ságrada Congregação—de Propaganda Fide." — (Title transcribed.) There is a reprint of this (apparently) of 1865, in the Catalogue of Garcin de Tassy's books.

c. 1830.—"Cet ignoble patois d'**Hindoustani**, qui ne servira jamais à rien quand je serai retourné en Europe, est difficile."—*V. Jacquemont, Correspondance*, i. 95.

1844.—"Hd. Quarters, Kurrachee, 12th February, 1844. The Governor unfortunately does not understand **Hindoostanee**, nor Persian, nor Mahratta, nor any other eastern dialect. He therefore will feel particularly obliged to Collectors, sub-

Collectors, and officers writing the proceedings of Courts-Martial, and all Staff Officers, to indite their various papers in English, larded with as small a portion of the to him unknown tongues as they conveniently can, instead of those he generally receives—namely, papers written in **Hindostanee** larded with occasional words in English.

"Any Indent made for English Dictionaries shall be duly attended to, if such be in the stores at Kurrachee; if not, gentlemen who have forgotten the vulgar tongue are requested to procure the requisite assistance from England." — *GG. OO.*, by *Sir Charles Napier*, 85.

[Compare the following:

[1617.—(In answer to a letter from the Court not now extant). "Wee have forbidden the severall Factoryes from wrighting words in this languadge and refrayned itt our selues, though in bookes of Coppies wee feare there are many which by wante of tyme for perusall wee cannot rectifie or expresse."—*Surat Factors* to *Court*, February 26, 1617. (*I.O. Records*: O. C., No. 450.)]

1856.—

"... they sound strange
As **Hindostanee** to an Ind-born man
Accustomed many years to English speech."

E. B. Browning, Aurora Leigh.

HING, s. Asafoetida. Skt. *hingu*, Hind. *hīng*, Dakh. *hīngu*. A repulsively smelling gum-resin which forms a favourite Hindu condiment, and is used also by Europeans in Western and Southern India as an ingredient in certain cakes eaten with curry. (See **POPPER-CAKE**). This product affords a curious example of the uncertainty which sometimes besets the origin of drugs which are the objects even of a large traffic. Hanbury and Flückiger, whilst describing Falconer's *Narthex Asafoetida* (*Ferula Narthex*, Boiss.) and *Scorodosma foetidum*, Bunge; (*F. asafoetida*, Boiss.) two umbelliferous plants, both cited as the source of this drug, say that neither has been proved to furnish the *asafoetida* of commerce. Yet the plant producing it has been described and drawn by Kaempfer, who saw the gum-resin collected in the Persian Province of Lāristān (near the eastern shore of the P. Gulf); and in recent years (1857) Surgeon-Major Bellew has described the collection of the drug near Kandahar. Asafoetida has been identified with the *σίλφιον* or *laserpitium* of the ancients. The substance is probably yielded not only by the species mentioned above, but by other allied plants, *e.g. Ferula Jaeschkiana*, Vatke, of Kashmīr and Turkistan. The *hing* of the Bombay market is the produce of F. *alliacea*, Boiss. [See *Watt, Econ. Dict.* iii. 328 *seqq.*]

c. 645.—"This kingdom of Tsao-kiu-tcha (Tsāukūta ?) has about 7000 *li* of compass,—the compass of the capital called *Ho-si-na* (Ghazna) is 30 *li*. . . . The soil is favourable to the plant *Yo-Kin* (Curcuma, or turmeric) and to that called **Hing-kiu**."—*Pèlerins Boudd.*, iii. 187.

1563.—"A Portuguese in Bisnagar had a horse of great value, but which exhibited a deal of flatulence, and on that account the King would not buy it. The Portuguese cured it by giving it this **ymgu** mixt with flour: the King then bought it, finding it thoroughly well, and asked him how he had cured it. When the man said it was with **ymgu**, the King replied: ''Tis nothing then to marvel at, for you have given it to eat the food of the gods' (or, as the poets say, nectar). Whereupon the Portuguese made answer *sotto voce* and in Portuguese: 'Better call it the food of the devils!'"—*Garcia*, f. 21*b*. The Germans do worse than this Portuguese, for they call the drug *Teufels dreck, i.e. diaboli non cibus sed stercus!*

1586.—"I went from *Agra* to *Satagam* (see **CHITTAGONG**) in *Bengale* in the companie of one hundred and four score Boates, laden with Salt, *Opium*, **Hinge**, Lead, Carpets, and divers other commodities down the River Jemena."—*R. Fitch*, in *Hakl.* ii. 386.

1611.—"In the Kingdom of Gujarat and Cambaya, the natives put in all their food **Ingu**, which is Assafetida." — *Teixeira, Relaciones*, 29.

1631. — ". . . ut totas aedas foetore replerent, qui insuetis vix tolerandus esset. Quod Javani et Malaii et caeteri Indiarum incolae negabant se quicquam odoratius naribus unquam percepisse. Apud hos **Hin** hic succus nominatur."—*Jac. Bontii*, lib. iv. p. 41.

1638.—"Le **Hingh**, que nos droguistes et apoticaires appellent *Assa foetida*, vient la plus part de Perse, mais celle que la Province d'Vtrad (?) produit dans les Indes est bien meilleur."—*Mandelslo*, 230.

1673.—"In this Country *Assa Foetida* is gathered at a place called *Descoon*; some deliver it to be the Juice of a Cane or Reed inspissated; others, of a Tree wounded: It differs much from the stinking Stuff called **Hing**, it being of the Province of *Carmania*; this latter is that the *Indians* perfume themselves with, mixing it in all their Pulse, and make it up in Wafers to correct the Windiness of their Food."—*Fryer*, 239.

1689.—"The Natives at Suratt are much taken with *Assa Foetida*, which they call **Hin**, and mix a little with the Cakes that they eat."—*Ovington*, 397.

1712.—". . . substantiam obtinet ponderosam, instar rapae solidam candidissimamque, plenam succi pinguis, albissimi, foetidissimi, porraceo odore nares horridé ferientis; qui ex eâ collectus, Persis Indisque Hingh, Europaeis Asa foetida appellatur." —*Eng. Kaempfer Amoen. Exotic.* 537.

1726.—"**Hing** or *Assa Foetida*, otherwise called Devil's-dung (*Duivelsdrek*)."—*Valentijn*, iv. 146.

1857.—"Whilst riding in the plain to the N.E. of the city (Candahar) we noticed several assafœtida plants. The assafœtida, called **hang or hing** by the natives, grows wild in the sandy or gravelly plains that form the western part of Afghanistan. It is never cultivated, but its peculiar gum-resin is collected from the plants on the deserts where they grow. The produce is for the most part exported to Hindustan." —*Bellew, Journal of a Pol. Mission*, &c., p. 270.

HIRAVA, n.p. Malayāl. *Iraya*. The name of a very low caste in Malabar. [The *Iraya* form one section of the *Cherumar*, and are of slightly higher social standing than the *Pulayar* (see **POLEA**). "Their name is derived from the fact that they are allowed to come only as far as the eaves (*ira*) of their employers' houses." (*Logan, Malabar*, i. 148.)]

1510.—"La sexta sorte (de' Gentili) se chiamão **Hirava**, e questi seminano e raccoglieno il riso."—*Varthema* (ed. 1517, f. 43*v*).

[**HIRRAWEN**, s. The Musulman pilgrim dress; a corruption of the Ar. *iḥrām*. Burton writes: "*Al-Iḥrām*, literally meaning 'prohibition' or 'making unlawful,' equivalent to our 'mortification,' is applied to the ceremony of the toilette, and also to the dress itself. The vulgar pronounce the word '*herām*,' or '*l'ehrām*.' It is opposed to *ihlāl*, 'making lawful,' or 'returning to laical life.' The further from Mecca it is assumed, provided that it be during the three months of Hajj, the greater is the religious merit of the pilgrim; consequently some come from India and Egypt in the dangerous attire" (*Pilgrimage*, ed. 1893, ii. 138, note).

[1813. — ". . . the ceremonies and penances mentioned by Pitts, when the *hajes*, or pilgrims, enter into **Hirrawen**, a ceremony from which the females are exempted; but the men, taking off all their clothes, cover themselves with two **hirrawens** or large white wrappers. . . ."—*Forbes, Or. Mem.* ii. 101, 2nd ed.]

HOBSON-JOBSON, s. A native festal excitement; a *tamāsha* (see **TUMASHA**); but especially the **Moharram** ceremonies. This phrase may be taken as a typical one of the most highly assimilated class of Anglo-Indian *argot*, and we have ventured to borrow from it a concise alternative title for this Glossary. It is peculiar to the British soldier and his surroundings, with whom it probably originated, and with whom it is by no means obsolete, as we once supposed. My friend Major John Trotter tells me that he has repeatedly heard it used by British soldiers in the Punjab; and has heard it also from a regimental Moonshee. It is in fact an Anglo-Saxon version of the wailings of the Mahommedans as they beat their breasts in the procession of the *Moharram*—"**Yā Hasan! Yā Hosain!**' It is to be remembered that these observances are *in India* by no means confined to Shī'as. Except at Lucknow and Murshīdābād, the great majority of Mahommedans in that country are professed Sunnis. Yet here is a statement of the facts from an unexceptionable authority:

"The commonalty of the Mussalmans, and especially the women, have more regard for the memory of Hasan and Husein, than for that of Muhammad and his khalifs. The heresy of making Ta'ziyas (see **TAZEEA**) on the anniversary of the two latter imáms, is most common throughout India: so much so that opposition to it is ascribed by the ignorant to blasphemy. This example is followed by many of the Hindus, especially the Mahrattas. The Muharram is celebrated throughout the Dekhan and Malwa, with greater enthusiasm than in other parts of India. Grand preparations are made in every town on the occasion, as if for a festival of rejoicing, rather than of observing the rites of mourning, as they ought. The observance of this custom has so strong a hold on the mind of the commonalty of the Mussulmans that they believe Muhammadanism to depend merely on keeping the memory of the imáms in the above manner." —*Mīr Shahāmat 'Ali*, in *J.R. As. Soc.* xiii. 369.

We find no literary quotation to exemplify the phrase as it stands. [But see those from the *Orient. Sporting Mag.* and *Nineteenth Century* below.] Those which follow show it in the process of evolution:

1618.—". . . . e particolarmente delle donne che, battendosi il petto e facendo gesti di grandissima compassione replicano spesso con gran dolore quegli ultimi versi di certi loro cantici: **Vah Hussein! sciah Hussein!**"—*P. della Valle*, i. 552.

c. 1630.—"Nine dayes they wander up and downe (shaving all that while neither head nor beard, nor seeming joyfull), incessantly calling out **Hussan, Hussan!** in a melancholy note, so long, so fiercely, that many can neither howle longer, nor for a month's space recover their voices."—*Sir T. Herbert*, 261.

1653.—". . . ils dressent dans les rues des Sepulchres de pierres, qu'ils couronnent de Lampes ardentes, et les soirs ils y vont dancer et sauter crians **Hussan, Houssain, Houssain, Hassan.** . . ."—*De la Boullaye-le-Gouz*, ed. 1657, p. 144.

c. 1665.—". . . ainsi j'eus tout le loisir dont j'eus besoin pour y voir celebrer la Fête de Hussein Fils d'Aly. . . . Les Mores de Golconde le celebrent avec encore beaucoup plus de folies qu'en Perse . . . d'autres font des dances en rond, tenant des épées nües là pointe en haut, qu'ils touchent les unes contre les autres, en criant de toute leur force **Hussein.**"—*Thevenot*, v. 320.

1673.—"About this time the Moors solemnize the Exequies of **Hosseen Gosseen,** a time of ten days Mourning for two Unfortunate Champions of theirs."—*Fryer*, p. 108.

,, "On the Days of their Feasts and Jubilees, Gladiators were approved and licensed; but feeling afterwards the Evils that attended that Liberty, which was chiefly used in their **Hossy Gossy,** any private Grudge being then openly revenged: it never was forbid, but it passed into an Edict by the following King, that it should be lawfull to Kill any found with Naked Swords in that Solemnity."—*Ibid.* 357.

[1710.—"And they sing around them **Saucem Saucem.**"—*Oriente Conquistado*, vol. ii.; *Conquista*, i. Div. 2, sec. 59.]

1720.—"Under these promising circumstances the time came round for the Mussulman feast called **Hossein Jossen** . . . better known as the Mohurrum."—In *Wheeler*, ii. 347.

1726.—"In their month Moharram they have a season of mourning for the two brothers Hassan and Hossein. . . . They name this mourning-time in Arabic *Ashur*, or the 10 days; but the Hollanders call it **Jaksom Baksom.**"—*Valentijn, Choro.* 107.

1763.—"It was the 14th of November, and the festival which commemorates the murder of the brothers **Hassein** and **Jassein** happened to fall out at this time."—*Orme*, i. 193.

[1773.—"The Moors likewise are not without their feasts and processions . . . particularly of their **Hassan Hassan.** . . ."—*Ives*, 28.

[1829.—"Them paper boxes are purty looking consarns, but then the folks makes sich a noise, firing and troompeting and shouting **Hobson Jobson, Hobson Jobson.**"—*Oriental Sporting Mag.*, reprint 1873, i. 129.

[1830.—"The ceremony of **Husen Hasen** . . . here passes by almost without notice."—*Raffles, Hist. Java*, 2nd ed. ii. 4.]

1832.—". . . they kindle fires in these pits every evening during the festival; and the ignorant, old as well as young, amuse themselves in fencing across them with sticks or swords; or only in running and playing round them, calling out, *Ya Allee! Ya Allee!* . . . **Shah Hussun! Shah Hussun!** . . . **Shah Hosein! Shah Hosein!** . . . *Doolha! Doolha!* (bridegroom! . . .); *Haee dost! Haee dost!* (alas, friend! . . .); *Ruheeo! Ruheeo!* (Stay! Stay!). Every two of these words are repeated probably a hundred times over as loud as they can bawl out."—*Jaffur Shureef*, *Qanoon-e-Islam*, tr. by *Herklots*, p. 173.

1883.—". . . a long procession . . . followed and preceded by the volunteer mourners and breast-beaters shouting their cry of **Hous-s-e-i-n H-as-san Houss-e-i-n H-a-s-san,** and a simultaneous blow is struck vigorously by hundreds of heavy hands on the bare breasts at the last syllable of each name."—*Wills' Modern Persia*, 282.

[1902.—"The **Hobson-Jobson.**" By Miss A. Goodrich-Freer, in *The Nineteenth Century and After*, April 1902.]

HODGETT, s. This is used among the English in Turkey and Egypt for a title-deed of land. It is Arabic *ḥujjat*, 'evidence.' *Hojat*, perhaps a corruption of the same word, is used in Western India for an account current between landlord and tenant. [Molesworth, *Mahr. Dict.*, gives "*Hujjat*, Ar., a Government acknowledgment or receipt."]

[1871.—". . . the Ḳadee attends, and writes a document (**hogget**-*el-buhr*) to attest the fact of the river's having risen to the height sufficient for the opening of the Canal. . . ."—*Lane, Mod. Egypt.*, 5th ed. ii. 233.]

[**HOG-BEAR,** s. Another name for the sloth-bear, *Melursus ursinus* (*Blanford, Mammalia*, 201). The word does not appear in the *N.E.D.*

[1895.—"Between the tree-stems he heard a **hog-bear** digging hard in the moist warm earth."—*R. Kipling, The Jungle Book*, 171.]

HOG-DEER, s. The Anglo-Indian popular name of the *Axis porcinus*, Jerd.; [*Cervus porcinus* (*Blanford, Mammalia*, 549)], the *Pārā* of Hindustan. The name is nearly the same as that which Cosmas (c. 545) applies to an animal (Χοιρέλαφος) which he draws (see under **BABI-ROUSSA**), but the two have no other relation. The Hog-deer is abundant in the grassy openings of forests throughout the Gangetic valley and further east. "It runs with its head low, and in a somewhat ungainly manner; hence its popular appellation."—*Jerdon, Mammals*, 263.

[1885.—"Two **hog-deer** were brought forward, very curious-shaped animals that I had never seen before."—*Lady Dufferin, Viceregal Life*, 146.]

HOG-PLUM, s. The austere fruit of the *amrā* (Hind.), *Spondias mangifera*, Pers. (Ord. *Terebinthaceae*), is sometimes so called; also called the wild mango. It is used in curries, pickles, and tarts. It is a native of various parts of India, and is cultivated in many tropical climates.

1852.—"The Karens have a tradition that in those golden days when God dwelt with men, all nations came before him on a certain day, each with an offering from the fruits of their lands, and the Karens selected the **hog's plum** for this oblation; which gave such offence that God cursed the Karen nation and placed it lowest. . . ."—*Mason's Burmah*, ed. 1860, p. 461.

HOKCHEW, HOKSIEU, AUCHEO, etc., n.p. These are forms which the names of the great Chinese port of *Fuh-chau*, the capital of Fuh-kien, takes in many old works. They, in fact, imitate the pronunciation in the Fuh-kien dialect, which is *Hok-chiu*; Fuh-kien similarly being called *Hoh-kien*.

1585.—"After they had travelled more than halfe a league in the suburbs of the cittie of **Aucheo**, they met with a post that came from the vizroy."—*Mendoza*, ii. 78.

1616.—"Also this day arrived a small China bark or *soma* from **Hochchew**, laden with silk and stuffes."—*Cocks*, i. 219.

HOME. In Anglo-Indian and colonial speech this means England.

1837.—"**Home** always means **England**; nobody calls India *home*—not even those who have been here thirty years or more, and are never likely to return to Europe."—*Letters from Madras*, 92.

1865.—"You may perhaps remember how often in times past we debated, with a seriousness becoming the gravity of the subject, what article of food we should each of us respectively indulge in, on our first arrival at **home**."—*Waring, Tropical Resident*, 154.

So also in the West Indies:

c. 1830.—". . . 'Oh, your cousin Mary, I forgot—fine girl, Tom—may do for you at **home** yonder' (all Creoles speak of England as **home**, although they may never have seen it)."—*Tom Cringle*, ed. 1863, 238.

HONG, s. The Chinese word is *hang*, meaning 'a row or rank'; a house of business; at Canton a warehouse, a factory, and particularly applied to the establishments of the European nations ("Foreign Hongs"), and to those of the so-called "**Hong-Merchants**." These were a body of merchants who had the monopoly of trade with foreigners, in return for which privilege they became security for the good behaviour of the foreigners, and for their payment of dues. The guild of these merchants was called 'The **Hong**.' The monopoly seems to have been first established about 1720-30, and it was terminated under the Treaty of Nanking, in 1842. The *Hong* merchants are of course not mentioned in Lockyer (1711), nor by A. Hamilton (in China previous to and after 1700, pubd. 1727). The latter uses the word, however, and the rudiments of the institution may be traced not only in this narrative, but in that of Ibn Batuta.

c. 1346.—"When a Musulman trader arrives in a Chinese city, he is allowed to choose whether he will take up his quarters with one of the merchants of his own faith settled in the country, or will go to an inn. If he prefers to go and lodge with a merchant, they count all his money and confide it to the merchant of his choice; the latter then takes charge of all expenditure on account of the stranger's wants, but acts with perfect integrity. . . ."—*Ibn Batuta*, iv. 265-6.

1727.—"When I arrived at *Canton* the *Hapoa* (see **HOPPO**) ordered me lodgings for myself, my Men, and Cargo, in (a) **Haung** or Inn belonging to one of his Merchants . . . and when I went abroad, I had always some Servants belonging to the **Haung** to follow me at a Distance."—*A. Hamilton*, ii. 227; [ed. 1744].

1782.—". . . *l'Opeou* (see **HOPPO**) . . . s'embarque en grande ceremonie dans une galère pavoisée, emmenant ordinairement avec lui trois ou quatre **Hanistes**."—*Sonnerat*, ii. 236.

" ". . . Les loges Européennes s'appellent **hams**."—*Ibid.* 245.

1783.—"It is stated indeed that a monopolizing Company in Canton, called the **Cohong**, had reduced commerce there to a desperate state."—*Report of Com. on Affairs of India, Burke*, vi. 461.

1797.—"A Society of **Hong**, or united merchants, who are answerable for one another, both to the Government and the foreign nations."—*Sir G. Staunton, Embassy to China*, ii. 565.

1882.—"The **Hong** merchants (collectively the **Co-hong**) of a body corporate, date from 1720."—*The Fankwae at Canton*, p. 34.

Cohong is, we believe, though speaking with diffidence, an exogamous union between the Latin *co-* and the Chinese *hong*. [Mr. G. T. Gardner confirms this explanation, and writes: "The term used in Canton itself is invariable: 'The Thirteen *Hong*,' or 'The Thirteen Firms'; and as these thirteen firms formed an association that had at one time the monopoly of the foreign trade, and as they were collectively responsible to the Chinese Government for the conduct of the trade, and to the foreign merchants for goods supplied to any one of the firms, some collective expression was required to denote the co-operation of the Thirteen Firms, and the word **Co-hang**, I presume, was found most expressive."]

HONG-BOAT, s. A kind of **sampan** (q.v.) or boat, with a small wooden house in the middle, used by foreigners at Canton. "A public passenger-boat (all over China, I believe) is called **Hang-chwen**, where *chwen* is generically 'vessel,' and *hang* is perhaps used in the sense of '*plying* regularly.' Boats built for this purpose, used as private boats by merchants and others, probably gave the English name **Hong-boat** to those used by our countrymen at Canton" (Note by *Bp. Moule*).

[1878.—"The *Koong-Sze Teng*, or *Hong-Mee-Teng*, or **hong boats** are from thirty to forty feet in length, and are somewhat like the gondolas of Venice. They are in many instances carved and gilded, and the saloon is so spacious as to afford sitting room for eight or ten persons. Abaft the saloon there is a cabin for the boatmen. The boats are propelled by a large scull, which works on a pivot made fast in the stern post."—*Gray, China*, ii. 273.]

HONG KONG, n.p. The name of this flourishing settlement is *hiang-kiang*, 'fragrant waterway' (*Bp. Moule*).

HONORE, ONORE, n.p. *Honāvar*, a town and port of Canara, of ancient standing and long of piratical repute. The etymology is unknown to us (see what Barbosa gives as the native name below). [A place of the same name in the Bellary District is said to be Can. *Honnūru*, *honnu*, 'gold,' *ūru*, 'village.'] Vincent has supposed it to be the Νάουρα of the *Periplus*, "the first part of the pepper-country Λιμυρική,"—for which read Διμυρική, the *Tamil* country or Malabar. But this can hardly be accepted, for Honore is less than 5000 stadia from Barygaza, instead of being 7000 as it ought to be by the *Periplus*, nor is it in the Tamil region. The true Νάουρα must have been Cannanore, or Pudopatana, a little south of the last. [The *Madras Gloss.* explains Νάουρα as the country of the Nairs.] The long defence of Honore by Captain Torriano, of the Bombay Artillery, against the forces of Tippoo, in 1783-1784, is one of the most noble records of the Indian army. (See an account of it in *Forbes, Or. Mem.* iv. 109 *seqq.*; [2nd ed. ii. 455 *seqq.*]).

c. 1343.—"Next day we arrived at the city of **Hinaur**, beside a great estuary which big ships enter. . . . The women of Hinaur are beautiful and chaste . . . they all know the Ḳurān al-'Azīm by heart. I saw at Hinaur 13 schools for the instruction of girls and 23 for boys,—such a thing as I have seen nowhere else. The inhabitants of Maleibār pay the Sultan . . . a fixed annual sum from fear of his maritime power."—*Ibn Batuta*, iv. 65-67.

1516.—". . . there is another river on which stands a good town called **Honor**; the inhabitants use the language of the country, and the Malabars call it *Ponouaram* (or *Ponaram*, in *Ramusio*); here the Malabars carry on much traffic. . . . In this town of **Onor** are two Gentoo corsairs patronised by the Lord of the Land, one called Timoja and the other Raogy, each of whom has 5 or 6 very big ships with large and well-armed crews."—*Barbosa*, Lisbon, ed. 291.

1553.—"This port (Onor) and that of Baticalá . . . belonged to the King of Bisnaga, and to this King of **Onor** his tributary, and these ports, less than 40 years before were the most famous of all that coast, not only for the fertility of the soil and its abundance in provisions . . . but for being the ingress and egress of all merchandize for the kingdom of Bisnaga, from which the King had a great revenue; and principally of horses from Arabia. . . ."—*Barros*, I. viii. cap. x. [And see *P. della Valle*, Hak. Soc. ii. 202; *Comm. Dalboquerque*, Hak. Soc. i. 148.]

HOOGLY, HOOGHLEY, n.p. Properly *Hūglī*, [and said to take its name from Beng. *hoglā*, 'the elephant grass' (*Typha angustifolia*)]: a town on the right bank of the Western Delta Branch of the Ganges, that which has long been known from this place as the **Hoogly River**, and on which Calcutta also stands, on the other bank, and 25 miles nearer the sea. Hoogly was one of the first places occupied by Europeans in the interior of Bengal; first by the Portuguese in the first half of the 16th century. An English factory was established here in 1640; and it was for some time their chief settlement in Bengal. In 1688 a quarrel with the Nawab led to armed action, and the English abandoned Hoogly; but on the arrangement of peace they settled at Chatānatī (**Chuttanutty**), now **Calcutta**.

[c. 1590.—"In the Sarkár of Satgáon, there are two ports at a distance of half a *kos* from each other; the one is Sátgáon, the other **Húglí**: the latter the chief; both are in possession of the Europeans."—*Āīn*, ed. *Jarrett*, ii. 125.]

1616.—"After the force of dom Francisco de Menezes arrived at Sundiva as we have related, there came a few days later to the same island 3 *sanguicels*, right well equipped with arms and soldiers, at the charges of Manuel Viegas, a householder and resident of **Ogolim**, or Porto Pequeno, where dwelt in Bengala many Portuguese, 80 leagues up the Ganges, in the territory of the Mogor, under his ill faith that every hour threatened their destruction."—*Bocarro, Decada*, 476.

c. 1632.—"Under the rule of the Bengális a party of Frank merchants . . . came trading to Sátgánw (see **PORTO PEQUENO**); one *kos* above that place they occupied some ground on the bank of the estuary. . . . In course of time, through the ignorance and negligence of the rulers of Bengal, these Europeans increased in number, and erected substantial buildings, which they fortified. . . . In due course a considerable place grew up, which was known by the name of the Port of **Húglí**. . . . These proceedings had come to the notice of the Emperor (Sháh Jehán), and he resolved to put an end to them," &c.—*'Abdul Ḥamīd Lāhorī*, in *Elliot*, vii. 31-32.

1644.—"The other important voyage which used to be made from Cochim was that to Bengalla, when the port and town of **Ugolim** were still standing, and much more when we had the **Porto Grande** (q.v.) and the town of *Diangâ*; this used to be made by so many ships that often in one monsoon there came 30 or more from Bengalla to Cochim, all laden with rice, sugar, lac, iron, salt-petre, and many kinds of cloths both of grass and cotton, ghee (*manteyga*), long pepper, a great quantity of wax, besides wheat and many things besides, such as quilts and rich bedding; so that every ship brought a capital of more than 20,000 xerafins. But since these two possessions were lost, and the two ports were closed, there go barely one or two vessels to *Orixa*."—*Bocarro, MS.*, f. 315.

1665.—"O Rey de Arracão nos tomou a fortaleza de Sirião em Pegû; O grão Mogor a cidade do **Golim** em Bengala."—*P. Manoel Godinho, Relação*, &c.

c. 1666.—"The rest they kept for their service to make Rowers of them; and such Christians as they were themselves, bringing them up to robbing and killing; or else they sold them to the Portugueses of *Goa*, *Ceilan*, *St. Thomas*, and others, and even to those that were remaining in *Bengall* at **Ogouli**, who were come thither to settle themselves there by favour of *Jehan-Guyre*, the Grandfather of *Aureng-Zebe*. . . ."—*Bernier*, E.T. 54; [ed. *Constable*, 176].

1727.—"**Hughly** is a Town of large Extent, but ill built. It reaches about 2 Miles along the River's Side, from the *Chinchura* before mentioned to the **Bandel**, a Colony formerly settled by the *Portuguese*, but the *Mogul's Fouzdaar* governs both at present."—*A. Hamilton*, ii. 19; [ed. 1744].

1753.—"**Ugli** est une forteresse des Maures. . . . Ce lieu étant le plus considérable de la contrée, des Européens qui remontent le Gange, lui ont donné le nom de **rivière d'Ugli** dans sa partie inférieure. . . ."—*D'Anville*, p. 64.

HOOGLY RIVER, n.p. See preceding. The stream to which we give this name is formed by the combination of the delta branches of the Ganges, viz., the Baugheruttee, Jalinghee, and Matabanga (*Bhāgirathī*, *Jalangī*, and *Mātābhāngā*), known as the **Nuddeea** (Nadiyā) **Rivers**.

HOOKA, s. Hind. from Arab. *ḥukkah*, properly 'a round casket.' The Indian pipe for smoking through water, the elaborated **hubble-bubble** (q.v.). That which is smoked in the *hooka* is a curious compound of tobacco, spice, molasses, fruit, &c. [See *Baden-Powell, Panjab Products*, i. 290.] In 1840 the *hooka* was still very common at Calcutta dinner-tables, as well as regimental mess-tables, and its *bubble-bubble-bubble* was heard from various quarters before the cloth was removed—as was customary in those days. Going back further some twelve or fifteen years it was not very uncommon to see the use of the *hooka* kept up by old Indians after their return to Europe; one such at least, in the recollection of the elder of the present writers in his childhood, being a lady who continued its use in Scotland for several years. When the second of the present writers landed first at Madras, in 1860, there were perhaps half-a-dozen Europeans at the Presidency who still used the *hooka*; there is not one now (c. 1878). A few gentlemen at Hyderabad are said still to keep it up. [Mrs. Mackenzie writing in 1850 says: "There was a dinner party in the evening (at Agra), mostly civilians, as I quickly discovered by their *huqas*. I have never seen the *huqa* smoked save at Delhi and Agra, except by a very old general officer at Calcutta." (*Life in the Mission*, ii. 196). In 1837 Miss Eden says: "the aides-de-camp and doctor get their newspapers and *hookahs* in a cluster on their side of the street." (*Up the Country*, i. 70). The rules for the Calcutta Subscription Dances in 1792 provide: "That *hookers* be not admitted to the ball room during any part of the night. But *hookers* might be admitted to the supper rooms, to the card rooms, to the boxes in the theatre, and to each side of the assembly room, between the large pillars and the walls."—*Carey, Good Old Days*, i. 98.] "In former days it was a dire offence to step over another person's *hooka*-carpet and *hooka*-snake. Men who did so intentionally were called out." (*M.-Gen. Keatinge*).

1768.—"This last Season I have been without Company (except that of my Pipe or **Hooker**), and when employed in the innocent diversion of smoaking it, have often thought of you, and Old England."—*MS. Letter of James Rennell*, July 1.

1782.—"When he observes that the gentlemen introduce their **hookas** and smoak in the company of ladies, why did he not add that the mixture of sweet-scented Persian tobacco, sweet herbs, coarse sugar, spice, etc., which they inhale . . . comes through clean water, and is so very pleasant, that many ladies take the tube, and draw a little of the smoak into their mouths."—*Price's Tracts*, vol. i. p. 78.

1783.—"For my part, in thirty years' residence, I never could find out one single luxury of the East, so much talked of here, except sitting in an arm-chair, smoaking a **hooka**, drinking cool water (when I could get it), and wearing clean linen."—(*Jos. Price*), *Some Observations on a late Publication*, &c., 79.

1789.—"When the cloth is removed, all the servants except the **hookerbedar** retire, and make way for the sea breeze to circulate, which is very refreshing to the Company, whilst they drink their wine, and smoke the **hooker**, a machine not easily described. . . ."—*Munro's Narrative*, 53.

1828.—"Every one was hushed, but the noise of that wind . . . and the occasional bubbling of my own **hookah**, which had just been furnished with another chillum."—*The Kuzzilbash*, i. 2.

c. 1849.—See Sir C. Napier, quoted under **GRAM-FED**.

c. 1858.—

"Son **houka** bigarré d'arabesques fleuries."
Leconte de Lisle, Poëmes Barbares.

1872.—". . . in the background the carcase of a boar with a cluster of villagers sitting by it, passing a **hookah** of primitive form round, for each to take a pull in turn."—*A True Reformer*, ch. i.

1874.—". . . des **houkas** d'argent emaillé et ciselé. . . ."—*Franz, Souvenir d'une Cosaque*, ch. iv.

HOOKA-BURDAR, s. Hind. from Pers. *huḳḳa-bardār*, 'hooka-bearer'; the servant whose duty it was to attend to his master's hooka, and who considered that duty sufficient to occupy his time. See *Williamson, V.M.* i. 220.

[1779.—"Mr. and Mrs. Hastings present their compliments to Mr. —— and request the favour of his company to a concert and supper on Thursday next. Mr. —— is requested to bring no servants except his **Houccaburdar**."—In *Carey, Good Old Days*, i. 71.]

1789.—"**Hookerbedar**." (See under **HOOKA**.)

1801.—"The Resident . . . tells a strange story how his **hookah-burdar**, after cheating and robbing him, proceeded to England, and set up as the Prince of Sylhet, took in everybody, was waited upon by Pitt, dined with the Duke of York, and was presented to the King."—*Elphinstone*, in *Life*, i. 34.

HOOKUM, s. An order; Ar.—H. *ḥukm*. (See under **HAKIM**.)

[1678.—"The King's **hookim** is of as small value as an ordinary Governour's."—In *Yule, Hedges' Diary*, Hak. Soc. ii. xlvi.

[1880.—"Of course Raja Joe **Hookham** will preside."—*Ali Baba*, 106.]

HOOLUCK, s. Beng. *hūlak?* The word is not in the Dicts., [but it is possibly connected with *ulūk*, Skt. *ulūka*, 'an owl,' both bird and animal taking their name from their wailing note]. The black gibbon (*Hylobates hoolook, Jerd.*; [*Blanford, Mammalia*, 5]), not unfrequently tamed on our E. frontier, and from its gentle engaging ways, and plaintive cries, often becoming a great pet. In the forests of the Kasia Hills, when there was neither sound nor sign of a living creature, by calling out hoo! hoo! one sometimes could wake a clamour in response from the *hoolucks*, as if hundreds had suddenly started to life, each shouting hoo! hoo! hoo! at the top of his voice.

c. 1809.—"The **Hulluks** live in considerable herds; and although exceedingly noisy, it is difficult to procure a view, their activity in springing from tree to tree being very great; and they are very shy."—*Buchanan's Rungpoor*, in *Eastern India*, iii. 563.

1868.—"Our only captive this time was a **huluq** monkey, a shy little beast, and very rarely seen or caught. They have black fur with white breasts, and go about usually in pairs, swinging from branch to branch with incredible agility, and making the forest resound with their strange cachinatory cry. . . ."—*T. Lewin, A Fly on the Wheel*, 374.

1884.—"He then . . . describes a gibbon he had (not an historian nor a book, but a specimen of *Hylobates* **hooluck**) who must have been wholly delightful. This engaging anthropoid used to put his arm through Mr. Sterndale's, was extremely clean in his habits ('which,' says Mr. Sterndale thoughtfully and truthfully, 'cannot be said of all the monkey tribe'), and would not go to sleep without a pillow. Of course he died of consumption. The gibbon, however, as a pet has one weakness, that of 'howling in a piercing and somewhat hysterical fashion for some minutes till exhausted.'"—*Saty. Review*, May 31, on *Sterndale's Nat. Hist. of Mammalia of India*, &c.

HOOLY, s. Hind. *holī* (Skt. *holākā*), [perhaps from the sound made in singing]. The spring festival, held at the approach of the vernal equinox, during the 10 days preceding the full moon of the month *P'hālguṇa*. It is a sort of carnival in honour of Kṛishna and the milkmaids. Passers-by are chaffed, and pelted with red powder, or drenched with yellow liquids from squirts. Songs, mostly obscene, are sung in praise of Kṛishna, and dances performed round fires. In Bengal the feast is called *dol jātrā*, or 'Swing-cradle festival.' [On the idea underlying the rite, see *Frazer, Golden Bough*, 2nd ed. iii. 306 *seq.*]

c. 1590.—"Here is also a place called Cheramutty, where, during the feast of the **Hooly**, flames issue out of the ground in a most astonishing manner."—*Gladwin's Ayeen Akbery*, ii. 34; [ed. *Jarrett*, ii. 173].

[1671.—"In Feb. or March they have a feast the Romanists call Carnival, the Indians **Whoolye**."—In *Yule, Hedges' Diary*, Hak. Soc. ii. cccxiv.]

1673.—". . . their **Hooly**, which is at their other Seed-Time."—*Fryer*, 180.

1727.—"One (Feast) they kept on Sight of a New Moon in February, exceeded the rest in ridiculous Actions and Expense; and this they called the Feast of **Wooly**, who was . . . a fierce fellow in a War with some Giants that infested Sindy. . . ."—*A. Hamilton*, i. 128; [ed. 1744, i. 129].

1808.—"I have delivered your message to Mr. H. about April day, but he says he understands the learned to place the **Hooly** as according with May day, and he believes they have no occasion in India to set apart a particular day in the year for the manufacture. . . ."—Letter from *Mrs. Halhed* to *W. Hastings*, in *Cal. Review*, xxvi. 93.

1809.—". . . We paid the Muha Raj (Sindhia) the customary visit at the **Hohlee**. Everything was prepared for playing; but at Captain C.'s particular request, that part of the ceremony was dispensed with. Playing the **Hohlee** consists in throwing about a quantity of flour, made from a water-nut called **singara**, and dyed with red sanders; it is called *abeer;* and the principal sport is to cast it into the eyes, mouth, and nose of the players, and to splash them all over with water tinged of an orange colour with the flowers of the *dak* (see **DHAWK**) tree."—*Broughton's Letters*, p. 87; [ed. 1892, p. 65 *seq.*].

HOON, s. A gold **Pagoda** (coin), q.v. Hind. *hūn*, "perhaps from Canar. *honnu* (gold)"—*Wilson*. [See *Rice, Mysore*, i. 801.]

1647.—"A wonderfully large diamond from a mine in the territory of Golkonda had fallen into the hands of Kutbu-l-Mulk; whereupon an order was issued, directing him to forward the same to Court; when its estimated value would be taken into account as part of the two *lacs* of **huns** which was the stipulated amount of his annual tribute."—*'Ināyat Khān*, in *Elliot*, vii. 84.

1879.—"In Exhibit 320 Ramji engages to pay five **hons** (=Rs. 20) to Vithoba, besides paying the Government assessment."—*Bombay High Court Judgment*, Jan. 27, p. 121.

HOONDY, s. Hind. *hunḍī, hundavī;* Mahr. and Guj. *hunḍī*. A bill of exchange in a native language.

1810.—"**Hoondies** (*i.e.* bankers' drafts) would be of no use whatever to them."—*Williamson, V. M.* ii. 530.

HOONIMAUN, s. The great ape; also called **Lungoor**.

1653.—"**Hermand** est vn singe que les Indou tiennent pour Sainct."—*De la Boullaye-le-Gouz*, p. 541.

HOOWA. A peculiar call (*hūwa*) used by the Singhalese, and thence applied to the distance over which this call can be heard. Compare the Australian *coo-ee*.

HOPPER, s. A colloquial term in S. India for cakes (usually of rice-flour), somewhat resembling the wheaten **chupatties** (q.v.) of Upper India. It is the Tamil *appam*, [from *appu*, 'to clap with the hand.' In Bombay the form used is **ap**.]

1582.—"Thus having talked a while, he gave him very good entertainment, and commanded to give him certaine cakes, made of the flower of Wheate, which the Malabars do call **Apes**, and with the same honnie."—*Castañeda* (by N.L.), f. 38.

1606.—"Great dishes of **apas**."—*Gouvea*, f. 48*v*.

1672.—"These cakes are called **Apen** by the Malabars."—*Baldaeus, Afgoderye* (Dutch ed.), 39.

c. 1690.—"Ex iis (the chestnuts of the Jack fruit) in sole siccatis farinam, ex eaque placentas, **apas** dictas, conficiunt."—*Rheede*, iii.

1707.—"Those who bake **oppers** without permission will be subject to severe penalty."—*Thesavaleme* (Tamil Laws of Jaffna), 700.

[1826.—"He sat down beside me, and shared between us his coarse brown **aps**."—*Pandurang Hari*, ed. 1873, i. 81.]

1860.—"*Appas* (called **hoppers** by the English) . . . supply their morning repast."—*Tennent's Ceylon*, ii. 161.

HOPPO, s. The Chinese Superintendent of Customs at Canton. Giles says: "The term is said to be a corruption of *Hoo poo*, the Board of Revenue, with which office the *Hoppo*, or Collector of duties, is in direct communication." Dr. Williams gives a different account (see below). Neither affords much satisfaction. [The *N.E.D.* accepts the account given in the quotation from Williams.]

1711.—"The **Hoppos**, who look on Europe Ships as a great Branch of their Profits, will give you all the fair words imaginable."—*Lockyer*, 101.

1727.—"I have staid about a Week, and found no Merchants come near me, which made me suspect, that there were some underhand dealings between the **Hapoa** and his Chaps, to my Prejudice."—*A. Hamilton*, ii. 228; [ed. 1744, ii. 227]. (See also under **HONG**.)

1743.—". . . just as he (Mr. Anson) was ready to embark, the **Hoppo** or *Chinese* Custom-house officer of *Macao* refused to grant a permit to the boat."—*Anson's Voyage*, 9th ed. 1756, p. 355.

1750-52.—"The **hoppo, happa**, or first inspector of customs . . . came to see us to-day."—*Osbeck*, i. 359.

1782.—"La charge d'**Opeou** répond à celle d'intendant de province."—*Sonnerat*, ii. 236.

1797.—". . . the **Hoppo** or mandarine more immediately connected with Europeans."—*Sir G. Staunton*, i. 239.

1842 (?).—"The term **hoppo** is confined to Canton, and is a corruption of the term *hoi-po-sho*, the name of the officer who has control over the boats on the river, strangely applied to the Collector of Customs by foreigners."—*Wells Williams, Chinese Commercial Guide*, 221.

[1878.—"The second board or tribunal is named **hoopoo**, and to it is entrusted the care and keeping of the imperial revenue."—*Gray, China*, i. 19.]

1882.—"It may be as well to mention here that the '**Hoppo**' (as he was incorrectly styled) filled an office especially created for the foreign trade at Canton. . . . The Board of Revenue is in Chinese 'Hoo-poo,' and the office was locally misapplied to the officer in question."—*The Fankwae at Canton*, p. 36.

HORSE-KEEPER, s. An old provincial English term, used in the Madras Presidency and in Ceylon, for 'groom.' The usual corresponding words are, in N. India, **syce** (q.v.), and in Bombay *ghorāwālā* (see **GORAWALLAH**).

1555.—"There in the reste of the Cophine made for the nones thei bewrie one of his dierest lemmans, a waityng manne, a Cooke, a **Horse-keeper**, a Lacquie, a Butler, and a Horse, whiche thei al at first strangle, and thruste in."—*W. Watreman, Fardle of Faciouns*, N. 1.

1609.—"Watermen, Lackeyes, **Horse-keepers**."—*Hawkins*, in *Purchas*, i. 216.

1673.—"On St. George's Day I was commanded by the Honourable *Gerald Aungier* . . . to embarque on a Bombaim Boat . . . waited on by two of the Governor's servants . . . an **Horsekeeper**. . . ."—*Fryer*, 123.

1698.—". . . followed by his boy . . . and his **horsekeeper**."—In *Wheeler*, i. 300.

1829.—"In my English buggy, with lamps lighted and an English sort of a nag, I might almost have fancied myself in England, but for the black **horse-keeper** alongside of me."—*Mem. of Col. Mountain*, 87.

1837.—"Even my horse pretends he is too fine to switch off his own flies with his own long tail, but turns his head round to order the **horsekeeper** . . . to wipe them off for him."—*Letters from Madras*, 50.

HORSE-RADISH TREE, s. This is a common name, in both N. and S. India, for the tree called in Hind. *sahajnā*; *Moringa pterygosperma*, Gaertn., *Hyperanthera Moringa*, Vahl. (N. O. *Moringaceae*), in Skt. *sobhānjana*. Sir G. Birdwood says: "A marvellous tree botanically, as no one knows in what order to put it; it has links with so many; and it is evidently a 'head-centre' in the progressive development of forms." The name is given because the scraped root is used in place of horse-radish, which it closely resembles in flavour. In S. India the same plant is called the **Drumstick-tree** (q.v.), from the shape of the long slender fruit, which is used as a vegetable, or in curry, or made into a native pickle "most nauseous to Europeans" (*Punjab Plants*). It is a native of N.W. India, and also extensively cultivated in India and other tropical countries, and is used also for many purposes in the native pharmacopœia. [See **MYROBALAN.**]

HOSBOLHOOKUM, &c. Properly (Ar. used in Hind.) *ḥasb-ul-ḥukm*, literally 'according to order'; these words forming the initial formula of a document issued by officers of State on royal authority, and thence applied as the title of such a document.

[1678.—"Had it bin another King, as Shajehawn, whose phirmaund (see **FIRMAUN**) and **hasbullhookims** were of such great force and binding."—In *Yule, Hedges' Diary*, Hak. Soc. ii. xlvi.]

" "... the other given in the 10th year of Oranzeeb, for the English to pay 2 per cent. at Surat, which the Mogul interpreted by his order, and **Husbull Hookum** (*id est*, a word of command by word of mouth) to his Devan in Bengall, that the English were to pay 2 per cent. custom at Surat, and in all other his dominions to be custom free."—*Ft. St. Geo. Consns.*, 17th Dec., in *Notes and Exts.*, Pt. I. pp. 97-98.

1702.—"The Nabob told me that the great God knows that he had ever a hearty respect for the English ... saying, here is the **Hosbulhocum**, which the king has sent me to seize Factories and all their effects."—In *Wheeler*, i. 387.

1727.—"The *Phirmaund* is presented (by the *Goosberdaar* (**Goorzburdar**), or **Hosbalhouckain**, or, in *English*, the King's Messenger) and the Governor of the Province or City makes a short speech."—*A. Hamilton*, i. 230; [ed. 1744, i. 233].

1757.—"This Treaty was conceived in the following Terms. I. Whatever Rights and Privileges the King had granted the English Company, in their Phirmaund, and the **Hushulhoorums** (*sic*), sent from Delly, shall not be disputed."—*Mem. of the Revolution in Bengal*, pp. 21-22.

1759.—"**Housbul-hookum** (*under the great seal of the Nabob Vizier, Ulmah Maleck, Nizam al Mulack Bahadour*. Be peace unto the high and renowned Mr. John Spencer ..." —In *Cambridge's Acct. of the War*, &c., 229.

1761.—"A grant signed by the Mogul is called a Phirmaund (*farmān*). By the Mogul's Son, a Nushawn (*nishān*). By the Nabob a Perwanna (*parwāna*). By the Vizier, a **Housebul-hookum**."—*Ibid.* 226.

1769.—"Besides it is obvious, that as great a sum might have been drawn from that Company without affecting property ... or running into his golden dream of cockets on the Ganges, or visions of Stamp duties, *Perwannas, Dusticks, Kistbundees* and **Husbulhookums**."—*Burke, Obsns. on a late Publication called* "The Present State of the Nation."

HOT-WINDS, s. This may almost be termed the name of one of the seasons of the year in Upper India, when the hot dry westerly winds prevail, and such aids to coolness as the **tatty** and **thermantidote** (q.v.) are brought into use. May is the typical month of such winds.

1804.—"Holkar appears to me to wish to avoid the contest at present; and so does Gen. Lake, possibly from a desire to give his troops some repose, and not to expose the Europeans to the **hot winds** in Hindustan." —*Wellington*, iii. 180.

1873.—"It's no use thinking of lunch in this roaring **hot wind** that's getting up, so we shall be all light and fresh for another shy at the pigs this afternoon."—*The True Reformer*, i. p. 8.

HOWDAH, vulg. **HOWDER,** &c., s. Hind. modified from Ar. *haudaj*. A great chair or framed seat carried by an elephant. The original Arabic word *haudaj* is applied to litters carried by camels.

c. 1663.—"At other times he rideth on an Elephant in a *Mik-dember* or **Hauze** ... the *Mik-dember* being a little square House or Turret of Wood, is always painted and gilded; and the **Hauze**, which is an Oval seat, having a Canopy with Pillars over it, is so likewise."—*Bernier*, E.T. 119; [ed. *Constable*, 370].

c. 1785.—"Colonel Smith ... reviewed his troops from the **houdar** of his elephant." —*Carraccioli's L. of Clive*, iii. 133.

A popular rhyme which was applied in India successively to Warren Hastings' escape from Benares in 1781, and to Col. Monson's retreat from Malwa in 1804, and which was perhaps much older than either, runs:

"Ghoṛe par **hauda**, hāthī par jīn
Jaldī bhāg-gāyā { Warren Hastīn!
Kornail Munsīn!"

which may be rendered with some anachronism in expression:

"Horses with **howdahs**, and elephants saddled
Off helter skelter the Sahibs skedaddled."

[1805. — "**Houza, howda.**" See under **AMBAREE.**]

1831.—
"And when they talked of Elephants,
And riding in my **Howder**,
(So it was called by all my aunts)
I prouder grew and prouder."
H. M. Parker, in *Bengal Annual*, 119.

1856.—
"But she, the gallant lady, holding fast
With one soft arm the jewelled **howdah's**
side,
Still with the other circles tight the babe
Sore smitten by a cruel shaft . . ."
The Banyan Tree, a Poem.

1863.—"Elephants are also liable to be disabled . . . ulcers arise from neglect or carelessness in fitting on the **howdah**."—*Sat. Review*, Sept. 6, 312.

HUBBA, s. A grain; a jot or tittle. Ar. *ḥabba*.

1786—"For two years we have not received a **hubba** on account of our **tunkaw**, though the ministers have annually charged a lac of rupees, and never paid us anything."—In *Art. agst. Hastings, Burke*, vii. 141.

[1836.—"The **habbeh** (or grain of barley) is the 48th part of dirhem, or third of a keerat . . . or in commerce fully equal to an English grain."—*Lane, Mod. Egypt.*, ii. 326.]

HUBBLE-BUBBLE, s. An onomatopoeia applied to the *hooka* in its rudimentary form, as used by the masses in India. Tobacco, or a mixture containing tobacco amongst other things, is placed with embers in a terra-cotta **chillum** (q.v.), from which a reed carries the smoke into a coconut shell half full of water, and the smoke is drawn through a hole in the side, generally without any kind of mouth-piece, making a bubbling or gurgling sound. An elaborate description is given in Terry's *Voyage* (see below), and another in *Govinda Samanta*, i. 29 (1872).

1616.—". . . they have little Earthen Pots . . . having a narrow neck and an open round top, out of the belly of which comes a small spout, to the lower part of which spout they fill the Pot with water: then putting their *Tobacco* loose in the top, and a burning coal upon it, they having first fastned a very small strait hollow Cane or Reed . . . within that spout . . . the Pot standing on the ground, draw that smoak into their mouths, which first falls upon the Superficies of the water, and much discolours it. And this way of taking their *Tobacco*, they believe makes it much more cool and wholsom."—*Terry*, ed. 1665, p. 363.

c. 1630.—"Tobacco is of great account here; not strong (as our men love), but weake and leafie; suckt out of long canes call'd **hubble-bubbles** . . ."—*Sir. T. Herbert*, 28.

1673.—"Coming back I found my troublesome Comrade very merry, and packing up his Household Stuff, his *Bang* bowl, and **Hubble-bubble**, to go along with me."—*Fryer*, 127.

1673.—". . . bolstered up with embroidered Cushions, smoaking out of a silver **Hubble-bubble**."—*Fryer*, 131.

1697.—". . . Yesterday the King's Dewan, and this day the King's Buxee . . . arrived . . . to each of whom sent two bottles of Rose-water, and a glass **Hubble-bubble**, with a compliment."—In *Wheeler*, i. 318.

c. 1760.—See *Grose*, i. 146.

1811.—"Cette manière de fumer est extrêmement commune . . . on la nomme **Hubbel de Bubbel**."—*Solvyns*, tom. iii.

1868.—"His (the Dyak's) favourite pipe is a huge **Hubble-bubble**."—*Wallace, Mal. Archip.*, ed. 1880, p. 80.

HUBSHEE, n.p. Ar. *Ḥabashī*, P. *Ḥabshī*, 'an Abyssinian,' an Ethiopian, a negro. The name is often specifically applied to the chief of Jinjīra on the western coast, who is the descendant of an Abyssinian family.

1298.—"There are numerous cities and villages in this province of **Abash**, and many merchants."—*Marco Polo*, 2nd ed. ii. 425.

[c. 1346.—"**Habshis**." See under **COLOMBO**.]

1553.—"At this time, among certain Moors, who came to sell provisions to the ships, had come three **Abeshis** (*Abexijs*) of the country of the Prester John . . ."—*Barros*, I. iv. 4.

[1612.—"Sent away the Thomas towards the **Habash** coast."—*Danvers, Letters*, i. 166; "The **Habesh** shore."—*Ibid.* i. 131.

[c. 1661.—". . . on my way to Gonder, the capital of **Habech**, or Kingdom of Ethiopia."—*Bernier*, ed. *Constable*, 2.]

1673.—"Cowis Cawn, an **Hobsy** or Arabian *Coffery* (**Caffer**)."—*Fryer*, 147.

1681.—"*Habessini* . . . nunc passim nominantur; vocabulo ab Arabibus indito, quibus **Habesh** colluviem vel mixturam gentium denotat."—*Ludolphi, Hist. Aethiop.* lib. i. c. i.

1750-60.—"The Moors are also fond of having Abyssinian slaves known in India by the name of **Hobshy** Coffrees."—*Grose*, i. 148.

1789.—"In India Negroes, *Habissinians*, *Nobis* (*i.e.* Nubians) &c. &c. are promiscuously called **Habashies** or *Habissians*, although the two latter are no negroes; and the *Nobies* and **Habashes** differ greatly from one another."—*Note to Seir Mutaqherin*, iii. 36.

[1813.—". . . the master of a family adopts a slave, frequently a **Haffshee** Abyssinian, of the darkest hue, for his heir."—*Forbes, Or. Mem.* 2nd ed. ii. 473.]

1884.—"One of my Tibetan ponies had short curly brown hair, and was called both by my servants, and by Dr. Campbell, 'a **Hubshee**.'

"I understood that the name was specific for that description of pony amongst the traders."—*Note by Sir Joseph Hooker.*

HUCK. Properly Ar. *hakk.* A just right; a lawful claim; a perquisite claimable by established usage.

[1866.—"The difference between the bazar price, and the amount price of the article sold, is the **huq** of the Dullal (**Deloll**)."—*Confessions of an Orderly*, 50.]

HUCKEEM, s. Ar.—H. *ḥakīm*; a physician. (See note under **HAKIM.**)

1622.—"I, who was thinking little or nothing about myself, was forthwith put by them into the hands of an excellent physician, a native of Shiraz, who then happened to be at Lar, and whose name was *Hekim Abu'l fetab.* The word **hekim** signifies 'wise'; it is a title which it is the custom to give to all those learned in medical matters."—*P. della Valle*, ii. 318.

1673.—"My Attendance is engaged, and a Million of Promises, could I restore him to his Health, laid down from his Wives, Children, and Relations, who all (with the Citizens, as I could hear going along) pray to God that the **Hackin** *Fringi*, the *Frank* Doctor, might kill him . . ."—*Fryer*, 312.

1837.—"I had the native works on Materia Medica collated by competent **Hakeems** and Moonshees."—*Royle, Hindoo Medicine*, 25.

HULLIA, s. Canarese *Holeya*; the same as **Polea** (*pulayan*) (q.v.), equivalent to **Pariah** (q.v.). ["*Holeyas* field-labourers and agrestic serfs of S. Canara; *Pulayan* being the Malayālam and *Paraiyan* the Tamil form of the same word. Brahmans derive it from *hole*, 'pollution'; others from *hola*, 'land' or 'soil,' as being thought to be autochthones" (*Sturrock, Man. of S. Canara*, i. 173). The last derivation is accepted in the *Madras Gloss.* For an illustration of these people, see *Richter, Man. of Coorg*, 112.]

1817.—". . . a **Hulliá** or Pariar King."—*Wilks, Hist. Sketches*, i. 151.

1874.—"At Melkotta, the chief seat of the followers of Râmanya [Rāmānuja] Achârya, and at the Brâhman temple at Bailur, the **Hŏlĕyars** or Pareyars have the right of entering the temple on three days in the year, specially set apart for them."—*M. J. Walhouse, in Ind. Antiq.* iii. 191.

HULWA, s. Ar. *ḥalwā* and *ḥalāwa* is generic for sweetmeat, and the word is in use from Constantinople to Calcutta. In H. the word represents a particular class, of which the ingredients are milk, sugar, almond paste, and ghee flavoured with cardamom. "The best at Bombay is imported from Muskat" (*Birdwood*).

1672.—"Ce qui estoit plus le plaisant, c'estoit un homme qui précédoit le corps des confituriers, lequel avoit une chemise qui luy descendoit aux talons, toute couverte **d'alva**, c'est à dire, de confiture."—*Journ. d'Ant. Galland*, i. 118.

1673.—". . . the Widow once a Moon (to) go to the Grave with her Acquaintance to repeat the doleful Dirge, after which she bestows **Holway**, a kind of Sacramental Wafer; and entreats their Prayers for the Soul of the Departed."—*Fryer*, 94.

1836.—"A curious cry of the seller of a kind of sweetmeat ('**haláweh**'), composed of treacle fried with some other ingredients, is 'For a nail! O sweetmeat! . . .' children and servants often steal implements of iron, &c., from the house . . . and give them to him in exchange. . . ."—*Lane, Mod. Egypt.*, ed. 1871, ii. 15.

HUMMAUL, s. Ar. *ḥammāl*, a porter. The use of the word in India is confined to the west, and there now commonly indicates a palankin-bearer. The word still survives in parts of Sicily in the form **camallu**=It. 'facchino,' a relic of the Saracenic occupation. In Andalusia **alhamel** now means a man who lets out a baggage horse; and the word is also used in Morocco in the same way (*Dozy*).

c. 1350.—"Those rustics whom they call **camalls** (*camallos*), whose business it is to carry burdens, and also to carry men and women on their shoulders in litters, such as are mentioned in Canticles: '*Ferculum fecit sibi Solomon de lignis Libani*,' whereby is meant a portable litter such as I used to be carried in at Zayton, and in India."—*John de' Marignolli*, in *Cathay*, &c., 366.

1554.—"To the Xabandar (see **SHABUNDER**) (at Ormuz) for the vessels employed in discharging stores, and for the **amals** who serve in the custom-house."—*S. Botelho, Tombo*, 103.

1691.—"His honour was carried by the **Amaals**, *i.e.* the Palankyn bearers 12 in number, sitting in his Palankyn."—*Valentijn*, v. 266.

1711.—"**Hamalage**, or Cooley-hire, at 1 *coz* (see **GOSBECK**) for every maund Tabrees."—Tariff in *Lockyer*, 243.

1750-60.—"The **Hamauls** or porters, who make a livelihood of carrying goods to and from the warehouses."—*Grose*, i. 120.

1809.—"The palankeen-bearers are here called **hamauls** (a word signifying carrier) . . . these people come chiefly from the Mahratta country, and are of the *coombie* or agricultural caste."—*Maria Graham*, 2.

1813.—For **Hamauls** at Bussora, see *Milburn*, i. 126.

1840.—"The **hamals** groaned under the weight of their precious load, the Apostle of the Ganges" (Dr. Duff to wit).—*Smith's Life of Dr. John Wilson*, 1878, p. 282.

1877.—"The stately iron gate enclosing the front garden of the Russian Embassy was beset by a motley crowd. . . . **Hamals**, or street porters, bent double under the burden of heavy trunks and boxes, would come now and then up one or other of the two semicircular avenues."—*Letter from Constantinople*, in *Times*, May 7.

HUMMING-BIRD, s. This name is popularly applied in some parts of India to the sun-birds (sub-fam. *Nectarininae*).

HUMP, s. 'Calcutta humps' are the salted humps of Indian oxen exported from that city. (See under **BUFFALO.**)

HURCARRA, HIRCARA, &c., s. Hind. *harkārā*, 'a messenger, a courier; an emissary, a spy' (*Wilson*). The etymology, according to the same authority, is *har*, 'every,' *kār*, 'business.' The word became very familiar in the Gilchristian spelling *Hurkaru*, from the existence of a Calcutta newspaper bearing that title (*Bengal Hurkaru*, generally enunciated by non-Indians as *Hurkĕroō*), for the first 60 years of last century, or thereabouts.

1747.—"Given to the **Ircaras** for bringing news of the Engagement. (Pag.) 4 3 0."—*Fort St David, Expenses of the Paymaster*, under January. MS. Records in India Office.

1748.—"The city of Dacca is in the utmost confusion on account of . . . advices of a large force of Mahrattas coming by way of the Sunderbunds, and that they were advanced as far as Sundra Col, when first descried by their **Hurcurrahs**."—In *Long*, 4.

1757.—"I beg you to send me a good **alcara** who understands the Portuguese language."—Letter in *Ives*, 159.

,, "**Hircars** or Spies."—*Ibid.* 161; [and comp. 67].

1761.—"The head **Harcar** returned, and told me this as well as several other secrets very useful to me, which I got from him by dint of money and some rum."—Letter of *Capt. Martin White*, in *Long*, 260.

[1772.—"**Hercarras.**" (See under **DALOYET.**)]

1780.—"One day upon the march a **Hircarrah** came up and delivered him a letter from Colonel Baillie."—Letter of *T. Munro*, in *Life*, i. 26.

1803.—"The **hircarras** reported the enemy to be at Bokerdun."—Letter of *A. Wellesley, ibid.* 348.

c. 1810.—"We were met at the entrance of Tippoo's dominions by four **hircarrahs**, or soldiers, whom the Sultan sent as a guard to conduct us safely."—*Miss Edgeworth, Lame Jervas.* Miss Edgeworth has oddly misused the word here.

1813.—"The contrivances of the native **halcarrahs** and spies to conceal a letter are extremely clever, and the measures they frequently adopt to elude the vigilance of an enemy are equally extraordinary."—*Forbes, Or. Mem.* iv. 129; [compare 2nd ed. i. 64; ii. 201].

HURTAUL, s. Hind. from Skt. *haritalaka, hartāl, haritāl*, yellow arsenic, orpiment.

c. 1347.—Ibn Batuta seems oddly to confound it with camphor. "The best (camphor) called in the country itself *al-***hardāla**, is that which attains the highest degree of cold."—iv. 241.

c. 1759.—". . . **hartal** and *Cotch*, Earth-Oil and Wood-Oil. . . ."—List of Burmese Products, in *Dalrymple's Or. Reper.* i. 109.

HUZĀRA, n.p. This name has two quite distinct uses.

(a.) Pers. *Hazāra*. It is used as a generic name for a number of tribes occupying some of the wildest parts of Afghanistan, chiefly N.W. and S.W. of Kabul. These tribes are in no respect Afghan, but are in fact most or all of them Mongol in features, and some of them also in language. The term at one time appears to have been used more generally for a variety of the wilder clans in the higher hill countries of Afghanistan and the Oxus basin, much as in Scotland of a century and a half ago they spoke of "the clans." It appears to be merely from the Pers. *hazār*, 1000. The regiments, so to speak, of the Mongol hosts of Chinghiz and his immediate successors were called **hazāras**, and if we accept the belief that the *Hazāras* of Afghanistan were predatory bands of those hosts who settled in that region (in favour of which there is a good deal to be said), this name is intelligible. If so, its application to the non-Mongol people of Wakhān, &c., must have been a later transfer. [See the discussion by Bellew, who points out that "amongst themselves this people never use the term *Hazārah* as their national appellation, and yet they have no name for their people as a nation.

They are only known amongst themselves by the names of their principal tribes and the clans subordinate to them respectively." (*Races of Afghanistan*, 114.)]

c. 1480.—"The **Hazāra**, Takdari, and all the other tribes having seen this, quietly submitted to his authority."—*Tarkhán-Náma*, in *Elliot*, i. 303. For *Takdari* we should probably read *Nakudari;* and see *Marco Polo*, Bk. I. ch. 18, note on *Nigudaris.*

c. 1505.—Kabul "on the west has the mountain districts, in which are situated Karnûd and Ghûr. This mountainous tract is at present occupied and inhabited by the **Hazâra** and Nukderi tribes."—*Baber*, p. 136.

1508.—"Mirza Ababeker, the ruler and tyrant of Káshghar, had seized all the Upper **Hazáras** of Badakhshán."—*Erskine's Baber and Humáyun*, i. 287. "*Hazáraját báládest.* The upper districts in Badakhshán were called *Hazáras.*" Erskine's note. He is using the *Tarīkh Rashīdī.* But is not the word *Hazáras* here, 'the clans,' used elliptically for the highland districts occupied by them?

[c. 1590.—"The **Hazárahs** are the descendants of the Chaghatai army, sent by Manku Ḳáán to the assistance of Huláku Khán. . . . They possess horses, sheep and goats. They are divided into factions, each covetous of what they can obtain, deceptive in their common intercourse and their conventions of amity savour of the wolf."—*Āīn*, ed. *Jarrett*, ii. 402.]

(b.) A mountain district in the extreme N.W. of the Punjab, of which *Abbottābād*, called after its founder, General James Abbott, is the British head-quarter. The name of this region apparently has nothing to do with *Hazāras* in the tribal sense, but is probably a survival of the ancient name of a territory in this quarter, called in Sanskrit *Abhisāra*, and figuring in Ptolemy, Arrian and Curtius as the kingdom of King *Abisarēs.* [See *M'Crindle, Invasion of India*, 69.]

HUZOOR, s. Ar. *ḥuzūr*, 'the presence'; used by natives as a respectful way of talking of or to exalted personages, to or of their master, or occasionally of any European gentleman in presence of another European. [The allied words *ḥazrat* and *ḥuzūrī* are used in kindred senses as in the examples.]

[1787.—"You will send to the **Huzzoor** an account particular of the assessment payable by each ryot."—*Parwana of Tippoo*, in *Logan, Malabar*, iii. 125.

[1813.—"The Mahratta cavalry are divided into several classes: the **Husserat**, or household troops called the *kassey-pagah*, are reckoned very superior to the ordinary horse. . . ."—*Forbes, Or. Mem.* 2nd ed. i. 344.

[1824.—"The employment of that singular description of officers called **Huzooriah**, or servants of the presence, by the Mahratta princes of Central India, has been borrowed from the usages of the Poona court. *Huzooriahs* are personal attendants of the chief, generally of his own tribe, and are usually of respectable parentage; a great proportion are hereditary followers of the family of the prince they serve. . . . They are the usual envoys to subjects on occasions of importance. . . . Their appearance supersedes all other authority, and disobedience to the orders they convey is termed an act of rebellion."—*Malcolm, Central India*, 2nd ed. i. 536 *seq.*

[1826.—"These men of authority being aware that I was a **Hoogorie**, or one attached to the suite of a great man, received me with due respect."—*Pandurang Hari*, ed. 1873, i. 40.]

HYSON. (See under **TEA**.)

I

IDALCAN, HIDALCAN, and sometimes **IDALXA**, n.p. The title by which the Portuguese distinguished the kings of the Mahommedan dynasty of Bījapūr which rose at the end of the 15th century on the dissolution of the Bahmani kingdom of the Deccan. These names represented *'Adil Khān*, the title of the founder before he became king, more generally called by the Portuguese the **Sabaio** (q.v.), and *'Adil Shāh*, the distinctive style of all the kings of the dynasty. The Portuguese commonly called their kingdom **Balaghaut** (q.v.).

1510.—"The **Hidalcan** entered the city (Goa) with great festivity and rejoicings, and went to the castle to see what the ships were doing, and there, inside and out, he found the dead Moors, whom Timoja had slain; and round about them the brothers and parents and wives, raising great wailings and lamentations, thus the festivity of the **Hidalcan** was celebrated by weepings and wailings . . . so that he sent João Machado to the Governor to speak about terms of peace. . . . The Governor replied that Goa belonged to his lord the K. of Portugal, and that he would hold no peace with him (Hidalcan) unless he delivered up the city with all its territories. . . . With which reply back went João Machado, and the **Hidalcan** on hearing it was left amazed, saying that our people were sons of the devil. . . ."—*Correa*, ii. 98.

1516.—"**Hydalcan.**" See under **SABAIO.**

1546.—"Trelado de contrato que ho Gouernador Dom Johão de Crastro ffeez com o **Idalxaa**, que d'antes se chamava **Idalcão.**"—*Tombo*, in *Subsidios*, 39.

1563.—"And as those Governors grew weary of obeying the King of Daquem (**Deccan**), they conspired among themselves that each should appropriate his own lands . . . and the great-grandfather of this **Adelham** who now reigns was one of those captains who revolted; he was a Turk by nation and died in the year 1535; a very powerful man he was always, but it was from him that we twice took by force of arms this city of Goa. . . ."—*Garcia*, f. 35*v*. [And comp. *Linschoten*, Hak. Soc. ii. 199.] N.B.—It was the *second* of the dynasty who died in 1535; the original **'Adil Khān** (or **Sabaio**) died in 1510, just before the attack of Goa by the Portuguese.

1594-5.—"There are three distinct States in the Dakhin. The **Nizám-ul-Mulkiya, 'Adil Kháníya,** and **Kutbu-l-Mulkiya.** The settled rule among them was, that if a foreign army entered their country, they united their forces and fought, notwithstanding the dissensions and quarrels they had among themselves. It was also the rule, that when their forces were united, Nizám-ul-Mulk commanded the centre, **'Adil Khán** the right, and Kutbu-l-Mulk the left. This rule was now observed, and an immense force had been collected."—*Akbar-Nāma*, in *Elliot*, vi. 131.

IMAUM, s. Ar. *Imām*, 'an exemplar, a leader' (from a root signifying 'to aim at, to follow after'), a title technically applied to the Caliph (*Khalīfa*) or 'Vicegerent,' or Successor, who is the head of Islām. The title "is also given—in its religious import only—to the heads of the four orthodox sects . . . and in a more restricted sense still, to the ordinary functionary of a mosque who leads in the daily prayers of the congregation" (*Dr. Badger, Omân*, App. A.). The title has been perhaps most familiar to Anglo-Indians as that of the Princes of 'Omān, or "**Imaums** of Muscat," as they were commonly termed. This title they derived from being the heads of a sect (*Ibādhiya*) holding peculiar doctrine as to the Imamate, and rejecting the Caliphate of Ali or his successors. It has not been assumed by the Princes themselves since Sa'īd bin Ahmad who died in the early part of last century, but was always applied by the English to Saiyid Sa'īd, who reigned for 52 years, dying in 1856. Since then, and since the separation of the dominions of the dynasty in Omān and in Africa, the title **Imām** has no longer been used.

It is a singular thing that in an article on Zanzibar in the *J. R. Geog. Soc.* vol. xxiii. by the late Col. Sykes, the Sultan is always called the *Imaun*, [of which other examples will be found below].

1673.—"At night we saw *Muschat*, whose vast and horrid Mountains no Shade but Heaven does hide. . . . The Prince of this country is called **Imaum**, who is guardian at *Mahomet's* Tomb, and on whom is devolved the right of *Caliphship* according to the Ottoman belief."—*Fryer*, 220.

[1753.—"These people are Mahommedans of a particular sect . . . they are subject to an **Iman**, who has absolute authority over them."—*Hanway*, iii. 67.

[1901.—Of the Bombay Kojas, "there were only 12 **Imans**, the last of the number . . . having disappeared without issue."—*Times*, April 12.]

IMAUMBARRA, s. This is a hybrid word *Imām-bāṛā*, in which the last part is the Hindī *bāṛā*, 'an enclosure,' &c. It is applied to a building maintained by Shī'a communities in India for the express purpose of celebrating the **mohurrum** ceremonies (see **HOBSON-JOBSON**). The sepulchre of the Founder and his family is often combined with this object. The Imāmbāṛā of the Nawāb Āsaf-ud-daula at Lucknow is, or was till the siege of 1858, probably the most magnificent modern Oriental structure in India. It united with the objects already mentioned a mosque, a college, and apartments for the members of the religious establishment. The great hall is "conceived on so grand a scale," says Fergusson, "as to entitle it to rank with the buildings of an earlier age." The central part of it forms a vaulted apartment of 162 feet long by 53½ wide.

[1837.—"In the afternoon we went to see the **Emaunberra.**"—*Miss Eden, Up the Country*, i. 87.]

IMPALE, v. It is startling to find an injunction to impale criminals given by an English governor (Vansittart, apparently) little more than a century ago. [See **CALUETE.**]

1764.—"I request that you will give orders to the Naib of Dacca to send some of the Factory Sepoys along with some of his own people, to apprehend the said murderers and to **impale** them, which will be very serviceable to traders."—*The Governor of Fort William* to the Nawab; in *Long*, 389.

1768-71.—"The punishments inflicted at Batavia are excessively severe, especially such as fall upon the Indians. **Impalement** is the chief and most terrible."—*Stavorinus*, i. 288. This writer proceeds to give a description of the horrible process, which he witnessed.

INAUM, ENAUM, s. Ar. *in'ām*, 'a gift' (from a superior), 'a favour,' but especially in India a gift of rent-free land: also land so held. **In'āmdār**, the holder of such lands. A full detail of the different kinds of *in'ām*, especially among the Mahrattas, will be found in *Wilson*, s.v. The word is also used in Western India for **bucksheesh** (q.v.). This use is said to have given rise to a little mistake on the part of an English political traveller some 30 or 40 years ago, when there had been some agitation regarding the **in'am** lands and the alleged harshness of the Government in dealing with such claims. The traveller reported that the public feeling in the west of India was so strong on this subject that his very palankin-bearers at the end of their stage invariably joined their hands in supplication, shouting, "**In'am! In'am!** Sahib!"

INDIA, INDIES, n.p. A book might be written on this name. We can only notice a few points in connection with it.

It is not easy, if it be possible, to find a truly native (*i.e.* Hindu) name for the whole country which we call India; but the *conception* certainly existed from an early date. *Bhāratavarsha* is used apparently in the Purānas with something like this conception. *Jambudwīpa*, a term belonging to the mythical cosmography, is used in the Buddhist books, and sometimes, by the natives of the south, even now. The accuracy of the definitions of India in some of the Greek and Roman authors shows the existence of the same conception of the country that we have now; a conception also obvious in the modes of speech of Hwen T'sang and the other Chinese pilgrims. The Aśoka inscriptions, c. B.C. 250, had enumerated Indian kingdoms covering a considerable part of the conception, and in the great inscription at Tanjore, of the 11th century A.D., which incidentally mentions the conquest (real or imaginary) of a great part of India, by the king of Tanjore, Vīra-Chola, the same system is followed. In a copperplate of the 11th century, by the Chalukya dynasty of Kalyāna, we find the expression "from the Himālaya to the Bridge" (*Ind. Antiq.* i. 81), *i.e.* the Bridge of Rāma, or 'Adam's Bridge,' as our maps have it. And Mahommedan definitions as old, and with the name, will be found below. Under the Hindu kings of Vijayanagara also (from the 14th century) inscriptions indicate all India by like expressions.

The origin of the name is without doubt (Skt.) *Sindhu*, 'the sea,' and thence the Great River on the West, and the country on its banks, which we still call *Sindh*.* By a change common in many parts of the world, and in various parts of India itself, this name exchanged the initial sibilant for an aspirate, and became (eventually) in Persia *Hindū*, and so passed on to the Greeks and Latins, viz. Ἰνδοί for the people, Ἰνδός for the river, Ἰνδική and India for the country on its banks. Given this name for the western tract, and the conception of the country as a whole to which we have alluded, the name in the mouths of foreigners naturally but gradually spread to the whole.

Some have imagined that the name of the land of *Nod* ('wandering'), to which Cain is said to have migrated, and which has the same consonants, is but a form of this; which is worth noting, as this idea may have had to do with the curious statement in some medieval writers (*e.g.* John Marignolli) that certain eastern races were "the descendants of Cain." In the form *Hidhu* [*Hindus*, see *Encycl. Bibl.* ii. 2169] India appears in the great cuneiform inscription on the tomb of Darius Hystaspes near Persepolis, coupled with *Gadāra* (*i.e. Gandhāra*, or the Peshawar country), and no doubt still in some degree restricted in its application. In the Hebrew of Esther i. 1, and viii. 9, the form is *Hōd(d)ū*, or perhaps rather *Hiddū* (see also *Peritsol* below). The first Greek writers to speak of India and the Indians were Hecataeus of Miletus, Herodotus, and Ctesias (B.C. c. 500, c.

* In most of the important Asiatic languages the same word indicates the Sea or a River of the first class; *e.g. Sindhu* as here; in Western Tibet *Gyamtso* and *Samandrang* (corr. of Skt. *samundra*) 'the Sea,' which are applied to the Indus and Sutlej (see *J. R. Geog. Soc.* xxiii. 34-35); Hebrew *yam*, applied both to the sea and to the Nile; Ar. *bahr*; Pers. *daryā*; Mongol. *dalai*, &c. Compare the Homeric Ὠκεανός.

440, c. 400). The last, though repeating more fables than Herodotus, shows a truer conception of what India was.

Before going further, we ought to point out that **India** itself is a Latin form, and does not appear in a Greek writer, we believe, before Lucian and Polyænus, both writers of the middle of the 2nd century. The Greek form is ἡ 'Ινδική, or else 'The Land of the Indians.'

The name of 'India' spread not only from its original application, as denoting the country on the banks of the Indus, to the whole peninsula between (and including) the valleys of Indus and Ganges; but also in a vaguer way to all the regions beyond. The compromise between the vaguer and the more precise use of the term is seen in Ptolemy, where the boundaries of the true India are defined, on the whole, with surprising exactness, as 'India within the Ganges,' whilst the darker regions beyond appear as 'India beyond the Ganges.' And this double conception of India, as 'India Proper' (as we may call it), and India in the vaguer sense, has descended to our own time.

So vague became the conception in the 'dark ages' that the name is sometimes found to be used as synonymous with Asia, 'Europe, Africa, and India,' forming the three parts of the world. Earlier than this, however, we find a tendency to discriminate different Indias, in a form distinct from Ptolemy's *Intra et extra Gangem*; and the terms *India Major*, *India Minor* can be traced back to the 4th century. As was natural where there was so little knowledge, the application of these terms was various and oscillating, but they continued to hold their ground for 1000 years, and in the later centuries of that period we generally find a third India also, and a tendency (of which the roots go back, as far at least as Virgil's time) to place one of the three in Africa.

It is this conception of a twofold or threefold India that has given us and the other nations of Europe the vernacular expressions in plural form which hold their ground to this day: the *Indies*, les *Indes*, (It.) le *Indie*, &c.

And we may add further, that China is called by Friar Odoric Upper India (*India Superior*), whilst Marignolli calls it *India Magna* and *Maxima*, and calls Malabar *India Parva*, and *India Inferior*.

There was yet another, and an Oriental, application of the term India to the country at the mouth of the Tigris and Euphrates, which the people of Basra still call *Hind*; and which Sir H. Rawlinson connects with the fact that the Talmudic writers confounded Obillah in that region with the *Havila* of Genesis. (See *Cathay*, &c., 55, note.)

In the work of the Chinese traveller Hwen T'sang again we find that by him and his co-religionists a plurality of Indias was recognised, *i.e.* five, viz. North, Central, East, South, and West.

Here we may remark how two names grew out of the original *Sindhu*. The aspirated and Persianised form *Hind*, as applied to the great country beyond the Indus, passed to the Arabs. But when they invaded the valley of the Indus and found it called *Sindhu*, they adopted that name in the form *Sind*, and thenceforward '*Hind* and *Sind*' were habitually distinguished, though generally coupled, and conceived as two parts of a great whole.

Of the application of *India* to an Ethiopian region, an application of which indications extend over 1500 years, we have not space to speak here. On this and on the medieval plurality of Indias reference may be made to two notes on *Marco Polo*, 2nd ed. vol. ii. pp. 419 and 425.

The vague extension of the term India to which we have referred, survives in another form besides that in the use of '*Indies.*' *India*, to each European nation which has possessions in the East, may be said, without much inaccuracy, to mean in colloquial use that part of the East in which their own possessions lie. Thus to the Portuguese, *India* was, and probably still is, the West Coast only. In their writers of the 16th and 17th century a distinction is made between *India*, the territory of the Portuguese and their immediate neighbours on the West Coast, and *Mogor*, the dominions of the Great Mogul. To the Dutchman *India* means Java and its dependencies. To the Spaniard, if we mistake not, *India* is Manilla. To the Gaul are not *les Indes* Pondicherry, Chandernagore, and Réunion?

As regards the **West Indies**, this expression originates in the misconception of the great Admiral himself, who in his memorable enterprise was seeking, and thought he had found, a new route to the 'Indias' by sailing west instead of east. His discoveries were to Spain *the* Indies, until it gradually became manifest that they were not identical with the ancient lands of the east, and then they became the *West-Indies.*

Indian is a name which has been carried still further abroad; from being applied, as a matter of course, to the natives of the islands, supposed of India, discovered by Columbus, it naturally passed to the natives of the adjoining continent, till it came to be the familiar name of all the tribes between (and sometimes even including) the Esquimaux of the North and the Patagonians of the South.

This abuse no doubt has led to our hesitation in applying the term to a native of India itself. We use the adjective *Indian,* but no modern Englishman who has had to do with India ever speaks of a man of that country as 'an Indian.' Forrest, in his *Voyage to Mergui,* uses the inelegant word *Indostaners;* but in India itself a **Hindustani** means, as has been indicated under that word, a native of the upper Gangetic valley and adjoining districts. Among the Greeks 'an Indian' (Ἰνδὸς) acquired a notable specific application. viz. to an elephant driver or **mahout** (q.v.).

B.C. c. 486.—"Says Darius the King: By the grace of Ormazd these (are) the countries which I have acquired besides Persia. I have established my power over them. They have brought tribute to me. That which has been said to them by me they have done. They have obeyed my law. Medea . . . Arachotia (*Harauvatish*), Sattagydia (*Thatagush*), Gandaria (*Gadára*), India (**Hidush**). . . ."—On the Tomb of Darius at Nakhsh-i-Rustam, see *Rawlinson's Herod.* iv. 250.

B.C. c. 440.—"Eastward of **India** lies a tract which is entirely sand. Indeed, of all the inhabitants of Asia, concerning whom anything is known, the **Indians** dwell nearest to the east, and the rising of the Sun."—*Herodotus,* iii. c. 98 (*Rawlinson*).

B.C. c. 300.—"**India** then (ἡ τοίνυν Ἰνδικὴ) being four-sided in plan, the side which looks to the Orient and that to the South, the Great Sea compasseth; that towards the Arctic is divided by the mountain chain of Hēmōdus from Scythia, inhabited by that tribe of Scythians who are called Sakai; and on the fourth side, turned towards the West, the Indus marks the boundary, the biggest or nearly so of all rivers after the Nile."—*Megasthenes,* in *Diodorus,* ii. 35. (From Müller's *Fragm. Hist. Graec.,* ii. 402.)

A.D. c. 140.—"Τὰ δὲ ἀπὸ τοῦ Ἰνδοῦ πρὸς ἕω, τοῦτό μοι ἔστω ἡ τῶν Ἰνδῶν γῆ, καὶ Ἰνδοὶ οὗτοι ἔστωσαν."—*Arrian, Indica,* ch. ii.

c. 590.—"As for the land of the Hind it is bounded on the East by the Persian Sea (*i.e.* the Indian Ocean), on the W. and S. by the countries of Islām, and on the N. by the Chinese Empire. . . . The length of the land of the Hind from the government of Mokrān, the country of Mansūra and Bodha and the rest of Sind, till thou comest to Ḳannūj and thence passest on to Tobbat (see **TIBET**), is about 4 months, and its breadth from the Indian Ocean to the country of Ḳannūj about three months."—*Istakhri,* pp. 6 and 11.

c. 650.—"The name of *T'ien-chu* (India) has gone through various and confused forms. . . . Anciently they said *Shin-tu;* whilst some authors called it *Hien-teou.* Now conforming to the true pronunciation one should say **In-tu**."—*Hwen T'sang,* in *Pèl. Bouddh.,* ii. 57.

c. 944.—"For the nonce let us confine ourselves to summary notices concerning the kings of **Sind** and **Hind**. The language of Sind is different from that of **Hind**. . . ." *Maṣ'ūdī,* i. 381.

c. 1020.—"**India (Al-Hind)** is one of those plains bounded on the south by the Sea of the Indians. Lofty mountains bound it on all the other quarters. Through this plain the waters descending from the mountains are discharged. Moreover, if thou wilt examine this country with thine eyes, if thou wilt regard the rounded and worn stones that are found in the soil, however deep thou mayest dig,—stones which near the mountains, where the rivers roll down violently, are large; but small at a distance from the mountains, where the current slackens; and which become mere sand where the currents are at rest, where the waters sink into the soil, and where the sea is at hand—then thou wilt be tempted to believe that this country was at a former period only a sea which the debris washed down by the torrents hath filled up. . . ."—*Al-Bīrūnī,* in *Reinaud's Extracts, Journ. As.* ser. 4. 1844.

,, "**Hind** is surrounded on the East by Chín and Máchín, on the West by Sind and Kábul, and on the South by the Sea."—*Ibid.* in *Elliot,* i. 45.

1205.—"The whole country of **Hind**, from Pershaur to the shores of the Ocean, and in the other direction, from Siwistán to the hills of Chín. . . ."—*Hasan Nizāmī,* in *Elliot,* ii. 236. That is, from Peshawar in the north, to the Indian Ocean in the south; from Sehwan (on the west bank of the Indus) to the mountains on the east dividing from China.

c. 1500.—"**Hodu** quae est **India** extra et intra Gangem."—*Itinera Mundi* (in Hebrew), by *Abr. Peritsol,* in *Hyde, Syntagma Dissertt.,* Oxon, 1767, i. 75.

1553.—"And had Vasco da Gama belonged to a nation so glorious as the Romans he would perchance have added to the style of his family, noble as that is, the surname '**Of India**,' since we know that those symbols of honour that a man wins are more glorious than those that he inherits, and that Scipio gloried more in the achievement which gave him the surname of '*Africanus*,' than in the name of Cornelius, which was that of his family."—*Barros*, I. iv. 12.

1572.—Defined, without being named, by Camoens:

"Alem do Indo faz, e aquem do Gange
Hu terreno muy grãde, e assaz famoso,
Que pela parte Austral o mar abrange,
E para o Norte o Emodio cavernoso."
Lusiadas, vii. 17.

Englished by Burton:

"Outside of Indus, inside Ganges, lies
a wide-spread country, famed enough of yore;
northward the peaks of caved Emódus rise,
and southward Ocean doth confine the shore."

1577.—"**India** is properly called that great Province of Asia, in the whiche great Alexander kepte his warres, and was so named of the ryuer Indus."—*Eden, Hist. of Trauayle*, f. 3v.

The *distinct* **Indias**.

c. 650.—"The circumference of the Five Indies is about 90,000 *li*; on three sides it is bounded by a great sea; on the north it is backed by snowy mountains. It is wide at the north and narrow at the south; its figure is that of a half-moon." — *Hwen T'sang*, in *Pèl. Bouddh.*, ii. 58.

1298.—"**India the Greater** is that which extends from Maabar to Kesmacoran (*i.e.* from Coromandel to Mekran), and it contains 13 great kingdoms. . . . **India the Lesser** extends from the Province of Champa to Mutfili (*i.e.* from Cochin-China to the Kistna Delta), and contains 8 great Kingdoms. . . . Abash (Abyssinia) is a very great province, and you must know that it constitutes the **Middle India**."—*Marco Polo*, Bk. iii. ch. 34, 35.

c. 1328.—"What shall I say? The greatness of this **India** is beyond description. But let this much suffice concerning **India the Greater** and **the Less**. Of **India Tertia** I will say this, that I have not indeed seen its many marvels, not having been there. . . ."—*Friar Jordanus*, p. 41.

India Minor, in *Clavijo*, looks as if it were applied to Afghanistan:

1404.—"And this same Thursday that the said Ambassadors arrived at this great River (the Oxus) they crossed to the other side. And the same day . . . came in the evening to a great city which is called *Tenmit* (Termedh), and this used to belong to **India Minor**, but now belongs to the empire of Samarkand, having been conquered by Tamurbec."—*Clavijo*, § ciii. (*Markham*, 119).

Indies.

c. 1601.—"He does smile his face into more lines than are in the new map with the augmentation of the **Indiaes**."—*Twelfth Night*, Act iii. sc. 2.

1653.—"I was thirteen times captive and seventeen times sold in the **Indies**."—*Trans. of Pinto*, by *H. Cogan*, p. 1.

1826.—". . . Like a French lady of my acquaintance, who had so general a notion of the East, that upon taking leave of her, she enjoined me to get acquainted with a friend of hers, living as she said *quelque part dans* **les Indes**, and whom, to my astonishment, I found residing at the Cape of Good Hope."—*Hajji Baba*, Introd. Epistle, ed. 1835, p. ix.

India of the **Portuguese**.

c. 1567.—"Di qui (Coilan) a Cao Comeri si fanno settanta due miglia, *e qui si finisse la costa* **dell' India**." — *Ces. Federici*, in *Ramusio*, iii. 390.

1598.—"At the ende of the countrey of *Cambaia* beginneth **India** and the lands of Decam and Cuncam . . . from the island called Das Vaguas (read *Vaquas*) . . . which is the righte coast that in all the East Countries is called **India**. . . . Now you must vnderstande that this coast of **India** beginneth at *Daman*, or the Island Das Vaguas, and stretched South and by East, to the Cape of *Comorin*, where it endeth."—*Linschoten*, ch. ix.-x.; [Hak. Soc. i. 62. See also under **ABADA**].

c. 1610.—"Il y a grand nombre des Portugais qui demeurent ès ports du cette coste de Bengale . . . ils n'osoient retourner **en l'Inde**, pour quelques fautes qu'ils y ont commis."—*Pyrard de Laval*, i. 239; [Hak. Soc. i. 334].

1615. — "Sociorum literis, qui Mogoris Regiam incolunt auditum est in **India** de celeberrimo Regno illo quod Saraceni Cataium vocant."—*Trigautius, De Christianâ Expeditione apud Sinas*, p. 544.

1644.—(Speaking of the Daman district above Bombay.—"The fruits are nearly all the same as those that you get in **India**, and especially many *Mangas* and *Cassaras* (?), which are like chestnuts."—*Bocarro, MS.*

It is remarkable to find the term used, in a similar restricted sense, by the Court of the E.I.C. in writing to Fort St. George. They certainly mean some part of the west coast.

1670.—They desire that **dungarees** may be supplied thence if possible, as "they were not procurable on the **Coast of India**, by reason of the disturbances of Sevajee."—*Notes and Exts.*, Pt. i. 2.

1673.—"The Portugals . . . might have subdued **India** by this time, had not we fallen out with them, and given them the first Blow at Ormuz . . . they have added some Christians to those formerly converted by St. Thomas, but it is a loud Report to say all India."—*Fryer*, 137.

1881.—In a correspondence with Sir R. Morier, we observe the Portuguese Minister of Foreign Affairs calls their Goa Viceroy "The Governor General of India."

India of the **Dutch**.

1876.—The Dorian "is common throughout all India."—*Filet, Plant-Kunding Woordenboek*, 196.

Indies applied to **America**.

1563.—"And please to tell me . . . which is better, this (*Radix Chinae*) or the *guiacão* of our **Indies** as we call them. . . ."—*Garcia*, f. 177.

INDIAN. This word in English first occurs, according to Dr. Guest, in the following passage :—

A.D. 433-440.
"Mid israelum ic waes
Mid ebreum and **indeum**, and mid egyptum."
In *Guest's English Rhythms*, ii. 86-87.

But it may be queried whether *indeum* is not here an error for *iudeum* ; the converse error to that supposed to have been made in the printing of Othello's death-speech—
"of one whose hand
Like the base *Judean* threw a pearl away."

Indian *used for* **Mahout**.

B.C. ? 116-105.—"And upon the beasts (the elephants) there were strong towers of wood, which covered every one of them, and were girt fast unto them with devices: there were also upon every one two and thirty strong men, that fought upon them, beside the **Indian** that ruled them."—*I. Maccabees*, vi. 37.

B.C. c. 150.—"Of Beasts (*i.e.* elephants) taken with all their **Indians** there were ten ; and of all the rest, which had thrown their **Indians**, he got possession after the battle by driving them together."—*Polybius*, Bk. i. ch. 40 ; see also iii. 46, and xi. 1. It is very curious to see the drivers of *Carthaginian* elephants thus called *Indians*, though it may be presumed that this is only a Greek application of the term, not a Carthaginian use.

B.C. c. 20.—"Tertio die . . . ad Thabusion castellum imminens fluvio Indo ventum est ; cui fecerat nomen **Indus** ab elephanto dejectus."—*Livy*, Bk. xxxviii. 14. This Indus or "Indian" river, named after the Mahout thrown into it by his elephant, was somewhere on the borders of Phrygia.

A.D. c. 210.—"Along with this elephant was brought up a female one called Nikaia. And the wife of their **Indian** being near death placed her child of 30 days old beside this one. And when the woman died a certain marvellous attachment grew up of the Beast towards the child. . . ."—*Athenaeus*, xiii. ch. 8.

Indian, for *Anglo-Indian*.

1816.—". . . our best **Indians**. In the idleness and obscurity of home they look back with fondness to the country where they have been useful and distinguished, like the ghosts of Homer's heroes, who prefer the exertions of a labourer on the earth to all the listless enjoyments of Elysium."—*Elphinstone*, in *Life*, i. 367.

INDIGO, s. The plant *Indigofera tinctoria*, L. (N.O. *Leguminosae*), and the dark blue dye made from it. Greek Ἰνδικὸν. This word appears from Hippocrates to have been applied in his time to *pepper*. It is also applied by Dioscorides to the mineral substance (a variety of the red oxide of iron) called Indian red (*F. Adams*, Appendix to *Dunbar's Lexicon*). [*Liddell & Scott* call it "a dark-blue dye, indigo." The dye was used in Egyptian mummy-cloths (*Wilkinson*, *Ancient Egypt*, ed. 1878, ii. 163).]

A.D. c. 60.—"Of that which is called Ἰνδικὸν one kind is produced spontaneously, being as it were a scum thrown out by the Indian reeds ; but that used for dyeing is a purple efflorescence which floats on the brazen cauldrons, which the craftsmen skim off and dry. That is deemed best which is blue in colour, succulent, and smooth to the touch."—*Dioscorides*, v. cap. 107.

c. 70.—"After this . . . **Indico** (*Indicum*) is a colour most esteemed ; out of India it commeth ; whereupon it tooke the name ; and it is nothing els but a slimie mud cleaving to the foame that gathereth about canes and reeds : whiles it is punned or ground, it looketh blacke ; but being dissolved it yeeldeth a woonderfull lovely mixture of purple and azur . . . **Indico** is valued at 20 denarii the pound. In physicke there is use of this **Indico** ; for it doth assuage swellings that doe stretch the skin."—*Plinie*, by *Ph. Holland*, ii. 531.

c. 80-90. — "This river (*Sinthus*, *i.e.* Indus) has 7 mouths . . . and it has none of them navigable except the middle one only, on which there is a coast mart called Barbaricon. . . . The articles imported into this mart are. . . . On the other hand there are exported *Costus*, *Bdellium* . . . and *Indian Black* (Ἰνδικὸν μέλαν, *i.e.* **Indigo**)."—*Periplus*, 38, 39.

1298.—(At Coilum) "They have also abundance of very fine **indigo** (*ynde*). This is made of a certain herb which is gathered and [after the roots have been removed] is put into great vessels upon which they pour water, and then leave it till the whole of the plant is decomposed. . . ." — *Marco Polo*, Bk. iii. ch. 22.

1584.—"**Indico** from Zindi and Cambaia."—*Barrett*, in *Hakl.* ii. 413.

[1605-6.—". . . for all which we shall buie Ryse, **Indico**, Lapes Bezar which theare in aboundance are to be hadd."—*Birdwood, First Letter Book*, 77.

[1609.—". . . . to buy such Comodities as they shall finde there as **Indico**, of Laher (Lahore), here worth viij[s] the pounde *Serchis* and the best *Belondri*. . . ."—*Ibid.* 287. *Serchis* is Sarkhej, the *Sercaze* of Forbes (*Or. Mem.*, 2nd ed. ii. 204) near Ahmadābād: Sir G. Birdwood with some hesitation identifies *Belondri* with Valabhi, 20 m. N.W. of Bhāvnagar.

[1610.—"*Anil* or **Indigue**, which is a violet-blue dye."—*Pyrard de Laval*, Hak. Soc. ii. 246.]

1610.—"In the country thereabouts is made some **Indigo**."—*Sir H. Middleton*, in *Purchas*, i. 259.

[1616.—"**Indigo** is made thus. In the prime June they sow it, which the rains bring up about the prime September: this they cut and it is called the *Newty* (H. *naudhā*, 'a young plant'), formerly mentioned, and is a good sort. Next year it sprouts again in the prime August, which they cut and is the best **Indigo**, called *Jerry* (H. *jaṛī*, 'growing from the root (*jaṛ*).'"—*Foster, Letters*, iv. 241.]

c. 1670.—Tavernier gives a detailed account of the manufacture as it was in his time. "They that sift this **Indigo** must be careful to keep a Linnen-cloath before their faces, and that their nostrils be well stopt. . . . Yet . . . they that have sifted **Indigo** for 9 or 10 days shall spit nothing but blew for a good while together. Once I laid an egg in the morning among the sifters, and when I came to break it in the evening it was all blew within."—*E.T.* ii. 128-9; [ed. *Ball*, ii. 11].

We have no conception what is meant by the following singular (apparently sarcastic) entry in the *Indian Vocabulary*:—

1788.—"**Indergo**—a drug of no estimation that grows wild in the woods." [This is H. *indarjau*, Skt. *indra-yava*, "barley of Indra," the *Wrightia tinctoria*, from the leaves of which a sort of indigo is made. See *Watt, Econ. Dict.* VI. pt. iv. 316. "**Inderjò** of the species of warm bitters."—*Halhed, Code*, ed. 1781, p. 9.]

1881.—"Découvertes et Inventions.—Décidément le cabinet Gladstone est poursuivi par la malechance. Voici un savant chimiste de Munich qui vient de trouver le moyen se preparer artificiellement et à très bon marché le bleu **Indigo**. Cette découverte peut amener la ruine du gouvernement des Indes anglaises, qui est déjà menacé de la banqueroute. **L'indigo**, en effet, est le principal article de commerce des Indes (!); dans l'Allemagne, seulement, on en importe par an pour plus de cent cinquante millions de francs."—*Havre Commercial Paper*, quoted in *Pioneer Mail*, Feb. 3.

INGLEES, s. Hind. *Inglīs* and *Inglis*. Wilson gives as the explanation of this: "Invalid soldiers and *sipahis*, to whom allotments of land were assigned as pensions; the lands so granted." But the word is now used as the equivalent of (sepoy's) *pension* simply. Mr. Carnegie, [who is followed by Platts], says the word is "probably a corruption of *English*, as pensions were unknown among native Governments, whose rewards invariably took the shape of land assignments." This, however, is quite unsatisfactory; and Sir H. Elliot's suggestion (mentioned by Wilson) that the word was a corruption of *invalid* (which the sepoys may have confounded in some way with *English*) is most probable.

INTERLOPER, s. One in former days who traded without the license, or outside the service, of a company (such as the E.I.C.) which had a charter of monopoly. The etymology of the word remains obscure. It *looks* like Dutch, but intelligent Dutch friends have sought in vain for a Dutch original. *Onderloopen*, the nearest word we can find, means 'to be inundated.' The hybrid etymology given by Bailey, though allowed by Skeat, seems hardly possible. Perhaps it is an English corruption from *ontloopen*, 'to evade, escape, run away from.' [The *N.E.D.* without hesitation gives *interlope*, a form of *leap*. Skeat, in his *Concise Dict.*, 2nd ed., agrees, and quotes Low Germ. and Dutch *enterloper*, 'a runner between.']

1627.—"**Interlopers** in trade, ¶ Attur Acad. pa. 54."—*Minsheu.* (What is the meaning of the reference?) [It refers to "The *Atturneyes Academie*" by Thomas Powell or Powel, for which see 9 ser. *Notes and Queries*, vii. 198, 392].

1680.—"The commissions relating to the **Interloper**, or private trader, being considered, it is resolved that a notice be fixed up warning all the Inhabitants of the Towne, not, directly or indirectly, to trade, negotiate, aid, assist, countenance, or hold any correspondence, with Captain William Alley or any person belonging to him or his ship without the license of the Honorable Company. Whoever shall offend herein shall answeare it at their Perill."—*Notes and Exts.*, Pt. iii. 29.

1681.—"The Shippe Expectation, Capt. Ally Comand[r], an **Interloper**, arrived in ye Downes from Porto Novo."—*Hedges, Diary*, Jan. 4; [Hak. Soc. i. 15].

[1682.—"The Agent having notice of an **Interloper** lying in Titticorin Bay, immediately sent for ye Councell to consult about it. . . ."—*Pringle, Diary of Ft. St. Geo.* 1st ser. i. 69.]

" "The Spirit of Commerce, which sees its drifts with eagle's eyes, formed associations at the risque of trying the consequence at law . . . since the statutes did not authorize the Company to seize or stop the ships of these adventurers, whom they called **Interlopers**."—*Orme's Fragments*, 127.

1683.—"If God gives me life to get this *Phirmaund* into my possession, ye Honble. Compy. shall never more be much troubled with **Interlopers**."—*Hedges, Diary*, Jan. 6; [Hak. Soc. i. 62].

" "*May* 28. About 9 this morning Mr. Littleton, Mr. Nedham, and Mr. Douglass came to ye factory, and being sent for, were asked 'Whether they did now, or ever intended, directly or indirectly, to trade with any **Interlopers** that shall arrive in the Bay of Bengall?'

"Mr. Littleton answered that, 'he did not, nor ever intended to trade with any **Interloper**.'

"Mr. Nedham answered, 'that at present he did not, and that he came to gett money, and if any such offer should happen, he would not refuse it.'

"Mr. Douglass answered, he did not, nor ever intended to trade with them; but he said 'what Estate he should gett here he would not scruple to send it home upon any **Interloper**.'

"And having given their respective answers they were dismist."—*Ibid.* Hak. Soc. i. 90-91.

1694.—"Whether ye souldiers lately sent up hath created any jealousye in ye **Interlopr**s: or their own Actions or guilt I know not, but they are so cautious yt every 2 or 3 bales yt are packt they immediately send on board."—MS. Letter from *Edwd. Hern* at *Hugley* to the Rt. Worshpll *Charles Eyre Esq. Agent for Affaires of the Rt. Honble. East India Compa.* in *Bengall*, &ca. (9th Sept.). *MS. Record in India Office.*

1719.—". . . their business in the *South Seas* was to sweep those coasts clear of the *French* **interlopers**, which they did very effectually."—*Shelvocke's Voyage*, 29.

" "I wish you would explain yourself; I cannot imagine what reason I have to be afraid of any of the Company's ships, or Dutch ships, I am no **interloper**."—*Robinson Crusoe*, Pt. ii.

1730.—"To **Interlope** [of *inter*, L. between, and loopen, *Du.* to run, q. d. to run in between, and intercept the Commerce of others], to trade without proper Authority, or interfere with a Company in Commerce."—*Bailey's English Dict.* s.v.

1760.—"**Enterlooper**. Terme de Commerce de Mer, fort en usage parmi les Compagnies des Pays du Nord, comme l'Angleterre, la Hollande, Hambourg, le Danemark, &c. Il signifie un vaisseau d'un particulier qui pratique et fréquente les Côtes, et les Havres ou Ports de Mer éloignés, pour y faire un commerce clandestin, au préjudice des Compagnies qui sont autorisées elles seules à le faire dans ces mêmes lieux. . . . Ce mot se prononce comme s'il étoit écrit **Eintrelopre**. Il est emprunté de l'Anglois, de *enter* qui signifie entrer et entreprendre, et de *Looper*, Courreur."—*Savary des Bruslons, Dict. Univ. de Commerce*, Nouv. ed., Copenhague, s.v.

c. 1812.—"The fault lies in the clause which gives the Company power to send home **interlopers** . . . and is just as reasonable as one which should forbid all the people of England, except a select few, to look at the moon."—*Letter of Dr. Carey*, in *William Carey*, by James Culross, D.D., 1881, p. 165.

IPECACUANHA (WILD), s. The garden name of a plant (*Asclepias curassavica*, L.) naturalised in all tropical countries. It has nothing to do with the true ipecacuanha, but its root is a powerful emetic, whence the name. The true ipecacuanha is cultivated in India.

IRON-WOOD. This name is applied to several trees in different parts; *e.g.* to *Mesua ferrea*, L. (N.O. *Clusiaceae*), Hind. *nagkesar;* and in the Burmese provinces to *Xylia dolabriformis*, Benth.

I-SAY. The Chinese mob used to call the English soldiers *A'says* or *Isays*, from the frequency of this apostrophe in their mouths. (The French gamins, it is said, do the same at Boulogne.) At Amoy the Chinese used to call out after foreigners **Akee! Akee!** a tradition from the Portuguese *Aqui!* 'Here!' In Java the French are called by the natives *Orang* **deedong**, *i.e.* the *dites-donc* people. (See *Fortune's Two Visits to the Tea Countries*, 1853, p. 52; and *Notes and Queries in China and Japan*, ii. 175.)

[1863.—"The Sepoys were . . . invariably called '**Achas**.' *Acha* or good is the constantly recurring answer of a Sepoy when spoken to. . . ."—*Fisher, Three Years in China*, 146.]

ISKAT, s. Ratlines. A marine term from Port. *escada* (*Roebuck*).

[**ISLAM**, s. Infn. of Ar. *salm*, 'to be or become safe'; the word generally used by Mahommedans for their religion.

[1616.—"Dated in Achen 1025 according to the rate of **Slam**."—*Foster, Letters*, iv. 125.

[1617.—"I demanded the debts . . . one [of the debtors] for the valew of 110 r[ials] is termed **Slam**."—*Letter of E. Young*, from Jacatra, Oct. 3, I.O. Records: O.C. No. 541.]

ISTOOP, s. Oakum. A marine term from Port. *estopa* (*Roebuck*).

ISTUBBUL, s. This usual Hind. word for 'stable' may naturally be imagined to be a corruption of the English word. But it is really Ar. *iṣṭabl*, though that no doubt came in old times from the Latin *stabulum* through some Byzantine Greek form.

ITZEBOO, s. A Japanese coin, the smallest silver denomination. *Itsi-bū*, 'one drachm.' [The *N.E.D.* gives *itse*, *itche*, 'one,' *bū*, 'division, part, quarter']. Present value about 1*s*. Marsden says: "**Itzebo**, a small gold piece of oblong form, being 0·6 inch long, and 0·3 broad. Two specimens weighed 2 dwt. 3 grs. only" (*Numism. Orient.*, 814-5). See *Cocks's Diary*, i. 176, ii. 77. [The coin does not appear in the last currency list; see *Chamberlain, Things Japanese*, 3rd ed. 99.]

[1616.—"**Ichibos.**" (See under **KOBANG.**)

[1859.—"We found the greatest difficulty in obtaining specimens of the currency of the country, and I came away at last the possessor of a solitary **Itzibu**. These are either of gold or silver: the gold **Itzibu** is a small oblong piece of money, intrinsically worth about seven and sixpence. The intrinsic value of the gold **half-itzibu**, which is not too large to convert into a shirt-stud, is about one and tenpence."—*L. Oliphant, Narr. of Mission*, ii. 232.]

IZAM MALUCO, n.p. We often find this form in Correa, instead of **Nizamaluco** (q.v.).

J

JACK, s. Short for **Jack-Sepoy**; in former days a familiar style for the native soldier; kindly, rather than otherwise.

1853.—". . . he should be leading the **Jacks**."—*Oakfield*, ii. 66.

JACK, s. The tree called by botanists *Artocarpus integrifolia*, L. fil., and its fruit. The name, says Drury, is "a corruption of the Skt. word *Tchackka*, which means the fruit of the tree" (*Useful Plants*, p. 55). There is, however, no such Skt. word; the Skt. names are *Kantaka*, *Phala*, *Panasa*, and *Phalasa*. [But the Malayāl. *chakka* is from the Skt. *chakra*, 'round.'] Rheede rightly gives *Tsjaka* (*chăkka*) as the Malayālam name, and from this no doubt the Portuguese took *jaca* and handed it on to us. "They call it," says Garcia Orta, "in Malavar *jacas*, in Canarese and Guzerati *panas*" (f. 111). "The Tamil form is *sākkei*, the meaning of which, as may be adduced from various uses to which the word is put in Tamil, is 'the fruit abounding in rind and refuse.'" (*Letter from Bp. Caldwell.*)

We can hardly doubt that this is the fruit of which Pliny writes: "Major alia pomo et suavitate praecellentior; quo sapientiores Indorum vivunt. (Folium alas avium imitatur longitudine trium cubitorum, latitudine duum). *Fructum e cortice mittit admirabilem succi dulcedine; ut uno quaternos satiet.* Arbori nomen *palae*, pomo *arienae*; plurima est in Sydracis, expeditionum Alexandri termino. Est et alia similis huic; dulcior pomo; sed interaneorum valetudini infesta" (*Hist. Nat.* xii. 12). Thus rendered, not too faithfully, by Philemon Holland: "Another tree there is in India, greater yet than the former; bearing a fruit much fairer, bigger, and sweeter than the figs aforesaid; and whereof the Indian Sages and Philosophers do ordinarily live. The leaf resembleth birds' wings, carrying three cubits in length, and two in breadth. The fruit it putteth forth at the bark, having within it a wonderfull pleasant juice: insomuch as one of them is sufficient to give four men a competent and full refection. The tree's name is *Pala*, and the fruit is called *Ariena*. Great plenty of them is in the country of the Sydraci, the utmost limit of *Alexander* the Great his expeditions and voyages. And yet there is another tree much like to this, and beareth a fruit more delectable that this *Ariena*, albeit the guts in a man's belly it wringeth and breeds the bloudie flix" (i. 361).

Strange to say, the fruit thus described has been generally identified with the plantain: so generally that (we presume) the Linnaean name of the plantain *Musa sapientum*, was founded upon the interpretation of this passage. (It was, I find, the excellent Rumphius who originated the erroneous identification of the *ariena* with the plantain). Lassen, at first hesitatingly (i. 262), and then more positively (ii. 678), adopts this interpretation, and seeks *ariena* in the Skt. *vāraṇa*. The shrewder Gildemeister does the like, for he, *sans phrase*, uses *arienae* as Latin for 'plantains.' Ritter, too, accepts it, and is not staggered even by the *uno quaternos satiet*. Humboldt, quoth he, often saw Indians make their meal with a very little manioc and three bananas of the big kind (*Platano-arton*). Still less sufficed the Indian Brahmins (*sapientes*), when one fruit was enough for four of them (v. 876, 877). Bless the venerable Prince of Geographers! Would one *Kartoffel*, even "of the big kind," make a dinner for four German Professors? Just as little would one plantain suffice four Indian Sages.

The words which we have italicised in the passage from Pliny are quite enough to show that the *jack* is intended; the fruit growing *e cortice* (*i.e.* piercing the bark of the stem, not pendent from twigs like other fruit), the sweetness, the monstrous size, are in combination infallible. And as regards its being the fruit of the sages, we may observe that the *jack* fruit is at this day in Travancore one of the staples of life. But that Pliny, after his manner, has jumbled things, is also manifest. The first two clauses of his description (*Major alia*, &c.; *Folium alas*, &c.) are found in Theophrastus, but apply to *two different trees*. Hence we get rid of the puzzle about the big leaves, which led scholars astray after plantains, and originated *Musa sapientum*. And it is clear from Theophrastus that the fruit which caused dysentery in the Macedonian army was yet another. So Pliny has rolled three plants into one. Here are the passages of Theophrastus:—

"(1) And there is another tree which is both itself a tree of great size, and produces a fruit that is wonderfully big and sweet. This is used for food by the Indian Sages, who wear no clothes. (2) And there is yet another which has the leaf of a very long shape, and resembling the wings of birds, and this they set upon helmets; the length is about two cubits. . . . (3) There is another tree the fruit of which is long, and not straight but crooked, and sweet to the taste. But this gives rise to colic and dysentery ("Ἄλλο τέ ἐστιν οὗ ὁ καρπὸς μακρὸς καὶ οὐκ εὐθὺς ἀλλὰ σκολιὸς, ἐσθιόμενος δὲ γλυκύς. Οὗτος ἐν τῇ κοιλίᾳ δηγμὸν ποιεῖ καὶ δυσεντέριαν . . .") wherefore Alexander published a general order against eating it."—(*Hist. Plant.* iv. 4-5).

It is plain that Pliny and Theophrastus were using the same authority, but neither copying the whole of what he found in it.

The second tree, whose leaves were like birds' wings and were used to fix upon helmets, is hard to identify. The first was, when we combine the additional characters quoted by Pliny but omitted by Theophrastus, certainly the *jack*; the third was, we suspect, the **mango** (q.v.). The terms long and crooked would, perhaps, answer better to the plantain, but hardly the unwholesome effect. As regards the *uno quaternos satiet*, compare Friar Jordanus below, on the *jack*: "Sufficiet circiter pro quinque personis." Indeed the whole of the Friar's account is worth comparing with Pliny's. Pliny says that it took four men *to eat* a *jack*, Jordanus says five. But an Englishman who had a plantation in Central Java told one of the present writers that he once cut a *jack* on his ground which took three men—not to eat—but to carry!

As regards the names given by Pliny it is hard to say anything to the purpose, because we do not know to which of the three trees jumbled together the names really applied. If *pala* really applied to the *jack*, possibly it may be the Skt. *phalasa*, or *panasa*. Or it may be merely *p'hala*, 'a fruit,' and the passage would then be a comical illustration of the persistence of Indian habits of mind. For a stranger in India, on asking the question, 'What on earth is that?' as he well might on his first sight of a *jack*-tree with its fruit, would at the present day almost certainly receive for answer: '*Phal hai khudāwand!*'—'It is a fruit, my lord!' *Ariena* looks like *hiraṇya*, 'golden,' which *might* be an epithet of the *jack*, but we find no such specific application of the word.

Omitting Theophrastus and Pliny, the oldest foreign description of the *jack* that we find is that by Hwen T'sang, who met with it in Bengal:

c. A.D. 650.—"Although the fruit of the *pan-wa-so* (*panasa*) is gathered in great quantities, it is held in high esteem. These fruits are as big as a pumpkin; when ripe they are of a reddish yellow. Split in two they disclose inside a quantity of little fruits as big as crane's eggs; and when these are broken there exudes a juice of reddish-yellow colour and delicious flavour. Sometimes the fruit hangs on the branches, as with other trees; but sometimes it grows from the roots, like the *fo-ling* (*Radix Chinae*), which is found under the ground."—*Julien*, iii. 75.

c. 1328.—"There are some trees that bear a very big fruit called **chaqui**; and the fruit is of such size that one is enough for about five persons. There is another tree that has a fruit like that just named, and it is called *Bloqui* [a corruption of *Malayāl. varikka*, 'superior fruit'], quite as big and as sweet, but not of the same species. These fruits never grow upon the twigs, for these are not able to bear their weight, but only from the main branches, and even from the trunk of the tree itself, down to the very roots."—*Friar Jordanus*, 13-14.

A unique MS. of the travels of Friar Odoric, in the Palatine Library at Florence, contains the following curious passage:—

c. 1330.—"And there be also trees which produce fruits so big that two will be a load for a strong man. And when they are eaten you must oil your hands and your mouth; they are of a fragrant odour and very savoury; the fruit is called *chabassi*." The name is probably corrupt (perhaps *chacassi*?). But the passage about oiling the hands and lips is aptly elucidated by the description in Baber's *Memoirs* (see below), a description matchless in its way, and which falls off sadly in the new translation by M. Pavet de Courteille, which quite omits the "haggises."

c. 1335.—"The **Shakī** and *Barkī*. This name is given to certain trees which live to a great age. Their leaves are like those of the walnut, and the fruit grows direct out of the stem of the tree. The fruits borne nearest to the ground are the *barkī*; they are sweeter and better-flavoured than the **Shakī** . . ." etc. (much to the same effect as before).—*Ibn Batuta*, iii. 127; see also iv. 228.

c. 1350.—"There is again another wonderful tree called **Chake**-*Baruke*, as big as an oak. Its fruit is produced from the trunk, and not from the branches, and is something marvellous to see, being as big as a great lamb, or a child of three years old. It has a hard rind like that of our pine-cones, so that you have to cut it open with a hatchet; inside it has a pulp of surpassing flavour, with the sweetness of honey, and of the best Italian melon; and this also contains some 500 chestnuts of like flavour, which are capital eating when roasted."—*John de' Marignolli*, in *Cathay*, &c., 363.

c. 1440.—"There is a tree commonly found, the trunk of which bears a fruit resembling a pine-cone, but so big that a man can hardly lift it; the rind is green and hard, but still yields to the pressure of the finger. Inside there are some 250 or 300 pippins, as big as figs, very sweet in taste, and contained in separate membranes. These have each a kernel within, of a windy quality, of the consistence and taste of chestnuts, and which are roasted like chestnuts. And when cast among embers (to roast), unless you make a cut in them they will explode and jump out. The outer rind of the fruit is given to cattle. Sometimes the fruit is also found growing from the roots of the tree underground, and these fruits excel the others in flavour, wherefore they are sent as presents to kings and petty princes. These (moreover) have no kernels inside them. The tree itself resembles a large fig-tree, and the leaves are cut into fingers like the hand. The wood resembles box, and so it is esteemed for many uses. The name of the tree is **Cachi**" (*i.e. Çachi* or **Tzacchi**).—*Nicolo de' Conti*.

The description of the leaves . . . "*foliis da modum palmi intercisis*"—is the only slip in this admirable description. Conti must, in memory, have confounded the Jack with its congener the bread-fruit (*Artocarpus incisa* or *incisifolia*). We have translated from Poggio's Latin, as the version by Mr. Winter Jones in *India in the XVth Century* is far from accurate.

1530.—"Another is the *kadhil*. This has a very bad look and flavour (odour ?). It looks like a sheep's stomach stuffed and made into a haggis. It has a sweet sickly taste. Within it are stones like a filbert. . . . The fruit is very adhesive, and on account of this adhesive quality many rub their mouths with oil before eating them. They grow not only from the branches and trunk, but from its root. You would say that the tree was all hung round with haggises!"—*Leyden and Erskine's Baber*, 325. Here *kadhil* represents the Hind. name *kaṭhal*. The practice of oiling the lips on account of the "adhesive quality" (or as modern mortals would call it, 'stickiness') of the jack, is still usual among natives, and is the cause of a proverb on premature precautions: *Gāch'h meṅ Kaṭhal, honṭh meṅ tel!* "You have oiled your lips while the jack still hangs on the tree!" We may observe that the call of the Indian cuckoo is in some of the Gangetic districts rendered by the natives as *Kaṭhal pakkā! Kaṭhal pakkā! i.e.* "Jack's ripe," the bird appearing at that season.

[1547.—"I consider it right to make over to them in perpetuity . . . one palm grove and an area for planting certain mango trees and **jack** trees (mangueiras e **jaqueiras**) situate in the village of Calangute. . . ."—*Archiv. Port. Orient.*, fasc. 5, No. 88.]

c. 1590.—"In Sircar Hajypoor there are plenty of the fruits called *Kathul* and

Budhul; some of the first are so large as to be too heavy for one man to carry."—*Gladwin's Ayeen*, ii. 25. In Blochmann's ed. of the Persian text he reads *barhal*, [and so in Jarrett's trans. (ii. 152),] which is a Hind. name for the *Artocarpus Lakoocha* of Roxb.

1563. — "*R.* What fruit is that which is as big as the largest (coco) nuts?

"*O.* You just now ate the *chestnuts* from inside of it, and you said that roasted they were like real chestnuts. Now you shall eat the envelopes of these . . .

"*R.* They taste like a melon; but not so good as the better melons.

"*O.* True. And owing to their viscous nature they are ill to digest; or say rather they are not digested at all, and often issue from the body quite unchanged. I don't much use them. They are called in Malavar **jacas**; in Canarin and Guzerati *panâs*. . . . The tree is a great and tall one; and the fruits grow from the wood of the stem, right up to it, and not on the branches like other fruits."—*Garcia*, f. 111.

[1598.—"A certain fruit that in Malabar is called **iaca**, in Canara and Gusurate *Panar* and *Panasa*, by the Arabians *Panax*, by the Persians *Fanax*."—*Linschoten*, Hak. Soc. ii. 20.

[c. 1610.—"The **Jaques** is a tree of the height of a chestnut."—*Pyrard de Laval*, Hak. Soc. ii. 366.

[1623.—"We had **Ziacche**, a fruit very rare at this time."—*P. della Valle*, Hak. Soc. ii. 264.]

1673.—"Without the town (Madras) grows their Rice . . . **Jawks**, a Coat of Armour over it, like an Hedg-hog's, guards its weighty Fruit."—*Fryer*, 40.

1810. — "The **jack**-wood . . . at first yellow, becomes on exposure to the air of the colour of mahogany, and is of as fine a grain."—*Maria Graham*, 101.

1878.—"The monstrous **jack** that in its eccentric bulk contains a whole magazine of tastes and smells."—*Ph. Robinson, In My Indian Garden*, 49-50.

It will be observed that the older authorities mention two varieties of the fruit by the names of *shakī* and *barkī*, or modifications of these, different kinds according to Jordanus, only from different parts of the tree according to Ibn Batuta. P. Vincenzo Maria (1672) also distinguishes two kinds, one of which he calls **Giacha** *Barca*, the other **Giacha** *papa* or *girasole*. And Rheede, the great authority on Malabar plants, says (iii. 19):

"Of this tree, however, they reckon more than 30 varieties, distinguished by the quality of their fruit, but all may be reduced to two kinds; the fruit of one kind distinguished by plump and succulent pulp of delicious honey flavour, being the *varaka*; that of the other, filled with softer and more flabby pulp of inferior flavour, being the *Tsjakapa*."

More modern writers seem to have less perception in such matters than the old travellers, who entered more fully and sympathetically into native tastes. Drury says, however, "There are several varieties, but what is called the Honey-jack is by far the sweetest and best."

"He that desireth to see more hereof let him reade Ludovicus Romanus, in his fifth Booke and fifteene Chapter of his Navigaciouns, and Christopherus a Costa in his cap. of **Iaca**, and Gracia ab Horto, in the Second Booke and fourth Chapter," saith the learned Paludanus . . . And if there be anybody so unreasonable, so say we too—by all means let him do so! [A part of this article is derived from the notes to Jordanus by one of the present writers. We may also add, in aid of such further investigation, that Paludanus is the Latinised name of v.d. Broecke, the commentator on Linschoten. "Ludovicus Romanus" is our old friend Varthema, and "Gracia ab Horto" is Garcia De Orta.]

JACKAL, s. The *Canis aureus*, L., seldom seen in the daytime, unless it be fighting with the vultures for carrion, but in shrieking multitudes, or rather what seem multitudes from the noise they make, entering the precincts of villages, towns, of Calcutta itself, after dark, and startling the newcomer with their hideous yells. Our word is not apparently Anglo-Indian, being taken from the Turkish *chakāl*. But the Pers. *shaghāl* is close, and Skt. *srigāla*, 'the howler,' is probably the first form. The common Hind. word is *gīdar*, ['the greedy one,' Skt. *gridh*]. The jackal takes the place of the fox as the object of hunting 'meets' in India; the indigenous fox being too small for sport.

1554.—"Non procul inde audio magnum clamorem et velut hominum irridentium insultantiumque voces. Interrogo quid sit; . . . narrant mihi ululatum esse bestiarum, quas Turcae **Ciacales** vocant. . . ."—*Busbeq. Epist.* i. p. 78.

1615.—"The inhabitants do nightly house their goates and sheepe for feare of **Iaccals** (in my opinion no other than Foxes), whereof an infinite number do lurke in the obscure vaults."—*Sandys, Relation*, &c., 205.

1616.—". . . those **jackalls** seem to be wild Doggs, who in great companies run up and down in the silent night, much disquieting the peace thereof, by their most hideous noyse."—*Terry*, ed. 1665, p. 371.

1653.—"Le **schekal** est vn espèce de chien sauvage, lequel demeure tout le jour en terre, et sort la nuit criant trois ou quatre fois à certaines heures."—*De la Boullaye-le-Gouz*, ed. 1657, p. 254.

1672:—"There is yet another kind of beast which they call **Jackhalz**; they are horribly greedy of man's flesh, so the inhabitants beset the graves of their dead with heavy stones."—*Baldaeus* (Germ. ed.), 422.

1673.—"An Hellish concert of **Jackals** (a kind of Fox)."—*Fryer*, 53.

1681.—"For here are many **Jackalls**, which catch their Henes, some *Tigres* that destroy their Cattle; but the greatest of all is the King; whose endeavour is to keep them poor and in want."—*Knox, Ceylon*, 87. On p. 20 he writes *Jacols*.

1711.—"**Jackcalls** are remarkable for Howling in the Night; one alone making as much noise as three or four Cur Dogs, and in different Notes, as if there were half a Dozen of them got together."—*Lockyer*, 382.

1810.—Colebrooke (*Essays*, ii. 109, [*Life*, 155]) spells **shakal**. But *Jackal* was already English.

c. 1816.—
"The **jackal's** troop, in gather'd cry,
Bayed from afar, complainingly."
Siege of Corinth, xxxiii.

1880.—"The mention of **Jackal**-hunting in one of the letters (of Lord Minto) may remind some Anglo-Indians still living, of the days when the Calcutta hounds used to throw off at gun-fire."—*Sat. Rev.* Feb. 14.

JACK-SNIPE of English sportsmen is *Gallinago gallinula*, Linn., smaller than the common snipe, *G. scolopacinus*, Bonap.

JACKASS COPAL. This is a trade name, and is a capital specimen of *Hobson-Jobson*. It is, according to Sir R. Burton, [*Zanzibar*, i. 357], a corruption of *chakāzi*. There are three qualities of copal in the Zanzibar market. 1. *Sandarusi m'ti*, or 'Tree Copal,' gathered directly from the tree which exudes it (*Trachylobium Mossambicense*). 2. *Chakāzi* or *chakazzi*, dug from the soil, but seeming of recent origin, and priced on a par with No. 1. 3. The genuine *Sandarusi*, or true Copal (the *Animé* of the English market), which is also fossil, but of ancient production, and bears more than twice the price of 1 and 2 (see *Sir J. Kirk* in *J. Linn. Soc.* (Botany) for 1871). Of the meaning of *chakāzi* we have no authentic information. But considering that a pitch made of copal and oil is used in Kutch, and that the cheaper copal would naturally be used for such a purpose, we may suggest as probable that the word is a corr. of *jahāzi*, and ='*ship*-copal.'

JACQUETE, Town and Cape, n.p. The name, properly **Jakad**, formerly attached to a place at the extreme west horn of the Kāthiawār Peninsula, where stands the temple of **Dwarka** (q.v.). Also applied by the Portuguese to the Gulf of Cutch. (See quotation from Camoens under **DIUL-SIND**.) The last important map which gives this name, so far as we are aware, is Aaron Arrowsmith's great Map of India, 1816, in which Dwarka appears under the name of **Juggut**.

1525.—(Melequyaz) "holds the revenue of Crystna, which is in a town called **Zaguete** where there is a place of Pilgrimage of gentoos which is called *Crysna*. . . ."—*Lembrança das Cousas da India*, 35.

1553.—"From the Diul estuary to the Point of **Jaquete** 38 leagues; and from the same **Jaquete**, which is the site of one of the principal temples of that heathenism, with a noble town, to our city Diu of the Kingdom of Guzarat, 58 leagues."—*Barros*, I. ix. 1.

1555.—"Whilst the tide was at its greatest height we arrived at the gulf of **Chakad**, where we descried signs of fine weather, such as sea-horses, great snakes, turtles, and sea-weeds."—*Sidi 'Ali*, p. 77.

[1563.—"Passed the point of **Jacquette**, where is that famous temple of the Resbutos (see **RAJPOOT**)."—*Barros*, IV. iv. 4.]

1726.—In Valentyn's map we find **Jaquete** marked as a town (at the west point of Kāthiawār) and *Enceada da* **Jaquete** for the Gulf of Cutch.

1727.—"The next sea-port town to *Baet*, is **Jigat**. It stands on a Point of low Land, called Cape **Jigat**. The City makes a good Figure from the Sea, showing 4 or 5 high Steeples."—*A. Hamilton*, i. 135; [ed. 1744].

1813.—"**Jigat** *Point* . . . on it is a pagoda; the place where it stands was formerly called **Jigat** *More*, but now by the Hindoos *Dorecur* (*i.e.* **Dwarka**, q.v.). At a distance the pagoda has very much the appearance of a ship under sail. . . . Great numbers of pilgrims from the interior visit **Jigat** pagoda. . . ."—*Milburn*, i. 150.

1841.—"**Jigat** *Point* called also Dwarka, from the large temple of Dwarka standing near the coast."—*Horsburgh, Directory*, 5th ed., i. 480.

JADE, s. The well-known mineral, so much prized in China, and so wonderfully wrought in that and other Asiatic countries; the *yashm* of the Persians; *nephrite* of mineralogists.

The derivation of the word has been the subject of a good deal of controversy. We were at one time inclined to connect it with the *yada-tāsh*, the *yada* stone used by the nomads of Central Asia in conjuring for rain. The stone so used was however, according to P. Hyakinth, quoted in a note with which we were favoured by the lamented Prof. Anton Schiefner, a **bezoar** (q.v.).

Major Raverty, in his translation of the *Tabaķāt-i-Nāṣirī*, in a passage referring to the regions of Tukhāristān and Bāmiān, has the following: "That tract of country has also been famed and celebrated, to the uttermost parts of the countries of the world, for its mines of gold, silver, rubies, and crystal, bejādah [jade], and other [precious] things" (p. 421). On *bejādah* his note runs: "The name of a gem, by some said to be a species of ruby, and by others a species of sapphire; but **jade** is no doubt meant." This interpretation seems however chiefly, if not altogether, suggested by the name; whilst the epithets compounded of *bejāda*, as given in dictionaries, suggest a red mineral, which jade rarely is. And Prof. Max Müller, in an interesting letter to the *Times*, dated Jan. 10, 1880, states that the name *jade* was not known in Europe till after the discovery of America, and that the jade brought from America was called by the Spaniards *piedra de* **ijada**, because it was supposed to cure pain in the groin (Sp. *ijada*); for like reasons to which it was called *lapis nephriticus*, whence *nephrite* (see *Bailey*, below). Skeat, s.v. says: "It is of unknown origin; but probably Oriental. Prof. Cowell finds *yedā* a material out of which ornaments are made, in the *Divyāvadāna;* but it does not seem to be Sanskrit." Prof. Müller's etymology seems incontrovertible; but the present work has afforded various examples of curious etymological coincidences of this kind. [Prof. Max Müller's etymology is now accepted by the *N.E.D.* and by Prof. Skeat in the new edition of his *Concise Dict.* The latter adds that **ijada** is connected with the Latin *ilia*.]

[1595.—"A kinde of greene stones, which the Spaniards call Piedras **hijadas**, and we vse for spleene stones."—*Raleigh, Discov. Guiana*, 24 (quoted in *N.E.D.*).]

1730.—"**Jade**, a greenish Stone, bordering on the colour of Olive, esteemed for its Hardness and Virtues by the *Turks* and *Poles*, who adorn their fine Sabres with it; and said to be a preservative against the nephritick Colick."—*Bailey's Eng. Dict.* s.v.

JADOO, s. Hind. from Pers. *jādū*, Skt. *yātu;* conjuring, magic, hocus-pocus.

[1826.—"'Pray, sir,' said the barber, 'is that Sanscrit, or what language?' 'May be it is **jadoo**,' I replied, in a solemn and deep voice."—*Pandurang Hari*, ed. 1873, i. 127.]

JADOOGUR, s. Properly Hind. *jādūghar*, 'conjuring-house' (see the last). The term commonly applied by natives to a Freemasons' Lodge, when there is one, at an English station. On the Bombay side it is also called *Shaitān khāna* (see Burton's *Sind Revisited*), a name consonant to the ideas of an Italian priest who intimated to one of the present writers that he had heard the raising of the devil was practised at Masonic meetings, and asked his friend's opinion as to the fact. In S. India the Lodge is called *Talai-vĕṭṭa-Kovil*, 'Cut-head Temple,' because part of the rite of initiation is supposed to consist in the candidate's head being cut off and put on again.

JAFNA, JAFNAPATÁM, n.p. The very ancient Tamil settlement, and capital of the Tamil kings on the singular peninsula which forms the northernmost part of Ceylon. The real name is, according to Emerson Tennent, *Yalpannan*, and it is on the whole probable that this name is identical with the *Galiba* (Prom.) of Ptolemy. [The *Madras Gloss.* gives the Tamil name as *Yāzhppānam*, from *yazh-pānan*, 'a lute-player'; "called after a blind minstrel of that name from the Chola country, who by permission of the Singhalese king obtained possession of Jaffna, then uninhabited, and introduced there a colony of the Tamul people."]

1553.—". . . the Kingdom Triquinamalé, which at the upper end of its coast adjoins another called **Jafanapatam**, which stands at the northern part of the island."—*Barros*, III. ii. cap. i.

c. 1566.—In Cesare de' Federici it is written **Gianifanpatan**.—*Ramusio*; iii. 390*v*.

[**JAFFRY**, s. A screen or lattice-work, made generally of bamboo, used for various purposes, such as a fence, a support for climbing plants, &c. The ordinary Pers. *ja'farī* is derived from a person of the name of *Ja'far;* but Mr. Platts suggests that in the sense under consideration it may be a corr. of Ar. *ẓafirat*, *ẓafir*, 'a braided lock.'

[1832.—"Of vines, the branches must also be equally spread over the **jaffry**, so that light and heat may have access to the whole."—*Trans. Agri. Hort. Soc. Ind.* ii. 202.]

JAGGERY, s. Coarse brown (or almost black) sugar, made from the sap of various palms. The wild date tree (*Phoenix sylvestris*, Roxb.), Hind. *khajūr*, is that which chiefly supplies palm-sugar in Guzerat and Coromandel, and almost alone in Bengal. But the palmyra, the caryota, and the coco-palm all give it; the first as the staple of Tinnevelly and northern Ceylon; the second chiefly in southern Ceylon, where it is known to Europeans as the **Jaggery** *Palm* (*kitūl* of natives); the third is much drawn for **toddy** (q.v.) in the coast districts of Western India, and this is occasionally boiled for sugar. Jaggery is usually made in the form of small round cakes. Great quantities are produced in Tinnevelly, where the cakes used to pass as a kind of currency (as cakes of salt used to pass in parts of Africa, and in Western China), and do even yet to some small extent. In Bombay all rough unrefined sugar-stuff is known by this name; and it is the title under which all kinds of half-prepared sugar is classified in the tariff of the Railways there. The word *jaggery* is only another form of **sugar** (q.v.), being like it a corr. of the Skt. *śarkarā*, Konkani *sakkarā*, [Malayāl. *chakkarā*, whence it passed into Port. *jagara, jagra*].

1516.—"Sugar of palms, which they call **xagara**."—*Barbosa*, 59.

1553.—Exports from the Maldives "also of fish-oil, coco-nuts, and **jágara**, which is made from these after the manner of sugar."—*Barros*, Dec. III. liv. iii. cap. 7.

1561.—"**Jagre**, which is sugar of palm-trees."—*Correa, Lendas*, i. 2, 592.

1563.—"And after they have drawn this pot of *çura*, if the tree gives much they draw another, of which they make sugar, prepared either by sun or fire, and this they call **jagra**."—*Garcia*, f. 67.

c. 1567.—"There come every yeere from Cochin and from Cananor tenne or fifteene great Shippes (to Chaul) laden with great nuts . . . and with sugar made of the selfe same nuts called **Giagra**."—*Caesar Frederike*, in *Hakl.* ii. 344.

1598.—"Of the aforesaid *sura* they likewise make sugar, which is called **Iagra**; they seeth the water, and set it in the sun, whereof it becometh sugar, but it is little esteemed, because it is of a browne colour."—*Linschoten*, 102; [Hak. Soc. ii. 49].

1616.—"Some small quantity of wine, but not common, is made among them; they call it *Raak* (see **ARRACK**), distilled from Sugar, and a spicy rinde of a tree called **Jagra**."—*Terry*, ed. 1665, p. 365.

1727.—"The Produce of the Samorin's Country is . . . Cocoa-Nut, and that tree produceth **Jaggery**, a kind of sugar, and Copera (see **COPRAH**), or the kernels of the Nut dried."—*A. Hamilton*, i. 306; [ed. 1744, i. 308].

c. 1750-60.—"Arrack, a coarse sort of sugar called **Jagree**, and vinegar are also extracted from it" (coco-palm).—*Grose*, i. 47.

1807.—"The *Tari* or fermented juice, and the **Jagory** or inspissated juice of the Palmira tree . . . are in this country more esteemed than those of the wild date, which is contrary to the opinion of the Bengalese."—*F. Buchanan, Mysore*, &c., i. 5.

1860.—"In this state it is sold as **jaggery** in the bazaars, at about three farthings per pound."—*Tennent's Ceylon*, iii. 524.

JAGHEER, JAGHIRE, s. Pers. *jāgīr*, lit. 'place-holding.' A hereditary assignment of land and of its rent as annuity.

[c. 1590.—"*Farmán-i-zabits* are issued for . . . appointments to **jágírs**, without military service."—*Āīn*, i. 261.

[1617.—"Hee quittes diuers small **Jaggers** to the King."—*Sir T. Roe*, Hak. Soc. ii. 449.]

c. 1666.—". . . Not to speak of what they finger out of the Pay of every Horseman, and of the number of the Horses; which certainly amounts to very considerable Pensions, especially if they can obtain good **Jah-ghirs**, that is, good Lands for their Pensions."—*Bernier*, E.T. 66; [ed. *Constable*, 213].

1673.—"It (Surat) has for its Maintenance the Income of six Villages; over which the Governor sometimes presides, sometimes not, being in the **Jaggea**, or diocese of another."—*Fryer*, 120.

" "**Jageah**, an Annuity."—*Ibid. Index*, vi.

1768.—"I say, Madam, I know nothing of books; and yet I believe upon a land-carriage fishery, a stamp act, or a **jaghire**, I can talk my two hours without feeling the want of them."—Mr. Lofty, in *The Good-Natured Man*, Act ii.

1778.—"Should it be more agreeable to the parties, Sir Matthew will settle upon Sir John and his Lady, for their joint lives, a **jagghire**.

"*Sir John.*—A **Jagghire**?

"*Thomas.*—The term is Indian, and means an annual Income."—*Foote, The Nabob*, i. 1.

We believe the traditional stage pronunciation in these passages is **Jag Hire** (assonant in both syllables to *Quag Mire*); and this is also the pronunciation given in some dictionaries.

1778.—". . . **Jaghires**, which were always rents arising from lands."—*Orme*, ed. 1803, ii. 52.

1809.—"He was nominally in possession of a larger **jaghire**."—*Ld. Valentia*, i. 401.

A territory adjoining Fort St. George was long known as the **Jaghire**, or *the Company's* **Jaghire**, and is often so mentioned in histories of the 18th century. This territory, granted to the Company by the Nabob of Arcot in 1750 and 1763, nearly answers to the former Collectorate of Chengalput and present Collectorate of Madras.

[In the following the reference is to the *Jirgah* or tribal council of the Pathan tribes on the N.W. frontier.

[1900.—"No doubt upon the occasion of Lord Curzon's introduction to the Waziris and the Mohmunds, he will inform their **Jagirs** that he has long since written a book about them."—*Contemporary Rev.* Aug. p. 282.]

JAGHEERDAR, s. P.—H. *jāgīrdār*, the holder of a **jagheer**.

[1813.—". . . in the Mahratta empire the principal **Jaghiredars**, or nobles, appear in the field. . . ."—*Forbes, Or. Mem.* 2nd ed. i. 328.]

1826.—"The Resident, many officers, men of rank . . . **jagheerdars**, Brahmins, and Pundits, were present, assembled round my father."—*Pandurang Hari*, 389; [ed. 1873, ii. 259].

1883.—"The Sikhs administered the country by means of **jagheerdars**, and paid them by their **jagheers**: the English administered it by highly paid British officers, at the same time that they endeavoured to lower the land-tax, and to introduce grand material reforms."—*Bosworth Smith, L. of Ld. Lawrence*, i. 378.

JAIL-KHANA, s. A hybrid word for 'a gaol,' commonly used in the Bengal Presidency.

JAIN, s. and adj. The non-Brahmanical sect so called; believed to represent the earliest heretics of Buddhism, at present chiefly to be found in the Bombay Presidency. There are a few in Mysore, Canara, and in some parts of the Madras Presidency, but in the Middle Ages they appear to have been numerous on the coast of the Peninsula generally. They are also found in various parts of Central and Northern India and Behar. The Jains are generally merchants, and some have been men of enormous wealth (see *Colebrooke's Essays*, i. 378 *seqq.*; [Lassen, in *Ind. Antiq.* ii. 193 *seqq.*, 258 *seqq.*]). The name is Skt. **jaina**, meaning a follower of **jina**. The latter word is a title applied to certain saints worshipped by the sect in the place of gods; it is also a name of the Buddhas. An older name for the followers of the sect appears to have been *Nirgrantha*, 'without bond,' properly the title of Jain *ascetics* only (otherwise *Yatis*), [and in particular of the *Digambara* or 'sky-clad,' naked branch]. (*Burnell, S. Indian Palaeography*, p. 47, note.)

[c. 1590.—"**Jaina**. The founder of this wonderful system was Jina, also called Arhat, or Arhant."—*Āīn*, ed. *Jarrett*, iii. 188.]

JALEEBOTE, s. *Jālībōt*. A marine corruption of *jolly-boat* (*Roebuck*). (See **GALLEVAT**.)

JAM, s. *Jām*.

a. A title borne by certain chiefs in Kutch, in Kāthiāwāṛ, and on the lower Indus. The derivation is very obscure (see *Elliot*, i. 495). The title is probably Bilūch originally. There are several **Jāms** in Lower Sind and its borders, and notably the *Jām* of Las Bela State, a well-known dependency of Kelat, bordering the sea. [Mr. Longworth Dames writes: "I do not think the word is of Balochi origin, although it is certainly made use of in the Balochi language. It is rather Sindhi, in the broad sense of the word, using Sindhi as the natives do, referring to the tribes of the Indus valley without regard to the modern boundaries of the province of Sindh. As far as I know, it is used as a title, not by Baloches, but by indigenous tribes of Rājput or Jat origin, now, of course, all Musulmans. The Jām of Las Bela belongs to a tribe of this nature known as the Jāmhat. In the Dera Ghāzī Khān District it is used by certain local notables of this class, none of them Baloches. The principal tribe there using it is the Udhāna. It is also an honorific title among the Mochis of Dera Ghāzī Khān town."]

[c. 1590.—"On the Gujarat side towards the south is a Zamíndár of note whom they call Jám. . . ."—*Āīn*, ed. *Jarrett*, ii. 250.

[1843.—See under **DAWK.**]

b. A nautical measure, Ar. *zām*, pl. *azwām*. It occurs in the form geme in a quotation of 1614 under **JASK**. It is repeatedly used in the *Mohit* of Sidi 'Ali, published in the *J. As. Soc. Bengal*. It would appear from J. Prinsep's remarks there that the word is used in various ways. Thus Baron J. Hammer writes to Prinsep: "Concerning the measure of *azwām* the first section of the IIId. chapter explains as follows: 'The *zām* is either the practical one (*'ārfī*), or the rhetorical (*iṣṭilāḥī*—but this the acute Prinsep suggests should be *aṣṭarlābī*, 'pertaining to the divisions of the astrolabe'). The *practical* is one of the 8 parts into which day and night are divided; the rhetorical (but read the *astrolabic*) is the 8th part of an inch (*iṣāba*) in the ascension and descension of the stars; . . . an explanation which helps me not a bit to understand the true measure of a *zām*, in the reckoning of a ship's course." Prinsep then elucidates this: The *zām* in practical parlance is said to be the 8th part of day and night; it is in fact a nautical *watch* or Hindu *pahar* (see **PUHUR**). Again, it is the 8th part of the ordinary inch, like the *jau* or barleycorn of the Hindus (the 8th part of an *angul* or digit), of which *jau*, *zām* is possibly a corruption. Again, the *iṣāba* or inch, and the *zām* or $\frac{1}{8}$ of an inch, had been transferred to the rude angle-instruments of the Arab navigators; and Prinsep deduces from statements in Sidi 'Ali's book that the *iṣāba*' was very nearly equal to 96′ and the *zām* to 12′. Prinsep had also found on enquiry among Arab mariners, that the term **zām** was still well known to nautical people as $\frac{1}{8}$ of a geographical degree, or 12 nautical miles, quite confirmatory of the former calculation; it was also stated to be still applied to terrestrial measurements (see *J.A.S.B.* v. 642-3).

1013.—"J'ai déjà parlé de Sérira (read *Sarbaza*) qui est située à l'extremité de l'île de Lâmeri, à cent-vingt **zâmâ** de Kala."—*Ajāib-al-Hind*, ed. *Van der Lith et Marcel Devic*, 176.

" "Un marin m'a rapporté qu'il avait fait la traversée de Sérira (*Sarbaza*) à la Chine dans un *Sambouq* (see **SAMBOOK**). 'Nous avions parcouru,' dit-il, 'un espace de cinquante **zâmâ**, lorsqu'une tempête fondit sur notre embarcation. . . . Ayant fait de l'eau, nous remîmes à la voile vers le Senf, suivant ses instructions, et nous y abordâmes sains et saufs, après un voyage de quinze **zâmâ**."—*Ibid.* pp. 190-91.

1554.—"26th VOYAGE *from Calicut* to *Kardafun*" (see **GUARDAFUI**).

". . . you run from *Calicut* to *Kolfaini* (*i.e.* Kalpeni, one of the Laccadive Ids.) two **zāms** in the direction of W. by S., the 8 or 9 **zāms** W.S.W. (this course is in the 9 degree channel through the Laccadives), then you may rejoice as you have got clear of the islands of *Fúl*, from thence W. by N. and W.N.W. till the pole is 4 inches and a quarter, and then true west to *Kardafún*."

* * * * *

"27th VOYAGE, *from Diû to Malacca*.

"Leaving Diû you go first S.S.E. till the pole is 5 inches, and side then towards the land, till the distance between it and the ship is six **zāms**; from thence you steer S.S.E. . . . you must not side all at once but by degrees, first till the *farkadain* (β and γ in the Little Bear) are made by a quarter less than 8 inches, from thence to S.E. till the *farkadain* are $7\frac{1}{2}$ inches, from thence true east at a rate of 18 **zāms**, then you have passed Ceylon."—*The Mohit*, in *J.A.S.B.* v. 465.

The meaning of this last *routier* is: "Steer S.S.E. till you are in 8° N. Lat. (lat. of Cape Comorin); make then a little more easting, but keep 72 miles between you and the coast of Ceylon till you find the β and γ of Ursa Minor have an altitude of only 12° 24′ (*i.e.* till you are in N. Lat. 6° or 5°), and then steer due east. When you have gone 216 miles you will be quite clear of Ceylon."

1625.—"We cast anchor under the island of Kharg, which is distant from Cais, which we left behind us, 24 **giam**. **Giam** is a measure used by the Arab and Persian pilots in the Persian Gulf; and every **giam** is equal to 3 leagues; insomuch that from Cais to Kharg we had made 72 leagues."—*P. della Valle*, ii. 816.

JAMBOO, JUMBOO, s. The Rose-apple, *Eugenia jambos*, L. *Jambosa vulgaris*, Decand.; Skt. *jambū*, Hind. *jam*, *jambū*, *jamrūl*, &c. This is the use in Bengal, but there is great confusion in application, both colloquially and in books. The name *jambū* is applied in some parts of India to the exotic **guava** (q.v.), as well as to other species of *Eugenia*; including the *jāmun* (see **JAMOON**), with which the rose-apple is often confounded in books. They are very different fruits, though they have both been classed by Linnaeus under the genus *Eugenia* (see further remarks under **JAMOON**). [Mr. Skeat notes that the word is applied by the Malays both to the rose-apple and the guava, and Wilkinson (*Dict.* s.v.) notes a large number of fruits to which the name *jambū* is applied.]

Garcia de Orta mentions the rose-apple under the name **Iambos**, and says (1563) that it had been recently introduced into Goa from Malacca. This may have been the *Eugenia Malaccensis*, L., which is stated in Forbes Watson's Catalogue of nomenclature to be called in Bengal *Malāka Jamrūī*, and in Tamil *Malākā maram i.e.* 'Malacca tree.' The Skt. name *jambū* is, in the Malay language, applied with distinguishing adjectives to all the species.

[1598.—"The trees whereon the **Iambos** do grow are as great as Plumtrees."—*Linschoten*, Hak. Soc. ii. 31.]

1672. — P. Vincenzo Maria describes the **Giambo d'India** with great precision, and also the **Giambo di China**—no doubt *J. malaccensis*—but at too great length for extract, pp. 351-352.

1673.—"In the South a Wood of **Jamboes**, Mangoes, Cocoes."—*Fryer*, 46.

1727.—"Their **Jambo** *Malacca* (at Goa) is very beautiful and pleasant."—*A. Hamilton*, i. 255; [ed. 1744, i. 258].

1810.—"The **jumboo**, a species of rose-apple, with its flower like crimson tassels covering every part of the stem."—*Maria Graham*, 22.

JAMES AND MARY, n.p. The name of a famous sand-bank in the Hoogly R. below Calcutta, which has been fatal to many a ship. It is mentioned under 1748, in the record of a survey of the river quoted in *Long*, p. 10. It is a common allegation that the name is a corruption of the Hind. words *jal mari*, with the supposed meaning of 'dead water.' But the real origin of the name dates, as Sir G. Birdwood has shown, out of India Office records, from the wreck of a vessel called the "*Royal James and Mary*," in September 1694, on that sand-bank (*Letter to the Court, from Chuttanuttee*, Dec. 19, 1694). [*Report on Old Records*, 90.] This shoal appears by name in a chart belonging to the *English Pilot*, 1711.

JAMMA, s. P.—H. *jāma*, a piece of native clothing. Thus, in composition, see **PYJAMMAS**. Also stuff for clothing, &c., *e.g. mom*-**jama**, wax-cloth. ["The **jama** may have been brought by the Aryans from Central Asia, but as it is still now seen it is thoroughly Indian and of ancient date" (*Rajendralala Mitra, Indo-Aryans*, i. 187 *seq.*]

[1813.—"The better sort (of Hindus) wear . . . a **jama**, or long gown of white calico, which is tied round the middle with a fringed or embroidered sash."—*Forbes, Or. Mem.* 2nd ed. i. 52].

JAMOON, s. Hind. *jāmun*, *jāman*, *jāmlī*, &c. The name of a poor fruit common in many parts of India, and apparently in E. Africa, the *Eugenia jambolana*, Lamk. (*Calyptranthes jambolana* of Willdenow, *Syzygium jambolanum* of Decand.) This seems to be confounded with the *Eugenia jambos*, or Rose-apple (see **JAMBOO**, above), by the author of a note on Leyden's *Baber* which Mr. Erskine justly corrects (Baber's own account is very accurate), by the translators of Ibn Batuta, and apparently, as regards the botanical name, by Sir R. Burton. The latter gives *jamli* as the Indian, and *zam* as the Arabic name. The name *jambū* appears to be applied to this fruit at Bombay, which of course promotes the confusion spoken of. In native practice the stones of this fruit have been alleged to be a cure for diabetes, but European trials do not seem to have confirmed this.

c. 13**.—"The inhabitants (of Mombasa) gather also a fruit which they call **jamūn**, and which resembles an olive; it has a stone like the olive, but has a very sweet taste."—*Ibn Batuta*, ii. 191. Elsewhere the translators write *tchoumoûn* (iii. 128, iv. 114, 229), a spelling indicated in the original, but surely by some error.

c. 1530.—"Another is the **jaman**. . . . It is on the whole a fine looking tree. Its fruit resembles the black grape, but has a more acid taste, and is not very good."—*Baber*, 325. The note on this runs: "This, Dr. Hunter says, is the *Eugenia Jambolana*, the rose-apple (*Eugenia jambolana*, but not the rose-apple, which is now called *Eugenia jambu*.—D.W.). The *jâman* has no resemblance to the rose-apple; it is more like an oblong sloe than anything else, but grows on a tall tree."

1563.—"I will eat of those olives,——, at least they look like such; but they are very astringent (*ponticas*) as if binding,——, and yet they do look like ripe Cordova olives.

"*O.* They are called **jambolones**, and grow wild in a wood that looks like a myrtle grove; in its leaves the tree resembles the arbutus; but like the jack, the people of the country don't hold this fruit for very wholesome."—*Garcia*, f. 111*v*.

1859.—"The Indian **jamli**. . . . It is a noble tree, which adorns some of the coast villages and plantations, and it produces a damson-like fruit, with a pleasant sub-acid flavour."—*Burton*, in *J.R.G.S.* ix. 36.

JANCADA, s. This name was given to certain responsible guides in the Nair country who escorted travellers from one inhabited place to another, guaranteeing their security with their own lives, like the Bhāts of Guzerat. The word is Malayāl. *chaṅṅāḍam* (*i.e.* *changngāḍam*, [the *Madras Gloss.* writes *channātam*, and derives it from Skt. *sanghāta*, 'union']), with the same spelling as that of the word given as the origin of **jangar** or **jangada**, 'a raft.' These *jancadas* or *jangadas* seem also to have been placed in other confidential and dangerous charges. Thus:

1543.—"This man who so resolutely died was one of the **jangadas** of the Pagode. They are called **jangades** because the kings and lords of those lands, according to a custom of theirs, send as guardians of the houses of the Pagodes in their territories, two men as captains, who are men of honour and good cavaliers. Such guardians are called **jangadas**, and have soldiers of guard under them, and are as it were the Counsellors and Ministers of the affairs of the pagodes, and they receive their maintenance from the establishment and its revenues. And sometimes the king changes them and appoints others."—*Correa*, iv. 328.

c. 1610.—"I travelled with another Captain . . . who had with him these **Jangai**, who are the Nair guides, and who are found at the gates of towns to act as escort to those who require them. . . . Every one takes them, the weak for safety and protection, those who are stronger, and travel in great companies and well armed, take them only as witnesses that they are not aggressors in case of any dispute with the Nairs."—*Pyrard de Laval*, ch. xxv.; [Hak. Soc. i. 339, and see Mr. Gray's note *in loco*].

1672.—"The safest of all journeyings in India are those through the Kingdom of the Nairs and the Samorin, if you travel with **Giancadas**, the most perilous if you go alone. These **Giancadas** are certain heathen men, who venture their own life and the lives of their kinsfolk for small remuneration, to guarantee the safety of travellers."—*P. Vincenzo Maria*, 127.

See also *Chungathum*, in *Burton's Goa*, p. 198.

JANGAR, s. A raft. Port. *jangada*. ["A double platform canoe made by placing a floor of boards across two boats, with a bamboo railing." (*Madras Gloss.*).] This word, chiefly colloquial, is the Tamil-Malayāl. *shangāḍam*, *channātam* (for the derivation of which see **JANCADA**). It is a word of particular interest as being one of the few Dravidian words, [but perhaps ultimately of Skt. origin], preserved in the remains of classical antiquity, occurring in the *Periplus* as our quotation shows. Bluteau does not call the word an Indian term.

c. 80-90.—"The vessels belonging to these places (*Camara*, *Poducē*, and *Sopatma* on the east coast) which hug the shore to Limyricē (*Dimyricē*), and others also called Σάγγαρα, which consist of the largest canoes of single timbers lashed together; and again those biggest of all which sail to Chryse and Ganges, and are called Κολανδιοφωντα."—*Periplus*, in *Müller's Geog. Gr. Min.*, i. "The first part of this name for boats or ships is most probably the Tam. *kulinda*= hollowed: the last *ōdam*=boat."—*Burnell*, *S.I. Palaeography*, 612.

c. 1504.—"He held in readiness many **jangadas** of timber."—*Correa*, *Lendas*, I. i. 476.

c. 1540.—". . . and to that purpose had already commanded two great Rafts (**jãgadas**), covered with dry wood, barrels of pitch and other combustible stuff, to be placed at the entering into the Port."—*Pinto* (orig. cap. xlvi.), in *Cogan*, p. 56.

1553.—". . . the fleet . . . which might consist of more than 200 rowing vessels of all kinds, a great part of them combined into **jangadas** in order to carry a greater mass of men, and among them two of these contrivances on which were 150 men."—*Barros*, II. i. 5.

1598.—"Such as stayed in the ship, some tooke bords, deals, and other peeces of wood, and bound them together (which ye Portingals cal **Iangadas**) every man what they could catch, all hoping to save their lives, but of all those there came but two men safe to shore."—*Linschoten*, p. 147; [Hak. Soc. ii. 181; and see Mr. Gray on *Pyrard de Laval*, Hak. Soc. i. 53 *seq.*].

1602.—"For his object was to see if he could rescue them in **jangadas**, which he ordered him immediately to put together of baulks, planks, and oars."—*Couto*, Dec. IV. liv. iv. cap. 10.

1756.—". . . having set fire to a **jungodo** of Boats, these driving down towards the Fleet, compelled them to weigh."—*Capt. Jackson*, in *Dalrymple's Or. Rep.* i. 199.

c. 1790.—"**Sangarie.**" See quotation under **HACKERY**.

c. 1793.—"Nous nous remîmes en chemin à six heures du matin, et passâmes la rivière dans un **sangarie** ou canot fait d'un palmier creusé."—*Haafner*, ii. 77.

JANGOMAY, ZANGOMAY, JAMAHEY, &c., n.p. The town and state of Siamese Laos, called by the Burmese *Zimmé*, by the Siamese *Xieng-*

mai or *Kiang-mai*, &c., is so called in narratives of the 17th century. Serious efforts to establish trade with this place were made by the E.I. Company in the early part of the 17th century, of which notice will be found in Purchas, *Pilgrimage*, and Sainsbury, *e.g.* in vol. i. (1614), pp. 311, 325; (1615) p. 425; (1617) ii. p. 90. The place has again become the scene of commercial and political interest; an English Vice-Consulate has been established; and a railway survey undertaken. [See *Hallett, A Thousand Miles on an Elephant*, 74 *seqq.*]

c. 1544.—"Out of this Lake of *Singapamor* . . . do four very large and deep rivers proceed, whereof the first . . . runneth Eastward through all the Kingdoms of *Sornau* and *Siam* . . . ; the Second, **Jangumaa** . . . disimboking into the Sea by the Bar of *Martabano* in the Kingdom of *Pegu*. . . ."—*Pinto* (in *Cogan*, 165).

1553.—(Barros illustrates the position of the different kingdoms of India by the figure of a (left) hand, laid with the palm downwards) "And as regards the western part, following always the sinew of the forefinger, it will correspond with the ranges of mountains running from north to south along which lie the kingdom of Avá, and Bremá, and **Jangomá**."—III. ii. 5.

c. 1587.—"I went from *Pegu* to **Iamayhey**, which is in the Countrey of the *Langeiannes*, whom we call **Iangomes**; it is five and twentie dayes iourney to Northeast from Pegu. . . . Hither to **Iamayhey** come many Merchants out of *China*, and bring great store of Muske, Gold, Silver, and many things of *China* worke."—*R. Fitch*, in *Hakl.* ii.

c. 1606.—"But the people, or most part of them, fled to the territories of the King of **Jangoma**, where they were met by the Padre Friar Francisco, of the Annunciation, who was there negotiating . . ."—*Bocarro*, 136.

1612.—"The Siamese go out with their heads shaven, and leave long mustachioes on their faces; their garb is much like that of the Peguans. The same may be said of the **Jangomas** and the Laojoes" (see **LAN JOHN**).—*Couto*, V. vi. 1.

c. 1615.—"The King (of Pegu) which now reigneth . . . hath in his time recovered from the King of *Syam* . . . the town and kingdom of **Zangomay**, and therein an Englishman called *Thomas Samuel*, who not long before had been sent from *Syam* by Master *Lucas Anthonison*, to discover the Trade of that country by the sale of certaine goods sent along with him for that purpose."—*W. Methold*, in *Purchas*, v. 1006.

[1617.—"**Jangama.**" See under **JUDEA**.

[1795.—"**Zemee.**" See under **SHAN**.]

JAPAN, n.p. Mr. Giles says: "Our word is from *Jeh-pun*, the Dutch orthography of the Japanese *Ni-pon*." What the Dutch have to do with the matter is hard to see. ["Our word '*Japan*' and the Japanese *Nihon* or *Nippon*, are alike corruptions of *Jih-pen*, the Chinese pronunciation of the characters (meaning) literally 'sun-origin.'" (*Chamberlain, Things Japanese*, 3rd ed. 221).] A form closely resembling *Japăn*, as we pronounce it, must have prevailed, among foreigners at least, in China as early as the 13th century; for Marco Polo calls it *Chipan*-gu or *Jipan*-ku, a name representing the Chinese *Zhi-păn-Kwe* ('Sun-origin-Kingdom'), the Kingdom of the Sunrise or Extreme Orient, of which the word *Nipon* or *Niphon*, used in Japan, is said to be a dialectic variation. But as there was a distinct gap in Western tradition between the 14th century and the 16th, no doubt we, or rather the Portuguese, acquired the name from the traders at Malacca, in the Malay forms, which Crawfurd gives as *Jăpung* and *Jăpang*.

1298.—"**Chipangu** is an Island towards the east in the high seas, 1,500 miles distant from the Continent; and a very great Island it is. The people are white, civilized, and well-favoured. They are Idolaters, and dependent on nobody. . . ."—*Marco Polo*, bk. iii. ch. 2.

1505.—". . . and not far off they took a ship belonging to the King of Calichut; out of which they have brought me certain jewels of good value; including Mccccc. pearls worth 8,000 ducats; also three astrological instruments of silver, such as are not used by our astrologers, large and well-wrought, which I hold in the highest estimation. They say that the King of Calichut had sent the said ship to an island called **Saponin** to obtain the said instruments. . . ."—*Letter from the K. of Portugal* (Dom Manuel) *to the K. of Castille* (Ferdinand). Reprint by *A. Burnell*, 1881, p. 8.

1521.—"In going by this course we passed near two very rich islands; one is in twenty degrees latitude in the antarctic pole, and is called **Cipanghu**."—*Pigafetta, Magellan's Voyage*, Hak. Soc., 67. Here the name appears to be taken from the chart or Mappe-Monde which was carried on the voyage. **Cipanghu** appears by that name on the globe of Martin Behaim (1492), but 20 degrees *north*, not south, of the equator.

1545.—"Now as for us three *Portugals*, having nothing to sell, we employed our time either in fishing, hunting, or seeing the Temples of these *Gentiles*, which were very sumptuous and rich, whereinto the *Bonzes*, who are their priests, received us very courteously, for indeed it is the custom of those of **Jappon** (*do Japão*) to be exceeding kind and courteous."—*Pinto* (orig. cap. cxxxiv.), in *Cogan*, E.T. p. 173.

1553.—"After leaving to the eastward the isles of the Lequios (see **LEW CHEW**) and of the **Japons** (*dos Japões*), and the great province of Meaco, which for its great size we know not whether to call it Island or Continent, the coast of China still runs on, and those parts pass beyond the antipodes of the meridian of Lisbon."—*Barros*, I. ix. 1.

1572.—
"Esta meia escondida, que responde
De longe a China, donde vem buscar-se,
He **Japão**, onde nasce la prata fina,
Que illustrada será co' a Lei divina."
Camões, x. 131.

By Burton:
"This Realm, half-shadowed, China's empery
afar reflecting, whither ships are bound,
is the **Japan**, whose virgin silver mine
shall shine still sheenier with the Law Divine."

1727.—"**Japon**, with the neighbouring Islands under its Dominions, is about the magnitude of Great Britain."—*A. Hamilton*, ii. 306; [ed. 1744, ii. 305].

JARGON, JARCOON, ZIRCON, s. The name of a precious stone often mentioned by writers of the 16th century, but respecting the identity of which there seems to be a little obscurity. The *English Encyclopaedia*, and the *Times* Reviewer of Emanuel's book *On Precious Stones* (1866), identify it with the hyacinth or jacinth; but Lord Stanley of Alderley, in his translation of Barbosa (who mentions the stone several times under the form *giagonza* and *jagonza*), on the authority of a practical jeweller identifies it with corundum. This is probably an error. *Jagonza* looks like a corruption of *jacinthus*. And Haüy's *Mineralogy* identifies *jargon* and *hyacinth* under the common name of *zircon*. Dana's *Mineralogy* states that the term *hyacinth* is applied to these stones, consisting of a *silicate of zirconia*, "which present bright colours, considerable transparency, and smooth shining surfaces. . . . The variety from Ceylon, which is colourless, and has a smoky tinge, and is therefore sold for inferior diamonds, is sometimes called *jargon*" (*Syst. of Mineral.*, 3rd ed., 1850, 379-380; [*Encycl. Britt.* 9th ed. xxiv. 789 *seq.*]).

The word probably comes into European languages through the Span. *azarcon*, a word of which there is a curious history in *Dozy and Engelmann*. Two Spanish words and their distinct Arabic originals have been confounded in the *Span. Dict.* of Cobarruvias (1611) and others following him. Sp. *zarca* is 'a woman with *blue* eyes,' and this comes from Ar. *zarkā*, fem. of *azrak*, 'blue.' This has led the lexicographers above referred to astray, and *azarcon* has been by them defined as a 'blue earth, made of burnt lead.' But *azarcon* really applies to 'red-lead,' or vermilion, as does the Port. *zarcão*, *azarcão*, and its proper sense is as the *Dict. of the Sp. Academy* says (after repeating the inconsistent explanation and etymology of Cobarruvias), "an intense orange-colour, Lat. *color aureus*." This is from the Ar. *zarkūn*, which in Ibn Baithar is explained as synonymous with *salīkūn*, and *asranj*, "which the Greeks call *sandix*," *i.e.* cinnabar or vermilion (see Sontheimer's *Ebn Beithar*, i. 44, 530). And the word, as Dozy shows, occurs in Pliny under the form *syricum* (see quotations below). The eventual etymology is almost certainly Persian, either *zargūn*, 'gold colour,' as Marcel Devic suggests, or *āzargūn* (perhaps more properly *āzargūn*, from *āzar*, 'fire'), 'flame-colour,' as Dozy thinks.

A.D. c. 70.—"Hoc ergo adulteratur minium in officinis sociorum, et ubivis **Syrico.** Quonam modo **Syricum** fiat suo loco docebimus, sublini autem **Syrico** minium conpendi ratio demonstrat."—*Plin. N. H.* XXXIII. vii.

" "Inter facticios est et **Syricum,** quo minium sublini diximus. Fit autem Sinopide et sandyce mixtis."—*Ibid.* XXXV. vi.

1796.—"The artists of Ceylon prepare rings and heads of canes, which contain a complete assortment of all the precious stones found in that island. These assemblages are called **Jargons** *de Ceilan*, and are so called because they consist of a collection of gems which reflect various colours."—*Fra Paolino*, Eng. ed. 1800, 393. (This is a very loose translation. Fra Paolino evidently thought *Jargon* was a figurative name applied to this mixture of stones, as it is to a mixture of languages).

1813.—"The colour of **Jargons** is grey, with tinges of green, blue, red, and yellow."—*I. Mawe*, [*A Treatise on Diamonds*, &c. 119.

1860.—"The 'Matura Diamonds,' which are largely used by the native jewellers, consist of **zircon**, found in the syenite, not only uncoloured, but also of pink and yellow tints, the former passing for rubies."—*Tennent's Ceylon*, i. 38.

JAROOL, s. The *Lagerstroemia reginae*, Roxb. H.-Beng. *jarūl*, *jāral*. A tree very extensively diffused in the forests of Eastern and Western India and Pegu. It furnishes excellent boat-timber, and is a splendid flowering tree. "An exceeding glorious tree of the Concan jungles, in the month of May robed as in imperial purple, with its terminal panicles of large showy purple flowers. I for the first time introduced it largely into Bombay gardens, and called it *Flos reginae*"—*Sir G. Birdwood, MS.*

1850.—"Their forests are frequented by timber-cutters, who fell **jarool**, a magnificent tree with red wood, which, though soft, is durable under water, and therefore in universal use for boat building."—*Hooker, Him. Journals*, ed. 1855, ii. 318.

1855.—"Much of the way from Rangoon also, by the creeks, to the great river, was through actual dense forest, in which the **jarool**, covered with purple blossoms, made a noble figure."—*Blackwood's Mag.*, May 1856, 538.

JASK, JASQUES, CAPE-, n.p. Ar. *Rās Jāshak*, a point on the eastern side of the Gulf of Omān, near the entrance to the Persian Gulf, and 6 miles south of a port of the same name. The latter was frequented by the vessels of the English Company whilst the Portuguese held Ormus. After the Portuguese were driven out of Ormus (1622) the English trade was moved to **Gombroon** (q.v.). The peninsula of which Cape Jask is the point, is now the terminus of the submarine cable from Bushire; and a company of native infantry is quartered there. *Jāsak* appears in Yāḳūt as "a large island between the land of Omān and the Island of Kish." No island corresponds to this description, and probably the reference is an incorrect one to *Jask* (see *Dict. de la Perse*, p. 149). By a curious misapprehension, Cape Jasques seems to have been Englished as *Cape James* (see *Dunn's Or. Navigator*, 1780, p. 94).

1553.—"Crossing from this Cape Moçandan to that opposite to it called **Jasque**, which with it forms the mouth of the strait, we enter on the second section (of the coast) according to our division. . . ."—*Barros*, I. ix. i.

1572.—
"Mas deixemos o estreito, e o conhecido
Cabo de Jasque, dito já Carpella,
Com todo o seu terreno mal querido
Da natura, e dos dons usados della. . . ."
Camões, x. 105.

By Burton:
"But now the Narrows and their noted head
Cape Jask, Carpella called by those of yore,
quit we, the dry terrene scant favourèd
by Nature niggard of her normal store. . . ."

1614.—"*Per Postscript*. If it please God this Persian business fall out to y^r^ contentt, and y^t^ you thinke fitt to adventure thither, I thinke itt not amisse to sett you downe as ye Pilotts have informed mee of **Jasques**, wch is a towne standinge neere ye edge of a straightte Sea Coast where a ship may ride in 8 fathome water a Sacar shotte from ye shoar and in 6 fathome you maye bee nearer. **Jasque** is 6 *Gemes* (see **JAM, b**) from Ormus southwards and six *Gemes* is 60 cosses makes 30 leagues. **Jasques** lieth from Muschet east. From **Jasques to Sinda** is 200 cosses or 100 leagues. At **Jasques** co͞monly they have northe winde wch blowethe trade out of ye Persian Gulfe. Mischet is on ye Arabian Coast, and is a little portte of Portugalls."—MS. Letter from *Nich. Downton*, dd. November 22, 1614, in India Office; [Printed in *Foster, Letters*, ii. 177, and compare ii. 145].

1617.—"There came news at this time that there was an English ship lying inside the Cape of Rosalgate (see **ROSALGAT**) with the intention of making a fort at **Jasques** in Persia, as a point from which to plunder our cargoes. . . ."—*Bocarro*, 672.

[1623.—"The point or peak of **Giasck**."—*P. della Valle*, Hak. Soc. i. 4.

[1630.—"**Iasques**." (See under **JUNK**.)]

1727.—"I'll travel along the Sea-coast, towards *Industan*, or the *Great Mogul's* Empire. All the Shore from **Jasques** to *Sindy*, is inhabited by uncivilized People, who admit of no Commerce with Strangers. . . ."—*A. Hamilton*, i. 115; [ed. 1744].

JASOOS, s. Ar.-H. *jāsūs*, 'a spy.'

1803.—"I have some **Jasooses**, selected by Col. C——'s brahmin for their stupidity, that they might not pry into state secrets, who go to Sindia's camp, remain there a *phaur* (see **PUHUR**) in fear . . ."—*M. Elphinstone*, in *Life*, i. 62.

JAUN, s. This is a term used in Calcutta, and occasionally in Madras, of which the origin is unknown to the present writers. [Mr. H. Beveridge points out that it is derived from H.—Beng. *yān*, defined by Sir G. Haughton: "a vehicle, any means of conveyance, a horse, a carriage, a *palkee*." It is Skt. *yāna*, with the same meaning. The initial *ya* in Bengali is usually pronounced *ja*. The root is *yā*, 'to go.'] It is, or was, applied to a small palankin carriage, such as is commonly used by business men in going to their offices, &c.

c. 1836.—
"Who did not know that office **Jaun** of pale Pomona green,
With its drab and yellow lining, and picked out black between,
Which down the Esplanade did go at the ninth hour of the day. . . ."—
Bole-Ponjis, by *H. M. Parker*, ii. 215.

[The **Jaun** Bazar is a well-known low quarter of Calcutta.]

[1892.—
"From Tarnau in Galicia
To **Jaun** Bazar she came."
R. Kipling, Ballad of Fisher's Boarding House.]

JAVA, n.p. This is a geographical name of great antiquity, and occurs, as our first quotation shows, in Ptolemy's Tables. His Ἰαβαδίου represents with singular correctness what was probably the Prakrit or popular form of *Yava-dvīpa* (see under **DIU** and **MALDIVES**), and his interpretation of the Sanskrit is perfectly correct. It will still remain a question whether *Yava* was not applied to some cereal more congenial to the latitude than barley,* or was (as is possible) an attempt to give an Indian meaning to some aboriginal name of similar sound. But the sixth of our quotations, the transcript and translation of a Sanskrit inscription in the Museum at Batavia by Mr. Holle, which we owe to the kindness of Prof. Kern, indicates that a signification of wealth in cereals was attached to the name in the early days of its Indian civilization. This inscription is most interesting, as it is the oldest *dated* inscription yet discovered upon Javanese soil. Till a recent time it was not known that there was any mention of Java in Sanskrit literature, and this was so when Lassen published the 2nd vol. of his *Indian Antiquities* (1849). But in fact Java was mentioned in the *Rāmāyana*, though a perverted reading disguised the fact until the publication of the Bombay edition in 1863. The passage is given in our second quotation; and we also give passages from two later astronomical works whose date is approximately known. The *Yava-Koṭi*, or *Java Point* of these writers is understood by Prof. Kern to be the eastern extremity of the island.

We have already (see **BENJAMIN**) alluded to the fact that the terms *Jāwa*, *Jāwi* were applied by the Arabs to the Archipelago generally, and often with specific reference to Sumatra. Prof. Kern, in a paper to which we are largely indebted, has indicated that this larger application of the term was originally Indian. He has discussed it in connection with the terms "Golden and Silver Islands" (*Suvarṇa dvīpa* and *Rūpya dvīpa*), which occur in the quotation from the *Rāmāyana*, and elsewhere in Sanskrit literature, and which evidently were the basis of the Chrysē and Argyrē, which take various forms in the writings of the Greek and Roman geographers. We cannot give the details of his discussion, but his condensed conclusions are as follows:—(1.) *Suvarṇa-dvīpa* and *Yava-dvīpa* were according to the prevalent representations the same; (2.) Two names of islands originally distinct were confounded with one another; (3.) *Suvarṇa-dvīpa* in its proper meaning is Sumatra, *Yava-dvīpa* in its proper meaning is Java; (4.) Sumatra, or a part of it, and Java were regarded as one whole, doubtless because they were politically united; (5.) By *Yava-koṭi* was indicated the east point of Java.

This Indian (and also insular) identification, in whole or in part, of Sumatra with Java explains a variety of puzzles, *e.g.* not merely the Arab application of *Java*, but also the ascription, in so many passages, of great wealth of gold to Java, though the island, to which that name properly belongs, produces no gold. This tradition of gold-produce we find in the passages quoted from Ptolemy, from the *Rāmāyana*, from the Holle inscription, and from Marco Polo. It becomes quite intelligible when we are taught that Java and Sumatra were at one time both embraced under the former name, for Sumatra has always been famous for its gold-production. [Mr. Skeat notes as an interesting fact that the standard Malay name *Jāwă* and the Javanese *Jāwa* preserve the original form of the word.]

* The Teutonic word *Corn* affords a handy instance of the varying application of the name of a cereal to that which is, or has been, the staple grain of each country. *Corn* in England familiarly means 'wheat'; in Scotland 'oats'; in Germany 'rye'; in America 'maize.'

(*Ancient*).—"Search carefully **Yava dvīpa**, adorned by seven Kingdoms, the Gold and Silver Island, rich in mines of gold. Beyond **Yava dvīpa** is the Mountain called Sisira, whose top touches the sky, and which is visited by gods and demons."—*Rāmāyana*, IV. xl. 30 (from Kern).

A.D. c. 150.—"**Iabadiu** (Ἰαβαδίου), which means 'Island of Barley,' most fruitful the island is said to be, and also to produce much gold; also the metropolis is said to have the name Argyrē (Silver), and to stand at the western end of the island."—*Ptolemy*, VII. ii. 29.

414.—"Thus they voyaged for about ninety days, when they arrived at a country called **Ya-va-di** [*i.e. Yava-dvīpa*]. In this country heretics and Brahmans flourish, but the Law of Buddha hardly deserves mentioning."—*Fahian*, ext. in *Groeneveldt's Notes from Chinese Sources*.

A.D. c. 500.—"When the sun rises in Ceylon it is sunset in the City of the Blessed (*Siddha-pura, i.e.* The Fortunate Islands), noon at **Yava-koti**, and midnight in the Land of the Romans."—*Aryabhata*, IV. v. 13 (from Kern).

A.D. c. 650.—"Eastward by a fourth part of the earth's circumference, in the world-quarter of the Bhadrāśvas lies the City famous under the name of **Yava koti** whose walls and gates are of gold."—*Suryā-Siddhānta*, XII. v. 38 (from Kern).

Saka, 654, *i.e.* A.D. 762.—"Dvīpavaram **Yavākhyam** atulan dhân-yādivājâihikam sampannam kanakākaraih" . . . *i.e.* the incomparable splendid island called **Java**, excessively rich in grain and other seeds, and well provided with gold-mines."—*Inscription in Batavia Museum* (see above).

943.—"Eager . . . to study with my own eyes the peculiarities of each country, I have with this object visited Sind and Zanj, and Sanf (see **CHAMPA**) and Sīn (China), and **Zābaj**."—*Maṣ'ūdī*, i. 5.

,, "This Kingdom (India) borders upon that of **Zābaj**, which is the empire of the *Mahrāj*, King of the Isles."—*Ibid.* 163.

992.—"**Djava** is situated in the Southern Ocean. . . . In the 12th month of the year (992) their King *Maradja* sent an embassy . . . to go to court and bring tribute."—*Groeneveldt's Notes from Chinese Sources*, pp. 15-17.

1298.—"When you sail from Ziamba (Chamba) 1500 miles in a course between south and south-east, you come to a very great island called **Java**, which, according to the statement of some good mariners, is the greatest Island that there is in the world, seeing that it has a compass of more than 3000 miles, and is under the dominion of a great king. . . . Pepper, nutmegs, spike, galanga, cubebs, cloves, and all the other good spices are produced in this island, and it is visited by many ships with quantities of merchandise from which they make great profits and gain, for such an amount of gold is found there that no one would believe it or venture to tell it."—*Marco Polo*, in *Ramusio*, ii. 51.

c. 1330.—"In the neighbourhood of that realm is a great island, **Java** by name, which hath a compass of a good 3000 miles. Now this island is populous exceedingly, and is the second best of all islands that exist. . . . The King of this island hath a palace which is truly marvellous. . . . Now the great Khan of Cathay many a time engaged in war with this King; but this King always vanquished and got the better of him."—*Friar Odoric*, in *Cathay*, &c., 87-89.

c. 1349.—"She clandestinely gave birth to a daughter, whom she made when grown up Queen of the finest island in the world, **Saba** by name. . . ."—*John de' Marignolli*, *ibid.* 391.

c. 1444.—"Sunt insulae duae in interiori India, e pene extremis orbis finibus, ambae **Java** nomine, quarum altera tribus, altera duobus millibus milliarum protenditur orientem versus; sed Majoris, Minorisque cognomine discernuntur."—*N. Conti*, in *Poggius, De Var. Fortunae*.

1503.—The Syrian Bishops Thomas, Jaballaha, Jacob, and Denha, sent on a mission to India in 1503 by the (Nestorian) Patriarch Elias, were ordained to go "to the land of the Indians and the islands of the seas which are between **Dabag** and Sin and Masin (see **MACHEEN**)."—*Assemani*, III. Pt. i. 592. This *Dabag* is probably a relic of the *Zābaj* of the *Relation*, of Maṣ'ūdī, and of Al-birūnī.

1516.—"Further on . . . there are many islands, small and great, amongst which is one very large which they call **Java** the Great. . . . They say that this island is the most abundant country in the world. . . . There grow pepper, cinnamon, ginger, bamboos, cubebs, and gold. . . ."—*Barbosa*, 197.

Referring to Sumatra, or the Archipelago in general.

Saka, 578, *i.e.* A.D. 656.—"The Prince Adityadharma is the Deva of the First **Java** Land (*prathama* **Yava**-*bhū*). May he be great! Written in the year of Saka, 578. May it be great!"—From a *Sanskrit Inscription from* Pager-Ruyong, *in* Menang Karbau (Sumatra), publd. by *Friedrich*, in the *Batavian Transactions*, vol. xxiii.

1224.—"**Ma'bar** (q.v.) is the last part of India; then comes the country of China (*Sīn*), the first part of which is **Jāwa**, reached by a difficult and fatal sea."—*Yākūt*, i. 516.

,, "This is some account of remotest *Sīn*, which I record without vouching for its truth . . . for in sooth it is a far off land. I have seen no one who had gone to it and penetrated far into it; only the merchants seek its outlying parts, to wit the country known as **Jāwa** on the sea-coast, like to India; from it are brought Aloeswood (*'ūd*), camphor, and nard (*sunbul*), and clove, and mace (*basbāsa*), and China drugs, and vessels of china-ware."—*Ibid.* iii. 445.

Kazwīnī speaks in almost the same words of **Jāwa**. He often copies Yākūt, but perhaps he really means his own time (for he uses different words) when he says: "Up to this time the merchants came no further into China than to this country (**Jāwa**) on account of the distance and difference of religion"—ii. 18.

1298.—"When you leave this Island of Pentam and sail about 100 miles, you reach the Island of **Java** the Less. For all its name 'tis none so small but that it has a compass of 2000 miles or more. . . ." &c.—*Marco Polo*, bk. iii. ch. 9.

c. 1300.—". . . In the mountains of **Jáva** scented woods grow. . . . The mountains of **Jáva** are very high. It is the custom of the people to puncture their hands and entire body with needles, and then rub in some black substance."—*Rashīd-uddīn*, in *Elliot*, i. 71.

1328.—"There is also another exceeding great island, which is called **Jaua**, which is in circuit more than seven [thousand?] miles as I have heard, and where are many world's wonders. Among which, besides the finest aromatic spices, this is one, to wit, that there be found pygmy men. . . . There are also trees producing cloves, which when they are in flower emit an odour so pungent that they kill every man who cometh among them, unless he shut his mouth and nostrils. . . . In a certain part of that island they delight to eat white and fat men when they can get them. . . ."—*Friar Jordanus*, 30-31.

c. 1330.—"Parmi les isles de la Mer de l'Inde il faut citer celle de **Djâwah**, grande isle célèbre par l'abondance de ses drogues . . . au sud de l'isle de **Djâwah** on remarque la ville de Fansour, d'où le camphre Fansoûri tire son nom."—*Géog. d'Aboulfeda*, II. pt. ii. 127. [See **CAMPHOR**].

c. 1346.—"After a passage of 25 days we arrived at the Island of **Jāwa**, which gives its name to the *lubān jāwiy* (see **BENJAMIN**). . . . We thus made our entrance into the capital, that is to say the city of Sumatra; a fine large town with a wall of wood and towers also of wood."—*Ibn Batuta*, iv. 228-230.

1553.—"And so these, as well as those of the interior of the Island (Sumatra), are all dark, with lank hair, of good nature and countenance, and not resembling the Javanese, although such near neighbours, indeed it is very notable that at so small a distance from each other their nature should vary so much, all the more because all the people of this Island call themselves by the common name of **Jawis** (*Jaüijs*), because they hold it for certain that the Javanese (*os* **Jāos**) were formerly lords of this great Island. . . ."—*Barros*, III. v. 1.

1555.—"Beyond the Island of **Iaua** they sailed along by another called Bali; and then came also vnto other called Aujaue, Cambaba, Solor. . . . The course by these Islands is about 500 leagues. The ancient cosmographers call all these Islands by the name **Iauos**; but late experience hath found the names to be very diuers as you see."—*Antonio Galvano*, old E.T. in *Hakl.* iv. 423.

1856.—
"It is a saying in Goozerat,—
'Who goes to **Java**
Never returns.
If by chance he return,
Then for two generations to live upon,
Money enough he brings back.'"
Râs Mâlâ, ii. 82; [ed. 1878, p. 418].

JAVA-RADISH, s. A singular variety (*Raphanus caudatus*, L.) of the common radish (*R. sativus*, L.), of which the pods, which attain a foot in length, are eaten and not the root. It is much cultivated in Western India, under the name of *mugra* [see *Baden-Powell, Punjab Products*, i. 260]. It is curious that the Hind. name of the common radish is *mūlī*, from *mūl*, 'root,' exactly analogous to *radish* from *radix*.

[**JAVA-WIND**, s. In the Straits Settlements an unhealthy south wind blowing from the direction of Java is so called. (Compare **SUMATRA**, b.)]

JAWAUB, s. Hind. from Ar. *jawāb*, 'an answer.' In India it has besides this ordinary meaning, that of 'dismissal.' And in Anglo-Indian colloquial it is especially used for a lady's refusal of an offer; whence the verb passive '*to be jawaub'd*.' [The **Jawaub** Club consisted of men who had been at least half a dozen times '*jawaub'd*.'

1830.—"'The **Juwawb'd Club**,' asked Elsmere, with surprise, 'what is that?'
"''Tis a fanciful association of those melancholy candidates for wedlock who have fallen in their pursuit, and are smarting under the sting of rejection.'"—*Orient. Sport. Mag.*, reprint 1873, i. 424.]

Jawāb among the natives is often applied to anything erected or planted for a symmetrical double, where

"Grove nods at grove, each alley has a brother,
And half the platform just reflects the other."

"In the houses of many chiefs every picture on the walls has its **jawab** (or duplicate). The portrait of Scindiah now in my dining-room was the **jawab** (copy in fact) of Mr. C. Landseer's picture, and hung opposite to the original in the Darbar room" (*M.-Gen. Keatinge*). ["The masjid with three domes of white marble occupies the left wing and has a counterpart (**jawāb**) in a precisely similar building on the right hand side of the Tāj. This last is sometimes called the false masjid; but it is in no sense dedicated to religious purposes."—*Führer, Monumental Antiquities, N.W.P.*, p. 64.]

JAY, s. The name usually given by Europeans to the *Coracias Indica*, Linn., the *Nīlkanṭh*, or 'blue-throat' of the Hindus, found all over India.

[1878.—"They are the commonality of birddom, who furnish forth the mobs which bewilder the drunken-flighted **jay** when he jerks, shrieking in a series of blue hyphen-flashes through the air. . . ."—*Ph. Robinson, In My Indian Garden*, 3.]

JEEL, s. Hind. *jhīl*. A stagnant sheet of inundation; a mere or lagoon. Especially applied to the great sheets of remanent inundation in Bengal. In Eastern Bengal they are also called **bheel** (q.v).

[1757.—"Towards five the guard waked me with notice that the Nawab would presently pass by to his palace of Mootee **jeel**."—*Holwell's Letter* of Feb. 28, in *Wheeler, Early Records*, 250.]

The *Jhīls* of Silhet are vividly and most accurately described (though the word is not used) in the following passage:—

c. 1778.—"I shall not therefore be disbelieved when I say that in pointing my boat towards Sylhet I had recourse to my compass, the same as at sea, and steered a straight course through a lake not less than 100 miles in extent, occasionally passing through villages built on artificial mounds: but so scanty was the ground that each house had a canoe attached to it."—*Hon. Robert Lindsay*, in *Lives of the Lindsays*, iii. 166.

1824.—"At length we . . . entered what might be called a sea of reeds. It was, in fact, a vast **jeel** or marsh, whose tall rushes rise above the surface of the water, having depth enough for a very large vessel. We sailed briskly on, rustling like a greyhound in a field of corn."—*Heber*, i. 101.

1850.—"To the geologist the **Jheels** and Sunderbunds are a most instructive region, as whatever may be the mean elevation of their waters, a permanent depression of 10 to 15 feet would submerge an immense tract."—*Hooker's Himalayan Journals*, ed. 1855, ii. 265.

1885.—"You attribute to me an act, the credit of which was due to Lieut. George Hutchinson, of the late Bengal Engineers.* That able officer, in company with the late Colonel Berkley, H.M. 32nd Regt., laid out the defences of the Alum Bagh camp, remarkable for its bold plan, which was so well devised that, with an apparently dangerous extent, it was defensible at every point by the small but ever ready force under Sir James Outram. A long interval . . . was defended by a post of support called 'Moir's Picket' . . . covered by a wide expanse of **jheel**, or lake, resulting from the rainy season. Foreseeing the probable drying up of the water, Lieut. Hutchinson, by a clever inspiration, marched all the transport elephants through and through the lake, and when the water disappeared, the dried clay-bed, pierced into a honey-combed surface of circular holes a foot in diameter and two or more feet deep, became a better protection against either cavalry or infantry than the water had been. . . ."—*Letter* to Lt.-Col. P. R. Innes from *F. M. Lord Napier of Magdāla*, dd. April 15.

Jeel and **bheel** are both applied to the artificial lakes in Central India and Bundelkhand.

JEETUL, s. Hind. *jītal*. A very old Indian denomination of copper coin, now entirely obsolete. It long survived on the western coast, and the name was used by the Portuguese for one of their small copper coins in the forms *ceitils* and *zoitoles*. It is doubtful, however, if *ceitil* is the same word. At least there is a medieval Portuguese coin called *ceitil* and *ceptil* (see *Fernandes*, in *Memorias da Academia Real das Sciencias de Lisboa*, 2da Classe, 1856); this may have got confounded with the Indian **Jital**. The *jītal* of the Delhi coinage of Alā-ud-dīn (c. 1300) was, according to Mr. E. Thomas's calculations, $\frac{1}{64}$ of the silver *tanga*, the coin called in later days the rupee. It was therefore just the equivalent of our modern *pice*. But of course, like most modern denominations of coin, it has varied greatly.

c. 1193-4.—"According to Ḳutb-ud-Dīn's command, Nizam-ud-Dīn Mohammad, on his return, brought them [the two slaves] along with him to the capital, Dihli; and Malik Ḳutb-ud-Dīn purchased both the Turks for the sum of 100,000 **jitals**."—*Raverty, Ṭabaḳāt-i-Nāṣiri*, p. 603.

c. 1290.—"In the same year . . : there was dearth in Dehli, and grain rose to a **jital** per sír (see **SEER**)."—*Ẓiāh-ud-dín Barní*, in *Elliot*, iii. 146.

* Afterwards M.-Gen. G. Hutchinson, C.B., C.S.I., Sec. to the Ch. Missy. Society.

c. 1340.—"The dirhem *sultānī* is worth ⅛ of the dirhem *shashtānī* . . . and is worth 3 *fals*, whilst the **jītal** is worth 4 *fals*; and the dirhem *hashtkānī*, which is exactly the silver dirhem of Egypt and Syria, is worth 32 *fals*."—*Shihābuddīn*, in *Notices et Extraits*, xiii. 212.

1554.—In Sunda. "The cash (*caixas*) here go 120 to the tanga of silver; the which *caixas* are a copper money larger than **ceitils**, and pierced in the middle, which they say have come from China for many years, and the whole place is full of them."—*A. Nunes*, 42.

c. 1590.—"For the purpose of calculation the dam is divided into 25 parts, each of which is called a **jétal**. This imaginary division is only used by accountants."—*Āīn*, ed. *Blochmann*, i. 31.

1678.—"48 **Juttals**, 1 *Pagod*, an Imaginary Coin."—*Fryer* (at Surat), 206.

c. 1750-60.—"At Carwar 6 pices make the **juttal**, and 48 **juttals** a Pagoda."—*Grose*, i. 282.

JEHAUD, s. Ar. *jihād*, ['an effort, a striving']; then a sacred war of Musulmans against the infidel; which Sir Herbert Edwardes called, not very neatly, 'a crescentade.'

[c. 630 A.D.—"Make war upon such of those to whom the Scriptures have been given who believe not in God, or in the last day, and who forbid not that which God and his Prophet have forbidden, and who profess not the profession of the truth, until they pay tribute (*jizyah*) out of hand, and they be humbled."—*Korān*, Surah ix. 29.]

1880.—"When the Athenians invaded Ephesus, towards the end of the Peloponnesian War, Tissaphernes offered a mighty sacrifice at Artemis, and raised the people in a sort of **Jehad**, or holy war, for her defence."—*Sat. Review*, July 17, 84*b*.

[1901.—"The matter has now assumed the aspect of a '**Schad**,' or holy war against Christianity."—*Times*, April 4.]

JELAUBEE, s. Hind. *jalebī*, [which is apparently a corruption of the Ar. *zalābiya*, P. *zalībiya*]. A rich sweetmeat made of sugar and ghee, with a little flour, melted and trickled into a pan so as to form a kind of interlaced work, when baked.

[1870.—"The poison is said to have been given once in sweetmeats, **Jelabees**."—*Chevers, Med. Jurisp.* 178.]

JELLY, s. In South India this is applied to vitrified brick refuse used as metal for roads. [The *Madras Gloss.* gives it as a synonym for **kunkur**.] It would appear from a remark of C. P. Brown (MS. notes) to be Telugu *zalli*, Tam. *shalli*, which means properly '*shivers*, bits, pieces.'

[1868.—". . . anicuts in some instances coated over the crown with **jelly** in chunam."—*Nelson, Man. of Madura*, Pt. v. 53.]

JELUM, n.p. The most westerly of the "Five Rivers" that give their name to the **Punjab** (q.v.), (among which the Indus itself is not usually included). Properly *Jailam* or *Jīlam*, now apparently written *Jhīlam*, and taking this name from a town on the right bank. The Jhilam is the Ὑδάσπης of Alexander's historians, a name corrupted from the Skt. *Vitastā*, which is more nearly represented by Ptolemy's Βιδάσπης. A still further (Prakritic) corruption of the same is *Behat* (see **BEHUT**).

1037.—"Here he (Mahmūd) fell ill, and remained sick for fourteen days, and got no better. So in a fit of repentance he forswore wine, and ordered his servants to throw all his supply . . . into the **Jailam** . . ."—*Baihaķī*, in *Elliot*, ii. 139.

c. 1204.—". . . in the height of the conflict, Shams-ud-dīn, in all his panoply, rode right into the water of the river **Jīlam** . . . and his warlike feats while in that water reached such a pitch that he was despatching those infidels from the height of the waters to the lowest depths of Hell . . ."—*Ṭabaķāt*, by *Raverty*, 604-5.

1856.—
"Hydaspes! often have thy waves run tuned
To battle music, since the soldier King,
The Macedonian, dipped his golden casque
And swam thy swollen flood, until the time
When Night the peace-maker, with pious hand,
Unclasping her dark mantle, smoothed it soft
O'er the pale faces of the brave who slept
Cold in their clay, on Chillian's bloody field."
The Banyan Tree.

JEMADAR, JEMAUTDAR, &c. Hind. from Ar.—P. *jama'dar*, *jama'* meaning 'an aggregate,' the word indicates generally, a leader of a body of individuals. [Some of the forms are as if from Ar.—P. *jamā'at*, 'an assemblage.'] Technically, in the Indian army, it is the title of the second rank of native officer in a company of sepoys, the Sūbadār (see **SOUBADAR**) being the first. In this sense the word dates from the re-organisation of the army in 1768. It is also applied to certain officers of police (under the *dārogha*), of the customs, and of other civil departments. And in larger domestic establishments there is often a *jemadār*, who is over the servants generally, or over the stables, camp service and orderlies. It is also an honorific title often used by the other household servants in addressing the *bihishtī* (see **BHEESTY**).

1752.—"The English battalion no sooner quitted Tritchinopoly than the regent set about accomplishing his scheme of surprising the City, and . . . endeavoured to gain 500 of the Nabob's best peons with firelocks. The **jemautdars**, or captains of these troops, received his bribes and promised to join." —*Orme*, ed. 1803, i. 257.

1817.—". . . Calliaud had commenced an intrigue with some of the **jematdars**, or captains of the enemy's troops, when he received intelligence that the French had arrived at Trichinopoly."—*Mill*, iii. 175.

1824. — "'Abdullah' was a Mussulman convert of Mr. Corrie's, who had travelled in Persia with Sir Gore Ouseley, and accompanied him to England, from whence he was returning . . . when the Bishop took him into his service as a '**jemautdar**,' or head officer of the peons."—Editor's note to *Heber*, ed. 1844, i. 65.

[1826.—"The principal officers are called **Jummahdars**, some of whom command five thousand horse." — *Pandurang Hari*, ed. 1873, i. 56.]

JENNYE, n.p. Hind. *Janaī*. The name of a great river in Bengal, which is in fact a portion of the course of the Brahmaputra (see **BURRAMPOOTER**), and the conditions of which are explained in the following passage written by one of the authors of this Glossary many years ago: "In Rennell's time, the Burrampooter, after issuing westward from the Assam valley, swept south-eastward, and forming with the Ganges a fluvial peninsula, entered the sea abreast of that river below Dacca. And so almost all English maps persist in representing it, though this eastern channel is now, unless in the rainy season, shallow and insignificant; the vast body of the Burrampooter cutting across the neck of the peninsula under the name of **Jenai**, and uniting with the Ganges near Pubna (about 150 miles N.E. of Calcutta), from which point the two rivers under the name of Pudda (*Padda*) flow on in mighty union to the sea." (*Blackwood's Mag.*, March 1852, p. 338.)

The river is indicated as an offshoot of the Burrampooter in Rennell's Bengal Atlas (Map No. 6) under the name of **Jenni**, but it is not mentioned in his *Memoir of the Map of Hindostan*. The great change of the river's course was palpably imminent at the beginning of the last century; for Buchanan (c. 1809) says: "The river threatens to carry away all the vicinity of Dewangunj, and perhaps to force its way into the heart of Nator." (*Eastern India*, iii. 394; see also 377.) Nator or Nattore was the territory now called Rajshāhī District. The real direction of the change has been further south. The Janai is also called the *Jamunā* (see under **JUMNA**). Hooker calls it *Jummal* (?) noticing that the maps still led him to suppose the Burrampooter flowed 70 miles further east (see *Him. Journals*, ed. 1855, ii. 259).

JENNYRICKSHAW, s. Read Capt. Gill's description below. Giles states the word to be taken from the Japanese pronunciation of three characters, reading *jin-riki-sha*, signifying '*Man—Strength—Cart*.' The term is therefore, observes our friend E. C. Baber, an exact equivalent of "*Pullman-Car*"! The article has been introduced into India, and is now in use at Simla and other hill-stations. [The invention of the vehicle is attributed to various people—to an Englishman known as "Public-spirited Smith" (8 ser. *Notes and Queries*, viii. 325); to native Japanese about 1868-70, or to an American named Goble, "half-cobbler and half-missionary." See *Chamberlain, Things Japanese*, 3rd ed. 236 *seq.*]

1876.—"A machine called a **jinnyrickshaw** is the usual public conveyance of Shanghai. This is an importation from Japan, and is admirably adapted for the flat country, where the roads are good, and coolie hire cheap. . . . In shape they are like a buggy, but very much smaller, with room inside for one person only. One coolie goes into the shafts and runs along at the rate of 6 miles an hour; if the distance is long, he is usually accompanied by a companion who runs behind, and they take it in turn to draw the vehicle."—*W. Gill, River of Golden Sand*, i. 10. See also p. 163.

1880. — "The Kuruma or **jin-ri-ki-sha** consists of a light perambulator body, an adjustable hood of oiled paper, a velvet or cloth lining and cushion, a well for parcels under the seat, two high slim wheels, and a pair of shafts connected by a bar at the ends." —*Miss Bird, Japan*, i. 18.

[1885. — "We . . . got into **rickshaws** to make an otherwise impossible descent to the theatre." — *Lady Dufferin, Viceregal Life*, 89.]

JEZYA, s. Ar. *jizya*. The poll-tax which the Musulman law imposes on subjects who are not Moslem.

[c. 630 A.D. See under **JEHAUD**.]

c. 1300. — "The Kázi replied . . . 'No doctor but the great doctor (Hanifa) to whose school we belong, has assented to the imposition of **Jizya** on Hindus. Doctors of other schools allow of no alternative but "Death or Islam."'"—*Ẓiā-ud-dīn Barnī*, in *Elliot*, iii. 184.

1683. — "Understand what custome ye English paid formerly, and compare ye difference between that and our last order for taking custome and **Jidgea**. If they pay no more than they did formerly, they complain without occasion. If more, write what it is, and there shall be an abatement." —*Vizier's Letter to Nabob*, in *Hedges, Diary*, July 18; [Hak. Soc. i. 100].

1686.—"Books of accounts received from Dacca, with advice that it was reported at the Court there that the Poll-money or **Judgeea** lately ordered by the Mogul would be exacted of the English and Dutch. . . . Among the orders issued to Pattana Cossumbazar, and Dacca, instructions are given to the latter place not to pay the **Judgeea** or Poll-tax, if demanded."—*Ft. St. Geo. Consns.* (on Tour) Sept. 29 and Oct. 10; *Notes and Extracts*, No. i. p. 49.

1765.—"When the *Hindoo* Rajahs . . . submitted to *Tamarlane;* it was on these capital stipulations: That . . . the emperors should never impose the **jesserah** (or poll-tax) upon the Hindoos."—*Holwell, Hist. Events*, i. 37.

JHAUMP, s. A hurdle of matting and bamboo, used as a shutter or door. Hind. *jhānp*, Mahr. *jhānpa;* in connection with which there are verbs, Hind. *jhānp-nā*, *jhāpnā*, *ḍhānpnā*, 'to cover.' See *jhoprā*, s.v. **ak**; [but there seems to be no etymological connection].

JHOOM, s. *jhūm*. This is a word used on the eastern frontiers of Bengal for that kind of cultivation which is practised in the hill forests of India and Indo-China, under which a tract is cleared by fire, cultivated for a year or two, and then abandoned for another tract, where a like process is pursued. This is the *Kumari* (see **COOMRY**) of S.W. India, the *Chena* of Ceylon (see *Emerson Tennent*, ii. 463), the *toung-gyan* of Burma [*Gazetteer*, ii. 72, 757, the *dahya* of North India (Skt. *dah*, 'to burn'), *ponam* (Tam. *pun*, 'inferior'), or *ponacaud* (Mal. *punakkātu*, *pun*, 'inferior,' *kātu*, 'forest') of Malabar]. In the Philippine Islands it is known as *gainges;* it is practised in the Ardennes, under the name of *sartage*, and in Sweden under the name of *svedjande* (see *Marsh, Earth as Modified by Human Action*, 346).

[1800.—"In this hilly tract are a number of people . . . who use a kind of cultivation called the *Cotucadu*, which a good deal resembles that which in the Eastern parts of Bengal is called **Jumea**."—*Buchanan, Mysore*, ii. 177.]

1883. — "It is now many years since Government, seeing the waste of forest caused by **juming**, endeavoured to put a stop to the practice. . . . The people **jumed** as before, regardless of orders."—*Indian Agriculturist*, Sept. (Calcutta).

1885. — "**Juming** disputes often arose, one village against another, both desiring to **jum** the same tract of jungle, and these cases were very troublesome to deal with. The **juming** season commences about the middle of May, and the air is then darkened by the smoke from the numerous clearings. . . ." (Here follows an account of the process).—*Lt.-Col. Lewin, A Fly on the Wheel*, 348 *seqq.*

JIGGY-JIGGY, adv. Japanese equivalent for 'make haste!' The Chinese syllables *chih-chih*, given as the origin, mean 'straight, straight!' Qu. 'right ahead'? (*Bp. Moule*).

JILLMILL, s. Venetian shutters, or as they are called in Italy, *persiane*. The origin of the word is not clear. The Hind. word '*jhilmilā*' seems to mean 'sparkling,' and to have been applied to some kind of gauze. Possibly this may have been used for blinds, and thence transferred to shutters. [So Platts in his *H. Dict.*] Or it may have been an *onomatopoeia*, from the rattle of such shutters; or it may have been corrupted from a Port. word such as *janella*, 'a window.' All this is conjecture.

[1832.—"Besides the purdahs, the openings between the pillars have blinds neatly made of bamboo strips, wove together with coloured cords: these are called **jhillmuns** or cheeks" (see **CHICK, a**).—*Mrs. Meer Hassan Ali, Observations*, i. 306.]

1874.—"The front (of a Bengal house) is generally long, exhibiting a pillared verandah, or a row of French casements, and **jillmilled** windows."—*Calc. Review*, No. cxvii. 207.

JOCOLE, s. We know not what this word is; perhaps 'toys'? [Mr.

W. Foster writes: "On looking up the I.O. copy of the *Ft. St. George Consultations* for Nov. 22, 1703, from which Wheeler took the passage, I found that the word is plainly not **jocoles**, but **jocolet**, which is a not unusual form of **chocolate**." The *N.E.D.* s.v. *Chocolate*, gives as other forms *jocolatte*, *jacolatt*, *jocalat*.]

1703.—". . . sent from the Patriarch to the Governor with a small present of **jocoles**, oil, and wines."—In *Wheeler*, ii. 32.

JOGEE, s. Hind. *jogī*. A Hindu ascetic; and sometimes a 'conjuror.' From Skt. *yogīn*, one who practises the *yoga*, a system of meditation combined with austerities, which is supposed to induce miraculous power over elementary matter. In fact the stuff which has of late been propagated in India by certain persons, under the names of theosophy and esoteric Buddhism, is essentially the doctrine of the Jogis.

1298.—"There is another class of people called **Chughi** who . . . form a religious order devoted to the Idols. They are extremely long-lived, every man of them living to 150 or 200 years . . . there are certain members of the Order who lead the most ascetic life in the world, going stark naked."—*Marco Polo*, 2nd ed. ii. 351.

1343.—"We cast anchor by a little island near the main, **Anchediva** (q.v.), where there was a temple, a grove, and a tank of water. . . . We found a **jogī** leaning against the wall of a *budkhāna* or temple of idols" (respecting whom he tells remarkable stories).—*Ibn Batuta*, iv. 62-63, and see p. 275.

c. 1442.—"The Infidels are divided into a great number of classes, such as the Bramins, the **Joghis** and others."—*Abdurrazzāk*, in *India in the XVth Cent.*, 17.

1498.—"They went and put in at Angediva . . . there were good water-springs, and there was in the upper part of the island a tank built with stone, with very good water and much wood . . . there were no inhabitants, only a beggar-man whom they call **joguedes**."—*Correa*, by *Lord Stanley*, 239. Compare Ibn Batuta above. After 150 years, tank, grove, and **jogi** just as they were!

1510.—"The King of the **Ioghe** is a man of great dignity, and has about 30,000 people, and he is a pagan, he and all his subjects; and by the pagan Kings he and his people are considered to be saints, on account of their lives, which you shall hear . . ."—*Varthema*, p. 111. Perhaps the chief of the *Gorakhnātha* Gosains, who were once very numerous on the West Coast, and have still a settlement at Kadri, near Mangalore. See *P. della Valle's* notice below.

1516.—"And many of them noble and respectable people, not to be subject to the Moors, go out of the Kingdom, and take the habit of poverty, wandering the world . . . they carry very heavy chains round their necks and waists, and legs; and they smear all their bodies and faces with ashes. . . . These people are commonly called **jogues**, and in their own speech they are called *Zoame* (see **SWAMY**) which means Servant of God. . . . These **jogues** eat all meats, and do not observe any idolatry."—*Barbosa*, 99-100.

1553.—"Much of the general fear that affected the inhabitants of that city (Goa before its capture) proceeded from a Gentoo, of Bengal by nation, who went about in the habit of a **Jogue**, which is the straitest sect of their Religion . . . saying that the City would speedily have a new Lord, and would be inhabited by a strange people, contrary to the will of the natives."—*De Barros*, Dec. II. liv. v. cap. 3.

" "For this reason the place (Adam's Peak) is so famous among all the Gentiledom of the East yonder, that they resort thither as pilgrims from more than 1000 leagues off, and chiefly those whom they call **Jógues**, who are as men who have abandoned the world and dedicated themselves to God, and make great pilgrimages to visit the Temples consecrated to him."—*Ibid.* Dec. III. liv. ii. cap. 1.

1563.—". . . to make them fight, like the *cobras de capello* which the **jogues** carry about asking alms of the people, and these **jogues** are certain heathen (*Gentios*) who go begging all about the country, powdered all over with ashes, and venerated by all the poor heathen, and by some of the Moors also. . . ."—*Garcia*, f. 156*v*, 157.

[1567.—"**Jogues**." See under **CASIS**.

[c. 1610.—"The Gentiles have also their Abedalles (*Abd-Allah*), which are like to our hermits, and are called **Joguies**."—*Pyrard de Laval*, Hak. Soc. i. 343.]

1624.—"Finally I went to see the King of the **Jogis** (Gioghi) where he dwelt at that time, under the shade of a cottage, and I found him roughly occupied in his affairs as a man of the field and husbandman . . . they told me his name was *Batinata*, and that the hermitage and the place generally was called Cadira (*Kadrī*)."—*P. della Valle*, ii. 724; [Hak. Soc. ii. 350, and see i. 37, 75].

[1667.—"I allude particularly to the people called **Jauguis**, a name which signifies 'united to God.'"—*Bernier*, ed. *Constable*, 316.]

1673.—"Near the Gate in a Choultry sate more than Forty naked **Jougies**, or men united to God, covered with Ashes and pleited Turbats of their own Hair."—*Fryer*, 160.

1727.—"There is another sort called **Jougies**, who . . . go naked except a bit of Cloth about their Loyns, and some deny themselves even that, delighting in Nastiness, and an holy Obscenity, with a great

Show of Sanctity."—*A. Hamilton*, i. 152; [ed. 1744, i. 153].

1809.—

"Fate work'd its own the while. A band
Of **Yoguees**, as they roamed the land
Seeking a spouse for Jaga-Naut their God,
Stray'd to this solitary glade."
Curse of Kehama, xiii. 16.

c. 1812.—"Scarcely . . . were we seated when behold, there poured into the space before us, not only all the **Yogees**, Fakeers, and rogues of that description . . . but the King of the Beggars himself, wearing his peculiar badge."—*Mrs. Sherwood*, (describing a visit to Henry Martyn at Cawnpore), *Autobiog.*, 415.

"*Apnē gānw kā* **jogī** *ān gānw kā sidh.*" Hind. proverb: "The man who is a **jogi** in his own village is a deity in another."—Quoted by *Elliot*, ii. 207.

JOHN COMPANY, n.p. An old personification of the East India Company, by the natives often taken seriously, and so used, in former days. The term **Company** is still applied in Sumatra by natives to the existing (Dutch) Government (see *H. O. Forbes, Naturalist's Wanderings*, 1885, p. 204). [*Dohāī* **Company** *Bahādur kī* is still a common form of native appeal for justice, and **Company** *Bāgh* is the usual phrase for the public garden of a station. It has been suggested, but apparently without real reason, that the phrase is a corruption of **Company Jahān**, "which has a fine sounding smack about it, recalling Shāh Jehān and Jehāngīr, and the golden age of the Moguls" (*G. A. Sala*, quoted in *Notes and Queries*, 8 ser. ii. 37). And Sir G. Birdwood writes: "The earliest coins minted by the English in India were of copper, stamped with a figure of an irradiated *lingam*, the phallic 'Roi Soleil.' The mintage of this coin is unknown (? Madras), but without doubt it must have served to ingratiate us with the natives of the country, and may have given origin to their personification of the Company under the potent title of **Kumpani Jehan**, which, in English mouths, became 'John Company'" (*Report on Old Records*, 222, note).]

[1784.—"Further, I knew that as simple Hottentots and Indians could form no idea of the Dutch Company and its government and constitution, the Dutch in India had given out that this was one mighty ruling prince who was called **Jan** or **John**, with the surname Company, which also procured for them more reverence than if they could have actually made the people understand that they were, in fact, ruled by a company of merchants."—*Andreas Spurrmann, Travels to the Cape of Good Hope, the South-Polar Lands, and round the World*, p. 347; see 9 ser. *Notes and Queries*, vii. 34.]

1803.—(The Nawab) "much amused me by the account he gave of the manner in which my arrival was announced to him. . . . '*Lord Sahab Ka bhānja, Company ki nawasa teshrīf laid*'; literally translated, 'The Lord's sister's son, and the grandson of the **Company**, has arrived."—*Lord Vālentia*, i. 137.

1808.—"However the business is pleasant now, consisting principally of orders to countermand military operations, and preparations to save **Johnny Company's** cash."—*Lord Minto in India*, 184.

1818-19.—"In England the ruling power is possessed by two parties, one the King, who is Lord of the State, and the other the Honourable **Company**. The former governs his own country; and the latter, though only subjects, exceed the King in power, and are the directors of mercantile affairs."—*Sadāsukh*, in *Elliot*, viii. 411.

1826.—"He said that according to some accounts, he had heard the Company was an old Englishwoman . . . then again he told me that some of the Topee wallas say '**John Company**,' and he knew that *John* was a man's name, for his master was called John Brice, but he could not say to a certainty whether '*Company*' was a man's or a woman's name."—*Pandurang Hari*, 60; [ed. 1873, i. 83, in a note to which the phrase is said to be a corruption of *Joint Company*].

1836.—"The jargon that the English speak to the natives is most absurd. I call it '**John Company's English**,' which rather affronts Mrs. Staunton."—*Letters from Madras*, 42.

1852.—"**John Company**, whatever may be his faults, is infinitely better than Downing Street. If India were made over to the Colonial Office, I should not think it worth three years' purchase."—*Mem. Col. Mountain*, 293.

1888.—"It fares with them as with the sceptics once mentioned by a South-Indian villager to a Government official. Some men had been now and then known, he said, to express doubt if there were any such person as **John Company**; but of such it was observed that something bad soon happened to them."—*Sat. Review*, Feb. 14, p. 220.

JOMPON, s. Hind. *jānpān*, *japān*, [which are not to be found in Platt's *Dict.*]. A kind of sedan, or portable chair used chiefly by the ladies at the Hill Sanitaria of Upper India. It is carried by two pairs of men (who are called *Jomponnies, i.e. jānpānī* or *japānī*), each pair bearing on their shoulders a short bar from which the shafts of the chair are slung. There is some perplexity as to the origin of the word. For we find in Crawfurd's *Malay Dict.* "*Jampana* (Jav. *Jampona*), a kind of litter." Also the *Javanese Dict.* of P. Jansz (1876) gives: "*Djempånå*—dragstoel (*i.e.* portable chair), or sedan of a person of rank." [Klinkert has *jempana*, *djempana*, *sempana* as a State sedan-chair, and he connects *sempana* with Skt. *sam-panna*, 'that which has turned out well, fortunate.' Wilkinson has: "*jempana*, Skt.? a kind of State carriage or sedan for ladies of the court."] The word cannot, however, have been introduced into India by the officers who served in Java (1811-15), for its use is much older in the Himālaya, as may be seen from the quotation from P. Desideri.

It seems just possible that the name may indicate the thing to have been borrowed from *Japan*. But the fact that *dpyān* means 'hang' in Tibetan may indicate another origin.

Wilson, however, has the following: "*Jhámpán*, Bengali. A stage on which snake-catchers and other juggling vagabonds exhibit; a kind of sedan used by travellers in the Himalaya, written *Jámpaun* (?)." [Both Platts and Fallon give the word *jhappān* as Hind.; the former does not attempt a derivation; the latter gives Hind. *jhānp*, 'a cover,' and this on the whole seems to be the most probable etymology. It may have been originally in India, as it is now in the Straits, a closed litter for ladies of rank, and the word may have become appropriated to the open conveyance in which European ladies are carried.]

1716.—"The roads are nowhere practicable for a horseman, or for a **Jampan**, a sort of palankin."—Letter of *P. Ipolito Desideri*, dated April 10, in *Lettres Edif.* xv. 184.

1783.—(After a description) "... by these central poles the litter, or as it is here called, the **Sampan**, is supported on the shoulders of four men."—*Forster's Journey*, ed. 1808, ii. 3.

[1822.—"The **Chumpaun**, or as it is more frequently called, the **Chumpala**, is the usual vehicle in which persons of distinction, especially females, are carried...."—*Lloyd, Gerard, Narr.* i. 105.

[1842.—"... a conveyance called a **Jaumpaun**, which is like a short palankeen, with an arched top, slung on three poles (like what is called a **Tonjon** in India)...."—*Elphinstone, Caubul*, ed. 1842, i. 137.

[1849.—"A **Jhappan** is a kind of arm chair with a canopy and curtains; the canopy, &c., can be taken off."—*Mrs. Mackenzie, Life in the Mission*, ii. 103.]

1879.—"The gondola of Simla is the '**jampan**' or 'jampot, as it is sometimes called, on the same linguistic principle ... as that which converts asparagus into sparrow-grass.... Every lady on the hills keeps her **jampan** and **jampanees** ... just as in the plains she keeps her carriage and footmen."—Letter in *Times*, Aug. 17.

JOOL, JHOOL, s. Hind. *jhūl*, supposed by Shakespear (no doubt correctly) to be a corrupt form of the Ar. *jull*, having much the same meaning; [but Platts takes it from *jhūlnā*, 'to dangle']. Housings, body clothing of a horse, elephant, or other domesticated animal; often a quilt, used as such. In colloquial use all over India. The modern Arabs use the plur. *jilāl* as a singular. This Dozy defines as "couverture en laine plus ou moins ornée de dessins, très large, très chaude et enveloppant le poitrail et la croupe du cheval" (exactly the Indian *jhūl*)—also "ornement de soie qu'on étend sur la croupe des chevaux aux jours de fête."

[1819.—"Dr. Duncan ... took the **jhool**, or broadcloth housing from the elephant. ..."—*Tod. Personal Narr.* in *Annals*, Calcutta reprint, i. 715.]

1880.—"Horse **Jhools**, &c., at shortest notice."—Advt. in *Madras Mail*, Feb. 13.

JOOLA, s. Hind. *jhūlā*. The ordinary meaning of the word is 'a swing'; but in the Himālaya it is specifically applied to the rude suspension bridges used there.

[1812.—"There are several kinds of bridges constructed for the passage of strong currents and rivers, but the most common are the *Sángha* and **Jhula**" (a description of both follows).—*Asiat. Res.* xi. 475.]

1830.—"Our chief object in descending to the Sutlej was to swing on a **Joolah** bridge. The bridge consists of 7 grass ropes, about twice the thickness of your thumb, tied to a single post on either bank. A piece of the hollowed trunk of a tree, half a yard long, slips upon these ropes, and from this 4 loops from the same grass rope depend. The passenger hangs in the loops, placing a couple of ropes under each thigh, and holds on by pegs in the block over his head; the signal is given, and he is drawn over by an eighth rope."—*Mem. of Col. Mountain*, 114.

JOSS, s. An idol. This is a corruption of the Portuguese *Deos*, 'God,' first taken up in the 'Pidgin' language of the Chinese ports from the Portuguese, and then adopted from that jargon by Europeans as if they had got hold of a Chinese word. [See **CHIN-CHIN.**]

1659.—"But the Devil (whom the Chinese commonly called **Joosje**) is a mighty and powerful Prince of the World."—*Walter Schulz*, 17.

" "In a four-cornered cabinet in their dwelling-rooms, they have, as it were, an altar, and thereon an image . . . this they call **Josin.**"—*Saar*, ed. 1672, p. 27:

1677.—"All the Sinese keep a limning of the Devil in their houses. . . . They paint him with two horns on his head, and commonly call him **Josie** (Joosje)."—*Gerret Vermeulen, Oost Indische Voyagie*, 33.

1711.—"I know but little of their Religion, more than that every Man has a small **Joss** or God in his own House."—*Lockyer*, 181.

1727.—"Their **Josses** or Demi-gods some of human shape, some of monstrous Figure."—*A. Hamilton*, ii. 266; [ed. 1744, ii. 265].

c. 1790.—

"Down with dukes, earls, and lords, those pagan **Josses**,
False gods! away with stars and strings and crosses."
Peter Pindar, Ode to Kien Long.

1798.—"The images which the Chinese worship are called **joostje** by the Dutch, and **joss** by the English seamen. The latter is evidently a corruption of the former, which being a Dutch nickname for the devil, was probably given to these idols by the Dutch who first saw them."—*Stavorinus*, E.T. i. 173.

This is of course quite wrong.

JOSS-HOUSE, s. An idol temple in China or Japan. From **joss**, as explained in the last article.

1750-52.—"The sailors, and even some books of voyages . . . call the pagodas **Yoss-houses**, for on enquiring of a Chinese for the name of the idol, he answers *Grande* **Yoss**, instead of *Gran Dios*."—*Olof. Toreen*, 232.

1760-1810.—"On the 8th, 18th, and 28th day of the Moon those foreign barbarians may visit the Flower Gardens, and the Honam **Joss-house**, but not in *droves* of over ten at a time."—'8 Regulations' at Canton, from *The Fankwae at Canton* (1882), p. 29.

1840.—"Every town, every village, it is true, abounds with **Joss-houses**, upon which large sums of money have been spent."—*Mem. Col. Mountain*, 186.

1876.—". . . the fantastic gables and tawdry ornaments of a large **joss-house**, or temple."—*Fortnightly Review*, No. cliii. 222.

1876:—

"One Tim Wang he makee-tlavel,
Makee stop one night in **Joss-house**."
Leland, Pidgin-English Sing-Song, p. 42.

Thus also in "pidgin," **Joss-house**-*man* or **Joss**-*pidgin-man* is a priest, or a missionary.

JOSTICK, JOSS-STICK, s. A stick of fragrant tinder (powdered *costus*, sandalwood, &c.) used by the Chinese as incense in their temples, and formerly exported for use as cigar-lights. The name appears to be from the temple use. (See **PUTCHOCK.**)

1876.—"Burnee **joss-stick**, talkee plitty."—*Leland, Pidgin-English Sing-Song*, p. 43.

1879.—"There is a recess outside each shop, and at dusk the **joss-sticks** burning in these fill the city with the fragrance of incense."—*Miss Bird, Golden Chersonese*, 49.

JOW, s. Hind. *jhāū*. The name is applied to various species of the shrubby tamarisk which abound on the low alluvials of Indian rivers, and are useful in many ways, for rough basket-making and the like. It is the usual material for gabions and fascines in Indian siege-operations.

[c. 1809.—". . . by the natives it is called **jhau**; but this name is generic, and is applied not only to another species of Tamarisk, but to the *Casuarina* of Bengal, and to the cone-bearing plants that have been introduced by Europeans."—*Buchanan-Hamilton, Eastern India*, iii. 597.

[1840.—". . . on the opposite **Jhow**, or bastard tamarisk jungle . . . a native . . . had been attacked by a tiger. . . ."—*Davidson, Travels*, ii. 326.]

JOWAULLA MOOKHEE, n.p. Skt.—Hind. *Jwālā-mukhī*, 'flame-mouthed'; a generic name for quasi-volcanic phenomena, but particularly applied to a place in the Kangra district of the Punjab mountain country, near the Biās River, where jets of gas issue from the ground and are kept constantly burning. There is a shrine of Devī, and it is a place of pilgrimage famous all over the Himālaya as well as in the plains of India. The famous fire-jets at Baku are sometimes visited by more adventurous Indian pilgrims, and known as the *Great* **Jwālā-mukhī**. The author of the following passage was evidently ignorant of the phenomenon worshipped, though the name indicates its nature.

c. 1360.—"Sultán Fíroz . . . marched with his army towards Nagarkot (see **NUGGURCOTE**) . . . the idol **Jwálá-mukhí**, much worshipped by the infidels, was situated on the road to Nagarkot. . . . Some of the infidels have reported that Sultán Fíroz went specially to see this idol, and held a golden umbrella over its head. But . . . the infidels slandered the Sultán. . . . Other infidels said that Sultán Muhammad Sháh bin Tughlik Sháh held an umbrella over this same idol, but this also is a lie. . . ."—*Shams-i-Siráj Afif*, in *Elliot*, iii. 318.

1616.—". . . a place called **Ialla mokee**, where out of cold Springs and hard Rocks, there are daily to be seene incessant Eruptions of Fire, before which the Idolatrous people fall doune and worship."—*Terry*, in *Purchas*, ii. 1467.

[c. 1617.—In *Sir T. Roe's* Map, "**Jallamakee**, the Pilgrimage of the Banians."—Hak. Soc. ii. 535.]

1783.—"At **Taullah Mhokee** (*sic*) a small volcanic fire issues from the side of a mountain, on which the Hindoos have raised a temple that has long been of celebrity, and favourite resort among the people of the Punjab."—*G. Forster's Journey*, ed. 1798, i. 308.

1799.—"Prason Poory afterwards travelled . . . to the Maha or Buree (*i.e.* larger) **Jowalla Mookhi** or Juâla Mûchi, terms that mean a 'Flaming Mouth,' as being a spot in the neighbourhood of Bakee (*Baku*) on the west side of the (Caspian) Sea . . . whence fire issues; a circumstance that has rendered it of great veneration with the Hindus."—*Jonathan Duncan*, in *As. Res.* v. 41.

JOWAUR, JOWARREE, s. Hind. *jawār*, *juār*, [Skt. *yava-prakāra* or *akāra*, 'of the nature of barley';] *Sorghum vulgare*, Pers. (*Holcus sorghum*, L.) one of the best and most frequently grown of the tall millets of southern countries. It is grown nearly all over India in the unflooded tracts; it is sown about July and reaped in November. The reedy stems are 8 to 12 feet high. It is the *cholam* of the Tamil regions. The stalks are **Kirbee**. The Ar. *dura* or *dhura* is perhaps the same word ultimately as *jawār;* for the old Semitic name is *dokn*, from the smoky aspect of the grain. It is an odd instance of the looseness which used to pervade dictionaries and glossaries that R. Drummond (*Illus. of the Gram. Parts of Guzerattee*, &c., Bombay, 1808) calls "**Jooar**, a kind of *pulse*, the food of the common people."

[c. 1590.—In Khandesh "**Jowári** is chiefly cultivated of which, in some places, there are three crops in a year, and its stalk is so delicate and pleasant to the taste that it is regarded in the light of a fruit."—*Āīn*, ed. *Jarrett*, ii. 223.]

1760.—"En suite mauvais chemin sur des levées faites de boue dans des quarrés de **Jouari** et des champs de *Nelis* (see **NELLY**) remplis d'eau."—*Anquetil du Perron*, I. ccclxxxiii.

1800.—". . . My industrious followers must live either upon **jowarry**, of which there is an abundance everywhere, or they must be more industrious in procuring rice for themselves."—*Wellington*, i. 175.

1813.—Forbes calls it "**juarree** or *cush-cush*" (?). [See **CUSCUS**.]—*Or. Mem.* ii. 406; [2nd ed. ii. 35, and i. 23].

1819.—"In 1797-8 **joiwaree** sold in the Muchoo Kaunta at six rupees per *culsee* (see **CULSEY**) of 24 maunds."—*Macmurdo*, in *Tr. Lit. Soc. Bo.* i. 287.

[1826.—"And the sabre began to cut away upon them as if they were a field of **Joanee** (standing corn)."—*Pandurang Hari*, ed. 1873 i. 66.]

JOY, s. This seems from the quotation to have been used on the west coast for *jewel* (Port. *joia*).

1810.—"The vanity of parents sometimes leads them to dress their children, even while infants, in this manner, which affords a temptation . . . to murder these helpless creatures for the sake of their ornaments or **joys**."—*Maria Graham*, 3.

JUBTEE, JUPTEE, &c., s. Guz. *japtī*, &c. Corrupt forms of *zabtī*. ["*Watan-zabtī*, or *-japtī*, Mahr., Produce of lands sequestered by the State, an item of revenue; in Guzerat the lands once exempt, now subject to assessment" (*Wilson*).] (See **ZUBT**.)

1808.—"The Sindias as Sovereigns of Broach used to take the revenues of *Moojmooadars* and *Desoys* (see **DESSAYE**) of that district every third year, amounting to Rs. 58,390, and called the periodical confiscation **Juptee**."—*R. Drummond*. [*Majmūadār* "in Guzerat the title given to the keepers of the pargana revenue records, who have held the office as a hereditary right since the settlement of Todar Mal, and are paid by fees charged on the villages." (*Wilson*)].

JUDEA, ODIA, &c., n.p. These names are often given in old writers to the city of *Ayuthia*, or *Ayodhya*, or *Yuthia* (so called apparently after the Hindu city of Rāma, *Ayodhya*, which we now call **Oudh**), which was the capital of Siam from the 14th century down to about 1767, when it was destroyed by the Burmese, and the Siamese royal residence was transferred to Bangkock [see **BANCOCK**.]

1522.—"All these cities are constructed like ours, and are subject to the King of Siam, who is named Siri Zacabedera, and who inhabits **Iudia**."—*Pigafetta*, Hak. Soc. 156.

c. 1546.—"The capitall City of all this Empire is **Odiaa**, whereof I haue spoken heretofore: it is fortified with walls of brick and mortar, and contains, according to some, foure hundred thousand fires, whereof an hundred thousand are strangers of divers countries."—*Pinto*, in *Cogan's* E.T. p. 285; orig. cap. clxxxix.

1553.—"For the Realm is great, and its Cities and Towns very populous; insomuch that the city **Hudia** alone, which is the capital of the Kingdom of Siam (*Sião*), and the residence of the King, furnishes 50,000 men of its own."—*Barros*, III. ii. 5.

1614.—"As regards the size of the City of **Odia** . . . it may be guessed by an experiment made by a curious engineer with whom we communicated on the subject. He says that . . . he embarked in one of the native boats, small, and very light, with the determination to go all round the City (which is entirely compassed by water), and that he started one day from the Portuguese settlement, at dawn, and when he got back it was already far on in the night, and he affirmed that by his calculation he had gone more than 8 leagues."—*Couto*, VI. vii. 9.

1617.—"The merchants of the country of **Lan John**, a place joining to the country of Jangama (see **JANGOMAY**) arrived at 'the city of **Judea**' before Eaton's coming away from thence, and brought great store of merchandize."—*Sainsbury*, ii. 90.

" "1 (letter) from Mr. Benjamyn Farry in **Judea**, at Syam."—*Cocks's Diary*, Hak. Soc. i. 272.

[1639.—"The chief of the Kingdom is **Iudia** by some called **Odia** . . . the city of **Iudia**, the ordinary Residence of the Court is seated on the Menam."—*Mandelslo, Travels*, E.T. ii. 122.

[1693.—"As for the City of Siam, the Siamese do call it **Si-yo-thi-ya**, the *o* of the syllable *yo* being closer than our (French) Diphthong *au*."—*La Loubère, Siam*, E.T. i. 7.]

1727.—". . . all are sent to the City of *Siam* or **Odia** for the King's Use. . . . The City stands on an Island in the River *Memnon*, which by Turnings and Windings, makes the distance from the Bar about 50 Leagues."—*A. Hamilton*, ii. 160; [ed. 1744].

[1774.—"**Ayuttaya** with its districts Dvaravati, **Yodaya** and Kamanpaik."—*Insc.* in *Ind. Antiq.* xxii. 4.

[1827.—"The powerful Lord . . . who dwells over every head in the city of the sacred and great kingdom of **Si-a-yoo-tha-ya**."—Treaty between E.I.C. and King of Siam, in *Wilson, Documents of the Burmese War*, App. lxxvii.]

JUGBOOLAK, s. Marine Hind. for *jack-block* (*Roebuck*).

JUGGURNAUT, n.p. A corruption of the Skt. *Jagannātha*, 'Lord of the Universe,' a name of Krishṇa worshipped as Vishṇu at the famous shrine of Pūrī in Orissa. The image so called is an amorphous idol, much like those worshipped in some of the South Sea Islands, and it has been plausibly suggested (we believe first by Gen. Cunningham) that it was in reality a Buddhist symbol, which has been adopted as an object of Brahmanical worship, and made to serve as the image of a god. The idol was, and is, annually dragged forth in procession on a monstrous car, and as masses of excited pilgrims crowded round to drag or accompany it, accidents occurred. Occasionally also persons, sometimes sufferers from painful disease, cast themselves before the advancing wheels. The testimony of Mr. Stirling, who was for some years Collector of Orissa in the second decade of the last century, and that of Sir W. W. Hunter, who states that he had gone through the MS. archives of the province since it became British, show that the popular impression in regard to the continued frequency of immolations on these occasions—a belief that has made *Juggurnaut* a standing metaphor—was greatly exaggerated. The belief indeed in the custom of such immolation had existed for centuries, and the rehearsal of these or other cognate religious suicides at one or other of the great temples of the Peninsula, founded partly on fact, and partly on popular report, finds a place in almost every old narrative relating to India. The really great mortality from hardship, exhaustion, and epidemic disease which frequently ravaged the crowds of pilgrims on such occasions, doubtless aided in keeping up the popular impressions in connection with the Juggurnaut festival.

[1311.—"**Jagnár.**" See under **MADURA**.]

c. 1321.—"Annually on the recurrence of the day when that idol was made, the folk of the country come and take it down, and put it on a fine chariot; and then the King and Queen, and the whole body of the people, join together and draw it forth from the church with loud singing of songs, and all kinds of music . . . and many pilgrims who have come to this feast cast themselves under the chariot, so that its wheels may go over them, saying that they desire to die for their god. And the car passes over them, and crushes them, and cuts them in sunder, and so they perish on the spot."—*Friar Odoric*, in *Cathay*, &c. i. 83.

c. 1430. — "In Bizenegalia (see **BISNAGAR**) also, at a certain time of the year, this idol is carried through the city, placed between two chariots . . . accompanied by a great concourse of people. Many, carried away by the fervour of their faith, cast themselves on the ground before the wheels, in order that they may be crushed to death, —a mode of death which they say is very acceptable to their god."—*N. Conti*, in *India in XVth Cent.*, 28.

c. 1581.—"All for devotion attach themselves to the trace of the car, which is drawn in this manner by a vast number of people . . . and on the annual feast day of the Pagod this car is dragged by crowds of people through certain parts of the city (Negapatam), some of whom from devotion, or the desire to be thought to make a devoted end, cast themselves down under the wheels of the cars, and so perish, remaining all ground and crushed by the said cars."—*Gasparo Balbi*, f. 84. The preceding passages refer to scenes in the south of the Peninsula.

c. 1590.—"In the town of Pursotem on the banks of the sea stands the temple of **Jagnaut**, near to which are the images of Kishen, his brother, and their sister, made of Sandal-wood, which are said to be 4,000 years old. . . . The Brahmins . . . at certain times carry the image in procession upon a carriage of sixteen wheels, which in the Hindooee language is called *Rahth* (see **RUT**); and they believe that whoever assists in drawing it along obtains remission of all his sins."—*Gladwin's Ayeen*, ii. 13-15; [ed. *Jarrett*, ii. 127].

[1616.—"The chief city called **Jekanat**." —*Sir T. Roe*, Hak. Soc. ii. 538.]

1632.—"Vnto this Pagod or house of Sathen . . . doe belong 9,000 Brammines or Priests, which doe dayly offer sacrifice vnto their great God **Iaggarnat**, from which Idoll the City is so called. . . . And when it (the chariot of *Iaggarnat*) is going along the city, there are many that will offer themselves a sacrifice to this Idoll, and desperately lye downe on the ground, that the Chariott wheeles may runne over them, whereby they are killed outright; some get broken armes, some broken legges, so that many of them are destroyed, and by this meanes they thinke to merit Heauen."—*W. Bruton*, in *Hakl.* v. 57.

1667.—"In the town of **Jagannat**, which is seated upon the Gulf of *Bengala*, and where is that famous Temple of the Idol of the same name, there is yearly celebrated a certain Feast. . . . The first day that they shew this Idol with Ceremony in the Temple, the Crowd is usually so great to see it, that there is not a year, but some of those poor Pilgrims, that come afar off, tired and harassed, are suffocated there; all the people blessing them for having been so happy. . . . And when this Hellish Triumphant Chariot marcheth, there are found (which is no Fable) persons so foolishly credulous and superstitious as to throw themselves with their bellies under those large and heavy wheels, which bruise them to death. . . ."—*Bernier, a Letter to Mr. Chapelain*, in Eng. ed. 1684, 97; [ed. *Constable*, 304 *seq.*].

[1669-79.—"In that great and Sumptuous Diabolicall Pagod, there Standeth theere gretest God **Jn°. Gernaet**, whence ye Pagod receued that name alsoe."—*MS. Asia*, &c., by *T. B.* f. 12. Col. Temple adds: "Throughout the whole MS. *Jagannāth* is repeatedly called *Jn°. Gernaet*, which obviously stands for the common transposition *Janganāth*.]

1682.—". . . We lay by last night till 10 o'clock this morning, ye Captain being desirous to see ye **Jagernot** Pagodas for his better satisfaction. . . ."—*Hedges, Diary*, July 16; [Hak. Soc. i. 30].

1727.—"His (**Jagarynat's**) Effigy is often carried abroad in Procession, mounted on a Coach four stories high . . . they fasten small Ropes to the Cable, two or three Fathoms long, so that upwards of 2,000 People have room enough to draw the Coach, and some old Zealots, as it passes through the Street, fall flat on the Ground, to have the Honour to be crushed to Pieces by the Coach Wheels."—*A. Hamilton*, i. 387; [ed. 1744].

1809.—

"A thousand pilgrims strain
Arm, shoulder, breast, and thigh, with might and main,
To drag that sacred wain,
And scarce can draw along the enormous load.
Prone fall the frantic votaries on the road,
And calling on the God
Their self-devoted bodies there they lay
To pave his chariot way.
On **Jaga-Naut** they call,
The ponderous car rolls on, and crushes all,
Through flesh and bones it ploughs its dreadful path.
Groans rise unheard; the dying cry.
And death, and agony
Are trodden under foot by yon mad throng,
Who follow close and thrust the deadly wheels along."

Curse of Kehama, xiv. 5.

1814.—"The sight here beggars all description. Though **Juggernaut** made some progress on the 19th, and has travelled daily ever since, he has not yet reached the place of his destination. His brother is ahead of him, and the lady in the rear. One woman has devoted herself under the wheels, and a shocking sight it was. Another also intended to devote herself, missed the wheels with her body, and had her arm broken. Three people lost their lives in the crowd."—In *Asiatic Journal*—quoted in *Beveridge, Hist. of India*, ii. 54, without exacter reference.

c. 1818. — "That excess of fanaticism which formerly prompted the pilgrims to court death by throwing themselves in crowds under the wheels of the car of

Jagannáth has happily long ceased to actuate the worshippers of the present day. During 4 years that I have witnessed the ceremony, three cases only of this revolting species of immolation have occurred, one of which I may observe is doubtful, and should probably be ascribed to accident; in the others the victims had long been suffering from some excruciating complaints, and chose this method of ridding themselves of the burthen of life in preference to other modes of suicide so prevalent with the lower orders under similar circumstances."—*A. Stirling*, in *As. Res.* xv. 324.

1827.—March 28th in this year, Mr. Poynder, in the E. I. Court of Proprietors, stated that "about the year 1790 no fewer than 28 Hindus were crushed to death at Ishera on the Ganges, under the wheels of **Juggurnaut.**"—*As. Journal*, 1821, vol. xxiii. 702.

[1864.—"On the 7th July 1864, the editor of the Friend of India mentions that, a few days previously, he had seen, near Serampore, two persons crushed to death, and another frightfully lacerated, having thrown themselves under the wheels of a car during the Rath Jatra festival. It was afterwards stated that this occurrence was accidental."—*Chevers, Ind. Med. Jurispr.* 665.]

1871.—". . . poor Johnny Tetterby staggering under his Moloch of an infant, the **Juggernaut** that crushed all his enjoyments."—*Forster's Life of Dickens*, ii. 415.

1876.—"Le monde en marchant n'a pas beaucoup plus de souci de ce qu'il écrase que le char de l'idole de **Jagarnata.**"—*E. Renan*, in *Revue des Deux Mondes*, 3e Série, xviii. p. 504.

JULIBDAR, s. Pers. *jilaudār*, from *jilau*, the string attached to the bridle by which a horse is led, the servant who leads a horse, also called *janībahdār*, *janībahkash*. In the time of Hedges the word must have been commonly used in Bengal, but it is now quite obsolete.

[c. 1590.—"For some time it was a rule that, whenever he (Akbar) rode out on a *khâçah* horse, a rupee should be given, viz., one dám to the Âtbegi, two to the **Jilaudár.** . . ."—*Āīn*, ed. *Blochmann*, i. 142. (And see under **PYKE.**)]

1673.—"In the heart of this Square is raised a place as large as a Mountebank's Stage, where the **Gelabdar**, or Master Muliteer, with his prime Passengers or Servants, have an opportunity to view the whole *Caphala.*"—*Fryer*, 341.

1683.—"Your **Jylibdar**, after he had received his letter would not stay for the Genll, but stood upon departure."—*Hedges, Diary*, Sept. 15; [Hak. Soc. i. 112].

,, "We admire what made you send peons to force our **Gyllibdar** back to your Factory, after he had gone 12 *cosses* on his way, and dismisse him again without any reason for it."—*Hedges, Diary*, Sept. 26; [Hak. Soc. i. 120].

1754.—"100 **Gilodar**; those who are charged with the direction of the couriers and their horses."—*Hanway's Travels*, i. 171; 252.

[1812.—"I have often admired the courage and dexterity with which the Persian **Jelowdars** or grooms throw themselves into the thickest engagement of angry horses."—*Morier, Journey through Persia*, 63 *seq.*]

1880.—"It would make a good picture, the surroundings of camels, horses, donkeys, and men. . . . Pascal and Remise cooking for me; the **Jellaodars**, enveloped in felt coats, smoking their kalliúns, amid the half-light of fast fading day. . . ."—*MS. Journal in Persia* of *Capt. W. Gill, R.E.*

JUMBEEA, s. Ar. *janbiya*, probably from *janb*, 'the side'; a kind of dagger worn in the girdle, so as to be drawn across the body. It is usually in form slightly curved. Sir R. Burton (*Camões, Commentary*, 413) identifies it with the *agomia* and *gomio* of the quotations below, and refers to a sketch in his *Pilgrimage*, but this we cannot find, [it is in the Memorial ed. i. 236], though the *jambiyah* is several times mentioned, *e.g.* i. 347, iii. 72. The term occurs repeatedly in Mr. Egerton's catalogue of arms in the India Museum. **Janbwa** occurs as the name of a dagger in the *Āīn* (orig. i. 119); why Blochmann in his translation [i. 110] spells it *jhanbwah* we do not know. See also Dozy and Eng. s.v. *jambette*. It seems very doubtful if the latter French word has anything to do with the Arabic word.

c. 1328.—"Takī-ud-dīn refused roughly and pushed him away. Then the maimed man drew a dagger (*khanjar*) such as is called in that country **janbiya**, and gave him a mortal wound."—*Ibn Batuta*, i. 534.

1498.—"The Moors had erected palisades of great thickness, with thick planking, and fastened so that we could not see them within. And their people paraded the shore with targets, azagays, **agomias**, and bows and slings from which they slung stones at us."—*Roteiro de Vasco da Gama*, 32.

1516.—"They go to fight one another bare from the waist upwards, and from the waist downwards wrapped in cotton cloths drawn tightly round, and with many folds, and with their arms, which are swords, bucklers, and daggers (**gomios**)."—*Barbosa*, p. 80.

1774.—"Autour du corps ils ont un ceinturon de cuir brodé, ou garni d'argent, au milieu duquel sur le devant ils passent un couteau large recourbé, et pointu (**jambea**), dont la pointe est tournée du côté droit."—*Niebuhr, Desc. de l'Arabie*, 54.

JUMDUD, s. H. *jamdad, jamdhar*. A kind of dagger, broad at the base and slightly curved, the hilt formed with a cross-grip like that of the *Katār* (see **KUTTAUR**). [A drawing of what he calls a *jamdhar katārī* is given in Egerton's *Catalogue* (Pl. IX. No. 344-5).] F. Johnson's Dictionary gives *jamdar* as a Persian word with the suggested etymology of *janb-dar*, 'flank-render.' But in the *Āīn* the word is spelt *jamdhar*, which seems to indicate Hind. origin; and its occurrence in the poem of Chand Bardāi (see *Ind. Antiq.* i. 281) corroborates this. Mr. Beames there suggests the etymology of *Yama-dant* 'Death's Tooth.' The drawings of the *jamdhad* or *jamdhar* in the *Āīn* illustrations show several specimens with double and triple toothed points, which perhaps favours this view; but *Yama-dhāra*, 'death-wielder,' appears in the Sanskrit dictionaries as the name of a weapon. [Rather, perhaps, *yama-dhara*, 'death-bearer.']

c. 1526.—"**Jamdher.**" See quotation under **KUTTAUR**.

[1813.—". . . visited the **jamdar** *khana*, or treasury containing his jewels . . . curious arms. . . ."—*Forbes, Or. Mem.* 2nd ed. ii. 469.]

JUMMA, s. Hind. from Ar. *jama'*. The total assessment (for land revenue) from any particular estate, or division of country. The Arab. word signifies 'total' or 'aggregate.'

1781.—"An increase of more than 26 *lacks* of rupees (was) effected on the former **jumma**."—*Fifth Report*, p. 8.

JUMMABUNDEE, s. Hind. from P.—Ar. *jama'bandī*. A **settlement** (q.v.), *i.e.* the determination of the amount of land revenue due for a year, or a period of years, from a village, estate, or parcel of land. [In the N.W.P. it is specially applied to the annual village rent-roll, giving details of the holding of each cultivator.]

[1765.—"The rents of the province, according to the **jumma-bundy**, or rent-roll . . . amounted to. . . ."—*Verelst, View of Bengal*, App. 214.

[1814.—"**Jummabundee.**" See under **PATEL**.]

JUMNA, n.p. The name of a famous river in India which runs by Delhi and Agra. Skt. *Yamunā*, Hind. *Jamunā* and *Jamnā*, the Διαμούνα of Ptolemy, the Ἰωβαρής of Arrian, the *Jomanes* of Pliny. The spelling of Ptolemy almost exactly expresses the modern Hind. form *Jamunā*. The name *Jamunā* is also applied to what was in the 18th century, an unimportant branch of the Brahmaputra R. which connected it with the Ganges, but which has now for many years been the main channel of the former great river. (See **JENNYE**.) *Jamunā* is the name of several other rivers of less note.

[1616-17.—"I proposed for a water worke, wch might giue the Chief Cittye of the *Mogores* content . . . wch is to be don vppon the Riuer **Ieminy** wch passeth by *Agra*. . . ."—*Birdwood, First Letter Book*, 460.

[1619.—"The river **Gemini** was vnfit to set a Myll vppon."—*Sir T. Roe*, Hak. Soc. ii. 477.

[1663.—". . . the **Gemna**, a river which may be compared to the Loire. . . ."—*Bernier, Letter to M. De la Mothe le Vayer*, ed. *Constable*, 241.]

[**JUMNA MUSJID**, n.p. A common corruption of the Ar. *jāme' masjid*, 'the cathedral or congregational mosque,' Ar. *jama'*, 'to collect.' The common form is supposed to represent some great mosque on the **Jumna** R.

[1785.—"The **Jumna**-musjid is of great antiquity. . . ."—*Diary*, in *Forbes, Or. Mem.* 2nd ed. ii. 448.

[1849.—"In passing we got out to see the **Jamna** Masjid, a very fine building now used as a magazine."—*Mrs. Mackenzie, Life in the Mission*, ii. 170.

[1865.—". . . the great mosque or **Djamia** '. . . this word **Djamia**' means literally 'collecting' or 'uniting,' because here attends the great concourse of Friday worshippers. . . ."—*Palgrave, Central and E. Arabia*, ed. 1868, 266.]

JUNGEERA, n.p., *i.e. Janjīrā*. The name of a native State on the coast, south of Bombay, from which the Fort and chief place is 44 m. distant. This place is on a small island, rising in the entrance to the Rājpurī inlet, to which the name Janjīrā properly pertains, believed to be a local corruption of the Ar. *jazīra*, 'island.' The State is also called *Habsān*, meaning '**Hubshee's** land,' from the fact that for 3 or 4 centuries its chief has been of that race. This was not at first continuous, nor have the chiefs, even when of African blood, been always of one family; but they have apparently been so for the last 200 years. 'The *Sīdī'* (see **SEEDY**) and 'The *Habshī*,' are titles popularly applied to this chief. This State has a port and some land in Kāthiāwār. Gen. Keatinge writes: "The members of the Sidi's family whom I saw were, for natives of India, particularly fair." The old Portuguese writers call this harbour *Danda* (or as they write it *Damda*), *e.g.* João de Castro in *Primeiro Roteiro*, p. 48. His rude chart shows the island-fort.

JUNGLE, s. Hind. and Mahr. *jangal*, from Skt. *jangala* (a word which occurs chiefly in medical treatises). The native word means in strictness only waste, uncultivated ground; then, such ground covered with shrubs, trees or long grass; and thence again the Anglo-Indian application is to forest, or other wild growth, rather than to the fact that it is not cultivated. A forest; a thicket; a tangled wilderness. The word seems to have passed at a rather early date into Persian, and also into use in Turkistan. From Anglo-Indian it has been adopted into French as well as in English. The word does not seem to occur in *Fryer*, which rather indicates that its use was not so extremely common among foreigners as it is now.

c. 1200.—". . . Now the land is humid, **jungle** (*jangalah*), or of the ordinary kind." —*Susruta*, i. ch. 35.

c. 1370.—"Elephants were numerous as sheep in the **jangal** round the Rái's dwelling."—*Tárikh-i-Firoz-Sháhi*, in *Elliot*, iii. 314.

c. 1450.—"The Kings of India hunt the elephant. They will stay a whole month or more in the wilderness, and in the **jungle** (*Jangal*)."—*Abdurrazāk*, in *Not. et Ext.* xiv. 51.

1474.—". . . Bicheneger. The vast city is surrounded by three ravines, and intersected by a river, bordering on one side on a dreadful **Jungel**."—*Ath. Nikitin*, in *India in XVth Cent.*, 29.

1776.—"Land waste for five years . . . is called **Jungle**."—*Halhed's Gentoo Code*, 190.

1809. — "The air of Calcutta is much affected by the closeness of the **jungle** around it."—*Ld. Valentia*, i. 207.

1809.—
"They built them here a bower of jointed cane,
Strong for the needful use, and light and long
Was the slight framework rear'd, with little pain;
Lithe creepers then the wicker sides supply,
And the tall **jungle** grass fit roofing gave
Beneath the genial sky."
Curse of Kehama, xiii. 7.

c. 1830.—"C'est là que je rencontrai les **jungles** . . . j'avoue que je fus très désappointé."—*Jacquemont, Correspond.* i. 134.

c. 1833-38.—
"L'Hippotame au large ventre
Habite aux **Jungles** de Java,
Où grondent, au fond de chaque antre
Plus de monstres qu'on ne rêva."
Theoph. Gautier, in *Poësies Complètes*, ed. 1876, i. 325.

1848.—"But he was as lonely here as in his **jungle** at Boggleywala." — *Thackeray, Vanity Fair*, ch. iii.

" " 'Was there ever a battle won like Salamanca? Hey, Dobbin? But where was it he learnt his art? In India, my boy. The **jungle** is the school for a general, mark me that.' "—*Ibid.*, ed. 1863, i. 312.

c. 1858.—
"La bête formidable, habitante des **jungles**
S'endort, le ventre en l'air, et dilate ses ongles."—*Leconte de Lisle.*

" "
"Des **djungles** du Pendj-Ab
Aux sables du Karnate."—*Ibid.*

1865.—"To an eye accustomed for years to the wild wastes of the **jungle**, the whole country presents the appearance of one continuous well-ordered garden." — *Waring, Tropical Resident at Home*, 7.

1867.—". . . here are no cobwebs of plea and counterplea, no **jungles** of argument and brakes of analysis."—*Swinburne, Essays and Studies*, 133.

1873.—"**Jungle**, derived to us, through the living language of India, from the Sanskrit, may now be regarded as good English." — *Fitz-Edward Hall, Modern English*, 306.

1878.—"Cet animal est commun dans les forêts, et dans les **djengles**."—*Marre, Kata-Kata-Malayou*, 83.

1879.—"The owls of metaphysics hooted from the gloom of their various **jungles**."—*Fortnightly Rev.* No. clxv., N.S., 19.

JUNGLE-FEVER, s. A dangerous remittent fever arising from the malaria of forest or jungle tracts.

1808.—"I was one day sent to a great distance, to take charge of an officer who had been seized by **jungle-fever**."—Letter in *Morton's L. of Leyden*, 43.

JUNGLE-FOWL, s. The popular name of more than one species of those birds from which our domestic poultry are supposed to be descended; especially *Gallus Sonneratii*, Temminck, the Grey *Jungle-fowl*, and *Gallus ferrugineus*, Gmelin, the Red *Jungle-fowl*. The former belongs only to Southern India; the latter from the Himālaya, south to the N. Circārs on the east, and to the Rājpīpla Hills south of the Nerbudda on the west.

1800.—". . . the thickets bordered on the village, and I was told abounded in **jungle-fowl**."—*Symes, Embassy to Ava*, 96.

1868.—"The common **jungle-cock** . . . was also obtained here. It is almost exactly like a common game-cock, but the voice is different."—*Wallace, Malay Archip.*, 108.

The word *jungle* is habitually used adjectively, as in this instance, to denote wild species, *e.g.* **jungle**-*cat*, **jungle**-*dog*, **jungle**-*fruit*, &c.

JUNGLE-MAHALS, n.p. Hind. *Jangal-Mahāl*. This, originally a vague name of sundry tracts and chieftainships lying between the settled districts of Bengal and the hill country of Chutiā Nāgpūr, was constituted a regular district in 1805, but again broken up and redistributed among adjoining districts in 1833 (see *Imperial Gazetteer*, s.v.).

JUNGLE-TERRY, n.p. Hind. *Jangal-tarāi* (see **TERAI**). A name formerly applied to a border-tract between Bengal and Behar, including the inland parts of Monghyr and Bhāgalpūr, and what are now termed the *Santāl Parganās*. Hodges, below, calls it to the "westward" of Bhāgalpūr; but Barkope, which he describes as near the centre of the tract, lies, according to Rennell's map, about 35 m. S.E. of Bhāgalpūr town; and the Cleveland inscription shows that the term included the tract occupied by the Rājmahāl hill-people. The Map No. 2 in Rennell's Bengal Atlas (1779) is entitled "the **Jungleterry** District, with the adjacent provinces of Birbhoom, Rajemal, Boglipour, &c., comprehending the countries situated between Moorshedabad and Bahar." But the map itself does not show the name *Jungle Terry* anywhere.

1781.—"Early in February we set out on a tour through a part of the country called the **Jungle-Terry**, to the westward of Bauglepore . . . after leaving the village of Barkope, which is nearly in the centre of the **Jungle Terry**, we entered the hills. . . . In the great famine which raged through Indostan in the year 1770 . . . the Jungle Terry is said to have suffered greatly."—*Hodges*, pp. 90-95.

1784.—"To be sold . . . that capital collection of Paintings, late the property of A. Cleveland, Esq., deceased, consisting of the most capital views in the districts of Monghyr, Rajemehal, Boglipoor, and the **Jungleterry**, by Mr. Hodges. . . ."—In *Seton-Karr*, i. 64.

c. 1788.—

"To the Memory of
Augustus Cleveland, Esq.,
Late Collector of the Districts of Bhaugulpore and Rajamahall,
Who without Bloodshed or the Terror of Authority,
Employing only the Means of Conciliation, Confidence, and Benevolence,
Attempted and Accomplished
The entire Subjection of the Lawless and Savage Inhabitants of the
Jungleterry of Rajamahall. . . ." (etc.)

Inscription on the Monument *erected by* Government *to* Cleveland, *who died in* 1784.

1817.—"These hills are principally covered with wood, excepting where it has been cleared away for the natives to build their villages, and cultivate *janaira* (**Jowaur**), plantains and yams, which together with some of the small grains mentioned in the account of the **Jungleterry**, constitute almost the whole of the productions of these hills."—*Sutherland's Report on the Hill People* (in App. to *Long*, 560).

1824.—"This part, I find (he is writing at Monghyr), is not reckoned either in Bengal or Bahar, having been, under the name of the **Jungleterry** district, always regarded, till its pacification and settlement, as a sort of border or debateable land."—*Heber*, i. 131.

JUNGLO, s. Guz. *Janglo*. This term, we are told by R. Drummond, was used in his time (the beginning of the 19th century), by the less polite, to distinguish Europeans; "wild men of the woods," that is, who did not understand Guzerati!

1808.—"Joseph Maria, a well-known scribe of the order of Topeewallas . . . was actually mobbed, on the first circuit of 1806, in the town of Pitlaud, by parties of curious old women and young, some of whom gazing upon him put the question, *Arê* **Jungla**, *too munne pirrneesh?* 'O wild one, wilt thou marry me?' He knew not what they asked, and made no answer, whereupon they declared that he was indeed a very *Jungla*, and it required all the address of Kripram (the worthy Brahmin who related this anecdote to the writer, uncontradicted in the presence of the said Senhor) to draw off the dames and damsels from the astonished Joseph."—*R. Drummond, Illns.* (s.v.).

JUNK, s. A large Eastern ship; especially (and in later use exclusively) a Chinese ship. This indeed is the earliest application also; any more general application belongs to an intermediate period. This is one of the oldest words in the Europeo-Indian vocabulary. It occurs in the travels of Friar Odorico, written down in 1331, and a few years later in the rambling reminiscences of John de' Marignolli. The great Catalan World-map of 1375 gives a sketch of one of those ships with their sails of bamboo matting and calls them **Inchi**, no doubt a clerical error for **Iūchi**. Dobner, the original editor of Marignolli, in the 18th century, says of the word (*junkos*): "This word I cannot find in any medieval glossary. Most probably we are to understand vessels of platted reeds (*a* juncis *texta*) which several authors relate to be used in India." It is notable that the same erroneous suggestion is made by Amerigo Vespucci in his curious letter to one of the Medici, giving an account of the voyage of Da Gama, whose squadron he had met at C. Verde on its way home.

The French translators of Ibn Batuta derive the word from the Chinese *tchouen* (*chwen*), and Littré gives the same etymology (s.v. *jonque*). It is possible that the word may be eventually traced to a Chinese original, but not very probable. The old Arab traders must have learned the word from Malay pilots, for it is certainly the Javanese and Malay *jong* and *ajong*, 'a ship or large vessel.' In Javanese the Great Bear is called *Lintang jong*, 'The Constellation *Junk*,' [which is in Malay *Bintang Jong*. The various forms in Malay and cognate languages, with the Chinese words which have been suggested as the origin, are very fully given by *Scott*, *Malayan Words in English*, p. 59 *seq.*].

c. 1300.—"Large ships called in the language of China '**Junks**' bring various sorts of choice merchandize and cloths from Chín and Máchín, and the countries of Hind and Sind."—*Rashíduddín*, in *Elliot*, i. 69.

1331.—"And when we were there in harbour at Polumbum, we embarked in another ship called a **Junk** (*aliam navim nomine* **Zuncum**). . . . Now on board that ship were good 700 souls, what with sailors and with merchants. . . ."—*Friar Odoric*, in *Cathay*, &c., 73.

c. 1343.—"They make no voyages on the China Sea except with Chinese vessels . . . of these there are three kinds; the big ones which are called **junk**, in the plural *junūk*. . . . Each of these big ships carries from three up to twelve sails. The sails are made of bamboo slips, woven like mats; they are never hauled down, but are shifted round as the wind blows from one quarter or another."—*Ibn Batuta*, iv. 91. The French translators write the words as *gonk* (and *gonoûk*). Ibn Batuta really indicates *chunk* (and *chunūk*); but both must have been quite wrong.

c. 1348.—"Wishing them to visit the shrine of St. Thomas the Apostle . . . we embarked on certain *Junks* (*ascendentes* **Junkos**) from Lower India, which is called Minubar."—*Marignolli*, in *Cathay*, &c., 356.

1459.—"About the year of Our Lord 1420, a Ship or **Junk** of India, in crossing the Indian Sea, was driven . . . in a westerly and south-westerly direction for 40 days, without seeing anything but sky and sea. . . . The ship having touched on the coast to supply its wants, the mariners beheld there the egg of a certain bird called *chrocho*, which egg was as big as a butt. . . ."—*Rubric* on *Fra Mauro's Great Map at Venice.*

" "The Ships or *junks* (**Zonchi**) which navigate this sea, carry 4 masts, and others besides that they can set up or strike (at will); and they have 40 to 60 little chambers for the merchants, and they have only one rudder. . . ."—*Ibid.*

1516.—"Many Moorish merchants reside in it (Malacca), and also Gentiles, particularly *Chetis* (see **CHETTY**), who are natives of Cholmendel; and they are all very rich, and have many large ships which they call **jungos**."—*Barbosa*, 191.

1549.—"Exclusus isto concilio, applicavit animum ad navem Sinensis formae, quam **Iuncum** vocant."—*Scti. Franc. Xaverii Epist.* 337.

[1554.—". . . in the many ships and *junks* (**Jugos**) which certainly passed that way."—*Castanheda*, ii. c. 20.]

1563.—"**Juncos** are certain long ships that have stern and prow fashioned in the same way."—*Garcia*, f. 58*b*.

1591.—"By this Negro we were advertised of a small Barke of some thirtie tunnes (which the Moors call a **Iunco**)."—*Barker's Acc. of Lancaster's Voyage*, in *Hakl.* ii. 589.

1616.—"And doubtless they had made havock of them all, had they not presently been relieved by two Arabian **Junks** (for so their small ill-built ships are named. . . .)"—*Terry*, ed. 1665, p. 342.

[1625.—"An hundred Prawes and **Iunkes.**"—*Purchas*, *Pilgrimage*, i. 2, 43.

[1627.—"China also, and the great Atlantis (that you call America), which have now but **Iunks** and Canoas, abounded then in tall Ships."—*Bacon*, *New Atlantis*, p. 12.]

1630.—"So repairing to *Iasques* (see **JASK**), a place in the *Persian* Gulph, they obtained a fleete of Seaven **Iuncks**, to convey them and theirs as Merchantmen bound for the Shoares of India."—*Lord*, *Religion of the Persees*, 3.

1673.—Fryer also speaks of "Portugal **Junks.**" The word had thus come to mean any large vessel in the Indian Seas. Barker's use for a small vessel (above) is exceptional.

JUNKAMEER, s. This word occurs in *Wheeler*, i. 300, where it should certainly have been written **Juncaneer.** It was long a perplexity, and as it was the subject of one of Dr. Burnell's latest, if not the very last, of his contributions to this work, I transcribe the words of his communication:

"Working at improving the notes to v. Linschoten, I have accidentally cleared up the meaning of a word you asked me about long ago, but which I was then obliged to give up—'Jonkamīr.' It = 'a collector of customs.'

"(1745). — Notre Supérieur qui sçavoit qu'à moitié chemin certains **Jonquaniers*** mettoient les passans à contribution, nous avoit donné un ou deux *fanons* (see **FANAM**) pour les payer en allant et en revenant, au cas qu'ils l'exigeassent de nous."—*P. Norbert, Memoires*, pp. 159-160.

"The original word is in Malayālam *chungakāran*, and do. in Tamil, though it does not occur in the Dictionaries of that language; but *chungam* (= 'Customs') does.

"I was much pleased to settle this curious word; but I should never have thought of the origin of it, had it not been for that rascally old Capuchin P. Norbert's note."

My friend's letter (from West Stratton) has no date, but it must have been written in July or August 1882. —[H.Y.] (See **JUNKEON.**)

1680.—"The *Didwan* (see **DEWAUN**) returned with Lingapas *Ruccas* (see **ROOCKA**) upon the *Avaldar* (see **HAVILDAR**) at St. Thoma, and upon the two chief **Juncaneers** in this part of the country, ordering them not to stop goods or provisions coming into the town."—*Fort St. Geo. Consn.*, Nov. 22, *Notes and Exts.*, iii. 39.

1746.—"Given to the Governor's Servants, **Juncaneers**, &c., as usual at Christmas, *Salampores* (see **SALEMPOORY**) 18Ps. P. 13."—*Acct. of Extra Charges at Fort St. David*, to Dec. 31. *MS. Report*, in India Office.

JUNK-CEYLON, n.p. The popular name of an island off the west coast of the Malay Peninsula. Forrest (*Voyage to Mergui*, pp. iii. and 29-30) calls it *Jan-Sylan*, and says it is properly *Ujong* (*i.e.* in Malay, 'Cape') *Sylang*. This appears to be nearly right. The name is, according to Crawfurd (*Malay Dict.* s.v. *Salang*, and *Dict. Ind. Archip.* s.v. *Ujung*) *Ujung Salang*, 'Salang Headland.' [Mr. Skeat doubts the correctness of this. "There is at least one quite possible alternative, *i.e. jong salang*, in which *jong* means 'a junk,' and *salang*, when applied to vessels, 'heavily tossing' (see *Klinkert, Dict.* s.v. *salang*). Another meaning of *salang* is 'to transfix a person with a dagger,' and is the technical term for Malay executions, in which the kris was driven down from the collar-bone to the heart. *Parles* in the first quotation is now known as *Perlis*."]

1539.—"There we crost over to the firm Land, and passing by the Port of **Junçalan** (*Iuncalão*) we sailed two days and a half with a favourable wind, by means whereof we got to the River of *Parles* in the Kingdom of *Queda*. . . ."—*Pinto* (orig. cap. xix.) in *Cogan*, p. 22.

1592.—"We departed thence to a Baie in the Kingdom of **Iunsalaom**, which is betweene Malacca and Pegu, 8 degrees to the Northward."—*Barker*, in *Hakl.* ii. 591.

1727.—"The North End of **Jonk Ceyloan** lies within a mile of the Continent."—*A. Hamilton*, 69; [ed. 1744, ii. 67].

JUNKEON, s. This word occurs as below. It is no doubt some form of the word *chungam*, mentioned under **JUNKAMEER.** Wilson gives Telugu *Sunkam*, which might be used in Orissa, where Bruton was. [*Shungum* (Mal. *chunkam*) appears in the sense of toll or customs duties in many of the old treaties in *Logan, Malabar*, vol. iii.]

1638.—"Any **Iunkeon** or Custome."—*Bruton's Narrative*, in *Hakl.* v. 53.

1676.—"These practices (claims of perquisite by the factory chiefs) hath occasioned some to apply to the Governour for relief, and chosen rather to pay **Juncan** than submit to the unreasonable demands aforesaid."—*Major Puckle's Proposals*, in *Fort St. Geo. Consn.*, Feb. 16. *Notes and Exts.*, i. 39.

[1727.—". . . at every ten or twelve Miles end, a Fellow to demand **Junkaun** or Poll-Money for me and my Servants. . . ." —*A. Hamilton*, ed. 1744, i. 392.]

JURIBASSO, s. This word, meaning 'an interpreter,' occurs constantly in the Diary of Richard Cocks, of the

* "Ce sont des Maures qui exigent de l'argent sur les grands chemins, de ceux qui passent avec quelques merchandises; souvent ils en demandent à ceux mêmes qui n'en portent point. On regarde ces gens-là à peu pres comme des voleurs."

English Factory in Japan, admirably edited for the Hakluyt Society by Mr. Edward Maunde Thompson (1883). The word is really Malayo-Javanese *jurubahāsa*, lit. 'language-master,' *juru* being an expert, 'a master of a craft,' and *bahāsa* the Skt. *bhāshā*, 'speech.' [*Wilkinson, Dict.*, writes *Juru-bĕhasa*; Mr. Skeat prefers *juru-bhasa.*]

1603.—At Patani the Hollanders having arrived, and sent presents—"ils furent pris par un officier nommé *Orankaea* (see **ORANKAY**) **Jurebassa**, qui en fit trois portions."—In *Rec. du Voyages*, ed. 1703, ii. 667. See also pp. 672, 675.

1613.—"(Said the Mandarin of Ancão) . . . 'Captain-major, Auditor, residents, and **jerubaças**, for the space of two days you must come before me to attend to these instructions (*capitulos*), in order that I may write to the Aitão.' . . .

"These communications being read in the Chamber of the City of Macau, before the Vereadores, the people, and the Captain-Major then commanding in the said city, João Serrão da Cunha, they sought for a person who might be charged to reply, such as had knowledge and experience of the Chinese, and of their manner of speech, and finding Lourenço Carvalho . . . he made the reply in the following form of words '. . . To this purpose we the Captain-Major, the Auditor, the Vereadores, the Padres, and the **Jurubaça**, assembling together and beating our foreheads before God. . . .'"—*Bocarro*, pp. 725-729.

" "The foureteenth, I sent M. Cockes, and my **Iurebasso** to both the Kings to entreat them to prouide me of a dozen Seamen."—*Capt. Saris*, in *Purchas*, 378.

1615.—". . . his desire was that, for his sake, I would geve over the pursute of this matter against the sea *bongew*, for that yf it were followed, of force the said *bongew* must cut his bellie, and then my **jurebasso** must do the lyke. Unto which his request I was content to agree. . . ."—*Cocks's Diary*, i. 33.

[" "This night we had a conference with our **Jurybassa**."—*Foster, Letters*, iii. 167].

JUTE, s. The fibre (**gunny**-fibre) of the bark of *Corchorus capsularis*, L., and *Corchorus olitorius*, L., which in the last 45 years has become so important an export from India, and a material for manufacture in Great Britain as well as in India. "At the last meeting of the Cambridge Philosophical Society, Professor Skeat commented on various English words. *Jute*, a fibrous substance, he explained from the Sanskrit *jūṭa*, a less usual form of *jaṭa*, meaning, 1st, the matted hair of an ascetic; 2ndly, the fibrous roots of a tree such as the banyan; 3rdly, any fibrous substance" (*Academy*, Dec. 27, 1879). The secondary meanings attributed here to *jaṭa* are very doubtful.* The term *jute* appears to have been first used by Dr. Roxburgh in a letter dated 1795, in which he drew the attention of the Court of Directors to the value of the fibre "called *jute* by the natives." [It appears, however, as early as 1746 in the Log of a voyage quoted by Col. Temple in *J.R.A.S.*, Jan. 1900, p. 158.] The name in fact appears to be taken from the vernacular name in Orissa. This is stated to be properly *jhōṭŏ*, but *jhūṭŏ* is used by the uneducated. See *Report of the Jute Commission*, by Babu Hemchundra Kerr, Calcutta, 1874; also a letter from Mr. J. S. Cotton in the *Academy*, Jan. 17, 1880.

JUTKA, s. From Dak.—Hind. *jhaṭkā*, 'quick.' The native cab of Madras, and of Mofussil towns in that Presidency; a conveyance only to be characterised by the epithet *ramshackle*, though in that respect equalled by the Calcutta **cranchee** (q.v.). It consists of a sort of box with venetian windows, on two wheels, and drawn by a miserable pony. It is entered by a door at the back. (See **SHIGRAM**, with like meanings).

JUZAIL, s. This word *jazāil* is generally applied to the heavy Afghan rifle, fired with a forked rest. If it is Ar. it must be *jazā'il*, the plural of *jazīl*, 'big,' used as a substantive. *Jazīl* is often used for a big, thick thing, so it looks probable. (See **GINGALL.**) Hence *jazā'ilchī*, one armed with such a weapon.

[1812.—"The **jezaerchi** also, the men who use blunderbusses, were to wear the new Russian dress."—*Morier, Journey through Persia*, 30.

[1898.—

"All night the cressets glimmered pale
On Ulwur sabre and Tonk **jezail**."
R. Kipling, Barrack-room Ballads, 84.

[1900.—"Two companies of Khyber **Jezailchies**."—*Warburton, Eighteen Years in the Khyber*, 78.]

JYEDAD, s. P.—H. *jāidād*. Territory assigned for the support of troops.

[1824.—"Rampoora on the Chumbul . . . had been granted to Dudernaic, as **Jaidad**,

* This remark is from a letter of Dr. Burnell's dd. Tanjore, March 16, 1880.

or temporary assignment for the payment of his troops."—*Malcolm, Central India*, i. 223.]

JYSHE, s. This term, Ar. *jaish*, 'an army, a legion,' was applied by Tippoo to his regular infantry, the body of which was called the *Jaish Kachari* (see under **CUTCHERRY**).

c. 1782.—"About this time the *Bar* or regular infantry, Kutcheri, were called the **Jysh Kutcheri**."—*Hist. of Tipú Sultán*, by *Hussein Ali Khân Kermâni*, p. 32.

1786.—"At such times as new levies or recruits for the **Jyshe** and *Piadehs* are to be entertained, you two and Syed Peer assembling in *Kuchurry* are to entertain none but proper and eligible men."—*Tippoo's Letters*, 256.

K

KAJEE, s. This is a title of Ministers of State used in Nepaul and Sikkim. It is no doubt the Arabic word (see **CAZEE** for quotations). *Kājī* is the pronunciation of this last word in various parts of India.

[**KALA JUGGAH**, s. Anglo-H. *kālā jagah* for a 'dark place,' arranged near a ball-room for the purpose of flirtation.

[1885.—"At night it was rather cold, and the frequenters of the **Kala Jagah** (or dark places) were unable to enjoy it as much as I hoped they would."—*Lady Dufferin, Viceregal Life*, 91.

KALINGA, n.p. (See **KLING**.)

KALLA-NIMMACK, s. Hind. *kālā-namak*, 'black salt,' a common mineral drug, used especially in horse-treatment. It is muriate of soda, having a mixture of oxide of iron, and some impurities. (*Royle*.)

KAPAL, s. *Kāpăl*, the Malay word for a ship, [which seems to have come from the Tam. *kappal*,] "applied to any square-rigged vessel, with top and top-gallant masts" (*Marsden, Memoirs of a Malay Family*, 57).

KARBAREE, s. Hind. *kārbārī*, 'an agent, a manager.' Used chiefly in Bengal Proper.

[c. 1857.—"The Foujdar's report stated that a police **Carbaree** was sleeping in his own house."—*Chevers, Ind. Med. Jurisp.* 467.]

1867.—"The Lushai **Karbaris** (literally men of business) duly arrived and met me at Kassalong."—*Lewin, A Fly on the Wheel*, 293.

KARCANNA, s. Hind. from Pers. *kār-khāna*, 'business-place.' We cannot improve upon Wilson's definition: "An office, or place where business is carried on; but it is in use more especially applied to places where mechanical work is performed; a workshop, a manufactory, an arsenal; also, fig., to any great fuss or bustle." The last use seems to be obsolete.

[1663.—"Large halls are seen in many places, called **Kar-Kanays** or workshops for the artizans."—*Bernier*, ed. *Constable*, 258 *seq.* Also see **CARCANA**.]

KARDAR, s. P.—H. *kārdār*, an agent (of the Government) in Sindh.

[1842.—"I further insist upon the offending **Kardar** being sent a prisoner to my head-quarters at Sukkur within the space of five days, to be dealt with as I shall determine."—*Sir C. Napier*, in *Napier's Conquest of Scinde*, 149.]

KAREETA, s. Hind. from Ar. *kharīṭa*, and in India also *khalīṭa*. The silk bag (described by Mrs. Parkes, below) in which is enclosed a letter to or from a native noble; also, by transfer, the letter itself. In 2 Kings v. 23, the bag in which Naaman bound the silver is *kharīt*; also in Isaiah iii. 22, the word translated 'crisping-pins' is *kharīṭim*, rather 'purses.'

c. 1350.—"The Sherīf Ibrāhīm, surnamed the **Khāritadār**, *i.e.* the Master of the Royal Paper and Pens, was governor of the territory of Hānsī and Sarsatī."—*Ibn Batuta*, iii. 337.

1838.—"Her Highness the Bāiza Bā'i did me the honour to send me a **Kharītā**, that is a letter enclosed in a long bag of *Kim-khwāb* (see **KINCOB**), crimson silk brocaded with flowers in gold, contained in another of fine muslin: the mouth of the bag was tied with a gold and tasseled cord, to which was appended the great seal of her Highness."—*Wanderings of a Pilgrim* (Mrs. Parkes), ii. 250.

In the following passage the *thing* is described (at Constantinople).

1673.—". . . le Visir prenant un sachet de beau brocard d'or à fleurs, long tout au moins d'une demi aulne et large de cinq ou six doigts, lié et scellé par le haut avec une inscription qui y estoit attachée, et disant que c'estoit une lettre du Grand Seigneur. . . ."—*Journal d'Ant. Galland*, ii. 94.

KAUL, s. Hind. *Kāl*, properly 'Time,' then a period, death, and popularly the visitation of famine. Under this word we read:

1808.—"Scarcity, and the scourge of civil war, embittered the Mahratta nation in A.D. 1804, of whom many emigrants were supported by the justice and generosity of neighbouring powers, and (a large number) were relieved in their own capital by the charitable contributions of the English at Bombay alone. This and opening of Hospitals for the sick and starving, within the British settlements, were gratefully told to the writer afterwards by many Mahrattas in the heart, and from distant parts, of their own country."—*R. Drummond, Illustrations*, &c.

KAUNTA, CAUNTA, s. This word, Mahr. and Guz. *kāntha*, 'coast or margin,' [Skt. *kantha*, 'immediate proximity,' *kanthī*, 'the neck,'] is used in the northern part of the Bombay Presidency in composition to form several popular geographical terms, as *Mahi Kānthā*, for a group of small States on the banks of the Mahi River; *Rewā Kānthā*, south of the above; *Sindhu Kānthā*, the Indus Delta, &c. The word is no doubt the same which we find in Ptolemy for the Gulf of Kachh, Κάνθι κόλπος. Kānthī-Kot was formerly an important place in Eastern Kachh, and *Kānthī* was the name of the southern coast district (see *Ritter*, vi. 1038).

KEBULEE. (See **MYROBOLANS.**)

KEDDAH, s. Hind. *Khedā* (*khednā*, 'to chase,' from Skt. *ākheta*, 'hunting'). The term used in Bengal for the enclosure constructed to entrap elephants. [The system of hunting elephants by making a trench round a space and enticing the wild animals by means of tame decoys is described by Arrian, *Indika*, 13.] (See **CORRAL.**)

[c. 1590. — "There are several modes of hunting elephants. 1. **k'hedah**" (then follows a description).—*Āīn*, i. 284.]

1780-90.—"The party on the plain below have, during this interval, been completely occupied in forming the **Keddah** or enclosure."—*Lives of the Lindsays*, iii. 191.

1810. — "A trap called a **Keddah**." — *Williamson, V. M.* ii. 436.

1860.—"The custom in Bengal is to construct a strong enclosure (called a **Keddah**) in the heart of the forest." — *Tennent's Ceylon*, ii. 342.

KEDGEREE, KITCHERY, s. Hind. *khichṛī*, a mess of rice, cooked with butter and *dāl* (see **DHALL**), and flavoured with a little spice, shred onion, and the like; a common dish all over India, and often served at Anglo-Indian breakfast tables, in which very old precedent is followed, as the first quotation shows. The word appears to have been applied metaphorically to mixtures of sundry kinds (see *Fryer*, below), and also to mixt jargon or *lingua franca*. In England we find the word is often applied to a mess of re-cooked fish, served for breakfast; but this is inaccurate. Fish is frequently eaten *with kedgeree*, but is no part of it. ["Fish *Kitcherie*" is an old Anglo-Indian dish, see the recipe in *Riddell, Indian Domestic Economy*, p. 437.]

c. 1340.—"The munj (**Moong**) is boiled with rice, and then buttered and eaten. This is what they call **Kishrī**, and on this dish they breakfast every day."—*Ibn Batuta*, iii. 131.

c. 1443.—"The elephants of the palace are fed upon **Kitchri**."—*Abdurrazzāk*, in *India in XVth Cent.* 27.

c. 1475.—"Horses are fed on pease; also on **Kichiris**, boiled with sugar and oil; and early in the morning they get *shishenivo*" (?).—*Athan. Nikitin*, in *do.*, p. 10.

The following recipe for **Kedgeree** is by Abu'l Fazl:—

c. 1590.—"**Khichri**, Rice, split *dāl*, and *ghī*, 5 *ser* of each; ½ *ser* salt; this gives 7 dishes."—*Āīn*, i. 59.

1648.—"Their daily gains are very small, . . . and with these they fill their hungry bellies with a certain food called **Kitserye**."—*Van Twist*, 57.

1653.—"**Kicheri** est vne sorte de legume dont les Indiens se nourissent ordinairement."—*De la Boullaye-le-Gouz*, ed. 1657, p. 545.

1672.—Baldaeus has **Kitzery**, Tavernier **Quicheri** [ed. *Ball*, i. 282, 391].

1673.—"The Diet of this Sort of People admits not of great Variety or Cost, their delightfullest Food being only **Cutcherry** a sort of Pulse and Rice mixed together, and boiled in Butter, with which they grow fat."—*Fryer*, 81.

Again, speaking of pearls in the Persian Gulf, he says: "Whatever is of any Value is very dear. Here is a great Plenty of what they call **Ketchery**, a mixture of all together, or Refuse of Rough, Yellow, and Unequal, which they sell by Bushels to the Russians."—*Ibid.* 320.

1727.—"Some Doll and Rice, being mingled together and boiled make **Kitcheree**, the common Food of the Country. They eat it with Butter and Atchar (see **ACHAR**)."—*A. Hamilton*, i. 161 ; [ed. 1744, i. 162].

1750-60.—"**Kitcharee** is only rice stewed, with a certain pulse they call Dholl, and is generally eaten with salt-fish, butter, and pickles of various sorts, to which they give the general name of *Atchar*."—*Grose*, i. 150.

[1813.—"He was always a welcome guest . . . and ate as much of their rice and **Cutcheree** as he chose."—*Forbes, Or. Mem.* 2nd ed. i. 502.]

1880.—"A correspondent of the *Indian Mirror*, writing of the annual religious fair at Ajmere, thus describes a feature in the proceedings: "There are two tremendous copper pots, one of which is said to contain about eighty maunds of rice and the other forty maunds. To fill these pots with rice, sugar, and dried fruits requires a round sum of money, and it is only the rich who can afford to do so. This year His Highness the Nawab of Tonk paid Rs. 3,000 to fill up the pots. . . . After the pots filled with **khichri** had been inspected by the Nawab, who was accompanied by the Commissioner of Ajmere and several Civil Officers, the distribution, or more properly the plunder, of **khichri** commenced, and men well wrapped up with clothes, stuffed with cotton, were seen leaping down into the boiling pot to secure their share of the booty."—*Pioneer Mail*, July 8. [See the reference to this custom in *Sir T. Roe*, Hak. Soc. ii. 314, and a full account in *Rajputana Gazetteer*, ii. 63.]

KEDGEREE, n.p. *Khijirī* or *Kijarī*, a village and police station on the low lands near the mouth of the Hoogly, on the west bank, and 68 miles below Calcutta. It was formerly well known as a usual anchorage of the larger Indiamen.

1683.—"This morning early we weighed anchor with the tide of Ebb, but having little wind, got no further than the Point of **Kegaria** Island."—*Hedges, Diary*, Jan. 26 ; [Hak. Soc. i. 64].

1684.—"Signr Nicolo Pareres, a Portugall Merchant, assured me their whole community had wrott ye Vice King of Goa . . . to send them 2 or 3 Frigates with . . . Soldiers to possess themselves of ye Islands of **Kegeria** and *Ingellee*."—*Ibid.* Dec. 17 ; [Hak. Soc. i. 172].

1727.—"It is now inhabited by Fishers, as are also *Ingellie* and **Kidgerie**, two neighbouring Islands on the West Side of the Mouth of the Ganges."—*A. Hamilton*, ii. 2 ; [ed. 1744]. (See **HIDGELEE**.)

1753.—"De l'autre côté de l'entré, les rivières de **Cajori** et de l'*Ingeli* (see **HIDGELEE**), puis plus au large la rivière de Pipli et celle de Balasor (see **BALASORE**), sont avec *Tombali* (see **TUMLOOK**), rivière mentionné plus haut, et qu'on peut ajouter ici, des dérivations d'un grand fleuve, dont le nom de Ganga lui est commun avec le Gange. . . . Une carte du Golfe de Bengale inserée dans Blaeu, fera même distinguer les rivières d'*Ingeli* et de **Cajori** (si on prend la peine de l'examiner) comme des bras du Ganga."—*D'Anville*, p. 66.

As to the origin of this singular error, about a river Ganga flowing across India from W. to E., see some extracts under **GODAVERY**. The Rupnarain River, which joins the Hoogly from the W. just above Diamond Harbour, is the *grand fleuve* here spoken of. The name *Gunga* or *Old Gunga* is applied to this in charts late in the 18th century. It is thus mentioned by A. Hamilton, 1727: "About five leagues farther up on the West Side of the River of *Hughly*, is another Branch of the *Ganges*, called *Ganga*, it is broader than that of the *Hughly*, but much shallower."—ii. 3 ; [ed. 1744].

KEDGEREE-POT, s. A vulgar expression for a round pipkin such as is in common Indian use, both for holding water and for cooking purposes. (See **CHATTY, GHURRA.**)

1811.—"As a memorial of such misfortunes, they plant in the earth an oar bearing a **cudgeri**, or earthen pot."—*Solvyns, Les Hindous*, iii.

1830.—"Some natives were in readiness with a small raft of **Kedgeree-pots**, on which the palkee was to be ferried over."—*Mem. of Col. Mountain*, 110.

KENNERY, n.p. The site of a famous and very extensive group of cave-temples on the Island of **Salsette**, near Bombay, properly *Kāṇherī*.

1602.—"Holding some conversation with certain very aged Christians, who had been among the first converts there of Padre Fr. Antonio do Porto, . . . one of them, who alleged himself to be more than 120 years old, and who spoke Portuguese very well, and read and wrote it, and was continually reading the *Flos Sanctorum*, and the Lives of the Saints, assured me that without doubt the work of the Pagoda of **Canari** was made under the orders of the father of Saint Josafat the Prince, whom Barlaam converted to the Faith of Christ. . . ."—*Couto*, VII. iii. cap. 10.

1673.—"Next Morn before Break of Day we directed our steps to the anciently fam'd, but now ruin'd City of **Canorein** . . . all cut out of a Rock," &c.—*Fryer*, 71-72.

1825.—"The principal curiosities of Salsette . . . are the cave temples of **Kennery**. These are certainly in every way remarkable, from their number, their beautiful situation, their elaborate carving, and their marked connection with Buddh and his religion."—*Heber*, ii. 130.

KERSEYMERE, s. This is an English draper's term, and not Anglo-

Indian. But it is through forms like *cassimere* (also in English use), a corruption of *cashmere*, though the corruption has been shaped by the previously existing English word *kersey* for a kind of woollen cloth, as if *kersey* were one kind and *kerseymere* another, of similar goods. *Kersey* is given by Minsheu (2nd ed. 1627), without definition, thus: "Kersie *cloth*, G. (*i.e.* French) *carizé*." The only word like the last given by Littré is "*Carisil*, sorte de canevas." . . . This does not apply to *kersey*, which appears to be represented by "*Creseau*—Terme de Commerce; étoffe de laine croissée à deux envers; etym. *croiser*." Both words are probably connected with *croiser* or with *carré*. Planché indeed (whose etymologies are generally worthless) says: "made originally at Kersey, in Suffolk, whence its name." And he adds, equal to the occasion, "*Kerseymere*, so named from the position of the original factory on the *mere*, or water which runs through the village of Kersey" (!) Mr. Skeat, however, we see, thinks that Kersey, in Suffolk, is perhaps the origin of the word *Kersey*: [and this he repeats in the new ed. (1901) of his *Concise Etym. Dict.*, adding, "Not from Jersey, which is also used as the name of a material." *Kerseymere*, he says, is "a corruption of *Cashmere* or *Cassimere*, by confusion with *kersey*"].

1495.—"Item the xv day of Februar, bocht fra Jhonne Andersoun x ellis of quhit **Caresay**, to be tua coitis, ane to the King, and ane to the Lard of Balgony; price of ellne vjs.; summa . . . iij. *li.*"—*Accts. of the Ld. H. Treasurer of Scotland*, 1877, p. 225.

1583.—"I think cloth, **Kerseys** and tinne have never bene here at so lowe prices as they are now."—*Mr. John Newton*, from Babylon (*i.e.* Bagdad) July 20, in *Hakl.* 378.

1603.—"I had as lief be a list of an English **kersey**, as be pil'd as thou art pil'd, for a French velvet."—*Measure for Measure*, i. 2.

1625.—"Ordanet the thesaurer to tak aff to ilk ane of the officeris and to the drummer and pyper, ilk ane of thame, fyve elne of reid **Kairsie** claithe."—*Exts. from Recds. of Glasgow*, 1876, p. 347.

1626.—In a contract between the Factor of the King of Persia and a Dutch "Opper Koopman" for goods we find: "2000 Persian ells of **Carsay** at 1 *eocri* (?) the ell."—*Valentijn*, v. 295.

1784.—"For sale—superfine cambrics and edgings . . . scarlet and blue **Kassimeres**."—In *Seton-Karr*, i. 47.

c. 1880.—(no date given) "**Kerseymere.** *Cassimere.* A finer description of kersey . . : (then follows the absurd etymology as given by Planché). . . . It is principally a manufacture of the west of England, and except in being tweeled (*sic*) and of narrow width it in no respect differs from superfine cloth."—*Draper's Dict.* s.v.

KHADIR, s. H. *khādar*; the recent alluvial bordering a large river. (See under **BANGUR**).

[1828.—"The river . . . meanders fantastically . . . through a **Khader**, or valley between two ranges of hills."—*Mundy, Pen and Pencil Sketches*, ed. 1858, p. 130.

[The **Khadir** Cup is one of the chief racing trophies open to pig-stickers in upper India.]

KHAKEE, vulgarly **KHARKI**, **KHARKEE**, s. or adj. Hind. *khākī*, 'dusty or dust-coloured,' from Pers. *khāk*, 'earth,' or 'dust'; applied to a light drab or chocolate-coloured cloth. This was the colour of the uniform worn by some of the Punjab regiments at the siege of Delhi, and became very popular in the army generally during the campaigns of 1857-58, being adopted as a convenient material by many other corps. [Gubbins (*Mutinies in Oudh*, 296) describes how the soldiers at Lucknow dyed their uniforms a light brown or dust colour with a mixture of black and red office inks, and Cave Brown (*Punjab and Delhi*, ii. 211) speaks of its introduction in place of the red uniform which gave the British soldier the name of "*Lal Coortee Wallahs*."]

[1858.—A book appeared called "Service and Adventures with the **Khakee** Ressalah, or Meerut Volunteer Horse during the Mutinies in 1857-8," by *R. H. W. Dunlop*.

[1859.—"It has been decided that the full dress will be of dark blue cloth, made up, not like the tunic, but as the native ungreekah (*angarkha*), and set off with red piping. The undress clothing will be entirely of **Khakee**."—*Madras Govt. Order*, Feb. 18, quoted in *Calcutta Rev.* ciii. 407.

[1862.—"**Kharkee** does not catch in brambles so much as other stuffs."—*Brinckman, Rifle in Cashmere*, 136.]

1878.—"The Amir, we may mention, wore a **khaki** suit, edged with gold, and the well-known Herati cap."—*Sat. Review*, Nov. 30, 683.

[1899.—"The batteries to be painted with the **Kirkee** colour, which being similar to the roads of the country, will render the vehicles invisible."—*Times*, July 12.

[1890-91.—The newspapers have constant references to a **khaki** election, that is an election started on a war policy, and the War Loan for the Transvaal Campaign has been known as "**khakis**."]

Recent military operations have led to the general introduction of **khaki** as the service uniform. Something like this has been used in the East for clothing from a very early time:—

[1611.—"See if you can get me a piece of very fine brown calico to make me clothes."—*Danvers, Letters*, i. 109.]

KHALSA, s. and adj. Hind. from Ar. *khālṣa* (properly *khāliṣa*) 'pure, genuine.' It has various technical meanings, but, as we introduce the word, it is applied by the Sikhs to their community and church (so to call it) collectively.

1783.—"The *Sicques* salute each other by the expression *Wah Gooroo*, without any inclination of the body, or motion of the hand. The Government at large, and their armies, are denominated **Khalsa**, and **Khalsajee**."—*Forster's Journey*, ed. 1808, i. 307.

1881.—
"And all the Punjab knows me, for my father's name was known
In the days of the conquering **Khalsa**, when I was a boy half-grown."
Attar Singh loquitur, by *Sowar*, in an Indian paper; name and date lost.

KHAN, s. **a**. Turki through Pers. *Khān*. Originally this was a title, equivalent to Lord or Prince, used among the Mongol and Turk nomad hordes. Besides this sense, and an application to various other chiefs and nobles, it has still become in Persia, and still more in Afghanistan, a sort of vague title like "Esq.," whilst in India it has become a common affix to, or in fact part of, the name of Hindustānis out of every rank, properly, however of those claiming a Pathān descent. The tendency of swelling titles is always thus to degenerate, and when the value of *Khān* had sunk, a new form, *Khān-Khānān* (Khān of Khāns) was devised at the Court of Delhi, and applied to one of the high officers of State.

[c. 1610.—The "*Assant* **Caounas**" of Pyrard de Laval, which Mr. Gray fails to identify, is probably *Hasan-Khan*, Hak. Soc. i. 69.

[1616.—"All the Captayens, as **Channa Chana** (Khān-Khānān), Mahobet **Chan**, **Chan** John (Khān Jahān)."—*Sir T. Roe*, Hak. Soc. i. 192.

[1675.—"**Cawn**." See under **GINGI**.]

b. Pers. *khān*. A public building for the accommodation of travellers, a caravanserai. [The word appears in English as early as about 1400; see *Stanf. Dict.* s.v.]

1653.—"**Han** est vn Serrail ou enclos que les Arabes appellent *fondoux* où se retirent les Carauanes, ou les Marchands Estrangers, . . . ce mot de **Han** est Turq, et est le mesme que *Kiarauansarai* ou *Karbasara* (see **CARAVANSERAY**) dont parle Belon. . . ."—*De la Boullaye-le-Gouz*, ed. 1657, p. 540.

1827.—"He lost all hope, being informed by his late fellow-traveller, whom he found at the **Khan**, that the Nuwaub was absent on a secret expedition."—*W. Scott, The Surgeon's Daughter*, ch. xiii.

KHANNA, CONNAH, &c. s. This term (Pers. *khāna*, 'a house, a compartment, apartment, department, receptacle,' &c.) is used almost *ad libitum* in India in composition, sometimes with most incongruous words, as *bobachee* (for *bāwarchī*) **connah**, 'cook-house,' **buggy-connah**, 'buggy, or coach-house,' **bottle-khanna**, **tosha-khana** (q.v.), &c. &c.

1784.—"The house, cook-room, **bottle-connah**, godown, &c., are all pucka built."—In *Seton-Karr*, i. 41.

KHANSAMA. See **CONSUMAH**.

KHANUM, s. Turki, through Pers. *khānum* and *khānim*, a lady of rank; the feminine of the title **Khān**, **a** (q.v.)

1404.—". . . la mayor delles avia nõbre **Cañon**, que quiere dezir Reyna, o Señora grande."—*Clavijo*, f. 52*v*.

" "The great wall and tents were for the use of the chief wife of the Lord, who was called **Caño**, and the other was for the second wife, called *Quinchi* **Caño**, which means 'the little lady.'"—*Markham's Clavijo*, 145.

1505.—"The greatest of the Begs of the Sagharichi was then Shīr Haji *Beg*, whose daughter, Ais-doulet *Begum*, Yunīs Khan married. . . . The *Khan* had three daughters by Ais-doulet Begum. . . . The second daughter, Kullûk Nigar **Khânum**, was my mother. . . . Five months after the taking of Kabul she departed to God's mercy, in the year 911" (1505).—*Baber*, p. 12.

1619.—"The King's ladies, when they are not married to him . . . and not near relations of his house, but only concubines or girls of the Palace, are not called *begum*, which is a title of queens and princesses, but only **canum**, a title given in Persia to all noble ladies."—*P. della Valle*, ii. 13.

KHASS, KAUSS, &c., adj. Hind. from Ar. *khāṣṣ*, 'special, particular, Royal.' It has many particular applications, one of the most common being to estates retained in the hands of Government, which are said to be held *khāṣṣ*. The *khāṣṣ-mahal* again, in a native house, is the women's apartment. Many years ago a white-bearded *khānsamān* (see **CONSUMAH**), in the service of one of the present writers, indulging in reminiscences of the days when he had been attached to Lord Lake's camp, in the beginning of the last century, extolled the *sāhibs* of those times above their successors, observing (in his native Hindustani): "In those days I think the Sahibs all came from London *khāṣṣ*; now a great lot of *Liverpoolwālās* come to the country!"

There were in the Palaces of the Great Mogul and other Mahommedan Princes of India always two Halls of Audience, or Durbar, the *Dewān-i-'Ām*, or Hall of the Public, and the *Dewān-i-Khāṣṣ*, the Special or Royal Hall, for those who had the *entrée*, as we say.

In the *Indian Vocabulary*, 1788, the word is written *Coss*.

KHĀSYA, n.p. A name applied to the oldest existing race in the cis-Tibetan Himālaya, between Nepal and the Ganges, *i.e.* in the British Districts of Kumāun and Garhwāl. The Khāsyas are Hindu in religion and customs, and probably are substantially Hindu also in blood; though in their aspect there is some slight suggestion of that of their Tibetan neighbours. There can be no ground for supposing them to be connected with the Mongoloïd nation of Kasias (see **COSSYA**) in the mountains south of Assam.

[1526.—"About these hills are other tribes of men. With all the investigation and enquiry I could make. . . . All that I could learn was that the men of these hills were called **Kas**. It struck me that as the Hindustanis frequently confound *shīn* and *sīn* and as Kashmīr is the chief . . . city in those hills, it may have taken its name from that circumstance."—*Leyden's Baber*, 313.]

1799.—"The Vakeel of the rajāh of *Comanh* (i.e. *Kumāun*) of *Almora*, who is a learned Pandit, informs me that the greater part of the zemindars of that country are **C'hasas**. . . . They are certainly a very ancient tribe, for they are mentioned as such in the Institutes of MENU; and their great ancestor C'HASA or C'HASYA is mentioned by Sanchoniathon, under the name of CASSIUS. He is supposed to have lived before the Flood, and to have given his name to the mountains he seized upon."—*Wilford* (Wilfordizing!), in *As. Res.* vi. 456.

1824.—"The **Khasya** nation pretend to be all Rajpoots of the highest caste . . . they will not even sell one of their little mountain cows to a stranger. . . . They are a modest, gentle, respectful people, honest in their dealings."—*Heber*, i. 264.

KHELÁT, n.p. The capital of the Bilūch State upon the western frontier of Sind, which gives its name to the State itself. The name is in fact the Ar. *ḳal'a*, 'a fort.' (See under **KILLADAR**.) The terminal *t* of the Ar. word (written *ḳal'at*) has for many centuries been pronounced only when the word is the first half of a compound name meaning 'Castle of ——.' No doubt this was the case with the Bilūch capital, though in its case the second part has been completely dropt out of use. *Khelát* (*Ḳal'at*)-*i-Ghiljī* is an example where the second part remains, though sometimes dropt.

KHIRÁJ, s. Ar. *kharāj* (usually pron. in India *khirāj*), is properly a tribute levied by a Musulman lord upon conquered unbelievers, also land-tax; in India it is almost always used for the land-revenue paid to Government; whence a common expression (also Ar.) *lā khirāj*, treated as one word, *lākhirāj*, 'rent-free.'

[c. 1590.—"In ancient times a capitation tax was imposed, called **khiráj**."—*Āīn*, ed. *Jarrett*, ii. 55. "Some call the whole produce of the revenue **khiráj**."—*Ibid.* ii. 57.]

1653.—"Le Sultan souffre les Chrétiens, les Iuifs, et les Indou sur ses terres, auec toute liberté de leur Loy, en payant cinq Reales d'Espagne ou plus par an, et ce tribut s'appelle **Karache**. . . ."—*De la Boullaye-le-Gouz*, ed. 1657, p. 48.

1784.—". . . 136 beegahs, 18 of which are **Lackherage** land, or land paying no rent."—In *Seton-Karr*, i. 49.

KHOA, s. Hind. and Beng. *khoā*, a kind of concrete, of broken brick, lime, &c., used for floors and terrace-roofs.

KHOT, s. This is a Mahrātī word, *khot*, in use in some parts of the Bombay Presidency as the designation of persons holding or farming villages on a peculiar tenure called *khotī*, and coming under the class legally defined as 'superior holders.'

The position and claims of the *khots* have been the subject of much debate and difficulty, especially with regard to the rights and duties of the tenants under them, whose position takes various forms; but to go into these questions would carry us much more deeply into local technicalities than would be consistent with the scope of this work, or the knowledge of the editor. Practically it would seem that the *khot* is, in the midst of provinces where **ryotwarry** is the ruling system, an exceptional person, holding much the position of a petty zemindar in Bengal (apart from any question of permanent settlement); and that most of the difficult questions touching *khotī* have arisen from this its exceptional character in Western India.

The **khot** occurs especially in the Konkan, and was found in existence when, in the early part of the last century, we occupied territory that had been subject to the Mahratta power. It is apparently traceable back at least to the time of the 'Adil Shāhī (see **IDALCAN**) dynasty of the Deccan. There are, however, various denominations of *khot*. In the Southern Konkan the *khoti* has long been a hereditary zemindar, with proprietary rights, and also has in many cases replaced the ancient **patel** as headman of the village; a circumstance that has caused the *khoti* to be sometimes regarded and defined as the holder of an office, rather than of a property. In the Northern Konkan, again, the *Khotis* were originally mere revenue-farmers, without proprietary or hereditary rights, but had been able to usurp both.

As has been said above, administrative difficulties as to the *Khotis* have been chiefly connected with their rights over, or claims from, the ryots, which have been often exorbitant and oppressive. At the same time it is in evidence that in the former distracted state of the country, a **Khoti** was sometimes established in compliance with a petition of the cultivators. The *Khoti* "acted as a *buffer* between them and the extortionate demands of the revenue officers under the native Government. And this is easily comprehended, when it is remembered that formerly districts used to be farmed to the native officials, whose sole object was to squeeze as much revenue as possible out of each village. The *Khot* bore the brunt of this struggle. In many cases he prevented a new survey of his village, by consenting to the imposition of some new *patti*.* This no doubt he recovered from the ryots, but he gave them their own time to pay, advanced them money for their cultivation, and was a milder master than a rapacious revenue officer would have been" (*Candy*, pp. 20-21). See *Selections from Records of Bombay Government*, No. cxxxiv., N.S., viz., *Selections with Notes, regarding the Khoti Tenure*, compiled by *E. T. Candy*, Bo. C. S. 1873; also *Abstract of Proceedings of the Govt. of Bombay in the Revenue Dept.*, April 24, 1876, No. 2474.

KHOTI, s. The holder of the peculiar **khot** tenure in the Bombay Presidency.

KHUDD, KUDD, s. This is a term chiefly employed in the Himālaya, *khadd*, meaning a precipitous hill-side, also a deep valley. It is not in the dictionaries, but is probably allied to the Hind. *khāt*, 'a pit,' Dakh.—Hind. *khaddā*. [Platts gives Hind. *khad*. This is from Skt. *khaṇḍa*, 'a gap, a chasm,' while *khāt* comes from Skt. *khāta*, 'an excavation.'] The word is in constant Anglo-Indian colloquial use at Simla and other Himālayan stations.

1837.—"The steeps about Mussoori are so very perpendicular in many places, that a person of the strongest nerve would scarcely be able to look over the edge of the narrow footpath into the **Khud**, without a shudder." —*Bacon, First Impressions*, ii. 146.

1838.—"On my arrival I found one of the ponies at the estate had been killed by a fall over the precipice, when bringing up water from the **khud**."—*Wanderings of a Pilgrim*, ii. 240.

1866.—"When the men of the 43d Regt. refused to carry the guns any longer, the **Eurasian** gunners, about 20 in number, accompanying them, made an attempt to bring them on, but were unequal to doing so, and under the direction of this officer (Capt. Cockburn, R.A.) threw them down a **Khud**, as the ravines in the Himalaya are called. . . ."—*Bhotan and the H. of the Dooar War*, by *Surgeon Rennie*, M.D. p. 199.

1879.—"The commander-in-chief . . . is perhaps alive now because his horse so judiciously chose the spot on which suddenly

* *Patti* is used here in the Mahratti sense of a 'contribution' or extra cess. It is the regular Mahratti equivalent of the *abwāb* of Bengal, on which see Wilson, s.v.

to swerve round that its hind hoofs were only half over the **chud**" (*sic*).—*Times Letter*, from Simla, Aug. 15.

KHURREEF, s. Ar. *kharīf*, 'autumn'; and in India the crop, or harvest of the crop, which is sown at the beginning of the rainy season (April and May) and gathered in after it, including rice, the tall millets, maize, cotton, rape, sesamum, &c. The obverse crop is **rubbee** (q.v.).

[1809.—"Three weeks have not elapsed since the **Kureef** crop, which consists of *Bajru* (see **BAJRA**), *Jooar* (see **JOWAUR**), several smaller kinds of grain, and cotton, was cleared from off the fields, and the same ground is already ploughed . . . and sown for the great **Rubbee** crop of wheat, barley and *chunu* (see **GRAM**)."—*Broughton, Letters from a Mahratta Camp*, ed. 1892, p. 215.]

KHUTPUT, s. This is a native slang term in Western India for a prevalent system of intrigue and corruption. The general meaning of *khaṭpaṭ* in Hind. and Mahr. is rather 'wrangling' and 'worry,' but it is in the former sense that the word became famous (1850-54) in consequence of Sir James Outram's struggles with the rascality, during his tenure of the Residency of Baroda.

[1881.—"**Khutput**, or court intrigue, rules more or less in every native State, to an extent incredible among the more civilised nations of Europe."—*Frazer, Records of Sport*, 204.]

KHUTTRY, KHETTRY, CUTTRY, s. Hind. *Khattrī*, *Khatrī*, Skt. *Kshatriya*. The second, or military caste, in the theoretical or fourfold division of the Hindus. [But the word is more commonly applied to a mercantile caste, which has its origin in the Punjab, but is found in considerable numbers in other parts of India. Whether they are really of Kshatriya descent is a matter on which there is much difference of opinion. See *Crooke, Tribes and Castes of N.W.P.*, iii. 264 *seqq.*] The Χατριαῖοι whom Ptolemy locates apparently towards Rājputānā are probably *Kshatriyas*.

[1623.—"They told me **Ciautru** was a title of honour."—*P. della Valle*, Hak. Soc. ii. 312.

1630.—"And because **Cuttery** was of a martiall temper God gave him power to sway Kingdomes with the scepter."—*Lord, Banians*, 5.

1638.—"Les habitans . . . sont la pluspart *Benyans* et **Ketteris**, tisserans, teinturiers, et autres ouuriers en coton."—*Mandelslo*, ed. 1659, 130.

[1671.—"There are also **Cuttarees**, another Sect Principally about Agra and those parts up the Country, who are as the Banian Gentoos here."—In *Yule, Hedges' Diary*, Hak. Soc. ii. cccxi.]

1673.—"Opium is frequently eaten in great quantities by the Rashpoots, **Queteries**, and Patans."—*Fryer*, 193.

1726.—"The second generation in rank among these heathen is that of the **Settre-'as**."—*Valentijn, Chorom.* 87.

1782.—"The **Chittery** occasionally betakes himself to traffic, and the Sooder has become the inheritor of principalities."—*G. Forster's Journey*, ed. 1808, i. 64.

1836.—"The Banians are the mercantile caste of the original Hindoos. . . . They call themselves **Shudderies**, which signifies innocent or harmless (!)"—*Sir R. Phillips, Million of Facts*, 322.

KHYBER PASS, n.p. The famous gorge which forms the chief gate of Afghanistan from Peshawar, properly *Khaibar*. [The place of the same name near Al-Madinah is mentioned in the *Āīn* (iii. 57), and Sir R. Burton writes: "Khaybar in Hebrew is supposed to mean a castle. D'Herbelot makes it to mean a pact or association of the Jews against the Moslems." (*Pilgrimage*, ed. 1893, i. 346, note).]

1519.—"Early next morning we set out on our march, and crossing the **Kheiber Pass**, halted at the foot of it. The Khizer-Khail had been extremely licentious in their conduct. Both on the coming and going of our army they had shot upon the stragglers, and such of our people as lagged behind, or separated from the rest, and carried off their horses. It was clearly expedient that they should meet with a suitable chastisement."—*Baber*, p. 277.

1603.—

"On Thursday Jamrúd was our encamping ground.

"On Friday we went through the **Khaibar Pass**, and encamped at 'Alí Musjid."—*Jahángír*, in *Elliot*, vi. 314.

1783.—"The stage from Timrood (read *Jimrood*) to Dickah, usually called the **Hyber-pass**, being the only one in which much danger is to be apprehended from banditti, the officer of the escort gave orders to his party to . . . march early on the next morning. . . . Timur Shah, who used to pass the winter at Peshour . . . never passed through the territory of the **Hybers**, without their attacking his advanced or rear guard."—*Forster's Travels*, ed. 1808, ii. 65-66.

1856.—

". . . See the booted Moguls, like a pack
Of hungry wolves, burst from their desert lair,
And crowding through the **Khyber's** rocky strait,
Sweep like a bloody harrow o'er the land."
The Banyan Tree, p. 6.

KIDDERPORE, n.p. This is the name of a suburb of Calcutta, on the left bank of the Hoogly, a little way south of Fort William, and is the seat of the Government Dockyard. This establishment was formed in the 18th century by Gen. Kyd, "after whom," says the *Imperial Gazetteer*, "the village is named." This is the general belief, and was mine [H.Y.] till recently, when I found from the chart and directions in the *English Pilot* of 1711 that the village of Kidderpore (called in the same chart *Kitherepore*) then occupied the same position, *i.e.* immediately below "*Gobarnapore*" and that immediately below "*Chittanutte*" (*i.e.* Govindpūr, and Chatānatī (see **CHUTTANUTTY**).

1711.—"... then keep Rounding *Chitti Poe* (Chitpore) Bite down to *Chitty Nutty* Point (see **CHUTTANUTTY**). ... The Bite below *Gover Napore* (*Govindpūr*) is Shoal, and below the Shoal is an Eddy; therefore from Gover Napore, you must stand over to the Starboard-Shore, and keep it aboard till you come up almost with the Point opposite to **Kiddery-pore**, but no longer. ..."—*The English Pilot*, p. 65.

KIL, s. Pitch or bitumen. Tam. and Mal. *kīl*, Ar. *ḳīr*, Pers. *ḳīr* and *ḳīl*.

c. 1330.—"In Persia are some springs, from which flows a kind of pitch which is called *kic* (read **kir**) (*pix dico seu pegua*), with which they smear the skins in which wine is carried and stored."—*Friar Jordanus*, p. 10.

c. 1560.—"These are pitched with a bitumen which they call **quil**, which is like pitch."—*Correa*, Hak. Soc. 240.

KILLADAR, s. P.—H. *ḳil'adār*, from Ar. *ḳal'a*, 'a fort.' The commandant of a fort, castle, or garrison. The Ar. *ḳal'a* is always in India pronounced *ḳil'a*. And it is possible that in the first quotation Ibn Batuta has misinterpreted an Indian title; taking it as from Pers. *kilīd*, 'a key.' It may be noted with reference to *ḳal'a* that this Ar. word is generally represented in Spanish names by *Alcala*, a name borne by nine Spanish towns entered in K. Johnstone's *Index Geographicus*; and in Sicilian ones by *Calata*, e.g. *Calatafimi*, *Caltanissetta*, *Caltagirone*.

c. 1340.—"... Kādhī Khān, Sadr-al-Jihān, who became the chief of the Amīrs, and had the title of **Kalīt-dār**, *i.e.* Keeper of the keys of the Palace. This officer was accustomed to pass every night at the Sultan's door, with the bodyguard."—*Ibn Batuta*, iii. 196.

1757.—"The fugitive garrison ... returned with 500 more, sent by the **Kellidar** of Vandiwash."—*Orme*, ed. 1803, ii. 217.

1817.—"The following were the terms ... that Arni should be restored to its former governor or **Killedar**."—*Mill*, iii. 340.

1829.—"Among the prisoners captured in the Fort of Hattrass, search was made by us for the **Keeledar**."—*Mem. of John Shipp*, ii. 210.

KILLA-KOTE, s. pl. A combination of Ar.—P. and Hind. words for a fort (*kil'a* for *ḳal'a*, and *kōt*), used in Western India to imply the whole fortifications of a territory (*R. Drummond*).

KILLUT, KILLAUT, &c., s. Ar.—H. *khil'at*. A dress of honour presented by a superior on ceremonial occasions; but the meaning is often extended to the whole of a ceremonial present of that nature, of whatever it may consist. [The Ar. *khil-a'h* properly means 'what a man strips from his person.' "There were (among the later Moguls) five degrees of *khila't*, those of three, five, six, or seven pieces; or they might as a special mark of favour consist of clothes that the emperor had actually worn." (See for further details Mr. Irvine in *J.R.A.S.*, N.S., July 1896, p. 533).] The word has in Russian been degraded to mean the long loose gown which forms the most common dress in Turkistan, called generally by Schuyler 'a dressing-gown' (Germ. *Schlafrock*). See *Fraehn*, *Wolga Bulgaren*, p. 43.

1411.—"Several days passed in sumptuous feasts. **Khil'ats** and girdles of royal magnificence were distributed."—*Abdurazzāk*, in *Not. et Exts.* xiv. 209.

1673.—"Sir George Oxenden held it. ... He defended himself and the Merchants so bravely, that he had a **Collat** or **Seerpaw**, (q.v.) a Robe of Honour from Head to Foot, offered him from the *Great Mogul*."—*Fryer*, 87.

1676.—"This is the Wardrobe, where the Royal Garments are kept; and from whence the King sends for the **Calaat**, or a whole Habit for a Man, when he would honour any Stranger. ..."—*Tavernier*, E.T. ii. 46; [ed. *Ball*, ii. 98].

1774.—"A flowered satin gown was brought me, and I was dressed in it as a **khilat**."—*Bogle*, in *Markham's Tibet*, 25.

1786.—"And he the said Warren Hastings did send **kellauts**, or robes of honour (the most public and distinguished mode of acknowledging merit known in India) to the said ministers in testimony of his approbation of their services."—*Articles of Charge against Hastings*, in *Burke's Works*, vii. 25.

1809.—"On paying a visit to any Asiatic Prince, an inferior receives from him a complete dress of honour, consisting of a **khelaut**, a robe, a turban, a shield and sword, with a string of pearls to go round the neck."—*Ld. Valentia*, i. 99.

1813.—"On examining the **khelauts** . . . from the great Maharajah Madajee Sindia, the serpeych (see **SIRPECH**) . . . presented to Sir Charles Malet, was found to be composed of false stones."—*Forbes, Or. Mem.* iii. 50; [2nd ed. ii. 418].

KINCOB, s. Gold brocade. P.—H. *kamkhāb*, *kamkhwāb*, vulgarly *kimkhwāb*. The English is perhaps from the Gujarātī, as in that language the last syllable is short.

This word has been twice imported from the East. For it is only another form of the medieval name of an Eastern damask or brocade, **cammocca**. This was taken from the medieval Persian and Arabic forms *kamkhā* or *kīmkhwā*, 'damasked silk,' and seems to have come to Europe in the 13th century. F. Johnson's Dict. distinguishes between *kamkhā*, 'damask silk of one colour,' and *kimkhā*, 'damask silk of different colours.' And this again, according to Dozy, quoting Hoffmann, is originally a Chinese word *kin-kha*; in which doubtless *kin*, 'gold,' is the first element. *Kim* is the Fuhkien form of the word; qu. *kim-hoa*, 'gold-flower'? We have seen *kimkhwāb* derived from Pers. *kam-khwāb*, 'less sleep,' because such cloth is rough and prevents sleep! This is a type of many etymologies. ["The ordinary derivation of the word supposes that a man could not even dream of it who had not seen it (*kam*, 'little,' *khwab*, 'dream')" (*Yusuf Ali, Mono. on Silk*, 86). Platts and the *Madras Gloss.* take it from *kam*, 'little,' *khwāb*, 'nap.'] Ducange appears to think the word survived in the French *mocade* (or *moquette*); but if so the application of the term must have degenerated in England. (See in *Draper's Dict.* *mockado*, the form of which has suggested a sham stuff.)

c. 1300.—"Παιδὸς γὰρ εὐδαιμονοῦντος, καὶ τὸν πάτερα δεῖ συνευδαιμονεῖν· κατὰ τὴν ὑμνουμένην ἀντιπελάργωσιν. Ἐσθῆτα πηνοϋφῆ πεπομφῶς ἣν καμχᾶν ἡ Περσῶν φησι γλῶττα, δράσων εὖ ἴσθι, οὐ δίπλακα μὲν οὐδὲ μαρμαρέην οἵαν Ἑλένη ἐξύφαινεν, ἀλλ' ἠερειδῆ καὶ ποικίλην."—Letter of *Theodorus the Hyrtacenian* to *Lucites*, Protonotary and Protovestiary of the Trapezuntians. In *Notices et Extraits*, vi. 38.

1330.—"Their clothes are of Tartary cloth, and **camocas**, and other rich stuffs ofttimes adorned with gold and silver and precious stones."—*Book of the Estate of the Great Kaan*, in *Cathay*, 246.

c. 1340.—"You may reckon also that in Cathay you get three or three and a half pieces of damasked silk (**cammocca**) for a *sommo*."—*Pegolotti, ibid.* 295.

1342.—"The King of China had sent to the Sultan 100 slaves of both sexes for 500 pieces of **kamkhā**, of which 100 were made in the City of Zaitūn. . . ."—*Ibn Batuta*, iv. 1.

c. 1375.—"Thei setten this Ydole upon a Chare with gret reverence, wel arrayed with Clothes of Gold, of riche Clothes of Tartarye, of **Camacaa**, and other precious Clothes."—*Sir John Maundevill*, ed. 1866, p. 175.

c. 1400.—"In kyrtle of **Cammaka** kynge am I cladde."—*Coventry Mystery*, 163.

1404.—". . . é quando se del quisieron partir los Embajadores, fizo vestir al dicho Ruy Gonzalez una ropa de **camocan**, e dióle un sombrero, e dixole, que aquello tomase en señal del amor que el Tamurbec tenia al Señor Rey."—*Clavijo*, § lxxxviii.

1411.—"We have sent an ambassador who carries you from us **kīmkhā**."—Letter from *Emp. of Chian* to Shah Rukh, in *Not. et Ext.* xiv. 214.

1474.—"And the King gave a signe to him that wayted, comaunding him to give to the dauncer a peece of **Camocato**. And he taking this peece threwe it about the heade of the dauncer, and of the men and women: and useing certain wordes in praiseng the King, threwe it before the mynstrells."—*Josafa Barbaro, Travels in Persia*, E.T. Hak. Soc. p. 62.

1688.—"Καμουχᾶς, Χαμουχᾶς, Pannus sericus, sive ex bombyce confectus, e\ more Damasceno contextus, Italis *Damasco*, nostris olim Camocas, de quâ voce diximus in Gloss. Mediæ Latinit. hodie etiamnum *Mocade*." This is followed by several quotations from Medieval Greek MSS.—*Du Cange, Gloss. Med. et Inf. Graecitatis*, s.v.

1712.—In the *Spectator* under this year see an advertisement of an 'Isabella-coloured **Kincob** gown flowered with green and gold."—Cited in *Malcolm's Anecdotes of Manners*, &c., 1808, p. 429.

1733.—"Dieser mal waren von Seiten des Bräutigams ein Stück rother **Kamka** . . . und eine rothe Pferdehaut; von Seiten der Braut aber ein Stück violet **Kamka**."—u. s. w.—*Gmelin, Reise durch Siberien*, i. 137-138.

1781.—"My holiday suit, consisting of a flowered Velvet Coat of the Carpet Pattern, with two rows of broad Gold Lace, a rich **Kingcob** Waistcoat, and Crimson Velvet Breeches with Gold Garters, is now a butt to the shafts of Macaroni ridicule."—Letter from *An Old Country Captain*, in *India Gazette*, Feb. 24.

1786.—". . . . but not until the nabob's mother aforesaid had engaged to pay for the said change of prison, a sum of £10,000 . . . and that she would ransack the *zenanah* . . . for **Kincobs**, muslins, cloths, &c. &c. &c. . . ."—*Articles of Charge against Hastings*, in *Burke's Works*, 1852, vii. 23.

1809.—"Twenty trays of shawls, **kheenkaubs** . . . were tendered to me."—*Ld. Valentia*, i. 117.

[1813.—Forbes writes **keemcob, keemcab**, *Or. Mem.* 2nd i. 311 ; ii. 418.]

1829.—"Tired of this service we took possession of the town of Muttra, driving them out. Here we had glorious plunder—shawls, silks, satins, **khemkaubs**, money, &c."—*Mem. of John Shipp*, i. 124.

KING-CROW, s. A glossy black bird, otherwise called Drongo shrike, about as large as a small pigeon, with a long forked tail, *Dicrurus macrocercus*, Vieillot, found all over India. "It perches generally on some bare branch, whence it can have a good look-out, or the top of a house, or post, or telegraph-wire, frequently also on low bushes, hedges, walks, or ant-hills" (*Jerdon*).

1883.—". . . the **King-crow** . . . leaves the whole bird and beast tribe far behind in originality and force of character. . . . He does not come into the house, the telegraph wire suits him better. Perched on it he can see what is going on . . . drops, beak foremost, on the back of the kite . . . spies a bee-eater capturing a goodly moth, and after a hot chase, forces it to deliver up its booty."—*The Tribes on My Frontier*, 143.

KIOSQUE, s. From the Turki and Pers. *kūshk* or *kushk*, 'a pavilion, a villa,' &c. The word is not Anglo-Indian, nor is it a word, we think, at all common in modern native use.

c. 1350.—"When he was returned from his expedition, and drawing near to the capital, he ordered his son to build him a palace, or as those people call it a **kushk**, by the side of a river which runs at that place, which is called Afghanpūr."—*Ibn Batuta*, iii. 212.

1623.—"There is (in the garden) running water which issues from the entrance of a great **kiosck**, or covered place, where one may stay to take the air, which is built at the end of the garden over a great pond which adjoins the outside of the garden, so that, like the one at Surat, it serves also for the public use of the city."—*P. della Valle*, i. 535 ; [Hak. Soc. i. 68].

KIRBEE, KURBEE, s. Hind. *karbī, kirbī*, Skt. *kaḍamba*, 'the stalk of a pot-herb.' The stalks of *juār* (see **JOWAUR**), used as food for cattle.

[1809.—"We also fell in with large ricks of **kurbee**, the dried stalks of *Bajru* and *Jooar*, two inferior kinds of grain ; an excellent fodder for the camels."—*Broughton, Letters from a Mahratta Camp*, ed. 1892, p. 41.

[1823.—"Ordinary price of the straw (**kirba**) at harvest-time Rs. $1\frac{1}{2}$ per hundred sheaves. . . ."—*Trans. Lit. Soc. Bombay*, iii. 243.]

KISHM, n.p. The largest of the islands in the Persian Gulf, called by the Portuguese *Queixome* and the like, and sometimes by our old travellers, *Kishmish*. It is now more popularly called *Jazīrat-al-ṭawīla*, in Pers. *Jaz. darāz*, 'the Long Island' (like the Lewes), and the name of Kishm is confined to the chief town, at the eastern extremity, where still remains the old Portuguese fort taken in 1622, before which William Baffin the Navigator fell. But the oldest name is the still not quite extinct *Brokht*, which closely preserves the Greek *Oaracta*.

B.C. 325.—"And setting sail (from Harmozeia), in a run of 300 *stadia* they passed a desert and bushy island, and moored beside another island which was large and inhabited. The small desert island was named Organa (no doubt *Gerun*, afterwards the site of N. Hormuz—see **ORMUS**); and the one at which they anchored 'Οάρακτα, planted with vines and date-palms, and with plenty of corn."—*Arrian, Voyage of Nearchus*, ch. xxxvii.

1538.—" . . . so I hasted with him in the company of divers merchants for to go from Babylon (orig. *Babylonia*) to **Caixem**, whence he carried me to Ormuz. . . ."—*F. M. Pinto*, chap. vi. (*Cogan*, p. 9).

1553.—"Finally, like a timorous and despairing man . . . he determined to leave the city (Ormuz) deserted, and to pass over to the Isle of **Queixome**. That island is close to the mainland of Persia, and is within sight of Ormuz at 3 leagues distance."—*Barros*, III. vii. 4.

1554.—"Then we departed to the Isle of Kais or Old Hormuz, and then to the island of **Brakhta**, and some others of the Green Sea, *i.e.* in the Sea of Hormuz, without being able to get any intelligence."—*Sidi 'Ali*, 67.

[1600.—"**Queixiome**." See under **RESHIRE**.

[1623.—"They say likewise that *Ormuz* and **Keschiome** are extremely well fortified by the *Moors*."—*P. della Valle*, Hak. Soc. i. 188 ; in i. 2, **Kesom**.

[1652.—"**Keckmishe**." See under **CONGO BUNDER**.]

1673. — "The next morning we had brought *Loft* on the left hand of the Island of **Kismash**, leaving a woody Island uninhabited between **Kismash** and the Main." —*Fryer*, 320.

1682.—"The Island **Queixome**, or **Queixume**, or **Quizome**, otherwise called by travellers and geographers **Kechmiche**, and by the natives **Brokt**. . . ."—*Nieuhof*, *Zee en Lant-Reize*, ii. 103.

1817.—

"... Vases filled with **Kishmee's** golden wine
And the red weepings of the Shiraz vine."—*Moore*, *Mokanna*.

1821.—"We are to keep a small force at **Kishmi**, to make descents and destroy boats and other means of maritime war, whenever any symptoms of piracy reappear."—*Elphinstone*, in *Life*, ii. 121.

See also **BASSADORE**.

KISHMISH, s. Pers. Small stoneless raisins originally imported from Persia. Perhaps so called from the island **Kishm**. Its vines are mentioned by Arrian, and by T. Moore! (See under **KISHM**.) [For the manufacture of *Kishmish* in Afghanistan, see *Watt*, *Econ. Dict.* VI. pt. iv. 284.]

[c. 1665.—"*Usbec* being the country which principally supplies Delhi with these fruits. . . . **Kichmiches**, or raisins, apparently without stones. . . ."—*Bernier*, ed. *Constable*, 118.]

1673.—"We refreshed ourselves an entire Day at *Gerom*, where a small White Grape, without any Stone, was an excellent Cordial . . . they are called **Kismas Grapes**, and the Wine is known by the same Name farther than where they grow."—*Fryer*, 242.

1711.—"I could never meet with any of the **Kishmishes** before they were turned. These are Raisins, a size less than our Malagas, of the same Colour, and without Stones."—*Lockyer*, 233.

1883.—"**Kishmish**, a delicious grape, of white elongated shape, also small and very sweet, both eaten and used for wine-making. When dried this is the Sultana raisin. . . ."—*Wills*, *Modern Persia*, 171.

KISSMISS, s. Native servant's word for *Christmas*. But that festival is usually called *Barā din*, 'the great day.' (See **BURRA DIN**.)

KIST, s. Ar. *kist*. The yearly land revenue in India is paid by instalments which fall due at different periods in different parts of the country; each such instalment is called a *kist*, or quota. [The settlement of these instalments is *kist-bandī*.]

[1767.—"This method of comprising the whole estimate into so narrow a compass . . . will convey to you a more distinct idea . . . than if we transmitted a monthly account of the deficiency of each person's **Kistbundee**."— *Verelst*, *View of Bengal*, App. 56.]

1809.—"Force was always requisite to make him pay his **Kists** or tribute."—*Ld. Valentia*, i. 347.

1810.—"The heavy **Kists** or collections of Bengal are from August to September." —*Williamson*, *V. M.* ii. 498.

1817.—"'So desperate a malady,' said the President, 'requires a remedy that shall reach its source. And I have no hesitation in stating my opinion that there is no mode of eradicating the disease, but by removing the original cause; and placing these districts, which are pledged for the security of the **Kists**, beyond the reach of his Highness's management.'"—*Mill*, vi. 55.

KITMUTGAR, s. Hind. *khidmatgār*, from Ar.—P. *khidmat*, 'service,' therefore 'one rendering service.' The Anglo-Indian use is peculiar to the Bengal Presidency, where the word is habitually applied to a Musulman servant, whose duties are connected with serving meals and waiting at table under the **Consumah**, if there be one. *Kismutgar* is a vulgarism, now perhaps obsolete. The word is spelt by Hadley in his *Grammar* (see under **MOORS**) *khuzmutgār*. In the word *khidmat*, as in *khil'at* (see **KILLUT**), the terminal *t* in uninflected *Arabic* has long been dropt, though retained in the form in which these words have got into foreign tongues.

1759.—The wages of a **Khedmutgar** appear as 3 Rupees a month.—In *Long*, p. 182.

1765.—". . . they were taken into the service of *Soujah Dowlah* as immediate attendants on his person; *Hodjee* (see **HADJEE**) in capacity of his first **Kistmutgar** (or valet)."—*Holwell*, *Hist. Events*, &c., i. 60.

1782. — "I therefore beg to caution strangers against those race of vagabonds who ply about them under the denomination of **Consumahs** and **Kismutdars**."—*Letter in India Gazette*, Sept. 28.

1784. — "The Bearer . . . perceiving a quantity of blood . . . called to the Hookaburdar and a **Kistmutgar**."—In *Seton-Karr*, i. 13.

1810.—"The **Khedmutgar**, or as he is often termed, the *Kismutgar*, is with very few exceptions, a Mussulman; his business is to . . . wait at table." — *Williamson*, *V. M.* i. 212.

c. 1810.—"The **Kitmutgaur**, who had attended us from Calcutta, had done his work, and made his harvests, though in no very large way, of the '*Tazee Willaut*' or white people."—*Mrs. Sherwood, Autobiog.* 283. The phrase in italics stands for *tāzī Wilāyatī* (see **BILAYUT**), "fresh or green Europeans"—**Griffins** (q.v.).

1813.—"We . . . saw nothing remarkable on the way but a **Khidmutgar** of Chimnagie Appa, who was rolling from Poona to Punderpoor, in performance of a vow which he made for a child. He had been a month at it, and had become so expert that he went on smoothly and without pausing, and kept rolling evenly along the middle of the road, over stones and everything. He travelled at the rate of two coss a day."—*Elphinstone*, in *Life*, i. 257-8.

1878. — "We had each our own . . . **Kitmutgar** or table servant. It is the custom in India for each person to have his own table servant, and when dining out to take him with him to wait behind his chair." —*Life in the Mofussil*, i. 32.

[1889.—"Here's the **Khit** coming for the late change."—*R. Kipling, The Gadsbys*, 24.]

KITTYSOL, KITSOL, s. This word survived till lately in the Indian Tariff, but it is otherwise long obsolete. It was formerly in common use for 'an umbrella,' and especially for the kind, made of bamboo and paper, imported from China, such as the English fashion of to-day has adopted to screen fire-places in summer. The word is Portuguese, *quita-sol*, 'bar-sun.' Also *tirasole* occurs in Scot's *Discourse of Java*, quoted below from *Purchas*. See also *Hulsius, Coll. of Voyages*, in German, 1602, i. 27. [Mr. Skeat points out that in Howison's *Malay Dict.* (1801) we have, s.v. *Payong*: "A **kittasol**, sombrera," which is nearer to the Port. original than any of the examples given since 1611. This may be due to the strong Portuguese influence at Malacca.]

1588.—"The present was fortie peeces of silke . . . a litter chaire and guilt, and two **quitasoles** of silke."—*Parkes's Mendoza*, ii. 105.

1605.—". . . Before the shewes came, the King was brought out vpon a man's shoulders, bestriding his necke, and the man holding his legs before him, and had many rich **tyrasoles** carried ouer and round about him."—*E. Scot*, in *Purchas*, i. 181.

1611.—"Of **Kittasoles** of State for to shaddow him, there bee twentie" (in the Treasury of Akbar).—*Hawkins*, in *Purchas*, i. 215.

[1614.—"**Quitta solls** (or sombreros)."—*Foster, Letters*, ii. 207.]

1615.—"The China Capt., Andrea Dittis, retorned from Langasaque and brought me a present from his brother, viz., 1 faire **Kitesoll**. . . ."—*Cocks's Diary*, i. 28.

1648.—". . . above his head was borne two **Kippe-soles**, or Sun-skreens, made of Paper."—*Van Twist*, 51.

1673.—"Little but rich **Kitsolls** (which are the names of several Countries for Umbrelloes)."—*Fryer*, 160.

1687.—"They (the Aldermen of Madras) may be allowed to have **Kettysols** over them." — *Letter of Court of Directors*, in *Wheeler*, i. 200.

1690.—"nomen . . . vulgo effertur *Peritsol* . . . aliquando paulo aliter scribitur . . . et utrumque rectius pronuntiandum est *Paresol* vel potius *Parasol* cujus significatio Appellativa est, *i. q.* **Quittesol** seu *une Ombrelle*, quâ in calidioribus regionibus utuntur homines ad caput a sole tuendum." — *Hyde's* Preface to *Travels of Abraham Peritsol*, p. vii., in *Syntag. Dissertt.* i.

" "No Man in India, no not the *Mogul's* Son, is permitted the Priviledge of wearing a **Kittisal** or Umbrella. . . . The use of the Umbrella is sacred to the Prince, appropriated only to his use."—*Ovington*, 315.

1755.—"He carries a *Roundell*, or **Quit de Soleil** over your head."—*Ives*, 50.

1759.—In Expenses of Nawab's entertainment at Calcutta, we find: "A China **Kitysol** . . . Rs. 3½."—*Long*, 194.

1761.—A chart of Chittagong, by Barth. Plaisted, marks on S. side of Chittagong R., an umbrella-like tree, called "**Kittysoll** Tree."

[1785.—"To finish the whole, a **Kittesaw** (a kind of umbrella) is suspended not infrequently over the lady's head."—*Diary*, in *Busteed, Echoes*, 3rd ed. 112.]

1792.—"In those days the **Ketesal**, which is now sported by our very Cooks and Boatswains, was prohibited, as I have heard, d'you see, to any one below the rank of field officer."—*Letter*, in *Madras Courier*, May 3.

1813.—In the table of exports from Macao, we find:—

"**Kittisolls**, large, 2,000 to 3,000,
do. small, 8,000 to 10,000,"
Milburn, ii. 464.

1875.—"Umbrellas, Chinese, of paper, or **Kettysolls**."—*Indian Tariff*.

In another table of the same year "Chinese paper **Kettisols**, valuation Rs. 30 for a box of 110, duty 5 per cent." (See **CHATTA, ROUNDEL, UMBRELLA.**)

KITTYSOL-BOY, s. A servant who carried an umbrella over his master. See *Milburn*, ii. 62. (See examples under **ROUNDEL**.)

KLING, n.p. This is the name (*Kăling*) applied in the Malay countries, including our Straits Settlements, to the people of Continental India who trade thither, or are settled in those regions, and to the descendants of those settlers. [Mr. Skeat remarks: "The standard Malay form is not *Kāling*, which is the Sumatran form, but *Kĕling* (*K'ling* or *Kling*). The Malay use of the word is, as a rule, restricted to Tamils, but it is very rarely used in a wider sense."]

The name is a form of **Kalinga**, a very ancient name for the region known as the "**Northern Circars**," (q.v.), *i.e.* the Telugu coast of the Bay of Bengal, or, to express it otherwise in general terms, for that coast which extends from the Kistna to the Mahānadī. "The *Kalingas*" also appear frequently, after the Pauranic fashion, as an ethnic name in the old Sanskrit lists of races. *Kalinga* appears in the earliest of Indian inscriptions, viz. in the edicts of Aśoka, and specifically in that famous edict (XIII.) remaining in fragments at Girnār and Kapurdi-giri, and more completely at Khālsī, which preserves the link, almost unique from the Indian side, connecting the histories of India and of the Greeks, by recording the names of Antiochus, Ptolemy, Antigonus, Magas, and Alexander.

Kalinga is a kingdom constantly mentioned in the Buddhist and historical legends of Ceylon; and we find commemoration of the kingdom of **Kalinga** and of the capital city of **Kalinga***nagara* (*e.g.* in *Ind. Antiq.* iii. 152, x. 243). It was from a daughter of a King of Kalinga that sprang, according to the Mahawanso, the famous Wijayo, the civilizer of Ceylon and the founder of its ancient royal race.

Kalinga*patam*, a port of the Ganjam district, still preserves the ancient name of Kalinga, though its identity with the Kalinganagara of the inscriptions is not to be assumed. The name in later, but still ancient, inscriptions appears occasionally as *Tri-Kalinga*, "the Three Kalingas"; and this probably, in a Telugu version *Mūdu-Kalinga*, having that meaning, is the original of the *Modogalinga* of Pliny in one of the passages quoted from him. (The possible connection which obviously suggests itself of this name *Trikalinga* with the names *Tilinga* and *Tilingāna*, applied, at least since the Middle Ages, to the same region, will be noticed under **TELINGA**).

The coast of Kalinga appears to be that part of the continent whence commerce with the Archipelago at an early date, and emigration thither, was most rife; and the name appears to have been in great measure adopted in the Archipelago as the designation of India in general, or of the whole of the Peninsular part of it. Throughout the book of Malay historical legends called the *Sijara Malayu* the word *Kaling* or *Kling* is used for India in general, but more particularly for the southern parts (see *Journ. Ind. Archip.* v. 133). And the statement of Forrest (*Voyage to Mergui Archip.* 1792, p. 82) that Macassar "Indostan" was called "*Neegree Telinga*" (i.e. *Nagara Telinga*) illustrates the same thing and also the substantial identity of the names Telinga, Kalinga.

The name *Kling*, applied to settlers of Indian origin, makes its appearance in the Portuguese narratives immediately after the conquest of Malacca (1511). At the present day most, if not all of the Klings of Singapore come, not from the "Northern Circars," but from Tanjore, a purely Tamil district. And thus it is that so good an authority as Roorda van Eijsinga translates *Kalīng* by 'Coromandel people.' They are either Hindūs or Labbais (see **LUBBYE**). The latter class in British India never take domestic service with Europeans, whilst they seem to succeed well in that capacity in Singapore. "In 1876," writes Dr. Burnell, "the head-servant at Bekker's great hotel there was a very good specimen of the Nagūr Labbais; and to my surprise he recollected me as the head assistant-collector of Tanjore, which I had been some ten years before." The Hindu Klings appear to be chiefly drivers of hackney carriages and keepers of eating-houses. There is a Siva temple in Singapore, which is served by **Pandārāms** (q.v.). The only Brahmans there in 1876 were certain convicts. It may be noticed that Calingas is the name of a heathen tribe of (alleged) Malay origin in the east of N. Luzon (Philippine Islands).

B.C. c. 250. — "Great is **Kaliñga** conquered by the King Piyadasi, beloved of the Devas. There have been hundreds of thousands of creatures carried off. . . . On learning it the King . . . has immediately after the acquisition of **Kaliñga**, turned to religion, he has occupied himself with religion, he has conceived a zeal for religion, he applies himself to the spread of religion.

. . ."—Edict XIII. of Piyadasi (*i.e.* Aśoka), after *M. Senart*, in *Ind. Antiq.* x. 271. [And see *V. A. Smith, Asoka*, 129 *seq.*]

A.D. 60-70.—". . . multarumque gentium cognomen Bragmanae, quorum *Macco* (or *Macto*) **Calingae** . . . gentes **Calingae** mari proximi, et supra Mandaei, Malli quorum Mons Mallus, finisque tractus ejus Ganges . . . novissima gente Gangaridum **Calingarum**. Regia Pertalis vocatur . . . Insula in Gange est magnae amplitudinis gentem continens unam, nomine *Modo*galingam.

"Ab ostio Gangis ad promontorium **Calingon** et oppidum Dandaguda DCXXV. mil. passuum."—*Pliny, Hist. Nat.* vi. 18, 19, 20.

"In **Calingis** ejusdem Indiae gente quinquennes concipere feminas, octavum vitae annum non excedere."—*Ibid.* vii. 2.

c. 460.—"In the land of Wango, in the capital of Wango, there was formerly a certain Wango King. The daughter of the King of **Kalinga** was the principal queen of that monarch.

"That sovereign had a daughter (named Suppadewi) by his queen. Fortune-tellers predicted that she would connect herself with the king of animals (the lion), &c."—*Mahawanso*, ch. vi. (*Turnour*, p. 43).

c. 550.—In the "Brhat-Sañhitâ" of Varāhamihira, as translated by Prof. Kern in the *J.R. As. Soc.*, **Kalinga** appears as the name of a country in iv. 82, 86, 231, and "the **Kalingas**" as an ethnic name in iv. 461, 468, v. 65, 239.

c. 640. — "After having travelled from 1400 to 1500 *li*, he (Hwen Thsang) arrived at the Kingdom of **Kielingkia** (*Kaliñga*). Continuous forests and jungles extend for many hundreds of *li*. The kingdom produces wild elephants of a black colour, which are much valued in the neighbouring realms.* In ancient times the kingdom of **Kalinga** possessed a dense population, insomuch that in the streets shoulders rubbed, and the naves of waggon-wheels jostled; if the passengers but lifted their sleeves an awning of immense extent was formed . . ." —*Pèlerins Bouddh.* iii. 92-93.

c. 1045.—"Bhíshma said to the prince: 'There formerly came, on a visit to me, a Brahman, from the **Kalinga** country. . . .'" —*Vishnu Purāna*, in *H. H. Wilson's Works*, viii. 75.

(*Trikalinga*).

A.D. c. 150.—". . . Τρίγλυπτον, το καὶ **Τρίλιγγον**, Βασιλεῖον· ἐν ταύτῃ ἀλεκτρυόνες λέγονται εἶναι πωγωνίαι, καὶ κόρακες καὶ ψιττακοὶ λευκοί."—*Ptolemy*, vi. 2, 23.

(A.D. —?). — Copper Grant of which a summary is given, in which the ancestors of the Donors are Vijáya Krishna and Siva Gupta Deva, monarch of the **Three Kalingas**. — *Proc. As. Soc. Bengal*, 1872, p. 171.

A.D. 876.—". . . a god amongst principal and inferior kings—the chief of the devotees of Siva—Lord of **Trikalinga**—lord of the three principalities of the Gajapati (see **COSPETIR**) Aswapati, and Narapati. . . ." — *Copper Grant from near Jabalpur*, in *J.A.S.B.*, viii. Pt. i. p. 484.

c. 12th century. — ". . . The devout worshipper of Maheçvara, most venerable, great ruler of rulers, and Sovereign Lord, the glory of the Lunar race, and King of the **Three Kalingas**, Çri Mahábhava Gupta Deva. . . ."—*Copper Grant from Sambulpur*, in *J.A.S.B.* xlvi. Pt. i. p. 177.

". . . the fourth of the *Agasti* family, student of the *Kánva* section of the Yajur Veda, emigrant from **Tríkalinga** . . . by name Koṇḍadeva, son of Rámaçarmá."—*Ibid.*

(*Kling*).

1511.—". . . And beyond all these arguments which the merchants laid before Afonso Dalboquerque, he himself had certain information that the principal reason why this Javanese (*este Iao*) practised these doings was because he could not bear that the **Quilins** and *Chitims* (see **CHETTY**) who were Hindoos (*Gentios*) should be out of his jurisdiction." — *Alboquerque, Commentaries*, Hak. Soc. iii. 146.

" "For in Malaca, as there was a continual traffic of people of many nations, each nation maintained apart its own customs and administration of justice, so that there was in the city one **Bendará** (q.v.) of the natives, of Moors and heathen severally; a Bendará of the foreigners; a Bendará of the foreign merchants of each class severally; to wit, of the Chins, of the Leqeos (**Loo-choo** people), of the people of Siam, of Pegu, of the **Quelins**, of the merchants from within Cape Comorin, of the merchants of India (*i.e.* of the Western Coast), of the merchants of Bengala. . . ."—*Correa*, ii. 253.

[1533.—"**Quelys.**" See under **TUAN.**]

1552.—"E repartidos os nossos em quadrilhas roubarão a cidade, et com quāto se não buleo com as casas dos **Quelins**, nem dos Pegus, nem dos Jaos . . ."—*Castanheda*, iii. 208; see also ii. 355.

De Bry terms these people **Quillines** (iii. 98, &c.)

1601.—"5. His Majesty shall repopulate the burnt suburb (of Malacca) called *Campo* **Clin** . . ."—Agreement between the King of Johore and the Dutch, in *Valentijn* v. 332. [In Malay *Kampong* **K'ling** or **Kling**, 'Kling village.']

1602.—"About their loynes they weare a kind of Callico-cloth, which is made at **Clyn** in manner of a silke girdle."—*E. Scot*, in *Purchas*, i. 165.

1604.—"If it were not for the *Sabindar* (see **SHABUNDER**), the Admirall, and one or two more which are **Clyn**-men borne, there were no living for a Christian among them. . . ."—*Ibid.* i. 175.

* The same breed of elephants perhaps that is mentioned on this part of the coast by the author of the *Periplus*, by whom it is called ἡ Δησαρήνη χώρα φέρουσα ἐλέφαντα τὸν λεγόμενον Βωσαρή.

1605.—"The fifteenth of Iune here arrived *Nockhoda* (**Nacoda**) *Tingall*, a **Cling**-man from Banda. . . ."—*Capt. Saris*, in *Purchas*, i. 385.

1610.—"His Majesty should order that all the Portuguese and **Quelins** merchants of San Thomé, who buy goods in Malacca and export them to India, San Thomé, and Bengala should pay the export duties, as the Javanese (*os Juos*) who bring them in pay the import duties." — *Livro das Monções*, 318.

1613.—See remarks under **Cheling**, and, in the quotation from Godinho de Eredia, "**Campon Chelim**" and "**Chelis** of Coromandel."

1868.—"The **Klings** of Western India are a numerous body of Mahometans, and . . . are petty merchants and shopkeepers."—*Wallace, Malay Archip.*, ed. 1880, p. 20.

,, "The foreign residents in Singapore mainly consist of two rival races . . . viz. **Klings** from the Coromandel Coast of India, and Chinese. . . . The **Klings** are universally the hack-carriage (gharry) drivers, and private grooms (syces), and they also monopolize the washing of clothes. . . . But besides this class there are **Klings** who amass money as tradesmen and merchants, and become rich."—*Collingwood, Rambles of a Naturalist*, 268-9.

KOBANG, s. The name (lit. 'greater division') of a Japanese gold coin, of the same form and class as the **obang** (q.v.). The coin was issued occasionally from 1580 to 1860, and its most usual weight was 222 grs. troy. The shape was oblong, of an average length of $2\frac{1}{2}$ inches and width of $1\frac{1}{2}$.

[1599.—"**Cowpan.**" See under **TAEL.**]

1616.—"Aug. 22.—About 10 a clock we departed from Shrongo, and paid our host for the howse a bar of **Coban** gould, vallued at 5 *tais* 4 *mas*. . . ."—*Cocks's Diary*, i. 165.

,, Sept. 17.—"I received two bars **Coban** gould with two ichibos (see **ITZEBOO**) of 4 to a **coban**, all gould, of Mr. Eaton to be acco. for as I should have occasion to use them."—*Ibid.* 176.

1705.—"Outre ces roupies il y a encore des pièces d'or qu'on appelle **coupans**, qui valent dix-neuf roupies. . . . Ces pièces s'appellant coupans parce-qu'elles sont longues, et si plates qu'on en pourroit *couper*, et c'est par allusion à notre langue qu'on les appellent ainsi."—*Luillier*, 256-7.

1727.—"My friend took my advice and complimented the Doctor with five *Japon* **Cupangs**, or fifty Dutch Dollars."—*A. Hamilton*, ii. 86; [ed. 1744, ii. 85].

1726.—"1 gold **Koebang** (which is no more seen now) used to make 10 ryx dollars, 1 Itzebo making $2\frac{1}{2}$ ryx dollars."—*Valentijn*, iv. 356.

1768-71.—"The coins current at Batavia are the following:—The milled Dutch gold ducat, which is worth 6 gilders and 12 stivers; the Japan gold **coupangs**, of which the old go for 24 gilders, and the new for 14 gilders and 8 stivers."—*Stavorinus*, E.T. i. 307.

[1813.—"**Copang.**" See under **MACE.**]

1880.—"Never give a **Kobang** to a cat." —*Jap. Proverb*, in *Miss Bird*, i. 367.

KOËL, s. This is the common name in northern India of *Eudynamys orientalis*, L. (Fam. of *Cuckoos*), also called *kokilā* and *koklā*. The name *koīl* is taken from its cry during the breeding season, "*ku-il, ku-il*, increasing in vigour and intensity as it goes on. The male bird has also another note, which Blyth syllables as *Ho-whee-ho*, or *Ho-a-o*, or *Ho-y-o*. When it takes flight it has yet another somewhat melodious and rich liquid call; all thoroughly cuculine." (*Jerdon.*)

c. 1526.—"Another is the **Koel**, which in length may be equal to the crow, but is much thinner. It has a kind of song, and is the nightingale of Hindustan. It is respected by the natives of Hindustan as much as the nightingale is by us. It inhabits gardens where the trees are close planted."—*Baber*, p. 323.

c. 1590.—"The **Koyil** resembles the myneh (see **MYNA**), but is blacker, and has red eyes and a long tail. It is fabled to be enamoured of the rose, in the same manner as the nightingale."—*Ayeen*, ed. *Gladwin*, ii. 381; [ed. *Jarrett*, iii. 121].

c. 1790.—"Le plaisir que cause la fraîcheur dont on jouit sous cette belle verdure est augmenté encore par le gazouillement des oiseaux et les cris clairs et perçans du **Koewil**. . . ."—*Haafner*, ii. 9.

1810.—"The **Kokeela** and a few other birds of song."—*Maria Graham*, 22.

1883.—"This same crow-pheasant has a second or third cousin called the **Koel**, which deposits its eggs in the nest of the crow, and has its young brought up by that discreditable foster-parent. Now this bird supposes that it has a musical voice, and devotes the best part of the night to vocal exercise, after the manner of the nightingale. You may call it the Indian nightingale if you like. There is a difference however in its song . . . when it gets to the very top of its pitch, its voice cracks and there is an end of it, or rather there is not, for the persevering musician begins again. . . . Does not the Maratha novelist, dwelling on the delights of a spring morning in an Indian village, tell how the air was filled with the dulcet melody of the **Koel**, the green parrot, and the peacock?"—*Tribes on My Frontier*, 156.

KOHINOR, n.p. Pers. *Koh-i-nūr*, 'Mountain of Light'; the name of one of the most famous diamonds in the world. It was an item in the Deccan booty of Alāuddīn Khiljī (dd. 1316), and was surrendered to Baber (or more precisely to his son Humāyūn) on the capture of Agra (1526). It remained in the possession of the Moghul dynasty till Nādir extorted it at Delhi from the conquered Mahommed Shāh (1739). After Nādir's death it came into the hands of Ahmed Shāh, the founder of the Afghān monarchy. Shāh Shujā', Ahmed's grandson, had in turn to give it up to Ranjīt Singh when a fugitive in his dominions. On the annexation of the Punjab in 1849 it passed to the English, and is now among the Crown jewels of England. Before it reached that position it ran through strange risks, as may be read in a most diverting story told by Bosworth Smith in his *Life of Lord Lawrence* (i. 327-8). In 1850-51, before being shown at the Great Exhibition in Hyde Park, it went through a process of cutting which, for reasons unintelligible to ordinary mortals, reduced its weight from $186\frac{1}{16}$ carats to $106\frac{1}{16}$. [See an interesting note in *Ball's Tavernier*, ii. 431 *seqq.*]

1526.—"In the battle in which Ibrâhim was defeated, Bikermâjit (Raja of Gwalior) was sent to hell. Bikermâjit's family . . . were at this moment in Agra. When Hûmâiûn arrived . . . (he) did not permit them to be plundered. Of their own free will they presented to Hûmâiûn a *peshkesh* (see **PESHCUSH**), consisting of a quantity of jewels and precious stones. Among these was one famous diamond which had been acquired by Sultân Alâeddîn. It is so valuable that a judge of diamonds valued it at half the daily expense of the whole world. It is about eight mishkals. . . ."—*Baber*, p. 308.

1676.—(With an engraving of the stone.) "This diamond belongs to the Great Mogul . . . and it weighs 319 *Ratis* (see **RUTTEE**) and a half, which make 279 and nine 16ths of our Carats; when it was rough it weigh'd 907 *Ratis*, which make 793 carats."—*Tavernier*, E.T. ii. 148; [ed. *Ball*, ii. 123].

[1842.—"In one of the bracelets was the **Cohi Noor**, known to be one of the largest diamonds in the world."—*Elphinstone, Caubul*, i. 68.]

1856.—
"He (Akbar) bears no weapon, save his dagger, hid
Up to the ivory haft in muslin swathes;
No ornament but that one famous gem,
Mountain of Light! bound with a silken thread
Upon his nervous wrist; more used, I ween,
To feel the rough strap of his buckler there."
The Banyan Tree.

See also (1876) Browning, Epilogue to *Pacchiarotto*, &c.

KOOKRY, s. Hind. *kukrī*, [which originally means 'a twisted skein of thread,' from *kūknā*, 'to wind'; and then anything curved]. The peculiar weapon of the Goorkhas, a bill, admirably designed and poised for hewing a branch or a foe. [See engravings in *Egerton, Handbook of Indian Arms*, pl. ix.]

1793.—"It is in felling small trees or shrubs, and lopping the branches of others for this purpose that the dagger or knife worn by every Nepaulian, and called **khookheri**, is chiefly employed."—*Kirkpatrick's Nepaul*, 118.

[c. 1826.—"I hear my friend means to offer me a **Cuckery**."—*Ld. Combermere*, in *Life*, ii. 179.

[1828.—"We have seen some men supplied with **Cookeries**, and the curved knife of the Ghorka."—*Skinner, Excursions*, ii. 129.]

1866.—"A dense jungle of bamboo, through which we had to cut a way, taking it by turns to lead, and hew a path through the tough stems with my '**kukri**,' which here proved of great service."—*Lt.-Col. T. Lewin, A Fly on the Wheel*, p. 269.

KOOMKY, s. (See **COOMKY**.)

KOONBEE, KUNBEE, KOOLUMBEE, n.p. The name of the prevalent cultivating class in Guzerat and the Konkan, the Kurmī of N. India. Skt. *kuṭumba*. The *Kunbī* is the pure Sudra, [but the N. India branch are beginning to assert a more respectable origin]. In the Deccan the title distinguished the cultivator from him who wore arms and preferred to be called a *Mahratta* (*Drummond*).

[1598.—"The Canarijns and **Corumbijns** are the Countrimen."—*Linschoten*, Hak. Soc. i. 260.

[c. 1610.—"The natives are the Bramenis, Canarins and **Coulombins**."—*Pyrard de Laval*, Hak. Soc. ii. 35.

[1813.—"A Sepoy of the Mharatta or **Columbee** tribe."—*Forbes, Or. Mem.* 2nd ed. i. 27.]

KOOT, s. Hind. *kuṭ*, from Skt. *kushṭa*, the *costum* and *costus* of the Roman writers. (See under **PUTCHOCK**.)

B.C. 16.—
"**Costum** molle date, et blandi mihi thuris honores."—*Propertius*, IV. vi. 5.

c. 70-80.—"Odorum causâ unguentorumque et deliciarum, si placet, etiam superstitionis gratiâ emantur, quoniam tunc supplicamus et **costo**."—*Pliny, Hist. Nat.* xxii. 56.

c. 80-90.—(From the Sinthus or Indus) "ἀντιφορτίζεται δὲ **κόστος**, βδέλλα, λύκιον, νάρδος. . . ."—*Periplus*.

1563.—"*R.* And does not the Indian **costus** grow in Guzarate?

"*O.* It grows in territory often subject to Guzarat, *i.e.* lying between Bengal and Dely and Cambay, I mean the lands of Mamdou and Chitor. . . ."—*Garcia*, f. 72.

1584.—"**Costo** *dulce* from Zindi and Cambaia."—*Barret*, in *Hakl.* ii. 413.

KOOZA, s. A **goglet**, or pitcher of porous clay; corr. of Pers. *kūza*. Commonly used at Bombay.

[1611.—"One sack of **cusher** to make coho."—*Danvers, Letters*, i. 128.]

1690.—"Therefore they carry about with them **Kousers** or Jarrs of Water, when they go abroad, to quench their thirst. . . ."—*Ovington*, 295.

[1871.—"Many parts of India are celebrated for their **Coojahs** or guglets, but the finest are brought from Bussorah, being light, thin, and porous, made from a whitish clay."—*Riddell, Ind. Domest. Econ.*, 362.]

KOSHOON, s. This is a term which was affected by Tippoo Sahib in his military organisation, for a brigade, or a regiment in the larger Continental use of that word. His *Piādah 'askar*, or Regular Infantry, was formed into 5 *Kachahris* (see **CUTCHERRY**), composed in all of 27 *Kushūns*. A MS. note on the copy of Kirkpatrick's *Letters* in the India Office Library says that *Kushoon* was properly Skt. *kshuni* or *kshauni*, 'a grand division of the force of an Empire, as used in the *Mahābhārata*. But the word adopted by Tippoo appears to be Turki. Thus we read in Quatremère's transl. from Abdurrazzāk: "He (Shāh Rukh) distributed to the emirs who commanded the *tomāns* (corps of 10,000), the **koshūn** (corps of 1000), the *sadeh* (of 100), the *deheh* (of 10), and even to the private soldiers, presents and rewards" (*Nots. et Exts.* xiv. 91; see also p. 89). Again: "The soldiers of Isfahan having heard of the amnesty accorded them, arrived, **koshūn** by **koshūn**." (*Ibid.* 130.) Vambéry gives **ḳoshūn** as Or. Turki for an army, a troop (literally whatever is composed of several parts).

[1753.—". . . Kara-**kushun**, are also foot soldiers . . . the name is Turkish and signifies black guard."—*Hanway*, I. pt. ii. 252.]

c. 1782.—"In the time of the deceased Nawab, the exercises . . . of the regular troops were . . . performed, and the word given according to the French system . . . but now, the Sultan (Tippoo) . . . changed the military code . . . and altered the technical terms or words of command . . . to words of the Persian and Turkish languages. . . . From the regular infantry 5000 men being selected, they were named **Kushoon**, and the officer commanding that body was called a Sipahdar. . . ."—*Hist. of Tipu Sultan*, p. 31.

[1810.—". . . with a division of five regular **cushoons**. . . ."—*Wilks, Mysore*, reprint 1869, ii. 218.]

KOTOW, KOWTOW, s. From the Chinese *k'o-t'ou*, lit. 'knock-head'; the salutation used in China before the Emperor, his representatives, or his symbols, made by prostrations repeated a fixed number of times, the forehead touching the ground at each prostration. It is also used as the most respectful form of salutation from children to parents, and from servants to masters on formal occasions, &c.

This mode of homage belongs to old Pan-Asiatic practice. It was not, however, according to M. Pauthier, of indigenous antiquity at the Court of China, for it is not found in the ancient Book of Rites of the Cheu Dynasty, and he supposes it to have been introduced by the great destroyer and reorganiser, Tsin shi Hwangti, the Builder of the Wall. It had certainly become established by the 8th century of our era, for it is mentioned that the Ambassadors who came to Court from the famous Hārūn-al-Rashīd (A.D. 798) had to perform it. Its nature is mentioned by Marco Polo, and by the ambassadors of Shāh Rukh (see below). It was also the established ceremonial in the presence of the Mongol Khāns, and is described by Baber under the name of *kornish*. It was probably introduced into Persia in the time of the Mongol Princes of the house of Hulākū, and it continued to be in use in the time of Shāh 'Abbās. The custom indeed in Persia may possibly have come down from time immemorial, for, as the classical quotations show, it was of very ancient prevalence in that country. But the interruptions to Persian monarchy are perhaps against this. In English the term, which was made familiar by Lord Amherst's refusal to perform it at Pekin in 1816, is frequently used for servile acquiescence or adulation.

K'o-tou-k'o-tou! is often colloquially used for 'Thank you' (*E. C. Baber*).

c. B.C. 484.—"And afterwards when they were come to Susa in the king's presence, and the guards ordered them to fall down and do obeisance, and went so far as to use force to compel them, they refused, and said they would never do any such thing, even were their heads thrust down to the ground, for it was not their custom to worship men, and they had not come to Persia for that purpose."—*Herodotus*, by *Rawlinson*, vii. 136.

c. B.C. 464.—"Themistocles . . . first meets with Artabanus the Chiliarch, and tells him that he was a Greek, and wished to have an interview with the king. . . . But quoth he; 'Stranger, the laws of men are various. . . . You Greeks, 'tis said, most admire liberty and equality, but to us of our many and good laws the best is to honour the king, and adore him by prostration, as the Image of God, the Preserver of all things.' . . . Themistocles, on hearing these things, says to him: 'But I, O Artabanus, . . . will myself obey your laws.' . . ."—*Plutarch*, *Themistoc.*, xxvii.

c. B.C. 390.—"Conon, being sent by Pharnabazus to the king, on his arrival, in accordance with Persian custom, first presented himself to the Chiliarch Tithraustes who held the second rank in the empire, and stated that he desired an interview with the king; for no one is admitted without this. The officer replied: 'It can be at once; but consider whether you think it best to have an interview, or to write the business on which you come. For if you come into the presence you must needs worship the king (what they call προσκυνεῖν). If this is disagreeable to you you may commit your wishes to me, without doubt of their being as well accomplished.' Then Conon says: 'Indeed it is not disagreeable to me to pay the king any honour whatever. But I fear lest I bring discredit upon my city, if belonging to a state which is wont to rule over other nations I adopt manners which are not her own, but those of foreigners.' Hence he delivered his wishes in writing to the officer."—*Corn. Nepos*, *Conon*, c. iv.

B.C. 324.—"But he (Alexander) was now downhearted, and beginning to be despairing towards the divinity, and suspicious towards his friends. Especially he dreaded Antipater and his sons. Of these Iolas was the Chief Cupbearer, whilst Kasander had come but lately. So the latter, seeing certain Barbarians prostrating themselves (προσκυνοῦντας), a sort of thing which he, having been brought up in Greek fashion, had never witnessed before, broke into fits of laughter. But Alexander in a rage gript him fast by the hair with both hands, and knocked his head against the wall."—*Plutarch*, *Alexander*, lxxiv.

A.D. 798.—"In the 14th year of Tchin-yuan, the Khalif Galun (*Hārūn*) sent three ambassadors to the Emperor; they performed the ceremony of kneeling and beating the forehead on the ground, to salute the Emperor. The earlier ambassadors from the Khalifs who came to China had at first made difficulties about performing this ceremony. The Chinese history relates that the Mahomedans declared that they knelt only to worship Heaven. But eventually, being better informed, they made scruple no longer."—*Gaubil*, *Abrégé de l'Histoire des Thangs*, in *Amyot*, *Mémoires conc. les Chinois*, xvi. 144.

c. 1245.—"Tartari de mandato ipsius principes suos Baiochonoy et Bato violenter ab omnibus nunciis ad ipsos venientibus faciunt adorari cum triplici genuum flexione, triplici quoque capitum suorum in terram allisione."—*Vincent Bellovacensis*, *Spec. Historiale*, l. xxix. cap. 74.

1298.—"And when they are all seated, each in his proper place, then a great prelate rises and says with a loud voice: 'Bow and adore!' And as soon as he has said this, the company bow down until their foreheads touch the earth in adoration towards the Emperor as if he were a god. And this adoration they repeat four times."—*Marco Polo*, Bk. ii. ch. 15.

1404.—"E ficieronle vestir dos ropas de *camocan* (see **KINCOB**), é la usanza era, quando estas roupat ponian por el Señor, de facer un gran yantar, é despues de comer de les vestir de las ropas, é entonces de fincar los finojos tres veces in tierra por reverencia del gran Señor."—*Clavijo*, § xcii.

,, "And the custom was, when these robes were presented as from the Emperor, to make a great feast, and after eating to clothe them with the robes, and then that they should touch the ground three times with the knees to show great reverence for the Lord."—See *Markham*, p. 104.

1421.—"His worship Hajji Yusuf the Kazi, who was . . . chief of one of the twelve imperial Councils, came forward accompanied by several Mussulmans acquainted with the languages. They said to the ambassadors: 'First prostrate yourselves, and then touch the ground three times with your heads.'"—*Embassy from Shāh Rukh*, in *Cathay*, p. ccvi.

1502.—"My uncle the elder Khan came three or four farsangs out from Tashkend, and having erected an awning, seated himself under it. The younger Khan advanced . . . and when he came to the distance at which the *kornish* is to be performed, he knelt nine times. . . ."—*Baber*, 106.

c. 1590.—The *kornish* under Akbar had been greatly modified:

"His Majesty has commanded the palm of the right hand to be placed upon the forehead, and the head to be bent downwards. This mode of salutation, in the language of the present age, is called *Kornish*."—*Āīn*, ed. *Blochmann*, i. 158.

But for his position as the head of religion, in his new faith he permitted, or claimed prostration (*sijda*) before him:

"As some perverse and dark-minded men look upon prostration as blasphemous man-worship, His Majesty, from practical wisdom, has ordered it to be discontinued by the ignorant, and remitted it to all ranks. . . . However, in the private assembly, when any of those are in waiting, upon whom the star of good fortune shines, and they receive the order of seating themselves, they certainly perform the prostration of gratitude by bowing down their foreheads to the earth."—*Ibid.* p. 159.

[1615.—". . . Whereatt some officers called me to *size-da* (*sij-dah*), but the King answered no, no, in Persian."—*Sir T. Roe*, Hak. Soc. i. 244; and see ii. 296.]

1618.—"The King (Shāh 'Abbās) halted and looked at the Sultan, the latter on both knees, as is their fashion, near him, and advanced his right foot towards him to be kissed. The Sultan having kissed it, and touched it with his forehead . . . made a circuit round the king, passing behind him, and making way for his companions to do the like. This done the Sultan came and kissed a second time, as did the other, and this they did three times."—*P. della Valle*, i. 646.

[c. 1686.—"Job (Charnock) made a salam *Koornis*, or low obeisance, every second step he advanced."—*Orme*, *Fragments*, quoted in *Yule, Hedges' Diary*, Hak. Soc. ii. xcvii.]

1816.—"Lord Amherst put into my hands . . . a translation . . . by Mr. Morrison of a document received at Tongchow with some others from Chang, containing an official description of the ceremonies to be observed at the public audience of the Embassador. . . . The Embassador was then to have been conducted by the Mandarins to the level area, where kneeling . . . he was next to have been conducted to the lower end of the hall, where facing the upper part . . . he was to have performed the **ko-tou** with 9 prostrations; afterwards he was to have been led out of the hall, and having prostrated himself once behind the row of Mandarins, he was to have been allowed to sit down; he was further to have prostrated himself with the attendant Princes and Mandarins when the Emperor drank. Two other prostrations were to have been made, the first when the milk-tea was presented to him, and the other when he had finished drinking."—*Ellis's Journal of* (Lord Amherst's) *Embassy to China*, 213-214.

1824.—"The first ambassador, with all his following, shall then perform the ceremonial of the three kneelings and the nine prostrations; they shall then rise and be led away in proper order."—*Ceremonial observed at the Court of Peking for the Reception of Ambassadors*, ed. 1824, in *Pauthier*, 192.

1855.—". . . The spectacle of one after another of the aristocracy of nature making the **kotow** to the aristocracy of the accident."—*H. Martineau*, *Autobiog.* ii. 377.

1860.—"Some Seiks, and a private in the Buffs having remained behind with the grog-carts, fell into the hands of the Chinese. On the next morning they were brought before the authorities, and commanded to perform the **kotou**. The Seiks obeyed; but Moyse, the English soldier, declaring that he would not prostrate himself before any Chinaman alive, was immediately knocked upon the head, and his body thrown upon a dunghill" (see China Correspondent of the *Times*). This passage prefaces some noble lines by Sir F. Doyle, ending:

"Vain mightiest fleets, of iron framed;
  Vain those all-shattering guns;
Unless proud England keep, untamed,
  The strong heart of her sons.
So let his name through Europe ring—
  A man of mean estate,
Who died, as firm as Sparta's king,
  Because his soul was great."
Macmillan's Mag. iii. 130.

1876.—"Nebba more **kowtow** big people."—*Leland*, 46.

1879.—"We know that John Bull adores a lord, but a man of Major L'Estrange's social standing would scarcely **kowtow** to every shabby little title to be found in stuffy little rooms in Mayfair."—*Sat. Review*, April 19, p. 505.

KOTUL, s. This appears to be a Turki word, though adopted by the Afghans. *Kotal*, 'a mountain pass, a *col*.' Pavet de Courteille quotes several passages, in which it occurs, from Baber's original Turki.

[1554.—"**Koutel**." See under **RHINOCEROS**.

[1809.—"We afterwards went on through the hills, and crossed two **Cotuls** or passes."—*Elphinstone*, *Caubul*, ed. 1842, i. 51.]

KUBBER, KHUBBER, s. Ar.—P.—H. *khabar*, 'news,' and especially as a sporting term, news of game, *e.g.* "There is **pucka khubber** of a tiger this morning."

[1828.—". . . the servant informed us that there were some gongwalas, or villagers, in waiting, who had some **khubber** (news about tigers) to give us."—*Mundy*, *Pen and Pencil Sketches*, ed. 1858, p. 53.]

1878.—"**Khabar** of innumerable black partridges had been received."—*Life in the Mofussil*, i. 159.

1879.—"He will not tell me what **khabbar** has been received."—'*Vanity Fair*,' Nov. 29, p. 299.

KUBBERDAUR. An interjectional exclamation, 'Take care!' Pers. *khabar-dār!* 'take heed!' (see **KUBBER**). It is the usual cry of chokidārs to show that they are awake. [As a substantive it has the sense of a 'scout' or 'spy.']

c. 1664.—"Each *omrah* causeth a guard to be kept all the night long, in his particular camp, of such men that perpetually go the round, and cry **Kaber-dar**, have a care."—*Bernier*, E.T. 119; [ed. *Constable*, 369].

c. 1665.—"Les archers crient ensuite a pleine tête, **Caberdar**, c'est à dire prends garde."—*Thevenot*, v. 58.

[1813.—"There is a strange custom which prevails at all Indian courts, of having a servant called a **khubur-dar**, or newsman, who is an admitted spy upon the chief, about whose person he is employed."—*Broughton*, *Letters from a Mahratta Camp*, ed. 1892, p. 25.]

KUHÁR, s. Hind. *Kahār*, [Skt. *skandha-kāra*, 'one who carries loads on his shoulders']. The name of a Sūdra caste of cultivators, numerous in Bahār and the N.W. Provinces, whose speciality is to carry palankins. The name is, therefore, in many parts of India synonymous with 'palankin-bearer,' and the Hindu body-servants called **bearers** (q.v.) in the Bengal Presidency are generally of this caste.

c. 1350.—"It is the custom for every traveller in India . . . also to hire **kahārs**, who carry the kitchen furniture, whilst others carry himself in the palankin, of which we have spoken, and carry the latter when it is not in use."—*Ibn Batuta*, iii. 415.

c. 1550.—"So saying he began to make ready a present, and sent for bulbs, roots, and fruit, birds and beasts, with the finest of fish . . . which were brought by **kahārs** in basketfuls."—*Rāmāyana of Tulsi Dās*, by *Growse*, 1878, ii. 101.

1673.—"He (the President of Bombay) goes sometimes in his Coach, drawn by large Milk-white Oxen, sometimes on Horseback, other times in Palankeens, carried by **Cohors**, *Musselmen* Porters."—*Fryer*, 68.

1810.—"The **Cahar**, or palanquin-bearer, is a servant of peculiar utility in a country where, for four months, the intense heat precludes Europeans from taking much exercise."—*Williamson*, *V.M.* i. 209.

1873.—"*Bhui* **Kahár**. A widely spread caste of rather inferior rank, whose occupation is to carry *palkis*, *dolis*, water-skins, &c.; to act as Porters . . . they eat flesh and drink spirits: they are an ignorant but industrious class. Buchanan describes them as of Telinga descent. . . ."—Dr. H. V. Carter's *Notices of Castes in Bombay Pry.*, quoted in *Ind. Antiq.* ii. 154.

KULÁ, KLÁ, n.p. Burmese name of a native of Continental India; and hence misapplied also to the English and other Westerns who have come from India to Burma; in fact used generally for a Western foreigner.

The origin of this term has been much debated. Some have supposed it to be connected with the name of the Indian race, the *Kols;* another suggestion has connected it with *Kalinga* (see **KLING**); and a third with the Skt. *kula*, 'caste or tribe'; whilst the Burmese popular etymology renders it from *kū*, 'to cross over,' and *la*, 'to come,' therefore 'the people that come across (the sea).' But the true history of the word has for the first time been traced by Professor Forchhammer, to **Gola**, the name applied in old Pegu inscriptions to the Indian Buddhist immigrants, a name which he identifies with the Skt. *Gauḍa*, the ancient name of Northern Bengal, whence the famous city of Gauṛ (see **GOUR, c**).

14th cent.—"The Heroes Sona and Uttara were sent to Rāmañña, which forms a part of Suvannabhūmi, to propagate the holy faith. . . . This town is called to this day **Gola***mattikanagara*, because of the many houses it contained made of earth in the fashion of houses of the **Gola** people."—*Inscr. at Kalyāni near Pegu*, in *Forchhammer*, ii. 5.

1795.—"They were still anxious to know why a person consulting his own amusement, and master of his own time, should walk so fast; but on being informed that I was a '**Colar**,' or stranger, and that it was the custom of my country, they were reconciled to this. . . ."—*Symes*, *Embassy*, p. 290.

1855.—"His private dwelling was a small place on one side of the court, from which the women peeped out at the **Kalás**; . . ."—*Yule*, *Mission to the Court of Ava* (*Phayre's*), p. 5.

,, "By a curious self-delusion, the Burmans would seem to claim that in theory at least they are white people. And what is still more curious, the Bengalees appear indirectly to admit the claim; for our servants in speaking of themselves and their countrymen, as distinguished from the Burmans, constantly made use of the term *kálá admi*—'black man,' as the representative of the Burmese **kālá**, a foreigner."—*Ibid.* p. 37.

KUMPÁSS, s. Hind. *kampās*, corruption of English *compass*, and hence applied not only to a marine or a surveying compass, but also to theodolites, levelling instruments, and other elaborate instruments of observation, and even to the shaft of a carriage. Thus the sextant used to be called *tikunta kampāss*, "the 3-cornered compass."

[1866.—"Many an amusing story did I hear of this wonderful **kumpass**. It possessed the power of reversing everything observed. Hence if you looked through the *doorbeen* at a fort, everything inside was revealed. Thus the Feringhees so readily took forts, not by skill or by valour, but by means of the wonderful power of the *doorbeen*."—*Confess. of an Orderly*, 175.]

KUNKUR, CONKER, &c., s. Hind. *kankar*, 'gravel.' As regards the definition of the word in Anglo-Indian usage it is impossible to improve on Wilson: "A coarse kind of limestone found in the soil, in large tabular strata, or interspersed throughout the superficial mould, in nodules of various sizes, though usually small." Nodular *kunkur*, wherever it exists, is the usual material for road metalling, and as it binds when wetted and rammed into a compact, hard, and even surface, it is an admirable material for the purpose.

c. 1781.—"Etaya is situated on a very high bank of the river Jumna, the sides of which consist of what in India is called **concha**, which is originally sand, but the constant action of the sun in the dry season forms it almost into a vitrification" (!)—*Hodges*, 110.

1794.—"**Konker**" appears in a Notification for tenders in Calcutta Gazette.—In *Seton-Karr*, ii. 135.

c. 1809.—"We came within view of Cawnpore. Our long, long voyage terminated under a high **conkur** bank."—*Mrs. Sherwood, Autobiog.* 381.

1810.—". . . a weaker kind of lime is obtained by burning a substance called **kunkur**, which, at first, might be mistaken for small rugged flints, slightly coated with soil."—*Williamson, V. M.* ii. 13.

KUREEF, KHURREEF, s. Hind. adopted from Ar. *kharīf* ('autumn'). The crop sown just before, or at the beginning of, the rainy season, in May or June, and reaped after the rains in November—December. This includes rice, maize, the tall millets, &c. (See **RUBBEE**).

[1824.—"The basis on which the settlements were generally founded, was a measurement of the **Khureef**, or first crop, when it is cut down, and of the **Rubbee**, or second, when it is about half a foot high. . . ."—*Malcolm, Central India*, ii. 29.]

KURNOOL, n.p. The name of a city and territory in the Deccan, *Karnūl* of the *Imp. Gazetteer*; till 1838 a tributary Nawabship; then resumed on account of treason; and now since 1858 a collectorate of Madras Presidency. Properly *Kandanūr; Canoul* of Orme. Kirkpatrick says that the name *Kurnool, Kunnool*, or *Kundnool* (all of which forms seem to be applied corruptly to the place) signifies in the language of that country 'fine spun, clear thread,' and according to Meer Husain it has its name from its beautiful cotton fabrics. But we presume the town must have existed before it made cotton fabrics? This is a specimen of the stuff that men, even so able as Kirkpatrick, sometimes repeat after those native authorities who "ought to know better," as we are often told. [The *Madras Gloss.* gives the name as Tam. *karnūlu*, from *kandena*, 'a mixture of lamp-oil and burnt straw used in greasing cart-wheels' and *prolu*, 'village,' because when the temple at Alampur was being built, the wheels of the carts were greased here, and thus a settlement was formed.]

KUTTAUR, s. Hind. *kaṭār*, Skt. *kaṭṭāra*, 'a dagger,' especially a kind of dagger peculiar to India, having a solid blade of diamond-section, the handle of which consists of two parallel bars with a cross-piece joining them. The hand grips the cross-piece, and the bars pass along each side of the wrist. [See a drawing in *Egerton, Handbook, Indian Arms*, pl. ix.] Ibn Batuta's account is vivid, and perhaps in the matter of size there may be no exaggeration. Through the kindness of Col. Waterhouse I have a phototype of some Travancore weapons shown at the Calcutta Exhibition of 1883-4; among them two great *kaṭārs*, with sheaths made from the snouts of two saw-fishes (with the teeth remaining in). They are done to scale, and one of the blades is 20 inches long, the other 26. There is also a plate in the *Ind. Antiq.* (vii. 193) representing some curious weapons from the Tanjore Palace Armoury, among which are *kaṭār*-hilted daggers evidently of great length, though the entire length is not shown. The plate accompanies interesting notes by Mr. M. J. Walhouse, who states the curious fact that many of the blades mounted *kaṭār*-fashion were of European manufacture, and that one of these bore the famous name of Andrea Ferara. I add an extract. Mr. Walhouse accounts for the adoption of these blades in a country possessing the far-famed Indian steel, in that the latter was excessively brittle. The passage from Stavorinus describes the weapon, without giving a native name. We do not know what name is indicated by 'belly piercer.'

c. 1343.—"The villagers gathered round him, and one of them stabbed him with a **kattāra.** This is the name given to an iron weapon resembling a plough-share; the hand is inserted into it so that the fore-arm is shielded; but the blade beyond is two cubits in length, and a blow with it is mortal."—*Ibn Batuta*, iv. 31-32.

1442.—"The blacks of this country have the body nearly naked. . . . In one hand they hold an Indian poignard (**katārah-i-***Hindī*), and in the other a buckler of ox-hide . . . this costume is common to the king and the beggar."—*Abdurrazzāk*, in *India in the XVth Cent.*, p. 17.

c. 1526.—"On the whole there were given one tipchâk horse with the saddle, two pairs of swords with the belts, 25 sets of enamelled daggers (*khanjar*—see **HANGER**), 16 enamelled **kitârehs**, two daggers (*jamdher*—see **JUMDUD**) set with precious stones."—*Baber*, 338.

[c. 1590.—In the list of the Moghul arms we have: "10. **Katárah**, price ½ R. to 1 Muhur."—*Āīn*, ed. *Blochmann*, i. 110, with an engraving, No. 9, pl. xii.]

1638.—"Les personnes de qualité portēt dans la ceinture vne sorte d'armes, ou de poignards, courte et large, qu'ils appellent *ginda* (?) ou **Catarre**, dont la garde et la gaine sont d'or."—*Mandelslo*, Paris, 1659, 223.

1673.—"They go rich in Attire, with a Poniard, or **Catarre**, at their girdle."—*Fryer*, 93.

1690.—". . . which chafes and ferments him to such a pitch; that with a **Catarry** or Bagonet in his hands he first falls upon those that are near him . . . killing and stabbing as he goes. . . ."—*Ovington*, 237.

1754.—"To these were added an enamelled dagger (which the Indians call **cuttarri**) and two swords. . . ."—*H. of Nadir*, in *Hanway's Travels*, ii. 386.

1768-71.—"They (the Moguls) on the left side . . . wear a weapon which they call by a name that may be translated *belly-piercer*; it is about 14 inches long; broad near the hilt, and tapering away to a sharp point; it is made of fine steel; the handle has, on each side of it, a catch, which, when the weapon is griped by the hand, shuts round the wrist, and secures it from being dropped."—*Stavorinus*, E.T. i. 457.

1813.—"After a short silent prayer, Lullabhy, in the presence of all the company, waved his **catarra**, or short dagger, over the bed of the expiring man. . . . The patient continued for some time motionless: in half an hour his heart appeared to beat, circulation quickened, . . . at the expiration of the third hour Lullabhy had effected his cure."—*Forbes, Or. Mem.* iii. 249; [2nd ed. ii. 272, and see i. 69].

1856.—"The manners of the bardic tribe are very similar to those of their Rajpoot clients; their dress is nearly the same, but the bard seldom appears without the '**Kutâr**,' or dagger, a representation of which is scrawled beside his signature, and often rudely engraved upon his monumental stone, in evidence of his death in the sacred duty of **Trâgâ**" (q.v.).—*Forbes, Râs Mâlâ*, ed. 1878, pp. 559-560.

1878.—"The ancient Indian smiths seem to have had a difficulty in hitting on a medium between this highly refined brittle steel and a too soft metal. In ancient sculptures, as in Srirangam near Trichinapalli, life-sized figures of armed men are represented, bearing **Kuttars** or long daggers of a peculiar shape; the handles, not so broad as in the later **Kuttars**, are covered with a long narrow guard, and the blades 2¼ inches broad at bottom, taper very gradually to a point through a length of 18 inches, more than ¾ of which is deeply channelled on both sides with 6 converging grooves. There were many of these in the Tanjor armoury, perfectly corresponding . . . and all were so soft as to be easily bent."—*Ind. Antiq.* vii.

KUZZANNA, s. Ar.—H. *khizāna*, or *khazāna*, 'a treasury.' [In Ar. *khazīnah*, or *khaznah*, means 'a treasure,' representing 1000 *kis* or purses, each worth about £5 (see *Burton, Ar. Nights*, i. 405).] It is the usual word for the district and general treasuries in British India; and *khazānchī* for the treasurer.

1683.—"Ye King's Duan (see **DEWAUN**) had demanded of them 8000 Rupees on account of remains of last year's Tallecas (see **TALLICA**) . . . ordering his Peasdast (*Peshdast*, an assistant) to see it suddenly paid in ye King's **Cuzzanna**."—*Hedges, Diary*, Hak. Soc. i. 103.

[1757.—"A mint has been established in Calcutta; continue coining gold and silver into **Siccas** and **Mohurs** . . . they shall pass current in the provinces of Bengal, Bahar and Orissa, and be received into the **Cadganna**. . . ."—Perwannah from *Jaffier Ally Khan*, in *Verelst*, App. 145.]

KUZZILBASH, n.p. Turki *kizilbāsh*, 'red-head.' This title has been since the days of the Safavi (see **SOPHY**) dynasty in Persia, applied to the Persianized Turks, who form the ruling class in that country, from the red caps which they wore. The class is also settled extensively over Afghanistan. ["At Kābul," writes Bellew (*Races of Afghanistan*, 107), "he (Nādir) left as *chandaul*, or 'rear guard,' a detachment of 12,000 of his Kizilbāsh (so named from the red caps they wore), or Mughal Persian troops. After the death of Nādir they remained at Kābul as a military colony, and their descendants occupy a distinct quarter of the city, which is called *Chandaul*. These Kizilbāsh hold their own ground here, as a distinct Persian community of the Shia persuasion, against the native population of the Sunni profession. They constitute an important element in the general population of the city, and exercise a considerable influence in its local politics. Owing to their isolated position and antagonism to the native population, they are favourably inclined to the British authority."] Many of them used to take service with the Delhi emperors; and not a few do so now in our frontier cavalry regiments.

c. 1510.—"L'vsanza loro è di portare vna **berretta rossa**, ch'auanza sopra la testa mezzo braccio, a guisa d'vn zon ('like a top'), che dalla parte, che si mette in testa, vine a essar larga, ristringendosi tuttauia sino in cima, et è fatta con dodici coste grosse vn dito . . . ne mai tagliano barba ne mostacchi."—*G. M. Angiolello*, in *Ramusio*, ii. f. 74.

1550.—"Oltra il deserto che è sopra il Corassam fino à Samarcand . . . signorreggiano *Iescil bas*, cioè le berrette verdi, le quali benette verdi sono alcuni Tartari Musulmani che portano le loro berrette di feltro verde acute, e cosi si fanno chiamare à differentia de Soffiani suoi capitali nemici che signoreggiano la Persia, pur anche essi Musulmani, i quali portano le **berrette rosse**, quali berrette verdi e rosse, hanno continuamente hauuta fra se guerra crudelissima per causa di diversità di opinione nella loro religione."—*Chaggi Memet*, in *Ramusio*, ii. f. 16*v*. "Beyond the desert above Corassam, as far as Samarkand and the idolatrous cities, the *Yeshilbas* (*Iescilbas*) or 'Green-caps,' are predominant. These Green-caps are certain Musulman Tartars who wear pointed caps of green felt, and they are so called to distinguish them from their chief enemies the Soffians, who are predominant in Persia, who are indeed also Musulmans, but who wear **red caps**."

1574.—"These Persians are also called *Red Turks*, which I believe is because they have behind on their Turbants, Red Marks, as Cotton Ribbands &c. with Red Brims, whereby they are soon discerned from other Nations."—*Rauwolff*, 173.

1606.—"**Cocelbaxas**, who are the soldiers whom they esteem most highly."—*Gouvea*, f. 143.

1653.—"Ie visité le **keselbache** qui y commande vne petite forteresse, duquel ie receu beaucoup de civilitez."—*De La Boullaye-le-Gouz*, ed. 1657, pp. 284-5.

" "**Keselbache** est vn mot composé de *Kesel*, qui signifie rouge, et *bachi*, teste, comme qui diroit **teste rouge**, et par ce terme s'entendent les gens de guerre de Perse, à cause du bonnet de Sophi qui est rouge."—*Ibid.* 545.

1673.—"Those who compose the Main Body of the Cavalry, are the **Cusle-Bashees**, or with us the Chevaliers."—*Fryer*, 356. Fryer also writes **Cusselbash** (Index).

1815.—"The seven Turkish tribes, who had been the chief promoters of his (Ismail's) glory and success, were distinguished by a particular dress; they wore a red cap, from which they received the Turkish name of **Kuzelbash**, or 'golden heads,' which has descended to their posterity." — *Malcolm*, *H. of Persia*, ii. 502-3.

1828.—"The **Kuzzilbash**, a Tale of Khorasan. By James Baillie Fraser."

1883.—"For there are rats and rats, and a man of average capacity may as well hope to distinguish scientifically between Ghilzais, Kuki Kheyls, Logar Maliks, Shigwals, Ghazis, Jezailchis, Hazaras, Logaris, Wardaks, Mandozais, Lepel-Griffin, and **Kizilbashes**, as to master the division of the great race of rats."—*Tribes on My Frontier*, 15.

KYFE, n. One often meets with this word (Ar. *kaif*) in books about the Levant, to indicate the absolute enjoyment of the *dolce far niente*. Though it is in the Hindustāni dictionaries, we never remember to have heard it used in India; but the first quotation below shows that it is, or has been, in use in Western India, in something like the Turkish sense. The proper meaning of the Ar. word is 'how?' 'in what manner?' the secondary is 'partial intoxication.' This looks almost like a parallel to the English vulgar slang of 'how comed you so?' But in fact a man's *kaif* is his 'howness,' *i.e.* what pleases him, his humour; and this passes into the sense of gaiety caused by *ḥashīsh*, &c.

1808.—". . . a kind of *confectio Japonica* loaded with opium, *Gānja* or *Bang*, and causing **keif**, or the first degree of intoxication, lulling the senses and disposing to sleep."—*R. Drummond*.

KYOUNG, s. Burm. *kyaung*. A Buddhist monastery. The term is not employed by Padre Sangermano, who uses **bao**, a word, he says, used by the

Portuguese in India (p. 88). I cannot explain it. [See **BAO.**]

1799.—"The **kioums** or convents of the Rhahaans are different in their structure from common houses, and much resemble the architecture of the Chinese; they are made entirely of wood; the roof is composed of different stages, supported by strong pillars," &c.—*Symes*, p. 210.

KYTHEE, s. Hind. *Kaithī*. A form of cursive Nagari character, used by Bunyas, &c., in Gangetic India. It is from *Kāyath* (Skt. *Kāyastha*), a member of the writer-caste.

L

LAC, s. Hind. *lākh*, from Skt. *lākshā*, for *rākshā*. The resinous incrustation produced on certain trees (of which the *dhāk* (see **DHAWK**) is one, but chiefly **Peepul**, and *khossum* [*kusum*, *kusumb*], *i.e.* *Schleichera bijuga*, *trijuga*) by the puncture of the Lac insect (*Coccus Lacca*, L.). See *Roxburgh*, in Vol. III. *As. Res.*, 384 *seqq*; [and a full list of the trees on which the insect feeds, in *Watt*, *Econ. Dict.* ii. 410 *seq.*]. The incrustation contains 60 to 70 per cent. of resinous *lac*, and 10 per cent. of dark red colouring matter from which is manufactured *lac-dye*. The material in its original crude form is called *stick-lac*; when boiled in water it loses its red colour, and is then termed *seed-lac*; the melted clarified substance, after the extraction of the dye, is turned out in thin irregular laminae called *shell-lac*. This is used to make sealing-wax, in the fabrication of varnishes, and very largely as a stiffening for men's hats.

Though *lāk* bears the same sense in Persian, and *lak* or *luk* are used in modern Arabic for sealing-wax, it would appear from Dozy (*Glos.*, pp. 295-6, and *Oosterlingen*, 57), that identical or approximate forms are used in various Arabic-speaking regions for a variety of substances giving a red dye, including the *coccus ilicis* or Kermes. Still, we have seen no evidence that in India the word was applied otherwise than to the *lac* of our heading. (Garcia says that the Arabs called it *loc-sumutri*, 'lac of Sumatra'; probably because the Pegu lac was brought to the ports of Sumatra, and purchased there.) And this the term in the *Periplus* seems unquestionably to indicate; whilst it is probable that the passage quoted from Aelian is a much misconceived account of the product. It is not nearly so absurd as De Monfart's account below. The English word *lake* for a certain red colour is from this. So also are *lacquer* and *lackered* ware, because *lac* is used in some of the varnishes with which such ware is prepared.

c. A.D. 80-90.—These articles are imported (to the ports of *Barbaricē*, on the W. of the Red Sea) from the interior parts of Ariakē:—

"Σίδηρος Ἰνδικὸς καὶ στόμωμα (Indian iron and steel)

* * * * *

Λάκκος χρωμάτινος (Lac-*dye*)."

Periplus, § 6.

c. 250.—"There are produced in India animals of the size of a beetle, of a red colour, and if you saw them for the first time you would compare them to cinnabar. They have very long legs, and are soft to the touch; they are produced on the trees that bear *electrum*, and they feed on the fruit of these. The Indians catch them and crush them, and with these dye their red cloaks, and the tunics under these, and everything else that they wish to turn to this colour, and to dye. And this kind of clothing is carried also to the King of Persia."—*Aelian, de Nat. Animal.* iv. 46.

c. 1343.—The notice of *lacca* in Pegolotti is in parts very difficult to translate, and we do not feel absolutely certain that it refers to the Indian product, though we believe it to be so. Thus, after explaining that there are two classes of *lacca*, the *matura* and *acerba*, or ripe and unripe, he goes on: "It is produced attached to stalks, *i.e.* to the branches of shrubs, but it ought to be clear from stalks, and earthy dust, and sand, and from *costiere* (?). The stalks are the twigs of the wood on which it is produced, the *costiere* or *figs*, as the Catalans call them, are composed of the dust of the thing, which when it is fresh heaps together and hardens like pitch; only that pitch is black, and those *costiere* or figs are red and of the colour of unripe **lacca**. And more of these *costiere* is found in the unripe than the ripe **lacca**," and so on.—*Della Decima*, iii. 365.

1510.—"There also grows a very large quantity of **lacca** (or *lacra*) for making red colour, and the tree of this is formed like our trees which produce walnuts."—*Varthema*, 238.

1516.—"Here (in Pegu) they load much fine **laquar**, which grows in the country."—*Barbosa*, *Lisbon Acad.*, 366.

1519.—"And because he had it much in charge to get all the *lac* (**alacre**) that he could, the governor knowing through information of the merchants that much came to the Coast of Choromandel by the ships of Pegu and Martaban that frequented that coast. . . ."—*Correa*, ii. 567.

1563.—"Now it is time to speak of the **lacre**, of which so much is consumed in this country in closing letters, and for other seals, in the place of wax."—*Garcia*, f. 112*v*.

1582.—"**Laker** is a kinde of gum that procedeth of the ant."—*Castañeda*, tr. by N.L., f. 33.

c. 1590.—(Recipe for *Lac* varnish). "**Lac** is used for *chighs* (see **CHICK, a**). If red, 4 *ser* of **lac**, and 1 *s.* of vermilion; if yellow, 4 *s.* of **lac**, and 1 *s. zarnīkh.*"—*Āīn*, ed. *Blochmann*, i. 226.

1615.—"In this Iland (Goa) is the hard Waxe made (which we call Spanish Waxe), and is made in the manner following. They inclose a large plotte of ground, with a little trench filled with water; then they sticke up a great number of small staues vpon the sayd plot, that being done they bring thither a sort of pismires, farre biggar than ours, which beeing debar'd by the water to issue out, are constrained to retire themselves vppon the said staues, where they are kil'd with the Heate of the Sunne, and thereof it is that **Lacka** is made."—*De Monfart*, 35-36.

c. 1610.—". . . Vne manière de boëte ronde, vernie, et **lacrée**, qui est vne ouurage de ces isles."—*Pyrard de Laval*, i. 127; [Hak. Soc. i. 170].

1627.—"**Lac** is a strange drugge, made by certain winged Pismires of the gumme of Trees."—*Purchas, Pilgrimage*, 569.

1644.—"There are in the territories of the *Mogor*, besides those things mentioned, other articles of trade, such as **Lacre**, both the insect lacre and the cake" (*de formiga e de pasta*).—*Bocarro, MS.*

1663.—"In one of these Halls you shall find Embroiderers . . . in another you shall see Goldsmiths . . . in a fourth Workmen in **Lacca**."—*Bernier* E.T. 83; [ed. *Constable*, 259].

1727.—"Their **lackt** or *japon'd* Ware is without any Doubt the best in the World."—*A. Hamilton*, ii. 305; [ed. 1744].

LACCADIVE ISLANDS, n.p. Probably Skt. *Lakśadvīpa*, '100,000 Islands'; a name however which would apply much better to the Maldives, for the former are not really very numerous. There is not, we suspect, any ancient or certain native source for the name as specifically applied to the northern group of islands. Barbosa, the oldest authority we know as mentioning the group (1516), calls them *Malandiva*, and the Maldives *Palandiva*. Several of the individual islands are mentioned in the *Tuhfat-al-Majāhidīn* (E.T. by *Rowlandson*, pp. 150-52), the group itself being called "the islands of Malabar."

LACK, s. One hundred thousand, and especially in the Anglo-Indian colloquial 100,000 Rupees, in the days of better exchange the equivalent of £10,000. Hind. *lākh*, *lak*, &c., from Skt. *laksha*, used (see below) in the same sense, but which appears to have originally meant "a mark." It is necessary to explain that the term does not occur in the earlier Skt. works. Thus in the *Talavakāra Brāhmaṇā*, a complete series of the higher numerical terms is given. After *śata* (10), *sahasra* (1000), comes *ayuta* (10,000), *prayuta* (*now* a million), *niyuta* (*now* also a million), *arbuda* (100 millions), *nyarbuda* (not now used), *nikharṇa* (do.), and *padma* (now 10,000 millions). *Laksha* is therefore a modern substitute for *prayuta*, and the series has been expanded. This was probably done by the Indian astronomers between the 5th and 10th centuries A.D.

The word has been adopted in the Malay and Javanese, and other languages of the Archipelago. But it is remarkable that in all of this class of languages which have adopted the word it is used in the sense of 10,000 instead of 100,000 with the sole exception of the Lampungs of Sumatra, who use it correctly. (*Crawfurd*). (See **CRORE.**)

We should observe that though a *lack*, used absolutely for a sum of money, in modern times always implies rupees, this has not always been the case. Thus in the time of Akbar and his immediate successors the revenue was settled and reckoned in *laks* of **dams** (q.v.). Thus:

c. 1594.—"In the 40th year of his majesty's reign (Akbar's), his dominions consisted of 105 *Sircars*, subdivided into 2737 *Kusbahs* (see **CUSBAH**), the revenue of which he settled for ten years, at the annual rent of 3 *Arribs*, 62 *Crore*, 97 **Lacks**, 55,246 *Dams.* . . ."—*Ayeen*, ed. *Gladwin*, ii. 1; [ed. *Jarrett*, ii. 115].

At Ormuz again we find another **lack** in vogue, of which the unit was apparently the *dīnār*, not the old gold coin, but a degenerate *dīnār* of small value. Thus:

1554.—"(Money of Ormuz).—A **leque** is equivalent to 50 pardaos of *çadis*, which is called 'bad money,' (and this *leque* is not a coin but a number by which they reckon at Ormuz): and each of these pardaos is equal to 2 *azares*, and each *azar* to 10 *çadis*, each *çadi* to 100 *dinars*, and after this fashion they calculate in the books of the Custom-house. . . ."—*Nunez, Lyvro dos Pesos*, &c., in *Subsidios*, 25.

Here the *azar* is the Persian *hazār* or 1000 (*dīnārs*); the *çadi* Pers. *sad* or 100 (*dīnārs*); the **leque** or **lak**, 100,000 (*dīnārs*); and the *tomān* (see **TOMAUN**), which does not appear here, is 10,000 (*dīnārs*).

c. 1300.—"They went to the *Kāfir's* tent, killed him, and came back into the town, whence they carried off money belonging to the Sultan amounting to 12 **laks**. The **lak** is a sum of 100,000 (silver) *dīnārs*, equivalent to 10,000 Indian gold *dīnārs*."—*Ibn Batuta*, iii. 106.

c. 1340.—"The Sultan distributes daily two **lāks** in alms, never less; a sum of which the equivalent in money of Egypt and Syria would be 160,000 pieces of silver."—*Shihābuddīn Dimishki*, in *Notes and Exts.*, xiii. 192.

In these examples from Pinto the word is used apart from money, in the Malay form, but not in the Malay sense of 10,000:

c. 1540.—"The old man desiring to satisfie *Antonio de Faria's* demand, *Sir*, said he . . . *the chronicles of those times affirm, how in only four yeares and an half sixteen* **Lacazaas** (*lacasā*) *of men were slain, every* **Lacazaa** *containing an hundred thousand*."—*Pinto* (orig. cap. xlv.) in *Cogan*, p. 53.

c. 1546.—". . . he ruined in 4 months space all the enemies countries, with such a destruction of people as, if credit may be given to our histories . . . there died fifty **Laquesaas** of persons."—*Ibid.* p. 224.

1615.—"And the whole present was worth ten of their **Leakes**, as they call them; a **Leake** being 10,000 pounds sterling; the whole 100,000 pounds sterling."—*Coryat's Letters from India* (*Crudities*, iii. f. 25*v*).

1616.—"He received twenty **lecks** of roupies towards his charge (two hundred thousand pounds sterling)."—*Sir T. Roe*, reprint, p. 35; [Hak. Soc. i. 201, and see i. 95, 183, 238].

1651.—"Yeder **Lac** is hondert duysend."—*Rogerius*, 77.

c. 1665.—"Il faut cent mille roupies pour faire un **lek**, cent mille **leks** pour faire un *courou*, cent mille *courous* pour faire un *padan*, et cent mille *padan* pour faire un *nil*."—*Thevenot*, v. 54.

1673.—"In these great Solemnities, it is usual for them to set it around with Lamps to the number of two or three **Leaques**, which is so many hundred thousand in our account."—*Fryer*, [p. 104, reading **Lecques**].

1684.—"They have by information of the servants dug in severall places of the house, where they have found great summes of money. Under his bed were found **Lacks** 4½. In the House of Office two **Lacks**. They in all found Ten **Lacks** already, and make no doubt but to find more."—*Hedges, Diary*, Jan. 2; [Hak. Soc. i. 145].

1692.—". . . a **lack** of Pagodas. . . ."—In *Wheeler*, i. 262.

1747.—"The Nabob and other Principal Persons of this Country are of such an extreme lacrative (*sic*) Disposition, and . . . are so exceedingly avaritious, occasioned by the large Proffers they have received from the French, that nothing less than **Lacks** will go near to satisfie them."—*Letter from Ft. St. David to the Court*, May 2 (MS. Records in India Office).

1778.—"Sir Matthew Mite will make up the money already advanced in another name, by way of future mortgage upon his estate, for the entire purchase, 5 **lacks** of roupees."—*Foote, The Nabob*, Act I. sc. i.

1785.—"Your servants have no Trade in this country; neither do you pay them high wages, yet in a few years they return to England with many **lacs** of pagodas."—*Nabob of Arcot*, in Burke's Speech on his Debts, *Works*, iv. 18.

1833.—"Tout le reste (et dans le reste il y a des intendants riches de plus de vingt **laks**) s'assied par terre." — *Jacquemont, Correspond.* ii. 120.

1879.—"In modern times the only numbers in practical use above 'thousands' are *laksa* ('**lac**' or '**lakh**') and *koṭi* ('crore'); and an Indian sum is wont to be pointed thus: 123, 45, 67, 890, to signify 123 crores, 45 **lakhs**, + 67 thousand, eight hundred and ninety."—*Whitney, Sansk. Grammar*, 161.

The older writers, it will be observed (c. 1600-1620), put the **lakh** at £10,000; Hamilton (c. 1700) puts it at £12,500; Williamson (c. 1810) at the same; then for many years it stood again as the equivalent of £10,000; now (1880) it is little more than £8000; [now (1901) about £6666].

LACKERAGE. (See **KHIRAJ.**)

LALL-SHRAUB, s. Englishman's Hind. *lāl-sharāb*, 'red wine.' The universal name of claret in India.

[c. 1780.—"To every plate are set down two glasses; one pyramidal (like hobnob glasses in England) for **Loll Shrub** (*scilicet*, claret); the other a common sized wineglass for whatever beverage is most agreeable."—*Diary of Mrs. Fay*, in *Busteed, Echoes*, 123.]

LALLA, s. P.—H. *lālā*. In Persia this word seems to be used for a kind of domestic tutor; now for a male nurse, or as he would be called in India, 'child's bearer.' In N. India it is usually applied to a native clerk writing the vernacular, or to a respectable merchant. [For the Pers. usage see *Blochmann, Āīn*, i. 426 note.]

[1765.—"Amongst the first to be considered, I would recommend Juggut Seet, and one Gurdy **Loll**."—*Verelst*, App. 218.

[1841.—"Where there are no tigers, the **Lalla** (scribe) becomes a shikaree."—*Society in India*, ii. 176.]

LAMA, s. A Tibetan Buddhist monk. Tibet. *bLama* (*b* being silent). The word is sometimes found written *Llama;* but this is nonsense. In fact it seems to be a popular confusion, arising from the name of the S. American quadruped which is so spelt. See quotation from *Times* below.

c. 1590.—"Fawning Court doctors . . . said it was mentioned in some holy books that men used to live up to the age of 1000 years . . . and in Thibet there were even now a class of **Lāmahs** or Mongolian devotees, and recluses, and hermits that live 200 years and more. . . ."—*Badāonī*, quoted by *Blochmann, Āīn*, i. 201.

1664.—"This Ambassador had in his suit a Physician, which was said to be of the Kingdom of Lassa, and of the Tribe *Lamy* or **Lama**, which is that of the men of the Law in that country, as the *Brahmans* are in the Indies . . . he related of his great **Lama** that when he was old, and ready to die, he assembled his council, and declared to them that now he was passing into the Body of a little child lately born. . . ."—*Bernier*, E.T. 135; [ed. *Constable*, 424].

1716.—"Les Thibetaines ont des Religieux nommés **Lamas**."—In *Lettres Edif.* xii. 438.

1774.—". . . ma questo primo figlio . . . rinunziò la corona al secondo e lui difatti si fece religioso o **lama** del paese."—*Della Tomba*, 61.

c. 1818.—

"The Parliament of Thibet met—
The little **Lama**, called before it,
Did there and then his whipping get,
And, as the Nursery Gazette
Assures us, like a hero bore it."
T. Moore, The Little Grand Lama.

1876.—". . . Hastings . . . touches on the analogy between Tibet and the high valley of Quito, as described by De la Condamine, an analogy which Mr. Markham brings out in interesting detail. . . . But when he enlarges on the wool which is a staple of both countries, and on the animals producing it, he risks confirming in careless readers that popular impression which might be expressed in the phraseology of Fluelen—"'Tis all one; 'tis alike as my fingers is to my fingers, and there is **Llamas** in both."—*Rev. of Markham's Tibet*, in *Times*, May 15.

The passage last quoted is in jesting vein, but the following is serious and delightful:—

1879.—"The landlord prostrated himself as reverently, if not as lowly, as a Peruvian before his *Grand* **Llama**."—*Patty's Dream*, a novel reviewed in the *Academy*, May 17.

LAMASERY, LAMASERIE, s. This is a word, introduced apparently by the French R. C. Missionaries, for a **lama** convent. Without being positive, I would say that it does not represent any Oriental word (*e.g.* compound of *lami* and **serai**), but is a factitious French word analogous to *nonnerie, vacherie, laiterie*, &c.

[c. 1844.—"According to the Tartars, the **Lamasery** of the Five Towers is the best place you can be buried in."—*Huc, Travels in Tartary*, i. 78.]

LAMBALLIE, LOMBALLIE, LOMBARDIE, LUMBANAH, &c., s. Dakh. Hind. *Lāmbārā*, Mahr. *Lambān*, with other forms in the languages of the Peninsula. [Platts connects the name with Skt. *lamba*, 'long, tall'; the *Madras Gloss.* with Skt. *lampata*, 'greedy.'] A wandering tribe of dealers in grain, salt, &c., better known as *Banjārās* (see **BRINJARRY**). As an Anglo-Indian word this is now obsolete. It was perhaps a corruption of *Lubhāna*, the name of one of the great clans or divisions of the Banjārās. [Another suggestion made is that the name is derived from their business of carrying salt (Skt. *lavana*); see *Crooke, Tribes of N.W.P.* i. 158.]

1756.—"The army was constantly supplied . . . by bands of people called **Lamballis**, peculiar to the Deccan, who are constantly moving up and down the country, with their flocks, and contract to furnish the armies in the field."—*Orme*, ii. 102.

1785.—"What you say of the scarcity of grain in your army, notwithstanding your having a **cutwâl** (see **COTWAL**), and so many **Lumbânehs** with you, has astonished us."—*Letters of Tippoo*, 49.

LANCHARA, s. A kind of small vessel often mentioned in the Portuguese histories of the 16th and 17th centuries. The derivation is probably Malay *lanchār*, 'quick, nimble.' [Mr. Skeat writes: "The real Malay form is *Lanchar-an*, which is regularly formed from Malay *lanchār*, 'swift,' and **lanchara** I believe to be a Port. form of *lanchar-an*, as **lanchara** could not possibly, in Malay, be formed from *lanchār*, as has hitherto been implied or suggested."]

c. 1535.—"In questo paese di Cambaia (read Camboja) vi sono molti fiumi, nelli quali vi sono li nauili detti **Lancharas**, cõ li quali vanno nauigando la costa di Siam. . . ." —*Sommario de' Regni*, &c., in *Ramusio*, i. f. 336.

c. 1539.—"This King (of the Batas) understanding that I had brought him a letter and a Present from the Captain of Malaca, caused me to be entertained by the *Xabundar* (see **SHABUNDER**). . . . This General, accompanied with five **Lanchares** and twelve Ballons, came to me to the Port where I rode at anchor."—*Pinto*, E.T. p. 81.

LANDWIND, s. Used in the south of India. A wind which blows seaward during the night and early morning. [The dangerous effects of it are described in *Madras Gloss.* s.v.] In Port. *Terrenho*.

1561.—"Correndo a costa com **terrenhos**." —*Correa, Lendas*, I. i. 115.

[1598.—"The East winds beginne to blow from off the land into the seas, whereby they are called **Terreinhos**."—*Linschoten*, Hak. Soc. i. 234.

[1612.—"Send John Dench . . . that in the morning he may go out with the **landtorne** and return with the seatorne."—*Danvers, Letters*, i. 206.]

1644.—"And as it is between monsoon and monsoon (*monsam*) the wind is quite uncertain only at the beginning of summer. The N.W prevails more than any other wind . . . and at the end of it begin the **land winds** (*terrenhos*) from midnight to about noon, and these are E. winds."—*Bocarro, MS.*

1673.—". . . we made for the Land, to gain the **Land Breezes**. They begin about Midnight, and hold till Noon, and are by the Portugals named **Terrhenoes**."—*Fryer*, 23.

[1773.—See the account in *Ives*, 76.]

1838.—"We have had some very bad weather for the last week; furious **landwind**, very fatiguing and weakening. . . . Everything was so dried up, that when I attempted to walk a few yards towards the beach, the grass crunched under my feet like snow."—*Letters from Madras*, 199-200.

LANGASAQUE, n.p. The most usual old form for the Japanese city which we now call *Nagasaki* (see *Sainsbury, passim*).

1611.—"After two or three dayes space a Iesuite came vnto vs from a place called **Langesacke**, to which place the Carake of *Macao* is yeerely wont to come."—*W. Adams*, in *Purchas*, i. 126.

1613.—The Journal of Capt. John Saris has both **Nangasaque** and **Langasaque**.—*Ibid.* 366.

1614.—"Geve hym counsell to take heed of one Pedro Guzano, a papist Christian, whoe is his hoste at Miaco; for a lyinge fryre (or Jesuit) tould Mr. Peacock at **Langasaque** that Capt. Adams was dead in the howse of the said Guzano, which now I know is a lye per letters I received. . . ."—*Cocks, to Wickham*, in *Diary*, &c., ii. 264.

1618.—"It has now com to passe, which before I feared, that a company of rich usurers have gotten this sentence against us, and com doune together every yeare to **Langasaque** and this place, and have allwais byn accustomed to buy by the *pancado* (as they call it), or whole sale, all the goodes which came in the carick from Amacan, the Portingales having no prevelegese as we have."—The same to the E.I. Co., ii. 207-8.

Two years later Cocks changes his spelling and adopts **Nangasaque** (*Ibid.* 300 and to the end).

LAN JOHN, LANGIANNE, &c., n.p. Such names are applied in the early part of the 17th century to the Shan or Laos State of *Luang Praban* on the Mekong. *Lan-chan* is one of its names signifying in Siamese, it is said, 'a million of elephants.' It is known to the Burmese by the same name (*Len-Shen*). It was near this place that the estimable French traveller Henri Mouhot died, in 1861.

1587.—"I went from Pegu to *Iamahey* (see **JANGOMAY**), which is in the country of the **Langeiannes**; it is fiue and twentie dayes iourney North-east from Pegu."—*Fitch*, in *Hakl.* ii.

c. 1598.—"Thus we arrived at **Lanchan**, the capital of the Kingdom (Lao) where the King resides. It is a Kingdom of great extent, but thinly inhabited, because it has been frequently devastated by Pegu."—*De Morga*, 98.

1613.—"There reigned in Pegu in the year 1590 a King called Ximindo ginico, Lord reigning from the confines and roots of Great Tartary, to the very last territories bordering on our fortress of Malaca. He kept at his court the principal sons of the Kings of Ová, Tangu, Porão, Lanjão (*i.e.* Ava, Taungu, Prome, **Lanjang**), Jangomá, Siam, Camboja, and many other realms, making two and thirty of the white umbrella."—*Bocarro*, 117.

1617.—"The merchants of the country of **Lan John**, a place joining to the country of *Jangoma* (**JANGOMAY**) arrived at the city of **Judea** . . . and brought great store of merchandize."—*Sainsbury*, ii. 90.

1663.—"Entre tant et de si puissans Royaumes du dernier Orient, desquels on n'a presque iamais entendu parler en Europe, il y en a vn qui se nomme **Lao**, et plus proprement le Royaume des **Langiens** . . . le Royaume n'a pris son nom que du grand nombre d'Elephants qui s'y rencontrent: do vray ce mot de **Langiens** signifie proprement, miliers d'Elephants."—*Marini, H. Norvelle et Curievse des Royaumes de Tunquin et de Lao* (Fr. Tr., Paris, 1666), 329, 337.

1668.—**Lanchang** appears in the Map of Siam in De la Loubère's work, but we do not find it in the book itself.

c. 1692.—"**Laos** est situé sous le même Climat que Tonquin; c'est un royaume grand et puissant, separé des Etats voisins par des forets et par des deserts. . . . Les principales villes sont **Landjam** et *Tsiamaja*."—*Kaempfer, H. du Japon*, i. 22-3.

LANTEA, s. A swift kind of boat frequently mentioned by F. M. Pinto and some early writers on China; but we are unable to identify the word.

c. 1540.—". . . that . . . they set sail from *Liampoo* for *Malaca*, and that being advanced as far as the Isle of *Sumbor* they had been set upon by a Pyrat, a *Guzarat* by Nation, called *Coia Acem*, who had three Junks, and four **Lanteeas**. . . ."—*Pinto*, E.T. p. 69.

c. 1560.—"There be other lesser shipping than Iunkes, somewhat long, called *Bancones*, they place three Oares on a side, and rowe very well, and load a great deal of goods; there be other lesse called **Lanteas**, which doe rowe very swift, and beare a good burthen also: and these two sorts of Ships, viz., *Bancones* and **Lanteas**, because they are swift, the theeues do commonly vse."—*Caspar da Cruz*, in *Purchas*, iii. 174.

LAOS, n.p. A name applied by the Portuguese to the civilised people who occupied the inland frontier of Burma and Siam, between those countries on the one hand and China and Tongking on the other; a people called by the Burmese **Shans**, a name which we have in recent years adopted. They are of the same race of *Thai* to which the Siamese belong, and which extends with singular identity of manners and language, though broken into many separate communities, from Assam to the Malay Peninsula. The name has since been frequently used as a singular, and applied as a territorial name to the region occupied by this people immediately to the North of Siam. There have been a great number of separate principalities in this region, of which now one and now another predominated and conquered its neighbours. Before the rise of Siam the most important was that of which Sakotai was the capital, afterwards represented by Xieng-mai, the Zimmé of the Burmese and the **Jangomay** of some old English documents. In later times the chief States were *Muang Luang Praban* (see **LAN JOHN**) and *Vien-shan*, both upon the Mekong. It would appear from Lieut. Macleod's narrative, and from Garnier, that the name of **Lao** is that by which the branch of these people on the Lower Mekong, *i.e.* of those two States, used to designate themselves. Muang Praban is still quasi independent; Vien-Shan was annexed with great cruelties by Siam, c. 1828.

1553.—"Of silver of 11 dinheiros alloy he (Alboquerque) made only a kind of money called *Malaquezes*, which silver came thither from Pegu, whilst from Siam came a very pure silver of 12 dinheiros assay, procured from certain people called **Laos**, lying to the north of these two kingdoms."—*Barros*, II. vi. 6.

1553.—". . . certain very rugged mountain ranges, like the Alps, inhabited by the people called Gueos who fight on horseback, and with whom the King of Siam is continually at war. They are near him only on the north, leaving between the two the people called **Laos**, who encompass this Kingdom of Siam, both on the North, and on the East along the river Mecon . . . and on the south adjoin these **Laos** the two Kingdoms of **Camboja** and Choampa (see **CHAMPA**), which are on the sea-board. These **Laos** . . . though they are lords of so great territories, are all subject to this King of Siam, though often in rebellion against him."—*Ibid.* III. ii. 5.

" "Three Kingdoms at the upper part of these, are those of the **Laos**, who (as we have said) obey Siam through fear: the first of these is called *Jangoma* (see **JANGOMAY**), the chief city of which is called Chiamay . . . the second *Chancray Chencran*: the third Lanchaa (see **LAN JOHN**) which is below the others, and adjoins the Kingdom of Cacho, or Cauchichina. . . ."—*Ibid.*

c. 1560.—"These **Laos** came to Camboia, downe a River many daies Iournie, which they say to have his beginning in *China* as many others which runne into the Sea of India; it hath eight, fifteene, and twentie fathome water, as myselfe saw by experience in a great part of it; it passeth through manie vnknowne and desart Countries of great Woods and Forests where there are innumerable Elephants, and many Buffes . . . and certayne beastes which in that Countrie they call *Badas* (see **ABADA**)."—*Gaspar da Cruz*, in *Purchas*, iii. 169.

c. 1598.—". . . I offered to go to the **Laos** by land, at my expense, in search of the King of Cambodia, as I knew that that was the road to go by. . . ."—*Blas de Herman Gonzalez*, in *De Morga* (E.T. by Hon. H. Stanley, Hak. Soc.), p. 97.

1641.—"*Concerning the Land of the* **Louwen**, *and a Journey made thereunto by our Folk in Anno* 1641" (&c.).—*Valentijn*, III. Pt. ii. pp. 50 *seqq.*

1663.—"*Relation Novvele et Cvrievse dv Royavme de* **Lao**.—Traduite de l'Italien du P. de Marini, Romain. Paris, 1666."

1766.—"Les peuples de **Lao**, nos voisins, n'admittent ni la question ni les peines arbitraires . . . ni les horribles supplices qui sont parmi nous en usage ; mais aussi nous les regardons comme de barbares. . . . Toute l'Asie convient que nous dansons beaucoup mieux qu'eux."—*Voltaire, Dialogue XXI., André des Couches à Siam.*

LAR, n.p. This name has had several applications.

(a). To the region which we now call Guzerat, in its most general application. In this sense the name is now quite obsolete ; but it is that used by most of the early Arab geographers. It is the Λαρικὴ of Ptolemy ; and appears to represent an old Skt. name *Laṭa*, adj. *Laṭaka*, or *Laṭika*. ["The name *Lâṭa* appears to be derived from some local tribe, perhaps the *Lattas*, who, as *r* and *l* are commonly used for each other, may possibly be the well-known Rashṭrakúṭas since their great King Amoghavarsha (A.D. 851-879) calls the name of the dynasty Ratta."—*Bombay Gazetteer*, I. pt. i. 7.]

c. A.D. 150.—"Τῆς δὲ 'Ινδοσκυθίας τὰ ἀπὸ ἀνατολῶν τὰ μεν ἀπὸ θαλάσσης κατέχει ἡ Λαρικὴ χώρα, ἐν ᾗ μεσόγειοι ἀπὸ μεν δύσεως τοῦ Ναμάδου ποταμοῦ πόλις ἥδε. . . . Βαρύγαζα ἐμπόριον."—*Ptolemy*, VII. ii. 62.

c. 940.—"On the coast, *e.g.* at Ṣaimūr, at Sūbāra, and at Tāna, they speak **Lārī** ; these provinces give their name to the Sea of **Lār** (**Lārawī**) on the coast of which they are situated."—*Maṣ'ūdi*, i. 381.

c. 1020.—" . . . to Kach the country producing gum (*mokl*, *i.e.* **Bdellium**, q.v.), and *bárdrúd* (?) . . . to Somnát, fourteen (parasangs) ; to Kambáya, thirty . . . to Tána five. There you enter the country of **Lárán**, where is Jaimúr" (i.q. *Ṣaimúr*, see **CHOUL**).—*Al-Birūni*, in *Elliot*, i. 66.

c. 1190.—"Udaya the Parmâr mounted and came. The Dors followed him from **Lār**. . . ."—The Poem of *Chand Bardai*, E.T. by *Beames*, in *Ind. Antiq.* i. 275.

c. 1330.—"A certain Traveller says that Tāna is a city of Guzerat (*Juzrāt*) in its eastern part, lying west of Malabar (*Munībār*) ; whilst Ibn Sa'yid says that it is the furthest city of **Lār** (*Al-Lār*), and very famous among traders."—*Abulfeda*, in *Gildemeister*, p. 188.

(b). To the Delta region of the Indus, and especially to its western part. Sir H. Elliot supposes the name in this use, which survived until recently, to be identical with the preceding, and that the name had originally extended continuously over the coast, from the western part of the Delta to beyond Bombay (see his *Historians*, i. 378). We have no means of deciding this question (see **LARRY BUNDER**).

c. 1820.—"Díwal . . . was reduced to ruins by a Muhammedan invasion, and another site chosen to the eastward. The new town still went by the same name . . . and was succeeded by *Lári Bandar* or the port of **Lár**, which is the name of the country forming the modern *delta*, particularly the western part."—*M'Murdo*, in *J.R. As. Soc.* i. 29.

(c). To a Province on the north of the Persian Gulf, with its capital.

c. 1220.—**Lar** is erroneously described by Yakūt as a great island between Sirāf and Kish. But there is no such island.* It is an extensive province of the continent. See *Barbier de Meynard, Dict. de la Perse*, p. 501.

c. 1330.—"We marched for three days through a desert . . . and then arrived at **Lār**, a big town having springs, considerable streams, and gardens, and fine bazars. We lodged in the hermitage of the pious Shaikh Abu Dulaf Muḥammad. . . ."—*Ibn Batuta*, ii. 240.

c. 1487.—"Retorneing alongest the coast, forneagainst Ormuos there is a towne called **Lar**, a great and good towne of merchaundise, about ij[ml]. houses. . . ."—*Josafa Barbaro*, old E.T. (Hak. Soc.) 80.

[c. 1590.—"**Lár** borders on the mountains of *Great Tibet*. To its north is a lofty mountain which dominates all the surrounding country, and the ascent of which is arduous. . . ."—*Āīn*, ed. *Jarrett*, ii. 363.]

1553.—"These benefactions the Kings of Ormuz . . . pay to this day to a mosque which that Caciz (see **CASIS**) had made in a district called Hongez of Sheikh Doniar, adjoining the city of **Lara**, distant from Ormuz over 40 leagues."—*Barros*, II. ii. 2.

1602.—"This man was a Moor, a native of the Kingdom of **Lara**, adjoining that of Ormuz : his proper name was Cufo, but as he was a native of the Kingdom of **Lara** he took a surname from the country, and called himself Cufo **Larym**."—*Couto*, IV. vii. 6.

1622.—"**Lar**, as I said before, is capital of a great province or kingdom, which till our day had a prince of its own, who rightfully or wrongfully reigned there absolutely ; but about 23 years since, for reasons rather generous than covetous, as it would seem, it was attacked by Abbas K. of Persia, and the country forcibly taken. . . . Now **Lar** is the seat of a Sultan dependent on the Khan of Shiraz. . . ."—*P. della Valle*, ii. 322.

1727.—"And 4 Days Journey within Land, is the City of **Laar**, which according to their fabulous tradition is the Burying-

* It is possible that the island called Shaikh Shu'aib, which is off the coast of Lār, and not far from Sirāf, may be meant. Barbosa also mentions *Lār* among the islands in the Gulf subject to the K. of Ormuz (p. 37).

place of Lot. . . ."—*A. Hamilton*, i. 92; [ed. 1744].

LARĀI, s. This Hind. word, meaning 'fighting,' is by a curious idiom applied to the biting and annoyance of fleas and the like. [It is not mentioned in the dictionaries of either Fallon or Platts.] There is a similar idiom (*jang kardan*) in Persian.

LAREK, n.p. *Lārak*; an island in the Persian Gulf, not far from the island of Jerun or **Ormus**.

[1623.—"At noon, being near **Lareck**, and no wind stirring, we cast Anchor."—*P. della Valle*, Hak. Soc. i. 3.]

1685.—"We came up with the Islands of Ormus and **Arack** . . ." (called **Lareck** afterwards).—*Hedges, Diary*, May 23; [Hak. Soc. i. 202].

LARIN, s. Pers. *lārī*. A peculiar kind of money formerly in use on the Persian Gulf, W. Coast of India, and in the Maldive Islands, in which last it survived to the last century. The name is there retained still, though coins of the ordinary form are used. It is sufficiently described in the quotations, and representations are given by De Bry and Tavernier. The name appears to have been derived from the territory of **Lar** on the Persian Gulf. (See under that word, [and Mr. Gray's note on *Pyrard de Laval*, Hak. Soc. i. 232 *seq.*].)

1525.—"As tamgas **larys** valem cada hũa sesẽmta reis. . . ."—*Lembrança, das Cousas da India*, 38.

c. 1563.—"I have seen the men of the Country who were Gentiles take their children, their sonnes and their daughters, and have desired the Portugalls to buy them, and I have seene them sold for eight or ten **larines** apiece, which may be of our money x *s.* or xiii *s.* iiii *d.*"—*Master Caesar Frederike*, in *Hakl.* ii. 343.

1583.—Gasparo Balbi has an account of the **Larino**, the greater part of which seems to be borrowed *literatim* by Fitch in the succeeding quotation. But Balbi adds: "The first who began to strike them was the King of **Lar**, who formerly was a powerful King in Persia, but is now a small one."—f. 35.

1587.—"The said **Larine** is a strange piece of money, not being round, as all other current money in Christianitie, but is a small rod of silver, of the greatnesse of the pen of a goose feather . . . which is wrested so that two endes meet at the just half part, and in the head thereof is a stamp *Turkesco*, and these be the best current money in all the Indias, and 6 of these **Larines** make a duckat."—*R. Fitch*, in *Hakl.* ii. 407.

1598.—"An Oxe or a Cowe is there to be bought for one **Larijn**, which is as much as halfe a Gilderne."—*Linschoten*, 28; [Hak. Soc. i. 94; in i. 48 **Larynen**; see also i. 242].

c. 1610.—"La monnoye du Royaume n'est que d'argent et d'vne sorte. Ce sont des pieces d'argent qu'ils appellent **larins**, de valeur de huit sols ou enuiron de nostre monnoye . . . longues comme le doigt mais redoublées. . . ."—*Pyrard de Laval*, i. 163; [Hak. Soc. i. 232].

1613.—"We agreed with one of the Governor's kinred for twenty **laries** (twenty shillings) to conduct us. . . ."—*N. Whithington*, in *Purchas*, i. 484.

1622.—"The **lari** is a piece of money that I will exhibit in Italy, most eccentric in form, for it is nothing but a little rod of silver of a fixed weight, and bent double unequally. On the bend it is marked with some small stamp or other. It is called **Lari** because it was the peculiar money of the Princes of **Lar**, invented by them when they were separated from the Kingdom of Persia. . . . In value every 5 **lari** are equal to a piastre or patacca of reals of Spain, or 'piece of eight' as we choose to call it."—*P. della Valle*, ii. 434.

LARKIN, s. (obsolete). A kind of drink—apparently a sort of **punch**—which was popular in the Company's old factories. We know the word only on the authority of Pietro della Valle; but he is the most accurate of travellers. We are in the dark as to the origin of the name. On the one hand its form suggests an *eponymus* among the old servants of the Company, such as Robert *Larkin*, whom we find to have been engaged for the service in 1610, and to have died chief of the Factory of Patani, on the E. coast of the Malay Peninsula, in 1616. But again we find in a Vocabulary of "Certaine Wordes of the Naturall Language of Iaua," in Drake's *Voyage* (Hak. iv. 246): "*Larnike*=Drinke." Of this word we can trace nothing nearer than (Javan.) *larih*, 'to pledge, or invite to drink at an entertainment,' and (Malay) *larih-larahan*, 'mutual pledging to drink.' It will be observed that della Valle assigns the drink especially to Java.

1623.—"Meanwhile the year 1622 was drawing near its close, and its last days were often celebrated of an evening in the House of the English, with good fellowship. And on one of these occasions I learned from them how to make a beverage called

Larkin, which they told me was in great vogue in Java, and in all those other islands of the Far East. This said beverage seemed to me in truth an admirable thing,—not for use at every meal (it is too strong for that), —but as a tonic in case of debility, and to make tasty possets, much better than those we make with Muscatel wines or Cretan malmseys. So I asked for the recipe; and am taking it to Italy with me. . . . It seemed odd to me that those hot southern regions, as well as in the environs of Hormuz here, where also the heat is great, they should use both spice in their food and spirits in their drink, as well as sundry other hot beverages like this **larkin**."—*P. della Valle*, ii. 475.

LARRY-BUNDER, n.p. The name of an old seaport in the Delta of the Indus, which succeeded Daibul (see **DIUL-SIND**) as the chief haven of Sind. We are doubtful of the proper orthography. It was in later Mahommedan times called *Lāhorī-bandar*, probably from presumed connection with Lahore as the port of the Punjab (*Elliot*, i. 378). At first sight M'Murdo's suggestion that the original name may have been *Lārī-bandar*, from **Lār**, the local name of the southern part of Sind, seems probable. M'Murdo, indeed, writing about 1820, says that the name *Lārī-Bandar* was not at all familiar to natives; but if accustomed to the form *Lāhorī-bandar* they might not recognize it in the other. The shape taken however by what is apparently the same name in our first quotation is adverse to M'Murdo's suggestion.

1030.—"This stream (the Indus) after passing (Alor) . . . divides into two streams; one empties itself into the sea in the neighbourhood of the city of **Lūharānī**, and the other branches off to the East, to the borders of Kach, and is known by the name of *Sind Sāgar*, *i.e.* Sea of Sind."—*Al-Birūnī*, in *Elliot*, i. 49.

c. 1333.—"I travelled five days in his company with Alā-ul-Mulk, and we arrived at the seat of his Government, *i.e.* the town of **Lāhari**, a fine city situated on the shore of the great Sea, and near which the River Sind enters the sea. Thus two great waters join near it; it possesses a grand haven, frequented by the people of Yemen, of Fārs (etc.). . . . The Amir Alā-ul-Mulk . . . told me that the revenue of this place amounted to 60 *laks* a year."—*Ibn Batuta*, iii. 112.

1565.—"Blood had not yet been spilled, when suddenly, news came from Thatta, that the Firingis had passed **Lāhorī-bandar**, and attacked the city."—*Tārīkh-i-Tāhirī*, in *Elliot*, i. 277.

[1607.—"Then you are to saile for **Lawrie** in the Bay of the River Syndus."—*Birdwood, First Letter-book*, 251.

[1611.—"I took . . . **Larree**, the port town of the River Sinda."—*Danvers, Letters*, i. 162.]

1613.—"In November 1613 the Expedition arrived at **Laurebunder**, the port of Sinde, with Sir Robert Shirley and his company."—*Sainsbury*, i. 321.

c. 1665.—"Il se fait aussi beaucoup de trafic au **Loure-bender**, qui est à trois jours de Tatta sur la mer, où la rade est plus excellente pour Vaisseaux, qu'en quelque autre lieu que ce soit des Indes."—*Thevenot*, v. 159.

1679.—". . . If Suratt, Baroach, and **Bundurlaree** in Scinda may be included in the same Phyrmaund to be customs free . . . then that they get these places and words inserted."—*Ft. St. Geo. Consns.*, Feb. 20. In *Notes and Exts.*, No. 1. Madras, 1871.

1727.—"It was my Fortune . . . to come to **Larribunder**, with a Cargo from *Mallebar*, worth above £10,000."—*A. Hamilton*, i. 116; [ed. 1744, i. 117, **Larribundar**].

1739.—"But the Castle and town of **Lohre Bender**, with all the country to the eastward of the river ATTOK, and of the waters of the SCIND, and NALA SUNKHRA, shall, as before, belong to the Empire of Hindostan."—*H. of Nadir*, in *Hanway*, ii. 387.

1753.—"Le bras gauche du Sind se rend à **Laheri**, où il s'épanche en un lac; et ce port, qui est celui de Tattanagar, communément est nommé **Laûrébender**."—*D'Anville*, p. 40.

1763.—"Les Anglois ont sur cette côte encore plusieurs petits établissement (*sic*) où ils envoyent des premiers Marchands, des sous-Marchands, ou des Facteurs, comme en *Scindi*, à trois endroits, à *Tatta*, une grande ville et la résidence du Seigneur du païs, à **Lar Bunder**, et à *Schah-Bunder*."—*Niebuhr, Voyage*, ii. 8.

1780.—"The first place of any note, after passing the bar, is **Laribunda**, about 5 or 6 leagues from the sea."—*Dunn's Oriental Navigator*, 5th ed. p. 96.

1813.—"**Laribunder**. This is commonly called Scindy River, being the principal branch of the Indus, having 15 feet water on the bar, and 6 or 7 fathoms inside; it is situated in latitude about 24° 30′ north. . . . The town of **Laribunder** is about 5 leagues from the sea, and vessels of 200 tons used to proceed up to it."—*Milburn*, i. 146.

1831.—"We took the route by Durajee and Meerpoor. . . . The town of **Lahory** was in sight from the former of these places, and is situated on the same, or left bank of the Pittee."—*A. Burnes*, 2nd. ed. i. 22.

LASCAR, s. The word is originally from Pers. *lashkar*, 'an army,' 'a camp.' This is usually derived from Ar. *al'askar*, but it would rather seem that

Ar. *'askar*, 'an army' is taken from this Pers. word: whence *lashkarī*, 'one belonging to an army, a soldier.' The word *lascár* or *láscár* (both these pronunciations are in vogue) appears to have been corrupted, through the Portuguese use of *lashkarī* in the forms *lasquarin*, *lascari*, &c., either by the Portuguese themselves, or by the Dutch and English who took up the word from them, and from these *laskār* has passed back again into native use in this corrupt shape. The early Portuguese writers have the forms we have just named in the sense of 'soldier'; but *lascar* is never so used now. It is in general the equivalent of *khalāsī*, in the various senses of that word (see **CLASSY**), viz. (1) an inferior class of artilleryman ('*gun-lascar*'); (2) a tent-pitcher, doing other work which the class are accustomed to do; (3) a sailor. The last is the most common Anglo-Indian use, and has passed into the English language. The use of *lascar* in the modern sense by Pyrard de Laval shows that this use was already general on the west coast at the beginning of the 17th century, [also see quotation from Pringle below]; whilst the curious distinction which Pyrard makes between *Lascar* and *Lascari*, and Dr. Fryer makes between *Luscar* and *Lascar* (accenting probably *Lúscar* and *Lascár*) shows that *lashkarī* for a soldier was still in use. In Ceylon the use of the word *lascareen* for a local or civil soldier long survived; perhaps is not yet extinct. The word *lashkari* does not seem to occur in the *Āīn*.

[1523.—"Fighting men called **Lascaryns**."—*Alguns documentos, Tombo*, p. 479.

[1538.—"My mother only bore me to be a Captain, and not your **Lascar** (**lascarin**)."—Letter of *Nuno da Cunha*, in *Barros*, Dec. IV. bk. 10, ch. 21.]

1541.—"It is a proverbial saying all over **India** (*i.e. Portuguese India*, see s.v.) that the good **Lasquarim**, or 'soldier' as we should call him, must be an Abyssinian."—*Castro, Roteiro*, 73.

1546.—"Besides these there were others (who fell at Diu) whose names are unknown, being men of the lower rank, among whom I knew a **lascarym** (a man getting only 500 reis of pay!) who was the first man to lay his hand on the Moorish wall, and shouted aloud that they might see him, as many have told me. And he was immediately thrown down wounded in five places with stones and bullets, but still lived; and a noble gentleman sent and had him rescued and carried away by his slaves. And he survived, but being a common man he did not even get his pay!"—*Correa*, iv. 567.

1552.—"... eles os reparte polos **lascarins** de suas capitanias, q̃ assi chamão soldados."—*Castanheda*, ii. 67. [Mr. Whiteway notes that in the orig. *repartem* for *reparte*, and the reference should be ii. 16.]

1554.—"Moreover the Senhor Governor conceded to the said ambassador that if in the territories of Idalshaa (see **IDALCAN**), or in those of our Lord the King there shall be any differences or quarrels between any Portuguese **lascarins** or **peons** (*piães*) of ours, and **lascarins** of the territories of Idalshaa and peons of his, that the said Idalshaa shall order the delivery up of the Portuguese and peons that they may be punished if culpable. And in like manner ..."—*S. Botelho, Tombo*, 44.

1572.—"Erant in eo praesidio **Lasquarini** circiter septingenti artis scolopettariae peritissimi."—*E. Acosta*, f. 236*v*.

1598.—"The soldier of *Ballagate*, which is called **Lascarin**. ..."—*Linschoten*, 74; [in Hak. Soc. i. 264, **Lascariin**].

1600.—"Todo a mais churma e meneyo das naos são Mouros que chamão **Laschãres**. ..."—*Lucena, Life of St. Franc. Xav.*, liv. iv. p. 223.

[1602.—"... because the **Lascars** (**lascaris**), for so they call the Arab sailors."—*Couto*, Dec. X. bk. 3, ch. 13.]

c. 1610.—"Mesmes tous les mariniers et les pilotes sont Indiens, tant Gentils que Mahometans. Tous ces gens de mer les appellent **Lascars**, et les soldats **Lascarits**."—*Pyrard de Laval*, i. 317; [Hak. Soc. i. 438; also see ii. 3, 17].

[1615.—"... two horses with six **Lasceras** and two caffres (see **CAFFER**)."—*Foster, Letters*, iv. 112.]

1644.—"... The *aldeas* of the jurisdiction of Damam, in which district there are 4 fortified posts defended by *Lascars* (**Lascarīs**) who are mostly native Christian soldiers, though they may be heathen as some of them are."—*Bocarro*, MS.

1673.—"The Seamen and Soldiers differ only in a Vowel, the one being pronounced with an *u*, the other with an *a*, as **Luscar**, a soldier, **Lascar**, a seaman."—*Fryer*, 107.

[1683-84.—"The Warehousekeeper having Seaverall dayes advised the Council of Ship Welfares tardynesse in receiving & stowing away the Goods, ... alledging that they have not hands Sufficient to dispatch them, though we have spared them tenn **Laskars** for that purpose. ..."—*Pringle, Diary Ft. St. Geo.*, 1st ser. iii. 7 *seq.*; also see p. 43.]

1685.—"They sent also from Sofragan D. Antonio da Motta Galvaon with 6 companies, which made 190 men; the Dissava (see **DISSAVE**) of the adjoining provinces joined him with 4000 **Lascarins**."—*Ribeyro, H. of the I. of Ceylan* (from French Tr., p. 241).

1690.—"For when the *English* Sailers at that time perceiv'd the softness of the Indian **Lascarrs**; how tame they were . . . they embark'd again upon a new Design . . . to . . . rob these harmless Traffickers in the *Red Sea*."—*Ovington*, 464.

1726.—"**Lascaryns**, or Loopers, are native soldiers, who have some regular maintenance, and in return must always be ready."—*Valentijn, Ceylon*, Names of Offices, &c., 10.

1755.—"Some **Lascars** and Sepoys were now sent forward to clear the road."—*Orme*, ed. 1803, i. 394.

1787.—"The Field Pieces attached to the Cavalry draw up on the Right and Left Flank of the Regiment; the Artillery **Lascars** forming in a line with the Front Rank the full Extent of the Drag Ropes, which they hold in their hands."—*Regns. for the Hon. Company's Troops on the Coast of Coromandel*, by *M.-Gen. Sir Archibald Campbell*, K.B. Govr. & C. in C. Madras, p. 9.

1803.—"In those parts (of the low country of Ceylon) where it is not thought requisite to quarter a body of troops, there is a police corps of the natives appointed to enforce the commands of Government in each district; they are composed of *Conganies*, or sergeants, *Aratjies*, or corporals, and **Lascarines**, or common soldiers, and perform the same office as our Sheriff's men or constables."—*Percival's Ceylon*, 222.

1807.—"A large open boat formed the van, containing his excellency's guard of **lascoreens**, with their spears raised perpendicularly, the union colours flying, and Ceylon drums called **tomtoms** beating."—*Cordiner's Ceylon*, 170.

1872.—"The **lascars** on board the steamers were insignificant looking people."—*The Dilemma*, ch. ii.

In the following passages the original word *lashkar* is used in its proper sense for 'a camp.'

[1614.—"He said he bought it of a banyan in the **Lasker**."—*Foster, Letters*, ii. 142.

[1615.—"We came to the **Lasker** the 7th of February in the evening."—*Ibid.* iii. 85.]

1616.—"I tooke horse to auoyd presse, and other inconvenience, and crossed out of the **Leskar**, before him."—*Sir T. Roe*, in *Purchas*, i. 559; see also 560; [Hak. Soc. ii. 324].

[1682.—". . . presents to the Seir **Lascarr** (*sar-i-lashkar*, 'head of the army') this day received."—*Pringle, Diary Ft. St. Geo.*, 1st ser. i. 84.]

LĀT, LĀT SĀHIB, s. This, a popular corruption of *Lord Sahib*, or *Lārd Sāhib*, as it is written in Hind., is the usual form from native lips, at least in the Bengal Presidency, of the title by which the Governor-General has long been known in the vernaculars. The term also extends nowadays to Lieutenant-Governors, who in contact with the higher authority become *Chhoṭā* ('Little') **Lāt**, whilst the Governor-General and the Commander-in-Chief are sometimes discriminated as the *Mulkī* **Lāt Sāhib** [or **Barē Lāt**], and the *Jangī* **Lāt Sāhib** ('territorial' and 'military'), the Bishop as the **Lāt Pādrē Sāhib**, and the Chief Justice as the **Lāt Justy Sāhib**. The title is also sometimes, but very incorrectly, applied to minor dignitaries of the supreme Government, [whilst the common form of blessing addressed to a civil officer is "*Huzūr* **Lāt Guvnar, Lāt Sikritar** *ho-jāeṅ*."

1824.—"He seemed, however, much puzzled to make out my rank, never having heard (he said) of any '**Lord Sahib**' except the Governor-General, while he was still more perplexed by the exposition of '**Lord** *Bishop* **Sahib**,' which for some reason or other my servants always prefer to that of **Lord Padre**."—*Heber*, i. 69.

1837.—"The Arab, thinking I had purposely stolen his kitten, ran after the buggy at full speed, shouting as he passed Lord Auckland's tents, 'Dohā'ī, dohā'ī, Sāhib! dohā'ī, **Lord Sāhib**!' (see **DOAI**). 'Mercy, mercy, sir! mercy, Governor-General!' The faster the horse rushed on, the faster followed the shouting Arab."—*Wanderings of a Pilgrim*, ii. 142.

1868.—"The old barber at Roorkee, after telling me that he had known Strachey when he first began, added, 'Ab **Lāt-Sekretur** hai! Ah! hum bhi boodda hogya!' ('Now he is *Lord Secretary!* Ah! I too have become old!')"—*Letter from the late M.-Gen. W. W. H. Greathed.*

1877.—". . . in a rare but most valuable book (*Galloway's Observations on India*, 1825, pp. 254-8), in which the author reports, with much quiet humour, an aged native's account of the awful consequences of contempt of an order of the (as he called the Supreme Court) '*Shubreem Koorut*,' the order of Impey being '**Lord Justey Sahib**-*kahookm*,' the instruments of whose will were '*abidabis*' or affidavits."—Letter from *Sir J. F. Stephen*, in *Times*, May 31.

LAT, s. Hind. *lāt*, used as a corruption of the English *lot*, in reference to an auction (*Carnegie*).

LĀṬ, LĀṬH, s. This word, meaning a staff or pole, is used for an obelisk or columnar monument; and is specifically used for the ancient Buddhist columns of Eastern India.

[1861-62.—"The pillar (at **Besarh**) is known by the people as *Bhīm-Sen-kā*-**lāt** and *Bhīm-Sen-ka-ḍanḍā*."—*Cunningham, Arch. Rep.* i. 61.]

LATERITE, s. A term, first used by Dr. Francis Buchanan, to indicate a reddish brick-like argillaceous formation much impregnated with iron peroxide, and hardening on exposure to the atmosphere, which is found in places all over South India from one coast to the other, and the origin of which geologists find very obscure. It is found in two distinct types: viz. (1) *High-level Laterite*, capping especially the trap-rocks of the Deccan, with a bed from 30 or 40 to 200 feet in thickness, which perhaps at one time extended over the greater part of Peninsular India. This is found as far north as the Rajmahal and Monghyr hills. (2). *Low-level Laterite*, forming comparatively thin and sloping beds on the plains of the coast. The origin of both is regarded as being, in the most probable view, modified volcanic matter; the low-level laterite having undergone a further rearrangement and deposition; but the matter is too complex for brief statement (see *Newbold*, in *J.R.A.S.*, vol. viii.; and the *Manual of the Geol. of India*, pp. xlv. *seqq.*, 348 *seqq.*). Mr. King and others have found flint weapons in the low-level formation. Laterite is the usual material for road-metal in S. India, as **kunkur** (q.v.) is in the north. In Ceylon it is called **cabook** (q.v.).

1800.—"It is diffused in immense masses, without any appearance of stratification, and is placed over the granite that forms the basis of *Malayala*. . . . It very soon becomes as hard as brick, and resists the air and water much better than any brick I have seen in India. . . . As it is usually cut into the form of bricks for building, in several of the native dialects it is called the brick-stone (*Iticacullee*) [Malayāl. *vettukal*]. . . . The most proper English name would be **Laterite**, from *Lateritis*, the appellation that may be given it in science."—*Buchanan, Mysore*, &c., ii. 440-441.

1860.—"Natives resident in these localities (Galle and Colombo) are easily recognisable elsewhere by the general hue of their dress. This is occasioned by the prevalence along the western coast of **laterite**, or, as the Singhalese call it, **cabook**, a product of disintegrated gneiss, which being subjected to detrition communicates its hue to the soil."—*Tennent's Ceylon*, i. 17.

LATTEE, s. A stick; a bludgeon, often made of the male bamboo (*Dendrocalamus strictus*), and sometimes bound at short intervals with iron rings, forming a formidable weapon. The word is Hind. *lāṭhī* and *lathī*, Mahr. *laththa*. This is from Prakrit *laṭṭhī*, for Skt. *yashṭi*, 'a stick,' according to the Prakrit grammar of Vavaruchi (ed. *Cowell*, ii. 32); see also *Lassen, Institutiones, Ling. Prakrit*, 195. *Jiskī lāṭhī, us kī bhains*, is a Hind. proverb (*cujus baculum ejus bubalus*), equivalent to the "good old rule, the simple plan."

1830.—"The natives use a very dangerous weapon, which they have been forbidden by Government to carry. I took one as a curiosity, which had been seized on a man in a fight in a village. It is a very heavy **lāthi**, a solid male bamboo, 5 feet 5 inches long, headed with iron in a most formidable manner. There are 6 jagged semicircular irons at the top, each 2 inches in length, 1 in height, and it is shod with iron bands 16 inches deep from the top."—*Wanderings of a Pilgrim*, i. 133.

1878.—"After driving some 6 miles, we came upon about 100 men seated in rows on the roadside, all with **latties**."—*Life in the Mofussil*, i. 114.

LATTEEAL, s. Hind. *lāṭhīyāl*, or, more cumbrously, *lāṭhīwālā*, 'a clubman,' a hired ruffian. Such gentry were not many years ago entertained in scores by planters in some parts of Bengal, to maintain by force their claims to lands for sowing indigo on.

1878.—"Doubtless there were hired **lattials** . . . on both sides."—*Life in the Mofussil*, ii. 6.

LAW-OFFICER. This was the official designation of a Mahommedan officer learned in the (Mahommedan) law, who was for many years of our Indian administration an essential functionary of the judges' Courts in the districts, as well as of the Sudder or Courts of Review at the Presidency.

It is to be remembered that the law administered in Courts under the Company's government, from the assumption of the Dewanny of Bengal, Bahar, and Orissa, was the Mahommedan law; at first by the hands of native **Cazees** and **Mufties**, with some superintendence from the higher European servants of the Company; a superintendence which, while undergoing sundry vicissitudes of system during the next 30 years, developed gradually into a European judiciary, which again was set on an extended and quasi-permanent footing by Lord Cornwallis's Government, in Regulation IX. of 1793 (see **ADAWLUT**). The Mahommedan law continued, however, to be the professed basis of criminal jurisprudence, though modified more and more, as years went on, by new **Regulations**, and by the recorded constructions and circular orders of the superior Courts, until the accomplishment of the great changes which followed the Mutiny, and the assumption of the direct government of India by the Crown (1858). The landmarks of change were (*a*) the enactment of the Penal Code (Act XLV. of 1860), and (*b*) that of the Code of Criminal Procedure (Act. XXV. of 1861), followed by (*c*) the establishment of the High Court (July 1, 1862), in which became merged both the **Supreme Court** with its peculiar jurisdiction, and the (quondam-Company's) Sudder Courts of Review and Appeal, civil and criminal (*Dewanny* **Adawlvt**, and *Nizamat* **Adawlut**).

The authoritative exposition of the Mahommedan Law, in aid and guidance of the English judges, was the function of the Mahommedan **Law-officer**. He sat with the judge on the bench at Sessions, *i.e.* in the hearing of criminal cases committed by the magistrate for trial; and at the end of the trial he gave in his written record of the proceedings with his **Futwa** (q.v.) (see Regn. IX. 1793, sect. 47), which was his judgment as to the guilt of the accused, as to the definition of the crime, and as to its appropriate punishment according to Mahommedan Law. The judge was bound attentively to consider the *futwa*, and if it seemed to him to be consonant with natural justice, and also in conformity with the Mahommedan Law, he passed sentence (save in certain excepted cases) in its terms, and issued his warrant to the magistrate for execution of the sentence, unless it were one of death, in which case the proceedings had to be referred to the Sudder Nizamut for confirmation. In cases also where there was disagreement between the civilian judge and the Law-officer, either as to finding or sentence, the matter was referred to the Sudder Court for ultimate decision.

In 1832, certain modifications were introduced by law (*Regn.* VI. of that year), which declared that the *futwa* might be dispensed with either by referring the case for report to a **punchayet** (q.v.), which sat apart from the Court; or by constituting assessors in the trial (generally three in number). The frequent adoption of the latter alternative rendered the appearance of the Law-officer and his *futwa* much less universal as time went on. The post of **Law-officer** was indeed not actually abolished till 1864. But it would appear from enquiry that I have made, among friends of old standing in the Civil Service, that for some years before the issue of the Penal Code and the other reforms already mentioned, the **Moolvee** (*maulavī*) or Mahommedan **Law-officer** had, in some at least of the Bengal districts, practically ceased to sit with the judge, even in cases where no assessors were summoned.* I cannot trace any legislative authority for this, nor any Circular of the Sudder Nizamut; and it is not easy, at this time of day, to obtain much personal testimony. But Sir George Yule (who was Judge of Rungpore and Bogra about 1855-56) writes thus:

> "The **Moulvee**-ship . . . must have been abolished before I became a judge (I think), which was 2 or 3 years before the Mutiny; for I have *no* recollection of *ever* sitting with a *Moulvee*, and I had a great number of heavy criminal cases to try in Rungpore and Bogra. Assessors were substituted for the *Moulvee* in some cases, but I have no recollection of employing these either."

Mr. Seton-Karr, again, who was Civil and Sessions Judge of Jessore (1857-1860), writes:

> "I am quite certain of my own practice . . . and I made deliberate choice of native assessors, whenever the law required me to have such functionaries. I determined *never* to sit with a *Maulavi*, as, even before the Penal Code was passed, and came into operation, I wished to get rid of **futwas** and differences of opinion."

The office of Law-officer was formally abolished by Act XI. of 1864.

In respect of civil litigation, it had been especially laid down (*Regn.* of April 11, 1780, quoted below) that in suits regarding successions, inheritance, marriage, caste, and all religious usages

* Reg. I. of 1810 had empowered the Executive Government, by an official communication from its Secretary in the Judicial Department, to dispense with the attendance and futwa of the Law officers of the courts of circuit, when it seemed advisable. But in such case the judge of the court passed no sentence, but referred the proceedings with an opinion to the *Nizamut Adawlut*.

and institutions, the Mahommedan laws with respect to Mahommedans, and the Hindū laws with respect to Hindūs, were to be considered as the general rules by which the judges were to form their decisions. In the respective cases, it was laid down, the *Mahommedan and Hindū* **law-officers** of the court were to attend and expound the law.

In this note I have dealt only with the Mahommedan law-officer, whose presence and co-operation was so long (it has been seen) essential in a criminal trial. In civil cases he did not sit with the judge (at least in memory of man now living), but the judge could and did, in case of need, refer to him on any point of Mahommedan Law. The Hindū **law-officer (Pundit)** is found in the legislation of 1793, and is distinctly traceable in the Regulations down at least to 1821. In fact he is named in the Act XI. of 1864 (see quotation under **CAZEE**) abolishing Law-officers. But in many of the districts it would seem that he had very long before 1860 practically ceased to exist, under what circumstances exactly I have failed to discover. He had nothing to do with criminal justice, and the occasions for reference to him were presumably not frequent enough to justify his maintenance in every district. A *Pundit* continued to be attached to the Sudder Dewanny, and to him questions were referred by the District Courts when requisite. Neither *Pundit* nor *Moolvee* is attached to the High Court, but native judges sit on its Bench. It need only be added that under Regulation III. of 1821, a magistrate was authorized to refer for trial to the Law-officer of his district a variety of complaints and charges of a trivial character. The designation of the Law-officer was *Maulavi.* (See **ADAWLUT, CAZEE, FUTWA, MOOLVEE, MUFTY.**)

1780.—"That in all suits regarding inheritance, marriage, and caste, and other religious usages or institutions, the laws of the Koran with respect to Mahommedans, and those of the Shaster with respect to Gentoos, shall be invariably adhered to. On all such occasions the **Molavies** or Brahmins shall respectively attend to expound the law; and they shall sign the report and assist in passing the decree."—*Regulation passed by the G.-G. and Council*, April 11, 1780.

1793.—"II. The **Law Officers** of the Sudder Dewanny Adawlut, the Nizamut Adawlut, the provincial Courts of Appeal, the courts of circuit, and the zillah and city courts . . . shall not be removed but for incapacity or misconduct. . . ."—*Reg. XII.* of 1793.

In §§ iv., v., vi. **Cauzy** and **Mufty** are substituted for **Law-Officer**, but referring to the same persons.

1799.—"IV. If the **futwa** of the **law officers** of the Nizamut Adawlut declare any person convicted of wilful murder not liable to suffer death under the Mahomedan law on the ground of . . . the Court of *Nizamut Adawlut* shall notwithstanding sentence the prisoner to suffer death. . . ."—*Reg. VIII.* of 1799.

LAXIMANA, LAQUESIMENA, &c., s. Malay *Laksamana*, from Skt. *lakshmana*, 'having fortunate tokens' (which was the name of a mythical hero, brother of *Rāma*). This was the title of one of the highest dignitaries in the Malay State, commander of the forces.

1511.—"There used to be in Malaca five principal dignities . . . the third is **Lassamane**; this is Admiral of the Sea. . . ."—*Alboquerque*, by *Birch*, iii. 87.

c. 1539.—"The King accordingly set forth a Fleet of two hundred Sails. . . . And of this Navy he made General the great **Laque Xemena**, his Admiral, of whose Valor the History of the *Indiaes* hath spoken in divers places."—*Pinto*, in *Çogan*, p. 38.

1553.—"**Lacsamana** was harassed by the King to engage Dom Garcia; but his reply was: *Sire, against the Portuguese and their high-sided vessels it is impossible to engage with low-cut* **lancharas** *like ours. Leave me (to act) for I know this people well, seeing how much blood they have cost me; good fortune is now with thee, and I am about to avenge you on them.* And so he did."—*Barros*, III. viii. 7.

[1615.—"On the morrow I went to take my leave of **Laxaman**, to whom all strangers' business are resigned."—*Foster, Letters*, iv. 6.]

LEAGUER, s. The following use of this word is now quite obsolete, we believe, in English; but it illustrates the now familiar German use of *Lager-Bier*, *i.e.* 'beer for laying down, for keeping' (primarily in cask). The word in this sense is neither in Minshew (1627), nor in Bayley (1730).

1747.—"That the Storekeeper do provide **Leaguers** of good Columbo or Batavia arrack."—*Ft. St. David Consn.*, May 5 (MS. Record in India Office).

1782.—"Will be sold by Public Auction by Mr. Bondfield, at his Auction Room, formerly the Court of Cutcherry . . . Square and Globe Lanthorns, a quantity of Country Rum in **Leaguers**, a Slave Girl, and a variety of other articles."—*India Gazette*, Nov. 23.

LECQUE, s. We do not know what the word used by the Abbé Raynal in the following extract is meant for. It is perhaps a mistake for *last*, a Dutch weight.

1770.—"They (Dutch at the Cape) receive a still smaller profit from 60 **lecques** of red wine, and 80 or 90 of white, which they carry to Europe every year. The **lecque** weighs about 1,200 pounds."—*Raynal*, E.T. 1777, i. 231.

LEE, s. Chin. *lī*. The ordinary Chinese itinerary measure. Books of the Jesuit Missionaries generally interpret the modern *lī* as $\frac{1}{10}$ of a league, which gives about 3 *lī* to the mile; more exactly, according to Mr. Giles, 27$\frac{4}{5}$ *lī*=10 miles; but it evidently varies a good deal in different parts of China, and has also varied in the course of ages. Thus in the 8th century, data quoted by M. Vivien de St. Martin, from Père Gaubil, show that the *lī* was little more than $\frac{1}{5}$ of an English mile. And from several concurrent statements we may also conclude that the *lī* is generalised so that a certain number of *lī*, generally 100, stand for a day's march. [Archdeacon Gray (*China*, ii. 101) gives 10 *lī* as the equivalent of 3$\frac{1}{3}$ English miles; Gen. Cunningham (*Arch. Rep.* i. 305) asserts that Hwen Thsang converts the Indian *yojanas* into Chinese *lī* at the rate of 40 *lī* per *yojana*, or of 10 *lī* per *kos*.]

1585.—"By the said booke it is found that the Chinos haue amongst them but only three kind of measures; the which in their language are called **lii**, *pu*, and *icham*, which is as much as to say, or in effect, as a forlong, league, or iorney: the measure, which is called *lii*, hath so much space as a man's voice on a plaine grounde may bee hearde in a quiet day, halowing or whoping with all the force and strength he may; and ten of these **liis** maketh a *pu*, which is a great Spanish league; and ten *pus* maketh a daye's iourney, which is called *icham*, which maketh 12 (*sic*) long leagues."—*Mendoza*, i. 21.

1861.—"In this part of the country a day's march, whatever its actual distance, is called 100 **li**; and the **li** may therefore be taken as a measure of time rather than of distance."—*Col. Sarel*, in *J.R. Geog. Soc.* xxxii. 11.

1878.—"D'après les clauses du contrat le voyage d'une longueur totale de 1,800 **lis**, ou 180 lieues, devait s'effectuer en 18 jours."—*L. Rousset, A Travers la Chine*, 337.

LEECHEE, LYCHEE, s. Chin. *li-chi*, and in S. China (its native region) *lai-chi*; the beautiful and delicate fruit of the *Nephelium litchi*, Cambessèdes (N. O. *Sapindaceae*), a tree which has been for nearly a century introduced into Bengal with success. The dried fruit, usually ticketed as *lychee*, is now common in London shops.

c. 1540.—". . . outra verdura muito mais fresca, e de melhor cheiro, que esta, a que os naturaes da terra chamão **lechias**. . . ."—*Pinto*, ch. lxviii.

1563.—"*R.* Of the things of China you have not said a word; though there they have many fruits highly praised, such as are **lalichias** (*lalixias*) and other excellent fruits.

"*O.* I did not speak of the things of China, because China is a region of which there is so much to tell that it never comes to an end. . . ."—*Garcia*, f. 157.

1585. — "Also they have a kinde of plummes that they doo call **lechias**, that are of an exceeding gallant tast, and never hurteth anybody, although they should eate a great number of them."—*Parke's Mendoza*, i. 14.

1598.—"There is a kind of fruit called **Lechyas**, which are like Plums, but of another taste, and are very good, and much esteemed, whereof I have eaten."—*Linschoten*, 38; [Hak. Soc. i. 131].

1631.—"Adfertur ad nos præterea fructus quidam *Lances* (read **Laices**) vocatus, qui racematim, ut uvæ, crescit."—*Jac. Bontii*, Dial. vi. p. 11.

1684.—"**Latsea**, or Chinese Chestnuts."—*Valentijn*, iv. (China) 12.

1750-52.—"**Leicki** is a species of trees which they seem to reckon equal to the sweet orange trees. . . . It seems hardly credible that the country about Canton (in which place only the fruit grows) annually makes 100,000 *tel* of dried **leickis**."—*Olof Toreen*, 302-3.

1824.—"Of the fruits which this season offers, the finest are **leeches** (*sic*) and mangoes; the first is really very fine, being a sort of plum, with the flavour of a Frontignac grape."—*Heber*, i. 60.

c. 1858.—

"Et tandis que ton pied, sorti de la babouche,
Pendait, rose, au bord du **manchy** (see **MUNCHEEL**)
À l'ombre des bois noirs touffus, et du **Letchi**,
Aux fruits moins pourpres que ta bouche."
Leconte de Lisle.

1878.—". . . and the **lichi** hiding under a shell of ruddy brown its globes of translucent and delicately fragrant flesh."—*Ph. Robinson, In My Indian Garden*, 49.

1879.—". . . Here are a hundred and sixty **lichi** fruits for you. . . ."—*M. Stokes, Indian Fairy Tales* (Calc. ed.) 51.

LEMON, s. *Citrus medica*, var. *Limonum*, Hooker. This is of course not an Anglo-Indian word. But it has come into European languages through the Ar. *leimūn*, and is, according to Hehn, of Indian origin. In Hind. we have both *līmū* and *nīmbū*, which last, at least, seems to be an indigenous form. The Skt. dictionaries give *nimbūka*. In England we get the word through the Romance languages, Fr. *limon*, It. *limone*, Sp. *limon*, &c., perhaps both from the Crusades and from the Moors of Spain. [Mr. Skeat writes: "The Malay form is *limau*, 'a lime, lemon, or orange.' The Port. *limão* may possibly come from this Malay form. I feel sure that *limau*, which in some dialects is *limar*, is an indigenous word which was transferred to Europe."] (See **LIME**.)

c. 1200.—"Sunt praeterea aliae arbores fructus acidos, pontici videlicet saporis, ex se procreantes, quos appellant **limones**."—*Jacobi de Vitriaco, Hist. Iherosolym*, cap. lxxxv. in *Bongars*.

c. 1328.—"I will only say this much, that this India, as regards fruit and other things, is entirely different from Christendom; except, indeed, that there be **lemons** in some places, as sweet as sugar, whilst there be other **lemons** sour like ours."—*Friar Jordanus*, 15.

1331.—"Profunditas hujus aquae plena est lapidibus preciosis. Quae aqua multum est yrudinibus et sanguisugis plena. Hos lapides non accipit rex, sed pro animâ suâ semel vel bis in anno sub aquas ipsos pauperes ire permittit. . . . Et ut ipsi pauperes ire sub aquam possint accipiunt **limonem** et quemdam fructum quem bene pistant, et illo bene se ungunt. . . . Et cum sic sint uncti yrudines et sanguisugæ illos offendere non valent."—*Fr. Odoric*, in *Cathay*, &c., App., p. xxi.

c. 1333.—"The fruit of the mango-tree (*al-'anba*) is the size of a great pear. When yet green they take the fallen fruit and powder it with salt and preserve it, as is done with the sweet citron and the *lemon* (*al*-**leimūn**) in our country."—*Ibn Batuta*, iii. 126.

LEMON-GRASS, s. *Andropogon citratus*, D.C., a grass cultivated in Ceylon and Singapore, yielding an oil much used in perfumery, under the name of *Lemon-Grass Oil, Oil of Verbena*, or *Indian Melissa Oil*. Royle (*Hind. Medicine*, 82) has applied the name to another very fragrant grass, *Andropogon schoenanthus*, L., according to him the *σχοῖνος* of Dioscorides. This last, which grows wild in various parts of India, yields *Rūsa Oil*, alias *O. of Ginger-grass* or *of Geranium*, which is exported from Bombay to Arabia and Turkey, where it is extensively used in the adulteration of "Otto of Roses."

LEOPARD, s. We insert this in order to remark that there has been a great deal of controversy among Indian sportsmen, and also among naturalists, as to whether there are or are not two species of this Cat, distinguished by those who maintain the affirmative, as panther (*F. pardus*) and leopard (*Felis leopardus*), the latter being the smaller, though by some these names are reversed. Even those who support this distinction of species appear to admit that the markings, habits, and general appearance (except size) of the two animals are almost identical. Jerdon describes the two varieties, but (with Blyth) classes both as one species (*Felis pardus*). [Mr. Blanford takes the same view: "I cannot help suspecting that the difference is very often due to age. . . . I have for years endeavoured to distinguish the two forms, but without success." (*Mammalia of India*, 68 *seq.*)]

LEWCHEW, LIU KIU, LOO-CHOO, &c., n.p. The name of a group of islands to the south of Japan, a name much more familiar than in later years during the 16th century, when their people habitually navigated the China seas, and visited the ports of the Archipelago. In the earliest notices they are perhaps mixt up with the Japanese. [Mr. Chamberlain writes the name *Luchu*, and says that it is pronounced *Dūchū* by the natives and *Ryūkyū* by the Japanese (*Things Japanese*, 3rd ed. p. 267). Mr. Pringle traces the name in the "Gold flowered **loes**" which appear in a Madras list of 1684, and which he supposes to be "a name invented for the occasion to describe some silk stuff brought from the Liu Kiu islands." (*Diary Ft. St. Geo.* 1st ser. iii. 174).]

1516.—"Opposite this country of China there are many islands in the sea, and beyond them at 175 leagues to the east there is one very large, which they say is the mainland, from whence there come in each year to Malaca 3 or 4 ships like those of the Chinese, of white people whom they describe as great and wealthy merchants. . . . These islands are called **Lequeos**, the people of Malaca say they are better men, and greater and wealthier merchants, and better dressed and adorned, and more honourable than the Chinese." — *Barbosa*, 207.

1540.—"And they, demanding of him whence he came, and what he would have, he answered them that he was of the Kingdom of *Siam* [of the settlement of the Tanaucarim foreigners, and that he came from Veniaga] and as a merchant was going to traffique in the Isle of **Lequios**."—*Pinto* (orig. cap. x. xli), in *Cogan*, 49.

1553.—"Fernao Peres . . . whilst he remained at that island of Beniaga, saw there certain junks of the people called **Lequios**, of whom he had already got a good deal of information at Malaca, as that they inhabited certain islands adjoining that coast of China; and he observed that the most part of the merchandize that they brought was a great quantity of gold . . . and they appeared to him a better disposed people than the Chinese. . . ."—*Barros*, III. ii. 8. See also II. vi. 6.

1556.—(In this year) "a Portugal arrived at *Malaca*, named *Pero Gomez d'Almeyda*, servant to the Grand Master of *Santiago*, with a rich Present, and letters from the *Nautaquim*, Prince of the Island of *Tanixumaa*, directed to King *John* the third . . . to have five hundred *Portugals* granted to him, to the end that with them, and his own Forces, he might conquer the Island of **Lequio**, for which he would remain tributary to him at 5000 Kintals of Copper and 1000 of Lattin, yearly. . . ."—*Pinto*, in *Cogan*, p. 188.

1615. — "The King of Mashona (qu. *Shashma ?*) . . . who is King of the westermost islands of Japan . . . has conquered the **Leques** Islands, which not long since were under the Government of China."—*Sainsbury*, i. 447.

" "The King of Shashma . . . a man of greate power, and hath conquered the islandes called the **Leques**, which not long since were under the government of China. **Leque** Grande yeeldeth greate store of amber greece of the best sorte, and will vent 1,000 or 15,000 (*sic*) ps. of coarse cloth, as dutties and such like, per annum."—*Letter of Raphe Coppindall*, in *Cocks*, ii. 272.

[" "They being put from **Liquea**. . . ."—*Ibid*. i. 1.]

LIAMPO, n.p. This is the name which the older writers, especially Portuguese, give to the Chinese port which we now call *Ning-Po*. It is a form of corruption which appears in other cases of names used by the Portuguese, or of those who learned from them. Thus *Nanking* is similarly called *Lanchin* in the publications of the same age, and *Yunnan* appears in Mendoza as *Olam*.

1540.—"Sailing in this manner we arrived six dayes after at the Ports of **Liampoo**, which are two Islands one just against another, distant three Leagues from the place, where at that time the *Portugals* used their commerce; There they had built above a thousand houses, that were governed by Sheriffs, Auditors, Consuls, Judges, and 6 or 7 other kinde of Officers [*com governança de* Vereadores, & Ouvidor, & Alcaides, *& outras seis ou sete Varas de Justiça & Officiaes de Republica*], where the Notaries underneath the publique Acts which they made, wrote thus, *I, such a one, publique Notarie of this Town of* **Liampoo** *for the King our Soveraign Lord*. And this they did with as much confidence and assurance as if this Place had been scituated between *Santarem* and *Lisbon*; so that there were houses there which cost three or four thousand Duckats the building, but both they and all the rest were afterwards demolished for our sins by the *Chineses*. . . ."—*Pinto* (orig. cap. lxvi.), in *Cogan*, p. 82.

What Cogan renders '*Ports of* **Liampoo**' is *portas, i.e. Gates*. And the expression is remarkable as preserving a very old tradition of Eastern navigation; the oldest document regarding Arab trade to China (the *Relation*, tr. by Reinaud) says that the ships after crossing the Sea of *Sanji* 'pass the *Gates of China*. These Gates are in fact mountains washed by the sea; between these mountains is an opening, through which the ships pass' (p. 19). This phrase was perhaps a translation of a term used by the Chinese themselves—see under **BOCCA TIGRIS**.

1553.—"The eighth (division of the coasts of the Indies) terminates in a notable cape, the most easterly point of the whole continent so far as we know at present, and which stands about midway in the whole coast of that great country China. This our people call Cabo de **Liampo**, after an illustrious city which lies in the bend of the cape. It is called by the natives **Nimpo**, which our countrymen have corrupted into **Liampo**."—*Barros*, i. ix. 1.

1696.—"Those Junks commonly touch at **Lympo**, from whence they bring *Petre, Geelongs*, and other Silks."—*Bowyear*, in *Dalrymple*, i. 87.

1701.—"The Mandarine of Justice arrived late last night from **Limpo**."—*Fragmentary MS. Records of China Factory* (at Chusan ?), in India Office, Oct. 24.

1727.—"The Province of *Chequiam*, whose chief city is **Limpoa**, by some called *Nimpoa*, and by others *Ningpoo*."—*A. Hamilton*, ii. 283; [ed. 1744, ii. 282].

1770.—"To these articles of importation may be added those brought every year, by a dozen Chinese Junks, from Emoy, **Limpo**, and Canton."—*Raynal*, tr. 1777, i. 249.

LIKIN, LEKIN, s. We borrow from Mr. Giles: "An arbitrary tax, originally of one cash per tael on all kinds of produce, imposed with a view of making up the deficiency in the land-tax of China caused by the T'aiping and Nienfei troubles. It was to be set aside for military purposes only — hence its common name of 'war tax'. . . The Chefoo Agreement makes the area of the Foreign concessions at the various Treaty Ports exempt from the tax of Lekin" (*Gloss. of Reference*, s.v.). The same authority explains the term as "*li* (*le*, *i.e.* a cash or $\frac{1}{1000}$ of a tael)-money," because of the original rate of levy. The **likin** is professedly not an imperial customs-duty, but a provincial tax levied by the governors of the provinces, and at their discretion as to amount; hence varying in local rate, and from time to time changeable. This has been a chief difficulty in carrying out the Chefoo Agreement, which as yet has never been authoritatively interpreted or finally ratified by England. [It was ratified in 1886. For the conditions of the Agreement see *Ball, Things Chinese*, 3rd ed. 629 *seqq.*] We quote the article of the Agreement which deals with opium, which has involved the chief difficulties, as leaving not only the amount to be paid, but the line at which this is to be paid, undefined.

1876.—"Sect. III. . . . (iii). On Opium Sir Thomas Wade will move his Government to sanction an arrangement different from that affecting other imports. British merchants, when opium is brought into port, will be obliged to have it taken cognizance of by the Customs, and deposited in Bond . . . until such time as there is a sale for it. The importer will then pay the tariff duty upon it, and the purchasers the **likin**: in order to the prevention of the evasion of the duty. The amount of **likin** to be collected will be decided by the different Provincial Governments, according to the circumstances of each."—*Agreement of Chefoo.*

1878.—"La Chine est parsemée d'une infinité de petits bureaux d'octroi échelonnés le long des voies commerciales; les Chinois les nomment **Li-kin**. C'est la source la plus sure, et la plus productive des revenus." —*Rousset, A Travers la Chine*, 221.

LILAC, s. This plant-name is eventually to be identified with **anil** (q.v.), and with the Skt. *nīla*, 'of a dark colour (especially dark blue or black)'; a fact which might be urged in favour of the view that the ancients in Asia, as has been alleged of them in Europe, belonged to the body of the colour-blind (like the writer of this article). The Indian word takes, in the sense of indigo, in Persian the form *līlang*; in Ar. this, modified into *līlak* and *līlāk*, is applied to the lilac (*Syringa* spp.). Marcel Devic says the Ar. adj. *līlak* has the modified sense 'bleuâtre.' See a remark under **BUCKYNE**. We may note that in Scotland the 'striving after meaning' gives this familiar and beautiful tree the name among the uneducated of '*lily-oak*.'

LIME, s. The fruit of the small *Citrus medica*, var. *acida*, Hooker, is that generally called *lime* in India, approaching as it does very nearly to the fruit of the West India Lime. It is often not much bigger than a pigeon's egg, and one well-known miniature lime of this kind is called by the natives from its thin skin *kāghazī nīmbū*, or 'paper lime.' This seems to bear much the same relation to the lemon that the miniature thin-skinned orange, which in London shops is called *Tangerine*, bears to the "China orange." But lime is also used with the characterising adjective for the *Citrus medica*, var. *Limetta*, Hooker, or Sweet Lime, an insipid fruit.

The word no doubt comes from the Sp. and Port. *lima*, which is from the Ar. *līma*; Fr. *lime*, Pers. *līmū*, *līmūn* (see **LEMON**). But probably it came into English from the Portuguese in India. It is not in Minsheu (2nd ed. 1727).

1404.—"And in this land of Guilan snow never falls, so hot is it; and it produces abundance of citrons and **limes** and oranges (*cidras ē* **limas** *ē naranjas*)."—*Clavijo*, § lxxxvi.

c. 1526.—"Another is the **lime** (*līmū*), which is very plentiful. Its size is about that of a hen's egg, which it resembles in shape. If one who is poisoned boils and eats its fibres, the injury done by the poison is averted."—*Baber*, 328.

1563.—"It is a fact that there are some Portuguese so pig-headed that they would rather die than acknowledge that we have here any fruit equal to that of Portugal; but there are many fruits here that bear the bell, as for instance all the *fructas de espinho*. For the **lemons** of those parts are so big that they look like citrons, besides being very tender and full of flavour, especially those of *Baçaim*; whilst the citrons themselves are much better and more tender (than those of Portugal); and the **limes** (*limas*) vastly better. . . ."—*Garcia*, f. 133.

c. 1630.—"The Ile inricht us with many good things; Buffolls, Goats, Turtle, Hens, huge Batts . . . also with Oranges, **Lemons**, **Lymes**. . . ."—*Sir T. Herbert*, 28.

1673.—"Here Asparagus flourish, as do **Limes**, Pomegranates, Genetins. . . ."—*Fryer*, 110. ("Jenneting" from Fr. *genêtin*, [or, according to Prof. Skeat, for *jeanneton*, a dimin. from Fr. *pomme de S. Jean*.]

1690.—"The Island (Johanna) abounds with Fowls and Rice, with Pepper, Yams, Plantens, Bonanoes, Potatoes, Oranges, **Lemons**, **Limes**, Pine-apples, &c. . . ."—*Ovington*, 109.

LINGAIT, LINGAYET, LINGUIT, LINGAVANT, LINGADHARI, s. Mahr. *Liñgā-īt*, Can. *Lingāyata*, a member of a Śivaite sect in W. and S. India, whose members wear the *liñga* (see **LINGAM**) in a small gold or silver box suspended round the neck. The sect was founded in the 12th century by Bāsava. They are also called *Jangama*, or *Vīra Śaiva*, and have various subdivisions. [See *Nelson, Madura*, pt. iii. 48 *seq.*; *Monier Williams, Brahmanism*, 88.]

1673.—"At *Hubly* in this Kingdom are a caste called **Linguits**, who are buried upright." — *Fryer*, 153. This is still their practice.

Lingua is given as the name or title of the King of Columbum (see **QUILON**) in the 14th century, by Friar Jordanus (p. 41), which might have been taken to denote that he belonged to this sect; but this seems never to have had followers in Malabar.

LINGAM, s. This is taken from the S. Indian form of the word, which in N. India is Skt. and Hind. *liñga*, 'a token, badge,' &c., thence the symbol of Śiva which is so extensively an object of worship among the Hindus, in the form of a cylinder of stone. The great idol of Somnāth, destroyed by Mahmūd of Ghazni, and the object of so much romantic narrative, was a colossal symbol of this kind. In the quotation of 1838 below, the word is used simply for a badge of caste, which is certainly the original Skt. meaning, but is probably a mistake as attributed in that sense to modern vernacular use. The man may have been a **lingait** (q.v.), so that his badge was actually a figure of the lingam. But this clever authoress often gets out of her depth.

1311. — "The stone idols called **Ling** Mahádeo, which had been a long time established at that place . . . these, up to this time, the kick of the horse of Islam had not attempted to break. . . . Deo Narain fell down, and the other gods who had seats there raised their feet, and jumped so high, that at one leap they reached the foot of Lanka, and in that affright the **lings** themselves would have fled, had they had any legs to stand on."—*Amír Khusrú*, in *Elliot*, iv. 91.

1616.—". . . above this there is elevated the figure of an idol, which in decency I abstain from naming, but which is called by the heathen **Linga**, and which they worship with many superstitions; and indeed they regard it to such a degree that the heathen of Canara carry well-wrought images of the kind round their necks. This abominable custom was abolished by a certain Canara King, a man of reason and righteousness."—*Couto*, Dec. VII. iii. 11.

1726.—"There are also some of them who wear a certain stone idol called **Lingam** . . . round the neck, or else in the hair of the head. . . ."—*Valentijn, Choro.* 74.

1781.—"These Pagodas have each a small chamber in the center of twelve feet square, with a lamp hanging over the **Lingham**."—*Hodges*, 94.

1799.—"I had often remarked near the banks of the rivulet a number of little altars, with a **linga** of Mahádeva upon them. It seems they are placed over the ashes of Hindus who have been burnt near the spot."—*Colebrooke*, in *Life*, p. 152.

1809.—"Without was an immense **lingam** of black stone."—*Ld. Valentia*, i. 371.

1814.—". . . two respectable Brahmuns, a man and his wife, of the secular order; who, having no children, had made several religious pilgrimages, performed the accustomed ceremonies to the **linga**, and consulted the divines." — *Forbes, Or. Mem.* ii. 364; [2nd ed. ii. 4; in ii. 164, **lingam**].

1838.—"In addition to the preaching, Mr. G. got hold of a man's **Lingum**, or badge of caste, and took it away."—*Letters from Madras*, 156.

1843.—"The homage was paid to **Lingamism**. The insult was offered to Mahometanism. *Lingamism* is not merely idolatry, but idolatry in its most pernicious form."—*Macaulay, Speech on Gates of Somnauth*.

LINGUIST, s. An old word for an interpreter, formerly much used in the East. It long survived in China, and is there perhaps not yet obsolete. Probably adopted from the Port. *lingua*, used for an interpreter.

1554.—"To a **llingua** of the factory (at Goa) 2 pardaos monthly. . . ."—*S. Botelho, Tombo*, 63.

" "To the **linguoa** of this kingdom (Ormuz) a Portuguese . . . To the **linguoa** of the custom-house, a bramen."—*Ibid.* 104.

[1612. — "Did Captain Saris' **Linguist** attend?"—*Danvers, Letters*, i. 68.]

1700.—"I carried the **Linguist** into a Merchant's House that was my Acquaintance to consult with that Merchant about removing that *Remora*, that stop'd the Man of War from entring into the Harbour."—*A. Hamilton*, iii. 254; [ed. 1744].

1711.—"**Linguists** require not too much haste, having always five or six to make choice of, never a Barrel the better Herring."—*Lockyer*, 102.

1760.—"I am sorry to think your Honour should have reason to think, that I have been anyway concerned in that unlucky affair that happened at the *Negrais*, in the month of October 1759; but give me leave to assure your Honour that I was no further concerned, than as a **Linguister** for the *King's Officer* who commanded the Party."—Letter to the Gov. of Fort St. George, from *Antonio the Linguist*, in *Dalrymple*, i. 396.

1760-1810.—"If the ten should presume to enter villages, public places, or bazaars, punishment will be inflicted on the **linguist** who accompanies them."—*Regulations at Canton*, from *The Fankwae at Canton*, p. 29.

1882.—"As up to treaty days, neither Consul nor Vice-Consul of a foreign nation was acknowledged, whenever either of these officers made a communication to the Hoppo, it had to be done through the Hong merchants, to whom the dispatch was taken by a **Linguist**."—*The Fankwae at Canton*, p. 50.

LIP-LAP, s. A vulgar and disparaging nickname given in the Dutch Indies to Eurasians, and corresponding to Anglo-Indian **chee-chee** (q.v.). The proper meaning of *lip-lap* seems to be the uncoagulated pulp of the coco-nut (see *Rumphius*, bk. i. ch. 1). [Mr. Skeat notes that the word is not in the dicts., but Klinkert gives Jav. *lap-lap*, 'a dish-clout.']

1768-71.—"Children born in the Indies are nicknamed **liplaps** by the Europeans, although both parents may have come from Europe."—*Stavorinus*, E.T. i. 315.

LISHTEE, LISTEE, s. Hind. *lishtī*, English word, 'a *list*.'

LONG-CLOTH, s. The usual name in India for (white) cotton shirtings, or Lancashire calico; but first applied to the Indian cloth of like kind exported to England, probably because it was made of length unusual in India; cloth for native use being ordinarily made in pieces sufficient only to clothe one person. Or it is just possible that it may have been a corruption or misapprehension of *lungi* (see **LOONGHEE**). [This latter view is accepted without question by Sir G. Birdwood (*Rep. on Old Rec.*, 224), who dates its introduction to Europe about 1675.]

1670.—"We have continued to supply you . . . in reguard the Dutch do so fully fall in with the Calicoe trade that they had the last year 50,000 pieces of **Long-cloth**."—*Letter from Court of E.I.C.* to Madras, Nov. 9th. In *Notes and Exts.*, No. i. p. 2.

[1682.—". . . for **Long cloth** brown English 72: Coveds long & $2\frac{1}{4}$ broad No. I. . . ."—*Pringle, Diary, Ft. St. Geo.* 1st ser. i. 40.]

1727.—"*Saderass*, or *Saderass Patam*, a small Factory belonging to the *Dutch*, to buy up **long cloth**."—*A. Hamilton*, i. 358; [ed. 1744].

1785.—"The trade of Fort St. David's consists in **long cloths** of different colours."—*Carraccioli's Life of Clive*, i. 5.

1865.—"**Long-cloth**, as it is termed, is the material principally worn in the Tropics."—*Waring, Tropical Resident*, p. 111.

1880.—"A Chinaman is probably the last man in the world to be taken in twice with a fraudulent piece of **long-cloth**."—*Pall Mall Budget*, Jan. 9, p. 9.

LONG-DRAWERS, s. This is an old-fashioned equivalent for **pyjamas** (q.v.). Of late it is confined to the Madras Presidency, and to outfitters' lists. [*Mosquito drawers* were probably like these.]

[1623.—"They wear a pair of **long Drawers** of the same Cloth, which cover not only their Thighs, but legs also to the Feet."—*P. della Valle*, Hak. Soc. i. 43.]

1711.—"The better sort wear **long Drawers**, and a piece of Silk, or wrought Callico, thrown loose over the Shoulders."—*Lockyer*, 57.

1774.—". . . gave each private man a frock and **long drawers** of chintz."—*Forrest, V. to N. Guinea*, 100.

1780.—"Leroy, one of the French hussars, who had saved me from being cut down by Hyder's horse, gave me some soup, and a shirt, and **long-drawers**, which I had great want of."—*Hon. John Lindsay* in *Lives of the Lindsays*, iv. 266.

1789.—"It is true that they (the *Sycs*) wear only a short blue jacket, and blue **long draws**."—Note by Translator of *Seir Mutaqherin*, i. 87.

1810.—"For wear on board ship, pantaloons . . . together with as many pair of wove cotton **long-drawers**, to wear under them."—*Williamson, V. M.* i. 9.

[1853.—"The Doctor, his gaunt figure very scantily clad in a dirty shirt and a pair of **mosquito drawers**."—*Campbell, Old Forest Ranger*, 3rd ed. 108.]

(See **PYJAMAS, MOGUL BREECHES, SHULWAURS, SIRDRARS.**)

LONG-SHORE WIND, s. A term used in Madras to designate the damp, unpleasant wind that blows in some seasons, especially July to September, from the south.

1837.—"This **longshore wind** is very disagreeable—a sort of sham sea-breeze blowing from the south; whereas the real sea-breeze blows from the east; it is a regular cheat upon the new-comers, feeling damp and fresh as if it were going to cool one."—*Letters from Madras*, 73.

[1879.—"Strong winds from the south known as **Alongshore winds**, prevail especially near the coast."—*Stuart, Tinnevelly*, 8.]

LONTAR, s. The palm leaves used in the Archipelago (as in S. India) for writing on are called *lontar*-leaves. Filet (No. 5179, p. 209) gives *lontar* as the Malay name of two palms, viz. *Borassus flabelliformis* (see **PALMYRA, BRAB**), and *Livistona tundifolia*. [See **CADJAN**.] [Mr. Skeat notes that Klinkert gives—"*Lontar*, metathesis of *ron-tal*, leaf of the *tal* tree, a fan-palm whose leaves were once used for writing on, *borassus flabelliformis*." *Ron* is thus probably equivalent to the Malay *daun*, or in some dialects *don*, 'leaf.' The tree itself is called *p'hun* (*pohun*) *tar* in the E. coast of the Malay Peninsula, *tar* and *tal* being only variants of the same word. Scott, *Malayan Words in English*, p. 121, gives: "*Lontar*, a palm, dial. form of *dāun tāl* (*tāl*, Hind.)." (See **TODDY**.]

LOOCHER, s. This is often used in Anglo-Ind. colloquial for a blackguard libertine, a lewd loafer. It is properly Hind. *luchchā*, having that sense. Orme seems to have confounded the word, more or less, with *lūṭiya* (see under **LOOTY**). [A rogue in *Pandurang Hari* (ed. 1873, ii. 168) is *Loochajee*. The place at Matheran originally called "*Louisa* Point" has become "*Loocha* Point!"]

[1829.—". . . nothing-to-do **lootchas** of every sect in Camp. . . ."—*Or. Sport. Mag.* ed. 1873, i. 121.]

LOONGHEE, s. Hind. *lungī*, perhaps originally Pers. *lung* and *lunggī*; [but Platts connects it with *linga*]. A scarf or web of cloth to wrap round the body, whether applied as what the French call *pagne*, *i.e.* a cloth simply wrapped once or twice round the hips and tucked in at the upper edge, which is the proper Mussulman mode of wearing it; or as a cloth tucked between the legs like a **dhoty** (q.v.), which is the Hindu mode, and often followed also by Mahommedans in India. The *Qanoon-e-Islam* further distinguishes between the *lunggī* and *dhotī* that the former is a coloured cloth worn as described, and the latter a cloth with only a coloured border, worn by Hindus alone. This explanation must belong to S. India. ["The *lungi* is really meant to be worn round the waist, and is very generally of a checked pattern, but it is often used as a *paggri* (see **PUGGRY**), more especially that known as the Kohat *lungi*" (*Cookson, Mon. on Punjab Silk*, 4). For illustrations of various modes of wearing the garment, see *Forbes Watson, Textile Manufactures and Costumes*, pl. iii. iv.]

1653.—"**Longui** est vne petite pièce de linge, dont les Indiens se servent à cacher les parties naturelles."—*De la Boullaye-le-Gouz*, 529. But in the edition of 1657 it is given: "**Longui** est vn morceau de linge dont l'on se sert au bain en Turquie" (p. 547).

1673.—"The Elder sat in a Row, where the Men and Women came down together to wash, having **Lungies** about their Wastes only."—*Fryer*, 101. In the Index, Fryer explains as a "Waste-Clout."

1726.—"Silk **Longis** with red borders, 160 pieces in a pack, 14 *cobidos* long and 2 broad."—*Valentijn*, v. 178.

1727.—". . . For some coarse chequered Cloth, called *Cambaya* (see **COMBOY**), **Lungies**, made of Cotton-Yarn, the Natives would bring Elephant's Teeth."—*A. Hamilton*, i. 9; [ed. 1744].

„ (In Pegu) "Under the Frock they have a Scarf or **Lungee** doubled fourfold, made fast about the Middle. . . ."—*Ibid.* ii. 49.

c. 1760.—"Instead of petticoats they wear what they call a **loongee**, which is simply a long piece of silk or cotton stuff."—*Grose*, i. 143.

c. 1809-10.—"Many use the **Lunggi**, a piece of blue cotton cloth, from 5 to 7 cubits long and 2 wide. It is wrapped simply two or three times round the waist, and hangs down to the knee."—*F. Buchanan*, in *Eastern India*, iii. 102.

LOOT, s. & v. Plunder; Hind. *lūṭ*, and that from Skt. *lotra*, for *loptra*, root *lup*, 'rob, plunder'; [rather *luṇṭ*, 'to rob']. The word appears in Stockdale's *Vocabulary*, of 1788, as "**Loot**—plunder, pillage." It has thus long been a familiar item in the Anglo-

Indian colloquial. But between the Chinese War of 1841, the Crimean War (1854-5), and the Indian Mutiny (1857-8), it gradually found acceptance in England also, and is now a recognised constituent of the English *Slang Dictionary*. Admiral Smyth has it in his *Nautical Glossary* (1867) thus: "**Loot**, plunder, or pillage, a term adopted from China."

1545.—St. Francis Xavier in a letter to a friend in Portugal admonishing him from encouraging any friend of his to go to India seems to have the thing *Loot* in his mind, though of course he does not use the word: "Neminem patiaris amicorum tuorum in Indiam cum Praefectura mitti, ad regias pecunias, et negotia tractanda. Nam de illis vere illud scriptum capere licet: 'Deleantur de libro viventium et cum justis non scribantur.' . . . Invidiam tantum non culpam usus publicus detrahit, dum vix dubitatur fieri non malè quod impunè fit. Ubique, semper, rapitur, congeritur, aufertur. Semel captum nunquam redditur. Quis enumeret artes et nomina, praedarum? Equidem mirari satis nequeo, quot, praeter usitatos modos, insolitis flexionibus inauspicatum illud **rapiendi** verbum quaedam avaritiae barbaria conjuget!"—*Epistolae, Prague*, 1667, Lib. V. Ep. vii.

1842.—"I believe I have already told you that I did not take any **loot**—the Indian word for plunder—so that I have nothing of that kind, to which so many in this expedition helped themselves so bountifully."—*Colin Campbell* to his Sister, in *L. of Ld. Clyde*, i. 120.

,, "In the Saugor district the plunderers are beaten whenever they are caught, but there is a good deal of burning and '**looting**,' as they call it."—*Indian Administration of Ld. Ellenborough. To the D. of Wellington*, May 17, p. 194.

1847.—"Went to see Marshal Soult's pictures which he **looted** in Spain. There are many Murillos, all beautiful."—*Ld. Malmesbury, Mem. of an Ex-Minister*, i. 192.

1858.—"There is a word called '**loot**,' which gives, unfortunately, a venial character to what would in common English be styled robbery."—*Ld. Elgin, Letters and Journals*, 215.

1860.—"**Loot**, swag or plunder."—*Slang Dict.* s.v.

1864.—"When I mentioned the '**looting**' of villages in 1845, the word was printed in italics as little known. Unhappily it requires no distinction now, custom having rendered it rather common of late."—*Admiral W. H. Smyth, Synopsis*, p. 52.

1875.—"It was the Colonel Sahib who carried off the **loot**."—*The Dilemma*, ch. xxxvii.

1876.—"Public servants (in Turkey) have vied with one another in a system of universal **loot**."—*Blackwood's Mag.* No. cxix. p. 115.

1878.—"The city (Hongkong) is now patrolled night and day by strong parties of marines and Sikhs, for both the disposition to **loot** and the facilities for **looting** are very great."—*Miss Bird, Golden Chersonese*, 34.

1883.—"'**Loot**' is a word of Eastern origin, and for a couple of centuries past . . . the **looting** of Delhi has been the day-dream of the most patriotic among the Sikh race."—*Bos. Smith's Life of Ld. Lawrence*, ii. 245.

,, "At Ta li fu . . . a year or two ago, a fire, supposed to be an act of incendiarism, broke out among the Tibetan encampments which were then **looted** by the Chinese."—*Official Memo. on Chinese Trade with Tibet*, 1883.

LOOTY, LOOTIEWALLA, s.

a. A plunderer. Hind. *lūṭī*, *lūṭīyā*, *lūṭīwālā*.

1757.—"A body of their **Louchees** (see **LOOCHER**) or plunderers, who are armed with clubs, passed into the Company's territory."—*Orme*, ed. 1803, ii. 129.

1782.—"Even the rascally **Looty wallahs**, or Mysorean hussars, who had just before been meditating a general desertion to us, now pressed upon our flanks and rear."—*Munro's Narrative*, 295.

1792.—"The Colonel found him as much dismayed as if he had been surrounded by the whole Austrian army, and busy in placing an ambuscade to catch about six **looties**."—*Letter of T. Munro*, in *Life*.

,, "This body (horse plunderers round Madras) had been branded generally by the name of **Looties**, but they had some little title to a better appellation, for they were . . . not guilty of those sanguinary and inhuman deeds. . . ."—*Madras Courier*, Jan. 26.

1793.—"A party was immediately sent, who released 27 half-starved wretches in heavy irons; among them was Mr. Randal Cadman, a midshipman taken 10 years before by Suffrein. The remainder were private soldiers; some of whom had been taken by the **Looties**; others were deserters. . . ."—*Dirom's Narrative*, p. 157.

b. A different word is the Ar.—Pers. *lūṭīy*, bearing a worse meaning, 'one of the people of Lot,' and more generally 'a blackguard.'

[1824.—"They were singing, dancing, and making the **luti** all the livelong day."—*Hajji Baba*, ed. 1851, p. 444.

[1858.—"The **Loutis**, who wandered from town to town with monkeys and other animals, taught them to cast earth upon their heads (a sign of the deepest grief among Asiatics) when they were asked whether they would be governors of Balkh or Akhcheh."—*Ferrier, H. of the Afghans*, 101.

[1883.—"Monkeys and baboons are kept and trained by the **Lūtis**, or professional buffoons."—*Will's Modern Persia*, ed. 1891, p. 306.]

The people of Shiraz are noted for a fondness for jingling phrases, common enough among many Asiatics, including the people of India, where one constantly hears one's servants speak of *chaukī-aukī* (for chairs and tables), *naukar-chākar* (where both are however real words), 'servants,' *lakrī-akrī*, 'sticks and staves,' and so forth. Regarding this Mr. Wills tells a story (*Modern Persia*, p. 239). The late Minister, Kawām-ud-Daulat, a Shirāzi, was asked by the Shāh:

"Why is it, Kawām, that you Shīrāzīs always talk of *Kabob-mabob* and so on? You always add a nonsense-word; is it for euphony?"

"Oh, Asylum of the Universe, may I be your sacrifice! No respectable person in Shīrāz does so, only the lūtī-pūtī says it!"

LOQUOT, LOQUAT, s. A sub-acid fruit, a native of China and Japan, which has been naturalised in India and in Southern Europe. In Italy it is called *nespola giapponese* (Japan medlar). It is *Eriobotrya japonica*, Lindl. The name is that used in S. China, *lu-küh*, pron. at Canton *lu-kwat*, and meaning 'rush-orange.' Elsewhere in China it is called *pi-pa*.

[1821.—"The **Lacott**, a Chinese fruit, not unlike a plum, was produced also in great plenty (at Bangalore); it is sweet when ripe, and both used for tarts, and eaten as dessert."—*Hoole, Missions in Madras and Mysore*, 2nd ed. 159.]

1878.—". . . the yellow **loquat**, peach-skinned and pleasant, but prodigal of stones."—*Ph. Robinson, In My Indian Garden*, 49.

c. 1880.—"A **loquat** tree in full fruit is probably a sight never seen in England before, but 'the phenomenon' is now on view at Richmond. (This was in the garden of Lady Parker at Stawell House.) We are told that it has a fine crop of fruit, comprising about a dozen bunches, each bunch being of eight or ten beautiful berries. . . ."—*Newspaper cutting* (*source lost*).

LORCHA, s. A small kind of vessel used in the China coasting trade. Giles explains it as having a hull of European build, but the masts and sails Chinese fashion, generally with a European skipper and a Chinese crew. The word is said to have been introduced by the Portuguese from S. America (*Giles*, 81). But Pinto's passage shows how early the word was used in the China seas, a fact which throws doubt on that view. [Other suggestions are that it is Chinese *low-chuen*, a sort of fighting ship, or Port. *lancha*, our *launch* (2 *N. & Q.* iii. 217, 236).]

1540.—"Now because the **Lorch** (*lorcha*), wherein *Antonio de Faria* came from *Patana* leaked very much, he commanded all his soldiers to pass into another better vessel . . . and arriving at a River that about evening we found towards the East, he cast anchor a league out at Sea, by reason his Junk . . . drew much water, so that fearing the Sands . . . he sent *Christovano Borralho* with 14 Soldiers in the **Lorch** up the River. . . ."—*Pinto* (orig. cap. xlii.), *Cogan*, p. 50.

" "Cõ isto nos partemos deste lugar de Laito muyto embandeirados, com as gavias toldadas de paños de seda, et os juncos e **lorchas** cõ duas ordens de paveses por banda"—*Pinto*, ch. lviii. *i.e.* "And so we started from Laito all dressed out, the tops draped with silk, and the junks and lorchas with two tiers of banners on each side."

1613.—"And they use smaller vessels called **lorchas** and *lyolyo* (?), and these never use more than 2 oars on each side, which serve both for rudders and for oars in the river traffic."—*Godinho de Eredia*, f. 26*v*.

1856.—". . . Mr. Parkes reported to his superior, Sir John Bowring, at Hong Kong, the facts in connexion with an outrage which had been committed on a British-owned **lorcha** at Canton. The **lorcha** 'Arrow,' employed in the river trade between Canton and the mouth of the river, commanded by an English captain and flying an English flag, had been boarded by a party of Mandarins and their escort while at anchor near Dutch Folly."—*Boulger, H. of China*, 1884, iii. 396.

LORY, s. A name given to various brilliantly-coloured varieties of parrot, which are found in the Moluccas and other islands of the Archipelago. The word is a corruption of the Malay *nūri*, 'a parrot'; but the corruption seems not to be very old, as Fryer retains the correct form. Perhaps it came through the French (see *Luillier* below). [Mr. Skeat writes: "*Lūri* is hardly a corruption of *nūri*; it is rather a parallel form. The two forms appear in different dialects. *Nūri* may have been first introduced, and *lūri* may be some dialectic form of it."] The first quotation shows that *lories* were imported into S. India as early as the 14th century. They are still imported thither, where they are called in the vernacular by a name signifying 'Five-coloured parrots.' [Can. *panchavarna-gini.*]

c. 1330.—"Parrots also, or popinjays, after their kind, of every possible colour, except black, for black ones are never found; but white all over, and green, and red, and also of mixed colours. The birds of this India seem really like the creatures of Paradise."—*Friar Jordanus*, 29.

c. 1430.—"In Bandan three kinds of parrot are found, some with red feathers and a yellow beak, and some parti-coloured which are called **Nori**, that is brilliant."—*Conti*, in *India in the XVth Cent.*, 17. The last words, in Poggio's original Latin, are: "quos *Noros* appellant hoc est *lucidos*," showing that Conti connected the word with the Pers. *nūr*="*lux*."

1516.—"In these islands there are many coloured parrots, of very splendid colours; they are tame, and the Moors call them **nure**, and they are much valued."—*Barbosa*, 202.

1555.—"There are hogs also with hornes (see **BABI-ROUSSA**), and parats which prattle much, which they call **Noris**."—*Galvano*, E.T. in *Hakl.* iv. 424.

[1598.—"There cometh into India out of the Island of Molucas beyond Malacca a kind of birdes called **Noyras**; they are like Parrattes. . . ."—*Linschoten*, Hak. Soc. i. 307.]

1601.—"Psittacorum passim in sylvis multae turmae obvolitant. Sed in Moluccanis Insulis per Malaccam avis alia, **Noyra** dicta, in Indiam importatur, quae psittaci faciem universim exprimit, quem cantu quoque adamussim aemulatur, nisi quod pennis rubicundis crebrioribus vestitur."—*De Bry*, v. 4.

1673.—". . . Cockatooas and **Newries** from Bantam."—*Fryer*, 116.

1682.—"The **Lorys** are about as big as the parrots that one sees in the Netherlands. . . . There are no birds that the Indians value more: and they will sometimes pay 30 rix dollars for one. . . ."—*Nieuhof*, *Zee en Lant-Reize*, ii. 287.

1698.—"Brought ashore from the Resolution . . . a **Newry** and four yards of broad cloth for a present to the Havildar."—In *Wheeler*, i. 333.

1705.—"On y trouve de quatre sortes de perroquets, sçavoir, perroquets, **lauris**, perruches, & cacatoris."—*Luillier*, 72.

1809.—

"'Twas Camdeo riding on his **lory**,
'Twas the immortal Youth of Love."
Kehama, x. 19.

1817.—

"Gay sparkling **loories**, such as gleam between
The crimson blossoms of the coral-tree
In the warm isles of India's summer sea."
Mokanna.

LOTA, s. Hind. *loṭā*. The small spheroidal brass pot which Hindus use for drinking, and sometimes for cooking. This is the exclusive Anglo-Indian application; but natives also extend it to the spherical pipkins of earthenware (see **CHATTY** or **GHURRA**.)

1810.—". . . a **lootah**, or brass water vessel."—*Williamson, V. M.* ii. 284.

LOTE, s. Mod. Hind. *lōṭ*, being a corruption of Eng. '*note*.' A bank-note; sometimes called *bănklōṭ*.

LOTOO, s. Burm. *Hlwat-d'hau*, 'Royal Court or Hall'; the Chief Council of State in Burma, composed nominally of four Wungyīs (see **WOON**) or Chief Ministers. Its name designates more properly the place of meeting; compare *Star-Chamber*.

1792.—". . . in capital cases he transmits the evidence in writing, with his opinion, to the **Lotoo**, or grand chamber of consultation, where the council of state assembles. . . ."—*Symes*, 307.

1819.—"The first and most respectable of the tribunals is the **Luttò**, comprised of four presidents called *Vunghì*, who are chosen by the sovereign from the oldest and most experienced Mandarins, of four assistants, and a great chancery."—*Sangermano*, 164.

1827.—"Every royal edict requires by law, or rather by usage, the sanction of this council: indeed, the King's name never appears in any edict or proclamation, the acts of the **Lut-d'hau** being in fact considered his acts."—*Crawfurd's Journal*, 401.

LOUTEA, LOYTIA, &c. s. A Chinese title of respect, used by the older writers on China for a Chinese official, much as we still use *mandarin*. It is now so obsolete that Giles, we see, omits it. "It would almost seem certain that this is the word given as follows in C. C. Baldwin's *Manual of the Foochow Dialect*: '*Lo-tia*.' . . . (in Mandarin *Lao-tye*) a general appellative used for an officer. It means 'Venerable Father' (p. 215). In the Court dialect *Ta-lao-yé*, 'Great Venerable Father' is the appellative used for any officer, up to the 4th rank. The *ye* of this expression is quite different from the *tyé* or *tia* of the former" (*Note by M. Terrien de la Couperie*). Mr. Baber, after giving the same explanation from Carstairs Douglas's *Amoy Dict.*, adds: "It would seem ludicrous to a Pekingese. Certain local functionaries (Prefects, Magistrates, &c.) are, however, universally known in China as *Fu-mu-kuan*, 'Parental Officers' (lit. 'Father-and-

Mother Officers') and it is very likely that the expression 'Old Papa' is intended to convey the same idea of paternal government."

c. 1560.—"Everyone that in China hath any office, command, or dignitie by the King, is called **Louthia**, which is to say with us *Señor*."—*Gaspar da Cruz*, in *Purchas*, iii. 169.

,, "I shall have occasion to speake of a certain Order of gentlemen that are called **Loutea**; I will first therefor expound what this word signifieth. *Loutea* is as muche as to say in our language as Syr. . . ."—*Galeotto Pereyra*, by *R. Willes*, in *Hakl.* ii.; [ed. 1810, ii. 548].

1585.—"And although all the Kinge's officers and justices of what sort of administration they are, be generally called by the name of **Loytia**; yet euerie one hath a speciall and a particular name besides, according vnto his office."—*Mendoza*, tr. by *R. Parke*, ii. 101.

1598.—"Not any Man in *China* is esteemed or accounted of, for his birth, family, or riches, but onely for his learning and knowledge, such as they that serve at every towne, and have the government of the same. They are called **Loitias** and Mandorijns."—*Linschoten*, 39; [Hak. Soc. i. 133].

1618.—"The China Capt. had letters this day per way of Xaxma (see **SATSUMA**) . . . that the letters I sent are received by the noblemen in China in good parte, and a mandarin, or **loytea**, appointed to com for Japon. . . ."—*Cocks, Diary*, ii. 44.

1681.—"They call . . . the lords and gentlemen **Loytias**. . . ."—*Martinez de la Puente, Compendio*, 26.

LOVE-BIRD, s. The bird to which this name is applied in Bengal is the pretty little lorikeet, *Loriculus vernalis*, Sparrman, called in Hind. *latkan* or 'pendant,' because of its quaint habit of sleeping suspended by the claws, head downwards.

LUBBYE, LUBBEE, s. [Tel. *Labbi*, Tam. *Ilappai*]; according to C. P. Brown and the *Madras Gloss.* a Dravidian corruption of *'Arabī*. A name given in S. India to a race, Mussulmans in creed, but speaking Tamil, supposed to be, like the **Moplahs** of the west coast, the descendants of Arab emigrants by inter-marriage with native women. "There are few classes of natives in S. India, who in energy, industry, and perseverance, can compete with the Lubbay"; they often, as pedlars, go about selling beads, precious stones, &c.

1810.—"Some of these (early emigrants from Kufa) landed on that part of the Western coast of India called the Concan; the others to the eastward of C. Comorin; the descendants of the former are the *Nevayets*; of the latter the **Lubbè**; a name probably given to them by the natives, from that Arabic particle (a modification of *Lubbeik*) corresponding with the English *here I am*, indicating attention on being spoken to. The **Lubbè** pretend to one common origin with the *Nevayets*, and attribute their black complexion to inter-marriage with the natives; but the *Nevayets* affirm that the **Lubbè** are the descendants of their domestic slaves, and there is certainly in the physiognomy of this very numerous class, and in their stature and form, a strong resemblance to the natives of Abyssinia."—*Wilks, Hist. Sketches*, i. 243.

1836.—"Mr. Boyd . . . describes the Moors under the name of *Cholias* (see **CHOOLIA**); and Sir Alexander Johnston designates them by the appellation of **Lubbes**. These epithets are however not admissible; for the former is only confined to a particular sect among them, who are rather of an inferior grade; and the latter to the priests who officiate in their temples; and also as an honorary affix to the proper names of some of their chief men."—*Simon Casie Chitty on the Moors of Ceylon*, in *J.R. As. Soc.* iii. 338.

1868.—"The **Labbeis** are a curious caste, said by some to be the descendants of Hindus forcibly converted to the Mahometan faith some centuries ago. It seems most probable, however, that they are of mixed blood. They are, comparatively, a fine strong active race, and generally contrive to keep themselves in easy circumstances. Many of them live by traffic. Many are smiths, and do excellent work as such. Others are fishermen, boatmen and the like. . . ."—*Nelson, Mudura Manual*, Pt. ii. 86.

1869.—In a paper by Dr. Shortt it is stated that the **Lubbays** are found in large numbers on the East Coast of the Peninsula, between Pulicat and Negapatam. Their headquarters are at Nagore, the burial place of their patron saint *Nagori Mīr Ṣāhib*. They excel as merchants, owing to their energy and industry.—In *Trans. Ethn. Soc. of London*, N.S. vii. 189-190.

LUCKERBAUG, s. Hind. *lakṛā*, *lagṛā*, *lakaṛbagghā*, *lagaṛbagghā*, 'a hyena.' The form *lakaṛbaghā* is not in the older dicts. but is given by Platts. It is familiar in Upper India, and it occurs in *Hickey's Bengal Gazette*, June 24, 1781. In some parts the name is applied to the leopard, as the extract from Buchanan shows. This is the case among the Hindi-speaking people of the Himālaya also (see *Jerdon*). It is not clear what the etymology of the name is, *lakaṛ*, *lakṛā* meaning in their everyday sense, a stick or piece of timber. But both in

Hind. and Mahr., in an adjective form, the word is used for 'stiff, gaunt, emaciated,' and this may be the sense in which it is applied to the hyena. [More probably the name refers to the bar-like stripes on the animal.] Another name is *harvāgh*, or (apparently) 'bone-tiger,' from its habit of gnawing bones.

c. 1809.—"It was said not to be uncommon in the southern parts of the district (Bhāgalpur) . . . but though I have offered ample rewards, I have not been able to procure a specimen, dead or alive; and the *leopard* is called at Munngger **Lakravagh.**"

,, "The hyaena or **Lakravagh** in this district has acquired an uncommon degree of ferocity."—*F. Buchanan, Eastern India*, iii. 142-3.

[1849.—"The man seized his gun and shot the hyena, but the '**lakkabakka**' got off."—*Mrs. Mackenzie, Life in the Mission*, ii. 152.]

LUCKNOW, n.p. Properly *Lakhnau;* the well-known capital of the Nawābs and Kings of Oudh, and the residence of the Chief Commissioner of that British Province, till the office was united to that of the Lieut.-Governor of the N.W. Provinces in 1877. [The name appears to be a corruption of the ancient *Lakshmanāvatī*, founded by *Lakshmana*, brother of Rāmachandra of Ayodhya.]

1528.—"On Saturday the 29th of the latter Jemādi, I reached **Luknow**; and having surveyed it, passed the river Gūmti and encamped."—*Baber*, p. 381.

[c. 1590.—"**Lucknow** is a large city on the banks of the Gūmti, delightful in its surroundings."—*Āīn*, ed. *Jarrett*, ii. 173.]

1663.—"In *Agra* the Hollanders have also an House. . . . Formerly they had a good trade there in selling Scarlet . . . as also in buying those cloths of Jelapour and **Laknau**, at 7 or 8 days journey from *Agra*, where they also keep an house. . . ." —*Bernier*, E.T. 94; [ed. *Constable*, 292, who identifies *Jelapour* with Jalālpur-Nāhir in the Fyzābād district.]

LUDDOO, s. H. *laḍḍū*. A common native sweetmeat, consisting of balls of sugar and ghee, mixt with wheat and gram flour, and with cocoanut kernel rasped.

[1826.—"My friends . . . called me *boor ke* **luddoo**, or the great man's sport."—*Pandurang Hari*, ed. 1873, i. 197.

[1828.—"When at large we cannot even get *rabri* (porridge), but in prison we eat **ladoo** (a sweetmeat)."—*Tod, Annals*, Calcutta reprint, ii. 185.]

LUGOW, TO, v. This is one of those imperatives transformed, in Anglo-Indian jargon, into infinitives, which are referred to under **BUNOW, PUCKEROW**. H. inf. *lagā-nā*, imperative *lagā-o*. The meanings of *lagānā*, as given by Shakespear, are: "to apply, close, attach, join, fix, affix, ascribe, impose, lay, add, place, put, plant, set, shut, spread, fasten, connect, plaster, put to work, employ, engage, use, impute, report anything in the way of scandal or malice"—in which long list he has omitted one of the most common uses of the verb, in its Anglo-Indian form *lugow*, which is "to lay a boat alongside the shore or wharf, to moor." The fact is that *lagānā* is the active form of the neuter verb *lag-nā*, 'to touch, lie, to be in contact with,' and used in all the neuter senses of which *lagānā* expresses the transitive senses. Besides neuter *lagnā*, active *lagānā*, we have a secondary casual verb, *lagwānā*, 'to cause to apply,' &c. *Lagnā, lagānā* are presumably the same words as our *lie*, and *lay*, A.-S. *licgan*, and *lecgan*, mod. Germ. *liegen* and *legen*. And the meaning 'lay' underlies all the senses which Shakespear gives of *lagā-nā*. [See *Skeat, Concise Etym. Dict.* s.v. *lie.*]

[1839.—"They **lugāoed**, or were fastened, about a quarter of a mile below us. . . ."—*Davidson, Travels in Upper India*, ii. 20.]

LUMBERDAR, s. Hind. *lambardār*, a word formed from the English word '*number*' with the Pers. termination *-dār*, and meaning properly 'the man who is registered by a number.' "The registered representative of a coparcenary community, who is responsible for Government revenue." (*Carnegy*). "The cultivator who, either on his own account or as the representative of other members of the village, pays the Government dues and is registered in the Collector's Roll according to his number; as the representative of the rest he may hold the office by descent or by election." (*Wilson*).

[1875. — ". . . Chota Khan . . . was exceedingly useful, and really frightened the astonished **Lambadars**."—*Wilson, Abode of Snow*, 97.]

LUNGOOR, s. Hind. *langūr*, from Skt. *lāngūlin*, 'caudatus.' The great white-bearded ape, much patronized by Hindus, and identified with the monkey-god Hanumān. The genus is *Presbytes*, Illiger, of which several species are now discriminated, but the differences are small. [See *Blanford, Mammalia*, 27, who classes the *Langūr* as *Semnopithecus entellus.*] The animal is well described by Aelian in the following quotation, which will recall to many what they have witnessed in the suburbs of Benares and other great Hindu cities. The *Langūr* of the *Prasii* is *P. Entellus*.

c. 250.—"Among the Prasii of India they say that there exists a kind of ape with human intelligence. These animals seem to be about the size of Hyrcanian dogs. Their front hair looks all grown together, and any one ignorant of the truth would say that it was dressed artificially. The beard is like that of a satyr, and the tail strong like that of a lion. All the rest of the body is white, but the head and the tail are red. These creatures are tame and gentle in character, but by race and manner of life they are wild. They go about in crowds in the suburbs of *Latagē* (now Latagē is a city of the Indians) and eat the boiled rice that is put out for them by the King's order. Every day their dinner is elegantly set out. Having eaten their fill it is said that they return to their parents in the woods in an orderly manner, and never hurt anybody that they meet by the way."—*Aelian, De Nat. Animal.* xvi. 10.

1825.—"An alarm was given by one of the sentries in consequence of a baboon drawing near his post. The character of the intruder was, however, soon detected by one of the Suwarrs, who on the Sepoy's repeating his exclamation of the broken English 'Who goes 'ere?' said with a laugh, 'Why do you challenge the **lungoor**? he cannot answer you.'"—*Heber*, ii. 85.

1859.—"I found myself in immediate proximity to a sort of parliament or general assembly of the largest and most human-like monkeys I had ever seen. There were at least 200 of them, great **lungoors**, some quite four feet high, the jetty black of their faces enhanced by a fringe of snowy whisker."—*Lewin, A Fly on the Wheel*, 49.

1884.—"Less interesting personally than the gibbon, but an animal of very developed social instincts, is *Semnopithecus entellus*, otherwise the Bengal **langur**. (He) fights for his wives according to a custom not unheard of in other cases; but what is peculiar to him is that the vanquished males 'receive charge of all the young ones of their own sex, with whom they retire to some neighbouring jungle.' Schoolmasters and private tutors will read this with interest, as showing the origin and early disabilities of their profession."—*Saturday Rev.*, May 31, on *Sterndale's Nat. Hist. of Mammalia of India*, &c.

LUNGOOTY, s. Hind. *langoṭī*. The original application of this word seems to be the scantiest modicum of covering worn for decency by some of the lower classes when at work, and tied before and behind by a string round the waist; but it is sometimes applied to the more ample *dhotī* (see **DHOTY**). According to R. Drummond, in Guzerat the "**Langoth** or **Lungota**" (as he writes) is "a pretty broad piece of cotton cloth, tied round the breech by men and boys bathing. . . . The diminutive is **Langotee**, a long slip of cloth, stitched to a loin band of the same stuff, and forming exactly the T bandage of English Surgeons. . . ." This distinction is probably originally correct, and the use of *langūta* by Abdurrazzāk would agree with it. The use of the word has spread to some of the Indo-Chinese countries. In the quotation from Mocquet it is applied in speaking of an American Indian near the R. Amazon. But the writer had been in India.

c. 1422.—"The blacks of this country have the body nearly naked; they wear only bandages round the middle called **lankoutah**, which descend from the navel to above the knee."—*Abdurrazzāk*, in *India in XV. Cent.* 17.

1526.—"Their peasants and the lower classes all go about naked. They tie on a thing which they call a **langoti**, which is a piece of clout that hangs down two spans from the navel, as a cover to their nakedness. Below this pendant modesty-clout is another slip of cloth, one end of which they fasten before to a string that ties on the **langoti**, and then passing the slip of cloth between the two legs, bring it up and fix it to the string of the **langoti** behind."—*Baber*, 333.

c. 1609.—"Leur capitaine auoit fort bonne façon, encore qu'il fust tout nud et luy seul auoit vn **langoutin**, qui est vne petite pièce de coton peinte."—*Mocquet*, 77.

1653.—"**Langouti** est une pièce de linge dont les Indou se seruent à cacher les parties naturelles."—*De la Boullaye-le-Gouz*, ed. 1657, p. 547.

[1822.—"The boatmen go nearly naked, seldom wearing more than a **langutty**. . . ."—*Wallace, Fifteen Years in India*, 410.]

1869.—"Son costume se compose, comme celui de tous les Cambodgiens, d'une veste courte et d'un **langouti**."—*Rev. des Deux Mondes*, lxxix. 854.

"They wear nothing but the **langoty**, which is a string round the loins, and a piece of cloth about a hand's breadth fastened to it in front."—(*Ref. lost*), p. 26.

LUNKA, n.p. Skt. *Lañka*. The oldest name of Ceylon in the literature both of Buddhism and Brahmanism. Also 'an island' in general.

——, s. A kind of strong cheroot much prized in the Madras Presidency, and so called from being made of tobacco grown in the 'islands' (the local term for which is *lañka*) of the Godavery Delta.

M

MĀ-BĀP, s. '*Āp* mā-bāp *hai khudāwand!*' 'You, my Lord, are my mother and father!' This is an address from a native, seeking assistance, or begging release from a penalty, or reluctant to obey an order, which the young *ṣāhib* hears at first with astonishment, but soon as a matter of course.

MABAR, n.p. The name given in the Middle Ages by the Arabs to that coast of India which we call Coromandel. The word is Ar. *ma'bar*, 'the ferry or crossing-place.' It is not clear how the name came to be applied, whether because the Arab vessels habitually touched at its ports, or because it was the place of crossing to Ceylon, or lastly whether it was not an attempt to give meaning to some native name. [The *Madras Gloss.* says it was so called because it was the place of crossing from Madura to Ceylon; also see *Logan, Malabar*, i. 280.] We know no occurrence of the term earlier than that which we give from Abdallatīf.

c. 1203.—"I saw in the hands of an Indian trader very beautiful mats, finely woven and painted on both sides with most pleasing colours. . . . The merchant told me . . . that these mats were woven of the Indian plantain . . . and that they sold in **Mabar** for two dinars apiece."—*Abd-Allatīf, Relation de l'Egypte*, p. 31.

1279-86.—In M. Pauthier's notes on Marco Polo very curious notices are extracted from Chinese official annals regarding the communications, in the time of Kublai Kaan, between that Emperor and Indian States, including **Ma-pa-'rh**.—(See pp. 600-605).

c. 1292.—"When you leave the Island of Seilan and sail westward about 60 miles, you come to the great province of **Maabar**, which is styled India the Greater: it is the best of all the Indies, and is on the mainland."—*Marco Polo*, Bk. iii. ch. 16.

c. 1300.—"The merchants export from **Ma'bar** silken stuffs, aromatic roots; large pearls are brought from the sea. The productions of this country are carried to 'Irák, Khorásán, Syria, Russia and Europe."—*Rashīduddīn*, in *Elliot*, i. 69.

1303.—"In the beginning of this year (703 H.), the Maliki-'Azam, Takiú-d-dín . . . departed from the country of Hind to the passage (*ma'bar*) of corruption. The King of **Ma'bar** was anxious to obtain his property and wealth, but Malik Mu'azzam Siráju-d-dín, son of the deceased, having secured his goodwill, by the payment of 200,000 dínárs, not only obtained the wealth, but rank also of his father."—*Wassáf*, in *Elliot*, iii. 45.

1310.—"The country of **Ma'bar**, which is so distant from Dehli that a man travelling with all expedition could only reach it after a journey of 12 months, there the arrow of any holy warrior had not yet reached."—*Amír Khusrú*, in *Elliot*, iii. 85.

c. 1330.—"The third part (of India) is *Ma'bar*, which begins some three or four days journey to the eastward of Kaulam; this territory lies to the east of Malabar. . . . It is stated that the territory **Ma'bar** begins at the Cape Kumhari, a name which applies both to a mountain and a city. . . . Biyyardāwal is the residence of the Prince of **Ma'bar**, for whom horses are imported from foreign countries."—*Abulfeda*, in *Gildemeister*, p. 185. We regret to see that M. Guyard, in his welcome completion of Reinaud's translation of Abulfeda, absolutely, in some places, substitutes "Coromandel" for "Ma'bar." It is French fashion, but a bad one.

c. 1498.—"Zo deser stat Kangera anlenden alle Kouffschyff die in den landen zo doyn hauen, ind lijcht in eyner provincie **Moabar** genant."—*Pilgerfahrt des Ritters Arnold von Harff* (a fiction-monger), p. 140.

1753.—"Selon cet autorité le pays du continent qui fait face à l'île de Ceïlan est **Maabar**, ou le grande Inde: et cette interpretation de Marc-Pol est autant plus juste, que *maha* est un terme Indien, et propre même à quelques langues Scythiques ou Tartares, pour signifier *grand*. Ainsi, **Maabar** signifie la grande region."—*D'Anville*, p. 105. The great Geographer is wrong!

MACAO, n.p.

a. The name applied by the Portuguese to the small peninsula and the city built on it, near the mouth of Canton River, which they have occupied since 1557. The place is called by the Chinese *Ngao-măn* (*Ngao*, 'bay or inlet,' *Măn*, 'gate'). The Portuguese name is alleged to be taken from *A-mā-ngao*, 'the Bay of Ama,' *i.e.* of the Mother, the so-called

'Queen of Heaven,' a patroness of seamen. And indeed *Amacao* is an old form often met with.

c. 1567.—"Hanno i Portoghesi fatta vna picciola cittáde in vna Isola vicina a' i liti della China chiamato **Machao** . . . ma i datii sono del Rè della China, e vanno a pagarli a Canton, bellissima cittáde, e di grande importanza, distante da *Machao* due giorni e mezzo." — *Cesare de' Federici*, in *Ramusio*, iii. 391.

c. 1570.—"On the fifth day of our voyage it pleased God that we arrived at . . . Lampacau, where at that time the *Portugals* exercised their commerce with the *Chineses*, which continued till the year 1557, when the *Mandarins* of *Canton*, at the request of the Merchants of that Country, gave us the port of **Macao**, where the trade now is; of which place (that was but a desart Iland before) our countrymen made a very goodly plantation, wherein there were houses worth three or four thousand Duckats, together with a Cathedral Church. . . ."—*Pinto*, in *Cogan*, p. 315.

1584.—"There was in **Machào** a religious man of the order of the barefoote friars of S. Francis, who vnderstanding the great and good desire of this king, did sende him by certaine Portugal merchants . . . a cloth whereon was painted the day of iudgement and hell, and that by an excellent workman."—*Mendoza*, ii. 394.

1585.—"They came to **Amacao**, in Iuly, 1585. At the same time it seasonably hapned that *Linsilan* was commanded from the court to procure of the Strangers at **Amacao**, certaine goodly feathers for the King." — From the *Jesuit Accounts*, in *Purchas*, iii. 330.

1599 . . . — "**Amacao**." See under **MONSOON**.

1602. — "Being come, as heretofore I wrote your Worship, to **Macao** a city of the Portugals, adjoyning to the firme Land of China, where there is a Colledge of our Company."—Letter from *Diego de Pantoia*, in *Purchas*, iii. 350.

[1611.—"There came a Jesuit from a place called Langasack (see **LANGASAQUE**), which place the Carrack of **Amakau** yearly was wont to come."—*Danvers, Letters*, i. 146.]

1615.—"He adviseth me that 4 juncks are arrived at **Langasaque** from Chanchew, which with this ship from **Amacau**, will cause all matters to be sould chepe."—*Cocks's Diary*, i. 35.

[,, ". . . carried them prisoners aboard the great ship of **Amacan**."—*Foster, Letters*, iv. 46.]

1625. — "That course continued divers yeeres till the *Chinois* growing lesse fearefull, granted them in the greater Iland a little *Peninsula* to dwell in. In that place was an Idoll, which still remained to be seene, called *Ama*, whence the Peninsula was called **Amacao**, that is Amas Bay."—*Purchas*, iii. 319.

b. **MACAO, MACCAO**, was also the name of a place on the Pegu River which was the port of the city so called in the day of its greatness. A village of the name still exists at the spot.

1554.—"The *baar* (see **BAHAR**) of **Macao** contains 120 biças, each biça 100 **ticals** (q.v.) . . ."—*A. Nunes*, p. 39.

1568.—"Si fa commodamente il viaggio sino a **Maccao** distante da Pegu dodeci miglia, e qui si sbarca."—*Ces. Federici*, in *Ramusio*, iii. 395.

1587.—"From Cirion we went to **Macao**, &c."—*R. Fitch*, in *Hakl.* ii. 391. (See **DELING**).

1599. — "The King of *Arracan* is now ending his business at the Town of **Macao**, carrying thence the Silver which the King of *Tangu* had left, exceeding three millions." —*N. Pimenta*, in *Purchas*, iii. 1748.

MACAREO, s. A term applied by old voyagers to the phenomenon of the *bore*, or great tidal wave as seen especially in the Gulf of Cambay, and in the Sitang Estuary in Pegu. The word is used by them as if it were an Oriental word. At one time we were disposed to think it might be the Skt. word *makara*, which is applied to a mythological sea-monster, and to the Zodiacal sign Capricorn. This might easily have had a mythological association with the furious phenomenon in question, and several of the names given to it in various parts of the world seem due to associations of a similar kind. Thus the old English word *Oegir* or *Eagre* for the bore on the Severn, which occurs in Drayton, "seems to be a reminiscence of the old Scandinavian deity *Oegir*, the god of the stormy sea."* [This theory is rejected by *N.E.D.* s.v. *Eagre.*] One of the Hindi names for the phenomenon is *Mendhā*, 'The Ram'; whilst in modern Guzerat, according to R. Drummond, the natives call it *ghoṛā*, "likening it to the war horse, or a squadron of them."† But nothing could illustrate the *naturalness* of such a figure as *makara*, applied to the bore, better than the following paragraph in the review-article just quoted (p. 401), which was evidently penned without any allusion to or suggestion of such an

* See an interesting paper in the *Saturday Review* of Sept. 29, 1883, on *Le Mascaret*.

† Other names for the bore in India are: Hind. *hummā*, and in Bengal *bān*.

origin of the name, and which indeed makes no reference to the Indian name, but only to the French names of which we shall presently speak :

"Compared with what it used to be, if old descriptions may be trusted, the Mascaret is now stripped of its terrors. It resembles the great nature-force which used to ravage the valley of the Seine, *like one of the mythical dragons which, as legends tell, laid whole districts waste*, about as much as a lion confined in a cage resembles the free monarch of the African wilderness."

Take also the following :

1885.—"Here at his mouth Father Meghna is 20 miles broad, with islands on his breast as large as English counties, and a great tidal bore which made a daily and ever-varying excitement. . . . In deep water, it passed merely as a large rolling billow; but in the shallows it rushed along, roaring like a crested and devouring monster, before which no small craft could live."—*Lt.-Col. T. Lewin, A Fly on the Wheel*, 161-162.

But unfortunately we can find no evidence of the designation of the phenomenon in India by the name of *makara* or the like; whilst both *mascaret* (as indicated in the quotation just made) and *macrée* are found in French as terms for the bore. Both terms appear to belong properly to the Garonne, though *mascaret* has of late began on the Seine to supplant the old term *barre*, which is evidently the same as our *bore*. [The *N.E.D.* suggests O. N. *bára*, 'wave.'] Littré can suggest no etymology for *mascaret;* he mentions a whimsical one which connects the word with a place on the Garrone called St. *Macaire*, but only to reject it. There would be no impossibility in the transfer of an Indian word of this kind to France, any more than in the other alternative of the transfer of a French term to India in such a way that in the 16th century visitors to that country should have regarded it as an indigenous word, if we had but evidence of its Indian existence. The date of Littré's earliest quotation, which we borrow below, is also unfavourable to the probability of transplantation from India. There remains the possibility that the word is *Basque*. The Saturday Reviewer already quoted says that he could find nothing approaching to *Mascaret* in a Basque French Dict., but this hardly seems final.

The vast rapidity of the flood-tide in the Gulf of Cambay is mentioned by Maṣ'ūdī, who witnessed it in the year H. 303 (A.D. 915) i. 255 ; also less precisely by Ibn Batuta (iv. 60). There is a paper on it in the *Bo. Govt. Selections*, N.S. No. xxvi., from which it appears that the bore wave reaches a velocity of 10½ knots. [See also *Forbes, Or. Mem.* 2nd. ed. i. 313.]

1553.—"In which time there came hither (to Diu) a concourse of many vessels from the Red Sea, the Persian Gulf, and all the coast of Arabia and India, so that the places within the Gulf of Cambaya, which had become rich and noble by trade, were by this port undone. And this because it stood outside of the **Macareos** of the Gulf of Cambaya, which were the cause of the loss of many ships."—*Barros*, II. ii. cap 9.

1568.—"These Sholds (G. of Cambay) are an hundred and foure-score miles about in a straight or gulfe, which they call **Macareo** (*Maccareo* in orig.) which is as much as to say a race of a Tide."—*Master C. Frederick, Hakl.* ii. 342 ; [and comp. ii. 362].

1583.—"And having sailed until the 23d of the said month, we found ourselves in the neighbourhood of the **Macareo** (of Martaban) which is the most marvellous thing that ever was heard of in the way of tides, and high waters. . . . The water in the channel rises to the height of a high tree, and then the boat is set to face it, waiting for the fury of the tide, which comes on with such violence that the noise is that of a great earthquake, insomuch that the boat is soused from stem to stern, and carried by that impulse swiftly up the channel."—*Gasparo Balbi*, ff. 91*v*, 92.

1613.—"The **Macareo** of waves is a disturbance of the sea, like water boiling, in which the sea casts up its waves in foam. For the space of an Italian mile, and within that distance only, this boiling and foaming occurs, whilst all the rest of the sea is smooth and waveless as a pond. . . . And the stories of the Malays assert that it is caused by souls that are passing the Ocean from one region to another, or going in *cafilas* from the Golden Chersonesus . . . to the river Ganges."—*Godinho de Eredia*, f. 41*v*. [See *Skeat, Malay Magic*, 10 *seq.*]

1644.—". . . thence to the Gulf of Cambaya with the impetuosity of the currents which are called **Macareo**, of whose fury strange things are told, insomuch that a stone thrown with force from the hand even in the first speed of its projection does not move more swiftly than those waters run."—*Bocarro, MS.*

1727.—"A Body of Waters comes rolling in on the Sand, whose Front is above two Fathoms high, and whatever Body lies in its Way it overturns, and no Ship can evade its Force, but in a Moment is overturned, this violent Boer the Natives called a **Mackrea**."—*A. Hamilton*, ii. 33 ; [ed. 1744, ii. 32].

1811.—Solvyns uses the word **Macrée** as French for 'Bore,' and in English describes his print as ". . . the representation of a phenomenon of Nature, the **Macrée** or tide, at the mouth of the river Ougly."—*Les Hindous*, iii.

MACASSAR, n.p. In Malay *Mangkasar*, properly the name of a people of **Celebes** (q.v.), but now the name of a Dutch seaport and seat of Government on the W. coast of the S.W. peninsula of that spider-like island. The last quotation refers to a time when we occupied the place, an episode of Anglo-Indian history almost forgotten.

[1605-6.—"A description of the Iland Selebes or **Makasser**."—*Birdwood, Letter Book*, 77.

[1610.—"Selebes or **Makassar**, wherein are spent and uttered these wares following."—*Danvers, Letters*, i. 71.

[1664-5.—". . . and anon to Gresham College, where, among other good discourse, there was tried the great poyson of **Maccassa** upon a dogg, but it had no effect all the time we sat there."—*Pepys, Diary*, March 15; ed. *Wheatley*, iv. 372.]

1816.—"Letters from **Macassar** of the 20th and 27th of June (1815), communicate the melancholy intelligence of the death of Lieut. T. C. Jackson, of the 1st Regt. of Native Bengal Infantry, and Assistant Resident of **Macassar**, during an attack on a fortified village, dependent on the dethroned Raja of Boni."—*As. Journal*, i. 297.

MACE, s.

a. The crimson net-like mantle, which envelops the hard outer shell of the nutmeg, when separated and dried constitutes the *mace* of commerce. Hanbury and Flückiger are satisfied that the attempt to identify the *Macir*, *Macer*, &c., of Pliny and other ancients with mace is a mistake, as indeed the sagacious Garcia also pointed out, and Chr. Acosta still more precisely. The name does not seem to be mentioned by Maṣ'ūdī; it is not in the list of aromatics, 25 in number, which he details (i. 367). It is mentioned by Edrisi, who wrote c. 1150, and whose information generally was of much older date, though we do not know what word he uses. The fact that nutmeg and mace are the product of one plant seems to have led to the fiction that clove and cinnamon also came from that same plant. It is, however, true that a kind of aromatic bark was known in the Arab pharmacopœia of the Middle Ages under the name of *ḳirfat-al-ḳaranful* or 'bark of clove,' which may have been either a cause of the mistake or a part of it. The mistake in question, in one form or another, prevailed for centuries. One of the authors of this book was asked many years ago by a respectable Mahommedan of Delhi if it were not the case that cinnamon, clove, and nutmeg were the produce of one tree. The prevalence of the mistake in Europe is shown by the fact that it is contradicted in a work of the 16th century (*Bodaei, Comment. in Theophrastum*, 992); and by the quotation from Funnel.

The name mace may have come from the Ar. *basbāsa*, possibly in some confusion with the ancient *macir*. [See Skeat, *Concise Dict.* who gives F. *macis*, which was confused with M. F. *macer*, probably Lat. *macer*, *macir*, doubtless of Eastern origin.]

c. 1150.—"On its shores (*i.e.* of the sea of Sanf or **Champa**), are the dominions of a King called Mihrāj, who possesses a great number of populous and fertile islands, covered with fields and pastures, and producing ivory, camphor, nutmeg, **mace**, clove, aloeswood, cardamom, cubeb, &c."—*Edrisi*, i. 89; see also 51.

c. 1347.—"The fruit of the clove is the nutmeg, which we know as the scented nut. The flower which grows upon it is the **mace** (*basbāsa*). And this is what I have seen with my own eyes."—*Ibn Batuta*, iv. 243.

c. 1370.—"A gret Yle and great Contree, that men clepen Java. . . . There growen alle manere of Spicerie more plentyfous liche than in any other contree, as of Gyngevere, Clowegylofres, Canelle, Zedewalle, Notemuges, and **Maces**. And wytethe wel, that the Notemuge bereth the **Maces**. For righte as the Note of the Haselle hath an Husk withouten, that the Note is closed in, til it be ripe, and after falleth out; righte so it is of the Notemuge and of the **Maces**."—*Sir John Maundeville*, ed. 1866, p. 187-188. This is a remarkable passage for it is interpolated by Maundeville, from superior information, in what he is borrowing from Odoric. The comparison to the hazel-nut husk is just that used by Hanbury & Flückiger (*Pharmacographia*, 1st ed. 456).

c. 1430.—"Has (insulas Java) ultra xv dierum cursu duae reperiuntur insulae, orientem versus. Altera Sandai appellata, in quâ nuces muscatae et **maces**, altera Bandam nomine, in quâ solâ gariofali producuntur."—*Conti*, in *Poggius, De Var Fortunae.*

1514.—"The tree that produces the nut (meg) and **macis** is all one. By this ship I send you a sample of them in the green state."—*Letter of Giov. da Empoli*, in *Archiv. Stor. Ital.* 81.

1563.—"It is a very beautiful fruit, and pleasant to the taste; and you must know that when the nut is ripe it swells, and the first cover bursts as do the husks of our chestnuts, and shows the **maça**, of a bright vermilion like fine grain (*i.e. coccus*); it is the most beautiful sight in the world when the trees are loaded with it, and sometimes the mace splits off, and that is why the nutmegs often come without the mace."—*Garcia*, f. 129*v*-130.

[1602-3.—"In yor Provision you shall make in Nutmeggs and **Mace** haue you a greate care to receiue such as be good."—*Birdwood, First Letter Book*, 36; also see 67.]

1705.—"It is the commonly received opinion that Cloves, Nutmegs, **Mace**, and Cinnamon all grow upon one tree; but it is a great mistake."—*Funnel*, in *Dampier*, iv. 179.

MACE, s.

b. Jav. and Malay *mās*. [Mr. Skeat writes: "*Mās* is really short for *amās* or *emās*, one of those curious forms with prefixed *a*, as in the case of **abada**, which are probably native, but may have been influenced by Portuguese."] A weight used in Sumatra, being, according to Crawfurd, 1-16th of a Malay **tael** (q.v.), or about 40 grains (but see below). *Mace* is also the name of a small gold coin of Achīn, weighing 9 grs. and worth about 1*s.* 1*d.* And *mace* was adopted in the language of European traders in China to denominate the tenth part of the Chinese *liang* or *tael* of silver; the 100th part of the same value being denominated in like manner **candareen** (q.v.). The word is originally Skt. *māsha*, 'a bean,' and then 'a particular weight of gold' (comp. **CARAT, RUTTEE**).

1539.—". . . by intervention of this thirdsman whom the Moor employed as broker they agreed on my price with the merchant at seven **mazes** of gold, which in our money makes a 1400 reys, at the rate of a half cruzado the **maz**."—*Pinto*, cap. xxv. Cogan has, "the fishermen sold me to the merchant for seven *mazes* of gold, which amounts in our money to seventeen shillings and sixpence."—p. 31.

1554.—"The weight with which they weigh (at Malaca) gold, musk, seed-pearl, coral, calambuco . . . consists of *cates* which contain 20 *tael*, each *tael* 16 **mazes**, each **maz** 20 *cumduryns*. Also one *paual* 4 **mazes**, one **maz** 4 *cupões* (see **KOBANG**), one *cupão* 5 *cumduryns* (see **CANDAREEN**)."—*A. Nunez*, 39.

1598.—"Likewise a Tael of Malacca is 16 **Mases**."—*Linschoten*, 44; [Hak. Soc. i. 149].

1599.—"*Bezar* sive *Bazar* (*i.e.* **Bezoar**, q.v.) per **Masas** venditur."—*De Bry*, ii. 64.

1625.—"I have also sent by Master Tomkins of their coine (Achin) . . . that is of gold named a **Mas**, and is ninepence halfpenie neerest."—*Capt. T. Davis*, in *Purchas*, i. 117.

1813.—"Milburn gives the following table of weights used at Achin, but it is quite inconsistent with the statements of Crawfurd and Linschoten above.

4	copangs	=	1 mace
5	mace	=	1 mayam
16	mayam	=	1 tale
5	tales	=	1 bancal
20	bancals	=	1 catty.
200	catties	=	1 bahar."

Milburn, ii. 329. [Mr. Skeat notes that here "copang" is Malay *kupang*; tale, *tali*; bancal, *bongkal*.]

MACHEEN, MAHACHEEN, n.p. This name, *Mahā-chīna*, "Great China," is one by which China was known in India in the early centuries of our era, and the term is still to be heard in India in the same sense in which Al-Birūnī uses it, saying that all beyond the great mountains (Himālaya) is *Mahā-chīn*. But "in later times the majority, not knowing the meaning of the expression, seem to have used it pleonastically coupled with *Chīn*, to denote the same thing, *Chīn* and *Māchīn*, a phrase having some analogy to the way *Sind* and *Hind* was used to express all India, but a stronger one to *Gog* and *Magog*, as applied to the northern nations of Asia." And eventually *Chīn* was discovered to be the eldest son of Japhet, and *Māchīn* his grandson; which is much the same as saying that Britain was the eldest son of Brut the Trojan, and Great Britain his grandson! (*Cathay and the Way Thither*, p. cxix.).

In the days of the Mongol supremacy in China, when Chinese affairs were for a time more distinctly conceived in Western Asia, and the name of *Manzi* as denoting Southern China, unconquered by the Mongols till 1275, was current in the West, it would appear that this name was confounded with *Māchīn*, and the latter thus acquired a specific but erroneous application. One author of the 16th century also (quoted by *Klaproth, J. As. Soc.* ser. 2, tom. i. 115) distinguishes *Chīn* and *Māchīn* as N. and S. China, but this distinction seems never to have been entertained by the Hindus. Ibn Batuta sometimes distinguishes *Sīn* (*i.e. Chīn*) as South China from *Khitāi* (see **CATHAY**) as North China. In times when intimacy with

China had again ceased, the double name seems to have recovered its old vagueness as a rotund way of saying China, and had no more plurality of sense than in modern parlance *Sodor and Man*. But then comes an occasional new application of *Māchīn* to Indo-China, as in Conti (followed by Fra Mauro). An exceptional application, arising from the Arab habit of applying the name of a country to the capital or the chief port frequented by them, arose in the Middle Ages, through which *Canton* became known in the West as the city of *Māchīn*, or in Persian translation *Chīnkalān*, *i.e.* Great Chīn.

Mahāchīna as applied to China :

636.—" 'In what country exists the kingdom of the Great *Thang?*' asked the king (Sīlāditya of Kanauj), 'how far is it from this?'

" 'It is situated,' replied he (Hwen T'sang), 'to the N.E. of this kingdom, and is distant several ten-thousands of *li*. It is the country which the Indian people call **Mahāchīna.**' "—*Pèl. Bouddh.* ii. 254-255.

c. 641.—"**Mohochintan.**" See quotation under **CHINA**.

c. 1030.—"Some other mountains are called Harmakūt, in which the Ganges has its source. These are impassable from the side of the cold regions, and beyond them lies **Māchīn.**"—*Al-Birūnī*, in *Elliot*, i. 46.

1501.—In the Letter of Amerigo Vespucci on the Portuguese discoveries, written from C. Verde, 4th June, we find mention among other new regions of **Marchin.** Published in Baldelli Boni's *Il Milione*, p. ciii.

c. 1590.—"Adjoining to Asham is Tibet, bordering upon Khatai, which is properly **Mahacheen,** vulgarly called **Macheen.** The capital of Khatai is Khan Baleegh, 4 days' journey from the sea."—*Ayeen*, by *Gladwin*, ed. 1800, ii. 4 ; [ed. *Jarrett*, ii. 118].

[c. 1665.—". . . you told me . . . that Persia, Usbec, Kachguer, Tartary, and Catay, Pegu, Siam, China and **Matchine** (in orig. *Tchine et* **Matchine**) trembled at the name of the Kings of the Indies."—*Bernier*, ed. *Constable*, 155 *seq.*]

Applied to Southern China.

c. 1300.—"Khatāi is bounded on one side by the country of Māchīn, which the Chinese call Manzi. . . . In the Indian language S. China is called **Mahā-chīn,** *i.e.* 'Great China,' and hence we derive the word Manzi."—*Rashīd-uddīn*, in *H. des Mongols* (*Quatremère*), xci.-xciii.

c. 1348.—"It was the Kaam's orders that we should proceed through Manzi, which was formerly known as *India Maxima*" (by which he indicates **Mahā-Chīnā**, see below, in last quotation).—*John Marignolli*, in *Cathay*, p. 354.

Applied to Indo-China :

c. 1430.—"Ea provincia (Ava)—**Macinum** incolae dicunt— . . . referta est elephantis."—*Conti*, in *Poggius, De Var. Fortunae.*

Chin and Machin :

c. 1320.—"The curiosities of **Chín and Machín,** and the beautiful products of Hind and Sind."—*Wassāf*, in *Elliot*, iii. 32.

c. 1440.—"Poi si retrova in quella istessa provincia di Zagatai Sanmarcant città grandissima e ben popolata, por la qual vanno e vengono tutti quelli di **Cini e Macini** e del Cataio, o mercanti o viandanti che siano."—*Barbaro*, in *Ramusio*, ii. f. 106*v*.

c. 1442.—"The merchants of the 7 climates from Egypt . . . from the whole of the realms of **Chīn and Māchīn,** and from the city of Khānbālik, steer their course to this port."—*Abdurrazāk*, in *Notices et Extraits*, xiv. 429.

[1503.—"**Sin and Masin.**" See under **JAVA.**]

Mahāchīn or Chīn Kalān, for Canton.

c. 1030.—In Sprenger's extracts from Al-Birūnī we have "*Sharghūd*, in Chinese *Sanfū*. This is Great China (**Māhāsīn**)."—*Post und Reise-routen des Orients*, 90.

c. 1300.—"This canal extends for a distance of 40 days' navigation from Khānbāligh to Khingsai and Zaitūn, the ports frequented by the ships that come from India, and from the city of **Māchīn.**"—*Rashīd-uddin*, in *Cathay*, &c., 259-260.

c. 1332.—". . . after I had sailed eastward over the Ocean Sea for many days I came to that noble province Manzi. . . . The first city to which I came in this country was called **Cens-Kalan,** and 'tis a city as big as three Venices."—*Odoric*, in *Cathay*, &c., 103-105.

c. 1347.—"In the evening we stopped at another village, and so on till we arrived at **Sīn-Kalān,** which is the city of Ṣīn-ul-Ṣīn . . . one of the greatest of cities, and one of those that has the finest of bazaars. One of the largest of these is the porcelain bazaar, and from it china-ware is exported to the other cities of China, to India, and to Yemen."—*Ibn Batuta*, iv. 272.

c. 1349.—"The first of these is called Manzi, the greatest and noblest province in the world, having no paragon in beauty, pleasantness, and extent. In it is that noble city of Campsay, besides Zayton, **Cynkalan,** and many other cities."—*John Marignolli*, in *Cathay*, &c., 373.

MĀCHIS, s. This is recent Hind. for 'lucifer matches.' An older and purer phrase for sulphur-matches is *dīwā-*, *dīyā-salāī*.

MADAPOLLAM, n.p. This term, applying to a particular kind of cotton cloth, and which often occurs in prices current, is taken from the name of a place on the Southern Delta-branch of the Godavery, properly *Mādhava-palam*, [Tel. *Mādhavayya-pālemu*, 'fortified village of Mādhava']. This was till 1833 [according to the *Madras Gloss.* 1827] the seat of one of the Company's Commercial Agencies, which was the chief of three in that Delta; the other two being Bunder Malunka and Injeram. *Madapollam* is now a staple export from England to India; it is a finer kind of white piece-goods, intermediate between calico and muslin.

[1610.—"**Madafunum** is chequered, somewhat fine and well requested in Pryaman." —*Danvers, Letters*, i. 74.]

1673.—"The *English* for that cause (the unhealthiness of Masulipatam), only at the time of shipping, remove to **Medopollon**, where they have a wholesome Seat Forty Miles more North."—*Fryer*, 35.

[1684-85.—"Mr. Benj[a] Northey having brought up Musters of the **Madapoll[m]** Cloth, Itt is thought convenient that the same be taken of him. . . ."—*Pringle, Diary Ft. St. Geo.* 1st ser. iv. 49.]

c. 1840.—"Pierrette eût de jolies chemises en **Madapolam**."—*Balzac, Pierrette.*

1879.—". . . liveliness seems to be the unfailing characteristic of autographs, fans, Cremona fiddles, Louis Quatorze snuff-boxes, and the like, however sluggish pig-iron and **Madapollams** may be."—*Sat. Review*, Jan. 11, p. 45.

MADRAFAXAO, s. This appears in old Portuguese works as the name of a gold coin of Guzerat; perhaps representing *Muzaffar-shāhī*. There were several kings of Guzerat of this name. The one in question was probably Muzaffar-Shah II. (1511-1525), of whose coinage Thomas mentions a gold piece of 185 grs. (*Pathān Kings*, 353).

1554.—"There also come to this city **Madrafaxaos**, which are a money of Cambaya, which vary greatly in price; some are of 24 tangas of 60 reis the tanga, others of 23, 22, 21, and other prices according to time and value."—*A. Nunez*, 32.

MADRAS, n.p. This alternative name of the place, officially called by its founders Fort St. George, first appears about the middle of the 17th century. Its origin has been much debated, but with little result. One derivation, backed by a fictitious legend, derives the name from an imaginary Christian fisherman called *Madarasen*; but this may be pronounced philologically impossible, as well as otherwise unworthy of serious regard.* Lassen makes the name to be a corruption of *Manda-rājya*, 'Realm of the Stupid!' No one will suspect the illustrious author of the *Indische Alterthumskunde* to be guilty of a joke; but it does look as if some malign Bengalee had suggested to him this gibe against the "Benighted"! It is indeed curious and true that, in Bengal, sepoys and the like always speak of the Southern Presidency as *Mandrāj*. In fact, however, all the earlier mentions of the name are in the form of *Madraspatanam*, 'the city of the *Madras*,' whatever the *Madras* may have been. The earliest maps show *Madraspatanam* as the Mahommedan settlement corresponding to the present Triplicane and Royapettah. The word is therefore probably of Mahommedan origin; and having got so far we need not hesitate to identify it with *Madrasa*, 'a college.' The Portuguese wrote this *Madaraza* (see *Faria y Sousa, Africa Portuguesa*, 1681, p. 6); and the European name probably came from them, close neighbours as they were to Fort St. George, at Mylapore or San Thomé. That there was such a *Madràsa* in existence is established by the quotation from Hamilton, who was there about the end of the 17th century.† Fryer's Map (1698, but illustrating 1672-73) represents the Governor's House as a building of Mahommedan architecture, with a dome. This may have been the *Madrasa* itself. Lockyer also (1711) speaks of a "College," of which the building was "very ancient"; formerly a hospital, and then used apparently as a residence for young writers. But it is not clear whether the name "College" was not given on this last account. [The *Madras Admin. Man.* says: "The origin of this name has been much discussed. *Madrissa*, a Mahommedan school, has been suggested, which considering the date at which the name is first found seems fanciful. *Manda* is in Sanscrit 'slow.' *Mandarāz* was a king of the lunar race.

* It is given in No. II. of *Selections from the Records of S. Arcot District*, p. 107.

† In a letter from poor Arthur Burnell, on which this paragraph is founded, he adds: "It is sad that the most Philistine town (in the German sense) in all the East should have such a name."

The place was probably called after this king" (ii. 91). The *Madras Gloss.* again writes: "Hind. *Madrās*, Can. *Madarāsu*, from Tel. *Mandaradzu*, name of a local Telegu Royer," or ruler. The whole question has been discussed by Mr. Pringle (*Diary Ft. St. Geo.*, 1st ser. i. 106 *seqq.*). He points out that while the earliest quotation given below is dated 1653, the name, in the form *Madrazpatam*, is used by the President and Council of Surat in a letter dated 29th December, 1640 (*I. O. Records*, O. C. No. 1764); "and the context makes it pretty certain that Francis Day or some other of the factors at the new Settlement must have previously made use of it in reference to the place, or 'rather,' as the Surat letter says, 'plot of ground' offered to him. It is no doubt just possible that in the course of the negotiations Day heard or caught up the name from the Portuguese, who were at the time in friendly relations with the English; but the probabilities are certainly in the opposite direction. The *nayak* from whom the plot was obtained must almost certainly have supplied the name, or what Francis Day conceived to be the name. Again, as regards Hamilton's mention of a 'college,' Sir H. Yule's remark certainly goes too far. Hamilton writes, 'There is a very Good Hospital in the Town, and the Company's Horse-stables are neat, but the old College where a good many Gentlemen Factors are obliged to lodge, is ill-kept in repair.' This remark taken together with that made by Lockyer . . . affords proof, indeed, that there was a building known to the English as the 'College.' But it does not follow that this, or any, building was distinctively known to Musulmans as the '*madrasa*.' The 'old College' of Hamilton may have been the successor of a Musulman '*madrasa*' of some size and consequence, and if this was so the argument for the derivation would be strengthened. It is however equally possible that some old buildings within the plot of territory acquired by Day, which had never been a '*madrasa*,' was turned to use as a College or place where the young writers should live and receive instruction; and in this case the argument, so far as it rests on a mention of 'a College' by Hamilton and Lockyer, is entirely destroyed. Next as regards the probability that the first part of '*Madraspatanam*' is 'of Mahommedan origin.' Sir H. Yule does not mention that date of the maps in which *Madraspatanam* is shown 'as the Mahommedan settlement corresponding to the present Triplicane and Royapettah'; but in Fryer's map, which represents the fort as he saw it in 1672, the name '*Madirass*'—to which is added 'the Indian Town with flat houses'—is entered as the designation of the collection of houses on the north side of the English town, and the next makes it evident that in the year in question the name of *Madras* was applied chiefly to the crowded collection of houses styled in turn the 'Heathen,' the 'Malabar,' and the 'Black' town. This consideration does not necessarily disprove the supposed Musulman origin of 'Madras,' but it undoubtedly weakens the chain of Sir H. Yule's argument." Mr. Pringle ends by saying: "On the whole it is not unfair to say that the chief argument in favour of the derivation adopted by Sir H. Yule is of a negative kind. There are fatal objections to whatever other derivations have been suggested, but if the mongrel character of the compound '*Madrasapatanam*' is disregarded, there is no fatal objection to the derivation from '*madrasa*.' . . . If however that derivation is to stand, it must not rest upon such accidental coincidences as the use of the word 'College' by writers whose knowledge of Madras was derived from visits made from 30 to 50 years after the foundation of the colony."]

1653.—"Estant desbarquez le R. P. Zenon reçut lettres de **Madraspatan** de la detention du Rev. P. Ephraim de Neuers par l'Inquisition de Portugal, pour avoir presché a **Madraspatan** que les Catholiques qui foüetoient et trampoient dans des puys les images de Sainct Antoine de Pade, et de la Vierge Marie, estoient impies, et que les Indous à tout le moins honorent ce qu'ils estiment Sainct. . . ."—*De la Boullaye-le-Gouz*, ed. 1657, 244.

c. 1665.—"Le Roi de Golconde a de grands Revenus. . . . Les Douanes des marchandises qui passent sur ses Terres, et celles des Ports de Masulipatan et de **Madrespatan**, lui rapportent beaucoup."—*Thevenot*, v. 306.

1672.—". . . following upon **Madraspatan**, otherwise called *Chinnepatan*, where the English have a Fort called St. George, chiefly garrisoned by *Toepasses* and *Mistices*; from this place they annually send forth their ships, as also from Suratte."—*Baldaeus*, Germ. ed. 152.

1673.—"Let us now pass the Pale to the Heathen Town, only parted by a wide Parrade, which is used for a *Buzzar*, or Mercate-place. **Maderas** then divides itself into divers long streets, and they are chequered by as many transverse. It enjoys some *Choultries* for Places of Justice; one Exchange; one *Pagod*. . . ."—*Fryer*, 38-39.

1726.—"The Town or Place, anciently called *Chinapatnam*, now called **Madras-patnam**, and Fort St. George."—*Letters Patent*, in *Charters of E.I. Company*, 368-9.

1727.—"Fort St. George or **Maderass**, or as the Natives call it, *China Patam*, is a Colony and City belonging to the *English East India Company*, situated in one of the most incommodious Places I ever saw. . . . There is a very good Hospital in the Town, and the Company's Horse-Stables are neat, but the Old College, where a great many Gentlemen Factors are obliged to lodge, is kept in ill Repair."—*A. Hamilton*, i. 364, [ed. 1744, ii. 182]. (Also see **CHINAPATAM.**)

MADRAS, s. This name is applied to large bright-coloured handkerchiefs, of silk warp and cotton woof, which were formerly exported from Madras, and much used by the negroes in the W. Indies as head-dresses. The word is preserved in French, but is now obsolete in England.

c. 1830.—". . . We found President Petion, the black Washington, sitting on a very old ragged sofa, amidst a confused mass of papers, dressed in a blue military undress frock, white trowsers, and the ever-lasting **Madras** handkerchief bound round his brows."—*Tom Cringle*, ed. 1863, p. 425.

1846.—"Et Madame se manifesta! C'était une de ces vieilles dévinées par Adrien Brauwer dans ses sorcières pour le Sabbat . . . coiffée d'un **Madras**, faisant encore papillottes avec les imprimés, que recevait gratuitement son maître."—*Balzac, Le Cousin Pons*, ch. xviii.

MADREMALUCO, n.p. The name given by the Portuguese to the Mahommedan dynasty of Berar, called *'Imād-shāhī*. The Portuguese name represents the title of the founder *'Imād-ul-Mulk*, ('Pillar of the State'), otherwise Fath Ullah 'Imād Shāh. The dynasty was the most obscure of those founded upon the dissolution of the Bāhmanī monarchy in the Deccan. (See **COTAMALUCO, IDALCAN, MELIQUE VERIDO, NIZAMALUCO, SABAIO.**) It began about 1484, and in 1572 was merged in the kingdom of Ahmednagar. There is another Madremaluco (or 'Imād-ul-Mulk) much spoken of in Portuguese histories, who was an important personage in Guzerat, and put to death with his own hand the king Sikandar Shāh (1526) (*Barros*, IV. v. 3; *Correa*, ii. 272, 344, &c.; *Couto*, Decs. v. and vi. *passim*).

[1543.—See under **COTAMALUCO.**]

1553.—"The **Madre Maluco** was married to a sister of the Hidalchan (see **IDALCAN**), and the latter treated this brother-in-law of his, and **Meleque Verido** as if they were his vassals, especially the latter."—*Barros*, IV. vii. 1.

1563.—"The Imademaluco or **Madremaluco**, as we corruptly style him, was a Circassian (*Cherques*) by nation, and had originally been a Christian, and died in 1546. . . . *Imad* is as much as to say 'prop,' and thus the other (of these princes) was called *Imadmaluco*, or 'Prop of the Kingdom.' . . ."—*Garcia*, f. 36v.

Neither the chronology of De Orta here, nor the statement of Imād-ul-Mulk's Circassian origin, agree with those of Firishta. The latter says that Fath-Ullah 'Imād Shāh was descended from the heathen of Bijanagar (iii. 485).

MADURA, n.p., properly *Madurei*, Tam. *Mathurai*. This is still the name of a district in S. India, and of a city which appears in the Tables of Ptolemy as "Μόδουρα βασίλειον Πανδιόνος." The name is generally supposed to be the same as that of *Mathurā*, the holy and much more ancient city of Northern India, from which the name was adopted (see **MUTTRA**), but modified after Tamil pronunciation.* [On the other hand, a writer in *J.R. As. Soc.* (xiv. 578, n. 3) derives *Madura* from the Dravidian *Madur* in the sense of 'Old Town,' and suggests that the northern Mathura may be an offshoot from it.] *Madura* was, from a date, at least as early as the Christian era, the seat of the Pāndya sovereigns. These, according to Tamil tradition, as stated by Bp. Caldwell, had previously held their residence at *Kolkei* on the Tamraparni, the Κόλχοι of Ptolemy. (See *Caldwell*, pp. 16, 95, 101). The name of *Madura*, probably as adopted from the holier northern Muttra, seems to have been a favourite among the Eastern settlements under Hindu influence. Thus we have

* This *perhaps* implies an earlier spread of northern influence than we are justified in assuming.

Matura in Ceylon; the city and island of *Madura* adjoining Java; and a town of the same name (*Madura*) in Burma, not far north of Mandalé, *Madeya* of the maps.

A.D. c. 70-80.—"Alius utilior portus gentis Neacyndon qui vocatur Becare. Ibi regnabat Pandion, longe ab emporio mediterraneo distante oppido quod vocatur **Modura**."—*Pliny*, vi. 26.

[c. 1315.—"**Mardi.**" See **CRORE.**]

c. 1347.—"The Sultan stopped a month at Fattan, and then departed for his capital. I stayed 15 days after his departure, and then started for his residence, which was at **Mutra**, a great city with wide streets. . . . I found there a pest raging of which people died in brief space . . . when I went out I saw only the dead and dying."—*Ibn Batuta*, iv. 200-1.

1311.—". . . the royal canopy moved from Bírdhúl . . . and 5 days afterwards they arrived at the city of **Mathra** . . . the dwelling-place of the brother of the Rái Sundar Pándya. They found the city empty, for the Rái had fled with the Ránís, but had left two or three elephants in the temple of Jagnár (Jaganāth)."—*Amír Khusrú*, in *Elliot*, iii. 91.

MADURA FOOT, s. A fungoidal disease of the foot, apparently incurable except by amputation, which occurs in the Madura district, and especially in places where the 'Black soil' prevails. Medical authorities have not yet decided on the causes or precise nature of the disease. See *Nelson*, *Madura*, Pt. i. pp. 91-94; [*Gribble, Cuddapah*, 193].

MAGADOXO, n.p. This is the Portuguese representation, which has passed into general European use, of *Makdashau*, the name of a town and State on the Somālī coast in E. Africa, now subject to Zanzibar. It has been shown by one of the present writers that Marco Polo, in his chapter on Madagascar, has made some confusion between Magadoxo and that island, mixing up particulars relating to both. It is possible that the name of Madagascar was really given from Makdashau, as Sir R. Burton supposes; but he does not give any authority for his statement that the name of Madagascar "came from Makdishú (Magadoxo) . . . . . whose Sheikh invaded it" (*Comment. on Camões*, ii. 520). [Owen (*Narrative*, i. 357) writes the name *Mukdeesha*, and Boteler (*Narrative*, ii. 215) says it is pronounced by the Arabs *Mŭkŏdĭsha*. The name is said to be *Magaad-el-Shata*, "Harbour of the Sheep," and the first syllable has been identified with that of *Magdala* and is said to mean "door" in some of the Galla dialects (*Notes & Queries*, 9 ser. ii. 193, 310. Also see Mr. Gray's note on *Pyrard*, Hak. Soc. i. 29, and Dr. Burnell on *Linschoten*, Hak. Soc. i. 19.]

c. 1330.—"On departing from Zaila, we sailed on the sea for 15 days, and then arrived at **Makdashau**, a town of great size. The inhabitants possess a great number of camels, and of these they slaughter (for food) several hundreds every day."—*Ibn Batuta*, ii. 181.

1498.—"And we found ourselves before a great city with houses of several stories, and in the midst of the city certain great palaces; and about it a wall with four towers; and this city stood close upon the sea, and the Moors call it **Magadoxó**. And when we were come well abreast of it, we discharged many bombards (at it), and kept on our way along the coast with a fine wind on the poop."—*Roteiro*, 102.

1505.—"And the Viceroy (Don Francisco D'Almeida) made sail, ordering the course to be made for **Magadaxo**, which he had instructions also to make tributary. But the pilots objected saying that they would miss the season for crossing to India, as it was already the 26th of August. . . ."—*Correa*, i. 560.

1514.—". . . The most of them are Moors such as inhabit the city of Zofalla . . . and these people continue to be found in Mazambic, Melinda, **Mogodecio**, Marachilue (read Brava Chilve, *i.e. Brava* and *Quiloa*), and Mombazza; which are all walled cities on the main land, with houses and streets like our own; except Mazambich."—*Letter of Giov. da Empoli*, in *Archiv. Stor. Ital.*

1516.—"Further on towards the Red Sea there is another very large and beautiful town called **Magadoxo**, belonging to the Moors, and it has a King over it, and is a place of great trade and merchandise."—*Barbosa*, 16.

1532.—". . . and after they had passed Cape Guardafu, Dom Estevão was going along in such depression that he was like to die of grief, on arriving at **Magadoxo**, they stopped to water. And the King of the country, hearing that there had come a son of the Count Admiral, of whom all had ample knowledge as being the first to discover and navigate on that coast, came to the shore to see him, and made great offers of all that he could require."—*Couto*, IV. viii. 2.

1727.—"**Magadoxa**, or as the Portuguese call it, **Magadocia**, is a pretty large City, about 2 or 3 Miles from the Sea, from whence it has a very fine Aspect, being adorn'd with many high Steeples and Mosques."—*A. Hamilton*, i. 12-13, [ed. 1744].

MAGAZINE, s. This word is, of course, not Anglo-Indian, but may find a place here because of its origin from Ar. *makhāzin*, plur. of *al-makhzan*, whence Sp. *almacen*, *almagacen*, *magacen*, Port. *almazem*, *armazem*, Ital. *magazzino*, Fr. *magazin*.

c. 1340.—"The Sultan . . . made him a grant of the whole city of Sīrī and all its houses with the gardens and fields of the treasury (**makhzan**) adjacent to the city (of Delhi)."—*Ibn Batuta*, iii. 262.

1539.—"A que Pero de Faria respondea, que lhe desse elle commissão per mandar nos **almazēs**, et que logo proveria no socorro que entendia ser necessario."—*Pinto*, cap. xxi.

MAHÁJUN, s. Hind. from Skt. *mahā-jan*, 'great person.' A banker and merchant. In Southern and Western India the vernacular word has various other applications which are given in *Wilson*.

[1813.—"**Mahajen, Mahajanum**, a great person, a merchant."—*Gloss. to 5th Rep.* s.v.]

c. 1861.—

"Down there lives a **Mahajun**—my father gave him a bill,
I have paid the knave thrice over, and here I'm paying him still.
He shows me a long stamp paper, and must have my land—must he?
If I were twenty years younger, he should get six feet by three."
Sir A. C. Lyall, The Old Pindaree.

1885.—"The **Mahajun** hospitably entertains his victim, and speeds his homeward departure, giving no word or sign of his business till the time for appeal has gone by, and the decree is made absolute. Then the storm bursts on the head of the luckless hill-man, who finds himself loaded with an overwhelming debt, which he has never incurred, and can never hope to discharge; and so he practically becomes the **Mahajun's** slave for the rest of his natural life."—*Lt.-Col. T. Lewin, A Fly on the Wheel*, 339.

MAHANNAH, s. (See **MEEANA**.)

MAHÉ, n.p. Properly *Māyēli*. [According to the *Madras Gloss.* the Māl. name is *Mayyazhi*, *mai*, 'black,' *azhi*, 'river mouth'; but the title is from the French *Mahé*, being one of the names of Labourdonnais.] A small settlement on the Malabar coast, 4 m. S.E. of Tellicherry, where the French established a factory for the sake of the pepper trade in 1722, and which they still retain. It is not now of any importance.

MAHI, n.p. The name of a considerable river flowing into the upper part of the Gulf of Cambay. ["The height of its banks, and the fierceness of its floods; the deep gullies through which the traveller has to pass on his way to the river, and perhaps, above all, the bad name of the tribes on its banks, explain the proverb: 'When the Mahi is crossed, there is comfort'" (*Imp. Gazetteer*, s.v.).]

c. A.D. 80-90.—"Next comes another gulf . . . extending also to the north, at the mouth of which is an island called *Baiōnēs* (**Perim**), and at the innermost extremity a great river called **Maïs**."—*Periplus*, ch. 42.

MAHOUT, s. The driver and tender of an elephant. Hind. *mahāwat*, from Skt. *mahā-mātra*, 'great in measure,' a high officer, &c., so applied. The Skt. term occurs in this sense in the *Mahābhārata* (*e.g.* iv. 1761, &c.). The *Mahout* is mentioned in the 1st Book of Maccabees as 'the **Indian**.' It is remarkable that we find what is apparently *mahā-mātra*, in the sense of a high officer in Hesychius:

"Μαμάτραι, οἱ στρατηγοὶ παρ' Ἰνδοῖς."—*Hesych.* s.v.

c. 1590.—"*Mast* elephants (see **MUST**). There are five and a half servants to each, viz., first a **Mahawat**, who sits on the neck of the animal and directs its movements. . . . He gets 200 *dāms* per month. . . . Secondly a *Bhōi*, who sits behind, upon the rump of the elephant, and assists in battle, and in quickening the speed of the animal; but he often performs the duties of the **Mahawat**. . . . Thirdly the *Met'hs* (see **MATE**). . . . A *Met'h* fetches fodder, and assists in caparisoning the elephant. . . ."—*Āīn*, ed. *Blochmann*, i. 125.

1648.—". . . and **Mahouts** for the elephants. . . ."—*Van Twist*, 56.

1826.—"I will now pass over the term of my infancy, which was employed in learning to read and write—my preceptor being a **mahouhut**, or elephant-driver—and will take up my adventures."—*Pandurang Hari*, 21; [ed. 1873, i. 28].

1848.—"Then he described a tiger hunt, and the manner in which the **Mahout** of his elephant had been pulled off his seat by one of the infuriate animals."—*Thackeray, Vanity Fair*, ch. iv.

MAHRATTA, n.p. Hind. *Marhaṭā*, *Marhaṭṭā*, *Marhāṭā* (*Marhaṭī*, *Marahṭī*, *Mārhaiṭī*), and *Marāṭhā*. The name of a famous Hindu race, from the old Skt. name of their country, *Mahā-rāshṭra*, 'Magna Regio.' [On the other hand H. A. Acworth (*Ballads of the Marathas*, Intro. vi.) derives the word from a tribal name

Rathī or *Rathā*, 'chariot fighters,' from *rath*, 'a chariot,' thus *Mahā-Rathā* means 'Great Warrior.' This was transferred to the country and finally Sanskritised into *Mahā-rāshtra*. Again some authorities (Wilson, *Indian Caste*, ii. 48; Baden-Powell, *J. R. As. Soc.*, 1897, p. 249, note) prefer to derive the word from the *Mhār* or *Mahār*, a once numerous and dominant race. And see the discussion in the *Bombay Gazetteer*, I. pt. ii. 143 *seq.*]

c. 550.—"The planet (Saturn's) motion in Açleshâ causes affliction to aquatic animals or products, and snakes . . . in Pûrva Phalgunî to vendors of liquors, women of the town, damsels, and the **Mahrattas.** . . ."—*Bṛhat Sanhitâ*, tr. by *Kern*, *J.R. As. Soc.* 2nd ser. v. 64.

640.—"De là il prit la direction du Nord-Ouest, traversa une vaste forêt, et . . . il arriva au royaume de *Mo-ho-la-to* (**Mahârâshtra**). . . ."—*Pèl. Bouddh.* i. 202; [*Bombay Gazetteer*, I. pt. ii. 353].

c. 1030.—"De Dhar, en se dirigeant vers le midi, jusqu'à la rivière de Nymyah on comte 7 parasanges; de là à **Mahrat-dessa** 18 paras."—*Albirûni*, in *Reinaud's Fragmens*, 109.

c. 1294-5. — "Alá-ud-dín marched to Elichpúr, and thence to Ghati-lajaura . . . the people of that country had never heard of the Mussulmans; the **Mahratta** land had never been punished by their armies; no Mussulman King or Prince had penetrated so far."—*Ziá-ud-dín Barní*, in *Elliot*, iii. 150.

c. 1328.—"In this Greater India are twelve idolatrous Kings, and more. . . . There is also the Kingdom of **Maratha** which is very great."—*Friar Jordanus*, 41.

1673.—"They tell their tale in **Moratty**; by Profession they are Gentues."—*Fryer*, 174.

1747.—"Agreed on the arrival of these Ships that We take Five Hundred (500) Peons more into our Service, that the 50 **Moratta** Horses be augmented to 100 as We found them very usefull in the last Skirmish. . . . ."—*Consn. at Ft. St. David*, Jan. 6 (MS. Record in India Office).

1748.—"That upon his hearing the **Mirattoes** had taken Tanner's Fort . . ." —In *Long*, p. 5.

c. 1760.—". . . those dangerous and powerful neighbors the **Morattoes**; who being now masters of the contiguous island of Salsette . . ."—*Grose*, ii. 44.

" "The name of **Morattoes**, or **Marattas**, is, I have reason to think, a derivation in their country-language, or by corruption, from *Mar-Rajah*."—*Ibid.* ii. 75.

1765.—"These united princes and people are those which are known by the general name of **Maharattors**; a word compounded of *Rattor* and *Maahah*; the first being the name of a particular *Raazpoot* (or *Rajpoot*) tribe; and the latter, signifying great or mighty (as explained by Mr. Fraser). . . ." —*Holwell, Hist. Events*, &c., i. 105.

c. 1769.—Under a mezzotint portrait: "*The Right Honble* George Lord Pigot, *Baron* Pigot *of* Patshul *in the Kingdom of* Ireland, *President and Governor of and for all the Affairs of the United Company of Merchants of* England *trading to the* East Indies, *on the Coast of* Choromandel, *and* Orixa, *and of the* Chingee *and* **Moratta** *Countries*, &c., &c., &c."

c. 1842.—

". . . Ah, for some retreat
Deep in yonder shining Orient, where my life began to beat;
Where in wild **Mahratta** battle fell my father evil starr'd."
—*Tennyson, Locksley Hall.*

The following is in the true **Hobson-Jobson** manner:

[1859.—"This term **Marhatta** or **Mârhutta**, is derived from the mode of warfare adopted by these men. *Mar* means to strike, and *hutna*, to get out of the way, *i.e.* those who struck a blow suddenly and at once retreated out of harm's way."—*H. Dundas Robertson, District Duties during the Revolt in* 1857, p. 104, note.]

MAHRATTA DITCH, n.p. An excavation made in 1742, as described in the extract from Orme, on the landward sides of Calcutta, to protect the settlement from the Mahratta bands. Hence the term, or for shortness 'The *Ditch*' simply, as a disparaging name for Calcutta (see **DITCHER**). The line of the Ditch corresponded nearly with the outside of the existing Circular Road, except at the S.E. and S., where the work was never executed. [There is an excavation known by the same name at Madras excavated in 1780. (*Murray, Handbook*, 1859, p. 43).]

1742.—"In the year 1742 the Indian inhabitants of the Colony requested and obtained permission to dig a ditch at their own expense, round the Company's bounds, from the northern parts of Sootanatty to the southern part of Govindpore. In six months three miles were finished: when the inhabitants . . . discontinued the work, which from the occasion was called the **Morattoe ditch**."—*Orme*, ed. 1803, ii. 45.

1757.—"That the Bounds of *Calcutta* are to extend the whole Circle of *Ditch* dug upon the Invasion of the **Marattes**; also 600 yards without it, for an Esplanade."—*Articles of Agreement sent by Colonel Clive* (previous to the Treaty with the Nabob of May 14). In *Memoirs of the Revolution in Bengal*, 1760, p. 89.

1782.—"To the Proprietors and Occupiers of Houses and other Tenements within the

Mahratta Entrenchment."—*India Gazette*, Aug. 10.

[1840.—"Less than a hundred years ago, it was thought necessary to fortify Calcutta against the horsemen of Berar, and the name of the **Mahratta Ditch** still preserves the memory of the danger."—*Macaulay, Essay on Clive.*]

1872. — "The Calcutta cockney, who glories in the **Mahratta Ditch**. . . ."—*Govinda Samanta*, i. 25.

MAHSEER, MASEER, MASAL, &c. Hind. *mahāsir, mahāser, mahāsaulā*, s. The name is applied to perhaps more than one of the larger species of *Barbus* (N.O. *Cyprinidae*), but especially to *B. Mosul* of Buchanan, *B. Tor*, Day, *B. megalepis*, McLelland, found in the larger Himālayan rivers, and also in the greater perennial rivers of Madras and Bombay. It grows at its largest, to about the size of the biggest salmon, and more. It affords also the highest sport to Indian anglers; and from these circumstances has sometimes been called, misleadingly, the 'Indian salmon.' The origin of the name *Mahseer*, and its proper spelling, are very doubtful. It may be Skt. *mahā-śiras*, 'big-head,' or *mahā-śalka*, 'large-scaled.' The latter is most probable, for the scales are so large that Buchanan mentions that playing cards were made from them at Dacca. Mr. H. S. Thomas suggests *mahā-āsya*, 'great mouth.' [The word does not appear in the ordinary dicts.; on the whole, perhaps the derivation from *mahā-śiras* is most probable.]

c. 1809.—"The **Masal** of the Kosi is a very large fish, which many people think still better than the Robu, and compare it to the salmon."—*Buchanan, Eastern India*, iii. 194.

1822.—"**Mahasaula** and *Tora*, variously altered and corrupted, and with various additions may be considered as genuine appellations, amongst the natives for these fishes, all of which frequent large rivers."—*F. Buchanan Hamilton, Fishes of the Ganges*, 304.

1873.—"In my own opinion and that of others whom I have met, the **Mahseer** shows more sport for its size than a salmon."—*H. S. Thomas, The Rod in India*, p. 9.

MAINATO, s. Tam. Mal. *Maināttā*, a washerman or **dhoby** (q.v.).

1516.—"There is another sect of Gentiles which they call **Mainatos**, whose business it is to wash the clothes of the Kings, Bramins, and Naires; and by this they get their living; and neither they nor their sons can take up any other business."—*Barbosa*, Lisbon ed., 334.

c. 1542.—"In this inclosure do likewise remain all the Landresses, by them called **Maynates**, which wash the linnen of the City (Pequin), who, as we were told, are above an hundred thousand."—*Pinto*, in *Cogan*, p. 133. The original (cap. cv.) has *todos os* **mainatos**, whose sex Cogan has changed.

1554.—"And the farm (*renda*) of **mainatos**, which farm prohibits any one from washing clothes, which is the work of a **mainato**, except by arrangement with the farmer (Rendeiro). . . ."—*Tombo*, &c., 53.

[1598.—"There are some among them that do nothing els but wash cloathes: . . . they are called **Maynattos**."—*Linschoten*, Hak. Soc. i. 260.

[c. 1610.—"These folk (the washermen) are called **Menates**."—*Pyrard de Laval*, Hak. Soc. ii. 71.]

1644.—(Expenses of Daman) "For two **maynatos**, three water *boys* (*bois de agoa*), one *sombreyro boy*, and 4 torch bearers for the said Captain, at 1 xerafim each a month, comes in the year to 36,000 *rēs* or xns. 00120.0.00."—*Bocarro, MS.* f. 181.

MAISTRY, MISTRY, sometimes even **MYSTERY**, s. Hind. *mistrī*. This word, a corruption of the Portuguese *mestre*, has spread into the vernaculars all over India, and is in constant Anglo-Indian use. Properly 'a foreman,' 'a master-workman'; but used also, at least in Upper India, for any artizan, as *rāj-mistrī* (properly Pers. *rāz*), 'a mason or bricklayer,' *lohār-mistrī*, 'a blacksmith,' &c. The proper use of the word, as noted above, corresponds precisely to the definition of the Portuguese word, as applied to artizans in Bluteau: "Artifice que sabe bem o seu officio. *Peritus artifex . . . Opifex, alienorum operum inspector*." In W. and S. India **maistry**, as used in the household, generally means the cook, or the tailor. (See **CALEEFA**.) **Mastèr** (Мастеръ) is also the Russian term for a skilled workman, and has given rise to several derived adjectives. There is too a similar word in modern Greek, *μαγίστωρ*.

1404.—"And in these (chambers) there were works of gold and azure and of many other colours, made in the most marvellous way; insomuch that even in Paris whence come the subtle **maestros**, it would be reckoned beautiful to see."—*Clavijo*, § cv. (Comp. *Markham*, p. 125).

1524.—"And the Viceroy (D. Vasco da Gama) sent to seize in the river of the Culymutys four newly-built **caturs**, and fetched them to Cochin. These were built very light for fast rowing, and were greatly admired. But he ordered them to be burned, saying that he intended to show the Moors that we knew how to build better **caturs** than they did; and he sent for Mestre Vyne the Genoese, whom he had brought to build galleys, and asked him if he could build boats that would row faster than the Malabar paraos (see **PROW**). He answered: 'Sir, I'll build you brigantines fast enough to catch a mosquito. . . .'"—*Correa*, ii. 830.

[1548.—"He ordered to be collected in the smithies of the dockyard as many smiths as could be had, for he had many **misteres**." —*Ibid.* iv. 663.]

1554.—"To the **mestrè** of the smith's shop (*ferraria*) 30,000 reis of salary and 600 reis for maintenance" (see **BATTA**).—*S. Botelho, Tombo*, 65.

1800.—". . . I have not yet been able to remedy the mischief done in my absence, as we have the advantage here of the assistance of some Madras **dubashes** and **maistries**" (ironical).—*Wellington*, i. 67.

1883.—". . . My mind goes back to my ancient Goanese cook. He was only a **maistry**, or more vulgarly a *bobberjee* (see **BOBACHEE**), yet his sonorous name recalled the conquest of Mexico, or the doubling of the Cape."—*Tribes on My Frontier*, 35.

[1900.—"**Mystery** very sick, Mem Sahib, very sick all the night."—*Temple Bar*, April.]

MAJOON, s. Hind. from Ar. *ma'jūn*, lit. 'kneaded,' and thence what old medical books call 'an electuary' (*i.e.* a compound of medicines kneaded with syrup into a soft mass), but especially applied to an intoxicating confection of hemp leaves, &c., sold in the bazar. [*Burton, Ar. Nights*, iii. 159.] In the Deccan the form is *ma'jūm*. Moodeen Sheriff, in his Suppt. to the *Pharmac. of India*, writes *maghjūn*. "The chief ingredients in making it are *ganja* (or hemp) leaves, milk, *ghee*, poppy-seeds, flowers of the thorn-apple (see **DATURA**), the powder of nux vomica, and sugar" (*Qanoon-e-Islam*, Gloss. lxxxiii).

1519.—"Next morning I halted . . . and indulging myself with a **maajûn**, made them throw into the water the liquor used for intoxicating fishes, and caught a few fish."—*Baber*, 272.

1563.—"And this they make up into an electuary, with sugar, and with the things above-mentioned, and this they call **maju**." —*Garcia*, f. 27v.

1781.—"Our ill-favoured guard brought in a dose of **majum** each, and obliged us to eat it . . . a little after sunset the surgeon came, and with him 30 or 40 Caffres, who seized us, and held us fast till the operation (circumcision) was performed."—*Soldier's letter* quoted in *Hon. John Lindsay's Journal of Captivity in Mysore, Lives of Lindsays*, iii. 293.

1874.—". . . it (Bhang) is made up with flour and various additions into a sweetmeat or **majum** of a green colour."—*Hanbury and Flückiger*, 493.

MALABAR, n.p.

a. The name of the sea-board country which the Arabs called the 'Pepper-Coast,' the ancient *Kerala* of the Hindus, the Λιμύρικη, or rather Διμύρικη, of the Greeks (see **TAMIL**), is not in form indigenous, but was applied, apparently, first by the Arab or Arabo-Persian mariners of the Gulf. The substantive part of the name, *Malai*, or the like, is doubtless indigenous; it is the Dravadian term for 'mountain' in the Sanskritized form *Malaya*, which is applied specifically to the southern portion of the Western Ghauts, and from which is taken the indigenous term *Malayālam*, distinguishing that branch of the Dravidian language in the tract which we call *Malabar*. This name—*Male* or *Malai*, *Malīah*, &c.,—we find in the earlier post-classic notices of India; whilst in the great Temple-Inscription of Tanjore (11th century) we find the region in question called *Malai-nādu* (*nādu*, 'country'). The affix *bār* appears attached to it first (so far as we are aware) in the Geography of Edrisi (c. 1150). This (Persian?) termination, *bār*, whatever be its origin, and whether or no it be connected either with the Ar. *barr*, 'a continent,' on the one hand, or with the Skt. *vāra*, 'a region, a slope,' on the other, was most assuredly applied by the navigators of the Gulf to other regions which they visited besides Western India. Thus we have *Zangī-bār* (mod. **Zanzibar**), 'the country of the Blacks'; *Kalāh-bār*, denoting apparently the coast of the Malay Peninsula; and even according to the dictionaries, *Hindū-bār* for India. In the Arabic work which affords the second of these examples (*Relation*, &c., tr. by *Reinaud*, i. 17) it is expressly explained: "The word *bār* serves to indicate that which is both a coast and a kingdom." It will be seen from the quotations below that in the Middle Ages, even after the establishment of the use of this termination, the exact form of the name as given by foreign travellers and writers, varies considerably. But, from the time of the Portuguese discovery of the Cape route, *Malavar*, or *Malabar*, as we have it now, is the persistent form. [Mr. Logan (*Manual*, i. 1) remarks that the name is not in use in the district itself except among foreigners and English-speaking natives; the ordinary name is *Malayālam* or *Malāyam*, 'the Hill Country.']

c. 545.—"The imports to Taprobane are silk, aloeswood, cloves, sandalwood. . . . These again are passed on from Sielediba to the marts on this side, such as Μαλὲ, where the pepper is grown. . . . And the most notable places of trade are these, Sindu . . . and then the five marts of Μαλὲ, from which the pepper is exported, viz., *Parti*, *Mangaruth*, *Salopatana*, *Nalopatana*, and *Pudopatana*."—*Cosmas*, Bk. xi. In *Cathay*, &c., p. clxxviii.

c. 645.—"To the south this kingdom is near the sea. There rise the mountains called **Mo-la-ye** (*Malaya*), with their precipitous sides, and their lofty summits, their dark valleys and their deep ravines. On these mountains grows the white sandalwood."—*Hwen T'sang*, in *Julien*, iii. 122.

851.—"From this place (Maskat) ships sail for India, and run for Kaulam-**Malai**; the distance from Maskat to Kaulam-**Malai** is a month's sail with a moderate wind."—*Relation*, &c., tr. by *Reinaud*, i. 15. The same work at p. 15 uses the expression "Country of Pepper" (*Balad-ul-falfal*).

890.—"From Sindán to **Malí** is five days' journey; in the latter pepper is to be found, also the bamboo."—*Ibn Khurdâdba*, in *Elliot*, i. 15.

c. 1030.—"You enter then on the country of Lárán, in which is Jaimúr (see under **CHOUL**), then **Maliah**, then Kánchí, then Dravira (see **DRAVIDIAN**)."—*Al-Birûnî*, in *Reinaud*, *Fragmens*, 121.

c. 1150.—"Fandarina (see **PANDARANI**) is a town built at the mouth of a river which comes from **Manibár**, where vessels from India and Sind cast anchor."—*Idrisi*, in *Elliot*, i. 90.

c. 1200.—"Hari sports here in the delightful spring . . . when the breeze from **Malaya** is fragrant from passing over the charming *lavanga*" (cloves).—*Gîta Govinda*.

1270.—"**Malibar** is a large country of India, with many cities, in which pepper is produced."—*Kazwînî*, in *Gildemeister*, 214.

1293.—"You can sail (upon that sea) between these islands and Ormes, and (from Ormes) to those parts which are called (**Minibar**), is a distance of 2,000 miles, in a direction between south and south-east; then 300 miles between east and south-east from **Minibar** to Maabar" (see **MABAR**).—Letter of *Fr. John of Montecorvino*, in *Cathay*, i. 215.

1298.—"**Melibar** is a great kingdom lying towards the west. . . . There is in this kingdom a great quantity of pepper."—*Marco Polo*, Bk. iii. ch. 25.

c. 1300.—"Beyond Guzerat are Kankan (see **CONCAN**) and **Tāna**; beyond them the country of **Malíbár**, which from the boundary of Karoha to Kúlam (probably from *Gheriah* to **Quilon**) is 300 parasangs in length."—*Rashiduddin*, in *Elliot*, i. 68.

c. 1320.—"A certain traveller states that India is divided into three parts, of which the first, which is also the most westerly, is that on the confines of Kerman and Sind, and is called Gūzerāt; the second **Manībār**, or the Land of Pepper, east of Gūzerāt."—*Abulfeda*, in *Gildemeister*, 184.

c. 1322.—"And now that ye may know how pepper is got, let me tell you that it groweth in a certain empire, whereunto I came to land, the name whereof is **Minibar**."—*Friar Odoric*, in *Cathay*, &c., 74.

c. 1343.—"After 3 days we arrived in the country of the **Mulaibār**, which is the country of Pepper. It stretches in length a distance of two months' march along the sea-shore."—*Ibn Batuta*, iv. 71.

c. 1348-49.—"We embarked on board certain junks from Lower India, which is called **Minubar**."—*John de' Marignolli*, in *Cathay*, 356.

c. 1420-30.—". . . Departing thence he . . . arrived at a noble city called Coloen. . . . This province is called **Melibaria**, and they collect in it the ginger called by the natives *colombi*, pepper, brazil-wood, and the cinnamon, called *canella grossa*."—*Conti*, corrected from Jones's tr. in *India in XVth Cent.* 17-18.

c. 1442. — "The coast which includes Calicut with some neighbouring ports, and which extends as far as (Kael), a place situated opposite to the Island of Serendib . . . bears the general name of **Melībār**."—*Abdurrazzāk*, *ibid.* 19.

1459.—Fra Mauro's great Map has **Milibar**.

1514.—"In the region of India called **Melibar**, which province begins at Goa, and extends to Cape Comedis (**Comorin**). . . ."—Letter of *Giov. da Empoli*, 79. It is remarkable to find this Florentine using this old form in 1514.

1516.—"And after that the Moors of Meca discovered India, and began to navigate near it, which was 610 years ago, they used to touch at this country of **Malabar** on account of the pepper which is found there."—*Barbosa*, 102.

1553. — "We shall hereafter describe particularly the position of this city of Calecut, and of the country of **Malauar** in which it stands."—*Barros*, Dec. I. iv. c. 6. In the following chapter he writes **Malabar**.

1554.—"*From Diu to the Islands of Dib.* Steer first S.S.E., the pole being made by five inches, side towards the land in the direction of E.S.E. and S.E. by E. till you see the mountains of **Monibár**."—*The Mohit*, in *J. As. Soc. Ben.* v. 461.

1572.—
"Esta provincia cuja porto agora
Tomado tendes, **Malabar** se chama:
Do culto antiguo os idolos adora,
Que cà por estas partes se derrama."
Camões, vii. 32.

By Burton:
"This province, in whose Ports your ships have tane
refuge, the **Malabar** by name is known;
its ántique rite adoreth idols vain,
Idol-religion being broadest sown."

Since De Barros **Malabar** occurs almost universally.

[1623.—". . . **Mahabar** Pirates. . . ."—*P. della Valle*, Hak. Soc. i. 121.]

1877.—The form **Malibar** is used in a letter from Athanasius Peter III., "Patriarch of the Syrians of Antioch" to the Marquis of Salisbury, dated Cairo, July 18.

MALABAR, n.p.

b. This word, through circumstances which have been fully elucidated by Bishop Caldwell in his *Comparative Grammar* (2nd ed. 10-12), from which we give an extract below,* was applied by the Portuguese not only to the language and people of the country thus called, but also to the *Tamil* language and the people speaking Tamil. In the quotations following, those under *A* apply, or may apply, to the proper people or language of Malabar (see **MALAYALAM**); those under *B* are instances of the misapplication to Tamil, a misapplication which was general (see *e.g.* in *Orme, passim*) down to the beginning of the last century, and which still holds among the more ignorant Europeans and Eurasians in S. India and Ceylon.

(*A*.)

1552.—"A lingua dos Gentios de Canara e **Malabar**."—*Castanheda*, ii. 78.

1572.—
"Leva alguns **Malabares**, que tomou
Por força, dos que o Samorim mandara."
Camões, ix. 14.

[By Aubertin:
"He takes some **Malabars** he kept on board
By force, of those whom Samorin had sent . . ."]

1582.—"They asked of the **Malabars** which went with him what he was?"—*Castañeda*, (tr. by N. L.) f. 37*v*.

1602.—"We came to anchor in the Roade of Achen . . . where we found sixteene or eighteene saile of shippes of diuers Nations, some *Goserats*, some of *Bengala*, some of *Calecut*, called **Malabares**, some *Pegues*, and some *Patanyes*."—*Sir J. Lancaster*, in *Purchas*, i. 153.

1606.—In *Gouvea* (*Synodo*, ff. 2*v*, 3, &c.) **Malavar** means the *Malayālam* language.

(*B*.)

1549.—"Enrico Enriques, a Pórtuguese priest of our Society, a man of excellent virtue and good example, who is now in the Promontory of Comorin, writes and speaks the **Malabar** tongue very well indeed." — Letter of *Xavier*, in Coleridge's *Life*, ii. 73.

1680.—"Whereas it hath been hitherto accustomary at this place to make sales and alienations of houses in writing in the Portuguese, Gentue, and **Mallabar** languages, from which some inconveniences have arisen. . . ."—*Ft. St. Geo. Consn.*, Sept 9, in *Notes and Extracts*, No. iii. 33.

[1682.—"An order in English Portuguez Gentue & **Mallabar** for the preventing the transportation of this Countrey People and makeing them slaves in other Strange Countreys. . . ."—*Pringle, Diary Ft. St. Geo.*, 1st ser. i. 87.]

1718.—"This place (Tranquebar) is altogether inhabited by **Malabarian** Heathens."—*Propn. of the Gospel in the East*, Pt. i. (3rd ed.), p. 18.

" "Two distinct languages are necessarily required; one is the *Damulian*, commonly called **Malabarick**."—*Ibid.* Pt. iii. 33.

1734.—"Magnopere commendantes zelum, ac studium Missionariorum, qui libros sacram Ecclesiae Catholicae doctrinam, rerumque sacrarum monumenta continentes, pro Indorum Christi fidelium eruditione in linguam **Malabaricam** seu Tamulicam transtulere."—*Brief of Pope Clement XII.*, in *Norbert*, ii. 432-3. These words are adopted from Card. Tournon's decree of 1704 (see *ibid.* i. 173).

c. 1760.—"Such was the ardent zeal of M. Ziegenbalg that in less than a year he attained a perfect knowledge of the **Malabarian** tongue. . . . He composed also a **Malabarian** dictionary of 20,000 words."—*Grose*, i. 261.

1782. — "Les habitans de la côte de Coromandel sont appellés *Tamouls;* les Européens les nomment improprement **Malabars**."—*Sonnerat*, i. 47.

1801.—"From Niliseram to the Chandergerry River no language is understood but the **Malabars** of the Coast."—*Sir T. Munro*, in *Life*, i. 322.

* "The Portuguese . . . sailing from Malabar on voyages of exploration . . . made their acquaintance with various places on the eastern or Coromandel Coast . . . and finding the language spoken by the fishing and sea-faring classes on the eastern coast similar to that spoken on the western, they came to the conclusion that it was identical with it, and called it in consequence by the same name—viz. Malabar. . . . A circumstance which naturally confirmed the Portuguese in their notion of the identity of the people and language of the Coromandel Coast with those of Malabar was that when they arrived at Cael, in Tinnevelly, on the Coromandel Coast . . . they found the King of Quilon (one of the most important places on the Malabar Coast) residing there."—*Bp. Caldwell*, u.s.

In the following passage the word **Malabars** is misapplied still further, though by a writer usually most accurate and intelligent:

1810.—"The language spoken at Madras is the *Talinga*, here called **Malabars**."—*Maria Graham*, 128.

1860.—"The term '**Malabar**' is used throughout the following pages in the comprehensive sense in which it is applied in the Singhalese Chronicles to the continental invaders of Ceylon; but it must be observed that the adventurers in these expeditions, who are styled in the *Mahawanso 'damilos*,' or Tamils, came not only from . . . '**Malabar**,' but also from all parts of the Peninsula as far north as Cuttack and Orissa."—*Tennent's Ceylon*, i. 353.

MALABAR-CREEPER, s. *Argyreia malabarica*, Choisy.

[**MALABAR EARS**, s. The seed vessels of a tree which Ives calls *Codaga palli*.

1773.—"From their shape they are called **Malabar-Ears**, on account of the resemblance they bear to the ears of the women of the Malabar coast, which from the large slit made in them and the great weight of ornamental rings put into them, are rendered very large, and so long that sometimes they touch the very shoulders."—*Ives*, 465.

MALABAR HILL, n.p. This favourite site of villas on Bombay Island is stated by Mr. Whitworth to have acquired its name from the fact that the Malabar pirates, who haunted this coast, used to lie behind it.

[1674.—"On the other side of the great Inlet, to the Sea, is a great Point abutting against Old Woman's Island, and is called **Malabar-Hill** . . . the remains of a stupendous Pagod, near a Tank of Fresh Water, which the Malabars visited it mostly for."—*Fryer*, 68 *seq*.]

[**MALABAR OIL**, s. "The ambiguous term '**Malabar Oil**' is applied to a mixture of the oil obtained from the livers of several kinds of fishes frequenting the Malabar Coast of India and the neighbourhood of Karachi."—*Watt, Econ. Dict.* v. 113.

MALABAR RITES. This was a name given to certain heathen and superstitious practices which the Jesuits of the Madura, Carnatic, and Mysore Missions permitted to their converts, in spite of repeated prohibitions by the Popes. And though these practices were finally condemned by the Legate Cardinal de Tournon in 1704, they still subsist, more or less, among native Catholic Christians, and especially those belonging to the (so-called) Goa Churches. These practices are generally alleged to have arisen under Father de' Nobili ("Robertus de Nobilibus"), who came to Madura about 1606. There can be no doubt that the aim of this famous Jesuit was to present Christianity to the people under the form, as it were, of a Hindu translation!

The nature of the practices of which we speak may be gathered from the following particulars of their prohibition. In 1623 Pope Gregory XV., by a constitution dated 31st January, condemned the following:—1. The investiture of Brahmans and certain other castes with the sacred thread, through the agency of Hindu priests, and with Hindu ceremonies. For these Christian ceremonies were to be substituted; and the thread was to be regarded as only a civil badge. 2. The ornamental use of sandalwood paste was permitted, but not its superstitious use, *e.g.*, in mixture with cowdung ashes, &c., for ceremonial purification. 3. Bathing as a ceremonial purification. 4. The observance of caste, and the refusal of high-caste Christians to mix with low-caste Christians in the churches was disapproved.

The quarrels between Capuchins and Jesuits later in the 17th century again brought the Malabar Rites into notice, and Cardinal de Tournon was sent on his unlucky mission to determine these matters finally. His decree (June 23, 1704) prohibited:—1. A mutilated form of baptism, in which were omitted certain ceremonies offensive to Hindus, specifically the use of '*saliva, sal, et insufflatio*.' 2. The use of Pagan names. 3. The Hinduizing of Christian terms by translation. 4. Deferring the baptism of children. 5. Infant marriages. 6. The use of the Hindu *tali* (see **TALEE**). 7. Hindu usages at marriages. 8. Augury at marriages, by means of a coco-nut. 9. The exclusion of women from churches during certain periods. 10. Ceremonies on a girl's attainment of puberty. 11. The making distinctions between Pariahs and others. 12. The assistance of Christian musicians at heathen ceremonies. 13. The use of ceremonial washings and bathings. 14. The use of cowdung-ashes. 15. The reading and use of Hindu books.

With regard to No. 11 it may be observed that in South India the distinction of castes still subsists, and the only Christian Mission in that quarter which has really succeeded in abolishing caste is that of the Basel Society.

MALABATHRUM, s. There can be very little doubt that this classical export from India was the dried leaf of various species of Cinnamomum, which leaf was known in Skt. as *tamāla-pattra*. Some who wrote soon after the Portuguese discoveries took, perhaps not unnaturally, the *pān* or betel-leaf for the *malabathrum* of the ancients; and this was maintained by Dean Vincent in his well-known work on the *Commerce and Navigation of the Ancients*, justifying this in part by the Ar. name of the betel, *tambūl*, which is taken from Skt. *tāmbūla*, betel; *tāmbūla-pattra*, betel-leaf. The *tamāla-pattra*, however, the produce of certain wild spp. of Cinnamomum, obtained both in the hills of Eastern Bengal and in the forests of Southern India, is still valued in India as a medicine and aromatic, though in no such degree as in ancient times, and it is usually known in domestic economy as **tejpāt**, or corruptly *tezpāt*, *i.e.* 'pungent leaf.' The leaf was in the Arabic Materia Medica under the name of *sādhaj* or *sādhajī Hindī*, as was till recently in the English Pharmacopœia as *Folium indicum*, which will still be found in Italian drug-shops. The matter is treated, with his usual lucidity and abundance of local knowledge, in the *Colloquios* of Garcia de Orta, of which we give a short extract. This was evidently unknown to Dean Vincent, as he repeats the very errors which Garcia dissipates. Garcia also notes that confusion of *Malabathrum* and *Folium indicum* with spikenard, which is traceable in Pliny as well as among the Arab pharmacologists. The ancients did no doubt apply the name *Malabathrum* to some other substance, an unguent or solid extract. Rheede, we may notice, mentions that in his time in Malabar, oils in high medical estimation were made from both leaves and root of the "wild cinnamon" of that coast, and that from the root of the same tree a *camphor* was extracted, having several of the properties of real camphor and more fragrance. (See a note by one of the present writers in *Cathay*, &c., pp. cxlv.-xlvi.) The name *Cinnamon* is properly confined to the tree of Ceylon (*C. Zeylanicum*). The other *Cinnamoma* are properly *Cassia barks*. [See *Watt. Econ. Dict.* ii. 317 *seqq.*]

c. A.D. 60.—"Μαλάβαθρον ἔνιοι ὑπολάμβάνουσιν εἶναι τῆς Ἰνδικῆς νάρδου φύλλον, πλανώμενοι ὑπὸ τῆς κατὰ τὴν ὀσμὴν, ἐμφερειας, . . . ἴδιον γαρ ἐστι γένος φυόμενον ἐν τοῖς Ἰνδικοῖς τέλμασι, φύλλον ὂν ἐπινηχόμενον ὕδατι."—*Dioscorides, Mat. Med.* i. 11.

c. A.D. 70.—"We are beholden to Syria for Malabathrum. This is a tree that beareth leaves rolled up round together, and seeming to the eie withered. Out of which there is drawn and pressed an Oile for perfumers to use. . . . And yet there commeth a better kind thereof from India. . . . The rellish thereof ought to resemble Nardus at the tongue end. The perfume or smell that . . . the leafe yeeldeth when it is boiled in wine, passeth all others. It is straunge and monstrous which is observed in the price; for it hath risen from one denier to three hundred a pound."—*Pliny*, xii. 26, in *Ph. Holland.*

c. A.D. 90. — ". . . Getting rid of the fibrous parts, they take the leaves and double them up into little balls, which they stitch through with the fibres of the withes. And these they divide into three classes. . . . And thus originate the three qualities of **Malabathrum**, which the people who have prepared them carry to India for sale."—*Periplus*, near the end. [Also see *Yule, Intro. Gill, River of Golden Sand*, ed. 1883, p. 89.]

1563.—"*R.* I remember well that in speaking of betel you told me that it was not *folium indu*, a piece of information of great value to me; for the physicians who put themselves forward as having learned much from these parts, assert that they are the same; and what is more, the modern writers . . . call betel in their works *tembul*, and say that the Moors give it this name. . . .

"*O.* That the two things are different as I told you is clear, for Avicenna treats them in two different chapters, viz., in 259, which treats of *folium indu*, and in 707, which treats of *tambul* . . . and the *folium indu* is called by the Indians **Tamalapatra**, which the Greeks and Latins corrupted into **Malabathrum**," &c.—*Garcia*, ff. 95*v*, 96.

c. 1690.—"Hoc Tembul seu Sirium, licet vulgatissimum in India sit folium, distinguendum est a *Folio Indo* seu **Malabathro**, Arabibus *Cadegi Hindi*, in Pharmacopoeis, et Indis, *Tamala-patra* et *folio Indo* dicto, . . . A nostra autem natione intellexi **Malabathrum** nihil aliud esse quam folium canellae, seu cinnamomi sylvestris."—*Rumphius*, v. 337.

c. 1760.—". . . quand l'on considère que les Indiens appellent notre feuille Indienne **tamalapatra** on croit d'apercevoir que le mot Grec μαλάβαθρον en a été anciennement dérivé."—(*Diderot*) *Encyclopédie*, xx. 846.

1837. — (**Malatroon** is given in Arabic works of Materia Medica as the Greek of *Sādhaj*, and *tuj* and *tej-pat* as the Hindi synonymes). "By the latter names may be obtained everywhere in the bazars of India, the leaves of *Cinn. Tamala* and of *Cinn. albiflorum*."—*Royle, Essay on Antiq. of Hindoo Medicine*, 85.

MALACCA, n.p. The city which gives its name to the Peninsula and the Straits of Malacca, and which was the seat of a considerable Malay monarchy till its capture by the Portuguese under D'Alboquerque in 1511. One naturally supposes some etymological connection between *Malay* and *Malacca*. And such a connection is put forward by De Barros and D'Alboquerque (see below, and also under **MALAY**). The latter also mentions an alternative suggestion for the origin of the name of the city, which evidently refers to the Ar. *mulākāt*, 'a meeting.' This last, though it appears also in the *Sijara Malayu*, may be totally rejected. Crawfurd is positive that the place was called from the word *malaka*, the Malay name of the *Phyllanthus emblica*, or emblic **Myrobalan** (q.v.), "a tree said to be abundant in that locality"; and this, it will be seen below, is given by Godinho de Eredia as the etymology. *Malaka* again seems to be a corruption of the Skt. *amlaka*, from *amla*, 'acid.' [Mr. Skeat writes: "There can be no doubt that Crawfurd is right, and that the place was named from the tree. The suggested connection between *Malayu* and *Malaka* appears impossible to me, and, I think, would do so to any one acquainted with the laws of the language. I have seen the *Malāka* tree myself and eaten its fruit. Ridley in his Botanical Lists has *laka-laka* and *malaka* which he identifies as *Phyllanthus emblica*, L. and *P. pectinatus Hooker* (*Euphorbiaceae*). The two species are hardly distinct, but the latter is the commoner form. The fact is that the place, as is so often the case among the Malays, must have taken its name from the Sungei *Malaka*, or *Malaka* River."]

1416.—"There was no King but only a chief, the country belonging to Siam. . . . In the year 1409, the imperial envoy Cheng Ho brought an order from the emperor and gave to the chief two silver seals, . . . he erected a stone and raised the place to a city, after which the land was called the Kingdom of **Malacca** (*Moa-la-ka*). . . . Tin is found in the mountains . . . it is cast into small blocks weighing 1 catti 8 taels . . . ten pieces are bound together with rattan and form a small bundle, whilst 40 pieces make a large bundle. In all their trading . . . they use these pieces of tin instead of money."—*Chinese Annals*, in *Groenveldt*, p. 123.

1498.—"**Melequa** . . . is 40 days from Qualecut with a fair wind . . . hence proceeds all the clove, and it is worth there 9 crusados for a **bahar** (q.v.), and likewise nutmeg other 9 crusados the bàhar; and there is much porcelain and much silk, and much tin, of which they make money, but the money is of large size and little value, so that it takes 3 farazalas (see **Frazala**) of it to make a crusado. Here too are many large parrots all red like fire."—*Roteiro de V. da Gama*, 110-111.

1510.—"When we had arrived at the city of **Melacha**, we were immediately presented to the Sultan, who is a Moor . . . I believe that more ships arrive here than in any other place in the world. . . ."—*Varthema*, 224.

1511.—"This Paremiçura gave the name of **Malaca** to the new colony, because in the language of Java, when a man of Palimbão flees away they call him *Malayo*. . . . Others say that it was called Malaca because of the number of people who came there from one part and the other in so short a space of time, for the word *Malaca* also signifies to *meet*. . . . Of these two opinions let each one accept that which he thinks to be the best, for this is the truth of the matter."—*Commentaries of Alboquerque*, E.T. by Birch, iii. 76-77.

1516.—"The said Kingdom of Ansyane (see **Siam**) throws out a great point of land into the sea, which makes there a cape, where the sea returns again towards China to the north; in this promontory is a small kingdom in which there is a large city called **Malaca**."—*Barbosa*, 191.

1553.—"A son of Paramisora called Xaquem Darxa, (*i.e. Sikandar Shāh*) . . . to form the town of **Malaca**, to which he gave that name in memory of the banishment of his father, because in his vernacular tongue (Javanese) this was as much as to say 'banished,' and hence the people are called **Malaios**."—*De Barros*, II. vi. 1.

" "That which he (Alboquerque) regretted most of all that was lost on that vessel, was two lions cast in iron, a first-rate work, and most natural, which the King of China had sent to the King of **Malaca**, and which King Mahamed had kept, as an honourable possession, at the gate of his Palace, whence Affonso Alboquerque carried them off, as the principal item of his triumph on the capture of the city."—*Ibid.* II. vii. 1.

1572.—
"Nem tu menos fugir poderás deste
Postoque rica, e postoque assentada
Là no gremio da Aurora, onde nasceste,
Opulenta **Malaca** nomeada!
Assettas venenosas, que fizeste,
Os crises, com que j'á te vejo armada,
Malaios namorados, Jaos valentes,
Todos farás ao Luso obedientes."
Camões, x. 44.

By Burton:

"Nor shalt thou 'scape the fate to fall his prize,
albeit so wealthy, and so strong thy site
there on Aurora's bosom, whence thy rise,
thou Home of Opulence, Malacca hight!
The poysoned arrows which thine art supplies,
the Krises thirsting, as I see, for fight,
th' enamoured Malay-men, the Javan braves,
all of the Lusian shall become the slaves."

1612.—"The Arabs call it *Malakat*, from collecting all merchants."—*Sijara Malayu*, in *J. Ind. Arch.* v. 322.

1613.—"Malaca significa *Mirabolanos*, fructa de huá arvore, plantada ao longo de hum ribeiro chamado Aerlele."—*Godinho de Eredia*, f. 4.

MALADOO, s. *Chicken maladoo* is an article in the Anglo-Indian menu. It looks like a corruption from the French *cuisine*, but of what? [*Maladoo* or *Manadoo*, a lady informs me, is cold meat, such as chicken or mutton, cut into slices, or pounded up and re-cooked in batter. The Port. *malhado*, 'beaten-up,' has been suggested as a possible origin for the word.]

MALAY, n.p. This is in the Malay language an adjective, *Malāyu*; thus *orang Malāyu*, 'a Malay'; *tāna* [*tānah*] *Malāyu*, 'the Malay country'; *bahāsa* [*bhāsa*] *Malāyu*, 'the Malay language.'

In Javanese the word *malāyu* signifies 'to run away,' and the proper name has traditionally been derived from this, in reference to the alleged foundation of **Malacca** by Javanese fugitives; but we can hardly attach importance to this. It may be worthy at least of consideration whether the name was not of foreign, *i.e.* of S. Indian origin, and connected with the *Malāya* of the Peninsula (see under **MALABAR**). [Mr. Skeat writes: "The tradition given me by Javanese in the Malay States was that the name was applied to Javanese refugees, who peopled the S. of Sumatra. Whatever be the original meaning of the word, it is probable that it started its life-history as a river-name in the S. of Sumatra, and thence became applied to the district through which the river ran, and so to the people who lived there; after which it spread with the Malay dialect until it included not only many allied, but also many foreign, tribes; all Malay-speaking tribes being eventually called Malays without regard to racial origin. A most important passage in this connection is to be found in Leyden's Tr. of the '*Malay Annals*' (1821), p. 20, in which direct reference to such a river is made: 'There is a country in the land of Andalás named Paralembang, which is at present denominated Palembang, the raja of which was denominated Damang Lebar Dawn (chieftain Broad-leaf), who derived his origin from Raja Sulan (Chulan?), whose great-grandson he was. The name of its river Muartatang, into which falls another river named Sungey **Malayu**, near the source of which is a mountain named the mountain Sagantang Maha Miru.' Here Palembang is the name of a well-known Sumatran State, often described as the original home of the Malay race. In standard Malay '*Damang Lebar Dawn*' would be '*Děmang Lebar Daun.*' Raja Chulan is probably some mythical Indian king, the story being evidently derived from Indian traditions. 'Muartatang' may be a mistake for *Muar Tenang*, which is a place one heard of in the Peninsula, though I do not know for certain where it is. 'Sungey Malayu' simply means 'River Malayu.' 'Sagantang Maha Miru' is, I think, a mistake for *Sa-guntang Maha Miru*, which is the name used in the Peninsula for the sacred central mountain of the world on which the episode related in the *Annals* occurred" (see Skeat, *Malay Magic*, p. 2).]

It is a remarkable circumstance, which has been noted by Crawfurd, that a name which appears on Ptolemy's Tables as on the coast of the Golden Chersonese, and which must be located somewhere about Maulmain, is Μαλεοῦ Κῶλον, words which in Javanese (*Malāyu-Kulon*) would signify "Malays of the West." After this the next (possible) occurrence of the name in literature is in the *Geography* of Edrisi, who describes *Malai* as a great island in the eastern seas, or rather as occupying the position of the *Lemuria* of Mr. Sclater, for (in partial accommodation to the Ptolemaic theory of the Indian Sea) it stretched eastward nearly from the coast of Zinj, *i.e.* of Eastern Africa, to the vicinity of China. Thus it must be uncertain without further accounts whether it is an adumbration of the great Malay islands (as is on the whole probable) or of the Island of the Malagashes (Madagascar), if it is either. We then come to Marco Polo, and after him there is, we believe, no mention of the Malay name till the Portuguese entered the seas of the Archipelago.

[A.D. 690.—Mr. Skeat notes: "I Tsing speaks of the '**Molo-yu** country,' *i.e.* the district W. or N.W. of Palembang in Sumatra."]

c. 1150.—"The Isle of **Malai** is very great. . . . The people devote themselves to very profitable trade; aud there are found here elephants, rhinoceroses, and various aromatics and spices, such as clove, cinnamon, nard . . . and nutmeg. In the mountains are mines of gold, of excellent quality . . . the people also have windmills."—*Edrisi*, by *Jaubert*, i. 945.

c. 1273.—A Chinese notice records under this year that tribute was sent from Siam to the Emperor. "The Siamese had long been at war with the **Maliyi**, or **Maliurh**, but both nations laid aside their feud and submitted to China."—Notice by Sir T. Wade, in *Bowring's Siam*, i. 72.

c. 1292.—"You come to an Island which forms a kingdom, and is called **Malaiur**. The people have a king of their own, and a peculiar language. The city is a fine and noble one, and there is a great trade carried on there. All kinds of spicery are to be found there."—*Marco Polo*, Bk. iii. ch. 8.

c. 1539.—". . . as soon as he had delivered to him the letter, it was translated into the *Portugal* out of the **Malayan** tongue wherein it was written."—*Pinto*, E.T. p. 15.

1548.—". . . having made a breach in the wall twelve fathom wide, he assaulted it with 10,000 strangers, *Turks*, *Abyssins*, *Moors*, *Malauares*, *Achems*, *Jaos*, and **Malayos**."—*Ibid.* p. 279.

1553.—"And so these Gentiles like the Moors who inhabit the sea-coasts of the Island (Sumatra), although they have each their peculiar language, almost all can speak the **Malay** of Malacca as being the most general language of those parts."—*Barros*, III. v. 1.

,, "Everything with them is to be a gentleman; and this has such prevalence in those parts that you will never find a native **Malay**, however poor he may be, who will set his hand to lift a thing of his own or anybody else's; every service must be done by slaves."—*Ibid.* II. vi. 1.

1610.—"I cannot imagine what the *Hollanders* meane, to suffer these **Malaysians**, *Chinesians*, and *Moores* of these countries, and to assist them in their free trade thorow all the *Indies*, and forbid it their owne seruants, countrymen, and Brethern, upon paine of death and losse of goods."—*Peter Williamson Floris*, in *Purchas*, i. 321.

[Mr. Skeat writes: "The word *Malaya* is now often applied by English writers to the Peninsula as a whole, and from this the term **Malaysia** as a term of wider application (*i.e.* to the Archipelago) has been coined (see quotation of 1610 above). The former is very frequently miswritten by English writers as '*Malay*,' a barbarism which has even found place on the title-page of a book—'Travel and Sport in Burma, Siam and **Malay**, by John Bradley, London, 1876.'"]

MALAYĀLAM. This is the name applied to one of the cultivated Dravidian languages, the closest in its relation to the Tamil. It is spoken along the Malabar coast, on the Western side of the **Ghauts** (or *Malāya* mountains), from the Chandragiri River on the North, near Mangalore (entering the sea in 12° 29′), beyond which the language is, for a limited distance, *Tulu*, and then Canarese, to Trevandrum on the South (lat. 8° 29′), where Tamil begins to supersede it. Tamil, however, also intertwines with Malayālam all along Malabar. The term *Malayālam* properly applies to territory, not language, and might be rendered "Mountain region." [See under **MALABAR**, and *Logan*, *Man. of Malabar*, i. 90.]

MALDIVES, MALDIVE ISLDS., n.p. The proper form of this name appears to be *Male-dīva*; not, as the estimable Garcia de Orta says, *Nale-dīva*; whilst the etymology which he gives is certainly wrong, hard as it may be to say what is the right one. The people of the islands formerly designated themselves and their country by a form of the word for 'island' which we have in the Skt. *dvīpa* and the Pali *dīpo*. We find this reflected in the *Divi* of Ammianus, and in the *Dīva* and *Dība*-jāt (Pers. plural) of old Arab geographers, whilst it survives in letters of the 18th century addressed to the Ceylon

Government (Dutch) by the Sultan of the Isles, who calls his kingdom *Divehi Rajjé*, and his people *Divehe mīhun*. Something like the modern form first appears in Ibn Batuta. He, it will be seen, in his admirable account of these islands, calls them, as it were, *Mahal*-dives, and says they were so called from the chief group *Mahal*, which was the residence of the Sultan, indicating a connection with *Mahal*, 'a palace.' This form of the name looks like a foreign 'striving after meaning.' But Pyrard de Laval, the author of the most complete account in existence, also says that the name of the islands was taken from *Malé*, that on which the King resided. Bishop Caldwell has suggested that these islands were the *dives*, or islands, of *Malé*, as *Malebār* (see **MALABAR**) was the coast-tract or continent, of *Malé*. It is, however, not impossible that the true etymology was from *mālā*, 'a garland or necklace,' of which their configuration is highly suggestive. [The *Madras Gloss.* gives Malayāl. *māl*, 'black,' and *dvīpa*, 'island,' from the dark soil. For a full account of early notices of the Maldives, see Mr. Gray's note on *Pyrard de Laval*, Hak. Soc. ii. 423 *seqq.*] Milburn (*Or. Commmerce*, i. 335) says: "This island was (these islands were) discovered by the Portuguese in 1507." Let us see!

A.D. 362.—"Legationes undique solito ocius concurrebant; hinc Transtigritanis pacem obsecrantibus et Armeniis, inde nationibus Indicis certatim cum donis optimates mittentibus ante tempus, ab usque **Divis** et Serendivis."—*Ammian. Marcellinus*, xxii. 3.

c. 545.—"And round about it (*Sielediba* or *Taprobane*, *i.e.* Ceylon) there are a number of small islands, in all of which you find fresh water and coco-nuts. And these are almost all set close to one another."—*Cosmas*, in *Çathay*, &c., clxxvii.

851.—"Between this Sea (of Horkand) and the Sea called Lāravi there is a great number of isles; their number, indeed, it is said, amounts to 1,900; . . . the distance from island to island is 2, 3, or 4 parasangs. They are all inhabited, and all produce coco-palms. . . . The last of these islands is Serendīb, in the Sea of Horkand; it is the chief of all; they give the islands the name of **Dībajāt**" (*i.e. Dibas*).—*Relation*, &c., tr. by *Reinaud*, i. 4-5.

c. 1030.—"The special name of **Dīva** is given to islands which are formed in the sea, and which appear above water in the form of accumulations of sand; these sands continually augment, spread, and unite, till they present a firm aspect . . . these islands are divided into two classes, according to the nature of their staple product. Those of one class are called **Dīva**-*Kūzah* (or the Cowry Divahs), because of the cowries which are gathered from coco-branches planted in the sea. The others are called **Dīva**-*Kanbar*, from the word *kanbar* (see **COIR**), which is the name of the twine made from coco-fibres, with which vessels are stitched."—*Al-Birūnī*, in *Reinaud, Fragmens*, 124.

1150.—See also *Edrisi*, in Jaubert's Transl. i. 68. But the translator prints a bad reading, *Raibihāt*, for **Dībajāt**.

c. 1343.—"Ten days after embarking at Calecut we arrived at the Islands called **Dhībat-al-Mahal**. . . . These islands are reckoned among the wonders of the World; there are some 2000 of them. Groups of a hundred, or not quite so many, of these islands are found clustered into a ring, and each cluster has an entrance like a harbour-mouth, and it is only there that ships can enter. . . . Most of the trees that grow on these islands are coco-palms. . . . They are divided into regions or groups . . . among which are distinguished . . . 3° **Mahal**, the group which gives a name to the whole, and which is the residence of the Sultans."—*Ibn Batuta*, iv. 110 *seqq.*

1442.—Abdurrazzak also calls them "the isles of **Dīva-Mahal**."—In *Not. et Exts.* xiv. 429.

1503.—"But Dom Vasco . . . said that things must go on as they were to India, and there he would inquire into the truth. And so arriving in the Gulf (*golfão*) where the storm befel them, all were separated, and that vessel which steered badly, parted company with the fleet, and found itself at one of the first islands of **Maldiva**, at which they stopped some days enjoying themselves. For the island abounded in provisions, and the men indulged to excess in eating cocos, and fish, and in drinking bad stagnant water, and in disorders with women; so that many died."—*Correa*, i. 347.

[1512.—"Mafamede Maçay with two ships put into the **Maldive** islands (ilhas de **Maldiva**)."—*Albuquerque, Cartas*, p. 30.]

1563.—"*R.* Though it be somewhat to interrupt the business in hand,—why is that chain of islands called 'Islands of **Maldiva**'?

"*O.* In this matter of the nomenclature of lands and seas and kingdoms, many of our people make gerat mistakes even in regard to our own lands; how then can you expect that one can give you the rationale of etymologies of names in foreign tongues? But, nevertheless, I will tell you what I have heard say. And that is that the right name is not **Maldiva**, but *Naledira;* for *nale* in Malabar means 'four,' and *diva* 'island,' so that in the Malabar tongue the name is as much as to say 'Four Isles.' . . . And in the same way we call a certain island that is 12 leagues from Goa *Angediva* (see **ANCHEDIVA**), because there are five in the group, and so the name in Malabar means 'Five Isles,' for *ange* is 'five.' But these derivations rest on common report, I don't detail them to you as demonstrable facts."—*Garcia, Colloquios*, f. 11.

1572.—"Nas ilhas de **Maldiva**." (See **COCO-DE-MER.**)

c. 1610.—"Ce Royaume en leur langage s'appelle **Malé**-*ragué*, Royaume de Malé, et des autres peuples de l'Inde il s'appelle **Malé-divar**, et les peuples **diues** . . . L'Isle principale, comme j'ay dit, s'appelle **Malé**, qui donne le nom à tout le reste des autres; car le mot **Diues** signifie vn nombre de petites isles amassées."—*Pyrard de Laval*, i. 63, 68, ed. 1679. [Hak. Soc. i. 83, 177.]

1683.—"Mr. Beard sent up his Couries, which he had received from ye **Mauldivas**, to be put off and passed by Mr. Charnock at Cassumbazar."—*Hedges, Diary*, Oct. 2; [Hak. Soc. i. 122].

MALUM, s. In a ship with English officers and native crew, the mate is called *mālum sāhib*. The word is Ar. *mu'allim*, literally 'the Instructor,' and is properly applied to the pilot or sailing-master. The word may be compared, thus used, with our 'master' in the Navy. In regard to the first quotation we may observe that *Nākhuda* (see **NACODA**) is, rather than *Mu'allim*, 'the captain'; though its proper meaning is the owner of the ship; the two capacities of owner and skipper being doubtless often combined. The distinction of *Mu'allim* from *Nākhuda* accounts for the former title being assigned to the mate.

1497.—"And he sent 20 cruzados in gold, and 20 testoons in silver for the **Malemos**, who were the pilots, for of these coins he would give each month whatever he (the Sheikh) should direct."—*Correa*, i. 38 (E.T. by *Ld. Stanley of Alderley*, 88). On this passage the Translator says: "The word is perhaps the Arabic for an instructor, a word in general use all over Africa." It is curious that his varied experience should have failed to recognise the habitual marine use of the term.

1541.—"Meanwhile he sent three **caturs** (q.v.) to the Port of the **Malems** (*Porto dos Malemos*) in order to get some pilot. . . . In this Port of the *Bandel of the* **Malems** the ships of the Moors take pilots when they enter the Straits, and when they return they leave them here again."*—*Correa*, iv. 168.

1553.—". . . among whom (at Melinda) came a Moor, a Guzarate by nation, called **Malem** Cana, who, as much for the satisfaction he had in conversing with our people, as to please the King, who was inquiring for a pilot to give them, agreed to accompany them."—*Barros*, I. iv. 6.

c. 1590.—"**Mu'allim** or Captain. He must be acquainted with the depths and shallow places of the Ocean, and must know astronomy. It is he who guides the ship to her destination, and prevents her falling into dangers."—*Āīn*, ed. *Blochmann*, i. 280.

[1887.—"The second class, or **Malumis**, are sailors."—*Logan, Malabar*, ii. ccxcv.]

MAMIRAN, MAMIRA, s. A medicine from old times of much repute in the East, especially for eye-diseases, and imported from Himalayan and Trans-Himalayan regions. It is a popular native drug in the Punjab bazars, where it is still known as *mamīra*, also as *pīlīdārī*. It seems probable that the name is applied to bitter roots of kindred properties but of more than one specific origin. Hanbury and Flückiger describe it as the rhizome of *Coptis Teeta*, Wallich, *tīta* being the name of the drug in the Mishmi country at the head of the Assam Valley, from which it is imported into Bengal. But Stewart states explicitly that the *mamīra* of the Punjab bazars is now "known to be" mostly, if not entirely, derived from *Thalictrum foliosum* D.C., a tall plant which is common throughout the temperate Himālaya (5000 to 8000 feet) and on the Kasia Hills, and is exported from Kumaun under the name of **Momiri**. [See *Watt, Econ. Dict.* vi. pt. iv. 42 *seq.*] "The **Mamira** of the old Arab writers was identified with *Χελιδόνιον μέγα*, by which, however, Löw (*Aram. Pflanzennamen*, p. 220) says they understood *curcuma longa*." W.R.S.

c. A.D. 600–700.—"**Μαμιράς**, *οἷον ῥιζίον τι πόας ἐστὶν ἔχον ὥσπερ κονδύλους πυκνοὺς, ὅπος οὐλάς τε καὶ λευκώματα λεπτύνειν πεπιστεύεται, δηλονότι ῥυπτικῆς ὑπάρχον δυνάμεως.*"—*Pauli Aeginetae Medici*, Libri vii., Basileae 1538. Lib. vii. cap. iii. sect. 12 (p. 246).

c. 1020.—"**Memirem** quid est? Est lignum sicut nodi declinans ad nigredinem . . .

* This Port was immediately outside the Straits, as appears from the description of Dom João de Castro (1541): "Now turning to the 'Gates' of the Strait, which are the chief object of our description, we remark that here the land of Arabia juts out into the sea, forming a prominent Point, and very prolonged. . . . This is the point or promontory which Ptolemy calls *Possidium*. . . . In front of it, a little more than a gunshot off, is an islet called the *Ilheo dos Roboeens*; because *Robodo* in Arabic means a pilot; and the pilots living here go aboard the ships which come from outside, and conduct them," &c.—*Roteiro do Mar Roxo*, &c., 35.

The Island retains its name, and is mentioned as *Pilot Island* by Capt. Haines in *J. R. Geog. Soc.* ix. 126. It lies about 1½ m. due east of Perim.

mundificat albuginem in oculis, et acuit visum: quum ex eo fit collyrium et abstergit humiditatem grossam. . . ." &c.—*Avicennae Opera*, Venet. 1564, p. 345 (lib. ii. tractat. ii.).

The glossary of Arabic terms by Andreas de Alpago of Belluno, attached to various early editions of Avicenna, gives the following interpretation: "**Memirem** est radix nodosa, non multum grossa, citrini coloris, sicut curcuma; minor tamen est et subtilior, et asportatur ex Indiâ, et apud physicos orientales est valde nota, et usitatur in passionibus oculi."

c. 1100.—"**Memiram** Arabibus, χελιδόνιον μέγα Graecis," &c.—*Io. Serapionis de Simpl. Medicam. Historia*, Lib. iv. cap. lxxvi. (ed. Ven. 1552, f. 106).

c. 1200.—"Some maintain that this plant (*'urūk al-ṣâbaghīn*) is the small *kurkum* (**turmeric**), and others that it is **mamīrān**. . . . The *kurkum* is brought to us from India. . . . The **mamīrān** is imported from China, and has the same properties as *kurkum*."—*Ibn Baithar*, ii. 186-188.

c. 1550.—"But they have a much greater appreciation of another little root which grows in the mountains of Succuir (*i.e.* Suchau in Shensi), where the rhubarb grows, and which they call **Mambroni**-Chini (*i.e.* **Mamīrān**-*i-Chīnī*). This is extremely dear, and is used in most of their ailments, but especially when the eyes are affected. They grind it on a stone with rose water, and anoint the eyes with it. The result is wonderfully beneficial."—*Hajji Mahommed's Account of Cathay*, in *Ramusio*, ii. f. 15*v*.

c. 1573.—(At Aleppo). "**Mamiranitchini**, good for eyes as they say."—*Rauwolff*, in Ray's 2nd ed. p. 114.

Also the following we borrow from Dozy's *Suppl. aux Dictt. Arabes*:—

1582.—"Mehr haben ihre Krämer kleine würtzelein zu verkaufen **mamirani** tchini genennet, in gebresten der Augen, wie sie fürgeben ganz dienslich; diese seind gelblecht wie die Curcuma umb ein zimlichs lenger, auch dünner und knopffet das solche unseren weisz wurtzlen sehr ehnlich, und wol für das rechte mamiran mögen gehalten werden, dessen sonderlich Rhases an mehr orten gedencket."—*Rauwolff, Aigentliehe Beschreibung der Raisz*, 126.

c. 1665.—"These caravans brought back *Musk, China-wood, Rubarb*, and **Mamiron**, which last is a small root exceeding good for ill eyes."—*Bernier*, E.T. 136; [ed. *Constable*, 426].

1862.—"Imports from Yarkand and Changthan, through Leh to the Punjab . . . **Mamiran**-*i-Chini* (a yellow root, medicine for the eyes) . . ."—*Punjaub Trade Report*, App. xxiv. p. ccxxxiii.

MAMLUTDAR, s. P.—H. *mu'āmalatdār* (from Ar. *mu'āmala*, 'affairs, business'), and in Mahr. *māmlatdār*. Chiefly used in Western India. Formerly it was the designation, under various native governments, of the chief civil officer of a district, and is now in the Bombay Presidency the title of a native civil officer in charge of a **Talook**, corresponding nearly to the **Tahseeldar** of a pergunna in the Bengal Presidency, but of a status somewhat more important.

[1826.—"I now proceeded to the **Maamulut-dar**, or farmer of the district. . . ."—*Pandurang Hari*, ed. 1873, i. 42.]

MAMOOL, s.; **MAMOOLEE**, adj. Custom, Customary. Ar.—H. *ma'mūl*. The literal meaning is 'practised,' and then 'established, customary.' *Ma'mūl* is, in short, 'precedent,' by which all Orientals set as much store as English lawyers, *e.g.* "And Laban said, It must not so be done in our country (*lit.* It is not so done in our place) to give the younger before the firstborn."—*Genesis* xxix. 26.

MAMOOTY, MAMOTY, MOMATTY, s. A digging tool of the form usual all over India, *i.e.* not in the shape of a spade, but in that of a hoe, with the helve at an acute angle with the blade. [See **FOWRA**.] The word is of S. Indian origin, Tamil *manvĕtti*, 'earth-cutter'; and its vernacular use is confined to the Tamil regions, but it has long been an established term in the list of ordnance stores all over India, and thus has a certain prevalence in Anglo-Indian use beyond these limits.

[1782.—"He marched . . . with two battalions of sepoys . . . who were ordered to make a show of entrenching themselves with **mamuties**. . . ."—Letter of *Ld. Macartney*, in *Forrest, Selections*, iii. 855.]

[1852.—". . . by means of a **mometty** or hatchet, which he ran and borrowed from a husbandman . . . this fellow dug . . . a reservoir. . . ."—*Neale, Narrative of Residence in Siam*, 138.]

MANCHUA, s. A large cargo-boat, with a single mast and a square sail, much used on the Malabar coast. This is the Portuguese form; the original Malayālam word is *manji*, [*manchi*, Skt. *mancha*, 'a cot,' so called apparently from its raised platform for cargo,] and nowadays a nearer approach to this, *manjee*, &c., is usual.

c. 1512.—"So he made ready two **manchuas**, and one night got into the house of the King, and stole from him the most beautiful woman that he had, and, along with her, jewels and a quantity of money."—*Correa*, i. 281.

1525.—"Quatro **lancharas** (q.v.) grandes e seis *qualaluzes* (see **CALALUZ**) e **manchuas** que se remam muyto."—*Lembrança das Cousas de India*, p. 8.

1552.—"**Manchuas** que sam navios de remo."—*Castanheda*, ii. 362.

c. 1610.—"Il a vne petite Galiote, qu'ils appellent **Manchouës**, fort bien couverte . . . et faut huit ou neuf hommes seulement pour la mener."—*Pyrard de Laval*, ii. 26; [Hak. Soc. ii. 42].

[1623.—". . . boats which they call **Maneive**, going with 20 or 24 Oars."—*P. della Valle*, Hak. Soc. ii. 211; **Mancina** in ii. 217.

[1679.—"I commanded the **shibbars** and **manchuas** to keepe a little ahead of me."—*Yule, Hedges' Diary*, Hak. Soc. ii. clxxxiv.]

1682.—"Ex hujusmodi arboribus excavatis naviculas Indi conficiunt, quas **Mansjoas** appellant, quarum nonullae longitudine 80, latitudine 9 pedum mensuram superant."—*Rheede, Hort. Malabar*, iii. 27.

[1736.—"All ships and vessels . . . as well as the **munchuas** appertaining to the Company's officers."—Treaty, in *Logan, Malabar*, ii. 31.

MANDADORE, s. Port. *mandador*, 'one who commands.'

1673.—"Each of which Tribes have a **Mandadore** or Superintendent."—*Fryer*, 67.

MANDALAY, MANDALÉ, n.p. The capital of the King of Burmah, founded in 1860, 7 miles north of the preceding capital Amarapura, and between 2 and 3 miles from the left bank of the Irawadi. The name was taken from that of a conical isolated hill, rising high above the alluvial plain of the Irawadi, and crowned by a gilt pagoda. The name of the hill (and now of the city at its base) probably represents *Mandara*, the sacred mountain which in Hindu mythology served the gods as a churning-staff at the churning of the sea. The hill appears as *Mandiye-taung* in Major Grant Allan's Map of the Environs of Amarapura (1855), published in the Narrative of Major Phayre's Mission, but the name does not occur in the Narrative itself.

[1860.—See the account of **Mandelay** in *Mason, Burmah*, 14 *seqq.*]

1861.—"Next morning the son of my friendly host accompanied me to the **Mandalay** Hill, on which there stands in a gilt chapel the image of Shwesayatta, pointing down with outstretched finger to the Palace of **Mandalay**, interpreted as the divine command there to build a city . . . on the other side where the hill falls in an abrupt precipice, sits a gigantic Buddha gazing in motionless meditation on the mountains opposite. There are here some caves in the hard rock, built up with bricks and whitewashed, which are inhabited by eremites. . . ."—*Bastian's Travels* (German), ii. 89-90.

MANDARIN, s. Port. *Mandarij*, *Mandarim*. Wedgwood explains and derives the word thus: "A Chinese officer, a name first made known to us by the Portuguese, and like the Indian *caste*, erroneously supposed to be a native term. From Portuguese *mandar*, to hold authority, command, govern, &c." So also T. Hyde in the quotation below. Except as regards the word having been first made known to us by the Portuguese, this is an old and persistent mistake. What sort of form would *mandarij* be as a derivative from *mandar?* The Portuguese might have applied to Eastern officials some such word as *mandador*, which a preceding article (see **MANDADORE**) shows that they did apply in certain cases. But the parallel to the assumed origin of *mandarin* from *mandar* would be that English voyagers on visiting China, or some other country in the far East, should have invented, as a title for the officials of that country, a new and abnormal derivation from 'order,' and called them *orderumbos*.

The word is really a slight corruption of Hind. (from Skt.) *mantri*, 'a counsellor, a Minister of State,' for which it was indeed the proper old pre-Mahommedan term in India. It has been adopted, and specially affected in various Indo-Chinese countries, and particularly by the Malays, among whom it is habitually applied to the highest class of public officers (see *Crawfurd's Malay Dict.* s.v. [and Klinkert, who writes *manteri*, colloquially *mentri*]). Yet Crawfurd himself, strange to say, adopts the current explanation as from the Portuguese (see *J. Ind. Archip.* iv. 189). [Klinkert adopts the Skt. derivation.] It is, no doubt, probable that the instinctive "striving after meaning" may have shaped the corruption of *mantri* into a semblance of *mandar*. Marsden is still more oddly perverse, *videns meliora, deteriora secutus*, when he says: "The officers next in rank to the Sultan are *Mantree*,

Mangălor next September. . . ."—*Correa*, iv. 701.

1648.—This place is called **Mangerol** by *Van Twist*, p. 13.

1727.—"The next maritime town is **Mangaroul.** It admits of Trade, and affords coarse Callicoes, white and died, Wheat, Pulse, and Butter for export."—*A. Hamilton*, i. 136, [ed. 1744].

c. **Manglavar** in Swat.

c. 630.—"Le royaume de Ou-tchang-na (Oudyâna) a environ 5000 *li* de tour . . . on compte 4 ou 5 villes fortifiées. La plus-part des rois de ce pays ont pris pour capitale la ville de **Moung-kie-li** (Moungali). . . . La population est fort nombreuse."—*Hwen T'sang*, in *Pèl. Bouddh.* ii. 131-2.

1858.—"Mongkieli se retrouve dans **Manglavor** (in Sanskrit Mañgala-poura) . . . ville située près de la rive gauche de la rivière de Svat, et qui a été longtemps, au rapport des indigènes, la capitale du pays." —*Vivien de St. Martin, Ibid.* iii. 314-315.

MANGELIN, s. A small weight, corresponding in a general way to a **carat** (q.v.), used in the S. of India and in Ceylon for weighing precious stones. The word is Telegu *manjāli*; in Tamil *manjādi*, [from Skt. *manju*, 'beautiful']; the seed of the *Adenanthera pavonina* (Compare **RUTTEE**). On the origin of this weight see Sir W. Elliot's *Coins of S. India*. The *manjādi* seed was used as a measure of weight from very early times. A parcel of 50 taken at random gave an average weight of 4·13 grs. Three parcels of 10 each, selected by eye as large, gave average 5·02 and 5·03 (*op. cit.* p. 47).

1516.—Diamonds ". . . sell by a weight which is called a **Mangiar**, which is equal to 2 *tare* and ⅔, and 2 *tare* make a carat of good weight, and 4 *tare* weigh one fanam." —*Barbosa*, in *Ramusio*, i. f. 321*v*.

1554.—(In Ceylon) "A *calamja* contains 20 **mamgelins**, each **mamgelim** 8 grains of rice; a Portugues of gold weighs 8 calamjas and 2 **mangelins**."—*A. Nunez*, 35.

1584.—"There is another sort of weight called **Mangiallino**, which is 5 graines of Venice weight, and therewith they weigh diamants and other jewels."—*Barret*, in *Hakl.* ii. 409.

1611.—"Quem não sabe a grandeza das minas de finissimos diamantes do Reyno de Bisnaga, donde cada dia, e cada hora se tiram peças de tamanho de hum ovo, e muitas de sessenta e oitenta **mangelins**."—*Couto, Dialogo do Soldato Pratico*, 154.

1665.—"Le poids principal des Diamans est le **mangelin**; il pèse cinq grains et trois cinquièmes."—*Thevenot*, v. 293.

1676.—"At the mine of *Raolconda* they weigh by **Mangelins**, a **Mangelin** being one *Carat* and three quarters, that is 7 grains. . . . At the Mine of Soumelpore in Bengal they weigh by *Rati's* (see **RUTTEE**), and the *Rati* is ⅞ of a *Carat*, or 3½ grains. In the Kingdoms of *Golconda* and *Visapour*, they make use of **Mangelins**, but a **Mangelin** in those parts is not above 1 carat and ⅜. The *Portugals* in *Goa* make use of the same Weights in *Goa*; but a **Mangelin** there is not above 5 grains."—*Tavernier*, E.T. ii. 141; [ed. *Ball*, ii. 87, and see ii. 433.]

MANGO, s. The royal fruit of the *Mangifera indica*, when of good quality is one of the richest and best fruits in the world. The original of the word is Tamil *mān-kāy* or *mān-gāy*, *i.e.* *mān* fruit (the tree being *māmarum*, '*mān*-tree'). The Portuguese formed from this *manga*, which we have adopted as *mango*. The tree is wild in the forests of various parts of India; but the fruit of the wild tree is uneatable.

The word has sometimes been supposed to be Malay; but it was in fact introduced into the Archipelago, along with the fruit itself, from S. India. Rumphius (*Herb. Amboyn.* i. 95) traces its then recent introduction into the islands, and says that it is called (*Malaicè*) "*mangka*, vel vulgo *Manga* et *Mapelaam*." This last word is only the Tamil *Māpaḷam*, *i.e.* '*mān* fruit' again. The close approximation of the Malay *mangka* to the Portuguese form might suggest that the latter name was derived from Malacca. But we see *manga* already used by Varthema, who, according to Garcia, never really went beyond Malabar. [Mr. Skeat writes: "The modern standard Malay word is *mangga*, from which the Port. form was probably taken. The other Malay form quoted from Rumphius is in standard Malay *mapĕlam*, with *mĕpĕlam*, *hĕmpĕlam*, *ampĕlam*, and *'pĕlam* or *'plam* as variants. The Javanese is *pĕlĕm*."]

The word has been taken to Madagascar, apparently by the Malayan colonists, whose language has left so large an impression there, in the precise shape *mangka*. Had the fruit been an Arab importation it is improbable that the name would have been introduced in that form.

The N. Indian names are *Ām* and *Amba*, and variations of these we find in several of the older European writers. Thus Fr. Jordanus, who had been in the Konkan, and appreciated the progenitors of the Goa and

Bombay Mango (c. 1328), calls the fruit *Aniba*. Some 30 years later John de' Marignolli calls the tree "*amburan*, having a fruit of excellent fragrance and flavour, somewhat like a peach" (*Cathay*, &c., ii. 362). Garcia de Orta shows how early the Bombay fruit was prized. He seems to have been the owner of the parent tree. The Skt. name is *Amra*, and this we find in Hwen T'sang (c. 645) phoneticised as *'An-mo-lo.*

The mango is probably the fruit alluded to by Theophrastus as having caused dysentery in the army of Alexander. (See the passage s.v. **JACK**).

c. 1328.—"Est etiam alia arbor quae fructus facit ad modum pruni, grosissimos, qui vocantur *Aniba*. Hi sunt fructus ita dulces et amabiles, quod ore tenus exprimi hoc minimè possit."—*Fr. Jordanus*, in *Rec. de Voyages*, &c., iv. 42.

c. 1334.—"The mango tree (*'anba*) resembles an orange-tree, but is larger and more leafy; no other tree gives so much shade, but this shade is unwholesome, and whoever sleeps under it gets fever."—*Ibn Batuta*, iii. 125. At ii. 185 he writes *'anbā*. [The same charge is made against the tamarind; see *Burton, Ar. Nights*, iii. 81.]

c. 1349.—"They have also another tree called *Amburan*, having a fruit of excellent fragrance and flavour, somewhat like a peach."—*John de' Marignolli*, in *Cathay*, &c., 362.

1510.—"Another fruit is also found here, which is called *Amba*, the stem of which is called **Manga**," &c.—*Varthema*, 160-161.

c. 1526.—"Of the vegetable productions peculiar to Hindustân one is the mango (*ambeh*). . . . Such mangoes as are good are excellent. . . ." &c.—*Baber*, 324.

1563.—"*O*. Boy! go and see what two vessels those are coming in—you see them from the varanda here—and they seem but small ones.

"*Servant*. I will bring you word presently.

* * * * *

"*S*. Sir! it is Simon Toscano, your tenant in Bombay, and he brings this hamper of **mangas** for you to make a present to the Governor, and says that when he has moored the boat he will come here to stop.

"*O*. He couldn't have come more à propos. I have a **manga**-tree (*mangueira*) in that island of mine which is remarkable for both its two crops, one at this time of year, the other at the end of May, and much as the other crop excels this in quality for fragrance and flavour, this is just as remarkable for coming out of season. But come, let us taste them before His Excellency. Boy! take out six **mangas**."—*Garcia*, ff. 134*v*, 135. This author also mentions that the **mangas** of Ormuz were the most celebrated; also certain **mangas** of Guzerat, not large, but of surpassing fragrance and flavour, and having a very small stone. Those of Balaghat were both excellent and big; the Doctor had seen two that weighed 4 *arratel* and a half (4½ lbs.); and those of Bengal, Pegu, and Malacca were also good.

[1569.—"There is much fruit that comes from Arabia and Persia, which they call mangoes (**mangas**), which is very good fruit."—*Cronica dos Reys Dormuz*, translated from the Arabic in 1569.]

c. 1590.—"The Mangoe (*Anba*). . . . This fruit is unrivalled in colour, smell, and taste; and some of the *gourmands* of Túrán and Irán place it above musk melons and grapes. . . . If a half-ripe mango, together with its stalk to a length of about two fingers, be taken from the tree, and the broken end of its stalk be closed with warm wax, and kept in butter or honey, the fruit will retain its taste for two or three months."—*Āīn*, ed. *Blochmann*, i. 67-68.

[1614.—"Two jars of **Manges** at rupees 4½."—*Foster, Letters*, iii. 41.

[1615.—"George Durois sent in a present of two pottes of **Mangeas**."—*Cocks's Diary*, Hak. Soc. i. 79.]

" "There is another very licquorish fruit called **Amangues** growing on trees, and it is as bigge as a great quince, with a very great stone in it."—*De Monfart*, 20.

1622.—P. della Valle describes the tree and fruit at Miná (*Minao*) near Hormuz, under the name of *Amba*, as an exotic introduced from India. Afterwards at Goa he speaks of it as "**manga** or *amba*."—ii. pp. 313-14, and 581; [Hak. Soc. i. 40].

1631.—"Alibi vero commemorat **mangae** speciem fortis admodum odoris, Terebinthinam scilicet, et Piceae arboris lacrymam redolentes, quas propterea nostri *stinkers* appellant."—*Piso* on *Bontius, Hist. Nat.* p. 95.

[1663.—"*Ambas*, or **Mangues**, are in season during two months in summer, and are plentiful and cheap; but those grown at Delhi are indifferent. The best come from *Bengale*, Golkonda, and Goa, and these are indeed excellent. I do not know any sweet-meat more agreeable."—*Bernier*, ed. *Constable*, 249.]

1673.—Of the Goa **Mango**,* Fryer says justly: "When ripe, the Apples of the *Hesperides* are but Fables to them; for Taste, the Nectarine, Peach, and Apricot fall short. . . ."—p. 182.

1679.—"**Mango** and **saio** (see **SOY**), two sorts of sauces brought from the East Indies."—*Locke's Journal*, in *Ld. King's Life*, 1830, i. 249.

* The excellence of the Goa Mangoes is stated to be due to the care and skill of the Jesuits (*Annaes Maritimos*, ii. 270). In S. India all good kinds have Portuguese or Mahommedan names. The author of *Tribes on My Frontier*, 1883, p. 148, mentions the luscious *peirie* and the delicate *afoos* as two fine varieties, supposed to bear the names of a certain *Peres* and a certain *Affonso*.

1727.—"The *Goa* **mango** is reckoned the largest and most delicious to the taste of any in the world, and I may add, the wholesomest and best tasted of any Fruit in the World."—*A. Hamilton*, i. 255, [ed. 1744, i. 258].

1883.—". . . the unsophisticated ryot . . . conceives that cultivation could only emasculate the pronounced flavour and firm fibrous texture of that prince of fruits, the wild **mango**, likest a ball of tow soaked in turpentine."—*Tribes on My Frontier*, 149.

The name has been carried with the fruit to Mauritius and the West Indies. Among many greater services to India the late Sir Proby Cautley diffused largely in Upper India the delicious fruit of the Bombay mango, previously rare there, by creating and encouraging groves of grafts on the banks of the Ganges and Jumna canals. It is especially true of this fruit (as Sultan Baber indicates) that excellence depends on the variety. The common mango is coarse and strong of turpentine. Of this only an evanescent suggestion remains to give peculiarity to the finer varieties. [A useful account of these varieties, by Mr. Maries, will be found in *Watt, Econ. Dict.* v. 148 *seqq.*]

MANGO-BIRD, s. The popular Anglo-Indian name of the beautiful golden oriole (*Oriolus aureus*, Jerdon). Its "loud mellow whistle" from the mango-groves and other gardens, which it affects, is associated in Upper India with the invasion of the hot weather.

1878.—"The **mango-bird** glances through the groves, and in the early morning announces his beautiful but unwelcome presence with his merle melody."—*Ph. Robinson, In My Indian Garden*, 59.

MANGO-FISH, s. The familiar name of an excellent fish (*Polynemus Visua* of Buchanan, *P. paradiseus* of Day), in flavour somewhat resembling the smelt, but, according to Dr. Mason, nearly related to the mullets. It appears in the Calcutta market early in the hot season, and is much prized, especially when in roe. The Hindustani name is *tapsī* or *tapassī*, 'an ascetic,' or 'penitent,' but we do not know the *rationale* of the name. Buchanan says that it is owing to the long fibres (or free rays), proceeding from near the head, which lead the natives to associate it with penitents who are forbidden to shave. [Dr. Grierson writes: "What the connection of the fish with a hermit was I never could ascertain, unless it was that like wandering Fakīrs, they disappear directly the rains begin. Compare the *uposatha* of the Buddhists." But *tapasya* means '-produced by heat,' and is applied to the month Phāgun (Feb.-March) when the fish appears; and this may be the origin of the name.]

1781.—"The BOARD OF TRUSTIES Assemble on Tuesday at the New Tavern, where the Committee meet to eat **Mangoe Fish** for the benefit of the Subscribers and on other special affairs."—*Hickey's Bengal Gazette*, March 3.

[1820.—". . . the **mangoe fish** (so named from its appearing during the mangoe season). . . . By the natives they are named the *Tapaswi* (penitent) fish, (abbreviated by Europeans to *Tipsy*) from their resembling a class of religious penitents, who ought never to shave."—*Hamilton, Des. of Hindostan*, i. 58.]

MANGO-SHOWERS, s. Used in Madras for showers which fall in March and April, when the mangoes begin to ripen.

MANGO-TRICK. One of the most famous tricks of Indian jugglers, in which they plant a mango-stone, and show at brief intervals the tree shooting above ground, and successively producing leaves, flowers, and fruit. It has often been described, but the description given by the Emperor Jahāngīr in his *Autobiography* certainly surpasses all in its demand on our belief.

c. 1610.—". . . Khaun-e-Jehaun, one of the nobles present, observed that if they spoke truly he should wish them to produce for his conviction a mulberry-tree. The men arose without hesitation, and having in ten separate spots set some seed in the ground, they recited among themselves . . . when instantly a plant was seen springing from each of the ten places, and each proved the tree required by Khaun-e-Jehaun. In the same manner they produced a mango, an apple-tree, a cypress, a pine-apple, a fig-tree, an almond, a walnut . . . open to the observation of all present, the trees were perceived gradually and slowly springing from the earth, to the height of one or perhaps of two cubits. . . . Then making a sort of procession round the trees as they stood . . . in a moment there appeared on the respective trees a sweet mango without the rind, an almond fresh and ripe, a large fig of the most delicious kind . . . the fruit being pulled in my presence, and every one present was allowed to taste it. This, however, was not all; before the trees were removed there appeared among the foliage birds of such surpassing beauty, in colour and shape, and melody and song, as the world never saw before. . . . At the close of the operation, the foliage, as in autumn, was seen to put on its variegated tints, and the trees gradually disappeared into the earth. . . ."—*Mem. of the Emp. Jehanguier*, tr. by *Major D. Price*, pp. 96-97.

c. 1650.—"Then they thrust a piece of stick into the ground, and ask'd the Company what Fruit they would have. One told them he would have *Mengues;* then one of the Mountebanks hiding himself in the middle of a Sheet, stoopt to the ground five or six times one after another. I was so curious to go upstairs, and look out of a window, to see if I could spy what the Mountebank did, and perceived that after he had cut himself under the armpits with a Razor, he rubb'd the stick with his Blood. After the two first times that he rais'd himself, the stick seemed to the very eye to grow. The third time there sprung out branches with young buds. The fourth time the tree was covered with leaves; and the fifth time it bore flowers. . . . The English Minister protested that he could not give his consent that any Christian should be Spectator of such delusions. So that as soon as he saw that these Mountebanks had of a dry stick, in less than half-an-hour, made a Tree four or five foot high, that bare leaves and flowers as in the Spring-time: he went about to break it, protesting that he would not give the Communion to any person that should stay any longer to see those things."—*Tavernier, Travels made English*, by J.P., ii. 36; [ed. *Ball*, i. 67, *seq.*].

1667.—"When two of these *Jauguis* (see **JOGEE**) that are eminent, do meet, and you stir them up on the point and power of their knowledge or *Jauguisme*, you shall see them do such tricks out of spight to one another, that I know not if *Simon Magus* could have outdone them. For they divine what one thinketh, make the Branch of a Tree blossome and bear fruit in less than an hour, hatch eggs in their bosome in less than half a quarter of an hour, and bring forth such birds as you demand: . . . *I mean, if what is said of them is true*. . . . For, as for me, I am with all my curiosity none of those happy Men, that are present at, and see these great feats."—*Bernier*, E.T. 103; [ed. *Constable*, 321].

1673.—"Others presented a Mock-Creation of a Mango-Tree, arising from the Stone in a short space (which they did in Hugger-Mugger, being very careful to avoid being discovered) with Fruit Green and Ripe; so that a Man must stretch his Fancy, to imagine it Witchcraft; though the common Sort think no less."—*Fryer*, 192.

1690.—"Others are said to raise a Mango-Tree, with ripe Fruit upon its Branches, in the space of one or two Hours. To confirm which Relation, it was affirmed confidently to me, that a Gentleman who had pluckt one of these Mangoes, fell sick upon it, and was never well as long as he kept it 'till he consulted a *Bramin* for his Health, who prescrib'd his only Remedy would be the restoring of the Mango, by which he was restor'd to his Health again."—*Ovington*, 258-259.

1726.—"They have some also who will show you the kernel of a mango-fruit, or may be only a twig, and ask if you will see the fruit or this stick planted, and in a short time see a tree grow from it and bear fruit: after they have got their answer the jugglers (*Koorde-danssers*) wrap themselves in a blanket, stick the twig into the ground, and then put a basket over them (&c. &c.).

"There are some who have prevailed on these jugglers by much money to let them see how they have accomplished this.

"These have revealed that the jugglers made a hole in their bodies under the armpits, and rubbed the twig with the blood from it, and every time that they stuck it in the ground they wetted it, and in this way they clearly saw it to grow and to come to the perfection before described.

"This is asserted by a certain writer who has seen it. But this can't move me to believe it!"—*Valentijn*, v. (*Chorom.*) 53.

Our own experience does not go beyond Dr. Fryer's, and the hugger-mugger performance that he disparages. But many others have testified to more remarkable skill. We once heard a traveller of note relate with much spirit such an exhibition as witnessed in the Deccan. The narrator, then a young officer, determined with a comrade, at all hazards of fair play or foul, to solve the mystery. In the middle of the trick one suddenly seized the conjuror, whilst the other uncovered and snatched at the mango-plant. But lo! it came from the earth *with a root*, and the mystery was darker than ever! We tell the tale as it was told.

It would seem that the trick was not unknown in European conjuring of the 16th or 17th centuries, *e.g.*

1657.—". . . trium horarum spatio arbusculam veram spitamae longitudine e mensâ facere enasci, ut et alias arbores frondiferas et fructiferas."—*Magia Universalis*, of *P. Gaspar Schottus e Soc. Jes.*, Herbipoli, 1657, i. 32.

MANGOSTEEN, s. From Malay *manggusta* (Crawfurd), or *manggistan* (Favre), in Javanese *Manggis*. [Mr. Skeat writes: "The modern standard Malay form used in the W. coast of the Peninsula is *manggis*, as in Javanese, the forms *manggusta* and *manggistan* never being heard there. The Siamese form *maangkhut* given in M'Farland's *Siamese Grammar* is probably from the Malay *manggusta*. It was very interesting to me to find that some distinct trace of this word was still preserved in the name of this fruit at Patani-Kelantan on the E. coast, where it was called *bawah 'seta* (or *'setar*), *i.e.* the '*setar* fruit,' as well as occasionally *mestar* or *mesetar*, clearly a corruption of some such old form as *manggistar*."] This delicious fruit is known throughout the Archipelago, and in Siam, by modifications of the same name; the delicious fruit of the *Garcinia Mangostana* (Nat. Ord. *Guttiferae*). It is strictly a tropical fruit, and, in fact, near the coast does not bear fruit further north than lat. 14°. It is a native of the Malay Peninsula and the adjoining islands.

1563.—"*R.* They have bragged much to me of a fruit which they call **mangostans**; let us hear what you have to say of these.

"*O.* What I have heard of the **mangostan** is that 'tis one of the most delicious fruits that they have in these regions. . . ."—*Garcia*, f. 151*v*.

1598.—"There are yet other fruites, as . . . **Mangostaine** [in Hak. Soc. **Mangestains**] . . . . but because they are of small account I thinke it not requisite to write severallie of them."—*Linschoten*, 96; [Hak. Soc. ii. 34].

1631.—

"Cedant Hesperii longe hinc, mala aurea, fructus,
Ambrosiâ pascit **Mangostan** et nectare divos——
. . . Inter omnes Indiae fructus longe sapidissimus."
Jac. Bontii, lib. vi. cap. 28, p. 115.

1645.—"Il s'y trouue de plus vne espece de fruit propre du terroir de Malaque, qu'ils nomment **Mangostans**."—*Cardim, Rel. de la Prov. de Japon*, 162.

[1662.—"The **Mangosthan** is a Fruit growing by the Highwayes in *Java*, upon bushes, like our Sloes."—*Mandelslo*, tr. *Davies*, Bk. ii. 121 (*Stanf. Dict.*).]

1727.—"The **Mangostane** is a delicious Fruit, almost in the Shape of an Apple, the Skin is thick and red, being dried it is a good Astringent. The Kernels (if I may so call them) are like Cloves of Garlick, of a very agreeable Taste, but very cold."—*A. Hamilton*, ii. 80 [ed. 1744].

MANGROVE, s. The sea-loving genera *Rhizophora* and *Avicennia* derive this name, which applies to both, from some happy accident, but from which of two sources may be doubtful. For while the former genus is, according to Crawfurd, called by the Malays *mànggi-manggi*, a term which he supposes to be the origin of the English name, we see from Oviedo that one or other was called *mangle* in S. America, and in this, which is certainly the origin of the French *manglier*, we should be disposed also to seek the derivation of the English word. Both genera are universal in the tropical tidal estuaries of both Old World and New. Prof. Sayce, by an amusing slip, or oversight probably of somebody else's slip, quotes from Humboldt that "maize, *mangle*, hammock, canoe, tobacco, are all derived through the medium of the Spanish from the Haytian *mahiz*, mangle, *hamaca*, *canoa*, and *tabaco*." It is, of course, the French and not the English *mangle* that is here in question. [Mr. Skeat observes: "I believe the old English as well as French form was *mangle*, in which case Prof. Sayce would be perfectly right. Mangrove is probably *mangle-grove*. The Malay *manggi-manggi* is given by Klinkert, and is certainly on account of the reduplication, native. But I never heard it in the Peninsula, where *mangrove* is always called *bakau*."] The mangrove abounds on nearly all the coasts of further India, and also on the sea margin of the Ganges Delta, in the backwaters of S. Malabar, and less luxuriantly on the Indus mouths.

1535.—"Of the Tree called **Mangle**. . . . These trees grow in places of mire, and on the shores of the sea, and of the rivers, and streams, and torrents that run into the sea. They are trees very strange to see . . . they grow together in vast numbers, and many of their branches seem to turn down and change into roots . . . and these plant themselves in the ground like stems, so that the tree looks as if it had many legs joining one to the other."—*Oviedo*, in *Ramusio*, iii. f. 145*v*.

,, "So coming to the coast, embarked in a great Canoa with some 30 Indians, and 5 Christians, whom he took with him, and coasted along amid solitary places and islets, passing sometimes into the sea itself for 4 or 5 leagues,—among certain trees, lofty, dense and green, which grow in the very sea-water, and which they call **mangle**."—*Ibid.* f. 224.

1553.—". . . . by advice of a Moorish pilot, who promised to take the people by night to a place where water could be got . . . and either because the Moor desired to land many times on the shore by which he was conducting them, seeking to get away from the hands of those whom he was conducting, or because he was really perplext by its being night, and in the middle of a great growth of *mangrove* (**mangues**) he never succeeded in finding the wells of which he spoke."—*Barros*, I. iv. 4.

c. 1830.—"'Smite my timbers, do the trees bear shellfish?' The tide in the Gulf of Mexico does not ebb and flow above two feet except in the springs, and the ends of the drooping branches of the **mangrove** trees that here cover the shore, are clustered, within the wash of the water, with a small well-flavoured oyster."—*Tom Cringle*, ed. 1863, 119.

MANILLA-MAN, s. This term is applied to natives of the Philippines, who are often employed on shipboard, and especially furnish the quarter-masters (**Seacunny**, q.v.) in Lascar crews on the China voyage. But *Manilla-man* seems also, from Wilson, to be used in S. India as a hybrid from Telug. *manelā vādu*, 'an itinerant dealer in coral and gems'; perhaps in this sense, as he says, from Skt. *maṇi*, 'a jewel,' but with some blending also of the Port. *manilha*, 'a bracelet.' (Compare **COBRA-MANILLA**.)

MANJEE, s. The master, or steersman, of a boat or any native river-craft; Hind. *mānjhī*, Beng. *mājī* and *mājhī*, [all from Skt. *madhya*, 'one who stands in the middle']. The word is also a title borne by the head men among the Pahāris or Hill-people of Rājmahal (*Wilson*), [and as equivalent for *Majhwār*, the name of an important Dravidian tribe on the borders of the N.W. Provinces and Chota Nāgpur].

1683.—"We were forced to track our boat till 4 in the Afternoon, when we saw a great black cloud arise out of ye North with much lightning and thunder, which made our **Mangee** or Steerman advise us to fasten our boat in some Creeke."—*Hedges, Diary*, Hak. Soc. i. 88.

[1706.—"**Manjee.**" See under **HARRY**.]

1781.—"This is to give notice that the principal Gaut **Mangies** of Calcutta have entered into engagements at the Police Office to supply all Persons that apply there with Boats and *Budgerows*, and to give security for the *Dandies*."—*India Gazette*, Feb. 17.

1784.—"Mr. Austin and his head bearer, who were both in the room of the budgerow, are the only persons known to be drowned. The **manjee** and dandees have not appeared."—In *Seton-Karr*, i. 25.

1810.—"Their **manjies** will not fail to take every advantage of whatever distress, or difficulty, the passenger may labour under."—*Williamson, V. M.* i. 148.

For the Pahari use, see *Long's Selections*, p. 561.

[1864.—"The Khond chiefs of villages and Mootas are termed **Maji** instead of Mulliko as in Goomsur, or Khonro as in Boad. . . ."—*Campbell, Wild Tribes of Khondistan*, 120.]

MANNICKJORE, s. Hind. *mānik-jor*; the white-necked stork (*Ciconia leucocephala*, Gmelin); sometimes, according to Jerdon, called in Bengal the 'Beef-steak bird,' because palatable when cooked in that fashion. "The name of *Manikjor* means the companion of Manik, a Saint, and some Mussulmans in consequence abstain from eating it" (*Jerdon*). [Platts derives it from *mānik*, 'a ruby.']

[1840.—"I reached the jheel, and found it to contain many **manickchors**, ibis, paddy birds, &c. . . ."—*Davidson, Travels in Upper India*, ii. 165.]

MANUCODIATA. (See **BIRD OF PARADISE**.)

MARAMUT, MURRUMUT, s. Hind. from Ar. *maramma(t)*, 'repair.' In this sense the use is general in Hindustani (in which the terminal *t* is always pronounced, though not by the Arabs), whether as applied to a stocking, a fortress, or a ship. But in Madras Presidency the word had formerly a very specialised sense as the recognised title of that branch of the Executive which included the conservation of irrigation tanks and the like, and which was worked under the District Civil Officers, there being then no separate department of the State in charge of Civil Public Works. It is a curious illustration of the wide spread at one time of Musulman power that the same Arabic word, in the form **Marama**, is still applied in Sicily to a standing committee charged with repairs to the Duomo or Cathedral of Palermo. An analogous instance of the wide grasp of the Saracenic power is mentioned by one of the Musulman authors whom Amari quotes in his History of the Mahommedan rule in Sicily. It is that the Caliph Al-Māmūn, under whom conquest was advancing in India and in Sicily simultaneously, ordered that the idols taken from the infidels in India should be sent for sale to the infidels in Sicily!

[1757.—"On the 6th the Major (Eyre Coote) left *Muxadabad* with . . . 10 **Marmutty** men, or pioneers to clear the road."—*Ives*, 156.

[1873.—"For the actual execution of works there was a **Maramat** Department constituted under the Collector."—*Boswell, Man. of Nellore*, 642.]

MARGOSA, s. A name in the S. of India and Ceylon for the *Nīm* (see **NEEM**) tree. The word is a corruption of Port. *amargosa*, 'bitter,' indicating the character of the tree. This gives rise to an old Indian proverb, traceable as far back as the *Jātakas*, that you cannot sweeten the *nīm* tree though you water it with syrup and ghee (*Naturam expellas furcâ*, &c.).

1727.—"The wealth of an evil man shall another evil man take from him, just as the crows come and eat the fruit of the **margoise** tree as soon as it is ripe."—Apophthegms translated in *Valentijn*, v. (Ceylon) 390.

1782.—". . . ils lavent le malade avec de l'eau froide, ensuite ils le frottent rudement avec de la feuille de **Margosier**."—*Sonnerat*, i. 208.

1834.—"Adjacent to the Church stand a number of tamarind and **margosa** trees."—*Chitty, Ceylon Gazetteer*, 183.

MARKHORE, s. Pers. *mār-khōr*, 'snake-eater.' A fine wild goat of the Western Himālaya; *Capra megaceros*, Hutton.

[1851.—"Hence the people of the country call it the **Markhor** (eater of serpents)."—*Edwardes, A Year on the Punjab Frontier*, i. 474.

[1895.—"Never more would he chase the ibex and **makor**."—*Mrs. Croker, Village Tales*, 112.]

MARTABAN, n.p. This is the conventional name, long used by all the trading nations, Asiatic and European, for a port on the east of the Irawadi Delta and of the Sitang estuary, formerly of great trade, but now in comparative decay. The original name is Talaing, *Mūt-ta-man*, the meaning of which we have been unable to ascertain.

1514.—". . . passed then before **Martaman**, the people also heathens; men expert in everything, and first-rate merchants; great masters of accounts, and in fact the greatest in the world. They keep their accounts in books like us. In the said country is great produce of lac, cloths, and provisions."—*Letter of Giov. da Empoli*, p. 80.

1545.—"At the end of these two days the King . . . caused the Captains that were at the Guard of the Gates to leave them and retire; whereupon the miserable City of **Martabano** was delivered to the mercy of the Souldiers . . . and therein showed themselves so cruel-minded, that the thing they made least reckoning of was to kill 100 men for a crown."—*Pinto*, in *Cogan*, 203.

1553. — "And the towns which stand outside this gulf of the Isles of Pegu (of which we have spoken) and are placed along the coast of that country, are Vagara, **Martaban**, a city notable in the great trade that it enjoys, and further on Rey, Talaga, and Tavay."—*Barros*, I. ix. 1.

1568.—"Trouassimo nella città di **Martauan** intorno a nouanta Portoghesi, tra mercadanti e huomini vagabondi, li quali stauano in gran differenza co' Rettori della città."—*Ces. Federici*, in *Ramusio*, iii. 393.

1586.—"The city of **Martaban** hath its front to the south-east, south, and south-west, and stands on a river which there enters the sea . . . it is a city of Mauparagia, a Prince of the King of Pegu's."—*Gasparo Balbi*, f. 129*v*, 130*v*.

1680. — "That the English may settle ffactorys at Serian, Pegu, and Ava . . . and alsoe that they may settle a ffactory in like manner at **Mortavan**. . . ."—*Articles to be proposed to the King of Barma and Pegu* in *Notes and Exts.*, No. iii. p. 8.

1695.—"Concerning *Bartholomew Rodrigues*. . . . I am informed and do believe he put into **Mortavan** for want of *wood* and *water*, and was there seized by the *King's officers*, because not bound to that Place."—*Governor Higginson*, in *Dalrymple, Or. Repert.* ii. 342-3.

MARTABAN, s. This name was given to vessels of a peculiar pottery, of very large size, and glazed, which were famous all over the East for many centuries, and were exported from Martaban. They were sometimes called *Pegu jars*, and under that name specimens were shown at the Great Exhibition of 1851. We have not been able to obtain recent information on the subject of this manufacture. The word appears to be now obsolete in India, except as a colloquial term in Telegu. [The word is certainly not obsolete in Upper India: "The *martaban'* (Plate ii. fig. 10) is a small deep jar with an elongated body, which is used by Hindus and Muhammadans to keep pickles and acid articles" (*Hallifax, Mono. of Punjab Pottery*, p. 9). In the endeavour to supply a Hindi derivation it has been derived from *imrita-bān*, 'the holder of the water of immortality.' In the *Arabian Nights* the word appears in the form *bartaman*, and is used for a crock in which gold is buried. (*Burton*, xi. 26). Mr. Bell saw some large earthenware jars at Malé, some about 2 feet high, called *rumba;* others larger and barrel-shaped, called **mātabān**. (*Pyrard*, Hak. Soc. i. 259.) For the modern manufacture, see *Scott*, *Gazetteer of Upper Burma*, 1900, Pt. i. vol. ii. 399 *seq.*]

c. 1350.—"Then the Princess made me a present consisting of dresses, of two elephant-loads of rice, of two she-buffaloes, ten sheep, four *rotls* of cordial syrup, and four **Martabāns**, or huge jars, filled with pepper, citron, and mango, all prepared with salt, as for a sea-voyage." — *Ibn Batuta*, iv. 253.

(?).—"Un grand bassin de **Martabani**."—1001 *Jours*, ed. Paris 1826, ii. 19. We do not know the date of these stories. The French translator has a note explaining "porcelaine verte."

1508. — "The lac (*làcre*) which your Highness desired me to send, it will be a piece of good lùck to get, because these ships depart early, and the vessels from Pegu and **Martaban** come late. But I hope for a good quantity of it, as I have given orders for it."—*Letter* from the Viceroy *Dom Francisco Almeida* to the King. In *Correa*, i. 900.

1516.—"In this town of **Martaban** are made very large and beautiful porcelain vases, and some of glazed earthenware of a black colour, which are highly valued among the Moors, and they export them as merchandize."—*Barbosa*, 185.

1598.—"In this towne many of the great earthen pots are made, which in India are called **Martauanas**, and many of them carryed throughout all India, of all sortes both small and great; some are so great that they will hold full two pipes of water. The cause why so many are brought into India is for that they vse them in every house, and in their shippes insteede of caskes."—*Linschoten*, p. 30; [Hak. Soc. i. 101; see also i. 28, 268].

c. 1610.—". . . des iarres les plus belles, les mieux vernis et les mieux façonnées que j'aye veu ailleurs. Il y en a qui tiennent autant qu'vne pippe et plus. Elles se font au Royaume de **Martabane**, d'ou on les apporte, et d'où elles prennent leur nom par toute l'Inde."—*Pyrard de Laval*, i. 179; [Hak. Soc. i. 259].

1615.—"Vasa figulina quae vulgo **Martabania** dicuntur per Indiam nota sunt. . . . Per Orientem omnem, quin et Lusitaniam, horum est usus." — *Jarric, Thesaurus Rer. Indic.* pt. ii. 389.

1673.—"Je vis un vase d'une certaine terre verte qui vient des Indes, dont les Turcs . . . font un grand estime, et qu'ils acheptent bien cher à cause de la propriété qu'elle a de se rompre à la présence du poison. . . . Ceste terre se nomme **Merdebani**."—*Journal d'Ant. Galland*. ii. 110.

1673.—". . . to that end offer Rice, Oyl, and Cocoe-Nuts in a thick Grove, where they piled an huge Heap of long Jars like **Mortivans**."—*Fryer*, 180.

1688.—"They took it out of the cask, and put it into earthen Jars that held about eight Barrels apiece. These they call **Montaban** Jars, from a town of that name in Pegu, whence they are brought, and carried all over India."—*Dampier*, ii. 98.

c. 1690.—"Sunt autem haec vastissimae ac turgidae ollae in regionibus **Martavana** et Siama confectae, quae per totam transferuntur Indiam ad varios liquores conservandos."—*Rumphius*, i. ch. iii.

1711.—". . . *Pegu, Quedah, Jahore* and all their own Coasts, whence they are plentifully supply'd with several Necessarys, they otherwise must want; As Ivory, Beeswax, **Mortivan** and small Jars, Pepper, &c."—*Lockyer*, 35.

1726.—". . . and the **Martavaans** containing the water to drink, when empty require two persons to carry them." — *Valentijn*, v. 254.

" "The goods exported hitherward (from Pegu) are . . . glazed pots (called **Martavans** after the district where they properly belong), both large and little."—*Ibid.* v. 128.

1727.—"**Martavan** was one of the most flourishing Towns for Trade in the East. . . . They make earthen Ware there still, and glaze them with Lead-oar. I have seen some Jars made there that could contain two Hogsheads of Liquor."—*A. Hamilton*, i. 63, [ed. 1744, ii. 62].

1740. — "The Pay Master is likewise ordered . . . to look out for all the **Pegu Jars** in Town, or other vessels proper for keeping water."—In *Wheeler*, iii. 194.

Such jars were apparently imitated in other countries, but kept the original name. Thus Baillie Fraser says that "certain jars called **Martaban** were manufactured in Oman."—*Journey into Khorasan*, 18.

1851.—"Assortment of **Pegu Jars** as used in the Honourable Company's Dispensary at Calcutta."

"Two large **Pegu Jars** from Moulmein." —*Official Catal.* Exhibition of 1851, ii. 921.

MARTIL, MARTOL, s. A hammer. Hind *mārtol*, from Port. *martello*, but assisted by imaginary connection with Hind *mār-nā*, 'to strike.'

MARTINGALE, s. This is no specially Anglo-Indian word; our excuse for introducing it is the belief that it is of Arabic origin. Popular assumption, we believe, derives the name from a mythical Colonel Martingale. But the word seems to come to us from the French, in which language, besides the English use,

Littré gives *chauses à la martingale* as meaning "culottes dont le pont était placé par derriere," and this he strangely declares to be the true and original meaning of the word. His etymology, after Ménage, is from *Martigues* in Provence, where, it is alleged, breeches of this kind were worn. Skeat seems to accept these explanations. [But see his *Concise Dict.*, where he inclines to the view given in this article, and adds: "I find Arab. *rataka* given by Richardson as a verbal root, whence *ratak*, going with a short quick step."] But there is a Span. word *al-martaga*, for a kind of bridle, which Urrea quoted by Dozy derives from verb Arab. *rataka*, "qui, à la IVe forme signifie 'effecit ut brevibus assibus incederet.'" This is precisely the effect of a martingale. And we venture to say that probably the word bore its English meaning originally also in French and Spanish, and came from Arabic direct into the latter tongue. Dozy himself, we should add, is inclined to derive the Span. word from *al-mirta'a*, 'a halter.'

MARWÁREE, n.p. and s. This word *Mārwāṛī*, properly a man of the Mārwār [Skt. *maru*, 'desert'], or Jodhpur country in Rājputāna, is used in many parts of India as synonymous with Banya (see **BANYAN**) or **Sowcar**, from the fact that many of the traders and money-lenders have come originally from Mārwār, most frequently Jains in religion. Compare the Lombard of medieval England, and the *caorsino* of Dante's time.

[1819.—"Miseries seem to follow the footsteps of the **Marwarees**."—*Tr. Lit. Soc. Bo.* i. 297.

[1826—"One of my master's under-shopmen, Sewchund, a **Marwarry**."—*Pandurang Hari*, ed. 1873, i. 233.]

MARYACAR, n.p. According to R. Drummond and a MS. note on the India Library copy of his book R. Catholics in Malabar were so called. *Marya Karar*, or 'Mary's People.' [The word appears to be really *marakkar*, of which two explanations are given. Logan (*Malabar*, i. 332 note) says that *Marakkar* means 'doer or follower of the Law' (*marggam*), and is applied to a foreign religion, like that of Christians and Mohammedans. The *Madras Gloss.* (iii. 474) derives it from Mal. *marakkalam*, 'boat,' and *kar*, a termination showing possession, and defines it as a "titular appellation of the **Moplah** Mahommedans on the S.W. coast."]

MASCABAR, s. This is given by C. P. Brown (MS. notes) as an Indo-Portuguese word for 'the last day of the month,' quoting *Calcutta Review*, viii. 345. He suggests as its etymon Hind. *mās-ke-ba'ad*, 'after a month.' [In N. Indian public offices the *māskabār* is well known as the monthly statement of cases decided during the month. It has been suggested that it represents the Port. *mes-acabar*, 'end of the month'; but according to Platts, it is more probably a corruption of Hind. *māsik-wār* or *mās-kā-wār*.]

MASH, s. Hind. *māsh*, [Skt. *māsha*, 'a bean']; *Phaseolus radiatus*, Roxb. One of the common Hindu pulses. [See **MOONG**.]

MASKEE. This is a term in Chinese "pigeon," meaning 'never mind,' '*n'importe*,' which is constantly in the mouths of Europeans in China. It is supposed that it may be the corruption or ellipsis of a Portuguese expression, but nothing satisfactory has been suggested. [Mr. Skeat writes: "Surely this is simply Port. *mas que*, probably imported direct through Macao, in the sense of 'although, even, in spite of,' like French *malgre*. And this seems to be its meaning in 'pigeon':

"That nightey tim begin chop-chop,
One young man walkee—no can stop.
Maskee snow, **maskee** ice!
He cally flag with chop so nice—
Topside Galow!
'*Excelsior*,' in 'pigeon.'"]

MASULIPATAM, n.p. This coast town of the Madras Presidency is sometimes vulgarly called *Machhlipatan* or *Machhli-bandar*, or simply *Bandar* (see **BUNDER**, 2); and its name explained (Hind. *machhlī*, 'fish') as Fish-town, [the *Madras Gloss.* says from an old tradition of a whale being stranded on the shore.] The etymology may originally have had such a connection, but there can be no doubt that the name is a trace of the Μαισωλία and Μαισώλου ποταμοῦ ἐκβολαί which we find in Ptolemy's

maṇi yakkāran, 'an overseer,' *maniyam*, 'superintendence.'

1707.—"Ego Petrus **Manicaren**, id est *Villarum Inspector*. . . ."—In *Norbert, Mem.* i. 390, note.

1717.—"Towns and villages are governed by inferior Officers . . . **maniakarer** (Mayors or Bailiffs) who hear the complaints."—*Phillips, Account*, &c., 83.

1800.—"In each *Hobly*, for every thousand *Pagodas* (335*l.* 15*s.* 10¼*d.*) rent that he pays, there is also a **Munegar**, or a Tahsildar (see **TAHSEELDAR**) as he is called by the Mussulmans."—*Buchanan's Mysore*, &c., i. 276.

MONKEY-BREAD TREE, s. The Baobab, *Adansonia digitata*, L. "a fantastic-looking tree with immense elephantine stem and small twisted branches, laden in the rains with large white flowers; found all along the coast of Western India, but whether introduced by the Mahommedans from Africa, or by ocean-currents wafting its large light fruit, full of seed, across from shore to shore, is a nice speculation. A sailor once picked up a large seedy fruit in the Indian Ocean off Bombay, and brought it to me. It was very rotten, but I planted the seeds. It turned out to be *Kigelia pinnata* of E. Africa, and propagated so rapidly that in a few years I introduced it all over the Bombay Presidency. The Baobab however is generally found most abundant about the old ports frequented by the early Mahommedan traders" (*Sir G. Birdwood, MS.*) We may add that it occurs sparsely about Allahabad, where it was introduced apparently in the Mogul time; and in the Gangetic valley as far E. as Calcutta, but always *planted*. There are, or were, noble specimens in the Botanic Gardens at Calcutta, and in Mr. Arthur Grote's garden at Alipūr. [See *Watt, Econ. Dict.* i. 105.]

MONSOON, s. The name given to the periodical winds of the Indian seas, and of the seasons which they affect and characterize. The original word is the Ar. *mausim*, 'season,' which the Portuguese corrupted into *monção*, and our people into *monsoon*. Dictionaries (except Dr. Badger's) do not apparently give the Arabic word *mausim* the technical sense of *monsoon*. But there can be no doubt that it had that sense among the Arab pilots from whom the Portuguese adopted the word. This is shown by the quotations from the Turkish Admiral Sidi 'Ali. "The rationale of the term is well put in the *Beirūt Moḥīt*, which says: '*Mausim* is used of anything that comes round but once a year, like the festivals. In Lebanon the *mausim* is the season of working with the silk,'—which is the important season there, as the season of navigation is in Yemen." (*W. R. S.*)

The Spaniards in America would seem to have a word for *season* in analogous use for a recurring wind, as may be gathered from *Tom Cringle*.* The Venetian, Leonardo Ca' Masser (below) calls the monsoons *li tempi*. And the quotation from *Garcia De Orta* shows that in his time the Portuguese sometimes used the word for *season* without any apparent reference to the wind. Though **monção** is general with the Portuguese writers of the 16th century, the historian Diogo de Couto always writes **moução**, and it is possible that the *n* came in, as in some other cases, by a habitual misreading of the written *u* for *n*. Linschoten in Dutch (1596) has **monssoyn** and **monssoen** (p. 8; [Hak. Soc. i. 33]). It thus appears probable that we get our *monsoon* from the Dutch. The latter in modern times seem to have commonly adopted the French form **mousson**. [Prof. Skeat traces our *monsoon* from Ital. *monsone*.] We see below (*Ces. Feder.*) that **Monsoon** was used as synonymous with "the half year," and so it is still in S. India.

1505.—"De qui passano el colfo de Colocut che sono leghe 800 de pacizo (? passeggio): aspettano *li tempi* che sono nel principio dell' Autuno, e con le cole fatte (?) passano."—*Leonardo di Ca' Masser*, 26.

[1512.—". . . because the **mauçam** for both the voyages is at one and the same time."—*Albuquerque, Cartas*, p. 30.]

1553.—". . . and the more, because the voyage from that region of Malaca had to be made by the prevailing wind, which they call **monção**, which was now near its end. If they should lose eight days they would have to wait at least three months for the return of the time to make the voyage."—*Barros*, Dec. II. liv. ii. cap. iv.

* "Don Ricardo began to fret and fidget most awfully—'Beginning of the *seasons*'—why, we may not get away for a week, and all the ships will be kept back in their loading."—Ed. 1863, p. 309.

1554.—"The principal winds are four, according to the Arabs, . . . but the pilots call them by names taken from the rising and setting of certain stars, and assign them certain limits within which they begin or attain their greatest strength, and cease. These winds, limited by space and time, are called **Mausim**."—*The Mohit*, by *Sidi 'Ali Kapudān*, in *J. As. Soc. Beng.* iii. 548.

" "Be it known that the ancient masters of navigation have fixed the time of the **monsoon** (in orig. doubtless *mausim*), that is to say, the time of voyages at sea, according to the year of Yazdajird, and that the pilots of recent times follow their steps. . . ." (*Much detail on the* **monsoons** *follows.*)—*Ibid.*

1563.—"The season (**monção**) for these (*i.e.* mangoes) in the earlier localities we have in April, but in the other later ones in May and June; and sometimes they come as a *rodolho* (as we call it in our own country) in October and November."—*Garcia*, f. 134*v*.

1568.—"Come s'arriua in vna città la prima cosa si piglia vna casa a fitto, ò per mesi ò per anno, seconda che si disegnà di starui, e nel Pegù è costume di pigliarla per **Moson**, cioè per sei mesi."—*Ces. Federici*, in *Ramusio*, iii. 394.

1585-6.—"But the other goods which come by sea have their fixed season, which here they call **Monzão**."—*Sassetti*, in *De Gubernatis*, p. 204.

1599. — "Ora nell anno 1599, essendo venuta la **Mansone** a proposito, si messero alla vela due navi Portoghesi, le quali eran venute dalla città di Goa in Amacao (see **MACAO**)."—*Carletti*, ii. 206.

c. 1610.—"Ces **Monssons** ou **Muessons** sont vents qui changent pour l'Esté ou pour l'Hyver de six mois en six mois."—*Pyrard de Laval*, i. 199; see also ii. 110; [Hak. Soc. i. 280; in i. 257 **Monsons**; in ii. 175, 235, **Muesons**].

[1615.—"I departed for Bantam having the time of the year and the opportunity of the **Monethsone**."—*Foster, Letters*, iii. 268.

[" "The **Monthsone** will else be spent."—*Sir T. Roe*, Hak. Soc. i. 36.]

1616.—". . . quos Lusitani patriâ voce **Moncam** indigetant."—*Jarric*, i. 46.

" Sir T. Roe writes **Monson**.

1627.—"Of *Corea* hee was also told that there are many bogges, for which cause they have Waggons with broad wheeles, to keepe them from sinking, and obseruing the **Monson** or season of the wind . . . they have sayles fitted to these waggons, and so make their Voyages on land."—*Purchas, Pilgrimage*, 602.

1634.—

"Partio, vendo que o tempo em vao gastava,
E que a **monção** di navegar passava."
Malaca, Conquistada, iv. 75.

1644.—"The winds that blow at Diu from the commencement of the change of season in September are sea-breezes, blowing from time to time from the S., S.W., or N.W., with no certain **Monsam** wind, and at that time one can row across to Dio with great facility."—*Bocarro*, MS.

c. 1665.—". . . and it would be true to say, that the sun advancing towards *one* Pole, causeth on that side two great regular currents, viz., that of the Sea, and that of the Air which maketh the **Mounson**-*wind*, as he causeth two opposite ones, when he returns towards the other Pole."—*Bernier*, E.T. 139-40; [ed. *Constable*, 436; see also 109].

1673.—"The northern **Monsoons** (if I may so say, being the name imposed by the first Observers, *i.e.* **Motiones**) lasting hither."—*Fryer*, 10.

" "A constellation by the Portugals called *Rabo del Elephanto* (see **ELEPHANTA, b.**) known by the breaking up of the **Munsoons**, which is the last Flory this Season makes."—*Ibid.* 48. He has also **Mossoons** or **Monsoons**, 46.

1690.—"Two **Mussouns** are the Age of a Man."—Bombay Proverb in *Ovington's Voyage*, 142.

[" "**Mussoans**." See under **ELEPHANTA, b.**]

1696.—"We thought it most advisable to remain here, till the next **Mossoon**."—*Bowyear*, in *Dalrymple*, i. 87.

1783.—"From the Malay word **moossin**, which signifies season."—*Forrest, V. to Mergui*, 95.

" "Their prey is lodged in England; and the cries of India are given to seas and winds, to be blown about, in every breaking up of the **monsoon**, over a remote and unhearing ocean."—*Burke's Speech on Fox's E.I. Bill*, in *Works*, iii. 468.

[**MOOBAREK**, adj. Ar. *mubārak*, 'blessed, happy'; as an interjection, 'Welcome!' 'Congratulations to you!'

[1617. — ". . . a present . . . is called **Mombareck**, good Newes, or good Successe."—*Sir T. Roe*, Hak. Soc. ii. 413.

[1812.—"*Bombareek* . . . which by sailors is also called **Bombay Rock**, is derived originally from '**moobarek**,' 'happy, fortunate.'"—*Morier, Journey through Persia*, 6.]

MOOCHULKA, s. Hind. *muchalkā* or *muchalka*. A written obligation or bond. For technical uses see *Wilson*. The word is apparently Turki or Mongol.

c. 1267.—"Five days thereafter judgment was held on Husamuddin the astrologer, who had executed a **muchilkai** that the death of the Khalif would be the calamity of the world."—*Hammer's Golden Horde*, 166.

c. 1280.—"When he (Kubilai Kaan) approached his 70th year, he desired to raise in his own lifetime, his son Chimkin to be his representative and declared successor. . . . The chiefs . . . represented

. . . that though the measure . . . was not in accordance with the Yasa and customs of the world-conquering hero Chinghiz Kaan, yet they would grant a **muchilka** in favour of Chimkin's Kaanship."—*Wassāf's History*, Germ. by *Hammer*, 46.

c. 1360.—"He shall in all divisions and districts execute **muchilkas** to lay no burden on the subjects by extraordinary imposts, and irregular exaction of supplies."—Form of the Warrant of a Territorial Governor under the Mongols, in the above, *App.* p. 468.

1818.—"You were present at the India Board when Lord B—— told me that I should have 10,000 pagodas per annum, and all my expenses paid. . . . I never thought of taking a **muchalka** from Lord B——, because I certainly never suspected that my expenses would . . . have been restricted to 500 pagodas, a sum which hardly pays my servants and equipage."—*Munro to Malcolm*, in *Munro's Life*, &c., iii. 257.

MOOCHY, s. One who works in leather, either as shoemaker or saddler. It is the name of a low caste, Hind. *mochī*. The name and caste are also found in S. India, Telug. *muchche*. These, too, are workers in leather, but also are employed in painting, gilding, and upholsterer's work, &c.

[1815.—"Cow-stealing . . . is also practised by . . . the **Mootshee** or Shoemaker cast."—*Tytler, Considerations*, i. 103.]

MOOKTEAR, s. Properly Hind. from Ar. *mukhtār*, 'chosen,' but corruptly *mukhtyār*. An authorised agent; an attorney. *Mukhtyār-nāma*, 'a power of attorney.'

1866.—"I wish he had been under the scaffolding when the roof of that new Cutcherry he is building fell in, and killed two **mookhtars**."—*The Dawk Bungalow* (by G. O. Trevelyan), in *Fraser's Mag.* lxxiii. p. 218.

1878.—"These were the **mookhtyars**, or Criminal Court attorneys, teaching the witnesses what to say in their respective cases, and suggesting answers to all possible questions, the whole thing having been previously rehearsed at the **mookhtyar's** house."—*Life in the Mofussil*, f. 90.

1885.—"The wily Bengali **muktears**, or attorneys, were the bane of the Hill Tracts, and I never relaxed in my efforts to banish them from the country."—*Lt.-Col. T. Lewin, A Fly on the Wheel*, p. 336.

MOOLLAH, s. Hind. *mullā*, corr. from Ar. *maulā*, a der. from *wilā*, 'propinquity.' This is the legal bond which still connects a former owner with his manumitted slave; and in virtue of this bond the patron and client are both called *maulā*. The idea of patronage is in the other senses; and the word comes to mean eventually 'a learned man, a teacher, a doctor of the Law.' In India it is used in these senses, and for a man who reads the Korān in a house for 40 days after a death. When oaths were administered on the Korān, the servitor who held the book was called *Mullā Ḳorānī*. *Mullā* is also in India the usual Mussulman term for 'a schoolmaster.'

1616.—"Their **Moolaas** employ much of their time like Scriueners to doe businesse for others."—*Terry*, in *Purchas*, ii. 1476.

[1617. — "He had shewed it to his **Mulaies**."—*Sir T. Roe*, Hak. Soc. ii. 417.]

1638.—"While the Body is let down into the grave, the kindred mutter certain Prayers between their Teeth, and that done all the company returns to the house of the deceased, where the **Mollas** continue their Prayers for his Soul, for the space of two or three days. . . ."—*Mandelslo*, E.T. 63.

1673.—"At funerals, the **Mullahs** or Priests make Orations or Sermons, after a Lesson read out of the *Alchoran*."—*Fryer*, 94.

1680.—"The old **Mulla** having been discharged for misconduct, another by name Cozzee (see **CAZEE**) Mahmud entertained on a salary of 5 Pagodas per mensem, his duties consisting of the business of writing letters, &c., in Persian, besides teaching the Persian language to such of the Company's servants as shall desire to learn it."—*Ft. St. Geo. Consn.* March 11. *Notes and Exts.* No. iii. p. 12; [also see *Pringle, Diary, Ft. St. Geo.*, 1st ser. ii. 2, with note].

1763.—"The **Mulla** in Indostan superintends the practice, and punishes the breach of religious duties."—*Orme*, reprint, i. 26.

1809. — "The British Government have, with their usual liberality, continued the allowance for the **Moolahs** to read the Koran."—*Ld. Valentia*, i. 423.

[1842.—See the classical account of the **Moollahs** of Kabul in *Elphinstone's Caubul*, ed. 1842, i. 281 *seqq.*]

1879.—". . . struck down by a fanatical crowd impelled by a fierce **Moola**."—*Sat. Rev.* No. 1251, p. 484.

MOOLVEE, s. Popular Hind. *mulvī*, Ar. *maulavī*, from same root as *mullā* (see **MOOLLAH**). A Judge, Doctor of the Law, &c. It is a usual prefix to the names of learned men and professors of law and literature. (See **LAW-OFFICER**.)

1784.—
"A Pundit in Bengal or **Molavee**
May daily see a carcase burn;
But you can't furnish for the soul of ye
A dirge sans ashes and an urn."
N. B. Halhed, see *Calc. Review*, xxvi. 79.

MOONAUL, s. Hind. *munāl* or *monāl* (it seems to be in no dictionary); [Platts gives "*Munāl* (dialec.)]. The *Lopophorus Impeyanus*, most splendid perhaps of all game-birds, rivalling the brilliancy of hue, and the metallic lustre of the humming-birds on the scale of the turkey. "This splendid pheasant is found throughout the whole extent of the Himalayas, from the hills bordering Afghanistan as far east as Sikkim, and probably also to Bootan" (*Jerdon*). "In the autumnal and winter months numbers are generally collected in the same quarter of the forest, though often so widely scattered that each bird appears to be alone" (*Ibid.*). Can this last circumstance point to the etymology of the name as connected with Skt. *muni*, 'an eremite'?

It was pointed out in a note on *Marco Polo* (1st ed. i. 246, 2nd ed. i. 272), that the extract which is given below from Aelian undoubtedly refers to the *Munāl*. We have recently found that this indication had been anticipated by G. Cuvier, in a note on Pliny (tom. vii. p. 409 of ed. Ajasson de Grandsagne, Paris, 1830). It appears from Jerdon that *Monaul* is popularly applied by Europeans at Darjeeling to the Sikkim horned pheasant *Ceriornis satyra*, otherwise sometimes called '**Argus Pheasant**' (q.v.).

c. A.D. 350.—"Cocks too are produced there of a kind bigger than any others. These have a crest, but instead of being red like the crest of our cocks, this is variegated like a coronet of flowers. The tail-feathers moreover are not arched, or bent into a curve (like a cock's), but flattened out. And this tail they trail after them as a peacock does, unless when they erect it, and set it up. And the plumage of these Indian cocks is golden, and dark blue, and of the hue of the emerald."—*De Nat. Animal.* xvi. 2.

MOON BLINDNESS. This affection of the eyes is commonly believed to be produced by sleeping exposed to the full light of the moon. There is great difference of opinion as to the facts, some quoting experience as incontrovertible, others regarding the thing merely as a vulgar prejudice, without substantial foundation. Some remarks will be found in *Collingwood's Rambles of a Naturalist*, pp. 308-10. The present writer has in the East twice suffered from a peculiar affection of the eyes and face, after being in sleep exposed to a bright moon, but he would hardly have used the term *moon-blindness*.

MOONG, MOONGO, s. Or. 'green-gram'; Hind. *mūng*, [Skt. *mudga*]. A kind of vetch (*Phaseolus Mungo*, L.) in very common use over India; according to Garcia the *mesce* (*māsh?*) of Avicenna. Garcia also says that it was popularly recommended as a diet for fever in the Deccan; [and is still recommended for this purpose by native physicians (*Watt, Econ. Dict.* vi. pt. i. 191)].

c. 1336.—"The **munj** again is a kind of *māsh*, but its grains are oblong and the colour is light green. **Munj** is cooked along with rice, and eaten with butter. This is what they call *Kichrī* (see **KEDGEREE**), and it is the diet on which one breakfasts daily."—*Ibn Batuta*, iii. 131.

1557.—"The people were obliged to bring hay, and corn, and **mungo**, which is a certain species of seed that they feed horses with."—*Albuquerque*, Hak. Soc. ii. 132.

1563.—

"*Servant-maid.*—That girl that you brought from the Deccan asks me for **mungo**, and says that in her country they give it them to eat, husked and boiled. Shall I give it her?

"*Orta.*—Give it her since she wishes it; but bread and a boiled chicken would be better. For she comes from a country where they eat bread, and not rice."—*Garcia*, f. 145.

[1611.—". . . for 25 maunds **Moong**, 28m. 09 p."—*Danvers, Letters*, i. 141.]

MOONGA, MOOGA, s. Beng. *mūgā*. A kind of wild silk, the produce of *Antheraea assama*, collected and manufactured in Assam. ["Its Assamese name is said to be derived from the amber *munga*, 'coral' colour of the silk, and is frequently used to denote silk in general" (*B. C. Allen, Mono. on the Silk Cloths of Assam*, 1899, p. 10).] The quotations in elucidation of this word may claim some peculiar interest. That from Purchas is a modern illustration of the legends which reached the Roman Empire in classic times, of the growth of silk in the Seric jungles ("*velleraque ut foliis depectunt tenuia Seres*"); whilst that from Robert Lindsay may possibly throw light on the statements in the *Periplus* regarding an overland importation of silk from *Thin* into Gangetic India.

1626.—". . . **Moga** which is made of the bark of a certaine tree."—*Purchas, Pilgrimage*, 1005.

c. 1676.—"The kingdom of *Asem* is one of the best countries of all Asia. . . . There is a sort of Silk that is found under the trees, which is spun by a Creature like our Silk-worms, but rounder, and which lives all the year long under the trees. The Silks which are made of this Silk glist'n very much, but they fret presently."—*Tavernier*, E.T. ii. 187-8; [ed. *Ball*, ii. 281].

1680.—"The Floretta yarn or **Muckta** examined and priced. . . . The Agent informed 'that 'twas called *Arundee*, made neither with cotton nor silke, but of a kind of Herba spun by a worme that feeds upon the leaves of a stalke or tree called *Arundee* which bears a round prickly berry, of which oyle is made; vast quantitys of this cloth is made in the country about Goora Ghaut beyond Seripore Mercha; where the wormes are kept as silke wormes here; twill never come white, but will take any colour'" &c. —*Ft. St. Geo. Agent on Tour, Consn.*, Nov. 19. In *Notes and Exts.*, No. iii. p. 58. *Arandī* or *rendī* is the castor-oil plant, and this must be the *Attacus ricini*, Jones, called in *H. Arrindi, Arrindiaria* (?) and in Bengali *Eri, Eria, Erindy*, according to *Forbes Watson's Nomenclature*, No. 8002, p. 371. [For full details see *Allen, Mono.* pp. 5, *seqq.*].

1763.—"No duties have ever yet been paid on Lacks, **Mugga**-*dooties*, and other goods brought from *Assam*."—In *Van Sittart*, i. 249.

c. 1778.—". . . Silks of a coarse quality, called **Moonga** dutties, are also brought from the frontiers of China for the Malay trade."—*Hon. R. Lindsay*, in *Lives of the Lindsays*, iii. 174.

MOONSHEE, s. Ar. *munshi*, but written in Hind. *munshī*. The verb *insha*, of which the Ar. word is the participle, means 'to educate' a youth, as well as 'to compose' a written document. Hence 'a secretary, a reader, an interpreter, a writer.' It is commonly applied by Europeans specifically to a native teacher of languages, especially of Arabic, Persian, and Urdū, though the application to a native amanuensis in those tongues, and to any respectable, well-educated native gentleman is also common. The word probably became tolerably familiar in Europe through a book of instruction in Persian bearing the name (viz. "*The Persian Moonshee, by F. Gladwyn*," 1st ed. s.a., but published in Calcutta about 1790-1800).

1777.—"**Moonshi**. A writer or secretary."—*Halhed, Code*, 17.

1782.—"The young gentlemen exercise themselves in translating . . . they reason and dispute with their **munchees** (tutors) in Persian and Moors. . . ."—*Price's Tracts*, i. 89.

1785.—"Your letter, requiring our authority for engaging in your service a **Mûnshy**, for the purpose of making out passports, and writing letters, has been received."—*Tippoo's Letters*, 67.

,, "A lasting friendship was formed between the pupil and his **Moonshee**. . . . The **Moonshee**, who had become wealthy, afforded him yet more substantial evidence of his recollection, by earnestly requesting him, when on the point of leaving India, to accept a sum amounting to £1600, on the plea that the latter (*i.e.* Shore) had saved little."—*Mem. of Lord Teignmouth*, i. 32-33.

1814.—"They presented me with an address they had just composed in the Hindoo language, translated into Persian by the Durbar **munsee**."—*Forbes, Or. Mem.* iii. 365; [2nd ed. ii. 344].

1817.—"Its authenticity was fully proved by . . . and a Persian **Moonshee** who translated."—*Mill, Hist.* v. 127.

1828.—". . . the great **Moonshi** of State himself had applied the whole of his genius to selecting such flowers of language as would not fail to diffuse joy, when exhibited in those dark and dank regions of the north."—*Hajji Baba in England*, i. 39.

1867.—"When the Mirza grew up, he fell among English, and ended by carrying his rupees as a **Moonshee**, or a language-master, to that infidel people."—*Select Writings of Viscount Strangford*, i. 265.

MOONSIFF, s. Hind. from Ar. *munṣif*, 'one who does justice' (*inṣāf*), a judge. In British India it is the title of a native civil judge of the lowest grade. This office was first established in 1793.

1812.—". . . **munsifs**, or native justices." —*Fifth Report*, p. 32.

[1852.—"'I wonder, Mr. Deputy, if Providence had made you a **Moonsiff**, instead of a Deputy Collector, whether you would have been more lenient in your strictures upon our system of civil justice?'"—*Raikes, Notes on the N. W. Provinces*, 155.]

MOOR, MOORMAN, s. (and adj. **MOORISH**). A Mahommedan; and so from the habitual use of the term (*Mouro*), by the Portuguese in India, particularly a Mahommedan inhabitant of India.

In the Middle Ages, to Europe generally, the Mahommedans were known as the *Saracens*. This is the word always used by Joinville, and by Marco Polo. Ibn Batuta also mentions the fact in a curious passage (ii. 425-6). At a later day, when the fear of the

Ottoman had made itself felt in Europe, the word *Turk* was that which identified itself with the Moslem, and thus we have in the Collect for Good Friday,—"Jews, *Turks*, Infidels, and Heretics." But to the Spaniards and Portuguese, whose contact was with the Musulmans of Mauritania who had passed over and conquered the Peninsula, all Mahommedans were **Moors**. So the Mahommedans whom the Portuguese met with on their voyages to India, on what coast soever, were alike styled *Mouros*; and from the Portuguese the use of this term, as synonymous with Mahommedan, passed to Hollanders and Englishmen.

The word then, as used by the Portuguese discoverers, referred to religion, and implied no nationality. It is plain indeed from many passages that the *Moors* of Calicut and Cochin were in the beginning of the 16th century people of mixt race, just as the **Moplahs** (q.v.) are now. The Arab, or Arabo-African occupants of Mozambique and Melinda, the Sumālis of Magadoxo, the Arabs and Persians of Kalhāt and Ormuz, the Boras of Guzerat, are all **Mouros** to the Portuguese writers, though the more intelligent among these are quite conscious of the impropriety of the term. The *Moors* of the Malabar coast were middlemen, who had adopted a profession of Islam for their own convenience, and in order to minister for their own profit to the constant traffic of merchants from Ormuz and the Arabian ports. Similar influences still affect the boatmen of the same coast, among whom it has become a sort of custom in certain families, that different members should profess respectively Mahommedanism, Hinduism, and Christianity.

The use of the word *Moor* for Mahommedan died out pretty well among educated Europeans in the Bengal Presidency in the beginning of the last century, or even earlier, but probably held its ground a good deal longer among the British soldiery, whilst the adjective *Moorish* will be found in our quotations nearly as late as 1840. In Ceylon, the Straits, and the Dutch Colonies, the term *Moorman* for a Musalman is still in common use. Indeed the word is still employed by the servants of Madras officers in speaking of Mahommedans, or of a certain class of these. **Moro** is still applied at Manilla to the Musulman Malays.

1498.—". . . the **Moors** never came to the house when this trading went on, and we became aware that they wished us ill, insomuch that when any of us went ashore, in order to annoy us they would spit on the ground, and say 'Portugal, Portugal.'"—*Roteiro de V. da Gama*, p. 75.

" "For you must know, gentlemen, that from the moment you put into port here (Calecut) you caused disturbance of mind to the **Moors** of this city, who are numerous and very powerful in the country."—*Correa*, Hak. Soc. 166.

1499.—"We reached a very large island called Sumatra, where pepper grows in considerable quantities. . . . The Chief is a **Moor**, but speaking a different language."—*Santo Stefano*, in *India in the XVth Cent.* [7].

1505.—"Adì 28 zugno vene in Venetia insieme co Sier Alvixe de Boni un sclav **moro** el qual portorono i spagnoli da la insula spagniola."—*MS.* in *Museo Civico* at Venice. Here the term **Moor** is applied to a native of Hispaniola!

1513.—"Hanc (Malaccam) rex **Maurus** gubernabat."—*Emanuelis Regis Epistola*, f. 1.

1553.—"And for the hatred in which they hold them, and for their abhorrence of the name of *Frangue*, they call in reproach the Christians of our parts of the world *Frangues* (see **FIRINGHEE**), just as we improperly call *them* again **Moors**."—*Barros*, IV. iv. 16.

c. 1560.—"When we lay at Fuquien, we did see certain **Moores**, who knew so little of their secte that they could say nothing else but that Mahomet was a **Moore**, my father was a **Moore**, and I am a **Moore**."—*Reports of the Province of China*, done into English by *R. Willes*, in *Hakl.* ii. 557.

1563.—"And as to what you say of Ludovico Vartomano, I have spoken both here and in Portugal, with people who knew him here in India, and they told me that he went about here in the garb of a **Moor**, and that he came back among us doing penance for his sins; and that the man never went further than Calecut and Cochin, nor indeed did we at that time navigate those seas that we now navigate."—*Garcia*, f. 30.

1569.—". . . always whereas I have spoken of Gentiles is to be understood Idolaters, and whereas I speak of **Moores**, I mean Mahomets secte."—*Caesar Frederike*, in *Hakl.* ii. 359.

1610.—"The King was fled for feare of the King of Makasar, who . . . would force the King to turne **Moore**, for he is a Gentile."—*Midleton*, in *Purchas*, i. 239.

1611.—"Les **Mores** du pay faisoiēt courir le bruict, que les notres avoient esté battus."—*Wytfliet*, *H. des Indes*, iii. 9.

1648.—"King Jangier (Jehāngīr) used to make use of a reproach: That one *Portugees* was better than three **Moors**, and one Hollander or Englishman better than two Portugees."—*Van Twist*, 59.

c. 1665.—"Il y en a de **Mores** et de Gentils *Raspoutes* (see **RAJPOOT**) parce que je savois qu'ils servent mieux que les **Mores** qui sont superbes, and ne veulent pas qu'on se plaigne d'eux, quelque sotise ou quelque tromperie qu'ils fassent."—*Thevenot*, v. 217.

1673.—"Their Crew were all **Moors** (by which Word hereafter must be meant those of the Mahometan faith) apparell'd all in white."—*Fryer*, p. 24.

" "They are a Shame to our Sailors, who can hardly ever work without horrid Oaths and hideous Cursing and Imprecations; and these **Moormen**, on the contrary, never set their Hands to any Labour, but that they sing a Psalm or Prayer, and conclude at every joint Application of it, 'Allah, Allah,' invoking the Name of God."—*Ibid.* pp. 55-56.

1685.—"We putt out a peece of a Red Ancient to appear like a **Moor's** Vessel: not judging it safe to be known to be English; Our nation having lately gott an ill name by abusing ye Inhabitants of these Islands: but no boat would come neer us . . ." (in the Maldives).—*Hedges, Diary*, March 9; [Hak. Soc. i. 190].

1688. — "**Lascars**, who are **Moors** of India."—*Dampier*, ii. 57.

1689.—"The place where they went ashore was a Town of the **Moors**: Which name our Seamen give to all the Subjects of the great Mogul, but especially his *Mahometan* Subjects; calling the Idolators, Gentous or *Rashboots* (see **RAJPOOT**)."—*Dampier*, i. 507.

1747.—"We had the Misfortune to be reduced to almost inevitable Danger, for as our Success chiefly depended on the assistance of the **Moors**, We were soon brought to the utmost Extremity by being abandoned by them."—*Letter from Ft. St. Geo. to the Court*, May 2 (India Office MS. Records).

1752.—"His successor Mr. Godehue . . . even permitted him (Dupleix) to continue the exhibition of those marks of **Moorish** dignity, which both Murzafa-jing and Sallabad-jing had permitted him to display."—*Orme*, i. 367.

1757.—In Ives, writing in this year, we constantly find the terms **Moormen** and **Moorish**, applied to the forces against which Clive and Watson were acting on the Hoogly.

1763.—"From these origins, time has formed in India a mighty nation of near ten millions of Mahomedans, whom Europeans call **Moors**."—*Orme*, ed. 1803, i. 24.

1770.—"Before the Europeans doubled the Cape of Good Hope, the **Moors**, who were the only maritime people of India, sailed from Surat and Bengal to Malacca."—*Raynal* (tr. 1777), i. 210.

1781.—"Mr. Hicky thinks it a Duty incumbent on him to inform his friends in particular, and the Public in General, that an attempt was made to Assassinate him last Thursday Morning between the Hours of One and two o'Clock, by two armed Europeans aided and assisted by a **Moorman**. . ."—*Hicky's Bengal Gazette*, April 7.

1784.—"Lieutenants Speediman and Rutledge . . . were bound, circumcised, and clothed in **Moorish** garments."—In *Seton-Karr*, i. 15.

1797.—"Under the head of castes entitled to a favourable term, I believe you comprehend Brahmans, **Moormen**, merchants, and almost every man who does not belong to the Sudra or cultivating caste. . . ."—*Minute of Sir T. Munro*, in *Arbuthnot*, i. 17.

1807.—"The rest of the inhabitants, who are **Moors**, and the richer Gentoos, are dressed in various degrees and fashions."—*Ld. Minto in India*, p. 17.

1829.—"I told my **Moorman**, as they call the Mussulmans here, just now to ask the drum-major when the mail for the *Pradwan* (?) was to be made up."—*Mem. of Col. Mountain*, 2nd ed. p. 80.

1839.—"As I came out of the gate I met some young **Moorish** dandies on horseback; one of them was evidently a 'crack-rider,' and began to show off."—*Letters from Madras*, p. 290.

MOORA, s. Sea Hind. *mūrā*, from Port. *amura*, Ital. *mura*; a tack (*Roebuck*).

MOORAH, s. A measure used in the sale of paddy at Bombay and in Guzerat. The true form of this word is doubtful. From Molesworth's *Mahr. Dict.* it would seem that *mudā* and *mudī* are properly cases of rice-straw bound together to contain certain quantities of grain, the former larger and the latter smaller. Hence it would be a vague and varying measure. But there is a land measure of the same name. See *Wilson*, s.v. *Múdi*. [The *Madras Gloss.* gives **mooda**, Mal. *mūta*, from *mūtu*, 'to cover,' "a fastening package; especially the packages in a circular form, like a Dutch cheese, fastened with wisps of straw, in which rice is made up in Malabar and Canara." The **mooda** is said to be 1 cubic foot and 1,116 cubic inches, and equal to 3 Kulsies (see **CULSEY**).]

1554.—"(At Baçaim) the *Mura* of *batee* (see **BATTA**) contains 3 candis (see **CANDY**), which (*batee*) is rice in the husk, and after it is stript it amounts to a candy and a half, and something more."—*A. Nunes*, p. 30.

[1611.—"I send your worship by the bearer 10 **moraes** of rice."—*Danvers, Letters*, i. 116.]

1813.—"Batty Measure.—

* * * * *

25 parahs ......make 1 **moorah**.*
4 candies...... „ 1 **moorah**."
Milburn, 2nd ed. p. 143.

MOORPUNKY, s. Corr. of *Morpankhī*, 'peacock-tailed,' or 'peacock-winged'; the name given to certain state pleasure-boats on the Gangetic rivers, now only (if at all) surviving at Murshīdābād. They are a good deal like the Burmese 'war-boats;' see cut in *Mission to Ava* (Major Phayre's), p. 4. [A similar boat was the *Feelchehra* (Hind. *fīl-chehra*, 'elephant-faced'). In a letter of 1784 Warren Hastings writes: "I intend to finish my voyage to-morrow in the *feelchehra*" (*Busteed, Echoes*, 3rd ed. 291).]

1767.—"Charges Dewanny, viz. :—

"A few **moorpungkeys** and *beauleahs* (see **BOLIAH**) for the service of Mahomed Reza Khan, and on the service at the city some are absolutely necessary . . . 25,000 : 0 : 0."—*Dacca Accounts*, in *Long*, 524.

1780.—"Another boat . . . very curiously constructed, the **Moor-punky**: these are very long and narrow, sometimes extending to upwards of 100 feet in length, and not more than 8 feet in breadth; they are always paddled, sometimes by 40 men, and are steered by a large paddle from the stern, which rises in the shape of a peacock, a snake, or some other animal."—*Hodges*, 40.

[1785.—". . . **moor-punkees**, or peacock-boats, which are made as much as possible to resemble the peacock."—*Diary*, in *Forbes, Or. Mem.* 2nd ed. ii. 450.]

MOORS, THE, s. The Hindustani language was in the 18th century commonly thus styled. The idiom is a curious old English one for the denomination of a language, of which 'broad Scots' is perhaps a type, and which we find exemplified in 'Malabars' (see **MALABAR**) for Tamil, whilst we have also met with *Bengals* for Bengālī, with *Indostans* for Urdū, and with *Turks* for Turkish. The term *Moors* is probably now entirely obsolete, but down to 1830, at least, some old officers of the Royal army and some old Madras civilians would occasionally use the term as synonymous with what the former would also call 'the black language.' [**Moors** for Urdū was certainly in use among the old European pensioners at Chunār as late as 1892.]

* Equal to 863 lbs. 12 oz. 12 drs.

The following is a transcript of the title-page of Hadley's Grammar, the earliest English Grammar of Hindustani: *

"Grammatical Remarks | on the | Practical and Vulgar Dialect | Of the | Indostan Language | commonly called **Moors** | with a Vocabulary | English and **Moors**. The Spelling according to | The Persian Orthography | Wherein are | References between Words resembling each other in | Sound and different in Significations | with Literal Translations and Explanations of the Com- | pounded Words and Circumlocutory Expressions | For the more easy attaining the Idiom of the Language | The whole calculated for
The Common Practice in Bengal.

"—— Si quid novisti rectius istis,
Candidus imperti; si non his utere mecum."

By Capt. George Hadley.
London:
Printed for T. Cadell in the Strand.
MDCCLXXII."

Captain Hadley's orthography is on a detestable system. He writes *chookerau, chookeree*, for *chhokrā, chhokrī* ('boy, girl'); *dolchinney* for *dāl-chīnī* ('cinnamon'), &c. His etymological ideas also are loose. Thus he gives 'shrimps=*chînghra mutchee*, 'fish with legs and claws,' as if the word was from *chang* (Pers.), 'a hook or claw.' *Bāgḍor*, 'a halter,' or as he writes, *baug-doore*, he derives from *dūr*, 'distance,' instead of *dor*, 'a rope.' He has no knowledge of the instrumental case with terminal *ne*, and he does not seem to be aware that *ham* and *tum* (*hum* and *toom*, as he writes) are in reality plurals ('we' and 'you'). The grammar is altogether of a very primitive and tentative character, and far behind that of the R. C. Missionaries, which is referred to s.v. **Hindostanee**. We have not seen that of Schulz (1745) mentioned under the same.

1752.—"The Centinel was sitting at the top of the gate, singing a **Moorish** song."—*Orme*, ed. 1803, i. 272.

1767.—"In order to transact Business of any kind in this Countrey, you must at least have a smattering of the Language for few of the Inhabitants (except in great Towns) speak English. The original Language, of this Countrey (or at least the earliest we know of) is the Bengala or Gentoo. . . . But the politest Language is the **Moors** or Mussulmans and Persian. . . . The only Language that I know anything of is the

* Hadley, however, mentions in his preface that a small pamphlet had been received by Mr. George Bogle in 1770, which he found to be the mutilated embryo of his own grammatical scheme. This was circulating in Bengal "at his expence."

Bengala, and that I do not speak perfectly, for you may remember that I had a very poor knack at learning Languages."—*MS. Letter of James Rennell*, March 10.

1779.—
"*C.* What language did Mr. Francis speak?
W. (*Meerum Kitmutgar*). The same as I do, in broken **Moors.**"—*Trial of* Grand *v.* Philip Francis, quoted in *Echoes of Old Calcutta*, 226.

1783.—"**Moors**, by not being written, bars all close application."—Letter in *Life of Colebrooke*, 13.

,, "The language called '**Moors**' has a written character differing both from the Sanskrit and Bengalee character, it is called *Nagree*, which means 'writing.'"—Letter in *Mem. of Ld. Teignmouth*, i. 104.

1784.—
"Wild perroquets first silence broke,
Eager of dangers near to prate;
But they in English never spoke,
And she began her **Moors** of late."
Plassey Plain, a Ballad by *Sir W. Jones*, in *Works*, ii. 504.

1788.—"*Wants Employment.* A young man who has been some years in Bengal, used to common accounts, understands *Bengallies*, **Moors**, Portuguese. . . ."—In *Seton-Karr*, i. 286.

1789.—". . . sometimes slept half an hour, sometimes not, and then wrote or talked Persian or **Moors** till sunset, when I went to parade."—Letter of *Sir T. Munro*, i. 76.

1802.—"All business is transacted in a barbarous mixture of **Moors**, Mahratta, and Gentoo."—*Sir T. Munro*, in *Life*, i. 333.

1803.—"Conceive what society there will be when people speak what they don't think, in **Moors**."—*M. Elphinstone*, in *Life*, i. 108.

1804.—"She had a **Moorish** woman interpreter, and as I heard her give orders to her interpreter in the **Moorish** language . . . I must consider the conversation of the first authority."—*Wellington*, iii. 290.

,, "*The Stranger's Guide to the* Hindoostanic, *or Grand Popular Language of India, improperly called* **Moorish**; *by* J. Borthwick Gilchrist: *Calcutta.*"

MOORUM, s. A word used in Western India for gravel, &c., especially as used in road-metal. The word appears to be Mahratti. Molesworth gives "*murūm*, a fissile kind of stone, probably decayed Trap." [*Murukallu* is the Tel. name for **Laterite**. (Also see **CABOOK**.)]

[1875.—"There are few places where **Morram**, or decomposed granite, is not to be found."—*Gribble, Cuddapah*, 247.

[1883.—"Underneath is **Morambu**, a good filtering medium."—*Le Fanu, Salem*, ii. 43.]

MOOTSUDDY, s. A native accountant. Hind. *mutaṣaddī* from Ar. *mutaṣaddi*.

1683.—"Cossadass ye Chief Secretary, **Mutsuddies**, and ye Nabobs Chief Eunuch will be paid all their money beforehand."—*Hedges, Diary*, Jan. 6; [Hak. Soc. i. 61].

[1762.—"**Muttasuddies.**" See under **GOMASTA**.]

1785.—"This representation has caused us the utmost surprise. Whenever the **Mutsuddies** belonging to your department cease to yield you proper obedience, you must give them a severe flogging."—*Tippoo's Letters*, p. 2.

,, "Old age has certainly made havock on your understanding, otherwise you would have known that the **Mutusuddies** here are not the proper persons to determine the market prices there."—*Ibid.* p. 118.

[1809.—"The regular battalions have also been riotous, and confined their **Mootusudee**, the officer who keeps their accounts, and transacts the public business on the part of the commandant."—*Broughton, Letters*, ed. 1892, p. 135.]

MOPLAH, s. Malayāl. *māppila*. The usual application of this word is to the indigenous Mahommedans of Malabar; but it is also applied to the indigenous (so-called) Syrian Christians of Cochin and Travancore. In Morton's *Life of Leyden* the word in the latter application is curiously misprinted as *madilla*. The derivation of the word is very obscure. Wilson gives *mā-pilla*, 'mother's son, "as sprung from the intercourse of foreign colonists, who were persons unknown, with Malabar women." Nelson, as quoted below interprets the word as 'bridegroom' (it should however rather be 'son-in-law').* Dr. Badger suggests that it is from the Arabic verb *falaḥa*, and means 'a cultivator' (compare the *fellah* of Egypt), whilst Mr. C. P. Brown expresses his conviction that it was a Tamil mispronunciation of the Arabic *mu'abbar*, 'from over the water.' No one of these greatly commends itself. [Mr. Logan (*Malabar*, ii. ccviii.) and the *Madras Glossary* derive it from Mal. *ma*, Skt. *maha*, 'great,' and Mal. *pilla*, 'a child.' Dr. Gundert's view is that *Māpilla* was an honorary title given to colonists from

* The husband of the existing Princess of Tanjore is habitually styled by the natives "*Mapillai Sāhib*" ("il Signor Genero"), as the son-in-law of the late Raja.

the W., perhaps at first only to their representatives.]

1516.—"In all this country of Malabar there are a great quantity of Moors, who are of the same language and colour as the Gentiles of the country. . . . They call these Moors **Mapulers**; they carry on nearly all the trade of the seaports."—*Barbosa*, 146.

1767.—"Ali Raja, the Chief of Cananore, who was a Muhammadan, and of the tribe called **Mapilla**, rejoiced at the success and conquests of a Muhammadan Chief."—*H. of Hydur*, p. 184.

1782.—". . . les **Maplets** reçurent les coutumes et les superstitions des Gentils, sous l'empire des quels ils vivoient. C'est pour se conformer aux usages des Malabars, que les enfans des **Maplets** n'héritent point de leurs pères, mais des frères de leurs mères."—*Sonnerat*, i. 193.

1787.—

"Of **Moplas** fierce your hand has tam'd,
And monsters that your sword has maim'd."
Life and Letters of J. Ritson, 1833, i. 114.

1800.—"We are not in the most thriving condition in this country. Polegars, nairs, and **moplas** in arms on all sides of us."—*Wellington*, i. 43.

1813. — "At one period the **Moplahs** created great commotion in Travancore, and towards the end of the 17th century massacred the chief of Anjengo, and all the English gentlemen belonging to the settlement, when on a public visit to the Queen of Attinga."—*Forbes, Or. Mem.* i. 402; [2nd ed. i. 259].

1868. — "I may add in concluding my notice that the Kallans alone of all the castes of Madura call the Mahometans '*māpilleis*' or bridegrooms (**Moplahs**)."—*Nelson's Madura*, Pt. ii. 55.

MORA, s. Hind. *morhā*. A stool (*tabouret*); a footstool. In common colloquial use.

[1795.—"The old man, whose attention had been chiefly attracted by a Ramnaghur **morah**, of which he was desirous to know the construction, . . . departed." — *Capt. Blunt*, in *Asiat. Res.*, vii. 92.

[1843.—"Whilst seated on a round stool, or **mondah**, in the thanna, . . . I entered into conversation with the thannadar. . . ." —*Davidson, Travels in Upper India*, i. 127.]

MORCHAL, s. A fan, or a fly-whisk, made of peacock's feathers. Hind. *morch'hal*.

1673. — "All the heat of the Day they idle it under some shady Tree, at night they come in troops, armed with a great Pole, a **Mirchal** or Peacock's Tail, and a Wallet."—*Fryer*, 95.

1690.—(The heat) "makes us Employ our Peons in Fanning of us with **Murchals** made of Peacock's Feathers, four or five Foot long, in the time of our Entertainments, and when we take our Repose."—*Ovington*, 335.

[1826.—"They (Gosseins) are clothed in a ragged mantle, and carry a long pole, and a **mirchal**, or peacock's tail."—*Pandurang Hari*, ed. 1873, i. 76.]

MORT-DE-CHIEN, s. A name for cholera, in use, more or less, up to the end of the 18th century, and the former prevalence of which has tended probably to the extraordinary and baseless notion that epidemic cholera never existed in India till the governorship of the Marquis of Hastings. The word in this form is really a corruption of the Portuguese **mordexim**, shaped by a fanciful French etymology. The Portuguese word again represents the Konkani and Mahratti *moḍachī*, *moḍshī*, or *moḍwashī*, 'cholera,' from a Mahr. verb *moḍnen*, 'to break up, to sink' (as under infirmities, in fact 'to collapse'). The Guzaratī appears to be *morchi* or *moṛachi*.

[1504. — Writing of this year Correa mentions the prevalence of the disease in the Samorin's army, but he gives it no name. "Besides other illness there was one almost sudden, which caused such a pain in the belly that a man hardly survived 8 hours of it."—*Correa*, i. 489.]

1543.—Correa's description is so striking that we give it almost at length: "This winter they had in Goa a mortal distemper which the natives call **morxy**, and attacking persons of every quality, from the smallest infant at the breast to the old man of fourscore, and also domestic animals and fowls, so that it affected every living thing, male and female. And this malady attacked people without any cause that could be assigned, falling upon sick and sound alike, on the fat and the lean; and nothing in the world was a safeguard against it. And this malady attacked the stomach, caused as some experts affirmed by chill; though later it was maintained that no cause whatever could be discovered. The malady was so powerful and so evil that it immediately produced the symptoms of strong poison; *e.g.*, vomiting, constant desire for water, with drying of the stomach; and cramps that contracted the hams and the soles of the feet, with such pains that the patient seemed dead, with the eyes broken and the nails of the fingers and toes black and crumpled. And for this malady our physicians never found any cure; and the patient was carried off in one day, or at the most in a day and night; insomuch that not ten in a hundred recovered, and those who did recover were such as were healed in haste with medicines of little importance known to the natives. So great was the mortality this season that the bells were tolling all day . . . insomuch that the governor forbade the tolling of the church bells, not to frighten the people . . . and when a man died in the hospital of this malady of **morexy** the Governor ordered all the experts to come together and open the body. But they found nothing wrong except that the paunch was shrunk up like a hen's gizzard, and wrinkled like a piece of scorched leather. . . ."—*Correa*, iv. 288-289.

1563.—

"*Page.*—Don Jeronymo sends to beg that you will go and visit his brother immediately, for though this is not the time of day for visits, delay would be dangerous, and he will be very thankful that you come at once.

"*Orta.* — What is the matter with the patient, and how long has he been ill?

"*Page.*—He has got **morxi**; and he has been ill two hours.

"*Orta.*—I will follow you.

"*Ruano.*—Is this the disease that kills so quickly, and that few recover from? Tell me how it is called by our people, and by the natives, and the symptoms of it, and the treatment you use in it.

"*Orta.* — Our name for the disease is *Collerica passio;* and the Indians call it *morxi;* whence again by corruption we call it **mordexi**. . . . It is sharper here than in our own part of the world, for usually it kills in four and twenty hours. And I have seen some cases where the patient did not live more than ten hours. The most that it lasts is four days; but as there is no rule without an exception, I once saw a man with great constancy of virtue who lived twenty days continually throwing up ("*curginosa*"?) . . . bile, and died at last. Let us go and see this sick man; and as for the symptoms you will yourself see what a thing it is."—*Garcia*, ff. 74*v*, 75.

1578.—"There is another thing which is useless called by them *canarin*, which the Canarin Brahman physicians usually employ for the *collerica passio* sickness, which they call **morxi**; which sickness is so sharp that it kills in fourteen hours or less."—*Acosta, Tractado*, 27.

1598.—"There reigneth a sicknesse called **Mordexijn** which stealeth uppon men, and handleth them in such sorte, that it weakeneth a man, and maketh him cast out all that he hath in his bodie, and many times his life withall."—*Linschoten*, 67; [Hak. Soc. i. 235; **Morxi** in ii. 22].

1599.—"The disease which in India is called **Mordicin**. This is a species of Colic, which comes on in those countries with such force and vehemence that it kills in a few hours; and there is no remedy discovered. It causes evacuations by stool or vomit, and makes one burst with pain. But there is a herb proper for the cure, which bears the same name of **mordescin**."—*Carletti*, 227.

1602.—"In those islets (off Aracan) they found bad and brackish water, and certain beans like ours both green and dry, of which they ate some, and in the same moment this gave them a kind of dysentery, which in India they corruptly call **mordexim**, which ought to be *morxis*, and which the Arabs call *sachaiza* (Ar. *hayzat*), which is what Rasis calls *sahida*, a disease which kills in 24 hours. Its action is immediately to produce a sunken and slender pulse, with cold sweat, great inward fire, and excessive thirst, the eyes sunken, great vomitings, and in fact it leaves the natural power so collapsed (*derribada*) that the patient seems like a dead man."—*Couto*, Dec. IV. liv. iv. cap. 10.

c. 1610.—"Il regne entre eux vne autre maladie qui vient a l'improviste, ils la nomment **Mordesin**, et vient auec grande douleur des testes, et vomissement, et crient fort, et le plus souvent en meurent."—*Pyrard de Laval*, ii. 19; [Hak. Soc. ii. 13].

1631.—"Pulvis ejus (Calumbac) ad scrup. unius pondus sumptus cholerae prodest, quam **Mordexi** incolae vocant."—*Jac. Bontii*, lib. iv. p. 43.

1638.—". . . celles qui y regnent le plus, sont celles qu'ils appellent **Mordexin**, qui tue subitement."—*Mandelslo*, 265.

1648.—See also the (questionable) *Voyages Fameux du Sieur Victor le Blanc*, 76.

c. 1665.—"Les Portugais appellent **Mordechin** les quatre sortes de Coliques qu'on souffre dans les Indes ou elles sont frequentes . . . ceux qui ont la quatrième soufrent les trois maux ensemble, à savoir le vomissement, le flux de ventre, les extremes douleurs, et je crois que cette derniere est le Colera-Morbus."—*Thevenot*, v. 324.

1673.—"They apply Cauteries most unmercifully in a **Mordisheen**, called so by the Portugals, being a Vomiting with Looseness."—*Fryer*, 114.

[1674. — "The disease called **Mordechi** generally commences with a violent fever, accompanied by tremblings, horrors and vomitings; these symptoms are generally followed by delirium and death." He prescribes a hot iron applied to the soles of the feet. He attributes the disease to indigestion, and remarks bitterly that at least the prisoners of the Inquisition were safe from this disease.—*Dellon, Relation de l'Inquisition de Goa*, ii. ch. 71.]

1690. — "The **Mordechine** is another Disease . . . which is a violent Vomiting and Looseness."—*Ovington*, 350.

c. 1690. — *Rumphius*, speaking of the **Jack-fruit** (q.v.): "Non nisi vacuo stomacho edendus est, alias enim . . . plerumque oritur *Passio Cholerica*, Portugallis **Mordexi** dicta."—*Herb. Amb.*, i. 106.

1702.—"Cette grande indigestion qu'on appelle aux Indes **Mordechin**, et que quelques uns de nos Français ont appellée **Mort-de-Chien**."—*Lettres Édif.*, xi. 156.

Bluteau (s.v.) says **Mordexim** is properly a failure of digestion which is very perilous in those parts, unless the native remedy be used. This is to apply a thin rod, like a spit, and heated, under the heel, till the patient screams with pain, and then to slap the same part with the sole of a shoe, &c.

1705.—"Ce mal s'appelle **mort-de-chien.**" —*Luillier*, 113.

The following is an example of literal translation, as far as we know, unique :

1716.—"The extraordinary distempers of this country (I. of Bourbon) are the *Cholick*, and what they call the *Dog's Disease*, which is cured by burning the heel of the patient with a hot iron."—*Acct. of the I. of Bourbon*, in *La Roque's Voyage to Arabia the Happy*, &c., E.T. London, 1726, p. 155.

1727.—". . . the **Mordexin** (which seizes one suddenly with such oppression and palpitation that he thinks he is going to die on the spot)."—*Valentijn*, v. (Malabar) 5.

c. 1760.—"There is likewise known, on the Malabar coast chiefly, a most violent disorder they call the **Mordechin**; which seizes the patient with such fury of purging, vomiting, and tormina of the intestines, that it will often carry him off in 30 hours."—*Grose*, i. 250.

1768.—"This (cholera morbus) in the East Indies, where it is very frequent and fatal, is called **Mort-de-chien.**"—*Lind, Essay on Diseases incidental to Hot Climates*, 248.

1778.—In the Vocabulary of the Portuguese *Grammatica Indostana*, we find **Mordechim**, as a Portuguese word, rendered in Hind. by the word *badazmi, i.e. bad-hazmī*, 'dyspepsia' (p. 99). The most common modern Hind. term for cholera is Arab. *haizah*. The latter word is given by Garcia de Orta in the form *hachaiza*, and in the quotation from Couto as *sachaiza* (?). Jahāngīr speaks of one of his nobles as dying in the Deccan, of *haizah*, in A.D. 1615 (see note to *Elliot*, vi. 346). It is, however, perhaps not to be assumed that *haizah* always means cholera. Thus Macpherson mentions that a violent epidemic, which raged in the Camp of Aurangzīb at Bījapur in 1689, is called so. But in the history of Khāfi Khān (*Elliot*, vii. 337) the general phrases *ta'ūn* and *wabā* are used in reference to this disease, whilst the description is that of bubonic plague.

1781.—"Early in the morning of the 21st June (1781) we had two men seized with the **mort-de-chien.**"—*Curtis, Diseases of India*, 3rd ed., Edinb., 1807.

1782.—"Les indigestions appellées dans l'Inde **Mort-de-chien**, sont fréquentes. Les Castes qui mangent de la viande, nourriture trop pesante pour un climat si chaud, en sont souvent attaquées. . . ."—*Sonnerat*, i. 205. This author writes just after having described two epidemics of cholera under the name of *Flux aigu*. He did not apprehend that this was in fact the real **Mort-de-chien.**

1783.—"A disease generally called '**Mort-de-chien**' at this time (during the defence of Onore) raged with great violence among the native inhabitants."—*Forbes, Or. Mem.* iv. 122.

1796.—"Far more dreadful are the consequences of the above-mentioned intestinal colic, called by the Indians *shani*, **mordexim** and also *Nircomben*. It is occasioned, as I have said, by the winds blowing from the mountains . . . the consequence is that malignant and bilious slimy matter adheres to the bowels, and occasions violent pains, vomiting, fevers, and stupefaction ; so that persons attacked with the disease die very often in a few hours. It sometimes happens that 30 or 40 persons die in this manner, in one place, in the course of the day. . . . In the year 1782 this disease raged with so much fury that a great many persons died of it."—*Fra Paolino*, E.T. 409-410 (orig. see p. 358). As to the names used by Fra Paolino, for his *Shani* or *Ciani*, we find nothing nearer than Tamil and Mal. *sanni*, 'convulsion, paralysis.' (Winslow in his *Tamil Dict*. specifies 13 kinds of *sanni*. *Komben* is explained as 'a kind of cholera or smallpox' (!) ; and *nir-komben* ('water-k.') as a kind of cholera or bilious diarrhœa.) Paolino adds: "La *droga amara* costa assai, e non si poteva amministrare a tanti miserabili che perivano. Adunque in mancanza di questa droga amara noi distillacimo in *Tágara*, o acqua vite di coco, molto sterco di cavalli (!), e l'amministrammo agl' infermi. Tutti quelli che prendevano questa guarivano."

1808.—"**Mōrchee** or **Mortshee** (Guz.) and *Mōdee* (Mah.). A morbid affection in which the symptoms are convulsive action, followed by evacuations of the first passage up and down, with intolerable tenesmus, or twisting-like sensation in the intestines, corresponding remarkably with the cholera-morbus of European synopsists, called by the country people in England (?) **mortisheen**, and by others **mord-du-chien** and **Maua des chienes**, as if it had come from France."—*R. Drummond, Illustrations*, &c. A curious notice ; and the author was, we presume, from his title of "Dr.," a medical man. We suppose for *England* above should be read *India*.

The next quotation is the latest instance of the *familiar* use of the word that we have met with :

1812.—"General M—— was taken very ill three or four days ago ; a kind of fit—**mort de chien**—the doctor said, brought on by eating too many radishes."—*Original Familiar Correspondence between Residents in India*, &c., Edinburgh, 1846, p. 287.

1813.—"**Mort de chien** is nothing more than the highest degree of Cholera Morbus." —*Johnson, Infl. of Tropical Climate*, 405.

The second of the following quotations evidently refers to the outbreak of cholera mentioned, after Macpherson, in the next paragraph.

1780.—"I am once or twice a year (!) subject to violent attacks of **cholera morbus**, here called **mort-de-chien**. . . ."—*Impey to Dunning*, quoted by *Sir James Stephen*, ii. 339.

1781.—"The Plague is now broke out in Bengal, and rages with great violence; it has swept away already above 4000 persons. 200 or upwards have been buried in the different Portuguese churches within a few days."—*Hicky's Bengal Gazette*, April 21.

These quotations show that cholera, whether as an epidemic or as sporadic disease, is no new thing in India. Almost in the beginning of the Portuguese expeditions to the East we find apparent examples of the visitations of this terrible scourge, though no precise name is given in the narratives. Thus we read in the Life of Giovanni da Emboli, an adventurous young Florentine who served with the Portuguese, that, arriving in China in 1517, the ships' crews were attacked by a *pessima malatia di frusso* (virulent flux) of such kind that there died thereof about 70 men, and among these Giovanni himself, and two other Florentines (*Vita*, in *Archiv. Stor. Ital.* 33). Correa says that, in 1503, 20,000 men died of a like disease in the army of the Zamorin. We have given above Correa's description of the terrible Goa pest of 1543, which was most evidently cholera. Madras accounts, according to Macpherson, first mention the disease at Arcot in 1756, and there are frequent notices of it in that neighbourhood between 1763 and 1787. The Hon. R. Lindsay speaks of it as raging at Sylhet in 1781, after carrying off a number of the inhabitants of Calcutta (*Macpherson*, see the quotation of 1781 above). It also raged that year at Ganjam, and out of a division of 5000 Bengal troops under Col. Pearse, who were on the march through that district, 1143 were in a few days sent into hospital, whilst "death raged in the camp with a horror not to be described." The earliest account from the pen of an English physician is by Dr. Paisley, and is dated Madras, Feby. 1774. In 1783 it broke out at Hardwār Fair, and is said, in less than 8 days, to have carried off 20,000 pilgrims. The paucity of cases of cholera among European troops in the returns up to 1817, is ascribed by Dr. Macnamara to the way in which facts were disguised by the current nomenclature of disease. It need not perhaps be denied that the outbreak of 1817 marked a great recrudescence of the disease. But it is a fact that some of the more terrible features of the epidemic, which are then spoken of as quite new, had been prominently described at Goa nearly three centuries before.

See on this subject an article by Dr. J. Macpherson in *Quarterly Review*, for Jany. 1867, and a *Treatise on Asiatic Cholera*, by C. Macnamara, 1876. To these, and especially to the former, we owe several facts and references; though we had recorded quotations relating to **mordexin** and its identity with cholera some years before even the earlier of these publications.

MORDEXIM, MORDIXIM, s. Also the name of a sea-fish. Bluteau says 'a fish found at the Isle of Quixembe on the Coast of Mozambique, very like *bogas* (?) or river-pikes.'

MOSELLAY, n.p. A site at Shīrāz often mentioned by Hāfiz as a favourite spot, and near which is his tomb.

c. 1350.—
"Boy! let yon liquid ruby flow,
And bid thy pensive heart be glad,
Whate'er the frowning zealots say;
Tell them that Eden cannot show
A stream so clear as Rocnabad;
A bower so sweet as **Mossellay**."
Hafiz, rendered by *Sir W. Jones.*

1811.—"The stream of Rúknabád murmured near us; and within three or four hundred yards was the **Mossellá** and the Tomb of Hafiz."—*W. Ouseley's Travels*, i. 318.

1813.—"Not a shrub now remains of the bower of **Mossella**, the situation of which is now only marked by the ruins of an ancient tower."—*Macdonald Kinneir's Persia*, 62.

MOSQUE, s. There is no room for doubt as to the original of this word being the Ar. *masjid*, 'a place of worship,' literally the place of *sujūd*, *i.e.* 'prostration.' And the probable course is this. *Masjid* becomes (1) in Span. *mezquita*, Port. *mesquita*;* (2)

* According to Pyrard *mesquite* is the word used in the Maldive Islands. It is difficult to suppose the people would adopt such a word from the Portuguese. And probably the form both in east and west is to be accounted for by a hard pronunciation of the Arabic *j*, as in Egypt now; the older and probably the most widely diffused. [See Mr. Gray's note in Hak. Soc. ii. 417.]

Ital. *meschita, moschea;* French (old) *mosquete, mosquée;* (3) Eng. *mosque.* Some of the quotations might suggest a different course of modification, but they would probably mislead.

Apropos of *masjid* rather than of mosque we have noted a ludicrous misapplication of the word in the advertisement to a newspaper story. "*Musjeed* the Hindoo: Adventures with the Star of India in the Sepoy Mutiny of 1857." The *Weekly Detroit Free Press, London,* July 1, 1882.

1336. — "Corpusque ipsius perditissimi Pseudo-prophetae . . . in civitate quae Mecha dicitur . . . pro maximo sanctuario conservatur in pulchrâ ipsorum Ecclesiâ quam **Mulscket** vulgariter dicunt."—*Gul. de Boldensele,* in *Canisii Thesaur. ed. Basnage,* iv.

1384.—"Sonvi le **mosquette**, cioe chiese de' Saraceni . . . dentro tutte bianche ed intonicate ed ingessate."—*Frescobaldi,* 29.

1543. — "And with the stipulation that the 5000 *larin tangas* which in old times were granted, and are deposited for the expenses of the **mizquitas** of Baçaim, are to be paid from the said duties as they always have been paid, and in regard to the said **mizquitas** and the prayers that are made in them there shall be no innovation whatever."—Treaty at Baçaim of the Portuguese with King Bador of Çanbaya (Bahādur Shāh of Guzerat) in *S. Botelho, Tombo,* 137.

1553.—". . . but destined yet to unfurl that divine and royal banner of the Soldiery of Christ . . . in the Eastern regions of Asia, amidst the infernal **mesquitas** of Arabia and Persia, and all the **pagodes** of the heathenism of India, on this side and beyond the Ganges."—*Barros,* I. i. 1.

[c. 1610.—"The principal temple, which they call *Oucourou* **misquitte**" (*Hukuru miskitu,* 'Friday mosque').—*Pyrard de Laval,* Hak. Soc. i. 72.]

1616.—"They are very jealous to let their women or **Moschees** be seen."—*Sir T. Roe,* in *Purchas,* i. 537; [Hak. Soc. ii. 21].

[1623.—"We went to see upon the same Lake a **meschita**, or temple of the Mahometans."—*P. della Valle,* Hak. Soc. i. 69.]

1634.—

"Que a de abominação **mesquita** immũda
Casa, a Deos dedicada hoje se veja."
Malaca Conquistada, l. xii. 43.

1638. — Mandelslo unreasonably applies the term to all sorts of pagan temples, *e.g.*—

"Nor is it only in great Cities that the *Benjans* have their many **Mosqueys**. . . ." —E.T. 2nd ed. 1669, p. 52.

"The King of *Siam* is a *Pagan,* nor do his Subjects know any other Religion. They have divers **Mosquees**, Monasteries, and Chappels."—*Ibid.* p. 104.

c. 1662.—". . . he did it only for love to their Mammon; and would have sold afterwards for as much more St. Peter's . . . to the Turks for a **Mosquito**."—*Cowley,* Discourse concerning the Govt. of O. Cromwell.

1680.—Consn. Ft. St. Geo. March 28: "Records the death of Cassa Verona . . . and a dispute arising as to whether his body should be burned by the *Gentues* or buried by the *Moors,* the latter having stopped the procession on the ground that the deceased was a Mussleman and built a **Musseet** in the Towne to be buried in, the Governor with the advice of his Council sent an order that the body should be burned as a *Gentue,* and not buried by the *Moors,* it being apprehended to be of dangerous consequence to admit the Moors such pretences in the Towne."—*Notes and Exts.* No. iii. p. 14.

1719.—"On condition they had a **Cowle** granted, exempting them from paying the Pagoda or **Musqueet** duty."—In *Wheeler,* ii. 301.

1727.—"There are no fine Buildings in the City, but many large Houses, and some Caravanserays and **Muscheits**."—*A. Hamilton,* i. 161; [ed. 1774, i. 163].

c. 1760.—"The Roman Catholic Churches, the Moorish **Moschs**, the Gentoo Pagodas, the worship of the Parsees, are all equally unmolested and tolerated."—*Grose,* i. 44.

[1862.—". . . I slept at a **Musheed**, or village house of prayer."—*Brinckman, Rifle in Cashmere,* 78.]

MOSQUITO, s. A gnat is so called in the tropics. The word is Spanish and Port. (dim. of *mosca,* 'a fly'), and probably came into familiar English use from the East Indies, though the earlier quotations show that it was *first* brought from S. America. A friend annotates here: "Arctic mosquitoes are worst of all; and the Norfolk ones (in the Broads) beat Calcutta!"

It is related of a young Scotch lady of a former generation who on her voyage to India had heard formidable, but vague accounts of this terror of the night, that on seeing an elephant for the first time, she asked: "Will yon be what's called a **musqueetae**?"

1539.—"To this misery was there adjoyned the great affliction, which the Flies and Gnats (*por parte dos atabões e* **mosquitos**), that coming out of the neighbouring Woods, bit and stung us in such sort, as not one of us but was gore blood."—*Pinto* (orig. cap. xxiii.), in *Cogan,* p. 29.

1582. — "We were oftentimes greatly annoyed with a kind of flie, which in the Indian tongue is called *Tiquari,* and the Spanish call them **Muskitos**." — *Miles Phillips,* in *Hakl.* iii. 564.

1584.—"The 29 Day we set Saile from Saint Iohns, being many of vs stung before upon Shoare with the **Muskitos**; but the same night we tooke a Spanish Frigat."—

Sir Richard Greenevile's Voyage, in *Hakl.* iii. 308.

1616 and 1673.—See both *Terry* and *Fryer* under **Chints.**

1662.—"At night there is a kind of insect that plagues one mightily; they are called **Muscieten**,—it is a kind that by their noise and sting cause much irritation." —*Saar*, 68-69.

1673.—"The greatest Pest is the **Mosquito**, which not only wheals, but domineers by its continual Hums."—*Fryer*, 189.

1690.—(The Governor) "carries along with him a *Peon* or Servant to Fan him, and drive away the busie Flies, and troublesome **Musketoes**. This is done with the Hair of a Horse's Tail."—*Ovington*, 227-8.

1740.—". . . all the day we were pestered with great numbers of **muscatos**, which are not much unlike the gnats in *England*, but more venomous. . . ."—*Anson's Voyage*, 9th ed., 1756, p. 46.

1764.—

"**Mosquitos**, sandflies, seek the sheltered roof,
And with full rage the stranger guest assail,
Nor spare the sportive child."
—*Grainger*, bk. i.

1883.—"Among rank weeds in deserted Bombay gardens, too, there is a large, speckled, unmusical **mosquito**, raging and importunate and thirsty, which will give a new idea in pain to any one that visits its haunts."—*Tribes on My Frontier*, 27.

MOTURPHA, s. Hind. from Ar. *muḥtarafa*, but according to C. P. B. *mu'tarifa*; [rather Ar. *muḥtarifa*, *muḥtarif*, 'an artizan']. A name technically applied to a number of miscellaneous taxes in Madras and Bombay, such as were called **sayer** (q.v.), in Bengal.

[1813.—"**Mohterefa**. An artificer. Taxes, personal and professional, on artificers, merchants and others; also on houses, implements of agriculture, looms, &c., a branch of the **sayer**."—*Gloss. 5th Report*, s.v.

1826.—". . . for example, the tax on merchants, manufacturers, &c. (called **mohturfa**). . . ."—*Grant Duff*, *H. of the Mahrattas*, 3rd ed. 356.]

MOULMEIN, n.p. This is said to be originally a Talaing name *Mutmwoa-lem*, syllables which mean (or may be made to mean) 'one-eye-destroyed'; and to account for which a cock-and-bull legend is given (probably invented for the purpose): "Tradition says that the city was founded . . . by a king with three eyes, having an extra eye in his forehead, but that by the machinations of a woman, the eye in his forehead was destroyed. . . ." (*Mason's Burmah*, 2nd ed. p. 18). The Burmese corrupted the name into *Maula-yaing*, whence the foreign (probably Malay) form *Maulmain*. The place so called is on the opposite side of the estuary of the Salwin R. from **Martaban** (q.v.), and has entirely superseded that once famous port. Moulmein, a mere site, was chosen as the headquarters of the Tenasserim provinces, when those became British in 1826 after the first Burmese War. It has lost political importance since the annexation of Pegu, 26 years later, but is a thriving city which numbered in 1881, 53,107 inhabitants; [in 1891, 55,785].

MOUNT DELY, n.p. (See **DELLY, MOUNT**.)

MOUSE-DEER, s. The beautiful little creature, *Meminna indica* (Gray), [*Tragulus meminna*, the Indian Chevrotain (*Blanford*, *Mammalia*, 555),] found in various parts of India, and weighing under 6 lbs., is so called. But the name is also applied to several pigmy species of the genus *Tragulus*, found in the Malay regions, [where, according to Mr. Skeat, it takes in popular tradition the place of Brer Rabbit, outwitting even the tiger, elephant, and crocodile.] All belong to the family of Musk-deer.

MUCHÁN, s. Hind. *machān*, Dekh. *manchān*, Skt. *mañcha*. An elevated platform; such as the floor of huts among the Indo-Chinese races; or a stage or scaffolding erected to watch a tiger, to guard a field, or what not.

c. 1662.—"As the soil of the country is very damp, the people do not live on the ground-floor, but on the **machán**, which is the name for a raised floor."—*Shiháhuddin Tálish*, by *Blochmann*, in *J. A. S. B.* xli. Pt. i. 84.

[1882.—"In a shady green **mechan** in some fine tree, watching at the cool of evening. . . ."—*Sanderson*, *Thirteen Years*, 3rd ed. 284.]

MUCHWA, s. Mahr. *machwā*, Hind. *machuā*, *machwā*. A kind of boat or barge in use about Bombay.

MUCKNA, s. Hind. *makhnā*, [which comes from Skt. *matkuna*, 'a bug, a flea, a beardless man, an elephant without tusks']. A male elephant without tusks or with only rudimentary tusks. These latter are familiar in Bengal, and still more so in Ceylon, where according to Sir S. Baker, "not more than one in 300 has tusks; they are merely provided with short grubbers, projecting generally about 3 inches from the upper jaw, and about 2 inches in diameter." (*The Rifle and Hound in Ceylon*, 11.) Sanderson (13 *Years among the Wild Beasts of India*, [3rd ed. 66]) says: "On the Continent of India *mucknas*, or elephants *born* without tusks, are decidedly rare . . . *Mucknas* breed in the herds, and the peculiarity is not hereditary or transmitted." This author also states that out of 51 male elephants captured by him in Mysore and Bengal only 5 were *mucknas*. But the definition of a *makhnā* in Bengal is that which we have given, including those animals which possess only feminine or rudimentary tusks, the 'short grubbers' of Baker; and these latter can hardly be called rare among domesticated elephants. This may be partially due to a preference in purchasers.* The same author derives the term from *mukh*, 'face'; but the reason is obscure. Shakespear and Platts give the word as also applied to 'a cock without spurs.'

c. 1780.—"An elephant born with the left tooth only is reckoned sacred; with black spots in the mouth unlucky, and not saleable; the **mukna** or elephant born without teeth is thought the best."—*Hon. R. Lindsay* in *Lives of the Lindsays*, iii. 194.

MUCOA, MUKUVA, n.p. Malayal. and Tamil, *mukkuvan* (sing.), 'a diver,' and *mukkuvar* (pl.). [Logan (*Malabar*, ii. Gloss. s.v.) derives it from Drav. *mukkuha*, 'to dive'; the *Madras Gloss.* gives Tam. *muzhugu*, with the same meaning.] A name applied to the fishermen of the western coast of the Peninsula near C. Comorin. [But Mr. Pringle (*Diary, Ft. St. Geo.* 1st ser. iii. 187) points out that formerly as now, the word was of much more general application. Orme in a passage quoted below employs it of boatmen at Karikal. The use of the word extended as far N. as Madras, and on the W. coast; it was not confined to the extreme S.] It was among these, and among the corresponding class of **Paravars** on the east coast, that F. Xavier's most noted labours in India occurred.

1510.—"The fourth class are called **Mechua**, and these are fishers."—*Varthema*, 142.

1525.—"And Dom João had secret speech with a married Christian whose wife and children were inside the fort, and a valiant man, with whom he arranged to give him 200 **pardaos** (and that he gave him on the spot) to set fire to houses that stood round the fort. . . . So this Christian, called Duarte Fernandes . . . put on a lot of old rags and tags, and powdered himself with ashes after the fashion of *jogues* (see **JOGEE**) . . . also defiling his hair with a mixture of oil and ashes, and disguising himself like a regular *jogue*, whilst he tied under his rags a parcel of gunpowder and pieces of slow-match, and so commending himself to God, in which all joined, slipped out of the fort by night, and as the day broke, he came to certain huts of **macuas**, which are fishermen, and began to beg alms in the usual palaver of the *jogues*, *i.e.* prayers for their long life and health, and the conquest of enemies, and easy deliveries for their womenkind, and prosperity for their children, and other grand things."—*Correa*, ii. 871.

1552.—Barros has **mucuaria**, 'a fisherman's village.'

1600.—"Those who gave the best reception to the Gospel were the **Macóas**; and, as they had no church in which to assemble, they did so in the fields and on the shores, and with such fervour that the Father found himself at times with 5000 or 6000 souls about him."—*Lucena, Vida do P. F. Xavier*, 117.

[c. 1610.—"These mariners are called **Moucois**."—*Pyrard de Laval*, Hak. Soc. i. 314.]

1615.—"Edixit ut **Macuae** omnes, id est vilissima plebecula et piscatu vivens, Christiana sacra susciperent."—*Jarric*, i. 390.

1626.—"The **Muchoa** or **Mechoe** are Fishers . . . the men Theeues, the women Harlots, with whom they please. . . ."—*Purchas, Pilgrimage*, 553.

1677.—Resolved "to raise the rates of hire of the *Mesullas* (see **MUSSOOLA**) boatmen called **Macquars**."—*Ft. St. Geo. Consn.*, Jan 12, in *Notes and Exts.* No. i. 54.

[1684.—"The **Maquas** or Boatmen ye Ordinary Astralogers (*sic*) for weather did . . . prognosticate great Rains. . . ."—*Pringle, Diary, Ft. St. Geo.*, 1st ser. iii. 131.]

1727.—"They may marry into lower Tribes . . . and so may the **Muckwas**, or Fishers, who, I think, are a higher tribe than the *Poulias* (see **POLEA**)."—*A. Hamilton*, i. 310, [ed. 1744, i. 312].

* Sir George Yule notes: "I can distinctly call to mind 6 mucknas that I had (I may have had more) out of 30 or 40 elephants that passed through my hands." This would give 15 or 20 per cent. of *mucknas*, but as the stud included females, the result would rather consist with Mr. Sanderson's 5 out of 51 males.

[1738. — "Gastos com Nairos, Tibas, **Maquas**."—Agreement, in *Logan, Malabar*, ii. 36.]

1745.—"The **Macoas**, a kind of Malabars, who have specially this business, and, as we might say, the exclusive privilege in all that concerns sea-faring."—*Norbert*, i. 227-8.

1746.—"194 **Macquars** attending the sea-side at night . . . (P.) 8 : 8 : 40."—*Account of Extraordinary Expenses, at Ft. St. David* (India Office MS. Records).

1760. — "Fifteen *massoolas* (see **MUSSOOLA**) accompanied the ships; they took in 170 of the troops, besides the **Macoas**, who are the black fellows that row them." —*Orme*, ed. 1803, iii. 617.

[1813.—"The **Muckwas** or **Macuars** of Tellicherry are an industrious, useful set of people."—*Forbes, Or. Mem.* 2nd ed. i. 202.]

MUDDÁR, s. Hind. *madār*, Skt. *mandāra*; *Calotropis procera*, R. Brown, N.O. *Asclepiadaceae*. One of the most common and widely diffused plants in uncultivated plains throughout India. In Sind the bark fibre is used for halters, &c., and experiment has shown it to be an excellent material worth £40 a ton in England, if it could be supplied at that rate; but the cost of collection has stood in the way of its utilisation. The seeds are imbedded in a silky floss, used to stuff pillows. This also has been the subject of experiment for textile use, but as yet without practical success. The plant abounds with an acrid milky juice which the Rājputs are said to employ for infanticide. (*Punjab Plants.*) The plant is called **Ak** in Sind and throughout N. India.

MUDDLE, s. (?) This word is only known to us from the clever—perhaps too clever—little book quoted below. The word does not seem to be known, and was probably a misapprehension of **budlee**. [Even Mr. Brandt and Mrs. Wyatt are unable to explain this word. The former does not remember hearing it. Both doubt its connection with **budlee**. Mrs. Wyatt suggests with hesitation Tamil *muder*, "boiled rice," *mudei-palli*, "the cook-house."]

1836-7.—"Besides all these acknowledged and ostensible attendants, each servant has a kind of **muddle** or double of his own, who does all the work that can be put off upon him without being found out by his master or mistress."—*Letters from Madras*, 38.

" "They always come accompanied by their Vakeels, a kind of Secretaries, or interpreters, or flappers,—their **muddles** in short; everybody here has a **muddle**, high or low."—*Letters from Madras*, 86.

MUFTY, s.

a. Ar. *Muftī*, an expounder of the Mahommedan Law, the utterer of the *fatwā* (see **FUTWAH**). Properly the *Muftī* is above the *Kāẓī* who carries out the judgment. In the 18th century, and including Regulation IX. of 1793, which gave the Company's Courts in Bengal the reorganization which substantially endured till 1862, we have frequent mention of both *Cauzies* and *Mufties* as authorized expounders of the Mahommedan Law; but, though Kāẓīs were nominally maintained in the Provincial Courts down to their abolition (1829-31), practically the duty of those known as Kāẓīs became limited to quite different objects and the designation of the Law-officer who gave the *futwā* in our District Courts was *Maulavī*. The title *Muftī* has been long obsolete within the limits of British administration, and one might safely say that it is practically unknown to any surviving member of the Indian Civil Service, and never was heard in India as a living title by any Englishman now surviving. (See **CAZEE, LAW-OFFICER, MOOLVEE**).

b. A slang phrase in the army, for 'plain clothes.' No doubt it is taken in some way from **a**, but the transition is a little obscure. [It was perhaps originally applied to the attire of dressing - gown, smoking - cap, and slippers, which was like the Oriental dress of the *Muftī* who was familiar in Europe from his appearance in Moliere's *Bourgeois Gentilhomme*. Compare the French *en Pekin*.]

a.—

1653.—"Pendant la tempeste vne femme **Indûstani** mourut sur notre bord; vn **Moufti** Persan de la Secte des Schaï (see **SHEEAH**) assista à cette derniere extrémité, luy donnant esperance d'vne meilleure vie que celle-cy, et d'vn Paradis, où l'on auroit tout ce que l'on peut desirer . . . et la fit changer de Secte. . . ."—*De la Boullaye-le-Gouz*, ed. 1657, p. 281.

1674.—"Resolve to make a present to the Governors of Changulaput and Pallaveram, old friends of the Company, and now about to go to Golcondah, for the marriage of the former with the daughter of the King's **Mufti** or Churchman."—*Fort St. Geo. Consn.*, March 26. In *Notes and Exts.*, No. i. 30.

1767.—"3d. You will not let the **Cauzy** or **Mufty** receive anything from the tenants unlawfully." — *Collectors' Instructions*, in *Long*, 511.

1777.—"The **Cazi** and **Muftis** now deliver in the following report, on the right of inheritance claimed by the widow and nephew of Shabaz Beg Khan. . : ."—*Report on the Patna Cause*, quoted in *Stephen's Nuncomar and Impey*, ii. 167.

1793.—"§ XXXVI. The **Cauzies** and **Muftis** of the provincial Courts of Appeal, shall also be **cauzies** and **mufties** of the courts of circuit in the several divisions, and shall not be removable, except on proof to the satisfaction of the Governor-General in Council that they are incapable, or have been guilty of misconduct. . . ."—*Reg. IX. of* 1793.

[c. 1855.—
"Think'st thou I fear the dark vizier,
Or the **mufti's** vengeful arm?"
Bon Gaultier, The Cadi's Daughter.]

MUGG, n.p. Beng. *Magh*. It is impossible to deviate without deterioration from Wilson's definition of this obscure name: "A name commonly applied to the natives of Arakan, particularly those bordering on Bengal, or residing near the sea; the people of Chittagong." It is beside the question of its origin or proper application, to say, as Wilson goes on to say, on the authority of Lieut. (now Sir Arthur) Phayre, that the Arakanese disclaim the title, and restrict it to a class held in contempt, viz. the descendants of Arakanese settlers on the frontier of Bengal by Bengali mothers. The proper names of foreign nations in any language do not require the sanction of the nation to whom they are applied, and are often not recognised by the latter. German is not the German name for the Germans, nor Welsh the Welsh name for the Welsh, nor Hindu (originally) a Hindu word, nor China a Chinese word. The origin of the present word is very obscure. Sir A. Phayre kindly furnishes us with this note: "There is good reason to conclude that the name is derived from *Maga*, the name of the ruling race for many centuries in *Magadha* (modern Behar). The kings of Arakan were no doubt originally of this race. For though this is not distinctly expressed in the histories of Arakan, there are several legends of Kings from Benares reigning in that country, and one regarding a Brahman who marries a native princess, and whose descendants reign for a long period. I say this, although Buchanan appears to reject the theory (see *Montg. Martin*, ii. 18 *seqq.*)" The passage is quoted below.

On the other hand the Mahommedan writers sometimes confound Buddhists with fire-worshippers, and it seems possible that the word may have been Pers. *magh*='magus.' [See *Risley, Tribes and Castes*, ii. 28 *seq.*] The Chittagong Muggs long furnished the best class of native cooks in Calcutta; hence the meaning of the last quotation below.

1585.—"The **Mogen**, which be of the kingdom of Recon (see **ARAKAN**) and Rame, be stronger than the King of Tipara; so that Chatigam or **Porto Grande** (q.v.) is often under the King of Recon."—*R. Fitch*, in *Hakl.* ii. 389.

c. 1590.—(In a country adjoining Pegu) "there are mines of ruby and diamond and gold and silver and copper and petroleum and sulphur and (the lord of that country) has war with the tribe of **Magh** about the mines; also with the tribe of Tipara there are battles."—*Āīn* (orig.) i. 388; [ed. *Jarrett*, ii. 120].

c. 1604.—"*Defeat of the* **Magh** *Rájá*.—This short-sighted Rájá . . . became elated with the extent of his treasures and the number of his elephants. . . . He then openly rebelled, and assembling an army at Sunárgánw laid seige to a fort in that vicinity . . . Rájá Mán Singh . . . despatched a force. . . . These soon brought the **Magh** Rájá and all his forces to action . . . regardless of the number of his boats and the strength of his artillery."—*Ináyatullah*, in *Elliot*, vi. 109.

1638.—"Submission of Manek Rái, the **Mag** Rájá of Chittagong."—*Abdul-Hamid Lahori*, in do. vii. 66.

c. 1665.—"These many years there have always been in the Kingdom of *Rakan* or *Moy* (read **Mog**) some *Portuguese*, and with them a great number of their *Christian* Slaves, and other *Franguis*. . . . *That* was the refuge of the Run-aways from *Goa*, *Ceilan*, *Cochin*, *Malague* (see **MALACCA**), and all these other places which the Portugueses formerly held in the *Indies*."—*Bernier*, E.T. p. 53; [ed. *Constable*, 109].

1676.—"In all *Bengala* this King (of *Arakan*) is known by no other name but the King of **Mogue**."—*Tavernier*, E.T. i. 8.

1752.—". . . that as the time of the **Mugs** draws nigh, they request us to order the pinnace to be with them by the end of next month."—In *Long*, p. 87.

c. 1810.—"In a paper written by Dr. Leyden, that gentleman supposes . . . that Magadha is the country of the people whom we call **Muggs**. . . . The term **Mugg**, these people assured me, is never used by either themselves or by the Hindus, except when speaking the jargon commonly called Hindustani by Europeans. . . ."—*F. Buchanan*, in *Eastern India*, ii. 18.

1811.—"**Mugs**, a dirty and disgusting people, but strong and skilful. They are somewhat of the Malayan race."—*Solvyns*, iii.

1866.—"That vegetable curry was excellent. Of course your cook is a **Mug**?"—*The Dawk Bungalow*, 389.

MUGGUR, s. Hind. and Mahr. *magar* and *makar*, from Skt. *makara* 'a sea-monster' (see **MACAREO**). The destructive broad-snouted crocodile of the Ganges and other Indian rivers, formerly called *Crocodilus biporcatus*, now apparently subdivided into several sorts or varieties.

1611.—"Alagaters or Crocodiles there called **Murgur** *match*. . . ."—*Hawkins*, in *Purchas*, i. 436. The word is here intended for *magar-mats* or *machh*, 'crocodile-fish.'

[1876.—See under **NUZZER**.]

1878.—"The **muggur** is a gross pleb, and his features stamp him as low-born. His manners are coarse."—*Ph. Robinson, In My Indian Garden*, 82-3.

1879.—"En route I killed two crocodiles; they are usually called alligators, but that is a misnomer. It is the **mugger** . . . these **muggers** kill a good many people, and have a playful way of getting under a boat, and knocking off the steersman with their tails, and then swallowing him afterwards."—*Pollok, Sport*, &c., i. 168.

1881.—"Alligator leather attains by use a beautiful gloss, and is very durable . . . and it is possible that our rivers contain a sufficient number of the two varieties of crocodile, the **muggar** and the *garial* (see **GAVIAL**) for the tanners and leather-dressers of Cawnpore to experiment upon."—*Pioneer Mail*, April 26.

MUGGRABEE, n.p. Ar. *maghrabī*, 'western.' This word, applied to western Arabs, or Moors proper, is, as might be expected, not now common in India. It is the term that appears in the Hayraddin **Mograbbin** of *Quentin Durward*. From *gharb*, the root of this word, the Spaniards have the province of **Algarve**, and both Spanish and Portuguese have **garbin**, a west wind. [The magician in the tale of Alaeddin is a *Maghrabī*, and to this day in Languedoc and Gascony *Maugraby* is used as a term of cursing. (*Burton*, *Ar. Nights*, x. 35, 379). **Muggerbee** is used for a coin (see **GUBBER**).]

1563.—"The proper tongue in which Avicena wrote is that which is used in Syria and Mesopotamia and in Persia and in Tartary (from which latter Avicena came) and this tongue they call *Araby*; and that of our Moors they call **Magaraby**, as much as to say Moorish of the West. . . ."—*Garcia*, f. 19*v*.

MULL, s. A contraction of **Mulligatawny**, and applied as a distinctive sobriquet to members of the Service belonging to the Madras Presidency, as Bengal people are called **Qui-his**, and Bombay people **Ducks** or **Benighted**.

[1837.—"The **Mulls** have been excited also by another occurrence . . . affecting rather the trading than fashionable world."—*Asiatic Journal*, December, p. 251.]

[1852.—". . . residents of Bengal, Bombay, and Madras are, in Eastern parlance, designated 'Qui Hies,' 'Ducks,' and '**Mulls**.'"—*Notes and Queries*, 1st ser. v. 165.]

1860.—"It ys ane darke Londe, and ther dwellen ye *Cimmerians* whereof speketh *Homerus Poeta* in his *Odysseia*, and to thys Daye thei clepen *Tenebrosi* or 'ye Benyghted ffolke.' Bot thei clepen hemselvys **Mullys** from *Mulligatawnee* wh[ch] ys ane of theyr goddys from w[ch] thei ben ysprong."—Ext. from a lately discovered MS. of *Sir John Maundeville*.

MULLIGATAWNY, s. The name of this well-known soup is simply a corruption of the Tamil *milagu-tannīr*, 'pepper-water'; showing the correctness of the popular belief which ascribes the origin of this excellent article to Madras, whence—and not merely from the complexion acquired there—the sobriquet of the preceding article.

1784.—
"In vain our hard fate we repine;
  In vain on our fortune we rail;
On **Mullaghee-tawny** we dine,
  Or **Congee**, in Bangalore Jail."
Song by a Gentleman of the Navy (one of Hyder's Prisoners), in *Seton-Karr*, i. 18.

[1823.— . . . in a brasen pot was **mulugu tanni**, a hot vegetable soup, made chiefly from pepper and capsicums."—*Hoole, Missions in Madras*, 2nd ed. 249.]

MULMULL, s. Hind. *malmal*; Muslin.

[c. 1590.—"**Malmal**, per piece . . . 4 R."—*Āīn*, ed. *Blochmann*, i. 94.]

1683.—"Ye said Ellis told your Petitioner that he would not take 500 Pieces of your Petitioner's **mulmulls** unless your Petitioner gave him 200 Rups. which your Petitioner being poor could not do."—

Petition of *Rogoodee,* Weaver of Hugly, in *Hedges, Diary,* March 26; [Hak. Soc. i. 73].

1705.—"**Malle-molles** et autre diverses sortes de toiles . . . stinquerques et les belles mousselines."—*Luillier,* 78.

MUNCHEEL, MANJEEL, s. This word is proper to the S.W. coast; Malayal. *manjīl, mañchal,* from Skt. *mañcha.* It is the name of a kind of hammock-litter used on that coast as a substitute for palankin or dooly. It is substantially the same as the **dandy** of the Himālaya, but more elaborate. Correa describes but does not name it.

1561.—". . . He came to the factory in a litter which men carried on their shoulders. These are made with thick canes, bent upwards and arched, and from them are suspended some clothes half a fathom in width, and a fathom and a half in length; and at the extremities pieces of wood to sustain the cloth hanging from the pole; and upon this cloth a mattress of the same size as the cloth . . . the whole very splendid, and as rich as the gentlemen . . . may desire."—*Correa, Three Voyages,* &c., p. 199.

1811.—"The Inquisition is about a quarter of a mile distant from the convent, and we proceeded thither in **manjeels**."—*Buchanan, Christian Researches,* 2nd ed., 171.

1819.—"**Muncheel,** a kind of litter resembling a sea-cot or hammock, hung to a long pole, with a moveable cover over the whole, to keep off the sun or rain. Six men will run with one from one end of the Malabar coast to the other, while twelve are necessary for the lightest palanquin."—*Welsh,* ii. 142.

1844.—"**Muncheels,** with poles complete. . . . Poles, **Muncheel-,** Spare."—*Jameson's Bombay Code, Ordnance Nomenclature.*

1862.—"We . . . started . . . in **Munsheels** or hammocks, slung to bamboos, with a shade over them, and carried by six men, who kept up unearthly yells the whole time."—*Markham, Peru and India,* 353.

c. 1886.—"When I landed at Diu, an officer met me with a **Muncheel** for my use, viz. a hammock slung to a pole, and protected by an awning."—*M.-Gen. R. H. Keatinge.*

A form of this word is used at Réunion, where a kind of palankin is called "le **manchy.**" It gives a title to one of Leconte de Lisle's Poems:

c. 1858.—
"Sous un nuage frais de claire mousseline
Tous les dimanches au matin,
Tu venais à la ville en **manchy** de rotin,
Par les rampes de la colline."
Le **Manchy.**

The word has also been introduced by the Portuguese into Africa in the forms *maxilla,* and *machilla.*

1810.—". . . tangas, que elles chamão **maxilas.**"—*Annaes Maritimas,* iii. 434.

1880.—"The Portuguese (in Quilliman) seldom even think of walking the length of their own street, and . . . go from house to house in a sort of palanquin, called here a **machilla** (pronounced *masheela*). This usually consists of a pole placed upon the shoulders of the natives, from which is suspended a long plank of wood, and upon that is fixed an old-fashioned-looking chair, or sometimes two. Then there is an awning over the top, hung all round with curtains. Each **machilla** requires about 6 to 8 bearers, who are all dressed alike in a kind of livery."—*A Journey in E. Africa,* by *M. A. Pringle,* p. 89.

MUNGOOSE, s. This is the popular Anglo-Indian name of the Indian ichneumons, represented in the South by *Mangusta Mungos* (Elliot), or *Herpestes griseus* (Geoffroy) of naturalists, and in Bengal by *Herpestes malaccensis.* [Blanford (*Mammalia,* 119 *seqq.*) recognises eight species, the "Common Indian Mungoose" being described as *Herpestes mungo.*] The word is Telugu, *mangīsu,* or *mungīsa.* In Upper India the animal is called *newal, neolā,* or *nyaul.* Jerdon gives *mangūs* however as a Deccani and Mahr. word; [Platts gives it as dialectic, and very doubtfully derives it from Skt. *makshu,* 'moving quickly.' In Ar. it is *bint-'arūs,* 'daughter of the bridegroom,' in Egypt *kitt* or *katt Farāūn,* 'Pharaoh's cat' (*Burton, Ar. Nights,* ii. 369].

1673.—". . . a **Mongoose** is akin to a Ferret. . . ."—*Fryer,* 116.

1681.—"The knowledge of these antidotal herbs they have learned from the **Moung-gutia,** a kind of Ferret."—*Knox,* 115.

1685.—"They have what they call a **Mangus,** creatures something different from ferrets; these hold snakes in great antipathy, and if they once discover them never give up till they have killed them."—*Ribeyrô,* f. 56*v.*

Bluteau gives the following as a quotation from a *History of Ceylon,* tr. from Portuguese into French, published at Paris in 1701, p. 153. It is in fact the gist of an anecdote in Ribeyro.

"There are persons who cherish this animal and have it to sleep with them, although it is ill-tempered, for they prefer to be bitten by a **mangus** to being killed by a snake."

1774.—"He (the Dharma Raja of Bhootan) has got a little lap-dog and a **Mungoos,** which he is very fond of."—*Bogle's Diary,* in *Markham's Tibet,* 27.

1790. — "His (Mr. Glan's) experiments have also established a very curious fact, that the ichneumon, or **mungoose**, which is very common in this country, and kills snakes without danger to itself, does not use antidotes . . . but that the poison of snakes is, to this animal, innocent."—Letter in *Colebrooke's Life*, p. 40.

1829.—"Il **Mongùse** animale simile ad una donnola."—*Papi*, in *de Gubernatis, St. dei Viagg. Ital.*, p. 279.

MUNJEET, s. Hind. *majīṭh*, Skt. *mañjishṭha;* a dye-plant (*Rubia cordifolia*, L., N.O. *Cinchonaceae*); 'Bengal Madder.'

MUNNEEPORE, n.p. Properly *Manipūr;* a quasi-independent State lying between the British district of Cachar on the extreme east of Bengal, and the upper part of the late kingdom of Burma, and in fact including a part of the watershed between the tributaries of the Brahmaputra and those of the Irawadi. The people are of genuinely Indo-Chinese and Mongoloid aspect, and the State, small and secluded as it is, has had its turn in temporary conquest and domination, like almost all the States of Indo-China from the borders of Assam to the mouth of the Mekong. Like the other Indo-Chinese States, too, Manipūr has its royal chronicle, but little seems to have been gathered from it. The Rājas and people have, for a period which seems uncertain, professed Hindu religion. A disastrous invasion of Manipūr by Alompra, founder of the present Burmese dynasty, in 1755, led a few years afterwards to negotiations with the Bengal Government, and the conclusion of a treaty, in consequence of which a body of British sepoys was actually despatched in 1763, but eventually returned without reaching Manipūr. After this, intercourse practically ceased till the period of our first Burmese War (1824-25), when the country was overrun by the Burmese, who also entered Cachar; and British troops, joined with a Manipūrī force, expelled them. Since then a British officer has always been resident at Manipūr, and at one time (c. 1838-41) a great deal of labour was expended on opening a road between Cachar and Manipūr. [The murder of Mr. Quinton, Chief-Commissioner of Assam, and other British officers at Manipūr, in the close of 1890, led to the infliction of severe punishment on the leaders of the outbreak. The Mahārāja, whose abdication led to this tragedy, died in Calcutta in the following year, and the State is now under British management during the minority of his successor.]

This State has been called by a variety of names. Thus, in Rennell's *Memoir* and maps of India it bears the name of **Meckley**. In Symes's *Narrative*, and in maps of that period, it is **Cassay**; names, both of which have long disappeared from modern maps. *Meckley* represents the name (*Makli?*) by which the country was known in Assam; *Mogli* (apparently a form of the same) was the name in Cachar; *Ka-sé* or *Ka-thé* (according to the Ava pronunciation) is the name by which it is known to the Shans or Burmese.

1755.—"I have carried my Arms to the *confines* of CHINA . . . on the other quarter I have reduced to my subjection the major part of the Kingdom of **Cassay**; whose Heir I have taken captive, see there he sits behind you. . . ."—Speech of *Alompra* to *Capt. Baker* at *Momchabue. Dalrymple, Or. Rep.* i. 152.

1759.—"**Cassay**, which . . . lies to the N. Westward of AVA, is a Country, so far as I can learn, hitherto unheard of in Europe. . . ."—*Letter*, dd. 22 June 1759, in *ibid.* 116.

[1762. — ". . . the President sent the Board a letter which he had received from Mr. Verelst at Chittagong, containing an invitation which had been made to him and his Council by the Rajah of **Meckley** to assist him in obtaining redress . . . from the Burmas. . . ." — Letter, in *Wheeler, Early Records*, 291.]

1763.—"**Meckley** is a Hilly Country, and is bounded on the North, South, and West by large tracts of *Cookie Mountains*, which prevent any intercourse with the countries beyond them; and on the East* by the Burampoota (see **BURRAMPOOTER**); beyond the Hills, to the North by Asam and *Poong;* to the West Cashar; to the South and East the BURMAH Country, which lies between Meckley and China. . . . The *Burampoota* is said to divide, somewhere to the north of *Poong*, into two large branches, one of which passes through ASAM, and down by the way of *Dacca*, the other through POONG into the Burma Country."—*Acct. of Meckley*, by *Nerher Doss Gosseen*, in *Dalrymple's Or. Rep.*, ii. 477-478.

". . . there is about *seven days plain" country* between **Moneypoor** and **Burampoota**, after crossing which, about

* Here the Kyendwen R. is regarded as a branch of the Brahmaputra. See further on.

seven days, Jungle and Hills, to the inhabited border of the Burmah country."—*Ibid.* 481.

1793.—". . . The first ridge of mountains towards Thibet and Bootan, forms the limit of the survey to the north; to which I may now add, that the surveys extend no farther eastward, than the frontiers of Assam and Meckley. . . . The space between Bengal and China, is occupied by the province of Meckley and other districts, subject to the King of Burmah, or Ava. . . ."—*Rennell's Memoir,* 295.

1799.—(Referring to 1757). "Elated with success Alompra returned to Monchaboo, now the seat of imperial government. After some months . . . he took up arms against the **Cassayers.** . . . Having landed his troops, he was preparing to advance to **Munnepoora,** the capital of **Cassay,** when information arrived that the Peguers had revolted. . . ."—*Symes, Narrative,* 41-42.

" "All the troopers in the King's service are natives of **Cassay,** who are much better horsemen than the Birmans." —*Ibid.* 318.

1819.—"Beyond the point of Negraglia (see **NEGRAIS**), as far as Azen (see **ASSAM**), and even further, there is a small chain of mountains that divides Aracan and **Cassé** from the Burmese. . . ."—*Sangermano,* p. 33.

1827.—"The extensive area of the Burman territory is inhabited by many distinct nations or tribes, of whom I have heard not less than eighteen enumerated. The most considerable of these are the proper Burmans, the Peguans or Talains, the Shans or people of Lao, the **Cassay,** or more correctly Kathé. . . ."—*Crawfurd's Journal,* 372.

1855.—"The weaving of these silks . . . gives employment to a large body of the population in the suburbs and villages round the capital, especially to the **Munnipoorians,** or **Kathé,** as they are called by the Burmese.

"These people, the descendants of unfortunates who were carried off in droves from their country by the Burmans in the time of King Mentaragyi and his predecessors, form a very great proportion . . . of the metropolitan population, and they are largely diffused in nearly all the districts of Central Burma. . . . Whatever work is in hand for the King or for any of the chief men near the capital, these people supply the labouring hands; if boats have to be manned they furnish the rowers; and whilst engaged on such tasks any remuneration they may receive is very scanty and uncertain."—*Yule, Mission to Ava,* 153-154.

MUNSUBDAR. Hind. from Pers. *mansabdār,* 'the holder of office or dignity' (Ar. *mansab*). The term was used to indicate quasi-feudal dependents of the Mogul Government who had territory assigned to them, on condition of their supplying a certain number of horse, 500, 1000 or more. In many cases the title was but nominal, and often it was assumed without warrant. [Mr. Irvine discusses the question at length and represents *mansab* by "the word '*rank,*' as its object was to settle precedence and fix gradation of pay; it did not necessarily imply the exercise of any particular office, and meant nothing beyond the fact that the holder was in the employ of the State, and bound in return to yield certain services when called upon." (*J.R.A.S.,* July 1896, pp. 510 *seqq.*)]

[1617.—". . . slew one of them and twelve **Maancipdares.**"—*Sir T. Roe,* Hak. Soc. ii. 417; in ii. 461, "**Mancipdaries.**"

[1623. — ". . . certain Officers of the Militia, whom they call **Mansubdàr.**"—*P. della Valle,* Hak. Soc. i. 97.]

c. 1665.—"**Mansebdars** are Cavaliers of *Manseb,* which is particular and honourable Pay; not so great indeed as that of the *Omrahs* . . . they being esteemed as little *Omrahs,* and of the rank of those, that are advanced to that dignity."—*Bernier,* E.T. p. 67; [ed. *Constable,* 215].

1673.—"**Munsubdars** or petty *omrahs.*" —*Fryer,* 195.

1758.—". . . a **munsubdar** or commander of 6000 horse."—*Orme,* ed. 1803, ii. 278.

MUNTRA, s. Skt. *mantra,* 'a text of the Vedas; a magical formula.'

1612.—". . . Trata da causa primeira, segundo os livros que tem, chamados Terum **Mandra** mole" (*mantra-mūla, mūla* 'text').—*Couto,* Dec. V. liv. vi. cap. 3.

1776.—"**Mantur**—a text of the Shaster." —*Halhed, Code,* p. 17.

1817.—". . . he is said to have found the great **mantra,** spell or talisman."—*Mill, Hist.* ii. 149.

MUNTREE, s. Skt. *Mantri.* A minister or high official. The word is especially affected in old Hindu States, and in the Indo-Chinese and Malay States which derive their ancient civilisation from India. It is the word which the Portuguese made into **mandarin** (q.v.).

1810.—"When the Court was full, and Ibrahim, the son of Candu the merchant, was near the throne, the Raja entered. . . . But as soon as the Rajah seated himself, the **muntries** and high officers of state arrayed themselves according to their rank."—In a Malay's account of Government House at Calcutta, transl. by Dr. Leyden, in *Maria Graham,* p. 200.

[1811.—"**Mantri.**" See under **ORANKAY.**

[1829.—"The **Mantris** of Mewar prefer estates to pecuniary stipend, which gives more consequence in every point of view."—*Tod, Annals*, Calcutta reprint, i. 150.]

MUNZIL, s. Ar. *manzil*, 'descending or alighting,' hence the halting place of a stage or march, a day's stage.

1685.—"We were not able to reach Obdeen-deen (ye usual **Menzill**) but lay at a sorry **Caravan Sarai**."—*Hedges, Diary*, July 30; [Hak. Soc. i. 203. In i. 214, **manzeill**].

MUSCÁT, n.p., properly *Măskăt*. A port and city of N.E. Arabia; for a long time the capital of 'Omān. (See **IMAUM**.)

[1659.—"The Governor of the city was Chah-Navaze-kan . . . descended from the ancient Princes of **Machate**. . . ."—*Bernier*, ed. *Constable*, 73.]

1673.—"**Muschat**." See under **IMAUM**.

MUSIC. There is no matter in which the sentiments of the people of India differ more from those of Englishmen than on that of music, and curiously enough the one kind of Western music which they appreciate, and seem to enjoy, is that of the bagpipe. This is testified by Captain Munro in the passage quoted below; but it was also shown during Lord Canning's visit to Lahore in 1860, in a manner which dwells in the memory of one of the present writers. The escort consisted of part of a Highland regiment. A venerable Sikh chief who heard the pipes exclaimed: 'That is indeed music! it is like that which we hear of in ancient story, which was so exquisite that the hearers became insensible (*behosh*).'

1780.—"The bagpipe appears also to be a favourite instrument among the natives. They have no taste indeed for any other kind of music, and they would much rather listen to this instrument a whole day than to an organ for ten minutes."—*Munro's Narrative*, 33.

MUSK, s. We get this word from the Lat. *muschus*, Greek *μόσχος*, and the latter must have been got, probably through Persian, from the Skt. *mushka*, the literal meaning of which is rendered in the old English phrase 'a cod of musk.' The oldest known European mention of the article is that which we give from St. Jerome; the oldest medical prescription is in a work of Aetius, of Amida (c. 540). In the quotation from Cosmas the word used is *μόσχος*, and *kastūri* is a Skt. name, still, according to Royle, applied to the musk-deer in the Himālaya. The transfer of the name to (or from) the article called by the Greeks *καστόριον*, which is an analogous product of the beaver, is curious. The Musk-deer (*Moschus moschiferus*, L.) is found throughout the Himālaya at elevations rarely (in summer) below 8000 feet, and extends east to the borders of Szechuen, and north to Siberia.

c. 390.—"Odoris autem suavitas, et diversa thymiamata, et amomum, et cyphi, oenanthe, **muscus**, et peregrini muris pellicula, quod dissolutis et amatoribus conveniat, nemo nisi dissolutus negat."—*St. Jerome*, in Lib. Secund. *adv. Jovinianum*, ed. *Vallarsii*, ii. col. 337.

c. 545.—"This little animal is the **Musk** (*μόσχος*). The natives call it in their own tongue *καστοῦρι*. They hunt it and shoot it, and binding tight the blood collected about the navel they cut this off, and this is the sweet smelling part of it, and what we call **musk**."—*Cosmas Indicopleustes*, Bk. xi.

["**Muske** commeth from Tartaria. . . . There is a certaine beast in Tartaria, which is wilde and big as a wolfe, which beast they take aliue, and beat him to death with small staues y^t his blood may be spread through his whole body, then they cut it in pieces, and take out all the bones, and beat the flesh with the blood in a mortar very smal, and dry it, and make purses to put it in of the skin, and these be the Cods of **Muske**."—*Caesar Frederick*, in *Hakl*. ii. 372.]

1673.—"**Musk**. It is best to buy it in the Cod . . . that which openeth with a bright *Mosk* colour is best."—*Fryer*, 212.

MUSK-RAT, s. The popular name of the *Sorex caerulescens*, Jerdon, [*Crocidura caerulea*, Blanford], an animal having much the figure of the common shrew, but nearly as large as a small brown rat. It diffuses a strong musky odour, so penetrative that it is commonly asserted to affect bottled beer by running over the bottles in a cellar. As Jerdon judiciously observes, it is much more probable that the corks have been affected before being used in bottling; [and Blanford (*Mammalia*, 237) writes that "the absurd story . . . is less credited in India than it formerly was, owing to the discovery that liquors bottled in Europe and exported to India are not liable to be tainted."] When the female is in heat she is often seen to be followed by a string of males giving out the odour strongly. Can this be the *mus peregrinus* mentioned by St. Jerome (see **MUSK**), as P. Vincenzo supposes?

c. 1590.—"Here (in Tooman Bekhrad, n. of Kabul R.) are also **mice** that have a fine **musky scent**."—*Ayeen*, by *Gladwin* (1800) ii. 166; [ed. *Jarrett*, ii. 406].

[1598.—"They are called sweet smelling **Rattes**, for they have a smell as if they were full of **Muske**."—*Linschoten*, Hak. Soc. i. 303.]

1653.—"Les rats d'Inde sont de deux sortes. . . . La deuxiesme espece que les Portugais appellent *cheroso* ou odoriferant est de la figure d'vn furet" (a ferret), "mais extremement petit, sa morseure est veneneuse. Lorsqu'il entre en vne chambre l'on le sent incontinent, et l'on l'entend crier *krik, krik, krik*."—*De la Boullaye-le-Gouz*, ed. 1657, p. 256. I may note on this that Jerdon says of the *Sorex murinus*,—the large musk-rat of China, Burma, and the Malay countries, extending into Lower Bengal and Southern India, especially the Malabar coast, where it is said to be the common species (therefore probably that known to our author),—that the bite is considered venomous by the natives (*Mammals*, p. 54), [a belief for which, according to Blanford (*l.c.* p. 236), there is no foundation].

1672.—P. Vincenzo Maria, speaking of his first acquaintance with this animal (*il ratto del musco*), which occurred in the Capuchin Convent at Surat, says with simplicity (or malignity?): "I was astonished to perceive an odour so fragrant* in the vicinity of those most religious Fathers, with whom I was at the moment in conversation."—*Viaggio*, p. 385.

1681.—"This country has its vermin also. They have a sort of Rats they call **Muskrats**, because they smell strong of musk. These the inhabitants do not eat of, but of all other sorts of Rats they do."—*Knox*, p. 31.

1789.—H. Munro in his *Narrative* (p. 34) absurdly enough identifies this animal with the **Bandicoot**, q.v.

1813.—See *Forbes, Or. Mem.* i. 42; [2nd. ed. i. 26].

MUSLIN, s. There seems to be no doubt that this word is derived from Mosul (Mauṣal or Mauṣil) on the Tigris,† and it has been from an old date the name of a texture, but apparently not always that of the thin semi-transparent tissue to which we now apply it. Dozy (p. 323) says that the Arabs employ *mauṣili* in the same sense as our word, quoting the *Arabian Nights* (Macnaghten's ed., i. 176, and ii. 159), in both of which the word indicates the material of a *fine* turban. [Burton (i. 211) translates 'Mosul stuff,' and says it may mean either of 'Mosul fashion,' or muslin.] The quotation from Ives, as well as that from Marco Polo, seems to apply to a different texture from what we call muslin.

1298.—"All the cloths of gold and silk that are called **Mosolins** are made in this country (Mausul)."—*Marco Polo*, Bk. i. chap. 5.

c. 1544.—"*Almussoli* est regio in Mesopotamia, in qua texuntur telae ex bombyce valde pulchrae, quae apud Syros et Aegyptios et apud mercatores Venetos appellantur **mussoli**, ex hoc regionis nomine. Et principes Aegyptii et Syri, tempore aestatis sedentes in loco honorauiliori induunt vestes ex hujusmodi **mussoli**."—*Andreae Bellunensis*, Arabicorum nominum quae in libris *Avicennae* sparsim legebantur *Interpretatio*.

1573.—". . . you have all sorts of Cotton-works, Handkerchiefs, long Fillets, Girdles . . . and other sorts, by the *Arabians* called **Mossellini** (after the Country *Mussoli*, from whence they are brought, which is situated in Mesopotamia), by us **Muslin**."—*Rauwolff*, p. 84.

c. 1580.—"For the rest the said Agiani (misprint for Bagnani, **Banyans**) wear clothes of white **mussolo** or *sessa* (?); having their garments very long and crossed over the breast."—*Gasparo Balbi*, f. 33*b*.

1673.—"Le drap qu'on estend sur les matelas est d'une toille aussy fine que de la **mousceline**."—App. to *Journal d'Ant. Galland*, ii. 198.

1685.—"I have been told by several, that **muscelin** (so much in use here for cravats) and *Calligo* (!), and the most of the Indian linens, are made of nettles, and I see not the least improbability but that they may be made of the fibres of them."—*Dr. Hans Sloane to Mr. Ray*, in *Ray Correspondence*, 1848, p. 163.

c. 1760.—"This city (Mosul)'s manufacture is **Mussolin** [read **Mussolen**] (a cotton cloth) which they make very strong and pretty fine, and sell for the European and other markets."—*Ives, Voyage*, p. 324.

MUSNUD, s. H.—Ar. *masnad*, from root *sanad*, 'he leaned or rested upon it.' The large cushion, &c., used by native Princes in India, in place of a throne.

1752.—"Salabat-jing . . . went through the ceremony of sitting on the **musnud** or throne."—*Orme*, ed. 1803, i. 250.

1757.—"On the 29th the Colonel went to the Soubah's Palace, and in the presence of all the Rajahs and great men of the court,

* "*Stupiva* d'vdire tanta fragranza." The Scotchman is laughed at for "feeling" a smell, but here the Italian *hears* one!

† We have seen, however, somewhere an ingenious suggestion that the word really came from *Maisolia* (the country about Masulipatam, according to Ptolemy), which even in ancient times was famous for fine cotton textures.

led him to the **Musland**. . . ."—*Reflexions by Luke Scrafton, Esq.*, ed. 1770, p. 93.

1803.—"The Peshwah arrived yesterday, and is to be seated on the **musnud**."—*A. Wellesley*, in *Munro's Life*, i. 343.

1809. — "In it was a **musnud**, with a carpet, and a little on one side were chairs on a white cloth."—*Ld. Valentia*, i. 346.

1824.—"They spread fresh carpets, and prepared the royal **musnud**, covering it with a magnificent shawl."—*Hajji Baba*, ed. 1835, p. 142.

1827.—"The Prince Tippoo had scarcely dismounted from his elephant, and occupied the **musnud**, or throne of cushions."—*Sir W. Scott, Surgeon's Daughter*, ch. xiv.

MUSSALLA, s. P.—H. (with change of sense from Ar. *maṣāliḥ*, pl. of *maṣlaḥa*) 'materials, ingredients,' lit. 'things for the good of, or things or affairs conducive to good.' Though sometimes used for the ingredients of any mixture, *e.g.* to form a cement, the most usual application is to spices, curry-stuffs and the like. There is a tradition of a very gallant Governor-General that he had found it very tolerable, on a sharp but brief campaign, to "rough it on **chuprassies** and **mussaulchees**" (qq.v.), meaning *chupatties* and *mussalla*.

1780.—"A dose of **marsall**, or purgative spices."—*Munro, Narrative*, 85.

1809.—"At the next hut the woman was grinding **missala** or curry-stuff on a flat smooth stone with another shaped like a rolling pin."—*Maria Graham*, 20.

MUSSAUL, s. Hind. from Ar. *mash'al*, 'a torch.' It is usually made of rags wrapt round a rod, and fed at intervals with oil from an earthen pot.

c. 1407.—"Suddenly, in the midst of the night they saw the Sultan's camp approaching, accompanied by a great number of **mashal**."—*Abdurazzāk*, in *N. & Exts.* xiv. Pt. i. 153.

1673.—"The *Duties* * march like Furies with their lighted **mussals** in their hands, they are Pots filled with Oyl in an Iron Hoop like our Beacons, and set on fire by stinking rags."—*Fryer*, 33.

1705.—". . . flambeaux qu'ils appellent **Mansalles**."—*Luillier*, 89.

1809.—"These **Mussal** or link-boys."—*Ld. Valentia*, i. 17.

* *Deotī*, a torch-bearer. Thus Baber: "If the emperor or chief nobility (in India) at any time have occasion for a light by night, these filthy *Deuties* bring in their lamps, which they carry up to their master, and stand holding it close by his side "—*Baber*, 333.

1810.—"The **Mosaul**, or flambeau, consists of old rags, wrapped very closely round a small stick."—*Williamson, V. M.* i. 219.

[1813.—"These nocturnal processions illumined by many hundred **massauls** or torches, illustrate the parable of the ten virgins. . . ."—*Forbes, Or. Mem.* 2nd ed. ii. 274.

[1857.—"Near him was another Hindoo . . . he is called a **Mussal**; and the lamps and lights are his special department."—*Lady Falkland, Chow-Chow*, 2nd ed. i. 35.]

MUSSAULCHEE, s. Hind. *mash'-alchī* from *mash'al* (see **MUSSAUL**), with the Turkish termination *chī*, generally implying an agent. [In the *Arabian Nights* (*Burton*, i. 239) *al-masha'ilī* is the executioner.] The word properly means a link-boy, and was formerly familiar in that sense as the epithet of the person who ran alongside of a palankin on a night journey, bearing a **mussaul**. "In Central India it is the special duty of the barber (*nāī*) to carry the torch; hence *nāī* commonly = 'torch-bearer'" (*M.-Gen. Keatinge*). The word [or sometimes in the corrupt form **mussaul**] is however still more frequent as applied to a humble domestic, whose duty was formerly of a like kind, as may be seen in the quotation from Ld. Valentia, but who now looks after lamps and washes dishes, &c., in old English phrase 'a scullion.'

1610.—"He always had in service 500 **Massalgees**."—*Finch*, in *Purchas*, i. 432.

1662.—(In Asam) "they fix the head of the corpse rigidly with poles, and put a lamp with plenty of oil, and a **mash'alchi** [torch-bearer] alive into the vault, to look after the lamp." — *Shihābuddīn Tālish*, tr. by *Blochmann*, in *J.A.S.B.* xli. Pt. i. 82.

[1665.—"They (flambeaux) merely consist of a piece of iron hafted in a stick, and surrounded at the extremity with linen rags steeped in oil, which are renewed . . . by the **Masalchis**, or link boys, who carry the oil in long narrow-necked vessels of iron or brass."—*Bernier*, ed. *Constable*, 361.]

1673.—"Trois **Massalgis** du Grand Seigneur vinrent faire honneur à M. l'Ambassadeur avec leurs feux allumés."—*Journal d'Ant. Galland*, ii. 103.

1686. — "After strict examination he chose out 2 persons, the *Chout* (*Chous?*), an Armenian, who had charge of watching my tent that night, and my **Mossalagee**, a person who carries the light before me in the night."—*Hedges, Diary*, July 2; [Hak. Soc. i. 232].

[1775. — ". . . **Mashargues**, Torch-bearers." — Letter of *W. Mackrabie*, in *Francis, Letters*, i. 227.]

1791.—". . . un **masolchi**, ou porte-flambeau, pour la nuit."—*B. de St. Pierre, La Chaumière Indienne*, 16.

1809.—"It is universally the custom to drive out between sunset and dinner. The **Massalchees**, when it grows dark, go out to meet their masters on their return, and run before them, at the full rate of eight miles an hour, and the numerous lights moving along the esplanade produce a singular and pleasing effect."—*Ld. Valentia*, i. 240.

1813.—"The occupation of **massaulchee**, or torch-bearer, although generally allotted to the village barber, in the purgannas under my charge, may vary in other districts."—*Forbes, Or. Mem.* ii. 417; [2nd ed. ii. 43].

1826.—"After a short conversation, they went away, and quickly returned at the head of 200 men, accompanied by **Mussalchees** or torch-bearers." — *Pandurang Hari*, 557; [ed. 1873, ii. 69].

[1831.—". . . a **mossolei**, or man to light up the place."—*Asiatic Journal*, N.S. v. 197.]

MUSSENDOM, CAPE, n.p. The extreme eastern point of Arabia, at the entrance of the Persian Gulf. Properly speaking, it is the extremity of a small precipitous island of the name, which protrudes beyond the N.E. horn of 'Omān. The name is written *Masăndim* in the map which Dr. Badger gives with his *H. of 'Oman.* But it is *Rās Masandam* (or possibly *Masandum*) in the *Mohit* of Sidi 'Ali Kapudān (*J. As. Soc. Ben.*, v. 459). Sprenger writes *Mosandam* (*Alt. Geog. Arabiens*, p. 107). [Morier gives another explanation (see the quotation below).]

1516.—". . . it (the coast) trends to the N.E. by N. 30 leagues until Cape **Mocondon**, which is at the mouth of the Sea of Persia."—*Barbosa*, 32.

1553.—". . . before you come to Cape **Moçandan**, which Ptolemy calls *Asaboro* (Ἀσαβῶν ἄκρον) and which he puts in 23½°, but which we put in 26°; and here terminates our first division" (of the Eastern Coasts).—*Barros*, I. ix. 1.

1572.—

"Olha o cabo Asabóro que chamado
Agora he **Moçandão** dos navegantes:
Por aqui entra o lago, que he fechado
De Arabia, e Persias terras abundantes."
Camões, x. 102.

By Burton:

"Behold of Asabón the Head, now hight
Mosandam, by the men who plough the Main:
Here lies the Gulf whose long and lake-like Bight,
parts Araby from fertile Persia's plain."

The fact that the poet copies the misprint or mistake of Barros in *Asaboro*, shows how he made use of that historian.

1673.—"On the one side St. Jaques (see **JASK**) his Headland, on the other that of **Mussendown** appeared, and afore Sunset we entered the Straights Mouth."—*Fryer*, 221.

1727.—"The same Chain of rocky Mountains continue as high as Zear, above Cape **Musenden**, which Cape and Cape Jaques begin the Gulf of Persia."—*A. Hamilton*, i. 71; [ed. 1744, i. 73].

1777.—"At the mouth of the Strait of **Mocandon**, which leads into the Persian gulph, lies the island of **Gombroon**" (?)—*Raynal*, tr. 1777, i. 86.

[1808.—"**Musseldom** is a still stronger instance of the perversion of words. The genuine name of this head-land is *Mama Selemeh*, who was a female saint of Arabia, and lived on the spot or in its neighbourhood."—*Morier, Journey through Persia*, p. 6.]

MUSSOOLA, MUSSOOLAH, BOAT, s. The surf boat used on the Coromandel Coast; of capacious size, and formed of planks sewn together with coir-twine; the open joints being made good with a caulking or wadding of twisted coir. The origin of the word is very obscure. Leyden thought it was derived from "*masoula* . . . the Mahratta term for fish" (*Morton's Life of Leyden*, 64). As a matter of fact the Mahr. word for fish is *māsolī*, Konk. *māsūlī*. This etymology is substantially adopted by Bp. Heber (see below); [and by the compiler of the *Madras Gloss.*, who gives Tel. *māsūla*, Hind. *machhlī*]. But it may be that the word is some Arabic sea-term not in the dictionaries. Indeed, if the term used by C. Federici (below) be not a clerical error, it suggests a possible etymology from the Ar. *masad*, 'the fibrous bark of the palm-tree, a rope made of it.' Another suggestion is from the Ar. *mauṣūl*, 'joined,' as opposed to 'dug-out,' or canoes; or possibly it may be from *maḥṣūl*, 'tax,' if these boats were subject to a tax. Lastly it is possible that the name may be connected with **Masulipatam** (q.v.), where similar boats would seem to have been in use (see *Fryer*, 26). But these are conjectures. The quotation from Gasparo Balbi gives a good account of the handling of these boats, but applies no name to them.

c. 1560.—"Spaventosa cosa'è chi nõ ha più visto, l'imbarcare e sbarcar le mercantie e le persone a San Tomè . . . adoperano certe barchette fatte aposta molto alte e larghe, ch' essi chiamano **Masudi**, e sono fatte con tauole sottili, e con corde sottili cusite insieme vna tauola con l'altre," &c. (there follows a very correct description of their use).—*C. Federici*, in *Ramusio*, iii. 391.

c. 1580.—". . . where (Negapatam) they cannot land anything but in the **Maçules** of the same country."—*Primor e Honra*, &c., f. 93.

c. 1582.—". . . There is always a heavy sea there (San Thomé), from swell or storm; so the merchandise and passengers are transported from shipboard to the town by certain boats which are sewn with fine cords, and when they approach the beach, where the sea breaks with great violence, they wait till the perilous wave has past, and then, in the interval between one wave and the next, those boatmen pull with great force, and so run ashore; and being there overtaken by the waves they are carried still further up the beach. And the boats do not break, because they give to the wave, and because the beach is covered with sand, and the boats stand upright on their bottoms."—*G. Balbi*, f. 89.

1673.—"I went ashore in a **Mussoola**, a Boat wherein ten Men paddle, the two aftermost of whom are Steersmen, using their Paddles instead of a Rudder. The Boat is not strengthened with Knee-Timbers, as ours are; the bended Planks are sowed together with Rope-Yarn of the Cocoe, and calked with *Dammar* (see **DAMMER**) (a sort of Resin taken out of the Sea), so artificially that it yields to every ambitious Surf."—*Fryer*, 37.

[1677.—"**Mesullas**." See **MUCOA**.]

1678.—"Three Englishmen drowned by upsetting of a **Mussoola** boat. The fourth on board saved with the help of the *Muckwas*" (see **MUCOA**).—*Ft. St. Geo. Consn.*, Aug. 13. *Notes and Exts.*, No. i. p. 78.

1679.—"A **Musseolee** being overturned, although it was very smooth water and no surf, and one Englishman being drowned, a Dutchman being with difficulty recovered, the Boatmen were seized and put in prison, one escaping."—*Ibid.* July 14. In No. ii. p. 16.

[1683.—"This Evening about seven a Clock a **Mussula** coming ashoar . . . was oversett in the Surf and all four drowned."—*Pringle, Diary, Ft. St. Geo.* 1st ser. ii. 54.]

1685.—"This morning two **Musoolas** and two *Cattamarans* came off to ye Shippe."—*Hedges, Diary*, Feb. 3; [Hak. Soc. i. 182].

1760.—"As soon as the yawls and pinnaces reached the surf they dropped their graplings, and cast off the **masoolas**, which immediately rowed ashore, and landed the troops."—*Orme*, iii. 617.

1762.—"No European boat can land, but the natives make use of a boat of a particular construction called a **Mausolo**," &c.—*MS. Letter of James Rennell*, April 1.

[1773.—". . . the governor . . . sent also four **Mossulas**, or country boats, to accommodate him. . . ."—*Ives*, 182.]

1783.—"The want of **Massoola** boats (built expressly for crossing the surf) will be severely felt."—In *Life of Colebrooke*, 9.

1826.—"The **masuli**-boats (which first word is merely a corruption of 'muchli,' fish) have been often described, and except that they are sewed together with coco-nut twine, instead of being fastened with nails, they very much resemble the high, deep, charcoal boats . . . on the Ganges."—*Heber*, ed. 1844, ii. 174.

1879.—"Madras has no harbour; nothing but a long open beach, on which the surf dashes with tremendous violence. Unlucky passengers were not landed there in the ordinary sense of the term, but were thrown violently on the shore, from springy and elastic **Masulah** boats, and were occasionally carried off by sharks, if the said boats chanced to be upset in the rollers."—*Saty. Review*, Sept. 20.

MUSSUCK, s. The leathern water-bag, consisting of the entire skin of a large goat, stript of the hair and dressed, which is carried by a *bhishtī* (see **BHEESTY**). Hind. *mashak*, Skt. *maśaka*.

[1610.—"**Mussocke**." See under **RUPEE**.

[1751.—"7 hands of **Musuk**" (probably meaning *Bhistis*).—In *Yule, Hedges' Diary*, Hak. Soc. II. xi.]

1842.—"Might it not be worth while to try the experiment of having '**mussucks**' made of waterproof cloth in England?"—*Sir G. Arthur*, in *Ind. Adm. of Lord Ellenborough*, 220.

MUSSULMAN, adj. and s. Mahommedan. *Muslim*, 'resigning' or 'submitting' (*sc.* oneself to God), is the name given by Mahommed to the Faithful. The Persian plural of this is *Muslimân*, which appears to have been adopted as a singular, and the word *Muslimān* or *Musalmān* thus formed. [Others explain it as either from Ar. pl. *Muslimīn*, or from *Muslim-mān*, 'like a Muslim,' the former of which is adopted by Platts as most probable.]

1246.—"Intravimus terram **Bisermino-rum**. Isti homines linguam Comanicam loquebantur, et adhuc loquuntur; sed legem Sarracenorum tenent."—*Plano Carpini*, in *Rec. de Voyages*, &c. iv. 750.

c. 1540.—". . . disse por tres vezes, *Lah, hilah, hilah, lah Muhamed roçol halah*, o **Massoleymoens** *e homes justos da santa ley de Mafamede.*"—*Pinto*, ch. lix.

1559.—"Although each horde (of Tartars) has its proper name, *e.g.* particularly the horde of the Savolhensians . . . and many others, which are in truth Mahometans; yet do they hold it for a grievous insult and reproach to be called and styled *Turks*; they wish to be styled **Besermani**, and by this name the Turks also desire to be styled."—*Herberstein*, in *Ramusio*, ii. f. 171.

[1568.—"I have noted here before that if any Christian will become a **Busorman**, . . . and be a Mahumetan of their religion, they give him any gifts . . ."—*A. Edward*, in *Hakl*. i. 442.]

c. 1580.—"Tutti sopradetti Tartari seguitano la fede de' Turchi et alla Turchesca credono, ma si tẽgono a gran vergogna, e molto si corrociano l'esser detti Turchi, secondo che all' incontro godono d'esser **Besurmani**, cioè gẽte eletta, chiamati."—*Descrittione della Sarmatia Evropea* del magn. caval. *Aless. Gvagnino*, in *Ramusio*, ii. Pt. ii. f. 72.

1619.—". . . i **Musulmani**, cioè i salvati: che cosa pazzamente si chiamano fra di loro i maomettani."—*P. della Valle*, i. 794.

,, "The precepts of the **Moslemans** are first, circumcision . . ."—*Gabriel Sionita*, in *Purchas*, ii. 1504.

1653.—". . . son infanterie d'Indistannis **Mansulmans**, ou Indiens de la secte des Sonnis."—*De la Boullaye-le-Gouz*, ed. 1657, 233.

1673.—"Yet here are a sort of bold, lusty, and most an end, drunken Beggars of the **Musslemen** Cast, that if they see a Christian in good clothes, mounted on a stately horse . . . are presently upon their Punctilio's with God Almighty, and interrogate him, Why he suffers him to go a Foot, and in Rags, and this *Coffery* (see **CAFFER**) (Unbeliever) to vaunt it thus?"—*Fryer*, 91.

1788.—"We escape an ambiguous termination by adopting *Moslem* instead of **Musulman** in the plural number."—*Gibbon*, pref. to vol. iv.

MUST, adj. Pers. *mast*, 'drunk.' It is applied in Persia also, and in India specially, to male animals, such as elephants and camels, in a state of periodical excitement.

[1882.—"Fits of **Must** differ in duration in different animals (elephants); in some they last for a few weeks, in others for even four or five months."—*Sanderson, Thirteen Years*, 3rd ed., 59.]

MUSTEES, MESTIZ, &c., s. A **half-caste**. A corruption of the Port. *mestiço*, having the same meaning; "a mixling; applied to human beings and animals born of a father and mother of different species, like a mule" (*Bluteau*); French, *métis* and *métif*.

1546.—"The Governor in honour of this great action (the victory at Diu) ordered that all the **mestiços** who were in Dio should be inscribed in the Book, and that pay and subsistence should be assigned to them,—subject to the King's confirmation. For a regulation had been sent to India that no **mestiço** of India should be given pay or subsistence: for, as it was laid down, it was their duty to serve for nothing, seeing that they had their houses and heritages in the country, and being on their native soil were bound to defend it."—*Correa*, iv. 580.

1552.—". . . the sight of whom as soon as they came, caused immediately to gather about them a number of the natives, Moors in belief, and Negroes with curly hair in appearance, and some of them only swarthy, as being **mistiços**."—*Barros*, I. ii. 1.

1586.—". . . che se sono nati qua di donne indiane, gli domandano **mestizi**."—*Sassetti*, in *De Gubernatis*, 188.

1588.—". . . an Interpretour . . . which was a **Mestizo**, that is halfe an Indian, and halfe a Portugall."—*Candish*, in *Hakl*. iv. 337.

c. 1610.—"Le Capitaine et les Marchands estoient **Mestifs**, les autres Indiens Christianisez."—*Pyrard de Laval*, i. 165; [Hak. Soc. i. 78; also see i. 240]. This author has also **Métifs** (ii. 10; [Hak. Soc. i. 373]), and again: ". . : qu'ils appellent **Metices**, c'est à dire **Metifs**, meslez" (ii. 23; [Hak. Soc. ii. 38]).

,, "Ie vy vne moustre generalle de tous les Habitans portans armes, tant Portugais que **Metices** et Indiens, and se trouuerent environ 4000."—*Moquet*, 352.

[1615.—"A **Mestiso** came to demand passage in our junck."—*Cocks's Diary*, Hak. Soc. i. 216.]

1653.—(At Goa) "Les **Mestissos** sont de plusieurs sortes, mais fort mesprisez des **Reinols** et Castissos (see **CASTEES**), parce qu'il y a eu vn peu de sang noir dans la generation de leurs ancestres . . . la tache d'auoir eu pour ancestre une Indienne leur demeure iusques à la centiesme generation: ils peuuent toutesfois estre soldats et Capitaines de forteresses ou de vaisseaux, s'ils font profession de suiure les armes, et s'ils se iettent du costé de l'Eglise ils peuuent estre Lecteurs, mais non Prouinciaux."—*De la Boullaye-le-Gouz*, ed. 1657, p. 226.

c. 1665.—"And, in a word, *Bengale* is a country abounding in all things; and 'tis for this very reason that so many *Portuguese*, **Mesticks**, and other Christians are fled thither."—*Bernier*, E.T. 140; [ed. *Constable*, 438].

[1673.—"Beyond the Outworks live a few Portugals **Musteroes** or **Misteradoes**."—*Fryer*, 57.]

1678.—"Noe Roman Catholick or Papist, whether English or of any other nation shall bear office in this Garrison, and shall have no more pay than 80 **fanams** per mensem, as private centinalls, and the pay of those of the Portuguez nation, as Europeans, **Musteeses**, and **Topasees**, is from 70 to 40 **fanams** per mensem."—*Articles and Orders . . . of Ft. St. Geo.*, Madraspatam. In *Notes and Exts.*, i. 88.

1699.—"Wives of Freemen, **Mustees**."—Census of Company's Servants on the Coast, in *Wheeler*, i. 356.

1727.—"A poor Seaman had got a pretty **Mustice** Wife."—*A. Hamilton*, ii. 10; [ed. 1744, ii. 8].

1781.—"Eloped from the service of his Mistress a Slave Boy aged 20 years, or thereabouts, pretty white or colour of **Musty**, tall and slinder."—*Hicky's Bengal Gazette*, Feb. 24.

1799.—"August 13th. . . . Visited by appointment . . . Mrs. Carey, the last survivor of those unfortunate persons who were imprisoned in the Black Hole of Calcutta. . . . This lady, now fifty-eight years of age, as she herself told me, is . . . of a fair **Mesticia** colour. . . . She confirmed all which Mr. Holwell has said. . . ."—*Note by* Thomas Boileau (an attorney in Calcutta, the father of Major-Generals John Theophilus and A. H. E. Boileau, R.E. (Bengal)), quoted in *Echoes of Old Calcutta*, 34.

1834.—"You don't know these Baboos. . . . Most of them now-a-days have their **Misteesa** *Beebees*, and their Moosulmaunees, and not a few their *Gora* Beebees likewise."—*The Baboo*, &c., 167-168.

1868.—"These **Mestizas**, as they are termed, are the native Indians of the Philippines, whose blood has to a great extent perhaps been mingled with that of their Spanish rulers. They are a very exclusive people . . . and have their own places of amusement . . . and **Mestiza** balls, to which no one is admitted who does not don the costume of the country."—*Collingwood, Rambles of a Naturalist*, p. 296.

MUSTER, s. A pattern, or a sample. From Port. *mostra* (Span. *muestra*, Ital. *mostra*). The word is current in China, as well as India. See *Wells Williams's Guide*, 237.

c. 1444.—"Vierão as nossas Galés por commissão sua com algunas **amostras** de açucar, da Madeira, de Sangue de Drago, e de outras cousas."—*Cadamosta, Navegação primeira*, 6.

1563.—"And they gave me a **mostra** of *amomum*, which I brought to Goa, and showed to the apothecaries here; and I compared it with the drawings of the simples of Dioscorides."—*Garcia*, f. 15.

1601.—"**Musters** and Shewes of Gold."—*Old Transl. of Galvano*, Hak. Soc. p. 83.

1612.—"A Moore came aboord with a **muster** of Cloves."—*Saris*, in *Purchas*, i. 357.

[1612-13.—"**Mustraes**." See under **CORGE**.]

1673.—"Merchants bringing and receiving **Musters**."—*Fryer*, 84.

1702.—". . . Packing Stuff, Packing Materials, **Musters**."—Quinquepartite Indenture, in *Charters of the E.I. Co.*, 325.

1727.—"He advised me to send to the King . . . that I designed to trade with his Subjects . . . which I did, and in twelve Days received an Answer that I might, but desired me to send some person up with **Musters** of all my Goods."—*A. Hamilton*, ii. 200; [ed. 1744].

c. 1760.—"He (the tailor) never measures you; he only asks *master for* **muster**, as he terms it, that is for a pattern."—*Ives*, 52.

1772.—"The Governor and Council of Bombay must be written to, to send round **Musters** of such kinds of silk, and silk piece-goods, of the manufacture of Bengal, as will serve the market of Surat and Bombay."—*Price's Travels*, i. 39.

[1846.—"The above **muster** was referred to a party who has lately arrived from . . . England. . . ."—*J. Agri. Hort. Soc.*, in *Watt, Econ. Dict.* vi. pt. ii. 601.]

MUTLUB, s. Hind. from Ar. *matlab*. The Ar. from *ṭalab*, 'he asked,' properly means a question, hence intention, wish, object, &c. In Anglo-Indian use it always means 'purpose, gist,' and the like. Illiterate natives by a common form of corruption turn the word into *matbal*. In the Punjab this occurs in printed books; and an adjective is formed, *matbalī*, 'opinionated,' and the like.

MUTT, MUTH, s. Skt. *maṭha*; a sort of convent where a celibate priest (or one making such profession) lives with disciples making the same profession, one of whom becomes his successor. Buildings of this kind are very common all over India, and some are endowed with large estates.

[1856.—". . . a Gosaeen's **Mut** in the neighbourhood . . ."—*Rās Mālā*, ed. 1878, p. 527.]

1874.—"The monastic Order is celibate, and in a great degree erratic and mendicant, but has anchorage places and head-quarters in the **maths**."—*Calc. Review*, cxvii. 212.

MUTTONGOSHT, s. (*i.e.* 'Mutton-flesh.') Anglo-Indian domestic Hind. for 'Mutton.'

MUTTONGYE, s. Sea-Hind. *matangai*, a (nautical) martingale; a corruption of the Eng. word.

MUTTRA, n.p. A very ancient and holy Hindu city on the Jumna, 30 miles above Agra. The name is *Mathura*, and it appears in *Ptolemy* as Μόδουρα ἡ τῶν Θεῶν. The sanctity of the name has caused it to be applied in numerous new localities; see under **MADURA**. [Tavernier (ed. *Ball*, ii. 240) calls it **Matura**, and Bernier (ed. *Constable*, 66), **Maturas**.]

MUXADABAD, n.p. Ar.—P. *Maksūdābād*, a name that often occurs in books of the 18th century. It pertains to the same city that has latterly been called *Murshidābād*, the capital of the Nawābs of Bengal since the beginning of the 18th century. The town *Maksūdābād* is stated by Tiefenthaler to have been founded by Akbar. The Governor of Bengal, Murshid Kulī Khān (also called in English histories Jafier Khan), moved the seat of Government hither in 1704, and gave the place his own name. It is written *Muxudavad* in the early English records down to 1760 (*Sir W. W. Hunter*).

[c. 1670.—"**Madesou Bazarki,**" in *Tavernier*, ed. *Ball*, i. 132.]

1684.—"Dec. 26.—In ye morning I went to give Bulchund a visit according to his invitation, who rose up and embraced me when I came near him, enquired of my health and bid me welcome to **Muxoodavad**. . . ."—*Hedges, Diary*, Hak. Soc. i. 59.

1703-4.—"The first act of the Nuwab, on his return to Bengal, was to change the name of the city of **Makhsoosabad** to Moorshudabad; and by establishing in it the mint, and by erecting a palace . . . to render it the capital of the Province."—*Stewart, H. of Bengal*, 309.

1726.—"**Moxadabath.**"—*Valentijn, Chorom.*, &c., 147.

1727.—"**Muxadabaud** is but 12 miles from it (Cossimbazar), a Place of much greater Antiquity, and the Mogul has a Mint there; but the ancient name of *Muxadabaud* has been changed for Rajahmal, for above a Century."—*A. Hamilton*, ii. 20; [ed. 1744]. (There is great confusion in this.)

1751.—"I have heard that Ram Kissen Seat, who lives in Calcutta, has carried goods to that place without paying the **Muxidavad** Syre (see **SAYER**) Chowkey duties. I am greatly surprised, and send a Chubdar to bring him, and desire you will be speedy in delivering him over."—Letter from *Nawab Allyverdi Caun* to the Prest. of Council, dated **Muxidavad**, May 20.

1753.—"En omettant quelques lieux de moindre considération, je m'arrête d'abord à **Mocsudabad**. Ce nom signifie ville de la monnoie. Et en effet c'est là où se frappe celle du pays; et un grand fauxbourg de cette ville, appelé *Azingonge*, est la résidence du Nabab, qui gouverne le Bengale presque souverainement."—*D'Anville*, 63.

1756.—"The Nabob, irritated by the disappointment of his expectations of immense wealth, ordered Mr. Holwell and the two other prisoners to be sent to **Muxadavad**."—*Orme*, iii. 79.

1782.—"You demand an account of the East Indies, the Mogul's dominions and **Muxadabad**. . . . I imagine when you made the above requisition that you did it with a view rather to try my knowledge than to increase your own, for your great skill in geography would point out to you that **Muxadabad** is as far from Madras, as Constantinople is from Glasgow."—*T. Munro* to his brother William, in *Life*, &c. iii. 41.

1884.—It is alleged in a passage introduced in Mrs. C. Mackenzie's interesting memoir of her husband, *Storms and Sunshine of a Soldier's Life*, that "Admiral Watson used to sail up in his ships to Moorshedabad." But there is no ground for this statement. So far as I can trace, it does not appear that the Admiral's flag-ship ever went above Chandernagore, and the largest of the vessels sent to Hoogly even was the *Bridgewater* of 20 guns. No vessel of the fleet appears to have gone higher.

MUZBEE, s. The name of a class of Sikhs originally of low caste, vulg. *mazbī*, apparently *mazhabī* from Ar. *mazhab*, 'religious belief.' Cunningham indeed says that the name was applied to Sikh converts from Mahommedanism (*History*, p. 379). But this is not the usual application now. ["When the sweepers have adopted the Sikh faith they are known as **Mazhabis**. . . . When the *Chuhra* is circumcised and becomes a Musulman, he is known as a *Musalli* or a *Kotána*" (*Maclagan, Panjab Census Rep.*, 1891, p. 202).] The original corps of **Muzbees**, now represented by the 32nd Bengal N.I. (Pioneers) was raised among the men labouring on the Baree Doab Canal.

1858.—"On the 19th June (1857) I advocated, in the search for new Military classes, the raising of a corps of **Muzzubees**. . . . The idea was ultimately carried out, and improved by making them pioneers."—*Letter from Col. H. B. Edwardes* to *R. Montgomery, Esq.*, March 23.

" "To the same destination (Delhi) was sent a strong corps of **Muzhubee** (low-caste) Sikhs, numbering 1200 men, to serve as pioneers."—*Letter from R. Temple, Secretary to Punjab Govt.*, dd. *Lahore*, May 25, 1858.

MYDAN, MEIDAUN, s. Hind. from Pers. *maidān*. An open space, an esplanade, parade-ground or green, in or adjoining a town; a *piazza* (in the Italian sense); any open plain with grass on it; a *chaugān* (see **CHICANE**) ground; a battle-field. In Ar., usually, a hippodrome or racecourse.

c. 1330.—"But the brethren were meanwhile brought out to the **Medan**, *i.e.*, the piazza of the City, where an exceeding great fire had been kindled. And Friar Thomas went forward to cast himself into the fire, but as he did so a certain Saracen caught him by the hood . . ."—*Friar Odoric*, in *Cathay*, 63.

1618.—"When it is the hour of complines, or a little later to speak exactly, it is the time for the promenade, and every one goes on horseback to the **meidan**, which is always kept clean, watered by a number of men whose business this is, who water it carrying the water in skins slung over the shoulder, and usually well shaded and very cool."—*P. della Valle*, i. 707.

c. 1665.—"Celui (Quervansera) des Étrangers est bien plus spacieux que l'autre et est quarré, et tous deux font face au **Meidan**." —*Thevenot*, v. 214.

1670.—"Before this house is a great square **meidan** or promenade, planted on all sides with great trees, standing in rows." —*Andriesz*, 35.

1673.—"The **Midan**, or open Space before the Caun's Palace, is an Oblong and Stately Piatzo, with real not belied Cloisters."—*Fryer*, 249.

1828.—"All this was done with as much coolness and precision, as if he had been at exercise upon the **maidaun**."—*The Kuzzilbash*, i. 223.

[1859. -"A 24-pound howitzer, hoisted on to the maintop of the Shannon, looked menacingly over the **Maidan** (at Calcutta) . . ."—*Oliphant, Narrative of Ld. Elgin's Mission*, i. 60.

MYNA, MINA, &c. s. Hind. *mainā*. A name applied to several birds of the family of starlings. The common *myna* is the *Acridotheres tristis* of Linn.; the southern Hill-Myna is the *Gracula*, also *Eulabes religiosa* of Linn.; the Northern Hill-Myna, *Eulabes intermedia* of Hay (see *Jerdon's Birds*, ii. Pt. i. 325, 337, 339). Of both the first and last it may be said that they are among the most teachable of imitative birds, articulating words with great distinctness, and without Polly's nasal tone. We have heard a wild one (probably the first), on a tree in a field, spontaneously echoing the very peculiar call of the black partridge from an adjoining jungle, with unmistakable truth. There is a curious description in Aelian (*De Nat. An.* xvi. 2) of an Indian talking bird which we thought at one time to be the *Myna;* but it seems to be nearer the **Shāmā**, and under that head the quotation will be found. [Mr. M'Crindle (*Invasion of India*, 186) is in favour of the *Myna*.]

[1590.—"The **Mynah** is twice the size of the *Shārak*, with glossy black plumage, but with the bill, wattles and tail coverts yellow. It imitates the human voice and speaks with great distinctness."—*Āīn*, ed. *Jarrett*, iii. 121.]

1631.—Jac. Bontius describes a kind of **Myna** in Java, which he calls *Pica, seu potius Sturnus Indicus*. "The owner, an old Mussulman woman, only lent it to the author to be drawn, after great persuasion, and on a stipulation that the beloved bird should get no swine's flesh to eat. And when he had promised accordingly, the *avis pessima* immediately began to chaunt: *Orang Nasarani catjor macan babi!* i.e. 'Dog of a Christian, eater of swine!'"—Lib. v. cap. 14, p. 67.

[1664.—"In the Duke's chamber there is a bird, given him by Mr. Pierce, the surgeon, comes from the East Indys, black the greatest part, with the finest collar of white about the neck; but talks many things and neyes like the horse, and other things, the best almost that ever I heard bird in my life."—*Pepys, Diary*, April 25. Prof. Newton in Mr. Wheatley's ed. (iv. 118) is inclined to identify this with the Myna, and notes that one of the earliest figures of the bird is by Eleazar Albin (*Nat. Hist. of Birds*, ii. pl. 38) in 1738.

[1703. — "Among singing birds that which in Bengall is called the **Minaw** is the only one that comes within my knowledge."—In *Yule, Hedges' Diary*, Hak. Soc. ii. cccxxxiv.]

1803.—"During the whole of our stay two **minahs** were talking almost incessantly, to the great delight of the old lady, who often laughed at what they said, and praised their talents. Her hookah filled up the interval." —*Ld. Valentia*, i. 227-8.

1813.—"The **myneh** is a very entertaining bird, hopping about the house, and articulating several words in the manner of the starling."—*Forbes, Or. Mem.* i. 47; [2nd ed. i. 32.]

1817.—"Of all birds the *chiong* (**miner**) is the most highly prized."—*Raffles, Java*, i. 260.

1875.—"A talking **mina** in a cage, and a rat-trap, completed the adornments of the veranda."—*The Dilemma*, ch. xii.

1878.—"The **myna** has no wit. . . . His only way of catching a worm is to lay hold of its tail and pull it out of its hole,—generally breaking it in the middle and losing the bigger half."—*Ph. Robinson, In My Indian Garden*, 28.

1879.—"So the dog went to a **mainá**, and said: 'What shall I do to hurt this cat!'"—*Miss Stokes, Indian Fairy Tales*, 18.

" ". . . beneath
Striped squirrels raced, the **mynas** perked and picked.
The **nine brown sisters** chattered in the thorn . . ."
E. Arnold, The Light of Asia, Book. i.

See **SEVEN SISTERS** in Gloss. Mr. Arnold makes too many!

MYROBALAN, s. A name applied to certain dried fruits and **kernels** of astringent flavour, but of several species, and not even all belonging to the same Natural Order, which were from an early date exported from India, and had a high reputation in the medieval pharmacopoeia. This they appear (some of them) to retain in native Indian medicine; though they seem to have disappeared from English use and have no place in Hanbury and Flückiger's great work, the *Pharmacographia*. They are still, to some extent, imported into England, but for use in tanning and dyeing, not in pharmacy.

It is not quite clear how the term *myrobalan*, in this sense, came into use. For the people of India do not seem to have any single name denoting these fruits or drugs as a group; nor do the Arabic dictionaries afford one either (but see further on). Μυροβάλανος is spoken of by some ancient authors, *e.g.* Aristotle, Dioscorides and Pliny, but it was applied by them to one or more fruits * entirely unconnected with the subjects of this article. This name had probably been preserved in the laboratories, and was applied by some early translator of the Arabic writers on Materia Medica to these Indian products. Though we have said that (so far as we can discover) the dictionaries afford no word with the comprehensive sense of *Myrobalan*, it is probable that the physicians had such a word, and Garcia de Orta, who is trustworthy, says explicitly that the Arab practitioners whom he had consulted applied to the whole class the name *delegi*, a word which we cannot identify, unless it originated in a clerical error for *alelegi*, i.e. *ihlīlaj*. The last word may perhaps be taken as covering all myrobalans; for according to the Glossary to Rhazes at Leyden (quoted by Dozy, *Suppt.* i. 43) it applies to the *Kābulī*, the *yellow*, and the *black* (or Indian), whilst the *Emblic* is also called *Ihlīlaj amlaj*.

In the Kashmīr Customs Tariff (in *Punjab Trade Report*, ccxcvi.) we have entries of

"*Hulela* (Myrobalan).
Bulela (Bellerick ditto).
Amla (Emblica Phyllanthus)."

* One of them is generally identified with the seeds of *Moringa pterygosperma*—see HORSE RADISH TREE—the Ben-nuts of old writers, and affording *Oil of Ben*, used as a basis in perfumery.

The kinds recognised in the Medieval pharmacopoeia were five, viz.:—

(1) The *Emblic myrobalan*; which is the dried astringent fruit of the *Ānwulā, ānwlā* of Hind., the *Emblica officinalis* of Gaertner (*Phyllanthus Emblica*, L., N. O. *Euphorbiaceae*). The Persian name of this is *āmlah*, but, as the Arabic *amlaj* suggests, probably in older Persian *amlag*, and hence no doubt *Emblica*. Garcia says it was called by the Arab physicians *embelgi* (which we should write *ambaljī*).

(2) The *Belleric Myrobalan*; the fruit of *Terminalia Bellerica*, Roxb. (N.O. *Combretaceae*), consisting of a small nut enclosed in a thin exterior rind. The Arabic name given in Ibn Baithar is *balīlij*; in the old Latin version of Avicenna *belilegi*; and in Persian it is called *balīl* and *balīla*. Garcia says the Arab physicians called it *beleregi* (*balīrij*, and in old Persian probably *balīrig*) which accounts for *Bellerica*.

(3) The *Chebulic Myrobalan*; the fruit of *Terminalia Chebula*, Roxb. The derivation of this name which we have given under CHEBULI is confirmed by the Persian name, which is *Halīla-i-Kābulī*. It can hardly have been a product of Kabul, but may have been imported into Persia by that route, whence the name, as calicoes got their name from Calicut. Garcia says these myrobalans were called by his Arabs *quebulgi*. Ibn Baithar calls them *halīlaj*, and many of the authorities whom he quotes specify them as *Kābulī*.

(4) and (5). The *Black Myrobalan*, otherwise called '*Indian*,' and the *Yellow* or *Citrine*. These, according to Royle (*Essay on Antiq. of Hindoo Medicine*, pp. 36-37), were both products of *T. Chebula* in different states; but this does not seem quite certain. Further varieties were sometimes recognised, and *nine* are said to be specified in a paper in an early vol. of the *Philos. Transactions*.* One kind

* This article we have been unable to find. Dr. Hunter in *As. Res.* (xi. 182) quotes from a Persian work of Mahommed Husain Shirāzi, communicated to him by Mr. Colebrooke, the names of 6 varieties of *Halīla* (or Myrobalan) as afforded in different stages of maturity by the *Terminalia Chebula*:—1. *H. Zīra*, when just set (from *Zīra*, cummin-seed). 2. *H. Jawī* (from *Jau*, barley). 3. *Zangī* or *Hindī* (The Black M.). 4. *H. Chīnī*. 5. *H. 'Asfar*, or Yellow. 6. *H. Kābulī*, the mature fruit. [See Dr. Murray's article in *Watt, Econ. Dict.* vi. pt. iv. 33 *seqq.*]

called *Ṣīnī* or Chinese, is mentioned by one of the authorities of Ibn Baithar, quoted below, and is referred to by Garcia.

The virtues of Myrobalans are said to be extolled by Charaka, the oldest of the Sanskrit writers on Medicine. Some of the Arabian and Medieval Greek authors, referred to by Royle, also speak of a combination of different kinds of Myrobalan called *Tryphera* or *Tryphala;* a fact of great interest. For this is the *triphala* ('Three-fruits') of Hindu medicine, which appears in *Amarakosha* (c. A.D. 500), as well as in a prescription of Susruta, the disciple of Charaka, and which is still, it would seem, familiar to the native Indian practitioners. It is, according to Royle, a combination of the black, yellow and *Chebulic;* but Garcia, who calls it *tinepala* (*tīn-phal* in Hind. = 'Three-fruits'), seems to imply that it consisted of the three kinds known in Goa, viz. *citrine* (or yellow), the *Indian* (or black), and the *belleric.* [*Watt, Econ. Dict.* vi. pt. iv. 32 *seqq.*] The *emblic*, he says, were not used in medicine there, only in tanning, like sumach. The Myrobalans imported in the Middle Ages seem often to have been preserved (in syrup ?).

c. B.C. 340.—"διότι ἡ γέννησις τοῦ καρποῦ ἐν τῇ ἀρχῇ ἐστὶ χωρὶς γλυκύτητος. Τῶν μυραβαλάνων δὲ δένδρων ἐν τῇ ἀρχῇ, ὅταν φανῶσιν, οἱ καρποὶ εἰσι γλυκεῖς· κοινῶς δὲ εἰσι στρυφνοὶ καὶ ἐν τῇ κράσει αὐτῶν πικροί . . ."—*Aristoteles, De Plantis,* ii. 10.

c. A.D. 60.—"φοῖνιξ ἐν Αἰγύπτῳ γίνεται· τρυγᾶται δε μετοπωρούσης τῆς κατὰ τὴν ὀπώραν ἀκμῆς, παρεμφέρων τῇ 'Αραβικῇ μυροβαλάνῳ, πόμα δὲ λέγεται."—*Dioscorides, de Mat. Medica,* i. cxlviii.

c. A.D. 70.—"**Myrobalanum** Troglodytis et Thebaidi et Arabiae quae Iudaeam ab Aegypto disterminat commune est, nascens unguento, ut ipso nomine apparet, quo item indicatur et glandem esse. Arbor est heliotropio . . . simili folio, fructus magnitudine abellanae nucis," &c.—*Pliny,* xii. 21 (46).

c. 540.—A prescription of Aëtius of Amida, which will be found transcribed under **ZEDOARY**, includes **myrobalan** among a large number of ingredients, chiefly of Oriental origin; and one doubts whether the word may not here be used in the later sense.

c. 1343.—"Preserved **Mirabolans** (*mirabolani conditi*) should be big and black, and the envelope over the nut tender to the tooth; and the bigger and blacker and tenderer to the tooth (like candied walnuts), the better they are. . . . Some people say that in India they are candied when unripe (*acerbe*), just as we candy * the unripe tender walnuts, and that when they are candied in this way they have no nut within, but are all through tender like our walnut-comfits. But if this is really done, anyhow none reach us except those with a nut inside, and often very hard nuts too. They should be kept in brown earthen pots glazed, in a syrop made of *cassia fistula* † and honey or sugar; and they should remain always in the syrop, for they form a moist preserve and are not fit to use dry."—*Pegolotti,* p. 377.

c. 1343.—(At Alexandria) "*are sold by the ten* mans (*mene,* see **MAUND**), . . . amomum, **mirobalans** of every kind, camphor, castor. . . ."—*Ibid.* 57.

1487.—". . . Vasi grandi di confectione, **mirobolani** e gengiovo."—*Letter* on presents sent by the Sultan to L. de' Medici, in *Roscoe's Lorenzo,* ed. 1825, ii. 372.

1505.—In Calicut) "li nasce **mirabolani**, emblici e chebali, li quali valeno ducati do' el *baar* (see **BAHAR**.)" — *Lionardo Ca' Masser,* p. 27.

1552. — "La campagne de Iericho est entournée de mõtaignes de tous costez: poignant laquelle, et du costé de midy est la mer morte. . . . Les arbres qui portent le Licion, naissent en ceste plaine, et aussi les arbres qui portent les **Myrobalans** *Citrins,* du noyau desquels les habitants font de l'huille."‡—*P. Belon, Observations,* ed. 1554, f. 144.

1560.—"Mais pource que le Ben, que les Grecz appellent Balanus Myrepsica, m'a fait souvenir des **Myrabolans** des Arabes, dont y en a cinq especes: et que d'ailleurs, on en vse ordinairement en Medecine, encores que les anciens Grecz n'en ayent fait aucune mention: il m'a semblé bon d'en toucher mot: car i'eusse fait grand tort à ces Commentaires de les priuer d'vn

* "*Confettiamo,*" "make comfits of"; "preserve," but the latter word is too vague.

† This is surely not what we now call *Cassia Fistula,* the long cylindrical pod of a leguminous tree, affording a mild laxative? But Hanbury and Flückiger (pp. 195, 475) show that some *Cassia bark* (of the cinnamon kind) was known in the early centuries of our era as κασία συριγγώδης and *cassia fistularis;* whilst the drug now called *Cassia Fistula,* L., is first noticed by a medical writer of Constantinople towards A.D. 1300. Pegolotti, at p. 366, gives a few lines of instruction for judging of *cassia fistula:* "It ought to be black, and thick, and unbroken (*salda*), and heavy, and the thicker it is, and the blacker the outside rind is, the riper and better it is; and it retains its virtue well for 2 years." This is not very decisive, but on the whole we should suppose Pegolotti's *cassia fistula* to be either a spice-bark, or solid twigs of a like plant (H. & F. 476).

‡ This is probably *Balanitis aegyptiaca,* Delile, the *zak* of the Arabs, which is not unlike myrobalan fruit and yields an oil much used medicinally. The negroes of the Niger make an intoxicating spirit of it.

fruict si requis en Medecine. Il y a donques cinq especes de **Myrabolans**."—*Matthioli, Com. on Dioscorides*, old Fr. Tr. p. 394.

1610.—
" *Kastril.* How know you?
Subtle. By inspection on her forehead;
And subtlety of lips, which must be tasted
Often, to make a judgment.
[*Kisses her again.*]
'Slight, she melts
Like a **Myrabolane**."—*The Alchemist*, iv. 1.

[c. 1665.—"Among other fruits, they preserve (in Bengal) large citrons . . . small **Mirobolans**, which are excellent. . . ."—*Bernier*, ed. *Constable*, 438.]

1672.—"Speaking of the *Glans Unguentaria*, otherwise call'd *Balanus Mirepsica* or *Ben Arabum*, a very rare Tree, yielding a most fragrant and highly esteem'd Oyl; he is very particular in describing the extraordinary care he used in cultivating such as were sent to him in Holland."—*Notice of a Work by Abraham Munting, M.D.*, in *Philosoph. Trans.* ix. 249.

MYSORE, n.p. Tam. *Maisūr*, Can. *Maisūru*. The city which was the capital of the Hindu kingdom, taking its name, and which last was founded in 1610 by a local chief on the decay of the Vijayanagar (see **BISNAGAR, NARSINGA**) dynasty. C. P. Brown gives the etym. as *Maisi-ūr*, *Maisi* being the name of a local goddess like Pomona or Flora; *ūr*, 'town, village.' It is however usually said to be a corruption of *Mahish-āsura*, the buffalo demon slain by the goddess Durga or Kali. [Rice (*Mysore*, i. 1) gives Can. *Maisa*, from Skt. *Mahisha*, and *ūru*, 'town.']

[1696.—"Nabob Zulphecar Cawn is gone into the **Mizore** country after the Mahratta army. . . ."—Letter in *Wilks, Hist. Sketches*, Madras reprint, i. 60.]

MYSORE THORN. The *Caesalpinia sepiaria*, Roxb. It is armed with short, sharp, recurved prickles; and is much used as a fence in the Deccan. Hyder Ali planted it round his strongholds in Mysore, and hence it is often called "Hyder's Thorn," *Haidar kā jhār*.

[1857.—"What may be termed the underwood consisted of **milk bushes, prickly pears, mysore thorn**, intermingled in wild confusion. . . ."—*Lady Falkland, Chow-chow*, 2nd ed. i. 300.]

N

NABÓB, s. Port. *Nabâbo*, and Fr. *Nabab*, from Hind. *Nawāb*, which is the Ar. pl. of sing. *Nāyab* (see **NAIB**), 'a deputy,' and was applied in a singular sense* to a delegate of the supreme chief, viz. to a Viceroy or chief Governor under the Great Mogul, *e.g.* the *Nawāb* of Surat, the *Nawāb* of Oudh, the *Nawāb* of Arcot, the *Nawāb Nāzim* of Bengal. From this use it became a title of rank without necessarily having any office attached. It is now a title occasionally conferred, like a peerage, on Mahommedan gentlemen of distinction and good service, as *Rāī* and *Rājā* are upon Hindus.

Nabob is used in two ways: (a) simply as a corruption and representative of *Nawāb*. We get it direct from the Port. *nabâbo*, see quotation from Bluteau below. (b) It began to be applied in the 18th century, when the transactions of Clive made the epithet familiar in England, to Anglo-Indians who returned with fortunes from the East; and Foote's play of 'The **Nabob**' (*Nābob*) (1768) aided in giving general currency to the word in this sense.

a.—

1604.—". . . delante del **Nauabo** que es justicia mayor."—*Guerrero, Relacion*, 70.

1615.—"There was as **Nababo** in Surat a certain Persian Mahommedan (*Mouro Parsio*) called Mocarre Bethião, who had come to Goa in the time of the Viceroy Ruy Lourenço de Tavora, and who being treated with much familiarity and kindness by the Portuguese . . . came to confess that it could not but be that truth was with their Law. . . ."—*Bocarro*, p. 354.

1616.—"Catechumeni ergo parentes viros aliquot inducunt honestos et assessores **Nauabi**, id est, judicis supremi, cui consiliarii erant, uti et Proregi, ut libellum famosum adversus Pinnerum spargerent."—*Jarric, Thesaurus*, iii. 378.

1652. — "The **Nahab**† was sitting, ac-

* Dozy says (2nd ed. 323) that the plural form has been adopted by mistake. Wilson says 'honorifically.' Possibly in this and other like cases it came from popular misunderstanding of the Arabic plurals. So we have omra, *i.e. umarā*, pl. of *amīr* used singularly and forming a plural *umrāyān*. (See also **OMLAH** and **MEHAUL**.)

† The word is so misprinted throughout this part of the English version.

cording to the custom of the Country, barefoot, like one of our Taylors, with a great number of Papers sticking between his Toes, and others between the Fingers of his left hand, which Papers he drew sometimes from between his Toes, sometimes from between his Fingers, and order'd what answers should be given to every one."—*Tavernier*, E. T. ii. 99; [ed. *Ball*, i. 291].

1653.—". . . il prend la qualité de **Nabab** qui vault autant à dire que monseigneur."—*De la Boullaye-le-Gouz* (ed. 1657), 142.

1666.—"The ill-dealing of the **Nahab** proceeded from a scurvy trick that was play'd me by three Canary-birds at the Great Mogul's Court. The story whereof was thus in short . . ."—*Tavernier*, E.T. ii. 57; [ed. *Ball*, i. 134].

1673.—"Gaining by these steps a nearer intimacy with the **Nabob**, he cut the new Business out every day."—*Fryer*, 183.

1675.—"But when we were purposing next day to depart, there came letters out of the Moorish Camp from the **Nabab**, the field-marshal of the Great Mogul. . . ."—*Heiden Vervaarlijke Schip-Breuk*, 52.

1682.—". . . Ray Nundelall ye **Nábabs** *Duan*, who gave me a most courteous reception, rising up and taking of me by ye hands, and ye like at my departure, which I am informed is a greater favour than he has ever shown to any *Franke*. . . ."—*Hedges, Diary*, Oct. 27; [Hak. Soc. i. 42]. Hedges writes *Nabob, Nabab, Navab, Navob*.

1716.—"**Nabâbo**. Termo do Mogol. He o Titolo do Ministro que he Cabeca."—*Bluteau*, s.v.

1727.—"A few years ago, the **Nabob** or Vice-Roy of *Chormondel*, who resides at *Chickakal*, and who superintends that Country for the Mogul, for some Disgust he had received from the Inhabitants of Diu Islands, would have made a Present of them to the Colony of Fort St. George."—*A. Hamilton*, i. 374; [ed. 1744].

1742.—"We have had a great man called the **Nabob** (who is the next person in dignity to the Great Mogul) to visit the Governor. . . . His lady, with all her women attendance, came the night before him. All the guns fired round the fort upon her arrival, as well as upon his; *he* and *she* are **Moors**, whose women are never seen by any man upon earth except their husbands."—Letter from Madras in *Mrs. Delany's Life*, ii. 169.

1743.—"Every governor of a fort, and every commander of a district had assumed the title of **Nabob** . . . one day after having received the homage of several of these little lords, Nizam ul muluck said that he had that day seen no less than eighteen **Nabobs** in the Carnatic."—*Orme*, Reprint, Bk. i. 51.

1752.—"Agreed . . . that a present should be made the **Nobab** that might prove satisfactory."—In *Long*, 33.

1773.—
"And though my years have passed in this
hard duty,
No Benefit acquired—no **Nabob's** booty."
Epilogue at Fort Marlborough, by *W. Marsden*, in *Mem*. 9.

1787.—
"Of armaments by flood and field;
Of **Nabobs** you have made to yield."
Ritson, in *Life and Letters*, i. 124.

1807.—"Some say that he is a Tailor who brought out a long bill against some of Lord Wellesley's staff, and was in consequence provided for; others say he was an adventurer, and sold knicknacks to the **Nabob** of Oude."—*Sir T. Munro*, in *Life*, i. 371.

1809.—"I was surprised that I had heard nothing from the **Nawaub** of the Carnatic."—*Ld. Valentia*, i. 381.

c. 1858.—
"Le vieux **Nabab** et la Begum d'Arkate."
Leconte de Lisle, ed. 1872, p. 156.

b.—

[1764.—"Mogul Pitt and **Nabob** Bute."—*Horace Walpole, Letters*, ed. 1857, iv. 222 (*Stanf. Dict.*).]

1773.—"I regretted the decay of respect for men of family, and that a **Nabob** would not carry an election from them.

"JOHNSON: Why, sir, the **Nabob** will carry it by means of his wealth, in a country where money is highly valued, as it must be where nothing can be had without money; but if it comes to personal preference, the man of family will always carry it."—*Boswell, Journal of a Tour to the Hebrides*, under Aug. 25.

1777.—"In such a revolution . . . it was impossible but that a number of individuals should have acquired large property. They did acquire it; and with it they seem to have obtained the detestation of their countrymen, and the appellation of **nabobs** as a term of reproach.—*Price's Tracts*, i. 13.

1780.—"The Intrigues of a **Nabob**, or Bengal the Fittest Soil for the Growth of Lust, Injustice, and Dishonesty. Dedicated to the Hon. the Court of Directors of the East India Company. By Henry Fred. Thompson. Printed for the Author." (A base book).

1783.—"The office given to a young man going to India is of trifling consequence. But he that goes out an insignificant boy, in a few years returns a great **Nabob**. Mr. Hastings says he has two hundred and fifty of that kind of raw material, who expect to be speedily manufactured into the merchantlike quality I mention."—*Burke, Speech on Fox's E.I. Bill*, in *Works and Corr.*, ed. 1852, iii. 506.

1787.—"The speakers for him (Hastings) were Burgess, who has completely done for himself in one day; Nichols, a lawyer; Mr. Vansittart, a **nabob**; Alderman Le Mesurier, a smuggler from Jersey; . . . and Dempster, who is one of the good-natured candid men who connect themselves with every bad man they can find."—*Ld. Minto*, in *Life*, &c., i. 126.

1848. — "'Isn't he very rich?' said Rebecca.

"'They say all Indian **Nabobs** are enormously rich.'"—*Vanity Fair*, ed. 1867, i. 17.

1872.—"Ce train de vie facile . . . suffit à me faire décerner . . . le surnom de **Nabob** par les bourgeois et les visiteurs de la petite ville."—*Rev. des Deux Mondes*, xcviii. 938.

1874.—"At that time (c. 1830) the Royal Society was very differently composed from what it is now. Any wealthy or well-known person, any M.P. . . . or East Indian **Nabob**, who wished to have F.R.S. added to his name, was sure to obtain admittance."—*Geikie, Life of Murchison*, i. 197.

1878.—". . . A Tunis?—interrompit le duc. . . . Alors pourquoi ce nom de **Nabab**? —Bah! les Parisiens n'y regardent pas de si près. Pour eux tout riche étranger est un **Nabab**, n'importe d'où il vienne."—*Le* **Nabab**, par *Alph. Daudet*, ch. i.

It is purism quite erroneously applied when we find **Nabob** in this sense miswritten *Nawab;* thus:

1878. — "These were days when India, little known still in the land that rules it, was less known than it had been in the previous generation, which had seen Warren Hastings impeached, and burghs* bought and sold by Anglo-Indian **Nawabs**."—*Smith's Life of Dr John Wilson*, 30.

But there is no question of purism in the following delicious passage:

1878.—"If . . . the spirited proprietor of the Daily Telegraph had been informed that our aid of their friends the Turks would have taken the form of a tax upon paper, and a concession of the Levis to act as Commanders of Regiments of Bashi-Bozouks, with a request to the Generalissimo to place them in as forward a position as **Nabob** was given in the host of King David, the harp in Peterborough Court would not have twanged long to the tune of a crusade in behalf of the Sultan of Turkey."—*Truth*, April 11, p. 470. In this passage in which the wit is equalled only by the scriptural knowledge, observe that *Nabob*=Naboth, and *Naboth*=Uriah.

NACODA, NACODER, &c., s. Pers. *nā-khudā* (*navis dominus*) 'a skipper'; the master of a native vessel. (Perhaps the original sense is rather the owner of the ship, going with it as his own supercargo.) It is hard to understand why Reinaud (*Relation*, ii. 42) calls this a "Malay word . . . derived from the Persian," especially considering that he is dealing with a book of the 9th and 10th centuries. [Mr. Skeat notes that the word is sometimes, after the manner of *Hobson-Jobson*, corrupted by the Malays into *Anak kuda*, 'son of a horse.']

c. 916.—"Bientôt l'on ne garda pas même de ménagements pour les patrons de navires (*nawākhuda*, pl. of **nākhudā**) Arabes, et les maîtres de batiments marchands furent en butte à des pretensions injustes."—*Relation*, &c., i. 68.

c. 1348. — "The second day after our arrival at the port of Kailūkarī, this princess invited the **nākhodha**, or owner of the ship (*sāhib-al-markab*), the *karānī* (see **CRANNY**) or clerk, the merchants, the chief people, the *tandail* (see **TINDAL**) or commander of the crew, the *sipasalār* (see **SIPAHSELAR**) or commander of the fighting men."—*Ibn Batuta*, iv. 250.

1502. — "But having been seen by our fleet, the caravels made for them, and the Moors being laden could no longer escape. So they brought them to the Captain General, and all struck sail, and from six of the *Zambucos* (see **SAMBOOK**) the **nacodas** came to the Captain General."—*Correa*, i. 302.

1540. — "Whereupon he desired us that the three **necodas** of the Junks, so are the commanders of them calledi n that country . . ."—*Pinto*, (orig. cap. xxxv.) in *Cogan*, p. 42.

[c. 1590. — "In large ships there are twelve classes. 1. The **Nakhuda**, or owner of the ship. This word is evidently a short form of *Nāvkhudā*. He fixes the course of the ship."—*Āīn*, ed. *Blochmann*, i. 280.]

1610. — "The sixth **Nohuda** Melech Ambor, Captaine of a great ship of *Dabull* (see **DABUL**), came ashore with a great many of Merchants with him, he with the rest were carried about the Towne in pompe."—*Sir H. Middleton*, in *Purchas*, i. 260.

[1616.—"**Nohody** Chinhonne's voyage for Syam was given over."—*Foster*, *Letters*, iv. 187.]

1623. — "The China **Nocheda** hath too long deluded you through your owne simplicitie to give creditt unto him."—*Council at Batavia, to Rich. Cocks*, in his *Diary*, ii. 341.

1625. — Purchas has the word in many forms; **Nokayday, Nahoda, Nohuda,** &c.

1638. — "Their **nockado** or India Pilot was stab'd in the Groyne twice."—In *Hakl.* iv. 48.

1649.—"In addition to this a receipt must be exacted from the **Nachodas**."—Secret Instructions in *Baldaeus* (Germ.), p. 6.

1758.—"Our *Chocarda* * (?) assured us they

* Qu. *boroughs?* The writer does injustice to his country when he speaks of *burghs* being bought and sold. The representation of Scotch *burghs* before 1832 was bad, but it never was purchasable. There are no *burghs* in England.

[* The late Mr. E. J. W. Gibb pointed out that *Chocarda* is Turkish *Chokadār*, a name given to a great man's lackey or footman. "High were rogues; but our **Knockaty** or pilot told us he knew them."—*Ives*, 248. This word looks like confusion, in the manner of the poet of the "Snark," between *nākhuda* and (Hind.) *arkātī*, "a pilot," [so called because many came from **Arcot**.]

[1822. — "The **Knockada** was very attentive to Thoughtless and his family. . . ." —*Wallace, Fifteen Years in India*, 241.

[1831. — "The Roban (Ar. *rubbān*, 'the master of a ship') and **Nockader** being afraid to keep at sea all night . . ."—*Life and Adventures of Nathaniel Pearce, written by himself*, ii. 303.]

1880. — "That a pamphlet should be printed, illustrated by diagrams, and widely circulated, commends itself to the Government of India . . . copies being supplied to **Nakhudas** and tindals of native craft at small cost."—*Resn. of Govt. of India* as to Lights for Shipping, 28 Jan.

NAGA, n.p. The name applied to an extensive group of uncivilised clans of warlike and vindictive character in the eastern part of the hill country which divides Assam Proper (or the valley of the Brahmaputra) from Kachār and the basin of the Surma. A part of these hills was formed into a British district, now under Assam, in 1867, but a great body of the Nāga clans is still independent. The etymology of the name is disputed; some identifying it with the *Nāga* or Snake Aborigines, who are so prominent in the legends and sculptures of the Buddhists. But it is, perhaps, more probable that the word is used in the sense of 'naked' (Skt. *nagna*, Hind. *nangā*, Beng. *nengṭā*, &c.), which, curiously enough, is that which Ptolemy attributes to the name, and which the spelling of Shihābuddīn also indicates. [The word is also used for a class of ascetics of the Dādupanthī sect, whose head-quarters are at Jaypur.]

c. A.D. 50.—"Καὶ μέχρι τοῦ Μαιάνδρου, . . . Ναγγα λόγαι ὃ σημαίνει γυμνῶν κόσμος."—*Ptol.* VII. ii. 18.

c. 1662.—"The Rájah had first intended to fly to the **Nágá** Hills, but from fear of our army the **Nágás** * would not afford him an asylum. 'The Nágás live in the southern mountains of Asám, have a light brown complexion, are well built, but treacherous. In number they equal the helpers of Yagog and Magog, and resemble, in hardiness and physical strength the 'Ádis (an ancient Arabian tribe). They go about naked like beasts. . . . Some of their chiefs came to see the Nawáb. They wore dark hip-clothes (*lung*), ornamented with cowries, and round about their heads they wore a belt of boar's tusks, allowing their black hair to hang down their neck.'"—*Shihābuddīn Tālish*, tr. by *Prof. Blochmann*, in *J. As. Soc. Beng.*, xli. Pt. i. p. 84. [See Plate xvi. of *Dalton's Descriptive Ethnology of Bengal; Journ. Anthrop. Inst.* xxvi. 161 *seqq.*]

1883.—A correspondent of the "Indian Agriculturist" (Calcutta), of Sept. 1, dates from the Naga Hills, which he calls "**Noga**, from *Nok*, not *Naga*, . . ." an assertion which one is not bound to accept. "One on the Spot" is not bound to know the etymology of a name several thousand years old.

[Of the ascetic class:

[1879.—"The **Nágás** of Jaipur are a sect of militant devotees belonging to the Dádú Panthi sect, who are enrolled in regiments to serve the State; they are vowed to celibacy and to arms, and constitute a sort of military order in the sect."—*Rajputana Gazetteer*, ii. 147.]

NAGAREE, s. Hind. from Skt. *nāgarī*. The proper Sanskrit character, meaning literally 'of the city'; and often called *deva-nāgarī*, 'the divine city character.'

[1623.—"An antique character . . . us'd by the Brachmans, who in distinction from other vulgar Characters . . . call it **Nagheri**." —*P. della Valle*, Hak. Soc. i. 75.

[1781.—"The Shanskrit alphabet . . . is now called **Diewnāgar**, or the Language of Angels. . . ."—*Halhed, Code*, Intro. xxiii.]

[c. 1805.—"As you sometimes see Mr. Wilkins, who was the inventor of printing with Bengal and **Nagree** types. . . ."—Letter of *Colebrooke*, in *Life*, 227.]

NAIB, s. Hind. from Ar. *nāyab*, a deputy; (see also under **NABOB**).

[c. 1610.—In the Maldives, "Of these are constituted thirteen provinces, over each of which is a chief called a **Naybe**."—*Pyrard de Laval*, Hak. Soc. i. 198.]

1682.—"Before the expiration of this time we were overtaken by ye *Caddie's* **Neip**, ye *Meerbar's* (see **MEARBAR**) deputy, and ye Dutch Director's *Vakill* (see **VAKEEL**) (by the way it is observable ye Dutch omit no opportunity to do us all the prejudice that lyes in their power)."—*Hedges, Diary*, Oct. 11; [Hak. Soc. i. 35].

functionaries have many *Chokadārs* attached to their establishments. In this case, probably the Pasha of the province through which Ives was travelling, or perhaps some functionary at Constantinople, appointed one of his *Chokadārs* to look after the traveller. The word literally means 'cloth-keeper,' and it is probable that the name was originally given to a servant who had charge of his master's wardrobe. But it has long been applied to a lackey who walks beside his master's horse when his master is out riding."]

* The word *Nágá* is spelt with a nasal *n*, "*Náñgá*" (p. 76).

1765.—"... this person was appointed **Niab**, or deputy governor of Orissa."—*Holwell, Hist. Events*, i. 53.

[1856.—"The **Naib** gave me letters to the chiefs of several encampments, charging them to provide me with horses."—*Ferrier, Caravan Journeys*, 237.]

NAIK, NAIQUE, &c. s. Hind. *nāyak.* A term which occurs in nearly all the vernacular languages; from Skt. *nāyaka*, 'a leader, chief, general.' The word is used in several applications among older writers (Portuguese) referring to the south and west of India, as meaning a native captain or headman of some sort **(a)**. It is also a title of honour among Hindus in the Deccan **(b)**. It is again the name of a Telugu caste, whence the general name of the Kings of Vijayanagara (A.D. 1325-1674), and of the Lords of Madura (1559-1741) and other places **(c)**. But its common Anglo-Indian application is to the non-commissioned officer of Sepoys who corresponds to a corporal, and wears the double chevron of that rank **(d)**.

(a)—

c. 1538.—"Mandou tambem hũ **Nayque** com vinti Abescins, que nos veio guardando dos ladrões."—*Pinto*, ch. iv.

1548.—"With these four captains there are 12 **naiques**, who receive as follows—to wit, for 7 **naiques** who have 37 pardaos and 1 tanga a year ... 11,160 reis. For Cidi **naique**, who has 30 pardaos, 4 tangas ... and Madguar **naique** the same ... and Salgy **naique** 24 pardaos a year, and two *nafares* [Ar. *nafar*, 'servant'] who have 8 vintens a month, equal to 12 pardaos 4 tangas a year."—*S. Botelho, Tombo*, 215.

1553.—"To guard against these he established some people of the same island of the Canarese Gentoos with their **Naiques**, who are the captains of the footmen and of the horsemen."—*Barros*, Dec. II. Liv. v. cap. 4.

c. 1565.—"Occorse l'anno 1565, se mi ricordo bene, che il **Naic** cioè il Signore della Città li mandi a domandami certi caualli Arabi."—*C. Federici*, in *Ramusio*, iii. 391.

c. 1610.—"Ie priay donc ce capitaine ... qu'il me fit bailler vne almadie ou basteau auec des mariniers et vn **Naique** pour truchement."—*Mocquet*, 289.

1646.—"Il s'appelle **Naique**, qui signifie Capitaine, doutant que c'est vn Capitaine du Roy du Narzingue."—*Barretto, Rel. du Prov. de Malabar*, 255.

(b)—

1598.—"The Kings of *Decam* also have a custome when they will honour a man or recompense [recompence] their service done, and rayse him to dignitie and honour. They give him the title of **Naygue**, which signifieth a Capitaine."—*Linschoten*, 51; [Hak. Soc. i. 173].

1673.—"The Prime Nobility have the title of **Naiks** or **Naigs**."—*Fryer*, 162.

c. 1704.—"Hydur Sáhib, the son of Muhammad Ilias, at the invitation of the Ministers of the Polygar of Mysore, proceeded to that country, and was entertained by them in their service ... he also received from them the honourable title of **Naik**, a term which in the Hindu dialect signifies an officer or commander of foot soldiers."—*H. of Hydur Naik*, p. 7. This was the uncle of the famous Haidar Naik or Hyder Ali Khan.

(c)—

1604.—"Maduré; corte del **Naygue** Señor destas terras."—*Guerrero, Relacion*, 101.

1616.—"... and that orders should be given for issuing a proclamation at Negapatam that no one was to trade at Tevenapatam, Porto Novo, or other port belonging to the **Naique** of Ginja or the King of Massulapatam."—*Bocarro*, 619.

1646.—"Le **Naique** de Maduré, à qui appartient la coste de la pescherie, a la pesche d'vn jour par semaine pour son tribut."—*Barretto*, 248.

c. 1665.—"Il y a plusieurs **Naiques** au Sud de Saint-Thomé, qui sont Souverains: Le **Naique** de Madure en est un."—*Thevenot*, v. 317.

1672.—"The greatest Lords and **Naiks** of this kingdom (Carnataca) who are subject to the Crown of Velour ... namely Vitipa **naik** of Madura, the King's Cuspidore- (see **CUSPADORE**) bearer ... and Cristapa **naik** of Chengier, the King's Betel-holder ... the **naik** of Tanjower the King's Shield-bearer."—*Baldaeus* (Germ.), p. 153.

1809.—"All I could learn was that it was built by a **Naig** of the place."—*Ld. Valentia*, i. 398.

(d)—

[c. 1610.—"These men are hired, whether Indians or Christians, and are called **Naicles**."—*Pyrard de Laval*, Hak. Soc. ii. 42.]

1787.—"A Troop of Native Cavalry on the present Establishment consists of 1 European subaltern, 1 European sergeant, 1 Subidar, 3 Jemidars, 4 Havildars, 4 **Naigues**, 1 Trumpeter, 1 Farrier, and 68 Privates."—*Regns. for H. Co.'s Troops on the Coast of Coromandel*, &c., 6.

1834.—"... they went gallantly on till every one was shot down except the one **naik**, who continued hacking at the gate with his axe ... at last a shot from above ... passed through his body. He fell, but in dying hurled his axe against the enemy."—*Mrs. Mackenzie, Storms and Sunshine of a Soldier's Life*, i. 37-38.

We may add as a special sense that in West India *Naik* is applied to the head-man of a hamlet (*Kūrī*) or camp (*Tānda*) of **Brinjarries** (q.v.). [Bhangi and Jhangi Naiks, the famous Banjāra leaders, are said to have had 180,000 bullocks in their camp. See *Berar Gazetteer*, 196.]

NAIR, s. Malayal. *nāyar;* from the same Skt. origin as **Naik**. Name of the ruling caste in Malabar. [The Greek *νάουρα* as a tract stood for the country of the Nairs. For their customs, see *Logan*, *Malabar*, i. 131.]

1510.—"The first class of Pagans in Calicut are called Brahmins. The second are **Naeri**, who are the same as the gentlefolks amongst us; and these are obliged to bear sword and shield or bows and lances."—*Varthema*, pp. 141-142.

1516.—"These kings do not marry . . . only each has a mistress, a lady of great lineage and family, which is called **nayre**."—*Barbosa*, 165.

1553.—"And as . . . the Gentiles of the place are very superstitious in dealing with people foreign to their blood, and chiefly those called Brammanes and **Naires**."—*Barros*, Dec. I. liv. iv. cap. 7.

1563.—". . . The **Naires** who are the Knights."—*Garcia*.

1582.—"The Men of Warre which the King of Calicut and the other Kings have, are **Nayres**, which be all Gentlemen."—*Castañeda* (by N. L.), f. 35*b*.

1644.—"We have much Christian people throughout his territory, not only the Christians of St. Thomas, who are the best soldiers that he (the King of Cochin) has, but also many other vassals who are converts to our Holy Catholic Faith, through the preaching of the Gospel, but none of these are **Nayres**, who are his fighting men, and his nobles or gentlemen."—*Bocarro, MS.*, f. 315.

1755.—"The king has disciplined a body of 10,000 **Naires**; the people of this denomination are by birth the Military tribe of the Malabar coast."—*Orme*, i. 400.

1781.—"The soldiers preceded the **Nairs** or nobles of Malabar."—*Gibbon*, ch. xlvii.

It may be added that *Nāyar* was also the term used in Malabar for the mahout of an elephant; and the fact that *Nāyar* and *Nāyaka* are of the same origin may be considered with the etymology which we have given of **Cornac** (see *Garcia*, 85*v*).

NALKEE, s. Hind. *nālkī*. A kind of litter formerly used by natives of rank; the word and thing are now obsolete. [It is still the name of the bride's litter in Behar (*Grierson*, *Bihār Peasant Life*, 45).] The name was perhaps a factitious imitation of *pālkī?* [Platts suggests Skt. *nalika*, 'a tube.']

1789.—"A **naleky** is a *paleky*, either opened or covered, but it bears upon two bamboos, like a sedan in Europe, with this difference only, that the poles are carried by four or eight men, and upon the shoulders."—Note by Tr. of *Seir Mutaqherin*, iii. 269.

[1844.—"This litter is called a '**nalki**.' It is one of the three great insignia which the Mogul emperors of Delhi conferred upon independent princes of the first class, and could never be used by any person upon whom, or upon whose ancestors, they had not been so conferred. These were the **nalki**, the order of the Fish, and the fan of peacock's feathers."—*Sleeman*, *Rambles*, ed. *V. A. Smith*, i. 165.]

NAMBEADARIM, s. Malayāl. *nambiyadiri*, *nambiyattiri*, a general, a prince. [See *Logan*, *Malabar*, i. 121.]

1503.—"Afterwards we were presented to the King called **Nambiadora**; who received us with no small gladness and kindness."—*Giov. da Empoli*, in *Ramusio*, i. f. 146.

1552.—"This advice of the **Nambeadarim** was disapproved by the kings and lords."—*Castanheda;* see also Transl. by N. L., 1582, f. 147.

1557.—"The **Nambeadarim** who is the principal governor."—*D'Alboquerque*, Hak. Soc. i. 9. The word is, by the translator, erroneously identified with *Nambūdiri* (see **NAMBOOREE**), a Malabar Brahman.

1634.—

"Entra em Cochim no thalamo secreto
Aonde **Nambeoderá** dorme quieto."
Malaca Conquist. i. 50.

NAMBOOREE, Malayāl. *nambūdiri*, Tam. *nambūri;* [*Logan* (*Malabar*, ii. Gloss. ccxi.) gives *nambūtiri*, *nambūri*, from Drav. *nambuka*, 'to trust,' *tiri*, Skt. *śrī*, 'blessed.' The *Madras Gloss.* has Mal. *nambu*, 'the Veda,' *ōthu*, 'to teach,' *tiri*, 'holy.'] A Brahman of Malabar. (See *Logan*, i. 118 *seqq.*].

1644.—"No more than any of his **Nambures** (among Christian converts) who are his *padres*, for you would hardly see any one of them become converted and baptized because of the punishment that the king has attached to that."—*Bocarro, MS.*, f. 313.

1727.—"The **Nambouries** are the first in both Capacities of Church and State, and some of them are Popes, being sovereign Princes in both."—*A. Hamilton*, i. 312; [ed. 1744].

[1800.—"The **Namburis** eat no kind of animal food, and drink no spirituous liquors."—*Buchanan*, *Mysore*, ii. 426.]

NANKEEN, s. A cotton stuff of a brownish yellow tinge, which was originally imported from China, and derived its name from the city of Nanking. It was not dyed, but made from a cotton of that colour, the *Gossypium religiosum* of Roxb., a variety of *G. herbaceum.* It was, however, imitated with dyed cotton in England, and before long exports of this imitation were made to China. Nankeen appears to be known in the Central Asia markets under the modified name of **Nanka** (see below).

1793-4.—"The land in this neighbourhood produces the cloth usually called **Nankeens** in Europe . . . in that growing in the province of Kiangnan, of which the city of Nan-kin is the capital, the down is of the same yellow tinge which it possesses when spun and woven into cloth."—*Staunton's Narr. of Ld. Macartney's Embassy*, ii. 425.

1794-5.—"The colour of **Nam-King** is thus natural, and not subject to fade. . . . The opinion (that it was dyed) that I combat was the cause of an order being sent from Europe a few years ago to dye the pieces of **Nam-King** of a deeper colour, because of late they had grown paler."—*Van Braam's Embassy*, E.T. ii. 141.

1797.—"*China Investment per Upton Castle.* . . . Company's broad and narrow **Nankeen**, brown **Nankeen.**"—In *Seton-Karr*, ii. 605.

c. 1809.—"Cotton in this district (*Puraniya* or *Purneea*) is but a trifling article. There are several kinds mentioned. . . . The *Kukti* is the most remarkable, its wool having the colour of **nankeen** cloth, and it seems in fact to be the same material which the Chinese use in that manufacture." —*F. Buchanan*, in *Eastern India*, iii. 244. [See *Watt, Econ. Dict.* iv. 16, 29.]

1838.—"**Nanka** is imported in the greatest quantity (to Kabul) from Russia, and is used for making the outer garments for the people, who have a great liking to it. It is similar to **nankeen** cloth that comes to India from China, and is of a strong durable texture."—*Report by Baines*, in *Punjab Trade Report*, App. p. ix. See also p. clxvii.

1848.—"'Don't be trying to deprecate the value of the lot, Mr. Moss,' Mr. Hammerdown said; 'let the company examine it as a work of art—the attitude of the gallant animal quite according to natur, the gentleman in a **nankeen**-jacket, his gun in hand, is going to the chase; in the distance a *banyhann* tree (see **BANYAN-TREE**) and a **pagody.**"—*Vanity Fair*, i. 178.

NANKING, n.p. The great Chinese city on the lower course of the Yangtse-kiang, which was adopted as capital of the Empire for a brief space (1368-1410) by the (native) Ming dynasty on the expulsion of the Mongol family of Chinghiz. The city, previously known as *Kin-ling-fu*, then got the style of *Nan-king*, or 'South Court.' Peking ('North Court') was however re-occupied as imperial residence by the Emperor Ching-su in 1410, and has remained such ever since. Nanking is mentioned as a great city called *Chilenfu* (Kin-ling), whose walls had a circuit of 40 miles, by Friar Odoric (c. 1323). And the province bears the same name (*Chelim*) in the old notices of China translated by R. Willes in *Hakluyt* (ii. 546).

It appears to be the city mentioned by Conti (c. 1430), as founded by the emperor: "Hinc prope XV. dierum itinere (*i.e.* from Cambalec or Peking), alia civitas *Nemptai* nomine, ab imperatore condita, cujus ambitus patet triginta milliaribus, eaque est popolosissima omnium." This is evidently the same name that is coupled with Cambalec, in Petis de la Croix's translation of the *Life of Timour* (iii. 218) under the form *Nemnai.* The form *Lankin*, &c., is common in old Portuguese narratives, probably, like **Liampo** (q.v.), a Fuhkien form.

c. 1520.—"After that follows Great China, the king of which is the greatest sovereign in the world. . . . The port of this kingdom is called Guantan, and among the many cities of this empire two are the most important, namely **Nankin** and Comlaka (read *Combalak*), where the king usually resides."—*Pigafetta's Magellan* (Hak. Soc.), p. 156.

c. 1540.—"Thereunto we answered that we were strangers, natives of the Kingdom of *Siam*, and that coming from the port of *Liampoo* to go to the fishing of **Nanquin**, we were cast away at sea . . . that we purposed to go to the city of **Nanquin** there to imbarque ourselves as rowers in the first *Lanteaa* (see **LANTEAS**) that should put to sea, for to pass unto Cantan. . . ."—*Pinto*, E.T. p. 99 (orig. cap. xxxi.).

1553.—"Further, according to the Cosmographies of China . . . the maritime provinces of this kingdom, which run therefrom in a N.W. direction almost, are these three: **Nanquij**, Xanton (*Shantung*), and Quincij" (*Kingsze* or capital, *i.e.* Pecheli).—*Barros*, I. ix: 1.

1556.—"Ogni anno va di Persia alla China vna grossa Carauana, che camina sei mesi prima ch'arriui alla Città de **Lanchin**, Città nella quale risiede il Re con la sua Corte."—*Ces. Federici*, in *Ramusio*, iii. 391*v.*

[1615.—"678⅛ Catties China of raw **Lankine** silk."—*Foster, Letters*, iii. 137.]

NARCONDAM, n.p. The name of a strange weird-looking volcanic cone, which rises, covered with forest, to a height of some 2,330 feet straight out of the deep sea, to the eastward of the Andamans. One of the present writers has observed (*Marco Polo*, Bk. III. ch. 13, note) that in the name of *Narkandam* one cannot but recognise *Narak*, 'Hell'; perhaps *Naraka-kundam*, 'a pit of hell'; adding: "Can it be that in old times, but still contemporary with Hindu navigation, this volcano was active, and that some Brahmin St. Brandon recognised in it the mouth of Hell, congenial to the Rakshasas of the adjacent group" of the Andamans? We have recently received an interesting letter from Mr. F. R. Mallet of the Geological Survey of India, who has lately been on a survey of Narcondam and Barren Island. Mr. Mallet states that Narcondam is "without any crater, and has certainly been extinct for many thousand years. Barren Island, on the other hand, forms a complete amphitheatre, with high precipitous encircling walls, and the volcano has been in violent eruption within the last century. The term 'pit of hell,' therefore, while quite inapplicable to Narcondam, applies most aptly to Barren Island." Mr. Mallet suggests that there may have been some confusion between the two islands, and that the name *Narcondam* may have been really applicable to Barren Island. [See the account of both islands in *Ball, Jungle Life*, 397 *seqq.*] The name Barren Island is quite modern. We are told in Purdy's *Or. Navigator* (350) that Barren Island was called by the Portuguese *Ilha alta*, a name which again would be much more apt for Narcondam, Barren Island being only some 800 feet high. Mr. Mallet mentions that in one of the charts of the *E.I. Pilot or Oriental Navigator* (1781) he finds "Narcondam according to the Portuguese" in 13° 45′ N. lat. and 110° 35′ E. long. (from Ferro) and "Narcondam or *High Island*, according to the French," in 12° 50′ N. lat. and 110° 55′ E. long. This is valuable as showing both that there may have been some confusion between the islands, and that *Ilha alta* or High Island has been connected with the name of Narcondam. The real positions by our charts are of *Narcondam*, N. lat. 13° 24′, E. long. 94° 12′. *Barren Island*, N. lat. 12° 16′, E. long. 93° 54′.

The difference of lat. (52 miles) agrees well with that between the Portuguese and French Narcondam, but the difference in long., though approximate in amount (18 or 20 miles), is in one case *plus* and in the other *minus*; so that the discrepancies may be due merely to error in the French reckoning. In a chart in the *E.I. Pilot* (1778) "Monday or Barren Island, called also High Island" and "Ayconda or Narcondam," are marked approximately in the positions of the present Barren Island and Narcondam. Still, we believe that Mr. Mallet's suggestion is likely to be well founded. The form *Ayconda* is nearer that found in the following:

1598.—". . . as you put off from the Ilandes of *Andeman* towards the Coast . . . there lyeth onely in the middle way an Ilande which the inhabitantes call **Viacondam**, which is a small Iland having faire ground round about it, but very little fresh water."—*Linschoten*, p. 328.

The discrepancy in the position of the islands is noticed in D'Anville:

1753.—"Je n'oublierai pas **Narcondam**, et d'autant moins que ce que j'en trouve dans les Portugais ne repond point à la position que nos cartes lui donnent. Le routier de Gaspar Pereira de los Reys indique l'île **Narcodão** ou Narcondam à 6 lieues des îles Cocos, 12 de la tête de l'Andaman; et le rhumb de vent à l'égard de ce point il le determine, *leste quarta da nordeste, meya quarta mais para les nordestes*, c'est à dire à peu-près 17 degrés de l'est au nord. Selon les cartes Françoises, **Narcondam** s'écarte environ 25 lieues marines de la tête d'Andaman; et au lieu de prendre plus du nord, cette île baisse vers le sud d'une fraction de degré plus ou moins considérable selon differéntes cartes."—*D'Anville, Eclairc.*, 141-142.

I may add that I find in a French map of 1701 (*Carte Marine depuis Suratte jusqu'au Detroit de Malaca, par le Père* P. P. Tachard) we have, in the (approximately) true position of Narcondam, *Isle Haute*, whilst an islet without name appears in the approximate position of Barren Island.

NARD, s. The rhizome of the plant *Nardostachys Jatamansi*, D.C., a native of the loftier Himālaya (allied to Valerian). This is apparently an Indian word originally, but, as we have it, it has come from the Skt. *nalàda* through Semitic media, whence the change of *l* into *r*; and in this form it is found both in Hebrew and Greek. [Prof. Skeat gives: "F. *nard*, L. *nardus*. Greek νάρδος, Pers. *nard* (whence Skt. *nalada*), spikenard. Skt. *nada*, a reed."] The plant was first identified in modern times by Sir W. Jones. See in Canticles, i. 12, and iv. 13, 14.

B.C. c. 25.—

"Cur non sub altâ vel platano, vel hac
Pinu jacentes sic temere, et rosâ
Canos odorati capillos,
Dum licet, Assyriâque **nardo**
Potamus uncti?"

Horace, Odes, II. xi.

A.D. 29.—"Καὶ ὄντος αὐτοῦ ἐν Βηθανίᾳ, ἐν τῇ οἰκίᾳ Σίμωνος . . . ἦλθε γυνὴ ἔχουσα ἀλάβαστρον μύρου, νάρδου πιστικῆς πολυτελοῦς. . . ."—*St. Mark*, xiv. 3.

c. A.D. 70.—"As touching the leafe of **Nardus**, it were good that we discoursed thereof at large, seeing that it is one of the principal ingredients aromaticall that goe to the making of most costly and precious ointments. . . . The head of **Nardus** spreadeth into certain spikes and ears, whereby it hath a twofold use both as spike and also as leafe."—*Pliny* (Ph. Holland), xii. 12.

c. A.D. 90.—"Κατάγεται δὲ δι' αὐτῆς (Οζηνῆς) καὶ ἀπὸ τῶν ἄνω τόπων, ἡ διὰ Πωκλαΐδος καταφερομένη νάρδος, ἡ Κασπαπυρηνή, καὶ ἡ Παροπανισηνή, καὶ ἡ Καβολίτη, καὶ ἡ διά τῆς παρακειμένης Σκυθίας."—*Periplus*, § 48 (corrected by Fabricius).

c. A.D. 545.—". . . also to Sindu, where you get the musk or castorin, and *androstachyn*" (for **nardostachys**, *i.e.* spikenard).—*Cosmas*, in *Cathay*, p. clxxviii.

1563.—"I know no other spikenard (*espiquenardo*) in this country, except what I have already told you, that which comes from Chitor and Mandou, regions on the confines of Deli, Bengala, and the Decan."—*Garcia*, f. 191.

1790.—"We may on the whole be assured that the **nardus** of Ptolemy, the *Indian Sumbul* of the Persians and Arabs, the *Jatámánsì* of the Hindus, and the *spikenard* of our shops, are one and the same plant."—*Sir W. Jones*, in *As. Res.* ii. 410.

c. 1781.—

"My *first* shuts out thieves from your house
or your room,
My *second* expresses a Syrian perfume;
My *whole* is a man in whose converse is
shared
The strength of a *Bar* and the sweetness
of **Nard**."—

Charade on Bishop Barnard by *Dr. Johnson*.

NARGEELA, NARGILEH, s. Properly the coco-nut (Skt. *nārikera*, *-kela*, or *-keli*; Pers. *nārgīl*; Greek of Cosmas, Ἀργέλλιον); thence the **hubble-bubble**, or **hooka** in its simplest form, as made from a coco-nut shell; and thence again, in Persia, a **hooka** or water-pipe with a glass or metal vase.

[c. 545.—"**Argell**." See under **SURA**.

[1623.—"**Narghil**, like the palm in the leaves also, and is that which we call *Nux Indica*."—*P. della Valle*, Hak. Soc. i. 40.

[1758.—"An **Argile**, or smoking tube, and coffee, were immediately brought us . . ."—*Ives*, 271.

[1813.—". . . the Persians smoked their culloons and **nargills**. . . ."—*Forbes*, *Or. Mem.* 2nd ed. ii: 173.]

NARROWS, THE, n.p. A name applied by the Hoogly pilots for at least two centuries to the part of the river immediately below Hoogly Point, now known as 'Hoogly Bight.' See Mr. Barlow's note on *Hedges' Diary*, i. 64.

1684.—"About 11 o'clock we met with ye *Good-hope*, at an anchor in ye **Narrows**, without Hugly River,* and ordered him upon ye first of ye flood to weigh, and make all haste he could to Hugly . . ."—*Hedges*, *Diary*, Hak. Soc. i. 64.

1711.—"From the lower Point of the **Narrows** on the Starboard-side . . . the Eastern Shore is to be kept close aboard, until past the said Creek, afterwards allowing only a small Birth for the Point off the **River of Rogues**, commonly called by the Country People, Adegom. . . . From the **River of Rogues**, the Starboard Shore, with a great Ship, ought to be kept close aboard down to the Channel Trees, for in the Offing lies the Grand middle Ground. . . ."—*English Pilot*, p. 57.

NARSINGA, n.p. This is the name most frequently applied in the 16th and 17th centuries to the kingdom in Southern India, otherwise termed Vijayanagara or **Bisnagar** (q.v.), the latest powerful Hindu kingdom in the Peninsula. This kingdom was founded on the ruins of the Belāla dynasty reigning at Dwāra Samudra, about A.D. 1341 [see *Rice*, *Mysore*, i. 344 *seqq.*]. The original dynasty of Vijayanagara became extinct about 1487, and was replaced by *Narasinha*, a prince of Telugu origin, who reigned till 1508. He was therefore reigning at the time of the first arrival of the Portuguese, and the

* The "Hugly" River was then considered (in ascending) to begin at Hooghly Point, and the confluence of the Rupnarain R., often called the *Gunga* (see under **GODAVERY**).

name of Narsinga, which they learned to apply to the kingdom from his name, continued to be applied to it for nearly two centuries.

1505.—"Hasse notizia delli maggiori Re che hanno nell' India, che è el Re de **Narsin**, indiano zentil; confina in Estremadura con el regno de Comj (qu. *regno Deconij?*), el qual Re si è Moro. El qual Re de **Narsin** tien grande regno; sarà (harà?) ad ogni suo comando 10 mila elefanti, 30 mila cavalli, e infinito numero di genti."—*Lionardo Ca' Masser*, 35.

1510.—"The Governor . . . learning of the embassy which the King of Bisnega was sending to Cananore to the Viceroy, to offer firm friendship, he was most desirous to make alliance and secure peace . . . principally because the kingdom of **Narsinga** extends in the interior from above Calecut and from the Balagate as far as Cambaya, and thus if we had any wars in those countries by sea, we might by land have the most valuable aid from the King of Bisnega."—*Correa*, ii. 30.

1513.—"Aderant tunc apud nostrũ praefectũ a **Narsingae** rege legati."—*Emanuel. Reg. Epist.* f. 3*v*.

1516.—"45 leagues from these mountains inland, there is a very large city which is called Bijanaguer, very populous. . . . The King of **Narsinga** always resides there."—*Barbosa*, 85.

c. 1538.—"And she (the Queen of Onor) swore to him by the golden sandals of her pagod that she would rejoice as much should God give him the victory over them (the Turks) as if the King of **Narsinga**, whose slave she was, should place her at table with his wife."—*F. Mendez Pinto*, ch. ix.; see also *Cogan*, p. 11.

1553.—"And they had learned besides from a Friar who had come from *Narsinga* to stay at Cananor, how that the King of **Narsinga**, who was as it were an Emperor of the Gentiles of India in state and riches, was appointing ambassadors to send him . . ."—*Barros*, I. viii. 9.

1572.—

"... O Reyno **Narsinga** poderoso
Mais de ouro e de pedras, que de forte gente." *Camões*, vii. 21.

By Burton:

"Narsinga's Kingdom, with her rich display
Of gold and gems, but poor in martial vein . . ."

1580.—"In the Kingdom of **Narsingua** to this day, the wives of their priests are buried alive with the bodies of their husbands; all other wives are burnt at their husbands' funerals."—*Montaigne*, by *Cotton*, ch. xi. (What is here said about priests applies to **Lingaits**, q.v.).

1611.—"... the Dutch President on the coast of *Choromandell*, shewed us a *Caul* (see **COWLE**) from the King of **Narsinga**, *Wencapati, Raia*, wherein was granted that it should not be lawfull for any one that came out of Europe to trade there, but such as brought Prince *Maurice* his Patent, and therefore desired our departure."—*P. W. Floris*, in *Purchas*, i. 320.

1681.—"Coromandel. Ciudad muy grande, sugeta al Rey de **Narsinga**, el qual Reyno e llamado por otre nombre *Bisnaga*."—*Martinez de la Puente, Compendio*, 16.

NASSICK, n.p. *Nāsik*; Νασικα of *Ptolemy* (vii. i. 63); an ancient city of Hindu sanctity on the upper course of the Godavery R., and the head-quarter of a district of the same name in the Bombay Presidency. A curious discussion took place at the R. Geog. Society in 1867, arising out of a paper by Mr. (afterwards Sir) George Campbell, in which the selection of a capital for British India was determined on logical principles in favour of Nassick. But logic does not decide the site of capitals, though government by logic is quite likely to lose India. Certain highly elaborated magic squares and magic cubes, investigated by the Rev. A. H. Frost (*Cambridge Math. Jour.*, 1857) have been called by him *Nasik* squares, and Nasik cubes, from his residence in that ancient place (see *Encyc. Britan.* 9th ed. xv. 215).

NAT, s. Burmese *nāt*, [apparently from Skt. *nātha*, 'lord']; a term applied to all spiritual beings, angels, elfs, demons, or what not, including the gods of the Hindus.

[1878.—"Indeed, with the country population of Pegu the worship, or it should rather be said the propitiation of the '**Náts**' or spirits, enters into every act of their ordinary life, and Buddha's doctrine seems kept for sacred days and their visits to the **kyoung** (monastery) or to the pagoda."—*Forbes, British Burma*, 222.]

NAUND, s. Hind. *nānd*. A coarse earthen vessel of large size, resembling in shape an inverted bee-hive, and useful for many economic and domestic purposes. The dictionary definition in Fallon, 'an earthen trough,' conveys an erroneous idea.

[1832.—"The ghuri (see **GHURRY**), or copper cup, floats usually in a vessel of coarse red pottery filled with water, called a **nān**."—*Wanderings of a Pilgrim*, i. 250.

[1899.—"To prevent the crickets from wandering away when left, I had a large earthen pan placed over them upside down. These pans are termed **nands**. They are made of the coarsest earthenware, and are very capacious. Those I used were nearly a yard in diameter and about eighteen inches deep."—*Thornhill, Haunts and Hobbies of an Indian Official*, 79.]

NAUTCH, s. A kind of ballet-dance performed by women; also any kind of stage entertainment; an European ball. Hind. and Mahr. *nāch*, from Skt. *nṛitya*, dancing and stage-playing, through Prakrit *nachcha*. The word is in European use all over India. [A *poggly nautch* (see **POGGLE**) is a fancy-dress ball. Also see **POOTLY NAUTCH.**] Browning seems fond of using this word, and persists in using it wrongly. In the first of the quotations below he calls Fifine the 'European *nautch*,' which is like calling some Hindu dancing-girl 'the Indian ballet.' He repeats the mistake in the second quotation.

[1809.—"You Europeans are apt to picture to yourselves a **Nach** as a most attractive spectacle, but once witnessed it generally dissolves the illusion."—*Broughton, Letters from a Mahratta Camp*, ed. 1892, p. 142.]

1823.—"I joined Lady Macnaghten and a large party this evening to go to a **nâch** given by a rich native, Rouplall Mullich, on the opening of his new house."—*Mrs. Heber*, in *Heber*, ed. 1844, i. 37.

[1829.—". . . a dance by black people which they calls a **Notch**. . . ."—*Oriental Sport. Mag.* ed. 1873, i. 129.]

c. 1831.—"Elle (Begum Sumrou) fit enterrer vivante une jeune esclave, dont elle était jalouse, et donna à son mari un **nautch** (bal) sur cette horrible tombe."—*Jacquemont, Correspondance*, ii. 221.

1872.—
". . . let be there was no worst
Of degradation spared Fifine; ordained from first
To last, in body and soul, for one life-long debauch,
The Pariah of the North, the European **Nautch**!"
Fifine at the Fair, 31.

1876.—
". . . I locked in the swarth little lady—I swear,
From the head to the foot of her,—well quite as bare!
'No **Nautch** shall cheat me,' said I, taking my stand
At this bolt which I draw. . . ."
Natural Magic, in *Pacchiarotto*, &c.

NAUTCH-GIRL, s. (See **BAYADÈRE, DANÇING-GIRL.**) The last quotation is a glorious jumble, after the manner of the compiler.

[1809.—"**Nach Girls** are exempted from all taxes, though they pay a kind of voluntary one monthly to a Fuqeer. . . ."—*Broughton, Letters from a Mahratta Camp*, ed. 1892, p. 113-4.]

1825.—"The **Nâch women** were, as usual, ugly, huddled up in huge bundles of red petticoats; and their exhibition as dull and insipid to an European taste, as could well be conceived."—*Heber*, ii. 102.

1836.—"In India and the East dancing-girls are trained called *Almeh*, and they give a fascinating entertainment called a **natch**, for which they are well paid."—In *R. Phillips, A Million of Facts*, 322.

NAVAIT, NAITEA, NEVOYAT, &c., n.p. A name given to Mahommedans of mixt race in the Konkan and S. Canara, corresponding more or less to **Moplahs** (q.v.) and **Lubbyes** of Malabar and the Coromandel coast. [The head-quarters of the Navayats are in N. Canara, and their traditions state that their ancestors fled from the Persian Gulf about the close of the 7th century, to escape the cruelty of a Governor of Irān. See *Sturrock, Man. of S. Canara*, i. 181.] It is apparently a Konkani word connected with Skt. *nava*, 'new,' and implying 'new convert.' [The *Madras Gloss.* derives the word from Pers. *nāiṭī*, from *Nāiṭ*, the name of an Arab clan.]

1552.—"Sons of Moors and of Gentile women, who are called **Neiteas**. . . ."—*Castanheda*, iii. 24.

1553.—"**Naiteas** que são mestiços: quanto aos padres de geração dos Arabios . . . e perparte das madres das Gentias."—*Barros*, I. ix. 3.

" And because of this fertility of soil, and of the trade of these ports, there was here a great number of Moors, natives of the country, whom they call **Naiteas**, who were accustomed to buy the horses and sell them to the Moors of the Decan. . . ."—*Ibid.* I. viii. 9.

c. 1612.—"From this period the Mahomedans extended their religion and their influence in Malabar, and many of the princes and inhabitants, becoming converts to the true faith, gave over the management of some of the seaports to the strangers, whom they called **Nowayits** (literally the New Race). . . ."—*Firishta*, by *Briggs*, iv. 533.

1615.—". . . et passim infiniti Mahometani reperiebantur, tum indigenae quos **naiteas** vocabant, tum externi. . . ."—*Jarric*, i. 57.

1626.—"There are two sorts of Moors, one *Mesticos* of mixed seed of Moore-fathers and Ethnike-mothers, called **Naiteani**, Mungrels also in their religion, the other Forreiners . . ."—*Purchas, Pilgrimage*, 554.

NAZIR, s. Hind. from Ar. *nāzir*, 'inspector' (*nazr*, 'sight'). The title of a native official in the Anglo-Indian Courts, sometimes improperly rendered 'sheriff,' because he serves processes, &c.

1670.—"The Khan . . . ordered his **Nassir**, or Master of the Court, to assign something to the servants. . . ."—*Andriesz*, 41.

[1708.—"He especially, who is called **Nader**, that is the chief of the Mahal . . ." —*Catrou, H. of the Mogul Dynasty*, E.T. 295.

[1826.—"The **Nazir** is a perpetual sheriff, and executes writs and summonses to all the parties required to attend in civil and criminal cases."—*Pandurang Hari*, ed. 1873, ii. 118.]

1878.—"The **Nazir** had charge of the treasury, stamps, &c., and also the issue of summonses and processes."—*Life in the Mofussil*, i. 204.

[In the following the word represents *nakkāra*, 'a kettle-drum.'

1763.—"His Excellency (Nawab Meer Cossim) had not eaten for three days, nor allowed his **Nazir** to be beaten."—*Diary of a Prisoner at Patna*, in *Wheeler, Early Records*, 323.]

NEELÁM, LEELÁM, s. Hind. *nīlām*, from Port. *leilão*. An auction or public **outcry**, as it used to be called in India (corresponding to Scotch *roup*; comp. Germ. *rufen*, and *outroop* of Linschoten's translator below). The word is, however, Oriental in origin, for Mr. C. P. Brown (MS. notes) points out that the Portuguese word is from Ar. *i'lām* (*al-i'lām*), 'proclamation, advertisement.' It is omitted by Dozy and Engelmann. How old the custom in India of prompt disposal by auction of the effects of a deceased European is, may be seen in the quotation from Linschoten.

1515.—"Pero d'Alpoym came full of sorrow to Cochin with all the apparel and servants of Afonso d'Alboquerque, all of which Dom Gracia took charge of; but the Governor (Lopo Soares) gave orders that there should be a **leilão** (auction) of all the wardrobe, which indeed made a very poor show. Dom Gracia said to D. Aleixo in the church, where they met: The Governor your uncle orders a **leilão** of all the old wardrobe of Afonso d'Alboquerque. I can't praise his intention, but what he has done only adds to my uncle's honour; for all the people will see that he gathered no rich Indian stuffs, and that he despised everything but to be foremost in honour."—*Correa*, ii. 469.

[1527.—"And should any man die, they at once make a **Leylam** of his property."—India Office MSS., *Corpo Chronologico*, vol. i. Letter of *Fernando Nunes* to the King, Sept. 7.

[1554.—"All the spoil of Mombasa that came into the general stock was sold by **leilão**."—*Castanheda*, Bk. ii. ch. 13.]

1598.—"In Goa there is holden a daylie assemblie . . . which is like the meeting upõ the burse in Andwarpe . . . and there are all kindes of Indian commodities to sell, so that in a manner it is like a Faire . . . it beginneth in ye morning at 7 of the clocke, and continueth till 9 . . . in the principal streete of the citie . . . and is called the **Leylon**, which is as much as to say, as an *outroop* . . . and when any man dieth, all his goods are brought thether and sold to the last pennieworth, in the same outroop, whosoever they be, yea although they were the Viceroyes goodes. . . ."—*Linschoten*, ch. xxix.; [Hak. Soc. i. 184; and compare *Pyrard de Laval*, Hak. Soc. ii. 52, who spells the word **Laylon**].

c. 1610.—". . . le mary vient frapper à la porte, dont la femme faisant fort l'estonnée, prie le Portugais de se cacher dans vne petite cuue à pourcelaine, et l'ayant fait entrer là dedans, et ferme tres bien à clef, ouurit la porte a son mary, qui . . . le laissa tremper là iusqu'au lendemain matin, qu'il fit porter ceste cuue au marché, ou **lailan** ainsi qu'ils appellent. . . ."—*Mocquet*, 344.

Linschoten gives an engraving of the *Rua Direita* in Goa, with many of these auctions going on, and the superscription: "*O* **Leilao** *que se faz cada dia pola menhã na Rua direita de Goa.*" The Portuguese word has taken root at Canton Chinese in the form *yélang*; but more distinctly betrays its origin in the Amoy form *lé-lang* and Swatow *loylang* (see *Giles*; also *Dennys's Notes and Queries*, vol. i.).

NEELGYE, NILGHAU, &c., s. Hind. *nīlgāū*, *nīlgāī*, *līlgāī*, *i.e.* 'blue cow'; the popular name of the great antelope, called by Pallas *Antilope tragocamelus* (*Portax pictus*, of Jerdon, [*Boselaphus tragocamelus* of Blanford, *Mammalia*, 517]), given from the slaty blue which is its predominant colour. The proper Hind. name of the animal is *rojh* (Skt. *ṛiśya*, or *ṛishya*).

1663.—"After these Elephants are brought divers tamed *Gazelles*, which are made to fight with one another; as also some **Nil-gaux**, or grey oxen, which in my opinion are a kind of *Elands*, and *Rhinoceross*, and those great *Buffalos* of *Bengala* . . . to combat with a Lion or Tiger."—*Bernier*, E.T. p. 84; [ed. *Constable*, 262; in 218 **nilsgaus**; in 364, 377, **nil-ghaux**].

1773.—"Captain Hamilton has been so obliging as to take charge of two deer, a male and a female, of a species which is called **neelgow**, and is, I believe, unknown in Europe, which he will deliver to you in my name."—*Warren Hastings* to *Sir G. Colebrooke*, in *Gleig*, i. 288.

1824.—"There are not only **neelghaus**, and the common Indian deer, but some noble red-deer in the park" (at Lucknow).—*Heber*, ed. 1844, i. 214.

1882.—"All officers, we believe, who have served, like the present writers, on the canals of Upper India, look back on their peripatetic life there as a happy time . . . occasionally on a winding part of the bank one intruded on the solitude of a huge **nīlgai**."—*Mem. of General Sir W. E. Baker*, p. 11.

NEEM, s. The tree (N.O. *Meliaceae*) *Azadirachta indica*, Jussieu ; Hind. *nīm* (and *nīb*, according to Playfair, *Taleef Shereef*, 170), Mahr. *nimb*, from Skt. *nimba*. It grows in almost all parts of India, and has a repute for various remedial uses. Thus poultices of the leaves are applied to boils, and their fresh juice given in various diseases ; the bitter bark is given in fevers ; the fruit is described as purgative and emollient, and as useful in worms, &c., whilst a medicinal oil is extracted from the seeds ; and the gum also is reckoned medicinal. It is akin to the *bakain* (see **BUCKYNE**), on which it grafts readily.

1563.—"*R.* I beg you to recall the tree by help of which you cured that valuable horse of yours, of which you told me, for I wish to remember it.

"*O.* You are quite right, for in sooth it is a tree that has a great repute as valuable and medicinal among nations that I am acquainted with, and the name among them all is **nimbo**. I came to know its virtues in the Balaghat, because with it I there succeeded in curing sore backs of horses that were most difficult to clean and heal ; and these sores were cleaned very quickly, and the horses very quickly cured. And this was done entirely with the leaves of this tree pounded and put over the sores, mixt with lemon-juice. . . ."—*Garcia*, f. 153.

1578.—"There is another tree highly medicinal . . . which is called **nimbo** ; and the Malabars call it *Bepole* [Malayāl. *vēppu*]."—*Acosta*, 284.

[1813.—". . . the principal square . . . regularly planted with beautiful **nym** or **lym**-trees."—*Forbes, Or. Mem.* 2nd ed. ii. 445.

[1856.—"Once on a time Guj Singh . . . said to those around him, 'Is there any one who would leap down from that **limb** tree into the court?'"—*Forbes, Rās Mālā*, ed. 1878, p. 465.]

1877.—"The elders of the Clans sat every day on their platform, under the great **neem** tree in the town, and attended to all complaints."—*Meadows Taylor, Story*, &c., ii. 85.

NEGAPATAM, n.p. A seaport of Tanjore district in S. India, written *Nāgai-ppaṭṭanam*, which may mean 'Snake Town.' It is perhaps the Νίγαμα Μητρόπολις of Ptolemy ; and see under **COROMANDEL**.

1534.—"From this he (Cunhall Marcar, a Mahommedan corsair) went plundering the coast as far as **Negapatão**, where there were always a number of Portuguese trading, and Moorish merchants. These latter, dreading that this pirate would come to the place and plunder them, to curry favour with him, sent him word that if he came he would make a famous haul, because the Portuguese had there a quantity of goods on the river bank, where he could come up. . . ."—*Correa*, iii. 554.

[1598.—"The coast of Choramandel beginneth from the Cape of **Negapatan**."—*Linschoten*, Hak. Soc. i. 82.

[1615.—"Two (ships) from **Negapotan**, one from Cullmat and Messepotan."—*Foster, Letters*, iv. 6.]

NEGOMBO, n.p. A pleasant town and old Dutch fort nearly 20 miles north of Colombo in Ceylon ; formerly famous for the growth of the best cinnamon. The etymology is given in very different ways. We read recently that the name is properly (Tamil) *Nīr-Koḷumbu*, *i.e.* 'Columbo in the water.' But, according to Emerson Tennent, the ordinary derivation is *Mi-gamoa*, the 'Village of bees' ; whilst Burnouf says it is properly *Nāga-bhu*, 'Land of Nagas,' or serpent worshippers (see *Tennent*, ii. 630).

1613.—"On this he cast anchor ; but the wind blowing very strong by daybreak, the ships were obliged to weigh, as they could not stand at their moorings. The vessel of Andrea Coelho and that of Nuno Alvares Teixeira, after weighing, not being able to weather the reef of **Negumbo**, ran into the bay, where the storm compelled them to be beached : but as there were plenty of people there, the vessels were run up by hand and not wrecked."—*Bocarro*, 42.

NEGRAIS, CAPE, n.p. The name of the island and cape at the extreme south end of Arakan. In the charts the extreme south point of the mainland is called Pagoda Point, and the seaward promontory, N.W. of this, *Cape Negrais*. The name is a Portuguese corruption probably of the Arab or Malay form of the native name which the Burmese express as *Naga-rīt*, 'Dragon's whirlpool.' The set of the tide here is very apt to carry vessels ashore, and thus the locality is famous for wrecks. It is possible, however, that the Burmese name is only an effort at interpretation, and that the locality was called in old times by some name like *Nāgarāshtra*. Ibn Batuta touched at a continental coast occupied by uncivilised people having elephants, between Bengal and Sumatra, which he calls *Baranagār*. From the intervals given, the place must have been near Negrais, and it is just possible that the term *Barra de Negrais*, which frequently occurs in the old writers (*e.g.* see Balbi, Fitch, and Bocarro below) is a misinterpretation of the old name used by Ibn Batuta (iv. 224-228).

1553.—"Up to the Cape of **Negrais**, which stands in 16 degrees, and where the Kingdom of Pegu commences, the distance may be 100 leagues."—*Barros*, I. ix. 1.

1583.—"Then the wind came from the S.W., and we made sail with our stern to the N.E., and running our course till morning we found ourselves close to the *Bar of* **Negrais**, as in their language they call the port which runs up into Pegu."—*Gasparo Balbi*, f. 92.

1586.—"We entered the *barre of* **Negrais**, which is a braue barre," &c. (see **COSMIN**). —*R. Fitch*, in *Hakl.* ii. 390.

1613.—"Philip de Brito having sure intelligence of this great armament . . . ordered the arming of seven ships and some *sanguicels*, and appointing as their commodore Paulo de Rego Pinheiro, gave him precise orders to engage the prince of Arracan at sea, before he should enter the *Bar* and rivers of **Negrais**, which form the mouth of all those of the kingdom of Pegù."—*Bocarro*, 137.

1727.—"The Sea Coast of Arackan reaches from Xatigam (see **CHITTAGONG**) to Cape **Negrais**, about 400 Miles in length, but few places inhabited . . ." (after speaking of "the great Island of Negrais") . . . he goes on. . . . "The other Island of Negrais, which makes the Point called the Cape . . . is often called *Diamond* Island, because its Shape is a Rhombus. . . . Three Leagues to the Southward of *Diamond* Island lies a Reef of Rocks a League long . . . conspicuous at all Times by the Sea breaking over them . . . the Rocks are called the *Legarti*, or in English, the *Lizard*."—*A. Hamilton*, ii. 29. This reef is the *Alguada*, on which a noble lighthouse was erected by Capt. (afterwards Lieut.-Gen.) Sir A. Fraser, C.B., of the Engineers, with great labour and skill. The statement of Hamilton suggests that the original name may have been *Lagarto*. But *Alagada*, "overflowed," is the real origin. It appears in the old French chart of d'Après as *Ile Noyée*. In Dunn it is *Negada* or *Neijada*, or *Lequado*, or Sunken Island (*N. Dir.* 1780, 325).

1759.—"The Dutch by an Inscription in *Teutonic Characters*, lately found at **Negrais**, on the Tomb of a *Dutch Colonel*, who died in 1607 (qu. if not 1627 ?), appear then to have had Possession of that Island."—Letter in *Dalrymple, Or. Rep.* i. 98.

1763.—"It gives us pleasure to observe that the King of the Burmahs, who caused our people at **Negrais** to be so cruelly massacred, is since dead, and succeeded by his son, who seems to be of a more friendly and humane disposition."—*Fort William Consns.*, Feb. 19. In *Long*, 288.

[1819.—"**Negraglia.**" See under **MUNNEEPORE.**]

NELLY, NELE. s. Malayāl. *nel*, 'rice in the husk'; [Tel. and Tam. *nelli*, 'rice-like']. This is the Dravidian equivalent of **paddy** (q.v.), and is often used by the French and Portuguese in South India, where Englishmen use the latter word.

1606.—". . . when they sell **nele**, after they have measured it out to the purchaser, for the seller to return and take out two grains for himself for luck (*com superstição*), things that are all heathen vanities, which the synod entirely prohibits, and orders that those who practise them shall be severely punished by the Bishop."—*Gouvea, Synodo*, f. 52*b*.

1651.—"**Nili**, that is unpounded rice, which is still in the husk."—*Rogerius*, p. 95.

1760.—"Champs de **nelis**." See under **JOWAUR.**

[1796.—"75 parahs **Nelly**."—List of Export Duties, in *Logan, Malabar*, iii. 265.]

NELLORE, n.p. A town and district north of Madras. The name may be Tamil. *Nall-ūr*, 'Good Town.' But the local interpretation is from *nel* (see **NELLY**); and in the local records it is given in Skt. as *Dhānya-puram*, meaning 'rice-town' (*Seshagiri Sāstri*). [The *Madras Man.* (ii. 214) gives *Nall-ūr*, 'Good-town'; but the *Gloss.* (s.v.) has *nellu*, 'paddy,' *ūru*, 'village.' Mr. Boswell (*Nellore*, 687) suggests that it is derived from a *nelli chett* tree under which a famous *lingam* was placed.]

c. 1310.—"Ma'bar extends in length from Kulam to **Niláwar**, nearly 300 parasangs along the sea coast."—*Wassáf*, in *Elliot*, iii. 32.

NERBUDDA R., n.p. Skt. *Narmadā*, 'causing delight'; *Ptol.* Νάμαδος; *Peripl.* Λαμναῖος (amended by Fabricius to Νάμμαδος). Dean Vincent's conjectured etymology of *Nahr-Budda*, 'River of Budda,' is a caution against such guesses.

c. 1020.—"From Dhár southwards to the R. **Nerbadda** nine (parasangs); thence to Mahrat-des . . . eighteen . . ."—*Al-Birūnī*, in *Elliot*, i. 60. The reading of Nerbadda is however doubtful.

c. 1310.—"There were means of crossing all the rivers, but the **Nerbádda** was such that you might say it was a remnant of the universal deluge."—*Amír Khusrú*, in *Elliot*, i. 79.

[1616.—"The King rode to the riuer of **Darbadath**."—*Sir T. Roe*, Hak. Soc. ii. 413. In his list (ii. 539) he has **Narbadah**.]

1727.—"The next Town of Note for Commerce is Baroach . . . on the Banks of the River **Nerdaba**."—*A. Hamilton*, ed. 1744, i. 145.]

NERCHA, s. Malayāl. *nerchcha*, 'a vow,' from verb *neruγa*, 'to agree or promise.'

1606.—"They all assemble on certain days in the porches of the churches and dine together . . . and this they call **nercha**."—*Gouvea*, *Synodo*, f. 63. See also f. 11. This term also includes offerings to saints, or to temples, or particular forms of devotion. Among Hindus a common form is to feed a lamp before an idol with *ghee* instead of oil.

NERRICK, NERRUCK, NIRK, &c., s. Hind. from Pers. *nirkh*, vulgarly *nirakh*, *nirikh*. A tariff, rate, or price-current, especially one established by authority. The system of publishing such rates of prices and wages by local authority prevailed generally in India a generation or two back, and is probably not quite extinct even in our own territories. [The provincial Gazettes still publish periodical lists of current prices, but no attempt is made to fix such by authority.] It is still in force in the French settlements, and with no apparent ill effects.

1799.—"I have written to Campbell a long letter about the **nerrick** of exchange, in which I have endeavoured to explain the principles of the whole system of *shroffing* (see **SHROFF**). . . ."—*Wellington*, i. 56.

1800.—"While I was absent with the army, Col. Sherbrooke had altered the **nerrick** of artificers, and of all kinds of materials for building, at the instigation of Capt. Norris . . . and on the examination of the subject a system of engineering came out, well worthy of the example set at Madras."—*Ibid*. i. 67.

[„ "Here is established a **niruc**, or regulation, by which all coins have a certain value affixed to them; and at this rate they are received in the payment of the revenue; but in dealings between private persons attention is not paid to this rule."—*F. Buchanan*, *Mysore*, ii. 279.]

1878.—"On expressing his surprise at this, the man assured him that it was really the case that the bazar '**nerik**' or market-rate, had so risen."—*Life in the Mofussil*, i. p. 33.

NGAPEE, s. The Burmese name, *ngapi*, 'pressed fish,' of the odorous delicacy described under **BALACHONG**. [See *Forbes*, *British Burma*, 83.]

1855.—"Makertich, the Armenian, assured us that the jars of **ngapé** at Amarapoora exhibited a flux and reflux of tide with the changes of the moon. I see this is an old belief. De la Loubère mentions it in 1688 as held by the Siamese."—*Yule*, *Mission to Ava*, p. 160.

NICOBAR ISLANDS, n.p. The name for centuries applied to a group of islands north of Sumatra. They appear to be the βάρουσσαι of Ptolemy, and the Lankha Bālus of the oldest Arab *Relation*. [Sir G. Birdwood identifies them with the Island of the Bell (*Nakūs*) to which Sindbad, the Seaman, is carried in his fifth voyage. (*Report on Old Records*, 108; *Burton*, *Arabian Nights*, iv. 368).] The Danes attempted to colonize the islands in the middle of the 18th century, and since, unsuccessfully. An account of the various attempts will be found in the *Voyage of the Novara*. Since 1869 they have been partially occupied by the British Government, as an appendage of the Andaman settlement. Comparing the old forms *Lankha* and *Nakkavāram*, and the nakedness constantly attributed to the people, it seems possible that the name may have had reference to this (*nañgā*). [Mr. Man (*Journn. Anthrop. Institute*, xviii. 359) writes: "A possible derivation may be suggested by the following extract from a paper by A. de Candolle (1885) on 'The Origin of Cultivated Plants': 'The presence of the coconut in Asia three or four thousand years ago is proved by several Sanskrit names. . . . The Malays have a name widely diffused in the Archipelago, *kalapa*, *klapa*, *klopo*. At Sumatra and Nicobar we find the name *njior*, *nieor*, in the Philippines *niog*, at Bali, *nioh*, *njo*. . .' While the Nicobars have long been famed for the excellence of their coconuts, the only words which bear any resemblance to the forms above given are *ngoât*, 'a ripe nut,' and *ñi-ndu*, 'a half-ripe nut.'"]

c. 1050.—The name appears as **Nakkavāram** in the great Tanjore Inscription of the 11th century.

c. 1292.—"When you leave the island of Java (the Less) and the Kingdom of Lambri, you sail north about 150 miles, and then you come to two Islands, one of which is called **Necuveran.** In this island they have no king nor chief, but live like beasts. . . ."—*Marco Polo*, Bk. III. ch. 12.

c. 1300.—"Opposite Lámúri is the island of Lákwáram (probably to read **Nákwáram**), which produces plenty of red amber. Men and women go naked, except that the latter cover the pudenda with cocoanut leaves. They are all subject to the Káán."—*Rashíd-uddín*, in *Elliot*, i. 71.

c. 1322.—"Departing from that country, and sailing towards the south over the Ocean Sea, I found many islands and countries, where among others was one called **Nicoveran** . . . both the men and women there have faces like dogs, etc. . . ."—*Friar Odoric*, in *Cathay*, &c., 97.

1510.—"In front of the before named island of Samatra, across the Gulf of the Ganges, are 5 or 6 small islands, which have very good water and ports for ships. They are inhabited by Gentiles, poor people, and are called **Niconvar** (*Nacabar* in Lisbon ed.), and they find in them very good amber, which they carry thence to Malaca and other parts."—*Barbosa*, 195.

1514.—"Seeing the land, the pilot said it was the land of **Nicubar**. . . . The pilot was at the top to look out, and coming down he said that this land was all cut up (*i.e.* in islands), and that it was possible to pass through the middle; and that now there was no help for it but to chance it or turn back to Cochin. . . . The natives of the country had sight of us and suddenly came forth in great boats full of people. . . . They were all *Caffres*, with fish-bones inserted in their lips and chin: big men and frightful to look on; having their boats full of bows and arrows poisoned with herbs."—*Giov. da Empoli*, in *Archiv. Stor.* pp. 71-72.

NIGGER, s. It is an old brutality of the Englishman in India to apply this title to the natives, as we may see from Ives quoted below. The use originated, however, doubtless in following the old Portuguese use of *negros* for "the **blacks**" (q.v.), with no malice prepense, without any intended confusion between Africans and Asiatics.

1539.—See quot. from Pinto under **COBRA DE CAPELLO**, where **negroes** is used for natives of Sumatra.

1548.—"Moreover three blacks (**negros**) in this territory occupy lands worth 3000 or 4000 pardaos of rent; [they are related to one another, and are placed as guards in the outlying parts."—*S. Botelho, Cartas*, 111.

1582.—"A **nigroe** of John *Cambrayes*, Pilot to *Paulo de la Gama*, was that day run away to the Moores."—*Castañeda*, by N. L., f. 19.

[1608.—"The King and people **niggers**." —*Danvers, Letters*, i. 10.]

1622.—Ed. Grant, purser of the Diamond, reports capture of vessels, including a junk "with some stoor of **negers**, which was devided bytwick the Duch and the English." —*Sainsbury*, iii. p. 78.

c. 1755.—"You cannot affront them (the natives) more than to call them by the name of **negroe**, as they conceive it implies an idea of slavery."—*Ives, Voyage*, p. 23.

c. 1757.—"Gli Gesuiti sono missionarii e parocchi de' **negri** detti Malabar."—*Della Tomba*, 3.

1760.—"The Dress of this Country is entirely linnen, save Hats and Shoes; the latter are made of tanned Hides as in England . . . only that they are no thicker than coarse paper. These shoes are neatly made by **Negroes**, and sold for about 10*d.* a Pr. each of which will last two months with care."—*MS. Letter of James Rennell*, Sept. 30.

1866.—"Now the political creed of the frequenters of dawk bungalows is too uniform . . . it consists in the following tenets . . . that Sir Mordaunt Wells is the greatest judge that ever sat on the English bench; and that when you hit a **nigger** he dies on purpose to spite you."—*The Dawk Bungalow*, p. 225.

NILGHERRY, NEILGHERRY, &c., n.p. The name of the Mountain Peninsula at the end of the Mysore table land (originally known as *Malai-nāḍu*, 'Hill country'), which is the chief site of hill sanataria in the Madras Presidency. Skt. *Nīlagiri*, 'Blue Mountain.' The name *Nīla* or *Nīlādri* (synonymous with *Nīlagiri*) belongs to one of the mythical or semi-mythical ranges of the Puranic Cosmography (see *Vishnu Purāna*, in *Wilson's Works*, by *Hall*, ii. 102, 111, &c.), and has been applied to several ranges of more assured locality, *e.g.* in Orissa as well as in S. India. The name seems to have been fancifully applied to the Ootacamund range about 1820, by some European. [The name was undoubtedly applied by natives to the range before the appearance of Europeans, as in the *Kongu-deśa Rajākal*, quoted by Grigg (*Nilagiri Man.* 363), and the name appears in a letter of Col. Mackenzie of about 1816 (*Ibid.* 278). Mr. T. M. Horsfall writes:

"The name is in common use among all classes of natives in S. India, but when it may have become specific I cannot say. Possibly the solution may be that the Nilgiris being the first large mountain range to become familiar to the English, that name was by them caught hold of, but not *coined*, and stuck to them by mere priority. It is on the face of it improbable that the Englishmen who early in the last century discovered these Hills, that is, explored and shot over them, would call them by a long Skt. name."]

Probably the following quotation from Dampier refers to Orissa, as does that from Hedges:

"One of the English ships was called the *Nellegree*, the name taken from the **Nellegree** Hills in Bengal, as I have heard."—*Dampier*, ii. 145.

1683.—"In ye morning early I went up the **Nilligree** Hill, where I had a view of a most pleasant fruitfull valley."—*Hedges, Diary*, March 2; [Hak. Soc. i. 67].

The following also refers to the Orissa Hills:

1752.—"Weavers of Balasore complain of the great scarcity of rice and provisions of all kinds occasioned by the devastations of the Mahrattas, who, 600 in number, after plundering Balasore, had gone to the **Nelligree** Hills."—In *Long*, 42.

NIPA, s. Malay *nīpah*.

a. The name of a stemless palm (*Nipa fruticans*, Thunb.), which abounds in estuaries from the Ganges delta eastwards, through Tenasserim and the Malay countries, to N. Australia, and the leaves of which afford the chief material used for thatch in the Archipelago. "In the Philippines," says Crawfurd, "but not that I am aware of anywhere else, the sap of the *Nipa*. . . is used as a beverage, and for the manufacture of vinegar, and the distillation of spirits. On this account it yields a considerable part of the revenue of the Spanish Government" (*Desc. Dict.* p. 301). But this fact is almost enough to show that the word is the same which is used in sense **b**; and the identity is placed beyond question by the quotations from Teixeira and Mason.

b. Arrack made from the sap of a palm tree, a manufacture by no means confined to the Philippines. The Portuguese, appropriating the word *Nipa* to this spirit, called the tree itself *nipeira*.

a.—

1611.—"Other wine is of another kind of palm which is called **Nipa** (growing in watery places), and this is also extracted by distillation. It is very mild and sweet, and clear as pure water; and they say it is very wholesome. It is made in great quantities, with which ships are laden in Pegu and Tanasarim, Malaca, and the Philippines or Manila; but that of Tanasarim exceeds all in goodness."—*Teixeira, Relaciones*, i. 17.

1613.—"And then on from the marsh to the **Nypeiras** or wild-palms of the rivulet of Paret China."—*Godinho de Eredia*, 6.

" "And the wild palms called **Nypeiras** . . . from those flowers is drawn the liquor which is distilled into wine by an alembic, which is the best wine of India."—*Ibid.* 16*v*.

[1817.—"In the maritime districts, *atap*, or thatch, is made almost exclusively from the leaves of the **nipa** or *bûyu*."—*Raffles, H. of Java*, 2nd ed. i. 185.]

1848.—"Steaming amongst the low swampy islands of the Sunderbunds . . . the paddles of the steamer tossed up the large fruits of the **Nipa** *fruticans*, a low stemless palm that grows in the tidal waters of the Indian ocean, and bears a large head of nuts. It is a plant of no interest to the common observer, but of much to the geologist, from the nuts of a similar plant abounding in the tertiary formations at the mouth of the Thames, having floated about there in as great profusion as here, till buried deep in the silt and mud that now form the island of Sheppey."—*Hooker, Himalayan Journals*, i. 1-2.

1860.—"The **Nipa** is very extensively cultivated in the Province of Tavoy. From incisions in the stem of the fruit, toddy is extracted, which has very much the flavour of mead, and this extract, when boiled down, becomes sugar."—*Mason's Burmah*, p. 506.

1874.—"It (sugar) is also got from **Nipa** *fruticans*, Thunb., a tree of the low coast-regions, extensively cultivated in Tavoy."—*Hanbury and Flückiger*, 655.

These last quotations confirm the old travellers who represent Tenasserim as the great source of the **Nipa** spirit.

b.—

c. 1567.—"Euery yeere is there lade (at Tenasserim) some ships with Verzino, **Nipa**, and Benjamin."—*Ces. Federici* (E.T. in *Hakl.*), ii. 359.

1568.—"**Nipa**, qual' è vn Vino eccellentissimo che nasce nel fior d'vn arbore chiamato **Niper**, il cui liquor si distilla, e se ne fa vna beuanda eccellentissima."—*Ces. Federici*, in *Ramusio*, iii. 392*v*.

1583.—"I Portoghesi e noi altri di queste bande di quà non mangiamo nel Regno di Pegù pane di grano . . . ne si beve vino;

ma una certa acqua lambiccata da vn albero detto **Annippa**, ch' è alla bocca assai gustevole; ma al corpo giova e nuoce, secondo le complessioni de gli huomini."—*G. Balbi*, f. 127.

1591.—"Those of Tanaseri are chiefly freighted with Rice and **Nipar** wine, which is very strong."—*Barker's Account of Lancaster's Voyage*, in *Hakl.* ii. 592.

In the next two quotations *nipe* is confounded with coco-nut spirit.

1598.—"Likewise there is much wine brought thether, which is made of Cocus or Indian Nuttes, and is called **Nype** *de Tanassaria*, that is *Aqua - Composita of Tanassaria*."—*Linschoten*, 30; [Hak. Soc. i. 103].

,, "The Sura, being distilled, is called *Fula* (see **FOOL'S RACK**) or **Nipe**, and is an excellent *Aqua Vitae* as any is made in Dort."—*Ibid.* 101; [Hak. Soc. ii. 49].

[1616.—"One jar of **Neepe**."—*Foster, Letters*, iv. 162].

1623.—"In the daytime they did nothing but talk a little with one another, and some of them get drunk upon a certain wine they have of raisins, or on a kind of aqua vitæ with other things mixt in it, in India called **nippa**, which had been given them."—*P. della Valle*, ii. 669; [Hak. Soc. ii. 272].

We think there can be little doubt that the slang word **nip**, for a small dram of spirits, is adopted from **nipa**. [But compare Dutch *nippen*, 'to take a dram.' The old word *nippitatum* was used for 'strong drink'; see *Stanf. Dict.*]

NIRVÁNA, s. Skt. *nirvāṇa*. The literal meaning of this word is simply 'blown out,' like a candle. It is the technical term in the philosophy of the Buddhists for the condition to which they aspire as the crown and goal of virtue, viz. the cessation of sentient existence. On the exact meaning of the term see Childer's *Pali Dictionary*, s.v. *nibbāna*, an article from which we quote a few sentences below, but which covers ten double-column pages. The word has become common in Europe along with the growing interest in Buddhism, and partly from its use by Schopenhauer. But it is often employed very inaccurately, of which an instance occurs in the quotation below from Dr. Draper. The oldest European occurrence of which we are aware is in *Purchas*, who had met with it in the Pali form common in Burma, &c., *nibban.*

1626.—"After death they (the Talapoys) beleeve three Places, one of Pleasure *Scuum* (perhaps *sukham*) like the Mahumitane Paradise; another of Torment *Naxac* (read *Narac*); the third of Annihilation which they call **Niba**."—*Purchas, Pilgrimage*, 506.

c. 1815.—". . . the state of **Niban**, which is the most perfect of all states. This consists in an almost perpetual extacy, in which those who attain it are not only free from troubles and miseries of life, from death, illness and old age, but are abstracted from all sensation; they have no longer either a thought or a desire."—*Sangermano, Burmese Empire*, p. 6.

1858.—". . . Transience, Pain, and Unreality . . . these are the characters of all existence, and the only true good is exemption from these in the attainment of **nirwâna**, whether that be, as in the view of the Brahmin or the theistic Buddhist, absorption into the supreme essence; or whether it be, as many have thought, absolute nothingness; or whether it be, as Mr. Hodgson quaintly phrases it, the *ubi* or the *modus* in which the infinitely attenuated elements of all things exist, in this last and highest state of abstraction from all particular modifications such as our senses and understandings are cognisant of."—*Yule, Mission to Ava*, 236.

,, "When from between the sál trees at Kusinára he passed into **nirwána**, he (Buddha) ceased, as the extinguished fire ceases."—*Ibid.* 239.

1869.—"What Bishop Bigandet and others represent as the popular view of the **Nirvâna**, in contradistinction to that of the Buddhist divines, was, in my opinion, the conception of Buddha and his disciples. It represented the entrance of the soul into rest, a subduing of all wishes and desires, indifference to joy and pain, to good and evil, an absorption of the soul into itself, and a freedom from the circle of existences from birth to death, and from death to a new birth. This is still the meaning which educated people attach to it, whilst **Nirvâna** suggests rather a kind of Mohammedan Paradise or of blissful Elysian fields to the minds of the larger masses."—*Prof. Max Müller, Lecture on Buddhistic Nihilism*, in *Trübner's Or. Record*, Oct. 16.

1875.—"**Nibbānam.** Extinction; destruction; annihilation; annihilation of being, **Nirvāṇa**; annihilation of human passion, Arhatship or final sanctification. . . . In Trübner's Record for July, 1870, I first propounded a theory which meets all the difficulties of the question, namely, that the word **Nirvāṇa** is used to designate two different things, the state of blissful sanctification called Arhatship, and the annihilation of existence in which Arhatship ends."—*Childers, Pali Dictionary*, pp. 265-266.

,, "But at length reunion with the universal intellect takes place; **Nirwana** is reached, oblivion is attained . . . the state in which we were before we were born."—*Draper, Conflict*, &c., 122.

1879.—
"And how—in fulness of the times—it fell
That Buddha died . . .
And how a thousand thousand crores since then
Have trod the Path which leads whither he went
Unto **Nirvâna** where the Silence lives."
Sir E. Arnold, Light of Asia, 237.

NIZAM, THE, n.p. The hereditary style of the reigning prince of the Hyderabad Territories; 'His Highness the Nizám,' in English official phraseology. This in its full form, *Niẓām-ul-Mulk*, was the title of Aṣaf Jāh, the founder of the dynasty, a very able soldier and minister of the Court of Aurangzīb, who became Sūbadār (see **SOUBADAR**) of the Deccan in 1713. The title is therefore the same that had pertained to the founder of the Ahmednagar dynasty more than two centuries earlier, which the Portuguese called that of **Nizamaluco**. And the circumstances originating the Hyderabad dynasty were parallel. At the death of Aṣaf Jāh (in 1748) he was independent sovereign of a large territory in the Deccan, with his residence at Hyderabad, and with dominions in a general way corresponding to those still held by his descendant.

NIZAMALUCO, n.p. **Izam Maluco** is the form often found in Correa. One of the names which constantly occur in the early Portuguese writers on India. It represents *Niẓām-ul-Mulk* (see **NIZAM**). This was the title of one of the chiefs at the court of the Bāhmani king of the Deccan, who had been originally a Brahman and a slave. His son Ahmed set up a dynasty at Ahmednagar (A.D. 1490), which lasted for more than a century. The sovereigns of this dynasty were originally called by the Portuguese *Nizamaluco*. Their own title was *Niẓām Shāh*, and this also occurs as *Nizamoxa*. [Linschoten's etymology given below is an incorrect guess.]

1521.—"Meanwhile (the Governor Diego Lopes de Sequeira) . . . sent Fernão Camello as ambassador to the **Nizamaluco**, Lord of the lands of Choul, with the object of making a fort at that place, and arranging for an expedition against the King of Cambaya, which the Governor thought the **Nizamaluco** would gladly join in, because he was in a quarrel with that King. To this he made the reply that I shall relate hereafter."—*Correa*, ii. 623.

c. 1539. — "*Trelado do Contrato que o Viso Rey* Dom Garcia de Noronha *fez com hu* **Niza Muxaa**, *que d'antes se chamava Hu* **Niza Maluquo**."—*Tombo*, in *Subsidios*, 115.

1543. — "**Izam maluco**." See under **COTAMALUCO**.

1553. — "This city of Chaul . . . is in population and greatness of trade one of the chief ports of that coast; it was subject to the **Nizamaluco**, one of the twelve Captains of the Kingdom of Decan (which we corruptly call *Daquem*). . . . The **Nizamaluco** being a man of great estate, although he possessed this maritime city, and other ports of great revenue, generally in order to be closer to the Kingdom of the Decan, held his residence in the interior in other cities of his dominion; instructing his governors in the coast districts to aid our fleets in all ways and content their captains, and this was not merely out of dread of them, but with a view to the great revenue that he had from the ships of Malabar. . . ."—*Barros*, II. ii. 7.

1563.—". . . This King of Dely conquered the Decam (see **DECCAN**) and the Cuncam (see **CONCAM**); and retained the dominion a while; but he could not rule territory at so great a distance, and so placed in it a nephew crowned as king. This king was a great favourer of foreign people, such as Turks, Rumis, Coraçonis, and Arabs, and he divided his kingdom into captaincies, bestowing upon *Adelham* (whom we call *Idalcam*—see **IDALCAN**) the coast from Angediva to Cifardam . . . and to **Nizamoluco** the coast from Cifardam to Negotana. . . ."—*Garcia*, f. 34*v*.

,, "*R.* Let us mount and ride in the country; and by the way you shall tell me who is meant by **Nizamoxa**, as you often use that term to me.

"*O.* At once I tell you he is a king in the Balaghat (see **BALAGHAUT**) (*Bagalate* for *Balagate*), whose father I have often attended, and sometimes also the son. . . ." —*Ibid.* f. 33*v*.

[1594-5. — "**Nizám-ul-Mulkhiya**." See under **IDALCAN**.

[1598.—"*Maluco* is a Kingdome, and *Nisa* a Lance or Speare, so that *Nisa Maluco* is as much as to say as the Lance or Speare of the Kingdom."—*Linschoten*, Hak. Soc. i. 172. As if *Neza-ul-mulk*, 'spear of the kingdom.']

NOKAR, s. A servant, either domestic, military, or civil, also pl. *Nokar-logue*, 'the servants.' Hind. *naukar*, from Pers. and *naukar-lōg*. Also *naukar-chākar*, 'the servants,' one of those jingling double-barrelled phrases in which Orientals delight even more than Englishmen (see **LOOTY**). As regards Englishmen, compare hugger-mugger, hurdy-gurdy, tip-top, highty-tighty, higgledy-piggledy, hocus-pocus, tit for tat, topsy-turvy, harum-scarum, roly-poly, fiddle-faddle, rump and stump, slip-slop. In this case *chākar* (see **CHACKUR**) is also Persian. *Naukar* would seem to be a Mongol word introduced into Persia by the hosts of Chinghiz. According to I. J. Schmidt, *Forschungen im Gebiete der Volker Mittel Asiens*, p. 96, **nükur** is in Mongol, 'a comrade, dependent, or friend.'

c. 1407.—"L'Emir Khodaidad fit partir avec ce député son serviteur (**naukar**) et celui de Mirza Djihanghir. Ces trois personnages joignent la cour auguste. . . ."—*Abdurrazzāk*, in *Notices et Extraits*, XIV. i. 146.

c. 1660.—"Mahmúd Sultán . . . understood accounts, and could reckon very well by memory the sums which he had to receive from his subjects, and those which he had to pay to his '**naukars**' (apparently armed followers)."—*Abulghāzi*, by *Desmaisons*, 271.

[1810.—"**Noker.**" See under **CHACKUR**.

[1834.—"Its (Balkh) present population does not amount to 2000 souls; who are chiefly . . . the remnant of the Kara **Noukur**, a description of the militia established here by the Afgans."—*Burnes, Travels into Bokhara*, i. 238.]

1840.—"**Noker**, 'the servant'; this title was borne by Tuli the fourth son of Chenghiz Khan, because he was charged with the details of the army and the administration."—*Hammer, Golden Horde*, 460.

NOL-KOLE, s. This is the usual Anglo-Indian name of a vegetable a good deal grown in India, perhaps less valued in England than it deserves, and known here (though rarely seen) as *Kol-rabi, kohl-rabi*, 'cabbage-turnip.' It is the *Brassica oleracea*, var. *caulorapa*. The stalk at one point expands into a globular mass resembling a turnip, and this is the edible part. I see my friend Sir G. Birdwood in his *Bombay Products* spells it *Knolkhol*. It is apparently Dutch, '*Knollkool*' 'Turnip-cabbage; *Chouxrave* of the French.'

NON-REGULATION, adj. The style of certain Provinces of British India (administered for the most part under the more direct authority of the Central Government in its Foreign Department), in which the ordinary Laws (or **Regulations**, as they were formerly called) are not in force, or are in force only so far as they are specially declared by the Government of India to be applicable. The original theory of administration in such Provinces was the union of authority in all departments under one district chief, and a kind of paternal despotism in the hands of that chief. But by the gradual restriction of personal rule, and the multiplication of positive laws and rules of administration, and the division of duties, much the same might now be said of the difference between *Regulation* and *Non-regulation* Provinces that a witty Frenchman said of Intervention and Non-intervention:—"La *Non-intervention* est une phrase politique et technique qui veut dire enfin à-peu-près la même chose que *l'Intervention.*"

Our friend Gen. F. C. Cotton, R.E., tells us that on Lord Dalhousie's visit to the Neilgherry Hills, near the close of his government, he was riding with the Governor-General to visit some new building. Lord Dalhousie said to him: "It is not a thing that one must say in public, but I would give a great deal that the whole of India should be *Non-regulation.*"

The Punjab was for many years the greatest example of a Non-regulation Province. The chief survival of that state of things is that there, as in Burma and a few other provinces, military men are still eligible to hold office in the civil administration.

1860.—". . . Nowe what ye ffolke of Bengala worschyppen Sir Jhone discourseth lityl. This moche wee gadere. Some worschyppin ane Idole yclept **Regulacioun** and some worschyppen **Non-regulacion** (*veluti* **Gog et Magog**). . . ."—Ext. from a MS. of *The Travels of Sir John Mandevill in the E. Indies*, lately discovered.

1867.—". . . We believe we should indicate the sort of government that Sicily wants, tolerably well to Englishmen who know anything of India, by saying that it should be treated in great measure as a '**non-regulation**' province."—*Quarterly Review*, Jan. 1867, p. 135.

1883.—"The Delhi district, happily for all, was a **non-regulation** province."—*Life of Ld. Lawrence*, i. 44.

NORIMON, s. Japanese word. A sort of portable chair used in Japan.

[1615.—"He kept himselfe close in a **neremon**."—*Cocks's Diary*, i. 164.]

1618.—"As we were going out of the towne, the street being full of hackneymen and horses, they would not make me way to passe, but fell a quarreling with my **neremoners**, and offred me great abuse. . . ."—*Cocks's Diary*, ii. 99; [**neremonnears** in ii. 23].

1768-71.—"Sedan-chairs are not in use here (in Batavia). The ladies, however, sometimes employ a conveyance that is somewhat like them, and is called a **norimon**."—*Stavorinus*, E.T. i. 324.

NOR'-WESTER, s. A sudden and violent storm, such as often occurs in the hot weather, bringing probably a 'dust-storm' at first, and culminating in hail or torrents of rain. (See **TYPHOON**.)

1810.—". . . those violent squalls called '**north-westers**,' in consequence of their usually either commencing in, or veering round to that quarter. . . . The force of these **north-westers** is next to incredible."—*Williamson, V. M.* ii. 35.

[1827.—"A most frightful **nor' wester** had come on in the night, every door had burst open, the peals of thunder and torrents of rain were so awful. . . ."—*Mrs. Fenton, Diary*, 98.]

NOWBEHAR, n.p. This is a name which occurs in various places far apart, a monument of the former extension of Buddhism. Thus, in the early history of the Mahommedans in Sind, we find repeated mention of a temple called *Nauvihār* (*Nava-vihāra*, 'New Monastery'). And the same name occurs at Balkh, near the Oxus. (See **VIHARA**).

NOWROZE, s. Pers. *nau-rōz*, 'New (Year's) Day'; *i.e.* the first day of the Solar Year. In W. India this is observed by the Parsees. [For instances of such celebrations at the vernal equinox, see *Frazer, Pausanias*, iv. 75.]

c. 1590.—"This was also the cause why the **Naurúz** *i Jalálí* was observed, on which day, since his Majesty's accession, a great feast was given. . . . The **New Year's Day** *feast* . . . commences on the day when the Sun in his splendour moves to Aries, and lasts till the 19th day of the month (Farwardīn)."—*Āīn*, ed. *Blochmann*, i. 183, 276.

[1614.—"Their **Noroose**, which is an annual feast of 20 days continuance kept by the Moors with great solemnity."—*Foster, Letters*, iii. 65.

[1615.—"The King and Prince went a hunting . . . that his house might be fitted against the **Norose**, which began the first Newe Moon in March."—*Sir T. Roe*, Hak. Soc. i. 138; also see 142.]

1638.—"There are two Festivals which are celebrated in this place with extraordinary ceremonies; one whereof is that of the first day of the year, which, with the Persians, they call **Naurus**, **Nauros**, or **Norose**, which signifies *nine dayes*, though now it lasts *eighteen* at least, and it falls at the moment that the Sun enters Aries."—*Mandelslo*, 41.

1673.—"On the day of the Vernal *Equinox*, we returned to *Gombroon*, when the *Moores* introduced their New-Year *Æde* (see **EED**) or **Noe Rose**, with Banqueting and great Solemnity."—*Fryer*, 306.

1712.—"Restat **Nauruus**, *i.e.* vertentis anni initium, incidens in diem aequinoctii verni. Non legalis est, sed ab antiquis Persis haereditate accepta festivitas, omnium caeterarum maxima et solennissima."—*Kaempfer, Am. Exot.* 162.

1815.—"Jemsheed also introduced the solar year; and ordered the first day of it, when the sun entered Aries, to be celebrated by a splendid festival. It is called **Nauroze**, or new year's day, and is still the great festival in Persia."—*Malcolm, H. of Persia*, i. 17.

1832.—"**Now-roz** (new year's day) is a festival or **eed** of no mean importance in the estimation of Mussulman society. . . . The trays of presents prepared by the ladies for their friends are tastefully set out, and the work of many days' previous arrangement. Eggs are boiled hard, some of these are stained in colours resembling our mottled papers; others are neatly painted in figures and devices; many are ornamented with gilding; every lady evincing her own peculiar taste in the prepared eggs for **now-roz**."—*Mrs. Meer Hassan Ali, Obsns. on the Mussulmans of India*, 283-4.

NOWSHADDER, s. Pers. *naushādar* (Skt. *narasāra*, but recent), Sal-ammoniac, *i.e.* chloride of ammonium.

c. 1300.—We find this word in a medieval list of articles of trade contained in Capmany's *Memorias de Barcelona* (ii. App. 74) under the form **noxadre**.

1343.—"Salarmoniaco, cioè **lisciadro**, e non si dà nè sacco ne cassa con essa."—*Pegolotti*, p. 17; also see 57, &c.

[1834.—"Sal ammoniac (**nouchadur**) is found in its native state among the hills near Juzzak."—*Burnes, Travels into Bokhara*, ii. 166.]

NUDDEEA RIVERS, n.p. See under **HOOGLY RIVER**, of which these are branches, intersecting the *Nadiya* District. In order to keep open navigation by the directest course from the Ganges to Calcutta, much labour is, or was, annually expended, under a special officer, in endeavouring during the dry season to maintain sufficient depth in these channels.

NUGGURKOTE, n.p. *Nagarkoṭ*. This is the form used in olden times, and even now not obsolete, for the name of the ancient fortress in the Punjab Himālaya which we now usually know by the name of *Koṭ-kāngra*, both being substantially the same name, *Nagarkoṭ*, 'the fortress town,' or *Koṭ-kā-nagara*, 'the town of the fortress.' [If it be implied that *Kāngra* is a corruption of *Koṭ-kā-nagara*, the idea may be dismissed as a piece of folk-etymology. What the real derivation of *Kāngra* is is unknown. One explanation is that it represents the Hind. *khankhara*, 'dried up, shrivelled.'] In yet older times, and in the history of Mahmūd of Ghazni, it is styled Bhīm-nagar. The name *Nagarkoṭ* is sometimes used by older European writers to designate the Himalayan mountains.

1008.—"The Sultan himself (Mahmūd) joined in the pursuit, and went after them as far as the fort called *Bhīm-nagar*, which is very strong, situated on the promontory of a lofty hill, in the midst of impassable waters."—*Al-'Utbi*, in *Elliot*, i. 34.

1337.—"When the sun was in Cancer, the King of the time (Mahommed Tughlak) took the stone fort of **Nagarkot** in the year 738. . . . It is placed between rivers like the pupil of an eye . . . and is so impregnable that neither Sikandar nor Dara were able to take it."—*Badr-i-chach*, *ibid.* iii. 570.

c. 1370.—"Sultan Firoz . . . marched with his army towards **Nagarkot**, and passing by the valleys of Nákhach-nuhgarhí, he arrived with his army at **Nagarkot**, which he found to be very strong and secure. The idol Jwálámukhi (see **JOWAULLA MOOKHEE**), much worshiped by the infidels, was situated in the road to Nagarkot. . . ."—*Shams-i-Siráj*, *ibid.* iii. 317-318.

1398.—"When I entered the valley on that side of the Siwálik, information was brought to me about the town of **Nagarkot**, which is a large and important town of Hindustán, and situated in these mountains. The distance was 30 *kos*, but the road lay through jungles, and over lofty and rugged hills."—*Autobiog. of Timur*, *ibid.* 465.

1553.—"But the sources of these rivers (Indus and Ganges) though they burst forth separately in the mountains which Ptolemy calls Imaus, and which the natives call *Dalanguer* and **Nangracot**, yet are these mountains so closely joined that it seems as if they sought to hide these springs."—*Barros*, I. iv. 7.

c. 1590.—"**Nagerkote** is a city situated upon a mountain, with a fort called Kangerah. In the vicinity of this city, upon a lofty mountain, is a place called Mahamaey (*Mahāmāyā*), which they consider as one of the works of the Divinity, and come in pilgrimage to it from great distances, thereby obtaining the accomplishment of their wishes. It is most wonderful that in order to effect this, they cut out their tongues, which grow again in the course of two or three days. . . ."—*Ayeen*, ed. *Gladwin*, ii. 119; [ed. *Jarrett*, ii. 312].

1609.—"Bordering to him is another great *Raiaw* called *Tulluck Chand*, whose chiefe City is **Negercoat**, 80 c. from *Lahor*, and as much from *Syrinan*, in which City is a famous Pagod, called *Ie* or *Durga*, vnto which worlds of People resort out of all parts of *India*. . . . Diuers *Moores* also resorte to this Peer. . . ."—*W. Finch*, in *Purchas*, i. 438.

1616.—"27. **Nagra Cutt**, the chiefe Citie so called. . . ."—*Terry*, in *Purchas*, ii.; [ed. 1777, p. 82].

[c. 1617.—"**Nakarkutt**."—*Sir T. Roe*, Hak. Soc. ii. 534.]

c. 1676.—"The caravan being arriv'd at the foot of the Mountains which are call'd at this day by the name of **Naugrocot**, abundance of people come from all parts of the Mountain, the greatest part whereof are women and maids, who agree with the Merchants to carry them, their Goods and provisions cross the Mountains. . . ."—*Tavernier*, E.T. ii. 183; [ed. *Ball*, ii. 263].

1788.—"Kote Kangrah, the fortress belonging to the famous temple of **Nagorcote**, is given at 49 royal cosses, equal to 99 G. miles, from Sirhind (northward)."—*Rennell*, *Memoir*, ed. 1793, p. 107.

1809.—"At Patancote, where the Padshah (so the Sikhs call Runjeet) is at present engaged in preparations and negotiations for the purpose of obtaining possession of **Cote Çaungrah** (or **Nagar Çote**), which place is besieged by the Raja of Nepaul. . . ."—*Elphinstone*, in *Life*, i. 217.

NUJEEB, s. Hind. from Ar. *najīb*, 'noble.' A kind of half-disciplined infantry soldiers under some of the native Governments; also at one time a kind of militia under the British; receiving this honorary title as being gentlemen volunteers.

[c. 1790.—"There were 1000 men, **nudjeeves**, sword men. . . ." Evidence of Sheikh Mohammed, quoted by Mr. Plumer, in Trial of W. Hastings, in *Bond*, iii. 393.

1796.—"The **Nezibs** are Matchlock men."—*W. A. Tone*, *A Letter on the Mahratta People*, Bombay, 1798, p. 50.]

1813.—"There are some corps (Mahratta) styled **Nujeeb** or men of good family. . . . These are foot soldiers invariably armed with a sabre and matchlock, and having adopted some semblance of European discipline are much respected."—*Forbes*, *Or. Mem.* ii. 46; [2nd ed. i. 343].

[,, "A corps of **Nujeebs**, or infantry with matchlocks. . . ."—*Broughton*, *Letters from a Mahratta Camp*, ed. 1892, p. 11.

[1817.—"In some instances they are called **Nujeeb** (literally, Noble) and would not deign to stand sentry or perform any fatiguing duty."—*V. Blacker, Mem. of the Operations in India* in 1817-19, p. 22.]

NULLAH, s. Hind. *nālā*. A watercourse; not necessarily a dry watercourse, though this is perhaps more frequently indicated in the Anglo-Indian use.

1776.—"When the water falls in all the **nullahs**. . . ."—*Halhed's Code*, 52.

c. 1785.—"Major Adams had sent on the 11th Captain Hebbert . . . to throw a bridge over Shinga **nullah**."—*Carraccioli, Life of Clive*, i. 93.

1789.—"The ground which the enemy had occupied was entirely composed of sandhills and deep **nullahs**. . . ."—*Munro, Narrative*, 224.

1799.—"I think I can show you a situation where two embrasures might be opened in the bank of the **nullah** with advantage."—*Wellington, Despatches*, i. 26.

1817.—"On the same evening, as soon as dark, the party which was destined to open the trenches marched to the chosen spot, and before daylight formed a **nullah** . . . into a large parallel."—*Mill's Hist.* v. 377.

1843.—"Our march tardy because of the **nullahs**. Watercourses is the right name, but we get here a slip-slop way of writing quite contemptible."—*Life of Sir C. Napier*, ii. 310.

1860.—"The real obstacle to movement is the depth of the **nullahs** hollowed out by the numerous rivulets, when swollen by the rains."—*Tennent's Ceylon*, ii. 574.

NUMDA, NUMNA, s. Hind. *namda, namdā*, from Pers. *namad*, [Skt. *namata*]. Felt; sometimes a woollen saddle-cloth, properly made of felt. The word is perhaps the same as Ar. *namaṭ*, 'a coverlet,' spread on the seat of a sovereign, &c.

[1774.—"The apartment was full of people seated on **Næmets** (felts of camel hair) spread round the sides of the room. . . ."—*Hanway, Hist. Account of British Trade*, i. 226.]

1815.—"That chief (Temugin or Chingiz), we are informed, after addressing the Khans in an eloquent harangue, was seated upon a black felt or **nummud**, and reminded of the importance of the duties to which he was called."—*Malcolm, H. of Persia*, i. 410.

[1819.—"A Kattie throws a **nunda** on his mare."—*Trans. Lit. Soc. Bo.* i. 279.]

1828.—"In a two-poled tent of a great size, and lined with yellow woollen stuff of Europe, sat Nader Koolee Khan, upon a coarse **numud**. . . ."—*The Kuzzilbash*, i. 254.

[1850.—"The natives use (for their tents) a sort of woollen stuff, about half an inch thick, called '**numbda**.' . . . By the bye, this word '**numbda**' is said to be the origin of the word *nomade*, because the nomade tribes used the same material for their tents" (!)—Letter in *Notes and Queries*, 1st ser. i. 342.]

NUMERICAL AFFIXES, CO-EFFICIENTS, or DETERMINATIVES.* What is meant by these expressions can perhaps be best elucidated by an extract from the *Malay Grammar* of the late venerable John Crawfurd:

"In the enumeration of certain objects, the Malay has a peculiar idiom which, as far as I know, does not exist in any other language of the Archipelago. It is of the same nature as the word 'head,' as we use it in the tale of cattle, or 'sail' in the enumeration of ships; but in Malay it extends to many familiar objects. *Alai*, of which the original meaning has not been ascertained, is applied to such tenuous objects as leaves, grasses, &c.; *Batang*, meaning 'stem,' or 'trunk,' to trees, logs, spears, and javelins; *Bantak*, of which the meaning has not been ascertained, to such objects as rings; *Bidang*, which means 'spreading' or 'spacious,' to mats, carpets, thatch, sails, skins, and hides; *Biji*, 'seeds,' to corn, seeds, stones, pebbles, gems, eggs, the eyes of animals, lamps, and candlesticks," and so on. Crawfurd names 8 or 9 other terms, one or other of which is always used in company with the numeral, in enumerating different classes of objects, as if, in English, idiom should compel us to say 'two *stems* of spears,' 'four *spreads* of carpets,' 'six *corns* of diamonds.' As a matter of fact we do speak of 20 *head* of cattle, 10 *file* of soldiers, 100 *sail* of ships, 20 *pieces* of cannon, a dozen *stand* of rifles. But still the practice is in none of these cases obligatory, it is technical and exceptional; insomuch that I remember, when a boy, in old Reform-Bill days, and when disturbances were expected in a provincial town, hearing it stated by a well-informed lady that a great proprietress in the neighbourhood was so alarmed that she had ordered from town *a whole stand of muskets!*

To some small extent the idiom occurs also in other European languages,

* Other terms applied have been *Numeralia*, Quantitative Auxiliaries, Numeral Auxiliaries, Segregatives, &c.

including French and German. Of French I don't remember any example now except *tête* (de betail), nor of German except *Stück*, which is, however, almost as universal as the Chinese *piecey*. A quaint example dwells in my memory of a German courier, who, when asked whether he had any employer at the moment, replied: '*Ja freilich! dreizehn* Stück *Amerikaner!*'

The same peculiar idiom that has been described in the extract from Crawfurd as existing in Malay, is found also in Burmese. The Burmese affixes seem to be more numerous, and their classification to be somewhat more arbitrary and sophisticated. Thus *oos*, a root implying 'chief' or 'first,' is applied to kings, divinities, priests, &c.; *Yauk*, 'a male,' to rational beings not divine; *Gaung*, 'a brute beast,' to irrational beings; *Pya* implying superficial extent, to dollars, countries, dishes, blankets, &c.; *Lun*, implying rotundity, to eggs, loaves, bottles, cups, toes, fingers, candles, bamboos, hands, feet, &c.; *Tseng* and *Gyaung*, 'extension in a straight line,' to rods, lines, spears, roads, &c.

The same idiom exists in Siamese, and traces of it appear in some of the vocabularies that have been collected of tribes on the frontier of China and Tibet, indicated by the fact that the numerals in such vocabularies in various instances show identity of origin in the essential part of the numeral, whilst a different aspect is given to the whole word by a variation in what appears to be the numeral-affix* (or what Mr. Brian Hodgson calls the 'servile affix'). The idiom exists in the principal vernaculars of China itself, and it is a transfer of this idiom from Chinese dialects to Pigeon-English which has produced the *piecey*, which in that quaint jargon seems to be used as the universal numerical affix ("Two *piecey* cooly," "three *piecey* dollar," &c.).

This one **pigeon** phrase represents scores that are used in the vernaculars. For in some languages the system has taken what seems an extravagant development, which must form a great difficulty in the acquisition of colloquial use by foreigners. Some approximate statistics on this subject will be given below.

* See Sir H. Yule's *Introductory Essay* to Capt. Gill's *River of Golden Sand*, ed. 1883, pp. [127], [128].

The idiom is found in Japanese and Corean, but it is in these cases possibly not indigenous, but an adoption from the Chinese.

It is found in several languages of C. America, *i.e.* the Quiché of Guatemala, the Nahault of Mexico Proper; and in at least two other languages (Tep and Pirinda) of the same region. The following are given as the coefficients or determinatives chiefly used in the (Nahualt or) Mexican. Compare them with the examples of Malay and Burmese usage already given:

Tetl (a stone) used for roundish or cylindrical objects; *e.g.* eggs, beans, cacao beans, cherries, prickly-pears, Spanish loaves, &c., also for books, and fowls:

Pantli (?) for long rows of persons and things; also for walls and furrows:

Tlamantli (from *mana*, to spread on the ground), for shoes, dishes, basins, paper, &c., also for speeches and sermons:

Olotl (maize-grains) for ears of maize, cacao-pods, bananas: also for flint arrow-heads (see *W. v. Humboldt, Kawi-Sprache*, ii. 265).

I have, by the kind aid of my friend Professor Terrien de la Couperie, compiled a list of nearly fifty languages in which this curious idiom exists. But it takes up too much space to be inserted here. I may, however, give his statistics of the number of such determinatives, as assigned in the grammars of some of these languages In Chinese vernaculars, from 33 in the Shanghai vernacular to 110 in that of Fuchau. In Corean, 12; in Japanese, 16; in Annamite, 106; in Siamese, 24; in Shan, 42; in Burmese, 40; in Malay and Javanese, 19.

If I am not mistaken, the propensity to give certain technical and appropriated titles to couples of certain beasts and birds, which had such an extensive development in old English sporting phraseology, and still partly survives, had its root in the same state of mind, viz. difficulty in grasping the idea of abstract numbers, and a dislike to their use. Some light to me was, many years ago, thrown upon this feeling, and on the origin of the idiom of which we have been speaking, by a passage in a modern book, which is the more noteworthy as the author does not make any reference to the existence of this idiom in any language, and possibly was not aware of it:

"On entering into conversation with the (Red) Indian, it becomes speedily apparent that he is unable to comprehend the idea of abstract numbers. They exist in his mind only as associated ideas. He has a distinct conception of five dogs or five deer, but he is so unaccustomed to the idea of number as a thing apart from specific objects, that I have tried in vain to get an Indian to admit that the idea of the number five, as associated in his mind with five dogs, is identical, as far as number is concerned, with that of five fingers."—(*Wilson's Prehistoric Man*, 1st ed. ii. 470.) [Also see *Tylor, Primitive Culture*, 2nd ed. i. 252 *seqq.*].

Thus it seems probable that the use of the *numeral* co-efficient, whether in the Malay idiom or in our old sporting phraseology, is a kind of *survival* of the effort to bridge the difficulty felt, in identifying abstract numbers as applied to different objects, by the introduction of a common concrete term.

Traces of a like tendency, though probably grown into a mere fashion and artificially developed, are common in Hindustani and Persian, especially in the official written style of *munshīs*, who delight in what seemed to me, before my attention was called to the Indo-Chinese idiom, the wilful surplusage (*e.g.*) of two 'sheets' (*fard*) of letters, also used with quilts, carpets, &c.; three 'persons' (*nafar*) of barḳandāzes; five 'rope' (*rās*) of buffaloes; ten 'chains' (*zanjīr*) of elephants; twenty 'grips' (*ḳabẓa*) of swords, &c. But I was not aware of the extent of the idiom in the *munshī's* repertory till I found it displayed in Mr. Carnegy's *Kachahri Technicalities*, under the head of *Muḥāwara* (Idioms or Phrases). Besides those just quoted, we there find *'adad* ('number') used with coins, utensils, and sleeveless garments; *dāna* ('grain') with pearls and coral beads; *dast* ('hand') with falcons, &c., shields, and robes of honour; *jild* (volume, lit. 'skin') with books; *muhār* ('nose-bit') with camels; *ḳiṭa* ('portion,' *piecey!*) with precious stones, gardens, tanks, fields, letters; *manzil* ('a stage on a journey, an alighting place') with tents, boats, houses, carriages, beds, howdas, &c.; *sāz* ('an instrument') with guitars, &c.; *silk* ('thread') with necklaces of all sorts, &c. Several of these, with others purely Turkish, are used also in Osmanli Turkish.*

NUNCATIES, s. Rich cakes made by the Mahommedans in W. India chiefly imported into Bombay from Surat. [There is a Pers. word, *nān-khatāi*, 'bread of Cathay or China,' with which this word has been connected. But Mr. Weir, Collector of Surat, writes that it is really *nankhaṭāī*, Pers. *nān*, 'bread,' and Mahr. *khaṭ*, *shaṭ*, 'six'; meaning a special kind of cake composed of six ingredients—wheat-flour, eggs, sugar, butter or ghee, leaven produced from toddy or grain, and almonds.]

[**NUT**, s. Hind. *nath*, Skt. *nastā*, 'the nose.' The nose-ring worn by Indian women.

[1819.—"An old fashioned **nuth** or nose-ring, stuck full of precious or false stones."—*Trans. Lit. Soc. Bo.* i. 284.

[1832.—"The **nut** (nose-ring) of gold wire, on which is strung a ruby between two pearls, worn only by married women."—*Mrs. Meer Hassan Ali, Obsns.* i. 45.]

NUT PROMOTION, s. From its supposed indigestible character, the kernel of the **cashew**-nut is so called in S. India, where, roasted and hot, it is a favourite dessert dish. [See *Linschoten*, Hak. Soc. ii. 28.]

NUZZER, s. Hind. from Ar. *nazr* or *nazar* (prop. *nadhr*), primarily 'a vow or votive offering'; but, in ordinary use, a ceremonial present, properly an offering from an inferior to a superior, the converse of *in'ām*. The root is the same as that of *Nazarite* (Numbers, vi. 2).

[1765.—"The congratulatory **nazirs**, &c., shall be set opposite my ordinary expenses; and if ought remains, it shall go to Poplar, or some other hospital."—Letter of *Ld. Clive*, Sept. 30, in *Verelst, View of Bengal*, 127.

* Some details on the subject of these determinatives, in reference to languages on the eastern border of India, will be found in Prof. Max Müller's letter to Bunsen in the latter's *Outlines of the Phil. of Universal History*, i. 396 *seqq.*; as well as in W. von Humboldt, quoted above. Prof. Max Müller refers to Humboldt's *Complete Works*, vi. 402; but this I have not been able to find, nor, in either writer, any suggested *rationale* of the idiom.

[c. 1775.—"The Governor lays before the board two bags . . . which were presented to him in **nizzers**. . . ."—*Progs. of Council*, quoted by Fox in speech against W. Hastings, in *Bond*, iv. 201.]

1782.—"Col. Monson was a man of high and hospitable household expenses; and so determined against receiving of presents, that he would not only not touch a **nazier** (a few silver rupees, or perhaps a gold mohor) always presented by **country** gentlemen, according to their rank. . . ."—*Price's Tracts*, ii. 61.

1785. — "Presents of ceremony, called **nuzzers**, were to many a great portion of their subsistence. . . ."—Letter in *Life of Colebrooke*, 16.

1786.—Tippoo, even in writing to the French Governor of Pondichery, whom it was his interest to conciliate, and in acknowledging a present of 500 muskets, cannot restrain his insolence, but calls them "sent by way of **nuzr**."—*Select Letters of Tippoo*, 377.

1809.—"The Aumil himself offered the **nazur** of fruit."—*Ld. Valentia*, i. 453.

[1832. — "I . . . looked to the Meer for explanation; he told me to accept Muckabeg's '**nuzza**.'"—*Mrs. Meer Hassan Ali, Observns.* i. 193.]

1876.—"The Standard has the following curious piece of news in its Court Circular of a few days ago:—

'Sir Salar Jung was presented to the Queen by the Marquis of Salisbury, and offered his **Muggur** as a token of allegiance, which her Majesty touched and returned.'"—*Punch*, July 15.

For the true sense of the word so deliciously introduced instead of **Nuzzer**, see **MUGGUR**.

O

OART, s. A coco-nut garden. The word is peculiar to Western India, and is a corruption of Port. *orta* (now more usually *horta*). "Any man's particular allotment of coco-nut trees in the groves at Mahim or Girgaum is spoken of as his **oart**." (*Sir G. Birdwood*).

1564.—". . . e me praz de fazer merce a dita cidade emfatiota para sempre que a ortaliça des **ortas** dos moradores Portuguezes o christãos que nesta cidade de Goa e ilha tẽ . . . possão vender. . . ." &c.—*Proclamation of Dom Sebastian*, in *Archiv. Port. Orient.* fasc. 2, 157.

c. 1610.—"Il y a vn grand nombre de *Palmero* ou **orta**, comme vous diriez ici de nos vergers, pleins d'arbres de Cocos, plantez bien pres à pres; mais ils ne viennent qu'ès lieux aquatiques et bas. . . ."—*Pyrard de Laval*, ii. 17-18; [Hak. Soc. ii. 28].

1613.—"E os naturaes habitão ao longo do ryo de Malaca, em seus pomares e **orthas**."—*Godinho de Eredia*, 11.

1673.—"Old Goa . . . her Soil is luxurious and Campaign, and abounds with Rich Inhabitants, whose Rural Palaces are immured with Groves and **Hortos**."—*Fryer*, 154.

[1749. — ". . . as well *Vargems* (Port. *vargem*, 'a field') lands as **Hortas**."—Letter in *Logan, Malabar*, iii. 48.]

c. 1760.—"As to the **Oarts**, or Coco-nut groves, they make the most considerable part of the landed property."—*Grose*, i. 47.

1793.—"For sale. . . . That neat and commodious Dwelling House built by Mr. William Beal; it is situated in a most lovely **Oart**. . . ."—*Bombay Courier*, Jan. 12.

OBANG, s. Jap. *Oh'o-ban*, lit. 'greater division.' The name of a large oblong Japanese gold piece, similar to the **kobang** (q.v.), but of 10 times the value; 5 to 6 inches in length and 3 to 4 inches in width, with an average weight of 2564 grs. troy. First issued in 1580, and last in 1860. Tavernier has a representation of one.

[1662. — "A thousand **Oebans** of gold, which amount to forty seven thousand *Thayls*, or Crowns."—*Mandelslo*, E.T. Bk. ii. 147 (*Stanf. Dict.*).

[1859.—"The largest gold coin known is the **Obang**, a most inconvenient circulating medium, as it is nearly six inches in length, and three inches and a half in breadth."—*Oliphant, Narrative of Mission*, ii. 232.]

OLD STRAIT, n.p. This is an old name of the narrow strait between the island of Singapore and the mainland, which was the old passage followed by ships passing towards China, but has long been abandoned for the wider strait south of Singapore and north of Bintang. It is called by the Malays *Salāt Tambrau*, from an edible fish called by the last name. It is the Strait of Singapura of some of the old navigators; whilst the wider southern strait was known as New Strait or **Governor's Straits** (q.v.).

1727. — ". . . . *Johore Lami*, which is sometimes the Place of that King's Residence, and has the Benefit of a fine deep large River, which admits of two Entrances into it. The smallest is from the Westward, called by *Europeans* the Streights of *Sincapore*, but by the Natives *Salleta de Brew*" (*i.e. Salāt Tambrau*, as above).—*A. Hamilton*, ii. 92; [ed. 1744].

1860.—"The **Old Straits**, through which formerly our Indiamen passed on their way to China, are from 1 to 2 miles in width, and except where a few clearings have been made . . . with the shores on both sides covered with dense jungle . . . doubtless, in old times, an isolated vessel . . . must have kept a good look out against attack from piratical *prahus* darting out from one of the numerous creeks."—*Cavenagh, Rem. of an Indian Official*, 285-6.

OLLAH, s. Tam. *ōlai*, Mal. *ōla*. A palm-leaf; but especially the leaf of the **Palmyra** (*Borassus flabelliformis*) as prepared for writing on, often, but incorrectly, termed **cadjan** (q.v.). In older books the term *ola* generally means a native letter; often, as in some cases below, a written order. A very good account of the royal scribes at Calicut, and their mode of writing, is given by Barbosa as follows :—

1516.—"The King of Calecut keeps many clerks constantly in his palace; they are all in one room, separate and far from the king, sitting on benches, and there they write all the affairs of the king's revenue, and his alms, and the pay which is given to all, and the complaints which are presented to the king, and, at the same time, the accounts of the collectors of taxes. All this is on broad stiff leaves of the palm-tree, without ink, with pens of iron; they write their letters in lines drawn like ours, and write in the same direction as we do. Each of these clerks has great bundles of these written leaves, and wherever they go they carry them under their arms, and the iron pen in their hands . . . and amongst these are 7 or 8 who are great confidants of the king, and men held in great honour, who always stand before him with their pens in their hand and a bundle of paper under their arm; and each of them has always several of these leaves in blank but signed at the top by the king, and when he commands them to despatch any business they write it on these leaves."—Pp. 110-111, Hak. Soc., but translation modified.

1553.—"All the Gentiles of India . . . when they wish to commit anything to written record, do it on certain palm-leaves which they call **olla**, of the breadth of two fingers."—*Barros*, I. ix. 3.

„ "All the rest of the town was of wood, thatched with a kind of palm-leaf, which they call **ola**."—*Ibid.* I. iv. vii.

1561. — "All this was written by the king's writer, whose business it is to prepare his **olas**, which are palm-leaves, which they use for writing-paper, scratching it with an iron point." — *Correa*, i. 212-213. Correa uses the word in three applications: (*a*) for a palm-leaf as just quoted; (*b*) for a palm-leaf letter; and (*c*) for (Coco) palm-leaf thatch.

1563. — ". . . in the Maldiva Islands they make a kind of vessel which with its nails, its sails, and its cordage is all made of palm; with the fronds (which we call **olla** in Malavar) they cover houses and vessels."—*Garcia*, f. 67.

1586. — "I answered that I was from Venice, that my name was Gasparo Balbi . . . and that I brought the emeralds from Venice expressly to present to his majesty, whose fame for goodness, courtesy, and greatness flew through all the world . . . and all this was written down on an **olla**, and read by the aforesaid 'Master of the Word' to his Majesty."—*G. Balbi*, f. 104.

„ "But to show that he did this as a matter of justice, he sent a further order that nothing should be done till they received an **olla**, or letter of his sign manual written in letters of gold; and so he (the King of Pegù) ordered all the families of those nobles to be kept prisoners, even to the women big with child, and the infants in bands, and so he caused the whole of them to be led upon the said scaffolding; and then the king sent the **olla**, ordering them to be burnt; and the Decagini executed the order, and burned the whole of them."—*Ibid.* f. 112-113.

[1598.—"Sayles which they make of the leaves, which leaves are called **Olas**." — *Linschoten*, Hak. Soc. ii. 45.

[1611. — "Two **Ollahs**, one to Gimpa Raya. . . ."—*Danvers, Letters*, i. 154.]

1626. — "The writing was on leaves of Palme, which they call **Olla**." — *Purchas, Pilgrimage*, 554.

1673.—"The houses are low, and thatched with **ollas** of the Cocoe-Trees."—*Fryer*, 66.

c. 1690. — ". . . **Ola** peculiariter Malabaris dicta, et inter alia Papyri loco adhibetur."—*Rumphius*, i. 2.

1718. — ". . . Damulian Leaves, commonly called **Oles**."—*Prop. of the Gospel*, &c., iii. 37.

1760.—"He (King Alompra) said he would give orders for **Olios** to be made out for delivering of what Englishmen were in his *Kingdom* to me."—*Capt. Alves*, in *Dalrymple, Or. Rep.* i. 377.

1806.—"Many persons had their **Ollahs** in their hands, writing the sermon in Tamil shorthand."—*Buchanan, Christian Res.* 2nd ed. 70.

1860. — "The books of the Singhalese are formed to-day, as they have been for ages past, of **olas**, or strips taken from the young leaves of the Talipot or the Palmyra palm."—*Tennent, Ceylon*, i. 512.

1870. — ". . . Un manuscrit sur **olles**. . . ."—*Revue Critique*, June 11, 374.

OMEDWAUR, s. Hind. from Pers. *ummedwār* (*ummed*, *umed*, 'hope'); literally, therefore, 'a hopeful one'; *i.e.* "an expectant, a candidate for employment, one who awaits a favourable answer to some representation or request." (*Wilson.*)

1816.—"The thoughts of being three or four years an **omeedwar**, and of staying out here till fifty deterred me."—*M. Elphinstone*, in *Life*, i. 344.

OMLAH, s. This is properly the Ar. pl. *'amalat, 'amalā*, of *'āmil* (see **AUMIL**). It is applied on the Bengal side of India to the native officers, clerks, and other staff of a civil court or **cutcherry** (q.v.) collectively.

c. 1778.—"I was at this place met by the **Omlah** or officers belonging to the establishment, who hailed my arrival in a variety of boats dressed out for the occasion."—*Hon. R. Lindsay*, in *Lives of the Lindsays*, iii. 167.

1866.—"At the worst we will hint to the **Omlahs** to discover a fast which it is necessary they shall keep with great solemnity." —*Trevelyan, The Dawk Bungalow*, in *Fraser*, lxxiii. 390.

The use of an English plural, *omlahs*, here is incorrect and unusual; though *omrahs* is used (see next word).

1878.—". . . the subordinate managers, young, inexperienced, and altogether in the hands of the **Omlah**."—*Life in the Mofussil*, ii. 6.

OMRAH, s. This is properly, like the last word, an Ar. pl. (*Umarā*, pl. of *Amīr*—see **AMEER**), and should be applied collectively to the higher officials at a Mahommedan Court, especially that of the Great Mogul. But in old European narratives it is used as a singular for a lord or grandee of that Court; and indeed in Hindustani the word was similarly used, for we have a Hind. plural *umarāyān*, 'omrahs.' From the remarks and quotations of Blochmann, it would seem that *Manṣabdārs* (see **MUNSUBDAR**), from the commandant of 1000 upwards, were styled *umarā-i-kabār*, or *umara-i-'izām*, 'Great Amīrs'; and these would be the *Omrahs* properly. Certain very high officials were styled *Amīr-ul-Umarā* (*Āīn*, i. 239-240), a title used first at the Court of the Caliphs.

1616.—"Two **Omrahs** who are great Commanders."—*Sir T. Roe*.

[,, "The King lately sent out two **Vmbras** with horse to fetch him in."—*Ibid.* Hak. Soc. ii. 417; in the same page he writes *Vmreis*, and in ii. 445, *Vmraes*.]

c. 1630.—"Howbeit, out of this prodigious rent, goes yearely many great payments: to his Leiftenants of Provinces, and **Vmbrayes** of Townes and Forts."—*Sir T. Herbert*, p. 55.

1638.—"Et sous le commandement de plusieurs autres seigneurs de ceux qu'ils appellent **Ommeraudes**."—*Mandelslo*, Paris, 1659, p. 174.

1653.—"Il y a quantité d'elephans dans les Indes . . . les **Omaras** s'en seruent par grandeur."—*De la Boullaye-le-Gouz*, ed. 1657, p. 250.

c. 1664.—"It is not to be thought that the **Omrahs**, or Lords of the Mogul's Court, are sons of great Families, as in *France* . . . these **Omrahs** then are commonly but Adventurers and Strangers of all sorts of Nations, some of them slaves; most of them without instruction, which the Mogul thus raiseth to Dignities as he thinks good, and degrades them again, as he pleaseth."—*Bernier*, E.T. 66; [ed. *Constable*, 211].

c. 1666.—"Les **Omras** sont les grand seigneurs du Roiaume, qui sont pour la plupart Persans ou fils de Persans."—*Thevenot*, v. 307.

1673.—"The President . . . has a Noise of Trumpets . . . an Horse of State led before him, a *Mirchal* (see **MORCHAL**) (a Fan of Ostrich Feathers) to keep off the Sun, as the **Ombrahs** or Great Men have."—*Fryer*, 86.

1676.—

"Their standard, planted on the battlement,
Despair and death among the soldiers sent;
You the bold **Omrah** tumbled from the wall,
And shouts of victory pursued the fall."
Dryden, Aurengzebe, ii. 1.

1710.—"Donna Juliana . . . let the Heer Ambassador know . . . that the Emperor had ordered the **Ammaraws** Enay Ullah Chan (&c.) to take care of our interests."—*Valentijn*, iv. *Suratte*, 284.

1727.—"You made several complaints against former Governors, all of which I have here from several of my **Umbras**."—*Firmān of Aurangzīb*, in *A. Hamilton*, ii. 227; [ed. 1744, i. 231].

1791.—". . . les **Omrahs** ou grands seigneurs Indiens. . . ."—*B. de St. Pierre, La Chaumière Indienne*, 32.

OMUM WATER, s. A common domestic medicine in S. India, made from the strong-smelling carminative seeds of an umbelliferous plant, *Carum copticum*, Benth. (*Ptychotis coptica*, and *Ptych. Ajowan* of Decand.), called in Tamil *omam*, [which comes from the Skt. *yamānī, yavānī*, in Hind. *ajwān*.] See *Hanbury and Flückiger*, 269.

OOJYNE, n.p. *Ujjayanī*, or, in the modern vernacular, *Ujjain*, one of the most ancient of Indian cities, and one of their seven sacred cities. It was the capital of King Vikramaditya, and was the first meridian of Hindu astronomers, from which they calculated their longitudes.

The name of Ujjain long led to a curious imbroglio in the interpretation of the Arabian geographers. Its meridian, as we have just mentioned, was the zero of longitude among the Hindus. The Arab writers borrowing from the Hindus wrote the name apparently *Azīn*, but this by the mere omission of a diacritical point became *Arīn*, and from the Arabs passed to medieval Christian geographers as the name of an imaginary point on the equator, the intersection of the central meridian with that circle. Further, this point, or transposed city, had probably been represented on maps, as we often see cities on medieval maps, by a cupola or the like. And hence the "Cupola of *Arin* or *Arym*," or the "Cupola of the Earth" (*Al-ḳubba al-arḍh*) became an established commonplace for centuries in geographical tables or statements. The idea was that just 180° of the earth's circumference was habitable, or at any rate cognizable as such, and this meridian of *Arin* bisected this habitable hemisphere. But as the western limit extended to the Fortunate Isles, it became manifest to the Arabs that the central meridian could not be so far east as the Hindu meridian of *Arin* (or of *Lanka*, *i.e.* Ceylon). (See quotation from the *Aryabhatta*, under **JAVA**.) They therefore shifted it westward, but shifted the mystic *Arin* along the equator westward also. We find also among medieval European students (as with Roger Bacon, below), a confusion between Arin and Syene. This Reinaud supposes to have arisen from the Ἐσσινὰ ἐμπόριον of Ptolemy, a place which he locates on the Zanzibar coast, and approximating to the shifted position of Arin. But it is perhaps more likely that the confusion arose from some survival of the real name *Azīn*. Many conjectures were vainly made as to the origin of *Arym*, and M. Sedillot was very positive that nothing more could be learned of it than he had been able to learn. But the late M. Reinaud completely solved the mystery by pointing out that *Arin* was simply a corruption of *Ujjain*. Even in Arabic the mistake had been thoroughly ingrained, insomuch that the word *Arīn* had been adopted as a generic name for a place of medium temperature or qualities (see *Jorjānī*, quoted below).

c. A.D. 150.—"Ὀζηνὴ βασίλειον Τιαστανοῦ."—*Ptol.* VII. i. 63.

c. 930.—"The Equator passes between east and west through an island situated between Hind and Habash (Abyssinia), and a little south of these two countries. This point, half way between north and south is cut by the point (meridian?) half way between the Eternal Islands and the extremity of China; it is what is called *The Cupola of the Earth*."—*Maṣ'ūdī*, i. 180-181.

c. 1020.—"Les Astronomes . . . ont fait correspondre la ville d'**Odjein** avec le lieu qui dans le tableau des villes inséré dans les tables astronomiques a reçu le nom d'**Arin**, et qui est supposé situé sur les bords de la mer. Mais entre **Odjein** et la mer, il y a près de cent *yodjanas*."—*Al-Birūnī*, quoted by *Reinaud, Intro. to Abulfeda*, p. ccxlv.

c. 1267.—"Meridianum vero latus Indiae descendit a tropico Capricorni, et secat aequinoctialem circulum apud Montem Maleum et regiones ei conterminos et transit per *Syenem*, quae nunc **Arym** vocatur. Nam in libro cursuum planetarum dicitur quod duplex est *Syene*; una sub solstitio . . . alia sub aequinoctiali circulo, de quâ nunc est sermo, distans per xc gradus ab occidente, sed magis ab oriente elongatur propter hoc, quod longitudo habitabilis major est quam medietas coeli vel terrae, et hoc versus orientem."—*Roger Bacon, Opus Majus*, ed. London, 1633, p. 195.

c. 1300.—"Sous la ligne équinoxiale, au milieu du monde, là où il n'y a pas de latitude, se trouve le point de la corrélation servant de centre aux parties que se coupent entre elles. . . . Dans cet endroit et sur ce point se trouve le lieu nommé *Coupole de* **Azin** ou *Coupole de* **Arin**. Là est un château grand, élevé et d'un accès difficile. Suivant Ibn-Alaraby, c'est le séjour des démons et la trône d'Eblis. . . . Les Indiens parlent également de ce lieu, et débitent des fables à son sujet."—*Arabic Cosmography*, quoted by *Reinaud*, p. ccxliii.

c. 1400.—"**Arin** (*al-arīn*. Le lieu d'une proportion moyenne dans les choses . . . un point sur la terre à une hauteur égale des deux poles, en sorte que la nuit n'y empiète point sur la durée du jour, ni le jour sur la durée de la nuit. Ce mot a passé dans l'usage ordinaire, pour signifier d'une manière générale un lieu d'une temperature moyenne."—Livre de *Definitions* du *Seïd Scherif Zeineddin* . . . fils de *Mohammed Djordjani*, trad. de *Silv. de Sacy*, *Not. et Extr.* x. 39.

1498.—"Ptolemy and the other philosophers, who have written upon the globe, thought that it was spherical, believing that this hemisphere was round as well as that in which they themselves dwelt, the centre of which was in the island of **Arin**, which is under the equinoctial line, between the Arabian Gulf and the Gulf of Persia."—*Letter of Columbus*, on his Third Voyage, to the King and Queen. *Major's Transl.*, Hak. Soc. 2nd ed. 135.

[c. 1583.—"From thence we went to **Vgini** and Serringe. . . ."—*R. Fitch*, in *Hakl.* ii. 385.

[1616.—"**Vgen**, the Cheefe Citty of Malwa."—*Sir T. Roe*, Hak. Soc. ii. 379.]

c. 1659.—"Dara having understood what had passed at **Eugenes**, fell into that choler against *Kasem Kan*, that it was thought he would have cut off his head."—*Bernier*, E.T. p. 13; [ed. *Constable*, 41].

1785.—"The *City* of **Ugen** is very ancient, and said to have been the *Residence* of the Prince Bicker Majit, whose Æra is now Current among the Hindus."—*Sir C. Malet*, in *Dalrymple*, *Or. Rep.* i. 268.

OOOLOOBALLONG, s. Malay, *Ulubalang*, a chosen warrior, a champion. [Mr. Skeat notes: "*hulu* or *ulu* certainly means 'head,' especially the head of a Raja, and *balang* probably means 'people'; hence *ulu-balang*, 'men of the head,' or 'body-guard.']

c. 1546.—"Four of twelve gates that were in the Town were opened, thorough each of the which sallied forth one of the four Captaines with his company, having first sent out for Spies into the Camp six **Orobalons** of the most valiant that were about the King. . . ."—*Pinto* (in *Cogan*), p. 260.

1688.—"The 500 gentlemen **Orobalang** were either slain or drowned, with all the Janizaries."—*Dryden*, *Life of Xavier*, 211.

1784.—(At Acheen) "there are five great officers of state who are named Maha Rajah, Laxamana (see **LAXIMANA**), Raja Oolah, **Ooloo Ballang**, and Parkah Rajah."—*Forrest*, *V. to Mergui*, 41.

1811.—"The **ulu balang** are military officers, forming the body-guard of the Sultan, and prepared on all occasions to execute his orders."—*Marsden*, *H. of Sumatra*, 3rd ed. 351.

OOPLAH, s. Cow dung patted into cakes, and dried and stacked for fuel. Hind. *uplā*. It is in S. India called **bratty** (q.v.).

1672.—"The allowance of cowdunge and wood was—for every basket of cowdunge, 2 cakes for the Gentu Pagoda; for Peddinagg the watchman, of every baskett of cowdunge, 5 cakes."—*Orders at Ft. St. Geo.*, *Notes and Exts.* i. 56.

[Another name for the fuel is *kaṇḍā*.

[1809.—". . . small flat cakes of cow-dung, mixed with a little chopped straw and water, and dried in the sun, are used for fuel; they are called **kundhas**. . . ."—*Broughton*, *Letters from a Mahratta Camp*, ed. 1892, p. 158.]

This fuel which is also common in Egypt and Western Asia, appears to have been not unknown even in England a century ago, thus:—

1789.—"We rode about 20 miles that day (near Woburn), the country . . . is very open, with little or no wood. They have even less fuel than we (*i.e.* in Scotland), and the poor burn *cow-dung*, which they scrape off the ground, and set up to burn as we do *divots* (*i.e.* turf)."—*Lord Minto*, in *Life*, i. 301.

1863.—A passage in Mr. Marsh's *Man and Nature*, p. 242, contains a similar fact in reference to the practice, in consequence of the absence of wood, in France between Grenoble and Briançon.

[For the use of this fuel, in Tartary under the name of **argols**, see *Huc*, *Travels*, 2nd ed. i. 23. Numerous examples of its use are collected in 8 ser. *Notes and Queries*, iv. 226, 277, 377, 417.

[c. 1590.—"The plates (in refining gold) having been washed in clean water, are . . . covered with cowdung, which in Hindi is called **uplah**."—*Āīn*, ed. *Blochmann*, i. 21.

1828.—"We next proceeded to the **Ooplee** Wallee's Bastion, as it is most erroneously termed by the Mussulmans, being literally in English a '**Brattee**,' or 'dried cowdung—Woman's Tower.' . . ." (This is the *Upri* Burj, or 'Lofty Tower' of Bijapur, for which see *Bombay Gazetteer*, xxiii. 638).—*Welsh*, *Military Reminiscences*, ii. 318 *seq*.]

[**OORD, OORUD**, s. Hind. *uṛad*. A variety of *dāl* (see **DHALL**) or pulse, the produce of Phaseolus radiatus. "*Urd* is the most highly prized of all the pulses of the genus *Phaseolus*, and is largely cultivated in all parts of India" (*Watt*, *Econ. Dict.* vi. pt. i. 102, *seqq.*).

[1792.—"The stalks of the **oord** are hispid in a lesser degree than those of **moong**."—*Asiat. Res.* vi. 47.

[1814.—"**Oord.**" See under **POPPER**.

[1857.—"The **Oordh** Dal is in more common use than any other throughout the country."—*Chevers*, *Man. of Medical Jurisprudence*, 309.]

OORDOO, s. The Hindustani language. The (Turki) word *urdū* means properly the camp of a Tartar Khān, and is, in another direction, the original of our word *horde* (Russian *orda*), [which, according to Schuyler (*Turkistan*, i. 30, note), "is now commonly used by the Russian soldiers and Cossacks in a very amusing manner as a contemptuous term for an Asiatic"]. The 'Golden Horde' upon the Volga was not properly (*pace* Littré) the name of a tribe of Tartars, as is often supposed, but was the style of the Royal Camp, eventually Palace, of the Khāns of the House of Batu at

Sarai. *Horde* is said by Pihan, quoted by Dozy (*Oosterl.* 43) to have been introduced into French by Voltaire in his *Orphelin de la Chine.* But Littré quotes it as used in the 16th century. *Urda* is now used in Turkistan, *e.g.* at Tashkend, Khokhand, &c., for a 'citadel' (*Schuyler, loc. cit.* i. 30). The word *urdū*, in the sense of a royal camp, came into India probably with Baber, and the royal residence at Delhi was styled *urdū-i-mu'allā*, 'the Sublime Camp.' The mixt language which grew up in the court and camp was called *zabān-i-urdū*, 'the Camp Language,' and hence we have elliptically *Urdū.* On the Peshawar frontier the word *urdū* is still in frequent use as applied to the camp of a field-force.

1247.—"Post haec venimus ad primam **ordam** Imperatoris, in quâ erat una de uxoribus suis; et quia nondum videramus Imperatorem, noluerint nos vocare nec intromittere ad **ordam** ipsius."—*Plano Carpini*, p. 752.

1254.—"Et sicut populus Israel sciebat, unusquisque ad quam regionem tabernaculi deberet figere tentoria, ita ipsi sciunt ad quod latus curie debeant se collocare. . . . Unde dicitur curia **Orda** lingua eorum, quod sonat medium, quia semper est in medio hominum suorum. . . ."—*William of Rubruk*, p. 267.

1404.—"And the Lord (Timour) was very wroth with his Mirassaes (Mirzas), because he did not see the Ambassador at this feast, and because the *Truximan* (Interpreter) had not been with them . . . and he sent for the *Truximan* and said to him: 'How is it that you have enraged and vexed the Lord? Now since you were not with the Frank ambassadors, and to punish you, and ensure your always being ready, we order your nostrils to be bored, and a cord put through them, and that you be led through the whole **Ordo** as a punishment.'"—*Clavijo*, § cxi.

c. 1440.—"What shall I saie of the great and innumerable moltitude of beastes that are in this **Lordo**? . . . if you were disposed in one daie to bie a thousande or ij.ml horses you shulde finde them to sell in this **Lordo**, for they go in heardes like sheepe. . . ."—*Josafa Barbaro*, old E.T. Hak. Soc. 20.

c. 1540.—"Sono diuisi i Tartari in **Horde**, e **Horda** nella lor lingua significa ragunãza di popolo vnito e concorde a similitudine d'vna città."—*P. Jovio, delle Cose della Moscovia*, in *Ramusio*, ii. f. 133.

1545.—"The Tartars are divided into certain groups or congregations, which they call **hordes.** Among which the Savola **horde** or group is the first in rank."—*Herberstein*, in *Ramusio*, ii. 171.

[1560.—"They call this place (or camp) **Ordu** bazaar."—*Tenreiro*, ed. 1829, ch. xvii. p. 45.]

1673.—"**L'Ourdy** sortit d'Andrinople pour aller au camp. Le mot *ourdy* signifie camp, et sous ce nom sont cõmpris les mestiers que sont necessaires pour la commodité du voyage."—*Journal d'Ant. Galland*, i. 117.

[1753.—"That part of the camp called in Turkish the **Ordubazar** or camp-market, begins at the end of the square fronting the guard-rooms. . . ."—*Hanway, Hist. Account*, i. 247.]

OORIAL, Panj. *ūrīal*, *Ovis cycloceros*, Hutton, [*Ovis vignei*, Blanford (*Mammalia*, 497), also called the *Shā*;] the wild sheep of the Salt Range and Sulimānī Mountains.

OORIYA, n.p. The adjective 'pertaining to **Orissa**' (native, language, what not); Hind. *Uṛiya.* The proper name of the country is *Odra-deśa*, and *Oṛ-deśa*, whence *Oṛ-iya* and *Uṛ-iya.* ["The Ooryah bearers were an old institution in Calcutta, as in former days palankeens were chiefly used. From a computation made in 1776, it is stated that they were in the habit of carrying to their homes every year sums of money sometimes as much as three lakhs made by their business" (*Carey, Good Old Days of Honble. John Company*, ii. 148).]

OOTACAMUND, n.p. The chief station in the Neilgherry Hills, and the summer residence of the Governor of Madras. The word is a corruption of the Badaga name of the site of 'Stone-house,' the first European house erected in those hills, properly *Hottaga-mand* (see *Metz, Tribes of the Neilgherries*, 6). [Mr. Grigg (*Man. of the Nilagiris*, 6, 189), followed by the *Madras Gloss.*, gives Tam. *Ottagaimandu*, from Can. *ottai*, 'dwarf bamboo,' Tam. *kay*, 'fruit,' *mandu*, 'a Toda village.']

OPAL, s. This word is certainly of Indian origin: Lat. *opalus*, Greek, *ὀπάλλιος*, Skt. *upala*, 'a stone.' The European word seems first to occur in Pliny. We do not know how the Skt. word received this specific meaning, but there are many analogous cases.

OPIUM, s. This word is in origin Greek, not Oriental. [The etymology accepted by Platts, Skt. *ahiphena*, 'snake venom' is not probable.] But from the Greek *ὄπιον* the Arabs took *afyūn* which has sometimes reacted on old spellings of the word. The collection of the ὀπὸς, or juice of the poppy-capsules, is mentioned by Dioscorides (c. A.D. 77), and Pliny gives a pretty full account of the drug as *opion* (see *Hanbury and Flückiger*, 40). The Opium-poppy was introduced into China, from Arabia, at the beginning of the 9th century, and its earliest Chinese name is **A-fu-yung**, a representation of the Arabic name. The Arab. *afyūn* is sometimes corruptly called *afīn*, of which *afīn*, 'imbecile,' is a popular etymology. Similarly the Bengalees derive it from *afi-heno*, 'serpent-home.' [A number of early references to opium smoking have been collected by Burnell, *Linschoten*, Hak. Soc. ii. 113.]

c. A.D. 70.—". . . which juice thus drawne, and thus prepared, hath power not onely to provoke sleepe, but if it be taken in any great quantitie, to make men die in their sleepe: and this our Physicians call **opion**. Certes I have knowne many come to their death by this meanes; and namely, the father of Licinius Cecinna late deceased, a man by calling a Pretour, who not being able to endure the intollerable pains and torments of a certaine disease, and being wearie of his life, at Bilbil in Spaine, shortened his owne daies by taking **opium**." —*Pliny*, in *Holland's* transl. ii. 68.

(*Medieval*).—

"Quod venit a Thebis, **opio** laudem perhibebis;
Naribus horrendum, rufum laus dictat emendum."

Otho Cremonensis.

1511.—"Next day the General (Alboquerque) sent to call me to go ashore to speak to the King; and that I should say on his part . . . that he had got 8 Guzzarate ships that he had taken on the way because they were enemies of the King of Portugal; and that these had many rich stuffs and much merchandize, and **arfiun** (for so they call *opio tebaico*) which they eat to cool themselves; all which he would sell to the King for 300,000 ducats worth of goods, cheaper than they could buy it from the Moors, and more such matter."—Letter of *Giovanni da Empoli*, in *Archivio Storico Italiano*, 55.

[1513.—"Opium (**oafyam**) is nothing else than the milk of poppies."—*Alboquerque, Cartas*, p. 174.]

1516.—"For the return voyage (to China) they ship there (at Malacca) Sumatra and Malabar pepper, of which they use a great deal in China, and drugs of Cambay, much *anfiam*, which we call **opium**. . . ."—*Barbosa*, 206.

1563.—"*R.* I desire to know for certain about **amfiao**, what it is, which is used by the people of this country; if it is what we call **opium**, and whence comes such a quantity as is expended, and how much may be eaten every day?

* * * * *

"*O.* . . . that which I call of Cambaia come for the most part from one territory which is called Malvi (*Mālwā*). . . . I knew a secretary of Nizamoxa (see **NIZAMALUCO**), a native of Coraçon, who every day eat three *tôllas* (see **TOLA**), or a weight of 10½ cruzados . . . though he was a well educated man, and a great scribe and notary, he was always dozing or sleeping; yet if you put him to business he would speak like a man of letters and discretion; from this you may see what habit will do."—*Garcia*, 153*v* to 155*v*.

1568.—"I went then to Cambaya . . . and there I bought 60 parcels of **Opium**, which cost me two thousand and a hundreth duckets, every ducket at foure shillings two pence."—*Master C. Frederike*, in *Hakl.* ii. 371. The original runs thus, showing the looseness of the translation: ". . . comprai sessanta *man* **d'Anfion**, che mi costò 2100 ducati serafini (see **XERAFINE**), che a nostro conto possono valere 5 lire l'vno."—In *Ramusio*, iii. 396*v*.

1598.—"**Amfion**, so called by the Portingales, is by Arabians, Mores, and Indians called **Affion**, in latine **Opio** or **Opium**. . . . The Indians use much to eat *Amfion*. . . . Hee that useth to eate it, must eate it daylie, otherwise he dieth and consumeth himselfe . . . likewise hee that hath never eaten it, and will venture at the first to eate as much as those that dayly use it, it will surely kill him. . . ."—*Linschoten*, 124; [Hak. Soc. ii. 112].

[c. 1610.—"Opium, or as they (in the Maldives) call it, **Aphion**."—*Pyrard de Laval*, Hak. Soc. i. 195.

[1614.—"The waster washer who to get **Affanan** hires them (the cloths) out a month."—*Foster, Letters*, ii. 127.

[1615.—". . . Coarse chintz, and **ophyan**." —*Ibid.* iv. 107].

1638.—"Turcae **opium** experiuntur, etiam in bona quantitate, innoxium et confortativum; adeo ut etiam ante praelia ad fortitudinem illud sumant; nobis vero, nisi in parvâ quantitate, et cum bonis correctivis lethale est."—*Bacon, H. Vitae et Mortis* (ed. Montague) x. 188.

1644.—"The principal cause that this monarch, or rather say, this tyrant, is so powerful, is that he holds in his territories, and especially in the kingdom of Cambaya, those three plants of which are made the **Anfiam**, and the anil (see **ANILE**), and that which gives the *Algodam*" (Cotton).—*Bocarro*, MS.

1694.—"This people, that with *amphioen* or **opium**, mixed with tobacco, drink themselves not merely drunk but mad, are wont to fall furiously upon any one whom they meet, with a naked *kris* or dagger in the hand, and to stab him, though it be but a child, in their mad passion, with the cry of *Amock* (see **A MUCK**), that is 'strike dead,' or 'fall on him.' . . ."—*Valentijn*, iv. (*China*, &c.) 124.

1726.—"It will hardly be believed . . . that Java alone consumes monthly 350 packs of **opium**, each being of 136 *catis* (see **CATTY**), though the E. I. Company make 145 catis out of it. . . ."—*Valentijn*, iv. 61.

1727.—"The Chiefs of Calecut, for many years had vended between 500 and 1000 chests of *Bengal* **Ophium** yearly up in the inland Countries, where it is very much used."—*A. Hamilton*, i. 315; [ed. 1744, i. 317 *seq.*].

1770.—"Patna . . . is the most celebrated place in the world for the cultivation of **opium**. Besides what is carried into the inland parts, there are annually 3 or 4000 chests exported, each weighing 300 lbs. . . . An excessive fondness for opium prevails in all the countries to the east of India. The Chinese emperors have suppressed it in their dominions, by condemning to the flames every vessel that imports this species of poison."—*Raynal* (tr. 1777), i. 424.

ORANGE, s. A good example of plausible but entirely incorrect etymology is that of orange from Lat. *aurantium*. The latter word is in fact an ingenious medieval fabrication. The word doubtless came from the Arab. *nāranj*, which is again a form of Pers. *nārang*, or *nārangī*, the latter being still a common term for the orange in Hindustan. The Persian indeed may be traced to Skt. *nāgarañga*, and *nārañga*, but of these words no satisfactory etymological explanation has been given, and they have perhaps been Sanscritized from some southern term. Sir W. Jones, in his article on the Spikenard of the Ancients, quotes from Dr. Anderson of Madras, "a very curious philological remark, that in the Tamul dictionary, most words beginning with *nar* have some relation to fragrance; as *narukeradu*, to yield an odour; *nārtum pillei*, lemon-grass; *nārtei*, citron; *nārta manum* (read *mārum*), the wild orange-tree; *nārum panei*, the Indian jasmine; *nārum alleri*, a strong smelling flower; and *nārtu*, which is put for *nard* in the Tamul version of our scriptures." (See *As. Res.* vol. ii. 414). We have not been able to verify many of these Tamil terms. But it is true that in both Tamil and Malayalam *naru* is 'fragrant.' See, also, on the subject of this article, *A. E. Pott*, in Lassen's *Zeitschrift f. d. Kunde des Morgenlandes*, vii. 114 *seqq.*

The native country of the orange is believed to be somewhere on the northern border of India. A wild orange, the supposed parent of the cultivated species, both sweet and bitter, occurs in Garhwāl and Sikkim, as well as in the Kāsia (see **COSSYA**) country, the valleys of which last are still abundantly productive of excellent oranges. [See *Watt, Econ. Dict.* ii. 336 *seqq.*] It is believed that the orange first known and cultivated in Europe was the bitter or Seville orange (see *Hanbury and Flückiger*, 111-112).

From the Arabic, Byzantine Greek got *νεράντζιον*, the Spaniards *naranja*, old Italian *narancia*, the Portuguese *laranja*, from which last, or some similar form, by the easy detachment of the *l* (taken probably, as in many other instances, for an article), we have the Ital. *arancio*, L. Latin *aurantium*, French *orange*, the modification of these two being shaped by *aurum* and *or*. Indeed, the quotation from Jacques de Vitry possibly indicates that some form like *al-arangi* may have been current in Syria. Perhaps, however, his phrase *ab indigenis nuncupantur* may refer only to the Frank or quasi-Frank settlers, in which case we should have among them the birthplace of our word in its present form. The reference to this passage we derived in the first place from Hehn, who gives a most interesting history of the introduction of the various species of *citrus* into Europe. But we can hardly think he is right in supposing that the Portuguese first brought the sweet orange (*Citrus aurantium dulce*) into Europe from China, c. 1548. No doubt there may have been a re-introduction of some fine varieties at that time.* But as early as the beginning of the 14th century we find Abulfeda extolling the fruit of Cintra. His words, as rendered by M. Reinaud, run: "Au nombre des dependances de Lisbonne est la ville de Schintara; à Schintara on recueille des pommes admirables pour la grosseur et le gout" (244 †). That these *pommes* were the famous Cintra oranges can hardly be

* There seems to have been great oscillation of traffic in this matter. About 1878, one of the present writers, then resident at Palermo, sent, in compliance with a request from Lahore, a collection of plants of many (about forty) varieties of *citrus* cultivated in Sicily, for introduction into the Punjab. This despatch was much aided by the kindness of Prof. Todaro, in charge of the Royal Botanic Garden at Palermo.

† In Reiske's version "poma stupendae molis et excellentissima."—*Büsching's Magazin*, iv. 230.

doubted. For Baber (*Autobiog.* 328) describes an orange under the name of *Sangtarah,* which is, indeed, a recognised Persian and Hind. word for a species of the fruit. And this early propagation of the sweet orange in Portugal would account not only for such wide diffusion of the name of *Cintra,* but for the persistence with which the alternative name of *Portugals* has adhered to the fruit in question. The familiar name of the large sweet orange in Sicily and Italy is *portogallo,* and nothing else; in Greece *πορτογαλέα,* in Albanian *protokale,* among the Kurds *portoghāl;* whilst even colloquial Arabic has *burtukān.* The testimony of Maṣʻūdī as to the introduction of the orange into Syria before his time (c. A.D. 930), even if that were (as it would seem) the Seville orange, renders it quite possible that better qualities should have reached Lisbon or been developed there during the Saracenic occupation. It was indeed suggested in our hearing by the late Sir Henry M. Elliot that *sangtarah* might be interpreted as *sang-tar,* 'green stones' (or in fact 'moist pips'); but we hardly think he would have started this had the passage in Abulfeda been brought to his notice. [In the *Āīn* (ed. *Gladwin,* 1800, ii. 20) we read: "Sircar Silhet. . . . Here grows a delicious fruit called *Soontara,* in colour like an orange, but of an oblong form." This passage reads in Col. Jarrett's translation (ii. 124): "There is a fruit called *Sūntarah* in colour like an orange but large and very sweet." Col. Jarrett disputes the derivation of *Sangtarah* from *Cintra,* and he is followed by Mr. H. Beveridge, who remarks that Humayun calls the fruit *Sanatra.* Mr. Beveridge is inclined to think that *Santra* is the *Indian* hill name of the fruit, of which *Sangtarah* is a corruption, and refers to a village at the foot of the Bhutan Hills called *Santrabārī,* because it had orange groves.]

A.D. c. 930.—"The same may be said of the orange-tree (*Shajr-ul-***nāranj**) and of the round citron, which were brought from India after the year (A.H.) 300, and first sown in 'Omān. Thence they were transplanted to Basra, to 'Irāk, and to Syria . . . but they lost the sweet and penetrating odour and beauty that they had in India, having no longer the benefits of the climate, soil, and water peculiar to that country."—*Maṣʻūdi,* ii. 438-9.

c. 1220.—"In parvis autem arboribus quaedam crescunt alia poma citrina, minoris quantitatis frigida et acidi seu pontici (*bitter*) saporis, quae poma **orenges** ab indigenis nuncupantur."—*Jacobus Vitriacus,* in *Bongars.* These were apparently our Seville oranges.

c. 1290.—"In the 18th of Edward the first a large Spanish Ship came to Portsmouth; out of the cargo of which the Queen bought one frail (see **FRAZALA**) of Seville figs, one frail of raisins or grapes, one bale of dates, two hundred and thirty pomegranates, fifteen citrons, and seven oranges (*Poma de* **orenge**)."—*Manners and Household Expenses of England in the 13th and 15th Centuries,* Roxb. Club, 1841, p. xlviii. The Editor deigns only to say that 'the MS. is in the Tower.' [Prof. Skeat writes (9 ser. *Notes and Queries,* v. 321): "The only known allusion to oranges, previously to 1400, in any piece of English literature (I omit household documents) is in the '*Alliterative Poems,*' edited by Dr. Morris, ii. 1044. The next reference, soon after 1400, is in Lydgate's '*Minor Poems,*' ed. Halliwell, p. 15. In 1440 we find **oronge** in the '*Promptorium Parvulorum,*' and in 1470 we find **orenges** in the '*Paston Letters,*' ed. Gairdner, ii. 394."]

1481.—"Item to the galeman (galley man) brought the lampreis and **oranges** . . . iiij*d.*" —*Household Book* of John D. of Norfolk, Roxb. Club, 1844, p. 38.

c. 1526.—"They have besides (in India) the **nâranj** [or Seville orange, Tr.] and the various fruits of the orange species. . . . It always struck me that the word **nâranj** was accented in the Arab fashion; and I found that it really was so; the men of Bajour and Siwâd call *nâranj nârank*" (or perhaps rather **nârang**). — *Baber,* 328. In this passage Baber means apparently to say that the right name was *nārang,* which had been changed by the usual influence of Arabic pronunciation into *nāranj.*

1883.—"Sometimes the foreign products thus cast up (on Shetland) at their doors were a new revelation to the islanders, as when a cargo of **oranges** was washed ashore on the coast of Delting, the natives boiled them as a new kind of potatoes." — *Saty. Review,* July 14, p. 57.

ORANG-OTANG, ORANG-OUTAN, &c. s. The great man-like ape of Sumatra and Borneo; *Simia Satyrus,* L. This name was first used by Bontius (see below). It is Malay, *ŏrăng-ūtăn,* 'homo sylvaticus.' The proper name of the animal in Borneo is *mias.* Crawfurd says that it is never called *orang-utan* by 'the natives.' But that excellent writer is often too positive—especially in his negatives! Even if it be not (as is probable) anywhere a recognised specific name, it is hardly possible that the name should not be sometimes applied popularly. We remember a tame **hooluck** belonging to a gentleman in E. Bengal, which was habitually known to the natives as *janglī ādmī*, literally = *orang-utan*. [There seems reason to believe that Crawfurd was right after all. Mr. Scott (*Malayan Words in English*, p. 87) writes: "But this particular application of *ōrang ūtan* to the ape does not appear to be, or ever to have been, familiar to the Malays generally; Crawfurd (1852) and Swettenham (1889) omit it, Pijnappel says it is 'Low Malay,' and Klinkert (1893) denies the use entirely. This uncertainty is explained by the limited area in which the animal exists within even native observation. Mr. Wallace could find no natives in Sumatra who 'had ever heard of such an animal,' and no 'Dutch officials who knew anything about it.' Then the name came to European knowledge more than 260 years ago; in which time probably more than one Malay name has faded out of general use or wholly disappeared, and many other things have happened." Mr. Skeat writes: "I believe Crawfurd is absolutely right in saying that it is never called *ōrang-ūtan* by the natives. It is much more likely to have been a sailor's mistake or joke than an error on the part of the Malays who know better. Throughout the Peninsula *ōrang-ūtan* is the name applied to the wild tribes, and though the *mawas* or *mias* is known to the Malays only by tradition, yet in tradition the two are never confused, and in those islands where the *mawas* does exist he is never called *ōrang-ūtan*, the word *ōrang* being reserved exclusively to describe the human species."]

1631.—"Loqui vero eos easque posse Iavani aiunt, sed non velle, ne ad labores cogantur; ridicule mehercules. Nomen ei induunt **Ourang Outang**, quod 'hominem silvae' significat, eosque nasci affirmant e libidine mulierum Indarum, quae se Simiis et Cercopithecis detestanda libidine uniunt." —*Bontii, Hist. Nat.* v. cap. 32, p. 85.

1668.—"Erat autem hic satyrus quadrupes: sed ab humanâ specie quam prae se fert, vocatur Indis **Ourang-outang**: sive homo silvestris."—*Licetus de Monstris*, 338.

[1701. — "**Orang-outang** sive Homo Sylvestris: or the Anatomy of a Pygmie compared with that of a Monkey, an Ape, and a Man. . . ."—Title of work by *E. Tyson* (*Scott*).]

1727.—"As there are many species of wild Animals in the Woods (of Java) there is one in particular called the **Ouran-Outang**." —*A. Hamilton*, ii. 131; [ed. 1744, ii. 136].

1783.—"Were we to be driven out of India this day, nothing would remain to tell that it had been possessed, during the inglorious period of our dominion, by any thing better than the **ourang-outang** or the tiger."—*Burke, Sp. on Fox's E. India Bill, Works*, ed. 1852, iii. 468.

1802.—"Man, therefore, in a state of nature, was, if not the **ourang-outang** of the forests and mountains of Asia and Africa at the present day, at least an animal of the same family, and very nearly resembling it."—*Ritson, Essay on Abstinence from Animal Food*, pp. 13-14.

1811.—"I have one slave more, who was given me in a present by the Sultan of Pontiana. . . . This gentleman is Lord Monboddo's genuine **Orang-outang**, which in the Malay language signifies literally *wild man*. . . . Some people think seriously that the **oran-outang** was the original patriarch and progenitor of the whole Malay race." —*Lord Minto, Diary in India*, 268-9.

1868.—"One of my chief objects . . . was to see the **Orang-utan** . . . in his native haunts."—*Wallace, Malay Archip.* 39.

In the following passage the term is applied to a tribe of men:

1884.—"The Jacoons belong to one of the wild aboriginal tribes . . . they are often styled **Orang Utan**, or men of the forest." —*Cavenagh, Rem. of an Indian Official*, 293.

ORANKAY, ARANGKAIO, &c. s. Malay *Orang kāya*. In the Archipelago, a person of distinction, a chief or noble, corresponding to the Indian **omrah**; literally 'a rich man,' analogous therefore to the use of *riche-homme* by Joinville and other old French authors. [Mr. Skeat notes that the terminal *o* in **arangkaio** represents a dialectical form used in Sumatra and Java. The Malay leader of the Pahang rising in 1891-2, who was supposed to bear a charmed life, was called by the title of *Orang Kāya Pahlawan* (see **PULWAUN**).]

c. 1612.—"The Malay officers of state are classified as 1. *Bandahara*; 2. *Ferdana Mantri*; 3. *Punghulu Bandari*; 4. the chief *Hulubalang* or champion (see **OOLOO-BALLONG**); 5. the *Paramantris*; 6. **Orang Kayas**; 7. *Chatriyas* (Kshatriyas); 8. *Seda Sidahs*; 9. *Bentaras* or heralds; 10. *Hulubalangs*."—*Sijara Malayu*, in *J. Ind. Arch.* v. 246.

1613.—"The nobler **Orancayas** spend their time in pastimes and recreations, in music and in cock fighting, a royal sport. . . ." —*Godinho de Eredia* f. 31*v*.

1613.—"An **Oran Caya** came aboord, and told me that a *Curra Curra* (see **CARACOA**) of the Flemmings had searched three or foure Praws or Canoas comming aboord vs with Cloues, and had taken them from them, threatening death to them for the next offence."—*Saris*, in *Purchas*, i. 348.

[„ ". . . gave him the title of **Orancaya Pute**, which is white or clear hearted lord."—*Danvers, Letters*, i. 270.]

1615.—"Another conference with all the **Arrankayos** of Lugho and Cambello in the hills among the bushes: their reverence for the King and the honourable Company."—*Sainsbury*, i. 420.

[„ "Presented by Mr. Oxwicke to the **Wrankiaw**."—*Foster, Letters*, iii. 96.

[„ ". . . a nobleman called **Aron Caie** Hettam."—*Ibid.* iii. 128.]

1620.—"Premierement sur vn fort grand Elephant il y auoit vne chaire conuerte, dans laquelle s'est assis vn des principaux **Orangcayes** ou Seigneurs."—*Beaulieu*, in *Thevenot's Collection*, i. 49.

1711.—"Two Pieces of Callico or Silk to the *Shabander* (see **SHABUNDER**), and head **Oronkoy** or Minister of State."—*Lockyer*, 36.

1727.—"As he was entering at the Door, the **Orankay** past a long Lance through his Heart, and so made an end of the Beast."—*A. Hamilton*, ii. 97; [ed. 1744, ii. 96].

„ "However, the reigning King not expecting that his Customs would meet with such Opposition, sent an **Orangkaya** aboard of my Ship, with the Linguist, to know why we made War on him."—*Ibid.* 106; [ed. 1744].

1784.—"Three or four days before my departure, Posally signified to me the King meant to confer on me the honour of being made Knight of the Golden Sword, **Orang Kayo** *derry piddang mas*" (*orang kaya dari pădang mas*).—*Forrest, V. to Mergui*, 54.

1811.—"From amongst the **orang kayas** the Sultan appoints the officers of state, who as members of Countil are called *mantri* (see **MUNTREE, MANDARIN**)."—*Marsden, H. of Sumatra*, 350.

[**ORGAN**, s. An Oriental form of mitrailleuse. Steingass (*Dict.* 38) has Pers. *arghan, arghon*, from the Greek *ὄργανον*, 'an organ.'

1790.—"A weapon called an **organ**, which is composed of about thirty-six gun barrels so joined as to fire at once."—Letter from De Boigne's Camp at Mairtha, dated Sept. 13, in *H. Compton, A particular Account of the European Military Adventurers of Hindustan, from* 1784 to 1803, p. 61.]

ORISSA, n.p. [Skt. *Odrāshtra*, 'the land of the Odras' (see **OORIYA**). The word is said to be the Prakrit form of *uttara*, 'north,' as applied to the N. part of Kalinga.] The name of the ancient kingdom and modern province which lies between Bengal and the Coromandel Coast.

1516.—"*Kingdom of* **Orisa**. Further on towards the interior there is another kingdom which is conterminous with that of Narsynga, and on another side with Bengala, and on another with the great Kingdom of Dely. . . ."—*Barbosa*, in Lisbon ed. 306.

c. 1568.—"**Orisa** fu già vn Regno molto bello e securo . . . sina che regnò il suo Rè legitimo, qual era Gentile."—*Ces. Federici, Ramusio*, iii. 392.

[c. 1616.—"**Vdeza**, the Chiefe Citty called Iekanat (**Juggurnaut**)."—*Sir T. Roe*, Hak. Soc. ii. 538.]

ORMESINE, s. A kind of silk texture, which we are unable to define. The name suggests derivation from Ormus. [The *Draper's Dict.* defines "**Armozeen**, a stout silk, almost invariably black. It is used for hatbands and scarfs at funerals by those not family mourners. Sometimes sold for making clergymen's gowns." The *N.E.D.* s.v. **Armozeen**, leaves the etymology doubtful. The *Stanf. Dict.* gives **Ormuzine**, "a fabric exported from *Ormuz*."]

c. 1566.—". . . a little Island called Tana, a place very populous with Portugals, Moores and Gentiles: these have nothing but Rice; they are makers of **Armesie** and weavers of girdles of wooll and bumbast."—*Caes. Fredericke*, in *Hakl.* ii. 344.

1726.—"Velvet, Damasks, **Armosyn**, Sattyn."—*Valentijn*, v. 183.

ORMUS, ORMUZ, n.p. Properly *Hurmuz* or *Hurmūz*, a famous maritime city and minor kingdom near the mouth of the Persian Gulf. The original place of the city was on the northern shore of the Gulf, some 30 miles east of the site of Bandar Abbās or **Gombroon** (q.v.); but about A.D. 1300, apparently to escape from Tartar raids, it was transferred to the small island of Gerūn or Jerūn, which may be identified with the *Organa* of Nearchus, about 12 m. westward, and five miles from the shore, and this was the seat of the kingdom when first visited and attacked by the Portuguese under Alboquerque in 1506. It was taken by them about 1515, and occupied permanently (though the nominal reign of the native kings was maintained), until wrested from them by Shāh 'Abbās, with the assistance of an English squadron from Surat, in 1622. The place was destroyed by the Persians, and the island has since remained desolate, and all but uninhabited, though the Portuguese citadel and water-tanks remain. The islands of Hormuz, Kishm, &c., as well as Bandar 'Abbās and other ports on the coast of Kerman, had been held by the Sultans of Omān as fiefs of Persia, for upwards of a century, when in 1854 the latter State asserted its dominion, and occupied those places in force (see *Badger's Imams of Omān*, &c., p. xciv.).

B.C. c. 325.—"They weighed next day at dawn, and after a course of 100 stadia anchored at the mouth of the river Anamis, in a country called **Harmozeia.**"—*Arrian, Voyage of Nearchus*, ch. xxxiii., tr. by *M'Crindle*, p. 202.

c. A.D. 150.—(on the coast of Carmania)

"Ἄρμουζα πόλις.
Ἄρμοζον ἄκρον."
Ptol. VI. viii. 5.

c. 540.—At this time one Gabriel is mentioned as (Nestorian) Bishop of **Hormuz** (see *Assemani*, iii. 147-8).

c. 655.—"Nobis . . . visum est nihilominus velut ad sepulchra mortuorum, quales vos esse video, geminos hosce Dei Sacerdotes ad vos allegare; Theodorum videlicet Episcopum **Hormuzdadschir** et Georgium Episcopum Susatrae."—Syriac Letter of the *Patriarch Jesujabus, ibid.* 133.

1298.—"When you have ridden these two days you come to the Ocean Sea, and on the shore you find a City with a harbour, which is called **Hormos.**"—*Marco Polo*, Bk. i. ch. xix.

c. 1330.—". . . I came to the Ocean Sea. And the first city on it that I reached is called **Ormes**, a city strongly fenced and abounding in costly wares. The city is on an island some five miles distant from the main; and on it there grows no tree, and there is no fresh water."—*Friar Odoric*, in *Cathay*, &c., 56.

c. 1331.—"I departed from 'Omān for the country of **Hormuz.** The city of Hormuz stands on the shore of the sea. The name is also called Moghistān. The new city of **Hormuz** rises in face of the first in the middle of the sea, separated from it only by a channel 3 parasangs in width. We arrived at New **Hormuz**, which forms an island of which the capital is called Jaraun. . . . It is a mart for Hind and Sind."—*Ibn Batuta*, ii. 230.

1442.—"**Ormus** (qu. *Hurmūz?*), which is now called Djerun, is a port situated in the middle of the sea, and which has not its equal on the face of the globe."—*Abdurrazzāk*, in *India in XV. Cent.* p. 5.

c. 1470.—"**Hormuz** is 4 miles across the water, and stands on an Island."—*Athan. Nikitin, ibid.* p. 8.

1503.—"Habitant autem ex eorum (Francorum) gente homines fere viginti in urbe Cananoro: ad quos profecti, postquam ex **Hormizda** urbe ad eam Indorum civitatem Cananorum venimus, significavimus illis nos esse Christianos, nostramque conditionem et gradum indicavimus; et ab illis magno cum gaudio suscepti sumus. . . . Eorundem autem Francorum regio Portugallus vocatur, una ex Francorum regionibus; eorumque Rex Emanuel appellatur; Emmanuelem oramus ut illum custodiat."—Letter from *Nestorian Bishops* on Mission to India, in *Assemani*, iii. 591.

1505.—"In la bocha di questo mare (di Persia) è vn altra insula chiamata **Agramuzo** doue sono perle infinite: (e) caualli che per tutte quelle parti sono in gran precio."—Letter of *K. Emanuel*, p. 14.

1572.—

"Mas vê a illa Gerum, como discobre
O que fazem do tempo os intervallos;
Que da cidade **Armuza**, que alli esteve
Ella o nome despois, e gloria teve."
Camões, x. 103.

By Burton:

"But see yon Gerum's isle the tale unfold
of mighty things which Time can make or mar;
for of **Armuza**-town yon shore upon
the name and glory this her rival won."

1575.—"Touchant le mot **Ormuz**, il est moderne, et luy a esté imposé par les Portugais, le nom venant de l'accident de ce qu'ils cherchoient que c'estoit que l'Or; tellement qu'estant arrivez là, et voyans le trafic de tous biens, auquel le pais abonde, ils dirent *Vssi esta Or mucho*, c'est à dire, Il y a force d'Or; et pource ils donnerēt le nom d'**Ormucho** à la dite isle."—*A. Thevet, Cosmographie Univ.*, liv. x. i. 329.

1623.—"Non volli lasciar di andare con gl' Inglesi in **Hormuz** a veder la forteza, la città, e ciò che vi era in fine di notabile in quell' isola."—*P. della Valle*, ii. 463. Also see ii. 61.

1667.—

"High on a throne of royal state, which far
Outshone the wealth of **Ormus** and of Ind,
Or where the gorgeous East with richest hand
Showers on her kings barbaric pearl and gold."
Paradise Lost, ii. 1-4.

OROMBARROS, s. This odd word seems to have been used as **griffin** (q.v.) now is. It is evidently the Malay *orang-baharu*, or *orang bharu*, 'a new man, a novice.' This is interesting as showing an unquestionable instance of an expression imported from the Malay factories to Continental India. [Mr. Skeat remarks that the form of the word shows that it came from the Malay under Portuguese influence.]

1711.—At Madras . . . "refreshments for the Men, which they are presently supply'ed with from Country Boats and Cattamarans, who make a good Peny at the first coming of **Orombarros**, as they call those who have not been there before."—*Lockyer*, 28.

ORTOLAN, s. This name is applied by Europeans in India to a small lark, *Calandrella brachydactyla*, Temm., in Hind. *bargel* and *bageri*, [Skt. *varga*, 'a troop']. Also sometimes in S. India to the finch-lark, *Pyrrhalauda grisea*, Scopoli.

OTTA, OTTER, s. Corruption of *āṭā*, 'flour,' a Hindi word having no Skt. original; [but Platts gives Skt. *ārdra*, 'soft']. Popular rhyme:

"Aī terī Shekhāwati
Ādhā āṭā ādhā matī!"

"Confound this Shekhawati land,
My bread's half wheat-meal and half sand."

Boileau, Tour through Rajwara, 1837, p. 274.

[1853.—"After travelling three days, one of the prisoners bought some **ottah**. They prepared bread, some of which was given him; after eating it he became insensible. . . ."—*Law Report*, in *Chevers, Ind. Med. Jurispr.* 166.]

OTTO, OTTER, s. Or usually 'Otto of Roses,' or by imperfect purists '*Attar* of Roses,' an essential oil obtained in India from the petals of the flower, a manufacture of which the chief seat is at Ghāzipur on the Ganges. The word is the Arab. *'itr*, 'perfume.' From this word are derived *'aṭṭār*, a 'perfumer or druggist,' *'aṭṭārī*, adj., 'pertaining to a perfumer.' And a relic of Saracen rule in Palermo is the *Via Latterini*, 'the street of the perfumers' shops.' We find the same in an old Spanish account of Fez;

1573.—"Issuing thence to the Cayzerie by a gate which faces the north there is a handsome street which is called *of the* **Atarin**, which is the Spicery."—*Marmol, Affrica*, ii. f. 88.

[*'Itr* of roses is said to have been discovered by the Empress Nūr-jahān on her marriage with Jahāngīr. A canal in the palace garden was filled with rose-water in honour of the event, and the princess, observing a scum on the surface, caused it to be collected, and found it to be of admirable fragrance, whence it was called *'iṭr-i-Jahāngīrī*.]

1712.—Kaempfer enumerating the departments of the Royal Household in Persia names: "*Pharmacopoeia* . . . **Atthaar** *choneh*, in quâ medicamenta, et praesertim variae virtutis opiata, pro Majestate et aulicis praeparantur. . . ."—*Am. Exot.* 124.

1759.—"To presents given, &c.

* * * * * *

"1 **otter** box set with diamonds
"*Sicca Rs.* 3000 ... ... 3222 3 6."
Accts. of Entertainment to Jugget Set, in *Long*, 89.

c. 1790.—"Elles ont encore une prédilection particulière pour les huiles oderiferantes, surtout pour celle de rose, appelée **otta**."—*Haafner*, ii. 122.

1824.—"The **attar** is obtained after the rose-water is made, by setting it out during the night and till sunrise in the morning in large open vessels exposed to the air, and then skimming off the essential oil which floats at the top."—*Heber*, ed. 1844, i. 154.

OUDH, OUDE, n.p. *Awadh*; properly the ancient and holy city of *Ayodhyā* (Skt. 'not to be warred against'), the capital of Rāma, on the right bank of the river Sarayū, now commonly called the Gogra. Also the province in which Ayodhya was situated, but of which **Lucknow** for about 170 years (from c. 1732) has been the capital, as that of the dynasty of the Nawābs, and from 1814 kings, of Oudh. Oudh was annexed to the British Empire in 1856 as a Chief Commissionership. This was re-established after the Mutiny was subdued and the country reconquered, in 1858. In 1877 the Chief Commissionership was united to the Lieut.-Governorship of the N.W. Provinces. (See **JUDEA**.)

B. C. *x*.—"The noble city of **Ayodhyā** crowned with a royal highway had already cleaned and besprinkled all its streets, and spread its broad banners. Women, children, and all the dwellers in the city eagerly looking for the consecration of *Rāma*, waited with impatience the rising of the morrow's sun."—*Rāmāyaṇa*, Bk. iii. (*Ayodhya Kanda*), ch. 3.

636.—"Departing from this Kingdom (*Kanyākubja* or Kanauj) he (Hwen T'sang) travelled about 600 *li* to the S.E., crossed the Ganges, and then taking his course southerly he arrived at the Kingdom of '**Oyut'o** (Ayōdhyā)."—*Pèlerins Bouddh.* ii. 267.

1255.—"A peremptory command had been issued that Malik Kutlugh Khān . . . should leave the province of **Awadh**, and proceed to the fief of Bharā'ij, and he had not obeyed. . . ."—*Tabaḳāt-i-Nāsirī*, E.T. by *Raverty*, 107.

1289.—"Mu'izzu-d dīn Kai-Kubād, on his arrival from Dehli, pitched his camp at

Oudh (Ajudhya) on the bank of the Ghagra. Nasiru-d dín, from the opposite side, sent his chamberlain to deliver a message to Kai-Kubád, who by way of intimidation himself discharged an arrow at him. . . ."—*Amīr Khusrū*, in *Elliot*, iii. 530.

c. 1335.—"The territories to the west of the Ganges, and where the Sultan himself lived, were afflicted by famine, whilst those to the east of it enjoyed great plenty. These latter were then governed by 'Ain-ul-Mulk . . . and among their chief towns we may name the city of **Awadh**, and the city of Ẓafarābād and the city of *Laknau*, et cetera."—*Ibn Batuta*, iii. 342.

c. 1340.—The 23 principal provinces of India under Mahommed Tughlak are thus stated, on the authority of Sirājuddīn Abu'l-fatah Omah, a native of **'Awadh**: "(1) *Aḳlīm Dihlī*, (2) *Multān*, (3) *Kahrān* (Guhrām), and (4) *Samān* (both about Sirhind), (5) *Siwastān* (Sehwān in Sind), (6) *Waju* (Ūja, *i.e.* Ūch), (7) *Hāsī* (Hānsī), (8) *Sarsati* (Sirsa), (9) *Ma'bar* (Coromandel), (10) *Tiling* (Kalinga), (11) *Gujrāt*, (12) *Badāūn*, (13) **'Awadh**, (14) *Kanauj*, (15) *Laknautī* (N. Bengal), (16) *Bahār*, (17) *Karra* (Lower Doāb), (18) *Malāwa* (Malwa), (19) *Lahāwar* (Lahore), (20) *Kalanūr* (E. Punjab), (21) *Jajnagar* (Orissa), (22) *Tilinj* (?), (23) *Dursamand* (Mysore)."—*Shihābuddīn*, in *Notices et Exts.* xiii. 167-171.

OUTCRY, s. Auction. This term seems to have survived a good deal longer in India than in England. (See **NEELAM**). The old Italian expression for auction seems to be identical in sense, viz. *gridaggio*, and the auctioneer *gridatore*, thus:

c. 1343.—"For jewels and plate; and (other) merchandize that is sold by **outcry** (*gridaggio*), *i.e.* by auction (*oncanto*) in Cyprus, the buyer pays the crier (*gridatore*) one quarter *carat* per bezant on the price bid for the thing bought through the crier, and the seller pays nothing except," &c.—*Pegolotti*, 74.

1627.—"Out-crie *of goods to be sold.* G(allicè) Encánt. Incánt. (I(talicè).—Incánto. . . . H(ispanicè). Almoneda, *ab* Al. *articulus, et Arab.* nedeye, *clamare, vocare.* . . . B(atavicè). Ut-roep."—*Minsheu*, s.v.

[1700.—"The last week Mr. Proby made a **outcry** of lace."—In *Yule, Hedges' Diary*, Hak. Soc. ii. cclix.]

1782.—"On Monday next will be sold by Public **Outcry** . . . large and small China silk Kittisals (**KITTYSOL**). . . ."—*India Gazette*, March 31.

1787. — "Having put up the Madrass Galley at **Outcry** and nobody offering more for her than 2300 Rupees, we think it more for the Company's Int. to make a Sloop of Her than let Her go at so low a price."—*Ft. William MS. Reports*, March.

[1841.—"When a man dies in India, we make short work with him; . . . an '**outcry**' is held, his goods and chattels are brought to the hammer. . . ."—*Society in India*, ii. 227.]

OVERLAND. Specifically applied to the Mediterranean route to India, which in former days involved usually the land journey from Antioch or thereabouts to the Persian Gulf; and still in vogue, though any land journey may now be entirely dispensed with, thanks to M. Lesseps.

1612.—"His Catholic Majesty the King Philip III. of Spain and II. of Portugal, our King and Lord, having appointed Dom Hieronymo de Azevedo to succeed Ruy Lourenço de Tavira . . . in January 1612 ordered that a courier should be despatched **overland** (*por terra*) to this Government to carry these orders and he, arriving at Ormuz at the end of May following. . . ."—*Bocarro, Decada*, p. 7.

1629.—"The news of his Exploits and Death being brought together to King *Philip* the Fourth, he writ with his own hand as follows. *Considering the two Pinks that were fitting for* India *may be gone without an account of my Concern for the Death of* Nunno Alvarez Botello, *an Express shall immediately be sent* **by Land** with advice."—*Faria y Sousa* (Stevens), iii. 373.

1673. — "French and Dutch Jewellers coming **overland** . . . have made good Purchase by buying Jewels here, and carrying them to Europe to Cut and Set, and returning thence sell them here to the Ombrahs (see **OMRAH**), among whom were Monsieur Tavernier. . . . "—*Fryer*, 89.

1675.—"Our last to you was dated the 17th August past, **overland**, transcripts of which we herewith send you."—*Letter from Court to Ft. St. Geo.* In *Notes and Exts.* No. i. p. 5.

1676.—"Docket Copy of the Company's General **Overland**.

"'Our Agent and Councel Fort St. George.

* * * * * *

"'The foregoing is copy of our letter of 28th June **overland**, which we sent by three several conveyances for Aleppo.'"—*Ibid.* p. 12.

1684. — "That all endeavors would be used to prevent my going home the way I intended, by Persia, and so **overland**."—*Hedges, Diary*, Aug. 19; [Hak. Soc. i. 155].

c. 1686.—"Those Gentlemen's Friends in the Committee of the Company in *England*, acquainted them by Letters **over Land**, of the Danger they were in, and gave them Warning to be on their guard." — *A. Hamilton*, i. 196; [ed. 1744, i. 195].

1737.—"Though so far apart that we can only receive letters from Europe once a year, while it takes 18 months to get an answer, we Europeans get news almost every year **over land** by Constantinople, through Arabia or Persia. . . . A few days ago we received the news of the Peace in Europe; of the death of Prince Eugene; of the marriage of the P. of Wales with the Princess of Saxe-Gotha. . . ."—Letter of the *Germ. Missionary Sartorius*, from Madras, Feb. 16. In *Notices of Madras, and Cuddalore*, &c. 1858, p. 159.

1763.—"We have received **Overland** the news of the taking of Havannah and the Spanish Fleet, as well as the defeat of the Spaniards in Portugall. We must surely make an advantageous Peace, however I'm no Politician."—*MS. Letter of James Rennell*, June 1, fr. Madras.

1774.—"Les Marchands à Bengale envoyèrent un Vaisseau à *Suès* en 1772, mais il fut endommagé dans le Golfe de Bengale, et obligé de retourner; en 1773 le Sr. *Holford* entreprit encore ce voyage, réussit cette fois, et fut ainsi le premier Anglois qui eut conduit un vaisseau à *Suès*. . . . On s'est déjà servi plusieurs fois de cette route comme d'un chemin de poste; car le Gouvernement des Indes envoye actuellement dans des cas d'importance ses Couriers par *Suès* en Angleterre, et peut presqu'avoir plutôt reponse de *Londres* que leurs lettres ne peuvent venir en Europe par le Chemin ordinaire du tour du Cap de bonne esperance."—*Niebuhr, Voyage*, ii. 10.

1776.—"We had advices long ago from England, as late as the end of May, by way of Suez. This is a new Route opened by Govr. Hastings, and the Letters which left Marseilles the 3rd June arrived here the 20th August. This, you'll allow, is a ready communication with Europe, and may be kept open at all times, if we chuse to take a little pains."—*MS. Letter from James Rennell*, Oct. 16, "from Islamabad, capital of Chittigong."

1781.—"On Monday last was Married Mr. George Greenley to Mrs. Anne Barrington, relict of the late Capt. William B——, who unfortunately perished on the Desart, in the attack that was made on the Carravan of Bengal Goods under his and the other Gentlemen's care between Suez and Grand Cairo."—*India Gazette*, March 7.

1782.—"When you left England with an intention to pass **overland** and by the route of the Red Sea into India, did you not know that no subject of these kingdoms can lawfully reside in India . . . without the permission of the United Company of Merchants? . . ."—*Price, Tracts*, i. 130.

1783.—". . . Mr. Paul Benfield, a gentleman whose means of intelligence were known to be both extensive and expeditious, publicly declared, from motives the most benevolent, that he had just received **overland** from England certain information that Great Britain had finally concluded a peace with all the belligerent powers in Europe."—*Munro's Narrative*, 317.

1786.—"The packet that was coming to us **overland**, and that left England in July, was cut off by the wild Arabs between Aleppo and Bussora."—*Lord Cornwallis*, Dec. 28, in *Correspondence*, &c., i. 247.

1793.—"Ext. of a letter from Poonamallee, dated 7th June.

'The dispatch by way of Suez has put us all in a commotion.'"—*Bombay Courier*, June 29.

1803.—"From the Governor General to the Secret Committee, dated 24th Decr. 1802. Recd. **Overland**, 9th May 1803."—*Mahratta War Papers* (Parliamentary).

OVIDORE, s Port. *Ouvidor*, *i.e.* 'auditor,' an official constantly mentioned in the histories of Portuguese India. But the term is also applied in an English quotation below to certain Burmese officials, an application which must have been adopted from the Portuguese. It is in this case probably the translation of a Burmese designation, perhaps of *Nekhan-dau*, 'Royal Ear,' which is the title of certain Court officers.

1500.—"The Captain-Major (at Melinde) sent on board all the ships to beg that no one when ashore would in any way misbehave or produce a scandal; any such offence would be severely punished. And he ordered the mariners of the ships to land, and his own Provost of the force, with an **Ouvidor** that he had on board, that they might keep an eye on our people to prevent mischief."—*Correa*, i. 165.

1507.—"And the Viceroy ordered the **Ouvidor General** to hold an inquiry on this matter, on which the truth came out clearly that the Holy Apostle (Sanctiago) showed himself to the Moors when they were fighting with our people, and of this he sent word to the King, telling him that such martyrs were the men who were serving in these parts that our Lord took thought of them and sent them a Helper from Heaven."—*Ibid.* i. 717.

1698.—(At Syriam) "**Ovidores** (Persons appointed to take notice of all passages in the *Runday* (office of administration) and advise them to Ava. . . . Three **Ovidores** that always attend the *Runday*, and are sent to the King, upon errands, as occasion obliges."—*Fleetwood's Diary*, in *Dalrymple, Or. Rep.* i. 355, 360.

[**OWL**, s. Hind. *aul*, 'any great calamity, as a plague, cholera,' &c.

[1787.—"At the foot of the hills the country is called Teriani (see **TERAI**) . . . and people in their passage catch a disorder, called in the language of that country **aul**, which is a putrid fever, and of which the generality of persons who are attacked with it die in a few days. . . ."—*Asiat. Res.* ii. 307.

1816.—". . . rain brings alone with it the local malady called the **Owl**, so much dreaded in the woods and valleys of Nepaul."—*Asiatic Journal*, ii. 405.

1858.—"I have known European officers, who were never conscious of having drunk either of the waters above described, take the fever (owl) in the month of May in the Tarae."—*Sleeman, Journey in Oudh*, ii. 103.]

P

PADDY, s. Rice in the husk; but the word is also, at least in composition, applied to growing rice. The word appears to have in some measure, a double origin.

There is a word *batty* (see **BATTA**) used by some writers on the west coast of India, which has probably helped to propagate our uses of *paddy*. This seems to be the Canarese *batta* or *bhatta*, 'rice in the husk,' which is also found in Mahr. as *bhāt* with the same sense, a word again which in Hind. is applied to 'cooked rice.' The last meaning is that of Skt. *bhaktā*, which is perhaps the original of all these forms.

But in Malay *pādī* [according to Mr. Skeat, usually pronounced *pădi*] Javan. *pārī*, is 'rice in the straw.' And the direct parentage of the word in India is thus apparently due to the Archipelago; arising probably out of the old importance of the export trade of rice from Java (see *Raffles, Java*, i. 239-240, and *Crawfurd's Hist.* iii. 345, and *Descript. Dict.*, 368). Crawfurd, (*Journ. Ind. Arch.*, iv. 187) seems to think that the Malayo-Javanese word may have come from India with the Portuguese. But this is impossible, for as he himself has shown (*Desc. Dict.*, u.s.), the word *pārī*, more or less modified, exists in all the chief tongues of the Archipelago, and even in Madagascar, the connection of which last with the Malay regions certainly was long prior to the arrival of the Portuguese.

1580.—"Certaine Wordes of the naturall language of Jaua . . . **Paree**, ryce in the huske."—*Sir F. Drake's Voyage*, in *Hakl.* iv. 246.

1598.—"There are also divers other kinds of Rice, of a lesse price, and slighter than the other Ryce, and is called **Batte** . . ."—*Linschoten*, 70; [Hak. Soc. i. 246].

1600.—"In the fields is such a quantity of rice, which they call **bate**, that it gives its name to the kingdom of Calou, which is called on that account *Batecalou*."—*Lucena, Vida do Padre F. Xavier*, 121.

1615.—". . . oryzae quoque agri feraces quam **Batum** incolae dicunt."—*Jarric, Thesaurus*, i. 461.

1673.—"The Ground between this and the great Breach is well ploughed, and bears good **Batty**."—*Fryer*, 67, see also 125. But in the Index he has **Paddy**.

1798.—"The **paddie** which is the name given to the rice, whilst in the husk, does not grow . . . in compact ears, but like oats, in loose spikes."—*Stavorinus*, tr. i. 231.

1837.—"Parrots brought 900,000 loads of hill-**paddy** daily, from the marshes of Chandata,—mice husking the hill-**paddy**, without breaking it, converted it into riçe."—*Turnour's Mahawanso*, 22.

1871.—"In Ireland Paddy makes riots, in Bengal raiyats make **paddy**; and in this lies the difference between the **paddy** of green Bengal, and the Paddy of the Emerald Isle."—*Govinda Samanta*, ii. 25.

1878.—"Il est établi un droit sur les riz et les **paddys** exportés de la Colonie, excepté pour le Cambodge par la voie du fleuve."—*Courrier de Saigon*, Sept. 20.

PADDY-BIRD, s. The name commonly given by Europeans to certain baser species of the family *Ardeidae* or Herons, which are common in the rice-fields, close in the wake of grazing cattle. Jerdon gives it as the European's name for the *Ardeola leucoptera*, Boddaert, *andhā baglā* ('blind heron') of the Hindus, a bird which is more or less coloured. But in Bengal, if we are not mistaken, it is more commonly applied to the pure white bird—*Herodias alba*, L., or *Ardea Torra*, Buch. Ham., and *Herodias egrettoides*, Temminck, or *Ardea putea*, Buch. Ham.

1727.—"They have also Store of wild Fowl; but who have a Mind to eat them must shoot them. Flamingoes are large and good Meat. The **Paddy-bird** is also good in their season."—*A. Hamilton*, i. 161; [ed. 1744, i. 162-3].

1868.—"The most common bird (in Formosa) was undoubtedly the **Padi bird**, a species of heron (*Ardea prasinosceles*), which was constantly flying across the padi, or rice-fields."—*Collingwood, Rambles of a Naturalist*, 44.

PADDY-FIELD, s. A rice-field, generally in its flooded state.

1759.—"They marched onward in the plain towards Preston's force, who, seeing them coming, halted on the other side of a long morass formed by **paddy-fields**."—*Orme*, ed. 1803, iii. 430.

1800.—"There is not a single **paddy-field** in the whole county, but plenty of cotton ground (see **REGUR**) swamps, which in this wet weather are delightful."—*Wellington* to *Munro*, in *Despatches*, July 3.

1809.—"The whole country was in high cultivation, consequently the **paddy-fields** were nearly impassable."—*Ld. Valentia*, i. 350.

PADRE, s. A priest, clergyman, or minister, of the Christian Religion; when applied by natives to their own priests, as it sometimes is when they speak to Europeans, this is only by way of accommodation, as 'church' is also sometimes so used by them.

The word has been taken up from the Portuguese, and was of course applied originally to Roman Catholic priests only. But even in that respect there was a peculiarity in its Indian use among the Portuguese. For P. della Valle (see below) notices it as a singularity of their practice at Goa that they gave the title of *Padre* to secular priests, whereas in Italy this was reserved to the *religiosi* or regulars. In Portugal itself, as Bluteau's explanation shows, the use is, or was formerly, the same as in Italy; but, as the first ecclesiastics who went to India were monks, the name apparently became general among the Portuguese there for all priests.

It is a curious example of the vitality of words that this one which had thus already in the 16th century in India a kind of abnormally wide application, has now in that country a still wider, embracing all Christian ministers. It is applied to the Protestant clergy at Madras early in the 18th century. A bishop is known as **Lord** (see **LAT**) **padre**. See **LAT** *Sahib*.

According to Leland the word is used in China in the form *pa-ti-li*.

1541.—"Chegando á Porta da Igreja, o sahirão a receber oito **Padres**."—*Pinto*, ch. lxix. (see *Cogan*, p. 85).

1584.—"It was the will of God that we found there two **Padres**, the one an Englishman, and the other a Flemming."—*Fitch*, in *Hakl.* ii. 381.

" "... had it not pleased God to put it into the minds of the archbishop and other two **Padres** of Jesuits of S. Paul's Colledge to stand our friends, we might have rotted in prison."—*Newberrie, ibid.* ii. 380.

c. 1590.—"Learned monks also come from Europe, who go by the name of **Pádre**. They have an infallible head called *Pápá*. He can change any religious ordinances as he may think advisable, and kings have to submit to his authority."—*Badāonī*, in *Blochmann's Āīn*, i. 182.

c. 1606.—"Et ut adesse **Patres** comperiunt, minor exclamat **Padrigi, Padrigi**, id est Domine Pater, Christianus sum."—*Jarric*, iii. 155.

1614.—"The **Padres** make a church of one of their Chambers, where they say Masse twice a day."—*W. Whittington*, in *Purchas*, i. 486.

1616.—"So seeing Master Terry whom I brought with me, he (the King) called to him, **Padre** you are very welcome, and this house is yours."—*Sir T. Roe*, in *Purchas*, i. 564; [Hak. Soc. ii. 385].

1623.—"I Portoghesi chiamano anche i preti secolari **padri**, come noi i religiosi ..."—*P. della Valle*, ii. 586; [Hak. Soc. i. 142].

1665.—"They (Hindu Jogis) are impertinent enough to compare themselves with our Religious Men they meet with in the *Indies*. I have often taken pleasure to catch them, using much ceremony with them, and giving them great respect; but I soon heard them say to one another, This *Franguis* knows who we are, he hath been a great while in the *Indies*, he knows that we are the **Padrys** of the *Indians*. A fine comparison, said I, within myself, made by an impertinent and idolatrous rabble of Men!"—*Bernier*, E.T. 104; [ed. *Constable*, 323].

1675.—"The **Padre** (or Minister) complains to me that he hath not that respect and place of preference at Table and elsewhere that is due unto him. ... At his request I promised to move it at ye next meeting of ye Councell. What this little Sparke may enkindle, especially should it break out in ye Pulpit, I cannot foresee further than the inflaming of ye dyning Roome wch sometimes is made almost intollerable hot upon other Accts."—*Mr. Puckle's Diary at Metchlapatam*, MS. in India Office.

1676.—"And whiles the French have no settlement near hand, the keeping French **Padrys** here instead of Portugueses, destroys the encroaching growth of the Portugall interest, who used to entail Portugalism as well as Christianity on all their converts."—*Madras Consns.*, Feb. 29, in *Notes and Exts.* i. p. 46.

1680.—"... where as at the Dedication of a New Church by the French **Padrys** and Portugez in 1675 guns had been fired from the Fort in honour thereof, neither **Padry** nor Portugez appeared at the Dedication of our Church, nor as much as gave the Governor a visit afterwards to give him joy of it."—*Ibid.* Oct. 28. No. III. p. 37.

c. 1692.—"But their greatest act of tyranny (at Goa) is this. If a subject of these misbelievers dies, leaving young children, and no grown-up son, the children are considered wards of the State. They take them to their places of worship, their churches ... and the **padris**, that is to say the priests, instruct the children in the

Christian religion, and bring them up in their own faith, whether the child be a Mussulman *saiyid* or a Hindú *bráhman*."—*Kháfi Khán*, in *Elliot*, vii. 345.

1711.—"The Danish **Padre** Bartholomew Ziegenbalgh, requests leave to go to Europe in the first ship, and in consideration that he is head of a Protestant Mission, espoused by the Right Reverend the Lord Archbishop of Canterbury . . . we have presumed to grant him his passage."—In *Wheeler*, ii. 177.

1726.—"May 14. Mr. Leeke went with me to St. Thomas's Mount. . . . We conversed with an old **Padre** from Silesia, who had been 27 years in India. . . ."—*Diary of the Missionary Schultze* (in *Notices of Madras*, &c., 1858), p. 14.

" "May 17. The minister of the King of Pegu called on me. From him I learned, through an interpreter, that Christians of all nations and professions have perfect freedom at Pegu; that even in the Capital two French, two Armenian, and two Portuguese **Patres**, have their churches. . . ."—*Ibid.* p. 15.

1803.—"Lord Lake was not a little pleased at the Begum's loyalty, and being a little elevated by the wine . . . he gallantly advanced, and to the utter dismay of her attendants, took her in his arms, and kissed her. . . . Receiving courteously the proffered attention, she turned calmly round to her astonished attendants—'It is,' said she, 'the salute of a **padre** (or priest) to his daughter.'"—*Skinner's Mil. Mem.* i. 293.

1809.—"The **Padre**, who is a half cast Portuguese, informed me that he had three districts under him."—*Ld. Valentia*, i. 329.

1830.—"Two fat naked Brahmins, bedaubed with paint, had been importuning me for money . . . upon the ground that they were **padres**."—*Mem. of Col. Mountain*, iii.

1876.—"There is **Padre** Blunt for example,—we always call them **Padres** in India, you know,—makes a point of never going beyond ten minutes, at any rate during the hot weather."—*The Dilemma*, ch. xliii.

PADSHAW, PODSHAW, s. Pers.—Hind. *pādishāh* (Pers. *pād*, *pāt* 'throne,' *shāh*, 'prince'), an emperor; the Great **Mogul** (q.v.); a king.

[1553.—"**Patxiah.**" See under **POORUB.**

[1612.—"He acknowledges no **Padenshawe** or King in Christendom but the Portugals' King."—*Danvers, Letters*, i. 175.]

c. 1630.—". . . round all the roome were placed tacite Mirzoes, Chauns, Sultans, and Beglerbegs, above threescore; who like so many inanimate Statues sat crosse-legg'd . . . their backs to the wall, their eyes to a constant object; not daring to speak to one another, sneeze, cough, spet, or the like, it being held in the **Potshaw's** presence a sinne of too great presumption."—*Sir T. Herbert*, ed. 1638, p. 169. At p. 171 of the same we have **Potshaugh**; and in the edition of 1677, in a vocabulary of the language spoken in Hindustan, we have "King, **Patchaw.**" And again: "Is the King at Agra? . . . **Punshaw** *Agrameha?*" (*Pādishāh Agrā men hai?*)—99-100.

1673.—"They took upon them without controul the Regal Dignity and Title of **Pedeshaw.**"—*Fryer*, 166.

1727.—"Aureng-zeb, who is now saluted **Pautshaw**, or Emperor, by the Army, notwithstanding his Father was then alive."—*A. Hamilton*, i. 175, [ed. 1744].

PAGAR, s.

a. This word, the Malay for a 'fence, enclosure,' occurs in the sense of 'factory' in the following passage:

1702.—"Some other out-**pagars** or Factories, depending upon the Factory of Bencoolen."—*Charters of the E.I. Co.* p. 324.

In some degree analogous to this use is the application, common among Hindustani-speaking natives, of the Hind.—Arab. word *iḥāṭa*, 'a fence, enclosure,' in the sense of *Presidency*: *Bombay kī* [*kā*] *iḥāṭa*, *Bangāl kī* [*kā*] *iḥāṭa*, a sense not given in Shakespear or Forbes; [it is given in Fallon and Platts. Mr. Skeat points out that the Malay word is *pāgar*, 'a fence,' but that it is not used in the sense of a 'factory' in the Malay Peninsula. In the following passage it seems to mean 'factory stock':

[1615.—"The King says that at her arrival he will send them their house and **pagarr** upon rafts to them."—*Foster, Letters*, iii. 151.]

b. (*pagār*). This word is in general use in the Bombay domestic dialect for wages, Mahr. *pagār*. It is obviously the Port. verb *pagar*, 'to pay,' used as a substantive.

[1875.—". . . the heavy-browed sultana of some Gangetic station, whose stern look palpably interrogates the amount of your monthly **paggar.**"—*Wilson, Abode of Snow*, 46.]

PAGODA, s. This obscure and remarkable word is used in three different senses.

a. An idol temple; and also specifically, in China, a particular form of religious edifice, of which the famous "Porcelain tower" of Nanking, now destroyed, may be recalled as typical. In the 17th century we find the word sometimes misapplied to places of Mahommedan worship, as by Faria-y-Sousa, who speaks of the "**Pagoda** of Mecca."

b. An idol.

c. A coin long current in S. India. The coins so called were both gold and silver, but generally gold. The gold *pagoda* was the *varāha* or *hūn* of the natives (see **HOON**); the former name (fr. Skt. for 'boar') being taken from the Boar avatār of Vishnu, which was figured on a variety of ancient coins of the South; and the latter signifying 'gold,' no doubt identical with *sonā*, and an instance of the exchange of *h* and *s*. (See also **PARDAO**.)

Accounts at Madras down to 1818 were kept in *pagodas*, *fanams*, and *kās* (see **CASH**); 8 *kās*=1 *fanam*, 42 *fanams* =1 *pagoda*. In the year named the rupee was made the standard coin.* The pagoda was then reckoned as equivalent to 3½ rupees.

In the suggestions of etymologies for this word, the first and most prominent meaning alone has almost always been regarded, and doubtless justly; for the other uses are deduceable from it. Such suggestions have been many.

Thus Chinese origins have been propounded in more than one form; *e.g.* *Pao-t'ah*, 'precious pile,' and *Poh-kuh-t'ah* ('white-bones-pile').† Anything can be made out of Chinese monosyllables in the way of etymology; though no doubt it is curious that the first at least of these phrases is actually applied by the Chinese to the polygonal towers which in China foreigners specially call *pagodas*. Whether it be possible that this phrase may have been in any measure formed in imitation of *pagoda*, so constantly in the mouth of foreigners, we cannot say (though it would not be a solitary example of such borrowing—see **NEELAM**); but we can say with confidence that it is impossible *pagoda* should have been taken from the Chinese. The quotations from Corsali and Barbosa set that suggestion at rest.

Another derivation is given (and adopted by so learned an etymologist as H. Wedgwood) from the Portuguese *pagão*, 'a pagan.' It is possible that this word may have helped to facilitate the Portuguese adoption of *pagoda*; it is not possible that it should have given rise to the word. A third theory makes *pagoda* a transposition of **dagoba**. The latter is a genuine word, used in Ceylon, but known in Continental India, since the extinction of Buddhism, only in the most rare and exceptional way.

A fourth suggestion connects it with the Skt. *bhagavat*, 'holy, divine,' or *Bhagavatī*, applied to Durgā and other goddesses; and a fifth makes it a corruption of the Pers. *but-kadah*, 'idol-temple'; a derivation given below by Ovington. There can be little doubt that the origin really lies between these two.

The two contributors to this book are somewhat divided on this subject:—

(1) Against the derivation from *bhagavat*, 'holy,' or the Mahr. form *bhagavant*, is the objection that the word *pagode* from the earliest date has the final *e*, which was necessarily pronounced. Nor is *bhagavant* a name for a temple in any language of India. On the other hand *but-kadah* is a phrase which the Portuguese would constantly hear from the Mahommedans with whom they chiefly had to deal on their first arrival in India. This is the view confidently asserted by Reinaud (*Mémoires sur l'Inde*, 90), and is the etymology given by Littré.

As regards the coins, it has been supposed, naturally enough, that they were called *pagoda*, because of the figure of a temple which some of them bear; and which indeed was borne by the *pagodas* of the Madras Mint, as may be seen in Thomas's *Prinsep*, pl. xlv. But in fact coins with this impress were first struck at Ikkeri at a date *after* the word *pagode* was already in use among the Portuguese. However, nearly all bore on one side a rude representation of a Hindu deity (see *e.g.* Krishṇarāja's pagoda, c. 1520), and sometimes two such images. Some of these figures are specified by Prinsep (*Useful Tables*, p. 41), and Varthema speaks of them: "These *pardai* . . . have two devils stamped upon one side of them, and certain letters on the other" (115-116). Here the name may have been appropriately taken from *bhagavat* (A. B.).

On the other hand, it may be urged that the resemblance between *but-kadah* and *pagode* is hardly close enough, and that the derivation from *but-kadah* does not easily account for all the uses of the word. Indeed, it seems admitted in the preceding para-

* Prinsep's *Useful Tables*, by E. Thomas, p. 19.
† Giles, *Glossary of Reference*, s.v.

graph that *bhagavat* may have had to do with the origin of the word in one of its meanings.

Now it is not possible that the word in all its applications may have had its origin from *bhagavat*, or some current modification of that word? We see from Marco Polo that such a term was currently known to foreign visitors of S. India in his day—a term almost identical in sound with *pagoda*, and bearing in his statement a religious application, though not to a temple.* We thus have four separate applications of the word *pacauta*, or *pagoda*, picked up by foreigners on the shores of India from the 13th century downwards, viz. to a Hindu ejaculatory formula, to a place of Hindu worship, to a Hindu idol, to a Hindu coin with idols represented on it. Is it not possible that *all* are to be traced to *bhagavat*, 'sacred,' or to *Bhagavat* and *Bhagavatī*, used as names of divinities—of Buddha in Buddhist times or places, of Kṛishṇa and Durgā in Brahminical times and places? (uses which are *fact*). How common was the use of *Bhagavatī* as the name of an object of worship in Malabar, may be seen from an example. Turning to Wilson's work on the Mackenzie MSS., we find in the list of local MS. tracts belonging to Malabar, the repeated occurrence of *Bhagavati* in this way. Thus in this section of the book we have at p. xcvi. (vol. ii.) note of an account "of a temple of *Bhagavati*"; at p. ciii. "Temple of Mannadi *Bhagavati* goddess . . ."; at p. civ. "Temple of Mangombu *Bhagavati* . . ."; "Temple of Paddeparkave *Bhagavati* . . ."; "Temple of the goddess Pannáyennar Kave *Bhagavati* . . ."; "Temple of the goddess Patáli *Bhagavati* . . ."; "Temple of *Bhagavati* . . ."; p. cvii., "Account of the goddess *Bhagavati* at, &c. . . ."; p. cviii., "Acc. of the goddess Yalanga *Bhagavati*," "Acc. of the goddess Vallur *Bhagavati*." The term *Bhagavati* seems thus to have been very commonly attached to objects of worship in Malabar temples (see also *Fra Paolino*, p. 79 and p. 57, quoted under **c.** below). And it is very interesting to observe that, in a paper on "Coorg Superstitions," Mr. Kittel notices parenthetically that Bhadrā Kālī (*i.e.* Durgā) is "also called **Pogŏdi**, *Pavodi*, a *tadbhava* of **Bagavati**" (*Ind. Antiq.* ii. 170)—an incidental remark that seems to bring us very near the possible origin of *pagode*. It is most probable that some form like *pogodi* or *pagode* was current in the mouths of foreign visitors before the arrival of the Portuguese; but if the word was of Portuguese origin there may easily have been some confusion in their ears between *Bagavati* and *but-kadah* which shaped the new word. It is no sufficient objection to say that *bhagavati* is not a term applied by the natives to a temple; the question is rather what misunderstanding and mispronunciation by foreigners of a native term may probably have given rise to the term?—(H. Y.)

Since the above was written, Sir Walter Elliot has kindly furnished a note, of which the following is an extract:—

"I took some pains to get at the origin of the word when at Madras, and the conclusion I came to was that it arose from the term used generally for the object of their worship, viz., *Bhagavat*, 'god'; *bhagavati*, 'goddess.'

"Thus, the Hindu temple with its lofty *gopuram* or propylon at once attracts attention, and a stranger enquiring what it was, would be told, 'the house or place of *Bhagavat*.' The village divinity throughout the south is always a form of *Durga*, or, as she is commonly called, simply '*Devi*' (or *Bhagavati*, 'the goddess'). . . . In like manner a figure of *Durga* is found on most of the gold *Huns* (*i.e. pagoda* coins) current in the Dakhan, and a foreigner inquiring what such a coin was, or rather what was the form stamped upon it, would be told it was 'the goddess,' *i.e.*, it was '*Bhagavati*.'"

As my friend, Dr. Burnell, can no longer represent his own view, it seems right here to print the latest remarks

* "The prayer that they say daily consists of these words: '*Pacauta! Pacauta! Pacauta!*' And this they repeat 104 times."—(Bk. iii. ch. 17.) The word is printed in Ramusio *pacauca*; but no one familiar with the constant confusion of *c* and *t* in medieval manuscript will reject this correction of M. Pauthier. Bishop Caldwell observes that the word was probably *Bagavā*, or *Pagavā*, the Tamil form of *Bhagavata*, "Lord"; a word reiterated in their sacred formulæ by Hindus of all sorts, especially Vaishnava devotees. The words given by Marco Polo, if written "*Pagoda! Pagoda! Pagoda!*" would be almost undistinguishable in sound from *Pacauta*.

of his on the subject that I can find. They are in a letter from Tanjore, dated March 10, 1880:—

"I think I overlooked a remark of yours regarding my observation that the *e* in *Pagode* was pronounced, and that this was a difficulty in deriving it from *Bhagavat*. In modern Portuguese *e* is *not* sounded, but verses show that it was in the 16th century. Now, if there is a final vowel in *Pagoda*, it must come from *Bhagavati;* but though the goddess is and was worshipped to a certain extent in S. India, it is by other names (*Amma*, &c.). Gundert and Kittel give '*Pogodi*' as a name of a Durga temple, but assuredly this is no corruption of *Bhagavati*, but *Pagoda!* Malayālam and Tamil are full of such adopted words. *Bhagavati* is little used, and the goddess is too insignificant to give rise to *pagoda* as a general name for a temple.

"*Bhagavat* can only appear in the S. Indian languages in its (Skt.) nominative form *bhagavān* (Tamil *paγuvān*). As such, in Tamil and Malayālam it equals Vishnu or Siva, which would suit. But *pagoda* can't be got out of *bhagavān;* and if we look to the N. Indian forms, *bhagavant*, &c., there is the difficulty about the *e*, to say nothing about the *nt*."

The use of the word by Barbosa at so early a date as 1516, and its application to a particular class of temples must not be overlooked.

a.—

1516.—"There is another sect of people among the Indians of Malabar, which is called *Cujaven* [*Kushavan*, *Logan*, *Malabar*, i. 115]. . . . Their business is to work at baked clay, and tiles for covering houses, with which the temples and Royal buildings are roofed. . . . Their idolatry and their idols are different from those of the others; and in their houses of prayer they perform a thousand acts of witchcraft and necromancy; they call their temples **pagodes**, and they are separate from the others."—*Barbosa*, 135. This is from Lord Stanley of Alderley's translation from a Spanish MS. The Italian of Ramusio reads: "nelle loro orationi fanno molte strigherie e necromãtie, le quali chiamano **Pagodes**, differenti assai dall' altre" (*Ramusio*, i. f. 308*v*.). In the Portuguese MS. published by the Lisbon Academy in 1812, the words are altogether absent; and in interpolating them from Ramusio the editor has given the same sense as in Lord Stanley's English.

1516.—"In this city of Goa, and all over India, there are an infinity of ancient buildings of the Gentiles, and in a small island near this, called Dinari, the Portuguese, in order to build the city, have destroyed an ancient temple called **Pagode**, which was built with marvellous art, and with ancient figures wrought to the greatest perfection in a certain black stone, some of which remain standing, ruined and shattered, because these Portuguese care nothing about them. If I can come by one of these shattered images I will send it to your Lordship, that you may perceive how much in old times sculpture was esteemed in every part of the world." — Letter of *Andrea Corsali* to *Giuliano de' Medici*, in *Ramusio*, i. f. 177.

1543.—"And with this fleet he anchored at Coulão (see **QUILON**) and landed there with all his people. And the Governor (Martim Afonso de Sousa) went thither because of information he had of a **pagode** which was quite near in the interior, and which, they said, contained much treasure. . . . And the people of the country seeing that the Governor was going to the **pagode**, they sent to offer him 50,000 pardaos not to go."—*Correa*, iv. 325-326.

1554.—"And for the monastery of Santa Fee 845,000 *reis* yearly, besides the revenue of the **Paguodes** which His Highness bestowed upon the said House, which gives 600,000 reis a year. . . ."—*Botelho, Tombo*, in *Subsidios*, 70.

1563.—"They have (at Baçaim) in one part a certain island called Salsete, where there are two **pagodes** or houses of idolatry."—*Garcia*, f. 211*v*.

1582.—". . . **Pagode**, which is the house of praiers to their Idolls."—*Castañeda* (by N. L.), f. 34.

1594.—"And as to what you have written to me, viz., that although you understand how necessary it was for the increase of the Christianity of those parts to destroy all the **pagodas** and mosques (*pagodes e mesquitas*), which the Gentiles and the Moors possess in the fortified places of this State. . . ." (The King goes on to enjoin the Viceroy to treat this matter carefully with some theologians and canonists of those parts, but not to act till he shall have reported to the King).—Letter from the *K. of Portugal* to the *Viceroy*, in *Arch. Port. Orient.*, Fasc. 3, p. 417.

1598.—". . . houses of Diuels [Divels] which they call **Pagodes**."—*Linschoten*, 22; [Hak. Soc. i. 70].

1606.—Gouvea uses **pagode** both for a temple and for an idol, *e.g.*, see f. 46*v*, f. 47.

1630.—"That he should erect **pagods** for God's worship, and adore images under green trees."—*Lord, Display*, &c.

1638.—"There did meet us at a great **Pogodo** or **Pagod**, which is a famous and sumptuous Temple (or Church)." — *W. Bruton*, in *Hakl.* v. 49.

1674.—"Thus they were carried, many flocking about them, to a **Pagod** or Temple" (*pagode* in the orig.).—*Steven's Faria y Sousa*, i. 45.

1674.—"**Pagod** (quasi Pagan-God), an Idol or false god among the Indians; also a kind of gold coin among them equivalent to our Angel."—*Glossographia*, &c., by T. S.

1689.—"A **Pagoda** . . . borrows its Name from the *Persian* word *Pout*, which signifies Idol; thence *Pout-Gheda*, a Temple of False Gods, and from thence **Pagode**."—*Ovington*, 159.

1696.—". . . qui eussent élévé des **pagodes** au milieu des villes."—*La Bruyère, Caractères*, ed. *Jouast*, 1881, ii. 306.

[1710.—"In India we use this word pagoda (**pagodes**) indiscriminately for idols or temples of the Gentiles."—*Oriente Conquistado*, vol. i. Conq. i. Div. i. 53.]

1717.—". . . the **Pagods**, or Churches."—*Phillip's Account*, 12.

1727.—"There are many ancient **Pagods** or Temples in this country, but there is one very particular which stands upon a little Mountain near *Vizagapatam*, where they worship living Monkies."—*A. Hamilton*, i. 380 [ed. 1744].

1736.—"**Págod** [incert. etym.], an idol's temple in China."—*Bailey's Dict.* 2nd ed.

1763.—"These divinities are worshipped in temples called **Pagodas** in every part of Indostan."—*Orme, Hist.* i. 2.

1781.—"During this conflict (at Chillumbrum), all the Indian females belonging to the garrison were collected at the summit of the highest **pagoda**, singing in a loud and melodious chorus hallelujahs, or songs of exhortation, to their people below, which inspired the enemy with a kind of frantic enthusiasm. This, even in the heat of the attack, had a romantic and pleasing effect, the musical sounds being distinctly heard at a considerable distance by the assailants."—*Munro's Narrative*, 222.

1809.—

"In front, with far stretch'd walls, and many a tower,
Turret, and dome, and pinnacle elate,
The huge **Pagoda** seemed to load the land."
Kehama, viii. 4.

[1830.—". . . **pagodas**, which are so termed from *paug*, an idol, and *ghoda*, a temple (!) . . ."—*Mrs. Elwood, Narrative of a Journey Overland from England*, ii. 27.]

1855.—". . . Among a dense cluster of palm-trees and small **pagodas**, rises a colossal Gaudama, towering above both, and, Memnon-like, glowering before him with a placid and eternal smile."—*Letters from the Banks of the Irawadee, Blackwood's Mag.*, May, 1856.

b.—

1498.—"And the King gave the letter with his own hand, again repeating the words of the oath he had made, and swearing besides by his **pagodes**, which are their idols, that they adore for gods. . . ."—*Correa, Lendas*, i. 119.

1582.—"The Divell is oftentimes in them, but they say it is one of their Gods or **Pagodes**."—*Castañeda* (tr. by N. L.), f. 37.

[In the following passage from the same author, as Mr. Whiteway points out, the word is used in both senses, a temple and an idol:

"In Goa I have seen this festival in a **pagoda**, that stands in the island of Divar, which is called Çapatu, where people collect from a long distance; they bathe in the arm of the sea between the two islands, and they believe . . . that on that day the idol (**pagode**) comes to that water, and they cast in for him much betel and many plantains and sugar-canes; and they believe that the idol (**pagode**) eats those things."—*Castanheda*, ii. ch. 34. In the orig., **pagode** when meaning a temple has a small, and when the idol, a capital, *P*.]

1584.—"La religione di queste genti non si intende per esser differenti sette fra loro; hanno certi lor **pagodi** che son gli idoli. . . ."—Letter of *Sassetti*, in *De Gubernatis*, 155.

1587.—"The house in which his **pagode** or idol standeth is covered with tiles of silver."—*R. Fitch*, in *Hakl.* ii. 391.

1598.—". . . The **Pagodes**, their false and divelish idols."—*Linschoten*, 26; [Hak. Soc. i. 86].

1630.—". . . so that the Bramanes under each green tree erect temples to **pagods**. . . ."—*Lord, Display*, &c.

c. 1630.—"Many deformed **Pagothas** are here worshipped; having this ordinary evasion that they adore not Idols, but the *Deumos* which they represent."—*Sir T. Herbert*, ed. 1665, p. 375.

1664.—

"Their classic model proved a maggot,
Their Directory an Indian **Pagod**."
Hudibras, Pt. II. Canto i.

1693.—". . . For, say they, what is the **Pagoda**? it is an image or stone. . . ."—In *Wheeler*, i. 269.

1727.—". . . the Girl with the Pot of Fire on her Head, walking all the Way before. When they came to the End of their journey . . . where was placed another black stone **Pagod**, the Girl set her Fire before it, and run stark mad for a Minute or so."—*A. Hamilton*, i. 274 [ed. 1744].

c. 1737.—

"See thronging millions to the **Pagod** run,
And offer country, Parent, wife or son."
Pope, Epilogue to Sat. I.

1814.—"Out of town six days. On my return, find my poor little **pagod**, Napoleon, pushed off his pedestal;—the thieves are in Paris."—Letter of *Byron's*, April 8, in *Moore's Life*, ed. 1832, iii. 21.

c.—

c. 1566.—"Nell' vscir poi li caualli Arabi di Goa, si paga di datio quaranta due **pagodi** per cauallo, et ogni **pagodo** val otto lire alla nostra moneta; e sono monete d'oro; de modo che li caualli Arabi sono in gran prezzo in que' paesi, come sarebbe trecento quattro cento, cinque cento, e fina mille ducati l'vno."—*C. Federici*, in *Ramusio*, iii. 388.

1597.—"I think well to order and decree that the **pagodes** which come from without shall not be current unless they be of forty and three points (assay?) conformable to the first issue, which is called of *Agra*, and which is of the same value as that of the *San Tomes*, which were issued in its likeness."—*Edict of the King*, in *Archiv. Port. Orient.* iii. 782.

1598.—"There are yet other sorts of money called **Pagodes**. . . . They are Indian and Heathenish money with the picture of a Diuell vpon them, and therefore are called **Pagodes**. . . ."—*Linschoten*, 54 and 69; [Hak. Soc. i. 187, 242].

1602.—"And he caused to be sent out for the Kings of the Decan and Canara two thousand horses from those that were in Goa, and this brought the King 80,000 **pagodes**, for every one had to pay forty as duty. These were imported by the Moors and other merchants from the ports of Arabia and Persia; in entering Goa they are free and uncharged, but on leaving that place they have to pay these duties."—*Couto*, IV. vi. 6.

[,, ". . . with a sum of gold **pagodes**, a coin of the upper country (Balagate), each of which is worth 500 *reis* (say 11s. 3d.; the usual value was 360 *reis*)."—*Ibid.* VII. i. 11.]

1623.—". . . An Indian Gentile Lord called Rama Rau, who has no more in all than 2000 **pagod** [**paygods**] of annual revenue, of which again he pays about 800 to Venktapà Naieka, whose tributary he is. . . ."—*P. della Valle*, ii. 692; [Hak. Soc. ii. 306].

1673.—"About this time the Rajah . . . was weighed in Gold, and poised about 16,000 **Pagods**."—*Fryer*, 80.

1676.—"For in regard these **Pagods** are very thick, and cannot be clipt, those that are Masters of the trade, take a Piercer, and pierce the **Pagod** through the side, halfway or more, taking out of one piece as much Gold as comes to two or three Sous."—*Tavernier*, E.T. 1684, ii. 4; [*Ball*, ii. 92].

1780.—"Sir Thomas Rumbold, Bart., resigned the Government of Fort St. George on the Mg. of the 9th inst., and immediately went on board the General Barker. It is confidently reported that he has not been able to accumulate a very large Fortune, considering the long time he has been at Madrass; indeed people say it amounts to only 17 Lacks and a half of **Pagodas**, or a little more than £600,000 sterling."—*Hicky's Bengal Gazette*, April 15.

1785.—"Your servants have no Trade in this country, neither do you pay them high wages, yet in a few years they return to England with many lacs of **pagodas**."—*Nabob of Arcot*, in *Burke's Speech on the Nabob's Debts*, *Works*, ed. 1852, iv. 18.

1796.—"La Bhagavadi, moneta d'oro, che ha l'immagine della dea Bhagavadi, nome corrotto in **Pagodi o Pagode** dagli Europei, è moneta rotonda, convessa in una parte . . ."—*Fra Paolino*, 57.

1803.—"It frequently happens that in the bazaar, the star **pagoda** exchanges for 4 rupees, and at other times for not more than 3."—*Wellington, Desp.*, ed. 1837, ii. 375.

PAGODA-TREE. A slang phrase once current, rather in England than in India, to express the openings to rapid fortune which at one time existed in India. [For the original meaning, see the quotation from Ryklof Van Goens under **BO TREE.** Mr. Skeat writes: "It seems possible that the idea of a coin tree may have arisen from the practice, among some Oriental nations at least, of making **cash** in moulds, the design of which is based on the plan of a tree. On the E. coast of the Malay Peninsula the name *cash-tree* (*poko' pitis*) is applied to cash cast in this form. Gold and silver tributary trees are sent to Siam by the tributary States: in these the leaves are in the shape of ordinary tree leaves."]

1877.—"India has been transferred from the regions of romance to the realms of fact . . . the mines of Golconda no longer pay the cost of working, and the **pagoda-tree** has been stripped of all its golden fruit."—*Blackwood's Magazine*, 575.

1881.—"It might be mistaken . . . for the work of some modern architect, built for the Nabob of a couple of generations back, who had enriched himself when the **pagoda-tree** was worth the shaking."—*Sat. Review*, Sept. 3, p. 307.

PAHLAVI, PEHLVI. The name applied to the ancient Persian language in that phase which prevailed from the beginning of the Sassanian monarchy to the time when it became corrupted by the influence of Arabic, and the adoption of numerous Arabic words and phrases. The name *Pahlavi* was adopted by Europeans from the Parsi use. The language of Western Persia in the time of the Achaemenian kings, as preserved in the cuneiform inscriptions of Persepolis, Behistun, and elsewhere, is nearly akin to the dialects of the **Zend-Avesta**, and is characterised by a number of inflections agreeing with those of the Avesta and of Sanskrit. The dissolution of inflectional terminations is already indicated as beginning in the later Achaemenian inscriptions, and in many parts of the Zend-Avesta, but its course cannot be traced, as there are no inscriptions in Persian language during the time of the Arsacidae; and it is in the inscriptions on rocks and coins of Ardakhshīr-i-Pāpakān (A.D. 226-240)—the Ardashīr Babagān of later Persian—that the language emerges in a form of that which is known as Pahlavi. "But, strictly speaking, the medieval Persian language is called Pahlavi when it is written in one of the characters used before the invention of the modern Persian alphabet, and in the peculiarly enigmatical mode adopted in Pahlavi writings. . . . Like the Assyrians of old, the Persians of Parthian times appear to have borrowed their writing from a foreign race. But, whereas the Semitic Assyrians adopted a Turanian syllabary, these later Aryan Persians accepted a Semitic alphabet. Besides the alphabet, however, which they could use for spelling their own words, they transferred a certain number of complete Semitic words to their writings as representatives of the corresponding words in their own language. . . . The use of such Semitic words, scattered about in Persian sentences, gives Pahlavi the motley appearance of a compound language. . . . But there are good reasons for supposing that the language was never spoken as it was written. The spoken language appears to have been pure Persian; the Semitic words being merely used as written representatives, or *logograms*, of the Persian words which were spoken. Thus, the Persians would write *malkân malkâ*, 'King of Kings,' but they would read *shâhân shâh*. . . . As the Semitic words were merely a Pahlavi mode of writing their Persian equivalents (just as 'viz.' is a mode of writing 'namely' in English*), they disappeared with the Pahlavi writing, and the Persians began at once to write all their words with their new alphabet, just as they pronounced them" (*E. W. West, Introd. to Pahlavi Texts*, p. xiii.; *Sacred Books of the East*, vol. v.).†

Extant Pahlavi writings are confined to those of the Parsis, translations from the Avesta, and others almost entirely of a religious character. Where the language is transcribed, either in the Avesta characters, or in those of the modern Persian alphabet, and freed from the singular system indicated above, it is called Pazand (see **PAZEND**); a term supposed to be derived from the language of the Avesta, *paitizanti*, with the meaning 're-explanation.'

Various explanations of the term *Pahlavi* have been suggested. It seems now generally accepted as a changed form of the *Parthva* of the cuneiform inscriptions, the Parthia of Greek and Roman writers. The Parthians, though not a Persian race, were rulers of Persia for five centuries, and it is probable that everything ancient, and connected with the period of their rule, came to be called by this name. It is apparently the same word that in the form *pahlav* and *pàhlavān*, &c., has become the appellation of a warrior or champion in both Persian and Armenian, originally derived from that most warlike people the Parthians. (See **PULWAUN**.) Whether there was any identity between the name thus used, and that of *Pahlava*, which is applied to a people mentioned often in Sanskrit books, is a point still unsettled.

The meaning attached to the term *Pahlavi* by Orientals themselves, writing in Arabic or Persian (exclusive of Parsis), appears to have been 'Old Persian' in general, without restriction to any particular period or dialect. It is thus found applied to the cuneiform inscriptions at Persepolis. (Derived from *West* as quoted above, and from *Haug's Essays*, ed. London, 1878.)

c. 930.—"Quant au mot *dirafeh*, en pehlvi (*al-fahlviya*) c'est à dire dans la langue primitive de la Perse, il signifie drapeau, pique et étendard."—*Maṣ'ūdī*, iii. 252.

c. A.D. 1000. — "Gayômarth, who was called *Girshâh*, because *Gir* means in Pahlavi *a mountain*. . . ."—*Albîrûnî, Chronology*, 108.

PAILOO, s. The so-called 'triumphal arches,' or gateways, which form so prominent a feature in Chinese landscape, really monumental erections in honour of deceased persons of eminent virtue. Chin. *pai*, 'a tablet,' and *lo*, 'a stage or erection.' Mr. Fergusson

* Or our symbol (&), now modified into (&), which is in fact Latin *et*, but is read 'and."

† "The peculiar mode of writing Pahlavi here alluded to long made the character of the language a standing puzzle for European scholars, and was first satisfactorily explained by Professor Haug, of Munich, in his admirable Essay on the Pahlavi Language, already cited" (*West*, p. xii.).

has shown the construction to have been derived from India with Buddhism (see *Indian and Eastern Architecture*, pp. 700-702). [So the *Torii* of Japan seem to represent Skt. *torana*, 'an archway' (see *Chamberlain, Things Japanese*, 3rd ed. 407 *seq.*).]

PÁLAGILÁSS, s. This is domestic Hind. for 'Asparagus' (*Panjab N. & Q.* ii. 189).

PALANKEEN, PALANQUIN, s. A box-litter for travelling in, with a pole projecting before and behind, which is borne on the shoulders of 4 or 6 men—4 always in Bengal, 6 sometimes in the Telugu country.

The origin of the word is not doubtful, though it is by no means clear how the Portuguese got the exact form which they have handed over to us. The nasal termination may be dismissed as a usual Portuguese addition, such as occurs in *mandarin*, *Baçaim* (*Wasai*), and many other words and names as used by them. The basis of all the forms is Skt. *paryañka*, or *palyañka*, 'a bed,' from which we have Hind. and Mahr. *palang*, 'a bed,' Hind. *pālkī*, 'a palankin,' [Telugu *pallakī*, which is perhaps the origin of the Port. word], Pali *pallanko*, 'a couch, bed, litter, or palankin' (*Childers*), and in Javanese and Malay *palañgki*, 'a litter or sedan' (*Crawfurd*).*

It is curious that there is a Spanish word *palanca* (L. Lat. *phalanga*) for a pole used to carry loads on the shoulders of two bearers (called in Sp. *palanquinos*); a method of transport more common in the south than in England, though even in old English the thing has a name, viz. 'a cowle-staff' (see *N.E.D.*). It is just possible that this word (though we do not find it in the Portuguese dictionaries) may have influenced the form in which the early Portuguese visitors to India took up the word.

The *thing* appears already in the *Rāmāyana*. It is spoken of by Ibn Batuta and John Marignolli (both c. 1350), but neither uses this Indian name; and we have not found evidence of *pālkī* older than Akbar (see *Elliot*, iv. 515, and *Āīn*, i. 254).

As drawn by Linschoten (1597), and as described by Grose at Bombay (c. 1760), the palankin was hung from a bamboo which bent in an arch over the vehicle; a form perhaps not yet entirely obsolete in native use. Williamson (*V. M.*, i. 316 *seqq.*) gives an account of the different changes in the fashion of palankins, from which it would appear that the present form must have come into use about the end of the 18th century. Up to 1840-50 most people in Calcutta kept a palankin and a set of bearers (usually natives of Orissa—see **OORIYA**), but the practice and the vehicle are now almost, if not entirely, obsolete among the better class of Europeans. Till the same period the palankin, carried by relays of bearers, laid out by the post-office, or by private **chowdries** (q.v.), formed the chief means of accomplishing extensive journeys in India, and the elder of the present writers has undergone hardly less than 8000 or 9000 miles of travelling in going considerable distances (excluding minor journeys) after this fashion. But in the decade named, the palankin began, on certain great roads, to be superseded by the *dawk-***garry** (a **Palkee-garry** or palankin-carriage, horsed by ponies posted along the road, under the post-office), and in the next decade to a large extent by railway, supplemented by other wheel-carriage, so that the palankin is now used rarely, and only in out-of-the-way localities.

c. 1340.—"Some time afterwards the pages of the Mistress of the Universe came to me with a *dūla*. . . . It is like a bed of state . . . with a pole of wood above . . . this is curved, and made of the Indian cane, solid and compact. Eight men, divided into two relays, are employed in turn to carry one of these; four carry the palankin whilst four rest. These vehicles serve in India the same purpose as donkeys in Egypt; most people use them habitually in going and coming. If a man has his own slaves, he is carried by them; if not he hires men to carry him. There are also a few found for hire in the city, which stand in the bazars, at the Sultan's gate, and also at the gates of private citizens."—*Ibn Batuta*, iii. 386.

c. 1350.—"Et eciam homines et mulieres portant super scapulas in lecticis de quibus in Canticis: *ferculum fecit sibi Salomon de*

* In *Canticles*, iii. 9, the "ferculum *quod fecit sibi rex Salomon de lignis Libani*" is in the Hebrew *appiryōn*, which has by some been supposed to be Greek φορεῖον; highly improbable, as the litter came to Greece from the East. Is it possible that the word can be in some way taken from *paryañka?* The R.V. has *palanquin*. [See the discussion in *Encyclopaedia Biblica*, iii. 2804 *seq.*].

lignis Libani, id est lectulum portatilem sicut portabar ego in Zayton et in India." —*Marignolli* (see *Cathay*, &c., p. 331).

1515.—"And so assembling all the people made great lamentation, and so did throughout all the streets the women, married and single, in a marvellous way. The captains lifted him (the dead Alboquerque), seated as he was in a chair, and placed him on a **palanquim**, so that he was seen by all the people; and João Mendes Botelho, a knight of Afonso d'Alboquerque's making (who was) his Ancient, bore the banner before the body." —*Correa, Lendas*, II. i. 460.

1563.—". . . and the branches are for the most part straight except some . . . which they twist and bend to form the canes for **palenquins** and portable chairs, such as are used in India."—*Garcia*, f. 194.

1567. — ". . . with eight Falchines (*fachini*), which are hired to carry the **palanchines**, eight for a **Palanchine** (*palanchino*), foure at a time."—*C. Frederike*, in *Hakl.* ii. 348.

1598.—". . . after them followeth the bryde between two *Commeres*, each in their **Pallamkin**, which is most costly made."—*Linschoten*, 56; [Hak. Soc. i. 196].

1606.—"The **palanquins** covered with curtains, in the way that is usual in this Province, are occasion of very great offences against God our Lord" . . . (the Synod therefore urges the Viceroy to prohibit them altogether, and) . . . "enjoins on all ecclesiastical persons, on penalty of sentence of excommunication, and of forfeiting 100 *pardaos* to the church court* not to use the said **palanquins**, made in the fashion above described."—4th Act of 5th Council of Goa, in *Archiv. Port. Orient.*, fasc. 4. (See also under **BOY**.)

The following is the remonstrance of the city of Goa against the ecclesiastical action in this matter, addressed to the King:

1606.—"Last year this City gave your Majesty an account of how the Archbishop Primate proposed the issue of orders that the women should go with their **palanquins** uncovered, or at least half uncovered, and how on this matter were made to him all the needful representations and remonstrances on the part of the whole community, giving the reasons against such a proceeding, which were also sent to Your Majesty. Nevertheless in a Council that was held this last summer, they dealt with this subject, and they agreed to petition Your Majesty to order that the said **palanquins** should travel in such a fashion that it could be seen who was in them.

"The matter is of so odious a nature, and of such a description that Your Majesty should grant their desire in no shape whatever, nor give any order of the kind, seeing this place is a frontier fortress. The reasons for this have been written to Your Majesty; let us beg Your Majesty graciously to make no new rule; and this is the petition of the whole community to Your Majesty."—*Carta, que a Cidade de Goa escrevea a Sua Magestade, o anno de* 1606. In *Archiv. Port. Orient.*, fasc. iº. 2ª. Edição, 2ª, Parte, 186.

1608-9.—"If comming forth of his Pallace, hee (Jahāngīr) get vp on a Horse, it is a signe that he goeth for the Warres; but if he be vp vpon an Elephant or **Palankine**, it will bee but an hunting Voyage."—*Hawkins*, in *Purchas*, i. 219.

1616.—". . . *Abdala Chan*, the great governour of *Amadauas*, being sent for to Court in disgrace, comming in Pilgrim's Clothes with fortie servants on foote, about sixtie miles in counterfeit humiliation, finished the rest in his **Pallankee**."—*Sir T. Roe*, in *Purchas*, i. 552; [Hak. Soc. ii. 278, which reads **Palanckee**, with other minor variances].

In Terry's account, in *Purchas*, ii. 1475, we have a **Pallankee**, and (p. 1481) **Palanka**; in a letter of Tom Coryate's (1615) **Palankeen**.

1623.—"In the territories of the Portuguese in India it is forbidden to men to travel in **palankin** (*Palanchino*) as in good sooth too effeminate a proceeding; nevertheless as the Portuguese pay very little attention to their laws, as soon as the rains begin to fall they commence getting permission to use the **palankin**, either by favour or by bribery; and so, gradually, the thing is relaxed, until at last nearly everybody travels in that way, and at all seasons."—*P. della Valle*, i. 611; [comp. Hak. Soc. i. 31].

1659. — "The designing rascal (Sivají) . . . conciliated Afzal Khán, who fell into the snare. . . . Without arms he mounted the **pálkí**, and proceeded to the place appointed under the fortress. He left all his attendants at the distance of a long arrow-shot. . . . Sivají had a weapon, called in the language of the Dakhin *bichúá* (*i.e.* 'scorpion') on the fingers of his hand, hidden under his sleeve. . . ."—*Kháfi Khán*, in *Elliot*, vii. 259. See also p. 509.

c. 1660.—". . . From *Golconda* to *Maslipatan* there is no travelling by waggons. . . . But instead of Coaches they have the convenience of **Pallekies**, wherein you are carried with more speed and more ease than in any part of India." — *Tavernier*, E.T. ii. 70; [ed. *Ball*, i. 175]. This was quite true up to our own time. In 1840 the present writer was carried on that road, a stage of 25 miles in little more than 5 hours, by 12 bearers, relieving each other by sixes.

1672. The word occurs several times in Baldaeus as **Pallinkijn**. Tavernier writes **Palleki** and sometimes **Pallanquin** [*Ball*, i. 45, 175, 390, 392]; Bernier has **Paleky** [ed. *Constable*, 214, 283, 372].

1673.—". . . ambling after these a great pace, the **Palankeen**-Boys support them four of them, two at each end of a *Bambo*,

* "*Pagos do aljube.*" We are not sure of the meaning.

which is a long hollow Cane . . . arched in the middle . . . where hangs the **Palenkeen**, as big as an ordinary Couch, broad enough to tumble in. . . ."—*Fryer*, 34.

1678.—"The permission you are pleased to give us to buy a **Pallakee** on the Company's Acct. Shall make use off as Soone as can possiblie meet wth one y[t] may be fitt for y[e] purpose. . . ."—MS. Letter from *Factory* at *Ballasore* to the *Council* (of Fort. St. George), March 9, in India Office.

1682.—Joan Nieuhof has **Palakijn.** *Zee en Lant-Reize*, ii. 78.

[„ "The Agent and Council . . . allowed him (Mr. Clarke) 2 pag[os] p. mensem more towards the defraying his **pallanquin** charges, he being very crazy and much weaken'd by his sicknesse."—*Pringle, Diary Ft. St. Geo.* 1st ser. i. 34.]

1720.—"I desire that all the free Merchants of my acquaintance do attend me in their **palenkeens** to the place of burial." — Will of *Charles Davers*, Merchant, in *Wheeler*, ii. 340.

1726.—". . . **Palangkyn** dragers" (palankin-bearers).—*Valentijn, Ceylon*, 45.

1736.—"**Palanquin**, a kind of chaise or chair, borne by men on their shoulders, much used by the Chinese and other Eastern peoples for travelling from place to place." —*Bailey's Dict.* 2nd ed.

1750-52. — "The greater nobility are carried in a **palekee**, which looks very like a hammock fastened to a pole."—*Toreen's Voyage to Suratte, China*, &c., ii. 201.

1754-58.—In the former year the Court of Directors ordered that Writers in their Service should "lay aside the expense of either horse, chair, or **Palankeen**, during their Writership." The Writers of Fort William (4th Nov. 1756) remonstrated, begging "to be indulged in keeping a **Palankeen** for such months of the year as the excessive heats and violent rains make it impossible to go on foot without the utmost hazard of their health." The Court, however, replied (11 Feb. 1756): "We very well know that the indulging Writers with **Palankeens** has not a little contributed to the neglect of business we complain of, by affording them opportunities of rambling"; and again, with an obduracy and fervour too great for grammar (March 3, 1758): "We do most positively order and direct (and will admit of no representation for postponing the execution of) that no Writer whatsoever be permitted to keep either **palankeen**, horse, or chaise, during his Writership, on pain of being immediately dismissed from our service." — In *Long*, pp. 54, 71, 130.

1780.—"The Nawaub, on seeing his condition, was struck with grief and compassion; but . . . did not even bend his eyebrow at the sight, but lifting up the curtain of the **Palkee** with his own hand, he saw that the eagle of his (Ali Ruza's) soul, at one flight had winged its way to the gardens of Paradise."—*H. of Hydur*, p. 429.

1784.—
"The Sun in gaudy **palanqueen**
Curtain'd with purple, fring'd with gold,
Firing no more heav'n's vault serene,
Retir'd to sup with Ganges old."
Plassy Plain, a ballad by *Sir W. Jones*; in *Life and Works*, ed. 1807, ii. 503.

1804.—"Give orders that a **palanquin** may be made for me; let it be very light, with the pannels made of canvas instead of wood, and the poles fixed as for a dooley. Your Bengally **palanquins** are so heavy that they cannot be used out of Calcutta." —*Wellington* (to Major Shaw), June 20.

The following measures a change in ideas. A palankin is now hardly ever used by a European, even of humble position, much less by the opulent:

1808.—"**Palkee.** A litter well known in India, called by the English **Palankeen.** A Guzerat punster (aware of no other) hazards the Etymology *Pa-lakhee* [*pāo-lākhī*] a thing requiring an annual income of a quarter Lack to support it and corresponding luxuries."—*R. Drummond, Illustrations*, &c.

„ "The conveyances of the island (Madeira) are of three kinds, viz.: horses, mules, and a litter, ycleped a **palanquin**, being a chair in the shape of a bathing-tub, with a pole across, carried by two men, as doolees are in the east."—*Welsh, Reminiscences*, i. 282.

1809.—
"Woe! Woe! around their **palankeen**,
As on a bridal day
With symphony and dance and song,
Their kindred and their friends come on,
The dance of sacrifice! The funeral song!"
Kehama, i. 6.

c. 1830.—"Un curieux indiscret reçut un galet dans la tête; on l'emporta baigné de sang, couché dans un **palanquin.**" — *V. Jacquemont, Corr.* i. 67.

1880.—"It will amaze readers in these days to learn that the Governor-General sometimes condescended to be carried in a **Palanquin**—a mode of conveyance which, except for long journeys away from railroads, has long been abandoned to portly Baboos, and Eurasian clerks."—*Sat. Rev.*, Feb. 14.

1881.—"In the great procession on Corpus Christi Day, when the Pope is carried in a **palanquin** round the Piazza of St. Peter, it is generally believed that the cushions and furniture of the **palanquin** are so arranged as to enable him to bear the fatigue of the ceremony by sitting whilst to the spectator he appears to be kneeling."—*Dean Stanley, Christian Institutions*, 231.

PALAVERAM, n.p. A town and cantonment 11 miles S.W. from Madras. The name is *Pallāvaram* probably *Palla-puram*, *Pallavapura* the 'town of the Pallas'; the latter a caste claiming descent from the Pallavas who reigned at Conjeveram (*Seshagiri Sāstrī*). [The *Madras Gloss.* derives their name from Tam. *pallam*, 'low land,' as they are commonly employed in the cultivation of wet lands.]

PALE ALE. The name formerly given to the beer brewed for Indian use. (See **BEER.**)

1784.—"London Porter and **Pale Ale**, light and excellent, Sicca Rupees 150 per hhd."—Advt. in *Seton-Karr*, i. 39.

1793.—"For sale . . . **Pale Ale** (per hhd.) . . . Rs. 80."—*Bombay Courier*, Jan. 19.

[1801.—"1. **Pale Ale**; 2. strong ale; 3. small beer; 4. brilliant beer; 5. strong porter; 6. light porter; 7. brown stout."—Advt. in *Carey, Good Old Days*, i. 147.]

1848.—"Constant dinners, tiffins, **pale ale**, and claret, the prodigious labour of cutchery, and the refreshment of brandy pawnee, which he was forced to take there, had this effect upon Waterloo Sedley."—*Vanity Fair*, ed. 1867, ii. 258.

1853.—"Parmi les cafés, les cabarets, les gargotes, l'on rencontre çà et là une taverne anglaise placardée de sa pancarte de porter simple et double, d'old Scotch ale, d'*East India* **Pale beer**."—*Th. Gautier, Constantinople*, 22.

1867.—

"Pain bis, galette ou panaton,
Fromage à la pie ou Stilton,
Cidre ou **pale-ale** de Burton,
Vin de brie, ou branne-mouton."
Th. Gautier à Ch. Garnier.

PALEMPORE, s. A kind of chintz bed-cover, sometimes made of beautiful patterns, formerly made at various places in India, especially at Sadras and Masulipatam, the importation of which into Europe has become quite obsolete, but under the greater appreciation of Indian manufactures has recently shown some tendency to revive. The etymology is not quite certain,—we know no place of the name likely to have been the eponymic,—and possibly it is a corruption of a hybrid (Hind. and Pers.) *palang-posh*, 'a bed-cover,' which occurs below, and which may have been perverted through the existence of **Salempore** as a kind of stuff. The probability that the word originated in a perversion of *palang-posh*, is strengthened by the following entry in Bluteau's *Dict.* (*Suppt.* 1727.)

"CHAUDUS or CHAUDEUS são huns panos grandes, que servem para cobrir camas e outras cousas. São pintados de cores muy vistosas, e alguns mais finos, a que chamão **palangapuzes**. Fabricão-se de algodão em Bengala e Choromandel,"—*i.e.* "*Chaudus* ou *Chaudeus*" (this I cannot identify, perhaps the same as *Choutar* among **Piece-goods**) "are a kind of large cloths serving to cover beds and other things. They are painted with gay colours, and there are some of a finer description which are called **palangposhes**," &c.

[For the mode of manufacture at Masulipatam, see *Journ. Ind. Art.* iii. 14. Mr. Pringle (*Madras Selections*, 4th ser. p. 71, and *Diary Ft. St. Geo.* 1st ser. iii. 173) has questioned this derivation. The word may have been taken from the State and town of *Pālanpur* in Guzerat, which seems to have been an emporium for the manufactures of N. India, which was long noted for chintz of this kind.]

1648.—"Int Governe van *Raga mandraga* . . . werden veel . . . **Salamporij** . . . gemaeckt."—*Van den Broecke*, 87.

1673.—"Staple commodities (at Masulipatam) are calicuts white and painted, **Palempores**, Carpets."—*Fryer*, 34.

1813.—

"A stain on every bush that bore
A fragment of his **palampore**,
His breast with wounds unnumber'd riven,
His back to earth, his face to heaven . . ."
Byron, The Giaour.

1814.—"A variety of tortures were inflicted to extort a confession; one was a sofa, with a platform of tight cordage in network, covered with a **palampore**, which concealed a bed of thorns placed under it: the collector, a corpulent Banian, was then stripped of his *jama* (see **JAMMA**), or muslin robe, and ordered to lie down."—*Forbes, Or. Mem.* ii. 429; [2nd ed. ii. 54].

1817.—". . . these cloths . . . serve as coverlids, and are employed as a substitute for the Indian **palempore**."—*Raffles, Java*, 171; [2nd ed. i. 191].

[1855.—

"The jewelled amaun of thy zemzem is bare,
And the folds of thy **palampore** wave in the air."
Bon Gaultier, Eastern Serenade.]

1862.—"Bala posh, or **Palang posh**, quilt or coverlet, 300 to 1000 rupees."—*Punjab Trade Report*, App. p. xxxviii.

1880.—". . . and third, the celebrated **palampores**, or 'bed-covers,' of Masulipatam, Fatehgarh, Shikarpur, Hazara, and other places, which in point of art decoration are simply incomparable."—*Birdwood, The Industrial Arts of India*, 260.

PALI, s. The name of the sacred language of the Southern Buddhists, in fact, according to their apparently well-founded tradition *Magadhī*, the dialect of what we now call South Bahar, in which Sakya Muni discoursed. It is one of the Prākrits (see **PRACRIT**) or Aryan vernaculars of India, and has probably been a dead language for nearly 2000 years. *Pāli* in Skt. means 'a line, row, series'; and by the Buddhists is used for the series of their Sacred Texts. *Pālī-bhāshā* is then 'the language of the Sacred Texts,' *i.e. Magadhī;* and this is called elliptically by the Singhalese **Pālī**, which we have adopted in like use. It has been carried, as the sacred language, to all the Indo-Chinese countries which have derived their religion from India through Ceylon. *Pālī* is "a sort of Tuscan among the Prākrits" from its inherent grace and strength (*Childers*). But the analogy to Tuscan is closer still in the parallelism of the modification of Sanskrit words, used in Pālī, to that of Latin words used in Italian.

Robert Knox does not apparently know by that name the Pālī language in Ceylon. He only speaks of the Books of Religion as "being in an eloquent style which the Vulgar people do not understand" (p. 75); and in another passage says: "They have a language something differing from the vulgar tongue (like *Latin* to us) which their books are writ in" (p. 109).

1689.—"Les uns font valoir le style de leur Alcoran, les autres de leur **Bâli**."—*Lettres Edif.* xxv. 61.

1690.—". . . this Doubt proceeds from the *Siameses* understanding two Languages, *viz.*, the Vulgar, which is a simple Tongue, consisting almost wholly of Monosyllables, without Conjugation or Declension; and another Language, which I have already spoken of, which to them is a dead Tongue, known only by the Learned, which is called the **Balie** Tongue, and which is enricht with the inflexions of words, like the Languages we have in Europe. The terms of Religion and Justice, the names of Offices, and all the Ornaments of the Vulgar Tongue are borrow'd from the **Balie**."—*De la Loubère's Siam*, E.T. 1693, p. 9.

1795.—"Of the ancient **Pállis**, whose language constitutes at the present day the sacred text of Ava, Pegue, and Siam, as well as of several other countries eastward of the Ganges: and of their migration from India to the banks of the Cali, the Nile of Ethiopia, we have but very imperfect information.* . . . It has been the opinion of some of the most enlightened writers on the languages of the East, that the **Pali**, the sacred language of the priests of Boodh, is nearly allied to the Shanscrit of the Bramins: and there certainly is much of that holy idiom engrafted on the vulgar language of Ava, by the introduction of the Hindoo religion."—*Symes*, 337-8.

1818.—"The **Talapoins** . . . do apply themselves in some degree to study, since according to their rules they are obliged to learn the Sadà, which is the grammar of the **Pali** language or Magatà, to read the Vini, the Padimot . . . and the sermons of Godama. . . . All these books are written in the **Pali** tongue, but the text is accompanied by a Burmese translation. They were all brought into the kingdom by a certain Brahmin from the island of Ceylon."—*Sangermano's Burmese Empire*, p. 141.

[1822.—". . . the sacred books of the Buddhists are composed in the **Balli** tongue. . . ."—*Wallace, Fifteen Years in India*, 187.]

1837.—"Buddhists are impressed with the conviction that their sacred and classical language, the Mágadhi or **Páli**, is of greater antiquity than the Sanscrit; and that it had attained also a higher state of refinement than its rival tongue had acquired. In support of this belief they adduce various arguments, which, in their judgment, are quite conclusive. They observe that the very word **Páli** signifies original, text, regularity; and there is scarcely a Buddhist scholar in Ceylon, who, in the discussion of this question, will not quote, with an air of triumph, their favourite verse,—

Sá Mágadhi; múla bhásá (&c.).

'There is a language which is the root; . . . men and bráhmans at the commencement of the creation, who never before heard nor uttered a human accent, and even the Supreme Buddhos, spoke it: it is Mágadhi.'

"This verse is a quotation from Kachcháyanó's grammar, the oldest referred to in the Páli literature of Ceylon. . . . Let me . . . at once avow, that, exclusive of all philological considerations, I am inclined, on primâ facie evidence—external as well as internal—to entertain an opinion adverse to the claims of the Buddhists on this particular point."—*George Turnour, Introd. to Mahâwanso*, p. xxii.

1874.—"The spoken language of Italy was to be found in a number of provincial dialects, each with its own characteristics, the Piedmontese harsh, the Neapolitan nasal, the Tuscan soft and flowing. These dialects had been rising in importance as Latin declined; the birth-time of a new literary language was imminent. Then came Dante, and choosing for his immortal Commedia the finest and most cultivated of the vernaculars, raised it at once to the position of dignity which it still retains. Read Sanskrit for Latin, Magadhese for Tuscan, and the Three Baskets for the Divina Commedia, and the parallel is complete. . . . Like Italian **Pali** is at once flowing and sonorous; it is a characteristic of both languages that nearly every word

* The writer is here led away by Wilford's nonsense.

ends in a vowel, and that all harsh conjunctions are softened down by assimilation, elision, or crasis, while on the other hand both lend themselves easily to the expression of sublime and vigorous thought."—*Childers, Preface to Pali Dict.* pp. xiii-xiv.

PALKEE-GARRY, s. A 'palankin-coach,' as it is termed in India; *i.e.* a carriage shaped somewhat like a palankin on wheels; Hind. *pālkī-gārī*. The word is however one formed under European influences. ["The system of conveying passengers by palkee carriages and trucks was first established between Cawnpore and Allahabad in May 1843, and extended to Allyghur in November of the same year; Delhi was included in June 1845, Agra and Meerut about the same time; the now-going line not being, however, ready till January 1846" (*Carey, Good Old Days*, ii. 91).]

1878.—"The Governor-General's carriage . . . may be jostled by the hired '**palki-gharry**,' with its two wretched ponies, rope harness, nearly naked driver, and wheels whose sinuous motions impress one with the idea that they must come off at the next revolution."—*Life in the Mofussil*, i. 38.

This description applies rather to the **cranchee** (q.v.) than to the palkee-garry, which is (or used to be) seldom so sordidly equipt. [Mr. Kipling's account of the Calcutta *palki gari* (*Beast and Man*, 192) is equally uncomplimentary.]

PALMYRA, s. The fan-palm (*Borassus flabelliformis*), which is very commonly cultivated in S. India and Ceylon (as it is also indeed in the Ganges valley from Farrukhābād down to the head of the Delta), and hence was called by the Portuguese *par excellence*, *palmeira* or 'the palm-tree.' Sir J. Hooker writes: "I believe this palm is nowhere wild in India; and have always suspected that it, like the tamarind, was introduced from Africa." [So *Watt, Econ. Dict.* i. 504.] It is an important tree in the economy of S. India, Ceylon, and parts of the Archipelago as producing **jaggery** (q.v.) or 'palm-sugar'; whilst the wood affords rafters and laths, and the leaf gives a material for thatch, mats, umbrellas, fans, and a substitute for paper. Its minor uses are many: indeed it is supposed to supply nearly all the wants of man, and a Tamil proverb ascribes to it 801 uses (see Ferguson's *Palmyra-Palm of Ceylon*, and *Tennent's Ceylon*, i. 111, ii. 519 *seqq.*; also see **BRAB**).

1563.—". . . A ilha de Ceilão . . . ha muitas **palmeiras**."—*Garcia*, ff. 65*v*-66.

1673.—"Their Buildings suit with the Country and State of the inhabitants, being mostly contrived for Conveniency: the Poorer are made of Boughs and *ollas* of the **Palmeroes**."—*Fryer*, 199.

1718.—". . . Leaves of a Tree called **Palmeira**."—*Prop. of the Gospel in the East*, iii. 85.

1756.—"The interval was planted with rows of **palmira**, and coco-nut trees."—*Orme*, ii. 90, ed. 1803.

1860.—"Here, too, the beautiful **palmyra** palm, which abounds over the north of the Island, begins to appear."—*Tennent's Ceylon*, ii. 54.

PALMYRA POINT, n.p. Otherwise called Pt. Pedro, [a corruption of the Port. *Punta das Pedras*, 'the rocky cape,' a name descriptive of the natural features of the coast (*Tennent*, ii. 535)]. This is the N.E. point of Ceylon, the high palmyra trees on which are conspicuous.

PALMYRAS, POINT, n.p. This is a headland on the Orissa coast, quite low, but from its prominence at the most projecting part of the combined Mahānadī and Brāhmaṇī delta an important landmark, especially in former days, for ships bound from the south for the mouth of the Hoogly, all the more for the dangerous shoal off it. A point of the Mahānadī delta, 24 miles to the south-west, is called *False Point*, from its liability to be mistaken for P. Palmyras.

1553.—". . . o **Cabo** Segógora, a que os nossos chamam **das Palmeiras** por humas que alli estam, as quaes os navigantes notam por lhes dar conhecimento da terra. E deste cabo . . . fazemos fim do Reyno Orixá."—*Barros*, I. ix. 1.

1598.—". . . 2 miles (Dutch) before you come to the **point of Palmerias**, you shall see certaine blacke houels standing vppon a land that is higher than all the land thereabouts, and from thence to the Point it beginneth againe to be low ground and . . . you shall see some small (but not ouer white) sandie Dŏwnes . . . you shall finde being right against the **point de Palmerias** . . . that vpon the point there is neyther tree nor bush, and although it hàth the name of the Point of Palm-trees, it hath notwithstanding right forth, but one Palme tree."—*Linschoten*, 3d Book, ch. 12.

[c. 1665.—"Even the *Portuguese* of *Ogouli* (see **HOOGLY**), in *Bengale*, purchased without scruple these wretched captives, and the horrid traffic was transacted in the vicinity of the island of *Galles*, near **Cape das Palmas**."—*Bernier*, ed. *Constable*, 176.]

1823.—"It is a large delta, formed by the mouths of the Maha-Nuddee and other rivers, the northernmost of which insulates **Cape Palmiras**."—*Heber*, ed. 1844, i. 88.

[**PAMBRE**, s. An article of dress which seems to have been used for various purposes, as a scarf, and perhaps as a turban. Mr. Yusuf Ali (*Monograph on Silk Fabrics*, 81) classes it among 'fabrics which are simply wrapped over the head and shoulders by men and women'; and he adds: "The **Pamri** is used by women and children, generally amongst Hindus." His specimens are some 3 yards long by 1 broad, and are made of pure silk or silk and cotton, with an ornamental border. The word does not appear in the Hind. dictionaries, but Molesworth has Mahr. *pāmarī*, 'a sort of silk cloth.'

[1616.—"He covered my head with his **Pambre**."—*Foster, Letters*, iv. 344.]

For some of the following quotations and notes I am indebted to Mr. W. Foster.

[1617.—"Antelopes and ramshelles,* which bear the finest wool in the world, with which they make very delicate mantles, called **Pawmmerys**."—*Joseph Salbank to the E. India Co.*, Agra, Nov. 22, 1617; India Office Records, O. C., No. 568.

[1627.—"L'on y [Kashmír] travaille aussi plusieurs **Vomeris** [misprint for **Pomeris**, which he elsewhere mentions as a stuff from Kashmir and Lahore], qui sont des pieces d'estoffes longues de trois, aulnes, et largers de deux, faite de laine de moutons, qui croit au derriere de ces bestes, et qui est aussi fine que de la soye: on tient ces estoffes exposées au froid pendant l'hyver: elles ont un beau lustre, semblables aux tabis de nos cartiers."—*François Pelsart*, in *Thevenot's Rélations de divers Voyages*, vol. i. pt. 2.

[1634.—A letter in the India Office of Dec. 29 mentions that the Governor of Surat presented to the two chief Factors a horse and "a coat and **pamorine**" apiece.

[,, O. C., No. 1543A (I. O. Records) mentions the presentation to the President of Surat of a "coat and **pamorine**."

[1673.—"A couple of **pamerins**, which are fine mantles."—*Fryer's New Account*, p. 79; also see 177; in 112 **ramerin**.

1766.—". . . a lungee (see **LOONGHEE**) or clout, barely to cover their nakedness, and a **pamree** or loose mantle to throw over their shoulders, or to lye on upon the ground."—*Grose*, 2nd ed. ii. 81.]

* Query (i.) *rámún* (Hind.) or *rama* (Ladakhi) *chhelli*=the *rama* (special variety of goat) -goat; (ii.) or is Salbank mixing *rama-shál* (goat-shawl), the product, with the name of the animal producing the raw material?

PANCHĀÑGAM, s. Skt.= 'quinque-partite.' A native almanac in S. India is called so, because it contains information on five subjects, viz. Solar Days, Lunar Days, Asterisms, Yogas, and *karaṇas* (certain astrological divisions of the days of a month). *Panchanga* is used also, at least by Buchanan below, for the Brahman who keeps and interprets the almanac for the villagers. [This should be Skt. *pañchāngī*.]

1612.—"Every year they make new almanacs for the eclipses of the Sun and of the Moon, and they have a perpetual one which serves to pronounce their auguries, and this they call **Panchagão**."—*Couto*, V. vi. 4.

1651.—"The Bramins, in order to know the good and bad days, have made certain writings after the fashion of our Almanacks, and these they call **Panjangam**."—*Rogerius*, 55. This author gives a specimen (pp. 63-69).

1800.—"No one without consulting the **Panchanga**, or almanac-keeper, knows when he is to perform the ceremonies of religion."—*Buchanan's Mysore*, &c., i. 234.

PANDAL, PENDAUL, s. A shed. Tamil. *pandal*, [Skt. *bandh*, 'to bind'].

1651.—". . . it is the custom in this country when there is a Bride in the house to set up before the door certain stakes somewhat taller than a man, and these are covered with lighter sticks on which foliage is put to make a shade. . . . This arrangement is called a **Pandael** in the country speech."—*Rogerius*, 12.

1717.—"Water-**Bandels**, which are little sheds for the Conveniency of drinking Water."—*Phillips's Account*, 19.

1745.—"Je suivis la procession d'un peu loin, et arrivé aux sepultures, j'y vis un **pandel** ou tente dressée, sur la fosse du defunt; elle était ornée de branches de figuier, de toiles peintes, &c. L'intérieur était garnie de petites lampes allumées."—*Norbert, Mémoires*, iii. 32.

1781.—"Les gens riches font construir devant leur porte un autre **pendal**."—*Sonnerat*, ed. 1782, i. 134.

1800.—"I told the farmer that, as I meant to make him pay his full rent, I could not take his fowl and milk without paying for them; and that I would not enter his **pundull**, because he had not paid the labourers who made it."—Letter of *Sir T. Munro*, in *Life*, i. 283.

1814.—"There I beheld, assembled in the same **pandaul**, or reposing under the friendly banian-tree, the *Gosannee* (see

GOSAIN) in a state of nudity, the *Yogee* (see JOGEE) with a lark or paroquet his sole companion for a thousand miles."—*Forbes, Or. Mem.* ii. 465; [2nd ed. ii. 72. In ii. 109 he writes **Pendall**].

1815.—"**Pandauls** were erected opposite the two principal fords on the river, where under my medical superintendence skilful natives provided with eau-de-luce and other remedies were constantly stationed."—*Dr. M'Kenzie*, in *Asiatic Researches*, xiii. 329.

PANDÁRAM, s. A Hindu ascetic mendicant of the (so-called) Śūdra, or even of a lower caste. A priest of the lower Hindu castes of S. India and Ceylon. Tamil, *pandāram*. C. P. Brown says the *Pandāram* is properly a Vaishnava, but other authors apply the name to Śaiva priests. [The *Madras Gloss.* derives the word from Skt. *pāndu-ranga*, 'white-coloured.' Messrs. Cox and Stuart (*Man of N. Arcot.* i. 199) derive it from Skt. *bhāndagāra*, 'a temple-treasury,' wherein were employed those who had renounced the world. "The Pandārams seem to receive numerous recruits from the Śaivite Súdra castes, who choose to make a profession of piety and wander about begging. They are, in reality, very lax in their modes of life, often drinking liquor and eating animal food furnished by any respectable Súdra. They often serve in Śiva temples, where they make up garlands of flowers to decorate the lingam, and blow brass trumpets when offerings are made or processions take place" (*ibid.*).]

1711.—". . . But the destruction of 50 or 60,000 pagodas worth of grain . . . and killing the **Pandarrum**; these are things which make his demands really carry too much justice with them."—Letter in *Wheeler*, ii. 163.

1717.—". . . Bramans, **Pantarongal**, and other holy men."—*Phillips's Account*, 18. The word is here in the Tamil plural.

1718.—"Abundance of Bramanes, **Pantares**, and Poets . . . flocked together."—*Propn. of the Gospel*, ii. 18.

1745.—"On voit ici quelquefois les **Pandarams** ou Penitens qui ont été en pélérinage à Bengale; quand ils retournent ils apportent ici avec grand soin de l'eau du *Gange* dans des pots ou vases bien formés."—*Norbert, Mém.* iii. 28.

c. 1760.—"The **Pandarams**, the Mahometan priests, and the Bramins themselves yield to the force of truth."—*Grose*, i. 252.

1781.—"Les **Pandarons** ne sont pas moins révérés que les *Saniasis*. Ils sont de la secte de Chiven, se barbouillent toute la figure, la poitrine, et les bras avec des cendres de bouze de vache," &c.—*Sonnerat*, 8vo. ed., ii. 113-114.

1798.—"The other figure is of a **Pandaram** or Senassey, of the class of pilgrims to the various pagodas."—*Pennant's View of Hindostan*, preface.

1800.—"In Chera the *Pújáris* (see POOJAREE) or priests in these temples are all **Pandarums**, who are the *Súdras* dedicated to the service of Siva's temples. . . ."—*Buchanan's Mysore*, &c., ii. 338.

1809.—"The chief of the pagoda (Rameswaram), or **Pandaram**, waiting on the beach."—*Ld. Valentia*, i. 338.

1860.—"In the island of Nainativoe, to the south-west of Jafna, there was till recently a little temple, dedicated to the goddess Naga Tambiran, in which consecrated serpents were tenderly reared by the **Pandarams**, and daily fed at the expense of the worshippers."—*Tennent's Ceylon*, i. 373.

PANDARĀNI, n. p. The name of a port of Malabar of great reputation in the Middle Ages, a name which has gone through many curious corruptions. Its position is clear enough from Varthema's statement that an uninhabited island stood opposite at three leagues distance, which must be the "Sacrifice Rock" of our charts. [The *Madras Gloss.* identifies it with Collam.] The name appears upon no modern map, but it still attaches to a miserable fishing village on the site, in the form **Pantalāni** (approx. lat. 11° 26′), a little way north of Koilandi. It is seen below in Ibn Batuta's notice that Pandarāni afforded an exceptional shelter to shipping during the S.W. monsoon. This is referred to in an interesting letter to one of the present writers from his friend Col. (now Lt.-Gen.) R. H. Sankey, C.B., R.E., dated Madras, 13th Feby., 1881: "One very extraordinary feature on the coast is the occurrence of mud-banks in from 1 to 6 fathoms of water, which have the effect of breaking both surf and swell to such an extent that ships can run into the patches of water so sheltered at the very height of the monsoon, when the elements are raging, and not only find a perfectly still sea, but are able to land their cargoes. . . . Possibly the snugness of some of the harbours frequented by the Chinese junks, such as **Pandarani**, may have been mostly due to banks of this kind? By the way, I suspect your 'Pandarani' was nothing but the roadstead of Coulete (Coulandi or

Quelande of our Atlas). The Master Attendant who accompanied me, appears to have a good opinion of it as an anchorage, and as well sheltered." [See *Logan*, *Malabar*, i. 72.]

c. 1150.—"**Fandarina** is a town built at the mouth of a river which comes from *Manībār* (see **MALABAR**), where vessels from India and Sind cast anchor. The inhabitants are rich, the markets well supplied, and trade flourishing."—*Edrisi*, in *Elliot*, i. 90.

1296.—"In the year (1296) it was prohibited to merchants who traded in fine or costly products with Maparh (Ma'bar or Coromandel), Peï-nan (?) and **Fantalaina**, three foreign kingdoms, to export any one of them more than the value of 50,000 *ting* in paper money."—*Chinese Annals of the Mongol Dynasty*, quoted by *Pauthier*, *Marc Pol*, 532.

c. 1300.—"Of the cities on the shore the first is Sindábúr, then Faknúr, then the country of Manjarúr, then the country of Hilí, then the country of (**Fandaraina***)."—*Rashīduddīn*, in *Elliot*, i. 68.

c. 1321.—"And the forest in which the pepper groweth extendeth for a good 18 days' journey, and in that forest there be two cities, the one whereof is called **Flandrina**, and the other *Cyngilin*" (see **SHINKALI**).—*Friar Odoric*, in *Cathay*, &c., 75.

c. 1343.—"From Boddfattan we proceeded to **Fandaraina**, a great and fine town with gardens and bazars. The Musulmans there occupy three quarters, each having its mosque. . . . It is at this town that the ships of China pass the winter" (*i.e.* the S.W. monsoon).—*Ibn Batuta*, iv. 88. (Compare *Roteiro* below.)

c. 1442.—"The humble author of this narrative having received his order of dismissal departed from Calicut by sea, after having passed the port of **Bendinaneh** (read **Bandarānah**, and see **MANGALORE**, a) situated on the coast of Melabar, (he) reached the port of Mangalor. . . ."—*Abdurrazzāk*, in *India in XVth Cent.*, 20.

1498.—". . . hum lugar que se chama **Pandarany** . . . por que alii estava bom porto, e que alii nos amarassemos . . . e que era costume que os navios que vinham a esta terra pousasem alii por estarem seguros. . . ."—*Roteiro de Vasco da Gama*, 53.

1503.—"Da poi feceno vela et in vn porto de dicto Re chiamato **Fundarane** amazorno molta gēte cō artelaria et deliberorno andare verso il regno de Cuchin. . . ."—*Letter of King Emanuel*, p. 5.

c. 1506.—"Questo capitanio si trovò nave 17 de mercadanti Mori in uno porto se chima **Panidarami**, e combattè con queste le quali se messeno in terra; per modo che questo capitanio mandò tutti li soi copani ben armadi con un baril de polvere per cadaun copano, e mise fuoco dentro dette navi de Mori; e tutte quelle brasolle, con tutte quelle spezierie che erano carghe per la Mecha, e s'intende ch' erano molto ricche. . . ."—*Leonardo Ca' Masser*, 20-21.

* This is the true reading, see note at the place, and *J. R. As. Soc.* N.S.

1510.—"Here we remained two days, and then departed, and went to a place which is called **Pandarani**, distant from this one day's journey, and which is subject to the King of Calicut. This place is a wretched affair, and has no port."—*Varthema*, 153.

1516.—"Further on, south south-east, is another Moorish place which is called **Pandarani**, in which also there are many ships."—*Barbosa*, 152.

In Rowlandson's Translation of the *Tohfat-ul-Majāhidīn* (*Or. Transl. Fund*, 1833), the name is habitually misread *Fundreeah* for **Fundaraina**.

1536.—"Martim Afonso . . . ran along the coast in search of the *paraos*, the galleys and caravels keeping the sea, and the foists hugging the shore. And one morning they came suddenly on Cunhalemarcar with 25 *paraos*, which the others had sent to collect rice; and on catching sight of them as they came along the coast towards the Isles of **Pandarane**, Diogo de Reynoso, who was in advance of our foists, he and his brother . . . and Diogo Corvo . . . set off to engage the Moors, who were numerous and well armed. And Cunhale, when he knew it was Martim Afonso, laid all pressure on his oars to double the Point of Tiracole. . . ."—*Correa*, iii. 775.

PANDY, s. The most current colloquial name for the Sepoy mutineer during 1857-58. The surname *Pāṇḍē* [Skt. *Paṇḍita*] was a very common one among the high-caste Sepoys of the Bengal army, being the title of a *Jōt* [*got*, *gotra*] or subdivisional branch of the Brahmins of the Upper Provinces, which furnished many men to the ranks. "The first two men hung" (for mutiny) "at Barrackpore were **Pandies** by caste, hence all sepoys were **Pandies**, and ever will be so called" (*Bourchier*, as below). "In the Bengal army before the Mutiny, there was a person employed in the quarter-guard to strike the gong, who was known as the *gunta* **Pandy**" (*M.-G. Keatinge*). *Ghaṇṭā*, 'a gong or bell.'

1857.—"As long as I feel the entire confidence I do, that we shall triumph over this iniquitous combination, I cannot feel gloom. I leave this feeling to the **Pandies**, who have sacrificed honour and existence to the ghost of a delusion."—*H. Greathed*, *Letters during the Siege of Delhi*, 99.

" "We had not long to wait before the line of guns, howitzers, and mortar carts, chiefly drawn by elephants, soon hove in sight. . . . Poor **Pandy**, what a pounding was in store for you! . . ."—*Bourchier, Eight Months' Campaign against the Bengal Sepoy Army*, 47.

PANGARA, PANGAIA, s. From the quotations, a kind of boat used on the E. coast of Africa. [Pyrard de Laval (i. 53, Hak. Soc.) speaks of a "kind of raft called a **panguaye**," on which Mr. Gray comments: "As Rivara points out, Pyrard mistakes the use of the word *panguaye*, or, as the Portuguese write it, *pangaio*, which was a small sailing canoe. . . . Rivara says the word is still used in Portuguese India and Africa for a two-masted barge with lateen sails. It is mentioned in Lancaster's *Voyages* (Hak. Soc. pp. 5, 6, and 26), where it is described as being like a barge with one mat sail of coco-nut leaves. 'The barge is sowed together with the rindes of trees and pinned with wooden pinnes.' See also *Alb. Comm.* Hak. Soc. iii. p. 60, note; and Dr. Burnell's note to Linschoten, Hak. Soc. i. p. 32, where it appears that the word is used as early as 1505, in Dom Manoel's letter."]

[1513.—**Pandejada** and **Panguagada** are used for a sort of boat near Malacca in D'Andrade's Letter to Alboquerque of 22 Feby.; and we have "a **Pandejada** laden with supplies and arms" in India Office MS., *Corpo Chronologico*, vol. i.]

1591.—". . . divers **Pangaras** or boates, which are pinned with wooden pinnes, and sowed together with Palmito cordes."—*Barker*, in *Hakluyt*, ii. 588.

1598.—"In this fortresse of Sofala the Captaine of *Mossambique* hath a Factor, and twice or thrice every yere he sendeth certaine boats called **Pangaios**, which saile along the shore to fetch gold, and bring it to *Mossambique*. These **Pangaios** are made of light planks, and sowed together with cords, without any nailes."—*Linschoten*, ch. 4; [Hak. Soc. i. 32].

1616.—"Each of these bars, of Quilimane, Cumama, and Luabo, allows of the entrance of vessels of 100 tons, viz., galeots and **pangaios**, loaded with cloth and provisions; and when they enter the river they discharge cargo into other light and very long boats called **almadias**. . . ."—*Bocarro, Decada*, 534.

[1766.—"Their larger boats, called **panguays**, are raised some feet from the sides with reeds and branches of trees, well bound together with small-cord, and afterwards made water-proof, with a kind of bitumen, or resinous substance."—*Grose*, 2nd ed. ii. 13.]

PANGOLIN, s. This book-name for the *Manis* is Malay *Pangūlang*, 'the creature that rolls itself up.' [Scott says: "The Malay word is *peng-goling*, transcribed also *peng-guling*; Katingan *pengiling*. It means 'roller,' or, more literally, 'roll up.' The word is formed from *goling*, 'roll, wrap,' with the denominative prefix *pe-*, which takes before *g* the form *peng*." Mr. Skeat remarks that the modern Malay form is *teng-giling* or *senggiling*, but the latter seems to be used, not for the *Manis*, but for a kind of centipede which rolls itself up. "The word **pangolin**, to judge by its form, should be derived from *guling*, which means to 'roll over and over.' The word *pangguling* or *pengguling* in the required sense of *Manis*, does not exist in standard Malay. The word was either derived from some out-of-the-way dialect, or was due to some misunderstanding on the part of the Europeans who first adopted it." Its use in English begins with Pennant (*Synopsis of Quadrupeds*, 1771, p. 329). Adam Burt gives a dissection of the animal in *Asiat. Res.* ii. 353 *seqq.*] It is the *Manis pentedactyla* of Linn.; called in Hind. *bajrkīt* (*i.e.* Skt. *vajra-kita* 'adamant reptile'). We have sometimes thought that the Manis might have been the creature which was shown as a gold-digging ant (see *Busbeck* below); was not this also the creature that Bertrandon de la Brocquière met with in the desert of Gaza? When pursued, "it began to cry like a cat at the approach of a dog. Pierre de la Vaudrei struck it on the back with the point of his sword, but it did no harm, from being covered with scales like a sturgeon." A.D. 1432. (*T. Wright's Early Travels in Palestine*, p. 290) (Bohn). It is remarkable to find the statement that these ants were found in the possession of the King of Persia recurring in Herodotus and in Busbeck, with an interval of nearly 2000 years! We see that the suggestion of the Manis being the gold-digging ant has been anticipated by Mr. Blakesley in his *Herodotus*. ["It is now understood that the gold-digging ants were neither, as ancients supposed, an extraordinary kind of real ants, nor, as many learned men have since supposed, large animals mistaken for ants, but Tibetan miners who, like their descendants of the present day, preferred working their mines in winter when the frozen soil stands well and is not likely to trouble them by falling in. The Sanskrit word *pipilika* denotes both an ant and a particular kind of gold" (*McCrindle, Ancient India, its Invasion by Alexander the Great*, p. 341 *seq.*]

c. B.C. 445.—"Here in this desert, there live amid the sand great ants, in size somewhat less than dogs, but bigger than foxes. The Persian King has a number of them, which have been caught by the hunters in the land whereof we are speaking. . . ."—*Herod.* iii. 102 (*Rawlinson's* tr.).

1562.—Among presents to the G. Turk from the King of Persia: "in his inusitati generis animantes, qualem memini dictum fuisse allatam *formicam Indicam* mediocris canis magnitudine, mordacem admodum et saevam."—*Busbequii Opera, Elzev.*, 1633, p. 343.

PANICALE, s. This is mentioned by Bluteau (vi. 223) as an Indian disease, a swelling of the feet. *Câle* is here probably the Tamil *kāl*, 'leg.' [*Anaikkāl* is the Tamil name for what is commonly called **Cochin Leg**.]

PANIKAR, PANYCA, &c., s. Malayāl. *panikan*, 'a fencing-master, a teacher' [Mal. *pani*, 'work,' *karan*, 'doer']; but at present it more usually means 'an astrologer.'

1518.—"And there are very skilful men who teach this art (fencing), and they are called **Panicars**."—*Barbosa*, 128.

1553.—"And when (the Naire) comes to the age of 7 years he is obliged to go to the fencing-school, the master of which (whom they call **Panical**) they regard as a father, on account of the instruction he gives them."—*Barros*, I. ix. 3.

1554.—"To the **panical** (in the Factory at Cochin) 300 *reis* a month, which are for the year 3600 *reis*."—*S. Botelho, Tombo*, 24.

1556.—". . . aho Rei arma caualleiro ho **Panica** q̃ ho ensinou."—*D. de Goes, Chron.* 51.

1583.—"The maisters which teach them, be graduats in the weapons which they teach, and they bee called in their language **Panycaes**."—*Castañeda* (by N. L.), f. 36*v*.

1599.—"L'Archidiacre pour assurer sa personne fit appeller quelques-uns des principaux Maitres d'Armes de sa Nation. On appelle ces Gens-là **Panicals**. . . . Ils sont extremement redoutez."—*La Croze*, 101.

1604.—"The deceased **Panical** had engaged in his pay many Nayres, with obligation to die for him."—*Guerrero, Relacion*, 90.

1606.—"**Paniquais** is the name by which the same Malauares call their masters of fence."—*Gouvea*, f. 28.

1644.—"To the cost of a **Penical** and 4 Nayres who serve the factory in the conveyance of the pepper on rafts for the year 12,960 *res*."—*Bocarro, MS.* 316.

PANTHAY, PANTHÉ, s. This is the name applied of late years in Burma, and in intelligence coming from the side of Burma, to the Mahommedans of Yunnan, who established a brief independence at Talifu, between 1867 and 1873. The origin of the name is exceedingly obscure. It is not, as Mr. Baber assures us, used or known in Yunnan itself (*i.e.* by the *Chinese*). It must be remarked that the usual Burmese name for a Mahommedan is *Pathí*, and one would have been inclined to suppose *Panthé* to be a form of the same; as indeed we see that Gen. Fytche has stated it to be (*Burma, Past and Present*, ii. 297-8). But Sir Arthur Phayre, a high authority, in a note with which he has favoured us, observes: '**Panthé**, I believe, comes from a Chinese word signifying 'native or indigenous.' It is quite a modern name in Burma, and is applied exclusively to the Chinese Mahommedans who come with caravans from Yunnan. I am not aware that they can be distinguished from other Chinese caravan traders, except that they *do not bring hams for sale* as the others do. In dress and appearance, as well as in drinking samshu (see **SAMSHOO**) and gambling, they are like the others. The word *Pa-thi* again is the old Burmese word for 'Mahommedan.' It is applied to all Mahommedans other than the Chinese *Panthé*. It is in no way connected with the latter word, but is, I believe, a corruption of *Pārsī* or *Fārsī*, *i.e.* Persian." He adds:—"The Burmese call their own indigenous Mahommedans '*Pathi-Kulà*,' and Hindus '*Hindu-Kulà*,' when they wish to distinguish between the two" (see **KULA**). The last suggestion is highly probable, and greatly to be preferred to that of M. Jacquet, who supposed that the word might be taken from *Pasei* in Sumatra, which was during part of the later Middle Ages a kind of metropolis of Islam, in the Eastern Seas.*

We may mention two possible origins for *Panthé*, as indicating lines for enquiry:—

* See *Journ. As.*, Ser. II., tom. viii. 352.

a. The title *Pathí* (or *Passí*, for the former is only the Burmese lisping utterance) is very old. In the remarkable Chinese Account of Camboja, dating from the year 1296, which has been translated by Abel-Rémusat, there is a notice of a sect in Camboja called *Pa-sse.* The author identifies them in a passing way, with the *Tao-sse*, but that is a term which Fah-hian also in India uses in a vague way, apparently quite inapplicable to the Chinese sect properly so called. These *Pa-sse*, the Chinese writer says, "wear a red or white cloth on their heads, like the head-dress of Tartar women, but not so high. They have edifices or towers, monasteries, and temples, but not to be compared for magnitude with those of the Buddhists. . . . In their temples there are no images . . . they are allowed to cover their towers and their buildings with tiles. The *Pa-sse* never eat with a stranger to their sect, and do not allow themselves to be seen eating; they drink no wine," &c. (*Rémusat, Nouv. Mél. As.*, i. 112). We cannot be quite sure that this applies to Mahommedans, but it is on the whole probable that the name is the same as the *Pathi* of the Burmese, and has the same application. Now the people from whom the Burmese were likely to adopt a name for the Yunnan Mahommedans are the Shans, belonging to the great Siamese race, who occupy the intermediate country. The question occurs:—Is *Panthé* a *Shan* term for Mahommedan? If so, is it not probably only a dialectic variation of the *Passe* of Camboja, the *Pathí* of Burma, but entering Burma from a new quarter, and with its identity thus disguised? (Cushing, in his *Shan Dict.* gives *Pasī* for Mahommedan. We do not find *Panthé*). There would be many analogies to such a course of things.

["The name Panthay is a purely Burmese word, and has been adopted by us from them. The Shan word Pang-hse is identical, and gives us no help to the origin of the term. Among themselves and to the Chinese they are known as Hui-hui or Hui-tzu (Mahomedans)."—*J. G. Scott, Gazetteer Upper Burma*, I. i. 606.]

b. We find it stated in Lieut. Garnier's narrative of his great expedition to Yunnan that there is a hybrid Chinese race occupying part of the plain of Tali-fu, who are called *Pen-ti* (see *Garnier, Voy. d'Expl.* i. 518). This name again, it has been suggested, may possibly have to do with *Panthé.* But we find that *Pen-tī* ('root-soil') is a generic expression used in various parts of S. China for 'aborigines'; it could hardly then have been applied to the Mahommedans.

PANWELL, n.p. This town on the mainland opposite Bombay was in pre-railway times a usual landing-place on the way to Poona, and the English form of the name must have struck many besides ourselves. [Hamilton (*Descr.* ii. 151) says it stands on the river *Pan*, whence perhaps the name]. We do not know the correct form; but this one has substantially come down to us from the Portuguese: *e.g.*

1644.—"This Island of Caranja is quite near, almost frontier-place, to six cities of the Moors of the Kingdom of the Melique, viz. *Carnalli, Drugo, Pene, Sabayo, Abitta*, and **Panoel**."—*Bocarro, MS.* f. 227.

1804.—"*P.S.* Tell Mrs. Waring that notwithstanding the debate at dinner, and her recommendation, we propose to go to Bombay, by **Panwell**, and in the balloon!"—*Wellington*, from "Candolla," March 8.

PAPAYA, PAPAW, s. This word seems to be from America like the insipid, not to say nasty, fruit which it denotes (*Carica papaya*, L.). A quotation below indicates that it came by way of the Philippines and Malacca. [The Malay name, according to Mr. Skeat, is *betik*, which comes from the same Ar. form as **pateca**, though *papaya* and *kapaya* have been introduced by Europeans.] Though of little esteem, and though the tree's peculiar quality of rendering fresh meat tender which is familiar in the W. Indies, is little known or taken advantage of, the tree is found in gardens and compounds all over India, as far north as Delhi. In the N.W. Provinces it is called by the native gardeners *arand-kharbūza*, 'castor-oil-tree-melon,' no doubt from the superficial resemblance of its foliage to that of the *Palma Christi*. According to Moodeen Sheriff it has a Perso-Arabic name *'anbah-i-Hindī*; in Canarese it is called *P'arangi-haṇṇu* or *-mara* ('Frank or Portuguese fruit, tree'). The name *papaya* according to Oviedo as quoted by Littré ("*Oviedo*, t. 1. p. 333, Madrid, 1851,"—we cannot find it in *Ramusio*) was that used in Cuba, whilst the Carib name was *ababai*.* [Mr. J. Platt, referring to his article in 9th Ser. *Notes & Queries*, iv. 515, writes: "Malay *papaya*, like the Accra term *kpakpa*, is a European loan word. The evidence for Carib origin is, firstly, Oviedo's *Historia*, 1535 (in the ed. of 1851, vol. i. 323): 'Del arbol que en esta isla Española llaman *papaya*, y en la tierra firme los llaman los Españoles los higos del mastuerço, y en la provincia de Nicaragua llaman a tal arbol *olocoton*.' Secondly, Breton, *Dictionnaire Caraibe*, has: '*Ababai*, papayer.' Gilij, *Saggio*, 1782, iii. 146 (quoted in *N. & Q.*, *u.s.*), says the Otamic word is *pappai*."] Strange liberties are taken with the spelling. Mr. Robinson (below) calls it *popeya;* Sir L. Pelly (*J.R.G.S.* xxxv. 232), *poppoi* (ὦ πόποι!). **Papaya** is applied in the Philippines to Europeans who, by long residence, have fallen into native ways and ideas.

c. 1550.—"There is also a sort of fruit resembling figs, called by the natives **Papaie** . . . peculiar to this kingdom" (Peru).—*Girol. Benzoni*, 242.

1598.—"There is also a fruite that came out of the Spanish Indies, brought from beyond ye *Philipinas* or *Lusons* to *Malacca*, and frõ thence to *India*, it is called **Papaios**, and is very like a *Mellon* . . . and will not grow, but alwaies two together, that is male and female . . . and when they are diuided and set apart one from the other, then they yield no fruite at all. . . . This fruite at the first for the strangeness thereof was much esteemed, but now they account not of it." —*Linschoten*, 97; [Hak. Soc. ii. 35].

c. 1630.—". . . **Pappaes**, Cocoes, and Plantains, all sweet and delicious. . . ."—*Sir T. Herbert*, ed. 1665, p. 350.

c. 1635.—

"The Palma Christi and the fair **Papaw**
Now but a seed (preventing Nature's Law)
In half the circle of the hasty year,
Project a shade, and lovely fruits do wear."

Waller, Battle of the Summer Islands.

1658.—"Utraque Pinoguaçu (mas. et fœmina), Mamoeira Lusitanis dicta, vulgò **Papay**, cujus fructum *Mamam* vocant a figura, quia mammae instar pendet in arbore . . . carne lutea instar melonum, sed sapore ignobiliori. . . ."—*Gul. Pisonis* . . . *de Indiae utriusque Re Naturali et Medicâ*, Libri xiv. 159-160.

1673.—"Here the flourishing **Papaw** (in Taste like our Melons, and as big, but growing on a Tree leaf'd like our Fig-tree. . . ."—*Fryer*, 19.

1705.—"Il y a aussi des ananas, des **Papées**. . . ."—*Luillier*, 33.

1764.—

"Thy temples shaded by the tremulous palm,
Or quick **papaw**, whose top is necklaced round
With numerous rows of particoloured fruit."

Grainger, Sugar Cane, iv.

[1773.—"**Paw Paw**. This tree rises to 20 feet, sometimes single, at other times it is divided into several bodies."—*Ives*, 480.]

1878.—". . . the rank **popeyas** clustering beneath their coronal of stately leaves."—*Ph. Robinson, In My Indian Garden*, 50.

* See also *De Candolle, Plantes Cultivées*, p. 234.

PAPUA, n.p. This name, which is now applied generically to the chief race of the island of New Guinea and resembling tribes, and sometimes (improperly) to the great island itself, is a Malay word *papuwah*, or sometimes *puwah-puwah*, meaning 'frizzle-haired,' and was applied by the Malays to the people in question.

1528.—"And as the wind fell at night the vessel was carried in among the islands, where there are strong currents, and got into the Sea of the Strait of Magalhães,* where he encountered a great storm, so that but for God's mercy they had all been lost, and so they were driven on till they made the land of the **Papuas**, and then the east winds began to blow so that they could not sail to the Moluccas till May 1527. And with their stay in these lands much people got ill and many died, so that they came to Molucca much shattered." — *Correa*, iii. 173-174.

1553.—(Referring to the same history.) "Thence he went off to make the islands of a certain people called **Papuas**, whom many on account of this visit of Don Jorge (de Menezes) call the Islands of Don Jorge, which lie east of the Moluccas some 200 leagues. . . ."—*Barros*, IV. i. 6.

PARABYKE, s. Burmese *pāra-beik*; the name given to a species of writing book which is commonly used in Burma. It consists of paper made from the bark of a spec. of *daphne*, which is agglutinated into a kind of pasteboard and blackened with a paste of charcoal. It is then folded, screen-fashion, into a note-book and written on with a steatite pencil. The same mode of writing has long been used in Canara; and from La Loubère we see

* "*E foy dar no golfam do* estreito de Magalhães." I cannot explain the use of this name. It must be applied here to the Sea between Banda and Timor.

that it is or was used also in Siam. The Canara books are called *kaḍatam*, and are described by Col. Wilks under the name of *cudduttum*, *carruttum*, or *currut* (*Hist. Sketches*, Pref. I. xii.). They appear exactly to resemble the Burmese *para-beik*, except that the substance blackened is cotton cloth instead of paper. "The writing is similar to that on a slate, and may be in like manner rubbed out and renewed. It is performed by a pencil of the *balapum* [Can. *balapa*] or *lapis ollaris;* and this mode of writing was not only in ancient use for records and public documents, but is still universally employed in Mysoor by merchants and shopkeepers, I have even seen a bond, regularly witnessed, entered in the *cudduttum* of a merchant, produced and received in evidence.

"This is the word *kirret*, translated 'palm-leaf' (of course conjecturally) in Mr. Crisp's translation of Tippoo's regulations. The Sultan prohibited its use in recording the public accounts; but altho' liable to be expunged, and affording facility to permanent entries, it is a much more durable material and record than the best writing on the best paper. . . . It is probable that this is the linen or cotton cloth described by Arrian, from Nearchus, on which the Indians wrote." (*Strabo*, XV. i. 67.)

1688.—"The Siamese make Paper of old Cotton rags, and likewise of the bark of a Tree named *Ton coi* . . . but these Papers have a great deal less Equality, Body and Whiteness than ours. The Siameses cease not to write thereon with China Ink. Yet most frequently they black them, which renders them smoother, and gives them a greater body; and then they write thereon with a kind of *Crayon*, which is made only of a clayish earth dry'd in the Sun. Their Books are not bound, and consist only in a very long Leaf . . . which they fold in and out like a Fan, and the way which the Lines are wrote, is according to the length of the folds. . . ."—*De la Loubère, Siam*, E.T. p. 12.

1855.—"Booths for similar goods are arrayed against the corner of the palace palisades, and at the very gate of the Palace is the principal mart for the stationers who deal in the **para-beiks** (or black books) and steatite pencils, which form the only ordinary writing materials of the Burmese in their transactions."—*Yule, Mission to Ava*, 139.

PARANGHEE, s. An obstinate chronic disease endemic in Ceylon. It has a superficial resemblance to syphilis; the whole body being covered with ulcers, while the sufferer rapidly declines in strength. It seems to arise from insufficient diet, and to be analogous to the *pellagra* which causes havoc among the peasants of S. Europe. The word is apparently **firinghee**, 'European,' or (in S. India) 'Portuguese'; and this would point perhaps to association with syphilis.

PARBUTTY, s. This is a name in parts of the Madras Presidency for a subordinate village officer, a writer under the **patel**, sometimes the village-crier, &c., also in some places a superintendent or manager. It is a corruption of Telug. and Canarese *pārapatti*, *pārupatti*, Mahr. and Konkani, *pārpatya*, from Skt. *pravṛitti*, 'employment.' The term frequently occurs in old Port. documents in such forms as *perpotim*, &c. We presume that the Great Duke (audax omnia *perpeti!*) has used it in the Anglicised form at the head of this article; for though we cannot find it in his Despatches, Gurwood's *Explanation of Indian Terms* gives "**Parbutty**, writer to the Patell." [See below.]

1567.—". . . That no unbeliever shall serve as scrivener, **shroff** (*xarrafo*), **mocuddum, naique** (see **NAIK**), **peon, parpatrim**, collector (*saccador*), constable (? *corrector*), interpreter, procurator, or solicitor in court, nor in any other office or charge by which they may in any way whatever exercise authority over Christians. . . ."—*Decree* 27 *of the Sacred Council of Goa*, in *Arch. Port. Orient.* fasc. 4.

1800.—"In case of failure in the payment of these instalments, the crops are seized, and sold by the **Parputty** or accomptant of the division."—*Buchanan's Mysore*, ii. 151-2. The word is elsewhere explained by Buchanan, as "the head person of a *Hobly* in Mysore." A *Hobly* [Canarese and Malayāl. *hobali*] is a sub-division of a **talook** (i. 270).

[1803.—"Neither has any one a right to compel any of the inhabitants, much less the particular servants of the government, to attend him about the country, as the soubahdar (see **SOUBADAR**) obliged the **parbutty** and pateel (see **PATEL**) to do, running before his horse."—*Wellington, Desp.* i. 323. (*Stanf. Dict.*).]

1878.—"The staff of the village officials . . . in most places comprises the following members . . . the crier (**parpoti**). . . ."—*Fonseca, Sketch of Goa*, 21-22.

PARDAO, s. This was the popular name among the Portuguese of a gold coin from the native mints of Western

India, which entered largely into the early currency of Goa, and the name of which afterwards attached to a silver money of their own coinage, of constantly degenerating value.

There could hardly be a better word with which to associate some connected account of the coinage of Portuguese India, as the *pardao* runs through its whole history, and I give some space to the subject, not with any idea of weaving such a history, but in order to furnish a few connected notes on the subject, and to correct some flagrant errors of writers to whose works I naturally turned for help in such a special matter, with little result except that of being puzzled and misled, and having time occupied in satisfying myself regarding the errors alluded to. The subject is in itself a very difficult one, perplexed as it is by the rarity or inaccessibility of books dealing with it, by the excessive rarity (it would seem) of specimens, by the large use in the Portuguese settlements of a variety of native coins in addition to those from the Goa mint,* by the frequent shifting of nomenclature in the higher coins and constant degeneration of value in the coins that retained old names. I welcomed as a hopeful aid the appearance of Dr. Gerson D'Acunha's *Contributions to the Study of Indo-Chinese Numismatics.* But though these contributions afford some useful facts and references, on the whole, from the rarity with which they give data for the intrinsic value of the gold and silver coins, and from other defects, they seem to me to leave the subject in utter chaos. Nor are the notes which Mr. W. de G. Birch appends, in regard to monetary values, to his translation of Alboquerque, more to be commended. Indeed Dr. D'Acunha, when he goes astray, seems sometimes to have followed Mr. Birch.

The word *pardao* is a Portuguese (or perhaps an indigenous) corruption of Skt. *pratāpa*, 'splendour, majesty,' &c., and was no doubt taken, as Dr. D'Acunha says, from the legend on some of the coins to which the name was applied, *e.g.* that of the Raja of Ikkeri in Canara: *Sri* **Pratāpa** *krishṇa-rāya.*

A little doubt arises at first in determining to what coin the name *pardao* was originally attached. For in the two earliest occurrences of the word that we can quote—on the one hand Abdurrazzāk, the Envoy of Shāh Rukh, makes the *partāb* (or *pardāo*) half of the *Varāha* ('boar,' so called from the Boar of Vishnu figured on some issues), *hūn*, or what we call **pagoda**;—whilst on the other hand, Ludovico Varthema's account seems to identify the *pardao* with the pagoda itself. And there can be no doubt that it was to the pagoda that the Portuguese, from the beginning of the 16th century, applied the name of *pardao d'ouro.* The money-tables which can be directly formed from the statements of Abdurrazzāk and Varthema respectively are as follows:*

ABDURRAZZAK (A.D. 1443).

3 Jitals (copper) .	= 1 Tar (silver).
6 Tars . . .	= 1 Fanam (gold).
10 Fanams . .	= 1 **Partāb.**
2 **Partābs** . .	= 1 Varāha.

And the *Varāha* weighed about 1 *Mithkāl* (see **MISCALL**), equivalent to 2 *dīnārs Kopekī.*

VARTHEMA (A.D. 1504-5).

16 Cas (see **CASH**)	= 1 Tare (silver).
16 Tare . .	= 1 Fanam (gold).
20 Fanams . .	= 1 **Pardao.**

And the **Pardao** was a gold ducat, smaller than the seraphim (see **XERAFINE**) of Cairo (gold dīnār), but thicker.

The question arises whether the *varāha* of Abdurrazzāk was the double pagoda, of which there are some examples in the S. Indian coinage, and his *partāb* therefore the same as Varthema's, *i.e.* the pagoda itself; or whether his *varāha* was the pagoda, and his *partāb* a half-pagoda. The weight which he assigns to the *varāha*, "about one *mithkāl*," a weight which may be taken at 73 grs., does not well suit either one or the other. I find the mean weight of 27 different issues of the (single) *hūn* or pagoda, given in Prinsep's *Tables*, to be 43 grs., the

* Antonio Nunez, "Comtador da Casa del Rey noso Senhor," who in 1554 compiled the *Livro dos Pesos da Ymdia e asy Medidas e Mohedas*, says of Diu in particular:

"The moneys here exhibit such variations and such differences, that it is impossible to write any thing certain about them; for every month, every 8 days indeed, they rise and fall in value, according to the money that enters the place" (p. 28).

* I invert the similar table given by Dr. Badger in his notes to Varthema.

maximum being 45 grs. And the fact that both the Envoy's *varāha* and the Italian traveller's *pardao* contain 20 fanams is a strong argument for their identity.*

In further illustration that the **pardao** was recognised as a half *hūn* or pagoda, we quote in a foot-note "the old arithmetical tables in which accounts are still kept" in the south, which Sir Walter Elliot contributed to Mr. E. Thomas's excellent *Chronicles of the Pathan Kings of Delhi, illustrated,* &c.†

Moreover, Dr. D'Acunha states that in the "New Conquests," or provinces annexed to Goa only about 100 years ago, "the accounts were kept until lately in *sanvoy* and *nixane* pagodas, each of them being divided into 2 **pratáps** . . . ." &c. (p. 46, *note*).

As regards the value of the *pardao d'ouro*, when adopted into the Goa currency by Alboquerque, Dr. D'Acunha tells us that it "was equivalent to 370 *reis*, or 1*s.* 6½*d.* ‡ English." Yet he accepts the identity of this *pardao d'ouro* with the *hūn* current in Western India, of which the Madras pagoda was till 1818 a living and unchanged representative, a coin which was, at the time of its abolition, the recognised equivalent of 3½ rupees, or 7 shillings. And doubtless this, or a few pence more, was the intrinsic value of the *pardao*. Dr. D'Acunha in fact has made his calculation from the *present* value of the (imaginary) *rei*. Seeing that a *milrei* is now reckoned equal to a dollar, or 50*d.*, we have a single *rei*=$\frac{1}{20}$*d.*, and 370 *reis*=1*s.* 6½*d.* It seems not to have occurred to the author that the *rei* might have degenerated in value as well as every other denomination of money with which he has to do, every other in fact of which we can at this moment remember anything, except the pagoda, the Venetian sequin, and the dollar.* Yet the fact of this degeneration everywhere stares him in the face. Correa tells us that the *cruzado* which Alboquerque struck in 1510 was the just equivalent of 420 *reis.* It was indubitably the same as the *cruzado* of the mother country, and indeed A. Nunez (1554) gives the same 420 *reis* as the equivalent of the *cruzado d'ouro de Portugal*, and that amount also for the Venetian sequin, and for the *sultani* or Egyptian gold dīnār. Nunez adds that a gold coin of Cambaya, which he calls **Madrafaxao** (q.v.), was worth 1260 to 1440 *reis*, according to variations in weight and exchange. We have seen that this must have been the gold-mohr of Muzaffar-Shāh II. of Guzerat (1511-1526), the weight of which we learn from E. Thomas's book.

From the Venetian sequin (content of pure gold 52·27 grs. value 111*d.*†) the value of the *rei* at $\frac{111}{420}$*d.* will be	·264*d.*
From the Muzaffar Shāhi mohr (weight 185 grs. value, if pure gold, 392·52*d.*) value of *rei* at 1440	0·272*d.*
Mean value of *rei* in 1513 . . .	0·268*d.*

i.e. more than five times its present value.

Dr. D'Acunha himself informs us (p. 56) that at the beginning of the 17th century the Venetian was worth 690 to 720 *reis* (mean 705 *reis*), whilst

* The issues of fanams, q.v., have been infinite; but they have not varied much in weight, though very greatly in alloy, and therefore in the number reckoned to a pagoda.

† "2 gunjās=1 dugala
2 dugalas = 1 chavula (= the panam or fanam),
2 chavalas=1 hoṇa (=the pratapa, máda, or *half pagoda*,
2 hoṇṇas=1 Varāha (the hūn or pagoda").

"The ganjā or unit (=¼ fanam) is the rati, or Sanskrit raktika, the seed of the *abrus*."—*Op. cit.* p. 224, *note.* See also Sir W. Elliot's *Coins of S. India*, p. 56.

‡ 360 *reis* is the equivalent in the authorities, so far as I know.

* Even the pound sterling, since it represented a pound of silver sterlings, has come down to one-third of that value; but if the value of silver goes on dwindling as it has done lately, our pound might yet justify its name again!

I have remarked elsewhere:

"Everybody seems to be tickled at the notion that the Scotch Pound or *Livre* was only 20 pence. Nobody finds it funny that the French or Italian *Livre* or Pound is only 20 halfpence or less!" I have not been able to trace how high the *rei* began, but the *maravedi* entered life as a gold piece, equivalent to the Saracen *mithkāl*, and ended—?

† I calculate all gold values in this paper at those of the present English coinage.

Besides the gradual depreciation of the Portugal *rei*, so prominently noticed in this paper, there was introduced in Goa a reduction of the *rei* locally below the *rei* of Portugal in the ratio of 15 to 8. I do not know the history or understand the object of such a change, nor do I see that it affects the calculations in this article. In a table of values of coins current in Portuguese India, given in the *Annaes Maritimos* of 1844, each coin is valued both in *Reis of Goa* and in *Reis of Portugal*, bearing the above ratio. My kind correspondent, Dr. J. N. Fonseca, author of the capital *History of Goa*, tells me that this was introduced in the beginning of the 17th century, but that he has yet found no document throwing light upon it. It is a matter quite apart from the secular depreciation of the *rei*.

the pagoda was worth 570 to 600 *reis* (mean 585 *reis*).

These statements, as we know the intrinsic value of the sequin, and the approximate value of the pagoda, enable us to calculate the value of the *rei* of about 1600 at . . . 0·16*d*. Values of the *milrei* given in Milburn's *Oriental Commerce*, and in Kelly's *Cambist*, enable us to estimate it for the early years of the last century. We have then the progressive deterioration as follows :

Value of *rei* in the beginning of the 16th century . . . . 0·268*d*.
Value of *rei* in the beginning of the 17th century . . . . 0·16*d*.
Value of *rei* in the beginning of the 19th century . . 0·06 to 0.066*d*.
Value of *rei* at present . . . . 0·06*d*.

Yet Dr. D'Acunha has valued the coins of 1510, estimated in *reis*, at the rate of 1880. And Mr. Birch has done the same.*

The Portuguese themselves do not seem ever to have struck gold *pardaos* or pagodas. The gold coin of Alboquerque's coinage (1510) was, we have seen, a *cruzado* (or *manuel*), and the next coinage in gold was by Garcia de Sá in 1548-9, who issued coins called *San Thomé*, worth 1000 *reis*, say about £1, 2*s*. 4*d*. ; with halves and quarters of the same. Neither, according to D'Acunha, was there silver money of any importance coined at Goa from 1510 to 1550, and the coins then issued were silver San Thomés, called also *patacões* (see **PATACA**). Nunez in his *Tables* (1554) does not mention these by either name, but mentions repeatedly *pardaos*, which represented 5 silver *tangas*, or 300 *reis*, and these D'Acunha speaks of as silver *coins*. Nunez, as far as I can make out, does not speak of them as coins, but rather implies that in account so many tangas of silver were reckoned as a *pardao*. Later in the century, however, we learn from Balbi (1580), Barrett * (1584), and Linschoten (1583-89), the principal currency of Goa consisted of a silver coin called *xerafin* (see **XERAFINE**) and *pardao-xerafin*, which was worth 5 *tangas*, each of 60 *reis*. (So these had been from the beginning, and so they continued, as is usual in such cases. The scale of sub-multiples remains the same, whilst the value of the divisible coin diminishes. Eventually the lower denominations become infinitesimal, like the *maravedis* and the *reis*, and either vanish from memory, or survive only as denominations of account). The data, such as they are, allow us to calculate the *pardao* or *xerafin* at this time as worth 4*s*. 2*d*. to 4*s*. 6*d*.

A century later, Fryer's statement of equivalents (1676) enables us to use the stability of the Venetian sequin as a gauge ; we then find the *tanga* gone down to 6*d*. and the *pardao* or *xerafin* to 2*s*. 6*d*. Thirty years later Lockyer (1711) tells us that one rupee was reckoned equal to 1½ *perdo*. Calculat-

* Thus Alboquerque, returning to Europe in 1504, gives a "Moorish" pilot, who carried him by a new course straight from Cannanore to Mozambique, a buckshish of 50 *cruzados;* this is explained as £5—a mild munificence for such a feat. In truth it was nearly £24, the *cruzado* being about the same as the sequin (see i. p. 17).

The mint at Goa was farmed out by the same great man, after the conquest, for 600,000 *reis*, amounting, we are told, to £125. It was really £670 (iii. 41).

Alboquerque demands as ransom to spare Muscat "10,000 xerafins of gold." And we are told by the translator that this ransom of a wealthy trading city like Muscat amounted to £625. The coin in question is the *ashrafi*, or gold dīnār, as much as, or more than the sequin in value, and the sum more than £5000 (i. p. 82).

In the note to the first of these cases it is said that the *cruzado* is "a silver coin (formerly gold), now equivalent to 480 *reis*, or about 2*s*. English money, but probably worth much more relatively in the time of Dalboquerque." "Much more relatively" means of course that the 2*s*. had much more purchasing power.

This is a very common way of speaking, but it is often very fallaciously applied. The change in purchasing power *in India* generally till the beginning of last century was probably not very great. There is a curious note by Gen. Briggs in his translation of Firishta, comparing the amount stated by Firishta to have been paid by the Bāhmanī King, about A.D. 1470, as the annual cost of a body of 500 horse, with the cost of a British corps of Irregular horse of the same strength in Briggs's own time (say about 1815). The Bāhmanī charge was 350,000 Rs. ; the British charge 219,000 Rs. A corps of the same strength would now cost the British Government, as near as I can calculate, 287,300 Rs.

The price of an Arab horse imported into India (then a great traffic) was in Marco Polo's time about three times what it was in our own, up to 1850.

The salary of the Governor at Goa, c. 1550, was 8000 *cruzados*, or nearly £4000 a year ; and the salaries of the commandants of the fortresses of Goa, of Malacca, of Dio, and of Bassain, 600,000 *reis*, or about £670.

The salary of Ibn Batuta, when Judge of Delhi, about 1340, was 1000 silver *tankas* or *dinārs* as he calls them (practically 1000 rupees) a month, which was in addition to an assignment of villages bringing in 5000 *tankas* a year. And yet he got into debt in a very few years to the tune of 55,000 *tankas*—say £5,500 !

* Dr. D'Acunha has set this English traveller down to 1684, and introduces a quotation from him in illustration of the coinage of the latter period, in his quasi-chronological notes, a new element in the confusion of his readers.

ing the Surat Rupee, which may have been probably his standard, still by help of the Venetian (p. 262) at about 2*s.* 3*d.*, the *pardao* would at this time be worth 1*s.* 6*d.* It must have depreciated still further by 1728, when the Goa mint began to strike rupees, with the effigy of Dom João V., and the half-rupee appropriated the denomination of *pardao.* And the half-rupee, till our own time, has continued to be so styled. I have found no later valuation of the Goa Rupee than that in *Prinsep's Tables* (Thomas's ed. p. 55), the indications of which, taking the Company's Rupee at 2*s.*, would make it 21*d.* The *pardao* therefore would represent a value of 10½*d.*, and there we leave it.

[On this Mr. Whiteway writes: "Should it be intended to add a note to this, I would suggest that the remarks on coinage commencing at page 67 of my *Rise of the Portuguese Power in India* be examined, as although I have gone to Sir H. Yule for much, some papers are now accessible which he does not appear to have seen. There were two *pardaos*, the *pardao d'ouro* and the *pardao de tanga*, the former of 360 *reals*, the latter of 300. This is clear from the *Foral* of Goa of Dec. 18, 1758 (India Office MSS. *Conselho Ultramarino*), which passage is again quoted in a note to Fasc. 5 of the *Archiv. Port. Orient.* p. 326. Apparently *patecoons* were originally coined in value equal to the *pardao d'ouro*, though I say (p. 71) their value is not recorded. The *patecoon* was a silver coin, and when it was tampered with, it still remained of the nominal value of the *pardao d'ouro*, and this was the cause of the outcry and of the injury the people of Goa suffered. There were monies in Goa which I have not shown on p. 69. There was the *tanga branca* used in revenue accounts (see *Nunez*, p. 31), nearly but not quite double the ordinary *tanga*. This money of account was of 4 *barganims* (see **BARGANY**) each of 24 *bazarucos* (see **BUDGROOK**), that is rather over 111 reals. The whole question of coinage is difficult, because the coins were continually being tampered with. Every ruler, and they were numerous in those days, stamped a piece of metal at his pleasure, and the trader had to calculate its value, unless as a subject of the ruler he was under compulsion."]

1444. — "In this country (Vijayanagar) they have three kinds of money, made of gold mixed with alloys: one called *varahah* weighs about one *mithkal*, equivalent to two dinars *kopeki;* the second, which is called **pertab**, is the half of the first; the third, called *fanom*, is equivalent in value to the tenth part of the last-mentioned coin. Of these different coins the *fanom* is the most useful. . . ."—*Abdurrazzāk*, in *India in the XVth Cent.* p. 26.

c. 1504-5; pubd. 1510. — "I departed from the city of Dabuli aforesaid, and went to another island, which . . . is called Goga (Goa) and which pays annually to the King of Decan 19,000 gold ducats, called by them **pardai**. These pardai are smaller than the seraphim of Cairo, but thicker, and have two devils stamped on one side, and certain letters on the other."—*Varthema*, pp. 115-116.

" ". . . his money consists of a **pardao**, as I have said. He also coins a silver money called tare (see **TARA**), and others of gold, twenty of which go to a *pardao*, and are called fanom. And of these small ones of silver, there go sixteen to a fanom. . . ."—*Ibid.* p. 130.

1510.—"Meanwhile the Governor (Albuquerque) talked with certain of our people who were goldsmiths, and understood the alligation of gold and silver, and also with goldsmiths and money-changers of the country who were well acquainted with that business. There were in the country **pardaos** of gold, worth in gold 360 *reys*, and also a money of good silver which they call *barganym* (see **BARGANY**) of the value of 2 *vintems*, and a money of copper which they call *bazaruqos* (see **BUDGROOK**), of the value of 2 *reis*. Now all these the Governor sent to have weighed and assayed. And he caused to be made *cruzados* of their proper weight of 420 *reis*, on which he figured on one side the cross of Christ, and on the other a sphere, which was the device of the King Dom Manuel; and he ordered that this *cruzado* should pass in the place (Goa) for 480 *reis*, to prevent their being exported . . . and he ordered silver money to be struck which was of the value of a **bargany**; on this money he caused to be figured on one side a Greek A, and on the other side a sphere, and gave the coin the name of *Espera;* it was worth 2 *vintems;* also there were half *esperas* worth one *vintem;* and he made *bazarucos* of copper of the weight belonging to that coin, with the A and the sphere; and each *bazaruco* he divided into 4 coins which they called *cepayquas* (see **SAPECA**), and gave the *bazarucos* the name of *leaes*. And in changing the cruzado into these smaller coins it was reckoned at 480 *reis*."—*Correa*, ii. 76-77.

1516.—"There are current here (in Baticala—see **BATCUL**) the **pardaos**, which are a gold coin of the kingdom, and it is worth here 360 *reis*, and there is another coin of silver, called *dama*, which is worth 20 *reis*. . . ."—*Barbosa*, Lisbon ed. p. 293.

1516.—"There is used in this city (Bisnagar) and throughout the rest of the Kingdom much pepper, which is carried hither from Malabar on oxen and asses; and it is all bought and sold for **pardaos**, which are made in some places of this Kingdom, and especially in a city called Hora (?), whence they are called *horãos*."—*Barbosa*, Lisbon ed. p. 297.

1552.—"Hic Sinam mercatorem indies exspecto, quo cum, propter atroces poenas propositas iis qui advenam sine fide publica introduxerint, **Pirdais** ducentis transegi, ut me in Cantonem trajiciat."—*Scti. Franc. Xaverii Epistt.*, Pragae, 1667, IV. xiv.

1553.—

"*R.* Let us mount our horses and take a ride in the country, and as we ride you shall tell me what is the meaning of *Nizamoxa* (see **NIZAMALUCO**), as you have frequently mentioned such a person.

"*O.* I can tell you that at once; it is the name of a King in the Bagalat (read Balagat, **Balaghaut**), whose father I often attended, and the son also not so often. I received from him from time to time more than 12,000 **pardaos**; and he offered me an income of 40,000 *pardaos* if I would pay him a visit of several months every year, but this I did not accept."—*Garcia*, f. 33*v*.

1584.—"For the money of Goa there is a kind of money made of lead and tin mingled, being thicke and round, and stamped on the one side with the spheare or globe of the world, and on the other side two arrows and five rounds;* and this kind of money is called *Basaruchi*, and 15 of them make a vinton of naughty money, and 5 *vintons* make a tanga, and 4 *vintenas* make a tanga of base money . . . and 5 *tangas* make a seraphine of gold† (read 'of silver'), which in marchandize is worth 5 tangas good money: but if one would change them into *basaruchies*, he may have 5 tangas, and 16 basaruchies, which matter they call *cerafaggio*, and when the bargain of the **pardaw** is gold, each *pardaw* is meant to be 6 tangas good money,‡ but in murchandize, the vse is not to demaund *pardawes* of gold in Goa, except it be for jewels and horses, for all the rest they take of seraphins of silver, per aduiso. . . . The ducat of gold is worth 9 *tangas* and a halfe good money, and yet not stable in price, for that when the ships depart from Goa to Cochin, they pay them at 9 *tangas* and 3 fourth partes, and 10 *tangas*, and that is the most that they are worth. . . ."—*W. Barret*, in *Hakl.* ii. 410. I retain this for the old English, but I am sorry to say that I find it is a mere translation of the notes of Gasparo Balbi, who was at Goa in 1580. We learn from Balbi that there were at Goa *tangas* not only of good money worth 75 *basarucchi*, and of bad money worth 60 *basarucchi*, but also of another kind of bad money used in buying wood, worth only 50 *basarucchi!*

* "3 *plaghe*" in Balbi.
† "*Serafinno di argento*" (*ibid.*).
‡ "*Quando si parla di pardai d'oro s'intendono, tanghe 6, di buona moneta*" (Balbi). This does not mean the old *pardao d'ouro* or golden pagoda, a sense which apparently had now become obsolete, but that in dealing in jewels, &c., it was usual to settle the price in pardaos of 6 good tangas instead of 5 (as we give doctors guineas instead of pounds). The actual *pagodas of gold* are also mentioned by Balbi, but these were worth, new ones 7½ and old ones 8 tangas of good money.

1598.—"The principall and commonest money is called **Pardaus Xeraphiins**, and is silver, but very brasse (read 'base'), and is coyned in Goa. They have Saint Sebastian on the one side, and three or four arrows in a bundle on the other side, which is as much as three Testones, or three hundred *Reijs* Portingall money, and riseth or falleth little lesse or more, according to the exchange. There is also a kind of money which is called **Tangas**, not that there is any such coined, but are so named onely in telling, five Tangas is one **Pardaw** or **Xeraphin**, badde money, for you must understande that in telling they have two kinds of money, good and badde. . . . Wherefore when they buy and sell, they bargain for good or badde money," &c. — *Linschoten*, ch. 35; [Hak. Soc. i. 241, and for another version see **XERAPHINE**].

" "They have a kind of money called **Pagodes** which is of Gold, of two or three sortes, and are above 8 **tangas** in value. They are Indian and Heathenish money, with the feature of a Devill upon them, and therefore they are called Pagodes. There is another kind of gold money, which is called *Venetianders;* some of Venice, and some of Turkish coine, and are commonly (worth) 2 **Pardawe Xeraphins**. There is yet another kind of golde called S. Thomas, because Saint Thomas is figured thereon and is worth about 7 and 8 *Tangas:* There are likewise Rialles of 8 which are brought from Portingall, and are *Pardawes de Reales*. . . . They are worth at their first coming out 436 Reyes of Portingall; and after are raysed by exchaunge, as they are sought for when men travell for China. . . . They use in Goa in their buying and selling a certaine maner of reckoning or telling. There are *Pardawes Xeraphins*, and these are silver. They name likewise *Pardawes* of Gold, and those are not in kinde or in coyne, but onely so named in telling and reckoning: for when they buy and sell Pearles, stones, golde, silver and horses, they name but so many *Pardawes*, and then you must understand that one *Pardaw* is sixe *Tangas:* but in other ware, when you make not your bargaine before hand, but plainely name Pardawes, they are *Pardawes Xeraphins* of 5 *Tangas* the peece. They use also to say a *Pardaw* of *Lariins* (see **LARIN**), and are five Lariins for every Pardaw. . . ."—*Ibid.*; [Hak. Soc. i. 187].

This extract is long, but it is the completest picture we know of the Goa currency. We gather from the passage (including a part that we have omitted) that in the latter part of the 16th century there were really no national *coins* there used intermediate between the *basaruccho*, worth at this time 0·133*d.*, and the **pardao xerafin** worth 50*d*.* The *vintens* and *tangas* that were nominally interposed were mere names for certain quantities of basaruccos, or rather of *reis* represented by basaruccos. And our interpretation of the statement about pardaos of gold in a note above is here expressly confirmed.

[1599.—"**Perdaw.**" See under **TAEL.**]

c. 1620.—"The gold coin, struck by the rāis of Bijanagar and Tiling, is called *hūn* and **partāb.**"—*Firishta*, quoted by *Quatremère*, in *Notices et Exts.* xiv. 509.

1643.—". . . estant convenu de prix auec luy à sept **perdos** et demy par mois tant pour mon viure que pour le logis. . . ."—*Mocquet*, 284.

PARELL, n.p. The name of a northern suburb of Bombay where stands the residence of the Governor. The statement in the *Imperial Gazetteer* that Mr. W. Hornby (1776) was the first Governor who took up his residence at Parell requires examination, as it appears to have been so occupied in Grose's time. The 2nd edition of Grose, which we use, is dated 1772, but he appears to have left India about 1760. It seems probable that in the following passage Niebuhr speaks of 1763-4, the date of his stay at Bombay, but as the book was not published till 1774, this is not absolutely certain. Evidently Parell was occupied by the Governor long before 1776.

"Les Jesuites avoient autrefois un beau couvent aupres du Village de **Parell** au milieu de l'Isle, mais il y a déjà plusieurs années, qu'elle est devenue la maison de campagne du Gouverneur, et l'Eglise est actuellement une magnifique salle à manger et de danse, qu'on n'en trouve point de pareille en toutes les Indes." — *Niebuhr, Voyage*, ii. 12.

[Mr. Douglas (*Bombay and W. India*, ii. 7, note) writes: "High up and outside the dining-room, and which was the chapel when Parel belonged to the Jesuits, is a plaque on which is printed: — 'Built by Honourable Hornby, 1771.'"]

1554.—*Parell* is mentioned as one of 4 aldeas, "**Parell**, Varella, Varell, and Siva, attached to the *Kasbah* (*Caçabe*—see **CUSBAH**) of Maim."—*Botelho, Tombo*, 157, in *Subsidios*.

c. 1750-60. — "A place called **Parell**, where the Governor has a very agreeable country-house, which was originally a Romish chapel belonging to the Jesuits, but confiscated about the year 1719, for some foul practices against the English interest."—*Grose*, i. 46; [1st ed. 1757, p. 72].

* No doubt, however, foreign coins were used to make up sums, and reduce the bulk of small change.

PARIAH, PARRIAR, &c., s.

a. The name of a low caste of Hindus in Southern India, constituting one of the most numerous castes, if not *the* most numerous, in the Tamil country. The word in its present shape means properly 'a drummer.' Tamil *paṛai* is the large drum, beaten at certain festivals, and the hereditary beaters of it are called (sing.) *paṛaiyan*, (pl.) *paṛaiyar*. [Dr. Oppert's theory (*Orig. Inhabitants*, 32 *seq.*) that the word is a form of *Pahariyā*, 'a mountaineer' is not probable.] In the city of Madras this caste forms one fifth of the whole population, and from it come (unfortunately) most of the domestics in European service in that part of India. As with other castes low in caste-rank they are also low in habits, frequently eating carrion and other objectionable food, and addicted to drink. From their coming into contact with and under observation of Europeans, more habitually than any similar caste, the name *Pariah* has come to be regarded as applicable to the whole body of the lowest castes, or even to denote outcastes or people without any caste. But this is hardly a correct use. There are several castes in the Tamil country considered to be lower than the *Pariahs*, *e.g.* the caste of shoemakers, and the lowest caste of washermen. And the *Pariah* deals out the same disparaging treatment to these that he himself receives from higher castes. The Pariahs "constitute a well-defined, distinct, ancient caste, which has 'subdivisions' of its own, its own peculiar usages, its own traditions, and its own jealousy of the encroachments of the castes which are above it and below it. They constitute, perhaps, the most numerous caste in the Tamil country. In the city of Madras they number 21 per cent. of the Hindu people."—*Bp. Caldwell, u. i.*, p. 545. Sir Walter Elliot, however, in the paper referred to further on includes under the term *Paraiya* all the servile class not recognised by Hindus of caste as belonging to their community.

A very interesting, though not conclusive, discussion of the ethnological position of this class will be found in Bp. Caldwell's *Dravidian Grammar* (pp. 540-554). That scholar's deduction is, on the whole, that they are probably Dravidians, but he states, and recognises force in, arguments for believing that they may have descended from a race older in the country than the proper Dravidian, and reduced to slavery by the first Dravidians. This last is the view of Sir Walter Elliot, who adduces a variety of interesting facts in its favour, in his paper on the *Characteristics of the Population of South India.**

Thus, in the celebration of the Festival of the Village Goddess, prevalent all over Southern India, and of which a remarkable account is given in that paper, there occurs a sort of Saturnalia in which the Pariahs are the officiating priests, and there are several other customs which are most easily intelligible on the supposition that the Pariahs are the representatives of the earliest inhabitants and original masters of the soil. In a recent communication from this venerable man he writes: 'My brother (Col. C. Elliot, C.B.) found them at Raipur, to be an important and respectable class of cultivators. The Pariahs have a sacerdotal order amongst themselves.' [The view taken in the *Madras Gloss.* is that "they are distinctly Dravidian without fusion, as the Hinduized castes are Dravidian with fusion."]

The mistaken use of *pariah*, as synonymous with out-caste, has spread in English parlance over all India. Thus the lamented Prof. Blochmann, in his *School Geography of India:* "Outcasts are called **pariahs**." The name first became generally known in Europe through Sonnerat's *Travels* (pub. in 1782, and soon after translated into English). In this work the **Parias** figure as the lowest of castes. The common use of the term is however probably due, in both France and England, to the appearance in the Abbé Raynal's famous *Hist. Philosophique des Établissements dans les Indes*, formerly read very widely in both countries, and yet more perhaps to its use in Bernardin de St. Pierre's preposterous though once popular tale, *La Chaumière Indienne*, whence too the misplaced halo of sentiment which reached its acme in the drama of Casimir Delavigne, and which still in some degree adheres to the name. It should be added that Mr. C. P. Brown says expressly: "The word *Paria* is unknown" (in *our* sense?) "to all natives, unless as learned from us."

b. See **PARIAH-DOG.**

1516.—"There is another low sort of Gentiles, who live in desert places, called **Pareas**. These likewise have no dealings with anybody, and are reckoned worse than the devil, and avoided by everybody; a man becomes contaminated by only looking at them, and is excommunicated. . . . They live on the *imane* (*iname*, *i.e.* **yams**), which are like the root of *iucca* or *batate* found in the West Indies, and on other roots and wild fruits."—*Barbosa*, in *Ramusio*, i. f. 310. The word in the Spanish version transl. by Lord Stanley of Alderley is *Pareni*, in the Portuguese of the Lisbon Academy, *Parcens*. So we are not quite sure that *Pareas* is the proper reading, though this is probable.

1626.—". . . The **Pareas** are of worse esteeme."—(*W. Methold*, in) *Purchas, Pilgrimage*, 553.

" ". . . the worst whereof are the abhorred **Piriawes** . . . they are in publike Justice the hateful executioners, and are the basest, most stinking, ill-favored people that I have seene."—*Ibid.* 998-9.

1648.—". . . the servants of the factory even will not touch it (beef) when they put it on the table, nevertheless there is a caste called **Pareyaes** (they are the most contemned of all, so that if another Gentoo touches them, he is compelled to be dipt in the water) who eat it freely."—*Van de Broecke*, 82.

1672.—"The **Parreas** are the basest and vilest race (accustomed to remove dung and all uncleanness, and to eat mice and rats), in a word a contemned and stinking vile people."—*Baldaeus* (Germ. ed.), 410.

1711.—"The Company allow two or three Peons to attend the Gate, and a **Parrear** Fellow to keep all clean."—*Lockyer*, 20.

" "And there . . . is such a resort of basket-makers, Scavengers, people that look after the buffaloes, and other **Parriars**,

* Sir W. Elliot refers to the Aśoka inscription (Edict II.) as bearing *Palaya* or *Paraya*, named with Choḍa (or Chola), Kerala, &c., as a country or people "in the very centre of the Dravidian group . . . a reading which, if it holds good, supplies a satisfactory explanation of the origin of the Paria name and nation" (in *J. Ethnol. Soc.* N.S., 1869, p. 103). But apparently the reading has not held good, for M. Senart reads the name *Pāṁdya* (see *Ind. Ant.* ix. 287). [Mr. V. A. Smith writes: "The Girnar text is very defective in this important passage, which is not in the Dhauli text; that text gives only 11 out of the 14 edicts. The capital of the *Pāṁdiyan* Kingdom was Madura. The history of the kingdom is very imperfectly known. For a discussion of it see *Sewell, Lists of Antiquities, Madras*, vol. ii. Of course it has nothing to do with Parias."]

to drink Toddy, that all the Punch-houses in Madras have not half the noise in them." —*Wheeler*, ii. 125.

1716.—"A young lad of the Left-hand Caste having done hurt to a **Pariah** woman of the Right-Hand Caste (big with child), the whole caste got together, and came in a tumultuous manner to demand justice."—*Ibid.* 230.

1717.—". . . **Barrier**, or a sort of poor people that eat all sort of Flesh and other things, which others deem unclean."—*Phillips, Account*, &c., 127.

1726.—"As for the separate generations and sorts of people who embrace this religion, there are, according to what some folks say, only 4; but in our opinion they are 5 in number, viz.:

α. The Bramins.
β. The Settreas.
γ. The Weynyas or Veynsyas.
δ. The Sudras.
ε. The **Perrias**, whom the High-Dutch and Danes call **Barriars**."—*Valentijn, Chorom.* 73.

1745.—"Les **Parreas** . . . sont regardés comme gens de la plus vile condition, exclus de tous les honneurs et prérogatives. Jusques-là qu'on ne sçauroit les souffrir, ni dans les Pagodes des Gentils, ni dans les Eglises des Jesuites."—*Norbert*, i. 71.

1750.—"*K.* Es ist der Mist von einer Kuh, denselben nehmen die **Parreyer**-Weiber, machen runde Kuchen daraus, und wenn sie in der Sonne genug getrocken sind, so verkauffen sie dieselbigen (see **OOPLAH**). *Fr.* O Wunder! Ist das das Feuerwerk, das ihr hier halt?"—*Madras*, &c., *Halle*, p. 14.

1770. — "The fate of these unhappy wretches who are known on the coast of Coromandel by the name of **Parias**, is the same even in those countries where a foreign dominion has contributed to produce some little change in the ideas of the people."—*Raynal, Hist.* &c., see ed. 1783, i. 63.

" "The idol is placed in the centre of the building, so that the **Parias** who are not admitted into the temple may have a sight of it through the gates."—*Raynal* (tr. 1777), i. p. 57.

1780.—"If you should ask a common *cooly*, or porter, what cast he is of, he will answer, 'the same as master, **pariar**-*cast*.'" —*Munro's Narrative*, 28-9.

1787.—". . . I cannot persuade myself that it is judicious to admit **Parias** into battalions with men of respectable casts. . . ."—*Col. Fullarton's View of English Interests in India*, 222.

1791.—"Le *masalchi* y courut pour allumer un flambeau; mais il revient un peu après, pris d'haleine, criant: 'N'approchez pas d'ici; il y a un **Paria**!' Aussitôt la troupe effrayée cria: 'Un **Paria**! Un **Paria**!' Le docteur, croyant que c'était quelque animal féroce, mit la main sur ses pistolets. 'Qu'est ce que qu'un **Paria**?' demanda-t-il à son porte-flambeau."—*B. de St. Pierre, La Chaumière Indienne*, 48.

1800.—"The **Parriar**, and other impure tribes, comprising what are called the *Punchum Bundum*, would be beaten, were they to attempt joining in a Procession of any of the gods of the Brahmins, or entering any of their temples."—*Buchanan's Mysore*, i. 20.

c. 1805-6. — "The Dubashes, then all powerful at Madras, threatened loss of cast and absolute destruction to any Brahmin who should dare to unveil the mysteries of their language to a **Pariar** *Frengi*. This reproach of *Pariar* is what we have tamely and strangely submitted to for a long time, when we might with a great facility have assumed the respectable character of *Chatriya*."—*Letter of Leyden*, in *Morton's Memoir*, ed. 1819, p. lxvi.

1809.—"Another great obstacle to the reception of Christianity by the Hindoos, is the admission of the **Parias** in our Churches. . . ."—*Ld. Valentia*, i. 246.

1821.—

"Il est sur ce rivage une race flètrie,
Une race étrangère au sein de sa patrie.
Sans abri protecteur, sans temple hospitalier,
Abominable, impie, horrible au peuple entier.
Les **Parias**; le jour à regret les éclaire,
La terre sur son sein les porte avec colère.
* * * * * *
Eh bien! mais je frémis; tu vas me fuir peut-être;
Je suis un **Paria**. . . ."
Casimir Delavigne, Le Paria, Acte 1. Sc. 1.

1843. — "The Christian **Pariah**, whom both sects curse, Does all the good he can and loves his brother."—*Forster's Life of Dickens*, ii. 31.

1873.—"The Tamilas hire a **Pariya** (*i.e.* drummer) to perform the decapitation at their Badra Kâli sacrifices."—*Kittel*, in *Ind. Ant.* ii. 170.

1878. — "L'hypothèse la plus vraisemblable, en tout cas la plus heureuse, est celle qui suppose que le nom propre et spécial de cette race [*i.e.* of the original race inhabiting the Deccan before contact with northern invaders] était le mot '**paria**'; ce mot dont l'orthographe correcte est **pareiya**, derivé de *par'ei*, 'bruit, tambour,' et à très-bien, pu avoir le sens de 'parleur, doué de la parole'" (?)—*Hovelacque et Vinson, Etudes de Linguistique*, &c., Paris, 67.

1872.—

"Fifine, ordained from first to last,
In body and in soul
For one life-long debauch,
The **Pariah** of the north,
The European *nautch*."
Browning, Fifine at the Fair.

Very good rhyme, but no reason. See under **NAUTCH**.

The word seems also to have been adopted in Java, *e.g.*:

1860.—"We Europeans . . . often . . . stand far behind compared with the poor **pariahs**."—*Max Havelaar*, ch. vii.

PARIAH-ARRACK, s. In the 17th and 18th centuries this was a name commonly given to the poisonous native spirit commonly sold to European soldiers and sailors. [See **FOOL'S RACK.**]

1671-72.—"The unwholesome liquor called **Parrier-arrack.** . . ."—*Sir W. Langhorne*, in *Wheeler*, iii. 422.

1711.—"The Tobacco, Beetle, and **Pariar Arack,** on which such great profit arises, are all expended by the Inhabitants."—*Lockyer*, 13.

1754.—"I should be very glad to have your order to bring the ship up to Calcutta . . . as . . . the people cannot here have the opportunity of intoxicating and killing themselves with **Pariar Arrack.**"—In *Long*, 51.

PARIAH-DOG, s. The common ownerless yellow dog, that frequents all inhabited places in the East, is universally so called by Europeans, no doubt from being a low-bred casteless animal; often elliptically '**pariah**' only.

1789.—". . . A species of the common cur, called a **pariar-dog.**"—*Munro, Narr.* p. 36.

1810. — "The nuisance may be kept circling for days, until forcibly removed, or until the **pariah dogs** swim in, and draw the carcase to the shore."—*Williamson, V. M.* ii. 261.

1824.—"The other beggar was a **Pariah dog,** who sneaked down in much bodily fear to our bivouac."—*Heber*, ed. 1844, i. 79.

1875.—"Le Musulman qui va prier à la mosquée, maudit les **parias** honnis."—*Rev. des Deux Mondes*, April, 539.

[1883.—"**Paraya Dogs** are found in every street."—*T. V. Row, Man. of Tanjore Dist.* 104.]

PARIAH-KITE, s. The commonest Indian kite, *Milvus Govinda*, Sykes, notable for its great numbers, and its impudence. "They are excessively bold and fearless, often snatching morsels off a dish *en route* from kitchen to hall, and even, according to Adams, seizing a fragment from a man's very mouth" (*Jerdon*). Compare quotation under **BRAHMINY KITE.**

[1880.—"I had often supposed that the scavenger or **Pariah Kites** (*Milvus govinda*), which though generally to be seen about the tents, are not common in the jungles, must follow the camp for long distances, and today I had evidence that such was the case. . . ."—*Ball, Jungle Life*, 655.]

PARSEE, n.p. This name, which distinguishes the descendants of those emigrants of the old Persian stock, who left their native country, and, retaining their Zoroastrian religion, settled in India to avoid Mahommedan persecution, is only the old form of the word for a Persian, viz., *Pārsī*, which Arabic influences have in more modern times converted into *Fārsī*. The Portuguese have used both *Parseo* and *Perseo*. From the latter some of our old travellers have taken the form *Persee*; from the former doubtless we got *Parsee*. It is a curious example of the way in which different accidental mouldings of the same word come to denote entirely different ideas, that Persian, in this form, in Western India, means a Zoroastrian fire-worshipper, whilst *Pathi* (see **PANTHAY**), a Burmese corruption of the same word, in Burma means a Mahommedan.

c. 1328. — "There be also other pagan-folk in this India who worship fire; they bury not their dead, neither do they burn them, but cast them into the midst of a certain roofless tower, and there expose them totally uncovered to the fowls of heaven. These believe in two First Principles, to wit, of Evil and of Good, of Darkness and of Light."—*Friar Jordanus*, 21.

1552.—"In any case he dismissed them with favour and hospitality, showing himself glad of the coming of such personages, and granting them protection for their ships as being (**Parseos**) Persians of the Kingdom of Ormuz."—*Barros*, I. viii. 9.

" ". . . especially after these were induced by the Persian and Guzerati Moors (*Mouros*, **Parseos** *e Guzarates*) to be converted from heathen (*Gentios*) to the sect of Mahamed."—*Ibid.* II. vi. i.

[1563. — "There are other herb-sellers (*mercadores de boticas*) called Coaris, and in the Kingdom of Cambay they call them **Esparcis,** and we Portuguese call them Jews, but they are not, only Hindus who came from Persia and have their own writing."—*Garcia*, p. 213.]

1616. — "There is one sect among the Gentiles, which neither burne nor interre their dead (they are called **Parcees**) who incircle pieces of ground with high stone walls, remote from houses or Road-wayes, and therein lay their Carcasses, wrapped in Sheetes, thus having no other Tombes but the gorges of rauenous Fowles."—*Terry*, in *Purchas*, ii. 1479.

1630.—"Whilst my observation was bestowed on such inquiry, I observed in the town of Surrat, the place where I resided, another Sect called the **Persees.** . . ."—*Lord, Two Forraigne Sects.*

1638.—"Outre les Benjans il y a encore vne autre sorte de Payens dans le royaume de *Gusuratte*, qu'ils appellent **Parsis**. Ce sont des Perses de Fars, et de Chorasan."—*Mandelslo* (Paris, 1659), 213.

1648.—"They (the **Persians** of India, *i.e.* *Parsees*) are in general a fast-gripping and avaricious nation (not unlike the Benyans and the Chinese), and very fraudulent in buying and selling."—*Van Twist*, 48.

1653.—"Les Ottomans appellent *gueuure* vne secte de Payens, que nous connaissons sous le nom d'adorateurs du feu, les Persans sous celuy d'*Atechperés*, et les Indous sous celuy de **Parsi**, terme dont ils se nomment eux-mesmes."—*De la Boullaye-le-Gouz*, ed. 1657, p. 200.

1672.—"Non tutti ancora de' Gentili sono d' vna medesima fede. Alcuni descendono dalli **Persiani**, li quali si conoscono dal colore, ed adorano il fuoco. . . . In Suratte ne trouai molti. . . ."—*P. F. Vincenzo Maria, Viaggio*, 234.

1673.—"On this side of the Water are people of another Offspring than those we have yet mentioned, these be called **Parseys** . . . these are somewhat white, and I think nastier than the Gentues. . . ."—*Fryer*, 117.

,, "The **Parsies**, as they are called, are of the old Stock of the Persians, worship the Sun and Adore the Elements; are known only about Surat."—*Ibid.* p. 197.

1689.—". . . the **Persies** are a Sect very considerable in India. . . ."—*Ovington*, 370.

1726.—". . . to say a word of a certain other sort of Heathen who have spread in the City of Suratte and in its whole territory, and who also maintain themselves in Agra, and in various places of Persia, especially in the Province of Kerman, at Yezd, and in Ispahan. They are commonly called by the Indians **Persees or Parsis**, but by the Persians *Gaurs* or *Gebbers*, and also *Atech Peres* or adorers of Fire."—*Valentijn*, iv. (*Suratte*) 153.

1727.—"The **Parsees** are numerous about Surat and the adjacent Countries. They are a remnant of the ancient Persians."—*A. Hamilton*, ch. xiv; [ed. 1744, i. 159].

1877.—". . . en se levant, le **Parsi**, après s'être lavé les mains et la figure avec l'urine du taureau, met sa ceinture en disant: Souverain soit Ormuzd, abattu soit Ahrimān."—*Darmesteter, Ormuzd et Ahriman*, p. 2.

PARVOE, PURVO, s. The popular name of the writer-caste in Western India, *Prabhū* or *Parbhū*, 'lord or chief' (Skt. *prabhu*), being an honorific title assumed by the caste of *Kāyath* or *Kāyastha*, one of the mixt castes which commonly furnished writers. A Bombay term only.

1548.—"And to the **Parvu** of the *Tenadar Mor* 1800 reis a year, being 3 *pardaos* a month. . . ."—*S. Botelho, Tombo*, 211.

[1567.—See *Paibus* under **CASIS**.

[1676-7. — ". . . the same guards the **Purvos** y^t^ look after ye Customes for the same charge can receive ye passage boats rent. . . ."—*Forrest, Bombay Letters, Home Series*, i. 125.

[1773.—"*Conucopola* (see **CONICOPOLY**). . . . At Bombay he is stiled **Purvo**, and is of the Gentoo religion."—*Ives*, 49 *seq.*]

1809. — "The Bramins of this village speak and write English; the young men are mostly **parvoes**, or writers."—*Maria Graham*, 11.

1813. — "These writers at Bombay are generally called **Purvoes**; a faithful diligent class."—*Forbes, Or. Mem.* i. 156-157; [2nd ed. i. 100].

1833. — "Every native of India on the Bombay Establishment, who can write English, and is employed in any office, whether he be a Brahman, Goldsmith, Parwary, Portuguese, or of English descent, is styled a **Purvoe**, from several persons of a caste of Hindoos termed *Prubhoe* having been among the first employed as English writers at Bombay." — *Mackintosh on the Tribe of Ramoosies*, p. 77.

PASADOR, s. A marlin-spike. Sea-Hind., from Port. *passador*.—*Roebuck*.

PASEI, PACEM, n.p. The name of a Malay State near the N.E. point of Sumatra, at one time predominant in those regions, and reckoned, with Malacca and Majapahit (the capital of the Empire of Java), the three greatest cities of the Archipelago. It is apparently the *Basma* of Marco Polo, who visited the coast before Islam had gained a footing.

c. 1292.—"When you quit the kingdom of Ferlec you enter upon that of **Basma**. This also is an independent kingdom, and the people have a language of their own; but they are just like beasts, without laws or religion."—*Marco Polo*, Bk. iii. ch. 9.

1511.—"Next day we departed with the plunder of the captured vessel, which also we had with us; we took our course forward until we reached another port in the same island Trapobana (Sumatra), which was called **Pazze**; and anchoring in the said port we found at anchor there several junks and ships from divers parts."—*Empoli*, p. 53.

1553.—"In the same manner he (Diogo Lopes) was received in the kingdom of **Pacem** . . . and as the King of Pedir had given him a cargo of pepper . . . he did not think well to go further . . . in case . . . they should give news of his coming at Malaca, those two ports of Pedir and **Pacem** being much frequented by a multitude of ships that go there for cargoes."—*Barros*, II. iv. 31.

1726.—"Next to this and close to the East-point of Sumatra is the once especially famous city **Pasi (or Pacem)**, which in old times, next to Magapahit and Malakka, was one of the three greatest cities of the East . . . but now is only a poor open village with not more than 4 or 500 families, dwelling in poor bamboo cottages."—*Valentijn*, (v.) *Sumatra*, 10.

1727.—"And at **Pissang**, about 10 Leagues to the Westward of Diamond Point, there is a fine deep River, but not frequented, because of the treachery and bloody disposition of the Natives."—*A. Hamilton*, ii. 125; [ed. 1744].

PĀT, s. A can or pot. Sea-Hind. from English.—*Roebuck*.

PATACA, PATACOON, s. Ital. *patacco;* Provenc. *patac;* Port. *patàca* and *patação;* also used in Malayālam. A term, formerly much diffused, for a dollar or piece of eight. Littré connects it with an old French word *patard*, a kind of coin, "du reste, origine inconnue." But he appears to have overlooked the explanation indicated by Volney (*Voyage en Egypte*, &c., ch. ix. note) that the name *abūṭāka* (or corruptly *bāṭāka*, see also *Dozy & Eng.* s.v.) was given by the Arabs to certain coins of this kind with a scutcheon on the reverse, the term meaning 'father of the window, or niche'; the scutcheon being taken for such an object. Similarly, the pillar-dollars are called in modern Egypt *abū medfa'*, 'father of a cannon'; and the Maria Theresa dollar *abū tēra*, 'father of the bird.' But on the Red Sea, where only the coinage of one particular year (or the modern imitation thereof, still struck at Trieste from the old die), is accepted, it is *abū nukāṭ*, 'father of dots,' from certain little points which mark the right issue.

[1528.—"Each of the men engaged in the attack on Purakkat received no less than 800 gold **Pattaks** (ducats) as his share."—*Logan, Malabar*, i. 329.

[1550.—"And afterwards while Viceroy Dom Affonso Noronha ordered silver coins to be made, which were patecoons (**patecoes**)."—*Arch. Port. Orient.*, Fasc. ii. No. 54 of 1569.]

PATCH, s. "Thin pieces of cloth at Madras" (*Indian Vocabulary*, 1788). Wilson gives **patch** as a vulgar abbreviation for Telug. *pach'chadamu*, 'a particular kind of cotton cloth, generally 24 cubits long and 2 broad; two cloths joined together.'

[1667.—"Pray if can procuer a good Pallenkeen bambo and 2 **patch** of ye finest with what colours you thinke hansome for my own wear, chockoloes and susaes (see **SOOSIE**)."—In *Yule, Hedges' Diary*, Hak. Soc. ii. cclxii.]

PATCHARÉE, PATCHERRY, PARCHERRY, s. In the Bengal Presidency, before the general construction of 'married quarters' by Government, *patcharée* was the name applied in European corps to the cottages which used to form the quarters of married soldiers. The origin of the word is obscure, and it has been suggested that it was a corruption of Hind. *pichch'hāṛī*, 'the rear,' because these cottages were in rear of the barracks. But we think it most likely that the word was brought, with many other terms peculiar to the British soldier in India, from Madras, and is identical with a term in use there, *parcherry* or *patcherry*, which represents the Tam. *parash'shēri*, *paraiççeri*, 'a Pariah village,' or rather the quarter or outskirts of a town or village where the Pariahs reside. Mr. Whitworth (s.v. *Patcherry*) says that "in some native regiments the term denotes the married sepoys' quarters, possibly because Pariah sepoys had their families with them, while the higher castes left them at home." He does not say whether Bombay or Madras sepoys are in question. But in any case what he states confirms the origin ascribed to the Bengal Presidency term *Patcharée*.

1747.—"**Patcheree Point**, mending Platforms and Gunports . . . (Pgs.) 4 : 21 : 48."—*Accounts from Ft. St. David*, under Feb. 21. MS. Records, in India Office.

1781.—"Leurs maisons (c.-à.-d. des *Parias*) sont des cahutes où un homme peut à peine entrer, et elles forment de petits villages qu'on appelle **Paretcheris**."—*Sonnerat*, ed. 1782, i. 98.

1878.—"During the greater portion of the year extra working gangs of scavengers were kept for the sole purpose of going from **Parcherry** to **Parcherry** and cleaning them."—*Report of Madras Municipality*, p. 24.

c. 1880.—"Experience obtained in Madras some years ago with reconstructed **parcherries**, and their effect on health, might be imitated possibly with advantage in Calcutta."—*Report by Army Sanitary Commission*.

PATCHOULI, PATCH-LEAF, also **PUTCH** and **PUTCHA-LEAF**, s. In Beng. *pachapāt;* Deccani Hind.

pacholī. The latter are trade names of the dried leaves of a labiate plant allied to mint (*Pogostemon patchouly*, Pelletier). It is supposed to be a cultivated variety of *Pogostemon Heyneanus*, Bentham, a native of the Deccan. It is grown in native gardens throughout India, Ceylon, and the Malay Islands, and the dried flowering spikes and leaves of the plant, which are used, are sold in every bazar in Hindustan. The *pacha-pāt* is used as an ingredient in tobacco for smoking, as hair-scent by women, and especially for stuffing mattresses and laying among clothes as we use lavender. In a fluid form *patchouli* was introduced into England in 1844, and soon became very fashionable as a perfume.

The origin of the word is a difficulty. The name is alleged in Drury, and in Forbes Watson's *Nomenclature* to be Bengāli. Littré says the word *patchouli* is *patchey-elley*, 'feuille de patchey'; in what language we know not; perhaps it is from Tamil *pachcha*, 'green,' and *ĕlâ*, *ĕlam*, an aromatic perfume for the hair. [The *Madras Gloss.* gives Tamil *paççilai*, *paççai*, 'green,' *ilai*, 'leaf.']

1673.—"*Note*, that if the following Goods from *Acheen* hold out the following *Rates*, the Factor employed is no further responsible.

* * * * *

Patch Leaf, 1 *Bahar Maunds* 7 20 *sear*."—*Fryer*, 209.

PATECA, s. This word is used by the Portuguese in India for a water-melon (*Citrullus vulgaris*, Schrader; *Cucurbita Citrullus*, L.). It is from the Ar. *al-baṭṭīkh* or *al-biṭṭīkh*. F. Johnson gives this 'a melon, musk-melon. A pumpkin; a cucurbitaceous plant.' We presume that this is not merely the too common dictionary looseness, for the chaos of cucurbitaceous nomenclature, both vulgar and scientific, is universal (see *A. De Candolle, Origine des Plantes cultivées*). In Lane's *Modern Egyptians* (ed. 1837, i. 200) the word *butteekh* is rendered explicitly 'water-melon.' We have also in Spanish *albadeca*, which is given by Dozy and Eng. as 'espèce de melon'; and we have French *pastèque*, which we believe always means a water-melon. De Candolle seems to have no doubt that the water-melon was cultivated in ancient Egypt, and believes it to have been introduced into the Graeco-Roman world about the beginning of our era; whilst Hehn carries it to Persia from India, 'whether at the time of the Arabian or of the Mongol domination, (and then) to Greece, through the medium of the Turks, and to Russia, through that of the Tartar States of Astrakan and Kazan.'

The name **pateca**, looking to the existence of the same word in Spanish, we should have supposed to have been Portuguese long before the Portuguese establishment in India; yet the whole of what is said by Garcia de Orta is inconsistent with this. In his *Colloquio XXXVI.* the gist of the dialogue is that his visitor from Europe, Ruano, tells how he had seen what seemed a most beautiful melon, and how Garcia's housekeeper recommended it, but on trying it, it tasted only of mud instead of melon! Garcia then tells him that at Diu, and in the Bālaghāt, &c., he would find excellent melons with the flavour of the melons of Portugal but "those others which the Portuguese here in India call **patecas** are quite another thing—huge round or oval fruits, with black seeds—not sweet (*doce*) like the Portugal melons, but bland (*suave*), most juicy and cooling, excellent in bilious fevers, and congestions of the liver and kidneys, &c." Both name and thing are represented as novelties to Ruano. Garcia tells him also that the Arabs and Persians call it *batiec indi*, *i.e.* melon of India (F. Johnson gives '*biṭṭīkh-i-hindī*, the citrul'; whilst in Persian *hinduwāna* is also a word for water-melon) but that the real Indian country name was (*calangari* Mahr. *kālingar*, [perhaps that known in the N.W.P. as *kalindā*, 'a water-melon']). Ruano then refers to the *budiecas* of Castille of which he had heard, and queries if these were not the same as these Indian **patecas**, but Garcia says they are quite different. All this is curious as implying that the water-melon was strange to the Portuguese at that time (1563; see *Colloquios*, f. 141v. *seqq.*).

[A friend who has Burnell's copy of Garcia De Orta tells me that he finds a note in the writing of the former on *bateca*: "*i.e.* the Arabic term. As this is used all over India, water-melons must have been imported by the Mahommedans." I believe it to be a mistake that the word is in use all over India. I do not think the word is ever used in Upper India, nor is it (in that sense) in either Shakespear or Fallon. [Platts gives: A. *biṭṭīkh*, s.m. The melon (*kharbūza*); the water-melon, *Cucurbita citrullus.*] The most common word in the N.W.P. for a water-melon is Pers. *tarbūz*, whilst the musk-melon is Pers. *kharbūza*. And these words are so rendered from the *Āīn* respectively by Blochmann (see his E.T. i. 66, "melons. . . water-melons," and the original i. 67, "*kharbuza. . . tarbuz*"). But with the usual chaos already alluded to, we find both these words interpreted in F. Johnson as "water-melon." And according to Hehn the latter is called in the Slav tongues *arbuz* and in Mod. Greek *καρπούσια*, the first as well as the last probably from the Turkish *ḳārpūz*, which has the same meaning, for this hard *ḳ* is constantly dropt in modern pronunciation.—H. Y.]

We append a valuable note on this from Prof. Robertson-Smith:

"(1) The classical form of the Ar. word is *biṭṭīkh*. *Baṭṭīkh* is a widely-spread vulgarism, indeed now, I fancy, universal, for I don't think I ever heard the first syllable pronounced with an *i*.

"(2) The term, according to the law-books, includes all kinds of melons (*Lane*); but practically it is applied (certainly at least in Syria and Egypt) almost exclusively to the water-melon, unless it has a limiting adjective. Thus "the wild *biṭṭīkh*" is the colocynth, and with other adjectives it may be used of very various cucurbitaceous fruits (see examples in Dozy's *Suppt.*)

"(6) The biblical form is *ăbaṭṭīkh* (*e.g.* Numbers xi. 5, where the E.V. has 'melons'). But this is only the 'water-melon'; for in the Mishna it is distinguished from the sweet melon, the latter being named by a mere transcription in Hebrew letters of the Greek *μηλοπέπων*. Löw justly concludes that the Palestinians (and the Syrians, for their name only differs slightly) got the sweet melon from the Greeks, whilst for the water-melon they have an old and probably true Semitic word. For *baṭṭīkh* Syriac has *paṭṭīkh*, indicating that in literary Arabic the *a* has been changed to *i*, only to agree with rules of grammar. Thus popular pronunciation seems always to have kept the old form, as popular usage seems always to have used the word mainly in its old specific meaning. The Bible and the Mishna suffice to refute Hehn's view (of the introduction of the water-melon from India). Old Kimḥi, in his *Miklol*, illustrates the Hebrew word by the Spanish *budiecas*."

1598.—". . . ther is an other sort like *Melons*, called **Patecas** or *Angurias*, or *Melons of India*, which are outwardlie of a darke greene colour; inwardlie white with blacke kernels; they are verie waterish and hard to byte, and so moyst, that as a man eateth them his mouth is full of water, but yet verie sweet and verie cold and fresh meat, wherefore manie of them are eaten after dinner to coole men."—*Linschoten*, 97; [Hak. Soc. ii. 35].

c. 1610.—"Toute la campagne est couverte d'arbres fruitiers . . . et d'arbres de coton, de quantité de melons et de **pateques**, qui sont espèce de citrouilles de prodigieuse grosseur. . . ."—*Pyrard de Laval*, ed. 1679, i. 286; [Hak. Soc. i. 399, and see i. 33].

,, A few pages later the word is written **Pasteques.**—*Ibid.* 301; [Hak. Soc. i. 417].

[1663.—"**Pateques**, or water-melons, are in great abundance nearly the whole year round: but those of *Delhi* are soft, without colour or sweetness. If this fruit be ever found good, it is among the wealthy people, who import the seed and cultivate it with much care and expense."—*Bernier*, ed. *Constable*, 250.]

1673.—"From hence (Elephanta) we sailed to the *Putachoes*, a Garden of Melons (**Putacho** being a Melon) were there not wild Rats that hinder their growth, and so to *Bombaim.*"—*Fryer*, 76.

PATEL, POTAIL, s. The head-man of a village, having general control of village affairs, and forming the medium of communication with the officers of Government. In Mahr. *paṭīl*, Hind. *paṭel*. The most probable etym. seems to be from *paṭ*, Mahr. 'a roll or. register,' Skt.—Hind. *paṭṭa*. The title is more particularly current in territories that are or have been subject to the Mahrattas, "and appears to be an essentially Maráthi word, being used as a respectful title in addressing one of that nation, or a Súdra in general" (*Wilson*). The office is hereditary, and is often held under a Government grant. The title is not used in the Gangetic Provinces, but besides its use in Central and W. India it has been commonly employed in S. India, probably as a Hindustani word, though *Monigar* (see **MONEGAR**)

(*Maniyakāram*), *adhikārī* (see **ADIGAR**), &c., are appropriate synonyms in Tamil and Malabar districts.

[1535.—"The **Tanadars** began to come in and give in their submission, bringing with them all the patels (**pateis**) and renters with their payments, which they paid to the Governor, who ordered fresh records to be prepared."—*Couto*, Dec. IV. Bk. ix. ch. 2 (description of the commencement of Portuguese rule in Bassein).

[1614.—"I perceive that you are troubled with a bad commodity, wherein the desert of **Patell** and the rest appeareth."—*Foster, Letters*, ii. 281.]

1804.—"The **Patel** of Beitculgaum, in the usual style of a Mahratta **patel**, keeps a band of plunderers for his own profit and advantage. You will inform him that if he does not pay for the horses, bullocks, and articles plundered, he shall be hanged also." —*Wellington*, March 27.

1809.—". . . **Pattels**, or headmen."—*Lord Valentia*, i. 415.

1814.—"At the settling of the *jummabundee*, they pay their proportion of the village assessment to government, and then dispose of their grain, cotton, and fruit, without being accountable to the **patell**."—*Forbes, Or. Mem.* ii. 418; [2nd ed. ii. 44].

1819.—"The present system of Police, as far as relates to the villagers may easily be kept up; but I doubt whether it is enough that the village establishment be maintained, and the whole put under the **Mamlutdar**. The **Potail's** respectability and influence in the village must be kept up."—*Elphinstone*, in *Life*, ii. 81.

1820.—"The **Patail** holds his office direct of Government, under a written obligation . . . which specifies his duties, his rank, and the ceremonies of respect he is entitled to; and his perquisites, and the quantity of freehold land allotted to him as wages." —*T. Coats*, in *Tr. Bo. Lit. Soc.* iii. 183.

1823.—"The heads of the family . . . have purchased the office of **Potail**, or headman."—*Malcolm, Central India*, i. 99.

1826.—"The **potail** offered me a room in his own house, and I very thankfully accepted it."—*Pandurang Hari*, ed. 1877, p. 241; [ed. 1873, ii. 45].

1851.—"This affected humility was in fact one great means of effecting his elevation. When at Poonah he (Madhajee Sindea) . . . instead of arrogating any exalted title, would only suffer himself to be called **Pateil**. . . ."—*Fraser, Mil. Mem. of Skinner*, i. 33.

1870.—"The **Potail** accounted for the revenue collections, receiving the perquisites and percentages, which were the accustomed dues of the office."—*Systems of Land Tenure* (Cobden Club), 163.

PATNA, n.p. The chief city of Bahar; and the representative of the *Palibothra* (*Pātaliputra*) of the Greeks. Hind. *Paṭṭana*, "the city." [See quotation from D'Anville under **ALLAHABAD**.]

1586. — "From Bannaras I went to **Patenaw** downe the riuer of Ganges. . . . **Patenaw** is a very long and a great towne. In times past it was a kingdom, but now it is vnder Zelabdim Echebar, the great Mogor. . . . In this towne there is a trade of cotton, and cloth of cotton, much sugar, which they carry from hence to Bengala and India, very much Opium, and other commodities."—*R. Fitch*, in *Hakl.* ii. 388.

1616.—"*Bengala*, a most spacious and fruitful Province, but more properly to be called a kingdom, which hath two very large Provinces within it, *Purb* (see **POORUB**) and **Patan**, the one lying on the east, and the other on the west side of the River Ganges."—*Terry*, ed. 1665, p. 357.

[1650.—"**Patna** is one of the largest towns in India, on the margin of the Ganges, on its western side, and it is not less than two *coss* in length."—*Tavernier*, ed. *Ball*. i. 121 *seq.*]

1673. — "*Sir William Langham* . . . is Superintendent over all the Factories on the coast of *Coromandel*, as far as the Bay of *Bengala*, and up Huygly River . . . viz. *Fort St. George*, alias *Maderas, Pettipolee, Mechlapatan, Gundore, Medapollon, Balasore, Bengala, Huygly, Castle Buzzar*, **Pattanaw**." —*Fryer*, 38.

1726.—"If you go higher up the Ganges to the N. W. you come to the great and famous trading city of **Pattena**, capital of the Kingdom of Behar, and the residence of the Vice-roy."—*Valentijn*, v. 164.

1727.—"**Patana** is the next Town frequented by Europeans . . . for Saltpetre and raw Silk. It produces also so much Opium, that it serves all the Countries in India with that commodity."—*A. Hamilton*, ii. 21; [ed. 1744].

PATOLA, s. Canarese and Malayāl. *paṭṭuda*, 'a silk-cloth.' In the fourth quotation it is rather misapplied to the Ceylon dress (see **COMBOY**).

1516.—"Coloured cottons and silks which the Indians call **patola**."—*Barbosa*, 184.

1522.—". . . **Patolos** of silk, which are cloths made at Cambaya that are highly prized at Malaca."—*Correa, Lendas*, ii. 2, 714.

1545.—". . . homems . . . enchachados com **patolas** de seda." — *Pinto*, ch. clx. (*Cogan*, p. 219).

1552.—"They go naked from the waist upwards, and below it they are clothed with silk and cotton which they call **patolas**."—*Castanheda*, ii. 78.

[1605. — "**Pattala**." — *Birdwood, Letter Book*, 74.]

1614.—". . . **Patollas**. . . ."—*Peyton*, in *Purchas*, i. 530.

PATTAMAR, PATIMAR, &c. This word has two senses :

a. A foot-runner, a courier. In this use the word occurs only in the older writers, especially Portuguese.

b. A kind of lateen-rigged ship, with one, two, or three masts, common on the west coast. This sense seems to be comparatively modern. In both senses the word is perhaps the Konkani *path-mār*, 'a courier.' C. P. Brown, however, says that *patta-mar*, applied to a vessel, is Malayāl. signifying "goose-wing." Molesworth's *Mahr. Dict.* gives both *patemārī* and *phatemārī* for "a sort of swift-sailing vessel, a *pattymar*," with the etym. "tidings-bringer." *Patta* is 'tidings,' but the second part of the word so derived is not clear. Sir. J. M. Campbell, who is very accurate, in the *Bo. Gazetteer* writes of the vessel as *pātimār*, though identifying, as we have done, both uses with *pathmār*, 'courier.' The Moslem, he says, write *phatemārī* quasi *fath-mār*, 'snake of victory' (?). [The *Madras Gloss.* gives Mal. *pattamāri*, Tam. *pāttimār*, from *patār*, Hind. 'tidings' (not in Platts), *māri*, Mahr. 'carrier.'] According to a note in *Notes and Extracts*, No. 1 (Madras, 1871), p. 27, under a Ft. St. Geo. Consultation of July 4, 1673, *Pattamar* is therein used "for a native vessel on the Coromandel Coast, though now confined to the Western Coast." We suspect a misapprehension. For in the following entry we have no doubt that the parenthetical gloss is wrong, and that *couriers* are meant :

"A letter sent to the President and Councell at Surratt by a Pair of **Pattamars** (native craft) express. . . ."—*Op. cit.* No. ii. p. 8. [On this word see further Sir H. Yule's note on *Linschoten*, Hak. Soc. ii. 165.]

a.—

1552.—". . . But Lorenço de Brito, seeing things come to such a pass that certain Captains of the King (of Cananor) with troops chased him to the gates, he wrote to the Viceroy of the position in which he was by **Patamares**, who are men that make great journeys by land."—*De Barros*, II. i. 5.

The word occurs repeatedly in *Correa, Lendas, e.g.* III. i. 108, 149, &c.

1598.—". . . There are others that are called **Patamares**, which serue onlie for Messengers or Posts, to carie letters from place to place by land in winter-time when men cannot travaile by sea."—*Linschoten*, 78 ; [Hak. Soc. i. 260, and see ii. 165].

1606.—"The eight and twentieth, a **Pattemar** told that the Governor was a friend to us only in shew, wishing the *Portugalls* in our roome ; for we did no good in the Country, but brought Wares which they were forced to buy. . . ."—*Roger Hawes*, in *Purchas*, i. 605.

[1616.—"The **Patamar** (for so in this country they call poor footmen that are letter-bearers). . . ."—*Foster*, *Letters*, iv. 227.]

1666.—"Tranquebar, qui est eloigné de Saint Thomé de cinq journées d'un Courier à pié, qu'on appelle **Patamar**."—*Thevenot*, v. 275.

1673.—"After a month's Stay here a **Patamar** (a Foot Post) from *Fort St. George* made us sensible of the Dutch being gone from thence to Ceylon."—*Fryer*, 36.

[1684.—"The **Pattamars** that went to Codaloor by reason of the deepness of the Rivers were forced to Return. . . ."—*Pringle*, *Diary Ft. St. Geo.* 1st ser. iii. 133.]

1689.—"A **Pattamar**, *i.e.* a Foot Messenger, is generally employ'd to carry them (letters) to the remotest Bounds of the Empire."—*Ovington*, 251.

1705.—"Un **Patemare** qui est un homme du Pais ; c'est ce que nous appellons un exprès. . . ."—*Luillier*, 43.

1758.—"Yesterday returned a **Pattamar** or express to our Jew merchant from Aleppo, by the way of the Desert. . . ."—*Ives*, 297.

c. 1760.—"Between Bombay and Surat there is a constant intercourse preserved, not only by sea . . . but by **Pattamars**, or foot-messengers overland."—*Grose*, i. 119. This is the last instance we have met of the word in this sense, which is now quite unknown to Englishmen.

b.—

1600.—". . . Escrevia que hum barco pequeno, dos que chamam **patamares**, se meteria. . . ."—*Lucena*, *Vida do P. F. Xavier*, 185.

[1822.—"About 12 o'clock on the same night they embarked in **Paddimars** for Cochin."—*Wallace*, *Fifteen Years*, 206.]

1834.—A description of the **Patamárs**, with a plate, is given in Mr. John Edye's paper on Indian coasting vessels, in vol. i. of the *R. As. Soc. Journal*.

1860.—"Among the vessels at anchor lie the dows (see **DHOW**) of the Arabs, the **petamares** of Malabar, and the dhoneys (see **DONEY**) of Coromandel."—*Tennent's Ceylon*, ii. 103.

PATTELLO, PATELLEE, s. A large flat-bottomed boat on the Ganges ; Hind. *paṭelā*. [Mr. Grierson gives among the Behar boats "the *paṭelī* or *pataili*, also called in Sāran *katrā*, on which the boards forming the sides overlap and are not joined edge to edge," with an illustration (*Bihar Peasant Life*, 42).]

[1680.—"The **Patella**; the boats that come down from Pattana with Saltpeeter or other goods, built of an Exceeding Strength and are very flatt and burthensome."—*Yule, Hedges' Diary*, Hak. Soc. ii. 15.]

1685.—"We came to a great *Godowne*, where . . . this Nabob's Son has laid in a vast quantity of Salt, here we found divers great **Patellos** taking in their lading for Pattana."—*Ibid.* Jan 6; [Hak. Soc. i. 175].

1860.—"The **Putelee** (or Kutora), or Baggage-boat of Hindostan, is a very large, flat-bottomed, clinker-built, unwieldy-looking piece of rusticity of probably . . . about 35 tons burthen; but occasionally they may be met with double this size."—*Colesworthy Grant, Rural Life in Bengal*, p. 6.

PAULIST, n.p. The Jesuits were commonly so called in India because their houses in that country were formerly always dedicated to St. Paul, the great Missionary to the Heathen. They have given up this practice since their modern re-establishment in India. They are still called *Paolotti* in Italy, especially by those who don't like them.

c. 1567.—". . . e vi sono assai Chiese dei **padri di San Paulo** i quali fanno in quei luoghi gran profitto in conuertire quei popoli."—*Federici*, in *Ramusio*, iii. 390.

1623.—"I then went to the College of the Jesuit Fathers, the Church of which, like that at Daman, at Bassaim, and at almost all the other cities of the Portuguese in India, is called **San Paolo**; whence it happens that in India the said Fathers are known more commonly by the name of **Paolisti** than by that of Jesuits."—*P. della Valle*, April 27; [iii. 135].

c. 1650.—"The *Jesuits* at *Goa* are known by the name of **Paulists**; by reason that their great Church is dedicated to St. *Paul*. Nor do they wear Hats, or Corner-Caps, as in *Europe*, but only a certain Bonnet, resembling the Skull of a Hat without the Brims."—*Tavernier*, E.T. 77; [ed. *Ball*, i. 197].

1672.—"There was found in the fortress of Cranganor a handsome convent, and Church of the **Paulists**, or disciples and followers of Ignatius Loyola. . . ."—*Baldaeus, Germ.*, p. 110. In another passage this author says they were called **Paulists** because they were first sent to India by Pope Paul III. But this is not the correct reason.

1673.—"St. Paul's was the first Monastery of the Jesuits in *Goa*, from whence they receive the name **Paulistins**."—*Fryer*, 150.

[1710.—See quotation under **COBRA DE CAPELLO**.]

1760.—"The Jesuits, who are better known in India by the appellation of **Paulists**, from their head church and convent of St. Paul's in Goa."—*Grose*, i. 50.

PAUNCHWAY, s. A light kind of boat used on the rivers of Bengal; like a large **dingy** (q.v.), with a tilted roof of matting or thatch, a mast and four oars. Beng. *panšī*, and *pansoī*. [Mr. Grierson (*Peasant Life*, 43) describes the *pansūhī* as a boat with a round bottom, but which goes in shallow water, and gives an illustration.]

[1757.—"He was then beckoning to his servant that stood in a **Ponsy** above the Gaut."—*A. Grant, Account of the Loss of Calcutta*, ed. by *Col. Temple*, p. 7.]

c. 1760.—"**Ponsways**, Guard-boats."—*Grose* (Glossary).

1780.—"The **Paunchways** are nearly of the same general construction (as budgerows), with this difference, that the greatest breadth is somewhat further aft, and the stern lower."—*Hodges*, 39-40.

1790.—"Mr. Bridgwater was driven out to sea in a common **paunchway**, and when every hope forsook him the boat floated into the harbour of Masulipatam."—*Calcutta Monthly Review*, i. 40.

1823.—". . . A **panchway**, or passage-boat . . . was a very characteristic and interesting vessel, large and broad, shaped like a snuffer-dish; a deck fore-and-aft, and the middle covered with a roof of palm-branches. . . ."—*Heber*, ed. 1844, i. 21.

1860.—". . . You may suppose that I engage neither pinnace nor *bujra* (see **BUDGEROW**), but that comfort and economy are sufficiently obtained by hiring a small *bhouliya* (see **BOLIAH**) . . . what is more likely at a fine weather season like this, a small native **punsóee**, which, with a double set of hands, or four oars, is a lighter and much quicker boat."—*C. Grant, Rural Life in Bengal*, 10 [with an illustration].

PAWL, s. Hind. *pāl*, [Skt. *paṭala*, 'a roof']. A small tent with two light poles, and steep sloping sides; no walls, or ridge-pole. I believe the statement 'no ridge-pole,' is erroneous. It is difficult to derive from memory an exact definition of tents, and especially of the difference between **pawl** and **shooldarry**. A reference to India failed in getting a reply. The **shooldarry** is not essentially different from the **pawl**, but is trimmer, tauter, better closed, and sometimes has two **flies**. [The names of tents are used in various senses in different parts. The *Madras Gloss.* defines a **paul** as "a small tent with two light poles, a ridge-bar, and steep sloping sides; the walls, if any, are very short, often not more than 6 inches high. Sometimes a second ridge above carries a second roof over the first; this makes a common shooting tent." Mr. G. R. Dampier writes: "These terms are, I think, used rather loosely in the N.W.P. **Sholdārī** generally means a servant's tent, a sort of *tente d'abri*, with very low sides: the sides are generally not more than a foot high; there are no doors only flaps at one end. **Pāl** is generally used to denote a sleeping tent for Europeans; the roof slopes on both sides from a longitudinal ridge-pole; the sides are much higher than in the **sholdārī**, and there is a door at one end; the **fly** is almost invariably single. The Raoti (see **ROWTEE**) is incorrectly used in some places to denote a sleeping **pāl**; it is, properly speaking, I believe, a larger tent, of the same kind, but with doors in the side, not at the end. In some parts I have found they use the word **pāl** as equivalent to **sholdārī** and **biltaṇ** (*? bell-tent*)."]

1785.—"Where is the great quantity of baggage belonging to you, seeing that you have nothing besides tents, **pawls**, and other such necessary articles?"—*Tippoo's Letters*, p. 49.

1793.—"There were not, I believe, more than two small **Pauls**, or tents, among the whole of the deputation that escorted us from Patna."—*Kirkpatrick's Nepaul*, p. 118.

[1809.—"The shops which compose the Bazars, are mostly formed of blankets or coarse cloth stretched over a bamboo, or some other stick for a ridge-pole, supported at either end by a forked stick fixed in the ground. These habitations are called **pals.**"—*Broughton, Letters*, ed. 1892, p. 20.]

1827.—"It would perhaps be worth while to record . . . the matériel and personnel of my camp equipment; an humble captain and single man travelling on the most economical principles. One double-poled tent, one routee (see **ROWTEE**), or small tent, a **pâl** or servants' tent, 2 elephants, 6 camels, 4 horses, a pony, a buggy, and 24 servants, besides mahouts, serwâns or camel-drivers, and tent pitchers."—*Mundy, Journal of a Tour in India*, [3rd ed. p. 8]. We may note that this is an absurd exaggeration of any equipment that, even seventy-five years since, would have characterised the march of a "humble captain travelling on economical principles," or any one under the position of a highly-placed civilian. Captain Mundy must have been enormously extravagant.

[1849.—". . . we breakfasted merrily under a **paul** (a tent without walls, just like two cards leaning against each other)."—*Mrs. Mackenzie, Life in the Mission*, ii. 141.]

PAWN, s. The **betel**-leaf (q.v.) Hind. *pān*, from Skt. *parṇa*, 'a leaf.' It is a North Indian term, and is generally used for the combination of betel, areca-nut, lime, &c., which is politely offered (along with otto of roses) to visitors, and which intimates the termination of the visit. This is more fully termed **pawn-sooparie** (*supārī*, [Skt. *supriya*, 'pleasant,'] is Hind. for areca). "These leaves are not vsed to bee eaten alone, but because of their bitternesse they are eaten with a certaine kind of fruit, which the *Malabars* and *Portugalls* call *Arecca*, the *Gusurates* and *Decanijns Suparijs*. . . ." (In *Purchas*, ii. 1781).

1616.—"The King giving mee many good words, and two pieces of his **Pawne** out of his Dish, to eate of the same he was eating. . . ."—*Sir T. Roe*, in *Purchas*, i. 576; [Hak. Soc. ii. 453].

[1623.—". . . a plant, whose leaves resemble a Heart, call'd here **pan**, but in other parts of India, Betle."—*P. della Valle*, Hak. Soc. i. 36.]

1673.—". . . it is the only Indian entertainment, commonly called **Pawn.**"—*Fryer*, p. 140.

1809.—"On our departure **pawn** and roses were presented, but we were spared the *attar*, which is every way detestable."—*Ld. Valentia*, i. 101.

PAWNEE, s. Hind. *pānī*, 'water.' The word is used extensively in Anglo-Indian compound names, such as **bilayutee pawnee**, 'soda-water,' brandy-**pawnee**, *Khush-bo* **pawnee** (for European scents), &c., &c. An old friend, Gen. J. T. Boileau, R.E. (Bengal), contributes from memory the following Hindi ode to Water, on the Pindaric theme ἄριστον μὲν ὕδωρ, or the Thaletic one ἀρχὴ δὲ τῶν πάντων ὕδωρ!

"**Pānī** kūā, pānī tāl;
Pānī āṭā, pānī dāl;
Pānī bāgh, pānī ramnā;
Pānī Gangā, pānī Jumnā;
Pānī haṅstā, pānī rotā;
Pānī jagtā, pānī sotā;
Pānī bāp, pānī mā;
Barā nām **Pānī** kā!"

Thus rudely done into English:

"Thou, Water, stor'st our Wells and Tanks,
Thou fillest Gunga's, Jumna's banks;
Thou Water, sendest daily food,
And fruit and flowers and needful wood;
Thou, Water, laugh'st, thou, Water, weepest;
Thou, Water, wak'st, thou, Water, sleepest;
—Father, Mother, in thee blent,—
Hail, O glorious element!"

PAWNEE, KALLA, s. Hind. *kālā pānī*, *i.e.* 'Black Water'; the name of dread by which natives of the interior of India designate the Sea, with especial reference to a voyage across it, and to transportation to penal settlements beyond it. "Hindu servants and sepoys used to object to cross the Indus, and called *that* the **kālā pānī**. I think they used to assert that they lost caste by crossing it, which might have induced them to call it by the same name as the ocean,—or possibly they believed it to be part of the river that flows round the world, or the country beyond it to be outside the limits of Aryavartta" (*Note by Lt.-Col. J. M. Trotter*).

1823.—"An agent of mine, who was for some days with Cheetoo" (a famous Pindārī leader), "told me he raved continually about **Kala Panee**, and that one of his followers assured him when the Pindarry chief slept, he used in his dreams to repeat these dreaded words aloud."—*Sir J. Malcolm, Central India* (2nd ed.), i. 446.

1833.—"**Kala Pany**, dark water, in allusion to the Ocean, is the term used by the Natives to express transportation. Those in the interior picture the place to be an island of a very dreadful description, and full of malevolent beings, and covered with snakes and other vile and dangerous nondescript animals."—*Mackintosh, Acc. of the Tribe of Ramoosies*, 44.

PAYEN-GHAUT, n.p. The country on the coast below the Ghauts or passes leading up to the table-land of the Deccan. It was applied usually on the west coast, but the expression *Carnatic* **Payen-ghaut** is also pretty frequent, as applied to the low country of Madras on the east side of the Peninsula, from Hind. and Mahr. *ghāt*, combined with Pers. *pāīn*, 'below.' [It is generally used as equivalent to *Talaghāt*, "but some Musalmans seem to draw the distinction that the Pāyīn-ghāt is nearer to the foot of the Ghāts than the Talaghāt" (*Le Fanu, Man. of Salem*, ii. 338).]

1629-30.—"But ('Azam Khán) found that the enemy having placed their elephants and baggage in the fort of Dhárúr, had the design of descending the **Páyín-ghát**."—*Abdu'l Hamid Lahori*, in *Elliot*, vii. 17.

1784.—"Peace and friendship . . . between the said Company and the Nabob Tippo Sultan Bahauder, and their friends and allies, particularly including therein the Rajahs of Tanjore and Travencore, who are friends and allies to the English and the Carnatic **Payen Ghaut**."—*Treaty of Mangalore*, in *Munro's Narr.*, 252.

1785.—"You write that the European taken prisoner in the **Pâyen-ghaut** . . . being skilled in the mortar practice, you propose converting him to the faith. . . . It is known (or understood)."—*Letters of Tippoo*, p. 12.

PAZEND, s. See for meaning of this term s.v. **Pahlavi**, in connection with **Zend**. (See also quotation from *Maṣ'ūdī* under latter.)

PECUL, PIKOL, s. Malay and Javanese *pikul*, 'a man's load.' It is applied as the Malay name of the Chinese weight of 100 *katis* (see **CATTY**), called by the Chinese themselves *shih*, and = 133⅓lb. *avoird.* Another authority states that the *shih* is = 120 *kin* or *katis*, whilst the 100 *kin* weight is called in Chinese *tan*.

1554.—"In China 1 tael weighs 7½ tangalarins of silver, and 16 taels=1 caté (see **CATTY**); 100 catés=1 **pico**=45 tangas of silver weigh 1 mark, and therefore 1 pico =133½ arratels (see **ROTTLE**)."—*A. Nunes*, 41.

" "And in China anything is sold and bought by *cates* and **picos** and *taels*, provisions as well as all other things."—*Ibid.* 42.

1613.—"Bantam pepper vngarbled . . . was worth here at our comming tenne Tayes the **Pecull** which is one hundred cattees, making one hundred thirtie pound *English* subtill."—*Saris*, in *Purchas*, i. 369.

[1616.—"The wood we have sold at divers prices from 24 to 28 mas per **Picoll**."—*Foster, Letters*, iv. 259.]

PEDIR, n.p. The name of a port and State of the north coast of Sumatra. Barros says that, before the establishment of Malacca, Pedir was the greatest and most famous of the States on that island. It is now a place of no consequence.

1498.—It is named as **Pater** in the *Roteiro* of Vasco da Gama, but with very incorrect information. See p. 113.

1510.—"We took a junk and went towards Sumatra, to a city called **Pider**. . . . In this country there grows a great quantity of pepper, and of long pepper which is called *Molaga* . . . in this port there are laden with it every year 18 or 20 ships, all of which go to Cathai."—*Varthema*, 233.

1511.—"And having anchored before the said **Pedir**, the Captain General (Alboquerque) sent for me, and told me that I should go ashore to learn the disposition of the people . . . and so I went ashore in the evening, the General thus sending me into a country of enemies,—people too whose vessels and goods we had seized, whose fathers, sons, and brothers we had killed;—into a country where even among themselves there is little justice, and treachery in plenty, still more as regards strangers; truly he acted as caring little what became of me! . . . The answer given me was this: that I should tell the Captain Major General that the city of **Pedir** had been for a long time noble and great in trade . . . that its port was always free for every man to come and go in security . . . that they were *men* and not *women*, and that they could hold for no friend one who seized the ships visiting their harbours; and that if the General desired the King's friendship let him give back what he had seized, and then his people might come ashore to buy and sell."—Letter of *Giov. da Empoli*, in *Archiv. Stor. Ital.* 54.

1516.—"The Moors live in the seaports, and the Gentiles in the interior (of Sumatra). The principal kingdom of the Moors is called **Pedir**. Much very good pepper grows in it, which is not so strong or so fine as that of Malabar. Much silk is also grown there, but not so good as the silk of China."—*Barbosa*, 196.

1538.—"Furthermore I told him what course was usually held for the fishing of seed-pearl between *Pullo Tiquos* and *Pullo Quenim*, which in time past were carried by the *Bataes* to *Pazem* (see **PASEI**) and **Pedir**, and exchanged with the *Turks* of the Straight of *Mecqua*, and the Ships of *Judaa* (see **JUDEA**) for such Merchandise as they brought from *Grand Cairo*." — *Pinto* (in *Cogan*), 25.

1553.—"After the foundation of Malaca, and especially after our entrance to the Indies, the Kingdom of Pacem began to increase, and that of **Pedir** to wane. And its neighbour of Achem, which was then insignificant, is now the greatest of all, so vast are the vicissitudes in States of which men make so great account."—*Barros*, iii. v. 1.

1615.—"Articles exhibited against John Oxwicke. That since his being in **Peedere** 'he did not entreate' anything for Priaman and Tecoe, but only an answer to King James's letter. . . ."—*Sainsbury*, i. 411.

" "**Pedeare**."—*Ibid.* p. 415.

PEEÁDA. See under **PEON**.

PEENUS, s. Hind. *pīnas*; a corruption of Eng. *pinnace*. A name applied to a class of budgerow rigged like a brig or brigantine, on the rivers of Bengal, for European use. Roebuck gives as the marine Hind. for pinnace, *p'hineez*. [The word has been adopted by natives in N. India as the name for a sort of palankin, such as that used by a bride.]

[1615.—"Soe he sent out a **Penisse** to look out for them."—*Cocks's Diary*, Hak. Soc. i. 22.]

1784.—"For sale . . . a very handsome **Pinnace** Budgerow."—In *Seton-Karr*, i. 45.

[1860. — "The **Pinnace**, the largest and handsomest, is perhaps more frequently a private than a hired boat—the property of the planter or merchant."—*C. Grant*, *Rural Life in Bengal*, 4 (with an illustration).]

PEEPUL, s. Hind. *pīpal*, Skt. *pippala*, *Ficus religiosa*, L.; one of the great fig-trees of India, which often occupies a prominent place in a village, or near a temple. The *Pīpal* has a strong resemblance, in wood and foliage, to some common species of poplar, especially the aspen, and its leaves with their long footstalks quaver like those of that tree. This trembling is popularly attributed to spirits agitating each leaf. And hence probably the name of 'Devil's tree' given to it, according to Rheede (*Hort. Mal.* i. 48), by Christians in Malabar. It is possible therefore that the name is identical with that of the poplar. Nothing would be more natural than that the Aryan immigrants, on first seeing this Indian tree, should give it the name of the poplar which they had known in more northern latitudes (*popul-us*, *pappel*, &c.). Indeed, in Kumāon, a true sp. of poplar (*Populus ciliata*) is called by the people *garpipal* (qu. *ghar*, or 'house'-peepul? [or rather perhaps as another name for it is *pahārī*, from *gir*, *giri*, 'a mountain']). Dr. Stewart also says of this *Populus*: "This tree grows to a large size, occasionally reaching 10 feet in girth, and from its leaves resembling those of the pipal . . . is frequently called by that name by plainsmen" (*Punjab Plants*, p. 204). A young *peepul* was shown to one of the present writers in a garden at Palermo as *populo delle Indie*. And the recognised name of the peepul in French books appears to be *peuplier d'Inde*. Col. Tod notices the resemblance (*Rajasthan*, i. 80), and it appears that Vahl called it *Ficus populifolia*. (See also *Geograph. Magazine*, ii. 50). In Balfour's *Indian Cyclopaedia* it is called by the same name in translation, 'the poplar-leaved Fig-tree.' We adduce these facts the more copiously perhaps because the suggestion of the identity of the names *pippala* and *populus* was somewhat scornfully rejected by a very learned scholar. The tree is peculiarly destructive to buildings, as birds drop the seeds in the joints of the masonry, which becomes thus penetrated by the spreading roots of the tree. This is alluded to in a quotation below. "I remember noticing among many Hindus, and especially among Hinduized Sikhs, that they often say *Pīpal ko jātā hūṅ* ('I am going to the Peepul Tree'), to express 'I am going to say my prayers.'" (*Lt.-Col. John Trotter.*) (See **BO-TREE.**)

c. 1550.—"His soul quivered like a **pipal** leaf."—*Rāmāyana of Tulsi Dás*, by *Growse* (1878), ii. 25.

[c. 1590.—"In this place an arrow struck Sri Kishn and buried itself in a **pipal** tree on the banks of the *Sarsuti*."—*Āīn*, ed. *Jarrett*, ii. 246.]

1806.—"Au sortir du village un **pipal** élève sa tête majestueuse. . . . Sa nombreuse posterité l'entoure au loin sur la plaine, telle qu'une armée de géans qui entrelacent fraternellement leurs bras informes."—*Haafner*, i. 149. This writer seems to mean a **banyan.** The *peepul* does not drop roots in that fashion.

1817.—"In the second ordeal, an excavation in the ground . . . is filled with a fire of **pippal** wood, into which the party must walk barefoot, proving his guilt if he is burned; his innocence, if he escapes unhurt."—*Mill* (quoting from Halhed), ed. 1830, i. 280.

1826.—"A little while after this he arose, and went to a **Peepul**-tree, a short way off, where he appeared busy about something, I could not well make out what."—*Pandurang Hari*, 26; [ed. 1873, i. 36, reading **Peepal**].

1836.—"It is not proper to allow the English, after they have made made war, and peace has been settled, to remain in the city. They are accustomed to act like the **Peepul** tree. Let not Younger Brother therefore allow the English to remain in his country."—Letter from *Court of China* to *Court of Ava*. See *Yule, Mission to Ava*, p. 265.

1854.—"Je ne puis passer sous silence deux beaux arbres . . . ce sont le **peuplier** *d'Inde* à larges feuilles, arbre reputé sacré. . . ."—*Pallegoix, Siam*, i. 140.

1861.—

". . . Yonder crown of umbrage hoar
Shall shield her well; the **Peepul** whisper a dirge
And Caryota drop her tearlike store
Of beads; whilst over all slim Casuarine
Points upwards, with her branchlets ever green,
To that remaining Rest where Night and Tears are o'er."

Barrackpore Park, 18th Nov. 1861.

PEER, *s.* Pers. *pīr*, a Mahommedan Saint or *Beatus*. But the word is used elliptically for the tombs of such personages, the circumstance pertaining to them which chiefly creates notoriety or fame of sanctity; and it may be remarked that **wali** (or *Wely* as it is often written), *Imāmzāda*, *Shaikh*, and *Marabout* (see **ADJUTANT**), are often used in the same elliptical way in Syria, Persia, Egypt, and Barbary respectively. We may add that *Nabī* (Prophet) is used in the same fashion.

[1609.—See under **NUGGURCOTE.**

[1623.—"Within the Mesquita (see **MOSQUE**) . . . is a kind of little Pyramid of Marble, and this they call **Pir**, that is *Old*, which they say is equivalent to Holy; I imagine it the Sepulchre of some one of their Sect accounted such."—*P. della Valle*, Hak. Soc. i. 69.]

1665.—"On the other side was the Garden and the chambers of the Mullahs, who with great conveniency and delight spend their lives there under the shadow of the miraculous Sanctity of this **Pire**, which they are not wanting to celebrate: But as I am always very unhappy on such occasions, he did no Miracle that day upon any of the sick."—*Bernier*, 133; [ed. *Constable*, 415].

1673.—"Hard by this is a **Peor**, or Burying place of one of the Prophets, being a goodly monument."—*Fryer*, 240.

1869.—"Certains **pirs** sont tellement renommés, qu'ainsi qu'on le verra plus loin, le peuple a donné leurs noms aux mois lunaires où se trouvent placées les fêtes qu'on celèbre en leur honneur."—*Garcin de Tassy, Rel. Musulm.* p. 18.

The following are examples of the parallel use of the words named:

Wali:

1841.—"The highest part (of Hermon) crowned by the **Wely**, is towards the western end."—*Robinson, Biblical Researches*, iii. 173.

" "In many of the villages of Syria the Traveller will observe small dome-covered buildings, with grated windows and surmounted by the crescent. These are the so-called **Welis**, mausolea of saints, or tombs of sheikhs."—*Baedeker's Egypt*, Eng. ed. Pt. i. 150.

Imamzada:

1864.—"We rode on for three farsakhs, or fourteen miles, more to another **Imámzádah**, called *Kafsh-girī*. . . ."—*Eastwick, Three Years' Residence in Persia*, ii. 46.

1883.—"The few villages . . . have numerous walled gardens, with rows of poplar and willow-trees and stunted mulberries, and the inevitable **Imamzadehs.**"—*Col. Beresford Lovett's Itinerary Notes of Route Surveys in N. Persia in* 1881 *and* 1882, *Proc. R.G.S.* (N.S.) v. 73.

Shaikh:

1817.—"Near the ford (on Jordan), half a mile to the south, is a tomb called '**Sheikh** Daoud,' standing on an apparent round hill like a barrow."—*Irby and Mangles, Travels in Egypt*, &c., 304.

Nabi:

1856. — "Of all the points of interest about Jerusalem, none perhaps gains so much from an actual visit to Palestine as the lofty-peaked eminence which fills up the north-west corner of the table-land. . . . At present it bears the name of **Nebi**-Samuel, which is derived from the Mussulman tradition—now perpetuated by a mosque and tomb—that here lies buried the prophet Samuel."—*Stanley's Palestine*, 165.

So also **Nabi**-*Yūnus* at Nineveh; and see **Nebi**-*Mousa* in *De Saulcy*, ii. 73.

PEGU, n.p. The name which we give to the Kingdom which formerly existed in the Delta of the Irawadi, to the city which was its capital, and to the British province which occupies its place. The Burmese name is *Bagó*. This name belongs to the Talaing language, and is popularly alleged to mean 'conquered by stratagem,' to explain which a legend is given; but no doubt this is mere fancy. The form *Pegu*, as in many other cases of our geographical nomenclature, appears to come through the Malays, who call it *Paigū*. The first European mention that we know of is in Conti's narrative (c. 1440) where Poggio has Latinized it as *Pauco-nia*; but Fra Mauro, who probably derived this name, with much other new knowledge, from Conti, has in his great map (c. 1459) the exact Malay form *Paigu*. Nikitin (c. 1475) has, if we may depend on his translator into English, *Pegu*, as has Hieronimo di S. Stefano (1499). The *Roteiro* of Vasco da Gama (1498) has *Pegúo*, and describes the land as Christian, a mistake arising no doubt from the use of the ambiguous term *Kāfir* by his Mahommedan informants (see under **CAFFER**). Varthema (1510) has *Pego*, and Giov. da Empoli (1514) *Pecù*; Barbosa (1516) again *Paÿgu*; but **Pegu** is the usual Portuguese form, as in Barros, and so passed to us.

1498.—"**Pegúo** is a land of Christians, and the King is a Christian; and they are all white like us. This King can assemble 20,000 fighting men, *i.e.* 10,000 horsemen, as many footmen, and 400 war elephants; here is all the musk in the world . . . and on the main land he has many rubies and much gold, so that for 10 cruzados you can buy as much gold as will fetch 25 in Calecut, and there is much lac (*lacra*) and benzoin. . . ."—*Roteiro*, 112.

1505.—"Two merchants of Cochin took on them to save two of the ships; one from **Pegú** with a rich cargo of lac (*lacre*), benzoin, and musk, and another with a cargo of drugs from Banda, nutmeg, mace, clove, and sandalwood; and they embarked on the ships with their people, leaving to chance their own vessels, which had cargoes of rice, for the value of which the owners of the ships bound themselves."—*Correa*, i. 611.

1514.—"Then there is **Pecù**, which is a populous and noble city, abounding in men and in horses, where are the true mines of *linoni* (? '*di* linoni *e perfetti rubini*,' perhaps should be 'di *buoni* e perfetti') and perfect rubies, and these in great plenty; and they are fine men, tall and well limbed and stout; as of a race of giants. . . ."—*Empoli*, 80.

[1516.—"**Peigu**." (See under **BURMA**).]

1541.—"**Bagou**." (See under **PEKING**.)

1542.—". . . and for all the goods which came from any other ports and places, viz. from **Peguu** to the said Port of Malaqua, from the Island of Çamatra and from within the Straits. . . ."—*Titolo of the Fortress and City of Malaqua*, in *Tombo*, p. 105 in *Subsidios*.

1568.—"Concludo che non è in terra Re di possãza maggiore del Re di **Pegù**, per ciòche ha sotto di se venti Re di corona."—*Ces. Federici*, in *Ramusio*, iii. 394.

1572.—

"Olha o reino Arracão, olha o assento
De **Pegú**, que já monstros povoaram,
Monstros filhos do feo ajuntamento
D'huma mulher e hum cão, que sos se acharam." *Camões*, x. 122.

By Burton:

"Arracan-realm behold, behold the seat
of **Pegu** peopled by a monster-brood;
monsters that gendered meeting most unmeet
of whelp and woman in the lonely wood. . . ."

1597.—". . . I recommend you to be very watchful not to allow the Turks to export any timber from the Kingdom of **Pegú** nor yet from that of Achin (*do Dachem*); and with this view you should give orders that this be the subject of treatment with the King of Dachem since he shows so great a desire for our friendship, and is treating in that sense."—*Despatch from the King to Goa*, 5th Feb. In *Archiv. Port. Orient.* Fasc. iii.

PEGU PONIES. These are in Madras sometimes termed elliptically **Pegus**, as Arab horses are universally termed Arabs. The ponies were much valued, and before the annexation of Pegu commonly imported into India; less commonly since, for the local demand absorbs them.

1880.—"For sale . . . also Bubble and Squeak, bay **Pegues**."—*Madras Mail*, Feb. 19.

[1890.—"Ponies, sometimes very good ones, were reared in a few districts in Upper Burma, but, even in Burmese times, the supply was from the Shan States. The so-called **Pegu Pony**, of which a good deal is heard, is, in fact, not a Pegu pony at all, for the justly celebrated animals called by that name were imported from the Shan States."—Report of *Capt. Evans*, in *Times*, Oct. 17.]

PEKING, n.p. This name means 'North-Court,' and in its present application dates from the early reigns of the Ming Dynasty in China. When they dethroned the Mongol descendants of Chinghiz and Kublai (1368) they removed the capital from Taitu or Khānbāligh (*Cambaluc* of Polo) to the great city on the Yangtsze which has since been known as *Nan-King* or 'South-Court.' But before many years the Mongol capital was rehabilitated as the imperial residence, and became *Pe-King* accordingly. Its preparation for reoccupation began in 1409. The first English mention that we have met with is that quoted by Sainsbury, in which we have the subjects of more than one allusion in Milton.

1520.—"Thomé Pires, quitting this pass, arrived at the Province of Nanquij, at its chief city called by the same name, where the King dwelt, and spent in coming thither always travelling north, four months; by which you may take note how vast a matter is the empire of this gentile prince. He sent word to Thomé Pires that he was to wait for him at **Pequij**, where he would despatch his affair. This city is in another province so called, much further north, in which the King used to dwell for the most part, because it was on the frontier of the Tartars. . . ."—*Barros*, III. vi. 1.

1541.—"This City of **Pequin** . . . is so prodigious, and the things therein so remarkable, as I do almost repent me for undertaking to discourse of it. . . . For one must not imagine it to be, either as the City of *Rome*, or *Constantinople*, or *Venice*, or *Paris*, or *London*, or *Sevill*, or *Lisbon*. . . . Nay I will say further, that one must not think it to be like to Grand *Cairo* in *Egypt*, *Tauris* in *Persia*, *Amadaba* (Amadabad, **Avadavat**) in *Cambaya*, *Bisnagu(r)* in *Narsingaa*, *Goura* (Gouro) in *Bengala*, *Ava* in *Chalen*, *Timplan* in *Calaminham*, *Martaban* (Martavão) and *Bagou* in *Pegu*, *Guimpel* and *Tinlau* in *Siammon*, *Odia* in the Kingdom of *Sornau*, *Passavan* and *Dema* in the Island of *Java*, *Pangor* in the Country of the *Lequiens* (no Lequio) *Usangea* (Uzãgnè) in the *Grand Cauchin*, *Lancama* (Laçame) in *Tartary*, and *Meaco* (Mioco) in *Jappun* . . . for I dare well affirm that all those same are not to be compared to the least part of the wonderful City of **Pequin**. . . ."—*Pinto* (in *Cogan*), p. 136 (orig. cap. cvii.).

[c. 1586.—"The King maketh alwayes his abode in the great city **Pachin**, as much as to say in our language . . . the towne of the kingdome."—*Reports of China*, in *Hakl.* ii. 546.]

1614.—"Richard Cocks writing from Ferando understands there are great cities in the country of Corea, and between that and the sea mighty bogs, so that no man can travel there; but great waggons have been invented to go upon broad flat wheels, under sail as ships do, in which they transport their goods . . . the deceased Emperor of Japan did pretend to have conveyed a great army in these sailing waggons, to assail the Emperor of China in his City of **Paquin**."—In *Sainsbury*, i. 343.

166*.—

"from the destined walls
Of Cambalu, seat of Cathaian Can,
And Samarchand by Oxus, Temer's throne,
To **Paquin** of Sinaean Kings. . . ."
Paradise Lost, xi. 387-390.

PELICAN, s. This word, in its proper application to the *Pelicanus onocrotalus*, L., is in no respect peculiar to Anglo-India, though we may here observe that the bird is called in Hindi by the poetical name *gagan-bher*, *i.e.* 'Sheep of the Sky,' which we have heard natives with their strong propensity to metathesis convert into the equally appropriate *Gangā-bheṛī* or 'Sheep of the Ganges.' The name may be illustrated by the old term 'Cape-sheep' applied to the albatross.* But *Pelican* is habitually misapplied by the British soldier in India to the bird usually called **Adjutant** (q.v.). We may remember how Prof. Max Müller, in his Lectures on Language, tells us that the Tahitians show respect to their sovereign by ceasing to employ in common language those words which form part or the whole of his name, and invent new terms to supply their place. "The object was clearly to guard against the name of the sovereign being ever used, even by accident, in ordinary conversation," 2nd ser. 1864, p. 35, [*Frazer, Golden Bough*, 2nd ed. i. 421 *seqq.*]). Now, by an analogous process, it is possible that

* ". . . great diversion is found . . . in firing balls at birds, particularly the *albitross*, a large species of the swan, commonly seen within two or three hundred miles round the Cape of Good Hope, and which the French call *Montons* (Moutons) du Cap."—*Munro's Narrative*, 13. The confusion of genera here equals that mentioned in our article above.

some martinet, holding the office of adjutant, at an early date in the Anglo-Indian history, may have resented the ludicrously appropriate employment of the usual name of the bird, and so may have introduced the entirely inappropriate name of *pelican* in its place. It is in the recollection of one of the present writers that a worthy northern matron, who with her husband had risen from the ranks in the —th Light Dragoons, on being challenged for speaking of "the *pelicans* in the barrack-yard," maintained her correctness, conceding only that "some ca'd them **paylicans**, some ca'd them **audjutants**."

1829.—"This officer . . . on going round the yard (of the military prison) . . . discovered a large beef-bone recently dropped. The sergeant was called to account for this ominous appearance. This sergeant was a shrewd fellow, and he immediately said,—'Oh Sir, the **pelicans** have dropped it.' This was very plausible, for these birds will carry enormous bones; and frequently when fighting for them they drop them, so that this might very probably have been the case. The moment the dinner-trumpet sounds, whole flocks of these birds are in attendance at the barrack-doors, waiting for bones, or anything that the soldiers may be pleased to throw to them."—*Mem. of John Shipp*, ii. 25.

PENANG, n.p. This is the proper name of the Island adjoining the Peninsula of Malacca (*Pulo*, properly *Pulau, Pinang*), which on its cession to the English (1786) was named 'Prince of Wales's Island.' But this official style has again given way to the old name. *Pinang* in Malay signifies an areca-nut or areca-tree, and, according to Crawfurd, the name was given on account of the island's resemblance in form to the fruit of the tree (*vulgo*, 'the betel-nut').

1592.—"Now the **winter** coming vpon vs with much contagious weather, we directed our course from hence with the Ilands of *Pulo* **Pinaou** (where by the way is to be noted that *Pulo* in the Malaian tongue signifieth an Iland) . . . where we came to an anker in a very good harborough betweene three Ilands. . . . This place is in 6 degrees and a halfe to the Northward, and some fiue leagues from the maine betweene Malacca and Pegu."—*Barker*, in *Hakl.* ii. 589-590.

PENANG LAWYER, s. The popular name of a handsome and hard (but sometimes brittle) walking-stick, exported from Penang and Singapore. It is the stem of a miniature palm (*Licuala acutifida*, Griffith). The sticks are prepared by scraping the young stem with glass, so as to remove the epidermis and no more. The sticks are then straightened by fire and polished (*Balfour*). The name is popularly thought to have originated in a jocular supposition that law-suits in Penang were decided by the *lex baculina*. But there can be little doubt that it is a corruption of some native term, and *pinang liyar*, 'wild areca' [or *pinang lāyor*, "fire-dried areca," which is suggested in *N.E.D.*], may almost be assumed to be the real name. [Dennys (*Descr. Dict.* s.v.) says from "*Layor*, a species of cane furnishing the sticks so named." But this is almost certainly wrong.]

1883.—(But the book—an excellent one—is without date—more shame to the *Religious Tract Society* which publishes it). "Next morning, taking my '**Penang lawyer**' to defend myself from dogs. . . ." The following note is added: "A **Penang lawyer** is a heavy walking-stick, supposed to be so called from its usefulness in settling disputes in Penang."—*Gilmour, Among the Mongols*, 14.

PENGUIN, s. Popular name of several species of birds belonging to the genera *Aptenodytes* and *Spheniscus*. We have not been able to ascertain the etymology of this name. It may be from the Port. *pingue*, 'fat.' See Littré. He quotes Clausius as picturing it, who says they were called a *pinguedine*. It is surely not that given by Sir Thomas Herbert in proof of the truth of the legend of Madoc's settlement in America; and which is indeed implied 60 years before by the narrator of Drake's voyage; though probably borrowed by Herbert direct from Selden.

1578.—"In these Islands we found greate relief and plenty of good victuals, for infinite were the number of fowle which the Welsh men named **Penguin**, and Magilanus tearmed them geese. . . ."—*Drake's Voyage*, by *F. Fletcher*, Hak. Soc. p. 72.

1593. — "The **pengwin** described."—*Hawkins, V. to S. Sea*, p. 111, Hak. Soc.

1606.—"The **Pengwines** bee as bigge as our greatest Capons we have in England, they have no winges nor cannot flye . . . they bee exceeding fatte, but their flesh is verie ranke. . . ."—*Middleton*, f. B. 4.

1609.—"Nous trouvâmes beaucoup de Chiẽs de Mer, et Oyseaux qu'on appelle **Penguyns**, dont l'Escueil en estait quasi couvert."—*Houtman*, p. 4.

c. 1610.—"... le reste est tout couvert ... d'vne quantité d'Oyseaux nommez **pinguy**, qui font là leurs oeufs et leurs petits, et il y en a une quantité si prodigieuse qu'on ne sçauroit mettre ... le pied en quelque endroit que ce soit sans toucher."—*Pyrard de Laval*, i. 73; [Hak. Soc. i. 97, also see i. 16].

1612.—"About the year CIↃ. C.LXX. Madoc brother to *David ap Owen*, prince of Wales, made this sea voyage (to *Florida*); and by probability these names of *Capo de Briton* in *Norumbeg*, and **Pengwin** in part of the Northern America, for a *white* rock, and a *white-headed* bird, according to the *British*, were relicks of this discovery."—*Selden, Notes on Drayton's Polyolbion*, in *Works* (ed. 1726), iii. col. 1802.

1616.—"The Island called **Pen-guin** Island, probably so named by some Welshman, in whose Language **Pen-guin** signifies a white head; and there are many great lazy fowls upon, and about, this Island, with great cole-black bodies, and very white heads, called **Penguins**."—*Terry*, ed. 1665, p. 334.

1638.—"... that this people (of the Mexican traditions) were Welsh rather than Spaniards or others, the Records of this Voyage writ by many Bardhs and Genealogists confirme it ... made more orthodoxall by Welsh names given there to birds, rivers, rocks, beasts, &c., as ... **Pengwyn**, refer'd by them to a bird that has a white head. ..."—*Herbert, Some Yeares Travels*, &c., p. 360.

Unfortunately for this etymology the head is precisely that part which seems in all species of the bird to be black! But M. Roulin, quoted by Littré, maintains the Welsh (or Breton) etymology, thinking the name was first given to some short-winged sea-bird with a white head, and then transferred to the penguin. And *Terry*, if to be depended on, supports this view. [So Prof. Skeat (*Concise Dict.*, s.v.): "In that case, it must first have been given to another bird, such as the auk (the puffin is common in Anglesey), since the penguin's head is black."]

1674.—
"So Horses they affirm to be
Mere Engines made by Geometry,
And were invented first from Engins,
As *Indian Britons* were from **Penguins**."
Hudibras, Pt. I. Canto ii. 57.

[1869.—In Lombock ducks "are very cheap and are largely consumed by the crews of the rice ships, by whom they are called Baly-soldiers, but are more generally known elsewhere as **penguin**-*ducks*."—*Wallace, Malay Archip.* ed. 1890, p. 135.]

PEON, s. This is a Portuguese word *peão* (Span. *peon*); from *pé*, 'foot,' and meaning a 'footman' (also a *pawn* at chess), and is not therefore a corruption, as has been alleged, of Hind. *piyāda*, meaning the same; though the words are, of course ultimately akin in root. It was originally used in the sense of 'a foot-soldier'; thence as 'orderly' or messenger. The word *Sepoy* was used within our recollection, and perhaps is still, in the same sense in the city of Bombay. The transition of meaning comes out plainly in the quotation from Ives. In the sense of 'orderly,' *peon* is the word usual in S. India, whilst **chuprassy** (q.v.) is more common in N. India, though *peon* is also used there. The word is likewise very generally employed for men on police service (see **BURKUNDAUZE**). [Mr. Skeat notes that *Piyun* is used in the Malay States, and *Tambi* or *Tanby* at Singapore]. The word had probably become unusual in Portugal by 1600; for Manoel Correa, an early commentator on the Lusiads (d. 1613), thinks it necessary to explain **piões** by 'gente de pé.'

1503. — "The Çamorym ordered the soldier (**pião**) to take the letter away, and strictly forbade him to say anything about his having seen it."—*Correa, Lendas*, I. i. 421.

1510.—"So the Sabayo, putting much trust in this (Rumi), made him captain within the city (Goa), and outside of it put under him a captain of his with two thousand soldiers (**piães**) from the Balagate. ..."—*Ibid.* II. i. 51.

1563.—"The pawn (**pião**) they call *Piada*, which is as much as to say a man who travels on foot."—*Garcia*, f. 37.

1575.—
"O Rey de Badajos era alto Mouro
Con quatro mil cavallos furiosos,
Innumeros **piões**, darmas e de ouro,
Guarnecidos, guerreiros, e lustrosos."
Camões, iii. 66.

By Burton:
"The King of Badajos was a Moslem bold,
with horse four thousand, fierce and furious knights,
and countless **Peons**, armed and dight with gold,
whose polisht surface glanceth lustrous light."

1609. — "The first of February the Capitaine departed with fiftie **Peons**. ..."—*W. Finch*, in *Purchas*, i. 421.

c. 1610.—"Les **Pions** marchent après le prisonnier, lié avec des cordes qu'ils tiennent."—*Pyrard de Laval*, ii. 11; [Hak. Soc. ii. 17; also i. 428, 440; ii. 16].

[1616.—"This Shawbunder (see **SHABUNDER**) imperiously by a couple of **Pyons** commanded him from me."—*Foster, Letters*, iv. 351.]

c. 1630.—"The first of *December*, with some **Pe-unes** (or black Foot-boyes, who can pratle some English) we rode (from Swally) to Surat."—*Sir T. Herbert*, ed. 1638, p. 35.

[For "black" the ed. of 1677 reads "olive-coloured," p. 42.]

1666.—". . . siete cientos y treinta y tres mil **peones**."—*Faria y Sousa*, i. 195.

1673.—"The Town is walled with Mud, and Bulwarks for Watch-Places for the English **peons**."—*Fryer*, 29.

,, ". . . **Peons** or servants to wait on us."—*Ibid.* 26.

1687.—"Ordered that ten **peons** be sent along the coast to Pulicat . . . and enquire all the way for goods driven ashore."—In *Wheeler*, i. 179.

1689.—"At this Moors Town, they got a **Peun** to be their guide to the Mogul's nearest Camp. . . . These **Peuns** are some of the Gentous or *Rashbouts* (see **RAJPOOT**), who in all places along the Coast, especially in Seaport Towns, make it their business to hire themselves to wait upon Strangers."—*Dampier*, i. 508.

,, "A **Peon** of mine, named *Gemal*, walking abroad in the Grass after the Rains, was unfortunately bit on a sudden by one of them" (a snake).—*Ovington*, 260.

1705.—". . . . **pions** qui sont ce que nous appellons ici des Gardes. . . ."—*Luillier*, 218.

1745.—"Dès le lendemain je fis assembler dans la Forteresse où je demeurois en qualité d'Aumonier, le Chef des **Pions**, chez qui s'étaient fait les deux mariages."—*Norbert, Mém.* iii. 129.

1746.—"As the Nabob's behaviour when Madras was attacked by De la Bourdonnais, had caused the English to suspect his assurances of assistance, they had 2,000 **Peons** in the defence of Cuddalore. . . ."—*Orme*, i. 81.

c. 1760.—"**Peon**. One who waits about the house to run on messages; and he commonly carries under his arm a sword, or in his sash a *krese*, and in his hand a ratan, to keep the rest of the servants in subjection. He also walks before your palanquin, carries **chits** (q.v.) or notes, and is your body-guard."—*Ives*, 50.

1763. — "Europeans distinguish these undisciplined troops by the general name of **Peons**."—*Orme*, ed. 1803, i. 80.

1772.—Hadley, writing in Bengal, spells the word **pune**; but this is evidently phonetic.

c. 1785.—". . . **Peons**, a name for the infantry of the Deckan."—*Carraccioli's Life of Clive*, iv. 563.

1780-90. — "I sent off annually from Sylhet from 150 to 200 (elephants) divided into 4 distinct flocks. . . . They were put under charge of the common **peon**. These people were often absent 18 months. On one occasion my servant Manoo . . . after a twelve-months' absence returned . . . in appearance most miserable; he unfolded his girdle, and produced a scrap of paper of small dimensions, which proved to be a banker's bill amounting to 3 or 4,000 pounds, —his own pay was 30 shillings a month. . . . When I left India Manoo was still absent on one of these excursions, but he delivered to my agents as faithful an account of the produce as he would have done to myself. . . ."—*Hon. R. Lindsay*, in *Lives of the Lindsays*, iii. 77.

1842.—". . . he was put under arrest for striking, and throwing into the Indus, an inoffensive **Peon**, who gave him no provocation, but who was obeying the orders he received from Captain ——. The Major General has heard it said that the supremacy of the British over the native must be maintained in India, and he entirely concurs in that opinion, but it must be maintained by justice."—*Gen. Orders*, &c., *of Sir Ch. Napier*, p. 72.

1873.—"Pandurang is by turns a servant to a shopkeeper, a **peon**, or orderly, a groom to an English officer . . . and eventually a pleader before an English Judge in a populous city."—*Saturday Review*, May 31, p. 728.

PEPPER, s. The original of this word, Skt. *pippali*, means not the ordinary pepper of commerce ('black pepper') but *long pepper*, and the Sanskrit name is still so applied in Bengal, where one of the long-pepper plants, which have been classed sometimes in a different genus (*Chavica*) from the black pepper, was at one time much cultivated. There is still indeed a considerable export of long pepper from Calcutta; and a kindred species grows in the Archipelago. Long pepper is mentioned by Pliny, as well as white and black pepper; the three varieties still known in trade, though with the kind of error that has persisted on such subjects till quite recently, he misapprehends their relation. The proportion of their ancient prices will be found in a quotation below.

The name must have been transferred by foreign traders to black pepper, the staple of export, at an early date, as will be seen from the quotations. *Pippalimūla*, the root of long pepper, still a stimulant medicine in the native pharmacopoeia, is probably the πεπέρεως ῥίζα of the ancients (*Royle*, p. 86).

We may say here that *Black pepper* is the fruit of a perennial climbing shrub, *Piper nigrum*, L., indigenous in the forests of Malabar and Travancore, and thence introduced into the Malay countries, particularly Sumatra.

White pepper is prepared from the black by removing the dark outer layer of pericarp, thereby depriving it of a part of its pungency. It comes chiefly *viâ* Singapore from the Dutch settlement of Rhio, but a small quantity of fine quality comes from Tellicherry in Malabar.

Long pepper is derived from two shrubby plants, *Piper officinarum*, C.D.C., a native of the Archipelago, and *Piper longum*, L., indigenous in Malabar, Ceylon, E. Bengal, Timor, and the Philippines. Long pepper is the fruit-spike gathered and dried when not quite ripe (*Hanbury and Flückiger, Pharmacographia*). All these kinds of pepper were, as has been said, known to the ancients.

c. 70 A.D.—"The cornes or graines . . . lie in certaine little huskes or cods. . . . If that be plucked from the tree before they gape and open of themselves, they make that spice which is called **Long pepper**; but if as they do ripen, they cleave and chawne by little and little, they shew within the **white pepper**: which afterwards beeing parched in the Sunne, chaungeth colour and waxeth blacke, and therewith riveled also . . . **Long pepper** is soone sophisticated, with the senvie or mustard seed of Alexandria: and a pound of it is worth fifteen Roman deniers. The **white** costeth seven deniers a pound, and the **black** is sold after foure deniers by the pound."—*Pliny*, tr. by *Phil. Holland*, Bk. xii. ch. 7.

c. 80-90.—"And there come to these marts great ships, on account of the bulk and quantity of **pepper** and **malabathrum**. . . . The **pepper** is brought (to market) here, being produced largely only in one district near these marts, that which is called *Kottonarikē*."—*Periplus*, § 56.

c. A.D. 100.—"The **Pepper-tree** (πέπερι δένδρον) is related to grow in India; it is short, and the fruit as it first puts it forth is long, resembling pods; and this **long pepper** has within it (grains) like small millet, which are what grow to be the perfect (**black**) **pepper**. At the proper season it opens and puts forth a cluster bearing the berries such as we know them. But those that are like unripe grapes, which constitute the **white pepper**, serve the best for eye-remedies, and for antidotes, and for theriacal potencies."—*Dioscorides, Mat. Med.* ii. 188.

c. 545.—"This is the **pepper-tree**" (there is a drawing). "Every plant of it is twined round some lofty forest tree, for it is weak and slim like the slender stems of the vine. And every bunch of fruit has a double leaf as a shield; and it is very green, like the green of rue."—*Cosmas*, Book xi.

c. 870.—"The mariners say every bunch of **pepper** has over it a leaf that shelters it from the rain. When the rain ceases the leaf turns aside; if rain recommences the leaf again covers the fruit."—*Ibn Khurdādba*, in *Journ. As.* 6th ser. tom. v. 284.

1166.—"The trees which bear this fruit are planted in the fields which surround the towns, and every one knows his plantation. The trees are small, and the **pepper** is originally white, but when they collect it they put it into basons and pour hot water upon it; it is then exposed to the heat of the sun, and dried . . . in the course of which process it becomes of a black colour."—*Rabbi Benjamin*, in *Wright*, p. 114.

c. 1330.—"L'albore che fa il **pepe** è fatto come l'elera che nasce su per gli muri. Questo pepe sale su per gli arbori che l'uomini piantano a modo de l'elera, e sale sopra tutti li arbori più alti. Questo pepe fa rami a modo dell' uve; . . . e maturo si lo vendemiano a modo de l'uve e poi pongono il pepe al sole a seccare come uve passe, e nulla altra cosa si fa del **pepe**."—*Odoric*, in *Cathay*, App. xlvii.

PERGUNNAH, s. Hind. *pargana* [Skt. *pragaṇ*, 'to reckon up'], a subdivision of a 'District' (see **ZILLAH**).

c. 1500.—"The divisions into *sûbas* (see **SOUBA**) and **parganas**, which are maintained to the present day in the province of Tatta, were made by these people" (the Samma Dynasty).—*Táríkh-i-Táhirí*, in *Elliot*, i. 273.

1535.—"Item, from the three **praguanas**, viz., Anzor, Cairena, Panchenaa 133,260 *fedeas*."—*S. Botelho, Tombo*, 139.

[1614. — "I wrote him to stay in the **Pregonas** near Agra."—*Foster, Letters*, ii. 106.]

[1617.—"For that Muckshud had also newly answered he had mist his **prigany**."—*Sir T. Roe*, Hak. Soc. ii. 415.]

1753.—"Masulipatnam . . . est capitale de ce qu'on appelle dans l'Inde un Sercar (see **SIRCAR**), qui comprend plusieurs **Pergанés**, ou districts particuliers."—*D'Anville*, 132.

1812. — "A certain number of villages with a society thus organised, formed a **pergunnah**."—*Fifth Report*, 16.

PERGUNNAHS, THE TWENTY-FOUR, n.p. The official name of the District immediately adjoining and inclosing, though not administratively including, Calcutta. The name is one of a character very ancient in India and the East. It was the original 'Zemindary of Calcutta' granted to the English Company by a 'Subadar's Perwana' in 1757-58. This grant was subsequently confirmed by the Great Mogul as an unconditional and rent-free **jagheer** (q.v.). The quotation from Sir Richard Phillips' *Million of Facts*, illustrates the development of 'facts' out of the moral consciousness. The book contains many of equal value. An approximate parallel to this statement would be that London is divided into Seven Dials.

1765.—"The lands of the **twenty-four Purgunnahs**, ceded to the Company by the treaty of 1757, which subsequently became Colonel *Clive's* jagghier, were rated on the King's books at 2 lac and 22,000 rupees." —*Holwell, Hist. Events*, 2nd ed., p. 217.

1812.—"The number of convicts confined at the six stations of this division (independent of *Zillah* **Twenty-four pergunnahs**, is about 4,000. Of them probably nine-tenths are dacoits."—*Fifth Report*, 559.

c. 1831. — "Bengal is divided in 24 **Pergunnahs**, each with its judge and magistrate, registrar, &c."—*Sir R. Phillips, Million of Facts*, stereot. ed. 1843, 927.

PERI, s. This Persian word for a class of imaginary sprites, rendered familiar in the verses of Moore and Southey, has no blood-relationship with the English *Fairy*, notwithstanding the exact compliance with Grimm's Law in the change of initial consonant. The Persian word is *parī*, from '*par*, 'a feather, or wing'; therefore 'the winged one'; [so F. Johnson, *Pers. Dict.*; but the derivation is very doubtful;] whilst the genealogy of *fairy* is apparently Ital. *fata*, French *fée*, whence *féerie* ('fay-dom') and thence *fairy*.

[c. 1500?—"I am the only daughter of a Jinn chief of noblest strain and my name is **Peri**-Banu."—*Arab. Nights, Burton*, x. 264.]

1800.—

"From cluster'd henna, and from orange groves,
That with such perfumes fill the breeze
As **Peris** to their Sister bear,
When from the summit of some lofty tree
She hangs encaged, the captive of the Dives." *Thalaba*, xi. 24.

1817.—

"But nought can charm the luckless **Peri**;
Her soul is sad—her wings are weary."
Moore, Paradise and the **Peri**.

PERPET, PERPETUANO, s. The name of a cloth often mentioned in the 17th and first part of the 18th centuries, as an export from England to the East. It appears to have been a light and glossy twilled stuff of wool, [which like another stuff of the same kind called '*Lasting*,' took its name from its durability. (See *Draper's Dict.* s.v.)]. In France it was called *perpétuanne* or *sempiterne*, in Ital. *perpetuana*.

[1609.—"Karsies, **Perpetuanos** and other woollen Comodities."—*Birdwood, Letter Book*, 288.

[1617.—"**Perpetuano**, 1 bale."—*Cocks's Diary*, Hak. Soc. i. 293.

[1630.—"... Devonshire kersies or **perpetuities** ..."—*Forrest, Bombay Letters*, i. 4.

[1680.—"**Perpetuances**."—*Ibid.* ii. 401.]

1711.—"Goods usually imported (to China) from *Europe* are Bullion Cloths, Clothrash **Perpetuano's**, and Camblets of Scarlet, black, blew, sad and violet Colours, which are of late so lightly set by; that to bear the Dutys, and bring the prime Cost, is as much as can reasonably be hoped for."—*Lockyer*, 147.

[1717.—"... a Pavilion lined with Imboss'd **Perpets**."—In *Yule, Hedges' Diary*, Hak. Soc. ii. ccclix.]

1754.—"Being requested by the Trustees of the Charity Stock of this place to make an humble application to you for an order that the children upon the Foundation to the number of 12 or 14 may be supplied at the expense of the Honorable Company with a coat of blue **Perpets** or some ordinary cloth. ..."—*Petition of Revd. R. Mapletoft*, in *Long*, p. 29.

1757.—Among the presents sent to the King of Ava with the mission of Ensign Robert Lester, we find:

"2 Pieces of ordinary Red Broad Cloth.
3 Do. of **Pérpetuánoes** Popingay."
In *Dalrymple, Or. Rep.* i. 203.

PERSAIM, n.p. This is an old form of the name of **Bassein** (q.v.) in Pegu. It occurs (*e.g.*) in *Milburn*, ii. 281.

1759.—"The Country for 20 miles round **Persaim** is represented as capable of producing Rice, sufficient to supply the Coast of CHOROMANDEL from *Pondicherry* to *Masulipatam*."—Letter in *Dalrymple, Or. Rep.* i. 110. Also in a Chart by Capt. G. Baker, 1754.

1795.—"Having ordered presents of a trivial nature to be presented, in return for those brought from Negrais, he referred the deputy ... to the Birman Governor of **Persaim** for a ratification and final adjustment of the treaty."—*Symes*, p. 40. But this author also uses *Bassien* (*e.g.* 32), and "**Persaim** or *Bassien*" (39), which alternatives are also in the chart by Ensign Wood.

PERSIMMON, s. This American name is applied to a fruit common in China and Japan, which in a dried state is imported largely from China into Tibet. The tree is the *Diospyros kaki*, L. fil., a species of the same genus which produces ebony. The word is properly the name of an American fruit and tree of the same genus (*D. virginiana*), also called date-plum, and, according to the Dictionary of Worcester, belonged to the Indian language of Virginia. [The word became familiar in 1896 as the name of the winner of the Derby.]

1878.—"The finest fruit of Japan is the *Kaki* or **persimmon** (*Diospyros Kaki*), a large golden fruit on a beautiful tree."—*Miss Bird's Japan*, i. 234.

PERUMBAUCUM, n.p. A town 14 m. N.W. of Conjevaram, in the district of Madras [Chingleput]. The name is perhaps *perum-pākkam*, Tam., 'big village.'

PESCARIA, n.p. The coast of Tinnevelly was so called by the Portuguese, from the great pearl 'fishery' there.

[c. 1566.—See under **BAZAAR**.]

1600.—"There are in the Seas of the East three principal mines where they fish pearls. . . . The third is between the Isle of Ceilon and Cape Comory, and on this account the Coast which runs from the said Cape to the shoals of Ramanancor and Manâr is called, in part, **Pescaria**. . . ."—*Lucena*, 80.

[1616.—"**Pesqueria**." See under **CHILAW**.]

1615.—"Iam nonnihil de orâ **Piscariâ** dicamus quae iam inde a promontorio Commorino in Orientem ad usque breuia Ramanancoridis extenditur, quod haud procul inde celeberrimus, maximus, et copiosissimus toto Oriente Margaritarum piscatus instituitur. . . ."—*Jarric, Thes.* i. 445.

1710.—"The Coast of the **Pescaria** of the mother of pearl which runs from the Cape of Camorim to the Isle of Manar, for the space of seventy leagues, with a breadth of six inland, was the first debarcation of this second conquest."—*Sousa, Orient. Conquist.* i. 122.

PESHAWUR, n.p. *Peshāwar*. This name of what is now the frontier city and garrison of India towards Kābul, is sometimes alleged to have been given by Akbar. But in substance the name is of great antiquity, and all that can be alleged as to Akbar is that he is said to have modified the old name, and that since his time the present form has been in use. A notice of the change is quoted below from Gen. Cunningham; we cannot give the authority on which the statement rests. Peshāwar could hardly be called a frontier town in the time of Akbar, standing as it did according to the administrative division of the *Āīn*, about the middle of the Sūba of Kābul, which included Kashmīr and all west of it. We do not find that the modern form occurs in the text of the *Āīn* as published by Prof. Blochmann. In the translation of the *Ṭabakāt-i-Akbarī* of Nizāmu-d-din Ahmad (died 1594-95), in Elliot, we find the name transliterated variously as *Peshâwar* (v. 448), *Parshâwar* (293), *Parshor* (423), *Pershor* (424). We cannot doubt that the Chinese form *Folausha* in Fah-hian already expresses the name *Parashāwar*, or *Parshāwar*.

c. 400.—"From Gandhâra, going south 4 days' journey, we arrive at the country of **Fo-lau-sha**. In old times Buddha, in company with all his disciples, travelled through this country."—*Fah-hian*, by *Beal*, p. 34.

c. 630.—"The Kingdom of Kien-to-lo (Gândhâra) extends about 1000 *li* from E. to W. and 800 *li* from S. to N. On the East it adjoins the river *Sin* (Indus). The capital of this country is called **Pu-lu-sha-pu-lo** (Purashapura). . . . The towns and villages are almost deserted. . . . There are about a thousand convents, ruined and abandoned; full of wild plants, and presenting only a melancholy solitude. . . ."—*Hwen T'sang, Pèl. Boud.* ii. 104-105.

c. 1001.—"On his (Mahmúd's) reaching **Purshaur**, he pitched his tent outside the city. There he received intelligence of the bold resolve of Jaipál, the enemy of God, and the King of Hind, to offer opposition."—*Al-Utbi*, in *Elliot*, ii. 25.

c. 1020.—"The aggregate of these waters forms a large river opposite the city of **Parsháwar**."—*Al-Birūnī*, in *Elliot*, i. 47. See also 63.

1059.—"The Amír ordered a letter to be despatched to the minister, telling him 'I have determined to go to Hindustán, and pass the winter in Waihind, and Marminára, and **Barshúr**. . . ."—*Baihaki*, in *Elliot*, ii. 150.

c. 1220.—"**Farshābūr**. The vulgar pronunciation is **Barshāwūr**. A large tract between Ghazna and Lahor, famous in the history of the Musulman conquest."—*Yāḳūt*, in *Barbier de Maynard, Dict. de la Perse*, 418.

1519.—"We held a consultation, in which it was resolved to plunder the country of the Aferîdî Afghâns, as had been proposed by Sultan Bayezîd, to fit up the fort of **Pershâwer** for the reception of their effects and corn, and to leave a garrison in it."—*Baber*, 276.

c. 1555.—"We came to the city of **Purshawar**, and having thus fortunately passed the *Kotal* we reached the town of Joshāya. On the Kotal we saw rhinoceroses, the size of a small elephant."—*Sidi 'Ali*, in *J. As. Ser.* i. tom. ix. 201.

c. 1590.—"Tumān Bagrām, which they call **Parshāwar**; the spring here is a source of delight. There is in this place a great place of worship which they call Gorkhatri, to which people, especially Jogis, resort from great distances."—*Āīn* (orig.), i. 592; [ed. *Jarrett*, ii. 404. In iii. 69, **Parasháwar**].

1754.—"On the news that **Peishor** was taken, and that Nadir Shah was preparing to pass the Indus, the Moghol's court, already in great disorder, was struck with terror."—*H. of Nadir Shah*, in *Hanway*, ii. 363.

1783.—"The heat of **Peshour** seemed to me more intense, than that of any country I have visited in the upper parts of India. Other places may be warm; hot winds blowing over tracts of sand may drive us under the shelter of a wetted skreen; but at **Peshour**, the atmosphere, in the summer solstice, becomes almost inflammable."—*G. Forster*, ed. 1808, ii. 57.

1863.—"Its present name we owe to Akbar, whose fondness for innovation led him to change the ancient **Parashâwara**, of which he did not know the meaning, to **Peshâwar**, or the 'frontier town.' Abul Fazl gives both names." — *Cunningham, Arch. Reports*, ii. 87. Gladwin does in his translation give both names; but see above.

PESHCUBZ, s. A form of dagger, the blade of which has a straight thick back, while the edge curves inwardly from a broad base to a very sharp point. Pers. *pesh-kabz*, 'fore-grip.' The handle is usually made of *shir-māhī*, 'the white bone (tooth?) of a large cetacean'; probably morse-tooth, which is repeatedly mentioned in the early English trade with Persia as an article much in demand (*e.g.* see *Sainsbury*, ii. 65, 159, 204, 305; iii. 89, 162, 268, 287, &c.). [The *peshkubz* appears several times in Mr. Egerton's *Catalogue of Indian Arms*, and one is illustrated, Pl. xv. No. 760.]

1767.—
"Received for sundry jewels, &c. . . . (Rs.) 7326 0 0
Ditto for knife, or **peshcubz** (misprinted *pesheolz*). . 3500 0 0."
Lord Clive's Accounts, in *Long*, 497.

PESHCUSH, s. Pers. *pesh-kash*. Wilson interprets this as literally 'first-fruits.' It is used as an offering or tribute, but with many specific and technical senses which will be found in Wilson, *e.g.* a fine on appointment, renewal, or investiture; a quit-rent, a payment exacted on lands formerly rent-free, or in substitution for service no longer exacted; sometimes a present to a great man, or (loosely) for the ordinary Government demand on land. **Peshcush**, in the old English records, is most generally used in the sense of a present to a great man.

1653.—"**Pesket** est vn presant en Turq." —*De la Boullaye-le-Gouz*, ed. 1657, p. 553.

1657.—"As to the **Piscash** for the King of Golcundah, if it be not already done, we do hope with it you may obteyn our liberty to coyne silver Rupees and copper Pice at the Fort, which would be a great accommodation to our Trade. But in this and all other **Piscashes** be as sparing as you can."—*Letter of Court to Ft. St. Geo.*, in *Notes and Exts.*, No. i. p. 7.

1673.—"Sometimes sending **Pishcashes** of considerable value."—*Fryer*, 166.

1675.—"Being informed that Mr. Mohun had sent a **Piscash** of Persian Wine, Cases of Stronge Water, &c. to ye Great Governour of this Countrey, that is 2*d*. or 3*d*. pson in ye kingdome, I went to his house to speake abt. it, when he kept me to dine with him." —*Puckle's Diary*, MS. in India Office.

[1683. — "**Piscash**." (See under **FIRMAUN**.)]

1689.—"But the **Pishcushes** or Presents expected by the *Nabobs* and *Omrahs* retarded our Inlargement for some time notwithstanding."—*Ovington*, 415.

1754.—"After I have refreshed my army at DELHIE, and received the subsidy (*Note*. —'This is called a **Peischcush**, or present from an inferior to a superior. The sum agreed for was 20 crores') which must be paid, I will leave you in possession of his dominion."—*Hist. of Nadir Shah*, in *Hanway*, ii. 371.

1761.—"I have obtained a promise from his Majesty of his royal confirmation of all your possessions and priviledges, provided you pay him a proper **pishcush**. . . ."—*Major Carnac* to the Governor and Council, in *Van Sittart*, i. 119.

1811.—"By the *fixed or regulated sum* . . . the Sultan . . . means the **Paishcush**, or tribute, which he was bound by former treaties to pay to the Government of Poonah; but which he does not think proper to . . . designate by any term denotive of inferiority, which the word *Paishcush* certainly is."—*Kirkpatrick*, Note on *Tippoo's Letters*, p. 9.

PESH-KHĀNA, PESH-KHIDMAT, ss. Pers. 'Fore-service.' The tents and accompanying retinue sent on over-night, during a march, to the new camping ground, to receive the master on his arrival. A great personage among the natives, or among ourselves, has a complete double establishment, one portion of which goes thus every night in advance. [Another term used is **peshkhaima** Pers. 'advance tents,' as below.]

1665.—"When the King is in the field, he hath usually two Camps . . . to the end that when he breaketh up and leaveth one, the other may have passed before by a day and be found ready when he arriveth at the place design'd to encamp at; and 'tis therefore that they are called **Peiche-kanes**, as if you should say, Houses going before. . . ."—*Bernier*, E.T. 115; [ed. *Constable*, 359].

[1738.—"**Peish-khanna** is the term given to the royal tents and their appendages in India."—*Hanway*, iv. 153.

[1862.—"The result of all this uproarious bustle has been the erection of the Sardár's **peshkhaima**, or advanced tent."—*Bellew, Journal of Mission*, 409.]

PESHWA, s. from Pers. 'a leader, a guide.' The chief minister of the Mahratta power, who afterwards, supplanting his master, the descendant of Sivaji, became practically the prince of an independent State and chief of the Mahrattas. The Peshwa's power expired with the surrender to Sir John Malcolm of the last Peshwa, Bājī Rāo, in 1817. He lived in wealthy exile, and with a *jāgīr* under his own jurisdiction, at Bhitūr, near Cawnpoor, till January 1851. His adopted son, and the claimant of his honours and allowances, was the infamous Nānā Sāhib.

Mr C. P. Brown gives a feminine *peshwīn*: "The princess Gangā Bāī was *Peshwīn* of Purandhar." (MS. notes).

1673.—"He answered, it is well, and referred our Business to *Moro Pundit* his **Peshua**, or Chancellour, to examine our Articles, and give an account of what they were."—*Fryer*, 79.

1803.—"But how is it with the **Peshwah**? He has no minister; no person has influence over him, and he is only guided by his own caprices."—*Wellington Desp.*, ed. 1837, ii. 177.

In the following passage (*quandoquidem dormitans*) the Great Duke had forgotten that things were changed since he left India, whilst the editor perhaps did not know:

1841.—"If you should draw more troops from the Establishment of Fort St. George, you will have to place under arms the subsidiary force of the Nizam, the **Peishwah**, and the force in Mysore, and the districts ceded by the Nizam in 1800-1801."—Letter from the *D. of Wellington*, in *Ind. Adm. of Lord Ellenborough*, 1874. (Dec. 29). The Duke was oblivious when he spoke of the Peshwa's Subsidiary Force in 1841.

PETERSILLY, s. This is the name by which 'parsley' is generally called in N. India. We have heard it quoted there as an instance of the absurd corruption of English words in the mouths of natives. But this case at least might more justly be quoted as an example of accurate transfer. The word is simply the Dutch term for 'parsley,' viz. **petersilie**, from the Lat. *petroselinum*, of which *parsley* is itself a double corruption through the French *persil*. In the Arabic of Avicenna the name is given as *fatrasiliūn*.

PETTAH, s. Tam. *pēṭṭai*. The extramural suburb of a fortress, or the town attached and adjacent to a fortress. The *pettah* is itself often separately fortified; the fortress is then its citadel. The Mahratti *peṭh* is used in like manner; [it is Skt. *peṭaka*, and the word possibly came to the Tamil through the Mahr.]. The word constantly occurs in the histories of war in Southern India.

1630.—"'Azam Khán, having ascended the Pass of Anjan-dúdh, encamped 3 *kos* from Dhárúr. He then directed Multafit Khán . . . to make an attack upon . . . Dhárúr and its **petta**, where once a week people from all parts, far and near, were accustomed to meet for buying and selling."—*Abdul Hamīd*, in *Elliot*, vii. 20.

1763.—"The pagoda served as a citadel to a large **pettah**, by which name the people on the Coast of Coromandel call every town contiguous to a fortress."—*Orme*, ed. 1803, i. 147.

1791.—". . . The **petta** or town (at Bangalore) of great extent to the north of the fort, was surrounded by an indifferent rampart and excellent ditch, with an intermediate berm . . . planted with impenetrable and well-grown thorns. . . . Neither the fort nor the **petta** had drawbridges."—*Wilks, Hist. Sketches*, iii. 123.

1803.—"The **pettah** wall was very lofty, and defended by towers, and had no rampart."—*Wellington*, ed. 1837, ii. 193.

1809.—"I passed through a country little cultivated . . . to Kingeri, which has a small mud-fort in good repair, and a **pettah** apparently well filled with inhabitants."—*Ld. Valentia*, i. 412.

1839.—"The English ladies told me this **Pettah** was 'a horrid place—quite native!' and advised me never to go into it; so I went next day, of course, and found it most curious—really *quite native*."—*Letters from Madras*, 289.

PHANSEEGAR, s. See under **THUG**.

[**PHOOLKAREE**, s. Hind. *phūlkārī*, 'flowered embroidery.' The term applied in N. India to the cotton sheets embroidered in silk by village women, particularly Jats. Each girl is supposed to embroider one of these for her marriage. In recent years a considerable demand has arisen for specimens of this kind of needlework among English ladies, who use them for screens and other decorative purposes. Hence a considerable manufacture has sprung up of which an account will be found in a note by Mrs. F. A. Steel, appended to Mr.

H. C. Cookson's *Monograph on the Silk Industry of the Punjab* (1886-7), and in the *Journal of Indian Art*, ii. 71 *seqq.*

[1887.—"They (native school girls) were collected in a small inner court, which was hung with the pretty **phulcarries** they make here (Rawal Pindi), and which . . . looked very Oriental and gay." — *Lady Dufferin, Viceregal Life*, 336.]

[**PHOORZA**, s. A custom-house; Gujarātī *phurjā*, from Ar. *furẓat* 'a notch,' then 'a bight,' 'river-mouth,' 'harbour'; hence 'a tax' or 'custom-duty.'

[1791.—The East India Calendar (p. 131) has "John Church, **Phoorza**-Master, Surat."

[1727. — "And the Mogul's **Furza** or custom-house is at this place (Hughly)."—*A. Hamilton*, ed. 1744, ii. 19.

[1772.—"But as they still insisted on their people sitting at the gates on the **Phoorzer** Coosky . . ."—*Forrest, Bombay Letters*, i. 386, and see 392, "**Phoorze** Master." *Coosky*= P.—Mahr. *Khushkī*, "inland transit-duties."

[1813.—". . . idols . . . were annually imported to a considerable number at the Baroche **Phoorza**, when I was custom-master at that settlement." — *Forbes, Or. Mem.* 2nd ed. ii. 334.]

PIAL, s. A raised platform on which people sit, usually under the verandah, or on either side of the door of the house. It is a purely S. Indian word, and partially corresponds to the N. Indian *chabūtra* (see **CHABOOTRA**). Wilson conjectures the word to be Telugu, but it is in fact a form of the Portuguese *poyo* and *poyal* (Span. *poyo*), 'a seat or bench.' This is again, according to Diez (i. 326), from the Lat. *podium*, 'a projecting base, a balcony.' Bluteau explains *poyal* as 'steps for mounting on horseback' (*Scoticè*, 'a louping-on stone') [see *Dalboquerque*, Hak. Soc. ii. 68]. The quotation from Mr. Gover describes the S. Indian thing in full.

1553.—". . . paying him his courtesy in Moorish fashion, which was seating himself along with him on a **poyal**."—*Castanheda*, vi. 3.

1578.—"In the public square at Goa, as it was running furiously along, an infirm man came in its way, and could not escape; but the elephant took him up in his trunk, and without doing him any hurt deposited him on a **poyo**."—*Acosta, Tractado*, 432.

1602.—"The natives of this region who are called Iaos, are men so arrogant that they think no others their superiors . . . insomuch that if a Iao in passing along the street becomes aware that any one of another nation is on a **poyal**, or any place above him, if the person does not immediately come down, . . . until he is gone by, he will kill him."—*Couto*, IV. iii. 1. [For numerous instances of this superstition, see *Frazer, Golden Bough*, 2nd ed. i. 360 *seqq.*]

1873.—"Built against the front wall of every Hindu house in southern India . . . is a bench 3 feet high and as many broad. It extends along the whole frontage, except where the house-door stands. . . . The posts of the **veranda** or **pandal** are fixed in the ground a few feet in front of the bench, enclosing a sort of platform: for the basement of the house is generally 2 or 3 feet above the street level. The raised bench is called the **Pyal**, and is the lounging-place by day. It also serves in the hot months as a couch for the night. . . . There the visitor is received; there the bargaining is done; there the beggar plies his trade, and the *Yogi* (see **JOGEE**) sounds his **conch**; there also the members of the household clean their teeth, amusing themselves the while with belches and other frightful noises. . . ."—*Pyal Schools in Madras*, by *E. C. Gover*, in *Ind. Antiq.* ii. 52.

PICAR, s. Hind. *paikār*, [which again is a corruption of Pers. *pā'e-kār*, *pā'e*, 'a foot'], a retail-dealer, an intermediate dealer or broker.

1680.—"**Picar.**" See under **DUSTOOR**.

1683.—"Ye said Naylor has always corresponded with Mr. Charnock, having been always his intimate friend; and without question either provides him goods out of the Hon. Comp.'s Warehouse, or connives at the Weavers and **Piccars** doing of it."—*Hedges, Diary*, Hak. Soc. i. 133.

[1772.—"**Pykârs** (*Dellols* (see **DELOLL**) and Gomastahs) are a chain of agents through whose hands the articles of merchandize pass from the loom of the manufacturer, or the store-house of the cultivator, to the public merchant, or exporter."—*Verelst, View of Bengal, Gloss.* s.v.]

PICE, s. Hind. *paisā*, a small copper coin, which under the Anglo-Indian system of currency is $\frac{1}{4}$ of an anna, $\frac{1}{64}$ of a rupee, and somewhat less than $\frac{3}{8}$ of a farthing. *Pice* is used slangishly for money in general. By Act XXIII. of 1870 (cl. 8) the following copper coins are current:—1. Double *Pice* or Half-anna, 2. *Pice* or $\frac{1}{4}$ anna. 3. *Half-pice* or $\frac{1}{8}$ anna. 4. *Pie* or $\frac{1}{12}$ anna. No. 2 is the only one in very common use. As with most other coins, weights, and measures, there used to be **pucka** pice, and **cutcha** pice. The distinction was sometimes between the regularly minted copper of the Government and certain amorphous pieces of copper which did duty for small change (*e.g.* in the N.W. Provinces within memory), or between single and double pice, *i.e.* $\frac{1}{4}$ anna-pieces and $\frac{1}{2}$ anna-pieces. [Also see **PIE.**]

c. 1590.—"The *dâm* . . . is the fortieth part of the rupee. At first this coin was called **Paisah.**"—*Āīn*, ed. *Blochmann*, i. 31.

[1614.—"Another coin there is of copper, called a **Pize**, whereof you have commonly 34 in the mamudo."—*Foster, Letters*, iii. 11.]

1615.—"**Pice**, which is a Copper Coyne; twelve Drammes make one **Pice**. The English Shilling, if weight, will yeeld thirtie three *Pice* and a halfe."—*W. Peyton*, in *Purchas*, i. 530.

1616.—"Brasse money, which they call **Pices**, whereof three or thereabouts countervail a Peny."—*Terry*, in *Purchas*, ii. 1471.

1648.—". . . de **Peysen** zijn kooper gelt. . . ."—*Van Twist*, 62.

1653.—"**Peça** est vne monnoye du Mogol de la valeur de 6 deniers."—*De la Boullaye-le-Gouz*, ed. 1657, p. 553.

1673.—"**Pice**, a sort of Copper Money current among the Poorer sort of People . . . the Company's Accounts are kept in Book-rate **Pice**, viz. 32 to the Mam. [i.e. *Mamoodee*, see **GOSBECK**], and 80 **Pice** to the Rupee."—*Fryer*, 205.

1676.—"The Indians have also a sort of small Copper-money; which is called **Pecha**. . . . In my last Travels, a *Roupy* went at Surat for nine and forty **Pecha's**."—*Tavernier*, E.T. ii. 22; [ed. *Ball*, i. 27].

1689.—"Lower than these (pice), bitter-Almonds here (at Surat) pass for Money, about Sixty of which make a **Pice**."—*Ovington*, 219.

1726.—"1 *Ana* makes 1½ stuyvers or 2 **peys**."—*Valentijn*, v. 179. [Also see under **MOHUR GOLD.**]

1768.—"Shall I risk my cavalry, which cost 1000 rupees each horse, against your cannon balls that cost two **pice**?—No.—I will march your troops until their legs become the size of their bodies."—*Hyder Ali*, Letter to *Col. Wood*, in *Forbes, Or. Mem.* iii. 287; [2nd ed. ii. 300].

c. 1816.—"'Here,' said he, 'is four **pucker-pice** for Mary to spend in the bazar; but I will thank you, Mrs. Browne, not to let her have any fruit. . . ."—*Mrs. Sherwood's Stories*, 16, ed. 1863.

PICOTA, s. An additional allowance or percentage, added as a handicap to the weight of goods, which varied with every description,—and which the editor of the *Subsidios* supposes to have lead to the varieties of **bahar** (q.v.). Thus at Ormuz the bahar was of 20 farazolas (see **FRAZALA**), to which was added, as *picota*, for cloves and mace 3 maunds (of Ormuz), or about $\frac{1}{7}$ additional; for cinnamon $\frac{1}{20}$ additional; for benzoin $\frac{1}{6}$ additional, &c. See the *Pesos*, &c. of *A. Nunes* (1554) *passim*. We have not been able to trace the origin of this term, nor any modern use.

[1554.—"**Picotaa.**" (See under **BRAZIL-WOOD, DOOCAUN.**)]

PICOTTAH, s. This is the term applied in S. India to that ancient machine for raising water, which consists of a long lever or yard, pivotted on an upright post, weighted on the short arm and bearing a line and bucket on the long arm. It is the *dhenklī* of Upper India, the *shādūf* of the Nile, and the old English *sweep*, *swape*, or *sway-pole*. The machine is we believe still used in the Terra Incognita of market-gardens S.E. of London. The name is Portuguese, *picota*, a marine term now applied to the handle of a ship's pump and post in which it works—a 'pump-brake.' The *picota* at sea was also used as a pillory, whence the employment of the word as quoted from Correa. The word is given in the Glossary attached to the "Fifth Report" (1812), but with no indication of its source. Fryer (1673, pub. 1698) describes the thing without giving it a name. In the following the word is used in the marine sense:

1524.—"He (V. da Gama) ordered notice to be given that no seaman should wear a cloak, except on Sunday . . . and if he did, that it should be taken from him by the constables (*lhe serra tomada polos meirinhos*), and the man put in the **picota** in disgrace, for one day. He found great fault with men of military service wearing cloaks, for in that guise they did not look like soldiers."—*Correa, Lendas*, II. ii. 822.

1782.—"Pour cet effet (arroser les terres) on emploie une machine appellée **Picôte**. C'est une bascule dressée sur le bord d'un puits ou d'un réservoir d'eaux pluviales, pour en tirer l'eau, et la conduire ensuite où l'on veut."—*Sonnerat, Voyage*, i. 188.

c. 1790.—"Partout les **pakotiés**, ou puits à bascule, étoient en mouvement pour fournir l'eau nécessaire aux plantes, et partout on entendoit les jardiniers égayer leurs travaux par des chansons."—*Haafner*, ii. 217.

1807.—"In one place I saw people employed in watering a rice-field with the *Yatam*, or **Pacota**, as it is called by the English."—*Buchanan, Journey through Mysore*, &c., i. 15. [Here *Yatam*, is Can. *yāta* Tel. *ētamu*, Mal. *ēttam*.]

[1871.—
"Aye, e'en **picotta**-work would gain
By using such bamboos."
Gover, Folk Songs of S. India, 184.]

PIE, s. Hind. *pā'ī*, the smallest copper coin of the Anglo-Indian currency, being $\frac{1}{12}$ of an anna, $\frac{1}{192}$ of a rupee, = about $\frac{1}{2}$ a farthing. This is now the authorised meaning of *pie*. But *pā'ī* was originally, it would seem, the fourth part of an anna, and in fact identical with **pice** (q.v.). It is the H.—Mahr. *pā'ī*, 'a quarter,' from Skt. *pad*, *pādikā* in that sense.

[1866.—". . . his father has a one pie share in a small village which may yield him perhaps 24 rupees per annum."—*Confessions of an Orderly*, 201.]

PIECE-GOODS. This, which is now the technical term for Manchester cottons imported into India, was originally applied in trade to the Indian cottons exported to England, a trade which appears to have been deliberately killed by the heavy duties which Lancashire procured to be imposed in its own interest, as in its own interest it has recently procured the abolition of the small import duty on English piece-goods in India.* [In 1898 a duty at the rate of 3 per cent. on cotton goods was reimposed.]

Lists of the various kinds of Indian piece-goods will be found in Milburn (i. 44, 45, 46, and ii. 90, 221), and we assemble them below. It is not in our power to explain their peculiarities, except in very few cases, found under their proper heading. [In the present edition these lists have been arranged in alphabetical order. The figures before each indicate that they fall into the following classes: 1. Piece-goods formerly exported from Bombay and Surat; 2. Piece-goods exported from Madras and the Coast; 3. Piece-goods: the kinds imported into Great Britain from Bengal. Some notes and quotations have been added. But it must be understood that the classes of goods now known under these names may or may not exactly represent those made at the time when these lists were prepared. The names printed in capitals are discussed in separate articles.]

1665.—"I have sometimes stood amazed at the vast quantity of Cotton-Cloth of all sorts, fine and others, tinged and white,

* It is an easy assumption that this export trade from India was killed by the development of machinery in England. We can hardly doubt that this cause would have killed it in time. But it was not left to any such lingering and natural death. Much time would be required to trace the whole of this episode of "ancient history." But it is certain that this Indian trade was not killed by natural causes: *it was killed by prohibitory duties*. These duties were so high in 1783 that they were declared to operate as a premium on smuggling, and they were *reduced* to 18 per cent. *ad valorem*. In the year 1796-97 the value of piece-goods from India imported into England was £2,776,682, or one-third of the whole value of the imports from India, which was £8,252,309. And in the sixteen years between 1793-4 and 1809-10 (inclusive) the imports of Indian piece-goods amounted in value to £26,171,125.

In 1799 the duties were raised. I need not give details, but will come down to 1814, just before the close of the war, when they were, I believe, at a maximum. The duties then, on "plain white calicoes," were:—

	£	s.	d.	
Warehouse duty . .	4	0	0	per cent.
War enhancement . .	1	0	0	,,
Customs duty . .	50	0	0	,,
War enhancement . .	12	10	0	,,
Total . . .	67	10	0	{ per cent. on value.

There was an Excise duty upon British manufactured and printed goods of 3½*d*. per square yard, and of twice that amount on foreign (Indian) calico and muslin printed in Great Britain, and the whole of both duty and excise upon such goods was recoverable as drawback upon re-exportation. But on the exportation of Indian white goods there was no drawback recoverable; and stuffs printed in India were at this time, so far as we can discern, *not admitted through the English Custom-house at all* until 1826, when they were admitted on a duty of 3½*d*. per square yard.

(See in the *Statutes*, 43 Geo. III. *capp.* 68, 69, 70; 54 Geo. III. *cap.* 36; 6 Geo. IV. *cap.* 3; also *Macpherson's Annals of Commerce*, iv. 426).

In Sir A. Arbuthnot's publication of *Sir T. Munro's Minutes* (*Memoir*, p. cxxix.) he quotes a letter of Munro's to a friend in Scotland, written about 1825, which shows him surprisingly before his age in the matter of Free Trade, speaking with reference to certain measures of Mr. Huskisson's. The passage ends thus: "India is the country that has been worst used in the new arrangements. All her products ought undoubtedly to be imported freely into England, upon paying the same duties, and no more, which English duties [? manufactures] pay in India. When I see what is done in Parliament against India, I think that I am reading about Edward III. and the Flemings."

Sir A. Arbuthnot adds very appropriately a passage from a note by the late Prof. H. H. Wilson in his continuation of James Mill's *History of India* (1845, vol. i. pp. 538-539), a passage which we also gladly insert here:

"It was stated in evidence (in 1813) that the cotton and silk goods of India, up to this period, could be sold for a profit in the British market at a price from 50 to 60 per cent. lower than those fabricated in England. It consequently became necessary to protect the latter by duties of 70 or 80 per cent. on their value, or by positive prohibition. Had this not been the case, had not such prohibitory duties and decrees existed, the mills of Paisley and of Manchester would have been stopped in their outset, and could hardly have been again set in motion, even by the powers of steam. They were created by the sacrifice of the Indian manufactures. Had India been independent, she would have retaliated; would have imposed preventive duties upon British goods, and would thus have preserved her own productive industry from annihilation. This act of self-defence was not permitted her; she was at the mercy of the stranger. British goods were forced upon her without paying any duty; and the foreign manufacturer employed the arm of political injustice to keep down and ultimately strangle a competitor with whom he could not contend on equal terms."

which the *Hollanders* alone draw from thence and transport into many places, especially into *Japan* and *Europe*; not to mention what the *English*, *Portingal* and *Indian* merchants carry away from those parts."—*Bernier*, E.T. 141; [ed. *Constable*, 439].

1785.—(Res[n]. of Court of Directors of the E.I.C., 8th October) ". . . that the Captains and Officers of all ships that shall sail from any part of India, after receiving notice hereof, shall be allowed to bring 8000 pieces of **piece-goods** and no more . . . that 5000 pieces and no more, may consist of white Muslins and Callicoes, stitched or plain, or either of them, of which 5000 pieces only 2000 may consist of any of the following sorts, viz., *Alliballies*, *Alrochs* (?), *Cossaes*, *Doreas*, *Jamdannies*, *Mulmuls*, *Nainsooks*, *Neckcloths*, *Tanjeebs*, and *Terrindams*, and that 3000 pieces and no more, may consist of coloured piece-goods. . . ." &c., &c.—In *Seton-Karr*, i. 83.

[**Abrawan**, P. *āb-i-ravān*, 'flowing water'; a very fine kind of Dacca muslin. 'Woven air' is the name applied in the *Arabian Nights* to the Patna gauzes, a term originally used for the produce of the Coan looms (*Burton*, x. 247.) "The Hindoos amuse us with two stories, as instances of the fineness of this muslin. One, that the Emperor Aurungzebe was angry with his daughter for exposing her skin through her clothes; whereupon the young princess remonstrated in her justification that she had seven *jamahs* (see **JAMMA**) or suits on; and another, in the Nabob Allaverdy Khawn's time a weaver was chastised and turned out of the city for his neglect, in not preventing his cow from eating up a piece of **abrooan**, which he had spread and carelessly left on the grass."—*Bolt*, *Considerations on Affairs of India*, 206.

3. **ADATIS.**
2. **ALLEJAS.**
3. **Alliballies.** — "*Alaballee* (signifying according to the weavers' interpretation of the word 'very fine') is a muslin of fine texture."—(*J. Taylor*, *Account of the Cotton Manufacture at Dacca*, 45). According to this the word is perhaps from Ar. *ā'lā*, 'superior,' H. *bhalā*, 'good.'
3. **Allibanees.**—Perhaps from *ā'lā*, 'superior,' *bānā*, 'woof.'
1. **Annabatchies.**
3. **Arrahs.**—Perhaps from the place of that name in Shahābād, where, according to Buchanan Hamilton (*Eastern India*, i. 548) there was a large cloth industry.
3. **Aubrahs.**
2. **Aunneketchies.**
3. **BAFTAS.**
3. **BANDANNAS.**
1. **Bejutapauts.** — H. *be-jūṛā*, 'without join,' *pāt*, 'a piece.'
1. **BETEELAS.**
3. **Blue cloth.**
1. **Bombay Stuffs.**
1. **Brawl.**—The *N.E.D.* describes Brawl as a 'blue and white striped cloth manufactured in India.' In a letter of 1616 (*Foster*, iv. 306) we have "Lolwee champell and **Burral**." The editor suggests H. *biral*, 'open in texture, fine.' But Roquefort (s.v.) gives: "*Bure*, *Burel*, grosse étoffe en laine de couleur rousse ou grisâtre, dont s'habillent ordinairement les ramoneurs; cette étoffe est faite de brebis noire et brune, sans aucune autre teinture." And see *N.E.D.* s.v. *Borrel*.
3. **Byrampauts.** (See **BEIRAMEE.**)
2. **Callawapores.**
3. **Callipatties.**—H. *Kālī*, 'black,' *paṭṭī*, 'strip.'
3. **CAMBAYS.**
3. **Cambrics.**
3. **Carpets.**
3. **Carridaries.**
2. **Cattaketchies.**
1. **Chalias.** (See under **SHALEE.**)
3. **Charconnaes.** — H. *chār-khāna*, 'chequered.' "The *charkana*, or chequered muslin, is, as regards manufacture, very similar to the *Doorea* (see **DOREAS** below). They differ in the breadth of the stripes, their closeness to each other, and the size of the squares." (*Forbes Watson*, *Textile Man.* 78). The same name is now applied to a silk cloth. "The word *chārkhāna* simply means 'a check,' but the term is applied to certain silk or mixed fabrics containing small checks, usually about 8 or 10 checks in a line to an inch." (*Yusuf Ali*, *Mon. on Silk*, 93. Also see *Journ. Ind. Art.* iii. 6.)

1683.—"20 yards of **charkonnas**."—In *Yule*, *Hedges' Diary*, Hak. Soc. i. 94.

2. **Chavonis.**
1. **Chelloes.** (See **SHALEE.**)
3. **Chinechuras.** — Probably cloth from **Chinsura.**
1. **CHINTZ**, of sorts.
3. **Chittabullies.**
3. **Chowtars.** — This is almost certainly not identical with **Chudder.** In a list of cotton cloths in the *Āīn* (i. 94) we have *chautār*, which may mean 'made with four threads or wires.' *Chautāhī*, 'four-fold,' is a kind of cloth used in the Punjab for counterpanes (*Francis*, *Man. Cotton*, 7). This cloth is frequently mentioned in the early letters.

1610.—"**Chautares** are white and well requested."—*Danvers*, *Letters*, i. 75.

1614.—"The **Chauters** of Agra and fine baftas nyll doth not here vend."—*Foster*, *Letters*, ii. 45.

1615.—"Four pieces fine white **Cowter**."—*Ibid.* iv. 51.

3. **Chuclaes.** — This may be H. *chaklā*, *chakrī*, which Platts defines as 'a kind of cloth made of silk and cotton.'
3. **Chunderbannies.**—This is perhaps H. *chandra*, 'the moon,' *bānā*, 'woof.'
3. **Chundraconaes.**—Forbes Watson has: "*Chunderkana*, second quality muslin for handkerchiefs": "Plain white bleached muslin called *Chunderkora*." The word is probably *chandrakhāna*, 'moon checks.'
3. **Clouts**, common coarse cloth, for which see *N.E.D.*
3. **Coopees.**—This is perhaps H. *kaupīn*, *kopīn*, 'the small **lungooty** worn by Fakirs.'
3. **Corahs.**—H. *korā*, 'plain, unbleached,

undyed.' What is now known as Kora silk is woven in pieces for waist-cloths (see *Yusuf Ali, op. cit.* 76).

3. **Cossaes.**—This perhaps represents Ar. *khāṣṣa* 'special.' In the *Āīn* we have *khāçah* in the list of cotton cloths (i. 94). Mr. Taylor describes it as a muslin of a close fine texture, and identifies it with the fine muslin which, according to the *Āīn* (ii. 124), was produced at Sonārgāon. The finest kind he says is "*jungle-khasu.*" (*Taylor, op. cit.* 45.)

3. **Cushtaes.**—These perhaps take their name from Kushtia, a place of considerable trade in the Nadiya District.

3. **Cuttannees.** (See **COTTON.**)

1. **Dhooties.** (See **DHOTY.**)

3. **Diapers.**

3. **Dimities.**

3. **Doreas.**—H. *doriyā*, 'striped cloth,' *dor*, 'thread.' In the list in the *Āīn* (i. 95), *Doriyah* appears among cotton stuffs. It is now also made in silk: "The simplest pattern is the stripe; when the stripes are longitudinal the fabric is a *doriya*. . . . The *doriya* was originally a cotton fabric, but it is now manufactured in silk, silk-and-cotton, *tasar*, and other combinations." (*Yusuf Ali, op. cit.* 57, 94.)

1683.—"3 pieces **Dooreas.**"—*Hedges, Diary*, Hak. Soc. i. 94.

3. **DOSOOTIES.**

3. **DUNGAREES.**

3. **Dysucksoys.**

3. **Elatches.**—Platts gives H. *Ilāchā*, 'a kind of cloth woven of silk and thread so as to present the appearance of cardamoms (*ilāchī*).' But it is almost certainly identical with **alleja.** It was probably introduced to Agra, where now alone it is made, by the Moghuls. It differs from *doriya* (see **DOREAS** above) in having a substantial texture, whereas the *doriya* is generally flimsy. (*Yusuf Ali, op. cit.* 95.)

3. **Emmerties.**—This is H. *amratī, imratī*, 'sweet as nectar.'

2. **GINGHAMS.**

2. **Gudelocr** (dimities).—There is a place of the name in the Neilgherry District, but it does not seem to have any cloth manufacture.

1. **GUINEA STUFFS.**

3. **Gurrahs.** — This is probably the H. *gārhā*: "unbleached fabrics which under names varying in different localities, constitute a large proportion of the clothing of the poor. They are used also for packing goods, and as a covering for the dead, for which last purpose a large quantity is employed both by Hindoos and Mahomedans. These fabrics in Bengal pass under the name of **garrha** and **guzee.**" (*Forbes Watson, op. cit.* 83.)

3. **Habassies.**—Probably P. *'abbāsī*, used of cloths dyed in a sort of magenta colour. The recipe is given by *Hadi, Mon. on Dyeing in the N.W.P.* p. 16.

3. **Herba Taffeties.** — These are cloths made of **Grass-cloth.**

3. **Humhums,** from Ar. *ḥammām*, 'a Turkish bath' "(apparently so named from its having been originally used at the bath), is a cloth of a thick stout texture, and generally worn as a wrapper in the cold season." (*Taylor, op. cit.* 63.)

2. **Izarees.**—P. *izār*, 'drawers, trousers.' Watson (*op. cit.* 57, note) says that in some places it is peculiar to men, the women's drawers being *Turwar*. Herklots (*Qanoon-e-Islam*, App. xiv.) gives *eezar* as equivalent to **shulwaur,** like the **pyjamma,** but not so wide.

3. **Jamdannies.** — P.-H. *jāmdānī*, which is said to be properly *jāmahdānī*, 'a box for holding a suit.' The *jāmdānī* is a loom-figured muslin, which Taylor (*op. cit.* 48) calls "the most expensive productions of the Dacca looms."

3. **Jamwars.** H. *jāmawār*, 'sufficient for a dress.' It is not easy to say what stuff is intended by this name. In the *Āīn* (ii. 240) we have *jamahwār*, mentioned among Guzerat stuffs worked in gold thread, and again (i. 95) *jāmahwār Parmnarm* among woollen stuffs. Forbes Watson gives among Kashmīr shawls: "*Jamewars*, or striped shawl pieces"; in the Punjab they are of a striped pattern made both in pashm and wool (*Johnstone, Mon. on Wool*, 9), and Mr. Kipling says, "the stripes are broad, of alternate colours, red and blue, &c." (*Mukharji, Art Manufactures of India*, 374.)

3. **Kincha cloth.**

3. **Kissorsoys.**

3. **Laccowries.**

1. **Lemmannees.**

3. **LONG CLOTHS.**

3. **LOONGHEES, HERBA.** (See **GRASS-CLOTH.**)

1. **LOONGHEE, MAGHRUB.** Ar. *maghrib, maghrab*, 'the west.'

3. **Mamoodeatis.**

3. **Mammoodies.** Platts gives *Maḥmūdī*, 'praised, fine muslin.' The *Āīn* (i. 94) classes the *Maḥmūdī* among cotton cloths, and at a low price. A cloth under this name is made at Shāhābād in the Hardoi District. (*Oudh Gazetteer*, ii. 25.)

2. **Monepore cloths.** (See **MUNNEPORE.**)

2. **Moorees.**—"*Moories* are blue cloths, principally manufactured in the districts of Nellore and at Canatur in the Chingleput collectorate of Madras. . . . They are largely exported to the Straits of Malacca." (*Balfour, Cycl.* ii. 982.)

1684-5.—"**Moorees** superfine, 1000 pieces."—*Pringle, Diary Ft. St. Geo.* iv. 41.

3. **Muggadooties.** (See **MOONGA.**)

3. **MULMULS.**

3. **Mushrues.**—P. *mashrū'*, 'lawful.' It is usually applied to a kind of silk or satin with a cotton back. "Pure silk is not allowed to men, but women may wear the most sumptuous silk fabrics" (*Yusuf Ali, op. cit.* 90, *seq.*). "All *Mushroos* wash well, especially the finer kinds, used for bodices, petticoats, and trousers of both sexes." (*Forbes Watson, op. cit.* 97.)

1832.—"... **Mussheroo** (striped washing silks manufactured at Benares) . . ."—*Mrs. Meer Hassan Ali, Observations*, i. 106.

1. **MUSTERS.**

3. **Naibabies.**

3. **Nainsooks.**—H. *nainsukh*, 'pleasure of the eye.' A sort of fine white calico. Forbes Watson (*op. cit.* 76) says it is used for neckerchiefs, and Taylor (*op. cit.* 46) defines it as "a thick muslin, apparently identical with the *tunsook* (*tansak'h*, *Blochmann*, i. 94) of the *Ayeen*." A cloth is made of the same name in silk, imitated from the cotton fabric. (*Yusuf Ali, op. cit.* 95.)

1. **Neganepauts.**

1. **Nicannees.**—Quoting from a paper of 1683, Orme (*Fragments*, 287) has "6000 **Niccanneers**, 13 yards long."

3. **Nillaes.**—Some kind of blue cloth, H. *nīlā*, 'blue.'

1. **Nunsarees.**—There is a place called Nansārī in the Bhandāra District (*Central Provinces Gazetteer*, 346).

2. **Oringal** (cloths). Probably take their name from the once famous city of Warangal in Hyderabad.

3. **PALAMPORES.**

3. **Peniascoes.**—In a paper quoted by Birdwood (*Report on Old Records*, 40) we have **Pinascos**, which he says are stuffs made of pine-apple fibre.

2, 3. **Percaulas.**—H. *parkālā*, 'a spark, a piece of glass.' These were probably some kind of spangled robe, set with pieces of glass, as some of the modern **Phoolkaris** are. In the *Madras Diaries* of 1684-5 we have "**Percollaes**," and "**percolles**, fine" (*Pringle*, i. 53, iii. 119, iv. 41.)

3. **Photaes.**—In a letter of 1615 we have "Lunges (see **LOONGHEE**) and **Footaes** of all sorts." (*Foster, Letters*, iv. 306), where the editor suggests H. *phūṭā*, 'variegated.' But in the *Āīn* we find "*Fautahs* (loin-bands)" (i. 93), which is the P. *foṭa*, and this is from the connection the word probably meant.

3. **Pulecat** handkerchiefs. (See **MADRAS** handkerchiefs and **BANDANNA.**)

2. **Punjum.**—The *Madras Gloss.* gives Tel. *punjamu*, Tam. *puñjam*, *lit.* 'a collection.' "In Tel. a collection of 60 threads and in Tam. of 120 threads skeined, ready for the formation of the warp for weaving. A cloth is denominated 10, 12, 14, up to 40 *poonjam*, according to the number of times 60, or else 120, is contained in the total number of threads in the warp. *Poonjam* thus also came to mean a cloth of the length of one *poonjam* as usually skeined; this usual length is 36 cubits, or 18 yards, and the width from 38 to 44 inches, 14 lbs. being the common weight; pieces of half length were formerly exported as **Salempoory.**" Writing in 1814, Heyne (*Tracts*, 347) says: "Here (in Salem) two punjums are designated by 'first call,' so that twelve punjums of cloth is called 'six call,' and so on."

3. **Puteahs.** (See **PUTTEE.**) In a letter of 1610 we have: "**Patta**, katuynen, with red stripes over thwart through." (*Danvers, Letters*, i. 72.)

2. **Putton Ketchies.** — Cloths which ossibly took their name from the city of Anhilwāra **Patan** in **Cutch.**

1727.—"That country (Tegnapatam) produces Pepper, and coarse Cloth called **catchas.**"—*A. Hamilton*, i. 335.

3. **Raings.**—"*Rang* is a muslin which resembles jhuna in its transparent gauze or net-like texture. It is made by passing a single thread of the warp through each division of the reed" (*Taylor, op. cit.* 44.) "1 Piece of **Raiglins.**"—*Hedges, Diary*, Hak. Soc. i. 94.

1. **Saloopauts.** (See **SHALEE.**)

3. **Sannoes.**

2. **Sassergates.** — Some kind of cloth called 'that of the 1000 knots,' H. *sahasra granṭhi.* "*Saserguntees*" (*Birdwood, Rep. on Old Records*, 63).

2. **Sastracundees.**—These cloths seem to take their name from a place called *Sāstra-kunḍa*, 'Pool of the Law.' This is probably the place named in the *Āīn* (ed. *Jarrett*, ii. 124): "In the township of *Kiyāra Sundar* is a large reservoir which gives a peculiar whiteness to the cloths washed in it." Gladwin reads the name *Catarashoonda*, or *Catarehsoonder* (see *Taylor, op. cit.* 91).

3. **Seerbands, Seerbetties.**—These are names for turbans, H. *sirband*, *sirbatti.* Taylor (*op. cit.* 47) names them as Dacca muslins under the names of *surbund* and *surbutee.*

3. **Seershauds.** — This is perhaps P. *sir-shād*, 'head-delighting,' some kind of turban or veil.

3. **Seersuckers.** — Perhaps, *sir*, 'head, *sukh*, 'pleasure.'

3. **Shalbaft.** — P. *shālbāft*, 'shawl-weaving.' (See **SHAWL.**)

3. **Sicktersoys.**

3. **SOOSIES.**

3. **Subnoms, Subloms.**—"*Shubnam* is a thin pellucid muslin to which the Persian figurative name of 'evening dew' (*shabnam*) is given, the fabric being, when spread over the bleaching-field, scarcely distinguishable from the dew on the grass." (*Taylor, op. cit.* 45.)

3. **Succatoons.** (See **SUCLAT.**)

3. **Taffaties** of sorts. "A name applied to plain woven silks, in more recent times signifying a light thin silk stuff with a considerable lustre or gloss" (*Drapers' Dict.* s.v.). The word comes from P. *tāftan*, 'to twist, spin.' The *Āīn* (i. 94) has *tāftah* in the list of silks.

3. **Tainsooks.**—H. *tansukh*, 'taking ease.' (See above under **NAINSOOKS.**)

3. **Tanjeebs.** P. *tanzeb*, 'body adorning.'—"A tolerably fine muslin" (*Taylor, op. cit.* 46; *Forbes Watson, op. cit.* 76). "The silk *tanzeb* seems to have gone out of fashion, but that in cotton is very commonly used for the **chicken** work in Lucknow." (*Yusuf Ali, op. cit.* 96.)

1. **Tapseils.** (See under **ALLEJA.**) In the *Āīn* (i. 94) we have: "*Tafçilah* (a stuff from Mecca)."

1670.—"So that in your house are only left some **Tapseiles** and cotton yarn."—In *Yule, Hedges' Diary*, Hak. Soc. ii. ccxxvi. Birdwood in *Report on Old Records*, 38, has **Topsails.**

2. **Tarnatannes.** — "There are various kinds of muslins brought from the East Indies, chiefly from Bengal, betelles (see **BETTEELA**) *tarnatans* . . ." (*Chambers' Cycl.* of 1788, quoted in 3rd ser. *N. & Q.*

iv. 135). It is suggested (*ibid.* 3rd ser. iv. 135) that this is the origin of English *tarletan*, Fr. *tarletane*, which is defined in the *Drapers' Dict.* as "a fine open muslin, first imported from India and afterwards imitated here."

3. **Tartorees.**
3. **Tepoys.**
3. **Terindams.**—"*Turundam* (said by the weavers to mean 'a kind of cloth for the body,' the name being derived from the Arabic word *turuh* (*tarh*, *tarah*) 'a kind,' and the Persian one *undam* (*andām*) 'the body,' is a muslin which was formerly imported, under the name of *terendam*, into this country." (*Taylor, op. cit.* 46.)
2. **Ventepollams.**

PIGDAUN, s. A spittoon; Hind. *pīkdān*. *Pīk* is properly the expectorated juice of chewed betel.

[c. 1665.—". . . servants . . . to carry the **Picquedent** or spittoon. . . ."—*Bernier*, ed. *Constable*, 214. In 283 **Piquedans.**]

1673. — "The Rooms are spread with Carpets as in *India*, and they have **Pigdans**, or Spitting pots of the Earth of this Place, which is valued next to that of China, to void their Spittle in."—*Fryer*, 223.

[1684.—Hedges speaks of purchasing a "Spitting Cup."—*Diary*, Hak. Soc. i. 149.]

PIGEON ENGLISH. The vile jargon which forms the means of communication at the Chinese ports between Englishmen who do not speak Chinese, and those Chinese with whom they are in the habit of communicating. The word "*business*" appears in this kind of talk to be corrupted into "*pigeon*," and hence the name of the jargon is supposed to be taken. [For examples see *Chamberlain, Things Japanese*, 3rd ed. pp. 321 *seqq.*; *Ball, Things Chinese*, 3rd ed. 430 *seqq.* (See **BUTLER ENGLISH.**)]

1880.—". . . the English traders of the early days . . . instead of inducing the Chinese to make use of correct words rather than the misshapen syllables they had adopted, encouraged them by approbation and example, to establish **Pigeon English**—a grotesque gibberish which would be laughable if it were not almost melancholy."—*Capt. W. Gill, River of Golden Sand*, i. 156.

1883.—"The '**Pidjun English**' is revolting, and the most dignified persons demean themselves by speaking it. . . . How the whole English-speaking community, without distinction of rank, has come to communicate with the Chinese in this baby talk is extraordinary."—*Miss Bird, Golden Chersonese*, 37.

PIG-STICKING. This is Anglo-Indian hog-hunting, or what would be called among a people delighting more in lofty expression, 'the chase of the Wild Boar.' When, very many years since, one of the present writers, destined for the Bengal Presidency, first made acquaintance with an Indian mess-table, it was that of a Bombay regiment at Aden — in fact of that gallant corps which is now known as the 103rd Foot, or Royal Bombay Fusiliers. Hospitable as they were, the opportunity of enlightening an aspirant Bengalee on the short-comings of his Presidency could not be foregone. The chief counts of indictment were three: 1st. The inferiority of the Bengal Horse Artillery system; 2nd. That the Bengalees were guilty of the base effeminacy of drinking beer out of champagne glasses; 3rd. That in pig-sticking they *threw* the spear at the boar. The two last charges were evidently ancient traditions, maintaining their ground as facts down to 1840 therefore; and showed how little communication practically existed between the Presidencies as late as that year. Both the allegations had long ceased to be true, but probably the second had been true in the 18th century, as the third certainly had been. This may be seen from the quotation from R. Lindsay, and by the text and illustrations of Williamson's *Oriental Field Sports* (1807), [and much later (see below)]. There is, or perhaps we should say more diffidently there was, still a difference between the Bengal practice in pig-sticking, and that of Bombay. The Bengal spear is about 6½ feet long, loaded with lead at the butt so that it can be grasped almost quite at the end and carried with the point down, inclining only slightly to the front; the boar's charge is received on the right flank, when the point, raised to 45° or 50° of inclination, if rightly guided, pierces him in the shoulder. The Bombay spear is a longer weapon, and is carried under the armpit like a dragoon's lance. Judging from Elphinstone's statement below we should suppose that the Bombay as well as the Bengal practice originally was to throw the spear, but that both independently discarded this, the **Qui-his** adopting the short overhand spear, the **Ducks** the long lance.

1679. — "In the morning we went a hunting of wild Hoggs with Kisna Reddy, the chief man of the Islands" (at mouth of the Kistna) "and about 100 other men of the island (Dio) with lances and Three score doggs, with whom we killed eight Hoggs great and small, one being a Bore very large and fatt, of greate weight."—*Consn. of Agent and Council of Fort St. Geo.* on Tour. In *Notes and Exts.* No. II.

The party consisted of Streynsham Master "Agent of the Coast and Bay;" with "Mr. Timothy Willes and Mr. Richard Mohun of the Councell, the Minister, the Chyrurgeon, the Schoolmaster, the Secretary, and two Writers, an Ensign, 6 mounted soldiers and a Trumpeter," in all 17 Persons in the Company's Service, and "Four Freemen, who went with the Agent's Company for their own pleasure, and at their own charges." It was a Tour of Visitation of the Factories.

1773.—The Hon. R. Lindsay *does* speak of the "Wild-boar chase"; but he wrote after 35 years in England, and rather eschews Anglo-Indianisms:

"Our weapon consisted only of a short heavy spear, three feet in length, and well poised; the boar being found and unkennelled by the spaniels, runs with great speed across the plain, is pursued on horseback, and the first rider who approaches him throws the javelin. . . ."—*Lives of the Lindsays*, iii. 161.

1807.—"When (the hog) begins to slacken, the attack should be commenced by the horseman who may be nearest pushing on to his left side; into which the spear should be thrown, so as to lodge behind the shoulder blade, and about six inches from the backbone."—*Williamson, Oriental Field Sports*, p. 9. (*Left* must mean hog's *right*.) This author says that the bamboo shafts were 8 or 9 feet long, but that *very short* ones had formerly been in use; thus confirming Lindsay.

1816.—"We hog-hunt till two, then tiff, and hawk or course till dusk . . . we do not throw our spears in the old way, but poke with spears longer than the common ones, and never part with them."—*Elphinstone's Life*, i. 311.

[1828.—". . . the boar who had made good the next cane with only a slight scratch from a spear thrown as he was charging the hedge."—*Orient. Sport. Mag.* reprint 1873, i. 116.]

1848.—"Swankey of the Body-Guard himself, that dangerous youth, and the greatest buck of all the Indian army now on leave, was one day discovered by Major Dobbin, *tête-à-tête* with Amelia, and describing the sport of **pigsticking** to her with great humour and eloquence."—*Vanity Fair*, ii. 288.

1866.—"I may be a young **pig-sticker**, but I am too old a sportsman to make such a mistake as that."—*Trevelyan, The Dawk Bungalow*, in *Fraser*, lxxiii. 387.

1873.—"**Pigsticking** may be very good fun. . . ."—*A True Reformer*, ch. i.

1876.—"You would perhaps like tiger-hunting or **pig-sticking**; I saw some of that for a season or two in the East. Everything here is poor stuff after that."—*Daniel Deronda*, ii. ch. xi.

1878.—"In the meantime there was a '**pig-sticking**' meet in the neighbouring district."—*Life in the Mofussil*, i. 140.

PIG-TAIL, s. This term is often applied to the Chinaman's long plait of hair, by transfer from the *queue* of our grandfathers, to which the name was much more appropriate. Though now universal among the Chinese, this fashion was only introduced by their Manchu conquerors in the 17th century, and was "long resisted by the natives of the Amoy and Swatow districts, who, when finally compelled to adopt the distasteful fashion, concealed the badge of slavery beneath cotton turbans, the use of which has survived to the present day" (*Giles, Glossary of Reference*, 32). Previously the Chinese wore their unshaven back hair gathered in a net, or knotted in a chignon. De Rhodes (Rome, 1615, p. 5) says of the people of Tongking, that "*like the Chinese* they have the custom of gathering the hair in fine nets under the hat."

1879.—"One sees a single Sikh driving four or five Chinamen in front of him, having knotted their **pigtails** together for reins."—*Miss Bird, Golden Chersonese*, 283.

PILAU, PILOW, PILÁF, &c., s. Pers. *pulāo*, or *pilāv*, Skt. *pulāka*, 'a ball of boiled rice.' A dish, in origin purely Mahommedan, consisting of meat, or fowl, boiled along with rice and spices. Recipes are given by Herklots, ed. 1863, App. xxix.; and in the *Āīn-i-Akbarī* (ed. *Blochmann*, i. 60), we have one for *kīma pulāo* (*kīma*='hash') with several others to which the name is not given. The *name* is almost as familiar in England as **curry**, but not the *thing*. It was an odd circumstance, some 45 years ago, that the two surgeons of a dragoon regiment in India were called *Currie* and *Pilleau*.

1616.—"Sometimes they boil pieces of flesh or hens, or other fowl, cut in pieces in their rice, which dish they call **pillaw**. As they order it they make it a very excellent and a very well tasted food."—*Terry*, in *Purchas*, ii. 1471.

c. 1630.—"The feast begins: it was compounded of a hundred sorts of **pelo** and candied dried meats."—*Sir T. Herbert*, ed. 1638, p. 138, [and for varieties, p. 310].

[c. 1660.—". . . my elegant hosts were fully employed in cramming their mouths with as much **Pelau** as they could contain. . . ."—*Bernier*, ed. *Constable*, 121.]

1673.—"The most admired Dainty wherewith they stuff themselves is **Pullow**, whereof they will fill themselves to the Throat and receive no hurt, it being so well prepared for the Stomach."—*Fryer*, 399. See also p. 93. At p. 404 he gives a recipe.

1682.—"They eate their **pilaw** and other spoone-meate withoute spoones, taking up their pottage in the hollow of their fingers."—*Evelyn, Diary*, June 19.

1687.—"They took up their Mess with their Fingers, as the Moors do their **Pilaw**, using no Spoons."—*Dampier*, i. 430.

1689.—"**Palau**, that is Rice boil'd . . . with Spices intermixt, and a boil'd Fowl in the middle, is the most common *Indian* Dish."—*Ovington*, 397.

1711.—"They cannot go to the Price of a **Pilloe**, or boil'd Fowl and Rice; but the better sort make that their principal Dish."—*Lockyer*, 231.

1793.—"On a certain day . . . all the Musulman officers belonging to your department shall be entertained at the charge of the *Sircar*, with a public repast, to consist of **Pullao** of the first sort."—*Select Letters of Tippoo S.*, App. xlii.

c. 1820.—

"And nearer as they came, a genial savour
Of certain stews, and roast-meats, and **pilaus**,
Things which in hungry mortals' eyes find favour."—*Don Juan*, v. 47.

1848.—"'There's a **pillau**, Joseph, just as you like it, and Papa has brought home the best turbot in Billingsgate.'"—*Vanity Fair*, i. 20.

PINANG, s. This is the Malay word for Areca, and it is almost always used by the Dutch to indicate that article, and after them by some Continental writers of other nations. The Chinese word for the same product—*pin-lang*—is probably, as Bretschneider says, a corruption of the Malay word. (See **PENANG**.)

[1603.—"They (the Javans) are very great eaters—and they haue a certaine hearbe called *bettaile* (see **BETEL**) which they vsually have carryed with them wheresouer they goe, in boxes, or wrapped vp in a cloath like a sugar loafe: and also a nut called **Pinange**, which are both in operation very hott, and they eate them continually to warme them within, and keepe them from the fluxe. They do likewise take much tabacco, and also opium."—*E. Scott, An Exact Discourse*, &c., *of the East Indies*, 1606, Sig. N. 2.

[1665.—"Their ordinary food . . . is Rice, Wheat, **Pinange**. . . ."—*Sir T. Herbert, Travels*, 1677, p. 365 (*Stanf. Dict.*).]

1726.—"But Shah Sousa gave him (viz. Van der Broek, an envoy to Rajmahal in 1655) good words, and regaled him with **Pinang** (a great favour), and promised that he should be amply paid for everything."—*Valentijn*, v. 165.

PINDARRY, s. Hind. *pinḍārī*, *pinḍārā*, but of which the more original form appears to be Mahr. *pendhārī*, a member of a band of plunderers called in that language *pendhār* and *pendhārā*. The etymology of the word is very obscure. We may discard as a curious coincidence only, the circumstance observed by Mr. H. T. Prinsep, in the work quoted below (i. 37, note), that "**Pindara** seems to have the same reference to *Pandour* that *Kuzāk* has to *Cossack*." Sir John Malcolm observes that the most popular etymology among the natives ascribes the name to the dissolute habits of the class, leading them to frequent the shops dealing in an intoxicating drink called *pinda*. (One of the senses of *penḍhā*, according to Molesworth's *Mahr. Dict.*, is 'a drink for cattle and men, prepared from *Holcus sorghum*' (see **JOWAUR**) 'by steeping it and causing it to ferment.') Sir John adds: 'Kurreem Khan' (a famous Pindarry leader) 'told me he had never heard of any other reason for the name; and Major Henley had the etymology confirmed by the most intelligent of the Pindarries of whom he enquired' (*Central India*, 2nd ed. i. 433). Wilson again considers the most probable derivation to be from the Mahr. *penḍhā*, but in the sense of a 'bundle of rice-straw,' and *hara*, 'who takes,' because the name was originally applied to horsemen who hung on to an army, and were employed in collecting forage. We cannot think either of the etymologies very satisfactory. We venture another, as a plausible suggestion merely. Both *pinḍ-parnā* in Hindi, and *pinḍās-basneṅ* in Mahr. signify 'to follow'; the latter being defined 'to stick closely to; to follow to the death; used of the adherence of a disagreeable fellow.' Such phrases would aptly apply to these hangers-on of an army in the field, looking out for prey. [The question has been discussed by Mr. W. Irvine in an elaborate note published in the *Indian Antiq.* of 1900. To the above three suggestions he adds two made by other authorities: 4. that the term was taken from the *Beder* race; 5. from *Pinḍārā*, *pinḍ*, 'a lump of food,' *ār*, 'bringer,' a plunderer. As to the fourth suggestion, he remarks that there was a Beder race dwelling in Mysore, Belary and the Nizam's territories. But the objection to this etymology is that as far back as 1748 both words, *Bedar* and *Pinḍārī*, are used by the native historian, Rām Singh Munshī, side by side, but applied to different bodies of men. Mr. Irvine's suggestion is that the word *Pinḍārī*, or more strictly *Pandhār*, comes from a place or region called *Pāndhār* or *Pandhār*. This place is referred to by native historians, and seems to have been situated between Burhānpur and Handiya on the Nerbudda. There is good evidence to prove that large numbers of Pindāris were settled in this part of the country. Mr. Irvine sums up by saying: "If it were not for a passage in Grant Duff (*H. of the Mahrattas*, Bombay reprint, 157), I should have been ready to maintain that I had proved my case. My argument requires two things to make it irrefutable: (1) a very early connection between Pandhār and the Pindhāris; (2) that the Pindhāris had no early home or settlement outside Pandhār. As to the first point, the recorded evidence seems to go no further back than 1794, when Sendhiah granted them lands in Nimār; whereas before that time the name had become fixed, and had even crept into Anglo-Indian vocabularies. As to the second point, Grant Duff says, and he if anybody must have known, that "there were a number of Pindhāris about the borders of Mahārāshtra and the Carnatic. . . ." Unless these men emigrated from Khandesh about 1726 (that is a hundred years before 1826, the date of Grant Duff's book), their presence in the South with the same name tends to disprove any special connection between their name, Pindhāri, and a place, Pindhār, several hundred miles from their country. On the other hand, it is a very singular coincidence that men known as Pindhāris should have been newly settled about 1794 in a country which had been known as Pandhār at least ninety years before they thus occupied it. Such a mere fortuitous connection between Pandhār and the Pindhāris is so extraordinary that we may call it an impossibility. A fair inference is that the region Pandhār was the original home of the Pindhāris, that they took their name from it, and that grants of land between Burhānpur and Handiya were made to them in what had always been their home-country, namely Pandhār."]

The Pinḍārīs seem to have grown up in the wars of the late Mahommedan dynasties in the Deccan, and in the latter part of the 17th century attached themselves to the Mahrattas in their revolt against Aurangzīb; the first mention which we have seen of the name occurs at this time. For some particulars regarding them we refer to the extract from Prinsep below. During and after the Mahratta wars of Lord Wellesley's time many of the Pinḍārī leaders obtained grants of land in Central India from Sindia and Holkar, and in the chaos which reigned at that time outside the British territory their raids in all directions, attended by the most savage atrocities, became more and more intolerable; these outrages extended from Bundelkhand on the N.E., Kadapa on the S., and Orissa on the S.E., to Guzerat on the W., and at last repeatedly violated British territory. In a raid made upon the coast extending from Masulipatam northward, the Pinḍārīs in ten days plundered 339 villages, burning many, killing and wounding 682 persons, torturing 3600, and carrying off or destroying property to the amount of £250,000. It was not, however, till 1817 that the Governor-General, the Marquis of Hastings, found himself armed with permission from home, and in a position to strike at them effectually, and with the most extensive strategic combinations ever brought into action in India. The Pinḍārīs were completely crushed, and those of the native princes who supported them compelled to submit, whilst the British power for the first time was rendered truly paramount throughout India.

1706-7.—"Zoolfecar Khan, after the rains pursued Dhunnah, who fled to the Beejapore country, and the Khan followed him to the banks of the Kistnah. The Pinderrehs took Velore, which however was soon retaken. . . . A great caravan, coming from Aurungabad, was totally plundered and everything carried off, by a body of Mharattas, at only 12 coss distance from the imperial camp."—*Narrative of a Bondeela Officer*, app. to Scott's Tr. of Firishta's *H. of Deccan*, ii. 122. [On this see *Malcolm, Central India*, 2nd ed. i. 426. Mr. Irvine in the paper quoted above shows that it is doubtful if the author really used the word. "By a strange coincidence the very copy used by J. Scott is now in the British Museum. On turning to the passage I find 'Peḍā Badar,' a well-known man of the period, and not *Pindārā* or *Pinderreh* at all."]

1762.—"Siwaee Madhoo Rao . . . began to collect troops, stores, and heavy artillery, so that he at length assembled near 100,000 horse, 60,000 **Pindarehs**, and 50,000 matchlock foot. . . . In reference to the **Pindarehs**, it is not unknown that they are a low tribe of robbers entertained by some of the princes of the Dakhan, to plunder and lay waste the territories of their enemies, and to serve for guides."—*H. of Hydur Naik*, by *Meer Hassan Ali Khan*, 149. [Mr. Irvine suspects that this may be based on a misreading as in the former quotation. The earliest undoubted mention of the name in native historians is by Rām Singh (1748). There is a doubtful reference in the *Tārīkh-i-Muhammadī* (1722-23)].

1784.—"**Bindarras**, who receive no pay, but give a certain monthly sum to the commander-in-chief for permission to maraud, or plunder, under sanction of his banners." —*Indian Vocabulary*, s.v.

1803.—"Depend upon it that no **Pindarries** or straggling horse will venture to your rear, so long as you can keep the enemy in check, and your detachment well in advance."—*Wellington*, ii. 219.

1823.—"On asking an intelligent old **Pindarry**, who came to me on the part of Kurreem Khan, the reason of this absence of high character, he gave me a short and shrewd answer: 'Our occupation' (said he) 'was incompatible with the fine virtues and qualities you state; and I suppose if any of our people ever had them, the first effect of such good feeling would be to make him leave our community.'"—*Sir John Malcolm, Central India*, i. 436.

[,, "He had ascended on horseback . . . being mounted on a **Pindaree** pony, an animal accustomed to climbing."—*Hoole, Personal Narrative*, 292.]

1825.—"The name of **Pindara** is coeval with the earliest invasion of Hindoostan by the Mahrattas. . . . The designation was applied to a sort of sorry cavalry that accompanied the Pêshwa's armies in their expeditions, rendering them much the same service as the Cossacks perform for the armies of Russia. . . . The several leaders went over with their bands from one chief to another, as best suited their private interests, or those of their followers. . . . The rivers generally became fordable by the close of the **Dussera**. The horses then were shod, and a leader of tried courage and conduct having been chosen as *Luhbureea*, all that were inclined set forth on a foray or *Luhbur*, as it was called in the **Pindaree** nomenclature; all were mounted, though not equally well. Out of a thousand, the proportion of good cavalry might be 400: the favourite weapon was a bamboo spear . . . but . . . it was a rule that every 15th or 20th man of the fighting **Pindarees** should be armed with a matchlock. Of the remaining 600, 400 were usually common *looteas* (see **LOOTY**), indifferently mounted, and armed with every variety of weapon, and the rest, slaves, attendants, and camp-followers, mounted on **tattoos**, or wild ponies, and keeping up with the *luhbur* in the best manner they could."—*Prinsep, Hist. of Pol. and Mil. Transactions* (1813-1823), i. 37, note.

1829.—"The person of whom she asked this question said '*Brinjaree*' (see **BRINJARRY**) . . . but the lady understood him **Pindaree**, and the name was quite sufficient. She jumped out of the palanquin and ran towards home, screaming, '**Pindarees, Pindarees.**'"—*Mem. of John Shipp*, ii. 281.

[1861.—
"So I took to the hills of Malwa, and the
free **Pindaree** life."]
Sir A. Lyall, The Old Pindaree.

PINE-APPLE. (See **ANANAS.**) [The word has been corrupted by native weavers into **pinaphal** or **minaphal**, as the name of a silk fabric, so called because of the pine-apple pattern on it. (See *Yusuf Ali, Mon. on Silk*, 99.)]

PINJRAPOLE, s. A hospital for animals, existing perhaps only in Guzerat, is so called. Guz. *pinjrāpor* or *pinjrapol*, [properly a cage (*pinjra*) for the sacred bull (*pola*) released in the name of Siva]. See *Heber*, ed. 1844, ii. 120, and *Ovington*, 300-301; [*P. della Valle*, Hak. Soc. i. 67, 70. *Forbes* (*Or. Mem.* 2nd ed. i. 156) describes "the Banian hospital" at Surat; but they do not use this word, which Molesworth says is quite modern in Mahr.]

1808.—"Every marriage and mercantile transaction among them is taxed with a contribution for the **Pinjrapole** ostensibly." —*R. Drummond.*

PINTADO. From the Port.

a. A 'painted' (or 'spotted') cloth, *i.e.* **chintz** (q.v.). Though the word was applied, we believe, to all printed goods, some of the finer Indian chintzes were, at least in part, finished by hand-painting.

1579.—"With cloth of diverse colours, not much unlike our vsuall **pentadoes**."—*Drake, World Encompassed*, Hak. Soc. 143.

[1602.—". . . some fine **pinthadoes**."—*Birdwood, First Letter Book*, 34.]

1602-5.—". . . about their loynes a fine **Pintadoe.**"—*Scot's Discourse of Iava*, in *Purchas*, i. 164.

1606.—"Heare the Generall deliuered a Letter from the KINGS MAIESTIE of ENGLAND, with a fayre standing Cuppe, and a cover double gilt, with divers of the choicest **Pintadoes**, which hee kindly accepted of."—*Middleton's Voyage*, E. 3.

[1610.—"**Pintadoes** of divers sorts will sell. . . . The names are Sarassa, Berumpury, large Chaudes, Selematt Cambaita, Selematt white and black, Cheat Betime and divers others."—*Danvers, Letters*, i. 75.

c. 1630.—"Also they stain Linnen cloth, which we call **pantadoes.**"—*Sir T. Herbert*, ed. 1677, p. 304.]

1665.—"To Woodcott . . . where was a roome hung with **Pintado**, full of figures greate and small, prettily representing sundry trades and occupations of the Indians."—*Evelyn's Diary*, Dec. 30.

c. 1759.—"The chintz and other fine **painted goods**, will, if the market is not overstocked, find immediate vent, and sell for 100 p. cent."—*Letter from Pegu*, in *Dalrymple, Or. Rep.* i. 120.

b. A name (not Anglo-Indian) for the Guinea-fowl. This *may* have been given from the resemblance of the speckled feathers to a chintz. But in fact *pinta* in Portuguese is 'a spot,' or fleck, so that probably it only means speckled. This is the explanation of *Bluteau*. [The word is more commonly applied to the cape Pigeon. See Mr. Gray's note on *Pyrard de Laval*, Hak. Soc. i. 21, who quotes from Fryer, p. 12.]

PISACHEE, Skt. *piśāchī*, a she-demon, m. *piśācha*. In S. India some of the demons worshipped by the ancient tribes are so called. The spirits of the dead, and particularly of those who have met with violent deaths, are especially so entitled. They are called in Tamil *pey*. Sir Walter Elliot considers that the *Piśāchīs* were (as in the case of *Rākshasas*) a branch of the aboriginal inhabitants. In a note he says: 'The *Piśāchī* dialect appears to have been a distinct Dravidian dialect, still to be recognised in the speech of the *Paraiya*, who cannot pronounce distinctly some of the pure Tamil letters.' There is, however, in the Hindu drama a *Piśāchā bhāshā*, a gibberish or corruption of Sanskrit, introduced. [This at the present day has been applied to English.] The term *piśāchī* is also applied to the small circular storms commonly by Europeans called **devils** (q.v.). We do not know where Archdeacon Hare (see below) found the *Piśāchī* to be a *white* demon.

1610.—"The fifth (mode of Hindu marriage) is the *Pisácha-viváha*, when the lover, without obtaining the sanction of the girl's parents, takes her home by means of talismans, incantations, and such like magical practices, and then marries her. **Pisách**, in Sanskrit, is the name of a demon, which takes whatever person it fixes on, and as the above marriage takes place after the same manner, it has been called by this name."—*The Dabistān*, ii. 72; [See *Manu*, iii. 34].

c. 1780.—"'Que demandez-vous?' leur criai-je d'un ton de voix rude. 'Pourquoi restez-vous là à m'attendre? et d'où vient que ces autres femmes se sont enfuies, comme si j'étois un **Péschaseh** (esprit malin), ou une bête sauvage qui voulût vous devorer?'"—*Haafner*, ii. 287.

1801.—"They believe that such men as die accidental deaths become **Pysáchi**, or evil spirits, and are exceedingly troublesome by making extraordinary noises, in families, and occasioning fits and other diseases, especially in women."—*F. Buchanan's Mysore*, iii. 17.

1816.—"Whirlwinds . . . at the end of March, and beginning of April, carry dust and light things along with them, and are called by the natives **peshashes** or devils."—*Asiatic Journal*, ii. 367.

1819.—"These demons or **peisaches** are the usual attendants of Shiva."—*Erskine* on *Elephanta*, in *Bo. Lit. Soc. Trans.* i. 219.

1827.—"As a little girl was playing round me one day with her white frock over her head, I laughingly called her **Pisashee**, the name which the Indians give to their white devil. The child was delighted with so fine a name, and ran about the house crying out to every one she met, *I am the* **Pisashee**, *I am the* **Pisashee**. Would she have done so, had she been wrapt in black, and called *witch* or *devil* instead? No: for, as usual, the reality was nothing, the sound and colour everthing."—*J. C. Hare*, in *Guesses at Truth, by Two Brothers*, 1st Series, ed. 1838, p. 7.

PISANG, s. This is the Malay word for **plantain** or **banana** (q.q.v.). It is never used by English people, but is the usual word among the Dutch, and common also among the Germans, [Norwegians and Swedes, who probably got it through the Dutch.]

1651.—"Les *Cottewaniens* vendent des fruits, come du **Pisang**, &c."—*A. Roger, La Porte Ouverte*, p. 11.

c. 1785.—"Nous arrivâmes au grand village de *Colla*, où nous vîmes de belles allées de bananiers ou **pisang**. . . ."—*Haafner*, ii. 85

[1875.—"Of the **pisang** or plantain . . . there are over thirty kinds, of which, the *Pisang-mas*, or golden plantain, so named from its colour, though one of the smallest, is nevertheless most deservedly prized."—*Thomson, The Straits of Malacca*, 8.]

PISHPASH, s. Apparently a factitious Anglo-Indian word, applied to a slop of rice-soup with small pieces of meat in it, much used in the Anglo-Indian nursery. [It is apparently P. *pash-pash*, 'shivered or broken in pieces'; from Pers. *pashīdan*.]

1834.—"They found the Secretary disengaged, that is to say, if surrounded with huge volumes of Financial Reports on one side, and a small silver tray holding a mess of **pishpash** on the other, can be called disengaged."—*The Baboo*, &c. i. 85.

PITARRAH, s. A coffer or box used in travelling by palankin, to carry the traveller's clothes, two such being slung to a **banghy** (q.v.). Hind. *piṭārā*, *peṭārā*, Skt. *piṭaka*, 'a basket.' The thing was properly a basket made of cane; but in later practice of tin sheet, with a light wooden frame.

[1833.—". . . he sat in the palanquin, which was filled with water up to his neck, whilst everything he had in his **batara** (or 'trunk') was soaked with wet. . . ."—*Travels of Dr. Wolff*, ii. 198.]

1849.—"The attention of the staff was called to the necessity of putting their **pitarahs** and property in the Bungalow, as thieves abounded. 'My dear Sir,' was the reply, 'we are quite safe; we have nothing.'"—*Delhi Gazette*, Nov. 7.

1853.—"It was very soon settled that Oakfield was to send to the dâk bungalow for his **petarahs**, and stay with Staunton for about three weeks."—*W. D. Arnold, Oakfield*, i. 223.

PLANTAIN, s. This is the name by which the *Musa sapientum* is universally known to Anglo-India. Books distinguish between the *Musa sapientum* or plantain, and the *Musa paradisaica* or banana; but it is hard to understand where the line is supposed to be drawn. Variation is gradual and infinite.

The botanical name *Musa* represents the Ar. *mauz*, and that again is from the Skt. *mocha*. The specific name *sapientum* arises out of a misunderstanding of a passage in Pliny, which we have explained under the head **Jack**. The specific *paradisaica* is derived from the old belief of Oriental Christians (entertained also, if not originated by the Mahommedans) that this was the tree from whose leaves Adam and Eve made themselves aprons. A further mystical interest attached also to the fruit, which some believed to be the forbidden apple of Eden. For in the pattern formed by the core or seeds, when the fruit was cut across, our forefathers discerned an image of the Cross, or even of the Crucifix. Medieval travellers generally call the fruit either *Musa* or 'Fig of Paradise,' or sometimes 'Fig of India,' and to this day in the W. Indies the common small plantains are called 'figs.' The Portuguese also habitually called it 'Indian Fig.' And this perhaps originated some confusion in Milton's mind, leading him to make the **Banyan** (*Ficus Indica* of Pliny, as of modern botanists) the Tree of the aprons, and greatly to exaggerate the size of the leaves of that *ficus*.

The name **banana** is never employed by the English in India, though it is the name universal in the London fruit-shops, where this fruit is now to be had at almost all seasons, and often of excellent quality, imported chiefly, we believe, from Madeira, [and more recently from Jamaica. Mr. Skeat adds that in the Strait Settlements the name **plantain** seems to be reserved for those varieties which are only eatable when cooked, but the word **banana** is used indifferently with **plantain**, the latter being on the whole perhaps the rarer word].

The name *plantain* is no more originally Indian than is *banana*. It, or rather *platano*, appears to have been the name under which the fruit was first carried to the W. Indies, according to Oviedo, in 1516; the first edition of his book was published in 1526. That author is careful to explain that the plant was *improperly* so called, as it was quite another thing from the *platanus* described by Pliny. Bluteau says the word is Spanish. We do not know how it came to be applied to the *Musa*. [Mr. Guppy (8 ser. *Notes & Queries*, viii. 87) suggests that "the Spaniards have obtained *platano* from the Carib and Galibi words for *banana*, viz., *balatanna* and *palatana*, by the process followed by the Australian colonists when they converted a native name for the casuarina trees into 'she-oak'; and that we can thus explain how *platano* came in Spanish to signify both the plane-tree and the banana." Prof. Skeat (*Concise Dict.* s.v.) derives plantain from Lat. *planta*, 'a plant'; properly 'a spreading sucker or shoot'; and says that the plantain took its name from its spreading leaf.] The rapid spread of the plantain or banana in the West, whence both names were carried back to India, is a counterpart to the rapid diffusion of the **ananas** in the Old World of Asia. It would seem from the translation of Mendoça that in his time (1585) the Spaniards had come to use the form *plantano*, which our Englishmen took up as *plantan* and *plantain*. But even in the 1736 edition of Bailey's Dict. the only explanation of plantain given is as the equivalent of the Latin *plantago*, the field-weed known by the former name. *Platano* and *Plantano* are used in the Philippine Islands by the Spanish population.

1336.—"Sunt in Syriâ et Aegypto poma oblonga quae Paradisi nuncupantur optimi saporis, mollia, in ore cito dissolubilia: per transversum quotiescumque ipsa incideris invenies *Crucifixum* . . . diu non durant, unde per mare ad nostras partes duci non possunt incorrupta."—*Gul. de Boldensele.*

c. 1350.—"Sunt enim in orto illo Adae de Seyllano primo *musae*, quas incolae ficus vocant . . . et istud vidimus oculis nostris quod ubicunque inciditur per transversum, in utrâque parte incisurae videtur ymago hominis *crucifixi* . . . et de istis foliis ficûs Adam et Eva fecerunt sibi perizomata. . . ." —*John de' Marignolli*, in *Cathay*, &c. p. 352.

1384.—"And there is again a fruit which many people assert to be that regarding which our first father Adam sinned, and this fruit they call *Muse* . . . in this fruit you see a very great miracle, for when you divide it anyway, whether lengthways or across, or cut it as you will, you shall see inside, as it were, the image of the *Crucifix*; and of this we comrades many times made proof."—*Viaggio di Simone Sigoli* (Firenze, 1862, p. 160).

1526 (tr. 1577).—"There are also certayne plantes whiche the Christians call **Platani**. In the myddest of the plant, in the highest part thereof, there groweth a cluster with fourtie or fiftie **platans** about it. . . . This cluster ought to be taken from the plant, when any one of the **platans** begins to appeare yelowe, at which time they take it, and hang it in their houses, where all the cluster waxeth rype, with all his **platans**." —*Oviedo*, transl. in *Eden's Hist. of Travayle*, f. 208.

1552 (tr. 1582).—"Moreover the Ilande (of Mombas) is verye pleasaunt, having many orchards, wherein are planted and are groweing. . . . Figges of the Indias. . . ." —*Castañeda*, by N. L., f. 22.

1579.—". . . a fruit which they call *Figo* (Magellane calls it a figge of a span long, but it is no other than that which the Spaniards and Portingalls have named **Plantanes**)."—*Drake's Voyage*, Hak. Soc. p. 142.

1585 (tr. 1588).—"There are mountaines very thicke of orange trees, siders [*i.e. cedras*, 'citrons'], limes, **plantanos**, and palmas."—*Mendoça*, by *R. Parke*, Hak. Soc. ii. 330.

1588.—"Our Generall made their wiues to fetch vs **Plantans**, Lymmons, and Oranges, Pine-apples, and other fruits."—*Voyage of Master Thomas Candish*, in *Purchas*, i. 64.

1588 (tr. 1604).—". . . the first that shall be needefulle to treate of is the **Plantain** (*Platano*), or **Plantano**, as the vulgar call it. . . . The reason why the Spaniards call it **platano** (for the Indians had no such name), was, as in other trees for that they have found some resemblance of the one with the other, even as they called some fruites prunes, pines, and cucumbers, being far different from those which are called by those names in Castille. The thing wherein was most resemblance, in my opinion, between the **platanos** at the Indies and those which the ancients did celebrate, is the greatnes of the leaves. . . . But, in truth, there is no more comparison nor resemblance of the one with the other than there is, as the Proverb saith, betwixt an egge and a chesnut."—*Joseph de Acosta*, transl. by E. G., Hak. Soc. i. 241.

1593.—"The **plantane** is a tree found in most parts of Afrique and America, of which two leaves are sufficient to cover a man from top to toe."—*Hawkins, Voyage into the South Sea*, Hak. Soc. 49.

1610.—". . . and every day failed not to send each man, being one and fiftie in number, two cakes of white bread, and a quantitie of Dates and **Plantans**. . . ."—*Sir H. Middleton*, in *Purchas*, i. 254.

c. 1610.—"Ces Gentils ayant pitié de moy, il y eut vne femme qui me mit . . . vne seruiete de feuilles de **plantane** accommodées ensemble auec des espines, puis meietta dessus du rys cuit auec vne certaine sauce qu'ils appellent *caril* (see **CURRY**). . . ."—*Mocquet, Voyages*, 292.

[„ "They (elephants) require . . . besides leaves of trees, chiefly of the Indian fig, which we call Bananes and the Turks **plantenes**."—*Pyrard de Laval*, Hak. Soc. ii. 345.]

1616.—"They have to these another fruit we English there call a **Planten**, of which many of them grow in clusters together . . . very yellow when they are Ripe, and then they taste like unto a *Norwich* Pear, but much better."—*Terry*, ed. 1665, p. 360.

c. 1635.—

". . . with candy **Plantains** and the juicy Pine,
On choicest Melons and sweet Grapes they dine,
And with Potatoes fat their wanton Swine."

Waller, Battle of the Summer Islands.

c. 1635.—
"Oh how I long my careless Limbs to lay
Under the **Plantain's** Shade; and all the Day
With amorous Airs my Fancy entertain."
Waller, Battle of the Summer Islands.

c. 1660.—
"The Plant (at Brasil *Bacone* call'd) the Name
Of the Eastern **Plane-tree** takes, but not the same:
Bears leaves so large, one single Leaf can shade
The Swain that is beneath her Covert laid;
Under whose verdant Leaves fair Apples grow,
Sometimes two Hundred on a single Bough. . . ."
Cowley, of Plants, Bk. v.

1664—
"Wake, Wake Quevera! Our soft rest must cease,
And fly together with our country's peace.
No more must we sleep under **plantain** shade,
Which neither heat could pierce nor cold invade;
Where bounteous Nature never feels decay,
And opening buds drive falling fruits away."
Dryden, Prologue to the Indian Queen.

1673.—"Lower than these, but with a Leaf far broader, stands the curious **Plantan**, loading its tender Body with a Fruit, whose clusters emulate the Grapes of *Canaan*, which burthened two men's shoulders."—*Fryer*, 19.

1686.—"The **Plantain** I take to be King of all Fruit, not except the Coco itself."—*Dampier*, i. 311.

1689.—". . . and now in the Governour's Garden (at St. Helena) and some others of the Island are quantities of **Plantins**, **Bonanoes**, and other delightful Fruits brought from the East. . . ."—*Ovington*, 100.

1764.—
"But round the upland huts, **bananas** plant;
A wholesome nutriment bananas yield,
And sunburnt labour loves its breezy shade,
Their graceful screen let kindred **plantanes** join,
And with their broad vans shiver in the breeze."
Grainger, Bk. iv.

1805.—"The **plantain**, in some of its kinds, supplies the place of bread."—*Orme, Fragments*, 479.

PLASSEY, n.p. The village *Palāsī*, which gives its name to Lord Clive's famous battle (June 23, 1757). It is said to take its name from the *pālas* (or **dhawk**) tree.

1748.—". . . that they have great reason to complain of Ensign English's conduct in not waiting at **Placy** . . . and that if he had staid another day at **Placy**, as Tullerooy Caun was marching with a large force towards Cutway, they presume the Mahrattas would have retreated inland on their approach and left him an open passage. . . ."—*Letter from Council at Cossimbazar*, in *Long*, p. 2.

[1757.—Clive's original report of the battle is dated on the "plain of **Placis**."—*Birdwood, Report on Old Records*, 57.]

1768-71. — "General CLIVE, who should have been the leader of the English troops in this battle (**Plassy**), left the command to Colonel COOTE, and remained hid in his palankeen during the combat, out of the reach of the shot, and did not make his appearance before the enemy were put to flight."—*Stavorinus*, E.T. i. 486. This stupid and inaccurate writer says that several English officers who were present at the battle related this "anecdote" to him. This, it may be hoped, is as untrue as the rest of the story. Even to such a writer one would have supposed that Clive's mettle would be familiar.

PODÁR, s. Hind. *poddār*, corrn. of Pers. *fotadār*, from *fota*, 'a bag of money.' A cash-keeper, or especially an officer attached to a treasury, whose business it is to weigh money and bullion and appraise the value of coins.

[c. 1590.—"The Treasurer. Called in the language of the day **Fotadar**."—*Āīn*, ed. *Jarrett*, ii. 49.]

1680.—"**Podar**." (See under **DUSTOOR.**)

1683.—"The like losses in proportion were preferred to be proved by Ramchurne **Podar**, Bendura bun **Podar**, and Mamoobishwas who produced their several books for evidence."—*Hedges, Diary*, Hak. Soc. i. 84.

[1772. — "**Podār**, a money-changer or teller, under a **shroff**."—*Verelst, View of Bengal*, Gloss. s. v.]

POGGLE, PUGGLY, &c., s. Properly Hind. *pāgal*; 'a madman, an idiot'; often used colloquially by Anglo-Indians. A friend belonging to that body used to adduce a macaronic adage which we fear the non-Indian will fail to appreciate: "**Pagal** *et pecunia jaldè separantur!*" [See **NAUTCH.**]

1829.—"It's true the people call me, I know not why, the **pugley**."—*Mem. John Shipp*, ii. 255.

1866. — "I was foolish enough to pay these **budmashes** beforehand, and they have thrown me over. I must have been a **paugul** to do it."—*Trevelyan, The Dawk Bungalow*, 385.

[1885. — "He told me that the native name for a regular picnic is a '**Poggle**-

khana,' that is, a fool's dinner." — *Lady Dufferin, Viceregal Life*, 88.]

POISON-NUT, s. *Strychnos nux vomica*, L.

POLEA, n.p. Mal. *pulayan*, [from Tam. *pulam*, 'a field,' because in Malabar they are occupied in rice cultivation]. A person of a low or impure tribe, who causes pollution (*pula*) to those of higher caste, if he approaches within a certain distance. [The rules which regulate their meeting with other people are given by Mr. Logan (*Malabar*, i. 118).] From *pula* the Portuguese formed also the verbs *empolear-se*, 'to become polluted by the touch of a low-caste person,' and *desempolear-se*, 'to purify oneself after such pollution' (*Gouvea*, f. 97, and *Synod.* f. 52*v*), superstitions which Menezes found prevailing among the Christians of Malabar. (See **HIRAVA**.)

1510.—"The fifth class are called **Poliar**, who collect pepper, wine, and nuts . . . the **Poliar** may not approach either the Naeri (see **NAIR**) or the Brahmins within 50 paces, unless they have been called by them. . . ."—*Varthema*, 142.

1516.—"There is another lower sort of gentiles called **puler**. . . . They do not speak to the nairs except for a long way off, as far as they can be heard speaking with a loud voice. . . . And whatever man or woman should touch them, their relations immediately kill them like a contaminated thing. . . ."—*Barbosa*, 143.

1572.—

"A ley, da gente toda, ricca e pobre,
De fabulas composta se imagina:
Andão nus, e somente hum pano cobre
As partes que a cubrir natura ensina.
Dous modos ha de gente; porque a nobre
Nayres chamados são, e a minos dina
Poleas tem por nome, a quem obriga
A ley não misturar a casta antiga."

Camões, vii. 37.

By Burton:

"The Law that holds the people high and low,
is fraught with false phantastick tales long past;
they go unclothèd, but a wrap they throw
for decent purpose round the loins and waist:
Two modes of men are known: the nobles know
the name of Nayrs, who call the lower caste
Poléas, whom their haughty laws contain
from intermingling with the higher strain. . . ."

1598.—"When the Portingales came first into India, and made league and composition with the King of *Cochin*, the *Nayros* desired that men shovld give them place, and turne out of the Way, when they mette in the Streetes, as the **Polyas** . . ." (used to do).—*Linschoten*, 78; [Hak. Soc. i. 281; also see i. 279].

1606.—". . . he said by way of insult that he would order him to touch a **Poleaa**, which is one of the lowest castes of Malauar."—*Gouvea*, f. 76.

1626.—"These **Puler** are Theeves and Sorcerers."—*Purchas, Pilgrimage*, 553.

[1727.—"**Poulias**." (See under **MUCOA**.)

[1754.—"Niadde and **Pullie** are two low castes on the *Malabar* coast. . . ."—*Ives*, 26.

[1766.—". . . **Poolighees**, a cast hardly suffered to breathe the common air, being driven into the forrests and mountains out of the commerce of mankind. . . ."—*Grose*, 2nd ed. ii. 161 *seq.*]

1770.—"Their degradation is still more complete on the Malabar coast, which has not been subdued by the Mogul, and where they (the pariahs) are called **Pouliats**."—*Raynal*, E.T. 1798, i. 6.

1865.—"Further south in India we find polyandry among . . . **Poleres** of Malabar."—*McLennan, Primitive Marriage*, 179.

POLIGAR, s. This term is peculiar to the Madras Presidency. The persons so called were properly subordinate feudal chiefs, occupying tracts more or less wild, and generally of predatory habits in former days; they are now much the same as **Zemindars** in the highest use of that term (q.v.). The word is Tam. *pālaiyakkāran*, 'the holder of a *pālaiyam*,' or feudal estate; Tel. *palegāḍu*; and thence Mahr. *pālegār*; the English form being no doubt taken from one of the two latter. The southern Poligars gave much trouble about 100 years ago, and the "Poligar wars" were somewhat serious affairs. In various assaults on Pānjālamkurichi, one of their forts in Tinnevelly, between 1799 and 1801 there fell 15 British officers. Much regarding the Poligārs of the south will be found in Nelson's *Madura*, and in Bishop Caldwell's very interesting *History of Tinnevelly*. Most of the quotations apply to those southern districts. But the term was used north to the Mahratta boundary.

1681.—"They pulled down the **Polegar's** houses, who being conscious of his guilt, had fled and hid himself."—*Wheeler*, i. 118.

1701.—"Le lendemain je me rendis à Tailur, c'est une petite ville qui appartient à un autre **Paleagaren**."—*Lett. Edif.* x. 269.

1745.—"J'espère que Votre Eminence agréera l'établissement d'une nouvelle Mission près des Montagnes appellées vulgairement des **Palleagares**, où aucun Missionnaire n'avait paru jusqu'à présent. Cette contrée est soumise à divers petits Rois appellés également **Palleagars**, qui sont independans du Grand Mogul quoique placés presque au milieu de son Empire."—*Norbert, Mem.* ii. 406-7.

1754. — "A **Polygar** . . . undertook to conduct them through defiles and passes known to very few except himself."—*Orme*, i. 373.

1780.—"He (Hyder) now moved towards the pass of Changana, and encamped upon his side of it, and sent ten thousand **polygàrs** to clear away the pass, and make a road sufficient to enable his artillery and stores to pass through." — *Hon. James Lindsay*, in *Lives of the Lindsays*, iii. 233.

,, "The matchlock men are generally accompanied by **poligars**, a set of fellows that are almost savage, and make use of no other weapon than a pointed bamboo spear, 18 or 20 feet long."—*Munro's Narrative*, 131.

1783.—"To Mahomet Ali they twice sold the Kingdom of Tanjore. To the same Mahomet Ali they sold at least twelve sovereign Princes called the **Polygars**."—*Burke's Speech on Fox's India Bill*, in *Works*, iii. 458.

1800. — "I think Pournaya's mode of dealing with these rajahs . . . is excellent. He sets them up in palankins, elephants, &c., and a great **sowarry**, and makes them attend to his person. They are treated with great respect, which they like, but can do no mischief in the country. Old Hyder adopted this plan, and his operations were seldom impeded by **polygar** wars." — *A. Wellesley* to *T. Munro*, in *Arbuthnot's Mem.* xcii.

1801.—"The southern **Poligars**, a race of rude warriors habituated to arms of independence, had been but lately subdued."—*Welsh*, i. 57.

1809.—"Tondiman is an hereditary title. His subjects are **Polygars**, and since the late war . . . he is become the chief of those tribes, among whom the singular law exists of the female inheriting the sovereignty in preference to the male."—*Ld. Valentia*, i. 364.

1868.—"There are 72 bastions to the fort of Madura; and each of them was now formally placed in charge of a particular chief, who was bound for himself and his heirs to keep his post at all times, and under all circumstances. He was also bound to pay a fixed annual tribute; to supply and keep in readiness a quota of troops for the Governor's armies; to keep the Governor's peace over a particular tract of country. . . . A grant was made to him of a tract of a country . . . together with the title of *Pâleiya Kâran* (**Poligar**). . . ."—*Nelson's Madura*, Pt. iii. p. 99.

,, "Some of the **Poligars** were placed in authority over others, and in time of war were answerable for the good conduct of their subordinates. Thus the Sethupati was chief of them all; and the **Poligar** of Dindigul is constantly spoken of as being the chief of eighteen **Poligars** . . . when the levying of troops was required the Delavay (see **DALAWAY**) sent requisitions to such and such **Poligars** to furnish so many armed men within a certain time. . . ."—*Nelson's Madura*, Pt. iii. p. 157.

The word got transferred in English parlance to the people *under* such Chiefs (see quotations above, 1780-1809); and especially, it would seem, to those whose habits were predatory:

1869.—"There is a third well-defined race mixed with the general population, to which a common origin may probably be assigned. I mean the predatory classes. In the south they are called **Poligars**, and consist of the tribes of Marawars, Kallars (see **COLLERY**), Bedars (see **BYDE**), Ramuses (see **RAMOOSY**): and in the North are represented by the Kolis (see **COOLY**) of Guzerat, and the Gujars (see **GOOJUR**) of the N.W. Provinces." — *Sir Walter Elliot*, in *J. Ethn. Soc. L.*, N.S. i. 112.

[**POLIGAR DOG**, s. A large breed of dogs found in S. India. "The Polygar dog is large and powerful, and is peculiar in being without hair" (*Balfour, Cycl.* i. 568).]

[1853.—"It was evident that the original breed had been crossed with the bull-dog, or the large **Poligar dog** of India." — *Campbell, Old Forest Ranger*, 3rd ed. p. 12.]

POLLAM, s. Tam. *pālaiyam*; Tel. *pālemu*; (see under **POLIGAR**).

1783.—"The principal reason which they assigned against the extirpation of the **polygars** (see **POLIGAR**) was that the weavers were protected in their fortresses. They might have added, that the Company itself which stung them to death, had been warmed in the bosom of these unfortunate princes; for on the taking of Madras by the French, it was in their hospitable **pollams** that most of the inhabitants found refuge and protection."—*Burke's Speech on Fox's E. I. Bill*, in *Works*, iii. 488.

1795.—"Having submitted the general remarks on the **Pollams** I shall proceed to observe that in general the conduct of the **Poligars** is much better than could be expected from a race of men, who have hitherto been excluded from those advantages, which almost always attend conquered countries, an intercourse with their conquerors. With the exception of a very few, when I arrived they had never seen a European. . . ."—*Report on Dindigal*, by *Mr. Wynch*, quoted in *Nelson's Madura*, Pt. iv. p. 15.

POLO, s. The game of hockey on horseback, introduced of late years into England, under this name, which comes from Baltī; *polo* being properly in the language of that region the ball used in the game. The game thus lately revived was once known and practised (though in various forms) from Provence to the borders of China (see **CHICANE**). It had continued to exist down to our own day, it would seem, only near the extreme East and the extreme West of the Himālaya, viz. at Manipur in the East (between Cachar and Burma), and on the West in the high valley of the Indus (in Ladāk, Balti, Astōr and Gilgit, and extending into Chitrāl). From the former it was first adopted by our countrymen at Calcutta, and a little later (about 1864) it was introduced into the Punjab, almost simultaneously from the Lower Provinces and from Kashmīr, where the summer visitors had taken it up. It was first played in England, it would seem at Aldershot, in July 1871, and in August of the same year at Dublin in the Phœnix Park. The next year it was played in many places.* But the first mention we can find in the *Times* is a notice of a match at Lillie-Bridge, July 11, 1874, in the next day's paper. There is mention of the game in the *Illustrated London News* of July 20, 1872, where it is treated as a new invention by British officers in India. [According to the author of the *Badminton Library* treatise on the game, it was adopted by Lieut. Sherer in 1854, and a club was formed in 1859. The same writer fixes its introduction into the Punjab and N.W.P. in 1861-62. See also an article in *Baily's Magazine* on "The Early History of Polo" (June 1890). The Central Asian form is described, under the name of *Baiga* or *Kok-büra*, 'grey wolf,' by Schuyler (*Turkistan*, i. 268 *seqq.*) and that in Dardistan by Biddulph (*Tribes of the Hindoo Koosh*, 84 *seqq.*).] In Ladāk it is not indigenous, but an introduction from Baltistan. See a careful and interesting account of the game of those parts in Mr. F. Drew's excellent book, *The Jummoo and Kashmir Territories*, 1875, pp. 380-392.

We learn from Professor Tylor that the game exists still in Japan, and a very curious circumstance is that the polo *racket*, just as that described by Jo. Cinnamus in the extract under **CHICANE** has survived there. [See *Chamberlain, Things Japanese*, 3rd ed. 333 *seqq.*]

1835.—"The ponies of Muneepoor hold a very conspicuous rank in the estimation of the inhabitants. . . . The national game of Hockey, which is played by every male of the country capable of sitting a horse, renders them all expert equestrians; and it was by men and horses so trained, that the princes of Muneepoor were able for many years not only to repel the aggressions of the Burmahs, but to save the whole country . . . and plant their banners on the banks of the Irrawattee."—*Pemberton's Report on the E. Frontier of Br. India*, 31-32.

1838.—"At Shighur I first saw the game of the Chaughán, which was played the day after our arrival on the **Mydan** or plain laid out expressly for the purpose. . . . It is in fact hocky on horseback. The ball, which is larger than a cricket ball, is only a globe made of a kind of willow-wood, and is called in Tibeti '**Pulu.**' . . . I can conceive that the Chaughán requires only to be seen to be played. It is the fit sport of an equestrian nation. . . . The game is played at almost every valley in Little Tibet and the adjoining countries . . . Ladakh, Yessen, Chitral, &c.; and I should recommend it to be tried on the Hippodrome at Bayswater. . . ."—*Vigne, Travels in Kashmir, Ladakh, Iskardo*, &c. (1842), ii. 289-392.

1848.—"An assembly of all the principal inhabitants took place at Iskardo, on some occasion of ceremony or festivity. . . . I was thus fortunate enough to be a witness of the chaugan, which is derived from Persia, and has been described by Mr. Vigne as hocky on horseback. . . . Large quadrangular enclosed meadows for this game may be seen in all the larger villages of Balti, often surrounded by rows of beautiful willow and poplar trees."—*Dr. T. Thomson, Himalaya and Tibet*, 260-261.

1875.—

"**Polo**, Tent-pegging, Hurlingham, the Rink,
I leave all these delights."

Browning, Inn Album, 23.

POLLOCK-SAUG, s. Hind. *pālak*, *pālak-sāg*; a poor vegetable, called also 'country spinach' (*Beta vulgaris*, or *B. Bengalensis*, Roxb.). [Riddell (*Domest. Econ.* 579) calls it 'Bengal Beet.']

POLONGA, TIC-POLONGA, s. A very poisonous snake, so called in Ceylon (*Bungarus?* or *Daboia elegans?*); Singh. *poloṅgarā*. [The *Madras Gloss.* identifies it with the *Daboia elegans*, and calls it 'Chain viper, 'Necklace snake,' 'Russell's viper,' or **cobra manilla**. The Singh. name is said

* See details in the *Field* of Nov. 15, 1884, p. 667, courteously given in reply to a query from the present writer.

to be **titpolanga**, *tit*, 'spotted,' *polanga*, 'viper.']

1681.—"There is another venomous snake called **Polongo**, the most venomous of all, that kills cattel. Two sorts of them I have seen, the one green, the other of reddish gray, full of white rings along the sides, and about five or six feet long."—*Knox*, 29.

1825.—"There are only four snakes ascertained to be poisonous; the **cobra de capello** is the most common, but its bite is not so certainly fatal as that of the **tic polonga**, which destroys life in a few minutes."—*Mrs. Heber*, in *H.'s Journal*, ed. 1844, ii. 167.

POMFRET, POMPHRET, s. A genus of sea-fish of broad compressed form, embracing several species, of good repute for the table on all the Indian coasts. According to Day they are all reducible to *Stromateus sinensis*, 'the white Pomfret,' *Str. cinereus*, which is, when immature, 'the silver Pomfret,' and when mature, 'the gray Pomfret,' and *Str. niger*, 'the black P.' The French of Pondicherry call the fish *pample*. We cannot connect it with the πομπίλος of *Aelian* (xv. 23) and Athenaeus (Lib. VII. cap. xviii. *seqq.*) which is identified with a very different fish, the 'pilot-fish' (*Naucrates ductor* of Day). The name is probably from the Portuguese, and a corruption of *pampano*, 'a vine-leaf,' from supposed resemblance; this is the Portuguese name of a fish which occurs just where the *pomfret* should be mentioned. Thus:

[1598.—"The best fish is called Mordexiin, **Pampano**, and Tatiingo."—*Linschoten*, Hak. Soc. ii. 11.]

1613.—"The fishes of this Mediterranean (the Malayan sea) are very savoury **sables**, and **seer fish** (*serras*) and **pampanos**, and rays. . . ."—*Godinho de Eredia*, f. 33*v*.

[1703.—". . . Albacores, Daulphins, **Paumphlets**."—In *Yule, Hedges' Diary*, Hak. Soc. ii. cccxxxiv.]

1727.—"Between *Cunnaca* and *Ballasore* Rivers . . . a very delicious Fish called the **Pamplee**, come in Sholes, and are sold for two Pence per Hundred. Two of them are sufficient to dine a moderate Man."—*A. Hamilton*, i. 396; [ed. 1744].

1810.—
"Another face look'd broad and bland
Like **pamplet** floundering on the sand;
Whene'er she turned her piercing stare,
She seemed alert to spring in air."—
Malay verses, rendered by *Dr. Leyden*, in *Maria Graham*, 201.

1813.—"The **pomfret** is not unlike a small turbot, but of a more delicate flavour; and epicures esteem the **black pomfret** a great dainty."—*Forbes, Or. Mem.* i. 52-53; [2nd ed. i. 36].

[1822.—". . . the lad was brought up to catch **pamphlets** and bombaloes. . . ."—*Wallace, Fifteen Years in India*, 106.]

1874.—"The greatest pleasure in Bombay was eating a fish called '**pomfret**.'"—*Sat. Rev.*, 30th May, 690.

[1896.—"Another account of this sort of seine fishing, for catching **pomfret** fish, is given by Mr. Gueritz."—*Ling Roth, Natives of Sarawak*, i. 455.]

POMMELO, PAMPELMOOSE, &c., s. *Citrus decumana*, L., the largest of the orange-tribe. It is the same fruit as the **shaddock** of the West Indies; but to the larger varieties some form of the name Pommelo seems also to be applied in the West. A small variety, with a fine skin, is sold in London shops as "the Forbidden fruit." The fruit, though grown in gardens over a great part of India, really comes to perfection only near the Equator, and especially in Java, whence it was probably brought to the continent. For it is called in Bengal *Batāvī nimbū* (*i.e. Citrus Bataviana*). It probably did not come to India till the 17th century; it is not mentioned in the *Āīn*. According to Bretschneider the Pommelo is mentioned in the ancient Chinese Book of the *Shu-King*. Its Chinese name is *Yu*.

The form of the name which we have put first is that now general in Anglo-Indian use. But it is probably only a modern result of 'striving after meaning' (quasi *Pomo-melone?*). Among older authors the name goes through many strange shapes. Tavernier calls it *pompone* (*Voy. des Indes*, liv. iii. ch. 24; [ed. *Ball*, ii. 360]), but the usual French name is *pampel-mousse*. Dampier has *Pumplenose* (ii. 125); Lockyer, *Pumplemuse* (51); Forrest, *Pummel-nose* (32); Ives, '*pimple-noses*, called in the West Indies *Chadocks*' [19]. Maria Graham uses the French spelling (22). *Pompoleon* is a form unknown to us, but given in the *Eng. Cyclopaedia*. Molesworth's *Marāṭhi Dict.* gives "*papannas, papanas*, or *papanis* (a word of. S. America)." We are unable to give the true etymology, though Littré says boldly "Tamoul, *bambolimas*." Ainslie (*Mat. Medica*, 1813) gives *Poomlimas* as the Tamil, whilst Balfour (*Cycl. of India*) gives *Pumpalimas* and *Bambulimas* as Tamil,

Bombarimasa and *Pampara-panasa* as Telugu, *Bambali naringi* as Malayālim. But if these are real words they appear to be corruptions of some foreign term. [Mr. F. Brandt points out that the above forms are merely various attempts to transliterate a word which is in Tamil *pambalimāsu*, while the Malayālim is *bambāli-nārakam* '*bambili* tree.' According to the *Madras Gloss.* all these, as well as the English forms, are ultimately derived from the Malay *pumpulmas.* Mr. Skeat writes: "In an obsolete Malay dict., by Howison (1801) I find '*poomplemoos,* a fruit brought from India by Captain Shaddock, the seeds of which were planted at Barbadoes,' and afterwards obtained his name: the affix *moos* appears to be the Dutch *moes,* 'vegetable.'" If this be so, the Malay is not the original form.]

1661.—"The fruit called by the Netherlanders **Pumpelmoos**, by the Portuguese *Jamboa,* grows in superfluity outside the city of Batavia. . . . This fruit is larger than any of the lemon-kind, for it grows as large as the head of a child of 10 years old. The core or inside is for the most part reddish, and has a kind of sourish sweetness, tasting like unripe grapes."—*Walter Schulzen,* 236

PONDICHERRY, n.p. This name of what is now the chief French settlement in India, is *Pudu-ch'chēri,* or *Puthuççēri,* 'New Town,' more correctly *Pudu-vai, Puthuvai,* meaning 'New Place.' C. P. Brown, however, says it is *Pudi-cherū,* 'New Tank.' The natives sometimes write it *Phulcheri.* [Mr. Garstin (*Man. S. Arcot,* 422) says that Hindus call it *Puthuvai* or *Puthuççeri,* while Musulmans call it *Pulcheri,* or as the *Madras Gloss.* writes the word, *Pulchari.*]

1680.—"Mr. Edward Brogden, arrived from Porto Novo, reports arrival at **Puddicherry** of two French ships from Surat, and the receipt of advices of the death of Sevajie."—*Fort St. Geo. Consn.*, May 23. In *Notes and Exts.* No. iii. p. 20.

[1683.—". . . Interlopers intend to settle att Verampatnam, a place neer **Pullicherry**. . . ."—*Pringle, Diary Ft. St. Geo.*, 1st ser. ii. 41. In iv. 113 (1685) we have **Pondicherry**.]

1711.—"The French and Danes likewise hire them (Portuguese) at **Pont de Cheree** and Trincombar."—*Lockyer,* 286.

1718.—"The Fifth Day we reached **Budulscheri**, a French Town, and the chief Seat of their Missionaries in India."—*Prop. of the Gospel,* p. 42.

1726.—"**Poedechery**," in *Valentijn, Choro.* 11.

1727.—"**Punticherry** is the next Place of Note on this Coast, a colony settled by the French."—*A. Hamilton,* i. 356; [ed. 1744].

1753.—"L'établissement des François à **Pondicheri** remonte jusqu'en l'année 1674; mais par de si foibles commencements, qu'on n'auroit eu de la peine à imaginer, que les suites en fussent aussi considerables."—*D'Anville,* p. 121.

1780.—"An English officer of rank, General Coote, who was unequalled among his compeers in ability and experience in war, and who had frequently fought with the French of **Phoolcheri** in the Karnatic and . . . had as often gained the victory over them. . . ."—*H. of Hyder Naik,* 413.

PONGOL, s. A festival of S. India, observed early in January. Tam. *pŏngăl,* 'boiling'; *i.e.* of the rice, because the first act in the feast is the boiling of the new rice. It is a kind of harvest-home. There is an interesting account of it by the late Mr. C. E. Gover (*J. R. As. Soc.* N.S. v. 91), but the connection which he traces with the old Vedic religion is hardly to be admitted. [See the meaning of the rite discussed by *Dr. Fraser, Golden Bough,* 2nd ed. iii. 305 *seq.*]

1651.—". . . nous parlerons maintenant du **Pongol**, qui se celebre le 9 de Janvier en l'honneur du Soleil. . . . Ils cuisent du ris avec du laict. . . . Ce ris se cuit hors la maison, afin que le Soleil puisse luire dessus . . . et quand ils voyent, qu'il semble le vouloir retirer, ils crient d'une voix intelligible, **Pongol, Pongol, Pongol, Pongol**. ."—*Abr. Roger,* Fr. Tr. 1670, pp. 237-8.

1871.—"Nor does the gentle and kindly influence of the time cease here. The files of the Munsif's Court will have been examined with cases from litigious enemies or greedy money lenders. But as **Pongol** comes round many of them disappear. . . . The creditor thinks of his debtor, the debtor of the creditor. The one relents, the other is ashamed, and both parties are saved by a compromise. Often it happens that a process is postponed 'till after **Pongol**!'"—*Gover,* as above, p. 96.

POOJA, s. Properly applied to the Hindu ceremonies in idol-worship; Skt. *pūjā;* and colloquially to any kind of rite. Thus *jhandā kī pūjā,* or 'Pooja of the flag,' is the sepoy term for what in St. James's Park is called 'Trooping of the colours.' [Used in the plural, as in the quotation of 1900, it means the holidays of the Durgā Pūjā or **Dussera**.]

[1776.—". . . the occupation of the *Bramin* should be . . . to cause the performance of the **poojen**, *i.e.* the worship to *Dewtàh*. . . ."—*Halhed, Code*, ed. 1781, Pref. xcix.

[1813.—". . . the Pundits in attendance commenced the **pooja**, or sacrifice, by pouring milk and curds upon the branches, and smearing over the leaves with wetted rice."—*Broughton, Letters*, ed. 1892, p. 214.]

1826.—"The person whose steps I had been watching now approached the sacred tree, and having performed **puja** to a stone deity at its foot, proceeded to unmuffle himself from his shawls. . . ."—*Pandurang Hari*, 26; [ed. 1873, i. 34].

1866.—"Yes, Sahib, I Christian boy. Plenty **poojah** do. Sunday time never no work do."—*Trevelyan, The Dawk Bungalow*, in *Fraser*, lxxiii. 226.

1874.—"The mass of the ryots who form the population of the village are too poor to have a family deity. They are forced to be content with . . . the annual **pujahs** performed . . . on behalf of the village community."—*Cal. Rev.* No. cxvii. 195.

1879.—"Among the curiosities of these lower galleries are little models of costumes and country scenes, among them a grand **pooja** under a tree."—*Sat. Rev.* No. 1251, p. 477.

[1900.—"Calcutta has been in the throes of the **Pujahs** since yesterday."—*Pioneer Mail*, 5 Oct.].

POOJAREE, s. Hind. *pujārī*. An officiating priest in an idol temple.

1702.—"L'office de **poujari** ou de Prêtresse de la Reine mère était incompatible avec le titre de servante du Seigneur."—*Lett. Edif.* xi. 111.

[1891.—"Then the **Pūjāri**, or priest, takes the Bhuta sword and bell in his hands. . . ." —*Monier-Williams, Brahmanism and Hinduism*, 4th ed. 249.]

POOL, s. P.—H. *pul*, 'a bridge.' Used in two of the quotations under the next article for 'embankment.'

[1812.—"The bridge is thrown over the river . . . it is called the **Pool** Khan. . . ." —*Morier, Journey through Persia*, 124.]

POOLBUNDY, s. P.—H. *pulbandī*, 'Securing of bridges or embankments.' A name formerly given in Bengal to a civil department in charge of the embankments. Also sometimes used improperly for the embankment itself.

[1765.—"Deduct **Poolbundy** advanced for repairs of dykes, roads, &c."—*Verelst, View of Bengal*, App. 213.

[c. 1781.—"Pay your constant devoirs to Marian Allypore, or sell yourself soul and body to **Poolbundy**."—Ext. from *Hicky's Gazette*, in *Busteed, Echoes of Old Calcutta*, 3rd ed. 178. This refers to Impey, who was called by this name in allusion to a lucrative contract given to his relative, a Mr. Fraser.]

1786. — "That the Superintendent of **Poolbundy** Repairs, after an accurate and diligent survey of the **bunds** and **pools**, and the provincial Council of Burdwan . . . had delivered it as their opinion. . . ."—*Articles of Charge against Warren Hastings*, in *Burke*, vii. 98.

1802.—"The Collector of Midnapore has directed his attention to the subject of **poolbundy**, and in a very ample report to the Board of Revenue, has described certain abuses and oppressions, consisting chiefly of pressing ryots to work on the **pools**, which call aloud for a remedy."—*Fifth Report*, App. p. 558.

1810.—". . . the whole is obliged to be preserved from inundation by an embankment called the **pool bandy**, maintained at a very great and regular expense."—*Williamson, V. M.*, ii. 365.

POON, PEON, &c., s. Can. *ponne*, [Mal. *punna*, Skt. *punnāga*]. A timber tree (*Calophyllum inophyllum*, L.) which grows in the forests of Canara, &c., and which was formerly used for masts, whence also called *mast-wood*. [Linschoten refers to this tree, but not by name (Hak. Soc. i. 67).]

[1727.—". . . good **Poon**-masts, stronger but heavier than Firr."—*A. Hamilton*, ed. 1744, i. 267.

[1776.—". . . **Pohoon**-masts, chiefly from the Malabar coast."—*Grose*, 2nd ed. ii. 109.]

[1773.—"**Poon** tree . . . the wood light but tolerably strong; it is frequently used for masts, but unless great care be taken to keep the wet from the ends of it, it soon rots."—*Ives*, 460.]

1835.—"**Peon**, or **Puna** . . . the largest sort is of a light, bright colour, and may be had at Mangalore, from the forests of Corumcul in Canara, where it grows to a length of 150 feet. At Mangalore I procured a tree of this sort that would have made a foremast for the Leander, 60-gun ship, in one piece, for 1300 Rupees."—*Edye*, in *J. R. As. Soc.* ii. 354.

POONAMALEE, n.p. A town, and formerly a military station, in the Chingleput Dist. of Madras Presidency, 13 miles west of Madras. The name is given in the *Imp. Gazetteer* as *Pūnamallu* (?), and *Ponda malāi*, whilst Col. Branfill gives it as "*Pūntha malli* for *Pūvirunthamalli*," without further explanation. [The *Madras Gloss.* gives Tam. *Pundamalli*, 'town of the jasmine-creeper,' which is largely grown there for the supply of the Madras markets.

[1876.—"The dog, a small piebald cur, with a short tail, not unlike the '**Poonamallee** terrier,' which the British soldier is wont to manufacture from **Pariah** dogs for '**Griffins**' with sporting proclivities, was brought up for inspection."—*McMahon, Karens of the Golden Chersonese*, 236.]

POONGEE, PHOONGY, s. The name most commonly given to the Buddhist *religieux* in British Burma. The word (*p'hun-gyi*) signifies 'great glory.'

1782.—". . . leurs Prêtres . . . sont moins instruits que les Brames, et portent le nom de **Ponguis**."—*Sonnerat*, ii. 301.

1795.—"From the many convents in the neighbourhood of Rangoon, the number of Rhahans and **Phongis** must be very considerable; I was told it exceeded 1500."—*Symes, Embassy to Ava*, 210.

1834.—"The **Talapoins** are called by the Burmese **Phonghis**, which term means great glory, or *Rahans*, which means perfect."—*Bp. Bigandet*, in *J. Ind. Archip.* iv. 222-3.

[1886. — "Every Burman has for some time during his life to be a **Pohngee**, or monk."—*Lady Dufferin, Viceregal Life*, 177.]

POORÁNA, s. Skt. *purāṇa*, 'old,' hence 'legendary,' and thus applied as a common name to 18 books which contain the legendary mythology of the Brahmans.

1612.—". . . These books are divided into bodies, members, and joints (*cortos, membros, e articulos*) . . . six which they call *Xastra* (see **SHASTER**), which are the bodies; eighteen which they call **Puraná**, which are the members; twenty-eight called *Agamon*, which are the joints."—*Couto*, Dec. V. liv. vi. cap. 3.

1651. — "As their **Poranas**, *i.e.* old histories, relate."—*Rogerius*, 153.

[1667. — "When they have acquired a knowledge of Sanscrit . . . they generally study the **Purana**, which is an abridgment and interpretation of the Beths" (see **VEDAS**).—*Bernier*, ed. *Constable*, p. 335.]

c. 1760.—"Le **puran** comprend dix-huit livres qui renferment l'histoire sacrée, qui contient les dogmes de la religion des Bramines."—*Encyclopédie*, xxvii. 807.

1806. — "Ceux-ci, calculoient tout haut de mémoire tandis que d'autres, plus avancés, lisoient, d'un ton chantant, leurs **Pourans**."—*Haafner*, i. 130.

POORUB, and **POORBEEA**, ss. Hind. *pūrab, pūrb*, 'the East,' from Skt. *pūrva* or *pūrba*, 'in front of,' as *paścha* (Hind. *pachham*) means 'behind' or 'westerly' and *dakshina*, 'right-hand' or southerly. In Upper India the term means usually Oudh, the Benares division, and Behar. Hence **Poorbeea** (*pūrbiya*), a man of those countries, was, in the days of the old Bengal army, often used for a sepoy, the majority being recruited in those provinces.

1553.—"Omaum (Humāyūn) Patxiah . . . resolved to follow Xerchan (Sher Khān) and try his fortunes against him . . . and they met close to the river Ganges before it unites with the river Jamona, where on the West bank of the river there is a city called Canose (Canauj), one of the chief of the kingdom of Dely. Xerchan was beyond the river in the tract which the natives call **Purba**. . . ."—*Barros*, IV. ix. 9.

[1611. — "**Pierb** is 400 cose long." — *Jourdain*, quoted in *Sir T. Roe*, Hak. Soc. ii. 538.]

1616. — "Bengala, a most spacious and fruitful province, but more properly to be called a kingdom, which hath two very large provinces within it, **Purb** and Patan, the one lying on the east, the other on the west side of the river."—*Terry*, ed. 1665, p. 357.

1666.—"La Province de Halabas s'appelloit autrefois **Purop**. . . ."—*Thevenot*, v. 197.

[1773.—"Instead of marching with the great army he had raised into the **Purbunean** country . . . we were informed he had turned his arms against us. . . ."—*Ives*, 91.]

1881.—

". . . My lands were taken away,
And the Company gave me a pension of just eight annas a day;
And the **Poorbeahs** swaggered about our streets as if they had done it all. . . ."
Attar Singh loquitur, by '*Sowar*,' Sir M. Durand in an Indian paper, the name and date lost.

POOTLY NAUTCH, s. Properly Hind. *kāṭh-putlī-nāch*, 'wooden-puppet-dance.' A puppet show.

c. 1817.—"The day after tomorrow will be my lad James Dawson's birthday, and we are to have a **puttully-nautch** in the evening."—*Mrs. Sherwood's Stories*, 291.

POPPER-CAKE, in Bombay, and in Madras **popadam**, ss. These are apparently the same word and thing, though to the former is attributed a Hind. and Mahr. origin *pāpar*, Skt. *parpaṭa*, and to the latter a Tamil one, *pappaḍam*, as an abbreviation of *paruppu-adam*, 'lentil cake.' [The *Madras Gloss.* gives Tel. *appadam*, Tam. *appalam* (see **HOPPER**), and Mal. *pappatam*, from *parippu*, '**dhall**,' *ata*, 'cake.'] It is a kind of thin scone or wafer, made of any kind of pulse or lentil flour, seasoned with assafoetida, &c., fried in oil, and in W. India baked crisp, and often eaten at European tables as an accompaniment to curry. It is not bad, even to a novice.

1814.—"They are very fond of a thin cake, or wafer, called **popper**, made from the flour of *oord* or *mash* . . . highly seasoned with assa-foetida; a salt called **popper**-*khor;* and a very hot massaula (see **MUSSALLA**), compounded of turmeric, black pepper, ginger, garlic, several kinds of warm seeds, and a quantity of the hottest Chili pepper."—*Forbes, Or. Mem.* ii. 50; [2nd ed. i. 347].

1820.—"**Papadoms** (fine cakes made of gram-flour and a fine species of alkali, which gives them an agreeable salt taste, and serves the purpose of yeast, making them rise, and become very crisp when fried. . . ."—*As. Researches,* xiii. 315.

,, "**Paper**, the flour of *ooreed* (see **OORD**), salt, assa-foetida, and various spices, made into a paste, rolled as thin as a wafer, and dried in the sun, and when wanted for the table baked crisp. . . ."—*T. Coates,* in *Tr. Lit. Soc. Bo.* iii. 194.

PORCA, n.p. In *Imp. Gazetteer Porakād,* also called *Piracada;* properly *Puṟakkāḍŭ,* [or according to the *Madras Gloss. Purakkātu,* Mal. *pura,* 'outside,' *kātu,* 'jungle']. A town on the coast of Travancore, formerly a separate State. The Portuguese had a fort here, and the Dutch, in the 17th century, a factory. Fra Paolina (1796) speaks of it as a very populous city full of merchants, Mahommedan, Christian, and Hindu. It is now insignificant. [See *Logan, Malabar,* i. 338.]

[1663-4.—"Your ffactories of Carwarr and **Porquatt** are continued but to very little purpose to you."—*Forrest, Bombay Letters,* i. 18.]

PORCELAIN, s. The history of this word for China-ware appears to be as follows. The family of univalve mollusks called *Cypraeidae,* or **Cowries**, (q.v.) were in medieval Italy called *porcellana* and *porcelletta,* almost certainly from their strong resemblance to the body and back of a pig, and not from a grosser analogy suggested by Mahn (see in Littré *sub voce*). That this is so is strongly corroborated by the circumstance noted by Dr. J. E. Gray (see *Eng. Cyc. Nat. Hist.* s.v. *Cypraeidae*) that *Pig* is the common name of shells of this family on the English coast; whilst *Sow* also seems to be a name of one or more kinds. The enamel of this shell seems to have been used in the Middle Ages to form a coating for ornamental pottery, &c., whence the early application of the term *porcellana* to the fine ware brought from the far East. Both applications of the term, viz. to cowries and to China-ware, occur in *Marco Polo* (see below). The quasi-analogous application of *pig* in Scotland to earthen-ware, noticed in an imaginary quotation below, is probably quite an accident, for there appears to be a Gaelic *pige,* 'an earthen jar,' &c. (see *Skeat,* s.v. *piggin*). We should not fail to recall Dr. Johnson's etymology of *porcelaine* from "*pour cent années,*" because it was believed by Europeans that the materials were matured under ground 100 years! (see quotations below from Barbosa, and from Sir Thomas Brown).

c. 1250.—Capmany has the following passage in the work cited. Though the same writer published the Laws of the Consulado del Mar in 1791, he has deranged the whole of the chapters, and this, which he has quoted, is omitted altogether!

"In the XLIVth chap. of the maritime laws of Barcelona, which are undoubtedly not later than the middle of the 13th century, there are regulations for the return cargoes of the ships trading with Alexandria. . . . In this are enumerated among articles brought from Egypt . . . cotton in bales and spun wool *de capells* (for hats?), **porcelanas**, alum, elephants' teeth. . . ."—*Memorias, Hist. de Barcelona,* I. Pt. ii. p. 44.

1298.—"Il ont monoie en tel mainere con je voz dirai, car il espendent **porcelaine** blance, celle qe se trovent en la mer et qe se metent au cuel des chienz, et vailent les quatre-vingt **porcelaines** un saic d'arjent qe sunt deus venesians gros. . . ."—*Marco Polo,* oldest French text, p. 132.

,, "Et encore voz di qe en ceste provence, en une cité qe est apellé Tinugui, se font escuelle de **porcellaine** grant et pitet les plus belles qe l'en peust deviser."—*Ibid.* 180.

c. 1328.—"Audivi quòd ducentas civitates habet sub se imperator ille (Magnus Tartarus) majores quàm Tholosa; et ego certè credo quòd plures habeant homines. . . . Alia non sunt quae ego sciam in isto imperio digna relatione, nisi vasa pulcherrima, et nobilissima, atque virtuosa **porseleta**."—*Jordani Mirabilia,* p. 59.

In the next passage it seems probable that the shells, and not China dishes, are intended.

c. 1343.—". . . ghomerabica, vernice, armoniaco, zaffiere, coloquinti, **porcellane**, mirra, mirabolani . . . si vendono a Vinegia a cento di peso sottile" (*i.e.* by the **cutcha** hundredweight).—*Pegolotti, Practica della Mercatura,* p. 134.

c. 1440.—". . . this Cim and Macinn that I haue before named arr ii verie great provinces, thinhabitants whereof arr idolaters, and there make they vessells and disshes of **Porcellana**."—*Giosafa Barbaro,* Hak. Soc. 75.

In the next the shells are clearly intended:

1442.—"*Gabelle di Firenze* . . . **Porcielette** marine, la libra . . . soldi . . . denari 4."—*Uzzano, Prat. della Mercatura*, p. 23.

1461. — "**Porcellane** pezzi 20, cioè 7 piattine, 5 scodelle, 4 grandi e una piccida, piattine 5 grandi, 3 scodelle, una biava, e due bianche."—*List of Presents sent by the* Soldan of Egypt *to the Doge* Pasquale Malepiero. In *Muratori, Rerum Italicarum Scriptores*, xxi. col. 1170.

1475. — "The seaports of Cheen and Machin are also large. **Porcelain** is made there, and sold by the weight and at a low price." — *Nikitin*, in *India in the XVth Cent.*, 21.

1487.—". . . le mando lo inventario del presente del Soldano dato a Lorenzo . . . vasi grandi di **Porcellana** mai più veduti simili ne meglio lavorati. . . ."—*Letter of P. da Bibbieno to Clar. de' Medici*, in *Roscoe's Lorenzo*, ed. 1825, ii. 371.

1502.—"In questo tempo abrusiorno xxi nave sopra il porto di Calechut; et de epse hebbe tãte drogarie e speciarie che caricho le dicte sei nave. Praeterea me ha mandato sei vasi di **porzellana** excellitissimi et grãdi: quatro bochali de argento grandi cõ certi altri vasi al modo loro per credentia."—*Letter of K. Emanuel*, 13.

1516. — "They make in this country a great quantity of **porcelains** of different sorts, very fine and good, which form for them a great article of trade for all parts, and they make them in this way. They take the shells of sea-snails (? *caracoli*), and eggshells, and pound them, and with other ingredients make a paste, which they put underground to refine for the space of 80 or 100 years, and this mass of paste they leave as a fortune to their children. . . ."—*Barbosa*, in *Ramusio*, i. 320*v*.

1553.—(In China) "The service of their meals is the most elegant that can be, everything being of very fine **procelana** (although they also make use of silver and gold plate), and they eat everything with a fork made after their fashion, never putting a hand into their food, much or little."—*Barros*, III. ii. 7.

1554.—(After a suggestion of the identity of the *vasa murrhina* of the ancients): "Ce nom de **Porcelaine** est donné à plusieurs coquilles de mer. Et pource qu'vn beau Vaisseau d'vne coquille de mer ne se pourroit rendre mieux à propos suyuãt le nom antique, que de l'appeller de **Porceláine** i'ay pensé que les coquilles polies et luysantes, resemblants à Nacre de perles, ont quelque affinité auec la matière des vases de **Porcelaine** antiques: ioinct aussi que le peuple Frãçois nomme les patesnostres faictes de gros vignols, patenostres de **Porcelaine**. Les susdicts vases de **Porcelaine** sont transparents, et coustent bien cher au Caire, et disent mesmement qu'ilz les apportent des Indes. Mais cela ne me sembla vraysemblable: car on n'en voirroit pas si grande quantité, ne de si grãdes pieces, s'il failloit apporter de si loing. Vne esguiere, vn pot, ou vn autre vaisseau pour petite qu'elle soit, couste vn ducat: si c'est quelque grãd vase, il coustera d'auantage."—*P. Belon, Observations*, f. 134.

c. 1560.—"And because there are many opinions among the Portugals which have not beene in *China*, about where this **Porcelane** is made, and touching the substance whereof it is made, some saying, that it is of oysters shels, others of dung rotten of a long time, because they were not enformed of the truth, I thought it conuenient to tell here the substance. . . ."—*Gaspar da Cruz*, in *Purchas*, iii. 177.

[1605-6.—". . . China dishes or **Puselen.**" —*Birdwood, First Letter Book*, 77.

[1612.—"Balanced one part with sandal wood, **Porcelain** and pepper."—*Danvers, Letters*, i. 197.]

1615.—"If we had in England beds of **porcelain** such as they have in China,—which **porcelain** is a kind of plaster buried in the earth, and by length of time congealed and glazed into that substance; this were an artificial mine, and part of that substance. . . ."—*Bacon, Argument on Impeachment of Waste; Works*, by *Spedding*, &c., 1859, vii. 528.

c. 1630.—"The *Bannyans* all along the sea-shore pitch their Booths . . . for there they sell Callicoes, China-satten, **Purcellain**-ware, scrutores or Cabbinets. . . ."—*Sir T. Herbert*, ed. 1665, p. 45.

1650.—"We are not thoroughly resolved concerning **Porcellane** or China dishes, that according to common belief they are made of earth, which lieth in preparation about an hundred years underground; for the relations thereof are not only divers but contrary; and Authors agree not herein. . . ."—*Sir Thomas Browne, Vulgar Errors*, ii. 5.

[1652.—"Invited by Lady Gerrard I went to London, where we had a greate supper; all the vessels, which were innumerable, were of **Porcelan**, she having the most ample and richest collection of that curiositie in England."—*Evelyn, Diary*, March 19.]

1726.—In a list of the treasures left by Akbar, which is given by Valentijn, we find:

"In **Porcelyn**, &c., Ropias 2507747."—iv. (*Suratte*), 217.

1880.—"'Vasella quidem delicatiora et caerulea et venusta, quibus inhaeret nescimus quid elegantiae, **porcellana** vocantur, quasi (sed nescimus quare) a *porcellis*. In partibus autem Britanniae quae septentrionem spectant, vocabulo forsan analogo, vasa grossiora et fusca *pigs* appellant barbari, quasi (sed quare iterum nescimus) a *porcis*.' *Narrischchen und Weitgeholt, Etymol. Universale*, s.v. 'Blue China.'"—Motto to *An Ode in Brown Pig, St. James's Gazette*, July 17.

PORGO, s. We know this word only from its occurrence in the passage quoted; and most probably the explanation suggested by the editor of the *Notes* is correct, viz. that it represents Port. *peragua*. This word is perhaps the same as *pirogue*, used by the French for a canoe or 'dug-out'; a term said by Littré to be (*piroga*) Carib. [On the passage from T. B. quoted below Sir H. Yule has the following note: "J. (*i.e.* T.) B., the author, gives a rough drawing. It represents the *Purgoe* as a somewhat high-sterned lighter, not very large, with five oar-pins a side. I cannot identify it exactly with any kind of modern boat of which I have found a representation. It is perhaps most like the *palwār*. I think it must be an Orissa word, but I have not been able to trace it in any dictionary, Uriya or Bengali." On this Col. Temple says: "The modern Indian *palwār* (Malay *palwa*) is a skiff, and would not answer the description." Anderson (*loc. cit.*) mentions that in 1685 several "well-laden *Purgoes*" and boats had put in for shelter at Rameswaram to the northward of Madapollam, *i.e.* on the Coromandel Coast. There seems to be no such word known there now. I think, however, that the term *Purgoo* is probably an obsolete Anglo-Indian corruption of an Indian corruption of the Port. term *barco*, *barca*, a term used for any kind of sailing boat by the early Portuguese visitors to the East (*e.g. D'Alboquerque*, Hak. Soc. ii. 230; *Vasco da Gama*, Hak. Soc. 77, 240).]

[1669-70.—"A **Purgoo**: These Vse for the most part between Hugly and Pyplo and Ballasore: with these boats they carry goods into ye Roads on board English and Dutch, &c. Ships, they will liue a longe time in ye Sea, beinge brought to anchor by ye Sterne, as theire Vsual way is."—MS. by T. B.[ateman], quoted by *Anderson, English Intercourse with Siam*, p. 266.]

1680.—Ft. St. Geo. Consn., Jany. 30, "records arrival from the Bay of the 'Success,' the Captain of which reports that a **Porgo** [*Peragua* ?, a fast-sailing vessel, Clipper] drove ashore in the Bay about Peply. . . ."—*Notes and Exts.* No. iii. p. 2.

[1683.—"The Thomas arrived with ye 28 bales of Silk taken out of the **Purga**."—*Hedges, Diary*, Hak. Soc. i. 65.

[1685.—"In Hoogly letter to Fort St. George, dated February 6 **Porgo** occurs coupled with 'bora' (Hind. *bhar*, 'a lighter')."—*Pringle, Diary Ft. St. Geo.* 1st ser. iii. 165.

PORTIA, s. In S. India the common name of the *Thespesia populnea*, Lam. (N.O. *Malvaceae*), a favourite ornamental tree, thriving best near the sea. The word is a corruption of Tamil *Puarassu*, 'Flower-king; [*puvarasu*, from *pu*, 'flower,' *arasu*, '**peepul** tree']. In Ceylon it is called *Suria gansuri*, and also the Tulip-tree.

1742.—"Le bois sur lequel on les met (les toiles), et celui qu'on employe pour les battre, sont ordinairement de tamarinier, ou d'un autre arbe nommé **porchi**."—*Lett. Edif.* xiv. 122.

1860.—"Another useful tree, very common in Ceylon, is the *Suria*, with flowers so like those of a tulip that Europeans know it as the tulip tree. It loves the sea air and saline soils. It is planted all along the avenues and streets in the towns near the coast, where it is equally valued for its shade and the beauty of its yellow flowers, whilst its tough wood is used for carriage-shafts and gun-stocks."—*Tennent's Ceylon*, i. 117.

1861.—"It is usual to plant large branches of the **portia** and banyan trees in such a slovenly manner that there is little probability of the trees thriving or being ornamental."—*Cleghorn, Forests and Gardens of S. India*, 197.

PORTO NOVO, n.p. A town on the coast of South Arcot, 32 m. S. of Pondicherry. The first mention of it that we have found is in Bocarro, *Decada*, p. 42 (c. 1613). The name was perhaps intended to mean 'New Oporto,' rather than 'New Haven,' but we have not found any history of the name. [The Tamil name is *Parangipēttai*, 'European town,' and it is called by Mahommedans *Maḥmūd-bandar*.]

1718.—"At Night we came to a Town called **Porta Nova**, and in Malabarish *Pirenki Potei* (*Parangipēṭṭai*)."—*Propagation of the Gospel*, &c., Pt. ii. 41.

1726.—"The name of this city (*Porto Novo*) signifies in Portuguese **New Haven**, but the Moors call it *Mohhammed Bendar* . . . and the Gentoos *Perringepeente*."—*Valentijn, Choromandel*, 8.

PORTO PIQUENO, PORTO GRANDE, nn. pp. 'The Little Haven and the Great Haven'; names by which the Bengal ports of **Satigam** (q.v.) and *Chatigam* (see **CHITTAGONG**) respectively were commonly known to the Portuguese in the 16th century.

1554.—"**Porto Pequeno** *de Bemgala* . . . **Cowries** are current in the country; 80 cowries make 1 *pone* (see **PUN**); of these *pones* 48 are equal to 1 **larin** more or less."—*A. Nunes*, 37.

1554.—"**Porto Grande** *de Bengala*. The **maund** (*mão*), by which they weigh all goods, contains 40 **seers** (*ceros*), each seer 18⅔ ounces. . . ."—*A. Nunes*, 37.

1568.—"Io mi parti d'Orisa per Bengala al **Porto Picheno** . . . s'entra nel fiume Ganze, dalla bocca del qual fiume sino a *Satagan* (see **SATIGAM**) città, oue si fanno negotij, et oue i mercadanti si riducono, sono centi e venti miglia, che si fanno in diciotto hore a remi, cioè, in tre crescenti d'acqua, che sono di sei hore l'uno."—*Ces. Federici*, in *Ramusio*, iii. 392.

1569.—"Partissemo di Sondiua, et giungessemo in Chitigan il **gran porto** di Bengala, in tempo che già i Portoghesi haueuano fatto pace o tregua con i Rettori."—*Ibid.* 396.

1595.—"Besides, you tell me that the traffic and commerce of the **Porto Pequeno** of Bemguala being always of great moment, if this goes to ruin through the Mogors, they will be the masters of those tracts."—*Letter of the K. of Portugal*, in *Archiv. Port. Orient.*, Fascic. 3, p. 481.

1596.—"And so he wrote me that the Commerce of **Porto Grande** of Bengala is flourishing, and that the King of the Country had remitted to the Portuguese 3 per cent. of the duties that they used to pay."—*Ibid.* p. 580.

1598.—"When you thinke you are at the point de Gualle, to be assured thereof, make towards the Iland, to know it . . . where commonlie all the shippes know the land, such I say as we sayle to *Bengalen*, or to any of the Hauens thereof, as **Porto Pequeno** or **Porto Grande**, that is the small, or the great Haven, where the Portingalles doe traffique. . . ." — *Linschoten*, Book III. p. 324.

[c. 1617.—"**Port Grande, Port Pequina**," in *Sir T. Roe's List*, Hak. Soc. ii. 538.]

POSTEEN, s. An Afghan leathern pelisse, generally of sheep-skin with the fleece on. Pers. *postīn*, from *post*, 'a hide.'

1080.—"Khwája Ahmad came on some Government business to Ghaznín, and it was reported to him that some merchants were going to Turkistán, who were returning to Ghaznín in the beginning of winter. The Khwája remembered that he required a certain number of **postins** (great coats) every year for himself and sons. . . ."—*Nizám-ul-Mulk*, in *Elliot*, ii. 497.

1442. — "His Majesty the Fortunate Khākān had sent for the Prince of Kālikūt, horses, pelisses (**postīn**) and robes woven of gold. . . ."—*Abdurazzāk*, in *Not. et Extr.* xiv. Pt. i. 437.

[c. 1590.—"In the winter season there is no need of **poshtins** (fur-lined coats). . . ." —*Āīn*, ed. *Jarrett*, ii. 337.]

1862.—"Otter skins from the Hills and Kashmir, worn as **Postīns** by the Yarkandis."—*Punjab Trade Report*, p. 65.

POTTAH, s. Hind. and other vernaculars, *paṭṭā*, &c. A document specifying the conditions on which lands are held; a lease or other document securing rights in land or house property.

1778.—"I am therefore hopeful you will be kindly pleased to excuse me the five lacs now demanded, and that nothing may be demanded of me beyond the amount expressed in the **pottah**."—*The Rajah of Benares* to Hastings, in *Articles of Charge against H.*, Burke, vi. 591.

[1860.—"By the Zumeendar, then, or his under tenant, as the case may be, the land is farmed out to the Ryuts by **pottahs**, or agreements. . . ."—*Grant, Rural Life in Bengal*, 67.]

PRA, PHRA, PRAW, s. This is a term constantly used in Burma, familiar to all who have been in that country, in its constant application as a style of respect, addressed or applied to persons and things of especial sanctity or dignity. Thus it is addressed at Court to the King; it is the habitual designation of the Buddha and his images and dagobas; of superior ecclesiastics and sacred books; corresponding on the whole in use, pretty closely to the Skt. *Śrī*. In Burmese the word is written *bhurā*, but pronounced (in Arakan) *p'hrā*, and in modern Burma Proper, with the usual slurring of the *r*, *P'hyā* or *Pyā*. The use of the term is not confined to Burma; it is used in quite a similar way in Siam, as may be seen in the quotation below from Alabaster; the word is used in the same form *P'hra* among the Shans; and in the form *Prea*, it would seem, in Camboja. Thus Garnier speaks of Indra and Vishnu under their Cambojan epithets as *Prea* En and *Prea* Noreai (Nārāyaṇa); of the figure of Buddha entering *nirvāna*, as *Prea* Nippan; of the King who built the great temple of Angkor Wat as *Prea* Kot Melea, of the King reigning at the time of the expedition as *Prea* Ang Reachea Vodey, of various sites of temples as *Preacon*, *Preacan*, *Prea* Pithu, &c. (*Voyage d'Exploration*, i. 26, 49, 388, 77, 85, 72).

The word **p'hrā** appears in composition in various names of Burmese kings, as of the famous *Alom***p'hra** (1753-60), founder of the late dynasty, and of his son *Bodoah*-**p'hra** (1781-1819). In the former instance the name is, according to Sir A. Phayre, Alaung-*p'hrā*, *i.e.* the embryo Buddha, or Bodisatva. A familiar Siamese example of use is in the **Phrā** *Bāt*, or sacred foot-mark of Buddha, a term which represents the *Śṛi Pada* of Ceylon.

The late Prof. H. H. Wilson, as will be seen, supposed the word to be a corruption of Skt. *prabhu* (see **PARVOE**). But Mr. Alabaster points, under the guidance of the Siamese spelling, rather to Skt. *vara*, 'pre-eminent, excellent.' This is in Pali *varo*, "excellent, best, precious, noble" (*Childers*). A curious point is that, from the prevalence of the term **phrā** in all the Indo-Chinese kingdoms, we must conclude that it was, at the time of the introduction of Buddhism into those countries, in predominant use among the Indian or Ceylonese propagators of the new religion. Yet we do not find any evidence of such a use of either *prabhu* or *vara*. The former would in Pali be *pabbho*. In a short paper in the *Bijdragen* of the Royal Institute of the Hague (Dl. X. 4de Stuk, 1885), Prof. Kern indicates that this term was also in use in Java, in the forms *Bra* and *pra*, with the sense of 'splendid' and the like; and he cites as an example **Bra**-*Wijaya* (the style of several of the medieval kings of Java), where **Bra** is exactly the representative of Skt. *Śrī*.

1688.—"I know that in the country of *Laos* the Dignities of *Pa-ya* and *Meuang*, and the honourable Epithets of **Pra** are in use; it may be also that the other terms of Dignity are common to both Nations, as well as the Laws."—*De la Loubère, Siam*, E.T. 79.

" "The **Pra**-Clang, or by a corruption of the *Portugueses*, the *Barcalon*, is the officer, who has the appointment of the Commerce, as well within as without the Kingdom. . . . His name is composed of the Balie word **Pra**, which I have so often discoursed of, and of the word *Clang*, which signifies Magazine."—*Ibid.* 93.

" "Then *Sommona-Codom* (see **GAUTAMA**) they call **Pra**-*Boute-Tchaou*, which verbatim signifies the *Great and Excellent Lord.*"—*Ibid.* 134.

1795.—"At noon we reached Meeaday, the personal estate of the Magwoon of Pegue, who is oftener called, from this place, Meeaday **Praw**, or Lord of Meeaday."—*Symes, Embassy to Ava*, 242.

1855.—"The epithet **Phra**, which occupies so prominent a place in the ceremonial and religious vocabulary of the Siamese and Burmese, has been the subject of a good deal of nonsense. It is unfortunate that our Burmese scholars have never (I believe) been Sanskrit scholars, nor *vice versâ*, so that the Palee terms used in Burma have had little elucidation. On the word in question, Professor H. H. Wilson has kindly favoured me with a note: '**Phrá** is no doubt a corruption of the Sanskrit *Prabhu*, a Lord or Master; the *h* of the aspirate *bh* is often retained alone, leaving *Prahu* which becomes **Práh** or **Phra**.'"—*Sir H. Yule, Mission to Ava*, 61.

1855.—"All these readings (of documents at the Court) were intoned in a high recitative, strongly resembling that used in the English cathedral service. And the long-drawn **Phyá-á-á-á**! (My Lord), which terminated each reading, added to the resemblance, as it came in exactly like the Amen of the Liturgy."—*Ibid.* 88.

1859.—"The word **Phra**, which so frequently occurs in this work, here appears for the first time; I have to remark that it is probably derived from, or of common origin with, the Pharaoh of antiquity. It is given in the Siamese dictionaries as synonymous with God, ruler, priest, and teacher. It is in fact the word by which sovereignty and sanctity are associated in the popular mind."—*Bowring, Kingdom and People of Siam*, [i. 35].

1863.—"The title of the First King (of Siam) is **Phra**-*Chom-Klao-Yu-Hua* and spoken as **Phra** *Phutthi-Chao-Yu-Hua*. . . . His Majesty's nose is styled in the Pali form **Phra**-*Nasa*. . . . The Siamese term the (Catholic) missionaries, the Preachers of the **Phra**-*Chao Phu-Sang*, *i.e.* of God the Creator, or the Divine Lord Builder. . . . The Catholic missionaries express 'God' by **Phra**-*Phutthi-Chao* . . . and they explain the Eucharist as **Phra**-*Phutthi-Kaya* (*Kaya*='Body')."—*Bastian, Reise*, iii. 109, and 114-115.

1870.—"The most excellent **Parā**, brilliant in his glory, free from all ignorance, beholding Nibbāna the end of the migration of the soul, lighted the lamp of the law of the Word."—*Rogers, Buddhagosha's Parables*, tr. from the Burmese, p. 1.

1871.—"**Phra** is a Siamese word applied to all that is worthy of the highest respect, that is, everything connected with religion and royalty. It may be translated as 'holy.' The Siamese letters *p—h—r* commonly represent the Sanskrit *v—r*. I therefore presume the word to be derived from the Sanskrit '*vri*'—'to choose, or to be chosen,' and '*vara*—better, best, excellent,' the root of ἄριστος."—*Alabaster, The Wheel of the Law*, 164.

PRAAG, sometimes **PIAGG**, n.p. Properly *Prayāga*, 'the place of sacrifice,' the old Hindu name of **Allahabad**, and especially of the river confluence, since remote ages a place of pilgrimage.

c. A.D. 638.—"Le royaume de *Polo-ye-kia* (**Prayâga**) a environ 5000 *li* de tour. La capitale, qui est située au confluent de deux fleuves, a environ 20 *li* de tour. . . . Dans la ville, il y a un temple des dieux qui est d'une richesse éblouissante, et où éclatent une multitude de miracles. . . . Si quel qu'un est capable de pousser le mépris de la vie jusqu' à se donner la mort dans ce temple, il obtient le bonheur eternel et les joies infinies des dieux. . . . Depuis l'antiquité jusqu' à nos jours, cette coutume insensée n'a pas cessé un instant." —*Hiouen-Thsang*, in *Pèl. Boudd.* ii. 276-79.

c. 1020.—". . . thence to the tree of **Barāgi**, 12 (parasangs). This is at the confluence of the Jumna and Ganges."—*Al-Birūnī*, in *Elliot*, i. 55.

1529.—"The same day I swam across the river Ganges for my amusement. I counted my strokes, and found that I crossed over at 33 strokes. I then took breath and swam back to the other side. I had crossed by swimming every river that I had met with, except the Ganges. On reaching the place where the Ganges and Jumna unite, I rowed over in the boat to the **Piâg** side. . . ."—*Baber*, 406.

1585.—". . . Frō Agra I came to **Prage**, where the riuer Jemena entreth into the mightie riuer Ganges, and Iemena looseth his name."—*R. Fitch*, in *Hakl.* ii. 386.

PRACRIT, s. A term applied to the older vernacular dialects of India, such as were derived from, or kindred to, Sanskrit. Dialects of this nature are used by ladies, and by inferior characters, in the Sanskrit dramas. These dialects, and the modern vernaculars springing from them, bear the same relation to Sanskrit that the "Romance" languages of Europe bear to Latin, an analogy which is found in many particulars to hold with most surprising exactness. The most completely preserved of old Prakrits is that which was used in Magadha, and which has come down in the Buddhist books of Ceylon under the name of **Pali** (q.v.). The first European analysis of this language bears the title "*Institutiones Linguae* **Pracriticae**. *Scripsit Christianus Lassen*, Bonnae ad Rhenum, 1837." The term itself is Skt. *prākrita*, 'natural, unrefined, vulgar,' &c.

1801.—"*Sanscrita* is the speech of the Celestials, framed in grammatical institutes, **Pracrita** is similar to it, but manifold as a provincial dialect, and otherwise."—*Sanskrit Treatise*, quoted by *Colebrooke*, in *As. Res.* vii. 199.

PRAYA, s. This is in Hong-Kong the name given to what in most foreign settlements in China is called the **Bund**; *i.e.* the promenade or drive along the sea. It is Port. *praia*, 'the shore.'

[1598.—"Another towne towards the North, called Villa de **Praya** (for **Praya** is as much as to say, as strand)."—*Linschoten*, Hak. Soc. ii. 278.]

PRESIDENCY (and **PRESIDENT**), s. The title 'President,' as applied to the Chief of a principal Factory, was in early popular use, though in the charters of the E.I.C. its first occurrence is in 1661 (see *Letters Patent*, below). In Sainsbury's *Calendar* we find letters headed "to Capt. Jourdain, president of the English at Bantam" in 1614 (i. 297-8); but it is to be doubted whether this wording is in the original. A little later we find a "proposal by Mr. Middleton concerning the appointment of two especial factors, at Surat and Bantam, to have authority over all other factors; Jourdain named." And later again he is styled "John Jourdain, Captain of the house" (at Bantam; see pp. 303, 325), and "Chief Merchant at Bantam" (p. 343).

1623.—"Speaking of the Dutch Commander, as well as of the English **President**, who often in this fashion came to take me for an airing, I should not omit to say that both of them in Surat live in great style, and like the grandees of the land. They go about with a great train, sometimes with people of their own mounted, but particularly with a great crowd of Indian servants on foot and armed, according to custom, with sword, target, bow and arrows."—*P. della Valle*, ii. 517.

,, "Our boat going ashore, the **President** of the English Merchants, who usually resides in Surat, and is chief of all their business in the E. Indies, Persia, and other places dependent thereon, and who is called Sign. Thomas Rastel* . . . came aboard in our said boat, with a minister of theirs (so they term those who do the priest's office among them)."—*Ibid.* ii. 501-2; [Hak. Soc. i. 19].

1638.—"As soon as the Commanders heard that the (English) **President** was come to Suhaly, they went ashore. . . . The two dayes following were spent in feasting, at which the Commanders of the two Ships treated the **President**, who afterwards returned to *Suratta*. . . . During my abode at *Suratta*, I wanted for no divertisement; for I . . . found company at the *Dutch* **President's**, who had his Farms there . . .

* Thomas Rastall or Rastell went out apparently in 1615, in 1616 is mentioned as a "chief merchant of the fleet at Swally Road," and often later as chief at Surat (see *Sainsbury*, i. 476, and ii. *passim*).

inasmuch as I could converse with them in their own Language."—*Mandelslo*, E.T., ed. 1669, p. 19.

1638.—"Les Anglois ont bien encore vn bureau à Bantam, dans l'Isle de Jaua, mais il a son **President** particulier, qui ne depend point de celuy de *Suratta*." — *Mandelslo*, French ed. 1659, p. 124.

" "A mon retour à *Suratta* ie trouvay dans la loge des Anglois plus de cinquante marchands, que le **President** auoit fait venir de tous les autres Bureaux, pour rendre compte de leur administration, et pour estre presens à ce changement de Gouuernement."—*Ibid.* 188.

1661.—"And in case any Person or Persons, being convicted and sentenced by the **President** and Council of the said Governor and Company, in the said East Indies, their Factors or Agents there, for any Offence by them done, shall appeal from the same, that then, and in every such case, it shall and may be lawful to and for the said **President** and Council, Factor or Agent, to seize upon him or them, and to carry him or them home Prisoners to England."—*Letters Patent to the Governor and Company of Merchants of London, trading with the E. Indies*, 3d April.

1670.—The Court, in a letter to Fort St. George, fix the amount of tonnage to be allowed to their officers (for their private investments) on their return to Europe:

"**Presidents** and Agents, at Surat, Fort St. George, and Bantam . 5 *tonns.*
Chiefes, at Persia, the **Bay** (q.v.), Mesulapatam, and Macassar: Deputy at Bombay, and Seconds at Surat, Fort St. George, and Bantam . 3 *tonns.*"
In *Notes and Exts.*, No. i. p. 3.

1702.—"Tuesday 7th Aprill. . . . In the morning a Councill . . . afterwards having some Discourse arising among us whether the charge of hiring Calashes, &c., upon Invitations given us from the Shabander or any others to go to their Countrey Houses or upon any other Occasion of diverting our Selves abroad for health, should be charged to our Honble Masters account or not, the **President** and Mr. Loyd were of opinion to charge the same. . . . But Mr. Rouse, Mr. Ridges, and Mr. Master were of opinion that Batavia being a place of extraordinary charge and Expense in all things, the said Calash hire, &c., ought not to be charged to the Honourable Company's Account."—*MS. Records in India Office.*

The book containing this is a collocation of fragmentary MS. diaries. But this passage pertains apparently to the proceedings of President Allen Catchpole and his council, belonging to the Factory of Chusan, from which they were expelled by the Chinese in 1701-2; they stayed some time at Batavia on their way home. Mr. Catchpole (or Ketchpole) was soon afterwards chief of an English settlement made upon Pulo Condore, off the Cambojan coast. In 1704-5, we read that he reported favourably on the prospects of the settlement, requesting a supply of young **writers**, to learn the Chinese language, anticipating that the island would soon become an important station for Chinese trade. But Catchpole was himself, about the end of 1705, murdered by certain people of Macassar, who thought he had broken faith with them, and with him all the English but two (see *Bruce's Annals*, 483-4, 580, 606, and *A. Hamilton*, ii. 205 [ed. 1744]). The Pulo Condore enterprise thus came to an end.

1727.—"About the year 1674, **President** Aungier, a gentleman well qualified for governing, came to the Chair, and leaving Surat to the Management of Deputies, came to *Bombay*, and rectified many things."—*A. Hamilton*, i. 188.

PRICKLY-HEAT, s. A troublesome cutaneous rash (*Lichen tropicus*) in the form of small red pimples, which itch intolerably. It affects many Europeans in the hot weather. Fryer (pub. 1698) alludes to these "fiery pimples," but gives the disease no specific name. Natives sometimes suffer from it, and (in the south) use a paste of sandal-wood to alleviate it. Sir Charles Napier in Sind used to suffer much from it, and we have heard him described as standing, when giving an interview during the hot weather, with his back against the edge of an open door, for the convenience of occasional friction against it. [See **RED-DOG**.]

1631.—"Quas Latinus Hippocrates *Cornelius Celsus* papulas, Plinius sudamina vocat . . . ita crebra sunt, ut ego adhuc neminem noverim qui molestias has effugerit, non magis quam morsas culicum, quos Lusitani *Mosquitas* vocant. Sunt autem haec papulae rubentes, et asperae aliquantum, per sudorem in cutem ejectæ; plerumque a capite ad calcem usque, cum summo pruritu, et assiduo scalpendi desiderio erumpentes."—*Jac. Bontii, Hist., Nat.* &c., ii. 18, p. 33.

1665.—"The Sun is but just now rising, yet he is intolerable; there is not a Cloud in the Sky, not a breath of Wind; my horses are spent, they have not seen a green Herb since we came out of *Lahor*; my *Indians*, for all their black, dry, and hard skin, sink under it. My face, hands and feet are peeled off, and my body is covered all over with **pimples that prick me**, as so many needles." — *Bernier*, E.T. 125; [ed. *Constable*, 389].

[1673.—"This Season . . . though moderately warm, yet our Bodies broke out into small **fiery Pimples** (a sign of a prevailing *Crasis*) augmented by MUSKEETOE-Bites, and *Chinces* raising Blisters on us."—*Fryer*, 35.]

1807.—"One thing I have forgotten to tell you of—the **prickly heat**. To give you some notion of its intensity, the placid Lord William (Bentinck) has been found sprawling on a table on his back; and Sir Henry Gwillin, one of the Madras Judges, who is a Welshman, and a fiery Briton in all senses, was discovered by a visitor rolling on his own floor, roaring like a baited bull."—*Lord Minto in India*, June 29.

1813.—"Among the primary effects of a hot climate (for it can hardly be called a disease) we may notice **prickly heat**."—*Johnson, Influence of Trop. Climates*, 25.

PRICKLY-PEAR, s. The popular name, in both E. and W. Indies, of the *Opuntia Dillenii*, Haworth (*Cactus Indica*, Roxb.), a plant spread all over India, and to which Roxburgh gave the latter name, apparently in the belief of its being indigenous in that country. Undoubtedly, however, it came from America, wide as has been its spread over Southern Europe and Asia. On some parts of the Mediterranean shores (*e.g.* in Sicily) it has become so characteristic that it is hard to realize the fact that the plant had no existence there before the 16th century. Indeed at Palermo we have heard this scouted, and evidence quoted in the supposed circumstance that among the mosaics of the splendid Duomo of Monreale (12th century) the fig-leaf garments of Adam and Eve are represented as of this uncompromising material. The mosaic was examined by one of the present writers, with the impression that the belief has no good foundation. [See 8th ser. *Notes and Queries*, viii. 254.] The cactus fruit, yellow, purple, and red, which may be said to form an important article of diet in the Mediterranean, and which is now sometimes seen in London shops, is not, as far as we know, anywhere used in India, except in times of famine. No cactus is named in Drury's *Useful Plants of India*. And whether the Mediterranean plants form a different species, or varieties merely, as compared with the Indian *Opuntia*, is a matter for inquiry. The fruit of the Indian plant is smaller and less succulent. There is a good description of the plant and fruit in *Oviedo*, with a good cut (see Ramusio's Ital. version, bk. viii. ch. xxv.). That author gives an amusing story of his first making acquaintance with the fruit in S. Domingo, in the year 1515.

Some of the names by which the *Opuntia* is known in the Punjab seem to belong properly to species of *Euphorbia*. Thus the *Euphorbia Royleana*, Bois., is called *tsūī*, *chū*, &c.; and the *Opuntia* is called *Kābulī tsūī*, *Gangi sho*, *Kanghi chū*, &c. *Gangi chū* is also the name of an *Euphorbia* sp. which Dr. Stewart takes to be the *E. Neriifolia*, L. (*Punjab Plants*, pp. 101 and 194-5). [The common name in Upper India for the prickly pear is *nāgphanī*, 'snake-hood,' from its shape.] This is curious; for although certain cactuses are very like certain *Euphorbias*, there is no *Euphorbia* resembling the *Opuntia* in form.

The *Zakūm* mentioned in the *Āīn* (*Gladwin*, 1800, ii. 68; [*Jarrett*, ii. 239; *Sidi Ali*, ed. *Vambery*, p. 31] as used for hedges in Guzerat, is doubtless *Euphorbia* also. The *Opuntia* is very common as a hedge plant in cantonments, &c., and it was much used by Tippoo as an obstruction round his fortifications. Both the *E. Royleana* and the *Opuntia* are used for fences in parts of the Punjab. The latter is objectionable, from harbouring dirt and reptiles; but it spreads rapidly both from birds eating the fruit, and from the facility with which the joints take root.

1685.—"The **Prickly-Pear**, Bush, or Shrub, of about 4 or 5 foot high . . . the Fruit at first is green, like the Leaf. . . . It is very pleasant in taste, cooling and refreshing; but if a Man eats 15 or 20 of them they will colour his water, making it look like Blood."—*Dampier*, i. 223 (in W. Indies).

1764.—

"On this lay cuttings of the **prickly pear**;
They soon a formidable fence will shoot."
Grainger, Bk. i.

[1829.—"The castle of Bunai . . . is covered with the *cactus*, or **prickly pear**, so abundant on the east side of the Aravali."—*Tod, Annals*, Calcutta reprint, i. 826.]

1861.—"The use of the **prickly pear**" (for hedges) "I strongly deprecate; although impenetrable and inexpensive, it conveys an idea of sterility, and is rapidly becoming a nuisance in this country."—*Cleghorn, Forests and Gardens*, 285.

PROME, n.p. An important place in Pegu above the Delta. The name is Talaing, properly *Brun*. The Burmese call it *Pyé* or (in the Aracanese form in which the *r* is pronounced) *Pré* and *Pré-myo* ('city').

1545.—"When he (the K. of *Bramaa*) was arrived at the young King's pallace, he caused himself to be crowned King of **Prom**, and during the Ceremony . . . made that poor Prince, whom he had deprived of his Kingdom, to continue kneeling before him, with his hands held up. . . . This done he went into a Balcone, which looked on a great Market-place, whither he commanded all the dead children that lay up and down the streets, to be brought, and then causing them to be hacked very small, he gave them, mingled with Bran, Rice, and Herbs, to his Elephants to eat."—*Pinto*, E.T. 211-212 (orig. clv.).

c. 1609.—". . . this quarrel was hardly ended when a great rumour of arms was heard from a quarter where the Portuguese were still fighting. The cause of this was the arrival of 12,000 men, whom the King of **Pren** sent in pursuit of the King of Arracan, knowing that he had fled that way. Our people hastening up had a stiff and well fought combat with them; for although they were fatigued with the fight which had been hardly ended, those of **Pren** were so disheartened at seeing the Portuguese, whose steel they had already felt, that they were fain to retire."—*Bocarro*, 142. This author has **Prom** (p. 132) and **Porão** (p. 149). [Also see under **AVA.**]

1755.—"**Prone** . . . has the ruins of an *old brick wall round it*, and immediately without *that*, another with *Teak Timber*."—*Capt. G. Baker*, in *Dalrymple*, i. 173.

1795.—"In the evening, my boat being ahead, I reached the city of *Peeaye-mew*, or **Prome**, . . . renowned in Birman history."—*Symes*, pp. 238-9.

PROW, PARAO, &c., s. This word seems to have a double origin in European use; the Malayāl. *pāru*, 'a boat,' and the Island word (common to Malay, Javanese, and most languages of the Archipelago) *prāū* or *prāhū*. This is often specifically applied to a peculiar kind of galley, "Malay Prow," but Crawfurd defines it as "a general term for any vessel, but generally for small craft." It is hard to distinguish between the words, as adopted in the earlier books, except by considering date and locality.

1499.—"The King despatched to them a large boat, which they call **paráo**, well manned, on board which he sent a Naire of his with an errand to the Captains. . . ."—*Correa, Lendas*, I. i. 115.

1510.—(At Calicut) "Some other small ships are called **Parao**, and they are boats of ten paces each, and are all of a piece, and go with oars made of cane, and the mast also is made of cane."—*Varthema*, 154.

1510.—"The other Persian said: 'O Sir, what shall we do?' I replied: 'Let us go along this shore till we find a **parao**, that is, a small bark.'"—*Ibid.* 269.

1518.—"Item; that any one possessing a zambuquo (see **SAMBOOK**) or a **parao** of his own and desiring to go in it may do so with all that belongs to him, first giving notice two days before to the Captain of the City."—*Livro dos Privilegios da Cidade de Goa*, in *Archiv. Port. Orient.* Fascic. v. p. 7.

1523.—"When Dom Sancho (Dom Sancho Anriquez; see *Correa*, ii. 770) went into Muar to fight with the fleet of the King of Bintam which was inside the River, there arose a squall which upset all our **paraos** and **lancharas** at the bar mouth. . . ."—*Lembrança, de Cousas de India*, p. 5.

1582.—"Next daye after the Capitaine Generall with all his men being a land, working upon the ship called Berrio, there came in two little **Paraos**."—*Castañeda* (tr. by N. L.), f. 62*v*.

1586.—"The fifth and last festival, which is called *Sapan Donon*, is one in which the King (of Pegu) is embarked in the most beautiful **paro**, or boat. . . ."—*G. Balbi*, f. 122.

1606.—Gouvea (f. 27*v*) uses **paro**.

" "An howre after this comming a board of the hollanders came a **prawe** or a canow from Bantam."—*Middleton's Voyage*, c. 3 (*v*).

[1611.—"The Portuguese call their own galiots Navires (*navios*) and those of the Malabars, **Pairaus**. Most of these vessels were Chetils (see **CHETTY**), that is to say merchantmen. Immediately on arrival the Malabars draw up their **Pados** or galliots on the beach."—*Pyrard de Laval*, Hak. Soc. i. 345.

[1623.—"In the Morning we discern'd four ships of Malabar Rovers near the shore (they called them **Paroes** and they goe with Oars like our Galeots or Foists."—*P. della Valle*, Hak. Soc. ii. 201.]

1666.—"Con secreto previno Lope de Soarez veinte bateles, y gobernandolo y entrando por un rio, hallaron el peligro de cinco naves y ochenta **paraos** con mucha gente resuelta y de valor."—*Faria y Sousa*, *Asia*, i. 66.

1673.—"They are owners of several small **Provoes**, of the same make, and Canooses, cut out of one entire Piece of Wood."—*Fryer*, 20. Elsewhere (*e.g.* 57, 59) he has **Proes**.

1727.—"The *Andemaners* had a yearly Custom to come to the *Nicobar* Islands, with a great number of small **Praws**, and kill or take Prisoners as many of the poor Nicobareans as they could overcome."—*A. Hamilton*, ii. 65 [ed. 1744].

1816.—". . . **Prahu**, a term under which the Malays include every description of vessel."—*Raffles*, in *As. Res.* xii. 132.

1817.—"The Chinese also have many brigs . . . as well as native-built **prahus**."—*Raffles*, *Java*, i. 203.

1868.—"On December 13th I went on board a **prau** bound for the Aru Islands."—— *Wallace, Malay Archip.* 227.

PUCKA, adj. Hind. *pakkā*, 'ripe, mature, cooked'; and hence substantial, permanent, with many specific applications, of which examples have been given under the habitually contrasted term **cutcha** (q.v.). One of the most common uses in which the word has become specific is that of a building of brick and mortar, in contradistinction to one of inferior material, as of mud, matting, or timber. Thus:

[1756.—". . . adjacent houses; all of them of the strongest **Pecca** work, and all most proof against our Mettal on ye Bastions." *Capt. Grant, Report on Siege of Calcutta*, ed. by Col. Temple, *Ind. Ant.*, 1890, p. 7.]

1784.—"The House, Cook-room, bottle-connah, godown, &c., are all **pucka**-built."—In *Seton-Karr*, i. 41.

1824.—"A little above this beautiful stream, some miserable **pucka** sheds pointed out the Company's warehouses."—*Heber*, ed. 1844, i. 259-60.

1842.—"I observe that there are in the town (Dehli) many buildings **pucka**-built, as it is called in India."—*Wellington* to Ld. Ellenborough, in *Indian Adm.* of *Ld. E.*, p. 306.

1857.—"Your Lahore men have done nobly. I should like to embrace them; Donald, Roberts, Mac, and Dick are, all of them, **pucca** trumps."—*Lord Lawrence*, in *Life*, ii. 11.

1869.—". . . there is no surer test by which to measure the prosperity of the people than the number of **pucka** houses that are being built."—*Report of a Sub-Committee* on Proposed Indian Census.

This application has given rise to a substantive **pucka**, for work of brick and mortar, or for the composition used as cement and plaster.

1727.—"Fort William was built on an irregular Tetragon of Brick and Mortar, called **Puckah**, which is a Composition of Brick-dust, Lime, Molasses, and cut Hemp, and when it comes to be dry, it is as hard and tougher than firm Stone or Brick."—*A. Hamilton*, ii. 19; [ed. 1744, ii. 7].

The word was also sometimes used substantively for "*pucka pice*" (see **CUTCHA**).

c. 1817.—"I am sure I strive, and strive, and yet last month I could only lay by eight rupees and four **puckers**."—*Mrs. Sherwood's Stories*, 66.

In (Stockdale's) *Indian Vocabulary* of 1788 we find another substantive use, but it was perhaps even then inaccurate.

1788.—"**Pucka**.—A putrid fever, generally fatal in 24 hours."

Another habitual application of **pucka** and **cutcha** distinguishes between two classes of weights and measures. The existence of twofold weight, the **pucka** ser and the **cutcha**, used to be very general in India. It was equally common in Medieval Europe. Almost every city in Italy had its libra *grossa* and libra *sottile* (*e.g.* see *Pegolotti*, 4, 34, 153, 228, &c.), and we ourselves still have them, under the names of *pound avoirdupois* and *pound troy*.

1673.—"The **Maund Pucka** at *Agra* is double as much (as the Surat *Maund*)."—*Fryer*, 205.

1760.—"Les **pacca** cosses . . . repondent à une lieue de l'Isle de France."—*Lett. Edif.* xv. 189.

1803.—"If the rice should be sent to Coraygaum, it should be in sufficient quantities to give 72 **pucca** seers for each load."—*Wellington, Desp.* (ed. 1837), ii. 43.

In the next quotation the terms apply to the temporary or permanent character of the appointments held.

1866.—"*Susan.* Well, Miss, I don't wonder you're so fond of him. He is such a sweet young man, though he is **cutcha**. Thank goodness, my young man is **pucka**, though he is only a subordinate Government Salt Chowkee."—*Trevelyan, The Dawk Bungalow*, 222.

The remaining quotations are examples of miscellaneous use:

1853.—"'Well, Jenkyns, any news?' 'Nothing **pucka** that I know of.'"—*Oakfield*, ii. 57.

1866.—"I cannot endure a swell, even though his whiskers are **pucka**."—*Trevelyan, The Dawk Bungalow*, in *Fraser*, lxxiii. 220.

The word has spread to China:

"Dis **pukka** sing-song makee show
How smart man make mistake, galow."
Leland, Pidgin English Sing-Song, 54.

PUCKAULY, s.; also **PUCKAUL**. Hind. *pakhālī*, 'a water-carrier.' In N. India the *pakhāl* [Skt. *payas*, 'water,' *khalla*, 'skin'] is a large water-skin (an entire ox-hide) of some 20 gallons content, of which a pair are carried by a bullock, and the *pakhālī* is the man who fills the skins, and supplies the water thus. In the Madras Drill Regulations for 1785 (33), ten **puckalies** are allowed to a battalion. (See also Williamson's *V. M.* (1810), i. 229.)

[1538.—Referring to the preparations for the siege of Diu, "which they brought from all the wells on the island by all the bullocks they could collect with their water-skins, which they call **pacals** (*Pacais*)."—*Couto*, Dec. V. Bk. iii. ch. 2.]

1780.—"There is another very necessary establishment to the European corps, which is two **buccalies** to each company; these are two large leathern bags for holding water, slung upon the back of a bullock. . . ."—*Munro's Narrative*, 183.

1803.—"It (water) is brought by means of bullocks in leathern bags, called here **puckally** bags, a certain number of which is attached to every regiment and garrison in India. Black fellows called **Puckauly-boys** are employed to fill the bags, and drive the bullocks to the quarters of the different Europeans."—*Percival's Ceylon*, 102.

1804.—"It would be a much better arrangement to give the adjutants of corps an allowance of 26 rupees per mensam, to supply two **puckalie** men, and two bullocks with bags, for each company."—*Wellington*, iii. 509.

1813.—"In cities, in the armies, and with Europeans on country excursions, the water for drinking is usually carried in large leather bags called **pacaulies**, formed by the entire skin of an ox."—*Forbes*, *Or. Mem.* ii. 140; [2nd ed. i. 415].

1842.—"I lost no time in confidentially communicating with Capt. Oliver on the subject of trying some experiments as to the possibility of conveying empty '**puckalls**' and '**mussucks**' by sea to Suez."—*Sir G. Arthur*, in *Ellenborough's Ind. Admin.* 219.

[1850.—"On the reverse flank of companies march the **Pickalliers**, or men driving bullocks, carrying large leather bags filled with water. . . ."—*Hervey*, *Ten Years in India*, iii. 335.]

PUCKEROW, v. This is properly the imperative of the Hind. verb *pakṛānā*, 'to cause to be seized,' *pakṛāo*, 'cause him to be seized'; or perhaps more correctly of a compound verb *pakaṛāo*, 'seize and come,' or in our idiom, 'Go and seize.' But *puckerow* belongs essentially to the dialect of the European soldier, and in that becomes of itself a verb 'to *puckerow*,' *i.e.* to lay hold of (generally of a recalcitrant native). The conversion of the Hind. imperative into an Anglo-Indian verb infinitive, is not uncommon; compare **bunow, dumbcow, gubbrow, lugow**, &c.

1866.—"Fanny, I am **cutcha** no longer. Surely you will allow a lover who is **pucka** to **puckero**!"—*Trevelyan*, *The Dawk Bungalow*, 390.

PUDIPATAN, n.p. The name of a very old seaport of Malabar, which has now ceased to have a place in the Maps. It lay between Cannanore and Calicut, and must have been near the Waddakaré of K. Johnston's Royal Atlas. [It appears in the map in Logan's *Malabar* as *Putuppatanam* or *Putappanam.*] The name is Tamil, *Pudupaṭṭana*, 'New City.' Compare true form of **Pondicherry**.

c. 545.—"The most notable places of trade are these . . . and then five marts of Malé from which pepper is exported, to wit, Parti, Mangaruth (see **MANGALORE**) Salopatana, Nalopatana, **Pudopatana**. . . ."—*Cosmas Indicopleustes*, Bk. xi. (see in *Cathay*, &c. p. clxxviii.).

c. 1342.—"**Buddfattan**, which is a considerable city, situated upon a great estuary. . . . The haven of this city is one of the finest; the water is good, the betel-nut is abundant, and is exported thence to India and China."—*Ibn Batuta*, iv. 87.

c. 1420.—"A quâ rursus se diebus viginti terrestri viâ contulit ad urbem portumque maritimum nomine **Pudifetaneam**."—*Conti*, in *Poggio*, *de Var. Fort.*

1516.—". . . And passing those places you come to a river called **Pudripatan**, in which there is a good place having many Moorish merchants who possess a multitude of ships, and here begins the Kingdom of Calicut."—*Barbosa*, in *Ramusio*, i. f. 311*v*. See also in Stanley's Barbosa **Pudopatani**, and in *Tohfat-ul-Mujahideen*, by Rowlandson, pp. 71, 157, where the name (*Budfattan*) is misread **Buduftun**.

[**PUG**, s. Hind. *pag*, Skt. *padaka*, 'a foot'; in Anglo-Indian use the footmarks of an animal, such as a tiger.

[1831.—". . . sanguine we were sometimes on the report of a *bura* **pug** from the **shikaree**."—*Orient. Sport. Mag.* reprint 1873, ii. 178.

[1882.—"Presently the large square '**pug**' of the tiger we were in search of appeared."—*Sanderson*, *Thirteen Years*, 30.]

PUGGRY, PUGGERIE, s. Hind. *pagṛī*, 'a turban.' The term being often used in colloquial for a scarf of cotton or silk wound round the hat in turban-form, to protect the head from the sun, both the thing and name have of late years made their way to England, and may be seen in London shop-windows.

c. 1200.—"Prithirâja . . . wore a **pagari** ornamented with jewels, with a splendid *toro*. In his ears he wore pearls; on his neck a pearl necklace."—*Chand Bardai* E.T. by *Beames*, *Ind. Ant.* i. 282.

[1627.—". . . I find it is the common mode of the Eastern People to shave the head all save a long lock which superstitiously they leave at the very top, such especially as wear **Turbans**, Mandils, Dustars, and **Puggarees.**"—*Sir T. Herbert*, ed. 1677, p. 140.]

1673.—"They are distinguished, some according to the consanguinity they claim with Mahomet, as a Siad is akin to that Imposture, and therefore only assumes to himself a Green Vest and **Puckery** (or Turbat). . . ."—*Fryer*, 93; [comp. 113].

1689.—". . . with a **Puggaree** or Turbant upon their Heads."—*Ovington*, 314.

1871. — "They (the Negro Police in Demarara) used frequently to be turned out to parade in George Town streets, dressed in a neat uniform, with white **puggries** framing in their ebony faces."—*Jenkins, The Coolie.*

PUGGY, s. Hind. *pagī* (not in Shakespear's Dict., nor in Platts), from *pag* (see **PUG**), 'the foot.' A professional tracker; the name of a caste, or rather an occupation, whose business is to track thieves by footmarks and the like. On the system, see *Burton, Sind Revisited*, i. 180 *seqq.*

[1824.—"There are in some of the districts of Central India (as in Guzerat) **puggees**, who have small fees on the village, and whose business it is to trace thieves by the print of their feet."—*Malcolm, Central India*, 2nd ed. ii. 19.]

1879.—"Good **puggies** or trackers should be employed to follow the dacoits during the daytime."—*Times of India*, Overland Suppt., May 12, p. 7.

PUHUR, PORE, PYRE, &c., s. Hind. *pahar*, *pahr*, from Skt. *prahara*. 'A fourth part of the day and of the night, a watch' or space of 8 *gharīs* (see **GHURRY**).

c. 1526. — "The natives of Hindostân divide the night and day into 60 parts, each of which they denominate a *Gheri*; they likewise divide the night into 4 parts, and the day into the same number, each of which they call a **Pahar** or watch, which the Persians call a *Pâs*."—*Baber*, 331.

[c. 1590.—"The Hindu philosophers divide the day and night into four parts, each of which they call a **pahr.**"—*Āīn*, ed. *Jarrett*, iii. 15.]

1633.—"**Par.**" See under **GHURRY.**

1673.—"**Pore.**" See under **GONG.**

1803.—"I have some **Jasooses** selected by Col. C's brahmin for their stupidity, that they might not pry into state secrets, who go to Sindia's camp, remain there a **phaur** in fear. . . ."—*M. Elphinstone*, in *Life*, i. 62.

PULÁ, s. In Tamil *pillai*, Malayāl. *pilla*, 'child'; the title of a superior class of (so-called) Śūdras, [especially **curnums**]. In Cochin and Travancore it corresponds with *Nāyar* (see **NAIR**). It is granted by the sovereign, and carries exemption from customary manual labour.

1553.—". . . **pulas**, who are the gentlemen" (*fidalgos*).—*Castanheda*, iv. 2.

[1726.—"O Saguate que o Commendor tinha remetido como gristnave amim e as **Pulamares** temos ca recebid."—*Ratification*, in *Logan*, *Malabar*, iii. 13.]

PULICAT, n.p. A town on the Madras coast, which was long the seat of a Dutch factory. Bp. Caldwell's native friend Seshagiri Śāstri gives the proper name as *pala-Vēlkāḍu*, 'old Velkāḍu or Verkāḍu,' the last a place-name mentioned in the Tamil Sivaite *Tevāram* (see also Valentijn below). [The *Madras Gloss.* gives *Pazhäverk-kādu*, 'old acacia forest,' which is corroborated by Dr. Hultzsch (*Epigraphia Indica*, i. 398).]

1519.—"And because he had it much in charge to obtain all the lac (*alacre*) that he could, the Governor learning from merchants that much of it was brought to the Coast of Choromandel by the vessels of Pegu and Martaban which visited that coast to procure painted cloths and other coloured goods, such as are made in **Paleacate**, which is on the coast of Choromandel, whence the traders with whom the Governor spoke brought it to Cochin; he, having got good information on the whole matter, sent a certain Frolentine (*sic, frolentim*) called Pero Escroco, whom he knew, and who was good at trade, to be factor on the coast of Choromandel. . . ."—*Correa*, ii. 567.

1533. — "The said Armenian, having already been at the city of **Paleacate**, which is in the Province of Choromandel and the Kingdom of Bisnaga, when on his way to Bengal, and having information of the place where the body of S. Thomas was said to be, and when they arrived at the port of **Paleacate** the wind was against their going on. . . ."—*Barros*, III. vii. 11.

[1611.—"The Dutch had settled a factory at **Pellacata.**"—*Danvers, Letters*, i. 133; in *Foster*, ii. 83, **Pollicat.**]

1726.—"Then we come to *Palleam Wedam Caddoe*, called by us for shortness **Palleacatta**, which means in Malabars 'The old Fortress,' though most commonly we call it *Castle Geldria*."—*Valentijn, Chorom.* 13.

" "The route I took was along the strip of country between **Porto Novo** and **Paleiacatta.** This long journey I travelled on foot; and preached in more than a hundred places. . . ."—*Letter of the Missionary Schultze*, July 19, in *Notices of Madras*, &c., p. 20.

1727.—"**Policat** is the next Place of Note to the City and Colony of Fort St *George.*

. . . It is strengthned with two Forts, one contains a few Dutch soldiers for a Garrison, the other is commanded by an Officer belonging to the *Mogul.*"—*A. Hamilton*, i. 372, [ed. 1744].

[1813.—"**Pulecat** handkerchiefs." See under **PIECE-GOODS.**]

PULTUN, s. Hind. *palṭan*, a corruption of *Battalion*, possibly with some confusion of *platoon* or *péloton*. The S. India form is *pataulam*, *patālam*. It is the usual native word for a regiment of native infantry; it is never applied to one of Europeans.

1800.—"All I can say is that I am ready primed, and that if all matters suit I shall go off with a dreadful explosion, and shall probably destroy some **campoos** and **pultons** which have been indiscreetly pushed across the Kistna."—*A. Wellesley* to *T. Munro*, in *Mem. of Munro*, by *Arbuthnot*, lxix.

[1895.—"I know lots of Sahibs in a **pultoon** at Bareilly."—*Mrs Croker, Village Tales and Jungle Tragedies*, 60.]

PULWAH, PULWAR, s. One of the native boats used on the rivers of Bengal, carrying some 12 to 15 tons. Hind. *palwār*. [For a drawing see *Grierson, Bihar Village Life*, p. 42.]

1735.—". . . We observed a boat which had come out of *Samboo* river, making for *Patna*: the commandant detached two light **pulwaars** after her. . . ."—*Holwell, Hist. Events*, &c., i. 69.

[1767.—". . . a Peon came twice to Noon-golah, to apply for **polwars**. . . ."—*Verelst, View of Bengal*, App. 197.]

1780.—"Besides this boat, a gentleman is generally attended by two others; a **pulwah** for the accommodation of the kitchen, and a smaller boat, a **paunchway**" (q.v.).—*Hodges*, p. 39.

1782.—"To be sold, Three New Dacca **Pulwars**, 60 feet long, with Houses in the middle of each."—*India Gazette*, Aug. 31.

1824.—"The ghât offered a scene of bustle and vivacity which I by no means expected. There were so many budgerows and **pulwars**, that we had considerable difficulty to find a mooring place."—*Heber*, ed. 1844, i. 131.

1860.—"The **Pulwar** is a smaller description of native travelling boat, of neater build, and less rusticity of character, sometimes used by a single traveller of humble means, and at others serves as *cook-boat* and accommodation for servants accompanying one of the large kind of boats. . . ."—*Grant, Rural Life in Bengal*, p. 7, with an illustration.

PULWAUN, s. P.—H. *pahlwān*, [which properly means 'a native of ancient Persia' (see **PAHLAVI**). Mr. Skeat notes that in Malay the word becomes *pahlāwan*, probably from a confusion with Malay *āwan*, 'to fight']. A champion; a professed wrestler or man of strength.

[1753.—". . . the fourth, and least numerous of these bodies, were choice men of the **Pehlevans**. . . ."—*Hanway*, iii. 104.

[1813.—"When his body has by these means imbibed an additional portion of vigour, he is dignified by the appellation of **Puhlwan**."—*Broughton, Letters*, ed. 1892, p. 165.]

1828.—"I added a **pehlivân** or prize-fighter, a negro whose teeth were filed into saws, of a temper as ferocious as his aspect, who could throw any man of his weight to the ground, carry a jackass, devour a sheep whole, eat fire, and make a fountain of his inside, so as to act as a spout."—*Hajji Baba in England*, i. 15.

PUN, s. A certain number of cowries, generally 80; Hind. *paṇa*. (See under **COWRY**). The Skt. *paṇa* is 'a stake played for a price, a sum,' and hence both a coin (whence **fanam**, q.v.) and a certain amount of cowries.

1554.—"**Pone**." (See under **PORTO PIQUENO.**)

1683.—"I was this day advised that Mr. Charnock putt off Mr. Ellis's Cowries at 34 **pund** to ye Rupee in payment of all ye Peons and Servants of the Factory, whereas 38 **punds** are really bought by him for a Rupee. . . ."—*Hedges, Diary*, Oct. 2; [Hak. Soc. i. 122].

1760.—"We now take into consideration the relief of the menial servants of this Settlement, respecting the exorbitant price of labor exacted from them by tailors, washermen, and barbers, which appear in near a quadruple (pro)portion compared with the prices paid in 1755. Agreed, that after the 1st of April they be regulated as follows:

"No tailor to demand for making:
 1 **Jamma**, more than 3 annas.
 * * * * *
 1 pair of drawers, 7 **pun** of cowries.
No washerman:
 1 corge of pieces, 7 **pun** of cowries.
No barber for shaving a single person, more than 7 gundas" (see **COWRY**).—*Ft. William Consns.*, March 27, in *Long*, 209.

PUNCH, s. This beverage, according to the received etymology, was named from the Pers. *panj*, or Hind. and Mahr. *pānch*, both meaning 'five'; because composed of five ingredients, viz. arrack, sugar, lime-juice, spice, and water. Fryer may be considered to give something like historical evidence of its origin; but there is also something of Indian idiom in the suggestion. Thus a famous horse-medicine in Upper India is known as *battīsī*, because it is supposed to contain 32 ('*battīs*') ingredients. Schiller, in his *Punschlied*, sacrificing truth to trope, omits the spice and makes the ingredients only 4: "*Vier* Elemente Innig gesellt, Bilden das Leben, Bauen die Welt."

The Greeks also had a "Punch," πενταπλόα, as is shown in the quotation from Athenaeus. Their mixture does not sound inviting. Littré gives the etymology correctly from the Pers. *panj*, but the 5 elements *à la française*, as tea, sugar, spirit, cinnamon, and lemon-peel,—no water therefore!

Some such compound appears to have been in use at the beginning of the 17th century under the name of **Larkin** (q.v.). Both Dutch and French travellers in the East during that century celebrate the beverage under a variety of names which amalgamate the drink curiously with the vessel in which it was brewed. And this combination in the form of **Bole-ponjis** was adopted as the title of a Miscellany published in 1851, by H. Meredith Parker, a Bengal civilian, of local repute for his literary and dramatic tastes. He had lost sight of the original authorities for the term, and his quotation is far astray. We give them correctly below.

c. 210.—"On the feast of the Scirrha at Athens he (Aristodemus on Pindar) says a race was run by the young men. They ran this race carrying each a vine-branch laden with grapes, such as is called *ōschus;* and they ran from the temple of Dionysus to that of Athena Sciras. And the winner receives a cup such as is called '**Five-fold**,' and of this he partakes joyously with the band of his comrades. But the cup is called πενταπλόα because it contains wine and honey and cheese and flour, and a little oil."—*Athenaeus*, XI. xcii.

1638.—"This voyage (Gombroon to Surat) . . . we accomplished in 19 days. . . . We drank English beer, Spanish sack, French wine, Indian spirit, and good English water, and made good **Palepunzen**."—*Mandelslo*, (Dutch ed. 1658), p. 24. The word **Palepunzen** seems to have puzzled the English translator (John Davis, 2nd ed. 1669), who has "excellent good sack, *English* beer, *French* wines, *Arak, and other refreshments.*" (p. 10).

1653.—"**Bolleponge** est vn mot Anglois, qui signifie vne boisson dont les Anglois vsent aux Indes faite de sucre, suc de limon, eau de vie, fleur de muscade, et biscuit roty."—*De la Boullaye-le-Gouz*, ed. 1657, p. 534.

[1658.—"Arriued this place where found the Bezar almost Burnt and many of the People almost starued for want of Foode which caused much Sadnes in Mr. Charnock and my Selfe, but not soe much as the absence of your Company, which wee haue often remembered in a bowle of the cleerest **Punch**, hauing noe better Liquor."—*Hedges*, *Diary*, Hak. Soc. iii. cxiv.]

1659.—"Fürs Dritte, **Pale bunze** getituliret, von halb Wasser, halb Brantwein, dreyssig, vierzig Limonien, deren Körnlein ausgespeyet werden, und ein wenig Zucker eingeworfen; wie dem Geschmack so angenehm nicht, also auch der Gesundheit nicht."—*Saar*, ed. 1672, 60.

[1662.—"Amongst other spirituous drinks, as **Punch**, &c., they gave us Canarie that had been carried to and fro from the Indies, which was indeed incomparably good."—*Evelyn*, *Diary*, Jan. 16.]

c. 1666.—"Neánmoins depuis qu'ils (les Anglois) ont donné ordre, aussi bien que les Hollandois, que leurs equipages ne boivent point tant de **Bouleponges** . . . il n'y a pas tant de maladies, et il ne leur meurt plus tant de monde. **Bouleponge** est un certain breuvage composé d'arac . . . avec du suc de limons, de l'eau, et un peu de muscade rapée dessus: il est assez agréable au gout, mais c'est la peste du corps et de la santé."—*Bernier*, ed. 1723, ii. 335 (Eng. Tr. p. 141); [ed. *Constable*, 441].

1670. — "Doch als men zekere andere drank, die zij **Paleponts** noemen, daartusschen drinkt, zo word het quaat enigsins geweert." — *Andriesz*, 9. Also at p. 27, "**Palepunts**."

We find this blunder of the compound word transported again to England, and explained as a 'hard word.'

1672. — Padre Vincenzo Maria describes the thing, but without a name:

"There are many fruites to which the Hollanders and the English add a certain beverage that they compound of lemon-juice, aqua-vitae, sugar, and nutmegs, to quench their thirst, and this, in my belief, augments not a little the evil influence."—*Viaggio*, p. 103.

1673.—"At Nerule is the best *Arach* or *Nepa* (see **NIPA**) *de Goa*, with which the *English* on this Coast make that enervating Liquor called **Paunch** (which is *Indostan* for Five), from Five Ingredients; as the Physicians name their Composition *Diapente;* or from four things, *Diatessaron*."—*Fryer*, 157.

1674. — "**Palapuntz**, a kind of Indian drink, consisting of *Aqua-vitae*, Rose-water, juyce of Citrons and Sugar."—*Glossographia*, &c., by T. E.

[1675.—"Drank part of their boules of **Punch** (a liquor very strange to me)."—*H. Teonge*, *Diary*, June 1.]

1682.—"Some (of the Chinese in Batavia) also sell Sugar-beer, as well as cooked dishes and Sury (see **SURA**), arak or Indian brandy; wherefrom they make *Mussak* and **Follepons**, as the Englishmen call it."—*Nieuhoff, Zee en Lant-Reize*, ii. 217.

1683.—". . . Our owne people and mariners who are now very numerous, and insolent among us, and (by reason of **Punch**) every day give disturbance." — *Hedges, Diary*, Oct. 8; [Hak. Soc. i. 123].

1688.—". . . the soldiers as merry as **Punch** could make them."—In *Wheeler*, i. 187.

1689.—"Bengal (Arak) is much stronger spirit than that of Goa, tho' both are made use of by the Europeans in making **Punch**." —*Ovington*, 237-8.

1694.—"If any man comes into a victualling house to drink **punch**, he may demand one quart good Goa *arak*, half a pound of sugar, and half a pint of good lime water, and make his own **punch**. . . ." —*Order Book of Bombay Govt.*, quoted by *Anderson*, p. 281.

1705.—"Un bon repas chez les Anglais ne se fait point sans *bonne* **ponse** qu'on sert dans un grand vase."—*Sieur Luillier, Voy. aux Grandes Indes*, 29.

1771.—"Hence every one (at Madras) has it in his Power to eat well, tho' he can afford no other Liquor at Meals than **Punch**, which is the common Drink among Europeans, and here made in the greatest Perfection."—*Lockyer*, 22.

1724.—"Next to *Drams*, no Liquor deserves more to be stigmatised and banished from the Repasts of the *Tender, Valetudinary*, and *Studious*, than **Punch**." — *G. Cheyne, An Essay on Health and Longevity*, p. 58.

1791.—"Dès que l'Anglais eut cessé de manger, le Paria . . . fit un signe à sa femme, qui apporta . . . une grande calebasse pleine de **punch**, qu'elle avoit preparé, pendant le souper, avec de l'eau, et du jus de citron, et du jus de canne de sucre. . . ."—*B. de St. Pierre, Chaumière Indienne*, 56.

PUNCH-HOUSE, s. An Inn or Tavern; now the term is chiefly used by natives (sometimes in the hybrid form **Punch-ghar**, [which in Upper India is now transferred to the meeting-place of a Municipal Board]) at the Presidency towns, and applied to houses frequented by seamen. Formerly the word was in general Anglo-Indian use. [In the Straits the Malay *Panchaus* is, according to Mr. Skeat, still in use, though obolescent.]

[1661.—". . . the Commandore visiting us, wee delivering him another examination of a Persee (**Parsee**), who kept a **Punch house**, where the murder was committed. . . ."—*Forrest, Bombay Letters, Home Series*, i. 189.]

1671-2.—"It is likewise enordered and declared hereby that no Victuallar, **Punch-house**, or other house of Entertainment shall be permitted to make stoppage at the pay day of their wages. . . ."—*Rules*, in *Wheeler*, iii. 423.

1676.—Major Puckle's "Proposals to the Agent about the young men at Metchlepatam.

"That some pecuniary mulct or fine be imposed . . . for misdemeanours.

* * * * *

"6. Going to **Punch** or **Rack-houses** without leave or warrantable occasion.

"Drubbing any of the Company's **Peons** or servants."

* * * * *

—In *Notes and Exts.*, No. I. p. 40.

1688.—". . . at his return to Achen he constantly frequented an English **Punch-house**, spending his Gold very freely."—*Dampier*, ii. 134.

" "Mrs. Francis, wife to the late Lieutenant Francis killed at Hoogly by the Moors, made it her petition that she might keep a **Punch-house** for her maintenance." —In *Wheeler*, i. 184.

1697.—"Monday, 1st April . . . Mr. Cheesely having in a **Punch-house**, upon a quarrel of words, drawn his Sword . . . and being taxed therewith, he both doth own and justify the drawing of the sword . . . it thereupon ordered not to wear a sword while here."—In *Wheeler*, i. 320.

1727.—". . . Of late no small Pains and Charge have been bestowed on its Buildings (of the Fort at Tellichery); but for what Reason I know not . . . unless it be for small Vessels . . . or to protect the Company's Ware-house, and a small **Punch-house** that stands on the Sea-shore. . . ." —*A. Hamilton*, i. 299 [ed. 1744].

1789.—"Many . . . are obliged to take up their residence in dirty **punch-houses**." —*Munro's Narrative*, 22.

1810.—"The best house of that description which admits boarders, and which are commonly called **Punch-houses**."—*Williamson, V.M.* i. 135.

PUNCHAYET, s. Hind. *panchāyat*, from *pānch*, 'five.' A council (properly of 5 persons) assembled as a Court of Arbiters or Jury; or as a committee of the people of a village, of the members of a Caste, or whatnot, to decide on questions interesting the body generally.

1778.—"*The Honourable* WILLIAM HORNBY, Esq., *President and Governor of His Majesty's Castle and Island of Bombay*, &c.

"The humble Petition of the Managers of the **Panchayet** of Parsis at Bombay. . . ." —*Dosambhai Framji, H. of the Parsis*, 1884, ii. 219.

1810.—"The Parsees . . . are governed by their own **panchait** or village Council.

The word **panchait** literally means a Council of five, but that of the Guebres in Bombay consists of thirteen of the principal merchants of the sect."—*Maria Graham*, 41.

1813.—"The carpet of justice was spread in the large open hall of the durbar, where the arbitrators assembled: there I always attended, and agreeably to ancient custom, referred the decision to a **panchaeet** or jury of five persons."—*Forbes, Or. Mem.*, ii. 359; [in 2nd ed. (ii. 2) **Panchaut**].

1819.—"The **punchayet** itself, although in all but village causes it has the defects before ascribed to it, possesses many advantages. The intimate acquaintance of the members with the subject in dispute, and in many cases with the characters of the parties, must have made their decisions frequently correct, and . . . the judges being drawn from the body of the people, could act on no principles that were not generally understood."—*Elphinstone*, in *Life*, ii. 89.

1821.—"I kept up **punchayets** because I found them . . . I still think that the **punchayet** should on no account be dropped, that it is an excellent institution for dispensing justice, and in keeping up the principles of justice, which are less likely to be observed among a people to whom the administration of it is not at all intrusted."—*Ibid.* 124.

1826.—". . . when he returns assemble a **punchayet**, and give this cause patient attention, seeing that Hybatty has justice." —*Pandurang Hari*, 31; [ed. 1873, i. 42].

1832.—Bengal Regn. VI. of this year allows the judge of the Sessions Court to call in the alternative aid of a **punchayet**, in lieu of assessors, and so to dispense with the **futwa**. See **LAW-OFFICER**.

1853.—"From the death of Runjeet Singh to the battle of Sobraon, the Sikh Army was governed by '**Punchayets**' or '**Punches**' —committees of the soldiery. These bodies sold the Government to the Sikh chief who paid the highest, letting him command until murdered by some one who paid higher."—*Sir C. Napier, Defects of Indian Government*, 69.

1873.—"The Council of an Indian Village Community most commonly consists of five persons . . . the **panchayet** familiar to all who have the smallest knowledge of India." —*Maine, Early Hist. of Institutions*, 221.

PUNDIT, s. Skt. *paṇḍita*, 'a learned man.' Properly a man learned in Sanskrit lore. The Pundit of the Supreme Court was a Hindu **Law-Officer**, whose duty it was to advise the English Judges when needful on questions of Hindu Law. The office became extinct on the constitution of the 'High Court,' superseding the Supreme Court and Sudder Court, under the Queen's Letters Patent of May 14, 1862.

In the Mahratta and Telegu countries, the word *Paṇḍit* is usually pronounced *Pant* (in English colloquial *Punt*); but in this form it has, as with many other Indian words in like case, lost its original significance, and become a mere personal title, familiar in Mahratta history, *e.g.* the Nānā Dhundo*pant* of evil fame.

Within the last 30 or 35 years the term has acquired in India a peculiar application to the natives trained in the use of instruments, who have been employed beyond the British Indian frontier in surveying regions inaccessible to Europeans. This application originated in the fact that two of the earliest men to be so employed, the explorations by one of whom acquired great celebrity, were masters of village schools in our Himālayan provinces. And the title *Pundit* is popularly employed there much as *Dominie* used to be in Scotland. The *Pundit* who brought so much fame on the title was the late Nain Singh, C.S.I. [See Markham, *Memoir of Indian Surveys*, 2nd ed. 148 *seqq.*]

1574.—"I hereby give notice that . . . I hold it good, and it is my pleasure, and therefore I enjoin on all the **pandits** (*panditos*) and Gentoo physicians (*phisicos gentios*) that they ride not through this City (of Goa) or the suburbs thereof on horseback, nor in **andors** and palanquins, on pain of paying, on the first offence 10 *cruzados*, and on the second 20, *pera o sapal*,* with the forfeiture of such horses, **andors**, or palanquins, and on the third they shall become the galley-slaves of the King my Lord. . . ." —*Procl.* of the Governor *Antonio Moriz Barreto*, in *Archiv. Port. Orient.* Fascic. 5, p. 899.

1604.—". . . llamando tãbien en su compania los **Pōditos**, le presentaron al Nauabo." —*Guerrero, Relaçion*, 70.

1616.—". . . Brachmanae una cum **Panditis** comparentes, simile quid iam inde ab orbis exordio in Indostane visum negant." —*Jarric, Thesaurus*, iii. 81-82.

* *Pera o sapal*, *i.e.* 'for the marsh.' We cannot be certain of the meaning of this; but we may note that in 1543 the King, as a favour to the city of Goa, and for the commodity of its shipping and the landing of goods, &c., makes a grant "of the marsh inundated with sea-water (*do* sapal *alagado dagoa salgada*) which extends along the river-side from the houses of Antonio Correa to the houses of Afonso Piquo, which grant is to be perpetual . . . to serve for a landing-place and quay for the merchants to moor and repair their ships, and to erect their **bankshalls** (*bangaçaes*), and never to be turned away to any other purpose." Possibly the fines went into a fund for the drainage of this *sapal* and formation of landing-places. See *Archiv. Port. Orient.*, Fasc. 2, pp. 130-131.

1663.—"A **Pendet** Brachman or *Heathen* Doctor whom I had put to serve my Agah . . . would needs make his Panegyrick . . . and at last concluded seriously with this: *When you put your Foot into the Stirrup, My Lord, and when you march on Horseback in the front of the Cavalry, the Earth trembleth under your Feet, the eight Elephants that hold it up upon their Heads not being able to support it.*" — *Bernier*, E.T., 85; [ed. *Constable*, 264].

1688.—"Je feignis donc d'être malade, et d'avoir la fièvre on fit venir aussitôt un **Pandite** ou médicin Gentil."—*Dellon, Rel. de l'Inq. de Goa*, 214.

1785.—"I can no longer bear to be at the mercy of our **pundits**, who deal out Hindu law as they please; and make it at reasonable rates, when they cannot find it ready made."—Letter of *Sir W. Jones*, in Mem. by *Ld. Teignmouth*, 1807, ii. 67.

1791.—"Il était au moment de s'embarquer pour l'Angleterre, plein de perplexité et d'ennui, lorsque les brames de Bénarés lui apprirent que le brame supérieur de la fameuse pagode de Jagrenat . . . était seul capable de resoudre toutes les questions de la Société royale de Londres. C'était en effet le plus fameux **pandect**, ou docteur, dont on eût jamais oui parler."—*B. de St. Pierre, La Chaumière Indienne.* The preceding exquisite passage shows that the blunder which drew forth Macaulay's flaming wrath, in the quotation lower down, was not a new one.

1798.—". . . the most learned of the **Pundits** or Bramin lawyers, were called up from different parts of Bengal."—*Raynal, Hist.* i. 42.

1856.—"Besides . . . being a **Pundit** of learning, he (Sir David Brewster) is a bundle of talents of various kinds."—*Life and Letters of Sydney Dobell*, ii. 14.

1860.—"Mr. Vizetelly next makes me say that the principle of limitation is found 'amongst the **Pandects** of the Benares. . . .' The Benares he probably supposes to be some Oriental nation. What he supposes their Pandects to be I shall not presume to guess. . . . If Mr. Vizetelly had consulted the Unitarian Report, he would have seen that I spoke of the **Pundits** of Benares, and he might without any very long and costly research have learned where Benares is and what a Pundit is."—*Macaulay*, Preface to his *Speeches*.

1877. — "Colonel Y——. Since Nain Singh's absence from this country precludes my having the pleasure of handing to him in person, this, the Victoria or Patron's Medal, which has been awarded to him, . . . I beg to place it in your charge for transmission to the **Pundit**."—*Address* by *Sir R. Alcock*, Prest. R. Geog. Soc., May 28.

"Colonel Y—— in reply, said: . . . Though I do not know Nain Singh personally, I know his work. . . . He is not a topographical automaton, or merely one of a great multitude of native employés with an average qualification. His observations have added a larger amount of important knowledge to the map of Asia than those of any other living man, and his journals form an exceedingly interesting book of travels. It will afford me great pleasure to take steps for the transmission of the Medal through an official channel to the **Pundit**."—*Reply to the President*, same date.

PUNJAUB, n.p. The name of the country between the Indus and the Sutlej. The modern Anglo-Indian province so-called, now extends on one side up beyond the Indus, including Peshāwar, the Derajāt, &c., and on the other side up to the Jumna, including Delhi. [In 1901 the Frontier Districts were placed under separate administration.] The name is Pers. *Panj-āb*, 'Five Rivers.' These rivers, as reckoned, sometimes include the Indus, in which case the five are (1) Indus, (2) Jelam (see **JELUM**) or Behat, the ancient *Vitasta* which the Greeks made Ὑδάσπης (*Strabo*) and Βιδάσπης (*Ptol.*), (3) Chenāb, ancient *Chandrabāgha* and *Asiknī*. Ptolemy preserves a corruption of the former Sanskrit name in Σανδαβάλ, but it was rejected by the older Greeks because it was of ill omen, *i.e.* probably because Grecized it would be Ξανδροφάγος, 'the devourer of Alexander.' The alternative *Āsiknī* they rendered Ἀκεσίνης. (4) Rāvī, the ancient *Airāvatī*, Ὑάρωτης (*Strabo*), Ὑδραώτης (*Arrian*), Ἄδρις or Ῥούαδις (*Ptol.*). (5) Biās, ancient *Vipāsā*, Ὕφασις (Arrian), Βιβάσιος (*Ptol.*). This excluded the Sutlej, *Satadru*, *Hesydrus* of Pliny, Ζαράδρος or Ζαδάδρης (*Ptol.*), as Timur excludes it below. We may take in the Sutlej and exclude the Indus, but we can hardly exclude the Chenāb as Wassāf does below.

No corresponding term is used by the Greek geographers. "Putandum est nomen **Panchanadae** Graecos aut omnino latuisse, aut casu quodam non ad nostra usque tempora pervenisse, quod in tanta monumentorum ruina facile accidere potuit" (*Lassen, Pentapotamia*, 3). Lassen however has termed the country *Pentepotamia* in a learned Latin dissertation on its ancient geography. Though the actual word *Panjāb* is Persian, and dates from Mahommedan times, the corresponding Skt. *Panchanada* is ancient and genuine, occurring in the *Mahābhārata* and *Rāmāyaṇa*. The name *Panj-āb* in older Mahommedan writers is applied to the Indus river, after receiving the rivers of the country which we call *Punjaub*. In that sense *Panj-nad*, of equivalent meaning, is still occasionally used. [In S. India the term is sometimes applied to the country watered by the Tumbhadra, Wardha, Malprabha, Gatprabha and Kistna (*Wilks, Hist. Sketches*, Madras reprint, i. 405).]

We remember in the newspapers, after the second Sikh war, the report of a speech by a clergyman in England, who spoke of the deposition of "the bloody **Punjaub** of Lahore."

B.C. *x*.—"Having explored the land of the Pahlavi and the country adjoining, there had then to be searched **Panchanada** in every part; the monkeys then explore the region of Kashmīr with its woods of acacias."—*Rāmāyana*, Bk. iv. ch. 43.

c. 940.—Mas'ūdī details (with no correctness) the five rivers that form the Mihrān or Indus. He proceeds: "When the **Five Rivers** which we have named have past the House of Gold which is Mūltān, they unite at a place three days distant from that city, between it and Manṣūra at a place called Doshāb."—i. 377-8.

c. 1020.—"They all (Sind, Jhailam, Irāwa, Biah) combine with the Satlader (Sutlej) below Múltán, at a place called **Panjnad**, or 'the junction of the five rivers.' They form a very wide stream."—*Al-Birūnī*, in *Elliot*, i. 48.

c. 1300.—"After crossing the **Panj-āb**, or five rivers, namely Sind, Jelam, the river of Loháwar (*i.e.* of *Lahore*, viz. the Rāvī), Satlút, and Bīyah. . . ."—*Wassāf*, in *Elliot*, iii. 36.

c. 1333.—"By the grace of God our caravan arrived safe and sound at **Banj-āb**, *i.e.* at the River of the Sind. *Banj* (*panj*) signifies 'five,' and *āb*, 'water;' so that the name signifies 'the Five Waters.' They flow into this great river, and water the country."—*Ibn Batuta*, iii. 91.

c. 1400.—"All these (united) rivers (Jelam, Chenáb, Rávī, Bíyáh, Sind) are called the Sind or **Panj-áb**, and this river falls into the Persian Gulf near Thatta."—*The Emp. Timur*, in *Elliot*, iii. 476.

[c. 1630.—"He also takes a Survey of **Pang-ob** . . ."—*Sir T. Herbert*, ed. 1677, p. 63. He gives a list of the rivers in p. 70.]

1648.—". . . **Pang-ab**, the chief city of which is Labor, is an excellent and fruitful province, for it is watered by the five rivers of which we have formerly spoken."—*Van Twist*, 3.

" "The River of the ancient Indus, is by the Persians and Magols called **Pang-ab**, *i.e.* the Five Waters."—*Ibid.* i.

1710.—"He found this ancient and famous city (Lahore) in the Province **Panschaap**, by the side of the broad and fish-abounding river Rari (for *Ravi*)."—*Valentijn*, iv. (*Suratte*), 282.

1790.—"Investigations of the religious ceremonies and customs of the Hindoos, written in the Carnatic, and in the **Punjab**, would in many cases widely differ."—*Forster*, Preface to *Journey*.

1793.—"The Province, of which Lahore is the capital, is oftener named **Panjab** than Lahore."—*Rennell's Memoir*, 3rd ed. 82.

1804.—"I rather think . . . that he (Holkar) will go off to the **Punjaub**. And what gives me stronger reason to think so is, that on the seal of his letter to me he calls himself '*the Slave of Shah Mahmoud, the King of Kings.*' Shah Mahmoud is the brother of Zemaun Shah. He seized the musnud and government of Caubul, after having defeated Zemaun Shah two or three years ago, and put out his eyes."—*Wellington, Desp.* under March 17.

1815.—"He (Subagtageen) . . . overran the fine province of the **Punjaub**, in his first expedition."—*Malcolm, Hist. of Persia*, i. 316.

PUNKAH, s. Hind. *pankhā*.

a. In its original sense a portable fan, generally made from the leaf of the **palmyra** (*Borassus flabelliformis*, or 'fan-shaped'), the natural type and origin of the fan. Such *pankhās* in India are not however formed, as Chinese fans are, like those of our ladies; they are generally, whether large or small, of a bean-shape, with a part of the dried leaf-stalk adhering, which forms the handle.

b. But the specific application in Anglo-Indian colloquial is to the large fixed and swinging fan, formed of cloth stretched on a rectangular frame, and suspended from the ceiling, which is used to agitate the air in hot weather. The date of the introduction of this machine into India is not known to us. The quotation from Linschoten shows that some such apparatus was known in the 16th century, though this comes out clearly in the French version alone; the original Dutch, and the old English translation are here unintelligible, and indicate that Linschoten (who apparently never was at Ormuz) was describing, from hearsay, something that he did not understand. More remarkable passages are those which we take from Dozy, and from El-Fakhrī, which show that the true Anglo-Indian *punka* was known to the Arabs as early as the 8th century.

a.—

1710.—"Aloft in a Gallery the King sits in his chaire of State, accompanied with his

Children and chiefe Vizier . . . no other without calling daring to goe vp to him, saue onely two **Punkaws** to gather wind."—*W. Finch*, in *Purchas*, i. 439. The word seems here to be used improperly for the men who plied the fans. We find also in the same writer a verb to **punkaw**:

". . . behind one **punkawing**, another holding his sword."—*Ibid.* 433.

Terry does not use the word:

1616.—". . . the people of better quality, lying or sitting on their Carpets or Pallats, have servants standing about them, who continually beat the air upon them with *Flabella's*, or Fans, of stiffned leather, which keepe off the flyes from annoying them, and cool them as they lye."—Ed. 1665, p. 405.

1663.—"On such occasions they desire nothing but . . . to lie down in some cool and shady place all along, having a servant or two to fan one by turns, with their great **Pankas**, or Fans."—*Bernier*, E.T., p. 76; [ed. *Constable*, 241].

1787.—"Over her head was held a **punker**."—*Sir C. Malet*, in Parl. Papers, 1821, '*Hindoo Widows.*'

1809.—"He . . . presented me . . . two **punkahs**."—*Lord Valentia*, i. 428.

1881.—"The chair of state, the *sella gestatoria*, in which the Pope is borne aloft, is the ancient palanquin? of the Roman nobles, and, of course, of the Roman Princes . . . the fans which go behind are the **punkahs** of the Eastern Emperors, borrowed from the Court of Persia."—*Dean Stanley, Christian Institutions*, 207.

b.—

c. 1150-60.—"Sous le nom de *Khaich* on entend des étoffes de mauvais toile de lin qui servent à différents usages. Dans ce passage de Rhazès (c. A.D. 900) ce sont des ventilateurs faits de cet étoffe. Ceci se pratique de cette manière: on en prend un morceau de la grandeur d'un tapis, un peu plus grand ou un peu plus petit selon les dimensions de la chambre, et on le rembourre avec des objets qui ont de la consistance et qui ne plient pas facilement, par exemple avec du sparte. L'ayant ensuite suspendu au milieu de la chambre, on le fait tirer et lacher doucement et continuellement par un homme placé dans le haut de l'appartement. De cette manière il fait beaucoup de vent et rafraichit l'air. Quelquefois on le trempe dans de l'eau de rose, et alors il parfume l'air en même temps qu'il le rafraichit."—*Glossaire sur le Mançouri*, quoted in *Dozy et Engelmann*, p. 342. See also *Dozy, Suppt. aux Dictt. Arabes*, s.v. *Khaich*.

1166.—"He (Ibn Hamdun the Kātib) once recited to me the following piece of his composition, containing an enigmatical description of a linen fan: (1)

"'Fast and loose, it cannot touch what it tries to reach; though tied up it moves swiftly, and though a prisoner it is free. Fixed in its place it drives before it the gentle breeze; though its path lie closed up it moves on in its nocturnal journey.'"—Quoted by *Ibn Khallikan*, E.T. iii. 91.

"(1) The *linen fan* (*Mirwaha-t al Khaish*) is a large piece of linen, stretched on a frame, and suspended from the ceiling of the room. They make use of it in Irâk. See de Sacy's *Hariri*, p. 474."—Note by *MacGuckin de Slane, ibid.* p. 92.

c. 1300.—"One of the innovations of the Caliph Mansūr (A.D. 753-774) was the *Khaish* of linen in summer, a thing which was not known before his time. But the Sāsānian Kings used in summer to have an apartment freshly plastered (with clay) every day, which they inhabited, and on the morrow another apartment was plastered for them."—*El-Fakhrī*, ed. *Ahlwardt*, p. 188.

1596.—"And (they use) instruments like swings with fans, to rock the people in, and to make wind for cooling, which they call *cattaventos*."—Literal Transln. from *Linschoten*, ch. 6.

1598.—"And they vse certaine instruments like Waggins, with bellowes, to beare all the people in, and to gather winde to coole themselves withall, which they call *Cattaventos*."—*Old English Translation*, by W. P., p. 16; [Hak. Soc. i. 52].

The French version is really a brief description of the punka:

1610.—"Ils ont aussi du Cattaventos qui sont certains instruments pendus en l'air es quels se faisant donner le bransle ils font du vent qui les rafraichit."—Ed. 1638, p. 17.

The next also perhaps refers to a suspended punka:

1662.—". . . furnished also with good Cellars with great *Flaps* to stir the Air, for reposing in the fresh Air from 12 till 4 or 5 of the Clock, when the Air of these Cellars begins to be hot and stuffing."—*Bernier*, p. 79; [ed. *Constable*, 247].

1807.—"As one small concern succeeds another, the **punkah** vibrates gently over my eyes."—*Lord Minto in India*, 27.

1810.—"Were it not for the **punka** (a large frame of wood covered with cloth) which is suspended over every table, and kept swinging, in order to freshen the air, it would be scarcely possible to sit out the melancholy ceremony of an Indian dinner."—*Maria Graham*, 30.

,, Williamson mentions that **punkahs** "were suspended in most dining halls."—*Vade Mecum*, i. 281.

1823.—"**Punkas**, large frames of light wood covered with white cotton, and looking not unlike enormous fire-boards, hung from the ceilings of the principal apartments."—*Heber*, ed. 1844, i. 28.

1852.—

"Holy stones with scrubs and slaps
(Our Christmas waits!) prelude the day;
For holly and festoons of bay
Swing feeble **punkas**,—or perhaps
A windsail dangles in collapse."
Christmas on board a P. and O., near the Equator.

1875.—"The **punkah** flapped to and fro lazily overhead."—*Chesney, The Dilemma*, ch. xxxviii.

Mr. Busteed observes: "It is curious that in none of the lists of servants and their duties which are scattered through the old records in the last century (18th), is there any mention of the **punka**, nor in any narratives referring to domestic life in India then, that have come under our notice, do we remember any allusion to its use. . . . The swinging **punka**, as we see it to-day, was, as every one knows, an innovation of a later period. . . . This dates from an early year in the present century."—*Echoes of Old Calcutta*, p. 115. He does not seem, however, to have found any positive evidence of the date of its introduction. ["Hanging punkahs are said by one authority to have originated in Calcutta by accident towards the close of the last (18th) century. It is reported that a clerk in a Government office suspended the leaf of a table, which was accidentally waved to and fro by a visitor. A breath of cool air followed the movement, and suggested the idea which was worked out and resulted in the present machine" (*Carey, Good Old Days of John Company*, i. 81). Mr. Douglas says that punkahs were little used by Europeans in Bombay till 1810. They were not in use at Nuncomar's trial in Calcutta (1775), *Bombay and W. India*, ii. 253.]

PUNSAREE, s. A native drug-seller; Hind. *pansārī*. We place the word here partly because C. P. Brown says 'it is certainly a foreign word,' and assigns it to a corruption of *dispensarium;* which is much to be doubted. [The word is really derived from Skt. *paṇyaśāla*, 'a market, warehouse.']

[1830.—"Beside this, I purchased from a **pansaree** some application for relieving the pain of a bruise."—*Frazer, The Persian Adventurer*, iii. 23.]

PURDAH, s. Hind. from Pers. *parda*, 'a curtain'; a *portière;* and especially a curtain screening women from the sight of men; whence a woman of position who observes such rules of seclusion is termed *parda-nishīn*, 'one who sits behind a curtain.' (See **GOSHA**.)

1809.—"On the fourth (side) a **purdah** was stretched across."—*Ld. Valentia*, i. 100.

1810.—"If the disorder be obstinate, the doctor is permitted to approach the **purdah** (*i.e.* curtain, or screen) and to put *the hand* through a small aperture . . . in order to feel the patient's pulse."—*Williamson, V. M.* i. 130.

[1813.—"My travelling palankeen formed my bed, its **purdoe** or chintz covering my curtains."—*Forbes, Or. Mem.* 2nd ed. ii. 109.]

1878.—"Native ladies look upon the confinement behind the **purdah** as a badge of rank, and also as a sign of chastity, and are exceedingly proud of it."—*Life in the Mofussil*, i. 113.

[1900.—"Charitable aid is needed for the **purdah** women."—*Pioneer Mail*, Jan. 21.]

PURDESEE, s. Hind. *paradeśī* usually written *pardesī*, 'one from a foreign country.' In the Bombay army the term is universally applied to a sepoy from N. India. [In the N.W.P. the name is applied to a wandering tribe of swindlers and coiners.]

PURWANNA, PERWAUNA, s. Hind. from Pers. *parwāna*, 'an order; a grant or letter under royal seal; a letter of authority from an official to his subordinate; a license or pass.'

1682.—". . . we being obliged at the end of two months to pay Custom for the said goods, if in that time we did not procure a **Pherwanna** for the *Duan* of Decca to excuse us from it."—*Hedges, Diary*, Oct. 10; [Hak. Soc. i. 34].

1693.—". . . Egmore and Pursewaukum were lately granted us by the Nabob's **purwannas**."—*Wheeler*, i. 281.

1759.—"**Perwanna**, under the Coochuck (or the small seal) of the Nabob Vizier Ulma Maleck, Nizam ul Muluck Bahadour, to Mr. John Spenser."—In *Cambridge's Acct. of the War*, 230. (See also quotation under **HOSBOLHOOKUM**.)

1774.—"As the peace has been so lately concluded, it would be a satisfaction to the Rajah to receive your **parwanna** to this purpose before the departure of the caravan."—*Bogle's Diary*, in *Markham's Tibet*, p. 50. But Mr. Markham changes the spelling of his originals.

PUTCHOCK, s. This is the trade-name for a fragrant root, a product of the Himālaya in the vicinity of Kashmīr, and forming an article of export from both Bombay and Calcutta to the Malay countries and to China, where it is used as a chief ingredient of the Chinese pastille-rods commonly called **jostick**. This root was recognised by the famous Garcia de Orta as the *Costus* of the ancients. The latter took their word from the Skt. *kustha*, by a modification of which name—*kut*—it is still known and used as a medicine in Upper India. De Orta speaks of the plant as growing about Mandu and Chitore, whence it was brought for sale to Ahmadābād; but his informants misled him. The true source was traced *in situ* by two other illustrious men, Royle and Falconer, to a plant belonging to the N. O. *Compositae, Saussurea Xappe*, Clarke, for which Dr. Falconer, not recognising the genus, had proposed the name of *Aucklandia Costus verus*, in honour of the then Governor-General. The *Costus* is a gregarious plant, occupying open, sloping sides of the mountains, at an elevation of 8000 to 9000 feet. See article by Falconer in *Trans. Linn. Soc.* xix. 23-31.

The trade-name is, according to Wilson, the Telugu *păch'chăku*, 'green leaf,' but one does not see how this applies. (Is there, perhaps, some confusion with *Patch?* see **PATCHOULI**). De Orta speaks as if the word, which he writes *pucho*, were Malay. Though neither Crawfurd nor Favre gives the word, in this sense, it is in Marsden's earlier *Malay Dict.*: "**Pūchok**, a plant, the aromatic leaves of which are an article of trade; said by some to be *Costus indicus*, and by others the *Melissa*, or *Laurus*." [On this Mr. Skeat writes: "**Puchok** is the Malay word for a young sprout, or the growing shoot of a plant. **Puchok** in the special sense here used is also a Malay word, but it may be separate from the other. Klinkert gives **puchok** as a sprout or shoot and also as a radish-like root (indigenous in China (*sic*), used in medicine for fumigation, &c.). Apparently it is always the root and not the leaves of the plant that are used, in which case Marsden may have confused the two senses of the word."] In the year 1837-38 about 250 tons of this article, valued at £10,000, were exported from Calcutta alone. The annual import into China at a later date, according to Wells Williams, was 2,000 *peculs* or 120 tons (*Middle Kingdom*, ed. 1857, ii. 308). In 1865-66, the last year for which the details of such minor exports are found in print, the quantity exported from Calcutta was only 492½ cwt., or 24⅝ tons. In 1875 the value of the imports at Hankow and Chefoo was £6,421. [*Watt, Econ. Dict.* vi. pt. ii. p. 482, *Bombay Gazetteer*, xi. 470.]

1516.—See Barbosa under **CATECHU**.

1520.—"We have prohibited (the export of) pepper to China . . . and now we prohibit the export of **pucho** and incense from these parts of India to China."—*Capitulo de hum Regimento del Rey* a Diogo Ayres, Feitor da China, in *Arch. Port. Orient.*, Fasc. v. 49.

1525.—"**Pucho** of Cambaya worth 35 tangas a maund."—*Lembranças*, 50.

[1527.—Mr. Whiteway notes that in a letter of Diogo Calvo to the King, dated Jan. 17, **pucho** is mentioned as one of the imports to China.—*India Office MS. Corpo Chronologico*, vol. i.]

1554.—"The *baar* (see **BAHAR**) of **pucho** contains 20 *faraçolas* (see **FRAZALA**), and an additional 4 of **picota** (q.v.), in all 24 *faraçolas*. . . ."—*A. Nunes*, 11.

1563.—"I say that *costus* in Arabic is called *cost* or *cast*; in Guzarate it is called *uplot* (*upaleta*); and in Malay, for in that region there is a great trade and consumption thereof, it is called **pucho**. I tell you the name in Arabic, because it is called by the same name by the Latins and Greeks, and I tell it you in Guzerati, because that is the land to which it is chiefly carried from its birth-place; and I tell you the Malay name because the greatest quantity is consumed there, or taken thence to China."—*Garcia*, f. 72.

c. 1563.—". . . Opium, Assa Fetida, **Puchio**, with many other sortes of Drugges."—*Caesar Frederike*, in *Hakl.* ii. 343.

[1609.—"Costus of 2 sorts, one called **pokermore**, the other called *Uplotte* (see *Garcia*, above)."—*Danvers, Letters*, i. 30.]

1617.—"5 hampers **pochok**. . . ."—*Cocks, Diary*, i. 294.

1631.—"Caeterum Costus vulgato vocabulo inter mercatores Indos **Pucho**, Chinensibus **Potsiock**, vocatur . . . vidi ego integrum *Picol*, quod pondus centum et viginti in auctione decem realibus distribui."—*Jac. Bontii, Hist. Nat.*, &c., lib. iv. p. 46.

1711.—In Malacca *Price Currant*, July 1704: "**Putchuck** or Costus dulcis."—*Lockyer*, 77.

1726.—"**Patsjaak** (a leaf of Asjien (Acheen?) that is pounded to powder, and used in incense). . . ."—*Valentijn, Choro.* 34.

1727.—"The Wood *Ligna dulcis* grows only in this country (Sind). It is rather a Weed than a Wood, and nothing of it is useful but the Root, called **Putchock**, or *Radix dulcis*. . . . There are great quantities exported from *Surat*, and from thence to *China*, where it generally bears a good Price. . . ."—*A. Hamilton*, i. 126; [ed. 1744, i. 127].

1808.—"Elles emploient ordinairement . . . une racine aromatique appelée **pieschtok**, qu'on coupe par petits morceaux, et fait bouillir dans de l'huile de noix de coco. . C'est avec cette huile que les danseuses se graissent . . ."—*Haafner*, ii. 117.

1862.—"*Koot* is sent down country in large quantities, and is exported to China, where it is used as incense. It is in Calcutta known under the name of '**Patchuk.**'"—*Punjab Trade Report*, cvii.

PUTLAM, n.p. A town in Ceylon on the coast of the bay or estuary of Calpentyn; properly *Puttalama;* a Tamil name, said by Mr. Fergusson to be *puthu-* (*pudu?*) *alam*, 'New Saltpans.' Ten miles inland are the ruins of Tammana Newera, the original Tambapanni (or *Taprobane*), where Vijaya, the first Hindu immigrant, established his kingdom. And Putlam is supposed to be the place where he landed.

1298.—"The pearl-fishers . . . go post to a place callen **Bettelar**, and (then) go 60 miles into the gulf."—*Marco Polo*, Bk. iii. ch. 16.

c. 1345.—"The natives went to their King and told him my reply. He sent for me, and I proceeded to his presence in the town of **Baṭṭāla**, which was his capital, a pretty little place, surrounded by a timber wall and towers."—*Ibn Batuta*, iv. 166.

1672.—"**Putelaon**. . ."—*Baldaeus* (Germ.), 373.

1726.—"**Portaloon** or **Putelan**."—*Valentijn*, *Ceylon*, 21.

PUTNEE, PUTNEY, s.

a. Hind. and Beng. *paṭṭanī*, or *paṭnī*, from v. *paṭ-nā*, 'to be agreed or closed' (*i.e.* a bargain). Goods commissioned or manufactured to order.

1755.—"A letter from Cossimbazar mentions they had directed Mr. Warren Hastings to proceed to the **Putney aurung** (q.v.) in order to purchase **putney** on our Honble. Masters' account, and to make all necessary enquiries."—*Fort William Consns.*, Nov. 10. In *Long*, 61.

b. A kind of sub-tenure existing in the Lower Provinces of Bengal, the **patnīdār**, or occupant of which "holds of a Zemindar a portion of the Zemindari in perpetuity, with the right of hereditary succession, and of selling or letting the whole or part, so long as a stipulated amount of rent is paid to the Zemindar, who retains the power of sale for arrears, and is entitled to a regulated fee or fine upon transfer" (*Wilson*, q.v.). Probably both **a** and **b** are etymologically the same, and connected with *paṭṭā* (see **POTTAH**).

[1860.—"A perpetual lease of land held under a Zumeendar is called a **putnee**,—and the holder is called a **putneedar**, who not only pays an advanced rent to the Zumeendar, but a handsome price for the same."—*Grant, Rural Life in Bengal*, 64.]

PUTTÁN, PATHÁN, n.p. Hind. *Paṭhān*. A name commonly applied to Afghans, and especially to people in India of Afghan descent. The derivation is obscure. Elphinstone derives it from *Pushtūn* and *Pukhtūn*, pl. *Pukhtāna*, the name the Afghans give to their own race, with which Dr. Trumpp [and Dr. Bellew (*Races of Afghanistan*, 25) agree. This again has been connected with the *Pactyica* of Herodotus (iii. 102, iv. 44).] The Afghans have for the name one of the usual fantastic etymologies which is quoted below (see quotation, c. 1611). The Mahommedans in India are sometimes divided into four classes, viz. *Paṭhāns; Mughals* (see **MOGUL**), *i.e.* those of Turki origin; *Shaikhs*, claiming Arab descent; and *Saiyyids*, claiming also to be descendants of Mahommed.

1553.—"This State belonged to a people called **Patane**, who were lords of that hill-country. And as those who dwell on the skirts of the Pyrenees, on this side and on that, are masters of the passes by which we cross from Spain to France, or vice versâ, so these **Patan** people are the masters of the two entrances to India, by which those who go thither from the landward must pass. . . ."—*Barros*, IV. vi. 1.

1563.—". . . This first King was a **Patane** of certain mountains that march with Bengala."—*Garcia, Coll.* f. 34.

1572.—

"Mas agora de nomes, et de usança,
Novos, et varios são os habitantes,
Os Delijs, os **Patãnes** que em possança
De terra, e gente são mais abundantes."
Camões, vii. 20.

[By Aubertin:

"But now inhabitants of other name
And customs new and various there are found,
The Delhis and **Patans**, who in the fame
Of land and people do the most abound."]

1610.—"A **Pattan**, a man of good stature."—*Hawkins*, in *Purchas*, i. 220.

c. 1611.—". . . the mightiest of the Afghan people was Kais. . . . The Prophet gave Kais the name of Abd Ulrasheed . . . and . . . predicted that God would make his issue so numerous that they, with respect to the establishment of the Faith, would outvie all other people; the angel Gabriel having revealed to him that their attachment to the Faith would, in strength, be like the wood upon which they lay the keel when constructing a ship, which wood the seamen call *Pathan;* on this account he conferred upon Abd Ulrasheed the title of **Pathan*** also."—*Hist. of the Afghans*, E.T., by *Dorn*, i. 38.

[1638.—"... Ozmanchan a **Puttanian** ..."—*Sir T. Herbert*, ed. 1677, p. 76.]

1648.—"In general the Moors are a haughty and arrogant and proud people, and among them the **Pattans** stand out superior to the others in dress and manners."—*Van Twist*, 58.

1666.—"Martin Affonso and the other Portuguese delivered them from the war that the **Patanes** were making on them."—*Faria y Sousa, Asia Portuguesa*, i. 343.

1673.—"They are distinguished, some according to the Consanguinity they claim with *Mahomet;* as a *Siad* is a kin to that Imposture. . . . A *Shiek* is a Cousin too, at a distance, into which Relation they admit all new made Proselytes. *Meer* is somewhat allied also. . . . The rest are adopted under the Name of the Province . . . as *Mogul*, the Race of the *Tartars* . . . **Patan**, *Duccan*."—*Fryer*, 93.

1681.—"En estas regiones ay vna cuyas gentes se dizen los **Patanes**."—*Martinez de la Puente, Compendio*, 21.

1726.—"... The *Patans* (**Patanders**) are very different in garb, and surpass in valour and stout-heartedness in war."—*Valentijn, Choro*. 109.

1757.—"The Colonel (Clive) complained bitterly of so many insults put upon him, and reminded the Soubahdar how different his own conduct was, when called upon to assist him against the **Pytans**."—*Ives*, 149.

1763.—"The northern nations of India, although idolaters . . . were easily induced to embrace Mahomedanism, and are at this day the Affghans or **Pitans**."—*Orme*, i. 24, ed. 1803.

1789.—"Moormen are, for the most part, soldiers by profession, particularly in the cavalry, as are also . . . **Pitans**."—*Munro, Narr*. 49.

1798.—"... Afghans, or as they are called in India, **Patans**." — *G. Forster, Travels*, ii. 47.

[**PUTTEE, PUTTY**, s. Hind. *paṭṭī*.

a. A piece or strip of cloth, bandage; especially used in the sense of a ligature round the lower part of the leg used in lieu of a gaiter, originally introduced from the Himālaya, and now commonly used by sportsmen and soldiers. A special kind of cloth appears in the old trade-lists under the name of **puteahs** (see **PIECE GOODS**).

1875.—"Any one who may be bound for a long march will put on leggings of a peculiar sort, a bandage about 6 inches wide and four yards long, wound round from the ankle up to just below the knee, and then fastened by an equally long string, attached to the upper end, which is lightly wound many times round the calf of the leg. This, which is called **patawa**, is a much cherished piece of dress."—*Drew, Jummoo*, 175.

1900.—"The **Puttee** leggings are excellent for peace and war, on foot or on horseback."—*Times*, Dec. 24.

b. In the N.W.P. "an original share in a joint or coparcenary village or estate comprising many villages; it is sometimes defined as the smaller subdivision of a mahal or estate" (*Wilson*). Hence **Putteedaree**, *paṭṭīdārī* used for a tenure of this kind.

1852. — "Their names were forthwith scratched off the collector's books, and those of their eldest sons were entered, who became forthwith, in village and cutcherry parlance, **lumberdars** of the shares of their fathers, or in other words, of **puttee** Shere Singh and **puttee** Baz Singh."—*Raikes, Notes on the N.W.P.* 94.

c. In S. India, soldiers' pay.

1810.—"... hence in ordinary acceptation, the pay itself was called **puttee**, a Canarese word which properly signifies a written statement of any kind."—*Wilks, Hist. Sketches*, Madras reprint, i. 415.]

PUTTYWALLA, s. Hind. *paṭṭā-wālā, paṭṭī-wālā* (see **PUTTEE**), 'one with a belt.' This is the usual Bombay term for a messenger or orderly attached to an office, and bearing a belt and brass badge, called in Bengal **chuprassy** or **peon** (qq.v.), in Madras usually by the latter name.

1878.—"Here and there a belted Government servant, called a **Puttiwālā**, or **Pattawālā**, because distinguished by a belt. . . ."—*Monier Williams, Modern India*, 34.

PUTWA, s. Hind. *patwā*. The *Hibiscus sabdariffa*, L., from the succulent acid flowers of which very fair jelly is made in Anglo-Indian households. [It is also known as the Rozelle or Red Sorrel (*Watt, Econ. Dict.* iv. 243). Riddell (*Domest. Econ.* 337) calls it "Oseille or **Roselle** jam and jelly."]

PYE, s. A familiar designation among British soldiers and young officers for a **Pariah-dog** (q.v.); a

* We do not know what word is intended, unless it be a special use of Ar. *baṭan*, 'the interior or middle of a thing.' Dorn refers to a note, which does not exist in his book. Bellew gives the title conferred by the Prophet as "*Pihtān* or *Pāthān*, a term which in the Syrian language signifies a rudder." Somebody else interprets it as 'a mast.

contraction, no doubt, of the former word.

[1892.—"We English call him a **pariah**, but this word, belonging to a low, yet by no means degraded class of people in Madras, is never heard on native lips as applied to a dog, any more than our other word '**pie**.'" —*L. Kipling, Beast and Man*, 266.]

PYJAMMAS, s. Hind. *pāē-jāma* (see **JAMMA**), lit. 'leg-clothing.' A pair of loose drawers or trowsers, tied round the waist. Such a garment is used by various persons in India, *e.g.* by women of various classes, by Sikh men, and by most Mahommedans of both sexes. It was adopted from the Mahommedans by Europeans as an article of *dishabille* and of night attire, and is synonymous with **Long Drawers, Shulwáurs**, and **Mogul-breeches**. [For some distinctions between these various articles of dress see Forbes-Watson, (*Textile Manufactures*, 57).] It is probable that we English took the habit like a good many others from the Portuguese. Thus Pyrard (c. 1610) says, in speaking of Goa Hospital: "Ils ont force *calsons* sans quoy ne couchent iamais les Portugais des Indes" (ii. p. 11; [Hak. Soc. ii. 9]). The word is now used in London shops. A friend furnishes the following reminiscence: "The late Mr. B——, tailor in Jermyn Street, some 40 years ago, in reply to a question why **pyjammas** had feet sewn on to them (as was sometimes the case with those furnished by London outfitters) answered: 'I believe, Sir, it is because of the **White Ants**!'"

[1828.—
"His chief joy smoking a cigar
In loose **Paee-jams** and native slippers."
Orient. Sport. Mag., reprint 1873, i. 64.]

1881.—"The rest of our attire consisted of that particularly light and airy white flannel garment, known throughout India as a **pajama** suit."—*Haekel, Ceylon*, 329.

PYKE, PAIK, s. Wilson gives only one original of the term so expressed in Anglo-Indian speech. He writes: "*Pāīk* or *Pāyik*, corruptly *Pyke*, Hind. &c. (from S. *padātika*), *Pāīk* or *Pāyak*, Mar. A footman, an armed attendant, an inferior police and revenue officer, a messenger, a courier, a village watchman: in Cuttack the *Pāīks* formerly constituted a local militia, holding land of the Zamindárs or Rájas by the tenure of military service," &c., quoting Bengal Regulations. [Platts also treats the two words as identical.] But it seems clear to us that there are here two terms rolled together:

a. Pers. *Paik*, 'a foot-runner or courier.' We do not know whether this is an old Persian word or a Mongol introduction. According to Hammer Purgstall it was the term in use at the Court of the Mongol princes, as quoted below. Both the words occur in the *Āīn*, but differently spelt, and that with which we now deal is spelt *paik* (with the *fatḥa* point).

c. 1590.—"The *Jilaudār* (see under **JULIBDAR**) and the **Paik** (a runner). Their monthly pay varies from 1200 to 120*d.* (*dāms*), according to their speed and manner of service. Some of them will run from 50 to 100 *kroh* (**Coss**) per day."—*Āīn*, E.T. by *Blochmann*, i. 138 (see orig. i. 144).

1673.—At the Court of Constantinople: "Les **Peiks** venoient ensuite, avec leurs bonnets d'argent doré ornés d'un petit plumage de héron, un arc et un carquois chargé de flèches."—*Journal d'A. Galland*, i. 98.

1687.—". . . the under officers and servants called *Agiam-Oglans*, who are designed to the meaner uses of the Seraglio . . . most commonly the sons of Christians taken from their Parents at the age of 10 or 12 years. . . . These are: 1, *Porters*, 2, *Bostangies* or Gardiners . . . 5, **Paicks** and *Solacks*. . . ." —*Sir Paul Rycaut, Present State of the Ottoman Empire*, 19.

1761.—"Ahmad Sultán then commissioned Sháh Pasand Khán . . . the *harkāras* (see **HURCARRA**) and the **Paiks**, to go and procure information as to the state and strength of the Mahratta army."—*Muhammad Jáfar Shāmlu*, in *Elliot*, viii. 151-2.

1840.—"The express-riders (*Eilbothen*) accomplished 50 *farsangs* a-day, so that an express came in 4 days from Khorasan to Tebris (*Tabrīz*). . . . The Foot-runners carrying letters (**Peik**), whose name at least is maintained to this day at both the Persian and Osmanli Courts, accomplished 30 *farsangs* a-day."—*Hammer Purgstall, Gesch. der Golden Horde*, 243.

[1868.—"The **Payeke** is entrusted with the *tchilim* (see **CHILLUM**) (pipe), which at court (Khiva) is made of gold or silver, and must be replenished with fresh water every time it is filled with tobacco."—*Vambery, Sketches*, 89.]

b. Hind *pāīk* and *pāyik* (also Mahr.) from Skt. *padātika*, and *padika*, 'a foot-soldier,' with the other specific application given by Wilson, exclusive of 'courier.' In some narratives the word seems to answer exactly to **peon**.

In the first quotation, which is from the *Āīn*, the word, it will be seen, is different from that quoted under (a) from the same source.

c. 1590.—"It was the custom in those times, for the palace (of the King of Bengal) to be guarded by several thousand **pykes** (*pāyak*), who are a kind of infantry. An eunuch entered into a confederacy with these guards, who one night killed the King, Futteh Shah, when the Eunuch ascended the throne, under the title of Barbuck Shah."—*Gladwin's* Tr., ed. 1800, ii. 19 (orig. i. 415; [*Jarrett* (ii. 149) gives the word as **Páyiks**].

In the next quotation the word seems to be the same, though used for 'a seaman.' Compare uses of **Lascar**.

c. 1615.—"(His fleet) consisted of 20 beaked vessels, all well manned with the sailors whom they call **paiques**, as well as with Portuguese soldiers and **topazes** who were excellent musketeers; 50 hired *jalias* (see **GALLEVAT**) of like sort and his own (Sebastian Gonçalves's) galliot (see **GALLEVAT**), which was about the size of a *patacho*, with 14 demi-falcons on each broadside, two pieces of 18 to 20 lbs. calibre in the forecastle, and 60 Portuguese soldiers, with more than 40 **topazes** and Cafres (see **CAFFER**)."—*Bocarro, Decada*, 452.

1722.—Among a detail of charges at this period in the **Zemindárry** of Rājshāhī appears:

"9. *Paikan*, or the **pikes**, guard of villages, everywhere necessary . . . 2,161 rupees."—*Fifth Report*, App. p. 345.

The following quotation from an Indian Regulation of Ld. Cornwallis's time is a good example of the extraordinary multiplication of terms, even in one Province in India, denoting approximately the same thing:

1792.—"All **Pykes**, Chokeydars (see **CHOKIDAR**), *Pasbans, Dusauds, Nigabans*,* Harees (see **HARRY**), and other descriptions of village watchmen are declared subject to the orders of the Darogah (see **DAROGA**) . . ."—*Regns. for the Police* . . . passed by the G.-G. in C., Dec. 7.

" "The army of Assam was a militia organised as follows. The whole male population was bound to serve either as soldiers or labourers, and was accordingly divided into sets of four men each, called *gotes*, the individuals comprising the gotes being termed **pykes**."—*Johnstone's Acct. of Welsh's Expedition to Assam*, 1792-93-94 (commd. by Gen. Keatinge).

* P. *pāsbān* and *nigabān*, both meaning literally 'watch-keeper,' the one from *pās*, 'a watch,' in the sense of a division of the day, the other from *nigah*, 'watch,' in the sense of 'heed' or 'observation.' [*Dusaud*=*Dosādh*, a low caste often employed as watchmen.]

1802.—After a detail of persons of rank in Midnapore:

"None of these entertain armed followers except perhaps ten or a dozen Peons for state, but some of them have **Pykes** in considerable numbers, to keep the peace on their estates. These **Pykes** are under the magistrate's orders."—*Fifth Report*, App. p. 535.

1812.—"The whole of this last-mentioned numerous class of **Pykes** are understood to have been disbanded, in compliance with the new Police regulations."—*Fifth Report*, 71.

1872.—". . . *Dalais* or officers of the peasant militia (**Paiks**). The **Paiks** were settled chiefly around the fort on easy tenures."—*Hunter's Orissa*, ii. 269.

PYSE! interjection. The use of this is illustrated in the quotations. Notwithstanding the writer's remark (below) it is really Hindustani, viz. *po'is*, 'look out!' or 'make way!' apparently from Skt. *paśya*, 'look! see!' (see Molesworth's *Mahr. Dict.* p. 529, col. *c*; Fallon's *Hind. Dict.*, p. 376, col. *a*; [*Platts*, 282*b*].

[1815.—". . . three men came running up behind them, as if they were clearing the road for some one, by calling out '**pice! pice!**' (make way, make way) . . ."—*Elphinstone's Report on Murder of Gungadhur Shastry*, in *Papers relating to E.I. Affairs*, p. 14.]

1883.—"Does your correspondent Col. Prideaux know the origin of the warning called out by buggy drivers to pedestrians in Bombay, '**Pyse**'? It is not Hindustani."—*Letter in N. & Q.*, Ser. VI. viii. p. 388.

[Other expressions of the same kind are Malayāl. *po*, 'Get out of the way!' and Hind. Mahr. *khis, khis*, from *khisnā*, 'to drop off.'

1598.—"As these hayros goe in the streetes, they crie **po, po**, which is to say, take heede."—*Linschoten*, Hak. Soc. i. 280.

1826.—"I was awoke from disturbed rest by cries of **kis! kis!** (clear the way)."—*Pandurang Hari*, ed. 1873, i. 46.]

Q

[**QUAMOCLIT**, s. The *Ipomaea* **quamoclitis**, the name given by Linnaeus to the Red Jasmine. The word is a corruption of Skt. *Kāma-latā*, 'the creeper of Kāma, god of love.'

1834.—"This climber, the most beautiful and luxuriant imaginable, bears also the name of **Kamalāta** 'Love's Creeper.' Some have flowers of snowy hue, with a delicate fragrance. . . ."—*Wanderings of a Pilgrim*, i. 310-11.]

QUEDDA, n.p. A city, port, and small kingdom on the west coast of the Malay Peninsula, tributary to Siam. The name according to Crawfurd is Malay *kadāh*, 'an elephant-trap' (see **KEDDAH**). [Mr. Skeat writes: "I do not know what Crawfurd's authority may be, but *kedah* does not appear in Klinkert's *Dict.* . . . In any case the form taken by the name of the country is *Kĕdah.* The coralling of elephants is probably a Siamese custom, the method adopted on the E. coast, where the Malays are left to themselves, being to place a decoy female elephant near a powerful noose."] It has been supposed sometimes that *Kadāh* is the Κῶλι or Κῶλις of Ptolemy's sea-route to China, and likewise the *Kalah* of the early Arab voyagers, as in the Fourth Voyage of Sindbad the Seaman (see *Procgs. R. Geog. Soc.* 1882, p. 655; *Burton, Arabian Nights,* iv. 386). It is possible that these old names however represent *Kwala,* 'a river mouth,' a denomination of many small ports in Malay regions. Thus the port that we call *Quedda* is called by the Malays *Kwala Batrang.*

1516.—"Having left this town of Tanassary, further along the coast towards Malaca, there is another seaport of the Kingdom of Ansiam, which is called **Queda**, in which also there is much shipping, and great interchange of merchandise." — *Barbosa*, 188-189.

1553.—". . . The settlements from Tavay to Malaca are these: Tenassary, a notable city, Lungur, Torrão, **Queda**, producing the best pepper on all that coast, Pedão, Perá, Solungor, and our City of Malaca. . . ."—*Barros*, I. ix. 1.

1572.—

"Olha Tavai cidade, onde começa
De Sião largo o imperio tão comprido:
Tenassarí, **Quedá**, que he so cabeça
Das que pimenta alli tem produzido."
Camões, x. 123.

By Burton:

"Behold Taváí City, whence begin
Siam's dominions, Reign of vast extent;
Tenassarí, **Quedá** of towns the Queen
that bear the burthen of the hot piment."

1598.—". . . to the town and Kingdome of **Queda** . . . which lyeth under 6 degrees and a halfe; this is also a Kingdome like *Tanassaria*, it hath also some wine, as *Tanassaria* hath, and some small quantitie of Pepper."—*Linschoten*, p. 31; [Hak. Soc. i. 103].

1614.—"And so . . . Diogo de Mendonça . . . sending the *galliots* (see **GALLEVAT**) on before, embarked in the *jalia* (see **GALLEVAT**) of João Rodriguez de Paiva, and coming to **Queda**, and making an attack at daybreak, and finding them unprepared, he burnt the town, and carried off a quantity of provisions and some tin" (*calaim*, see **CALAY**).—*Bocarro, Decada*, 187.

1838.—"Leaving Penang in September, we first proceeded to the town of **Quedah** lying at the mouth of a river of the same name." — **Quedah**, &c., by *Capt. Sherard Osborne*, ed. 1865.

QUEMOY, n.p. An island at the east opening of the Harbour of **Amoy.** It is a corruption of *Kin-măn*, in Chang-chau dialect *Kin-muiⁿ*, meaning 'Golden-door.'

QUI-HI, s. The popular distinctive nickname of the Bengal Anglo-Indian, from the usual manner of calling servants in that Presidency, viz. '*Koī hai?*' 'Is any one there?' The Anglo-Indian of Madras was known as a **Mull**, and he of Bombay as a **Duck** (qq.v.).

1816.—"The Grand Master, or Adventures of **Qui Hi** in Hindostan, a Hudibrastic Poem; with illustrations by Rowlandson."

1825.—"Most of the household servants are Parsees, the greater part of whom speak English. . . . Instead of '**Koee hue**,' Who's there? the way of calling a servant is 'boy,' a corruption, I believe, of '*bhae*,' brother."—*Heber*, ed. 1844, ii. 98. [But see under **BOY**.]

c. 1830.—"J'ai vu dans vos gazettes de Calcutta les clameurs des **quoihaés** (sobriquet des Européens Bengalis de ce côté) sur la chaleur."—*Jacquemont, Corresp.* ii. 308.

QUILOA, n.p. *i.e. Kilwa*, in lat. 9° 0′ S., next in remoteness to Sofāla, which for a long time was the *ne plus ultra* of Arab navigation on the East Coast of Africa, as Capt. Boyados was that of Portuguese navigation on the West Coast. Kilwa does not occur in the Geographies of Edrisi or Abulfeda, though Sofāla is in both. It is mentioned in the *Roteiro*, and in Barros's account of Da Gama's voyage. Barros had access to a native chronicle of Quiloa, and says it was founded about A.H. 400, and a little more than 70 years after Magadoxo and Brava, by a Persian Prince from Shiraz.

1220.—"**Kilwa**, a place in the country of Zenj, a city."—*Yākūt*, (orig.), iv. 302.

c. 1330.—"I embarked at the town of *Makdashau* (**Magadoxo**), making for the country of the Sawāhil, and the town of **Kulwā**, in the country of the Zenj. . . ."—*Ibn Batuta*, ii. 191. [See under **SOFALA.**]

1498.—"Here we learned that the island of which they told us in Mocombiquy as being peopled by Christians is an island at which dwells the King of Mocombiquy himself, and that the half is of Moors, and the half of Christians, and in this island is much seed-pearl, and the name of the island is **Quyluee**. . . ."—*Roteiro da Viagem de Vasco da Gama*, 48.

1501.—"**Quilloa** è cittade in Arabia in vna insuletta giunta a terra firma, ben popolata de homini negri et mercadanti: edificata al modo nr̃o: Quiui hanno abundantia de auro: argento: ambra: muschio: et perle: ragionevolmente vesteno panni de sera: et bambaxi fini."—*Letter of K. Emanuel*, 2.

1506.—"Del 1502 . . . mandò al viaggio naue 21, Capitánio Don Vasco de Gamba, che fu quello che discoperse l'India . . . e nell' andar de li, del Cao de Bona Speranza, zonse in uno loco chiamato **Ochilia**; la qual terra e dentro uno rio. . . ."—*Leonardo Ca' Masser*, 17.

1553.—"The Moor, in addition to his natural hatred, bore this increased resentment on account of the chastisement inflicted on him, and determined to bring the ships into port at the city of **Quiloa**, that being a populous place, where they might get the better of our ships by force of arms. To wreak this mischief with greater safety to himself he told Vasco da Gama, as if wishing to gratify him, that in front of them was a city called **Quiloa**, half peopled by Christians of Abyssinia and of India, and that if he gave the order the ships should be steered thither."—*Barros*, I. iv. 5.

1572.—

"Esta ilha pequena, que habitamos,
He em toda esta terra certa escala
De todos os que as ondas navegamos
De **Quilóa**, de Mombaça, a de Sofala."
Camões, i. 54.

By Burton:

"This little island, where we now abide,
of all this seaboard is the one sure place
for ev'ry merchantman that stems the tide
from **Quiloa**, or Sofala, or Mombas. . . ."

QUILON, n.p. A form which we have adopted from the Portuguese for the name of a town now belonging to Travancore; once a very famous and much frequented port of Malabar, and known to the Arabs as *Kaulam*. The proper name is Tamil, *Kollam*, of doubtful sense in this use. Bishop Caldwell thinks it may be best explained as 'Palace' or 'royal residence,' from *Kolu*, 'the royal Presence,' or Hall of Audience. [Mr. Logan says: "*Kollam* is only an abbreviated form of *Koyilagam* or *Kovilagam*, 'King's house'" (*Malabar*, i. 231, note).] For ages *Kaulam* was known as one of the greatest ports of Indian trade with Western Asia, especially trade in pepper and brazil-wood. It was possibly the *Malé* of Cosmas in the 6th century (see **MALABAR**), but the first mention of it by the present name is about three centuries later, in the *Relation* translated by Reinaud. The 'Kollam era' in general use in Malabar dates from A.D. 824; but it does not follow that the city had no earlier existence. In a Syriac extract (which is, however, modern) in *Land's Anecdota Syriaca* (Latin, i. 125; Syriac, p. 27) it is stated that three Syrian missionaries came to Kaulam in A.D. 823, and got leave from King *Shakīrbīrtī* to build a church and city at Kaulam. It would seem that there is some connection between the date assigned to this event, and the 'Kollam era'; but what it is we cannot say. *Shakīrbīrtī* is evidently a form of *Chakravartti Rāja* (see under **CHUCKERBUTTY**). Quilon, as we now call it, is now the 3rd town of Travancore, pop. (in 1891) 23,380; there is little trade. It had a European garrison up to 1830, but now only one Sepoy regiment.

In ecclesiastical narratives of the Middle Ages the name occurs in the form *Columbum*, and by this name it was constituted a See of the Roman Church in 1328, suffragan of the Archbishop of Sultaniya in Persia; but it is doubtful if it ever had more than one bishop, viz. Jordanus of Severac, author of the *Mirabilia* often quoted in this volume. Indeed we have no knowledge that he ever took up his bishopric, as his book was written, and his nomination occurred, both during a visit to Europe. The Latin Church however which he had founded, or obtained the use of, existed 20 years later, as we know from John de' Marignolli, so it is probable that he had reached his See. The form *Columbum* is accounted for by an inscription (see *Ind. Antiq.* ii. 360) which shows that the city was called *Kolamba*, [other forms being *Kelambapaṭṭana*, or *Kālambapaṭṭana* (*Bombay Gazetteer*, vol. i. pt. i. 183)]. The form *Palumbum* also occurs in most of the MSS. of Friar Odoric's Journey; this is the more difficult to account for, unless it was a mere play (or a trick of memory) on the kindred meanings of *columba* and *palumbes.* A passage in a letter from the Nestorian Patriarch Yeshu'-yab (c. 650-60) quoted in *Assemani* (iii. pl. i. 131), appears at that date to mention **Colon**. But this is an arbitrary and erroneous rendering in Assemani's Latin. The Syriac has *Kalah*, and probably therefore refers to the port of the Malay regions noticed under **CALAY** and **QUEDDA**.

851.—"De ce lieu (Mascate) les navires mettent la voile pour l'Inde, et se dirigent vers **Koulam**-*Malay;* la distance entre Mascate et Koulam-Malay est d'un mois de marche, avec un vent modéré."—*Relation*, &c., tr. by *Reinaud*, i. 15.

1166.—"Seven days from thence is **Chulam**, on the confines of the country of the sun-worshippers, who are descendants of Kush . . . and are all black. This nation is very trustworthy in matters of trade. . . . Pepper grows in this country. . . . Cinnamon, ginger, and many other kinds of spices also grow in this country."—*Benjamin of Tudela*, in *Early Travels in Palestine*, 114-115.

c. 1280-90.—"Royaumes de Ma-pa-'rh. Parmi tous les royaumes étrangers d'au-de-là des mers, il n'y eut que Ma-pa-'rh et **Kiu-lan (Mabar and Quilon)** sur lesquels on ait pu parvenir à établir une certaine sujétion; mais surtout Kiu-lan. . . . (Année 1282). Cette année . . . **Kiu-lan** a envoyé un ambassadeur à la cour (mongole) pour présenter en tribut des marchandises precieuses et un singe noir."—*Chinese Annals*, quoted by *Pauthier, Marc Pol*, ii. 603, 643.

1298.—"When you quit Maabar and go 500 miles towards the S.W. you come to the Kingdom of **Coilum**. The people are idolators, but there are also some Christians and some Jews," &c.—*Marco Polo*, Bk. iii. ch. 22.

c. 1300.—"Beyond Guzerat are Kankan and Tána; beyond them the country of Malibár, which from the boundary of Karoha to **Kúlam**, is 300 parasangs in length. . . . The people are all Samánis, and worship idols. . . ."—*Rashíduddin*, in *Elliot*, i. 68.

c. 1310.—"Ma'bar extends in length from **Kúlam** to *Nîláwar* **(Nellore)** nearly 300 parasangs along the sea-coast. . . ."—*Wassáf*, in *Elliot*, iii. 32.

c. 1322.—". . . as I went by the sea . . . towards a certain city called **Polumbum** (where groweth the pepper in great store). . . ."—*Friar Odoric*, in *Cathay*, p. 71.

c. 1322.—"Poi venni a **Colonbio**, ch' è la migliore terra d'India per mercatanti. Quivi è il gengiovo in grande copia e del bueno del mondo. Quivi vanno tutti ignudi salvo che portano un panno innanzi alla vergogna, . . . e legalosi di dietro."—*Palatine MS.* of *Odoric*, in *Cathay*, App., p. xlvii.

c. 1328.—"In India, whilst I was at **Columbum**, were found two cats having wings like the wings of bats. . . ."—*Friar Jordanus*, p. 29.

1330.—"Joannes, &c., nobili viro domino Nascarenorum et universis sub eo Christianis Nascarenis de **Columbo** gratiam in praesenti, quae ducat ad gloriam in futuro . . . quatenus venerabilem Fratrem nostrum Jordanum Catalani episcopum Columbensem . . . quem nuper ad episcopalis dignatatis apicem auctoritate apostolica diximus promovendum. . . ."—*Letter of Pope John XXII.* to the Christians of Coilon, in *Odorici Raynaldi Ann. Eccles.* v. 495.

c. 1343.—"The 10th day (from Calicut) we arrived at the city of **Kaulam**, which is one of the finest of Malībār. Its markets are splendid, and its merchants are known under the name of *Sūlī* (see **CHOOLIA**). They are rich; one of them will buy a ship with all its fittings and load it with goods from his own store."—*Ibn Batuta*, iv. 10.

c. 1348.—"And sailing on the feast of St. Stephen, we navigated the Indian Sea until Palm Sunday, and then arrived at a very noble city of India called **Columbum**, where the whole world's pepper is produced. . . . There is a church of St. George there, of the Latin communion, at which I dwelt. And I adorned it with fine paintings, and taught there the holy Law."—*John Marignolli*, in *Cathay*, &c., pp. 342-344.

c. 1430.—". . . **Coloen**, civitatem nobilem venit, cujus ambitus duodecim millia passuum amplectitur. Gingiber qui *colobi* **(colombi)** dicitur, piper, verzinum, cannellae quae crassae appellantur, hac in provincia, quam vocant Melibariam, leguntur."—*Conti*, in *Poggius de Var. Fortunae*.

c. 1468-9.—"In the year *Bhavati* (644) of the **Kolamba** era, King Adityavarmâ the ruler of Vânchi . . . who has attained the sovereignty of Cherabaya Mandalam, hung up the bell. . . ."—*Inscr.* in *Tinnevelly*, see *Ind. Antiq.* ii. 360.

1510.—". . . we departed . . . and went to another city called **Colon**. . . . The King of this city is a Pagan, and extremely powerful, and he has 20,000 horsemen, and many archers. This country has a good port near to the sea-coast. No grain grows here, but fruits as at Calicut, and pepper in great quantities."—*Varthema*, 182-3.

1516.—"Further on along the same coast towards the south is a great city and good sea-port which is named **Coulam**, in which dwell many Moors and Gentiles and Christians. They are great merchants and very rich, and own many ships with which they trade to Cholmendel, the Island of Ceylon, Bengal, Malaca, Samatara, and Pegu. . . . There is also in this city much pepper."—*Barbosa*, 157-8.

1572.—

"A hum Cochim, e a outro Cananor
A qual Chalé, a qual a ilha da Pimenta,
A qual **Coulao**, a qual da Cranganor,
E os mais, a quem o mais serve, e contenta. . . ."— *Camões*, vii. 35.

By Burton:

"To this Cochim, to that falls Cananor,
one hath **Chalé**, another th' Isle Piment,
a third **Coulam**, a fourth takes Cranganor,
the rest is theirs with whom he rests content."

1726.—"... **Coylang.**"—*Valentijn, Choro.*, 115.

1727.—"**Coiloan** is another small principality. It has the Benefit of a River, which is the southermost Outlet of the *Couchin* Islands; and the *Dutch* have a small Fort, within a Mile of it on the Sea-shore. . . . It keeps a Garrison of 30 Men, and its trade is inconsiderable."—*A. Hamilton*, i. 333 [ed. 1744].

QUIRPELE, s. This Tamil name of the **mungoose** (q.v.) occurs in the quotation which follows: properly *Kīrippiḷḷai*, ['little squeaker'].

1601.—"... bestiolia quaedam **Quil** sive **Quirpele** vocata, quae aspectu primo viverrae. . . ."—*De Bry*, iv. 63.

R

RADAREE, s. P.—H. *rāh-dārī*, from *rāh-dār*, 'road-keeper.' A transit duty; sometimes 'black-mail.' [*Rāhdārī* is very commonly employed in the sense of sending prisoners, &c., by escort from one police post to another, as along the Grand Trunk road].

1620.—"Fra Nicolo Ruigiola Francescano genovese, il quale, passagiero, che d'India andava in Italia, partito alcuni giorni prima da Ispahan . . . poco di qua lontano era stato trattenuto dai **rahdari**, o custodi delle strade. . . ."—*P. della Valle*, ii. 99.

1622.—"At the garden Pelengon we found a **rahdar** or guardian of the road, who was also the chief over certain other **rahdari**, who are usually posted in another place 2 leagues further on."—*Ibid.* ii. 285.

1623.—"For **Rahdars**, the Khan has given them a firman to free them, also firmans for a house. . . ."—*Sainsbury*, iii. p. 163.

[1667.—". . . that the goods . . . may not be stopped . . . on pretence of taking **Rhadaryes**, or other dutyes. . . ."—*Phirmaan of Shaw Orung Zeeb*, in *Forrest, Bombay Letters, Home Series*, i. 213.]

1673.—"This great officer, or Farmer of the Emperor's Custom (the Shawbunder [see **SHABUNDER**]), is obliged on the Roads to provide for the safe travelling for Merchants by a constant Watch . . . for which **Rhadorage**, or high Imposts, are allowed by the Merchants, both at Landing and in their passage inland."—*Fryer*, 222.

1685.—"Here we were forced to compound with the **Rattaree** men, for ye Dutys on our goods."—*Hedges, Diary*, Dec. 15; [Hak. Soc. i. 213. In i. 100, **Rawdarrie**].

c. 1731.—"Nizámu-l Mulk . . . thus got rid of . . . the **ráhdárí** from which latter impost great annoyance had fallen upon travellers and traders."—*Kháfi Khán*, in *Elliot*, vii. 531.

[1744.—"Passing the river Kizilazan we ascended the mountains by the **Rahdar** (a Persian toll) of Noglabar. . . ."—*Hanway*, i. 226.]

RAGGY, s. *Rāgī* (the word seems to be Dec. Hindustani, [and is derived from Skt. *rāga*, 'red,' on account of the colour of the grain]. A kind of grain, *Eleusine Coracana*, Gaertn.; *Cynosurus Coracanus*, Linn.; largely cultivated, as a staple of food, in Southern India.

1792.—"The season for sowing **raggy**, rice, and bajera from the end of June to the end of August."—*Life of T. Munro*, iii. 92.

1793.—"The Mahratta supplies consisting chiefly of **Raggy**, a coarse grain, which grows in more abundance than any other in the Mysore Country, it became necessary to serve it out to the troops, giving rice only to the sick."—*Dirom*, 10.

[1800.—"The Deccany Mussulmans call it **Ragy**. In the Tamil language it is called *Kevir* (*kēzhvaragu*)."—*Buchanan, Mysore*, i. 100.]

RAINS, THE, s. The common Anglo-Indian colloquial for the Indian rainy season. The same idiom, *as chuvas*, had been already in use by the Portuguese. (See **WINTER**).

c. 1666.—"Lastly, I have imagined that if in *Delhi*, for example, the **Rains** come from the East, it may yet be that the Seas which are Southerly to it are the origin of them, but that they are forced by reason of some Mountains . . . to turn aside and discharge themselves another way. . . ."—*Bernier*, E.T., 138; [ed. *Constable*, 433].

1707.—"We are heartily sorry that the **Rains** have been so very unhealthy with you."—Letter in *Orme's Fragments*.

1750.—"The **Rains** . . . setting in with great violence, overflowed the whole country."—*Orme, Hist.*, ed. 1803, i. 153.

1868.—"The place is pretty, and although it is '**the Rains**,' there is scarcely any day when we cannot get out."—*Bp. Milman*, in *Memoir*, p. 67.

[**RAIS**, s. Ar. *ra'īs*, from *ra's*, 'the head,' in Ar. meaning 'the captain, or master, not the owner of a ship;' in

India it generally means 'a native gentleman of respectable position.'

1610.—"... **Reyses** of all our Nauyes." —*Birdwood, First Letter Book*, 435.

1785.—"... their chief (more worthless in truth than a **horsekeeper**)." In note—"In the original the word **syse** is introduced for the sake of a jingle with the word **Ryse** (a chief or leader)."—*Tippoo's Letters*, 18.

1870.—"**Raees.**" See under **RYOT**.

1900.—"The petition was signed by representative landlords, **raises**." — *Pioneer Mail*, April 13.]

RAJA, RAJAH, s. Skt. *rājā*, 'king.' The word is still used in this sense, but titles have a tendency to degenerate, and this one is applied to many humbler dignitaries, petty chiefs, or large Zemindars. It is also now a title of nobility conferred by the British Government, as it was by their Mahommedan predecessors, on Hindus, as Nawāb is upon Moslem. *Rāī, Rāo, Rānā, Rāwal, Rāya* (in S. India), are other forms which the word has taken in vernacular dialects or particular applications. The word spread with Hindu civilisation to the eastward, and survives in the titles of Indo-Chinese sovereigns, and in those of Malay and Javanese chiefs and princes.

It is curious that the term *Rājā* cannot be traced, so far as we know, in any of the Greek or Latin references to India, unless the very questionable instance of Pliny's *Rachias* be an exception. In early Mahommedan writers the now less usual, but still Indian, forms *Rāō* and *Rāī*, are those which we find. (Ibn Batuta, it will be seen, regards the words for king in India and in Spain as identical, in which he is fundamentally right.) Among the English vulgarisms of the 18th century again we sometimes find the word barbarised into *Roger*.

c. 1338.—"... Bahā-uddīn fled to one of the heathen Kings called the Rāī Kanbīlah. The word **Rāī** among those people, just as among the people of Rūm, signifies 'King.'"—*Ibn Batuta*, iii. 318. The traveller here refers, as appears by another passage, to the Spanish *Rey*.

[1609.—"**Raiaw.**" See under **GOONT**.]

1612.—"In all this part of the East there are 4 castes. ... The first caste is that of the **Rayas**, and this is a most noble race from which spring all the Kings of Canara. ..."—*Couto*, V. vi. 4.

[1615.—"According to your direction I have sent per Orincay (see **ORANKAY**) Beege **Roger's** junk six peccules (see **PECUL**) of lead."—*Foster, Letters*, iv. 107.

[1623. — "A **Ragia**, that is an Indian Prince."—*P. della Valle*, Hak. Soc. i. 84.]

1683.—"I went a hunting with ye **Ragea**, who was attended with 2 or 300 men, armed with bows and arrows, swords and targets." —*Hedges, Diary*, March 1; [Hak. Soc. i. 66].

1786. — Tippoo with gross impropriety addresses Louis XVI. as "the **Rajah** of the French."—*Select Letters*, 369.

RAJAMUNDRY, n.p. A town, formerly head-place of a district, on the lower Godavery R. The name is in Telegu *Rājamahendravaramu*, 'King-chief('s)-Town,' [and takes its name from Mahendradeva of the Orissa dynasty; see *Morris, Godavery Man.* 23].

RAJPOOT, s. Hind. *Rājpūt*, from Skt. *Rājaputra*, 'King's Son.' The name of a great race in India, the hereditary profession of which is that of arms. The name was probably only a honorific assumption; but no race in India has furnished so large a number of princely families. According to Chand, the great medieval bard of the Rājpūts, there were 36 clans of the race, issued from four *Kshatriyas* (Parihār, Pramār, Solankhī, and Chauhān) who sprang into existence from the sacred *Agnikuṇḍa* or Firepit on the summit of Mount Abū. Later bards give five eponyms from the firepit, and 99 clans. The Rājpūts thus claim to be true *Kshatriyas*, or representatives of the second of the four fundamental castes, the Warriors; but the Brahmans do not acknowledge the claim, and deny that the true Kshatriya is extant. Possibly the story of the fireborn ancestry hides a consciousness that the claim is factitious. "The Rajpoots," says Forbes, "use animal food and spirituous liquors, both unclean in the last degree to their puritanic neighbours, and are scrupulous in the observance of only two rules,—those which prohibit the slaughter of cows, and the remarriage of widows. The clans are not forbidden to eat together, or to intermarry, and cannot be said in these respects to form separate castes" (*Rās-mālā*, reprint 1878, p. 537).

An odd illustration of the fact that to partake of animal food, and especially of the heroic repast of the flesh of the wild boar killed in the chase (see Terry's representation of this below), is a Rājpūt characteristic, occurs to the memory of one of the present writers. In Lord Canning's time the young Rājpūt Rāja of Alwar had betaken himself to degrading courses, insomuch that the Viceroy felt constrained, in open **durbar** at Agra, to admonish him. A veteran political officer, who was present, inquired of the agent at the Alwar Court what had been the nature of the conduct thus rebuked. The reply was that the young prince had become the habitual associate of low and profligate Mahommedans, who had so influenced his conduct that among other indications, he *would not eat wild pig.* The old Political, hearing this, shook his head very gravely, saying, 'Would not eat *Wild Pig!* Dear! Dear! Dear!' It seemed the *ne plus ultra* of Rājpūt degradation! The older travellers give the name in the quaint form *Rashboot*, but this is not confined to Europeans, as the quotation from Sidi 'Alī shows; though the aspect in which the old English travellers regarded the tribe, as mainly a pack of banditti, might have made us think the name to be shaped by a certain sense of aptness. The Portuguese again frequently call them *Reys Butos*, a form in which the true etymology, at least partially, emerges.

1516.—"There are three qualities of these Gentiles, that is to say, some are called **Razbutes**, and they, in the time that their King was a Gentile, were Knights, the defenders of the Kingdom, and governors of the Country."—*Barbosa*, 50.

1533.—"Insomuch that whilst the battle went on, Saladim placed all his women in a large house, with all that he possessed, whilst below the house were combustibles for use in the fight; and Saladim ordered them to be set fire to, whilst he was in it. Thus the house suddenly blew up with great explosion and loud cries from the unhappy women; whereupon all the people from within and without rushed to the spot, but the **Resbutos** fought in such a way that they drove the Guzarat troops out of the gates, and others in their hasty flight cast themselves from the walls and perished."—*Correa*, iii. 527.

" "And with the stipulation that the 200 *pardaos*, which are paid as allowance to the *lascarins* of the two small forts which stand between the lands of Baçaim and the **Reys buutos**, shall be paid out of the revenues of Baçaim as they have been paid hitherto."—*Treaty* of *Nuno da Cunha* with the *K. of Cambaya*, in *Subsidios*, 137.

c. 1554.—"But if the caravan is attacked, and the *Bāts* (see **BHAT**) kill themselves, the **Rashbūts**, according to the law of the *Bāts*, are adjudged to have committed a crime worthy of death."—*Sidi 'Ali Kapudān*, in *J. As.*, Ser. I., tom. ix. 95.

[1602.—"**Rachebidas.**"—*Couto*, Dec. viii. ch. 15.]

c. 1614.—"The next day they embarked, leaving in the city, what of those killed in fight and those killed by fire, more than 800 persons, the most of them being **Regibutos**, *Moors* of great valour; and of ours fell eighteen. . . ."—*Bocarro*, *Decada*, 210.

[1614.—". . . in great danger of thieves called **Rashbouts**. . . ."—*Foster*, *Letters*, ii. 260.]

1616.—". . . it were fitter he were in the Company of his brother . . . and his safetie more regarded, then in the hands of a **Rashboote** Gentile. . . ."—*Sir T. Roe*, i. 553-4; [Hak. Soc. ii. 282].

" "The **Rashbootes** eate Swines-flesh most hateful to the Mahometans."—*Terry*, in *Purchas*, ii. 1479.

1638.—"These **Rasboutes** are a sort of Highway men, or Tories."—*Mandelslo*, Eng. by *Davies*, 1669, p. 19.

1648.—"These **Resbouts** (Resbouten) are held for the best soldiers of Gusuratta."—*Van Twist*, 39.

[c. 1660.—"The word **Ragipous** signifies *Sons of Rajas.*"—*Bernier*, ed. *Constable*, 39.]

1673.—"Next in esteem were the *Rashwaws*, **Rashpoots**, or Souldiers."—*Fryer*, 27.

1689.—"The place where they went ashore was at a Town of the *Moors*, which name our Seamen give to all the Subjects of the Great Mogul, but especially his Mahometan Subjects; calling the Idolaters *Gentous* or **Rashbouts**."—*Dampier*, i. 507.

1791.—". . . Quatre cipayes ou **reispoutes** montés sur des chevaux persans, pour l'escorter."—*B. de St. Pierre*, *Chaumière Indienne*.

RAMASAMMY, s. This corruption of *Rāmaswāmi* ('Lord Rāma'), a common Hindū proper name in the South, is there used colloquially in two ways:

(a). As a generic name for Hindūs, like 'Tommy Atkins' for a British soldier. Especially applied to Indian coolies in Ceylon, &c.

(b). For a twisted roving of cotton in a tube (often of wrought silver) used to furnish light for a cigar (see **FULEETA**). Madras use:

a.—

[1843.—"I have seen him almost swallow it, by Jove, like **Ramo Samee**, the Indian juggler."—*Thackeray*, *Book of Snobs*, ch. i.]

1880.—". . . if you want a clerk to do your work or a servant to attend on you, . . . you would take on a saponaceous Bengali Baboo, or a servile abject Madrasi **Ramasammy**. . . . A Madrasi, even if wrongly abused, would simply call you his father, and his mother, and his aunt, defender of the poor, and epitome of wisdom, and would take his change out of you in the bazaar accounts."—*Cornhill Mag.*, Nov., pp. 582-3.

RAMBOTANG, s. Malay, *rambūtan* (*Filet*, No. 6750, p. 256). The name of a fruit (*Nephelium lappaceum*, L.), common in the Straits, having a thin luscious pulp, closely adhering to a hard stone, and covered externally with bristles like those of the external envelope of a chestnut. From *rambūt*, 'hair.'

1613.—"And other native fruits, such as *bachoes* (perhaps *bachang*, the *Mangifera foetida*?) **rambotans**, *rambes*,* *buasducos*,* and pomegranates, and innumerable others. . . ."—*Godinho de Eredia*, 16.

1726.—". . . the **ramboetan**-tree (the fruit of which the Portuguese call *froeta dos caffaros* or *Caffer's fruit*)."—*Valentijn* (v.) *Sumatra*, 3.

1727.—"The **Rambostan** is a Fruit about the Bigness of a Walnut, with a tough Skin, beset with Capillaments; within the Skin is a very savoury Pulp."—*A. Hamilton*, ii. 81; [ed. 1744, ii. 80].

1783.—"Mangustines, **rambustines**, &c." —*Forrest, Mergui*, 40.

[1812.—". . . mangustan, **rhambudan**, and dorian . . ."—*Heyne, Tracts*, 411.]

RAMDAM, s. Hind. from Ar. *ramazān* (*ramadhān*). The ninth Mahommedan lunar month, viz. the month of the Fast.

1615.—". . . at this time, being the preparation to the **Ramdam** or Lent."—*Sir T. Roe*, in *Purchas*, i. 537; [Hak. Soc. i. 21; also 58, 72, ii. 274].

1623.—"The 29th June: I think that (to-day?) the Moors have commenced their **ramadhan**, according to the rule by which I calculate."—*P. della Valle*, ii. 607; [Hak. Soc. i. 179].

1686.—"They are not . . . very curious or strict in observing any Days or Times of particular Devotions, except it be **Ramdam** time as we call it. . . . In this time they fast all Day. . . ."—*Dampier*, i. 343.

* Favre gives (*Dict. Malay-Français*): "*Duku*" (*buwa* is=fruit). "Nom d'un fruit de la grosseur d'un œuf de poule; il parait être une grosse espèce de *Lansium*." (It is *L. domesticum*.) The *Rambeh* is figured by Marsden in Atlas to *Hist. of Sumatra*, 3rd ed. pl. vi. and pl. ix. It seems to be *Baccaurea dulcis*, Müll. (*Pierardia dulcis*, Jack).

RAMOOSY, n.p. The name of a very distinct caste in W. India, Mahr. *Rāmosī*, [said to be from Mahr. *ranavāsī*, 'jungle-dweller']; originally one of the thieving castes. Hence they came to be employed as hereditary watchmen in villages, paid by cash or by rent-free lands, and by various petty dues. They were supposed to be responsible for thefts till the criminals were caught; and were often themselves concerned. They appear to be still commonly employed as hired **chokidars** by Anglo-Indian households in the west. They come chiefly from the country between Poona and Kolhapūr. The surviving traces of a Ramoosy dialect contain Telegu words, and have been used in more recent days as a secret slang. [See an early account of the tribe in: "An Account of the Origin and Present condition of the tribe of **Ramoosies**, including the Life of the Chief Oomíah Naik, by *Capt. Alexander Mackintosh* of the Twenty-seventh Regiment, Madras Army," Bombay 1833.]

[1817.—"His Highness must long have been aware of **Ramoosees** near the Mahadeo pagoda."—*Elphinstone's Letter* to *Peshwu*, in *Papers relating to E.I. Affairs*, 23.]

1833.—"There are instances of the **Ramoosy** Naiks, who are of a bold and daring spirit, having a great ascendancy over the village **Patells** (**Patel**) and *Koolkurnies* (**Coolcurnee**), but which the latter do not like to acknowledge openly . . . and it sometimes happens that the village officers participate in the profits which the **Ramoosies** derive from committing such irregularities."—*Macintosh, Acc. of the Tribe of Ramoossies*, p. 19.

1883.—"Till a late hour in the morning he (the chameleon) sleeps sounder than a **ramoosey** or a chowkeydar; nothing will wake him."—*Tribes on My Frontier*.

RAM-RAM! The commonest salutation between two Hindus meeting on the road; an invocation of the divinity.

[1652.—". . . then they approach the idol waving them (their hands) and repeating many times (the words) **Ram, Ram**, *i.e.* God, God."—*Tavernier*, ed. *Ball*, i. 263.]

1673.—"Those whose Zeal transports them no further than to die at home, are immediately Washed by the next of Kin, and bound up in a Sheet; and as many as go with him carry them by turns on a Colt-staff; and the rest run almost naked and shaved, crying after him **Ram, Ram**."—*Fryer*, 101.

1726.—"The wives of Bramines (when about to burn) first give away their jewels and ornaments, or perhaps a **pinang**, (q.v.), which is under such circumstances a great present, to this or that one of their male or female friends who stand by, and after taking leave of them, go and lie over the corpse, calling out only **Ram, Ram**."—*Valentijn*, v. 51.

[1828.—See under **SUTTEE.**]

c. 1885.—Sir G. Birdwood writes: "In 1869-70 I saw a green parrot in the Crystal Palace aviary very doleful, dull, and miserable to behold. I called it 'pretty poll,' and coaxed it in every way, but no notice of me would it take. Then I bethought me of its being a Mahratta *poput*, and hailed it **Ram Ram!** and spoke in Mahratti to it; when at once it roused up out of its lethargy, and hopped and swung about, and answered me back, and cuddled up close to me against the bars, and laid its head against my knuckles. And every day thereafter, when I visited it, it was always in an eager flurry to salute me as I drew near to it."

RANEE, s. A Hindu queen; *rānī*, fem. of *rājā*, from Skt. *rājnī* (= *regina*).

1673.—"*Bedmure* (Bednūr) . . . is the Capital City, the Residence of the **Ranna**, the Relict of *Sham Shunker Naig*."—*Fryer*, 162.

1809.—"The young **Rannie** may marry whomsoever she pleases."—*Lord Valentia*, i. 364.

1879.—"There were once a Raja and a **Ráné** who had an only daughter."—*Miss Stokes, Indian Fairy Tales*, 1.

RANGOON, n.p. Burm. *Ran-gun*, said to mean 'War-end'; the chief town and port of Pegu. The great Pagoda in its immediate neighbourhood had long been famous under the name of **Dagon** (q.v.), but there was no town in modern times till Rangoon was founded by Alompra during his conquest of Pegu, in 1755. The name probably had some kind of intentional assonance to *Da-gun*, whilst it "proclaimed his forecast of the immediate destruction of his enemies." Occupied by the British forces in May 1824, and again, taken by storm, in 1852, Rangoon has since the latter date been the capital, first of the British province of Pegu, and latterly of British Burma. It is now a flourishing port with a population of 134,176 (1881); [in 1891, 180,324].

RANJOW, s. A Malay term, *ranjau*. Sharp-pointed stakes of bamboo of varying lengths stuck in the ground to penetrate the naked feet or body of an enemy. See *Marsden, H. of Sumatra*, 2nd ed., 276. [The same thing on the Assam frontier is called a *poee* (*Lewin, Wild Races*, 308), or *panji* (*Sanderson, Thirteen Years*, 233).]

RASEED, s. Hind. *rasīd*. A native corruption of the English 'receipt,' shaped, probably, by the Pers. *rasīda*, 'arrived'; viz. an acknowledgment that a thing has 'come to hand.'

1877.—"There is no Sindi, however wild, that cannot now understand '**Rasíd**' (receipt), and '*Apil*' (appeal)."—*Burton, Sind Revisited*, i. 282.

RAT-BIRD, s. The striated bush-babbler (*Chattarhoea caudata*, Dumeril); see *Tribes on My Frontier*, 1883, p. 3.

RATTAN, s. The long stem of various species of Asiatic climbing palms, belonging to the genus *Calamus* and its allies, of which canes are made (not 'bamboo-canes,' improperly so called), and which, when split, are used to form the seats of cane-bottomed chairs and the like. From Malay *rotan*, [which Crawfurd derives from *rawat*, 'to pare or trim'], applied to various species of *Calamus* and *Daemonorops* (see *Filet*, No. 696 *et seq.*). Some of these attain a length of several hundred feet, and are used in the Himālaya and the Kāsia Hills for making suspension bridges, &c., rivalling rope in strength.

1511.—"The Governor set out from Malaca in the beginning of December, of this year, and sailed along the coast of Pedir. . . . He met with such a contrary gale that he was obliged to anchor, which he did with a great anchor, and a cable of **rótas**, which are slender but tough canes, which they twist and make into strong cables."—*Correa, Lendas*, ii. 269.

1563.—"They took thick ropes of **rotas** (which are made of certain twigs which are very flexible) and cast them round the feet, and others round the tusks."—*Garcia*, f. 90.

1598.—"There is another sorte of the same reedes which they call **Rota**: these are thinne like twigges of Willow for baskets. . . ."—*Linschoten*, 28; [Hak. Soc. i. 97].

c. 1610.—"Il y a vne autre sorte de canne qui ne vient iamais plus grosse que le petit doigt . . . et il ploye comme osier. Ils l'appellent **Rotan**. Ils en font des cables de nauire, et quantité de sortes de paniers gentiment entre lassez."—*Pyrard de Laval*, i. 237; [Hak. Soc. i. 331, and see i. 207].

1673.—"... The Materials Wood and Plaister, beautified without with folding windows, made of Wood and latticed with **Rattans**. . . ."—*Fryer*, 27.

1844.—"In the deep vallies of the south the vegetation is most abundant and various. Amongst the most conspicuous species are . . . the **rattan** winding from trunk to trunk and shooting his pointed head above all his neighbours."—*Notes on the Kasia Hills and People*, in *J.A.S.B.* vol. xiii. pt. ii. 615.

RAVINE-DEER. The sportsman's name, at least in Upper India, for the Indian gazelle (*Gazella Bennettii*, Jerdon, [Blanford, *Mammalia*, 526 *seqq.*]).

RAZZIA, s. This is Algerine-French, not Anglo-Indian, meaning a sudden raid or destructive attack. It is in fact the Ar. *ghāziya*, 'an attack upon infidels,' from *ghāzī*, 'a hero.'

REAPER, s. The small laths, laid across the rafters of a sloping roof to bear the tiles, are so called in Anglo-Indian house-building. We find no such word in any Hind. Dictionary; but in the Mahratti Dict. we find *rīp* in this sense.

[1734-5.—See under **BANKSHALL**.]

REAS, REES, s. Small money of account, formerly in use at Bombay, the 25th part of an anna, and 400th of a rupee. Port. *real*, pl. *réis*. Accounts were kept at Bombay in rupees, quarters, and *reas*, down at least to November 1834, as we have seen in accounts of that date at the India Office.

1673.—(In Goa) "The *Vinteen* . . . 15 *Basrooks* (see **BUDGROOK**), whereof 75 make a *Tango* (see **TANGA**), and 60 **Rees** make a *Tango*."—*Fryer*, 207.

1727.—"Their Accounts (Bombay) are kept by **Rayes** and *Rupees*. 1 *Rupee* is . . . 400 **Rayes**."—*A. Hamilton*, ii. App. 6; [ed. 1744, ii. 315].

RED CLIFFS, n.p. The nautical name of the steep coast below Quilon. This presents the only bluffs on the shore from Mt. Dely to Cape Comorin, and is thus identified, by character and name, with the Πυῤῥὸν ὄρος of the *Periplus*.

c. 80-90.—"Another village, Bakarē, lies by the mouth of the river, to which the ships about to depart descend from Nelkynda. . . . From Bakarē extends the **Red-Hill** (πυῤῥὸν ὄρος) and then a long stretch of country called Paralia."—*Periplus*, §§ 55-58.

1727.—"I wonder why the English built their Fort in that place (Anjengo), when they might as well have built it near the **Red Cliffs** to the Northward, from whence they have their Water for drinking."—*A. Hamilton*, i. 332; [ed. 1744, i. 334].

1813.—"Water is scarce and very indifferent; but at the **red cliffs**, a few miles to the north of Anjengo, it is said to be very good, but difficult to be shipped."—*Milburn, Or. Comm.* i. 335. See also *Dunn's New Directory*, 5th ed. 1780, p. 161.

1814.—"From thence (Quilone) to Anjengo the coast is hilly and romantic; especially about the **red cliffs** at *Boccoli* (qu. Βακαρὴ as above?); where the women of Anjengo daily repair for water, from a very fine spring."—*Forbes, Or. Mem.*, i. 334; [2nd ed. i. 213].

1841.—"There is said to be fresh water at the **Red Cliffs** to the northward of Anjengo, but it cannot be got conveniently; a considerable surf generally prevailing on the coast, particularly to the southward, renders it unsafe for ships' boats to land."—*Horsburgh's Direc.* ed. 1841, i. 515.

RED-DOG, s. An old name for **Prickly-heat** (q.v.).

c. 1752.—"The **red-dog** is a disease which affects almost all foreigners in hot countries, especially if they reside near the shore, at the time when it is hottest."—*Osbeck's Voyage*, i. 190.

REGULATION, s. A law passed by the Governor-General in Council, or by a Governor (of Madras or Bombay) in Council. This term became obsolete in 1833, when legislative authority was conferred by the Charter Act (3 & 4 Will. IV. cap. 85) on those authorities; and thenceforward the term used is *Act*. By 13 Geo. III. cap. 63, § xxxv., it is enacted that it shall be lawful for the G.-G. and Council of Fort William in Bengal to issue Rules or Decrees and Regulations for the good order and civil government of the Company's settlements, &c. This was the same Charter Act that established the Supreme Court. But the authorised compilation of "*Regulations of the Govt. of Fort William in force at the end of* 1853," begins only with the Regulations of 1793, and makes no allusion to the earlier Regulations. No more does Regulation XLI. of 1793, which prescribes the form, numbering, and codifying of the

Regulations to be issued. The fact seems to be that prior to 1793, when the enactment of Regulations was systematized, and the Regulations began to be regularly numbered, those that were issued partook rather of the character of resolutions of Government and circular orders than of Laws.

1868.—"The new Commissioner . . . could discover nothing prejudicial to me, except, perhaps, that the **Regulations** were not sufficiently observed. The sacred **Regulations!** How was it possible to fit them on such very irregular subjects as I had to deal with?"—*Lt.-Col. Lewin, A Fly on the Wheel*, p. 376.

1880.—"The laws promulgated under this system were called **Regulations**, owing to a lawyer's doubts as to the competence of the Indian authorities to infringe on the legislative powers of the English Parliament, or to modify the 'laws and customs' by which it had been decreed that the various nationalities of India were to be governed."—*Saty. Review*, March 13, p. 335.

REGULATION PROVINCES. See this explained under **NON-REGULATION.**

REGUR, s. Dakh. Hind. *regaṛ*, also *legaṛ*. The peculiar black loamy soil, commonly called by English people in India 'black cotton soil.' The word may possibly be connected with H.—P. *reg*, 'sand'; but *regaḍa* and *regaḍi* is given by Wilson as Telugu. [Platts connects it with Skt. *rekha*, 'a furrow.'] This soil is not found in Bengal, with some restricted exception in the Rājmahal Hills. It is found everywhere on the plains of the Deccan trap-country, except near the coast. Tracts of it are scattered through the valley of the Krishna, and it occupies the flats of Coimbatore, Madura, Salem, Tanjore, Ramnād, and Tinnevelly. It occurs north of the Nerbudda in Saugor, and occasionally on the plain of the eastern side of the Peninsula, and composes the great flat of Surat and Broach in Guzerat. It is also found in Pegu. The origin of *regar* has been much debated. We can only give the conclusion as stated in the *Manual of the Geology of India*, from which some preceding particulars are drawn: "**Regur** has been shown on fairly trustworthy evidence to result from the impregnation of certain argillaceous formations with organic matter, but . . . the process which has taken place is imperfectly understood, and . . . some peculiarities in distribution yet require explanation."—*Op. cit.* i. 434.

REH, s. [Hind. *reh*, Skt. *rej*, 'to shine, shake, quiver.'] A saline efflorescence which comes to the surface in extensive tracts of Upper India, rendering the soil sterile. The salts (chiefly sulphate of soda mixed with more or less of common salt and carbonate of soda) are superficial in the soil, for in the worst *reh* tracts sweet water is obtainable at depths below 60 or 80 feet. [Plains infested with these salts are very commonly known in N. India as *Oosur* Plains (Hind. *ūsar*, Skt. *ūshara*, 'impregnated with salt.')] The phenomenon seems due to the climate of Upper India, where the ground is rendered hard and impervious to water by the scorching sun, the parching winds, and the treeless character of the country, so that there is little or no water-circulation in the subsoil. The salts in question, which appear to be such of the substances resulting from the decomposition of rock, or of the detritus derived from rock, and from the formation of the soil, as are not assimilated by plants, accumulate under such circumstances, not being diluted and removed by the natural purifying process of percolation of the rain-water. This accumulation of salts is brought to the surface by capillary action after the rains, and evaporated, leaving the salts as an efflorescence on the surface. From time to time the process culminates on considerable tracts of land, which are thus rendered barren. The canal-irrigation of the Upper Provinces has led to some aggravation of the evil. The level of the canal-waters being generally high, they raise the level of the *reh*-polluted water in the soil, and produce in the lower tracts a great increase of the efflorescence. A partial remedy for this lies in the provision of drainage for the subsoil water, but this has only to a small extent been yet carried out. [See a full account in *Watt, Econ. Dict.* VI. pt. i. 400 *seqq.*]

REINOL, s. A term formerly in use among the Portuguese at Goa, and applied apparently to 'Johnny Newcomes' or **Griffins** (q.v.). It is from *reino*, 'the Kingdom' (viz. of Portugal). The word was also sometimes used to distinguish the European Portuguese from the country-born.

1598.—". . . they take great pleasure and laugh at him, calling him **Reynol**, which is a name given in iest to such as newly come from *Portingall*, and know not how to behave themselves in such grave manner, and with such ceremonies as the *Portingales* use there in *India*."—*Linschoten*, ch. xxxi. ; [Hak. Soc. i. 208].

c. 1610.—". . . quand ces soldats Portugais arriuent de nouueau aux Indes portans encor leurs habits du pays, ceux qui sont là de long tẽs quand ils les voyent par les ruës les appellent **Renol**, chargez de poux, et mille autres iniures et mocqueries."—*Mocquet*, 304.

[,, "When they are newly arrived in the Indies, they are called **Raignolles**, that is to say 'men of the Kingdom,' and the older hands mock them until they have made one or two voyages with them, and have learned the manners and customs of the Indies; this name sticks to them until the fleet arrives the year following."—*Pyrard de Laval*, Hak. Soc. ii. 123.

[1727. — "The **Reynolds** or European fidalgos."—*A. Hamilton*, ed. 1744, i. 251.]

At a later date the word seems to have been applied to Portuguese deserters who took service with the E.I. Co. Thus:

c. 1760.—"With respect to the military, the common men are chiefly such as the Company sends out in their ships, or deserters from the several nations settled in India, Dutch, French, or Portuguese, which last are commonly known by the name of **Reynols**."—*Grose*, i. 38.

RESHIRE, n.p. *Rīshihr*. A place on the north coast of the Persian Gulf, some 5 or 6 miles east of the modern port of **Bushire** (q.v.). The present village is insignificant, but it is on the site of a very ancient city, which continued to be a port of some consequence down to the end of the 16th century. I do not doubt that this is the place intended by **Reyxel** in the quotation from A. Nunes under **Dubber**. The spelling **Raxet** in Barros below is no doubt a clerical error for **Raxel**.

c. 1340.—"**Rishihr**. . . . This city built by Lohrasp, was rebuilt by Shapūr son of Ardeshīr Babegān; it is of medium size, on the shore of the sea. The climate is very hot and unhealthy. . . . The inhabitants generally devote themselves to sea-trade, but poor and feeble that they are, they live chiefly in dependence on the merchants of other countries. Dates and the cloths called *Rīschihrī* are the chief productions."—*Hamdalla Mastūfī*, quoted in *Barbier de Meynard, Dict. de la Perse*.

1514. — "And thereupon Pero Dalboquerque sailed away . . . and entered through the straits of the Persian sea, and explored all the barbours, islands, and villages which are contained in it . . . and when he was as far advanced as Bárem, the winds being now westerly—he tacked about, and stood along in the tack for a two days voyage, and reached **Raxel**, where he found Mirbuzaca, Captain of the Xeque Ismail, (Shāh Ismaīl Sūfī, of Persia), who had captured 20 *tarradas* from a Captain of the King of Ormuz."—*Alboquerque*, Hak. Soc. iv. 114-115.

,, "On the Persian side (of the Gulf) is the Province of **Raxel**, which contains many villages and fortresses along the sea, engaged in a flourishing trade."—*Ibid*. 186-7.

1534.—"And at this time insurrection was made by the King of **Raxel**, (which is a city on the coast of Persia); who was a vassal of the King of Ormuz, so the latter King sought help from the Captain of the Castle, Antonio da Silveira. And he sent down Jorge de Crasto with a galliot and two foists and 100 men, all well equipt, and good musketeers; and bade him tell the King of **Raxel** that he must give up the fleet which he kept at sea for the purpose of plundering, and must return to his allegiance to the K. of Ormuz."—*Correa*, iii. 557.

1553.—". . . And Francisco de Gouvea arrived at the port of the city of **Raxet**, and having anchored, was forthwith visited by a Moor on the King's part, with refreshments and compliments, and a message that . . . he would make peace with us, and submit to the King of Ormuz."—*Barros*, IV. iv. 26.

1554.—"**Reyxel**." See under **DUBBER**, as above.

1600.—"Reformados y proueydos en Harmuz de lo necessario, nos tornamos a partir . . . fuymos esta vez por fuera de la isla Queixiome (see **KISHM**) corriendo la misma costa, como de la primera, passamos . . . mas adelante la fortaleza de **Rexel**, celebre por el mucho y perfetto pan y frutos, que su territorio produze."—*Teixeira*, *Viage*, 70.

1856.—"48 hours sufficed to put the troops in motion northwards, the ships of war, led by the Admiral, advancing along the coast to their support. This was on the morning of the 9th, and by noon the enemy was observed to be in force in the village of **Reshire**. Here amidst the ruins of old houses, garden-walls, and steep ravines, they occupied a formidable position; but notwithstanding their firmness, wall after wall was surmounted, and finally they were driven from their last defence (the old fort of **Reshire**) bordering on the cliffs at the margin of the sea."—*Despatch* in *Lowe's H. of the Indian Navy*, ii. 346.

RESIDENT, s. This term has been used in two ways which require distinction. Thus (**a**) up to the organization of the Civil Service in Warren Hastings's time, the chiefs of the Company's commercial establishments in the provinces, and for a short time the European chiefs of districts, were termed *Residents.* But later the word was applied (**b**) also to the representative of the Governor-General at an important native Court, *e.g.* at Lucknow, Delhi, Hyderabad, and Baroda. And this is the only meaning that the term now has in British India. In Dutch India the term is applied to the chief European officer of a province (corresponding to an Indian **Zillah**) as well as to the Dutch representative at a native Court, as at Solo and Djokjocarta.

a.—

1748.—"We received a letter from Mr. Henry Kelsall, **Resident** at Ballasore."—*Ft. William Consn.*, in *Long*, 3.

1760.—"*Agreed*, Mr. Howitt the present **Resident** in Rajah Tillack Chund's country (*i.e.* Burdwan) for the collection of the tuncahs (see **TUNCA**), be wrote to. . . ."—*Ibid.* March 29, *ibid.* 244.

c. 1778.—"My pay as **Resident** (at Sylhet) did not exceed 500*l.* per annum, so that fortune could only be acquired by my own industry."—*Hon. R. Lindsay*, in *Lives of the L.'s*, iii. 174.

b.—

1798.—"Having received overtures of a very friendly nature from the Rajah of Berar, who has requested the presence of a British **Resident** at his Court, I have despatched an ambassador to Nagpore with full powers to ascertain the precise nature of the Rajah's views."—*Marquis Wellesley, Despatches*, i. 99.

RESPONDENTIA, s. An old trade technicality, thus explained: "Money which is borrowed, not upon the vessel as in bottomry, but upon the goods and merchandise contained in it, which must necessarily be sold or exchanged in the course of the voyage, in which case the borrower personally is bound to answer the contract" (*Wharton's Law Lexicon*, 6th ed., 1876; [and see *N.E.D.* under *Bottomry*]). What is now a part of the Calcutta Course, along the bank of the Hoogly, was known down to the first quarter of the last century, as **Respondentia** Walk. We have heard this name explained by the supposition that it was a usual scene of proposals and contingent **jawaubs**, (q.v.); but the name was no doubt, in reality, given because this walk by the river served as a sort of 'Change, where bargains in **Respondentia** and the like were made.

[1685.—". . . Provided he gives his Bill to repay itt in Syam, . . . with 20 p. Ct. **Respondentia** on the Ship. . . ."—*Pringle, Diary Ft. St. Geo.*, 1st ser. iv. 123.]

1720.—"I am concerned with Mr. Thomas Theobalds in a **respondentia** Bond in the 'George' Brigantine."—*Testament of Ch. Davers*, Merchant. In *Wheeler*, ii. 340.

1727.—"There was one Captain Perrin Master of a Ship, who took up about 500 L. on **respondentia** from Mr. Ralph Sheldon . . . payable at his Return to Bengal."—*A. Hamilton*, ii. 14; [ed. 1744, ii. 12].

" ". . . which they are enabled to do by the Money taken up here on **Respondentia** bonds. . . ."—In *Wheeler*, ii. 427.

1776.—"I have desired my Calcutta Attorney to insure some Money lent on **Respondentia** on Ships in India. . . . I have also subscribed £500 towards a China Voyage."—*MS. Letter* of *James Rennell*, Feb. 20.

1794.—"I assure you, Sir, Europe articles, especially good wine, are not to be had for love, money, or **respondentia**."—*The Indian Observer*, by *Hugh Boyd*, &c., p. 206.

[1840.—"A Grecian ghat has been built at the north end of the old **Respondentia** walk. . . ."—*Davidson, Diary of Travels*, ii. 209.]

RESSAIDAR, s. P.—H. *Rasāīdār.* A native subaltern of irregular cavalry, under the **Ressaldar** (q.v.). It is not clear what sense *rasāī* has in the formation of this title (which appears to be of modern devising). The meaning of that word is 'quickness of apprehension; fitness, perfection.'

RESSALA, s. Hind. from Ar. *risāla.* A troop in one of our regiments of native (so-called) Irregular Cavalry. The word was in India applied more loosely to a native corps of horse, apart from English regimental technicalities. The Arabic word properly means the charge or commission of a *rasūl*, *i.e.* of a civil officer employed to make arrests (*Dozy*), [and in the passage from the *Āīn*, quoted under **RESSALDAR**, the original text has *Risalah*]. The transition of meaning, as with many other words of Arabic origin, is very obscure.

1758.—"Presently after Shokum Sing and Harroon Cawn (formerly of Roy Dullub's

Rissalla) came in and discovered to him the whole affair."—*Letter* of *W. Hastings*, in *Gleig*, i. 70.

[1781.—"The enemy's troops before the place are five **Rosollars** of infantry . . ."—*Sir Eyre Coote*, letter of July 6, in *Progs. of Council*, September 7, *Forrest*, *Letters*, vol. iii.]

RESSALDAR, Ar.—P.—H. *Risāladār* (**Ressala**). Originally in Upper India the commander of a corps of Hindustani horse, though the second quotation shows it, in the south, applied to officers of infantry. Now applied to the native officer who commands a **ressala** in one of our regiments of "Irregular Horse." This title is applied honorifically to overseers of post-horses or stables. (See *Panjab Notes & Queries*, ii. 84.)

[c. 1590.—"Besides, there are several copyists who write a good hand and a lucid style. They receive the *yāddāsht* (memorandum) when completed, keep it with themselves, and make a proper abridgement of it. After signing it, they return this instead of the *yaddāsht*, when the abridgement is signed and sealed by the Wāqi'ahnawīs, and the **Risalahdar** (in orig. *risālah*). . . ."—*Āīn*, i. 259.]

1773.—"The Nawaub now gave orders to the **Risaladárs** of the regular and irregular infantry, to encircle the fort, and then commence the attack with their artillery and musketry."—*H. of Hydur Naik*, 327.

1803.—"The **rissaldars** finding so much money in their hands, began to quarrel about the division of it, while Perron crossed in the evening with the bodyguard."—*Mil. Mem. of James Skinner*, i. 274.

c. 1831.—"Le lieutenant de ma troupe a bonne chance d'être fait Capitaine (**resseldar**)."—*Jacquemont, Corresp.* ii. 8.

REST-HOUSE, s. Much the same as **Dawk Bungalow** (q.v.). Used in Ceylon only. [But the word is in common use in Northern India for the **chokies** along roads and canals.]

[1894.—"'**Rest-Houses**' or 'staging bungalows' are erected at intervals of twelve or fifteen miles along the roads."—*G. W. MacGeorge, Ways and Works in India*, p. 78.]

RESUM, s. Lascar's Hind. for *ration* (*Roebuck*).

RHINOCEROS, s. We introduce this word for the sake of the quotations, showing that even in the 16th century this animal was familiar not only in the Western Himālaya, but in the forests near Peshāwar. It is probable that the nearest rhinoceros to be found at the present time would be not less than 800 miles, as the crow flies, from Peshāwar. See also **GANDA**, [and for references to the animal in Greek accounts of India, *McCrindle, Ancient India, its Invasion by Alexander*, 186].

c. 1387.—"In the month of Zī-l Ka'da of the same year he (Prince Muhammed Khan) went to the mountains of Sirmor (W. of the Jumna) and spent two months in hunting the **rhinoceros** and the elk."—*Tārīkh-i-Mubārak-Shāhī*, in *Elliot*, iv. 16.

1398.—(On the frontier of Kashmīr). "Comme il y avoit dans ces Pays un lieu qui par sa vaste étendue, et la grande quantité de gibiers, sembloit inviter les passans à chasser. . . . Timur s'en donna le divertissement . . . ils prisent une infinité de gibiers, et l'on tua plusiers **rhinoceros** à coups de sabre et de lances, quoique cet animal . . . a la peau si ferme, qu'on ne peut la percer que par des efforts extraordinaires."—*Petis de la Croix, H. de Timur-Bec*, iii. 159.

1519.—"After sending on the army towards the river (Indus), I myself set off for Sawâti, which they likewise call Karak-Khaneh (*kark-khāna*, 'the rhinoceros-haunt'), to hunt the **rhinoceros**. We started many **rhinoceroses**, but as the country abounds in brushwood, we could not get at them. A she rhinoceros, that had whelps, came out, and fled along the plain; many arrows were shot at her, but . . . she gained cover. We set fire to the brushwood, but the rhinoceros was not to be found. We got sight of another, that, having been scorched in the fire, was lamed and unable to run. We killed it, and every one cut off a bit as a trophy of the chase."—*Baber*, 253.

1554.—"Nous vinmes à la ville de *Pourschewer* (**Peshawur**), et ayant heureusement passe le *Koutel* (**Kotul**), nous gagnâmes la ville de Djouschayeh. Sur le *Koutel* nous aperçûmes des **rhinoceros**, dont la grosseur approchait celle d'un elephant. . . ."—*Sidi 'Ali*, in *J. As.*, 1st ser. tom. ix. 201-202.

RHOTASS, n.p. This (*Rohtās*) is the name of two famous fortresses in India, viz. **a.** a very ancient rock-fort in the Shāhābād district of Behar, occupying part of a tabular hill which rises on the north bank of the Sōn river to a height of 1490 feet. It was an important stronghold of Sher Shāh, the successful rival of the Mogul Humāyūn: **b.** A fort at the north end of the Salt-range in the Jhelum District, Punjab, which was built by the same king, named by him after the ancient Rohtās. The ruins are very picturesque.

a.—

c. 1560.—"Sher Shâh was occupied night and day with the business of his kingdom, and never allowed himself to be idle. . . . He kept money (*khazâna*) and revenue (*kharâj*) in all parts of his territories, so that, if necessity required, soldiers and money were ready. The chief treasury was in **Rohtás** under the care of Ikhtiyár Khán."—*Wakí'at-i-Mushtaki*, in *Elliot*, iv. 551.

[c. 1590.—"**Rohtas** is a stronghold on the summit of a lofty mountain, difficult of access. It has a circumference of 14 *kos* and the land is cultivated. It contains many springs, and whenever the soil is excavated to the depth of 3 or 4 yards, water is visible. In the rainy season many lakes are formed, and more than 200 waterfalls gladden the eye and ear."—*Āīn*, ed. *Jarrett*, ii. 152 *seq.*]

1665.—". . . You must leave the great road to *Patna*, and bend to the South through *Exberbourgh* (?) [Akbarpur] and the famous Fortress of **Rhodes**."—*Tavernier*, E.T. ii. 53; [ed. *Ball*, i. 121].

[1764.—"From Shaw Mull, Kelladar of **Rotus** to Major Munro."—In *Long*, 359.]

b.—

c. 1540.—"Sher Shâh . . . marched with all his forces and retinue through all the hills of Padmán and Garjhák, in order that he might choose a fitting site, and build a fort there to keep down the Ghakkars. . . . Having selected **Rohtás**, he built there the fort which now exists."—*Táríkh-i-Sher Sháhí*, in *Elliot*, iv. 390.

1809.—"Before we reached the Hydaspes we had a view of the famous fortress of **Rotas**; but it was at a great distance. . . . **Rotas** we understood to be an extensive but strong fort on a low hill."—*Elphinstone, Caubul*, ed. 1839, i. 108.

RICE, s. The well-known cereal, *Oryza sativa*, L. There is a strong temptation to derive the Greek ὀρύζα, which is the source of our word through It. *riso*, Fr. *riz*, etc., from the Tamil *arisi*, 'rice deprived of husk,' ascribed to a root *ari*, 'to separate.' It is quite possible that Southern India was the original seat of rice cultivation. Roxburgh (*Flora Indica*, ii. 200) says that a wild rice, known as *Newaree* [Skt. *nīvāra*, Tel. *nivvāri*] by the Telinga people, grows abundantly about the lakes in the Northern Circars, and he considers this to be the original plant.

It is possible that the Arabic *al-ruzz* (*arruzz*) from which the Spaniards directly take their word *arroz*, may have been taken also directly from the Dravidian term. But it is hardly possible that ὀρύζα can have had that origin. The knowledge of rice apparently came to Greece from the expedition of Alexander, and the mention of ὀρύζα by Theophrastus, which appears to be the oldest, probably dates almost from the lifetime of Alexander (d. B.C. 323). Aristobulus, whose accurate account is quoted by Strabo (see below), was a companion of Alexander's expedition, but seems to have written later than Theophrastus. The term was probably acquired on the Oxus, or in the Punjab. And though no Skt. word for rice is nearer ὀρύζα than *vrīhi*, the very common exchange of aspirant and sibilant might easily give a form like *vrīsi* or *brīsi* (comp. *hindū*, *sindū*, &c.) in the dialects west of India. Though no such exact form seems to have been produced from old Persian, we have further indications of it in the Pushtu, which Raverty writes, sing. 'a grain of rice' *w'rijza'h*, pl. 'rice' *w'rijzey*, the former close to *oryza*. The same writer gives in *Barakai* (one of the uncultivated languages of the Kabul country, spoken by a 'Tajik' tribe settled in Logar, south of Kabul, and also at Kanigoram in the Waziri country) the word for rice as *w'rizza*, a very close approximation again to *oryza*. The same word is indeed given by Leech, in an earlier vocabulary, largely coincident with the former, as *rizza*. The modern Persian word for husked rice is *birinj*, and the Armenian *brinz*. A nasal form, deviating further from the hypothetical *brīsi* or *vrīsi*, but still probably the same in origin, is found among other languages of the Hindū Kūsh tribes, *e.g.* Burishki (Khajuna of Leitner) *bron*; Shina (of Gilgit), *briūn*; Khowar of the Chitral Valley (Arniyah of Leitner), *grinj* (*Biddulph, Tribes of Hindoo Koosh*, App., pp. xxxiv., lix., cxxxix.).

1298.—"Il hi a forment et **ris** asez, mès il ne menuient pain de forment por ce que il est en cele provence enferme, mès menuient **ris** et font poison (*i.e.* drink) de **ris** con especes qe molt e(s)t biaus et cler et fait le home evre ausi con fait le vin."—*Marc Pol.* Geo. Text, 132.

B.C. c. 320–300.—"Μᾶλλον δὲ σπείρουσι τὸ καλούμενον ὄρυζον, ἐξ οὗ το ἕψημα· τοῦτο δὲ ὅμοιον τῇ ζειᾷ, καὶ περιπτισθὲν οἷον χόνδρος, ευπεπτον δὲ τὴν ὄψιν πεφυκὸς ὅμοιον ταῖς αἴραις, καὶ τὸν πολύν χρόνον ἐν ὕδατι. Ἀποχεῖται δὲ οὐκ εἰς στάχυν, ἀλλ' οἷον φόβην ὥσπερ ὁ κέγχρος καὶ ὁ ἔλυμος."—*Theophrast. de Hist. Plantt.*, iv. c. 4.

B.C. c. 20.—"The rice (ὄρυζα), according to Aristobulus, stands in water, in an enclosure. It is sowed in beds. The plant is 4 cubits in height, with many ears, and yields a large produce. The harvest is about the time of the setting of the Pleiades, and the grain is beaten out like barley.

"It grows in Bactriana, Babylonia, Susis, and in the Lower Syria."—*Strabo*, xv. i. § 18, in Bohn's E.T. iii. 83.

B.C. 300.—"Megasthenes writes in the second Book of his *Indica:* The Indians, says he, at their banquets have a table placed before each person. This table is made like a buffet, and they set upon it a golden bowl, into which they first help boiled rice (ὄρυζαν), as it might be boiled groats, and then a variety of cates dressed in Indian fashions."—*Athenaeus*, iv. § 39.

A.D. c. 70.—"Hordeum Indis sativum et silvestre, ex quo panis apud eos praecipuus et alica. Maxime quidem **oryza** gaudent, ex qua tisanam conficiunt quam reliqui mortales ex hordeo. . . ."—*Pliny*, xviii. 13. Ph. Holland has here got so wrong a reading that we abandon him.

A.D. c. 80-90.—"Very productive is this country (*Syrastrēnē* or Penins. Guzerat) in wheat and rice (ὀρύζης) and sessamin oil and butter * (see **GHEE**) and cotton, and the abounding Indian piece-goods made from it."—*Periplus*, § 41.

ROC, s. The *Rukh* or fabulous colossal bird of Arabian legend. This has been treated of at length by one of the present writers in *Marco Polo* (Bk. iii. ch. 33, notes); and here we shall only mention one or two supplementary facts.

M. Marre states that *rūk-rūk* is applied by the Malays to a bird of prey of the vulture family, a circumstance which *possibly* may indicate the source of the Arabic name, as we know it to be of some at least of the legends. [See Skeat, *Malay Magic*, 124.]

In one of the notes just referred to it is suggested that the roc's quills, spoken of by Marco Polo in the passage quoted below (a passage which evidently refers to some real object brought to China), might possibly have been some vegetable production such as the great frond of the *Ravenala* of Madagascar (*Urania speciosa*), cooked to pass as a bird's quill. Mr. Sibree, in his excellent book on Madagascar (*The Great African Island*, 1880), noticed this, but pointed out that the object was more probably the immensely long midrib of the *rofia* palm (*Sagus Raphia*). Sir John Kirk, when in England in 1882, expressed entire confidence in this identification, and on his return to Zanzibar in 1883 sent four of these midribs to England. These must have been originally from 36 to 40 feet in length. The leaflets were all stript, but when entire the object must have strongly resembled a Brobdingnagian feather. These roc's quills were shown at the Forestry Exhibition in Edinburgh, 1884. Sir John Kirk wrote:

"I send to-day per S.S. Arcot . . . four fronds of the Raphia palm, called here *Moale.* They are just as sold and shipped up and down the coast. No doubt they were sent in Marco Polo's time in exactly the same state — *i.e.* stripped of their leaflets and with the tip broken off. They are used for making stages and ladders, and last long if kept dry. They are also made into doors, by being cut into lengths, and pinned through."

Some other object has recently been shown at Zanzibar as part of the wings of a great bird. Sir John Kirk writes that this (which he does not describe particularly) was in the possession of the R. C. priests at Bagamoyo, to whom it had been given by natives of the interior, and these declared that they had brought it from Tanganyika, and that it was part of the wing of a gigantic bird. On another occasion they repeated this statement, alleging that this bird was known in the Udoe (?) country, near the coast. The priests were able to communicate directly with their informants, and certainly believed the story. Dr. Hildebrand also, a competent German naturalist, believed in it. But Sir John Kirk himself says that 'what the priests had to show was most undoubtedly the whalebone of a comparatively small whale' (see letter of the present writer in *Athenaeum*, March 22nd, 1884).

(c. 1000 ?).—"El Haçan fils d'Amr et d'autres, d'après ce qu'ils tenaient de maint-personnages de l'Inde, m'ont rapporté des choses bien extraordinaires, au sujet des oiseaux du pays de Zabedj, de Khmêr (*Kumār*) du Senf et autres regions des

* Müller and (very positively) Fabricius discard Βουτύρου for Βοσμόρου, which "no fellow understands." A. Hamilton (i. 136) mentions "Wheat, Pulse, and *Butter*" as exports from *Mangaroul* on this coast. He does *not* mention *Bosmoron!*

parages de l'Inde. Ce que j'ai vu de plus grand, en fait de plumes d'oiseaux, c'est un tuyau que me montra Abou' l-Abbas de Siraf. Il était long de deux aunes environs capable, semblait-il, de contenir une outre d'eau.

"'J'ai vu dans l'Inde, me dit le capitaine Ismaïlawéih, chez un des principaux marschands, un tuyau de plume qui était près de sa maison, et dans lequel on versait de l'eau comme dans une grande tonne. . . . Ne sois pas étonné, me dit-il, car un capitaine du pays des Zindjs m'a conté qu'il avait vu chez le roi de Sira un tuyau de plume qui contenait vingt-cinq outres d'eau.'"—*Livre des Merveilles d'Inde.* (*Par Van der Lith* et *Marcel Devic*, pp. 62-63.)

ROCK-PIGEON. The bird so called by sportsmen in India is the *Pterocles exustus* of Temminck, belonging to the family of sand-grouse (*Pteroclidae*). It occurs throughout India, except in the more wooded parts. In their swift high flight these birds look something like pigeons on the wing, whence perhaps the misnomer.

ROGUE (Elephant), s. An elephant (generally, if not always a male) living in apparent isolation from any herd, usually a bold marauder, and a danger to travellers. Such an elephant is called in Bengal, according to Williamson, *saun*, *i.e.* *sān* [Hind. *sānd*, Skt. *shanda*]; sometimes it would seem *gundā* [Hind. *gundā*, 'a rascal']; and by the Sinhalese *hora*. The term *rogue* is used by Europeans in Ceylon, and its origin is somewhat obscure. Sir Emerson Tennent finds such an elephant called, in a curious book of the 18th century, *ronkedor* or *runkedor*, of which he supposes that *rogue* may perhaps have been a modification. That word looks like Port. *roncador*, 'a snorer, a noisy fellow, a bully,' which gives a plausible sense. But Littré gives *rogue* as a colloquial French word conveying the idea of arrogance and rudeness. In the following passage which we have copied, unfortunately without recording the source, the word comes still nearer the sense in which it is applied to the elephant: "On commence à s'apperceuoir dés Bayonne, que l'humeur de ces peuples tient vn peu de celle de ses voisins, et qu'ils sont *rogues* et peu communicatifs avec l'Estranger." After all however it is most likely that the word is derived from an English use of the word. For Skeat shows that *rogue*, from the French sense of 'malapert, saucy, rude, surly,' came to be applied as a cant term to beggars, and is used, in some old English passages which he quotes, exactly in the sense of our modern 'tramp.' The transfer to a vagabond elephant would be easy. Mr. Skeat refers to Shakspeare:—

"And wast thou fain, poor father,
To hovel thee with swine, and **rogues** forlorn?"
K. Lear, iv. 7.

1878.—"Much misconception exists on the subject of **rogue** or solitary elephants. The usually accepted belief that these elephants are turned out of the herds by their companions or rivals is not correct. Most of the so-called solitary elephants are the lords of some herds near. They leave their companions at times to roam by themselves, usually to visit cultivation or open country . . . sometimes again they make the expedition merely for the sake of solitude. They, however, keep more or less to the jungle where their herd is, and follow its movements."—*Sanderson*, p. 52.

ROGUE'S RIVER, n.p. The name given by Europeans in the 17th and 18th centuries to one of the Sunderbund channels joining the Lower Hoogly R. from the eastward. It was so called from being frequented by the Arakan Rovers, sometimes Portuguese vagabonds, sometimes native **Muggs**, whose vessels lay in this creek watching their opportunity to plunder craft going up and down the Hoogly.

Mr. R. Barlow, who has partially annotated *Hedges' Diary* for the Hakluyt Society, identifies Rogue's River with Channel Creek, which is the channel between Saugor Island and the Delta. Mr. Barlow was, I believe, a member of the Bengal Pilot service, and this, therefore, must have been the application of the name in recent tradition. But I cannot reconcile this with the sailing directions in the *English Pilot* (1711), or the indications in Hamilton, quoted below.

The *English Pilot* has a sketch chart of the river, which shows, just opposite Buffalo Point, "*R. Theeves*," then, as we descend, the *R. Rangafula*, and, close below that, "*Rogues*" (without the word *River*), and still further below, *Chanell Creek* or *R. Jessore*. Rangafula R. and Channel Creek we still have in the charts.

After a careful comparison of all the notices, and of the old and modern charts, I come to the conclusion that the R. of Rogues must have been either what is now called *Chingrī Khāl*, entering immediately below **Diamond Harbour**, or *Kalpī* Creek, about 6 m. further down, but the preponderance of argument is in favour of *Chingrī Khāl*. The position of this quite corresponds with the *R. Theeves* of the old English chart; it corresponds in distance from Saugor (the *Gunga Saugor* of those days, which forms the extreme S. of what is styled *Saugor Island* now) with that stated by Hamilton, and also in being close to the "first safe anchoring place in the River," viz. Diamond Harbour. The Rogue's River was apparently a little 'above the head of the Grand Middle Ground' or great shoals of the Hoogly, whose upper termination is now some 7½ m. below Chingrī Khāl. One of the extracts from the *English Pilot* speaks of the "R. of Rogues, commonly called by the Country People, *Adegom*." Now there is a town on the Chingrī Khāl, a few miles from its entrance into the Hoogly, which is called in Rennell's Map *Ottogunge*, and in the *Atlas of India* Sheet *Huttoogum*. Further, in the tracing of an old Dutch chart of the 17th century, in the India Office, I find in a position corresponding with Chingrī Khāl, *D'Roevers Spruit*, which I take to be 'Robber's (or **Rogue's**) **River**.'

1683.—"And so we parted for this night, before which time it was resolved by ye Councill that if I should not prevail to go this way to Decca, I should attempt to do it with ye Sloopes by way of the **River of Rogues**, which goes through to the great River of Decca."—*Hedges, Diary*, Hak. Soc. i. 36.

1711.—"*Directions to go up along the Western Shore.* . . . The nearer the Shore the better the Ground until past the River of Tygers.* You may begin to edge over towards the **River of Rogues** about the head of the Grand Middle Ground; and when the *Buffalow* Point bears from you ¼ N. ¾ of a Mile, steer directly over for the East Shore E.N.E."—*The English Pilot*, Pt. iii. p. 54.

,, "*Mr. Herring, the Pilot's Directions for bringing of Ships down the River of Hughley.* . . . From the lower point of the *Narrows* on the Starboard side . . . the Eastern Shore is to be kept close aboard, until past the said Creek, afterwards allowing only a small Birth for the Point off the **River of Rogues**, commonly called by the Country People, Adegom. . . . From the **River Rogues**, the Starboard (qu. larboard?) shore with a great ship ought to be kept close aboard all along down to Channel Trees, for in the offing lies the Grand Middle Ground."—*Ibid.* p. 57.

1727.—"The first safe anchoring Place in the River, is off the Mouth of a River about 12 Leagues above Sagor,* commonly known by the Name of **Rogues River**, which had that Appellation from some *Banditti Portuguese*, who were followers of *Shah Sujah* . . . for those Portuguese . . . after their Master's Flight to the Kingdom of *Arackan*, betook themselves to Piracy among the Islands at the Mouth of the *Ganges*, and this River having communication with all the Channels from *Xatigam* (see **CHITTAGONG**) to the Westward, from this River they used to sally out."—*A. Hamilton*, ii. 3 [ed. 1744].

1752.—". . . 'On the receipt of your Honors' orders per *Dunnington*, we sent for Capt. Pinson, the Master Attendant, and directed him to issue out fresh orders to the Pilots not to bring up any of your Honors' Ships higher than **Rogues River**.'"*—*Letter to Court*, in *Long*, p. 32.

ROHILLA, n.p. A name by which Afghāns, or more particularly Afghāns settled in Hindustan, are sometimes known, and which gave a title to the province *Rohilkand*, and now, through that, to a Division of the N.W. Provinces embracing a large part of the old province. The word appears to be Pushtu, *rōhēlah* or *rōhēlai*, adj., formed from *rōhu*, 'mountain,' thus signifying 'mountaineer of Afghānistān.' But a large part of E. Afghānistān specifically bore the name of *Roh*. Keene (*Fall of the Moghul Monarchy*, 41) puts the rise of the Rohillas of India in 1744, when 'Ali Mahommed revolted, and made the territory since called Rohilkhand independent. A very comprehensive application is given to the term *Roh* in the quotation from Firishta. A friend (Major J. M. Trotter) notes here: "The word **Rohilla** is little, if at all, used now in Pushtu, but I remember a line of an ode in that language, '*Sādik* **Rohilai** *yam pa Hindubār gad*,' meaning, 'I am a simple mountaineer, compelled to live in Hindustan'; *i.e.* 'an honest man among knaves.'"

* This is shown by a 17th century Dutch chart in I.O. to be a creek on the west side, very little below Diamond Point. It is also shown in Tassin's *Maps of the R. Hoogly*, 1835; not later.

* This also points to the locality of Diamond Harbour, and the Chingrī Khāl.

c. 1452.—"The King . . . issued *farmáns* to the chiefs of the various Afghán Tribes. On receipt of the *farmáns*, the Afgháns of **Roh** came as is their wont, like ants and locusts, to enter the King's service. . . . The King (Bahlol Lodi) commanded his nobles, saying,—'Every Afghán who comes to Hind from the country of **Roh** to enter my service, bring him to me. I will give him a *jágír* more than proportional to his deserts.'"—*Táríkh-i-Shír-Sháhí*, in *Elliot*, iv. 307.

c. 1542.—"Actuated by the pride of power, he took no account of clanship, which is much considered among the Afghans, and especially among the **Rohilla** men."—*Ibid.* 428.

c. 1612.—"**Roh** is the name of a particular mountain [-country], which extends in length from Swád and Bajaur to the town of Siwí belonging to Bhakar. In breadth it stretches from Hasan Abdál to Kábul. Kandahár is situated in this territory."—*Firishta's Introduction*, in *Elliot*, vi. 568.

1726.—". . . 1000 other horsemen called **Ruhelahs**."—*Valentijn*, iv. (*Suratte*), 277.

1745.—"This year the Emperor, at the request of Suffder Jung, marched to reduce Ali Mahummud Khan, a **Rohilla** adventurer, who had, from the negligence of the Government, possessed himself of the district of Kutteer (*Kathehar*), and assumed independence of the royal authority."—In Vol. II. of *Scott's* E.T. of *Hist. of the Dekkan*, &c., p. 218.

1763.—"After all the **Rohilas** are but the best of a race of men, in whose blood it would be difficult to find one or two single individuals endowed with good nature and with sentiments of equity; in a word they are **Afghans**."—*Seir Mutaqherin*, iii. 240.

1786.—"That the said Warren Hastings . . . did in September, 1773, enter into a private engagement with the said Nabob of Oude . . . to furnish them, for a stipulated sum of money to be paid to the E. I. Company, with a body of troops for the declared purpose of 'thoroughly extirpating the nation of the **Rohillas**'; a nation from whom the Company had never received, or pretended to receive, or apprehend, any injury whatever."—*Art. of Charge against Hastings*, in *Burke*, vi. 568.

ROLONG, s. Used in S. India, and formerly in W. India, for fine flour; semolina, or what is called in Bengal **soojee** (q.v.). The word is a corruption of Port. *rolão* or *ralão*. But this is explained by Bluteau as *farina secunda*. It is, he says (in Portuguese), that substance which is extracted between the best flour and the bran.

1813.—"Some of the greatest delicacies in India are now made from the **rolong**-flour, which is called the heart or kidney of the wheat."—*Forbes*, *Or. Mem.* i. 47; [2nd ed. i. 32].

ROOCKA, ROCCA, ROOKA, s.

a. Ar. *ruk'a*. A letter, a written document; a note of hand.

1680.—"One Sheake Ahmud came to Towne slyly with several peons dropping after him, bringing letters from Futty Chaun at Chingalhatt, and **Ruccas** from the Ser Lascar. . . ."—*Fort St. Geo. Consns.* May 25. In *Notes and Exts.* iii. 20. [See also under **AUMILDAR** and **JUNCAMEER**.]

" ". . . proposing to give 200 Pagodas Madaras Brahminy to obtain a **Rocca** from the Nabob that our business might go on Salabad (see **SALLABAD**)."—*Ibid.* Sept. 27, p. 35.

[1727.—"Swan . . . holding his Petition or **Rocca** above his head . . ."—*A. Hamilton*, ed. 1744, i. 199.]

[**b**. An ancient coin in S. India; Tel. *rokkam*, *rokkamu*, Skt. *roka*, 'buying with ready money,' from *ruch*, 'to shine.'

[1875.—"The old native coins seem to have consisted of Varaghans, **rookas** and Doodoos. The Varaghan is what is now generally called a **pagoda**. . . . The **rookas** have now entirely disappeared, and have probably been melted into rupees. They varied in value from 1 to 2 Rupees. Though the coins have disappeared, the name still survives, and the ordinary name for silver money generally is **rookaloo**."—*Gribble*, *Man. of Cuddapah*, 296 *seq*.]

ROOK, s. In chess the *rook* comes to us from Span. *roque*, and that from Ar. and Pers. *rukh*, which is properly the name of the famous gryphon, the **roc** of Marco Polo and the *Arabian Nights*. According to Marcel Devic it meant 'warrior.' It is however generally believed that this form was a mistake in transferring the Indian *rath* (see **RUT**) or 'chariot,' the name of the piece in India.

ROOM, n.p. 'Turkey' (*Rūm*); **ROOMEE**, n.p. (*Rūmī*); 'an Ottoman Turk.' Properly 'a Roman.' In older Oriental books it is used for an European, and was probably the word which Marco Polo renders as '*a Latin*'—represented in later times by **firinghee** (*e.g.* see quotation from Ibn Batuta under **RAJA**). But *Rūm*, for the Roman Empire, continued to be applied to what had been part of the Roman Empire after it had fallen into the hands of the Turks, first to the Seljukian Kingdom in Anatolia, and afterwards to the Ottoman Empire seated at Constantinople. Garcia de Orta and Jarric deny the name of *Rūmī*, as used in India, to the Turks of Asia, but they are apparently wrong in their expressions. What they seem to mean is that Turks of the Ottoman Empire were called *Rūmī*; whereas those others in Asia of Turkish race (whom we sometimes call *Toorks*), as of Persia and Turkestan, were excluded from the name.

c. 1508.—"Ad haec, trans euripum, seu fretum, quod insulam fecit, in orientali continentis plaga oppidum condidit, receptaculum advenis militibus, maximo Turcis; ut ab Diensibus freto divisi, rixandi cum iis . . . causas procul haberent. Id oppidum primo Gogola (see **GOGOLLA**), dein **Rumepolis** vocitatum ab ipsa re. . . ."—*Maffei*, p. 77.

1510.—"When we had sailed about 12 days we arrived at a city which is called *Diuobandier***rumi**, that is '**Diu**, the port of the Turks.' . . . This city is subject to the Sultan of Combeia . . . 400 Turkish merchants reside here constantly."—*Varthema*, 91-92.

Bandar-i-Rūmī is, as the traveller explains, the 'Port of the Turks.' Gogola, a suburb of Diu on the mainland, was known to the Portuguese some years later, as *Villa dos Rumes* (see **GOGOLLA**, and quotation from Maffei above). The quotation below from Damian a Goes alludes apparently to Gogola.

1513.—". . . Vnde **Ruminū** Turchorūque sex millia nostros continue infestabāt."—*Emanuelis Regis Epistola*, p. 21.

1514.—"They were ships belonging to Moors, or to **Romi** (there they give the name of **Romi** to a white people who are, some of them, from Armenia the Greater and the Less, others from Circassia and Tartary and Rossia, Turks and Persians of Shaesmal called the *Soffi*, and other renegades from all) countries."—*Giov. da Empoli*, 38.

1525.—In the expenditure of Malik Aiaz we find 30 **Rumes** at the pay (monthly) of 100 *fedeas* each. The *Arabis* are in the same statement paid 40 and 50 **fedeas**, the *Coraçones* (Khorāsānīs) the same; Guzerates and *Cymdes* (*Sindis*) 25 and 30 *fedeas*; *Fartaquis*, 50 *fedeas*.—*Lembrança*, 37.

1549.—". . . in nova civitate quae **Rhomaeum** appellatur. Nomen inditum est **Rhomaeis**, quasi Rhomanis, vocantur enim in totâ Indiâ **Rhomaei** ii, quos nos communi nomine *Geniceros* (*i.e.* Janisaries) vocamus. . . ."—*Damiani a Goes, Diensis Oppugnatio*—in *De Rebus Hispanicis Lusitanicis, Aragonicis, Indicis et Aethiopicis*. . . . Opera, Colon. Agr., 1602, p. 281.

1553.—"The Moors of India not understanding the distinctions of those Provinces of Europe, call the whole of Thrace, Greece, Sclavonia, and the adjacent islands of the Mediterranean **Rum**, and the men thereof **Rumi**, a name which properly belongs to that part of Thrace in which lies Constantinople: from the name of New Rome belonging to the latter, Thrace taking that of Romania."—*Barros*, IV. iv. 16.

1554.—"Also the said ambassador promised in the name of Idalshaa (see **IDALCAN**) his lord, that if a fleet of **Rumes** should invade these parts, Idalshaa should be bound to help and succour us with provisions and mariners at our expense. . . ."—*S. Botelho, Tombo*, 42.

c. 1555.—"One day (the Emp. Humāyūn) asked me: 'Which of the two countries is greatest, that of **Rūm** or of Hindustan?' I replied: . . . 'If by **Rūm** you mean all the countries subject to the Emperor of Constantinople, then India would not form even a sixth part thereof.' . . ."—*Sidi 'Ali*, in *J. As.*, ser. I. tom. ix. 148.

1563.—"The *Turks* are those of the province of Natolia, or (as we now say) Asia Minor; the **Rumes** are those of Constantinople, and of its empire."—*Garcia De Orta*, f. 7.

1572.—

"Persas feroces, Abassis, e **Rumes**,
Que trazido de Roma o nome tem. . . ."
Camões, x. 68.

[By Aubertin:

"Fierce Persians, Abyssinians, **Rumians**,
Whose appellation doth from Rome descend. . . ."]

1579.—"Without the house . . . stood foure ancient comely hoare-headed men, cloathed all in red downe to the ground, but attired on their heads not much vnlike the Turkes; these they call **Romans**, or strangers. . . ."—*Drake, World Encompassed*, Hak. Soc. 143.

1600.—"A nation called **Rumos** who have traded many hundred years to Achen. These **Rumos** come from the Red Sea."—*Capt. J. Davis*, in *Purchas*, i. 117.

1612.—"It happened on a time that Rajah Sekunder, the Son of Rajah Darab, a *Roman* (**Rumi**), the name of whose country was Macedonia, and whose title was Zul-Karneini, wished to see the rising of the sun, and with this view he reached the confines of India."—*Sijara Malayu*, in *J. Indian Archip.* v. 125.

1616.—"**Rumae**, id est Turcae Europaei. In India quippe duplex militum Turcaeorum genus, quorum primi, in Asia orti, qui *Turcae* dicuntur; alii in Europa qui Constantinopoli quae olim Roma Nova, advocantur, ideoque **Rumae**, tam ab Indis quam a Lusitanis nomine Graeco 'Ρωμαῖοι in **Rumas** depravato dicuntur."—*Jarric, Thesaurus*, ii. 105.

1634.—

"Alli o forte Pacheco se eterniza
Sustentando incansavel o adquirido;
Depois Almeida, que as Estrellas piza
Se fez do **Rume**, e Malavar temido."
Malaca Conquistada, ii. 18.

1781. — "These Espanyols are a very western nation, always at war with the **Roman** Emperors (*i.e.* the Turkish Sultans); since the latter took from them the city of Ashtenbol (*Istambūl*), about 500 years ago, in which time they have not ceased to wage war with the **Roumees**."—*Seir Mutaqherin*, iii. 336.

1785. — "We herewith transmit a letter . . . in which an account is given of the conference going on between the Sultan of **Room** and the English ambassador." —*Letters of Tippoo*, p. 224.

ROOMAUL, s. Hind. from Pers. *rūmāl* (lit. 'face-rubber,') a towel, a handkerchief. ["In modern native use it may be carried in the hand by a high-born *parda* lady attached to her *batwa* or tiny silk handbag, and ornamented with all sorts of gold and silver trinkets; then it is a handkerchief in the true sense of the word. It may be carried by men, hanging on the left shoulder, and used to wipe the hands or face; then, too, it is a handkerchief. It may be as big as a towel, and thrown over both shoulders by men, the ends either hanging loose or tied in a knot in front; it then serves the purpose of a *gulūband* or muffler. In the case of children it is tied round the neck as a neckkerchief, or round the waist for mere show. It may be used by women much as the 18th century tucker was used in England in Addison's time" (*Yusuf Ali*, *Mon. on Silk*, 79; for its use to mark a kind of shawl, see Forbes Watson, *Textile Manufactures*, 123).] In ordinary Anglo-Indian Hind. it is the word for a 'pocket handkerchief.' In modern trade it is applied to thin silk piece-goods with handkerchief-patterns. We are not certain of its meaning in the old trade of piece-goods, *e.g.*:

[1615. — "2 handkerchiefs **Rumall** cottony."—*Cocks's Diary*, Hak. Soc. i. 179.

[1665.—"Towel, **Rumale**."—*Persian Glossary*, in *Sir T. Herbert*, ed. 1677, p. 100.

[1684. — "**Romalls** Courge . . . 16."—*Pringle, Diary Ft. St. Geo.*, 1st ser. iii. 119.]

1704. — "Price Currant (Malacca) . . . **Romalls**, Bengall ordinary, per Corge, 26 Rix Dlls."—*Lockyer*, 71.

1726.—"**Roemaals**, 80 pieces in a pack, 45 ells long, $1\frac{1}{2}$ broad."—*Valentijn*, v. 178.

Rūmāl was also the name technically used by the **Thugs** for the handkerchief with which they strangled their victims.

[c. 1833.—"There is no doubt but that all the Thugs are expert in the use of the handkerchief, which is called **Roomal** or *Paloo*. . . ."—*Wolff, Travels*, ii. 180.]

ROSALGAT, CAPE, n.p. The most easterly point of the coast of Arabia; a corruption (originally Portuguese) of the Arabic name *Rās-al-ḥadd*, as explained by P. della Valle, with his usual acuteness and precision, below.

1553. — "From **Curia Muria** to Cape **Rosalgate**, which is in $22\frac{1}{2}°$, an extent of coast of 120 leagues, all the land is barren and desert. At this Cape commences the Kingdom of Ormus."—*Barros*, I. ix. 1.

,, "Affonso d'Alboquerque . . . passing to the Coast of Arabia ran along till he doubled **Cape Roçalgate**, which stands at the beginning of that coast . . . which Cape Ptolemy calls *Siragros Promontory* (Συαγρος ἄκρα). . . ."—*Ibid.* II. ii. 1.

c. 1554.—"We had been some days at sea, when near **Rā'is-al-hadd** the *Damani*, a violent wind so called, got up. . . ."—*Sidi 'Ali, J. As. S.* ser. I. tom. ix. 75.

,, "If you wish to go from **Rásolhadd** to *Dûlsind* (see **DIUL-SIND**) you steer E.N.E. till you come to Pasani . . . from thence . . . E. by S. to *Rás Karáshi* (*i.e.* Karāchī), where you come to an anchor. . . ."—*The Mohit* (by *Sidi 'Ali*), in *J.A.S.B.*, v. 459.

1572.—

"Olha Dofar insigne, porque manda
O mais cheiroso incenso para as aras;
Mas attenta, já cá est' outra banda
De **Roçalgate**, o praias semper avaras,
Começa o regno Ormus. . . ."
Camões, x. 101.

By Burton:

"Behold insign Dofar that doth command
for Christian altars sweetest incense-store;
But note, beginning now on further band
of **Roçalgaté's** ever greedy shore,
yon Hormus Kingdom. . . ."

1623.—"We began meanwhile to find the sea rising considerably; and having by this time got clear of the Strait . . . and having past not only Cape Iasck on the Persian side, but also that cape on the Arabian side which the Portuguese vulgarly call **Rosalgate**, as you also find it marked in maps, but the proper name of which is **Ras el had**, signifying in the Arabic tongue Cape of the End or Boundary, because it is in fact the extreme end of that Country . . . just as in our own Europe the point of Galizia is called by us for a like reason *Finis Terrae*." —*P. della Valle*, ii. 496; [Hak. Soc. ii. 11].

[1665.—". . . **Rozelgate** formerly *Corodamum* and *Maces* in *Amian. lib.* 23, almost *Nadyr* to the Tropick of *Cancer*."—*Sir T. Herbert*, ed. 1677, p. 101.]

1727.—"*Maceira*, a barren uninhabited Island . . . within 20 leagues of Cape

Rasselgat."—*A. Hamilton*, i. 56; [ed. 1744, i. 57].

[1823.—". . . it appeared that the whole coast of Arabia, from **Ras al had**, or Cape **Raselgat**, as it is sometimes called by the English, was but little known. . . ."—*Owen, Narr.* i. 333.]

ROSE-APPLE. See **JAMBOO.**

ROSELLE, s. The Indian Hibiscus or *Hib. sabdariffa*, L. The fleshy calyx makes an excellent sub-acid jelly, and is used also for tarts; also called 'Red Sorrel.' The French call it 'Guinea Sorrel,' *Oseille* de Guinée, and *Roselle* is probably a corruption of *Oseille*. [See **PUTWA.**]

[**ROSE-MALLOWS**, s. A semi-fluid resin, the product of the *Liquidambar altingia*, which grows in Tenasserim; also known as Liquid Storax, and used for various medicinal purposes. (See *Hanbury and Flückiger, Pharmacog.* 271, *Watt, Econ. Dict.* V. 78 *seqq.*). The Burmese name of the tree is *nan-ta-yoke* (*Mason, Burmah*, 778). The word is a corruption of the Malay-Javanese *rasamalla*, Skt. *rasa-mālā*, 'Perfume garland,' the gum being used as incense (*Encycl. Britann.* 9th ed. xii. 718.)

1598.—"**Rosamallia.**"—*Linschoten*, Hak. Soc. i. 150.]

ROTTLE, RATTLE, s. Arab. *raṭl* or *riṭl*, the Arabian pound, becoming in S. Ital. *rotolo*; in Port. *arratel*; in Span. *arrelde*; supposed to be originally a transposition of the Greek λίτρα, which went all over the Semitic East. It is in Syriac as *lītrā*; and is also found as *lītrīm* (pl.) in a Phoenician inscription of Sardinia, dating c. B.C. 180 (see *Corpus Inscriptt. Semitt.* i. 188-189.)

c. 1340.—"The **ritl** of India which is called *sīr* (see **SEER**) weighs 70 *mithkāls* . . . 40 *sīrs* form a *mann* (see **MAUND**)."—*Shihābuddīn Dimishkī*, in *Notes and Exts.* xiii. 189.

[c. 1590.—"*Kafīz* is a measure, called also *sāā'* weighing 8 **ratl**, and, some say, more."—*Āīn*, ed. *Jarrett*, ii. 55.

[1612.—"The **bahar** is 360 **rottolas** of Moha."—*Danvers, Letters*, i. 193.]

1673.—". . . Weights in Goa:
1 *Baharr* is ... 3½ *Kintal.*
1 *Kintal* is ... 4 *Arobel* or *Rovel.*
1 *Arobel* is ... 32 **Rotolas.**
1 **Rotola** is ... 16 Ounc. or 1*l. Averd.*"
Fryer, 207.

1803.—"At Judda the weights are:
15 Vakeeas = 1 **Rattle.**
2 **Rattles** = 1 maund."
Milburn, i. 88.

ROUND, s. This is used as a Hind. word, *raund*, or corruptly *raun gasht*, a transfer of the English, in the sense of patrolling, or 'going the rounds.' [And we find in the Madras Records the grade of 'Rounder,' or 'Gentlemen of the Round,' officers whose duty it was to visit the sentries.

[1683.—". . . itt is order'd that 18 Souldiers, 1 Corporall & 1 **Rounder** goe upon the Sloop Conimer for Hugly. . . ."—*Pringle, Diary Ft. St. Geo.* 1st ser. ii. 33.]

ROUNDEL, s. An obsolete word for an umbrella, formerly in use in Anglo-India. [In 1676 the use of the *Roundell* was prohibited, except in the case of "the Councell and Chaplaine" (*Hedges, Diary*, Hak. Soc. ii. ccxxxii.)] In old English the name *roundel* is applied to a variety of circular objects, as a mat under a dish, a target, &c. And probably this is the origin of the present application, in spite of the circumstance that the word is sometimes found in the form *arundel*. In this form the word also seems to have been employed for the conical hand-guard on a lance, as we learn from Bluteau's great *Port. Dictionary*: "**Arundela**, or **Arandella**, is a guard for the right hand, in the form of a funnel. It is fixed to the thick part of the lance or mace borne by men at arms. The Licentiate Covarrubias, who piques himself on finding etymologies for every kind of word, derives *Arandella* from *Arundel*, a city (so he says) of the Kingdom of England." Cobarruvias (1611) gives the above explanation; adding that it also was applied to a kind of smooth collar worn by women, from its resemblance to the other thing. Unless historical proof of this last etymology can be traced, we should suppose that *Arundel* is, even in this sense, probably a corruption of *roundel*. [The *N.E.D.* gives *arrondell*, *arundell* as forms of *hirondelle*, 'a swallow.']

1673.—"Lusty Fellows running by their Sides with **Arundels** (which are broad Umbrelloes held over their Heads)."—*Fryer*, 30.

1676.—"Proposals to the Agent, &c., about the young men in Metchlipatam.
"*Generall.* I.—Whereas each hath his peon and some more with their **Rondells**,

that none be permitted but as at the Fort." —*Ft. St. Geo. Consn.*, Feb. 16. In *Notes and Exts.* No. I. p. 43.

1677-78.—". . . That except by the Members of this Councell, those that have formerly been in that quality, Cheefes of Factorys, Commanders of Shipps out of England, and the Chaplains, **Rundells** shall not be worne by any Men in this Towne, and by no Woman below the Degree of Factors' Wives and Ensigns' Wives, except by such as the Governour shall permit." —*Madras Standing Orders*, in *Wheeler*, iii. 438.

1680.—"To Verona (the Company's Chief Merchant)'s adopted son was given the name of Muddoo Verona, and a **Rundell** to be carried over him, in respect to the memory of Verona, eleven cannon being fired, that the Towne and Country might take notice of the honour done them."—*Ft. St. Geo. Consn.* In *Notes and Exts.* No. II. p. 15.

1716.—"All such as serve under the Honourable Company and the English Inhabitants, deserted their Employs; such as Cooks, Water bearers, Coolies, Palankeen-boys, **Roundel** men. . . ."—In *Wheeler*, ii. 230.

1726.—"Whenever the magnates go on a journey they go not without a considerable train, being attended by their pipers, horn-blowers, and **Rondel** bearers, who keep them from the Sun with a **Rondel** (which is a kind of little round sunshade)."—*Valentijn*, *Chor.* 54.

" "Their Priests go like the rest clothed in yellow, but with the right arm and breast remaining uncovered. They also carry a **rondel**, or parasol, of a *Tallipot* (see **TALIPOT**) leaf. . . ."—*Ibid.* v. (*Ceylon*), 408.

1754.—"Some years before our arrival in the country, they (the E. I. Co.) found such sumptuary laws so absolutely necessary, that they gave the strictest orders that none of these young gentlemen should be allowed even to hire a **Roundel-boy**, whose business it is to walk by his master, and defend him with his **Roundel** or Umbrella from the heat of the sun. A young fellow of humour, upon this last order coming over, altered the form of his Umbrella from a round to a square, called it a *Squaredel* instead of a **Roundel**, and insisted that no order yet in force forbad him the use of it."—*Ives*, 21.

1785.—"He (Clive) enforced the Sumptuary laws by severe penalties, and gave the strictest orders that none of these young gentlemen should be allowed even to have a **roundel-boy**, whose business is to walk by his master, and defend him with his **roundel** or umbrella from the heat of the sun."—*Carraccioli*, i. 283. This ignoble writer has evidently copied from Ives, and applied the passage (untruly, no doubt) to Clive.

ROWANNAH, s. Hind. from Pers. *rawānah*, from *rawā*, 'going.' A pass or permit.

[1764.—". . . that the English shall carry on their trade . . . free from all duties . . . excepting the article of salt, . . . on which a duty is to be levied on the **Rowana** or Houghly market-price. . . ."—*Letter from Court*, in *Verelst, View of Bengal*, App. 127.]

ROWCE, s. Hind. *raus, rois, rauns.* A Himālayan tree which supplies excellent straight and strong alpenstocks and walking-sticks, *Cotoneaster bacillaris*, Wall., also *C. acuminata* (N.O. *Rosaceae*). [See Watt, *Econ. Dict.* ii. 581.]

1838.—"We descended into the **Khud**, and I was amusing myself jumping from rock to rock, and thus passing up the centre of the brawling mountain stream, aided by my long *pahārī* pole of **rous** wood." —*Wanderings of a Pilgrim*, ii. 241; [also i. 112].

ROWNEE, s.

a. A fausse-braye, *i.e.* a subsidiary enceinte surrounding a fortified place on the outside of the proper wall and on the edge of the ditch; Hind. *raonī*. The word is not in Shakespear, Wilson, Platts or Fallon. But it occurs often in the narratives of Anglo-Indian siege operations. The origin of the word is obscure. [Mr. Irvine suggests Hind. *rūndhnā*, 'to enclose as with a hedge,' and says: "Fallon evidently knew nothing of the word *raunī*, for in his *E. H. Dict.* he translates fausse-braye by *dhus, mattī kā pushtah;* which also shows that he had no definite idea of what a fausse-braye was, *dhus* meaning simply an earthen or mud fort." Dr. Grierson suggests Hind. *ramanā*, 'a park,' of which the fem., *i.e.* diminutive, would be *ramanī* or *rāonī;* or possibly the word may come from Hind. *rev*, Skt. *reṇu*, 'sand,' meaning "an entrenchment of sand."]

1799.—"On the 20th I ordered a mine to be carried under (the glacis) because the guns could not bear on the **rounee**."—*Jas. Skinner's Mil. Memoirs*, i. 172. J. B. Fraser, the editor of Skinner, parenthetically interprets *rounee* here as 'counterscarp'; but that is nonsense, as well as incorrect.

[1803.—Writing of Hathras, "**Renny** wall, with a deep, broad, dry ditch behind it surrounds the fort."—*W. Thorn, Mem. of the War in India*, p. 400.]

1805.—In a work by Major L. F. Smith (*Sketch of the Rise, &c., of the Regular Corps in the Service of the Native Princes of India*) we find a plan of the attack of Aligarh, in which is marked "Lower Fort or **Renny**, well supplied with grape," and again, "Lower Fort, **Renny** or Faussebraye."

[1819.—". . . they saw the necessity of covering the foot of the wall from an enemy's fire, and formed a defence, similar to our fausse-braye, which they call **Rainee**."—*Fitzclarence, Journal of a Route to England*, p. 245; also see 110.]

b. This word also occurs as representative of the Burmese *yo-wet-ni*, or (in Arakan pron.) *ro-wet-ni*, 'red-leaf,' the technical name of the standard silver of the Burmese ingot currency, commonly rendered **Flowered-silver**.

1796.—"**Rouni** or fine silver, Ummerapoora currency."—*Notification* in *Seton-Karr*, ii. 179.

1800.—"The quantity of alloy varies in the silver current in different parts of the empire; at Rangoon it is adulterated 25 per cent.; at Ummerapoora, pure, or what is called **flowered silver**, is most common; in the latter all duties are paid. The modifications are as follows:

"**Rouni**, or pure silver.
Rounika, 5 per cent. of alloy."
Symes, 327.

ROWTEE, s. A kind of small tent with pyramidal roof, and no projection of fly, or eaves. Hind. *rāoṭī*.

[1813.—". . . the military men, and others attached to the camp, generally possess a dwelling of somewhat more comfortable description, regularly made of two or three folds of cloth in thickness, closed at one end, and having a flap to keep out the wind and rain at the opposite one: these are dignified with the name of **ruotees**, and come nearer (than the **pawl**) to our ideas of a tent."—*Broughton, Letters*, ed. *Constable*, p. 20.

[1875.—"For the servants I had a good **rauti** of thick lined cloth."—*Wilson, Abode of Snow*, 90.]

ROY, s. A common mode of writing the title *rāī* (see **RAJA**); which sometimes occurs also as a family name, as in that of the famous Hindu Theist Rammohun **Roy**.

ROZA, s. Ar. *rauḍa*, Hind. *rauza*. Properly a garden; among the Arabs especially the *rauḍa* of the great mosque at Medina. In India it is applied to such mausolea as the **Taj** (generally called by the natives the *Tāj-rauza*); and the mausoleum built by Aurungzīb near Aurungābād.

1813.—". . . the **roza**, a name for the mausoleum, but implying something saintly or sanctified."—*Forbes, Or. Mem.* iv. 41; [2nd ed. ii. 413].

ROZYE, s. Hind. *razāī* and *rajāī*; a coverlet quilted with cotton. The etymology is very obscure. It is spelt in Hind. with the Ar. letter *zwād*; and F. Johnson gives a Persian word so spelt as meaning 'a cover for the head in winter.' The kindred meaning of *mirzāī* is apt to suggest a connection between the two, but this may be accidental, or the latter word factitious. We can see no likelihood in Shakespear's suggestion that it is a corruption of an alleged Skt. *rañjika*, 'cloth.' [Platts gives the same explanation, adding "probably through Pers. *razā'i*, from *razīdan*, 'to dye.'"] The most probable suggestion perhaps is that *razāī* was a word taken from the name of some person called *Razā*, who may have invented some variety of the article; as in the case of *Spencer*, *Wellingtons*, &c. A somewhat obscure quotation from the Pers. Dict. called *Bahār-i-Ajam*, extracted by Vüllers (s.v.), seems to corroborate the suggestion of a *personal* origin of the word.

1784.—"I have this morning . . . received a letter from the Prince addressed to you, with a present of a **rezy** and a shawl handkerchief."—*Warren Hastings to his Wife*, in *Busteed, Echoes of Old Calcutta*, 195.

1834.—"I arrived in a small open pavilion at the top of the building, in which there was a small Brahminy cow, clothed in a wadded **resai**, and lying upon a carpet."—*Mem. of Col. Mountain*, 135.

1857. — (Imports into Kandahar, from Mashad and Khorasan) "**Razaies** from Yezd. . . ."—*Punjab Trade Report*, App. p. lxviii.

1867.—"I had brought with me a soft quilted **rezai** to sleep on, and with a rug wrapped round me, and sword and pistol under my head, I lay and thought long and deeply upon my line of action on the morrow."—*Lieut.-Col. Lewin, A Fly on the Wheel*, 301.

RUBBEE, s. Ar. *rabi*, 'the Spring.' In India applied to the crops, or harvest of the crops, which are sown after the rains and reaped in the following spring or early summer. Such crops are wheat, barley, **gram**, linseed, tobacco, onions, carrots and turnips, &c. (See **KHURREEF**.)

[1765.—". . . we have granted them the Dewannee (see **DEWAUNY**) of the provinces of Bengal, Bahar, and Orissa, from the beginning of the Fussul **Rubby** of the Bengal year 1172. . . ."—*Firmaun of Shah Aaalum*, in *Verelst, View of Bengal*, App. 167.

[1866.—"It was in the month of November, when, if the rains closed early, irrigation is resorted to for producing the young **rubbee** crops."—*Confessions of an Orderly*, 179.]

RUBLE, s. Russ. The silver unit of Russian currency, when a coin (not paper) equivalent to 3*s.* 1½*d.*; [in 1901 about 2*s.* 1½*d.*]. It was originally a silver ingot; see first quotation and note below.

1559.—"Vix centum annos vtuntur moneta argentea, praesertim apud illos cusa. Initio cum argentum in provinciam inferebatur, fundebantur portiunculae oblongae argenteae, sine imagine et scriptura, aestimatione vnius **rubli**, quarum nulla nunc apparet." * *Herberstein*, in *Rerum Moscovit. Auctores*, Francof. 1600, p. 42.

1591.—"This penaltie or mulct is 20 *dingoes* (see **TANGA**) or pence upon every **rubble** or mark, and so ten in the hundred. . . . Hee (the Emperor) hath besides for every name conteyned in the writs that passe out of their courts, five *alteens*, an alteen 5 pence sterling or thereabouts."—*Treatise of the Russian Commonwealth*, by *Dr. Giles Fletcher*, Hak. Soc. 51.

c. 1654-6. — "Dog dollars they (the Russians) are not acquainted with, these being attended with loss . . . their own *dinârs* they call **Roubles**."—*Macarius*, E.T. by *Balfour*, i. 280.

[**RUFFUGUR**, s. P.—H. *rafūgar*, Pers. *rafū*, 'darning.' The modern *rafūgar* in Indian cities is a workman who repairs rents and holes in Kashmīr shawls and other woollen fabrics. Such workmen were regularly employed in the cloth factories of the E.I. Co., to examine the manufactured cloths and remove petty defects in the weaving.

1750.—"On inspecting the Dacca goods, we found the Seerbetties (see **PIECE-GOODS**) very much frayed and very badly **raffa-gūrr'd** or joined."—*Bengal Letter to E.I. Co.*, Feb. 25, India Office MSS.

1851. — "**Rafu-gars** are darners, who repair the cloths that have been damaged during bleaching. They join broken threads, remove knots from threads, &c."—*Taylor, Cotton Manufacture of Dacca*, 97.]

RUM, s. This is not an Indian word. The etymology is given by Wedgwood as from a slang word of the 16th century, *rome* for 'good'; *rome-booze*, 'good drink'; and so, *rum*. The English word has always with us a note of vulgarity, but we may note here that Gorresio in his Italian version of the Rāmāyaṇa, whilst describing the Palace of Rāvaṇa, is bold enough to speak of its being pervaded by "an odoriferous breeze, perfumed with sandalwood, and bdellium, with *rum* and with sirop" (iii. 292). "Mr. N. Darnell Davis has put forth a derivation of the word *rum*, which gives the only probable history of it. It came from Barbados, where the planters first distilled it, somewhere between 1640 and 1645. A MS. 'Description of Barbados,' in Trinity College, Dublin, written about 1651, says: 'The chief fudling they make in the Island is *Rumbullion*, alias *Kill-Divil*, and this is made of sugar-canes distilled, a hot, hellish, and terrible liqour.' G. Warren's *Description of Surinam*, 1661, shows the word in its present short term: '**Rum** is a spirit extracted from the juice of sugar-canes . . . called *Kill-Devil* in New England!' '*Rambullion*' is a Devonshire word, meaning 'a great tumult,' and may have been adopted from some of the Devonshire settlers in Barbados; at any rate, little doubt can exist that it has given rise to our word **rum**, and the longer name *rumbowling*, which sailors give to their grog."—*Academy*, Sept. 5, 1885.

RUM-JOHNNY, s. Two distinct meanings are ascribed to this vulgar word, both, we believe, obsolete.

a. It was applied, according to Williamson, (*V.M.*, i. 167) to a low class of native servants who plied on the wharves of Calcutta in order to obtain employment from new-comers. That author explains it as a corruption of *Ramazānī*, which he alleges to be one of the commonest of Mahommedan names. [The *Meery-jhony Gully* of Calcutta (*Carey, Good Old Days*, i.

* These ingots were called *saum*. Ibn Batuta says: "At one day's journey from Ukak are the hills of the Rūs, who are Christians; they have red hair and blue eyes, they are ugly in feature and crafty in character. They have silver mines, and they bring from their country *saum*, *i.e.* ingots of silver, with which they buy and sell in that country. The weight of each ingot is five ounces."—ii. 414. Pegolotti (c. 1340), speaking of the land-route to Cathay, says that on arriving at Cassai (*i.e. Kinsay* of Marco Polo or Hang-chau-fu) "you can dispose of the *sommi* of silver that you have with you . . . and you may reckon the *sommo* to be worth 5 golden florins" (see in *Cathay*, &c., ii. 288-9, 293). It would appear from Wasāf, quoted by Hammer (*Geschichte der Goldenen Horde*, 224), that gold ingots also were called *sum* or *saum*. The ruble is still called *sūm* in Turkestan.

139) perhaps in the same way derived its name from one *Mīr Jān*.]

1810.—"Generally speaking, the present *banians*, who attach themselves to the captains of European ships, may without the least hazard of controversion, be considered as nothing more or less than **Rum-johnnies** 'of a larger growth.'"—*Williamson, V.M.*, i. 191.

b. Among soldiers and sailors, 'a prostitute'; from Hind. *rāmjanī*, Skt. *rāmā-janī*, 'a pleasing woman,' 'a dancing-girl.'

[1799.—". . . and the **Rámjenís** (Hindu dancing women) have been all day dancing and singing before the idol."—*Colebrooke*, in *Life*, 153.]

1814.—"I lived near four years within a few miles of the solemn groves where those voluptuous devotees pass their lives with the **ramjannies** or dancing-girls attached to the temples, in a sort of luxurious superstition and sanctified indolence unknown in colder climates."—*Forbes, Or. Mem.* iii. 6; [2nd ed. ii. 127].

[1816.—"But we must except that class of females called **ravjannees**, or dancing-girls, who are attached to the temples."—*Asiatic Journal*, ii. 375, quoting *Wathen, Tour to Madras and China*.]

RUMNA, s. Hind. *ramnā*, Skt. *ramaṇa*, 'causing pleasure,' a chase, or reserved hunting-ground.

1760.—"Abdal Chab Cawn murdered at the **Rumna** in the month of March, 1760, by some of the Hercarahs. . . ."—*Van Sittart*, i. 63.

1792.—"The Peshwa having invited me to a novel spectacle at his **runma** (read *rumna*), or park, about four miles from Poonah. . . ."—*Sir C. Malet*, in *Forbes, Or. Mem.* [2nd ed. ii. 82]. (See also verses quoted under **PAWNEE**.)

RUNN (OF CUTCH), n.p. Hind. *raṉ*. This name, applied to the singular extent of sand-flat and salt-waste, often covered by high tides, or by land-floods, which extends between the Peninsula of Cutch and the mainland, is a corruption of the Skt. *irina* or *īriṇa*, 'a salt-swamp, a desert,' [or of *araṇya*, 'a wilderness']. The Runn is first mentioned in the *Periplus*, in which a true indication is given of this tract and its dangers.

c. A.D. 80-90.—"But after passing the Sinthus R. there is another gulph running to the north, not easily seen, which is called **Irinon**, and is distinguished into the Great and the Little. And there is an expanse of shallow water on both sides, and swift continual eddies extending far from the land."—*Periplus*, § 40.

c. 1370.—"The guides had maliciously misled them into a place called the **Kúnchi-ran**. In this place all the land is impregnated with salt, to a degree impossible to describe."—*Shams-i-Sirāj-Afīf*, in *Elliot*, iii. 324.

1583.—"Muzaffar fled, and crossed the **Ran**, which is an inlet of the sea, and took the road to Jessalmír. In some places the breadth of the water of the **Ran** is 10 *kos* and 20 *kos*. He went into the country which they call **Kach**, on the other side of the water."—*Tabaḳāt-i-Akbarī*, *Ibid.* v. 440.

c. 1590.—"Between Chalwaneh, Sircar Ahmedabad, Putten, and Surat, is a low tract of country, 90 cose in length, and in breadth from 7 to 30 cose, which is called **Run**. Before the commencement of the periodical rains, the sea swells and inundates this spot, and leaves by degrees after the rainy season."—*Ayeen*, ed. *Gladwin*, 1800, ii. 71; [ed. *Jarrett*, ii. 249].

1849.—"On the morning of the 24th I embarked and landed about 6 p.m. in the **Runn** of Sindh.

". . . a boggie syrtis, neither sea
Nor good dry land. . ."

Dry Leaves from Young Egypt, 14.

RUPEE, s. Hind. *rūpiya*, from Skt. *rūpya*, 'wrought silver.' The standard coin of the Anglo-Indian monetary system, as it was of the Mahommedan Empire that preceded ours. It is commonly stated (as by Wilson, in his article on this word, which contains much valuable and condensed information) that the rupee was introduced by Sher Shāh (in 1542). And this is, no doubt, formally true; but it is certain that a coin substantially identical with the rupee, *i.e.* approximating to a standard of 100 *ratis* (or 175 grains troy) of silver, an ancient Hindu standard, had been struck by the Mahommedan sovereigns of Delhi in the 13th and 14th centuries, and had formed an important part of their currency. In fact, the capital coins of Delhi, from the time of Iyaltimish (A.D. 1211-1236) to the accession of Mahommed Tughlak (1325) were gold and silver pieces, respectively of the weight just mentioned. We gather from the statements of Ibn Batuta and his contemporaries that the gold coin, which the former generally calls **tanga** and sometimes *gold* **dīnār**, was worth 10 of the silver coin, which he calls **dīnār**, thus indicating that the relation of gold to silver value was, or had recently been, as

10 : 1. Mahommed Tughlak remodelled the currency, issuing gold pieces of 200 grs. and silver pieces of 140 grs. —an indication probably of a great "depreciation of gold" (to use our modern language) consequent on the enormous amount of gold bullion obtained from the plunder of Western and Southern India. Some years later (1330) Mahommed developed his notable scheme of a forced currency, consisting entirely of copper tokens. This threw everything into confusion, and it was not till six years later that any sustained issues of ordinary coin were recommenced. From about this time the old standard of 175 grs. was readopted for gold, and was maintained till the time of Sher Shāh. But it does not appear that the old standard was then resumed for silver. In the reign of Mahommed's successor Feroz Shāh, Mr. E. Thomas's examples show the gold coin of 175 grs. standard running parallel with continued issues of a silver (or professedly silver) coin of 140 grs.; and this, speaking briefly, continued to be the case to the end of the Lodi dynasty (*i.e.* 1526). The coinage seems to have sunk into a state of great irregularity, not remedied by Baber (who struck *ashrafīs* (see **ASHRAFEE**) and *dirhams*, such as were used in Turkestan) or Humāyūn, but the reform of which was undertaken by Sher Shāh, as above mentioned.

His silver coin of 175-178 grs. was that which popularly obtained the name of *rūpiya*, which has continued to our day. The weight, indeed, of the coins so styled, never very accurate in native times, varied in different States, and the purity varied still more. The former never went very far on either side of 170 grs., but the quantity of pure silver contained in it sunk in some cases as low as 140 grs., and even, in exceptional cases, to 100 grs. Variation however was not confined to native States. Rupees were struck in Bombay at a very early date of the British occupation. Of these there are four specimens in the Br. Mus. The first bears *obv.* 'THE RVPEE OF BOMBAIM. 1677. BY AUTHORITY OF CHARLES THE SECOND; *rev.* KING OF GREAT BRITAINE . FRANCE . AND . IRELAND .' Wt. 167·8 gr. The fourth bears *obv.* 'HON . SOC . ANG . IND . ORI.' with a shield; *rev.* 'A . DEO . PAX . ET . INCREMENTUM :—MON . BOMBAY . ANGLIC . REGIM^{s}. A° 7°.' Weight 177·8 gr. Different *Rupees* minted by the British Government were current in the three Presidencies, and in the Bengal Presidency several were current; viz. the *Sikka* (see **SICCA**) Rupee, which latterly weighed 192 grs., and contained 176 grs. of pure silver; the *Farrukhābād*, which latterly weighed 180 grs.,* containing 165·215 of pure silver; the *Benares* Rupee (up to 1819), which weighed 174·76 grs., and contained 168·885 of pure silver. Besides these there was the *Chalānī* or 'current' rupee of account, in which the Company's accounts were kept, of which 116 were equal to 100 *sikkas*. ["The *bharī* or Company's Arcot rupee was coined at Calcutta, and was in value 3½ per cent. less than the Sikka rupee" (*Beveridge, Bakarganj*, 99).] The Bombay Rupee was adopted from that of Surat, and from 1800 its weight was 178·32 grs.; its pure silver 164·94. The Rupee at Madras (where however the standard currency was of an entirely different character, see **PAGODA**) was originally that of the Nawāb of the Carnatic (or 'Nabob of Arcot') and was usually known as the *Arcot* Rupee. We find its issues varying from 171 to 177 grs. in weight, and from 160 to 170 of pure silver; whilst in 1811 there took place an abnormal coinage, from Spanish dollars, of rupees with a weight of 188 grs. and 169·20 of pure silver.

Also from some reason or other, perhaps from commerce between those places and the '**Coast**,' the Chittagong and Dacca currency (*i.e.* in the extreme east of Bengal) "formerly consisted of Arcot rupees; and they were for some time coined expressly for those districts at the Calcutta and

* The term *Sonaut* rupees, which was of frequent occurrence down to the reformation and unification of the Indian coinage in 1833, is one very difficult to elucidate. The word is properly *sanwāt*, pl. of Ar. *sana(t)*, a year. According to the old practice in Bengal, coins deteriorated in value, in comparison with the rupee of account, when they passed the third year of their currency, and these rupees were termed *Sanwāt* or *Sonaut*. But in 1773, to put a stop to this inconvenience, Government determined that all rupees coined in future should bear the impression of the 19th *san* or year of Shāh 'Alam (the Mogul then reigning). And in all later uses of the term *Sonaut* it appears to be equivalent in value to the Farrukhābād rupee, or the modern "Company's Rupee" (which was of the same standard).

Dacca Mints.' (!) (*Prinsep, Useful Tables*, ed. by *E. Thomas*, 24.)

These examples will give some idea of the confusion that prevailed (without any reference to the vast variety besides of native coinages), but the subject is far too complex to be dealt with minutely in the space we can afford to it in such a work as this. The first step to reform and assimilation took place under Regulation VII. of 1833, but this still maintained the exceptional **Sicca** in Bengal, though assimilating the rupees over the rest of India. The *Sicca* was abolished as a coin by Act XIII. of 1836; and the universal rupee of British territory has since been the "Company's Rupee," as it was long called, of 180 grs. weight and 165 pure silver, representing therefore in fact the *Farrukhābād* Rupee.

1610.—"This armie consisted of 100,000 horse at the least, with infinite number of Camels and Elephants: so that with the whole baggage there could not bee lesse than fiue or sixe hundred thousand persons, insomuch that the waters were not sufficient for them; a **Mussocke** (see **MUSSUCK**) of water being sold for a **Rupia**, and yet not enough to be had."—*Hawkins*, in *Purchas*, i. 427.

[1615.—"**Roupies** Jangers (*Jahāngīrī*) of 100 *pisas*, which goeth four for five ordinary roupies of 80 *pisas* called *Cassanes* (see **KUZZANNA**), and we value them at 2*s*. 4*d*. per piece: *Cecaus* (see **SICCA**) of Amadavrs which goeth for 86 *pisas; Challennes* of Agra, which goeth for 83 *pisas*."—*Foster, Letters*, iii. 87.]

1616.—"**Rupias** monetae genus est, quarum singulae xxvi assibus gallicis aut circiter aequivalent."—*Jarric*, iii. 83.

" "... As for his Government of Patan onely, he gave the King eleven Leckes of **Rupias** (the **Rupia** is two shillings, twopence sterling) ... wherein he had Regall Authoritie to take what he list, which was esteemed at five thousand horse, the pay of every one at two hundred Rupias by the yeare."—*Sir T. Roe*, in *Purchas*, i. 548; [Hak. Soc. i. 239, with some differences of reading].

" "They call the peeces of money **roopees**, of which there are some of divers values, the meanest worth two shillings and threepence, and the best two shillings and ninepence sterling."—*Terry*, in *Purchas*, ii. 1471.

[" "This money, consisting of the two-shilling pieces of this country called **Roopeas**."—*Foster, Letters*, iv. 229.]

1648.—"Reducing the **Ropie** to four and twenty Holland Stuyvers."—*Van Twist*, 26.

1653.—"**Roupie** est vne mõnoye des Indes de la valeur de 30*s*." (*i.e. sous*).—*De la Boullaye-le-Gouz*, ed. 1657, p. 355.

c. 1666.—"And for a **Roupy** (in Bengal) which is about half a Crown, you may have 20 good Pullets and more; Geese and Ducks, in proportion."—*Bernier*, E.T. p. 140; [ed. *Constable*, 438].

1673.—"The other was a Goldsmith, who had coined copper **Rupees**."—*Fryer*, 97.

1677.—"We do, by these Presents ... give and grant unto the said Governor and Company ... full and free Liberty, Power, and Authority ... to stamp and coin ... Monies, to be called and known by the Name or Names of **Rupees**, **Pices**, and **Budgrooks**, or by such other Name or Names ..."—*Letters Patent of Charles II.* In *Charters of the E.I. Co.*, p. 111.

1771.—"We fear the worst however; that is, that the Government are about to interfere with the Company in the management of Affairs in India. Whenever that happens it will be high Time for us to decamp. I know the Temper of the King's Officers pretty well, and however they may decry our manner of acting they are ready enough to grasp at the **Rupees** whenever they fall within their Reach."—*MS. Letter* of *James Rennell*, March 31.

RUSSUD, s. Pers. *rasad*. The provisions of grain, forage, and other necessaries got ready by the local officers at the camping ground of a military force or official cortège. The vernacular word has some other technical meanings (see *Wilson*), but this is its meaning in an Anglo-Indian mouth.

[c. 1640-50.—**Rasad**. (See under **TANA**.)

RUT, s. Hind. *rath*, 'a chariot.' Now applied to a native carriage drawn by a pony, or oxen, and used by women on a journey. Also applied to the car in which idols are carried forth on festival days. [See **ROOK**.]

[1810-17.—"Tippoo's **Aumil** ... wanted iron, and determined to supply himself from the **rut**, (a temple of carved wood fixed on wheels, drawn in procession on public occasions, and requiring many thousand persons to effect its movement)."—*Wilks, Sketches*, Madras reprint, ii. 281.

[1813.—"In this camp **hackeries** and **ruths**, as they are called when they have four wheels, are always drawn by bullocks, and are used, almost exclusively, by the *Baees*, the Nach girls, and the bankers."—*Broughton, Letters*, ed. 1892, p. 117.]

1829.—"This being the case I took the liberty of taking the **rut** and horse to camp as prize property."—*Mem. of John Shipp*, ii. 183.

RUTTEE, RETTEE, s. Hind. *rattī*, *ratī*, Skt. *raktikā*, from *rakta*, 'red.' The seed of a leguminous creeper

(*Abrus precatorius*, L.) sometimes called country liquorice—a pretty scarlet pea with a black spot—used from time immemorial in India as a goldsmith's weight, and known in England as 'Crab's eyes.' Mr. Thomas has shown that the ancient *rattī* may be taken as equal to 1·75 grs. Troy (*Numismata Orientalia*, New ed., Pt. I. pp. 12-14). This work of Mr. Thomas's contains interesting information regarding the old Indian custom of basing standard weights upon the weight of seeds, and we borrow from his paper the following extract from Manu (viii. 132): "The very small mote which may be discerned in a sunbeam passing through a lattice is the first of quantities, and men call it a *trasareṇu*. 133. Eight of these *trasareṇus* are supposed equal in weight to one minute poppy-seed (*likhyā*), three of those seeds are equal to one black mustard-seed (*raja-sarshapa*), and three of these last to a white mustard-seed (*gaura-sarshapa*). 134. Six white mustard-seeds are equal to a middle-sized barley-corn (*yava*), three such barley-corns to one *krishṇala* (or **raktika**), five *krishṇalas* of gold are one *másha*, and sixteen such *máshas* one *suvarna*," &c. (*ibid.* p. 13). In the *Āīn*, Abul Fazl calls the **ratti** *surkh*, which is a translation (Pers. for 'red'). In Persia the seed is called *chashm-i-khurūs*, 'Cock's eye' (see *Blochmann's* E.T., i. 16 n., and *Jarrett*, ii. 354). Further notices of the *ratī* used as a weight for precious stones will be found in Sir W. Elliot's *Coins of Madras* (p. 49). Sir Walter's experience is that the *ratī* of the gem-dealers is a *double ratī*, and an approximation to the *manjādi* (see **MANGELIN**). This accounts for Tavernier's valuation at 3½ grs. [Mr. Ball gives the weight at 2·66 Troy grs. (*Tavernier*, ii. 448).]

c. 1676.—"At the mine of *Soumelpour* in *Bengala*, they weigh by **Rati's**, and the **Rati** is seven eighths of a Carat, or three grains and a half."—*Tavernier*, E.T. ii. 140; [ed. *Ball*, ii. 89].

RYOT, s. Ar. *ra'īyat*, from *ra'ā*, 'to pasture,' meaning originally, according to its etymology, 'a herd at pasture'; but then 'subjects' (collectively). It is by natives used for 'a subject' in India, but its specific Anglo-Indian application is to 'a tenant of the soil'; an individual occupying land as a farmer or cultivator. In Turkey the word, in the form *raiya*, is applied to the Christian subjects of the Porte, who are not liable to the conscription, but pay a poll-tax in lieu, the *Kharāj*, or *Jizya* (see **JEZYA**).

[1609.—"**Riats** or clownes." (See under **DOAI.**)]

1776. — "For some period after the creation of the world there was neither Magistrate nor Punishment . . . and the **Ryots** were nourished with piety and morality."—*Halhed, Gentoo Code*, 41.

1789.—
"To him in a body the **Ryots** complain'd
That their houses were burnt, and their cattle distrain'd."
The Letters of Simpkin the Second, &c. 11.

1790.—"A **raiyot** is rather a farmer than a husbandman."—*Colebrooke*, in *Life*, 42.

1809.—"The **ryots** were all at work in their fields."—*Lord Valentia*, ii. 127.

1813.—
"And oft around the cavern fire
On visionary schemes debate,
To snatch the **Rayahs** from their fate."
Byron, Bride of Abydos.

1820.—"An acquaintance with the customs of the inhabitants, but particularly of the **rayets**, the various tenures . . . the agreements usual among them regarding cultivation, and between them and soucars (see **SOWCAR**) respecting loans and advances . . . is essential to a judge."—*Sir T. Munro*, in *Life*, ii. 17.

1870.—"**Ryot** is a word which is much . . . misused. It is Arabic, but no doubt comes through the Persian. It means 'protected one,' 'subject,' 'a commoner,' as distinguished from '*Raees*' or 'noble.' In a native mouth, to the present day, it is used in this sense, and not in that of tenant."—*Systems of Land Tenure* (Cobden Club), 166.

The title of a newspaper, in English but of native editing, published for some years back in Calcutta, corresponds to what is here said; it is *Raees and* **Raiyat**.

1877.—"The great financial distinction between the followers of Islam . . . and the **rayahs** or infidel subjects of the Sultan, was the payment of *haratch* or capitation tax."—*Finlay, H. of Greece*, v. 22 (ed. 1877).

1884.—"Using the rights of conquest after the fashion of the Normans in England, the Turks had everywhere, except in the Cyclades, . . . seized on the greater part of the most fertile lands. Hence they formed the landlord class of Greece; whilst the **Rayahs**, as the Turks style their non-Mussulman subjects, usually farmed the territories of their masters on the *metayer* system." — *Murray's Handbook for Greece* (by A. F. Yule), p. 54.

RYOTWARRY, adj. A technicality of modern coinage. Hind. from Pers. *ra'iyatwār*, formed from the preceding. The *ryotwarry* system is that under which the settlement for land revenue is made directly by the Government agency with each individual cultivator holding land, not with the village community, nor with any middleman or landlord, payment being also received directly from every such individual. It is the system which chiefly prevails in the Madras Presidency; and was elaborated there in its present form mainly by Sir T. Munro.

1824.—"It has been objected to the **ryotwári** system that it produces unequal assessment and destroys ancient rights and privileges: but these opinions seem to originate in some misapprehension of its nature."—*Minutes*, &c., of *Sir T. Munro*, i. 265. We may observe that the spelling here is not Munro's. The Editor, Sir A. Arbuthnot, has followed a system (see Preface, p. x.); and we see in *Gleig's Life* (iii. 355) that Munro wrote '**Rayetwar.**'

S

SABAIO, ÇABAIO, &c., n.p. The name generally given by the Portuguese writers to the Mahommedan prince who was in possession of Goa when they arrived in India, and who had lived much there. He was in fact that one of the captains of the Bāhmanī kingdom of the Deccan who, in the division that took place on the decay of the dynasty towards the end of the 15th century, became the founder of the 'Adil Shāhī family which reigned in Bijapur from 1489 to the end of the following century (see **IDALCAN**). His real name was Abdul Muzaffar Yūsuf, with the surname *Sabāī* or *Savāī*. There does not seem any ground for rejecting the intelligent statement of De Barros (II. v. 2) that he had this name from being a native of *Sāvā* in Persia [see *Bombay Gazetteer*, xxiii. 404]. Garcia de Orta does not seem to have been aware of this history, and he derives the name from *Sāhib* (see below), apparently a mere guess, though not an unnatural one. Mr. Birch's surmise (*Alboquerque*, ii. 82), with these two old and obvious sources of suggestion before him, that "the word may possibly be connected with *sipāhī*, Arabic, a soldier," is quite inadmissible (nor is *sipāhī* Arabic). [On this word Mr. Whiteway writes: "In his explanation of this word Sir H. Yule has been misled by Barros. Couto (Dec. iv. Bk. 10 ch. 4) is conclusive, where he says: 'This Çufo extended the limits of his rule as far as he could till he went in person to conquer the island of Goa, which was a valuable possession for its income, and was in possession of a lord of Canara, called *Savay*, a vassal of the King of Canara, who then had his headquarters at what we call Old Goa. . . . As there was much jungle here, *Savay*, the lord of Goa, had certain houses where he stayed for hunting. . . . These houses still preserve the memory of the Hindu *Savay*, as they are called the **Savayo's** house, where for many years the Governors of India lived. As our João de Barros could not get true information of these things, he confounded the name of the Hindu *Savay* with that of *Çufo* (? Yūsuf) Adil Shāh, saying in the 5th Book of his 2nd Decade that when we went to India a Moor called **Soay** was lord of Goa, that we ordinarily called him **Sabayo**, and that he was a vassal of the King of the Deccan, a Persian, and native of the city of *Sawa*. At this his sons laughed heartily when we read it to them, saying that their father was anything but a Turk, and his name anything but Çufo.' This passage makes it clear that the origin of the word is the Hindu title *Siwāī*, Hind. *Sawāī*, 'having the excess of a fourth,' 'a quarter better than other people,' which is one of the titles of the Mahārājā of Jaypur. To show that it was more or less well known, I may point to the little State of Sunda, which lay close to Goa on the S.E., of which the Rāja was of the Vijayanagar family. This little State became independent after the destruction of Vijayanagar, and remained in existence till absorbed by Tippoo Sultan. In this State *Siwāī* was a common honorific of the ruling family. At the same time Barros was not alone in calling Adil Shāh the **Sabaio** (see *Alboquerque*, *Cartas*, p. 24), where the name occurs. The mistake having been made, everyone accepted it."]

There is a story, related as unquestionable by Firishta, that the Sabaio was in reality a son of the Turkish Sultan Agā Murād (or 'Amurath') II., who was saved from murder at his father's death, and placed in the hands of 'Imād-ud-dīn, a Persian merchant of Sāvā, by whom he was brought up. In his youth he sought his fortune in India, and being sold as a slave, and going through a succession of adventures, reached his high position in the Deccan (*Briggs, Firishta*, iii. 7-8).

1510.—"But when Afonso Dalboquerque took Goa, it would be about 40 years more or less since the **Çabaio** had taken it from the Hindoos."—*Dalboquerque*, ii. 96.

,, "In this island (Goa called *Goga*) there is a fortress near the sea, walled round after our manner, in which there is sometimes a captain called **Savaiu**, who has 400 Mamelukes, he himself being also a Mameluke. . . ."—*Varthema*, 116.

1516.—"Going further along the coast there is a very beautiful river, which sends two arms into the sea, making between them an island, on which stands the city of Goa belonging to *Daquem* (**Deccan**), and it was a principality of itself with other districts adjoining in the interior; and in it there was a great Lord, as vassal of the said King (of Deccan) called **Sabayo**, who being a good soldier, well mannered and experienced in war, this lordship of Goa was bestowed upon him, that he might continually make war on the King of Narsinga, as he did until his death. And then he left this city to his son **Çabaym Hydalçan**. . . ." —*Barros*, Lisbon ed. 287.

1563.—"*O.* . . . And returning to our subject, as Adel in Persian means 'justice,' they called the prince of these territories **Adelham**, as it were 'Lord of Justice.'

"*R.* A name highly inappropriate, for neither he nor the rest of them are wont to do justice. But tell me also why in Spain they call him the **Sabaio**?

"*O.* Some have told me that he was so called because they used to call a Captain by this name; but I afterwards came to know that in fact *saibo* in Arabic means 'lord.' . . ."—*Garcia*, f. 36.

SABLE-FISH. See **HILSA**.

SADRAS, SADRASPATÁM, n.p. This name of a place 42 m. south of Madras, the seat of an old Dutch factory, was probably shaped into the usual form in a sort of conformity with **Madras** or *Madraspatam*. The correct name is *Sadurai*, but it is sometimes made into *Sadrang-* and *Shatranj-patam*. [The *Madras Gloss.* gives Tam. *Shathurangappaṭanam*, Skt. *chatur-anga*, 'the four military arms, infantry, cavalry, elephants and cars.'] Fryer (p. 28) calls it *Sandraslapatam*, which is probably a misprint for *Sandrastapatam*.

1672.—"From Tirepoplier you come . . . to **Sadraspatam**, where our people have a Factory."—*Baldaeus*, 152.

1726.—"The name of the place is properly **Sadrangapatam**; but for short it is also called **Sadrampatam**, and most commonly **Sadraspatam**. In the Tellinga it indicates the name of the founder, and in Persian it means 'thousand troubles' or the Shahboard which we call chess."—*Valentijn, Choromandel*, 11. The curious explanation of *Shatranj* or 'chess,' as 'a thousand troubles,' is no doubt some popular etymology; such as P. *sad-ranj*, 'a hundred griefs.' The word is really of Sanskrit origin, from *Chaturangam*, literally, 'quadripartite'; the four constituent parts of an army, viz. horse, foot, chariots and elephants.

[1727.—"**Saderass, or Saderass Patam.**" (See under **LONG-CLOTH**.)]

c. 1780.—"J'avois pensé que **Sadras** auroit été le lieu où devoient finir mes contrarietés et mes courses."—*Haafner*, i. 141.

,, "'Non, je ne suis point Anglois,' m'écriai-je avec indignation et transport; 'je suis un Hollandois de **Sadringapatnam**.'"—*Ibid.* 191.

1781.—"The chief officer of the French now despatched a summons to the English commandant of the Fort to surrender, and the commandant, not being of opinion he could resist . . . evacuated the fort, and proceeded by sea in boats to **Sudrung Puttun**."—*H. of Hydur Naik*, 447.

SAFFLOWER, s. The flowers of the annual *Carthamus tinctorius*, L. (N.O. *Compositae*), a considerable article of export from India for use of a red dye, and sometimes, from the resemblance of the dried flowers to saffron, termed 'bastard saffron.' The colouring matter of safflower is the basis of *rouge*. The name is a curious modification of words by the 'striving after meaning.' For it points, in the first half of the name, to the analogy with saffron, and in the second half, to the object of trade being a flower. But neither one nor the other of these meanings forms any real element in the word. *Safflower* appears to be an eventual corruption of the Arabic name of the thing, *'uṣfūr*. This word we find in medieval trade-lists (*e.g.* in Pegolotti) to take various forms such as *asfiore, asfrole, astifore, zaffrole, saffiore;* from the last of which the transition to *safflower* is natural. In the old Latin translation of Avicenna it seems to be called *Crocus hortulanus*, for the corresponding Arabic is given *hasfor*. Another Arabic name for this article is *ḳurṭum*, which we presume to be the origin of the botanist's *carthamus*. In Hind. it is called *kusumbha* or *kusum*. Bretschneider remarks that though the two plants, saffron and safflower, have not the slightest resemblance, and belong to two different families and classes of the nat. system, there has been a certain confusion between them among almost all nations, including the Chinese.

c. 1200. — "'**Usfur** . . . *Abu Hanifa*. This plant yields a colouring matter, used in dyeing. There are two kinds, cultivated and wild, both of which grow in Arabia, and the seeds of which are called *al-ḳurṭum*."—*Ibn Baithar*, ii. 196.

c. 1343.—"**Affiore** vuol esser fresco, e asciutto, e colorito rosso in colore di buon zafferano, e non giallo, e chiaro a modo di femminella di zafferano, e che non sia trasandato, che quando è vecchio e trasandato si spolverizza, e fae vermini."—*Pegolotti*, 372.

1612.—"The two Indian ships aforesaid did discharge these goods following . . . **oosfar**, which is a red die, great quantitie." —*Capt. Saris*, in *Purchas*, i. 347.

[1667-8.—". . . madder, **safflower**, argoll, castoreum. . . ."—*List of Goods imported*, in *Birdwood*, *Report on Old Records*, 76.]

1810.—"Le safran bâtard ou carthame, nommé dans le commerce *safranon*, est appelé par les Arabes . . . **osfour** ou . . . *Kortom*. Suivant M. Sonnini, le premier nom désigne la plante; et le second, ses graines."—*Silv. de Sacy*, Note on *Abdallatif*, p. 123.

1813.—"**Safflower** (*Cussom*, Hind., *Asfour* Arab.) is the flower of an annual plant, the *Carthamus tinctorius*, growing in Bengal and other parts of India, which when well-cured is not easily distinguishable from saffron by the eye, though it has nothing of its smell or taste."—*Milburn*, ii. 238.

SAFFRON, s. Arab. *za'farān*. The true saffron (*Crocus sativus*, L.) in India is cultivated in Kashmīr only. In South India this name is given to *turmeric*, which the Portuguese called *açafrão da terra* ('country saffron.') The Hind. name is *haldī*, or in the Deccan *halad*, [Skt. *haridra*, *hari*, 'green, yellow']. Garcia de Orta calls it *croco Indiaco*, 'Indian saffron.' Indeed, Dozy shows that the Arab. *kurkum* for turmeric (whence the bot. Lat. *curcuma*) is probably taken from the Greek κρόκος or obl. κρόκον. Moodeen Sherif says that *kurkum* is applied to saffron in many Persian and other writers.

c. 1200.—"The Persians call this root *al-Hard*, and the inhabitants of Basra call it *al-Kurkum*, and *al-Kurkum* is **Saffron**. They call these plants **Saffron** because they dye yellow in the same way as Saffron does."—*Ibn Baithar*, ii. 370.

1563.—"*R*. Since there is nothing else to be said on this subject, let us speak of what we call 'country **saffron**.'

"*O*. This is a medicine that should be spoken of, since it is in use by the Indian physicians; it is a medicine and article of trade much exported to Arabia and Persia. In this city (Goa) there is little of it, but much in Malabar, *i.e.* in Cananor and Calecut. The Canarins call the root *alad*; and the Malabars sometimes give it the same name, but more properly call it *mangale*, and the Malays *cunhet*; the Persians, *darzard*, which is as much as to say 'yellow-wood.' The Arabs call it *habet*; and all of them, each in turn, say that this saffron does not exist in Persia, nor in Arabia, nor in Turkey, except what comes from India."—*Garcia*, f. 78*v*. Further on he identifies it with *curcuma*.

1726.—"Curcuma, or Indian **Saffron**."—*Valentijn*, *Chor*. 42.

SAGAR-PESHA, s. Camp-followers, or the body of servants in a private establishment. The word, though usually pronounced in vulgar Hind. as written above, is Pers. *shāgird-pesha* (lit. *shāgird*, 'a disciple, a servant,' and *pesha*, 'business').

[1767.—"**Saggur Depessah**-pay. . . ."—In *Long*, 513.]

SAGO, s. From Malay *sāgū*. The farinaceous pith taken out of the stem of several species of a particular genus of palm, especially *Metroxylon laeve*, Mart., and *M. Rumphii*, Willd., found in every part of the Indian Archipelago, including the Philippines, wherever there is proper soil. They are most abundant in the eastern part of the region indicated, including the Moluccas and N. Guinea, which probably formed the original habitat; and in these they supply the sole bread of the natives. In the remaining parts of the Archipelago, *sago* is the food only of certain wild tribes, or consumed (as in Mindanao) by the poor only, or prepared (as at Singapore, &c.) for export. There are supposed to be five species producing the article.

1298.—"They have a kind of trees that produce flour, and excellent flour it is for food. These trees are very tall and thick, but have a very thin bark, and inside the bark they are crammed with flour."—*Marco Polo*, Bk. iii. ch. xi.

1330.—"But as for the trees which produce flour, tis after this fashion. . . . And the result is the best *pasta* in the world, from which they make whatever they choose, cates of sorts, and excellent bread, of which I, Friar Odoric, have eaten."—*Fr. Odoric*, in *Cathay*, &c., 32.

1522.—"Their bread (in Tidore) they make of the wood of a certain tree like a palm-tree, and they make it in this way. They take a piece of this wood, and extract from it certain long black thorns which are situated there; then they pound it, and make bread of it which they call **sagu**. They make provision of this bread for their sea voyages."—*Pigafetta*, Hak. Soc. p. 136. This is a bad description, and seems to refer to the **Sagwire**, not the true sago-tree.

1552.—"There are also other trees which are called **çagus**, from the pith of which bread is made."—*Castanheda*, vi. 24.

1553.—"Generally, although they have some millet and rice, all the people of the Isles of Maluco eat a certain food which they call **Sagum**, which is the pith of a tree like a palm-tree, except that the leáf is softer and smoother, and the green of it is rather dark."—*Barros*, III. v. 5.

1579.—". . . and a Kind of meale which they call **Sago**, made of the toppes of certaine trees, tasting in the Mouth like some curds, but melts away like sugar."—*Drake's Voyage*, Hak. Soc. p. 142.

" Also in a list of "Certaine Wordes of the Naturall Language of Iaua"; "**Sagu**, bread of the Countrey."—*Hakl.* iv. 246.

c. 1690.—"Primo **Sagus** genuina, Malaice **Sagu**, sive *Lapia tuni*, h.e. vera *Sagu*."—*Rumphius*, i. 75. (We cannot make out the language of *lapia tuni*.)

1727.—"And the inland people subsist mostly on **Sagow**, the Pith of a small Twig split and dried in the Sun."—*A. Hamilton*, ii. 93; [ed. 1744].

SAGWIRE, s. A name applied often in books, and, formerly at least, in the colloquial use of European settlers and traders, to the **Gomuti** palm or *Arenga saccharifera*, Labill., which abounds in the Ind. Archipelago, and is of great importance in its rural economy. The name is Port. *sagueira* (analogous to *palmeira*), in Span. of the Indies *saguran*, and no doubt is taken from *sagu*, as the tree, though not the **Sago**-palm of commerce, affords a sago of inferior kind. Its most important product, however, is the sap, which is used as **toddy** (q.v.), and which in former days also afforded almost all the sugar used by natives in the islands. An excellent cordage is made from a substance resembling black horse-hair, which is found between the trunk and the fronds, and this is the **gomuti** of the Malays, which furnished one of the old specific names (*Borassus Gomutus*, Loureiro). There is also found in a like position a fine cotton-like substance which makes excellent tinder, and strong stiff spines from which pens are made, as well as arrows for the blow-pipe, or Sumpitan (see **SARBATANE**). "The seeds have been made into a confection, whilst their pulpy envelope abounds in a poisonous juice—used in the barbarian wars of the natives—to which the Dutch gave the appropriate name of 'hell-water'" (*Crawfurd, Desc. Dict.* p. 145). The term *sagwire* is sometimes applied to the toddy or palm-wine, as will be seen below.

1515.—"They use no sustenance except the meal of certain trees, which trees they call **Sagur**, and of this they make bread."—*Giov. da Empoli*, 86.

1615.—"Oryza tamen magna hic copia, ingens etiam modus arborum quas **Saguras** vocant, quaeque varia suggerunt commoda."—*Jarric*, i. 201.

1631.—". . . tertia frequens est in Banda ac reliquis insulis Moluccis, quae distillat ex arbore non absimili Palmae Indicae, isque potus indigenis **Saguër** vocatur. . . ."—*Jac. Bontii, Dial.* iv. p. 9.

1784.—"The natives drink much of a liquor called **saguire**, drawn from the palm-tree."—*Forrest, Mergui*, 73.

1820.—"The Portuguese, I know not for what reason, and other European nations who have followed them, call the tree and the liquor **sagwire**."—*Crawfurd, Hist.* i. 401.

SAHIB, s. The title by which, all over India, European gentlemen, and it may be said Europeans generally, are addressed, and spoken of, when no disrespect is intended, by natives. It is also the general title (at least where Hindustani or Persian is used) which is affixed to the name or office of a European, corresponding thus rather to *Monsieur* than to Mr. For *Colonel Ṣāḥib, Collector Ṣāḥib, Lord Ṣāḥib*, and even *Sergeant Ṣāḥib* are thus used, as well as the general vocative *Ṣāḥib!* 'Sir!' In other Hind. use the word is equivalent to 'Master'; and it is occasionally used as a specific title both among Hindus and Musulmans, *e.g. Appa Ṣāḥib, Tīpū Ṣāḥib*; and generically is affixed to the titles of men of rank when indicated by those titles, as *Khān Ṣāḥib*, *Nawāb Ṣāḥib*, *Rāja Ṣāḥib*. The word is Arabic, and originally means 'a companion'; (sometimes a companion of Mahommed). [In the *Arabian Nights* it is the title of a Wazīr (*Burton*, i. 218).]

1673.—". . . To which the subtle Heathen replied, **Sahab** (i.e. Sir), why will you do more than the Creator meant?"—*Fryer*, 417.

1689.—"Thus the distracted Husband in his *Indian* English confest, *English fashion*, **Sab**, best fashion, have one Wife best for one Husband."—*Ovington*, 326.

1853.—"He was told that a '**Sahib**' wanted to speak with him."—*Oakfield*, ii. 252.

1878.—". . . forty Elephants and five **Sahibs** with guns and innumerable followers."—*Life in the Mofussil*, i. 194.

[**ST. DEAVES**, n.p. A corruption of the name of the island of *Sandwīp* in the Bay of Bengal, situated off the coast of Chittagong and Noakhālī, which is best known in connection with the awful loss of life and property in the cyclone of 1876.

[1688.—"From Chittagaum we sailed away the 29th January, after had sent small vessels to search round the Island **St. Deaves**."—In *Yule, Hedges' Diary*, Hak. Soc. II. lxxx.]

SAINT JOHN'S, n.p.

a. An English sailor's corruption, which for a long time maintained its place in our maps. It is the *Sindān* of the old Arab Geographers, and was the first durable settling-place of the Parsee refugees on their emigration to India in the 8th century. [Dosabhai Framji, *Hist. of the Parsis*, i. 30.] The proper name of the place, which is in lat. 20° 12′ and lies 88 m. north of Bombay, is apparently *Sajām* (see *Hist. of Cambay*, in *Bo. Govt. Selections*, No. xxvi., N.S., p. 52), but it is commonly called *Sanjān*. E. B. Eastwick in *J. Bo. As. Soc. R.* i. 167, gives a Translation from the Persian of the "*Kiṣṣah-i-***Sanjân**, or History of the arrival and settlement of the Parsees in India." Sanjān is about 3 m. from the little river-mouth port of Umbargām. "Evidence of the greatness of Sanjān is found, for miles around, in old foundations and bricks. The bricks are of very superior quality."—*Bomb. Gazetteer*, vol. xiv. 302, [and for medieval references to the place, *ibid.* I. Pt. i. 262, 520 *seq.*].

c. 1150.—"**Sindān** is 1½ mile from the sea. . . . The town is large and has an extensive commerce both in exports and imports."—*Edrisi*, in *Elliot*, i. 85.

c. 1599.—

"When the Dastur saw the soil was good,
He selected the place for their residence:
The Dastur named the spot **Sanjan**,
And it became populous as the Land of
Iran."—*Kiṣṣah*, &c., as above, p. 179.

c. 1616.—"The aldea Nargol . . . in the lands of Daman was infested by Malabar Moors in their *parós*, who commonly landed there for water and provisions, and plundered the boats that entered or quitted the river, and the passengers who crossed it, with heavy loss to the aldeas adjoining the river, and to the revenue from them, as well as to that from the custom-house of **Sangens**."—*Bocarro, Decada*, 670.

1623.—"La mattina seguente, fatto giorno, scoprimmo terra di lontano . . . in un luogo poco discosto da Bassain, che gl' Inglesi chiamano *Terra di* **San Giovanni**; ma nella carta da navigare vidi esser notato, in lingua Portoghese, col nome *d'ilhas das vaccas*, o 'isole delle vacche' al modo nostro."—*P. della Valle*, ii. 500; [Hak. Soc. i. 16].

1630.—"It happened that in safety they made to the land of **St. Iohns** on the shoares of India."—*Lord, The Religion of the Persees*, 3.

1644.—"Besides these four posts there are in the said district four *Tanadarias* (see **TANADAR**), or different Captainships, called **Samgês** (St. John's), Danū, Maim, and Trapor."—*Bocarro* (Port. MS.).

1673.—"In a Week's Time we turned it up, sailing by Baçein, Tarapore, Valentine's Peak, **St. John's**, and Daman, the last City northward on the Continent, belonging to the Portuguese."—*Fryer*, 82.

1808. — "They (the Parsee emigrants) landed at Dieu, and lived there 19 years; but, disliking the place . . . the greater part of them left it and came to the Guzerat coast, in vessels which anchored off **Seyjan**, the name of a town."—*R. Drummond*.

1813.—"The Parsees or Guebres . . . continued in this place (Diu) for some time, and then crossing the Gulph, landed at **Suzan**, near Nunsaree, which is a little to the southward of Surat."—*Forbes, Or. Mem.* i. 109; [2nd ed. i. 78].

1841.—"The high land of **St. John**, about 3 leagues inland, has a regular appearance. . . ."—*Horsburgh's Directory*, ed. 1841, i. 470.

1872.—"In connexion with the landing of the Parsis at **Sanjân**, in the early part of the 8th century, there still exist copies of the 15 Sanskrit *Ślokas*, in which their Mobeds explained their religion to Jadé Rânâ, the Râja of the place, and the reply he gave them."—*Ind. Antiq.* i. 214. The Ślokas are given. See them also in *Dosabhai Framji's Hist. of the Parsees*, i. 31.

b. **ST. JOHN'S ISLAND**, n.p. This again is a corruption of *San-*

Shan, or more correctly *Shang-chuang*, the Chinese name of an island about 60 or 70 miles S.W. of Macao, and at some distance from the mouth of the Canton River, the place where St. Francis Xavier died, and was originally buried.

1552.—"Inde nos ad **Sancianum**, Sinarum insulam a Cantone millia pas. circiter cxx Deus perduxit incolumes."—*Scti. Franc. Xaverii Epistt.*, Pragae 1667, IV. xiv.

1687.—"We came to Anchor the same Day, on the N.E. end of **St. John's** Island. This Island is in Lat. about 32 d. 30 min. North, lying on the S. Coast of the Province of Quantung or Canton in *China*."—*Dampier*, i. 406.

1727.—"A Portuguese Ship . . . being near an Island on that Coast, called after **St. Juan**, some Gentlemen and Priests went ashore for Diversion, and accidentally found the Saint's Body uncorrupted, and carried it Passenger to Goa."—*A. Hamilton*, i. 252; [ed. 1744, ii. 255].

1780.—"**St. John's**," in *Dunn's New Directory*, 472.

c. **ST. JOHN'S ISLANDS**. This is also the chart-name, and popular European name, of two islands about 6 m. S. of Singapore, the chief of which is properly Pulo *Sikajang*, [or as Dennys (*Desc. Dict.* 321) writes the word, Pulo *Skijang*].

SAIVA, s. A worshipper of *Śiva*; Skt. *Śaiva*, adj., 'belonging to Siva.'

1651.—"The second sect of the Bramins, '**Seiviá**' . . . by name, say that a certain *Eswara* is the supreme among the gods, and that all the others are subject to him."—*Rogerius*, 17.

1867.—"This temple is reckoned, I believe, the holiest shrine in India, at least among the **Shaivites**."—*Bp. Milman*, in *Memoirs*, p. 48.

SALA, s. Hind. *sālā*, 'brother-in-law,' *i.e.* wife's brother; but used elliptically as a low term of abuse.

[1856.—"Another reason (for infanticide) is the blind pride which makes them hate that any man should call them **sala**, or Sussoor—brother-in-law, or father-in-law."—*Forbes, Rās Mālā*, ed. 1878, 616.]

1881.—"Another of these popular Paris sayings is '*et ta sœur?*' which is as insulting a remark to a Parisian as the apparently harmless remark **sālā**, 'brother-in-law,' is to a Hindoo."—*Sat. Rev.*, Sept. 10, 326.

SALAAM, s. A salutation; properly oral salutation of Mahommedans to each other. Arab. *salām*, 'peace.' Used for any act of salutation; or for 'compliments.'

[c. 60 B.C.—

"'Αλλ' εἰ μὲν Σύρος ἐσσὶ "Σαλάμ," εἰ δ' οὖν σύ γε φοῖνιξ
"Ναίδιος," εἰ δ' Ἕλλην "Χαῖρε"· τὸ δ' αὐτὸ φράσον."

—*Meleagros*, in *Anthologia Palatina*, vii. 149.

The point is that he has been a bird of passage, and says good-bye now to his various resting-places in their own tongue.]

1513.—"The ambassador (of Bisnagar) entering the door of the chamber, the Governor rose from the chair on which he was seated, and stood up while the ambassador made him great **çalema**."—*Correa, Lendas*, II. i. 377. See also p. 431.

1552.—"The present having been seen he took the letter of the Governor, and read it to him, and having read it told him how the Governor sent him his **çalema**, and was at his command with all his fleet, and with all the Portuguese. . . ."—*Castanheda*, iii. 445.

1611.—"**Çalema**. The salutation of an inferior."—*Cobarruvias, Sp. Dict.* s.v.

1626.—"Hee (Selim *i.e.* Jahāngīr) turneth ouer his Beades, and saith so many words, to wit three thousand and two hundred, and then presenteth himself to the people to receive their **salames** or good morrow. . . ."—*Purchas, Pilgrimage*, 523.

1638.—"En entrant ils se salüent de leur **Salom** qu'ils accompagnent d'vne profonde inclination."—*Mandelslo*, Paris, 1659, 223.

1648.—". . . this salutation they call **salam**; and it is made with bending of the body, and laying of the right hand upon the head."—*Van Twist*, 55.

1689.—"The **Salem** of the Religious Bramins, is to join their Hands together, and spreading them first, make a motion towards their Head, and then stretch them out."—*Ovington*, 183.

1694.—"The Town **Conicopolies**, and chief inhabitants of Egmore, came to make their **Salaam** to the President."—*Wheeler*, i. 281.

1717.—"I wish the Priests in Tranquebar a Thousand fold **Schalam**."—*Philipp's Acct.* 62.

1809.—"The old priest was at the door, and with his head uncovered, to make his **salaams**."—*Ld. Valentia*, i. 273.

1813.—

"'Ho! who art thou?'—'This low **salam**
Replies, of Moslem faith I am.'"
Byron, The Giaour.

1832.—"Il me rendit tous les **salams** que je fis autrefois au Grand Mogol."—*Jacquemont, Corresp.* ii. 137.

1844.—"All chiefs who have made their **salam** are entitled to carry arms personally."—*G. O. of Sir C. Napier*, 2.

SALAK, s. A singular-looking fruit, sold and eaten in the Malay regions, described in the quotation.

It is the fruit of a species of ratan (*Salacca edulis*), of which the Malay name is *rotan-salak*.

1768-71. — "The **salac** (*Calamus rotang zalacca*) which is the fruit of a prickly bush, and has a singular appearance, being covered with scales, like those of a lizard; it is nutritious and well tasted, in flavour somewhat resembling a raspberry." — *Stavorinus*, E.T. i. 241.

SALEB, SALEP, s. This name is applied to the tubers of various species of *orchis* found in Europe and Asia, which from ancient times have had a great reputation as being restorative and highly nutritious. This reputation seems originally to have rested on the 'doctrine of signatures,' but was due partly no doubt to the fact that the mucilage of saleb has the property of forming, even with the addition of 40 parts of water, a thick jelly. Good modern authorities quite disbelieve in the virtues ascribed to *saleb*, though a decoction of it, spiced and sweetened, makes an agreeable drink for invalids. Saleb is identified correctly by Ibn Baithar with the Satyrium of Dioscorides and Galen. The full name in Ar. (analogous to the Greek *orchis*) is *Khuṣī-al-tha'lab*, i.e. '*testiculus vulpis*'; but it is commonly known in India as *ṣa'lab miṣrī*, i.e. Salep of Egypt, or popularly *salep-misry*. In Upper India *saleb* is derived from various species of *Eulophia*, found in Kashmīr and the Lower Himālaya. **Saloop**, which is, or used to be, supplied hot in winter mornings by itinerant vendors in the streets of London, is, we believe, a representative of Saleb; but we do not know from what it is prepared. [In 1889 a correspondent to *Notes & Queries* (7 ser. vii. 35) stated that "within the last twenty years **saloop** vendors might have been seen plying their trade in the streets of London. The term **saloop** was also applied to an infusion of the sassafras bark or wood. In Pereira's *Materia Medica*, published in 1850, it is stated that 'sassafras tea, flavoured with milk and sugar, is sold at daybreak in the streets of London under the name of **saloop**.' **Saloop** in balls is still sold in London, and comes mostly from Smyrna."]

In the first quotation it is doubtful what is meant by *salīf;* but it seems possible that the traveller may not have recognised the *tha'lab, ṣa'lab* in its Indian pronunciation.

c. 1340. — "After that, they fixed the amount of provision to be given by the Sultan, viz. 1000 Indian *riṭls* of flour . . . 1000 of meat, a large number of *riṭls* (how many I don't now remember) of sugar, of ghee, of **salīf**, of areca, and 1000 leaves of betel."—*Ibn Batuta*, iii. 382.

1727.—"They have a fruit called **Salob**, about the size of a Peach, but without a stone. They dry it hard . . . and being beaten to Powder, they dress it as Tea and Coffee are. . . . They are of opinion that it is a great restorative."—*A. Hamilton*, i. 125; [ed. 1744, i. 126].

[1754.—In his list of Indian drugs Ives (p. 44) gives "Rad. **Salop**, Persia Rs. 35 per maund."]

1838.—"**Saleb Misree**, a medicine, comes (a little) from Russia. It is considered a good nutritive for the human constitution, and is for this purpose powdered and taken with milk. It is in the form of flat oval pieces of about 80 grains each. . . . It is sold at 2 or 3 Rupees per ounce."—*Desc. of articles found in Bazars of Cabool*. In *Punjab Trade Report*, 1862, App. vi.

1882 (?).—"Here we knock against an ambulant **salep**-shop (a kind of tea which people drink on winter mornings); there against roaming oil, salt, or water-vendors, bakers carrying brown bread on wooden trays, pedlars with cakes, fellows offering dainty little bits of meat to the knowing purchaser."—*Levkosia, The Capital of Cyprus*, ext. in *St. James's Gazette*, Sept. 10.

SALEM, n.p. A town and inland district of S. India. Properly *Shelam*, which is perhaps a corruption of *Chera*, the name of the ancient monarchy in which this district was embraced. ["According to one theory the town of Salem is said to be identical with Seran or Sheran, and occasionally to have been named Sheralan; when S. India was divided between the three dynasties of Chola, Sera and Pandia, according to the generally accepted belief, Karur was the place where the three territorial divisions met; the boundary was no doubt subject to vicissitudes, and at one time possibly Salem or Serar was a part of Sera."—*Le Fanu, Man. of Salem*, ii. 18.]

SALEMPOORY, s. A kind of chintz. See allusions under **PALEMPORE**. [The *Madras Gloss.*, deriving the word from Tel. *sāle*, 'weaver,' *pura*, Skt. 'town,' describes it as "a kind of cotton cloth formerly manufactured at Nellore; half the length of ordinary

Punjums" (see **PIECE-GOODS**). The third quotation indicates that it was sometimes white.]

[1598. — " **Sarampuras.**" — *Linschoten*, Hak. Soc. i. 95.

[1611.—" I . . . was only doubtful about the white **Betteelas** and **Salempurys.**"—*Danvers, Letters*, i. 155.

[1614.—" **Salampora**, being a broad white cloth."—*Foster, ibid.* ii. 32.]

1680.—" Certain goods for Bantam priced as follows :—

" **Salampores**, Blew, at 14 Pagodas per corge. . . ."—*Ft. St. Geo. Consn.*, April 22. In *Notes and Exts.* iii. 16 ; also *ibid.* p. 24.

1747.—" The Warehousekeeper reported that on the 1st inst. when the French entered our Bounds and attacked us . . . it appeared that 5 Pieces of Long Cloth and 10 Pieces of **Salampores** were stolen, That Two Pieces of **Salampores** were found upon a Peon . . . and the Person detected is ordered to be severely whipped in the Face of the Publick. . . ."—*Ft. St. David Consn.*, March 30 (MS. Records in India Office).

c. 1780.—" . . . en l'on y fabriquoit différentes espèces de toiles de coton, telles que **salempouris.**"—*Haafner*, ii. 461.

SALIGRAM, s. Skt. *Śālagrāma* (this word seems to be properly the name of a place, 'Village of the Sāl-tree'—a real or imaginary *tīrtha* or place of sacred pilgrimage, mentioned in the *Mahābhārata*). [Other and less probable explanations are given by Oppert, *Anc. Inhabitants*, 337.] A pebble having mystic virtues, found in certain rivers, *e.g.* Gandak, Son, &c. Such stones are usually marked by containing a fossil ammonite. The *śālagrāma* is often adopted as the representative of some god, and the worship of any god may be performed before it.* It is daily worshipped by the Brahmans ; but it is especially connected with Vaishnava doctrine. In May 1883 a *śālagrāma* was the ostensible cause of great popular excitement among the Hindus of Calcutta. During the proceedings in a family suit before the High Court, a question arose regarding the identity of a *śālagrāma*, regarded as a household god. Counsel on both sides suggested that the thing should be brought into court. Mr. Justice Norris hesitated to give this order till he had taken advice. The attorneys on both sides, Hindus, said there could be no objection ; the Court interpreter, a high-caste Brahman, said it could not be brought into Court, *because of the coir-matting*, but it might with perfect propriety be brought into the corridor for inspection ; which was done. This took place during the excitement about the " Ilbert Bill," giving natives magisterial authority in the provinces over Europeans ; and there followed most violent and offensive articles in several native newspapers reviling Mr. Justice Norris, who was believed to be hostile to the Bill. The editor of the *Bengallee* newspaper, an educated man, and formerly a member of the covenanted Civil Service, the author of one of the most unscrupulous and violent articles, was summoned for contempt of court. He made an apology and complete retractation, but was sentenced to two months' imprisonment.

c. 1590.—" **Salgram** is a black stone which the Hindoos hold sacred. . . . They are found in the river Sown, at the distance of 40 cose from the mouth."—*Ayeen, Gladwin's* E.T. 1800, ii. 25 ; [ed. *Jarrett*, ii. 150].

1782. — " Avant de finir l'histoire de Vichenou, je ne puis me dispenser de parler de la pierre de **Salagraman.** Elle n'est autre chose qu'une coquille petrifiée du genre des *cornes d'Ammon :* les Indiens prétendent qu'elle represente Vichenou, parcequ'ils en ont découvert de neuf nuances différentes, ce qu'ils rapportent aux neuf incarnations de ce Dieu. . . . Cette pierre est aux sectateurs de Vichenou ce que le Lingam est à ceux de Chiven."—*Sonnerat*, i. 307.

[1822. — " In the Nerbuddah are found those types of Shiva, called **Solgrammas**, which are sacred pebbles held in great estimation all over India."—*Wallace, Fifteen Years in India*, 296.]

1824.—" The **shalgramŭ** is black, hollow, and nearly round ; it is found in the Gunduk River, and is considered a representation of Vishnoo. . . . The **Shalgramŭ** is the only stone that is naturally divine ; all the other stones are rendered sacred by incantations."—*Wanderings of a Pilgrim*, i. 43.

1885.—" My father had one (a **Salagram**). It was a round, rather flat, jet black, small, shining stone. He paid it the greatest reverence possible, and allowed no one to touch it, but worshipped it with his own hands. When he became ill, and as he would not allow a woman to touch it, he

* Like the Βαιτύλιον which the Greeks got through the Semitic nations. In Photius there are extracts from Damascius (*Life of Isidorus the Philosopher*), which speak of the stones called *Baitulos* and *Baitulion*, which were objects of worship, gave oracles, and were apparently used in healing. These appear, from what is stated, to have been meteoric stones. There were many in Lebanon (see *Phot. Biblioth.*, ed. 1653, pp. 1047, 1062-3).

made it over to a Brahman ascetic with a money present." — *Sundrâbâi*, in *Punjab Notes and Queries*, ii. 109. The **sālagrāma** is in fact a Hindu fetish.

SALLABAD, s. This word, now quite obsolete, occurs frequently in the early records of English settlements in India, for the customary or prescriptive exactions of the native Governments, and for native prescriptive claims in general. It is a word of Mahratti development, *sālābād*, 'perennial,' applied to permanent collections or charges; apparently a factitious word from Pers. *sāl*, 'year,' and Ar. *ābād*, 'ages.'

[1680.—"**Salabad.**" See under **ROOCKA.**]

1703.—". . . although these are hardships, yet by length of time become **Sallabad** (as we esteem them), there is no great demur made now, and are not recited here as grievances."—In *Wheeler*, ii. 19.

1716.—"The Board upon reading them came to the following resolutions:—That for anything which has yet appeared the Comatees (**Comaty**) may cry out their Pennagundoo Nagarum . . . at their houses, feasts, and weddings, &c., according to **Salabad** but not before the Pagoda of Chindy Pillary. . . ."—*Ibid.* 234.

1788. — "**Sallabaud.** (Usual Custom). A word used by the Moors Government to enforce their demand of a present."—*Indian Vocabulary* (*Stockdale*).

SALOOTREE, SALUSTREE, s. Hind. *Sālotar*, *Sālotrī*. A native farrier or horse-doctor. This class is now almost always Mahommedan. But the word is taken from the Skt. name *Sālihotra*, the original owner of which is supposed to have written in that language a treatise on the Veterinary Art, which still exists in a form more or less modified and imperfect. "A knowledge of Sanskrit must have prevailed pretty generally about this time (14th century), for there is in the Royal Library at Lucknow a work on the veterinary art, which was translated from the Sanskrit by order of Ghiyásu-d dín Muhammad Sháh Khiljí. This rare book, called *Kurrutu-l-Mulk*, was translated as early as A.H. 783 (A.D. 1381), from an original styled *Sálotar*, which is the name of an Indian, who is said to have been a Bráhman, and the tutor of Susruta. The Preface says the translation was made 'from the barbarous Hindi into the refined Persian, in order that there may be no more need of a reference to infidels.'"* (*Elliot*, v. 573-4.)

[1831.—"'. . . your aloes are not genuine.' 'Oh yes, they are,' he exclaimed. 'My **salutree** got them from the Bazaar."—*Or. Sport. Mag.*, reprint 1873, ii. 223.]

SALSETTE, n.p.

a. A considerable island immediately north of Bombay. The island of Bombay is indeed naturally a kind of pendant to the island of Salsette, and during the Portuguese occupation it was so in every sense. That occupation is still marked by the remains of numerous villas and churches, and by the survival of a large R. Catholic population. The island also contains the famous and extensive caves of Kāṇhērī (see **KENNERY**). The old city of **Tana** (q.v.) also stands upon Salsette. Salsette was claimed as part of the Bombay dotation of Queen Catherine, but refused by the Portuguese. The Mahrattas took it from them in 1739, and it was taken from these by us in 1774. The name has been by some connected with the salt-works which exist upon the islands (*Salinas*). But it appears in fact to be the corruption of a Mahratti name *Shāshtī*, from *Shāshashṭī*, meaning 'Sixty-six' (Skt. *Shaṭ-shashṭi*), because (it is supposed) the island was alleged to contain that number of villages. This name occurs in the form **Shatsashti** in a stone inscription dated Sak. 1103 (A.D. 1182). See *Bo. J. R. As. Soc.* xii. 334. Another inscription on copper plates dated Sak. 748 (A.D. 1027) contains a grant of the village of Naura, "one of the 66 of *Śri Sthānaka* (Thana)," thus entirely confirming the etymology (*J.R. As. Soc.* ii. 383). I have to thank Mr. J. M. Campbell, C.S.I., for drawing my attention to these inscriptions.

b. Salsette is also the name of the three provinces of the Goa territory which constituted the *Velhas Conquistas* or Old Conquests. These lay all along the coast, consisting of (1)

* "It is curious that without any allusion to this work, another on the Veterinary Art, styled *Sálotari*, and said to comprise in the Sanskrit original 16,000 *slokas*, was translated in the reign of Sháh Jahán . . . by Saiyad 'Abdulla Khán Bahádur Firoz Jang, who had found it among some other Sanskrit books which . . . had been plundered from Amar Singh, Ráná of Chitor."

the *Ilhas* (viz. the island of Goa and minor islands divided by rivers and creeks), (2) *Bardez* on the northern mainland, and (3) *Salsette* on the southern mainland. The port of Marmagaon, which is the terminus of the Portuguese Indian Railway, is in this Salsette. The name probably had the like origin to that of the Island Salsette; a parallel to which was found in the old name of the Island of Goa, *Tiçoari*, meaning (Mahr.) *Tīs-wādī*, "30 hamlets." [See **BARGANY**.]

A.D. 1186.—"I, Aparāditya ("the paramount sovereign, the Ruler of the Konkana, the most illustrious King") have given with a libation of water 24 drachms, after exempting other taxes, from the fixed revenue of the oart in the village of Mahauli, connected with **Shaṭ-shashṭi**." — *Inscription* edited by *Pandit Bhagavānlāl Indraji*, in *J. Bo. Br. R. A. S.* xii. 332. [And see *Bombay Gazetteer*, I. Pt. ii. 544, 567.]

a.—

1536. — "Item — Revenue of the Cusba (Caçabe—see **CUSBAH**) of Maym:

R~b^c lxbj *fedeas* (40,567)
And the custom-house (*Mandovim*) of the said Maym . ,, (48,000)
And **Mazagong** (*Mazaguão*) . ,, (11,500)
And **Bombay** (*Monbaym*) . ,, (23,000)
And the *Cusba* and Customs of Caranja . . . . ,, (94,700)
And in **paddy** (*batê*) . . xxi *muras* (see **MOORAH**) 1 *candil* (see **CANDY**)
And the Island of **Salsete** fedeas (319,000)
And in paddy . . xxi *muras* 1 *candil*."
S. Botelho, Tombo, 142.

1538.—"Beyond the Isle of **Elephanta** (*do Alifante*) about a league distant is the island of **Salsete**. This island is seven leagues long by 5 in breadth. On the north it borders the Gulf of Cambay, on the south it has the I. of Elephanta, on the east the mainland, and on the west the I. of **Bombai** or of *Boa Vida*. This island is very fertile, abounding in provisions, cattle, and game of sorts, and in its hills is great plenty of timber for building ships and galleys. In that part of the island which faces the S.W. wind is built a great and noble city called Thana; and a league and a half in the interior is an immense edifice called the Pagoda of **Salsete**; both one and the other objects most worthy of note; Thana for its decay (*destroição*) and the Pagoda as a work unique in its way, and the like of which is nowhere to be seen."—*João de Castro, Primo Roteiro da India*, 69-70.

1554.—

"And to the **Tanadar** (*tenadar*) of **Salsete** 30,000 *reis*.

"He has under him 12 **peons** (*piães*) of whom the said governor takes 7; leaving him 5, which at the aforesaid rate amount to 10,800 *reis*.

"And to a *Parvu* (see **PARVOE**) that he has, who is the country writer . . . and having the same pay as the Tenadar Mor, which is 3 pardaos a month, amounting in a year at the said rate to 10,800 *reis*."—*Botelho, Tombo*, in *Subsidios*, 211-212.

1610. — "Frey Manuel de S. Mathias, guardian of the convent of St. Francis in Goa, writes to me that . . . in Goa alone there are 90 resident friars; and besides in Baçaim and its adjuncts, viz., in the island of **Salsete** and other districts of the north they have 18 parishes (**Freguezias**) of native Christians with vicars; and five of the convents have colleges, or seminaries where they bring up little orphans; and that the said Ward of Goa extends 300 leagues from north to south."—*Livros das Monções*, 298.

[1674. — "From whence these Pieces of Land receive their general Name of **Salset** . . . either because it signifies in *Canorein* a Granary. . . ."—*Fryer*, 62.]

c. 1760.—"It was a melancholy sight on the loss of **Salsett**, to see the many families forced to seek refuge on Bombay, and among them some Portuguese Hidalgos or noblemen, reduced of a sudden from very flourishing circumstances to utter beggary."—*Grose*, i. 72.

[1768. — "Those lands are comprised in 66 villages, and from this number it is called **Salsette**." — *Foral of Salsette*, India Office MS.]

1777.—"The acquisition of the Island of **Salset**, which in a manner surrounds the Island of Bombay, is sufficient to secure the latter from the danger of a famine."—*Price's Tracts*, i. 101.

1808.—"The island of *Sashty* (corrupted by the Portuguese into **Salsette**) was conquered by that Nation in the year of Christ 1534, from the Mohammedan Prince who was then its Sovereign; and thereupon parcelled out, among the European subjects of Her Most Faithful Majesty, into village allotments, at a very small Foro or quit-rent."—*Bombay, Regn.* I. of 1808, sec. ii.

b.—

1510.—"And he next day, by order of the Governor, with his own people and many more from the Island (Goa) passed over to the mainland of **Salsete** and Antruz, scouring the districts and the **tanadaris**, and placing in them by his own hand **tanadars** and collectors of revenue, and put all in such order that he collected much money, insomuch that he sent to the factor at Goa very good intelligence, accompanied by much money."—*Correa*, ii. 161.

1546.—"We agree in the manner following, to wit, that I Idalxaa (**Idalcan**) promise and swear on our Koran (*no noso moçaffo*), and by the head of my eldest son, that I will remain always firm in the said amity with the King of Portugal and with his governors of India, and that the lands of **Salsete** and Bardees, which I have made contract and donation of to His Highness,

I confirm and give anew, and I swear and promise by the oath aforesaid never to reclaim them or make them the Subject of War."—*Treaty* between *D. John de Castro* and *Idalxaa*, who was formerly called *Idalção* (*Adil Khān*).—*Botelho, Tombo*, 40.

1598.—"On the South side of the Iland of *Goa*, wher the riuer runneth againe into the Sea, there cometh euen out with the coast a land called **Salsette**, which is also vnder the subiection of the Portingales, and is . . . planted both with people and fruite." —*Linschoten*, 51; [Hak. Soc. i. 177].

1602. — "Before we treat of the Wars which in this year (c. 1546) Idalxa (Adil Shāh) waged with the State about the mainland provinces of **Salsete** and Bardés, which caused much trouble to the Government of India, it seems well to us to give an account of these Moor Kings of Visiapor."—*Couto*, IV. x. 4.

SALWEN, n.p. The great river entering the sea near Martaban in British Burma, and which the Chinese in its upper course call *Lu-kiang*. The Burmese form is *Than-lwen*, but the original form is probably Shān. ["The **Salween** River, which empties itself into the sea at Maulmain, rivals the Irrawaddy in length but not in importance" (*Forbes, British Burma*, 8).]

SAMBOOK, s. Ar. *sanbuk*, and *sunbūk* (there is a Skt. word *śambūka*, 'a bivalve shell, but we are unable to throw any light on any possible transfer); a kind of small vessel formerly used in Western India and still on the Arabian coast. [See *Bombay Gazetteer*, xiii. Pt. ii. 470.] It is smaller than the *bagalā* (see **BUGGALOW**), and is chiefly used to communicate between a roadstead and the shore, or to go inside the reefs. Burton renders the word 'a foyst,' which is properly a smaller kind of galley. See description in the last but one quotation below.

c. 330.—"It is the custom when a vessel arrives (at Makdashau) that the Sultan's **sunbūk** boards her to ask whence the ship comes, who is the owner, and the skipper (or pilot), what she is laden with, and what merchants or other passengers are on board." — *Ibn Batuta*, ii. 183; also see pp. 17, 181, &c.

1498.—"The **Zambuco** came loaded with doves'-dung, which they have in those islands, and which they were carrying, it being merchandize for Cambay, where it is used in dyeing cloths." — *Correa, Lendas*, i. 33-34.

,, In the curious Vocabulary of the language of Calicut, at the end of the *Roteiro* of Vasco da Gama, we find: "Barcas; **Cambuco**."

[1502. — "**Zambucos**." See under **NACODA**.]

1506. — "Questo Capitanio si prese uno **sambuco** molto ricco, veniva dalla Mecha per Colocut."—*Leonardo Ca' Masser*, 17.

1510.—"As to the names of their ships, some are called **Sambuchi**, and these are flat-bottomed."—*Varthema*, 154.

1516. — "Item — our Captain Major, or Captain of Cochim shall give passes to secure the navigation of the ships and **zanbuqos** of their ports . . . provided they do not carry spices or drugs that we require for our cargoes, but if such be found, for the first occasion they shall lose all the spice and drugs so loaded, and on the second they shall lose both ship and cargo, and all may be taken as prize of war."—*Treaty* of *Lopo Soares* with *Coulão* (**Quilon**), in *Botelho, Tombo, Subsidios*, p. 32.

[1516.—"**Zambucos**." See under **ARECA**.]

1518.—"**Zambuquo**." See under **PROW**.

1543. — "Item — that the **Zanbuquos** which shall trade in his port in rice or *nele* (paddy) and cottons and other matters shall pay the customary dues."—*Treaty* of *Martin Affonso de Sousa* with *Coulam*, in *Botelho, Tombo*, 37.

[1814.—"**Sambouk**." See under **DHOW**.]

1855.—"Our pilgrim ship . . . was a **Sambuk** of about 400 *ardēbs* (50 tons), with narrow wedge-like bows, a clean water-line, a sharp keel, undecked except upon the poop, which was high enough to act as a sail in a gale of wind. We carried 2 masts, imminently raking forward, the main considerably longer than the mizen, and the former was provided with a large triangular latine. . . ." — *Burton, Pilgrimage to El Medinah and Meccah*, i. 276; [Memorial ed. i. 188].

1858.—"The vessels of the Arabs called **Sembuk** are small Baggelows of 80 to 100 tons burden. Whilst they run out forward into a sharp prow, the after part of the vessel is disproportionately broad and elevated above the water, in order to form a counterpoise to the colossal triangular sail which is hoisted to the masthead with such a spread that often the extent of the yard is greater than the whole length of the vessel." — *F. von Neimans*, in *Zeitschr. der Deutsch. Morgenl. Gesellsch.* xii. 420.

1880.—"The small sailing boat with one sail, which is called by the Arabs '**Jâmbook**' with which I went from Hodeida to Aden." — Letter in *Athenaeum*, March 13, p. 346.

[1900.—"We scrambled into a **sambouka** crammed and stuffed with the baggage."— *Bent, Southern Arabia*, 220.]

SAMBRE, SAMBUR, s. Hind. *sābar, sāmbar*; Skt. *śambara*. A kind of stag (*Rusa Aristotelis*, Jerdon; [Blanford, *Mammalia*, 543 *seqq.*]) the

elk of S. Indian sportsmen; *ghaus* of Bengal; jerrow (*jarāo*) of the Himālaya; the largest of Indian stags, and found in all the large forests of India. The word is often applied to the soft leather, somewhat resembling chamois leather, prepared from the hide.

1673. — "... Our usual diet was of spotted deer, **Sabre**, wild Hogs and sometimes wild Cows."—*Fryer*, 175.

[1813.—"Here he saw a number of deer, and four large **sabirs** or **samboos**, one considerably bigger than an ox. ..."—*Diary*, in *Forbes, Or. Mem.* 2nd ed. ii. 400.]

1823.—"The skin of the **Sambre**, when well prepared, forms an excellent material for the military accoutrements of the soldiers of the native Powers."—*Malcolm, Central India*, i. 9.

[1900.—"The **Sambu** stags which Lord Powerscourt turned out in his glens. ..."—*Spectator*, December 15, p. 883.]

SAMPAN, s. A kind of small boat or skiff. The word appears to be Javanese and Malay. It must have been adopted on the Indian shores, for it was picked up there at an early date by the Portuguese; and it is now current all through the further East. [The French have adopted the Annamite form *tamban*.] The word is often said to be originally Chinese, '*sanpan*,' ='three boards,' and this is possible. It is certainly one of the most ordinary words for a boat in China. Moreover, we learn, on the authority of Mr. E. C. Baber, that there is another kind of boat on the Yangtse which is called *wu-pan*, 'five boards.' Giles however says: "From the Malay *sampan*=three boards"; but in this there is some confusion. The word has no such meaning in Malay.

1510. — "My companion said, 'What means then might there be for going to this island?' They answered: 'That it was necessary to purchase a **chiampana**,' that is a small vessel, of which many are found there."—*Varthema*, 242.

1516. — "They (the Moors of Quilacare) perform their voyages in small vessels which they call **champana**."—*Barbosa*, 172.

c. 1540. — "In the other, whereof the captain was slain, there was not one escaped, for *Quiay Panian* pursued them in a **Champana**, which was the Boat of his Junk."—*Pinto* (*Cogan*, p. 79), orig. ch. lix.

1552.—"... **Champanas**, which are a kind of small vessels."—*Castanheda*, ii. 76; [rather, Bk. ii. ch. xxii. p. 76].

1613. — "And on the beach called the Bazar of the *Jaos* ... they sell every sort of provision in rice and grain for the Jaos merchants of Java Major, who daily from the dawn are landing provisions from their junks and ships in their boats or **Champenas** (which are little skiffs). ..."—*Godinho de Eredia*, 6.

[1622.—"Yt was thought fytt ... to trym up a China **Sampan** to goe with the fleete. ..."—*Cocks's Diary*, Hak. Soc. ii. 122.]

1648. — In *Van Spilbergen's Voyage* we have **Champane**, and the still more odd **Champaigne**. [See under **TOPAZ.**]

1702.—"**Sampans** being not to be got we were forced to send for the Sarah and Eaton's Long-boats."—*MS. Correspondence in I. Office from China Factory* (at Chusan), Jan. 8.

c. 1788.—"Some made their escape in prows, and some in **sampans**."—*Mem. of a Malay Family*, 3.

1868. — "The harbour is crowded with men-of-war and trading vessels ... from vessels of several hundred tons burthen down to little fishing-boats and passenger **sampans**."—*Wallace, Malay Archip.* 21.

SAMSHOO, s. A kind of ardent spirit made in China from rice. Mr. Baber doubts this being Chinese; but according to Wells Williams the name is *san-shao*, 'thrice fired' (*Guide*, 220). 'Distilled liquor' is *shao-siu*, 'fired liquor.' Compare Germ. *Brantwein*, and XXX beer. Strabo says: 'Wine the Indians drink not except when sacrificing, and that is made of rice in lieu of barley" (xv. c. i. § 53).

1684.—"... **sampsoe**, or Chinese Beer."—*Valentijn*, iv. (*China*) 129.

[1687.—"**Samshu.**" See under **ARRACK.**]

1727.—"... **Samshew** or Rice Arrack."—*A. Hamilton*, ii. 222; [ed. 1744, ii. 224].

c. 1752.—"... the people who make the *Chinese* brandy called **Samsu**, live likewise in the suburbs."—*Osbeck's Voyage*, i. 235.

[1852.—"... **samshoe**, a Chinese invention, and which is distilled from rice, after the rice has been permitted to foment (?) in ... vinegar and water."—*Neale, Residence in Siam*, 75.

SANDAL, SANDLE, SANDERS, SANDAL-WOOD, s. From Low Latin santalum, in Greek σάνταλον, and in later Greek σάνδανον; coming from the Arab. *sandal*, and that from Skt. *chandana*. The name properly belongs to the fragrant wood of the *Santalum album*, L. Three woods bearing the name *santalum*, white, yellow, and red, were in officinal use in the Middle Ages. But the name Red Sandalwood, or Red Sanders, has been long applied, both in English and in the Indian vernaculars, to the wood of *Pterocarpus santalina*, L., a tree of S. India, the wood of which is inodorous, but which is valued for various purposes in India (pillars, turning, &c.), and is exported as a dye-wood. According to Hanbury and Flückiger this last was the *sanders* so much used in the cookery of the Middle Ages for colouring sauces, &c. In the opinion of those authorities it is doubtful whether the red sandal of the medieval pharmacologists was a kind of the real odorous sandal-wood, or was the wood of *Pteroc. santal.* It is possible that sometimes the one and sometimes the other was meant. For on the one hand, even in modern times, we find Milburn (see below) speaking of the three colours of the real sandal-wood; and on the other hand we find Matthioli in the 16th century speaking of the red sandal as inodorous.

It has been a question how the *Pterocarpus santalina* came to be called sandal-wood at all. We may suggest, as a possible origin of this, the fact that its powder "mixed with oil is used for bathing and purifying the skin" (*Drury*, s.v.), much as the true sandal-wood powder also is used in the East.

c. 545.—"And from the remoter regions, I speak of Tzinista and other places of export, the imports to Taprobane are silk, aloeswood, cloves, **Sandalwood** (τζάνδανη), and so forth. . . ."—*Cosmas*, in *Cathay*, &c., clxxvii.

1298.—"Encore sachiez que en ceste ysle a arbres de **sandal** vermoille ausi grant come sunt les arbres des nostre contrée . . . et il en ont bois come nos avuns d'autres arbres sauvajes."—*Marco Polo*, Geog. Text, ch. cxci.

c. 1390.—"Take powdered rice and boil it in almond milk . . . and colour it with **Saunders.**"—Recipe quoted by *Wright, Domestic Manners*, &c., 350.

1554.—"Le **Santal** donc croist es Indes Orientales et Occidentales: en grandes Forestz, et fort espesses. Il s'en treuue trois especes: mais le plus pasle est le meilleur: le blanc apres: le rouge est mis au dernier ranc, pource qu'il n'a aucune odeur: mais les deux premiers sentent fort bon."—*Matthioli* (old Fr. version), liv. i. ch. xix.

1563.—"The **Sandal** grows about Timor, which produces the largest quantity, and it is called **chundana**; and by this name it is known in all the regions about Malaca; and the Arabs, being those who carried on the trade of those parts, corrupted the word and called it **sandal**. Every Moor, whatever his nation, calls it thus . . ."—*Garcia*, f. 185*v*. He proceeds to speak of the **sandalo** *vermelho* as quite a different product, growing in Tenasserim and on the Coromandel Coast.

1584.—". . . **Sandales** wilde from Cochin. **Sandales** domestick from Malacca. . . ."—*Wm. Barrett*, in *Hakl.* ii. 412.

1613.—". . . certain renegade Christians of the said island, along with the Moors, called in the Hollanders, who thinking it was a fine opportunity, went one time with five vessels, and another time with seven, against the said fort, at a time when most of the people . . . were gone to Solor for the **Sandal** trade, by which they had their living."—*Bocarro, Decada*, 723.

1615.—"Committee to procure the commodities recommended by Capt. Saris for Japan, viz. . . . pictures of wars, steel, skins, **sanders-wood.**"—*Sainsbury*, i. 380.

1813.—"When the trees are felled, the bark is taken off; they are then cut into billets, and buried in a dry place for two months, during which period the white ants will eat the outer wood without touching the **sandal**; it is then taken up and . . . sorted into three kinds. The deeper the colour, the higher is the perfume; and hence the merchants sometimes divide **sandal** into red, yellow, and white; but these are all different shades of the same colour."—*Milburn*, i. 291.

1825.—"Redwood, properly Red **Saunders**, is produced chiefly on the Coromandel Coast, whence it has of late years been imported in considerable quantity to England, where it is employed in dyeing. It . . . comes in round billets of a thickish red colour on the outside, a deep brighter red within, with a wavy grain; no smell or taste."—*Ibid.* ed. 1825, p. 249.

SANDOWAY, n.p. A town of Arakan, the Burmese name of which is *Thandwé* (Sand-wé), for which an etymology ('iron-tied'), and a corresponding legend are invented, as usual [see *Burmah Gazetteer*, ii. 606]. It is quite possible that the name is ancient, and represented by the *Sada* of Ptolemy.

1553.—"In crossing the gulf of Bengal there arose a storm which dispersed them in such a manner that Martin Affonso found himself alone, with his ship, at the island called Negamale, opposite the town of **Sodoe**, which is on the mainland, and there was wrecked upon a reef . . ."—*Barros*, IV. ii. 1.

In I. ix. 1, it is called **Sedoe**.

1696.—"Other places along this Coast subjected to this King (of Arracan) are *Coromoria*, **Sedoa**, *Zara*, and *Port Magaoni*."—Appendix to *Ovington*, p. 563.

SANGUICEL, s. This is a term (pl. *sanguiceis*) often used by the Portuguese writers on India for a kind of boat, or small vessel, used in war. We are not able to trace any origin in a vernacular word. It is perhaps taken from the similar proper name which is the subject of the next article. [This supposition is rendered practically certain from the quotation from Albuquerque below, furnished by Mr. Whiteway.] Bluteau gives "**Sanguicel**; termo da India. He hum genero de embarcação pequena q̃ serve na costa da India para dar alcanse aos paròs dos Mouros," 'to give chase to the prows of the Moors.'

[1512.—"Here was Nuno Vaz in a ship, the St. John, which was built in **Çamguicar**."—*Albuquerque, Cartas*, p. 99. In a letter of Nov. 30, 1513, he varies the spelling to **Çamgicar**. There are many other passages in the same writer which make it practically certain that **Sanguicels** were the vessels built at Sanguicer.]

1598.—"The Conde (Francisco da Gama) was occupied all the **winter** (q.v.) in reforming the fleets . . . and as the time came on he nominated his brother D. Luiz da Gama to be Captain-Major of the Indian Seas for the expedition to Malabar, and wrote to Baçaim to equip six very light **Sanguicels** according to instructions which should be given by Sebastian Botelho, a man of great experience in that craft. . . . These orders were given by the Count Admiral because he perceived that big fleets were not of use to guard convoys, and that it was light vessels like these alone which could catch the paraos and vessels of the pirates . . . for these escaped our fleets, and got hold of the merchant vessels at their pleasure, darting in and out, like light horse, where they would. . . ."—*Couto*, Dec. XII. liv. i. ch. 18.

1605.—"And seeing that I am informed that . . . the incursions of certain pirates who still infest that coast might be prevented with less apparatus and expense, if we had light vessels which would be more effective than the foists and galleys of which the fleets have hitherto been composed, seeing how the enemy use their **sanguicels**, which our ships and galleys cannot overtake, I enjoin and order you to build a quantity of light vessels to be employed in guarding the coast in place of the fleet of galleys and foists. . . ."—*King's Letter* to *Dom Affonso de Castro*, in *Livros das Monções*, i. 26.

[1612.—See under **GALLIVAT**, b.]

1614.—"The eight Malabaresque **Sanguicels** that Francis de Miranda despatched to the north from the bar of Goa went with three chief captains, each of them to command a week in turn. . . ."—*Bocarro, Decada*, 262.

SANGUICER, SANGUEÇA, ZINGUIZAR, &c., n.p. This is a place often mentioned in the Portuguese narratives, as very hostile to the Goa Government, and latterly as a great nest of corsairs. This appears to be *Sangameshvar*, lat. 17° 9′, formerly a port of Canara on the River Shāstrī, and standing 20 miles from the mouth of that river. The latter was navigable for large vessels up to Sangameshvar, but within the last 50 years has become impassable. [The name is derived from Skt. *sangama-īśvara*, 'Siva, Lord of the river confluence.']

1516.—"Passing this river of Dabul and going along the coast towards Goa you find a river called **Cinguiçar**, inside of which there is a place where there is a traffic in many wares, and where enter many vessels and small *Zambucos* (**Sambook**) of Malabar to sell what they bring, and buy the products of the country. The place is peopled by Moors, and Gentiles of the aforesaid Kingdom of Daquem" (**Deccan**).—*Barbosa*, Lisbon ed. p. 286.

1538.—"Thirty-five leagues from Guoa, in the middle of the Gulf of the Malabars there runs a large river called **Zamgizara**. This river is well known and of great renown. The bar is bad and very tortuous, but after you get within, it makes amends for the difficulties without. It runs inland for a great distance with great depth and breadth."—*De Castro, Primeiro Roteiro*, 36.

1553.—De Barros calls it **Zingaçar** in II. i. 4, and **Sangaça** in IV. i. 14.

1584.—"There is a Haven belonging to those ryvers (rovers), distant from Goa about 12 miles, and is called **Sanguiseo**, where many of those Rovers dwell, and doe so much mischiefe that no man can passe by, but they receive some wrong by them. . . . Which the Viceroy understanding, prepared an armie of 15 Foists, over which he made chiefe Captaine a Gentleman, his Nephew called Don Iulianes Mascharenhas, giving him expresse commandement first to goe unto the Haven of **Sanguiseu**, and utterly to raze the same downe to the ground."—*Linschoten*, ch. 92; [Hak. Soc. ii. 170].

1602.—"Both these projects he now began to put in execution, sending all his treasures (which they said exceeded ten millions in gold) to the river of **Sanguicer**, which was also within his jurisdiction, being a seaport, and there embarking it at his pleasure."—*Couto*, ix. 8. See also Dec. X. iv.:

"*How D. Gileanes Mascarenhas arrived in Malabar, and how he entered the river of* **Sanguicer** *to chastise the Naique of that place; and of the disaster in which he met his death.*" (This is the event of 1584 related by Linschoten); also Dec. X. vi. 4: "*Of the things that happened to D. Jeronymo Mascarenhas in Malabar, and how he had a* *meeting with the Zamorin, and swore peace with him; and how he brought destruction on the Naique of* **Sanguicer.**"

1727.—"There is an excellent Harbour for Shipping 8 Leagues to the Southward of *Dabul*, called **Sanguseer**, but the Country about being inhabited by *Raparees*, it is not frequented."—*A. Hamilton*, [ed. 1744] i. 244.

SANSKRIT, s. The name of the classical language of the Brahmans, *Samskrita*, meaning in that language 'purified' or 'perfected.' This was obviously at first only an epithet, and it is not of very ancient use in this specific application. To the Brahmans Sanskrit was the *bhāsha*, or language, and had no particular name. The word Sanskrit is used by the proto-grammarian Pāṇini (some centuries before Christ), but not as a denomination of the language. In the latter sense, however, both 'Sanskrit' and 'Prakrit' (**Pracrit**) are used in the *Brihat Samhitā* of Varāhamihira, c. A.D. 504, in a chapter on omens (lxxxvi. 3), to which Prof. Kern's translation does not extend. It occurs also in the *Mrichch'hakatikā*, translated by Prof. H. H. Wilson in his *Hindu Theatre*, under the name of the 'Toy-cart'; in the works of Kumārila Bhatta, a writer of the 7th century; and in the *Pāṇinīyā Śikshā*, a metrical treatise ascribed by the Hindus to Pāṇini, but really of comparatively modern origin.

There is a curiously early mention of Sanskrit by the Mahommedan poet Amīr Khusrū of Delhi, which is quoted below. The first mention (to our knowledge) of the word in any European writing is in an Italian letter of Sassetti's, addressed from Malabar to Bernardo Davanzati in Florence, and dating from 1586. The few words on the subject, of this writer, show much acumen.

In the 17th and 18th centuries such references to this language as occur are found chiefly in the works of travellers to Southern India, and by these it is often called *Grandonic*, or the like, from *grantha*, 'a book' (see **GRUNTH, GRUNTHUM**) *i.e.* a book of the classical Indian literature. The term *Sanskrit* came into familiar use after the investigations into this language by the English in Bengal (viz. by Wilkins, Jones, &c.) in the last quarter of the 18th century. [See Macdonell, *Hist. of Sanskrit Lit.* ch. i.]

A.D. *x* ?—"*Maitreya.* Now, to me, there are two things at which I cannot choose but laugh, a woman reading **Sanskrit**, and a man singing a song: the woman snuffles like a young cow when the rope is first passed through her nostrils; and the man wheezes like an old Pandit repeating his bead-roll."—*The Toy-Cart*, E.T. in *Wilson's Works*, xi. 60.

A.D. *y* ?—"Three-and-sixty or four-and-sixty sounds are there originally in Prakrit (**PRACRIT**) even as in **Sanskrit**, as taught by the Svayambhū."—*Pāṇinīyā Śikshā*, quoted in *Weber's Ind. Studien* (1858), iv. 348. But see also *Weber's Akadem. Vorlesungen* (1876), p. 194.

1318.—"But there is another language, more select than the other, which all the Brahmans use. Its name from of old is **Sahaskrit**, and the common people know nothing of it."—*Amīr Khusrū*, in *Elliot*, iii. 563.

1586.—"Sono scritte le loro scienze tutte in una lingua che dimandano **Samscruta**, che vuol dire 'bene articolata': della quale non si ha memoria quando fusse parlata, con avere (com' io dico) memorie antichissime. Imparanla come noi la greca e la latina, e vi pongono molto maggior tempo, si che in 6 anni o 7 sene fanno padroni: et ha la lingua d'oggi molte cose comuni con quella, nella quale sono molti de' nostri nomi, e particularmente de numeri il 6, 7, 8, e 9, *Dio, serpe*, et altri assai."—*Sassetti*, extracted in *De Gubernatis, Storia*, &c., Livorno, 1875, p. 221.

c. 1590.—"Although this country (Kashmīr) has a peculiar tongue, the books of knowledge are **Sanskrit** (or Sahanskrit). They also have a written character of their own, with which they write their books. The substance which they chiefly write upon is *Tūs*, which is the bark of a tree,* which with a little pains they make into leaves, and it lasts for years. In this way ancient books have been written thereon, and the ink is such that it cannot be washed out."—*Āīn* (orig.), i. p. 563; [ed. *Jarrett*, ii. 351].

1623.—"The Jesuites conceive that the Bramenes are of the dispersion of the Israelites, and their Bookes (called **Samescretan**) doe somewhat agree with the Scriptures, but that they understand them not."—*Purchas, Pilgrimage*, 559.

1651.—". . . *Souri* signifies the Sun in **Samscortam**, which is a language in which all the mysteries of Heathendom are written, and which is held in esteem by the Bramines just as Latin is among the Learned in Europe."—*Rogerius*, 4.

In some of the following quotations we have a form which it is difficult to account for:

c. 1666.—"Their first study is in the **Hanscrit**, which is a language entirely

* Of the birch-tree, Sansk. *bhurja, Betula Bhojpattra*, Wall., the exfoliating outer bark of which is called *tōz*.

different from the common *Indian*, and which is only known by the *Pendets*. And this is that Tongue, of which Father *Kircher* hath published the Alphabet received from Father *Roa*. It is called **Hanscrit**, that is, a pure Language; and because they believe this to be the Tongue in which God, by means of *Brahma*, gave them the four *Beths* (see **VEDA**), which they esteem *Sacred Books*, they call it a Holy and Divine Language."—*Bernier*, E.T. 107; [ed. *Constable*, 335].

1673.—"... who founded these, their Annals nor their **Sanscript** deliver not."—*Fryer*, 161.

1689.—"... the learned Language among them is called the **Sanscreet**."—*Ovington*, 248.

1694.—"Indicus ludus *Tchûpur*, sic nominatus veterum Brachmanorum linguâ Indicè dictâ **Sanscroot**, seu, ut vulgo, exiliori sono elegantiae causâ **Sanscreet**, non autem **Hanscreet** ut minus recte eam nuncupat Kircherus."—*Hyde, De Ludis Orientt.*, in *Syntagma Diss.* ii. 264.

1726.—"Above all it would be a matter of general utility to the Coast that some more chaplains should be maintained there for the sole purpose of studying the *Sanskrit* tongue (*de* **Sanskritze** *taal*) the head-and-mother tongue of most of the Eastern languages, and once for all to make an exact translation of the *Vedam* or Law book of the Heathen...."—*Valentijn, Choro.* p. 72.

1760.—"They have a learned language peculiar to themselves, called the **Hanscrit**...."—*Grose*, i. 202.

1774.—"This code they have written in their own language, the **Shanscrit**. A translation of it is begun under the inspection of one of the body, into the Persian language, and from that into English."—*W. Hastings*, to *Lord Mansfield*, in *Gleig*, i. 402.

1778.—"The language as well as the written character of Bengal are familiar to the Natives ... and both seem to be base derivatives from the **Shanscrit**."—*Orme*, ed. 1803, ii. 5.

1782.—"La langue **Samscroutam**, *Samskret*, **Hanscrit** ou *Grandon*, est la plus étendue: ses caractères multipliés donnent beaucoup de facilité pour exprimer ses pensées, ce qui l'a fait nommer langue divine par le P. Pons."—*Sonnerat*, i. 224.

1794.—
"With Jones, a linguist, **Sanskrit**, Greek,
or Manks."
Pursuits of Literature, 6th ed. 286.

1796.—"La madre di tutte le lingue Indiane è la **Samskrda**, cioè, *lingua perfetta*, piena, *ben digerita*. *Krda* opera perfetta o compita, *Sam*, simul, *insieme*, e vuol dire lingua tutta insieme *ben digerita*, legata, *perfetta*."—*Fra Paolino*, p. 258.

SAPECA, SAPÈQUE, s. This word is used at Macao for what we call **cash** (q.v.) in Chinese currency; and it is the word generally used by French writers for that coin. Giles says: "From *sapek*, a coin found in Tonquin and Cochin-China, and equal to about half a pfennig ($\frac{1}{600}$ Thaler), or about one-sixth of a German Kreutzer" (*Gloss. of Reference*, 122). We cannot learn much about this coin of Tonquin. Milburn says, under 'Cochin China': "The only currency of the country is a sort of cash, called **sappica**, composed chiefly of tutenague (see **TOOTNAGUE**), 600 making a *quan*: this is divided into 10 mace of 60 cash each, the whole strung together, and divided by a knot at each mace" (ed. 1825, pp. 444-445). There is nothing here inconsistent with our proposed derivation, given later on. *Mace* and *Sappica* are equally Malay words. We can hardly doubt that the true origin of the term is that communicated by our friend Mr. E. C. Baber: "Very probably from Malay *sa*, 'one,' and *păku*, 'a string or file of the small coin called pichis.' *Pichis* is explained by Crawfurd as 'Small coin ... money of copper, brass, or tin.... It was the ancient coin of Java, and also the only one of the Malays when first seen by the Portuguese.' *Păku* is written by Favre *pekū* (*Dict. Malais-Français*) and is derived by him from Chinese *pé-ko*, 'cent.' In the dialect of Canton *pak* is the word for 'a hundred,' and one *pak* is the colloquial term for a string of one hundred cash." **Sapeku** would then be properly a string of 100 cash, but it is not difficult to conceive that it might through some misunderstanding (*e.g.* a confusion of *peku* and *pichis*) have been transferred to the single coin. There is a passage in Mr. Gerson da Cunha's *Contributions to the Study of Portuguese Numismatics*, which may seem at first sight inconsistent with this derivation. For he seems to imply that the smallest denomination of coin struck by Albuquerque at Goa in 1510 was called **cepayqua**, *i.e.* in the year before the capture of Malacca, and consequent familiarity with Malay terms. I do not trace his authority for this; the word is not mentioned in the Commentaries of Alboquerque, and it is quite possible that the *dinheiros*, as these small copper coins were also called, only received the name *cepayqua* at a later date, and some time after the occupation of Malacca (see *Da Cunha*, pp. 11-12, and 22). [But also see the quotation of 1510 from Correa under **PARDAO**. This word has been discussed by Col. Temple (*Ind. Antiq.*, August 1897, pp. 222 *seq.*), who gives quotations establishing the derivation from the Malay *sapaku.*

[1639.—"It (*caxa*, cash) hath a four-square hole through it, at which they string them on a Straw; a String of two hundred *Caxaes*, called *Sata*, is worth about three farthings sterling, and five *Satas* tyed together make a **Sapocon**. The Javians, when this money first came amongst them, were so cheated with the Novelty, that they would give six bags of Pepper for ten **Sapocons**, thirteen whereof amount to but a Crown."—*Mandelslo, Voyages*, E.T. p. 117.

[1703.—"This is the reason why the *Caxas* are valued so little: they are punched in the middle, and string'd with little twists of Straw, two hundred in one Twist, which is called Santa, and is worth nine Deniers. Five Santas tied together make a thousand *Caxas*, or a **Sapoon (? Sapocon)**."—*Collection of Dutch Voyages*, 199.

[1830.—"The money current in Bali consists solely of Chinese pice with a hole in the centre. . . . They however put them up in hundreds and thousands; two hundred are called *satah*, and are equal to one rupee copper, and a thousand called **Sapaku**, are valued at five rupees."—*Singapore Chronicle*, June 1830, in *Moor, Indian Archip.* p. 94.

[1892.—"This is a brief history of the **Sapec** (more commonly known to us as the **cash**), the only native coin of China, and which is found everywhere from Malaysia to Japan."—*Ridgeway, Origin of Currency*, 157.]

SAPPAN-WOOD, s. The wood of *Caesalpina sappan*; the *bakkam* of the Arabs, and the **Brazil-wood** of medieval commerce. Bishop Caldwell at one time thought the Tamil name, from which this was taken, to have been given because the wood was supposed to come from *Japan*. Rumphius says that Siam and Champa are the original countries of the Sappan, and quotes from Rheede that in Malabar it was called *Tsajampangan*, suggestive apparently of a possible derivation from *Champa*. The mere fact that it does not come from Japan would not disprove this derivation any more than the fact that turkeys and maize did not originally come from Turkey would disprove the fact of the birds and the grain (*gran turco*) having got names from such a belief. But the tree appears to be indigenous in Malabar, the Deccan, and the Malay Peninsula; whilst the Malayāl. *shappaṅṅam*, and the Tamil *shappu*, both signifying 'red (wood),' are apparently derivatives from *shawa*, 'to be red,' and suggest another origin as most probable. [The *Mad. Gloss.* gives Mal. *chappannam*, from *chappu*, 'leaf,' Skt. *anga*, 'body'; Tam. *shappangam*.] The Malay word is also *sapang*, which Crawfurd supposes to have originated the trade-name. If, however, the etymology just suggested be correct, the word must have passed from Continental India to the Archipelago. For curious particulars as to the names of this dye-wood, and its vicissitudes, see **BRAZIL**; [and Burnell's note on *Linschoten*, Hak. Soc. i. 121].

c. 1570.—
"O rico Sião ja dado ao Bremem,
O Cochim de Calemba que deu mana
De **sapão**, chumbo, salitre e vitualhas
Lhe apercebem celleiros e muralhas."
A de Abreu, Desc. de Malaca.

1598.—"There are likewise some Diamants and also . . . the wood **Sapon**, whereof also much is brought from *Sian*, it is like Brasill to die withall."—*Linschoten*, 36; [Hak. Soc. i. 120].

c. 1616.—"There are in this city of Ová (read *Odia*, **Judea**), capital of the kingdom of Siam, two factories; one of the Hollanders with great capital, and another of the English with less. The trade which both drive is in deer-skins, shagreen **sappan** (*sapão*) and much silk which comes thither from Chincheo and Cochinchina. . . ."—*Bocarro, Decadă*, 530.

[1615.—"Hindering the cutting of **baccam** or brazill wood."—*Foster, Letters*, iii. 158.]

1616.—"I went to Sapàn Dono to know whether he would lend me any money upon interest, as he promised me; but . . . he drove me afe with wordes, ofring to deliver me money for all our **sappon** which was com in this junk, at 22 *mas* per *pico*."—*Cocks's Diary*, i. 208-9.

1617.—Johnson and Pitts at **Judea** in Siam "are glad they can send a **junk** well laden with **sapon**, because of its scarcity."—*Sainsbury*, ii. 32.

1625.—". . . a wood to die withall called **Sapan** wood, the same we here call Brasill."—*Purchas, Pilgrimage*, 1004.

1685.—"Moreover in the whole Island there is a great plenty of Brazill wood, which in India is called **sapão**."—*Ribeiro, Fat. Hist.* f. 8.

1727.—"It (the Siam Coast) produces good store of **Sapan** and Agala-woods, with Gumlack and Sticklack, and many Drugs that I know little about."—*A. Hamilton*, ii. 194; [ed. 1744].

1860. — "The other productions which constituted the exports of the island were **Sapan** wood to Persia. . . ."—*Tennent, Ceylon*, ii. 54.

SARBATANE, SARBACANE, s. This is not Anglo-Indian, but it often occurs in French works on the East, as applied to the blowing-tubes used by various tribes of the Indian Islands for discharging small arrows, often poisoned. The same instrument is used among the tribes of northern South America, and in some parts of Madagascar. The word comes through the Span. *cebratana, cerbatana, zarbatana*, also Port. *sarabatana*, &c., Ital. *cerbotana*, Mod. Greek *ζαροβοτάνα*, from the Ar. *zabaṭāna*, 'a tube for blowing pellets' (a pea-shooter in fact!). Dozy says that the *r* must have been sounded in the Arabic of the Spanish Moors, as Pedro de Alcala translates *zebratana* by Ar. *zarbatāna*. The resemblance of this to the Malay **sumpitan** (q.v.) is curious, though it is not easy to suggest a transition, if the Arabic word is, as it appears, old enough to have been introduced into Spanish. There is apparently, however, no doubt that in Arabic it is a borrowed word. The Malay word seems to be formed directly from *sumpit*, 'to discharge from the mouth by a forcible expiration' (*Crawfurd, Mal. Dict.*).

[1516.—". . . the force which had accompanied the King, very well armed, many of them with bows, others carrying blowing tubes with poisoned arrows (*Zarvatanas com setas ervadas*. . . ."—*Comm. of Dalboquerque*, Hak. Soc. iii. 104.]

SARBOJI, s. This is the name of some weapon used in the extreme south of India; but we have not been able to ascertain its character or etymology. We conjecture, however, that it may be the long lance or pike, 18 or 20 feet long, which was the characteristic and formidable weapon of the Marava **Colleries** (q.v.). See *Bp. Caldwell's H. of Tinnevelly*, p. 103 and *passim*; [*Stuart, Man. of Tinnevelly*, 50. This explanation is probably incorrect. Welsh (*Military Rem.* i. 104) defines **sarabogies** as "a species of park guns, for firing salutes at feasts, &c.; but not used in war." It has been suggested that the word is simply Hind. *sirbojha*, 'a head-load,' and Dr. Grierson writes: "'Laden with a head' may refer to a head carried home on a spear." Dr. Pope writes: "*Sarboji* is not found in any Dravidian dialect, as far as I know. It is a synonym for Sivaji. *Sarva (sarbo)-ji* is honorific. In the Tanjore Inscription it is *Serfogi*. In mythology Siva's name is 'arrow,' 'spear,' and 'head-burthen,' of course by metonomy." Mr. Brandt suggests Tam. *sĕrŭ*, "war," *bŭgei*, "a tube." No weapon of the name appears in Mr. Egerton's *Hand-book of Indian Arms*.]

1801.—"The Rt. Hon. the Governor in Council . . . orders and directs all persons, whether Polygars (see **BOLIGAR**), **Colleries**, or other inhabitants possessed of arms in the Provinces of Dindigul, Tinnevelly, Ramnadpuram, Sivagangai, and Madura, to deliver the said arms, consisting of Muskets, Matchlocks, Pikes, Gingauls (see **GINGALL**), and **Sarabogoi** to Lieut.-Col. Agnew. . . ."—*Procl. by Madras Govt.*, dd. 1st Decr., in *Bp. Caldwell's Hist.* p. 227.

c. 1814.—"Those who carry spear and sword have land given them producing 5 *kalams* of rice; those bearing muskets, 7 *kalams*; those bearing the **sarboji**, 9 *kalams*; those bearing the *sanjali* (see **GINGALL**), or gun for two men, 14 *kalams*. . . ."—*Account of the Maravas*, from *Mackenzie MSS.* in *Madras Journal*, iv. 360.

SAREE, s. Hind. *sāṛī, sāṛhī*. The cloth which constitutes the main part of a woman's dress in N. India, wrapt round the body and then thrown over the head.

1598.—". . . likewise they make whole pieces or webbes of this hearbe, sometimes mixed and woven with silke. . . . Those webs are named **sarijn** . . ."—*Linschoten*, 28; [Hak. Soc. i. 96].

1785.—". . . Her clothes were taken off, and a red silk covering (a **saurry**) put upon her."—*Acct. of a Suttee*, in *Seton-Karr*, i. 90.

SARNAU, SORNAU, n.p. A name often given to Siam in the early part of the 16th century; from *Shahr-i-nao*, Pers. 'New-city'; the name by which Yuthia or Ayodhya (see **JUDEA**), the capital founded on the Menam about 1350, seems to have become known to the traders of the Persian Gulf. Mr. Braddell (*J. Ind. Arch.* v. 317) has suggested that the name (*Sheher-al-nawi*, as he calls it) refers to the distinction spoken of by La Loubère between the **Thai-Yai**, an older people of the race, and the Thai-*Noi*, the people known to us as Siamese. But this is less probable.

We have still a city of Siam called *Lophaburī*, anciently a capital, and the name of which appears to be a Sanskrit or Pali form, *Nava-pura*, meaning the same as *Shahr-i-nao;* and this indeed may have first given rise to the latter name. The *Cernove* of Nicolo Conti (c. 1430) is generally supposed to refer to a city of Bengal, and one of the present writers has identified it with Lakhnāotī or Gauṛ, an official name of which in the 14th cent. was *Shahr-i-nao.* But it is just possible that Siam was the country spoken of.

1442.—"The inhabitants of the sea-coasts arrive here (at Ormuz) from the counties of Chín, Java, Bengal, the cities of Zirbád, Tenásiri, Sokotora, **Shahr-i-nao.** . . ."—*Abdurrazzāk*, in *Not. et Exts.*, xiv. 429.

1498.—"**Xarnauz** is of Christians, and the King is Christian; it is 50 days voyage with a fair wind from Calicut. The King . . . has 400 elephants of war; in the land is much benzoin . . . and there is aloes-wood . . ."—*Roteiro de Vasco da Gamá*, 110.

1510.—". . . They said they were from a city called **Sarnau**, and had brought for sale silken stuffs, and aloeswood, and benzoin, and musk."—*Varthema*, 212.

1514.—". . . Tannazzari, **Sarnau**, where is produced all the finest white benzoin, storax, and lac finer than that of Martaman." —Letter of *Giov. d'Empoli*, in *Arch. Storico Italiano*, App. 80.

1540.—". . . all along the coast of *Malaya*, and within the Land, a great King commands, who for a more famous and recommendable Title above all other Kings, causeth himself to be called *Prechau Saleu*, Emperor of all **Sornau**, which is a Country wherein there are thirteen kingdoms, by us commonly called **Siam**" (Sião).—*Pinto* (orig. cap. xxxvi.), in *Cogan*, p. 43.

c. 1612.—"It is related of Siam, formerly called **Sheher-al-Nawi**, to which Country all lands under the wind here were tributary, that there was a King called Bubannia, who when he heard of the greatness of Malacca sent to demand submission and homage of that kingdom."—*Sijara Malayu*, in *J. Ind. Arch.* v. 454.

1726.—"About 1340 reigned in the kingdom of **Siam** (then called **Sjaharnouw** or **Sornau**), a very powerful Prince."—*Valentijn*, v. 319.

SARONG, s. Malay. *sārung;* the body-cloth, or long kilt, tucked or girt at the waist, and generally of coloured silk or cotton, which forms the chief article of dress of the Malays and Javanese. The same article of dress, and the name (*saran*) are used in Ceylon. It is an old Indian form of dress, but is now used only by some of the people of the south; *e.g.* on the coast of Malabar, where it is worn by the Hindus (white), by the Mappilas (**Moplah**) of that coast, and the Labbais (**Lubbye**) of Coromandel (coloured), and by the *Bants* of Canara, who wear it of a dark blue. With the Labbais the coloured *sarong* is a modern adoption from the Malays. Crawfurd seems to explain *sarung* as Javanese, meaning first 'a case or sheath,' and then a wrapper or garment. But, both in the Malay islands and in Ceylon, the word is no doubt taken from Skt. *sāranga*, meaning 'variegated' and also 'a garment.'

[1830.—". . . the cloth or **sarong**, which has been described by Mr. Marsden to be 'not unlike a Scots highlander's plaid in appearance, being a piece of party-coloured cloth, about 6 or 8 feet long, and 3 or 4 feet wide, sewed together at the ends, forming, as some writers have described it, a wide sack without a bottom.' With the *Malâyus*, the **sarong** is either worn slung over the shoulders as a sash, or tucked round the waist and descending to the ankles, so as to enclose the legs like a petticoat."—*Raffles, Java*, i. 96.]

1868.—"He wore a **sarong** or Malay petticoat, and a green jacket."—*Wallace, Mal. Arch.* 171.

SATIGAM, n.p. *Sātgāon*, formerly and from remote times a port of much trade on the right bank of the Hoogly R., 30 m. above Calcutta, but for two and a half centuries utterly decayed, and now only the site of a few huts, with a ruined mosque as the only relique of former importance. It is situated at the bifurcation of the Saraswati channel from the Hoogly, and the decay dates from the silting up of the former. It was commonly called by the Portuguese **Porto Pequeno** (q.v.).

c. 1340.—"About this time the rebellion of Fakhrá broke out in Bengal. Fakhrá and his Bengali forces killed Kádar Khán (Governor of Lakhnauti). . . . He then plundered the treasury of Lakhnauti, and secured possession of that place and of **Satgánw** and Sunárgánw."—*Ziā-ud-dīn Barnī*, in *Elliot*, iii. 243.

1535.—"In this year Diogo Rabello, finishing his term of service as Captain and Factor of the Choromandel fishery, with license from the Governor went to Bengal in a vessel of his . . . and he went well armed along with two foists which equipped with his own money, the Governor only lending him artillery and nothing more. . . . So this

Diogo Rabello arrived at the Port of **Satigaon**, where he found two great ships of Cambaya which three days before had arrived with great quantity of merchandise, selling and buying: and these, without touching them, he caused to quit the port and go down the river, forbidding them to carry on any trade, and he also sent one of the foists, with 30 men, to the other port of **Chatigaon**, where they found three ships from the Coast of Choromandel, which were driven away from the port. And Diogo Rabello sent word to the Gozil that he was sent by the Governor with choice of peace or war, and that he should send to ask the King if he chose to liberate the (Portuguese) prisoners, in which case he also would liberate his ports and leave them in their former peace. . . ."—*Correa*, iii. 649.

[c. 1590.—"In the Sarkár of **Sátgáon**, there are two ports at a distance of half a *kos* from each other; the one is **Sátgáon**, the other Hugli: the latter the chief; both are in the possession of the Europeans. Fine pomegranates grow here."—*Āīn*, ed. *Jarrett*, ii. 125.]

SATIN, s. This is of course English, not Anglo-Indian. The common derivation [accepted by Prof. Skeat (*Concise Dict.* 2nd ed. s.v.] is with Low Lat. *seta*, 'silk,' Lat. *seta*, *saeta*, 'a bristle, a hair,' through the Port. *setim*. Dr. Wells Williams (*Mid. King.*, ii. 123) says it is probably derived eventually from the Chinese *sz'-tün*, though intermediately through other languages. It is true that *sz'tün* or *sz'-twan* is a common (and ancient) term for this sort of silk texture. But we may remark that trade-words adopted directly from the Chinese are comparatively rare (though no doubt the intermediate transit indicated would meet this objection, more or less). And we can hardly doubt that the true derivation is that given in *Cathay and the Way Thither*, p. 486; viz. from *Zaitun* or *Zayton*, the name by which Chwan-chau (**Chinchew**), the great medieval port of western trade in Fokien, was known to western traders. We find that certain rich stuffs of damask and satin were called from this place, by the Arabs, *Zaitūnia;* the Span. *aceytuni* (for 'satin'), the medieval French *zatony*, and the medieval Ital. *zetani*, afford intermediate steps.

c. 1350.—"The first city that I reached after crossing the sea was *Zaitūn*. . . . It is a great city, superb indeed; and in it they make damasks of velvet as well as those of satin (*kimkhā*—see **KINCOB, ATLAS**), which are called from the name of the city **zaitūnia**."—*Ibn Batuta*, iv. 269.

1352.—In an inventory of this year in *Douet d'Arcq* we have: "**Zatony** at 4 *écus* the ell" (p. 342).

1405.—"And besides, this city (Samarkand) is very rich in many wares which come to it from other parts. From Russia and Tartary come hides and linens, and from Cathay silk-stuffs, the best that are made in all that region, especially the **setunis**, which are said to be the best in the world, and the best of all are those that are without pattern."—*Clavijo* (translated anew—the passage corresponding to Markham's at p. 171). The word **setuni** occurs repeatedly in Clavijo's original.

1440.—In the *Libro de Gabelli*, &c., of Giov. da Uzzano, we have mention among silk stuffs, several times, of "**zetani** *vellutati*, and other kinds of **zetani**."—*Della Decima*, iv. 58, 107, &c.

1441.—"Before the throne (at Bijanagar) was placed a cushion of **zaitūnī** satin, round which three rows of the most exquisite pearls were sewn."—*Abdurrazzāk*, in *Elliot*, iv. 120. (The original is "*darpesh-i-takht bālishī az* **atlas-i-zaitūnī**"; see *Not. et Exts.* xiv. 376. Quatremère (*ibid.* 462) translated '*un carreau de satin* olive,' taking *zaitūn* in its usual Arabic sense of 'an olive tree.') Also see *Elliot*, iv. 113.

SATRAP, s. Anc. Pers. *khshatrapa*, which becomes *satrap*, as *khshāyathiya* becomes *shāh*. The word comes to us direct from the Greek writers who speak of Persia. But the title occurs not only in the books of Ezra, Esther, and Daniel, but also in the ancient inscriptions, as used by certain lords in Western India, and more precisely in Surāshtra or Peninsular Guzerat. Thus, in a celebrated inscription regarding a dam, near Girnār:

c. A.D. 150.—". . . he, the Mahā-**Khshatrapa** Rudradāman . . . for the increase of his merit and fame, has rebuilt the embankment three times stronger." — In *Indian Antiquary*, vii. 262. The identity of this with *satrap* was pointed out by James Prinsep, 1838 (*J. As. Soc. Ben.* vii. 345). [There were two Indian satrap dynasties, viz. the Western Satraps of Saurāshtra and Gujarāt, from about A.D. 150 to A.D. 388; for which see *Rapson and Indraji*, *The Western Kshatrapas* (*J. R. A. S.*, *N. S.*, 1890, p. 639); and the Northern Kshatrapas of Mathura and the neighbouring territories in the 1st cent. A.D. See articles by *Rapson and Indraji* in *J. R. A. S.*, *N. S.*, 1894, pp. 525, 541.]

1883.—"An eminent Greek scholar used to warn his pupils to beware of false analogies in philology. 'Because,' he used to say, 'σατράπης is the Greek for **satrap**, it does not follow that ῥατράπης is the Greek for rat-trap.'"—*Sat. Rev.* July 14, p. 53.

SATSUMA, n.p. Name of a city and formerly of a principality (daimioship) in Japan, the name of which is familiar not only from the deplorable necessity of bombarding its capital Kagosima in 1863 (in consequence of the murder of Mr. Richardson, and other outrages, with the refusal of reparation), but from the peculiar cream-coloured pottery made there and now well known in London shops.

1615.—"I said I had receued suffition at his highnes hands in havinge the good hap to see the face of soe mightie a King as the King of **Shashma**; whereat he smiled."—*Cocks's Diary*, i. 4-5.

1617.—"Speeches are given out that the *caboques* or Japon players (or whores) going from hence for Tushma to meete the Corean ambassadors, were set on by the way by a boate of **Xaxma** theeves, and kild all both men and women, for the money they had gotten at Firando."—*Ibid.* 256.

SAUGOR, SAUGOR ISLAND, n.p. A famous island at the mouth of the Hoogly R., the site of a great fair and pilgrimage—properly *Ganga Sāgara* ('Ocean Ganges'). It is said once to have been populous, but in 1688 (the date is clearly wrong) to have been swept by a cyclone-wave. It is now a dense jungle haunted by tigers.

1683.—"We went in our Budgeros to see ye Pagodas at **Sagor**, and returned to ye Oyster River, where we got as many Oysters as we desired."—*Hedges*, March 12; [Hak. Soc. i. 68].

1684.—"James Price assured me that about 40 years since, when ye Island called **Gonga Sagur** was inhabited, ye Raja of ye Island gathered yearly Rent out of it, to ye amount of 26 Lacks of Rupees." — *Ibid.* Dec. 15; [Hak. Soc. i. 172].

1705.—"**Sagore** est une Isle où il y a une Pagode très-respectée parmi les Gentils, où ils vont en pelerinage, et où il y a deux Faquers qui y font leur residence. Ces Faquers sçavent charmer les bêtes feroces, qu'on y trouve en quantité, sans quoi ils seroient tous les jours exposés à estre devorez."—*Luillier*, p. 123.

1727.—". . . among the *Pagans*, the Island **Sagor** is accounted holy, and great numbers of *Jougies* go yearly thither in the Months of *November* and *December*, to worship and wash in Salt-Water, tho' many of them fall Sacrifices to the hungry Tigers."—*A. Hamilton*, ii. 3; [ed. 1744].

SAUL-WOOD, s. Hind. *sāl*, from Skt. *śāla;* the timber of the tree *Shorea robusta*, Gaertner, N.O. *Dipterocarpeae*, which is the most valuable building timber of Northern India. Its chief habitat is the forest immediately under the Himālaya, at intervals throughout that region from the Brahmaputra to the Biās; it abounds also in various more southerly tracts between the Ganges and the Godavery. [The botanical name is taken from Sir John Shore. For the peculiar habitat of the Sāl as compared with the Teak, see *Forsyth, Highlands of C.I.* 25 *seqq.*] It is strong and durable, but very heavy, so that it cannot be floated without more buoyant aids, and is, on that and other accounts, inferior to teak. It does not appear among eight kinds of timber in general use, mentioned in the *Āīn*. The *saul* has been introduced into China, perhaps at a remote period, on account of its connection with Buddha's history, and it is known there by the Indian name, *so-lo* (*Bretschneider* on *Chinese Botan. Works*, p. 6).

c. 650.—"L'Honorable du siècle, animé d'une grande pitié, et obéissant à l'ordre des temps, jugea utile de paraitre dans le monde. Quand il eut fini de convertir les hommes, il se plongea dans les joies du Nirvâna. Se plaçant entre deux arbres **Sâlas**, il tourna sa tête vers le nord et s'endormit."—*Hiouen Thsang, Mémoires* (*Voyages des Pèl. Bouddh.* ii. 340).

1765.—"The produce of the country consists of **shaal** timbers (a wood equal in quality to the best of our oak)."—*Holwell, Hist. Events*, &c., i. 200.

1774.—"This continued five *kos;* towards the end there are **sāl** and large forest trees."—*Bogle*, in *Markham's Tibet*, 19.

1810.—"The **saul** is a very solid wood . . . it is likewise heavy, yet by no means so ponderous as teak; both, like many of our former woods, sink in fresh water."—*Williamson, V.M.* ii. 69.

SAYER, SYRE, &c., s. Hind. from Arab. *sā'ir*, a word used technically for many years in the Indian accounts to cover a variety of items of taxation and impost, other than the Land Revenue.

The transitions of meaning in Arabic words are (as we have several times had occasion to remark) very obscure; and until we undertook the investigation of the subject for this article (a task in which we are indebted to the kind help of Sir H. Waterfield, of the India Office, one of the busiest men in the public service, but, as so often happens, one of the readiest to render assistance) the obscurity attaching to the word *sayer* in this sense was especially great.

Wilson, s.v. says: "In its original purport the word signifies moving, walking, or the whole, the remainder; from the latter it came to denote the remaining, or all other, sources of revenue accruing to the Government in addition to the land-tax." In fact, according to this explanation, the application of the term might be illustrated by the ancient story of a German Professor lecturing on botany in the pre-scientific period. He is reported to have said: 'Every plant, gentlemen, is divided into two parts. *This* is the *root*,—and *this* is the *rest of it!*' Land revenue was the root, and all else was 'the rest of it.'

Sir C. Trevelyan again, in a passage quoted below, says that the Arabic word has "the same meaning as 'miscellaneous.'" Neither of these explanations, we conceive, *pace tantorum virorum*, is correct.

The term **Sayer** in the 18th century was applied to a variety of inland imposts, but especially to local and arbitrary charges levied by zemindars and other individuals, with a show of authority, on all goods passing through their estates by land or water, or sold at markets (**bazar, haut, gunge**) established by them, charges which formed in the aggregate an enormous burden upon the trade of the country.

Now the fact is that in *sā'ir* two old Semitic forms have coalesced in sound though coming from different roots, viz. (in Arabic) *sair*, producing *sā'ir*, 'walking, current,' and *sā'r*, producing *sā'ir*, 'remainder,' the latter being a form of the same word that we have in the Biblical *Shear-jashub*, 'the remnant shall remain' (*Isaiah*, vii. 3). And we conceive that the true sense of the Indian term was 'current or customary charges'; an idea that lies at the root of sundry terms of the same kind in various languages, including our own *Customs*, as well as the **dustoory** which is so familiar in India. This interpretation is aptly illustrated by the quotation below from Mr. Stuart's Minute of Feb. 10, 1790.

At a later period it seems probable that some confusion arose with the other sense of *sā'ir*, leading to its use, more or less, for 'et ceteras,' and accounting for what we have indicated above as erroneous explanations of the word.

I find, however, that the *Index and Glossary to the Regulations*, ed. 1832 (vol. iii.), defines: "**Sayer.** What moves. Variable imports, distinct from land-rent or revenue, consisting of customs, tolls, licenses, duties on merchandise, and other articles of personal moveable property; as well as mixed duties, and taxes on houses shops, bazars, &c." This of course throws some doubt on the rationale of the Arabic name as suggested above.

In a despatch of April 10, 1771, to Bengal, the Court of Directors drew attention to the private Bazar charges, as "a great detriment to the public collections, and a burthen and oppression to the inhabitants"; enjoining that no *Buzars* or *Gunges* should be kept up but such as particularly belonged to the Government. And in such the duties were to be rated in such manner as the respective positions and prosperity of the different districts would admit.

In consequence of these instructions it was ordered in 1773 that "all duties coming under the description of **sayer** *Chelluntah* (H. *chalantā*, 'in transit'), and *Rah-darry* (**radaree**) . . . and other oppressive impositions on the foreign as well as the internal trade of the country" should be abolished; and, to prevent all pretext of injustice, proportional deductions of rent were conceded to the zemindars in the annual collections. Nevertheless the exactions went on much as before, in defiance of this and repeated orders. And in 1786 the Board of Revenue issued a proclamation declaring that any person levying such duties should be subject to corporal punishment, and that the zemindar in whose zemindarry such an offence might be committed, should forfeit his lands.

Still the evil practices went on till 1790, when Lord Cornwallis took up the matter with intelligence and determination. In the preceding year he had abolished all **radaree** duties in Behar and Benares, but the abuses in Bengal Proper seem to have been more swarming and persistent. On June 11, 1790, orders were issued resuming the collection of all duties indicated into the hands of Government; but this was followed after a few weeks (July 28) by an order abolishing them altogether, with some exceptions, which will be presently alluded to. This double step is explained by the Governor-General in a Minute dated July 18: "When I first proposed the resumption of the **Sayer** from the Landholders, it appeared to me advisable to continue the former collection (the unauthorised articles excepted) for the current year, in order that by the necessary accounts [we might have the means] for making a fair adjustment of the compensation, and at the same time acquire sufficient knowledge of the collections to enable us to enter upon the regulation of them from the commencement of the ensuing year. . . . The collections appear to be so numerous, and of so intricate a nature, as to preclude the possibility of regulating them all; and as the establishment of new rates for such articles as it might be thought advisable to continue would require much consideration, . . . I recommend that, instead of continuing the collection . . . for the current year . . . all the existing articles of **Sayer** collection (with the exception of the Abkarry (**Abcarree**) . . .) be immediately abolished; and that the Collectors be directed to withdraw their officers from the **Gunges, Bazars** and **Hauts**," compensation being duly made. The Board of Revenue could then consider on what few articles of luxury in general consumption it might be proper to reimpose a tax.

The Order of July 28 abolished "all duties, taxes, and collections coming under the denomination of **Sayer** (with the exception of the Government and Calcutta Customs, the duties levied on pilgrims at Gya, and other places of pilgrimage,—the *Abkarry* . . . which is to be collected on account of the Government . . . the collections made in the **Gunges, Bazars** and **Hauts** situated within the limits of Calcutta, and such collections as are confirmed to the landholders and the holders of **Gunges** &c. by the published Resolutions of June 11, 1790, namely, rent paid for the use of land (and the like) . . . or for orchards, pasture-ground, or fisheries sometimes included in the sayer under the denomination of *phulkur* (Hind. *phalkar*, from *phal*, 'fruit'), *bunkur* (from Hind. *ban*, 'forest or pasture-ground'), and *julkur* (Hind. *jalkar*, from *jal*, 'water') . . . ." These Resolutions are printed with Regn. XXVII. of 1793.

By an order of the Board of Revenue of April 28, 1790, correspondence regarding **Sayer** was separated from 'Land Revenue'; and on the 16th *idem* the Abkarry was separately regulated.

The amount in the Accounts credited as Land Revenue in Bengal seems to have included both *Sayer* and *Abkarry* down to the Accts. presented to Parliament in 1796. In the "Abstract Statement of Receipts and Disbursements of the Bengal Government" for 1793-94, the "Collections under head of **Syer** and Abkarry" amount to Rs. 10,98,256. In the Accounts, printed in 1799, for 1794-5 to 1796-7, the "Land and **Sayer** Revenues" are given, but Abkārī is not mentioned. Among the Receipts and Disbursements for 1800-1 appears "**Syer** Collections, including Abkaree, 7,81,925."

These forms appear to have remained in force down to 1833. In the accounts presented in 1834, from 1828-9, to 1831-2, with Estimate for 1832-3, Land Revenue is given separately, and next to it **Syer** and Abkaree Revenue. Except that the spelling was altered back to *Sayer* and *Abkarry*, this remained till 1856. In 1857 the accounts for 1854-5 showed in separate lines,—

> Land Revenue,
> Excise Duties, in Calcutta,
> **Sayer** Revenue,
> Abkarry ditto.

In the accounts for 1861-2 it became—

> Land Revenue,
> **Sayer** and Miscellaneous,
> Abkaree,

and in those for 1863-4 **Sayer** vanished altogether.

The term Sayer has been in use in Madras and Bombay as well as in Bengal. From the former we give an example under 1802; from the latter we have not met with a suitable quotation.

The following entries in the Bengal accounts for 1858-59 will exemplify the application of **Sayer** in the more recent times of its maintenance :—

Under Bengal, Behar and Orissa :

Sale of Trees and Sunken Boats	Rs. 555	0	0

Under Pegu and Martaban Provinces :

Fisheries	Rs. 1,22,874	0	2
Tax on **Birds' nests** (q.v.)	7,449	0	0
,, on Salt . .	43,061	3	10
Fees for fruits and gardens . . .	7,287	9	1
Tax on Bees' wax .	1,179	8	0
Do. Collections . .	8,050	0	0
Sale of Government Timbers, &c. . .	4,19,141	12	8
	6,09,043	1	9

Under the same :

Sale proceeds of unclaimed and confiscated Timbers, ...	Rs. 146	11	10
Net Salvage on Drift Timbers	2,247	10	0
	2,394	5	10

c. 1580.—"**Sāir** *az Gangāpat o aṭrāf-i-Hindowi waghaira* . . ." *i.e.* "**Sayer** from the Ganges . . . and the Hindu districts, &c. . . 170,800 *dams*."—*Āīn-i-Akbarī*, orig. i. 395, in detailed Revenues of *Sirkar Jannatābād* or *Gaur ;* [ed. *Jarrett*, ii. 131].

1751.—"I have heard that Ramkissen Seat who lives in Calcutta has carried goods to that place without paying the Muxidavad **Syre** chowkey (**choky**) duties." — *Letter from Nawāb to Prest. Ft. William*, in *Long*, 25.

1788.—"**Sairjat**—All kinds of taxation besides the land-rent. **Sairs**.—Any place or office appointed for the collection of duties or customs."—*The Indian Vocabulary*, 112.

1790.—"Without entering into a discussion of privileges founded on Custom, and of which it is easier to ascertain the abuse than the origin, I shall briefly remark on the Collections of **Sayer**, that while they remain in the hands of the Zemindars, every effort to free the internal Commerce from the baneful effects of their vexatious impositions must necessarily prove abortive."—*Minute by the Hon. C. Stuart*, dd. Feb. 10, quoted by Lord Cornwallis in his Minute of July 18.

,, "The Board last day very humanely and politically recommended unanimously the abolition of the **Sayr**.

"The statement of Mr. Mercer from Burdwan makes all the **Sayr** (consisting of a strange medley of articles taxable, not omitting even Hermaphrodites) amount only to 58,000 Rupees. . . ."—*Minute by Mr. Law of the Bd. of Revenue*, forwarded by the Board, July 12.

1792.—"The **Jumma** on which a settlement for 10 years has been made is about (current Rupees) 3,01,00,000 . . . which is 9,35,691 Rupees less than the Average Collections of the three preceding Years. On this Jumma, the Estimate for 1791-2 is formed, and the **Sayer** Duties, and some other extra Collections, formerly included in the Land Revenue, being abolished, accounts for the Difference. . . ."—*Heads of Mr. Dundas's Speech on the Finances of the E.I. Company*, June 5, 1792.

1793.—"A Regulation for re-enacting with alterations and modifications, the Rules passed by the Governor General in Council on 11th June and 28th July, 1790, and subsequent dates, for the resumption and abolition of **Sayer**, or internal Duties and Taxes throughout Bengal, Bahar, and Orissa," &c. "Passed by the Governor General in Council on the 1st May, 1793. . . ."—*Title of Regulation*, XXVII. of 1793.

1802.—"The Government having reserved to itself the entire exercise of its discretion in continuing or abolishing, temporarily or permanently, the articles of revenue included according to the custom and practice of the country, under the several heads of salt and saltpetre—of the **sayer** or duties by sea or land—of the **abkarry** . . .—of the excise . . .—of all takes personal and professional, as well as those derived from markets, fairs and bazaars—of *lakhiraj* (see **LACKERAGE**) lands. . . . The permanent land-tax shall be made exclusively of the said articles now recited."—*Madras Regulation*, XXV. § iv.

1817.—"Besides the land-revenue, some other duties were levied in India, which were generally included under the denomination of **Sayer**."—*Mill, H. of Br. India*, v. 417.

1863.—"The next head was '**Sayer**,' an obsolete Arabic word, which has the same meaning as 'miscellaneous.' It has latterly been composed of a variety of items connected with the Land Revenue, of which the Revenue derived from Forests has been the most important. The progress of improvement has given a value to the Forests which they never had before, and it has been determined . . . to constitute the Revenue derived from them a separate head of the Public Accounts. The other Miscellaneous Items of Land Revenue which appeared under '**Sayer**,' have therefore been added to Land Revenue, and what remains has been denominated 'Forest Revenue.'"—*Sir C. Trevelyan, Financial Statement*, dd. April 30.

SCARLET. See **SUCLAT**.

SCAVENGER, s. We have been rather startled to find among the MS. records of the India Office, in certain "*Lists of Persons in the Service of the Right. Honble.* the East India Company, in Fort St. George, *and the other Places on the Coast of* Choromandell," beginning with Feby. 170½, and in the entries for that year, the following:

"*Fort St. David.*

"5. *Trevor Gaines*, Land **Customer** and **Scavenger** of Cuddalore, 5th Councl. . . .

"6. *Edward Bawgus*, Translator of Country Letters, *Sen. Mercht.*

"7. *John Butt*, **Scavenger** and Cornmeeter, Tevenapatam, *Mercht.*"

Under 1714 we find again, at Fort St. George:

"*Joseph Smart*, Rentall General and **Scavenger**, *8th of Council*,"

and so on, in the entries of most years down to 1761, when we have, for the last time:

"*Samuel Ardley, 7th of Council*, Masulipatam, Land - Customer, Military Storekeeper, Rentall General, and **Scavenger**."

Some light is thrown upon this surprising occurrence of such a term by a reference to *Cowel's Law Dictionary, or The Interpreter* (published originally in 1607) new ed. of 1727, where we read:

"**Scabage**, Scavagium. It is otherwise called *Schevage, Shewage*, and *Scheauwing;* maybe deduced from the Saxon *Seawian* (Sceawian?) *Ostendere*, and is a kind of Toll or Custom exacted by Mayors, Sheriffs, &c., of Merchant-strangers, for Wares *shewed* or offered to Sale within their Precincts, which is prohibited by the Statute 19 H. 7, 8. In a Charter of *Henry* the Second to the City of *Canterbury* it is written *Scewinga*, and (in Mon. Ang. 2, per fol. 890 b.) *Sceawing;* and elsewhere I find it in Latin *Tributum Ostensorium.* The City of London still retains the Custom, of which in *An old printed Book of the Customs of London*, we read thus, *Of which Custom halfen del appertaineth to the Sheriffs, and the other halfen del to the Hostys in whose Houses the Merchants been lodged; And it is to wet that* Scavage *is the Shew by cause that Merchanties* (sic) *shewn unto the Sheriffs Merchandizes, of the which Customs ought to be taken ere that ony thing thereof be sold, &c.*

"**Scabenger**, From the Belgick *Scavan*, to scrape. Two of every Parish within London and the suburbs are yearly chosen into this Office, who hire men called Rakers, and carts, to cleanse the streets, and carry away the Dirt and Filth thereof, mentioned in 14 Car. 2, cap. 2. The Germans call him a *Drecksimon*, from one *Simon*, a noted Scavenger of Marpurg.

* * * * *

"**Schabaldus**, The officer who collected the Scavage-Money, which was sometimes done with Extortion and great Oppression." (Then quotes Hist. of Durham from Wharton, *Anglia Sacra*, Pt. i. p. 75; "Anno 1311. Schavaldos insurgentes in Episcopatu (Richardus episcopus) fortiter composuit. Aliqui suspendebantur, aliqui extra Episcopatum fugabantur.")

In *Spelman* also (*Glossarium Archaiologicum*, 1688) we find:—

"*Scavagium.*] Tributum quod a mercatoribus exigere solent nundinarum domini, ob licentiam proponendi ibidem venditioni mercimonia, a Saxon (sceawian) id est, Ostendere, inspicere, Angl. **schewage** and **shewage**." Spelman has no *Scavenger* or *Scavager*.

The *scavage* then was a tax upon goods for sale which were liable to duty, the word being, as Skeat points out, a Law French (or Low Latin?) formation from *shew*. ["From O.F. *escauw-er*, to examine, inspect. O. Sax. *skawon*, to behold; cognate with A.S. *sceawian*, to look at." (*Concise Dict.* s.v.)] And the **scavager** or **scavenger** was originally the officer charged with the inspection of the goods and collection of this tax. Passages quoted below from the *Liber Albus* of the City of London refer to these officers, and Mr. Riley in his translation of that work (1861, p. 34) notes that they were "Officers whose duty it was originally to take custom upon the *Scavage, i.e.* inspection of the opening out, of imported goods. At a later date, part of their duty was to see that the streets were kept clean; and hence the modern word '**scavenger**,' whose office corresponds with the *rakyer* (raker) of former times." [The meaning and derivation of this word have been discussed in *Notes & Queries*, 2 ser. ix. 325; 5 ser. v. 49, 452.]

We can hardly doubt then that the office of the Coromandel **scavenger** of the 18th century, united as we find it with that of "Rentall General," or of **Land-customer**," and held by a senior member of the Company's Covenanted Service, must be understood in the older sense of Visitor or Inspector of Goods subject to duties, but (till we can find more light) we should suppose rather duties of the nature of bazar tax, such as at a later date we find classed as **sayer** (q.v.), than customs on imports from seaward.

It still remains an obscure matter how the charge of the scavagers or scavengers came to be transferred to the oversight of streets and street-cleaning. That this must have become a predominant part of their duty at an early period is shown by the Scavager's Oath which we quote below from the *Liber Albus*. In *Skinner's Etymologicon*, 1671, the definition is *Collector sordium abrasarum* (erroneously connecting the word with *shaving* and scraping), whilst he adds: "*Nostri* Scabengers vilissimo omnium ministerio sordes et purgamenta urbis auferendi funguntur." In *Cotgrave's English-French Dict.*, ed. by Howel, 1673, we have: "Scabinger. Boueur. Gadouard" — agreeing precisely with our modern use. Neither of these shows any knowledge of the less sordid office attaching to the name. The same remark applies to Lye's *Junius*, 1743. It is therefore remarkable to find such a *survival* of the latter sense in the service of the Company, and coming down so late as 1761. It must have begun with the very earliest of the Company's establishments in India, for it is probable that the denomination was even then only a survival in England, due to the Company's intimate connection with the city of London. Indeed we learn from Mr. Norton, quoted below, that the term *scavage* was still alive within the City in 1829.

1268. — "Walterus Hervy et Willelmus de Dunolmo, Ballivi, ut Custodes . . . de Lxxv.*l.* vj.*s.* & x*d.* de consuetudinibus omnemodarum mercandisarum venientium de partibus transmarinis ad Civitatem praedictam, de quibus consuetudo debetur quae vocatur **Scavagium**. . . ."—*Mag. Rot.* 59. Hen. III., extracted in *T. Madox, H. and Ant. of the Exchequer*, 1779, i. 779.

Prior to 1419. — "Et debent ad dictum Wardemotum per Aldermannum et probos Wardae, necnon per juratores, eligi Constabularii, **Scavegeours**, Aleconners, Bedelle, et alii Officiarii."—*Liber Albus*, p. 38.

" "SEREMENT DE **Scawageours**. Vous jurrez qe vous surverrez diligientiement qe lez pavimentz danz vostre Garde soient bien et droiturelement reparaillez et nyent enhaussez a nosance dez veysyns; et qe lez chemyns, ruwes, et venelles soient nettez dez fiens et de toutz maners dez ordures, pur honestee de la citee; et qe toutz les chymyneys, fournes, terrailles soient de piere, et suffisantement defensables encontre peril de few; et si vous trovez rien a contraire vous monstrez al Alderman, issint qe l'Alderman ordeigne pur amendement de celle. Et ces ne lerrez—si Dieu vous eyde et lez Saintz."—*Ibid.* p. 313.

1594. — Letter from the Lords of the Council to the Lord Mayor and Aldermen, requesting them to admit John de Cardenas to the office of Collector of **Scavage**, the reversion of which had . . . been granted to him.—*Index* to the *Remembrancia* of the C. of London (1878), p. 284.

1607. — Letter from the Lord Mayor to the Lord Treasurer . . . enclosing a Petition from the Ward of Aldersgate, complaining that William Court, an inhabitant of that Ward for 8 or 10 years past, refused to undergo the office of **Scavenger** in the Parish, claiming exemption . . . being privileged as Clerk to Sir William Spencer, Knight, one of the Auditors of the Court of Exchequer, and praying that Mr. Court, although privileged, should be directed to find a substitute or deputy and pay him.—*Ibid.* 288.

1623.—Letter . . . reciting that the City by ancient Charters held . . . "the office of Package and **Scavage** of Strangers' goods, and merchandise carried by them by land or water, out of the City and Liberties to foreign parts, whereby the Customs and Duties due to H.M. had been more duly paid, and a stricter oversight taken of such commodities so exported."—*Remembrancia*, p. 321.

1632.—Order in Council, reciting that a Petition had been presented to the Board from divers Merchants born in London, the sons of Strangers, complaining that the "Packer of London required of them as much fees for Package, Balliage, **Shewage**, &c., as of Strangers not English-born. . . ."—*Ibid.* 322.

1760. — "Mr. Handle, applying to the Board to have his allowance of **Scavenger** increased, and representing to us the great fatigue he undergoes, and loss of time, which the Board being very sensible of. Agreed we allow him Rs. 20 per month more than before on account of his diligence and assiduity in that post."—*Ft. William Consn.*, in *Long*, 245. It does not appear from this what the duties of the scavenger in Mr. Handle's case were.

1829. — "The oversight of customable goods. This office, termed in Latin *supervisus*, is translated in another charter by the words search and surveying, and in the 2nd Charter of Charles I. it is termed the **scavage**, which appears to have been its most ancient and common name, and that which is retained to the present day. . . . The real nature of this duty is not a toll for *showing*, but a toll paid for the *oversight of showing;* and under that name (*supervisus apertionis*) it was claimed in an action of debt in the reign of Charles II. . . . The duty performed was seeing and knowing the merchandize on which the King's import customs were paid, in order that no concealment, or fraudulent practices . . . should deprive the King of his just dues . . . (The duty) was well known under the name of **scavage**, in the time of Henry III., and it seems at that time to have been a franchise of the commonalty."—*G. Norton, Commentaries on the Hist., &c., of the City of London*, 3rd ed. (1869), pp. 380-381.

Besides the books quoted, see *H. Wedgewood's Etym. Dict.* and *Skeat's* do., which have furnished useful light, and some references.

SCRIVAN, s. An old word for a clerk or writer, from Port. *escrivão*.

[1616.—"He desired that some English might early on the Morow come to his howse, wher should meete a **Scriuano** and finish that busines."—*Sir T. Roe*, Hak. Soc. i. 173. On the same page "The **Scriuane** of Zulpheckcarcon."]

1673.—"In some Places they write on Cocoe-Leafes dried, and then use an Iron Style, or else on Paper, when they use a Pen made with a Reed, for which they have a Brass Case, which holds them and the Ink too, always stuck at the Girdles of their **Scrivans**."—*Fryer*, 191.

1683.—"Mr. Watson in the Taffaty warehouse without any provocation called me Pittyful Prodigall **Scrivan**, and told me my Hatt stood too high upon my head. . . ."—Letter of *S. Langley*, in *Hedges' Diary*, Sept. 5; [Hak. Soc. i. 108].

SCYMITAR, s. This is an English word for an Asiatic sabre. The common Indian word is *talwār* (see **TULWAUR**). We get it through the French *cimiterre*, Ital. *scimeterra*, and according to Marcel Devic originally from Pers. *shamshīr* (*chimchīr* as he writes it). This would be still very obscure unless we consider the constant clerical confusion in the Middle Ages between *c* and *t*, which has led to several metamorphoses of words; of which a notable example is Fr. *carquois* from Pers. *tīrkash*. *Scimecirra* representing *shimshīr* might easily thus become *scimetirra*. But we cannot *prove* this to have been the real origin. This word (*shamshīr*) was known to Greek writers. Thus:

A.D. 93.—" . . . *Καὶ καθίστησι τὸν πρεσβύτατον παῖδα Μορόβαζον βασιλέα περιθεῖσα τὸ διάδημα καὶ δοῦσα τὸν σημαντῆρα τοῦ πατρὸς δακτύλιον, τήντε σαμψηρὰν ὀνομαζομένην παρ' αὐτοῖς.*"—*Joseph. Antiqq.* xx. ii. 3.

c. A.D. 114.—"*Δῶρα φέρει Τραιανῷ ὑφάσματα σηρικὰ καὶ σαμψήρας αἱ δέ εἰσι σπάθαι βαρβαρικαί.*"—Quoted in *Suidas Lexicon*, s.v.

1595.—

" . . . By this **scimitar**,
That slew the Sophy, and a Persian prince
That won three fields of Sultan Soliman
. . ."*
Merchant of Venice, ii. 1.

* In a Greek translation of Shakspere, published some years ago at Constantinople, *this line is omitted!*

1610.—" . . . Anon the Patron starting up, as if of a sodaine restored to life; like a mad man skips into the boate, and drawing a Turkise **Cymiter**, beginneth to lay about him (thinking that his vessell had been surprised by Pirats), when they all leapt into the sea; and diuing vnder water like so many Diue-dappers, ascended without the reach of his furie."—*Sandys, Relation*, &c., 1615, p. 28.

1614.—"Some days ago I visited the house of a goldsmith to see a **scimitar** (*scimitarra*) that Nasuhbashá the first vizir, whom I have mentioned above, had ordered as a present to the Grand Signor. Scabbard and hilt were all of gold; and all covered with diamonds, so that little or nothing of the gold was to be seen."—*P. della Valle*, i. 43.

c. 1630.—"They seldome go without their swords (**shamsheers** they call them) form'd like a cresent, of pure metall, broad, and sharper than any rasor; nor do they value them, unlesse at one blow they can cut in two an Asinego. . . ."—*Sir T. Herbert*, ed. 1638, p. 228.

1675.—"I kept my hand on the Cock of my Carabine; and my Comrade followed a foote pace, as well armed; and our Janizary better than either of us both: but our Armenian had only a **Scimeter**."—(Sir) *George Wheler, Journey into Greece*, London, 1682, p. 252.

1758.—"The Captain of the troop . . . made a cut at his head with a **scymetar** which Mr. Lally parried with his stick, and a *Coffree* (**Caffer**) servant who attend him shot the Tanjerine dead with a pistol."—*Orme*, i. 328.

SEACUNNY, s. This is, in the phraseology of the Anglo-Indian marine, a steersman or quartermaster. The word is the Pers. *sukkānī*, from Ar. *sukkān*, 'a helm.'

c. 1580.—"Aos Mocadões, **Socões**, e Vogas."—*Primor e Honra*, &c. f. 68*v*. ("To the **Mocuddums**, **Seacunnies**, and oarsmen.")

c. 1590.—"**Sukkāngīr**, or helmsman. *He* steers the ship according to the orders of the *Mu'allim*."—*Āīn*, i. 280.

1805.—"I proposed concealing myself with 5 men among the bales of cloth, till it should be night, when the Frenchmen being necessarily divided into two watches might be easily overpowered. This was agreed to . . . till daybreak, when unfortunately descrying the masts of a vessel on our weather beam, which was immediately supposed to be our old friend, the sentiments of every person underwent a most unfortunate alteration, and the Nakhoda, and the **Soucan**, as well as the Supercargo, informed me that they would not tell a lie for all the world, even to save their lives; and in short, that they would neither be *airt nor pairt* in the business."—Letter of *Leyden*, dd. Oct. 4-7, in *Morton's Life*.

1810.—"The gunners and quartermasters . . . are Indian Portuguese; they are called **Secunnis**."—*Maria Graham*, 85.

[1855.—". . . the **Seacunnies**, or helmsmen, were principally Manilla men."—*Neale, Residence in Siam*, 45.]

SEBUNDY, s. Hind. from Pers. *sihbandī* (*sih*, 'three'). The *rationale* of the word is obscure to us. [Platts says it means 'three-monthly or quarterly payment.' The *Madras Gloss.* less probably suggests Pers. *sipāhbandī* (see **SEPOY**), 'recruitment.'] It is applied to irregular native soldiery, a sort of militia, or imperfectly disciplined troops for revenue or police duties, &c. Certain local infantry regiments were formerly officially termed *Sebundy*. The last official appearance of the title that we can find is in application to "The *Sebundy* Corps of Sappers and Miners" employed at Darjeeling. This is in the E.I. Register down to July, 1869, after which the title does not appear in any official list. Of this corps, if we are not mistaken, the late Field-Marshal Lord Napier of Magdala was in charge, as Lieut. Robert Napier, about 1840. An application to Lord Napier, for corroboration of this reminiscence of many years back, drew from him the following interesting note:—

"Captain Gilmore of the (Bengal) Engineers was appointed to open the settlement of Darjeeling, and to raise two companies of **Sebundy** Sappers, in order to provide the necessary labour.

"He commenced the work, obtained some (Native) officers and N.C. officers from the old Bengal Sappers, and enlisted about half of each company.

"The first season found the little colony quite unprepared for the early commencement of the **Rains**. All the **Coolies**, who did not die, fled, and some of the Sappers deserted. Gilmore got sick; and in 1838 I was suddenly ordered from the extreme border of Bengal—Nyacollee—to relieve him for one month. I arrived somehow, with a pair of **pitarahs** as my sole possession.

"Just then, our relations with Nepaul became strained, and it was thought desirable to complete the **Sebundy** Sappers with men from the Border Hills unconnected with Nepaul—Garrows and similar tribes. Through the Political Officer the necessary number of men were enlisted and sent to me.

"When they arrived I found, instead of the 'fair recruits' announced, a number of most unfit men; some of them more or less crippled, or with defective sight. It seemed probable that, by the process known to us in India as *uddlee buddlee* (see **BUDLEE**), the original recruits had managed to insert substitutes during the journey! I was much embarrassed as to what I should do with them; but night was coming on, so I encamped them on the newly opened road, the only clear space amid the dense jungle on either side. To complete my difficulty it began to rain, and I pitied my poor recruits! During the night there was a storm—and in the morning, to my intense relief, they had all disappeared!

"In the expressive language of my sergeant, there was not a '*visage*' of the men left.

"The **Sebundies** were a local corps, designed to furnish a body of labourers fit for mountain-work. They were armed, and expected to fight if necessary. Their pay was 6rs. a month, instead of a Sepoy's 7½. The pensions of the Native officers were smaller than in the regular army, which was a ground of complaint with the Bengal Sappers, who never expected in accepting the new service that they would have lower pensions than those they enlisted for.

"I eventually completed the corps with Nepaulese, and, I think, left them in a satisfactory condition.

"I was for a long time their only sergeant-major. I supplied the Native officers and N.C. officers from India with a good pea-jacket each, out of my private means, and with a little gold-lace made them smart and happy.

"When I visited Darjeeling again in 1872, I found the remnant of my good Sapper officers living as pensioners, and waiting to give me an affectionate welcome.

* * * * *

"My month's acting appointment was turned into four years. I walked 30 miles to get to the place, lived much in hovels and temporary huts thrown up by my Hill-men, and derived more benefit from the climate than from my previous visit to England. I think I owe much practical teaching to the Hill-men, the Hills and the Climate. I learnt the worst the elements could do to me—very nearly—excepting earthquakes! And I think I was thus prepared for any hard work."

c. 1778.—"At Dacca I made acquaintance with my venerable friend John Cowe. He had served in the Navy so far back as the memorable siege of Havannah, was reduced when a lieutenant, at the end of the American War, went out in the Company's military service, and here I found him in command of a regiment of **Sebundees**, or native militia."—*Hon. R. Lindsay*, in *L. of the Lindsays*, iii. 161.

1785.—"The Board were pleased to direct that in order to supply the place of the **Sebundy** corps, four regiments of Sepoys be employed in securing the collection of the revenues."—In *Seton-Karr*, i. 92

" "One considerable charge upon the Nabob's country was for extraordinary **sibbendies**, sepoys and horsemen, who appear to us to be a very unnecessary incumbrance upon the revenue."—Append. to

Speech on Nab. of Arcot's Debts, in *Burke's Works*, iv. 18, ed. 1852.

1796.—"The Collector at Midnapoor having reported the **Sebundy** Corps attached to that Collectorship, Sufficiently Trained in their Exercise; the Regular Sepoys who have been Employed on that Duty are to be withdrawn."—G. O. Feb. 23, in *Suppt.* to *Code of Military Regs.*, 1799, p. 145.

1803.—"The employment of these people therefore . . . as **sebundy** is advantageous . . . it lessens the number of idle and discontented at the time of general invasion and confusion."—*Wellington, Desp.* (ed. 1837), ii. 170.

1812.—"**Sebundy**, or provincial corps of native troops."—*Fifth Report*, 38.

1861.—"Sliding down Mount Tendong, the summit of which, with snow lying there, we crossed, the **Sebundy** Sappers were employed cutting a passage for the mules; this delayed our march exceedingly."—*Report* of *Capt. Impey, R.E.*, in *Gawler's Sikhim*, p. 95.

SEEDY, s. Hind. *sīdī;* Arab. *saiyid*, 'lord' (whence the *Cid* of Spanish romantic history), *saiyidī*, 'my lord'; and Mahr. *siddhī*. Properly an honorific name given in Western India to African Mahommedans, of whom many held high positions in the service of the kings of the Deccan. Of these at least one family has survived in princely position to our own day, viz. the Nawāb of Jangīra (see **JUNGEERA**), near Bombay. The young heir to this principality, Siddhī Ahmad, after a minority of some years, was installed in the Government in Oct., 1883. But the proper application of the word in the ports and on the shipping of Western India is to negroes in general. [It "is a title still applied to holy men in Marocco and the Maghrib; on the East African coast it is assumed by negro and negroid Moslems, *e.g.* Sidi Mubarak Bombay; and 'Seedy boy' is the Anglo-Indian term for a Zanzibar-man" (*Burton, Ar. Nights*, iv. 231).]

c. 1563.—"And among these was an Abyssinian (*Abexim*) called **Cide** Meriam, a man reckoned a great cavalier, and who entertained 500 horse at his own charges, and who greatly coveted the city of Daman to quarter himself in, or at the least the whole of its pergunnas (*parganas*—see **PERGUNNAH**) to devour."—*Couto*, VII. x. 8.

[c. 1610.—"The greatest insult that can be passed upon a man is to call him **Cisdy**—that is to say 'cook.'"—*Pyrard de Laval*, Hak. Soc. i. 173.]

1673.—"An *Hobsy* or African Coffery (they being preferred here to chief employments, which they enter on by the name of **Siddies**)."—*Fryer*, 147.

" "He being from a *Hobsy Caphir* made a free Denizen . . . (who only in this Nation arrive to great Preferment, being the Frizled Woolly-pated Blacks) under the known style of **Syddies**. . . ."—*Ibid.* 168.

1679.—"The protection which the **Siddees** had given to Gingerah against the repeated attacks of Sevagi, as well as their frequent annoyance of their country, had been so much facilitated by their resort to Bombay, that Sevagi at length determined to compel the English Government to a stricter neutrality, by reprisals on their own port."—*Orme, Fragments*, 78.

1690.—"As he whose Title is *most Christian*, encouraged him who is its principal Adversary to invade the Rights of Christendom, so did Senor Padre *de Pandara*, the Principal Jesuite and in an adjacent Island to *Bombay*, invite the **Síddy** to exterminate all the Protestants there."—*Ovington*, 157.

1750-60.—"These (islands) were formerly in the hands of Angria and the **Siddies** or Moors."—*Grose*, i. 58.

1759.—"The Indian seas having been infested to an intolerable degree by pirates, the Mogul appointed the **Siddee**, who was chief of a colony of Coffrees (**Caffer**), to be his Admiral. It was a colony which, having been settled at Dundee-Rajapore, carried on a considerable trade there, and had likewise many vessels of force."—*Cambridge's Account of the War*, &c., p. 216.

1800.—"I asked him what he meant by a **Siddee**. He said a *hubshee*. This is the name by which the Abyssinians are distinguished in India."—*T. Munro*, in *Life*, i. 287.

1814.—"Among the attendants of the Cambay Nabob . . . are several Abyssinian and Caffree slaves, called by way of courtesy **Seddees** or Master."—*Forbes, Or. Mem.* iii. 167; [2nd ed. ii. 225].

1832.—"I spoke of a **Sindhee**" (*Siddhee*) "or *Habshee*, which is the name for an Abyssinian in this country lingo."—*Mem. of Col. Mountain*, 121.

1885.—"The inhabitants of this singular tract (Soopah plateau in N. Canara) were in some parts Mahrattas, and in others of Canarese race, but there was a third and less numerous section, of pure African descent called **Sidhis** . . . descendants of fugitive slaves from Portuguese settlements . . . the same ebony coloured, large-limbed men as are still to be found on the African coast, with broad, good-humoured, grinning faces."—*Gordon S. Forbes, Wild Life in Canara*, &c., 32-33.

[1896.—
"We've shouted on seven-ounce nuggets,
We've starved on a **Seedee** boy's pay."
R. Kipling, The Seven Seas.]

SEEMUL, SIMMUL, &c. (sometimes we have seen **Symbol,** and **Cymbal**), s. Hind. *semal* and *sembhal;* [Skt. *śālmali*]. The (so-called) cotton-tree *Bombax Malabaricum,* D.C. (N.O. *Malvaceae*), which occurs sporadically from Malabar to Sylhet, and from Burma to the Indus and beyond. It is often cultivated. "About March it is a striking object with its immense buttressed trunks, and its large showy red flowers, 6 inches in breadth, clustered on the leafless branches. The flower-buds are used as a potherb and the gum as a medicine" (*Punjab Plants*). We remember to have seen a giant of this species near Kishnagarh, the buttresses of which formed chambers, 12 or 13 feet long and 7 or 8 wide. The silky cotton is only used for stuffing pillows and the like. The wood, though wretched in quality for any ordinary purpose, lasts under water, and is commonly the material for the curbs on which wells are built and sunk in Upper India.

[c. 1807.—". . . the Salmoli, or **Simul** . . . is one of the most gaudy ornaments of the forest or village. . . ."—*Buchanan Hamilton, E. India,* ii. 789.]

SEER, s. Hind. *ser;* Skt. *seṭak.* One of the most generally spread Indian denominations of weight, though, like all Indian measures, varying widely in different parts of the country. And besides the variations of local *ser* and *ser* we often find in the same locality a *pakkā* **(pucka)** and a *kachchhā* **(cutcha)** ser; a state of things, however, which is human, and not Indian only (see under **PUCKA**). The *ser* is generally (at least in upper India) equivalent to 80 *tolas* or rupee-weights; but even this is far from universally true. The heaviest *ser* in the *Useful Tables* (see Thomas's ed. of *Prinsep*) is that called "Coolpahar," equivalent to **123** *tolas,* and weighing **3** lbs. 1 oz. 6¼ dr. avoird.; the lightest is the *ser* of Malabar and the S. Mahratta country, which is little more than 8 oz. [The Macleod *ser* of Malabar, introduced in 1802, is of 130 *tolas;* 10 of these weigh **33** *lb.* (*Madras Man.* ii. 516).]

Regulation VII. of the Govt. of India of 1833 is entitled "A Reg. for altering the weight of the Furruckabad Rupee (see **RUPEE**) and for assimilating it to the legal currency of the Madras and Bombay Presidencies; for adjusting the weight of the Company's sicca Rupee, *and for fixing a standard unit of weight for India.*" This is the nearest thing to the establishment of standard weights that existed up to 1870. The preamble says: "It is further convenient to introduce the weight of the Furruckabad Rupee as the unit of a general system of weights for Government transactions throughout India." And Section IV. contains the following:

"The *Tola* or **Sicca** weight to be equal to 180 grains troy, and the other denominations or weights to be derived from this unit, according to the following scale:—

8 **Rutties** = 1 Masha = 15 troy grains.
12 Mashas = 1 **Tola** = 180 ditto.
80 **Tolas** (or sicca weight) = 1 **Seer**= 2½ lbs. troy.
40 **Seers** = 1 *Mun* or *Bazar* **Maund** = 100 lbs. troy."

Section VI. of the same Regulation says:

"The system of weights and measures (?) described in Section IV. is to be adopted at the mints and assay offices of Calcutta and Saugor respectively in the adjustment and verification of all weights for government or public purposes sent thither for examination."

But this does not go far in establishing a standard unit of weight *for India:* though the weights detailed in § iv. became established for Government purposes in the Bengal Presidency. The *seer* of this Regulation was thus 14,400 grains troy—2½ lbs. troy, 2·057 lbs. avoirdupois.

In 1870, in the Government of Lord Mayo, a strong movement was made by able and influential men to introduce the metrical system, and an Act was passed called "*The Indian Weights and Measures Act*" (Act XI. of 1870) to pave the way for this. The preamble declares it expedient to provide for the ultimate adoption of an uniform system of weights and measures thoughout British India, and the Act prescribes certain standards, with powers to the Local Governments to declare the adoption of these.

Section II. runs:

"*Standards.*—The primary standard of weight shall be called **ser,** and shall be a weight of metal in the possession of the Government of India, which weight, when weighed in a vacuum, is equal to the weight known in France as the kilogramme des Archives."

Again, Act XXXI. of 1872, called "*The Indian Weights and Measures of Capacity Act*," repeats in substance the same preamble and prescription of standard weight. It is not clear to us what the separate object of this second Act was. But with the death of Lord Mayo the whole scheme fall to the ground. The *ser* of these Acts would be=2·2 lbs. avoirdupois, or 0·143 of a pound greater than the 80 tola *ser*.

1554.—"*Porto Grande de Bemgala.*—'The **maund** (*mão*) with which they weigh all merchandize is of 40 **ceres**, each **cer** 18¾ ounces; the said **maund** weighs 46½ *arratels* **(rottle)**."—*A. Nunes*, 37.

1648.—"One **Ceer** weighs 18 *peysen* . . . and makes ¾ pound troy weight."—*Van Twist*, 62.

1748.—"Enfin on verse le tout un serre de l'huile."—*Lett. Edif.* xiv. 220.

SEER-FISH, s. A name applied to several varieties of fish, species of the genus *Cybium*. When of the right size, neither too small nor too big, these are reckoned among the most delicate of Indian sea-fish. Some kinds salt well, and are also good for preparing as **Tamarind-Fish**. The name is sometimes said to be a corruption of Pers. *sīah* (qu. Pers. 'black?') but the quotations show that it is a corruption of Port. *serra*. That name would appear to belong properly to the well-known saw-fish (*Pristis*)—see *Bluteau*, quoted below; but probably it may have been applied to the fish now in question, because of the serrated appearance of the rows of finlets, behind the second dorsal and anal fins, which are characteristic of the genus (see *Day's Fishes of India*, pp. 254-256, and plates lv., lvi.).

1554.—"E aos Marinheiros hum **peixe cerra** par mes, a cada hum."—*A. Nunez, Livro dos Pesos*, 43.

,, "To Lopo Vaaz, Mestre of the firearms (*espingardes*), his pay and provisions. . . . And for his three workmen, at the rate of 2 measures of rice each daily, and half a **seer fish** (*peixe serra*) each monthly, and a maund of firewood each monthly."—*S. Botelho, Tombo*, 235.

1598.—"There is a fish called **Piexe Serra**, which is cut in round pieces, as we cut Salmon and salt it. It is very good."—*Linschoten*, 88; [Hak. Soc. ii. 11].

1720.—"**Peyxe Serra** is ordinarily produced in the Western Ocean, and is so called" etc. (describing the *Saw-fish*) . . . "But in the Sea of the Islands of Quirimba (*i.e.* off Mozambique) there is a different **peyxe serra** resembling a large *corvina*,* but much better, and which it is the custom to pickle. When cured it seems just like ham."—*Bluteau, Vocab.* vii. 606-607.

1727.—"They have great Plenty of **Seer-fish**, which is as savoury as any Salmon or Trout in Europe."—*A. Hamilton*, i. 379; [ed. 1744, i. 382].

[1813.—". . . the robal, the **seir-fish**, the grey mullet . . . are very good."—*Forbes, Or. Mem.* 2nd ed. i. 36.]

1860.—"Of those in ordinary use for the table the finest by far is the **Seir-fish**,† a species of Scomber, which is called *Toramalu* by the natives. It is in size and form very similar to the salmon, to which the flesh of the female fish, notwithstanding its white colour, bears a very close resemblance, both in firmness and in flavour."—*Tennent's Ceylon*, i. 205.

SEERPAW, s. Pers. through Hind. *sar-ā-pā*—'cap-a-pie.' A complete suit, presented as a *Khilat* (**Killut**) or dress of honour, by the sovereign or his representative.

c. 1666.—"He . . . commanded, there should be given to each of them an embroider'd Vest, a Turbant, and a Girdle of Silk Embroidery, which is that which they call **Ser-apah**, that is, an Habit from head to foot."—*Bernier*, E.T. 37; [ed. *Constable*, 147].

1673.—"Sir George Oxendine . . . had a *Collat* (**Killut**) or **Serpaw**, a Robe of Honour from Head to Foot, offered him from the Great Mogul."—*Fryer*, 87.

1680.—"Answer is returned that it hath not been accustomary for the Governours to go out to receive a bare *Phyrmaund* (**Firmaun**), except there come therewith a **Serpow** or a Tasheriffe (**Tashreef**)."—*Ft. St. Geo. Consn.* Dec. 2, in *N. & E.* No. iii. 40.

1715.—"We were met by Padre Stephanus, bringing two **Seerpaws**."—In *Wheeler*, ii. 245.

1727.—"As soon as he came, the King embraced him, and ordered a **serpaw** or a royal Suit to be put upon him."—*A. Hamilton*, i. 171 [ed. 1744].

1735.—"The last Nabob (Sadatulla) would very seldom suffer any but himself to send a **Seerpaw**; whereas in February last Sunta Sahib, Subder Ali Sahib, Jehare Khan and Imaum Sahib, had all of them taken upon them to send distinct **Seerpaws** to the President."—In *Wheeler*, iii. 140.

1759.—"Another deputation carried six costly **Seerpaws**; these are garments which are presented sometimes by superiors in token of protection, and sometimes by inferiors in token of homage."—*Orme*, i. 159.

* *Corvina* is applied by Cuvier, Cantor and others to fish of the genus *Sciaena* of more recent ichthyologists.

† "*Cybium* (*Scomber*, Linn.) *guttatum*."—*Tennent.*

SEETULPUTTY, s. A fine kind of mat made especially in Eastern Bengal, and used to sleep on in the cold weather. [They are made from the split stems of the *mukta pata*, *Phrynium dichotomum*, Roxb. (see *Watt, Econ. Dict.* vi. pt. i. 216 *seq.*).] Hind. *sītalpattī*, 'cold-slip.' Williamson's spelling and derivation (from an Arab. word impossibly used, see **SICLEEGUR**) are quite erroneous.

1810.—"A very beautiful species of mat is made . . . especially in the south-eastern districts . . . from a kind of reedy grass. . . . These are peculiarly slippery, whence they are designated '**seekul-putty**' (*i.e.* polished sheets). . . . The principal uses of the '**seekul-putty**' are to be laid under the lower sheet of a bed, thereby to keep the body cool."—*Williamson, V.M.* ii. 41.

[1818.—"Another kind (of mat) the **shēētŭlŭpatēēs**, laid on beds and couches on account of their coolness, are sold from one roopee to five each."—*Ward, Hindoos*, i. 106.]

1879.—In *Fallon's Dicty.* we find the following Hindi riddle :—

"*Chīnī kā piyālā ṭūṭā, koī joṛtā nahīn ;*
Mālī jī kā bāg lagā, koī toṛtā nahīn ;
Sītal-pāṭī bichhī, koī sotā nāhīn ;
Rāj-bansī mūā, koī rotā nāhīn."

Which might be rendered :

"A china bowl that, broken, none can join ;
A flowery field, whose blossoms none purloin ;
A royal scion slain, and none shall weep ;
A **sītalpaṭṭī** spread where none shall sleep."

The answer is an Egg ; the Starry Sky ; a Snake (*Rāj-bansī*, 'royal scion,' is a placatory name for a snake) ; and the Sea.

SEMBALL, s. Malay-Javan. *sāmbil, sāmbal.* A spiced condiment, the *curry* of the Archipelago. [Dennys (*Descr. Dict.* p. 337) describes many varieties.]

1817.—"The most common seasoning employed to give a relish to their insipid food is the *lombock* (*i.e.* red-pepper) ; triturated with salt it is called **sambel**."—*Raffles, H. of Java*, i. 98.

SEPOY, SEAPOY, s. In Anglo-Indian use a native soldier, disciplined and dressed in the European style. The word is Pers. *sipāhī*, from *sipāh*, 'soldiery, an army'; which J. Oppert traces to old Pers. *spāda*, 'a soldier' (*Le peuple et la Langue des Mèdes*, 1879, p. 24). But *Sbah* is a horseman in Armenian ; and sound etymologists connect *sipāh* with *asp*, 'a horse'; [others with Skt. *padāti*, 'a foot-soldier']. The original word *sipāhī* occurs frequently in the poems of Amīr Khusrū (c. A.D. 1300), bearing always probably the sense of a 'horse-soldier,' for all the important part of an army then consisted of horsemen. See *spāhī* below.

The word *sepoy* occurs in Southern India before we had troops in Bengal ; and it was probably adopted from Portuguese. We have found no English example in print older than 1750, but probably an older one exists. The India Office record of 1747 from Fort St. David's is the oldest notice we have found in extant MS. [But see below.]

c. 1300.—"Pride had inflated his brain with wind, which extinguished the light of his intellect, and a few **sipāhīs** from Hindustan, without any religion, had supported the credit of his authority."—*Amīr Khusrū*, in *Elliot*, iii. 536.

[1665.—"Souldier—**Suppya** and Haddee."—*Persian Gloss.* in *Sir T. Herbert*, ed. 1677, p. 99.]

1682.—"As soon as these letters were sent away, I went immediately to Ray Nundelall's to have ye **Seapy**, or Nabob's horseman, consigned to me, with order to see ye *Perwanna* put in execution ; but having thought better of it, ye Ray desired me to have patience till tomorrow morning. He would then present me to the Nabob, whose commands to ye **Seapy** and Bulchunds *Vekeel* would be more powerfull and advantageous to me than his own."—*Hedges, Diary*, Hak. Soc. i. 55, *seq.* Here we see the word still retaining the sense of 'horseman' in India.

[1717.—"A Company of **Sepoys** with the colours."—*Yule*, in *ditto*, II. ccclix. On this Sir H. Yule notes : "This is an occurrence of the word **sepoy**, in its modern signification, 30 years earlier than any I had been able to find when publishing the A.-I. Gloss. I have one a year earlier, and expect now to find it earlier still."

[1733.—"You are next . . . to make a complete survey . . . of the number of fighting **Sepoys**. . . ."—*Forrest, Bombay Letters*, ii. 55.]

1737.—"Elle com tota a força desponivel, que eram 1156 soldados pagos em que entraram 281 chegados na não Mercês, e 780 **sypaes** ou *lascarins* (**lascar**), recuperon o territorio."—*Bosquejo das Possessões Portuguezas no Oriente*, &c., *por Joaquim Pedro Celestino Soares*, Lisboa, 1851, p. 58.

1746.—"The Enemy, by the best Intelligence that could be got, and best Judgment that could be formed, had or would have on Shore next Morning, upwards of 3000 *Europeans*, with at least 500 *Coffrys*, and a number of **Cephoys** and Peons."—*Ext. of Diary*, &c., in App. to *A Letter to a Propr. of the E.I. Co.*, London, 1750, p. 94.

[1746.—Their strength on shore I compute 2000 Europeans **Seapiahs** and 300 Coffrees."—*Letter from Madras*, Oct. 9, in *Bengal Consultations. Ibid.* p. 600, we have **Seapies.**]

1747.—"At a Council of War held at Fort St. David the 25th December, 1747.

Present:—
Charles Floyer, Esq., Governor.
George Gibson John Holland
John Crompton John Rodolph de Gingens
William Brown John Usgate
Robert Sanderson.

* * *

"It is further ordered that Captn. Crompton keep the Detachment under his Command at Cuddalore, in a readiness to march to the **Choultry** over against the Fort as soon as the Signal shall be made from the Place, and then upon his firing two Muskets, Boats shall be sent to bring them here, and to leave a serjeant at Cuddalore Who shall conduct his **Seapoys** to the Garden Guard, and the Serjeant shall have a Word by which He shall be received at the Garden."—*Original MS. Proceedings* (in the India Office).

" The Council of Fort St. David write to Bombay, March 16th, "if they could not supply us with more than 300 Europeans, We should be glad of Five or Six Hundred of the best Northern People their way, as they are reported to be much better than ours, and not so liable to Desertion."

In Consn. May 30th they record the arrival of the ships Leven, Warwick, and Ilchester, Princess Augusta, "on the 28th inst., from Bombay, (bringing) us a General from that Presidency,* as entered No. 38, advising of having sent us by them sundry stores and a Reinforcement of Men, consisting of 70 European Soldiers, 200 *Topasses* **(Topaz)**, and 100 well-trained **Seapoys**, all of which under the command of Capt. Thomas Andrews, a Good Officer. . . ."

And under July 13th. ". . . The Reinforcement of **Sepoys** having arrived from Tellicherry, which, with those that were sent from Bombay, making a formidable Body, besides what are still expected; and as there is far greater Dependance to be placed on those People than on our own **Peons** . . . many of whom have a very weakly Appearance, AGREED, that a General Review be now had of them, that all such may be discharged, and only the Choicest of them continued in the Service."—*MS. Records in India Office.*

1752.—". . . they quitted their entrenchments on the first day of March, 1752, and advanced in order of battle, taking possession of a rising ground on the right, on which they placed 50 Europeans; the front consisted of 1500 **Sipoys**, and one hundred and twenty or thirty French."—*Complete Hist. of the War in India*, 1761, pp. 9-10.

* Not a general officer, but a letter from the body of the Council.

1758.—A Tabular Statement (*Mappa*) of the Indian troops, 20th Jan. of this year, shows "Corpo de **Sipaes**" with 1162 "**Sipaes** promptos."—*Bosquejo*, as above.

" "A stout body of near 1000 **Sepoys** has been raised within these few days."—In *Long*, 134.

[1759.—"Boat rice extraordinary for the Gentoo **Seapois**. . . ."—*Ibid.* 174.]

1763.—"The Indian natives and Moors, who are trained in the European manner, are called **Sepoys**."—*Orme*, i. 80.

1763.—"Major Carnac . . . observes that your establishment is loaded with the expense of more Captains than need be, owing to the unnecessarily making it a point that they should be Captains who command the **Sepoy** Battalions, whereas such is the nature of **Sepoys** that it requires a peculiar genius and talent to be qualified for that service, and the Battalion should be given only to such who are so without regard to rank."—*Court's Letter*, of March 9. In *Long*, 290.

1770.—"England has at present in India an establishment to the amount of 9800 European troops, and 54,000 **sipahis** well armed and disciplined."—*Raynal* (tr. 1777), i. 459.

1774.—"**Sipai** sono li soldati Indiani."—*Della Tomba*, 297.

1778.—"La porta del Ponente della città si custodiva dalli **sipais** soldati Indiani radunati da tutte le tribù, e religioni."—*Fra Paolino, Viaggio*, 4.

1780.—"Next morning the **sepoy** came to see me. . . . I told him that I owed him my life. . . . He then told me that he was not very rich himself, as his pay was only a pagoda and a half a month—and at the same time drew out his purse and offered me a rupee. This generous behaviour, so different to what I had hitherto experienced, drew tears from my eyes, and I thanked him for his generosity, but I would not take his money."—*Hon. J. Lindsay's Imprisonment, Lives of Lindsays*, iii. 274.

1782.—"As to Europeans who run from their natural colours, and enter into the service of the country powers, I have heard one of the best officers the Company ever had . . . say that he considered them no otherwise than as so many **Seapoys**; for acting under blacks they became mere blacks in spirit."—*Price, Some Observations*, 95-96.

1789.—
"There was not a captain, nor scarce a **seapoy**,
But a Prince would depose, or a Bramin destroy."
Letter of Simpkin the Second, &c., 8.

1803.—"Our troops behaved admirably; the **sepoys** astonished me."—*Wellington* ii. 384

1827.—"He was betrothed to the daughter of a **Sipahee**, who served in the mud-fort which they saw at a distance rising above the jungle."—*Sir W. Scott, The Surgeon's Daughter*, ch. xiii.

1836.—"The native army of the E. I. Company. . . . Their formation took place in 1757. They are usually called **sepoys**, and are light and short."—In *R. Phillips, A Million of Facts*, 718.

1881.—"As early as A.D. 1592 the chief of Sind had 200 natives dressed and armed like Europeans: these were the first '**sepoys**.'"—*Burton's Camoens, A Commentary*, ii. 445.

The French write *cipaye* or *cipai*:

1759.—"De quinze mille **Cipayes** dont l'armée est censée composée, j'en compte à peu près huit cens sur la route de Pondichery, chargé de sucre et de poivre et autres marchandises, quant aux Coulis, ils sont tous employés pour le même objet."—*Letter of Lally to the Governor of Pondicherry*, in *Cambridge's Account*, p. 150.

c. 1835-38.—

"Il ne criant ni Kriss ni zagaies,
Il regarde l'homme sans fuir,
Et rit des balles des **cipayes**
Qui rebondissent sur son cuir."
Th. Gautier, L'Hippopotame.

Since the conquest of Algeria the same word is common in France under another form, viz., *spāhī*. But the *Spāhī* is totally different from the *sepoy*, and is in fact an irregular horseman. With the Turks, from whom the word is taken, the *spāhī* was always a horseman.

1554.—"Aderant magnis muneribus praepositi multi, aderant praetoriani equites omnes **Sphai**, Garipigi, Ulufagi, Gianizarorum magnus numerus, sed nullus in tanto conventu nobilis nisi ex suis virtutibus et fortibus factis."—*Busbeq, Epistolae*, i. 99.

[1562.—"The **Spachi**, and other orders of horsemen."—*J. Shute, Two Comm.* (Tr.) fol. 53 ro. *Stanf. Dict.* where many early instances of the word will be found.]

1672.—"Mille ou quinze cents **Spahiz**, tous bien équippés et bien montés . . . terminoient toute ceste longue, magnifique, et pompeuse cavalcade."—*Journal d'Ant. Galland*, i. 142.

1675.—"The other officers are the *sardar* (**Sirdar**), who commands the Janizaries . . . the **Spahi** *Aga*, who commands the **Spahies** or *Turkish* Horse."—*Wheeler's Journal*, 348.

[1686.—"I being providentially got over the river before the **Spie** employed by them could give them intelligence."—*Hedges, Diary*, Hak. Soc. i. 229.]

1738.—"The Arab and other inhabitants are obliged, either by long custom . . . or from fear and compulsion, to give the **Spahees** and their company the *mounah* . . . which is such a sufficient quantity of provision for ourselves, together with straw and barley for our mules and horses."—*Shaw's Travels in Barbary*, ed. 1757, p. xii.

1786.—"Bajazet had two years to collect his forces . . . we may discriminate the janizaries . . . a national cavalry, the **Spahis** of modern times."—*Gibbon*, ch. lxv.

1877.—"The regular cavalry was also originally composed of tribute children. . . . The **sipahis** acquired the same pre-eminence among the cavalry which the janissaries held among the infantry, and their seditious conduct rendered them much sooner troublesome to the Government."—*Finlay, H. of Greece*, ed. 1877, v. 37.

SERAI, SERYE, s. This word is used to represent two Oriental words entirely different.

a. Hind. from Pers. *sarā*, *sarāī*. This means originally an edifice, a palace. It was especially used by the Tartars when they began to build palaces. Hence *Sarāī*, the name of more than one royal residence of the Mongol Khāns upon the Volga, the *Sarra* of Chaucer. The Russians retained the word from their Tartar oppressors, but in their language *sarai* has been degraded to mean 'a shed.' The word, as applied to the Palace of the Grand Turk, became, in the language of the Levantine Franks, *serail* and *serraglio*. In this form, as P. della Valle lucidly explains below, the "striving after meaning" connected the word with Ital. *serrato*, 'shut up'; and with a word *serraglio* perhaps previously existing in Italian in that connection. [*Seraglio*, according to Prof. Skeat (*Concise Dict.* s.v.) is "formed with suffix-*aglio* (L. -*aculum*) from Late Lat. *serare*, 'to bar, shut in' —Lat. *sera*, a 'bar, bolt'; Lat. *serere*, 'to join together.'] It is this association that has attached the meaning of 'women's apartments' to the word. *Sarai* has no such specific sense.

But the usual modern meaning in Persia, and the only one in India, is that of a building for the accommodation of travellers with their pack-animals; consisting of an enclosed yard with chambers round it.

Recurring to the Italian use, we have seen in Italy the advertisement of a travelling menagerie as *Serraglio di Belve*. A friend tells us of an old Scotchman whose ideas must have run in this groove, for he used to talk of 'a *Serragle* of blackguards.' In the

Diary in England of Annibale Litolfi of Mantua the writer says: "On entering the tower there is a *Serraglio* in which, from grandeur, they keep lions and tigers and cat-lions." (See *Rawdon Brown's Calendar of Papers in Archives of Venice*, vol. vi. pt. iii. 1557-8. App.) [The *Stanf. Dict.* quotes Evelyn as using the word of a place where persons are confined: 1644. "I passed by the Piazza Judea, where their *seraglio* begins" (*Diary*, ed. 1872, i. 142).]

c. 1584.—"At **Saraium** Turcis palatium principis est, vel aliud amplum aedificium, non a *Czar** voce Tatarica, quae regem significat, dictum; vnde Reineccius **Saragliam** Turcis vocari putet, ut *regiam*. Nam aliae quoque domus, extra Sultani regiam, nomen hoc ferunt . . . vt ampla Turcorum hospitia, sive diversoria publica, quae vulgo *Caravasarias* (**Caravanseray**) nostri vocant."—*Leunclavius*, ed. 1650, p. 403.

1609.—". . . by it the great **Suray**, besides which are diuers others, both in the city and suburbs, wherein diuers neate lodgings are to be let, with doores, lockes, and keys to each."—*W. Finch*, in *Purchas*, i. 434.

1614.—"This term **serraglio**, so much used among us in speaking of the Grand Turk's dwelling . . . has been corrupted into that form from the word **serai**, which in their language signifies properly 'a palace.' . . . But since this word *serai* resembles *serraio*, as a Venetian would call it, or *seraglio* as we say, and seeing that the palace of the Turk is (*serrato* or) shut up all round by a strong wall, and also because the women and a great part of the courtiers dwell in it barred up and shut in, so it may perchance have seemed to some to have deserved such a name. And thus the real term **serai** has been converted into **serraglio**."—*P. della Valle*, i. 36.

1615.—"Onely from one dayes Journey to another the *Sophie* hath caused to bee erected certaine kind of great harbours, or huge lodgings (like hamlets) called *caravansara*, or **surroyes**, for the benefite of *Caravanes*. . . ."—*De Montfart*, 8.

1616.—"In this kingdome there are no Innes to entertaine strangers, only in great Townes and Cities are faire Houses built for their receit, which they call **Sarray**, not inhabited, where any Passenger may haue roome freely, but must bring with him his Bedding, his Cooke, and other necessaries."—*Terry*, in *Purchas*, ii. 1475.

1638.—"Which being done we departed from our **Serray** (or Inne)."—*W. Bruton*, in *Hakl.* v. 49.

* On another B.M. copy of an earlier edition than that quoted, and which belonged to Jos. Scaliger, there is here a note in his autograph: "Id est *Caesar*, non est vox Tatarica, sed Vindica seu Illyrica, ex Latino detorta."

1648.—"A great **sary** or place for housing travelling folk."—*Van Twist*, 17.

[1754.—". . . one of the Sciddees (**seedy**) officers with a party of men were lodged in the **Sorroy**. . . ."—*Forrest, Bombay Letters*, i. 307.]

1782.—"The stationary tenants of the Serauee, many of them women, and some of them very pretty, approach the traveller on his entrance, and in alluring language describe to him the varied excellencies of their several lodgings."—*Forster, Journey*, ed. 1808, i. 86.

1825.—"The whole number of lodgers in and about the **serai**, probably did not fall short of 500 persons. What an admirable scene for an Eastern romance would such an inn as this afford!"—*Heber*, ed. 1844, ii. 122.

1850.—"He will find that, if we omit only three names in the long line of the Delhi Emperors, the comfort and happiness of the people were never contemplated by them; and with the exception of a few **saráis** and bridges,—and these only on roads traversed by the imperial camps—he will see nothing in which purely selfish considerations did not prevail."—*Sir H. M. Elliot*, Original Preface to *Historians of India, Elliot*, I. xxiii.

b. A long-necked earthenware (or metal) flagon for water; a **goglet** (q.v.). This is Ar.—P. *ṣurāḥī*. [This is the *dorak* or *kulleh* of Egypt, of which Lane (*Mod. Egypt.* ed. 1871, i. 186 *seq.*) gives an account with illustrations.]

c. 1666.—". . . my *Navab* having vouchsafed me a very particular favour, which is, that he hath appointed to give me every day a new loaf of his house, and a **Souray** of the water of *Ganges* . . . **Souray** is that Tin-flagon full of water, which the Servant that marcheth on foot before the Gentleman on horseback, carrieth in his hand, wrapt up in a sleeve of red cloath."—*Bernier*, E.T. 114; [ed. *Constable*, 356].

1808.—"We had some bread and butter, two **surahees** of water, and a bottle of brandy."—*Elphinstone*, in *Life*, i. 183.

[1880.—"The best known is the gilt silver work of Cashmere, which is almost confined to the production of the water-vessels or **sarais**, copied from the clay goblets in use throughout the northern parts of the Panjab."—*Birdwood, Indust. Arts of India*, 149.]

SERANG, s. A native boatswain, or chief of a **lascar** crew; the skipper of a small native vessel. The word is Pers. *sarhang*, 'a commander or overseer.' In modern Persia it seems to be used for a colonel (see *Wills*, 80).

1599.—". . . there set sail two Portuguese vessels which were come to Amacao

(Macao) from the City of Goa, as occurs every year. They are commanded by Captains, with Pilots, quartermasters, clerks, and other officers, who are Portuguese; but manned by sailors who are Arabs, Turks, Indians, and Bengalis, who serve for so much a month, and provide themselves under the direction and command of a chief of their own whom they call the **Saranghi**, who also belongs to one of these nations, whom they understand, and recognise and obey, carrying out the orders that the Portuguese Captain, Master, or Pilot may give to the said **Saranghi**."—*Carletti, Viaggi*, ii. 206.

1690.—"Indus quem de hoc Ludo consului fuit scriba satis peritus ab officio in nave suâ dictus *le* **sarang**, Anglicè Boatswain seu Boson."—*Hyde, De Ludis Orientt.* in *Syntagma*, ii. 264.

[1822.—". . . the ghaut **syrangs** (a class of men equal to the kidnappers of Holland and the crimps of England). . . ."—*Wallace, Fifteen Years in India*, 256.]

SERAPHIN. See **XERAFIN.**

SERENDĪB, n.p. The Arabic form of the name of Ceylon in the earlier Middle Ages. (See under **CEYLON.**)

SERINGAPATAM, n.p. The city which was the capital of the Kingdom of Mysore during the reigns of Hyder Ali and his son Tippoo. Written *Sri-ranga-pattana*, meaning according to vulgar interpretation 'Vishnu's Town.' But as both this and the other Srirangam (*Seringam* town and temple, so-called, in the Trichinopoly district) are on islands of the Cauvery, it is possible that *ranga* stands for *Lanka*, and that the true meaning is 'Holy-Isle-Town.'

[**SERPEYCH**, s. Pers. *sarpech, sarpesh*; an ornament of gold, silver or jewels, worn in front of the turban; it sometimes consists of gold plates strung together, each plate being set with precious stones. Also a band of silk and embroidery worn round the turban.

[1753.—". . . a fillet. This they call a **sirpeach**, which is wore round the turban; persons of great distinction generally have them set with precious stones."—*Hanway*, iv. 191.

[1786.—"**Surpaishes.**" See under **CULGEE.**

[1813.—"**Serpeych.**" See under **KILLUT.**]

SETT, s. Properly Hind. *seth*, which according to Wilson is the same word with the Chetti (see **CHETTY**) or *Shetti* of the Malabar Coast, the different forms being all from Skt. *śreshtha*, 'best, or chief,' *śresthi*, 'the chief of a corporation, a merchant or banker.' C. P. Brown entirely denies the identity of the S. Indian *shetti* with the Skt. word (see **CHETTY**).

1740.—"The **Sets** being all present at the Board inform us that last year they dissented to the employment of Fillick Chund (&c.), they being of a different caste; and consequently they could not do business with them."—In *Long*, p. 9.

1757.—"To the **Seats** Mootabray and Roopchund the Government of Chandunagore was indebted a million and a half Rupees."—*Orme*, ii. 138 of reprint (Bk. viii.).

1770.—"As soon as an European arrived the Gentoos, who know mankind better than is commonly supposed, study his character . . . and lend or procure him money upon bottomry, or at interest. This interest, which is usually 9 per cent. at this is higher when he is under a necessity of borrowing of the **Cheyks**.

"These **Cheyks** are a powerful family of Indians, who have, time immemorial, inhabited the banks of the Ganges. Their riches have long ago procured them the management of the bank belonging to the Court. . . ."—*Raynal*, tr. 1777, i. 427. Note that by *Cheyks* the Abbé means **Setts**.

[1883.—". . . from the Himalayas to Cape Comorin a security endorsed by the Mathura **Seth** is as readily convertible into cash as a Bank of England Note in London or Paris."—*F. S. Growse, Mathura*, 14.]

SETTLEMENT, s. In the Land Revenue system of India, an estate or district is said to be *settled*, when instead of taking a quota of the year's produce the Government has agreed with the cultivators, individually or in community, for a fixed sum to be paid at several periods of the year, and not liable to enhancement during the term of years for which the agreement or *settlement* is made. The operation of arranging the terms of such an agreement, often involving tedious and complicated considerations and enquiries, is known as the process of *settlement*. A *Permanent Settlement* is that in which the annual payment is fixed in perpetuity. This was introduced in Bengal by Lord Cornwallis in 1793, and does not exist except within that great Province, [and a few districts in the Benares division of the N.W.P., and in Madras.]

[**SEVEN PAGODAS**, n.p. The Tam. *Mavallipuram*, Skt. *Mahabalipura*, 'the City of the Great Bali,' a place midway between **Sadras** and Covelong. But in one of the inscriptions (about 620 A.D.) a King, whose name is said to have been Amara, is described as having conquered the chief of the Mahamalla race. Malla was probably the name of a powerful highland chieftain subdued by the Chalukyans. (See *Crole, Man. of Chingleput*, 92 *seq.*). Dr. Oppert (*Orig. Inhabit.*, 98) takes the name to be derived from the Malla or Palli race.

SEVEN SISTERS, or **BROTHERS**. The popular name (Hind. *sāt-bhāī*) of a certain kind of bird, about the size of a thrush, common throughout most parts of India, *Malacocercus terricolor*, Hodgson, 'Bengal babbler' of Jerdon. The latter author gives the native name as *Seven Brothers*, which is the form also given in the quotation below from *Tribes on My Frontier*. The bird is so named from being constantly seen in little companies of about that number. Its characteristics are well given in the quotations. See also *Jerdon's Birds* (Godwin-Austen's ed., ii. 59). In China certain birds of starling kind are called by the Chinese *pa-ko*, or "Eight Brothers," for a like reason. See *Collingwood's Rambles of a Naturalist*, 1868, p. 319. (See **MYNA**.)

1878. — "The **Seven Sisters** pretend to feed on insects, but that is only when they cannot get peas . . . sad-coloured birds hopping about in the dust, and incessantly talking whilst they hop."—*Ph. Robinson, In My Indian Garden*, 30-31.

1883.—". . . the **Satbhai** or 'Seven Brothers' . . . are too shrewd and knowing to be made fun of. . . . Among themselves they will quarrel by the hour, and bandy foul language like fishwives; but let a stranger treat one of their number with disrespect, and the other six are in arms at once. . . . Each Presidency of India has its own branch of this strange family. Here (at Bombay) they are brothers, and in Bengal they are sisters; but everywhere, like Wordsworth's opinionative child, they are seven."—*Tribes on My Frontier*, 143.

SEVERNDROOG, n.p. A somewhat absurd corruption, which has been applied to two forts of some fame, viz.:

a. *Suvarna-druga*, or *Suwandrug*, on the west coast, about 78 m. below Bombay (Lat. 17° 48′ N.). It was taken in 1755 by a small naval force from Tulajī Angria, of the famous piratical family. [For the commander of the expedition, Commodore James, and his monument on Shooter's Hill, see *Douglas, Bombay and W. India*, i. 117 *seq.*]

b. *Savandrug*; a remarkable double hill-fort in Mysore, standing on a two-topped bare rock of granite, which was taken by Lord Cornwallis's army in 1791 (Lat. 12° 55′). [Wilks (*Hist. Sketches*, Madras reprint, i. 228, ii. 232) calls it *Savendy Droog*, and *Savendroog*.]

SEYCHELLE ISLANDS, n.p. A cluster of islands in the Indian Ocean, politically subordinate to the British Government of Mauritius, lying be-between 3° 40′ & 4° 50′ S. Lat., and about 950 sea-miles east of Mombas on the E. African coast. There are 29 or 30 of the Seychelles proper, of which Mahé, the largest, is about 17 m. long by 3 or 4 wide. The principal islands are granitic, and rise "in the centre of a vast plateau of coral" of some 120 m. diameter.

These islands are said to have been visited by Soares in 1506, and were known vaguely to the Portuguese navigators of the 16th century as the Seven Brothers (*Os sete Irmanos* or *Hermanos*), sometimes Seven Sisters (*Sete Irmanas*), whilst in Delisle's Map of Asia (1700) we have both "les Sept Frères" and "les Sept Sœurs." Adjoining these on the W. or S.W. we find also on the old maps a group called the *Almirantes*, and this group has retained that name to the present day, constituting now an appendage of the Seychelles.

The islands remained uninhabited, and apparently unvisited, till near the middle of the 18th century. In 1742 the celebrated Mahé de la Bourdonnais, who was then Governor of Mauritius and the Isle of Bourbon, despatched two small vessels to explore the islands of this little archipelago, an expedition which was renewed by Lazare Picault, the commander of one of the two vessels, in 1774, who gave to the principal island the name of *Mahé*, and to the group the name of *Iles de Bourdonnais*, for which *Iles Mahé* (which is the name given in the

Neptune Orientale of D'Apres de Manneville, 1775, pp. 29-38, and the charts), seems to have been substituted. Whatever may have been La Bourdonnais' plans with respect to these islands, they were interrupted by his engagement in the Indian campaigns of 1745-46, and his government of Mauritius was never resumed. In 1756 the Sieur Morphey (Murphy ?), commander of the frigate *Le Cerf*, was sent by M. Magon, Governor of Mauritius and Bourbon, to take possession of the Island of Mahé. But it seems doubtful if any actual settlement of the islands by the French occurred till after 1769. [See the account of the islands in *Owen's Narrative*, ii. 158 *seqq.*]

A question naturally has suggested itself to us as to how the group came by the name of the *Seychelles Islands;* and it is one to which no trustworthy answer will be easily found in English, if at all. Even French works of pretension (*e.g.* the *Dictionnaire de la Rousse*) are found to state that the islands were named after the "Minister of Marine, Herault de Séchelles, who was eminent for his services and his able administration. He was the first to establish a French settlement there." This is quoted from La Rousse; but the fact is that the only man of the name known to fame is the Jacobin and friend of Danton, along with whom he perished by the guillotine. There never was a Minister of Marine so called! The name **Séchelles** first (so far as we can learn) appears in the *Hydrographie Française* of Belin, 1767, where in a map entitled *Carte réduite du Canal de Mozambique* the islands are given as *Les Iles* **Sécheyles**, with two enlarged plans *en cartouche* of the *Port de Sécheyles*. In 1767 also Chev. de Grenier, commanding the *Heure du Berger*, visited the Islands, and in his narrative states that he had with him the chart of Picault, "envoyé par La Bourdonnais pour reconnoître les isles des Sept Frères, *lesquelles ont été depuis nommée iles Mahé et ensuite* **iles Séchelles.**" We have not been able to learn by whom the latter name was given, but it was probably by Morphey of the *Cerf;* for among Dalrymple's Charts (pub. 1771), there is a "*Plan of the Harbour adjacent to* Bat River *on the Island* Seychelles, *from a French plan made in* 1756, *published by* Bellin." And there can be no doubt that the name was bestowed in honour of Moreau de Séchelles, who was *Contrôleur-Général des Finances* in France in 1754-56, *i.e.* at the very time when Governor Magon sent Capt. Morphey to take possession. One of the islands again is called *Silhouette*, the name of an official who had been *Commissaire du roi près la Compagnie des Indes*, and succeeded Moreau de Séchelles as Controller of Finance; and another is called *Praslin*, apparently after the Duc de Choiseul Praslin who was Minister of Marine from 1766 to 1770.

The exact date of the settlement of the islands we have not traced. We can only say that it must have been between 1769 and 1772. The quotation below from the Abbé Rochon shows that the islands were not settled when he visited them in 1769; whilst that from Capt. Neale shows that they were settled before his visit in 1772. It will be seen that both Rochon and Neale speak of Mahé as "the island Seychelles, or Sécheyles," as in Belin's chart of 1767. It seems probable that the cloud under which La Bourdonnais fell, on his return to France, must have led to the suppression of his name in connection with the group.

The islands surrendered to the English Commodore Newcome in 1794, and were formally ceded to England with Mauritius in 1815. **Seychelles** appears to be an erroneous English spelling, now however become established. (For valuable assistance in the preceding article we are indebted to the courteous communications of M. James Jackson, Librarian of the *Société de Géographie* at Paris, and of M. G. Marcel of the *Bibliothèque Nationale*. And see, besides the works quoted here, a paper by M. Elie Pujot, in *L'Explorateur*, vol. iii. (1876) pp. 523-526).

The following passage of Pyrard probably refers to the Seychelles:

c. 1610.—"Le Roy (des Maldives) enuoya par deux foys vn très expert pilote pour aller descouvrir vne certaine isle nommée *pollouoys*, qui leur est presque inconnuë. . . . Ils disent aussi que le diable les y tourmentoit visiblement, et que pour l'isle elle est fertile en toutes sortes de fruicts, et mesme ils ont opinion que ces gros Cocos medicinaux qui sont si chers-là en viennent. . . . Elle est sous la hauteur de dix degrés au delà de la ligne et enuiron six vingt lieuës des Maldiues. . . ."—(see **COCO-DE-MER**).—*Pyrard de Laval*, i. 212. [Also see Mr. Gray's note in Hak. Soc. ed. i. 296, where he explains the word *pollouoys* in the above quotation as the Malay *pulo*, 'an island,' Malé *Fōlávahi*.]

1769.—"The principal places, the situation of which I determined, are the **Secheyles islands**, the flat of Cargados, the Salha da Maha, the island of Diego Garcia, and the Adu isles. The island **Secheyles** has an exceedingly good harbour. . . . This island is covered with wood to the very summit of the mountains. . . . In 1769 when I spent a month here in order to determine its position with the utmost exactness, Secheyles and the adjacent isles were inhabited only by monstrous crocodiles; but a small establishment has since been formed on it for the cultivation of cloves and nutmegs."—*Voyage to Madagascar and the E. Indies by the Abbé Rochon*, E.T., London, 1792, p. liii.

1772.—"The island named **Seychelles** is inhabited by the French, and has a good harbour. . . . I shall here deliver my opinion that these islands, where we now are, are the Three Brothers and the adjacent islands . . . as there are no islands to the eastward of them in these latitudes, and many to the westward." — *Capt. Neale's Passage from Bencoolen to the Seychelles Islands in the Swift Grab.* In *Dunn's Directory*, ed. 1780, pp. 225, 232.

[1901.—"For a man of energy, perseverance, and temperate habits, **Seychelles** affords as good an opening as any tropical colony."—*Report of Administrator*, in *Times*, Oct. 2.]

SHA, SAH, s. A merchant or banker; often now attached as a surname. It is Hind. *sāh* and *sāhu* from Skt. *sādhu*, 'perfect, virtuous, respectable' ('*prudhomme*'). See **SOWCAR**.

[c. 1809.—". . . the people here called Mahajans (**Mahajun**), **Sahu**, and Bahariyas, live by lending money."—*Buchanan Hamilton, E. India*, ii. 573.]

SHABASH! interj. 'Well done!' 'Bravo!' Pers. *Shā-bāsh.* 'Rex fias!'* [Rather *shād-bāsh*, 'Be joyful.']

c. 1610.—"Le Roy fit rencontre de moy . . . me disant vn mot qui est commun en toute l'Inde, à savoir **Sabatz**, qui veut dire grand mercy, et sert aussi à louer vn homme pour quelque chose qu'il a bien fait."—*Pyrard de Laval*, i. 224.

[1843.—"I was awakened at night from a sound sleep by the repeated **savāshes**! *wāh! wāhs!* from the residence of the thanndar."—*Davidson, Travels in Upper India*, i. 209.]

* "At pueri ludentes, *Rex eris*, aiunt, Si recte facies."—*Hor. Ep.* I. i.

SHABUNDER, s. Pers. *Shāh-bandar*, lit. 'King of the Haven,' Harbour-Master. This was the title of an officer at native ports all over the Indian seas, who was the chief authority with whom foreign traders and ship-masters had to transact. He was often also head of the Customs. Hence the name is of prominent and frequent occurrence in the old narratives. Portuguese authors generally write the word *Xabander*; ours *Shabunder* or *Sabundar*. The title is not obsolete, though it does not now exist in India; the quotation from Lane shows its recent existence in Cairo, [and the Persians still call their Consuls *Shāh-bandar* (*Burton, Ar. Nights*, iii. 158)]. In the marine Malay States the *Shābandar* was, and probably is, an important officer of State. The passages from Lane and from Tavernier show that the title was not confined to seaports. At Aleppo Thevenot (1663) calls the corresponding official, perhaps by a mistake, '*Scheik* **Bandar**' (*Voyages*, iii. 121). [This is the office which King Mihrjān conferred upon Sindbad the Seaman, when he made him "his agent for the port and registrar of all ships that entered the harbour" (*Burton*, iv. 351)].

c. 1350.—"The chief of all the Musulmans in this city (*Kaulam*—see **QUILON**) is Mahommed **Shāhbandar**."—*Ibn Batuta*, iv. 100.

c. 1539.—"This King (of the Batas) understanding that I had brought him a Letter and a Present from the Captain of *Malaca*, caused me to be entertained by the **Xabandar**, who is he that with absolute Power governs all the affairs of the Army."—*Pinto* (orig. cap. xv.), in *Çogan's Transl.* p. 18.

1552.—"And he who most insisted on this was a Moor, **Xabandar** of the Guzarates" (at Malacca).—*Castanheda*, ii. 359.

1553.—"A Moorish lord called Sabayo (**Sabaio**) . . . as soon as he knew that our ships belonged to the people of these parts of Christendom, desiring to have confirmation on the matter, sent for a certain Polish Jew who was in his service as **Shabandar** (*Xabandar*), and asked him if he knew of what nation were the people who came in these ships. . . ."—*Barros*, I. iv. 11.

1561.—". . . a boatman, who, however, called himself **Xabandar**."—*Correa, Lendas*, ii. 80.

1599.—"The **Sabandar** tooke off my Hat, and put a Roll of white linnen about my head. . . ."—*J. Davis*, in *Purchas*, i. 12.

[1604.—"**Sabindar**." See under **KLING**.]

1606.—"Then came the **Sabendor** with light, and brought the Generall to his house." —*Middleton's Voyage*, E. (4).

1610.—"The **Sabander** and the Governor of *Mancock* (a place scituated by the River). . . ."—*Peter Williamson Floris*, in *Purchas*, i. 322.

[1615.—"The opinion of the **Sabindour** shall be taken."—*Foster*, *Letters*, iv. 79.]

c. 1650.—"Coming to Golconda, I found that the person whom I had left in trust with my chamber was dead: but that which I observ'd most remarkable, was that I found the door seal'd with two Seals, one being the Cadi's or chief Justice's, the other the **Sha-Bander's** or Provost of the Merchants."—*Tavernier*, E.T. Pt. ii. 136; [ed. *Ball*, ii. 70].

1673.—"The **Shawbunder** has his Grandeur too, as well as receipt of Custom, for which he pays the King yearly 22,000 *Thomands*."—*Fryer*, 222.

1688.—"When we arrived at Achin, I was carried before the **Shabander**, the chief Magistrate of the City. . . ."—*Dampier*, i. 502.

1711.—"The Duties the Honourable Company require to be paid here on Goods are not above one fifth Part of what is paid to the **Shabander** or Custom-Master."—*Lockyer*, 223.

1726.—Valentyn, v. 313, gives a list of the **Sjahbandars** of Malakka from 1641 to 1725. They are names of Dutchmen.

[1727.—"**Shawbandaar**." See under **TENASSERIM**.]

1759.—"I have received a long letter from the Shahzada, in which he complains that you have begun to carry on a large trade in salt, and betel nut, and refuse to pay the duties on those articles . . . which practice, if continued, will oblige him to throw up his post of **Shahbunder** Droga (**Daroga**)."—*W. Hastings* to the Chief at Dacca, in *Van Sittart*, i. 5.

1768.—". . . two or three days after my arrival (at Batavia), the landlord of the hotel where I lodged told me he had been ordered by the **shebandar** to let me know that my carriage, as well as others, must stop, if I should meet the Governor, or any of the council; but I desired him to acquaint the **shebandar** that I could not consent to perform any such ceremony." —*Capt. Carteret*, quoted by transl. of *Stavorinus*, i. 281.

1795.—"The descendant of a Portuguese family, named Jaunsee, whose origin was very low . . . was invested with the important office of **Shawbunder**, or intendant of the port, and receiver of the port customs."—*Symes*, p. 160.

1837.—"The Seyd Mohammad El Mahroockee, the **Shahbendar** (chief of the Merchants of Cairo) hearing of this event, suborned a common fellah. . . ."—*Lane's Mod. Egyptians*, ed. 1837, i. 157.

3 F

SHADDOCK, s. This name properly belongs to the West Indies, having been given, according to Grainger, from that of the Englishman who first brought the fruit thither from the East, and who was, according to Crawfurd, an interloper captain, who traded to the Archipelago about the time of the Revolution, and is mentioned by his contemporary Dampier. The fruit is the same as the **pommelo** (q.v.). And the name appears from a modern quotation below to be now occasionally used in India. [Nothing definite seems to be known of this Capt. Shaddock. Mr. R. C. A. Prior (7 ser. *N. & Q.*, vii. 375) writes: "Lunan, in '*Hortus Jamaicensis*,' vol. ii. p. 171, says, 'This fruit is not near so large as the shaddock, which received its name from a Capt. Shaddock, who first brought the plant from the East Indies.' The name of the captain is believed to have been Shattock, one not uncommon in the west of Somersetshire. Sloane, in his 'Voyage to Jamaica,' 1707, vol. i. p. 41 says, 'The seed of this was first brought to Barbados by one Capt. Shaddock, commander of an East Indian ship, who touch'd at that island in his passage to England, and left its seed there.'" Watt (*Econ. Dict.* ii. 349) remarks that the Indian vernacular name *Batāvī nībū*, 'Batavian lime,' suggests its having been originally brought from Batavia.]

[1754.—". . . pimple-noses (**pommelo**), called in the West Indies, **Chadocks**, a very fine large fruit of the citron-kind, but of four or five times its size. . . ."—*Ives*, 19.]

1764.—

"Nor let thy bright impatient flames destroy
The golden **Shaddock**, the forbidden fruit. . . ."—*Grainger*, Bk. I.

1803.—"The **Shaddock**, or pumpelmos (**pommelo**), often grows to the size of a man's head."—*Percival's Ceylon*, 313.

[1832.—"Several trays of ripe fruits of the season, viz., kurbootahs (**shadock**), kabooza (melons). . . ."—*Mrs. Meer Hassan Ali, Observations*, i. 365.]

1878.—". . . the splendid **Shaddock** that, weary of ripening, lays itself upon the ground and swells at ease. . . ."—*In My Indian Garden*, 50.

[1898.—

"He has stripped my rails of the **shaddock** frails and the green unripened pine."
R. Kipling, Barrack Room Ballads, p. 130.]

SHADE (TABLE-SHADE, WALL-SHADE), s. A glass guard to protect a candle or simple oil-lamp from the wind. The oldest form, in use at the beginning of the last century, was a tall glass cylinder which stood on the table, the candlestick and candle being placed bodily within in. In later days the universal form has been that of an inverted dome fitting into the candlestick, which has an annular socket to receive it. The *wall-shade* is a bracket attached to the wall, bearing a candle or cocoa-nut oil lamp, protected by such a shade. In the wine-drinking days of the earlier part of last century it was sometimes the subject of a challenge, or forfeit, for a man to empty a wall-shade filled with claret. The second quotation below gives a notable description of a captain's outfit when taking the field in the 18th century.

1780.—"Borrowed last Month by a Person or Persons unknown, out of a private Gentleman's House near the Esplanade, a very elegant Pair of Candle **Shades**. Whoever will return the same will receive a reward of 40 *Sicca Rupees*. — N.B. The Shades have private marks."—*Hicky's Bengal Gazette*, April 8.

1789.—"His tent is furnished with a good large bed, mattress, pillow, &c., a few campstools or chairs, a folding table, a pair of **shades** for his candles, six or seven trunks with table equipage, his stock of linen (at least 24 shirts); some dozens of wine, brandy, and gin; tea, sugar, and biscuit; and a hamper of live poultry and his milchgoat."—*Munro's Narrative*, 186.

1817.—"I am now finishing this letter by candle-light, with the help of a handkerchief tied over the **shade**."—*T. Munro*, in *Life*, i. 511.

[1838.—"We brought carpets, and chandeliers, and **wall shades** (the great staple commodity of Indian furniture), from Calcutta. . . ."—*Miss Eden, Up the Country*, 2nd ed. i. 182.]

SHAGREEN, s. This English word, —French *chagrin*; Ital. *zigrino*; Mid. High Ger. *Zager*,—comes from the Pers. *saghrī*, Turk. *ṣāghrī*, meaning properly the croupe or quarter of a horse, from which the peculiar granulated leather, also called *sāghrī* in the East, was originally made. Diez considers the French (and English adopted) *chagrin* in the sense of vexation to be the same word, as certain hard skins prepared in this way were used as files, and hence the word is used figuratively for gnawing vexation, as (he states) the Ital. *lima* also is (*Etym. Worterbuch*, ed. 1861, ii. 240). He might have added the figurative origin of *tribulation*. [This view is accepted by the *N.E.D.*; but Prof. Skeat (*Concise Dict.*) denies its correctness.]

1663.—". . . à Alep . . . on y travaille aussi bien qu'à Damas le **sagri**, qui est ce qu'on appelle **chagrin** en France, mais l'on en fait une bien plus grande quantité en Perse. . . . Le **sagri** sa fait de croupe d'âne," &c.—*Thevenot, Voyages*, iii. 115-116.

1862.—"**Saghree**, or *Keemookt*, Horse or Ass-Hide." — *Punjab Trade Report*, App. ccxx.; [For an account of the manufacture of *kimukht*, see *Hoey, Mon. on Trades and Manufactures of N. India*, 94.]

SHAITAN, Ar. 'The Evil One; Satan.' *Shaitān kā bhāī*, 'Brother of the Arch-Enemy,' was a title given to Sir C. Napier by the Amīrs of Sind and their followers. He was not the first great English soldier to whom this title had been applied in the East. In the romance of *Cœur de Lion*, when Richard entertains a deputation of Saracens by serving at table the head of one of their brethren, we are told:

"Every man sat stylle and pokyd othir;
They saide: 'This is the *Develys brothir*,
That sles our men, and thus hem eetes. . ."

[c. 1630.—"But a Mountebank or Impostor is nick-named **Shitan**. Tabib, *i.e.* the Devil's Chirurgion."—*Sir T. Herbert*, ed. 1677, p. 304.

1753. — "God preserve me from the **Scheithan** Alragim."—*Hanway*, iii. 90.]

1863.—"Not many years ago, an eccentric gentleman wrote from Sikkim to the Secretary of the Asiatic Society in Calcutta, stating that, on the snows of the mountains there were found certain mysterious footsteps, *more than* 30 *or* 40 *paces asunder*, which the natives alleged to be **Shaitan's**. The writer at the same time offered, if Government would give him leave of absence for a certain period, etc., to go and trace the author of these mysterious vestiges, and thus this strange creature would be discovered *without any expense to Government*. The notion of catching **Shaitan** *without any expense to Government* was a sublime piece of Anglo-Indian tact, but the offer was not accepted."—*Sir H. Yule, Notes to Friar Jordanus*, 37.

SHALEE, SHALOO, SHELLA, SALLO, &c., s. We have a little doubt as to the identity of all these words; the two latter occur in old works as names of cotton stuffs; the first two (Shakespear and Fallon give *sālū*) are names in familiar use for a soft twilled cotton stuff, of a Turkey-red colour, somewhat resembling what we call, by what we had judged to be a modification of the word, *shaloon*. But we find that Skeat and other authorities ascribe the latter word to a corruption of *Chalons*, which gave its name to certain stuffs, apparently bed-coverlets of some sort. Thus in Chaucer:

"With shétes and with **chalons** faire yspredde."—*The Reve's Tale.*

On which Tyrwhitt quotes from the *Monasticon*, "... *aut pannos pictos qui vocantur* **chalons** *loco lectisternii*." See also in *Liber Albus:*

"La charge de **chalouns** et draps de Reynes. ..."—p. 225, also at p. 231.

c. 1343.—"I went then to *Shāliyāt* (near Calicut—see **CHALIA**) a very pretty town, where they make the stuffs (qu. **shālī**?) that bear its name."—*Ibn Batuta*, iv. 109.

[It is exceedingly difficult to disentangle the meanings and derivations of this series of words. In the first place we have **saloo**, Hind. *sālū*, the Turkey-red cloth above described; a word which is derived by Platts from Skt. *śālū*, 'a kind of astringent substance,' and is perhaps the same word as the Tel. *sālū*, 'cloth.' This was originally an Indian fabric, but has now been replaced in the bazars by an English cloth, the art of dyeing which was introduced by French refugees who came over after the Revolution (see 7 ser. *N. & Q.* viii. 485 *seq.*). See **PIECE-GOODS, SALOO-PAUTS**.

[c. 1590.—"**Sálu**, per piece, 3 R. to 2 M."—*Āīn*, i. 94.

[1610.—"**Sallallo**, blue and black."—*Danvers, Letters*, i. 72.

[1672.—"**Salloos**, made at Gulcundah, and brought from thence to Surat, and go to England."—In *Birdwood, Report on Old Records*, 62.

[1896.—"**Salu** is another fabric of a red colour prepared by dyeing English cloth named *mārkīn* ('American') in the *āl* dye, and was formerly extensively used for turbans, curtains, borders of female coats and female dress."—*Muhammad Hadi, Mon. on Dyes*, 34.

Next we have **shelah**, which may be identical with Hind. *selā*, which Platts connects with Skt. *chela, chaila*, 'a piece of cloth,' and defines as "a kind of scarf or mantle (of silk, or lawn, or muslin; usually composed of four breadths depending from the shoulders loosely over the body: it is much worn and given as a present, in the Dakkhan); silk turban." In the Deccan it seems to be worn by men (*Herklots, Qanoon-e-Islam*, Madras reprint, 18). The *Madras Gloss.* gives **sheelay**, Mal. *shīla*, said to be from Skt. *chīra*, 'a strip of cloth,' in the sense of clothes; and **sullah**, Hind. *sela*, 'gauze for turbans.'

[c. 1590.—"**Shelah**, from the Dek'han, per piece, ½ to 2 M."—*Āīn*, i. 95.

[1598.—"**Cheyla**," in *Linschoten*, i. 91.

[1800.—"**Shillas**, or thin white muslins. ... They are very coarse, and are sometimes striped, and then called *Dupattas* (see **DOOPUTTY**)."—*Buchanan, Mysore*, ii. 240.]

1809.—"The **shalie**, a long piece of coloured silk or cotton, is wrapped round the waist in the form of a petticoat, which leaves part of one leg bare, whilst the other is covered to the ancle with long and graceful folds, gathered up in front, so as to leave one end of the **shalie** to cross the breast, and form a drapery, which is sometimes thrown over the head as a veil."—*Maria Graham*, 3. [But, as Sir H. Yule suggested, in this form the word may represent **Saree**.]

1813.—"Red **Shellas** or **Salloes**. ..."—*Milburne*, i. 124.

[,, "His **shela**, of fine cloth, with a silk or gold thread border. ..."—*Trans. Lit. Soc. Bo.* iii. 219 *seq.*

[1900.—"**Sela** *Dupatta*—worn by men over shoulders, tucked round waist, ends hanging in front ... plain body and borders richly ornamented with gold thread; white, yellow, and green; worn in full dress, sometimes merely thrown over shoulders, with the ends hanging in front from either shoulder.'—*Yusuf Ali, Mon. on Silk*, 72.

The following may represent the same word, or be perhaps connected with P.—H. *chilla*, 'a selvage, gold threads in the border of a turban, &c.'

[1610.—"**Tsyle**, the corge, Rs. 70."—*Danvers, Letters*, i. 72.]

1615.—"320 pieces red **zelas**."—*Foster, Letters*, iv. 129. The same word is used by *Cocks, Diary*, Hak. Soc. i. 4.]

SHAMA, s. Hind. *shāmā* [Skt. *syāma*, 'black, dark-coloured.'] A favourite song-bird and cage-bird, *Kitta cincla macrura*, Gmel. "In confinement it imitates the notes of other birds, and of various animals, with ease and accuracy" (*Jerdon*). The long tail seems to indicate the identity of this bird rather than the *mainā* (see **MYNA**) with that described by Aelian. [Mr. M'Crindle (*Invasion of India*, 186) favours the identification of the bird with the *Mainā*.]

c. A.D. 250.—"There is another bird found among the Indians, which is of the size of a starling. It is particoloured; and in imitating the voice of man it is more loquacious and clever than a parrot. But it does not readily bear confinement, and yearning for liberty, and longing for intercourse with its kind, it prefers hunger to bondage with fat living. The Macedonians who dwell among the Indians, in the city of Bucephala and thereabouts . . . call the bird *κερκίων* ('Taily'); and the name arose from the fact that the bird twitches his tail just like a wagtail."—*Aelian, de Nat. Anim.* xvi. 3.

SHAMAN, SHAMANISM, s. These terms are applied in modern times to superstitions of the kind that connects itself with exorcism and "devil-dancing" as their most prominent characteristic, and which are found to prevail with wonderful identity of circumstance among non-Caucasian races over parts of the earth most remote from one another; not only among the vast variety of Indo-Chinese tribes, but among the Dravidian tribes of India, the Veddahs of Ceylon, the races of Siberia, and the red nations of N. and S. America. "Hinduism has assimilated these 'prior superstitions of the sons of Tur,' as Mr. Hodgson calls them, in the form of Tantrika mysteries, whilst, in the wild performance of the Dancing Dervishes at Constantinople, we see, perhaps, again, the infection of Turanian blood breaking out from the very heart of Mussulman orthodoxy" (see *Notes to Marco Polo*, Bk. II. ch. 50). The characteristics of Shamanism is the existence of certain sooth-sayers or medicine-men, who profess a special art of dealing with the mischievous spirits who are supposed to produce illness and other calamities, and who invoke these spirits and ascertain the means of appeasing them, in trance produced by fantastic ceremonies and convulsive dancings.

The immediate origin of the term is the title of the spirit-conjuror in the Tunguz language, which is *shaman*, in that of the Manchus becoming *saman*, pl. *samasa*. But then in Chinese *Sha-măn* or *Shi-măn* is used for a Buddhist ascetic, and this would seem to be taken from the Skt. *śramana*, Pali *samana*. Whether the Tunguz word is in any way connected with this or adopted from it, is a doubtful question. W. Schott, who has treated the matter elaborately (*Über den Doppelsinn des Wortes* Schamane *und über den tungusichen* Schamanen-*Cultus am Hofe der Mandju Kaisern*, Berlin Akad. 1842), finds it difficult to suppose any connection. We, however, give a few quotations relating to the two words in one series. In the first two the reference is undoubtedly to Buddhist ascetics.

c. B.C. 320.—"Τοὺς δὲ Σαρμάνας, τοὺς μὲν ἐντιμοτάτους Ὑλοβίους φησὶν ὀνομάζεσθαι, ζῶντας ἐν ταῖς ὕλαις ἀπὸ φύλλων καὶ καρπῶν ἀγρίων, ἐσθῆτας δ' ἔχειν ἀπὸ φλοιῶν δενδρείων, ἀφροδισίων χωρὶς καὶ οἴνου."—From *Megasthenes*, in *Strabo*, xv.

c. 712.—"All the **Samanís** assembled and sent a message to Bajhrá, saying, "We are *násik* devotees. Our religion is one of peace and quiet, and fighting and slaying is prohibited, as well as all kinds of shedding of blood."—*Chach Náma*, in *Elliot*, i. 158.

1829.—"*Kami* is the Mongol name of the spirit-conjuror or sorcerer, who before the introduction of Buddhism exercised among the Mongols the office of Sacrificer and Priest, as he still does among the Tunguzes, Manjus, and other Asiatic tribes. . . . In Europe they are known by the Tunguz name **schaman**; among the Manjus as **saman**, and among the Tibetans as *Hlaba*. The Mongols now call them with contempt and abhorrence *Böh* or *Böghe*, *i.e.* 'Sorcerer,' 'Wizard,' and the women who give themselves to the like fooleries *Udugun*."—*I. J. Schmidt, Notes to Sanang Setzen*, p. 416.

1871. — "Among Siberian tribes, the **shamans** select children liable to convulsions as suitable to be brought up to the profession, which is apt to become hereditary with the epileptic tendencies it belongs to."—*Tylor, Primitive Culture*, ii. 121.

SHAMBOGUE, s. Canar. *shāna-* or *sāna-bhoga*; *shanāya*, 'allowance of grain paid to the village accountant,' Skt. *bhoga*, 'enjoyment.' A village clerk or accountant.

[c. 1766.—". . . this order to be enforced in the accounts by the **shanbague**."—*Logan, Malabar*, iii. 120.

[1800.—"**Shanaboga**, called **Shanbogue** by corruption, and **Curnum** by the Musulmans, is the village accountant."—*Buchanan's Mysore*, i. 268.]

1801.—"When the whole **kist** is collected, the **shanbogue** and potail (see **PATEL**) carry it to the teshildar's cutcherry."—*T. Munro*, in *Life*, i. 316.

SHAMEEANA, SEMIANNA, s. Pers. *shamiyāna* or *shāmiyāna* [very doubtfully derived from Pers. *shāh*, 'king,' *miyāna*, 'centre'], an awning or flat tent-roof, sometimes without sides, but often in the present day with **canauts**; sometimes pitched like a porch before a large tent; often used by civil officers, when on tour, to hold their court or office proceedings *coram populo*, and in a manner generally accessible. [In the early records the word is used for a kind of striped calico.]

c. 1590.—"The **Shāmyānah**-awning is made of various sizes, but never more than of 12 yards square."—*Āīn*, i. 54.

[1609.—"A sort of Calico here called **semi-janes** are also in abundance, it is broader than the Calico."—*Danvers, Letters*, i. 29.]

[1613. — "The Hector having certain chueckeros (**chucker**) of fine **Semian** chowters."—*Ibid.* i. 217. In *Foster*, iv. 239, **semanes.**]

1616.—". . . there is erected a throne foure foote from the ground in the Durbar Court from the backe whereof, to the place where the King comes out, a square of 56 paces long, and 43 broad was rayled in, and covered with fair **Semiaenes** or Canopies of Cloth of Gold, Silke, or Velvet ioyned together, and sustained with Canes so covered."—*Sir T. Roe*, in *Purchas*, i.; Hak. Soc. i. 142.

[1676.—"We desire you to furnish him with all things necessary for his voyage, . . . with bridle and sadle, **Semeanoes**, canatts (**Canaut**). . . ."—*Forrest, Bombay Letters*, i. 89.]

1814.—"I had seldom occasion to look out for gardens or pleasure grounds to pitch my tent or erect my **Summiniana** or **Shamyana**, the whole country being generally a garden."—*Forbes, Or. Mem.* ii. 455; 2nd ed. ii. 64. In ii. 294 he writes **Shumeeana**].

1857.—"At an early hour we retired to rest. Our beds were arranged under large canopies, open on all sides, and which are termed by the natives '**Shameanahs**.'"—*M. Thornhill, Personal Adventures*, 14.

SHAMPOO, v. To knead and press the muscles with the view of relieving fatigue, &c. The word has now long been familiarly used in England. The Hind. verb is *chāmpnā*, from the imperative of which, *chāmpō*, this is most probably a corruption, as in the case of **Bunow, Puckerow,** &c. The process is described, though not named, by Terry, in 1616: "Taking thus their ease, they often call their Barbers, who tenderly gripe and smite their Armes and other parts of their bodies instead of exercise, to stirre the bloud. It is a pleasing wantonnesse, and much valued in these hot climes." (In *Purchas*, ii. 1475). The process was familiar to the Romans under the Empire, whose slaves employed in this way were styled *tractator* and *tractatrix*. [Perhaps the earliest reference to the practice is in Strabo (*McCrindle, Ancient India*, 72).] But with the ancients it seems to have been allied to vice, for which there is no ground that we know in the Indian custom.

1748.—"**Shampooing** is an operation not known in Europe, and is peculiar to the Chinese, which I had once the curiosity to go through, and for which I paid but a trifle. However, had I not seen several China merchants **shampooed** before me, I should have been apprehensive of danger, even at the sight of all the different instruments. . . ." (The account is good, but too long for extract.)—*A Voyage to the E. Indies in* 1747 *and* 1748. London, 1762, p. 226.

1750-60.—"The practice of **champing**, which by the best intelligence I could gather is derived from the Chinese, may not be unworthy particularizing, as it is little known to the modern Europeans. . . ."—*Grose*, i. 113. This writer quotes *Martial*, iii. Ep. 82, and *Seneca*, Epist. 66, to show that the practice was known in ancient Rome.

1800.—"The Sultan generally rose at break of day: after being **champoed**, and rubbed, he washed himself, and read the Koran for an hour."—*Beatson, War with Tippoo*, p. 159.

[1810.—"**Shampoeing** may be compared to a gentle kneading of the whole person, and is the same operation described by the voyagers to the Southern and Pacific ocean."—*Wilks, Hist. Sketches*, Madras [reprint, i. 276.]

" 'Then whilst they fanned the children, or **champooed** them if they were restless, they used to tell stories, some of which dealt of marvels as great as those recorded in the 1001 Nights."—*Mrs. Sherwood, Autobiog.* 410.

" "That considerable relief is obtained from **shampoing**, cannot be doubted; I have repeatedly been restored surprisingly from severe fatigue. . . ."—*Williamson, V. M.* ii. 198.

1813.—"There is sometimes a voluptuousness in the climate of India, a stillness in nature, an indescribable softness, which soothes the mind, and gives it up to the most delightful sensations: independent of the effects of opium, **champoing**, and other luxuries indulged in by oriental sensualists.'—*Forbes, Or. Mem.* i. 35; [2nd ed. i. 25.]

SHAN, n.p. The name which we have learned from the Burmese to apply to the people who call themselves the *great T'ai*, kindred to the Siamese, and occupying extensive tracts in Indo-China, intermediate between Burma, Siam, and China. They are the same people that have been known, after the Portuguese, and some of the early R. C. Missionaries, as **Laos** (q.v.); but we now give the name an extensive signification covering the whole race. The Siamese, who have been for centuries politically the most important branch of this race, call (or did call themselves—see De la Loubère, who is very accurate) *T'ai-Noe* or 'Little T'ai,' whilst they applied the term *T'ai-Yai*, or 'Great T'ai,' to their northern kindred or some part of these;* sometimes also calling the latter *T'ai-gŭt*, or the 'Ta'i left behind.' The T'ai or Shan are certainly the most numerous and widely spread race in Indo-China, and innumerable petty Shan States exist on the borders of Burma, Siam, and China, more or less dependent on, or tributary to, their powerful neighbours. They are found from the extreme north of the Irawadi Valley, in the vicinity of Assam, to the borders of Camboja; and in nearly all we find, to a degree unusual in the case of populations politically so segregated, a certain homogeneity in language, civilisation, and religion (Buddhist), which seems to point to their former union in considerable States.

One branch of the race entered and conquered Assam in the 13th century, and from the name by which they were known, *Ahom* or *Aham*, was derived, by the frequent exchange of aspirant and sibilant, the name, just used, of the province itself. The most extensive and central Shan State, which occupied a position between Ava and Yunnan, is known in the Shan traditions as Mung-*Mau*, and in Burma by the Buddhisto-classical name of *Kauśāmbi* (from a famous city of that name in ancient India) corrupted by a usual process into *Ko-Shan-pyi* and interpreted to mean 'Nine-Shan-States.' Further south were those T'ai States which have usually been called **Laos**, and which formed several considerable kingdoms, going through many vicissitudes of power. Several of their capitals were visited and their ruins described by the late Francis Garnier, and the cities of these and many smaller States of the same race, all built on the same general quadrangular plan, are spread broadcast over that part of Indo-China which extends from Siam north of Yunnan.

Mr. Cushing, in the Introduction to his *Shan Dictionary* (Rangoon, 1881), divides the Shan family by dialectic indications into the *Ahoms*, whose language is now extinct, the *Chinese Shan* (occupying the central territory of what was *Mau* or Kauśāmbi), the *Shan* (*Proper*, or Burmese Shan), *Laos* (or Siamese Shan), and Siamese.

The term **Shan** is borrowed from the Burmese, in whose peculiar orthography the name, though pronounced *Shān*, is written *rham*. We have not met with its use in English prior to the Mission of Col. Symes in 1795. It appears in the map illustrating his narrative, and once or twice in the narrative itself, and it was frequently used by his companion, F. Buchanan, whose papers were only published many years afterwards in various periodicals difficult to meet with. It was not until the Burmese war of 1824-1826, and the active investigation of our Eastern frontier which followed, that the name became popularly known in British India. The best notice of the Shans that we are acquainted with is a scarce pamphlet by Mr. Ney Elias, printed by the Foreign Dept. of Calcutta in 1876 (*Introd. Sketch of the Hist. of the Shans, &c.*). [The ethnology of the race is discussed by J. G. Scott, *Upper Burma Gazetteer*, i. pt. i. 187 *seqq.* Also see *Prince Henri d'Orleans, Du Tonkin aux Indes*, 1898; *H. S. Hallett, Among the Shans*, 1885, and *A Thousand Miles on an Elephant*, 1890.]

Though the name as we have taken it is a Burmese oral form, it seems to be essentially a genuine ethnic name for the race. It is applied in the form **Sam** by the Assamese, and the Kakhyens; the Siamese themselves have an obsolete **Siēm** (written *Sieyam*) for themselves, and **Sieng** (*Sieyang*) for the Laos. The former word is evidently the *Sien*, which the Chinese used in the compound *Sien-lo* (for Siam,—see *Marco Polo*, 2nd ed. Bk. iii. ch. 7, note 3), and from which we got, probably through a Malay

* On the probable indication of Great and Little used in this fashion, see remarks in notes on *Marco Polo*, bk. iii. ch. 9.

medium, our **Siam** (q.v.). The Burmese distinguish the Siamese Shans as *Yudia* (see **JUDEA**) Shans, a term perhaps sometimes including Siam itself. Symes gives this (through Arakanese corruption) as 'Yoodra-Shaan,' and he also (no doubt improperly) calls the Manipūr people 'Cassay Shaan' (see **CASSAY**).

1795.—"These events did not deter Shanbuan from pursuing his favourite scheme of conquest to the westward. The fertile plains and populous towns of Munnipoora and the **Cassay Shaan**, attracted his ambition."—*Symes*, p. 77.

" "Zemee (see **JANGOMAY**), Sandapoora, and many districts of the **Yoodra Shaan** to the eastward, were tributary, and governed by **Chobwas**, who annually paid homage to the Birman king."—*Ibid.* 102.

" "**Shaan**, or **Shan**, is a very comprehensive term given to different nations, some independent, others the subjects of the greater states."—*Ibid.* 274.

c. 1818.—". . . They were assisted by many of the *Zabod* (see **CHOBWA**) or petty princes of the **Sciam**, subject to the Burmese, who, wearied by the oppressions and exactions of the Burmese Mandarins and generals, had revolted, and made common cause with the enemies of their cruel masters. . . . The war which the Burmese had to support with these enemies was long and disastrous . . . instead of overcoming the **Sciam** (they) only lost day by day the territories . . . and saw their princes range themselves . . . under the protection of the King of Siam."—*Sangermano*, p. 57.

1861.—
"Fie, Fie! Captain Spry!
You are surely in joke
With your wires and your trams,
Going past all the **Shams**
With branches to *Bam-you* (see **BAMO**), and
end in **A-smoke**."
Ode on the proposed Yunnan Railway.

Bhamo and *Esmok* were names constantly recurring in the late Capt. Spry's railway projects.

SHANBAFF, SINABAFF, &c., s. Pers. *shānbāft*. A stuff often mentioned in the early narratives as an export from Bengal and other parts of India. Perhaps indeed these names indicate two different stuffs, as we do not know what they were, except that (as mentioned below) the *sinabaff* was a fine white stuff. *Sīnabāff* is not in Vuller's *Lexicon*. *Shānabāf* is, and is explained as *genus panni grossioris, sic descripta* (E. T.): "A very coarse and cheap stuff which they make for the sleeves of *kabās* (see **CABAYA**) for sale."—*Bāhār-i-'Ajam*. But this cannot have been the character of the stuffs sent by Sultan Mahommed Tughlak (as in the first quotation) to the Emperor of China. [Badger (quoted by *Birdwood*, *Report on Old Records*, 153) identifies the word with *sīna-bāfta*, 'China-woven' cloths.]

1343.—"When the aforesaid present came to the Sultan of India (from the Emp. of China) . . . in return for this present he sent another of greater value . . . 100 pieces of **shīrīnbāf**, and 500 pieces of **shānbāf**."—*Ibn Batuta*, iv. 3.

1498.—"The overseer of the Treasury came next day to the Captain-Major, and brought him 20 pieces of white stuff, very fine, with gold embroidery which they call *beyramies* (**beiramee**), and other 20 large white stuffs, very fine, which were named **sinabafos**. . . ."—*Correa*, E.T. b. *Ld. Stanley*, 197.

[1508.—See under **ALJOFAR**.]

1510.—"One of the Persians said: 'Let us go to our house, that is, to Calicut.' I answered, 'Do not go, for you will lose these fine **sinabaph**' (which were pieces of cloth we carried)."—*Varthema*, 269.

1516.—"The quintal of this sugar was worth two ducats and a half in Malabar, and a good **Sinabáffo** was worth two ducats."—*Barbosa*, 179.

[" "Also they make other stuffs which they call *Mamonas* (*Maḥmūdīs*?), others *duguazas* (*dogazīs*?), others *chautares* (see **chowtars**, under **PIECE-GOODS**), others **sinabafas**, which last are the best, and which the Moors hold in most esteem to make shirts of."—*Ibid.*, Lisbon ed. 362.]

SHASTER, s. The Law books or Sacred Writings of the Hindus. From Skt. *śāstra*, 'a rule,' a religious code, a scientific treatise.

1612.—". . . They have many books in their Latin. . . . Six of these they call **Xastra**, which are the bodies; eighteen which they call *Purāna* (**Poorana**), which are the limbs."—*Couto*, V. vi. 3.

1630.—". . . The Banians deliver that this book, by them called the **Shaster**, or the Book of their written word, consisted of these three tracts."—*Lord's Display*, ch. viii.

1651.—In *Rogerius*, the word is everywhere misprinted **Iastra**.

1717.—"The six **Sastrangól** contain all the Points and different Ceremonies in Worship. . . ."—*Phillips's Account*, 40.

1765.—". . . at the capture of *Calcutta*, A.D. 1756, I lost many curious *Gentoo* manuscripts, and among them two very correct and valuable copies of the *Gentoo* **Shastah**.'—*J. Z. Holwell*, *Interesting Hist. Events*, &c., 2d ed., 1766, i. 3.

1770.—"The **Shastah** is looked upon by some as a commentary on the *vedam*, and by others as an original work."—*Raynal* (tr. 1777), i. 50.

1776.—"The occupation of the Bramin should be to read the *Beids*, and other **Shasters**."—*Halhed, Gentoo Çode*, 39.

[**SHASTREE**, s. Hind. *śāstrī* (see **SHASTER**). A man of learning, one who teaches any branch of Hindu learning, such as law.

[1824.—"Gungadhur **Shastree**, the minister of the Baroda state, . . . was murdered by Trimbuckjee under circumstances which left no doubt that the deed was perpetrated with the knowledge of Bajerow."—*Malcolm, Central India*, 2nd ed. i. 307.]

SHAWL, s. Pers. and Hind. *shāl*, also *doshāla*, 'a pair of shawls.' The Persian word is perhaps of Indian origin, from Skt. *śavala*, 'variegated.' Sir George Birdwood tells us that he has found among the old India records "Carmania **shells**" and "Carmania **shawools**," meaning apparently *Kermān shawls*. He gives no dates unfortunately. [In a book of 1685 he finds "**Shawles** Carmania" and "Carmania Wooll"; in one of 1704, "**Chawools**" (*Report on Old Records*, 27, 40). Carmania goats are mentioned in a letter in *Forrest, Bombay Letters*, i. 140.] In Meninski (published in 1680) *shāl* is defined in a way that shows the humble sense of the word originally:

"Panni viliores qui partim albi, partim cineritii, partim nigri esse solent ex lana et pillis caprinis; hujusmodi pannum seu telam injiciunt humeris Dervisii . . . instar stolae aut pallii." To this he adds, "Datur etiam sericea ejusmodi tela, fere instar nostri multitii, sive simplicis sive duplicati." For this the 2nd edition a century later substitutes: "*Shāl-i-Hindī*" (Indian shawl). "Tela *sericea* subtilissima ex India adferri solita."

c. 1590.—"In former times **shawls** were often brought from Kashmír. People folded them in four folds, and wore them for a very long time. . . . His Majesty encourages in every possible way the (*shāl-bāfī*) manufacture of **shawls** in Kashmír. In Lahór also there are more than 1000 workshops."—*Āīn* i. 92. [Also see ed. *Jarrett*, ii. 349, 355.]

c. 1665.—"Ils mettent sur eux a toute saison, lorsqu'ils sortent, une **Chal**, qui est une maniere de toilette d'une laine très-fine qui se fait a Cachmír. Ces **Chals** ont environ deux aunes (the old French *aune*, nearly 47 inches English) de long sur une de large. On les achete vingt-cinq ou trente écus si elles sont fines. Il y en a même qui coûtent cinquante écus, mais ce sont les trés-fines."—*Thevenot*, v. 110.

c. 1666.—"Ces **chales** sont certaines pièces d'étoffe d'une aulne et demie de long, et d'une de large ou environ, qui sont brodées aux deux bouts d'une espèce de broderie, faite au métier, d'un pied ou environ de large. . . . J'en ai vu de ceux que les *Omrahs* font faire exprès, qui coutoient jusqu'à cent cinquante Roupies; des autres qui sont de cette laine du pays, je n'en ai pas vu qui passaient 50 Roupies."—*Bernier*, ii. 280-281; [ed. *Constable*, 402].

1717.—". . . Con tutto ciò preziosissime nobilissime e senza comparazione magnifiche sono le tele che si chiamano **Scial**, si nella lingua Hindustana, come ancora nella lingua Persiana. Tali **Scial** altro non sono, che alcuni manti, che si posano sulla testa, e facendo da man destra, e da man sinistra scendere le due metà, con queste si cinge. . . ."—*MS. Narrative of Padre Ip. Desideri.*

[1662.—"Another rich Skarf, which they call **schal**, made of a very fine stuff."—*J. Davies, Ambassador's Trav.*, Bk. vi. 235, *Stanf. Dict.*]

1727.—"When they go abroad they wear a **Shawl** folded up, or a piece of White Cotton Cloth lying loose on the Top of their Heads."—*A. Hamilton*, ii. 50; [**Shaul** in ed. 1744, ii. 49].

c. 1760.—"Some **Shawls** are manufactured there. . . . Those coming from the province of Cachemire on the borders of Tartary, being made of a peculiar kind of silky hair, that produces from the loom a cloth beautifully bordered at both ends, with a narrow flowered selvage, about two yards and a half long, and a yard and a half wide . . . and according to the price, which is from ten pounds and upwards to fifteen shillings, join, to exquisite fineness, a substance that renders them extremely warm, and so pliant that the fine ones are easily drawn through a common ring on the finger."—*Grose*, i. 118.

1781.—Sonnerat writes **challes**. He says: "Ces étoffes (faites avec la laine des moutons de Tibet) surpassent nos plus belles soieries en finesse."—*Voyage*, i. 52.

It seems from these extracts that the large and costly shawl, woven in figures over its whole surface, is a modern article. The old shawl, we see, was from 6 to 8 feet long, by about half that breadth; and it was most commonly white, with only a *border* of figured weaving at each end. In fact what is now called a **Rampoor Chudder** when made with figured ends is probably the best representation of the old shawl.

SHEEAH, SHIA, s. Arab. *shī'a*, *i.e.* 'sect.' A follower (more properly the followers collectively) of the Mahommedan 'sect,' or sects rather, which specially venerate 'Ali, and regard the Imāms (see **IMAUM**), his descendants, as the true successors to the Caliphate. The Persians (since the accession of the '**Sophy**' dynasty, (q.v.)) are *Shīʿas*, and a good many of the Moslems in India. The sects which have followed more or less secret doctrines, and the veneration of hereditary quasi-divine heads, such as the Karmathites and Ismaelites of Musulman history, and the modern **Bohras** (see **BORA**) and "Mulāhis," may generally be regarded as *Shīʿa*. [See the elaborate article on the sect in *Hughes, Dict. of Islām*, 572 *seqq.*]

c. 1309.—". . . dont encore il est ainsi, que tuit cil qui croient en la loy Haali dient que cil qui croient en la loy Mahommet sont mescréant; et aussi tuit cil qui croient en la loy Mahommet dient que tuit cil qui croient en la loy Haali sont mescréant."—*Joinville*, 252.

1553.—"Among the Moors have always been controversies . . . which of the four first Caliphs was the most legitimate successor to the Caliphate. The Arabians favoured Bubac, Homar, and Otthoman, the Persians (*Parseos*) favoured Alle, and held the others for usurpers, and as holding it against the testament of Mahamed . . . to the last this schism has endured between the Arabians aud the Persians. The latter took the appellation **Xiá**, as much as to say 'Union of one Body,' and the Arabs called them in reproach *Raffady* [*Rāfiḍī*, a heretic (lit. 'deserter')], as much as to say 'People astray from the Path,' whilst they call themselves **Çuny** (see **SUNNEE**), which is the contrary."—*Barros*, II. x. 6.

1620.—"The Sonnite adherents of tradition, like the Arabs, the Turks, and an infinite number of others, accept the primacy of those who actually possess it. The Persians and their adherents who are called *Shias* (**Sciai**), *i.e.* 'Sectaries,' and are not ashamed of the name, believe in the primacy of those who have only claimed it (without possessing it), and obstinately contend that it belongs to the family of Alì only."—*P. della Valle*, ii. 75; [conf. Hak. Soc. i. 152].

1626.—"He is by Religion a Mahumetan, descended from Persian Ancestors, and retaineth their opinions, which differing in many points from the Turkes, are distinguished in their Sectes by tearmes of **Seaw** and *Sunnee*."—*Purchas, Pilgrimage*, 995.

1653.—"Les Persans et *Keselbaches* (**Kuzzilbash**) se disent **Schai** . . . si les Ottomans estoient **Schais**, ou de la Secte de Haly, les Persans se feroient *Sonnis* qui est la Secte des Ottomans."—*De la Boullaye-le-Gouz*, ed. 1657, 106.

1673.—"His Substitute here is a **Chias** Moor."—*Fryer*, 29.

1798.—"In contradistinction to the *Soonis*, who in their prayers cross their hands on the lower part of the breast, the **Schiahs** drop their arms in straight lines."—*G. Forster, Travels*, ii. 129.

1805.—"The word **Sh'eeah**, or **Sheeut**, properly signifies a troop or sect . . . but has become the distinctive appellation of the followers of Aly, or all those who maintain that he was the first legitimate *Khuleefah*, or successor to Moohummad."—*Baillie, Digest of Mah. Law*, II. xii.

1869.—"La tolerance indienne est venue diminuer dans l'Inde le fanatisme Musulman. Là *Sunnites* et **Schiites** n'ont point entre eux cette animosité qui divise les Turcs et les Persans . . . ces deux sectes divisent les musulmans de l'Inde; mais comme je viens de dire, elles n'excitent généralement entre eux aucune animosité."—*Garcin de Tassy, Rel. Mus.*, p. 12.

SHEERMAUL, s. Pers.—Hind. *shīrmāl*, a cake made with flour, milk and leaven; a sort of *brioche*. [The word comes from Pers. *shīr*, 'milk,' *māl*, 'crushing.' Riddell (*Domest. Econ.* 461) gives a receipt for what he calls "*Nauna Sheer Mhal*," *nān* being Pers., 'bread.']

[1832.—"The dishes of meetah (*miṭhā*, 'sweet') are accompanied with the many varieties of bread common to Hindoostaun, without leaven, as **Sheah-maul**, *bacherkaunie* (**bakir-khani**), *chapaatie* (**chupatty**), &c.; the first two have milk and ghee mixed with the flour, and nearly resemble our pie-crust."—*Mrs. Meer Hassan Ali, Observations*, i. 101.

[**SHEIKH**, s. Ar. *shaikh*; an old man, elder, chief, head of an Arab tribe. The word should properly mean one of the descendants of tribes of genuine Arab descent, but at the present day, in India, it is often applied to converts to Islam from the lower Hindu tribes. For the use of the word in the sense of a saint, see under **PEER**.

[1598.—"Lieftenant (which the Arabians called **zequen**)."—*Linschoten*, Hak. Soc. i. 24.

[1625.—"They will not haue them iudged by any Custome, and they are content that their **Xeque** doe determine them as he list."—*Purchas, Pilgrimage*, ii. 1146.

1727.—". . . but if it was so, that he (Abraham) was their **Sheek**, as they alledge, they neither follow him in Morals or Religion."—*A. Hamilton*, ed. 1744, i. 37.

[1835.—"Some parents employ a **sheykh** or fikee to teach their boys at home."—*Lane, Mod. Egypt.*, ed. 1871, i. 77.]

SHERBET, s. Though this word is used in India by natives in its native (Arab. and Pers.) form *sharbat*,*

* In both written alike, but the final *t* in Arabic is generally silent, giving *sharba*, in Persian *sharbat*. So we get *minaret* from Pers. and Turk. *munārat*, in Ar. (and in India) *munāra* [*manār*, *manāra*].

'draught,' it is not a word now specially in Anglo-Indian use. The Arabic seems to have entered Europe by several different doors. Thus in Italian and French we have *sorbetto* and *sorbet*, which probably came direct from the Levantine or Turkish form *shurbat* or *shorbat*; in Sp. and Port. we have *xarabe*, *axarabe* (*ash-sharāb*, the standard Ar. *sharāb*, 'wine or any beverage'), and *xarope*, and from these forms probably Ital. *sciroppo*, *siroppo*, with old French *ysserop* and mod. French *sirop*; also English *syrup*, and more directly from the Spanish, *shrub*. Mod. Span. again gets, by reflection from French or Italian, *sorbete* and *sîrop* (see *Dozy*, 17, and *Marcel Devic*, s.v. *sirop*). Our *sherbet* looks as if it had been imported direct from the Levant. The form *shrāb* is applied in India to all wines and spirits and prepared drinks, *e.g.* Port-*shraub*, Sherry-*shraub*, **Lall-shraub**, Brandy-*shraub*, Beer-*shraub*.

c. 1334.—". . . They bring cups of gold, silver, and glass, filled with sugar-candy-water; *i.e.* syrup diluted with water. They call this beverage **sherbet**" (*ash-shurbat*).—*Ibn Batuta*, iii. 124.

1554.—". . . potio est gratissima praesertim ubi multa nive, quae Constantinopoli nullo tempore deficit, fuerit refrigerata, *Arab* **Sorbet** vocant, hoc est, potionem Arabicam."—*Busbeq*. Ep. i. p. 92.

1578. — "The physicians of the same country use this **xarave** (of tamarinds) in bilious and ardent fevers."—*Acosta*, 67.

c. 1580.—"Et saccharo potum jucundissimum parant quem **Sarbet** vocant." — *Prosper Alpinus*, Pt. i. p. 70.

1611.—"In Persia there is much good wine of grapes which is called **Xaràb** in the language of the country."—*Teixeira*, i. 16.

c. 1630. — "Their liquor may perhaps better delight you; 'tis faire water, sugar, rose-water, and juyce of Lemons mixt, call'd **Sherbets or Zerbets**, wholsome and potable."—*Sir T. Herbert*, ed. 1638, p. 241.

1682.—"The Moores . . . dranke a little milk and water, but not a drop of wine; they also dranke a little **sorbet**, and *jacolatt* (see **JOCOLE**)."—*Evelyn's Diary*, Jan 24.

1827.—"On one occasion, before Barak-el-Hadgi left Madras, he visited the Doctor, and partook of his **sherbet**, which he preferred to his own, perhaps because a few glasses of rum or brandy were usually added to enrich the compound."—*Sir W. Scott*, *The Surgeon's Daughter*, ch. x.

1837. — "The Egyptians have various kinds of **sherbets**. . . . The most common kind (called simply **shurbát** or **shurbát** *sook'har* . . .) is merely sugar and water . . . lemonade (*ley'moónáteh*, or **sharáb** *el-leymoón*) is another."—*Lane, Mod. Egypt.*, ed. 1837, i. 206.

1863.—"The Estate overseer usually gave a dance to the people, when the most dissolute of both sexes were sure to be present, and to indulge too freely in the **shrub** made for the occasion."—*Waddell*, 29 *Years in the W. Indies*, 17.

SHEREEF, s. Ar. *sharīf*, 'noble.' A dignitary descended from Mahommed.

1498. — "The ambassador was a white man who was **Xarife**, as much as to say a *creligo*" (*i.e. clerigo*).—*Roteiro*, 2nd ed. 30.

[1672.—"**Schierifi.**" See under **CASIS**.

[c. 1666. — "The first (embassage) was from the **Cherif** of Meca. . . ."—*Bernier*, ed. *Constable*, 133.

1701.—". . . ye **Shreif** of Judda. . . ." —*Forrest*, *Bombay Letters*, i. 232.]

SHERISTADAR, s. The head ministerial officer of a Court, whose duty it is to receive plaints, and see that they are in proper form and duly stamped, and generally to attend to routine business. Properly H.—P. from *sar-rishtā-dār* or *sarishta-dār*, 'register-keeper.' *Sar-rishtā*, an office of registry, literally means 'head of the string.' C. P. Brown interprets *Sarrishtadār* as "he who holds the end of the string (on which puppets dance)"—satirically, it may be presumed. Perhaps 'keeper of the clue,' or 'of the file' would approximately express the idea.

1786.—(With the object of establishing) "the officers of the **Canongoe's** Department upon its ancient footing, altogether independent of the Zemindars . . . and to prevent confusion in the time to come. . . . For these purposes, and to avail ourselves as much as possible of the knowledge and services of Mr. James Grant, we have determined on the institution of an office well-known in this country under the designation of Chief **Serrishtadar**, with which we have invested Mr. Grant, to act in that capacity under your Board, and also to attend as such at your deliberations, as well as at our meetings in the Revenue Department."—*Letter from G. G. in C. to Board of Revenue*, July 19 (Bengal Rev. Regulation xix.).

1878. — "Nowadays, however, the **Serishtadar's** signature is allowed to authenticate copies of documents, and the Assistant is thus spared so much drudgery."—*Life in the Mofussil*, i. 117.

[**SHEVAROY HILLS**, n.p. The name applied to a range of hills in the Salem district of Madras. The origin of the name has given rise to much difference of opinion. Mr. Lefanu (*Man. of Salem*, ii. 19 *seq.*) thinks that the original name was possibly *Sivarayan*, whence the German name *Shivarai* and the English **Shevaroys**; or that *Sivarayan* may by confusion have become *Sherarayan*, named after the Raja of *Sera;* lastly, he suggests that it comes from *sharpu* or *sharvu*, 'the slope or declivity of a hill,' and *vay*, 'a mouth, passage, way.' This he is inclined to accept, regarding *Shervarayan* or *Sharvayrayan*, as 'the cliff which dominates (*rayan*) the way (*vay*) which leads through or under the declivity (*sharvu*).' The *Madras Gloss.* gives the Tam. form of the name as *Shervarayanmalai*, from *Sheran*, 'the Chera race,' *irayan*, 'king,' and *malai*, 'mountain.'

[1823.—"Mr. Cockburn . . . had the kindness to offer me the use of a bungalow on the **Shervaraya** hills. . . ."—*Hoole, Missions in Madras*, 282.

[SHIBAR, SHIBBAR, s. A kind of coasting vessel, sometimes described as a great **pattamar**. Molesworth (*Mahr. Dict.* s.v.) gives *shibāṛ* which, in the usual dictionary way, he defines as 'a ship or large vessel of a particular description.' The *Bombay Gazetteer* (x. 171) speaks of the '*shibādi*, a large vessel, from 100 to 300 tons, generally found in the Ratnagiri sub-division ports'; and in another place (xiii. Pt. ii. 720) says that it is a large vessel chiefly used in the Malabar trade, deriving the name from Pers. *shāhī-bār*, 'royal-carrier.'

[1684.—"The Mucaddam (**MOCUDDUM**) of this **shibar** bound for Goa."—*Yule*, in *Hedges' Diary*, Hak. Soc. II. clxv.; also see clxxxiv.

[1727.—". . . the other four were **Grabs** or Gallies, and **Sheybars**, or half Gallies."—*A. Hamilton*, ed. 1744, i. 134.

[1758.—". . . then we cast off a boat called a large **seebar**, bound to Muscat. . . ."—*Ives*, 196.]

SHIGRAM, s. A Bombay and Madras name for a kind of hack palankin carriage. The camel-*shigram* is often seen on roads in N. India. The name is from Mahr. *śighr*, Skt. *śighra*, 'quick or quickly.' A similar carriage is the *Jutkah*, which takes its name from Hind. *jhaṭkā*, 'swift.'

[1830.—At Bombay, "In heavy coaches, lighter landaulets, or singular-looking **shigrampoes**, might be seen bevies of British fair . . ."—*Mrs. Elwood, Narr.* ii. 376.

[1875.—"As it is, we have to go . . . 124 miles in a dak gharri, bullock **shigram**, or mail-cart. . . ."—*Wilson, Abode of Snow* 18.]

SHIKAR, s. Hind. from Pers. *shikār*, 'la chasse'; sport (in the sense of shooting and hunting); game.

c. 1590.—"*Āīn*, 27. *Of Hunting* (orig. *Āīn-i-***Shikār**). Superficial worldly observers see in killing an animal a sort of pleasure, and in their ignorance stride about, as if senseless, on the field of their passions. But deep enquirers see in hunting a means of acquisition of knowledge. . . . This is the case with His Majesty."—*Āīn*, i. 282.

1609-10. — "**Sykary**, which signifieth, seeking, or hunting."—*W. Finch*, in *Purchas*, i. 428.

1800.—"250 or 300 horsemen . . . divided into two or three small parties, supported by our infantry, would give a proper **shekar**; and I strongly advise not to let the Mahratta boundary stop you in the pursuit of your game."—*Sir A. Wellesley* to *T. Munro*, in *Life of Munro*, iii. 117.

1847. — "Yet there is a charm in this place for the lovers of **Shikar**."—*Dry Leaves from Young Egypt*, 3.

[1859. — "Although the jungles literally swarm with tigers, a **shickar**, in the Indian sense of the term, is unknown."—*Oliphant, Narr. of Mission*, i. 25.]

1866.—"May I ask what has brought you out to India, Mr. Cholmondeley? Did you come out for **shikar**, eh?"—*Trevelyan, The Dawk Bungalow*, in *Fraser*, lxxiii. 222.

In the following the word is wrongly used in the sense of **Shikaree**.

[1900.—"That so experienced a **shikar** should have met his death emphasises the necessity of caution."—*Field*, Sept. 1.]

SHIKAREE, SHEKARRY, s. Hind. *shikārī*, a sportsman. The word is used in three ways:

a. As applied to a native expert, who either brings in game on his own account, or accompanies European sportsmen as guide and aid.

[1822.—"**Shecarries** are generally Hindoos of low cast, who gain their livelihood entirely by catching birds, hares, and all sorts of animals."—*Johnson, Sketches of Field Sports*, 25.]

1879. — "Although the province (Pegu) abounds in large game, it is very difficult to discover, because there are no regular **shikarees** in the Indian acceptation of the word. Every village has its local **shikaree**, who lives by trapping and killing game. Taking life as he does, contrary to the principles of his religion, he is looked upon as damned by his neighbours, but that does not prevent their buying from him the spoils of the chase."—*Pollok, Sport in Br. Burmah*, &c., i. 13.

b. As applied to the European sportsman himself; *e.g.* "Jones is well known as a great *Shikaree.*" There are several books of sporting adventure written *circa* 1860-75 by Mr. H. A. Leveson under the name of 'The Old **Shekarry.**'

[c. A shooting-boat used in the Cashmere lakes.

[1875.—"A **shikārī** is a sort of boat, that is in daily use with the English visitors; a light boat manned, as it commonly is, by six men, it goes at a fast pace, and, if well fitted with cushions, makes a comfortable conveyance. A *bandūqī* (see **BUNDOOK**) *shikārī* is the smallest boat of all; a shooting punt, used in going after wild fowl on the lakes."—*Drew, Jummoo*, &c., 181.]

SHIKAR-GĀH, s. Pers. A hunting ground, or enclosed preserve. The word has also a technical application to patterns which exhibit a variety of figures and groups of animals, such as are still woven in brocade at Benares, and in shawl-work in Kashmir and elsewhere (see *Marco Polo*, Bk. I. ch. 17, and notes). [The great areas of jungle maintained by the Amīrs of Sind and called *Shikārgāhs* are well known.

[1831.—"Once or twice a month when they (the Ameers) are all in good health, they pay visits to their different **shikargahs** or preserves for game."—*J. Burnes, Visit to the Court of Sinde*, 103.]

SHIKHÓ, n. and v. Burmese word. The posture of a Burmese in presence of a superior, *i.e.* kneeling with joined hands and bowed head in an attitude of worship. Some correspondence took place in 1883, in consequence of the use of this word by the then Chief Commissioner of British Burma, in an official report, to describe the attitude used by British envoys at the Court of Ava. The statement (which was grossly incorrect) led to remonstrance by Sir Arthur Phayre. The fact was that the envoy and his party sat on a carpet, but the attitude had no analogy whatever to that of *shikho*, though the endeavour of the Burmese officials was persistent to involve them in some such degrading attitude. (See **KOWTOW.**)

1855.—"Our conductors took off their shoes at the gate, and the Woondouk made an ineffectual attempt to induce the Envoy to do likewise. They also at four different places, as we advanced to the inner gate, dropt on their knees and **shikhoed** towards the palace."—*Yule, Mission to Ava*, 82.

1882.—"Another ceremony is that of **shekhoing** to the spire, the external emblem of the throne. All Burmans must do this at each of the gates, at the foot of the steps, and at intervals in between. . . ."—*The Burman, His Life and Notions*, ii. 206.

SHINBIN, SHINBEAM, &c., s. A term in the Burmese teak-trade; apparently a corruption from Burm. *shīn-byīn.* The first monosyllable (*shīn*) means 'to put together side by side,' and *byīn*, 'plank,' the compound word being used in Burmese for 'a thick plank used in constructing the side of a ship.' The *shinbin* is a thick plank, about 15″ wide by 4″ thick, and running up to 25 feet in length (see *Milburn*, i. 47). It is not sawn, but split from green trees.

1791.—"Teak Timber for sale, consisting of

Duggis (see **DUGGIE**).	Maguire planks (?)
Shinbeens.	Joists and Sheathing Boards."
Coma planks (?).	

Madras Courier, Nov. 10.

SHINKALI, SHIGALA, n.p. A name by which the City and Port of **Cranganore** (q.v.) seems to have been known in the early Middle Ages. The name was probably formed from Tiruvan-*jiculam*, mentioned by Dr. Gundert below. It is perhaps the Gingaleh of Rabbi Benjamin in our first quotation; but the data are too vague to determine this, though the position of that place seems to be in the vicinity of Malabar.

c. 1167.—"**Gingaleh** is but three days distant by land, whereas it requires a journey of fifteen days to reach it by the sea; this place contains about 1,000 Israelites."—*Benjamin of Tudela*, in *Wright's Early Travels*, p. 117.

c. 1300.—"Of the cities on the shore (of Malībār) the first is **Sindábúr** (Goa), then Faknúr (see **BACANORE**), then the country of Manjarúr (see **MANGALORE**) . . . then **Chinkalī** (or **Jinkalī**), then Kúlam (see **QUILON**)."—*Rashīduddīn*, see *J. R. As. Soc.*, N.S., iv. pp. 342, 345.

c. 1320.—"Le pays de Manîbâr, appelè pays du Poivre, comprend les villes suivantes.

* * * * * * *

"La ville de **Shinkli**, dont la majeure partie de la population est composée de Juifs.

"KAULAM est la dernière ville de la côte de Poivre." — *Shemseddin Dimishqui*, by *Mehren* (Cosmographie du Moyen Age), p. 234.

c. 1328.—". . . there is one very powerful King in the country where the pepper grows, and his kingdom is called Molebar. There is also the King of **Singuyli**. . . ."—*Fr. Jordanus*, p. 40.

1330. — "And the forest in which the pepper groweth extendeth for a good 18 days' journey, and in that forest there be two cities, the one whereof is called Flandrina (see **PANDARANI**), and the other **Cyngilin**. . . ."—*Fr. Odoric*, in *Cathay*, &c., 75-76.

c. 1330.—"Etiam Shâliyât (see **CHALIA**) et **Shinkala** urbes Malabaricae sunt, quarum alteram Judaei incolunt. . . ."—*Abulfeda*, in *Gildemeister*, 185.

c. 1349. — "And in the second India, which is called Mynibar, there is **Cynkali**, which signifieth Little India" (Little China) "for *Kali* is 'little.'"—*John Marignolli*, in *Cathay*, &c., 373.

1510.—"**Sciglà** alias et Chrongalor vocatur, ea quam Cranganorium dicimus Malabariae urbem, ut testatur idem Jacobus Indiarum episcopus ad calcem Testamenti Novi ab ipso exarati anno Graecorum 1821, Christi 1510, et in fine Epistolarum Pauli, Cod. Syr. Vat. 9 et 12."—In *Assemani*, *Diss. de Syr. Nest.*, pp. 440, 732.

1844.—"The place (Codungalur) is identified with *Tiruvan*-**jiculam** river-harbour, which Cheraman Perumal is said to have declared the best of the existing 18 harbours of Kerala. . . ."—*Dr. Gundert*, in *Madras Journal*, xiii. 120.

" "One *Kerala Ulpatti* (*i.e.* legendary history of Malabar) of the Nasrani, says that their forefathers . . . built Codangalur, as may be learned from the granite inscription at the northern entrance of the *Tiruvan*-**jiculam** temple. . . ."—*Ibid.* 122.

SHINTOO, SINTOO, s. Japanese *Shintau*, 'the Way of the Gods.' The primitive relation of Japan. It is described by Faria y Sousa and other old writers, but the name does not apparently occur in those older accounts, unless it be in the *Seuto* of Couto. According to Kaempfer the philosophic or Confucian sect is called in Japan *Siuto*. But that hardly seems to fit what is said by Couto, and his *Seuto* seems more likely to be a mistake for *Sento*. [See Lowell's articles on *Esoteric Shintoo*, in *Proc. As. Soc. Japan*, 1893.]

1612.—"But above all these idols they adore one **Seutó**, of which they say that it is the substance and principle of All, and that its abode is in the Heavens."—*Couto*, V. viii. 12.

1727. — "Le **Sinto** qu'on appelle aussi Sinsju et Kamimitsi, est le Culte des Idoles, établi anciennement dans le pays. Sin et Kami sont les noms des Idoles qui font l'object de ce Culte. Siu (*sic*) signifie la Foi, ou la Religion. Sinsja et au pluriel Sinsju, ce sont les personnes qui professent cette Religion."—*Kaempfer, Hist. de Japon*, i. 176; [E.T. 204].

1770. — "Far from encouraging that gloomy fanaticism and fear of the gods, which is inspired by almost all other religions, the **Xinto** sect had applied itself to prevent, or at least to moderate that disorder of the imagination."—*Raynal* (E.T. 1777), i. 137.

1878. — "The indigenous religion of the Japanese people, called in later times by the name of **Shintau** or Way of the Gods, in order to distinguish it from the way of the Chinese moral philosophers, and the way of Buddha, had, at the time when Confucianism and Buddhism were introduced, passed through the earliest stages of development."—*Westminster Rev.*, N.S., No. cvii. 29.

[**SHIRAZ**, n.p. The wine of Shiraz was much imported and used by Europeans in India in the 17th century, and even later.

[1627.—"**Sheraz** then probably derives it self either from *sherab* which in the *Persian* Tongue signifies a Grape here abounding . . . or else from *sheer* which in the Persian signifies Milk."—*Sir T. Herbert*, ed. 1677, p. 127.

[1685.—". . . three Chests of **Sirash** wine. . . ."—*Pringle, Diary Ft. St. Geo.*, 1st ser. iv. 109, and see ii. 148.

[1690.—"Each Day there is prepar'd (at Surrat) a Publick Table for the Use of the President and the rest of the Factory. . . . The Table is spread with the choicest Meat Surrat affords . . . and equal plenty of generous **Sherash** and **Arak Punch**. . . ." —*Ovington*, 394.

[1727.—"**Shyrash** is a large City on the Road, about 550 Miles from *Gombroon*."—*A. Hamilton*, ed. 1744, i. 99.

[1813.—"I have never tasted this (pomegranate wine), nor any other Persian wine, except that of **Schiraz**, which, although much extolled by poets, I think inferior to many wines in Europe." — *Forbes, Or. Mem.* 2nd ed. i. 468.]

SHIREENBAF, s. Pers. *Shīrīnbāf*, 'sweet-woof.' A kind of fine cotton stuff, but we cannot say more precisely what.

c. 1343.—". . . one hundred pieces o **shīrīnbāf**. . . ."—*Ibn Batuta*, iv. 3.

[1609.—"**Serribaff**, a fine light stuff or cotton whereof the Moors make their **cabayes** or clothing."—*Danvers, Letters*, i. 29.]

1673.—". . . **siring** chintz, Broad Baftas. . . ."—*Fryer*, 88.

SHISHAM. See under **SISSOO.**

SHISHMUHULL, s. Pers. *shīsha-mahal*, lit. 'glass apartment' or palace. This is or was a common appendage of native palaces, viz. a hall or suite of rooms lined with mirror and other glittering surfaces, usually of a gimcrack aspect. There is a place of exactly the same description, now gone to hideous decay, in the absurd Villa Palagonia at Bagheria near Palermo.

1835.—"The **Shīsha-mahal**, or house of glass, is both curious and elegant, although the material is principally pounded talc and looking-glass. It consists of two rooms, of which the walls in the interior are divided into a thousand different panels, each of which is filled up with raised flowers in silver, gold, and colours, on a ground-work of tiny convex mirrors."—*Wanderings of a Pilgrim*, i. 365.

SHOE OF GOLD (or of Silver). The name for certain ingots of precious metal, somewhat in the form of a Chinese shoe, but more like a boat, which were formerly current in the trade of the Far East. Indeed of silver they are still current in China, for Giles says: "The common name among foreigners for the Chinese silver ingot, which bears some resemblance to a native shoe. May be of any weight from 1 oz. and even less, to 50 and sometimes 100 oz., and is always stamped by the assayer and banker, in evidence of purity" (*Gloss. of Reference*, 128). [In Hissar the Chinese silver is called *sillī* from the slabs (*sil*) in which it is sold (*Maclagan, Mon. on Gold and Silver Work in Punjab*, p. 5).] The same form of ingot was probably the *bālish* (or *yāstok*) of the Middle Ages, respecting which see *Cathay*, &c., 115, 481, &c. Both of these latter words mean also 'a cushion,' which is perhaps as good a comparison as either 'shoe' or 'boat.' The word now used in C. Asia is *yambū*. There are cuts of the gold and silver ingots in Tavernier, whose words suggest what is probably the true origin of the popular English name, viz. a corruption of the Dutch *Goldschuyt*.

1566.—". . . valuable goods exported from this country (China) . . . are first, a quantity of gold, which is carried to India, in **loaves** in the shape of **boats**. . . ."—*C. Federici*, in *Ramusio*, iii. 391*b*.

1611.—"Then, I tell you, from China I could load ships with **cakes of gold** fashioned like **boats**, containing, each of them, roundly speaking, 2 marks weight, and so each cake will be worth 280 pardaos."—*Couto, Dialogo do Soldado Pratico*, p. 155.

1676.—"The Pieces of Gold mark'd Fig. 1, and 2, are by the Hollanders called **Goltschut**, that is to say, a Boat of Gold, because they are in the form of a Boat. Other Nations call them Loaves of Gold. . . . The Great Pieces come to 12 hundred Gilders of *Holland* Money, and thirteen hundred and fifty Livres of our Money."—*Tavernier*, E.T. ii. 8.

1702.—"Sent the Moolah to be delivered the Nabob, Dewan, and Buxie 48 China Oranges . . . but the Dewan bid the Moolah write the Governor for a hundred more that he might send them to Court; which is understood to be One Hundred **shoes of gold**, or so many thousand pagodas or rupees."—In *Wheeler*, i. 397.

1704.—"Price Currant, July, 1704, (at Malacca) . . . **Gold**, *China*, in **Shoos** 94 Touch."—*Lockyer*, 70.

1862.—"A silver ingot '*Yambu*' weighs about 2 (Indian) *seers* . . . = 4 lbs., and is worth 165 Co.'s rupees. *Koomoosh*, also called '*Yambucha*,' or small silver ingot, is worth 33 Rs. . . . 5 *yambuchas*, being equal to 1 *yambu*. There are two descriptions of '*yambucha*'; one is a square piece of silver, having a Chinese stamp on it; the other . . . in the form of a boat, has no stamp. The *Yambu* is *in the form of a boat*, and has a Chinese stamp on it."—*Punjab Trade Report*, App. ccxxvi.-xxviii. 1.

1875.—"The *yâmbû* or *kûrs* is a silver ingot something the shape of a deep boat with projecting bow and stern. The upper surface is lightly hollowed, and stamped with a Chinese inscription. It is said to be pure silver, and to weigh 50 (Cashghar) *ser* = 30,000 grains English."—Report of *Forsyth's Mission to Kashghar*, 494.

[1876.—". . . he received his pay in Chinese *yambs* (gold coins), at the rate of 128 rubles each, while the real commercial value was only 115 rubles."—*Schuyler, Turkistan*, ii. 322.

[1901.—A piece of Chinese **shoe money**, value 10 taels, was exhibited before the Numismatic Society.—*Athenaeum*, Jan. 26, p. 118. Perhaps the largest specimen known of Chinese "boat-money" was exhibited. It weighed 89¼ ounces troy, and represented 50 taels, or £8, 8*s*. 0*d*. English.—*Ibid*. Jan. 25, 1902, p. 120].

SHOE-FLOWER, s. A name given in Madras Presidency to the flower of the *Hibiscus Rosa-sinensis*, L. It is a literal translation of the Tam. *shapāttu-pu*, Singh. *sappattumala*, a name given because the flowers are used at Madras to blacken shoes. The Malay name *Kempang sapatu* means the same. Voigt gives **shoe-flower** as the English name, and adds: "Petals astringent, used by the Chinese to blacken their shoes (?) and eyebrows" (*Hortus Suburbanus Calcuttensis*, 116-7); see also *Drury*, s.v. The notion of the Chinese blackening their shoes is surely an error, but perhaps they use it to blacken leather for European use.

[1773.—"The flower (*Trepalta*, or *Morroock*) (which commonly by us is called **Shoe-flower**, because used to black our shoes) is very large, of a deep but beautiful crimson colour."—*Ives*, 475.]

1791.—"La nuit suivante . . . je joignis aux pavots . . . une fleur de **foule sapatte**, qui sert aux cordonniers à teindre leurs cuirs en noir."—*B. de St. Pierre, Chaumière Indienne.* This *foule-sapatte* is apparently some quasi Hindustani form of the name (*phul-sabāt ?*) used by the Portuguese.

SHOE-GOOSE, s. This ludicrous corruption of the Pers. *siyāh-gosh*, lit. 'black-ear,' *i.e.* lynx (*Felis Caracal*) occurs in the passage below from A. Hamilton. [The corruption of the same word by the *Times*, below, is equally amusing.]

[c. 1330.—". . . ounces, and another kind something like a greyhound, having only the ears black, and the whole body perfectly white, which among these people is called **Siagois**."—*Friar Jordanus*, 18.]

1727.—"Antelopes, Hares and Foxes, are their wild game, which they hunt with Dogs, Leopards, and a small fierce creature called by them a **Shoe-goose**."—*A. Hamilton*, i. 124; [ed. 1744, i. 125].

1802.—". . . between the cat and the lion, are the . . . **syagush**, the lynx, the tiger-cat. . . ."—*Ritson, Essay on Abstinence from Animal Food*, 12.

1813.—"The Moguls train another beast for antelope-hunting called the **Syah-gush**, or black-ears, which appears to be the same as the caracal, or Russian lynx."—*Forbes, Or. Mem.* i. 277; [2nd ed. i. 175 and 169].

[1886.—"In 1760 a Moor named Abdallah arrived in India with a '**Shah Goest**' (so spelt, evidently a **Shawl Goat**) as a present for Mr. Secretary Pitt."—*Account of I. O. Records*, in *Times*, Aug. 3.]

SHOKE, s. A hobby, a favourite pursuit or whim. Ar.—*shauḳ*.

1796.—"This increased my **shouq** . . . for soldiering, and I made it my study to become a proficient in all the Hindostanee modes of warfare."—*Mily. Mem. of Lt.-Col. J. Skinner*, i. 109.

[1866.—"One Hakim has a **shoukh** for turning everything *ooltapoolta*."—*Confessions of an Orderly*, 94.]

SHOLA, s. In S. India, a wooded ravine; a thicket. Tam. *sholāi*.

1862.—"At daylight . . . we left the Sisipara bungalow, and rode for several miles through a valley interspersed with **sholas** of rhododendron trees."—*Markham, Peru and India*, 356.

1876.—"Here and there in the hollows were little jungles; **sholas**, as they are called."—*Sir M. E. Grant-Duff, Notes of Indian Journey*, 202.

SHOOCKA, s. Ar.—H. *shuḳḳa* (properly 'an oblong strip'), a letter from a king to a subject.

1787.—"I have received several melancholy **Shukhas** from the King (of Dehli) calling on me in the most pressing terms for assistance and support."—*Letter of Lord Cornwallis*, in *Corresp.* i. 307.

SHOOLDARRY, s. A small tent with steep sloping roof, two poles and a ridge-piece, and with very low side walls. The word is in familiar use, and is habitually pronounced as we have indicated. But the first dictionary in which we have found it is that of Platts. This author spells the word *chholdārī*, identifying the first syllable with *jhol*, signifying 'puckering or bagging.' In this light, however, it seems possible that it is from *jhūl* in the sense of a bag or wallet, viz. a tent that is crammed into a bag when carried. [The word is in Fallon, with the rather doubtful suggestion that it is a corruption of the English '*soldier's*' tent. See **PAWL**.]

1808.—"I have now a **shoaldarree** for myself, and a long *paul* (see **PAWL**) for my people."—*Elphinstone*, in *Life*, i. 183.

[1869.—". . . the men in their **suldaris**, or small single-roofed tents, had a bad time of it. . . ."—*Ball, Jungle Life*, 156.]

SHRAUB, SHROBB, s. Ar. *sharāb*; Hind. *sharāb*, *shrāb*, 'wine.' See under **SHERBET**.

SHROFF, s. A money-changer, a banker. Ar. *ṣarrāf*, *ṣairafi*, *ṣairaf*. The word is used by Europeans in China as well as in India, and is there applied to the experts who are employed by banks and mercantile firms to check the quality of the dollars that pass into the houses (see *Giles* under next word). Also **shroffage**, for money-dealer's commission. From the same root comes the Heb. *sōrēf*, 'a goldsmith.' Compare the figure in *Malachi*, iii. 3: "He shall sit as a refiner and purifier of silver;

and he shall purify the sons of Levi." Only in Hebrew the goldsmith tests metal, while the *ṣairaf* tests *coins*. The Arab poet says of his mare: "Her forefeet scatter the gravel every midday, as the dirhams are scattered at their testing by the *ṣairaf*" (W. R. S.)

1554.—"*Salaries of the officers of the Custom Houses, and other charges for these which the Treasurers have to pay.* . . . Also to the **Xarrafo**, whose charge it is to see to the money, two *pardaos* a month, which make for a year seven thousand and two hundred *reis*."—*Botelho, Tombo*, in *Subsidios*, 238.

1560.—"There are in the city many and very wealthy **çarafos** who change money."—*Tenreiro*, ch. i.

1584.—"5 **tangas** make a *seraphin* (see **XERAFINE**) of gold; but if one would change them into *basaruchies* (see **BUDGROOK**) he may have 5 tangas and 16 *basaruchies*, which ouerplus they call **cerafagio**. . . ."—*Barret*, in *Hakl.* ii. 410.

1585.—"This present year, because only two ships came to Goa, (the *reals*) have sold at 12 per cent. of **Xarafaggio** (shroffage), as this commission is called, from the word **Xaraffo**, which is the title of the banker."—*Sassetti*, in *De Gubernatis, Storia*, p. 203.

1598.—"There is in every place of the street exchangers of money, by them called **Xaraffos**, which are all christian Jewes."—*Linschoten*, 66; [Hak. Soc. i. 231, and see 244.]

c. 1610.—"Dans ce Marché . . . aussi sont les changeurs qu'ils nomment **Cherafes**, dont il y en a en plusieurs autres endroits; leurs boutiques sont aux bouts des ruës et carrefours, toutes couuertes de monnoye, dont ils payent tribut au Roy."—*Pyrard de Laval*, ii. 39; [Hak. Soc. ii. 67].

[1614.—". . . having been borne in hand by our **Sarafes** to pay money there."—*Foster, Letters*, iii. 282. The "**Sheriff** of Bantam" (*ibid.* iv. 7) may perhaps be a **shroff**, but compare **Shereef**.]

1673.—"It could not be improved till the Governor had released the **Shroffs** or Bankers."—*Fryer*, 413.

1697-8.—"In addition to the cash and property which they had got by plunder, the enemy fixed two *lacs* of rupees as the price of the ransom of the prisoners. . . . To make up the balance, the **Sarráfs** and merchants of Nandurbár were importuned to raise a sum, small or great, by way of loan. But they would not consent."—*Kháfi Khán*, in *Elliot*, vii. 362.

1750.—". . . the Irruption of the *Morattoes* into *Carnatica*, was another event that brought several eminent **Shroffs** and wealthy Merchants into our Town; insomuch, that I may say, there was hardly a **Shroff** of any Note, in the *Mogul* empire but had a House in it; in a word, *Madrass* was become the Admiration of all the Country People, and the Envy of all our *European* Neighbours."—*Letter to a Proprietor of the E. I. Co.* 53-54.

1809.—"I had the satisfaction of hearing the Court order them (*i.e.* Gen. Martin's executors) to pay two lacs and a half to the plaintiff, a **shroff** of Lucknow."—*Ld. Valentia*, i. 243.

[1891.—"The banker in Persia is looked on simply as a small tradesman—in fact the business of the **Serof** is despised."—*Wills, in the Land of the Lion and the Sun*, 192].

SHROFF, TO, v. This verb is applied properly to the sorting of different rupees or other coins, so as to discard refuse, and to fix the various amounts of discount or *agio* upon the rest, establishing the value in standard coin. Hence figuratively 'to sift,' choosing the good (men, horses, facts, or what not) and rejecting the inferior.

[1554.—(See under **BATTA, b.**)]

1878.—"**Shroffing** schools are common in Canton, where teachers of the art keep bad dollars for the purpose of exercising their pupils; and several works on the subject have been published there, with numerous illustrations of dollars and other foreign coins, the methods of scooping out silver and filling up with copper or lead, comparisons between genuine and counterfeit dollars, the difference between native and foreign milling, etc., etc."—*Giles, Glossary of Reference*, 129.

1882.—(The **Compradore**) "derived a profit from the process of **shroffing** which (the money received) underwent before being deposited in the Treasury."—*The Fankwae at Canton*, 55.

SHRUB, s. See under **SHERBET**.

SHULWAURS, s. Trousers, or drawers rather, of the Oriental kind, the same as **pyjammas, long-drawers**, or **mogul-breeches** (qq.v). The Persian is *shalwār*, which according to Prof. Max Müller is more correctly *shulvār*, from *shul*, 'the thigh,' related to Latin *crus, cruris*, and to Skt. *kshura* or *khura*, 'hoof' (see *Pusey* on *Daniel*, 570). Be this as it may, the Ar. form is *sirwāl* (vulg. *sharwāl*), pl. *sarāwīl*, [which Burton (*Arab. Nights*, i. 205) translates 'bag-trousers' and 'petticoat-trousers,' "the latter being the divided skirt of the future."] This appears in the ordinary editions of the Book of Daniel in Greek, as *σαράβαρα*, and also in the Vulgate, as follows: "Et capillus capitis eorum non esset adustus, et **sarabala** eorum non fuissent immutata, et odor ignis non transisset per eos" (iii. 27). The original word is *sarbālīn*, pl. of *sarbāla*. Luther, however, renders this *Mantel;* as the A.V. also does by *coats;* [the R.V. *hosen*]. On this Prof. Robertson-Smith writes:

"It is not certain but that Luther and the A.V. are right. The word *sarbālīn* means 'cloak' in the Gemara; and in Arabic *sirbāl* is 'a garment, a coat of mail.' Perhaps quite an equal weight of scholarship would now lean (though with hesitation) towards the cloak or coat, and against the breeches theory.

"The Arabic word occurs in the Traditions of the Prophet (*Bokhāri*, vii. 36).

"Of course it is certain that σαράβαρα comes from the Persian, but not through Arabic. The Bedouins did not wear trowsers in the time of Ammianus, and don't do so now.

"The ordinary so-called LXX. editions of Daniel contain what is really the post-Christian version of Theodotion. The true LXX. text has ὑποδήματα.

"It may be added that Jerome says that both Aquila and Symmachus wrote *saraballa*." [The *Encycl. Biblica* also prefers the rendering of the A.V. (i. 607), and see iii. 2934.]

The word is widely spread as well as old; it is found among the Tartars of W. Asia as *jālbār*, among the Siberians and Bashkirds as *sālbār*, among the Kalmaks as *shālbūr*, whilst it reached Russia as *sharawari*, Spain as *zaraguelles*, and Portugal as *zarelos*. A great many Low Latin variations of the word will be found in Ducange, *serabula*, *serabulla*, *sarabella*, *sarabola*, *sarabura*, and more! [And Crawfurd (*Desc. Dict.* 124) writes of Malay dress: "Trowsers are occasionally used under the *sarung* by the richer classes, and this portion of dress, like the imitation of the turban, seems to have been borrowed from the Arabs, as is implied by its Arabic name, *sarual*, corrupted *saluwar*."]

In the second quotation from Isidore of Seville below it will be seen that the word had in some cases been interpreted as 'turbans.'

A.D. (?).—"Καὶ ἐθεώρουν τοὺς ἄνδρας ὅτι οὐκ ἐκυρίευσε τὸ πῦρ τοῦ σώματος αὐτῶν καὶ ἡ θρὶξ τῆς κεφαλῆς αὐτῶν οὐκ ἐφλογίσθη καὶ τα σαράβαρα αὐτῶν οὐκ ἠλλοιώθη, καὶ ὀσμὴ πυρὸς οὐκ ἦν ἐν αὐτοῖς."—Gr. Tr. of *Dan.* iii. 27.

c. A.D. 200.—"Ἐν δὲ τοῖς Σκύθαις Ἀντιφάνης ἔφη Σαράβαρα καὶ χιτῶνας πάντας ἐνδεδυκότας."—*Julius Pollux, Onomast.* vii. 13, sec. 59.

c. A.D. 500.—"Σαράβαρα, τὰ περὶ τὰς κνημῖδας (sic) ἐνδύματα."—*Hesychius*, s.v.

c. 636.—"**Sarabara** sunt fluxa ac sinuosa vestimenta de quibus legitur in Daniele. . . . Et Publius: Vt quid ergo in ventre tuo Parthi **Sarabara** suspenderunt? Apud quosdam autem **Sarabarae** quaedã capitum tegmina nuncupantur qualia videmus in capite Magorum picta."—*Isidorus Hispalensis, Orig. et Etym.*, lib. xix., ed. 1601, pp. 263-4.

c. 1000?—"Σαράβαρα,—ἐσθὴς Περσική ἔνιοι δὲ λέγουσι βρακία."—*Suidas*, s.v.

which may be roughly rendered:

"A garb outlandish to the Greeks,
Which some call **Shalwārs**, some call
Breeks!"

c. 900.—"The deceased was unchanged, except in colour. They dressed him then with **sarāwīl**, overhose, boots, a *ḳurṭak* and *khaftān* of gold-cloth, with golden buttons, and put on him a golden cap garnished with sable."—*Ibn Foszlān*, in *Fraehn*, 15.

c. 1300.—"Disconsecratur altare eorum, et oportet reconciliari per episcopum . . . si intraret ad ipsum aliquis qui non esset Nestorius; si intraret eciam ad ipsum quicumque sine **sorrabulis** vel capite cooperto."—*Ricoldo of Monte Croce*, in *Peregrinatores Quatuor*, 122.

1330.—"Haec autem mulieres vadunt discalceatae portantes **sarabulas** usque ad terram."—*Friar Odoric*, in *Cathay*, &c., App. iv.

c. 1495.—"The first who wore **sarāwīl** was Solomon. But in another tradition it is alleged that Abraham was the first."—The '*Beginnings*,' by *Soyuti*, quoted by *Fraehn*, 113.

1567.—"Portauano braghesse quasi alla turchesca, et anche **saluarī**."—*C. Federici*, in *Ramusio*, iii. f. 389.

1824.—". . . tell me how much he will be contented with? Can I offer him five *Tomauns*, and a pair of crimson **Shulwaurs**?"—*Hajji Baba*, ed. 1835, p. 179.

1881.—"I used to wear a red shirt and velveteen **sharovary**, and lie on the sofa like a gentleman, and drink like a Swede."—*Ten Years of Penal Servitude in Siberia*, by *Fedor Dostoyeffski*, E.T. by Maria v. Thilo, 191.

SIAM, n.p. This name of the Indo-Chinese Kingdom appears to come to us through the Malays, who call it *Siyăm*. From them we presume the Portuguese took their Reyno de *Sião* as Barros and Couto write it, though we have in Correa *Siam* precisely as we write it. Camões also writes *Syão* for the kingdom; and the statement of De la Loubère quoted below that the Portuguese used Siam as a national, not a geographical, expression cannot be accepted in its generality, accurate as that French writer usually is. It is true that both Barros and F. M. Pinto use *os Siames* for the nation, and the latter also uses the adjective form *o reyno Siame*. But he also constantly says *rey de Sião*. The origin of the name would seem to be a term **Sien**, or *Siam*, identical with **Shan** (q.v.). "The kingdom of Siam is known to the Chinese by the name *Sien-lo*. . . . The supplement to Matwanlin's *Encyclopædia* describes *Sien-lo* as on the seaboard, to the extreme south of Chen-ching (or Cochin China). 'It originally consisted of two kingdoms, **Sien** and *Lo-hoh*. The Sien people are the remains of a tribe which in the year (A.D. 1341) began to come down upon the Lo-hoh and united with the latter into one nation.'" See *Marco Polo*, 2nd ed., Bk. iii. ch. 7, note 3. The considerations there adduced indicate that the *Lo* who occupied the coast of the Gulf before the descent of the *Sien*, belonged to the Laotian Shans, *Thainyai*, or Great T'ai, whilst the *Sien* or Siamese Proper were the *T'ai Noi*, or Little T'ai. (See also **SARNAU**.) ["The name *Siam* . . . whether it is 'a barbarous Anglicism derived from the Portuguese or Italian word *Sciam*,' or is derived from the Malay *Sayam*, which means 'brown.'"—*J. G. Scott, Upper Burma Gazetteer*, i. pt. i. 205.]

1516.—"Proceeding further, quitting the kingdom of Peeguu, along the coast over against Malaca there is a very great kingdom of pagans which they call Danseam (of **Anseam**); the king of which is a pagan also, and a very great lord."—*Barbosa* (Lisbon, Acad.), 369. It is difficult to interpret this *An*seam, which we find also in C. Federici below in the form **Asion**. But the *An* is probably a Malay prefix of some kind. [Also see **ansyane** in quotation from the same writer under **MALACCA**.]

c. 1522.—"The king (of Zzuba) answered him that he was welcome, but that the custom was that all ships which arrived at his country or port paid tribute, and it was only 4 days since that a ship called the Junk of **Ciama**, laden with gold and slaves, had paid him his tribute, and to verify what he said, he showed them a merchant of the said **Ciama**, who had remained there to trade with the gold and slaves."—*Pigafetta*, Hak. Soc. 85.

" "All these cities are constructed like ours, and are subject to the king of **Siam**, who is named Siri Zacebedera, and who inhabits Iudia (see **JUDEA**)."—*Ibid.* 156.

1525.—"In this same Port of Pam (Pahang), which is in the kingdom of **Syam**, there was another junk of Malaqua, the captain whereof was Alvaro da Costaa, and it had aboard 15 Portuguese, at the same time that in Joatane (Patane) they seized the ship of Andre de Bryto, and the junk of Gaspar Soarez, and as soon as this news was known they laid hands on the junk and the crew and the cargo; it is presumed that the people were killed, but it is not known for certain."—*Lembrança das Cousas da India*, 6.

1572.—

"Vês Pam, Patâne, reinos e a longura
De **Syão**, que estes e outros mais sujeita;
Olho o rio Menão que se derrama
Do grande lago, que Chiamay se chiama."
Camões, x. 25.

By Burton:

"See Pam, Patane and in length obscure,
Siam that ruleth all with lordly sway;
behold Menam, who rolls his lordly tide
from source Chiámái called, lake long and wide."

c. 1567.—"Va etiandio ogn' anno per l'istesso Capitano (di Malacca) vn nauilio in **Asion**, a caricare di *Verzino*" (Brazilwood).—*Ces. Federici*, in *Ramusio*, iii. 396.

" "Fu già **Sion** vna grandissima Città e sedia d'Imperio, ma l'anno MDLXVII fu pressa dal Re del Pegu, qual caminando per terra quattro mesi di viaggio, con vn esercito d'vn million, e quattro cento mila uomini da guerra, la venne ad assediare . . . e lo so io percioche mi ritrouai in Pegù sei mesi dopo la sua partita."—*Ibid.*

1598.—". . . The King of **Sian** at this time is become tributarie to the king of Pegu. The cause of this most bloodie battaile was, that the king of **Sian** had a white Elephant."—*Linschoten*, p. 30; [Hak. Soc. i. 102. In ii. 1 **Sion**].

[1611.—"We have news that the Hollanders were in **Shian**."—*Danvers, Letters*, i. 149.]

1688.—"The Name of **Siam** is unknown to the *Siamese*. 'Tis one of those words which the *Portugues* of the *Indies* do use, and of which it is very difficult to discover the Original. They use it as the Name of the Nation and not of the Kingdom: And the Names of *Pegu*, *Lao*, *Mogul*, and most of the Names which we give to the Indian Kingdoms, are likewise National Names."—*De la Loubère*, E.T. p. 6.

SICCA, s. As will be seen by reference to the article **RUPEE**, up to 1835 a variety of rupees had been coined in the Company's territories. The term *sicca* (*sikkā*, from Ar. *sikka*, 'a coining die,'—and 'coined money,'—whence Pers. *sikka zadan*, 'to coin') had been applied to newly coined rupees, which were at a **batta** or premium over those worn, or assumed to be worn, by use. In 1793 the Government of Bengal, with a view to terminating, as far as that Presidency was concerned, the confusion and abuses engendered by this system, ordered that all rupees coined for the future should bear the impress of the 19th year of Shāh 'Alam (the "Great Mogul" then reigning), and this rupee, "19 *San* **Sikkah**," 'struck in the 19th year,' was to be the legal tender in Bengal, Bahar, and Orissa. This rupee, which is the Sicca of more recent monetary history, weighed 192 grs. troy, and then contained 176·13 grs. of pure silver. The "Company's Rupee," which introduced uniformity of coinage over British India in 1835, contained only 165 grs. silver. Hence the *Sicca* bore to the Company's Rupee (which was based on the old Farrukhābād rupee) the proportion of 16 : 15 nearly. The *Sicca* was allowed by Act VII. of 1833 to survive as an exceptional coin in Bengal, but was abolished as such in 1836. It continued, however, a ghostly existence for many years longer in the form of certain Government Book-debts in that currency. (See also **CHICK.**)

1537.—". . . Sua senhoria avia d'aver por bem que as **siquas** das moedas corressem em seu nome per todo o Reino do Guzerate, asy em Dio como nos otros luguares que forem del Rey de Portuguall."—*Treaty of Nuno da Cunha with Nizamamede Zamom* (*Mahommed Zamam*) *concerning Cambaya*, in *Botelho, Tombo*, 225.

1537.—". . . e quoanto á moeda ser chapada de sua *sita* (read **sica**) pois já lhe concedia."—*Ibid.* 226.

[1615.—". . . **cecaus** of Amadavrs which goeth for eighty-six *pisas* (see **PICE**). . . ."—*Foster, Letters*, iii. 87.]

1683.—"Having received 25,000 Rupees **Siccas** for Rajamaul."—*Hedges, Diary*, April 4; [Hak. Soc. i. 75].

1705.—"Les roupies **Sicca** valent à Bengale 39 sols."—*Luillier*, 255.

1779.—"In the 2nd Term, 1779, on Saturday, March 6th: Judgment was pronounced for the plaintiff. Damages fifty thousand **sicca rupees**.

" ". . . 50,000 **Sicca Rupees** are equal to five thousand one hundred and nine pounds, two shillings and elevenpence sterling, reckoning according to the weight and fineness of the silver."—*Notes of Mr. Justice Hyde* on the case *Grand v. Francis*, in *Echoes of Old Calcutta*, 243. [To this Mr. Busteed adds: "Nor does there seem to be any foundation for the other time-honoured story (also repeated by Kaye) in connection with this judgment, viz., the alleged interruption of the Chief Justice, while he was delivering judgment, by Mr. Justice Hyde, with the eager suggestion or reminder of '**Siccas, Siccas**, Brother Impey,' with the view of making the damages as high at the awarded figure as possible. Mr. Merivale says that he could find no confirmation of the old joke. . . . The story seems to have been first promulgated in a book of 'Personal Recollections' by John Nicholls, M.P., published in 1822."—*Ibid.* 3rd ed. 229].

1833.— * * *

"III.—The weight and standard of the Calcutta **sicca** rupee and its sub-divisions, and of the Furruckabad rupee, shall be as follows:—

	Weight. Grains.	*Fine.* Grains.	*Alloy.* Grains.
Calcutta sicca rupee	192	176	16

* * * * *

"IV.—The use of the **sicca** weight of 179·666 grains, hitherto employed for the receipt of bullion at the Mint, being in fact the weight of the Moorshedabad rupee of the old standard . . . shall be discontinued, and in its place the following unit to be called the **Tola** (q.v.) shall be introduced."—*India Regulation VII.* of 1833.

[**SICKMAN**, s. adj. The English *sick man* has been adopted into Hind. sepoy patois as meaning 'one who has to go to hospital,' and generally *sikmān ho jānā* means 'to be disabled.'

[1665.—"That **sickman** Chaseman."—In *Yule, Hedges' Diary*, Hak. Soc. II. cclxxx.

[1843.—". . . my hired cart was broken—(or, in the more poetical garb of the sepahee, '**seek mān** *hogya*,' *i.e.* become a sick man)."—*Davidson, Travels*, i. 251.]

SICLEEGUR, s. Hind. *saiḳalgar*, from Ar. *saiḳal*, 'polish.' A furbisher of arms, a sword-armourer, a sword- or knife-grinder. [This, in Madras, is turned into **Chickledar**, Tel. *chikilidarudu.*]

[1826.—"My father was a **shiekul-ghur**, or sword-grinder."—*Pandurang Hari*, ed. 1873, i. 216.]

SIKH, SEIKH, n.p. Panjābi-Hind. *Sikh*, 'a disciple,' from Skt. *Śishya*; the distinctive name of the disciples of Nānak Shāh who in the 16th century established that sect, which eventually rose to warlike predominance in the Punjab, and from which sprang Ranjīt Singh, the founder of the brief Kingdom of Lahore.

c. 1650-60.—"The Nanac-Panthians, who are known as composing the nation of the **Sikhs**, have neither idols, nor temples of idols. . . ." (Much follows.)—*Dabistān*, ii. 246.

1708-9.—"There is a sect of infidels called *Gurū* (see **GOOROO**), more commonly known as **Sikhs**. Their chief, who dresses as a fakir, has a fixed residence at Lāhore. . . . This sect consists principally of *Jāts* and *Khatrīs* of the Panjāb and of other tribes of infidels. When Aurangzeb got knowledge of these matters, he ordered these deputy *Gurūs* to be removed and the temples to be pulled down."—*Khāfi Khān*, in *Elliot*, vii. 413.

1756.—"April of 1716, when the Emperor took the field and marched towards Lahore, against the **Sykes**, a nation of Indians lately reared to power, and bearing mortal enmity to the Mahomedans."—*Orme*, ii. 22. He also writes **Sikes**.

1781.—"Before I left *Calcutta*, a gentleman with whom I chanced to be discoursing of that sect who are distinguished from the worshippers of *Brăhm*, and the followers of MAHOMMED by the appellation **Seek**, informed me that there was a considerable number of them settled in the city of *Patna*, where they had a College for teaching the tenets of their philosophy."—*Wilkins*, in *As. Res.* i. 288.

1781-2.—"In the year 1128 of the Hedjra" (1716) "a bloody action happened in the plains of the Pendjab, between the **Sycs** and the Imperialists, in which the latter, commanded by Abdol-semed-Khan, a famous Viceroy of that province, gave these inhuman freebooters a great defeat, in which their General, Benda, fell into the victors' hands. . . . He was a **Syc** by profession, that is one of those men attached to the tenets of Guru-Govind, and who from their birth or from the moment of their admission never cut or shave either their beard or whiskers or any hair whatever of their body. They form a particular Society as well as a sect, which distinguishes itself by wearing almost always blue cloaths, and going armed at all times. . . ." &c.—*Seir Mutaqherin*, i. 87.

1782.—"News was received that the **Seiks** had crossed the Jumna."—*India Gazette*, May 11.

1783.—"Unhurt by the **Sicques**, tigers, and thieves, I am safely lodged at Nourpour."—*Forster*, *Journey*, ed. 1808, i. 247.

1784.—"The **Seekhs** are encamped at the distance of 12 cose from the Pass of Dirderry, and have plundered all that quarter."—In *Seton-Karr*, i. 13.

1790.—"Particulars relating to the seizure of Colonel Robert Stewart by the **Sicques**."—*Calc. Monthly Register*, &c., i. 152.

1810.—Williamson (*V.M.*) writes **Seeks**.

The following extract indicates the prevalence of a very notable error :—

1840.—"Runjeet possesses great personal courage, a quality in which the **Sihks** (*sic*) are supposed to be generally deficient."—*Osborne, Court and Camp of Runjeet Singh*, 83.

We occasionally, about 1845-6 saw the word written by people in Calcutta, who ought to have known better, **Sheiks**.

SILBOOT, SILPET, SLIPPET, s. Domestic Hind. corruptions of 'slipper.' The first is an instance of "striving after meaning" by connecting it in some way with 'boot.' [The Railway 'sleeper' is in the same way corrupted into *silīpat*.]

SILLADAR, adj. and s. Hind. from Pers. *silaḥ-dār*, 'bearing or having arms,' from Ar. *silaḥ*, 'arms.' [In the *Arabian Nights* (*Burton*, ii. 114) it has the primary sense of an 'armour-bearer.'] Its Anglo-Indian application is to a soldier, in a regiment of irregular cavalry, who provides his own arms and horse; and sometimes to regiments composed of such men—"a corps of **Silladar** Horse." [See Irvine, *The Army of the Indian Moghuls*, (*J. R. As. Soc.*, July 1896, p. 549).]

1766.—"When this intelligence reached the Nawaub, he leaving the whole of his troops and baggage in the same place, with only 6000 stable horse, 9000 **Sillahdārs**, 4000 regular infantry, and 6 guns . . . fell bravely on the Mahrattas. . . ."—*Mir Hussein Ali*, *H. of Hydur Naik*, 173.

1804.—"It is my opinion, that the arrangement with the Soubah of the Deccan should be, that the whole of the force . . . should be **silladar** horse."—*Wellington*, iii. 671.

1813.—"Bhàou . . . in the prosecution of his plan, selected Malhar Row Holcar, a **Silledar** or soldier of fortune."—*Forbes*, *Or. Mem.* iii. 349.

[**SILLAPOSH**, s. An armour-clad warrior; from Pers. *silaḥ*, 'body armour,' *posh*, Pers. *poshīdan*, 'to wear.'

[1799.—"The **Sillah posh** or body-guard of the Rajah (of Jaipur)."—*W. Francklin*, *Mil. Mem. of Mr. George Thomas*, ed. 1805, p. 165.

[1829.—". . . he stood two assaults, in one of which he slew thirty **Sillehposh**, or men in armour, the body-guard of the prince."—*Tod*, *Annals*, Calcutta reprint, ii. 462.]

SILMAGOOR, s. Ship Hind. for 'sail-maker' (*Roebuck*).

SIMKIN, s. Domestic Hind. for champagne, of which it is a corruption; sometimes **samkīn**.

1853.—"'The dinner was good, and the iced **simkin**, Sir, delicious.'"—*Oakfield*, ii. 127.

SIND, SCINDE, &c., n.p. The territory on the Indus below the Punjab. [In the early inscriptions the two words *Sindhu-Sauvīra* are often found conjoined, the latter probably part of Upper Sind (see *Bombay Gazetteer*, i. pt. i. 36).] The earlier Mahommedans hardly regarded Sind as part of India, but distinguished sharply between *Sind* and *Hind*, and denoted the whole region that we call India by the copula 'Hind and Sind.' We know that originally these were in fact but diverging forms of one word; the aspirant and sibilant tending in several parts of India (includ- the extreme east—compare **ASSAM**, *Ahom*—and the extreme west), as in some other regions, to exchange places.

c. 545.—"Σινδοῦ, Ὄρροθα, Καλλιάνα, Σιβὼρ καὶ Μαλὲ πέντε ἐμπόρια ἔχουσα."—*Cosmas*, lib. xi.

770.—"Per idem tempus quingenti circiter ex Mauris, **Sindis**, et Chazaris servi in urbe Haran rebellarunt, et facto agmine regium thesaurum diripere tentarunt." — *Dionysii Patriarchae Chronicon*, in *Assemani*, ii. 114. But from the association with the Khazars, and in a passage on the preceding page with Alans and Khazars, we may be almost certain that these *Sindi* are not Indian, but a Sarmatic people mentioned by Ammianus (xxii. 8), Valerius Flaccus (vi. 86), and other writers.

c. 1030.—"**Sind** and her sister (*i.e. Hind*) trembled at his power and vengeance."—*Al 'Utbi*, in *Elliot*, ii. 32.

c. 1340.—"Mohammed-ben-Iousouf Thakafi trouva dans la province de **Sind** quarante behar (see **BAHAR**) d'or, et chaque behar comprend 333 *mann*."—*Shihābuddīn Dimishḳi*, in *Not. et Ext.* xiii. 173.

1525.—"*Expenses of Melyquyaz* (*i.e.* Malik Ayāz of Diu):—1,000 foot soldiers (*lasquarys*), viz., 300 Arabs, at 40 and 50 *fedeas* each; also 200 *Coraçones* (Khorāsānīs) at the wage of the Arabs; also 200 Guzarates and **Cymdes** at 25 to 30 *fedeas* each; also 30 Rumes at 100 *fedeas* each; 120 *Fartaquys* at 50 *fedeas* each. Horse soldiers (*Lasquarys a quaualo*), whom he supplies with horses, 300 at 70 *fedeas* a month. . . ."—*Lembrança*, p. 37. The preceding extract is curious as showing the comparative value put upon Arabs, Khorāsānīs (qu. Afghāns?), Sindīs, Rūmīs (*i.e.* Turks), Fartakīs (Arabs of Hadramaut?), &c.

1548. — "And the rent of the shops (*buticas*) of the Guzaratis of **Cindy**, who prepare and sell parched rice (*avel*), paying 6 bazarucos (see **BUDGROOK**) a month."—*Botelho, Tombo*, 156.

1554.—"Towards the Gulf of Chakad, in the vicinity of **Sind**."—*Sidi' Ali*, in *J. As.* Ser. I. tom. ix. 77.

1583.—"The first citie of India . . . after we had passed the coast of **Zindi** is called Diu."—*Fitch*, in *Hakl.* p. 385.

1584.—"Spicknard from **Zindi** and Lahor."—*W. Barret*, in *Hakl.* ii. 412.

1598.—"I have written to the said Antonio d'Azevedo on the ill treatment experienced by the Portuguese in the kingdom of **Cimde**."—King's Letter to Goa, in *Archiv. Port. Orient.* Fascic. iii. 877.

[1610.—"**Tzinde**, are silk cloths with red stripes."—*Danvers, Letters*, i. 72.]

1611.—"*Cuts-nagore*, a place not far from the River of **Zinde**."—*N. Downton*, in *Purchas*, i. 307.

1613.—". . . considering the state of destitution in which the fortress of Ormuz had need be,—since it had no other resources but the revenue of the custom-house, and there could now be returning nothing, from the fact that the ports of Cambaia and **Sinde** were closed, and that no ship had arrived from Goa in the current monsoon of January and February, owing to the news of the English ships having collected at Suratte. . . ."—*Bocarro, Decada*, 379.

[c. 1665.—". . . he (Dara) proceeded towards **Scimdy**, and sought refuge in the fortress of *Tatabakar*. . . ."—*Bernier*, ed. *Constable*, 71.]

1666.—"De la Province du **Sinde** ou **Sindy** . . . que quelques-uns nomment le Tatta."—*Thevenot*, v. 158.

1673.—". . . Retiring with their ill got Booty to the Coasts of **Sindu**."—*Fryer*, 218.

1727.—"**Sindy** is the westmost Province of the Mogul's Dominions on the Sea-coast, and has Larribunder (see **LARRY-BUNDER**) to its Mart."—*A. Hamilton*, i. 114; [ed. 1744, i. 115].

c. 1760.—"**Scindy**, or Tatta."—*Grose*, i. 286.

SINDĀBŪR, SANDĀBŪR, n.p. This is the name by which Goa was known to the old Arab writers. The identity was clearly established in *Cathay and the Way Thither*, pp. 444 and ccli. We will give the quotations first, and then point out the grounds of identification.

A.D. 943.—"Crocodiles abound, it is true, in the *ajwān* or bays formed by the Sea of India, such as that of **Sindābūra** in the Indian Kingdom of Bāghira, or in the bay of Zābaj (see **JAVA**) in the dominion of the Maharāj."—*Maṣ'ūdi*, i. 207.

1013.—"I have it from Ābū Yūsaf bin Muslim, who had it from Ābū Bakr of Fasā at Saimūr, that the latter heard told by Mūsa the **Sindābūri**: 'I was one day conversing with the Sahib of **Sindābūr**, when suddenly he burst out laughing. . . . It was, said he, because there is a lizard on the wall, and it said, 'There is a guest coming to-day. . . . Don't you go till you see what comes of it.' So we remained talking till one of his servants came in and said 'There is a ship of Oman come in.' Shortly after, people arrived, carrying hampers with various things, such as cloths, and rose-water. As they opened one, out came a long lizard, which instantly clung to the wall and went to join the other one. It was the same person, they say, who enchanted the crocodiles in the estuary of **Sindābūr**, so that now they hurt nobody." —*Livre des Merveilles de l'Inde. V. der Lith et Devic*, 157-158.

c. 1150. — "From the city of Barūh (Barūch, *i.e.* **Broach**) following the coast, to **Sindābūr** 4 days.

"**Sindābūr** is on a great inlet where ships anchor. It is a place of trade, where one sees fine buildings and rich bazars."—*Edrisi*, i. 179. And see *Elliot*, i. 89.

c. 1300.—"Beyond Guzerat are Konkan and Tána; beyond them the country of Malibár. . . . The people are all Samanís (Buddhists), and worship idols. Of the cities on the shore the first is **Sindabūr**, then Faknūr, then the country of Manjarūr, then the country of Hílí. . . ."—*Rashīd-uddīn*, in *Elliot*, i. 68.

c. 1330. — "A traveller states that the country from **Sindāpūr** to Hanāwar towards its eastern extremity joins with Malabar. . . ."—*Abulfeda*, Fr. tr., II. ii. 115. Further on in his Tables he jumbles up (as Edrisi has done) **Sindāpūr** with Sindān (see **ST. JOHN**).

" "The heat is great at Aden. This is the port frequented by the people of India; great ships arrive there from Cambay, Tāna, Kaulam, Calicut, Fandarāina, Shāliyāt, Manjarūr, Fākanūr, Hanaur, **Sandābūr**, et cetera."—*Ibn Batuta*, ii. 177.

c. 1343-4.—"Three days after setting sail we arrived at the Island of **Sandābūr**, within which there are 36 villages. It is surrounded by an inlet, and at the time of ebb the water of this is fresh and pleasant, whilst at flow it is salt and bitter. There are in the island two cities, one ancient, built by the pagans; the second built by the Musulmans when they conquered the island the first time. . . . We left this island behind us and anchored at a small island near the mainland, where we found a temple, a grove, and a tank of water. . . ."—*Ibid.* iv. 61-62.

1350, 1375.—In the Medicean and the Catalan maps of those dates we find on the coast of India **Cintabor** and **Chintabor** respectively, on the west coast of India.

c. 1554. — "*24th Voyage: from* **Guvah-Sindābūr** *to Aden.* If you start from **Guvah-Sindābūr** at the end of the season, take care not to fall on Cape Fāl," &c.—*Mohit*, in *J.A.S.B.* v. 564.

The last quotation shows that Goa was known even in the middle of the 16th century to Oriental seamen as Goa-Sindābūr, whatever Indian name the last part represented; probably, from the use of the *ṣwād* by the earlier Arab writers, and from the **Chintabor** of the European maps, *Chandāpur* rather than *Sundāpur*. No Indian name like this has yet been recovered from inscriptions as attaching to Goa; but the Turkish author of the Mohit supplies the connection, and Ibn Batuta's description even without this would be sufficient for the identification. His description, it will be seen, is that of a delta-island, and Goa is the only one partaking of that character upon the coast. He says it contained 36 villages; and Barros tells us that Goa Island was known to the natives as *Tīsvādī*, a name signifying "Thirty villages." (See **SALSETTE.**) Its vicinity to the island where Ibn Batuta proceeded to anchor, which we have shown to be **Anchediva** (q.v.), is another proof. Turning to Rashīduddīn, the order in which he places **Sindābūr**, Faknūr (**Baccanore**), Manjarūr(**Mangalore**), **Hīlī (Mt. D'Ely)**, is perfectly correct, if for Sindābūr we substitute Goa. The passage from Edrisi and one indicated from Abulfeda only show a confusion which has misled many readers since.

SINGALESE, CINGHALESE, n.p. Native of Ceylon; pertaining to Ceylon. The word is formed from *Sinhala*, 'Dwelling of Lions,' the word used by the natives for the Island, and which is the origin of most of the names given to it (see **CEYLON**). The explanation given by De Barros and Couto is altogether fanciful, though it leads them to notice the curious and obscure fact of the introduction of Chinese influence in Ceylon during the 15th century.

1552.—"That the Chinese (*Chijs*) were masters of the Choromandel Coast, of part of Malabar, and of this Island of Ceylon, we have not only the assertion of the Natives of the latter, but also evidence in the buildings, names, and language that they left in it . . . and because they were in the vicinity of this Cape Galle, the other people who lived from the middle of the Island upwards called those dwelling about there **Chingálla**, and their language the same, as much as to say the language, or the people of the **Chins of Galle.**"—*Barros*, III. ii. 1.

1583.—(The Cauchin Chineans) "are of the race of the **Chingalays**, which they say are the best kinde of all the Malabars."—*Fitch*, in *Hakl.* ii. 397.

1598.—". . . inhabited with people called **Cingalas**. . . ."—*Linschoten*, 24; [Hak. Soc. i. 77; in i. 81, **Chingalas**].

c. 1610.—"Ils tiennent donc que . . . les premiers qui y allerent, et qui les peuplerent (les Maldives) furent . . . les **Cingalles** de l'Isle de Ceylan."—*Pyrard de Laval*, i. 185; [Hak. Soc. i. 105, and see i. 266].

1612.—Couto, after giving the same explanation of the word as Barros, says: "And as they spring from the Chins, who are the falsest heathen of the East . . . so are they of this island the weakest, falsest, and most tricky people in all India, insomuch that, to this day, you never find faith or truth in a Chingalla."—V. i. 5.

1681.—"The **Chingûleys** are naturally a people given to sloth and laziness: if they can but anyways live, they abhor to work." . . . .—*Knox*, 32.

SINGAPORE, SINCAPORE, n.p. This name was adopted by Sir Stamford Raffles in favour of the city which he founded, February 23, 1819, on the island which had always retained the name since the Middle Ages. This it derived from *Sinhapura*, Skt. 'Lion-city,' the name of a town founded by Malay or Javanese settlers from Sumatra, probably in the 14th century, and to which Barros ascribes great commercial importance. The Indian origin of the name, as of many other names and phrases which survive from the old Indian civilisation of the Archipelago, had been forgotten, and the origin which Barros was taught to ascribe to it is on a par with his etymology of **Singalese** quoted in the preceding article. The words on which his etymology is founded are no doubt Malay: *singah*, 'to tarry, halt, or lodge,' and *pora-pora*, 'to pretend'; and these were probably supposed to refer to the temporary occupation of Sinhapura, before the chiefs who founded it passed on to Malacca. [It may be noted that Dennys (*Desc. Dict.* s.v.) derives the word from *singha*, 'a place of call,' and *pura*, 'a city.' In Dalboquerque's *Comm.* Hak. Soc. iii. 73, we are told: "Singapura, whence the city takes its name, is a channel through which all the shipping of those parts passes, and signifies in his Malay language, '*treacherous delay*'" See quotation from Barros below.]

The settlement of Hinduized people on the site, if not the name, is probably as old as the 4th century, A.D., for inscriptions have been found there in a very old character. One of these, on a rock at the mouth of the little river on which the town stands, was destroyed some 40 or 50 years ago for the accommodation of some wretched bungalow.

The modern Singapore and its prosperity form a monument to the patriotism, sagacity, and fervid spirit of the founder. According to an article in the *Geogr. Magazine* (i. 107) derived from Mr. Archibald Ritchie, who was present with the expedition which founded the colony, Raffles, after consultation with Lord Hastings, was about to establish a settlement for the protection and encouragement of our Eastern trade, in the Nicobar Islands, when his attention was drawn to the superior advantages of Singapore by Captains Ross and Crawford of the Bombay Marine, who had been engaged in the survey of those seas. Its great adaptation for a mercantile settlement had been discerned by the shrewd, if somewhat vulgar, Scot, Alexander Hamilton, 120 years earlier. It seems hardly possible, we must however observe, to reconcile the *details* in the article cited, with the letters and facts contained in the *Life of Raffles;* though probably the latter had, at some time or other, received information from the officers named by Mr. Ritchie.

1512.—"And as the enterprise was one to make good booty, everybody was delighted to go on it, so that they were more than 1200 men, the soundest and best armed of the garrison, and so they were ready incontinently, and started for the Strait of **Cincapura**, where they were to wait for the junks."—*Correa*, ii. 284-5.

1551.—"Sed hactenus Deus nobis adsit omnibus. Amen. Anno post Christum natum, MDLI. *Ex Freto* **Syncapurano**."—*Scti. Franc. Xaverii* Epistt. Pragae, 1667, Lib. III. viii.

1553.—"Anciently the most celebrated settlement in this region of Malaca was one called **Cingapura**, a name which in their tongue means 'pretended halt' (*falsa dimora*); and this stood upon a point of that country which is the most southerly of all Asia, and lies, according to our graduation, in half a degree of North Latitude . . . before the foundation of Malaca, at this same **Cingapura** . . . flocked together all the navigators of the Seas of India from West and East. . . ."—*Barros*, II. vi. 1. [The same derivation is given in the *Comm. of Dalboquerque*, Hak. Soc. iii. 73.]

1572.—

"Mas na ponta da terra **Cingapura**
Verás, onde o caminho as naos se estreita;
Daqui, tornando a costa á Cynosura,
Se incurva, e para a Aurora se endireita."
Camões, x. 125.

By Burton:

"But on her Lands-end throned see **Cingapúr**,
where the wide sea-road shrinks to narrow way:
Thence curves the coast to face the Cynosure,
and lastly trends Aurora-wards its lay."

1598.—". . . by water the coast stretcheth to the Cape of **Singapura**, and from thence it runneth upwards [inwards] againe. . . .—" *Linschoten*, 30; [Hak. Soc. i. 101].

1599.—"In this voyage nothing occurred worth relating, except that, after passing the Strait of **Sincapura**, situated in one degree and a half, between the main land and a variety of islands . . . with so narrow a channel that from the ship you could jump ashore, or touch the branches of the trees on either side, our vessel struck on a shoal."—*Viaggi di Carletti*, ii. 208-9.

1606.—"The 5th May came there 2 Prows from the King of Johore, with the Shahbander (**Shabunder**) of **Singapoera**, called Siri Raja Nagara. . . ."—*Valentijn*, v. 331.

1616.—"Found a Dutch man-of-war, one of a fleet appointed for the siege of Malaca, with the aid of the King of Acheen, at the entrance of the Straits of **Singapore**."—*Sainsbury*, i. 458.

1727.—"In anno 1703 I called at *Johore* on my Way to China, and he treated me very kindly, and made me a Present of the Island of **Sincapure**, but I told him it could be of no use to a private Person, tho' a proper Place for a Company to settle a Colony in, lying in the Center of Trade, and being accommodated with good Rivers and safe Harbours, so conveniently situated that all Winds served Shipping, both to go out and come in."—*A. Hamilton*, ii. 98; [ed. 1744, ii. 97].

1818.—"We are now on our way to the eastward, in the hope of doing something, but I much fear the Dutch have hardly left us an inch of ground. . . . My attention is principally turned to Johore, and you must not be surprised if my next letter to you is dated from the site of the ancient city of **Singapura**."—*Raffles*, Letter to Marsden, dated *Sandheads*, Dec. 12.

SINGARA, s. Hind. *singhārā*, Skt. *sringāttaka*, *sringa*, 'a horn.' The caltrop or water-chestnut; *Trapa bispinosa*, Roxb. (N.O. *Haloragaceae*).

[c. 1590. — The *Āīn* (ed. *Jarrett*, ii. 65) mentions it as one of the crops on which revenue was levied in cash.

[1798.—In Kashmīr "many of them . . . were obliged to live on the Kernel of the **singerah**, or water-nut. . . ." — *Forster*, *Travels*, ii. 29.

[1809.—Buchanan-Hamilton writes **singghara**.—*Eastern India*, i. 241.]

1835.—"Here, as in most other parts of India, the tank is spoiled by the water-chestnut, **singhara** (*Trapa bispinosa*), which is everywhere as regularly planted and cultivated in fields under a large surface of water, as wheat or barley is in the dry plains. . . . The nut grows under the water after the flowers decay, and is of a triangular shape, and covered with a tough brown integument adhering strongly to the kernel, which is wholly esculent, and of a fine cartilaginous texture. The people are very fond of these nuts, and they are carried often upon bullocks' backs two or three hundred miles to market."—*Sleeman*, *Rambles*, &c. (1844), i. 101; [ed. *Smith*, i. 94.]

1839.—"The nuts of the *Trapa bispinosa*, called **Singhara**, are sold in all the Bazaars of India; and a species called by the same name, forms a considerable portion of the food of the inhabitants of Cashmere, as we learn from Mr. Forster [*loc. cit.*] that it yields the Government 12,000*l.* of revenue; and Mr. Moorcroft mentions nearly the same sum as Runjeet Sing's share, from 96,000 to 128,000 ass-loads of this nut, yielded by the Lake of Oaller."—*Royle*, *Him. Plants*, i. 211.

SIPAHSELAR, s. A General-in-chief; Pers. *sipāh-sālār*, 'army-leader,' the last word being the same as in the title of the late famous Minister-Regent of Hyderabad, Sir Sālār Jang, *i.e.* 'the leader in war.'

c. 1000-1100.—"Voici quelle étoit alors la gloire et la puissance des Orpélians dans le royaume. Ils possédoient la charge de **sbasalar**, ou de généralissime de toute la Georgie. Tous les officiers du palais étoient de leur dependance."—*Hist. of the Orpélians*, in *St. Martin*, *Mem. sur l'Arménie*, ii. 77.

c. 1358.—"At 16 my father took me by the hand, and brought me to his own Monastery. He there addressed me: 'My boy, our ancestors from generation to generation have been commanders of the armies of the Jagtay and the Berlas family. The dignity of (**Sepah Salar**) Commander-in-Chief has now descended to me, but as I am tired of this world . . . I mean therefore to resign my public office. . . ."—*Autob. Mem. of Timour*, E.T. p. 22.

1712.—"Omnibus illis superior est . . . **Sipah Salaar**, sive *Imperator Generalis* Regni, Praesidem dignitate excipiens. . . ." —*Kaempfer*, *Amoen. Exot.* 73.

1726.—A letter from the Heer Van Maatzuiker "to His Highness Chan Chanaan, **Sapperselaar**, Grand Duke, and General in Chief of the Great Mogol in Assam, Bengal, &c."—*Valentijn*, v. 173.

1755.—"After the **Sipahsalar** Hydur, by his prudence and courage, had defeated the Mahrattas, and recovered the country taken by them, he placed the government of Seringaputtun on a sure and established basis. . . ."—*Meer Hussein Ali Khan*, *H. of Hydur Naik*, O. T. F. p. 61.

[c. 1803.—In a collection of native letters, the titles of Lord Lake are given as follows: "*Ashja-ul-Mulk Khān Daurān*, General Gerard Lake Bahādur, **Sipahsalar**-i-kishwar-i-Hind," "Valiant of the Kingdom, Lord of the Cycle, Commander-in-chief of the Territories of Hindustan."—*North Indian Notes and Queries*, iv. 17.]

SIRCAR, s. Hind. from Pers. *sarkār*, 'head (of) affairs.' This word has very divers applications; but its senses may fall under three heads.

a. The State, the Government, the Supreme authority; also 'the Master' or head of the domestic government. Thus a servant, if asked 'Whose are those horses?' in replying 'They are the *sarkār's*,' may mean according to circumstances, that they are Government horses, or that they belong to his own master.

b. In Bengal the word is applied to a domestic servant who is a kind of house-steward, and keeps the accounts of household expenditure, and makes miscellaneous purchases for the family; also, in merchants' offices, to any native accountant or native employed in making purchases, &c.

c. Under the Mahommedan Governments, as in the time of the Mogul Empire, and more recently in the Deccan, the word was applied to certain extensive administrative divisions of territory. In its application in the Deccan it has been in English generally spelt **Circar** (q.v.).

a.—

[1759.—". . . there is no separation between your Honour . . . and this **Sircar**. . . ."—*Forrest, Bombay Letters*, ii. 129.]

1800.—"Would it not be possible and proper to make people pay the **circar** according to the exchange fixed at Seringapatam?"—*Wellington*, i. 60.

[1866.—". . . the **Sirkar** Buhadoor gives me four rupees a month. . . ."—*Confessions of an Orderly*, 43.]

b.—

1777.—"There is not in any country in the world, of which I have any knowledge, a more pernicious race of vermin in human shape than are the numerous cast of people known in Bengal by the appellation of **Sircars**; they are educated and trained to deceive."—*Price's Tracts*, i. 24.

1810.—"The **Sircar** is a genius whose whole study is to handle money, whether receivable or payable, and who contrives either to confuse accounts, when they are adverse to his view, or to render them most expressively intelligible, when such should suit his purpose."—*Williamson, V.M.* i. 200.

1822.—"One morning our **Sircar**, in answer to my having observed that the articles purchased were highly priced, said, 'You are my father and my mother, and I am your poor little child. I have only taken 2 annas in the rupee dustoorie'" (**dustoor**).—*Wanderings of a Pilgrim*, i. 21-22.

1834.—"'And how the deuce,' asked his companion, 'do you manage to pay for them?' 'Nothing so easy,—I say to my **Sirkar**: 'Baboo, go pay for that horse 2000 rupees, and it is done, Sir, as quickly as you could dock him.'"—*The Baboo and Other Tales*, i. 13.

c.—

c. 1590.—"In the fortieth year of his majesty's reign, his dominions consisted of 105 **Sircars**, subdivided into 2737 kusbahs" (**cusba**), "the revenue of which he settled for ten years at 3 **Arribs**, 62 **Crore**, 97 **Lacks**, 55,246 **Dams**" (q.v. 3,62,97,55,246 *dāms* = about 9 millions sterling).—*Ayeen*, E.T. by Gladwin, 1800, ii. 1; [ed. *Jarrett*, ii. 115.]

SIRDAR, s. Hind. from Pers. *sardār*, and less correctly *sirdār*, 'leader, a commander, an officer'; a chief, or lord; the head of a set of palankin-bearers, and hence the '*sirdār-bearer*,' or elliptically 'the *Sirdār*,' is in Bengal the style of the valet or body-servant, even when he may have no others under him (see **BEARER**). [**Sirdār** is now the official title of the Commander-in-Chief of the Egyptian army; **Sirdār** *Bahādur* is an Indian military distinction.]

[c. 1610.—". . . a captain of a company, or, as they call it, a **Sardare**."—*Pyrard de Laval*, Hak. Soc. i. 254.

[1675.—"**Sardar**." See under **SEPOY**.]

1808.—"I, with great difficulty, knocked up some of the villagers, who were nearly as much afraid as Christie's Will, at the visit of a **Sirdār**" (here an *officer*).—*Life of Leyden*.

[c. 1817.—". . . the bearers, with their **Sirdaur**, have a large room with a verandah before it."—*Mrs. Sherwood, Last Days of Boosy*, 63.]

1826.—"Gopee's father had been a **Sirdar** of some consequence."—*Pandurang Hari*, 174; [ed. 1873, i. 252].

SIRDRÁRS, s. This is the name which native valets (**bearer**) give to common drawers (underclothing). A friend (Gen. R. Maclagan, R.E.) has suggested the origin, which is doubtless "short drawers" in contradistinction to **Long-drawers**, or **Pyjamas** (qq.v.). A common bearer's pronunciation is *sirdrāj*; as a chest of drawers is also called '**Drāj** *kā almairā*' (see **ALMYRA**).

SIRKY, s. Hind. *sirkī*. A kind of unplatted matting formed by laying the fine cylindrical culms from the upper part of the *Saccharum sara*, Roxb. (see **SURKUNDA**) side by side, and binding them in single or double layers. This is used to lay under the thatch of a house, to cover carts and palankins, to make **Chicks** (q.v.) and table-mats, and for many other purposes of rural and domestic economy.

1810.—"It is perhaps singular that I should have seen **seerky** in use among a group of gypsies in Essex. In India these itinerants, whose habits and characters correspond with this intolerable species of banditti, invariably shelter themselves under **seerky**."—*Williamson, V.M.* ii. 490.

[1832.—". . . neat little huts of **sirrakee**, a reed or grass, resembling bright straw."—*Mrs. Meer Hassan Ali, Observations*, i. 23.]

SIRRIS, s. Hind. *siris*, Skt. *shirisha*, *shri*, 'to break,' from the brittleness of its branches; the tree *Acacia Lebbek*, Benth., indigenous in S. India, the Sātpura range, Bengal, and the sub-Himālayan tract; cultivated in Egypt and elsewhere. A closely kindred sp., *A. Julibrissin*, Boivin, affords a specimen of scientific 'Hobson-Jobson'; the specific name is a corruption of *Gulāb-reshm*, 'silk-flower.'

1808.—"Quelques anneés après le mort de Dariyaî, des charpentiers ayant abattu un arbre de **Seris**, qui croissoit auprès de son tombeau, le coupèrent en plusieurs pièces pour l'employer à des constructions. Tout-à-coup une voix terrible se fit entendre, la terre se mit à trembler et le tronc de cet arbre se releva de lui-même. Les ouvriers épouvantés s'enfuirent, et l'arbre ne tarda pas à reverdir."—*Afsōs, Arāyish-i-Mahfil*, quoted by *Garcin de Tassy, Rel. Mus.* 88.

[c. 1890.—
"An' it fell when **sirris**-shaws were sere,
And the nichts were long and mirk."
R. Kipling, Departmental Ditties, The Fall of Jock Gillespie.]

SISSOO, SHISHAM, s. Hind. *sīsū*, *sīsūn*, *shīsham*, Skt. *śinśapā*; Ar. *sāsam*, *sāsim*; the tree *Dalbergia Sissoo*, Roxb. (N.O. *Leguminosae*) and its wood. This is excellent, and valuable for construction, joinery, boat- and carriage-building, and furniture. It was the favourite wood for gun-carriages as long as the supply of large timber lasted. It is now much cultivated in the Punjab plantations. The tree is indigenous in the sub-Himālayan tracts; and believed to be so likewise in Beluchistan, Guzerat, and Central India. Another sp. of *Dalbergia* (*D. latifolia*) affords the **Black Wood** (q.v.) of S. and W. India. There can be little doubt that one or more of these species of *Dalbergia* afforded the *sesamine* wood spoken of in the *Periplus*, and in some old Arabic writers. A quotation under **Black Wood** shows that this wood was exported from India to Chaldaea in remote ages. Sissoo has continued in recent times to be exported to Egypt, (see *Forskal*, quoted by *Royle, Hindu Medicine*, 128). Royle notices the resemblance of the Biblical *shittim* wood to *shīsham*.

c. A.D. 80.—". . . Thither they are wont to despatch from Barygaza (**Broach**) to both these ports of Persia, great vessels with brass, and timbers, and beams of teak (ξύλων σαγαλίνων καὶ δοκῶν) . . . and logs of **shīsham** (φαλάγγων σασαμίνων) . . ."—*Periplus, Maris Erythr.*, cap 36.

c. 545.—"These again are passed on from Sielediba to the marts on this side, such as Malé, where the pepper is grown, and Kalliana, whence are exported brass, and **shīsham** logs (σησαμίνα ξύλα), and other wares."—*Cosmas*, lib. xi.

? before 1200.—
"There are the wolf and the parrot, and the peacock, and the dove,
And the plant of Zinj, and al-**sāsim**, and pepper. . . ."
Verses on India by *Abu'l-dhal'i, the Sindi*, quoted by *Kazvīnī*, in *Gildemeister*, p. 218.

1810.—"**Sissoo** grows in most of the great forests, intermixed with **saul**. . . . This wood is extraordinarily hard and heavy, of a dark brown, inclining to a purple tint when polished."—*Williamson, V.M.* ii. 71.

1839.—"As I rode through the city one day I saw a considerable quantity of timber lying in an obscure street. On examining it I found it was **shīsham**, a wood of the most valuable kind, being not liable to the attacks of white ants."—*Dry Leaves from Young Egypt*, ed. 1851, p. 102.

SITTING-UP. A curious custom, in vogue at the Presidency towns more than a century ago, and the nature of which is indicated by the quotations. Was it of Dutch origin?

1777.—"Lady Impey **sits up** with Mrs. Hastings; *vulgo* toad-eating."—*Ph. Francis's Diary*, quoted in *Busteed, Echoes of Old Calcutta*, 124; [3rd ed. 125].

1780.—"When a young lady arrives at Madras, she must, in a few days afterwards **sit up** to receive company, attended by some beau or master of the ceremonies, which perhaps continues for a week, or until she has seen all the fair sex, and gentlemen of the settlement." — *Munro's Narr.*, 56.

1795.—"You see how many good reasons there are against your scheme of my taking horse instantly, and hastening to throw myself at the lady's feet; as to the other, of proxy, I can only agree to it under certain conditions. . . . I am not to be forced to **sit up**, and receive male or female visitors. . . . I am not to be obliged to deliver my opinion on patterns for caps or petticoats for any lady. . . ."—*T. Munro to his Sister*, in *Life*, i. 169.

1810. — "Among the several justly exploded ceremonies we may reckon that . . . of '**Sitting up.**' . . . This '**Sitting up,**' as it was termed, generally took place at the house of some lady of rank or fortune, who, for three successive nights, threw open her mansion for the purpose of receiving all . . . who chose to pay their respects to such ladies as might have recently arrived in the country."—*Williamson, V.M.* i. 113.

SITTRINGY, s. Hind. from Ar. *shiṭranjī*, *shaṭranjī*, and that from Pers. *shaṭrang*, 'chess,' which is again of Skt. origin, *chaturanga*, 'quadripartite' (see **SADRAS**). A carpet of coloured cotton, now usually made in stripes, but no doubt originally, as the name implies, in chequers.

1648. — ". . . Een andere soorte van slechte Tapijten die mē noemt **Chitrenga.**" —*Van Twist*, 63.

1673. — "They pull off their Slippers, and after the usual **Salams**, seat themselves in **Choultries**, open to some **Tank** of purling Water; commonly spread with Carpets or **Siturngees.**"—*Fryer*, 93.

[1688. — "2 **citterengees.**" — In *Yule, Hedges' Diary*, Hak. Soc. ii. cclxv.]

1785.—"To be sold by public auction . . . the valuable effects of Warren Hastings, Esquire . . . carpets and **sittringees.**"— In *Seton-Karr*, i. 111.

SIWALIK, n.p. This is the name now applied distinctively to that outer range of tertiary hills which in various parts of the Himālaya runs parallel to the foot of the mountain region, separated from it by valleys known in Upper India as *dūns* (see **DHOON**). But this special and convenient sense **(d)** has been attributed to the term by modern Anglo-Indian geographers only. Among the older Mahommedan historians the term *Siwālikh* is applied to a territory to the west of and perhaps embracing the Aravalli Hills, but certainly including specifically Nagore (*Nāgaur*) and Mandāwar the predecessor of modern Jodhpūr, and in the vicinity of that city. This application is denoted by **(a)**.

In one or two passages we find the application of the name (Siwālikh) extending a good deal further south, as if reaching to the vicinity of Mālwā. Such instances we have grouped under **(b)**. But it is possible that the early application **(a)** habitually extended thus far.

At a later date the name is applied to the Himālaya; either to the range in its whole extent, as in the passages from *Chereffedin* (Sharīffuddīn 'Ali of Yezd) and from Baber; sometimes with a possible limitation to that part of the mountains which overlooks the Punjab; or, as the quotation from Rennell indicates, with a distinction between the less lofty region nearest the plains, and the Alpine summits beyond, Siwālik applying to the former only.

The true Indian form of the name is, we doubt not, to be gathered from the occurrence, in a list of Indian national names, in the *Vishnu Purāna*, of the **Saivālas**. But of the position of these we can only say that the nations, with whom the context immediately associates them, seem to lie towards the western part of Upper India. (See *Wilson's Works, Vishnu Purāna*, ii. 175.) The popular derivation of Siwālik as given in several of the quotations below, is from *sawalākh*, 'One lākh and a quarter'; but this is of no more value than most popular etymologies.

We give numerous quotations to establish the old application of the term, because this has been somewhat confused in Elliot's extracts by the interpolated phrase '**Siwálik** *Hills*,' where it is evident from Raverty's version of the *Ṭabakāt-i-Nāsirī* that there is no such word as *Hills* in the original.

We have said that the special application of the term to the detached sub-Himālayan range is quite modern. It seems in fact due to that very eminent investigator in many branches of natural science, Dr. Hugh Falconer; at least we can find no trace of it before the use of the term by him in papers presented to the Asiatic Society of Bengal. It is not previously used, so far as we can discover, even by Royle; nor is it known to Jacquemont, who was intimately associated with Royle and Cautley, at Sahāranpūr, very shortly before Falconer's arrival there. Jacquemont (*Journal*, ii. 11) calls the range: "la première chaine de montagnes que j'appellerai *les montagnes de Dehra.*" The first occurrence that we can find is in a paper by Falconer on the 'Aptitude of the Himālayan Range for the Culture of the Tea Plant,' in vol. iii. of the *J. As. Soc. Bengal*, which we quote below. A year later, in the account of the *Sivatherium* fossil, by Falconer and Cautley, in the *As. Researches*, we have a fuller explanation of the use of the term *Siwālik*, and its alleged etymology.

It is probable that there may have been some real legendary connection of the hills in the vicinity with the name of *Śiva*. For in some of the old maps, such as that in Bernier's *Travels*, we find *Siba* given as the name of a province about Hurdwār; and the same name occurs in the same connection in the Mem. of the Emperor Jahāngīr (*Elliot*, vi. 382). [On the connection of Siva worship with the lower Himālaya, see *Atkinson, Himalayan Gazetteer*, ii. 743.]

a.—

1118.—"Again he rebelled, and founded the fortress of Nāghawr, in the territory of **Siwālikh**, in the neighbourhood of Bīrah(?)."—*Ṭabaḳāt-i-Nāṣirī*, E.T. by *Raverty*, 110.

1192.—"The seat of government, Ajmīr, with the whole of the **Siwālikh** [territory], such as (?) Hānsi, Sursutī, and other tracts, were subjugated."—*Ibid.* 468-469.

1227.—"A year subsequent to this, in 624 H., he (Sultan Iyaltimish) marched against the fort of Mandawar within the limits of the **Siwālikh** [territory], and its capture, likewise the Almighty God facilitated for him."—*Ibid.* 611.

c. 1247.—". . . When the Sultan of Islam, Nāṣir-ud Dunyā-wa-ud-Dīn, ascended the throne of sovereignty . . . after Malik Balban had come [to Court ?] he, on several occasions made a request for Uchchah together with Multan. This was acquiesced in, under the understanding that the **Siwālikh** [territory] and Nāg-awr should be relinquished by him to other Maliks. . . ."—*Ibid.* 781.

1253.—"When the new year came round, on Tuesday, the 1st of the month of Muharram, 651 H., command was given to Ulugh Khān-i-A'ẓam . . . to proceed to his fiefs, the territory of **Siwālikh** and Hānsī."—*Ibid.* 693.

1257.—"Malik Balban . . . withdrew (from Dehli), and by way of the **Siwālikh** [country], and with a slight retinue, less than 200 or 300 in number, returned to Uchchah again."—*Ibid.* 786.

1255.—"When the royal tent was pitched at Talh-pat, the [contingent] forces of the **Siwālikh** [districts], which were the fiefs of Ulugh Khān-i-A'ẓam, had been delayed . . . (he) set out for Hānsī . . . (and there) issued his mandate, so that, in the space of 14 days, the troops of the **Siwālikh**, Hānsī, Sursutī, Jīnd [Jhīnd], and Barwālah . . . assembled. . . ."—*Ibid.* 837.

1260.—"Ulugh Khān-i-A'ẓam resolved upon making a raid upon the Koh-pāyah [hill tracts of Mewāt] round about the capital, because in this . . . there was a community of obdurate rebels, who, unceasingly, committed highway robbery, and plundered the property of Musalmāns . . . and destruction of the villages in the districts of Hariānah, the **Siwālikh**, and Bhiānah, necessarily followed their outbreaks."—*Ibid.* 850.

1300-10.—"The Mughals having wasted the **Siwálik**, had moved some distance off. When they and their horses returned weary and thirsty to the river, the army of Islám, which had been waiting for them some days, caught them as they expected. . . ."—*Ziā-uddīn Barnī*, in *Elliot*, iii. 199.

b.—

c. 1300.—"Of the cities on the shore the first is Sandabúr, then Faknúr, then the country of Manjarúr, then the country of (Fandarainá), then Jangli (Jinkali), then Kúlam. . . . After these comes the country of **Sawálak**, which comprises 125,000 cities and villages. After that comes Málwála" (but in some MSS. *Málwá*).—*Rashīduddīn*, in *Elliot*, i. 68. *Rashīduddīn* has got apparently much astray here, for he brings in the Siwālik territory at the far end of Malabar. But the mention of Mālwā as adjoining is a probable indication of the true position. (Elliot imagines here some allusion to the Maldives and Laccadives. All in that way that seems possible is that Rashīduddīn may have heard of the Maldives and made some jumble between them and Mālwā). And this is in a manner confirmed by the next quotation from a Portuguese writer who places the region inland from Guzerat.

1644.—"It confines . . . on the east with certain kingdoms of heathen, which are called **Saualacca** *prabatta* (Skt. *parvata*), as much as to say 120,000 mountains."—*Bocarro, MS.*

c.—

1399.—"Le Détroit de Coupelé est situé au pied d'une montagne par où passe le Gange, et à quinze milles plus haut que ce Détroit il y a une pierre en forme de Vache, de laquelle sort la source de ce grand Fleuve; c'est la cause pour laquelle les Indous adorent cette pierre, et dans tous les pays circonvoisins jusques à une année de chemin, ils se tournent pour prier du côté de ce Détroit et de cette Vache de pierre. . . . Cependant on eut avis que dans la montagne de **Soüalec**, qui est une des plus considerables de l'Inde, et qui s'étend dans le deux tiers de ce grand Empire, il s'étoit assemblé un grand nombre d'Indiens qui cherchoient à nous faire insulte."—*H. de Timur-Bec*, par *Chereffedin Ali d'Yezd* (Fr. Tr. by *Petis de la Croix*), Delf, 1723, iii. ch. xxv.-xxvi.

1528.—"The northern range of hills has been mentioned . . . after leaving Kashmîr, these hills contain innumerable tribes and states, pergannahs and countries, and extend all the way to Bengal and the shores of the Great Ocean. . . . The chief trade of the inhabitants of these hills is in musk-bags, the tails of the mountain cow, saffron, lead, and copper. The natives of Hind call these hills **Sewâlik**-*Parbat*. In the language of Hind **Sawalâk** means a lak and a quarter (or 125,000), and *Parbat* means a *hill*, that is, the 125,000 hills. On these hills the snow never melts, and from some parts of Hindustán, such as Lahore, Sehrend, and Sambal, it is seen white on them all the year round."—*Baber*, p. 313.

c. 1545.—"*Sher Sháh's dying regrets.*

"On being remonstrated with for giving way to low spirits, when he had done so much for the good of the people during his short reign, after earnest solicitation, he said, 'I have had three or four desires on my heart, which still remain without accomplishment. . . . One is, I wished to have depopulated the country of Roh, and to have transferred its inhabitants to the tract between the Niláb and Lahore, including the hills below Nindūna as far as the **Siwálik**.'" — *Táríkh-Khán Jahán Lodí*, in *Elliot*, v. 107-8. Nindūna was on Balnāth, a hill over the Jelam (compare *Elliot*, ii. 450-1).

c. 1547-8. — "After their defeat the Níázís took refuge with the Ghakkars, in the hill-country bordering on Kashmír. Islám Sháh . . . during the space of two years was engaged in constant conflicts with the Ghakkars, whom he desired to subdue. . . . Skirting the hills he went thence to Múrín (?), and all the Rájás of the **Siwálik** presented themselves. . . . Parsurám, the Rájá of Gwálior, became a staunch servant of the King . . . Gwálior is a hill, which is on the right hand towards the South, amongst the hills, as you go to Kángra and Nagarkot." (See **NUGGUR-COTE**).—*Táríkh-i-Dáúdí*, in *Elliot*, iv. 493-4.

c. 1555. — "The Imperial forces encountered the Afghans near the **Siwálik** mountains, and gained a victory which elicited gracious marks of approval from the Emperor. Sikandar took refuge in the mountains and jungles. . . . Rájá Rám Chand, Rájá of Nagarkot, was the most renowned of all the Rájás of the hills, and he came and made his submission." — *Ṭabaḳát-i-Akbarí*, in *Elliot*, v. 248.

c. 1560. — "The Emperor (Akbar) then marched onwards towards the **Siwálik** hills, in pursuit of the Khán-Khánán. He reached the neighbourhood of Talwára, a district in the Siwálik, belonging to Rájá Gobind Chand. . . . A party of adventurous soldiers dashed forward into the hills, and surrounding the place put many of the defenders to the sword."—*Ibid*. 267.

c. 1570.—"Husain Khán . . . set forth from Lucknow with the design of breaking down the idols, and demolishing the idol temples. For false reports of their unbounded treasures had come to his ears. He proceeded through Oudh, towards the **Siwálik** hills. . . . He then ravaged the whole country, as far as the *Kasbah* of Wajráíl, in the country of Rájá Ranka, a powerful *zamíndár*, and from that town to Ajmír which is his capital."—*Badáúni*, in *Elliot*, iv. 497.

1594-5. — "The force marched to the **Siwálik** hills, and the *Bakhshí* resolved to begin by attacking Jammú, one of the strongest forts of that country." — *Akbar Náma*, in *Elliot*, v. 125.

c. ,, "Rám Deo . . . returned to Kanauj . . . after that he marched into the **Siwálik** hills, and made all the zamíndárs tributary. The Rájá of Kamáún . . . came out against Rám Deo and gave him battle." — *Firishta's Introduction*, in *Elliot*, vi. 561.

1793.—"Mr. Daniel, with a party, also visited Sirinagur the same year [1789]: . . . It is situated in an exceedingly deep and very narrow valley; formed by Mount **Sewalick**,* the northern boundary of Hindoostan, on the one side; and the vast range of snowy mountains of HIMMALEH or IMAUS, on the other; and from the report of the natives, it would appear, that the nearest part of the base of the latter (on which snow was actually falling in the month of May), was not more than 14 or 15 G. miles in direct distance to the N. or N.E. of Sirinagur town.

"In crossing the mountains of **Sewalick**, they met with vegetable productions, proper to the temperate climates."—*Rennell's Mem.*, ed. 1793, pp. [368-369].

d.—

1834.—"On the flank of the great range there is a line of low hills, the **Sewalik**, which commence at Roopur, on the Satlej, and run down a long way to the south, skirting the great chain. In some places they run up to, and rise upon, the Himálayas; in others, as in this neighbourhood (Seháranpur), they are separated by an intermediate valley. Between the Jumna and Ganges they attain their greatest height, which Capt. Herbert estimates at 2,000 feet above the plains at their foot, or 3,000 above the sea. Seháranpur is about 1,000 feet above the sea. About 25 miles north are the **Sewálik** hills."—*Falconer*, in *J.A.S.B.* iii. 182.

1835.—"We have named the fossil *Sivatherium* from *Siva* the Hindu god, and *θηρίον*, *bellua*. The **Siválik**, or Sub-Himalayan range of hills, is considered, in the Hindu mythology, as the *Látiah* or edge of the roof of SIVA's dwelling on the Himálaya, and hence they are called the *Siva-ala* or *Sib-ala*, which by an easy transition of sound became the **Sewálik** of the English.

"The fossil has been discovered in a tract which may be included in the **Sewálik**

* "Sewalick is the term, according to the common acceptation; but Capt. Kirkpatrick proves, from the evident etymology of it, that it should be Sewa-luck."—*Note by Rennell.*

range, and we have given the name of Sivatherium to it, to commemorate the remarkable formation, so rich in new animals. Another derivation of the name of the hills, as explained by the *Mahant*, or High Priest at Dehra, is as follows:—

"**Sewálik**, a corruption of *Siva-wála*, a name given to the tract of mountains between the Jumna and Ganges, from having been the residence of ISWARA SIVA and his son GANES."—*Falconer and Cautley*, in *As. Res.*, xix. p. 2.

1879.—"These fringing ranges of the later formations are known generally as the Sub-Himalayas. The most important being the **Siwálik** hills, a term especially applied to the hills south of the Deyra Dún, but frequently employed in a wider sense."—*Medlicott and Blanford, Man. of the Geology of India, Intro.* p. x.

[1899.—Even so late as this year the old inaccurate etymology of the word appears: "The term **Shewalic** is stated by one of the native historians to be a combination of two Hindee words '*sewa*' and '*lae*' (*sic*), the word '*sewa*' signifying one and a quarter, and the word '*lae*' being the term which expresses the number of one hundred thousand."—*Thornhill, Haunts and Hobbies*, 213.]

SKEEN, s. Tib. *skyin*. The Himalayan Ibex; (*Capra Sibirica*, Meyer). [See *Blanford, Mammalia*, 503.]

SLAVE. We cannot now attempt a history of the former tenure of slaves in British India, which would be a considerable work in itself. We only gather a few quotations illustrating that history.

1676.—"Of three Theeves, two were executed and one made a **Slave**. We do not approve of putting any to death for theft, nor that any of our own nation should be made a **Slave**, a word that becomes not an Englishman's mouth."—*The Court to Ft. St. Geo.*, March 7. In *Notes and Exts.* No. i. p. 18.

1682.—". . . making also proclamation by beat of drum that if any **Slave** would run away from us he should be free, and liberty to go where they pleased."—*Hedges, Diary*, Oct. 14; [Hak. Soc. i. 38].

[„ "There being a great number of **Slaves** yearly exported from this place, to ye great grievance of many persons whose Children are very commonly stollen away from them, by those who are constant traders in this way, the Agent, &c., considering the Scandall that might accrue to ye Government, &c:, the great losse that many parents may undergoe by such actions, have order'd that noe more **Slaves** be sent off the shoare again."—*Pringle, Diary, Ft. St. Geo.*, 1st ser. i. 70.]

1752.—"Sale of **Slaves** . . . Rs. 10 : 1 : 3."—Among Items of Revenue. In *Long*, 34.

1637.—"We have taken into consideration the most effectual and speedy method for supplying our settlements upon the West Coast with **slaves**, and we have therefore fixed upon two ships for that purpose . . . to proceed from hence to Madagascar to purchase as many as can be procured, and the said ships conveniently carry, who are to be delivered by the captains of those ships to our agents at Fort Marlborough at the rate of £15 a head."—*Court's Letter* of Dec. 8. In *Long*, 293.

1764.—"That as an inducement to the Commanders and Chief Mates to exert themselves in procuring as large a number of **Slaves** as the Ships can conveniently carry, and to encourage the Surgeons to take proper care of them in the passage, there is to be allowed 20 shillings for every **slave** shipped at Madagascar, to be divided, viz., 13s. 4d. a head to the Commander, and 6s. 8d. to the Chief Mate, also for every one delivered at Fort Marlborough the Commander is to be allowed the further sum of 6s. 8d. and the Chief Mate 3s. 4d. The Surgeon is likewise to be allowed 10s. for each **slave** landed at Fort Marlborough."—*Court's Letter*, Feb. 22. In *Long*, 366.

1778.—Mr. Busteed has given some curious extracts from the charge-sheet of the Calcutta Magistrate in this year, showing **slaves** and **slave-girls**, of Europeans, Portuguese, and Armenians, sent to the magistrate to be punished with the rattan for running away and such offences.—*Echoes of Old Calcutta*, 117 *seqq.* [Also see extracts from newspapers, &c., in *Carey, Good Old Days*, ii. 71 *seqq.*].

1782.—"On Monday the 29th inst. will be sold by auction . . . a bay Buggy Horse, a Buggy and Harness . . . some cut Diamonds, a quantity of China Sugarcandy . . . a quantity of the best Danish Claret . . . deliverable at Serampore; two **Slave Girls** about 6 years old; and a great variety of other articles."—*India Gazette*, July 27.

1785.—"Malver. Hair-dresser from Europe, proposes himself to the ladies of the settlement to dress hair daily, at two gold mohurs per month, in the latest fashion, with gauze flowers, &c. He will also instruct the **slaves** at a moderate price."—In *Seton-Karr*, i. 119. This was surely a piece of slang. Though we hear occasionally, in the advertisements of the time, of slave boys and girls, the domestic servants were not usually of that description.

1794.—"50 Rupees Reward for Discovery. "RUN OFF about four Weeks ago from a Gentleman in Bombay, A Malay **Slave** called Cambing or Rambing. He stole a Silk Purse, with 45 Venetians, and some Silver Buttons. . . ."—*Bombay Courier*, Feb. 22.

SLING, SELING, n.p. This is the name used in the Himalayan regions for a certain mart in the direction of

China which supplies various articles of trade. Its occurrence in Trade Returns at one time caused some discussion as to its identity, but there can be no doubt that it is Si-ning (Fu) in Kan-su. The name **Sling** is also applied, in Ladak and the Punjab, to a stuff of goat's wool made at the place so called.

c. 1730.—"Kokonor is also called *Tzongombo*, which means blue lake. . . . The Tibetans pretend that this lake belongs to them, and that the limits of Tibet adjoin those of the town of **Shilin** or **Shilingh**."—*P. Orazio della Penna*, E.T. in *Markham's Tibet*, 2d ed. 314.

1774.—"The natives of Kashmir, who like the Jews of Europe, or the Armenians in the Turkish Empire, scatter themselves over the Eastern kingdoms of Asia . . . have formed extensive establishments at Lhasa and all the principal towns in the country. Their agents, stationed on the coast of Coromandel, in Bengal, Benares, Nepal, and Kashmir, furnish them with the commodities of these different countries, which they dispose of in Tibet, or forward to their associates at **Seling**, a town on the borders of China."—*Bogle's Narrative*, in *Markham's Tibet*, 124.

1793.—". . . it is certain that the product of their looms (*i.e.* of Tibet and Nepaul) is as inconsiderable in quantity as it is insignificant in quality. The *Joos* (read **TOOS**) or flannel procured from the former, were it really a fabric of Tibet, would perhaps be admitted as an exception to the latter part of this observation; but the fact is that it is made at **Siling**, a place situated on the western borders of China."—*Kirkpatrick's Acc. of Nepaul* (1811), p. 134.

1854.—"*List of Chinese Articles brought to India.* . . . **Siling**, a soft and silky woollen of two kinds—1. *Shirán*. 2. *Gorán*."—*Cunningham's Ladak*, 241-2.

1862.—"**Sling** is a '*Pushmina*' (fine wool) cloth, manufactured of goat-wool, taken from Karashahr and Urumchi, and other districts of Turkish China, in a Chinese town called **Sling**."—*Punjab Trade Report*, App. p. ccxxix.

1871.—"There were two Calmucks at Yârkand, who had belonged to the suite of the Chinese Ambân. . . . Their own home they say is **Zilm**" (qu. *Zilin?*) "a country and town distant 1½ month's journey from either Aksoo or Khoten, and at an equal distance in point of time from Lhassa . . . **Zilm** possesses manufactures of carpets, horse-trappings, pen-holders, &c. . . . This account is confirmed by the fact that articles such as those described are imported occasionally into Ladâk, under the name of **Zilm** or **Zirm** goods.

"Now if the town of **Zilm** is six weeks journey from either Lhassa or Aksoo, its position may be guessed at."—*Shaw, Visits to High Tartary*, 38.

SLOTH, s. In the usual way of transferring names which belong to other regions, this name is sometimes applied in S. India to the Lemur (*Loris gracilis*, Jerdon).

SNAKE-STONE, s. This is a term applied to a substance, the application of which to the part where a snake-bite has taken effect, is supposed to draw out the poison and render it innocuous. Such applications are made in various parts of the Old and New Worlds. The substances which have this reputation are usually of a porous kind, and when they have been chemically examined have proved to be made of charred bone, or the like. There is an article in the 13th vol. of the *Asiatic Researches* by Dr. J. Davy, entitled *An Analysis of the Snake-Stone*, in which the results of the examination of three different kinds, all obtained from Sir Alex. Johnstone, Chief Justice of Ceylon, is given. (1) The first kind was of round or oval form, black or brown in the middle, white towards the circumference, polished and somewhat lustrous, and pretty enough to be sometimes worn as a neck ornament; easily cut with a knife, but not scratched by the nail. When breathed on it emitted an earthy smell, and when applied to the tongue, or other moist surface, it adhered firmly. This kind proved to be of bone partially calcined. (2) We give below a quotation regarding the second kind. (3) The third was apparently a **bezoar**, (q.v.), rather than a snake-stone. There is another article in the *As. Res.* xvi. 382 *seqq.* by Captain J. D. Herbert, on *Zehr Mohereh, or* **Snake-Stone.** Two kinds are described which were sold under the name given (*Zahr muhra*, where *zahr* is 'poison,' *muhra*, 'a kind of polished shell,' 'a bead,' applied to a species of bezoar). Both of these were mineral, and not of the class we are treating of.

c. 1666.—"C'est dans cette Ville de Diu que se font les **Pierres de Cobra** si renommées: elles sont composées de racines qu'on brûle, et dont on amasse les cendres pour les mettre avec une sorte de terre qu'ils ont, et les brûler encore une fois avec cette terre; et après cela on en fait la pâte dont ces Pierres sont formées. . . . Il faut faire sortir avec une éguille, un peu de sang de la plaie, y appliquer la Pierre, et l'y laisser jusqu'à ce qu'elle tombe d'elle même."—*Thevenot*, v. 97.

1673. — "Here are also those Elephant Legged St. *Thomeans*, which the unbiassed Enquirers will tell you chances to them two ways: By the Venom of a certain Snake, by which the *Jaugies* (see **JOGEE**) or Pilgrims furnish them with a Factitious Stone (which we call a **snake-stone**), and is a Counter-poyson of all deadly Bites; if it stick, it attracts the Poyson; and put into Milk it recovers itself again, leaving its virulency therein, discovered by its Greenness."—*Fryer*, 53.

c. 1676.—"There is the **Serpent's stone** not to be forgot, about the bigness of a *double* (doubloon?); and some are almost oval, thick in the middle and thin about the sides. The Indians report that it is bred in the head of certain Serpents. But I rather take it to be a story of the Idoloter's Priests, and that the Stone is rather a composition of certain Drugs. . . . If the Person bit be not much wounded, the place must be incis'd; and the Stone being appli'd thereto, will not fall off till it has drawn all the poison to it: To cleanse it you must steep it in Womans-milk, or for want of that, in Cows-milk. . . . There are two ways to try whether the **Serpent-stone** be true or false. The first is, by putting the Stone in your mouth, for there it will give a leap, and fix to the Palate. The other is by putting it in a glass full of water; for if the Stone be true, the water will fall a boyling, and rise in little bubbles. . . ."—*Tavernier*, E.T., Pt. ii. 155; [ed. *Ball*, ii. 152]. Tavernier also speaks of another **snake-stone** alleged to be found behind the hood of the Cobra: "This Stone being rubb'd against another Stone, yields a slime, which being drank in water," &c. &c.—*Ibid.*

1690.—"The thing which he carried . . . is a Specific against the Poison of Snakes . . . and therefore obtained the name of **Snake-stone**. It is a small artificial Stone. . . . The Composition of it is Ashes of burnt Roots, mixt with a kind of Earth, which is found at Diu. . . ."—*Ovington*, 260-261.

1712. — "**Pedra de Cobra**: ita dictus lapis, vocabulo a Lusitanis imposito, adversus viperarum morsus praestat auxilium, externè applicatus. In serpente, quod vulgò credunt, non invenitur, sed arte secretâ fabricatur à Brahmanis. Pro dextro et felici usu, oportet adesse geminos, ut cum primus veneno saturatus vulnusculo decidit, alter surrogari illico in locum possit. . . . Quo ipso feror, ut istis lapidibus nihil efficaciæ inesse credam, nisi quam actuali frigiditate suâ, vel absorbendo praestant."—*Kaempfer, Amoen. Exot.* 395-7.

1772.—"Being returned to Roode-Zand, the much celebrated **Snake-stone** (*Slangesteen*) was shown to me, which few of the farmers here could afford to purchase, it being sold at a high price, and held in great esteem. It is imported from the *Indies*, especially from Malabar, and cost several, frequently 10 or 12, rix dollars. It is round, and convex on one side, of a black colour, with a pale ash-grey speck in the middle, and tubulated with very minute pores. . . . When it is applied to any part that has been bitten by a serpent, it sticks fast to the wound, and extracts the poison; as soon as it is saturated, it falls off of itself. . . ."—*Thunberg, Travels*, E.T. i. 155 (*A Journey into Caffraria*).

1796.—"Of the remedies to which cures of venomous bites are often ascribed in India, some are certainly not less frivolous than those employed in Europe for the bite of the viper; yet to infer from thence that the effects of the poison cannot be very dangerous, would not be more rational than to ascribe the recovery of a person bitten by a **Cobra de Capello**, to the application of a **snake-stone**, or to the words muttered over the patient by a Bramin."—*Patrick Russell, Account of Indian Serpents*, 77.

1820. — "Another kind of **snake-stone** . . . was a small oval body, smooth and shining, externally black, internally grey; it had no earthy smell when breathed on, and had no absorbent or adhesive power. By the person who presented it to Sir Alexander Johnstone it was much valued, and for adequate reason if true, 'it had saved the lives of four men.'"—*Dr. Davy*, in *As. Res.* xiii. 318.

1860.—"The use of the *Pamboo-Kaloo*, or **snake-stone**, as a remedy in cases of wounds by venomous serpents, has probably been communicated to the Singhalese by the itinerant snake-charmers who resort to the island from the Coast of Coromandel; and more than one well-authenticated instance of its successful application has been told to me by persons who had been eye-witnesses." . . . (These follow.) ". . . As to the **snake-stone** itself, I submitted one, the application of which I have been describing, to Mr. Faraday, and he has communicated to me, as the result of his analysis, his belief that it is 'a piece of charred bone which has been filled with blood, perhaps several times, and then charred again.' . . . The probability is, that the animal charcoal, when instantaneously applied, may be sufficiently porous and absorbent to extract the venom from the recent wound, together with a portion of the blood, before it has had time to be carried into the system. . . ."—*Tennent, Ceylon*, i. 197-200.

1861.—"'Have you been bitten?' 'Yes, Sahib,' he replied, calmly; 'the last snake was a vicious one, and it has bitten me. But there is no danger,' he added, extracting from the recesses of his mysterious bag a small piece of white stone. This he wetted, and applied to the wound, to which it seemed to adhere . . . he apparently suffered no . . . material hurt. I was thus effectually convinced that snake-charming is a real art, and not merely clever conjuring, as I had previously imagined. These so-called **snake stones** are well known throughout India."—*Lt.-Col. T. Lewin, A Fly on the Wheel*, 91-92.

1872.—"With reference to the **snake-stones**, which, when applied to the bites, are said to absorb and suck out the poison,

. . . I have only to say that I believe they are perfectly powerless to produce any such effect . . . when we reflect on the quantity of poison, and the force and depth with and to which it is injected . . . and the extreme rapidity with which it is hurried along in the vascular system to the nerve centres, I think it is obvious that the application of one of these stones can be of little use in a real bite of a deadly snake, and that a belief in their efficacy is a dangerous delusion."—*Fayrer, Thanatophidia of India*, pp. 38, 40.

[1880.—"It is stated that in the pouch-like throat appendages of the older birds (**adjutants**), the fang of a snake is sometimes to be found. This, if rubbed above the place where a poisonous snake has bitten a man, is supposed to prevent the venom spreading to the vital parts of the body. Again, it is believed that a so-called '**snake-stone**' is contained within the head of the adjutant. This, if applied to a snake-bite, attaches itself to the punctures, and extracts all the venom. . . ."—*Ball, Jungle Life*, 82.]

SNEAKER, s. A large cup (or small basin) with a saucer and cover. The native servants call it *sīnīgar*. We had guessed that it was perhaps formed in some way from *ṣīnī* in the sense of 'china-ware,' or from the same word, used in Ar. and Pers., in the sense of 'a salver' (see **CHINA**, s.). But we have since seen that the word is not only in Grose's *Lexicon Balatronicum*, with the explanation 'a small bowl,' but is also in *Todd*: 'A small vessel of drink.' A *sneaker of punch* is a term still used in several places for a small bowl; and in fact it occurs in the *Spectator* and other works of the 18th century. So the word is of genuine English origin; no doubt of a semi-slang kind.

1714.—"Our little burlesque authors, who are the delight of ordinary readers, generally abound in these pert phrases, which have in them more vivacity than wit. I lately saw an instance of this kind of writing, which gave me so truly an idea of it, that I could not forbear begging a copy of the letter. . . .

"Past 2 o'clock and
"DEAR JACK, a frosty morning.

"I have just left the Right Worshipful and his myrmidons about a **sneaker** of 5 gallons. The whole magistracy was pretty well disguised before I gave them the slip."
The Spectator, No. 616.

1715.—
"Hugh Peters is making
A **sneaker** within
For Luther, Buchanan,
John Knox, and Calvin;
And when they have toss'd off
A brace of full bowls,
You'll swear you ne'er met
With honester souls."
Bp. Burnett's Descent into Hell. In *Political Ballads of the 17th and 18th centuries.* Annotated by *W. W. Wilkins*, 1860, ii. 172.

1743.—"Wild . . . then retired to his seat of contemplation, a night-cellar, where, without a single farthing in his pocket, he called for a **sneaker** of punch, and placing himself on a bench by himself, he softly vented the following soliloquy."—*Fielding, Jonathan Wild*, Bk. ii. ch. iv.

1772. — "He received us with great cordiality, and entreated us all, five in number, to be seated in a bungalow, where there were only two broken chairs. This compliment we could not accept of; he then ordered five **sneakers** of a mixture which he denominated punch."—Letter in *Forbes, Or. Mem.* iv. 217.

[**SNOW RUPEE**, s. A term in use in S. India, which is an excellent example of a corruption of the 'Hobson-Jobson' type. It is an Anglo-Indian corruption of the Tel. *tsanauvu*, 'authority, currency.']

SOFALA, n.p. Ar. *Sufāla*, a district and town of the East African coast, the most remote settlement towards the south made upon that coast by the Arabs. The town is in S. Lat. 20° 10′, more that 2° south of the Zambesi delta. The territory was famous in old days for the gold produced in the interior, and also for iron. It was not visited by V. da Gama either in going or returning.

c. 1150.—"This section embraces the description of the remainder of the country of **Sofāla**. . . . The inhabitants are poor, miserable, and without resources to support them except iron; of this metal there are numerous mines in the mountains of **Sofāla**. The people of the islands . . . come hither for iron, which they carry to the continent and islands of India . . . for although there is iron in the islands and in the mines of that country, it does not equal the iron of **Sofāla**."—*Edrisi*, i. 65.

c. 1220.—"**Sofāla** is the most remote known city in the country of the Zenj . . . wares are carried to them, and left by the merchants who then go away, and coming again find that the natives have laid down the price [they are willing to give] for every article beside it. . . . *Sofālī* gold is well-known among the Zenj merchants."—*Yākūt, Mu'jam al-Buldān*, s.v.

In his article on the gold country, Yākūt describes the kind of dumb trade in which the natives decline to come face to face with the merchants at greater length. It is a practice that has been ascribed to a great variety of uncivilized races; *e.g.* in various parts of Africa; in the extreme north of Europe and of Asia; in the Clove Islands; to the Veddas of Ceylon, to the Poliars of Malabar, and (by Pliny, surely under some mistake) to the Seres or Chinese. See on this subject a note in *Marco Polo*, Bk. iv. ch. 21; a note by *Mr. De B. Priaulx*, in *J. R. As. Soc.*, xviii. 348 (in which several references are erroneously printed); *Tennent's Ceylon*, i. 593 *seqq.*; *Rawlinson's Herodotus*, under Bk. iv. ch. 196.

c. 1330.—"**Sofāla** is situated in the country of the Zenj. According to the author of the *Kānūn*, the inhabitants are Muslim. Ibn Sayd says that their chief means of subsistence are the extraction of gold and of iron, and that their clothes are of leopard-skin."—*Abulfeda*, Fr. Tr. i. 222.

" "A merchant told me that the town of **Sofāla** is a half month's march distant from Culua (**Quiloa**), and that from **Sofāla** to Yūfī (Nūfī) . . . is a month's march. From Yūfī they bring gold-dust to **Sofāla**."—*Ibn Batuta*, ii. 192-3.

1499.—"Coming to Moçambique (*i.e.* Vasco and his squadron on their return) they did not desire to go in because there was no need, so they kept their course, and being off the coast of **Çofala**, the pilots warned the officers that they should be alert and ready to strike sail, and at night they should keep their course, with little sail set, and a good look-out, for just thereabouts there was a river belonging to a place called **Çofala**, whence there sometimes issued a tremendous squall, which tore up trees and carried cattle and all into the sea. . . ."—*Correa, Lendas*, i. 134-135.

1516.—". . . at xviii. leagues from them there is a river, which is not very large, whereon is a town of the Moors called **Sofala**, close to which town the King of Portugal has a fort. These Moors established themselves there a long time ago on account of the great trade in gold, which they carry on with the Gentiles of the mainland."—*Barbosa*, 4.

1523.—"Item—that as regards all the ships and goods of the said Realm of Urmuz, and its ports and vassals, they shall be secure by land and by sea, and they shall be as free to navigate where they please as vassals of the King our lord, save only that they shall not navigate inside the Strait of Mecca, nor yet to **Çoffala** and the ports of that coast, as that is forbidden by the King our lord. . . ."—Treaty of *Dom Duarto de Menezes*, with the *King of Ormuz*, in *Botelho, Tombo*, 80.

1553.—"Vasco da Gama . . . was afraid that there was some gulf running far inland, from which he would not be able to get out. And this apprehension made him so careful to keep well from the shore that he passed without even seeing the town of **Çofala**, so famous in these parts for the quantity of gold which the Moors procured there from the Blacks of the country by trade. . . ."—*Barros*, I. iv. 3.

1572.—
". . . Fizemos desta costa algum desvio
Deitando para o pégo toda a armada:
Porque, ventando Noto manso e frio,
Não nos apanhasse a agua da enseada,
Que a costa faz alli daquella banda,
Donde a rica **Sofala** o ouro manda."
Camões, v. 73.

By Burton:
"off from the coast-line for a spell we stood,
till deep blue water 'neath our kelsons lay;
for frigid Notus, in his fainty mood,
was fain to drive us leewards to the Bay
made in that quarter by the crookèd shore,
whence rich **Sofála** sendeth golden ore."

1665.—
"Mombaza and Quiloa and Melind,
And **Sofala**, thought Ophir, to the realm
Of Congo, and Angola farthest south."
Paradise Lost, xi. 399 *seqq.*

Milton, it may be noticed, misplaces the accent, reading *Sófala*.

1727.—"Between *Delagoa* and *Mosambique* is a dangerous Sea-coast, it was formerly known by the names of **Suffola** and *Cuama*, but now by the *Portuguese*, who know that country best, is called *Sena*."—*A. Hamilton*, i. 8 [ed. 1744].

SOLA, vulg. **SOLAR**, s. This is properly Hind. *sholā*, corrupted by the Bengālī inability to utter the shibboleth, to *solā*, and often again into *solar* by English people, led astray by the usual "striving after meaning." *Sholā* is the name of the plant *Aeschynomene aspera*, L. (N.O. *Leguminosae*), and is particularly applied to the light pith of that plant, from which the light thick Sola **topees**, or pith hats, are made. The material is also used to pad the roofs of palankins, as a protection against the sun's power, and for various minor purposes, *e.g.* for slips of tinder, for making models, &c. The word, until its wide diffusion within the last 45 years, was peculiar to the Bengal Presidency. In the Deccan the thing is called *bhend*, Mahr. *bhenda*, and in Tamil. *netti*, ['breaking with a crackle.'] **Solar** hats are now often advertised in London. [Hats made of elder pith were used in S. Europe in the early 16th century. In Albert Dürer's *Diary in the Netherlands* (1520-21) we find: "Also Tomasin has given me a plaited hat of elder-pith" (*Mrs. Heaton, Life of Albrecht Dürer*, 269). Miss Eden, in 1839, speaks of Europeans wearing "broad white feather hats to keep off the sun" (*Up the Country*, ii. 56).

Illustrations of the various shapes of Sola hats used in Bengal about 1854 will be found in *Grant, Rural Life in Bengal*, 105 *seq.*]

1836.—"I stopped at a fisherman's, to look at the curiously-shaped floats he used for his very large and heavy fishing-nets; each float was formed of eight pieces of **sholā**, tied together by the ends. . . . When this light and spongy pith is wetted, it can be cut into thin layers, which pasted together are formed into hats; Chinese paper appears to be made of the same material."—*Wanderings of a Pilgrim*, ii. 100.

1872.—"In a moment the flint gave out a spark of fire, which fell into the **solá**; the sulphur match was applied; and an earthen lamp. . . ."—*Govinda Samanta*, i. 10.

1878.—"My **solar** topee (pith hat) was whisked away during the struggle."—*Life in the Mofussil*, i. 164.

1885.—"I have slipped a pair of galoshes over my ordinary walking-boots; and, with my **solar topee** (or sun helmet) on, have ridden through a mile of deserted streets and thronged bazaars, in a grilling sunshine."—*A Professional Visit in Persia, St. James's Gazette*, March 9.

[**SOMBA, SOMBAY**, s. A present. Malay *sambah-an*.

[1614.—"**Sombay** or presents."—*Foster, Letters*, ii. 112.

[1615.—". . . concluded rather than pay the great **Somba** of eight hundred reals."—*Ibid.* iv. 43.]

SOMBRERO, s. Port. *sumbreiro*. In England we now understand by this word a broad-brimmed hat; but in older writers it is used for an *umbrella*. **Summerhead** is a name in the Bombay Arsenal (as M.-Gen. Keatinge tells me) for a great umbrella. I make no doubt that it is a corruption (by 'striving after meaning') of **Sombreiro**, and it is a capital example of **Hobson-Jobson**.

1503.—"And the next day the Captain-Major before daylight embarked armed with all his people in the boats, and the King (of Cochin) in his boats which they call *tones* (see **DONEY**) . . . and in the *tone* of the King went his **Sombreiros**, which are made of straw, of a diameter of 4 palms, mounted on very long canes, some 3 or 4 fathoms in height. These are used for state ceremonial, showing that the King is there in person, as it were his pennon or royal banner, for no other lord in his realm may carry the like."—*Correa*, i. 378.

1516.—"And besides the page I speak of who carries the sword, they take another page who carries a **sombreiro** with a stand to shade his master, and keep the rain off him; and some of these are of silk stuff finely wrought, with many fringes of gold, and set with stones and seed pearl. . . ."—*Barbosa*, Lisbon ed. 298.

1553.—"At this time Dom Jorge discerned a great body of men coming towards where he was standing, and amid them a **sombreiro** on a lofty staff, covering the head of a man on horseback, by which token he knew it to be some noble person. This **sombreiro** is a fashion in India coming from China, and among the Chinese no one may use it but a gentleman, for it is a token of nobility, which we may describe as a one-handed *pallium* (having regard to those which we use to see carried by four, at the reception of some great King or Prince on his entrance into a city). . . ."—*Barros*, III. x. 9. Then follows a minute description of the **sombreiro** or **umbrella**.

[1599.—". . . a great broad **sombrero** or shadow in their hands to defend them in the Summer from the Sunne, and in the Winter from the Raine."—*Hakl.* II. i. 261 (*Stanf. Dict.*).

[1602.—In his character of D. Pedro Mascarenhas, the Viceroy, Couto says he was anxious to change certain habits of the Portuguese in India: "One of these was to forbid the tall **sombreiros** for warding off the rain and sun, to relieve men of the expence of paying those who carried them; he himself did not have one, but used a woollen umbrella with small cords (?), which they called for many years *Mascarenhas*. Afterwards finding the sun intolerable and the rain immoderate, he permitted the use of tall umbrellas, on the condition that private slaves should bear them, to save the wages of the Hindus who carry them, and are called **boys de sombreiro** (see **BOY**)."—*Couto*, Dec. VII. Bk. i. ch. 12.]

c. 1630.—"Betwixt towns men usually travel in Chariots drawn by Oxen, but in Towns upon **Palamkeens**, and with **Sombreros** *de Sol* over them."—*Sir T. Herbert*, ed. 1665, p. 46.

1657.—"A costé du cheval il y a un homme qui esvente *Wistnou*, afin qu'il ne reçoive point d'incommodité soit par les mouches, ou par la chaleur; et à chaque costé on porte deux **Zombreiros**, afin que le Soleil ne luise pas sur luy. . . ."—*Abr. Roger*, Fr. Tr. ed. 1670, p. 223.

1673.—"None but the Emperor have a **Sumbrero** among the *Moguls*."—*Fryer*, 36.

1727.—"The *Portuguese* ladies . . . sent to beg the Favour that he would pick them out some lusty *Dutch* men to carry their *Palenqueens* and **Somereras** or **Umbrellas**."—*A. Hamilton*, i. 338; [ed. 1744, i. 340].

1768-71.—"Close behind it, followed the heir-apparent, on foot, under a **sambreel**, or sunshade, of state."—*Stavorinus*, E.T. i. 87.

[1845.—"No open umbrellas or **summerheads** allowed to pass through the gates."—*Public Notice on Gates of Bombay Town*, in *Douglas, Glimpses of Old Bombay*, 86.]

SOMBRERO, CHANNEL OF THE, n.p. The channel between the northern part of the Nicobar group, and the southern part embracing the Great and Little Nicobar, has had this name since the early Portuguese days. The origin of the name is given by A. Hamilton below. The indications in C. Federici and Hamilton are probably not accurate. They do not agree with those given by Horsburgh.

1566.—"Si passa per il canale di Nicubar, ouero per quello del **Sombrero**, li quali son per mezzo l'isola di Sumatra. . . ."—*C. Federici*, in *Ramusio*, iii. 391.

1727.—"The Islands off this Part of the Coast are the *Nicobars*. . . . The northernmost Cluster is low, and are called the *Carnicubars*. . . . The middle Cluster is fine champain Ground, and all but one, well inhabited. They are called the **Somerera** Islands, because on the South End of the largest Island, is an Hill that resembleth the top of an Umbrella or **Somerera**."—*A. Hamilton*, ii. 68 [ed. 1744].

1843.—"**Sombrero Channel**, bounded on the north by the Islands of Katchull and Noncowry, and by Merve or Passage Island on the South side, is very safe and about seven leagues wide."—*Horsburgh*, ed. 1843, ii. 59-60.

SONAPARANTA, n.p. This is a quasi-classical name, of Indian origin, used by the Burmese Court in State documents and formal enumerations of the style of the King, to indicate the central part of his dominions; Skt. *Suvarna* (Pali *Sona*) *prānta* (or perhaps *aparānta*), 'golden frontier-land,' or something like that. There can be little doubt that it is a survival of the names which gave origin to the *Chrysē* of the Greeks. And it is notable, that the same series of titles embraces *Tambadīpa* ('Copper Island' or Region) which is also represented by the *Chalcitis* of Ptolemy. [Also see J. G. Scott, *Upper Burma Gazetteer*, i. pt. i. 103.]

(Ancient). — "There were two brothers resident in the country called **Sunáparanta**, merchants who went to trade with 500 wagons. . . ."—*Legends of Gotama Buddha*, in *Hardy's Manual of Buddhism*, 259.

1636.—"All comprised within the great districts . . . of Tsa-Koo, Tsa-lan, Laygain, Phoung-len, Kalé, and Thoung-thwot is constituted the Kingdom of **Thuna-paranta**. All within the great districts of Pagán, Ava, Penya, and Myen-Zain, is constituted the Kingdom of **Tampadewa**. . . ." (&c.)—From an *Inscription at the Great Pagoda* of Khoug-Mhoo-dau, near Ava; from the *MS. Journal of Major H. Burney*, accompanying a Letter from him, dated 11th September, 1830, in the Foreign Office, Calcutta. Burney adds: "The Ministers told me that by **Thunaparanta** they mean all the countries to the northward of Ava, and by **Tampadewa** all to the southward. But this inscription shows that the Ministers themselves do not exactly understand what countries are comprised in **Thunaparanta** and **Tāmpa-dewa**."

1767.—"The King despotick; of great Merit, of great Power, Lord of the Countries **Thonaprondah**, **Tompdevah**, and **Camboja**, Sovereign of the Kingdom of BURAGHMAGH (**Burma**), the Kingdom of **Siam** and Hughen (?), and the Kingdom of **Cassay**."—Letter from the *King of Burma*, in *Dalrymple*, *Or. Rep.* i. 106.

1795.—"The Lord of Earth and Air, the Monarch of extensive Countries, the Sovereign of the Kingdoms of **Sonahparindá**, **Tombadeva**. . . . etc. . . ."—Letter from *the King* to *Sir John Shore*, in *Symes*, 487.

1855. — "His great, glorious and most excellent Majesty, who reigns over the Kingdoms of **Thunaparanta**, **Tampadeeva**, and all the great umbrella-wearing chiefs of the Eastern countries, the King of the Rising Sun, Lord of the Celestial Elephants, and Master of many white Elephants, and great Chief of Righteousness. . . ."—*King's* Letter to the *Governor-General* (Lord Dalhousie), Oct. 2, 1855.

SONTHALS, n.p. Properly *Santāls*, [the name being said to come from a place called *Saont*, now Silda in Mednipur, where the tribe remained for a long time (*Dalton*, *Descr. Eth.* 210-11)]. The name of a non-Aryan people belonging to the Kolarian class, extensively settled in the hilly country to the west of the Hoogly R. and to the south of Bhāgalpur, from which they extended to Balasore at interval, sometimes in considerable masses, but more generally much scattered. The territory in which they are chiefly settled is now formed into a separate district called Santāl Parganas, and sometimes *Santalia*. Their settlement in this tract is, however, quite modern; they have emigrated thither from the S.W. In Dr. F. Buchanan's statistical account of Bhāgalpur and its Hill people the Santāls are not mentioned. The earliest mention of this tribe that we have found is in Mr. Sutherland's Report on the Hill People, which is printed in the Appendix to Long. No date is given there, but we learn from Mr. Man's book, quoted below, that the date is 1817. [The word is, however, much older than this. Forbes (*Or. Mem.* ii. 374 *seq.*) gives an account taken from Lord Teignmouth of witch tests among the **Soontaar**.

[1798.—". . . amongst a wild and unlettered tribe, denominated **Soontaar**, who have reduced the detection and trial of persons suspected of witchcraft to a system."—*As. Res.* iv. 359.]

1817.—"For several years many of the industrious tribes called **Sonthurs** have established themselves in these forests, and have been clearing and bringing into cultivation large tracts of lands. . . ."—*Sutherland's Report*, quoted in *Long*, 569.

1867.—"This system, indicated and proposed by Mr. Eden,* was carried out in its integrity under Mr. George Yule, C.B., by whose able management, with Messrs. Robinson and Wood as his deputies, the **Sonthals** were raised from misery, dull despair, and deadly hatred of the government, to a pitch of prosperity which, to my knowledge, has never been equalled in any other part of India under the British rule. The Regulation Courts, with their horde of leeches in the shape of badly paid, and corrupt Amlah (**Omlah**) and pettifogging **Mooktears**, were abolished, and in their place a Number of active English gentlemen, termed Assistant Commissioners, and nominated by Mr. Yule, were set down among the **Sonthals**, with a Code of Regulations drawn up by that gentleman, the pith of which may be summed up as follows:—

"'To have no medium between the **Sonthal** and the **Hakim**, *i.e.* Assistant Commissioner.

"'To patiently hear any complaint made by the **Sonthal** from his own mouth, without any written petition or charge whatever, and without any **Amlah** or Court at the time.

"'To carry out all criminal work by the aid of the villagers themselves, who were to bring in the accused, with the witnesses, to the **Hakim**, who should immediately attend to their statements, and punish them, if found guilty, according to the tenor of the law.'

"These were some of the most important of the golden rules carried out by men who recognised the responsibility of their situation; and with an adored chief, in the shape of Yule, for their ruler, whose firm, judicious, and gentlemanly conduct made them work with willing hearts, their endeavours were crowned with a success which far exceeded the expectations of the most sanguine. . . ."—*Sonthalia and the Sonthals*, by *E. G. Man*, Barrister-at-Law, &c. Calcutta, 1867, pp. 125-127.

SOODRA, SOODER, s. Skt. *śudra*, [usually derived from root. *śuć*, 'to be afflicted,' but probably of non-Aryan origin]. The (theoretical) Fourth Caste of the Hindus. In South India, there being no claimants of the 2nd or 3rd classes, the highest castes among the (so-called) *Śudras* come next after the Brahmans in social rank, and *śudra* is a note of respect, not of the contrary as in Northern India.

1630.—"The third Tribe or Cast, called the **Shudderies**."—*Lord, Display*, &c., ch. xii.

1651.—"La quatrième lignée est celle des **Soudraes**; elle est composée du commun peuple: cette lignée a sous soy beaucoup et diverses familles, dont une chacune prétend surpasser l'autre. . . ."—*Abr. Roger*, Fr. ed. 1670, p. 8.

[c. 1665.—"The fourth caste is called **Charados or Soudra**."—*Tavernier*, ed. *Ball*, ii. 184.

[1667.—". . . and fourthly, the tribe of **Seydra**, or artisans and labourers."—*Bernier*, ed. *Constable*, 325.]

1674.—"The . . . **Chudrer** (these are the Nayres)."—*Faria y Sousa*, ii. 710.

1717.—"The Brahmens and the **Tschuddirers** are the proper persons to satisfy your Enquiries."—*Phillips, An Account of the Religion*, &c., 14.

1858.—"Such of the Aborigines as yet remained were formed into a fourth class, the **Çudra**, a class which has no rights, but only duties."—*Whitney, Or. and Ling. Studies*, ii. 6.

1867.—"A Brahman does not stand aloof from a **Soudra** with a keener pride than a Greek Christian shows towards a Copt."—*Dixon, New America*, 7th ed. i. 276.

SOOJEE, SOOJY, s. Hind. *sūjī*, [which comes probably from Skt. *śuci*, 'pure']; a word curiously misinterpreted ("the coarser part of pounded wheat") by the usually accurate Shakespear. It is, in fact, the fine flour, made from the heart of the wheat, used in India to make bread for European tables. It is prepared by grinding between two millstones which are not in close contact. [*Sūjī* "is a granular meal obtained by moistening the grain overnight, then grinding it. The fine flour passes through a coarse sieve, leaving the **Suji** and bran above. The latter is got rid of by winnowing, and the round, granular meal or **Suji**, composed of the harder pieces of the grain, remains" (*Watt. Econ. Dict.* VI. pt. iv. 167).] It is the *semolina* of Italy. Bread made from this was called in Low Latin *simella*; Germ. *Semmelbrödchen*, and old English *simnel*-cakes. A kind of porridge made with *soojee*

* This is apparently a mistake. The proposals were certainly original with Mr. Yule.

is often called *soojee* simply. (See **ROLONG**.)

1810.—"Bread is not made of flour, but of the heart of the wheat, which is very fine, ground into what is called **soojy**. . . . **Soojy** is frequently boiled into 'stirabout' for breakfast, and eaten with milk, salt, and butter; though some of the more zealous may be seen to moisten it with porter."—*Williamson, V.M.* ii. 135-136.

1878.—"**Sujee** flour, ground coarse, and water."—*Life in the Mofussil*, i. 213.

SOORKY, s. Pounded brick used to mix with lime to form a hydraulic mortar. Hind. from Pers. *surkhī*, 'red-stuff.'

c. 1770.—"The terrace roofs and floors of the rooms are laid with fine pulverized stones, which they call **zurkee**; these are mixed up with lime-water, and an inferior kind of molasses, and in a short time grow as hard and as smooth, as if the whole were one large stone."—*Stavorinus*, E.T. i. 514.

1777.—"The inquiry verified the information. We found a large group of miserable objects confined by order of Mr. Mills; some were simply so; some under sentence from him to beat **Salkey**."—*Report of Impey and others*, quoted in *Stephen's Nuncomar and Impey*, ii. 201.

1784.—"One lack of 9-inch bricks, and about 1400 maunds of **soorky**."—*Notifn.* in *Seton-Karr*, i. 34; see also ii. 15.

1811.—"The road from Calcutta to Baracpore . . . like all the Bengal roads it is paved with bricks, with a layer of **sulky**, or broken bricks over them."—*Solvyns, Les Hindous*, iii. The word is misused as well as miswritten here. The substance in question is **khoa** (q.v.).

SOORMA, s. Hind. from Pers. *surma*. Sulphuret of antimony, used for the purpose of darkening the eyes, *kuḥl* of the Arabs, the *stimmi* and *stibium* of the ancients. With this Jezebel "painted her eyes" (2 *Kings*, ix. 30; *Jeremiah*, iv. 30 R.V.) "With it, I believe, is often confounded the sulphuret of lead, which in N. India is called *soormee* (*ee* is the feminine termination in Hindust.), and used as a substitute for the former: a mistake not of recent occurrence only, as Sprengel says, '*Distinguit vero Plinius marem a feminâ*'" (*Royle*, on *Ant. of Hindu Medicine*, 100). [See *Watt. Econ. Dict.* i. 271.]

[1766.—"The powder is called by them **surma**; which they pretend refreshes and cools the eye, besides exciting its lustre, by the ambient blackness."—*Grose*, 2nd ed. ii. 142.]

[1829.—"**Soorma**, or the oxide of antimony, is found on the western frontier."—*Tod, Annals*, Calcutta reprint, i. 13.

[1832.—"**Sulmah**—A prepared permanent black dye, from antimony. . . . ."—*Mrs. Meer Hassan Ali, Observations*, ii. 72.]

SOOSIE, s. Hind. from Pers. *sūsī*. Some kind of silk cloth, but we know not what kind. [Sir G. Birdwood (*Industr. Arts*, 246) defines *sūsīs* as "fine-coloured cloths, made chiefly at Battala and Sialkote, striped in the direction of the warp with silk, or cotton lines of a different colour, the cloth being called *dokanni* [*dokhānī*], 'in two stripes' if the stripe has two lines, if three, *tinkanni* [*tīnkhānī*], and so on." In the Punjab it is 'a striped stuff used for women's trousers. This is made of fine thread, and is one of the fabrics in which English thread is now largely used' (*Francis, Mon. on Cotton Manufactures*, 7). A silk fabric of the same name is made in the N.W.P., where it is classed as a variety of *chārkhāna*, or check (*Yusuf Ali, Mon. on Silk*, 93). Forbes Watson (*Textile Manufactures*, 85) speaks of *Sousee* as chiefly employed for trousering, being a mixture of cotton and silk. The word seems to derive its origin from *Susa*, the Biblical *Shushan*, the capital of Susiana or Elam, and from the time of Darius I. the chief residence of the Achaemenian kings. There is ample evidence to show that fabrics from Babylon were largely exported in early times. Such was perhaps the "Babylonish garment" found at Ai (*Josh.* vii. 21), which the R.V. marg. translates as a "mantle of Shinar"). This a writer in Smith's *Dict. of the Bible* calls "robes trimmed with valuable furs, or the skins themselves ornamented with embroidery" (i. 452). These Babylonian fabrics have been often described (see *Layard, Nineveh and Babylon*, 537; *Maspero, Dawn of Civ.*, 470, 758; *Encycl. Bibl.* ii. 1286 *seq.*; *Frazer, Pausanias*, iii. 545 *seq.*). An early reference to this old trade in costly cloths will be found in the quotation from the *Periplus* under **CHINA**, which has been discussed by Sir H. Yule (*Introd.* to *Gill, River of Golden Sand*, ed. 1883, p. 88 *seq.*). This *Sūsī* cloth appears in a log of 1746 as **Soacie**, and was known to the Portuguese in 1550 as **Soajes** (*J. R. As. Soc.*, Jan. 1900, p. 158.)]

[1667.—" . . . 2 patch of ye finest with what colours you thinke handsome for my own wear Chockoles and **susaes**."—In *Yule, Hedges' Diary*, Hak. Soc. ii. cclxii.

[1690.—" It (Suratt) is renown'd . . . for **Sooseys**. . . ."—*Ovington*, 218.

[1714-20.—In an inventory of Sir J. Fellowes: "A **Susa** window-curtain." — 2nd ser. *N. & Q.* vi. 244.]

1784. — " Four cassimeers of different colours; Patna dimity, and striped **Soosies**." —In *Seton-Karr*, i. 42.

SOPHY, n.p. The name by which the King of Persia was long known in Europe—"The *Sophy*," as the Sultan of Turkey was "The Turk" or "Grand Turk," and the King of Delhi the "Great Mogul." This title represented *Sūfī, Safavī*, or *Safī*, the name of the dynasty which reigned over Persia for more than two centuries (1449-1722, nominally to 1736). The first king of the family was Isma'il, claiming descent from 'Ali and the Imāms, through a long line of persons of saintly reputation at Ardebil. The surname of Sūfī or Safī assumed by Isma'il is generally supposed to have been taken from Shaikh Safī-ud-dīn, the first of his more recent ancestors to become famous, and who belonged to the class of Sūfīs or philosophic devotees. After Isma'il the most famous of the dynasty was Shāh Abbās (1585-1629).

c. 1524.—"Susiana, quae est Shushan Palatium illud regni **Sophii**."—*Abraham Peritsol*, in *Hyde, Syntagma Dissertt.* i. 76.

1560.—"De que o **Sufi** foy contente, e mandou gente em su ajuda."—*Terceiro*, ch. i.

" "Quae regiones nomine Persiae ei regnantur quem Turcae *Chislibas*, nos **Sophi** vocamus."—*Busbeq. Epist.* iii. (171).

1561.—"The Queenes Maiesties *Letters to the great* **Sophy** *of Persia, sent by* M. Anthonie Ienkinson.

"Elizabetha Dei gratia Angliae Franciae et Hiberinae Regina, &c. Potentissimo et inuictissimo Principi, Magno **Sophi** Persarum, Medorum, Hircanorum, Carmanorum, Margianorum, populorum cis et vltra Tygrim fluuium, et omnium intra Mare Caspium et Persicum Sinum nationum atque Gentium Imperatori salutem et rerum prosperarum foelicissimum incrementum."—In *Hakl.* i. 381.

[1568.—"The King of Persia (whom here we call the great **Sophy**) is not there so called, but is called the Shaugh. It were dangerous to call him by the name of **Sophy**, because that **Sophy** in the Persian tongue is a beggar, and it were as much as to call him The great beggar."—*Geffrey Ducket, ibid.* i. 447.]

1598.—"And all the Kings continued so with the name of Xa, which in Persia is a King, and Ishmael is a proper name, whereby Xa Ismael, and Xa Thamas are as much as to say King Ismael, and King Thamas, and of the Turkes and Rumes are called **Suffy** or **Soffy**, which signifieth a great Captaine." — *Linschoten*, ch. xxvii.; [Hak. Soc. i. 173].

1601.—

"*Sir Toby.* Why, man, he's a very devil: I have not seen such a firago . . .

"They say, he has been fencer to the **Sophy**."—*Twelfth Night*, III. iv.

[c. 1610.—"This King or **Sophy**, who is called the Great Chaa."—*Pyrard de Laval*, Hak. Soc. ii. 253.]

1619.—"Alla porta di Sciah **Sofi**, si sonarono nacchere tutto il giorno: ed insomma tutta la città e tutto il popolo andò in allegrezza, concorrendo infinita gente alla meschita di Schia **Sofi**, a far *Gratiarum actionem*."—*P. della Valle*, i. 808.

1626.—

" Were it to bring the Great Turk bound in chains
Through France in triumph, or to couple up
The **Sophy** and great Prester-John together;
I would attempt it."
Beaum. & Fletch., The Noble Gentleman, v. 1.

c. 1630.—"Ismael at his Coronation proclaim'd himself King of *Persia* by the name of *Pot-shaw* (**Padshaw**)-*Ismael*-**Sophy**. Whence that word **Sophy** was borrowed is much controverted. Whether it be from the Armenian idiom, signifying Wooll, of which the Shashes are made that ennobled his new order. Whether the name was from **Sophy** his grandsire, or from the Greek word *Sophos* imposed upon *Aydar* at his conquest of *Trebizond* by the Greeks there, I know not. Since then, many have called the Kings of Persia **Sophy's**: but I see no reason for it; since *Ismael's* son, grand and great grandsons Kings of *Persia* never continued that name, till this that now reigns, whose name indeed is *Soffee*, but casuall."—*Sir T. Herbert*, ed. 1638, 286.

1643.—"Y avoit vn Ambassadeur Persien qui auoit esté enuoyé en Europe de la part du Grand **Sophy** Roy de Perse."—*Mocquet, Voyages*, 269.

1665.—

" As when the Tartar from his Russian foe,
By Astracan, over the snowy plains
Retires; or Bactrian **Sophy**, from the horns
Of Turkish crescent, leaves all waste beyond
The realm of Aladule, in his retreat
To Tauris or Casbeen. . . ."
Paradise Lost, x. 431 *seqq.*

1673.—"But the **Suffee's** Vicar-General is by his Place the Second Person in the Empire, and always the first Minister of State."—*Fryer* 338.

1681.—"La quarta parte comprehende el Reyno de Persia, cuyo Señor se llama en estos tiempos, el Gran **Sophi**."—*Martinez, Compendio*, 6.

1711.—"In Consideration of the Company's good Services . . . they had half of the Customs of *Gombroon* given them, and their successors, by a Firman from the **Sophi** or Emperor."—*Lockyer*, 220.

1727.—"The whole Reign of the last **Sophi** or King, was managed by such Vermin, that the *Ballowches* and *Mackrans* . . . threw off the Yoke of Obedience first, and in full Bodies fell upon their Neighbours in *Caramania*."—*A. Hamilton*, i. 108; [ed. 1744, i. 105].

1815.—"The **Suffavean** monarchs were revered and deemed holy on account of their descent from a saint."—*Malcolm, H. of Pers.* ii. 427.

1828.—"It is thy happy destiny to follow in the train of that brilliant star whose light shall shed a lustre on Persia, unknown since the days of the earlier **Soofees**."—*J. B. Fraser, The Kuzzilbash*, i. 192.

SOUBA, SOOBAH, s. Hind. from Pers. *ṣūba*. A large Division or Province of the Mogul Empire (*e.g.* the *Ṣūbah* of the Deccan, the *Ṣūbah* of Bengal). The word is also frequently used as short for *Sūbadār* (see **SOUBADAR**), 'the Viceroy' (over a *ṣūba*). It is also "among the Marathas sometimes applied to a smaller division comprising from 5 to 8 *ṭarafs*" (*Wilson*).

c. 1594.—"In the fortieth year of his majesty's reign, his dominions consisted of 105 **Sircars**. . . . The empire was then parcelled into 12 grand divisions, and each was committed to the government of a **Soobadar** . . . upon which occasion the Sovereign of the world distributed 12 Lacks of beetle. The names of the **Soobahs** were Allahabad, Agra, Owdh, Ajmeer, Ahmedabad, Bahar, Bengal, Dehly, Cabul, Lahoor, Multan, and Malwa: when his majesty conquered Berar, Khandeess, and Ahmednagur, they were formed into three **Soobahs**, increasing the number to 15."—*Ayeen*, ed. *Gladwin*, ii. 1-5; [ed. *Jarrett*, ii. 115].

1753.—"Princes of this rank are called **Subahs**. *Nizam al muluck* was **Subah** of the *Decan* (or Southern) provinces. . . . The Nabobs of *Condanore, Cudapah, Carnatica, Yalore*, &c., the Kings of *Tritchinopoly, Mysore, Tanjore*, are subject to this **Subah**ship. Here is a subject ruling a larger empire than any in Europe, excepting that of the Muscovite."—*Orme, Fragments*, 398-399.

1760.—"Those Emirs or Nabobs, who govern great Provinces, are stiled **Subahs**, which imports the same as Lord-Lieutenants or Vice-Roys."—*Memoirs of the Revolution in Bengal*, p. 6.

1763.—"From the word **Soubah**, signifying a province, the Viceroy of this vast territory (the Deccan) is called **Soubahdar**, and by the Europeans improperly **Soubah**."—*Orme*, i. 35.

1765.—"Let us have done with this ringing of changes upon **Soubahs**; there's no end to it. Let us boldly dare to be **Soubah** ourselves. . . ."—*Holwell, Hist. Events*, &c., i. 183.

1783.—"They broke their treaty with him, in which they stipulated to pay 400,000*l.* a year to the **Subah** of Bengal."—*Burke's Speech on Fox's India Bill, Works*, iii. 468.

1804.—"It is impossible for persons to have behaved in a more shuffling manner than the **Soubah's** servants have. . . ."—*Wellington*, ed. 1837, iii. 11.

1809.—"These (pillars) had been removed from a sacred building by Monsieur Dupleix, when he assumed the rank of **Soubah**."—*Lord Valentia*, i. 373.

1823.—"The Delhi Sovereigns whose vast empire was divided into **Soubahs**, or Governments, each of which was ruled by a **Soubahdar** or Viceroy."—*Malcolm, Cent. India*, i. 2.

SOUBADAR, SUBADAR, s. Hind. from Pers. *ṣūbadār*, 'one holding a *ṣūba*' (see **SOUBA**).

a. The Viceroy, or Governor of a *ṣūba*.

b. A local commandant or chief officer.

c. The chief native officer of a company of Sepoys; under the original constitution of such companies, its actual captain.

a. See **SOUBA**.

b.—

1673.—"The **Subidar** of the Town being a Person of Quality . . . he (the Ambassador) thought good to give him a Visit."—*Fryer*, 77.

1805.—"The first thing that the **Subidar** of Vire Rajendra Pettah did, to my utter astonishment, was to come up and give me such a shake by the hand, as would have done credit to a Scotsman."—Letter in *Leyden's Life*, 49.

c.—

1747.—"14th September . . . Read the former from Tellicherry adviseing that . . . in a day or two they shall despatch another **Subidar** with 129 more Sepoys to our assistance."—MS. *Consultations at Fort St. David*, in *India Office*.

1760.—"One was the **Subahdar**, equivalent to the Captain of a Company."—*Orme*, iii. 610.

c. 1785.—". . . the **Subahdars** or commanding officers of the black troops."—*Carraccioli, L. of Clive*, iii. 174.

1787.—"A Troop of Native Cavalry on the present Establishment consists of 1 European Subaltern, 1 European Serjeant, 1 **Subidar**, 3 **Jemadars**, 4 **Havildars**, 4 Naiques (**naik**), 1 Trumpeter, 1 Farrier, and 68 Privates."—*Regns. for the Hon. Comp.'s Black Troops on the Coast of Coromandel*, &c., p. 6.

[**SOUDAGUR**, s. P.—H. *saudāgar*, Pers. *saudā*, 'goods for sale'; a merchant, trader; now very often applied to those who sell European goods in civil stations and cantonments.

[1608.—". . . and kill the merchants (**sodagares** mercadores)."—*Livras das Monções*, i. 183.

[c. 1809.—"The term **Soudagur**, which implies merely a principal merchant, is here (Behar) usually given to those who keep what the English of India call **Europe** shops; that is, shops where all sorts of goods imported from Europe, and chiefly consumed by Europeans, are retailed."—*Buchanan, Eastern India*, i. 375.

[c. 1817.—"This sahib was a very rich man, a **Soudagur**. . . ."—*Mrs. Sherwood, Last Days of Boosy*, 84.]

SOURSOP, s.

a. The fruit *Anona muricata*, L., a variety of the **Custard apple**. This kind is not well known on the Bengal side of India, but it is completely naturalised at Bombay. The terms *soursop* and *sweetsop* are, we believe, West Indian.

b. In a note to the passage quoted below, Grainger identifies the *soursop* with the *suirsack* of the Dutch. But in this, at least as regards use in the East Indies, there is some mistake. The latter term, in old Dutch writers on the East, seems always to apply to the Common **Jack** fruit, the 'sourjack,' in fact, as distinguished from the superior kinds, especially the *champada* of the Malay Archipelago.

a.—

1764.—

". . . a neighbouring hill
Which Nature to the **Soursop** had resigned."
Grainger, Bk. 2.

b.—

1659.—"There is another kind of tree (in Ceylon) which they call **Sursack** . . . which has leaves like a laurel, and bears its fruit, not like other trees on twigs from the branches, but on the trunk itself. . . ." &c.—*Saar*, ed. 1672, p. 84.

1661.—Walter Schulz says that the famous fruit Jaka was called by the Netherlanders in the Indies **Soorsack**.—p. 236.

1675.—"The whole is planted for the most part with coco-palms, mangoes, and **suursacks**."—*Ryklof van Goens*, in *Valentijn, Ceylon*, 223.

1768-71.—"The **Sursak**-tree has a fruit of a similar kind with the durioon (**durian**), but it is not accompanied by such a fetid smell."—*Stavorinus*, E.T. i. 236.

1778.—"The one which yields smaller fruit, without seed, I found at Columbo, Gale, and several other places. The name by which it is properly known here is the *Maldivian* **Sour Sack**, and its use here is less universal than that of the other sort, which . . . weighs 30 or 40 lbs."—*Thunberg*, E.T. iv. 255.

[1833.—"Of the eatable fruited kinds above referred to, the most remarkable are the **sweetsop**, **sour sop**, and cherimoyer. . . ."—*Penny Cycl.* ii. 54.]

SOWAR, SUWAR, s. Pers. *sawār*, 'a horseman.' A native cavalry soldier; a mounted orderly. In the Greek provinces in Turkey, the word is familiar in the form σουβάρις, pl. σουβαρίδες, for a mounted gendarme. [The regulations for *suwārs* in the Mogul armies are given by *Blochmann, Āīn*, i. 244 *seq.*]

1824-5.—". . . The **sowars** who accompanied him."—*Heber*, Orig. i. 404.

1827.—"Hartley had therefore no resource save to keep his eye steadily fixed on the lighted match of the **sowar** . . . who rode before him."—*Sir W. Scott, The Surgeon's Daughter*, ch. xiii.

[1830.—". . . Meerza, an **Asswar** well known on the Collector's establishment."—*Or. Sport. Mag.* reprint 1873, i. 390.]

SOWAR, SHOOTER-, s. Hind. from Pers. *shutur-sawār*, the rider of a dromedary or swift camel. Such riders are attached to the establishment of the Viceroy on the march, and of other high officials in Upper India. The word *sowar* is quite misused by the Great Duke in the passage below, for a camel-*driver*, a sense it never has. The word written, or intended, may however have been **surwaun** (q.v.)

[1815.—"As we approached the camp his oont-**surwars** (camel-riders) went ahead of us."—*Journal, Marquess of Hastings*, i. 337.]

1834.—"I . . . found a fresh horse at Sufter Jung's tomb, and at the Kutub (**cootub**) a couple of riding camels and an attendant **Shutur Suwar**."—*Mem. of Col. Mountain*, 129.

[1837.—"There are twenty **Shooter Suwars** (I have not an idea how I ought to spell those words), but they are native soldiers mounted on swift camels, very much *trapped*, and two of them always ride before our carriage."—*Miss Eden, Up the Country*, i. 31.]

1840.—"Sent a **Shuta Sarwar** (camel driver) off with an express to Simla."—*Osborne, Court and Camp of Runj. Singh*, 179.

1842.—"At Peshawur, it appears by the papers I read last night, that they have camels, but no **sowars**, or drivers."—Letter of *D. of Wellington*, in *Indian Administration of Ld. Ellenborough*, 228.

1857.—"I have given general notice of the **Shutur Sowar** going into Meerut to all the Meerut men."—*H. Greathed's Letters during Siege of Delhi*, 42.

SOWARRY, SUWARREE, s. Hind. from Pers. *sawārī*. A cavalcade, a cortège of mounted attendants.

1803.—"They must have tents, elephants, and other **sewary**; and must have with them a sufficient body of troops to guard their persons."—*A. Wellesley*, in *Life of Munro*, i. 346.

1809.—"He had no **sawarry**."—*Ld. Valentia*, i. 388.

1814.—"I was often reprimanded by the Zemindars and native officers, for leaving the **suwarree**, or state attendants, at the outer gate of the city, when I took my evening excursion."—*Forbes, Or. Mem.* iii. 420; [2nd ed. ii. 372].

[1826.—"The '**aswary**,' or suite of Trimbuckje, arrived at the palace."—*Pandurang Hari*, ed. 1873, i. 119.]

1827.—"Orders were given that on the next day all should be in readiness for the **Sowarree**, a grand procession, when the Prince was to receive the Begum as an honoured guest."—*Sir Walter Scott, The Surgeon's Daughter*, ch. xiv.

c. 1831.—"Je tâcherai d'éviter toute la poussière de ces immenses **sowarris**."—*Jacquemont, Corresp.* ii. 121.

[1837.—"The Raja of Benares came with a very magnificent **surwarree** of elephants and camels."—*Miss Eden, Up the Country*, i. 35.]

SOWARRY CAMEL, s. A swift or riding camel. See **SOWAR, SHOOTER-**.

1835.—"'I am told you dress a camel beautifully,' said the young Princess, 'and I was anxious to . . . ask you to instruct my people how to attire a **sawārī camel**.' This was flattering me on a very weak point: there is but one thing in the world that I perfectly understand, and that is how to dress a camel."—*Wanderings of a Pilgrim*, ii. 36.

SOWCAR, s. Hind. *sāhūkār*; alleged to be from Skt. *sādhu*, 'right,' with the Hind. affix *kār*, 'doer'; Guj. Mahr. *sāvakār*. A native banker; corresponding to the **Chetty** of S. India.

1803.—"You should not confine your dealings to one **soucar**. Open a communication with every **soucar** in Poonah, and take money from any man who will give it you for bills."—*Wellington, Desp.*, ed. 1837, ii. 1.

1826.—"We were also **sahoukars**, and granted bills of exchange upon Bombay and Madras, and we advanced moneys upon interest."—*Pandurang Hari*, 174; [ed. 1873, i. 251].

[In the following the word is confounded with **Sowar**:

[1877.—"It was the habit of the **sowars**, as the goldsmiths are called, to bear their wealth upon their persons."—*Mrs. Guthrie, My Year in an Indian Fort*, i. 294.]

SOY, s. A kind of condiment once popular. The word is Japanese *si-yau* (a young Japanese fellow-passenger gave the pronunciation clearly as *sho-yu*.—A. B.), Chin. *shi-yu*. [Mr. Platts (9 ser. *N. & Q.* iv. 475) points out that in Japanese as written with the native character *soy* would not be *siyau*, but *siyau-yu*; in the Romanised Japanese this is simplified to *shoyu* (colloquially this is still further reduced, by dropping the final vowel, to *shoy* or *soy*). Of this monosyllable only the *so* represents the classical *siyau*; the final consonant (*y*) is a relic of the termination *yu*. The Japanese word is itself derived from the Chinese, which at Shanghai is *sze-yu*, at Amoy, *si-iu*, at Canton, *shi-yau*, of which the first element means 'salted beans,' or other fruits, dried and used as condiments; the second element merely means 'oil.'] It is made from the beans of a plant common in the Himālaya and E. Asia, and much cultivated, viz. *Glycine Soja*, Sieb. and Zucc. (*Soya hispida*, Moench.), boiled down and fermented. [In India the bean is eaten in places where it is cultivated, as in Chutia Nāgpur (*Watt, Econ. Dict.* iii. 510 *seq.*)]

1679.—". . . Mango and **Saio**, two sorts of sauces brought from the East Indies."—*Journal of John Locke*, in *Ld. King's Life of L.*, i. 249.

1688.—"I have been told that **soy** is made with a fishy composition, and it seems most likely by the Taste; tho' a Gentleman of my Acquaintance who was very intimate with one that sailed often from Tonquin to Japan, from whence the true *Soy* comes, told me that it was made only with Wheat and a sort of Beans mixt with Water and Salt."—*Dampier*, ii. 28.

1690.—". . . **Souy**, the choicest of all Sawces."—*Ovington*, 397.

1712.—"Hoc legumen in coquinâ Japonicâ utramque replet paginam; ex eo namque conficitur: tum puls *Miso* dicta, quae ferculis pro consistentiâ, et butyri loco additur, butyrum enim hôc coelô res ignota est; tum **Sooju** dictum embamma, quod nisi ferculis, certè frictis et assatis omnibus affunditur."—*Kaempfer, Amoen. Exot.* p. 839.

1776.—An elaborate account of the preparation of Soy is given by *Thunberg, Travels*. E.T. iv. 121-122; and more briefly by Kaempfer on the page quoted above.

[1900.—"Mushrooms shred into small pieces, flavoured with *shoyu*" (**soy**).—*Mrs. Frazer, A Diplomatist's Wife in Japan*, i. 238.]

SPIN, s. An unmarried lady; popular abbreviation of 'Spinster.' [The Port. equivalent *soltera* (*soltiera*) was used in a derogatory sense (*Gray*, note on *Pyrard de Laval*, Hak. Soc. ii. 128).]

SPONGE-CAKE, s. This well-known form of cake is called throughout Italy *pane di Spagna*, a fact that suggested to us the possibility that the English name is really a corruption of *Spanish-cake*. The name in Japan tends to confirm this, and must be our excuse for introducing the term here.

1880.—"There is a cake called *kasateira* resembling **sponge-cake**. . . . It is said to have been introduced by the Spaniards, and that its name is a corruption of *Castilla*."—*Miss Bird's Japan*, i. 235.

SPOTTED-DEER, s. *Axis maculatus* of Gray; [*Cervus axis* of Blanford (*Mammalia*, 546)]; Hind. *chītal*, Skt. *chitra*, 'spotted.'

1673.—"The same Night we travelled easily to Megatana, using our Fowling-Pieces all the way, being here presented with Rich Game, as Peacocks, Doves, and Pigeons, *Chitrels*, or **Spotted Deer**."—*Fryer*, 71.

[1677.—"**Spotted Deare** we shall send home, some by ye Europe ships, if they touch here."—*Forrest, Bombay Letters*, i. 140.]

1679.—"There being conveniency in this place for ye breeding up of **Spotted Deer**, which the Hon'ble Company doe every yeare order to be sent home for His Majesty, it is ordered that care be taken to breed them up in this Factory (Madapollam), to be sent home accordingly."—*Ft. St. George Council* (on Tour), 16th April, in *Notes and Exts.*, *Madras*, 1871.

1682.—"This is a fine pleasant situation, full of great shady trees, most of them *Tamarins*, well stored with peacocks and **Spotted Deer** like our fallow-deer."—*Hedges, Diary*, Oct. 16; [Hak. Soc. i. 39].

SQUEEZE, s. This is used in Anglo-Chinese talk for an illegal exaction. It is, we suppose, the translation of a Chinese expression. It corresponds to the *malatolta* of the Middle Ages, and to many other slang phrases in many tongues.

1882.—"If the licence (of the Hong merchants) . . . was costly, it secured to them uninterrupted and extraordinary pecuniary advantages; but on the other hand it subjected them to 'calls' or '**squeezes**' for contributions to public works, . . . for the relief of districts suffering from scarcity . . . as well as for the often imaginary . . . damage caused by the overflowing of the 'Yangtse Keang' or the 'Yellow River.'"—*The Fankwae at Canton*, p. 36.

STATION, s. A word of constant recurrence in Anglo-Indian colloquial. It is the usual designation of the place where the English officials of a district, or the officers of a garrison (not in a fortress) reside. Also the aggregate society of such a place.

[1832.—"The nobles and gentlemen are frequently invited to witness a '**Station** ball.' . . ."—*Mrs. Meer Hassan Ali, Observations*, i. 196.]

1866.—
"And if I told how much I ate at one
Mofussil **station**,
I'm sure 'twould cause at home a most
extraordinary sensation."
Trevelyan, The Dawk Bungalow, in *Fraser*, lxxiii. p. 391.

" "Who asked the **Station** to dinner, and allowed only one glass of **Simkin** to each guest."—*Ibid.* 231.

STEVEDORE, s. One employed to stow the cargo of a ship and to unload it. The verb *estivar* [Lat. *stipare*] is used both in Sp. and Port. in the sense of stowing cargo, implying originally to pack close, as to press wool. *Estivador* in the sense of a wool-packer only is given in the Sp. Dictionaries, but no doubt has been used in every sense of *estivar*. See *Skeat*, s.v.

STICK-INSECT, s. The name commonly applied to certain orthopterous insects, of the family

Phasmidae, which have the strongest possible resemblance to dry twigs or pieces of stick, sometimes 6 or 7 inches in length.

1754.—"The other remarkable animal which I met with at *Cuddalore* was the **animated Stalk**, of which there are different kinds. Some appear like dried straws tied together, others like grass. . . ."—*Ives*, 20.

1860.—"The **Stick-insect**. — The *Phasmidae* or spectres . . . present as close a resemblance to small branches, or leafless twigs, as their congeners do to green leaves. . . ."—*Tennent, Ceylon*, i. 252.

[**STICKLAC**, s. **Lac** encrusted on sticks, which in this form is collected in the jungles of Central India.

[1880. — "Where, however, there is a regular trade in **stick-lac**, the propagation of the insect is systematically carried on by those who wish for a certain and abundant crop."—*Ball, Jungle Life*, 308.]

STINK-WOOD, s. *Foetidia Mauritiana*, Lam., a myrtaceous plant of Mauritius, called there *Bois puant*. "At the Carnival in Goa, one of the sports is to drop bits of this **stinkwood** into the pockets of respectable persons."—*Birdwood* (MS.).

STRIDHANA, STREEDHANA, s. Skt. *stri-dhana*, 'women's property.' A term of Hindu Law, applied to certain property belonging to a woman, which follows a law of succession different from that which regulates other property. The term is first to be found in the works of Jones and Colebrooke (1790-1800), but has recently been introduced into European scientific treatises. [See Mayne, *Hindu Law*, 541 *seqq.*]

1875.—"The settled property of a married woman . . . is well known to the Hindoos under the name of **stridhan**."—*Maine, Early Institutions*, 321.

STUPA. See **TOPE.**

SUÁKIN, n.p. This name, and the melancholy victories in its vicinity, are too familiar now to need explanation. Arab. *Sawākin*.

c. 1331.—"This very day we arrived at the island of **Sawākin**. It is about 6 miles from the mainland, and has neither drinkable water, nor corn, nor trees. Water is brought in boats, and there are cisterns to collect rain water. . . ."—*Ibn Batuta*, ii. 161-2.

1526.—"The Preste continued speaking with our people, and said to Don Rodrigo that he would have great pleasure and complete contentment, if he saw a fort of ours erected in Macuha, or in **Çuaquem**, or in Zyla."—*Correa*, iii. 42; [see *Dalboquerque, Comm.* ii. 229].

[c. 1590.—". . . thence it (the sea) washes both Persia and Ethiopia where are Dahlak and **Suakin**, and is called (the Gulf of) Omán and the Persian Sea."—*Āīn*, ed. *Jarrett*, ii. 121.]

SUCKER-BUCKER, n.p. A name often given in N. India to Upper Sind, from two neighbouring places, viz., the town of *Sakhar* on the right bank of the Indus, and the island fortress of *Bakkar* or *Bhakkar* in the river. An alternative name is *Roree-Bucker*, from *Rohrī*, a town opposite Bakkar, on the left bank, the name of which is probably a relic of the ancient town of *Arōr* or *Alōr*, though the site has been changed since the Indus adopted its present bed. [See *McCrindle, Invasion of India*, 352 *seqq.*]

c. 1333.—"I passed 5 days at Lāharī . . . and quitted it to proceed to **Bakār**. They thus call a fine town through which flows a canal derived from the river Sind."—*Ibn Batuta*, iii. 114-115.

1521. — Shah Beg "then took his departure for **Bhakkar**, and after several days' marching arrived at the plain surrounding **Sakhar**."—*Turkhān Nāma*, in *Elliot*, i. 311.

1554.—"After a thousand sufferings we arrived at the end of some days' journey, at Siāwan (*Sehwan*), and then, passing by Patara and Darilja, we entered the fortress of **Bakr**."—*Sidi 'Ali*, p. 136.

[c. 1590. — "**Bhakkar** (Bhukkar) is a notable fortress; in ancient chronicles it is called Mamṣūrah."—*Āīn*, ed. *Jarrett*, ii. 327.]

1616. — "**Buckor**, the Chiefe Citie, is called **Buckor Succor**."—*Terry*, [ed. 1777, p. 75].

1753.—"Vient ensuite **Bukor**, ou comme il est écrit dans la Géographie Turque, **Peker**, ville située sur une colline, entre deux bras de l'Indus, qui en font une île . . . la géographie . . . ajoute que *Louhri* (*i.e.* Rori) est une autre ville située vis-à-vis de cette île du côté meridional, et que **Sekar**, autrement **Sukor**, est en même position du côté septentrional."—*D'Anville*, p. 37.

SUCKET, s. Old English. Wright explains the word as 'dried sweetmeats or sugar-plums.' Does it not in the quotations rather mean *loaf-sugar?* [Palmer (*Folk Etymol.* 378) says that the original meaning was a 'slice of melon or gourd,' Ital. *zuccata*, 'a kind of meat made of Pumpions or

Gourdes' (Florio) from *zucca*, 'a gourd or pumpkin,' which is a shortened form of *cucuzza*, a corruption of Lat. *cucurbita* (*Diez*). This is perhaps the same word which appears in the quotation from Linschoten below, where the editor suggests that it is derived from Mahr *sukata*, 'slightly dried, desiccated,' and Sir H. Yule suggests a corruption of H. *sonṭh*, 'dried ginger.']

[1537.—"... packed in a fraile, two little barrels of **suckat**. ..."—*Letters and Papers of the Reign of Henry VIII*. xii. pt. i. 451.]

1584.—"White **sucket** from Zindi" (*i.e.* Sind) "Cambaia, and China."—*Barret*, in *Hakl*. ii. 412.

[1598.—"Ginger by the Arabians, Persians and Turkes is called Gengibil (see **GINGER**), in Gusurate, Decan, and Bengala, when it is fresh and green Adrac, and when dried **sukte**."—*Linschoten*, Hak. Soc. ii. 79.]

c. 1620-30.—
"...... For this,
This Candy wine, three merchants were undone;
These **suckets** brake as many more."
Beaum. and Fletch., *The Little French Lawyer*, i. 1.

SUCLÁT, SACKCLOTH, &c., s. Pers. *saḳallāt*, *saḳallaṭ*, *saḳlatīn*, *saḳlāṭūn*, applied to certain woollen stuffs, and particularly now to European broadcloth. It is sometimes defined as *scarlet* broad cloth; but though this colour is frequent, it does not seem to be essential to the name. [*Scarlet* was the name of a material long before it denoted a colour. In the Liberate Roll of 14 Hen. III. (1230, quoted in *N. & Q*. 8 ser. i. 129) we read of *sanguine scarlet*, brown, red, white and scarlet *coloris de Marble*.] It has, however, been supposed that our word *scarlet* comes from some form of the present word (see *Skeat*, s.v. *Scarlet*).* But the fact that the Arab. dictionaries give a form *saḳirlāṭ* must not be trusted to. It is a modern form, probably taken from the European word, [as according to Skeat, the Turkish *iskerlat* is merely borrowed from the Ital. *scarlatto*].

The word is found in the medieval literature of Europe in the form *siclatoun*, a term which has been the subject of controversy both as to etymology and to exact meaning (see *Marco Polo*, Bk. i. ch. 58, *notes*). Among the conjectures as to etymology are a derivation from Ar. *ṣaḳl*. 'polishing' (see **SICLEEGUR**); from Sicily (Ar. *Ṣiḳiliya*); and from the Lat. *cyclas*, *cycladatus*. In the Arabic *Vocabulista* of the 13th century (Florence, 1871), **siḳlaṭūn** is translated by *ciclas*. The conclusion come to in the note on *Marco Polo*, based, partly but not entirely, on the modern meaning of *saḳallāṭ*, was that *saḳlāṭūn* was probably a light woollen texture. But Dozy and De Jong give it as *étoffe de* soie, *brochée d'or*, and the passage from Edrisi supports this undoubtedly. To the north of India the name *suklāt* is given to a stuff imported from the borders of China.

1040.—"The robes were then brought, consisting of valuable frocks of **saklátún** of various colours. ..."—*Baihaki*, in *Elliot*, ii. 148.

c. 1150.—"Almeria (*Almarīa*) was a Musulman city at the time of the Moravidae. It was then a place of great industry, and reckoned, among others, 800 silk looms, where they manufactured costly robes, brocades, the stuffs known as **Saklātūn** *Isfahānī* ... and various other silk tissues."—*Edrisi* (Joubert), ii. 40.

c. 1220.—"Tabrīz. The chief city of Azarbaijān. ... They make there the stuffs called *'attābī* (see **TABBY**), **Siklātūn**, *Khiṭābī*, fine satins and other textures which are exported everywhere."—*Yāḳūt*, in *Barbier de Meynard*, i. 133.

c. 1370?—
"His heer, his berd, was lyk saffroun
That to his girdel raughte adoun
Hise shoos of Cordewane,
Of Brugges were his hosen broun
His Robe was of **Syklatoun**
That coste many a Jane."
Chaucer, *Sir Thopas*, 4 (*Furnival*, Ellesmere Text).

c. 1590.—
"**Suklāt**-*i-Rūmī o Farangī o Purtagālī*" (Broadcloth of Turkey, of Europe, and of Portugal). ...—*Āīn* (orig.) i. 110. Blochmann renders '*Scarlet* Broadcloth' (see above). [The same word, *suḳlāṭi*, is used later on of 'woollen stuffs' made in Kashmīr (*Jarrett*, *Āīn*, ii. 355).]

1673. — "*Suffahaun* is already full of London Cloath, or **Sackcloath** *Londre*, as they call it."—*Fryer*, 224.

" "His Hose of London **Sackcloth** of any Colour."—*Ibid*. 391.

[1840.—"... his simple dress of **sooklaat** and flat black woollen cap. ..."—*Lloyd*, *Gerard*, *Narr*. i. 167.]

* Here is an instance in which scarlet is used for 'scarlet broadcloth':

c. 1665.—"... they laid them out, partly in fine Cotton Cloth ... partly in Silken Stuffs streaked with Gold and Silver, to make Vests and Summer-Drawers of; partly in English Scarlet, to make two Arabian Vests of for their King ..."—*Bernier*, E.T. 43; [ed. *Constable*, 139].

1854.—"List of Chinese articles brought to India. . . . **Suklat**, a kind of camlet made of camel's hair."—*Cunningham's Ladak*, 242.

1862.—"In this season travellers wear garments of sheep-skin with sleeves, the fleecy side inwards, and the exterior covered with **Sooklat**, or blanket."—*Punjab Trade Report*, 57.

" "BROADCLOTH (Europe), ('**Suklat**,' 'Mahoot')."—*Ibid. App.* p. ccxxx.

SUDDEN DEATH. Anglo-Indian slang for a fowl served as a spatchcock, the standing dish at a dawk-bungalow in former days. The bird was caught in the yard, as the traveller entered, and was on the table by the time he had bathed and dressed.

[c. 1848.—"'**Sudden death**' means a young chicken about a month old, caught, killed, and grilled at the shortest notice."—*Berncastle, Voyage to China*, i. 193.]

SUDDER, adj., but used as s. Literally 'chief,' being Ar. *sadr*. This term had a technical application under Mahommedan rule to a chief Judge, as in the example quoted below. The use of the word seems to be almost confined to the Bengal Presidency. Its principal applications are the following:

a. **Sudder Board.** This is the 'Board of Revenue,' of which there is one at Calcutta, and one in the N.W. Provinces at Allahabad. There is a Board of Revenue at Madras, but not called '**Sudder** Board' there.

b. **Sudder Court**, *i.e.* 'Sudder **Adawlut** (*sadr 'adālat*). This was till 1862, in Calcutta and in the N.W.P., the chief court of appeal from the **Mofussil** or District Courts, the Judges being members of the Bengal Civil Service. In the year named the Calcutta Sudder Court was amalgamated with the Supreme Court (in which English Law had been administered by English Barrister-Judges), the amalgamated Court being entitled the *High Court of Judiciary*. A similar Court also superseded the Sudder Adawlut in the N.W.P.

c. **Sudder Ameen**, *i.e.* chief **Ameen** (q.v.). This was the designation of the second class of native Judge in the classification which was superseded in Bengal by Act XVI. of 1868, in Bombay by Act XIV. of 1869, and in Madras by Act III. of 1873. Under that system the highest rank of native Judge was **Principal Sudder Ameen**; the 2nd rank, **Sudder Ameen**; the 3rd, **Moonsiff**. In the new classification there are in Bengal Subordinate Judges of the 1st, 2nd and 3rd grade, and Munsiffs (see **MOONSIFF**) of 4 grades; in Bombay, Subordinate Judges of the 1st class in 3 grades, and 2nd class in 4 grades; and in Madras Subordinate Judges in 3 grades, and Munsiffs in 4 grades.

d. **Sudder Station.** The chief station of a district, viz. that where the Collector, Judge, and other chief civil officials reside, and where their Courts are.

c. 1340.—"The **Sadr**-*Jihān* ('Chief of the Word') *i.e.* the **Kadi**-*al-Kudāt* ('Judge of Judges') (**CAZEE**) . . . possesses ten townships, producing a revenue of about 60,000 **tankas**. He is also called **Sadr**-*al-Islām*."—*Shihābuddīn Dimishkī*, in *Notes et Exts.* xiii. 185.

SUFEENA, s. Hind. *sàfīna*. This is the native corr. of *subpoena*. It is shaped, but not much distorted, by the existence in Hind. of the Ar. word *safīna* for 'a blank-book, a note-book.'

SUGAR, s. This familiar word is of Skt. origin. *Sarkara* originally signifies 'grit or gravel,' thence crystallised sugar, and through a Prakrit form *sakkara* gave the Pers. *shakkar*, the Greek σάκχαρ and σάκχαρον, and the late Latin *saccharum*. The Ar. is *sukkar*, or with the article *as-sukkar*, and it is probable that our modern forms, It. *zucchero* and *succhero*, Fr. *sucre*, Germ. *Zucker*, Eng. *sugar*, came as well as the Sp. *azucar*, and Port. *assucar*, from the Arabic direct, and not through Latin or Greek. The Russian is *sakhar*; Polish *zukier*; Hung. *zukur*. In fact the ancient knowledge of the product was slight and vague, and it was by the Arabs that the cultivation of the sugar-cane was introduced into Egypt, Sicily, and Andalusia. It is possible indeed, and not improbable, that palm-sugar (see **JAGGERY**) is a much older product than that of the cane. [This is disputed by Watt (*Econ. Dict.* vi. pt. i. p. 31), who is inclined to fix the home of the cane in E. India.] The original habitat of the cane is not known; there is only a slight and doubtful statement of Loureiro, who, in speaking of Cochin-China, uses the words "habitat et colitur," which may imply its existence in a wild state, as well as under cultivation, in that country. De Candolle assigns its earliest production to the country extending from Cochin-China to Bengal.

Though, as we have said, the knowledge which the ancients had of sugar was very dim, we are disposed greatly to question the thesis, which has been so confidently maintained by Salmasius and later writers, that the original *saccharon* of Greek and Roman writers was not sugar but the siliceous concretion sometimes deposited in bamboos, and used in medieval medicine under the name **tabasheer** (q.v.) (where see a quotation from Royle, taking the same view). It is just possible that Pliny in the passage quoted below may have jumbled up two different things, but we see no sufficient evidence even of this. In White's Latin Dict. we read that by the word *saccharon* is meant (not sugar but) "a sweet juice distilling from the joints of the bamboo." This is nonsense. There is no such sweet juice distilled from the joints of the bamboo; nor is the substance *tabashīr* at all sweet. On the contrary it is slightly bitter and physicky in taste, with no approach to sweetness. It is a hydrate of silica. It could never have been called "honey" (see Dioscorides and Pliny below); and the name of *bamboo-sugar* appears to have been given it by the Arabs merely because of some resemblance of its concretions to lumps of sugar. [The same view is taken in the *Encycl. Brit.* 9th ed. xxii. 625, quoting *Not. et Extr.*, xxv. 267.] All the erroneous notices of σάκχαρον seem to be easily accounted for by lack of knowledge; and they are exactly paralleled by the loose and inaccurate stories about the origin of camphor, of lac, and what-not, that may be found within the boards of this book.

In the absence or scarcity of sugar, honey was the type of sweetness, and hence the name of *honey* applied to sugar in several of these early extracts. This phraseology continued down to the Middle Ages, at least in its application to uncrystallised products of the sugar-cane, and analogous substances. In the quotation from Pegolotti we apprehend that his three kinds of honey indicate honey, treacle, and a syrup or treacle made from the sweet pods of the carob-tree.

Sugar does not seem to have been in early Chinese use. The old Chinese books often mention *shi-mi* or 'stone-honey' as a product of India and Persia. In the reign of Taitsung (627-650) a man was sent to Gangetic India to learn the art of sugar-making; and Marco Polo below mentions the introduction from Egypt of the further art of refining it. In India now, *Chīnī* (**Cheeny**) (Chinese) is applied to the whiter kinds of common sugar; *Miṣrī* (**Misree**) or Egyptian, to sugar-candy; loaf-sugar is called *ḳand.*

c. A.D. 60.—

"Quâque ferens rapidum diviso gurgite fontem
Vastis Indus aquis mixtum non sentit Hydaspen:
Quique bibunt tenerâ dulcis ab arundine succos. . . ." *Lucan*, iii. 235.

" "Aiunt inveniri apud Indos mel in arundinum foliis, quod aut nos illius cœli, aut ipsius arundinis humor dulcis et pinguis gignat."—*Seneca, Epist.* lxxxiv.

c. A.D. 65.—"It is called σάκχαρον, and is a kind of honey which solidifies in India, and in Arabia Felix; and is found upon canes, in its substance resembling salt, and crunched by the teeth as salt is. Mixed with water and drunk, it is good for the belly and stomach, and for affections of the bladder and kidneys."—*Dioscorides, Mat. Med.* ii. c. 104.

c. A.D. 70.—"**Saccharon** et Arabia fert, sed laudatius India. Est autem mel in harundinibus collectum, cummium modo candidum, dentibus fragile, amplissimum nucis abellanae magnitudine, ad medicinae tantum usum."—*Plin. Hist. Nat.* xii. 8.

c. 170.—"But all these articles are hotter than is desirable, and so they aggravate fevers, much as wine would. But *oxymeli* alone does not aggravate fever, whilst it is an active purgative. . . . Not undeservedly, I think, that **saccharum** may also be counted among things of this quality. . . ." —*Galen, Methodus Medendi*, viii.

c. 636.—"In Indicis stagnis nasci arundines calamique dicuntur, ex quorum radicibus expressum suavissimum succum bibunt. Vnde et Varro ait:

Indica non magno in arbore crescit arundo;
Illius et lentis premitur radicibus humor,
Dulcia qui nequeant succo concedere mella."

Isidori Hispalensis Originum, Lib. xvii. cap. vii.

c. 1220.—"Sunt insuper in Terra (Sancta) *canamellae* de quibus **zucchara** ex compressione eliquatur." — *Jacobi Vitriaci, Hist. Jherosolym*, cap. lxxxv.

1298.—"Bangala est une provence vers midi. . . . Il font grant merchandie, car il ont espi e galanga e gingiber e **succare** et de maintes autres chieres espices."—*Marco Polo*, Geog. Text, ch. cxxvi.

1298.—"Je voz di que en ceste provences" (Quinsai or Chekiang) "naist et se fait plus **sucar** que ne fait en tout le autre monde, et ce est encore grandissime vente." —*Ibid.* ch. cliii.

1298.—"And before this city" (a place near Fu-chau) "came under the Great Can these people knew not how to make fine **sugar** (*zucchero*); they only used to boil and skim the juice, which, when cold, left a black paste. But after they came under the Great Can some men of Babylonia" (*i.e.* of Cairo) "who happened to be at the Court proceeded to this city and taught the people to refine **sugar** with the ashes of certain trees."—*Idem.* in *Ramusio*, ii. 49.

c. 1343. — "In Cyprus the following articles are sold by the hundred-weight (*cantara di peso*) and at a price in besants: Round pepper, sugar in powder (*polvere di* **zucchero**) . . . sugars in loaves (**zuccheri** *in pani*), bees' honey, sugar-cane honey, and carob-honey (*mele d'ape, mele di cannameli, mele di carrube*). . . ."—*Pegolotti*, 64.

,, "Loaf sugars are of several sorts, viz. **zucchero** *muchhera*, *caffettino*, and *bambillonia*; and *musciatto*, and *dommaschino*; and the *mucchera* is the best sugar there is; for it is more thoroughly boiled, and its paste is whiter, and more solid, than any other sugar; it is in the form of the *bambillonia* sugar like this Δ; and of this *mucchara* kind but little comes to the west, because nearly the whole is kept for the mouth and for the use of the Soldan himself.

"**Zucchero** *caffettino* is the next best after the *muccara* . . .

"**Zucchero** *Bambillonia* is the best next after the best *caffettino*.

"**Zucchero** *musciatto* is the best after that of *Bambillonia*.

* * * * *

"**Zucchero** *chandi*, the bigger the pieces are, and the whiter, and the brighter, so much is it the better and finer, and there should not be too much small stuff.

"Powdered sugars are of many kinds, as of Cyprus, of Rhodes, of the Cranco of Monreale, and of Alexandria; and they are all made originally in entire loaves; but as they are not so thoroughly done, as the other sugars that keep their loaf shape . . . the loaves tumble to pieces, and return to powder, and so it is called powdered sugar . . ." (and a great deal more).—*Ibid.* 362-365. We cannot interpret most of the names in the preceding extract. *Bambillonia* is 'Sugar of Babylon,' *i.e.* of Cairo, and *Dommaschino* of Damascus. *Mucchera* (see **CANDY (SUGAR)**, the second quotation), *Caffettino*, and *Musciatto*, no doubt all represent Arabic terms used in the trade at Alexandria, but we cannot identify them.

c. 1345.—"J'ai vu vendre dans le Bengale . . . un *rithl* (**rottle**) de sucre (**al-sukkar**), poids de Dihly, pour quatre drachmes."—*Ibn Batuta*, iv. 211.

1516.—"Moreover they make in this city (Bengala, *i.e.* probably Chittagong) much and good white cane **sugar** (**açuquere** *branco de canas*), but they do not know how to consolidate it and make loaves of it, so they wrap up the powder in certain wrappers of raw hide, very well stitched up; and make great loads of it, which are despatched for sale to many parts, for it is a great traffic."—*Barbosa*, Lisbon ed. 362.

[1630.—"Let us have a word or two of the prices of **suger** and **suger candy**."—*Forrest, Bombay Letters*, i. 5.]

1807.—"Chacun sait que par effet des regards de Farid, des monceaux de terre se changeaient en sucre. Tel est le motif du surnom de **Schakar** *ganj*, 'tresor de sucre' qui lui a été donné." — *Arāish-i-Mahfil*, quoted by *Garcin de Tassy, Rel. Mus.* 95. (This is the saint, Farīd-uddīn Shakarganj (d. A.D. 1268) whose shrine is at *Pāk Pattan* in the Punjab.) [See *Crooke, Popular Religion*, &c. i. 214 *seqq.*]

1810.—"Although the sugar cane is supposed by many to be indigenous in India, yet it has only been within the last 50 years that it has been cultivated to any great extent. . . . Strange to say, the only sugar-candy used until that time" (20 years before the date of the book) "was received from China; latterly, however, many gentlemen have speculated deeply in the manufacture. We now see sugar-candy of the first quality manufactured in various places of Bengal, and I believe that it is at least admitted that the raw sugars from that quarter are eminently good."—*Williamson, V.M.* ii. 133.

SULTAN, s. Ar. *sulṭān*, 'a Prince, a Monarch.' But this concrete sense is, in Arabic, post-classical only. The classical sense is abstract 'dominion.' The corresponding words in Hebrew and Aramaic have, as usual, *sh* or *s*. Thus *sholṭān* in Daniel (*e.g.* vi. 26—"in the whole dominion of my kingdom") is exactly the same word. The concrete word, corresponding to *sulṭān* in its post-classical sense, is *shallīṭ*, which is applied to Joseph in Gen. xlii. 6—"governor." So Saladin (Yūsuf Salāh-ad-dīn) was not the first Joseph who was *sultan* of Egypt. ["In Arabia it is a not uncommon proper name; and as a title it is taken by a host of petty kinglets. The Abbaside Caliphs (as Al-Wásik . . .) formerly created these Sultans as their regents. Al Tá'i bi'llah (A.D. 974) invested the famous Sabuktagin with the office . . . Sabuktagin's son, the famous Mahmúd of the Ghaznavite dynasty in 1002, was the first to adopt 'Sultán' as an independent title some 200 years after the death of Harún-al-Rashíd" (*Burton, Arab. Nights*, i. 188.)]

c. 950.—"Ἐπὶ δὲ τῆς Βασιλείας Μιχαὴλ τοῦ υἱοῦ Θεοφίλου ἀνῆλθεν ἀπὸ Ἀφρικῆς στόλος λϛ′ κομπαρίων, ἔχων κεφαλὴν τόν τε Σολδανὸν καὶ τὸν Σάμαν καὶ τὸν Καλφοῦς, καὶ ἐχειρώσαντο διαφόρους πόλεις τῆς Δαλματίας."—*Constant. Porphyrog.*, *De Thematibus*, ii. Thēma xi.

c. 1075 (written c. 1130).—". . . οἳ καὶ καθελόντες Πέρσας τε καὶ Σαρακηνοὺς αὐτοὶ κύριοι τῆς Περσίδος γεγόνασι σουλτάνον τὸν Στραγγολίπιδα * ὀνομάσαντες, ὅπερ σημαίνει παρ' αὐτοῖς Βασιλεὺς καὶ παντοκράτωρ."—*Nicephorus Bryennius*, *Comment*, i. 9.

c. 1124.—"De divitiis **Soldani** mira referunt, et de incognitis speciebus quas in oriente viderunt. **Soldanus** dicitur quasi *solus dominus*, quia cunctis praeest Orientis principibus."—*Ordericus Vitalis*, *Hist. Eccles.* Lib. xi. In Paris ed. of *Le Prevost*, 1852, iv. 256-7.

1165.—"Both parties faithfully adhered to this arrangement, until it was interrupted by the interference of Sanjar-Shah ben Shah, who governs all Persia, and holds supreme power over 45 of its Kings. This prince is called in Arabic **Sultan** ul-Fars-al-Khabir (supreme commander of Persia)."—*R. Benjamin*, in *Wright*, 105-106.

c. 1200.—"Endementres que ces choses coroient einsi en Antioche, li message qui par Aussiens estoient alé au **soudan** de Perse por demander aide s'en retournoient."—*Guillaume de Tyr*, Old Fr. Tr. i. 174.

1298.—"Et quaint il furent là venus, adonc Bondocdaire qe **soldan** estoit de Babelonie vent en Armenie con grande host, et fait grand domajes por la contrée."—*Marco Polo*, Geog. Text, ch. xiii.

1307.—"Post quam vero Turchi occupaverunt terrã illã et habitaverũt ibidem, elegerũt dominũ super eos, et illum vocaverunt **Soldã** quod idem est quod rex in idiomate Latinorũ."—*Haitoni Armeni de Tartaris Liber*, cap. xiii. in *Novus Orbis*.

1309.—"En icelle grant paour de mort où nous estiens, vindrent à nous jusques à treize ou quatorze dou consoil dou **soudan**, trop richement appareillé de dras d'or et de soie, et nous firent demander (par un frere de l'Ospital qui savoit sarrazinois), de par le **soudan**, se nous vorriens estre delivre, et nous deimes que oil, et ce pooient il bien savoir."—*Joinville*, *Credo*. Joinville often has **soudanc**, and sometimes **saudanc**.

1498.—"Em este lugar e ilha a que chamão Moncobiquy estava hum senhor a que elles chamavam **Colyytam** que era como visorrey."—*Roteiro de V. da Gama*, 26.

c. 1586.—
"Now Tamburlaine the mighty **Soldan** comes,
And leads with him the great Arabian King."
Marlowe, *Tamb. the Great*, iv. 3.

[1596.— ". . . this scimitar
That slew the Sophy and a Persian prince
That won three fields of **Sultan** Solyman."
Merchant of Venice, II. i. 26.]

SUMATRA, a. n.p. This name has been applied to the great island since about A.D. 1400. There can be no reasonable doubt that it was taken from the very similar name of one of the maritime principalities upon the north coast of the island, which seems to have originated in the 13th century. The seat of this principality, a town called *Samudra*, was certainly not far from **Pasei**, the *Pacem* of the early Portuguese writers, the *Passir* of some modern charts, and probably lay near the inner end of the Bay of Telo Samawe (see notes to *Marco Polo*, 2nd ed. ii. 276 *seqq.*). This view is corroborated by a letter from C. W. J. Wenniker (*Bijdragen tot de Taal-Land-en Volkenkunde van Nederlandsch Indie*, ser. iv. vol. 6. (1882), p. 298) from which we learn that in 1881 an official of Netherlands India, who was visiting Pasei, not far from that place, and on the left bank of the river (we presume the river which is shown in maps as entering the Bay of Telo Samawe near Pasei) came upon a *kampong*, or village, called Samudra. We cannot doubt that this is an indication of the site of the old capital.

The first mention of the name is probably to be recognised in **Samara**, the name given in the text of Marco Polo to one of the kingdoms of this coast, intervening between *Basma*, or Pacem, and Dagroian or Dragoian, which last seems to correspond with Pedir. This must have been the position of Samudra, and it is probable that *d* has disappeared accidentally from Polo's *Samara*. Malay legends give trivial stories to account for the etymology of the name, and others have been suggested; but in all probability it was the Skt. *Samudra*, the 'sea.' [See *Miscellaneous Papers relating to Indo-China*, 2nd ser. ii. 50; Leyden, *Malay Annals*, 65.] At the very time of the alleged foundation of the town a kingdom was flourishing at Dwāra Samudra in S. India (see **DOOR SUMMUND**).

The first authentic occurrence of the name is probably in the Chinese annals, which mention, among the Indian kingdoms which were prevailed on to

* Togrul Beg, founder of the Seljuk dynasty, called by various Western writers *Tangrolipix*, and (as here) *Strāngolipes*.

send tribute to Kublai Khan, that of *Sumutala*. The chief of this State is called in the Chinese record *Tu-han-pa-ti* (*Pauthier, Marc Pol*, 605), which seems to exactly represent the Malay words **Tuan**-*Pati*, 'Lord Ruler.'

We learn next from Ibn Batuta that at the time of his visit (about the middle of the 14th century) the State of *Sumutra*, as he calls it, had become important and powerful in the Archipelago; and no doubt it was about that time or soon after, that the name began to be applied by foreigners to the whole of the great island, just as *Lamori* had been applied to the same island some centuries earlier, from *Lāmbrī*, which was then the State and port habitually visited by ships from India. We see that the name was so applied early in the following century by Nicolo Conti, who was in those seas apparently c. 1420-30, and who calls the island *Shamuthera*. Fra Mauro, who derived much information from Conti, in his famous World-Map, calls the island *Isola Siamotra* or *Taprobane*. The confusion with *Taprobane* lasted long.

When the Portuguese first reached those regions Pedir was the leading State upon the coast, and certainly no State *known* as Samudra or Sumatra then continued to exist. Whether the *city* continued to exist, even in decay, is obscure. The *Āīn*, quoted below, refers to the "port of Sumatra," but this may have been based on old information. Valentijn seems to recognise the existence of a place called *Samudra* or *Samotdara*, though it is not entered in his map. A famous mystic theologian who flourished under the great King of Achīn, Iskandar Muda, and died in 1630, bore the name of Shamsuddīn Shamatrānī, which seems to point to a place called Shamatra as his birthplace. And a distinct mention of "the island of Samatra" as named from "a city of this northern part" occurs in the *soi-disant* "Voyage which Juan Serano made when he fled from Malacca" in 1512, published by Lord Stanley of Alderley at the end of his translation of Barbosa. This man, on leaving Pedir and going down the coast, says: "I drew towards the south and south-east direction, and reached to another country and city which is called Samatra," and so on. Now this indicates the position in which the city of Sumatra must really have been, if it continued to exist. But, though this passage is not, all the rest of the narrative seems to be mere plunder from Varthema. Unless, indeed, the plunder was the other way; for there is reason to believe that Varthema never went east of Malabar.

There is, however, a like intimation in a curious letter respecting the Portuguese discoveries, written from Lisbon in 1515, by a German, Valentino Moravia (the same probably who published a Portuguese version of Marco Polo, at Lisbon, in 1502) and who shows an extremely accurate conception of Indian geography. He says: "The greatest island is that called by Marco Polo the Venetian Java Minor, and at present it is called **Sumotra** from a port of the said island" (see in *De Gubernatis, Viagg. Ital.* 391).

It is probable that before the Portuguese epoch the adjoining States of Pasei and Sumatra had become united. Mr. G. Phillips, of the Consular Service in China, was good enough to send to one of the present writers, when engaged on Marco Polo, a copy of an old Chinese chart showing the northern coast of the island, and this showed the town of Sumatra (*Sumantala*). It seemed to be placed in the Gulf of Pasei, and very near where Pasei itself still exists. An extract of a Chinese account "of about A.D. 1413" accompanied the map. This was fundamentally the same as that quoted below from Groeneveldt. There was a village at the mouth of the river called *Talu-mangkin* (qu. Telu-Samawe?). A curious passage also will be found below, extracted by the late M. Pauthier from the great Chinese *Imperial Geography*, which alludes to the disappearance of Sumatra from knowledge.

We are quite unable to understand the doubts that have been thrown upon the derivation of the name, given to the island by foreigners, from that of the kingdom of which we have been speaking (see the letter quoted above from the *Bijdragen*).

1298.—"So you must know that when you leave the Kingdom of Basma (*Pacem*) you come to another Kingdom called **Samara** on the same Island."—*Marco Polo*, Bk. iii. ch. 10.

c. 1300.—"Beyond it (*Lāmūrī*, or *Lāmbrī*, near Achīn) lies the country of **Sūmūtra**, and beyond that Darband Niās, which is a dependency of Java."—*Rashīduddīn*, in *Elliot*, i. 71.

c. 1323.—"In this same island, towards the south, is another Kingdom by name **Sumoltra**, in which is a singular generation of people."—*Odoric*, in *Cathay*, &c., i. 277.

c. 1346.—". . . after a voyage of 25 days we arrived at the island of Jāwa" (*i.e.* the Java Minor of Marco Polo, or Sumatra). ". . . We thus made our entrance into the capital, that is to say into the city of **Sumuthra**. It is large and handsome, and is encompassed with a wall and towers of timber."—*Ibn Batuta*, iv. 228-230.

1416.—"SUMATRA [Su-men-ta-la]. This country is situated on the great road of western trade. When a ship leaves Malacca for the west, and goes with a fair eastern wind for five days and nights, it first comes to a village on the sea-coast called *Ta-lu-man;* and anchoring here and going south-east for about 10 *li* (3 miles) one arrives at the said place.

"This country has no walled city. There is a large brook running out into the sea, with two tides every day; the waves at the mouth of it are very high, and ships continually founder there. . . ."—Chinese work, quoted by *Groeneveldt*, p. 85.

c. 1430.—"He afterwards went to a fine city of the island Taprobana, which island is called by the natives **Sciamuthera**."—*Conti*, in *India in XVth. Cent.*, 9.

1459.—"Isola **Siamotra**."—*Fra Mauro*.

1498.—". . . **Camatarra** is of the Christians; it is distant from Calicut a voyage of 30 days with a good wind."—*Roteiro*, 109.

1510.—"Wherefore we took a junk and went towards **Sumatra** to a city called Pider."—*Varthema*, 228.

1522.—". . . We left the island of Timor, and entered upon the great sea called Lant Chidol, and taking a west-south-west course, we left to the right and the north, for fear of the Portuguese, the island of **Zumatra**, anciently called Taprobana; also Pegu, Bengala, Urizza, Chelim (see **KLING**) where are the Malabars, subjects of the King of **Narsinga**."—*Pigafetta*, Hak. Soc. 159.

1572.—

"Dizem, que desta terra, co' as possantes
Ondas o mar intrando, dividio
À nobre ilha **Samatra**, que já d'antes
Juntas ambas a gente antigua vio:
Chersoneso foi dita, e das prestantes
Veas d'ouro, que a terra produzio,
Aurea por epithéto lhe ajuntaram
Alguns que fosse Ophir imaginarám."
Camões, x. 124.

By Burton:

"From this Peninsula, they say, the sea
parted with puissant waves, and entering tore
Samatra's noble island, wont to be
joined to the Main as seen by men of yore.
'Twas callèd Chersonese, and such degree
it gained by earth that yielded golden ore,
they gave a golden epithet to the ground:
Some be who fancy Ophir here was found."

c. 1590.—"The *zabād* (*i.e.* civet) which i brought from the harbour, town of *Sumatra*), from the territory of Áchín, goes by the name of *Sumatra zabād* (chūn az bandar-i **Sāmatrāī** az muẓāfat-i Achīn awurdand, **Sāmatrāī** goyand)."—*Āīn*, *Blochmann*, i. 79, (orig. i. 93). [And see a reference to Lámri in *Āīn*, ed. *Jarrett*, iii. 48.]

1612.—"It is related that Raja *Shaher-ul-Nawi* (see **SARNAU**) was a sovereign of great power, and on hearing that **Samadra** was a fine and flourishing land he said to his warriors—which of you will take the Rajah of Samadra?"—*Sijara Malayu*, in *J. Ind. Archip.* v. 316.

c. **.—"**Sou-men-t'ala** est située au sud-ouest de *Tchen-tching* (la Cochin *Chine*) . . . jusqu'à la fin du règne de *Tching-tsou* (in 1425), ce roi ne cessa d'envoyer son tribut à la cour. Pendant les années *wen-hi* (1573-1615) ce royaume se partagea en deux, dont le nouveau se nomma *A-tchi*. . . . Par la suite on n'en entendit plus parler."—*Grande Geog. Impériale*, quoted by *Pauthier*, *Marc Pol*, 567.

b.—

SUMATRA, s. Sudden squalls, precisely such as are described by Lockyer and the others below, and which are common in the narrow sea between the Malay Peninsula and the island of Sumatra, are called by this name.

1616.—". . . it befel that the galliot of Miguel de Macedo was lost on the Ilha Grande of Malaca (?), where he had come to anchor, when a **Samatra** arose that drove him on the island, the vessel going to pieces, though the crew and most part of what she carried were saved."—*Bocarro*, *Decada*, 626.

1711.—"Frequent squalls . . . these are often accompanied with Thunder and Lightning, and continue very fierce for Half an Hour, more or less. Our English Sailors call them **Sumatras**, because they always meet with them on the Coasts of this Island."—*Lockyer*, 56.

1726.—"At Malacca the streights are not above 4 Leagues broad; for though the opposite shore on **Sumatra** is very low, yet it may easily be seen on a clear Day, which is the Reason that the Sea is always as smooth as a Mill-pond, except it is ruffled with Squalls of Wind, which seldom come without Lightning, Thunder, and Rain, and though they come with great Violence, yet they are soon over, not often exceeding an Hour."—*A. Hamilton*, ii. 79, [ed. 1744].

1843.—"**Sumatras**, or squalls from the S. Westward, are often experienced in the S.W. Monsoon. . . . **Sumatras** generally come off the land during the first part of the night, and are sometimes sudden and severe, accompanied with loud thunder, lightning, and rain."—*Horsburgh*, ed. 1843, ii. 215.

[**SUMJAO**, v. This is properly the imp. of the H. verb *samjhānā*, 'to cause to know, warn, correct,' usually with the implication of physical coercion. Other examples of a similar formation will be found under **PUCKEROW**.

[1826.—". . . in this case they apply themselves to **sumjao**, the defendant."—*Pandurang Hari*, ed. 1873, ii. 170.]

[**SUMPITAN**, s. The Malay blowing-tube, by means of which arrows, often poisoned, are discharged. The weapon is discussed under **SARBATANE**. The word is Malay *sumpitan*, properly 'a narrow thing,' from *sumpit*, 'narrow, strait.' There is an elaborate account of it, with illustrations, in *Ling Roth, Natives of Sarawak and Br. N. Borneo*, ii. 184 *seqq*. Also see *Scott, Malayan Words*, 104 *seqq*.

[c. 1630.—"**Sempitans**." See under **UPAS**.

[1841.—"In advancing, the **sumpitan** is carried at the mouth and elevated, and they will discharge at least five arrows to one compared with a musket."—*Brooke*, in *Narrative of Events in Borneo and Celebes*, i. 261.

[1883.—"Their (the Samangs') weapon is the **sumpitan**, a blow-gun, from which poisoned arrows are expelled."—*Miss Bird, The Golden Chersonese*, 16.]

SUNDA, n.p. The western and most mountainous part of the island of Java, in which a language different from the proper Javanese is spoken, and the people have many differences of manners, indicating distinction of race. In the 16th century, Java and Sunda being often distinguished, a common impression grew up that they were separate islands; and they are so represented in some maps of the 16th century, just as some medieval maps, including that of Fra Mauro (1459), show a like separation between England and Scotland. The name Sunda is more properly indeed that of the people than of their country. The Dutch call them *Sundanese* (Soendanezen). The Sunda country is considered to extend from the extreme western point of the island to Cheribon, *i.e.* embracing about one-third of the whole island of Java. Hinduism appears to have prevailed in the Sunda country, and held its ground longer than in "Java," a name which the proper Javanese restrict to their own part of the island. From this country the sea between Sumatra and Java got from Europeans the name of the Straits of Sunda. Geographers have also called the great chain of islands from Sumatra to Timor "the Sunda Islands."

[Mr. Whiteway adds: "There was another Sunda near Goa, but above the Ghāts, where an offspring of the Vijāyanagara family ruled. It was founded at the end of the 16th century, and in the 18th the Portuguese had much to do with it, till Tippoo Sultān absorbed it, and the ruler became a Portuguese pensioner."]

1516.—"And having passed Samatara towards Java there is the island of **Sunda**, in which there is much good pepper, and it has a king over it, who they say desires to serve the King of Portugal. They ship thence many slaves to China."—*Barbosa*, 196.

1526.—"Duarte Coelho in a ship, along with the galeot and a foist, went into the port of **Çunda**, which is at the end of the island of Çamatra, on a separate large island, in which grows a great quantity of excellent pepper, and of which there is a great traffic from this port to China, this being in fact the most important merchandize exported thence. The country is very abundant in provisions, and rich in groves of trees, and has excellent water, and is peopled with Moors who have a Moorish king over them."—*Correa*, iii. 92.

1553.—"Of the land of Jaüa we make two islands, one before the other, lying west and east as if both on one parallel. . . . But the Jaos themselves do not reckon two islands of Jaoa, but one only, of the length that has been stated . . . about a third in length of this island towards the west constitutes **Sunda**, of which we have now to speak. The natives of that part consider their country to be an island divided from Jaüa by a river, little known to our navigators, called by them Chiamo or Chenano, which cuts off right from the sea,* all that third part of the land in such a way that when these natives define the limits of Jaüa they say that on the west it is bounded by the Island of **Sunda**, and separated from it by this river Chiamo, and on the east by the island of Bale, and that on the north they have the island of Madura, and on the south the unexplored sea. . . ." &c.—*Barros*, IV. i. 12.

1554.—"The information we have of this port of Calapa, which is the same as **Çumda**, and of another port called *Bocaa*, these two being 15 leagues one from the other, and

* ". . . hum rio . . . que corta do mar todo aquelle terço de terra." . . . We are not quite sure how to translate. Crawfurd renders: "This (river) intersects the whole island from sea to sea," which seems very free. But it is true, as we have said, that several old maps show Java and Sunda thus divided from sea to sea.

both under one King, is to the effect that the supply of pepper one year with another will be xxx thousand quintals,* that is to say, xx thousand in one year, and x thousand the next year; also that it is very good pepper, as good as that of Malauar, and it is purchased with cloths of Cambaya, Bengalla, and Choromandel."—*A. Nunez*, in *Subsidios*, 42.

1566.—"**Sonda**, vn Isola de' Mori appresso la costa della Giava." — *Ces. Federici*, in *Ramusio*, iii. 391*v*.

c. 1570.—

"Os **Sundas** e Malaios con pimenta,
Con massa, e noz ricos Bandanezes,
Com roupa e droga Cambaia a opulenta,
E com cravo os longinquos Maluguezes."
Ant. desc Abreu, De. de Malaca.

1598.—Linschoten does not recognize the two islands. To him Sunda is only a place in Java :—

". . . there is a straight or narrow passage betweene *Sumatra* and *Iaua*, called the straight of **Sunda**, of a place so called, lying not far from thence within the Ile of *Iaua*. . . . The principall hauen in the Iland is **Sunda** Calapa,† whereof the straight beareth the name; in this place of **Sũda** there is much Pepper."—p. 34.

SUNDERBUNDS, n.p. The well-known name of the tract of intersecting creeks and channels, swampy islands, and jungles, which constitutes that part of the Ganges Delta nearest the sea. The limits of the region so-called are the mouth of the Hoogly on the west, and that of the Megna (*i.e.* of the combined great Ganges and Brahmaputra) on the east, a width of about 220 miles. The name appears not to have been traced in old native documents of any kind, and hence its real form and etymology remain uncertain. *Sundara-vana*, 'beautiful forest'; *Sundarī-vana*, or *-ban*, 'forest of the *Sundarī* tree'; *Chandra-ban*, and *Chandra-band*, 'moon-forest' or 'moon-embankment'; *Chanda-bhanda*, the name of an old tribe of salt-makers; ‡ *Chandra dīp-ban* from a large zemindary called Chandra-dīp in the Bakerganj district at the eastern extremity of the Sunderbunds; these are all suggestions that have been made. Whatever be the true etymology, we doubt if it is to be sought in *sundara* or *sundarī*. [As to the derivation from the *Sundarī* tree which is perhaps most usually accepted, Mr. Beveridge (*Man. of Bakarganj*, 24, 167, 32) remarks that this tree is by no means common in many parts of the Bakarganj Sunderbunds; he suggests that the word means 'beautiful wood' and was possibly given by the Brahmans.] The name has never (except in one quotation below) been in English mouths, or in English popular orthography, *Soonderbunds*, but *Sunderbunds*, which implies (in correct transliteration) an original *sandra* or *chandra*, not *sundara*. And going back to what we conjecture may be an early occurrence of the name in two Dutch writers, we find this confirmed. These two writers, it will be seen, both speak of a famous **Sandery**, or *Santry*, Forest in Lower Bengal, and we should be more positive in our identification were it not that in Van der Broucke's map (1660) which was published in Valentijn's *East Indies* (1726) this Sandery Forest is shown on the *west* side of the Hoogly R., in fact about due west of the site of Calcutta, and a little above a place marked as *Basanderi*, located near the exit into the Hoogly of what represents the old Saraswati R., which enters the former at Sānkrāl, not far below the Botanical Gardens, and 5 or 6 miles below Fort William. This has led Mr. Blochmann to identify the *Sanderi Bosch* with the old Mahall *Basandhari* which appears in the *Āīn* as belonging to the Sirkār of Sulīmānābād (*Gladwin's Ayeen*, ii. 207, *orig.* i. 407; *Jarrett*, ii. 140; *Blochm.* in *J.A.S.B.* xlii. pt. i. p. 232), and which formed one of the original "xxiv. Pergunnas."* Undoubtedly this is the *Basanderi* of V. den Broucke's map; but it seems possible that some confusion between *Basanderi* and Bosch Sandery (which would be *Sandarban* in the vernacular) may have led the map-maker to misplace the latter. We should gather from Schulz † that he passed the Forest of Sandry about a Dutch mile below Sankral, which he mentions. But his statement is so nearly identical with that in Valentijn that we appre-

* Apparently 30,000 quintals *every two years*.

† Sunda Kalapa was the same as Jacatra, on the site of which the Dutch founded Batavia in 1619.

‡ These are mentioned in a copper tablet inscription of A.D. 1136; see *Blochmann*, as quoted further on, p. 226.

* Basandhari is also mentioned by Mr. James Grant (1786) in his *View of the Revenues of Bengal*, as the Pergunna of *Belia-bussendry*; and by A. Hamilton as a place on the Damūdar, producing much good sugar (*Fifth Report*, p. 405; *A. Ham.* ii. 4). It would seem to have been the present Pergunna of Balia, some 13 or 14 miles west of the northern part of Calcutta. See *Hunter's Bengal Gaz.* i. 365.

† So called in the German version which we use; but in the Dutch original he is *Schouten*.

hend they have no *separate* value. Valentijn, in an earlier page, like Bernier, describes the Sunderbunds as the resort of the Arakan pirates, but does not give a name (p. 169).

1661.—"We got under sail again" (just after meeting the Arakan pirates) "in the morning early, and went past the **Forest of Santry**, so styled because (as has been credibly related) Alexander the Great with his mighty army was hindered by the strong rush of the ebb and flood at this place, from advancing further, and therefore had to turn back to Macedonia."—*Walter Schulz*, 155.

c. 1666.—"And thence it is" (from piratical raids of the Mugs, &c.) "that at present there are seen in the mouth of the *Ganges*, so many fine Isles quite deserted, which were formerly well peopled, and where no other Inhabitants are found but wild Beasts, and especially Tygers."—*Bernier*, E.T. 54; [ed. *Constable*, 442].

1726.—"This (Bengal) is the land wherein they will have it that Alexander the Great, called by the Moors, whether Hindostanders or Persians, *Sulthaan Iskender*, and in their historians *Iskender Doulcarnain*, was . . . they can show you the exact place where King Porus held his court. The natives will prate much of this matter; for example, that in front of the SANDERIE-WOOD (*Sanderie Bosch*, which we show in the map, and which they call properly after him *Iskenderie*) he was stopped by the great and rushing streams."—*Valentijn*, v. 179.

1728.—"But your petitioners did not arrive off **Sunderbund Wood** till four in the evening, where they rowed backward and forward for six days; with which labour and want of provisions three of the people died."—*Petition of Sheik Mahmud Ameen and others*, to Govr. of Ft. St. Geo., in *Wheeler*, iii. 41.

1764.—"On the 11th Bhaudan, whilst the Boats were at Kerma in **Soonderbund**, a little before daybreak, Captain Ross arose and ordered the **Manjee** to put off with the **Budgerow**. . . ."—*Native Letter regarding Murder of Captain John Ross by a Native Crew*. In *Long*, 383. This instance is an exception to the general remark made above that the English popular orthography has always been *Sunder*, and not *Soonder-bunds*.

1786.—"If the Jelinghy be navigable we shall soon be in Calcutta; if not, we must pass a second time through the **Sundarbans**."—Letter of *Sir W. Jones*, in *Life*, ii. 83.

„ "A portion of the **Sunderbunds** . . . for the most part overflowed by the tide, as indicated by the original Hindoo name of **Chunderbund**, signifying mounds, or offspring of the moon."—*James Grant*, in App. to *Fifth Report*, p. 260. In a note Mr. Grant notices the derivation from "Soondery wood," and "Soonder-ban," 'beautiful wood,' and proceeds: "But we adhere to our own etymology rather . . . above all, because the richest and greatest part of the **Sunderbunds** is still comprized in the ancient Zemindarry pergunnah of *Chunder deep*, or lunar territory."

1792.—"Many of these lands, what is called the **Sundra bunds**, and others at the mouth of the Ganges, if we may believe the history of Bengal, was formerly well inhabited."—*Forrest, V. to Mergui*, Pref. p. 5.

1793.—"That part of the delta bordering on the sea, is composed of a labyrinth of rivers and creeks, . . . this tract known by the name of the Woods, or **Sunderbunds**, is in extent equal to the principality of Wales."—*Rennell, Mem. of Map of Hind.*, 3rd ed., p. 359.

1853.—"The scenery, too, exceeded his expectations; the terrible forest solitude of the **Sunderbunds** was full of interest to an European imagination."—*Oakfield*, i. 38.

[**SUNGAR**, s. Pers. *sanga, sang*, 'a stone.' A rude stone breastwork, such as is commonly erected for defence by the Afrīdīs and other tribes on the Indian N.W. frontier. The word has now come into general military use, and has been adopted in the S. African war.

[1857.—". . . breastworks of wood and stone (*murcha* and **sanga** respectively). . . ."—*Bellew, Journal of Mission*, 127.

[1900. — "Conspicuous **sungars** are constructed to draw the enemy's fire."—*Pioneer Mail*, March 16.]

The same word seems to be used in the Hills in the sense of a rude wooden bridge supported by stone piers, used for crossing a torrent.

[1833.—"Across a deep ravine . . . his Lordship erected a neat **sangah**, or mountain bridge of pines."—*Mundy, Pen and Pencil Sketches*, ed. 1858, p. 117.

[1871.—"A **sungha** bridge is formed as follows: on either side the river piers of rubble masonry, laced with cross-beams of timber, are built up; and into these are inserted stout poles, one above the other in successively projecting tiers, the interstices between the latter being filled up with cross-beams," &c.—*Harcourt, Himalayan Districts of Kooloo*, p. 67 *seq.*]

SUNGTARA, s. Pers. *sangtara*. The name of a kind of orange, probably from *Cintra*. See under **ORANGE** a quotation regarding the fruit of Cintra, from Abulfeda.

c. 1526.—"The **Sengtereh** . . . is another fruit. . . . In colour and appearance it is like the citron (*Tāranj*), but the skin of the fruit is smooth."—*Baber*, 328.

c. 1590.—"Sirkar Silhet is very mountainous. . . . Here grows a delicious fruit called **Soontara** (*sūntara*) in colour like an orange, but of an oblong form."—*Ayeen*, by

Gladwin, ii. 10; [*Jarrett* (ii. 124) writes **Súntarah**].

1793.—"The people of this country have infinitely more reason to be proud of their oranges, which appear to me to be very superior to those of Silhet, and probably indeed are not surpassed by any in the world. They are here called *Santôla*, which I take to be a corruption of **Sengterrah**, the name by which a similar species of orange is known in the Upper Provinces of India."—*Kirkpatrick's Nepaul*, 129.

1835.—"The most delicious oranges have been procured here. The rind is fine and thin, the flavour excellent; the natives call them '**cintra.**'"—*Wanderings of a Pilgrim*, ii. 99.

SUNN, s. Beng. and Hind. *san*, from Skt. *śaṇa;* the fibre of the *Crotalaria juncea*, L. (N.O. *Leguminosae*); often called Bengal, or Country, hemp. It is of course in no way kindred to true hemp, except in its economic use. In the following passage from the *Āīn* the reference is to the *Hibiscus canabinus* (see *Watt*, *Econ. Dict.* ii. 597).

[c. 1590.—"Hemp grows in clusters like a nosegay. . . . One species bears a flower like the cotton-shrub, and this is called in Hindostan, **sun**-*paut*. It makes a very soft rope."—*Ayeen*, by *Gladwin*, ii. 89; in *Blochmann* (i. 87) *Pat***san.**]

1838.—"**Sunn** . . . a plant the bark of which is used as hemp, and is usually sown around cotton fields."—*Playfair*, *Taleef-i-Shereef*, 96.

[SUNNEE, SOONNEE, s. Ar. *sunnī*, which is really a Pers. form and stands for that which is expressed by the Ar. *Ahlu's-Sunnah*, 'the people of the Path,' a 'Traditionist.' The term applied to the large Mahommedan sect who acknowledge the first four Khalīfahs to have been the rightful descendants of the Prophet, and are thus opposed to the **Sheeahs**. The latter are much less numerous than the former, the proportion being, according to Mr. Wilfrid Blunt's estimate, 15 millions Shiahs to 145 millions of Sunnis.

[c. 1590.—"The Mahommedans (of Kashmīr) are partly **Sunnies**, and others of the sects of Aly and Noorbukhshy; and they are frequently engaged in wars with each other."—*Ayeen*, by *Gladwin*, ii. 125; ed. *Jarrett*, ii. 352.

[1623.—"The other two . . . are **Sonni**, as the Turks and Moghol."—*P. della Valle*, Hak. Soc. i. 152.

[1812.—"A fellow told me with the gravest face, that a lion of their own country would never hurt a **Sheyah** . . . but would always devour a **Sunni**."—*Morier*, *Journey through Persia*, 62.]

SUNNUD, s. Hind. from Ar. *sanad*. A diploma, patent, or deed of grant by the government of office, privilege, or right. The corresponding Skt.—H. is *śāsana*.

[c. 1590. — "A paper authenticated by proper signatures is called a **sunnud.** . . ."—*Ayeen*, by *Gladwin*, i. 214; ed. *Blochmann*, i. 259.]

1758.—"They likewise brought **sunnuds**, or the commission for the nabobship."—*Orme*, *Hist.*, ed. 1803, ii. 284.

1759.—"That your Petitioners, being the Bramins, &c. . . . were permitted by **Sunnud** from the President and Council to collect daily alms from each shop or doocan (**Doocaun**) of this place, at 5 cowries per diem."—In *Long*, 184.

1776.—"If the path to and from a House . . . be in the Territories of another Person, that Person, who always hath passed to and fro, shall continue to do so, the other Person aforesaid, though he hath a Right of Property in the Ground, and hath an attested **Sunnud** thereof, shall not have Authority to cause him any Let or Molestation."—*Halhed*, *Code*, 100-101.

1799.—"I enclose you **sunnuds** for pension for the **Killadar** of Chittledroog."—*Wellington*, i. 45.

1800.—"I wished to have traced the nature of landed property in Soondah . . . by a chain of **Sunnuds** up to the 8th century."—*Sir T. Munro*, in *Life*, i. 249.

1809.—"This **sunnud** is the foundation of all the rights and privileges annexed to a Jageer (**Jagheer**)."—*Harrington's Analysis*, ii. 410.

SUNYÁSEE, s. Skt. *sannyāsī*, lit. 'one who resigns, or abandons,' *scil.* 'wordly affairs'; a Hindu religious mendicant. The name of Sunnyásee was applied familiarly in Bengal, c. 1760-75, to a body of banditti claiming to belong to a religious fraternity, who, in the interval between the decay of the imperial authority and the regular establishment of our own, had their head-quarters in the forest-tracts at the foot of the Himālaya. From these they used to issue periodically in large bodies, plundering and levying exactions far and wide, and returning to their asylum in the jungle when threatened with pursuit. In the days of Nawāb Mīr Kāsim 'Ali (1760-64) they were bold enough to plunder the city of Dacca; and in 1766 the great geographer James

Rennell, in an encounter with a large body of them in the territory of Koch (see **COOCH**) Bihār, was nearly cut to pieces. Rennell himself, five years later, was employed to carry out a project which he had formed for the suppression of these bands, and did so apparently with what was considered at the time to be success, though we find the depredators still spoken of by W. Hastings as active, two or three years later.

[c. 200 A.D.—"Having thus performed religious acts in a forest during the third portion of his life, let him become a **Sannyasi** for the fourth portion of it, abandoning all sensual affection."—*Manu*, vi. 33.

[c. 1590.—"The fourth period is **Sannyása**, which is an extraordinary state of austerity that nothing can surpass. . . . Such a person His Majesty calls **Sannyásí**."—*Āīn*, ed. *Jarrett*, iii. 278.]

1616.—"Sunt autem **Sanasses** apud illos Brachmanes quidam, sanctimoniae opinione habentes, ab hominum scilicet consortio semoti in solitudine degentes et nonnunquã totũ nudi corpus in publicũ prodeuntes."—*Jarric, Thes.* i. 663.

1626.—"Some (an vnlearned kind) are called **Sannases**."—*Purchas, Pilgrimage*, 549.

1651.—"The **Sanyasys** are people who set the world and worldly joys, as they say, on one side. These are indeed more precise and strict in their lives than the foregoing."—*Rogerius*, 21.

1674.—"**Saniade, or Saniasi**, is a dignity greater than that of Kings."—*Faria y Sousa, Asia Port.* ii. 711.

1726.—"The **San-yasés** are men who, forsaking the world and all its fruits, betake themselves to a very strict and retired manner of life."—*Valentijn, Choro.* 75.

1766.—"The **Sanashy** Faquirs (part of the same Tribe which plundered Dacca in Cossim Ally's Time*) were in arms to the number of 7 or 800 at the Time I was surveying Báár (a small Province near Boutan), and had taken and plundered the Capital of that name within a few Coss of my route. . . . I came up with Morrison immediately after he had defeated the **Sanashys** in a pitched Battle. . . . Our Escorte, which were a few Horse, rode off, and the Enemy with drawn Sabres immediately surrounded us. Morrison escaped unhurt, Richards, my Brother officer, received only a slight Wound, and fought his Way off; my Armenian Assistant was killed, and the Sepoy Adjutant much wounded. . . . I was put in a Palankeen, and Morrison made an attack on the Enemy and cut most of them to Pieces. I was now in a most shocking Condition indeed, being deprived of the Use of both my Arms, . . . a cut of a Sable (*sic*) had cut through my right Shoulder Bone, and laid me open for nearly a Foot down the Back, cutting thro' and wounding some of my Ribs. I had besides a Cut on the left Elbow wh[ch] took off the Muscular part of the breadth of a Hand, a Stab in the Arm, and a large Cut on the head. . . ."—MS. Letter from *James Rennell*, dd. August 30, in possession of his grandson *Major Rodd*.

1767.—"A body of 5000 **Sinnasses** have lately entered the Sircar Sarong country; the Phousdar sent two companies of Sepoys after them, under the command of a serjeant . . . the **Sinnasses** stood their ground, and after the Sepoys had fired away their ammunition, fell on them, killed and wounded near 80, and put the rest to flight. . . ."—Letter to *President at Ft. William*, from *Thomas Rumbold, Chief at Patna*, dd. April 20, in *Long*, p. 526.

1773. — "You will hear of great disturbances committed by the **Sinassies**, or wandering Fackeers, who annually infest the provinces about this time of the year, in pilgrimage to Juggernaut, going in bodies of 1000 and sometimes even 10,000 men."—Letter of *Warren Hastings*, dd. February 2, in *Gleig*, i. 282.

" "At this time we have five battalions of Sepoys in pursuit of them."—Do. do., March 31, in *Gleig*, i. 294.

1774.—"The history of these people is curious. . . . They . . . rove continually from place to place, recruiting their numbers with the healthiest children they can steal. . . . Thus they are the stoutest and most active men in India. . . . Such are the **Senassies**, the gypsies of Hindostan."—Do. do., dd. August 25, in *Gleig*, 303-4. See the same vol., also pp. 284, 296-7-8, 395.

1826.—"Being looked upon with an evil eye by many persons in society, I pretended to bewail my brother's loss, and gave out my intention of becoming a **Sunyasse**, and retiring from the world."—*Pandurang Hari*, 394; [ed. 1873, ii. 267; also i. 189].

SUPÁRA, n.p. The name of a very ancient port and city of Western India; in Skt. *Sūrpāraka*,* popularly Supāra. It was near Wasāī (*Baçaim* of the Portuguese—see (1) **Bassein**)—which was for many centuries the chief city of the Konkan, where the name still survives as that of a well-to-do town of 1700 inhabitants, the channel by which vessels in former days reached

* This affair is alluded to in one of the extracts in *Long* (p. 342): "Agreed . . . that the Fakiers who were made prisoners at the retaking of Dacca may be employed as Coolies in the repair of the Factory."—*Procgs. of Council at Ft. William*, Dec. 5, 1769.

* Williams (*Skt. Dict.* s.v.) gives **Sūrpāraka** as "the name of a mythical country"; but it was real enough. There is some ground for believing that there was another *Sūrpāraka* on the coast of Orissa, Σιππάρα of Ptolemy.

it from the sea being now dry. The city is mentioned in the *Mahābhārata* as a very holy place, and in other old Sanskrit works, as well as in cave inscriptions at Kārlī and Nāsik, going back to the 1st and 2nd centuries of the Christian era. Excavations affording interesting Buddhist relics, were made in 1882 by Mr. (now Sir) J. M. Campbell (see his interesting notice in *Bombay Gazetteer*, xiv. 314-342; xvi. 125) and Pundit Indrajī Bhagwānlāl. The name of Supāra is one of those which have been plausibly connected, through *Sophir*, the Coptic name of India, with the *Ophir* of Scripture. Some Arab writers call it the Sofāla of India.

c. A.D. 80-90.—"Τοπικὰ δὲ ἐμπόρια κατὰ τὸ ἑξῆς κείμενα ἀπὸ Βαρυγάζων, Σούππαρα, καὶ Καλλιένα πόλις . . ."—*Periplus*, § 52, ed. *Fabricii.*

c. 150.—

"'Αριακῆς Σαδινῶν
Σουπάρα . . .
Γοάριος ποταμοῦ ἐκβολαι . . .
Δοῦγγα . . .
Βήνδα ποταμοῦ ἐκβολαί . . .
Σίμυλλα ἐμπόριον καὶ ἄκρα . . ."
Ptolemy, VII. i. f. § 6.

c. 460.—"The King compelling Wijayo and his retinue, 700 in number, to have the half of their heads shaved, and having embarked them in a vessel, sent them adrift on the ocean. . . . Wijayo himself landed at the port of **Suppâraka**. . . ."—*The Mahawanso*, by *Turnour*, p. 46.

c. 500.—"Σουφείρ, χώρα, ἐν ᾗ οἱ πολύτιμοι λίθοι, καὶ ὁ χρυσὸς, ἐν 'Ινδίᾳ."—*Hesychius*, s.v.

c. 951.—"Cities of Hind . . . Kambáya, **Subárá**, Sindán."—*Istakhri*, in *Elliot*, i. 27.

A.D. 1095.—"The Mahâmândalîka, the illustrious Anantadêva, the Emperor of the Koṅkan (**Concan**), has released the toll mentioned in this copper-grant given by the Sîlâras, in respect of every cart belonging to two persons . . . which may come into any of the ports, Sri Sthânaka (**Tana**), as well as Nâgapur, **Surpâraka**, Chemuli (**Chaul**) and others, included within the Koṅkan Fourteen Hundred. . . ."—*Copper-Plate Grant*, in *Ind. Antiq.* ix. 38.

c. 1150.—"**Súbára** is situated 1½ mile from the sea. It is a populous busy town, and is considered one of the entrepôts of India."—*Edrisi*, in *Elliot*, i. 85.

1321.—"There are three places where the Friars might reap a great harvest, and where they could live in common. One of these is **Supera**, where two friars might be stationed; and a second is in the district of Parocco (**Broach**), where two or three might abide; and the third is Columbus (**Quilon**)."—Letter of *Fr. Jordanus*, in *Cathay*, &c., 227.

c. 1330.—"**Sufâlah** Indica. Birunio nominatur **Sûfârah**. . . . De eo nihil commemorandum inveni."—*Abulfeda*, in *Gildemeister*, 189.

1538.—"Rent of the *caçabe* (**Cusbah**), of **Çupara** . . . 14,122 *fedeas*."—*S. Bothelho, Tombo*, 175.

1803.—Extract from a letter dated Camp **Soopara**, March 26, 1803.

"We have just been paying a formal visit to his highness the peishwa," &c.—In *Asiatic Annual Reg.* for 1803, *Chron.* p. 99.

1846.—"**Sopara** is a large place in the Agasee mahal, and contains a considerable Mussulman population, as well as Christian and Hindoo . . . there is a good deal of trade; and grain, salt, and garden produce are exported to Guzerat and Bombay."—*Desultory Notes*, by *John Vaupell, Esq.*, in *Trans. Bo. Geog. Soc.* vii. 140.

SUPREME COURT. The designation of the English Court established at Fort William by the Regulation Act of 1773 (13 Geo. III. c. 63), and afterwards at the other two Presidencies. Its extent of jurisdiction was the subject of acrimonious controversies in the early years of its existence; controversies which were closed by 21 Geo. III. c. 70, which explained and defined the jurisdiction of the Court. The use of the name came to an end in 1862 with the establishment of the 'High Court,' the bench of which is occupied by barrister judges, judges from the Civil Service, and judges promoted from the native bar.

The Charter of Charles II., of 1661, gave the Company certain powers to administer the laws of England, and that of 1683 to establish Courts of Judicature. That of Geo. I. (1726) gave power to establish at each Presidency Mayor's Courts for civil suits, with appeal to the Governor and Council, and from these, in cases involving more than 1000 **pagodas**, to the King in Council. The same charter constituted the Governor and Council of each Presidency a Court for trial of all offences except high treason. Courts of Requests were established by charter of Geo. II., 1753. The Mayor's Court at Madras and Bombay survived till 1797, when (by 37 Geo. III. ch. 142) a Recorder's Court was instituted at each. This was superseded at Madras by a Supreme Court in 1801, and at Bombay in 1823.

SURA, s. **Toddy** (q.v.), *i.e.* the fermented sap of several kinds of palm, such as coco, palmyra, and wild-date. It is the Skt. *sura*, 'vinous liquor,' which has passed into most of the vernaculars. In the first quotation we certainly have the word, though combined with other elements of uncertain identity, applied by Cosmas to the milk of the coco-nut, perhaps making some confusion between that and the fermented sap. It will be seen that Linschoten applies *sura* in the same way. Bluteau, curiously, calls this a *Caffre* word. It has in fact been introduced from India into Africa by the Portuguese (see *Ann. Marit.* iv. 293).

c. 545.—"The Argell" (*i.e. Nargil*, or **nargeela**, or coco-nut) "is at first full of very sweet water, which the Indians drink, using it instead of wine. This drink is called *Rhonco*-**sura**,* and is exceedingly pleasant."—*Cosmas*, in *Cathay*, &c., clxxvi.

[1554.—"**Cura.**" See under **ARRACK.**]

1563.—"They grow two qualities of palm-tree, one kind for the fruit, and the other to give **çura.**"—*Garcia*, f. 67.

1578.—"**Sura**, which is, as it were, *vino mosto.*"—*Acosta*, 100.

1598.—". . . in that sort the pot in short space is full of water, which they call **Sura**, and is very pleasant to drinke, like sweet whay, and somewhat better."—*Linschoten*, 101; [Hak. Soc. ii. 48].

1609-10.—". . . A goodly country and fertile . . . abounding with Date Trees, whence they draw a liquor, called *Tarree* (**Toddy**) or **Sure**. . . ."—*W. Finch*, in *Purchas*, i. 436.

1643.—"Là ie fis boire mes mariniers de telle sorte que peu s'en falut qu'ils ne renuersassent notre almadie ou batteau: Ce breuvage estoit du **sura**, qui est du vin fait de palmes."—*Mocquet, Voyages*, 252.

c. 1650.—"Nor could they drink either Wine, or **Sury**, or Strong Water, by reason of the great Imposts which he laid upon them."—*Tavernier*, E.T. ii. 86; [ed. *Ball*, i. 343].

1653.—"Les Portugais appelent ce *tari* ou vin des Indes, **Soure** . . . de cette liqueur le singe, et la grande chauue-souris . . . sont extremement amateurs, aussi bien que les Indiens Mansulmans (*sic*), Parsis, et quelque tribus d'Indou. . . ."—*De la Boullaye-le-Gouz*, ed. 1657, 263.

SURAT, n.p. In English use the name of this city is accented *Surătt*; but the name is in native writing and parlance generally *Sŭrăt*. In the *Āīn*, however (see below), it is written *Sūrat*; also in *Ṣādiķ Isfahānī* (p. 106). Surat was taken by Akbar in 1573, having till then remained a part of the falling Mahommedan kingdom of Guzerat. An English factory was first established in 1608-9, which was for more than half a century the chief settlement of the English Company in Continental India. The transfer of the Chiefs to Bombay took place in 1687.

We do not know the origin of the name. Various legends on the subject are given in Mr. (now Sir J.) Campbell's *Bombay Gazetteer* (vol. ii.), but none of them have any probability. The ancient Indian *Saurāshtra* was the name of the Peninsula of Guzerat or Kattywar, or at least of the maritime part of it. This latter name and country is represented by the differently spelt and pronounced *Sōrath* (see **SŪRATH**). Sir Henry Elliot and his editor have repeatedly stated the opinion that the names are identical. Thus: "The names 'Surat' and 'Sūrath' are identical, both being derived from the Sankrit *Surāshtra*; but as they belong to different places a distinction in spelling has been maintained. 'Surat' is the city; 'Súrath' is a *prānt* or district of Kattiwar, of which Junágarh is the chief town" (*Elliot*, v. 350; see also 197). Also: "The Sanskrit *Surāshtra* and *Gurjjara* survive in the modern names *Surat* and *Guzerat*, and however the territories embraced by the old terms have varied, it is hard to conceive that Surat was not in Surāshtra nor Guzerat in Gurjjara. All evidence goes to prove that the old and modern names applied to the same places. Thus Ptolemy's *Surastrene* comprises Surat. . . ." (*Dowson* (?) *ibid.* i. 359). This last statement seems distinctly erroneous. Surat is in Ptolemy's Λάρικη, not in Συραστρηνή, which represents, like Saurāshtra, the peninsula. It must remain doubtful whether there was any connection between the names, or the resemblance was accidental. It is possible that continental Surat may have originally had some name implying its being the place of passage to *Saurāshtra* or Sorath.

Surat is not a place of any antiquity. There are some traces of the existence of the name ascribed to the 14th century, in passages of uncertain value in certain native writers. But it only

* Ῥογχὸ perhaps is Tam. *lanha*, 'coco-nut.'

came to notice as a place of any importance about the very end of the 15th century, when a rich Hindu trader, Gopi by name, is stated to have established himself on the spot, and founded the town. The way, however, in which it is spoken of by Barbosa previous to 1516 shows that the rise of its prosperity must have been rapid.

[*Surat* in English slang is equivalent to the French *Rafiot*, in the sense of 'no great shakes,' an adulterated article of inferior quality (*Barrére*, s.v. *Rafiot*). This perhaps was accounted for by the fact that "until lately the character of Indian cotton in the Liverpool market stood very low, and the name '*Surats*,' the description under which the cotton of this province is still included, was a byword and a general term of contempt" (*Berar Gazetteer*, 226 *seq.*).]

1510.—"Don Afonso" (de Noronha, nephew of Alboquerque) "in the storm not knowing whither they went, entered the Gulf of Cambay, and struck upon a shoal in front of **Çurrate**. Trying to save themselves by swimming or on planks many perished, and among them Don Afonso."—*Correa*, ii. 29.

1516.—"Having passed beyond the river of Reynel, on the other side there is a city which they call **Çurate**, peopled by Moors, and close upon the river; they deal there in many kinds of wares, and carry on a great trade; for many ships of Malabar and other parts sail thither, and sell what they bring, and return loaded with what they choose. . . ."—*Barbosa*, Lisbon ed. 280.

1525.—"The corjaa (**Corge**) of cotton cloths of **Çuryate**, of 14 yards each, is worth . . . 250 *fedeas*."—*Lembrança*, 45.

1528.—"Heytor da Silveira put to sea again, scouring the Gulf, and making war everywhere with fire and sword, by sea and land; and he made an onslaught on **Çurrate** and Reynel, great cities on the sea-coast, and sacked them, and burnt part of them, for all the people fled, they being traders and without a garrison. . . ."—*Correa*, iii. 277.

1553.—"Thence he proceeded to the bar of the river Tapty, above which stood two cities the most notable on that gulf. The first they call **Surat**, 3 leagues from the mouth, and the other Reiner, on the opposite side of the river and half a league from the bank. . . . The latter was the most sumptuous in buildings and civilisation, inhabited by warlike people, all of them Moors inured to maritime war, and it was from this city that most of the foists and ships of the King of Cambay's fleet were furnished. **Surat** again was inhabited by an unwarlike people whom they call **Banyans**, folk given to mechanic crafts, chiefly to the business of weaving cotton cloths."—*Barros*, IV. iv. 8.

1554.—"So saying they quitted their rowing-benches, got ashore, and started for **Surrat**."—*Sidi 'Ali*, p. 83.

1573.—"Next day the Emperor went to inspect the fortress. . . . During his inspection some large mortars and guns attracted his attention. Those mortars bore the name of Sulaimání, from the name of Sulaimán Sultán of Turkey. When he made his attempt to conquer the ports of Gujarát, he sent these . . . with a large army by sea. As the Turks . . . were obliged to return, they left these mortars. . . . The mortars remained upon the sea-shore, until Khudáwand Khán built the fort of **Surat**, when he placed them in the fort. The one which he left in the country of **Súrath** was taken to the fort of Junágarh by the ruler of that country."—*Ṭabaḳāt-i-Akbarī*, in *Elliot*, v. 350.

c. 1590.—"**Sūrat** is among famous ports. The river Taptī runs hard by, and at seven coss distance joins the salt sea. Rānīr on the other side of the river is now a port dependent on **Sūrat**, but was formerly a big city. The ports of Khandevī and Balsār are also annexed to **Sūrat**. Fruit, and especially the **ananās**, is abundant. . . . The sectaries of Zardasht, emigrant from Fārs, have made their dwelling here; they revere the Zhand and Pazhand and erect their *dakhmas* (or places for exposing the dead). . . . Through the carelessness of the agents of Government and the commandants of the troops (*sipah-salārān*, **Sipah Selar**), a considerable tract of this Sirkār is at present in the hands of the Frank, *e.g.* Daman, Sanjān (**St. John's**), Tārāpūr, Māhim, and Basai (see (1) **Bassein**), that are both cities and forts."—*Āin*, orig. i. 488; [ed. *Jarrett*, ii. 243].

[1615.—"To the Right Honourable Sir Thomas Roe . . . these in **Zuratt**."—*Foster*, *Letters*, iii. 196.]

1638.—"Within a League of the Road we entred into the River upon which **Surat** is seated, and which hath on both sides a very fertile soil, and many fair gardens, with pleasant Country-houses, which being all white, a colour which it seems the *Indians* are much in love with, afford a noble prospect amidst the greenness whereby they are encompassed. But the River, which is the *Tapte* . . . is so shallow at the mouth of it, that Barks of 70 or 80 Tun can hardly come into it."—*Mandelslo*, p. 12.

1690.—"**Suratt** is reckon'd the most fam'd Emporium of the *Indian* Empire, where all Commodities are vendible. . . . And the River is very commodious for the Importation of Foreign Goods, which are brought up to the City in Hoys and Yachts, and Country Boats."—*Ovington*, 218.

1779.—"There is some report that he (Gen. Goddard) is gone to *Bender*-**Souret** . . . but the truth of this God knows."—*Seir Mutaq*. iii. 328.

SURATH, more properly **Sōrath**, and **Sōreth**, n.p. This name is the legitimate modern form and representative of the ancient Indian *Saurāshṭra* and Greek *Syrastrēnē*, names which applied to what we now call the Kattywar Peninsula, but especially to the fertile plains on the sea-coast. ["Suráshṭra, the land of the Sus, afterwards Sanskritized into Sauráshṭra the Goodly Land, preserves its name in **Sorath** the southern part of Káthiáváḍa. The name appears as *Suráshtra* in the *Mahábhárata* and Pánini's *Gaṇapátha*, in Rudradáman's (A.D. 150) and Skandagupta's (A.D. 456) Girnár inscriptions, and in several Valabhi copper-plates. Its Prákrit form appears as *Suraṭha* in the Násik inscription of Gotamiputra (A.D. 150) and in later Prákrit as *Suraṭhṭha* in the *Tírthakalpa* of Jinapra-bhásuri of the 13th or 14th century. Its earliest foreign mention is perhaps Strabo's *Saraostus* and Pliny's *Oratura*" (*Bombay Gazetteer*, i. pt. i. 6)]. The remarkable discovery of one of the great inscriptions of Aśoka (B.C. 250) on a rock at Girnār, near Junāgarh in Saurāshtra, shows that the dominion of that great sovereign, whose capital was at Pataliputra (Παλιμβόθρα) or **Patna**, extended to this distant shore. The application of the modern form Sūrath or Sōrath has varied in extent. It is now the name of one of the four *prānts* or districts into which the peninsula is divided for political purposes, each of these *prānts* containing a number of small States, and being partly managed, partly controlled by a Political Assistant. Sorath occupies the south-western portion, embracing an area of 5,220 sq. miles.

c. A.D. 80–90.—"Ταύτης τὰ μὲν μεσόγεια τῇ Σκυθίᾳ συνορίζοντα Ἀβιρία καλεῖται, τὰ δὲ παραθαλάσσια Συραστρήνη."—*Periplus*, § 41.

c. 150.—

"Συραστρηνῆς, * * *
Βαρδάξημα πόλις . . .
Συράστρα κώμη . . .
Μονόγλωσσον ἐμπόριον . . ."

Ptolemy, VII. i. 2-3.

" "Πάλιν ἡ μὲν παρὰ τὸ λοιπὸν μέρος τοῦ Ἰνδοῦ πᾶσα καλεῖται κοινῶς μὲν . . . Ἰνδοσκυθία

* * * * * *

καὶ ἡ περὶ τὸν Κάνθι κόλπον . . . Συραστρηνή."—*Ibid.* 55.

c. 545.—"Εἰσὶν οὖν τὰ λαμπρὰ ἐμπόρια τῆς Ἰνδικῆς ταῦτα, Σινδοῦ, Ὀῤῥοθὰ, Καλλιάνα, Σιβὼρ, ἡ Μαλὲ, πέντε ἐμπόρια ἔχουσα βάλλοντα τὸ πέπερι."—*Cosmas*, lib. xi. These names may be interpreted as **Sind, Sorath, Calyan, Choul** (?), **Malabar**.

c. 640.—"En quittant le royaume de *Fa-la-pi* (Vallabhi), il fit 500 *li* à l'ouest, et arriva au royaume de *Sou-la-tch'a* (**Sourâchtra**). . . . Comme ce royaume se trouve sur le chemin de la mer occidentale, tous les habitans profitent des avantages qu'offre la mer; ils se livrent au négoce, et à un commerce d'échange."—*Hiouen-Thsang*, in *Pèl. Bouddh.*, iii. 164-165.

1516.—"Passing this city and following the sea-coast, you come to another place which has also a good port, and is called **Çurati Mangalor**,* and here, as at the other, put in many vessels of Malabar for horses, grain, cloths, and cottons, and for vegetables and other goods prized in India, and they bring hither coco-nuts, Jagara (**Jaggery**), which is sugar that they make drink of, emery, wax, cardamoms, and every other kind of spice, a trade in which great gain is made in a short time."—*Barbosa*, in *Ramusio*, i. f. 296.

1573. — See quotation of this date under preceding article, in which both the names **Surat** and **Sūrath**, occur.

1584.—"After his second defeat Muzaffar Gujarátí retreated by way of Champánír, Bírpúr, and Jhaláwar, to the country of **Súrath**, and rested at the town of Gondal, 12 *kos* from the fort of Junágarh. . . . He gave a lac of *Mahmúdís* and a jewelled dagger to Amín Khán Ghorí, ruler of **Súrath**, and so won his support."—*Ṭabaḳāt-i-Akbarí*, in *Elliot*, v. 437-438.

c. 1590.—"Sircar *Surat* (**Sūrath**) was formerly an independent territory; the chief was of the Ghelolo tribe, and commanded 50,000 cavalry, and 100,000 infantry. Its length from the port of Ghogeh (**Gogo**) to the port of Aramroy (*Arāmrāī*) measures 125 *cose*; and the breadth from Sindehar (*Sirdhār*), to the port of **Diu**, is a distance of 72 *cose*."—*Ayeen*, by *Gladwin*, ii. 73; [ed. *Jarrett*, ii. 243].

1616.—"7 **Soret**, the chief city, is called *Janagar*; it is but a little Province, yet very rich; it lyes upon Guzarat; it hath the Ocean to the South."—*Terry*, ed. 1665, p. 354.

SURKUNDA, s. Hind. *sarkandā*, [Skt. *śara*, 'reed-grass,' *kāṇḍa*, 'joint, section']. The name of a very tall reed-grass, *Saccharum Sara*, Roxb., perhaps also applied to *Saccharum procerum*, Roxb. These grasses are often tall enough in the riverine plains of Eastern Bengal greatly to overtop a tall man standing in a

* **Mangalore** (q.v.) on this coast, no doubt called *Sorathī* Mangalor to distinguish it from the well-known Mangalor of Canara.

howda on the back of a tall elephant. It is from the upper part of the flower-bearing stalk of *surkunda* that **sirky** (q.v.) is derived. A most intelligent visitor to India was led into a curious mistake about the name of this grass by some official, who ought to have known better. We quote the passage. ———'s story about the main branch of a river channel probably rests on no better foundation.

1875.—"As I drove yesterday with ——, I asked him if he knew the scientific name of the tall grass which I heard called tiger-grass at Ahmedabad, and which is very abundant here (about Lahore). I think it is a *saccharum*, but am not quite sure. 'No,' he said, 'but the people in the neighbourhood call it **Sikunder's Grass**, as they still call the main branch of a river 'Sikander's channel.' Strange, is it not?—how that great individuality looms through history."—*Grant Duff, Notes of an Indian Journey*, 105.

SURPOOSE, s. Pers. *sar-posh*, 'head-cover,' [which again becomes corrupted into our *Tarboosh* (*tarbūsh*), and '*Tarbrush*' of the wandering Briton]. A cover, as of a basin, dish, hooka-bowl, &c.

1829.—"Tugging away at your hookah, find no smoke; a thief having purloined your silver **chelam** (see **CHILLUM**) and **surpoose**."—*Mem. of John Shipp*, ii. 159.

SURRAPURDA, s. Pers. *sarā-parda*. A canvas screen surrounding royal tents or the like (see **CANAUT**).

1404.—"And round this pavilion stood an enclosure, as it were, of a town or castle made of silk of many colours, inlaid in many ways, with battlements at the top, and with cords to strain it outside and inside, and with poles inside to hold it up. . . . And there was a gateway of great height forming an arch, with doors within and without made in the same fashion as the wall . . . and above the gateway a square tower with battlements: however fine the said wall was with its many devices and artifices, the said gateway, arch and tower, was of much more exquisite work still. And this enclosure they call **Zalaparda**."—*Clavijo*, s. cxvi.

c. 1590.—"The **Sarápardah** was made in former times of coarse canvass, but his Majesty has now caused it to be made of carpeting, and thereby improved its appearance and usefulness."—*Āīn*, i. 54.

[1839.—"The camp contained numerous enclosures of **serrapurdahs** or canvass skreens. . . ."—*Elphinstone, Caubul*, 2nd ed. i. 101.]

SURRINJAUM, s. Pers. *saranjām*, lit. 'beginning-ending.' Used in India for 'apparatus,' 'goods and chattels,' and the like. But in the Mahratta provinces it has a special application to grants of land, or rather assignments of revenue, for special objects, such as keeping up a contingent of troops for service; to civil officers for the maintenance of their state; or for charitable purposes.

[1823.—"It was by accident I discovered the deed for this tenure (for the support of troops), which is termed **serinjam**. The Pundit of Dhar shewed some alarm; at which I smiled, and told him that his master had now the best tenure in India. . . ." *Malcolm, Central India*, 2nd ed. i. 103.]

[1877.—"Government . . . did not accede to the recommendation of the political agent immediately to confiscate his **saringam**, or territories."—*Mrs. Guthrie, My Year in an Indian Fort*, i. 166.]

SURRINJAUMEE, GRAM, s. Hind. *grām-saranjāmī*; Skt. *grāma*, 'a village,' and *saranjām* (see **SURRINJAUM**); explained in the quotation.

1767. — "**Gram-serenjammee**, or peons and pykes stationed in every village of the province to assist the farmers in the collections, and to watch the villages and the crops on the ground, who are also responsible for all thefts within the village they belong to . . . (Rs.) 1,54,521 : 14." — *Revenue Accounts of Burdwan*. In *Long*, 507.

SURROW, SEROW, &c., s. Hind. *sarāo*. A big, odd, awkward-looking antelope in the Himālaya, 'something in appearance between a jackass and a *Tahir*' (**Tehr** or Him. wild goat).—*Col. Markham* in *Jerdon*. It is *Nemorhoedus bubalina*, Jerdon; [*N. bubalinus*, Blanford (*Mammalia*, 513)].

SURWAUN, s. Hind. from Pers. *sārwān*, *sārbān*, from *sār* in the sense of camel, a camel-man.

[1828.—". . . camels roaring and blubbering, and resisting every effort, soothing or forcible, of their **serwans** to induce them to embark." — *Mundy, Pen and Pencil Sketches*, ed. 1858, p. 185.]

1844.—". . . armed **Surwans**, or camel-drivers."—*G. O. of Sir C. Napier*, 93.

SUTLEDGE, n.p. The most easterly of the Five Rivers of the Punjab, the great tributaries of the Indus. Hind. *Satlaj*, with certain variations in spelling and pronunciation. It is in Skt. *Satadru*, 'flowing in a hundred channels,' *Sutudru*, *Sutudri*, *Sitadru*, &c., and is the Σαράδρος, Ζαράδρος, or Σαδάδρης of Ptolemy, the Sydrus (or *Hesudrus*) of Pliny (vi. 21).

c. 1020.—"The Sultán . . . crossed in safety the Síhún (Indus), Jelam, Chandráha, Ubrá (Rávi), Bah (Bíyáh), and **Sataldur.** . . ."—*Al-'Utbi*, in *Elliot*, ii. 41.

c. 1030.—"They all combine with the **Satlader** below Múltán, at a place called Panjnad, or 'the junction of the five rivers.'"—*Al-Birūnī*, in *Elliot*, i. 48. The same writer says: "(The name) should be written **Shataludr.** It is the name of a province in Hind. But I have ascertained from well-informed people that it should be *Sataludr*, not *Shataldudr*" (*sic*).—*Ibid.* p. 52.

c. 1310.—"After crossing the Panjáb, or five rivers, namely, Sind, Jelam, the river of Loháwar, **Satlút**, and Bíyah. . . ."—*Wassāf*, in *Elliot*, iii. 36.

c. 1380.—"The Sultán (Fíroz Sháh) . . . conducted two streams into the city from two rivers, one from the river Jumna, the other from the **Sutlej.**"—*Táríkh-i-Fíroz-Sháhí*, in *Elliot*, iii. 300.

c. 1450.—"In the year 756 H. (1355 A.D.) the Sultán proceeded to Díbálpúr, and conducted a stream from the river **Satladar**, for a distance of 40 *kos* as far as Jhajar."—*Táríkh-i-Mubárak Sháhí*, in *Elliot*, iv. 8.

c. 1582.—"Letters came from Lahore with the intelligence that Ibrahím Husain Mirzá had crossed the **Satlada**, and was marching upon Dipálpúr."—*Ṭabakāt-i-Akbarī*, in *Elliot*, v. 358.

c. 1590.—"*Sūbah Dihlī.* In the 3rd climate. The length (of this Sūbah) from Palwal to Lodhiāna, which is on the bank of the river **Satlaj**, is 165 *Kuroh.*"—*Āīn*, orig. i. 513; [ed. *Jarrett*, ii. 278].

1793.—"Near Moultan they unite again, and bear the name of **Setlege**, until both the substance and name are lost in the Indus."—*Rennell*, *Memoir*, 102.

In the following passage the great French geographer has missed the Sutlej:

1753.—"Les cartes qui ont précédé celles que j'ai composées de l'Arie, ou de l'Inde . . . ne marquoient aucune rivière entre l'Hyphasis, ou Hypasis, dernier des fleuves qui se rendent dans l'Indus, et le Gemné, qui est le *Jomanes* de l'Antiquité. . . . Mais la marche de Timur a indiqué dans cette intervalle deux rivières, celle de *Kehker* et celle de *Panipat.* Dans un ancien itineraire de l'Inde, que Pline nous a conservé, on trouve entre l'*Hyphasis* et le *Jomanes* une rivière sous le nom d'**Hesidrus** à égale distance d'Hyphasis et de Jomanes, et qu'on a tout lieu de prendre pour *Kehker.*"—*D'Anville*, p. 47.

SUTTEE, s. The rite of widow-burning; *i.e.* the burning of the living widow along with the corpse of her husband, as practised by people of certain castes among the Hindus, and eminently by the Rājpūts.

The word is properly Skt. *satī*, 'a good woman,' 'a true wife,' and thence specially applied, in modern vernaculars of Sanskrit parentage, to the wife who was considered to accomplish the supreme act of fidelity by sacrificing herself on the funeral pile of her husband. The application of this substantive to the suicidal act, instead of the person, is European. The proper Skt. term for the act is *sahagamana*, or 'keeping company,' [*sahamaraṇa*, 'dying together'].* A very long series of quotations in illustration of the practice, from classical times downwards, might be given. We shall present a selection.

We should remark that the word (*satī* or *suttee*) does not occur, so far as we know, in any European work older than the 17th century. And then it only occurs in a disguised form (see quotation from P. Della Valle). The term *masti* which he uses is probably *mahā-satī*, which occurs in Skt. Dictionaries ('a wife of great virtue'). Della Valle is usually eminent in the correctness of his transcriptions of Oriental words. This conjecture of the interpretation of *masti* is confirmed, and the traveller himself justified, by an entry in Mr. Whitworth's Dictionary of a word *Masti-kalla* used in Canara for a monument commemorating a *sati.* *Kalla* is stone and *masti*=*mahā-satī.* We have not found the term exactly in any European document older than Sir C. Malet's letter of 1787, and Sir W. Jones's of the same year (see below).

Suttee is a Brahmanical rite, and there is a Sanskrit ritual in existence (see *Classified Index to the Tanjore MSS.*, p. 135*a*). It was introduced into Southern India with the Brahman civilisation, and was prevalent there chiefly in the Brahmanical Kingdom of Vijayanagar, and among the Mahrattas. In Malabar, the most primitive part

* But it is worthy of note that in the Island of Bali one manner of accomplishing the rite is called **Satia** (Skt. *satyā*, 'truth,' from *sat*, whence also *satī*). See *Crawfurd*, *H. of Ind. Archip.* ii. 243, and *Friedrich*, in *Verhandelingen van het Batav. Genootschap.* xxiii. 10.

of S. India, the rite is forbidden (*Anāchāranirṇaya*, v. 26). The cases mentioned by Teixeira below, and in the *Lettres Édifiantes*, occurred at Tanjore and Madura. A (Mahratta) Brahman at Tanjore told one of the present writers that he had to perform commemorative funeral rites for his grandfather and grandmother on the same day, and this indicated that his grandmother had been a *satī*.

The practice has prevailed in various regions besides India. Thus it seems to have been an early custom among the heathen Russians, or at least among nations on the Volga called Russians by Maṣ'ūdī and Ibn Foẓlān. Herodotus (Bk. v. ch. 5) describes it among certain tribes of Thracians. It was in vogue in Tonga and the Fiji Islands. It has prevailed in the island of Bali within our own time, though there accompanying Hindu rites, and perhaps of Hindu origin,—certainly modified by Hindu influence. A full account of Suttee as practised in those Malay Islands will be found in Zollinger's account of the Religion of Sassak in *J. Ind. Arch.* ii. 166; also see Friedrich's *Bali* as in note preceding. [A large number of references to *Suttee* are collected in Frazer, *Pausanias*, iii. 198 *seqq.*]

In Diodorus we have a long account of the rivalry as to which of the two wives of Kēteus, a leader of the Indian contingent in the army of Eumenes, should perform **suttee**. One is rejected as with child. The history of the other terminates thus:

B.C. 317.—"Finally, having taken leave of those of the household, she was set upon the pyre by her own brother, and was regarded with wonder by the crowd that had run together to the spectacle, and heroically ended her life; the whole force with their arms thrice marching round the pyre before it was kindled. But she, laying herself beside her husband, and even at the violence of the flame giving utterance to no unbecoming cry, stirred pity indeed in others of the spectators, and in some excess of eulogy; not but what there were some of the Greeks present who reprobated such rites as barbarous and cruel. . . ."—*Diod. Sic. Biblioth.* xix. 33-34.

c. B.C. 30.

"Felix Eois lex funeris una maritis
  Quos Aurora suis rubra colorat equis;
Namque ubi mortifero jacta est fax ultima lecto
  Uxorum fusis stat pia turba comis;
Et certamen habet leti, quae viva sequatur
  Conjugium; pudor est non licuisse mori.
Ardent victrices; et flammae pectora praebent,
  Imponuntque suis ora perusta viris."
Propertius,* Lib. iii. xiii. 15-22.

c. B.C. 20.—"He (Aristobulus) says that he had heard from some persons of wives burning themselves voluntarily with their deceased husbands, and that those women who refused to submit to this custom were disgraced."—*Strabo*, xv. 62 (E.T. by *Hamilton and Falconer*, iii. 112).

A.D. c. 390.—"Indi, ut omnes fere barbari uxores plurimas habent. Apud eos lex est, ut uxor carissima cum defuncto marito cremetur. Hae igitur contendunt inter se de amore viri, et ambitio summa certantium est, ac testimonium castitatis, dignam morte decerni. Itaque victrix in habitu ornatuque pristino juxta cadaver accubat, amplexans illud et deosculans et suppositos ignes prudentiae laude contemnens."—*St. Jerome, Advers. Jovinianum*, in ed. *Vallars*, ii. 311.

c. 851.—"All the Indians burn their dead. Serendib is the furthest out of the islands dependent upon India. Sometimes when they burn the body of a King, his wives cast themselves on the pile, and burn with him; but it is at their choice to abstain."—*Reinaud, Relation*, &c. i. 50.

c. 1200.—"Hearing the Raja was dead, the Parmâri became a **satí**:—dying she said—The son of the Jadavanî will rule the country, may my blessing be on him!"—*Chand Bardai*, in *Ind. Ant.* i. 227. We cannot be sure that *sati* is in the original, as this is a *condensed* version by Mr. Beames.

1298.—"Many of the women also, when their husbands die and are placed on the pile to be burnt, do burn themselves along with the bodies."—*Marco Polo*, Bk. iii. ch. 17.

c. 1322.—"The idolaters of this realm have one detestable custom (that I must mention). For when any man dies they burn him; and if he leave a wife they burn her alive with him, saying that she ought to go and keep her husband company in the other world. But if the woman have sons by her husband she may abide with them, an she will."—*Odoric*, in *Cathay*, &c., i. 79.

" Also in Zampa or **Champa**: "When a married man dies in this country his body is burned, and his living wife along with it. For they say that she should go to keep company with her husband in the other world also."—*Ibid.* 97.

c. 1328.—"In this India, on the death of a noble, or of any people of substance, their bodies are burned; and eke their wives follow them alive to the fire, and for the sake of worldly glory, and for the love of their husbands, and for eternal life, burn along with them, with as much joy as if they were going to be wedded. And those

* The same poet speaks of Evadne, who threw herself at Thebes on the burning pile of her husband Capaneus (I. xv. 21), a story which Paley thinks must have come from some early Indian legend.

who do this have the higher repute for virtue and perfection among the rest."—*Fr. Jordanus*, 20.

c. 1343.—"The burning of the wife after the death of her husband is an act among the Indians recommended, but not obligatory. If a widow burns herself, the members of the family get the glory thereof, and the fame of fidelity in fulfilling their duties. She who does not give herself up to the flames puts on coarse raiment and abides with her kindred, wretched and despised for having failed in duty. But she is not compelled to burn herself." (There follows an interesting account of instances witnessed by the traveller.)—*Ibn Batuta*, ii. 138.

c. 1430.—"In Mediâ vero Indiâ mortui comburuntur, cumque his, ut plurimum vivae uxores . . . una pluresve, prout fuit matrimonii conventio. Prior ex lege uritur, etiam quae unica est. Sumuntur autem et aliae uxores quaedam eo pacto, ut morte funus suâ exornent, isque haud parvus apud eos honos ducitur . . . submisso igne uxor ornatiori cultu inter tubas tibicinasque et cantus, et ipsa psallentis more alacris rogum magno comitatu circuit. Adstat interea et sacerdos . . . hortando suadens. Cum circumierit illa saepius ignem prope suggestum consistit, vestesque exuens, loto de more prius corpore, tum sindonem albam induta, ad exhortationem dicentis in ignem prosilit."—*N. Conti*, in *Poggius de Var. Fort.* iv.

c. 1520.—"There are in this Kingdom (the Deccan) many heathen, natives of the country, whose custom it is that when they die they are burnt, and their wives along with them; and if these will not do it they remain in disgrace with all their kindred. And as it happens oft times that they are unwilling to do it, their Bramin kinsfolk persuade them thereto, and this in order that such a fine custom should not be broken and fall into oblivion."—*Sommario de' Genti*, in *Ramusio*, i. f. 329.

" "In this country of **Camboja** . . . when the King dies, the lords voluntarily burn themselves, and so do the King's wives at the same time, and so also do other women on the death of their husbands."—*Ibid.* f. 336.

1522.—"They told us that in Java Major it was the custom, when one of the chief men died, to burn his body; and then his principal wife, adorned with garlands of flowers, has herself carried in a chair by four men . . . comforting her relations, who are afflicted because she is going to burn herself with the corpse of her husband . . . saying to them, 'I am going this evening to sup with my dear husband and to sleep with him this night.' . . . After again consoling them (she) casts herself into the fire and is burned. If she did not do this she would not be looked upon as an honourable woman, nor as a faithful wife."—*Pigafetta*, E.T. by *Lord Stanley of A.*, 154.

c. 1566.—Cesare Federici notices the rite as peculiar to the Kingdom of "*Bezeneger*" (see **BISNAGAR**): "vidi cose stranie e bestiali di quella gentilitâ; vsano primamente abbrusciare i corpi morti cosi d'huomini come di donne nobili; e si l'huomo è maritato, la moglie è obligata ad abbrusciarsi viva col corpo del marito."—*Orig.* ed. p. 36. This traveller gives a good account of a Suttee.

1583.—"In the interior of Hindústán it is the custom when a husband dies, for his widow willingly and cheerfully to cast herself into the flames (of the funeral pile), although she may not have lived happily with him. Occasionally love of life holds her back, and then her husband's relations assemble, light the pile, and place her upon it, thinking that they thereby preserve the honour and character of the family. But since the country had come under the rule of his gracious Majesty [Akbar], inspectors had been appointed in every city and district, who were to watch carefully over these two cases, to discriminate between them, and to prevent any woman being forcibly burnt."—*Abu'l Fazl, Akbar Námah*, in *Elliot*, vi. 69.

1583.—"Among other sights I saw one I may note as wonderful. When I landed (at Negapatam) from the vessel, I saw a pit full of kindled charcoal; and at that moment a young and beautiful woman was brought by her people on a litter, with a great company of other women, friends of hers, with great festivity, she holding a mirror in her left hand, and a lemon in her right hand. . . ."—and so forth.—*G. Balbi*, f. 82*v*. 83.

1586.—"The custom of the countrey (Java) is, that whensoever the King doeth die, they take the body so dead and burne it, and preserve the ashes of him, and within five dayes next after, the wiues of the said King so dead, according to the custome and vse of their countrey, every one of them goe together to a place appointed, and the chiefe of the women which was nearest to him in accompt, hath a ball in her hand, and throweth it from her, and the place where the ball resteth, thither they goe all, and turne their faces to the Eastward, and every one with a dagger in their hand (which dagger they call a crise (see **CREASE**), and is as sharpe as a rasor), stab themselues in their owne blood, and fall a-groueling on their faces, and so ende their dayes."—*T. Candish*, in *Hakl.* iv. 338. This passage refers to Blambangan at the east end of Java, which till a late date was subject to Bali, in which such practices have continued to our day. It seems probable that the Hindu rite here came in contact with the old Polynesian practices of a like kind, which prevailed *e.g.* in Fiji, quite recently. The narrative referred to below under 1633, where the victims were the slaves of a deceased queen, points to the latter origin. W. Humboldt thus alludes to similar passages in old Javanese literature: "Thus we may reckon as one of the finest episodes in the *Brata Yuda*, the story how **Satya Wati**, when she had sought out her slain husband among the wide-spread heap of corpses on the battlefield, stabs herself by his side with a dagger."—*Kawi-Sprache*, i. 89 (and see the whole section, pp. 87-95).

[c. 1590. — "When he (the Rajah of Asham) dies, his principal attendants of both sexes voluntarily bury themselves alive in his grave."—*Āīn*, ed. *Jarrett*, ii. 118.]

1598.—The usual account is given by *Linschoten*, ch. xxxvi., with a plate; [Hak. Soc. i. 249].

[c. 1610.—See an account in *Pyrard de Laval*, Hak. Soc. i. 394.]

1611.—"When I was in India, on the death of the Naique (see **NAIK**) of Maduré, a country situated between that of Malauar and that of Choromandel, 400 wives of his burned themselves along with him."—*Teixeira*, i. 9.

c. 1620.—"The author . . . when in the territory of the Karnátik . . . arrived in company with his father at the city of Southern Mathura (Madura), where, after a few days, the ruler died and went to hell. The chief had 700 wives, and they all threw themselves at the same time into the fire."—*Muhammad Sharíf Hanafí*, in *Elliot*, vii. 139.

1623.—"When I asked further if force was ever used in these cases, they told me that usually it was not so, but only at times among persons of quality, when some one had left a young and handsome widow, and there was a risk either of her desiring to marry again (which they consider a great scandal) or of a worse mishap,—in such a case the relations of her husband, if they were very strict, would compel her, even against her will, to burn . . . a barbarous and cruel law indeed! But in short, as regarded Giaccamà, no one exercised either compulsion or persuasion; and she did the thing of her own free choice; both her kindred and herself exulting in it, as in an act magnanimous (which in sooth it was) and held in high honour among them. And when I asked about the ornaments and flowers that she wore, they told me this was customary as a sign of the joyousness of the **Masti** (*Masti* is what they call a woman who gives herself up to be burnt upon the death of her husband)."—*P. della Valle*, ii. 671; [Hak. Soc. ii. 275, and see ii. 266 *seq.*].

1633.—"The same day, about noon, the queen's body was burnt without the city, with two and twenty of her female slaves; and we consider ourselves bound to render an exact account of the barbarous ceremonies practised in this place on such occasions as we were witness to. . . ."—*Narrative of a Dutch Mission to Bali*, quoted by *Crawfurd*, *H. of Ind. Arch.*, ii. 244-253, from *Prevost*. It is very interesting, but too long for extract.

c. 1650.—"They say that when a woman becomes a **Sattee**, that is burns herself with the deceased, the Almighty pardons all the sins committed by the wife and husband and that they remain a long time in paradise; nay if the husband were in the infernal regions, the wife by this means draws him from thence and takes him to paradise. . . . Moreover the **Sattee**, in a future birth, returns not to the female sex . . . but she who becomes not a **Sattee**, and passes her life in widowhood, is never emancipated from the female state. . . . It is however criminal to force a woman into the fire, and equally to prevent her who voluntarily devotes herself."—*Dabistān*, ii. 75-76.

c. 1650-60.—Tavernier gives a full account of the different manners of *Suttee*, which he had witnessed often, and in various parts of India, but does not use the word. We extract the following:

c. 1648.—". . . there fell of a sudden so violent a Shower, that the Priests, willing to get out of the Rain, thrust the Woman all along into the Fire. But the Shower was so vehement, and endured so long, that the Fire was quench'd, and the Woman was not burn'd. About midnight she arose, and went and knock'd at one of her Kinsmen's Houses, where Father *Zenon* and many *Hollanders* saw her, looking so gastly and grimly, that it was enough to have scar'd them; however the pain she endur'd did not so far terrifie her, but that three days after, accompany'd by her Kindred, she went and was burn'd according to her first intention."—*Tavernier*, E.T. ii. 84; [ed. *Ball*, i. 219].

Again:

"In most places upon the Coast of Coromandel, the Women are not burnt with their deceas'd Husbands, but they are buried alive with them in holes, which the Bramins make a foot deeper than the tallness of the man and woman. Usually they chuse a Sandy place; so that when the man and woman are both let down together, all the Company with Baskets of Sand fill up the hole above half a foot higher than the surface of the ground, after which they jump and dance upon it, till they believe the woman to be stifl'd."—*Ibid.* 171; [ed. *Ball*, ii. 216].

c. 1667.—Bernier also has several highly interesting pages on this subject, in his "Letter written to M. Chapelan, sent from Chiras in Persia." We extract a few sentences: "Concerning the Women that have actually burn'd themselves, I have so often been present at such dreadful spectacles, that at length I could endure no more to see it, and I retain still some horrour when I think on't. . . . The Pile of Wood was presently all on fire, because store of Oyl and Butter had been thrown upon it, and I saw at the time through the Flames that the Fire took hold of the Cloaths of the Woman. . . . All this I saw, but observ'd not that the Woman was at all disturb'd; yea it was said, that she had been heard to pronounce with great force these two words, *Five*, *Two*, to signifie, according to the Opinion of those who hold the Souls Transmigration, that this was the 5th time she had burnt herself with the same Husband, and that there remain'd but *two* times for perfection; as if she had at that time this Remembrance, or some Prophetical Spirit."—E.T. p. 99; [ed. *Constable*, 306 *seqq.*].

1677.—Suttee, described by A. Bassing, in *Valentijn* v. (*Ceylon*) 300.

1713.—"Ce fut cette année de 1710, que mourut le Prince de Marava, âgé de plus de quatre-vingt-ans; ses femmes, en nombre de quarante sept, se brûlèrent avec le corps du Prince. . . ." (details follow). — *Père Martin* (of the Madura Mission), in *Lett. Edif.* ed. 1781, tom. xii., pp. 123 *seqq.*

1727. — "I have seen several burned several Ways. . . . I heard a Story of a Lady that had received Addresses from a Gentleman who afterwards deserted her, and her Relations died shortly after the Marriage . . . and as the Fire was well kindled . . . she espied her former Admirer, and beckned him to come to her. When he came she took him in her Arms, as if she had a Mind to embrace him; but being stronger than he, she carried him into the Flames in her Arms, where they were both consumed, with the Corpse of her Husband." —*A. Hamilton*, i. 278; [ed. 1744, i. 280].

" "The Country about (Calcutta) being overspread with *Paganisms*, the Custom of Wives burning themselves with their deceased Husbands, is also practised here. Before the *Mogul's* War, Mr. *Channock* went one time with his Ordinary Guard of Soldiers, to see a young Widow act that tragical Catastrophe, but he was so smitten with the Widow's Beauty, that he sent his Guards to take her by Force from her Executioners, and conducted her to his own Lodgings. They lived lovingly many Years, and had several Children; at length she died, after he had settled in *Calcutta*, but instead of converting her to *Christianity*, she made him a Proselyte to *Paganism*, and the only part of *Christianity* that was remarkable in him, was burying her decently, and he built a Tomb over her, where all his Life after her Death, he kept the anniversary Day of her Death by sacrificing a Cock on her Tomb, after the *Pagan* Manner." — *Ibid.* [ed. 1744], ii. 6-7. [With this compare the curious lines described as an Epitaph on "Joseph Townsend, Pilot of the Ganges" (5 ser. *Notes & Queries*, i. 466 *seq.*).]

1774.—"Here (in Bali) not only women often kill themselves, or burn with their deceased husbands, but men also burn in honour of their deceased masters."—*Forrest, V. to N. Guinea*, 170.

1787.—"Soon after I and my conductor had quitted the house, we were informed the **suttee** (for that is the name given to the person who so devotes herself) had passed. . . ." — *Sir C. Malet*, in *Parly. Papers of* 1821, p. 1 ("Hindoo Widows").

" "My Father, said he (Pundit Rhadacaunt), died at the age of one hundred years, and my mother, who was eighty years old, became a **sati**, and burned herself to expiate sins." — Letter of *Sir W. Jones*, in *Life*, ii. 120.

1792.—"In the course of my endeavours I found the poor **suttee** had no relations at Poonah."—Letter from *Sir C. Malet*, in *Forbes, Or. Mem.* ii. 394; [2nd ed. ii. 28, and see i. 178, in which the previous passage is quoted].

1808.—"These proceedings (Hindu marriage ceremonies in Guzerat) take place in the presence of a Brahmin. . . . And farther, now the young woman vows that her affections shall be fixed upon her Lord alone, not only in all this life, but will follow in death, or to the next, that she will die, that she may burn with him, through as many transmigrations as shall secure their joint immortal bliss. Seven successions of **suttees** (a woman seven times born and burning, thus, as often) secure to the loving couple a seat among the gods."—*R. Drummond.*

1809.—

"O sight of misery!
You cannot hear her cries . . . their sound
In that wild dissonance is drowned; . . .
But in her face you see
The supplication and the agony . . .
See in her swelling throat the desperate strength
That with vain effort struggles yet for life;
Her arms contracted now in fruitless strife,
Now wildly at full length,
Towards the crowd in vain for pity spread, . . .
They force her on, they bind her to the dead."

Kehama, i. 12.

In all the poem and its copious notes, the word **suttee** does not occur.

[1815.—"In reference to this mark of strong attachment (of Sati for Siva), a Hindoo widow burning with her husband on the funeral pile is called **sutee.**"—*Ward, Hindoos*, 2nd ed. ii. 25.]

1828.—"After having bathed in the river, the widow lighted a brand, walked round the pile, set it on fire, and then mounted cheerfully: the flame caught and blazed up instantly; she sat down, placing the head of the corpse on her lap, and repeated several times the usual form, 'Ram, Ram, **Suttee**; Ram, Ram, **Suttee.**'"—*Wanderings of a Pilgrim*, i. 91-92.

1829.—"*Regulation XVII.*

"A Regulation for declaring the practice of **Suttee**, or of burning or burying alive the widows of Hindoos, illegal, and punishable by the Criminal Courts." — Passed by the *G.-G. in C.*, Dec. 4.

1839.—"Have you yet heard in England of the horrors that took place at the funeral of that wretched old Runjeet Singh? *Four* wives, and *seven* slave-girls were burnt with him; not a word of remonstrance from the British Government."—*Letters from Madras*, 278.

1843.—"It is lamentable to think how long after our power was firmly established in Bengal, we, grossly neglecting the first and plainest duty of the civil magistrate, suffered the practices of infanticide and **suttee** to continue unchecked."—*Macaulay's Speech on Gates of Somnauth.*

1856.—"The pile of the **sutee** is unusually large; heavy cart-wheels are placed upon it, to which her limbs are bound, or sometimes a canopy of massive logs is raised above it, to crush her by its fall. . . . It is a fatal omen to hear the **sutee's** groan; therefore as the fire springs up from the pile, there rises simultaneously with it a deafening shout of 'Victory to Umbâ! Victory to Ranchor!' and the horn and the hard rattling drum sound their loudest, until the sacrifice is consumed."—*Râs Mâlâ*, ii. 435; [ed. 1878, p. 691].

[1870.—A case in this year is recorded by Chevers, *Ind. Med. Jurispr.* 665.]

1871.—"Our bridal finery of dress and feast too often proves to be no better than the Hindu woman's 'bravery,' when she comes to perform **suttee**."—*Cornhill Mag.* vol. xxiv. 675.

1872. — "La coutume du suicide de la **Satî** n'en est pas moins fort ancienne, puisque déjà les Grecs d'Alexandre la trouvèrent en usage chez un peuple au moins du Penjâb. Le premier témoignage brahmanique qu'on en trouve est celui de la *Brihaddevatâ* qui, peut-être, remonte tout aussi haut. A l'origine elle parait avoir été propre à l'aristocratie militaire." — *Barth, Les Religions de l'Inde*, 39.

SWALLOW, SWALLOE, s. The old trade-name of the sea-slug, or **tripang** (q.v.). It is a corruption of the Bugi (Makassar) name of the creature, *suwālā* (see *Crawfurd's Malay Dict.*; [Scott, *Malayan Words*, 107)].

1783. — "I have been told by several Buggesses that they sail in their Paduakans to the northern parts of New Holland . . . to gather **Swallow** (Biche de Mer), which they sell to the annual China junk at Macassar."—*Forrest, V. to Mergui*, 83.

SWALLY, SWALLY ROADS, SWALLY MARINE, SWALLY HOLE, n.p. *Suwālī*, the once familiar name of the roadstead north of the mouth of the Tapti, where ships for Surat usually anchored, and discharged or took in cargo. It was perhaps Ar. *sawāḥil*, 'the shores' (?). [Others suggest Skt. *Śivālaya*, 'abode of Siva.']

[1615.—"The Osiander proving so leaky through the worm through the foulness of the sea-water at **Sually**."—*Foster, Letters*, iv. 22. Also see *Birdwood, Report on Old Recs.* 209.]

1623.—"At the beach there was no kind of vehicle to be found; so the Captain went on foot to a town about a mile distant called **Sohali**. . . . The Franks have houses there for the goods which they continually despatch for embarkation."—*P. della Valle*, ii. 503.

1675. — "As also passing by . . . eight ships riding at *Surat* River's Mouth, we then came to **Swally Marine**, where were flying the Colours of the Three Nations, *English, French*, and *Dutch* . . . who here land and ship off all Goods, without molestation."—*Fryer*, 82.

1677.—"The 22d of February 167⅞ from **Swally hole** the Ship was despatched alone."—*Ibid.* 217.

1690. — "In a little time we happily arriv'd at **Sualybar**, and the Tide serving, came to an Anchor very near the *Shoar*."—*Ovington*, 163.

1727. — "One Season the *English* had eight good large Ships riding at **Swally** . . . the Place where all Goods were unloaded from the Shipping, and all Goods for Exportation were there shipp'd off."—*A. Hamilton*, i. 166; [ed. 1744].

1841.—"These are sometimes called the inner and the outer sands of **Swallow**, and are both dry at low water."—*Horsburgh's India Directory*, ed. 1841, i. 474.

SWAMY, SAMMY, s. This word is a corruption of Skt. *suāmin*, 'Lord.' It is especially used in S. India, in two senses: (a) a Hindu idol, especially applied to those of Śiva or Subramanyam; especially, as **Sammy**, in the dialect of the British soldier. This comes from the usual Tamil pronunciation *sāmi*. (b) The Skt. word is used by Hindus as a term of respectful address, especially to Brahmans.

a.—

1755.—"Towards the upper end there is a dark repository, where they keep their **Swamme**, that is their chief god."—*Ives*, 70.

1794.—"The gold might for us as well have been worshipped in the shape of a **Sawmy** at Juggernaut." — *The Indian Observer*, p. 167.

1838.—"The Government lately presented a shawl to a Hindu idol, and the Government officer . . . was ordered to superintend the delivery of it . . . so he went with the shawl in his **tonjon**, and told the Bramins that they might come and take it, for that he would not touch it with his fingers to present it to a **Swamy**." — *Letters from Madras*, 183.

b.—

1516.—"These people are commonly called **Jogues** (see **JOGEE**), and in their own speech they are called **Zoame**, which means Servant of God."—*Barbosa*, 99.

1615.—"Tunc ad suos conversus: Eia Brachmanes, inquit, quid vobis videtur? Illi mirabundi nihil praeter **Suami, Suami**, id est Domine, Domine, retulerunt."—*Jarric, Thes.*, i. 664.

SWAMY-HOUSE, SAMMY-HOUSE, s. An idol-temple, or

pagoda. The *Sammy-house* of the Delhi ridge in 1857 will not soon be forgotten.

1760.—"The French cavalry were advancing before their infantry; and it was the intention of Colliaud that his own should wait until they came in a line with the flank-fire of the field-pieces of the **Swamy-house**."—*Orme*, iii. 443.

1829.—"Here too was a little detached **Swamee-house** (or chapel) with a lamp burning before a little idol."—*Mem. of Col. Mountain*, 99.

1857.—"We met Wilby at the advanced post, the '**Sammy House**,' within 600 yards of the Bastion. It was a curious place for three brothers to meet in. The view was charming. Delhi is as green as an emerald just now, and the Jumma Musjid and Palace are beautiful objects, though held by infidels."—*Letters written during the Siege of Delhi*, by *Hervey Greathed*, p. 112.

[**SWAMY JEWELRY**, s. A kind of gold and silver jewelry, made chiefly at Trichinopoly, in European shapes covered with grotesque mythological figures.

[1880. — "In the characteristic **Swami** work of the Madras Presidency the ornamentation consists of figures of the Puranic gods in high relief, either beaten out from the surface, or affixed to it, whether by soldering, or wedging, or screwing them on."—*Birdwood, Industr. Arts*, 152.]

SWAMY-PAGODA, s. A coin formerly current at Madras; probably so called from the figure of an idol on it. Milburn gives 100 *Swamy Pagodas* =110 Star Pagodas. A "*three* **swāmi** pagoda" was a name given to a gold coin bearing on the obverse the effigy of Chenna Keswam **Swāmi** (a title of Krishna) and on the reverse Lakshmi and Rukmini (*C.P.B.*).

SWATCH, s. This is a marine term which probably has various applications beyond Indian limits. But the only two instances of its application are both Indian, viz. "the **Swatch** of No Ground," or elliptically "The **Swatch**," marked in all the charts just off the Ganges Delta, and a space bearing the same name, and probably produced by analogous tidal action, off the Indus Delta. [The word is not to be found in Smyth, *Sailor's Word-book*.]

1726.—In Valentijn's first map of Bengal, though no name is applied there is a space marked "no ground with 60 raam (fathoms?) of line."

1863. — (Ganges). "There is still one other phenomenon. . . . This is the existence of a great depression, or hole, in the middle of the Bay of Bengal, known in the charts as the '**Swatch** of No Ground.'"—*Fergusson, on Recent Changes in the Delta of the Ganges, Qy. Jour. Geol. Soc.*, Aug. 1863.

1877. — (Indus). "This is the famous **Swatch** of no ground where the lead falls at once into 200 fathoms."—*Burton, Sind Revisited*, 21.

[1878. — "He (Capt. Lloyd, in 1840) describes the remarkable phenomenon at the head of the Bay of Bengal, similar to that reported by Captain Selby off the mouths of the Indus, called 'the **Swatch** of no ground.' It is a deep chasm, open to seaward and very steep on the north-west face, with no soundings at 250 fathoms."—*Markham, Mem. of Indian Surveys*, 27.]

[**SWEET APPLE**, s. An Anglo-Indian corruption of *sītāphal*, 'the fruit of Sītā,' the Musk Melon, Fr. *Potiron*. *Cucurbita moschata* (see **CUSTARD-APPLE**).]

SWEET OLEANDER, s. This is in fact the common oleander, *Nerium odorum*, Ait.

1880.—"Nothing is more charming than, even in the upland valleys of the Mahratta country, to come out of a wood of all outlandish trees and flowers suddenly on the dry winter bed of some mountain stream, grown along the banks, or on the little islets of verdure in mid (shingle) stream, with clumps of mixed tamarisk and lovely blooming **oleander**."—*Birdwood, MS.* 9.

SWEET POTATO, s. The root of *Batatas edulis*, Choisy (*Convolvulus Batatas*, L.), N.O. *Convolvulaceae*; a very palatable vegetable, grown in most parts of India. Though extensively cultivated in America, and in the W. Indies, it has been alleged in various books (*e.g.* in *Eng. Cyclop.* Nat. Hist. Section, and in *Drury's Useful Plants of India*), that the plant is a native of the Malay islands. The *Eng. Cyc.* even states that *batatas* is the Malay name. But the whole allegation is probably founded in error. The Malay names of the plant, as given by Crawfurd, are *Kaledek*, *Ubi Jawa*, and *Ubi Kastila*, the last two names meaning 'Java yam,' and 'Spanish yam,' and indicating the foreign origin of the vegetable. In India, at least in the Bengal Presidency, natives commonly call it *shakarkand*, P.—Ar., literally 'sugar-candy,' a name equally suggesting that it is not indigenous among them. And in fact when we turn to Oviedo, we find the following distinct statement:

"**Batatas** are a staple food of the Indians, both in the Island of Spagnuola and in the others . . . and a ripe **Batata** properly dressed is just as good as a marchpane twist of sugar and almonds, and better indeed. . . . When *Batatas* are well ripened, they are often carried to Spain, *i.e.*, if the voyage be a quiet one; for if there be delay they get spoilt at sea. I myself have carried them from this city of S. Domingo to the city of Avila in Spain, and although they did not arrive as good as they should be, yet they were thought a great deal of, and reckoned a singular and precious kind of fruit."—In *Ramusio*, iii. f. 134.

It must be observed however that several distinct varieties are cultivated by the Pacific islanders even as far west as New Zealand. And Dr. Bretschneider is satisfied that the plant is described in Chinese books of the 3rd or 4th century, under the name of *Kan-chu* (the first syllable ='sweet'). See *B. on Chin. Botan. Words*, p. 13. This is the only good argument we have seen for Asiatic origin. The whole matter is carefully dealt with by M. Alph. De Candolle (*Origine des Plantes cultivées*, pp. 43-45), concluding with the judgment: "Les motifs sont beaucoup plus forts, ce me semble, en faveur de l'origine americaine."

The "Sanskrit name" *Ruktaloo*, alleged by Mr. Piddington, is worthless. *Ālū* is properly an esculent *Arum*, but in modern use is the name of the common potato, and is sometimes used for the sweet potato. *Raktālū*, more commonly *rat-ālū*, is in Bengal the usual name of the *Yam*, no doubt given first to a highly-coloured kind, such as *Dioscorea purpurea*, for *rakt-* or *rat-ālū* means simply 'red potato'; a name which might also be well applied to the *batatas*, as it is indeed, according to Forbes Watson, in the Deccan. There can be little doubt that this vegetable, or fruit as Oviedo calls it, having become known in Europe many years before the *potato*, the latter robbed it of its name, as has happened in the case of **brazil-wood** (q.v.). The *batata* is clearly the 'potato' of the fourth and others of the following quotations. [See *Watt, Econ. Dict.* iii. 117 *seqq.*]

1519.—"At this place (in Brazil) we had refreshment of victuals, like fowls and meat of calves, also a variety of fruits, called **batate**, pigne (pine-apples), sweet, of singular goodness. . . ."—*Pigafetta*, E.T. by *Lord Stanley of A.*, p. 43.

1540.—"The root which among the Indians of Spagnuola Island is called **Batata**, the negroes of St. Thomè (*C. Verde* group) called *Igname*, and they plant it as the chief staple of their maintenance; it is of a black colour, *i.e.* the outer skin is so, but inside it is white, and as big as a large turnip, with many branchlets; it has the taste of a chestnut, but much better."—*Voyage to the I. of San Tomè under the Equinoctial, Ramusio*, i. 117*v*.

c. 1550.—"They have two other sorts of roots, one called **batata**. . . . They generate windiness, and are commonly cooked in the embers. Some say they taste like almond cakes, or sugared chestnuts; but in my opinion chestnuts, even without sugar, are better."—*Girol. Benzoni*, Hak. Soc. 86.

1588.—"Wee met with sixtee or seventee sayles of Canoes full of Sauages, who came off to Sea vnto vs, and brought with them in their Boates, Plantans, Cocos, **Potato-rootes**, and fresh fish."—*Voyage of Master Thomas Candish, Purchas*, i. 66.

1600. — "The **Battatas** are somewhat redder of colour, and in forme almost like *Iniamas* (see **YAM**), and taste like Earthnuts."—In *Purchas*, ii. 957.

1615.—"I took a garden this day, and planted it with **Pottatos** brought from the Liquea, a thing not yet planted in Japan. I must pay a *tay*, or 5 shillings sterling, per annum for the garden."—*Cocks's Diary*, i. 11.

1645.—". . . **pattate**; c'est vne racine comme naueaux, mais plus longue et de couleur rouge et jaune: cela est de tres-bon goust, mais si l'on en mange souuent, elle degouste fort, et est assez venteuse."—*Mocquet, Voyages*, 83.

1764.—

"There let **Potatos** mantle o'er the ground,
Sweet as the cane-juice is the root they bear."—*Grainger*, Bk. iv.

SYCE, s. Hind. from Ar. *sāïs*. A groom. It is the word in universal use in the Bengal Presidency. In the South **horse-keeper** is more common, and in Bombay a vernacular form of the latter, viz. *ghorāwālā* (see **GORA-WALLAH**). The Ar. verb, of which *sāïs* is the participle, seems to be a loan-word from Syriac, *sausī*, 'to coax.'

[1759.—In list of servants' wages: "**Syce**, Rs. 2."—In *Long*, 182.]

1779.—"The bearer and **scise**, when they returned, came to the place where I was, and laid hold of Mr. Ducarell. I took hold of Mr. Shee and carried him up. The bearer and **scise** took Mr. Ducarell out. Mr. Keeble was standing on his own house looking, and asked, 'What is the matter?'

The bearer and **scise** said to Mr. Keeble, 'These gentlemen came into the house when my master was out.'"—*Evidence on Trial of* Grand *v.* Francis, in *Echoes of Old Calcutta*, 230.

1810.—"The **Syce**, or groom, attends but one horse."—*Williamson, V.M.* i. 254.

c. 1858 ?—

" Tandis que les **çais** veillent
les chiens rodeurs."
Leconte de Lisle.

SYCEE, s. In China applied to pure silver bullion in ingots, or **shoes** (q.v.). The origin of the name is said to be *si* (pron. at Canton *sai* and *sei*)= *sz'*, *i.e.* 'fine silk'; and we are told by Mr. Giles that it is so called because, if pure, it may be drawn out into fine threads. [Linschoten (1598) speaks of: "Peeces of cut silver, in which sort they pay and receive all their money" (Hak. Soc. i. 132).]

1711.—"Formerly they used to sell for **Sisee**, or Silver full fine; but of late the Method is alter'd."—*Lockyer*, 135.

SYRAS, CYRUS. See under **CYRUS.**

SYRIAM, n.p. A place on the Pegu R., near its confluence with the Rangoon R., six miles E. of Rangoon, and very famous in the Portuguese dealings with Pegu. The Burmese form is *Than-lyeng*, but probably the Talaing name was nearer that which foreigners give it. [See *Burma Gazetteer*, ii. 672. Mr. St John (*J. R. As. Soc.*, 1894, p. 151) suggests the Mwn word *sarang* or *siring*, 'a swinging cradle.'] Syriam was the site of an English factory in the 17th century, of the history of which little is known. See the quotation from Dalrymple below.

1587.—"To **Cirion** a Port of Pegu come ships from Mecca with woollen Cloth, Scarlets, Velvets, Opium, and such like."—*R. Fitch*, in *Hakl.* ii. 393.

1600.—"I went thither with Philip Brito, and in fifteene dayes arrived at **Sirian** the chiefe Port in Pegu. It is a lamentable spectacle to see the bankes of the Riuers set with infinite fruit-bearing trees, now ouerwhelmed with ruines of gilded Temples, and noble edifices; the wayes and fields full of skulls and bones of wretched Peguans, killed or famished, and cast into the River in such numbers that the multitude of carkasses prohibiteth the way and passage of ships."—The Jesuit *Andrew Boves*, in *Purchas* ii. 1748.

c. 1606.—"Philip de Brito issued an order that a custom-house should be planted at **Serian** (*Serião*), at which duties should be paid by all the vessels of this State which went to trade with the kingdom of Pegu, and with the ports of Martavan, Tavay, Tenasserim, and Juncalon. . . . Now certain merchants and shipowners from the Coast of Coromandel refused obedience, and this led Philip de Brito to send a squadron of 6 ships and galliots with an imposing and excellent force of soldiers on board, that they might cruise on the coast of Tenasserim, and compel all the vessels that they met to come and pay duty at the fortress of **Serian**."—*Bocarro*, 135.

1695.—"9th. That the *Old house* and *Ground* at **Syrian**, formerly belonging to the *English Company*, may still be continued to them, and that they may have liberty of building *dwelling-houses*, and *warehouses*, for the securing their *Goods*, as shall be necessary, and that more *Ground* be given them, if what they formerly had be not sufficient." Petition presented to the K. of Burma at Ava, by *Ed. Fleetwood*; in *Dalrymple, O.R.* ii. 374.

1726.—**Zierjang** (Syriam) in *Valentijn, Choro.*, &c., 127.

1727.—"About 60 Miles to the Eastward of China Backaar (see **CHINA-BUCKEER**) is the Bar of **Syrian**, the only port now open for Trade in all the *Pegu* Dominions. . . . It was many Years in Possession of the *Portugueze*, till by their Insolence and Pride they were obliged to quit it."—*A. Hamilton*, ii. 31-32; [ed. 1744].

SYUD, s. Ar. *saiyid*, 'a lord.' The designation in India of those who claim to be descendants of Mahommed. But the usage of *Saiyid* and *Sharīf* varies in different parts of Mahommedan Asia. ["As a rule (much disputed) the Sayyid is a descendant from Mahommed through his grandchild Hasan, and is a man of the pen; whereas the Sharīf derives from Husayn and is a man of the sword" (*Burton, Ar. Nights*, iv. 209).]

1404.—"On this day the Lord played at chess, for a great while, with certain **Zaytes**; and **Zaytes** they call certain men who come of the lineage of Mahomad."—*Clavijo*, § cxiv. (*Markham*, p. 141-2).

1869.—"Il y a dans l'Inde quatre classes de musulmans: les **Saiyids** ou descendants de Mahomet par Huçain, les *Schaikhs* ou Arabes, nommés vulgairement Maures, les **Pathans** ou Afgans, et les **Mogols**. Ces quatres classes ont chacune fourni à la religion de saints personnages, qui sont souvent designés par ces dénominations, et par d'autres spécialement consacrées à chacune d'elles, telles que *Mir* pour les **Saiyids**, *Khân* pour les Pathans, *Mirzâ*, *Beg*, *Agâ*, et *Khwâja* pour les Mogols."—*Garcin de Tassy, Religion Mus. dans l'Inde*, 22.

(The learned author is mistaken here in supposing that the obsolete term **Moor** was in India specially applied to Arabs. It was applied, following Portuguese custom, to all Mahommedans.)

T

TABASHEER, s. 'Sugar of Bamboo.' A siliceous substance sometimes found in the joints of the bamboo, formerly prized as medicine, [also known in India as *Bānslochan* or *Bānskapūr*]. The word is Pers. *tabāshīr*, but that is from the Skt. name of the article, *tvakkshīra*, and *tavakkshīra*. The substance is often confounded, in name at least, by the old Materia Medica writers, with *spodium* and is sometimes called *ispodio di canna*. See *Ces. Federici* below. Garcia De Orta goes at length into this subject (f. 193 *seqq.*). [See **SUGAR**.]

c. 1150.—"Tanah (miswritten *Banah*) est une jolie ville située sur un grand golfe. . . . Dans les montagnes environnantes croissent le . . . kana et le . . . **tabāshīr** . . . Quant au **tébachir**, on le falsifie en le mélangeant avec de la cendre d'ivoire; mais le veritable est celui qu'on extrait des racines du roseau dit . . . *al Sharkī*."—*Edrisi*, i. 179.

1563. — "And much less are the roots of the cane **tabaxer**; so that according to both the translations Avicena is wrong; and Averrois says that it is charcoal from burning the canes of India, whence it appears that he never saw it, since he calls such a white substance charcoal."—*Garcia*, f. 195*v*.

c. 1570.—"Il *Spodio* si congela d'acqua in alcune canne, e io n'ho trouato assai nel Pegù quando faceuo fabricar la mia casa." —*Ces. Federici*, in *Ramusio*, iii. 397.

1578.—"The *Spodium* or **Tabaxir** of the Persians . . . was not known to the Greeks."—*Acosta*, 295.

c. 1580.—"Spodium **Tabaxir** vocant, quo nomine vulgus pharmacopoeorum Spodium factitium, quippe metallicum, intelligunt. At eruditiores viri eo nomine lacrymam quandam, ex caudice arboris procerae in India nascentis, albicantem, odoratam, facultatis refrigeratoriae, et cor maxime roborantis itidem intelligunt."—*Prosper Alpinus, Rerum Ægyptiarum*, Lib. III. vii.

1598.—". . . these *Mambus* have a certain Matter within them, which is (as it were) the pith of it . . . the Indians call it *Sacar Mambu*, which is as much as to say, as Sugar of *Mambu*, and is a very deep Medicinable thing much esteemed, and much sought for by the Arabians, Persians, and Moores, that call it **Tabaxiir**."—*Linschoten*, p. 104; [Hak. Soc. ii. 56].

1837. — "Allied to these in a botanical point of view is *Saccharum officinarum*, which has needlessly been supposed not to have yielded *saccharum*, or the substance known by this name to the ancients; the same authors conjecturing this to be **Tabasheer**. . . . Considering that this substance is pure *silex*, it is not likely to have been arranged with the honeys and described under the head of περι Σακχαρον μελιτον." —*Royle on the Ant. of Hindoo Medicine*, p. 83. This confirms the views expressed in the article **SUGAR**.

1854.—"In the cavity of these cylinders water is sometimes secreted, or, less commonly, an opaque white substance, becoming opaline when wetted, consisting of a flinty secretion, of which the plant divests itself, called **Tabasheer**, concerning the optical properties of which Sir David Brewster has made some curious discoveries." — *Engl. Cycl.* Nat. Hist. Section, article *Bamboo*.

TABBY, s. Not Anglo-Indian. A kind of watered silk stuff; Sp. and Port. *tabi*, Ital. *tabino*, Fr. *tabis*, from Ar. *'attābī*, the name said to have been given to such stuffs from their being manufactured in early times in a quarter of Baghdad called *al-'attābīya*; and this derived its name from a prince of the 'Omaiyad family called 'Attāb. [See Burton, *Ar. Nights*, ii. 371.]

12th cent.—"The *'Attābīya* . . . here are made the stuffs, called **'Attābīya**, which are silks and cottons of divers colours."—*Ibn Jubair*, p. 227.

[c. 1220.—"**'Attabi.**" See under **SUCLAT**.]

TABOOT, s. The name applied in India to a kind of shrine, or model of a Mahommedan mausoleum, of flimsy material, intended to represent the tomb of Husain at Kerbela, which is carried in procession during the Moharram (see *Herklots*, 2nd ed. 119 *seqq.*, and *Garcin de Tassy, Rel. Musulm. dans l'Inde*, 36). [The word is Ar. *tabūt*, 'a wooden box, coffin.' The term used in N. India is *ta'ziya* (see **TAZEEA**).]

[1856.—"There is generally over the vaul in which the corpse is deposited an oblong monument of stone or brick (called '**tarkeebeh**') or wood (in which case it is called '**taboot**')." — *Lane, Mod. Egypt.*, 5th ed. i. 299.]

[**TACK-RAVAN**, s. A litter carried on men's shoulders, used only by royal personages. It is Pers. *takht-ravān*, 'travelling-throne.' In the Hindi of

Behar the word is corrupted into *tartarwān*.

[c. 1660.—"... several articles of *Chinese* and *Japan* workmanship; among which were a *paleky* and a **tack-ravan**, or travelling throne, of exquisite beauty, and much admired." — *Bernier*, ed. *Constable*, 128; in 370, **tact-ravan**.

[1753. — "Mahommed Shah, emperor of Hindostan, seated in a royal litter (**takht revan**, which signifies a moving throne) issued from his camp. . . ." — *Hanway*, iv. 169.]

TAEL, s. This is the trade-name of the Chinese ounce, viz., $\frac{1}{16}$ of a **catty** (q.v.); and also of the Chinese money of account, often called "the ounce of silver," but in Chinese called *liang*. The standard *liang* or *tael* is, according to Dr. Wells Williams, = 579·84 grs. troy. It was formerly equivalent to a string of 1000 *tsien*, or (according to the trade-name) **cash** (q.v.). The China *tael* used to be reckoned as worth 6*s.* 8*d.*, but the rate really varied with the price of silver. In 1879 an article in the *Fortnightly Review* puts it at 5*s.* 7½*d.* (Sept. p. 362); the exchange at Shanghai in London by telegraphic transfer, April 13, 1885, was 4*s.* 9⅝*d.*; [on Oct. 3, 1901, 2*s.* 7¼*d.*]. The word was apparently got from the Malays, among whom *taïl* or *tahil* is the name of a weight; and this again, as Crawfurd indicates, is probably from the India **tola** (q.v.). [Mr. Pringle writes: "Sir H. Yule does not refer to such forms as **tahe** (see below), **taies** (plural in Fryer's *New Account*, p. 210, sub *Machawo*), **Taye** (see quotation below from Saris), **tayes** (see quotation below from Mocquet), or **taey**, and **taeys** (Philip's translation of *Linschoten*, Hak. Soc. i. 149). These probably come through the medium of the Portuguese, in which the final *l* of the singular **tael** is changed into *s* in the plural. Such a form as **taeis** might easily suggest a singular wanting the final *s*, and from such a singular French and English plurals of the ordinary type would in turn be fashioned" (*Diary Ft. St. Geo.*, 1st ser. ii. 126).]

The Chinese scale of weight, with their trade-names, runs: 16 **taels** = 1 **catty**, 100 *catties* = 1 **pecul** = 133⅓ *lbs. avoird.* Milburn gives the weights of Achin as 4 *copangs* (see **KOPANG**) = 1 **mace**, 5 **mace** = 1 *mayam*, 16 *mayam* = 1 *tale* (see **TAEL**), 5 *tales* = 1 *buncal*, 20 *buncals* = 1 **catty**, 200 *catties* = 1 **bahar**; and the *catty* of Achīn as = 2 *lbs.* 1 *oz.* 13 *dr.* Of these names, **mace, tale** and **bahar** (qq.v.) seem to be of Indian origin, *mayam*, *bangkal*, and *katī* Malay.

1540. — "And those three junks which were then taken, according to the assertion of those who were aboard, had contained in silver alone 200,000 **taels** (*taeis*), which are in our money 300,000 *cruzados*, besides much else of value with which they were freighted."—*Pinto*, cap. xxxv.

1598.—"A **Tael** is a full ounce and a halfe Portingale weight."—*Linschoten*, 44; [Hak. Soc. i. 149].

1599.—"Est et ponderis genus, quod **Tael** vocant in Malacca. **Tael** unum in Malacca pendet 16 **masas**."—*De Bry*, ii. 64.

,, "Four hundred **cashes** make a *cowpan* (see **KOBANG**). Foure *cowpans* are one **mas**. Foure *masses* make a *Perdaw* (see **PARDAO**). Four *Perdaws* make a **Tayel**."—*Capt. T. Davis*, in *Purchas*, i. 123.

c. 1608.—"Bezar stones are thus bought by the **Taile** . . . which is one Ounce, and the third part English."—*Saris*, in *do.*, 392.

1613.—"A **Taye** is five shillinge sterling." —*Saris*, in *do.* 369.

1643.—"Les Portugais sont fort desireux de ces Chinois pour esclaves . . . il y a des Chinois faicts à ce mestier . . . quand ils voyent quelque beau petit garçon ou fille . . . les enleuent par force et les cachent . . . puis viennent sur la riue de la mer, ou ils sçauent que sont les trafiquans à qui ils les vendent 12 et 15 **tayes** chacun, qui est enuiron 25 escus."—*Mocquet*, 342.

c. 1656.—"Vn Religieux Chinois qui a esté surpris auec des femmes de debauche . . . l'on a percé le col avec vn fer chaud; à ce fer est attaché vne chaisne de fer d'enuiron dix brasses qu'il est obligé de traisner jusques à ce qu'il ait apporté au Couuent trente **theyls** d'argent qu'il faut qu'il amasse en demandant l'aumosne."—In *Thevenot*, *Divers Voyages*, ii. 67.

[1683. — "The abovesaid Musk weyes Cattee 10: **tahe** 14: Mas 03. . . ." — *Pringle*, *Diary Ft. St. Geo.*, 1st ser. ii. 34.]

TAHSEELDAR, s. The chief (native) revenue officer of a subdivision (*taḥsīl*, conf. **Pergunnah, Talook**) of a district (see **ZILLAH**). Hind. from Pers. *taḥṣīldār*, and that from Ar. *taḥṣīl*, 'collection.' This is a term of the Mahommedan administration which we have adopted. It appears by the quotation from Williamson that the term was formerly employed in Calcutta to designate the cash-keeper in a firm or private establishment, but this use is long obsolete.

[Possibly there was a confusion with *taḥvīldār*, 'a cashier.']

[1772. — "**Tahsildar**, or *Sezawaul*, an officer employed for a monthly salary to collect the revenues."—*Glossary*, in *Verelst, View of Bengal*, s.v.]

1799.—". . . He (Tippoo) divided his country into 37 Provinces under Dewans (see **DEWAUN**) . . . and he subdivided these again into 1025 inferior districts, having each a **Tisheldar**." — Letter of *Munro*, in *Life*, i. 215.

1808.—". . . he continues to this hour **tehsildar** of the petty pergunnah of Sheopore."—*Fifth Report*, 583.

1810.—". . . the sircar, or **tusseeldar** (cash-keeper) receiving one key, and the master retaining the other."—*Williamson, V.M.* i. 209.

[1826.—". . . I told him . . . that I was . . . the bearer of letters to his head collector or **T,huseeldam** (*sic*) there."—*Pandurang Hari*, ed. 1873, i. 155.]

TAILOR-BIRD, s. This bird is so called from the fact that it is in the habit of drawing together "one leaf or more, generally two leaves, on each side of the nest, and stitches them together with cotton, either woven by itself, or cotton thread picked up; and after putting the thread through the leaf, it makes a knot at the end to fix it" (*Jerdon*). It is *Orthrotomos longicauda*, Gmelin (sub-fam. *Drymoicinae*).

[1813.—"Equally curious in the structure of its nest, and far superior (to the **baya**) in the variety and elegance of its plumage, is the **tailor-bird** of Hindostan" (here follows a description of its nest).—*Forbes, Or. Mem.*, 2nd ed. i. 33.]

1883.—"Clear and loud above all . . . sounds the to-whee, to-whee, to-whee of the **tailor-bird**, a most plain-looking little greenish thing, but a skilful workman and a very Beaconsfield in the matter of keeping its own counsel. Aided by its industrious spouse, it will, when the monsoon comes on, spin cotton, or steal thread from the **durzee**, and sew together two broad leaves of the laurel in the pot on your very doorstep, and when it has warmly lined the bag so formed it will bring up therein a large family of little tailors." — *Tribes on My Frontier*, 145.

TAJ, s. Pers. *tāj*, 'a crown.' The most famous and beautiful mausoleum in Asia; the *Tāj Mahal* at Agra, erected by Shāh Jahān over the burial-place of his favourite wife Mumtāz-i-Mahal ('Ornament of the Palace') Banū Begam.

1663.—"I shall not stay to discourse of the Monument of *Ekbar*, because whatever beauty is there, is found in a far higher degree in that of **Taj Mehale**, which I am now going to describe to you . . . judge whether I had reason to say that the *Mausoleum*, or Tomb of **Taj-Mehale**, is something worthy to be admired. For my part I do not yet well know, whether I am somewhat infected still with Indianisme; but I must needs say, that I believe it ought to be reckoned amongst the Wonders of the World. . . ." — *Bernier*, E.T. 94-96; [ed. *Constable*, 293].

1665.—"Of all the Monuments that are to be seen at *Agra*, that of the Wife of *Cha-Jehan* is the most magnificent; she caus'd it to be set up on purpose near the *Tasimacan*, to which all strangers must come, that they should admire it. The *Tasimacan* [? Tāj-i-mukām, 'Place of the Tāj'] is a great *Bazar*, or Market-place, comprised of six great courts, all encompass'd with Portico's; under which there are Warehouses for Merchants. . . . The monument of this *Begum* or *Sultaness*, stands on the East side of the City. . . . I saw the beginning and com pleating of this great work, that cost two and twenty years labour, and 20,000 men always at work."—*Tavernier*, E.T. ii. 50; [ed. *Ball*, i. 109].

1856.—

"But far beyond compare, the glorious **Taj**,
Seen from old Agra's towering battlements,
And mirrored clear in Jumna's silent stream;
Sun-lighted, like a pearly diadem
Set royal on the melancholy brow
Of withered Hindostan; but, when the moon
Dims the white marble with a softer light,
Like some queened maiden, veiled in dainty lace,
And waiting for her bridegroom, stately, pale,
But yet transcendent in her loveliness."

The Banyan Tree.

TALAING, n.p. The name by which the chief race inhabiting Pegu (or the Delta of the Irawadi) is known to the Burmese. The Talaings were long the rivals of the Burmese, alternately conquering and conquered, but the Burmese have, on the whole, so long predominated, even in the Delta, that the use of the Talaing language is now nearly extinct in Pegu proper, though it is still spoken in Martaban, and among the descendants of emigrants into Siamese territory. We have adopted the name from the Burmese to designate the race, but their own name for their people is *Mōn* or *Mūn* (see **MONE**).

Sir Arthur Phayre has regarded the name *Talaing* as almost undoubtedly a form of **Telinga**. The reasons given are plausible, and may be briefly stated in two extracts from his Essay *On the History of Pegu* (*J. As. Soc. Beng.*, vol. xlii. Pt. i.): "The names given in the histories of Tha-htun and Pegu to the first Kings of those cities are Indian; but they cannot be accepted as historically true. The countries from which the Kings are said to have derived their origin . . . may be recognised as Karnáta, *Kalinga*, Venga and Vizianagaram . . . probably mistaken for the more famous Vijayanagar. . . . The word *Talingána* never occurs in the Peguan histories, but only the more ancient name Kalinga" (*op. cit.* pp. 32-33). "The early settlement of a colony or city for trade, on the coast of Rámanya by settlers from Talingána, satisfactorily accounts for the name **Talaing**, by which the people of Pegu are known to the Burmese and all peoples of the west. But the Peguans call themselves by a different name . . . *Mun*, *Mwun*, or *Mon*" (*ibid.* p. 34).

Prof. Forchhammer, however, who has lately devoted much labour to the study of Talaing archæology and literature, entirely rejects this view. He states that prior to the time of Alompra's conquest of Pegu (middle of 18th century) the name Talaing was entirely unknown as an appellation of the Muns, and that it nowhere occurs in either inscriptions or older palm-leaves, and that by all nations of Further India the people in question is known by names related to either *Mun* or *Pegu*. He goes on: "The word 'Talaing' is the term by which the Muns acknowledged their total defeat, their being vanquished and the slaves of their Burmese conqueror. They were no longer to bear the name of Muns or Peguans. Alompra stigmatized them with an appellation suggestive at once of their submission and disgrace. Talaing means" (in the Mun language) "'one who is trodden under foot, a slave.' . . . Alompra could not have devised more effective means to extirpate the national consciousness of a people than by burning their books, forbidding the use of their language, and by substituting a term of abject reproach for the name under which they had maintained themselves for nearly 2000 years in the marine provinces of Burma. The similarity of the two words 'Talaing' and 'Telingana' is purely accidental; and all deductions, historical or etymological . . . from the resemblance . . . must necessarily be void *ab initio*" (*Notes on Early Hist. and Geog. of Br. Burma*, Pt. ii. pp. 11-12, Rangoon, 1884).

Here we leave the question. It is not clear whether Prof. F. gives the story of Alompra as a historical fact, or as a probable explanation founded on the etymology. Till this be clear we cannot say that we are altogether satisfied. But the fact that we have been unable to find any occurrence of *Talaing* earlier than Symes's narrative is in favour of his view.

Of the relics of Talaing literature almost nothing is known. Much is to be hoped from the studies of Prof. Forchhammer himself.

There are linguistic reasons for connecting the *Talaing* or Mun people with the so-called Kolarian tribes of the interior of India, but the point is not yet a settled one. [Mr. Baines notes coincidences between the Mon and Munda languages, and accepts the connection of Talaing with Telinga (*Census Report*, 1891, i. p. 128).]

1795.—"The present King of the Birmans . . . has abrogated some severe penal laws imposed by his predecessors on the **Taliens**, or native Peguers. Justice is now impartially distributed, and the only distinction at present between a Birman and a **Talien**, consists in the exclusion of the latter from places of public trust and power."—*Symes*, 183.

TALAPOIN, s. A word used by the Portuguese, and after them by French and other Continental writers, as well as by some English travellers of the 17th century, to designate the Buddhist monks of Ceylon and the Indo-Chinese countries. The origin of the expression is obscure. Monseigneur Pallegoix, in his *Desc. du Royaume Thai ou Siam* (ii. 23) says: "Les Européens les ont appelés **talapoins**, probablement du nom de l'éventail qu'ils tiennent à la main, lequel s'appelle *talapat*, qui signifie *feuille de palmier*." Childers gives *Talapannam*, Pali, 'a leaf used in writing, &c.' This at first sight seems to have nothing to support it except similarity of sound; but the quotations from Pinto throw some possible light, and afford probability to this origin, which is also accepted by

Koeppen (*Rel. des Buddhas*, i. 331 *note*), and by Bishop Bigandet (*J. Ind. Archip.* iv. 220). [Others, however, derive it from Peguan *Tilapoin*, *tala* (not *tila*), 'lord,' *poin*, 'wealth.']

c. 1554.—". . . hũa procissão . . . na qual se affirmou . . . que hião quarenta mil Sacerdotes . . . dos quaes muytos tinhão differentes dignidades, come erão *Grepos* (?), **Talagrepos**, *Rolins*, *Neepois*, *Bicos*, *Sacareus* e *Chanfarauhos*, os quaes todas pelas vestiduras, de que hião ornados, *e pelas divisas, e insignias, que levarão nas mãos, se conhecião*, quaes erão huno, e quaes erão outros."—*F. M. Pinto*, ch. clx. Thus rendered by Cogan: "A Procession . . . it was the common opinion of all, that in this Procession were 40,000 Priests . . . most of them were of different dignities, and called Grepos, **Talagrepos** (&c.). Now by the ornaments they wear, as also by the devices and ensigns which they carry in their hands, they may be distinguished."—p. 218.

,, "O *Chaubainha* lhe mandou hũa carta por hum seu *Grepo* **Talapoy**, religioso já de idade de oitenta annos."—*Pinto*, ch. cxlix. By Cogan: "The *Chaubinhaa* sent the King a Letter by one of his Priests that was fourscore years of age."—*Cogan*, 199.

[1566.—"**Talapoins.**" See under **COSMIN.**]

c. 1583.—". . . Sì veggono le case di legno tutte dorate, et ornate di bellissimi giardini fatti alla loro vsanza, nelle quali habitano tutti i **Talapoi**, che sono i loro Frati, che stanno a gouerno del Pagodo."—*Gasparo Balbi*, f. 96.

1586.—"There are . . . many good houses for the **Tallapoies** to preach in."—*R. Fitch*, in *Hakl.* ii. 93.

1597.—"The **Talipois** persuaded the *Iangoman*, brother to the King of *Pegu*, to vsurpe the Kingdome, which he refused, pretending his Oath. They replied that no Religion hindered, if he placed his brother in the *Vahat*, that is, a *Golden Throne*, to be adored of the people for a God."—*Nicolas Pimenta*, in *Purchas*, ii. 1747.

1612.—"There are in all those Kingdoms many persons belonging to different Religious Orders; one of which in Pegu they call **Talapois.**"—*Couto*, V. vi. 1.

1659.—"Whilst we looked on these temples, wherin these horrid idols sat, there came the Aracan **Talpooys**, or Priests, and fell down before the idols."—*Walter Schulze, Reisen*, 77.

1689.—"S'il vous arrive de fermer la bouche aux **Talapoins** et de mettre en évidence leurs erreurs, ne vous attendez qu'à les avoir pour ennemis implacables."—*Lett. Edif.* xxv. 64.

1690.—"Their Religious they call **Telapoi**, who are not unlike mendicant *Fryers*, living upon the Alms of the People, and so highly venerated by them that they would be glad to drink the Water wherein they wash their Hands."—*Ovington*, 592.

1696.—". . . à permettre l'entrée de son royaume aux **Talapoins.**"—*La Bruyère, Caractères*, ed. Jouast, 1881, ii. 305.

1725.—"This great train is usually closed by the Priests or **Talapois** and Musicians."—*Valentijn*, v. 142.

1727.—"The other Sects are taught by the **Talapoins**, who . . . preach up Morality to be the best Guide to human Life, and affirm that a good Life in this World can only recommend us in the next to have our Souls transmigrated into the Body of some innocent Beast."—*A. Hamilton*, i. 151; [ed. 1744, i. 152].

,, "The great God, whose Adoration is left to their **Tallapoies** or Priests."—*Ibid.* ii.; [ed. 1744, ii. 54].

1759.—"When asked if they believed the existence of any SUPERIOR BEING, they (the *Carianners* (**Carens**)) replied that the Bûraghmahs and Pegu **Tallopins** told them so."—Letter in *Dalrymple, Or. Rep.* i. 100.

1766.—"*André Des Couches.* Combien avez-vous de soldats? *Croutef.* Quatre-vingt-mille, fort médiocrement payés. *A. des C.* Et de **talapoins**? *Cr.* Cent vingt mille, tous faineans et très riches. Il est vrai que dans la dernière guerre nous avons été bien battus; mais, en récompense, nos **talapoins** ont fait très grande chère," &c.—*Voltaire*, Dial. xxii. *André Des Couches à Siam.*

c. 1818.—"A certain priest or **Talapoin** conceived an inordinate affection for a garment of an elegant shape, which he possessed, and which he diligently preserved to prevent its wearing out. He died without correcting his irregular affection, and immediately becoming a louse, took up his abode in his favourite garment."—*Sangermano*, p. 20.

1880.—"The *Phongyies* (**Poongee**), or Buddhist Monks, sometimes called **Talapoins**, a name given to them, and introduced into Europe by the Portuguese, from their carrying a fan formed of *tâla-pat*, or palm-leaves."—*Saty. Rev.*, Feb. 21, p. 266, quoting *Bp. Bigandet*,

TALEE, s. Tam. *tāli*. A small trinket of gold which is fastened by a string round the neck of a married woman in S. India. It may be a curious question whether the word may not be an adaptation from the Ar. *tahlīl*, "qui signifie proprement: prononcer la formule *lâ ilâha illâ 'llâh*. . . . Cette formule, écrite sur un morceau de papier, servait d'amulette . . . le tout était renfermé dans un étui auquel on donnait le nom de *tahlīl*" (*Dozy & Engelmann*, 346). These Mahommedan *tahlīls* were worn by a band, and were the origin of the Span. word *tali*, 'a baldrick.' [But the *talee* is a Hindu, not a Mahommedan ornament, and there seems no doubt that it takes its name from Skt. *tāla*, 'the palmyra' (see **TALIPOT**), it being the original practice for women to wear this leaf dipped in saffron-water (*Mad. Gloss*, s.v. *Logan*, *Malabar*, i. 134).] The Indian word appears to occur first in Abraham Rogerius, but the custom is alluded to by early writers, *e.g.* Gouvea, *Synodo*, f. 43*v*.

1651.—"So the Bridegroom takes this **Tali**, and ties it round the neck of his bride."—*Rogerius*, 45.

1672.—"Among some of the Christians there is also an evil custom, that they for the greater tightening and fast-making of the marriage bond, allow the Bridegroom to tie a **Tali** or little band round the Bride's neck; although in my time this was as much as possible denounced, seeing that it is a custom derived from Heathenism."—*Baldaeus*, *Zeylon* (German), 408.

1674.—"The bridegroom attaches to the neck of the bride a line from which hang three little pieces of gold in honour of the three gods: and this they call **Tale**; and it is the sign of being a married woman."—*Faria y Sousa, Asia Port.*, ii. 707.

1704.—"Praeterea, quum moris hujus Regionis sit, ut infantes sex vel septem annorum, interdum etiam in teneriori aetate, ex genitorum consensu, matrimonium indissolubile de praesenti contrahant, per impositionem **Talii**, seu aureae tesserae nuptialis, uxoris collo pensilis: missionariis mandamus ne hujusmodi irrita matrimonia inter Christianos fieri permittant."—*Decree of Card. Tournon*, in *Norbert, Mem. Hist.* i. 155.

1726.—"And on the betrothal day the **Tali**, or bride's betrothal band, is tied round her neck by the Bramin . . . and this she must not untie in her husband's life."—*Valentijn, Choro.* 51.

[1813.—". . . the **tali**, which is a ribbon with a gold head hanging to it, is held ready; and, being shown to the company, some prayers and blessings are pronounced; after which the bridegroom takes it, and hangs it about the bride's neck."—*Forbes, Or. Mem.* 2nd ed. ii. 312.]

TALIAR, TARRYAR, s. A watchman (S. India). Tam. *talaiyāri*, [from *talai*, 'head,' a chief watchman].

1680.—"The Peons and **Tarryars** sent in quest of two soldiers who had deserted . . . returned with answer that they could not light of them, whereupon the Peons were turned out of service, but upon Verona's intercession were taken in again and fined each one month's pay, and to repay the money paid them for Battee (see **BATTA**); also the Pedda Naigu was fined in like manner for his **Tarryars**."—*Fort St. Geo. Consns.*, Feb. 10. In *Notes and Exts.*, Madras, 1873, No. III. p. 3.

1693.—"**Taliars** and Peons appointed to watch the Black Town. . . ."—In *Wheeler*, i. 267.

1707.—"Resolving to march 250 soldiers, 200 **talliars**, and 200 peons."—*Ibid.* ii. 74.

[1800.—"In every village a particular officer, called **Talliari**, keeps watch at night, and is answerable for all that may be stolen."—*Buchanan, Mysore*, i. 3.]

TALIPOT, s. The great-leaved fan-palm of S. India and Ceylon, *Corypha umbraculifera*, L. The name, from Skt. *tāla-pattra*, Hind. *tālpāt*, 'leaf of the *tāla* tree,' properly applies to the *leaf* of such a tree, or to the smaller leaf of the palmyra (*Borassus flabelliformis*), used for many purposes, *e.g.* for slips to write on, to make fans and umbrellas, &c. See **OLLAH, PALMYRA, TALAPOIN.** Sometimes we find the word used for an umbrella, but this is not common. The quotation from Jordanus, though using no name, refers to this tree. [Arrian says.: "These trees were called in Indian speech *tala*, and there grew on them, as there grows at the tops of the palm-trees, a fruit resembling balls of wool" (*Indika*, vii.).]

c. 1328.—"In this India are certain trees which have leaves so big that five or six men can very well stand under the shade of one of them."—*Fr. Jordanus*, 29-30.

c. 1430.—"These leaves are used in this country for writing upon instead of paper, and in rainy weather are carried on the head as a covering, to keep off the wet. Three or four persons travelling together can be covered by one of these leaves stretched out." And again: "There is also a tree called **tal**, the leaves of which are extremely large, and upon which they write."—*N. Conti*, in *India in the XV. Cent.*, 7 and 13.

1672.—"**Talpets** or sunshades."—*Baldaeus*, Dutch ed., 102.

1681.—"There are three other trees that must not be omitted. The first is **Talipot**. . . ."—*Knox*, 15.

" "They (the priests) have the honour of carrying the **Tallipot** with the broad end over their heads foremost; which none but the King does."—*Ibid.* 74. [See **TALAPOIN.**]

1803.—"The **talipot** tree . . . affords a prodigious leaf, impenetrable to sun or rain, and large enough to shelter ten men. It is a natural umbrella, and is of as eminent service in that country as a great-coat tree would be in this. A leaf of the **talipot**-tree is a tent to the soldier, a parasol to the traveller, and a book to the scholar."—*Sydney Smith, Works*, 3rd ed. iii. 15.

1874.—"... dans les embrasures ... s'étalaient des bananiers, des **tallipots**. ..." -*Franz, Souvenirs d'un Cosaque*, ch. iv.

1881.—"The lofty head of the **talipot** palm ... the proud queen of the tribe in Ceylon, towers above the scrub on every side. Its trunk is perfectly straight and white, like a slender marble column, and often more than 100 feet high. Each of the fans that compose the crown of leaves covers a semicircle of from 12 to 16 feet radius, a surface of 150 to 200 square feet."—*Haeckel's Visit to Ceylon*, E.T. p. 129.

TALISMAN, s. This word is used by many medieval and post-medieval writers for what we should now call a **moollah**, or the like, a member of the Mahommedan clergy, so to call them. It is doubtless the corruption of some Ar. term, but of *what* it is not easy to say. Qu. *talāmiza*, 'disciples, students'? [See *Burton*, *Ar. Nights*, ix. 165.] On this Prof. Robertson Smith writes: "I have got some fresh light on your *Talisman*.

"W. Bedwell, the father of English Arabists, in his *Catalogue of the Chapters of the Turkish Alkoran*, published (1615) along with the *Mohammedis Imposturaè*, and *Arabian Trudgman*, has the following, quoted from *Postellus de Orbis Concordia*, i. 13: 'Haec precatio (the *fātiḥa*) illis est communis ut nobis dominica: et ita quibusdum ad battologiam usque recitatur ut centies idem, aut duo aut tria vocabula repetant dicendo, *Alhamdu lillah, hamdu lillah, hamdu lillah*, et cetera ejus vocabula eodem modo. Idque facit in publicà oratione **Taalima**, id est sacrificulus, pro his qui negligenter orant ut aiunt, ut ea repititione suppleat eorum erroribus .... Quidam medio in campo tam assiduè, ut defessi considant; alii circumgirando corpus,' etc.

"Here then we have a form without the *s*, and one which from the vowels seem to be *tiʿlima*, 'a very learned man.' This, owing to the influence of the guttural, would sound in modern pronunciation nearly as *Taalima*. At the same time *tiʿlima* is not the name of an office, and prayers on behalf of others can be undertaken by any one who receives a mandate, and is paid for them; so it is very possible that Postellus, who was an Arabic scholar, made the pointing suit his idea of the word meant, and that the real word is *talāmi*, a shortened form, recognised by Jawhari, and other lexicographers, of **talāmidh**, 'disciples.' That students should turn a penny by saying prayers for others is very natural." This, therefore, confirms our conjecture of the origin.

1338.—"They treated me civilly, and set me in front of their mosque during their Easter; at which mosque, on account of its being their Easter, there were assembled from divers quarters a number of their *Cadini*, *i.e.* of their bishops, and of their **Talismani**, *i.e.* of their priests."—Letter of *Friar Pascal*, in *Cathay*, &c., p. 235.

1471.—"In questa città è vna fossa d'acqua nel modo di vna fontana, la qual' è guardata da quelli suoi **Thalassimani**, cioè preti; quest' acqua dicono che ha gran vertù contra la lebra, e contra le caualette."—*Giosafa Barbaro*, in *Ramusio*, ii. f. 107.

1535.—

"Non vi sarebbe più confusione
S'a Damasco il Soldan desse l'assalto;
Un muover d'arme, un correr di persone
E di **talacimanni** un gridar d'alto."
Ariosto, xviii. 7.

1554.—"**Talismánnos** habent hominum genus templorum ministerio dicatum. ..." *Busbeq. Epistola*. i. p. 40.

c. 1590.—"Vt **Talismanni**, qui sint commodius intelligatur: sciendum, certos esse gradus Mahumetanis eorum qui legum apud ipsos periti sunt, et partim jus dicunt, partim legem interpretantur. Ludovicus Bassanus Iadrensis in hunc modum comparat eos cum nostris Ecclesiasticis. ... *Muphtim* dicit esse inter ipsos instar vel Papae nostro, vel Patriarchae Graecorum. ... Huic proximi sunt *Cadilescheri*. ... Bassanus hos cum Archiepiscopis nostris comparat. Sequuntur **Cadij** ... locum obtinent Episcopi. Secundum hos sunt eis *Hoggiae*,* qui seniores dicuntur, vt Graecis et nostris Presbyteri. Excipiunt *Hoggias* **Talismani**, seu Presbyteros Diaconi. Vltimi sunt **Dervisii**, qui Calogeris Graecorum, monachis nostris respondent. **Talismani** Mahumetanis ad preces interdiu et noctu quinquis excitant."—*Leunclavius, Annales Sultanorum Othmanidarum*, ed. 1650, 414.

1610.—"Some hauing two, some foure, some sixe adioyning turrets, exceeding high, and exceeding slender: tarrast aloft on the outside like the maine top of a ship ... from which the **Talismanni** with elated voices (for they vse no bels) do congregate the people. ..."—*Sandys*, p. 31.

c. 1630.—"The *Fylalli* converse most in the Alcoran. The *Deruissi* are wandering wolves in sheepes clothing. The **Talismanni** regard the houres of prayer by turning the 4 hour'd glasse. The *Muyezini*

* *Hoggiae* is of course Khwājas (see **COJA**). But in the B. Museum there is a copy of Leunclavius, ed. of 1588, with MS. autograph remarks by Joseph Scaliger; and on the word in question he notes as its origin (in Arabic characters): "*Hujja(t)* Disputatio"—which is manifestly erroneous.

crie from the tops of Mosques, battologuizing Llala Hyllula."—*Sir T. Herbert*, 267; [and see ed. 1677, p. 323].

1678.—"If he can read like a Clerk a Chapter out of the Alcoran . . . he shall be crowned with the honour of being a Mullah or **Talman**. . . ."—*Fryer*, 368.

1687.—". . . It is reported by the Turks that . . . the victorious Sultan . . . went with all Magnificent pomp and solemnity to pay his thanksgiving and devotions at the church of Sancta Sophia; the Magnificence so pleased him, that he immediately added a yearly Rent of 10,000 zechins to the former Endowments, for the maintenance of Imaums or Priests, Doctours of their Law, **Talismans** and others who continually attend there for the education of youth. . . ."—*Sir P. Rycaut, Present State of the Ottoman Empire*, p. 54.

TĀLIYAMĀR, s. Sea-Hind. for 'cut-water.' Port. *talhamar*.—*Roebuck*.

TALLICA, s. Hind. from Ar *ta'līkah*. An invoice or schedule.

1682.—". . . that he . . . would send another Droga (**Daroga**) or **Customer** on purpose to take our **Tallicas**."—*Hedges, Diary*, Dec. 26; [Hak. Soc. i. 60. Also see under **KUZZANNA**].

TALOOK, s. This word, Ar. *ta'alluk*, from root *'alak*, 'to hang or depend,' has various shades of meaning in different parts of India. In S. and W. India it is the subdivision of a district, presided over as regards revenue matters by a **tahseeldar**. In Bengal it is applied to tracts of proprietary land, sometimes not easily distinguished from *Zemindaries*, and sometimes subordinate to or dependent on Zemindars. In the N.W. Prov. and Oudh the *ta'alluk* is an estate the profits of which are divided between different proprietors, one being superior, the other inferior (see **TALOOKDAR**). *Ta'alluk* is also used in Hind. for 'department' of administration.

1885.—"In October, 1779, the Dacca Council were greatly disturbed in their minds by the appearance amongst them of John Doe, who was then still in his prime. One Chundermonee demised to John Doe and his assigns certain lands in the pergunna Bullera . . . whereupon George III., by the Grace of God, of Great Britain, France, and Ireland, King, Defender of the Faith, and so forth, commanded the Sheriff of Calcutta to give John Doe possession. At this Mr. Shakspeare burst into fury, and in language which must have surprised John Doe, proposed 'that a *sezawul* be appointed for the collection of Patparrah **Talook**, with directions to pay the same into Bullera **cutcherry**.'"—*Sir J. Stephen, Nuncomar and Impey*, ii. 159-60. A *sazāwal* is "an officer specially appointed to collect the revenue of an estate, from the management of which the owner or farmer has been removed."—(*Wilson*).

TALOOKDĀR, s. Hind. from Pers. *ta'allukdār*, 'the holder of a *ta'alluk*' (see **TALOOK**) in either of the senses of that word; *i.e.* either a Government officer collecting the revenue of a *ta'alluk* (though in this sense it is probably now obsolete everywhere), or the holder of an estate so designated. The famous *Talookdars* of Oudh are large landowners, possessing both villages of which they are sole proprietors, and other villages, in which there are subordinate holders, in which the *Talookdar* is only the superior proprietor (see *Carnegie, Kachari Technicalities*).

[1769.—". . . inticements are frequently employed by the **Talookdars** to augment the concourse to their lands."—*Verelst, View of Bengal*, App. 233. In his *Glossary* he defines "*Talookdar*, the Zemeen-dar of a small district."]

TAMARIND, s. The pod of the tree which takes its name from that product, *Tamarindus indica*, L., N.O. *Leguminosae*. It is a tree cultivated throughout India and Burma for the sake of the acid pulp of the pod, which is laxative and cooling, forming a most refreshing drink in fever. The tree is not believed by Dr. Brandis to be indigenous in India, but is supposed to be so in tropical Africa. The origin of the name is curious. It is Ar. *tamar-u'l-Hind*, 'date of India,' or perhaps rather in Persian form, *tamar-i-Hindī*. It is possible that the original name may have been *thamar*, 'fruit' of India, rather than *tamar*, 'date.'

1298.—"When they have taken a merchant vessel, they force the merchants to swallow a stuff called **Tamarindi**, mixed in sea-water, which produces a violent purging."—*Marco Polo*, 2nd ed., ii. 383.

c. 1335.—"L'arbre appelé *ḥammar*, c'est à dire **al-tamar-al-Hindi**, est un arbre sauvage qui couvre les montagnes."—*Masālik-al-abṣar*, in *Not. et Ext.* xiii. 175.

1563.—"It is called in Malavar *puli*, and in Guzerat *ambili*, and this is the name they have among all the other people of this India; and the Arab calls it **tamarindi**, because *tamar*, as you well know, is our *tamara*, or, as the Castilians say, *datil* [*i.e.* date], so that **tamarindi** are 'dates of

India'; and this was because the Arabs could not think of a name more appropriate on account of its having stones inside, and not because either the tree or the fruit had any resemblance."—*Garcia*, f. 200. [*Puli* is the Malayāl. name; *ambilii* is probably Hind. *imlī*, Skt. *amlikā*, 'the tamarind.']

c. 1580.—"In febribus verò pestilentibus, atque omnibus aliis ex putridis, exurentibus, aquam, in qua multa copia **Tamarindorum** infusa fuerit cum saccharo ebibunt."—*Prosper Alpinus* (*De Plantis Aegypt.*) ed. Lugd. Bat. 1735, ii. 20.

1582.—"They have a great store of **Tamarindos**. . . ."—*Castañeda*, by N.L. f. 94.

[1598.—"**Tamarinde** is by the Aegyptians called *Derelside* (qu. *dār-al-sayyida*, 'Our Lady's tree'?)."—*Linschoten*, Hak. Soc. ii. 121.]

1611.—"That wood which we cut for firewood did all hang trased with cods of greene fruit (as big as a Bean-cod in England) called **Tamerim**; it hath a very soure tast, and by the Apothecaries is held good against the Scurvie."—*N. Dounton*, in *Purchas*, i. 277.

[1623.—"**Tamarinds**, which the Indians call *Hambele*" (*imlī*, as in quotation from Garcia above).—*P. della Valle*, Hak. Soc. i. 92.]

1829.—"A singularly beautiful **Tamarind** tree (ever the most graceful, and amongst the most magnificent of trees). . . ."—*Mem. of Col. Mountain*, 98.

1877.—"The natives have a saying that sleeping beneath the '**Date of Hind**' gives you fever, which you cure by sleeping under a *nim* tree (*Melia azedirachta*), the lilac of Persia."—*Burton, Sind Revisited*, i. 92. The *nim* (see **NEEM**) (*pace* Capt. Burton) is not the 'lilac of Persia' (see **BUCKYNE**). The prejudice against encamping or sleeping under a tamarind tree is general in India. But, curiously, Bp. Pallegoix speaks of it as the practice of the Siamese "to rest and play under the beneficent shade of the **Tamarind**."—(*Desc. du Royaume Thai ou Siam*, i. 136).

TAMARIND-FISH, s. This is an excellent zest, consisting, according to Dr. Balfour, of white **pomfret**, cut in transverse slices, and preserved in tamarinds. The following is a note kindly given by the highest authority on Indian fish matters, Dr. Francis Day:

"My account of **Tamarind fish** is very short, and in my *Fishes of Malabar* as follows:—

"'The best **Tamarind fish** is prepared from the Seir fish (see **SEER-FISH**), and from the *Lates calcarifer*, known as **Cockup** in Calcutta; and a rather inferior quality from the *Polynemus* (or Roe-ball, to which genus the **Mango-fish** belongs), and the more common from any kind of fish.' The above refers to Malabar, and more especially to Cochin. Since I wrote my *Fishes of Malabar* I have made many inquiries as to **Tamarind fish**, and found that the white pomfret, where it is taken, appears to be the best for making the preparation."

TAMBERANEE, s. Malayāl. *tamburān*, 'Lord; God, or King.' It is a title of honour among the **Nairs**, and is also assumed by Saiva monks in the Tamil countries. [The word is derived from Mal. *tam*, 'one's own,' *purān*, 'lord.' The junior male members of the Malayāli Rāja's family, until they come of age, are called *Tambān*, and after that *Tamburān*. The female members are similarly styled *Tambaṭṭi* and *Tamburaṭṭi* (*Logan, Malabar*, iii. *Gloss.* s.v.).]

1510.—"Dice l'altro **Tamarai**: zoe Per Dio? L'altro respõde **Tamarani**: zoe Per Dio."—*Varthema*, ed. 1517, f. 45.

[c. 1610.—"They (the Nairs) call the King in their language **Tambiraine**, meaning 'God.'"—*Pyrard de Laval*, Hak. Soc. i. 357.]

TANA, TANNA, n.p. *Thāna*, a town on the Island of Salsette on the strait ('River of Tana') dividing that island from the mainland and 20 m. N.E. of Bombay, and in the early Middle Ages the seat of a Hindu kingdom of the Konkan (see **CONCAN**), as well as a seaport of importance. It is still a small port, and is the chief town of the District which bears its name.

c. 1020.—"From Dhár southwards to the river Nerbudda, nine; thence to Mahratdes . . . eighteen; thence to Konkan, of which the capital is **Tana**, on the seashore, twenty-five parasangs."—*Al-Birūnī*, in *Elliot*, i. 60.

[c. 1150.—"**Tanah**," miswritten **Banah**. See under **TABASHEER**.]

1298.—"**Tana** is a great Kingdom lying towards the West. . . . There is much traffic here, and many ships and merchants frequent the place."—*Marco Polo*, Bk. III. ch. 27.

1321.—"After their blessed martyrdom, which occurred on the Thursday before Palm Sunday in **Thana** of India, I baptised about 90 persons in a certain city called Parocco, ten days' journey distant therefrom, and I have since baptised more than twenty, besides thirty-five who were baptised between **Thana** and Supera (**Supara**)."—*Letter of Friar Jordanus*, in *Cathay*, &c., 226.

c. 1323.—"And having thus embarked I passed over in 28 days to **Tana**, where for the faith of Christ four of our Minor Friars had suffered martyrdom. . . . The land is under the dominion of the Saracens. . . ."—*Fr. Odoric*, *Ibid.* i. 57-58.

1516.—"25 leagues further on the coast is a fortress of the before-named king, called **Tana**-*Mayambu*" (this is perhaps rather **Bombay**).—*Barbosa*, 68.

1529.—"And because the norwest winds blew strong, winds contrary to his course, after going a little way he turned and anchored in sight of the island, where were stationed the foists with their captain-in-chief Alixa, who seeing our fleet in motion put on his oars and assembled at the River of **Tana**, and when the wind came round our fleet made sail, and anchored at the mouth of the River of **Tana**, for the wind would not allow of its entering."—*Correa*, iii. 290.

1673.—"The Chief City of this Island is called **Tanaw**; in which are Seven Churches and Colleges, the chiefest one of the *Paulistines* (see **PAULIST**). . . . Here are made good Stuffs of Silk and Cotton."—*Fryer*, 73.

TANA, THANA, s. A Police station. Hind. *thāna*, *thānā*, [Skt. *sthāna*, 'a place of standing, a post']. From the quotation following it would seem that the term originally meant a fortified post, with its garrison, for the military occupation of the country; a meaning however closely allied to the present use.

c. 1640-50.—"**Thánah** means a corps of cavalry, matchlockmen, and archers, stationed within an enclosure. Their duty is to guard the roads, to hold the places surrounding the **Thánah**, and to despatch provisions (*rasad*, see **RUSSUD**) to the next **Thánah**."—*Pādishāh nāmah*, quoted by *Blochmann*, in *Āīn*, i. 345.

TANADAR, THANADAR, s. The chief of a police station (see **TANA**), Hind. *thānadār*. This word was adopted in a more military sense at an early date by the Portuguese, and is still in habitual use with us in the civil sense.

1516.—In a letter of 4th Feb. 1515 (*i.e.* 1516), the King Don Manoel constitutes João Machado to be **Tanadar** and captain of land forces in Goa.—*Archiv. Port. Orient.* fasc. 5, 1-3.

1519.—"Senhor Duarte Pereira; this is the manner in which you will exercise your office of **Tannadar** of this Isle of Tyçoari (*i.e.* Goa), which the Senhor Capitão will now encharge you with."—*Ibid.* p. 35.

c. 1548.—"In Aguaci is a great mosque (*mizquita*), which is occupied by the **tenadars**, but which belongs to His Highness; and certain *petayas*, (yards?) in which *bate* (**paddy**) is collected, which also belong to His Highness."—*Tombo* in *Subsidios*, 216.

1602.—"So all the force went aboard of the light boats, and the Governor in his bastard-galley entered the river with a grand clangour of music, and when he was in mid-channel there came to his galley a boat, in which was the **Tanadar** of the City (Dabul), and going aboard the galley presented himself to the Governor with much humility, and begged pardon of his offences. . . ."—*Couto*, IV. i. 9.

[1813.—"The third in succession was a **Tandar**, or petty officer of a district. . . ."—*Forbes, Or. Mem.* 2nd ed. ii. 5.]

TANGA, s. Mahr. *tānk*, Turki *tanga*. A denomination of coin which has been in use over a vast extent of territory, and has varied greatly in application. It is now chiefly used in Turkestan, where it is applied to a silver coin worth about 7½*d*. And Mr. W. Erskine has stated that the word *tanga* or *tanka* is of Chagatai Turki origin, being derived from *tang*, which in that language means 'white' (*H. of Baber and Humayun*, i. 546). Though one must hesitate in differing from one usually so accurate, we must do so here. He refers to Josafa Barbaro, who says this, viz. that certain silver coins are called by the Mingrelians *tetari*, by the Greeks *aspri*, by the Turks *akcha*, and by the Zagatais *tengh*, all of which words in the respective languages signify 'white.' We do not however find such a word in the dictionaries of either Vambéry or of Pavet de Courteille;—the latter only having *tangah*, 'fer-blanc.' And the obvious derivation is the Skt. *ṭaṅka*, 'a weight (of silver) equal to 4 *māshas* . . . a stamped coin.' The word in the forms *ṭakā* (see **TUCKA**) and *tanga* (for these are apparently identical in origin) is, "in all dialects, laxly used for money in general" (*Wilson*).

In the Lahore coinage of Mahmūd of Ghaznī, A.H. 418-419 (A.D. 1027-28), we find on the Skt. legend of the reverse the word *tanka* in correspondence with the *dirham* of the Ar. obverse (see *Thomas, Pathan Kings*, p. 49). *Tanka* or *Tanga* seems to have continued to be the popular name of the chief silver coin of the Delhi sovereigns during the 13th and first part of the 14th centuries, a coin which was substantially the same with the **rupee** (q.v.) of later days. In fact this application of the word in the form *ṭakā* (see **TUCKA**) is usual in Bengal down to our own day. Ibn Batuta indeed, who was in India in the time of Mahommed Tughlak, 1333-

1343 or thereabouts, always calls the gold coin then current a *tanka* or *dīnār* of gold. It was, as he repeatedly states, the equivalent of 10 silver *dīnārs*. These silver *dīnārs* (or rupees) are called by the author of the *Masālik-al-Absār* (c. 1340) the "silver *tanka* of India." The gold and silver *tanka* continue to be mentioned repeatedly in the history of Feroz Shāh, the son of Mahommed (1351-1388), and apparently with the same value as before. At a later period under Sikandar Buhlol (1488-1517), we find *black* (or copper) *tankas*, of which 20 went to the old silver *tanka*.

We cannot say when the coin, or its name rather, first appeared in Turkestan.

But the name was also prevalent on the western coast of India as that of a low denomination of coin, as may be seen in the quotations from Linschoten and Grose. Indeed the name still survives in Goa as that of a copper coin equivalent to 60 *reis* or about 2*d*. And in the 16th century also 60 *reis* appears from the papers of Gerson da Cunha to have been the equivalent of the silver *tanga* of Goa and Bassein, though all the equations that he gives suggest that the *rei* may have been more valuable then.

The denomination is also found in Russia under the form **dengi**. See a quotation under **COPECK**, and compare **PARDAO**.

c. 1335.—"According to what I have heard from the Shaikh Mubarak, the red *lak* (see **LACK**) contains 100,000 golden **tankahs**, and the white *lak* 100,000 (silver) **tankahs**. The golden **tanka**, called in this country the red *tanka*, is equivalent to three *mithkāls*, and the silver **tanka** is equivalent to 8 *hashtkānī dirhams*, this *dirham* being of the same weight as the silver *dirham* current in Egypt and Syria."—*Masālik-al-abṣār*, in *Not. et Exts.* xiii. 211.

c. 1340.—"Then I returned home after sunset and found the money at my house. There were 3 bags containing in all 6233 **tankas**, *i.e.* the equivalent of the 55,000 dīnārs (of silver) which was the amount of my debts, and of the 12,000 which the sultan had previously ordered to be paid me, after of course deducting the tenth part according to Indian custom. The value of the piece called **tanka** is 2½ dīnārs in gold of Barbary."—*Ibn Batuta*, iii. 426. (Here the gold **tanga** is spoken of.)

c. 1370.—"Sultán Fíroz issued several varieties of coins. There was the gold **tanka**, and the silver **tanka**," &c.—*Táríkh-i-Fíroz Sháhí*, in *Elliot*, iii. 357.

1404.—". . . vna sua moneda de plata que llaman **Tangaes**."—*Clavijo*, f. 46*b*.

1516.—". . . a round coin like ours, and with Moorish letters on both sides, and about the size of a *fanon* (see **FANAM**) of Calicut, . . . and its worth 55 maravedis; they call these **tanga**, and they are of very fine silver."—*Barbosa*, 45.

[1519.—Rules regulating ferry-dues at Goa: "they may demand for this one **tamgua** only."—*Archiv. Port. Orient.* fasc. 5, p. 18.]

c. 1541.—"Todar . . . fixed first a golden *ashrafi* (see **ASHRAFEE**) as the enormous remuneration for one stone, which induced the *Ghakkars* to flock to him in such numbers that afterwards a stone was paid with a rupee, and this pay gradually fell to 5 **tankas**, till the fortress (Rōhtās) was completed." — *Táríkh-i-Khán-Jahán Lodí*, in *Elliot*, v. 115. (These are the Bahlūlī or Sikandarī **tankas** of copper, as are also those in the next quotation from *Elliot*.)

1559.—"The old Muscovite money is not round but oblong or egg-shaped, and is called **denga**. . . . 100 of these coins make a Hungarian gold-piece; 6 **dengas** make an *altin*; 20 a *grifna*; 100 a *poltina*; and 200 a *ruble*."—*Herberstein*, in *Ramusio*, ii. f. 158*v*.

[1571. — "Gujarati **tankchahs** at 100 **tankchahs** to the rupee. At the present time the rupee is fixed at 40 dams. . . . As the current value of the **tankchah** of Pattan, etc., was less than that of Gujarat."—*Mirat-i-Ahmadī*, in *Bayley*, *Gujarat*, pp. 6, 11.

[1591.—"**Dingoes**." See under **RUBLE**.]

1592-3.—"At the present time, namely, A.H. 1002, Hindustan contains 3200 towns, and upon each town are dependent 200, 500, 1000, or 1500 villages. The whole yields a revenue of 640 *krors* (see **CRORE**) *murádi* **tankas**." — *Ṭabaḳāt-i-Akbarī*, in *Elliot*, v. 186.

1598.—"There is also a kinde of reckoning of money which is called **Tangas**, not that there is any such coined, but are so named onely in telling, five **Tangas** is one *Pardaw* (see **PARDAO**), or **Xeraphin** badde money, for you must understande that in telling they have two kinds of money, good and badde, for foure **Tangas** good money are as much as five **Tangas** badde money."—*Linschoten*, ch. 35; [Hak. Soc. i. 241].

[c. 1610.—"The silver money of Goa is perdos, larins, **Tangues**, the last named worth 7 sols, 6 deniers a piece."—*Pyrard de Laval*, Hak. Soc. ii. 69.]

1615.—"Their moneyes in Persia of silver, are the . . . the rest of copper, like the **Tangas** and Pisos (see **PICE**) of India."—*Richard Steele*, in *Purchas*, i. 543.

[c. 1630. — "There he expended fifty thousand Crow (see **CRORE**) of **tacks** . . . sometimes twenty **tack** make one Roopee."—*Sir T. Herbert*, ed. 1677, p. 64.]

1673.—"**Tango**." See under **REAS**.

[1638.—"Their (at Surat) ordinary way of accompting is by **lacs**, each of which is worth 100,000 *ropias* (see **RUPEE**), and 100 lacs make a *crou*, or *carroa* (see **CRORE**), and 10 *carroas* make an *Areb*. A *Theil* (see **TOLA, TAEL**) of silver (? gold) makes 11, 12, or 13 *ropias* ready money. A *massa* (*māshā*) and a half make a *Thiel* of silver, 10 whereof make a *Thiel* of gold. They call their brass and copper-money **Tacques**."—*Mandelslo*, 107.]

c. 1750-60.—"Throughout Malabar and Goa, they use **tangas**, vintins, and Pardoo (see **PARDAO**) **xeraphin**."—*Grose*, i. 283. The Goa **tanga** was worth 60 *reis*, that of Ormus 62 $\frac{14}{43}$ to 69 $\frac{33}{43}$ *reis*.

[1753.—In Khiva "... **Tongas**, a small piece of copper, of which 1500 are equal to a ducat."—*Hanway*, i. 351.]

1815.—"... one **tungah** ... a coin about the value of fivepence."—*Malcolm*, *H. of Persia*, ii. 250.

[1876.—"... it seemed strange to me to find that the Russian word for money, **denga** or **dengi**, in the form **tenga**, meant everywhere in Central Asia a coin of twenty kopeks. ..."—*Schuyler*, *Turkistan*, i. 153.]

TANGUN, TANYAN, s. Hind. *ṭānghan*, *ṭāngan*; apparently from Tibetan *rTanān*, the vernacular name of this kind of horse (*rTa*, 'horse'). The strong little pony of Bhutān and Tibet.

c. 1590.—"In the confines of Bengal, near Kuch [-Bahār], another kind of horses occurs, which rank between the *gūṭ* (see **GOONT**) and Turkish horses, and are called **táng'han**; they are strong and powerful."—*Āīn*, i. 133.

1774.—"2d. That for the possession of the Chitchanotta Province, the Deb Raja shall pay an annual tribute of five **Tangan** Horses to the Honorable Company, which was the acknowledgment paid to the Deb Raja."—*Treaty of Peace* between the H.E.I.C. and the *Rajah of Bootan*, in *Aitchison's Treaties*, i. 144.

" "We were provided with two **tangun** ponies of a mean appearance, and were prejudiced against them unjustly. On better acquaintance they turned out patient, sure-footed, and could climb the Monument."—*Bogle's Narrative*, in *Markham*, 17.

1780.—"... had purchased 35 Jhawah or young elephants, of 8 or 9 years old, 60 **Tankun**, or ponies of Manilla and Pegu."—*H. of Hydur Naik*, 383.

" "... small horses brought from the mountains on the eastern side of Bengal. These horses are called **tanyans**, and are mostly pyebald."—*Hodges*, *Travels*, 31.

1782.—"To be sold, a Phaeton, in good condition, with a pair of young **Tanyan** Horses, well broke."—*India Gazette*, Oct. 26.

1793.—"As to the **Tanguns** or **Tanyans**, so much esteemed in India for their hardiness, they come entirely from the Upper Tibet, and notwithstanding their make, are so sure footed that the people of Nepaul ride them without fear over very steep mountains, and along the brink of the deepest precipices."—*Kirkpatrick's Nepaul*, 135.

1854.—"These animals, called **Tanghan**, are wonderfully strong and enduring; they are never shod, and the hoof often cracks. ... The Tibetans give the foals of value messes of pig's blood and raw liver, which they devour greedily, and it is said to strengthen them wonderfully; the custom is, I believe, general in Central Asia."—*Hooker*, *Himalayan Journals*, 1st ed. ii. 131.

TANJORE, n.p. A city and District of S. India; properly *Tañjāvūr* ('Low Town'?), so written in the inscription on the great Tanjore Pagoda (11th century). [The *Madras Manual* gives two derivations: "*Tañjāvūr*, familiarly called *Tañjai* by the natives. It is more fully given as *Tañjai-mānagaram*, Tañjan's great city, after its founder. *Tañjam* means 'refuge, shelter'" (ii. 216). The Gloss. gives *Tañjāvūr*, Tam. *tañjam*, 'asylum,' *ūr*, 'village.']

[1816.—"The **Tanjore** Pill, it is said, is made use of with great success in India against the bite of mad dogs, and that of the most venemous serpents."—*Asiatic Journal*, ii. 381.]

TANK, s. A reservoir, an artificial pond or lake, made either by excavation or by damming. This is one of those perplexing words which seem to have a double origin, in this case one Indian, the other European.

As regards what appears to be the Indian word, Shakespear gives: "*Tānk'h* (in Guzerat), an underground reservoir for water." [And so Platts.] Wilson gives: "*Tánken* or *táken*, Mahr. ... *Tánkh* (said to be Guzeráthí). A reservoir of water, an artificial pond, commonly known to Europeans in India as a **Tank**. *Tánki*, Guz. A reservoir of water; a small well." R. Drummond, in his *Illustrations of Guzerattee*, &c., gives: "*Tanka* (Mah.) and *Tankoo* (Guz.) Reservoirs, constructed of stone or brick or lime, of larger and lesser size, generally inside houses. ... They are almost entirely covered at top, having but a small aperture to let a pot or bucket down." ... "In the towns of Bikaner," says Tod, "most families have large cisterns or reservoirs called *Tankas*, filled by the rains" (*Rajputana*, ii. 202). Again, speaking of towns in the desert of Márwár, he says; "they collect the rain water in reservoirs called *Tanka*, which they are obliged to use sparingly, as it is said to produce night blindness" (ii. 300). Again, Dr. Spilsbury (*J.A.S.B.* ix. pt. 2, 891), describing a journey in the Nerbudda Basin, cites the word, and notes: "I first heard this word used by a native in the Betool district; on asking him if at the top of Bowergurh there was any spring, he said No, but there was a *Tanka* or place made of *pukka* (stone and cement) for holding water." Once more, in an Appendix to the Report of the Survey of India for 1881-1882, Mr. G. A. MacGill, speaking of the rain cisterns in the driest part of Rajputana, says: "These cisterns or wells are called by the people *tánkás*" (*App.* p. 12). See also quotation below from a Report by Major Strahan. It is not easy to doubt the genuineness of the word, which may possibly be from Skt. *taḍaga*, *taṭāga*, *taṭāka*, 'a pond, pool, or tank.'

Fr. Paolino, on the other hand, says the word *tanque* used by the Portuguese in India was *Portoghesa corrotta*, which is vague. But in fact *tanque* is a word which appears in all Portuguese dictionaries, and which is used by authors so early after the opening of communication with India (we do not know if there is an instance actually earlier) that we can hardly conceive it to have been borrowed from an Indian language, nor indeed could it have been borrowed from Guzerat and Rajpūtāna, to which the quotations above ascribe the vernacular word. This Portuguese word best suits, and accounts for that application of *tank* to large sheets of water which is habitual in India. The indigenous Guzerati and Mahratti word seems to belong rather to what we now call a *tank* in England; *i.e.* a small reservoir for a house or ship. Indeed the Port. *tanque* is no doubt a form of the Lat. *stagnum*, which gives It. *stagno*, Fr. old *estang* and *estan*, mod. *étang*, Sp. *estanque*, a word which we have also in old English and in Lowland Scotch, thus:

1589.—"They had in them **stanges** or pondes of water full of fish of sundrie sortes."—*Parkes's Mendoza*, Hak. Soc. ii. 46.

c. 1785.—

"I never drank the Muses' **stank**,
Castalia's burn and a' that;
But there it streams, and richly reams,
My Helicon I ca' that."—*Burns.*

It will be seen that Pyrard de Laval uses *estang*, as if specifically, for the *tank* of India.

1498.—"And many other saints were there painted on the walls of the church, and these wore diadems, and their portraiture was in a divers kind, for their teeth were so great that they stood an inch beyond the mouth, and every saint had 4 or 5 arms, and below the church stood a great **tanque** wrought in cut stone like many others that we had seen by the way."—*Roteiro de Vasco da Gama*, 57.

" "So the Captain Major ordered Nicolas Coelho to go in an armed boat, and see where the water was, and he found in the said island (**Anchediva**) a building, a church of great ashlar work which had been destroyed by the Moors, as the country people said, only the chapel had been covered with straw, and they used to make their prayers to three black stones which stood in the midst of the body of the chapel. Moreover they found just beyond the church a **tanque** of wrought ashlar in which we took as much water as we wanted; and at the top of the whole island stood a great **tanque** of the depth of 4 fathoms, and moreover we found in front of the church a beach where we careened the ship Berrio."—*Ibid.* 95.

1510.—"Early in the morning these Pagans go to wash at a **tank**, which **tank** is a pond of still water (—*ad uno* **Tancho** *il qual* **Tancho** *è una fossa d'acqua morta*)."—*Varthema*, 149.

" "Near to Calicut there is a temple in the midst of a **tank**, that is, in the middle of a pond of water."—*Ibid.* 175.

1553.—"In this place where the King (Bahádur Sháh) established his line of battle, on one side there was a great river, and on the other a **tank** (*tanque*) of water, such as they are used to make in those parts. For as there are few streams to collect the winter's waters, they make these **tanks** (which might be more properly called lakes), all lined with stone. They are so big that many are more than a league in compass."—*Barros*, IV. vi. 5.

c. 1610.—"Son logis estoit éloigné près d'vne lieuë du palais Royal, situé sur vn **estang**, et basty de pierres, ayant bien demy lieuë de tour, comme tous les autres **estangs**."—*Pyrard de Laval*, ed. 1679, i. 262; [Hak. Soc. i. 367].

[1615.—"I rode early . . . to the **tancke** to take the ayre."—*Sir T. Roe*, Hak. Soc. i. 78.]

1616.—"Besides their Rivers . . . they have many Ponds, which they call **Tankes**."—*Terry*, in *Purchas*, ii. 1470.

1638.—"A very faire **Tanke**, which is a square pit paved with gray marble."—*W. Bruton*, in *Hakl.* v. 50.

1648.—". . . a standing water or **Tanck**. . . ."—*Van Twist*, *Gen. Beschr.* 11.

1672.—"Outside and round about Suratte, there are elegant and delightful houses for recreation, and stately cemeteries in the usual fashion of the Moors, and also divers **Tanks** and reservoirs built of hard and solid stone."—*Baldaeus*, p. 12.

1673.—"Within a square Court, to which a stately Gate-house makes a Passage, in the middle whereof a **Tank** vaulted. . . ." —*Fryer*, 27.

1754.—"The post in which the party intended to halt had formerly been one of those reservoirs of water called **tanks**, which occur so frequently in the arid plains of this country."—*Orme*, i. 354.

1799.—"One crop under a **tank** in Mysore or the Carnatic yields more than three here." —*T. Munro*, in *Life*, i. 241.

1809.—
"Water so cool and clear,
The peasants drink not from the humble well.

* * * * *

Nor **tanks** of costliest masonry dispense
To those in towns who dwell,
The work of kings in their beneficence."
Kehama, xiii. 6.

1883.—". . . all through sheets* 124, 125, 126, and 131, the only drinking water is from '**tankas**,' or from '*tobs*.' The former are circular pits puddled with clay, and covered in with wattle and daub domes, in the top of which are small trap doors, which are kept locked; in these the villages store rain-water; the latter are small and somewhat deep ponds dug in the valleys where the soil is clayey, and are filled by the rain; these latter of course do not last long, and then the inhabitants are entirely dependent on their **tankas**, whilst their cattle migrate to places where the well-water is fit for use."—*Report* on Cent. Ind. and Rajputana Topogr. Survey (Bickaneer and Jeysulmeer). By *Major C. Strachan*, R.E., in *Report of the Survey in India*, 1882-83, App. p. 4. [The writer in the *Rajputana Gazetteer* (Bikanir) (i. 182) calls these covered pits *kund*, and the simple excavations *sār*.]

TANOR, n.p. An ancient town and port about 22 miles south of Calicut. There is a considerable probability that it was the *Tyndis* of the Periplus. It was a small kingdom at the arrival of the Portuguese, in partial subjection to the Zamorin. [The name is Malayāl. *Tānūr*, *tanni*, the tree *Terminalis belerica*, *ūr*, village.]

1516.—"Further on . . . are two places of Moors 5 leagues from one another. One is called Paravanor, and the other **Tanor**, and inland from these towns is a lord to whom they belong; and he has many Nairs, and sometimes he rebels against the King of Calicut. In these towns there is much shipping and trade, for these Moors are great merchants."—*Barbosa*, Hak. Soc. 153.

1521.—"Cotate was a great man among the Moors, very rich, and lord of **Tanor**, who carried on a great sea-trade with many ships, which trafficked all about the coast of India with passes from our Governors, for he only dealt in wares of the country; and thus he was the greatest possible friend of the Portuguese, and those who went to his dwelling were entertained with the greatest honour, as if they had been his brothers. In fact for this purpose he kept houses fitted up, and both cots and bedsteads furnished in our fashion, with tables and chairs and casks of wine, with which he regaled our people, giving them entertainments and banquets, insomuch that it seemed as if he were going to become a Christian. . . ."—*Correa*, ii. 679.

1528.—"And in the year (A.H.) 935, a ship belonging to the Franks was wrecked off **Tanoor**. . . . Now the Ray of that place affording aid to the crew, the Zamorin sent a messenger to him demanding of him the surrender of the Franks who composed it, together with such parts of the cargo of the ship as had been saved, but that chieftain having refused compliance with this demand, a treaty of peace was entered into with the Franks by him; and from this time the subjects of the Ray of **Tanoor** traded under the protection of the passes of the Franks."—*Tohfut-ul-Mujahideen*, E.T. 124-125.

1553.—"For Lopo Soares having arrived at Cochin after his victory over the Çamorin, two days later the King of **Tanor**, the latter's vassal, sent (to Lopo) to complain against the Çamorin by ambassadors, begging for peace and help against him, having fallen out with him for reasons that touched the service of the King of Portugal."—*Barros*, I. vii. 10.

1727.—"Four leagues more southerly is **Tannore**, a Town of small Trade, inhabited by Mahometans."—*A. Hamilton*, i. 322; [ed. 1744].

TAPPAUL, s. The word used in S. India for 'post,' in all the senses in which **dawk** (q.v.) is used in Northern India. Its origin is obscure. C. P. Brown suggests connection with the Fr. *étape* (which is the same originally as the Eng. *staple*). It is sometimes found in the end of the 18th century written *tappa* or *tappy*. But this seems to have been derived from Telugu clerks, who sometimes write *tappā* as a singular of *tappālu*, taking the latter for a plural (*C.P.B.*). Wilson appears to give the word a southern origin. But though its use is confined to the South and West, Mr. Beames assigns to it an Aryan origin: "*ṭappā* 'post-office,' *i.e.* place where

* These are sheets of the *Atlas of India*, within Bhawalpur and Jeysalmīr, on the borders of Bikaner.

letters are stamped, *ṭappāl* 'letter-post' (*ṭappā* + *alya* = 'stamping-house')," connecting it radically with *ṭāpā* 'a coop,' *ṭāpnā* 'to tap,' 'flatten,' 'beat down,' *ṭapak* 'a sledge hammer,' *ṭīpnā* 'to press,' &c. [with which Platts agrees.]

1799.—"You will perceive that we have but a small chance of establishing the **tappal** to Poonah."—*Wellington*, i. 50.

1800.—"The **Tappal** does not go 30 miles a day."—*T. Munro*, in *Life*, i. 244.

1809. — "Requiring only two sets of bearers I knew I might go by **tappaul** the whole way to Seringapatam."—*Ld. Valentia*, i. 385.

TAPTEE R., n.p. *Tāptī*; also called *Tāpī*, [Skt. *Tāpī*, 'that which is hot']. The river that runs by the city of Surat.

[1538.—"**Tapi**." See under **GODAVERY**.]

c. 1630.—"*Surat* is . . . watered with a sweet River named **Tappee** (or *Tindy*), as broad as the *Thames* at *Windsor*."—*Sir T. Herbert*, ed. 1638, p. 36.

1813.—"The sacred groves of Pulparra are the general resort for all the Yogees (**Jogee**), Senassees (**Sunyasee**), and Hindoo pilgrims . . . the whole district is holy, and the **Tappee** in that part has more than common sanctity." — *Forbes*, *Or. Mem.* i. 286; [2nd ed. i. 184, and compare i. 176].

" "**Tappee** or **Tapty**."—*Ibid.* 244; [2nd ed. i. 146].

TARA, TARE, s. The name of a small silver coin current in S. India at the time of the arrival of the Portuguese. It seems to have survived longest in Calicut. The origin we have not traced. It is curious that the commonest silver coin in Sicily down to 1860, and worth about 4½*d.*, was a *tarì*, generally considered to be a corruption of *dirhem*. I see Sir Walter Elliot has mooted this very question in his *Coins of S. India* (p. 138). [The word is certainly Malayāl. *tāram*, defined in the *Madras Gloss.* as "a copper coin, value 1½ pies." Mr. Gray in his note to the passage from Pyrard de Laval quoted below, suggests that it took its name from *tāra*, 'a star.']

1442.—"They cast (at Vijayanagar), in pure silver a coin which is the sixth of the *fanom*, which they call **tar**."—*Abdurrazzāk*, in *India in the XV. Cent.* 26.

1506.—(The Viceroy, D. Francisco D'Almeida, wintering his fleet in Cochin). "As the people were numerous they made quite a big town with a number of houses covered with upper stories of timber, and streets also where the people of the country set up their stalls in which they sold plenty of victuals, and cheap. Thus for a vinten of silver you got in change 20 silver coins that they called **taras**, something like the scale of a sardine, and for such coin they gave you 12 or 15 figs, or 4 or 5 eggs, and for a single *vintem* 3 or 4 fowls, and for one **tara** fish enough to fill two men's bellies, or rice enough for a day's victuals, dinner and supper too. Bread there was none, for there was no wheat except in the territory of the Moors."—*Correa*, i. 624.

1510.—The King of Narsinga (or Vijayanagar) "coins a silver money called **tare**, and others of gold, twenty of which go to a **pardao**, and are called fanom. And of these small ones of silver, there go 16 to a fanom."—*Varthema*, 130.

[c. 1610. — "Each man receives four **tarents**, which are small silver coins, each of the value of one-sixteenth of a **larin**."—*Pyrard de Laval*, Hak. Soc. i. 344. Later on (i. 412) he says "16 **tarens** go to a Phanan"].

1673.—(at Calicut). "Their coin admits no Copper; Silver **Tarrs**, 28 of which make a *Fanam*, passing instead thereof."—*Fryer*, 55.

" "Calicut.

* * * * *

"**Tarrs** *are the peculiar Coin, the rest are common to* India."—*Ibid.* 207.

1727.—"*Calecut* . . . coins are 10 **Tar** to a Fanam, 4½ Fanams to a Rupee."—*A. Hamilton*, ii. 316; [ed. 1744].

[1737.—"We are to allow each man 4 measures of rice and 1 **tar** per diem."—*Agreement* in *Logan*, *Malabar*, iii. 95, and see "**tarrs**" in iii. 192. Mr. Logan (vol. iii. *Gloss.* s.v.) defines the *tara* as equal to 2 pies.]

TARE AND TRET. Whence comes this odd firm in the books of arithmetic? Both partners apparently through Italy. The first Fr. *tare*, It. *tara*, from Ar. *ṭaraḥa*, 'to reject,' as pointed out by Dozy. *Tret* is alleged to be from It. *tritare*, 'to crumble or grind,' perhaps rather from *trito*, 'ground or triturated.' [Prof. Skeat (*Concise Dict.* s.v.) derives it from Fr. *traite*, 'a draught,' and that from Lat. *tractus*, *trahere*, 'to draw.']

TAREGA, s. This represents a word for a broker (or person analogous to the **hong merchants** of Canton in former days) in Pegu, in the days of its prosperity. The word is from S. India. We have in Tel. *taraga*, 'the occupation of a broker'; Tam. *taragari*, 'a broker.'

1568.—"Sono in Pegu otto sensari del Re che si chiamano **Tarege** li quali sono obligati di far vendere tutte le mercantie . . . per il prezzo corrente."—*Ces. Federici*, in *Ramusio*, iii. 395.

1583.—". . . e se fosse alcuno che a tempo del pagamento per non pagar si absentasse dalla città, o si ascondesse, il **Tarrecà** e obligato pagar per lui . . . i **Tarrecà** cosi si demandano i sensari."—*G. Balbi*, f. 107*v*, 108.

1587.—"There are in Pegu eight Brokers, whom they call **Tareghe**, which are bound to sell your goods at the price they be Woorth, and you give them for their labour two in the hundred: and they be bound to make your debt good, because you sell your marchandises vpon their word."—*R. Fitch*, in *Hakl.* ii. 393.

TARIFF, s. This comes from Ar. *ta'rīf*, *ta'rīfa*, 'the making known.' Dozy states that it appears to be comparatively modern in Spanish and Port., and has come into Europe apparently through Italian.

[1591.—"So that helping your memorie with certain Tablei or **Tariffas** made of purpose to know the numbers of the souldiers that are to enter into ranke."—*Garrard, Art Warre*, p. 224 (*Stanf. Dict.*).

[1617.—". . . a brief **Tareg** of Persia." —*Birdwood, First Letter Book*, 462.]

TAROUK, TAROUP, n.p. Burm. *Tarūk*, *Tarūp*. This is the name given by the Burmese to the Chinese. Thus a point a little above the Delta of the Irawadi, where the invading army of Kublai Khan (c. 1285) is said to have turned back, is called *Tarūk-mau*, or Chinese Point. But the use of this name, according to Sir A. Phayre, dates only from the Middle Ages, and the invasion just mentioned. Before that the Chinese, as we understand him, are properly termed *Tsin*; though the coupled names *Tarūk* and *Taret*, which are applied in the chronicles to early invaders, "may be considered as designations incorrectly applied by later copyists." And Sir A. Phayre thinks *Tarūk* is a form of *Tūrk*, whilst *Taret* is now applied to the Manchus. It seems to us probable that *Taruk* and *Taret* are probably meant for 'Turk and Tartar' (see *H. of Burma*, pp. 8. 11, 56). [Mr. Scott (*Upper Burma Gazetteer*, i. pt. i. 193) suggests a connection with the *Teru* or *Tero* State, which developed about the 11th century, the race having been expelled from China in 778 A.D.]

TASHREEF, s. This is the Ar. *tashrīf*, 'honouring'; and thus "conferring honour upon anyone, as by paying him a visit, presenting a dress of honour, or any complimentary donation" (*Wilson*). In Northern India the general use of the word is as one of ceremonious politeness in speaking of a visit from a superior or from one who is treated in politeness as a superior; when such an one is invited to 'bring his *tashrīf*,' *i.e.* 'to carry the honour of his presence,' 'to condescend to visit '——. The word always implies superiority on the part of him to whom *tashrīf* is attributed. It is constantly used by polite natives in addressing Europeans. But when the European in return says (as we have heard said, through ignorance of the real meaning of the phrase), 'I will bring my *tashrīf*,' the effect is ludicrous in the extreme, though no native will betray his amusement. In S. India the word seems to be used for the dress of honour conferred, and in the old Madras records, rightly or wrongly, for any complimentary present, in fact a *honorarium*. Thus in Wheeler we find the following:

1674.—"He (Lingapa, naik of Poonamalee) had, he said, carried a **tasheriff** to the English, and they had refused to take it. . . ."—*Op. cit.* i. 84.

1680.—"It being necessary to appoint one as the Company's Chief Merchant (Verona being deceased), resolved Bera Pedda Vincatadry, do succeed and the **Tasheriffs** be given to him and the rest of the principal Merchants, viz., 3 yards Scarlett to Pedda Vincatadry, and 2½ yards each to four others. . . .

"The Governor being informed that Verona's young daughter was melancholly and would not eat because her husband had received no **Tasheriff**, he also is **Tasherifd** with 2½ yards Scarlet cloth."—*Fort St. Geo. Consns.*, April 6. In *Notes and Exts.*, Madras, 1873, p. 15.

1685.—"Gopall Pundit having been at great charge in coming hither with such a numerous retinue . . . that we may engage him . . . to continue his friendship, to attain some more and better privileges there (at Cuddalore) than we have as yet—It is ordered that he with his attendants be **Tasherift** as followeth" (a list of presents follows).—In *Wheeler*, i. 148. [And see the same phrase in *Pringle, Diary*, &c., i. 1].

TATTOO, and abbreviated, **TAT**, s. A native-bred pony. Hind. *ṭaṭṭū*, [which Platts connects with Skt. *tara*, 'passing over'].

c. 1324.—"Tughlak sent his son Mahommed to bring Khusrū back. Mahommed seized the latter and brought him to his father mounted on a **tātū**, *i.e.* a pack-horse."—*Ibn Batuta*, iii. 207.

1784.—"On their arrival at the Choultry they found a miserable dooley and 15 **tattoo** horses."—In *Seton-Karr*, i. 15.

1785.—"We also direct that strict injunctions be given to the baggage department, for sending all the lean **Tatoos**, bullocks, &c., to grass, the rainy season being now at hand."—*Tippoo's Letters*, 105.

1804.—"They can be got for 25 rupees each horseman upon an average; but, I believe, when they receive only this sum they muster **tattoos**. . . . From 30 to 35 rupees each horse is the sum paid to the best horsemen."—*Wellington*, iii. 174.

1808.—"These **tut,hoos** are a breed of small ponies, and are the most useful and hardy little animals in India."—*Broughton's Letters*, 156; [ed. 1892, 117].

1810.—"Every servant . . . goes share in some **tattoo** . . . which conveys his luggage."—*Williamson, V.M.* i. 311.

1824.—"**Tattoos**. These are a kind of small, cat-hammed, and ill-looking ponies; but they are hardy and walk faster than oxen."—*Seely, Wonders of Ellora*, ch. ii.

1826.—". . . when I mounted on my **tattoo**, or pony, I could at any time have commanded the attendance of a dozen grooms, so many pressed forward to offer me their services."—*Pandurang Hari*, 21; [ed. 1873, i. 28].

[1830.—"Mounting our **tats**, we were on the point of proceeding homewards. . . ."—*Oriental Sport. Mag.*, ed. 1873, i. 437.]

c. 1831.—". . . mon **tattou** est fort au dessous de la taille d'un arabe. . . ."—*Jacquemont, Corresp.* i. 347.

c. 1840.
"With its bright brass patent axles, and
its little hog-maned **tatts**,
And its ever jetty harness, which was
always made by Watts. . . ."
A few lines in honour of the late Mr. Simms, in *Parker's Bole Ponjis*, 1851, ii. 215.

1853.—". . . Smith's plucky proposal to run his notable **tat**, Pickles."—*Oakfield*, i. 94.

1875.—"You young Gentlemen rode over on your **tats**, I suppose? The Subaltern's **tat**—that is the name, you know, they give to a pony in this country—is the most useful animal you can imagine."—*The Dilemma*, ch. ii.

TATTY, s. Hind. *ṭaṭṭī* and *ṭaṭī*, [which Platts connects with Skt. *tantra*, 'a thread, the warp in a loom']. A screen or mat made of the roots of fragrant grass (see **CUSCUS**) with which door or window openings are filled up in the season of hot winds. The screens being kept wet, their fragrant evaporation as the dry winds blow upon them cools and refreshes the house greatly, but they are only efficient when such winds are blowing. See also **THERMANTIDOTE**. The principle of the *tatty* is involved in the quotation from Dr. Fryer, though he does not mention the grass-mats.

c. 1665.—". . . or having in lieu of Cellarage certain *Kas-Kanays*, that is, little Houses of Straw, or rather of odoriferous Roots, that are very neatly made, and commonly placed in the midst of a Parterre . . . that so the Servants may easily with their Pompion-bottles, water them from without."—*Bernier*, E.T. 79; [ed. *Constable*, 247].

1673.—"They keep close all day for 3 or 4 Months together . . . repelling the Heat by a coarse wet Cloath, continually hanging before the chamber-windows."—*Fryer*, 47.

[1789.—The introduction of **tatties** into Calcutta is mentioned in a letter from Dr. Campbell, dated May 10, 1789:—"We have had very hot winds and delightful cool houses. Everybody uses **tatties** now. . . . Tatties are however dangerous when you are obliged to leave them and go abroad, the heat acts so powerfully on the body that you are commonly affected with a severe catarrh."—In *Carey, Good Old Days*, i. 80.]

1808.—". . . now, when the hot winds have set in, and we are obliged to make use of **tattees**, a kind of screens made of the roots of a coarse grass called Kus."—*Broughton's Letters*, 110; [ed. 1892, p. 83].

1809.—"Our style of architecture is by no means adapted to the climate, and the large windows would be insufferable, were it not for the **tattyes** which are easily applied to a house one story high."—*Ld. Valentia*, i. 104.

1810.—"During the hot winds **tats** (a kind of mat), made of the root of the koosa grass, which has an agreeable smell, are placed against the doors and windows."—*Maria Graham*, 125.

1814.—"Under the roof, throughout all the apartments, are iron rings, from which the **tattees** or screens of sweet scented grass, were suspended."—*Forbes, Or. Mem.* iv. 6; [2nd ed. ii. 392].

1828.—"An early breakfast was over; the well watered **tatties** were applied to the windows, and diffused through the apartment a cool and refreshing atmosphere which was most comfortably contrasted with the white heat and roar of the fierce wind without."—*The Kuzzilbash*, I. ii.

TAUT, s. Hind. *ṭāṭ*, [Skt. *trātra*, 'defence,' or *tantrī*, 'made of threads']. Sackcloth.

[c. 1810.—"In this district (Dinajpoor) large quantities of this cloth (**Tat or Choti**) are made. . . ."—*Buchanan, Eastern India*, ii. 851.]

1820.—". . . made into coarse cloth **taut**, by the Brinjaries and people who use pack bullocks for making bags (gonies, see **GUNNY**) for holding grain, &c."—*Tr. Bo. Lit. Soc.* iii. 244.

TAVOY, n.p. A town and district of what we call the Tenasserim Province of B. Burma. The Burmese call it *Dha-wé;* but our name is probably adopted from a Malay form. The original name is supposed to be Siamese. [The *Burmah Gazetteer* (ii. 681) gives the choice of three etymologies: 'landing place of bamboos'; from its arms (*dha*, 'a sword,' *way*, 'to buy'); from *Hta-way*, taken from a cross-legged Buddha.]

1553.—"The greater part of this tract is mountainous, and inhabited by the nation of *Brammâs* and *Jangomas*, who interpose on the east of this kingdom (Pegu) between it and the great kingdom of Siam; which kingdom of Siam borders the sea from the city of **Tavay** downwards."—*Barros*, III. iii. 4.

1583.—"Also some of the rich people in a place subject to the Kingdom of Pegu, called **Tavae**, where is produced a quantity of what they call in their language *Calain*, but which in our language is called *Calaia* (see **CALAY**), in summer leave their houses and go into the country, where they make some sheds to cover them, and there they stop three months, leaving their usual dwellings with food in them for the devil, and this they do in order that in the other nine months he may give them no trouble, but rather be propitious and favourable to them."—*G. Balbi*, f. 125.

1587.—". . . Iland of **Tavi**, from which cometh great store of Tinne which serveth all India."—*R. Fitch*, in *Hakl.* ii. 395.

1695. — "10th. That your *Majesty*, of your wonted favour and charity to all distresses, would be pleased to look with Eyes of Pity, upon the poor *English Captive*, *Thomas Browne*, who is the only *one surviving* of four that were accidentally drove into **Tauwy** by *Storm*, as they were going for *Atcheen* about 10 years ago, in the *service* of the *English Company*."—*Petition to the King of Burma*, presented at Ava by *Edward Fleetwood*, in *Dalrymple, Or. Repert.* ii. 374.

[**TAWEEZ**, s. Ar. *ta'wīz*, lit. 'praying for protection by invoking God, or by uttering a charm'; then 'an amulet or phylactery'; and, as in the quotation from Herklots, 'a structure of brick or stone-work over a tomb.'

[1819.—"The Jemidar . . . as he is very superstitious, all his stud have **turveez** or charms. . . ."—*Lt.-Col. Fitzclarence, Journal of a Route across India*, 144.

[1826.—
"Let her who doth this **Taweey** wear,
Guard against the Gossein's snare."
Pandurang Hari, ed. 1873, i. 148.

[1832.—"The generality of people have tombs made of mud or stone . . . forming first three square **taweezes** or platforms. . . ."—*Herklots, Qanoon-e-Islam*, 2nd ed. 284.]

[**TAZEE**, s. Pers. *tāzī*, 'invading, invader,' from *tāz*, 'running.' A favourite variety of horse, usually of Indian breed. The word is also used of a variety of greyhound.

[c. 1590.—"Horses have been divided into seven classes. . . . Arabs, Persian horses, Mujannas, Turki horses, Yabus (see **YABOO**) and Janglah horses. . . . The last two classes are also mostly Indian breed. The best kind is called **Tází**. . . ."—*Āīn*, i. 234-5.

[1839.—"A good breed of the Indian kind, called **Tauzee**, is also found in Bunnoo and Damaun. . . ."—*Elphinstone, Caubul*, ed. 1842, i. 189.

[1883.—"The '**Tazzies**,' or greyhounds are not looked upon as unclean. . . ."—*Wills, Modern Persia*, ed. 1891, p. 306.]

TAZEEA, n. A.—P.—H. *ta'ziya*, 'mourning for the dead.' In India the word is applied to the **taboot**, or representations, in flimsy material, of the tombs of Hussein and Hassan which are carried about in the Muḥarram (see **MOHURRUM**) processions. In Persia it seems to be applied to the whole of the mystery-play which is presented at that season. At the close of the procession the *ta'ziyas* must be thrown into water; if there be no sufficient mass of water they should be buried. [See Sir L. Pelly, *The Miracle Play of Hasan and Husain.*] The word has been carried to the W. Indies by the coolies, whose great festival (whether they be Mahommedans or Hindus) the Muḥarram has become. And the attempt to carry the *Tazeeas* through one of the towns of Trinidad, in spite of orders to the contrary, led in the end of 1884 to a sad catastrophe. [Mahommedan Lascars have an annual celebration at the London Docks.]

1809.—"There were more than a hundred **Taziyus**, each followed by a long train of Fuqueers, dressed in the most extravagant manner, beating their breasts . . . such of the Mahratta Surdars as are not Brahmuns frequently construct **Taziyus** at their own tents, and expend large sums of money upon them."—*Broughton, Letters*, 72; [ed. 1892, 53].

1869. — "En lisant la description . . . de ces fêtes on croira souvent qu'il s'agit de fêtes hindous. Telle est par exemple la solennité du **ta'zia** ou *deuil*, établie en commemoration du martyre de Huçaïn, laquelle est semblable en bien de points à celle du *Durga-pujâ*. . . . Le **ta'ziya** dure dix jours comme le *Durga-pujâ*. Le dixième jour, les Hindous précipitent dans la rivière la statue de la déesse au milieu d'une foule immense, avec un grand appareil et au son de mille instruments de musique; la même chose a lieu pour les représentations du tombeau de Huçaïn."—*Garcin de Tassy, Rel. Musulm.* p. 11.

TEA, s. Crawfurd alleges that we got this word in its various European forms from the Malay *Te*, the Chinese name being *Chhâ*. The latter is indeed the pronunciation attached, when reading in the 'mandarin dialect,' to the character representing the tea-plant, and is the form which has accompanied the knowledge of tea to India, Persia, Portugal, Greece (τσάι) and Russia. But though it may be probable that *Te*, like several other names of articles of trade, may have come to us through the Malay, the word is, not the less, originally Chinese, *Tê* (or *Tay* as Medhurst writes it) being the utterance attached to the character in the Fuh-kien dialect. The original pronunciation, whether direct from Fuh-kien or through the Malay, accompanied the introduction of tea to England as well as other countries of Western Europe. This is shown by several couplets in Pope, *e.g.*

1711.—

" . . . There stands a structure of majestic frame
Which from the neighbouring Hampton takes its name.
* * * * *
Here thou, great ANNA, whom three Realms obey,
Dost sometimes counsel take, and sometimes tea."

Rape of the Lock, iii.

Here *tay* was evidently the pronunciation, as in Fuh-kien. The *Rape of the Lock* was published in 1711. In Gray's *Trivia*, published in 1720, we find *tea* rhyme to *pay*, in a passage needless to quote (ii. 296). Fifty years later there seems no room for doubt that the pronunciation had changed to that now in use, as is shown by Johnson's extemporised verses (c. 1770):

"I therefore pray thee, Renny, dear,
That thou wilt give to me
With cream and sugar soften'd well,
Another dish of **tea**"—and so on.

Johnsoniana, ed. *Boswell*, 1835, ix. 194.

The change must have taken place between 1720 and 1750, for about the latter date we find in the verses of Edward Moore:

" One day in July last at **tea**,
And in the house of Mrs. P."

The Trial of Sarah, &c.

[But the two forms of pronunciation seem to have been in use earlier, as appears from the following advertisement in *The Gazette* of Sept. 9, 1658 (quoted in 8 ser. *N. & Q.* vi. 266): "That excellent, and by all Physitians approved, China Drink, called by the Chineans Toha, by other nations Tay, alias Tee, is sold at the Sultaness Head, a coffee house in Sweetings Rents by the Royal Exchange, London."] And in *Zedler's Lexicon* (1745) it is stated that the English write the word either *Tee* or *Tea*, but pronounce it *Tiy*, which seems to represent our modern pronunciation. ["Strange to say, the Italians, however, have two names for tea, *cia* and *te*, the latter, of course, is from the Chinese word *te*, noticed above, while the former is derived from the word *ch'a*. It is curious to note in this connection that an early mention, if not the first notice, of the word in English is under the form *cha* (in an English Glossary of A.D. 1671); we are also told that it was once spelt *tcha*—both evidently derived from the Cantonese form of the word: but 13 years later we have the word derived from the Fokienese *te*, but borrowed through the French and spelt as in the latter language *the*; the next change in the word is early in the following century when it drops the French spelling and adopts the present form of *tea*, though the Fokienese pronunciation, which the French still retain, is not dropped for the modern pronunciation of the now wholly Anglicised word *tea* till comparatively lately. It will thus be seen that we, like the Italians, might have had two forms of the word, had we not discarded the first, which seemed to have made but little lodgement with us, for the second" (*Ball, Things Chinese*, 3rd ed. 583 *seq.*).]

Dr. Bretschneider states that the Tea-shrub is mentioned in the ancient Dictionary *Rh-ya*, which is believed to date long before our era, under the names *Kia* and *K'u-tu* (*K'u*='bitter'), and a commentator on this work who wrote in the 4th century A.D. describes it, adding "From the leaves can be made by boiling a hot beverage" (*On Chinese Botanical Works*, &c., p. 13). But the first distinct mention of tea-cultivation in Chinese history is said to be a record in the annals of the T'ang Dynasty under A.D. 793, which mentions the imposition in that year of a duty upon tea. And the first western mention of it occurs in the next century, in the notes of the Arab traders, which speak not only of tea, but of this fact of its being subject to a royal impost. Tea does not appear to be mentioned by the medieval Arab writers upon Materia Medica, nor (strange to say) do any of the European travellers to Cathay in the 13th and 14th centuries make mention of it. Nor is there any mention of it in the curious and interesting narrative of the Embassy sent by Shāh Rukh, the son of the great Timur, to China (1419-21).* The first European work, so far as we are aware, in which *tea* is named, is Ramusio's (posthumous) Introduction to Marco Polo, in the second volume of his great collection of *Navigationi e Viaggi.* In this he repeats the account of Cathay which he had heard from Hajji Mahommed, a Persian merchant who visited Venice. Among other matters the Hajji detailed the excellent properties of *Chiai-Catai* (*i.e.* Pers. *Chā-i-Khitāī*, 'Tea of China'), concluding with an assurance that if these were known in Persia and in Europe, traders would cease to purchase rhubarb, and would purchase this herb instead, a prophecy which has been very substantially verified. We find no mention of tea in the elaborate work of Mendoça on China. The earliest notices of which we are aware will be found below. Milburn gives some curious extracts from the E.I. Co.'s records as to the early importation of tea into England. Thus, 1666, June 30, among certain "raretys," chiefly the production of China, provided by the Secretary of the Company for His Majesty, appear:

"$22\frac{3}{4}$ *lbs.* of **thea** at 50*s.* per *lb.*=£56 17 6
For the two cheefe persons
that attended his Majesty,
thea . . . . . . 6 15 6"

In 1667 the E.I. Co.'s first order for the importation of tea was issued to their agent at Bantam: "to send home by these ships 100lb. weight of the best **tey** that you can get." The first importation actually made for the Co. was in 1669, when two canisters were received from Bantam, weighing $143\frac{1}{2}$ lbs. (*Milburn*, ii. 531.) [The earliest mention of tea in the Old Records of the India Office is in a letter from Mr. R. Wickham, the Company's Agent at Firando, in Japan, who, writing, June 27, 1615, to Mr. Eaton at Miaco, asks for "a pt. of the best sort of **chaw**" (see *Birdwood, Report on Old Records*, 26, where the early references are collected).]

A.D. 851.—"The King (of China) reserves to himself . . . a duty on salt, and also on a certain herb which is drunk infused in hot water. This herb is sold in all the towns at high prices; it is called **sākh.** It has more leaves than the *ratb'ah* (Medicago sativa recens) and something more of aroma, but its taste is bitter. Water is boiled and poured upon this herb. The drink so made is serviceable under all circumstances."—*Relation*, &c., trad. par *Reinaud*, i. 40.

c. 1545.—"Moreover, seeing the great delight that I above the rest of the party took in this discourse of his, he (Chaggi Memet, *i.e.* Hajji Mahommed) told me that all over the country of Cathay they make use of another plant, that is of its leaves, which is called by those people **Chiai** *Catai:* it is produced in that district of Cathay which is called Cachanfu. It is a thing generally used and highly esteemed in all those regions. They take this plant whether dry or fresh, and boil it well in water, and of this decoction they take one or two cups on an empty stomach; it removes fever, headache, stomach-ache, pain in the side or joints; taking care to drink it as hot as you can bear; it is good also for many other ailments which I can't now remember, but I know gout was one of them. And if any one chance to feel his stomach oppressed by overmuch food, if he will take a little of this decoction he will in a short time have digested it. And thus it is so precious and highly esteemed that every one going on a journey takes it with him,

* Mr. Major, in his Introduction to Parke's *Mendoza* for the Hak. Soc. says of this embassy, that at their halt in the desert 12 marches from Su-chau, they were regaled "with a variety of strong liquors, *together with a pot of Chinese tea.*" It is not stated by Mr. Major whence he took the account; but there is nothing about tea in the translation of M. Quatremère (*Not. et Ext.* xiv. pt. 1), nor in the Persian text given by him, nor in the translation by Mr. Rehatsek in the *Ind. Ant.* ii. 75 *seqq.*

and judging from what he said these people would at any time gladly swap a sack of rhubarb for an ounce of *Chiai Catai*. These people of Cathay say (he told us) that if in our country, and in Persia, and the land of the Franks, it was known, merchants would no longer invest their money in *Rauend Chini* as they call rhubarb."—*Ramusio, Dichiaratione*, in ii. f. 15.

c. 1560.—"Whatsoever person or persones come to any mans house of qualitee, hee hath a custome to offer him in a fine basket one Porcelane . . . with a kinde of drinke which they call **cha**, which is somewhat bitter, red, and medicinall, which they are wont to make with a certayne concoction of herbes."—*Da Cruz*, in *Purchas*, iii. 180.

1565. — "Ritus est Japoniorum . . . benevolentiae causâ praebere spectanda, quae apud se pretiosissima sunt, id est, omne instrumentum necessarium ad potionem herbae cujusdam in pulverem redactae, suavem gustu, nomine **Chia**. Est autem modus potionis ejusmodi: pulveris ejus, quantum uno juglandis putamine continetur, conjiciunt in fictile vas ex eorum genere, quae procellana (**Porcelain**) vulgus appellat. Inde calenti admodum aquâ dilutum ebibunt. Habent autem in eos usus ollam antiquissimi operis ferream, figlinum poculum, cochlearia, infundibulum eluendo figlino, tripodem, foculum denique potioni calefaciendae."—Letter from Japan, of *L. Almeida*, in *Maffei, Litt. Select. ex India*, Lib. iv.

1588. — "Caeterum (apud Chinenses) ex herba quadam expressus liquor admodum salutaris, nomine **Chia**, calidus hauritur, ut apud Iaponios."—*Maffei, Hist. Ind.* vi.

" "Usum vitis ignorant (Japonii): oryzâ exprimunt vinum: Sed ipsi quoque ante omnia delectantur haustibus aquae poene ferventis, insperso quem supra diximus pulvere **Chia**. Circa eam potionem diligentissimi sunt, ac principes interdum viri suis ipsi manibus eidem temperandae ac miscendae, amicorum honoris causae, dant operam."—*Ibid.* Lib. xii.

1598.—". . . the aforesaid warme water is made with the powder of a certaine hearbe called **chaa**."—*Linschoten*, 46; [Hak. Soc. i. 157].

1611.—"Of the same fashion is the **cha** of China, and taken in the same manner; except that the *Cha* is the small leaf of a herb, from a certain plant brought from Tartary, which was shown me when I was at Malaca."—*Teixeira*, i. 19.

1616.—"I bought 3 **chaw** cups covered with silver plates. . . ."—*Cocks, Diary*, Hak. Soc. i. 202, [and see ii. 11].

1626.—"They vse much the powder of a certaine Herbe called **Chia**, of which they put as much as a Walnut-shell may containe, into a dish of Porcelane, and drinke it with hot water."—*Purchas, Pilgrimage*, 587.

1631.—"*Dur.* You have mentioned the drink of the Chinese called **Thee**; what is your opinion thereof? . . . *Bont.* . . . The Chinese regard this beverage almost as something sacred . . . and they are not thought to have fulfilled the rites of hospitality to you until they have served you with it, just like the Mahometans with their Caveah (see **COFFEE**). It is of a drying quality, and banishes sleep . . . it is beneficial to asthmatic and wheezing patients."—*Jac. Bontius, Hist. Nat. et Med. Ind. Or.* Lib. i. Dial. vi. p. 11.

1638. — "Dans les assemblées ordinaires (à Sourat) que nous faisions tous les iours, nous ne prenions que du **Thè**, dont l'vsage est fort cummun par toutes les Indes."—*Mandelslo*, ed. Paris, 1659, p. 113.

1658. — "Non mirum est, multos etiam nunc in illo errore versari, quasi diversae speciei plantae essent **The** et **Tsia**, cum è contra eadem sit, cujus decoctum Chinensibus **The**, Iaponensibus **Tsia** nomen audiat; licet horum **Tsia**, ob magnam contributionem et coctionem, nigrum **The** appellatur."—*Bontii Hist. Nat.* Pisonis Annot. p. 87.

1660. — (September) "28th. . . . I did send for a cup of **tea** (a China drink) of which I never had drank before."—*Pepys's Diary*. [Both Ld. Braybrooke (4th ed. i. 110) and Wheatley (i. 249) read **tee**, and give the date as Sept. 25.]

1667. — (June) "28th. . . . Home and there find my wife making of **tea**; a drink which Mr. Pelling, the Potticary, tells her is good for her cold and defluxions."—*Ibid.* [*Wheatley*, vi. 398].

1672.—"There is among our people, and particularly among the womankind a great abuse of **Thee**, not only that too much is drunk . . . but this is also an evil custom to drink it with a full stomach; it is better and more wholesome to make use of it when the process of digestion is pretty well finished. . . . It is also a great folly to use sugar candy with **Thee**."—*Baldaeus*, Germ. ed. 179. (This author devotes five columns to tea, and its use and abuse in India).

1677.—"Planta dicitur **Chà**, vel . . . **Cià**, . . . cujus usus in *Chinae* claustris nescius in Europae quoque paulatim sese insinuare attentat. . . . Et quamvis Turcarum *Cave* (see **COFFEE**) et Mexicanorum *Ciocolata* eundem praestent effectum, **Cià** tamen, quam nonulli quoque **Te** vocant, ea multum superat," etc.—*Kircher, China Illust.* 180.

" "Maer de **Ciâ** (of **Thee**) sonder achting op eenije tijt te hebben, is novit schadelijk."—*Vermeulen*, 30.

1683.—"Lord Russell . . . went into his chamber six or seven times in the morning, and prayed by himself, and then came out to Tillotson and me; he drunk a little **tea** and some sherry."—*Burnet, Hist. of Own Time*, Oxford ed. 1823, ii. 375.

1683.—
"Venus her Myrtle, Phœbus has his Bays;
Tea both excels which She* vouchsafes to praise,
The best of Queens, and best of Herbs we owe

* Queen Catharine.

To that bold Nation which the Way did show
To the fair Region where the Sun does rise,
Whose rich Productions we so justly prize."—*Waller*.

1690.—". . . Of all the followers of *Mahomet* . . . none are so rigidly Abstemious as the *Arabians* of *Muscatt*. . . . For **Tea** and **Coffee**, which are judg'd the privileg'd Liquors of all the *Mahometans*, as well as *Turks*, as those of *Persia*, *India*, and other parts of *Arabia*, are condemned by them as unlawful. . . ."—*Ovington*, 427.

1726.—"I remember well how in 1681 I for the first time in my life drank **thee** at the house of an Indian Chaplain, and how I could not understand how sensible men could think it a treat to drink what tasted no better than hay-water."—*Valentijn*, v. 190.

1789.—
"And now her vase a modest Naiad fills
With liquid crystal from her pebbly rills;
Piles the dry cedar round her silver urn,
(Bright climbs the blaze, the crackling faggots burn).
Culls the green herb of China's envy'd bowers,
In gaudy cups the steaming treasure pours;
And sweetly smiling, on her bended knee,
Presents the fragrant quintessence of **Tea**."
Darwin, *Botanic Garden*, *Loves of the Plants*, Canto ii.

1844.—"The Polish word for tea, *Herbata*, signifies more properly 'herb,' and in fact there is little more of the genuine Chinese beverage in the article itself than in its name, so that we often thought with longing of the delightful Russian **Tshaï**, genuine in word and fact."—*J. I. Kohl*, *Austria*, p. 444.

The following are some of the names given in the market to different kinds of tea, with their etymologies.

1. **(TEA), BOHEA.** This name is from the *Wu-i* (dialectically *Bú-i*)-shan Mountains in the N.W. of Fuh-kien, one of the districts most famous for its black tea. In Pope's verse, as Crawfurd points out, *Bohea* stands for a tea in use among fashionable people. Thus:

"To part her time 'twixt reading and **bohea**,
To muse, and spill her solitary tea."
Epistle to Mrs Teresa Blount.

[The earliest examples in the *N.E.D.* carry back the use of the word to the first years of the 18th century.]

1711.—"There is a parcel of extraordinary fine **Bohee Tea** to be sold at 26*s*. per Pound, at the sign of the Barber's Pole, next door to the Brazier's Shop in Southampton Street in the Strand."—Advt. in the *Spectator* of April 2, 1711.

1711.—
"Oh had I rather unadmired remained
On some lone isle or distant northern land;
Where the gilt chariot never marks the way,
Where none learn ombre, none e'er taste **bohea**."
Belinda, in *Rape of the Lock*, iv. 153.

The last quotation, and indeed the first also, shows that the word was then pronounced *Bohay*. At a later date *Bohea* sank to be the market name of one of the lowest qualities of tea, and we believe it has ceased altogether to be a name quoted in the tea-market. The following quotations seem to show that it was the general name for "black-tea."

1711.—"**Bohea** is of little Worth among the *Moors* and *Gentoos* of India, *Arrabs* and *Persians* . . . that of 45 Tale (see **TAEL**) would not fetch the Price of green Tea of 10 Tale a **Pecull**."—*Lockyer*, 116.

1721.—
"Where Indus and the double Ganges flow,
On odorif'rous plains the leaves do grow,
Chief of the treat, a plant the boast of fame,
Sometimes called green, **Bohea's** the greater name."
Allan Ramsay's Poems, ed. 1800, i. 213-14.

1726.—"Anno 1670 and 1680 there was knowledge only of **Boey** Tea and Green-Tea, but later they speak of a variety of other sorts . . . **Congo** . . . **Pego** . . . *Tongge*, *Rosmaryn Tea*, rare and very dear."—*Valentijn*, iv. 14.

1727.—"In September they strip the Bush of all its Leaves, and, for Want of warm dry Winds to cure it, are forced to lay it on warm Plates of Iron or Copper, and keep it stirring gently, till it is dry, and that Sort is called **Bohea**."—*A. Hamilton*, ii. 289; [ed. 1744, ii. 288].

But Zedler's *Lexicon* (1745) in a long article on **Thee** gives **Thee Bohea** as "the worst sort of all." The other European trade-names, according to Zedler, were **Thee-Peco**, **Congo** which the Dutch called the best, but **Thee Cancho** was better still and dearer, and **Chaucon** best of all.

2. **(TEA) CAMPOY,** a black tea also. *Kam-pui*, the Canton pron. of the characters *Kien-pei*, "select-dry (over a fire)."

3. **(TEA) CONGOU** (a black tea). This is *Kang-hu* (**tê**) the Amoy pronunciation of the characters *Kung-fu*, 'work or labour.' [Mr. Pratt (9 ser. *N. & Q.* iv. 26) writes: "The *N.E.D.*

under *Congou* derives it from the standard Chinese *Kung-fu* (which happens also to be the Cantonese spelling); 'the omission of the *f*,' we are told, 'is the foreigner's corruption.' It is nothing of the kind. The Amoy name for this tea is *Kong-hu*, so that the omission of the *f* is due to the local Chinese dialect."]

4. **HYSON** (a green tea). This is *He-* (*hei* and *ai* in the south) *-ch'un*, 'bright spring,' [which Mr. Ball (*Things Chinese*, 586) writes *yu-ts'in*, 'before the rain'], characters which some say formed the **hong** name of a tea-merchant named Le, who was in the trade in the dist. of Hiu-ning (S.W. of Hang-chau) about 1700; others say that *He-chun* was Le's daughter, who was the first to separate the leaves, so as to make what is called **Hyson**. [Mr. Ball says that it is so called, "the young hyson being half-opened leaves plucked in April before the spring rains."]

c. 1772.—

"And Venus, goddess of the eternal smile,
Knowing that stormy brows but ill become
Fair patterns of her beauty, hath ordained
Celestial **Tea**;—a fountain that can cure
The ills of passion, and can free from frowns.
* * * * *
To her, ye fair! in adoration bow!
Whether at blushing morn, or dewy eve,
Her smoking cordials greet your fragrant board
With **Hyson**, or **Bohea**, or **Congo** crown'd."

R. Fergusson, Poems.

5. **OOLONG** (bl. tea). *Wu-lung*, 'black dragon'; respecting which there is a legend to account for the name. ["A black snake (and snakes are sometimes looked upon as dragons in China) was coiled round a plant of this tea, and hence the name" (*Ball, op. cit.* 586).]

6. **PEKOE** (do.). *Pak-ho*, Canton pron. of characters *pŏh-hao*, 'white-down.'

7. **POUCHONG** (do.). *Pao-chung*, 'fold-sort.' So called from its being packed in small paper packets, each of which is supposed to be the produce of one choice tea-plant. Also called **Padre**-*souchong*, because the priests in the Wu-i hills and other places prepare and pack it.

8. **SOUCHONG** (do.). *Siu-chung*, Canton for *Siao-chung*, 'little-sort.'

1781.—"Les Nations Européennes retirent de la Chine des thés connus sous les noms de thé **bouy**, thé vert, et **thé saothon**."—*Sonnerat*, ii. 249.

9. **TWANKAY** (green tea). From *T'un-k'i*, the name of a mart about 15 m. S.W. of Hwei-chau-fu in Nganhwei. Bp. Moule says (perhaps after W. Williams?) from *T'un-k'i*, name of a stream near Yen-shau-fu in Chikiang. [Mr. Pratt (*loc. cit.*) writes; "The Amoy *Tun-ke* is nearer, and the Cantonese *Tun-kei* nearer still, its second syllable being absolutely the same in sound as the English. The Twankay is a stream in the E. of the province of Nganhwui, where Twankay tea grows."] *Twankay* is used by Theodore Hook as a sort of slang for 'tea.'

10. **YOUNG HYSON**. This is called by the Chinese *Yü-t'sien*, 'rain-before,' or '*Yu-before*,' because picked before *Kuh-yu*, a term falling about 20th April (see **HYSON** above). According to Giles it was formerly called, in trade, *Uchain*, which seems to represent the Chinese name. In an "*Account of the Prices at which Teas have been put up to Sale, that arrived in England in* 1784, 1785" (MS. India Office Records) the Teas are (from cheaper to dearer):—

"**Bohea Tea.**	Singlo (?),
Congou,	**Hyson.**"
Souchong,	

TEA-CADDY, s. This name, in common English use for a box to contain tea for the daily expenditure of the household, is probably corrupted, as Crawfurd suggests, from **catty**, a weight of 1⅓ *lb.* (q.v.). A '*catty-box*,' meaning a box holding a *catty*, might easily serve this purpose and lead to the name. This view is corroborated by a quotation which we have given under **caddy** (q.v.) A friend adds the remark that in his youth 'Tea-caddy' was a Londoner's name for Harley Street, due to the number of E.I. Directors and proprietors supposed to inhabit that district.

TEAPOY, s. A small tripod table. This word is often in England imagined to have some connection with *tea*, and hence, in London shops for japanned ware and the like, a *teapoy* means a tea-chest fixed on legs. But this is quite erroneous. *Tipāī* is a Hindustāni, or perhaps rather an Anglo-Hindustāni word for a tripod, from Hind. *tīn*, 3, and Pers. *pāē*, 'foot.' The legitimate word from the Persian is *sipāī* (properly *sihpāya*), and the legitimate Hindi word *tirpad* or *tripad*, but *tipāī* or *tepoy* was probably originated by some European in analogy with the familiar **charpoy** (q.v.) or 'four-legs,' possibly from inaccuracy, possibly from the desire to avoid confusion with another very familiar word **sepoy, seapoy**. [Platts, however, gives *tipāī* as a regular Hind. word, Skt. *tri-pād-ikā*.] The word is applied in India not only to a three-legged table (or any very small table, whatever number of legs it has), but to any tripod, as to the tripod-stands of surveying instruments, or to trestles in carpentry. *Sihpāya* occurs in 'Ali of Yezd's history of Timur, as applied to the trestles used by Timur in bridging over the Indus (*Elliot*, iii. 482). A teapoy is called in Chinese by a name having reference to tea: viz. *Ch'a-chi'rh*. It has 4 legs.

[c. 1809.—"(Dinajpoor) **Sepaya**, a wooden stand for a lamp or candle with three feet." —*Buchanan, Eastern India*, ii. 945.]

1844.—"'Well, to be sure, it does seem odd—very odd;'—and the old gentleman chuckled,—'most odd to find a person who don't know what a **tepoy** is. . . . Well, then, a **tepoy** or *tinpoy* is a thing with three feet, used in India to denote a little table, such as that just at your right.'

"'Why, that table has four legs,' cried Peregrine.

"'It's a **tepoy** all the same,' said Mr. Havethelacks."—*Peregrine Pulteney*, i. 112.

TEAK, s. The tree, and timber of the tree, known to botanists as *Tectona grandis*, L., N.O. *Verbenaceae*. The word is Malayāl. *tekka*, Tam. *tekku*. No doubt this name was adopted owing to the fact that Europeans first became acquainted with the wood in Malabar, which is still one of the two great sources of supply; Pegu being the other. The Skt. name of the tree is *śāka*, whence the modern Hind. name *sāgwān* or *sāgūn* and the Mahr. *śāg*. From this last probably was taken *sāj*, the name of teak in Arabic and Persian. And we have doubtless the same word in the σαγαλίνα of the Periplus, one of the exports from Western India, a form which may be illustrated by the Mahr. adj. *sāgalī*, 'made of the teak, belonging to teak.' The last fact shows, in some degree, how old the export of teak is from India. Teak beams, still undecayed, exist in the walls of the great palace of the Sassanid Kings at Seleucia or Ctesiphon, dating from the middle of the 6th century. [See *Birdwood, First Letter Book*, Intro. XXIX.] Teak has continued to recent times to be imported into Egypt. See *Forskal*, quoted by Royle (*Hindu Medicine*, 128). The *gopher-wood* of Genesis is translated *sāj* in the Arabic version of the Pentateuch (Royle). [It was probably cedar (see *Encycl. Bibl.* s.v.)]

Teak seems to have been hardly known in Gangetic India in former days. We can find no mention of it in Baber (which however is indexless), and the only mention we can find in the *Āīn*, is in a list of the weights of a cubic yard of 72 kinds of wood, where the name "*Ságaun*" has not been recognised as teak by the learned translator (see *Blochmann's* E.T. i. p. 228).

c. A.D. 80.—"In the innermost part of this Gulf (the Persian) is the Port of Apologos, lying near Pasine Charax and the river Euphrates.

"Sailing past the mouth of the Gulf, after a course of 6 days you reach another port of Persia called Omana. Thither they are wont to despatch from Barygaza, to both these ports of Persia, great vessels with brass, and timbers and beams of **teak** (ξύλων σαγαλίνων καὶ δοκῶν), and horns and spars of shisham (see **SISSOO**) (σασαμίνων), and of ebony. . . ."—*Peripl. Maris Erythr.* § 35-36.

c. 800.—(under Hārūn al Rashīd) "Fazl continued his story '. . . I heard loud wailing from the house of Abdallah . . . they told me he had been struck with the *judām*, that his body was swollen and all black. . . . I went to Rashīd to tell him, but I had not finished when they came to say Abdallah was dead. Going out at once I ordered them to hasten the obsequies. . . . I myself said the funeral prayer. As they let down the bier a slip took place, and the bier and earth fell in together; an intolerable stench arose . . . a second slip took place. I then called for planks of *teak* (**sāj**). . . ."—Quotation in *Maṣ'ūdī*, *Prairies d'Or*, vi. 298-299.

c. 880.—"From Kol to Sindān, where they collect **teak**-*wood* (**sāj**) and cane, 18 farsakhs."—*Ibn Khurdādba*, in *J. As. S.* VI. tom. v. 284.

c. 940.—". . . The *teak-tree* (sāj). This tree, which is taller than the date-palm, and more bulky than the walnut, can shelter under its branches a great number of men and cattle, and you may judge of its dimensions by the logs that arrive, of their natural length, at the depôts of Basra, of 'Irāk, and of Egypt. . . ."—*Mas'ūdī*, iii. 12.

Before 1200.—Abu'l-dhali' the Sindian, describing the regions of Hind, has these verses:

* * * * *

"By my life! it is a land where, when the rain falls,
Jacinths and pearls spring up for him who wants ornaments.
There too are produced **musk** and **camphor** and *ambergris* and *agila*,
* * * * *
And ivory there, and *teak* (al-sāj) and aloeswood and sandal. . . ."

Quoted by *Kazwini*, in *Gildemeister*, 217-218.

The following order, in a King's Letter to the Goa Government, no doubt refers to Pegu teak, though not naming the particular timber:

1597.—"We enjoin you to be very vigilant not to allow the Turks to export any timber from the Kingdom of Pegu, nor from that of Achem (see **ACHEEN**), and you must arrange how to treat this matter, particularly with the King of Achem."—In *Archiv. Port. Orient.* fasc. ii. 669.

1602.—". . . It was necessary in order to appease them, to give a promise in writing that the body should not be removed from the town, but should have public burial in our church in sight of everybody; and with this assurance it was taken in solemn procession and deposited in a box of *teak* (**teca**), which is a wood not subject to decay. . . ."—*Sousa*, *Oriente Conquist.* (1710), ii. 265.

[,, "Of many of the roughest thickets of bamboos and of the largest and best wood in the world, that is **teca**."—*Couto*, Dec. VII. Bk. vi. ch. 6. He goes on to explain that all the ships and boats made either by Moors or Gentiles since the Portuguese came to India, were of this wood which came from the inexhaustible forests at the back of Damaun.]

1631.—Bontius gives a tolerable cut of the foliage, &c., of the Teak-tree, but writing in the Archipelago does not use that name, describing it under the title "*Quercus Indica*, Kiati Malaiis dicta."—Lib. vi. cap. 16. On this Rheede, whose plate of the tree is, as usual, excellent (*Hortus Malabaricus*, iv. tab. 27), observes justly that the teak has no resemblance to an oak-tree, and also that the Malay name is not *Kiati* but *Jati*: *Kiati* seems to be a mistake of some kind growing out of *Kayu-jati*, 'Teak-wood.

1644.—"Hã nestas terras de Damam muyta e boa madeyra de **Teca**, a milhor de toda a India, e tambem de muyta parte do mundo, porque com ser muy fasil de laurar he perduravel, e particullarmente nam lhe tocando agoa."—*Bocarro, MS.*

1675.—"At Cock-crow we parted hence and observed that the Sheds here were round thatched and lined with broad Leaves of **Teke** (the Timber Ships are built with) in Fashion of a Bee-hive."—*Fryer*, 142.

,, ". . . **Teke** by the Portuguese, **Sogwan** by the Moors, is the firmest Wood they have for Building . . . in Height the lofty Pine exceeds it not, nor the sturdy Oak in Bulk and Substance. . . . This Prince of the Indian Forest was not so attractive, though mightily glorious, but that . . ."—*Ibid.* 178.

1727.—"*Gundavee* is next, where good Quantities of **Teak** Timber are cut, and exported, being of excellent Use in building of Houses or Ships."—*A. Hamilton*, i. 178; [ed. 1744].

1744.—"**Tecka** is the name of costly wood which is found in the Kingdom of Martaban in the East Indies, and which never decays."—*Zeidler*, *Univ. Lexicon*, s.v.

1759.—"They had endeavoured to burn the **Teak** *Timbers* also, but they lying in a *swampy place*, could not take fire."—*Capt. Alves*, *Report on Loss of Negrais*, in *Dalrymple*, i. 349.

c. 1760.—"As to the wood it is a sort called **Teak**, to the full as durable as oak."—*Grose*, i. 108.

1777.—"Experience hath long since shewn, that ships built with oak, and joined together with wooden trunnels, are by no means so well calculated to resist the extremes of heat and damp, in the tropical latitudes of Asia, as the ships which are built in India of **tekewood**, and bound with iron spikes and bolts."—*Price's Tracts*, i. 191.

1793.—"The **teek** forests, from whence the marine yard at Bombay is furnished with that excellent species of ship-timber, lie along the western side of the Gaut mountains . . . on the north and north-east of Basseen. . . . I cannot close this subject without remarking the unpardonable negligence we are guilty of in delaying to build **teak** ships of war for the service of the Indian seas."—*Rennell*, *Memoir*, 3rd ed. 260.

[1800.—"**Tayca**, *Tectona Robusta*."—*Buchanan*, *Mysore*, i. 26.]

TEE, s. The metallic decoration, generally gilt and hung with tinkling bells, on the top of a dagoba in Indo-Chinese countries, which represents the *chatras* [*chhattras*] or umbrellas which in ancient times, as royal emblems, crowned these structures. Burm. *h'ti*, 'an umbrella.'

1800.—". . . In particular the **Tee**, or umbrella, which, composed of open iron-work, crowned the spire, had been thrown down."—*Symes*, i. 193.

1855.—". . . gleaming in its white plaster, with numerous pinnacles and tall central spire, we had seen it (Gaudapalen Temple at Pugan) from far down the Irawadi rising like a dim vision of Milan Cathedral. . . . It is cruciform in plan . . . exhibiting a massive basement with porches, and rising above in a pyramidal gradation of terraces, crowned by a spire and **htee**. The latter has broken from its stays at one side, and now leans over almost horizontally. . . ."—*Yule, Mission to Ava*, 1858, p. 42.

1876.—". . . a feature known to Indian archaeologists as a **Tee**. . . ."—*Fergusson, Ind. and East. Archit.* 64.

TEEK, adj. Exact, precise, punctual; also parsimonious, [a meaning which Platts does not record]. Used in N. India. Hind. *ṭhīk*.

[1843.—"They all feel that *the good old rule of right* (**teek**), as long as a man does his duty well, can no longer be relied upon."—*G. W. Johnson, Stranger in India*, i. 290.]

[1878.—". . . 'it is necessary to send an explanation to the magistrate, and the return does not look so **thêk**' (a word expressing all excellence)."—*Life in the Mofussil*, i. 253.]

TEERUT, TEERTHA, s. Skt. and Hind. *tīrth, tīrtha*. A holy place of pilgrimage and of bathing for the good of the soul, such as Hurdwar, or the confluence at **Praag** (Allahabad).

[1623.—"The Gentiles call it *Ram***tirt**, that is, Holy Water."—*P. della Valle*, Hak. Soc. ii. 205.]

c. 1790.—"Au temple l'enfant est reçue par les devedaschies (**Deva-dasi**) des mains de ses parens, et après l'avoir baignée dans le **tirtha** ou étang du temple, elles lui mettent des vêtemens neufs. . . ."—*Haafner*, ii. 114.

[1858.—"He then summoned to the place no less than three **crores** and half, or thirty millions and half of **teeruts**, or angels (*sic*) who preside each over his special place of religious worship."—*Sleeman, Journey through Oudh*, ii. 4.]

TEHR, TAIR, &c., s. The wild goat of the Himālaya; *Hemitragus jemlaicus*, Jerdon, [Blanford, *Mammalia*, 509]. In Nepāl it is called *jhāral*. (See **SURROW**).

TEJPAT, s. Hind. *tejpāt*, Skt. *tejapatra*, 'pungent leaf.' The native name for **malabathrum.**

1833.—"Last night as I was writing a long description of the **tēz-pāt**, the leaf of the cinnamon-tree, which humbly pickles beef, leaving the honour of crowning heroes to the *Laurus nobilis*. . . ."—*Wanderings of a Pilgrim*, i. 278.

1872. — **Tejpát** is mentioned as sold by the village shopkeeper, in *Govinda Samanta*, i. 223.

(1) **TELINGA,** n.p. Hind. *Tilangā*, Skt. *Tailanga*. One of the people of the country east of the Deccan, and extending to the coast, often called, at least since the Middle Ages, *Tiliñgāna* or *Tilangāna*, sometimes *Tiling* or *Tilang*. Though it has not, perhaps, been absolutely established that this came from a form *Triliñga*, the habitual application of *Tri-Kaliñga*, apparently to the same region which in later days was called **Tilinga**, and the example of actual use of *Triliñga*, both by Ptolemy (though he carries us beyond the Ganges) and by a Tibetan author quoted below, do make this a reasonable supposition (see *Bp. Caldwell's Dravidian Grammar*, 2nd ed. Introd. pp. 30 *seqq.*, and the article **KLING** in this book).

A.D. c. 150.—"Τρίγλυπτον, τὸ καὶ Τρίλιγγον Βασίλειον . . . κ. τ. λ."—*Ptolemy*, vi. 2, 23.

1309.—"On Saturday the 10th of Sha'bán, the army marched from that spot, in order that the pure tree of Islám might be planted and flourish in the soil of **Tilang**, and the evil tree which had struck its roots deep, might be torn up by force. . . . When the blessed canopy had been fixed about a mile from Arangal (Warangal, N.E. of Hyderabad), the tents around the fort were pitched so closely that the head of a needle could not get between them."—*Amīr Khusrū*, in *Elliot*, iii. 80.

1321.—"In the year 721 H. the Sultán (Ghiyásu-ddín) sent his eldest son, Ulugh Khán, with a canopy and an army against Arangal and **Tilang**."—*Ziá-uddín Barní*, *Ibid.* 231.

c. 1335.—"For every mile along the road there are three *dāwāt* (post stations) . . . and so the road continues for six months' marching, till one reaches the countries of **Tiling** and Ma'bar. . . ."—*Ibn Batuta*, iii. 192.

" In the list of provinces of India under the Sultan of Delhi, given by Shihāb-ud-dīn Dimishkī, we find both **Talang** and **Talanj**, probably through some mistake.—*Not. et Exts.* Pt. I. 170-171.

c. 1590.—"Sūba Berār. . . . Its length from Batāla (or Patiāla) to Bairāgarh is 200 *kuroh* (or kos); its breadth from Bīdar to Hindia 180. On the east of Bairāgarh it marches with Bastar; on the north with Hindia; on the south with **Tilingāna**; on the west with Mahkarābād. . . ."—*Āīn* (orig.) i. 476; [ed. *Jarrett*, ii. 228; and see 230, 237].

1608.—"In the southern lands of India since the day when the Turushkas (Turks, *i.e.* Mahommedans) conquered Magadha, many abodes of Learning were founded; and though they were inconsiderable, the continuance of instruction and exorcism was without interruption, and the Pandit who was called the Son of Men, dwelt in Kalinga, a part of **Trilinga**."—*Tāranātha's H. of Buddhism* (Germ. ed. of Schiefner), p. 264. See also 116, 158, 166.

c. 1614.—"Up to that time none of the *zamindārs* of distant lands, such as the Rājá of **Tilang**, Pegu, and Malabar, had ventured upon disobedience or rebellion."—*Firishta*, in *Elliot*, vi. 549.

1793.—"**Tellingana**, of which Warangoll was the capital, comprehended the tract lying between the Kistnah and Godavery Rivers, and east of Visiapour. . . ."—*Rennell's Memoir*, 3rd ed. p. [cxi.]

(2) **TELINGA**, s. This term in the 18th century was frequently used in Bengal as synonymous with **sepoy**, or a native soldier disciplined and clothed in quasi-European fashion, [and is still commonly used by natives to indicate a sepoy or armed policeman in N. India], no doubt because the first soldiers of that type came to Bengal from what was considered to be the Telinga country, viz. Madras.

1758.—". . . the latter commanded a body of Hindu soldiers, armed and accoutred and disciplined in the European manner of fighting; I mean those soldiers that are become so famous under the name of **Talingas**."—*Seir Mutaqherin*, ii. 92.

c. 1760.—". . . Sepoys, sometimes called **Tellingas**."—*Grose*, in his *Glossary*, see vol. I. xiv.

1760.—"300 **Telingees** are run away, and entered into the Beerboom Rajah's service."—In *Long*, 235; see also 236, 237, and (1761) p. 258, "**Tellingers.**"

c. 1765.—"Somro's force, which amounted to 15 or 16 field-pieces and 6000 or 7000 of those foot soldiers called **Talinghas**, and which are armed with flint muskets, and accoutred as well as disciplined in the *Frenghi* or European manner."—*Seir Mutaqherin*, iii. 254.

1786.—". . . *Gardi* (see **GARDEE**), which is now the general name of Sipahies all over India, save Bengal . . . where they are stiled **Talingas**, because the first Sipahees that came in Bengal (and they were imported in 1757 by Colonel Clive) were all **Talingas** or **Telougous** born . . . speaking hardly any language but their native. . . ."—Note by Tr. of *Seir Mutaqherin*, ii. 93.

c. 1805.—"The battalions, according to the old mode of France, were called after the names of cities and forts. . . . The **Telingas**, composed mostly of Hindoos, from Oude, were disciplined according to the old English exercise of 1780. . . ."—*Sketch of the Regular Corps, &c., in Service of Native Princes*, by *Major Lewis Ferdinand Smith*, p. 50.

1827.—"You are a Sahib Angrezie. . . . I have been a **Telinga** . . . in the Company's service, and have eaten their salt. I will do your errand."—*Sir W. Scott, The Surgeon's Daughter*, ch. xiii.

1883.—"We have heard from natives whose grandfathers lived in those times, that the Oriental portions of Clive's army were known to the Bengalis of Nuddea as **Telingas**, because they came, or were supposed to have accompanied him from Telingana or Madras."—*Saty. Review*, Jan. 29, p. 120.

TELOOGOO, n.p. The first in point of diffusion, and the second in culture and copiousness, of the Dravidian languages of the Indian Peninsula. It is "spoken all along the eastern coast of the Peninsula, from the neighbourhood of Pulicat" (24 m. N. of Madras) "where it supersedes Tamil, to Chicacole, where it begins to yield to the Oriya (see **OORIYA**), and inland it prevails as far as the eastern boundary of the Marâtha country and Mysore, including within its range the '**Ceded Districts**' and Karnûl (see **KURNOOL**), a considerable part of the territories of the Nizam . . . and a portion of the Nâgpûr country and Gonḍvâna" (*Bp. Caldwell's Dravid. Gram. Introd.* p. 29). *Telugu* is the name given to the language of the people themselves (other forms being, according to Bp. Caldwell, **Telunga, Telinga, Tailinga, Tenugu,** and **Tenungu**), as the language of Telingāna (see **TELINGA (1)**). It is this language (as appears in the passage from Fryer) that used to be, perhaps sometimes is, called **Gentoo** at Madras. [Also see **BADEGA**.]

1673.—"Their Language they call generally **Gentu** . . . the peculiar name of their speech is **Telinga**."—*Fryer*, 33.

1793.—"The **Tellinga** language is said to be in use, at present, from the River Pennar in the Carnatic, to Orissa, along the coast, and inland to a very considerable distance."—*Rennell, Memoir*, 3rd ed. p. [cxi].

TEMBOOL, Betel-leaf. Skt. *tāmbūla*, adopted in Pers. as *tāmbūl*, and in Ar. *al-tambūl*. [It gives its name to the Tambolis or Tamolis, sellers of betel in the N. Indian bazars.]

1298.—"All the people of this city, as well as the rest of India, have a custom of perpetually keeping in the mouth a certain leaf called **Tembul**. . . ."—*Marco Polo*, ii. 358.

1498.—"And he held in his left hand a very great cup of gold as high as a half *almude* pot . . . into which he spat a certain herb which the men of this country chew for solace, and which herb they call **atambor**."—*Roteiro de V. da Gama*, 59.

1510.—"He also eats certain leaves of herbs, which are like the leaves of the sour orange, called by some **tamboli**."—*Varthema*, 110.

1563. — "Only you should know that Avicenna calls the betre (**Betel**) **tembul**, which seems a word somewhat corrupted, since everybody pronounces it **tambul**, and not *tembul*."—*Garcia*, f. 37*h*.

TENASSERIM, n.p. A city and territory on the coast of the Peninsula of Further India. It belonged to the ancient kingdom of Pegu, and fell with that to Ava. When we took from the latter the provinces east and south of the Delta of the Irawadi, after the war of 1824-26, these were officially known as "the Martaban and Tenasserim Province," or often as "the Tenasserim Provinces." We have the name probably from the Malay form *Tanasari*. We do not know to what language the name originally belongs. The Burmese call it *Ta-nen-thā-ri*. ["The name Tenasserim (Malay *Tanah-sari*), 'the land of happiness or delight,' was long ago given by the Malays to the Burma province, which still keeps it, the Burmese corruption being *Tanang-sari*" (*Gray*, on *Pyrard de Laval*, quoted below).]

c. 1430.—"Relicta Taprobane ad urbem **Thenasserim** supra ostium fluvii eodem nomine vocitati diebus XVI tempestate actus est. Quae regio et elephantis et verzano (**brazil-wood**) abundat."—*Nic. Conti*, in *Poggio de Var. Fort.* lib. iv.

1442.—"The inhabitants of the shores of the Ocean come thither (to Hormuz) from the countries of Chīn (**China**), Jāvah, Bangāla, the cities of **Zirbād** (q.v.), of **Tenaseri**, of Sokotara, of *Shahrinao* (see **SARNAU**), of the Isles of Dīwah Mahal (**Maldives**)."—*Ābdur-razzāk*, in *Not. et Exts.* xiv. 429.

1498.—"**Tenaçar** is peopled by Christians, and the King is also a Christian . . . in this land is much brasyll, which makes a fine vermilion, as good as the grain, and it costs here 3 cruzados a **bahar**, whilst in Quayro (Cairo) it costs 60; also there is here aloes-wood, but not much."—*Roteiro de V. da Gama*, 110.

1501.—**Tanaser** appears in the list of places in the East Indies of which Amerigo Vespucci had heard from the Portuguese fleet at C. Verde. Printed in *Baldelli Boni's Il Milione*, pp. liii. *seqq.*

1506.—"At **Tenazar** grows all the *verzi* (**brazil**), and it costs $1\frac{1}{2}$ ducats the baar (**bahar**), equal to 4 *kantars*. This place, though on the coast, is on the mainland. The King is a Gentile; and thence come pepper, cinnamon, galanga, camphor that is eaten, and camphor that is not eaten. . . . This is indeed the first mart of spices in India."—*Leonardo Ca' Masser*, in *Archiv. Stor. Ital.* p. 28.

1510.—"The city of **Tarnassari** is situated near the sea, etc."—*Varthema*, 196. This adventurer's account of Tenasserim is an imposture. He describes it by implication as in India Proper, somewhere to the north of Coromandel.

1516.—"And from the Kingdom of Peigu as far as a city which has a seaport, and is named **Tanasery**, there are a hundred leagues. . . ."—*Barbosa*, 188.

1568.—"The Pilot told vs that wee were by his altitude not farre from a citie called **Tanasary**, in the Kingdom of Pegu."—*C. Frederike*, in *Hakl.* ii. 359. See *Lancaster*.

c. 1590.—"In *Kambayat* (**Cambay**) a Nákhuda (**Nacoda**) gets 800 R. . . . In Pegu and **Dahnasari**, he gets half as much again as in Cambay."—*Āīn*, i. 281.

[1598.—"Betweene two Islandes the coast runneth inwards like a bow, wherein lyeth the towne of **Tanassarien**."—*Linschoten*, Hak. Soc. i. 103. In the same page he writes **Tanassaria**.

[1608.—"The small quantities they have here come from **Tannaserye**."—*Danvers, Letters*, i. 22.

[c. 1610.—"Some Indians call it (Ceylon) **Tenasirin**, signifying land of delights, or earthly paradise."—*Pyrard de Laval*, ii. 140, with Gray's note (Hak. Soc.) quoted above.]

1727. — "Mr. *Samuel White* was made Shawbandaar (**Shabunder**) or Custom-Master at Merjee (**Mergui**) and **Tanacerin**, and Captain Williams was Admiral of the King's Navy."—*A. Hamilton*, ii. 64; [ed. 1744].

1783.—"**Tannaserim**. . . ."—*Forrest V. to Mergui*, 4.

TERAI, TERYE, s. Hind. *tarāī*, 'moist (land)' from *tar*, 'moist' or 'green.' [Others, however, connect it with *tara*, *tala*, 'beneath (the Himālaya).'] The term is specially applied to a belt of marshy and jungly land which runs along the foot of the Himālaya north of the Ganges, being that zone in which the moisture which has sunk into the talus of porous material exudes. A tract on the south side of the Ganges, now part of Bhāgalpūr, was also formerly known as the **Jungle-terry** (q.v.).

1793.—"Helloura, though standing very little below the level of Cheeria Ghat's top is nevertheless comprehended in the **Turry** or **Turryani** of Nepaul . . . **Turryani** properly signifies low marshy lands, and is sometimes applied to the flats lying below the hills in the interior of Nepaul, as well as the low tract bordering immediately on the Company's northern frontier."—*Kirkpatrick's Nepaul* (1811), p. 40.

1824.—"Mr. Boulderson said he was sorry to learn from the raja that he did not consider the unhealthy season of the **Terrai** yet over . . . I asked Mr. B. if it were true that the monkeys forsook these woods during the unwholesome months. He answered that not the monkeys only, but everything which had the breath of life instinctively deserts them from the beginning of April to October. The tigers go up to the hills, the antelopes and wild hogs make incursions into the cultivated plain . . . and not so much as a bird can be heard or seen in the frightful solitude."—*Heber*, ed. 1844, 250-251.

[The word is used as an adj. to describe a severe form of malarial fever, and also a sort of double felt hat, worn when the sun is not so powerful as to require the use of a **sola topee**.

[1879.—"Remittent has been called Jungle Fever, **Terai** Fever, Bengal Fever, &c., from the locality in which it originated. . . ."—*Moore, Family Med. for India*, 211.

[1880.—"A **Terai** hat is sufficient for a Collector."—*Ali Baba*, 85.]

THAKOOR, s. Hind. *thākur*, from Skt. *ṭhakkura*, 'an idol, a deity.' Used as a term of respect, Lord, Master, &c., but with a variety of specific applications, of which the most familiar is as the style of Rājpūt nobles. It is also in some parts the honorific designation of a barber, after the odd fashion which styles a tailor *khalīfa* (see **CALEEFA**); a *bihishtī*, *jama'-dār* (see **JEMADAR**); a sweeper, **mehtar**. And in Bengal it is the name of a Brahman family, which its members have Anglicised as *Tagore*, of whom several have been men of character and note, the best known being Dwārkanāth Tagore, "a man of liberal opinions and enterprising character" (*Wilson*), who died in London in 1840.

[c. 1610.—"The nobles in blood (in the Maldives) add to their name **Tacourou**."—*Pyrard de Laval*, Hak. Soc. i. 217.

[1798.—"The **Thacur** (so Rajput chieftains are called) was naked from the waist upwards, except the sacrificial thread or scarf on his shoulders and a turban on his head."—*L. of Colebrooke*, 462.

[1881.—"After the sons have gone to their respective offices, the mother changing her clothes retires into the **thakur***ghar* (the place of worship), and goes through her morning service. . . ."—*S. C. Bose, The Hindoos as they are*, 13.]

THERMANTIDOTE, s. This learned word ("heat-antidote") was applied originally, we believe, about 1830-32 to the invention of the instrument which it designates, or rather to the application of the instrument, which is in fact a winnowing machine fitted to a window aperture, and incased in wet **tatties** (q.v.), so as to drive a current of cooled air into a house during hot, dry weather. We have a dim remembrance that the invention was ascribed to Dr. Spilsbury.

1831.—"To the 21st of June, this oppressive weather held its sway; our only consolation grapes, iced-water, and the **thermantidote**, which answers admirably, almost too well, as on the 22d. I was laid up with rheumatic fever and lumbago, occasioned . . . by standing or sleeping before it."—*Wanderings of a Pilgrim*, i. 208.

[Mrs Parkes saw for the first time a **thermantidote** at Cawnpore in 1830.—*Ibid.* i. 134.]

1840.—". . . The thermometer at 112° all day in our tents, notwithstanding tatties, **phermanticlotes**,* and every possible invention that was likely to lessen the stifling heat."—*Osborne, Court and Camp of Runjeet Singh*, 132.

1853.—". . . then came punkahs by day, and next punkahs by night, and then tatties, and then **therm-antidotes**, till at last May came round again, and found the unhappy Anglo-Indian world once more surrounded with all the necessary but uncomfortable sweltering panoply of the hot weather."—*Oakfield*, i. 263-4.

1878.—"They now began (c. 1840) to have the benefit of **thermantidotes**, which however were first introduced in 1831; the name of the inventor is not recorded."—*Calcutta Rev.* cxxiv. 718.

1880.—". . . low and heavy punkahs swing overhead; a sweet breathing of wet *khaskhas* grass comes out of the **thermantidote**."—*Sir Ali Baba*, 112.

THUG, s. Hind. *ṭhag*, Mahr. *ṭhak*, Skt. *sthaga*, 'a cheat, a swindler.' And this is the only meaning given and illustrated in R. Drummond's *Illustrations of Guzerattee*, &c. (1808). But it has acquired a specific meaning, which cannot be exhibited more precisely or tersely than by Wilson:

* This book was printed in England, whilst the author was in India; doubtless he was innocent of this quaint error.

"Latterly applied to a robber and assassin of a peculiar class, who sallying forth in a gang . . . and in the character of wayfarers, either on business or pilgrimage, fall in with other travellers on the road, and having gained their confidence, take a favourable opportunity of strangling them by throwing their handkerchiefs round their necks, and then plundering them and burying their bodies." The proper specific designation of these criminals was *phānsīgar* or *phānsigar*, from *phansī*, 'a noose.'

According to Mackenzie (in *As. Res.* xiii.) the existence of gangs of these murderers was unknown to Europeans till shortly after the capture of Seringapatam in 1799, when about 100 were apprehended in Bangalore. But Fryer had, a century earlier, described a similar gang caught and executed near Surat. The *Phānsigars* (under that name) figured prominently in an Anglo-Indian novel called, we think, "The English in India," which one of the present writers read in early boyhood, but cannot now trace. It must have been published between 1826 and 1830.

But the name of *Thug* first became thoroughly familiar not merely to that part of the British public taking an interest in Indian affairs, but even to the mass of Anglo-Indian society, through the publication of the late Sir William Sleeman's book "*Ramaseeana; or a Vocabulary of the peculiar* language used by the **Thugs**, with an Introduction and Appendix, descriptive of that Fraternity, and of the Measures which have been adopted by the Supreme Government of India for its Suppression," Calcutta, 1836; and by an article on it which appeared in the *Edinburgh Review*, for Jan. 1837, (lxiv. 357). One of Col. Meadows Taylor's Indian romances also, *Memoirs of a Thug* (1839), has served to make the name and system familiar. The suppression of the system, for there is every reason to believe that it was brought to an end, was organised in a masterly way by Sir W. (then Capt.) Sleeman, a wise and admirable man, under the government and support of Lord William Bentinck. [The question of the Thugs and their modern successors has been again discussed in the *Quarterly Review*, Oct. 1901.]

c. 1665.—"Les Voleurs de ce pais-là sont les plus adroits du monde; ils ont l'usage d'un certain lasset à noeud coulant, qu'ils savent jetter si subtilement au col d'un homme, quand ils sont à sa portée, qu'ils ne le manquent jamais; en sorte qu'en un moment ils l'étranglent . . ." &c.—*Thevenot*, v. 123.

1673.—"They were Fifteen, all of a Gang, who used to lurk under Hedges in narrow Lanes, and as they found Opportunity, by a Device of a Weight tied to a Cotton Bow-string made of Guts, . . . they used to throw it upon Passengers, so that winding it about their Necks, they pulled them from their Beasts and dragging them upon the Ground strangled them, and possessed themselves of what they had . . . they were sentenced to *Lex Talionis*, to be hang'd; wherefore being delivered to the *Catwal* or Sheriff's Men, they led them two Miles with Ropes round their Necks to some Wild Date-trees: In their way thither they were chearful, and went singing, and smoaking Tobacco . . . as jolly as if going to a Wedding; and the Young Lad now ready to be tied up, boasted, That though he were not 14 Years of Age, he had killed his Fifteen Men. . . ."—*Fryer*, 97.

1785.—"Several men were taken up for a most cruel method of robbery and murder, practised on travellers, by a tribe called **phanseegurs**, or stranglers . . . under the pretence of travelling the same way, they enter into conversation with the strangers, share their sweetmeats, and pay them other little attentions, until an opportunity offers of suddenly throwing a rope round their necks with a slip-knot, by which they dexterously contrive to strangle them on the spot."—*Forbes, Or. Mem.* iv. 13; [2nd ed. ii. 397].

1808.—"**Phanseeo.** A term of abuse in Guzerat, applied also, truly, to thieves or robbers who strangle children in secret or travellers on the road."—*R. Drummond, Illustrations*, s.v.

1820.—"In the more northern parts of India these murderers are called **Thegs**, signifying deceivers."—*As. Res.* xiii. 250.

1823.—"The **Thugs** are composed of all castes, Mahommedans even were admitted: but the great majority are Hindus; and among these the Brahmins, chiefly of the Bundelcund tribes, are in the greatest numbers, and generally direct the operations of the different bands."—*Malcolm, Central India*, ii. 187.

1831.—"The inhabitants of Jubbulpore were this morning assembled to witness the execution of 25 **Thugs**. . . . The number of **Thugs** in the neighbouring countries is enormous; 115, I believe, belonged to the party of which 25 were executed, and the remainder are to be transported; and report says there are as many in Sauger Jail."—*Wanderings of a Pilgrim*, i. 201-202.

1843.—"It is by the command, and under the special protection of the most powerful goddesses that the **Thugs** join themselves to the unsuspecting traveller, make friends with him, slip the noose round his neck, plunge their knives in his eyes, hide him in the earth, and divide his money and baggage."—*Macaulay, Speech on Gates of Somnauth.*

1874.—"If a **Thug** makes strangling of travellers a part of his religion, we do not allow him the free exercise of it."—*W. Newman*, in *Fortnightly Rev.*, N.S. xv. 181.

[Tavernier writes: "The remainder of the people, who do not belong to either of these four castes, are called *Pauzecour*." This word Mr. Ball (ii. 185) suggests to be equivalent to either **pariah** or **phansigar**. Here he is in error. *Pauzecour* is really Skt. *Pancha-Gauḍa*, the five classes of northern Brahmans, for which see *Wilson*, (*Indian Caste*, ii. 124 *seqq.*).]

TIBET, n.p. The general name of the vast and lofty table-land of which the Himālaya forms the southern marginal range, and which may be said roughly to extend from the Indus elbow, N.W. of Kashmīr, to the vicinity of Sining-fu in Kansuh (see **SLING**) and to Tatsienlu on the borders of Szechuen, the last a distance of 1800 miles. The origin of the name is obscure, but it came to Europe from the Mahommedans of Western Asia; its earliest appearance being in some of the Arab Geographies of the 9th century.

Names suggestive of *Tibet* are indeed used by the Chinese. The original form of these (according to our friend Prof. Terrien de la Couperie) was *Tu-pot*; a name which is traced to a prince so called, whose family reigned at Liang-chau, north of the Yellow R. (in modern Kansuh), but who in the 5th century was driven far to the south-west, and established in eastern Tibet a State to which he gave the name of *Tu-pot*, afterwards corrupted into *Tu-poh* and *Tu-fan*. We are always on ticklish ground in dealing with derivations from or through the Chinese. But it is doubtless possible, perhaps even probable, that these names passed into the western form *Tibet*, through the communication of the Arabs in Turkestan with the tribes on their eastern border. This may have some corroboration from the prevalence of the name *Tibet*, or some proximate form, among the Mongols, as we may gather both from Carpini and Rubruck in the 13th century (quoted below), and from Sanang Setzen, and the Mongol version of the *Bodhimor* several hundred years later. These latter write the name (as represented by I. J. Schmidt), *Tūbet* and *Tōbōt*.

[c. 590.—"**Tobbat.**" See under **INDIA.**]

851.—"On this side of China are the countries of the Taghazghaz and the Khākān of **Tibbat**; and that is the termination of China on the side of the Turks."—*Relation*, &c., tr. par *Reinaud*, pt. i. p. 60.

c. 880.—"Quand un étranger arrive au *Tibet* (*al*-**Tibbat**), il éprouve, sans pouvoir s'en rendre compte, un sentiment de gaieté et de bien être qui persiste jusqu'au départ."—*Ibn Khurdādba*, in *J. As.* Ser. vi. tom. v. 522.

c. 910.—"The country in which lives the goat which produces the musk of China, and that which produces the musk of **Tibbat** are one and the same; only the Chinese get into their hands the goats which are nearest their side, and the people of **Tibbat** do likewise. The superiority of the musk of **Tibbat** over that of China is due to two causes; first, that the musk-goat on the **Tibbat** side of the frontier finds aromatic plants, whilst the tracts on the Chinese side only produce plants of a common kind."—*Relation*, &c., pt. 2, pp. 114-115.

c. 930.—"This country has been named **Tibbat** because of the establishment there of the Himyarites, the word *thabat* signifying to fix or establish oneself. That etymology is the most likely of all that have been proposed. And it is thus that Di'bal, son of 'Alī-al-Khuzā'ī, vaunts this fact in a poem, in which when disputing with Al-Kumair he exalts the descendants of Ḳaṭlān above those of Nizāar, saying:

"'Tis they who have been famous by their writings at the gate of Merv,
And who were writers at the gate of Chīn,
'Tis they who have bestowed on Samarkand the name of Shamr,
And who have transported thither the *Tibetans*" (*Al*-**Tubbatīna**).*
Mas'ūdī, i. 352.

c. 976.—"From the sea to **Tibet** is 4 months' journey, and from the sea of Fārs to the country of Kanauj is 3 months' journey."—*Ibn Haukal*, in *Elliot*, i. 33.

* This refers to an Arab legend that Samarkand was founded in very remote times by Tobba'-al-Akbar, Himyarite King of Yemen, (see *e.g. Edrisi*, by *Jaubert*, ii. 198), and the following: "The author of the *Treatise on the Figure of the Earth* says on this subject: "This is what was told me by Abu-Bakr-Dimashkī—'I have seen over the great gate of Samarkand an iron tablet bearing an inscription, which, according to the people of the place, was engraved in Himyarite characters, and as an old tradition related, had been the work of "Tobba."'"—*Shihābuddīn Dimashkī*, in *Not. et Ext.* xiii. 254.

c. 1020.—"Bhútesar is the first city on the borders of **Tibet**. There the language, costume, and appearance of the people are different. Thence to the top of the highest mountain, of which we spoke . . . is a distance of 20 parasangs. From the top of it **Tibet** looks red and Hind black."—*Al-Bīrūnī*, in *Elliot*, i. 57.

1075.—"Τοῦ *μόσχου, διάφορα εἴδη εἰσὶν· ὧν ὁ κρείττων γίνεται ἐν πόλει τινὶ πολὺ τοῦ* Χορ*άση ἀνατολικοτέρα, λεγομένη* Τουπάτα· *ἔστι δὲ τὴν χροιὰν ὑπόξανθον· τοῦτον δὲ ἧττον ὁ ἀπὸ τῆς* 'Ι*νδιάς μετακομιζόμενος· ῥέπει δὲ ἐπὶ τὸ μελάντερον· καὶ τούτου πάλιν ὑποδεέστερος ὁ ἀπὸ τῶν* Σ*ίνων ἀγόμενος· πάντες δε ἐν ὀμφαλῷ ἀπογεννῶνται ζώου τινὸς μονοκέρωτος μέγιστον ὁμοιόν δορκάδος.*" —*Symeon Seth*, quoted by *Bochart, Hieroz.* III. xxvi.

1165.—"This prince is called in Arabic Sultan-al-Fars-al-Kábar . . . and his empire extends from the banks of the Shat-al-Arab to the City of Samarkand . . . and reaches as far as **Thibet**, in the forests of which country that quadruped is found which yields the musk."—*Rabbi Benjamin*, in *Wright's Early Travels*, 106.

c. 1200.—

"He went from Hindustan to the **Tibat**-land. . . .
From **Tibat** he entered the boundaries of Chīn."

Sikandar Nāmah, E.T. by *Capt. H. W. Clarke*, R.E., p. 585.

1247.—"Et dum reverteretur exercitus ille, videlicet Mongalorum, venit ad terram Buri-**Thabet**, quos bello vicerunt: qui sunt pagani. Qui consuetudinem mirabilem imo potius miserabilem habent: quia cum alicujus pater humanae naturae debitum solvit, omnem congregant parentelam ut comedant eum, sicut nobis dicebatur pro certo."—*Joan. de Plano Carpini*, in *Rec. de Voyages*, iv. 658.

1253.—"Post istos sunt **Tebet**, homines solentes comedere parentes suos defunctos, ut causa pietatis non facerent aliud sepulchrum eis nisi viscera sua."—*Rubruq.* in *Recueil de Voyages*, &c. iv. 289.

1298.—"**Tebet** est une grandisime provence qve lengajes ont por elles, et sunt ydres. . . . Il sunt maint grant laironz . . . il sunt mau custumés; il ont grandismes chenz mastin qe sunt grant come asnes et sunt mout buen a prendre bestes sauvajes."—*Marco Polo*, Geog. Text. ch. cxvi.

1330.—"Passando questa provincia grande perveni a un altro gran regno che si chiama **Tibet**, ch'ene ne confini d'India ed e tutta al gran Cane . . . la gente di questa contrada dimora in tende che sono fatte di feltri neri. La principale cittade è fatta tutta di pietre bianche e nere, e tutte le vie lastricate. In questa cittade dimora il Atassi (Abassi ?) che viene a dire in nostro modo il Papa."—*Fr. Odorico*, Palatine MS., in *Cathay*, &c. App. p. lxi.

c. 1340.—"The said mountain (*Karāchīl*, the Himālaya) extends in length a space of 3 months' journey, and at the base is the country of **Thabbat**, which has the antelopes which give musk."—*Ibn Batuta*, iii. 438-439.

TICAL, s. This (*tikāl*) is a word which has long been in use by foreign traders to Burma, for the quasi-standard weight of (uncoined) current silver, and is still in general use in B. Burma as applied to that value. This weight is by the Burmese themselves called *kyat*, and is the hundredth part of the **viss** (q.v.), being thus equivalent to about 1¼ rupee in value. The origin of the word *tikāl* is doubtful. Sir A. Phayre suggests that possibly it is a corruption of the Burmese words *ta-kyat*, "one kyat." On the other hand perhaps it is more probable that the word may have represented the Indian *ṭakā* (see **TUCKA**). The word is also used by traders to Siam. But there likewise it is a foreign term; the Siamese word being *bat*. In Siam the *tikal* is according to Crawfurd a silver *coin*, as well as a weight equivalent to 225½ grs. English. In former days it was a short cylinder of silver bent double, and bearing two stamps, thus half-way between the Burmese bullion and proper coin.*

[1554.—"**Ticals**." See **MACAO** b. Also see **VISS**.]

1585.—"Auuertendosi che vna *bize* di peso è per 40 once Venetiane, e ogni *bize* è **teccali** cento, e vn *gito* val **teccali** 25, e vn *abocco* val **teccali** 12½."—*G. Balbi* (in Pegu), f. 108.

[1615.—"Cloth to the value of six cattes (**Catty**) less three **tiggalls**."—*Foster, Letters*, iv. 107.

[1639.—"Four **Ticals** make a Tayl (**Tael**)."—*Mandelslo*, E.T. ii. 130.]

1688.—"The proportion of their (Siamese) Money to ours is, that their **Tical**, which weighs no more than half a Crown, is yet worth three shillings and three half-pence." —*La Loubère*, E.T. p. 72.

1727.—"*Pegu* Weight.
1 *Viece* is . . . 39 ou. *Troy*,
or 1 *Viece* . . . 100 **Teculs**.
140 *Viece* . . a *Bahaar* (see **BAHAR**).
The *Bahaar* is 3 **Pecul** China."—*A. Hamilton*, ii. 317; [ed. 1744].

c. 1759.—". . . a dozen or 20 fowls may be bought for a **Tical** (little more than ½ a Crown)."—In *Dalrymple, Or. Rep.* i. 121.

* [Col. Temple notes that the pronunciation has always been twofold. At present in Burma it is usual to pronounce it like *tickle*, and in Siam like *tacawl*. He regards it as certain that it comes from *takā* through Talaing and Peguan *t'ke*.]

1775.—Stevens, *New and Complete Guide to E.I. Trade*, gives
"Pegu weight:
100 moo = 1 Tual (read **Tical**).
100 tual (**Tical**) = 1 vis (see **VISS**) = 3 lb. 5 oz. 5 dr. avr.
150 vis = 1 **candy**."
And under Siam:
"80 Tuals (**Ticals**) = 1 **Catty**.
50 **Catties** = 1 **Pecul**."

1783.—"The merchandize is sold for **tee-calls**, a round piece of silver, stamped and weighing about one rupee and a quarter."—*Forrest, V. to Mergui*, p. vii.

TICCA, and vulg. **TICKER**, adj. This is applied to any person or thing engaged by the job, or on contract. Thus a *ticca garry* is a hired carriage, a *ticca doctor* is a surgeon not in the regular service but temporarily engaged by Government. From Hind. *ṭhīka*, *ṭhīkah*, 'hire, fare, fixed price.'

[1813.—"**Teecka**, hire, fare, contract, job."—*Gloss. to Fifth Report*, s.v.]

1827.—"A Rule, Ordinance and Regulation for the good Order and Civil Government of the Settlement of Fort William in Bengal, and for regulating the number and fare of **Teeka Palankeens**, and **Teeka Bearers** in the Town of Calcutta . . . registered in the Supreme Court of Judicature, on the 27th June, 1827."—*Bengal Regulations* of 1827.

1878.—"Leaving our servants to jabber over our heavier baggage, we got into a '**ticca gharry**,' 'hired trap,' a bit of civilization I had hardly expected to find so far in the Mofussil."—*Life in the Mofussil*, ii. 94.

[**TICKA**, s. Hind. *ṭīkā*, Skt. *tilaka*, a mark on the forehead made with coloured earth or unguents, as an ornament, to mark sectarial distinction, accession to the throne, at betrothal, &c; also a sort of spangle worn on the forehead by women. The word has now been given the additional meaning of the mark made in vaccination, and the *ṭīkāwālā Ṣāḥib* is the vaccination officer.

[c. 1796.—". . . another was sent to Kutch to bring thence the **tika**. . . ."—*Mir Hussein Ali, Life of Tipu*, 251

[1832.—"In the centre of their foreheads is a **teeka** (or spot) of lamp-black."—*Herklots, Qanoon-e-Islam*, 2nd ed. 139.

[c. 1878.—"When a sudden stampede of the children, accompanied by violent yells and sudden falls, has taken place as I entered a village, I have been informed, by way of apology, that it was not I whom the children feared, but that they supposed that I was the **Tikawala** *Sahib*."—*Panjab Gazetteer, Rohtak*, p. 9.]

TICKY-TOCK. This is an unmeaning refrain used in some French songs, and by foreign singing masters in their scales. It would appear from the following quotations to be of Indian origin.

c. 1755.—"These gentry (the band with nautch-girls) are called **Tickytaw** boys, from the two words **Ticky** and **Taw**, which they continually repeat, and which they chaunt with great vehemence."—*Ives*, 75.

[c. 1883.—"Each pair of boys then, having privately arranged to represent two separate articles . . . comes up to the captains, and one of the pair says **dik dik, daun daun**, which apparently has about as much meaning as the analogous English nursery saying, 'Dickory, dickory dock.'"—*Panjab Gazetteer, Hoshiārpur*, p. 35.]

[**TIER-CUTTY**, s. This is Malayāl. *tiyar-katti*, the knife used by a Tiyan or toddy-drawer for scarifying the palm-trees. The Tiyan caste take their title from Malayal. *tíyyan*, which again comes from Malayal. *tívu*, Skt. *dvīpa*, 'an island,' and derive their name from their supposed origin in Ceylon.

[1792.—"12 **Tier Cutties**."—Account, in *Logan, Malabar*, iii. 169.

[1799.—"The negadee (*naqdī*, 'cash-payment') on houses, banksauls (see **BANKSHALL**), **Tiers' knives**."—*Ibid.* iii. 324.]

TIFFIN, s. Luncheon, Anglo-Indian and Hindustani, at least in English households. Also **to Tiff**, v. to take luncheon. Some have derived this word from Ar. *tafannun*, 'diversion, amusement,' but without history, or evidence of such an application of the Arabic word. Others have derived it from Chinese *ch'ih-fan*, 'eat-rice,' which is only an additional example that anything whatever may be plausibly resolved into Chinese monosyllables. We believe the word to be a local survival of an English colloquial or slang term. Thus we find in the *Lexicon Balatronicum*, compiled originally by Capt. Grose (1785): "*Tiffing*, eating or drinking out of meal-times," besides other meanings. Wright (*Dict. of Obsolete and Provincial English*) has: "*Tiff*, s. (1) a draught of liquor, (2) small beer;" and Mr. Davies (*Supplemental English Glossary*) gives some good quotations both of this substantive and of a verb "*to tiff*," in the sense of 'take off a draught.' We should conjecture that Grose's sense was a modification of this one, that his "*tiffing*" was a participial noun from the verb *to tiff*, and that the Indian **tiffin** is identical with the participial noun. This has perhaps some corroboration both from the form "*tiffing*" used in some earlier Indian examples, and from the Indian use of the verb "**to Tiff.**" [This view is accepted by Prof. Skeat, who derives *tiff* from Norweg. *tev*, 'a drawing in of the breath, sniff,' *teva*, 'to sniff' (*Concise Dict.* s.v.; and see 9 ser. *N. & Q.* iv. 425, 460, 506; v. 13).] Rumphius has a curious passage which we have tried in vain to connect with the present word; nor can we find the words he mentions in either Portuguese or Dutch Dictionaries. Speaking of **Toddy** and the like he says:

"Homines autem qui eas (potiones) colligunt ac praeparant, dicuntur Portugallico nomine *Tiffadores*, atque opus ipsum *Tiffar*; nostratibus Belgis *tyfferen*" (*Herb. Amboinense*, i. 5).

We may observe that the comparatively late appearance of the word **tiffin** in our documents is perhaps due to the fact that when dinner was early no lunch was customary. But the word, to have been used by an English novelist in 1811, could not then have been new in India.

We now give examples of the various uses:

TIFF, s. In the old English senses (in which it occurs also in the form *tip*, and is probably allied to *tipple* and *tipsy*); [see Prof. Skeat, quoted above].

(1) For a draught:

1758.—"*Monday . . . Seven.* Returned to my room. Made a **tiff** of warm punch, and to bed before nine."—*Journal of a Senior Fellow*, in the *Idler*, No. 33.

(2) For small beer:

1604.—

"... make waste more prodigal
Than when our beer was good, that John may float
To Styx in beer, and lift up Charon's boat
With wholsome waves: and as the conduits ran
With claret at the Coronation,
So let your channels flow with single **tiff**,
For John I hope is crown'd. . . ."

On John Dawson, Butler of Christ Church, in *Bishop Corbet's Poems*, ed. 1807, pp. 207-8.

TO TIFF, v. in the sense of taking off a draught.

1812.—
"He **tiff'd** his punch and went to rest."
Combe, Dr. Syntâx, I. Canto v.
(This is quoted by Mr. Davies.)

TIFFIN (the Indian substantive).

1807.—"Many persons are in the habit of sitting down to a repast at one o'clock, which is called **tiffen**, and is in fact an early dinner."—*Cordiner's Çeylon*, i. 83.

1810.—"The (Mahommedan) ladies, like ours, indulge in **tiffings** (slight repasts), it being delicate to eat but little before company."—*Williamson, V.M.* i. 352.

,, (published 1812) "The dinner is scarcely touched, as every person eats a hearty meal called **tiffin**, at 2 o'clock, at home."—*Maria Graham*, 29.

1811.—"Gertrude was a little unfortunate in her situation, which was next below Mrs. Fashionist, and who . . . detailed the delights of India, and the *routine* of its day; the changing linen, the *curry-combing* . . . the idleness, the dissipation, the sleeping and the necessity of sleep, the gay **tiffings**, were all delightful to her in reciting. . . ."—*The Countess and Gertrude, or Modes of Discipline*, by *Laetitia Maria Hawkins*, ii. 12.

1824.—"The entreaty of my friends compelled me to remain to breakfast and an early **tiffin**. . . ."—*Seely, Wonders of Ellora*, ch. iii.

c. 1832.—"Reader! I, as well as Pliny, had an uncle, an East Indian Uncle . . . everybody has an Indian Uncle. . . . He is not always so orientally rich as he is reputed; but he is always orientally munificent. Call upon him at any hour from two till five, he insists on your taking **tiffin**; and such a **tiffin**! The English corresponding term is luncheon: but how meagre a shadow is the European meal to its glowing Asiatic cousin."—*De Quincey, Casuistry of Roman Meals*, in *Works*, iii. 259.

1847.—"'Come home and have some **tiffin**, Dobbin,' a voice cried behind him, as a pudgy hand was laid on his shoulder. . . . But the Captain had no heart to go a-feasting with Joe Sedley."—*Vanity Fair*, ed. 1867, i. 235.

1850.—"A vulgar man who enjoys a champagne **tiffin** and swindles his servants . . . may be a pleasant companion to those who do not hold him in contempt as a vulgar knave, but he is not a gentleman."—*Sir C. Napier, Farewell Address.*

1853.—"This was the case for the prosecution. The court now adjourned for **tiffin**."—*Oakfield*, i. 319.

1882.—"The last and most vulgar form of 'nobbling' the press is well known as the luncheon or **tiffin** trick. It used to be confined to advertising tradesmen and hotel-keepers, and was practised on newspaper reporters. Now it has been practised on a loftier scale. . . ."—*Saty. Rev.*, March 25, 357.

TO TIFF, in the Indian sense.

1803.—"He hesitated, and we were interrupted by a summons to **tiff** at Floyer's. After **tiffin** Close said he should be glad to go."—*Elphinstone*, in *Life*, i. 116.

1814.—"We found a pool of excellent water, which is scarce on the hills, and laid down to **tiff** on a full soft bed, made by the grass of last year and this. After **tiffing**, I was cold and unwell."—*Ibid.* p. 283. *Tiffing* here is a participle, but its use shows how the noun **tiffin** would be originally formed.

1816.—

"The huntsman now informed them all
They were to **tiff** at Bobb'ry Hall.
Mounted again, the party starts,
Upsets the **hackeries** and carts,
Hammals (see **HUMMAUL**) and **palanquins** and **doolies**,
Dobies (see **DHOBY**) and burrawas (?) and **coolies**."

The Grand Master, or Adventures of Qui Hi, by *Quiz* (Canto viii.).

[Burrawa is probably H. *bharuā*, 'a pander.']

1829.—"I was **tiffing** with him one day, when the subject turned on the sagacity of elephants. . . ."—*John Shipp*, ii. 267.

1859.—"Go home, Jack. I will **tiff** with you to-day at half-past two."—*J. Lang, Wanderings in India*, p. 16.

The following, which has just met our eye, is bad grammar, according to Anglo-Indian use:

1885.—"'Look here, RANDOLPH, don't you know,' said Sir PEEL, . . . 'Here you've been gallivanting through India, riding on elephants, and **tiffining** with Rajahs. . . .'"—*Punch, Essence of Parliament*, April 25, p. 204.

TIGER, s. The royal tiger was apparently first known to the Greeks by the expedition of Alexander, and a little later by a live one which Seleucus sent to Athens. The animal became, under the Emperors, well known to the Romans, but fell out of the knowledge of Europe in later days, till it again became familiar in India. The Greek and Latin τίγρις, *tigris*, is said to be from the old Persian word for an arrow, *tigra*, which gives the modern Pers. (and Hind.) *tīr*.* Pliny says of the *River* Tigris: "*a celeritate* **Tigris** *incipit vocari. Ita appellant Medi sagittam*" (vi. 27). In speaking of the animal and its "*velocitatis tremendae,*" Pliny evidently glances at this etymology, real or imaginary. So does Pausanias probably, in his remarks on its colour. [This view of the origin of the name is accepted by Schrader (*Prehist. Ant. of the Aryan Peoples*, E.T. 250), who writes: "Nothing like so far back in the history of the Indo-Europeans does the lion's dreadful rival for supremacy over the beasts, the tiger, go. In India the songs of the Rigveda have nothing to say about him; his name (*vyāghrá*) first occurs in the Atharvaveda, *i.e.* at a time when the Indian immigration must have extended much farther towards the Ganges; for it is in the reeds and grasses of Bengal that we have to look for the tiger's proper home. Nor is he mentioned among the beasts of prey in the Avesta. The district of Hyrcania, whose numerous tigers the later writers of antiquity speak of with especial frequency, was then called *Vehrkana*, 'wolf-land.' It is, therefore, not improbable . . . that the tiger has spread in relatively late times from India over portions of W. and N. Asia."]

c. B.C. 325.—"The Indians think the **Tiger** (τὸν τίγριν) a great deal stronger than the elephant. Nearchus says he saw the skin of a tiger, but did not see the beast itself, and that the Indians assert the **tiger** to be as big as the biggest horse; whilst in swiftness and strength there is no creature to be compared to him. And when he engages the elephant he springs on its head, and easily throttles it. Moreover, the creatures which we have seen and call *tigers* are only jackals which are dappled, and of a kind bigger than ordinary jackals."—*Arrian, Indica*, xv. We apprehend that this big dappled jackal (θῶς) is meant for a *hyaena*.

c. B.C. 322.—"In the island of Tylos . . . there is also another wonderful thing they say . . . for there is a certain tree, from which they cut sticks, and these are very handsome articles, having a certain variegated colour, like the skin of a **tiger**. The wood is very heavy; but if it is struck against any solid substance it shivers like a piece of

* Sir H. Rawlinson gives *tigra* as old Persian for an arrow (see *Herod.* vol. iii. p. 552). Vüllers seems to consider it rather an induction than a known word for an arrow. He says: "Besides the name of that river (Tigris) *Arvand*, which often occurs in the *Shāhnāma*, and which properly signifies 'running' or 'swift'; another Medo-persic name *Tigra* is found in the cuneiform inscriptions, and is cognate with the Zend word *tedjao*, *tedjerem*, and Pehlvi *tedjera*, *i.e.* 'a running river,' which is entered in Anquetil's vocabulary. And these, along with the Persian *tej* 'an arrow,' *tegh* 'a sword,' *tekh* and *teg* 'sharp,' are to be referred to the Zend root *tikhsh*, Skt. *tij*, 'to sharpen.' The Persian word *tīr*, 'an arrow,' may be of the same origin, since its primitive form appears to be *tigra*, from which it seems to come by elision of the *g*, as the Skt. *tīr*, 'arrow,' comes from *tīvra* for *tīgra*, where *v* seems to have taken the place of *g*. From the word *tīgra* . . . seem also to be derived the usual names of the river Tigris, Pers. *Dizhla*, Ar. *Dijlah*" (Vüllers, s.v. *tīr*).

pottery."—*Theophrastus, H. of Plants*, Bk. v. c. 4.

c. B.C. 321.—"And Ulpianus . . . said: 'Do we anywhere find the word used a masculine, τὸν τίγριν? for I know that Philemon says thus in his Neaera:

'*A.* We've seen the **tigress** (τὴν τίγριν) that Seleucus sent us;
Are we not bound to send Seleucus back
Some beast in fair exchange?'"
In *Athenaeus*, xiii. 57.

c. B.C. 320.—"According to Megasthenes, the largest **tigers** are found among the Prasii, almost twice the size of lions, and of such strength that a tame one led by four persons seized a mule by its hinder leg, overpowered it, and dragged it to him."—*Strabo*, xv. ch. 1, § 37 (*Hamilton* and *Falconer's* E.T. iii. 97).

c. B.C. 19.—"And Augustus came to Samos, and again passed the winter there . . . and all sorts of embassies came to him; and the Indians who had previously sent messages proclaiming friendship, now sent to make a solemn treaty, with presents, and among other things including **tigers**, which were then seen for the first time by the Romans; and if I am not mistaken by the Greeks also."—*Dio Cassius*, liv. 9. [See *Merivale, Hist. Romans*, ed. 1865, iv. 176.]

c. B.C. 19.—
". . . duris genuit te cautibus horrens
Caucasus, Hyrcanaeque admôrunt ubera **tigres**."
Aen. iv. 366-7.

c. A.D. 70.—"The Emperor Augustus . . . in the yeere that Q. Tubero and Fabius Maximus were Consuls together . . . was the first of all others that shewed a tame **tygre** within a cage: but the Emperour Claudius foure at once. . . . **Tygres** are bred in Hircania and India: this beast is most dreadful for incomparable swiftness."—*Pliny*, by *Ph. Holland*, i. 204.

c. 80-90.—"Wherefore the land is called Dachanabadēs (see **DECCAN**), for the South is called *Dachanos* in their tongue. And the land that lies in the interior above this towards the East embraces many tracts, some of them of deserts or of great mountains, with all kinds of wild beasts, panthers and **tigers** (τίγρεις) and elephants, and immense serpents (δράκοντας) and hyenas (κροκόττας) and *cynocephala* of many species, and many and populous nations till you come to the Ganges."—*Periplus*, § 50.

c. A.D. 180.—"That beast again, in the talk of Ctesias about the Indians, which is alleged to be called by them *Martióra* (*Martichóra*), and by the Greeks *Androphagus* (Maneater), I am convinced is really the **tiger** (τὸν τίγριν. The story that he has a triple range of teeth in each jaw, and sharp prickles at the tip of his tail which he shoots at those who are at a distance, like the arrows of an archer,—I don't believe it to be true, but only to have been generated by the excessive fear which the beast inspires. They have been wrong also about his colour;—no doubt when they see him in the bright sunlight he takes that colour and looks red; or perhaps it may be because of his going so fast, and because even when not running he is constantly darting from side to side; and then (to be sure) it is always from a long way off that they see him."—*Pausanias*, IX. xxi. 4. [See Frazer's tr. i. 470; v. 86. *Martichoras* is here Pers. *mardumkhwūr*, 'eater of men.']

1298.—"Enchore sachiés qe le Grant Sire a bien leopars asez qe tuit sunt bon da chacer et da prendre bestes. . . . Il ha plosors lyons grandismes, greignors asez qe cele de Babilonie. Il sunt de mout biaus poil et de mout biaus coleor, car il sunt tout vergés por lonc, noir et vermoil et blance. Il sunt afaités a prandre sengler sauvajes et les bueff sauvajes, et orses et asnes sauvajes et cerf et cavriolz et autres bestes."—*Marco Polo, Geog. Text*, ch. xcii. Thus Marco Polo can only speak of this huge animal, striped black and red and white, as of a *Lion*. And a medieval Bestiary has a chapter on the **Tigre** which begins: "Une Beste est qui est apelée **Tigre**, c'est une maniere de serpent."—(In *Cahier et Martin, Mélanges d'Archéol.* ii. 140).

1474.—"This meane while there came in certein men sent from a Prince of India, wth certain strange beastes, the first whereof was a *leonza* ledde in a chayne by one that had skyll, which they call in their languaige *Babureth*. She is like vnto a lyonesse; but she is redde coloured, streaked all over wth black strykes; her face is redde wth certain white and blacke spottes, the bealy white, and tayled like the lyon: seemyng to be a marvailouse fiers beast."—*Josafa Barbaro*, Hak. Soc. pp. 53-54. Here again is an excellent description of a tiger, but that name seems unknown to the traveller. *Babureth* is in the Ital. original *Baburth*, Pers. *babr*, a **tiger**.

1553.—". . . Beginning from the point of Çingapura and all the way to Pulloçambilam, *i.e.* the whole length of the Kingdom of Malaca . . . there is no other town with a name except this City of Malaca, only some havens of fishermen, and in the interior a very few villages. And indeed the most of these wretched people sleep at the top of the highest trees they can find, for up to a height of 20 palms the **tigers** can seize them at a leap; and if anything saves the poor people from these beasts it is the bonfires they keep burning at night, which the tigers are much afraid of. In fact these are so numerous that many come into the city itself at night in search of prey. And it has happened, since we took the place, that a tiger leapt into a garden surrounded by a good high timber fence, and lifted a beam of wood with three slaves who were laid by the heels, and with these made a clean leap over the fence."—*Barros*, II. vi. 1. Lest I am doing the great historian wrong as to this Munchausen-like story, I give the original: "E jà aconteceo . . . saltar hum tigre em hum quintal cercado de madeira bem alto, e levou hum tronco de madeira com trez (tres?) escravos que estavam prezos nelle, com os quaes saltou de claro em claro per cima da cerca."

1583.—"We also escaped the peril of the multitude of **tigers** which infest those tracts" (the Pegu delta) "and prey on whatever they can get at. And although we were on that account anchored in midstream, nevertheless it was asserted that the ferocity of these animals was such that they would press even into the water to seize their prey." —*Gasparo Balbi*, f. 94*v*.

1586.—"We went through the wildernesse because the right way was full of thieves, when we passed the country of *Gouren*, where we found but few Villages, but almost all Wildernesse, and saw many Buffes, Swine, and Deere, Grasse longer than a man, and very many **Tigres**."—*R. Fitch*, in *Purchas*, ii. 1736.

1675.—"Going in quest whereof, one of our Soldiers, a Youth, killed a **Tigre-Royal**; it was brought home by 30 or 40 *Combies* (**Koonbee**), the Body tied to a long Bamboo, the Tail extended . . . it was a **Tigre** of the Biggest and Noblest Kind, Five Feet in Length beside the Tail, Three and a Half in Height, it was of a light Yellow, streaked with Black, like a Tabby Cat . . . the Visage Fierce and Majestick, the Teeth gnashing. . . ."—*Fryer*, 176.

1683.—"In ye afternoon they found a great **Tiger**, one of ye black men shot a barbed arrow into his Buttock. Mr. Frenchfeild and Capt. Raynes alighted off their horses and advanced towards the thicket where ye Tiger lay. The people making a great noise, ye Tiger flew out upon Mr. Frenchfeild, and he shot him with a brace of Bullets into ye breast: at which he made a great noise, and returned again to his den. The Black Men seeing of him wounded fell upon him, but the Tiger had so much strength as to kill 2 men, and wound a third, before he died. At Night ye Ragea sent me the Tiger."—*Hedges, Diary*, Hak. Soc. i. 66-67.

1754.—"There was a *Charter* granted to the *East India Company*. Many Disputes arose about it, which came before Parliament; all Arts were used to corrupt or delude the Members; among others a **Tyger** *was baited* with Solemnity, on the Day the great Question was to come on. This was such a Novelty, that several of the Members were drawn off from their Attendance, and absent on the Division. . . ."—*A Collection of Letters relating to the E.I. Company*, &c. (Tract), 1754, p. 13.

1869.—"Les **tigres** et les léopards sont considérés, autant par les Hindous que par les musalmans, comme étant la propriété des *pirs* (see **PEER**): aussi les naturels du pays ne sympathisent pas avec les Européens pour la chasse du **tigre**."—*Garcin de Tassy, Rel. Mus.* p. 24.

1872.—"One of the Frontier Battalion soldiers approached me, running for his life. . . . This was his story:—

'Sahib, I was going along with the letters . . . which I had received from your highness . . . a great **tiger** came out and stood in the path. Then I feared for my life; and the **tiger** stood, and I stood, and we looked at each other. I had no weapon but my kukri (**Kookry**) . . . and the Government letters. So I said, 'My lord **Tiger**, here are the Government letters, the letters of the Honourable Kumpany Bahadur . . . and it is necessary for me to go on with them.' The tiger never ceased looking at me, and when I had done speaking he growled, but he never offered to get out of the way. On this I was much more afraid, so I kneeled down and made obeisance to him; but he did not take any more notice of that either, so at last I told him I should report the matter to the Sahib, and I threw down the letters in front of him, and came here as fast as I was able. Sahib, I now ask for your justice against that **tiger**.'"—*Lt.-Col. T. Lewin, A Fly on the Wheel*, p. 444.

TINCALL, s. Borax. Pers. *tinkār*, but apparently originally Skt. *ṭaṅkana*, and perhaps from the people so called who may have supplied it, in the Himālaya—Τάγγανοι of Ptolemy. [Mr. Atkinson (*Himalayan Gazz.* ii. 357) connects the name of this people with that of the **tangun** pony.]

1525.—"**Tymquall**, small, 60 tangas a maund."—*Lembrança*, 50.

1563.—"It is called *borax* and *crisocola;* and in Arabic **tincar**, and so the Guzeratis call it. . . ."—*Garcia*, f. 78.

c. 1590.—"Having reduced the *k'haral* to small bits, he adds to every *man* of it 1¼ *sers* of **tangár** (borax) and 3 *sers* of pounded *natrum*, and kneads them together."—*Āīn*, i. 26.

[1757.—"A small quantity of *Tutenegg* (**Tootnague**), **Tinkal** and *Japan Copper* was also found here. . . ."—*Ives*, 105.]

TINDAL, s. Malayāl. *taṇḍal*, Telug. *taṇḍelu*, also in Mahr. and other vernaculars *ṭandel*, *ṭanḍail*, [which Platts connects with *ṭāṇḍā*, Skt. *tantra*, 'a line of men,' but the *Madras Gloss.* derives the S. Indian forms from Mal. *tandu*, 'an oar,' *valli*, 'to pull.'] The head or commander of a body of men; but in ordinary specific application a native petty officer of **lascars**, whether on board ship (boatswain) or in the ordnance department, and sometimes the head of a gang of labourers on public works.

c. 1348. — "The second day after our arrival at the port of Kailukari this princess invited the *nākhodah* (**Nacoda**) or owner of the ship, the *karānī* (see **CRANNY**) or clerk, the merchants, the persons of distinction, the **tandīl**. . . ."—*Ibn Batuta*, iv. 250. The Moorish traveller explains the word as *mukaddam* (**Mocuddum**, q.v.) *al-rajāl*, which the French translators render as "général des piĉtons," but we may hazard the correction of "Master of the crew."

c. 1590.—"In large ships there are twelve classes. 1. The *Nākhudā*, or owner of the ship. . . . 3. The **Tandīl**, or chief of the *khalāçis* (see **CLASSY**) or sailors. . . ."—*Āīn*, i. 280.

1673.—"The Captain is called **Nucquedah**, the boatswain **Tindal**. . . ."—*Fryer*, 107.

1758.—"One **Tindal**, or Corporal of Lascars."—*Orme*, ii. 339.

[1826.—"I desired the **tindal**, or steersman to answer, 'Bombay.'"—*Pandurang Hari*, ed. 1873, ii. 157.]

TINNEVELLY, n.p. A town and district of Southern India, probably *Tiru-nel-vēli*, 'Sacred Rice-hedge.' [The *Madras Gloss.* gives 'Sacred Paddy-village.'] The district formed the southern part of the Madura territory, and first became a distinct district about 1744, when the Madura Kingdom was incorporated with the territories under the Nawāb of Arcot (*Caldwell, H. of Tinnevelly*).

TIPARRY, s. Beng. and Hind. *tipārī, tepārī*, the fruit of *Physalis peruviana*, L., N.O. *Solanaceae*. It is also known in India as 'Cape gooseberry,' [which is usually said to take its name from the Cape of Good Hope, but as it is a native of tropical America, Mr. Ferguson (8 ser. *N. & Q.* xii. 106) suggests that the word may really be *cape* or *cap*, from the peculiarity of its structure noted below.] It is sometimes known as 'Brazil cherry.' It gets its generic name from the fact that the inflated calyx encloses the fruit as in a bag or bladder (φύσα). It has a slightly acid gooseberry flavour, and makes excellent jam. We have seen a suggestion somewhere that the Bengali name is connected with the word *ṭenpā*, 'inflated,' which gives its name to a species of *tetrodon* or globe-fish, a fish which has the power of dilating the œsophagus in a singular manner. The native name of the fruit in N.W. India is *māk* or *māko*, but *tipārī* is in general Anglo-Indian use. The use of an almost identical name for a gooseberry-like fruit, in a Polynesian Island (Kingsmill group) quoted below from Wilkes, is very curious, but we can say no more on the matter.

1845.—"On Makin they have a kind of fruit resembling the gooseberry, called by the natives '**teiparu**'; this they pound, after it is dried, and make with molasses into cakes, which are sweet and pleasant to the taste."—*U.S. Expedition*, by *C. Wilkes*, U.S.N., v. 81.

1878.—". . . The enticing **tipari** in its crackly covering. . . ."—*P. Robinson, In My Indian Garden*, 49-50.

TIPPOO SAHIB, n.p. The name of this famous enemy of the English power in India was, according to C. P. Brown, taken from that of *Tipū Sultān*, a saint whose tomb is near Hyderabad. [Wilks (*Hist. Sketches*, i. 522, ed. 1869), says that the tomb is at Arcot.]

TIRKUT, s. Foresail. Sea Hind. from Port. *triquette* (*Roebuck*).

TIYAN, n.p. Malayāl. *Tīyan*, or *Tīvan*, pl. *Tīyar* or *Tīvar*. The name of what may be called the third caste (in rank) of Malabar. The word signifies 'islander,' [from Mal. *tīvu*, Skt. *dvīpa*, 'an island']; and the people are supposed to have come from Ceylon (see **TIER CUTTY**).

1510.—"The third class of Pagans are called **Tiva**, who are artizans."—*Varthema*, 142.

1516.—"The cleanest of these low and rustic people are called *Tuias* (read **Tivas**), who are great labourers, and their chief business is to look after the palm-trees, and gather their fruit, and carry everything . . . for hire, because there are no draught cattle in the country."—*Barbosa*, Lisbon ed. 335.

[1800.—"All **Tirs** can eat together, and intermarry. The proper duty of the cast is to extract the juice from palm-trees, to boil it down to *Jagory* (**Jaggery**), and to distil it into spirituous liquors; but they are also very diligent as cultivators, porters, and cutters of firewood."—*Buchanan, Mysore*, ii. 415; and see *Logan, Malabar*, i. 110, 142.]

TOBACCO, s. On this subject we are not prepared to furnish any elaborate article, but merely to bring together a few quotations touching on the introduction of tobacco into India and the East, or otherwise of interest.

[? c. 1550.—". . . Abū Kīr would carry the cloth to the market-street and sell it, and with its price buy meat and vegetables and **tobacco**. . . ."—*Burton, Arab. Nights*, vii. 210. The only mention in the *Nights* and the insertion of some scribe.]

,, "It has happened to me several times, that going through the provinces of Guatemala and Nicaragua I have entered the house of an Indian who had taken this herb, which in the Mexican language is called **tabacco**, and immediately perceived the sharp fetid smell of this truly diabolical and stinking smoke, I was obliged to go away in haste, and seek some other place." —*Girolamo Benzoni*, Hak. Soc. p. 81. [The word *tabaco* is from the language of Hayti, and meant, first, the pipe, secondly, the plant, thirdly, the sleep which followed its use (*Mr. J. Platt*, 9 ser. *N. & Q.* viii. 322).]

1585.—"Et hi" (viz. Ralph Lane and the first settlers in Virginia) "reduces Indicam illam plantam quam **Tabaccam** vocant et *Nicotiam*, qua contra cruditates ab Indis edocti, usi erant, in Angliam primi, quod suam, intulerunt. Ex illo sane tempore usu cöepit esse creberrimo, et magno pretio, dum quam plurimi graveolentem illius fumum, alii lascivientes, alii valetudini consulentes, per tubulum testaceum inexplebili aviditate passim hauriunt, et mox e naribus efflant; adeo ut tabernae **Tabaccanae** non minus quam cervisiariae et vinariae passim per oppida habeantur. Ut Anglorum corpora (quod salse ille dixit) qui hac plantâ tantopere delectantur in Barbarorum naturam degenerasse videantur; quum iisdem quibus Barbari delectentur et sanari se posse credant." — *Gul. Camdeni, Annal. Rerum Anglicanum* . . . regn. *Elizabetha*, ed. 1717, ii. 449.

1592.—

"Into the woods thence forth in haste shee went
To seeke for hearbes that mote him remedy;
For shee of herbes had great intendiment,
Taught of the Nymphe which from her infancy
Her nourced had in true Nobility:
This whether yt divine **Tobacco** were,
Or Panachaea, or Polygony,
Shee fownd, and brought it to her patient deare
Who al this while lay bleding out his hart-blood neare."
The Faerie Queen, III. v. 32.

1597.—"His Lordship" (E. of Essex at Villafranca) "made no answer, but called for **tobacco**, seeming to give but small credit to this alarm; and so on horseback, with these noblemen and gentlemen on foot beside him, took **tobacco**, whilst I was telling his Lordship of the men I had sent forth, and the order I had given them. Within some quarter of an hour, we might hear a good round volley of shot betwixt the 30 men I had sent to the chapel, and the enemy, which made his Lordship cast his pipe from him, and listen to the shooting." —*Commentaries of Sir Francis Vere*, p. 62.

1598. — "*Cob.* Ods me I marle what pleasure or felicity they have in taking this roguish **tobacco**. It is good for nothing but to choke a man, and fill him full of smoke and embers: there were four died out of one house last week with taking of it, and two more the bell went for yesternight; one of them they say will never scape it; he voided a bushel of soot yesterday upward and downward . . . its little better than rats-bane or rosaker."—*Every Man in his Humour*, iii. 2.

1604.—"Oct. 19. Demise to Tho. Lane and Ph. Bold of the new Impost of 6*s.* 8*d.*, and the old Custom of 2*d.* per pound on **tobacco**." — *Calendar of State Papers, Domestic*, James I., p. 159.

1604 or 1605.—"In Bijápúr I had found some **tobacco**. Never having seen the like in India, I brought some with me, and prepared a handsome pipe of jewel work. . . . His Majesty (Akbar) was enjoying himself after receiving my presents, and asking me how I had collected so many strange things in so short a time, when his eye fell upon the tray with the pipe and its appurtenances: he expressed great surprise and examined the **tobacco**, which was made up in pipefuls; he inquired what it was, and where I had got it. The Nawab Khán-i-'Azam replied: 'This is **tobacco**, which is well known in Mecca and Medina, and this doctor has brought it as a medicine for your Majesty.' His Majesty looked at it, and ordered me to prepare and take him a pipeful. He began to smoke it, when his physician approached and forbade his doing so" . . . (omitting much that is curious). "As I had brought a large supply of tobacco and pipes, I sent some to several of the nobles, while others sent to ask for some; indeed all, without exception, wanted some, and the practice was introduced. After that the merchants began to sell it, so the custom of smoking spread rapidly."—*Asad Beg*, in *Elliot*, vi. 165-167.

1610. — "The *Turkes* are also incredible takers of Opium . . . carrying it about with them both in peace and in warre; which they say expelleth all feare, and makes them couragious; but I rather think giddy headed. . . . And perhaps for the self same cause they also delight in **Tobacco**; they take it through reeds that have ioyned vnto them great heads of wood to containe it: I doubt not but lately taught them, as brought them by the English: and were it not sometimes lookt into (for *Morat Bassa* not long since commanded a pipe to be thrust through the nose of a *Turke*, and so to be led in derision through the Citie,) no question but it would prove a principall commodity. Neverthelesse they will take it in corners, and are so ignorant therein, that that which in England is not saleable, doth passe here amongst them for most excellent."—*Sandys, Journey*, 66.

1615.—"Il **tabacco** ancora usano qui" (at Constantinople) "di pigliar in conversazione per gusto: ma io non ho voluto mai provarne, e ne avera cognizione in Italia che molti ne pigliano, ed in particolare il signore cardinale Crescenzio qualche volta per medicamento insegnatogli dal Signor don Virginio Orsino, che primo di tutti, se io non fallo, gli anni addietro lo portò in Roma d'Inghilterra."—*P. della Valle*, i. 76.

1616. — "Such is the miraculous omnipotence of our strong tasted **Tobacco**, as it cures al sorts of diseases (which neuer any drugge could do before) in all persons and at all times. . . . It cures the gout in the feet and (which is miraculous) in that very instant when the smoke thereof, as light, flies vp into the head, the virtue thereof, as heauy, runs down to the litle toe. It helps all sorts of agues. It refreshes a weary man, and yet makes a man hungry. Being taken when they goe to bed, it makes one sleepe soundly, and yet being taken when a man is sleepie and drousie, it will, as they say, awake his braine, and quicken his vnderstanding. . . . O omnipotent power of **Tobacco!** And if it could by the smoake thereof chase out deuils, as the smoake of *Tobias* fish did (which I am sure could smell no stronglier) it would serve for a precious Relicke, both for the Superstitious Priests, and the insolent Puritanes, to cast out deuils withall."—*K. James I., Counterblaste to Tobacco*, in *Works*, pp. 219-220.

1617. — "As the smoking of tobacco (**tambákú**) had taken very bad effect upon the health and mind of many persons, I ordered that no one should practise the habit. My brother Sháh 'Abbás, also being aware of its evil effects, had issued a command against the use of it in Irán. But Khán-i-'Alam was so much addicted to smoking, that he could not abstain from it, and often smoked."—*Memoirs of Jahángír*, in *Elliot*, v. 351. See the same passage rendered by *Blochmann*, in *Ind. Antiq.* i. 164.

1623.—"Incipit nostro seculo in immensum crescere usus **tobacco**, atque afficit homines occulta quidem delectatione, ut qui illi semel assueti sint, difficile postea abstinent."—*Bacon, H. Vitae et Mortis*, in *B. Montague's* ed. x. 189.

We are unable to give the date or Persian author of the following extract (though clearly of the 17th century), which with an introductory sentence we have found in a fragmentary note in the handwriting of the late Major William Yule, written in India about the beginning of last century: *

"Although **Tobacco** be the produce of an European Plant, it has nevertheless been in use by our Physicians medicinally for some time past. Nay, some creditable People even have been friendly to the use of it, though from its having been brought sparingly in the first instance from Europe, its rarity prevented it from coming into general use. The Culture of this Plant, however, became speedily almost universal, within a short period after its introduction into Hindostaun; and the produce of it rewarded the Cultivator far beyond every other article of Husbandry. This became more especially the case in the reign of Shah Jehaun (commenced A.H. 1037) when the Practice of Smoking pervaded all Ranks and Classes within the Empire. Nobles and Beggars, Pious and Wicked, Devotees and Free-thinkers, poets, historians, rhetoricians, doctors and patients, high and low, rich and poor, all! all seemed intoxicated with a decided preference over every other luxury, nay even often over the necessaries of life. To a stranger no offering was so acceptable as a Whiff, and to a friend one could produce nothing half so grateful as a **Chillum**. So rooted was the habit that the confirmed Smoker would abstain from Food and Drink rather than relinquish the gratification he derived from inhaling the Fumes of this deleterious Plant! Nature recoils at the very idea of touching the Saliva of another Person, yet in the present instance our Tobacco smokers pass the moistened Tube from one mouth to another without hesitation on the one hand, and it is received with complacency on the other! The more acrid the Fumes so much the more grateful to the Palate of the Connoisseur. The Smoke is a Collyrium to the Eyes, whilst the Fire, they will tell you, supplies to the Body the waste of radical Heat. Without doubt the **Hookah** is a most pleasing Companion, whether to the Wayworn Traveller or to the solitary Hermit. It is a Friend in whose Bosom we may repose our most confidential Secrets; and a Counsellor upon whose advice we may rely in our most important Concerns. It is an elegant Ornament in our private Appartments: it gives joy to the Beholder in our public Halls. The Music of its sound puts the warbling of the Nightingale to Shame, and the Fragrance of its Perfume brings a Blush on the Cheek of the Rose. Life in short is prolonged by the Fumes inhaled at each inspiration, whilst every expiration of them is accompanied with extatic delight. . . ."—(*cætera desunt*).

c. 1760.—"**Tambákú**. It is known from the *Maásir-i-Rahími* that the **tobacco** came from Europe to the Dakhin, and from the Dakhin to Upper India, during the reign of Akbar Sháh (1556-1605), since which time it has been in general use."—*Bahár-i'-Ajam*, quoted by *Blochmann*, in *Ind. Antiq.* i. 164.

1878.—It appears from Miss Bird's *Japan* that tobacco was not cultivated in that country till 1605. In 1612 and 1615 the Shogun prohibited both culture and use of **tabako**. — See the work, i. 276-77. [According to Mr. Chamberlain (*Things Japanese*, 3rd ed. p. 402) by 1651 the law was so far relaxed that smoking was permitted, but only out-of-doors.]

TOBRA, s. Hind. *tobrā*, [which, according to Platts, is Skt. *protha*, 'nose of a horse,' inverted]. The leather nose-bag in which a horse's feed is administered. "In the Nerbudda valley, in Central India, the women wear a profusion of toe-rings, some standing up an inch high. Their shoes are consequently curiously shaped, and are called **tobras**" (*M.-Gen. R. H.*

* Some notice of Major Yule, whose valuable Oriental MSS. were presented to the British Museum after his death, will be found in Dr. Rieu's Preface to the *Catalogue of Persian MSS.* (vol. iii. p. xviii.).

Keatinge). As we should say, 'buckets.' [The use of the nosebag is referred to by Sir T. Herbert (ed. 1634): "The horses (of the Persians) feed usually of barley and chopt-straw put into a bag, and fastened about their heads, which implyes the manger." Also see **TURA**.]

1808.—". . . stable-boys are apt to serve themselves to a part out of the poor beasts allowance; to prevent which a thrifty housewife sees it put into a **tobra**, or mouth bag, and spits thereon to make the Hostler loathe and leave it alone."—*Drummond, Illustrations*, &c.

[1875.—"One of the horsemen dropped his **tobra** or nose-bag."—*Drew, Jummoo*, 240.]

TODDY, s. A corruption of Hind. *tāṛī, i.e.* the fermented sap of the *tāṛ* or palmyra, Skt. *tāla*, and also of other palms, such as the date, the coco-palm, and the *Caryota urens;* palm-wine. *Toddy* is generally the substance used in India as yeast, to leaven bread. The word, as is well known, has received a new application in Scotland, the immediate history of which we have not traced. The *tāla*-tree seems to be indicated, though confusedly, in this passage of Megasthenes from Arrian:

c. B.C. 320.—"Megasthenes tells us . . . the Indians were in old times nomadic . . . were so barbarous that they wore the skins of such wild animals as they could kill, and subsisted (?) on the bark of trees; that these trees were called in the Indian speech **tala**, and that there grew on them as there grows at the tops of the (date) palm trees, a fruit resembling balls of wool."—*Arrian, Indica*, vii., tr. by McCrindle.

c. 1330.—". . . There is another tree of a different species, which . . . gives all the year round a white liquor, pleasant to drink, which tree is called **tari**." — *Fr. Jordanus*, 16.

[1554.—"There is in Gujaret a tree of the palm-tribe, called **tari** agadji (millet tree). From its branches cups are suspended, and when the cut end of a branch is placed into one of these vessels, a sweet liquid, something of the nature of **arrack**, flows out in a continuous stream . . . and presently changes into a most wonderful wine."—*Travels of Sidi Ali Reïs, trans. A. Vambéry*, p. 29.]

[1609-10. — "**Tarree**." See under **SURA**.]

1611.—"Palmiti Wine, which they call **Taddy**."—*N. Downton*, in *Purchas*, i. 298.

[1614.—"A sort of wine that distilleth out of the Palmetto trees, called **Tadie**."—*Foster, Letters*, iii. 4.]

1615.—
". . . And then more to glad yee
Weele have a health to al our friends in
Tadee."
Verses to T. Coryat, in *Crudities*, iii. 47.

1623.—". . . on board of which we stayed till nightfall, entertaining with conversation and drinking **tari**, a liquor which is drawn from the coco-nut trees, of a whitish colour, a little turbid, and of a somewhat rough taste, though with a blending in sweetness, and not unpalatable, something like one of our *vini piccanti*. It will also intoxicate, like wine, if drunk over freely."—*P. della Valle*, ii. 530; [Hak. Soc. i. 62].

[1634.—"The **Toddy**-tree is like the Date of Palm; the Wine called **Toddy** is got by wounding and piercing the Tree, and putting a Jar or Pitcher under it, so as the Liquor may drop into it."—*Sir T. Herbert*, in *Harris*, i. 408.]

1648.—"The country . . . is planted with palmito-trees, from which a sap is drawn called **Terry**, that they very commonly drink."—*Van Twist*, 12.

1653.—". . . le **tari** qui est le vin ordinaire des Indes."—*De la Boullaye-le-Gouz*, 246.

1673.—"The Natives singing and roaring all Night long; being drunk with **Toddy**, the Wine of the Cocoe."—*Fryer*, 53.

,, "As for the rest, they are very respectful, unless the Seamen and Soldiers get drunk, either with **Toddy** or Bang."—*Ibid.* 91.

1686.—"Besides the Liquor or Water in the Fruit, there is also a sort of Wine drawn from the Tree called **Toddy**, which looks like Whey."—*Dampier*, i. 293.

1705.—". . . cette liqueur s'appelle **tarif**."—*Luillier*, 43.

1710.—This word was in common use at Madras.—*Wheeler*, ii. 125.

1750. — "*J.* Was vor Leute trincken **Taddy**? *C.* Die Soldaten, die Land Portugiesen, die Parreier (see **PARIAH**) und Schiffleute trincken diesen **Taddy**."—*Madras, oder Fort St. George*, &c., Halle, 1750.

1857.—"It is the unfermented juice of the Palmyra which is used as food: when allowed to ferment, which it will do before midday, if left to itself, it is changed into a sweet, intoxicating drink called 'kal' or '**toddy**.'"—*Bp. Caldwell, Lectures on Tinnevelly Mission*, p. 33.

¶ "The Rat, returning home full of **Toddy**, said, If I meet the Cat, I will tear him in pieces."—Ceylon Proverb, in *Ind. Antiq.* i. 59.

Of the Scotch application of the word we can find but one example in Burns, and, strange to say, no mention in Jameson's Dictionary:

1785.—
"The lads an' lasses, blythely bent
To mind baith saul an' body,
Sit round the table, weel content
An' steer about the **toddy**. . . ."
Burns, The Holy Fair.

1798.—"Action of the case, for giving her a dose in some **toddy**, to intoxicate and inflame her passions."—*Roots's Reports*, i. 80.

1804.—
". . . I've nae fear for't;
For siller, faith, ye ne'er did care for't,
Unless to help a needful body,
An' get an antrin glass o' **toddy**."
Tannahill, Epistle to James Barr.

TODDY-BIRD, s. We do not know for certain what bird is meant by this name in the quotation. The nest would seem to point to the **Baya**, or Weaver-bird (*Ploceus Baya*, Blyth): but the *size* alleged is absurd; it is probably a blunder. [Another bird, the *Artamus fuscus*, is, according to Balfour (*Cycl.* s.v.) called the **toddy** shrike.]

[1673.—"For here is a Bird (having its name from the Tree it chuses for its Sanctuary, the **toddy-tree**). . . ."—*Fryer*, 76.]

c. 1750-60.—"It is in this tree (see **PALMYRA, BRAB**) that the **toddy-birds**, so called from their attachment to that tree, make their exquisitely curious nests, wrought out of the thinnest reeds and filaments of branches, with an inimitable mechanism, and are about the bigness of a partridge (?) The birds themselves are of no value. . . ."—*Grose*, i. 48.

TODDY-CAT, s. This name is in S. India applied to the *Paradoxurus Musanga*, Jerdon: [the *P. niger*, the Indian Palm-Civet of Blanford (*Mammalia*, 106).] It infests houses, especially where there is a ceiling of cloth (see **CHUTT**). Its name is given for its fondness, real or supposed, for palm-juice.

[**TOKO**, s. Slang for 'a thrashing.' The word is imper. of Hind. *ṭoknā*, 'to censure, blame,' and has been converted into a noun on the analogy of **bunnow** and other words of the same kind.

[1823.—"**Toco** *for yam*—Yams are food for negroes in the W. Indies . . . and if, instead of receiving his proper ration of these, blackee gets a whip (**toco**) about his back, why 'he has caught **toco**' instead of yam."—*John Bee, Slang Dict.*

[1867.—"**Toko for Yam.** An expression peculiar to negroes for crying out before being hurt."—*Smyth, Sailor's Word-Book*, s.v.]

TOLA, s. An Indian weight (chiefly of gold or silver), not of extreme antiquity. Hind. *tolā*, Skt. *tulā*, 'a balance,' *tul*, 'to lift up, to weigh.' The Hindu scale is 8 *rattīs* (see **RUTTEE**)=1 *māsha*, 12 *māshas*= 1 *tolā*. Thus the *tolā* was equal to 96 *rattīs*. The proper weight of the *rattī*, which was the old Indian unit of weight, has been determined by Mr. E. Thomas as 1·75 grains, and the medieval *tanga* which was the prototype of the rupee was of 100 *rattīs* weight. "But . . . the factitious *rattī* of the Muslims was merely an aliquot part—$\frac{1}{96}$ of the comparatively recent *tola*, and $\frac{1}{92}$ of the newly devised *rupee*." By the Regulation VII. of 1833, putting the British India coinage on its present footing (see under **SEER**) the *tolā* weighing 180 grs., which is also the weight of the rupee, is established by the same Regulation, as the unit of the system of weights, 80 *tolas*=1 *ser*, 40 *sers*=1 **Maund**.

1563.—"I knew a secretary of Nizamoxa (see **NIZAMALUCO**), a native of Coraçon, who ate every day three **tollas** (of opium), which is the weight of ten cruzados and a half; but this Coraçoni (*Khorasānī*), though he was a man of letters and a great scribe and official, was always nodding or sleeping."—*Garcia*, f. 155*b*.

1610.—"A **Tole** is a rupee *challany* of silver, and ten of these **Toles** are the value of one of gold."—*Hawkins*, in *Purchas*, i. 217.

1615-16.—"Two **tole** and a half being an ounce."—*Sir T. Roe*, in *Purchas*, i. 545; [Hak. Soc. i. 183].

1676.—"Over all the Empire of the Great *Mogul*, all the Gold and Silver is weigh'd with Weights, which they call **Tolla**, which amounts to 9 deniers and eight grains of our weight."—*Tavernier*, E.T. ii. 18; [ed. *Ball*, i. 14].

TOMAUN, s. A Mongol word, signifying 10,000, and constantly used in the histories of the Mongol dynasties for a division of an army theoretically consisting of that number. But its modern application is to a Persian money, at the present time worth about 7*s.* 6*d.* [In 1899 the exchange was about 53 **crans** to the £1; 10 *Crans*=1 tumān.] Till recently it was only a money of account, representing 10,000 *dīnārs*; the latter also having been in Persia for centuries only a money of account, constantly degenerating in value. The tomaun in Fryer's time (1677) is reckoned by him as equal to £3, 6*s.* 8*d.* P. della Valle's estimate 60 years earlier would give about £4, 10*s.* 0*d.*, and is perhaps loose and too high. Sir T. Herbert's valuation (5 × 13*s.* 8*d.*) is the same as Fryer's. In the first and third of the following quotations we have the word in the Tartar military sense, for a division of 10,000 men :

1298.—"You see when a Tartar prince goes forth to war, he takes with him, say, 100,000 horse . . . they call the corps of 100,000 men a *Tuc;* that of 10,000 they call a **Toman.**"—*Marco Polo*, Bk. i. ch. 54.

c. 1340. — "Ces deux portions réunies formaient un total de 800 **toumans,** dont chacun vaut 10,000 **dinars** courants, et le **dinar** 6 dirhems."—*Shihābuddīn, Masālak-al Abṣār*, in *Not. et Exts.* xiii. 194.

c. 1347.—"I was informed . . . that when the Kān assembled his troops, and called the array of his forces together, there were with him 100 divisions of horse, each composed of 10,000 men, the chief of whom was called Amīr **Tumān,** or lord of 10,000."—*Ibn Batuta*, iv. 299-300.

A form of the Tartar word seems to have passed into Russian :

c. 1559.—"One thousand in the language of the people is called *Tissutze:* likewise ten thousand in a single word **Tma:** twenty thousand *Duue***tma**: thirty thousand *Tri***tma.**"—*Herberstein, Della Moscovia, Ramusio,* iii. 159.

[c. 1590.—In the Sarkár of Kandahár "eighteen **dinárs** make a **tumán,** and each tumán is equivalent to 800 dáms. The tumán of Khurasán is equal in value to 30 rupees and the tumán of Irák to 40."—*Āīn*, ed. *Jarrett*, ii. 393-94.]

1619. — "L'ambasciadore Indiano . . . ordinò che donasse a tutti un **tomano,** cioè dieci zecchini per uno."—*P. della Valle*, ii. 22.

c. 1630.—"But how miserable so ere it seemes to others, the Persian King makes many happy harvests; filling every yeere his insatiate coffers with above 350,000 **Tomans** (a **Toman** is five markes sterlin)."—*Sir T. Herbert*, p. 225.

[c. 1665.—In Persia "the abási is worth 4 sháhis, and the **tomán** 50 *abásis* or 200 *sháhis.*"—*Tavernier*, ed. *Ball*, i. 24.]

1677. — ". . . Receipt of Custom (at Gombroon) for which he pays the King yearly Twenty-two thousand **Thomands,** every **Thomand** making Three pound and a Noble in our Accompt, Half which we have a Right to."—*Fryer*, 222.

1711.—"Camels, Houses, &c., are generally sold by the **Tomand,** which is 200 Shahees or 50 Abassees; and they usually reckon their Estates that way; such a man is worth so many **Tomands,** as we reckon by Pounds in England."—*Lockyer*, 229.

[1858.—"Girwur Singh, **Tomandar,** came up with a detachment of the special police."—*Sleeman, Journey through Oudh*, ii. 17.]

TOMBACK, s. An alloy of copper and zinc, *i.e.* a particular modification of brass, formerly imported from Indo-Chinese countries. Port. *tambaca*, from Malay *tămbaga* and *tămbaga*, 'copper,' which is again from Skt. *tamṛika* and *tāmra*.

1602.—"Their drummes are huge pannes made of a metall called **Tombaga,** which makes a most hellish sound."—*Scott, Discourse of Iaua*, in *Purchas*, i. 180.

1690.—"This **Tombac** is a kind of Metal, whose scarcity renders it more valuable than Gold. . . . 'Tis thought to be a kind of natural Compound of Gold, Silver, and Brass, and in some places the mixture is very Rich, as at *Borneo*, and the *Moneilloes*, in others more allayed, as at Siam."—*Ovington*, 510.

1759.—"The *Productions* of this *Country* (Siam) are prodigious quantities of Grain, Cotton, Benjamin . . . and **Tambanck.**"—In *Dalrymple*, i. 119.

TOM-TOM, s. *Ṭamṭam*, a native drum. The word comes from India, and is chiefly used there. Forbes (*Rās-Mālā*, ii. 401) [ed. 1878, p. 665] says the thing is so called because used by criers who beat it *tām-tām*, 'place by place,' *i.e.* first at one place, then at another. But it is rather an *onomatopoeia*, not belonging to any language in particular. In Ceylon it takes the form *tamaṭṭama*, in Tel. *tappeta*, in Tam. *tambaṭṭam;* in Malay it is *toṅtoṅ*, all with the same meaning. [When badminton was introduced at Satāra natives called it *Ṭamṭam phūl khel*, *ṭam-ṭam* meaning 'battledore,' and the shuttlecock looked like a flower (*phūl*). Tommy Atkins promptly turned this into "*Tom Fool*" (*Calcutta Rev.* xcvi. 346).] In French the word *tamtam* is used, not for a drum of any kind, but for a Chinese **gong** (q.v.). M. Littré, however, in the Supplement to his Dict., remarks that this use is erroneous.

1693. — "It is ordered that to-morrow morning the **Choultry** Justices do cause the **Tom Tom** to be beat through all the Streets of the Black Town. . . ."—In *Wheeler*, i. 268.

1711. — "Their small Pipes, and **Tom Toms,** instead of Harmony made the Discord the greater."—*Lockyer*, 235.

1755.—In the Calcutta Mayor's expenses we find :

"**Tom Tom,** R. 1 1 0."—In *Long*, 56.

1764.—"You will give strict orders to the Zemindars to furnish Oil and Musshauls, and **Tom Toms** and Pikemen, &c., according to custom."—*Ibid.* 391.

1770.—"... An instrument of brass which the Europeans lately borrowed from the Turks to add to their military music, and which is called a **tam**" (!).—*Abbé Raynal*, tr. 1777, i. 30.

1789.—"An harsh kind of music from a **tom-tom** or drum, accompanied by a loud rustic pipe, sounds from different parties throughout the throng. . . ."—*Munro, Narrative*, 73.

1804. — "I request that they may be hanged; and let the cause of their punishment be published in the bazar by beat of **tom-tom**."—*Wellington*, iii. 186.

1824. — "The Mahrattas in my vicinity kept up such a confounded noise with the **tamtams**, cymbals, and pipes, that to sleep was impossible."—*Seely, Wonders of Ellora*, ch. iv.

1836.—For the use of the word by Dickens, see under **GUM-GUM**.

1862. — "The first musical instruments were without doubt percussive sticks, calabashes, **tomtoms**."—*Herbert Spencer, First Principles*, 356.

1881.—"The **tom-tom** is ubiquitous. It knows no rest. It is content with depriving man of his. It selects by preference the hours of the night as the time for its malign influence to assert its most potent sway. It reverberates its dull unmeaning monotones through the fitful dreams which sheer exhaustion brings. It inspires delusive hopes by a brief lull only to break forth with refreshed vigour into wilder ecstacies of maniacal fury—accompanied with nasal incantations and protracted howls. . . ."—*Overland Times of India*, April 14.

TONGA, s. A kind of light and small two-wheeled vehicle, Hind. *tāngā*, [Skt. *tamanga*, 'a platform']. The word has become familiar of late years, owing to the use of the *tonga* in a modified form on the roads leading up to Simla, Darjeeling, and other hill-stations. [Tavernier speaks of a carriage of this kind, but does not use the word:

[c. 1665.—"They have also, for travelling, small, very light, carriages which contain two persons; but usually one travels alone . . . to which they harness a pair of oxen only. These carriages, which are provided, like ours, with curtains and cushions, are not slung. . . ."—*Tavernier*, ed. *Ball*, i. 44.]

1874.—"The villages in this part of the country are usually superior to those in Poona or Sholápur, and the people appear to be in good circumstances. . . . The custom too, which is common, of driving light **Tongas** drawn by ponies or oxen points to the same conclusion."—*Settlement Report of Násik*.

1879.—"A **tongha** dák has at last been started between Rajpore and Dehra. The first tongha took only 5½ hours from Rajpore to Saharunpore."—*Pioneer Mail*.

1880.—"In the (*Times*) of the 19th of April we are told that 'Syud Mahomed Padshah has repulsed the attack on his fort instigated by certain *moolahs* of **tonga** *dâk*.' . . . Is the relentless **tonga** a region of country or a religious organization? . . . The original telegram appears to have contemplated a full stop after 'certain *moollahs*.' Then came an independent sentence about the **tonga** *dâk* working admirably between Peshawur and Jellalabad, but the sub-editor of the *Times*, interpreting the message referred to, made sense of it in the way we have seen, associating the ominous mystery with the *moollahs*, and helping out the other sentence with some explanatory ideas of his own."—*Pioneer Mail*, June 10.

1881. — "Bearing in mind Mr. Framji's extraordinary services, notably those rendered during the mutiny, and . . . that he is crippled for life . . . by wounds received while gallantly defending the mail **tonga** cart in which he was travelling, when attacked by dacoits. . . ."—Letter from *Bombay Govt. to Govt. of India*, June 17, 1881.

TONICATCHY, TUNNYKETCH, s. In Madras this is the name of the domestic water-carrier, who is generally a woman, and acts as a kind of under housemaid. It is a corr. of Tamil *tannir-kāssi*, *tannikkāriççi*, an abbreviation of *tannīr-kāsatti*, 'water-woman.'

c. 1780.—"'Voudriez-vous me permettre de faire ce trajet avec mes gens et mes bagages, qui ne consistent qu'en deux malles, quatre caisses de vin, deux ballots de toiles, et deux femmes, dont l'une est ma cuisinière, et l'autre, ma **tannie karetje** ou porteuse d'eau.'"—*Haafner*, i. 242.

1792.—"The Armenian . . . now mounts a bit of blood . . . and . . . dashes the mud about through the streets of the *Black Town*, to the admiration and astonishment of the **Tawny-kertches**."—*Madras Courier*, April 26.

TONJON, and vulg. **TOMJOHN**, s. A sort of sedan or portable chair. It is (at least in the Bengal Presidency) carried like a palankin by a single pole and four bearers, whereas a **jompon** (q.v.), for use in a hilly country, has two poles like a European sedan, each pair of bearers bearing it by a stick between the poles, to which the latter are slung. We cannot tell what the origin of this word is, nor explain the etymology given by Williamson below, unless it is intended for *thām-jāngh*, which *might* mean 'support-thigh.' Mr. Platts gives as forms in Hind. *tāmjhām* and *thāmjān*. The word is perhaps adopted from some trans-gangetic language. A rude contrivance of this kind in Malabar is described by Col. Welsh under the name of a 'Tellicherry chair' (ii. 40).

c. 1804.—"I had a **tonjon**, or open palanquin, in which I rode."—*Mrs. Sherwood, Autobiog.* 283.

1810.—"About Dacca, Chittagong, Tipperah, and other mountainous parts, a very light kind of conveyance is in use, called a **taum-jaung**, *i.e.* 'a support to the feet.'"—*Williamson, V.M.* i. 322-23.

" "Some of the party at the tents sent a **tonjon**, or open chair, carried like a palankeen, to meet me."—*Maria Graham*, 166.

[1827.—"In accordance with Lady D'Oyly's earnest wish I go out every morning in her **tonjin**."—*Diary of Mrs. Fenton*, 100.]

1829.—"I had been conveyed to the hill in Hanson's **tonjon**, which differs only from a palanquin in being like the body of a gig with a head to it."—*Mem. of Col. Mountain*, 88.

[1832.—". . . I never seat myself in the palankeen or **thonjaun** without a feeling bordering on self-reproach. . . ."—*Mrs. Meer Hassan Ali, Observations*, i. 320.]

1839.—"He reined up his ragged horse, facing me, and dancing about till I had passed; then he dashed past me at full gallop, wheeled round, and charged my **tonjon**, bending down to his saddlebow, pretending to throw a lance, showing his teeth, and uttering a loud quack!"—*Letters from Madras*, 290.

[1849.—"We proceeded to Nawabgunge, the minister riding out with me, for some miles, to take leave, as I sat in my **tonjohn**."—*Sleeman, Journey through Oudh*, i. 2.]

TOOLSY, s. The holy Basil of the Hindus (*Ocimum sanctum*, L.), Skt. *tulsī* or *tulasī*, frequently planted in a vase upon a pedestal of masonry in the vicinity of Hindu temples or dwellings. Sometimes the ashes of deceased relatives are preserved in these domestic shrines. The practice is alluded to by Fr. Odoric as in use at Tana, near Bombay (see *Cathay*, i. 59, c. 1322); and it is accurately described by the later ecclesiastic quoted below. See also *Ward's Hindoos*, ii. 203. The plant has also a kind of sanctity in the Greek Church, and a character for sanitary value at least on the shores of the Mediterranean generally.

[c. 1650.—"They who bear the **tulasī** round the neck . . . they are Vaishnavas, and sanctify the world."—*Bhaktā Mālā*, in *H. H. Wilson's Works*, i. 41.]

1672.—"Almost all the Hindus . . . adore a plant like our *Basilico gentile*, but of more pungent odour. . . . Every one before his house has a little altar, girt with a wall half an ell high, in the middle of which they erect certain pedestals like little towers, and in these the shrub is grown. They recite their prayers daily before it, with repeated prostrations, sprinklings of water, &c. There are also many of these maintained at the bathing-places, and in the courts of the pagodas."—*P. Vincenzo Maria*, 300.

1673.—"They plaster Cow-dung before their Doors; and so keep themselves clean, having a little place or two built up a Foot Square of Mud, where they plant *Calaminth*, or (by them called) **Tulce**, which they worship every Morning, and tend with Diligence."—*Fryer*, 199.

1842.—"Veneram a planta chamada **Tulosse**, por dizerem é do pateo dos Deoses, e por isso é commun no pateo de suas casas, e todas as manhãs lhe vão tributar veneração."—*Annaes Maritimos*, iii. 453.

1872.—"At the head of the ghát, on either side, is a sacred **tulasi** plant . . . placed on a high pedestal of masonry."—*Govinda Samanta*, i. 18.

The following illustrates the esteem attached to Toolsy in S. Europe:

1885.—"I have frequently realised how much prized the basil is in Greece for its mystic properties. The herb, which they say grew on Christ's grave, is almost worshipped in the Eastern Church. On St. Basil's day women take sprigs of this plant to be blessed in church. On returning home they cast some on the floor of the house, to secure luck for the ensuing year. They eat a little with their household, and no sickness, they maintain, will attack them for a year. Another bit they put in their cupboard, and firmly believe that their embroideries and silken raiment will be free from the visitation of rats, mice, and moths, for the same period."—*J. T. Bent, The Cyclades*, p. 328.

TOOMONGONG, s. A Malay title, especially known as borne by one of the chiefs of Johōr, from whom the Island of Singapore was purchased. The Sultans of Johōr are the representatives of the old Mahommedan dynasty of Malacca, which took refuge in Johōr, and the adjoining islands (including Bintang especially), when expelled by Albuquerque in 1511, whilst the *Tumanggung* was a minister who had in Peshwa fashion appropriated the power of the Sultan, with hereditary tenure: and this chief now lives, we believe, at Singapore. Crawfurd says: "The word is most probably Javanese; and in Java is the title of a class of nobles, not of an office" (*Malay Dict.* s.v.)

[1774.—"Paid a visit to the Sultan . . . and Pangaram **Toomongong**. . . ."—*Diary* *of J. Herbert*, in *Forrest, Bombay Letters, Home Series*, ii. 438.

[1830.—"This (Bopáti), however, is rather a title of office than of mere rank, as these governors are sometimes **Tumúng'gungs**, *An'gebâis*, and of still inferior rank."—*Raffles, Java*, 2nd ed. i. 299.]

1884.—"Singapore had originally been purchased from two Malay chiefs; the Sultan and **Tumangong** of Johore. The former, when Sir Stamford Raffles entered into the arrangement with them, was the titular sovereign, whilst the latter, who held an hereditary office, was the real ruler."—*Cavenagh, Reminis. of an Indian Official*, 273.

TOON, TOON-WOOD, s. The tree and timber of the *Cedrela Toona*, Roxb. N.O. *Meliaceae*. Hind. *tun*, *tūn*, Skt. *tunna*. The timber is like a poor mahogany, and it is commonly used for furniture and fine joiner's work in many parts of India. It is identified by Bentham with the Red Cedar of N.S. Wales and Queensland (*Cedrela australis*, F. Mueller). See *Brandis, Forest Flora*, 73. A sp. of the same genus (*C. sinensis*) is called in Chinese *ch'un*, which looks like the same word.

[1798.—The tree first described by Sir W. Jones, *As. Res.* iv. 288.]

1810.—"The **toon**, or country mahogany, which comes from Bengal. . . ."—*Maria Graham*, 101.

1837.—"Rosellini informs us that there is an Egyptian harp at Florence, of which the wood is what is commonly called E. Indian mahogany (*Athenaeum*, July 22, 1837). This may be the *Cedrela* **Toona**."—*Royle's Hindu Medicine*, 30.

TOORKEY, s. A *Turkī* horse, *i.e.* from Turkestan. Marco Polo uses what is practically the same word for a horse from the Turcoman horse-breeders of Asia Minor.

1298.—". . . the Turcomans . . . dwell among mountains and downs where they find good pasture, for their occupation is cattle-keeping. Excellent horses, known as **Turquans**, are reared in their country. . . ."—*Marco Polo*, Bk. i. ch. 2.

[c. 1590.—"The fourth class (**Turkí**) are horses imported from Turán; though strong and well formed, they do not come up to the preceding (Arabs, Persian, Mujannas)."—*Áin*, i. 234.

[1663.—"If they are found to be **Turki** horses, that is from Turkistan or Tartary, and of a proper size and adequate strength, they are branded on the thigh with the King's mark. : . ."—*Bernier*, ed. *Constable*, 243.]

1678.—"Four horses bought for the Company—

	Pagodas.
One young Arab at . .	160
One old **Turkey** at . .	40
One old Atchein at . .	20
One of this country at . .	20
	240."

Ft. St. Geo. Consns., March 6, in *Notes and Exts.*, Madras, 1871.

1782.—"Wanted one or two Tanyans (see **TANGUN**) rising six years old, Wanted also a Bay **Toorkey**, or Bay *Tazzi* (see **TAZEE**) Horse for a Buggy. . . ."—*India Gazette*, Feb. 9.

" "To be disposed of at Ghyretty . . . a Buggy, almost new . . . a pair of uncommonly beautiful spotted **Toorkays**."—*Ibid.* March 2.

TOOTNAGUE, s. Port. *tutenaga*. This word appears to have two different applications. **a.** A Chinese alloy of copper, zinc, and nickel, sometimes called 'white copper' (*i.e. peh-tung* of the Chinese). The finest qualities are alleged to contain arsenic.* The best comes from Yunnan, and Mr. Joubert of the Garnier Expedition, came to the conclusion that it was produced by a direct mixture of the ores in the furnace (*Voyage d'Exploration*, ii. 160). **b.** It is used in Indian trade in the same loose way that *spelter* is used, for either *zinc* or *pewter* (*peh-yuen*, or 'white lead' of the Chinese). The base of the word is no doubt the Pers. *tūtiya*, Skt. *tuttha*, an oxide of zinc, generally in India applied to blue vitriol or sulphate of copper, but the formation of the word is obscure. Possibly the last syllable is merely an adjective affix, in which way *nāk* is used in Persian. Or it may be *nāga* in the sense of lead, which is one of the senses given by Shakespear. In one of the quotations given below, *tutenague* is confounded with *calin* (see **CALAY**). Moodeen Sheriff gives as synonyms for *zinc*, Tam. *tuttanāgam* [*tuttunāgam*], Tel. *tuttunāgam* [*tuttināgamu*], Mahr. and Guz. *tutti-nāga*. Sir G. Staunton is curiously wrong in supposing (as his mode of writing seems to imply) that *tutenague* is a Chinese word. [The word has been finally corrupted in

* *St. Julien et P. Champion, Industries Anciennes et Modernes de l'Empire Chinois*, 1869, p. 75. Wells Williams says: "The *peh-tung* argentan, or white copper of the Chinese, is an alloy of copper 40·4, zinc 25·4, nickel 31·6, and iron 2·6, and occasionally a little silver; and these proportions are nearly those of German silver."—*Middle Kingdom*, ed. 1883, ii. 19.

England into '*tooth and egg*' metal, as in a quotation below.]

1605.—"4500 Pikals (see **PECUL**) of *Tintenaga* (for **Tiutenaga**) or Spelter."—In *Valentijn*, v. 329.

1644.—"That which they export (from Cochin to Orissa) is pepper, although it is probibited, and all the drugs of the south, with Callaym (see **CALAY**), **Tutunaga**, wares of China and Portugal; jewelled ornaments; but much less nowadays, for the reasons already stated. . . ."—*Bocarro, MS.* f. 316.

1675.—" . . from thence with *Dollars* to *China* for *Sugar, Tea, Porcelane, Laccared Ware, Quicksilver*, **Tuthinag**, and Copper. . . ."—*Fryer*, 86.

[1676-7.—". . . supposing yor Honr may intend to send ye Sugar, Sugar-candy, and **Tutonag** for Persia. . . ."—*Forrest, Bombay Letters, Home Series*, i. 125.]

1679.—Letter from Dacca reporting . . . "that Dacca is not a good market for Gold, Copper, Lead, Tin or **Tutenague**."—*Ft. St. Geo. Consns.*, Oct. 31, in *Notes and Exts.* Madras, 1871.

[,, "In the list of commodities brought from the East Indies, 1678, I find among the drugs, tincal (see **TINCALL**) and **Toothanage** set doune. Enquire also what these are. . . ."—Letter of *Sir T. Browne*, May 29, in *N. & Q.* 2 ser. vii. 520.]

1727.—"Most of the Spunge in China had pernicious Qualities because the Subterraneous Grounds were stored with Minerals, as Copper, Quicksilver, Allom, **Toothenague**, &c."—*A. Hamilton*, ii. 223; [ed. 1744, ii. 222, for "Spunge" reading "Springs"].

1750.—"A sort of Cash made of **Toothenague** is the only Currency of the Country." —*Some Ac. of Cochin China*, by *Mr. Robert Kirsop*, in *Dalrymple, Or. Rep.* i. 245.

[1757.—Speaking of the freemen enrolled at Nottingham in 1757, Bailey (*Annals of Nottinghamshire*, iii. 1235) mentions as one of them William Tutin, buckle-maker, and then goes on to say: "It was a son of this latter person who was the inventor of that beautiful composite white metal, the introduction of which created such a change in numerous articles of ordinary table service in England. This metal, in honour of the inventor, was called **Tutinic**, but which word, by one of the most absurd perversions of language ever known, became transferred into '**Tooth and Egg**,' the name by which it was almost uniformly recognised in the shops."—Quoted in 2 ser. *N. & Q.* x. 144.]

1780.—"At Quedah, there is a trade for calin (see **CALAY**) or **tutenague** . . . to export to different parts of the Indies."—*Dunn, New Directory*, 5th ed. 338.

1797.—"**Tu-te-nag** is, properly speaking, zinc, extracted from a rich ore or calamine; the ore is powdered and mixed with charcoal dust, and placed in earthen jars over a slow fire, by means of which the metal rises in form of vapour, in a common distilling apparatus, and afterwards is condensed in water."—*Staunton's Acct. of Lord Macartney's Embassy*, 4to ed. ii. 540.

TOPAZ, TOPASS, &c., s. A name used in the 17th and 18th centuries for dark-skinned or half-caste claimants of Portuguese descent, and Christian profession. Its application is generally, though not universally, to soldiers of this class, and it is possible that it was originally a corruption of Pers. (from Turkish) *top-chī*, 'a gunner.' It may be a slight support to this derivation that Italians were employed to cast guns for the Zamorin at Calicut from a very early date in the 16th century, and are frequently mentioned in the annals of Correa between 1503 and 1510. Various other etymologies have however been given. That given by Orme below (and put forward doubtfully by Wilson) from *topī*, 'a hat,' has a good deal of plausibility, and even if the former etymology be the true *origin*, it is probable that this one was often in the minds of those using the term, as its true connotation. It may have some corroboration not only in the fact that Europeans are to this day often spoken of by natives (with a shade of disparagement) as **Topeewalas** (q.v.) or 'Hat-men,' but also in the pride commonly taken by all persons claiming European blood in wearing a hat; indeed Fra Paolino tells us that this class call themselves *gente de chapeo* (see also the quotation below from Ovington). Possibly however this was merely a misrendering of *topaz* from the assumed etymology. The same Fra Paolino, with his usual fertility in error, propounds in another passage that *topaz* is a corruption of *do-bhāshiya*, 'two-tongued' (in fact is another form of **Dubash**, q.v.), viz. using Portuguese and a debased vernacular (pp. 50 and 144). [The *Madras Gloss.* assumes Mal. *tópáshi* to be a corruption of **dubash**.] The *Topaz* on board ship is the sweeper, who is at sea frequently of this class.

1602.—"The 12th ditto we saw to seaward another *Champaigne* (**Sampan**) wherein were 20 men, Mestiços (see **MUSTEES**) and **Toupas**."—*Van Spilbergen's Voyage*, p. 34, pub. 1648.

[1672. — "**Toepasses**." See under **MADRAS**.]

1673.—"To the Fort then belonged 300 *English*, and 400 **Topazes**, or Portugal Firemen."—*Fryer*, 66. In his glossarial Index he gives "**Topazes**, Musketeers."

1680.—"It is resolved and ordered to entertain about 100 **Topasses**, or Black Portuguese, into pay."—In *Wheeler*, i. 121.

1686.—"It is resolved, as soon as English soldiers can be provided sufficient for the garrison, that all **Topasses** be disbanded, and no more entertained, since there is little dependence on them."—In *ditto*, 159.

1690.—"A Report spread abroad, that a Rich Moor Ship belonging to one *Abdal Ghaford*, was taken by *Hat-men*, that is, in their (the Moors) Dialect, Europeans."—*Ovington*, 411.

1705.—". . . **Topases**, qui sont des gens du pais qu'on élève et qu'on habille à la Françoise, lesquels ont esté instruits dans la Religion Catholique par quelques uns de nos Missionnaires."—*Luillier*, 45-46.

1711.—"The Garrison consists of about 250 Soldiers, at 91 Fanhams, or 1*l*. 2*s*. 9*d*. per Month, and 200 **Topasses**, or black Mungrel Portuguese, at 50, or 52 Fanhams per Month."—*Lockyer*, 14.

1727.—"Some Portuguese are called **Topasses** . . . will be served by none but Portuguese Priests, because they indulge them more and their Villany."—*A. Hamilton*, [ed. 1744, i. 326].

1745.—"Les Portugais et les autres Catholiques qu'on nomme Mestices (see **MUSTEES**) et **Topases**, également comme les naturels du Pays y viennent sans distinction pour assister aux Divins mystères."—*Norbert*, ii. 31.

1747.—"The officers upon coming in report their People in general behaved very well, and could not do more than they did with such a handful of men against the Force the Enemy had, being as they believe at least to be one thousand Europeans, besides **Topasses**, Coffrees (see **CAFFER**), and Seapoys (see **SEPOY**), altogether about Two Thousand (2000)."—*MS. Consns. at Ft. St. David*, March 1. (In India Office).

1749.—"600 effective *Europeans* would not have cost more than that Crowd of useless **Topasses** and *Peons* of which the Major Part of our Military has of late been composed."—In *A Letter to a Proprietor of the E.I. Co.* p. 57.

,, "The **Topasses** of which the major Part of the Garrison consisted, every one that knows *Madrass* knows it to be a black, degenerate, wretched Race of the antient *Portuguese*, as proud and bigotted as their Ancestors, lazy, idle, and vitious withal, and for the most Part as weak and feeble in Body as base in Mind, not one in ten possessed of any of the necessary Requisites of a Soldier."—*Ibid.* App. p. 103.

1756.—". . . in this plight, from half an hour after eleven till near two in the morning, I sustained the weight of a heavy man, with his knees on my back, and the pressure of his whole body on my head; a Dutch sergeant, who had taken his seat upon my left shoulder, and a **Topaz** bearing on my right."—*Holwell's Narr. of the Black Hole*, [ed. 1758, p. 19].

1758.—"There is a distinction said to be made by you . . . which, in our opinion, does no way square with rules of justice and equity, and that is the exclusion of Portuguese **topasses**, and other Christian natives, from any share of the money granted by the Nawab."—*Court's Letter*, in *Long*, 133.

c. 1785.—"**Topasses**, black foot soldiers, descended from Portuguese marrying natives, called **topasses** because they wear hats."—*Carraccioli's Clive*, iv. 564. The same explanation in *Orme*, i. 80.

1787.—". . . Assuredly the mixture of Moormen, Rajahpoots, Gentoos, and Malabars in the same corps is extremely beneficial. . . . I have also recommended the corps of **Topasses** or descendants of Europeans, who retain the characteristic qualities of their progenitors."—*Col. Fullarton's View of English Interests in India*, 222.

1789.—"**Topasses** are the sons of Europeans and black women, or low Portuguese, who are trained to arms."—*Munro, Narr.* 321.

1817.—"**Topasses**, or persons whom we may denominate Indo-Portuguese, either the mixed produce of Portuguese and Indian parents, or converts to the Portuguese, from the Indian, faith."—*J. Mill, Hist.* iii. 19.

TOPE, s. This word is used in three quite distinct senses, from distinct origins.

a. Hind. *top*, 'a cannon.' This is Turkish *tōp*, adopted into Persian and Hindustani. We cannot trace it further. [Mr. Platts regards T. *tob*, *top*, as meaning originally 'a round mass,' from Skt. *stūpa*, for which see below.]

b. A grove or orchard, and in Upper India especially a mango-orchard. The word is in universal use by the English, but is quite unknown to the natives of Upper India. It is in fact Tam. *tōppu*, Tel. *tōpu*, [which the *Madras Gloss.* derives from Tam. *togu*, 'to collect,'] and must have been carried to Bengal by foreigners at an early period of European traffic. But Wilson is curiously mistaken in supposing it to be in common use in Hindustan by natives. The word used by them is *bāgh*.

c. An ancient Buddhist monument in the form of a solid dome. The word *tōp* is in local use in the N.W. Punjab, where ancient monuments of this kind occur, and appears to come from Skt. *stūpa* through the Pali or

Prakrit *thūpo*. According to Sir H. Elliot (i. 505), *Stupa* in Icelandic signifies 'a Tower.' We cannot find it in Cleasby. The word was first introduced to European knowledge by Mr. Elphinstone in his account of the Tope of Manikyala in the Rawul Pindi district.

a.—

[1687. — "**Tope.**" See under **TOPE-KHANA**.

[1884.—"The big gun near the Central Museum of Lahor called the Zam-Zamah or Bhanjianvati **top**, seems to have held much the same place with the Sikhs as the Malik-i-Maidân held in Bijapur." — *Bombay Gazetteer*, xxiii. 642.]

b.—

1673.—". . . flourish pleasant **Tops** of Plantains, Cocoes, Guiavas."—*Fryer*, 40.

" "The Country is Sandy; yet plentiful in Provisions; in all places, **Tops** of Trees."—*Ibid*. 41.

1747.—"The **Topes** and Walks of Trees in and about the Bounds will furnish them with firewood to burn, and Clay for Bricks is almost everywhere."—*Report of a Council of War at Ft. St. David*, in *Consns*. of May 5, MS. in India Office.

1754.—"A multitude of People set to the work finished in a few days an entrenchment, with a stout mud wall, at a place called Facquire's **Tope**, or the grove of the Facquire."—*Orme*, i. 273.

1799.—"Upon looking at the **Tope** as I came in just now, it appeared to me, that when you get possession of the bank of the **Nullah**, you have the **Tope** as a matter of course."—*Wellington, Desp.* i. 23.

1809.—". . . behind that a rich country, covered with rice fields and **topes**."—*Ld. Valentia*, i. 557.

1814.—"It is a general practice when a plantation of mango trees is made, to dig a well on one side of it. The well and the **tope** are married, a ceremony at which all the village attends, and large sums are often expended."—*Forbes, Or. Mem.* iii. 56.

c.—

[1839.—"**Tope** is an expression used for a mound or barrow as far west as Peshawer. . . ."—*Elphinstone, Caubul*, 2nd ed. i. 108.]

TOPE-KHANA, s. The Artillery, Artillery Park, or Ordnance Department, Turco-Pers. *tōp-khāna*, 'cannon-house' or 'cannon-department.' The word is the same that appears so often in reports from Constantinople as the *Tophaneh*. Unless the traditions of Donna Tofana are historical, we are strongly disposed to suspect that *Aqua Tofana* may have had its name from this word.

1687.—"*The Toptchi*. These are Gunners, called so from the word *Tope*, which in Turkish signifies a Cannon, and are in number about 1200, distributed in 52 Chambers; their Quarters are at **Tophana**, or the place of Guns in the Suburbs of Constantinople."—*Rycaut's Present State of the Ottoman Empire*, p. 94.

1726. — "Isfandar Chan, chief of the Artillery (called the Daroger (see **DAROGA**) of the **Topscanna**)."—*Valentijn*, iv. (*Suratte*), 276.

1765.—"He and his troops knew that by the treachery of the **Tope Khonnah Droger** (see **DAROGA**), the cannon were loaded with powder only."—*Holwell, Hist. Events*, &c. i. 96.

TOPEE, s. A hat, Hind. *ṭopī*. This is sometimes referred to Port. *topo*, 'the top' (also *tope*, 'a top-knot,' and *topete*, a 'toupee'), which is probably identical with English and Dutch *top*, L. German *topp*, Fr. *topet*, &c. But there is also a simpler Hind. word *ṭop*, for a helmet or hat, and the quotation from the Roteiro Vocabulary seems to show that the word existed in India when the Portuguese first arrived. With the usual tendency to specialize foreign words, we find this word becomes specialized in application to the **sola** hat.

1498. — In the vocabulary ("*Este he a linguajem de Calicut*") we have: "barrete (*i.e.* a cap): **tupy**."—*Roteiro*, 118.

The following expression again, in the same work, seems to be Portuguese, and to refer to some mode in which the women's hair was dressed: "Trazem em a moleera huuns **topetes** por signall que sam Christãos."—*Ibid*. 52.

1849.—"Our good friend Sol came down in right earnest on the waste, and there is need of many a fold of twisted muslin round the white **topi**, to keep off his importunacy."—*Dry Leaves from Young Egypt*, 2.

1883.—"**Topee**, a solar helmet."—*Wills, Modern Persia*, 263.

TOPEEWALA, s. Hind. *ṭopīwālā*, 'one who wears a hat,' generally a European, or one claiming to be so. Formerly by Englishmen it was habitually applied to the dark descendants of the Portuguese. R. Drummond says that in his time (before 1808) *Topeewala* and **Puggry***wala* were used in Guzerat and the Mahratta country for 'Europeans' and 'natives.' [The S. Indian form is *Toppikār*.] The author of the Persian *Life of Hydur Naik* (Or. Tr. Fund, by Miles) calls

Europeans *Kalāh-posh*, *i.e.* 'hat-wearers' (p. 85).

1803.—"The descendants of the Portuguese . . . unfortunately the ideas of Christianity are so imperfect that the only mode they hit upon of displaying their faith is by wearing hats and breeches."—*Sydney Smith, Works*, 3d. ed. iii. 5.

[1826.—"It was now evident we should have to encounter the **Topee wallas**."—*Pandurang Hari*, ed. 1873, i. 71.]

1874.—". . . you will see that he will not be able to protect us. All **topiwálás** . . . are brothers to each other. The magistrates and the judge will always decide in favour of their white brethren."—*Govinda Samanta*, ii. 211.

TORCULL, s. This word occurs only in Castanheda. It is the Malayālam *tiru-koyil*, [Tam. *tiru*, Skt. *śri*, 'holy' *koyil*, 'temple']. See i. 253, 254; also the English Trans. of 1582, f. 151. In fact, in the 1st ed. of the 1st book of Castanheda *turcoll* occurs where *pagode* is found in subsequent editions. [*Tricalore* in S. Arcot is in Tam. *Tirukkoyilūr*, with the same meaning.]

TOSHACONNA, s. P.—H. *toshakhāna*. The repository of articles received as presents, or intended to be given as presents, attached to a government-office, or great man's establishment. The *tosha-khāna* is a special department attached to the Foreign Secretariat of the Government of India.

[1616.—"Now indeed the **atashckannoe** was become a right stage."—*Sir T. Roe*, Hak. Soc. ii. 300.]

[1742.—". . . the Treasury, Jewels, **toishik-khanna** . . . that belonged to the Emperor. . . ."—*Fraser, H. of Nadir Shah*, 173.]

1799.—"After the capture of Seringapatam, and before the country was given over to the Raja, some brass **swamies** (q.v.), which were in the **toshekanah** were given to the brahmins of different pagodas, by order of Macleod and the General. The prize-agents require payment for them."—*Wellington*, i. 56.

[1885.—"When money is presented to the Viceroy, he always 'remits' it, but when presents of jewels, arms, stuffs, horses, or other things of value are given him, they are accepted, and are immediately handed over to the **tosh khana** or Government Treasury. . . ."—*Lady Dufferin, Viceregal Life*, 75.]

TOSTDAUN, s. Military Hind. *tosdān* for a cartouche-box. The word appears to be properly Pers. *toshadān*, 'provision-holder,' a wallet.

[1841.—"This last was, however, merely '**tos-dan** *kee awaz*'—a cartouch-box report—as our sepoys oddly phrase a vague rumour."—*Society in India*, ii. 223.]

TOTY, s. Tam. *toṭṭi*, Canar. *toṭiga*, from Tam. *tondu*, 'to dig,' properly a low-caste labourer in S. India, and a low-caste man who in villages receives certain allowances for acting as messenger, &c., for the community, like the **gorayt** of N. India.

1730.—"Il y a dans chaque village un homme de service, appellé **Totti**, qui est chargé des impositions publiques."—*Lettr. Edif.* xiii. 371.

[1883.—"The name **Toty** being considered objectionable, the same officers in the new arrangements are called *Talaiaris* (see **TALIAR**) when assigned to Police, and *Vettians* when employed in Revenue duties."—*Le Fanu, Man. of Salem*, ii. 211.]

TOUCAN, s. This name is very generally misapplied by Europeans to the various species of Hornbill, formerly all styled *Buceros*, but now subdivided into various genera. Jerdon says: "They (the hornbills) are, indeed, popularly called Toucans throughout India; and this appears to be their name in some of the Malayan isles; the word signifying 'a worker,' from the noise they make." This would imply that the term did originally belong to a species of hornbill, and not to the S. American *Rhamphastes* or *Zygodactyle*. *Tukang* is really in Malay a 'craftsman or artificer'; but the dictionaries show no application to the bird. We have here, in fact, a remarkable instance of the coincidences which often justly perplex etymologists, or would perplex them if it were not so much their habit to seize on one solution and despise the others. Not only is *tukang* in Malay 'an artificer,' but, as Willoughby tells us, the Spaniards called the real S. American toucan '*carpintero*' from the noise he makes. And yet there seems no doubt that *Toucan* is a Brazilian name for a Brazilian bird. See the quotations, and especially Thevet's, with its date.

The Toucan is described by Oviedo (c. 1535), but he mentions only the name by which "the Christians" called it,—in Ramusio's Italian *Picuto* (?*Beccuto*; *Sommario*, in *Ramusio*, iii. f. 60). [Prof. Skeat (*Concise Dict.* s.v.) gives only the Brazilian derivation.

The question is still further discussed, without any very definite result, save that it is probably an imitation of the cry of the bird, in *N. & Q.* 9 ser. vii. 486 ; viii. 22, 67, 85, 171, 250.]

1556.—"Sur la coste de la marine, la plus frequête marchandise est le plumage d'vn oyseau, qu'ils appellent en leur langue **Toucan**, lequel descrivons sommairement puis qu'il vient à propos. Cest oyseau est de la grandeur d'vn pigeon. . . . Au reste cest oyseau est merveilleusement difforme et monstrueux, ayant le bec plus gros et plus long quasi que le reste du corps."—*Les Singularitez de la France Antarticque, autrement nommée Amerique. . . . Par T. André Theuet, Natif d'Angoulesme*, Paris, 1558, f. 91.

1648.—"**Tucana** sive **Toucan** Brasiliensibus: avis picae aut palumbi magnitudine. . . . Rostrum habet ingens et nonnumquam palmum longum, exterius flavam. . . . Mirum est autem videri possit quomodo tantilla avis tam grande rostrum ferat ; sed levissimum est." — *GeorgI MarcgravI de Liebstad, Hist. Rerum Natur. Brasiliae.* Lib. V. cap. xv., in *Hist. Natur. Brasil.* Lugd. Bat. 1648, p. 217.

See also (1599) *Aldrovandus, Ornitholog.* lib. xii. cap. 19, where the word is given **toucham**.

Here is an example of misapplication to the Hornbill, though the latter name is also given :

1885.—"Soopah (in N. Canara) is the only region in which I have met with the **toucan** or great hornbill. . . . I saw the comical looking head with its huge aquiline beak, regarding me through a fork in the branch ; and I account it one of the best shots I ever made, when I sent a ball . . . through the head just at its junction with the handsome orange-coloured helmet which surmounts it. Down came the **toucan** with outspread wings, dead apparently ; but when my peon Manoel raised him by the thick muscular neck, he fastened his great claws on his hand, and made the wood resound with a succession of roars more like a bull than a bird."—*Gordon Forbes, Wild Life in Canara*, &c. pp. 37-38.

TOWLEEA, s. Hind. *tauliyā*, 'a towel.' This is a corruption, however, not of the English form, but rather of the Port. *toalha* (*Panjab N. & Q.*, 1885, ii. 117).

TRAGA, s. [Molesworth gives "S. *trāgā*, Guz. *trāgu*"; *trāga* does not appear in Monier-Williams's Skt. Dict., and Wilson queries the word as doubtful. Dr. Grierson writes: "I cannot trace its origin back to Skt. One is tempted to connect it with the Skt. root *trai*, or *trā*, 'to protect,' but the termination *gā* presents difficulties which I cannot get over. One would expect it to be derived from some Skt. word like *trāka*, but no such word exists."] The extreme form of **dhurna** (q.v.) among the Rājputs and connected tribes, in which the complainant puts himself, or some member of his family, to torture or death, as a mode for bringing vengeance on the oppressor. The tone adopted by some persons and papers at the time of the death of the great Charles Gordon, tended to imply their view that his death was a kind of *traga* intended to bring vengeance on those who had sacrificed him. [For a case in Greece, see *Pausanias*, X. i. 6. Another name for this self-sacrifice is *Chandi*, which is perhaps Skt. *ćaṇḍa*, 'passionate' (see *Malcolm, Cent. India*, 2nd ed. ii. 137). Also compare the *jūhar* of the Rājputs (*Tod, Annals*, Calcutta reprint, i. 74). And for *Kūr*, see *As. Res.* iv. 357 *seqq.*]

1803.—A case of **traga** is recorded in Sir Jasper Nicoll's Journal, at the capture of Gawilgarh, by Sir A. Wellesley. See note to *Wellington*, ed. 1837, ii. 387.

1813.—"Every attempt to levy an assessment is succeeded by the **Tarakaw**, a most horrid mode of murdering themselves and each other."—*Forbes, Or. Mem.* ii. 91 ; [2nd ed. i. 378 ; and see i. 244].

1819.—For an affecting story of **Traga**, see *Macmurdo*, in *Bo. Lit. Soc. Trans.* i. 281.

[**TRANKEY**, s. A kind of boat used in the Persian Gulf and adjoining seas. All attempts to connect it with any Indian or Persian word have been unsuccessful. It has been supposed to be connected with the Port. *trincador*, a sort of flat-bottomed coasting vessel with a high stern, and with *trinquart*, a herring-boat used in the English Channel. Smyth (*Sailor's Word-book*, s.v.) has: "*Trankeh* or *Trankies*, a large boat of the Gulf of Persia." See *N. & Q.* 8 ser. vii. 167, 376.

[1554.—"He sent certain spies who went in **Terranquims** dressed as fishermen who caught fish inside the straits."—*Couto*, Dec. VI. Bk. x. ch. 20.

[c. 1750.—". . . he remained some years in obscurity, till an Arab **tranky** being driven in there by stress of weather, he made himself known to his countrymen. . . ."—*Grose*, 1st ed. 25.

[1753.—"Taghi Khan . . . soon after embarked a great number of men in small vessels." In the note **tarranquins**.—*Hanway*, iv. 181.

[1773.—"Accordingly we resolved to hire one of the common, but uncomfortable vessels of the Gulph, called a **Trankey**. . . ."—*Ives*, 203.]

TRANQUEBAR, n.p. A seaport of S. India, which was in the possession of the Danes till 1807, when it was taken by England. It was restored to the Danes in 1814, and purchased from them, along with Serampore, in 1845. The true name is said to be *Tarangambāḍi*, 'Sea-Town' or 'Wave-Town'; [so the *Madras Gloss.*; but in the *Man.* (ii. 216) it is interpreted 'Street of the Telegu people.']

1610.—"The members of the Company have petitioned me, that inasmuch as they do much service to God in their establishment at Negapatam, both among Portuguese and natives, and that there is a settlement of newly converted Christians who are looked after by the catechumens of the parish (**freguezia**) of **Trangabar**. . . ."—*King's Letter*, in *Livros das Monções*, p. 285.

[1683-4.—"This Morning the Portuguez ship that came from Vizagapatam Sailed hence for **Trangambar**."—*Pringle, Diary, Ft. St. Geo.* 1st ser. iii. 16.]

TRAVANCORE, n.p. The name of a village south of Trevandrum, from which the ruling dynasty of the kingdom which is known by the name has been called. The true name is said to be *Tiru-vidān-koḍu*, shortened to *Tiruvānkoḍu*. [The *Madras Gloss.* gives *Tiruvitānkūr*, *tiru*, Skt. *śrī*, 'the goddess of prosperity,' *vāzhu*, 'to reside,' *kūr*, 'part.']

[1514.—"As to the money due from the Raja of **Travamcor**. . . ."—*Albuquerque, Cartas*, p. 270.]

1553.—"And at the place called **Travancor**, where this Kingdom of Coulam terminates, there begins another Kingdom, taking its name from this very **Travancor**, the king of which our people call the *Rey Grande*, because he is greater in his dominion, and in the state which he keeps, than those other princes of Malabar; and he is subject to the King of **Narsinga**."—*Barros*, I. ix. 1.

1609.—"The said Governor has written to me that most of the kings adjacent to our State, whom he advised of the coming of the rebels, had sent replies in a good spirit, with expressions of friendship, and with promises not to admit the rebels into their ports, all but him of **Travancor**, from whom no answer had yet come."—*King of Spain's Letter*, in *Livros das Monções*, p. 257.

TRIBENY, n.p. Skt. *tri-veṇī*, 'threefold braid'; a name which properly belongs to Prayāga (Allahābād), where the three holy rivers, Ganges, Jumna, and (unseen) Sarasvatī are considered to unite. But local requirements have instituted another Tribeṇī in the Ganges Delta, by bestowing the name of Jumna and Sarasvatī on two streams connected with the Hugli. The Bengal Tribeni gives name to a village, which is a place of great sanctity, and to which the *melas* or religious fairs attract many visitors.

1682.—". . . if I refused to stay there he would certainly stop me again at **Trippany** some miles further up the River."—*Hedges, Diary*, Oct. 14; [Hak. Soc. i. 38].

1705.—". . . pendant la Lune de Mars . . . il arrive la Fête de **Tripigny**, c'est un Dieu enfermé dans une maniere de petite Mosquée, qui est dans le milieu d'une tres-grande pleine . . . au bord du Gange."—*Luillier*, 69.

1753.—"Au-dessous de Nudia, à **Tripini**, dont le nom signifie trois eaux, le Gange fait encore sortir du même côte un canal, qui par sa rentrée, forme une seconde île renfermée dans la première."—*D'Anville*, 64.

TRICHIES, TRITCHIES, s. The familiar name of the cheroots made at Trichinopoly; long, and rudely made, with a straw inserted at the end for the mouth. They are (or were) cheap and coarse, but much liked by those used to them. Mr. C. P. Brown, referring to his etymology of **Trichinopoly** under the succeeding article, derives the word *cheroot* from the form of the name which he assigns. But this, like his etymology of the place-name, is entirely wrong (see **CHEROOT**). Some excellent practical scholars seem to be entirely without the etymological sense.

1876. — "Between whiles we smoked, generally Manillas, now supplanted by foul Dindiguls and fetid **Trichies**." — *Burton, Sind Revisited*, i. 7.

TRICHINOPOLY, n.p. A district and once famous rock-fort of S. India. The etymology and proper form of the name has been the subject of much difference. Mr. C. P. Brown gives the true name as *Chiruta-paḷḷi*, 'Little-Town.' But this may be safely rejected as mere guess, inconsistent with facts. The earliest occurrence of the name on an inscription is (about 1520) as *Tiru-śśilla-paḷḷi*, apparently 'Holy-rock-town.' In the *Tevāram* the place is said to be mentioned under the name of *Sirapalli*. Some derive it from *Tri-sira-puram*, 'Three-head-town,' with allusion to a 'three-headed demon.' [The *Madras Gloss.* gives *Tiruččināppalli*, *tiru*, 'holy,' *shina*, 'the plant *cissampelos pareira*, L. *palli*, 'village.']

1677.—"**Tritchenapali.**"—*A. Bassing*, in *Valentijn*, v. (*Ceylon*), 300.

1741.—"The Maratas concluded the campaign by putting this whole Peninsula under contribution as far as C. Cumerim, attacking, conquering, and retaining the city of **Tiruxerapali**, capital of Madura, and taking prisoner the Nabab who governed it."—*Report of the Port. Viceroy*, in *Bosquejo das Possessões*, &c., *Documentos*, ed. 1853, iii. 19.

1753.—"Ces embouchûres sont en grand nombre, vû la division de ce fleuve en différens bras ou canaux, à remonter jusqu'à **Tirishirapali**, et à la pagode de Shiringham."—*D'Anville*, 115.

1761.—"After the battle Mahommed Ali Khan, son of the late nabob, fled to **Truchinapolli**, a place of great strength."—*Complete Hist. of the War in India*, 1761, p. 3.

TRINCOMALEE, n.p. A well-known harbour on the N.E. coast of Ceylon. The proper name is doubtful. It is alleged to be *Tirukko-nātha-malai*, or *Taranga-malai*. The last ('Sea-Hill') seems conceived to fit our modern pronunciation, but not the older forms. It is perhaps *Tri-kona-malai*, for 'Three-peak Hill.' There is a shrine of Siva on the hill, called *Trikoneśwara*; [so the *Madras Man.* (ii. 216)].

1553.—"And then along the coast towards the north, above Baticalou, there is the kingdom of **Triquinamalé**."—*Barros*, II. ii. cap. 1.

1602.—"This Prince having departed, made sail, and was driven by the winds unknowing whither he went. In a few days he came in sight of a desert island (being that of Ceilon), where he made the land at a haven called Preaturé, between **Triquillimalé** and the point of **Jafanapatam.**"—*Couto*, V. i. 5.

1672.—"**Trinquenemale** hath a surpassingly fine harbour, as may be seen from the draught thereof, yea one of the best and largest in all Ceylon, and better sheltered from the winds than the harbours of Belligamme, Gale, or Colombo."—*Baldaeus*, 413.

1675.—"The Cinghalese themselves oppose this, saying that they emigrated from another country . . . that some thousand years ago, a Prince of great piety, driven out of the land of Tanassery . . . came to land near the Hill of **Tricoenmale** with 1800 or 2000 men. . . ."—*Ryklof van Goens*, in *Valentijn* (*Ceylon*), 210.

1685.—"**Triquinimale.** . . ."—*Ribeyro*, Fr. Tr. 6.

1726.—"**Trinkenemale**, properly **Tricoenmale**" (*i.e. Trikunmalê*).—*Valentijn* (*Ceylon*), 19.

,, "**Trinkemale.** . . ."—*Ibid.* 103.

1727.—". . . that vigilant *Dutchman* was soon after them with his Fleet, and forced them to fight disadvantageously in **Trankamalaya** Bay, wherein the French lost one half of their Fleet, being either sunk or burnt."—*A. Hamilton*, i. 343, [ed. 1744].

1761.—"We arrived at **Trinconomale** in Ceylone (which is one of the finest, if not ye best and most capacious Harbours in ye World) the first of November, and employed that and part of the ensuing Month in preparing our Ships for ye next Campaign."—MS. Letter of *James Rennell*, Jan. 31.

TRIPANG, s. The sea-slug. This is the Malay name, *trīpang*, *tĕrīpang*. See **SWALLOW**, and **BECHE-DE-MER**.

[1817.—"Bich de mar is well known to be a dried sea slug used in the dishes of the Chinese; it is known among the Malayan Islands by the name of **Tripang**. . . ."—*Raffles, H. of Java*, 2nd ed. i. 232.]

TRIPLICANE, n.p. A suburb of Fort St. George; the part where the palace of the "Nabob of the Carnatic" is. It has been explained, questionably, as *Tiru-valli-kēdi*, 'sacred-creeper-tank.' Seshagiri Sastri gives it as *Tiru-alli-kēni*, 'sacred lily- (*Nymphaea rubea*) tank,' [and so the *Madras Gloss.* giving the word as *Tiruvallikkéni*.]

1674.—"There is an absolute necessity to go on fortifying this place in the best manner we can, our enemies at sea and land being within less than musket shot, and better fortified in their camp at **Trivelicane** than we are here."—*Ft. St. Geo. Consns.* Feb. 2. In *Notes and Exts.*, Madras, 1871, No. I. p. 28.

1679.—"The Didwan (**Dewaun**) from Conjeveram, who pretends to have come from Court, having sent word from **Treplicane** that unless the Governor would come to the garden by the river side to receive the Phyrmaund he would carry it back to Court again, answer is returned that it hath not been accustomary for the Governours to go out to receive a bare Phyrmaund except there come therewith a Serpow (see **SEERPAW**) or a Tasheriff" (see **TASHREEF**).—*Do., do.*, Dec. 2. *Ibid.* 1873, No. III. p. 40.

[1682-4.—"**Triblicane**, **Treblicane** Trivety."—*Diary Ft. St. Geo.* ed. *Pringle*, i. 63; iii. 154.]

TRIVANDRUM, n.p. The modern capital of the State now known as **Travancore** (q.v.) Properly *Tiru-(v)anantā-puram*, 'Sacred Vishnu-Town.'

TRUMPÁK, n.p. This is the name by which the site of the native suburb of the city of **Ormus** on the famous island of that name is known. The real name is shown by Lt. Stiffe's account of that island (*Geogr. Mag.* i. 13) to have been *Tūrūn-bāgh*, 'Garden of Tūrūn,' and it was properly the palace of the old Kings, of whom more than one bore the name of Tūrūn or Tūrūn Shāh.

1507.—"When the people of the city saw that they were so surrounded, that from no direction could water be brought, which was what they felt most of all, the principal Moors collected together and went to the king desiring him earnestly to provide a guard for the pools of **Turumbaque**, which were at the head of the island, lest the Portuguese should obtain possession of them. . . ."—*Comment. of Alboquerque*, E.T. by *Birch*, i. 175.

,, "Meanwhile the Captain-Major ordered Afonso Lopes de Costa and João da Nova, and Manuel Teles with his people to proceed along the water's edge, whilst he with all the rest of the force would follow, and come to a place called **Turumbaque**, which is on the water's edge, in which there were some palm-trees, and wells of brackish water, which supplied the people of the city with drink when the water-boats were not arriving, as sometimes happened owing to a contrary wind."—*Correa*, i. 830.

1610.—"The island has no fresh water . . . only in **Torunpaque**, which is a piece of white salt clay, at the extremity of the island, there is a well of fresh water, of which the King and the Wazir take advantage, to water the gardens which they have there, and which produce perfectly everything which is planted."—*Teixeira, Rel. de los Reyes de Harmuz*, 115.

1682.—"Behind the hills, to the S.S.W. and W.S.W. there is another part of the island, lying over against the anchorage that we have mentioned, and which includes the place called **Turumbake** . . . here one sees the ancient pleasure-house of the old Kings of Ormus, with a few small trees, and sundry date-palms. There are also here two great wells of water, called after the name of the place, 'The Wells of **Turumbake**'; which water is the most wholesome and the freshest in the whole island."—*Nieuhof, Zee en Lant-Reize*, ii. 86.

TUAN, s. Malay *tuan* and *tuwan*, 'lord, master.' The word is used in the English and Dutch settlements of the Archipelago exactly as **sahib** is in India. [An early Chinese form of the word is referred to under **SUMATRA**.]

1553.—"Dom Paulo da Gama, who was a worthy son of his father in his zeal to do the King good service . . . equipped a good fleet, of which the King of Ugentana (see **UJUNGTANAH**) had presently notice, who in all speed set forth his own, consisting of 30 **lancharas**, with a large force on board, and in command of which he put a valiant Moor called **Tuam**-bár, to whom the King gave orders that as soon as our force had quitted the fortress (of Malacca) not leaving enough people to defend it, he should attack the town of the *Queleys* (see **KLING**) and burn and destroy as much as he could."—*Correa*, iii. 486.

1553.—"For where this word **Raja** is used, derived from the kingly title, it attaches to a person on whom the King bestows the title, almost as among us that of Count, whilst the style **Tuam** is like our *Dom*; only the latter of the two is put before the person's proper name, whilst the former is put after it, as we see in the names of these two Javanese, Vtimuti **Raja**, and **Tuam** Colascar."—*Barros*, II. vi. 3.

[1893.—". . . the cooly talked over the affairs of the **Tuan** *Ingris* (English gentleman) to a crowd of natives."—*W. B. Worsfold, A Visit to Java*, 145.]

TUCKA, s. Hind. *takā*, Beng. *ṭākā*, [Skt. *ṭankaka*, 'stamped silver money']. This is the word commonly used among Bengalis for a rupee. But in other parts of India it (or at least *ṭakā*) is used differently; as for aggregates of 4, or of 2 pice (generally in N.W.P. *pānch ṭakā paisā* = five *ṭakā* of pice, 20 pice). Compare **TANGA**.

[1809.—"A requisition of four **tukhas**, or eight *pice*, is made upon each shop. . . ."—*Broughton, Letters from a Mahr. Camp*, ed. 1892, p. 84.]

1874.—"'. . . How much did my father pay for her?'

"'He paid only ten **tákás**.'

"I may state here that the word *rupeyā*, or as it is commonly written **rupee** or *rupi*, is unknown to the peasantry of Bengal, at least to Bengali Hindu peasants; the word they invariably use is **táká**."—*Govinda Samanta*, i. 209.

TUCKÁVEE, s. Money advanced to a ryot by his superior to enable him to carry on his cultivation, and recoverable with his quota of revenue. It is Ar.—H. *takāvī*, from Ar. *ḳavī*, 'strength,' thus literally 'a reinforcement.'

[1800.—"A great many of them, who have now been forced to work as labourers, would have thankfully received **tacavy**, to be repaid, by instalments, in the course of two or three years."—*Buchanan, Mysore*, ii. 188.]

1880.—"When the Sirkar disposed of lands which reverted to it . . . it sold them almost always for a *nazarána* (see **NUZZERANA**). It sometimes gave them gratis, but it never paid money, and seldom or ever advanced **takávi** to the tenant or owner."—*Minutes of Sir T. Munro,* i. 71. These words are not in Munro's spelling. The Editor has reformed the orthography.

TUCKEED, s. An official reminder. Ar.—H. *tākīd,* 'emphasis, injunction,' and verb *tākīd karnā,* 'to enjoin stringently, to insist.'

1862.—"I can hardly describe to you my life—work all day, English and Persian, scores of appeals and session cases, and a continual irritation of **tukeeds** and offensive remarks . . . these take away all the enjoyment of doing one's duty, and make work a slavery."—Letter from *Col. J. R. Becher,* in (unpublished) *Memoir,* p. 28.

[**TUCKIAH,** s. Pers. *takya,* literally 'a pillow or cushion'; but commonly used in the sense of a hut or hermitage occupied by a fakīr or holy man.

[1800.—"He declared . . . that two of the people charged . . . had been at his **tuckiah**."—*Wellington, Desp.* i. 78.

[1847.—"In the centre of the wood was a Faqir's **Talkiat** (*sic*) or Place of Prayer, situated on a little mound."—*Mrs. Mackenzie, Life in the Mission,* &c. ii. 47.]

TULWAUR, s. Hind. *talwār* and *tarwār,* 'a sabre.' Williams gives Skt. *taravāri* and *tarabālika.* ["*Talwār* is a general term applied to shorter or more or less curved side-arms, while those that are lighter and shorter still are often styled *nimchas*" (*Sir W. Elliot,* in *Ind. Antiq.* xv. 29). Also see *Egerton, Handbook,* 138.]

[1799.—". . . Ahmood Sollay . . . drew his **tolwa** on one of them."—*Jackson, Journey from India,* 49.

[1829.—". . . the *panchās huzār* **turwar** *Rahtorān,* meaning the 'fifty thousand Rahtore swords,' is the proverbial phrase to denote the muster of Maroo. . . ."—*Tod, Annals,* Calcutta reprint, ii. 179.]

1853.—"The old native officer who carried the royal colour of the regiments was cut down by a blow of a Sikh **tulwar**."—*Oakfield,* ii. 78.

TUMASHA, s. An entertainment, a *spectacle* (in the French sense), a popular excitement. It is Ar. *tamāshi,* 'going about to look at anything entertaining.' The word is in use in Turkestan (see *Schuyler,* below).

1610.—"Heere are also the ruines of *Ranichand* (*qu.* Ramchand's ?) Castle and Houses which the Indians acknowledge for the great God, saying that he took flesh vpon him to see the **Tamasha** of the World."—*Finch,* in *Purchas,* i. 436.

1631.—"Hic quoque meridiem prospicit, ut spectet **Thamasham** id est pugnas Elephantum Leonum Buffalorum et aliarum ferarum. . . ."—*De Laet, De Imperio Magni Mogolis,* 127. (For this quotation I am indebted to a communication from Mr. Archibald Constable of the Oudh and Rohilkund Railway.—*Y.*)

1673.—". . . We were discovered by some that told our Banyan . . . that two Englishmen were come to the **Tomasia,** or Sight. . . ."—*Fryer,* 159.

1705.—"**Tamachars.** Ce sont des réjouissances que les Gentils font en l'honneur de quelqu'unes de leurs divinitez."—*Luillier, Tab. des Matières.*

1840.—"Runjeet replied, 'Don't go yet; I am going myself in a few days, and then we will have *burra* **tomacha.**'"—*Osborne, Court and Camp of Runjeet Singh,* 120-121.

1876.—"If you told them that you did not want to buy anything, but had merely come for **tomasha,** or amusement, they were always ready to explain and show you everything you wished to see."—*Schuyler's Turkistan,* i. 176.

TUMLET, s. Domestic Hind. *tāmlet,* being a corruption of *tumbler.*

TUMLOOK, n.p. A town, and anciently a sea-port and seat of Buddhist learning on the west of the Hoogly near its mouth, formerly called *Tāmralipti* or *-lipta.* It occurs in the Mahābhārata and many other Sanskrit words. "In the *Dasa Kumāra* and *Vrihat Katha,* collections of tales written in the 9th and 12th centuries, it is always mentioned as a great port of Bengal, and the seat of an active and flourishing commerce with the countries and islands of the Bay of Bengal, and the Indian Ocean" (*Prof. H. H. Wilson,* in *J. R. As. Soc.* v. 135). [Also see *Cunningham, Anct. Geog.* p. 504.]

c. 150.—
". . . *καὶ πρὸς αὐτῷ τῷ ποταμῷ* (Γάγγῃ) *πολεις·*

* * * *

Παλιμβόθρα βασίλειον
Ταμαλίτης."
—*Ptolemy's Tables,* Bk. VII. i. 73.

c. 410.—"From this, continuing to go eastward nearly 50 *yôjanas,* we arrive at the Kingdom of **Tamralipti.** Here it is the river (Ganges) empties itself into the sea. Fah Hian remained here for two years, writing out copies of the Sacred Books. . . . He then shipped himself on board a great merchant vessel. . . ."—*Beal, Travels of Fah Hian,* &c. (1869), pp. 147-148.

[c. 1070.—". . . a merchant named Harshagupta, who had arrived from **Tamralipti,** having heard of that event, came there full of curiosity." — *Tawney, Katha Sarit Sāgara*, i. 329.]

1679.—In going down the Hoogly: "Before daybreak overtook the *Ganges* at Barnagur, met the *Arrival* 7 days out from Ballasore, and at night passed the *Lilly* at **Tumbalee**."—*Ft. St. Geo.* (Council on Tour). In *Notes & Exts.* No. II. p. 69.

1685. — "*January* 2. — We fell downe below **Tumbolee** River.

"*January* 3.—We anchored at the Channel Trees, and lay here ye 4th and 5th for want of a gale to carry us over to Kedgeria."—*Hedges, Diary*, Hak. Soc. i. 175.

[1694.—"The Royal James and Mary . . . fell on a sand on this side **Tumbolee** point. . . ."—*Birdwood, Report on Old Records*, 90.]

1726. — "**Tamboli** and Banzia are two Portuguese villages, where they have their churches, and salt business."—*Valentijn*, v. 159.

[1753.—"**Tombali**." See under **KEDGEREE**.]

TUMTUM, s. A dog-cart. We do not know the origin. [It is almost certainly a corr. of English *tandem*, the slang use of which in the sense of a conveyance (according to the *Stanf. Dict.*) dates from 1807. Even now English-speaking natives often speak of a dog-cart with a single horse as a *tandem*.]

1866.—"We had only 3 coss to go, and we should have met a pair of **tumtums** which would have taken us on."—*Trevelyan, The Dawk Bungalow*, 384.

[1889.—"A G.B.T. cart once married a bathing-machine, and they called the child **Tum-tum**."—*R. Kipling, The City of Dreadful Night*, 74.]

TUNCA, TUNCAW, &c., s. P.—H. *tankhwāh*, pron. *tankhā*. Properly an assignment on the revenue of a particular locality in favour of an individual; but in its most ordinary modern sense it is merely a word for the wages of a monthly servant. For a full account of the special older uses of the word see *Wilson*. In the second quotation the use is obscure; perhaps it means the villages on which assignments had been granted.

1758.—"Roydoolub . . . has taken the discharge of the **tuncaws** and the arrears of the Nabob's army upon himself."—*Orme*, iii.; [ii. 361].

1760.—"You have been under the necessity of writing to Mr. Holwell (who was sent to collect in the **tuncars**). . . . The low men that are employed in the **tuncars** are not to be depended on."—*The Nawab to the Prest. and Council of Ft. Wm.*, in *Long*, 233.

1778. — "These rescripts are called **tuncaws**, and entitle the holder to receive to the amount from the treasuries . . . as the revenues come in."—*Orme*, ii. 276.

[1823.—"The Grassiah or Rajpoot chiefs . . . were satisfied with a fixed and known **tanka**, or tribute from certain territories, on which they had a real or pretended claim." — *Malcolm, Cent. India*, 2nd. ed. i. 385.

[1851.—"The Sikh detachments . . . used to be paid by **tunkhwáhs**, or assignments of the provincial collectors of revenue."—*Edwardes, A Year on the Punjab Frontier*, i. 19.]

TURA, s. Or. Turk. *tūra*. This word is used in the Autobiography of Baber, and in other Mahommedan military narratives of the 16th century. It is admitted by the translators of Baber that it is rendered by them quite conjecturally, and we cannot but think that they have missed the truth. The explanation of *tūr* which they quote from Meninski is "*reticulatus*," and combining this with the manner in which the quotations show these *tūra* to have been employed, we cannot but think that the meaning which best suits is 'a gabion.' Sir H. Elliot, in referring to the first passage from Baber, adopts the reading *túbra*, and says: "*Túbras* are nose-bags, but . . . Badáúni makes the meaning plain, by saying that they were *filled with earth* (*Tārīkh-i-Badáúni*, f. 136). . . . The sacks used by Sher Sháh as temporary fortifications on his march towards Rájpútána were *túbras*" (*Elliot*, vi. 469). It is evident, however, that Baber's **tūras** were no **tobras**, whilst a reference to the passage (*Elliot*, iv. 405) regarding Sher Shāh shows that the use of bags filled with sand on that occasion was regarded as a new contrivance. The *túbra* of Badáúni may therefore probably be a misreading; whilst the use of gabions implies necessarily that they would be filled with earth.

1526. —(At the Battle of Pānipat) "I directed that, according to the custom of Rûm, the gun-carriages should be connected together with twisted bull-hides as with chains. Between every two gun-carriages were 6 or 7 **tûras** (or breastworks). The matchlockmen stood behind these guns and **tûras**, and discharged their matchlocks. . . . It was settled, that as Pânipat was a considerable city, it would cover one of our flanks by its buildings and houses while we might fortify our front by **tûras**. . . ."—*Baber*, p. 304.

1528.—(At the siege of Chānderī) "overseers and pioneers were appointed to construct works on which the guns were to be planted. All the men of the army were directed to prepare **tûras** and scaling-ladders, and to serve the **tûras** which are used in attacking forts. . . ."—*Ibid.* p. 376. The editor's note at the former passage is: "The meaning (viz. 'breastwork') assigned to **Tûra** here, and in several other places is merely conjectural, founded on Petis de la Croix's explanation, and on the meaning given by Meninski to **Tûr**, viz. *reticulatus.* The **Tûras** may have been formed by the branches of trees, interwoven like basket-work . . . or they may have been covered defences from arrows and missiles. . . ." Again: "These **Tûras**, so often mentioned, appear to have been a sort of *testudo*, under cover of which the assailants advanced, and sometimes breached the wall. . . ."

TURAKA, n.p. This word is applied both in Mahratti and in Telugu to the Mahommedans (*Turks*). [The usual form in the inscriptions is *Turushka* (see *Bombay Gazetteer*, i. pt. i. 189).] Like this is *Tarūk* (see **TAROUK**) which the Burmese now apply to the Chinese.

TURBAN, s. Some have supposed this well-known English word to be a corruption of the P.—H. *sirband*, 'head-wrap,' as in the following:

1727.—"I bought a few **seerbunds** and *sannoes* there (at Cuttack) to know the difference of the prices."—*A. Hamilton*, i. 394 (see **PIECE-GOODS**).

This, however, is quite inconsistent with the history of the word. Wedgewood's suggestion that the word may be derived from Fr. *turbin*, 'a whelk,' is equally to be rejected. It is really a corruption of one which, though it seems to be out of use in modern Turkish, was evidently used by the Turks when Europe first became familiar with the Ottomans and their ways. This is set forth in the quotation below from Zedler's *Lexicon*, which is corroborated by those from Rycaut and from Galland, &c. The proper word was apparently *dulband*. Some modern Persian dictionaries give the only meaning of this as 'a sash.' But Meninski explains it as 'a cloth of fine white muslin; a wrapper for the head'; and Vüllers also gives it this meaning, as well as that of a 'sash or belt.'* In doing so he quotes Shakespear's Dict., and marks the use as 'Hindustani-Persian.' But a merely Hindustani use of a Persian word could hardly have become habitual in Turkey in the 15th and 16th centuries. The use of *dulband* for a turban was probably genuine Persian, adopted by the Turks. Its etymology is apparently from Arab. *dul*, '*volvere*,' admitting of application to either a girdle or a head-wrap. From the Turks it passed in the forms *Tulipant*, *Tolliban*, *Turbant*, &c., into European languages. And we believe that the flower *tulip* also has its name from its resemblance to the old Ottoman turban, [a view accepted by Prof. Skeat (*Concise Dict.* s.v. *tulip*, *turban*)].*

1487.—". . . tele bambagine assai che loro chiamano **turbanti**; tele assai colla salda, che lor chiamano *sexe* (sash). . . ."—Letter on presents from the Sultan to L. de' Medici, in *Roscoe's Lorenzo*, ed. 1825, ii. 371-72.

c. 1490.—"Estradiots sont gens comme Genetaires: vestuz, à pied et à cheval, comme les Turcs, sauf la teste, où ils ne portent ceste toille qu'ils appellent **tolliban**, et sont durs gens, et couchent dehors tout l'an et leurs chevaulx."—*Ph. de Commynes*, Liv. VIII. ch. viii. ed. *Dupont* (1843), ii. 456. Thus given in Danett's translation (1595): "These Estradiots are soldiers like to the Turkes Ianizaries, and attired both on foote and on horsebacke like to the Turks, save that they weare not vpon their head such a great roule of linnen as the Turkes do called (*sic*) **Tolliban**."—p. 325.

1586-8.—". . . [the King's Secretarie, who had upon his head a peece of died linen cloth folded vp like vnto a Turkes **Tuliban**."—*Voyage of Master Thomas Candish*, in *Hakl.* iv. 33.

1588.—"In this canoa was the King's Secretarie, who had on his head a piece of died linen cloth folded vp like vnto a Turkes **Tuliban**."—*Cavendish, ibid.* iv. 337.

c. 1610.—". . . un gros **turban** blanc à la Turque."—*Pyrard de Laval*, i. 98; [Hak. Soc. i. 132 and 165].

1611.—Cotgrave's French Dict. has: "**Toliban**: m. A **Turbant** or Turkish hat.
"**Tolopan**, as **Turbant**.
"**Turban**: m. A **Turbant**; a Turkish hat, of white and fine linnen wreathed into a rundle; broad at the bottom to enclose the head, and lessening, for ornament, towards the top."

1615.—". . . se un Cristiano fosse trovato con **turbante** bianco in capo, sarebbe perciò costretto o a rinegare o a morire. Questo **turbante** poi lo portano Turchi, di varie forme."—*P. della Valle*, i. 96.

* The Pers. *partala* is always used for a 'waist-belt' in India, but in Persia also for a turban.

* Busbecq (1554) says: ". . . ingens ubique florum copia offerebatur, Narcissorum, Hyacinthorum, et eorum quos Turcae **Tulipan** vocant."—*Epist.* i. Elzevir ed. p. 47.

1615.—"The Sultan of Socotora . . . his clothes are *Surat* Stuffes, after the Arabs manner . . . a very good **Turbant**, but bare footed."—*Sir T. Roe*, [Hak. Soc. i. 32].

" "Their Attire is after the Turkish fashion, **Turbants** only excepted, insteed whereof they have a kind of Capp, rowled about with a black **Turbant**."—*De Monfart*, 5.

1619.—"Nel giorno della qual festa tutti Persiani più spensierati, e fin gli uomini grandi, e il medesimo rè, si vestono in abito succinto all uso di Mazanderan; e con certi berrettini, non troppo buoni, in testa, perchè i **turbanti** si guasterebbono e sarebbero di troppo impaccio. . . ."—*P. della Valle*, ii. 31; [Hak. Soc. comp. i. 43].

1630.—"Some indeed have sashes of silke and gold, **tulipanted** about their heads. . . ."—*Sir T. Herbert*, p. 128.

" "His way was made by 30 gallant young gentlemen vested in crimson saten; their **Tulipants** were of silk and silver wreath'd about with cheynes of gold."—*Ibid.* p. 139.

1672.—"On the head they wear great **Tulbands** (*Tulbande*) which they touch with the hand when they say *salam* to any one."—*Baldaeus* (Germ. version), 33.

" "Trois **Tulbangis** venoient de front après luy, et ils portoient chascun un beau **tulban** orné et enrichy d'aigrettes."—*Journ. d'Ant. Galland*, i. 139.

1673.—"The mixture of Castes or Tribes of all *India* are distinguished by the different Modes of binding their **Turbats**."—*Fryer*, 115.

1674.—"El **Tanadar** de un golpo cortò las repetidas bueltas del **turbante** a un Turco, y la cabeça asta la mitad, de que cayò muerte."—*Faria y Sousa, Asia Port.* ii. 179-180.

" "**Turbant**, a Turkish hat," &c.—*Glossographia, or a Dictionary interpreting the Hard Words of whatsoever language, now used in our refined English Tongue*, &c., the 4th ed., by *T.E.*, of the Inner Temple, Esq. In the Savoy, 1674.

1676.—"*Mahamed Alibeg* returning into *Persia* out of *India* . . . presented *Cha-Sefi* the second with a Coco-nut about the bigness of an Austrich-egg . . . there was taken out of it a **Turbant** that had 60 cubits of calicut in length to make it, the cloath being so fine that you could hardly feel it."—*Tavernier*, E.T. p. 127; [ed. *Ball*, ii. 7].

1687.—In a detail of the high officers of the Sultan's Court we find:

"5. The **Tulbentar** Aga, he that makes up his **Turbant**."

A little below another personage (apparently) is called **Tulban**-*oghlani* ('The Turban Page')—*Ricaut, Present State of the Ottoman Empire*, p. 14.

1711.—"Their common Dress is a piece of blew Callico, wrap'd in a Role round their Heads for a **Turbat**."—*Lockyer*, 57.

1745.—"The Turks hold the Sultan's **Turban** in honour to such a degree that they hardly dare touch it . . . but he himself has, among the servants of his privy chamber, one whose special duty it is to adjust his **Turban**, or head-tire, and who is thence called **Tulbentar** or **Dulbentar** *Aga*, or **Dulbendar** *Aga*, also called by some **Dulbend** *Oghani* (*Oghlani*), or Page of the Turban."—*Zedler, Universal Lexicon*, s.v.

c. 1760.—"They (the Sepoys) are chiefly armed in the country manner, with sword and target, and wear the Indian dress, the **turbant**, the cabay (**Cabaya**) or vest, and **long drawers**."—*Grose*, i. 39.

1843.—"The mutiny of Vellore was caused by a slight shown to the Mahomedan **turban**; the mutiny of Bangalore by disrespect said to have been shown to a Mahomedan place of worship."—*Macaulay, Speech on Gates of Somnauth.*

TURKEY, s. This fowl is called in Hindustani *perū*, very possibly an indication that it came to India, perhaps first to the Spanish settlements in the Archipelago, across the Pacific, as the red pepper known as **Chili** did. In Tamil the bird is called *vān-kōri*, 'great fowl.' Our European names of it involve a complication of mistakes and confusions. *We* name it as if it came from the Levant. But the name *turkey* would appear to have been originally applied to another of the *Pavonidae*, the **guinea-fowl**, *Meleagris* of the ancients. Minsheu's explanations (quoted below) show strange confusions between the two birds. The French *coq d'Inde* or *Dindon* points only ambiguously to India, but the German *Calecutische Hahn* and the Dutch *Kalkoen* (from *Calicut*) are specific in error as indicating the origin of the Turkey in the East. This misnomer may have arisen from the nearly simultaneous discovery of America and of the Cape route to Calicut, by Spain and Portugal respectively. It may also have been connected with the fact that Malabar produced domestic fowls of extraordinary size. Of these Ibn Batuta (quoted below) makes quaint mention. Zedler's great German *Lexicon of Universal Knowledge*, a work published as late as 1745, says that these birds (turkeys) were called *Calecutische* and *Indische* because they were brought by the Portuguese from the Malabar coast. Dr. Caldwell cites a curious disproof of the antiquity of certain Tamil verses from their containing a simile of which the turkey forms the subject. And native scholars, instead of admitting the anachronism, have boldly maintained that the turkey had always been found in India (*Dravidian Gramm.* 2nd ed. p. 137). Padre Paolino was apparently of the same opinion, for whilst explaining that the etymology of Calicut is "Castle of the Fowls," he asserts that Turkeys (*Galli d'India*) came originally from India; being herein, as he often is, positive and wrong. In 1615 we find W. Edwards, the E.I. Co.'s agent at Ajmir, writing to send the Mogul "three or four **Turkey** cocks and hens, for he hath three cocks but no hens' (*Colonial Paper*, E. i. c. 388). Here, however, the ambiguity between the real turkey and the guinea-fowl may possibly arise. In Egypt the bird is called *Dik-Rūmī*, 'fowl of Rūm' (*i.e.* of Turkey), probably a rendering of the English term.

c. 1347.—"The first time in my life that I saw a China cock was in the city of Kaulam. I had at first taken it for an ostrich, and I was looking at it with great wonder, when the owner said to me, 'Pooh! there are cocks in China much bigger than that!' and when I got there I found that he had said no more than the truth."—*Ibn Batuta*, iv. 257.

c. 1550.—"One is a species of peacock that has been brought to Europe, and commonly called the **Indian fowl**."—*Girolamo Benzoni*, 148.

1627.—"Turky *Cocke*, or *cocke of* India, *avis ita dicta, quod ex* Africa, *et vt nonulli volunt alii, ex* India *vel* Arabia *ad nos allata sit.* B. Indische haen. T. Indianisch hun, Calecuttisch hun. . . . H. Pavon de las Indias. G. Poulle d'Inde. H. 2. Gallepauo. L. Gallo-pauo, *quod de* vtriusque natura videtur participare . . . *aves* Numidicae, *à Numidia*, Meleagris . . . à *μέλας*, i. niger, and *ἄγρος*, ager, quod in Æthiopia praecipuè inveniuntur.

"A Turkie, or Ginnie Henne . . . I. *Gallina d'India.* H. Galina Morisca. G. Poulle d'Inde. L. Penélope. *Auis Pharaonis.* Meleágris. . . .

* * * * *

"A Ginnie *cocke or hen: ex* Guinea, *regione* Indica . . . *vnde fuerunt priùs ad alias regiones transportati.* vi. Turkie-cocke or hen."—*Minsheu's Guide into Tongues* (2d edition).

1623.—"33. **Gallus Indicus**, aut **Turcicus** (quem vocant), gallinacei aevum parum superat; iracundus ales, et carnibus valde albis."—*Bacon, Hist. Vitae et Mortis*, in *Montague's* ed. x. 140.

1653.—"Les François appellent *coq-d'Inde* vn oyseau lequel ne se trouue point aux Indes Orientales, les Anglois le nomment **turki-koq** qui signifie coq de Turquie, quoy qu'il n'y ait point d'autres en Turquie que ceux que l'on y a portez d'Europe. Ie croy que cet oyseau nous est venu de l'Amerique."—*De la Boullaye-le-Gouz*, ed. 1657, p. 259.

1750-52.—"Some Germans call the **turkeys** *Calcutta hens*; for this reason I looked about for them here, and to the best of my remembrance I was told they were foreign."—*Olof Toreen*, 199-200. We do not know whether the mistake of *Calcutta* for *Calicut* belongs to the original author or to the translator—probably to the proverbial *traditore*.

TURNEE, TUNNEE, s. An English supercargo, Sea-Hind., and probably a corruption of *attorney*. (*Roebuck*).

TURPAUL, s. Sea-Hind. A tarpaulin (*ibid.*). [The word (*tārpāl*) has now come into common native use.]

TUSSAH, TUSSER, s. A kind of inferior silk, the tissues of which are now commonly exported to England. Anglo-Indians generally regard the termination of this word in *r* as a vulgarism, like the use of *solar* for **sola** (q.v.); but it is in fact correct. For though it is written by Milburn (1813) *tusha*, and *tusseh* (ii. 158, 244), we find it in the *Āīn-i-Akbarī* as *tassar*, and in Dr. Buchanan as *tasar* (see below). The term is supposed to be adopted from Skt. *tasara, trasara*, Hind. *tasar*, 'a shuttle'; perhaps from the form of the cocoon? The moth whose worm produced this silk is generally identified with *Antheraea paphia*, but Capt. Hutton has shown that there are several species known as *tasar* worms. These are found almost throughout the whole extent of the forest tracts of India. But the chief seat of the manufacture of stuffs, wholly or partly of *tasar* silk, has long been Bhāgalpur on the Ganges. [See also *Allen, Mon. on Silk Cloths of Assam*, 1899; *Yusuf Ali, Silk Fabrics of N.W.P.*, 1900.] The first mention of *tasar* in English reports is said to be that by Michael Atkinson of Jangīpūr, as cited below in the *Linnœan Transactions* of 1804 by Dr. Roxburgh (see *Official Report on Sericulture in India*, by *J. Geoghegan*, Calcutta, 1872), [and the elaborate article in Watt, *Econ. Dict.* vi. pt. iii. 96 *seqq.*].

c. 1590.—"**Tassar**, per piece . . . ½ to 2 Rupees."—*Āīn*, i. 94.

[1591.—See the account by Rumphius, quoted by *Watt, loc. cit.* p. 99.]

1726.—"**Tessersse** . . . 11 ells long and 2 els broad. . . ."—*Valentijn*, v. 178.

1796.—". . . I send you herewith for Dr. Roxburgh a specimen of Bughy **Tusseh** silk. . . . There are none of the Palma Christi species of **Tusseh** to be had here. . . . I have heard that there is another variation of the Tusseh silk-worm in the hills near Bauglipoor."—Letter of *M. Atkinson*, as above, in *Linn. Trans.*, 1804, p. 41.

1802.—"They (the insects) are found in such abundance over many parts of Bengal and the adjoining provinces as to have afforded to the natives, from time immemorial, an abundant supply of a most durable, coarse, dark-coloured silk, commonly called **Tusseh** silk, which is woven into a cloth called **Tusseh** *doot'hies*, much worn by Bramins and other sects of Hindoos."—*Roxburgh, Ibid.* 34.

c. 1809.—"The chief use to which the tree (*Terminalia elata*, or *Asan*) is however applied, is to rear the **Tasar** silk."—*Buchanan, Eastern India*, ii. 157 *seqq.*

[1817.—"A thick cloth, called **tusuru**, is made from the web of the gootee insect in the district of Veerbhoomee."—*Ward, Hindoos*, 2d ed. i. 85.]

1876.—"The work of the **Tussur** silk-weavers has so fallen off that the Calcutta merchants no longer do business with them."—*Sat. Rev.*, 14 Oct., p. 468.

TUTICORIN, n.p. A sea-port of Tinnevelly, and long the seat of pearl-fishery, in Tamil *Tūttukkudi*, [which the *Madras Gloss.* derives from Tam. *tūttu*, 'to scatter,' *kudi*, 'habitation']. According to Fra Paolino the name is *Tutukodi*, 'a place where nets are washed,' but he is not to be trusted. Another etymology alleged is from *turu*, 'a bush.' But see Bp. Caldwell below.

1544.—"At this time the King of Cape Comorin, who calls himself the Great King (see **TRAVANCORE**), went to war with a neighbour of his who was king of the places beyond the Cape, called Manapá and **Totucury**, inhabited by the Christians that were made there by Miguel Vaz, Vicar General of India at the time."—*Correa*, iv. 403.

1610.—"And the said Captain and Auditor shall go into residence every three years, and to him shall pertain all the temporal government, without any intermeddling therein of the members of the Company . . . nor shall the said members (*religiosos*) compel any of the Christians to remain in the island unless it is their voluntary choice to do so, and such as wish it may live at **Tuttucorim**."—*King's Letter*, in *L. das Monções*, 386.

1644.—"The other direction in which the residents of Cochim usually go for their trading purchases is to **Tutocorim**, on the Fishery Coast (Costa da **Pescaria**), which gets that name from the pearl which is fished there."—*Bocarro*, MS.

[c. 1660.—". . . musk and porcelain from *China*, and pearls from Beharen (Bahrein), and **Tutucoury**, near Ceylon. . . ."—*Bernier*, ed. *Constable*, 204.]

1672.—"The pearls are publicly sold in the market at **Tutecoryn** and at Cailpatnam. . . . The **Tutecorinish** and Manaarish pearls are not so good as those of Persia and Ormus, because they are not so free from water or so white."—*Baldaeus* (Germ. ed.), 145.

1673.—". . . **Tutticaree**, a Portugal Town in time of Yore."—*Fryer*, 49.

[1682.—"The Agent having notice of an **Interloper** lying in **Titticorin** Bay, immediately sent for ye Councell to consult about it."—*Pringle, Diary Ft. St. Geo.* 1st ser. i. 69.]

1727.—"**Tutecareen** has a good safe harbour. . . . This colony superintends a Pearl-Fishery . . . which brings the Dutch Company 20,000L. yearly Tribute."—*A. Hamilton*, i. 334; [ed. 1744, i. 336].

1881.—"The final *n* in **Tuticorin** was added for some such euphonic reason as turned Kochchi into Cochin and Kumari into Comorin. The meaning of the name *Tūttukkudi* is said to be 'the town where the wells get filled up'; from *tūttu* (properly *tūrttu*), 'to fill up a well,' and *kudi*, 'a place of habitation, a town.' This derivation, whether the true one or not, has at least the merit of being appropriate. . . ."—*Bp. Caldwell, Hist. of Tinnevelly*, 75.

TYCONNA, TYEKANA, s. A room in the basement or cellarage, or dug in the ground, in which it has in some parts of India been the practice to pass the hottest part of the day during the hottest season of the year. Pers. *tah-khāna*, 'nether-house,' *i.e.* 'subterraneous apartment.' ["In the centre of the court is an elevated platform, the roof of a subterraneous chamber called a *zeera zemeon*, whither travellers retire during the great heats of the summer" (*Morier, Journey through Persia*, &c., 81). Another name for such a place is *sardābeh* (*Burton, Ar. Nights*, i. 314).]

1663.—". . . in these hot Countries, to entitle an House to the name of Good and Fair it is required it should be . . . furnish'd also with good **Cellars** with great Flaps to stir the Air, for reposing in the fresh Air from 12 till 4 or 5 of the Clock, when the Air of these Cellars begins to be hot and stuffing. . . ."—*Bernier*, E.T. 79; [ed. *Constable*, 247].

c. 1763.—"The throng that accompanied that minister proved so very great that the floor of the house, which happened to have a **Tah-Qhana**, and possibly was at that moment under a secret influence, gave way, and the body, the Vizir, and all his company fell into the apartment underneath."—*Seir Mutagherin*, iii. 19.

1842.—"The heat at Jellalabad from the end of April was tremendous, 105° to 110° in the shade. Everybody who could do so lived in underground chambers called **ty-khánás**. Broadfoot dates a letter 'from my den six feet under ground.'"—*Mrs. Mackenzie, Storms and Sunshine of a Soldier's Life*, i. 298. [The same author in her *Life in the Mission* (i. 330) writes **taikhana**.]

TUXALL, TAKSAUL, s. The Mint. Hind. *ṭaksāl*, from Skt. *ṭankaśālā*, 'coin-hall.'

[1757.—"Our provisions were regularly sent us from the Dutch **Tanksal**. . . ."—*Holwell's Narr. of Attack on Calcutta*, p. 34; in *Wheeler, Early Records*, 248.

[1811.—"The **Ticksali**, or superintendent of the mint. . . ."—*Kirkpatrick, Nepaul*, 201.]

TYPHOON, s. A tornado or cyclone-wind; a sudden storm, a '**nor-wester**' (q.v.). Sir John Barrow (see *Autobiog.* 57) ridicules "learned anti-quarians" for fancying that the Chinese took *typhoon* from the Egyptian *Typhon*, the word being, according to him, simply the Chinese syllables, *ta-fung*, 'Great Wind.' His ridicule is misplaced. With a monosyllabic language like the Chinese (as we have remarked elsewhere) you may construct a plausible etymology, to meet the requirements of the sound alone, from anything and for anything. And as there is no evidence that the word is in Chinese use at all, it would perhaps be as fair a suggestion to derive it from the English "*tough 'un.*" Mr. Giles, who seems to think that the balance of evidence is in favour of this (Barrow's) etymology, admits a serious objection to be that the Chinese have special names for the *typhoon*, and rarely, if ever, speak of it vaguely as a 'great wind.' The fact is that very few words of the class used by seafaring and trading people, even when they refer to Chinese objects, are directly taken from the Chinese language. *E.g. Mandarin, pagoda, chop, cooly, tutenague*;—none of these are Chinese. And the probability is that Vasco and his followers got the *tufão*, which our sailors made into *touffon* and then into *typhoon*, as they got the *monção* which our sailors made into *monsoon*, direct from the Arab pilots.

The Arabic word is *tūfān*, which is used habitually in India for a sudden and violent storm. Lane defines it as meaning 'an overpowering rain, . . . Noah's flood,' etc. And there can be little doubt of its identity with the Greek τυφῶν or τυφών. [But Burton (*Ar. Nights*, iii. 257) alleges that it is pure Arabic, and comes from the root *ṭauf*, 'going round.'] This word τυφών (the etymologists say, from τυφώ, 'I raise smoke') was applied to a demon-giant or Titan, and either directly from the etym. meaning or from the name of the Titan (as in India a whirlwind is called 'a **Devil** or **Pisachee**') to a 'waterspout,' and thence to analogous stormy phenomena. 'Waterspout' seems evidently the meaning of τυφών in the *Meteorologica* of Aristotle (γίγνεται μὲν οὖν τυφών . . . κ.τ.λ.) iii. 1; the passage is exceedingly difficult to render clearly); and also in the quotation which we give from Aulus Gellius. The word *may* have come to the Arabs either in maritime intercourse, or through the translations of Aristotle. It occurs (*al-ṭūfān*) several times in the Koran; thus in *sura*, vii. 134, for a flood or storm, one of the plagues of Egypt, and in s. xxix. 14 for the Deluge.

Dr. F. Hirth, again (*Journ. R. Geog. Soc.* i. 260), advocates the quasi-Chinese origin of the word. Dr. Hirth has found the word *T'ai* (and also with the addition of *fung*, 'wind') to be really applied to a certain class of cyclonic winds, in a Chinese work on Formosa, which is a re-issue of a book originally published in 1694. Dr. Hirth thinks *t'ai* as here used (which is not the Chinese word *ta* or *tai*, 'great,' and is expressed by a different character) to be a local Formosan term; and is of opinion that the combination *t'ai-fung* is "a sound so near that of *typhoon* as almost to exclude all other conjectures, if we consider that the writers using the term in European languages were travellers distinctly applying it to storms encountered in that part of the China Sea." Dr. Hirth also refers to F. Mendes Pinto and the passages (quoted below) in which he says *tufão* is the Chinese name for such storms. Dr. Hirth's paper is certainly worthy of much more attention than the scornful assertion of Sir John Barrow, but it does not induce us to change our view as to the origin of *typhoon*.

Observe that the Port. *tufão* distinctly represents *ṭūfān* and not *t'ai-fung*, and the oldest English form '*tuffon*' does the same, whilst it is not by any means unquestionable that these Portuguese and English forms were first applied in the China Sea, and not in the Indian Ocean. Observe also Lord Bacon's use of the word *typhones* in his Latin below; also that *ṭūfān* is an Arabic word, at least as old as the Koran, and closely allied in sound and meaning to τυφῶν, whilst it is habitually used for a storm in Hindustani. This is shown by the quotations below (1810-1836); and Platts defines *ṭūfān* as "a violent storm of wind and rain, a tempest, a **typhoon**; a flood, deluge, inundation, the universal deluge" etc.; also *ṭūfānī*, "stormy, tempestuous . . . boisterous, quarrelsome, violent, noisy, riotous."

Little importance is to be attached to Pinto's linguistic remarks such as that quoted, or even to the like dropt by Couto. We apprehend that Pinto made exactly the same mistake that Sir John Barrow did; and we need not wonder at it, when so many of our countrymen in India have supposed **hackery** to be a Hindustani word, and when we find even the learned H. H. Wilson assuming **tope** (in the sense of 'grove') to be in native Hindustani use. Many instances of such mistakes might be quoted. It is just possible, though not we think very probable, that some contact with the Formosan term may have influenced the modification of the old English form *tuffon* into *typhoon*. It is much more likely to have been influenced by the analogies of *monsoon, simoom;* and it is quite possible that the Formosan mariners took up their (unexplained) *t'ai-fung* from the Dutch or Portuguese.

On the origin of the Ar. word the late Prof. Robertson-Smith forwarded the following note:

"The question of the origin of *Ṭūfān* appears to be somewhat tangled.

"Τυφῶν, 'whirlwind, waterspout,' connected with τῦφος seems pure Greek; the combination in Baal-*Zephon*, Exod. xiv. 2, and *Sephōni*, the northern one, in Joel, ii. 20, suggested by Hitzig, appears to break down, for there is no proof of any Egyptian name for Set corresponding to Typhon.

"On the other hand *Ṭūfān*, the deluge, is plainly borrowed from the Aramaic. *Ṭūfān*, for Noah's flood, is both Jewish, Aramaic and Syriac, and this form is not borrowed from the Greek, but comes from a true Semitic root *ṭūf* 'to overflow.'

"But again, the sense of *whirlwind* is not recognised in classical Arabic. Even Dozy in his dictionary of later Arabic only cites a modern French-Arabic dictionary (Bocthor's) for the sense, *Tourbillon, trombe*. Bistánī in the *Moḥīt el Moḥīt* does not give this sense, though he is pretty full in giving modern as well as old words and senses. In Arabic the root *ṭūf* means 'to go round,' and a combination of this idea with the sense of sudden disaster might conceivably have given the new meaning to the word. On the other hand it seems simpler to regard this sense as a late loan from some modern form of τυφών, *typho*, or *tifone*. But in order finally to settle the matter one wants examples of this sense of *ṭūfān*."

[Prof. Skeat (*Concise Dict.* s.v.) gives: "Sometimes claimed as a Chinese word meaning 'a great wind' . . . but this seems to be a late mystification. In old authors the forms are *tuffon, tuffoon, tiphon*, &c.—Arab. *ṭūfān*, a hurricane, storm. Gk. τυφών, better τυφώς, a whirlwind. The close accidental coincidence of these words in sense and form is very remarkable, as Whitney notes."]

c. A.D. 160.—". . . dies quidem tandem illuxit: sed nichil de periculo, de saevitiâve remissum, quia turbines etiam crebriores, et coelum atrum et fumigantes globi, et figurae quaedam nubium metuendae, quas τυφῶνας vocabant, impendere, imminere, et depressurae navem videbantur."—*Aul. Gellius*, xix. 2.

1540.—"Now having . . . continued our Navigation within this Bay of *Cauchin-china* . . . upon the day of the nativity of our Lady, being the eight of *September*, for the fear that we were in of the new Moon, during the which there oftentimes happens in this Climate such a terrible storm of wind and rain, as it is not possible for ships to withstand it, which by the Chineses is named **Tufan**" (*o qual tormento os Chins chamão* **tufão**).—*Pinto* (orig. cap. I.) in *Cogan*, p. 60.

" ". . . in the height of forty and one degrees, there arose so terrible a South-wind, called by the Chineses **Tufaon** (*un tempo do Sul, a q̄ Chins chamão* **tufão**)."—*Ibid.* (cap. lxxix.), in *Cogan*, p. 97.

1554.—"Não se ouve por pequena maravilha cessarem os **tufões** na paragem da ilha de Sãchião."—Letter in *Sousa, Oriente Conquist.* i. 680.

[c. 1554.—". . . suddenly from the west arose a great storm known as fil **Tofani** [literally 'Elephant's flood, comp. **ELEPHANTA, b.**]."—*Travels of Sidi Ali, Reïs*, ed. *Vambéry*, p. 17.]

1567.—"I went aboorde a shippe of Bengala, at which time it was the yeere of **Touffon**, concerning which **Touffon** ye are to vnderstand that in the East Indies often times, there are not stormes as in other countreys; but every 10 or 12 yeeres there are such tempests and stormes that it is a thing incredible . . . neither do they know certainly what yeere they will come."—*Master Caesar Frederike*, in *Hakl.* ii. 370 [369].

1575.—"But when we approach'd unto it (Cyprus), a Hurricane arose suddenly, and blew so fiercely upon us, that it wound our great Sail round about our main Mast. . . . These Winds arise from a Wind that is called by the Greeks **Typhon**; and *Pliny* calleth it *Vertex* and *Vortex*; but as dangerous as they are, as they arise suddenly, so quickly are they laid again also."—*Rauwolff's Travels*, in *Ray's Collection*, ed. 1705, p. 320. Here the traveller seems to intimate (though we are not certain) that *Typhon* was then applied in the Levant to such winds; in any case it was exactly the *ṭūfān* of India.

1602.—"This Junk seeking to make the port of Chincheo met with a tremendous storm such as the natives call **Tufão**, a thing so overpowering and terrible, and bringing such violence, such earthquake as it were, that it appears as if all the spirits of the infernal world had got into the waves and seas, driving them in a whirl till their fury seems to raise a scud of flame, whilst in the space of one turning of the sand-glass the wind shall veer round to every point of the compass, seeming to blow more furiously from each in succession.

"Such is this phenomenon that the very birds of heaven, by some natural instinct, know of its coming 8 days beforehand, and are seen to take their nests down from the tree-tops and hide them in crevices of rock. Eight days before, the clouds also are seen to float so low as almost to graze men's heads, whilst in these days the seas seem beaten down as it were, and of a deep blue colour. And before the storm breaks forth, the sky exhibits a token well-known to all, a great object which seamen call the Ox-Eye (*Olho de Boi*) all of different colours, but so gloomy and appalling that it strikes fear in all who see it. And as the Bow of Heaven, when it appears, is the token of fair weather, and calm, so this seems to portend the Wrath of God, as we may well call such a storm. . . ." &c.—*Couto*, V. viii. 12.

1610.—"But at the breaking vp, commeth alway a cruell Storme, which they call the **Tuffon**, fearfull even to men on land; which is not alike extreame euery yeare."—*Finch*, in *Purchas*, i. 423.

1613.—"E porque a terra he salitrosa e ventosa, he muy sogeita a tempestades, ora menor aquella chamada Ecnephia (Εκνεφιας), ora maior chamada **Tiphon** (Τυφων), aquelle de ordinario chamamos **Tuphão** ou Tormenta desfeita . . . e corre com tanta furia e impeto que desfas os tectos das casas e aranca arvores, e as vezes do mar lança as embarcações em terra nos campos do sertão."—*Godinho de Eredia*, f. 36*v*.

1615.—"And about midnight Capt. Adams went out in a bark abord the *Hozeander* with many other barks to tow her in, we fearing a **tuffon**."—*Cocks's Diary*, i. 50.

1624.—"3. **Typhones** majores, qui per latitudinem aliquam corripiunt, et correpta sorbent in sursum, raro fiunt; at vortices, sive turbines exigui et quasi ludicri, frequenter.

"4. Omnes procellae et **typhones**, et turbines majores, habent manifestum motum praecipitii, aut vibrationis deorsum magis quam alii venti."—*Bacon, Hist. Ventorum*, in *B. Montagu's* ed. of Works, x. 49. In the translation by R. G. (1671) the words are rendered "the greater **typhones**."—*Ibid.* xiv. 268.

1626.—"*Francis Fernandez* writeth, that in the way from Malacca to Iapan they are encountred with great stormes which they call **Tuffons**, that blow foure and twentie houres, beginning from the North to the East, and so about the Compasse."—*Purchas, Pilgrimage*, 600.

1688.—"**Tuffoons** are a particular kind of violent Storms blowing on the Coast of Tonquin . . . it comes on fierce and blows very violent, at N.E. twelve hours more or less. . . When the Wind begins to abate it dies away suddenly, and falling flat calm it continues so an Hour, more or less; then the Wind comes round about to the S.W. and it blows and rains as fierce from thence, as it did before at N.E. and as long."—*Dampier*, ii. 36.

1712.—"Non v'è spavento paragonabile a quello de' naviganti, quali in mezzo all' oceano assaltati d'ogni intorno da turbini e da **tifoni**."—*P. Paolo Segnero, Mann. dell' Anima*, Ottobre 14. (Borrowed from Della Crusca Voc.).

1721.—"I told them they were all strangers to the nature of the **Moussoons** and **Tuffoons** on the coast of India and China."—*Shelvocke's Voyage*, 383.

1727.—". . . by the Beginning of *September*, they reacht the Coast of China, where meeting with a **Tuffoon**, or a North East Storm, that often blows violently about that Season, they were forced to bear away for Johore."—*A. Hamilton*, ii. 89; [ed. 1744, ii. 88].

1727.—

"In the dread Ocean, undulating wide,
Beneath the radiant line that girts the globe,
The circling **Typhon**, whirl'd from point to point,
Exhausting all the rage of all the Sky. . . ."
Thomson, Summer.

1780.—Appended to Dunn's New Directory, 5th ed. is:—

"PROGNOSTIC of a **Tuffoon** *on the Coast of China.* By ANTONIO PASCAL DE ROSA, *a Portuguese Pilot of* MACAO."

c. 1810.—(Mr. Martyn) "was with us during a most tremendous **touffan**, and no one who has not been in a tropical region can, I think, imagine what these storms are."—*Mrs. Sherwood's Autobiog.* 382.

1826.—"A most terrific **toofaun** . . . came on that seemed likely to tear the very trees up by the roots."—*John Shipp*, ii. 285.

" "I thanked him, and enquired how this **toofan** or storm had arisen."—*Pandurang Hari*, [ed. 1873, i. 50].

1836. — "A hurricane has blown ever since gunfire; clouds of dust are borne along upon the rushing wind; not a drop of rain; nothing is to be seen but the whirling clouds of the **tūfān**. The old peepul-tree moans, and the wind roars in it as if the storm would tear it up by the roots."—*Wanderings of a Pilgrim*, ii. 53.

1840.—"Slavers throwing overboard the Dead and Dying. **Typhoon** coming on.

"'Aloft all hands, strike the topmasts and belay;
Yon angry setting sun, and fierce-edge clouds
Declare the **Typhoon's** coming' &c. (*Fallacies of Hope*)."

J. M. W. Turner, in the R.A. Catalogue.

Mr. Ruskin appears to have had no doubt as to the etymology of **Typhoon**, for the rain-cloud from this picture is engraved in *Modern Painters*, vol. iv. as "The Locks of **Typhon.**" See Mr. Hamerton's *Life of Turner*, pp. 288, 291, 345.

Punch parodied Turner in the following imaginary entry from the R.A. Catalogue:

"34.—A **Typhoon** bursting in a Simoon over the Whirlpool of Maelstrom, Norway, with a ship on fire, an eclipse and the effect of a lunar rainbow."

1853.—". . . pointing as he spoke to a dark dirty line which was becoming more and more visible in the horizon:

"'By Jove, yes!' cried Stanton, 'that's a **typhaon** coming up, sure enough.'"—*Oakfield*, i. 122.

1859.—"The weather was sultry and unsettled, and my Jemadar, Ramdeen Tewarry . . . opined that we ought to make ready for the coming **tuphan** or tempest. . . . A darkness that might be felt, and that no lamp could illumine, shrouded our camp. The wind roared and yelled. It was a hurricane."—*Lt.-Col. Lewin, A Fly on the Wheel*, p. 62.

Compare the next quotation, from the same writer, with that given above from Couto respecting the *Olho de Boi*:

1885. — "The district was subject to cyclonic storms of incredible violence, fortunately lasting for a very short time, but which often caused much destruction. These storms were heralded by the appearance above the horizon of clouds known to the natives by the name of 'lady's eyebrows,' so called from their being curved in a narrow black-arched wisp, and these most surely foretold the approach of the tornado."—*Ibid.* 176.

TYRE, s. Tamil and Malayāl. *tayir*. The common term in S. India for curdled milk. It is the Skt. *dadhi*, Hind. *dahi* of Upper India, and probably the name is a corruption of that word.

1626.—"Many reasoned with the Iesuits, and some held vaine Discourses of the Creation, as that there were seuen seas; one of Salt water, the second of Fresh, the third of Honey, the fourth of Milke, the fift of **Tair** (which is Cream beginning to sowre). . . ."—*Purchas, Pilgrimage*, 561.

1651.—"**Tayer**, dat is dicke Melch, die wie *Saen* nommen."—*Rogerius*, 138.

1672.—"Curdled milk, **Tayer**, or what we call *Saane*, is a thing very grateful to them, for it is very cooling, and used by them as a remedy, especially in hot fevers and smallpox, which is very prevalent in the country."—*Baldaeus, Zeylon*, 403.

1776.—"If a Bramin applies himself to commerce, he shall not sell . . . Camphire and other aromaticks, or Honey, or Water, or Poison, or Flesh, or Milk, or **Tyer** (Sour Cream) or **Ghee**, or bitter Oil. . . ."—*Halhed, Code*, 41.

1782.—"Les uns en furent affligés pour avoir passé les nuits et dormi en plein air; d'autres pour avoir mangé du riz froid avec du **Tair**."—*Sonnerat*, i. 201.

c. 1784.—"The Saniassi (**Sunyasee**), who lived near the *chauderie* (see **CHOULTRY**), took charge of preparing my meals, which consisted of rice, vegetables, **tayar** (*lait caillé*), and a little *mologonier*" (*eau poivrée*—see **MULLIGATAWNY**).—*Haafner*, i. 147.

[1800.—"The boiled milk, that the family has not used, is allowed to cool in the same vessel; and a little of the former day's **tyre**, or curdled milk, is added to promote its coagulation. . . ."—*Buchanan, Mysore*, ii. 14.]

1822.—"He was indeed poor, but he was charitable; so he spread before them a repast, in which there was no lack of **ghee**, or milk, or **tyer**."—*The Gooroo Paramartan*, E.T. by *Babington*, p. 80.

U

UJUNGTANAH, n.p. This is the Malay name (nearly answering to 'Land's End,' from *Ujung*, 'point or promontory,' and *tanah*, 'land') of the extreme end of the Malay Peninsula terminating in what the maps call Pt. Romania. In Godinho de Eredia's *Declaracam de Malaca* the term is applied to the whole Peninsula, but owing to the interchangeable use of *u*, *v*, and of *j*, *i*, it appears there throughout as **Viontana**. The name is often applied by the Portuguese writers to the Kingdom of Johor, in which the Malay dynasty of Malacca established itself when expelled by Alboquerque in 1511; and it is even applied (as in the quotation from Barros) to their capital.

c. 1539.—"After that the King of **Jantana** had taken that oath before a great Cacis (**Casis**) of his, called *Raia Moulana*, upon a festival day when as they solemnized their Ramadan (**Ramdam**) . . ."—*Pinto*, in *Cogan's* E.T., p. 36.

1553.—"And that you may understand the position of the city of **Ujantana**, which Don Stephen went to attack, you must know that **Ujantana** is the most southerly and the most easterly point of the mainland of the Malaca coast, which from this Point (distant from the equator about a degree, and from Malaca something more than 40 leagues) turns north in the direction of the Kingdom of Siam. . . . On the western side of this Point a river runs into the sea, so deep that ships can run up it 4 leagues beyond the bar, and along its banks, well inland, King Alaudin had established a big town. . . ."—*Barros*, IV. xi. 13.

1554.—". . . en Muar, in **Ojantana**. . . ." —*Botelho, Tombo*, 105.

UMBRELLA, s. This word is of course not Indian or Anglo-Indian, but the *thing* is very prominent in India, and some interest attaches to the history of the word and thing in Europe. We shall collect here a few quotations bearing upon this. The knowledge and use of this serviceable instrument seems to have gone through extraordinary eclipses. It is frequent as an accompaniment of royalty in the Nineveh sculptures; it was in general Indian use in the time of Alexander; it occurs in old Indian inscriptions, on Greek vases, and in Greek and Latin literature; it was in use at the court of Byzantium, and at that of the Great Khan in Mongolia, in medieval Venice, and more recently in the semi-savage courts of Madagascar and Ashantee. Yet it was evidently a strange object, needing particular description, to John Marignolli (c. 1350), Ruy Clavijo (c. 1404), Barbosa (1516), John de Barros (1553), and Minsheu (1617). See also **CHATTA**, and **SOMBRERO**.

c. B.C. 325.—"Τοὺς δὲ πωγώνας λέγει Νέαρχος ὅτι βάπτονται Ἰνδοὶ . . . καὶ σκιάδια ὅτι προβάλλονται, τοῦ θέρεος, ὅσοι οὐκ ἠμελημένοι Ἰνδῶν."—*Arrian, Indica*, xvi.

c. B.C. 2.

"Ipse tene distenta suis **umbracula** virgis;
Ipse face in turba, qua venit illa, locum."
Ovid, Art. Amat. ii. 209-210.

c. A.D. 5.

"Aurea pellebant rapidos **umbracula** soles
Quae tamen Herculeae sustinuere manus." *Ibid. Fasti*, ii. 311-312.

c. A.D. 100.

"En, cui tu viridem **umbellam**, cui succina mittas
Grandia natalis quoties redit. . . ."
Juvenal, ix. 50-51.

c. 200.—". . . ἔπεμψε δὲ καὶ κλίνην αὐτῷ ἀργυρόποδα, καὶ στρωμνὴν, καὶ σκηνὴν οὐρανόροφον ἀνθίνην, καὶ θρόνον ἀργυροῦν, καὶ ἐπίχρυσον σκιάδιον . . ."—*Athenaeus*, Lib. ii. Epit. § 31.

c. 380.—"Ubi si inter aurata flabella laciniis sericis insiderint muscae, vel per foramen **umbraculi** pensilis radiolus irruperit solis, queruntur quod non sunt apud Cimmerios nati."—*Ammianus Marcellinus*, XXVIII. iv.

1248.—"Ibi etiam quoddam **Solinum** (*v.* **Soliolum**), sive tentoriolum, quod portatur super caput Imperatoris, fuit praesentatum eidem, quod totum erat praeparatum cum gemmis."—*Joan. de Plano Carpini*, in *Rec. de V.*, iv. 759-760.

c. 1292.—"Et a haute festes porte Monsignor le Dus une corone d'or . . . et la ou il vait a hautes festes si vait apres lui un damoiseau qui porte une **unbrele** de dras à or sur son chief . . ."

and again:

"Et apres s'en vet Monsignor li Dus desos l'**onbrele** que li dona Monsignor l'Apostoille; et cele **onbrele** est d'un dras (a) or, que la porte un damosiaus entre ses mains, que s'en vet totes voies apres Monsignor li Dus."—Venetian Chronicle of *Martino da Canale, Archiv. Stor. Ital.*, I. Ser. viii. 214, 560.

1298.—"Et tout ceus . . . ont par commandement que toutes fois que il chevauchent doivent avoir sus le chief un palieque que on dit **ombrel**, que on porte sur une lance en senefiance de grant seigneurie."—*Marco Polo*, Text of *Pauthier*, i. 256-7.

c. 1332.—(At Constantinople) "the inhabitants, military men or others, great and small, winter and summer, carry over their heads huge **umbrellas** (*ma hallāt*)."—*Ibn Batuta*, ii. 440.

c. 1335.—"Whenever the Sultan (of Delhi) mounts his horse, they carry an **umbrella** over his head. But when he starts on a march to war, or on a long journey, you see carried over his head seven umbrellas, two of which are covered with jewels of inestimable value."—*Shihābuddīn Dimishkī*, in *Not. et Exts.* xiii. 190.

1404.—"And over her head they bore a **shade (sombra)** carried by a man, on a shaft like that of a lance; and it was of white silk, made like the roof of a round tent, and stretched by a hoop of wood, and this shade they carry over the head to protect them from the sun."—*Clavijo*, § cxxii.

1541.—"Then next to them marches twelve men on horseback, called Peretandas, each of them carrying an **Umbrello** of carnation Sattin, and other twelve that follow with banners of white damask."—*Pinto*, in *Cogan's* E.T., p. 135.

In the original this runs:

"Vão doze homẽs a cavallo, que se chamão peretandas, cõ **sombreyros** de citim cramesim nas mãos *a modo de esparavels postos em cesteas muyto compridas* (like tents upon very long staves) et outros doze cõ bãdeyras de damasco branco."

[c. 1590.—"*The Ensigns of Royalty*. . . . 2. The *Chatr*, or **umbrella**, is adorned with the most precious jewels, of which there are never less than seven. 3. The *Sáibán* is of an oval form, a yard in length, and its handle, like that of the umbrella, is covered with brocade, and ornamented with precious stones. One of the attendants holds it, to keep off the rays of the sun. It is also called *Áftābgír*."—*Āīn*, i. 50.]

1617.—"An **Umbrell**, a *fashion of* round and broade fanne, wherewith the Indians, *and from them our great ones preserue themselves from the heate of the scorching sunne*. G. Ombrafre, m. Ombrelle, f. I. Ombrélla. L. Vmbella, *ab vmbra*, the shadow, *est enim* instrumentum quo solem à facie arcent ¶ Iuven. Gr. σκιάδιον, diminut. a σκία, i. vmbra. T. Schabhut, q. schathut, à schatten, i. *vmbra*, et hut, i. *pileus, à quo*, et B. Schinhoedt. Br. *Teggidel, à teg*. i. pulchrum forma, et *gidd*, pro *riddio*, i. protegere; *haec enim vmbellae finis*."—*Minsheu* (1st ed. s.v.).

1644.—"Here (at Marseilles) we bought **umbrellas** against the heats."—*Evelyn's Diary*, 7th Oct.

1677.—(In this passage the word is applied to an awning before a shop. "The Streets are generally narrow . . . the better to receive the advantages of **Umbrello's** extended from side to side to keep the sun's violence from their customers."—*Fryer*, 222.

1681.—"After these comes an Elephant with two Priests on his back; one whereof is the Priest before spoken of, carrying the painted Stick on his shoulder. . . . The other sits behind him, holding a round thing like an **Vmbrello** over his head, to keep off Sun or Rain."—*Knox's Ceylon*, 79.

1709.—". . . The Young Gentleman belonging to the Custom-house that for fear of rain borrowed the **Umbrella** at Will's Coffee-house in Cornhill of the Mistress, is hereby advertised that to be dry from head to foot in the like occasion he shall be welcome to the Maid's pattens."—*The Female Tatler*, Dec. 12, quoted in *Malcolm's Anecdotes*, 1808, p. 429.

1712.

"The tuck'd up semstress walks with hasty strides
While streams run down her oil'd **umbrella's** sides."

Swift, A City Shower.

1715.

"Good housewives all the winter's rage despise,
Defended by the riding hood's disguise;
Or underneath the **Umbrella's** oily shade
Safe through the wet on clinking pattens tread.

"Let Persian dames the **Umbrella's** ribs display
To guard their beauties from the sunny ray;
Or sweating slaves support the shady load
When Eastern monarchs show their state abroad;
Britain in winter only knows its aid
To guard from chilly showers the walking maid."

Gay, Trivia, i.

1850.—*Advertisement posted at the door of one of the Sections of the* British Association *meeting at* Edinburgh.

"The gentleman, who carried away a brown silk **umbrella** from the —— Section yesterday, may have the cover belonging to it, which is of no further use to the Owner, by applying to the Porter at the Royal Hotel."—(*From Personal Recollection.*)—It is a curious parallel to the advertisement above from the *Female Tatler*.

UPAS, s. This word is now, like **Juggernaut**, chiefly used in English as a customary metaphor, and to indicate some institution that the speaker wishes to condemn in a compendious manner. The word *upas* is Javanese for poison; [Mr. Scott writes: "The Malay word *ūpas*, means simply 'poison.' It is Javanese *hupas*, Sundanese *upas*, Balinese *hupas*, 'poison.' It commonly refers to vegetable poison, because such are more common. In the Lampong language *upas* means 'sickness.'"] It became familiar in Europe in connection with exaggerated and fabulous stories regarding the extraordinary and deadly character of a tree in Java, alleged to be so called. There are several trees in the Malay Islands producing deadly poisons, but the particular tree to which such stories were attached is one which has in the last century been described under the name of *Antiaris toxicaria*, from the name given to the poison by the Javanese proper, viz. *Antjar*, or *Anchar* (the name of the tree all over Java), whilst it is known to the Malays and people of Western Java as *Upas*, and in Celebes and the Philippine Islands as *Ipo* or *Hipo*.

[According to Mr. Scott "the Malay name for the 'poison-tree,' or any poison-tree, is *pōhun ūpas*, *pūhun ūpas*, represented in English by **bohon-upas**. The names of two poison-trees, the Javanese *anchar* (Malay also *anchar*) and *chetik*, appear occasionally in English books. . . The Sundanese name for the poison tree is *bulo ongko*."] It was the poison commonly used by the natives of Celebes and other islands for poisoning the small bamboo darts which they used (and in some islands still use) to shoot from the blow-tube (see **SUMPITAN, SARBATANE**).

The story of some deadly poison in these islands is very old, and we find it in the *Travels* of Friar Odoric, accompanied by the mention of the disgusting antidote which was believed to be efficacious, a genuine Malay belief, and told by a variety of later and independent writers, such as Nieuhof, Saar, Tavernier, Cleyer, and Kaempfer.

The subject of this poison came especially to the notice of the Dutch in connection with its use to poison the arrows just alluded to, and some interesting particulars are given on the subject by Bontius, from whom a quotation is given below, with others. There is a notice of the poison in De Bry, in Sir T. Herbert (whencesoever he borrowed it), and in somewhat later authors about the middle of the 17th century. In March 1666 the subject came before the young Royal Society, and among a long list of subjects for inquiry in the East occur two questions pertaining to this matter.

The illustrious Rumphius in his *Herbarium Amboinense* goes into a good deal of detail on the subject, but the tree does not grow in Amboyna where he wrote, and his account thus contains some ill-founded statements, which afterwards lent themselves to the fabulous history of which we shall have to speak presently. Rumphius however procured from Macassar specimens of the plant, and it was he who first gave the native name (*Ipo*, the Macassar form) and assigned a scientific name, *Arbor toxicaria*.* Passing over with simple mention the notices in the appendix to John Ray's *Hist. Plantarum*, and in Valentijn (from both of which extracts will be found below), we come to the curious compound of the loose statements of former writers magnified, of the popular stories current among Europeans in the Dutch colonies, and of pure romantic invention, which first appeared in 1783, in the *London Magazine*. The professed author of this account was one Foersch, who had served as a junior surgeon in the Dutch East Indies.* This person describes the tree, called **bohon-upas**, as situated "about 27 leagues † from Batavia, 14 from Soura Karta, the seat of the Emperor, and between 18 and 20 leagues from Tinkjoe" (probably for *Tjukjoe*, *i.e.* Djokjo-Karta), "the present residence of the Sultan of Java." Within a radius of 15 to 18 miles round the tree no human creature, no living thing could exist. Condemned malefactors were employed to fetch the poison; they were protected by special arrangements, yet not more than 1 in 10 of them survived the adventure. Foersch also describes executions by means of the Upas poison, which he says he witnessed at Sura Karta in February 1776.

The whole paper is a very clever piece of sensational romance, and has impressed itself indelibly, it would seem, on the English language; for to it is undoubtedly due the adoption of that standing metaphor to which we have alluded at the beginning of this article. This effect may, however, have been due not so much directly to the article in the *London Magazine* as to the adoption of the fable by the famous ancestor of a man still more famous, Erasmus Darwin, in his poem of the *Loves of the Plants*. In that work not only is the essence of Foersch's story embodied in the verse, but the story itself is quoted at length in the notes. It is said that Darwin was warned of the worthlessness of the narrative, but was unwilling to rob his poem of so sensational an episode.

Nothing appears to be known of Foersch except that there was really a person of that name in the medical

* It must be kept in mind that though Rumphius (George Everard Rumpf) died in 1693, his great work was not printed till nearly fifty years afterwards (1741).

* Foersch was a surgeon of the third class at Samarang in the year 1773.—*Horsfield*, in *Bat. Trans.* as quoted below.

† This distance is probably a clerical error. It is quite inconsistent with the other two assigned.

service in Java at the time indicated. In our article **ANACONDA** we have adduced some curious particulars of analogy between the Anaconda-myth and the Upas-myth, and intimated a suspicion that the same hand may have had to do with the spinning of both yarns.

The extraordinary *éclat* produced by the Foerschian fables led to the appointment of a committee of the Batavian Society to investigate the true facts, whose report was published in 1789. This we have not yet been able to see, for the report is not contained in the regular series of the *Transactions* of that Society ; nor have we found a refutation of the fables by M. Charles Coquebert referred to by Leschenault in the paper which we are about to mention. The poison tree was observed in Java by Deschamps, naturalist with the expedition of D'Entrecasteaux, and is the subject of a notice by him in the *Annales de Voyages*, vol. i., which goes into little detail, but appears to be correct as far as it goes, except in the statement that the Anchar was confined to Eastern Java. But the first thorough identification of the plant, and scientific account of the facts was that of M. Leschenault de la Tour. This French savant, when about to join a voyage of discovery to the South Seas, was recommended by Jussieu to take up the investigation of the Upas. On first enquiring at Batavia and Samarang, M. Leschenault heard only fables akin to Foersch's romance, and it was at Sura Karta that he first got genuine information, which eventually enabled him to describe the tree from actual examination.

The tree from which he took his specimens was more than 100 ft. in height, with a girth of 18 ft. at the base. A Javanese who climbed it to procure the flowers had to make cuts in the stem in order to mount. After ascending some 25 feet the man felt so ill that he had to come down, and for some days he continued to suffer from nausea, vomiting, and vertigo. But another man climbed to the top of the tree without suffering at all. On another occasion Leschenault, having had a tree of 4 feet girth cut down, walked among its broken branches, and had face and hands besprinkled with the gum-resin, yet neither did he suffer ; he adds, however, that he had washed immediately after. Lizards and insects were numerous on the trunk, and birds perched upon the branches. M. Leschenault gives details of the preparation of the poison as practised by the natives, and also particulars of its action, on which experiment was made in Paris with the material which he brought to Europe. He gave it the scientific name by which it continues to be known, viz. *Antiaris toxicaria* (N.O. *Artocarpeae*).*

M. Leschenault also drew the attention of Dr. Horsfield, who had been engaged in the botanical exploration of Java some years before the British occupation, and continued it during that period, to the subject of the Upas, and he published a paper on it in the *Batavian Transactions* for 1813 (vol. vii.). His account seems entirely in accordance with that of Leschenault, but is more detailed and complete, with the result of numerous observations and experiments of his own. He saw the *Antiaris* first in the Province of Poegar, on his way to Banyuwangi. In Blambangan (eastern extremity of Java) he visited four or five trees ; he afterwards found a very tall specimen growing at Passaruwang, on the borders of Malang, and again several young trees in the forests of Japāra, and one near Onārang. In all these cases, scattered over the length of Java, the people knew the tree as *anchar*.

Full articles on the subject are to be found (by Mr. J. J. Bennet) in Horsfield's *Plantae Javanicae Rariores*, 1838-52, pp. 52 *seqq.*, together with a figure of a flowering branch pl. xiii. ; and in Blume's *Rumphia* (Brussels, 1836), pp. 46 *seqq.*, and pls. xxii., xxiii. ; to both of which works we have been much indebted for guidance. Blume gives a drawing, for the truth of which he vouches, of a tall specimen of the trees. These he describes as "*vastas, arduas, et a ceteris segregatas,*"—solitary

* Leschenault also gives the description of another and still more powerful poison, used in a similar way to that of the *Antiaris*, viz. the *tieute*, called sometimes *Upas Raja*, the plant producing which is a *Strychnos*, and a creeper. Though, as we have said, the name *Upas* is generic, and is applied to this, it is not *the* Upas of English metaphor, and we are not concerned with it here. Both kinds are produced and prepared in Java. The *Ipo* (a form of *Upas*) of Macassar is the *Antiaris;* the *ipo* of the Borneo Dayaks is the *Tieute.*

and eminent, on account of their great longevity, (possibly on account of their being spared by the axe?), but not for any such reason as the fables allege. There is no lack of adjoining vegetation; the spreading branches are clothed abundantly with parasitical plants, and numerous birds and squirrels frequent them. The stem throws out 'wings' or buttresses (see Horsfield in the *Bat. Trans.*, and Blume's Pl.) like many of the forest trees of Further India. Blume refers, in connection with the origin of the prevalent fables, to the real existence of exhalations of carbonic acid gas in the volcanic tracts of Java, dangerous to animal life and producing sterility around, alluding particularly to a paper by M. Loudoun (a Dutch official of Scotch descent), in the *Edinburgh New Phil. Journal* for 1832, p. 102, containing a formidable description of the Guwo Upas or Poison Valley on the frontier of the Pekalongan and Banyumas provinces. We may observe, however, that, if we remember rightly, the exaggerations of Mr. Loudoun have been exposed and ridiculed by Dr. Junghuhn, the author of "*Java.*" And if the Foersch legend be compared with some of the particulars alleged by several of the older writers, *e.g.* Camell (in Ray), Valentijn, Spielman, Kaempfer, and Rumphius, it will be seen that the *basis* for a great part of that *putida commentatio*, as Blume calls it, is to be found in them.

George Colman the Younger founded on the Foerschian Upas-myth, a kind of melodrama, called the *Law of Java*, first acted at Covent Garden May 11, 1822. We give some quotations below.*

Lindley, in his *Vegetable Kingdom*, in a short notice of *Antiaris toxicaria*, says that, though the accounts are greatly exaggerated, yet the facts are notable enough. He says cloth made from the tough fibre is so acrid as to verify the Shirt of Nessus. My friend Gen. Maclagan, noticing Lindley's remark to me, adds: "Do you remember in our High School days (at Edinburgh) a grand Diorama called **The Upas Tree?** It showed a large wild valley, with a single tree in the middle, and illustrated the safety of approach on the windward side, and the desolation it dealt on the other."

[For some details as to the use of the Upas poison, and an analysis of the Arrow-poisons of Borneo by Dr. L. Lewin (from *Virchow's Archiv. fur Pathol. Anat.* 1894, pp. 317-25) see *Ling Roth, Natives of Sarawak*, ii. 188 *seqq.* and for superstitions connected with these poisons, *Skeat, Malay Magic*, 426.]

c. 1330.—"En queste isole sono molte cose maravigliose e strane. Onde alcuni arbori li sono . . . che fanno veleno pessimo . . . Quelli uomini sono quasi tutti corsali, e quando vanno a battaglia portano ciascuno uno canna in mano, di lunghezza d'un braccio e pongono in capo de la canna uno ago di ferro atossiato in quel veleno, e sofiano nella canna e l'ago vola e percuotelo dove vogliono, e'ncontinente quelli ch'è percosso muore. Ma egli hanno la tina piene di sterco d'uomo e una iscodella di sterco guarisce l'uomo da queste cotali ponture."—*Storia di Frate Odorigo*, from Palatina MS., in *Cathay, &c.*, App., p. xlix.

c. 1630.—"And (in Makasser) which is no lesse infernall, the men use long canes or truncks (cald Sempitans—see **SUMPITAN**), out of which they can (and use it) blow a little pricking quill, which if it draw the lest drop of blood from any part of the body, it makes him (though the strongest man living) die immediately; some venoms operate in an houre, others in a moment, the veynes and body (by the virulence of the poyson) corrupting and rotting presently, to any man's terrour and amazement, and feare to live where such abominations predominate."—*Sir T. Herbert*, ed. 1638, p. 329.

c. 1631.—"I will now conclude; but I first must say something of the poison used by the King of Macassar in the Island of Celebes to envenom those little arrows which they shoot through blowing-tubes, a poison so deadly that it causes death more rapidly than a dagger. For one wounded ever so lightly, be it but a scratch bringing blood, or a prick in the heel, immediately begins to nod like a drunken man, and falls dead to the ground. And within half an hour of death this putrescent poison so corrupts the flesh that it can be plucked from the bones like so much *mucus*. And what seems still more marvellous, if a man (*e.g.*) be scratched in the thigh, or higher in the body, by another point which is *not* poisoned, and the still warm blood as it flows down to the feet be merely touched by one of these poisoned little arrows, swift as wind the pestilent influence ascends to the wound, and with the same swiftness and other effects snatches the man from among the living.

"These are no idle tales, but the experience of eye-witnesses, not only among our countrymen, but among Danes and Englishmen."—*Jac. Bontii*, lib. v. cap. xxxiii.

* I remember when a boy reading the whole of Foersch's story in a fascinating book, called *Wood's Zoography*, which I have not seen for half a century, and which, I should suppose from my recollection, was more sensational than scientific. —*Y.*

1646.—"Es wachst ein Baum auf *Maccasser*, einer Cüst auf der Insul *Çelebes*, der ist treflich vergiftet, dass wann einer nur an einem Glied damit verletzet wird, und man solches nit alsbald wegschlägt, der Gift geschwind zum Hertzen eilet, und den Garaus machet" (then the antidote as before is mentioned). . . . "Mit solchem Gift schmieren die *Bandanesen* Ihre lange Pfeil, die Sie von grossen Bögen, einer Mannslāng hoch, hurtig schiessen; in *Banda* aber tähten Ihre Weiber grossen Schaden damit. Denn Sie sich auf die Bäume setzten, und kleine Fischgeräht damit schmierten, und durch ein gehöhlert Röhrlein, von einem Baum, auf unser Volck schossen, mit grossen machtigen Schaden."—*Saar, Ost-Indianische Funfzehen-Jahrige Kriegs-Dienste* . . . 1672, pp. 46-47.

1667.—"*Enquiries for* Suratt, *and other parts of the East Indies*.

* * * * *

"19. Whether it be true, that the only Antidote hitherto known, against the famous and fatal *macassar-poison*, is *human ordure*, taken inwardly? And what substance that poison is made of?"—*Phil. Trans.* vol. ii. Anno 1667 (Proceedings for March 11, 1666, *i.e.* N.S. 1667), d. 417.

1682.—"The especial weapons of the Makassar soldiers, which they use against their enemies, are certain pointed arrowlets about a foot in length. At the foremost end these are fitted with a sharp and pointed fish-tooth, and at the butt with a knob of spongy wood.

"The points of these arrows, long before they are to be used, are dipt in poison and then dried.

"This poison is a sap that drips from the bark of the branches of a certain tree, like resin, from pine-trees.

"The tree grows on the Island Makasser, in the interior, and on three or four islands of the Bugisses (see **BUGIS**), round about Makassar. It is about the height of the clove-tree, and has leaves very similar.

"The fresh sap of this tree is a very deadly poison; indeed its virulence is incurable.

"The arrowlets prepared with this poison are not, by the Makasser soldiers, shot with a bow, but blown from certain blow-pipes (*uit zekere spatten gespat*); just as here, in the country, people shoot birds by blowing round pellets of clay.

"They can with these in still weather hit their mark at a distance of 4 rods.

"They say the Makassers themselves know no remedy against this poison . . . for the poison presses swiftly into the blood and vital spirits, and causes a violent inflammation. They hold (however) that the surest remedy for this poison is . . ." (and so on, repeating the antidote already mentioned).—*Joan Nieuhof's Zee en Land Reize*, &c., pp. 217-218.

c. 1681.—"*Arbor Toxicaria*, **Ipo**.

"I have never yet met with any poison more horrible and hateful, produced by any vegetable growth, than that which is derived from this lactescent tree.

* * * * *

Moreover beneath this tree, and in its whole circumference to the distance of a stone-cast, no plant, no shrub, or herbage will grow; the soil beneath it is barren, blackened, and burnt as it were . . . and the atmosphere about it is so polluted and poisoned that the birds which alight upon its branches become giddy and fall dead. * * * all things perish which are touched by its emanations, insomuch that every animal shuns it and keeps away from it, and even the birds eschew flying by it.

"No man dares to approach the tree without having his arms, feet, and head wrapped round with linen . . . for Death seems to have planted his foot and his throne beside this tree. . . ." (He then tells of a venomous basilisk with two feet in front and fiery eyes, a crest, and a horn, that dwelt under this tree). * * *

"The Malays call it *Cayu* **Upas**, but in Macassar and the rest of Celebes it is called **Ipo**.

* * * * *

"It grows in desert places, and amid bare hills, and is easily discerned from afar, there being no other tree near it."

* * * * *

—*Rumphii, Herbarium Amboinense*, ii. 263-268.

1685.—"I cannot omit to set forth here an account of the poisoned missiles of the Kingdom of *Macassar*, which the natives of that kingdom have used against our soldiers, bringing them to sudden death. It is extracted from the Journal of the illustrious and gallant admiral, H. Cornelius Spielman. . . . The natives of the kingdom in question possess a singular art of shooting arrows by blowing through canes, and wounding with these, insomuch that if the skin be but slightly scratched the wounded die in a twinkling."

(Then the old story of the only antidote). . . .

The account follows extracted from the Journal.

* * * * *

"There are but few among the Macassars and Bugis who possess the real knowledge needful for selecting the poison, so as to distinguish between what is worthless and what is highest quality. . . . From the princes (or Rajas) I have understood that the soil in which the trees affording the poison grow, for a great space round about produces no grass nor any other vegetable growth, and that the poison is properly a water or liquid, flowing from a bruise or cut made in the bark of those trees, oozing out as sap does from plants that afford milky juices. . . . When the liquid is being drawn from the wounded tree, no one should carelessly approach it so as to let the liquid touch his hands, for by such contact all the joints become stiffened and contracted. For this reason the collectors make use of long bamboos, armed with sharp iron points. With these they stab the tree with great force, and so get the sap to flow into the canes, in which it speedily hardens."—Dn. Corn. Spielman . . . *de Telis deleterio Veneno infectis in* Macassar, *et aliis Regnis Insulae* Celebes; *ex ejus Diario extracta. Huic praemittitur brevis narratio de hac materia Dn.* Andreae Cleyeri. In *Miscellanea Curiosa, sive Ephemeridum. . . Academiae Naturae Curiosorum,* Dec. II. Annus Tertius. Anni MDCLXXXIV., Norimbergae (1685), pp. 127 *seqq.*

1704.—"Ipo seu **Hypo** arbor est mediocris, folio parvo, et obscure virenti, quae tam malignae et nocivae qualitatis, ut omne vivens umbrâ suâ interimat, unde narrant in circuitu, et umbrae distinctu, plurima ossium mortuorum hominum animaliumque videri. Circumvicinas etiam plantas enecat, et aves insidentes interficere ferunt, si Nucis Vomicae *Igasur,* plantam non invenerint, qua reperta vita quidem donantur et servantur, sed defluvium patiuntur plumarum. . . . **Hypo** lac Indi *Camucones* et *Sambales,* Hispanis infensissimi, longis, excipiunt arundineis perticis, sagittis intoxicandis deserviturum irremediabile venenum, omnibus aliis alexipharmacis superius, praeterquam stercore humano propinato. An Argensolae *arbor comosa,* quam *Insulae Celebes* ferunt, cujus umbra occidentalis mortifera, orientalis antidotum? . . ."—*De Quibusdam Arboribus Venenatis,* in *Herbarum aliarumque Stirpium in Insula Luzone* . . . a Revdo Patre Georgio Camello, S.J. *Syllabus ad* Joannem Raium *transmissus.* In Appendix, p. 87, of *Joan. Raii Hist. Plantarum.* Vol. III. (London 1704).

1712.—"Maxima autem celebritas radiculae enata est, ab eximia illa virtute, quam adversus toxicum Macassariense praestat, exitiale illud, et vix alio remedio vincibile. Est venenum hoc succus lacteus et pinguis, qui collegitur ex recens sauciata arbore quadam, indigenes **Ipu**, Malajis Javanisque **Upà** dictâ, in abditis locis sylvarum Insulae Celebes . . . crescente . . . cujus genuinum et in solâ Macassariâ germinantis succum, qui colligere suscipiunt, praesentissimis vitae periculis se exponant necesse est. Nam ad quaerendam arborem loca dumis beluisque infesta penetranda sunt, inventa vero, nisi eminus vulneretur, et ab eâ parte, a qua ventus adspirat, vel aura incumbit, aggressores erumpento halitu subito suffocabit. Quam sortem etiam experiri dicuntur volucres, arborem recens vulneratam transvolantes. Collectio exitiosi liquoris, morti ob patrata maleficia damnatis committitur, eo pacto, ut poena remittatur, si liquorem reportaverint . . . Sylvam ingrediuntur longâ instructi arundine . . . quam altera extremitate . . . ex asse acuunt, ut ad pertundendam arboris corticem valeat. . . . Quam longe possunt, ab arbore constituti, arundinis aciem arbori valide intrudunt, et liquoris, ex vulnere effluentis, tantum excipiunt, quantum arundinis cavo ad proximum usque internodium capi potest. . . . Reduces, supplicio et omni discrimine defuncti, hoc vitae suae λυτρον Regi offerunt. Ita narrarunt mihi populares Celebani, hodie Macassari dicti. Quis autem veri quicquam ex Asiaticorum ore referat, quod figmentis non implicatur . . . ?"—*Kaempfer, Amoen. Exot.*, 575-576.

1726.—"But among all sorts of trees, that occur here, or hereabouts, I know of none more pernicious than the sap of the Macassar Poison tree * * * They say that there are only a few trees of this kind, occuring in the district of *Turatte* on Celebes, and that none are employed except, at a certain time of the year when it is procurable, those who are condemned to death, to approach the trees and bring away the poison. . . . The poison must be taken with the greatest care in Bamboos, into which it drips slowly from the bark of the trees, and the persons collected for this purpose must first have their hands, heads, and all exposed parts, well wound round with cloths. . . ."—*Valentijn,* iii. 218.

1783.—"The following description of the BOHON **Upas**, or POISON TREE, which grows in the Island of Java, and renders it unwholesome by its noxious vapours, has been procured for the *London Magazine,* from Mr. Heydinger, who was employed to translate it from the original Dutch, by the author, Mr. Foersch, who, we are informed, is at present abroad, in the capacity of surgeon on board an English vessel. . . .

* * * * *

"'In the year 1774, I was stationed at Batavia, as a surgeon, in the service of the Dutch East India Company. During my residence there I received several different accounts of the *Bohon*-**Upas**, and the violent effects of its poison. They all then seemed incredible to me, but raised my curiosity in so high a degree, that I resolved to investigate this subject thoroughly. . . . I had procured a recommendation from an old Malayan priest to another priest, who lives on the nearest habitable spot to the tree, which is about fifteen or sixteen miles distant. The letter proved of great service to me on my undertaking, as that priest is employed by the Emperor to reside there, in order to prepare for eternity the souls of those who, for different crimes, are sentenced to approach the tree, and to procure the poison. . . . Malefactors, who, for their crimes, are sentenced to die, are the only persons to fetch the poison; and this is the only chance they have of saving their lives. . . . They are then provided with a silver or tortoise-shell box, in which they are to put the poisonous gum, and are properly instructed how to proceed, while they are upon their dangerous expedition. Among other particulars, they are always told to attend to the direction of the winds; as they are to go towards the tree before the wind, so that the effluvia from the tree are always blown from them. . . . They are afterwards sent to the house of the old priest, to which place they are commonly attended by their friends and relations. Here they generally remain some days, in expectation of a favourable breeze. During that time the ecclesiastic prepares them for their future fate by prayers and admonitions. When the hour of their departure arrives the priest puts them on a long leather cap with two glasses before their eyes, which comes down as far as their breast, and also provides them with a pair of leather gloves. . . .

"The worthy old ecclesiastic has assured me, that during his residence there, for upwards of thirty years, he had dismissed above seven hundred criminals in the manner which I have described; and that scarcely two out of twenty returned," . . . &c. &c.—*London Magazine*, Dec. 1783, pp. 512-517.

The paper concludes:

"[We shall be happy to communicate any authentic papers of Mr. Foersch to the public through the London Magazine.]"

1789.—

"No spicy nutmeg scents the vernal gales,
Nor towering plantain shades the midday vales,
* * * * *
No step retreating, on the sand impress'd,
Invites the visit of a second guest;
* * * * *
Fierce in dread silence on the blasted heath
Fell **Upas** sits, the Hydra Tree of death;
Lo! from one root, the envenom'd soil below,
A thousand vegetative serpents grow . . ." etc.

Darwin, Loves of the Plants; in The Botanic Garden, Pt. II.

1808. — "*Notice sur le* Pohon **Upas** *ou Arbre à* Poison; *Extrait d'un Voyage inédit dans l'Intérieur de l'Ile de Java, par* L. A. Deschamps, D.M.P., *l'un des compagnons du Voyage du Général d'Entrecasteaux.*

"C'est au fond des sombre forêts de l'ile de Java que la nature a caché le *pohun* **upas**, l'arbre le plus dangereux du règne végétal, pour le poison mortel qu'il renferme, et plus celèbre encore par les fables dont on l'a rendu le sujet. . . ."—*Annales des Voyages*, i. 69.

1810.—"Le poison fameux dont se servent les Indiens de l'Archipel des *Moluques*, et des iles de la *Sonde*, connu sous le nom d'**ipo** et **upas**, a interessé plus que tous les autres la curiosité des Européens, parce que les relations qu'on en a donné ont été exagérées et accompagnées de ce merveilleux dont les peuples de l'Inde aiment à orner leurs narrations. . . ."—*Leschenault de la Tour*, in Mémoire sur le Strychnos Tieute *et l'*Antiaris toxicaria, *plantes venimeuses de l'Ile de* Java. . . . In *Annales du Museum d'Histoire Naturelle*, Tom. XVIième, p. 459.

1813.—"The literary and scientific world has in few instances been more grossly imposed upon than in the account of the *Pohon* **Upas**, published in Holland about the year 1780. The history and origin of this forgery still remains a mystery. Foersch, who put his name to the publication, certainly was . . . a surgeon in the Dutch East India Company's service about the time. . . . I have been led to suppose that his literary abilities were as mean as his contempt for truth was consummate. Having hastily picked up some vague information regarding the **Oopas**, he carried it to Europe, where his notes were arranged, doubtless by a different hand, in such a form as by their plausibility and appearance of truth, to be generally credited. . . . But though the account just mentioned . . . has been demonstrated to be an extravagant forgery, the existence of a tree in Java, from whose sap a poison is prepared, equal in fatality, when thrown into the circulation, to the strongest animal poisons hitherto known, is a fact."—*Horsfield*, in *Batavian Trans.* vol. vii. art. x. pp. 2-4.

1822.—"The Law of Java," a Play . . . *Scene.* Kérta-Sûra, and a desolate Tract in the Island of Java.

* * * * *

"Act I. Sc. 2.

Emperor. The haram's laws, which cannot be repealed,
Had not enforced me to pronounce your death,
* * * * *
One chance, indeed, a slender one, for life,
All criminals may claim.
Parbaya. Aye, I have heard
Of this your cruel mercy;—'tis to seek
That tree of Java, which, for many a mile,
Sheds pestilence;—for where the **Upas** grows
It blasts all vegetation with its own;
And, from its desert confines, e'en those brutes
That haunt the desert most shrink off, and tremble.
Thence if, by miracle, a man condemned
Bring you the poison that the tree exudes,
In which you dip your arrows for the war,
He gains a pardon,—and the palsied wretch
Who scaped the **Upas**, has escaped the tyrant."
* * * * *

"Act II. Sc. 4.

Pengoose. Finely dismal and romantic, they say, for many miles round the **Upas**; nothing but poisoned air, mountains, and melancholy. A charming country for making *Mems* and *Nota benes!*"

* * * * *

"Act III. Sc. 1.

Pengoose. . . . That's the Divine, I suppose, who starts the poor prisoners, for the last stage to the **Upas tree**; an Indian Ordinary of Newgate.

Servant, your brown Reverence! There's no people in the parish, but, I believe, you are the rector?

(*Writing*). "The reverend Mister Orzinga U.C.J.—The **Upas** Clergyman of Java."

George Colman the Younger.

[1844.—"We landed in the Rajah's boat at the watering place, near the **Upas** tree. . . ."—Here follows an interesting account by Mr Adams, in which he describes how "the mate, a powerful person and of strong constitution, felt so much stupified as to be compelled to withdraw from his position on the tree."—*Capt. Sir E. Belcher, Narr. of the Voyage of H.M.S. Samarang*, i. 180 *seqq.*]

1868.—"The Church of Ireland offers to us, indeed, a great question, but even that question is but one of a group of questions. There is the Church of Ireland, there is the land of Ireland, there is the education of Ireland . . . they are all so many branches from one trunk, and that trunk is the Tree of what is called Protestant ascendancy. . . . We therefore aim at the destruction of that system of ascendancy, which, though it has been crippled and curtailed by former measures, yet still must be allowed to exist; it is still there like a tall tree of noxious growth, lifting its head to heaven, and darkening and poisoning the land as far as its shadow can extend; it is still there, gentlemen, and now at length the day has come when, as we hope, the axe has been laid to the root of that tree, and it nods and quivers from its top to its base. . . ."—Mr. GLADSTONE'S *Speech at Wigan*, Oct. 23. In this quotation the orator indicates the **Upas tree** without naming it. The name was supplied by some commentators referring to this indication at a later date:

1873.—"It was perfectly certain that a man who possessed a great deal of imagination might, if he stayed out sufficiently long at night, staring at a small star, persuade himself next morning that he had seen a great comet; and it was equally certain that such a man, if he stared long enough at a bush, might persuade himself that he had seen a branch of the **Upas Tree.**" —Speech of Lord EDMOND FITZMAURICE on the 2nd reading of the University Education (Ireland) Bill, March 3.

" "It was to regain office, to satisfy the Irish irreconcilables, to secure the Pope's brass band, and not to pursue 'the glorious traditions of English Liberalism,' that Mr. Gladstone struck his two blows at the **Upas tree.**"—Mr. JOSEPH CHAMBERLAIN, in *Fort. Rev.* Sept. pp. 289-90.

1876.—". . . the **Upas-tree** superstition." —*Contemp. Rev.* May.

1880.—"Lord Crichton, M.P. . . . last night said . . . there was one topic which was holding all their minds at present . . . what was this conspiracy which, like the **Upas-tree** of fable, was spreading over the land, and poisoning it? . . ."—In *St. James's Gazette*, Nov. 11, p. 7.

1885.—"The dread **Upas** dropped its fruits.

"Beneath the shady canopy of this tall fig no native will, if he knows it, dare to rest, nor will he pass between its stem and the wind, so strong is his belief in its evil influence.

"In the centre of a tea estate, not far off from my encampment, stood, because no one could be found daring enough to cut it down, an immense specimen, which had long been a nuisance to the proprietor on account of the lightning every now and then striking off, to the damage of the shrubs below, large branches, which none of his servants could be induced to remove. One day, having been pitchforked together and burned, they were considered disposed of: but next morning the whole of his labourers awoke, to their intense alarm, afflicted with a painful eruption. . . . It was then remembered that the smoke of the burning branches had been blown by the wind through the village. . . ." (Two Chinamen were engaged to cut down and remove the tree, and did not suffer; it was ascertained that they had smeared their bodies with coco-nut oil.)—*H. O. Forbes, A Naturalist's Wanderings*, 112-113.

[Mr. Bent (*Southern Arabia*, 72, 89) tells a similar story about the collection of frankincense, and suggests that it was based on the custom of employing slaves in this work, and on an interpretation of the name Hadrimaut, said to mean 'valley of death.']

UPPER ROGER, s. This happy example of the Hobson-Jobson dialect occurs in a letter dated 1755, from Capt. Jackson at Syrian in Burma, which is given in Dalrymple's *Oriental Repertory*, i. 192. It is a corruption of the Skt. *yuva-rāja*, 'young King,' the Caesar or Heir-Apparent, a title borrowed from ancient India by most of the Indo-Chinese monarchies, and which we generally render in Siam as the 'Second King.'

URZ, URZEE, and vulgarly **URJEE**, s. P.—H. *'arẕ* and *'arẕī*, from Ar. *'arẓ*, the latter a word having an extraordinary variety of uses even for Arabic. A petition or humble representation either oral or in writing; the technical term for a request from an inferior to a superior; 'a siffication' as one of Sir Walter Scott's characters calls it. A more elaborate form is *'arẕ-dāsht*, 'memorializing.' This is used in a very barbarous form of Hobson-Jobson below.

1606.—"Every day I went to the Court, and in every eighteen or twentie dayes I put up **Ars** or Petitions, and still he put mee off with good words. . . ."—*John Mildenhall*, in *Purchas*, i. (Bk. iii.) 115.

[1614.—"Until Mocrob Chan's **erzedach** or letter came to that purpose it would not be granted."—*Foster, Letters*, ii. 178. In p. 179 "By whom I **erzed** unto the King again."

[1687.—"The **arzdest** with the Estimauze (*Iltimās*, 'humble representation') concerning your twelve articles. . . ."—In *Yule, Hedges' Diary*, Hak. Soc. II. lxx.

[1688.—"Capt. Haddock desiered the Agent would write his **arzdost** in answer to the Nabob's Perwanna (**Purwanna**)."—*Ibid.* II. lxxxiii.]

1690.—"We think you should **Urzdaast** the Nabob to writt purposely for ye releasm[t] of Charles King, it may Induce him to put a great Value on him."—Letter from Factory at Chuttanutte to *Mr. Charles Eyre* at Ballasore, d. November 5 (MS. in India Office).

1782.—"Monsr. de Chemant refuses to write to Hyder by *arzoasht* (read **arzdasht**), and wants to correspond with him in the same manner as Mons. Duplex did with Chanda Sahib; but the Nabob refuses to receive any letter that is not in the stile of an **arzee** or petition."—*India Gazette*, June 22.

c. 1785.—". . . they (the troops) constantly applied to our colonel, who for presenting an **arzee** to the King, and getting him to sign it for the passing of an account of 50 lacks, is said to have received six lacks as a reward. . . ."—*Carraccioli, Life of Clive*, iii. 155.

1809.—"In the morning . . . I was met by a minister of the Rajah of Benares, bearing an **arjee** from his master to me. . . ."—*Ld. Valentia*, i. 104.

1817.—"The Governor said the Nabob's Vakeel in the **Arzee** already quoted, directed me to forward to the presence that it was his wish, that your Highness would write a letter to him."—*Mill's Hist.* iv. 436.

USHRUFEE. See **ASHRAFEE**.

USPUK, s. Hind. *aspak*. 'A handspike,' corr. of the English. This was the form in use in the Canal Department, N.W.P. Roebuck gives the Sea form as **hanspeek**.

[**UZBEG**, n.p. One of the modern tribes of the Turkish race. "Uzbeg is a political not an ethnological denomination, originating from Uzbeg Khān of the Golden Horde (1312-1340). It was used to distinguish the followers of Shaibāni Khān (16th century) from his antagonists, and became finally the name of the ruling Turks in the khanates as opposed to the Sarts, Tajiks, and such Turks as entered those regions at a later date. . . ." (*Encycl. Brit.* 9th ed. xxiii. 661). Others give the derivation from *uz*, 'self,' *bek*, 'a ruler,' in the sense of independent. (*Schuyler, Turkistan*, i. 106, *Vambéry, Sketches of C. Asia*, 301).

[c. 1330.—"But other two empires of the Tartars . . . that which was formerly of Cathay, but now is **Osbet**, which is called Gatzaria. . . ."—*Friar Jordanus*, 54.

[1616.—"He . . . intendeth the conquest of the **Vzbiques**, a nation between Samarchand and here."—*Sir T. Roe*, i. 113, Hak. Soc.

[c. 1660.—"There are probably no people more narrow-minded, sordid or uncleanly, than the **Usbec** Tartars."—*Bernier*, ed. *Constable*, 120.

[1727.—"The **Uspecks** entred the Provinces *Muschet* and *Yesd*. . . ."—*A. Hamilton*, ed. 1744, i. 108.

[1900.—"**Uz-beg** cavalry ('them Housebugs,' as the British soldiers at Rawal Pindi called them)."—*Sir R. Warburton, Eighteen Years in the Khyber*, 135.]

V

[**VACCA, VAKEA-NEVIS**, s. Ar. *wākia'h*, 'an event, news': *wāki'ah-navīs*, 'a news-writer.' These among the Moghuls were a sort of registrars or remembrancers. Later they became spies who were sent into the provinces to supply information to the central Government.

[c. 1590. — "*Regulations regarding the* **Waqi'ahnawís**. Keeping records is an excellent thing for a government. . . . His Majesty has appointed fourteen zealous, experienced, and impartial clerks. . . ."—*Āīn*, i. 258.

[c. 1662. — "It is true that the Great Mogul sends a **Vakea-nevis** to the various provinces; that is persons whose business it is to communicate every event that takes place."—*Bernier*, ed. *Constable*, 231.

[1673.—". . . Peta Gi Pundit **Vocanovice**, or Publick Intelligencer. . . ."—*Fryer*, 80.

[1687.—"Nothing appearing in the **Vacca** or any other Letters untill of late concerning these broils."—In *Yule, Hedges' Diary*, II. lxiii.]

VACCINATION. Vaccine was first imported into Bombay viâ Bussora in 1802. "Since then," says R. Drummond, "the British Governments in Asia have taken great pains to preserve and diffuse this mild instrument of salvation." [Also see *Forbes, Or. Mem.* 2nd ed. ii. 374.]

VAISHNAVA, adj. Relating to Vishnu; applied to the sectaries who especially worship him. In Bengālī the term is converted into *Boishnab*.

1672.—". . . also some hold *Wistnou* for the supreme god, and therefore are termed **Wistnouwaes**."—*Baldaeus*.

[1815.—"Many choose Vishnoo for their guardian deity. These persons are called **Voishnuvus**." — *Ward, Hindoos*, 2nd ed. ii. 13.

VAKEEL, s. An attorney; an authorised representative. Arab. *wakīl.*

[c. 1630.—"A Scribe, **Vikeel.**"—*Persian Gloss.* in *Sir T. Herbert*, ed. 1677, p. 316.]

1682.—"If Mr. Charnock had taken the paines to present these 2 Perwannas (**Purwanna**) himself, 'tis probable, with a small present, he might have prevailed with Bulchund to have our goods freed. However, at this rate any pitifull **Vekeel** is as good to act ye Company's Service as himself."—*Hedges, Diary*, Dec. 7; [Hak. Soc. i. 54].

[1683.—". . . a copy whereof your **Vackel** James Price brought you from Dacca."—In *Yule, ibid.* II. xxiii.]

1691.—"*November* the 1st, arriv'd a **Pattamar** or *Courrier*, from our **Fakeel**, or Sollicitor at Court. . . ."—*Orington*, 415.

1811.—"The Raja has sent two **Vakeels** or ambassadors to meet me here. . . ."—*Ld. Minto in India*, 268.

c. 1847.—"If we go into Court I suppose I must employ a **Vehicle.**"—Letter from an European subordinate to one of the present writers.

VARELLA, s. This is a term constantly applied by the old Portuguese writers to the pagodas of Indo-China and China. Of its origin we have no positive evidence. The most probable etymology is that it is the Malay *barāhlā* or *brāhlā*, [in Wilkinson's Dict. *bĕrhala*], 'an idol.' An idol temple is *rūmah-barāhlā*, 'a house of idols,' but *barāhlā* alone may have been used elliptically by the Malays or misunderstood by the Portuguese. We have an analogy in the double use of *pagoda* for temple and idol.

1555.—"Their temples are very large edifices, richly wrought, which they call **Valeras**, and which cost a great deal. . . ."—*Account of China* in a Jesuit's Letter appended to *Fr. Alvarez H. of Ethiopia*, translated by Mr. Major in his *Introd. to Mendoza*, Hak. Soc. I. xlviii.

1569.—"Gran quantità se ne consuma ancora in quel Regno nelle lor **Varelle**, che sono gli suo' pagodi, de' quali ve n'è gran quantità di grandi e di picciole, e sono alcune montagnuole fatte a mano, a giusa d'vn pan di zuccaro, e alcune d'esse alte quanti il campanile di S. Marco di Venetia . . . si consuma in queste istesse **varelle** anco gran quantità di oro di foglia. . . ."—*Ces. Federici*, in *Ramusio*, iii. 395; [in *Hakl.* ii. 368.]

1583.—". . . nauigammo fin la mattina, che ci trouammo alla Bara giusto di Negrais, che cosi si chiama in lor linguaggio il porto, che va in Pegu, oue discoprimmo a banda sinistra del riuo vn pagodo, ouer **varella** tutta dorata, la quale si scopre di lontano da' vascelli, che vengono d'alto mare, et massime quando il Sol percote in quell' oro, che la fà risplendere all' intorno. . . ."—*Gasparo Balbi*, f. 92.*

1587.—"They consume in these **Varellaes** great quantitie of Golde; for that they be all gilded aloft."—*Fitch*, in *Hakl.* ii. 393; [and see quotation from same under **DAGON**].

1614.—"So also they have many **Varelas**, which are monasteries in which dwell their *religiosos*, and some of these are very sumptuous, with their roofs and pinnacles all gilded."—*Couto*, VI. vii. 9.

More than one prominent geographical feature on the coast-navigation to China was known by this name. Thus in Linschoten's description of the route from Malacca to Macao, he mentions at the entrance to the 'Straits of Sincapura,' a rock having the appearance of an obelisk, called the **Varella** *del China;* and again, on the eastern coast of Champa, or Cochin China, we have frequent notice of a point (with a river also) called that of the **Varella.** Thus in Pinto:

1540.—"The Friday following we found ourselves just against a River called by the inhabitants of the Country *Tinacoreu*, and by us (the) **Varella.**"—*Pinto* (in *Cogan*), p. 48.

This Varella of Champa is also mentioned by Linschoten:

1598.—". . . from this thirde point to the **Varella** the coast turneth North. . . . This **Varella** is a high hill reaching into the Sea, and above on the toppe it hath a verie high stonie rock, like a tower or piller, which may be seen far off, therefore it is by the *Portingalles* called **Varella.**"—p. 342.

VEDAS. The Sacred Books of the Brahmans, *Veda* being 'knowledge.' Of these books there are nominally four, viz. the *Rig*, *Yajur*, *Sāma* and *Atharva* Vedas.

The earliest direct intimation of knowledge of the existence of the Vedas appears to be in the book called *De Tribus Impostoribus*, said to have been printed in 1598, in which they are mentioned.† Possibly this know-

* Compare this vivid description with a modern notice of the same pagoda:

1855. "This meridian range . . . 700 miles from its origin in the Naga wilds . . . sinks in the sea hard by Negrais, its last bluff crowned by the golden Pagoda of Modain, gleaming far to seaward, a Burmese Sunium."—*Yule, Mission to Ava*, 272. There is a small view of it in this work.

† So wrote A. B. I cannot find the book in the B. Museum Library.—*Y.* [A bibliographical account of this book will be found in "*Le Traité des Trois Imposteurs, et précédé d'une notice philologique et bibliographique par Philomneste Junior* (*i.e.* Brunet), Paris and Brussels, 1867. Also see 7 Ser. *N. & Q.* viii. 449 *seqq.*; 9 Ser. ix. 55. The passage about the Vedas seems to be the following: "Et Sectarii istorum, ut et *Vedae* et Brachmanorum ante MCCC retro secula obstant collectanea, ut de Sinensibus nil dicam. Tu, qui in angulo Europae hic delitescis, ista neglegis, negas; quam bene videas ipse. Eadem facilitate enim isti tua

ledge came through the Arabs. Though thus we do not trace back any direct allusion to the Vedas in European books, beyond the year 1600 or thereabouts, there seems good reason to believe that the Jesuit missionaries had information on the subject at a much earlier date. St. Francis Xavier had frequent discussions with Brahmans, and one went so far as to communicate to him the *mantra* "*Om śrīnārāyaṇanāmah.*" In 1559 a learned Brahman at Goa was converted by Father Belchior Carneyro, and baptized by the name of Manuel. He afterwards (with the Viceroy's sanction!) went by night and robbed a Brahman on the mainland who had collected many MSS., and presented the spoil to the Fathers, with great satisfaction to himself and them (*Sousa, Orient. Conquist.* i. 151-2).

It is probable that the information concerning the Hindu religion and sacred books which was attained even in Europe by the end of the 16th century was greater than is commonly supposed, and greater than what we find in print would warrant us to assume. A quotation from San Roman below illustrates this in a general way. And in a constitution of Gregory XV. dated January 31, 1623, there is mention of rites called *Haiteres* and *Tandié*, which doubtless represent the Vedic names *Aitareya* and *Tāṇḍya* (see *Norbert*, i. 39). Lucena's allusion below to the "four parts" of Hindu doctrine must have reference to the Vedas, and his information must have come from reports and letters, as he never was in India. In course of time, however, what had been known seems to have been forgotten, and even Halhed (1776) could write about 'Beids of the Shaster!' (see *Code*, p. xiii.). This shows that though he speaks also of the 'Four Beids' (p. xxxi.) he had no precise knowledge.

In several of the earlier quotations of the word it will be seen that the form used is *Vedam* or *Veidam*. This is the Tamil form. And it became prevalent during the 18th century in France from Voltaire's having constituted himself the advocate of a Sanskrit Poem, called by him *l'Ezour Vedam*, and which had its origin in S. India. This was in reality an imitation of an Indian *Purāna*, composed by some missionary in the 17th century (probably by R. de' Nobili), to introduce Christian doctrines; but Voltaire supposed it to be really an ancient Indian book. Its real character was first explained by Sonnerat (see the Essay by F. W. Ellis, in *As. Res.* xi.). The first information regarding the real Vedas was given by Colebrooke in 1805 (*As. Res.* viii.). Orme and some authors of the 18th and early part of the 19th century write *Bede*, which represents the N. Indian vernacular form *Bed*. Both forms, *Bed* and *Vedam*, are known to Fleury, as we see below.

On the subject of the Vedas, see *Weber's Hist. of Indian Lit.*, *Max Müller's Ancient Sanskrit Lit.*, *Whitney's Oriental and Linguistic Studies*, vol. i. [and *Macdonell's Hist. of Sanskrit Lit.*, pp. 29 *seqq.*].

c. 1590.—"*The Brahmins.* These have properly six duties. 1. The study of the **Bedes.**"—*Ayeen*, by *Gladwin*, ii. 393; [ed. *Jarrett*, iii. 115].

" "Philologists are constantly engaged in translating Hindí, Greek, Arabic, and Persian books . . . Hájí Ibrahím of Sarhind translated into Persian the *At'harban* (*i.e. Atharva* **Veda**) which, according to the Hindús is one of the four divine books."—*Ibid.* by *Blochmann*, i. 104-105.

1600.—". . . Consta esta doutrina de quatro partes. . . ."—*Lucena V. de P. Franc. Xavier*, 95.

1602.—"These books are divided into bodies, limbs, and joints; and their foundations are certain books which they call **Vedáos**, which are divided into four parts."—*Couto*, V. vi. 3.

1603.—"Tienen muchos libros, de mucha costa y escriptura, todos llenos de agueros y supersticiones, y de mil fabulas ridiculas que son sus evangelios. . . . Todo esto es tan sin fundamento, que algunos libros han llegado a Portugal, que se han traydo de la India, y han venido algunos Iogues que se convertieron à la Fè."—*San Roman, Hist. de la India Oriental*, 47.

1651.—"The **Vedam**, or the Heathen's book of the Law, hath brought great Esteem unto this Tribe (the Bramines)."—*Rogerius*, 3.

c. 1667.—"They say then that God, whom they call *Achar*, that is to say, Immoveable or Immutable, hath sent them four Books which they call **Beths**, a word signifying *Science*, because they pretend that in these Books all Sciences are comprehended. The first of these Books is called *Athenba-* (*Atherba-*)

negant. Et quid non miraculorum superesset ad convincendos orbis incolas, si mundum ex Scorpionis ovo conditum et progenitum terramque Tauri capiti impositam, et rerum prima fundamentis ex prioribus III. Vedae libris constarent, nisi invidus aliquis Deorum filius haec III. prima volumina furatus esset!"]

bed, the second *Zagur*-**bed**, the third *Rek*-**bed**, the fourth *Sama*-**bed**."—*Bernier*, E.T. 104; [ed. *Constable*, 325].

1672.—"Commanda primieramente il **Veda** (che è tutto il fondamento della loro fede) l'adoratione degli Idoli."—*P. Vincenzo*, 313.

" "Diese vier Theile ihres **Vedam** oder Gesetzbuchs werden genant *Roggo* **Vedam**, *Jadura* **Vedam**, *Sama* **Vedam**, und *Tarawana* **Vedam**. . . ."—*Baldaeus*, 556.

1689.—"Il reste maintenant à examiner sur quelles preuves les Siamois ajoutent foi à leur Bali, les Indiens à leur **Beth** ou **Vedam**, les Musulmans à leur Alcoran."—*Fleury*, in *Lett. Edif.* xxv. 65.

1726.—"Above all it would be a matter of general utility to the Coast that some more chaplains should be maintained there for the sole purpose of studying the Sanskrits tongue (*de Sanskritse taal*), the head and mother tongue of most eastern languages, and once for all to make a translation of the **Vedam**, or Lawbook of the Heathen (which is followed not only by the Heathen on this Coast, but also, in whole or in part, in Ceylon, Malabar, Bengal, Surat, and other neighbouring Kingdoms), and thereby to give such preachers further facilities for the more powerful conviction of the Heathen here and elsewhere, on their own ground, and for the disclosure of many mysteries and other matters, with which we are now unacquainted. . . . This Lawbook of the Heathen, called the **Vedam**, had in the very old times 4 parts, though one of these is now lost. . . . These parts were named *Roggo* **Vedam**, *Sadura* or *Issoure* **Vedam**, *Sama* **Vedam**, and *Tarawana* or *Adderawana* **Vedam**."—*Valentijn*, *Keurlijke Beschryving van Choromandel*, in his *East Indies*, v. pp. 72-73.

1745.—"Je commençais à douter si nous n'avions point été trompés par ceux qui nous avoient donné l'explication de ces cérémonies qu'ils nous avoient assurés être très-conformes à leur **Vedam**, c'est à dire au Livre de leur loi."—*Norbert*, iii. 132.

c. 1760.—"**Vedam**—s.m. *Hist. Superst.* C'est un livre pour qui les Brames ou Nations idolâtres de l'Indostan ont la plus grande vénération . . . en effet, on assure que le **Vedam** est écrit dans une langue beaucoup plus ancienne que le *Sanskrit*, qui est la langue savante, connue des bramines. Le mot **Vedam** signifie science."—*Encylopédie*, xxx. 32. This information was taken from a letter by Père Calmette, S.J. (see *Lett. Edif.*), who anticipated Max Müller's chronological system of Vedic literature, in his statement that some parts of the *Veda* are at least 500 years later than others.

1765.—"If we compare the great purity and chaste manners of the Shastah (**Shaster**), with the great absurdities and impurities of the **Viedam**, we need not hesitate to pronounce the latter a corruption of the former."—*J. Z. Holwell*, *Interesting Hist. Events*, &c., 2nd ed. i. 12. This gentleman also talks of the **Bhades** and the **Viedam** in the same line without a notion that the word was the same (see *ibid.* Pt. ii. 15, 1767).

c. 1770.—"The Bramin, bursting into tears, promised to pardon him on condition that he should swear never to translate the **Bedas** or sacred volumes. . . . From the Ganges to the Indus the **Vedam** is universally received as the book that contains the principles of religion."—*Raynal*, tr. 1777, i. 41-42.

c. 1774.—"Si crede poi como infallibile che dai quattro suddette **Bed**, che in Malabar chiamano **Vedam**, Bramah medesimo ne retirasse sei *Sustrah*, cioè scienze."—*Della Tomba*, 102.

1777.—"The word **Vēd**, or **Vēdă**, signifies Knowledge or Science. The sacred writings of the Hindoos are so distinguished, of which there are four books."—*C. Wilkins*, in his *Hēētopădēs*, 298.

1778.—"The natives of Bengal derive their religion from a Code called the **Shaster**, which they assert to be the genuine scripture of Bramah, in preference to the **Vedam**."—*Orme*, ed. 1803, ii. 5.

1778.—

"Ein indischer Brahman, geboren auf der Flur,
Der nichts gelesen als den **Weda** der Natur."
Rückert, *Weisheit der Bramanen*, i. 1.

1782.—". . . pour les rendre (les *Pouranons*) plus authentiques, ils ajoutèrent qu'ils étoient tirés du **Védam**; ce que n'étoit pas facile à vérifier, puisque depuis très longtems les Védams ne sont plus connus."—*Sonnerat*, ii. 21.

1789.—

"Then Edmund begg'd his Rev'rend Master
T'instruct him in the *Holy* **Shaster**.
No sooner does the Scholar ask,
Than *Goonisham* begins the task,
Without a book he glibly reads
Four of his own invented **Bedes**."
Simpkin the Second, 145.

1791.—"Toute verité . . . est renfermée dans les quatre **beths**."—*St. Pierre*, *Chaumière Indienne*.

1794-97.—". . . or Hindoo **Vedas** taught."
Pursuits of Literature, 6th ed. 359.

VEDDAS, n.p. An aboriginal—or at least a forest—people of Ceylon. The word is said to mean 'hunters,' [Tam. *vedu*, 'hunting'].

1675.—"The **Weddas** (who call themselves **Beddas**) are all original inhabitants from old time, whose descent no one is able to tell."—*Ryklof van Goens*, in *Valentijn*, *Ceylon*, 208.

1681.—"In this Land are many of these wild men they call **Vaddahs**, dwelling near no other Inhabitants. They speak the *Chingalayes* Language. They kill Deer, and dry the Flesh over the Fire . . . their Food being only Flesh. They are very expert with their Bows. . . . They have no Towns nor Houses, only live by the waters under a Tree."—*Knox*, 61-62.

1770.—"The **Bedas** who were settled in the northern part of the island (Ceylon)

. . . go almost naked, and, upon the whole, their manners and government are the same with that of the Highlanders of Scotland." (!) —*Raynal* (tr. 1777), i. 90.

VELLARD, s. This is a word apparently peculiar to the Island of Bombay, used in the sense which the quotation shows. We have failed to get any elucidation of it from local experience; but there can be little doubt that it is a corruption of the Port. *vallado*, 'a mound or embankment.' [It is generally known as 'Hornby's Vellard,' after the Governor of that name; but it seems to have been built about 1752, some 20 years before Hornby's time (see *Douglas, Bombay and W. India*, i. 140).]

1809.—"At the foot of the little hill of Sion is a causeway or **vellard**, which was built by Mr. Duncan, the present Governor, across a small arm of the sea, which separates Bombay from Salsette. . . . The **vellard** was begun A.D. 1797, and finished in 1805, at an expense of 50,575 rupees."—*Maria Graham*, 8.

VELLORE, n.p. A town, and formerly a famous fortress in the district of N. Arcot, 80 m. W. of Madras. It often figures in the wars of the 18th century, but is best known in Europe for the mutiny of the Sepoys there in 1806. The etym. of the name *Vellūr* is unknown to us. Fra Paolino gives it as *Velur*, 'the Town of the Lance'; and Col. Branfill as '*Vēlūr*, from *Vēl*, a benefit, benefaction.' [Cox-Stuart (*Man. N. Arcot*, ii. 417) and the writer of the *Madras Gloss.* agree in deriving it from Tam. *vel*, 'the **babool** tree, *Acacia arabica*,' and *ūr*, 'village.']

VENDU-MASTER, s. We know this word only from the notifications which we quote. It was probably taken from the name of some Portuguese office of the same kind. [In the quotation given below from Owen it seems that the word was in familiar use at Johanna, and the context shows that his duty was somewhat like that of the **chowdry**, as he provided fowls, cattle, fruit, &c., for the expedition.]

1781.—From an advertisement in the *India Gazette* of May 17th it appears to have been an euphemism for *Auctioneer*; [also see *Busteed, Echoes of Old Calcutta*, 3rd ed. p. 109].

,, "Mr. Donald . . . begs leave to acquaint them that the **Vendu** business will in future be carried on by Robert Donald, and W. Williams."—*India Gazette*, July 28.

1793.—"The Governor-General is pleased to notify that Mr. Williamson as the Company's **Vendu Master** is to have the superintendence and management of all Sales at the Presidency."—In *Seton-Karr*, ii. 99. At pp. 107, 114, also are notifications of sales by "G. Williamson, **Vendu Master**."

[1823.—"One of the chiefs, a crafty old rogue, commonly known by the name of 'Lord Rodney' . . . acted as captain of the port, interpreter, **Vendue-Master** and master of the ceremonies. . . ."—*Owen, Narrative of Voyages to explore the shores of Africa*, &c., i. 179.]

VENETIAN, s. This is sometimes in books of the 18th and preceding century used for *Sequins*. See under **CHICK**.

1542.—"At the bottom of the cargo (? *cifa*), among the ballast, she carried 4 big guns (*tiros*), and others of smaller size, and 60,000 **venetians** in gold, which were destined for Coje Çafar, in order that with this money he should in all speed provide necessaries for the fleet which was coming."—*Correa*, iv. 250.

1675.—Fryer gives among coins and weights at Goa:

"The **Venetian** . . . 18 Tangoes, 30 Rees."
—p. 206.

1752.—"At this juncture a gold mohur is found to be worth 14 Arcot Rupees, and a **Venetian** 4½ Arcot Rupees."—In *Long*, p. 32.

VERANDA, s. An open pillared gallery round a house. This is one of the very perplexing words for which at least two origins may be maintained, on grounds equally plausible. Besides these two, which we shall immediately mention, a third has sometimes been alleged, which is thus put forward by a well-known French scholar:

"Ce mot (**véranda**) n'est lui-même qu'une transcription inexacte du Persan *beramada*, perche, terrasse, balcon."—*C. Defrémery*, in *Revue Critique*, 1869, 1st Sem. p. 64.

Plausible as this is, it may be rejected. Is it not, however, possible that *barāmada*, the literal meaning of which is 'coming forward, projecting,' may be a Persian 'striving after meaning,' in explanation of the foreign word which they may have borrowed?

Williams, again, in his Skt. Dict. (1872) gives '*varaṇḍa* . . . a veranda, a portico. . . .' Moreover Beames in his *Comparative Grammar of Modern Aryan Languages*, gives Sansk. *baraṇḍa*, 'portico,' Bengali *bārāṇḍā*, Hind. *varaṇḍā*, adding: "Most of our wiseacre *literateurs* (qu. *littérateurs?*) in Hindustan now-a-days consider this word to be derived from Pers. *barā-madah*, and write it accordingly. It is, however, good Sanskrit" (i. 153). Fortunately we have in Bishop Caldwell a proof that comparative grammar does not preclude good manners. Mr. Beames was evidently in entire ignorance of the facts which render the origin of the Anglo-Indian word so curiously ambiguous; but we shall *not* call him the "wise-acre grammarian." *Varaṇḍa*, with the meaning in question, does not, it may be observed, belong to the older Sanskrit, but is only found in comparatively modern works.*

Littré also gives as follows (1874): "ETYM. *Verandah*, mot rapporté de l'Inde par les Anglais, est la simple dégénérescence, dans les langues modernes de l'Inde, du Sansc. *veranda*, colonnade, de *var*, couvrir."

That the word as used in England and in France was brought by the English from India need not be doubted. But either in the same sense, or in one closely analogous, it appears to have existed, quite independently, in Portuguese and Spanish; and the manner in which it occurs without explanation in the very earliest narrative of the adventure of the Portuguese in India, as quoted below, seems almost to preclude the possibility of their having learned it in that country for the first time; whilst its occurrence in P. de Alcala can leave no doubt on the subject. [Prof. Skeat says: "If of native Span. origin, it may be Span. *vara* a rod, rail. Cf. L. *uarus*, crooked" (*Concise Dict.* s.v.).]

1498.—"E vêo ter comnosco onde estavamos lançados, em huma **varanda** onde estava hum grande castiçall d'arame que nos alumeava."—*Roteiro da Viagem de Vasco da Gama*, 2nd ed., 1861, p. 62, *i.e.* ". . . and came to join us where we had been put in a **varanda**, where there was a great candlestick of brass that gave us light. . . ." And Correa, speaking of the same historical passage, though writing at a later date, says: "When the Captain-Major arrived, he was conducted through many courts and **verandas** (*muitos pateos e* **varandas**) to a dwelling opposite that in which the king was. . . ."—*Correa*, by *Stanley*, 193, compared with original *Lendas*, I. i. 98.

1505. — In Pedro de Alcala's Spanish-Arabic Vocabulary we have:

"**Varandas**—*Târbuç*.
Varandas assi *çârgaba*, *çârgab*."

Interpreting these Arabic words, with the assistance of Prof. Robertson Smith, we find that *târbuç* is, according to Dozy (*Suppt.* I. 430), *darbūz*, itself taken from *darābazīn* (τραπέζιον), 'a stair-railing, fireguard, balcony, &c.'; whilst *çârgab* stands for *sarjab*, a variant (*Abul W.*, p. 735, i.) of the commoner *sharjab*, 'a lattice, or anything latticed,' such as a window,—'a balcony, a balustrade.'

1540.—"This said, we entred with her into an outward court, all about invironed with Galleries (*cercado a roda de duas ordens de* **varandas**) as if it had been a Cloister of Religious persons. . . ."—*Pinto* (orig. cap. lxxxiii.), in *Cogan*, 102.

1553 (but relating events of 1511).
". . . assentou Affonso d'Alboquerque com elles, que primeiro que sabissem em terra, irem ao seguinte dia, quando agua estivesse estofa, dez bateis a queimar alguns baileus, que são como **varandas** sobre o mar."—*Barros*, II. vi. 3.

1563.—"*R.* . . . nevertheless tell me what the tree is like. *O.* From this **varanda** you can see the trees in my garden: those little ones have been planted two years, and in four they give excellent fruit. . . ."—*Garcia*, f. 112.

1602.—"De maneira, que quando ja El Rey (de Pegu) chegava, tinha huns formosos Paços de muitas camaras, **varandas**, retretes, cozinhas, em que se recolhia com suas mulheres. . . ."—*Couto*, Dec. vi. Liv. vii., cap. viii.

1611.—"**Varanda.** Lo entreado de los corridores, por ser como varas, per otro nombre vareastes quasi varafustes."— *Cobarruvias.*

1631.—In Haex, Malay-Latin Vocabulary, we have as a *Malay* word, "**Baranda**, Contignatio vel Solarium."

1644.—"The fort (at Cochin) has not now the form of a fortress, consisting all of houses; that in which the captain lives has a **Varanda** fronting the river, 15 paces long and 7 wide. . . ."—*Bocarro*, MS. f. 313.

1710.—"There are not wanting in Cambaya great buildings with their courts, **varandas**, and chambers." — *De Sousa, Oriente Conquist.* ii. 152.

1711.—"The Building is very ancient . . and has a paved Court, two large **Verandas** or Piazzas."—*Lockyer*, 20.

c. 1714.—"**Varanda.** Obra sacada do corpo do edificio, cuberta o descuberta, na qual se costuma passear, tomar o sol, o fresco, &c. *Pergula.*"—*Bluteau*, s.v.

1729.—"**Baranda.** Especie de corredor o balaustrada que ordinariamente se colocà debante de los altares o escaléras, compuesta de balaustres de hierro, bronce, madera, o otra materia, de la altura de un medio cuerpo, y su uso es para adorno y reparo. Algunos escriven esta voce con *b.* Lat. Peribolus, Lorica clathrata."—*Golis, Hist. de Nueva España*, lib. 3, cap. 15. "Alajábase la pieza por la mitad con un **baranda** o biombo que sin impedir la vista señalava

* This last remark is due to A. B.

termino al concorso."—*Dicc. de la Ling. Cast. por la R. Acad.*

1754.—Ives, in describing the Cave of Elephanta, speaks twice of "the **voranda** or open gallery."—p. 45.

1756.—". . . as soon as it was dark, we were all, without distinction, directed by the guard set over us to collect ourselves into one body, and sit down quietly under the arched **Veranda**, or Piazza, to the west of the Black-hole prison. . . ."—*Holwell's Narr. of the Black Hole* [p. 3]; [in *Wheeler, Early Records*, 229].

c. 1760.—". . . Small ranges of pillars that support a pent-house or shed, forming what is called, in the Portuguese lingua-franca, **Verandas**."—*Grose*, i. 53.

1781.—"On met sur le devant une petite galerie appellée **varangue**, et formée par le toit."—*Sonnerat*, i. 54. There is a French nautical term, *varangue*, 'the ribs or floor-timbers of a ship,' which seems to have led this writer astray here.

1783.—"You are conducted by a pretty steep ascent up the side of a rock, to the door of the cave, which enters from the North. By it you are led first of all into a **feerandah** (!) or piazza which extends from East to West 60 feet."—*Acct. of some Artificial Caves in the Neighbourhood of Bombay* (Elephanta), by *Mr. W. Hunter*, Surgeon in the E. Indies. In *Archaeologia*, vii. 287.

,, "The other gate leads to what in this country is called a **veranda or feranda** (printed *seranda*), which is a kind of piazza or landing-place before you enter the hall."—*Letter* (on Caves of Elephanta, &c.), from *Hector Macneil*, Esq., *ibid.* viii. 254.

1796.—". . . Before the lowest (storey) there is generally a small hall supported by pillars of teka (**Teak**) wood, which is of a yellow colour and exceedingly hard. This hall is called **varanda**, and supplies the place of a parlour."—*Fra Paolino*, E.T.

1809.—"In the same **verandah** are figures of natives of every cast and profession."—*Ld. Valentia*, i. 424.

1810.—"The **viranda** keeps off the too great glare of the sun, and affords a dry walk during the rainy season."—*Maria Graham*, 21.

c. 1816. — ". . . and when Sergeant Browne bethought himself of Mary, and looked to see where she was, she was conversing up and down the **verandah**, though it was Sunday, with most of the rude boys and girls of the barracks."—*Mrs. Sherwood's Stories*, p. 47, ed. 1873.

VERDURE, s. This word appears to have been used in the 18th century for vegetables, adapted from the Port. *verduras*.

1752.—Among minor items of revenue from duties in Calcutta we find:

	RS.	A.	P.
"**Verdure**, fish pots, firewood	216	10	6."

—In *Long*, 35.

[**VERGE**, s. A term used in S. India for rice lands. It is the Port. *Vársea*, *Varzia*, *Vargem*, which Vieyra defines as 'a plain field, or a piece of level ground, that is sowed and cultivated.'

[1749.—". . . as well as **vargems** lands as hortas" (see **OART**).—*Treaty*, in *Logan, Malabar*, iii. 48.

[1772.—"The estates and **verges** not yet assessed must be taxed at 10 per cent."—*Govt. Order, ibid.* i. 421.]

VETTYVER, s. This is the name generally used by the French for the fragrant grass which we call **cuscus** (q.v.). The word is Tamil *vettiver*, [from *vettu*, 'digging,' *ver*, 'root'].

1800.—"Europeans cool their apartments by means of wetted tats (see **TATTY**) made of straw or grass, and sometimes of the roots of the **wattie waeroo**, which, when wetted, exhales a pleasant but faint smell."—*Heyne's Tracts*, p. 11.

VIDANA, s. In Ceylon, the title of a village head man. "The person who conveys the orders of Government to the people" (*Clough*, s.v. *vidán*). It is apparently from the Skt. *vadana*, ". . . the act of speaking . . . the mouth, face, countenance . . . the front, point," &c. In Javanese *wadana* (or *wadono*, in Jav. pronunciation) is "the face, front, van; a chief of high rank: a Javanese title" (*Crawfurd*, s.v.). The Javanese title is, we imagine, now only traditional; the Ceylonese one has followed the usual downward track of high titles; we can hardly doubt the common Sanskrit origin of both (see *Athenaeum*, April 1, 1882, p. 413, and May 13, *ibid.* p. 602). The derivation given by Alwis is probably not inconsistent with this.

1681.—"The Dissauvas (see **DISSAVE**) by these *Courli* **vidani** their officers do oppress and squeez the people, by laying Mulcts upon them. . . . In *Fine* this officer is the **Dissauva's** chief Substitute, who orders and manages all affairs incumbent upon his master."—*Knox*, 51.

1726.—"**Vidanes**, the overseers of villages, who are charged to see that no inhabitant suffers any injury, and that the Land is sown betimes. . . ."—*Valentijn* (*Ceylon*), *Names of Officers*, &c., 11.

1756.—"Under each (chief) were placed different subordinate headmen, called **Vidána**-*Aratchies* and **Vidáns**. The last is derived from the word (*vidāna*), 'commanding,' or 'ordering,' and means, as Clough (p. 647) defines it, the person who conveys the orders of the Government to the People."—*J. de Alwis*, in *Ceylon Journal*, 8, p. 237.

VIHARA, WIHARE, &c., s. In Ceylon a Buddhist temple. Skt. *vihāra*, a Buddhist convent, originally the hall where the monks met, and thence extended to the buildings generally of such an institution, and to the shrine which was attached to them, much as *minster* has come from *monasterium*. Though there are now no Buddhist *vihāras* in India Proper, the former wide diffusion of such establishments has left its trace in the names of many noted places: *e.g. Bihār*, and the great province which takes its name; *Kuch Behār;* the *Vihār* water-works at Bombay; and most probably the City of *Bokhārā* itself. [Numerous ruins of such buildings have been unearthed in N. India, as, for instance, that at Sarnāth near Benares, of which an account is given by Gen. Cunningham (*Arch. Rep.* i. 121). An early use of the word (probably in the sense of a monastery) is found in the Mathura Jain inscription of the 2nd century, A.D. in the reign of Huvishka (*ibid.* iii. 33).]

1681.—"The first and highest order of priests are the *Tirinanxes*,* who are the priests of the *Buddou* God. Their temples are styled **Vehars**. . . . These . . . only live in the **Vihar**, and enjoy great Revenues."—*Knox, Ceylon*, 74.

[1821.—"The Malwatte and Asgirie **wihares** . . . are the two heads of the Boodhaical establishment in Ceylon."—*Davy, An Account of the Interior of Ceylon*, 369.]

1877.—"Twice a month, when the rules of the order are read, a monk who had broken them is to confess his crime; if it be slight, some slight penance is laid upon him, to sweep the court-yard of the **wihāra**, sprinkle the dust round the sacred bo-tree."—*Rhys Davids, Buddhism*, 169.

VISS, s. A weight used in S. India and in Burma; Tam. *vīsai*, 'division,' Skt. *vihita*, 'distributed.' In Madras it was ⅛ of a Madras maund, and=3lb. 2oz. avoirdupois. The old scale ran, 10 pagoda weights = 1 *pollam*, 40 *pollams*=1 **viss**, 8 **viss**=1 **maund** (of 25lbs.), 20 *maunds* = 1 *candy*. In Burma the *viss*=100 *tikals*=3lbs. 5 5⅓. **Viss** is used in Burma by foreigners, but the Burmese call the weight *peiktha*, probably a corruption of *vīsai*.

* [The first part of this word is *thera*, Skt. *sthavira*. Hardy (*E. Monachism*, p. 11) says the superior priests were called *terunnānses*, from Pali *thero*, "an elder."

1554.—"The baar (see **BAHAR**) of Peguu contains 120 **biças**; each **biça** weighs 40 ounces; the **biça** contains 100 **ticals**; the **tical** weighs 3½ *oitavas*."—*A. Nunes*, 38.

1568.—"This **Ganza** goeth by weight of **Byze** . . . and commonly a **Byza** of Ganza is worth (after our accompt) halfe a ducat."—*Caesar Frederike*, in *Hakl.* ii. 367.

1626.—"In anno 1622 the Myne was shut up . . . the comming of the Mogull's Embassadour to this King's Court, with his peremptory demand of a **Vyse** of the fairest diamonds, caused the cessation."—*Purchas, Pilgrimage*, 1003.

[1727.—"**Viece.**" See under **TICAL.**

[1807.—"**Visay.**" See under **GARCE.**]

1855.—"The King last year purchased 800,000 **viss** of lead, at 5 tikals (see **TICAL**) for 100 viss, and sold it at twenty tikals."—*Yule, Mission to Ava*, 256.

VIZIER, WUZEER, s. Ar.—H. *wazīr*, 'a minister,' and usually the principal minister, under a (Mahommedan) prince. [In the Koran (cap. xx. 30) Moses says: "Give a **wazir** of my family, Harūn (Aaron) my brother." In the *Āīn* we have a distinction drawn between the *Vakīl*, or prime minister, and the *Vazīr*, or minister of finance (ed. *Blochmann*, i. 527).] In India the Nawāb of Oudh was long known as the Nawāb Wazīr, the founder of the quasi-independent dynasty having been Sa'ādat 'Alī Khān, who became Sūbadār of Oudh, c. 1732, and was also Wazīr of the Empire, a title which became hereditary in his family. The title of Nawāb Wazīr merged in that of *pādshāh*, or King, assumed by Ghāzī-ud-dīn Haidar in 1820, and up to his death still borne or claimed by the ex-King Wājid 'Alī Shāh, under surveillance in Calcutta. As most titles degenerate, *Wazīr* has in Spain become *alguazil*, 'a constable,' in Port. *alvasil*, 'an alderman.'

[1612.—"Jeffer Basha **Vizier** and Viceroy of the Province."—*Danvers, Letters*, i. 173.]

1614.—"Il primo **visir**, sopra ogni altro, che era allora Nasuh bascià, genero del Gran Signore, venne ultimo di tutti, con grandissima e ben adorna cavalcata, enfin della quale andava egli solo con molta gravita."—*P. della Valle* (from Constantinople), i. 43.

W

[**WACADASH,** s. Japanese *wakizashi*, 'a short sword.'

[1613.—"The Captain Chinesa is fallen at square with his new wife and hath given her his **wacadash** bidding her cut off her little finger."—*Foster, Letters*, ii. 18.

[" "His **wacadash** or little cattan."—*Ibid.* ii. 20.

[1898.—"There is also the **wakizashi**, or dirk of about nine and a half inches, with which harikari was committed."—*Chamberlain, Things Japanese*, 3rd ed. 377.]

WALER, s. A horse imported from N. South Wales, or Australia in general.

1866.—"Well, young shaver, have you seen the horses? How is the **Waler's** off foreleg?"—*Trevelyan, Dawk Bungalow*, 223.

1873.—"For sale, a brown **Waler** gelding," &c.—*Madras Mail*, June 25.

WALI, s. Two distinct words are occasionally written in the same way.

(a). Ar. **wâli**. A Mahommedan title corresponding to Governor; ["the term still in use for the Governor-General of a Province as opposed to the Muḥāfiẓ, or district-governor. In E. Arabia the Wali is the Civil Governor as opposed to the Amīr or Military Commandant. Under the Caliphate the Wali acted also as Prefect of Police (the Indian *Faujdār*—see **FOUJDAR**), who is now called Ẓābiṭ" (*Burton, Ar. Nights*, i. 238)]. It became familiar some years ago in connection with Kandahar. It stands properly for a governor of the highest class, in the Turkish system superior to a Pasha. Thus, to the common people in Egypt, the Khedive is still the *Wālī*.

1298.—"Whenever he knew of anyone who had a pretty daughter, certain ruffians of his would go to the father and say: 'What say you? Here is this pretty daughter of yours; give her in marriage to the **Bailo** Achmath' (for they call him the *Bailo*, or, as we should say, 'the Viceregent')."—*Marco Polo*, i. 402.

1498.—". . . e mandou hum homem que se chama **Bale**, o qual he como alquaide."—*Roteiro de V. da Gama*, 54.

1727.—"As I was one morning walking in the Streets, I met accidentally the Governor of the City (Muscat), by them called the **Waaly**."—*A. Hamilton*, i. 70; [ed. 1744, i. 71.]

[1753.—In Georgia. "**Vali**, a viceroy descended immediately from the sovereigns of the country over which he presides."—*Hanway*, iii. 28.]

b. Ar. *walī*. This is much used in some Mahommedan countries (*e.g.* Egypt and Syria) for a saint, and by a transfer for the shrine of such a saint. ["This would be a separate building like our family tomb and probably domed. . . . Europeans usually call it 'a little *Wali*'; or, as they write it, '*Wely*'; the contained for the container; the 'Santon' for the 'Santon's tomb'" (*Burton, Ar. Nights*, i. 97).] See under **PEER**.

[c. 1590.—"The ascetics who are their repositaries of learning, they style **Wali**, whose teaching they implicitly follow."—*Āīn*, ed. *Jarrett*, ii. 119.]

1869.—"Quant au titre de pir (see **PEER**) . . . il signifie proprement *vieillard*, mais il est pris dans cette circonstance pour désigner une dignité spirituelle equivalente à celle des *Gurû* Hindous . . . Beaucoup de ces pirs sont à leur mort vénérés comme saints; de là le mot pir est synonyme de **Wali**, et signifie Saint aussi bien que ce dernier mot."—*Garcin de Tassy, Rel. Mus. dans l'Inde*, 23.

WALLA, s. This is a popular abridgment of **Competition-walla**, under which will be found remarks on the termination *wālā*, and illustrations of its use.

WANDEROO, s. In Ceylon a large kind of monkey, originally described under this name by Knox (*Presbytes ursinus*). The name is, however, the generic Singhalese word for 'a monkey' (*wanderu, vandura*), and the same with the Hind. *bandar*, Skt. *vānara*. Remarks on the disputed identity of Knox's *wanderoo*, and the different species to which the name has been applied, popularly, or by naturalists, will be found in Emerson Tennent, i. 129-130.

1681.—"*Monkeys* . . . Some so large as our *English Spaniel Dogs*, of a darkish gray colour, and black faces, with great white beards round from ear to ear, which makes them show just like old men. There is another sort just of the same bigness, but differ in colour, being milk white both in body and face, having great beards like the others . . . both these sorts do but little mischief. . . . This sort they call in their language **Wanderow**."—*Knox, Hist. Rel. of the I. of Ceylon*, 26.

[1803.—"The **wanderow** is remarkable for its great white beard, which stretches quite from ear to ear across its black face, while the body is of a dark grey."—*Percival, Acc. of the I. of Ceylon*, 290.]

1810.—"I saw one of the large baboons, called here **Wanderows**, on the top of a coco-nut tree, where he was gathering nuts. . . ."—*Maria Graham*, 97.

1874.—"There are just now some very remarkable monkeys. One is a Macaque . . . Another is the **Wanderoo**, a fellow with a great mass of hair round his face, and the most awful teeth ever seen in a monkey's mouth. This monkey has been credited with having killed two niggers before he was caught; he comes from Malabar."—*F. Buckland*, in *Life*, 289.

WANGHEE, WHANGEE, s. The trade name for a slender yellow bamboo with beautifully regular and short joints, imported from Japan. We cannot give the origin of the term with any conviction. The two following suggestions may embrace or indicate the origin. (1). Rumphius mentions a kind of bamboo called by him *Arundinarbor fera*, the native name of which is Bulu **swangy** (see in vol. iv. cap. vii. *et seqq.*). As *buluh* is Malay for bamboo, we presume that *swangi* is also Malay, but we do not know its meaning. (2). Our friend Professor Terrien de la Couperie notes: "In the *K'ang-hi tze-tien*, 118, 119, the **Huang-tchu** is described as follows: 'A species of bamboo, very hard, with the joints close together; the skin is as white as snow; the larger kind can be used for boats, and the smaller used for pipes, &c.' See also *Wells Williams, Syllabic Dict. of the Chinese Lang.* p. 251.

[On this Professor Giles writes: "'*Whang*' clearly stands for 'yellow,' as in *Whang*poo and like combinations. The difficulty is with *ee*, which should stand for some word of that sound in the Cantonese dialect. There is such a word in 'clothes, skin, sheath'; and 'yellow skin (or sheath)' would form just such a combination as the Chinese would be likely to employ. The suggestion of Terrien de la Couperie is not to the purpose." So Mr. C. M. Gardner writes: "The word *hwang* has many meanings in Chinese according to the tone in which it is said. *Hwang-chi têng* or *hwangee-têng* might be 'yellow-corticled cane.' The word *chuh* means 'bamboo,' and *hwang-chuh* might be 'yellow or Imperial bamboo.' *Wan* means a 'myriad,' *ch'i* 'utensil'; *wan-chi têng* might mean a kind of cane 'good for all kinds of uses.' *Wan-chuh* is a particular kind of bamboo from which paper is made in W. Hapei."

Mr. Skeat writes: "'*Buluh swangi*' is correct Malay. Favre in his *Malay-Fr. Dict.* has '*suwângi*, esprit, spectre, esprit mauvais.' '*Buluh swangi*' does not appear in Ridley's list as the name of a bamboo, but he does not profess to give all the Malay plant names."]

WATER-CHESTNUT. The *trapa bispinosa* of Roxb.; Hind. *singhārā*, 'the horned fruit.' See **SINGARA**.

WEAVER-BIRD, s. See **BAYA**.

WEST-COAST, n.p. This expression in Dutch India means the west coast of Sumatra. This seems also to have been the recognised meaning of the term at Madras in former days. See **SLAVE**.

[1685.—"Order'd that the following goods be laden aboard the Syam Merchant for the **West Coast** of Sumatra. . . ."—*Pringle, Diary Ft. St. Geo.* 1st ser. IV. 136; also see 136, 138, 163, &c.]

1747.—"The Revd. Mr. Francis Fordyce being entered on the Establishment . . . and having several months' allowance due to him for the **West Coast**, amounting to Pags. 371. 9. . . ."—*Ft. St. David's Consn.*, April 30, MS. in India Office. The letter appended shows that the chaplain had been attached to Bencoolen. See also *Wheeler*, i. 148.

WHAMPOA, n.p. In former days the anchorage of European ships in the river of Canton, some distance below that city. [The name is pronounced *Wongpo* (*Ball, Things Chinese*, 3rd ed. 631).]

1770.—"Now all European ships are obliged to anchor at **Houang-poa**, three leagues from the city" (Canton).—*Raynal*, tr. 1777, ii. 258.

WHISTLING TEAL, s. This in Jerdon is given as *Dendrocygna Awsuree* of Sykes. Latin names given to birds and beasts might at least fulfil one object of Latin names, in being intelligible and pronounceable by foreign nations. We have seldom met with a more barbarous combination of impossible words than this. A numerous flock of these whistlers is sometimes seen in Bengal sitting in a tree, a curious habit for ducks.

WHITE ANTS. See **ANTS, WHITE**.

WHITE JACKET, s. The old custom in the hot weather, in the family or at bachelor parties, was to wear this at dinner; and one or more dozens of white jackets were a regular item in an Indian outfit. They are now, we believe, altogether, and for many years obsolete. [They certainly came again into common use some 20 years ago.] But though one reads under every generation of British India that they had gone out of use, they did actually survive to the middle of the last century, for I can remember a white-jacket dinner in Fort William in 1849. [The late Mr. Bridgman of Gorakhpur, whose recollection of India dated from the earlier part of the last century told me that in his younger days the rule at Calcutta was that the guest always arrived at his host's house in the full evening-dress of the time, on which his host meeting him at the door expressed his regret that he had not chosen a cooler dress; on which the guest's Bearer always, as if by accident, appeared from round the corner with a nankeen jacket, which was then and there put on. But it would have been opposed to etiquette for the guest to appear in such a dress without express invitation.]

1803.—"It was formerly the fashion for gentlemen to dress in **white jackets** on all occasions, which were well suited to the country, but being thought too much an undress for public occasions, they are now laid aside for English cloth."—*Ld. Valentia*, i. 240.

[c. 1848.—". . . . a **white jacket** being evening dress for a dinner-party. . . ."—*Berncastle, Voyage to China, including a Visit to the Bombay Pres.* i. 93.]

WINTER, s. This term is constantly applied by the old writers to the *rainy season*, a usage now quite unknown to Anglo-Indians. It may have originated in the fact that winter is in many parts of the Mediterranean coast so frequently a season of rain, whilst rain is rare in summer. Compare the fact that *shitā* in Arabic is indifferently 'winter,' or 'rain'; the winter season being the rainy season. *Shitā* is the same word that appears in *Canticles* ii. 11: "The winter (*sethāv*) is past, the rain is over and gone."

1513.—"And so they set out, and they arrived at Surat (*Çurrate*) in May, when the **winter** had already begun, so they went into **winter-quarters** (*polo que envernarão*), and in September, when the **winter** was over, they went to Goa in two foists and other vessels, and in one of these was the **ganda** (rhinoceros), the sight of which made a great commotion when landed at Goa. . . ."—*Correa*, ii. 373.

1563.—"*R.* . . . In what time of the year does this disease (*morxi*, **Mort-de-chien**) mostly occur?

"*O.* . . . It occurs mostly in June and July (which is the **winter-time** in this country). . . ."—*Garcia*, f. 76*v*.

c. 1567. — "Da Bezeneger a Goa sono d'estate otto giornate di viaggio: ma noi lo facessimo di mezo **l'inverno**, il mese de Luglio."—*Cesare Federici*, in *Ramusio*, iii. 389.

1583.—"Il **uerno** in questo paese è il Maggio, Giugno, Luglio e Agosto, e il resto dell' anno è state. Ma bene è da notare che qui la stagione nõ si può chiamar **uerno** rispetto al freddo, che nõ vi regna mai, mà solo per cagione de' venti, e delle gran pioggie. . . ."—*Gasparo Balbi*, f. 67*v*.

1584.—"Note that the Citie of Goa is the principall place of all the Oriental India, and the **winter** thus beginneth the 15 of May, with very great raine."—*Barret*, in *Hakl.* ii. 413.

[1592.—See under **PENANG**.]

1610. — "The **Winter** heere beginneth about the first of Iune and dureth till the twentieth of September, but not with continuall raines as at Goa, but for some sixe or seuen dayes every change and full, with much wind, thunder and raine."—*Finch*, in *Purchas*, i. 423.

c. 1610.—"**L'hyver** commence au mois d'Avril, et dure six mois."—*Pyrard de Laval*, i. 78: [Hak. Soc. i. 104, and see i. 64, ii. 34].

1643.—". . . des Galiottes (qui sortent tous les ans pour faire la guerre aux Malabares . . . et cela est enuiron la May-Septembre, lors que leur **hyuer** est passé. . . ."—*Mocquet*, 347.

1653.—"Dans les Indes il y a deux Estez et deux **Hyuers**, ou pour mieux dire vn Printemps perpetuel, parce que les arbres y sont tousiours verds: Le premier Esté commance au mois de Mars, et finit au mois de May, que est la commancement de **l'hyuer** de pluye, qui continue iusques en Septembre pleuuant incessament ces quatre mois, en sorte que les Karauanes, ny les Patmars (see **PATTAMAR, a**) ne vont ne viennent: i'ay esté quarante iours sans pouuoir sortir de la maison. . . . Le second Esté est depuis Octobre iusques en Decembre, au quel mois il commance à faire froid . . . ce froid est le second **Hyuer** qui finit au mois de Mars."—*De la Boullaye-le-Gouz*, ed. 1657, p. 244-245.

1665.—"**L'Hyver** se sait sentir. El commença en Juin per quantité de pluies et de tonneres."—*Thevenot*, v. 311.

1678.—". . . In **Winter** (when they rarely stir) they have a *Mumjama*, or Wax Cloth to throw over it. . . ."—*Fryer*, 410.

1691.—"In orâ Occidentali, quae *Malabarorum* est, **hyems** à mense Aprili in Septembrem usque dominatur: in littore verò Orientali, quod Hollandi de Kust van Choromandel, *Oram Coromandellae* vocant trans illos montes, in iisdem latitudinis gradibus, contrariô planè modô à Septembri usque ad Aprilem **hyemem** habent."—*Iobi Lusdofi*, ad suam Historiam *Commentarius*, 101.

1770. — "The mere breadth of these mountains divides summer from winter, that is to say, the season of fine weather from the rainy . . . all that is meant by **winter** in India is the time of the year when the clouds . . . are driven violently by the winds against the mountains," &c.—*Raynal*, tr. 1777, i. 34.

WOOD-APPLE, s. [According to the *Madras Gloss.* also known as *Curd Fruit*, *Monkey Fruit*, and *Elephant Apple*, because it is like an elephant's skin.] A wild fruit of the N.O. *Aurantiaceae* growing in all the drier parts of India (*Feronia elephantum*, Correa). It is somewhat like the *bel* (see **BAEL**) but with a still harder shell, and possesses some of its medicinal virtue. In the native pharmacopœia it is sometimes substituted (*Moodeen Sherif*, [Watt, *Econ. Dict.* iii. 324 *seqq.*). Buchanan-Hamilton calls it the *Kot-bel* (*Kaṭhbel*), (*Eastern India*, ii. 787)].

1875. — "Once upon a time it was announced that the Pádsháh was about to pass through a certain remote village of Upper India. And the village heads gathered in pancháyat to consider what offering they could present on such an unexampled occasion. Two products only of the village lands were deemed fit to serve as nazráua. One was the **custard-apple**, the other was the **wood-apple** . . . a wild fruit with a very hard shelly rind, something like a large lemon or small citron converted into wood. After many *pros* and *cons*, the custard-apple carried the day, and the village elders accordingly, when the king appeared, made salám, and presented a large basket of custard-apples. His Majesty did not accept the offering graciously, but with much abusive language at being stopped to receive such trash, pelted the simpletons with their offering, till the whole basketful had been squashed upon their venerable heads. They retired, abashed indeed, but devoutly thanking heaven that the offering had not been of **wood-apples!**"—*Some Unscientific Notes on the History of Plants* (by H. Y.) in *Geog. Mag.*, 1875, pp. 49-50. The story was heard many years ago from Major William Yule, for whom see under **TOBACCO.**

WOOD-OIL, or **GURJUN OIL**, s. Beng.—H. *garjan*. A thin balsam oil drawn from a great forest tree (N.O. *Dipterocarpeae*) *Dipterocarpus turbinatus*, Gaertn., and from several other species of *Dipt.*, which are among the finest trees of Transgangetic India. Trees of this N.O. abound also in the Malay Archipelago, whilst almost unknown in other parts of the world. The celebrated Borneo camphor is the product of one such tree, and the **saul-wood** of India of another. Much wood-oil is exported from the Burmese provinces, the Malay Peninsula, and Siam. It is much used in the East as a natural varnish and preservative of timber; and in Indian hospitals it is employed as a substitute for copaiva, and as a remedy for leprosy (*Hanbury & Flückiger*, Watt, *Econ. Dict.* iii. 167 *seqq.*). The first mention we know of is c. 1759 in Dalrymple's *Or. Repertory* in a list of Burma products (i. 109).

WOOLOCK, OOLOCK, s. [Platts in his *Hind. Dict.* gives *ulāq*, *ulāk*, as Turkish, meaning 'a kind of small boat.' Mr. Grierson (*Bihar Peasant Life*, 42), among the larger kinds of boats, gives *ulānk*, "which has a long narrow bow overhanging the water in front." Both he and Mr. Grant (*Rural Life in Bengal*, 25) give drawings of this boat, and the latter writes: "First we have the bulky *Oolāk*, or baggage boat of Bengal, sometimes as gigantic as the *Putelee* (see **PATTELLO**), and used for much the same purposes. This last-named vessel is a clinker-built boat—that is having the planks overlapping each other, like those in a London wherry; whereas in the round smooth-sided *oolak* and most country boats, they are laid edge to edge, and fastened with iron clamps, having the appearance of being stitched."]

1679. — "Messrs. Vincent" (&c.) . . . "met the Agent (on the Hoogly R.) in Budgeroes and **Oolankes.**"—*Fort St. Geo. Consns.*, Sept. 14. In *Notes and Exts.*, Madras, 1871.

[1683.—". . . 10 **Ulocks** for Souldiers, etc."—*Hedges, Diary*, Hak. Soc. i. 76.

[1760.—"20 **Hoolucks** 6 Oars at 28 Rs. per month."—In *Long*, 227.]

1764. — "Then the Manjees went after him in a **wollock** to look after him."—*Ibid.* 383.

1781. — "The same day will be sold a twenty-oar'd **Wollock**-built Budgerow. . . ." —*India Gazette*, April 14.

1799.—"We saw not less than 200 large boats at the different quays, which on an average might be reckoned each at 60 tons burthen, all provided with good roofs, and masted after the country manner. They seemed much better constructed than the unwieldy **wullocks** of Bengal." — *Symes, Ava*, 233.

WOON, s. Burm. *wun*, 'a governor or officer of administration'; literally 'a burden,' hence presumably the 'Bearer of the Burden.' Of this there are various well-known compounds, *e.g.*:

Woon-gyee, *i.e.* '*Wun-gyī*' or Great Minister, a member of the High Council of State or Cabinet, called the Hlot-dau (see **LOTOO**).

Woon-douk, *i.e.* *Wun-dauk*, lit. 'the prop of the *Wun*'; a sort of Adlatus, or Minister of an inferior class. We have recently seen a Burmese envoy to the French Government designated as "M. Woondouk."

Atwen-wun, Minister of the Interior (of the Court) or Household.

Myo-wun, Provincial Governor (*Maywoon* of Symes).

Ye-wun, 'Water-Governor,' formerly Deputy of the Myo-wun of the Pr. of Pegu (*Ray-woon* of Symes).

Akaok-wun, Collector of Customs (*Akawoon* of Symes).

WOORDY-MAJOR, s. The title of a native adjutant in regiments of Indian Irregular Cavalry. Both the rationale of the compound title, and the etymology of *wardī*, are obscure. Platts gives Hind. *wardī* or *urdī*, 'uniform of a soldier, badge or dress of office,' as the first part of the compound, with a questionable Skt. etymology, *viruda*, 'crying, proclaiming, a panegyric.' But there is also Ar. *wird*, 'a flight of birds,' and then also 'a troop or squadron,' which is perhaps as probable. [Others, again, as many military titles have come from S. India, connect it with Can. *varadi*, 'news, an order.']

[1784.—". . . We made the **wurdee wollah** acquainted with the circumstance. . . ."—*Forrest, Bombay Letters*, ii. 323.

[1861. — "The senior **Ressaldar** (native captain) and the **Woordie Major** (native adjutant) . . . reported that the sepoys were trying to tamper with his men."—*Cave-Browne, Punjab and Delhi*, i. 120.]

WOOTZ, s. This is an odd name which has attached itself in books to the so-called 'natural steel' of S. India, made especially in Salem, and in some parts of Mysore. It is prepared from small bits of malleable iron (made from magnetic ore) which are packed in crucibles with pieces of a particular wood (*Cassia auriculata*), and covered with leaves and clay. The word first appears in a paper read before the Royal Society, June 11, 1795, called: "Experiments and observations to investigate the nature of a kind of Steel, manufactured at Bombay, and there called **Wootz** . . . by George Pearson, M.D." This paper is quoted below.

The word has never since been recognised as the name of steel in any language, and it would seem to have originated in some clerical error, or misreading, very possibly for *wook*, representing the Canarese *ukku* (pron. *wukku*) 'steel.' Another suggestion has been made by Dr. Edward Balfour. He states that *uchcha* and *nicha* (Hind. *ūncha-nīcha*, in reality for 'high' and 'low') are used in Canarese speaking districts to denote *superior* and *inferior* descriptions of an article, and supposes that **wootz** may have been a misunderstanding of *uchcha*, 'of superior quality.' The former suggestion seems to us preferable. [The *Madras Gloss.* gives as local names of steel, Can. *ukku*, Tel. *ukku*, Tam. and Malayāl. *urukku*, and derives **wootz** from Skt. *ucca*, whence comes H. *ūnchā*.]

The article was no doubt the famous 'Indian Steel,' the σίδηρος Ἰνδικὸς καὶ στόμωμα of the *Periplus*, the material of the Indian swords celebrated in many an Arabic poem, the *alhinde* of old Spanish, the *hundwānī* of the Persian traders, *ondanique* of Marco Polo, the *iron* exported by the Portuguese in the 16th century from Baticalà (see **BATCUL**) in Canara and other parts (see Correa *passim*). In a letter of the King to the Goa Government in 1591 he animadverts on the great amount of iron and steel permitted to be exported from Chaul, for sale on the African coast and to the Turks in the Red Sea (*Archiv. Port. Orient.*, Fasc. 3, 318).

1795. — "Dr. Scott, of Bombay, in a letter to the President, acquainted him that he had sent over specimens of a substance known by the name of **Wootz**; which is considered to be a kind of steel, and is in high esteem among the Indians."—*Phil. Trans.* for 1795, Pt. ii. p. 322.

[1814.—See an account of **wootz**, in *Heyne's Tracts*, 362 *seqq.*]

1841. — "The cakes of steel are called **Wootz**; they differ materially in quality, according to the nature of the ore, but are generally very good steel, and are sent into Persia and Turkey. . . . It may be rendered self-evident that the figure or pattern (of Damascus steel) so long sought after exists in the cakes of **Wootz**, and only requires to be produced by the action of diluted acids . . . it is therefore highly probable that the ancient blades (of Damascus) were made of this steel."—*Wilkinson, Engines of War*, pp. 203-206.

1864.—"Damascus was long celebrated for the manufacture of its sword blades, which it has been conjectured were made from the **wootz** of India."—*Percy's Metallurgy, Iron and Steel*, 860.

WRITER, s.

(a). The rank and style of the junior grade of covenanted civil servants of the E.I. Company. Technically it has been obsolete since the abolition of the old grades in 1833. The term no doubt originally described the duty of these young men; they were the clerks of the factories.

(b). A copying clerk in an office, native or European.

a.—

1673.—"The whole Mass of the Company's Servants may be comprehended in those Classes, viz., Merchants, Factors, and **Writers**."—*Fryer*, 84.

[1675-6.—See under **FACTOR**.]

1676.—"There are some of the **Writers** who by their lives are not a little scandalous."—*Letter from a Chaplain*, in *Wheeler*, i. 64.

1683.—"Mr. Richard More, one that came out a **Writer** on ye *Herbert*, left this World for a better. Ye Lord prepare us all to follow him!"—*Hedges, Diary*, Aug. 22; [Hak. Soc. i. 105].

1747.—"82. Mr. ROBERT CLIVE, Writer in the Service, being of a Martial Disposition, and having acted as a Volunteer in our late Engagements, We have granted him an Ensign's Commission, upon his Application for the same."—Letter from the *Council at Ft. St. David* to the *Honble. Court of Directors*, dd. 2d. May, 1747 (MS. in India Office).

1758.—"As we are sensible that our junior servants of the rank of **Writers** at Bengal are not upon the whole on so good a footing as elsewhere, we do hereby direct that the future appointments to a **Writer** for salary, diet money, and all allowances whatever, be 400 Rupees per annum, which mark of our favour and attention, properly attended to, must prevent their reflections on what we shall further order in regard to them as having any other object or foundation than their particular interest and happiness."—*Court's Letter*, March 3, in *Long*, 129. (The 'further order' is the prohibition of *palankins*, &c.—see **PALANKEEN**.)

c. 1760.—"It was in the station of a covenant servant and **writer**, to the East India Company, that in the month of March, 1750, I embarked."—*Grose*, i. 1.

1762.—"We are well assured that one great reason of the **Writers** neglecting the Company's business is engaging too soon in trade. . . . We therefore positively order that none of the **Writers** on your establishment have the benefit or liberty of Dusticks (see **DUSTUCK**) until the times of their respective writerships are expired, and they commence **Factors**, with this exception. . . ."—*Court's Letter*, Dec. 17, in *Long*, 287.

1765.—"Having obtained the appointment of a **Writer** in the East India Company's service at Bombay, I embarked with 14 other passengers . . . before I had attained my sixteenth year."—*Forbes, Or. Mem.* i. 5; [2nd ed. i. 1].

1769.—"The **Writers** of Madras are exceedingly proud, and have the knack of forgetting their old acquaintances."—*Ld. Teignmouth, Mem.* i. 20.

1788.—"In the first place all the persons who go abroad in the Company's civil service, enter as clerks in the counting-house, and are called by a name to correspond with it, **Writers**. In that condition they are obliged to serve five years."—*Burke, Speech on Hastings' Impeachment*, Feb. 1788. In *Works*, vii. 292.

b.—

1764.—"*Resolutions and orders.*—That no **Moonshee**, **Linguist**, Banian (see **BANYAN**), or **Writer** be allowed to any officer except the Commander-in-Chief and the commanders of detachments. . . ."—*Ft. William Consns.* In *Long*, 382.

[1860.—"Following him are the krānees (see **CRANNY**), or **writers**, on salaries varying, according to their duties and abilities, from five to thirty roopees."—*Grant, Rural L. in Bengal*, 138-9.]

WUG, s. We give this Belūch word for **loot** on the high authority quoted. [On this Mr. M. L. Dames writes: "This is not, strictly speaking, a Balochī word, but Sindhī, in the form *wag* or *wagu*. The Balochī word is *bag*, but I cannot say for certain whether it is borrowed from Sindhī by Balochi, or *vice versâ*. The meaning, however, is not **loot**, but 'a herd of camels.' It is probable that on the occasion referred to the *loot* consisted of a herd of camels, and this would easily give rise to the idea that the word meant *loot*. It is one of the commonest forms of plunder in those regions, and I have often heard Balochis, when narrating their raids, describe how they had carried off a '*bag*.'"]

1845.—"In one hunt after **wug**, as the Beloochees call plunder, 200 of that beautiful regiment, the 2nd Europeans, marched incessantly for 15 hours over such ground as I suppose the world cannot match for ravines, except in places where it is impossible to march at all."—*Letter of Sir C. Napier*, in *Life*, iii. 298.

X

XERAFINE, XERAFIM, &c., s. The word in this form represents a silver coin formerly current at Goa and several other Eastern ports, in value somewhat less than 1*s.* 6*d.* It varied in Portuguese currency from 300 to 360 *reis.* But in this case as in so many others the term is a corruption applied to a degenerated value. The original is the Arabic *ashrafī* (see **ASHRAFEE**) (or *sharīfī*, 'noble'—compare the medieval coin so called), which was applied properly to the gold *dīnār*, but was also in India, and still is occasionally by natives, applied to the gold **mohur.** *Ashrafī* for a gold *dīnār* (value in gold about 11*s.* 6*d.*) occurs frequently in the '1001 Nights,' as Dozy states, and he gives various other quotations of the word in different forms (pp. 353-354; [*Burton, Ar. Nights*, x. 160, 376]). *Aigrefin*, the name of a coin once known in France, is according to Littré also a corruption of *ashrafī.*

1498.—"And (the King of Calicut) said that they should tell the Captain that if he wished to go he must give him 600 **xarifes**, and that soon, and that this was the custom of that country, and of those who came thither."—*Roteiro de V. da G.* 79.

1510.—"When a new Sultan succeeds to the throne, one of his lords, who are called Amirra (**Ameer**), says to him: 'Lord, I have been for so long a time your slave, give me Damascus, and I will give you 100,000 or 200,000 **teraphim** of gold.'"—*Varthema*, 10.

" "Every Mameluke, great or little, has for his pay six **saráphi** per month."—*Ibid.* 13.

" "Our captain sent for the superior of the said mosque, to whom he said: that he should show him the body of *Nabi*—this Nabi means the Prophet Mahomet—that he would give him 3000 **seraphim** of gold."—*Ibid.* 29. This one eccentric traveller gives thus three different forms.

1513.—"... hunc regem Affonsus idem, urbe opulētissima et praecipuo emporio Armusio vi capto, quindecim milliū **Seraphinorū**, ea est aurea moneta ducatis equivalēs annuū nobis tributariū effecerat."—*Epistola Emmanuelis Regis*, 2*b*. In the preceding the word seems to apply to the gold dīnār.

1523.—"And by certain information of persons who knew the facts ... Antonio de Saldanha ... agreed with the said King Turuxa (Tūrūn Shāh), ... that the said King ... should pay to the King Our lord 10,000 **xarafins** more yearly ... in all 25,000 **xarafins.**"—*Tombo da India, Subsidios*, 79. This is the gold **mohur.**

1540.—"This year there was such a famine in Choromandel, that it left nearly the whole land depopulated with the mortality, and people ate their fellow men. Such a thing never was heard of on that Coast, where formerly there was such an abundance of rice, that in the port of Negapatam I have often seen more than 700 sail take cargoes amounting to more than 20,000 *moios* (the *moyo* = 29.39 bushels) of rice. ... This year of famine the Portuguese of the town of St. Thomé did much good to the people, helping them with quantities of rice and millet, and coco-nuts and jagra (see **JAGGERY**), which they imported in their vessels from other parts, and sold in retail to the people at far lower prices than they could have got if they wished it; and some rich people caused quantities of rice to be boiled in their houses, and gave it boiled down in the water to the people to drink, all for the love of God. ... This famine lasted a whole year, and it spread to other parts, but was not so bad as in Choromandel. The King of Bisnagar, who was sovereign of that territory, heard of the humanity and beneficence of the Portuguese to the people of the country, and he was greatly pleased thereat, and sent an *ola* (see **OLLAH**) of thanks to the residents of S. Thomé. And this same year there was such a scarcity of provisions in the harbours of the Straits, that in Aden a load (*fardo*) of rice fetched forty **xarafis**, each worth a *cruzado.* ..."—*Correa*, iv. 131-132.

1598.—"The chief and most common money (at Goa) is called Pardauue (**Pardao**) **Xeraphin.** It is of silver, but of small value. They strike it at Goa, and it is marked on one side with the image of St. Sebastian, on the other with 3 or 4 arrows in a sheaf. It is worth 3 testoons or 300 Reys (**Reas**) of Portugal, more or less."—*Linschoten* (from French ed. 71); [Hak. Soc. i. 241, and compare i. 190; and see another version of the same passage under **PARDAO**].

1610.—"Inprimis of **Seraffins** *Ecberi*, which be ten Rupias (**Rupee**) a piece, there are sixtie Leckes (**Lack**)."—*Hawkins*, in *Purchas*, i. 217. Here the gold **mohur** is meant.

c. 1610.—"Les pièces d'or sont **cherafins** à vingt-cinq sols pièce."—*Pyrard da Laval*, ii. 40; [Hak. Soc. ii. 69, reading **cherufins**].

1653.—"*Monnoyes courantes à Goa.*

"Sequin de Venise . 24 tangues (**Tanga**)
* * * * *
Reale d'Espagne . 12 tangues.
Abassis de Perse . 3 tangues.
Pardaux (**Pardao**) . 5 tangues.
Scherephi . . 6 tangues.
Roupies (**Rupee**) du Mogol . . . 6 tangues.
Tangue . . . 20 bousserouque (**Budgrook**)."

De la Boullaye-le-Gouz, 1657, 530.

c. 1675.—"Coins . . . of Rajapore. Imaginary Coins. The Pagod (**Pagoda**) is 3½ Rupees. 48 Juttals (see **JEETUL**) is one Pagod. 10 and ½ Larees (**Larin**) is 1 Pagod. **Zeraphins** 2½, 1 Old Dollar.

"Coins and weights of Bombaim. 3 Larees is 1 **Zeraphin**. 80 Raies (**Reas**) 1 Laree. 1 **Pice** is 10 Raies. The Raies are imaginary.

"Coins and weights in Goa. . . . The *Cruzado* of gold, 12 **Zeraphins**. The *Zeraphin*, 5 *Tangoes*. The *Tango* (**Tanga**), 5 *Vinteens*. The *Vinteen*, 15 *Basrooks* (**Budgrook**), whereof 75 make a *Tango*. And 60 *Rees* make a *Tango*."—*Fryer*, 206.

1690.—

	dw.	gr.
"The Gold St. Thoma	2	5¼
The Silv. **Sherephene**	7	4."

Table of Coins, in *Ovington*.

1727.—"Their Soldiers Pay (at Goa) is very small and ill paid. They have but six **Xerapheens** per Month, and two Suits of Calico, stript or checquered, in a Year . . . and a **Xerapheen** is worth about sixteen Pence half Peny *Ster*."—*A. Hamilton*, i. 249; [ed. 1744, i. 252].

1760.—"You shall coin Gold and silver of equal weight and fineness with the Ashrefees (**Ashrafee**) and Rupees of Moorshedabad, in the name of Calcutta."—*Nawab's Perwannah for Estabt. of a Mint in Calcutta*, in *Long*, 227.

c. 1844.—"Sahibs now are very different from what they once were. When I was a young man with an officer in the camp of Lāt Līk Sāhib (Lord Lake) the sahibs would give an *ashrafi* (**Ashrafee**), when now they think twice before taking out a rupee."—*Personal Reminiscences of an old Khansama's Conversation*. Here the gold **mohur** is meant.

XERCANSOR, n.p. This is a curious example of the manner in which the Portuguese historians represent Mahommedan names. Xercansor does really very fairly represent phonetically the name of *Sher Khān Sūr*, the famous rival and displacer of Humāyūn, under the title of Sher Shāh.

c. 1538.—"But the King of Bengal, seeing himself very powerful in the kingdom of the Patans, seized the king and took his kingdom from him . . . and made Governor of the kingdom a great lord, a vassal of his, called Cotoxa, and then leaving everything in good order, returned to Bengal. The administrator Cotoxa took the field with a great array, having with him a Patan Captain called **Xercansor**, a valiant cavalier, much esteemed by all."—*Correa*, ii. 719.

The kingdom of the Patans appears to be Behar, where various Afghan chiefs tried to establish themselves after the conquest of Delhi by Baber. It would take more search than it is worth to elucidate the story as told by Correa, but see *Elliot*, iv. 333. Cotoxa (Koto sha) appears to be *Kutb Khān* of the Mahommedan historian there.

Another curious example of Portuguese nomenclature is that given to the first Mahommedan king of Malacca by Barros, *Xaquem Darxá* (II. vi. 1), by Alboquerque *Xaquendarxa* (*Comm.* Pt. III. ch. 17). This name is rendered by Lassen's ponderous lore into Skt. *Sakanadhara*, "d. h. Besitzer kräftiger Besinnungen" (or "Possessor, of strong recollections."—*Ind. Alt.* iv. 546), whereas it is simply the Portuguese way of writing *Sikandar Shāh!* [So Linschoten (Hak. Soc. ii. 183) writes Xatamas for *Shāh Tamasp.*]. For other examples, see **Codovascam, Idalcan.**

Y

YABOO, s. Pers. *yābū*, which is perhaps a corruption of Ar. *ya'būb*, defined by Johnson as 'a swift and long horse.' A nag such as we call 'a galloway,' a large pony or small hardy horse; the term in India is generally applied to a very useful class of animals brought from Afghanistan.

[c. 1590.—"The fifth class (**yábú horses**) are bred in this country, but fall short in strength and size. Their performances also are mostly bad. They are the offspring of Turki horses with an inferior breed."—*Āīn*, ed. *Blochmann*, i. 234.]

1754.—"There are in the highland country of Kandahar and Cabul a small kind of horses called **Yabous**, which are very serviceable."—*Hanway, Travels*, ii. 367.

[1839.—"A very strong and useful breed of ponies, called **Yauboos**, is however reared, especially about Baumiaun. They are used to carry baggage, and can bear a great load, but do not stand a long continuance of hard work so well as mules."—*Elphinstone, Caubul*, ed. 1842, i. 189.]

YAK, s. The Tibetan ox (*Bos grunniens*, L., *Poëphagus* of Gray), belonging to the Bisontine group of *Bovinae*. It is spoken of in Bogle's Journal under the odd name of the "cow-tailed cow," which is a literal sort of translation of the Hind. name *chāorī gāo*, *chāorīs* (see **CHOWRY**), having been usually called "**cow-tails**" in the 18th century. [The usual native name for the beast in N. India is *suragā'o*, which comes from Skt. *surabhi*, 'pleasing.'] The name **yak** does not appear in Buffon, who calls it the 'Tartarian cow,' nor is it found in the 3rd ed. of Pennant's *H. of Quad-*

rupeds (1793), though there is a fair account of the animal as *Bos grunniens* of Lin., and a poor engraving. Although the word occurs in Della Penna's account of Tibet, written in 1730, as quoted below, its first appearance in print was, as far as we can ascertain, in Turner's *Mission to Tibet.* It is the Tib. *gYak*, Jäsche's Dict. *gyag*. The animal is mentioned twice, though in a confused and inaccurate manner, by Aelian; and somewhat more correctly by Cosmas. Both have got the same fable about it. It is in medieval times described by Rubruk. The domestic yak is in Tibet the ordinary beast of burden, and is much ridden. Its hair is woven into tents, and spun into ropes; its milk a staple of diet, and its dung of fuel. The wild yak is a magnificent animal, standing sometimes 18 hands high, and weighing 1600 to 1800 lbs., and multiplies to an astonishing extent on the high plateaux of Tibet. The use of the tame yak extends from the highlands of Khokand to Kukukhotan or Kwei-hwaching, near the great northern bend of the Yellow River.

c. A.D. 250. — "The Indians (at times) carry as presents to their King tame tigers, trained panthers, four-horned oryxes, and cattle of two different races, one kind of great swiftness, and another kind that are terribly wild, that kind of cattle from (the tails of) which they make fly-flaps. . . ."—*Aelian, de Animalibus*, xv. cap. 14.

Again:

"There is in India a grass-eating* animal, which is double the size of the horse, and which has a very bushy tail very black in colour.† The hairs of the tail are finer than human hair, and the Indian women set great store by its possession. . . . When it perceives that it is on the point of being caught, it hides its tail in some thicket . . . and thinks that since its tail is not seen, it will not be regarded as of any value, for it knows that the tail is the great object of fancy."—*Ibid.* xvi. 11.

c. 545.—"This Wild Ox is a great beast of India, and from it is got the thing called *Tupha*, with which officers in the field adorn their horses and pennons. They tell of this beast that if its tail catches in a tree he will not budge but stands stock-still, being horribly vexed at losing a single hair of its tail; so the natives come and cut his tail off, and then when he has lost it altogether, he makes his escape."—*Cosmas Indicopleustes*, Bk. xi. Transl. in *Cathay*, &c., p. clxxiv.

[c. 1590.—In a list of things imported from the "northern mountains" into Oudh, we have "tails of the *Kutās* cow."—*Āīn*, ed. *Jarrett*, ii. 172; and see 280.]

1730.—"Dopo di che per circa 40 giorni di camino non si trova più abitazioni di case, ma solo alcune tende con quantità di mandre di **Iak**, ossiano bovi pelosi, pecore, cavalli. . . ."—*Fra Orazio della Penna di Billi, Breve Notizia del Thibet* (published by Klaproth in *Journ. As.* 2d. ser.) p. 17.

1783.—". . . on the opposite side saw several of the black chowry-tailed cattle. . . . This very singular and curious animal deserves a particular description. . . . The **Yak** of Tartary, called *Soora Goy* in Hindostan. . . ."—*Turner's Embassy* (pubd. 1800), 185-6. [Sir H. Yule identifies *Soora Goy* with *Ch'āorī Gāī*; but, as will be seen above, the H. name is *surāgāo*.]

In the publication at the latter date appears the excellent plate after Stubbs, called "the **Yak** *of Tartary*," still the standard representation of the animal. [Also see Turner's paper (1794) in the *As. Res.*, London reprint of 1798, iv. 365 *seqq.*]

Though the two following quotations from Abbé Huc do not contain the word *yak*, they are pictures by that clever artist which we can hardly omit to reproduce:

1851.—"Les bœufs à long poils étaient de véritables caricatures; impossible de figurer rien de plus drôle; ils marchaient les jambes écartées, et portaient péniblement un énorme système de stalactites, qui leur pendaient sous le ventre jusqu'à terre. Ces pauvres bêtes étaient si informes et tellement recouvertes de glaçons qu'il semblait qu'on les eût mis confire dans du sucre candi."—*Huc et Gabet, Souvenirs d'un Voyage*, &c. ii. 201; [E.T. ii. 108].

,, "Au moment où nous passâmes le Mouroui Oussou sur la glace, un spectacle assez bizarre s'offrit à nos yeux. Déjà nous avions remarqué de loin . . . des objets informes et noirâtres rangés en file en travers de ce grand fleuve. . . . Ce fut seulement quand nous fûmes tout près, que nous pûmes reconnaître plus de 50 bœufs sauvages incrustés dans la glace. Ils avaient voulu, sans doute, traverser le fleuve à la nage, au moment de la concrétion des eaux, et ils s'étaient trouvés pris par les glaçons sans avoir la force de s'en débarrasser et de continuer leur route. Leur belle tête, surmontée de grandes cornes, était encore à découvert; mais la reste du corps était pris dans la glace, qui était si transparente qu'on pouvait distinguer facilement la position de ces imprudentes bêtes; on eût dit qu'elles étaient encore à nager. Les aigles et les corbeaux leur avaient arraché les yeux."—*Ibid.* ii. 219; [E.T. ii. 119 *seq.* and for a further account of the animal see ii. 81].

* Ποηφάγος, whence no doubt Gray took his name for the genus.

† The tails usually brought for sale are those of the tame Yak, and are *white*. The tail of the wild Yak is black, and of much greater size.

YAM, s. This general name in English of the large edible tuber *Dioscorea* seems to be a corruption of the name used in the W. Indies at the time of the discovery. [Mr. Platt (9 ser. *N. & Q.* v. 226 *seq.*) suggests that the original form was *nyam* or *nyami*, in the sense of 'food,' *nyami* meaning 'to eat' in the Fulah language of Senegal. The cannibal *Nyam-Nyams*, of whom Miss Kingsley gives an account (*Travels in W. Africa*, 330 *seq.*) appear to take their name from the same word.]

1600.—"There are great store of **Iniamas** growing in Guinea, in great fields."—*Purchas*, ii. 957.

1613.—". . . Moreover it produces great abundance of **inhames**, or large subterranean tubers, of which there are many kinds, like the *camottes* of America, and these *inhames* boiled or roasted serve in place of bread."—*Godinho de Eredia*, 19.

1764.—

"In meagre lands
'Tis known the **Yam** will ne'er to bigness swell."
Grainger, Bk. i.

Z

ZABITA, s. Hind. from Ar. *zābitā*. An exact rule, a canon, but in the following it seems to be used for a tariff of assessment :

1799.—"I have established the **Zabeta** for the shops in the Fort as fixed by Macleod. It is to be paid annually."—*Wellington*, i. 49.

ZAMORIN, s. The title for many centuries of the Hindu sovereign of Calicut and the country round. The word is Malayāl. *Sāmūtiri*, *Sāmūri*, *Tāmātiri*, *Tāmūri*, a *tadbhava* (or vernacular modification) of Skt. *Sāmundri*, 'the Sea-King.' (See also *Wilson*, *Mackenzie MSS.* i. xcvii.) [Mr. Logan (*Malabar*, iii. Gloss. s.v.) suggests that the title *Samudri* is a translation of the Rāja's ancient Malayāl. title of *Kunnalakkon*, *i.e.* 'King (*kon*) of the hills (*kunnu*) and waves (*ala*).' The name has recently become familiar in reference to the curious custom by which the Zamorin was attacked by one of the candidates for his throne (see the account by A. Hamilton (ed. 1744, i. 309 *seq.* *Pinkerton*, viii. 374) quoted by Mr. Frazer (*Golden Bough*, 2nd ed. ii. 14 *seq.*).]

c. 1343.—"The sultan is a Kāfir called the **Sāmarī**. . . . When the time of our departure for China came, the sultan, the **Sāmarī** equipped for us one of the 13 junks which were lying in the port of Calicut."—*Ibn Batuta*, iv. 89-94.

1442.—"I saw a man with his body naked like the rest of the Hindus. The sovereign of this city (Calicut) bears the title of **Sāmari**. When he dies it is his sister's son who succeeds him."—*Abdurrazzāk*, in *India in the XVth. Cent.* 17.

1498.—"First Calicut whither we went. . . . The King whom they call **Camolim** (for **Çamorim**) can muster 100,000 men for war, with the contingents that he receives, his own authority extending to very few."—*Roteiro de Vasco da Gama*.

1510.—"Now I will speak of the King here in Calicut, because he is the most important King of all those before mentioned, and is called **Samory**, which in the Pagan language means God on earth."—*Varthema*, 134. The traveller confounds the word with *tamburān*, which does mean 'Lord.' [Forbes (see below) makes the same mistake.]

1516.—"This city of Calicut is very large. . . . This King became greater and more powerful than all the others: he took the name of **Zomodri**, which is a point of honour above all other Kings."—*Barbosa*, 103.

[1552.—"**Samarao**." See under **CELEBES**.]

1553.—"The most powerful Prince of this Malebar was the King of Calecut, who *par excellence* was called **Camarij**, which among them is as among us the title Emperor."—*Barros*, I. iv. 7.

[1554.—Speaking of the Moluccas, "**Camarao**, which in their language means Admiral."—*Castanheda*, Bk. vi. ch. 66.]

,, "I wrote him a letter to tell him . . . that, please God, in a short time the imperial fleet would come from Egypt to the **Sāmari**, and deliver the country from the hands of the infidels."—*Sidi 'Ali*, p. 83. [Vambéry, who in his translation betrays a remarkable ignorance of Indian geography, speaks (p. 24) of "Samiri, the ruler of *Calcutta*, by which he means *Calicut*."]

1563.—"And when the King of Calecut (who has for title **Samorim** or Emperor) besieged Cochin. . . ."—*Garcia*, f. 58*b*.

1572.—

"Sentado o Gama junto ao rico leito
Os seus mais affastados, prompto em vista
Estava o **Samori** no trajo, e geyto
Da gente, nunca dantes delle vista."
Camões, vii. 59.

By Burton :

"When near that splendid couch took place the guest
and others further off, prompt glance and keen
the **Samorin** cast on folk whose garb and gest
were like to nothing he had ever seen."

1616.—Under this year there is a note of a Letter from Underecoon-Cheete the Great **Samorin** or K. of Calicut to K. James.—*Sainsbury*, i. 462.

1673.—"Indeed it is pleasantly situated under trees, and it is the Holy See of their **Zamerhin** or Pope."—*Fryer*, 52.

1781.—"Their (the Christians') hereditary privileges were respected by the **Zamorin** himself."—*Gibbon*, ch. xlvii.

1785.—A letter of Tippoo's applies the term to a tribe or class, speaking of '2000 **Samories**'; who are these?—*Select Letters*, 274.

1787.—"The **Zamorin** is the only ancient sovereign in the South of India."—*T. Munro*, in *Life*, i. 59.

1810.—"On our way we saw one of the **Zamorim's** houses, but he was absent at a more favoured residence of Paniany."—*Maria Graham*, 110.

[1814.—"The King of Calicut was, in the Malabar language, called **Samory**, or **Zamorine**, that is to say, God on the earth."—*Forbes, Or. Mem.* 2nd ed. i. 263. See quotation above from Varthema.]

,, ". . . nor did the conqueror (Hyder Ali) take any notice of the **Zamorine's** complaints and supplications. The unfortunate prince, after fasting three days, and finding all remonstrance vain, set fire to his palace, and was burned, with some of his women and their brahmins."—*Ibid.* iv. 207-8; [2nd ed. ii. 477]. This was a case of **Traga**.

[1900.—"The **Zamorin** of Calicut who succeeded to the gadi (**Guddy**) three months ago, has died."—*Pioneer Mail*, April 13.

ZANZIBAR, n.p. This name was originally general, and applied widely to the East African coast, at least south of the River Jubb, and as far as the Arab traffic extended. But it was also specifically applied to the island on which the Sultan of Zanzibar now lives (and to which we now generally restrict the name); and this was the case at least since the 15th century, as we see from the *Roteiro*. The Pers. *Zangī-bār*, 'Region of the Blacks,' was known to the ancients in the form *Zingis* (*Ptolemy*, i. 17, 9; iv. 7, 11) and *Zingium*. The Arab softening of the *g* made the name into *Zanjībār*, and this the Portuguese made into *Zanzibar*.

c. 545.—"And those who navigate the Indian Sea are aware that **Zingium**, as it is called, lies beyond the country where the incense grows, which is called Barbary."—*Cosmas*, in *Cathay*, &c., clxvii.

c. 940.—"The land of the **Zanj** begins at the channel issuing from the Upper Nile" (by this the Jubb seems meant) "and extends to the country of **Sofāla** and of the Wak-wak."—*Maṣ'ūdī, Prairies d'Or*, iii. 7.

c. 1190.—Alexander having eaten what was pretended to be the head of a black captive says:

". . . I have never eaten better food than this!
Since a man of **Zang** is in eating so heart-attracting,
To eat any other roast meat to me is not agreeable!"

Sikandar-Nāmah of Nizāmī, by *Wilberforce Clarke*, p. 104.

1298.—"**Zanghibar** is a great and noble Island, with a compass of some 2000 miles. The people . . . are all black, and go stark naked, with only a little covering for decency. Their hair is as black as pepper, and so frizzly that even with water you can scarcely straighten it," &c., &c.—*Marco Polo*, ii. 215. Marco Polo regards the coast of Zanzibar as belonging to a great island like Madagascar.

1440.—"Kalikut is a very safe haven . . . where one finds in abundance the precious objects brought from maritime countries, especially from Habshah (see **HUBSHEE, ABYSSINIA**), **Zirbad**, and **Zanzibar**." *Abdurrazzāk*, in *Not. et Exts.*, xiv. 436.

1498.—"And when the morning came, we found we had arrived at a very great island called **Jamgiber**, peopled with many Moors, and standing good ten leagues from the coast."—*Roteiro*, 105.

1516.—"Between this island of San Lorenzo (*i.e.* Madagascar) and the continent, not very far from it are three islands, which are called one Manfia, another **Zanzibar**, and the other Penda; these are inhabited by Moors; they are very fertile islands."—*Barbosa*, 14.

1553.—"And from the streams of this river Quilimance towards the west, as far as the Cape of Currents, up to which the Moors of that coast do navigate, all that region, and that still further west towards the Cape of Good Hope (as we call it), the Arabians and Persians of those parts call **Zanguebar**, and the inhabitants they call **Zanguy**."—*Barros*, I. viii. 4.

,, A few pages later we have "Isles of Pemba, *Zanzibar*, Monfia, Comoro," showing apparently that a difference had grown up, at least among the Portuguese, distinguishing **Zanguebar** the continental region from **Zanzibar** the Island.

c. 1586.

"And with my power did march to **Zanzibar**
The western (*sic*) part of Afric, where I view'd
The Ethiopian Sea, rivers, and lakes. . . ."

Marlowe's Tamburlane the Great, 2d. part, i. 3.

1592.—"From hence we went for the Isle of **Zanzibar** on the coast of **Melinde**, where at wee stayed and wintered untill the beginning of February following."—*Henry May*, in *Hakl.* iv. 53.

ZEBU, s. This whimsical name, applied in zoological books, English as well as French, to the humped domestic ox (or **Brahminy bull**) of India, was taken by Buffon from the exhibitors of such a beast at a French fair, who perhaps invented the word, but who told him the beast had been brought from Africa, where it was called by that name. We have been able to discover no justification for this in African dialects, though our friend Mr. R. Cust has kindly made search, and sought information from other philologists on our account. *Zebu* passes, however, with most people as an Indian word; thus *Webster's Dictionary*, says "**Zebu**, the native Indian name." The only word at all like it that we can discover is **zobo** (q.v.) or *zhobo*, applied in the semi-Tibetan regions of the Himālaya to a useful hybrid, called in Ladak by the slightly modified form *dsomo*. In Jäschke's *Tibetan Dict.* we find "*Ze'-ba* . . . . 1. hump of a camel, zebu, etc." This is curious, but, we should think, only one of those coincidences which we have had so often to notice.

Isidore Geoffroy de St. Hilaire, in his work *Acclimatation et Domestication des Animaux Utiles*, considers the ox and the *zebu* to be two distinct species. Both are figured on the Assyrian monuments, and both on those of ancient Egypt. The humped ox also exists in Southern Persia, as Marco Polo mentions. Still, the great naturalist to whose work we have referred is hardly justified in the statement quoted below, that the "zebu" is common to "almost the whole of Asia" with a great part of Africa. [Mr. Blanford writes: "The origin of *Bos indicus* (sometimes called **zebu** by European naturalists) is unknown, but it was in all probability tropical or sub-tropical, and was regarded by Blyth as probably African. No ancestral form has been discovered among Indian fossil bovines, which . . . comprise species allied to the gaur and buffalo" (*Mammalia*, 483 *seq.*).]

c. 1772.—"We have seen this small hunched ox alive. . . . It was shown at the fair in Paris in 1752 (*sic*, but a transcript from the French edition of 1837 gives 1772) under the name of **Zebu**; which we have adopted to describe the animal by, for it is a particular breed of the ox, and not a species of the buffalo."—*Buffon's Nat. Hist.*, E.T. 1807, viii. 19, 20; see also p. 33.

1861.—"Nous savons donc positivement qu'à une époque où l'occident était encore couvert de forêts, l'orient, déjà civilisé, possédait déjà le boeuf et le **Zebu**; et par consequent c'est de l'orient que ces animaux sont sortis, pour devenir, l'un (le boeuf) cosmopolite, l'autre commun à presque toute l'Asie et à une grande partie de l'Afrique."—*Geoffroy St. Hilaire* (work above referred to, 4th ed. 1861).

[1898.—"I have seen a herd of **Zebras** (*sic*) or Indian humped cattle, but cannot say where they are kept."—In 9 ser. *N. & Q.* i. 468.]

ZEDOARY, and **ZERUMBET**, ss. These are two aromatic roots, once famous in pharmacy and often coupled together. The former is often mentioned in medieval literature. The former is Arabic *jadwār*, the latter Pers. *zarambād*. There seems some doubt about the scientific discrimination of the two. Moodeen Sheriff says that Zedoary (*Curcuma zedoaria*) is sold in most bazars under the name of *anbe-haldī*, whilst *jadvār*, or *zhadvār*, is the bazar name of roots of varieties of non-poisonous aconites. There has been considerable confusion in the nomenclature of these drugs [see *Watt, Econ. Dict.* ii. 655, 670]. Dr. Royle, in his most interesting discourse on the *Antiquity of Hindoo Medicine* (p. 77), transcribes the following prescription of the physician Aetius, in which the name of Zedoary first occurs, along with many other Indian drugs:

c. A.D. 540.—"**Zador** (*i.e. zedoariae*), galangae, ligustici, seselis, cardamomi, piperis longi, piperis albi, cinnamomi, zingiberis, seminis Smyrnii, caryophylli, phylli, stachyos, **myrobalani**, phu, costi, scordii, silphii vel laserpitii, rhei barbarici, poeoniae; alii etiam arboris nucis viscum et paliuri semen, itemque saxifragum ac casiam addunt; ex his singulis stateres duos commisceto. . . ."

c. 1400.—"Canell and **setewale** of price."—*R. of the Rose.*

1516.—"In the Kingdom of Calicut there grows much pepper . . . and very much good ginger of the country, cardamoms, myrobolans of all kinds, bamboo canes, **zerumba**, **zedoary**, wild cinnamon."—*Barbosa*, 154.

1563.—". . . da **zedoaria** faz capitulo Avicena e de **Zerumbet**; e isto que chamamos **zedoaria**, chama Avicena *geiduar*, e o outro nome não lhe sei, porque o não ha senão nas terras confins á China e este *geiduar* e uma mézinha de muito preço, e não achada senão nas mãos dos que os

Gentios chamam *jogues*, ou outros a quem os Mouros chamam calandares."—*Garcia*, f. 216*v*-217.

[1605.—"**Setweth**," a copyist's error for *Setwall*.—*Birdwood, First Letter Book*, 200.]

ZEMINDAR, s. Pers. *zamīn-dār*, 'landholder.' One holding land on which he pays revenue to the Government direct, and not to any intermediate superior. In Bengal Proper the zemindars hold generally considerable tracts, on a permanent settlement of the amount to be paid to Government. In the N.W. Provinces there are often a great many zemindars in a village, holding by a common settlement, periodically renewable. In the N.W. Provinces the rustic pronunciation of the word *zamīndār* is hardly distinguishable from the ordinary Anglo-Indian pronunciation of *jama'-dār* (see **JEMADAR**), and the form given to *zamīndār* in early English records shows that this pronunciation prevailed in Bengal more than two centuries ago.

1683.—"We lay at Bogatchera, a very pleasant and delightfull Country, ye **Gemidar** invited us ashore, and showed us Store of Deer, Peacocks, &c., but it was not our good fortune to get any of them."—*Hedges, Diary*, April 11; [Hak. Soc. i. 77, also i. 89].

[1686.—"He has ordered downe 300 horse under the conduct of three **Jemidars**."—In ditto, II. lvi.]

1697.—"Having tried all means with the **Jemidar** of the Country adjacent to us to let us have the town of *De Calcutta* at the usual Hire or Rent, rather than fail, having promised him ¼ Part more than the Place at present brings him in, and all to no Purpose, he making frivolous and idle Objections, that he will not let us have any Part of the Country in the Right Honourable Company's name, but that we might have it to our use in any of the Natives Names; the Reason he gives for it is, that the Place will be wholly lost to him—that we are a Powerful People—and that he cannot be possessed of his Country again when he sees Occasion — whereas he can take it from any of the Natives that rent any Part of his Country at his Pleasure.

* * * * *

October 31st, 1698. "The Prince having given us the three towns adjacent to our Settlement, viz. *De Çalcutta, Chutanutte*, and *Gobinpore*, or more properly may be said the **Jemmidarship** of the said towns, paying the said Rent to the King as the **Jemidars** have successively done, and at the same time ordering the **Jemmidar** of the said towns to make over their Right and Title to the English upon their paying to the **Jemidar(s)** One thousand Rupees for the same, it was agreed that the Money should be paid, being the best Money that ever was spent for so great a Privilege; but the **Jemmidar(s)** making a great Noise, being unwilling to part with their Countrey . . . and finding them to continue in their averseness, notwithstanding the Prince had an officer upon them to bring them to a Compliance, it is agreed that 1,500 Rupees be paid them, provided they will relinquish their title to the said towns, and give it under their Hands in Writing, that they have made over the same to the Right Honourable Company."—*Ext of Consns. at Chuttanutte*, the 29th December (Printed for Parliament in 1788).

In the preceding extracts the *De* prefixed to Calcutta is Pers. *deh*. 'village,' or 'township,' a common term in the language of Indian Revenue administration. An 'Explanation of Terms' furnished by W. Hastings to the Fort William Council in 1759 thus explains the word:

"**Deeh**—the ancient limits of any village or parish. Thus, '**Deeh** Calcutta' means only that part which was originally inhabited."—(In *Long*, p. 176.)

1707-8.—In a "List of Men's Names, &c., immediately in the Service of the Honble Vnited Compy. in their Factory of Fort William, Bengal * * *

New Co. 1707/8

* * * * *

Mr. William Bugden . . . **Jemidar** or rent gatherer.

* *

1713. * *

Mr. Edward Page . . . **Jemendar**."

MS. Records in India Office.

1762.—"One of the articles of the Treaty with Meer Jaffier says the Company shall enjoy the **Zemidary** of the Lands from Calcutta down to Culpee, they paying what is paid in the King's Books."—*Holograph* (unpublished) *Letter of Ld. Clive*, in India Office Records, *dated* Berkeley Square, Jan. 21.

1776.—"The Countrey **Jemitdars** remote from Calcutta, treat us frequently with great Insolence; and I was obliged to retreat with only an officer and 17 Sepoys near 6 Miles in the face of 3 or 400 Burgundasses (see **BURKUNDAUZE**), who lined the Woods and Kept a straggling Fire all ye Way." — *MS. Letter of Major James Rennell*, dd. August 5.

1778.—"This avaricious disposition the English plied with presents, which in 1698 obtained his permission to purchase from the **Zemindar**, or Indian proprietor, the town of Sootanutty, Calcutta and Govindpore."—*Orme*, ii. 17.

1809.—"It is impossible for a province to be in a more flourishing state: and I must, in a great degree, attribute this to the total absence of **zemindars**." — *Ld. Valentia*, i. 456. He means *zemindars* of the Bengal description.

1812.—". . . the **Zemindars**, or hereditary Superintendents of Land."—*Fifth Report*, 13.

[1818.—"The Bengal farmers, according to some, are the tenants of the Honourable Company; according to others, of the **Jumidarus**, or land-holders."—*Ward, Hindoos*, i. 74.]

1822.—"Lord Cornwallis's system was commended in Lord Wellesley's time for some of its parts, which we now acknowledge to be the most defective. Surely you will not say it has no defects. The one I chiefly alluded to was its leaving the ryots at the mercy of the **zemindars**."—*Elphinstone*, in *Life*, ii. 182.

1843.—"Our plain clothing commands far more reverence than all the jewels which the most tawdry **Zemindar** wears."—*Macaulay, Speech on Gates of Somnauth*.

1871.—"The **Zemindars** of Lower Bengal, the landed proprietary established by Lord Cornwallis, have the worst reputation as landlords, and appear to have frequently deserved it."—*Maine, Village Communities*, 163.

ZENANA, s. Pers. *zanāna*, from *zan*, 'woman'; the apartments of a house in which the women of the family are secluded. This Mahommedan custom has been largely adopted by the Hindus of Bengal and the Mahrattas. **Zanāna** is also used for the women of the family themselves. The growth of the admirable Zenana Missions has of late years made this word more familiar in England. But we have heard of more than one instance in which the objects of this Christian enterprise have been taken to be an amiable aboriginal tribe—"the **Zenanas**."

[1760.—"I am informed the Dutch chief at Bimlipatam has . . . embarked his **jenninora** on board a sloop bound to Chinsurah. . . ."—In *Long*, 236.]

1761.—". . . I asked him where the Nabob was? Who replied, he was asleep in his **Zunana**."—*Col. Coote*, in *Van Sittart*, i. 111.

1780.—"It was an object with the Omrahs or great Lords of the Court, to hold captive in their **Zenanahs**, even hundreds of females."—*Hodges, Travels*, 22.

1782.—"Notice is hereby given that one *Zoraveer*, **consumah** to Hadjee Mustapha of Moorshedabad these 13 years, has absconded, after stealing. . . . He has also carried away with him two Women, heretofore of Sujah Dowlah's **Zenana**; purchased by Hadjee Mustapha when last at Lucknow, one for 300 and the other for 1200 Rupees."—*India Gazette*, March 9.

1786.—
"Within the **Zenana**, no longer would they
In a starving condition impatiently stay,
But break out of prison, and all run away."
Simpkin the Second, 42.

,, "Their behaviour last night was so furious, that there seemed the greatest probability of their proceeding to the uttermost extremities, and that they would either throw themselves from the walls, or force open the doors of the **zenanahs**."—*Capt. Jaques*, quoted in *Articles of Charge against Hastings*, in *Burke*, vii. 27.

1789.—"I have not a doubt but it is much easier for a gentleman to support a whole **zenana** of Indians than the extravagance of one English lady."—*Munro's Narr.* 50.

1790.—"In a Mussleman Town many complaints arise of the *Passys* or Toddy Collectors climbing the Trees and overlooking the **Jenanas** or Women's apartments of principal Natives."—*Minute* in a letter from *Bd. of Revenue* to Govt. of Bengal, July 12.—MS. in India Office.

1809.—"Musulmauns . . . even carried their depravity so far as to make secret enquiries respecting the females in their districts, and if they heard of any remarkable for beauty, to have them forcibly removed to their **zenanas**."—*Lord Valentia*, i. 415.

1817.—"It was represented by the Rajah that they (the bailiffs) entered the house, and endeavoured to pass into the **zenana**, or women's apartments."—*J. Mill, Hist.* iv. 294.

1826.—"The women in the **zananah**, in their impotent rage, flew at Captain Brown, who came off minus a considerable quantity of skin from his face."—*John Shipp*, iii. 49.

1828.—"'Thou sayest Tippoo's treasures are in the fort?' 'His treasures and his **Zenana**; I may even be able to secure his person.'"—*Sir W. Scott, The Surgeon's Daughter*, ch. xii.

ZEND, ZENDAVESTA, s. Zend is the name which has been commonly applied, for more than a hundred years to that dialect of the ancient Iranian (or Persian) language in which the Avesta or Sacred Books of Zorastrianism or the old Persian religion are written. The application of the name in this way was quite erroneous, as the word *Zand* when used alone in the Parsi books indicates a 'commentary or explanation,' and is in fact applied only to some **Pahlavi** translation, commentary, or gloss. If the name Zend were now to be used as the designation of any language it would more justly apply to the Pahlavi itself. At the same time Haug thinks it probable that the term Zand was originally applied to a commentary written in the same language as the Avesta itself, for in the Pahlavi translations of the Yasna, a part of the Avesta, where the scriptures are mentioned, Avesta and Zend are coupled together, as of equal authority, which could hardly have been the case if by Zend the translator meant his own work. No name for the language of the ancient scriptures has been found in the Parsi books; and *Avesta* itself has been adopted by scholars in speaking of the language. The fragments of these scriptures are written in two dialects of the Eastern Iranian, one, the more ancient, in which the *Gāthas* or hymns are written; and a later one which was for many centuries the spoken and written language of Bactria.

The word *Zand*, in Haug's view, may be referred to the root *zan*, 'to know'; Skt. *jnā*, Gr. *γνω*, Lat. *gno* (as in *agnosco*, *cognosco*), so that its meaning is 'knowledge.' Prof. J. Oppert, on the other hand, identifies it with old Pers. *zannda*, 'prayer.'

Zendavesta is the name which has been by Europeans popularly applied to the books just spoken of as the Avesta. The term is undoubtedly an inversion, as, according to Haug, "the Pahlavi books always style them *Avistâk va Zand* (Avesta and Zend)" *i.e.* the Law with its traditional and authoritative explanation. *Abastâ*, in the sense of law, occurs in the funeral inscription of Darius at Behistūn; and this seems now the most generally accepted origin of the term in its application to the Parsi sacred books. (This is not, however, the explanation given by Haug.) Thus, '*Avesta* and Zend' signify together 'The Law and the Commentary.'

The Avesta was originally much more extensive than the texts which now exist, which are only fragments. The Parsi tradition is that there were twenty-one books called *Nasks*, the greater part of which were burnt by Alexander in his conquest of Persia; possibly true, as we know that Alexander did burn the palace at Persepolis. The collection of fragments which remains, and is known as the Zend-avesta, is divided, in its usual form, into two parts. I. The Avesta properly so called, containing (*a*) the *Vendîdâd*, a compilation of religious laws and of mythical tales; (*b*) the *Vispêrad*, a collection of litanies for the sacrifice; and (*c*) the *Yasna*, composed of similar litanies and of 5 hymns or *Gâthas* in an old dialect. II. The *Khorda*, or small, *Avesta*, composed of short prayers for recitation by the faithful at certain moments of the day, month, or year, and in presence of the different elements, with which certain other hymns and fragments are usually included.

The term Zendavesta, though used, as we see below, by Lord in 1630, first became familiar in Europe through the labours of Anquetil du Perron, and his publication of 1771. [The Zend-Avesta has now been translated in *Sacred Books of the East*, by J. Darmesteter, L. H. Mills; *Pahlavī Texts*, by E. W. West.]

c. 930.—"Zarādasht, the son of Asbimām, . . . had brought to the Persians the book **al-Bastāh** in the old Fārsī tongue. He gave a commentary on this, which is the **Zand**, and to this commentary yet another explanation which was called **Bazand**. . . ." —*Maṣ'ūdi*, ii. 167. [See *Haug, Essays*, p. 11.]

c. 1030.—"The chronology of this same past, but in a different shape, I have also found in the book of Hamza ben Alhusain Alisfahâni, which he calls '*Chronology of great nations of the past and present.*' He says that he has endeavoured to correct his account by means of the **Abastâ**, which is the religious code (of the Zoroastrians). Therefore I have transferred it into this place of my book."—*Al-Birûni, Chronology of Ancient Nations*, by *Sachau*, p. 112.

,, "Afterwards the wife gave birth to six other children, the names of whom are known in the **Avastâ**."—*Ibid.* p. 108.

1630.—"Desirous to add anything to the ingenious that the opportunities of my Travayle might conferre vpon mee, I ioyned myselfe with one of their Church men called their *Daroo*, and by the interpretation of a *Parsee*, whose long imployment in the Companies Service, had brought him to mediocrity in the *English* tongue, and whose familiarity with me, inclined him to further my inquiries: I gained the knowledge of what hereafter I shall deliver as it was compiled in a booke writ in the Persian Characters containing their Scriptures, and in their own language called their ZVNDAVASTAVV."—*Lord, The Religion of the Persees, The Proeme.*

[c. 1630.—"Being past the Element of Fire and the highest Orbs (as saith their **Zundavastaio**) . . ."—*Sir T. Herbert*, 2nd ed. 1677, p. 54.]

1653.—"Les ottomans appellent *gueuures* vne secte de Payens que nous connoissons sous le nom d'adorateurs du feu, les Persans sous celuy d'*Atechperes*, et les Indou sous celuy de Parsi, terme dont ils se nommēt eux-mesmes. . . . Ils ont leur Saincte Escriture ou **Zundeuastavv**, en deux volumes composée par vn nommé Zertost, conduit par vn Ange nommé Abraham ou plus-tost Bahaman Vmshauspan. . . ."—*De la Boullaye-le-Gouz*, ed. 1657, pp. 200-201.

1700.—"Suo itaque Libro (Zerdusht) . . . alium affixit specialem Titulum **Zend**, seu alias **Zendavestâ**; vulgus sonat *Zund* et *Zundavastaw*. Ita ut quamvis illud ejus Opus variis Tomis, sub distinctis etiam nominibus, constet, tamen quidvis ex dictorum Tomorum quovis, satis propriè et legitimè citari possit, sub dicto generali nomine, utpote quod, hac ratione, in operum ejus complexu seu Syntagmate contineri intelligatur. . . . Est autem **Zend** nomen Arabicum: et **Zendavestâ** conflatum est ex superaddito nomine *Hebraeo - Chaldaico, Eshta, i.e.* ignis, unde Εστία . . . supra dicto nomine *Zend* apud Arabes, significatur *Igniarium* seu *Focile*. . . . Cum itaque nomine **Zend** significetur *Igniarium*, et **Zendavestâ** *Igniarium et Ignis*," &c.—*T. Hyde, Hist. Rel. Vet. Persarum eorumque Magorum*, cap. xxv., ed. Oxon. 1760, pp. 335-336.

1771. — "Persuadé que les usages modernes de l'Asie doivent leur origine aux Peuples et aux Religions qui l'ont subjuguée, je me suis proposé d'étudier dans les sources l'ancienne Théologie des Nations habituées dans les Contrées immenses qui sont à l'Est de l'Euphrate, et de consulter sur leur Histoire, les livres originaux. Ce plan m'a engagé à remonter aux Monumens les plus anciens. Je les ai trouvé de deux espèces: les prémiers écrits en Samskretan; ce sont les *Vedes*, Livres sacrés des Pays, qui de l'Indus s'étendent aux frontières de la Chine: les seconds écrits en **Zend**, ancienne Langue du Nord de la Perse; c'est le **Zend Avesta**, qui passe pour avoir été la Loi des Contrées bornées par l'Euphrate, le Caucase, l'Oxus, et la mer des Indes."—*Anquetil du Perron, Zend-Avesta, Ouvrage de Zoroastre—Documens Préliminaires*, p. iii.

,, "Dans deux cens ans, quand les Langues **Zend** et Pehlvie (**Pahlavi**) seront devenues en Europe familières aux Sçavans, on pourra, en rectifiant les endroits où je me serai trompé, donner une Traduction plus exacte du **Zend-Avesta**, et ci ce que je dis ici excitant l'émulation, avance le terme que je viens de fixer, mes fautes m'auront conduit au but que je me suis proposé."—*Ibid.* Preface, xvii.

1884.—"The supposition that some of the books were destroyed by Alexander the Great is contained in the introductory chapter of the Pehlevi *Viraf-Nama*, a book written in the Sassanian times, about the 6th or 7th century, and in which the event is thus chronicled:—'The wicked, accursed Guna Mino (the evil spirit), in order to make the people sceptical about their religion, instigated the accursed Alexiedar (Alexander) the Ruman, the inhabitant of Egypt, to carry war and hardships to the country of Iran (Persia). He killed the monarch of Iran, and destroyed and made desolate the royal court. And this religion, that is, all the books of **Avesta** and **Zend**, written with gold ink upon prepared cow-skins, was deposited in the archives of Stakhar (Istakhar or Persepolis) of Papak. The accursed, wretched, wicked *Ashmogh* (destroyer of the pious), Alexiedar the evildoer, took them (the books) out and burnt them."—*Dosabhai Framji, H. of the Parsis*, ii. 158-159.

ZERBAFT, s. Gold-brocade, Pers. *zar*, 'gold,' *bāft*, 'woven.'

[1900.—"Kamkwabs, or kimkhwabs (**Kincob**), are also known as **zar-baft** (gold-woven), and mushajjar (having patterns)."—*Yusuf Ali, Mon. on Silk Fabrics*, 86.]

ZILLAH, s. This word is properly Ar. (in Indian pron.) *ẓila*, 'a rib,' thence 'a side,' a district. It is the technical name for the administrative districts into which British India is divided, each of which has in the older provinces a Collector, or Collector and Magistrate combined, a Sessions Judge, &c., and in the newer provinces, such as the Punjab and B. Burma, a Deputy Commissioner.

[1772.—"With respect to the **Talookdarrys** and inconsiderable **Zemindarrys**, which formed a part of the Huzzoor (**Huzoor**) **Zilahs** or Districts which paid their rents immediately to the General **Cutcherry** at Moorshedabad. . . ."—*W. Hastings*, in *Hunter, Annals of Bengal*, 4th ed., 388.]

1817.—"In each district, that is in the language of the country, each **Zillah** . . . a **Zillah** Court was established."—*Mill's Hist.* v. 422.

ZINGARI, n.p. This is of course not Anglo-Indian, but the name applied in various countries of Europe, and in various modifications, *zincari*, *zingani*, *zincali*, *chingari*, *zigeuner*, &c., to the gypsies.

Various suggestions as to its derivation have been made on the supposition that it is of Indian origin. Borrow has explained the word as 'a person of mixt blood,' deriving it from the Skt. *sankara*, 'made up.' It is true that *varṅa sankara* is used for an admixture of castes and races (*e.g.* in *Bhāgavad Gītā*, i. 41, &c.), but it is not the name of any caste, nor would people to whom such an opprobrious epithet had been applied be likely to carry it with them to distant lands. A writer in the *Saturday Review* once suggested the Pers. *zīngar*, 'a saddler.' Not at all probable. In Sleeman's

Ramaseeana or Vocabulary of the peculiar Language used by the Thugs (Calcutta, 1836), p. 85, we find :

"**Chingaree**, a class of Multani Thugs, sometimes called *Nàiks*, of the Mussulman faith. They proceed on their expeditions in the character of Brinjaras, with cows and bullocks laden with merchandize, which they expose for sale at their encampments, and thereby attract their victims. They use the rope of their bullocks instead of the *roomal* in strangling. They are an ancient tribe of Thugs, and take their wives and children on their expeditions."

[These are the Chāngars of whom Mr. Ibbetson (*Panjab Ethnog.* 308) gives an account. A full description of them has been given by Dr. G. W. Leitner (*A Sketch of the Changars and of their Dialect*, Lahore, 1880), in which he shows reason to doubt any connection between them and the Zingari.] De Goeje (*Contributions to the Hist. of the Gypsies*) regards that people as the Indian *Zoṭṭ* (*i.e. Jatt* of Sind). He suggests as possible origins of the name first *shikārī* (see **SHIKAREE**), and then Pers. *changī*, 'harper,' from which a plural *changān* actually occurs in Lane's *Arabian Nights*, iii. 730, note 22. [These are the Al-Jink, male dancers (see *Burton*, *Ar. Nights*, viii. 18).]

If the name is to be derived from India, the term in Sleeman's *Vocabulary* seems a more probable origin than the others mentioned here. But is it not more likely that *zingari*, like Gipsy and Bohemian, would be a name given *ab extra* on their appearing in the West, and not carried with them from Asia ?

ZIRBAD, n.p. Pers. *zīr-bād*, 'below the wind,' *i.e.* leeward. This is a phrase derived from nautical use, and applied to the countries eastward of India. It appears to be adopted with reference to the S.W. Monsoon. Thus by the extracts from the *Mohit* or 'Ocean' of Sidi 'Ali Kapudān (1554), translated by Joseph V. Hammer in the *Journ. As. Soc. Bengal*, we find that one chapter (unfortunately not given) treats "Of the Indian Islands above and below the wind." The islands "above the wind" were probably Ceylon, the Maldives, Socotra, &c., but we find no extract with precise indication of them. We find however indicated as the "tracts situated below the wind" Malacca, Sumatra, Tenasserim, Bengal, Martaban, Pegu. The phrase is one which naturally acquires a specific meaning among sea-faring folk, of which we have an instance in the Windward and Leeward Islands of the W. Indies. But probably it was adopted from the Malays, who make use of the same nomenclature, as the quotations show.

1442.—"The inhabitants of the sea coasts arrive here (at Ormuz) from the countries of Tchin, Java, Bengal, the cities of **Zirbad.**"—*Abdurrazzāk*, in *India in the XVth Cent.* 6.

1553.—". . . Before the foundation of Malaca, in this Cingapura . . . met all the navigators of the seas to the West of India and of those to the East of it, which last embrace the regions of Siam, China, Choampa, Camboja, and the many thousand islands that lie in that Orient. And these two quarters the natives of the land distinguish as Dybananguim (*di-bāwa-angīn*) and Ataz Anguim (*ātas-angīn*) which are as much as to say '**below the winds**' and '*above the winds*,' below being West and above East."—*Barros*, Dec. II. Liv. vi. cap. i. In this passage De Barros goes unusually astray, for the use of the Malay expressions which he quotes, *bawa-angin* (or *di-bawah*) '**below the wind**,' and *ātas* (or *di-ātas*) *angīn*, 'above the wind,' is just the reverse of his explanation, the former meaning the east, and the latter the west (see below).

c. 1590.—"*Kalanbak* (see **CALAMBAK**) is the wood of a tree brought from **Zírbád** (?)"—*Āīn*, i. 81. A mistaken explanation is given in the foot-note from a native authority, but this is corrected by Prof. Blochmann at p. 616.

1726.—"The Malayers are also commonly called *Orang di Bawah Angin*, or 'people **beneath the wind**,' otherwise *Easterlings*, as those of the West, and particularly the Arabs, are called *Orang Atas Angin*, or 'people above the wind,' and known as Westerlings."—*Valentijn*, v. 310.

" "The land of the Peninsula, &c., was called by the geographers **Zierbaad**, meaning in Persian 'beneath the wind.'"—*Ibid.* 317.

1856.—"There is a peculiar idiom of the Malay language, connected with the monsoons. . . . The Malays call all countries west of their own 'countries above the wind,' and their own and all countries east of it 'countries **below the wind**.' . . . The origin of the phrase admits of no explanation, unless it have reference to the most important of the two monsoons, the western, that which brought to the Malayan countries the traders of India."—*Crawfurd's Desc. Dict.* 288.

ZOBO, ZHOBO, DSOMO, &c., s. Names used in the semi-Tibetan tracts of the Himālaya for hybrids between the yak bull and the ordinary hill cow, much used in transport and agriculture. See quotation under **ZEBU**. The following are the connected Tibetan terms, according to Jaeschke's Dict. (p. 463): "*mdzo*, a mongrel bred of Yak bull and common cow; *bri-mdzo*, a mongrel bred of common bull and yak cow; *m***dzopo**, a male; *m***dzo-mo**, a female animal of the kind, both valued as domestic cattle." [Writing of the Lower Himālaya, Mr. Atkinson says: "When the sire is a yak and the dam a hill cow, the hybrid is called **jubu;** when the parentage is reversed, the produce is called *garjo*. The *jubu* is found more valuable than the other hybrid or than either of the pure stocks" (*Himalayan Gazetteer*, ii. 38). Also see *Āīn*, ed. *Jarrett*, ii. 350.]

1298. — "There are wild cattle in that country almost as big as elephants, splendid creatures, covered everywhere but in the back with shaggy hair a good four palms long. They are partly black, partly white, and really wonderfully fine creatures, and the hair or wool is extremely fine and white, finer and whiter than silk. Messer Marco brought some to Venice as a great curiosity, and so it was reckoned by those who saw it. There are also plenty of them tame, which have been caught young. They also cross these with the common cow, and the cattle from this cross are wonderful beasts, and better for work than other animals. These the people use commonly for burden and general work, and in the plough as well; and at the latter they will do twice as much work as any other cattle, being such very strong beasts."—*Marco Polo*, Bk. i. ch. 57.

1854.—"The **Zobo**, or cross between the yak and the hill-cow (much resembling the English cow) is but rarely seen in these mountains (Sikkim), though common in the N.W. Himalaya."—*Hooker's Him. Journals*, 2d ed. i. 203.

[1871.—"The plough in Lahoul . . . is worked by a pair of **dzos** (hybrids between the cow and yak)."—*Harcourt, Him. Dists of Kooloo, Lahoul, and Spiti*, 180.

[1875.—"Ploughing is done chiefly with the hybrid of the yak bull and the common cow; this they call **zo** if male and **zomo** if female."—*Drew, Jummoo and Kashmir*, 246.]

ZOUAVE, s. This modern French term is applied to certain regiments of light infantry in a quasi-Oriental costume, recruited originally in Algeria, and from various races, but now only consisting of Frenchmen. The name *Zuawa*, *Zouaoua* was, according to Littré, that of a Kabyle tribe of the Jurjura which furnished the first soldiers so called.

[**ZUBT, ZUBTEE**, adj. and s. of which the corrupted forms are **JUBTEE, JUPTEE**. Ar. *ẓabṭ*, lit. 'keeping, guarding,' but more generally in India, in the sense of 'seizure, confiscation.' In the *Āīn* it is used in the sense which is still in use in the N.W.P., 'cash rents on the more valuable crops, such as sugar-cane, tobacco, etc., in those districts where rents in kind are generally paid.'

[c. 1590.—"Of these Parganahs, 138 pay revenue in cash from crops charged at special rates (in orig. *ẓabṭī*)."—*Āīn*, ed. *Jarret*, ii. 153.

[1813.—"**Zebt** . . . restraint, confiscation, sequestration. **Zebty**. Relating to restraint or confiscation; what has been confiscated. . . . Lands resumed by *Jaffier Khan* which had been appropriated in *Jaghire* (see **JAGHEER**)."—Glossary to *Fifth Report*.

[1851. — "You put down one hundred rupees. If the water of your land does not come . . . then my money shall be confiscated to the Sabib. If it does then your money shall be **zupt** (confiscated)."—*Edwardes, A Year on the Punjab Frontier*, i. 278.]

ZUMBOORUCK, s. Ar. Turk. Pers. *zambūrak* (spelt *zanbūrak*), a small gun or swivel usually carried on a camel, and mounted on a saddle;—a falconet. [See a drawing in R. Kipling's *Beast and Man in India*, 255.] It was, however, before the use of gunpowder came in, the name applied sometimes to a cross-bow, and sometimes to the *quarrel* or bolt shot from such a weapon. The word is in form a Turkish diminutive from Ar. *zambūr*, 'a hornet'; much as 'musket' comes from *mosquetta*. Quatremère thinks the name was given from the twang of the cross-bow at the moment of discharge (see *H. des Mongols*, 285-6; see also *Dozy, Suppt.* s.v.). This older meaning is the subject of our first quotation:

1848.—"Les écrivains arabes qui ont traité des guerres des croisades, donnent à l'arbalète, telle que l'employait les chrétiens, le nom de **zenbourek**. La première fois qu'ils en font mention, c'est en parlant du siège de Tyr par Saladin en 1187. . . . Suivant l'historien des patriarches d'Alexandrie, le **zenbourek** était une flèche de l'épaisseur du pouce, de la longueur d'une coudée, qui avait quatre faces . . . il traversait quelque fois au même coup deux hommes placés l'un derrière l'autre. . . . Les musulmans paraissent n'avoir fait usage qu'assez tard du **zenbourek**. Djèmal - Eddin est, à ma connaissance, le premier écrivain arabe qui, sous la date 643 (1245 de J.C.), cite cette arme comme servant aux guerriers de l'Islamisme; c'est à propos du siège d'Ascalon par le sultan d'Égypte. . . . Mais bientôt l'usage du **zenbourek** devint commun en Orient, et dans la suite des Turks ottomans entretinrent dans leurs armées un corps de soldats appelés **zenbourekdjis**. Maintenant . . . ce mot a tout à fait changé d'acception, et l'on donne en Perse le nom de **zenbourek** à une petite pièce d'artillerie légère."—*Reinaud, De l'Art Militaire chez les Arabes au moyen age. Journ. As.*, Ser. IV., tom. xii. 211-213.

1707.—"Prince Bedár Bakht . . . was killed by a cannon-ball, and many of his followers also fell. . . . His younger brother Wálájáh was killed by a ball from a **zambúrak**."—*Kháfí Khán*, in *Elliot*, vii. 398.

c. 1764.—"Mirza Nedjef Qhan, who was preceded by some **Zemberecs**, ordered that kind of artillery to stand in the middle of the water and to fire on the eminence."—*Seir Mutaqherin*, iii. 250.

1825.—"The reign of Futeh Allee Shah has been far from remarkable for its military splendour. . . . He has rarely been exposed to danger in action, but, early in his reign . . . he appeared in the field, . . . till at last one or two shots from **zumboorucks** dropping among them, he fell from his horse in a swoon of terror. . . ."—*J. B. Fraser, Journey into Khorasān* in 1821-22, pp. 197-8.

[1829. — "He had no cannon; but was furnished with a description of ordnance, or swivels, called **zumbooruk**, which were mounted on camels; and which, though useful in action, could make no impression on the slightest walls. . . ."—*Malcolm, H. of Persia*, i. 419.]

1846.—"So hot was the fire of cannon, musquetry, and **zambooraks**, kept up by the Khalsa troops, that it seemed for some moments impossible that the entrenchments could be won under it."—*Sir Hugh Gough's desp. on the Battle of Sobraon*, dd. Feb 13.

" "The flank in question (at Subrāon) was mainly guarded by a line of two hundred '**zumbooruks**,' or falconets; but it derived some support from a salient battery, and from the heavy guns retained on the opposite bank of the river."—*Cunningham's H. of the Sikhs*, 322.

INDEX.